Cornerst

C000130445

Electoral Legislation 2016

Cornerstone's

Electoral Legislation 2016

Philip Coppel QC

Bloomsbury Professional

Cornerstones

Electoral Legislation 2016

Published by:

Bloomsbury Professional Ltd, Maxwelton House, 41-43 Boltro Road, Haywards Heath, West Sussex, RH16 1BJ

© Bloomsbury Professional 2016

A CIP Catalogue record for this book is available from the British Library.

Whilst every care has been taken to ensure the accuracy of the content of this work, no responsibility for loss occasioned to any person acting or refraining from action as a result of the material in this publication can be accepted by the authors or by the publisher.

ISBN 978 1 78451 261 3

Printed in Great Britain by CPI Group (UK) Ltd, Croydon, CR0 4YY

Bloomsbury Professional

Preface

Unearthing the electoral legislation of this country reveals a vignette of its political history. Much has, of course, changed since the 1753 Oxfordshire election that inspired Hogarth's *The Humours of an Election* series of paintings. It had been a bitterly fought contest, widely reported in the London press. Treating was lavish, drunkenness widespread and physical violence not uncommon. The remainder of Hogarth's series depicts every corrupt and illegal electoral practice of the time. Given that there was an immediate demand for a scrutiny, we may question whether anyone was actually chaired. But it all makes for one of the masterpieces of English 18th century painting.

The current regime is more orderly, if altogether more complicated. Just this year the three Law Commissions of the United Kingdom jointly reported:

> "Electoral law in the UK has become complex, voluminous and fragmented. There is an enormous amount of primary and secondary legislative material governing elections and referendums." (*Electoral Law: An Interim Report*, 4 February 2016, §1.15)

Nobody could rationally suggest otherwise. The Law Commissions have for the past four years been undertaking a project to rationalise the legislation.

> "The twin aims of the project are to ensure, first, that electoral laws are presented within a rational, modern legislative framework, governing all elections and referendums within its scope; and secondly, that provisions of electoral law are modern, simple, and fit for purpose." (§1.15)

Both aims are laudable. Time will tell if they are attainable.

In the meantime, this work was born of an ambition to present the electoral laws of the country in an accessible, affordable and portable volume; none of which, it seemed to me, rival publications had managed.

The importance of ready access to the provisions governing election law can hardly be gainsaid. The procedures are necessarily highly prescriptive. So far as possible, it is desirable that decisions affecting the fortunes of candidates and the entitlements of electors are not left to subjective evaluation but are instead to be measured against objective criteria.

At one level, the productivity of those drafting the legislation has to be admired. Parliamentary, European, local government, regional assemblies and referendums are all given their own rules; then there are variations according to region; further variations according to whether different sorts of elections are held at the same time; some provisions are shared, with or without adaptations; some are time-limited. The strictures on funding brings its own weight of regulation. Lest it be thought that this is red-tape visited on the country from abroad, a casual examination of the contents of this book reveals it to have an autochthonous pedigree.

The selection of legislation and legislative provisions that needed inclusion in this work proved more difficult than I had anticipated. While some legislation obviously answered the description "electoral legislation", in other cases the connection was more tenuous — even though the title of the legislation might have suggested otherwise. On the other hand, some legislation that from its title might have been thought to have no relevance had provisions that on analysis were closely connected to electoral matters. Then again, there were other pieces of electoral legislation that I would have liked to include but simply could not: there is a limit to what a paper-bound book can physically contain. It may be that the dimensions of the work will be re-visited next year to accommodate these.

Until such time as the legislation steadies down, the proposal is to update this work annually. I hope in this way to maintain its currency and utility. I am grateful to my publishers for having priced it in a way that – for legal texts at least – should be attractive to all.

The reproduced legislation is as at 1 January 2016 – a little later in some cases. I have included all the principal legislation governing the EU referendum. Inevitably, provisions will continue to come into force, or be repealed or amended on a regular basis, sometimes throughout the country and on other occasions restricted to particular localities. Users should always check the current status of any provision, together with transitional arrangements that may apply.

Philip Coppel QC
2-3 Gray's Inn Square

21 March 2015

Table of Contents

WESTMINSTER SECONDARY LEGISLATION

Westminster Primary Legislation

Act of Settlement (1700)

3 Further provisions for securing the religions, laws, and liberties of these realms

And whereas it is requisite and necessary that some further provision be made for securing our religion laws and liberties from and after the death of his Majesty and the Princess Ann of Denmark and in default of issue of the body of the said princess and of his Majesty respectively Be it enacted by the Kings most excellent Majesty by and with the advice and consent of the lords spirituall and temporall and commons in Parliament and by the authority of the same

That whosoever shall hereafter come to the possession of this crown shall joyn in communion with the Church of England as by law established

That in case the crown and imperiall dignity of this realm shall hereafter come to any person not being a native of this kingdom of England this nation be not obliged to ingage in any warr for the defence of any dominions or territories which do not belong to the crown of England without the consent of Parliament

That after the said limitation shall take effect as aforesaid no person born out of the kingdoms of England Scotland or Ireland or the dominions thereunto belonging (although he be < . . . > made a denizen (except such as are born of English parents) shall be capable to be of the privy councill or a member of either House of Parliament or to enjoy any office or place of trust either civill or military or to have any grant of lands tenements or hereditaments from the Crown to himself or to any other or others in trust for him.

That no pardon under the great seal of England be pleadable to an impeachment by the commons in Parliament.

NOTES

Government of Wales Act 2006, s 17(2) provides that a citizen of the European Union who is resident in the United Kingdom is not disqualified from being an Assembly member merely because of the provisions in this section.

The Electoral Administration Act 2006, s 18 effects a modified disapplication of this provision for the purposes of s 18 of that Act.

Banking and Financial Dealings Act 1971

An Act to make new provision in place of the Bank Holidays Act 1871, to confer power to suspend financial and other dealings on bank holidays or other days, and to amend the law relating to bills of exchange and promissory notes with reference to the maturity of bills and notes and other matters affected by the closing of banks on Saturdays, and for purposes connected therewith

16th December 1971

1   Bank holidays
2-4   *Repealed*
5   Short title and extent
     SCHEDULES

1 Bank holidays

(1)   Subject to subsection (2) below, the days specified in Schedule 1 to this Act shall be bank holidays in England and Wales, in Scotland and in Northern Ireland as indicated in the Schedule.

(2)   If it appears to Her Majesty that, in the special circumstances of any year, it is inexpedient that a day specified in Schedule 1 to this Act should be a bank holiday, Her Majesty may by proclamation declare that that day shall not in that year be a bank holiday and appoint another day in place of it; and the day appointed by the proclamation shall, in that year, be a bank holiday under this Act instead of the day specified in Schedule 1.

(3)   Her Majesty may from time to time by proclamation appoint a special day to be, either throughout the United Kingdom or in any place or locality in the United Kingdom, a bank holiday under this Act.

(4)   No person shall be compellable to make any payment or to do any act on a bank holiday under this Act which he would not be compellable to make or do on Christmas Day or Good Friday; and where a person would, apart from this subsection, be compellable to make any payment or to do any act on a bank holiday under this Act, his obligation to make the payment or to do the act shall be deemed to be complied with if he makes or does it on the next following day on which he is compellable to make or do it.

(5)   The powers conferred on Her Majesty by subsections (2) and (3) above may, as respects Northern Ireland, be exercised by the Governor of Northern Ireland.

(6)   The provision made by this section for January 2nd or 3rd to be a bank holiday in Scotland shall have effect for the year 1973 and subsequent years.

NOTES

Since 1974, New Year's Day (or, as appropriate, 2 or 3 January) has each year been declared a bank holiday in England, Wales and Northern Ireland by proclamation in the London Gazette.

Since 1978 the first Monday in May has by royal proclamation been declared a bank holiday in England, Wales and Northern Ireland.

Definitions
England: Interpretation Act 1978 Sch 1
Great Britain: Interpretation Act 1978 Sch 1
United Kingdom: Interpretation Act 1978 s 5, Sch 1.
Wales: Interpretation Act 1978 Sch 1
Neither the Channel Islands nor the Isle of Man is within the United Kingdom.

5 Short title and extent

(1)   This Act may be cited as the Banking and Financial Dealings Act 1971.

(2)   It is hereby declared that this Act extends to Northern Ireland.

SCHEDULE 1
Bank Holidays

Section 1

1 The following are to be bank holidays in England and Wales:

Easter Monday.

The last Monday in May.

The last Monday in August.

26th December, if it be not a Sunday.

27th December in a year in which 25th or 26th December is a Sunday.

2 The following are to be bank holidays in Scotland:

New Year's Day, if it be not a Sunday or, if it be a Sunday, 3rd January.

2nd January, if it be not a Sunday or, if it be a Sunday, 3rd January.

Good Friday.

The first Monday in May.

The first Monday in August.

30th November, if it is not a Saturday or Sunday or, if it is a Saturday or Sunday, the first Monday following that day.

Christmas Day, if it be not a Sunday or, if it be a Sunday, 26th December.

3 The following are to be bank holidays in Northern Ireland:

17th March, if it be not a Sunday or, if it be a Sunday, 18th March.

Easter Monday.

The last Monday in May.

The last Monday in August.

26th December, if it be not a Sunday.

27th December in a year in which 25th or 26th December is a Sunday.

SCHEDULE 2

Enactments Repealed
Not reproduced

Bribery Act 2010

An Act to make provision about offences relating to bribery; and for connected purposes.

8th April 2010

General bribery offences

1 Offences of bribing another person

(1)   A person ("P") is guilty of an offence if either of the following cases applies.

(2)   Case 1 is where
   (a)   P offers, promises or gives a financial or other advantage to another person, and
   (b)   P intends the advantage
      (i) to induce a person to perform improperly a relevant function or activity, or
      (ii)   to reward a person for the improper performance of such a function or activity.

(3) Case 2 is where
   (a) P offers, promises or gives a financial or other advantage to another person, and
   (b) P knows or believes that the acceptance of the advantage would itself constitute the improper performance of a relevant function or activity.

(4) In case 1 it does not matter whether the person to whom the advantage is offered, promised or given is the same person as the person who is to perform, or has performed, the function or activity concerned.

(5) In cases 1 and 2 it does not matter whether the advantage is offered, promised or given by P directly or through a third party.

2 Offences relating to being bribed

(1) A person ("R") is guilty of an offence if any of the following cases applies.

(2) Case 3 is where R requests, agrees to receive or accepts a financial or other advantage intending that, in consequence, a relevant function or activity should be performed improperly (whether by R or another person).

(3) Case 4 is where
   (a) R requests, agrees to receive or accepts a financial or other advantage, and
   (b) the request, agreement or acceptance itself constitutes the improper performance by R of a relevant function or activity.

(4) Case 5 is where R requests, agrees to receive or accepts a financial or other advantage as a reward for the improper performance (whether by R or another person) of a relevant function or activity.

(5) Case 6 is where, in anticipation of or in consequence of R requesting, agreeing to receive or accepting a financial or other advantage, a relevant function or activity is performed improperly
   (a) by R, or
   (b) by another person at R's request or with R's assent or acquiescence.

(6) In cases 3 to 6 it does not matter
   (a) whether R requests, agrees to receive or accepts (or is to request, agree to receive or accept) the advantage directly or through a third party,
   (b) whether the advantage is (or is to be) for the benefit of R or another person.

(7) In cases 4 to 6 it does not matter whether R knows or believes that the performance of the function or activity is improper.

(8) In case 6, where a person other than R is performing the function or activity, it also does not matter whether that person knows or believes that the performance of the function or activity is improper.

3 Function or activity to which bribe relates

(1) For the purposes of this Act a function or activity is a relevant function or activity if
   (a) it falls within subsection (2), and
   (b) meets one or more of conditions A to C.

(2) The following functions and activities fall within this subsection
   (a) any function of a public nature,
   (b) any activity connected with a business,
   (c) any activity performed in the course of a person's employment,
   (d) any activity performed by or on behalf of a body of persons (whether corporate or unincorporate).

(3) Condition A is that a person performing the function or activity is expected to perform it in good faith.

(4) Condition B is that a person performing the function or activity is expected to perform it impartially.

(5) Condition C is that a person performing the function or activity is in a position of trust by virtue of performing it.

(6) A function or activity is a relevant function or activity even if it
    (a) has no connection with the United Kingdom, and
    (b) is performed in a country or territory outside the United Kingdom.

(7) In this section "business" includes trade or profession.

4 Improper performance to which bribe relates

(1) For the purposes of this Act a relevant function or activity
    (a) is performed improperly if it is performed in breach of a relevant expectation, and
    (b) is to be treated as being performed improperly if there is a failure to perform the function or activity and that failure is itself a breach of a relevant expectation.

(2) In subsection (1) "relevant expectation"
    (a) in relation to a function or activity which meets condition A or B, means the expectation mentioned in the condition concerned, and
    (b) in relation to a function or activity which meets condition C, means any expectation as to the manner in which, or the reasons for which, the function or activity will be performed that arises from the position of trust mentioned in that condition.

(3) Anything that a person does (or omits to do) arising from or in connection with that person's past performance of a relevant function or activity is to be treated for the purposes of this Act as being done (or omitted) by that person in the performance of that function or activity.

5 Expectation test

(1) For the purposes of sections 3 and 4, the test of what is expected is a test of what a reasonable person in the United Kingdom would expect in relation to the performance of the type of function or activity concerned.

(2) In deciding what such a person would expect in relation to the performance of a function or activity where the performance is not subject to the law of any part of the United Kingdom, any local custom or practice is to be disregarded unless it is permitted or required by the written law applicable to the country or territory concerned.

(3) In subsection (2) "written law" means law contained in
    (a) any written constitution, or provision made by or under legislation, applicable to the country or territory concerned, or
    (b) any judicial decision which is so applicable and is evidenced in published written sources.

Bribery of foreign public officials

6 Bribery of foreign public officials

(1) A person ("P") who bribes a foreign public official ("F") is guilty of an offence if P's intention is to influence F in F's capacity as a foreign public official.

(2) P must also intend to obtain or retain
    (a) business, or
    (b) an advantage in the conduct of business.

(3) P bribes F if, and only if

      (a) directly or through a third party, P offers, promises or gives any financial or other advantage
          (i) to F, or
          (ii) to another person at F's request or with F's assent or acquiescence, and
      (b) F is neither permitted nor required by the written law applicable to F to be influenced in F's capacity as a foreign public official by the offer, promise or gift.

(4)   References in this section to influencing F in F's capacity as a foreign public official mean influencing F in the performance of F's functions as such an official, which includes
      (a) any omission to exercise those functions, and
      (b) any use of F's position as such an official, even if not within F's authority.

(5)   "Foreign public official" means an individual who
      (a) holds a legislative, administrative or judicial position of any kind, whether appointed or elected, of a country or territory outside the United Kingdom (or any subdivision of such a country or territory),
      (b) exercises a public function
          (i) for or on behalf of a country or territory outside the United Kingdom (or any subdivision of such a country or territory), or
          (ii) for any public agency or public enterprise of that country or territory (or subdivision), or
      (c) is an official or agent of a public international organisation.

(6)   "Public international organisation" means an organisation whose members are any of the following
      (a) countries or territories,
      (b) governments of countries or territories,
      (c) other public international organisations,
      (d) a mixture of any of the above.

(7)   For the purposes of subsection (3)(b), the written law applicable to F is
      (a) where the performance of the functions of F which P intends to influence would be subject to the law of any part of the United Kingdom, the law of that part of the United Kingdom,
      (b) where paragraph (a) does not apply and F is an official or agent of a public international organisation, the applicable written rules of that organisation,
      (c) where paragraphs (a) and (b) do not apply, the law of the country or territory in relation to which F is a foreign public official so far as that law is contained in
          (i) any written constitution, or provision made by or under legislation, applicable to the country or territory concerned, or
          (ii) any judicial decision which is so applicable and is evidenced in published written sources.

(8)   For the purposes of this section, a trade or profession is a business.

Failure of commercial organisations to prevent bribery

7 Failure of commercial organisations to prevent bribery

(1)   A relevant commercial organisation ("C") is guilty of an offence under this section if a person ("A") associated with C bribes another person intending
      (a) to obtain or retain business for C, or
      (b) to obtain or retain an advantage in the conduct of business for C.

(2)   But it is a defence for C to prove that C had in place adequate procedures designed to prevent persons associated with C from undertaking such conduct.

(3)   For the purposes of this section, A bribes another person if, and only if, A
      (a) is, or would be, guilty of an offence under section 1 or 6 (whether or not A has been

prosecuted for such an offence), or

(b) would be guilty of such an offence if section 12(2)(c) and (4) were omitted.

(4) See section 8 for the meaning of a person associated with C and see section 9 for a duty on the Secretary of State to publish guidance.

(5) In this section

"partnership" means

(a) a partnership within the Partnership Act 1890, or

(b) a limited partnership registered under the Limited Partnerships Act 1907,

or a firm or entity of a similar character formed under the law of a country or territory outside the United Kingdom,

"relevant commercial organisation" means

(a) a body which is incorporated under the law of any part of the United Kingdom and which carries on a business (whether there or elsewhere),

(b) any other body corporate (wherever incorporated) which carries on a business, or part of a business, in any part of the United Kingdom,

(c) a partnership which is formed under the law of any part of the United Kingdom and which carries on a business (whether there or elsewhere), or

(d) any other partnership (wherever formed) which carries on a business, or part of a business, in any part of the United Kingdom,

and, for the purposes of this section, a trade or profession is a business.

8 Meaning of associated person

(1) For the purposes of section 7, a person ("A") is associated with C if (disregarding any bribe under consideration) A is a person who performs services for or on behalf of C.

(2) The capacity in which A performs services for or on behalf of C does not matter.

(3) Accordingly A may (for example) be C's employee, agent or subsidiary.

(4) Whether or not A is a person who performs services for or on behalf of C is to be determined by reference to all the relevant circumstances and not merely by reference to the nature of the relationship between A and C.

(5) But if A is an employee of C, it is to be presumed unless the contrary is shown that A is a person who performs services for or on behalf of C.

9 Guidance about commercial organisations preventing bribery

(1) The Secretary of State must publish guidance about procedures that relevant commercial organisations can put in place to prevent persons associated with them from bribing as mentioned in section 7(1).

(2) The Secretary of State may, from time to time, publish revisions to guidance under this section or revised guidance.

(3) The Secretary of State must consult the Scottish Ministers and the Department of Justice in Northern Ireland before publishing anything under this section.

(4) Publication under this section is to be in such manner as the Secretary of State considers appropriate.

(5) Expressions used in this section have the same meaning as in section 7.

Prosecution and penalties

10 Consent to prosecution

(1) No proceedings for an offence under this Act may be instituted in England and Wales except by or with the consent of

(a) the Director of Public Prosecutions, or

(b) the Director of the Serious Fraud Office,

(c) *Repealed*

(2) No proceedings for an offence under this Act may be instituted in Northern Ireland except by or with the consent of

(a) the Director of Public Prosecutions for Northern Ireland, or

(b) the Director of the Serious Fraud Office.

(3) No proceedings for an offence under this Act may be instituted in England and Wales or Northern Ireland by a person

(a) who is acting

(i) under the direction or instruction of the Director of Public Prosecutions or the Director of the Serious Fraud Office, or

(ii) on behalf of such a Director, or

(b) to whom such a function has been assigned by such a Director,

except with the consent of the Director concerned to the institution of the proceedings.

(4) The Director of Public Prosecutions and the Director of the Serious Fraud Office must exercise personally any function under subsection (1), (2) or (3) of giving consent.

(5) The only exception is if

(a) the Director concerned is unavailable, and

(b) there is another person who is designated in writing by the Director acting personally as the person who is authorised to exercise any such function when the Director is unavailable.

(6) In that case, the other person may exercise the function but must do so personally.

(7) Subsections (4) to (6) apply instead of any other provisions which would otherwise have enabled any function of the Director of Public Prosecutions or the Director of the Serious Fraud Office under subsection (1), (2) or (3) of giving consent to be exercised by a person other than the Director concerned.

(8) No proceedings for an offence under this Act may be instituted in Northern Ireland by virtue of section 36 of the Justice (Northern Ireland) Act 2002 (delegation of the functions of the Director of Public Prosecutions for Northern Ireland to persons other than the Deputy Director) except with the consent of the Director of Public Prosecutions for Northern Ireland to the institution of the proceedings.

(9) The Director of Public Prosecutions for Northern Ireland must exercise personally any function under subsection (2) or (8) of giving consent unless the function is exercised personally by the Deputy Director of Public Prosecutions for Northern Ireland by virtue of section 30(4) or (7) of the Act of 2002 (powers of Deputy Director to exercise functions of Director).

(10) Subsection (9) applies instead of section 36 of the Act of 2002 in relation to the functions of the Director of Public Prosecutions for Northern Ireland and the Deputy Director of Public Prosecutions for Northern Ireland under, or (as the case may be) by virtue of, subsections (2) and (8) above of giving consent.

11 Penalties

(1) An individual guilty of an offence under section 1, 2 or 6 is liable

(a) on summary conviction, to imprisonment for a term not exceeding 12 months, or to a fine not exceeding the statutory maximum, or to both,

(b) on conviction on indictment, to imprisonment for a term not exceeding 10 years, or to a fine, or to both.

(2) Any other person guilty of an offence under section 1, 2 or 6 is liable

(a) on summary conviction, to a fine not exceeding the statutory maximum,

(b)   on conviction on indictment, to a fine.

(3)   A person guilty of an offence under section 7 is liable on conviction on indictment to a fine.

(4)   The reference in subsection (1)(a) to 12 months is to be read

    (a)   in its application to England and Wales in relation to an offence committed before the commencement of section 154(1) of the Criminal Justice Act 2003, and

    (b)   in its application to Northern Ireland,

as a reference to 6 months.

Other provisions about offences

12   Offences under this Act: territorial application

(1)   An offence is committed under section 1, 2 or 6 in England and Wales, Scotland or Northern Ireland if any act or omission which forms part of the offence takes place in that part of the United Kingdom.

(2)   Subsection (3) applies if

    (a)   no act or omission which forms part of an offence under section 1, 2 or 6 takes place in the United Kingdom,

    (b)   a person's acts or omissions done or made outside the United Kingdom would form part of such an offence if done or made in the United Kingdom, and

    (c)   that person has a close connection with the United Kingdom.

(3)   In such a case

    (a)   the acts or omissions form part of the offence referred to in subsection (2)(a), and

    (b)   proceedings for the offence may be taken at any place in the United Kingdom.

(4)   For the purposes of subsection (2)(c) a person has a close connection with the United Kingdom if, and only if, the person was one of the following at the time the acts or omissions concerned were done or made

    (a)   a British citizen,

    (b)   a British overseas territories citizen,

    (c)   a British National (Overseas),

    (d)   a British Overseas citizen,

    (e)   a person who under the British Nationality Act 1981 was a British subject,

    (f) a British protected person within the meaning of that Act,

    (g)   an individual ordinarily resident in the United Kingdom,

    (h)   a body incorporated under the law of any part of the United Kingdom,

    (i) a Scottish partnership.

(5)   An offence is committed under section 7 irrespective of whether the acts or omissions which form part of the offence take place in the United Kingdom or elsewhere.

(6)   Where no act or omission which forms part of an offence under section 7 takes place in the United Kingdom, proceedings for the offence may be taken at any place in the United Kingdom.

(7)   Subsection (8) applies if, by virtue of this section, proceedings for an offence are to be taken in Scotland against a person.

(8)   Such proceedings may be taken

    (a)   in any sheriff court district in which the person is apprehended or in custody, or

    (b)   in such sheriff court district as the Lord Advocate may determine.

(9)   In subsection (8) "sheriff court district" is to be read in accordance with section 307(1) of the Criminal Procedure (Scotland) Act 1995.

13 Defence for certain bribery offences etc

(1) It is a defence for a person charged with a relevant bribery offence to prove that the person's conduct was necessary for
    (a) the proper exercise of any function of an intelligence service, or
    (b) the proper exercise of any function of the armed forces when engaged on active service.

(2) The head of each intelligence service must ensure that the service has in place arrangements designed to ensure that any conduct of a member of the service which would otherwise be a relevant bribery offence is necessary for a purpose falling within subsection (1)(a).

(3) The Defence Council must ensure that the armed forces have in place arrangements designed to ensure that any conduct of
    (a) a member of the armed forces who is engaged on active service, or
    (b) a civilian subject to service discipline when working in support of any person falling within paragraph (a),
which would otherwise be a relevant bribery offence is necessary for a purpose falling within subsection (1)(b).

(4) The arrangements which are in place by virtue of subsection (2) or (3) must be arrangements which the Secretary of State considers to be satisfactory.

(5) For the purposes of this section, the circumstances in which a person's conduct is necessary for a purpose falling within subsection (1)(a) or (b) are to be treated as including any circumstances in which the person's conduct
    (a) would otherwise be an offence under section 2, and
    (b) involves conduct by another person which, but for subsection (1)(a) or (b), would be an offence under section 1.

(6) In this section
"active service" means service in
    (a) an action or operation against an enemy,
    (b) an operation outside the British Islands for the protection of life or property, or
    (c) the military occupation of a foreign country or territory,
"armed forces" means Her Majesty's forces (within the meaning of the Armed Forces Act 2006),
"civilian subject to service discipline" and "enemy" have the same meaning as in the Act of 2006,
"GCHQ" has the meaning given by section 3(3) of the Intelligence Services Act 1994,
"head" means
    (a) in relation to the Security Service, the Director General of the Security Service,
    (b) in relation to the Secret Intelligence Service, the Chief of the Secret Intelligence Service, and
    (c) in relation to GCHQ, the Director of GCHQ,
"intelligence service" means the Security Service, the Secret Intelligence Service or GCHQ,
"relevant bribery offence" means
    (a) an offence under section 1 which would not also be an offence under section 6,
    (b) an offence under section 2,
    (c) an offence committed by aiding, abetting, counselling or procuring the commission of an offence falling within paragraph (a) or (b),
    (d) an offence of attempting or conspiring to commit, or of inciting the commission of, an offence falling within paragraph (a) or (b), or
    (e) an offence under Part 2 of the Serious Crime Act 2007 (encouraging or

assisting crime) in relation to an offence falling within paragraph (a) or (b).

14 Offences under sections 1, 2 and 6 by bodies corporate etc

(1) This section applies if an offence under section 1, 2 or 6 is committed by a body corporate or a Scottish partnership.

(2) If the offence is proved to have been committed with the consent or connivance of
   (a) a senior officer of the body corporate or Scottish partnership, or
   (b) a person purporting to act in such a capacity,
the senior officer or person (as well as the body corporate or partnership) is guilty of the offence and liable to be proceeded against and punished accordingly.

(3) But subsection (2) does not apply, in the case of an offence which is committed under section 1, 2 or 6 by virtue of section 12(2) to (4), to a senior officer or person purporting to act in such a capacity unless the senior officer or person has a close connection with the United Kingdom (within the meaning given by section 12(4)).

(4) In this section
   "director", in relation to a body corporate whose affairs are managed by its members, means a member of the body corporate,
   "senior officer" means
      (a) in relation to a body corporate, a director, manager, secretary or other similar officer of the body corporate, and
      (b) in relation to a Scottish partnership, a partner in the partnership.

15 Offences under section 7 by partnerships

(1) Proceedings for an offence under section 7 alleged to have been committed by a partnership must be brought in the name of the partnership (and not in that of any of the partners).

(2) For the purposes of such proceedings
   (a) rules of court relating to the service of documents have effect as if the partnership were a body corporate, and
   (b) the following provisions apply as they apply in relation to a body corporate
      (i) section 33 of the Criminal Justice Act 1925 and Schedule 3 to the Magistrates' Courts Act 1980,
      (ii) section 18 of the Criminal Justice Act (Northern Ireland) 1945 (c 15 (NI)) and Schedule 4 to the Magistrates' Courts (Northern Ireland) Order 1981 (SI 1981/1675 (NI 26)),
      (iii) section 70 of the Criminal Procedure (Scotland) Act 1995.

(3) A fine imposed on the partnership on its conviction for an offence under section 7 is to be paid out of the partnership assets.

(4) In this section "partnership" has the same meaning as in section 7.

Supplementary and final provisions

16 Application to Crown

This Act applies to individuals in the public service of the Crown as it applies to other individuals.

17 Consequential provision

(1) The following common law offences are abolished
   (a) the offences under the law of England and Wales and Northern Ireland of bribery and embracery,

    (b) the offences under the law of Scotland of bribery and accepting a bribe.

(2) Schedule 1 (which contains consequential amendments) has effect.

(3) Schedule 2 (which contains repeals and revocations) has effect.

(4) The relevant national authority may by order make such supplementary, incidental or consequential provision as the relevant national authority considers appropriate for the purposes of this Act or in consequence of this Act.

(5) The power to make an order under this section
    (a) is exercisable by statutory instrument (subject to subsection (9A)),
    (b) includes power to make transitional, transitory or saving provision,
    (c) may, in particular, be exercised by amending, repealing, revoking or otherwise modifying any provision made by or under an enactment (including any Act passed in the same Session as this Act).

(6) Subject to subsection (7), a statutory instrument containing an order of the Secretary of State under this section may not be made unless a draft of the instrument has been laid before, and approved by a resolution of, each House of Parliament.

(7) A statutory instrument containing an order of the Secretary of State under this section which does not amend or repeal a provision of a public general Act or of devolved legislation is subject to annulment in pursuance of a resolution of either House of Parliament.

(8) Subject to subsection (9), a statutory instrument containing an order of the Scottish Ministers under this section may not be made unless a draft of the instrument has been laid before, and approved by a resolution of, the Scottish Parliament.

(9) A statutory instrument containing an order of the Scottish Ministers under this section which does not amend or repeal a provision of an Act of the Scottish Parliament or of a public general Act is subject to annulment in pursuance of a resolution of the Scottish Parliament.

(9A) The power of the Department of Justice in Northern Ireland to make an order under this section is exercisable by statutory rule for the purposes of the Statutory Rules (Northern Ireland) Order 1979 (and not by statutory instrument).

(9B) Subject to subsection (9C), an order of the Department of Justice in Northern Ireland made under this section is subject to affirmative resolution (within the meaning of section 41(4) of the Interpretation Act (Northern Ireland) 1954).

(9C) An order of the Department of Justice in Northern Ireland made under this section which does not amend or repeal a provision of an Act of the Northern Ireland Assembly or of a public general Act is subject to negative resolution (within the meaning of section 41(6) of the Interpretation Act (Northern Ireland) 1954).

(10) In this section
    "devolved legislation" means an Act of the Scottish Parliament, a Measure of the National Assembly for Wales or an Act of the Northern Ireland Assembly,
    "enactment" includes an Act of the Scottish Parliament and Northern Ireland legislation,
    "relevant national authority" means
        (a) in the case of provision which would be within the legislative competence of the Scottish Parliament if it were contained in an Act of that Parliament, the Scottish Ministers,
        (aa) in the case of provision which could be made by an Act of the Northern Ireland Assembly without the consent of the Secretary of State (see sections 6 to 8 of the Northern Ireland Act 1998), the Department of Justice in Northern Ireland, and
        (b) in any other case, the Secretary of State.

18 Extent

(1) Subject as follows, this Act extends to England and Wales, Scotland and Northern Ireland.

(2) Subject to subsections (3) to (5), any amendment, repeal or revocation made by Schedule 1 or 2 has the same extent as the provision amended, repealed or revoked.

(3) The amendment of, and repeals in, the Armed Forces Act 2006 do not extend to the Channel Islands.

(4) The amendments of the International Criminal Court Act 2001 extend to England and Wales and Northern Ireland only.

(5) Subsection (2) does not apply to the repeal in the Civil Aviation Act 1982.

19 Commencement and transitional provision etc

(1) Subject to subsection (2), this Act comes into force on such day as the Secretary of State may by order made by statutory instrument appoint.

(2) Sections 16, 17(4) to (10) and 18, this section (other than subsections (5) to (7)) and section 20 come into force on the day on which this Act is passed.

(3) An order under subsection (1) may
   (a) appoint different days for different purposes,
   (b) make such transitional, transitory or saving provision as the Secretary of State considers appropriate in connection with the coming into force of any provision of this Act.

(4) The Secretary of State must consult the Scottish Ministers before making an order under this section in connection with any provision of this Act which would be within the legislative competence of the Scottish Parliament if it were contained in an Act of that Parliament.

(5) This Act does not affect any liability, investigation, legal proceeding or penalty for or in respect of
   (a) a common law offence mentioned in subsection (1) of section 17 which is committed wholly or partly before the coming into force of that subsection in relation to such an offence, or
   (b) an offence under the Public Bodies Corrupt Practices Act 1889 or the Prevention of Corruption Act 1906 committed wholly or partly before the coming into force of the repeal of the Act by Schedule 2 to this Act.

(6) For the purposes of subsection (5) an offence is partly committed before a particular time if any act or omission which forms part of the offence takes place before that time.

(7) Subsections (5) and (6) are without prejudice to section 16 of the Interpretation Act 1978 (general savings on repeal).

20 Short title

This Act may be cited as the Bribery Act 2010.

SCHEDULE 1
Consequential Amendments

Not reproduced

SCHEDULE 2
Repeals and Revocations

Not reproduced

City of London (Various Powers) Act 1957

An Act to make further provision with respect to ward elections in the city of London to confer further powers on the corporation of London with respect to the provision of garaging and parking accommodation for vehicles and for other purposes

6th June 1957

PART I
PRELIMINARY

1 Short title

This Act may be cited as the City of London (Various Powers) Act 1957.

2 Division of Act into Parts

This Act is divided into Parts as follows:

Part I.Preliminary.

Part II.Ward elections.

Part III.Miscellaneous.

3 Interpretation

(1) In this Act unless there be something in the subject or context repugnant to such construction

"city" means the city of London;

"common council" means the mayor aldermen and commons of the city in common council assembled;

"Corporation" means the mayor and commonalty and citizens of the city acting by the common council.

(2) Unless otherwise expressly stated any reference in this Act to any enactment shall be construed as a reference to that enactment as applied extended amended or varied by or by virtue of any subsequent enactment including this Act.

PART II
WARD ELECTIONS

4 Interpretation of Part II

(1)   In this Part of this Act unless there be something in the subject or context repugnant to such construction

"Act of 1983" means the Representation of the People Act 1983;

"citizen of the Union" shall be construed in accordance with Article 8.1 of the Treaty establishing the European Community (as amended by Title II of the Treaty on European Union) and "relevant citizen of the Union" means such a citizen who is not a Commonwealth citizen or a citizen of the Republic of Ireland;

"local elections rules" means the local elections rules made by the Secretary of State under section 36 of the Act of 1983 as applied and modified by virtue of subsection (4) of section 8 (Manner of voting at ward elections) of this Act;

"qualifying date" means the date determined in accordance with subsections (4) and (5) of section 3 (Qualification of voters at ward elections) of the City of London (Ward Elections) Act 2002;

"rateable" means liable for the time being to be rated to the poor rate of the city;

"regulations of 1950" means the Representation of the People Regulations 1950 or any other regulations from time to time amending or replacing those regulations;

"town clerk" means the town clerk of the city and includes any person duly appointed to discharge temporarily the duties of that officer;

"ward election" means an election for alderman or common councilman for any ward of the city;

"ward list" means the list of persons entitled to vote at any ward election prepared in accordance with section 7 (Ward lists) of this Act.

(2)   *Repealed*

5 Qualification of candidate for election to common council

(1)   A person shall unless disqualified by virtue of any enactment be qualified for election to the common council as a common councilman if at the date of nomination and at the date of election he is a freeman of the city and is of full age and a British subject or a citizen of the Republic of Ireland or a relevant citizen of the Union and

(a)   is registered in the list of persons entitled to vote at any ward election; or

(b)   owns freehold or leasehold land in the city; or

(c)   has during the whole of the twelve months preceding the date of nomination, and has until the date of election, resided in the city.

(2)   A person shall not be qualified for election to the common council as a common councilman otherwise than in accordance with this section.

NOTES

Defined terms
   city: s 3(1)
   common council: s 3(1)

relevant citizen of the Union: s 4(1)

6 Qualification of voters at ward elections

(1)   The persons entitled to vote in any ward of the city as electors at a ward election shall be those who on the qualifying date are of full age and

(a)   are occupying as owner or tenant the whole or part of a hereditament which is shown in a local non-domestic rating list, which is in that ward, and for which the rateable value shown in that list is not less than £10; or

(b)   are resident in that ward; or

(c)   are persons appointed in writing as voters by a qualifying body which ordinarily occupies as owner or tenant any premises situated in that ward, being premises in respect of which the right to appoint one or more voters depends on the size of the workforce there;

and who on that date and on the date of the poll are not subject to any legal incapacity to vote and are Commonwealth citizens or citizens of the Republic of Ireland or, in the case of a ward election for common councilmen, relevant citizens of the Union:

Provided that a person shall not be entitled to vote as an elector at a ward election unless registered in the ward list for that ward to be used at that election.

(2) *Repealed*

(3) In this section "occupies" shall be construed in accordance with subsection (1) of section 2 of the City of London (Ward Elections) Act 2002; and "qualifying body" and "workforce" have the respective meanings given by that subsection.

NOTES

Defined terms
city: s 3(1)
qualifying date: s 4(1)
rateable: s 4(1)
relevant citizen of the Union: s 4(1)

ward election: s 4(1)
ward list: s 4(1)

7 Ward lists

(1) It shall be the duty of the town clerk to prepare and publish with respect to each ward of the city a ward list of all persons entitled to vote in that ward as electors at a ward election.

(2) With a view to the preparation of such ward lists the town clerk shall have a house to house or other sufficient inquiry made as to the persons entitled to vote as electors at a ward election.

(3) On or before the 30th November in each year the town clerk shall prepare and publish provisional lists showing the persons appearing to him to be so entitled and such lists shall be made available for inspection and shall remain open for inspection until the date of publication of the ward lists.

(4) On or before the 16th December in each year any person whose name does not appear in any such provisional list may submit a claim to the town clerk for his name to be included in a ward list and any person appearing from any provisional list to be entitled to have his own name included in a ward list may submit an objection to the town clerk to the inclusion in such ward list of the name of any other person included in the provisional list relating thereto and the town clerk shall determine any such claim or objection in accordance with regulations 8 to 15 of the regulations of 1950 so far as material as if those regulations with any necessary modifications (including modifications of dates) applied to ward lists.

(5) On or before the 15th February in each year ward lists shall be published and such lists shall be the lists of all persons entitled to vote as electors at ward elections to be held between the said 15th February and the 16th February in the following year. The ward lists shall be made available for inspection and shall remain open for inspection between the date of publication and the 16th February in the following year.

(6) The provisional lists and the ward lists may be inspected by any person without payment at all reasonable hours at the offices of the town clerk and copies of the ward lists may be purchased thereat at a price of 5p for each list.

(7) The town clerk shall supply to each ward clerk a copy of the ward list relating to his ward as soon as such list is made available for inspection.

(8) For the purposes of this section regulations 22 and 70 of the regulations of 1950 shall so far as they are applicable for such purposes apply and have effect with any necessary modifications including the substitution of the words "the town clerk" for the words "the

registration officer" where they occur therein.

NOTES
Defined terms
  city: s 3(1)
  regulations of 1950: s 4(1)
  town clerk: s 4(1)

                                          ward election: s 4(1)

8 Manner of voting at ward elections

(1) Subject as hereinafter provided the following provisions of the Act of 1983 shall in addition to the provisions which apply by virtue of sections 191 to 196 of that Act apply to and in respect of ward elections:

  section 3 (disfranchisement of offenders in prison, etc);

  section 3A (disfranchisement of offenders detained in mental hospitals);

  section 6 (residence: merchant seamen);

  sections 14(1) and 15 to 17 (service qualifications and declarations for registration);

  section 46 (further provision as to local election voting);

  section 59 (supplemental provisions as to members of forces and service voters).

(2) Subject as hereinafter provided, Schedule 4 to the Representation of the People Act 2000 shall apply to and in respect of ward elections, but as if any reference to the polling station allotted or likely to be allotted to any person under rules made (or having effect as if made) under section 36 of the Representation of the People Act 1983 were a reference to the polling station provided or likely to be provided by the returning officer.

(4) For the purposes of the said provisions of the Act of 1983 or the Act of 2000 as applied to and in respect of ward elections by virtue of subsection (1) or (2) of this section the local elections rules and the regulations of 1950 shall so far as the same are applicable for such purposes apply and have effect with any necessary modifications:

  Provided that

  (i) for the purposes of rule 20 of the Local Elections (Principal Areas) Rules 1973 the town clerk shall act instead of the returning officer;

  (ii) for the purposes of regulations 36 to 48 of the regulations of 1950 the functions of the returning officer shall be performed by the town clerk and subsection (1) of regulation 38 thereof shall have effect as if the persons referred to therein included the town clerk; and

  (iii) regulation 49 of the said regulations shall have effect as if for subsection (1) thereof there were substituted the following subsections:

  "(1) When the postal voters' ballot box has been opened the town clerk shall count and note the number of covering envelopes. He shall then make up separate sealed packages containing the covering envelopes relating to each ward and shall deliver each such sealed package to the returning officer of the appropriate ward so that it shall be received by him before the count.

  (1A) The returning officer shall on receipt of the package containing the covering envelopes relating to his ward open each covering envelope separately."

(5) For the purposes of the provisions of the Act of 1983 or the Act of 2000 as applied to and in respect of ward elections by virtue of subsection (1) or (2) of this section and for the purposes of the local elections rules and the regulations of 1950 as so applied by virtue of subsection (4) of this section the following expressions shall have the following meanings:

  "day of election" means the day of the wardmote;

  "electoral area" means any ward in the city;

  "local government area" means the city;

  "local government election" includes a ward election;

  "qualifying address" means the address specified in respect of each person in the ward list;

"qualifying date" has the same meaning as in this Part of this Act;

"registration officer" means the town clerk;

"returning officer" means the presiding officer at the ward election;

"vote" does not include voting otherwise than on a poll.

NOTES

Defined terms

the Act of 1983: s 4(1)

city: s 3(1)

local elections rules: s 4(1)

qualifying date: s 4(1)

regulations of 1950: s 4(1)

town clerk: s 4(1)

ward election: s 4(1)

ward list: s 4(1)

9 Appeals relating to ward lists

(1) An appeal shall lie to the Mayor's and City of London Court from any decision of the town clerk under this Part of this Act or under any provision applied by virtue of this Part of this Act on any claim by any person for his name to be included in a ward list or in any special list prepared by the town clerk in accordance with the local elections rules or on any objection by another person made to and considered by the town clerk.

(2) No appeal shall lie from the decision of the Court of Appeal on appeal from a decision of the Mayor's and City of London Court under this section.

(3) Notice shall be sent to the town clerk in manner provided by the rules of court of the decision of the Mayor's and City of London Court or of the Court of Appeal on any appeal by virtue of this section and the town clerk shall make such alteration in the ward lists or the special lists (as the case may be) as may be required to give effect to the decision.

(4) The regulations and rules of court relating to appeals made in pursuance of the Act of 1983 shall with any necessary adaptations apply to appeals brought by virtue of this section.

NOTES

Defined terms

the Act of 1983: s 4(1)

local elections rules: s 4(1)

town clerk: s 4(1)

ward list: s 4(1)

10 Expenses of the town clerk

The expenses incurred by the town clerk in connection with his duties under this Part of this Act shall be paid by the Corporation out of the general rate of the city.

NOTES

Defined terms

city: s 3(1)

Corporation: s 3(1)

town clerk: s 4(1)

11 Repeal and amendment of enactments

(1) Part II (Ward elections) of the City of London (Various Powers) Act 1949 is hereby repealed and section 3 (Interpretation) of the said Act shall have effect as if the words therein after the words "in common council assembled" where those words secondly occur to the end of the section were omitted.

(2) Section 5 (Days and times for opening and closing the poll) of the City of London Ballot Act 1887 shall have effect in relation to ward elections

(i) as if for the words "hour of ten in the forenoon" there were substituted the words "hour of eight in the forenoon"; and

(ii) as if for the words "hour of six in the afternoon" there were substituted the words "hour of eight in the afternoon".

PART III
MISCELLANEOUS

These provisions are not relevant to elections and are not reproduced

City of London (Ward Elections) Act 2002

2002 CHAPTER vi

An Act to make further provision with respect to the qualification of voters at ward elections in the city of London; and for connected purposes.

Whereas
(1) The qualification of voters at ward elections in the city of London is governed by Part II of the City of London (Various Powers) Act 1957 (c x):
(2) It is expedient to alter the qualification for which that Act provides better to reflect the present nature of commercial occupation of premises in the city of London by extending the categories of persons entitled to vote at such elections:
(3) It is expedient that the other connected matters dealt with in this Act should be enacted:
(4) The objects of this Act cannot be attained without the authority of Parliament:
May it therefore please Your Majesty that it may be enacted, and be it enacted, by the Queen's most Excellent Majesty, by and with the advice and consent of the Lords Spiritual and Temporal, and Commons, in this present Parliament assembled, and by the authority of the same, as follows:

1 Short title

This Act may be cited as the City of London (Ward Elections) Act 2002.

2 Interpretation

(1) In this Act
"the 1957 Act" means the City of London (Various Powers) Act 1957 (c x);
"city" means city of London;
"occupying", in relation to any premises, means occupying for relevant purposes by personal physical presence there and, in the case of a qualifying body, includes such occupation
(a) through a director, officer, employee or agent of that body, or
(b) through a holder of any paid or unpaid office for the performance of whose functions accommodation is being provided by a qualifying body;
"qualifying body" means a body corporate or an unincorporated body other than a partnership within the meaning of section 1 of the Partnership Act 1890 (c 39);
"relevant purposes" means the carrying on of any trade, business, profession or other occupation or calling, or the performance of the functions of any paid or unpaid office, being functions for whose performance accommodation is being provided by a

qualifying body (whether or not they are functions of that body);

"workforce", in relation to a qualifying body, means all those persons whose principal or only place of work on the qualifying date is ordinarily the premises in respect of which that body's right to appoint voters arises, and who work for that body.

(2) For the purposes of this Act an unincorporated body which is occupying any premises shall be taken to be doing so as owner or tenant whether or not the person who is on its behalf the owner or tenant of those premises is occupying them.

(3) This Act shall be construed as one with Part II of the 1957 Act.

3 Qualification of voters at ward elections

(1) *Amends the 1957 Act: not reproduced here*

(2) The extent of the right to appoint mentioned in section 6(1)(c) of the 1957 Act as depending on the size of the workforce shall be

    (a) one for a workforce of up to 5, plus one for every 5 by which a workforce exceeds 5, up to a workforce of 50; and

    (b) for a workforce that exceeds 50, the number given by paragraph (a) of this subsection plus 1 for every 50 of that excess.

(3) In the case of a workforce of over 5 whose number is not exactly divisible by 5 or 50, as the case may be, the remainder shall be disregarded for the purposes of subsection (2) above.

(4) For ward elections to be held during the period of 12 months beginning with 16th February in the appointed year or during the period of 12 months beginning with that date in any subsequent year, the qualifying date is 1st September in the preceding year.

(5) For the purposes of subsection (4)

    (a) if this Act is passed before 1st September in the year in which it is passed, the appointed year is the year next after that year;

    (b) if not, the appointed year is the year next but one after the year in which it is passed.

(6) No person shall be entitled to vote in more than one ward or more than once in a ward at any ward elections; and accordingly no person shall be registered in more than one ward list or more than once in a ward list.

(7) For the purposes of section 6 of the 1957 Act, any premises partly situated in each of two or more wards of the city shall be treated as being situated wholly within the ward which appears to the town clerk to contain the greater or, as the case may be, the greatest part of the premises.

(8) Where, apart from this subsection, sections 6(1)(a) and 6(1)(c) of the 1957 Act would both apply in relation to the same premises, only section 6(1)(a) shall apply in relation to those premises.

4 Allocation of appointments

A qualifying body which is entitled to appoint more than one person as a voter pursuant to section 6(1)(c) of the 1957 Act shall ensure that the appointments which it makes reflect, so far as is reasonably practicable, the composition of the workforce.

5 Requirements as to connection of persons appointed with the city

(1) A person shall not be appointed as a voter pursuant to section 6(1)(c) of the 1957 Act unless on the qualifying date

    (a) the conditions specified in subsection (2) below are fulfilled in respect of him; or

    (b) one of the alternative conditions specified in subsection (3) below is fulfilled in respect of him and, if he no longer has his principal or only place of work within the city, the further condition specified in subsection (4) below is also fulfilled in respect of him.

(2) The conditions referred to in subsection (1)(a) above are that
   (a) the person's principal or only place of work is within the city and has been within the city for the whole of the twelve months preceding the qualifying date; and
   (b) he works for the qualifying body proposing to appoint him and has so worked throughout those twelve months.

(3) The alternative conditions referred to in subsection (1)(b) above are that the person's principal or only place of work has been within the city for an aggregate period
   (a) of at least five years, during the whole of which the person has worked exclusively for the qualifying body proposing to appoint him, or
   (b) of at least ten years in any other case.

(4) The further condition referred to in subsection (1)(b) above is that at least part of the period relied on under subsection (3) above falls within the 5 years preceding the qualifying date.

(5) A person who on the qualifying date is a member of a board of directors or other governing body of a qualifying body shall, for the purposes of this section, be treated as having his principal or only place of work on that date, and for the period during which he has been a member of that board or governing body, at the premises in respect of which the entitlement to appoint by that qualifying body arises.

6 Exclusion of Crown bodies

A government department or other body exercising on behalf of the Crown functions conferred by or under any Act shall not be treated as a qualifying body within the meaning of this Act.

7 Reports

(1) Not more than 5 years after 16th February in the appointed year, the Corporation shall submit to the Secretary of State a report on the working of the provisions of this Act in relation to those ward elections to which the provisions have applied; and the Secretary of State shall lay the report before Parliament.

(2) The Corporation shall submit further such reports, at such intervals, as the Secretary of State may require; and the Secretary of State shall lay any such report before Parliament.

(3) In this section "the appointed year" has the meaning given by section 3(5) above.

8 Ward lists: qualifying bodies

(1) The inquiries which the town clerk is required to have made under section 7(2) of the 1957 Act as to the persons entitled to vote at ward elections shall include inquiries for the purpose of identifying qualifying bodies; and such inquiries constitute registration duties for the purpose of regulation 29 of the Representation of the People Regulations 1986 (SI 1986/1081).

(2) Before 1st September next after the passing of this Act, and before each subsequent 1st September, the town clerk shall send to each qualifying body known to him to be occupying any premises in the city a notice
   (a) stating the maximum number of persons which that body may appoint as voters in accordance with the provisions of section 3(2) above; and
   (b) requesting the body to inform him, in writing, of the persons appointed by that body pursuant to section 6(1)(c) of the 1957 Act.

(3) The town clerk shall include in the provisional ward list prepared by him for any ward under section 7(3) of the 1957 Act the names of all persons appointed by each qualifying body from which he has received notice of appointment.

(4) The right to submit claims or objections with respect to the contents of ward lists shall include a right for any qualifying body to submit a claim or objection through a duly authorised person acting on behalf of that body, and sections 7(4) and 9 of the 1957 Act with any necessary modifications apply accordingly.

9 Minor and consequential amendments, and repeals

(1) The enactments specified in Schedule 1 to this Act shall have effect with the amendments there specified, being minor amendments and amendments consequential on the provisions of this Act.

(2) The enactments specified in Schedule 2 to this Act are repealed to the extent specified in the second column of that Schedule.

10 Interim saving for existing system of ward elections

Any ward election held before 16th February in the appointed year (as determined by section 3(5) above) shall in all respects (including the qualification of voters) be conducted as if this Act (except paragraph 1 of Schedule 1) had not been enacted.

SCHEDULE 1
MINOR AND CONSEQUENTIAL AMENDMENTS

Not reproduced

City of London (Various Powers) Act 1957

An Act to make further provision with respect to ward elections in the city of London to confer further powers on the corporation of London with respect to the provision of garaging and parking accommodation for vehicles and for other purposes

6th June 1957

PART I PRELIMINARY

PART II WARD ELECTIONS

PART III MISCELLANEOUS

PART I
PRELIMINARY

1 Short title

This Act may be cited as the City of London (Various Powers) Act 1957.

2 Division of Act into Parts

This Act is divided into Parts as follows:

Part I.Preliminary.

Part II.Ward elections.

Part III.Miscellaneous.

3 Interpretation

(1) In this Act unless there be something in the subject or context repugnant to such construction
  "city" means the city of London;
  "common council" means the mayor aldermen and commons of the city in common council assembled;
  "Corporation" means the mayor and commonalty and citizens of the city acting by the common council.

(2) Unless otherwise expressly stated any reference in this Act to any enactment shall be construed as a reference to that enactment as applied extended amended or varied by or by virtue of any subsequent enactment including this Act.

PART II
WARD ELECTIONS

4 Interpretation of Part II

(1) In this Part of this Act unless there be something in the subject or context repugnant to such construction

"Act of 1983" means the Representation of the People Act 1983;

"citizen of the Union" shall be construed in accordance with Article 8.1 of the Treaty establishing the European Community (as amended by Title II of the Treaty on European Union) and "relevant citizen of the Union" means such a citizen who is not a Commonwealth citizen or a citizen of the Republic of Ireland;

"local elections rules" means the local elections rules made by the Secretary of State under section 36 of the Act of 1983 as applied and modified by virtue of subsection (4) of section 8 (Manner of voting at ward elections) of this Act;

"qualifying date" means the date determined in accordance with subsections (4) and (5) of section 3 (Qualification of voters at ward elections) of the City of London (Ward Elections) Act 2002;

"rateable" means liable for the time being to be rated to the poor rate of the city;

"regulations of 1950" means the Representation of the People Regulations 1950 or any other regulations from time to time amending or replacing those regulations;

"town clerk" means the town clerk of the city and includes any person duly appointed to discharge temporarily the duties of that officer;

"ward election" means an election for alderman or common councilman for any ward of the city;

"ward list" means the list of persons entitled to vote at any ward election prepared in accordance with section 7 (Ward lists) of this Act.

(2) *Repealed*

5 Qualification of candidate for election to common council

(1) A person shall unless disqualified by virtue of any enactment be qualified for election to the common council as a common councilman if at the date of nomination and at the date of election he is a freeman of the city and is of full age and a British subject or a citizen of the Republic of Ireland or a relevant citizen of the Union and

(a) is registered in the list of persons entitled to vote at any ward election; or

(b) owns freehold or leasehold land in the city; or

(c) has during the whole of the twelve months preceding the date of nomination, and has until the date of election, resided in the city.

(2) A person shall not be qualified for election to the common council as a common councilman otherwise than in accordance with this section.

NOTES

Defined terms
city: s 3(1)
common council: s 3(1)
relevant citizen of the Union: s 4(1)

6 Qualification of voters at ward elections

(1) The persons entitled to vote in any ward of the city as electors at a ward election shall be those who on the qualifying date are of full age and

(a) are occupying as owner or tenant the whole or part of a hereditament which is shown in a local non-domestic rating list, which is in that ward, and for which the rateable value shown in that list is not less than £10; or

(b) are resident in that ward; or

(c) are persons appointed in writing as voters by a qualifying body which ordinarily occupies as owner or tenant any premises situated in that ward, being premises in respect of which the right to appoint one or more voters depends on the size of the workforce there;

and who on that date and on the date of the poll are not subject to any legal incapacity to vote and are Commonwealth citizens or citizens of the Republic of Ireland or, in the case of a ward election for common councilmen, relevant citizens of the Union:

Provided that a person shall not be entitled to vote as an elector at a ward election unless registered in the ward list for that ward to be used at that election.

(2) *Repealed*

(3) In this section "occupies" shall be construed in accordance with subsection (1) of section 2 of the City of London (Ward Elections) Act 2002; and "qualifying body" and "workforce" have the respective meanings given by that subsection.

NOTES

Defined terms
  city: s 3(1)
  qualifying date: s 4(1)
  rateable: s 4(1)
  relevant citizen of the Union: s 4(1)

ward election: s 4(1)
ward list: s 4(1)

7 Ward lists

(1) It shall be the duty of the town clerk to prepare and publish with respect to each ward of the city a ward list of all persons entitled to vote in that ward as electors at a ward election.

(2) With a view to the preparation of such ward lists the town clerk shall have a house to house or other sufficient inquiry made as to the persons entitled to vote as electors at a ward election.

(3) On or before the 30th November in each year the town clerk shall prepare and publish provisional lists showing the persons appearing to him to be so entitled and such lists shall be made available for inspection and shall remain open for inspection until the date of publication of the ward lists.

(4) On or before the 16th December in each year any person whose name does not appear in any such provisional list may submit a claim to the town clerk for his name to be included in a ward list and any person appearing from any provisional list to be entitled to have his own name included in a ward list may submit an objection to the town clerk to the inclusion in such ward list of the name of any other person included in the provisional list relating thereto and the town clerk shall determine any such claim or objection in accordance with regulations 8 to 15 of the regulations of 1950 so far as material as if those regulations with any necessary modifications (including modifications of dates) applied to ward lists.

(5) On or before the 15th February in each year ward lists shall be published and such lists shall be the lists of all persons entitled to vote as electors at ward elections to be held between the said 15th February and the 16th February in the following year. The ward lists shall be made available for inspection and shall remain open for inspection between the date of publication and the 16th February in the following year.

(6) The provisional lists and the ward lists may be inspected by any person without payment at all reasonable hours at the offices of the town clerk and copies of the ward lists may be purchased thereat at a price of 5p for each list.

(7) The town clerk shall supply to each ward clerk a copy of the ward list relating to his ward as soon as such list is made available for inspection.

(8) For the purposes of this section regulations 22 and 70 of the regulations of 1950 shall so far as they are applicable for such purposes apply and have effect with any necessary modifications including the substitution of the words "the town clerk" for the words "the

registration officer" where they occur therein.

NOTES
Defined terms
  city: s 3(1)
  regulations of 1950: s 4(1)
  town clerk: s 4(1)

ward election: s 4(1)

8 Manner of voting at ward elections

(1) Subject as hereinafter provided the following provisions of the Act of 1983 shall in addition to the provisions which apply by virtue of sections 191 to 196 of that Act apply to and in respect of ward elections:

    section 3 (disfranchisement of offenders in prison, etc);

    section 3A (disfranchisement of offenders detained in mental hospitals);

    section 6 (residence: merchant seamen);

    sections 14(1) and 15 to 17 (service qualifications and declarations for registration);

    section 46 (further provision as to local election voting);

    section 59 (supplemental provisions as to members of forces and service voters).

(2) Subject as hereinafter provided, Schedule 4 to the Representation of the People Act 2000 shall apply to and in respect of ward elections, but as if any reference to the polling station allotted or likely to be allotted to any person under rules made (or having effect as if made) under section 36 of the Representation of the People Act 1983 were a reference to the polling station provided or likely to be provided by the returning officer.

(4) For the purposes of the said provisions of the Act of 1983 or the Act of 2000 as applied to and in respect of ward elections by virtue of subsection (1) or (2) of this section the local elections rules and the regulations of 1950 shall so far as the same are applicable for such purposes apply and have effect with any necessary modifications:

    Provided that

    (i) for the purposes of rule 20 of the Local Elections (Principal Areas) Rules 1973 the town clerk shall act instead of the returning officer;

    (ii) for the purposes of regulations 36 to 48 of the regulations of 1950 the functions of the returning officer shall be performed by the town clerk and subsection (1) of regulation 38 thereof shall have effect as if the persons referred to therein included the town clerk; and

    (iii) regulation 49 of the said regulations shall have effect as if for subsection (1) thereof there were substituted the following subsections:

      "(1) When the postal voters' ballot box has been opened the town clerk shall count and note the number of covering envelopes. He shall then make up separate sealed packages containing the covering envelopes relating to each ward and shall deliver each such sealed package to the returning officer of the appropriate ward so that it shall be received by him before the count.

      (1A) The returning officer shall on receipt of the package containing the covering envelopes relating to his ward open each covering envelope separately."

(5) For the purposes of the provisions of the Act of 1983 or the Act of 2000 as applied to and in respect of ward elections by virtue of subsection (1) or (2) of this section and for the purposes of the local elections rules and the regulations of 1950 as so applied by virtue of subsection (4) of this section the following expressions shall have the following meanings:

    "day of election" means the day of the wardmote;

    "electoral area" means any ward in the city;

    "local government area" means the city;

    "local government election" includes a ward election;

    "qualifying address" means the address specified in respect of each person in the ward list;

"qualifying date" has the same meaning as in this Part of this Act;

"registration officer" means the town clerk;

"returning officer" means the presiding officer at the ward election;

"vote" does not include voting otherwise than on a poll.

NOTES

Defined terms

    the Act of 1983: s 4(1)

    city: s 3(1)

    local elections rules: s 4(1)

    qualifying date: s 4(1)

    regulations of 1950: s 4(1)

    town clerk: s 4(1)

    ward election: s 4(1)

    ward list: s 4(1)

9 Appeals relating to ward lists

(1) An appeal shall lie to the Mayor's and City of London Court from any decision of the town clerk under this Part of this Act or under any provision applied by virtue of this Part of this Act on any claim by any person for his name to be included in a ward list or in any special list prepared by the town clerk in accordance with the local elections rules or on any objection by another person made to and considered by the town clerk.

(2) No appeal shall lie from the decision of the Court of Appeal on appeal from a decision of the Mayor's and City of London Court under this section.

(3) Notice shall be sent to the town clerk in manner provided by the rules of court of the decision of the Mayor's and City of London Court or of the Court of Appeal on any appeal by virtue of this section and the town clerk shall make such alteration in the ward lists or the special lists (as the case may be) as may be required to give effect to the decision.

(4) The regulations and rules of court relating to appeals made in pursuance of the Act of 1983 shall with any necessary adaptations apply to appeals brought by virtue of this section.

NOTES

Defined terms

    the Act of 1983: s 4(1)

    local elections rules: s 4(1)

    town clerk: s 4(1)

    ward list: s 4(1)

10 Expenses of the town clerk

The expenses incurred by the town clerk in connection with his duties under this Part of this Act shall be paid by the Corporation out of the general rate of the city.

NOTES

Defined terms

    city: s 3(1)

    Corporation: s 3(1)

    town clerk: s 4(1)

11 Repeal and amendment of enactments

(1) Part II (Ward elections) of the City of London (Various Powers) Act 1949 is hereby repealed and section 3 (Interpretation) of the said Act shall have effect as if the words therein after the words "in common council assembled" where those words secondly occur to the end of the section were omitted.

(2) Section 5 (Days and times for opening and closing the poll) of the City of London Ballot Act 1887 shall have effect in relation to ward elections

    (i) as if for the words "hour of ten in the forenoon" there were substituted the words "hour of eight in the forenoon"; and

    (ii) as if for the words "hour of six in the afternoon" there were substituted the words "hour of eight in the afternoon".

PART III
MISCELLANEOUS

These provisions are not relevant to elections and are not reproduced

Communications Act 2003

PART 3
RADIO AND TELEVISION SERVICES

198-318 *Not reproduced*

Programme and fairness standards for television and radio

319 OFCOM's standards code

(1) It shall be the duty of OFCOM to set, and from time to time to review and revise, such standards for the content of programmes to be included in television and radio services as appear to them best calculated to secure the standards objectives.

(2) The standards objectives are
  (a) that persons under the age of eighteen are protected;
  (b) that material likely to encourage or to incite the commission of crime or to lead to disorder is not included in television and radio services;
  (c) that news included in television and radio services is presented with due impartiality and that the impartiality requirements of section 320 are complied with;
  (d) that news included in television and radio services is reported with due accuracy;
  (e) that the proper degree of responsibility is exercised with respect to the content of programmes which are religious programmes;
  (f) that generally accepted standards are applied to the contents of television and radio services so as to provide adequate protection for members of the public from the inclusion in such services of offensive and harmful material;
  (fa) that the product placement requirements referred to in section 321(3A) are met in relation to programmes included in a television programme service (other than advertisements);
  (g) that advertising that contravenes the prohibition on political advertising set out in section 321(2) is not included in television or radio services;
  (h) that the inclusion of advertising which may be misleading, harmful or offensive in television and radio services is prevented;
  (i) that the international obligations of the United Kingdom with respect to advertising included in television and radio services are complied with;
  (j) that the unsuitable sponsorship of programmes included in television and radio services is prevented;
  (k) that there is no undue discrimination between advertisers who seek to have advertisements included in television and radio services; and
  (l) that there is no use of techniques which exploit the possibility of conveying a message to viewers or listeners, or of otherwise influencing their minds, without their being aware, or fully aware, of what has occurred.

(3) The standards set by OFCOM under this section must be contained in one or more codes.

(4) In setting or revising any standards under this section, OFCOM must have regard, in particular and to such extent as appears to them to be relevant to the securing of the standards objectives, to each of the following matters
  (a) the degree of harm or offence likely to be caused by the inclusion of any particular sort of material in programmes generally, or in programmes of a particular description;
  (b) the likely size and composition of the potential audience for programmes included in television and radio services generally, or in television and radio services of a particular description;

(c) the likely expectation of the audience as to the nature of a programme's content and the extent to which the nature of a programme's content can be brought to the attention of potential members of the audience;
(d) the likelihood of persons who are unaware of the nature of a programme's content being unintentionally exposed, by their own actions, to that content;
(e) the desirability of securing that the content of services identifies when there is a change affecting the nature of a service that is being watched or listened to and, in particular, a change that is relevant to the application of the standards set under this section; and
(f) the desirability of maintaining the independence of editorial control over programme content.

(5) OFCOM must ensure that the standards from time to time in force under this section include
(a) minimum standards applicable to all programmes included in television and radio services; and
(b) such other standards applicable to particular descriptions of programmes, or of television and radio services, as appear to them appropriate for securing the standards objectives.

(6) Standards set to secure the standards objective specified in subsection (2)(e) shall, in particular, contain provision designed to secure that religious programmes do not involve
(a) any improper exploitation of any susceptibilities of the audience for such a programme; or
(b) any abusive treatment of the religious views and beliefs of those belonging to a particular religion or religious denomination.

(7) In setting standards under this section, OFCOM must take account of such of the international obligations of the United Kingdom as the Secretary of State may notify to them for the purposes of this section.

(8) In this section "news" means news in whatever form it is included in a service.

(9) Subsection (2)(fa) applies only in relation to programmes the production of which begins after 19th December 2009.

NOTES
Defined terms
contravention (and cognate expressions): s 405(1)
international obligation of the United Kingdom: s 405(1)
OFCOM: s 405(1)
product placement: s 362(1), Sch 11A, para 1

programme: s 405(1)
television and radio services: s 405(1)

320 Special impartiality requirements

(1) The requirements of this section are
(a) the exclusion, in the case of television and radio services (other than a restricted service within the meaning of section 245), from programmes included in any of those services of all expressions of the views or opinions of the person providing the service on any of the matters mentioned in subsection (2);
(b) the preservation, in the case of every television programme service, teletext service, national radio service and national digital sound programme service, of due impartiality, on the part of the person providing the service, as respects all of those matters;
(c) the prevention, in the case of every local radio service, local digital sound programme service or radio licensable content service, of the giving of undue prominence in the programmes included in the service to the views and opinions of particular persons or bodies on any of those matters.

(2) Those matters are
(a) matters of political or industrial controversy; and

(b) matters relating to current public policy.

(3) Subsection (1)(a) does not require

    (a) the exclusion from television programmes of views or opinions relating to the provision of programme services; or

    (b) the exclusion from radio programmes of views or opinions relating to the provision of programme services.

(4) For the purposes of this section

    (a) the requirement specified in subsection (1)(b) is one that (subject to any rules under subsection (5)) may be satisfied by being satisfied in relation to a series of programmes taken as a whole;

    (b) the requirement specified in subsection (1)(c) is one that needs to be satisfied only in relation to all the programmes included in the service in question, taken as a whole.

(5) OFCOM's standards code shall contain provision setting out the rules to be observed in connection with the following matters

    (a) the application of the requirement specified in subsection (1)(b);

    (b) the determination of what, in relation to that requirement, constitutes a series of programmes for the purposes of subsection (4)(a);

    (c) the application of the requirement in subsection (1)(c).

(6) Any provision made for the purposes of subsection (5)(a) must, in particular, take account of the need to ensure the preservation of impartiality in relation to the following matters (taking each matter separately)

    (a) matters of major political or industrial controversy, and

    (b) major matters relating to current public policy,

as well as of the need to ensure that the requirement specified in subsection (1)(b) is satisfied generally in relation to a series of programmes taken as a whole.

(7) In this section "national radio service" and "local radio service" mean, respectively, a sound broadcasting service which is a national service within the meaning of section 245 and a sound broadcasting service which is a local service within the meaning of that section.

NOTES

Defined terms

body: s 405(1)
local digital sound programme service: s 362(1)
national digital sound programme service: s 362(1)
OFCOM: s 405(1)
programme: s 405(1)
programme service: s 405(1)
provision (in relation to a service): s 362(1)-(3)

radio licensable content service: ss 247, 362(1)
sound broadcasting service: s 362(1)
television and radio services: s 405(1)
television programme: s 405(1)
television programme service: s 362(1)

321 Objectives for advertisements, sponsorship and product placement

(1) Standards set by OFCOM to secure the objectives mentioned in section 319(2)(a) and (fa) to (j)

    (a) must include general provision governing standards and practice in advertising and in the sponsoring of programmes and, in relation to television programme services, general provision governing standards and practice in product placement;

    (b) may include provision prohibiting advertisements and forms and methods of advertising or sponsorship (whether generally or in particular circumstances); and

    (c) in relation to television programme services, may include provision prohibiting forms and methods of product placement (including product placement of products, services or trade marks of any description) (whether generally or in particular circumstances).

(2)   For the purposes of section 319(2)(g) an advertisement contravenes the prohibition on political advertising if it is

    (a)   an advertisement which is inserted by or on behalf of a body whose objects are wholly or mainly of a political nature;

    (b)   an advertisement which is directed towards a political end; or

    (c)   an advertisement which has a connection with an industrial dispute.

(3)   For the purposes of this section objects of a political nature and political ends include each of the following

    (a)   influencing the outcome of elections or referendums, whether in the United Kingdom or elsewhere;

    (b)   bringing about changes of the law in the whole or a part of the United Kingdom or elsewhere, or otherwise influencing the legislative process in any country or territory;

    (c)   influencing the policies or decisions of local, regional or national governments, whether in the United Kingdom or elsewhere;

    (d)   influencing the policies or decisions of persons on whom public functions are conferred by or under the law of the United Kingdom or of a country or territory outside the United Kingdom;

    (e)   influencing the policies or decisions of persons on whom functions are conferred by or under international agreements;

    (f) influencing public opinion on a matter which, in the United Kingdom, is a matter of public controversy;

    (g)   promoting the interests of a party or other group of persons organised, in the United Kingdom or elsewhere, for political ends.

(3A)   For the purposes of section 319(2)(fa) the product placement requirements are the requirements set out in Schedule 11A.

(4)   OFCOM

    (a)   shall

      (i) in relation to programme services, have a general responsibility with respect to advertisements and methods of advertising and sponsorship; and

      (ii)   in relation to television programme services, have a general responsibility with respect to methods of product placement; and

    (b)   in the discharge of that responsibility may include conditions in any licence which is granted by them for any such service that enable OFCOM to impose requirements with respect to any of those matters that go beyond the provisions of OFCOM's standards code.

(5)   OFCOM must, from time to time, consult the Secretary of State about

    (a)   the descriptions of advertisements that should not be included in programme services;

    (b)   the forms and methods of advertising and sponsorship that should not be employed in, or in connection with, the provision of such services; and

    (c)   the forms and methods of product placement that should not be employed in the provision of a television programme service (including the descriptions of products, services or trade marks for which product placement should not be employed).

(6)   The Secretary of State may give OFCOM directions as to the matters mentioned in subsection (5); and it shall be the duty of OFCOM to comply with any such direction.

(7)   Provision included by virtue of this section in standards set under section 319 is not to apply to, or to be construed as prohibiting the inclusion in a programme service of

    (a)   an advertisement of a public service nature inserted by, or on behalf of, a government department; or

    (b)   a party political or referendum campaign broadcast the inclusion of which is required by a condition imposed under section 333 or by paragraph 18 of Schedule 12 to this Act.

(8) In this section "programme service" does not include a service provided by the BBC (except in the expression "television programme service").

NOTES

Defined terms
  the BBC: s 405(1)
  body: s 405(1)
  OFCOM: s 405(1)
  product placement: s 362(1), Sch 11A, para 1
  programme: s 405(1)

programme service: s 405(1) (and note sub-s (8) of this section)
provision (in relation to a service): s 362(1)-(3)

Party political broadcasts on television and radio

333 Party political broadcasts

(1) The regulatory regime for every licensed public service channel, and the regulatory regime for every national radio service, includes

  (a) conditions requiring the inclusion in that channel or service of party political broadcasts and of referendum campaign broadcasts; and

  (b) conditions requiring that licence holder to observe such rules with respect to party political broadcasts and referendum campaign broadcasts as may be made by OFCOM.

(2) The rules made by OFCOM for the purposes of this section may, in particular, include provision for determining

  (a) the political parties on whose behalf party political broadcasts may be made;

  (b) in relation to each political party on whose behalf such broadcasts may be made, the length and frequency of the broadcasts; and

  (c) in relation to each designated organisation on whose behalf referendum campaign broadcasts are required to be broadcast, the length and frequency of such broadcasts.

(3) Those rules are to have effect subject to sections 37 and 127 of the Political Parties, Elections and Referendums Act 2000 (c 41) (only registered parties and designated organisations to be entitled to party political broadcasts or referendum campaign broadcasts).

(4) Rules made by OFCOM for the purposes of this section may make different provision for different cases.

(5) Before making any rules for the purposes of this section, OFCOM must have regard to any views expressed by the Electoral Commission.

(6) In this section

"designated organisation", in relation to a referendum, means a person or body designated by the Electoral Commission under section 108 of the Political Parties, Elections and Referendums Act 2000 (c 41) in respect of that referendum;

"national radio service" means a national service within the meaning of section 245 of this Act; and

"referendum campaign broadcast" has the meaning given by section 127 of that Act.

NOTES

Defined terms
  body: s 405(1)
  frequency: s 405(1)
  licensed public service channel: s 362(1)

OFCOM: s 405(1)

Companies Act 2006

PART 14
CONTROL OF POLITICAL DONATIONS AND EXPENDITURE

Introductory

362 Introductory

This Part has effect for controlling
  (a) political donations made by companies to political parties, to other political organisations and to independent election candidates, and
  (b) political expenditure incurred by companies.

NOTES

Application
In relation to the application of this section to unregistered companies: the Unregistered Companies Regulations 2009, SI 2009/2436, regs 35, 7, 9, Sch 1, para 9(1), Sch 2, para 20(1).

Defined terms
company: s 1(1)

independent election candidate: s 363(3), (4)
organisation: s 379
political donation: s 364
political expenditure: ss 363(4), 365
political organisation: s 363(2), (4)
political party: s 363(1), (4)

Donations and expenditure to which this Part applies

363 Political parties, organisations etc to which this Part applies

(1) This Part applies to a political party if
  (a) it is registered under Part 2 of the Political Parties, Elections and Referendums Act 2000 (c 41), or
  (b) it carries on, or proposes to carry on, activities for the purposes of or in connection with the participation of the party in any election or elections to public office held in a member State other than the United Kingdom.

(2) This Part applies to an organisation (a "political organisation") if it carries on, or proposes to carry on, activities that are capable of being reasonably regarded as intended
  (a) to affect public support for a political party to which, or an independent election candidate to whom, this Part applies, or
  (b) to influence voters in relation to any national or regional referendum held under the law of the United Kingdom or another member State.

(3) This Part applies to an independent election candidate at any election to public office held in the United Kingdom or another member State.

(4) Any reference in the following provisions of this Part to a political party, political organisation or independent election candidate, or to political expenditure, is to a party, organisation, independent candidate or expenditure to which this Part applies.

NOTES

Application
In relation to the application of this section to unregistered companies: the Unregistered Companies Regulations 2009, SI 2009/2436, regs 35, 7, 9, Sch 1, para 9(1), Sch 2, para 20(1).

Defined terms
independent election candidate: s 363(3), (4)
organisation: s 379(1)
political party: s 363(1), (4)

364 Meaning of "political donation"

(1) The following provisions have effect for the purposes of this Part as regards the meaning

of "political donation".

(2)   In relation to a political party or other political organisation

    (a)   "political donation" means anything that in accordance with sections 50 to 52 of the Political Parties, Elections and Referendums Act 2000

        (i) constitutes a donation for the purposes of Chapter 1 of Part 4 of that Act (control of donations to registered parties), or

        (ii)   would constitute such a donation reading references in those sections to a registered party as references to any political party or other political organisation,

    and

    (b)   section 53 of that Act applies, in the same way, for the purpose of determining the value of a donation.

(3)   In relation to an independent election candidate

    (a)   "political donation" means anything that, in accordance with sections 50 to 52 of that Act, would constitute a donation for the purposes of Chapter 1 of Part 4 of that Act (control of donations to registered parties) reading references in those sections to a registered party as references to the independent election candidate, and

    (b)   section 53 of that Act applies, in the same way, for the purpose of determining the value of a donation.

(4)   For the purposes of this section, sections 50 and 53 of the Political Parties, Elections and Referendums Act 2000 (c 41) (definition of "donation" and value of donations) shall be treated as if the amendments to those sections made by the Electoral Administration Act 2006 (which remove from the definition of "donation" loans made otherwise than on commercial terms) had not been made.

NOTES

365 Meaning of "political expenditure"

(1)   In this Part "political expenditure", in relation to a company, means expenditure incurred by the company on

    (a)   the preparation, publication or dissemination of advertising or other promotional or publicity material

        (i) of whatever nature, and

        (ii)   however published or otherwise disseminated,

    that, at the time of publication or dissemination, is capable of being reasonably regarded as intended to affect public support for a political party or other political organisation, or an independent election candidate, or

    (b)   activities on the part of the company that are capable of being reasonably regarded as intended

        (i) to affect public support for a political party or other political organisation, or an independent election candidate, or

        (ii)   to influence voters in relation to any national or regional referendum held under the law of a member State.

(2)   For the purposes of this Part a political donation does not count as political expenditure.

NOTES

independent election candidate: s 363(3), (4)　　　political party: s 363(1), (4)
political donation: s 364
political organisation: ss 363(2), (4), 374(2)

Authorisation required for donations or expenditure

366 Authorisation required for donations or expenditure

(1)　A company must not
　　(a)　make a political donation to a political party or other political organisation, or to an independent election candidate, or
　　(b)　incur any political expenditure,
unless the donation or expenditure is authorised in accordance with the following provisions.

(2)　The donation or expenditure must be authorised
　　(a)　in the case of a company that is not a subsidiary of another company, by a resolution of the members of the company;
　　(b)　in the case of a company that is a subsidiary of another company by
　　　　(i) a resolution of the members of the company, and
　　　　(ii)　a resolution of the members of any relevant holding company.

(3)　No resolution is required on the part of a company that is a wholly-owned subsidiary of a UK-registered company.

(4)　For the purposes of subsection (2)(b)(ii) a "relevant holding company" means a company that, at the time the donation was made or the expenditure was incurred
　　(a)　was a holding company of the company by which the donation was made or the expenditure was incurred,
　　(b)　was a UK-registered company, and
　　(c)　was not a subsidiary of another UK-registered company.

(5)　The resolution or resolutions required by this section
　　(a)　must comply with section 367 (form of authorising resolution), and
　　(b)　must be passed before the donation is made or the expenditure incurred.

(6)　Nothing in this section enables a company to be authorised to do anything that it could not lawfully do apart from this section.

NOTES

Application
In relation to the application of this section to unregistered companies: the Unregistered Companies Regulations 2009, SI 2009/2436, regs 35, 7, 9, Sch 1, para 9(1), Sch 2, para 20(1).

Defined terms
company: s 1(1)
holding company: s 1159(1), (3), Sch 6
independent election candidate: s 363(3), (4)

member: ss 112, 122(3)
political donation: s 364
political expenditure: ss 363(4), 365
political organisation: s 363(2), (4)
political party: s 363(1), (4)
subsidiary: s 1159(1), (3), Sch 6
UK-registered company: s 1158
wholly-owned subsidiary: s 1159(2)

367 Form of authorising resolution

(1)　A resolution conferring authorisation for the purposes of this Part may relate to
　　(a)　the company passing the resolution,
　　(b)　one or more subsidiaries of that company, or
　　(c)　the company passing the resolution and one or more subsidiaries of that company.

(2)　A resolution may be expressed to relate to all companies that are subsidiaries of the company passing the resolution
　　(a)　at the time the resolution is passed, or
　　(b)　at any time during the period for which the resolution has effect,

without identifying them individually.

(3) The resolution may authorise donations or expenditure under one or more of the following heads
    (a) donations to political parties or independent election candidates;
    (b) donations to political organisations other than political parties;
    (c) political expenditure.

(4) The resolution must specify a head or heads
    (a) in the case of a resolution under subsection (2), for all of the companies to which it relates taken together;
    (b) in the case of any other resolution, for each company to which it relates.

(5) The resolution must be expressed in general terms conforming with subsection (3) and must not purport to authorise particular donations or expenditure.

(6) For each of the specified heads the resolution must authorise donations or, as the case may be, expenditure up to a specified amount in the period for which the resolution has effect (see section 368).

(7) The resolution must specify such amounts
    (a) in the case of a resolution under subsection (2), for all of the companies to which it relates taken together;
    (b) in the case of any other resolution, for each company to which it relates.

NOTES

Application
In relation to the application of this section to unregistered companies: the Unregistered Companies Regulations 2009, SI 2009/2436, regs 35, 7, 9, Sch 1, para 9(1), Sch 2, para 20(1).

Defined terms
company: s 1(1)

independent election candidate: s 363(3), (4)
political expenditure: ss 363(4), 365
political organisation: s 363(2), (4)
political party: s 363(1), (4)
subsidiary: s 1159(1), (3), Sch 6

368 Period for which resolution has effect

(1) A resolution conferring authorisation for the purposes of this Part has effect for a period of four years beginning with the date on which it is passed unless the directors determine, or the articles require, that it is to have effect for a shorter period beginning with that date.

(2) The power of the directors to make a determination under this section is subject to any provision of the articles that operates to prevent them from doing so.

NOTES

Application
In relation to the application of this section to unregistered companies: the Unregistered Companies Regulations 2009, SI 2009/2436, regs 35, 7, 9, Sch 1, para 9(1), Sch 2, para 20(1).

Defined terms
articles: s 18(4)
director: ss 250, 379(1)

Remedies in case of unauthorised donations or expenditure

369 Liability of directors in case of unauthorised donation or expenditure

(1) This section applies where a company has made a political donation or incurred political expenditure without the authorisation required by this Part.

(2) The directors in default are jointly and severally liable
    (a) to make good to the company the amount of the unauthorised donation or expenditure, with interest, and
    (b) to compensate the company for any loss or damage sustained by it as a result of the unauthorised donation or expenditure having been made.

(3)   The directors in default are
  (a)   those who, at the time the unauthorised donation was made or the unauthorised expenditure was incurred, were directors of the company by which the donation was made or the expenditure was incurred, and
  (b)   where
    (i) that company was a subsidiary of a relevant holding company, and
    (ii)   the directors of the relevant holding company failed to take all reasonable steps to prevent the donation being made or the expenditure being incurred,
  the directors of the relevant holding company.

(4)   For the purposes of subsection (3)(b) a "relevant holding company" means a company that, at the time the donation was made or the expenditure was incurred
  (a)   was a holding company of the company by which the donation was made or the expenditure was incurred,
  (b)   was a UKregistered company, and
  (c)   was not a subsidiary of another UKregistered company.

(5)   The interest referred to in subsection (2)(a) is interest on the amount of the unauthorised donation or expenditure, so far as not made good to the company
  (a)   in respect of the period beginning with the date when the donation was made or the expenditure was incurred, and
  (b)   at such rate as the Secretary of State may prescribe by regulations.
  Section 379(2) (construction of references to date when donation made or expenditure incurred) does not apply for the purposes of this subsection.

(6)   Where only part of a donation or expenditure was unauthorised, this section applies only to so much of it as was unauthorised.

NOTES

Application
In relation to the application of this section to unregistered companies: the Unregistered Companies Regulations 2009, SI 2009/2436, regs 35, 7, 9, Sch 1, para 9(1), Sch 2, para 20(1).

Subordinate legislation
Companies (Interest Rate for Unauthorised Political Donation or Expenditure) Regulations 2007, SI 2007/2242

Defined terms
company: s 1(1)
director: ss 250, 379(1)
holding company: s 1159(1), (3), Sch 6
political donation: s 364
political expenditure: ss 363(4), 365
subsidiary: s 1159(1), (3), Sch 6
UK-registered company: s 1158

370 Enforcement of directors' liabilities by shareholder action

(1)   Any liability of a director under section 369 is enforceable
  (a)   in the case of a liability of a director of a company to that company, by proceedings brought under this section in the name of the company by an authorised group of its members;
  (b)   in the case of a liability of a director of a holding company to a subsidiary, by proceedings brought under this section in the name of the subsidiary by
    (i) an authorised group of members of the subsidiary, or
    (ii)   an authorised group of members of the holding company.

(2)   This is in addition to the right of the company to which the liability is owed to bring proceedings itself to enforce the liability.

(3)   An "authorised group" of members of a company means
  (a)   the holders of not less than 5% in nominal value of the company's issued share capital,
  (b)   if the company is not limited by shares, not less than 5% of its members, or
  (c)   not less than 50 of the company's members.

(4)   The right to bring proceedings under this section is subject to the provisions of section

371.

(5) Nothing in this section affects any right of a member of a company to bring or continue proceedings under Part 11 (derivative claims or proceedings).

NOTES

Application

In relation to the application of this section to unregistered companies: the Unregistered Companies Regulations 2009, SI 2009/2436, regs 35, 7, 9, Sch 1, para 9(1), Sch 2, para 20(1).

Defined terms

company: s 1(1)

director: ss 250, 379(1)
holding company: s 1159(1), (3), Sch 6
issued share capital: s 546(1)(a), (2)
member: ss 112, 122(3)
share: ss 540(1), (4), 1161(2)
subsidiary: s 1159(1), (3), Sch 6

371 Enforcement of directors' liabilities by shareholder action: supplementary

(1) A group of members may not bring proceedings under section 370 in the name of a company unless
   (a) the group has given written notice to the company stating
      (i) the cause of action and a summary of the facts on which the proceedings are to be based,
      (ii) the names and addresses of the members comprising the group, and
      (iii) the grounds on which it is alleged that those members constitute an authorised group; and
   (b) not less than 28 days have elapsed between the date of the giving of the notice to the company and the bringing of the proceedings.

(2) Where such a notice is given to a company, any director of the company may apply to the court within the period of 28 days beginning with the date of the giving of the notice for an order directing that the proposed proceedings shall not be brought, on one or more of the following grounds
   (a) that the unauthorised amount has been made good to the company;
   (b) that proceedings to enforce the liability have been brought, and are being pursued with due diligence, by the company;
   (c) that the members proposing to bring proceedings under this section do not constitute an authorised group.

(3) Where an application is made on the ground mentioned in subsection (2)(b), the court may as an alternative to directing that the proposed proceedings under section 370 are not to be brought, direct
   (a) that such proceedings may be brought on such terms and conditions as the court thinks fit, and
   (b) that the proceedings brought by the company
      (i) shall be discontinued, or
      (ii)   may be continued on such terms and conditions as the court thinks fit.

(4) The members by whom proceedings are brought under section 370 owe to the company in whose name they are brought the same duties in relation to the proceedings as would be owed by the company's directors if the proceedings were being brought by the company.
   But proceedings to enforce any such duty may be brought by the company only with the permission of the court.

(5) Proceedings brought under section 370 may not be discontinued or settled by the group except with the permission of the court, which may be given on such terms as the court thinks fit.

NOTES

Application

In relation to the application of this section to unregistered companies: the Unregistered Companies

Regulations 2009, SI 2009/2436, regs 35, 7, 9, Sch 1, para 9(1), Sch 2, para 20(1).

372 Costs of shareholder action

(1)   This section applies in relation to proceedings brought under section 370 in the name of a company ("the company") by an authorised group ("the group").

(2)   The group may apply to the court for an order directing the company to indemnify the group in respect of costs incurred or to be incurred by the group in connection with the proceedings.
The court may make such an order on such terms as it thinks fit.

(3)   The group is not entitled to be paid any such costs out of the assets of the company except by virtue of such an order.

(4)   If no such order has been made with respect to the proceedings, then
    (a)   if the company is awarded costs in connection with the proceedings, or it is agreed that costs incurred by the company in connection with the proceedings should be paid by any defendant, the costs shall be paid to the group; and
    (b)   if any defendant is awarded costs in connection with the proceedings, or it is agreed that any defendant should be paid costs incurred by him in connection with the proceedings, the costs shall be paid by the group.

(5)   In the application of this section to Scotland for "costs" read "expenses" and for "defendant" read "defender".

NOTES

Application
In relation to the application of this section to unregistered companies: the Unregistered Companies Regulations 2009, SI 2009/2436, regs 35, 7, 9, Sch 1, para 9(1), Sch 2, para 20(1).

Defined terms
company: s 1(1)
the court: s 1156(1)
member: ss 112, 122(3)

373 Information for purposes of shareholder action

(1)   Where proceedings have been brought under section 370 in the name of a company by an authorised group, the group is entitled to require the company to provide it with all information relating to the subject matter of the proceedings that is in the company's possession or under its control or which is reasonably obtainable by it.

(2)   If the company, having been required by the group to do so, refuses to provide the group with all or any of that information, the court may, on an application made by the group, make an order directing
    (a)   the company, and
    (b)   any of its officers or employees specified in the application,
to provide the group with the information in question in such form and by such means as the court may direct.

NOTES

Application
In relation to the application of this section to unregistered companies: the Unregistered Companies Regulations 2009, SI 2009/2436, regs 35, 7, 9, Sch 1, para 9(1), Sch 2, para 20(1).

Defined terms
company: s 1(1)
the court: s 1156(1)
officer: s 1173(1)

Exemptions

374 Trade unions

(1) A donation to a trade union, other than a contribution to the union's political fund, is not a political donation for the purposes of this Part.

(2) A trade union is not a political organisation for the purposes of section 365 (meaning of "political expenditure").

(3) In this section
"trade union" has the meaning given by section 1 of Trade Union and Labour Relations (Consolidation) Act 1992 (c 52) or Article 3 of the Industrial Relations (Northern Ireland) Order 1992 (SI 1992/807 (NI 5));
"political fund" means the fund from which payments by a trade union in the furtherance of political objects are required to be made by virtue of section 82(1)(a) of that Act or Article 57(2)(a) of that Order.

NOTES
Application
In relation to the application of this section to unregistered companies: the Unregistered Companies Regulations 2009, SI 2009/2436, regs 35, 7, 9, Sch 1, para 9(1), Sch 2, para 20(1).

Defined terms
political donation: s 364
political organisation: s 363(2), (4)

375 Subscription for membership of trade association

(1) A subscription paid to a trade association for membership of the association is not a political donation for the purposes of this Part.

(2) For this purpose
"trade association" means an organisation formed for the purpose of furthering the trade interests of its members, or of persons represented by its members, and "subscription" does not include a payment to the association to the extent that it is made for the purpose of financing any particular activity of the association.

NOTES
Application
In relation to the application of this section to unregistered companies: the Unregistered Companies Regulations 2009, SI 2009/2436, regs 35, 7, 9, Sch 1, para 9(1), Sch 2, para 20(1).

Defined terms
organisation: s 379(1)
political donation: s 364

376 All-party parliamentary groups

(1) An all-party parliamentary group is not a political organisation for the purposes of this Part.

(2) An "all-party parliamentary group" means an all-party group composed of members of one or both of the Houses of Parliament (or of such members and other persons).

NOTES
Application
In relation to the application of this section to unregistered companies: the Unregistered Companies Regulations 2009, SI 2009/2436, regs 35, 7, 9, Sch 1, para 9(1), Sch 2, para 20(1).

Defined terms
political organisation: s 363(2), (4)

377 Political expenditure exempted by order

(1) Authorisation under this Part is not needed for political expenditure that is exempt by virtue of an order of the Secretary of State under this section.

(2) An order may confer an exemption in relation to
(a) companies of any description or category specified in the order, or

(b) expenditure of any description or category so specified (whether framed by reference to goods, services or other matters in respect of which such expenditure is incurred or otherwise),

or both.

(3) If or to the extent that expenditure is exempt from the requirement of authorisation under this Part by virtue of an order under this section, it shall be disregarded in determining what donations are authorised by any resolution of the company passed for the purposes of this Part.

(4) An order under this section is subject to affirmative resolution procedure.

NOTES

Application

In relation to the application of this section to unregistered companies: the Unregistered Companies Regulations 2009, SI 2009/2436, regs 35, 7, 9, Sch 1, para 9(1), Sch 2, para 20(1).

Subordinate legislation

Companies (Political Expenditure Exemption) Order

2007, SI 2007/2081.

Defined terms

affirmative resolution procedure: s 1290

company: s 1(1)

political expenditure: ss 363(4), 365

378 Donations not amounting to more than £5,000 in any twelve month period

(1) Authorisation under this Part is not needed for a donation except to the extent that the total amount of

(a) that donation, and

(b) other relevant donations made in the period of 12 months ending with the date on which that donation is made,

exceeds £5,000.

(2) In this section

"donation" means a donation to a political party or other political organisation or to an independent election candidate; and

"other relevant donations" means

(a) in relation to a donation made by a company that is not a subsidiary, any other donations made by that company or by any of its subsidiaries;

(b) in relation to a donation made by a company that is a subsidiary, any other donations made by that company, by any holding company of that company or by any other subsidiary of any such holding company.

(3) If or to the extent that a donation is exempt by virtue of this section from the requirement of authorisation under this Part, it shall be disregarded in determining what donations are authorised by any resolution passed for the purposes of this Part.

NOTES

Application

In relation to the application of this section to unregistered companies: the Unregistered Companies Regulations 2009, SI 2009/2436, regs 35, 7, 9, Sch 1, para 9(1), Sch 2, para 20(1).

Defined terms

company: s 1(1)

holding company: s 1159(1), (3), Sch 6

independent election candidate: s 363(3), (4)

political organisation: s 363(2), (4)

political party: s 363(1), (4)

subsidiary: s 1159(1), (3), Sch 6

Supplementary provisions

379 Minor definitions

(1) In this Part

"director" includes shadow director; and

"organisation" includes any body corporate or unincorporated association and any combination of persons.

(2) Except as otherwise provided, any reference in this Part to the time at which a donation is made or expenditure is incurred is, in a case where the donation is made or expenditure incurred in pursuance of a contract, any earlier time at which that contract is entered into by the company.

NOTES

Application

In relation to the application of this section to unregistered companies: the Unregistered Companies Regulations 2009, SI 2009/2436, regs 35, 7, 9, Sch 1, para 9(1), Sch 2, para 20(1).

Defined terms

body corporate: s 1173(1)

company: s 1(1)

shadow director: s 251

Constitutional Reform and Governance Act 2010

PART 7
MISCELLANEOUS AND FINAL PROVISIONS

47 Section 3 of the Act of Settlement

(1) For the avoidance of doubt, the repeal in section 18(7) of the Electoral Administration Act 2006 of the entry in Schedule 7 to the British Nationality Act 1981 (entry which modified certain disqualifications imposed by section 3 of the Act of Settlement) applied only so far as the modification made by that entry related to

    (a) membership of the House of Commons, or

    (b) anything from which a person is disqualified by virtue of a disqualification from membership of that House.

(2) Section 3 of the Act of Settlement has effect accordingly, and has done so since the coming into force of section 18 of the Electoral Administration Act 2006.

Defamation Act 1952

10 Limitation on privilege at elections

A defamatory statement published by or on behalf of a candidate in any election to a local government authority, to the National Assembly for Wales, to the Scottish Parliament or to Parliament shall not be deemed to be published on a privileged occasion on the ground that it is material to a question in issue in the election, whether or not the person by whom it is published is qualified to vote at the election.

Election Publications Act 2001

An Act to make provision for postponing the operation of certain enactments relating to election publications; and for connected purposes.

10th April 2001

1 Restoration of previous law relating to election publications

(1)   Despite the relevant commencement order
   (a)   section 143 of the Political Parties, Elections and Referendums Act 2000 (c 41) (details to appear on election material), and
   (b)   paragraph 14 of Schedule 18 to that Act (replacement of section 110 of the Representation of the People Act 1983 (c 2)),
   shall be deemed not to have come into force on the commencement date.

(2)   As a result of subsection (1)(b), section 110 of the 1983 Act (details to appear on candidates' election material)
   (a)   shall, as from the passing of this Act, have effect in the form in which it had effect immediately before the commencement date, and
   (b)   shall be deemed to have had effect in that form at all times on or after the commencement date and before the passing of this Act.

(3)   Subsection (2) has effect despite any repeal by the 2000 Act of any provision amending section 110 of the 1983 Act.

(4)   In this section
   "the commencement date" means 16th February 2001 (the date appointed by the relevant commencement order for the coming into force of the provisions mentioned in subsection (1));
   "the relevant commencement order" means the Political Parties, Elections and Referendums Act 2000 (Commencement No 1 and Transitional Provisions) Order 2001 (SI 2001/222).

NOTES
Defined terms
   the 1983 Act: s 3(2)
   the 2000 Act: s 3(2)

2 Introduction of new law relating to election publications

(1)   The Secretary of State may by order made by statutory instrument provide
   (a)   that either or both of the provisions of the 2000 Act mentioned in section 1(1) above shall come into force on a day appointed by the order;
   (b)   that any of the provisions of section 1 above specified in the order shall in consequence cease to have effect on that day to such extent as is so specified.

(2)   Different days may be appointed under subsection (1) for different purposes.

(3)   An order under subsection (1) may contain such transitional provisions and savings (including provisions modifying enactments) as the Secretary of State considers appropriate.

NOTES
Defined terms
   the 2000 Act: s 3(2)

3 Short title, construction, transitionals and extent

(1)   This Act may be cited as the Election Publications Act 2001.

(2)   In this Act
       "the 1983 Act" means the Representation of the People Act 1983 (c 2);
       "the 2000 Act" means the Political Parties, Elections and Referendums Act 2000 (c 41).

(3)   Where any act or omission occurring during the continuation period would, if section 1(1) and (2) above had not been enacted, have been lawful by reason of
       (a)   the act being done in compliance with, or
       (b)   the omission being made in reliance on,
       any provisions of the new section 110 (the "relevant provisions" of that section), it shall be deemed to be lawful despite section 1(1) and (2).

(4)   In subsection (3)
       "the continuation period" means the period beginning with the commencement date (within the meaning of section 1) and ending immediately before the day on which the relevant provisions of the new section 110 come into force by virtue of an order under section 2(1);
       "the new section 110" means the section 110 of the 1983 Act contained in paragraph 14 of Schedule 18 to the 2000 Act.

(5)   This Act extends to the whole of the United Kingdom.

(6)   However, so far as it relates in any way to section 110 of the 1983 Act, this Act does not have effect in relation to local government elections in Scotland (within the meaning of that Act).

Elections (Northern Ireland) Act 1985

An Act to make further provision for preventing personation at elections in Northern Ireland

24th January 1985

Parliamentary elections
1 Voters to produce specified documents
2 Further provisions
3 Offences relating to specified documents
4 Effect on the franchise

Other elections
5 Elections other than parliamentary

General
6 Expenses
7 Citation, commencement and extent

Parliamentary elections

1 Voters to produce specified documents
Makes amendments to other legislation: not reproduced here.

2 Further provisions
Makes amendments to other legislation: not reproduced here.

3 Offences relating to specified documents

(1) A person commits an offence if, on the day of or the day next preceding the poll for a parliamentary election, he has possession of a document to which this section applies, with the intention of committing or of enabling another person to commit the offence of personation at the election.

(2) This section applies to
(a) a document which is not, but purports to be, a specified document within the meaning of rule 37 of the parliamentary elections rules in Schedule 1 to the 1983 Act, and
(b) a specified document within the meaning of that rule which either falsely bears the name of the person in possession or does not bear that name.

(3) If a constable has reasonable grounds for suspecting that a person has possession of a document in contravention of subsection (1), the constable may
(a) search that person, and detain him for the purpose of searching him;
(b) search any vehicle in which the constable suspects that the document may be found, and for that purpose require the person in control of the vehicle to stop it;
(c) seize and retain, for the purpose of proceedings for an offence under subsection (1), any document found in the course of the search if there are reasonable grounds for suspecting that it is a document to which this section applies.

(4) If a resident magistrate is satisfied by complaint on oath that there are reasonable grounds for suspecting that a person has possession on any premises of a document in contravention of subsection (1), he may grant a warrant authorising any constable
(a) to enter, if need be by force, the premises named in the warrant,
(b) to search the premises and any person found there, and
(c) to seize and retain, for the purpose of proceedings for an offence under subsection (1), any document found in the course of the search if there are reasonable grounds

for suspecting that it is a document to which this section applies.

(5) A person commits an offence if he
    (a) intentionally obstructs a constable in the exercise of his powers under this section, or
    (b) conceals from a constable acting in the exercise of those powers any document to which this section applies.

(6) A constable may arrest without warrant a person who has committed, or whom the constable has reasonable grounds for suspecting to have committed, an offence under subsection (1) or (5) if
    (a) he has reasonable grounds for believing that that person will abscond unless arrested,
    (b) the name and address of that person are unknown to, and cannot be ascertained by, him, or
    (c) he is not satisfied that a name and address furnished by that person as his name and address are true.

(7) A person is guilty of a corrupt practice if he commits or aids, abets, counsels or procures the commission of an offence under subsection (1); and the provisions of the 1983 Act relating to corrupt practices shall apply in such a case, but reading for the words "one year" in section [168(1)(a)(ii)] (penalty on indictment) the words "two years".

(8) A person guilty of an offence under subsection (5) shall be liable on summary conviction to a fine not exceeding level 5 on the standard scale (as provided by Article 5 of the Fines and Penalties (Northern Ireland) Order 1984) or to imprisonment for a term not exceeding 6 months or to both.

(9) A prosecution shall not be instituted in respect of an offence under subsection (1) except by or with the consent of the Director of Public Prosecutions for Northern Ireland.

(10) In this section
    "premises" includes any place and, in particular, includes any movable structure, and "vehicle" means a vehicle intended or adapted for use on land (however propelled, and including a caravan or other vehicle intended or adapted to be drawn).

NOTES
Defined terms
1983 Act means RPA 1983

4 Effect on the franchise
Makes amendments to other legislation: not reproduced here.

5 Elections other than parliamentary

(1) Without prejudice to the generality of section 38(1) of the Northern Ireland Constitution Act 1973 (power by Order in Council to provide for local authority elections, but not the franchise) an Order in Council under it may contain provisions corresponding to any of those of sections 1 to 3 of this Act; and in section 38(1)(a) the words "(but not the franchise)", and the Electoral Law Act (Northern Ireland) 1962, shall have effect subject to that.

(2) Without prejudice to the generality of section 2(5) of the Northern Ireland Assembly Act 1973 (power to make by order provision concerning elections to Assembly, including provision as to franchise) an order under it may contain provisions corresponding to any of those of sections 1 to 3 of this Act.

(3) Paragraph 2(1) of Schedule 1 to the [European Parliamentary] Elections Act 1978 (person entitled to vote if he would be entitled at parliamentary or local election) shall have effect subject to anything in regulations under paragraph 2 (conduct of elections) which applies or corresponds to any of the provisions of sections 1 to 3 of this Act; but otherwise those

provisions, and any provision corresponding to any of them, shall be ignored in construing paragraph 2(1).

NOTES

The Northern Ireland Act 1998 makes new provision for the government of Northern Ireland for the purpose of implementing the Belfast Agreement (the agreement reached at multiparty talks on Northern Ireland and set out in Command Paper 3883). As a consequence of that Act, any reference in this section to the Parliament of Northern Ireland or the Assembly established under the Northern Ireland Assembly Act 1973, s 1, certain officeholders and Ministers, and any legislative act and certain financial dealings thereof, shall, for the period specified, be construed in accordance with Sch 12, paras 111 to the 1998 Act.

6 Expenses

Not reproduced

7 Citation, commencement and extent

(1)   This Act may be cited as the Elections (Northern Ireland) Act 1985, and shall be included among the Acts that may be cited as the Representation of the People Acts.

(2)   Subject to subsection (3), this Act shall come into force on such day as the Secretary of State may appoint by order made by statutory instrument.

(3)   Section 5(1), section 6 and this section (and sections 1 to 3 so far as necessary to give effect to section 5(1)) shall come into force on the day on which this Act is passed.

(4)   This Act extends to Northern Ireland only.

Electoral Administration Act 2006

An Act to make provision in relation to the registration of electors and the keeping of electoral registration information; standing for election; the administration and conduct of elections and referendums; and the regulation of political parties.

11th July 2006

PART 7
REGULATION OF PARTIES

PART 1

1–8   *Repealed*

PARTS 2-4

9–16   *Effect amendments to other legislation: not reproduced here*

PART 5
STANDING FOR ELECTION

Minimum age

17 (1)   A person is disqualified for membership of the House of Commons if, on the day on which he is nominated as a candidate, he has not attained the age of 18.

(2)   Subject to an order made by the House of Commons under section 6(2) of the House of Commons Disqualification Act 1975 (c 24) as applied by subsection (3), if a person disqualified by subsection (1) for membership of that House is elected as a member of that House his election is void.

(3)   Sections 6(2) to (4) and 7 of that Act apply in the case of a person disqualified by subsection (1) as they apply in the case of a person disqualified by that Act, and references in those sections to a person disqualified by that Act must be construed as including references to a person disqualified by subsection (1).

(4)   In section 79(1) of the Local Government Act 1972 (c 70) (qualifications for election and holding office as a member of a local authority) for "twenty-one" substitute "eighteen".

(5)   In section 20(3) of the Greater London Authority Act 1999 (c 29) (minimum age for election as Mayor or Assembly member) for "21" substitute "18".

(6)   In section 3(1) of the Local Government Act (Northern Ireland) 1972 (C 9) (qualifications for election and holding office as a councillor) for "twenty-one" substitute "eighteen".

(7)   The following enactments (which disqualify a person who has not attained the age of 21 for election as a Member of Parliament), so far as not previously repealed, cease to have effect
   (a)   section 7 of the Parliamentary Elections Act 1695 (c 25);
   (b)   the Election Act 1707 (cap 8);
   (c)   section 74 of the Parliamentary Elections (Ireland) Act 1823 (c 55).

(8)   In section 6 of the Union with Scotland Act 1706 (c 11) the words "It is always hereby expressly provided and declared that none shall be capable to elect or be elected for any of the said estates but such as are twenty one years complete" do not apply for the purpose of fixing the minimum age at which a person may be elected as a member of the House of Commons.

Certain Commonwealth citizens

18 (1)   In section 3 of the Act of Settlement (1700 c 2), the words from "That after the said limitation shall take effect" to "in trust for him." (which impose certain disqualifications) do not apply (so far as they relate to membership of the House of Commons) to a person

who is
- (a) a qualifying Commonwealth citizen, or
- (b) a citizen of the Republic of Ireland.

(2) For the purposes of subsection (1), a person is a qualifying Commonwealth citizen if he is a Commonwealth citizen who either
- (a) is not a person who requires leave under the Immigration Act 1971 (c 77) to enter or remain in the United Kingdom, or
- (b) is such a person but for the time being has (or is, by virtue of any enactment, to be treated as having) indefinite leave to remain within the meaning of that Act.

(3) But a person is not a qualifying Commonwealth citizen by virtue of subsection (2)(a) if he does not require leave to enter or remain in the United Kingdom by virtue only of section 8 of the Immigration Act 1971 (exceptions to requirement for leave in special cases).

(4) Subject to an order made by the House of Commons under section 6(2) of the House of Commons Disqualification Act 1975 (c 24) as applied by subsection (5)
- (a) if a person disqualified for membership of that House by virtue of section 3 of the Act of Settlement (1700 c.2) as modified by this section is elected as a member of that House his election is void;
- (b) if a person being a member of that House becomes so disqualified for membership his seat is vacated.

(5) Sections 6(2) to (4) and 7 of the House of Commons Disqualification Act 1975 apply in the case of a person disqualified as mentioned in subsection (4) as they apply in the case of a person disqualified by that Act, and references in those sections to a person disqualified by that Act must be construed as including references to a person disqualified as mentioned in subsection (4).

(6) Part 3 of Schedule 1 (which contains further amendments relating to standing for election) has effect.

(7) In Schedule 7 to the British Nationality Act 1981 (c 61), the entry relating to the Act of Settlement is omitted.

19 *Effects amendments to other legislation: not reproduced here*

PART 6
CONDUCT OF ELECTIONS ETC

20–31 *Effect amendments to other legislation: not reproduced here*

Photographs on ballot papers: piloting

32 (1) This section applies if a local authority makes a proposal that an order be made under subsection (2) applying to particular local government elections held in its area.

(2) The Secretary of State may by order (a pilot order) make provision for the purposes of enabling ballot papers issued at such local government elections as are specified in the order to contain photographs of the candidates.

(3) A pilot order may include such provision modifying or disapplying any enactment as the Secretary of State thinks is necessary or expedient for the purposes of the order.

(4) The Secretary of State must not make a pilot order unless he first consults the Electoral Commission.

(5) A pilot order may make provision implementing the local authority's proposal
- (a) without modification, or

    (b) with such modifications as the Secretary of State and the local authority agree between them.

(6) If the Secretary of State makes a pilot order
    (a) he must send a copy of it to the local authority and to the Electoral Commission, and
    (b) the local authority must publish the order in their area in such manner as they think fit.

(7) A pilot order may be amended or revoked by a further order.

(8) The Secretary of State may reimburse a returning officer for any expenditure necessarily incurred by him in consequence of the making of a pilot order.

(9) A local authority is
    (a) in England, a county council, a district council, a London borough council or the Greater London Authority;
    (b) in Wales, a county council or a county borough council.

(10) In this section
    (a) "local government election" must be construed in accordance with section 203(1) of the 1983 Act;
    (b) a reference to the area of a local authority must be construed in accordance with the definition of "local government area" in that subsection.

Evaluation of pilots under section 32

33 (1) After any elections specified in a pilot order have taken place, the Electoral Commission must prepare a report on the operation of the order.

(2) The report must contain, in particular
    (a) a description of the way in which the provision made by the order differed from the provisions which would otherwise have applied to the election or elections;
    (b) a copy of the order;
    (c) an assessment of the success or otherwise of the order in assisting voters to make informed decisions at the election or elections in question;
    (d) an assessment of the success or otherwise of the order in encouraging voting at the election or elections in question;
    (e) an assessment of whether the procedures provided for in the order operated satisfactorily.

(3) An assessment under subsection (2)(c) must include a statement of whether, in the opinion of the Commission, the inclusion of photographs on the ballot paper
    (a) assisted voters in marking their papers with a vote for a candidate (or with votes for candidates) for whom they had decided to vote on grounds other than the candidates' appearance;
    (b) resulted in voters being influenced (or more influenced) by the appearance of candidates in deciding for whom to vote.

(4) An assessment under subsection (2)(d) must include a statement of whether, in the opinion of the Commission, the turnout of voters was higher than it would have been if the order had not applied.

(5) An assessment under subsection (2)(e) must include a statement of
    (a) whether the candidates and their agents found the procedures provided for in the order easy to use;
    (b) whether the returning officer found those procedures easy to administer;
    (c) whether those procedures had any effect on the incidence of malpractice (whether or not amounting to an offence) in connection with elections;
    (d) the amount of any increase attributable to those procedures in the resources applied by the authority concerned to the election or elections.

(6)   In making an assessment under subsection (2)(c), (d) or (e), the Commission must also apply such other criteria as are specified in the order in relation to that assessment.

(7)   The local authority must give the Commission such assistance as the Commission may reasonably require in connection with the preparation of the report.

(8)   The assistance may include
   (a)   making arrangements for ascertaining the views of electors about the operation of the provisions of the order;
   (b)   reporting to the Commission allegations of electoral offences or other malpractice.

(9)   The Commission must, before the end of the period of three months beginning with the date of the declaration of the result of the election or elections in question, send a copy of the report
   (a)   to the Secretary of State, and
   (b)   to the local authority.

(10)   The local authority must publish the report in their area in such manner as they think fit.

(11)   In this section "pilot order" and "the local authority" must be construed in accordance with section 32.

Revision of electoral provisions in the light of pilot schemes

34 (1)   This section applies if the Secretary of State thinks, in the light of a report made under section 33 on the operation of a pilot order under section 32, that it would be desirable for provision similar to that made by the order to apply generally, and on a permanent basis, in relation to
   (a)   parliamentary elections;
   (b)   local government elections in England and Wales;
   (c)   any description of election falling within paragraph (a) or (b).

(2)   The Secretary of State may by order make provision for the purposes of enabling ballot papers issued at such elections (mentioned in subsection (1)) as are specified in the order to contain photographs of the candidates.

(3)   The Secretary of State must not make an order under subsection (2) unless he first consults the Electoral Commission.

(4)   An order under subsection (2) may
   (a)   include such provision modifying or disapplying any enactment as the Secretary of State thinks is necessary or expedient for the purposes of the order;
   (b)   create or extend the application of an offence.

(5)   An order under subsection (2) must not create an offence punishable
   (a)   on conviction on indictment, with imprisonment for a term exceeding one year;
   (b)   on summary conviction, with imprisonment for a term exceeding 51 weeks or with a fine exceeding the statutory maximum.

(6)   The power to make an order under subsection (2) is exercisable by statutory instrument, but no such order may be made unless a draft of the instrument containing the order has been laid before and approved by a resolution of each House of Parliament.

(7)   The reference to local government elections must be construed in accordance with section 32.

(8)   If an order under subsection (2) is made before the date of commencement of section 281(5) of the Criminal Justice Act 2003, then in relation to any offence committed before that date the reference in subsection (5)(b) to 51 weeks must be taken to be a reference to six months.

(9)   In its application to Scotland and Northern Ireland, the reference in subsection (5)(b) to 51 weeks must be taken to be a reference to six months.

Voting in person

35–41   *Effect amendments to other legislation: not reproduced here*

Access to other election documents

42 (1)   The relevant officer must
    (a)   make relevant election documents available for inspection by members of the public;
    (b)   supply, on request, copies of or extracts from such description of relevant election documents as is prescribed by regulations.

  (2)   In the case of an election other than a parliamentary election, a local government election in Scotland or a local election in Northern Ireland, each of the following must, on request, be supplied with a copy of the marked copies of the register, the postal voters list, the list of proxies and the proxy postal voters list
    (a)   a registered party;
    (b)   a person who was a candidate at the election in relation to the electoral area for which he was a candidate;
    (c)   in the case of an election at which a registered party submits a list of candidates, a person who was appointed as an agent for the candidates on the party's list.

  (3)   The Secretary of State may by regulations impose conditions in relation to
    (a)   the inspection of any document in pursuance of subsection (1)(a);
    (b)   the supply of any document or part of a document in pursuance of subsection (1)(b);
    (c)   the supply of any document or part of a document in pursuance of subsection (2).

  (4)   Regulations may also make provision
    (a)   as to the form in which any such document or part is supplied;
    (b)   for the payment of a fee in respect of the supply of a document or part.

  (5)   Conditions which may be imposed for the purposes of subsection (3)(a) or (b) include conditions as to
    (a)   whether a person may take any copy of a document he is permitted to inspect;
    (b)   the manner in which any such copy is to be taken;
    (c)   the purposes for which information contained in any document or part of a document which is inspected or supplied in pursuance of subsection (1) may be used.

  (6)   Conditions which may be imposed for the purposes of subsection (3)(b) or (c) include conditions as to the extent to which a person to whom a document or part of a document has been supplied may
    (a)   supply that document or part to any other person;
    (b)   disclose to any other person any information contained in the document or part;
    (c)   use any such information for a purpose other than that for which the document or part was supplied to him.

  (7)   Regulations may also impose conditions corresponding to those mentioned in subsection (6) in respect of persons who have obtained a document or part of a document mentioned in subsection (2)
    (a)   which was supplied to another person in pursuance of subsection (2), or
    (b)   otherwise than in accordance with regulations under this section.

  (8)   The power to make regulations under this section
    (a)   is exercisable by the Secretary of State by statutory instrument;
    (b)   includes power to make different provision for different purposes.

  (9)   The Secretary of State must not make regulations under this section unless he first

consults the Electoral Commission.

(10) No regulations may be made under this section unless a draft of the statutory instrument containing the regulations has been laid before, and approved by resolution of, each House of Parliament.

NOTES

Access to other election documents: contravention of regulations

43 (1) A person is guilty of an offence
    (a) if he fails to comply with any conditions imposed in pursuance of regulations under section 42, or
    (b) if he is an appropriate supervisor of a person (P) who fails to comply with such a condition and he failed to take appropriate steps.

(2) P is not guilty of an offence under subsection (1) if
    (a) he has an appropriate supervisor, and
    (b) he has complied with all the requirements imposed on him by his appropriate supervisor.

(3) A person who is not P or an appropriate supervisor is not guilty of an offence under subsection (1) if he takes all reasonable steps to ensure that he complies with the conditions.

(4) In subsections (1)(b) and (2)
    (a) an appropriate supervisor is a person who is a director of a company or concerned in the management of an organisation in which P is employed or under whose direction or control P is;
    (b) appropriate steps are such steps as it was reasonable for the appropriate supervisor to take to secure the operation of procedures designed to prevent, so far as reasonably practicable, the occurrence of a failure to comply with the conditions.

(5) A person guilty of an offence as mentioned in subsection (1) is liable on summary conviction to a fine not exceeding level 5 on the standard scale.

NOTES
See Further

Access to other election documents: supplementary

44 (1) This section applies for the purposes of section 42.

(2) The relevant officer is
    (a) in England and Wales, the relevant registration officer;
    (b) in Scotland, the relevant sheriff clerk;
    (c) in Northern Ireland, the Chief Electoral Officer for Northern Ireland.

(3) The relevant registration officer is
    (a) the registration officer of the local authority in whose area the election is held, or
    (b) if the election is held in respect of an electoral area which comprises any part of the area of more than one local authority, such registration officer as the Secretary of State by order appoints.

(4) The relevant sheriff clerk is
    (a) the sheriff clerk of the sheriff court district in which the election is held, or
    (b) if the election is held in respect of an electoral area which comprises any part of the area of more than one sheriff court district, the sheriff clerk of such of those districts as the Secretary of State by order appoints.

(5) The relevant election documents are such documents relating to an election (other than a parliamentary election, a local government election in Scotland or a local election in Northern Ireland) as the relevant officer is required by or under any enactment to retain for any period except

    (a) ballot papers;

    (b) completed corresponding number lists;

    (c) certificates as to employment on the day of the election.

(6) A party is a registered party if it is registered for the purposes of Part 2 of the 2000 Act (registration of political parties).

(7) An electoral area is

    (a) in relation to a local government election, an electoral area within the meaning of section 203(1) of the 1983 Act;

    (b) in relation to an election to the National Assembly for Wales, an Assembly constituency or an Assembly electoral region within the meaning of [section 2 of the Government of Wales Act 2006 (Assembly constituencies and electoral regions)];

    (c) in relation to an election to the Scottish Parliament, a constituency or a region within the meaning of Schedule 1 to the Scotland Act 1998 (c 46) (constituencies, regions and regional members);

    (d) in relation to an election to the Northern Ireland Assembly, a constituency for the purposes of section 33 of the Northern Ireland Act 1998 (c 47) (constituencies and numbers of members);

    (e) in relation to an election to the European Parliament, an electoral region within the meaning of section 1 of the European Parliamentary Elections Act 2002 (c 24) (electoral regions and number of MEPs).

(8) The marked register is the copy of the register of electors marked in accordance with provision corresponding to rule 37(1)(c) of the parliamentary elections rules.

(9) A marked copy of the list of proxies is the copy of that list marked in accordance with provision corresponding to rule 37(1)(e) of the parliamentary elections rules.

(10) A marked copy of the postal voters list or the proxy postal voters list is the copy of that list marked in accordance with provision corresponding to rule 31A(1) of the parliamentary elections rules.

(11) A completed corresponding number list is a list prepared under provision corresponding to rule 19A of the parliamentary elections rules which is completed in accordance with provision corresponding to rule 37(1)(b) and (d) of those rules.

(12) Expressions used in this section or section 42 or 43 and in the 1983 Act must (unless the context otherwise requires) be construed in accordance with that Act.

NOTES
See Further

45 *Effects amendments to other legislation: not reproduced here*

Correction of procedural errors

Returning officers: correction of procedural errors

46 (1) A returning officer for an election to which this section applies may take such steps as he thinks appropriate to remedy any act or omission on his part, or on the part of a relevant person, which

    (a) arises in connection with any function the returning officer or relevant person has in relation to the election, and

    (b)   is not in accordance with the rules or any other requirements applicable to the election.

(2)   But a returning officer may not under subsection (1) recount the votes given at an election after the result has been declared.

(3)   This section applies to
    (a)   a parliamentary election;
    (b)   a local government election in England and Wales (within the meaning of the 1983 Act).

(4)   These are the relevant persons
    (a)   an electoral registration officer;
    (b)   a presiding officer;
    (c)   a person providing goods or services to the returning officer;
    (d)   a deputy of any person mentioned in paragraph (a) to (c) or a person appointed to assist, or in the course of his employment assisting, such a person in connection with any function he has in relation to the election.

(5)   Subsections (1) to (4) must be construed as part of the Representation of the People Acts.

(6)   *Effects amendments to other legislation: not reproduced here*

NOTES
See

Miscellaneous amendments

Miscellaneous amendments of the 1983 Act

47   Part 5 of Schedule 1 (which contains miscellaneous amendments of the 1983 Act relating to the conduct of elections) has effect.

PART 7
REGULATION OF PARTIES

Registration of parties

48-54   *Effect amendments to other legislation: not reproduced here*

Control of donations

55-60   *Effect amendments to other legislation: not reproduced here*

Regulation of loans etc

Regulation of loans etc

61   *Effects amendments to other legislation: not reproduced here*

Regulation of loans: power to make provision for candidates, third parties, referendums and recall petitions

62 (1)   The Secretary of State may by order make in relation to a relevant matter such provision as he thinks appropriate which corresponds to or is similar to any provision of Part 4A of or Schedule 7A to the 2000 Act (the relevant transaction provisions).

(2)   A relevant matter is a loan, credit facility or any form of security (whether real or personal)

which benefits
(a) a candidate at [a relevant election];
(b) a recognised third party;
(c) a permitted participant in a referendum;
(d) an accredited campaigner in relation to a recall petition.

(3) An order under this section may
(a) amend or repeal any enactment (whenever passed);
(b) create an offence corresponding or similar to any offence created by the relevant transaction provisions;
(c) confer power on the Secretary of State to make provision by order corresponding to any such power in the relevant transaction provisions;
(d) make different provision for different purposes;
(e) make such supplemental, incidental, consequential, transitional or savings provision as the Secretary of State thinks necessary or expedient in connection with the order.

(3A) The provision that may be made by virtue of subsection (3)(e) includes, in particular, provision amending paragraph 1 of Schedule 19A to the 2000 Act (requirement for unincorporated associations to notify Commission of political contributions over £25,000) so that, in the case of a [relevant person], a "political contribution" includes a relevant matter.

(3B) In subsection (3A) "a relevant person" means
(a) a recognised third party,
(b) a permitted participant in a referendum, or
(c) an accredited campaigner in relation to a recall petition.

(4) An order under this section which confers power to make an order by virtue of subsection (3)(c) must require the order
(a) to be made by statutory instrument;
(b) not to be made unless a draft of the instrument containing the order has been laid before and approved by resolution of each House of Parliament.

(5) Subsection (4) does not apply to any power to make provision determining a rate of interest.

(6) The power to make an order under this section is exercisable by statutory instrument.

(7) No such order may be made unless a draft of the instrument containing the order has been laid before and approved by resolution of each House of Parliament.

(8) In this section

"accredited campaigner" has the same meaning as in Schedule 3 to the Recall of MPs Act 2015 (see Part 5 of that Schedule);

"candidate"
(a) in relation to a police and crime commissioner election, is to be construed in accordance with subsection (8A), and
(b) in relation to any other relevant election, has the same meaning as in Part 2 of the 1983 Act;]

"credit facility" must be construed in accordance with section 71F(11) of the 2000 Act;

"permitted participant" has the same meaning as in Part 7 of the 2000 Act;

"police and crime commissioner election" means an election of a police and crime commissioner in accordance with Chapter 6 of Part 1 of the Police Reform and Social Responsibility Act 2011;

"recall petition" has the same meaning as in the Recall of MPs Act 2015 (see section 1(2) of that Act);

"recognised third party" has the same meaning as in Part 6 of that Act;

"relevant election" means

    (a) an election within the meaning of the 1983 Act, or

    (b) a police and crime commissioner election.

(8A) For the purposes of this section, a person becomes a candidate at a police and crime commissioner election

    (a) on the last day for publication of notice of the election if on or before that day the person is declared by himself or herself or by others to be a candidate at the election, and

    (b) otherwise, on the day on which the person is so declared by himself or herself or by others or on which the person is nominated as a candidate at the election (whichever is the earlier).

(9) An order under this section must not make provision which is within the legislative competence of the Scottish Parliament.

(10) Subsection (9) does not apply to provision made by virtue of subsection (3)(e).

Regulation of loans etc: Northern Ireland

63 (1) The Secretary of State may, after consulting the Electoral Commission, by order make provision relating to regulated transactions, controlled transactions or relevant matters which corresponds to or is similar to any provision ("relevant provision") relating to donations for political purposes which is made by, or which may be made under, the Northern Ireland (Miscellaneous Provisions) Act 2006 ("the 2006 Act").

(2) But if a relevant provision has effect, or would have effect, subject to a temporal limitation, a provision of an order under this section which corresponds to or is similar to the relevant provision must be subject to the same temporal limitation.

(3) An order under this section may in particular

    (a) amend, repeal or revoke any provision made by or under an Act of Parliament or Northern Ireland legislation (whenever passed or made);

    (b) create an offence corresponding or similar to any offence relating to donations for political purposes created by the 2006 Act;

    (c) confer power on the Secretary of State to make provision by order corresponding or similar to any such power relating to donations for political purposes conferred by the 2006 Act;

    (d) make different provision for different purposes;

    (e) make such supplemental, incidental, consequential, transitional or savings provision as the Secretary of State thinks necessary or expedient in connection with the order.

(4) An order under this section which confers power to make an order by virtue of subsection (3)(c) must require the order

    (a) to be made only after consulting the Electoral Commission;

    (b) to be made by statutory instrument; and

    (c) not to be made unless a draft of the instrument containing the order has been laid before and approved by a resolution of each House of Parliament.

(5) The power to make an order under this section is exercisable by statutory instrument.

(6) No such order may be made unless a draft of the instrument containing the order has been laid before and approved by a resolution of each House of Parliament.

(7) In this section

"regulated transaction" has the same meaning as in Part 4A of the 2000 Act (see section 71F of that Act);

"controlled transaction" has the same meaning as in Schedule 7A to that Act (see paragraphs 1 and 2 of that Schedule);

"relevant matter" has the same meaning as in section 62 of this Act (see subsection (2) of that section).

(8)   For the purposes of this section, section 1(3) of the Northern Ireland (Miscellaneous Provisions) Act 2014 (which amends section 71E of the 2000 Act) is treated as provision made by the 2006 Act.

NOTES
Subordinate Legislation
Electoral Administration Act 2006 (Regulation of Loans etc:
Northern Ireland) Order 2008, SI 2008/1319

64-66   *Effect amendments to other legislation: not reproduced here*

PART 8
MISCELLANEOUS

67   *Effects amendments to other legislation: not reproduced here*

68   *Repealed*

Encouraging electoral participation

Encouraging electoral participation

69(1)   A local electoral officer must take such steps as he thinks appropriate to encourage the participation by electors in the electoral process in the area for which he acts.

(2)   A local electoral officer must have regard to any guidance issued by the Electoral Commission for the purposes of this section.

(3)   This section does not permit an electoral registration officer to undertake any activity in relation to a local government election in Scotland unless the activity relates to a matter falling within Section B3 (elections) of Schedule 5 to the Scotland Act 1998 (c 46) (reserved matters).

(4)   The Secretary of State may reimburse a local electoral officer in respect of any expenditure incurred by the officer for the purposes of this section.

(5)   The amount paid under subsection (4) must not in any year exceed such amount as is determined in accordance with regulations made by the Secretary of State.

(6)   The power to make regulations under subsection (5) is exercisable by statutory instrument subject to annulment in pursuance of a resolution of either House of Parliament.

(7)   The regulations may make different provision for different purposes.

(8)   A local electoral officer is
     (a)   an electoral registration officer;
     (b)   a returning officer for an election mentioned in subsection (9).

(9)   These are the elections
     (a)   parliamentary elections;
     (b)   local government elections in England and Wales and Northern Ireland;
     (c)   European Parliamentary elections;
     (d)   elections to the Scottish Parliament;

in connection with the consolidation of some or all of those enactments.

(2) The enactments relating to *the representation of the people are*

    (a) the Representation of the People Act 1983 (c 2);

    (b) the Representation of the People Act 1985 (c 50);

    (c) the Representation of the People Act 1989 (c 28);

    (d) the Representation of the People Act 1993 (c 29);

    (e) the Representation of the People Act 2000 (c 2);

    (f) the Electoral Administration Act 2006;

    (g) the Elections (Northern Ireland) Act 1985 (c 2);

    (h) the Electoral Fraud (Northern Ireland) Act 2002 (c 13);

    (i) the Northern Ireland (Miscellaneous Provisions) Act 2006;

    (j) an enactment referring to any enactment falling within paragraphs (a) to (i).

(3) An order under this section must not come into force unless an Act consolidating the enactments amended by the order (with or without other enactments relating to the representation of the people) has been passed.

(4) An order under this section must not come into force until immediately before that Act comes into force.

(5) Subsection (6) applies if the provisions of that Act come into force at different times.

(6) So much of an order under this section as amends an enactment repealed and reenacted by a provision of that Act comes into force immediately before that provision.

(7) An order under this section must not be made unless the Secretary of State first consults the Electoral Commission.

(8) An order under this section must be made by statutory instrument, but no such order may be made unless a draft of the statutory instrument containing the order has been laid before, and approved by a resolution of, each House of Parliament.

(9) An order under this section must not make any provision which would, if it were included in an Act of the Scottish Parliament, be within the legislative competence of that Parliament.

Legal incapacity to vote

Abolition of common law incapacity: mental state

72(1) Any rule of the common law which provides that a person is subject to a legal incapacity to vote by reason of his mental state is abolished.

(2) Accordingly, in section 202(1) of the 1983 Act (general provisions as to interpretation), in

Pre-consolidation amendments

72 (1) The Secretary of State may by order make such amendments of the enactments relating

Pre-consolidation amendments

70–71 *Effect amendments to other legislation: not reproduced here*

(10) References to a local government election must be construed in accordance with the 1983 Act.

Electoral Administration Act 2006

77 Not reproduced

Extent

78 (1) Subject to subsections (2) to (5), the extent of any amendment or repeal made by this Act is the same as that of the enactment amended or repealed.

(2) The following provisions do not extend to Northern Ireland

    (a) sections 9 and 11;

    (b) section 67;

    (c) section 70;

    (d) Part] 2 of Schedule 1.

(3) Section 70 does not extend to Scotland.

(4) A repeal of an enactment by Schedule 2 which corresponds to a repeal of that enactment by any other provision of this Act has the same extent as that other provision.

(5) The repeal in Schedule 2 relating to paragraph 86 of Schedule 4 to the Representation of the People Act 1985 (c 50) does not extend to Northern Ireland.

Short title

79 This Act may be cited as the Electoral Administration Act 2006.

SCHEDULE 1
Amendments

Not reproduced

SCHEDULE 2
Repeals

Not reproduced

Electoral Registration and Administration Act 2013

An Act to make provision about the registration of electors and the administration and conduct of elections; and to amend section 3(2)(a) of the Parliamentary Constituencies Act 1986.

31st January 2013

PART 1
INDIVIDUAL ELECTORAL REGISTRATION IN GREAT BRITAIN

1 Individual registration
Amends the Representation of the People Act 1983. Not reproduced here.

2 Applications for registration and verification of entitlement etc
Amends the Representation of the People Act 1983. Not reproduced here.

3 Proxies to be registered electors
Amends the Representation of the People Act 2000. Not reproduced here.

4 Annual canvass
Amends the Representation of the People Act 1983. Not reproduced here.

5 Invitations to register
Amends the Representation of the People Act 1983. Not reproduced here.

6 Amendment of Parliamentary Constituencies Act 1986
Amends the Parliamentary Constituencies Act 1986. Not reproduced here.

7 Power to amend or abolish the annual canvass

(1) The Minister may by order make provision for the purposes of assisting registration officers in Great Britain to ascertain
  (a) the names and addresses of persons who are not registered in a register but who are entitled to be registered;
  (b) those persons who are registered in a register but who are not entitled to be registered.

(2) The Minister may by order
  (a) modify section 9D of the Representation of the People Act 1983 or any other provision relating to a canvass under that section;
  (b) abolish the duty to conduct a canvass under that section.

(3) If the duty to conduct a canvass is abolished, the provision that may be made under subsection (1) includes provision reinstating the duty.

(4) An order under this section may create offences punishable on summary conviction by a fine not exceeding level 5 on the standard scale.

(5) An order under this section may confer power to make subordinate legislation and, if it does so, must provide
  (a) that the subordinate legislation is to be made by statutory instrument, and
  (b) that the instrument may not be made unless a draft of it has been laid before and approved by a resolution of each House of Parliament.

NOTES
Defined terms
  the Minister: s 25
  modify: s 12
  register: s 12

  registration officer: s 12
  subordinate legislation: s 12

8 Consulting Electoral Commission about proposals under section 7

(1) If the Minister consults the Electoral Commission about a proposal to make an order under section 7, the Commission must prepare a report assessing
  (a) the extent to which the objective in subsection (2) is met,
  (b) the extent to which the objective would be met if the order were made, and
  (c) the merits of alternative ways of achieving the objective.

(2) The objective is to assist registration officers in Great Britain to ascertain
  (a) the names and addresses of persons who are not registered in a register but who are entitled to be registered;
  (b) those persons who are registered in a register but who are not entitled to be

registered.

(3) The Electoral Commission must give a copy of the report to the Minister by the specified date.

(4) The "specified date" means a date to be specified by the Minister and the date must not be before the end of the period of 3 months beginning with the day on which the Commission is consulted.

(5) A registration officer in Great Britain must comply with any request made by the Electoral Commission for information that it reasonably requires in connection with the preparation of a report under this section.

(6) When a draft of a statutory instrument containing an order under section 7 is laid before Parliament (see section 11), it must be accompanied by a report under this section, unless the instrument contains provision only for the purpose of reinstating the duty to conduct a canvass as mentioned in section 7(3).

NOTES

Defined terms
   the Minister: s 25
  register: s 12

registration officer: s 12

9 Piloting of changes to the annual canvass

(1) An order under section 7 may be made so as to have effect in relation to a specified period.

(2) An order which, by virtue of subsection (1), is to have effect in relation to a limited period is referred to in this section as a "pilot scheme".

(3) The Minister may make a pilot scheme applying in relation to an area only if the registration officer for that area has
   (a) proposed the making of a pilot scheme in relation to that area, and
   (b) agreed to any modifications made by the Minister to the proposal.

(4) Section 8 does not apply in relation to a pilot scheme.

(5) The provision that may be made in a pilot scheme by virtue of section 11(3) includes, in particular, provision in connection with the expiry of the specified period.

(6) A pilot scheme may be replaced by a further pilot scheme.

(7) If a pilot scheme is made, the Electoral Commission must
   (a) prepare a report on the pilot scheme, and
   (b) by no later than a date to be specified in the pilot scheme, give a copy of the report to the Minister and to the registration officer for the area concerned (or the officer for each area concerned).

(8) The Electoral Commission's report must contain
   (a) a description of the pilot scheme,
   (b) an assessment of the extent to which the objective in section 8(2) was met in the area or areas concerned immediately before the specified period,
   (c) an assessment of the extent to which the objective was met in the area or areas concerned during the specified period, and
   (d) an assessment of the extent to which the scheme resulted in savings of time and costs, or the opposite.

(9) The Minister must publish the Electoral Commission's report.

(10) A registration officer in Great Britain must comply with any request made by the Electoral Commission for information that it reasonably requires in connection with the preparation of a report under this section.

NOTES

Defined terms

the Minister: s 25

10 Piloting registration provisions

(1) The Minister may by order make provision for the purpose of testing, for a specified period and in relation to a specified area, how the changes made by any registration provision work in practice.

(2) An order under this section may, in particular, make provision the effect of which corresponds to the effect of the amendments made by any registration provision (or the subordinate legislation that may be made by virtue of any registration provision).

(3) "Registration provision" means any provision of
   (a) section 1 and Schedule 1,
   (b) section 2 and Schedule 2, and
   (c) Schedule 4.

(4) The Minister may make an order under this section in relation to an area only if the registration officer for that area has
   (a) proposed the making of an order in relation to that area, and
   (b) agreed to any modifications made by the Minister to the proposal.

(5) The provision that may be made in an order under this section by virtue of section 11(3) includes, in particular, provision in connection with the expiry of the specified period.

(6) An order under this section may make provision modifying Schedule 5 (for example, to modify the meaning of "new application for registration").

NOTES

Subordinate legislation

Electoral Registration and Administration Act 2013 (Transitional Provisions) Order 2013, SI 2013/3197.
Electoral Registration and Administration Act 2013 (Transitional Provisions) (Amendment) Order 2014, SI 2014/449.
Electoral Registration Pilot Scheme Order 2014, SI 2014/3178.

Defined terms
the Minister: s 25
modify: s 12
registration officer: s 12
subordinate legislation: s 12

11 Orders under Part 1

(1) An order under this Part is to be made by statutory instrument.

(2) A statutory instrument containing an order under this Part (whether alone or with other provision) may not be made unless a draft of the instrument has been laid before and approved by a resolution of each House of Parliament (but paragraph 28 of Schedule 5 contains an exception to this).

(3) An order under this Part may make consequential, supplementary, incidental, transitional or saving provision.

(4) An order under this Part may modify any other Act or subordinate legislation (whenever passed or made).

(5) An order under this Part
   (a) may apply generally or only in specified cases, circumstances or areas;
   (b) may make different provision for different cases, circumstances or areas.

NOTES

Subordinate legislation

Electoral Registration and Administration Act 2013 (Transitional Provisions) Order 2013, SI 2013/3197.
Electoral Registration and Administration Act 2013 (Transitional Provisions) (Amendment) Order 2014, SI 2014/449.
Electoral Registration Pilot Scheme Order 2014, SI 2014/3178.

Defined terms
modify: s 12
subordinate legislation: s 12

12 Interpretation of Part 1

In this Part

"modify" includes amend, repeal or revoke;

"register" means a register of parliamentary electors or local government electors maintained by a registration officer in Great Britain;

"registration officer" has the same meaning as in the Representation of the People Act 1983 (see section 8 of that Act);

"subordinate legislation" has the same meaning as in the Interpretation Act 1978.

13 Amendments and transitional provision

(1) Schedule 4 contains amendments to do with this Part.

(2) Schedule 5 makes transitional provision to do with this Part.

(3) In relation to an offence committed in England and Wales before the commencement of section 154(1) of the Criminal Justice Act 2003, the reference to 12 months in paragraph 13(1ZD)(a) of Schedule 2 to the Representation of the People Act 1983 (inserted by Schedule 2 to this Act) is to be read as a reference to 6 months.

(4) In relation to an offence committed in England and Wales before the commencement of section 281(5) of the Criminal Justice Act 2003, the reference to 51 weeks in paragraph 13(1ZD)(b) of Schedule 2 to the Representation of the People Act 1983 (inserted by Schedule 2 to this Act) is to be read as a reference to 6 months.

NOTES
Subordinate legislation
Electoral Registration and Administration Act 2013 (Transitional Provisions) Order 2015, SI 2015/1520.

PART 2
ADMINISTRATION AND CONDUCT OF ELECTIONS ETC

14 Extension of timetable for parliamentary elections
Amends various election statutes. Not reproduced here.

15 Timing of parish and community council elections in England and Wales
Amends various election statutes. Not reproduced here.

16 Alteration of electoral registers: pending elections
Amends various election statutes. Not reproduced here.

17 Review of polling districts and places in Great Britain
Amends various election statutes. Not reproduced here.

18 Inadequate performance of returning officer: reduction of charges
Amends various election statutes. Not reproduced here.

19 Voters waiting at polling station at close of poll
Amends various election statutes. Not reproduced here.

20 Use of emblems on ballot papers
Amends various election statutes. Not reproduced here.

21 Community support officers
Amends various election statutes. Not reproduced here.

22 Notification of rejected postal vote
Amends various election statutes. Not reproduced here.

23 Repeal of powers to establish co-ordinated online record of electors
Amends various election statutes. Not reproduced here.

PART 3
FINAL PROVISIONS

24 Financial provisions
Not reproduced.

25 Meaning of "the Minister" etc

(1) In this Act "the Minister" means the Chancellor of the Duchy of Lancaster or the Secretary of State.

(2) In article 3(1) of the Lord President of the Council Order 2010 (SI 2010/1837) (which makes certain functions of the Secretary of State exercisable concurrently with the Lord President) a reference to an enactment that is amended by this Act is to that enactment as amended.

26 Extent

An amendment or repeal made by this Act has the same extent as the enactment (or part of an enactment) amended or repealed.

27 Commencement

(1) Subject as follows, Parts 1 and 2 of this Act come into force on such day as the Minister may by order made by statutory instrument appoint.

(2) Paragraph 28 of Schedule 5 comes into force at the end of the period of 2 months beginning with the day on which this Act is passed.

(3) This Part comes into force on the day on which this Act is passed.

(4) An order under subsection (1) may appoint different days for different purposes (including different days for different parts of the United Kingdom).

(5) An order under subsection (1) bringing into force any provision of section 19 may
    (a) make provision in consequence of, or for giving full effect to, that section, or
    (b) make supplementary or incidental provision for the purposes of that section.

(6) An order made by virtue of subsection (5) may
    (a) modify any Act (whenever passed), including any provision inserted by a provision of this Act apart from section 19, or
    (b) modify subordinate legislation (whenever made).

(7) An order made by virtue of subsection (5) that contains provision modifying an Act may not be made unless a draft of the statutory instrument containing it has been laid before and approved by a resolution of each House of Parliament.

(8) Any other order made by virtue of subsection (5) is subject to annulment in pursuance of a resolution of either House of Parliament.

(9) In this section
    "modify" includes amend, repeal or revoke;
    "subordinate legislation" has the same meaning as in the Interpretation Act 1978.

(10) The Minister may by order made by statutory instrument make transitional, transitory or

saving provision in connection with the coming into force of any provision of this Act or of any provision of an order made by virtue of subsection (5).

NOTES

Subordinate legislataion

Electoral Registration and Administration Act 2013 (Commencement No 1) Order 2013, SI 2013/219.

Electoral Registration and Administration Act 2013 (Commencement No 2) Order 2013, SI 2013/702.

Electoral Registration and Administration Act 2013 (Commencement No 3) Order 2013, SI 2013/969.

Electoral Registration and Administration Act 2013 (Commencement No 4 and Consequential Provision)

Order 2014, SI 2014/336.

Electoral Registration and Administration Act 2013 (Commencement No 5 and Transitory Provisions) Order 2014, SI 2014/414.

Electoral Registration and Administration Act 2013 (Commencement No 1) (Northern Ireland) Order 2014, SI 2014/2439.

28 Short title

This Act may be cited as the Electoral Registration and Administration Act 2013.

SCHEDULE 1
Amends various election statutes. Not reproduced here.

SCHEDULE 2
Amends various election statutes. Not reproduced here.

SCHEDULE 3
Amends various election statutes. Not reproduced here.

SCHEDULE 4
Amends various election statutes. Not reproduced here.

SCHEDULE 5
Transitional Provision to do with Part 1

Part 1
Introduction

Applications for registration etc made before commencement

1 The amendments made by Part 1 of this Act do not apply in relation to an application made before the commencement date (even if it is determined later).

Meaning of "commencement date"

2 In this Schedule "commencement date" means the date appointed for sections 1 and 4 and Schedule 1 to come fully into force.

Meaning of "new application for registration" and "successful" new application

3(1) For the purposes of this Schedule, a person ("P") makes a "new application for registration" in a register maintained by a registration officer in Great Britain if

    (a) an application for registration in the register under section 10ZC of the Representation of the People Act 1983 is made in respect of P, or

    (b) an application for alteration of the register under section 10ZD of that Act is made in respect of P.

(2) For the purposes of this Schedule, a new application for registration is "successful"

    (a) in the case of an application within sub-paragraph (1)(a), if the officer determines that P is to be entered in the register (or that P would be entered in the register had P not already been registered);

(b)   in the case of an application within sub-paragraph (1)(b), if the officer determines that P's entry in the register is to be altered.

Checking of old entries and meaning of "confirmation" of entitlement to remain registered

4(1)   The Minister may by order require a registration officer in Great Britain to take specified steps to check whether each person who has an entry in a register maintained by the officer is entitled to remain registered.

(2)   For the purposes of this Schedule a person's entitlement to remain registered has been "confirmed" if, having taken steps in accordance with an order under sub-paragraph (1), the registration officer is satisfied that there is evidence of a kind specified in the order to support the person's entitlement to be registered.

(3)   An order under this paragraph may make further provision about checking or confirming a person's entitlement to remain registered, including
   (a)   provision of the kind mentioned in paragraph 1A or 13(1ZB) to (1ZD) of Schedule 2 to the Representation of the People Act 1983 (inserted by Schedule 2 to this Act);
   (b)   provision requiring a registration officer to have regard to guidance given by the Minister (including guidance of the kind mentioned in section 1(4));
   (c)   provision requiring a registration officer who has confirmed a person's entitlement, to notify that person in a specified manner and within a specified period;
   (d)   provision requiring the notification to be accompanied by, or combined with, other documents.

(4)   Subsections (5) to (8) of section 53 of the Representation of the People Act 1983 (inserted by Schedule 2 to this Act) apply in relation to an order containing provision of the kind mentioned in sub-paragraph (3)(a) above as they apply in relation to the regulations mentioned in subsection (5) of that section.

(5)   Nothing in this paragraph requires a registration officer to take steps to check the entitlement of a person to remain registered in a register if
   (a)   the person's entry in the register was carried forward on the conclusion of the final old canvass (see paragraph 5(2)),
   (b)   the person has made a successful new application for registration in the register, or
   (c)   the person is a relevant person for the purposes of Part 5 or 6 of this Schedule.

NOTES

Subordinate legislation
Electoral Registration and Administration Act 2013 (Transitional Provisions) Order 2013, SI 2013/3197.
Electoral Registration and Administration Act 2013

(Transitional Provisions) (Amendment) Order 2014, SI 2014/449.

Part 2
Removal of Existing Registrations by End of the Third New Canvass

Removal of certain existing registrations after the first new canvass

5(1)   A registration officer in Great Britain must, immediately before the publication of a register following the first new canvass, remove the entry of a person ("P") if
   (a)   P's entry was carried forward on the conclusion of the final old canvass,
   (b)   P has not made a new application for registration in the register, and
   (c)   at the first new canvass, no canvass form has been completed and returned in respect of P and the address to which the entry relates.

(2)   For the purposes of sub-paragraph (1), P's entry on the register was carried forward on the conclusion of the final old canvass if
   (a)   P's entitlement to remain registered in the register terminated on the conclusion of the final old canvass by virtue of section 10A(5)(a) of the Representation of the

People Act 1983, but

    (b)   in accordance with regulations under section 10A(7) of that Act, P's entry was not removed from the register.

(3)   In this paragraph "the final old canvass" means the final canvass under section 10(1) of the Representation of the People Act 1983.

Removal of existing registrations after the third new canvass

6   A registration officer in Great Britain must, immediately before the publication of a register following the third new canvass, remove the entry of any person who has neither

(a)   had his or her entitlement to remain registered confirmed, nor

(b)   made a successful new application for registration in the register.

This Part not to apply to persons within Part 5 or 6 below

7   In this Part of this Schedule, references to a person who has an entry in a register do not include a person who is a relevant person for the purposes of Part 5 or 6 of this Schedule.

Part 3
Encouraging New Applications

Registration officers to invite applications in year of first new canvass from those with existing registrations

8(1)   A registration officer in Great Britain must, within a prescribed period, give an invitation to make a new application for registration in a register maintained by the officer to each person who

    (a)   has an entry in the register but has not had his or her entitlement to remain registered confirmed, and

    (b)   has not made a new application for registration.

(2)   But the officer need not give an invitation at a time when the officer has reason to believe, from records available to the officer, that the person is no longer resident at the address to which the entry relates.

(3)   The period prescribed for the purposes of this paragraph must begin in the year in which the first new canvass begins.

Powers to delay canvasses and timing of canvasses

9(1)   The Minister may by order

    (a)   postpone any canvass to be conducted under section 10(1) of the Representation of the People Act 1983;

    (b)   make provision about the period during which canvass forms to be used for the purpose of such a canvass are to be given.

(2)   The Minister may by order postpone the first new canvass.

(3)   Any canvass forms to be used by a registration officer for the purpose of the first new canvass must be given within the period prescribed for the purposes of paragraph 8.

(4)   The Minister may by order make provision about the period during which any canvass forms to be used for the purpose of the second new canvass are to be given.

(5)   A registration officer is not required, before the commencement date, to do anything for the purpose of conducting any canvass under section 10(1) of the Representation of the People Act 1983 by reference to residence on the 15 October after the commencement date.

(6)   An order under sub-paragraph (1) or (2) postponing a canvass must specify the period

during which it is to be conducted; and the period must not end later than the 1 April after it begins.

(7) An order under sub-paragraph (1) or (2) postponing a canvass does not postpone or remove a duty to conduct any other canvass.

Canvass forms need not be supplied to addresses to which invitations supplied

10(1) At the first new canvass, a registration officer is not required to supply a canvass form to an address if the officer thinks that it is unnecessary to do so and

    (a) the officer has given a person an invitation under paragraph 8 in respect of the address,

    (b) the officer has given a person an invitation under section 9E of the Representation of the People Act 1983 in respect of the address, or

    (c) a person is registered in respect of the address in a register maintained by the officer and the person's entitlement to remain registered in the register has been confirmed.

(2) In deciding whether it is necessary to supply a canvass form to an address the registration officer must, in particular, consider whether supplying the canvass form is likely to result in the officer finding out about people residing at the address whom the officer might not otherwise find out about.

Registration officers to invite applications in year of second new canvass from those with existing registrations

11(1) A registration officer in Great Britain must, on or as soon as reasonably practicable after the relevant date, give a person an invitation to make a new application for registration in a register maintained by the officer if the person

    (a) has an entry in the register but has not had his or her entitlement to remain registered confirmed, and

    (b) has not made a successful new application for registration in the register.

(2) "The relevant date" means whichever of the following comes first

    (a) the date on which, at the second new canvass, a canvass form is completed and returned in respect of the address to which the person's entry in the register relates;

    (b) the date on which it appears to the officer that, at the second new canvass, no canvass form will be completed and returned in respect of that address;

    (c) 31 October in the year of the second new canvass.

(3) But the officer need not give an invitation at a time when

    (a) the officer has reason to believe, from records available to the officer, that the person is no longer resident at that address, or

    (b) the person has made a new application for registration which has not been determined.

Invitations under paragraph 8 or 11 and power to require application following invitation

12 The Minister may by order make provision in connection with invitations under paragraph 8 or 11, including provision of the kind mentioned in

    (a) section 9E(2) and (3) of the Representation of the People Act 1983, or

    (b) paragraph 3C(2) of Schedule 2 to that Act.

13(1) A registration officer who gives a person an invitation under paragraph 8 or 11 may subsequently require the person to make an application for registration by a specified date.

(2) A requirement under sub-paragraph (1) is of no effect if the person is not entitled to be

registered.

(3)   The Minister may by order make provision of the kind mentioned in section 9E(6) of the Representation of the People Act 1983 in connection with requirements under sub-paragraph (1).

(4)   A registration officer may impose a civil penalty on a person who fails to comply with a requirement imposed by the officer under sub-paragraph (1).

(5)   The Minister
(a)   must by order make provision of the kind mentioned in paragraphs 2 and 3 of Schedule ZA1 to the Representation of the People Act 1983 in connection with a civil penalty under sub-paragraph (4), and
(b)   may by order make any other provision of the kind mentioned in that Schedule in connection with a civil penalty under that sub-paragraph.

(6)   A civil penalty under sub-paragraph (4) received by a registration officer is to be paid into the Consolidated Fund.

Power to require additional information on poll cards at 2014 European Parliamentary election

14   Regulations under section 7(1) of the European Parliamentary Elections Act 2002 may include provision for the purpose of requiring a poll card to be used at the 2014 European Parliamentary general election to include information relating to changes made by Part 1 of this Act.

Certain provisions of this Part not to apply to persons within Part 5 or 6 below

15   In this Part of this Schedule, references to a person who has an entry in a register do not include a person who is a relevant person for the purposes of Part 5 or 6 of this Schedule.

NOTES
Subordinate legislation

Electoral Registration (Postponement of 2013 Annual Canvass) Order 2013, SI 2013/794.
Electoral Registration and Administration Act 2013

(Transitional Provisions) Order 2013, SI 2013/3197.

Part 4
Absent Voting

Applicant for absent vote must have made successful new application for registration or had registration confirmed

16(1)   For the purposes of an absent voting application made on or after the commencement date, a person is to be regarded as registered in a register in Great Britain only if the person
(a)   was registered in the register immediately before the commencement date and has had his or her entitlement to remain registered confirmed, or
(b)   has made a successful new application for registration.

(2)   "Absent voting application" means an application under paragraph 3(1) or (2) or 4(1) or (2) of Schedule 4 to the Representation of the People Act 2000.

(3)   This paragraph does not apply in relation to a person who is a relevant person for the purposes of Part 5 or 6 of this Schedule.

Entitlement to absent vote ceases after first new canvass if no successful new application for *registration or confirmation of registration*

17(1)   Sub-paragraph (2) applies if, on the day on which a registration officer in Great Britain publishes a register following the first new canvass

date.

(4) For the purposes of this Schedule a document may be given to a person
   (a) by delivering it to the person,
   (b) by leaving it at the person's address, or
   (c) by sending it to the person by post.

(5) The Representation of the People Act 1983 and this Schedule are to have effect as if this Schedule were contained in Part 1 of that Act.

(6) References in an enactment other than one contained in this Schedule or the Representation of the People Act 1983 to Part 1 of that Act include a reference to this Schedule.

NOTES

Subordinate legislation

Electoral Registration and Administration Act 2013 (Transitional Provisions) Order 2013, SI 2013/3197.
Electoral Registration and Administration Act 2013 (Transitional Provisions) (Amendment) Order 2014, SI 2014/449.
Electoral Registration and Administration Act 2013 (Transitional Provisions) Order 2015, SI 2015/1520.

Equality Act 2010

PART 7
ASSOCIATIONS

Preliminary

100 Application of this Part

(1) This Part does not apply to the protected characteristic of marriage and civil partnership.

(2) This Part does not apply to discrimination, harassment or victimisation
   (a) that is prohibited by Part 3 (services and public functions), Part 4 (premises), Part 5 (work) or Part 6 (education), or
   (b) that would be so prohibited but for an express exception.

101 Members and associates

(1) An association (A) must not discriminate against a person (B)
   (a) in the arrangements A makes for deciding who to admit to membership;
   (b) as to the terms on which A is prepared to admit B to membership;
   (c) by not accepting B's application for membership.

(2) An association (A) must not discriminate against a member (B)
   (a) in the way A affords B access, or by not affording B access, to a benefit, facility or service;
   (b) by depriving B of membership;
   (c) by varying B's terms of membership;
   (d) by subjecting B to any other detriment.

(3) An association (A) must not discriminate against an associate (B)
   (a) in the way A affords B access, or by not affording B access, to a benefit, facility or service;
   (b) by depriving B of B's rights as an associate;
   (c) by varying B's rights as an associate;
   (d) by subjecting B to any other detriment.

(4) An association must not harass
   (a) a member;
   (b) a person seeking to become a member;
   (c) an associate.

(5) An association (A) must not victimise a person (B)
   (a) in the arrangements A makes for deciding who to admit to membership;
   (b) as to the terms on which A is prepared to admit B to membership;
   (c) by not accepting B's application for membership.

(6) An association (A) must not victimise a member (B)
   (a) in the way A affords B access, or by not affording B access, to a benefit, facility or service;
   (b) by depriving B of membership;
   (c) by varying B's terms of membership;
   (d) by subjecting B to any other detriment.

(7) An association (A) must not victimise an associate (B)
   (a) in the way A affords B access, or by not affording B access, to a benefit, facility or service;
   (b) by depriving B of B's rights as an associate;

(c)   by varying B's rights as an associate;

(d)   by subjecting B to any other detriment.

NOTES
Defined terms
  affording access to a benefit, facility or service: s 212(4)
  associate: s 107(1), (6)
  association: s 107(1), (2), (4)
  detriment: s 212(1), (5)

member: s 107(1), (5)
membership: s 107(1), (5)

102 Guests

(1)   An association (A) must not discriminate against a person (B)

    (a)   in the arrangements A makes for deciding who to invite, or who to permit to be invited, as a guest;

    (b)   as to the terms on which A is prepared to invite B, or to permit B to be invited, as a guest;

    (c)   by not inviting B, or not permitting B to be invited, as a guest.

(2)   An association (A) must not discriminate against a guest (B) invited by A or with A's permission (whether express or implied)

    (a)   in the way A affords B access, or by not affording B access, to a benefit, facility or service;

    (b)   by subjecting B to any other detriment.

(3)   An association must not harass

    (a)   a guest;

    (b)   a person seeking to be a guest.

(4)   An association (A) must not victimise a person (B)

    (a)   in the arrangements A makes for deciding who to invite, or who to permit to be invited, as a guest;

    (b)   as to the terms on which A is prepared to invite B, or to permit B to be invited, as a guest;

    (c)   by not inviting B, or not permitting B to be invited, as a guest.

(5)   An association (A) must not victimise a guest (B) invited by A or with A's permission (whether express or implied)

    (a)   in the way A affords B access, or by not affording B access, to a benefit, facility or service;

    (b)   by subjecting B to any other detriment.

NOTES
Defined terms
  affording access to a benefit, facility or service: s 212(4)
  association: s 107(1), (2), (4)

detriment: s 212(1), (5)

103 Sections 101 and 102: further provision

(1)   A duty to make reasonable adjustments applies to an association.

(2)   In the application of section 26 for the purposes of section 101(4) or 102(3), neither of the following is a relevant protected characteristic

    (a)   religion or belief;

    (b)   sexual orientation.

NOTES
Defined terms
  association: s 107(1), (2), (4)

Special provision for political parties

104 Selection of candidates

(1)   This section applies to an association which is a registered political party.

(2)   A person does not contravene this Part only by acting in accordance with selection arrangements.

(3)   Selection arrangements are arrangements
  (a)   which the party makes for regulating the selection of its candidates in a relevant election,
  (b)   the purpose of which is to reduce inequality in the party's representation in the body concerned, and
  (c)   which, subject to subsection (7), are a proportionate means of achieving that purpose.

(4)   The reference in subsection (3)(b) to inequality in a party's representation in a body is a reference to inequality between
  (a)   the number of the party's candidates elected to be members of the body who share a protected characteristic, and
  (b)   the number of the party's candidates so elected who do not share that characteristic.

(5)   For the purposes of subsection (4), persons share the protected characteristic of disability if they are disabled persons (and section 6(3)(b) is accordingly to be ignored).

(6)   Selection arrangements do not include shortlisting only such persons as have a particular protected characteristic.

(7)   But subsection (6) does not apply to the protected characteristic of sex; and subsection (3)(c) does not apply to shortlisting in reliance on this subsection.

(8)   The following elections are relevant elections
  (a)   Parliamentary Elections;
  (b)   elections to the European Parliament;
  (c)   elections to the Scottish Parliament;
  (d)   elections to the National Assembly for Wales;
  (e)   local government elections within the meaning of section 191, 203 or 204 of the Representation of the People Act 1983 (excluding elections for the Mayor of London).

NOTES
Defined terms
  association: s 107(1), (2), (4)
  registered political party: s 107(1), (7)

105 Time-limited provision

(1)   Section 104(7) and the words ", subject to subsection (7)," in section 104(3)(c) are repealed at the end of 2030 unless an order is made under subsection (2).

(2)   At any time before the end of 2030, a Minister of the Crown may by order provide that subsection (1) is to have effect with the substitution of a later time for that for the time being specified there.

(3)   In section 3 of the Sex Discrimination (Election Candidates) Act 2002 (expiry of that Act), in subsection (1) for "2015" substitute "2030".

(4)   The substitution made by subsection (3) does not affect the power to substitute a later time by order under section 3 of that Act.

NOTES
Defined terms   registered political party: s 107(1), (7)
  association: s 107(1), (2), (4)
  prescribed: s 212(1)

106 Information about diversity in range of candidates, etc

(1)   This section applies to an association which is a registered political party.

(2)   If the party had candidates at a relevant election, the party must, in accordance with regulations, publish information relating to protected characteristics of persons who come within a description prescribed in the regulations in accordance with subsection (3).

(3)   One or more of the following descriptions may be prescribed for the purposes of subsection (2)
    (a)   successful applicants for nomination as a candidate at the relevant election;
    (b)   unsuccessful applicants for nomination as a candidate at that election;
    (c)   candidates elected at that election;
    (d)   candidates who are not elected at that election.

(4)   The duty imposed by subsection (2) applies only in so far as it is possible to publish information in a manner that ensures that no person to whom the information relates can be identified from that information.

(5)   The following elections are relevant elections
    (a)   Parliamentary Elections;
    (b)   elections to the European Parliament;
    (c)   elections to the Scottish Parliament;
    (d)   elections to the National Assembly for Wales.

(6)   This section does not apply to the following protected characteristics
    (a)   marriage and civil partnership;
    (b)   pregnancy and maternity.

(7)   The regulations may provide that the information to be published
    (a)   must (subject to subsection (6)) relate to all protected characteristics or only to such as are prescribed;
    (b)   must include a statement, in respect of each protected characteristic to which the information relates, of the proportion that the number of persons who provided the information to the party bears to the number of persons who were asked to provide it.

(8)   Regulations under this section may prescribe
    (a)   descriptions of information;
    (b)   descriptions of political party to which the duty is to apply;
    (c)   the time at which information is to be published;
    (d)   the form and manner in which information is to be published;
    (e)   the period for which information is to be published.

(9)   Provision by virtue of subsection (8)(b) may, in particular, provide that the duty imposed by subsection (2) does not apply to a party which had candidates in fewer constituencies in the election concerned than a prescribed number.

(10)   Regulations under this section
    (a)   may provide that the duty imposed by subsection (2) applies only to such relevant elections as are prescribed;
    (b)   may provide that a by-election or other election to fill a vacancy is not to be treated as a relevant election or is to be so treated only to a prescribed extent;
    (c)   may amend this section so as to provide for the duty imposed by subsection (2) to apply in the case of additional descriptions of election.

(11)   Nothing in this section authorises a political party to require a person to provide information to it.

NOTES
Defined terms   association: s 107(1), (2), (4)

prescribed: s 212(1)
registered political party: s 107(1), (7)

Supplementary

107 Interpretation and exceptions

(1)   This section applies for the purposes of this Part.

(2)   An "association" is an association of persons
    (a)   which has at least 25 members, and
    (b)   admission to membership of which is regulated by the association's rules and involves a process of selection.

(3)   A Minister of the Crown may by order amend subsection (2)(a) so as to substitute a different number for that for the time being specified there.

(4)   It does not matter
    (a)   whether an association is incorporated;
    (b)   whether its activities are carried on for profit.

(5)   Membership is membership of any description; and a reference to a member is to be construed accordingly.

(6)   A person is an "associate", in relation to an association, if the person
    (a)   is not a member of the association, but
    (b)   in accordance with the association's rules, has some or all of the rights as a member as a result of being a member of another association.

(7)   A reference to a registered political party is a reference to a party registered in the Great Britain register under Part 2 of the Political Parties, Elections and Referendums Act 2000.

(8)   Schedule 15 (reasonable adjustments) has effect.

(9)   Schedule 16 (exceptions) has effect.

SCHEDULE 15
Associations: Reasonable Adjustments

Preliminary

1   This Schedule applies where a duty to make reasonable adjustments is imposed on an association (A) by this Part.

The duty

2(1)   A must comply with the first, second and third requirements.

(2)   For the purposes of this paragraph, the reference in section 20(3), (4) or (5) to a disabled person is a reference to disabled persons who
    (a)   are, or are seeking to become or might wish to become, members,
    (b)   are associates, or
    (c)   are, or are likely to become, guests.

(3)   Section 20 has effect as if, in subsection (4), for "to avoid the disadvantage" there were substituted
    "(a)   to avoid the disadvantage, or
    (b)   to adopt a reasonable alternative method of affording access to the benefit, facility or service or of admitting persons to membership or inviting persons as guests."

(4)   In relation to the first and third requirements, the relevant matters are

(a) access to a benefit, facility or service;

(b) members' or associates' retaining their rights as such or avoiding having them varied;

(c) being admitted to membership or invited as a guest.

(5) In relation to the second requirement, the relevant matters are

(a) access to a benefit, facility or service;

(b) being admitted to membership or invited as a guest.

(6) In relation to the second requirement, a physical feature includes a physical feature brought by or on behalf of A, in the course of or for the purpose of providing a benefit, facility or service, on to premises other than those that A occupies (as well as including a physical feature in or on premises that A occupies).

(7) Nothing in this paragraph requires A to take a step which would fundamentally alter

(a) the nature of the benefit, facility or service concerned, or

(b) the nature of the association.

(8) Nor does anything in this paragraph require a member or associate in whose house meetings of the association take place to make adjustments to a physical feature of the house.

NOTES

Defined terms

A: s 20(1)

affording access to a benefit, facility or service: s 212(4)

associate: s 107(1), (6)

association: s 107(1), (2), (4)

avoiding a substantial disadvantage: s 20(9)

first requirement: s 20(3), (8)

member: s 107(1), (5)

membership: s 107(1), (5)

occupation in relation to premises: s 212(6)

physical feature: s 20(10) (and para 2(6))

second requirement: s 20(4), (8)

third requirement: s 20(5), (8)

SCHEDULE 16
Associations: Exceptions

Single characteristic associations

1(1) An association does not contravene section 101(1) by restricting membership to persons who share a protected characteristic.

(2) An association that restricts membership to persons who share a protected characteristic does not breach section 101(3) by restricting the access by associates to a benefit, facility or service to such persons as share the characteristic.

(3) An association that restricts membership to persons who share a protected characteristic does not breach section 102(1) by inviting as guests, or by permitting to be invited as guests, only such persons as share the characteristic.

(4) Sub-paragraphs (1) to (3), so far as relating to race, do not apply in relation to colour.

(5) This paragraph does not apply to an association that is a registered political party.

Age

1A(1) An association does not contravene section 101(1) or (2), so far as relating to age discrimination, by giving a concession on admission to membership for

(a) persons of a particular age group, or

(b) persons who have been members of the association for more than a number of years specified by the association for this purpose.

(2) An association does not contravene section 101(2) or (3), so far as relating to age discrimination, by giving a concession on access to a benefit, facility or service for

(a) members of a particular age group, or

(b)   persons who have been members of the association for more than a number of years specified by the association for this purpose.

(3)   An association does not contravene section 102(1), so far as relating to age discrimination, by giving a concession on invitations of persons of a particular age group as guests.

(4)   An association does not contravene section 102(2), so far as relating to age discrimination, by giving a concession on access to a benefit, facility or service for guests of a particular age group.

(5)   For the purposes of this paragraph, affording only persons of a particular age group access to a benefit, facility or service for a limited time is to be regarded as a concession.

(6)   The reference to a concession in respect of something done by an association is a reference to a benefit, right or privilege having the effect that the manner in which, or the terms on which, it does it are more favourable than the manner in which, or the terms on which, it usually does the thing.]

Health and safety

2(1)   An association (A) does not discriminate against a pregnant woman in contravention of section 101(1)(b) because she is pregnant if
   (a)   the terms on which A is prepared to admit her to membership include a term intended to remove or reduce a risk to her health or safety,
   (b)   A reasonably believes that admitting her to membership on terms which do not include that term would create a risk to her health or safety,
   (c)   the terms on which A is prepared to admit persons with other physical conditions to membership include a term intended to remove or reduce a risk to their health or safety, and
   (d)   A reasonably believes that admitting them to membership on terms which do not include that term would create a risk to their health or safety.

(2)   Sub-paragraph (1) applies to section 102(1)(b) as it applies to section 101(1)(b); and for that purpose a reference to admitting a person to membership is to be read as a reference to inviting the person as a guest or permitting the person to be invited as a guest.

(3)   An association (A) does not discriminate against a pregnant woman in contravention of section 101(2)(a) or (3)(a) or 102(2)(a) because she is pregnant if
   (a)   the way in which A affords her access to a benefit, facility or service is intended to remove or reduce a risk to her health or safety,
   (b)   A reasonably believes that affording her access to the benefit, facility or service otherwise than in that way would create a risk to her health or safety,
   (c)   A affords persons with other physical conditions access to the benefit, facility or service in a way that is intended to remove or reduce a risk to their health or safety, and
   (d)   A reasonably believes that affording them access to the benefit, facility or service otherwise than in that way would create a risk to their health or safety.

(4)   An association (A) which does not afford a pregnant woman access to a benefit, facility or service does not discriminate against her in contravention of section 101(2)(a) or (3)(a) or 102(2)(a) because she is pregnant if
   (a)   A reasonably believes that affording her access to the benefit, facility or service would, because she is pregnant, create a risk to her health or safety,
   (b)   A does not afford persons with other physical conditions access to the benefit, facility or service, and

(c)   the reason for not doing so is that A reasonably believes that affording them access to the benefit, facility or service would create a risk to their health or safety.

(5)   An association (A) does not discriminate against a pregnant woman under section 101(2)(c) or (3)(c) because she is pregnant if

     (a)   the variation of A's terms of membership, or rights as an associate, is intended to remove or reduce a risk to her health or safety,

     (b)   A reasonably believes that not making the variation to A's terms or rights would create a risk to her health or safety,

     (c)   A varies the terms of membership, or rights as an associate, of persons with other physical conditions,

     (d)   the variation of their terms or rights is intended to remove or reduce a risk to their health or safety, and

     (e)   A reasonably believes that not making the variation to their terms or rights would create a risk to their health or safety.

NOTES

Defined terms

affording access to a benefit, facility or service: s 212(4)
associate: s 107(1), (6)
association: s 107(1), (2), (4)

membership: s 107(1), (5)
registered political party: s 107(1), (7)
woman: s 212(1)

Enterprise Act 2002

268 Disqualification from office: general

(1) The Secretary of State may make an order under this section in relation to a disqualification provision.

(2) A "disqualification provision" is a provision which disqualifies (whether permanently or temporarily and whether absolutely or conditionally) a bankrupt or a class of bankrupts from
   (a) being elected or appointed to an office or position,
   (b) holding an office or position, or
   (c) becoming or remaining a member of a body or group.

(3) In subsection (2) the reference to a provision which disqualifies a person conditionally includes a reference to a provision which enables him to be dismissed.

(4) An order under subsection (1) may repeal or revoke the disqualification provision.

(5) An order under subsection (1) may amend, or modify the effect of, the disqualification provision
   (a) so as to reduce the class of bankrupts to whom the disqualification provision applies;
   (b) so as to extend the disqualification provision to some or all individuals who are subject to a bankruptcy restrictions regime;
   (c) so that the disqualification provision applies only to some or all individuals who are subject to a bankruptcy restrictions regime;
   (d) so as to make the application of the disqualification provision wholly or partly subject to the discretion of a specified person, body or group.

(6) An order by virtue of subsection (5)(d) may provide for a discretion to be subject to
   (a) the approval of a specified person or body;
   (b) appeal to a specified person or body.

(7) An order by virtue of subsection (5)(d) may provide for a discretion to be subject to appeal to a specified court or tribunal ; but any such order must
   (a) if it relates to England and Wales, be made with the concurrence of the Lord Chief Justice of England and Wales;
   (b) if it relates to Northern Ireland, be made with the concurrence of the Lord Chief Justice of Northern Ireland .

(8) The Secretary of State may specify himself for the purposes of subsection (5)(d) or (6)(a) or (b).

(9) In this section "bankrupt" means an individual
   (a) who has been adjudged bankrupt by a court in England and Wales or in Northern Ireland,
   (b) whose estate has been sequestrated by a court in Scotland, or
   (c) who has made an agreement with creditors of his for a composition of debts, for a scheme of arrangement of affairs, for the grant of a trust deed or for some other kind of settlement or arrangement.

(10) In this section "bankruptcy restrictions regime" means an order or undertaking
   (a) under Schedule 4A to the Insolvency Act 1986 (c 45) (bankruptcy restrictions orders), or
   (b) under any system operating in Scotland or Northern Ireland which appears to the Secretary of State to be equivalent to the system operating under that Schedule.

(11) In this section
   "body" includes Parliament and any other legislative body, and
   "provision" means

(a) a provision made by an Act of Parliament passed before or in the same Session as this Act, and

(b) a provision made, before or in the same Session as this Act, under an Act of Parliament.

(12) An order under this section
    (a) may make provision generally or for a specified purpose only,
    (b) may make different provision for different purposes, and
    (c) may make transitional, consequential or incidental provision.

(13) An order under this section
    (a) must be made by statutory instrument, and
    (b) may not be made unless a draft has been laid before and approved by resolution of each House of Parliament.

(14) A reference in this section to the Secretary of State shall be treated as a reference to the National Assembly for Wales in so far as it relates to a disqualification provision which
    (a) is made by the National Assembly for Wales, or
    (b) relates to a function of the National Assembly.

(15) Provision made by virtue of subsection (7) is subject to any order of the Lord Chancellor under section 56(1) of the Access to Justice Act 1999 (c 22) (appeals: jurisdiction).

(16) The Lord Chief Justice may nominate a judicial office holder (as defined in section 109(4) of the Constitutional Reform Act 2005) to exercise his functions under subsection (7).

(17) The Lord Chief Justice of Northern Ireland may nominate any of the following to exercise his functions under subsection (7)
    (a) the holder of one of the offices listed in Schedule 1 to the Justice (Northern Ireland) Act 2002;
    (b) a Lord Justice of Appeal (as defined in section 88 of that Act).

NOTES
Subordinate Legislation   General) Order 2006
  Enterprise Act 2002 (Disqualification from Office:

European Parliament (Representation) Act 2003

An Act to make provision enabling alterations to be made to the total number of Members of the European Parliament to be elected for the United Kingdom and to their distribution between the electoral regions; to make provision for and in connection with the establishment of an electoral region including Gibraltar for the purposes of European Parliamentary elections; and for connected purposes.

8th May 2003

24   Effect of statutory powers on capacity of Gibraltar legislature

PART 3 SUPPLEMENTARY

25   Financial provisions
26   *Repealed*
26A   Functions of the Chancellor of the Duchy of Lancaster
27   Interpretation
28   Short title, extent and commencement

SCHEDULES

PART 1
CHANGES IN TOTAL NUMBER OF UNITED KINGDOM MEPS

Preliminary

1 Electoral regions in the United Kingdom
Amends the European Parliamentary Elections Act 2002. Not reproduced here

Electoral Commission recommendations relating to changes in total number of United Kingdom MEPs

2 References to changes under EU law

(1)   In this Part "change under EU law" (in relation to a change in the number of MEPs to be elected for the United Kingdom) means a change made by
   (a)   a treaty provision that is part of the EU Treaties; or
   (b)   any provision of a Council Decision, or of any other instrument, made under a treaty provision that is part of the EU Treaties.

(2)   In this Part a reference to a treaty provision being part of the EU Treaties is to it being, or being included in provisions which are, specified in section 1(2) of the European Communities Act 1972 (c 68) by virtue of an amendment made by an Act (whether passed before or after this Act).

(3)   In this Part "treaty" includes any international agreement (however described) and a protocol or annex to a treaty or other international agreement.

NOTES
Defined terms
   MEP: s 27(1)

3 Recommendations by Electoral Commission as to the distribution of United Kingdom MEPs

(1)   The Secretary of State may by notice require the Electoral Commission to make a recommendation to him as to the distribution between the electoral regions of
   (a)   a total number of MEPs specified in the notice; or
   (b)   if the notice specifies more than one total number of MEPs, each of the total numbers so specified.

(2)   The power to give such a notice is exercisable with a view to the implementation of any change or anticipated change under EU law in the total number of MEPs to be elected for the United Kingdom.

(3) The Electoral Commission must comply with such a notice within the period specified in the notice.

(4) In determining what recommendation to make for the distribution of any total number of MEPs, the Electoral Commission must ensure that
  (a) each electoral region is allocated at least three MEPs; and
  (b) the ratio of electors to MEPs is as nearly as possible the same in each electoral region.

(5) A recommendation under this section
  (a) must be published by the Electoral Commission and laid before Parliament by the Secretary of State; and
  (b) ceases to have effect at the end of the period of one year beginning with the day on which it is made.

NOTES
Defined terms   MEP: s 27(1)
  change under Community law: s 2(1)
  electoral region: s 27(1)

4 Section 3: meaning of "elector"

(1) For the purposes of section 3(4) an elector, in relation to an electoral region, is a person whose name appears on the relevant day in (or in any part of) a relevant register which relates to the region.

(2) In subsection (1)
  "relevant day" means 1st December preceding the day on which the notice under section 3 is given; and
  "relevant register" has the same meaning as in Schedule 1A to the 2002 Act (periodic reviews).

(3) In calculating the total number of electors for any electoral region
  (a) persons who are registered but have not attained the age of 18 are to be counted as electors;
  (b) a citizen of the European Union (not being a Commonwealth citizen or a citizen of the Republic of Ireland) who is registered only for the purposes of local government elections is to be disregarded; and
  (c) the Electoral Commission may assume that each relevant register is accurate and that names appearing more than once on registers (or parts of registers) which relate to an electoral region are the names of different electors.

NOTES
Defined terms
  the 2002 Act: s 27(1)
  electoral region: s 27(1)

Implementation of changes in total number of United Kingdom MEPs

5 Orders implementing changes

(1) The Secretary of State may by order give effect to a change under EU law in the number of MEPs to be elected for the United Kingdom by amending
  (a) the figure specified in section 1(1) of the 2002 Act (total number of MEPs to be elected for the United Kingdom); and
  (b) any of the figures specified in section 1(3) of that Act (numbers of MEPs to be elected in the electoral regions).

(2) The distribution of MEPs resulting from the provision made under subsection (1)(b) must (subject to section 6(6) to (8)) be the distribution proposed in a recommendation of the

Electoral Commission under section 3 which is effective on the day on which the order is made.

(3) An order making an amendment to section 1 of the 2002 Act may be made before the provision making the relevant change has entered into force.

(4) If the relevant change is made by a provision of a treaty, an order making such an amendment may also be made before that provision has become part of the EU Treaties and, if the treaty requires ratification, before it is ratified by the United Kingdom.

(5) But no amendment to section 1 of the 2002 Act may be made so as to come into force
    (a) if the relevant change is made by a provision mentioned in section 2(1)(b), before that provision has entered into force; and
    (b) if the relevant change is made by a treaty provision, before that provision has both entered into force and become part of the EU Treaties.

(6) In subsections (3) to (5) "the relevant change", in relation to an order under this section amending section 1 of the 2002 Act, means the change under EU law being implemented by the order.

(7) The Secretary of State must consult the Electoral Commission before making an order under this section.

NOTES

Subordinate legislation
European Parliament (Number of MEPs and Distribution between Electoral Regions) (United Kingdom and Gibraltar) Order 2008, SI 2008/1954.

Defined terms
the 2002 Act: s 27(1)

change under EU law: s 2(1)
electoral region: s 27(1)
MEP: s 27(1)
part of the EU Treaties: s 2(2)
treaty: s 2(3)

6 Section 5: supplementary

(1) This section applies to orders under section 5.

(2) The power to make such an order is exercisable by statutory instrument.

(3) Such an order may make consequential, transitional or saving provision.

(4) Provision made under subsection (3) may modify any enactment.

(5) An order which contains amendments to section 1 of the 2002 Act may not be made unless a draft of it has been laid before, and approved by a resolution of, each House of Parliament.

(6) If a motion for the approval of a draft order is rejected by either House or withdrawn by leave of the House the Secretary of State may, after consulting the Electoral Commission, alter the draft order.

(7) But the Secretary of State may not, without the consent of the Electoral Commission, alter any amendments to section 1(3) of the 2002 Act contained in the draft order.

(8) The Electoral Commission may not give its consent under subsection (7) unless it is satisfied that the distribution of MEPs proposed by the altered draft order could have been recommended under section 3.

(9) A statutory instrument containing an order that is not subject to approval in draft under subsection (5) is subject to annulment in pursuance of a resolution of either House of Parliament.

NOTES

Defined terms
the 2002 Act: s 27(1)
enactment: s 2(2)

MEP: s 27(1)

Supplementary

7 Periodic reviews of distribution of MEPs

Amends the European Parliamentary Elections Act 2002. Not reproduced here

8 Consequential amendments

Amends the European Parliamentary Elections Act 2002. Not reproduced here

PART 2
GIBRALTAR

New combined electoral region

9 Combination of Gibraltar with existing electoral region

Gibraltar is to be combined with an existing electoral region in England and Wales to form a new electoral region ("the combined region") for the purposes of European Parliamentary elections taking place after 1st April 2004.

NOTES
Defined terms
electoral region: s 27(1)
existing electoral region: s 27(1)

10 Electoral Commission recommendation as to the electoral region to be combined with Gibraltar

(1) The Electoral Commission must, before 1st September 2003
  (a) consider which of the existing electoral regions in England and Wales should be combined with Gibraltar; and
  (b) report its conclusions (with a recommendation as to which existing region should be so combined) to the Secretary of State.

(2) Before determining what recommendation to make under subsection (1)(b) the Electoral Commission must consult the Governor, the Chief Minister and the leader of each political party represented in the House of Assembly of Gibraltar.

(3) The report required by this section must be published by the Electoral Commission and laid before Parliament by the Secretary of State.

NOTES
Defined terms
existing electoral region: s 27(1)

11 Establishment of combined region

(1) The Secretary of State may by order
  (a) specify the existing electoral region to be combined with Gibraltar to form the combined region; and
  (b) make provision establishing the combined region.

(2) The existing electoral region specified under subsection (1)(a) must (subject to section 13(8)) be the one recommended by the Electoral Commission under section 10.

(3) The Secretary of State must consult the Electoral Commission before making an order under this section.

NOTES
Subordinate Legislation
European Parliamentary Elections (Combined Region and Campaign Expenditure) (United Kingdom and

Gibraltar) Order 2004, SI 2004/366.

Defined terms

combined region: s 27(1)
existing electoral region: s 27(1)

12 Power to make consequential etc provision

(1) The Secretary of State may by order make such provision as he considers necessary or expedient in consequence of, or in connection with, the inclusion of Gibraltar in an electoral region for the purposes of European Parliamentary elections.

(2) Such an order may be made before or after the combined region is established under section 11.

(3) Without prejudice to the generality of subsection (1), the provision which may be made under this section includes provision about
  (a) the registration of political parties established in Gibraltar (as a condition for nomination in relation to a European Parliamentary election in the combined region) and the obligations of registered parties in Gibraltar and their officers;
  (b) the control of any description of donation to registered parties in Gibraltar or to their members or officers;
  (ba) the regulation of loans or credit facilities which benefit, or any form of security (whether real or personal) which benefits, registered parties in Gibraltar or their members or officers;
  (c) the obligations of persons providing programme services in or to Gibraltar, and the functions of any public authority in Gibraltar responsible for the regulation of persons providing such services, in relation to European Parliamentary elections and election campaigns.

(4) In subsection (3)
    "credit facilities" must be construed in accordance with section 71F(11) of the Political Parties, Elections and Referendums Act 2000;
    "donation" includes anything which is (or corresponds to) a donation within the meaning of Part 4 of the Political Parties, Elections and Referendums Act 2000 (c 41); and
    "programme services" includes services which would, if Gibraltar were part of the United Kingdom, be programme services for the purposes of the Broadcasting Act 1990 (c 42).

(5) The Secretary of State must consult the Electoral Commission before making an order under this section.

(6) The power under this section is not restricted by any power conferred by section 17 (or any other power to make subordinate legislation which is exercisable by the Secretary of State).

NOTES

Subordinate Legislation
European Parliamentary Elections (Combined Region and Campaign Expenditure) (United Kingdom and Gibraltar) Order 2004, SI 2004/366.
European Parliamentary Elections (Loans and Related Transactions and Miscellaneous Provisions) (United Kingdom and Gibraltar) Order 2009, SI 2009/185.

Defined terms
combined region: s 27(1)
electoral region: s 27(1)

13 Sections 11 and 12: supplementary

(1) This section applies to orders under section 11 or 12.

(2) The power to make such an order is exercisable by statutory instrument.

(3) Such an order may
  (a) confer power to make subordinate legislation;
  (b) make consequential, supplementary, incidental, transitional or saving provision;

(c) make provision extending or applying to (or extending or applying only to) Gibraltar or any part of the United Kingdom; and

(d) make different provision for different electoral regions or for different parts of the combined region.

(4) Such an order may modify, exclude or apply (with or without modifications) any enactment.

(5) Such an order may not be made unless a draft of the order has been laid before and approved by a resolution of each House of Parliament.

(6) Subsection (5) does not apply to an order (not being an order which specifies the existing electoral region to be combined with Gibraltar) if it appears to the Secretary of State that by reason of urgency the order should be made without being approved in draft.

(7) Where an order is made without being approved in draft, by virtue of subsection (6)

(a) it must be laid before Parliament after being made; and

(b) if it is not approved by a resolution of each House of Parliament within the period of 40 days after the date on which it is made, the order shall cease to have effect at the end of that period.

(8) If a motion for the approval of a draft order which specifies the existing electoral region to be combined with Gibraltar is rejected by either House or withdrawn by leave of the House, the Secretary of State may, after consulting the Electoral Commission, alter the draft order.

(9) If, apart from this subsection, an order to which this section applies would be treated for the purposes of the standing orders of either House of Parliament as a hybrid instrument, it shall proceed as if it were not such an instrument.

NOTES

Subordinate Legislation
European Parliamentary Elections (Combined Region and Campaign Expenditure) (United Kingdom and Gibraltar) Order 2004, SI 2004/366.
European Parliamentary Elections (Loans and Related Transactions and Miscellaneous Provisions) (United Kingdom and Gibraltar) Order 2009, SI 2009/185.

Defined terms
combined region: s 27(1)
electoral region: s 27(1)
enactment: s 27(2), (3)
existing electoral region: s 27(1)

Electoral registration and voting in Gibraltar

14 The Gibraltar register

(1) There shall be a register of European Parliamentary electors in Gibraltar (referred to in this Act as "the Gibraltar register") maintained by the European electoral registration officer for Gibraltar.

(2) The Clerk of the House of Assembly of Gibraltar shall (by virtue of his office) be the European electoral registration officer for Gibraltar.

15 Gibraltar franchise for European Parliamentary elections

(1) A person is entitled to vote in Gibraltar as an elector at a European Parliamentary election if on the day of the poll he

(a) is registered in the Gibraltar register;

(b) is not subject to a legal incapacity to vote in Gibraltar at such an election (age apart);

(c) is a Commonwealth citizen or a citizen of the European Union (other than a Commonwealth citizen); and

(d) is at least 18 years of age.

(2) Subsection (1)(a) has effect subject to any enactment which provides for alterations made after a specified date in the register to be disregarded.

(3) In section 8 of the 2002 Act (persons entitled to vote), at the end there is added
"(8) The entitlement to vote under this section does not apply to voting in Gibraltar."

NOTES
Defined terms
enactment: s 27(2)
the Gibraltar register: s 14(1)

16 Entitlement to be registered in Gibraltar

(1) A person is entitled to be registered in the Gibraltar register if, on the relevant date, he

(a) is resident in Gibraltar;

(b) is not subject to a legal incapacity to vote in Gibraltar at a European Parliamentary election (age apart);

(c) is a qualifying Commonwealth citizen or a citizen of the European Union (other than a qualifying Commonwealth citizen); and

(d) is at least 18 years of age.

(2) A person is also entitled to be registered in the Gibraltar register if, on the relevant date, he
(a) is not resident in Gibraltar but qualifies for registration in Gibraltar as an overseas elector;
(b) is not subject to a legal incapacity to vote in Gibraltar at a European Parliamentary election (age apart);
(c) is a Commonwealth citizen; and
(d) is at least 18 years of age.

(3) Subsections (1) and (2) have effect subject to or in accordance with any provision made under section 17.

(4) In this section "the relevant date" is the date on which an application for registration in the Gibraltar register is made or treated (by virtue of any enactment) as having been made.

(5) In this section "qualifying Commonwealth citizen" means a Commonwealth citizen who
(a) does not, under the law of Gibraltar, require a permit or certificate to enter or remain in Gibraltar; or
(b) for the time being has (or is by virtue of any provision of the law of Gibraltar to be treated as having) a permit or certificate entitling him to enter or remain in Gibraltar.

NOTES
Defined terms
enactment: s 27(2)
the Gibraltar register: s 14(1)

17 Regulations relating to sections 14 to 16

(1) The Secretary of State may by regulations
(a) make provision about the Gibraltar register and the manner in which it is to be maintained;
(b) confer functions on the European electoral registration officer for Gibraltar;
(c) prescribe requirements to be complied with in connection with the registration of electors in the Gibraltar register;
(d) prescribe circumstances in which a person is legally incapable of voting in Gibraltar at a European Parliamentary election;

(e) make provision for determining whether a person is or may be treated as resident in Gibraltar for the purposes of section 16;

(f) prescribe conditions which must be satisfied by a person in order for him to qualify for registration in Gibraltar as an overseas elector;

(g) impose a disqualification for registration in Gibraltar as a European Parliamentary elector;

(h) make provision enabling a person who has not attained the age of 18 to be entered on the Gibraltar register with a view to his being able to vote at a European Parliamentary election in Gibraltar after he has attained that age; and

(i) amend the definition of "qualifying Commonwealth citizen" in section 16 if he considers it necessary or expedient to do so in consequence of developments in the law of Gibraltar relating to immigration control.

(2) The provision which may be made under subsection (1) includes anything which corresponds to any provision that may be made for the United Kingdom in regulations under section 53 of the Representation of the People Act 1983 (c 2) (regulations as to registration etc).

(3) Regulations under this section may (without prejudice to the generality of the paragraph in subsection (1) under which they are made) make provision corresponding to any provision of

(a) sections 3 and 3A of the Representation of the People Act 1983 (incapacity of offenders detained in prison or in a mental hospital) and any other provision relating to incapacity from voting;

(b) sections 5 to 7C and 14 to 17 of that Act (residence, declarations of local connection and service qualifications) and any other provision relating to residence for electoral purposes; and

(c) sections 1 and 2 of the Representation of the People Act 1985 (c 50) (registration of British citizens overseas) and any other provision relating to overseas electors.

(4) The Secretary of State must consult the Electoral Commission before making regulations under this section.

NOTES

Subordinate Legislation
European Parliamentary Elections Regulations 2004, SI 2004/293.
European Parliamentary Elections (Amendment) Regulations 2009, SI 2009/186.
European Parliamentary Elections (Amendment) (No 2) Regulations 2009, SI 2009/848.
European Parliamentary Elections (Anonymous Registration) (Northern Ireland) Regulations 2014, SI 2014/1803.

Defined terms
the Gibraltar register: s 14(1)
qualifying Commonwealth citizen: s 16(5)

18   Section 17: supplementary

(1) This section applies to regulations under section 17.

(2) The power to make such regulations is exercisable by statutory instrument.

(3) Such regulations may

(a) make consequential, supplementary, incidental, transitional or saving provision;

(b) make provision extending or applying to (or extending or applying only to) Gibraltar or any part of the United Kingdom; and

(c) modify, exclude or apply (with or without modifications) any enactment.

(4) Such regulations may not be made unless a draft of the regulations has been laid before, and approved by a resolution of, each House of Parliament.

(5) Subsection (4) does not apply to any regulations if it appears to the Secretary of State that by reason of urgency the regulations should be made without being approved in draft.

(6) Where regulations are made without being approved in draft, by virtue of subsection (5)

    (a) the regulations must be laid before Parliament after being made; and

    (b) if the regulations are not approved by a resolution of each House of Parliament within the period of 40 days after the date on which they are made, the regulations shall cease to have effect at the end of that period.

NOTES

Subordinate Legislation   enactment: s 27(2), (3)

European Parliamentary Elections (Anonymous Registration)(Northern Ireland) Regulations 2014, SI 2014/1803.

Defined terms

Miscellaneous provisions

19 Extension of 2002 Act to Gibraltar

The provisions of the 2002 Act, other than Schedules 3 and 4, extend to Gibraltar.

20 Returning officers

Amends the European Parliamentary Elections Act 2002. Not reproduced here

21 Disqualification from office of MEP

Amends the European Parliamentary Elections Act 2002. Not reproduced here

22 European Parliamentary elections regulations

Amends the European Parliamentary Elections Act 2002. Not reproduced here

23 Jurisdiction of courts

(1) Without prejudice to the generality of the power under which it is made, subordinate legislation to which this section applies

    (a) may make provision for a judge of the Supreme Court of Gibraltar to be appointed as an additional judge (with the two judges acting under section 123 of the Representation of the People Act 1983 (c 2) as applied for the purposes of European Parliamentary elections) for the trial of an election petition relating to the election of MEPs in the combined region; and

    (b) may, for the purposes of such an election petition

        (i) confer the powers, jurisdiction and authority of a judge of the High Court on any Gibraltar judge who is so appointed; and

        (ii) make any other provision necessary to secure that a Gibraltar judge so appointed is treated as if he were a judge of the High Court.

(2) Without prejudice to the generality of the power under which it is made, subordinate legislation to which this section applies may

    (a) confer jurisdiction over any matter connected with the election of MEPs in the combined region on an election court constituted under section 123 of the Representation of the People Act 1983 (as applied for the purposes of European Parliamentary elections);

    (b) confer jurisdiction over any such matter (not being a matter within the jurisdiction of the election court) on

        (i) one or more courts in the United Kingdom;

        (ii) one or more courts in Gibraltar (whether specified in the subordinate legislation or left to be determined by or under the law of Gibraltar); or

        (iii) one or more courts in the United Kingdom and one or more courts in Gibraltar.

(3) This section applies to

    (a) an order under section 12;

    (b) regulations under section 17; and

(c)   regulations under section 7 of the 2002 Act.

NOTES

Subordinate Legislation

European Parliamentary Elections (Combined Region and Campaign Expenditure) (United Kingdom and Gibraltar) Order 2004, SI 2004/366.
European Parliamentary Elections Regulations 2004, SI 2004/293.
European Parliamentary Elections (Loans and Related Transactions and Miscellaneous Provisions) (United Kingdom and Gibraltar) Order 2009, SI 2009/185.

European Parliamentary Elections (Amendment) Regulations 2009, SI 2009/186.

Defined terms
the 2002 Act: s 27(1)
combined region: s 27(1)
MEP: s 27(1)

24   Effect of statutory powers on capacity of Gibraltar legislature

(1)   The capacity (apart from this Act) of the Gibraltar legislature to make law for Gibraltar is not affected by the existence of a power under this Part or the 2002 Act to make subordinate legislation extending to Gibraltar.

(2)   Subsection (1) does not affect the operation of the Colonial Laws Validity Act 1865 (c 63) in relation to subordinate legislation made under such a power.

NOTES

Defined terms
the 2002 Act: s 27(1)

PART 3
SUPPLEMENTARY

25   Financial provisions

(1)   There shall be paid out of money provided by Parliament
(a)   any expenditure incurred by a Minister of the Crown in consequence of this Act;
(b)   any increase attributable to this Act in the sums so payable by virtue of paragraph 14 of Schedule 1 to the Political Parties, Elections and Referendums Act 2000 (c 41) (expenditure of the Electoral Commission in the performance of its functions); and
(c)   any other increase attributable to this Act in the sums payable out of money so provided by virtue of an Act other than this Act.

(2)   There shall be charged on and paid out of the Consolidated Fund any increase attributable to this Act in the sums to be charged on and paid out of that Fund under any other Act.

(3)   Subordinate legislation to which this subsection applies may make provision
(a)   for sums required to meet any expenditure (other than expenditure to be met from funds provided by Gibraltar) to be
(i) paid out of money provided by Parliament; or
(ii)   charged on and paid out of the Consolidated Fund; and
(b)   for the payment of sums into the Consolidated Fund.

(4)   Subsection (3) applies to
(a)   an order under section 12;
(b)   regulations under section 17; and
(c)   regulations under section 7 of the 2002 Act.

NOTES

Subordinate Legislation

European Parliamentary Elections (Combined Region and Campaign Expenditure) (United Kingdom and Gibraltar) Order 2004, SI 2004/366.
European Parliamentary Elections Regulations 2004, SI 2004/293.
European Parliamentary Elections (Amendment)

Regulations 2009, SI 2009/186.

Defined terms
the 2002 Act: s 27(1)

26

Repealed

26A Functions of the Chancellor of the Duchy of Lancaster

See the Chancellor of the Duchy of Lancaster Order 2015, by virtue of which functions of the Secretary of State under this Act are exercisable concurrently with the Chancellor of the Duchy of Lancaster.

27 Interpretation

(1) In this Act
"combined region" means the electoral region which includes Gibraltar;
"electoral region" means an electoral region of the United Kingdom established under the 2002 Act for the purposes of European Parliamentary elections;
"existing electoral region" means an electoral region existing immediately before the passing of this Act;
"MEP" means a member of the European Parliament; and
"the 2002 Act" means the European Parliamentary Elections Act 2002 (c 24).

(2) In this Act "enactment" means (subject to subsection (3))
    (a) a provision of an Act (whether passed before or after this Act), including a provision modified by this Act; or
    (b) a provision of subordinate legislation (whenever made).

(3) In sections 13(4) and 18(3)(c) "enactment" also includes a provision of law passed or made in or for Gibraltar (whenever passed or made) and in section 13(4) it also includes a provision of Part 1 or 3 of this Act.

28 Short title, extent and commencement

(1) This Act may be cited as the European Parliament (Representation) Act 2003.

(2) This Act extends to each part of the United Kingdom and to Gibraltar.

(3) Part 1, sections 9 and 10 and this Part come into force in each part of the United Kingdom on the passing of this Act but shall not come into force in Gibraltar until such day as the Secretary of State may appoint by order made by statutory instrument.

(4) Sections 11 to 24 shall not come into force until such day as the Secretary of State may appoint by order made by statutory instrument.

(5) Different days may be appointed under this section for different purposes.

NOTES

Subordinate Legislation

European Parliament (Representation) Act 2003 (Commencement No 1) Order 2003, SI 2003/1401.
European Parliament (Representation) Act 2003 (Commencement No 2) Order 2003, SI 2003/1402.
European Parliament (Representation) Act 2003 (Commencement No 3) Order 2004, SI 2004/24.
European Parliament (Representation) Act 2003

(Commencement No 4) Order 2004, SI 2004/320.
European Parliament (Representation) Act 2003 (Commencement No 5) Order 2004, SI 2004/700.
European Parliament (Representation) Act 2003 (Commencement No 6) Order 2004, SI 2004/1035.

SCHEDULE 1A

Amends the European Parliamentary Elections Act 2002. Not reproduced here.

European Parliamentary Elections Act 2002

An Act to consolidate the European Parliamentary Elections Acts 1978, 1993 and 1999.

24th July 2002

Introductory

1 Number of MEPs and electoral regions

(1) There shall be 73 members of the European Parliament ("MEPs") elected for the United Kingdom.

(2) For the purposes of electing those MEPs
   (a) the area of England and Gibraltar is divided into the nine electoral regions specified in Schedule 1; and
   (b) Scotland, Wales and Northern Ireland are each single electoral regions.

(3) The number of MEPs to be elected for each electoral region is as follows

East Midlands	5
Eastern	7
London	8
North East	3
North West	8
South East	10
South West	6
West Midlands	7
Yorkshire and the Humber	6
Scotland	6
Wales	4
Northern Ireland	3.

1A Periodic reviews of distribution of MEPs

Schedule 1A (which provides for periodic reviews by the Electoral Commission of the distribution of MEPs between the electoral regions) has effect.

NOTES
Defined terms
   MEPs: s 1(1)

General elections

2 Voting system in Great Britain and Gibraltar

(1) The system of election of MEPs in an electoral region other than Northern Ireland is to be a regional list system.

(2) The Secretary of State must by regulations
   (a) make provision for the nomination of registered parties in relation to an election in such a region, and
   (b) require a nomination under paragraph (a) to be accompanied by a list of candidates numbering no more than the MEPs to be elected for the region.

(3) The system of election must comply with the following conditions.

(4) A vote may be cast for a registered party or an individual candidate named on the ballot paper.

(5) The first seat is to be allocated to the party or individual candidate with the greatest number of votes.

(6) The second and subsequent seats are to be allocated in the same way, except that the number of votes given to a party to which one or more seats have already been allocated are to be divided by the number of seats allocated plus one.

(7) In allocating the second or any subsequent seat there are to be disregarded any votes given to

    (a)   a party to which there has already been allocated a number of seats equal to the number of names on the party's list of candidates, and

    (b)   an individual candidate to whom a seat has already been allocated.

(8)   Seats allocated to a party are to be filled by the persons named on the party's list of candidates in the order in which they appear on that list.

(9)   For the purposes of subsection (6) fractions are to be taken into account.

(10) In this section "registered party" means a party registered under Part 2 of the Political Parties, Elections and Referendums Act 2000 (c 41).

NOTES

Subordinate Legislation
European Parliamentary Elections (Amendment) Regulations 2009, SI 2009/186

Defined terms
MEPs: s 1(1)

3 Voting system in Northern Ireland

The system of election of MEPs in Northern Ireland is to be a single transferable vote system under which

    (a)   a vote is capable of being given so as to indicate the voter's order of preference for the candidates, and

    (b)   a vote is capable of being transferred to the next choice

        (i) when the vote is not required to give a prior choice the necessary quota of votes, or

        (ii) when, owing to the deficiency in the number of votes given for a prior choice, that choice is eliminated from the list of candidates.

NOTES

Defined terms
MEPs: s 1(1)

4 Date of elections

The poll at each general election of MEPs is to be held on a day appointed by order of the Secretary of State.

NOTES

Subordinate Legislation
European Parliamentary Elections (Appointed Day of Poll) Order 2004, SI 2004/217.
European Parliamentary Elections (Appointed Day of Poll) Order 2008, SI 2008/3102.
European Parliamentary Elections (Appointed Day of

Poll) Order 2013, SI 2013/2063.

Defined terms
MEPs: s 1(1)

Vacant seats

5 Filling vacant seats

(1)   The Secretary of State must by regulations make provision prescribing the procedure to be followed when a seat is or becomes vacant.

(2)   The regulations may

    (a)   include provision requiring a by-election to be held in specified circumstances (and provision modifying section 2 in its application to by-elections);

    (b)   require a seat last filled from a party's list of candidates to be filled, in specified circumstances, from such a list (without a by-election).

(3)   Where regulations provide for a by-election to be held

    (a)   the poll must take place on a day, appointed by order of the Secretary of State, within such period as may be specified in the regulations, but

(b) the regulations may enable the Secretary of State to decline to appoint a day in certain circumstances.

(4) As regards a seat in Northern Ireland, the regulations may, in specified circumstances, require it to be filled as follows
   (a) where the previous MEP stood in the name of a registered party when elected (or most recently elected), by a person nominated by the nominating officer of that party;
   (b) where the previous MEP stood in the names of two or more registered parties when elected (or most recently elected), by a person jointly nominated by the nominating officers of those parties;
   (c) where paragraph (a) or (b) does not apply but the previous MEP gave a notice in accordance with regulations under this Act naming one or more persons as substitutes, by a person so named.

(5) In subsection (4)
   "nominating officer", in relation to a registered party, means the person registered as its nominating officer under the Political Parties, Elections and Referendums Act 2000 in the Northern Ireland register (within the meaning of that Act);
   "registered party" means a party registered under that Act in that register;
   "the previous MEP", in relation to a vacancy, means the person who was the MEP immediately before the vacancy arose.

NOTES

Subordinate Legislation
European Parliamentary Elections Regulations 2004, SI 2004/293.
European Parliamentary Elections (Northern Ireland) Regulations 2004, SI 2004/1267.
European Parliamentary Elections (Amendment) Regulations 2009, SI 2009/186.

European Parliamentary Elections (Northern Ireland) (Amendment) Regulations 2010, SI 2010/1175.

Defined terms
MEPs: s 1(1)

Conduct of elections

6 Returning officers

(1) There is to be a returning officer for each electoral region.

(2) For a region in England and Wales (including the combined region), the returning officer is to be a person who
   (a) is an acting returning officer by virtue of section 28(1) of the Representation of the People Act 1983 (c 2) or is the proper officer of the Greater London Authority for the purposes of section 35(2C) of that Act, and
   (b) is designated for the purposes of this subsection by order of the Secretary of State.

(3) For Scotland the returning officer is to be a person who
   (a) is a returning officer by virtue of section 25 of that Act, and
   (b) is designated for the purposes of this subsection by order of the Secretary of State.

(4) For Northern Ireland the returning officer is to be the Chief Electoral Officer.

(5) The Secretary of State may by regulations confer functions on the returning officers for the electoral regions and on local returning officers.

(5A) For the purposes of subsection (5) "local returning officer" means
   (a) a person who, by virtue of section 35 of the Representation of the People Act 1983, is a returning officer for
      (i) elections of councillors of a district or London borough,
      (ii) elections of councillors of a county in which there are no district councils,
      (iii) elections to the Council of the Isles of Scilly, or
      (iv) elections of councillors of a county or county borough in Wales,

or who by virtue of section 41 of that Act is a returning officer for elections of councillors for a local authority in Scotland; or

    (b)   the European electoral registration officer for Gibraltar (within the meaning of section 14 of the European Parliament (Representation) Act 2003).

(6)   There are to be charged on, and paid out of, the Consolidated Fund

    (a)   charges to which persons on whom functions are conferred under subsection (5) are entitled under regulations under this Act, and

    (b)   any sums required by the Secretary of State for expenditure on the provision of training relating to functions conferred under subsection (5).

(7)   Where functions are conferred on a person under subsection (5) in relation to an electoral region

    (a)   in the case of an electoral region other than the combined region, the council of a relevant area falling wholly or partly within that region; and

    (b)   in the case of the combined region, the council of a relevant area falling wholly or partly within that region and the Government of Gibraltar,

must place the services of their officers at his disposal for the purpose of assisting him in the discharge of those functions.

(8)   In subsection (7), "relevant area" means

    (a)   a district or London borough in England,

    (b)   a county or county borough in Wales, and

    (c)   a local government area in Scotland.

(9)   Where functions are conferred on the proper officer of the Greater London Authority under subsection (5) in relation to the London electoral region, the Authority must place the services of its employees at his disposal for the purpose of assisting him in the discharge of those functions.

NOTES

Subordinate Legislation

European Parliamentary Elections Regulations 2004, SI 2004/293.

European Parliamentary Elections (Northern Ireland) Regulations 2004, SI 2004/1267.

European Parliamentary Elections (Amendment) Regulations 2009, SI 2009/186.

European Parliamentary Elections (Northern Ireland) (Amendment) Regulations 2009, SI 2009/813.

European Parliamentary Elections (Amendment) (No 2) Regulations 2009, SI 2009/848.

European Parliamentary Elections (Returning Officers) Order 2013, SI 2013/2064.

European Parliamentary Elections (Northern Ireland) (Amendment) Regulations 2013, SI 2013/2893.

European Parliamentary Elections (Amendment) Regulations 2014, SI 2014/923.

European Parliamentary Elections (Anonymous Registration) (Northern Ireland) Regulations 2014, SI 2014/1803.

Defined terms

combined region: s 17

7 Regulation-making powers: general

(1)   The Secretary of State may, subject to the provisions of this Act, by regulations make provision as to

    (a)   the conduct of elections to the European Parliament, and

    (b)   the questioning of such an election and the consequences of irregularities.

(2)   Regulations under this Act may make provision (including the creation of criminal offences)

    (a)   about the limitation of election expenses of candidates;

    (b)   for the allocation of seats in the case of an equality of votes;

    (c)   for securing that no person stands for election more than once at a general election (whether by being nominated as a candidate or by being included in a party's list of candidates).

(3)   Regulations under this Act may apply, with such modifications or exceptions as may be specified in the regulations

(a) any provision of the Representation of the People Acts or of any other enactment relating to parliamentary elections or local government elections, and

(b) any provision made under any enactment.

(4) Regulations under this Act may amend any form contained in regulations made under the Representation of the People Acts so far as may be necessary to enable it to be used both for the purpose indicated in regulations so made and for the corresponding purpose in relation to elections to the European Parliament.

(4A) Without prejudice to the generality of the power under which they are made, regulations under this Act may make different provision for different electoral regions and, in particular, for the part of the combined region which is in England and Wales and for Gibraltar.

(5) Section 26 of the Welsh Language Act 1993 (c 38) (power to prescribe Welsh version) applies in relation to regulations under this Act as it applies in relation to Acts of Parliament.

NOTES

Subordinate Legislation

European Parliamentary Elections Regulations 2004, SI 2004/293.

European Parliamentary Elections (Northern Ireland) Regulations 2004, SI 2004/1267.

Representation of the People (Northern Ireland) Regulations 2008, SI 2008/1741.

European Parliamentary Elections (Amendment) Regulations 2009, SI 2009/186.

European Parliamentary Elections (Northern Ireland) (Amendment) Regulations 2009, SI 2009/813.

European Parliamentary Elections (Amendment) (No 2) Regulations 2009, SI 2009/848.

Elections (Fresh Signatures for Absent Voters) Regulations 2013, SI 2013/1599.

European Parliamentary Elections (Northern Ireland) (Amendment) Regulations 2013, SI 2013/2893.

European Parliamentary Elections (Northern Ireland) (Amendment) (No 2) Regulations 2013, SI 2013/3114.

European Parliamentary Elections (Amendment) Regulations 2014, SI 2014/923.

European Parliamentary Elections (Anonymous Registration) (Northern Ireland) Regulations 2014, SI 2014/1803.

European Parliamentary Elections (Forms) (Northern Ireland) Regulations 2015, SI 2015/220.

European Parliamentary Elections (Amendment) Regulations 2015, SI 2015/459.

Defined terms

combined region: s 17

enactment: s 17

Entitlement to vote

8 Persons entitled to vote

(1) A person is entitled to vote as an elector at an election to the European Parliament in an electoral region if he is within any of subsections (2) to (5).

(2) A person is within this subsection if on the day of the poll he would be entitled to vote as an elector at a parliamentary election in a parliamentary constituency wholly or partly comprised in the electoral region, and

(a) the address in respect of which he is registered in the relevant register of parliamentary electors is within the electoral region, or

(b) his registration in the relevant register of parliamentary electors results from an overseas elector's declaration which specifies an address within the electoral region.

(3) A person is within this subsection if

(a) he is a peer who on the day of the poll would be entitled to vote at a local government election in an electoral area wholly or partly comprised in the electoral region, and

(b) the address in respect of which he is registered in the relevant register of local government electors is within the electoral region.

(4)   A person is within this subsection if he is entitled to vote in the electoral region by virtue of section 3 of the Representation of the People Act 1985 (c 50) (peers resident outside the United Kingdom).

(5)   A person is within this subsection if he is entitled to vote in the electoral region by virtue of the European Parliamentary Elections (Franchise of Relevant Citizens of the Union) Regulations 2001 (SI 2001/1184) (citizens of the European Union other than Commonwealth and Republic of Ireland citizens).

(6)   Subsection (1) has effect subject to any provision of regulations made under this Act which provides for alterations made after a specified date in a register of electors to be disregarded.

(7)   In subsection (3) "local government election" includes a municipal election in the City of London (that is, an election to the office of mayor, alderman, common councilman or sheriff and also the election of any officer elected by the mayor, aldermen and liverymen in common hall).

(8)   The entitlement to vote under this section does not apply to voting in Gibraltar.

NOTES
Defined terms
   citizen of the European Union: s 17

9 Double voting

(1)   A person is guilty of an offence if, on any occasion when elections to the European Parliament are held in all the member states under Article 10 of the Act annexed to Council Decision 76/787, he votes as an elector more than once in those elections, whether in the United Kingdom or elsewhere.

(2)   Subsection (1) is without prejudice to any enactment relating to voting offences, as applied by regulations under this Act to elections of MEPs held in the United Kingdom and Gibraltar.

(3)   The provisions of the Representation of the People Act 1983 (c 2), as applied by regulations under this Act, have effect in relation to an offence under this section as they have effect in relation to an offence under section 61(2) of that Act (double voting).

(4)   In particular, the following provisions of that Act apply
   (a)   section 61(7) (which makes an offence under section 61(2) an illegal practice but allows any incapacity resulting from conviction to be mitigated by the convicting court), and
   (b)   section 178 (prosecutions for offences committed outside the United Kingdom).

NOTES
Defined terms   MEPs: s 1(1)
   the Act annexed to Council Decision 76/787: s 17
   enactment: s 17

Entitlement to be MEP

10 Disqualification

(1)   A person is disqualified for the office of MEP if
   (a)   he is disqualified for membership of the House of Commons,
   (b)   *Repealed.*

(2)   But a person is not disqualified for the office of MEP under subsection (1)(a) merely because
   (a)   he is a peer,
   (b)   he is a Lord Spiritual,

(c) he holds an office mentioned in section 4 of the House of Commons Disqualification Act 1975 (c 24) (stewardship of Chiltern Hundreds etc), or

(d) he holds any of the offices described in Part 2 or 3 of Schedule 1 to that Act which are designated by order by the Secretary of State for the purposes of this section.

(3) A citizen of the European Union who is resident in the United Kingdom or Gibraltar is not disqualified for the office of MEP under subsection (1)(a) merely because he is disqualified for membership of the House of Commons under section 3 of the Act of Settlement (12&13 Will 3 c 2) (disqualification of persons, other than qualifying Commonwealth citizens and Republic of Ireland citizens, who are born outside Great Britain and Ireland and the dominions).

(3A) A Commonwealth citizen who is resident in Gibraltar and who

(a) does not, under the law of Gibraltar, require a permit or certificate to enter or remain there, or

(b) for the time being has (or is by virtue of any provision of the law of Gibraltar to be treated as having) a certificate of permanent residence issued under the Immigration Control Ordinance,

is not disqualified for the office of MEP under subsection (1)(a) merely because he is disqualified for membership of the House of Commons under section 3 of the Act of Settlement (12&13 Will 3 c. 2) (disqualification of persons, other than qualifying Commonwealth citizens and Republic of Ireland citizens, who are born outside Great Britain and Ireland and the dominions).

(3B) But subsection (3A)(a) does not cause a person to be qualified for the office of MEP if he does not require a permit or certificate to enter Gibraltar by virtue only of section 14(1) of the Immigration Control Ordinance (certain exemptions from requirement of permit or certificate).

(4) A person is disqualified for the office of MEP for a particular electoral region if, under section 1(2) of the House of Commons Disqualification Act 1975 (c 24), he is disqualified for membership of the House of Commons for any parliamentary constituency wholly or partly comprised in that region.

(4A) The Secretary of State may by order make such other provision as he thinks appropriate for persons of a description connected to Gibraltar (including any description of persons who are disqualified for membership of the Gibraltar House of Assembly) to be disqualified from the office of MEP.

(4B) The Secretary of State must consult the Electoral Commission before making an order under subsection (4A).

(5) A person who

(a) is a citizen of the European Union, and

(b) is not a Commonwealth citizen or a citizen of the Republic of Ireland,

is disqualified for the office of MEP if he is disqualified for that office through a relevant disqualifying decision under the law of the member state of which he is a national.

(5A) In this section "relevant disqualifying decision" means, in accordance with Article 6(1) of Council Directive 93/109/EC

(a) a judicial decision, or

(b) an administrative decision that can be subject to a judicial remedy.

(6) If a person who is returned as an MEP for an electoral region under section 2, 3 or 5

(a) is disqualified under this section for the office of MEP, or

(b) is disqualified under this section for the office of MEP for that region,

his return is void and his seat vacant.

(7) If an MEP becomes disqualified under this section for the office of MEP or for the office of MEP for the electoral region for which he was returned, his seat is to be vacated.

(7A) In this section "the Immigration Control Ordinance" means the Gibraltar Ordinance of that name (Ord. 1962 No 12).

(7B) The Secretary of State may by regulations amend this section if he considers it necessary or expedient to do so in consequence of developments in the law of Gibraltar relating to immigration control.

(7C) Such regulations may
  (a) make transitional or saving provision;
  (b) make provision extending or applying to (or extending or applying only to) Gibraltar or any part of the United Kingdom.

(8) Subsection (1) is without prejudice to Article 7(1) and (2) of the Act annexed to Council Decision 76/787 (incompatibility of office of MEP with certain offices in or connected with EU institutions).

NOTES
Subordinate Legislation
European Parliament (Disqualification) (United Kingdom and Gibraltar) Order 2009, SI 2009/190.

Defined terms
the Act annexed to Council Decision 76/787: s 17
citizen of the European Union: s 17
MEPs: s 1(1)

11 Judicial determination of disqualification

(1) Any person may apply to the appropriate court for a declaration or (in Scotland) declarator that a person who purports to be an MEP for a particular electoral region
  (a) is disqualified under section 10 (whether generally or for that region), or
  (b) was so disqualified at the time when, or at some time since, he was returned as an MEP under section 2, 3 or 5.

(2) For the purposes of subsection (1), the appropriate court is
  (a) the High Court, if the electoral region concerned is an electoral region in England and Wales or the combined region,
  (b) the Court of Session, if the electoral region concerned is Scotland, or
  (c) the High Court of Justice in Northern Ireland, if the electoral region concerned is Northern Ireland.

(3) The decision of the court on an application under this section is final.

(4) On an application under this section
  (a) the person in respect of whom the application is made is to be the respondent or (in Scotland) the defender, and
  (b) the applicant must give such security for the costs or expenses of the proceedings, not exceeding £5000, as the court may direct.

(5) The Secretary of State may by order
  (a) substitute another figure for the figure in subsection (4)(b); and
  (b) prescribe a different figure for applications where the electoral region concerned is the combined region.

(6) No declaration or declarator is to be made under this section in respect of any person on grounds which subsisted at the time of his election if there is pending, or has been tried, an election petition in which his disqualification on those grounds is, or was, in issue.

(7) Any declaration or declarator made by the court on an application under this section must be certified in writing to the Secretary of State immediately by the court.

NOTES
Defined terms
combined region: s 17
MEP: s 1(1)

12
Repealed

Supplementary

13 Regulations and orders

(1) Regulations and orders made under this Act must be made by statutory instrument.

(2) No regulations may be made under this Act unless a draft of the regulations has been laid before Parliament and approved by a resolution of each House of Parliament.

(3) A statutory instrument containing an order under
    (a) section 10(2)(d) or 11(5),
    (b) *Repealed*
is subject to annulment in pursuance of a resolution of either House of Parliament.

(3A) An order under section 10(4A) may not be made unless a draft of the order has been laid before, and approved by a resolution of, each House of Parliament.

(3B) Subsection (3A) does not apply if it appears to the Secretary of State that by reason of urgency the order should be made without being approved in draft.

(3C) Where an order is made without being approved in draft, by virtue of subsection (3A)
    (a) it must be laid before Parliament after being made; and
    (b) if it is not approved by a resolution of each House of Parliament within the period of 40 days after the date on which it is made, the order shall cease to have effect at the end of that period.

(4) A statutory instrument containing an order under section 4 or 5(3) is to be laid before Parliament after being made.

14 Transitional provisions

Schedule 2 (transitional provisions) has effect.

15 Consequential amendments

Schedule 3 (consequential amendments) has effect.

16 Repeals and revocation

The enactments and instrument specified in Schedule 4 are repealed or revoked to the extent specified.

General
16A
Repealed

16B Functions of the Chancellor of the Duchy of Lancaster

See the Chancellor of the Duchy of Lancaster Order 2015, by virtue of which functions of the Secretary of State under this Act are exercisable concurrently with the Chancellor of the Duchy of Lancaster.

17 Interpretation

In this Act
    "enactment" includes an enactment contained in
        (a) an Act of the Parliament of Northern Ireland,

      (b) an Order in Council made under the Northern Ireland (Temporary Provisions) Act 1972 (c 22), or

      (c) a Measure of the Northern Ireland Assembly;

"the Act annexed to Council Decision 76/787" is the Act concerning the election of MEPs annexed to Council Decision 76/787/ECSC, EEC, Euratom of 20th September 1976;

"citizen of the European Union" is to be determined in accordance with Article 17.1 of the Treaty establishing the European Community;

"combined region" means the electoral region which includes Gibraltar.

18 Short title and commencement

(1)   This Act may be cited as the European Parliamentary Elections Act 2002.

(2)   This Act comes into force at the end of the period of 3 months beginning with the day on which it is passed.

SCHEDULE 1
Electoral Regions in England and Gibraltar

Electoral regions

1   The electoral regions in England and Gibraltar are listed in column (1) of the Table below and comprise the areas specified in column (2) of the Table).

2(1)   A reference to an area specified in column (2) of the Table is a reference to that area as it is for the time being.

(2)   But where an area specified in column (2) of the Table is altered, the alteration does not have effect for the purposes of this Act until the first general election of MEPs at which the poll in the United Kingdom and Gibraltar takes place after the alteration comes into force for all other purposes.

3

    Repealed.

4

TABLE

(1)	(2)	(3)
Name of Region	Area Included	...
East Midlands	County of Derby	...
	County of Derbyshire	
	County of Leicester	
	County of Leicestershire	
	County of Lincolnshire	
	County of Northamptonshire	
	County of Nottingham	
	County of Nottinghamshire	
	County of Rutland	
Eastern	County of Bedford	...
	County of Central Bedfordshire	
	County of Cambridgeshire	
	County of Essex	
	County of Hertfordshire	
	County of Luton	
	County of Norfolk	

	County of Peterborough	
	County of SouthendonSea	
	County of Suffolk	
	County of Thurrock	
London	Greater London	...
North East	County of Darlington	...
	County of Durham	
	County of Hartlepool	
	County of Middlesbrough	
	County of Northumberland	
	County of Redcar and Cleveland	
	County of Stockton-on-Tees	
	County of Tyne and Wear	
North West	County of Blackburn with Darwen	...
	County of Blackpool	
	County of Cheshire East	
	County of Cheshire West and Chester	
	County of Cumbria	
	County of Greater Manchester	
	County of Halton	
	County of Lancashire	
	County of Merseyside	
	County of Warrington	
South East	County of Berkshire	...
	County of Brighton and Hove	
	County of Buckinghamshire	
	County of East Sussex	
	County of Hampshire	
	County of Isle of Wight	
	County of Kent	
	County of the Medway Towns	
	County of Milton Keynes	
	County of Oxfordshire	
	County of Portsmouth	
	County of Southampton	
	County of Surrey	
	County of West Sussex	
South West	County of Bath and North East Somerset	...
	County of Bournemouth	
	County of the City of Bristol	
	County of Cornwall	
	County of Devon	
	County of Dorset	
	County of Gloucestershire	
	County of North Somerset	
	County of Plymouth	
	County of Poole	
	County of Somerset	
	County of South Gloucestershire	
	County of Swindon	
	County of Torbay	
	County of Wiltshire	
	Isles of Scilly	
	Gibraltar	

West Midlands	County of Herefordshire	...
	County of Shropshire	
	County of Staffordshire	
	County of StokeonTrent	
	County of Telford and Wrekin	
	County of Warwickshire	
	County of West Midlands	
	County of Worcestershire	
Yorkshire and the Humber	County of the City of Kingston upon Hull	...
	County of the East Riding of Yorkshire	
	County of North East Lincolnshire	
	County of North Lincolnshire	
	County of North Yorkshire	
	County of South Yorkshire	
	County of West Yorkshire	
	County of York	

NOTES

Defined terms
  MEP: s 1(1)

SCHEDULE 1A
PERIODIC REVIEWS OF DISTRIBUTION OF MEPS

Electoral Commission review and recommendation

1(1)   As soon as possible after 1st May in a pre-election year the Electoral Commission ("the Commission") must, subject to paragraph 2

    (a)   carry out a review ("the periodic review") of the distribution of MEPs between the electoral regions; and

    (b)   report its conclusions to the Secretary of State.

(2)   In carrying out the periodic review the Commission must consider whether (assuming that each region is entitled to be allocated at least three MEPs) the ratio of electors to MEPs is as nearly as possible the same for every electoral region.

(3)   If the Commission concludes that the result mentioned in sub-paragraph (2) is not achieved by the current distribution of MEPs, it must include in its report a recommendation specifying a distribution that would achieve that result.

(4)   The report must be published by the Commission and laid before Parliament by the Secretary of State.

Exclusion or suspension of duties under paragraph 1

2(1)   The Commission may not take any step (or further step) under paragraph 1 if a 2003 Act order is made or a suspension notice is given to the Commission

    (a)   within the period of 12 months ending with 1st May in the preelection year in question or,

    (b)   after the end of that period but before the Commission makes its report,

unless and until the duties under paragraph 1 revive by virtue of sub-paragraph (2).

(2)   If the Secretary of State withdraws a suspension notice more than nine months before the date of the poll for the next general election of MEPs, the duties under paragraph 1 revive (but subject again to this paragraph).

(3)   In this Schedule

"2003 Act order" means an order under section 5 of the European Parliament (Representation) Act 2003 (orders implementing changes in the number of United Kingdom MEPs) which takes effect in relation to the next general election of MEPs after it is made; and

"suspension notice" means a notice stating that the Secretary of State considers it likely that a 2003 Act order will be made before the next general election of MEPs.

Implementation of Electoral Commission recommendation

3(1)   Where a recommendation under paragraph 1(3) is made to him, the Secretary of State must

    (a)   lay before Parliament a draft of an order giving effect to the recommendation by amending any of the numbers specified in section 1(3); and

    (b)   if the draft is approved by resolution of each House, make an order in the terms of the draft.

(2)   An order under this paragraph may make consequential, transitional or saving provision.

(3)   Provision made under sub-paragraph (2) may modify any enactment.

(4)   The Secretary of State must consult the Commission before laying an order under this paragraph before Parliament.

(5)   This paragraph has effect subject to paragraphs 4 and 5.

4(1)   If a motion for the approval of a draft of an order under paragraph 3 is rejected by either House or withdrawn by leave of the House, the Secretary of State may, after consulting the Commission, alter the draft order and lay it before Parliament for approval.

(2)   But the Secretary of State may not, without the consent of the Commission, alter a draft order so as to propose a distribution of MEPs other than that recommended under paragraph 1(3).

(3)   The Commission may not give its consent under sub-paragraph (2) unless it is satisfied that the distribution of MEPs could have been recommended under paragraph 1(3).

(4)   If an altered draft order is approved by both Houses the Secretary of State must make an order under paragraph 3 in the terms of the altered draft.

(5)   This paragraph has effect subject to paragraph 5.

Exclusion or suspension of duties and powers under paragraph 3 or 4

5(1)   The Secretary of State may not take any step (or further step) under paragraph 3 or 4 if a 2003 Act order is made before he would otherwise have taken it.

(2)   Subject to that, the Secretary of State is not required to take any step (or further step) under paragraph 3 or 4 if and so long as he is of the opinion that it is likely that a 2003 Act order will be made before the next general election of MEPs.

(3)   But if he ceases to be of that opinion, the Secretary of State

    (a)   may not make an order under paragraph 3 on or after the relevant day; and

    (b)   is not required to take any other step under paragraph 3 or 4 if he does not consider that it will be practicable to make an order under paragraph 3 before the relevant day.

(4)   In sub-paragraph (3) "the relevant day" means the first day of the period of four months ending with the day on which the poll for the next general election of MEPs is to be held.

Supplementary

6(1)   In this Schedule

"general election of MEPs" means an election required to be held in the United Kingdom by virtue of Article 11(2) of the Act annexed to Council Decision 76/787;

"pre-election year" means a year (including 2003) which immediately precedes a year in which a general election of MEPs is to be held; and

"relevant register" means

(a) a register of parliamentary electors;

(b) a register of local government electors;

(c) a register of peers maintained under section 3 of the Representation of the People Act 1985 (c 50) (peers resident outside the United Kingdom); and

(d) a register maintained under regulation 5 of the European Parliamentary Elections (Franchise of Relevant Citizens of the Union) Regulations 2001 (SI 2001/1184) (citizens of the European Union other than Commonwealth and Republic of Ireland citizens).

(2) For the purposes of paragraph 1(2) a person is an "elector", in relation to an electoral region, if his name appears on 1st May in the pre-election year concerned in (or in any part of) a relevant register which relates to the region.

(3) In calculating the total number of electors for any electoral region

(a) persons who are registered but have not attained the age of 18 are to be counted as electors;

(b) a citizen of the European Union (not being a Commonwealth citizen or a citizen of the Republic of Ireland) who is registered only for the purposes of local government elections is to be disregarded; and

(c) the Electoral Commission may assume that each relevant register is accurate and that names appearing more than once on registers (or parts of registers) which relate to an electoral region are the names of different electors.

NOTES

Defined terms   MEP: s 1(1)
   the Act annexed to Council Decision 76/787: s 17
   citizen of the European Union: s 17
   enactment: s 17

SCHEDULE 2
Transitional Provisions

1   The repeal and re-enactment of provisions in this Act does not affect the continuity of the law.

2   Anything done, or having effect as if done, under or for the purposes of a provision repealed by this Act (including subordinate legislation so made or having effect as if so made), and in force or effective immediately before the commencement of this Act, has effect after that commencement as if done under or for the purposes of the corresponding provision of this Act.

3   A reference, express or implied, in this Act, another enactment or an instrument or document, to a provision of this Act is, subject to its context, to be read as being or including a reference to the corresponding provision repealed by this Act, in relation to times, circumstances or purposes in relation to which the repealed provision had effect.

4(1)   A reference, express or implied, in any enactment, instrument or document, to a provision repealed by this Act is, subject to its context, to be read as being or including a reference to the corresponding provision of this Act, in relation to times, circumstances or purposes in relation to which that provision has effect.

(2) In particular, where a power conferred by an Act is expressed to be exercisable in relation to enactments contained in Acts passed before or in the same Session as the Act conferring the power, the power is also exercisable in relation to provisions of this Act that reproduce such enactments.

5 Paragraphs 1 to 4 have effect in place of section 17(2) of the Interpretation Act 1978 (c 30) (but are without prejudice to any other provision of that Act).

NOTES
Defined terms
enactment: s 17

SCHEDULE 3
Consequential Amendments

Not reproduced

SCHEDULE 4
Repeals and Revocations

Not reproduced

European Union Act 2011

An Act to make provision about treaties relating to the European Union and decisions made under them, including provision implementing the Protocol signed at Brussels on 23 June 2010 amending the Protocol (No 36) on transitional provisions annexed to the Treaty on European Union, to the Treaty on the Functioning of the European Union and to the Treaty establishing the European Atomic Energy Community; and to make provision about the means by which directly applicable or directly effective European Union law has effect in the United Kingdom.

19th July 2011

PART 1

RESTRICTIONS ON TREATIES AND DECISIONS RELATING TO EU

Introductory

1 Interpretation of Part 1

(1) This section has effect for the interpretation of this Part.

(2) "TEU" means the Treaty on European Union.

(3) "TFEU" means the Treaty on the Functioning of the European Union.

(4) A reference to a treaty which amends TEU or TFEU includes a reference to
   (a) a treaty resulting from the application of Article 48(2) to (5) of TEU (ordinary revision procedure);
   (b) an agreement under Article 49 of TEU (admission of new members).

(5) An "Article 48(6) decision" means a decision under Article 48(6) of TEU (simplified revision procedure).

(6) Except in a reference to "the European Council", "the Council" means the Council of the European Union.

(7) A reference to a Minister of the Crown voting in favour of or otherwise supporting a decision is a reference to a Minister of the Crown
   (a) voting in favour of the decision in the European Council or the Council, or
   (b) allowing the decision to be adopted by consensus or unanimity by the European Council or the Council.

Restrictions relating to amendments of TEU or TFEU

2 Treaties amending or replacing TEU or TFEU

(1) A treaty which amends or replaces TEU or TFEU is not to be ratified unless
   (a) a statement relating to the treaty was laid before Parliament in accordance with section 5,
   (b) the treaty is approved by Act of Parliament, and
   (c) the referendum condition or the exemption condition is met.

(2) The referendum condition is that
   (a) the Act providing for the approval of the treaty provides that the provision approving the treaty is not to come into force until a referendum about whether the treaty should be ratified has been held throughout the United Kingdom or, where the treaty also affects Gibraltar, throughout the United Kingdom and Gibraltar,
   (b) the referendum has been held, and
   (c) the majority of those voting in the referendum are in favour of the ratification of the treaty.

(3) The exemption condition is that the Act providing for the approval of the treaty states that the treaty does not fall within section 4.

NOTES
Defined terms
TEU: s 1(2)
TFEU: s 1(3)

treaty which amends TEU or TFEU: s 1(4)

3 Amendment of TFEU under simplified revision procedure

(1) Where the European Council has adopted an Article 48(6) decision subject to its approval by the member States, a Minister of the Crown may not confirm the approval of the decision by the United Kingdom unless

    (a) a statement relating to the decision was laid before Parliament in accordance with section 5,

    (b) the decision is approved by Act of Parliament, and

    (c) the referendum condition, the exemption condition or the significance condition is met.

(2) The referendum condition is that

    (a) the Act providing for the approval of the decision provides that the provision approving the decision is not to come into force until a referendum about whether the decision should be approved has been held throughout the United Kingdom or, where the decision also affects Gibraltar, throughout the United Kingdom and Gibraltar,

    (b) the referendum has been held, and

    (c) the majority of those voting in the referendum are in favour of the approval of the decision.

(3) The exemption condition is that the Act providing for the approval of the decision states that the decision does not fall within section 4.

(4) The significance condition is that the Act providing for the approval of the decision states that

    (a) the decision falls within section 4 only because of provision of the kind mentioned in subsection (1)(i) or (j) of that section, and

    (b) the effect of that provision in relation to the United Kingdom is not significant.

NOTES
Defined terms
Article 48(6) decision: s 1(5)

4 Cases where treaty or Article 48(6) decision attracts a referendum

(1) Subject to subsection (4), a treaty or an Article 48(6) decision falls within this section if it involves one or more of the following

    (a) the extension of the objectives of the EU as set out in Article 3 of TEU;

    (b) the conferring on the EU of a new exclusive competence;

    (c) the extension of an exclusive competence of the EU;

    (d) the conferring on the EU of a new competence shared with the member States;

    (e) the extension of any competence of the EU that is shared with the member States;

    (f) the extension of the competence of the EU in relation to

        (i) the co-ordination of economic and employment policies, or

        (ii) common foreign and security policy;

    (g) the conferring on the EU of a new competence to carry out actions to support, co-ordinate or supplement the actions of member States;

    (h) the extension of a supporting, co-ordinating or supplementing competence of the EU;

    (i) the conferring on an EU institution or body of power to impose a requirement or obligation on the United Kingdom, or the removal of any limitation on any such power of an EU institution or body;

> (j) the conferring on an EU institution or body of new or extended power to impose sanctions on the United Kingdom;
>
> (k) any amendment of a provision listed in Schedule 1 that removes a requirement that anything should be done unanimously, by consensus or by common accord;
>
> (l) any amendment of Article 31(2) of TEU (decisions relating to common foreign and security policy to which qualified majority voting applies) that removes or amends the provision enabling a member of the Council to oppose the adoption of a decision to be taken by qualified majority voting;
>
> (m) any amendment of any of the provisions specified in subsection (3) that removes or amends the provision enabling a member of the Council, in relation to a draft legislative act, to ensure the suspension of the ordinary legislative procedure.

(2) Any reference in subsection (1) to the extension of a competence includes a reference to the removal of a limitation on a competence.

(3) The provisions referred to in subsection (1)(m) are
   (a) Article 48 of TFEU (social security),
   (b) Article 82(3) of TFEU (judicial co-operation in criminal matters), and
   (c) Article 83(3) of TFEU (particularly serious crime with a cross-border dimension).

(4) A treaty or Article 48(6) decision does not fall within this section merely because it involves one or more of the following
   (a) the codification of practice under TEU or TFEU in relation to the previous exercise of an existing competence;
   (b) the making of any provision that applies only to member States other than the United Kingdom;
   (c) in the case of a treaty, the accession of a new member State.

NOTES

Defined terms
   Article 48(6) decision: s 1(5)
   the Council: s 1(6)
   TEU: s 1(2)

TFEU: s 1(3)

5 Statement to be laid before Parliament

(1) If a treaty amending TEU or TFEU is agreed in an inter-governmental conference, a Minister of the Crown must lay the required statement before Parliament before the end of the 2 months beginning with the date on which the treaty is agreed.

(2) If an Article 48(6) decision is adopted by the European Council subject to its approval by the member States, a Minister of the Crown must lay the required statement before Parliament before the end of the 2 months beginning with the date on which the decision is adopted.

(3) The required statement is a statement as to whether, in the Minister's opinion, the treaty or Article 48(6) decision falls within section 4.

(4) If the Minister is of the opinion that an Article 48(6) decision falls within section 4 only because of provision of the kind mentioned in subsection (1)(i) or (j) of that section, the statement must indicate whether in the Minister's opinion the effect of that provision in relation to the United Kingdom is significant.

(5) The statement must give reasons for the Minister's opinion under subsection (3) and, if relevant, subsection (4).

(6) In relation to an Article 48(6) decision adopted by the European Council before the day on which this section comes into force ("the commencement date"), the condition in section 3(1)(a) is to be taken to be complied with if a statement under this section is laid before Parliament before the end of the 2 months beginning with the commencement date.

NOTES

Defined terms
  Article 48(6) decision: s 1(5)
  TEU: s 1(2)
  TFEU: s 1(3)

treaty amending TEU or TFEU: s 1(4)

Restrictions relating to other decisions under TEU or TFEU

6 Decisions requiring approval by Act and by referendum

(1) A Minister of the Crown may not vote in favour of or otherwise support a decision to which this subsection applies unless
   (a) the draft decision is approved by Act of Parliament, and
   (b) the referendum condition is met.

(2) Where the European Council has recommended to the member States the adoption of a decision under Article 42(2) of TEU in relation to a common EU defence, a Minister of the Crown may not notify the European Council that the decision is adopted by the United Kingdom unless
   (a) the decision is approved by Act of Parliament, and
   (b) the referendum condition is met.

(3) A Minister of the Crown may not give a notification under Article 4 of Protocol (No 21) on the position of the United Kingdom and Ireland in respect of the area of freedom, security and justice annexed to TEU and TFEU which relates to participation by the United Kingdom in a European Public Prosecutor's Office or an extension of the powers of that Office unless
   (a) the notification has been approved by Act of Parliament, and
   (b) the referendum condition is met.

(4) The referendum condition is that set out in section 3(2), with references to a decision being read for the purposes of subsection (1) as references to a draft decision and for the purposes of subsection (3) as references to a notification.

(5) The decisions to which subsection (1) applies are
   (a) a decision under the provision of Article 31(3) of TEU that permits the adoption of qualified majority voting;
   (b) a decision under Article 48(7) of TEU which in relation to any provision listed in Schedule 1
      (i) adopts qualified majority voting, or
      (ii) applies the ordinary legislative procedure in place of a special legislative procedure requiring the Council to act unanimously;
   (c) a decision under Article 86(1) of TFEU involving participation by the United Kingdom in a European Public Prosecutor's Office;
   (d) where the United Kingdom has become a participant in a European Public Prosecutor's Office, a decision under Article 86(4) of TFEU to extend the powers of that Office;
   (e) a decision under Article 140(3) of TFEU which would make the euro the currency of the United Kingdom;
   (f) a decision under the provision of Article 153(2) of TFEU (social policy) that permits the application of the ordinary legislative procedure in place of a special legislative procedure;
   (g) a decision under the provision of Article 192(2) of TFEU (environment) that permits the application of the ordinary legislative procedure in place of a special legislative procedure;
   (h) a decision under the provision of Article 312(2) of TFEU (EU finance) that permits the adoption of qualified majority voting;
   (i) a decision under the provision of Article 333(1) of TFEU (enhanced co-operation) that permits the adoption of qualified majority voting, where the decision relates to a

provision listed in Schedule 1 and the United Kingdom is a participant in the enhanced co-operation to which the decision relates;

    (j) a decision under the provision of Article 333(2) of TFEU (enhanced co-operation) that permits the adoption of the ordinary legislative procedure in place of a special legislative procedure, where

        (i) the decision relates to a provision listed in Schedule 1,

        (ii) the special legislative procedure requires the Council to act unanimously, and

        (iii) the United Kingdom is a participant in the enhanced co-operation to which the decision relates;

    (k) a decision under Article 4 of the Schengen Protocol that removes any border control of the United Kingdom.

(6) In subsection (5)(k) "the Schengen Protocol" means the Protocol (No 19) on the Schengen acquis integrated into the framework of the European Union, annexed to TEU and TFEU.

NOTES

Defined terms
  the Council: s 1(6)
  Minister of the Crown voting in favour of or otherwise
  supporting a decision: s 1(7)

TEU: s 1(2)
TFEU: s 1(3)

7 Decisions requiring approval by Act

(1) A Minister of the Crown may not confirm the approval by the United Kingdom of a decision to which this subsection applies unless the decision is approved by Act of Parliament.

(2) The decisions to which subsection (1) applies are

    (a) a decision under the provision of Article 25 of TFEU that permits the adoption of provisions to strengthen or add to the rights listed in Article 20(2) of that Treaty (rights of citizens of the European Union);

    (b) a decision under the provision of Article 223(1) of TFEU that permits the laying down of the provisions necessary for the election of the members of the European Parliament in accordance with that Article;

    (c) a decision under the provision of Article 262 of TFEU that permits the conferring of jurisdiction on the Court of Justice of the European Union in disputes relating to the application of acts adopted on the basis of the EU Treaties which create European intellectual property rights;

    (d) a decision under the third paragraph of Article 311 of TFEU to adopt a decision laying down provisions relating to the system of own resources of the European Union.

(3) A Minister of the Crown may not vote in favour of or otherwise support a decision to which this subsection applies unless the draft decision is approved by Act of Parliament.

(4) The decisions to which subsection (3) applies are

    (a) a decision under the provision of Article 17(5) of TEU that permits the alteration of the number of members of the European Commission;

    (b) a decision under Article 48(7) of TEU which in relation to any provision not listed in Schedule 1

        (i) adopts qualified majority voting, or

        (ii) applies the ordinary legislative procedure in place of a special legislative procedure requiring the Council to act unanimously;

    (c) a decision under the provision of Article 64(3) of TFEU that permits the adoption of measures which constitute a step backwards in European Union law as regards the liberalisation of the movement of capital to or from third countries;

    (d) a decision under the provision of Article 126(14) of TFEU that permits the adoption of provisions to replace the Protocol (No 12) on the excessive deficit procedure annexed to TEU and TFEU;

(e) a decision under the provision of Article 333(1) of TFEU (enhanced co-operation) that permits the adoption of qualified majority voting, where the decision relates to a provision not listed in Schedule 1 and the United Kingdom is a participant in the enhanced co-operation to which the decision relates;

(f) a decision under the provision of Article 333(2) of TFEU (enhanced co-operation) that permits the adoption of the ordinary legislative procedure in place of a special legislative procedure, where

(i) the decision relates to a provision not listed in Schedule 1,

(ii) the special legislative procedure requires the Council to act unanimously, and

(iii) the United Kingdom is a participant in the enhanced co-operation to which the decision relates.

NOTES

Defined terms
  Minister of the Crown voting in favour of or otherwise
  supporting a decision: s 1(7)
  TEU: s 1(2)

TFEU: s 1(3)

8 Decisions under Article 352 of TFEU
Not relevant to election law and not reproduced

9 Approval required in connection with Title V of Part 3 of TFEU
Not relevant to election law and not reproduced

10 Parliamentary control of certain decisions not requiring approval by Act
Not relevant to election law and not reproduced

11 Persons entitled to vote in referendum

(1) The persons entitled to vote in any referendum held in pursuance of section 2, 3 or 6 are to be as follows

(a) the persons who, on the date of the referendum, would be entitled to vote as an elector at a parliamentary election in a constituency in the United Kingdom;

(b) the persons who, on that date, are disqualified by reason of being peers from voting as electors in parliamentary elections but

(i) would be entitled to vote as electors at a local government election in any electoral area in Great Britain,

(ii) would be entitled to vote as electors at a local election in any district electoral area in Northern Ireland, or

(iii) would be entitled to vote as electors at a European Parliamentary election in any electoral region by virtue of section 3 of the Representation of the People Act 1985 (peers resident outside the United Kingdom);

(c) if the referendum is also held in Gibraltar, the Commonwealth citizens who, on the date of the referendum, would be entitled to vote in Gibraltar at a European Parliamentary election in the combined electoral region in which Gibraltar is comprised.

(2) In subsection (1)(b)(i) "local government election" includes a municipal election in the City of London (that is, an election to the office of mayor, alderman, common councilman or sheriff and also the election of any officer elected by the mayor, aldermen and liverymen in common hall).

12 Separate questions

If a referendum is to be held in pursuance of any of sections 2, 3 and 6 in relation to two or more treaties or decisions, or in relation to one or more treaties and one or more decisions, a separate question must be included on the ballot paper in relation to each treaty or decision.

13 Role of Electoral Commission

Where an Act provides for a referendum to be held in pursuance of section 2, 3 or 6, the Electoral Commission

   (a) must take whatever steps they think appropriate to promote public awareness of the referendum and how to vote in it, and

   (b) may take whatever steps they think appropriate to promote public awareness of the subject-matter of the referendum.

Supplementary

14 Consequential amendments and repeals relating to Part 1
Not reproduced

PART 2
IMPLEMENTATION OF TRANSITIONAL PROTOCOL ON MEPS

15 Protocol on MEPs: approval, and addition to list of treaties
Not reproduced

16 Number of MEPs and electoral regions
Amends the European Parliamentary Elections Act 2002. Not reproduced here.

17 Election of additional MEP

(1) The additional seat allocated to the West Midlands electoral region by virtue of section 16 is to be filled by applying subsections (5) to (9) of section 2 of the 2002 Act (voting system in Great Britain and Gibraltar) to the results of the poll at the general election of members of the European Parliament held on 4 June 2009, as if the seat had been allocated to the region at that date.

(2) Subsection (1) is subject to Schedule 2 which makes further provision about the filling of the additional seat.

(3) This section and Schedule 2

   (a) cease to have effect on the date appointed under section 4 of the 2002 Act as the date of the poll at the next general election of members of the European Parliament after the passing of this Act, and

   (b) do not affect the procedure to be followed in accordance with regulations made under section 5 of the 2002 Act if, after being filled in accordance with this section and Schedule 2, the additional seat subsequently becomes vacant before that date.

(4) In this section and in Schedule 2 "the 2002 Act" means the European Parliamentary Elections Act 2002.

PART 3
GENERAL

Status of EU law

18 Status of EU law dependent on continuing statutory basis

Directly applicable or directly effective EU law (that is, the rights, powers, liabilities, obligations, restrictions, remedies and procedures referred to in section 2(1) of the European Communities Act 1972) falls to be recognised and available in law in the United Kingdom only by virtue of that Act or where it is required to be recognised and available in law by virtue of any other Act.

Final provisions
19 Financial provisions

(1) There is to be paid out of money provided by Parliament any increase attributable to this Act in the sums payable under any other Act out of money so provided.

(2) There is to be charged on and paid out of the Consolidated Fund any increase attributable to this Act in the sums charged on and paid out of that Fund under any other Act.

20 Extent

(1) This Act extends to the whole of the United Kingdom.

(2) Part 2 (and this section and sections 21 and 22 so far as relating to that Part) extend also to Gibraltar.

21 Commencement

(1) The following provisions come into force on the day on which this Act is passed
    (a) section 15;
    (b) this Part.

(2) The other provisions of this Act come into force on such day as the Secretary of State may by order made by statutory instrument appoint.

(3) Different days may be appointed for different purposes.

22 Short title

This Act may be cited as the European Union Act 2011.

SCHEDULE 1
Treaty Provisions where Amendment Removing Need for Unanimity, Consensus or Common Accord Would Attract Referendum

Part 1
Provisions of the Treaty on European Union
Not reproduced.

Part 2
Provisions of the Treaty on the Functioning of the European Union
Not reproduced

SCHEDULE 2
Election of Additional Mep

Interpretation

1   In this Schedule
     "list of candidates", in relation to a registered party, means the list of candidates that
     accompanied the party's nomination paper for the general election of members of the
     European Parliament held on 4 June 2009, in accordance with rules 6 and 7 of the
     European Parliamentary elections rules in Schedule 1 to the European Parliamentary
     Elections Regulations 2004 (SI 2004/293);
     "MEP" means a Member of the European Parliament;
     "nominating officer", in relation to a registered party, has the meaning given by section
     5(5) of the 2002 Act;
     "registered party" has the meaning given by section 2(10) of the 2002 Act.

Allocation to a registered party

2(1)   The returning officer for the West Midlands electoral region must ascertain the registered
        party to which the additional seat provided for by section 16 falls to be allocated in
        accordance with section 17(1).

 (2)   In the following provisions, that registered party is referred to as "the qualifying party".

3(1)   The returning officer must ascertain from the qualifying party's list of candidates the
        name and address of the person whose name appears highest on that list ("the first
        choice"), disregarding the name of any person who has been returned as an MEP or who
        has died.

 (2)   The returning officer must take such steps as the returning officer considers reasonable
        to contact the first choice to ask whether he or she will
        (a)   state in writing that he or she is willing and able to be returned as an MEP, and
        (b)   deliver a certificate, signed by or on behalf of the nominating officer of the
               qualifying party, stating that he or she may be returned as that party's MEP.

4(1)   This paragraph applies where
        (a)   within such period as the returning officer considers reasonable, the returning
               officer decides that steps taken to contact the first choice have been unsuccessful,
        (b)   the first choice has not provided to the returning officer, within such period as the
               returning officer considers reasonable, the statement and certificate referred to in
               paragraph 3(2), or
        (c)   the first choice has provided to the returning officer a statement in writing that he
               or she is not willing or able to be returned as an MEP.

 (2)   The returning officer must ascertain from the qualifying party's list of candidates the
        name and address of the person whose name appears next in the qualifying party's list of
        candidates ("the subsequent choice"), disregarding the name of any person who has died.

 (3)   The returning officer must take such steps as the returning officer considers reasonable
        to contact the subsequent choice to ask the question in paragraph 3(2)(a) and (b).

5(1)   This paragraph applies where
        (a)   within such period as the returning officer considers reasonable, the returning
               officer decides that the steps taken to contact the subsequent choice have been
               unsuccessful,
        (b)   the subsequent choice has not provided to the returning officer, within such period
               as the returning officer considers reasonable, the statement and certificate
               referred to in paragraph 3(2), or
        (c)   the subsequent choice has provided to the returning officer a statement in writing
               that he or she is not willing or able to be returned as an MEP.

(2) The returning officer must repeat the procedure under paragraph 4(2) and (3) until
    (a) the seat is filled, or
    (b) there are no more names on the qualifying party's list of candidates.

6 Where
    (a) the returning officer has, in accordance with this Schedule, asked a subsequent choice the questions in paragraphs 3(2)(a) and (b), and
    (b) a person who was previously asked those questions ("the prior choice") then provides the statement and certificate referred to in that paragraph,
the statement and certificate provided by the prior choice are to have no effect unless and until any of the circumstances described in paragraph 5(1)(a), (b) or (c) apply in respect of the subsequent choice.

7(1) Where, on being asked under paragraphs 3 to 5 by the returning officer, a person whose name appears on the qualifying party's list of candidates provides the statement and certificate referred to in paragraph 3(2)(a) and (b), the returning officer must
    (a) declare in writing that person to be returned as an MEP, and
    (b) prepare a statement containing the information specified in sub-paragraph (2).

(2) The statement must specify
    (a) the total number of valid votes (as notified to the returning officer) given to each registered party at the general election of members of the European Parliament held on 4 June 2009, and
    (b) the number of votes which each party to which a seat has been allocated had after the application of subsections (5) to (9) of section 2 of the 2002 Act (including that section as applied by section 17(1)) at any stage when a seat was allocated to the party.

(3) The returning officer must
    (a) give public notice of a declaration given and a statement prepared under this paragraph, and
    (b) send a copy of the notice and statement to the Secretary of State.

By-election if seat not filled from qualifying party's list of candidates

8(1) This paragraph applies where the additional seat cannot be filled in accordance with paragraphs 3 to 7.

(2) The returning officer must notify the Secretary of State that the seat cannot be filled in accordance with paragraphs 3 to 7.

(3) A by-election is to be held to fill the seat.

(4) The by-election is to take place on a day specified by order of the Secretary of State.

(5) The by-election is to be conducted in accordance with regulations made under the 2002 Act.

9(1) An order under paragraph 8(4) is to be made by statutory instrument.

(2) A statutory instrument containing such an order is to be laid before Parliament after being made.

NOTES
Defined terms   the 2002 Act: s 17(4)

European Union Referendum Act 2015

An Act to make provision for the holding of a referendum in the United Kingdom and Gibraltar on whether the United Kingdom should remain a member of the European Union.

17th December 2015

The Referendum

_____

SCHEDULES

The Referendum

The referendum

1(1)   A referendum is to be held on whether the United Kingdom should remain a member of the European Union.

(2)   The Secretary of State must, by regulations, appoint the day on which the referendum is to be held.

(3)   The day appointed under subsection (2)
    (a)   must be no later than 31 December 2017,
    (b)   must not be 5 May 2016, and
    (c)   must not be 4 May 2017.

(4)   The question that is to appear on the ballot papers is
"Should the United Kingdom remain a member of the European Union or leave the European Union?"

(5)   The alternative answers to that question that are to appear on the ballot papers are
"Remain a member of the European Union
Leave the European Union".

(6)   In Wales, there must also appear on the ballot papers
    (a)   the following Welsh version of the question

"A *ddylai'r Deyrnas Unedig aros yn aelod o'r Undeb Ewropeaidd neu adael yr Undeb Ewropeaidd?*", and

(b) the following Welsh versions of the alternative answers
"*Aros yn aelod o'r Undeb Ewropeaidd*
Gadael yr Undeb Ewropeaidd".

Entitlement to vote in the referendum

2(1) Those entitled to vote in the referendum are

    (a) the persons who, on the date of the referendum, would be entitled to vote as electors at a parliamentary election in any constituency,

    (b) the persons who, on that date, are disqualified by reason of being peers from voting as electors at parliamentary elections but

        (i) would be entitled to vote as electors at a local government election in any electoral area in Great Britain,

        (ii) would be entitled to vote as electors at a local election in any district electoral area in Northern Ireland, or

        (iii) would be entitled to vote as electors at a European Parliamentary election in any electoral region by virtue of section 3 of the Representation of the People Act 1985 (peers resident outside the United Kingdom), and

    (c) the persons who, on the date of the referendum

        (i) would be entitled to vote in Gibraltar as electors at a European Parliamentary election in the combined electoral region in which Gibraltar is comprised, and

        (ii) fall within subsection (2).

(2) A person falls within this subsection if the person is either

    (a) a Commonwealth citizen, or

    (b) a citizen of the Republic of Ireland.

(3) In subsection (1)(b)(i) "local government election" includes a municipal election in the City of London (that is, an election to the office of mayor, alderman, common councilman or sheriff and also the election of any officer elected by the mayor, aldermen and liverymen in common hall).

NOTES

Defined terms
the referendum: s 11(1)

Further provision about the referendum

3 Part 7 of the 2000 Act (general provision about referendums) applies to the referendum but see also

    (a) Schedules 1 and 2 (which make, in relation to the referendum, further provision about campaigning and financial controls, including provision modifying Part 7 of the 2000 Act), and

    (b) Schedule 3 (which makes further provision about the referendum, including provision modifying Part 7 of the 2000 Act).

NOTES

Defined terms
the 2000 Act: s 11(1)
the referendum: s 11(1)

Conduct regulations, etc

4(1) The Minister may by regulations

    (a) make provision about voting in the referendum and otherwise about the conduct of the referendum, which may include provision corresponding to any provision of Schedules 2 and 3 to the 2011 Act (with or without modifications);

    (b) apply for the purposes of the referendum, with or without modifications

        (i)   any provision of the 1983 Act, or

        (ii)   any other enactment relating to elections or referendums,

    including provisions creating offences;

    (c)   further modify the 2000 Act for the purposes of the referendum;

    (d)   modify or exclude any provision of any other enactment (other than this Act) that applies to the referendum.

(2)   The Minister may by regulations make provision for and in connection with the combination of the poll for the referendum with any one or more of the following

    (a)   the poll for any election specified in the regulations;

    (b)   the poll for any other referendum specified in the regulations.

Regulations under this subsection may amend or modify any enactment (but may not alter the date of the poll for any such election or other referendum).

(3)   The reference in subsection (2) to any enactment includes

    (a)   the definition of "counting officer" in section 11(1),

    (b)   section 11(2), and

    (c)   Schedule 3,

but does not include any other provision of this Act.

(4)   The Minister may by regulations make such amendments or modifications of this Act or any other enactment as appear to the Minister to be necessary because the referendum is to be held in Gibraltar as well as the United Kingdom.

(5)   Regulations under this section may, in particular

    (a)   make provision for disregarding alterations in a register of electors;

    (b)   make provision extending or applying to (or extending or applying only to) Gibraltar or any part of the United Kingdom;

    (c)   make different provision for different purposes.

(6)   Before making any regulations under this section, the Minister must consult the Electoral Commission.

(7)   Consultation carried out before the commencement of this section is as effective for the purposes of subsection (6) as consultation carried out after that commencement.

NOTES

Defined terms
  the 1983 Act: s 11(1)
  the 2000 Act: s 11(1)
  the 2011 Act: s 11(1)
  enactment: s 11(1)

the Minister: s 11(1)
the referendum: s 11(1)

Gibraltar

5(1)   Regulations under section 4 which extend to Gibraltar may extend and apply to Gibraltar, with or without modifications, any enactment relating to referendums or elections that applies in any part of the United Kingdom.

(2)   The capacity (apart from this Act) of the Gibraltar legislature to make law for Gibraltar is not affected by the existence of

    (a)   section 4, or

    (b)   anything in any other provision of this Act which enables particular provision to be made under section 4,

and in this Act "Gibraltar conduct law" means any provision of law made in and for Gibraltar which corresponds to any provision that has been or could be made for any part of the United Kingdom by regulations under section 4.

(3)   Subsection (2) does not affect the operation of the Colonial Laws Validity Act 1865 in relation to Gibraltar conduct law.

NOTES

Defined terms
enactment: s 11(1)

Duty to publish information on outcome of negotiations between member States

6(1) The Secretary of State must publish a report which contains (alone or with other material)

(a) a statement setting out what has been agreed by member States following negotiations relating to the United Kingdom's request for reforms to address concerns over its membership of the European Union, and

(b) the opinion of the Government of the United Kingdom on what has been agreed.

(2) The report must be published before the beginning of the final 10 week period.

(3) In this section "the final 10 week period" means the period of 10 weeks ending with the date of the referendum.

(4) A copy of the report published under this section must be laid before Parliament by the Secretary of State.

NOTES
Defined terms
the referendum: s 11(1)

Duty to publish information about membership of the European Union etc

7(1) The Secretary of State must publish a report which contains (alone or with other material)

(a) information about rights, and obligations, that arise under European Union law as a result of the United Kingdom's membership of the European Union, and

(b) examples of countries that do not have membership of the European Union but do have other arrangements with the European Union (describing, in the case of each country given as an example, those arrangements).

(2) The report must be published before the beginning of the final 10 week period.

(3) In this section "the final 10 week period" means the period of 10 weeks ending with the date of the referendum.

(4) A copy of the report published under this section must be laid before Parliament by the Secretary of State.

NOTES
Defined terms
the referendum: s 11(1)

Power to modify section 125 of the 2000 Act

8(1) In this section

(a) "section 125" means section 125 of the 2000 Act (restriction on publication etc of promotional material by central and local government etc), as modified by paragraph 38 of Schedule 1, and

(b) "section 125(2)" means subsection (2) of section 125 (which prevents material to which section 125 applies from being published by or on behalf of certain persons and bodies during the 28 days ending with the date of the poll).

(2) The Minister may by regulations make provision modifying section 125, for the purposes of the referendum, so as to exclude from section 125(2) cases where

(a) material is published

(i) in a prescribed way, or

(ii) by a communication of a prescribed kind, and

(b) such other conditions as may be prescribed are met.

(3) The communications that may be prescribed under subsection (2)(a)(ii) include, in particular, oral communications and communications with the media.

(4) Before making any regulations under this section, the Minister must consult the Electoral Commission.

(5) Consultation carried out before the commencement of this section is as effective for the purposes of subsection (4) as consultation carried out after that commencement.

(6) Any regulations under subsection (2) must be made not less than 4 months before the date of the referendum.

(7) In this section
"prescribed" means prescribed by the regulations;
"publish" has the same meaning as in section 125.

(8) This section does not affect the generality of section 4(1)(c).

NOTES
Defined terms
the 2000 Act: s 11(1)
the Minister: s 11(1)
the referendum: s 11(1)

Supplemental

Regulations

9(1) Any power under this Act to make regulations, apart from the power of the Electoral Commission under paragraph 16(10) of Schedule 3, is exercisable by statutory instrument.

(2) Subject to subsection (3), a statutory instrument containing regulations under this Act may not be made unless a draft of the instrument has been laid before, and approved by a resolution of, each House of Parliament.

(3) Subsection (2) does not apply to a statutory instrument containing only regulations within subsection (4).

(4) Regulations within this subsection are any of the following
(a) regulations under section 13;
(b) regulations made by the Minister under paragraph 16 of Schedule 3.

(5) Regulations under this Act, other than regulations under section 13 or paragraph 16 of Schedule 3, may contain supplemental, consequential, incidental, transitional or saving provision.

(6) Section 26 of the Welsh Language Act 1993 (power to prescribe Welsh forms) applies in relation to regulations under this Act as it applies in relation to Acts of Parliament.

NOTES
Defined terms
the Minister: s 11(1)

Financial provisions

10(1) The following are to be paid out of money provided by Parliament
(a) expenditure incurred under this Act by the Minister;
(b) any increase attributable to this Act in the sums payable under any other Act out of money so provided.

(2) There is to be paid into the Consolidated Fund any increase attributable to this Act in the sums payable into that Fund under any other Act.

NOTES
Defined terms
the Minister: s 11(1)

Definitions

11(1)   In this Act

"the 1983 Act" means the Representation of the People Act 1983;

"the 2000 Act" means the Political Parties, Elections and Referendums Act 2000;

"the 2011 Act" means the Parliamentary Voting System and Constituencies Act 2011;

"body", without more, means a body corporate or any combination of persons or other unincorporated association;

"Chief Counting Officer" means the Chief Counting Officer for the referendum (see section 128(2) of the 2000 Act);

"conduct regulations" means regulations under section 4(1)(a);

"counting officer" has the meaning given by paragraph 3 of Schedule 3;

"designated organisation" means a person or body designated under section 108 of the 2000 Act (designation of organisations to whom assistance is available) in respect of the referendum;

"document" means a document in whatever form;

"enactment" includes

(a)   any provision of an Act,

(b)   any provision of, or of any instrument made under, an Act of the Scottish Parliament,

(c)   any provision of, or of any instrument made under, Northern Ireland legislation, and

(d)   any provision of subordinate legislation (within the meaning of the Interpretation Act 1978);

"Gibraltar conduct law" has the meaning given by section 5(2);

"the Gibraltar standard scale" means the standard scale set out in Part A of Schedule 9 to the Criminal Procedure and Evidence Act;

"the Minister" means the Secretary of State or the Chancellor of the Duchy of Lancaster;

"permitted participant" means a person who, in relation to the referendum, is a permitted participant within the meaning given by section 105(1) of the 2000 Act (as modified by paragraph 2 of Schedule 1);

"the referendum" means the referendum under section 1;

"referendum expenses" has the meaning given by section 111 of the 2000 Act (see also paragraph 19 of Schedule 1);

"the referendum period" has the meaning given by paragraph 1 of Schedule 1;

"Regional Counting Officer" means an officer appointed under paragraph 5(1) of Schedule 3;

"registered party" and "minor party" have the same meaning as in the 2000 Act (see section 160(1) of that Act);

"registration officer" has the meaning given by section 8 of the 1983 Act;

"responsible person", in relation to a permitted participant, means the responsible person within the meaning given by section 105(2) of the 2000 Act (as modified by paragraph 5 of Schedule 1);

"voting area" has the meaning given by subsection (2).

(2)   Each of the following, as it exists on the day of the referendum, is a "voting area" for the purposes of this Act

(a)   a district in England for which there is a district council;

(b)   a county in England in which there are no districts with councils;

(c)   a London borough;

(d)   the City of London (including the Inner and Middle Temples);

(e)   the Isles of Scilly;

(f)   a county or county borough in Wales;

(g)   a local government area in Scotland;

(h)   Northern Ireland;

(i)   Gibraltar.

(3)   References in this Act to a named Act (with no date) are to the Gibraltar Act of that name.

Final Provisions

Extent

12(1)   This Act extends to the whole of the United Kingdom and to Gibraltar.

(2)   For the purposes of the referendum, Part 7 of the 2000 Act (whose extent is set out in section 163 of that Act) extends also to Gibraltar.

NOTES
Defined terms
  the 2000 Act: s 11(1)
  the referendum: s 11(1)

Commencement

13(1)   The following provisions come into force on the day on which this Act is passed
          sections 9 to 12;
          this section;
          section 14.

(2)   The remaining provisions of this Act come into force on such day as the Minister may by regulations appoint.

(3)   Different days may be appointed for different purposes.

Short title

14   This Act may be cited as the European Union Referendum Act 2015.

SCHEDULE 1
CAMPAIGNING AND FINANCIAL CONTROLS

Section 3

The referendum period

1(1)   For the purposes of Part 7 of the 2000 Act and this Act, the referendum period for the referendum is such period as may be prescribed by regulations made by the Minister.

(2)   The period prescribed under this paragraph must be a period which
        (a)   is at least 10 weeks, and
        (b)   ends with the date of the referendum.

Permitted participants

2   Section 105(1) of the 2000 Act (bodies and individuals who are "permitted participants" in relation to a referendum) has effect for the purposes of the referendum as if for paragraph (b) there were substituted
        "(b)   any of the following by whom a notification has been given under section 106 in relation to the referendum, namely
          (i)   any individual who is resident in the United Kingdom or registered in an electoral register as defined by section 54(8);
          (ii)   any individual who is resident in Gibraltar or is a Gibraltar elector;
          (iii)   any body falling within any of paragraphs (b) and (d) to (h) of section 54(2);
          (iv)   any body falling within any of paragraphs (b) and (d) to (g) of section 54(2A);
          (v)   any body incorporated by Royal Charter which does not fall within section 54(2);

(vi) any charitable incorporated organisation within the meaning of Part 11 of the Charities Act 2011 or Part 11 of the Charities Act (Northern Ireland) 2008;

(vii) any Scottish charitable incorporated organisation within the meaning of Chapter 7 of Part 1 of the Charities and Trustee Investment (Scotland) Act 2005 (asp 10);

(viii) any partnership constituted under the law of Scotland which carries on business in the United Kingdom."

Notifications and declarations for purpose of becoming permitted participant

3(1) Section 106 of the 2000 Act (declarations and notifications relating to section 105) has effect for the purposes of the referendum with the following modifications.

(2) Subsection (4)(b) has effect for those purposes as if after "54(2)" there were inserted "or any of paragraphs (b) and (d) to (g) of section 54(2A)".

(3) Subsection (4) has effect for those purposes as if after paragraph (b) there were inserted
"(c) if given by a body within any of sub-paragraphs (v) to (viii) of section 105(1)(b), state
(i) the details mentioned in subsection (4A), and
(ii) the name of the person or officer who will be responsible for compliance on the part of the body with the provisions of Chapter 2,
and be signed by the body's secretary or a person who acts in a similar capacity in relation to the body."

(4) For the purposes of the referendum the following subsection is to be treated as inserted after subsection (4)
"(4A) The details referred to in subsection (4)(c)(i) are
(a) in the case of a body within section 105(1)(b)(v) (body incorporated by Royal Charter)
(i) the name of the body, and
(ii) the address of its main office in the United Kingdom;
(b) in the case of a body within section 105(1)(b)(vi) or (vii) (charitable incorporated organisation)
(i) the name of the body, and
(ii) the address of its principal office;
(c) in the case of a body within section 105(1)(b)(viii) (Scottish partnership)
(i) the name of the body, and
(ii) the address of its main office in the United Kingdom."

(5) For the purposes of the referendum the following subsections are to be treated as inserted after subsection (6)
"(6A) A declaration or notification under this section must be accompanied by a statement by the person who is the responsible person which
(a) states that that person is willing to exercise, in relation to the referendum, the functions conferred by and under this Act and the European Union Referendum Act 2015 on the responsible person, and
(b) is signed by that person.

(6B) Subsection (6A) does not apply to a notification of alteration unless the notification replaces a statement under subsection (2)(b) or (4)(b)(ii) or (c)(ii)."

Registration under section 107 of the 2000 Act

4 Where a statement under 106(6A) of the 2000 Act (treated as inserted by paragraph 3 above) is given to the Electoral Commission with a declaration or notification, the information that must be entered in the register under section 107 of that Act in respect of the declaration or notification includes
(a) the fact that the statement was made, and

(b) the name of the person who made it.

Responsible person

5   Section 105(2) of the 2000 Act (meaning of "responsible person") has effect for the purposes of the referendum as if in paragraph (c) after "106(4)(b)(ii)" there were inserted "or (c)(ii)".

Person may not be responsible for compliance for two or more permitted participants

6(1)   A person who is the responsible person for a permitted participant may not give a notification under section 106(3) of the 2000 Act in relation to the referendum.

(2)   An individual who is a permitted participant ceases to be a permitted participant if he or she is the treasurer of a registered party (other than a minor party) that becomes a permitted participant.

(3)   The requirement in section 106(2)(b) or (4)(b)(ii) or (c)(ii) of the 2000 Act (declaration or notification must state the name of the person who will be responsible for compliance) is not complied with for the purposes of the referendum if the person whose name is stated

(a)   is already the responsible person for a permitted participant,

(b)   is an individual who gives a notification under section 106(3) of that Act at the same time, or

(c)   is the person whose name is stated, in purported compliance with the requirement in section 106(2)(b) or (4)(b)(ii) or (c)(ii) of that Act, in a notification given at the same time by another body.

(4)   Where a registered party (other than a minor party) makes a declaration under section 106 of the 2000 Act in relation to the referendum and the treasurer of the party ("the treasurer") is already the responsible person for a permitted participant ("the relevant participant")

(a)   the treasurer ceases to be the responsible person for the relevant participant at the end of the period of 14 days beginning with the day on which (by reason of the declaration) the treasurer becomes the responsible person for the party, and

(b)   the relevant participant must, before the end of that period, give a notice of alteration under section 106(5) of the 2000 Act stating the name of the person who is to replace the treasurer as the responsible person for the relevant participant.

(5)   In sub-paragraphs (3) and (4)(b) "the person", in relation to a body which is not a minor party, is to be read as "the person or officer".

(6)   In this paragraph "treasurer" has the same meaning as in the 2000 Act (see 160(1) of that Act), and section 25(6) of that Act (references to the treasurer to be read in certain cases as references to the campaigns officer) applies for the purposes of this paragraph as it applies for the purposes of Part 7 of that Act.

Unincorporated associations with offensive etc names

7(1)   This paragraph applies to a notification which, in relation to the referendum, is given to the Electoral Commission under section 106(3) of the 2000 Act by an unincorporated association falling within section 54(2)(h) or 54(2A)(g) of that Act.

(2)   A notification to which this paragraph applies is not to be treated for the purposes of section 105 or 107 of the 2000 Act as having been given unless the Electoral Commission have accepted the notification.

(3)   As soon as reasonably practicable after receiving a notification to which this paragraph applies the Electoral Commission must decide whether or not to accept the notification, and they must accept it unless in their opinion the name of the association

(a)   is obscene or offensive, or

(b) includes words the publication of which would be likely to amount to the commission of an offence.

(4) As soon as reasonably practicable after deciding whether to accept the notification the Electoral Commission must give written notice to the association

    (a) stating whether they accept the notification, and

    (b) if their decision is not to accept the notification, giving the reasons for that decision.

8(1) Where

    (a) a permitted participant is an unincorporated association falling within section 54(2)(h) or 54(2A)(g) of the 2000 Act,

    (b) the Electoral Commission is notified under section 106(5) of that Act of a change of name of the association, and

    (c) in the opinion of the Electoral Commission the new name is obscene or offensive or includes words the publication of which would be likely to amount to the commission of an offence,

the Electoral Commission does not have to enter the new name in the register under section 107 of that Act.

(2) If the Electoral Commission decide under this paragraph not to enter the new name of an unincorporated association in that register, the Electoral Commission

    (a) must as soon as reasonably practicable give written notice to the association of that decision and the reasons for it, and

    (b) in any case where they are required to make available for public inspection a document that uses the association's new name, may replace that name in the document with the name that appears on the register in respect of the association.

(3) The fact that the association's new name is not entered in the register does not cause the association to cease to be a permitted participant.

Designation of organisations: designation of one organisation only

9(1) Section 108 of the 2000 Act (designation of organisations to whom assistance is available) has effect for the purposes of the referendum with the following modifications.

(2) Subsection (2) has effect for those purposes as if for the words from "the Commission" to the end there were substituted "the Commission may

    (a) in relation to each of those outcomes, designate one permitted participant as representing those campaigning for the outcome in question; or

    (b) if the condition in subsection (2A) is met as regards one of those outcomes ("outcome A") but not the other ("outcome B"), designate one permitted participant as representing those campaigning for outcome B.

(2A) The condition in this subsection is met as regards an outcome if either

    (a) no permitted participant makes an application to be designated under section 109 as representing those campaigning for that outcome; or

    (b) the Commission are not satisfied that there is any permitted participant who has made an application under that section who adequately represents those campaigning for that outcome."

(3) For the purposes of the referendum subsections (3) and (4) are to be treated as omitted.

10 Accordingly, for the purposes of the referendum, section 109 of the 2000 Act (applying to become a designated organisation) has effect as if

    (a) in subsection (4) paragraph (b) (and the "or" before it) were omitted, and

    (b) in subsection (5) paragraph (b) (and the "or" before it) were omitted.

11(1) This paragraph applies if the Electoral Commission designate only one permitted participant under section 108(2) of the 2000 Act in respect of the referendum.

(2) If this paragraph applies, section 110 of the 2000 Act (assistance available to designated organisations) has effect for the purposes of the referendum as if
 (a) in subsection (1)
  (i) for "any designations" there were substituted "a designation", and
  (ii) for "the designated organisations" there were substituted "the designated organisation",
 (b) subsections (2) and (3) were omitted, and
 (c) for subsection (4) there were substituted the subsection set out in sub-paragraph (3) below.

(3) That subsection is
 "(4) The designated organisation (or, as the case may be, persons authorised by the organisation) shall have the rights conferred by paragraphs 1 to 3 of Schedule 12."

(4) If this paragraph applies, section 127(1) of the 2000 Act (referendum campaign broadcasts) has effect for the purposes of the referendum as if the words from "made" to the end were omitted.

Applying to become a designated organisation: period for making application

12 Subsections (2), (3) and (6) of section 109 of the 2000 Act (application by organisation for designation) have effect for the purposes of the referendum as if the reference in subsection (2)(b) of that section to the first day of the referendum period were a reference to the day prescribed under this paragraph by regulations made by the Minister.

Grants to designated organisations may be paid in instalments

13(1) This paragraph applies to a grant under section 110(2) of the 2000 Act (grants to designated organisations) made in respect of the referendum.

(2) The grant may be paid in whatever instalments the Electoral Commission consider appropriate.

(3) Instalments may be withheld if the Electoral Commission are satisfied that the designated organisation concerned has failed to comply with a condition imposed under section 110(3) of the 2000 Act.

(4) Section 110(2) of the 2000 Act, so far as it requires the grant to be of the same amount in the case of each designated organisation, has effect in relation to the referendum subject to sub-paragraph (3).

Assistance available to designated organisations

14(1) Schedule 12 to the 2000 Act (assistance available to designated organisations) has effect for the purposes of the referendum with the following modifications.

(2) Paragraph 2(2) has effect for those purposes as if after paragraph (b) there were inserted
 "(c) in Gibraltar, to a school the expense of maintaining which is payable wholly or partly out of Gibraltar public funds or out of any rate, or by a body whose expenses are so payable."

(3) Paragraph 3(2) has effect for those purposes as if after paragraph (b) there were inserted
 "or
 (c) in the case of a school in Gibraltar, with the Gibraltar Government Ministry of Education."

(4) Paragraph 3(3) has effect for those purposes as if at the end there were inserted "or, in the case of a school in Gibraltar, by the Government of Gibraltar".

Referendum agents

15(1)   A permitted participant may, in relation to any voting area, appoint an individual (who may be the responsible person) to be the permitted participant's referendum agent for that area.

   (2)   Regulations under section 4 may
      (a)   confer functions on a referendum agent appointed under this paragraph;
      (b)   make further provision (additional to the provision in paragraphs 16 and 17) in connection with referendum agents.

16(1)   If a permitted participant appoints a referendum agent for a voting area, the responsible person must give the counting officer for the area notification of the name and home or business address of
      (a)   the permitted participant, and
      (b)   the referendum agent.

   (2)   The notification must be given before noon on the 16th day before the date of the poll, disregarding for this purpose
      (a)   Saturdays and Sundays,
      (b)   Christmas Eve, Christmas Day, Good Friday and any other day that is a bank holiday under the Banking and Financial Dealings Act 1971 in any part of the United Kingdom,
      (c)   any day that is a bank or public holiday in Gibraltar under the Banking and Financial Dealings Act and the Interpretation and General Clauses Act, and
      (d)   any day appointed in any part of the United Kingdom or Gibraltar as a day of public thanksgiving or mourning.

   (3)   The notification must be in writing and signed by the responsible person.

   (4)   The duties imposed on a responsible person by this paragraph may be discharged by any person authorised in writing by the responsible person.

17   If a counting officer is notified under paragraph 16 that a permitted participant has appointed a referendum agent, the counting officer must as soon as practicable give public notice of
      (a)   the name and address of the referendum agent, and
      (b)   the name of the permitted participant.

Referendum expenses: definition

18   Schedule 13 to the 2000 Act (expenses that are referendum expenses where incurred for referendum purposes) has effect for the purposes of the referendum as if in paragraph 2(a) after "public funds" there were inserted "or Gibraltar public funds".

19(1)   In relation to the referendum, expenses mentioned in sub-paragraph (2) are not to be treated for any purpose of this Act or Part 7 of the 2000 Act as referendum expenses.

   (2)   Those expenses are
      (a)   expenses incurred in respect of the publication of any matter relating to the referendum, other than an advertisement, in
         (i)   a newspaper or periodical;
         (ii)   a broadcast made by the British Broadcasting Corporation, Sianel Pedwar Cymru or the Gibraltar Broadcasting Corporation;
         (iii)   a programme included in any service licensed under Part 1 or 3 of the Broadcasting Act 1990 or Part 1 or 2 of the Broadcasting Act 1996;

    (b)   expenses incurred in respect of, or in consequence of, the translation of anything from English into Welsh or from Welsh into English;

    (c)   reasonable expenses incurred that are reasonably attributable to an individual's disability;

    (d)   expenses incurred in providing for the protection of persons or property at rallies or other public events.

(3)   In sub-paragraph (2)(c) "disability" has the same meaning as in the Equality Act 2010 (see section 6 of that Act).

20(1)   In section 117(5) of the 2000 Act (certain expenditure incurred before the referendum period treated as incurred during that period), the reference to any time before the beginning of the referendum period is to be read for the purposes of the referendum as including any time before the day when section 3 of this Act (application of Part 7 of the 2000 Act to the referendum) is brought into force for the purposes of applying section 117 of the 2000 Act to the referendum.

(2)   This paragraph has effect in relation to section 117(5) of the 2000 Act as it applies for the purposes of section 117 of that Act and as applied by any provision of that Act or of this Schedule.

Creditors' rights

21(1)   This paragraph applies where

    (a)   a contract is made, or an expense is incurred, in connection with the referendum, and

    (b)   the contract or expense is in contravention of a relevant provision.

(2)   In this paragraph a "relevant provision" means a provision of Part 7 of the 2000 Act which prohibits

    (a)   payments or contracts for payments,

    (b)   the payment or incurring of referendum expenses in excess of the maximum amount allowed by that Part, or

    (c)   the incurring of referendum expenses without the authority mentioned in section 113(1) of the 2000 Act.

(3)   Nothing in any such provision affects the right of a creditor who, when the contract was made or the expense was incurred, was ignorant of the fact that the contract or expense was in contravention of the relevant provision.

Expenses incurred by persons acting in concert

22(1)   This paragraph applies where

    (a)   referendum expenses are incurred by or on behalf of an individual or body during the referendum period for the referendum, and

    (b)   those expenses are incurred in pursuance of a plan or other arrangement by which referendum expenses are to be incurred by or on behalf of

       (i)   that individual or body, and

       (ii)   one or more other individuals or bodies,

with a view to, or otherwise in connection with, promoting or procuring a particular outcome in relation to the question asked in the referendum.

(2)   In this paragraph references to "common plan expenses" of an individual or body are to referendum expenses which are incurred by or on behalf of that individual or body

    (a)   as mentioned in sub-paragraph (1)(a), and

    (b)   in pursuance of a plan or other arrangement mentioned in sub-paragraph (1)(b).

(3)   The common plan expenses of the individual or body which is mentioned in sub-paragraph (1)(a) are to be treated for the purposes of

    (a)   section 117 of the 2000 Act, and

    (b)   section 118 of and Schedule 14 to that Act,

as having also been incurred during the referendum period by or on behalf of the other individual or body (or, as the case may be, each of the other individuals or bodies) mentioned in sub-paragraph (1)(b)(ii); but this is subject to sub-paragraph (5).

(4)   This paragraph applies whether or not any of the individuals or bodies in question is a permitted participant.

(5)   But if any of the individuals or bodies in question ("the persons involved") is or becomes a designated organisation, the following referendum expenses are to be treated for the purposes of sections 117 and 118 of and Schedule 14 to the 2000 Act as having been incurred during the referendum period by or on behalf of the designated organisation only

    (a)   any referendum expenses incurred during the referendum period by or on behalf of the designated organisation;

    (b)   where any of the other persons involved is a permitted participant, any common plan expenses of that permitted participant;

    (c)   where any of the other persons involved is an individual or body which is not a permitted participant but is below the expenses threshold, any common plan expenses of that individual or body.

(6)   For the purposes of this paragraph an individual or body is "below the expenses threshold" if the total of the referendum expenses incurred during the referendum period by or on behalf of the individual or body does not exceed £10,000.

(7)   For the purposes of this paragraph

    (a)   section 112 of the 2000 Act (notional referendum expenses) applies as it applies for the purposes of Part 7 of that Act,

    (b)   section 113(3) of the 2000 Act (expenses incurred in contravention of section 113(1)) applies as it applies for the purposes of sections 117 to 123 of that Act, and

    (c)   subsections (5) and (6) of section 117 of the 2000 Act (certain expenditure incurred before the referendum period) apply as they apply for the purposes of that section.

(8)   In this paragraph any reference to referendum expenses incurred by or on behalf of a designated organisation, or a permitted participant, during the referendum period includes referendum expenses incurred during that period before the person by or on whose behalf the expenses were incurred became a designated organisation or, as the case may be, permitted participant.

23(1)   Section 120 of the 2000 Act (returns in respect of referendum expenses and donations) has effect for the purposes of the referendum with the following modifications (as well as with the modification in paragraph 2(1) of Schedule 2 to this Act).

(2)   Subsection (2) has effect for the purposes of the referendum as if the "and" after paragraph (c) were omitted and as if after paragraph (c) there were inserted

    "(ca)   a declaration under subsection (4A);

    (cb) a declaration under subsection (4B); and".

(3)   Subsection (4) has effect for those purposes as if for "(2)" there were substituted "(2)(a) to (c)".

(4)   For the purposes of the referendum the following subsections are to be treated as inserted after subsection (4)

    "(4A)   For the purposes of subsection (2)(ca), a declaration under this subsection is a declaration of

    (a)   whether there are any referendum expenses, incurred by or on behalf of an individual or body other than the permitted participant to which the return under this section relates, that must under paragraph 22 of Schedule 1 to the European Union Referendum Act 2015 be treated as having been incurred during the referendum period by or on behalf of the permitted participant; and

(b) if so, in the case of each individual or body concerned, its name and the amount of referendum expenses incurred by or on its behalf that must be treated as mentioned in paragraph (a).

(4B) For the purposes of subsection (2)(cb), a declaration under this subsection is a declaration of

(a) whether there are any referendum expenses incurred by or on behalf of the permitted participant that must under paragraph 22 of Schedule 1 to the European Union Referendum Act 2015 be treated as having been incurred during the referendum period by or on behalf of another individual or body; and

(b) if so, in the case of each such individual or body, its name and the amount of referendum expenses incurred by or on behalf of the permitted participant that must be treated as having been incurred during the referendum period by or on behalf of that individual or body.

(4C) The reference in subsection (4B) to referendum expenses incurred by or on behalf of the permitted participant includes referendum expenses incurred before the person by or on whose behalf the expenses were incurred became a permitted participant.

(4D) Any reference in subsection (4A) or (4B) to referendum expenses that must be treated under paragraph 22 of Schedule 1 to the European Union Referendum Act 2015 as having been incurred during the referendum period by or on behalf of a particular person includes

(a) referendum expenses that under that paragraph must be treated as having been incurred by or on behalf of that person only; and

(b) referendum expenses that, under that paragraph, must be treated as having also been incurred by or on behalf of that person.

(4E) Any reference in subsection (4A)(b) or (4B)(b) to the name of an individual or body is to be read, where the individual or body is a permitted participant, as a reference to the name under which that permitted participant is registered in the register under section 107."

Restriction on making claims in respect of referendum expenses

24. Section 115(7) of the 2000 Act (which applies subsections (7) to (10) of section 77 of that Act) has effect for the purposes of the referendum as if for "(10)" there were substituted "(12)".

Limits on referendum expenses by permitted participants

25(1) In Schedule 14 to the 2000 Act (limits on referendum expenses by permitted participants), any reference to a referendum falling within section 101(1)(a) includes a reference to the referendum.

(2) Paragraph 1(2) of that Schedule (limit on expenses incurred by permitted participants during referendum period) has effect for the purposes of the referendum as if

(a) in paragraph (a) (designated organisations) for "£5 million" there were substituted "£7 million",

(b) in paragraph (b) (registered parties that are not designated organisations)

(i) in sub-paragraph (i) for "£5 million" there were substituted "£7 million",

(ii) in sub-paragraph (ii) for "£4 million" there were substituted "£5.5 million",

(iii) in sub-paragraph (iii) for "£3 million" there were substituted "£4 million",

(iv) in sub-paragraph (iv) for "£2 million" there were substituted "£3 million", and

(v) in sub-paragraph (v) for "£500,000" there were substituted "£700,000", and

(c) in paragraph (c) (certain other persons and bodies) for "£500,000" there were substituted "£700,000".

Permissible donors: donations to registered parties other than minor parties

26(1) This paragraph applies in relation to a donation received by a permitted participant if
    (a) the permitted participant is a registered party that is not a minor party,
    (b) the donation is received from a person ("the donor") who in relation to that donation is not a permissible donor for the purposes of Part 4 of the 2000 Act by virtue of section 54 of that Act,
    (c) the donor is a person within sub-paragraph (3), and
    (d) the donation is received by the party within the referendum period.

(2) In relation to that donation, the donor is to be regarded for the purposes of Part 4 of the 2000 Act as a permissible donor.

(3) The persons within this sub-paragraph are
    (a) a Gibraltar elector;
    (b) a body falling within any of paragraphs (b) to (g) of section 54(2A) of the 2000 Act;
    (c) a body incorporated by Royal Charter which does not fall within section 54(2) of that Act;
    (d) a charitable incorporated organisation within the meaning of Part 11 of the Charities Act 2011 or Part 11 of the Charities Act (Northern Ireland) 2008;
    (e) a Scottish charitable incorporated organisation within the meaning of Chapter 7 of Part 1 of the Charities and Trustee Investment (Scotland) Act 2005 (asp 10);
    (f) a partnership constituted under the law of Scotland which carries on business in the United Kingdom.

(4) In relation to a donation in the form of a bequest sub-paragraph (3)(a) is to be read as referring to an individual who was, at any time within the period of 5 years ending with the date of the individual's death, a Gibraltar elector.

(5) In this paragraph
    (a) "donation" has the same meaning as in section 54 of the 2000 Act (see section 50 of that Act);
    (b) "Gibraltar elector" has the same meaning as in the 2000 Act (see section 160(1) of that Act).

27 Where paragraph 26 applies in relation to a donation received by a permitted participant, paragraph 2 of Schedule 6 to the 2000 Act (details to be given in donation reports) has effect as if
    (a) in sub-paragraph (1)(a) for "(10)" there were substituted "(10C)", and
    (b) the following sub-paragraphs were inserted after sub-paragraph (10)
"(10A) In the case of a body within paragraph 26(3)(c) of Schedule 1 to the European Union Referendum Act 2015 (body incorporated by Royal Charter) the report must give
    (a) the name of the body; and
    (b) the address of its main office in the United Kingdom.
(10B) In the case of a body within paragraph 26(3)(d) or (e) of that Schedule (charitable incorporated organisation) the report must give
    (a) the name of the body; and
    (b) the address of its principal office.
(10C) In the case of a body within paragraph 26(3)(f) of that Schedule (Scottish partnership) the report must give
    (a) the name of the body; and
    (b) the address of its main office in the United Kingdom."

Financial limit on certain donations etc to registered parties other than minor parties

28(1)   This paragraph applies where the permitted maximum is exceeded by the aggregate value of
    (a)   relevant donations which are received and accepted, and
    (b)   relevant regulated transactions which are entered into,
during the referendum period by a permitted participant that is a registered party other than a minor party.

(2)   Each of the relevant donations and relevant regulated transactions falling within sub-paragraph (3) is to be treated for the purposes of Parts 4 and 4A of the 2000 Act (as modified by paragraphs 26 and 27 of this Schedule and paragraphs 10 to 13 of Schedule 2) as if
    (a)   it had been received or entered into, as the case may be, at the end of the period of 3 months after the end of the referendum period,
    (b)   in the case of a relevant donation, it had been received from a person who was not a permissible donor at the time, and
    (c)   in the case of a relevant regulated transaction, it had been entered into with a person who was not an authorised participant at the time.

(3)   A relevant donation or relevant regulated transaction falls within this sub-paragraph
    (a)   if
        (i)   it is the first of the relevant donations received or is the only one,
        (ii)   no relevant regulated transaction has previously been entered into, and
        (iii) the value of the donation alone exceeds the permitted maximum,
    (b)   if it is the first of the relevant regulated transactions entered into or is the only one, and the value of the transaction alone exceeds the permitted maximum, or
    (c)   in a case not falling within paragraph (a) or (b), if the aggregate value of the relevant donation or relevant regulated transaction and the relevant donations and relevant regulated transactions previously received or entered into exceeds the permitted maximum.

(4)   But
    (a)   in the case of a relevant donation within sub-paragraph (3)(a), only so much of the donation as exceeds the permitted maximum is a donation falling within sub-paragraph (3), and
    (b)   in the case of a relevant donation within sub-paragraph (3)(c) where the aggregate value of the relevant donations and relevant regulated transactions previously received or entered into does not exceed the permitted maximum, only so much of the donation as exceeds the difference between that aggregate value and the permitted maximum is a donation falling within sub-paragraph (3).

(5)   In this paragraph
"authorised participant" means an authorised participant for the purposes of Part 4A of the 2000 Act;
"permissible donor" means a permissible donor for the purposes of Part 4 of the 2000 Act;
"permitted maximum", in relation to a permitted participant, means an amount equal to the limit imposed on that permitted participant by paragraph 1(2) of Schedule 14 to the 2000 Act (as modified by paragraph 25 of this Schedule);
"relevant donation" means a donation which is received from a person who is a permissible donor in relation to that donation by virtue of paragraph 26 of this Schedule;
"relevant regulated transaction" means a transaction which
    (a)   is a regulated transaction for the purposes of Part 4A of the 2000 Act (see section 71F of that Act), and
    (b)   is entered into with a person who is an authorised participant in relation to that transaction by virtue of paragraph 10 of Schedule 2.

(6)   In this paragraph

  (a)   references to a donation and to the value of a donation have the same meaning as in Part 4 of the 2000 Act (see sections 50 and 53 of that Act), and

  (b)   references to the value of a regulated transaction have the same meaning as in Part 4A of that Act (see section 71G of that Act).

Permissible donors: donations to minor parties and to persons who are not parties

29   Paragraph 1 of Schedule 15 to the 2000 Act (control of donations to permitted participants: operation and interpretation of Schedule) has effect for the purposes of the referendum as if the following sub-paragraphs were substituted for sub-paragraph (6)

  "(6) In relation to donations received by a permitted participant other than a designated organisation

   (a)   references to a permissible donor falling within section 54(2), and

   (b)   references to a person within paragraph 6(1A) of this Schedule,

   do not include a registered party and do not include a political party which is not a registered party but is established in Gibraltar.

  (7)   Sub-paragraph (6) applies also to references to a permissible donor, and references to a person within paragraph 6(1A) of this Schedule, in sections 56 and 61 as applied by paragraphs 7 and 8 of this Schedule."

30   Paragraph 4(1) of Schedule 15 to the 2000 Act (payments etc not to be regarded as donations) has effect for the purposes of the referendum as if after paragraph (a) there were inserted

  "(aa)   any grant provided out of Gibraltar public funds;".

31(1)   Paragraph 6 of Schedule 15 to the 2000 Act (prohibition on accepting donations from persons who are not permissible donors) has effect for the purposes of the referendum with the following modifications.

  (2)   Sub-paragraph (1)(a) has effect for those purposes as if after "a permissible donor falling within section 54(2)" there were inserted "or a person within sub-paragraph (1A)".

  (3)   For the purposes of the referendum the following sub-paragraph is to be treated as inserted after sub-paragraph (1)

   "(1A)   The persons within this sub-paragraph are

    (a)   a Gibraltar elector;

    (b)   a body falling within any of paragraphs (b) to (g) of section 54(2A);

    (c)   a body incorporated by Royal Charter which does not fall within section 54(2);

    (d)   a charitable incorporated organisation within the meaning of Part 11 of the Charities Act 2011 or Part 11 of the Charities Act (Northern Ireland) 2008;

    (e)   a Scottish charitable incorporated organisation within the meaning of Chapter 7 of Part 1 of the Charities and Trustee Investment (Scotland) Act 2005 (asp 10);

    (f)   a partnership constituted under the law of Scotland which carries on business in the United Kingdom."

  (4)   Sub-paragraph (3) has effect for those purposes as if after "exempt trust donation" there were inserted "or exempt Gibraltar trust donation".

  (5)   Sub-paragraph (4) has effect for those purposes as if

   (a)   in paragraph (a) after "exempt trust donation" there were inserted "or exempt Gibraltar trust donation",

   (b)   in paragraph (b)(i) after "permissible donors falling within section 54(2)" there were inserted "or persons within sub-paragraph (1A)",

   (c)   in paragraph (b)(ii) after "such a permissible donor" there were inserted "or such a person", and

(d) after "not such a permissible donor" there were inserted "and is not within sub-paragraph (1A)".

(6) For the purposes of the referendum the following sub-paragraph is to be treated as inserted after sub-paragraph (8)

"(9) In relation to a relevant donation in the form of a bequest sub-paragraph (1A)(a) is to be read as referring to an individual who was, at any time within the period of five years ending with the date of the individual's death, a Gibraltar elector."

Acceptance or return of donations

32 Paragraph 7(2) of Schedule 15 to the 2000 Act (application of sections 56 to 60 of the 2000 Act) has effect for the purposes of the referendum as if

(a) before paragraph (a) there were inserted

"(za) any reference in section 56 to a permissible donor is to be read as including a reference to a person within paragraph 6(1A) above;",

(b) before paragraph (b) there were inserted

"(ab) section 56(2) shall have effect as if for the words from "by virtue" to the end of paragraph (b) there were substituted "by virtue of paragraph 6(1) of Schedule 15, or which it is decided that the party should for any other reason refuse, then

(a) unless the donation falls within paragraph 6(1)(b) of Schedule 15, the donation, or a payment of an equivalent amount, must be sent back to the person who made the donation or any person appearing to be acting on his behalf, and

(b) if the donation falls within that provision, the required steps (as defined by section 57(1)) must be taken in relation to the donation,"", and; and

(c) at the end of paragraph (b) there were inserted "; and

(c) section 58(1) shall have effect as if in paragraph (a) for the words from "by virtue" to "party" there were substituted "by virtue of paragraph 6(1)(a) or (b) of Schedule 15, the party"."

Evasion of restrictions on donations

33. Paragraph 8 of Schedule 15 to the 2000 Act (application of section 61 of the 2000 Act) has effect for the purposes of the referendum as if for paragraph (c) (and the "and" preceding it) there were substituted

"(c) any reference to a permissible donor included a person within paragraph 6(1A) above; and

(d) any reference to the treasurer of a registered party were, in relation to a permitted participant, a reference to the responsible person."

Reporting of donations from permissible donors

34(1) Paragraph 10 of Schedule 15 to the 2000 Act (reporting of donations from permissible donors) has effect for the purposes of the referendum with the following modifications.

(2) Sub-paragraph (1)(c) has effect for those purposes as if at the end there were inserted "or, where the donor is within any of paragraphs (c) to (f) of paragraph 6(1A), the information mentioned in sub-paragraph (1A) below".

(3) For the purposes of the referendum the following sub-paragraph is to be treated as inserted after sub-paragraph (1)

"(1A) The information to be recorded in the case of a donor within any of paragraphs (c) to (f) of paragraph 6(1A) is

(a) where the donor is a body within paragraph 6(1A)(c) (body incorporated by Royal Charter)

(i) the name of the body, and

        (ii)   the address of its main office in the United Kingdom;

   (b)   where the donor is a body within paragraph 6(1A)(d) or (e) (charitable incorporated organisation)

        (i)   the name of the body, and

        (ii)   the address of its principal office;

   (c)   where the donor is a body within paragraph 6(1A)(f) (Scottish partnership)

        (i)   the name of the body, and

        (ii)   the address of its main office in the United Kingdom."

(4)   In paragraph 10(1)(c) of Schedule 15 to the 2000 Act as it applies for the purposes of the referendum, the reference to paragraph 2 of Schedule 6 to that Act is to be taken as a reference to that paragraph without the modifications of that paragraph made by this Schedule.

Returns in respect of referendum expenses and donations

35   For the purposes of the referendum, the following section is to be treated as inserted after section 120 of the 2000 Act (returns in respect of referendum expenses and donations)

   "**120A Full return not required if expenses do not exceed £10,000**

   (1)   A return under section 120 need not be made by the responsible person in relation to a permitted participant if, within 3 months beginning with the end of the referendum period, the responsible person

      (a)   makes a relevant declaration, and

      (b)   delivers that declaration to the Commission.

   (2)   A "relevant declaration" is a declaration that, to the best of the responsible person's knowledge and belief, the total amount of referendum expenses incurred by or on behalf of the permitted participant during the referendum period does not exceed £10,000.

   (3)   If a person who is the responsible person in relation to a permitted participant knowingly or recklessly makes a false declaration under this section, that person commits an offence.

   (4)   A person guilty of an offence under this section is liable

      (a)   on conviction on indictment, to imprisonment for a term not exceeding 12 months or to a fine, or to both;

      (b)   on summary conviction in England and Wales, to imprisonment for a term not exceeding 12 months or to a fine, or to both;

      (c)   on summary conviction in Scotland, to imprisonment for a term not exceeding 12 months or to a fine not exceeding the statutory maximum, or to both;

      (d)   on summary conviction in Northern Ireland, to imprisonment for a term not exceeding 6 months or to a fine not exceeding the statutory maximum, or to both;

      (e)   on summary conviction in Gibraltar, to imprisonment for a term not exceeding 12 months or to a fine not exceeding level 5 on the Gibraltar standard scale, or to both.

   (5)   The reference in subsection (4)(b) to 12 months is to be read as a reference to 6 months in relation to an offence committed before the commencement of section 154(1) of the Criminal Justice Act 2003.

   (6)   In subsection (4)(e) "the Gibraltar standard scale" means the standard scale set out in Part A of Schedule 9 to the Criminal Procedure and Evidence Act."

Declaration of responsible person as to donations

36(1)   Section 123 of the 2000 Act (declaration of responsible person as to return under section 120) has effect for the purposes of the referendum with the following modifications.

   (2)   For those purposes, the following subsection is to be treated as substituted for subsection (3)

"(3) In a case where the permitted participant either is not a registered party or is a minor party, the declaration must also, in relation to all relevant donations recorded in the return as having been accepted by the permitted participant

(a) state that they were all from permissible donors, or

(b) state whether or not section 56(2) was complied with in the case of each of those donations that was not from a permissible donor."

(3) For the purposes of the referendum, the following subsection is to be treated as inserted after subsection (5)

"(6) In this section "permissible donor" includes a person within paragraph 6(1A) of Schedule 15."

Declaration where no referendum expenses incurred in referendum period

37(1) For the purposes of the referendum, the following section is to be treated as inserted after section 124 of the 2000 Act

"124A Declaration where no expenses in referendum period

(1) Subsection (2) applies where, in relation to a referendum to which this Part applies

(a) a permitted participant incurs no referendum expenses during the referendum period (and no such expenses are incurred on behalf of that participant during that period), and

(b) accordingly, the responsible person in relation to the permitted participant is not required to make a return under section 120 or a declaration under section 120A.

(2) The responsible person must, within 3 months beginning with the end of the referendum period

(a) make a declaration under this section, and

(b) deliver that declaration to the Commission.

(3) A declaration under this section is a declaration that no referendum expenses were incurred by or on behalf of the permitted participant during the referendum period.

(4) The responsible person commits an offence if, without reasonable excuse, that person fails to comply with the requirements of subsection (2).

(5) If a person who is the responsible person in relation to a permitted participant knowingly or recklessly makes a false declaration in purported compliance with the requirement in subsection (2)(a), that person commits an offence.

(6) A person guilty of an offence under subsection (4) is liable

(a) on summary conviction in England and Wales, to a fine;

(b) on summary conviction in Scotland or Northern Ireland, to a fine not exceeding level 5 on the standard scale;

(c) on summary conviction in Gibraltar, to a fine not exceeding level 5 on the Gibraltar standard scale.

(7) A person guilty of an offence under subsection (5) is liable

(a) on conviction on indictment, to imprisonment for a term not exceeding 12 months or to a fine, or to both;

(b) on summary conviction in England and Wales, to imprisonment for a term not exceeding 12 months or to a fine, or to both;

(c) on summary conviction in Scotland, to imprisonment for a term not exceeding 12 months or to a fine not exceeding the statutory maximum, or to both;

(d) on summary conviction in Northern Ireland, to imprisonment for a term not exceeding 6 months or to a fine not exceeding the statutory maximum, or to both;

(e) on summary conviction in Gibraltar, to imprisonment for a term not exceeding 12 months or to a fine not exceeding level 5 on the Gibraltar standard scale, or to both.

(8) The reference in subsection (7)(b) to 12 months is to be read as a reference to 6 months in relation to an offence committed before the commencement of section 154(1) of the Criminal Justice Act 2003.

(9) In this section "the Gibraltar standard scale" means the standard scale set out in Part A of Schedule 9 to the Criminal Procedure and Evidence Act.

(10) Schedule 19C (civil sanctions), and any order under Part 5 of that Schedule, have effect as if the offence under subsection (4) of this section were an offence prescribed in an order under that Part.

(11) In
   (a) section 113(3) (treatment of expenses incurred in contravention of section 113(1)), and
   (b) section 118(4) and (5) (treatment of certain expenses incurred before referendum period or before becoming permitted participant),
the references to, respectively, sections 117 to 123 and sections 120 to 123 include references to this section."

(2) Nothing in subsection (10) of the section treated as inserted by this paragraph (read with section 12 of this Act) is to be taken to mean that Schedule 19C to the 2000 Act extends or applies to Gibraltar for the purposes of the referendum.

Application to Gibraltar public bodies of restriction on publication of promotional material

38(1) Section 125 of the 2000 Act (restriction on publication etc of promotional material by central and local government etc) has effect for the purposes of the referendum with the following modifications.

(2) Subsection (2) has effect for those purposes as if after paragraph (a) there were inserted "(aa) the Government of Gibraltar or any Gibraltar government department; or".

(3) Subsection (2)(b) has effect for those purposes as if for the words from "wholly or mainly" to the end there were substituted "wholly or mainly
   (i) out of public funds or by any local authority; or
   (ii) out of Gibraltar public funds."

(4) Subsection (3) has effect for those purposes as if after "Sianel Pedwar Cymru" there were inserted "or the Gibraltar Broadcasting Corporation".

Reporting of donations during referendum period

39(1) In this paragraph references to a permitted participant are to a permitted participant which either is not a registered party or is a minor party.

(2) In relation to the referendum, the responsible person in relation to a permitted participant must prepare reports under this paragraph in respect of
   (a) the period ("the first reporting period") beginning with the commencement day and ending with the 7th day of the referendum period, and
   (b) such other periods ending before the date of the referendum as may be prescribed by regulations made by the Minister;
and in paragraph (a) "the commencement day" means the day on which that paragraph comes into force.

(3) The report for a period must record, in relation to each relevant donation of more than £7,500 which is received by the permitted participant during the period
   (a) the amount of the donation (if it is a donation of money, in cash or otherwise) or (in any other case) the nature of the donation and its value as determined in accordance with paragraph 5 of Schedule 15 to the 2000 Act,
   (b) the date when the donation was received by the permitted participant, and
   (c) the information about the donor which is, in connection with recordable donations to registered parties, required to be recorded in weekly donation reports by virtue of paragraph 3 of Schedule 6 to the 2000 Act.

(4)   If during any period no relevant donations of more than £7,500 were received by the permitted participant, the report for the period must contain a statement of that fact.

(5)   A report under this paragraph in respect of a period must be delivered by the responsible person to the Electoral Commission
    (a)   in the case of the report for the first reporting period, within 7 days beginning with the end of that period;
    (b)   in the case of the report for a period prescribed under sub-paragraph (2)(b), within such time as may be prescribed by regulations made by the Minister.

(6)   If, in relation to a donation made by an individual who has an anonymous entry in an electoral register, a report under this paragraph contains a statement that the permitted participant has seen evidence that the individual has such an anonymous entry, the report must be accompanied by a copy of the evidence.

(7)   The Minister may by regulations modify the operation of sub-paragraphs (2) to (4) in relation to cases where an individual or body becomes a permitted participant during a period prescribed under sub-paragraph (2)(b).

(8)   Regulations under sub-paragraph (5) or (7) may make different provision for different cases.

(9)   The responsible person commits an offence if, without reasonable excuse, that person
    (a)   fails to comply with the requirements of sub-paragraph (5) in relation to a report under this paragraph, or
    (b)   delivers a report to the Electoral Commission that does not comply with the requirements of sub-paragraph (3), (4) or (6).

(10)   A person guilty of an offence under sub-paragraph (9)(a) is liable
    (a)   on summary conviction in England and Wales, to a fine;
    (b)   on summary conviction in Scotland or Northern Ireland, to a fine not exceeding level 5 on the standard scale;
    (c)   on summary conviction in Gibraltar, to a fine not exceeding level 5 on the Gibraltar standard scale.

(11)   A person guilty of an offence under sub-paragraph (9)(b) is liable
    (a)   on conviction on indictment, to imprisonment for a term not exceeding 12 months or to a fine, or to both;
    (b)   on summary conviction in England and Wales, to imprisonment for a term not exceeding 12 months or to a fine, or to both;
    (c)   on summary conviction in Scotland, to imprisonment for a term not exceeding 12 months or to a fine not exceeding the statutory maximum, or to both;
    (d)   on summary conviction in Northern Ireland, to imprisonment for a term not exceeding 6 months or to a fine not exceeding the statutory maximum, or to both;
    (e)   on summary conviction in Gibraltar, to imprisonment for a term not exceeding 12 months or to a fine not exceeding level 5 on the Gibraltar standard scale, or to both.

(12)   The reference in sub-paragraph (11)(b) to 12 months is to be read as a reference to 6 months in relation to an offence committed before the commencement of section 154(1) of the Criminal Justice Act 2003.

(13)   In this paragraph
    (a)   "electoral register" means
      (i)   an electoral register as defined by 54(8) of the 2000 Act, or
      (ii)   the Gibraltar register as defined by section 14 of the European Parliament (Representation) Act 2003,
    (b)   "relevant donation" has the same meaning as in Schedule 15 to the 2000 Act, and
    (c)   references to a relevant donation received by a permitted participant include any donation received at a time before the individual or body concerned became a

permitted participant, if the donation would have been a relevant donation had the individual or body been a permitted participant at that time.

(14) Section 161 of the 2000 Act (interpretation: donations) applies for the purposes of this paragraph as it applies for the purposes of the provisions of that Act relating to donations.

Declaration of responsible person as to donation reports under paragraph 39

40(1) Each report delivered under paragraph 39 must be accompanied by a declaration which complies with sub-paragraph (2) and is signed by the responsible person.

(2) The declaration must state
   (a) that the responsible person has examined the report, and
   (b) that to the best of the responsible person's knowledge and belief, it is a complete and correct report as required by law.

(3) A person commits an offence if
   (a) the person knowingly or recklessly makes a false declaration under this paragraph, or
   (b) sub-paragraph (1) is contravened at a time when the person is the responsible person in the case of the permitted participant to which the report relates.

(4) A person guilty of an offence under sub-paragraph (3) is liable
   (a) on conviction on indictment, to imprisonment for a term not exceeding 12 months or to a fine, or to both;
   (b) on summary conviction in England and Wales, to imprisonment for a term not exceeding 12 months or to a fine, or to both;
   (c) on summary conviction in Scotland, to imprisonment for a term not exceeding 12 months or to a fine not exceeding the statutory maximum, or to both;
   (d) on summary conviction in Northern Ireland, to imprisonment for a term not exceeding 6 months or to a fine not exceeding the statutory maximum, or to both;
   (e) on summary conviction in Gibraltar, to imprisonment for a term not exceeding 12 months or to a fine not exceeding level 5 on the Gibraltar standard scale, or to both.

(5) The reference in sub-paragraph (4)(b) to 12 months is to be read as a reference to 6 months in relation to an offence committed before the commencement of section 154(1) of the Criminal Justice Act 2003.

Public inspection of donation reports under paragraph 39

41(1) Where the Electoral Commission receive a report under paragraph 39 they must
   (a) as soon as is reasonably practicable after receiving the report, make a copy of the report and of any document accompanying it available for public inspection, and
   (b) keep any such copy available for public inspection for the period for which the report or other document is held by them.

(2) The Electoral Commission must secure that the copy of the report made available for public inspection does not include, in the case of any donation by an individual, the donor's address.

(3) At the end of the period of two years beginning with the date when any report under paragraph 39 or other document accompanying it is received by the Electoral Commission
   (a) they may cause the report or other document to be destroyed, or
   (b) if requested to do so by the responsible person in the case of the permitted participant concerned, they must arrange for the report or other document to be returned to that person.

42 Section 149(2) to (5) and (7) of the 2000 Act (inspection of Commission's documents) apply in relation to reports and documents which the Electoral Commission are required to

make available for public inspection under paragraph 41 as they apply to the documents which the Electoral Commission are required to make available for public inspection by virtue of the provisions of the 2000 Act mentioned in section 149(6) of that Act.

Referendum campaign broadcasts

43   Section 127 of the 2000 Act (referendum campaign broadcasts) has effect for the purposes of the referendum as if any reference to a broadcaster (within the meaning given by section 37(2) of that Act) included a reference to the Gibraltar Broadcasting Corporation.

Enforcement

44(1)   Section 145(1)(a) and (6A) of the 2000 Act (general functions of Electoral Commission with respect to compliance) apply in relation to the requirements imposed by this Schedule as they apply in relation to the requirements referred to in section 145(1)(a).

(2)   In section 148 of the 2000 Act (general offences), the references in each of subsections (1) to (3) to any of the provisions of that Act include any of the provisions of this Schedule.

(3)   Sections 151 and 154 of the 2000 Act (summary proceedings, and duty of court to report conviction to Electoral Commission) apply in relation to an offence under this Schedule as they apply in relation to an offence under that Act.

(4)   In paragraphs 3 to 5 of Schedule 19B to the 2000 Act (powers of Electoral Commission in relation to suspected offences or contraventions)
    (a)   the references to an offence under that Act include an offence under this Schedule, and
    (b)   the references to a restriction or other requirement imposed by or by virtue of that Act include a requirement or restriction imposed by or by virtue of this Schedule.

(5)   Schedule 19C to the 2000 Act (civil sanctions), and any order under Part 5 of that Schedule, have effect as if any reference in that Schedule to an offence under the 2000 Act, or to a prescribed offence under that Act, included a reference to an offence under paragraph 39(9) of this Schedule.

(6)   Nothing in sub-paragraph (4) or (5) (read with section 12) is to be taken to mean that Schedule 19B or 19C to the 2000 Act extends or applies to Gibraltar for the purposes of the referendum.

Interpretation

45   Section 160 of the 2000 Act (general interpretation) has effect for the purposes of the referendum as if the following subsection were inserted after subsection (4)
    "(4A)   References in this Act (in whatever terms) to expenses met, or things provided, out of "Gibraltar public funds" are references to expenses met, or things provided, by means of
        (a)   payments out of
            (i)   the Gibraltar consolidated fund; or
            (ii)   monies voted by the Gibraltar Parliament; or
        (b)   payments by the Government of Gibraltar or any Gibraltar government department."

NOTES

Defined terms
    the 2000 Act: s 11(1)
    bequest: Political Parties, Elections and Referendums Act 2000, s 160(1)
    body: s 11(1); Political Parties, Elections and Referendums Act 2000, s 160(1)
    the Commission: Political Parties, Elections and Referendums Act 2000, s 160(1)
    counting officer: s 11(1)

designated organisation: s 11(1)
document: s 11(1)
exempt Gibraltar trust donation: Political Parties, Elections and Referendums Act 2000, ss 160(1), 162
Gibraltar elector: Political Parties, Elections and Referendums Act 2000, s 160(1)
Gibraltar public funds: Political Parties, Elections and Referendums Act 2000, s 160(4A) (as inserted by para 45)
the Minister: s 11(1)

minor party: s 11(1)
permitted participant: s 11(1)
referendum expenses: s 11(1)
the referendum: s 11(1)
registered party: s 11(1)
responsible person: s 11(1)

treasurer: Political Parties, Elections and Referendums
Act 2000, s 160(1)
voting area: s 11(1), (2)

SCHEDULE 2
Control of Loans etc to Permitted Participants

Section 3

Control of loans etc to permitted participants

1   For the purposes of the referendum, the 2000 Act has effect as if after Schedule 15 (in Part 7 of that Act) there were inserted

"SCHEDULE 15A
CONTROL OF LOANS ETC TO CERTAIN PERMITTED PARTICIPANTS

Part 1
Introductory

Introductory

1(1)   This Schedule has effect for controlling regulated transactions entered into by permitted participants that either are not registered parties or are minor parties.

(2)   Accordingly, in the following provisions of this Schedule references to permitted participants do not include a permitted participant which is a registered party other than a minor party.

(3)   In this Schedule
"connected transaction" has the meaning given by paragraph 2(9);
"credit facility" has the meaning given by paragraph 2(11);
"nonqualifying person" means a person who is not a qualifying person;
"qualifying person" has the meaning given by paragraph 4(2);
"regulated transaction" has the meaning given by paragraph 2.

Regulated transactions

2(1)   An agreement between a permitted participant and another person by which the other person makes a loan of money to the permitted participant is a regulated transaction if the use condition is satisfied.

(2)   An agreement between a permitted participant and another person by which the other person provides a credit facility to the permitted participant is a regulated transaction if the use condition is satisfied.

(3)   Where
(a)   a permitted participant and another person ("A") enter into a regulated transaction of a description mentioned in sub-paragraph (1) or (2), or a transaction under which any property, services or facilities are provided for the use or benefit of the permitted participant (including the services of any person),
(b)   A also enters into an arrangement whereby another person ("B") gives any form of security (whether real or personal) for a sum owed to A by the permitted participant under the transaction mentioned in paragraph (a), and
(c)   the use condition is satisfied,

the arrangement mentioned in paragraph (b) is a regulated transaction.

(4) An agreement or arrangement is also a regulated transaction if

    (a) the terms of the agreement or arrangement as first entered into do not constitute a regulated transaction by virtue of sub-paragraph (1), (2) or (3), but

    (b) the terms are subsequently varied in such a way that the agreement or arrangement becomes a regulated transaction.

(5) "The use condition" is that the permitted participant intends at the time of entering into a transaction mentioned in sub-paragraph (1), (2) or (3)(a) to use any money or benefit obtained in consequence of the transaction for meeting referendum expenses incurred by or on behalf of the permitted participant.

(6) For the purposes of sub-paragraph (5), it is immaterial that only part of the money or benefit is intended to be used for meeting referendum expenses incurred by or on behalf of the permitted participant.

(7) References in sub-paragraphs (1) and (2) to a permitted participant include references to an officer, member, trustee or agent of the permitted participant if that person makes the agreement as such.

(8) References in sub-paragraph (3) to a permitted participant include references to an officer, member, trustee or agent of the permitted participant if the property, services or facilities are provided to that person as such, or the sum is owed by that person as such.

(9) A reference in this Schedule to a connected transaction is a reference to the arrangement mentioned in sub-paragraph (3)(b).

(10) In this paragraph a reference to anything being done by or in relation to a permitted participant or a person includes a reference to its being done directly or indirectly through a third person.

(11) A "credit facility" is an agreement whereby a permitted participant is enabled to receive from time to time from another party to the agreement a loan of money not exceeding such amount (taking account of any repayments made by the permitted participant) as is specified in or determined in accordance with the agreement.

(12) An agreement or arrangement is not a regulated transaction

    (a) to the extent that a payment made in pursuance of the agreement or arrangement falls, by virtue of paragraph 9 of Schedule 15, to be included in a return under section 120 (or would do so but for section 120A), or

    (b) if its value is not more than £500.

Valuation of regulated transaction

3(1) The value of a regulated transaction which is a loan is the value of the total amount to be lent under the loan agreement.

(2) The value of a regulated transaction which is a credit facility is the maximum amount which may be borrowed under the agreement for the facility.

(3) The value of a regulated transaction which is an arrangement by which any form of security is given is the contingent liability under the security provided.

(4) For the purposes of sub-paragraphs (1) and (2), no account is to be taken of the effect of any provision contained in a loan agreement or an agreement for a credit facility at the time it is entered into which enables outstanding interest to be added to any sum for the time being owed in respect of the loan or credit facility, whether or not any such interest has been so added.

Part 2
Controls on Regulated Transactions

Regulated transactions with non-qualifying persons

4(1)   A permitted participant must not
    (a) be a party to a regulated transaction to which a person who is not a qualifying person is also a party;
    (b) derive a benefit in consequence of a connected transaction if any of the parties to that transaction is not a qualifying person.

(2)   In this Schedule, "qualifying person" means
    (a) a permissible donor falling within section 54(2) (but see sub-paragraph (3));
    (b) a Gibraltar elector;
    (c) any body falling within any of paragraphs (b) to (g) of section 54(2A);
    (d) a body incorporated by Royal Charter which does not fall within section 54(2);
    (e) a charitable incorporated organisation within the meaning of Part 11 of the Charities Act 2011 or Part 11 of the Charities Act (Northern Ireland) 2008;
    (f) a Scottish charitable incorporated organisation within the meaning of Chapter 7 of Part 1 of the Charities and Trustee Investment (Scotland) Act 2005 (asp 10);
    (g) a partnership constituted under the law of Scotland which carries on business in the United Kingdom.

(3)   In relation to transactions entered into by a permitted participant other than a designated organisation, references in this Schedule to a qualifying person do not include
    (a) a registered party, or
    (b) a political party which is not a registered party but is established in Gibraltar,
and sub-paragraph (2)(a) and (c) have effect subject to this sub-paragraph.

(4)   In this paragraph "designated organisation" has the meaning given by section 110(5).

Effect of transaction with non-qualifying person

5(1)   This paragraph applies if a permitted participant is a party to a regulated transaction to which a nonqualifying person is also a party.

(2)   The transaction is void.

(3)   Despite sub-paragraph (2)
    (a) any money received by the permitted participant by virtue of the transaction must be repaid by the responsible person to the person from whom it was received, along with interest at the rate referred to in section 71I(3)(a);
    (b) the person from whom it was received is entitled to recover the money, along with such interest.

(4)   If
    (a) the money is not (for whatever reason) repaid as mentioned in sub-paragraph (3)(a), or
    (b) the person entitled to recover the money refuses or fails to do so,
the Commission may apply to the court to make such order as it thinks fit to restore (so far as is possible) the parties to the transaction to the position they would have been in if the transaction had not been entered into.

(5)   An order under sub-paragraph (4) may in particular

    (a)   where the transaction is a loan or credit facility, require that any amount owed by the permitted participant be repaid (and that no further sums be advanced under it);

    (b)   where any form of security is given for a sum owed under the transaction, require that security to be discharged.

(6)   In the case of a regulated transaction where a party other than a permitted participant

    (a)   at the time the permitted participant enters into the transaction, is a qualifying person, but

    (b)   subsequently, for whatever reason, ceases to be a qualifying person,

the transaction is void and sub-paragraphs (3) to (5) apply with effect from the time when the other party ceased to be a qualifying person.

Guarantees and securities involving nonqualifying persons

6(1)   This paragraph applies if

    (a)   a permitted participant and another person ("A") enter into a transaction of a description mentioned in paragraph 2(3)(a),

    (b)   A is party to a regulated transaction of a description mentioned in paragraph 2(3)(b) ("the connected transaction") with another person ("B"), and

    (c)   B is not a qualifying person.

(2)   Paragraph 5(2) to (5) applies to the transaction mentioned in sub-paragraph (1)(a).

(3)   The connected transaction is void.

(4)   Sub-paragraph (5) applies if (but only if) A is unable to recover from the permitted participant the whole of the money mentioned in paragraph 5(3)(a) (as applied by sub-paragraph (2) above), along with such interest as is there mentioned.

(5)   Despite sub-paragraph (3), A is entitled to recover from B any part of that money (and such interest) that is not recovered from the permitted participant.

(6)   Sub-paragraph (5) does not entitle A to recover more than the contingent liability under the security provided by virtue of the connected transaction.

(7)   In the case of a connected transaction where B

    (a)   at the time A enters into the transaction, is a qualifying person, but

    (b)   subsequently, for whatever reason, ceases to be a qualifying person,

sub-paragraphs (2) to (6) apply with effect from the time when B ceased to be a qualifying person.

(8)   If the transaction mentioned in paragraph 2(3)(a) is not a regulated transaction of a description mentioned in paragraph 2(1) or (2), references in this paragraph and paragraph 5(2) to (5) (as applied by sub-paragraph (2) above) to the repayment or recovery of money are to be construed as references to (as the case may be)

    (a)   the return or recovery of any property provided under the transaction,

    (b)   to the extent that such property is incapable of being returned or recovered or its market value has diminished since the time the transaction was entered into, the repayment or recovery of the market value at that time, or

    (c)   the repayment or recovery of the market value (at that time) of any facilities or services provided under the transaction.

Transfer to non-qualifying person

7   If a qualifying person purports to transfer the person's interest in a regulated transaction to a nonqualifying person, the purported transfer is of no effect.

Part 3

Offences

Offences of knowingly entering into certain transactions

8(1)   An individual who is a permitted participant commits an offence if

    (a)   the individual enters into a regulated transaction of a description mentioned in paragraph 2(1) or (2) to which a nonqualifying person is also a party, and

    (b)   the individual knew or ought reasonably to have known of the matters mentioned in paragraph (a).

(2)   A permitted participant that is not an individual commits an offence if

    (a)   it enters into a regulated transaction of a description mentioned in paragraph 2(1) or (2) to which a nonqualifying person is also a party, and

    (b)   an officer of the permitted participant knew or ought reasonably to have known of the matters mentioned in paragraph (a).

(3)   A person who is the responsible person in relation to a permitted participant that is not an individual commits an offence if

    (a)   the permitted participant enters into a regulated transaction of a description mentioned in paragraph 2(1) or (2) to which a nonqualifying person is also a party, and

    (b)   the responsible person knew or ought reasonably to have known of the matters mentioned in paragraph (a).

(4)   It is a defence for a person charged with an offence under sub-paragraph (3) to prove that the person took all reasonable steps to prevent the permitted participant from entering into the transaction.

Offences of failing to act on finding that transaction was not permitted

9(1)   An individual who is a permitted participant commits an offence if

    (a)   the individual has entered into a regulated transaction of a description mentioned in paragraph 2(1) or (2) to which a nonqualifying person is also a party,

    (b)   the individual neither knew nor ought reasonably to have known that the other party is a nonqualifying person,

    (c)   the individual comes to know of the matters mentioned in paragraph (a), and

    (d)   the individual does not take, as soon as practicable after coming to know of those matters, all reasonable steps to repay any money which he or she has received by virtue of the transaction.

(2)   A permitted participant that is not an individual commits an offence if

    (a)   it has entered into a regulated transaction of a description mentioned in paragraph 2(1) or (2) to which a nonqualifying person is also a party,

    (b)   no officer of the permitted participant knew or ought reasonably to have known that the other party is a nonqualifying person,

    (c)   the responsible person comes to know of the matters mentioned in paragraph (a), and

    (d)   the responsible person does not take, as soon as practicable after coming to know of those matters, all reasonable steps to repay any money which the permitted participant has received by virtue of the transaction.

(3)   A person who is the responsible person in relation to a permitted participant that is not an individual commits an offence if

(a) the permitted participant has entered into a regulated transaction of a description mentioned in paragraph 2(1) or (2) to which a nonqualifying person is also a party,

(b) paragraph 8(3)(b) does not apply to the responsible person,

(c) the responsible person comes to know of the matters mentioned in paragraph (a), and

(d) the responsible person does not take, as soon as practicable after coming to know of those matters, all reasonable steps to repay any money which the permitted participant has received by virtue of the transaction.

Offences of benefiting from certain connected transactions

10(1) An individual who is a permitted participant commits an offence if

(a) the individual benefits from, or falls to benefit in consequence of, a connected transaction to which a nonqualifying person is a party, and

(b) the individual knew or ought reasonably to have known of the matters mentioned in paragraph (a).

(2) A permitted participant that is not an individual commits an offence if

(a) it benefits from, or falls to benefit in consequence of, a connected transaction to which a nonqualifying person is a party, and

(b) an officer of the permitted participant knew or ought reasonably to have known of the matters mentioned in paragraph (a).

(3) A person who is the responsible person in relation to a permitted participant that is not an individual commits an offence if

(a) the permitted participant benefits from, or falls to benefit in consequence of, a connected transaction to which a nonqualifying person is a party, and

(b) the person knew or ought reasonably to have known of the matters mentioned in paragraph (a).

(4) It is a defence for a person charged with an offence under sub-paragraph (3) to prove that the person took all reasonable steps to prevent the permitted participant from benefiting in consequence of the connected transaction.

Offences of failing to act on finding connected transaction was not permitted

11(1) An individual who is a permitted participant commits an offence if

(a) the individual is a party to a transaction of a description mentioned in paragraph 2(3)(a),

(b) the individual benefits from, or falls to benefit in consequence of, a connected transaction to which a nonqualifying person is a party,

(c) the individual neither knew nor ought reasonably to have known of the matters mentioned in paragraphs (a) and (b),

(d) the individual comes to know of those matters, and

(e) the individual does not take, as soon as practicable after coming to know of those matters, all reasonable steps to pay to any person who has provided the individual with any benefit in consequence of the connected transaction the value of the benefit.

(2) A permitted participant that is not an individual commits an offence if

(a) it is a party to a transaction of a description mentioned in paragraph 2(3)(a),

(b) it benefits from, or falls to benefit in consequence of, a connected transaction to which a nonqualifying person is a party,

(c) no officer of the permitted participant knew or ought reasonably to have known of the matters mentioned in paragraphs (a) and (b),

(d) the responsible person comes to know of those matters, and

(e) the responsible person does not take, as soon as practicable after coming to know of those matters, all reasonable steps to pay to any person who has provided the permitted participant with any benefit in consequence of the connected transaction the value of the benefit.

(3) A person who is the responsible person in relation to a permitted participant that is not an individual commits an offence if
  (a) the permitted participant is a party to a transaction of a description mentioned in paragraph 2(3)(a),
  (b) the permitted participant benefits from, or falls to benefit in consequence of, a connected transaction to which a nonqualifying person is a party,
  (c) paragraph 10(3)(b) does not apply to the person,
  (d) the responsible person comes to know of the matters mentioned in paragraphs (a) and (b), and
  (e) the responsible person does not take, as soon as practicable after coming to know of those matters, all reasonable steps to pay to any person who has provided the permitted participant with any benefit in consequence of the connected transaction the value of the benefit.

Arrangements facilitating transactions with non-qualifying persons

12 A person commits an offence if the person
  (a) knowingly enters into, or
  (b) knowingly does any act in furtherance of,
any arrangement which facilitates or is likely to facilitate, whether by means of concealment or disguise or otherwise, the participation by a permitted participant in a regulated transaction with a non-qualifying person.

Offences: interpretation

13(1) A reference in this Part of this Schedule to a permitted participant entering into a regulated transaction includes a reference to any circumstances in which the terms of a regulated transaction are varied so as to increase the amount of money to which the permitted participant is entitled in consequence of the transaction.

(2) A reference in paragraph 8 or 9 to entering into a regulated transaction of a description mentioned in paragraph 2(1) or (2) to which a nonqualifying person is also a party includes receiving an amount of money under a regulated transaction of a description mentioned in paragraph 2(1) or (2) at a time when a person who is also a party to the transaction (and who was a qualifying person when the transaction was entered into) has ceased to be a qualifying person.

(3) It is a defence for a person charged with an offence under paragraph 8 by virtue of sub-paragraph (2) to prove that the person took all reasonable steps, as soon as practicable, to repay the money received as mentioned in sub-paragraph (2).

(4) Where a person is charged with an offence under paragraph 8(3) by virtue of sub-paragraph (2), paragraph 8(4) does not apply.

(5) In relation to a case where paragraph 9(1)(a) to (c), (2)(a) to (c) or (3)(a) to (c) apply by reason of sub-paragraph (2), the reference in paragraph 9(1)(d), (2)(d) or (3)(d) to any money received by virtue of the transaction is to be read as a reference to any money so received after the party in question ceased to be a qualifying person.

Penalties

14(1) A person guilty of an offence under paragraph 8(1) or (2), 9(1), 10(1) or (2) or 11(1) is liable
  (a) on conviction on indictment, to a fine;

(b)   on summary conviction in England and Wales, to a fine;

(c)   on summary conviction in Scotland or Northern Ireland, to a fine not exceeding the statutory maximum;

(d)   on summary conviction in Gibraltar, to a fine not exceeding level 5 on the Gibraltar standard scale.

(2)   A person guilty of an offence under paragraph 8(3), 9(2) or (3), 10(3), 11(2) or (3) or 12 is liable

(a)   on conviction on indictment, to imprisonment for a term not exceeding 12 months or to a fine, or to both;

(b)   on summary conviction in England and Wales, to imprisonment for a term not exceeding 12 months or to a fine, or to both;

(c)   on summary conviction in Scotland, to imprisonment for a term not exceeding 12 months or to a fine not exceeding the statutory maximum, or to both;

(d)   on summary conviction in Northern Ireland, to imprisonment for a term not exceeding 6 months or to a fine not exceeding the statutory maximum, or to both;

(e)   on summary conviction in Gibraltar, to imprisonment for a term not exceeding 12 months or to a fine not exceeding level 5 on the Gibraltar standard scale, or to both.

(3)   The reference in sub-paragraph (2)(b) to 12 months is to be read as a reference to 6 months in relation to an offence committed before the commencement of section 154(1) of the Criminal Justice Act 2003.

(4)   In this paragraph "the Gibraltar standard scale" means the standard scale set out in Part A of Schedule 9 to the Criminal Procedure and Evidence Act.

Part 4
Reporting of Regulated Transactions

Statement of regulated transactions

15(1)   The responsible person in relation to a permitted participant must include in any return required to be prepared under section 120 a statement of regulated transactions entered into by the permitted participant.

(2)   The statement must comply with paragraphs 16 to 20.

(3)   For the purposes of those paragraphs a regulated transaction is a "recordable transaction"

(a)   if the value of the transaction is more than £7,500, or

(b)   if the aggregate value of it and any other relevant benefit or benefits is more than that amount.

In paragraph (b) "relevant benefit" means any relevant donation (within the meaning of Schedule 15) or regulated transaction made by, or entered into with, the person with whom the regulated transaction was entered into.

Information about qualifying persons

16(1)   The statement must record, in relation to each recordable transaction to which a qualifying person was a party

(a)   the information about the qualifying person which is, in connection with transactions entered into by registered parties, required to be recorded in transaction reports by virtue of paragraph 2 of Schedule 6A (reading references in that paragraph to an authorised participant as references to a qualifying person who is a party to the transaction), or

      (b) where the qualifying person is within any of paragraphs (d) to (g) of paragraph 4(2), the information mentioned in sub-paragraph (2) below.

(2) The information referred to in sub-paragraph (1)(b) is
      (a) where the qualifying person is a body within paragraph 4(2)(d) (body incorporated by Royal Charter)
          (i) the name of the body, and
          (ii) the address of its main office in the United Kingdom;
      (b) where the qualifying person is a body within paragraph 4(2)(e) or (f) (charitable incorporated organisation)
          (i) the name of the body, and
          (ii) the address of its principal office;
      (c) where the qualifying person is a body within paragraph 4(2)(g) (Scottish partnership)
          (i) the name of the body, and
          (ii) the address of its main office in the United Kingdom.

(3) In sub-paragraph (1), the reference to paragraph 2 of Schedule 6A is to be taken as a reference to that paragraph without the modifications of that paragraph made by Schedule 2 to the European Union Referendum Act 2015.

Information about non-qualifying persons

17 The statement must record, in relation to each recordable transaction to which a non-qualifying person was a party
      (a) the name and address of the person;
      (b) the date when and the manner in which sub-paragraphs (3) to (5) of paragraph 5, or those sub-paragraphs as applied by paragraph 5(6) or 6(2), were complied with.

Details of transaction

18(1) The statement must record, in relation to each recordable transaction, the information about the transaction which is, in connection with transactions entered into by registered parties, required to be recorded in transaction reports by virtue of paragraph 5(2), (3) and (4) of Schedule 6A (read with the modifications mentioned in sub-paragraph (2) and any other necessary modifications).

(2) In relation to the statement
      (a) paragraph 5(4) of Schedule 6A has effect as if the reference to the relevant date for the transaction determined in accordance with paragraph 8 of that Schedule were a reference to the relevant date for the transaction determined in accordance with paragraph 8(1) of that Schedule, and
      (b) paragraph 8(1) of that Schedule has effect as if
          (i) the reference to a quarterly report were a reference to the statement,
          (ii) the reference to section 71M(4)(a) or (7)(a) were a reference to paragraph 15(3)(a) of this Schedule, and
          (iii) the reference to section 71M(4)(b) or (7)(b) were a reference to paragraph 15(3)(b) of this Schedule.

(3) The statement must record, in relation to each recordable transaction of a description mentioned in paragraph 2(1) or (2) above, the information about the transaction which is, in connection with transactions entered into by registered parties, required to be recorded in transaction reports by virtue of paragraph 6 of Schedule 6A.

(4) The statement must record, in relation to each recordable transaction of a description mentioned in paragraph 2(3)(b) above, the information about the transaction which is, in connection with transactions entered into by registered

parties, required to be recorded in transaction reports by virtue of paragraph 7(2)(b), (3) and (4) of Schedule 6A.

Changes

19(1) Where another qualifying person has become a party to a regulated transaction (whether in place of or in addition to any existing party), or there has been any other change in any of the information that is required by paragraphs 16 to 18 to be included in the statement, the statement must record
  (a) the information as it was both before and after the change;
  (b) the date of the change.

  (2) Where a recordable transaction has come to an end, the statement must
  (a) record that fact;
  (b) record the date when it happened;
  (c) in the case of a loan, state how the loan has come to an end.

  (3) For the purposes of sub-paragraph (2), a loan comes to an end if
  (a) the whole debt (or all the remaining debt) is repaid;
  (b) the creditor releases the whole debt.

Total value of non-recordable transactions

20 The statement must record the total value of any regulated transactions that are not recordable transactions.

Part 5
Supplemental

Non-disclosure with intent to conceal

21(1) This paragraph applies where, on an application made by the Commission, the court is satisfied that any failure to comply with a requirement of Part 4 of this Schedule in relation to
  (a) any transaction entered into by the permitted participant, or
  (b) any change made to a transaction to which the permitted participant is a party,
  was attributable to an intention on the part of any person to conceal the existence or true value of the transaction.

  (2) The court may make such order as it thinks fit to restore (so far as is possible) the parties to the transaction to the position they would have been in if the transaction had not been entered into.

  (3) An order under this paragraph may in particular
  (a) where the transaction is a loan or credit facility, require that any amount owed by the permitted participant be repaid (and that no further sums be advanced under it);
  (b) where any form of security is given for a sum owed under the transaction, or the transaction is an arrangement by which any form of security is given, require that the security be discharged.

Proceedings under paragraphs 5 and 21

22(1) This paragraph has effect in relation to proceedings on an application under paragraph 5(4) or 21.

  (2) The court referred to in paragraphs 5(4) and 21 is
  (a) in England and Wales or Northern Ireland, the county court;
  (b) in Gibraltar, the Gibraltar court.

In Scotland, the court is the sheriff and the proceedings are civil proceedings.

(3) The standard of proof is that applicable to civil proceedings.

(4) An order may be made whether or not proceedings are brought against any person for an offence under this Schedule or section 123.

(5) An appeal against an order made by the sheriff may be made to the Court of Session.

(6) Rules of court in any part of the United Kingdom may make provision
  (a) with respect to applications or appeals from proceedings on such applications;
  (b) for the giving of notice of such applications or appeals to persons affected;
  (c) for the joinder, or in Scotland sisting, of such persons as parties;
  (d) generally with respect to procedure in such applications or appeals.

(7) Sub-paragraph (6) does not affect any existing power to make rules.

Interpretation of provisions relating to reporting of transactions

23 For the purposes of any provision of this Schedule relating to the reporting of transactions, anything required to be done by a permitted participant in consequence of the participant's being a party to a regulated transaction must also be done by the participant, if the participant is a party to a transaction of a description mentioned in paragraph 2(3)(a), as if the participant were a party to the connected transaction."

Further modifications of 2000 Act relating to loans etc

2(1) Section 120 of the 2000 Act (returns in respect of referendum expenses and donations) has effect in relation to the referendum as if at the end of subsection (2)(d) there were inserted "and a statement of regulated transactions entered into in respect of the referendum which complies with the requirements of paragraphs 16 to 20 of Schedule 15A".

(2) Section 123 of the 2000 Act (declaration of responsible person as to return under section 120) has effect in relation to the referendum as if after subsection (3) (as modified by Schedule 1) there were inserted
  "(3A) In a case where the permitted participant either is not a registered party or is a minor party, the declaration must also, in relation to all regulated transactions recorded in the return as having been entered into by the permitted participant
    (a) state that none of the transactions was made void by paragraph 5(2) or (6) or 6(3) of Schedule 15A, or
    (b) state whether or not paragraph 5(3)(a) of that Schedule was complied with in the case of each of the transactions that was made void by paragraph 5(2) or (6) of that Schedule."

(3) Section 124 of the 2000 Act (public inspection of returns under section 120) has effect in relation to the referendum as if after subsection (2) there were inserted
  "(2A) If the return contains a statement of regulated transactions in accordance with section 120(2)(d), the Commission shall secure that the copy of the statement made available for public inspection does not include, in the case of a transaction entered into by the permitted participant with an individual, the individual's address."

(4) For the purposes of the referendum, the following provisions of Schedule 15 to the 2000 Act are to be treated as omitted
  (a) paragraph 2(1)(d),
  (b) in paragraph 2(3)
    (i) paragraph (a), and
    (ii) the words "the loan or", and

(c) in paragraph 5(4)

    (i) the words "(d) or",

    (ii) in paragraph (a) the words "the loan or", and

    (iii) paragraph (a)(i).

Accordingly, paragraph 2(3)(b) of that Schedule has effect for the purposes of the referendum as if for "such terms" there were substituted "commercial terms".

(5) Paragraph 10 of Schedule 15 to the 2000 Act, which is modified by paragraph 34 of Schedule 1, also has effect in relation to the referendum as if for paragraph (b) of sub-paragraph (2) there were substituted

> "(b) the value of it and any other relevant benefit or benefits is more than that amount; and "relevant benefit" here means any relevant donation or regulated transaction (within the meaning of Schedule 15A) made by, or entered into with, the person who made the donation."

(6) Paragraph 1 of Schedule 19A to the 2000 Act (requirement to notify Commission of certain political contributions) has effect in relation to the referendum as if

    (a) in sub-paragraph (2) after paragraph (f) there were inserted

> "(fa) it makes a loan of money to a permitted participant, or discharges (to any extent) a liability of a permitted participant, in pursuance of a regulated transaction (within the meaning of Schedule 15A);", and

    (b) in sub-paragraph (5)(e) for "sub-paragraph (2)(b) or (d)" there were substituted "sub-paragraph (2)(b), (d) or (fa)".

(7) Schedule 19C to the 2000 Act (civil sanctions), and any order under Part 5 of that Schedule, have effect as if offences under paragraphs 8 to 11 of the Schedule treated as inserted by paragraph 1 above were offences prescribed in an order under that Part.

(8) Nothing in sub-paragraph (6) or (7) (read with section 12) is to be taken to mean that Schedule 19A or 19C of the 2000 Act extends or applies to Gibraltar for the purposes of the referendum.

Transactions entered into before commencement: operation of paragraphs 1 and 2

3(1) In this paragraph and paragraph 4 "Schedule 15A" means the Schedule treated as inserted by paragraph 1.

(2) The following provisions of Schedule 15A

    (a) paragraphs 1 and 3, and

    (b) Parts 4 and 5, except paragraph 17(b),

apply to a relevant varied transaction as they apply to a regulated transaction within the meaning of Schedule 15A.

(3) Accordingly, any reference to a regulated transaction in a provision of the 2000 Act modified by paragraph 2 of this Schedule includes a relevant varied transaction.

(4) For the purposes of this paragraph and paragraph 4 a transaction is a "relevant varied transaction" if

    (a) the transaction was entered into, before or after the commencement of paragraph 1 of this Schedule, by a person who after entering into the transaction became a permitted participant,

    (b) the transaction would have been a regulated transaction within the meaning given by paragraph 2 of Schedule 15A if at the time when that person entered into the transaction

        (i) that person had been a permitted participant, and

        (ii) the use condition mentioned in paragraph 2(5) of Schedule 15A had been satisfied (if it was not in fact satisfied at the time the transaction was entered into),

    (c) at a time after the commencement of paragraph 1 of this Schedule, and after that person became a permitted participant, the terms of that transaction were varied so as to increase the amount of money or benefit to which the permitted participant is entitled in consequence of the transaction, and

    (d) at the time of that variation, the permitted participant intends to use any money or benefit obtained in consequence of the transaction for meeting referendum expenses incurred by or on behalf of the permitted participant.

(5) For the purposes of sub-paragraph (4)(d) it is immaterial whether only part of the money or benefit is intended to be used as mentioned there.

(6) In this paragraph "permitted participant" has the same meaning as it has in Schedule 15A (see paragraph 1(2) of that Schedule).

(7) In sub-paragraph (4)

    (a) the reference in paragraph (a) to a person who after entering into the transaction became a permitted participant includes an officer, member, trustee or agent of any such person, and

    (b) in relation to a case where such an officer, member, trustee or agent entered into the transaction, the references in paragraphs (b)(i) and (c) to "that person" are to be read as references to the person for whom the person who entered into the agreement is an officer, member, trustee or agent.

4   Parts 2 and 3 of Schedule 15A do not apply to a relevant varied transaction (or to any other transaction which was entered into before the commencement of paragraph 1 of this Schedule or before a party to the transaction became a permitted participant).

Reporting of regulated transactions during referendum period

5(1) In this paragraph references to a permitted participant are to a permitted participant which either is not a registered party or is a minor party.

(2) In relation to the referendum, the responsible person in relation to a permitted participant must prepare reports under this paragraph in respect of

    (a) the period ("the first reporting period") beginning with the commencement day and ending with the 7th day of the referendum period, and

    (b) such other periods ending before the date of the referendum as may be prescribed by regulations made by the Minister;

and in paragraph (a) "the commencement day" means the day on which that paragraph comes into force.

(3) The report for a period must record, in relation to each regulated transaction having a value exceeding £7,500 which is entered into by the permitted participant during the period

    (a) the nature of the transaction (that is to say whether it is a loan, a credit facility or an arrangement by which any form of security is given),

    (b) the value of the transaction (determined in accordance with paragraph 3 of the Schedule treated as inserted by paragraph 1 above ("Schedule 15A")) or, in the case of a credit facility or security to which no limit is specified, a statement to that effect,

    (c) the date when the transaction was entered into by the permitted participant,

    (d) the same information about the transaction as would be required by paragraph 18(3) and (4) of Schedule 15A to be recorded in the statement referred to in paragraph 15 of that Schedule,

    (e) the information about each qualifying person who is a party to the transaction which is, in connection with recordable transactions entered into by registered parties, required to be recorded in weekly transaction reports by paragraph 3 of Schedule 6A to the 2000 Act (reading references in that paragraph to an authorised participant as references to a qualifying person who is a party to the transaction), and

(f) in relation to a transaction to which a person who is not a qualifying person is a party, the information referred to in paragraph 17 of Schedule 15A.

(4) If during any period no regulated transactions having a value exceeding £7,500 were entered into by the permitted participant, the report for the period must contain a statement of that fact.

(5) A report under this paragraph in respect of a period must be delivered by the responsible person to the Electoral Commission

    (a) in the case of the report for the first reporting period, within 7 days beginning with the end of that period;

    (b) in the case of the report for a period prescribed under sub-paragraph (2)(b), within such time as may be prescribed by regulations made by the Minister.

(6) If, in relation to a regulated transaction entered into with an individual who has an anonymous entry in an electoral register, a report under this paragraph contains a statement that the permitted participant has seen evidence that the individual has such an anonymous entry, the report must be accompanied by a copy of the evidence.

(7) The Minister may by regulations modify the operation of sub-paragraphs (2) to (4) in relation to cases where an individual or body becomes a permitted participant during a period prescribed under sub-paragraph (2)(b).

(8) Regulations under sub-paragraph (5) or (7) may make different provision for different cases.

(9) The responsible person commits an offence if, without reasonable excuse, that person

    (a) fails to comply with the requirements of sub-paragraph (5) in relation to a report under this paragraph, or

    (b) delivers a report to the Electoral Commission that does not comply with the requirements of sub-paragraph (3), (4) or (6).

(10) A person guilty of an offence under sub-paragraph (9)(a) is liable

    (a) on summary conviction in England and Wales, to a fine;

    (b) on summary conviction in Scotland or Northern Ireland, to a fine not exceeding level 5 on the standard scale;

    (c) on summary conviction in Gibraltar, to a fine not exceeding level 5 on the Gibraltar standard scale.

(11) A person guilty of an offence under sub-paragraph (9)(b) is liable

    (a) on conviction on indictment, to imprisonment for a term not exceeding 12 months or to a fine, or to both;

    (b) on summary conviction in England and Wales, to imprisonment for a term not exceeding 12 months or to a fine, or to both;

    (c) on summary conviction in Scotland, to imprisonment for a term not exceeding 12 months or to a fine not exceeding the statutory maximum, or to both;

    (d) on summary conviction in Northern Ireland, to imprisonment for a term not exceeding 6 months or to a fine not exceeding the statutory maximum, or to both;

    (e) on summary conviction in Gibraltar, to imprisonment for a term not exceeding 12 months or to a fine not exceeding level 5 on the Gibraltar standard scale, or to both.

(12) The reference in sub-paragraph (11)(b) to 12 months is to be read as a reference to 6 months in relation to an offence committed before the commencement of section 154(1) of the Criminal Justice Act 2003.

(13) In this paragraph

    (a) "electoral register" means

        (i) an electoral register as defined by 54(8) of the 2000 Act, or

        (ii) the Gibraltar register as defined by section 14 of the European Parliament (Representation) Act 2003,

(b) the following expressions
"qualifying person", and
"regulated transaction",
have the same meaning as in the Schedule treated as inserted by paragraph 1, and

(c) references to a regulated transaction entered into by a permitted participant include any transaction entered into at a time before the individual or body concerned became a permitted participant, if the transaction would have been a regulated transaction had the individual or body been a permitted participant at that time.

(14) Paragraph 23 of the Schedule treated as inserted by paragraph 1 applies for the purposes of this paragraph as it applies for the purposes of the provisions of that Schedule relating to the reporting of transactions.

Declaration of responsible person as to reports under paragraph 5

6(1) Each report delivered under paragraph 5 must be accompanied by a declaration which complies with sub-paragraph (2) and is signed by the responsible person.

(2) The declaration must state
(a) that the responsible person has examined the report, and
(b) that to the best of the responsible person's knowledge and belief, it is a complete and correct report as required by law.

(3) A person commits an offence if
(a) the person knowingly or recklessly makes a false declaration under this paragraph, or
(b) sub-paragraph (1) is contravened at a time when the person is the responsible person in the case of the permitted participant to which the report relates.

(4) A person guilty of an offence under sub-paragraph (3) is liable
(a) on conviction on indictment, to imprisonment for a term not exceeding 12 months or to a fine, or to both;
(b) on summary conviction in England and Wales, to imprisonment for a term not exceeding 12 months or to a fine, or to both;
(c) on summary conviction in Scotland, to imprisonment for a term not exceeding 12 months or to a fine not exceeding the statutory maximum, or to both;
(d) on summary conviction in Northern Ireland, to imprisonment for a term not exceeding 6 months or to a fine not exceeding the statutory maximum, or to both;
(e) on summary conviction in Gibraltar, to imprisonment for a term not exceeding 12 months or to a fine not exceeding level 5 on the Gibraltar standard scale, or to both.

(5) The reference in sub-paragraph (4)(b) to 12 months is to be read as a reference to 6 months in relation to an offence committed before the commencement of section 154(1) of the Criminal Justice Act 2003.

Public inspection of reports under paragraph 5

7(1) Where the Electoral Commission receive a report under paragraph 5 they must
(a) as soon as is reasonably practicable after receiving the report, make a copy of the report and of any document accompanying it available for public inspection, and
(b) keep any such copy available for public inspection for the period for which the report or other document is held by them.

(2) The Electoral Commission must secure that the copy of the report made available for public inspection does not include, in the case of any transaction entered into by the permitted participant with an individual, the individual's address.

(3)   At the end of the period of two years beginning with the date when any report under paragraph 5 or other document accompanying it is received by the Electoral Commission

    (a)   they may cause the report or other document to be destroyed, or

    (b)   if requested to do so by the responsible person in the case of the permitted participant concerned, they must arrange for the report or other document to be returned to that person.

8   Section 149(2) to (5) and (7) of the 2000 Act (inspection of Commission's documents) apply in relation to reports and documents which the Electoral Commission are required to make available for public inspection under paragraph 7 as they apply to the documents which the Electoral Commission are required to make available for public inspection by virtue of the provisions of the 2000 Act mentioned in section 149(6) of that Act.

Enforcement

9(1)   Section 145(1)(a) and (6A) of the 2000 Act (general functions of Electoral Commission with respect to compliance) apply in relation to the requirements imposed by this Schedule as they apply in relation to the requirements referred to in section 145(1)(a).

(2)   In section 148 of the 2000 Act (general offences), the references in each of subsections (1) to (3) to any of the provisions of that Act include any of the provisions of this Schedule.

(3)   Sections 151 and 154 of the 2000 Act (summary proceedings, and duty of court to report conviction to Electoral Commission) apply in relation to an offence under this Schedule as they apply in relation to an offence under that Act.

(4)   In paragraphs 3 to 5 of Schedule 19B to the 2000 Act (powers of Electoral Commission in relation to suspected offences or contraventions)

    (a)   the references to an offence under that Act include an offence under this Schedule, and

    (b)   the references to a restriction or other requirement imposed by or by virtue of that Act include a requirement or restriction imposed by or by virtue of this Schedule.

(5)   Schedule 19C to the 2000 Act (civil sanctions), and any order under Part 5 of that Schedule, have effect as if any reference in that Schedule to an offence under the 2000 Act, or to a prescribed offence under that Act, included a reference to an offence under paragraph 5(9) of this Schedule.

(6)   Nothing in sub-paragraph (4) or (5) (read with section 12) is to be taken to mean that Schedule 19B or 19C to the 2000 Act extends or applies to Gibraltar for the purposes of the referendum.

Persons with whom certain registered parties may enter into loan agreements etc

10(1)   Sub-paragraph (2) applies if

    (a)   a permitted participant

        (i)   is a party to a transaction which is a regulated transaction for the purposes of Part 4A of the 2000 Act, or

        (ii)   derives a benefit from a transaction which is a connected transaction for the purposes of that Part,

    (b)   that transaction is entered into during the referendum period,

    (c)   the permitted participant is a registered party that is not a minor party,

    (d)   any of the other parties to the regulated transaction or any of the parties to the connected transaction (as the case may be) is a person ("the unauthorised person") who, in relation to that transaction, is not an authorised participant for the purposes of Part 4A of the 2000 Act by virtue of section 71H of that Act, and

    (e)   the unauthorised person is a person within sub-paragraph (3).

(2) In relation to the transaction mentioned in sub-paragraph (1)(a)(i) or (ii), the unauthorised person is to be regarded for the purposes of Part 4A of the 2000 Act as an authorised participant.

(3) The persons within this sub-paragraph are
    (a) a Gibraltar elector;
    (b) a body falling within any of paragraphs (b) to (g) of section 54(2A) of the 2000 Act;
    (c) a body incorporated by Royal Charter which does not fall within section 54(2) of that Act;
    (d) a charitable incorporated organisation within the meaning of Part 11 of the Charities Act 2011 or Part 11 of the Charities Act (Northern Ireland) 2008;
    (e) a Scottish charitable incorporated organisation within the meaning of Chapter 7 of Part 1 of the Charities and Trustee Investment (Scotland) Act 2005 (asp 10);
    (f) a partnership constituted under the law of Scotland which carries on business in the United Kingdom.

(4) In this paragraph "Gibraltar elector" has the same meaning as in the 2000 Act (see section 160(1) of that Act).

11 Where paragraph 10 applies in relation to a transaction to which a permitted participant is a party, or from which a permitted participant derives a benefit, paragraph 2 of Schedule 6A to the 2000 Act (details to be given in quarterly reports) has effect as if
    (a) in sub-paragraph (1) for "(10)" there were substituted "(10C)", and
    (b) the following sub-paragraphs were inserted after sub-paragraph (10)
    "(10A) In the case of a body within paragraph 10(3)(c) of Schedule 2 to the European Union Referendum Act 2015 (body incorporated by Royal Charter) the report must give
      (a) the name of the body, and
      (b) the address of its main office in the United Kingdom.
    (10B) In the case of a body within paragraph 10(3)(d) or (e) of that Schedule (charitable incorporated organisation) the report must give
      (a) the name of the body, and
      (b) the address of its principal office.
    (10C) In the case of a body within paragraph 10(3)(f) of that Schedule (Scottish partnership) the report must give
      (a) the name of the body, and
      (b) the address of its main office in the United Kingdom."

12(1) This paragraph applies to a variation of a regulated transaction if
    (a) the regulated transaction was entered into by a permitted participant during the referendum period,
    (b) the permitted participant is a registered party that is not a minor party,
    (c) one of the other parties to the regulated transaction is an authorised participant in relation to the transaction by virtue of paragraph 10 of this Schedule, and
    (d) the variation has the effect of increasing the value of the regulated transaction or enabling it to be increased.

(2) It does not matter for the purposes of sub-paragraph (1)(d) when the variation is entered into or when the increase takes effect or could take effect.

(3) The variation is to be treated for the purposes of sections 71I(2) to (4) of the 2000 Act as a regulated transaction in which another participant is not an authorised participant.

(4) An order made under section 71I(4) of the 2000 Act in relation to a variation to which this paragraph applies may in particular
    (a) require that any amount owed as a result of the variation be repaid (and that no further sums be advanced under the terms of the variation);

    (b) where any additional security is provided under the terms of the variation, require that security to be discharged.

(5) In this paragraph
    (a) "authorised participant" means an authorised participant for the purposes of Part 4A of the 2000 Act;
    (b) "regulated transaction" and references to the value of a regulated transaction have the same meaning as in Part 4A of the 2000 Act (see sections 71F and 71G of that Act).

13(1) Section 71L of the 2000 Act (offences relating to regulated transactions) has effect with the following modifications.

(2) In each of subsections (1)(a), (2)(b), (3)(a) and (4)(a), the reference to entering into a regulated transaction of a description mentioned in section 71F(2) or (3) in which another participant is not an authorised participant includes a reference to entering into a variation to which paragraph 12 of this Schedule applies.

(3) In relation to such a variation
    (a) subsection (3)(b) has effect as if for the words "that the other participant is not an authorised participant" there were substituted "of the matters mentioned in paragraph (a)", and
    (b) subsections (3)(c), (4)(c) and (10) each have effect as if the reference to the transaction were to the variation.

(4) In subsection (9), the reference to a regulated transaction with a person other than an authorised participant includes a reference to a variation to which paragraph 12 of this Schedule applies.

NOTES

Defined terms

the 2000 Act: s 11(1)	by para 1)
body: s 11(1)	Gibraltar elector: s 160(1)
document: s 11(1)	market value: s 160(1)
the Minister: s 11(1)	minor party: s 160(1)
minor party: s 11(1)	non-qualifying person: Sch 15A, Pt 1, para 1(3) (as inserted by para 1)
permitted participant: s 11(1)	permitted participant: s 105(1) (as read with Sch 1, para 2 to this Act)
the referendum: s 11(1)	property: s 160(1)
referendum expenses: s 11(1)	qualifying person: Sch 15A, Pt 1, para 1(3), Pt 2, para 4(2) (as inserted by para 1)
the referendum period: s 11(1)	the referendum: s 101(2)-(5) (as read with s 1 of this Act)
registered party: s 11(1)	referendum expenses: s 111(2) (see also Sch 1, para 19 to this Act)
responsible person: s 11(1)	registered party: s 160(1)
	regulated transaction: Sch 15A, Pt 1, paras 1(3), 2 (as inserted by para 1)
Terms defined in the Political Parties, Elections and Referendums Act 2000 picked up by s 11(1) of this Act	responsible person: s 105(2)
body: s 160(1)	
the Commission: s 160(1)	
connected transaction: Sch 15A, Pt 1, paras 1(3), 2(9) (as inserted by para 1)	
credit facility: Sch 15A, Pt 1, paras 1(3), 2(11) (as inserted	

SCHEDULE 3
FURTHER PROVISION ABOUT THE REFERENDUM

Section 3

Interpretation

1 In this Schedule a reference to functions includes functions conferred by any provision of law made in and for Gibraltar.

Appointment of Chief Counting Officer

2(1) Section 128 of the 2000 Act (Chief Counting Officers, and counting officers, for referendums) has effect for the purposes of the referendum with the following modifications.

(2) Subsection (2) has effect for those purposes as if
    (a) the words "(subject to subsection (8))" were omitted, and
    (b) in paragraph (b), after "appoints" there were inserted "in writing".

(3) For the purposes of the referendum subsection (8) is to be treated as omitted.

(4) See also paragraphs 4 and 6 (which contain additional modifications of section 128 of the 2000 Act for the purposes of the referendum).

Counting officers

3(1) This paragraph applies to determine, for the purposes of the referendum, who is a counting officer in relation to a voting area.

(2) The counting officer for a voting area that is
    (a) a district in England,
    (b) a county in England, or
    (c) a London borough,
is the person who, by virtue of section 35 of the 1983 Act, is the returning officer for elections of councillors of the district, county or borough.

(3) The counting officer for the City of London voting area is the person who, by virtue of that section, is the returning officer for elections of councillors of the London borough of Westminster.

(4) The counting officer for the Isles of Scilly voting area is the person who, by virtue of that section, is the returning officer for elections to the Council of the Isles of Scilly.

(5) The counting officer for a voting area that is a county or a county borough in Wales is the person who, by virtue of that section, is the returning officer for elections of councillors of the county or county borough.

(6) The counting officer for a voting area that is a local government area in Scotland is the person who, by virtue of section 41 of the 1983 Act, is the returning officer for elections of councillors of the local government area.

(7) The counting officer for the Northern Ireland voting area is the Chief Electoral Officer for Northern Ireland.

(8) The counting officer for the Gibraltar voting area is the Clerk to the Gibraltar Parliament.

4(1) Accordingly, section 128 of the 2000 Act (Chief Counting Officers, and counting officers, for referendums) has effect for the purposes of the referendum with the following modifications.

(2) For the purposes of the referendum subsection (3) is to be treated as omitted.

(3) Subsection (5) has effect for the purposes of the referendum as if for the words "the area for which he is appointed" there were substituted "the voting area for which the counting officer acts".

(4) Subsection (9) has effect for the purposes of the referendum as if
    (a) for paragraph (a) there were substituted
        "(a) voting area" has the meaning given by section 11 of the European Union Referendum Act 2015;",
    (b) paragraph (b) were omitted, and
    (c) for paragraph (c) there were substituted
        "(c) the referendum area" means the United Kingdom and Gibraltar."

Regional Counting Officers

5(1) For the purposes of the referendum, the Chief Counting Officer may appoint a Regional
Counting Officer for any of the following regions
East Midlands;
Eastern;
London;
North East;
North West;
South East;
South West and Gibraltar;
West Midlands;
Yorkshire and the Humber;
Scotland;
Wales.

(2) Where
(a) a region mentioned in sub-paragraph (1) (a "listed region"), and
(b) a region mentioned in the Table in Schedule 1 to the European Parliamentary
Elections Act 2002 (an "electoral region"),
have the same name, the listed region comprises the areas specified in relation to that
electoral region in that Table as they are for the time being.

(3) The South West and Gibraltar region mentioned in sub-paragraph (1) comprises the areas
specified in relation to the South West region in that Table as they are for the time being.

(4) In determining for the purposes of sub-paragraph (2) or (3) what the areas are that are
specified in that Table, paragraph 2(2) of Schedule 1 to the European Parliamentary
Elections Act 2002 is to be ignored.

Assistance to counting officers etc

6(1) A local authority whose area forms a particular voting area must place the services of their
officers at the disposal of
(a) the counting officer for the voting area, and
(b) the Regional Counting Officer (if any) appointed for the region that includes the
voting area,
for the purpose of assisting the officer in the discharge of his or her functions.

(2) In this paragraph "local authority"
(a) in the case of a voting area that is a district or county in England, or a London
borough, means the council for that district, county or borough;
(b) in the case of the City of London voting area, means the Common Council of the
City of London;
(c) in the case of the Isles of Scilly voting area, means the Council of the Isles of Scilly;
(d) in the case of a voting area in Wales, means the council of the county or county
borough;
(e) in the case of a voting area in Scotland, means the council of the local government
area.

(3) The Government of Gibraltar must place the services of its public officers at the disposal
of
(a) the Clerk to the Gibraltar Parliament, as counting officer for the Gibraltar voting
area, and
(b) the Regional Counting Officer (if any) appointed for the South West and Gibraltar
region,
for the purpose of assisting the officer in the discharge of his or her functions as counting
officer or as Regional Counting Officer (as the case may be).

(4) Accordingly, section 128 of the 2000 Act (Chief Counting Officers, and counting officers, for referendums) has effect for the purposes of the referendum as if subsection (4) were omitted.

General duties of counting officers etc

7(1) The Chief Counting Officer, Regional Counting Officers and counting officers must do whatever things are necessary for conducting the referendum in the manner provided

    (a) by and under this Act, and

    (b) in the case of the Chief Counting Officer, the Regional Counting Officer (if any) appointed for the South West and Gibraltar region and the counting officer for the Gibraltar voting area, by Gibraltar conduct law.

(2) The counting officer for a voting area is responsible, as regards that area, for

    (a) the conduct of the poll,

    (b) (subject to sub-paragraph (3)) the printing of the ballot papers,

    (c) the issue and receipt of postal ballot papers for persons entitled to vote on their own behalf in the referendum and for their proxies,

    (d) the counting of the votes cast, and

    (e) any other matters specified in conduct regulations or Gibraltar conduct law (as the case may be).

(3) Responsibility for the printing of the ballot papers for a voting area may be taken

    (a) by the Chief Counting Officer;

    (b) in the case of a voting area in a region for which a Regional Counting Officer is appointed, by the Chief Counting Officer or the Regional Counting Officer.

The Chief Counting Officer or Regional Counting Officer may direct the counting officer concerned accordingly.

(4) In the case of a region for which a Regional Counting Officer is appointed for the purposes of the referendum, the officer must certify as regards the votes cast in the region

    (a) the total number of ballot papers counted, and

    (b) the total number of votes cast in favour of each answer to the question asked in the referendum.

Where two or more forms of ballot paper are used in the referendum, a separate number must be certified under paragraph (a) in relation to each form of ballot paper used.

(5) The Chief Counting Officer may give Regional Counting Officers or counting officers

    (a) directions about the discharge of their functions;

    (b) directions requiring them to take specified steps in preparation for the referendum;

    (c) directions requiring them to provide the Chief Counting Officer with information that they have or are entitled to have.

(6) A Regional Counting Officer for a region may give counting officers for voting areas within that region

    (a) directions about the discharge of their functions;

    (b) directions requiring them to take specified steps in preparation for the referendum;

    (c) directions requiring them to provide the Regional Counting Officer with information that they have or are entitled to have.

(7) A power under this paragraph of a Regional Counting Officer to give a direction to a counting officer is exercisable only in accordance with a specific or general authorisation or direction given by the Chief Counting Officer.

(8) A person to whom a direction is given under this paragraph must comply with it.

(9) This paragraph applies in addition to section 128 of the 2000 Act (as modified by this Schedule).

(10)   The number of ballot papers or votes purportedly certified under this paragraph or section 128 of the 2000 Act is not liable to be questioned by reason of a defect in the title, or a lack of title, of any person purporting to exercise functions in relation to the referendum, if the person was then in actual possession of, or acting in, the office giving the right to exercise the functions.

Appointment of deputies and clerks

8(1)   The Chief Counting Officer or a Regional Counting Officer or counting officer may appoint deputies to carry out any or all of the officer's functions.

(2)   An appointment under sub-paragraph (1) must be in writing.

(3)   A Regional Counting Officer may appoint however many clerks are necessary to assist in carrying out the officer's functions.

Counting officers etc: correction of procedural errors

9(1)   A Regional Counting Officer or counting officer may take whatever steps the officer thinks appropriate to remedy any act or omission on the part of the officer or a relevant person that
   (a)   arises in connection with any function that the officer or relevant person has in relation to the referendum, and
   (b)   is not in accordance with any requirements applicable to the referendum imposed as described in sub-paragraph (4) or otherwise.

(2)   A recount of votes in reliance on sub-paragraph (1) may only be conducted in the circumstances (if any) specified in conduct regulations or Gibraltar conduct law (as the case may be).

(3)   For the purposes of this paragraph each of the following is a "relevant person"
   (a)   a registration officer;
   (b)   the European electoral registration officer for Gibraltar (within the meaning of section 14 of the European Parliament (Representation) Act 2003);
   (c)   a clerk of, or a person providing goods or services to, the Regional Counting Officer or the counting officer;
   (d)   any person designated by conduct regulations or Gibraltar conduct law as a relevant person for the purposes of this sub-paragraph;
   (e)   a deputy or assistant of
      (i)   the Regional Counting Officer or the counting officer, or
      (ii)   a person mentioned in paragraph (a), (b), (c) or (d).

(4)   For the purposes of sub-paragraph (1)(b) requirements are imposed as described in this sub-paragraph if they are imposed
   (a)   by or under this Act, or
   (b)   in the case of the Regional Counting Officer (if any) appointed for the South West and Gibraltar region, the counting officer for the Gibraltar voting area or a Gibraltar relevant person, by any provision of law made in and for Gibraltar.

(5)   For the purposes of sub-paragraph (4)(b) each of the following relevant persons is a "Gibraltar relevant person"
   (a)   the European electoral registration officer for Gibraltar (within the meaning of section 14 of the European Parliament (Representation) Act 2003);
   (b)   a clerk of the Regional Counting Officer (if any) appointed for the South West and Gibraltar region;
   (c)   a person providing goods or services to the Regional Counting Officer (if any) appointed for the South West and Gibraltar region or to the counting officer for the Gibraltar voting area;

(d) any person designated by conduct regulations or Gibraltar conduct law as a relevant person for the purposes of this sub-paragraph;

(e) a deputy or assistant of

(i) the Regional Counting Officer (if any) appointed for the South West and Gibraltar region or the counting officer for the Gibraltar voting area, or

(ii) a person mentioned in paragraph (a), (b), (c) or (d).

(6) For the purposes of sub-paragraph (3)(e) and (5)(e) a person ("A") is an assistant of another person ("P") if

(a) A is appointed to assist P, or

(b) in the course of employment A is assisting P,

in connection with any function in relation to the referendum.

Public notices

10 A public notice required by or under this Act or Gibraltar conduct law to be given by the Chief Counting Officer, a Regional Officer or a counting officer must be given

(a) by posting the notice in some conspicuous place in the area or region for which the officer acts, or

(b) in whatever other manner the officer thinks desirable for publicising it.

Role of Electoral Commission

11(1) The Electoral Commission must take whatever steps they think appropriate to promote public awareness about the referendum and how to vote in it.

(2) Following the referendum, the Electoral Commission must

(a) publish the most accurate estimate that it is reasonably possible to make of the turnout in each of England, Wales, Scotland, Northern Ireland and Gibraltar, and

(b) include that information in any report they submit under section 6(1)(b) of the 2000 Act which relates to the referendum.

(3) In sub-paragraph (2) "turnout" means the percentage of those entitled to vote in the referendum who did so.

(4) The reference in sub-paragraph (3) to those entitled to vote in the referendum who did so includes any persons entitled to vote who conduct regulations or Gibraltar conduct law provides are to be treated for the purposes of sub-paragraph (3) as having voted.

Encouraging participation

12(1) The Chief Counting Officer must take whatever steps the officer thinks appropriate to encourage participation in the referendum.

(2) An officer to whom sub-paragraph (3) applies must take whatever steps the officer thinks appropriate to encourage participation in the referendum in the area or region for which the officer acts.

(3) This sub-paragraph applies to

(a) a Regional Counting Officer;

(b) a counting officer;

(c) a registration officer.

(4) The Chief Counting Officer must take whatever steps the officer thinks appropriate to facilitate co-operation between that officer and the officers to whom sub-paragraph (3) applies in taking any steps under sub-paragraph (1) or (2).

(5) In discharging the duty imposed by sub-paragraph (1) or (2) an officer must have regard to any guidance issued by the Electoral Commission.

(6) The Minister may reimburse any expenditure incurred by an officer for the purposes of sub-paragraph (1) or (2).

(7)   A reference in this paragraph to "a registration officer" includes the European electoral registration officer for Gibraltar (within the meaning of section 14 of the European Parliament (Representation) Act 2003).

Supply and use of register of electors

13(1)   The Representation of the People (England and Wales) Regulations 2001 (SI 2001/341) have effect for the purposes of the referendum with the following modifications.

(2)   Regulation 106 (supply of full register etc to registered political parties etc and restrictions on use) has effect for those purposes as if
    (a)   in paragraph (1)(c), for ", other than a registered political party" there were substituted "which either is not a registered political party or is a minor party within the meaning of section 160(1) of that Act", and
    (b)   at the end of paragraph (4)(b)(ii) there were inserted ", and
       (iii)   the purposes of complying with the requirements of Schedule 15A to that Act (control of loans etc to certain permitted participants), and
       (iv)   the purposes of complying with the requirements of paragraphs 39 and 40 of Schedule 1 and paragraphs 5 and 6 of Schedule 2 to the European Union Referendum Act 2015."

14(1)   The Representation of the People (Scotland) Regulations 2001 (SI 2001/497) have effect for the purposes of the referendum with the following modifications.

(2)   Regulation 105 (supply of full register etc to registered political parties etc and restrictions on use) has effect for those purposes as if
    (a)   in paragraph (1)(c), for ", other than a registered political party" there were substituted "which either is not a registered political party or is a minor party within the meaning of section 160(1) of that Act", and
    (b)   at the end of paragraph (4)(b)(ii) there were inserted ", and
       (iii)   the purposes of complying with the requirements of Schedule 15A to that Act (control of loans etc to certain permitted participants), and
       (iv)   the purposes of complying with the requirements of paragraphs 39 and 40 of Schedule 1 and paragraphs 5 and 6 of Schedule 2 to the European Union Referendum Act 2015."

15(1)   The Representation of the People (Northern Ireland) Regulations 2008 (SI 2008/1741) have effect for the purposes of the referendum with the following modifications.

(2)   Regulation 105 (supply of full register etc to registered political parties etc and restrictions on use) has effect for those purposes as if
    (a)   in paragraph (1)(c), for ", other than a registered political party" there were substituted "which either is not a registered political party or is a minor party within the meaning of section 160(1) of that Act", and
    (b)   at the end of paragraph (4)(b)(ii) there were inserted "; and
       (iii)   the purposes of complying with the requirements of Schedule 15A to that Act (control of loans etc to certain permitted participants); and
       (iv)   the purposes of complying with the requirements of paragraphs 39 and 40 of Schedule 1 and paragraphs 5 and 6 of Schedule 2 to the European Union Referendum Act 2015."

Payments to counting officers and Regional Counting Officers

16(1)   Subject to sub-paragraphs (3) and (4), a counting officer or Regional Counting Officer is entitled to recover his or her charges in respect of services rendered, or expenses incurred, for or in connection with the referendum if

European Union Referendum Act 2015

(a) the services were necessarily rendered, or the expenses were necessarily incurred, for the efficient and effective conduct of the referendum, and

(b) the total of the officer's charges does not exceed the amount ("the overall maximum recoverable amount") specified in, or determined in accordance with, regulations made by the Minister, with the consent of the Treasury, for the purposes of this sub-paragraph.

(2) Sub-paragraph (3) applies to a service rendered by
(a) the counting officer for a voting area in England, Wales or Scotland,
(b) the Clerk to the Gibraltar Parliament, as counting officer for the Gibraltar voting area, or
(c) a Regional Counting Officer,
which in the opinion of the Electoral Commission was inadequately performed.

(3) In respect of a service to which this sub-paragraph applies, the officer is entitled under sub-paragraph (1) to no more than the amount (which may be nil) that seems reasonable in all the circumstances
(a) to the Commission, or
(b) on a taxation under paragraph 17, to the county court, the Auditor of the Court of Session or the Gibraltar court (as the case may be).

(4) Regulations under sub-paragraph (1) may specify, or make provision for determining in accordance with the regulations, a maximum recoverable amount for services or expenses of a specified description
(a) for counting officers;
(b) for Regional Counting Officers.
Subject to sub-paragraph (5), an officer may not recover more than the specified amount in respect of such services or expenses.

(5) In a particular case the Electoral Commission may, with the consent of the Treasury, authorise the payment of
(a) more than the overall maximum recoverable amount, or
(b) more than the amount specified as the maximum recoverable amount for services or expenses of a specified description,
if the Commission are satisfied that the conditions in sub-paragraph (6) are met.

(6) The conditions are
(a) that it was reasonable for the officer concerned to render the services or incur the expenses, and
(b) that the charges in question are reasonable.

(7) The Chief Counting Officer is entitled to recover expenses incurred by that officer for or in connection with the referendum if
(a) the expenses are of a kind that would otherwise have been incurred by counting officers or Regional Counting Officers, and
(b) the Chief Counting Officer considered that it would be more economical for the expenses to be incurred by that officer instead.

(8) The Electoral Commission must pay the amount of any charges recoverable in accordance with this paragraph on an account being submitted to them.

(9) At the request of a counting officer or Regional Counting Officer or the Chief Counting Officer, the Electoral Commission may make an advance on account of the officer's charges on such terms as they think fit.

(10) The Electoral Commission may by regulations make provision as to the time when and the manner and form in which accounts are to be rendered to the Commission for the purposes of the payment of the charges of a counting officer or Regional Counting Officer or the Chief Counting Officer.

(11) Regulations under this paragraph may make different provision for different cases or areas.

(12) Any sums required by the Electoral Commission for making payments under this paragraph are to be charged on and paid out of the Consolidated Fund.

Taxation of counting officer's or Regional Counting Officer's account

17(1) An application for the account of a counting officer or Regional Counting Officer to be taxed may be made
    (a) except where any of paragraphs (b) to (d) applies, to the county court;
    (b) in the case of the Chief Electoral Officer for Northern Ireland, to the county court that has jurisdiction at the place where the officer certified the number of ballot papers counted and votes cast;
    (c) where the officer is one who was appointed for an area in Scotland, or for the region of Scotland, to the Auditor of the Court of Session;
    (d) in the case of the Clerk to the Gibraltar Parliament, to the Gibraltar court.

(2) On any such application the court has jurisdiction to tax the account in whatever manner and at whatever time and place the court thinks fit, and finally to determine the amount payable to the officer.

(3) Where an application is made for the account of a counting officer or Regional Counting Officer to be taxed, the officer may apply to the court for it to examine any claim made by any person ("the claimant") against the officer in respect of matters charged in the account.

(4) On an application under sub-paragraph (3), after the claimant has been given notice and an opportunity to be heard and to tender any evidence, the court may allow, disallow or reduce the claim, with or without costs.

(5) A reference in this paragraph to "the court" includes a reference to the Auditor of the Court of Session.

(6) In this paragraph, "Gibraltar court" means the court determined by or under the law of Gibraltar to be the court for the purpose of this paragraph.

Electoral Commission accounts

18(1) If directed to do so by the Treasury, the Electoral Commission must prepare accounts in respect of their expenditure in relation to the referendum.

(2) Accounts under this paragraph must be prepared in accordance with directions given to the Commission by the Treasury.

(3) Directions under sub-paragraph (2) may include, in particular, directions as to
    (a) the information to be contained in the accounts and the manner in which it is to be presented,
    (b) the methods and principles in accordance with which the accounts are to be prepared, and
    (c) the additional information (if any) that is to accompany the accounts.

(4) Accounts under this paragraph must be submitted by the Commission to
    (a) the Comptroller and Auditor General, and
    (b) the Speaker's Committee,
as soon may be practicable after the giving of the direction under sub-paragraph (1).

Restriction on challenge to referendum result

19(1) No court may entertain any proceedings for questioning the number of ballot papers counted or votes cast in the referendum as certified by the Chief Counting Officer or a Regional Counting Officer or counting officer unless

191

    (a) the proceedings are brought by a claim for judicial review, and

    (b) the claim form is filed before the end of the permitted period.

(2) In sub-paragraph (1) "the permitted period" means the period of 6 weeks beginning with

    (a) the day on which the officer in question gives a certificate as to the number of ballot papers counted and votes cast in the referendum, or

    (b) if the officer gives more than one such certificate, the day on which the last is given.

(3) In the application of this paragraph to Scotland, sub-paragraph (1) has effect

    (a) with the substitution in paragraph (a) of "a petition" for "a claim";

    (b) with the substitution in paragraph (b) of "the petition is lodged" for "the claim form is filed".

(4) In the application of this paragraph to Northern Ireland, sub-paragraph (1) has effect

    (a) with the substitution in paragraph (a) of "an application" for "a claim";

    (b) with the substitution in paragraph (b) of "the application for leave to apply for judicial review is lodged" for "the claim form is filed".

(5) In the application of this paragraph to Gibraltar, sub-paragraph (1) has effect with the substitution in paragraph (a) of "an application" for "a claim".

NOTES

Defined terms

the 1983 Act: s 11(1)
the 2000 Act: s 11(1)
Chief Counting Officer: s 11(1)
conduct regulations: s 11(1)

Gibraltar conduct law: ss 5, 11(1)
the Minister: s 11(1)
the referendum: s 11(1)
registration officer: s 11(1) (and see para 12(7))
voting area: s 11(1), (2)

Fixed-term Parliaments Act 2011

An Act to make provision about the dissolution of Parliament and the determination of polling days for parliamentary general elections; and for connected purposes.

15th September 2011

1 Polling days for parliamentary general elections

(1) This section applies for the purposes of the Timetable in rule 1 in Schedule 1 to the Representation of the People Act 1983 and is subject to section 2.

(2) The polling day for the next parliamentary general election after the passing of this Act is to be 7 May 2015.

(3) The polling day for each subsequent parliamentary general election is to be the first Thursday in May in the fifth calendar year following that in which the polling day for the previous parliamentary general election fell.

(4) But, if the polling day for the previous parliamentary general election
    (a) was appointed under section 2(7), and
    (b) in the calendar year in which it fell, fell before the first Thursday in May,
subsection (3) has effect as if for "fifth" there were substituted "fourth".

(5) The Prime Minister may by order made by statutory instrument provide that the polling day for a parliamentary general election in a specified calendar year is to be later than the day determined under subsection (2) or (3), but not more than two months later.

(6) A statutory instrument containing an order under subsection (5) may not be made unless a draft has been laid before and approved by a resolution of each House of Parliament.

(7) The draft laid before Parliament must be accompanied by a statement setting out the Prime Minister's reasons for proposing the change in the polling day.

2 Early parliamentary general elections

(1) An early parliamentary general election is to take place if
    (a) the House of Commons passes a motion in the form set out in subsection (2), and
    (b) if the motion is passed on a division, the number of members who vote in favour of the motion is a number equal to or greater than two thirds of the number of seats in the House (including vacant seats).

(2) The form of motion for the purposes of subsection (1)(a) is
    "That there shall be an early parliamentary general election."

(3) An early parliamentary general election is also to take place if
    (a) the House of Commons passes a motion in the form set out in subsection (4), and
    (b) the period of 14 days after the day on which that motion is passed ends without the House passing a motion in the form set out in subsection (5).

(4) The form of motion for the purposes of subsection (3)(a) is
"That this House has no confidence in Her Majesty's Government."

(5) The form of motion for the purposes of subsection (3)(b) is
"That this House has confidence in Her Majesty's Government."

(6) Subsection (7) applies for the purposes of the Timetable in rule 1 in Schedule 1 to the Representation of the People Act 1983.

(7) If a parliamentary general election is to take place as provided for by subsection (1) or (3), the polling day for the election is to be the day appointed by Her Majesty by proclamation on the recommendation of the Prime Minister (and, accordingly, the appointed day replaces the day which would otherwise have been the polling day for the next election determined under section 1).

3 Dissolution of Parliament

(1) The Parliament then in existence dissolves at the beginning of the 25th working day before the polling day for the next parliamentary general election as determined under section 1 or appointed under section 2(7).

(2) Parliament cannot otherwise be dissolved.

(3) Once Parliament dissolves, the Lord Chancellor and, in relation to Northern Ireland, the Secretary of State have the authority to have the writs for the election sealed and issued (see rule 3 in Schedule 1 to the Representation of the People Act 1983).

(4) Once Parliament dissolves, Her Majesty may issue the proclamation summoning the new Parliament which may
    (a) appoint the day for the first meeting of the new Parliament;
    (b) deal with any other matter which was normally dealt with before the passing of this Act by proclamations summoning new Parliaments (except a matter dealt with by subsection (1) or (3)).

(5) In this section "working day" means any day other than
    (a) a Saturday or Sunday;
    (b) a Christmas Eve, Christmas Day or Good Friday;
    (c) a day which is a bank holiday under the Banking and Financial Dealings Act 1971 in any part of the United Kingdom;
    (d) a day appointed for public thanksgiving or mourning.

(6) But, if
    (a) on a day ("the relevant day") one or more working days are fixed or appointed as bank holidays or days for public thanksgiving or mourning, and
    (b) as a result, the day for the dissolution of a Parliament would (apart from this subsection) be brought forward from what it was immediately before the relevant day to a day that is earlier than 30 days after the relevant day,
the day or days in question are to continue to be treated as working days (even if the polling day is subsequently changed).

4 General election for Scottish Parliament not to fall on same date as parliamentary general election under section 1(2)

(1) This section applies in relation to the ordinary general election for membership of the Scottish Parliament the poll for which would, apart from this section and disregarding sections 2(5) and 3(3) of the Scotland Act 1998, be held on 7 May 2015 (that is, the date specified in section 1(2) of this Act).

(2) Section 2(2) of the 1998 Act has effect as if, instead of providing for the poll for that election to be held on that date, it provided (subject to sections 2(5) and 3(3) of that Act)

for the poll to be held on 5 May 2016 (and section 2(2) has effect in relation to subsequent ordinary general elections accordingly).

5 *Repealed*

6 **Supplementary provisions**

(1) This Act does not affect Her Majesty's power to prorogue Parliament.

(2) This Act does not affect the way in which the sealing of a proclamation summoning a new Parliament may be authorised; and the sealing of a proclamation to be issued under section 2(7) may be authorised in the same way.

(3) The Schedule (which contains consequential amendments etc) has effect.

7 **Final provisions**

(1) This Act may be cited as the Fixed-term Parliaments Act 2011.

(2) This Act comes into force on the day it is passed.

(3) An amendment or repeal made by this Act has the same extent as the enactment or relevant part of the enactment to which the amendment or repeal relates.

(4) The Prime Minister must make arrangements
    (a) for a committee to carry out a review of the operation of this Act and, if appropriate in consequence of its findings, to make recommendations for the repeal or amendment of this Act, and
    (b) for the publication of the committee's findings and recommendations (if any).

(5) A majority of the members of the committee are to be members of the House of Commons.

(6) Arrangements under subsection (4)(a) are to be made no earlier than 1 June 2020 and no later than 30 November 2020.

SCHEDULE
Consequential Amendments etc

Not reproduced

Forfeiture Act 1870

2 Conviction for treason or felony to be a disqualification for offices, etc

... if any person hereafter convicted of treason ... shall at the time of such conviction hold any military or naval office, or any civil office under the Crown or other public employment ... or any place, office, or emolument in any university, college, or other corporation, or be entitled to any pension or superannuation allowance payable by the public, or out of any public fund, such office ... employment, or place shall forthwith become vacant, and such pension or superannuation allowance or emolument shall forthwith determine and cease to be payable, unless such person shall receive a free pardon from Her Majesty, within two months after such conviction, or before the filling up of such office ... employment, or place if given at a later period; and such person shall become, and (until he shall have suffered the punishment to which he had been sentenced, or such other punishment as by competent authority may be substituted for the same, or shall receive a free pardon from Her Majesty), shall continue thenceforth incapable of holding any military or naval office, or any civil office under the Crown or other public employment ... or of being elected, or sitting, or voting as a member of either House of Parliament, or of exercising any right of suffrage or other parliamentary or municipal franchise whatever within England, Wales, or Ireland.

NOTES

Criminal Law Act 1967, s 1 abolished all distinction between felony and misdemeanour. The law and practice in relation to felonies became that previously applicable to misdemeanours.

Forgery and Counterfeiting Act 1981

Offences

The offence of forgery

1. A person is guilty of forgery if he makes a false instrument, with the intention that he or another shall use it to induce somebody to accept it as genuine, and by reason of so accepting it to do or not to do some act to his own or any other person's prejudice.

NOTES

Defined terms
  false: s 9(1)
  inducing somebody, etc: s 10(3)
  instrument: s 8

making a false instrument: s 9(2)
prejudice: s 10(1), (4)

The offence of copying a false instrument

2. It is an offence for a person to make a copy of an instrument which is, and which he knows or believes to be, a false instrument, with the intention that he or another shall use it to induce somebody to accept it as a copy of a genuine instrument, and by reason of so accepting it to do or not to do some act to his own or any other person's prejudice.

NOTES

Defined terms
  false: s 9(1)
  inducing somebody, etc: s 10(3)
  instrument: s 8

prejudice: s 10(1), (4)

The offence of using a false instrument

3. It is an offence for a person to use an instrument which is, and which he knows or believes to be, false, with the intention of inducing somebody to accept it as genuine, and by reason of so accepting it to do or not to do some act to his own or any other person's prejudice.

NOTES

Defined terms
  false: s 9(1)
  inducing somebody, etc: s 10(3)
  instrument: s 8

prejudice: s 10(1), (4)

The offence of using a copy of a false instrument

4. It is an offence for a person to use a copy of an instrument which is, and which he knows or believes to be, a false instrument, with the intention of inducing somebody to accept it as a copy of a genuine instrument, and by reason of so accepting it to do or not to do some act to his own or any other person's prejudice.

NOTES

Defined terms
  false: s 9(1)
  inducing somebody, etc: s 10(3)

instrument: s 8

5. *Not reproduced*

Penalties etc

Penalties for offences under Part I

6(1)   A person guilty of an offence under this Part of this Act shall be liable on summary conviction

    (a)   to a fine not exceeding the statutory maximum; or

    (b)   to imprisonment for a term not exceeding six months; or

    (c)   to both.

(2)   A person guilty of an offence to which this subsection applies shall be liable on conviction on indictment to imprisonment for a term not exceeding ten years.

(3)   The offences to which subsection (2) above applies are offences under the following provisions of this Part of this Act

    (a)   section 1;

    (b)   section 2;

    (c)   section 3;

    (d)   section 4;

    (e)   section 5(1); and

    (f)   section 5(3).

(4)   A person guilty of an offence under section 5(2) or (4) above shall be liable on conviction on indictment to imprisonment for a term not exceeding two years.

(5)   ......

7   *Not reproduced*

Interpretation of Part I

Meaning of "instrument"

8(1)   Subject to subsection (2) below, in this Part of this Act "instrument" means

    (a)   any document, whether of a formal or informal character;

    (b)   any stamp issued or sold by a postal operator;

    (c)   any Inland Revenue stamp; and

    (d)   any disc, tape, sound track or other device on or in which information is recorded or stored by mechanical, electronic or other means.

(2)   A currency note within the meaning of Part II of this Act is not an instrument for the purposes of this Part of this Act.

(3)   A mark denoting payment of postage which a postal operator authorises to be used instead of an adhesive stamp is to be treated for the purposes of this Part of this Act as if it were a stamp issued by the postal operator concerned.

(3A)   In this section "postal operator" has the meaning given by section 27 of the Postal Services Act 2011.

(4)   In this Part of this Act "Inland Revenue stamp" means a stamp as defined in section 27 of the Stamp Duties Management Act 1891.

Meaning of "false" and "making"

9(1)   An instrument is false for the purposes of this Part of this Act

    (a)   if it purports to have been made in the form in which it is made by a person who did not in fact make it in that form; or

    (b)   if it purports to have been made in the form in which it is made on the authority of a person who did not in fact authorise its making in that form; or

    (c)   if it purports to have been made in the terms in which it is made by a person who did not in fact make it in those terms; or

    (d)   if it purports to have been made in the terms in which it is made on the authority of a person who did not in fact authorise its making in those terms; or

(e)   if it purports to have been altered in any respect by a person who did not in fact alter it in that respect; or

(f)   if it purports to have been altered in any respect on the authority of a person who did not in fact authorise the alteration in that respect; or

(g)   if it purports to have been made or altered on a date on which, or at a place at which, or otherwise in circumstances in which, it was not in fact made or altered; or

(h)   if it purports to have been made or altered by an existing person but he did not in fact exist.

(2)   A person is to be treated for the purposes of this Part of this Act as making a false instrument if he alters an instrument so as to make it false in any respect (whether or not it is false in some other respect apart from that alteration).

Meaning of "prejudice" and "induce"

10(1)   Subject to subsections (2) and (4) below, for the purposes of this Part of this Act an act or omission intended to be induced is to a person's prejudice if, and only if, it is one which, if it occurs

(a)   will result

(i)   in his temporary or permanent loss of property; or

(ii)   in his being deprived of an opportunity to earn remuneration or greater remuneration; or

(iii)   in his being deprived of an opportunity to gain a financial advantage otherwise than by way of remuneration; or

(b)   will result in somebody being given an opportunity

(i)   to earn remuneration or greater remuneration from him; or

(ii)   to gain a financial advantage from him otherwise than by way of remuneration; or

(c)   will be the result of his having accepted a false instrument as genuine, or a copy of a false instrument as a copy of a genuine one, in connection with his performance of any duty.

(2)   An act which a person has an enforceable duty to do and an omission to do an act which a person is not entitled to do shall be disregarded for the purposes of this Part of this Act.

(3)   In this Part of this Act references to inducing somebody to accept a false instrument as genuine, or a copy of a false instrument as a copy of a genuine one, include references to inducing a machine to respond to the instrument or copy as if it were a genuine instrument or, as the case may be, a copy of a genuine one.

(4)   Where subsection (3) above applies, the act or omission intended to be induced by the machine responding to the instrument or copy shall be treated as an act or omission to a person's prejudice.

(5)   In this section "loss" includes not getting what one might get as well as parting with what one has.

11-30   *Not reproduced*

Extent

Scotland

31   The following provisions of this Act do not extend to Scotland, namely

(a)   Part I; and

(b)   Part I of the Schedule.

Northern Ireland

32 It is hereby declared that this Act extends to Northern Ireland.

Government of Wales Act 2006

An Act to make provision about the government of Wales.

25th July 2006

PART 1
NATIONAL ASSEMBLY FOR WALES

The Assembly

The Assembly

1(1)   There is to be an Assembly for Wales to be known as the National Assembly for Wales or Cynulliad Cenedlaethol Cymru (referred to in this Act as "the Assembly").

(2)   The Assembly is to consist of
  (a)   one member for each Assembly constituency (referred to in this Act as "Assembly constituency members"), and
  (b)   members for each Assembly electoral region (referred to in this Act as "Assembly regional members").

(3)   Members of the Assembly (referred to in this Act as "Assembly members") are to be returned in accordance with the provision made by and under this Act for
  (a)   the holding of general elections of Assembly members (for the return of the entire Assembly), and
  (b)   the filling of vacancies in Assembly seats.

(4)   The validity of any Assembly proceedings is not affected by any vacancy in its membership.

(5)   In this Act "Assembly proceedings" means any proceedings of
  (a)   the Assembly,
  (b)   committees of the Assembly, or

(c) subcommittees of such committees.

NOTES
Defined terms
  Assembly constituency: s 2(1)
  Assembly electoral region: s 2(2), (3)

Wales: s 158(1), (3), (4)

Assembly constituencies and electoral regions

2(1) The Assembly constituencies are the constituencies specified in the Parliamentary Constituencies and Assembly Electoral Regions (Wales) Order 2006 (SI 2006/1041) as amended by
    (a) the Parliamentary Constituencies and Assembly Electoral Regions (Wales) (Amendment) Order 2008 (SI 2008/1791), and
    (b) any Order in Council under the Parliamentary Constituencies Act 1986 giving effect (with or without modifications) to a report falling within section 13(3) or (4) of the Parliamentary Voting System and Constituencies Act 2011.

(2) There are five Assembly electoral regions.

(3) The Assembly electoral regions are as specified in the Parliamentary Constituencies and Assembly Electoral Regions (Wales) Order 2006.

(4) There are four seats for each Assembly electoral region.

(5) *Repealed*

(6) *Repealed*

General elections

Ordinary general elections

3(1) The poll at an ordinary general election is to be held on the first Thursday in May in the fifth calendar year following that in which the previous ordinary general election was held, unless provision is made for the day of the poll by an order under section 4.

(2) If the poll is to be held on the first Thursday in May, the Assembly
    (a) is dissolved by virtue of this section at the beginning of the minimum period which ends with that day, and
    (b) must meet within the period of seven days beginning immediately after the day of the poll.

(3) In subsection (2) "the minimum period" means the period determined in accordance with an order under section 13.

(4) In calculating any period of days for the purposes of subsection (2)(b), the following days are to be disregarded
    (a) Saturday and Sunday,
    (b) any day which is a bank holiday in Wales under the Banking and Financial Dealings Act 1971 (c 80), and
    (c) any day appointed for public thanksgiving or mourning.

NOTES
Defined terms
  the Assembly: s 1(1)
  Wales: s 158(1), (3), (4)

Power to vary date of ordinary general election

4(1) The Secretary of State may by order provide for the poll at an ordinary general election to be held on a day which is neither
    (a) more than one month earlier, nor
    (b) more than one month later,

than the first Thursday in May.

(2) An order under this section must make provision for the Assembly

    (a) to be dissolved on a day specified in the order, and

    (b) to meet within the period of seven days beginning immediately after the day of the poll.

(3) In calculating any period of days for the purposes of provision made by virtue of subsection (2)(b), the following days are to be disregarded

    (a) Saturday and Sunday,

    (b) Good Friday,

    (c) any day which is a bank holiday in Wales under the Banking and Financial Dealings Act 1971 (c 80), and

    (d) any day appointed for public thanksgiving or mourning.

(4) An order under this section may make provision for

    (a) any provision of, or made under, the Representation of the People Acts, or

    (b) any other enactment relating to the election of Assembly members,

to have effect with such modifications or exceptions as the Secretary of State considers appropriate in connection with the alteration of the day of the poll.

(5) No order is to be made under this section unless the Secretary of State has consulted the Welsh Ministers about it.

(6) A statutory instrument containing an order under this section is subject to annulment in pursuance of a resolution of either House of Parliament.

NOTES

Defined terms

  the Assembly: s 1(1)

  Assembly members: s 1(3)

  modifications: s 158(1)

Wales: s 158(1), (3), (4)

the Welsh Ministers: s 45(2)

Extraordinary general elections

5(1) The Secretary of State must propose a day for the holding of a poll at an extraordinary general election if subsection (2) or (3) applies.

(2) This subsection applies if

    (a) the Assembly resolves that it should be dissolved, and

    (b) the resolution of the Assembly is passed on a vote in which the number of Assembly members voting in favour of it is not less than two-thirds of the total number of Assembly seats.

(3) This subsection applies if any period during which the Assembly is required under section 47 to nominate an Assembly member for appointment as the First Minister ends without such a nomination being made.

(4) If the Secretary of State proposes a day under subsection (1), Her Majesty may by Order in Council

    (a) dissolve the Assembly and require an extraordinary general election to be held,

    (b) require the poll at the election to be held on the day proposed, and

    (c) require the Assembly to meet within the period of seven days beginning immediately after the day of the poll.

(5) If a poll is held under this section within the period of six months ending with the day on which the poll at the next ordinary general election would be held (disregarding section 4), that ordinary general election is not to be held.

(6) But subsection (5) does not affect the year in which the subsequent ordinary general election is to be held.

(7) In calculating any period of days for the purposes of subsection (4)(c), the following days are to be disregarded

(a) Saturday and Sunday,

(b) Christmas Eve, Christmas Day and Good Friday,

(c) any day which is a bank holiday in Wales under the Banking and Financial Dealings Act 1971 (c 80), and

(d) any day appointed for public thanksgiving or mourning.

NOTES

Defined terms   Wales: s 158(1), (3), (4)
  the Assembly: s 1(1)
  Assembly members: s 1(3)

Voting at general elections

6(1)   Each person entitled to vote at a general election in an Assembly constituency has two votes.

(2)   One (referred to in this Act as a "constituency vote") is a vote which may be given for a candidate to be the Assembly constituency member for the Assembly constituency.

(3)   The other (referred to in this Act as an "electoral region vote") is a vote which may be given for

(a) a registered political party which has submitted a list of candidates to be Assembly regional members for the Assembly electoral region in which the Assembly constituency is included, or

(b) an individual who is a candidate to be an Assembly regional member for that Assembly electoral region.

(4)   The Assembly constituency member for the Assembly constituency is to be returned under the simple majority system.

(5)   The Assembly regional members for the Assembly electoral region are to be returned under the additional member system of proportional representation provided for in this Part.

(6)   In this Act "registered political party" means a party registered under Part 2 of the Political Parties, Elections and Referendums Act 2000 (c 41).

NOTES

Defined terms   Assembly regional members: s 1(2)(b)
  Assembly constituency: s 2(1)
  Assembly constituency member: s 1(2)(a)
  Assembly electoral region: s 2(2), (3)

Candidates at general elections

7(1)   At a general election a person may not be a candidate to be the Assembly constituency member for more than one Assembly constituency.

(2)   Any registered political party may submit a list of candidates for return as Assembly regional members for a particular Assembly electoral region at a general election.

(3)   The list must be submitted to the regional returning officer.

(4)   The list must not include more than twelve persons (but may include only one).

(5)   The list must not include a person

(a) who is included on any other list submitted for the Assembly electoral region or any list submitted for another Assembly electoral region,

(b) who is an individual candidate to be an Assembly regional member for the Assembly electoral region or another Assembly electoral region,

(c) who is a candidate to be the Assembly constituency member for an Assembly constituency which is not included in the Assembly electoral region, or

   (d) who is a candidate to be the Assembly constituency member for an Assembly constituency included in the Assembly electoral region but is not a candidate of the party.

(6) A person may not be an individual candidate to be an Assembly regional member for the Assembly electoral region if that person is

   (a) included on a list submitted by a registered political party for the Assembly electoral region or another Assembly electoral region,

   (b) an individual candidate to be an Assembly regional member for another Assembly electoral region,

   (c) a candidate to be the Assembly constituency member for an Assembly constituency which is not included in the Assembly electoral region, or

   (d) a candidate of any registered political party to be the Assembly constituency member for an Assembly constituency included in the Assembly electoral region.

(7) In this Act "regional returning officer", in relation to an Assembly electoral region, means the person designated as the regional returning officer for the Assembly electoral region in accordance with an order under section 13.

NOTES

Defined terms

Assembly constituency: s 2(1)
Assembly constituency member: s 1(2)(a)
Assembly electoral region: s 2(2), (3)
Assembly members: s 1(3)

Assembly regional members: s 1(2)(b)
registered political party: s 6(6)

Calculation of electoral region figures

8(1) This section and section 9 are about the return of Assembly regional members for an electoral region at a general election.

(2) The person who is to be returned as the Assembly constituency member for each Assembly constituency in the Assembly electoral region is to be determined before it is determined who are to be returned as the Assembly regional members for the Assembly electoral region.

(3) For each registered political party by which a list of candidates has been submitted for the Assembly electoral region

   (a) there is to be added together the number of electoral region votes given for the party in the Assembly constituencies included in the Assembly electoral region, and

   (b) the number arrived at under paragraph (a) is then to be divided by the aggregate of one and the number of candidates of the party returned as Assembly constituency members for any of those Assembly constituencies.

(4) For each individual candidate to be an Assembly regional member for the Assembly electoral region there is to be added together the number of electoral region votes given for the candidate in the Assembly constituencies included in the Assembly electoral region.

(5) The number arrived at

   (a) in the case of a registered political party, under subsection (3)(b), or

   (b) in the case of an individual candidate, under subsection (4),

is referred to in this Act as the electoral region figure for that party or individual candidate.

NOTES

Defined terms

Assembly constituency: s 2(1)
Assembly constituency member: s 1(2)(a)
Assembly electoral region: s 2(2), (3)
Assembly regional members: s 1(2)(b)

electoral region votes: s 6(3)
registered political party: s 6(6)

Allocation of seats to electoral region members

9(1)   The first seat for the Assembly electoral region is to be allocated to the party or individual candidate with the highest electoral region figure.

(2)   The second and subsequent seats for the Assembly electoral region are to be allocated to the party or individual candidate with the highest electoral region figure after any recalculation required by subsection (3) has been carried out.

(3)   This subsection requires a recalculation under paragraph (b) of section 8(3) in relation to a party
   (a)   for the first application of subsection (2), if the application of subsection (1) resulted in the allocation of an Assembly seat to the party, or
   (b)   for any subsequent application of subsection (2), if the previous application of that subsection did so,
   and a recalculation is to be carried out after adding one to the aggregate mentioned in that paragraph.

(4)   An individual candidate already returned as an Assembly constituency member or Assembly regional member is to be disregarded.

(5)   Seats for the Assembly electoral region which are allocated to a party are to be filled by the persons on the party's list in the order in which they appear on the list (disregarding anyone already returned as an Assembly constituency member, including anyone whose return is void).

(6)   Once a party's list has been exhausted (by the return of persons included on it as Assembly constituency members or by the previous application of subsection (1) or (2)), the party is to be disregarded.

(7)   If (on the application of subsection (1) or any application of subsection (2)) the highest electoral region figure is the electoral region figure of two or more parties or individual candidates, the subsection applies to each of them.

(8)   However, if subsection (7) would mean that more than the full number of seats for the Assembly electoral region were allocated, subsection (1) or (2) does not apply until
   (a)   a recalculation has been carried out under section 8(3)(b) after adding one to the number of votes given for each party with that electoral region figure, and
   (b)   one has been added to the number of votes given for each individual candidate with that electoral region figure.

(9)   If, after that, the highest electoral region figure is still the electoral region figure of two or more parties or individual candidates, the regional returning officer must decide between them by lots.

NOTES

Defined terms
   Assembly electoral region: s 2(2), (3)
   Assembly regional members: s 1(2)(b)
   electoral region figure: s 8(5)

regional returning officer: s 7(7)

Vacancies

Constituency vacancies

10(1)   This section applies if the seat of an Assembly constituency member returned for an Assembly constituency is vacant.

(2)   Subject to subsection (7), an election must be held in the Assembly constituency to fill the vacancy.

(3)   At the election, each person entitled to vote only has a constituency vote; and the Assembly constituency member for the Assembly constituency is to be returned under the simple majority system.

(4) The date of the poll at the election must be fixed by the Presiding Officer.

(5) The date must fall within the period of three months beginning with the occurrence of the vacancy.

(6) But if the vacancy does not come to the Presiding Officer's notice within the period of one month beginning with its occurrence, the date must fall within the period of three months beginning when it does come to the Presiding Officer's notice.

(7) The election must not be held if it appears to the Presiding Officer that the latest date which may be fixed for the poll would fall within the period of three months ending with the day on which the poll at the next ordinary general election would be held (disregarding section 4).

(8) The standing orders must make provision for determining the date on which a vacancy occurs for the purposes of this section.

(9) A person may not be a candidate in an election to fill a vacancy if the person is
- (a) an Assembly member, or
- (b) a candidate in another such election.

NOTES

Defined terms

Assembly constituency: s 2(1)
Assembly constituency member: s 1(2)(a)
Assembly members: s 1(3)
constituency vote: s 6(2)
the Presiding Officer: s 25(1)(a)
the standing orders: s 31(1)

Electoral region vacancies

11(1) This section applies if the seat of an Assembly regional member returned for an Assembly electoral region is vacant.

(2) If the Assembly regional member was returned (under section 9 or this section) from the list of a registered political party, the regional returning officer must notify to the Presiding Officer the name of the person who is to fill the vacancy.

(3) A person's name may only be so notified if the person
- (a) is included on the list submitted by the registered political party for the last general election,
- (b) is willing to serve as an Assembly regional member for the Assembly electoral region, and
- (c) is not a person to whom subsection (4) applies.

(4) This subsection applies to a person if
- (a) the person is not a member of the registered political party, and
- (b) the registered political party gives notice to the regional returning officer that the person's name is not to be notified to the Presiding Officer as the name of the person who is to fill the vacancy.

(5) But if there is more than one person who satisfies the conditions in subsection (3), the regional returning officer may only notify the name of whichever of them was the higher, or the highest, on that list.

(6) A person whose name is notified under subsection (2) is to be treated as having been declared to be returned as an Assembly regional member for the Assembly electoral region on the day on which notification of the person's name is received by the Presiding Officer.

(7) The seat remains vacant until the next general election
- (a) if the Assembly regional member was returned as an individual candidate, or
- (b) if that Assembly regional member was returned from the list of a registered political party but there is noone who satisfies the conditions in subsection (3).

(8)   For the purposes of this section, a person included on the list submitted by a registered political party for the last general election who

    (a)   was returned as an Assembly member at that election (even if the return was void), or

    (b)   has subsequently been returned under section 10 or this section (even if the return was void),

is treated on and after the return of the person as not having been included on the list.

NOTES
Defined terms
  Assembly electoral region: s 2(2), (3)
  Assembly regional members: s 1(2)(b)
  the Presiding Officer: s 25(1)(a)

registered political party: s 6(6)

Franchise and conduct of elections

Entitlement to vote

12(1)   The persons entitled to vote at an election of Assembly members (or of an Assembly member) in an Assembly constituency are those who on the day of the poll

    (a)   would be entitled to vote as electors at a local government election in an electoral area wholly or partly included in the Assembly constituency, and

    (b)   are registered in the register of local government electors at an address within the Assembly constituency.

(2)   But a person is not entitled as an elector

    (a)   to cast more than one constituency vote, or more than one electoral region vote, in the same Assembly constituency at any general election,

    (b)   to vote in more than one Assembly constituency at any general election, or

    (c)   to cast more than one vote in any election held under section 10.

NOTES
Defined terms
  Assembly constituency: s 2(1)
  Assembly members: s 1(3)
  constituency vote: s 6(2)

electoral region vote: s 6(3)

Power to make provision about elections etc

13(1)   The Secretary of State may by order make provision as to

    (a)   the conduct of elections for the return of Assembly members,

    (b)   the questioning of an election for the return of Assembly members and the consequences of irregularities, and

    (c)   the return of an Assembly member otherwise than at an election.

(2)   The provision which may be made under subsection (1)(a) includes, in particular, provision

    (a)   about the registration of electors,

    (b)   for disregarding alterations in a register of electors,

    (c)   about the limitation of the election expenses of candidates (and the creation of criminal offences in connection with the limitation of such expenses),

    (d)   for the combination of polls at elections for the return of Assembly members and other elections, and

    (e)   for modifying the operation of sections 6 and 8(2) in a case where the poll at an election for the return of the Assembly constituency member for an Assembly constituency is abandoned (or notice of it is countermanded).

(3)   The provision that may be made under subsection (1)(c) includes, in particular, provision making modifications to section 11(3) to (5).

(4)   An order under this section may

(a) apply or incorporate, with or without modifications or exceptions, any provision of or made under the election enactments,

(b) modify any form contained in, or in regulations or rules made under, the Representation of the People Acts so far as may be necessary to enable it to be used both for the original purpose and in relation to elections for the return of Assembly members, and

(c) so far as may be necessary in consequence of any provision made by this Act or an order under this section, make modifications of any provision made by or under any enactment relating to the registration of parliamentary electors or local government electors.

(5) In subsection (4)(a) "the election enactments" means

(a) the Representation of the People Acts,

(b) the Political Parties, Elections and Referendums Act 2000 (c 41),

(c) the European Parliamentary Elections Act 2002 (c 24), and

(d) any other enactments relating to parliamentary elections, European Parliamentary elections or local government elections.

(6) No return of an Assembly member at an election may be questioned except by an election petition under the provisions of Part 3 of the Representation of the People Act 1983 (c 2) as applied by or incorporated in an order under this section.

(7) No order is to be made under this section unless a draft of the statutory instrument containing it has been laid before, and approved by a resolution of, each House of Parliament.

NOTES

Subordinate Legislation
National Assembly for Wales (Representation of the People) (Amendment) Order 2010, SI 2010/2931.
National Assembly for Wales (Representation of the People) (Fresh Signatures for Absent Voters) Order 2013, SI 2013/1514.

Defined terms
Assembly constituency: s 2(1)
Assembly constituency member: s 1(2)(a)
Assembly members: s 1(3)
enactment: s 158(1)
modifications: s 158(1)

Duration of membership

Term of office of Assembly members

14 The term of office of an Assembly member

(a) begins when the Assembly member is declared to be returned, and

(b) ends with the dissolution of the Assembly.

NOTES

Defined terms
the Assembly: s 1(1)
Assembly members: s 1(3)

Resignation of members

15 An Assembly member may at any time resign by giving notice in writing to the Presiding Officer.

NOTES

Defined terms
Assembly members: s 1(3)
the Presiding Officer: s 25(1)(a)

Disqualification

Disqualification from being Assembly member

16(1) A person is disqualified from being an Assembly member if that person (za) is a member of the House of Commons (but see sections 17A and 17B),

(a) is disqualified from being a member of the House of Commons under paragraphs (a) to (e) of section 1(1) of the House of Commons Disqualification Act 1975 (c 24) (judges, civil servants, members of the armed forces, members of police forces and members of foreign legislatures),

(b) holds any of the offices for the time being designated by Order in Council as offices disqualifying persons from being Assembly members,

(c) holds the office of Auditor General,

(d) holds the office of Public Services Ombudsman for Wales, or

(e) is employed as a member of the staff of the Assembly.

(2) Subject to section 17(1) and (2), a person is also disqualified from being an Assembly member if that person is disqualified otherwise than under the House of Commons Disqualification Act 1975 (c 24) (either generally or in relation to a particular constituency) from being a member of the House of Commons or from sitting and voting in it.

(3) For the purposes of subsection (2) the references to the Republic of Ireland in section 1 of the Representation of the People Act 1981 (c 34) (disqualification of offenders detained in, or unlawfully at large from detention in, the British Islands or the Republic of Ireland) are to be treated as references to any member State (other than the United Kingdom).

(4) A person who holds office as lord-lieutenant, lieutenant or high sheriff of any area in Wales is disqualified from being an Assembly member for any Assembly constituency or Assembly electoral region wholly or partly included in that area.

(5) An Order in Council under paragraph (b) of subsection (1)

(a) may designate particular offices or offices of any description, and

(b) may designate an office by reference to any characteristic of a person holding it,

and in that paragraph and this subsection "office" includes any post or employment.

(6) No recommendation is to be made to Her Majesty in Council to make an Order in Council under subsection (1)(b) unless a draft of the statutory instrument containing the Order in Council has been laid before, and approved by a resolution of, the Assembly.

NOTES

Subordinate legislation
National Assembly for Wales (Disqualification) Order 2015, SI 2015/1536

Defined terms
Assembly constituency: s 2(1)
Assembly electoral region: s 2(2), (3)

Assembly members: s 1(3)
the Auditor General: s 145(1)
member of the staff of the Assembly: Sch 2, para 3(2)
Wales: s 158(1), (3), (4)

Exceptions and relief from disqualification

17(1) A person is not disqualified from being an Assembly member merely because that person is

(a) a peer (whether of the United Kingdom, Great Britain, England or Scotland), or

(b) a Lord Spiritual.

(2) A citizen of the European Union who is resident in the United Kingdom is not disqualified from being an Assembly member merely because of section 3 of the Act of Settlement (1700 c 2) (disqualification of certain persons born outside United Kingdom).

(3) The Assembly may resolve that the disqualification of any person who was, or is alleged to have been, disqualified from being an Assembly member on a ground within section 16(1) or (4) is to be disregarded if it appears to the Assembly

(a) that the ground has been removed, and

(b) that it is proper so to resolve.

(4) A resolution under subsection (3) does not

(a) affect any proceedings under Part 3 of the Representation of the People Act 1983 (c 2) as applied by or incorporated in an order under section 13, or

(b) enable the Assembly to disregard any disqualification which has been established in such proceedings or in proceedings under section 19.

NOTES
Defined terms
  the Assembly: s 1(1)
  Assembly members: s 1(3)

Exception from disqualification by virtue of being an MP: recently elected members

17A(1) A person returned at an election as an Assembly member is not disqualified under section 16(1)(za) (disqualification by virtue of being an MP) at any time in the period of 8 days beginning with the day the person is so returned.

(2) Subsection (3) applies where a person
  (a) is returned at an election as an Assembly member,
  (b) on being so returned is a candidate for election to the House of Commons, and
  (c) is subsequently returned at that election as a member of that House.

(3) The person is not disqualified under section 16(1)(za) at any time in the period of 8 days beginning with the day the person is returned as a member of the House of Commons.

(4) A person is a "candidate for election to the House of Commons" if the person's nomination paper for election as a member of the House of Commons has been delivered to the returning officer under rule 6 of Schedule 1 to the Representation of the People Act 1983 (parliamentary election rules).

Exception from disqualification by virtue of being an MP: general election of Assembly members within 372 days

17B(1) This section applies if
  (a) an Assembly member is returned as a member of the House of Commons, and
  (b) the expected day of the next general election of Assembly members is within the period of 372 days beginning with the day the person is so returned ("the return day").

(2) The member is not disqualified under section 16(1)(za) (disqualification by virtue of being an MP) at any time in the period
  (a) beginning with the return day, and
  (b) ending immediately before the day of the next general election of Assembly members.

(3) For the purposes of subsection (1)(b) the expected day of the next general election of Assembly members is to be determined by reference to the circumstances as at the beginning of the return day ("the relevant time").

(4) Where, at the relevant time, section 5(2) or (3) (extraordinary general elections) applies
  (a) if an Order in Council under section 5(4) has been made, the expected day is the day on which the poll is required to be held in accordance with that Order;
  (b) if no Order in Council under section 5(4) has been made but a day has been proposed under section 5(1), that is the expected day;
  (c) otherwise, the expected day is to be treated as being within the period mentioned in subsection (1)(b).

(5) For the purpose of determining the expected day, no account is to be taken of the possibility of
  (a) an order under section 4 (power to vary date of ordinary general election) being made after the relevant time, or
  (b) section 5(2) or (3) (extraordinary general elections) first applying after that time.

(6)   References in this section to the "day" of the election are to the day on which the poll at the election is held.

Effect of disqualification

18(1)   If a person who is disqualified from being an Assembly member is returned as an Assembly member, the person's return is void and the person's seat is vacant.

(2)   If a person who is disqualified from being an Assembly member for a particular Assembly constituency or Assembly electoral region is returned as an Assembly member for that Assembly constituency or Assembly electoral region, the person's return is void and the person's seat is vacant.

(3)   If a person who is an Assembly member becomes disqualified
    (a)   from being an Assembly member, or
    (b)   from being an Assembly member for the Assembly constituency or Assembly electoral region for which the person is sitting,
the person ceases to be an Assembly member (so that the person's seat is vacant).

(4)   Subsections (1) to (3) have effect subject to any resolution of the Assembly under section 17(3).

(5)   In addition, subsection (3) has effect subject to
    (a)   *repealed*
    (b)   section 427 of the Insolvency Act 1986 (c 45) (bankruptcy etc).

(6)   If, in consequence of the provision mentioned in subsection (5), the seat of a person who is disqualified from being an Assembly member is not vacant, the person does not cease to be an Assembly member until the person's seat becomes vacant.

(7)   But for any period for which the person is disqualified but the person's seat is not vacant
    (a)   the person must not participate in any Assembly proceedings, and
    (b)   any of the person's other rights and privileges as an Assembly member may be withdrawn by the Assembly.

(8)   The validity of any Assembly proceedings is not affected by the disqualification of any person
    (a)   from being an Assembly member, or
    (b)   from being an Assembly member for the Assembly constituency or Assembly electoral region for which the person purports to sit.

NOTES

Defined terms
the Assembly: s 1(1)
Assembly constituency: s 2(1)
Assembly electoral region: s 2(2), (3)

Assembly members: s 1(3)
Assembly proceedings: s 1(5)

Judicial proceedings as to disqualification

19(1)   Any person who claims that a person purporting to be an Assembly member is, or at any time since being returned as an Assembly member has been, disqualified from being
    (a)   an Assembly member, or
    (b)   an Assembly member for the Assembly constituency or Assembly electoral region for which the person purports to sit,
may apply to the High Court for a declaration to that effect.

(2)   An application under subsection (1) in respect of any person may be made whether the grounds on which it is made are alleged to have subsisted at the time when the person was returned or to have arisen subsequently.

(3)   No declaration may be made under this section in respect of any person

    (a) on grounds which subsisted when the person was returned, if an election petition is pending or has been tried in which the person's disqualification on those grounds is or was in issue, or

    (b) on any ground, if a resolution of the Assembly under section 17(3) requires that any disqualification incurred by the person on that ground is to be disregarded.

(4)   On an application under this section

    (a) the person in respect of whom the application is made is to be the respondent, and

    (b) the applicant must give such security for the costs of the proceedings as the court may direct.

(5)   The amount of the security may not exceed £5,000 or such other sum as the Welsh Ministers may specify by order.

(6)   The decision of the court on an application under this section is final.

(7)   A statutory instrument containing an order under subsection (5) is subject to annulment in pursuance of a resolution of the Assembly.

NOTES

Defined terms
the Assembly: s 1(1)
Assembly constituency: s 2(1)
Assembly electoral region: s 2(2), (3)

Assembly members: s 1(3)
the Welsh Ministers: s 45(2)

20-63   *Not reproduced*

Polls for ascertaining views of the public

64(1)   The Welsh Ministers may hold a poll in an area consisting of Wales or any part (or parts) of Wales for the purpose of ascertaining the views of those polled about whether or how any of the functions of the Welsh Ministers (other than that under section 62) should be exercised.

(2)   The persons entitled to vote in a poll under this section are those who

    (a) would be entitled to vote as electors at a local government election in an electoral area wholly or partly included in the area in which the poll is held, and

    (b) are registered in the register of local government electors at an address within the area in which the poll is held.

(3)   The Welsh Ministers may by order make provision

    (a) as to the conduct of polls (or any poll) under this section, or

    (b) for the combination of polls (or any poll) under this section with polls at any elections.

(4)   An order under subsection (3) may apply or incorporate, with or without modifications or exceptions, any provision of or made under any enactment relating to elections or referendums; and the provision which may be made under paragraph (a) of that subsection includes, in particular, provision for disregarding alterations in a register of electors.

(5)   A statutory instrument containing an order under subsection (3) is subject to annulment in pursuance of a resolution of the Assembly.

NOTES

Defined terms
the Assembly: s 1(1)
enactment: s 158(1)
function: s 158(1)
modifications: s 158(1)

Wales: s 158(1), (3), (4) (and see also the note to s 1)
the Welsh Ministers: s 45(2)

65-157   *Not reproduced*

Interpretation

158(1)   In this Act (except where the context otherwise requires)
        "EU law" means
                (a)   all the rights, powers, liabilities, obligations and restrictions from time to time created or arising by or under the EU Treaties, and
                (b)   all the remedies and procedures from time to time provided for by or under the EU Treaties,
        "the Convention rights" has the same meaning as in the Human Rights Act 1998 (c 42),
        "cross-border body" means any body (including a government department) or undertaker exercising functions, or carrying on activities, in or with respect to Wales (or any part of Wales) and anywhere else,
        "enactment" includes an Assembly Measure, an Act of the Assembly and subordinate legislation (but see also subsection (2)),
        "English border area" means a part of England adjoining Wales (but not the whole of England),
        "financial year" means the twelve months ending with 31st March,
        "function" means power or duty,
        "government department" means any department of the Government of the United Kingdom,
        "international obligations" means any international obligations of the United Kingdom other than obligations to observe and implement EU law or the Convention rights,
        "Minister of the Crown" includes the Treasury,
        "modifications" includes amendments, repeals and revocations,
        "subordinate legislation" has the same meaning as in the Interpretation Act 1978 (c 30) (including an instrument made under an Assembly Measure or Act of the Assembly),
        "tribunal" means any tribunal in which legal proceedings may be brought,
        "Wales" includes the sea adjacent to Wales out as far as the seaward boundary of the territorial sea, and
        "Welsh zone" means the sea adjacent to Wales which is
                (a)   within British fishery limits (that is, the limits set by or under section 1 of the Fishery Limits Act 1976), and
                (b)   specified in an Order in Council under section 58 or an order under subsection (3).

(2)-(6)   *Not reproduced*

59-166   *Not reproduced*

SCHEDULES

Not reproduced

Greater London Authority Act 1999

An Act to establish and make provision about the Greater London Authority, the Mayor of London and the London Assembly; to make provision in relation to London borough councils and the Common Council of the City of London with respect to matters consequential on the establishment of the Greater London Authority; to make provision with respect to the functions of other local authorities and statutory bodies exercising functions in Greater London; to make provision about transport and road traffic in and around Greater London; to make provision about policing in Greater London and to make an adjustment of the metropolitan police district; and for connected purposes.

11th November 1999

PART I

THE GREATER LONDON AUTHORITY

PART I
THE GREATER LONDON AUTHORITY

The Authority

The Authority

1(1)   There shall be an authority for Greater London, to be known as the Greater London Authority.

(2)   The Authority shall be a body corporate.

(3)   The Authority shall have the functions which are transferred to, or conferred or imposed on, the Authority by or under this Act or any other Act.

NOTES
Defined terms
   the Authority: s 424(1)

Membership

Membership of the Authority and the Assembly

2(1)   The Authority shall consist of
   (a)   the Mayor of London; and
   (b)   an Assembly for London, to be known as the London Assembly.

(2)   The Assembly shall consist of twenty five members, of whom
   (a)   fourteen shall be members for Assembly constituencies ("constituency members"); and
   (b)   eleven shall be members for the whole of Greater London ("London members").

(3)   There shall be one constituency member for each Assembly constituency.

(4)   The Assembly constituencies shall be the areas, and shall be known by the names, specified in an order made by statutory instrument by the Local Government Boundary Commission for England.

(5)   Schedule 1 to this Act (which makes further provision about Assembly constituencies and orders under subsection (4) above) shall have effect.

(6)   The Mayor and the Assembly members shall be returned in accordance with the provision made in or by virtue of this Act for
   (a)   the holding of ordinary elections of the Mayor, the constituency members and the London members; and
   (b)   the filling of vacancies in the office of Mayor or among the constituency members or the London members.

(7)   An ordinary election involves the holding of
   (a)   an election for the return of the Mayor;
   (b)   an election for the return of the London members; and
   (c)   elections for the return of the constituency members.

(8)   The term of office of the Mayor and Assembly members returned at an ordinary election shall
   (a)   begin on the second day after the day on which the last of the successful candidates at the ordinary election is declared to be returned; and
   (b)   end on the second day after the day on which the last of the successful candidates at the next ordinary election is declared to be returned;

but this subsection is subject to the other provisions of this Act and, in particular, to any provision made by order by virtue of subsection (4) of section 3 below.

(9) If at any ordinary election the poll at the election of an Assembly member for an Assembly constituency is countermanded or abandoned for any reason, the day on which the last of the successful candidates at the ordinary election is declared to be returned shall be determined for the purposes of subsection (8) above without regard to the return of the Assembly member for that Assembly constituency.

(10) The validity of proceedings of the Assembly is not affected by any vacancy in its membership.

(11) The validity of anything done by the Authority is not affected by any vacancy in the office of Mayor or any vacancy in the membership of the Assembly.

NOTES

Subordinate legislation
   Greater London Authority (Assembly Constituencies and
   Returning Officers) Order 1999, SI 1999/3380

Assembly member: s 424(1)
the Authority: s 424(1)
Mayor: s 424(1)

Defined terms
   the Assembly: s 424(1)

Ordinary elections

Time of ordinary elections

3(1) The poll at the first ordinary election shall be held on 4th May 2000 or such later date as the Secretary of State may by order provide.

(2) The poll at each subsequent ordinary election shall be held on the first Thursday in May in the fourth calendar year following that in which the previous ordinary election was held.

(3) Subsection (2) above is subject to any order made by virtue of section 37(2) or 37A of the Representation of the People Act 1983 (power by order to fix a day other than the first Thursday in May).

(4) As respects the first ordinary election, the Secretary of State may by order make provision
   (a) modifying section 2(8) above in relation to the Mayor and Assembly members returned at that election;
   (b) for the returning officer at the election of the Mayor and the election of the London members to be a person, or a person of a description, designated in the order (instead of the person specified in section 35(2C) of the Representation of the People Act 1983);
   (c) for and in connection with modifying the entitlement to vote or the registration of electors, or with respect to the registers (or parts of registers) of electors to be used;
   (d) for or in connection with enabling electors to vote in the poll at such polling stations or other places as may be prescribed, at such times as may be prescribed, on such one or more days preceding the date specified in or provided under subsection (1) above for the poll as may be specified in the order.

(5) The provision that may be made by an order under paragraph (d) of subsection (4) above includes provision for such enactments or statutory instruments as may be specified in the order to have effect with such modifications as may be so specified.

(6) In this section "prescribed" means specified in, or determined in accordance with, an order under this section.

NOTES

Subordinate legislation
   Greater London Authority Election (Early Voting) Order

2000, SI 2000/826

Defined terms
Assembly member: s 424(1)
elector: s 29
London member: ss 2(2)(b), 424(1)
Mayor: s 424(1)

ordinary election: ss 2(7), 424(1)
vote: s 29

Voting at ordinary elections

4(1) Each person entitled to vote as an elector at an ordinary election shall have the following votes
  (a) one vote (referred to in this Part as a mayoral vote) which may be given for a candidate to be the Mayor;
  (b) one vote (referred to in this Part as a constituency vote) which may be given for a candidate to be the Assembly member for the Assembly constituency; and
  (c) one vote (referred to in this Part as a London vote) which may be given in accordance with subsection (5) below.

(2) The Mayor shall be returned under the simple majority system, unless there are three or more candidates.

(3) If there are three or more candidates to be the Mayor
  (a) the Mayor shall be returned under the supplementary vote system in accordance with Part I of Schedule 2 to this Act; and
  (b) a voter's mayoral vote shall accordingly be a supplementary vote, that is to say, a vote capable of being given to indicate the voter's first and second preferences from among the candidates.

(4) The Assembly member for an Assembly constituency shall be returned under the simple majority system.

(5) A London vote may be given for
  (a) a registered political party which has submitted a list of candidates to be London members; or
  (b) an individual who is a candidate to be a London member.

(6) The London members shall be returned in accordance with Part II of Schedule 2 to this Act.

(7) The persons who are to be returned as
  (a) the Mayor, and
  (b) the constituency members,
  must be determined before it is determined who are to be returned as the London members.

(8) But if the poll at the election of an Assembly member for an Assembly constituency is countermanded or abandoned for any reason, the persons who are to be returned as the London members shall be determined without regard to the determination of the Assembly member for that Assembly constituency.

(9) At an ordinary election, a person may not be a candidate to be the Assembly member for more than one Assembly constituency.

(10) If the person who is returned as the Mayor is also returned as an Assembly member for an Assembly constituency, a vacancy shall arise in the Assembly constituency.

(11) In this Part "registered political party" means a party registered under Part II of the Political Parties, Elections and Referendums Act 2000.

NOTES
Defined terms
Assembly member: s 424(1)
constituency member: ss 2(2)(a), 424(1)
elector: s 29
London member: ss 2(2)(b), 424(1)

Mayor: s 424(1)
ordinary election: ss 2(7), 424(1)
vote: s 29
voter: s 29

Vacancies in the Assembly

Resignation

5(1) An Assembly member may at any time resign his membership of the Assembly by giving notice to the proper officer of the Authority.

(2) Any such resignation shall take effect on the officer's receipt of the notice.

NOTES

Defined terms
  the Assembly: s 424(1)
  Assembly member: s 424(1)
  the Authority: s 424(1)

notice: s 424(1)
proper officer: s 424(1), (2)

Failure to attend meetings

6(1) If an Assembly member fails, throughout a period of six consecutive months from his last attendance, to attend any meeting of the Assembly, he shall cease to be a member of the Assembly.

(2) A person shall not cease to be a member by virtue of subsection (1) above if the failure to attend is due to some reason approved by the Assembly before the expiry of that period.

(3) For the purposes of this section, an Assembly member shall be deemed to have attended a meeting of the Assembly on any occasion on which he attended

    (a) as a member at a meeting of any committee or subcommittee of the Assembly; or

    (b) as a representative of the Assembly or the Authority at a meeting of any body of persons.

(4) A person shall not cease to be a member of the Assembly by reason only of a failure to attend meetings of the Assembly if

    (a) he is a member of any branch of Her Majesty's naval, military or air forces and is at the time employed during war or any emergency on any naval, military or air force service, or

    (b) he is a person whose employment in the service of Her Majesty in connection with war or any emergency is such as, in the opinion of the Secretary of State, to entitle him to relief from disqualification on account of absence,

and the failure to attend is due to that employment.

(5) Any period during which an Assembly member is suspended or partially suspended under section 66, 73, 78 or 79 of the Local Government Act 2000 shall be disregarded for the purpose of calculating the period of six consecutive months under subsection (1).

NOTES

Defined terms
  the Assembly: s 424(1)
  Assembly member: s 424(1)

the Authority: s 424(1)

Declaration of vacancy in certain cases

7 Where an Assembly member

    (a) ceases to be qualified to be a member of the Assembly, or

    (b) becomes disqualified from being a member otherwise than

        (i) *Repealed*

        (ia) under section 34 of the Localism Act 2011,

        (ii) by virtue of a conviction, or

        (iii) by virtue of a breach of any provision of Part II of the Representation of the People Act 1983, or

    (c) ceases to be a member of the Assembly by reason of failure to attend meetings of the Assembly, the proper officer of the Authority shall forthwith declare the member's office to be vacant, unless it has been declared vacant by the High Court.

NOTES

Defined terms
the Assembly: s 424(1)
Assembly member: s 424(1)
the Authority: s 424(1)

proper officer: s 424(1), (2)

Election of member as Mayor

8   If the person who is returned at an election under section 16 below to fill a vacancy in the office of Mayor is an Assembly member, a vacancy shall arise

(a)   if he is a member for an Assembly constituency, in that Assembly constituency; or

(b)   if he is a London member, in his office as a London member.

NOTES

Defined terms
Assembly member: s 424(1)
London member: ss 2(2)(b), 424(1)

Mayor: s 424(1)

Date of casual vacancies

9(1)   For the purpose of filling a casual vacancy in the membership of the Assembly, the date on which a vacancy is to be regarded as occurring shall be

(a)   in the case of any person being returned

(i)   at an ordinary election, as the Mayor and also as the Assembly member for an Assembly constituency, or

(ii)   at an election under section 16 below to fill a vacancy in the office of Mayor when he is an Assembly member,

on the date on which he is returned as the Mayor or, as the case may be, to fill the vacancy in that office;

(b)   in the case of any person being returned as mentioned in section 16(10) below, on the date on which he is returned to fill the vacancy in the Assembly constituency;

(c)   in the case of nonacceptance of office by any person who is required to make and deliver a declaration of acceptance of office, on the expiration of the period appointed under this Part of this Act for the delivery of the declaration;

(d)   in the case of resignation, upon the receipt of the notice of resignation by the proper officer of the Authority;

(e)   in the case of death, on the date of death;

(f)   in the case of disqualification under section 34 of the Localism Act 2011 or by virtue of a conviction

(i)   on the expiration of the ordinary period allowed for making an appeal or application with respect to the relevant order or decision under that section or (as the case may be) that conviction, or

(ii)   if an appeal or application is made, on the date on which that appeal or application is finally disposed of or abandoned or fails by reason of its non-prosecution;

(g)   in the case of an election being declared void on an election petition, on the date of the report or certificate of the election court;

(h)   in the case of a person

(i)   ceasing to be qualified to be an Assembly member, or becoming disqualified, for any reason other than one mentioned in paragraphs (a) to (g) above, or

(ii)   ceasing to be an Assembly member by reason of failure to attend meetings, on the date on which his office is declared to have been vacated either by the High Court or by the proper officer of the Authority as the case may be.

(2)   The proper officer of the Authority shall

    (a) give written notice of any casual vacancy among the London members to the Greater London returning officer; and

    (b) give public notice of any casual vacancy among the constituency members.

(3) Any public notice under subsection (2)(b) above shall be given

    (a) by posting the notice in some conspicuous place or places in the Assembly constituency concerned; and

    (b) in such other manner, if any, as the officer considers desirable for giving publicity to the notice.

(4) Any notice under subsection (2) above shall be given as soon as practicable after the date on which the vacancy is to be regarded under subsection (1) above as occurring.

NOTES

Defined terms

the Assembly: s 424(1)	Mayor: s 424(1)
Assembly member: s 424(1)	notice: s 424(1)
the Authority: s 424(1)	ordinary election: ss 2(7), 424(1)
constituency member: ss 2(2)(a), 424(1)	proper officer: s 424(1), (2)
Greater London returning officer: s 29	
London member: ss 2(2)(b), 424(1)	

Filling a vacancy in an Assembly constituency

10(1) This section applies where the office of an Assembly member returned for an Assembly constituency is vacant.

(2) Subject to subsection (8) below, an election shall be held in the Assembly to fill the vacancy.

(3) At the election to fill the vacancy

    (a) each person entitled to vote at the election shall have a constituency vote; and

    (b) the Assembly member for the Assembly constituency shall be returned under the simple majority system.

(4) The date of the poll at the election shall be fixed by the constituency returning officer in accordance with subsection (5) below.

(5) The date fixed shall be no later than 35 days after the date of the relevant event.

(6) In subsection (5) above, "the relevant event" means

    (a) in a case where the High Court or the proper officer of the Authority has declared the office to be vacant, the making of that declaration; or

    (b) in any other case, the giving of notice of the vacancy to the proper officer of the Authority by two or more local government electors for the Assembly constituency concerned.

(7) Section 243(4) of the Local Government Act 1972 shall apply for the purpose of computing the period of 35 days referred to in subsection (5) above as it applies for the purposes of section 89(1) of that Act.

(8) If the vacancy occurs within the period of six months preceding an ordinary election, it shall be left unfilled until that election unless subsection (9) below applies.

(9) This subsection applies if, on the occurrence of the vacancy (or, in the case of a number of simultaneous vacancies, the occurrence of the vacancies) the total number of unfilled vacancies in the membership of the Assembly exceeds onethird of the whole number of Assembly members.

(10) A person may not be a candidate at an election to fill a vacancy if he is

    (a) the Mayor;

    (b) an Assembly member; or

    (c) a candidate in another such election.

(11) The term of office of the person returned at the election

(a) shall begin immediately upon his being declared to be returned as the constituency member; and

(b) shall end at the time when it would have ended had he been returned as the constituency member at the previous ordinary election.

NOTES

Defined terms

the Assembly: s 424(1)

Assembly member: s 424(1)

the Authority: s 424(1)

constituency member: ss 2(2)(a), 424(1)

constituency returning officer: s 29

constituency vote: ss 4(1)(b), 29

local government elector: s 29

Mayor: s 424(1)

notice: s 424(1)

ordinary election: ss 2(7), 424(1)

proper officer: s 424(1), (2)

vote: s 29

Filling a vacancy among the London members

11(1) This section applies where the office of a London member is vacant.

(2) If the London member was returned as an individual candidate, or the vacancy is not filled in accordance with the following provisions, the vacancy shall remain unfilled until the next ordinary election.

(3) If the London member was returned (under Part II of Schedule 2 to this Act or this section) from a registered political party's list, the Greater London returning officer shall notify the Chair of the Assembly of the name of the person who is to fill the vacancy.

(4) The person who is to fill the vacancy must be one who

(a) is included in that list;

(b) is willing to serve as a London member; and

(c) is not a person to whom subsection (5) below applies.

(5) This subsection applies to a person if

(a) he is not a member of the party; and

(b) the party gives notice to the Greater London returning officer that his name is not to be notified under subsection (3) above as the name of the person who is to fill the vacancy.

(6) Where more than one person satisfies the conditions in subsection (4) above, the Greater London returning officer shall notify the name of whichever of them is higher, or highest, in the list.

(7) Where a person's name has been notified under subsection (3) above, his term of office as a London member

(a) shall begin on the day on which the notification is received under that subsection, and

(b) shall end at the time when it would have ended had he been returned as a London member at the previous ordinary election,

and this Act shall apply as if the person had been declared to be returned as a London member on the day on which the notification under subsection (3) above is so received.

NOTES

Defined terms

the Chair of the Assembly: s 50(1)

Greater London returning officer: s 29

London member: ss 2(2)(b), 424(1)

notify: s 424(1)

ordinary election: ss 2(7), 424(1)

registered political party: ss 4(11), 29

Vacancy in the office of Mayor

Resignation

12(1)   The Mayor may at any time resign his office by giving notice to the proper officer of the Authority.

(2)   Any such resignation shall take effect on the officer's receipt of the notice.

NOTES

Defined terms
   the Authority: s 424(1)
   Mayor: s 424(1)
   notice: s 424(1)

proper officer: s 424(1), (2)

Failure to attend meetings

13(1)   If the Mayor fails on six consecutive occasions to attend meetings of the Assembly held pursuant to section 52(3) below, he shall cease to be the Mayor.

(2)   Any meeting of the Assembly which the Mayor is unable to attend because he is suspended or partially suspended under section 66, 73, 78 or 79 of the Local Government Act 2000 shall be disregarded for the purposes of subsection (1) above.

NOTES

Defined terms
   the Assembly: s 424(1)
   Mayor: s 424(1)

Declaration of vacancy in certain cases

14   Where the Mayor
   (a)   ceases to be qualified to be the Mayor,
   (b)   becomes disqualified from being the Mayor otherwise than
      (i)   *Repealed*
      (ia)   under section 34 of the Localism Act 2011,
      (ii)   by virtue of a conviction, or
      (iii)   by virtue of a breach of any provision of Part II of the Representation of the People Act 1983, or
   (c)   ceases to be the Mayor by reason of failure to attend meetings of the Assembly,
the proper officer of the Authority shall forthwith declare his office to be vacant, unless it has been declared vacant by the High Court.

NOTES

Defined terms
   the Assembly: s 424(1)
   the Authority: s 424(1)
   Mayor: s 424(1)

proper officer: s 424(1), (2)

Date of casual vacancy

15(1)   Subsection (1) of section 9 above shall apply for the purpose of filling a casual vacancy in the office of Mayor as it applies for the purpose of filling a casual vacancy in the membership of the Assembly, but with the omission of paragraphs (a) and (b) and the substitution for paragraph (h) of
   "(h)   in the case of a person
      (i)   ceasing to be qualified to be the Mayor, or becoming disqualified, for any reason other than one mentioned in paragraphs (c) to (g) above, or
      (ii)   ceasing to be the Mayor by reason of failure to attend meetings of the Assembly,
   on the date on which his office is declared to have been vacated either by the High Court or by the proper officer of the Authority, as the case may be."

(2)   If a casual vacancy arises in the office of Mayor, the proper officer of the Authority shall give
   (a)   notice of the vacancy to the Greater London returning officer; and

(b) public notice of the vacancy in every Assembly constituency.

(3) Any public notice under subsection (2)(b) above shall be given

    (a) by posting the notice in some conspicuous place or places in each Assembly constituency; and

    (b) in such other manner, if any, as the officer considers desirable for giving publicity to the notice.

(4) Any notice under subsection (2) above shall be given as soon as practicable after the date on which the vacancy is to be regarded by virtue of subsection (1) above as occurring.

NOTES

Defined terms
  the Assembly: s 424(1)
  the Authority: s 424(1)
  Greater London returning officer: s 29
  Mayor: s 424(1)

notice: s 424(1)
proper officer: s 424(1), (2)

Filling a vacancy

16(1) This section applies where a vacancy occurs in the office of the Mayor.

(2) Subject to subsection (9) below, an election shall be held to fill the vacancy.

(3) At the election, each person entitled to vote as an elector at the election shall have a mayoral vote.

(4) Subsections (2) and (3) of section 4 above and Part I of Schedule 2 to this Act shall apply in relation to the election as they apply in relation to the election of the Mayor at an ordinary election.

(5) The date of the poll at the election shall be fixed by the Greater London returning officer in accordance with subsection (6) below.

(6) The date fixed shall be no later than 35 days after the date of the relevant event.

(7) In subsection (6) above, "the relevant event" means

    (a) in a case where the High Court or the proper officer of the Authority have declared the office to be vacant, the making of that declaration; or

    (b) in any other case, the giving of notice of the vacancy to the proper officer of the Authority by two or more local government electors for Greater London.

(8) Section 243(4) of the Local Government Act 1972 shall apply for the purpose of computing the period of 35 days referred to in subsection (6) above as it applies for the purposes of section 89(1) of that Act.

(9) If the vacancy occurs within the period of six months preceding an ordinary election, it shall be left unfilled until that election.

(10) If

    (a) a person who is a candidate in an election to fill a vacancy in the office of Mayor is also a candidate in an election to fill a vacancy in an Assembly constituency, and

    (b) that person is returned in both elections, but

    (c) the circumstances are such that a vacancy does not arise in the Assembly constituency by virtue of section 8 above,

a vacancy shall arise in the Assembly constituency.

(11) The term of office of the person returned as the Mayor at the election

    (a) shall begin immediately upon his being declared to be returned as the Mayor; and

    (b) shall end at the time when it would have ended had he been returned as the Mayor at the previous ordinary election.

NOTES

Defined terms
  the Authority: s 424(1)

elector: s 29
Greater London returning officer: s 29

local government elector: s 29   proper officer: s 424(1), (2)
Mayor: s 424(1)   vote: s 29
mayoral vote: ss 4(1)(a), (3), 29
notice: s 424(1)
ordinary election: ss 2(7), 424(1)

Franchise, conduct of elections etc

Franchise, conduct of elections etc

17   Schedule 3 to this Act (which, by amending the Representation of the People Acts, makes
      provision for and in connection with treating elections under this Act as local government
      elections for the purposes of those Acts) shall have effect.

Free delivery of election addresses

17A(1) Each candidate at the first election of the Mayor shall be entitled (subject to and in
        accordance with the provisions of Schedule 3A to this Act) to have an election address
        prepared on behalf of the candidate included in a booklet of election addresses
        (a)   prepared by the Greater London returning officer; and
        (b)   sent by that officer, by post, to each elector in Greater London.

   (2) In subsection (1) above "elector", in relation to the election mentioned in that subsection
        (a)   means a person who is registered in the register of local government electors for
              an electoral area in Greater London on the last day for publication of notice of the
              election; and
        (b)   includes a person then shown in any such register (or, in the case of a person who
              has an anonymous entry in any such register, in the record of anonymous entries
              for that electoral area) as below voting age if (but only if) it appears from the
              register (or from the record) that he will be of voting age on the day fixed for the
              poll.

   (2A) In subsection (2)(b), "anonymous entry" and "record of anonymous entries" have the
         meaning given in section 202(1) of the Representation of the People Act 1983.

   (3) The Secretary of State or the Chancellor of the Duchy of Lancaster may by order make
        such provision as he considers appropriate for and in connection with enabling
        candidates
        (a)   at ordinary elections other than the first such election, or
        (b)   at elections to fill vacancies in the office of Mayor or Assembly member,
        to have their election addresses (within the meaning of the order) delivered, at the
        Authority's expense, by a universal service provider (within the meaning of Part 3 of the
        Postal Services Act 2011) or by any other means specified in the order.

   (4) Without prejudice to the generality of subsection (3) above, an order under that
        subsection may make provision
        (a)   for free delivery of election addresses to be available under the order only in the
              case of any specified description of election falling within paragraph (a) or (b) of
              that subsection or within section 2(7) above;
        (b)   for enabling the Authority to determine the descriptions of elections (if any) in the
              case of which free delivery of election addresses is to be so available;
        (c)   for regulating in any respect the form and manner in which free delivery of election
              addresses is to be so available;
        (d)   for restricting the number of separate mailings in respect of the free delivery of
              election addresses, whether
              (i)   by limiting the number of separate election addresses by reference to any
                     specified circumstances, or
              (ii)   by requiring the preparation of a single document incorporating all the
                     election addresses to be delivered on behalf of candidates at a particular
                     election,

or otherwise;

    (e) for imposing conditions which must be satisfied by any candidate or candidates seeking to avail themselves of free delivery of election addresses under the order;

    (f) for authorising election addresses falling to be delivered under the order to be disseminated by such means (other than those by which they are to be so delivered) as may be specified;

    (g) for securing that civil or criminal liability in respect of material contained in any election address falling to be delivered under the order (including any such liability arising in connection with any dissemination of the material in pursuance of paragraph (f) above) is incurred only by the candidate on behalf of whom it falls to be so delivered or his election agent.

(5) In subsection (4) above

"free delivery of election addresses" means the delivery of election addresses, in accordance with an order under subsection (3) above, at the Authority's expense;

"specified" means specified in an order under subsection (3) above.

(6) Before making an order under subsection (3) above the Secretary of State or the Chancellor of the Duchy of Lancaster shall consult

    (a) the Mayor and the London Assembly; and

    (b) such other persons and bodies as he may determine to be appropriate.

(7) Schedule 3A to this Act (which makes provision supplementing subsection (1) above) shall have effect.

NOTES

Subordinate legislation
Greater London Authority Elections (Election Addresses) Order 2003, SI 2003/1907

Greater London returning officer: s 29
local government elector: s 29
Mayor: s 424(1)
ordinary election: ss 2(7), 424(1)

Defined terms
Assembly member: s 424(1)
the Authority: s 424(1)

Cost of holding the first ordinary elections

18(1) A returning officer shall be entitled to recover expenditure properly incurred by him in relation to the holding of the first ordinary election if the expenditure

    (a) is of a kind determined by the Secretary of State; and

    (b) is reasonable.

(2) The Secretary of State may determine a maximum recoverable amount for expenditure of such description as he may determine; and the returning officer may not recover more than that amount in respect of any such expenditure.

(3) The amount of any expenditure recoverable in accordance with this section shall be charged on and paid out of the Consolidated Fund on an account being submitted to the Secretary of State; but the Secretary of State must, before payment, satisfy himself that the expenditure in the account is properly payable.

(4) A returning officer must furnish the Secretary of State with such information or documents relating to an account submitted under subsection (3) above as the Secretary of State may require.

(5) The Secretary of State must prepare an account of any sums which are issued to him out of the Consolidated Fund by virtue of this section and of his use of those sums.

(6) The account required to be prepared under subsection (5) above must be audited by such body or person as the Treasury may determine.

(7) Any exercise by the Secretary of State of his functions under subsections (1) and (2) above shall require the consent of the Treasury.

(8) This section has effect in relation to the first ordinary election instead of section 36(4B) of the Representation of the People Act 1983.

NOTES
Defined terms
    ordinary election: ss 2(7), 424(1)

Expenditure of Secretary of State in connection with holding the first ordinary election

19(1) The Secretary of State may incur expenditure in doing anything which he considers expedient
    (a) in preparation for the holding of the first ordinary election,
    (b) for the purpose of facilitating the conduct of the first ordinary election, or
    (c) otherwise in connection with the holding of the first ordinary election.

(2) The Secretary of State must not, by virtue of subsection (1) above, incur expenditure of a kind which is recoverable by a returning officer under section 18 above.

NOTES
Defined terms
    ordinary election: ss 2(7), 424(1)

Qualifications and disqualifications

Qualification to be the Mayor or an Assembly member

20(1) Subject to any disqualification by virtue of this Act or any other enactment, a person is qualified to be elected and to be the Mayor or an Assembly member if he satisfies the requirements of subsections (2) to (4) below,

(2) The person must be
    (a) a qualifying Commonwealth citizen;
    (b) a citizen of the Republic of Ireland; or
    (c) a relevant citizen of the Union.

(3) On the relevant day, the person must have attained the age of 18 years.

(4) The person must satisfy at least one of the following conditions
    (a) on the relevant day he is, and from that day continues to be, a local government elector for Greater London;
    (b) he has, during the whole of the twelve months preceding that day, occupied as owner or tenant any land or other premises in Greater London;
    (c) his principal or only place of work during that twelve months has been in Greater London;
    (d) he has during the whole of that twelve months resided in Greater London.

(5) This section applies in relation to being returned as a London member under section 11 above otherwise than at an election as it applies in relation to being elected.

(6) References in this section to election shall accordingly be construed as if a London member so returned were elected at an election on the day on which he is to be treated as returned.

(7) In the application of this section by virtue of subsection (5) above, any reference to the day on which a person is nominated as a candidate shall be taken as a reference to the day on which notification of the person's name is given under section 11(3) above by the Greater London returning officer.

(7A) For the purposes of this section, a person is a qualifying Commonwealth citizen if he is a Commonwealth citizen who either

(a) is not a person who requires leave under the Immigration Act 1971 to enter or remain in the United Kingdom, or

(b) is such a person but for the time being has (or is, by virtue of any enactment, to be treated as having) indefinite leave to remain within the meaning of that Act.

(7B) But a person is not a qualifying Commonwealth citizen by virtue of subsection (7A)(a) if he does not require leave to enter or remain in the United Kingdom by virtue only of section 8 of the Immigration Act 1971 (exceptions to requirement for leave in special cases).

(8) In this section

"citizen of the Union" shall be construed in accordance with Article 20(1) of the Treaty on the Functioning of the European Union;

"relevant citizen of the Union" means a citizen of the Union who is not

(a) a qualifying Commonwealth citizen; or

(b) a citizen of the Republic of Ireland;

"the relevant day", in relation to any candidate, means

(a) the day on which he is nominated as a candidate and also, if there is a poll, the day of the election; or

(b) if the election is not preceded by the nomination of candidates, the day of the election.

NOTES

Defined terms
  Assembly member: s 424(1)
  Greater London returning officer: s 29
  local government elector: s 29

London member: ss 2(2)(b), 424(1)
Mayor: s 424(1)

Disqualification from being the Mayor or an Assembly member

21(1) A person is disqualified from being elected or being the Mayor or an Assembly member if

(a) he is a member of staff of the Authority;

(b) he holds any of the offices or appointments for the time being designated by the Secretary of State in an order as offices or appointments disqualifying persons from being the Mayor or an Assembly member;

(c) he is the subject of a bankruptcy restrictions order or an interim bankruptcy restrictions order, or a debt relief restrictions order or interim debt relief restrictions order under Schedule 4ZB of the Insolvency Act 1986;

(d) he has within five years before the day of the election, or since his election, been convicted in the United Kingdom, the Channel Islands or the Isle of Man of any offence and has had passed on him a sentence of imprisonment (whether suspended or not) for a period of not less than three months without the option of a fine; or

(e) he is disqualified under

(i) section 85A or Part III of the Representation of the People Act 1983,

(ii) *Repealed*

from being elected or being the Mayor or an Assembly member.

(2) A paid officer of a London borough council who is employed under the direction of

(a) any of that council's committees or subcommittees the membership of which includes the Mayor or one or more persons appointed on the nomination of the Authority acting by the Mayor, or

(b) a joint committee the membership of which includes one or more members appointed on the nomination of that council and one or more members appointed on the nomination of the Authority acting by the Mayor,

(c) the executive or any committee of the executive of that council, where that council are operating executive arrangements and the membership of that executive includes the Mayor or one or more persons appointed on the nomination of the Authority acting by the Mayor, or

    (d) a member of the executive of that council, where that council are operating executive arrangements and that member is also the Mayor or a person appointed on the nomination of the Authority acting by the Mayor,

shall be disqualified from being elected or being the Mayor or an Assembly member.

(2A) In this section "executive" and "executive arrangements" have the same meaning as in Part II of the Local Government Act 2000.

(3) *Repealed*

(4) *Repealed*

(5) For the purposes of subsection (1)(d) above
    (a) the ordinary date on which the period allowed for making an appeal or application with respect to the conviction expires, or
    (b) if such an appeal or application is made, the date on which the appeal or application is finally disposed of or abandoned or fails by reason of its nonprosecution,

shall be deemed to be the date of the conviction.

(6) This section shall apply in relation to being returned as a London member under section 11 above otherwise than at an election as it applies in relation to being elected.

(7) References in this section to election shall accordingly be construed as if a London member so returned were elected at an election on the day on which he is to be treated as returned.

NOTES

  Greater London Authority (Disqualification) Order 2000, SI 2000/432

Defined terms
  Assembly member: s 424(1)

the Authority: s 424(1)
London member: ss 2(2)(b), 424(1)
Mayor: s 424(1)
member of staff: s 424(1)

22-27 *Not reproduced*

Supplementary provisions

Declaration of acceptance of office

28(1) A person elected to the office of Mayor or of an Assembly member shall not act in that office unless
    (a) he has made a declaration of acceptance of the office in a form prescribed in an order made by the Secretary of State; and
    (b) within two months from the day of the election, the declaration has been delivered to the proper officer of the Authority.

(2) If such a declaration is not made and delivered to that officer within that time, the office of the person elected shall become vacant at the expiration of that time.

(3) The declaration shall be made before
    (a) two members of the Assembly;
    (b) the proper officer of the Authority;
    (c) a justice of the peace or magistrate in the United Kingdom, the Channel Islands or the Isle of Man; or
    (d) a commissioner appointed to administer oaths in the Senior Courts.

(4) Any person before whom a declaration is authorised to be made under this section may take the declaration.

(5)   In relation to the first ordinary election, an order under section 3(4) above may make provision with respect to the making and delivery of declarations of acceptance of office in the case of the persons elected as the Mayor or Assembly members.

(6)   An order made by virtue of subsection (5) above may (in particular) make provision
    (a)   permitting declarations to be made before such person (other than those specified in subsection (3) above) as may be specified or described in the order;
    (b)   authorising any person specified or described under paragraph (a) above to take declarations;
    (c)   requiring declarations to be delivered to such person as may be specified or described in the order instead of the officer mentioned in subsection (1)(b) above; and
    (d)   requiring declarations delivered in accordance with provision made under paragraph (c) above to be transmitted to the proper officer of the Authority when one has been appointed.

(7)   No salary, and no payment towards the provision of superannuation benefits, shall be paid under this Act to or in respect of the Mayor or an Assembly member until he has complied with the requirements of subsection (1) above.

(8)   Subsection (7) above does not affect any entitlement of the Mayor or an Assembly member to payments in respect of the period before he complies with the requirements of subsection (1) above once he has complied with those requirements.

(9)   This section applies in relation to a London member returned otherwise than at an election as if he had been elected on the day on which he is to be treated as returned.

NOTES

Subordinate legislation
Greater London Authority (Declaration of Acceptance of Office) Order 2002, SI 2002/1044

Defined terms
the Assembly: s 424(1)
Assembly member: s 424(1)

the Authority: s 424(1)
London member: ss 2(2)(b), 424(1)
Mayor: s 424(1)
ordinary election: ss 2(7), 424(1)
proper officer: s 424(1), (2)

Interpretation of Part I

29   In this Part, except where the context otherwise requires
    "constituency returning officer" means the returning officer at an election of an Assembly member for an Assembly constituency (see section 35(2B) of the Representation of the People Act 1983);
    "constituency vote" has the meaning given by section 4(1)(b) above;
    "elector" has the same meaning as in the Representation of the People Act 1983 (see section 202(1) of that Act);
    "Greater London returning officer" means the person who is for the time being the proper officer of the Authority for the purposes of section 35(2C) of the Representation of the People Act 1983 (returning officer at elections of Mayor and London members);
    "local government elector" means a person registered as a local government elector in the register of electors in accordance with the provisions of the Representation of the People Acts;
    "London vote" has the meaning given by section 4(1)(c) above;
    "mayoral vote" has the meaning given by subsection (1)(a) of section 4 above (as read with subsection (3) of that section);
    "registered political party" has the meaning given by section 4(11) above;
    "vote" and "voter" have the same meaning as in the Representation of the People Act 1983 (see section 202(1) of that Act).

Interpretation

424(1)   In this Act, unless the context otherwise requires,

"advisory committee" and "advisory subcommittee", in relation to the Assembly, shall be construed in accordance with section 55(4) and (5) above;

"the Assembly" means the London Assembly (but see also section 85(3A) above);

"Assembly member" means a member of the Assembly;

"the Authority" means the Greater London Authority;

"certify" means certify in writing; and related expressions shall be construed accordingly;

"the Common Council" means the Common Council of the City of London

"company" means any body corporate;

"constituency member" shall be construed in accordance with section 2(2)(a) above;

"Deputy Health Adviser" is to be read in accordance with sections 309C and 309D above;

"financial year" means a period of twelve months ending with 31st March;

"the Fire etc Authority" has the meaning given by section 328(2);

"functional body" means

(a)   Transport for London;

(aa) a Mayoral development corporation;

(b)   *Repealed*

(c)   the Mayor's Office for Policing and Crime; or

(d)   the London Fire and Emergency Planning Authority;

....

"guidance" means guidance in writing;

"Health Adviser" is to be read in accordance with sections 309A and 309B above;

....

"local authority" has the same meaning as in the Local Government Act 1972;

"London member" shall be construed in accordance with section 2(2)(b) above;

"Mayor" means Mayor of London (but see also section 85(3A) above);

"member of staff, in relation to the Authority, means a person appointed under section 67(1) or (2), 72(1), 73(1) or 127A(1) above;

"Minister of the Crown" has the same meaning as in the Ministers of the Crown Act 1975;

....

"notice" means notice in writing;

"notify" means notify in writing;

"ordinary committee" and "ordinary subcommittee", in relation to the Assembly, shall be construed in accordance with section 55(1) above;

"ordinary election" shall be construed in accordance with section 2(7) above;

"principal council" has the same meaning as in the Local Government Act 1972;

"principal purposes", in relation to the Authority, shall be construed in accordance with section 30(2) above;

"proper officer" shall be construed in accordance with subsection (2) below;

"standing orders", in relation to the Authority, shall be construed in accordance with subsection (3) below;

"statutory functions" means functions conferred or imposed by or under any enactment;

"subordinate legislation" has the same meaning as in the Interpretation Act 1978 (see section 21(1) of that Act);

"subsidiary" has the meaning given by section 1159 of the Companies Act 2006;

"transport subsidiary's agreement" has the meaning given by section 169 above.

(2)   In this Act, and in any enactment applied by this Act, any reference to a proper officer and any reference which by virtue of this Act is to be construed as such a reference, shall in

relation to the Authority or a functional body and any purpose or area be construed as a reference to an officer appointed by the Authority or body for that purpose or area.

(3) In this Act, or any other enactment which has effect in relation to the Authority, any reference to standing orders shall, in its application in relation to the Authority, have effect as a reference to standing orders of the Authority made under and in accordance with section 36 above.

(4) Any power conferred by this Act to affect enactments by subordinate legislation is exercisable notwithstanding that those enactments consist of or include
  (a) provisions contained in Part III above;
  (b) provisions relating to the subject matter of that Part; or
  (c) provisions creating or otherwise relating to offences.

(5) In subsection (4) above "affect", in relation to any enactment, includes make
  (a) incidental, consequential, transitional, supplemental or supplementary provision or savings; or
  (b) amendments, modifications or adaptations.

SCHEDULE 1
ASSEMBLY CONSTITUENCIES AND ORDERS UNDER SECTION 2(4)

Section 2

Part I
Assembly Constituencies

Changes to Assembly constituencies

1(1) This paragraph applies where the Secretary of State makes an order under section 10 of the Local Government and Public Involvement in Health Act 2007 which includes a boundary change (within the meaning of section 8(3) of that Act) affecting a London borough.

(2) Where this paragraph applies, the Local Government Boundary Commission for England must consider whether to conduct a review of Assembly constituencies for the purpose of making recommendations as to
  (a) whether the boundary change referred to in sub-paragraph (1) requires changes to Assembly constituencies in order to comply with the rules set out in paragraph 7 below, and
  (b) if so, what those changes should be.

Comprehensive review of Assembly constituencies

2(1) The Local Government Boundary Commission for England may at any time
  (a) conduct a review of Assembly constituencies, and
  (b) make recommendations as to
    (i) the area into which Greater London should be divided to form the Assembly constituencies, and
    (ii) the name by which each Assembly constituency should be known.

(2) No recommendations may be made by the Local Government Boundary Commission for England pursuant to a review under this paragraph unless the recommendations comply with the rules set out in paragraph 7 below.

Preparation and submission of report

3(1) As soon as reasonably practicable after deciding to conduct a review under paragraph 1 or 2, the Local Government Boundary Commission for England must take such steps as it considers sufficient to secure that persons who may be interested in the review are informed of

(a) the fact that the review is to take place, and

(b) any particular matters to which the review is to relate.

(2) In conducting a review under paragraph 1 or 2 the Local Government Boundary Commission for England must

    (a) prepare and publish draft recommendations,

    (b) take such steps as its considers sufficient to secure that persons who may be interested in the recommendations are informed of them and of the period within which representations with respect to them may be made, and

    (c) take into consideration any representations made to the Commission within that period.

(3) The Local Government Boundary Commission for England may at any time before publishing draft recommendations under sub-paragraph (2)(a) consult such persons as it considers appropriate.

(4) As soon as practicable after conducting a review under paragraph 1 or 2 the Local Government Boundary Commission for England must

    (a) publish a report stating its recommendations, and

    (b) take such steps as it considers sufficient to secure that persons who may be interested in the recommendations are informed of them.

4(1) Where a report under paragraph 3 contains recommendations for changes to any Assembly constituency or the name by which any Assembly constituency is known, an order under section 2(4) may give effect to the recommendations.

(2) An order under section 2(4) may contain incidental, consequential, supplementary or transitional provision, or savings.

(3) The provision referred to in sub-paragraph (2) may include provision

    (a) applying any instrument made under an enactment, with or without modifications,

    (b) extending, excluding or amending any such instrument, or

    (c) repealing or revoking any such instrument.

(4) Where the Local Government Boundary Commission for England is satisfied that

    (a) a mistake has occurred in the preparation of an order under section 2(4), and

    (b) the mistake is such that it cannot be rectified by a subsequent order under that section by virtue of section 14 of the Interpretation Act 1978 (c 30) (implied power to amend),

the Commission may by order under section 2(4) make such provision as it thinks necessary or expedient for rectifying the mistake.

(5) In sub-paragraph (4), "mistake", in relation to an order, includes a provision contained in or omitted from the order in reliance on inaccurate or incomplete information supplied by any public body.

(6) A draft of a statutory instrument containing an order under section 2(4) is to be laid before Parliament before the instrument is made.

6 *Repealed*

The rules about Assembly constituencies

7(1) The rules referred to in paragraphs 1(2) and 2(2) above are

    1 There shall be fourteen Assembly constituencies.

    2 Each Assembly constituency shall consist of two or more entire London boroughs.

    3 A part of the boundary of each London borough contained within an Assembly constituency shall adjoin a part of the boundary of at least one other London borough contained within that constituency.

    4 No London borough shall be included in more than one Assembly constituency.

5 The electorate for an Assembly constituency shall be as near the electorate for each other Assembly constituency as is reasonably practicable.

(2) For the purposes of the rules in sub-paragraph (1) above

    (a) any reference to a London borough includes a reference to the City of London, which for this purpose shall be taken to include the Inner Temple and the Middle Temple; and

    (b) a part of a boundary which would, except for the river Thames or a tributary of the river Thames, adjoin a part of another boundary is deemed to adjoin that part of that other boundary.

Part II

Repealed

SCHEDULE 2
VOTING AT ELECTIONS

Section 4

Part I
Election of the Mayor

Application

1 This Part of this Schedule applies where there are three or more candidates to be the Mayor.

First preference vote and second preference vote

2 In this Schedule

"first preference vote" means a mayoral vote to the extent that it is given so as to indicate a voter's first preference from among the candidates to be the Mayor;

"second preference vote" means a mayoral vote to the extent that it is given so as to indicate a voter's second preference from among the candidates to be the Mayor.

Candidate with overall majority of first preference votes

3 If one of the candidates to be the Mayor receives more than half of all the first preference votes given in the Assembly constituencies that candidate shall be returned as the Mayor.

No candidate with overall majority of first preference votes

4(1) If none of the candidates to be the Mayor receives more than half of all the first preference votes given in the Assembly constituencies, the following provisions of this paragraph shall have effect.

(2) The two candidates who received the greatest number of first preference votes given in the Assembly constituencies remain in the contest.

(3) If, by reason of an equality of first preference votes, three or more candidates are qualified to remain in the contest by virtue of sub-paragraph (2) above, all of them remain in the contest.

(4) The other candidates are eliminated from the contest.

(5) The number of second preference votes given in the Assembly constituencies for each of the candidates remaining in the contest by voters who did not give their first preference vote to any of those candidates shall be ascertained.

(6) That number shall be added to the number of first preference votes given for that candidate, to give his total number of preference votes.

(7) The person who is to be returned as the Mayor is that one of the candidates remaining in the contest who has the greatest total number of preference votes.

(8) If, by reason of an equality of total number of preference votes, two or more candidates remaining in the contest each have the greatest total number of preference votes, the Greater London returning officer shall decide by lots which of them is to be returned as the Mayor.

NOTES

Defined terms

Greater London returning officer: s 29

Mayor: s 424(1)

mayoral vote: ss 4(1)(a), (3), 29

voter: s 29

Part II
Return of London Members

Party lists and individual candidates

5(1) Any registered political party may submit a list of candidates to be London members.

(2) The list is to be submitted to the Greater London returning officer.

(3) The list has effect in relation to
   (a) the ordinary election; and
   (b) any vacancies among the London members which occur after that election and before the next ordinary election.

(4) The list must not include more than twenty five persons (but may include only one).

(5) The list must not include a person
   (a) who is a candidate to be a constituency member but who is not a candidate of that party;
   (b) who is included on any other list submitted for the election of London members; or
   (c) who is an individual candidate to be a London member.

(6) A person may not be an individual candidate to be a London member if
   (a) he is included on a list submitted by a registered political party for the election of London members; or
   (b) he is a candidate of any registered political party to be the Mayor or a constituency member.

Calculation of the London figure

6(1) For each registered political party by which a list of candidates has been submitted for the election of London members
   (a) there shall be added together the number of London votes given for the party in the Assembly constituencies; and
   (b) the number arrived at under paragraph (a) above shall then be divided by the aggregate of one and the number of candidates of the party returned as constituency members.

(2) For each individual candidate to be a London member there shall be added together the number of London votes given for that candidate in the Assembly constituencies.

(3) The number arrived at
   (a) in the case of a registered political party, under sub-paragraph (1)(b) above, or
   (b) in the case of an individual candidate, under sub-paragraph (2) above,
   is referred to in this Schedule as "the London figure" for that party or individual candidate.

(4) If a person who is a candidate of a registered political party in an Assembly constituency

(a)   is returned as the Assembly member for the constituency, and

(b)   is also returned as the Mayor,

that person counts for the purposes of sub-paragraph (1)(b) above as a candidate of the party returned as a constituency member, notwithstanding that a vacancy arises in the Assembly constituency by virtue of subsection (10) of section 4 of this Act.

No seats for party etc not polling prescribed percentage of total vote

7(1)   If the number arrived at under

(a)   paragraph 6(1)(a) above, in the case of a registered political party, or

(b)   paragraph 6(2) above, in the case of an individual candidate,

is not more than 5 per cent of the total number of London votes polled by all the registered political parties and all the individual candidates at the election, none of the seats for London members shall be allocated to that party or individual candidate.

(2)   That party or candidate shall accordingly be left out of account in applying paragraph 8 below.

Return of members

8(1)   The first of the seats for London members shall be allocated to the party or individual candidate with the highest London figure.

(2)   The second and subsequent seats for London members shall be allocated to the party or individual candidate with the highest London figure after any recalculation required by sub-paragraph (3) below has been carried out.

(3)   This sub-paragraph requires a recalculation under paragraph 6(1)(b) above in relation to a party

(a)   for the first application of sub-paragraph (2) above, if the application of sub-paragraph (1) above resulted in the allocation of a seat to the party, or

(b)   for any subsequent application of sub-paragraph (2) above, if the previous application of that sub-paragraph did so;

and a recalculation shall be carried out after adding one to the aggregate mentioned in paragraph 6(1)(b) above.

(4)   An individual candidate already returned as the Mayor or as an Assembly member shall be disregarded.

(5)   Seats for London members which are allocated to a party shall be filled by the persons on the party's list in the order in which they appear on the list.

(6)   Once a party's list has been exhausted (by the return of persons included on it as constituency members or by the previous application of sub-paragraph (1) or (2) above) the party shall be disregarded.

(7)   If (on the application of sub-paragraph (1) above or any application of sub-paragraph (2) above) the highest London figure is the London figure of two or more parties or individual candidates, the sub-paragraph shall apply to each of them.

(8)   However, where sub-paragraph (7) above would mean that more than the full number of seats for London members was allocated, sub-paragraph (1) or (2) above shall not apply until

(a)   a recalculation has been carried out under paragraph 6(1)(b) above after adding one to the number of votes given for each party with that London figure, and

(b)   one has been added to the number of votes given for each individual candidate with that London figure.

(9)   If, after that, the highest London figure is still the London figure of two or more parties or individual candidates, the Greater London returning officer shall decide between them by lots.

(10) For the purposes of sub-paragraph (5) above and section 11 of this Act, a person included on a list submitted by a registered political party who is returned as the Mayor or as an Assembly member shall be treated as ceasing to be on the list (even if his return is void).

NOTES

Defined terms

Assembly member: s 424(1)
constituency member: ss 2(2)(a), 424(1)
Greater London returning officer: s 29
London member: ss 2(2)(b), 424(1)

London vote: ss 4(1)(c), 29
Mayor: s 424(1)
ordinary election: ss 2(7), 424(1)
registered political party: ss 4(11), 29
vote: s 29

House of Commons Disqualification Act 1975

An Act to consolidate certain enactments relating to disqualification for membership of the House of Commons

8th May 1975

1 Disqualification of holders of certain offices and places

(1) Subject to the provisions of this Act, a person is disqualified for membership of the House of Commons who for the time being

    (za) is a Lord Spiritual;

    (a) holds any of the judicial offices specified in Part I of Schedule 1 to this Act;

    (b) is employed in the civil service of the Crown, whether in an established capacity or not, and whether for the whole or part of his time;

    (c) is a member of any of the regular armed forces of the Crown . . .;

    (d) is a member of any police force maintained by a local policing body or a police authority;

    (da) . . .

    (e) is a member of the legislature of any country or territory outside the Commonwealth (other than Ireland); or

    (f) holds any office described in Part II or Part III of Schedule 1.

(2) A person who for the time being holds any office described in Part IV of Schedule 1 is disqualified for membership of the House of Commons for any constituency specified in relation to that office in the second column of Part IV.

(3) In this section

    "civil service of the Crown" includes the civil service of Northern Ireland, the Northern Ireland Court Service, Her Majesty's Diplomatic Service and Her Majesty's Overseas Civil Service;

    "police authority" means any police authority within the meaning of the Police Act 1996 , the Scottish Police Authority, or the Northern Ireland Policing Board; and "member" in relation to a police force means a person employed as a fulltime constable;

"regular armed forces of the Crown" means the Royal Navy, the Royal Marines, the regular army (as defined by section 374 of the Armed Forces Act 2006) or the Royal Air Force.

(4) Except as provided by this Act, a person shall not be disqualified for membership of the House of Commons by reason of his holding an office or place of profit under the Crown or any other office or place; and a person shall not be disqualified for appointment to or for holding any office or place by reason of his being a member of that House.

2 Ministerial offices

(1) Not more than ninetyfive persons being the holders of offices specified in Schedule 2 to this Act (in this section referred to as Ministerial offices) shall be entitled to sit and vote in the House of Commons at any one time.

(2) If at any time the number of members of the House of Commons who are holders of Ministerial offices exceeds the number entitled to sit and vote in that House under subsection (1) above, none except any who were both members of that House and holders of Ministerial offices before the excess occurred shall sit or vote therein until the number has been reduced, by death, resignation or otherwise, to the number entitled to sit and vote as aforesaid.

(3) A person holding a Ministerial office is not disqualified by this Act by reason of any office held by him ex officio as the holder of that Ministerial office.

3 Reserve and auxiliary forces, etc

(1) Notwithstanding section 1(1)(c) above

    (a) a person who is an officer on the retired or emergency list of any of the regular armed forces of the Crown, or who holds an emergency commission in any of those forces, or belongs to any reserve of officers of any of those forces, is not disqualified as a member of those forces; and

    (b) a naval, army, marine or air force pensioner, or former soldier, who is recalled for service for which he is liable as such is not disqualified as a member of the regular armed forces of the Crown.

(2) A person is not disqualified under section 1(1)(c) above by reason of his being an Admiral of the Fleet, a Field Marshal or a Marshal of the Royal Air Force, if he does not for the time being hold an appointment in the naval, military or air force service of the Crown.

(3) A person is not disqualified under section 1(1)(b) above by reason of his being a member of the Royal Observer Corps unless he is employed as such for the whole of his time.

NOTES
Defined terms
  regular armed forces of the Crown: cf s 1(3)

4 Stewardship of Chiltern Hundreds, etc

For the purposes of the provisions of this Act relating to the vacation of the seat of a member of the House of Commons who becomes disqualified by this Act for membership of that House, the office of steward or bailiff of Her Majesty's three Chiltern Hundreds of Stoke, Desborough and Burnham, or of the Manor of Northstead, shall be treated as included among the offices described in Part III of Schedule 1 to this Act.

5 Power to amend Schedule 1

(1) If at any time it is resolved by the House of Commons that Schedule 1 to this Act be amended, whether by the addition or omission of any office or the removal of any office from one Part of the Schedule to another, or by altering the description of any office specified therein, Her Majesty may by Order in Council amend that Schedule accordingly.

(2) A copy of this Act as from time to time amended by Order in Council under this section or by or under any other enactment shall be prepared and certified by the Clerk of the Parliaments and deposited with the rolls of Parliament; and all copies of this Act thereafter to be printed by Her Majesty's printer shall be printed in accordance with the copy so certified.

NOTES

Subordinate Legislation

House of Commons Disqualification Order 1982, SI 1982/160.
House of Commons Disqualification Order 1983, SI 1983/608.
House of Commons Disqualification Order 1984, SI 1984/705.
House of Commons Disqualification Order 1985, SI 1985/1212.
House of Commons Disqualification Order 1986, SI 1986/2219.
House of Commons Disqualification Order 1987, SI 1987/449.

House of Commons Disqualification Order 1990, SI 1990/2585.
House of Commons Disqualification Order 1993, SI 1993/1572.
House of Commons Disqualification Order 1997, SI 1997/861.
House of Commons Disqualification Order 2010, SI 2010/762

6 Effects of disqualification and provision for relief

(1) Subject to any order made by the House of Commons under this section

(a) if any person disqualified by this Act for membership of that House, or for membership for a particular constituency, is elected as a member of that House, or as a member for that constituency, as the case may be, his election shall be void; and

(b) if any person being a member of that House becomes disqualified by this Act for membership, or for membership for the constituency for which he is sitting, his seat shall be vacated.

(2) If, in a case falling or alleged to fall within subsection (1) above, it appears to the House of Commons that the grounds of disqualification or alleged disqualification under this Act which subsisted or arose at the material time have been removed, and that it is otherwise proper so to do, that House may by order direct that any such disqualification incurred on those grounds at that time shall be disregarded for the purposes of this section.

(3) No order under subsection (2) above shall affect the proceedings on any election petition or any determination of an election court, and this subsection shall have effect subject to the provisions of section 144(7) of the Representation of the People Act 1983 (making of an order by the House of Commons when informed of a certificate and any report of an election court).

(4) In any case where, by virtue of the Recess Elections Act 1975, the Speaker of the House of Commons would be required to issue during a recess of that House a warrant for a new writ for election of a member, in the room of a member becoming disqualified by this Act, he may, if it appears to him that an opportunity should be given to that House to consider the making of an order under subsection (2) above, defer the issue of his warrant pending the determination of that House.

7 Jurisdiction of Privy Council as to disqualification

(1) Any person who claims that a person purporting to be a member of the House of Commons is disqualified by this Act, or has been so disqualified at any time since his election, may apply to Her Majesty in Council, in accordance with such rules as Her Majesty in Council may prescribe, for a declaration to that effect.

(2) Section 3 of the Judicial Committee Act 1833 (reference to the Judicial Committee of the Privy Council of appeals to Her Majesty in Council) shall apply to any application under this section as it applies to an appeal to Her Majesty in Council from a court.

(3) Upon any such application the person in respect of whom the application is made shall be the respondent; and the applicant shall give such security for the cost of the proceedings, not exceeding £200, as the Judicial Committee may direct.

(4) For the purpose of determining any issue of fact arising on an application under this section the Judicial Committee may direct the issue to be tried

> (a) if the constituency for which the respondent purports to be a member is in England or Wales, in the High Court;
>
> (b) if that constituency is in Scotland, in the Court of Session;
>
> (c) if that constituency is in Northern Ireland, in the High Court in Northern Ireland;
>
> and the decision of that Court shall be final.

(5) A declaration under this section may be made in respect of any person whether the grounds of the alleged disqualification subsisted at the time of his election or arose subsequently; but no such declaration shall be made

> (a) in the case of disqualification incurred by any person on grounds which subsisted at the time of his election, if an election petition is pending or has been tried in which his disqualification on those grounds is or was in issue;
>
> (b) in the case of disqualification incurred by any person on any grounds, if an order has been made by the House of Commons under section 6(2) above directing that any disqualification incurred by him on those grounds shall be disregarded for the purposes of that section.

8 Relaxation of obligation to accept office

(1) No person being a member of the House of Commons, or for the time being nominated as a candidate for election to that House, shall be required to accept any office or place by virtue of which he would be disqualified by this Act for membership of that House, or for membership of that House for the constituency for which he is sitting or is a candidate.

(2) This section does not affect any obligation to serve in the armed forces of the Crown, whether imposed by an enactment or otherwise.

9 Interpretation

In this Act

"Minister of State" means a member of Her Majesty's Government in the United Kingdom who neither has charge of any public department nor holds any other of the offices specified in Schedule 2 to this Act or any office in respect of which a salary is payable out of money provided by Parliament under section 3(1)(b) of the Ministerial and other Salaries Act 1975;

"Parliamentary Secretary" includes a person holding Ministerial office (however called) as assistant to a Member of Her Majesty's Government in the United Kingdom, but not having departmental responsibilities.

10
Repealed

11 Short title and extent

(1) This Act may be cited as the House of Commons Disqualification Act 1975.

(2) This Act extends to Northern Ireland.

SCHEDULE 1
Offices Disqualifying for Membership

Sections 1, 4, 5

Part I
Judicial Offices

Judge of the Supreme Court.
Judge of the High Court of Justice or Court of Appeal.

Judge of the Court of Session, or Temporary Judge appointed under the Law Reform (Miscellaneous Provisions) (Scotland) Act 1990.

Judge of the High Court of Justice or Court of Appeal in Northern Ireland.

Judge of the Court Martial Appeal Court.

Chairman of the Scottish Land Court.

Circuit Judge.

Sheriff Principal or Sheriff (other than Honorary Sheriff) appointed under the Sheriff Courts (Scotland) Act 1907, or Temporary Sheriff Principal or parttime sheriff appointed under the Sheriff Courts (Scotland) Act 1971.

County Court Judge or deputy County Court Judge in Northern Ireland.

District Judge (Magistrates' Courts) (but not Deputy District Judge (Magistrates' Courts)).

District judge (magistrates' courts), or deputy district judge (magistrates' courts), in Northern Ireland.

Stipendiary Magistrate in Scotland.

Chief or other Child Support Commissioner for Northern Ireland or deputy Child Support Commissioner for Northern Ireland.

Chief or other Social Security Commissioner (not including a deputy Commissioner).

Chief or other Social Security Commissioner for Northern Ireland or deputy Social Security Commissioner for Northern Ireland.

Part II
Bodies of which all Members are Disqualified

The Accounts Commission for Scotland.

The Advisory Council established under section 3 of the Scottish Qualification Authority Act 2002.

The Agriculture and Horticulture Development Board.

The Antarctic Act Tribunal established under regulations made under the Antarctic Act 1994.

The Appointments Commission.

An Arbitration Tribunal established under Schedule 3 to the Industry Act 1975.

The Armed Forces Pay Review Body.

The Arts Council of England.

The British Railways Board.

The British Transport Police Authority.

The British Waterways Board.

Bwrdd yr Iaith Gymraeg (Welsh Language Board).

The Care Council for Wales.

The Care Quality Commission and the Healthwatch England committee.

The Central Arbitration Committee.

The Channel Four Television Corporation.

The Charity Commission.

The Charity Commission for Northern Ireland.

The Children and Family Court Advisory and Support Service.

The Civil Aviation Authority.

The Civil Nuclear Police Authority.

The Civil Service Arbitration Tribunal.

The Civil Service Commission

The Coal Authority.

Commission for Architecture and the Built Environment.

The Commission for Equality and Human Rights.

The Commission on Human Medicines.

The Commission for Local Administration in England.

The Commission for Victims and Survivors for Northern Ireland.

The Committee on Climate Change.

The Office of Communications.

The Competition Appeal Tribunal.

The Competition and Markets Authority.

The Competition Service.

The Consumer Council for Water, and each regional committee of the Council established under section 27A of the Water Industry Act 1991.

The Copyright Tribunal.

The Council of the Advisory, Conciliation and Arbitration Service.

The Covent Garden Market Authority.

The Criminal Cases Review Commission.

The Crown Estate Commissioners.

The Development Commission.

A Development Corporation within the meaning of the New Towns Act 1981 or the New Towns (Scotland) Act 1968.

The Disability Living Allowance Advisory Board for Northern Ireland.

The Disclosure and Barring Service.

The Electoral Commission.

The Employment Appeal Tribunal.

The English Sports Council.

The Environment Agency.

The Equality Commission for Northern Ireland.

The Fair Employment Tribunal for Northern Ireland.

The First-tier Tribunal.

The Food Standards Agency.

The Foreign Compensation Commission.

The Forestry Commissioners.

The Gambling Commission.

Gangmasters Licensing Authority.

The Gas and Electricity Markets Authority.

The Health and Care Professions Council.

The Health and Safety Executive.

The Health and Social Care Information Centre.

The Health and Social Care Regulation and Quality Improvement Authority in Northern Ireland.

Health Education England.

Health Research Authority.

Healthcare Improvement Scotland.

Highlands and Islands Enterprise.

The Homes and Communities Agency.

The Horserace Betting Levy Appeal Tribunal for England and Wales.

The Human Fertilisation and Embryology Authority.

The Human Tissue Authority.

The Independent Commission for Police Complaints for Northern Ireland.

The Independent Parliamentary Standards Authority.

The Independent Police Complaints Commission.

An Industrial Court established in Northern Ireland.

The Industrial Injuries Advisory Council.

Invest Northern Ireland.

A Joint Planning Inquiry Commission constituted under Part III of the Town and Country Planning (Scotland) Act 1997.

The Judicial Appointments Commission.

The Labour Relations Agency.

The Lands Tribunal for Northern Ireland.

The Lands Tribunal for Scotland.

The Law Commission.

The Legal Services Board.

The Legal Services Commission.

The Local Government Boundary Commission for England.

The Local Government Boundary Commission for Scotland.

The Local Government Boundary Commission for Wales.

The Low Pay Commission appointed under section 8(9) of the National Minimum Wage Act 1998.

The Marine Management Organisation.

A Mayoral development corporation (see section 198 of the Localism Act 2011).

The Mental Health Review Tribunal for Wales.

The Mental Health Review Tribunal for Northern Ireland.

The Mental Welfare Commission for Scotland.

The National Audit Office.

The National Institute for Health and Care Excellence.

Natural England.

The Natural Resources Body for Wales.

The NHS Pay Review Body.

The Northern Ireland Housing Executive.

The Northern Ireland Judicial Appointments Commission.

The Northern Ireland Law Commission.

The Northern Ireland Legal Services Commission.

The Northern Ireland Social Care Council.

The Nuclear Decommissioning Authority.

The Office for Budget Responsibility.

The Office of Rail and Road.

The Office of the Renewable Fuels Agency.

The Office for Legal Complaints.

The Office for Nuclear Regulation.

The Office for Standards in Education, Children's Services and Skills.

The Oil and Pipelines Agency.

The Parades Commission for Northern Ireland.

The Parole Board.

The Parole Board for Scotland.

A Pensions Appeal Tribunal.

The Board of the Pension Protection Fund.

The Pensions Regulator.

The Planning Appeals Commission constituted under Article 110 of the Planning (Northern Ireland) Order 1991.

A Planning Inquiry Commission constituted under Part III of the Town and Country Planning Act 1990.

A Planning Inquiry Commission constituted under Part III of the Town and Country Planning (Scotland) Act 1997.

The Police Remuneration Review Body.

The Prison Service Pay Review Body.

The Professional Standards Authority for Health and Social Care.

A regional committee of the Gas and Electricity Consumer Council established under section 18(2) of the Utilities Act 2000.

A regional water authority established in accordance with section 2 of the Water Act 1973.

Revenue Scotland.

The Review Body on Doctors and Dentists Remuneration.

The Risk Management Authority established under the Criminal Justice (Scotland) Act 2003.

A Rural Development Board.

The School Teachers' Review Body.

The Scottish Charity Regulator.

The Scottish Criminal Cases Review Commission.

Scottish Enterprise.

The Scottish Environment Protection Agency.

The Scottish Further and Higher Education Funding Council.

The Scottish Housing Regulator

The Scottish Land Court.
The Scottish Law Commission.
The Scottish Legal Aid Board.
Scottish Natural Heritage.
The Scottish Qualifications Authority.
The Scottish Social Services Council.
Scottish Water.
The Sea Fish Industry Authority.
The Sea Fish Licence Tribunal.
The Security Industry Authority.
Seirbheis nam Meadhanan Gàidhlig.
The Senior Salaries Review Body.
Sianel Pedwar Cymru.
The Single Source Regulations Office.
Social Care and Social Work Improvement Scotland.
The Social Mobility and Child Poverty Commission.
The Social Security Advisory Committee.
The Standards Commission for Scotland.
The Statistics Board.
Strategic Rail Authority.
The Sustainable Development Commission (an advisory subcommittee of The Sustainable
    Development Commission Limited).
The Transport Tribunal.
The Tribunal established under section 91 of the Northern Ireland Act 1998.
The Tribunal established under section 65 of the Regulation of Investigatory Powers Act 2000.
The trustee corporation established by section 75 of the Pensions Act 2008.
The Trustees of the National Heritage Memorial Fund.
The United Kingdom Atomic Energy Authority.
The United Kingdom Sports Council.
The Upper Tribunal.
The Valuation Tribunal for England.
The Valuation Tribunal Service.
The Water Appeals Commission for Northern Ireland.
The Water Industry Commission for Scotland.
The Water Services Regulation Authority.
The Welsh Water Authority.
The Youth Justice Board for England and Wales

Part III
Other Disqualifying Offices

Adjudicator appointed under section 25 of the School Standards and Framework Act 1998.
Adjudicator appointed by the Commissioners for Her Majesty's Revenue and Customs.
Advocate Depute (not being the Solicitor General for Scotland) appointed by the Lord Advocate.
Ambassador or Permanent Representative to an international organisation representing Her
    Majesty's Government in the United Kingdom.
Appeal Officer for Community Interest Companies.
Assembly Ombudsman for Northern Ireland.
Assessor appointed for the purposes of paragraph 9 of schedule 1 to the Public Appointments
    and Public Bodies etc (Scotland) Act 2003.
Assessor appointed for the purposes of section 133 of the Criminal Justice Act 1988.
Assessor of Public Undertakings (Scotland).
Assistant Commissioner appointed under Part IV of the Local Government Act 1972.
Assistant Commissioner appointed under Part II of the Local Government (Scotland) Act 1973.
Assistant Electoral Commissioners.

Attorney General of the Duchy of Lancaster.

Attorney General for Northern Ireland.

Auditor General for Scotland.

Auditor of the Court of Session.

Auditor General for Wales.

Boundary Commissioner or assistant Commissioner appointed under Schedule 1 to the Parliamentary Constituencies Act 1986.

Certification officer or any assistant certification officer.

Certification Officer for Northern Ireland appointed under Article 69 of the Industrial Relations (Northern Ireland) Order 1992.

Chair of Creative Scotland.

Chair of the Northern Ireland Library Authority.

Chair or any member, not also being an employee, of the Patient Client Council established under section 16 of the Health and Social Care (Reform) Act (Northern Ireland) 2009.

Chair or any member, not also being an employee, of the Regional Agency for Public Health and Social Wellbeing established under section 12 of the Health and Social Care (Reform) Act (Northern Ireland) 2009.

Chair or any member, not also being an employee, of the Regional Business Services Organisation established under section 14 of the Health and Social Care (Reform) Act (Northern Ireland) 2009.

Chair or any member, not also being an employee, of the Regional Health and Social Care Board established under section 7 of the Health and Social Care (Reform) Act (Northern Ireland) 2009.

Chair or other member of Monitor.

Chair of the School Food Trust.

Chair or Chief Executive of the Science and Technology Facilities Council.

Chair, Deputy Chair or Chief Executive of the Technology Strategy Board.

Chairman or Medical Director of the Advisory Committee on Clinical Excellence Awards.

Chairman of an Agricultural Land Tribunal or member of a panel appointed under paragraph 14 or 15 of Schedule 9 to the Agriculture Act 1947.

Chairman or deputy chairman of the AgriFood and Biosciences Institute.

Chairman, Deputy Chairman or Chief Executive of the Arts and Humanities Research Council.

Chairman or Vice Chairman of the Arts Council of Northern Ireland.

Chairman, vicechairman or ordinary member of the BBC Trust.

Member of the Big Lottery Fund or of a committee established by the Fund under paragraph 7 of Schedule 4A to the National Lottery Act 1993.

Chairman, Deputy Chairman, or Chief Executive of the Biotechnology and Biological Sciences Research Council.

Chairman, or director appointed by the Secretary of State, of CDC Group plc (formerly the Commonwealth Development Corporation).

Chairman of the Board of Governors of the Commonwealth Institute.

Chairman or DirectorGeneral of the British Council.

Chairman of the British Library Board.

Chairman of the Chief Executives' Forum in Northern Ireland.

Chairman of the Committee on Standards in Public Life.

Chairman or Deputy Chairman of the Civil Service Appeal Board.

Chairman of the Crofters Commission.

Chairman of the Northern Ireland Clinical Excellence Awards Committee.

Chairman, Deputy Chairman or Chief Executive of the Economic and Social Research Council.

Chairman, Deputy Chairman or Chief Executive of the Engineering and Physical Sciences Research Council.

Chairman or Deputy Chairman of the Financial Reporting Council.

Chairman of the Fire and Rescue Service Board.

Chairman of the General Consumer Council for Northern Ireland.

Chairman or any member, not being also an employee, of any Special Health Authority

Chairman or any member, not being also an employee, of a Health Board or a Special Health Board constituted under the National Health Service (Scotland) Act 1978.

Chairman or any member, not being also an employee, of a Local Health Board established under section 11 of the National Health Service (Wales) Act 2006.

Chairman of the Health and Safety Agency for Northern Ireland.

Chairman of the Health and Safety Commission.

Chairman or nonexecutive director of a Health and Social Care trust established under the Health and Personal Social Services (Northern Ireland) Order 1991.

Chairman or Deputy Chairman, in receipt of remuneration, of the Historic Buildings and Monuments Commission for England.

Paid Chairman of an Industrial Training Board constituted under the Industrial Training Act 1964 or the Industrial Training Act 1982 or of a committee appointed under either of those Acts or paid Deputy Chairman of such a board.

Chairman of the Inland Waterways Advisory Council.

Chairman of Investors in People UK.

Chairman of the Joint Nature Conservation Committee.

Chairman, ViceChairman or member of the executive committee of the Land Settlement Association Limited appointed at a salary.

Chairman of Learning and Teaching Scotland.

Chairman of the Livestock and Meat Commission for Northern Ireland.

Chairman or Chief Executive of the Local Government Staff Commission for Northern Ireland.

Chairman or any member, not being also an employee, of the Management Committee of the Common Services Agency for the Scottish Health Service constituted under the National Health Service (Scotland) Act 1978.

Chairman, Deputy Chairman or Chief Executive of the Medical Research Council.

Chairman of the Museums, Libraries and Archives Council.

Chairman or Director of the National Forest Company.

Chairman or nonexecutive member of the National Health Service Commissioning Board.

Chairman or other nonexecutive director of an NHS foundation trust.

Chairman or nonexecutive member of a National Health Service trust established under the National Health Service Act 2006 or the National Health Service (Wales) Act 2006.

Chairman, Deputy Chairman or Chief Executive of the Natural Environment Research Council.

Chairman of the Northern Ireland Civil Service Appeal Board.

Chairman of the Northern Ireland Community Relations Council.

Chairman of the Northern Ireland Council for the Curriculum, Examinations and Assessment.

Chairman of the Northern Ireland Higher Education Council.

Chairman of, or secretary to, the Northern Ireland Local Government Officers' Superannuation Committee.

Chairman or vicechairman of the Northern Ireland Policing Board.

Chairman of the Northern Ireland Screen Commission.

Chairman of the Northern Ireland Tourist Board.

Chairman, or member in receipt of remuneration, of the Olympic Delivery Authority.

Chairman, or member in receipt of remuneration, of the Olympic Lottery Distributor.

Chairman of the Prescription Pricing Authority.

Chairman of the Probation Board for Northern Ireland.

Chairman of a probation trust.

Chairman of Quality Meat Scotland.

Chairman of a Regional Flood and Coastal Committee for any area of England and Wales.

Chairman of the Scottish Dental Practice Board or a member of that Board appointed at an annual salary.

Chairman . . . of the Scottish Sports Council.

A regional or other fulltime Chairman of Social Security Appeal Tribunals, Medical Appeal Tribunals and Disability Appeal Tribunals.

Chairman of a special health and social care agency established under Article 3 of the Health and Personal Social Services (Special Agencies) (Northern Ireland) Order 1990.

Chairman of the Special Hospitals Service Authority.

Chairman or ViceChairman of the Sports Council for Northern Ireland.

Chairman or ViceChairman of the Sports Council for Wales.

Chairman or Chief Executive of the Student Loans Company Limited.

Chairman or Chief Executive of the UK Commission for Employment and Skills or a Director or Commissioner of that Commission appointed by the First Minister in Scotland, the First Minister for Wales or a Northern Ireland Minister.

Chairman of the Women's Royal Voluntary Service.

Chairman or ViceChairman of the Youth Council for Northern Ireland.

Chief Adjudication Officer appointed under section 39 of the Social Security Administration Act 1992.

Chief Electoral Officer for Northern Ireland or any whole time officer appointed under section 14A(1) of the Electoral Law Act (Northern Ireland) 1962.

Chief executive of SITPRO Limited.

Chief Executive of The Sustainable Development Commission Limited or a Director appointed by the members of that company or by the Secretary of State, the First Minister in Scotland, the First Minister for Wales or the First Minister and deputy First Minister in Northern Ireland.

Chief Inspector of Criminal Justice in Northern Ireland.

Chief Inspector of the UK Border Agency.

Chief Investigating Officer appointed under section 9 of the Ethical Standards in Public Life etc (Scotland) Act 2000.

Chief Land Registrar.

Chief Officer of a community justice authority appointed under section 4(2) of the Management of Offenders etc (Scotland) Act 2005.

The Chief Ombudsman or an assistant ombudsman appointed under section 122 of the Legal Services Act 2007 (Chief Ombudsman and assistant ombudsmen appointed for the purposes of the ombudsman scheme).

The Chief Regulator of Qualifications and Examinations, the chair of the Office of Qualifications and Examinations Regulation and any member of the Office of Qualifications and Examinations Regulation in receipt of remuneration.

Children's Commissioner.

Children's Commissioner for Wales.

Civil Service Commissioner for Northern Ireland.

Clerk or deputy clerk of a district council in Northern Ireland.

Commissioner or Assistant Commissioner appointed under section 50(1) or (2) of, or Schedule 4 to, the Local Government Act (Northern Ireland) 1972.

Commissioner of the City of London Police.

Commissioner for Children and Young People for Northern Ireland.

Commissioner for Older People in Wales

Commissioner for Parliamentary Investigations.

Commissioner for Public Appointments.

Commissioner for Public Appointments for Northern Ireland.

Commissioner for the Retention and Use of Biometric Material

Commissioner for Victims and Witnesses.

Commons Commissioner.

Compliance Officer for the Independent Parliamentary Standards Authority.

Comptroller and Auditor General for Northern Ireland.

Controller of Audit appointed under section 97(4) of the Local Government (Scotland) Act 1973.

Coroner, deputy coroner or assistant deputy coroner appointed under the Coroners Act 1988.

Coroner or deputy coroner appointed under section 2(1) of the Coroners Act (Northern Ireland) 1959.

Coroner of the Queen's household.

Senior coroner, area coroner or assistant coroner appointed under Part 1 of the Coroners and Justice Act 2009.

Coroner for Treasure.

Deputy Chief Coroner appointed by the Lord Chancellor under that Part who is not also a senior coroner.

Counsel to the Secretary of State under the Private Legislation Procedure (Scotland) Act 1936.

Crown Solicitor for Northern Ireland.

Deputy Electoral Commissioners.

Director of the British Aerospace Public Limited Company appointed subject to the approval of a Minister or government department.

Director of British Nuclear Fuels Limited.

Director of Caledonian Maritime Assets Limited.

Director of Citybus Limited.

Director of any of the following

(a) a company which for the time being holds a licence under Chapter I of Part I of the Transport Act 2000 (a licence company);

(b) a company of which a licence company is a subsidiary (within the meaning given by section 1159 of the Companies Act 2006);

(c) a company which is a subsidiary (within the meaning so given) of a licence company.

Director of any company eligible for loans under section 13 of the Transport Act 1982 (loans to Government-controlled company interested in former Government testing stations).

Director of a company for the time being holding an appointment under Chapter I of Part II of the Water Industry Act 1991 or of such a company's holding company, being a director nominated or appointed by a Minister of the Crown or by a person acting on behalf of the Crown.

Director of any company in receipt of financial assistance under . . . Part III or section 13 of the Industrial Development Act 1982, being a director nominated by a Minister of the Crown or government department.

Director of a company

(a) which, within the meaning of Part II of the Railways Act 1993, is a successor company wholly owned by the Crown, (b)

being a director nominated or appointed by a Minister of the Crown, the Director of Passenger Rail Franchising or any other person acting on behalf of the Crown.

Director nominated by the Secretary of State of any company in respect of which an undertaking to make advances has been given by the Secretary of State under section 2 of the Highlands and Islands Shipping Services Act 1960 and is for the time being in force.

Director of David MacBrayne Limited.

Director of Fair Access to Higher Education.

Director of Flexibus Limited.

Director in receipt of remuneration of High Speed Two (HS2) Limited.

Director of Highlands and Islands Airports Limited.

Any Director of Horticulture Research International in receipt of remuneration.

Director of International Military Services Limited.

Director of a Local Healthwatch organisation.

Director of Middletown Centre for Autism (Holdings) Limited or of Middletown Centre for Autism Limited.

Director of Northern Ireland Railways Company Limited.

Director of the Northern Ireland Transport Holding Company.

Director of Northern Ireland Water Limited.

Director of Nuclear Electric plc.

Director of Partnerships for Schools Limited.

Director of the Pensions Advisory Service Limited.

Director of any of the following, being a director appointed or nominated by a Minister of the Crown or by a person acting on behalf of the Crown

(a) a Post Office company,

(b) a Royal Mail company,

(c) the original holding company, and

(d) a parent company of a company within any of paragraphs (a) to (c).

Expressions used in paragraphs (a) to (d) have the same meaning as in Part 1 of the Postal Services Act 2011.

Director, or Deputy Director, of Public Prosecutions for Northern Ireland.

Director of a publicly controlled company (within the meaning of Chapter 2 of Part 1 of the Energy Act 2004) to which transfers have been made in accordance with provisions of nuclear transfer schemes authorised by that Chapter.

Director of a publicly owned successor company (within the meaning of the Atomic Energy Authority Act 1995).

Director appointed at a salary of Remploy Limited.

Director of Scottish Futures Trust Limited.

Director of Scottish Nuclear Limited.

Director of Service Prosecutions.

Director of The Skills Development Scotland Co Limited.

Director of Strategic Investment Board Limited.

Director of the successor company (within the meaning of the Crown Agents Act 1995) being a director nominated or appointed by a Minister of the Crown or by a person acting on behalf of the Crown.

Director of UK Film Council.

Director in receipt of remuneration of UK Financial Investments Limited.

Director of United Kingdom AntiDoping Limited appointed by the members of the company.

Director of Ulsterbus Limited.

Director General or Deputy Director General of the Scottish Crime and Drug Enforcement Agency.

District Judge appointed under section 6 of the County Courts Act 1984.

Employee of the National Audit Office.

The Governor or Administrator of a British overseas territory within the meaning of section 50(1) of the British Nationality Act 1981.

Governor, Deputy Governor or nonexecutive director of the Bank of England.

Governor, Lieutenant Governor and Secretary, or Captain of Invalids of Chelsea Hospital.

Governor... or other officer or member of the staff of a prison to which the Prison Act (Northern Ireland) 1953 applies.

Groceries Code Adjudicator or Deputy Groceries Code Adjudicator.

Health Service Commissioner for England.

Her Majesty's Chief Inspector of Education and Training in Wales or Prif Arolygydd Ei Mawrhydi dros Addysg a Hyfforddiant yng Nghymru

Her Majesty's Chief Inspector of Prisons for England and Wales.

Her Majesty's Chief Inspector of Probation for England and Wales.

High Commissioner representing Her Majesty's Government in the United Kingdom.

The Immigration Services Commissioner.

The Deputy Immigration Services Commissioner.

Independent Antislavery Commissioner.

The Independent Case Examiner for the Department for Work and Pensions.

The Information Commissioner.

Investigating Commissioner of, or member of a decisionmaking committee of, the Commission for Equality and Human Rights.

Judge Advocate General, Vice Judge Advocate General or Assistant Judge Advocate General.

The Judicial Appointments and Conduct Ombudsman.

Lay observer appointed under Article 42 of the Solicitors (Northern Ireland) Order 1976.

The Legal Services Complaints Commissioner.

Lyon Clerk.

Lyon King of Arms.

Member of an Agricultural Marketing Board appointed by the Minister under Schedule 2 to the Agricultural Marketing Act 1958.

Member of an Agricultural Marketing Board appointed under section 3 of the Agricultural Marketing Act (Northern Ireland) 1964 or Schedule 2 to the Agricultural Marketing (Northern Ireland) Order 1982.

Member appointed by the Scottish Ministers of the Scottish Agricultural Wages Board.

Member appointed by the Head of the Department of Agriculture for Northern Ireland of the Agricultural Wages Board for Northern Ireland.

Member of Audit Scotland appointed under section 10(2)(c) of the Public Finance and Accountability (Scotland) Act 2000 or member of the staff of Audit Scotland.

Member of the staff of the Auditor General for Wales.

Any member in receipt of remuneration of the British Tourist Authority, the English Tourist Board or Visit-Scotland.

Member of staff of the Children's Commissioner.

Member of the staff of the Children's Commissioner for Wales.

Member of the staff of the Commissioner for Older People in Wales.

Member of the Determinations Panel established by the Pensions Regulator under section 9 of the Pensions Act 2004.

Any member of the Education Assets Board in receipt of remuneration.

Member of the staff of the Electoral Commission

Member of the Financial Policy Committee of the Bank of England appointed under section 9B(1)(d) or (e) of the Bank of England Act 1998.

Member of the governing body of the Financial Conduct Authority;

Member of the governing body of the Prudential Regulation Authority;

Member of the staff of the Forestry Commissioners.

Any member of the General Teaching Council for England in receipt of remuneration.

Any member of the General Teaching Council for Wales in receipt of remuneration.

Any member of the Higher Education Funding Council for England in receipt of remuneration.

Any member of the Higher Education Funding Council for Wales in receipt of remuneration.

Member appointed by the Secretary of State of the Horserace Betting Levy Board.

Member of the London Transport Users' Committee in receipt of remuneration.

Member of a Medical Appeal Tribunal appointed under section 50 of the Social Security Administration Act 1992.

Member of the Monetary Policy Committee of the Bank of England appointed under section 13(2)(b) or (c) of the Bank of England Act 1998.

Member of staff of the Commissioner for Older People in Wales

Member of the staff of the Northern Ireland Audit Office.

Member of staff of the Office for Nuclear Regulation (within the meaning of Part 3 of the Energy Act 2013).

Member of staff of the Pubs Code Adjudicator.

Member of the panel of persons available to serve as chairmen of the Care Tribunal in Northern Ireland.

Member of a panel of persons appointed to act as chairman or other members of industrial tribunals in Northern Ireland.

Any member of the Qualifications and Curriculum Development Agency (continued under section 175 of the Apprenticeships, Skills, Children and Learning Act 2009) in receipt of remuneration.

Member of the . . . Passengers' Council in receipt of remuneration.

Member of a panel of persons appointed under Schedule 10 to the Rent Act 1977 to act as chairmen and other members of rent assessment committees.

President or vicepresident of the panel of persons appointed under Schedule 4 to the Rent (Scotland) Act 1984 to act as chairmen and other members of private rented housing committees.

Member of a panel of persons appointed under section 6 of the Social Security Act 1998

Member of a panel of persons appointed under Article 7 of the Social Security (Northern Ireland) Order 1998 to act as members of appeal tribunals.

Member of a panel appointed under section 6 of the Tribunals and Inquiries Act 1992 of persons to act as chairmen of Social Security Appeal Tribunals, Medical Appeal Tribunals and Disability Appeal Tribunals.

Any member of the property commission established by virtue of section 19 of the Local Government etc (Scotland) Act 1994.

Any member of a residuary body established by Part VII of the Local Government Act 1985 who is in receipt of remuneration.

Any member of a residuary body established by virtue of section 18 of the Local Government etc (Scotland) Act 1994 who is in receipt of remuneration.

Any member, in receipt of remuneration, of a panel of persons who may be selected to act as members of the Pensions Regulator Tribunal.

Member, not being also a Forestry Commissioner or officer of the Forestry Commissioners, of a committee appointed for England, Scotland or Wales under section 2(3) of the Forestry Act 1967.

Any member of the staff commission established by virtue of section 12 of the Local Government etc (Scotland) Act 1994.

Member of the staff of the Disclosure and Barring Service.

Member of the staff of the State Pathology Service for Northern Ireland.

Any member of the Training and Development Agency for Schools in receipt of remuneration.

Any member, in receipt of remuneration, of an urban development corporation (within the meaning of Part XVI of the Local Government, Planning and Land Act 1980).

Any member of the Young People's Learning Agency for England in receipt of remuneration.

National Assembly for Wales Commissioner for Standards.

Northern Ireland Commissioner for Complaints.

Northern Ireland Human Rights Commissioner

The Northern Ireland Judicial Appointments Ombudsman.

Officer or servant of the Crown Estate Commissioners.

Officer, clerk or servant appointed or employed under section 20 of the Greenwich Hospital Act 1865.

Officer of the Senior Courts being the holder of any office listed in any Part of Schedule 2 to the Senior Courts Act 1981 or a district judge of the High Court.

Ombudsman for the Board of the Pension Protection Fund and any deputy to that Ombudsman appointed under section 210 of the Pensions Act 2004.

Ordinary member of BBC Audience Council England, BBC Audience Council Northern Ireland, BBC Audience Council Scotland or BBC Audience Council Wales.

Parliamentary Commissioner for Administration.

Parole Commissioner for Northern Ireland.

Pensions Ombudsman and any deputy to that Ombudsman appointed under section 145A of the Pension Schemes Act 1993.

Person appointed under section 3(1) of the Local Government and Housing Act 1989 to carry out functions relating to the political restriction of posts under local authorities, within the meaning of Part I of that Act.

Person appointed under section 27A of the Registered Designs Act 1949 to hear and determine appeals against decisions of the registrar under that Act.

Person appointed to chair the Sports Grounds Safety Authority.

Person appointed to hear and determine appeals under the Trade Marks Act 1994.

Person holding a politically restricted post, within the meaning of Part I of the Local Government and Housing Act 1989, under a local authority, within the meaning of that Part, or a National Park authority.

Person on the list of those eligible to sit as members of a Gender Recognition Panel.

The Police Ombudsman for Northern Ireland.

President of the Additional Support Needs Tribunal for Scotland.

President of appeal tribunals (within the meaning of Chapter I of Part I of the Social Security Act 1998) appointed under section 5 of that Act

President of the Employment Tribunals (England and Wales), President of the Employment Tribunals (Scotland), Employment Judge, or member of a panel of members of employment tribunals that is not a panel of Employment Judges.

President or member of the Mental Health Tribunal for Scotland.

President of Social Security Appeal Tribunals, Medical Appeal Tribunals and Disability Appeal Tribunals.

President of appeal tribunals appointed under Article 6 of the Social Security (Northern Ireland) Order 1998.

President, or member of a panel of persons appointed to act as chairman or other members, of the Special Educational Needs and Disability Tribunal for Northern Ireland.

President of the Special Educational Needs Tribunal for Wales, or member of a panel of persons appointed to act as chairman or other member of that Tribunal.

Prisoner Ombudsman for Northern Ireland.

Prisons and Probation Ombudsman for England and Wales.

Public Services Ombudsman for Wales.

Public Works Loan Commissioner.

Pubs Code Adjudicator or Deputy Pubs Code Adjudicator.

Receiver for the Metropolitan Police District.

A regional returning officer for the purposes of the Scotland Act 1998.

Registrar of the Privy Council.

Registration Officer appointed under section 8(2), (2A) or (3) of the Representation of the People Act 1983.

Regulator of Community Interest Companies.

Rent officer appointed in pursuance of a scheme under section 63 of the Rent Act 1977.

Returning Officer under section 25(1) of the Representation of the People Act 1983 and any Deputy Returning Officer appointed by him.

The reviewer appointed under section 40 of the Justice and Security (Northern Ireland) Act 2007.

Scottish Information Commissioner.

Scottish Parliamentary Standards Commissioner.

Scottish Public Services Ombudsman.

Scottish Road Works Commissioner.

Sentence Review Commissioner

Service Complaints Commissioner.

Service Complaints Ombudsman.

Social fund Commissioner in Northern Ireland.

Solicitor in Scotland to any department of Her Majesty's Government in the United Kingdom.

Standing Counsel to any department of Her Majesty's Government in the United Kingdom.

Statutory officer appointed under section 70 of the Judicature (Northern Ireland) Act 1978.

Surveillance Camera Commissioner.

Traffic commissioner for any area constituted for the purposes of the Public Passenger Vehicles Act 1981.

Trustee of the Independent Living Fund (2006).

Part IV
Offices Disqualifying for Particular Constituencies

Office	Constituency
Member of Her Majesty's Commission of Lieutenancy for the City of London.	Any constituency comprising the whole or part of the City of London.
Her Majesty's LordLieutenant or Lieutenant for Greater London.	Any constituency comprising any part of Greater London.
Her Majesty's LordLieutenant or Lieutenant for a county in England and Wales.	Any constituency comprising the whole or part of the area for which he is appointed.
Her Majesty's LordLieutenant or Lieutenant for an area in Scotland.	Any constituency comprising the whole or part of the area in which the Lord Lieutenant holds office or in which the Lord-Lieutenant or Lieutenant discharges his functions.

Her Majesty's Lord-Lieutenant or Lieutenant for the city of Aberdeen, Dundee, Edinburgh or Glasgow.	Any constituency comprising the whole or part of the city in which the Lord-Lieutenant holds office or for which the Lieutenant is appointed.
Her Majesty's Lord-Lieutenant or Lieutenant for a county or county borough in Northern Ireland.	Any constituency comprising the whole or part of the area for which he is appointed.
Governor of the Isle of Wight.	Any constituency comprising any part of the Isle of Wight
The High Sheriff of Greater London.	Any constituency comprising any part of Greater London.
The High Sheriff of a county in England and Wales.	Any constituency comprising the whole or part of the area for which he is appointed.

SCHEDULE 2

Ministerial Offices

Section 2

Prime Minister and First Lord of the Treasury.
Lord President of the Council.
Lord Privy Seal.
Chancellor of the Duchy of Lancaster.
Paymaster General.
Secretary of State.
Chancellor of the Exchequer.
President of the Board of Trade.
Minister of State.
Chief Secretary to the Treasury.
Minister in charge of a public department of Her Majesty's Government in the United Kingdom (if not within the other provisions of this Schedule).
Attorney General.
Solicitor General.
Advocate General for Scotland.
Parliamentary Secretary to the Treasury.
Financial Secretary to the Treasury.
Parliamentary Secretary in a Government Department other than the Treasury, or not in a department.
Junior Lord of the Treasury.
Treasurer of Her Majesty's Household.
Comptroller of Her Majesty's Household.
Vice-Chamberlain of Her Majesty's Household.
Assistant Government Whip.

House of Commons (Removal of Clergy Disqualification) Act 2001

An Act to remove any disqualification from membership of the House of Commons that arises by reason of a person having been ordained or being a minister of a religious denomination and to continue the disqualification of Lords Spiritual from such membership.

11th May 2001

BE IT ENACTED by the Queen's most Excellent Majesty, by and with the advice and consent of the Lords Spiritual and Temporal, and Commons, in this present Parliament assembled, and by the authority of the same, as follows:

1 Removal of disqualification of clergy
2 Short title and extent

1 Removal of disqualification of clergy

(1) A person is not disqualified from being or being elected as a member of the House of Commons merely because he has been ordained or is a minister of any religious denomination.

(2) But a person is disqualified from being or being elected as a member of that House if he is a Lord Spiritual.

(3) Accordingly

 (a) Schedule 1 (which makes amendments consequential on this section) has effect, and

 (b) the enactments mentioned in Schedule 2 (which relate to the disqualification of clergy from membership of the House of Commons) are repealed to the extent specified in that Schedule.

2 Short title and extent

(1) This Act may be cited as the House of Commons (Removal of Clergy Disqualification) Act 2001.

(2) Any amendment contained in Schedule 1 or repeal contained in Schedule 2 has the same extent as the enactment to which it relates.

(3) Subject to that, this Act extends to Northern Ireland.

SCHEDULE 1
Consequential Amendments
Not reproduced

SCHEDULE 2
Repeals
Not reproduced

House of Lords Act 1999

An Act to restrict membership of the House of Lords by virtue of a hereditary peerage; to make related provision about disqualifications for voting at elections to, and for membership of, the House of Commons; and for connected purposes.

11th November 1999

1 Exclusion of hereditary peers
2 Exception from section 1
3 Removal of disqualifications in relation to the House of Commons
4 Amendments and repeals
5 Commencement and transitional provision
6 Interpretation and short title

SCHEDULE 1 Amendments
SCHEDULE 2 Repeals

1 Exclusion of hereditary peers

No-one shall be a member of the House of Lords by virtue of a hereditary peerage.

NOTES
Defined terms
  hereditary peerage: s 6(1)

2 Exception from section 1

(1) Section 1 shall not apply in relation to anyone excepted from it by or in accordance with Standing Orders of the House.

(2) At any one time 90 people shall be excepted from section 1; but anyone excepted as holder of the office of Earl Marshal, or as performing the office of Lord Great Chamberlain, shall not count towards that limit.

(3) Once excepted from section 1, a person shall continue to be so throughout his life (until an Act of Parliament provides to the contrary).

(4) Standing Orders shall make provision for filling vacancies among the people excepted from section 1; and in any case where
   (a) the vacancy arises on a death occurring after the end of the first Session of the next Parliament after that in which this Act is passed, and
   (b) the deceased person was excepted in consequence of an election,
   that provision shall require the holding of a by-election.

(5) A person may be excepted from section 1 by or in accordance with Standing Orders made in anticipation of the enactment or commencement of this section.

(6) Any question whether a person is excepted from section 1 shall be decided by the Clerk of the Parliaments, whose certificate shall be conclusive.

3 Removal of disqualifications in relation to the House of Commons

(1) The holder of a hereditary peerage shall not be disqualified by virtue of that peerage for
   (a) voting at elections to the House of Commons, or
   (b) being, or being elected as, a member of that House.

(2) Subsection (1) shall not apply in relation to anyone excepted from section 1 by virtue of section 2.

NOTES
Defined terms   hereditary peerage: s 6(1)

4 Amendments and repeals

(1) The enactments mentioned in Schedule 1 are amended as specified there.

(2) The enactments mentioned in Schedule 2 are repealed to the extent specified there.

5 Commencement and transitional provision

(1) Sections 1 to 4 (including Schedules 1 and 2) shall come into force at the end of the Session of Parliament in which this Act is passed.

(2) Accordingly, any writ of summons issued for the present Parliament in right of a hereditary peerage shall not have effect after that Session unless it has been issued to a person who, at the end of the Session, is excepted from section 1 by virtue of section 2.

(3) The Secretary of State may by order make such transitional provision about the entitlement of holders of hereditary peerages to vote at elections to the House of Commons or the European Parliament as he considers appropriate.

(4) An order under this section

    (a) may modify the effect of any enactment or any provision made under an enactment, and

    (b) shall be made by statutory instrument which shall be subject to annulment in pursuance of a resolution of either House of Parliament.

NOTES

Defined terms

  hereditary peerage: s 6(1)

6 Interpretation and short title

(1) In this Act "hereditary peerage" includes the principality of Wales and the earldom of Chester.

(2) This Act may be cited as the House of Lords Act 1999.

SCHEDULE 1

Amendments

Not reproduced

SCHEDULE 2

Repeals

Not reproduced

House of Lords (Expulsion and Suspension) Act 2015

An Act to make provision empowering the House of Lords to expel or suspend members.

26th March 2015

1   Expulsion and suspension of members of the House of Lords
2   Entitlement to receive writs of summons to attend House of Lords
3   Effect of ceasing to be a member
4   Short title, commencement and extent

1 Expulsion and suspension of members of the House of Lords

(1)   Standing Orders of the House of Lords may make provision under which the House of Lords may by resolution
    (a)   expel a member of the House of Lords, or
    (b)   suspend a member of the House of Lords for the period specified in the resolution.

(2)   A person expelled by virtue of this section ceases to be a member.

(3)   A person suspended by virtue of this section remains a member during the period of suspension, but during that period the person
    (a)   is not entitled to receive writs of summons to attend the House of Lords, and
    (b)   despite any writ of summons previously issued to the person, is disqualified from sitting or voting in the House of Lords or a committee of the House of Lords.

(4)   A resolution passed by virtue of subsection (1) must state that, in the opinion of the House of Lords, the conduct giving rise to the resolution
    (a)   occurred after the coming into force of this Act, or
    (b)   occurred before the coming into force of this Act and was not public knowledge before that time.

2 Entitlement to receive writs of summons to attend House of Lords

Effects amendments: not reproduced

3 Effect of ceasing to be a member

A person expelled in accordance with section 1 is to be treated as if that person had ceased to be a member in accordance with the House of Lords Reform Act 2014, for the purposes of section 4(2) to (8) of that Act.

4 Short title, commencement and extent

(1)   This Act may be cited as the House of Lords (Expulsion and Suspension) Act 2015.

(2)   This Act shall come into force at the end of the period of three months beginning with the day on which this Act is passed.

(3)   This Act extends to England and Wales, Scotland and Northern Ireland.

House of Lords Reform Act 2014

An Act to make provision for resignation from the House of Lords; and to make provision for the expulsion of Members of the House of Lords in specified circumstances.

14 May 2014

1 Resignation

(1)   A member of the House of Lords who is a peer may retire or otherwise resign as a member of the House of Lords by giving notice in writing to the Clerk of the Parliaments.

(2)   The notice must
   (a)   specify a date from which the resignation is to take effect, and
   (b)   be signed by the peer and by a witness.

(3)   At the beginning of that date the peer ceases to be a member of the House of Lords.

(4)   Resignation may not be rescinded.

NOTES
Defined terms
   member of the House of Lords: s 6(1), (2)
   peer: s 6(3)

2 Nonattendance

(1)   A member of the House of Lords who is a peer and does not attend the House of Lords during a Session ceases to be a member of the House at the beginning of the following Session.

(2)   A peer "does not attend the House of Lords during a Session" if, and only if, the Lord Speaker certifies that the peer
   (a)   at no time during the Session attended the House, having regard to attendance records kept by officials of the House, and
   (b)   did not have leave of absence in respect of the Session, in accordance with Standing Orders of the House.

(3)   Subsection (1) does not apply to a peer in respect of attendance during a Session if
   (a)   the peer was disqualified from sitting or voting in the House, or suspended from its service, for the whole of the Session, or
   (b)   the House resolves that subsection (1) should not apply to the peer by reason of special circumstances.

(4)   Subsection (1) does not apply in respect of attendance during a Session that is less than six months long.

(5)   In this section a reference to attendance is a reference to attending the proceedings of the House (including the proceedings of a Committee of the House).

(6)   This section applies in respect of attendance during the first Session to begin after its coming into force and subsequent Sessions.

NOTES

3 Conviction of serious offence

(1) A member of the House of Lords who is convicted of a serious offence ceases to be a member of the House of Lords.

(2) A person "is convicted of a serious offence" if, and only if, the Lord Speaker certifies that the person, while a member of the House of Lords, has been
   (a) convicted of a criminal offence, and
   (b) sentenced or ordered to be imprisoned or detained indefinitely or for more than one year.

(3) It is irrelevant for the purposes of subsection (2)
   (a) whether the offence is committed at a time when the person is a member of the House of Lords;
   (b) whether any of the offence, conviction, sentence, order, imprisonment or detention occurs in the United Kingdom or elsewhere; (but see subsection (9)).

(4) The reference in subsection (2) to an offence is only to an offence committed on or after the day on which this section comes into force.

(5) The reference in subsection (2) to a person being sentenced or ordered to be imprisoned or detained indefinitely or for more than one year does not include such a sentence or order where the sentence or order is suspended.

(6) A certificate under subsection (2) takes effect when it is issued.

(7) If a person who has ceased to be a member of the House of Lords in accordance with this section is successful on appeal
   (a) the Lord Speaker must issue a further certificate to that effect, and
   (b) on the issue of that certificate, the original certificate under subsection (2) shall be treated for the purposes of this Act as never having had effect.

(8) A person who has ceased to be a member of the House of Lords in accordance with this section "is successful on appeal" if, and only if, the Lord Speaker certifies that
   (a) the conviction certified under subsection (2)(a) has been quashed, or
   (b) the sentence or order certified under subsection (2)(b) has been
      (i) varied so that it is no longer a sentence or order that the person be imprisoned or detained indefinitely or for more than one year within the meaning of subsection (2)(b), or
      (ii) replaced with another sentence or order that is not a sentence or order that the person be so imprisoned or detained.

(9) A certificate under subsection (2) in respect of a conviction outside the United Kingdom may be issued only if the House of Lords resolves that subsection (1) should apply; and where the House does so resolve the Lord Speaker must issue the certificate.

NOTES

4 Effect of ceasing to be a member

(1) This section applies where a person ceases to be a member of the House of Lords in accordance with this Act.

(2) The person becomes disqualified from attending the proceedings of the House of Lords (including the proceedings of a Committee of the House).

(3) Accordingly, the person shall not be entitled to receive a writ to attend the House (whether under section 1 of the Life Peerages Act 1958, by virtue of the dignity conferred

by virtue of appointment as a Lord of Appeal in Ordinary, by virtue of a hereditary peerage or as a Lord Spiritual) and may not attend the House in pursuance of a writ already received.

(4) If the person is a hereditary peer who is excepted from section 1 of the House of Lords Act 1999 by virtue of section 2 of that Act, the person ceases to be excepted from section 1 of that Act (and accordingly section 3 of that Act applies (removal of disqualification on voting in parliamentary elections or being an MP)).

(5) If the person is a peer other than a hereditary peer, the person is not, by virtue of that peerage, disqualified for
    (a) voting at elections to the House of Commons, or
    (b) being, or being elected as, a member of that House.

(6) In relation to a peer who ceases to be a member of the House of Lords in accordance with this Act, any reference in section 1(3) or (4)(b) of the Representation of the People Act 1985 to a register of parliamentary electors is to be read as including
    (a) any register of local government electors in Great Britain, and
    (b) any register of local electors in Northern Ireland,
which was required to be published on any date before the date on which the peer ceased to be a member.

(7) The Standing Orders of the House required by section 2(4) of the House of Lords Act 1999 (filling of vacancies) must make provision requiring the holding of a by-election to fill any vacancy which arises under this Act among the people excepted from section 1 of that Act in consequence of an election.

(8) Subject to section 3(7), a person who ceases to be a member of the House of Lords in accordance with this Act may not subsequently become a member of that House.

NOTES
Defined terms
   member of the House of Lords: s 6(1), (2)
   peer: s 6(3)

5 Certificate of Lord Speaker

(1) A certificate of the Lord Speaker under this Act shall be conclusive for all purposes.

(2) A certificate may be issued on the Lord Speaker's own initiative.

6 Interpretation

(1) For the purposes of this Act a person is a member of the House of Lords if the person is entitled to receive writs of summons to attend that House.

(2) In determining whether a person is so entitled, ignore
    (a) section 2 of the Forfeiture Act 1870 (disqualification on conviction of treason);
    (b) sections 426A and 427 of the Insolvency Act 1986 (disqualification on insolvency);
    (c) regulation 4 of the European Parliament (House of Lords Disqualification) Regulations 2008 (SI 2008/1647) (disqualification where MEP);
    (d) section 1(3) of the House of Lords (Expulsion and Suspension) Act 2015 (suspension).

(3) In this Act "peer" includes a person upon whom a dignity has been conferred by virtue of appointment as a Lord of Appeal in Ordinary.

7 Short title, commencement and extent

(1) This Act may be cited as the House of Lords Reform Act 2014.

(2) Sections 1 and 2 of this Act shall come into force at the end of the period of three months beginning with the day on which this Act is passed.

(3)   The remaining provisions of this Act shall come into force on the day on which this Act is passed.

(4)   This Act extends to England and Wales, Scotland and Northern Ireland.

Insolvency Act 1986
PART XVII

Miscellaneous and General

426 Co-operation between courts exercising jurisdiction in relation to insolvency
Not reproduced

426A Disqualification from Parliament (England and Wales and Northern Ireland)

(1) A person in respect of whom a bankruptcy restrictions order or a debt relief restrictions order has effect shall be disqualified
    (a) from membership of the House of Commons,
    (b) from sitting or voting in the House of Lords, and
    (c) from sitting or voting in a committee of the House of Lords or a joint committee of both Houses.

(2) If a member of the House of Commons becomes disqualified under this section, his seat shall be vacated.

(3) If a person who is disqualified under this section is returned as a member of the House of Commons, his return shall be void.

(4) No writ of summons shall be issued to a member of the House of Lords who is disqualified under this section.

(5) If a court makes a bankruptcy restrictions order or interim order, or a debt relief restrictions order or an interim debt relief restrictions order, in respect of a member of the House of Commons or the House of Lords the court shall notify the Speaker of that House.

(6) If the Secretary of State accepts a bankruptcy restrictions undertaking or a debt relief restrictions undertaking made by a member of the House of Commons or the House of Lords, the Secretary of State shall notify the Speaker of that House.

(7) If the Department of Enterprise, Trade and Investment for Northern Ireland accepts a bankruptcy restrictions undertaking made by a member of the House of Commons or the House of Lords under Schedule 2A to the Insolvency (Northern Ireland) Order 1989, the Department shall notify the Speaker of that House.

(8) In this section a reference to a bankruptcy restrictions order or an interim order includes a reference to a bankruptcy restrictions order or an interim order made under Schedule 2A to the Insolvency (Northern Ireland) Order 1989.

426B Devolution

(1) If a court in England and Wales makes a bankruptcy restrictions order or interim order in respect of a member of the Scottish Parliament, the Northern Ireland Assembly or the National Assembly for Wales, or makes a debt relief restrictions order or interim debt relief restrictions order in respect of such a member, the court shall notify the presiding officer of that body.

(1A) If the High Court in Northern Ireland makes a bankruptcy restrictions order or interim order under Schedule 2A to the Insolvency (Northern Ireland) Order 1989 in respect of a member of the Scottish Parliament or the National Assembly for Wales, the Court shall notify the presiding officer of that body.

(2) If the Secretary of State accepts a bankruptcy restrictions undertaking or a debt relief restrictions undertaking made by a member of the Scottish Parliament, the Northern Ireland Assembly or the National Assembly for Wales, the Secretary of State shall notify the presiding officer of that body.

(3) If the Department of Enterprise, Trade and Investment for Northern Ireland accepts a bankruptcy restrictions undertaking made by a member of the Scottish Parliament or the National Assembly for Wales under Schedule 2A to the Insolvency (Northern Ireland) Order 1989, the Department shall notify the presiding officer of that body.

426C Irrelevance of privilege

(1) An enactment about insolvency applies in relation to a member of the House of Commons or the House of Lords irrespective of any Parliamentary privilege.

(2) In this section "enactment" includes a provision made by or under
    (a) an Act of the Scottish Parliament, or
    (b) Northern Ireland legislation.

427 Disqualification from Parliament (Scotland)

(1) Where a court in Scotland awards sequestration of an individual's estate, the individual is disqualified
    (a) for sitting or voting in the House of Lords,
    (b) for being elected to, or sitting or voting in, the House of Commons, and
    (c) for sitting or voting in a committee of either House.

(2) Where an individual is disqualified under this section, the disqualification ceases
    (a) except where the award is recalled or reduced without the individual having been first discharged, on the discharge of the individual, and
    (b) in the excepted case, on the recall or reduction, as the case may be.

(3) No writ of summons shall be issued to any lord of Parliament who is for the time being disqualified under this section for sitting and voting in the House of Lords.

(4) Where a member of the House of Commons who is disqualified under this section continues to be so disqualified until the end of the period of 6 months beginning with the day of the award, his seat shall be vacated at the end of that period.

(5) A court which makes an award such as is mentioned in subsection (1) in relation to any lord of Parliament or member of the House of Commons shall forthwith certify the . . .award to the Speaker of the House of Lords or, as the case may be, to the Speaker of the House of Commons.

(6) Where a court has certified an award to the Speaker of the House of Commons under subsection (5), then immediately after it becomes apparent which of the following certificates is applicable, the court shall certify to the Speaker of the House of Commons
    (a) that the period of 6 months beginning with the day of the award has expired without the award having been recalled or reduced, or
    (b) that the award has been recalled or reduced before the end of that period.

(6A) Subsections (4) to (6) have effect in relation to a member of the Scottish Parliament but as if
    (a) references to the House of Commons were to the Parliament and references to the Speaker were to the Presiding Officer, and
    (b) in subsection (4), for "under this section" there were substituted "under section 15(1)(b) of the Scotland Act 1998 by virtue of this section".

(6B) Subsections (4) to (6) have effect in relation to a member of the National Assembly for Wales but as if
    (a) references to the House of Commons were to the Assembly and references to the Speaker were to the presiding officer, and
    (b) in subsection (4), for "under this section" there were substituted "under section 16(2) of the Government of Wales Act 2006 by virtue of this section".

(6C) Subsections (4) to (6) have effect in relation to a member of the Northern Ireland Assembly but as if
  (a) references to the House of Commons were to the Assembly and references to the Speaker were to the Presiding Officer; and
  (b) in subsection (4), for "under this section" there were substituted "under section 36(4) of the Northern Ireland Act 1998 by virtue of this section".
(7) *Repealed*

Interpretation Act 1978

An Act to consolidate the Interpretation Act 1889 and certain other enactments relating to the construction and operation of Acts of Parliament and other instruments, with amendments to give effect to recommendations of the Law Commission and the Scottish Law Commission

20th July 1978

Schedule 3 — Enactments Repealed

General provisions as to enactment and operation

Words of enactment

1 Every section of an Act takes effect as a substantive enactment without introductory words.

Amendment or repeal in same Session

2 Any Act may be amended or repealed in the Session of Parliament in which it is passed.

Judicial notice

3 Every Act is a public Act to be judicially noticed as such, unless the contrary is expressly provided by the Act.

Time of commencement

4 An Act or provision of an Act comes into force
   (a) where provision is made for it to come into force on a particular day, at the beginning of that day;
   (b) where no provision is made for its coming into force, at the beginning of the day on which the Act receives the Royal Assent.

Interpretation and construction

Definitions

5 In any Act, unless the contrary intention appears, words and expressions listed in Schedule 1 to this Act are to be construed according to that Schedule.

Gender and number

6 In any Act, unless the contrary intention appears,
   (a) words importing the masculine gender include the feminine;
   (b) words importing the feminine gender include the masculine;
   (c) words in the singular include the plural and words in the plural include the singular.

References to service by post

7 Where an Act authorises or requires any document to be served by post (whether the expression "serve" or the expression "give" or "send" or any other expression is used) then, unless the contrary intention appears, the service is deemed to be effected by properly addressing, prepaying and posting a letter containing the document and, unless the contrary is proved, to have been effected at the time at which the letter would be delivered in the ordinary course of post.

References to distance

8 In the measurement of any distance for the purposes of an Act, that distance shall, unless the contrary intention appears, be measured in a straight line on a horizontal plane.

References to time of day

9 Subject to section 3 of the Summer Time Act 1972 (construction of references to points of time during the period of summer time), whenever an expression of time occurs in an Act,

the time referred to shall, unless it is otherwise specifically stated, be held to be Greenwich mean time.

References to the Sovereign

10   In any Act a reference to the Sovereign reigning at the time of the passing of the Act is to be construed, unless the contrary intention appears, as a reference to the Sovereign for the time being.

Construction of subordinate legislation

11   Where an Act confers power to make subordinate legislation, expressions used in that legislation have, unless the contrary intention appears, the meaning which they bear in the Act.

Statutory powers and duties

Continuity of powers and duties

12(1)   Where an Act confers a power or imposes a duty it is implied, unless the contrary intention appears, that the power may be exercised, or the duty is to be performed, from time to time as occasion requires.

(2)   Where an Act confers a power or imposes a duty on the holder of an office as such, it is implied, unless the contrary intention appears, that the power may be exercised, or the duty is to be performed, by the holder for the time being of the office.

Anticipatory exercise of powers

13   Where an Act which (or any provision of which) does not come into force immediately on its passing confers power to make subordinate legislation, or to make appointments, give notices, prescribe forms or do any other thing for the purposes of the Act, then, unless the contrary intention appears, the power may be exercised, and any instrument made thereunder may be made so as to come into force, at any time after the passing of the Act so far as may be necessary or expedient for the purpose

(a)   of bringing the Act or any provision of the Act into force; or

(b)   of giving full effect to the Act or any such provision at or after the time when it comes into force.

Implied power to amend

14   Where an Act confers power to make

(a)   rules, regulations or bye-laws; or

(b)   Orders in Council, orders or other subordinate legislation to be made by statutory instrument,

it implies, unless the contrary intention appears, a power, exercisable in the same manner and subject to the same conditions or limitations, to revoke, amend or reenact any instrument made under the power.

Power to include sunset and review provisions in subordinate legislation

14A(1)   This section applies where an Act confers a power or a duty on a person to make subordinate legislation except to the extent that

(a)   the power or duty is exercisable by the Scottish Ministers, or

(b)   the power or duty is exercisable by any other person within devolved competence (within the meaning of the Scotland Act 1998).

(2)   The subordinate legislation may include

(a)   provision requiring the person to review the effectiveness of the legislation within a specified period or at the end of a specified period;

(b) provision for the legislation to cease to have effect at the end of a specified day or a specified period;

(c) if the power or duty is being exercised to amend other subordinate legislation, provision of the kind mentioned in paragraph (a) or (b) in relation to that other legislation.

(3) The provision that may be made by virtue of subsection (2)(a) includes provision requiring the person to consider whether the objectives which it was the purpose of the legislation to achieve remain appropriate and, if so, whether they could be achieved in another way.

(4) Subordinate legislation including provision of a kind mentioned in subsection (2) may make such provision generally or only in relation to specified provisions of the legislation or specified cases or circumstances.

(5) Subordinate legislation including provision of a kind mentioned in subsection (2) may make transitional, consequential, incidental or supplementary provision or savings in connection with such provision.

(6) In this section, "specified" means specified in the subordinate legislation.

Repealing enactments

Repeal of repeal

15 Where an Act repeals a repealing enactment, the repeal does not revive any enactment previously repealed unless words are inserted reviving it.

General savings

16(1) Without prejudice to section 15, where an Act repeals an enactment, the repeal does not, unless the contrary intention appears,

(a) revive anything not in force or existing at the time at which the repeal takes effect;

(b) affect the previous operation of the enactment repealed or anything duly done or suffered under that enactment;

(c) affect any right, privilege, obligation or liability acquired, accrued or incurred under that enactment;

(d) affect any penalty, forfeiture or punishment incurred in respect of any offence committed against that enactment;

(e) affect any investigation, legal proceeding or remedy in respect of any such right, privilege, obligation, liability, penalty, forfeiture or punishment;

and any such investigation, legal proceeding or remedy may be instituted, continued or enforced, and any such penalty, forfeiture or punishment may be imposed, as if the repealing Act had not been passed.

(2) This section applies to the expiry of a temporary enactment as if it were repealed by an Act.

Repeal and re-enactment

17(1) Where an Act repeals a previous enactment and substitutes provisions for the enactment repealed, the repealed enactment remains in force until the substituted provisions come into force.

(2) Where an Act repeals and reenacts, with or without modification, a previous enactment then, unless the contrary intention appears,

(a) any reference in any other enactment to the enactment so repealed shall be construed as a reference to the provision reenacted;

(b) in so far as any subordinate legislation made or other thing done under the enactment so repealed, or having effect as if so made or done, could have been made or done under the provision reenacted, it shall have effect as if made or done under that provision.

Miscellaneous

Duplicated offences

18   Where an act or omission constitutes an offence under two or more Acts, or both under an Act and at common law, the offender shall, unless the contrary intention appears, be liable to be prosecuted and punished under either or any of those Acts or at common law, but shall not be liable to be punished more than once for the same offence.

Citation of other Acts

19(1)   Where an Act cites another Act by year, statute, session or chapter, or a section or other portion of another Act by number or letter, the reference shall, unless the contrary intention appears, be read as referring

    (a)   in the case of Acts included in any revised edition of the statutes printed by authority, to that edition;

    (b)   in the case of Acts not so included but included in the edition prepared under the direction of the Record Commission, to that edition;

    (c)   in any other case, to the Acts printed by the Queen's Printer, or under the superintendence or authority of Her Majesty's Stationery Office.

  (2)   An Act may continue to be cited by the short title authorised by any enactment notwithstanding the repeal of that enactment.

References to other enactments

20(1)   Where an Act describes or cites a portion of an enactment by referring to words, sections or other parts from or to which (or from and to which) the portion extends, the portion described or cited includes the words, sections or other parts referred to unless the contrary intention appears.

  (2)   Where an Act refers to an enactment, the reference, unless the contrary intention appears, is a reference to that enactment as amended, and includes a reference thereto as extended or applied, by or under any other enactment, including any other provision of that Act.

References to EU instruments

20A   Where an Act passed after the commencement of this section refers to a EU instrument that has been amended, extended or applied by another such instrument, the reference, unless the contrary intention appears, is a reference to that instrument as so amended, extended or applied.

Supplementary

Interpretation etc

21(1)   In this Act "Act" includes a local and personal or private Act; and "subordinate legislation" means Orders in Council, orders, rules, regulations, schemes, warrants, byelaws and other instruments made or to be made under any Act.

  (2)   This Act binds the Crown.

Application to Acts and Measures

22(1) This Act applies to itself, to any Act passed after the commencement of this Act (subject, in the case of section 20A, to the provision made in that section) and, to the extent specified in Part I of Schedule 2, to Acts passed before the commencement of this Act.

(2) In any of the foregoing provisions of this Act a reference to an Act is a reference to an Act to which that provision applies; but this does not affect the generality of references to enactments or of the references in section 19(1) to other Acts.

(3) This Act applies to Measures of the General Synod of the Church of England (and, so far as it relates to Acts passed before the commencement of this Act, to Measures of the Church Assembly passed after 28th May 1925) as it applies to Acts.

Application to other instruments

23(1) The provisions of this Act, except sections 1 to 3 and 4(*b*), apply, so far as applicable and unless the contrary intention appears, to subordinate legislation made after the commencement of this Act and, to the extent specified in Part II of Schedule 2, to subordinate legislation made before the commencement of this Act, as they apply to Acts.

(2) In the application of this Act to Acts passed or subordinate legislation made after the commencement of this Act, all references to an enactment include an enactment comprised in subordinate legislation whenever made, and references to the passing or repeal of an enactment are to be construed accordingly.

(3) Sections 9 and 19(1) also apply to deeds and other instruments and documents as they apply to Acts and subordinate legislation; and in the application of section 17(2)(*a*) to Acts passed or subordinate legislation made after the commencement of this Act, the reference to any other enactment includes any deed or other instrument or document.

(4) Subsections (1) and (2) of this section do not apply to Orders in Council made under section 5 of the Statutory Instruments Act 1946, section 1(3) of the Northern Ireland (Temporary Provisions) Act 1972 or Schedule 1 to the Northern Ireland Act 1974.

Acts of the Scottish Parliament etc

23A(1) This Act applies in relation to an Act of the Scottish Parliament and an instrument made under such an Act only to the extent provided in this section.

(2) Except as provided in subsection (3) below, sections 15 to 18 apply to
  (a) an Act of the Scottish Parliament as they apply to an Act,
  (b) an instrument made under an Act of the Scottish Parliament as they apply to subordinate legislation.

(3) In the application of those sections to an Act and to subordinate legislation
  (a) references to an enactment include an enactment comprised in, or in an instrument made under, an Act of the Scottish Parliament, and
  (b) the reference in section 17(2)(b) to subordinate legislation includes an instrument made under an Act of the Scottish Parliament.

(4) In the application of section 20 to an Act and to subordinate legislation, references to an enactment include an enactment comprised in, or in an instrument made under, an Act of the Scottish Parliament.

Measures and Acts of the National Assembly for Wales etc

23B(1) Subject as follows, the provisions of this Act
  (a) apply to a Measure or Act of the National Assembly for Wales as they apply to an Act, and
  (b) apply to an instrument made under a Measure or Act of the National Assembly for Wales as they apply to other subordinate legislation.

(2) Sections 1 to 3 do not apply to a Measure or Act of the National Assembly for Wales.

(3) In this Act references to an enactment include an enactment comprised in, or in an instrument made under, a Measure or Act of the National Assembly for Wales.

(4) In the application of this Act to a Measure or Act of the National Assembly for Wales, references to the passing of an Act or an enactment are to be read as references to the enactment of the Measure or Act.

(5) Section 4(b) does not apply to a Measure of the National Assembly for Wales; but where such a Measure makes no provision for the coming into force of a provision contained in it, that provision comes into force at the beginning of the day on which the Measure is approved by Her Majesty in Council.

Application to Northern Ireland

24(1) This Act extends to Northern Ireland so far as it applies to Acts or subordinate legislation which so extend.

(2) In the application of this Act to Acts passed or subordinate legislation made after the commencement of this Act, all references to an enactment include an enactment comprised in Northern Ireland legislation whenever passed or made; and in relation to such legislation references to the passing or repeal of an enactment include the making or revocation of an Order in Council.

(3) In the application of section 14 to Acts passed after the commencement of this Act which extend to Northern Ireland, "statutory instrument" includes statutory rule for the purposes of the Statutory Rules Northern Ireland Order 1979.

(3A) Section 20A applies to Northern Ireland legislation as it applies to Acts.

(4) The following definitions contained in Schedule 1, namely those of
The Communities and related expressions;
The Corporation Tax Acts;
EEA agreement and EEA state;
The Income Tax Acts;
The Tax Acts,
apply unless the contrary intention appears, to Northern Ireland legislation as they apply to Acts.

(5) In this section "Northern Ireland legislation" means
(a) Acts of the Parliament of Ireland;
(b) Acts of the Parliament of Northern Ireland;
(c) Orders in Council under section 1(3) of the Northern Ireland (Temporary Provisions) Act 1972;
(d) Measures of the Northern Ireland Assembly established under section 1 of the Northern Ireland Assembly Act 1973;
(e) orders in Council under Schedule 1 to the Northern Ireland Act 1974;
(f) Acts of the Northern Ireland Assembly; and
(g) Orders in Council under section 85 of the Northern Ireland Act 1998.

Repeals and savings

25(1) The enactments described in Schedule 3 are repealed to the extent specified in the third column of that Schedule.

(2) Without prejudice to section 17(2)(*a*), a reference to the Interpretation Act 1889, to any provision of that Act or to any other enactment repealed by this Act, whether occurring in another Act, in subordinate legislation, in Northern Ireland legislation or in any deed or other instrument or document, shall be construed as referring to this Act, or to the corresponding provision of this Act, as it applies to Acts passed at the time of the reference.

(3) The provisions of this Act relating to Acts passed after any particular time do not affect the construction of Acts passed before that time, though continued or amended by Acts passed thereafter.

Commencement

26 This Act shall come into force on 1st January 1979.

Short title

27 This Act may be cited as the Interpretation Act 1978.

SCHEDULE 1
WORDS AND EXPRESSIONS DEFINED

Section 5

Note: The years or dates which follow certain entries in this Schedule are relevant for the purposes of paragraph 4 of Schedule 2 (application to existing enactments).

Definitions

"Act" means an Act of Parliament.

"Associated state" means a territory maintaining a status of association with the United Kingdom in accordance with the West Indies Act 1967. 16th February 1967

"Bank of England" means, as the context requires, the Governor and Company of the Bank of England or the bank of the Governor and Company of the Bank of England.

"Bank of Ireland" means, as the context requires, the Governor and Company of the Bank of Ireland or the bank of the Governor and Company of the Bank of Ireland.

"British Islands" means the United Kingdom, the Channel Islands and the Isle of Man. 1889

"British overseas territory" has the same meaning as in the British Nationality Act 1981;

"British possession" means any part of Her Majesty's dominions outside the United Kingdom; and where parts of such dominions are under both a central and a local legislature, all parts under the central legislature are deemed, for the purposes of this definition, to be one British possession. 1889

"Building regulations", in relation to England and Wales, has the meaning given by section 122 of the Building Act 1984.

"Central funds", in an enactment providing in relation to England and Wales for the payment of costs out of central funds, means money provided by Parliament.

"Charity Commission" means the Charity Commission for England and Wales (see section 13 of the Charities Act 2011).

"Church Commissioners" means the Commissioners constituted by the Church Commissioners Measure 1947.

"Civil partnership" means a civil partnership which exists under or by virtue of the Civil Partnership Act 2004 (and any reference to a civil partner is to be read accordingly).

"Colonial legislature", and "legislature" in relation to a British possession, mean the authority, other than the Parliament of the United Kingdom or Her Majesty in Council, competent to make laws for the possession.

"Colony" means any part of Her Majesty's dominions outside the British Islands except

(a) countries having fully responsible status within the Commonwealth;

(b) territories for whose external relations a country other than the United Kingdom is responsible;

(c) associated states;

and where parts of such dominions are under both a central and a local legislature, all parts under the central legislature are deemed for the purposes of this definition to be one colony. 1889

"Commencement", in relation to an Act or enactment, means the time when the Act or enactment comes into force.

"Committed for trial" means

    (a) *Repealed*

    (b) in relation to Northern Ireland, committed in custody or on bail by a magistrates' court pursuant to Article 37 of the Magistrates' Courts (Northern Ireland) Order 1981, or by a court, judge, resident magistrate or other authority having power to do so, with a view to trial on indictment. 1st January 1979

"The EU" or "the EU Treaties" and other expressions defined by section 1 of and Schedule 1 to the European Communities Act 1972 have the meanings prescribed by that Act.

"Comptroller and Auditor General" means the Comptroller-General of the receipt and issue of Her Majesty's Exchequer and Auditor-General of Public Accounts.

"Consular officer" has the meaning assigned by Article 1 of the Vienna Convention set out in Schedule 1 to the Consular Relations Act 1968.

"The Corporation Tax Acts" means the enactments relating to the taxation of the income and chargeable gains of companies and of company distributions (including provisions relating to income tax).

"County court" means

    (a) in relation to England and Wales, the county court established under section A1 of the County Courts Act 1984, 1846

    (b) in relation to Northern Ireland, a court held for a division under the County Courts (Northern Ireland) Order 1980. 1889

"Court of Appeal" means

    (a) in relation to England and Wales, Her Majesty's Court of Appeal in England;

    (b) in relation to Northern Ireland, Her Majesty's Court of Appeal in Northern Ireland.

"Court of Judicature" means the Court of Judicature of Northern Ireland.

"Court of summary jurisdiction", "summary conviction" and "Summary Jurisdiction Acts", in relation to Northern Ireland, have the same meanings as in Measures of the Northern Ireland Assembly and Acts of the Parliament of Northern Ireland.

"Crown Court" means

    (a) in relation to England and Wales, the Crown Court constituted by section 4 of the Courts Act 1971;

    (b) in relation to Northern Ireland, the Crown Court constituted by section 4 of the Judicature (Northern Ireland) Act 1978.

"Crown Estate Commissioners" means the Commissioners referred to in section 1 of the Crown Estate Act 1961.

"EEA agreement" means the agreement on the European Economic Area signed at Oporto on 2nd May 1992, together with the Protocol adjusting that Agreement signed at Brussels on 17th March 1993, as modified or supplemented from time to time. The date of the coming into force of this paragraph.

"EEA state", in relation to any time, means

    (a) a state which at that time is a member State; or

    (b) any other state which at that time is a party to the EEA agreement. The date of the coming into force of this paragraph.

"Enactment" does not include an enactment comprised in, or in an instrument made under, an Act of the Scottish Parliament.

"England" means, subject to any alteration of boundaries under Part IV of the Local Government Act 1972, the area consisting of the counties established by section 1 of that Act, Greater London and the Isles of Scilly. 1st April 1974

"Financial year" means, in relation to matters relating to the Consolidated Fund, the National Loans Fund, or moneys provided by Parliament, or to the Exchequer or to central taxes or finance, the twelve months ending with 31st March. 1889

"Governor-General" includes any person who for the time being has the powers of the Governor-General, and "Governor", in relation to any British possession, includes the officer for the time being administering the government of that possession. 1889

"Her Majesty's Revenue and Customs" has the meaning given by section 4 of the Commissioners for Revenue and Customs Act 2005.

"High Court" means

(a)   in relation to England and Wales, Her Majesty's High Court of Justice in England;

(b)   in relation to Northern Ireland, Her Majesty's High Court of Justice in Northern Ireland.

"The Immigration Acts" has the meaning given by section 61 of the UK Borders Act 2007.

"The Income Tax Acts" means all enactments relating to income tax, including any provisions of the Corporation Tax Acts which relate to income tax.

"Land" includes buildings and other structures, land covered with water, and any estate, interest, easement, servitude or right in or over land. 1st January 1979)

"Lands Clauses Acts" means

(a)   in relation to England and Wales, the Lands Clauses Consolidation Act 1845 and the Lands Clauses Consolidation Acts Amendment Act 1860, and any Acts for the time being in force amending those Acts; 1889

(b)   in relation to Scotland, the Lands Clauses Consolidation (Scotland) Act 1845 and the Lands Clauses Consolidation Acts Amendment Act 1860, and any Acts for the time being in force amending those Acts; 1889

(c)   in relation to Northern Ireland, the enactments defined as such by section 46 (1) of the Interpretation Act (Northern Ireland) 1954. 1889

"Local land charges register", in relation to England and Wales, means the register kept pursuant to section 3 of the Local Land Charges Act 1975.

"Local policing body" has the meaning given by section 101(1) of the Police Act 1996.

"London borough" means a borough described in Schedule 1 to the London Government Act 1963, "inner London borough" means one of the boroughs so described and numbered from 1 to 12 and "outer London borough" means one of the boroughs so described and numbered from 13 to 32, subject (in each case) to any alterations made under Part IV of the Local Government Act 1972, Part 2 of the Local Government Act 1992 or Part 1 of the Local Government and Public Involvement in Health Act 2007.

"Lord Chancellor" means the Lord High Chancellor of Great Britain.

"Magistrates' court" has the meaning assigned to it

(a)   in relation to England and Wales, by section 148 of the Magistrates' Courts Act 1980;

(b)   in relation to Northern Ireland, by Article 2(2) of the Magistrates' Courts (Northern Ireland) Order 1981.

"Month" means calendar month. 1850

"National Debt Commissioners" means the Commissioners for the Reduction of the National Debt.

"Northern Ireland legislation" has the meaning assigned by section 24(5) of this Act. 1st January 1979

"Oath" and "affidavit" include affirmation and declaration, and "swear" includes affirm and declare.

"Officer of a provider of probation services" in relation to England and Wales, has the meaning given by section 9(1) of the Offender Management Act 2007;

"Officer of Revenue and Customs" has the meaning given by section 2(1) of the Commissioners for Revenue and Customs Act 2005.

"Ordnance Map" means a map made under powers conferred by the Ordnance Survey Act 1841 or the Boundary Survey (Ireland) Act 1854.

"Parliamentary Election" means the election of a Member to serve in Parliament for a constituency. 1889

"PAYE income" has the meaning given by section 683 of the Income Tax (Earnings and Pensions) Act 2003.

"PAYE regulations" means regulations under section 684 of that Act.

"Person" includes a body of persons corporate or unincorporate. 1889

"Police and crime commissioner" means a police and crime commissioner established under section 1 of the Police Reform and Social Responsibility Act 2011.

"Police area" and other expressions relating to the police have the meaning or effect described

    (a)   in relation to England and Wales, by section 101(1) of the Police Act 1996;

    (b)   *Repealed*

"Police Service of Northern Ireland" and "Police Service of Northern Ireland Reserve" have the same meaning as in the Police (Northern Ireland) Act 2000;

"The Privy Council" means the Lords and others of Her Majesty's Most Honourable Privy Council.

"Provider of probation services", in relation to England and Wales, has the meaning given by section 3(6) of the Offender Management Act 2007;

"Registered" in relation to nurses and midwives, means registered in the register maintained under article 5 of the Nursing and Midwifery Order 2001 by virtue of qualifications in nursing or midwifery, as the case may be.

"Registered medical practitioner" means a fully registered person within the meaning of the Medical Act 1983 who holds a licence to practise under that Act.

"Registered provider of social housing" and "private registered provider of social housing" have the meanings given by section 80 of the Housing and Regeneration Act 2008 (and "nonprofit" and "profitmaking" in connection with a registered provider are to be read in accordance with section 115 of that Act).

"Rules of Court" in relation to any court means rules made by the authority having power to make rules or orders regulating the practice and procedure of that court, and in Scotland includes Acts of Adjournal and Acts of Sederunt; and the power of the authority to make rules of court (as above defined) includes power to make such rules for the purpose of any Act which directs or authorises anything to be done by rules of court. 1889

"Secretary of State" means one of Her Majesty's Principal Secretaries of State.

"Senior Courts" means the Senior Courts of England and Wales.

"Sent for trial" means, in relation to England and Wales, sent by a magistrates' court to the Crown Court for trial pursuant to section 51 or 51A of the Crime and Disorder Act 1998.

"Sewerage undertaker", in relation to England and Wales, shall be construed in accordance with section 6 of the Water Industry Act 1991.

"Sheriff" is to be construed in accordance with section 134(2) and (3) of the Courts Reform (Scotland) Act 2014.

"The standard scale", with reference to a fine or penalty for an offence triable only summarily,

    (a)   in relation to England and Wales, has the meaning given by section 37 of the Criminal Justice Act 1982;

    (b)   in relation to Scotland, has the meaning given by section 225(1) of the Criminal Procedure (Scotland) Act 1995;

    (c)   in relation to Northern Ireland, has the meaning given by Article 5 of the Fines and Penalties (Northern Ireland) Order 1984.

"Statutory declaration" means a declaration made by virtue of the Statutory Declarations Act 1835.

"Statutory maximum", with reference to a fine or penalty on summary conviction for an offence,

    (a)   in relation to England and Wales, means the prescribed sum within the meaning of section 32 of the Magistrates' Courts Act 1980;

    (b)   in relation to Scotland, means the prescribed sum within the meaning of section 225(8) of the Criminal Procedure (Scotland) Act 1995; and

    (c)   in relation to Northern Ireland, means the prescribed sum within the meaning of Article 4 of the Fines and Penalties (Northern Ireland) Order 1984.

"Supreme Court" means the Supreme Court of the United Kingdom.

"The Tax Acts" means the Income Tax Acts and the Corporation Tax Acts.

"The Treasury" means the Commissioners of Her Majesty's Treasury.

"Trust of land" and "trustees of land", in relation to England and Wales, have the same meanings as in the Trusts of Land and Appointment of Trustees Act 1996.

"United Kingdom" means Great Britain and Northern Ireland. 12th April 1927

"Wales" means the combined area of the counties which were created by section 20 of the Local Government Act 1972, as originally enacted, but subject to any alteration made under section 73 of that Act (consequential alteration of boundary following alteration of watercourse).

"Water undertaker", in relation to England and Wales, shall be construed in accordance with section 6 of the Water Industry Act 1991.

"Writing" includes typing, printing, lithography, photography and other modes of representing or reproducing words in a visible form, and expressions referring to writing are construed accordingly.

Construction of certain expressions relating to offences
In relation to England and Wales
  (a) "indictable offence" means an offence which, if committed by an adult, is triable on indictment, whether it is exclusively so triable or triable either way;
  (b) "summary offence" means an offence which, if committed by an adult, is triable only summarily;
  (c) "offence triable either way" means an offence, other than an offence triable on indictment only by virtue of Part V of the Criminal Justice Act 1988 which, if committed by an adult, is triable either on indictment or summarily;
and the terms "indictable", "summary" and "triable either way", in their application to offences, are to be construed accordingly.

In the above definitions references to the way or ways in which an offence is triable are to be construed without regard to the effect, if any, of section 22 of the Magistrates' Courts Act 1980 on the mode of trial in a particular case.

Construction of certain references to relationships
In relation to England and Wales
  (a) references (however expressed) to any relationship between two persons;
  (b) references to a person whose father and mother were or were not married to each other at the time of his birth; and
  (c) references cognate with references falling within paragraph (b) above,
shall be construed in accordance with section 1 of the Family Law Reform Act 1987. The date of the coming into force of that section.

Construction of certain expressions relating to the police: Scotland
In relation to Scotland
  (a) references to a police force include references to the Police Service of Scotland;
  (b) references to a chief officer of police include references to the chief constable of the Police Service of Scotland;
  (c) "police authority" means the Scottish Police Authority;
  (d) the "police area" of the Police Service of Scotland is Scotland and references to a police force or police authority for any area include references to the Police Service of Scotland or, as the case may be, the Scottish Police Authority;
  (e) references to a constable or chief constable of, or appointed for, any area are to be construed as references to a constable or, as the case may be, the chief constable of, or appointed for, the Police Service of Scotland.

Sections 22, 23

Part I

Acts

1   The following provisions of this Act apply to Acts whenever passed:
> Section 6(a) and (c) so far as applicable to enactments relating to offences punishable on indictment or on summary conviction
> Section 9
> Section 10
> Section 11 so far as it relates to subordinate legislation made after the year 1889
> Section 14A
> Section 18
> Section 19(2).

2   The following apply to Acts passed after the year 1850:
> Section 1
> Section 2
> Section 3
> Section 6(a) and (c) so far as not applicable to such Acts by virtue of paragraph 1
> Section 15
> Section 17(1).

3   The following apply to Acts passed after the year 1889:
> Section 4
> Section 7
> Section 8
> Section 12
> Section 13
> Section 14 so far as it relates to rules, regulations or byelaws
> Section 16(1)
> Section 17(2)(a)
> Section 19(1)
> Section 20(1).

4(1)   Subject to the following provisions of this paragraph
>(a) paragraphs of Schedule 1 at the end of which a year or date is specified or described apply, so far as applicable, to Acts passed on or after the date, or after the year, so specified or described; and
>(b) paragraphs of that Schedule at the end of which no year or date is specified or described apply, so far as applicable, to Acts passed at any time.

(2)   The definition of "British Islands", in its application to Acts passed after the establishment of the Irish Free State but before the commencement of this Act, includes the Republic of Ireland.

(3)   The definition of "colony", in its application to an Act passed at any time before the commencement of this Act, includes
>(a) any colony within the meaning of section 18(3) of the Interpretation Act 1889 which was excluded, but in relation only to Acts passed at a later time, by any enactment repealed by this Act;

(b) any country or territory which ceased after that time to be part of Her Majesty's dominions but subject to a provision for the continuation of existing law as if it had not so ceased;

and paragraph (b) of the definition does not apply.

(4) The definition of "Lord Chancellor" does not apply to Acts passed before 1st October 1921 in which that expression was used in relation to Ireland only.

(5) The definition of "person", so far as it includes bodies corporate, applies to any provision of an Act whenever passed relating to an offence punishable on indictment or on summary conviction.

(6) This paragraph applies to the Water Act 1973 as if they were passed after 1st April 1974.

5 The following definitions shall be treated as included in Schedule 1 for the purposes specified in this paragraph

(a) in any Act passed before 1st April 1974, a reference to England includes Berwick upon Tweed and Monmouthshire and, in the case of an Act passed before the Welsh Language Act 1967, Wales;

(b) in any Act passed before the commencement of this Act and after the year 1850, "land" includes messuages, tenements and hereditaments, houses and buildings of any tenure;

(c) in any Act passed before the commencement of the Criminal Procedure (Scotland) Act 1975, "the Summary Jurisdiction (Scotland) Acts" means Part II of that Act.

Part II
Subordinate Legislation

6 Sections 4, 9 and 19(1), and so much of Schedule 1 as defines the following expressions, namely

England;
Local land charges register and appropriate local land charges register;
In relation to Scotland, expressions relating to the police;
United Kingdom;
Wales,

apply to subordinate legislation made at any time before the commencement of this Act as they apply to Acts passed at that time.

7 The definition in Schedule 1 of "county court", in relation to England and Wales, applies to Orders in Council made after the year 1846.

SCHEDULE 3
ENACTMENTS REPEALED

Not reproduced

Local Democracy, Economic Development and Construction Act 2009

PART 3
LOCAL GOVERNMENT BOUNDARY AND ELECTORAL CHANGE

Establishment of the Local Government Boundary Commission for England

55 Local Government Boundary Commission for England

(1) The Local Government Boundary Commission for England is established as a body corporate.

(2) The Local Government Boundary Commission for England is not to be regarded as a servant or agent of the Crown or as enjoying any status, immunity or privilege of the Crown.

(3) Accordingly, the property of the Local Government Boundary Commission for England is not to be regarded as the property of the Crown or as property held on behalf of the Crown.

(4) The Local Government Boundary Commission for England may do anything, except borrow money, which is calculated to facilitate, or is incidental or conducive to, the exercise of its functions.

(5) Schedule 1 (which makes further provision about the constitution and administration of the Local Government Boundary Commission for England) is part of this Part.

Local Government Boundary Commission for England: functions relating to electoral change

Review of electoral arrangements

56(1) The Local Government Boundary Commission for England must from time to time
  (a) conduct a review of the area of each principal council, and
  (b) recommend whether a change should be made to the electoral arrangements for that area.

(2) The Local Government Boundary Commission for England may at any time
  (a) conduct a review of all or any part of the area of a principal council, and
  (b) recommend whether a change should be made to the electoral arrangements for the area of the principal council.

(3) In this Part "principal council" means
  (a) a county council in England;
  (b) a district council;
  (c) the Council of the Isles of Scilly;
  (d) a London borough council.

(4) In this Part "electoral arrangements", in relation to the area of a principal council, means
  (a) the total number of members of the council ("councillors"),
  (b) the number and boundaries of electoral areas for the purposes of the election of councillors,
  (c) the number of councillors to be returned by any electoral area in that area, and
  (d) the name of any electoral area.

(5) Where under this section the Local Government Boundary Commission for England recommends that a change should be made to the electoral arrangements for the area of

a principal council, the Commission must also recommend whether, in consequence, a change should be made to the electoral arrangements for the area of any parish council, where that area is within the area of the principal council.

(6) In this Part "electoral arrangements", in relation to the area of a parish council, means
    (a) the total number of members of the parish council ("parish councillors"),
    (b) arrangements for the division of the parish or (in the case of a common parish council) any of the parishes into wards for the purposes of the election of parish councillors,
    (c) the number and boundaries of any wards,
    (d) the number of parish councillors to be returned by any ward or, in the case of a common parish council, by each parish, and
    (e) the name of any ward.

(7) Section 6(2)(a) of the Local Government Act 1972 (c) 70) (electoral divisions of non-metropolitan county to return one councillor each) does not limit the recommendations that may be made under this section.

(8) Schedule 2 (which makes further provision relating to recommendations under this section) is part of this Part.

(9) A principal council or parish council must, if requested by the Local Government Boundary Commission for England to do so, provide the Commission, by such date as it may specify, with any information that it may reasonably require in connection with its functions under this section.

Requests for review of single-member electoral areas

57(1) A principal council which falls within subsection (3) may request the Local Government Boundary Commission for England to
    (a) conduct a review of the council's area under section 56(2)(a), and
    (b) make recommendations as to single-member electoral areas under section 56(2)(b).

(2) In this section "recommendations as to single-member electoral areas" means recommendations, for each electoral area in the area of a principal council, as to whether the electoral area should return one member of the council.

(3) A principal council falls within this subsection if
    (a) it is not the case that each of the electoral areas in the council's area returns one member of the council, and
    (b) the council is subject to a scheme for whole-council elections.

(4) For the purposes of subsection (3)(b) a principal council is "subject to a scheme for whole-council elections" if, in each year in which ordinary elections of members of the council are to be held, all the members of the council are to be elected.

(4A) A district council is also "subject to a scheme for whole-council elections" for those purposes if
    (a) section 34 of the Local Government and Public Involvement in Health Act 2007 (scheme for whole-council elections) applies to the council, but
    (b) by virtue of subsection (4A) of that section (temporary continuation of previous electoral scheme), not all the members of the council are to be elected in a year in which ordinary elections of members of the council are to be held.

(5) If the Local Government Boundary Commission for England grants a request under this section, in making its recommendations it must (in addition to the matters to be considered pursuant to Schedule 2) have regard to the desirability of securing that each electoral area in the principal council's area should return one member of the council.

(6) If the Local Government Boundary Commission for England decides not to grant a principal council's request under this section, it must notify the council of its decision and the reasons for it.

(7) Nothing in this section prevents the Local Government Boundary Commission for England, when making recommendations as to single-member electoral areas pursuant to subsection (1), from making other recommendations under section 56(2)(b).

(8) In subsections (2) and (5), references to electoral areas are, in relation to a case where the Local Government Boundary Commission for England makes recommendations for change to the number or boundaries of electoral areas in the area of a principal council, to the recommended electoral areas.

Review procedure

58(1) As soon as reasonably practicable after deciding to conduct a review under section 56, the Local Government Boundary Commission for England must take such steps as it considers sufficient to secure that persons who may be interested in the review are informed of
    (a) the fact that the review is to take place, and
    (b) any particular matters to which the review is to relate.

(2) In conducting a review under section 56, the Local Government Boundary Commission for England must
    (a) prepare and publish draft recommendations,
    (b) take such steps as its considers sufficient to secure that persons who may be interested in the recommendations are informed of them and of the period within which representations with respect to them may be made, and
    (c) take into consideration any representations made to the Local Government Boundary Commission for England within that period.

(3) The Local Government Boundary Commission for England may at any time before publishing draft recommendations under subsection (2)(a) consult such persons as it considers appropriate.

(4) As soon as practicable after conducting a review under section 56, the Local Government Boundary Commission for England must
    (a) publish a report stating its recommendations, and
    (b) take such steps as it considers sufficient to secure that persons who may be interested in the recommendations are informed of them.

Implementation of review recommendations

59(1) Where a report under section 58(4) contains recommendations for electoral changes, the Local Government Boundary Commission for England may by order give effect to all or any of the recommendations.

(2) An order under this section may in particular include provision as to
    (a) the total number of members of any principal council or parish council ("councillors");
    (b) the number and boundaries of electoral areas for the purposes of the election of councillors;
    (c) the number of councillors to be returned by any electoral area;
    (d) the name of any electoral area;
    (e) the election of councillors for any electoral area;
    (f) the order of retirement of councillors;
    (g) the ordinary year of election for a parish council.

(3) An order under this section may not require or authorise the holding of an election for membership of a principal council otherwise than at an ordinary election for that council.

(4) An order under this section may
  (a) contain incidental, consequential, supplementary or transitional provision, or savings;
  (b) make different provision for different cases, including different provision for different areas or councils.

(5) The provision referred to in subsection (4)(a) may include provision
  (a) applying any instrument made under an enactment, with or without modifications,
  (b) extending, excluding or amending any such instrument, or
  (c) repealing or revoking any such instrument.

(6) Where the Local Government Boundary Commission for England is satisfied that
  (a) a mistake has occurred in the preparation of an order under subsection (1), and
  (b) the mistake is such that it cannot be rectified by a subsequent order under this section by virtue of section 14 of the Interpretation Act 1978 (c) 30) (implied power to amend),
  the Local Government Boundary Commission for England may by order under this subsection make such provision as it thinks necessary or expedient for rectifying the mistake.

(7) In subsection (6), "mistake", in relation to an order, includes a provision contained in or omitted from the order in reliance on information supplied by any public body which is inaccurate or incomplete.

(8) An order under this section is to be made by statutory instrument.

(9) A draft of a statutory instrument containing an order under this section is to be laid before Parliament before the instrument is made.

Local Government Boundary Commission for England: functions relating to boundary change

Transfer of functions relating to boundary change

60(1) The functions of the Electoral Commission's Boundary Committee under Chapter 1 of Part 1 of the Local Government and Public Involvement in Health Act 2007 (c) 28) (structural and boundary change) are, subject to this Part, transferred to the Local Government Boundary Commission for England.

(2) The functions of the Electoral Commission under the enactments specified in subsection (3) are, subject to the following provisions of this Part, transferred to the Local Government Boundary Commission for England.

(3) Those enactments are
  (a) section 2(4) of the Greater London Authority Act 1999 (c) 29) (constituencies for the Greater London Assembly);
  (b) Chapter 1 of Part 2 of the Local Government and Public Involvement in Health Act 2007 (electoral arrangements);
  (c) section 59 of that Act (change of name of electoral area);
  (d) Chapter 3 of Part 4 of that Act (parish re-organization).

(4) In this Part, the "Electoral Commission's Boundary Committee" means the Boundary Committee for England constituted by the Electoral Commission under section 14 of the Political Parties, Elections and Referendums Act 2000 (c) 41).

Termination of involvement of Electoral Commission

Removal of functions relating to boundary and electoral change

61(1) The duty of the Electoral Commission under section 14 of the Political Parties, Elections and Referendums Act 2000 (c) 41) to establish Boundary Committees is abolished so far as relating to England.

(2) Accordingly, the following provisions of that Act are repealed
   (a) section 14 (Boundary Committees), so far as relating to England;
   (b) section 15 (Deputy Electoral Commissioners).

(3) In that Act, the following provisions (which provide for the transfer of functions etc to the Electoral Commission and which are not in force or in force only to a limited extent) are repealed
   (a) section 14 (Boundary Committees) so far as relating to Scotland, Wales and Northern Ireland;
   (b) sections 16 and 17 (transfer of functions and property etc of Boundary Commissions to the Electoral Commission);
   (c) sections 19 and 20 (transfer of functions of Local Government Boundary Commissions for Scotland and Wales to Electoral Commission);
   (d) Part 1 of Schedule 3 (amendments relating to the transfer of functions of Boundary Commissions);
   (e) in Schedule 22 (repeals), the entries relating to the Parliamentary Constituencies Act 1986 (c) 56) and the Boundary Commissions Act 1992 (c) 55).

Transfer schemes

62(1) For the purpose of the exercise of functions conferred on the Local Government Boundary Commission for England by or under this Part, the Electoral Commission must make one or more schemes for the transfer of property, rights and liabilities from the Electoral Commission to the Local Government Boundary Commission for England.

(2) The Electoral Commission may not make a scheme under this section
   (a) without consulting the Secretary of State;
   (b) without the consent of the Electoral Commission's Boundary Committee.

(3) If the Electoral Commission and the Electoral Commission's Boundary Committee fail to agree on the provision to be included in a scheme under this section, the Secretary of State may by order specify the provision to be included in the scheme.

(4) A scheme under this section must be made on or before
   (a) 31 December 2009, or
   (b) such later date as the Secretary of State may by order specify.

(5) A transfer under a scheme under this section has effect in accordance with the terms of the scheme.

(6) A transfer under a scheme under this section may have effect
   (a) whether or not the property, rights and liabilities would otherwise be capable of being transferred;
   (b) without any instrument or other formality being required.

(7) The rights and liabilities which may be transferred by a scheme under this section include rights and liabilities in relation to a contract of employment.

(8) The Transfer of Undertakings (Protection of Employment) Regulations 2006 (SI 2006/246) apply to the transfer under a scheme under this section (whether or not the transfer is a relevant transfer for the purposes of those regulations).

(9) A scheme under this section may define the property, rights and liabilities to be transferred by specifying or describing them.

(10) A scheme under this section may include supplementary, incidental, transitional and consequential provision and may in particular

(a) make provision for the continuing effect of things done by the Electoral Commission in relation to anything transferred by the scheme;

(b) make provision for the continuation of things (including legal proceedings) in the process of being done, by or on behalf of or in relation to the Electoral Commission in relation to anything transferred by the scheme;

(c) make provision for references to the Electoral Commission in an agreement (whether written or not), instrument or other document in relation to anything transferred by the scheme to be treated (so far as necessary for the purposes of or in consequence of the transfer) as references to the Local Government Boundary Commission for England;

(d) make provision for the shared ownership or use of any property or facilities.

(11) Where a scheme has been made under this section, the Electoral Commission and the Local Government Boundary Commission for England may (subject to any order under this section) agree in writing to modify the scheme; and any such modification is to have effect as from the date the original scheme came into effect.

(12) An order under this section is to be made by statutory instrument.

(13) A statutory instrument containing an order under this section is subject to annulment in pursuance of a resolution of either House of Parliament.

Transitional

Continuity of functions

63(1) Anything done before the relevant day by the Electoral Commission's Boundary Committee for the purposes of the discharge of its functions under Part 2 of the Local Government Act 1992 (c) 19) may for the purposes of the discharge of any function of the Local Government Boundary Commission for England under any of sections 56 to 59 be regarded as having been done by the Local Government Boundary Commission for England under that section.

(2) In subsection (1) "relevant day" means the day on which section 56 comes into force.

(3) Anything done before the relevant day by the Electoral Commission's Boundary Committee for the purposes of the discharge of any function referred to in section 60(1) may for the purposes of the discharge of that function by the Local Government Boundary Commission for England under Chapter 1 of Part 1 of the Local Government and Public Involvement in Health Act 2007 (c) 28) be regarded as having been done by the Local Government Boundary Commission for England under that Chapter.

(4) Anything done before the relevant day by the Electoral Commission for the purposes of the discharge of any function under an enactment specified in section 60(3) may for the purposes of the discharge of that function by the Local Government Boundary Commission for England under that enactment be regarded as having been done by the Local Government Boundary Commission for England under that enactment.

(5) In subsections (3) and (4), "relevant day" means the day on which section 60 comes into force.

Interim provision

64(1) Schedule 3 (which makes modifications to Part 2 of the Local Government Act 1992 (c) 19) for an interim period) is part of this Part.

(2) Where the Electoral Commission receives recommendations under Part 2 of the Local Government Act 1992 before the day on which this Act is passed, it must determine whether to give effect to any or all of those recommendations on or before 31 March 2010.

Miscellaneous

Electoral changes consequential on boundary change in England

65   *Amends Chapter 1 of Part 1 of the Local Government and Public Involvement in Health Act 2007: not reproduced*

Repeal of redundant provisions

66   *Not reproduced*

General

Consequential and supplementary provision

67   *Not reproduced*

Interpretation

68   In this Part

"the Electoral Commission's Boundary Committee" has the meaning given by section 60(4);

"electoral arrangements" has the meaning given in section 56(4) and (6);

"principal council" has the meaning given in section 56(3).

SCHEDULE 1

LOCAL GOVERNMENT BOUNDARY COMMISSION FOR ENGLAND

Section 55

Members

1(1)   The Local Government Boundary Commission for England ("the Commission") is to consist of
  (a)   the chair of the Commission, and
  (b)   at least four and no more than eleven other members ("ordinary members").

(2)   The ordinary members are to be appointed by Her Majesty on the recommendation of the Secretary of State.

(3)   The following may not be appointed as an ordinary member
  (a)   a member of a registered party;
  (b)   a person who is, or has at any time with the last ten years been, an officer or employee of a registered party or of any accounting unit of such a party;
  (c)   a person who holds, or has at any time within the last ten years held, a relevant elective office (within the meaning of Schedule 7 to the Political Parties, Elections and Referendums Act 2000 (c) 41) ("the 2000 Act"));
  (d)   a person who has at any time within the last ten years been named
    (i)   as a donor in the register of donations reported under Chapter 3 or 5 of Part 4 of the 2000 Act, or
    (ii)   as a participant in the register of recordable transactions reported under Part 4A of that Act.

(4)   A person may not be appointed as an ordinary member for a period of more than five years at any one time.

(5)   Subject to the provisions of this paragraph, an ordinary member holds office
  (a)   for the term for which the ordinary member is appointed, and
  (b)   otherwise in accordance with the terms of their appointment.

(6) An ordinary member ceases to hold office if
  (a) the ordinary member consents to being nominated as a candidate at a relevant election (within the meaning of Part 2 of the 2000 Act) or to being included in a registered party's list of candidates at such an election,
  (b) the ordinary member takes up any office or employment in or with
    (i) a registered party or any accounting unit of such a party,
    (ii) a recognised third party (within the meaning of Part 6 of the 2000 Act), or
    (iii) a permitted participant (within the meaning of Part 7 of that Act),
  (c) the ordinary member is named as a donor in the register of donations reported under Chapter 3 or 5 of Part 4 of the 2000 Act or in any statement of donations included in a return delivered to the Electoral Commission under section 98 or 122 of that Act,
  (d) the ordinary member is named as a participant in the register of recordable transactions reported under Part 4A of that Act, or
  (e) the ordinary member becomes a member of a registered party.

(7) An ordinary member may, on the member's request, be relieved of office by Her Majesty.

(8) An ordinary member may, on the recommendation of the Secretary of State, be removed from office by Her Majesty on any of the following grounds
  (a) failure to discharge the functions of membership for a continuous period of at least three months;
  (b) failure to comply with the terms of appointment;
  (c) conviction of a criminal offence;
  (d) being an undischarged bankrupt or having their estate sequestrated in Scotland and not being discharged;
  (e) making an arrangement or composition contract with, or granting a trust deed for, their creditors;
  (f) otherwise being unfit to hold office or unable to carry out the functions of membership.

(9) No-one may serve as an ordinary member for more than ten years (continuously or otherwise).

(10) Service as an ordinary member is not service in the civil service of the State.

Chair

2(1) The chair of the Commission is to be appointed by Her Majesty on an Address from the House of Commons.

(2) A motion for such an Address may be made only if
  (a) the Speaker of the House of Commons agrees that the motion may be made, and
  (b) the person whose appointment is proposed in the motion has been selected in accordance with a procedure put in place and overseen by the Speaker's Committee (see section 2 of the 2000 Act).

(3) Such an Address must specify the period, not exceeding five years, for which the proposed chair is to be appointed.

(4) A person may not be appointed as chair under sub-paragraph (1) if by virtue of paragraph 1(3)(a) to (d) that person may not be appointed as an ordinary member.

(5) Subject to the provisions of this paragraph, the chair holds office
  (a) for the period of their appointment (which is to be that specified under sub-paragraph (3)), and
  (b) otherwise in accordance with the terms of their appointment.

(6) The chair ceases to hold office on the occurrence of such an event as is mentioned in any of paragraphs (a) to (e) of paragraph 1(6).

(7)   The chair may, on the chair's request, be relieved of office as chair by Her Majesty.

(8)   The chair may be removed from office by Her Majesty on an Address from the House of Commons.

(9)   No motion may be made for such an Address unless the Speaker's Committee have presented a report to the House of Commons stating that the Speaker's Committee are satisfied that one or more of the following grounds is made out in relation to the chair

    (a)   failure to discharge the functions of their office for a continuous period of at least three months;

    (b)   failure to comply with the terms of appointment as chair;

    (c)   conviction of a criminal offence;

    (d)   being an undischarged bankrupt or having their estate sequestrated in Scotland and not being discharged;

    (e)   making an arrangement or composition contract with, or granting a trust deed for, their creditors;

    (f)   otherwise being unfit to hold office as chair or unable to carry out the functions of that office.

(10)   No-one may serve as chair for more than ten years (continuously or otherwise).

(11)   In the case of a reappointment, the reference in sub-paragraph (2)(b) to being selected in accordance with a procedure put in place and overseen by the Speaker's Committee is to be read as including a reference to being recommended for reappointment by the Speaker's Committee.

(12)   Service as chair is not service in the civil service of the State.

Deputy chair

3(1)   The Secretary of State may designate one of the ordinary members of the Commission to be the deputy chair.

(2)   The deputy chair is to act as chair

    (a)   in the event of a vacancy in the office of chair,

    (b)   if the chair is unable to act, and

    (c)   in such other circumstances as the Commission may determine.

(3)   The deputy chair may at any time resign as deputy chair by notice to the Secretary of State.

Remuneration

4   The Commission must pay to or in respect of the members (including the chair and deputy chair) such sums by way of or in respect of remuneration, allowances, expenses, pensions or gratuities as the Speaker of the House of Commons, after consulting the Speaker's Committee, may determine.

Committees

5(1)   The Commission may establish any committees which it considers appropriate.

(2)   A committee of the Commission may establish one or more subcommittees.

(3)   A committee established under this paragraph to review the economy, efficiency or effectiveness with which the Commission has used its resources, or any subcommittee of such a committee, may include up to two people who are not also members of the Commission ("independent members").

(4)   The Commission may not appoint as an independent member anyone who would be ineligible for appointment as a member of the Commission because of paragraph 1(3).

(5)   An independent member must be appointed on such terms and conditions, including terms and conditions as to remuneration, as the Commission may determine.

(6)   Except as provided by sub-paragraph (3), only a member of the Commission may be a member of one of its committees or subcommittees.

Proceedings

6(1)   Subject to this Schedule, the Commission may regulate its own proceedings and the proceedings of any of its committees or subcommittees (including quorum).

(2)   The validity of proceedings of the Commission, or of any of its committees or subcommittees, is not affected by
    (a)   a vacancy, or
    (b)   a defective appointment.

Chief executive and other employees

7(1)   The Commission
    (a)   must appoint a chief executive, and
    (b)   may appoint other employees.

(2)   A person may not be appointed
    (a)   as chief executive of the Commission if by virtue of paragraph 1(3)(a) to (d) that person may not be appointed as an ordinary member of the Commission;
    (b)   as any other member of staff of the Commission if by virtue of paragraph 1(3)(b) to (d) that person may not be appointed as an ordinary member of the Commission.

(3)   Service as chief executive or other employee of the Commission is not service in the civil service of the State.

(4)   Subject as follows, employees of the Commission must be appointed on such terms and conditions, including terms and conditions as to remuneration, as the Commission may determine.

(5)   The appointment of any member of staff of the Commission terminates
    (a)   if that person is the chief executive of the Commission, on the occurrence of such an event as is mentioned in any of paragraphs (a) to (e) of paragraph 1(6), and
    (b)   in any other case, on the occurrence of such an event as is mentioned in any of paragraphs (a) to (d) of paragraph 1(6).

(6)   For the purposes of determinations under sub-paragraph (4), the Commission must have regard to the desirability of keeping the remuneration and other terms or conditions of employment of its employees broadly in line with those applying to persons in the civil service of the State.

(7)   Service as an employee of the Commission is included in the kinds of employment to which a scheme under section 1 of the Superannuation Act 1972 (c 11) can apply; and accordingly, in Schedule 1 to that Act, "Local Government Boundary Commission for England" is to be inserted at the appropriate place in the list of "Other bodies".

(8)   The Commission must pay to the Minister for the Civil Service, at such times as the Minister may direct, such sums as the Minister may determine in respect of any increase attributable to sub-paragraph (7) in the sums payable out of money provided by Parliament under the Superannuation Act 1972 (c) 11).

Superannuation: supplementary

8(1)   Section 1(2) of the Superannuation Act 1972 (delegation of functions relating to civil service superannuation schemes by the Minister for the Civil Service to another office of the Crown etc) has effect as if the reference to an officer of the Crown other than a Minister included the chief executive of the Commission.

(2) An administration function conferred on the chief executive under section 1(2) of that Act by virtue of sub-paragraph (1) may be exercised by (or by employees of) such person as may be authorised in that behalf by the chief executive.

(3) For the purposes of this paragraph an "administration function" is a function of administering schemes
   (a) made under section 1 of the Superannuation Act 1972, and
   (b) for the time being in force.

(4) An authorisation given by virtue of sub-paragraph (2) may authorise the exercise of an administration function
   (a) wholly or to such extent as may be specified in the authorisation;
   (b) generally or in such cases as may be so specified;
   (c) unconditionally or subject to such conditions as may be so specified.

(5) An authorisation given by virtue of sub-paragraph (2)
   (a) is to be treated for all purposes as if it were given by virtue of an order under section 69 of the Deregulation and Contracting Out Act 1994 (c) 40) (contracting out of functions of Ministers and officeholders);
   (b) may be revoked at any time by the Commission (as well as by the chief executive).

Delegations

9(1) The Commission may delegate any of its functions to any of its members, employees, committees or subcommittees.

(2) Sub-paragraph (1) does not apply to any function of making an order by statutory instrument.

(3) The chief executive of the Commission may delegate any of the chief executive's functions to any other employee of the Commission.

(4) A committee of the Commission may delegate any of its functions to any of its subcommittees.

(5) A committee or subcommittee of the Commission may delegate any of its functions to any employee of the Commission.

Financial year

10(1) The financial year of the Commission is the period of twelve months ending on 31 March.

(2) But the first financial year of the Commission is the period
   (a) starting on the day on which section 55 comes into force, and
   (b) ending on the following 31 March.

Funding

11(1) The expenditure of the Commission is to be met, in accordance with this paragraph, out of money provided by Parliament.

(2) For each financial year of the Commission (other than the first) the Commission must prepare, and submit to the Speaker's Committee, an estimate of its income and expenditure.

(3) The Speaker's Committee must
   (a) examine each such estimate,
   (b) decide whether they are satisfied that the estimated level of income and expenditure is consistent with the economical, efficient and effective discharge by the Commission of its functions, and
   (c) if they are not so satisfied, must make such modifications to the estimate as they consider appropriate for the purpose of achieving such consistency.

(4) Before deciding whether they are so satisfied or making any such modification the Speaker's Committee must

    (a) have regard to the most recent report made to them by the Comptroller and Auditor General under paragraph 13 and to any recommendations contained in that report, and

    (b) consult the Treasury and have regard to any advice which the Treasury may give.

(5) The Speaker's Committee must, after concluding their examination and making their modifications (if any) to the estimate, lay the estimate before the House of Commons.

(6) If the Speaker's Committee, in the discharge of their functions under this paragraph

    (a) do not follow any recommendation contained in the report of the Comptroller and Auditor General,

    (b) do not follow any advice given to them by the Treasury, or

    (c) make any modification to the estimate,

they must include in the next report which they make to the House of Commons under paragraph 1 of Schedule 2 of the 2000 Act a statement of their reasons for so doing.

Five-year plan

12(1) An estimate under paragraph 11 in respect of the first financial year to begin after the day on which Parliament meets for the first time following a parliamentary general election is to be accompanied by a plan prepared by the Commission setting out its

    (a) aims and objectives for the period of five years beginning with the financial year to which the estimate relates, and

    (b) estimated requirements for resources during that Five-year period.

(1A) The Speaker's Committee may require the Commission to submit a plan under sub-paragraph (1) when the Commission submits such an estimate as is mentioned in paragraph 11 in respect of a financial year other than one mentioned in that sub-paragraph.

(2) The Speaker's Committee must

    (a) examine each such plan,

    (b) decide whether they are satisfied that the plan is consistent with the economical, efficient and effective discharge by the Commission of its functions, and

    (c) if they are not so satisfied, make such modifications to the plan as they consider appropriate for the purpose of achieving such consistency.

(3) Before deciding whether they are so satisfied or making any such modification the Speaker's Committee must

    (a) have regard to the most recent report made to them by the Comptroller and Auditor General under paragraph 13 and to any recommendations contained in that report, and

    (b) consult the Treasury and have regard to any advice which the Treasury may give.

(4) The Speaker's Committee must, after concluding their examination and making their modifications (if any) to the plan, lay the plan before the House of Commons.

(5) If the Speaker's Committee, in the discharge of their functions under this paragraph

    (a) do not follow any recommendation contained in the report of the Comptroller and Auditor General,

    (b) do not follow any advice given to them by the Treasury, or

    (c) make any modification to the plan,

they must include in the next report which they make to the House of Commons under paragraph 1 of Schedule 2 of the 2000 Act a statement of their reasons for so doing.

Examination by Comptroller and Auditor General

13(1)   For the purpose of assisting the Speaker's Committee to discharge their functions under paragraphs 11 and 12 in respect of any year when both an estimate under paragraph 11 and a Five-year plan under paragraph 12 are submitted to them, the Comptroller and Auditor General must before the Committee consider the estimate and plan

   (a)   carry out an examination into the economy, efficiency or effectiveness (or any combination thereof) with which the Commission has used its resources in discharging its functions (or, if the Comptroller and Auditor General so determines, any particular function),

   (b)   report to the Speaker's Committee the results of the examination, and

   (c)   include in the report such recommendations as the Comptroller and Auditor General considers appropriate in the light of the examination.

   (2)   Section 8 of the National Audit Act 1983 (c) 44) (right to obtain documents and information) applies in relation to any examination under this paragraph as it applies in relation to an examination under section 6 of that Act.

Accounts

14(1)   The Commission must keep accounting records.

   (2)   The Commission must, for each financial year, prepare accounts in accordance with directions given to it by the Treasury.

   (3)   Those directions may include directions as to

   (a)   the information to be contained in the accounts,

   (b)   the manner in which the information is to be presented,

   (c)   the methods and principles according to which the accounts are to be prepared, and

   (d)   the additional information (if any) that is to accompany the accounts.

Audit

15(1)   The Commission must send copies of its accounts to

   (a)   the Comptroller and Auditor General, and

   (b)   the Speaker's Committee,

as soon after the end of the financial year as may be practicable.

   (2)   The Comptroller and Auditor General must

   (a)   examine and certify accounts received under sub-paragraph (1),

   (b)   report on the accounts, and

   (c)   lay the certified accounts and report before Parliament.

Accounting officer

16(1)   The Speaker's Committee must designate an employee of the Commission as the Commission's accounting officer.

   (2)   The accounting officer is to have, in relation to the Commission's accounts and finance, the responsibilities that are from time to time specified by the Speaker's Committee.

   (3)   In this paragraph references to responsibilities include in particular

   (a)   responsibilities in relation to the signing of accounts;

   (b)   responsibilities for the propriety and regularity of the Commission's finances;

   (c)   responsibilities for the economy, efficiency and effectiveness with which the Commission's resources are used.

   (4)   The responsibilities which may be specified under this paragraph include responsibilities owed to the Commission, the Speaker's Committee or the House of Commons or its Committee of Public Accounts.

(5)   In this paragraph any reference to the Public Accounts Committee of the House of Commons is, if
  (a)   the name of that Committee is changed, or
  (b)   its functions at the passing of this Act (or functions substantially corresponding thereto) become functions of a different committee of the House of Commons,
to be taken to be references to the Committee by its new name or (as the case may be) to the committee by whom the functions are for the time being exercisable.

Annual report

17(1)   The Commission must, as soon after the end of each financial year as may be practicable, prepare and lay before Parliament a report about the performance of the Commission's functions during that financial year.

(2)   The Commission must, on so laying such a report, publish it in such manner as it may determine.

Instruments and authentication

18(1)   The fixing of the seal of the Commission is to be authenticated by the signature of the chair or of another person authorised by the Commission to act for that purpose.

(2)   A document purporting to be duly executed under the seal of the Commission, or to be signed on its behalf, is to be received in evidence and, unless the contrary is proved, is to be treated as having been so executed or signed.

Records

19   In the Public Records Act 1958 (c) 51), in Schedule 1 (definition of public records), in Part 2 of the Table at the end of paragraph 3, at the appropriate place insert
  "Local Government Boundary Commission for England."

Investigation

20   In the Parliamentary Commissioner Act 1967 (c) 13), in Schedule 2 (departments etc subject to investigation), at the appropriate place insert
  "Local Government Boundary Commission for England".

Freedom of information

21   In the Freedom of Information Act 2000 (c) 36), in Schedule 1, in Part 6 (other public bodies and offices: general), at the appropriate place insert
  "The Local Government Boundary Commission for England."

House of Commons disqualification

22   In the House of Commons Disqualification Act 1975 (c) 24), in Part 2 of Schedule 1 (bodies of which all members are disqualified), at the appropriate place insert
  "The Local Government Boundary Commission for England."

Transitional

23(1)   The Electoral Commissioner who immediately before the day on which section 55 comes into force is the chair of the Electoral Commission's Boundary Committee is to be treated
  (a)   as having been appointed as the chair of the Commission under paragraph 2(1), and
  (b)   as having been so appointed on the day on which, and for the term for which, that person was appointed as the chair of the Electoral Commission's Boundary Committee.

(2)　A Deputy Electoral Commissioner who immediately before the day on which section 55 comes into force is a member of the Electoral Commission's Boundary Committee is to be treated

　　(a)　as having been appointed as an ordinary member of the Commission under paragraph 1(2), and

　　(b)　as having been so appointed on the day on which, and for the term for which, that person was appointed as a member of the Electoral Commission's Boundary Committee.

Interpretation

24　In this Schedule

　　"the 2000 Act" means the Political Parties, Elections and Referendums Act 2000 (c) 41);

　　"accounting unit" and "registered party" have the same meanings as in the 2000 Act (see section 160 of that Act);

　　"the Commission" means the Local Government Boundary Commission for England;

　　"ordinary member" is to be construed in accordance with paragraph 1(1)(b).

SCHEDULE 2
ELECTORAL CHANGE IN ENGLAND: CONSIDERATIONS ON REVIEW

Section 56

County councils

1(1)　This paragraph applies where the Local Government Boundary Commission for England makes recommendations under section 56 in relation to the electoral arrangements for the area of a county council.

(2)　The recommendations must secure the following results

　　(a)　an electoral area of the county council must not fall partly inside and partly outside any district,

　　(b)　every ward of a parish having a parish council (whether separate or common) must lie wholly within a single electoral area of the county council, and

　　(c)　every parish which is not divided into parish wards must lie wholly within a single electoral area of the county council.

(3)　Subject to sub-paragraph (2), in making the recommendations the Local Government Boundary Commission for England must have regard to

　　(a)　the need to secure that the ratio of the number of local government electors to the number of members of the county council to be elected is, as nearly as possible, the same in every electoral area of the council,

　　(b)　the need to reflect the identities and interests of local communities and in particular

　　　(i)　the desirability of fixing boundaries which are and will remain easily identifiable, and

　　　(ii)　the desirability of not breaking local ties when fixing boundaries,

　　(c)　the need to secure effective and convenient local government, and

　　(d)　the boundaries of the electoral areas of any district council whose area is within the area of the county council.

(4)　For the purpose of sub-paragraph (3)(a) the Local Government Boundary Commission for England must have regard to any change in the number or distribution of local government electors in the area of the county council which is likely to take place within the period of five years immediately following the making of the recommendations.

District councils

2(1) This paragraph applies where the Local Government Boundary Commission for England makes recommendations under section 56 in relation to the electoral arrangements for the area of a district council.

(2) The recommendations must secure the following results

    (a) every ward of a parish having a parish council (whether separate or common) must lie wholly within a single electoral area of the district council, and

    (b) every parish which is not divided into parish wards must lie wholly within a single electoral area of the district council.

(3) Subject to sub-paragraph (2), in making the recommendations the Local Government Boundary Commission for England must have regard to

    (a) the need to secure that the ratio of the number of local government electors to the number of members of the district council to be elected is, as nearly as possible, the same in every electoral area of the council,

    (b) the need to reflect the identities and interests of local communities and in particular

        (i) the desirability of fixing boundaries which are and will remain easily identifiable, and

        (ii) the desirability of fixing boundaries so as not to break any local ties,

    (c) the need to secure effective and convenient local government, and

    (d) in the case of a district council that is subject to a scheme for elections by halves or by thirds, or that has resolved to revert to being subject to such a scheme under Chapter 1 of Part 2 of the Local Government and Public Involvement in Health Act 2007 (c 28), the desirability of securing that each electoral area of the district council returns an appropriate number of members of the council.

(4) For the purpose of sub-paragraph (3)(a) the Local Government Boundary Commission for England must have regard to any change in the number or distribution of local government electors in the area of the district council which is likely to take place within the period of five years immediately following the making of the recommendations.

(5) For the purposes of sub-paragraph (3)(d)

    (a) a district council is "subject to a scheme of elections by halves" if one half (or as nearly as may be) of its members are to be elected in each year in which it holds ordinary elections of members of the council;

    (b) a district council is "subject to a scheme of elections by thirds" if one third (or as nearly as may be) of its members are to be elected in each year in which it holds ordinary elections of members of the council;

    (c) the number of members of the district council returned by an electoral area of the council is "appropriate"

        (i) in the case of a scheme for elections by halves, if it is divisible by 2;

        (ii) in the case of a scheme for elections by thirds, if it is divisible by 3.

London borough councils

3(1) This paragraph applies where the Local Government Boundary Commission for England makes recommendations under section 56 in relation to the electoral arrangements for the area of a London borough council.

(2) The recommendations must secure the following results

    (a) every ward of a parish having a parish council (whether separate or common) must lie wholly within a single electoral area of the London borough council, and

    (b) every parish which is not divided into parish wards must lie wholly within a single electoral area of the London borough council.

(3) Subject to sub-paragraph (2), in making the recommendations the Local Government Boundary Commission for England must have regard to

    (a) the need to secure that the ratio of the number of local government electors to the number of members of the London borough council to be elected is, as nearly as possible, the same in every electoral area of the council,

    (b) the need to reflect the identities and interests of local communities and in particular

        (i) the desirability of fixing boundaries which are and will remain easily identifiable, and

        (ii) the desirability of fixing boundaries so as not to break any local ties, and

    (c) the need to secure effective and convenient local government.

(4) For the purpose of sub-paragraph (3)(a) the Local Government Boundary Commission for England must have regard to any change in the number or distribution of local government electors in the area of the London borough council which is likely to take place within the period of five years immediately following the making of the recommendations.

Parish councils

4(1) This paragraph applies where the Local Government Boundary Commission for England makes recommendations under section 56 in relation to the electoral arrangements for the area of a parish council (including a common parish council).

(2) In making any such recommendations, the Local Government Boundary Commission for England must have regard to

    (a) the need to reflect the identities and interests of local communities, and in particular

        (i) the desirability of fixing boundaries which are and will remain easily identifiable, and

        (ii) the desirability of fixing boundaries so as not to break any local ties,

    (b) the need to secure effective and convenient local government, and

    (c) the boundaries of the electoral areas of the principal council or councils in whose area the area of the parish council falls.

(3) In making any recommendations as to whether the area of the parish council is to be divided into wards for the election of members of the parish council, the Local Government Boundary Commission for England must have regard to

    (a) whether the number or distribution of the local government electors in the area is such as to make a single election of the members of the council impracticable or inconvenient, and

    (b) whether it is desirable for any parts of the area of the parish council to be separately represented on the council.

(4) In making any recommendations as to

    (a) the size and boundaries of wards, or

    (b) the number of members of a parish council to be elected for each ward,

the Local Government Boundary Commission for England must have regard to any change in the number or distribution of the local government electors in the area of the parish council which is likely to take place within the period of five years immediately following the making of the recommendations.

(5) In the case of the area of a parish council not divided into wards, in making recommendations as to the number of members to be elected for the parish council, the Local Government Boundary Commission for England must have regard to

    (a) the number and distribution of the local government electors in the area of the parish council, and

    (b) any change in such number or distribution which is likely to take place within the period of five years immediately following the making of the recommendations.

Interpretation

5 In this Schedule

"local government elector" has the meaning given in section 270(1) of the Local Government Act 1972 (c 70);

"electoral area", in relation to a principal council, means an area for which one or more members of the council are elected.

Local Government Act 1972

An Act to make provision with respect to local government and the functions of local authorities in England and Wales; to amend Part II of the Transport Act 1968; to confer rights of appeal in respect of decisions relating to licences under the Home Counties (Music and Dancing) Licensing Act 1926; to make further provision with respect to magistrates' courts committees; to abolish certain inferior courts of record; and for connected purposes

26th October 1972

PART I
LOCAL GOVERNMENT AREAS AND AUTHORITIES IN ENGLAND

New local government areas

PART II
LOCAL GOVERNMENT AREAS AND AUTHORITIES IN WALES

New local government areas

PART III

Repealed

PART IV

CHANGES IN LOCAL GOVERNMENT AREAS

PART V

GENERAL PROVISIONS AS TO MEMBERS AND PROCEEDINGS OF LOCAL AUTHORITIES

PART I
LOCAL GOVERNMENT AREAS AND AUTHORITIES IN ENGLAND

New local government areas

New local government areas in England

1(1)   For the administration of local government on and after 1st April 1974 England (exclusive of Greater London and the Isles of Scilly) shall be divided into local government areas to be known as counties and in those counties there shall be local government areas to be known as districts.

(2) The counties shall be the metropolitan counties named in Part I and the non-metropolitan counties named in Part II of Schedule 1 to this Act and shall comprise the areas respectively described (by reference to administrative areas existing immediately before the passing of this Act) in column 2 of each Part of that Schedule.

(3) The districts in the metropolitan counties shall be those respectively specified in column 2 of the said Part I and shall comprise the areas respectively described (by reference to administrative areas existing immediately before the passing of this Act) in that column, and the Secretary of State may by order provide a name for any such district.

(4) The districts in the non-metropolitan counties shall be those respectively specified in one or more orders made by the Secretary of State under paragraph 1 of Schedule 3 to this Act and having the names given to them by one or more orders so made.

(5) Part III of Schedule 1 to this Act shall have effect in relation to the boundaries of the new local government areas.

(6) Subject to Part IV of Schedule 1 to this Act and to any provision corresponding to that Part made by an order under section 254 below, the rural parishes existing immediately before 1st April 1974 shall continue to exist on and after that date by the name of parishes.

(7) The said Part IV shall have effect with respect to the existing rural parishes which by virtue of this Act are comprised in more than one county or more than one metropolitan district.

(8) Part V of Schedule 1 to this Act shall have effect for the purpose of constituting parishes the boundaries of which are determined by reference to those of existing boroughs and urban districts and also, in cases where the areas of such boroughs and urban districts are divided by or under this section between two or more new districts, by reference to the boundaries of the new districts.

(9) The boroughs which by virtue of section 141 of the 1933 Act or section 28 of the Local Government Act 1958 are included in rural districts immediately before the passing of this Act shall on the passing of this Act become parishes without ceasing to be boroughs, but shall cease to be boroughs on 1st April 1974.

(10) On that date the following local government areas existing immediately before that date outside Greater London and the Isles of Scilly, that is to say, all administrative counties, boroughs (except those in rural districts), urban districts, rural districts and urban parishes, shall cease to exist and the council of every such area which has a council shall also cease to exist.

(11) On that date the municipal corporation of every borough outside Greater London (and the corporation of a borough included in a rural district) shall cease to exist.

(12) In this section "England" does not include the administrative county of Monmouthshire or the county borough of Newport.

NOTES

Subordinate legislation
  Metropolitan Districts (Names) Order 1973, SI 1973/137

local government area: s 270(1)
new: s 270(1)

Defined terms
  1933 Act: s 270(1)

Principal councils

Constitution of principal councils in England

2(1) For every non-metropolitan county there shall be a council consisting of a chairman and councillors and the council shall have all such functions as are vested in them by this Act or otherwise.

(2) For every district there shall be a council consisting of a chairman and councillors and the council shall have all such functions as are vested in them by this Act or otherwise.

(2A) Where a council mentioned in subsection (1) or (2) above are operating executive arrangements which involve a mayor and cabinet executive , the council shall consist of an elected mayor, a chairman and councillors.

(2B) In such a case, a reference in this Act to a member of a council is a reference to
    (a) the elected mayor of the council,
    (b) the chairman of the council, or
    (c) a councillor of the council.

(3) Each council mentioned in subsection (1) or (2) above shall be a body corporate by the name "The County Council" or "The District Council", as the case may be, with the addition of the name of the particular county or district.

NOTES

Defined terms

district: s 270(1)
elected mayor: s 270(1)
executive arrangements: s 270(1)

mayor and cabinet executive: s 270(1)
non-metropolitan county: s 270(2)

Members of principal councils

Chairman

3(1) The chairman of a principal council shall be elected annually by the council from among the councillors.

(1A) A member of the executive of a principal council may not be elected as the chairman of the council.

(2) The chairman shall, unless he resigns or becomes disqualified, continue in office until his successor becomes entitled to act as chairman.

(3) During his term of office the chairman shall continue to be a member of the council notwithstanding the provisions of this Act relating to the retirement of councillors.

(4) The chairman of a district council shall have precedence in the district, but not so as prejudicially to affect Her Majesty's royal prerogative.

(4A) Subsection (4) above shall have effect in relation to a district council which are operating executive arrangements which involve a mayor and cabinet executive as if it provided for the elected mayor of the council to have precedence in the district, but this subsection shall not apply if the executive arrangements provide for it not to apply.

(5) A principal council may pay the chairman for the purpose of enabling him to meet the expenses of his office such allowance as the council think reasonable.

NOTES

Defined terms

elected mayor: s 270(1)
executive: s 270(1)
executive arrangements: s 270(1)

mayor and cabinet executive: s 270(1)
principal council: s 270(1)

Election of chairman

4(1) The election of the chairman shall be the first business transacted at the annual meeting of a principal council.

(2) If, apart from section 3(3) above or section 5(2) below, the person presiding at the meeting would have ceased to be a member of the council, he shall not be entitled to vote in the election except in accordance with subsection (3) below.

(3) In the case of an equality of votes the person presiding at the meeting shall give a casting vote in addition to any other vote he may have.

NOTES
Defined terms
    principal council: s 270(1)

Vice-chairman

5(1)   A principal council shall appoint a member of the council to be vice-chairman of the council.

(1A)   A member of the executive of a principal council may not be appointed as the vice-chairman of the council.

(2)   The vice-chairman shall, unless he resigns or becomes disqualified, hold office until immediately after the election of a chairman at the next annual meeting of the council and during that time shall continue to be a member of the council notwithstanding the provisions of this Act relating to the retirement of councillors.

(3)   Subject to any standing orders made by the council, anything authorised or required to be done by, to or before the chairman may be done by, to or before the vice-chairman.

(4)   A principal council may pay the vice-chairman for the purpose of enabling him to meet the expenses of his office such allowance as the council think reasonable.

NOTES
Defined terms
    executive: s 270(1)
    principal council: s 270(1)

Term of office and retirement of councillors

6(1)   Councillors for a principal area shall be elected by the local government electors for that area in accordance with this Act and Part I of the Representation of the People Act 1983.

(2)   For the purposes of the election of councillors
    (a)   every non-metropolitan county shall be divided into electoral divisions, each returning (subject to paragraph 3 of Schedule 3 to this Act and subject to section 56(8) of the Local Democracy, Economic Development and Construction Act 2009 and section 12(4) of the Local Government and Public Involvement in Health Act 2007) one councillor;
    (b)   every metropolitan district shall be divided into wards, each returning such number of councillors as may be provided as mentioned in subsection (3) below; and
    (c)   every non-metropolitan district shall be divided into wards, each returning such number of councillors as may be provided as mentioned in subsection (3) below;
    and there shall be a separate election for each electoral division or ward.

(3)   The number of councillors referred to in subsection (2)(b) or (c) above may be provided
    (a)   under or by virtue of the provisions of section 7 below;
    (b)   by an order under Part 2 of the Local Government Act 1992 (c 19) or Part 3 of the Local Democracy, Economic Development and Construction Act 2009;
    (c)   by an order under section 14 of the Local Government and Rating Act 1997 (c 29);
    (d)   by an order under Part 1 of the Local Government and Public Involvement in Health Act 2007.

NOTES
Defined terms
    local government elector: s 270(1)   principal area: s 270(1)
    non-metropolitan county: s 270(2)
    non-metropolitan district: s 270(2)

Elections of councillors

7(1) The ordinary elections of county councillors shall take place in 1973 and every fourth year thereafter, their term of office shall be four years and they shall retire together in every such fourth year on the fourth day after the ordinary day of election of county councillors, and in and after 1977 the newly elected councillors shall come into office on the day on which their predecessors retire.

 (2) The ordinary elections of metropolitan district councillors shall take place in 1973, 1975 and every year thereafter other than 1977 and every fourth year thereafter.

 (3) Subject to paragraph 4 of Schedule 3 to this Act, the term of office of metropolitan district councillors shall be four years and one-third of the whole number of councillors in each ward of a metropolitan district, being those who have been councillors for the longest time without reelection, shall retire in every ordinary year of election of such councillors on the fourth day after the ordinary day of election of such councillors, and in and after 1975 the newly elected councillors shall come into office on the day on which their predecessors retire.

(4)-(7) *Repealed*

 (8) The ordinary elections of non-metropolitan district councillors shall take place
    (a) except where an order is in force providing for the election of district councillors by thirds, in 1973, 1976, 1979 and every fourth year thereafter; and
    (b) where such an order is in force, in the year when the order comes into force and every year thereafter other than a year of election of county councillors.

 (9) The following provisions of this subsection shall, subject to the provisions of any order made under or by virtue of this section, have effect with respect to non-metropolitan district councillors:
    (a) their term of office shall be three years in the case of the councillors elected at the ordinary elections in 1973 and 1976 and four years in the case of those elected at ordinary elections held thereafter;
    (b) except where an order is in force providing for the election of councillors by thirds, the whole number of councillors shall retire together in every ordinary year of election of such councillors on the fourth day after the ordinary day of election of such councillors, and in and after 1976 the newly elected councillors shall come into office on the day on which their predecessors retire; and
    (c) where such an order is in force, one-third of the whole number of councillors in each ward returning a number of councillors which is divisible by three and, as nearly as may be, one-third of the whole number of the councillors in the other wards, being those who have been councillors of the district for the longest time without reelection, shall retire in every ordinary year of election of such councillors on the fourth day after the ordinary day of election of such councillors, and in every such year the newly elected councillors shall come into office on the day on which their predecessors retire.

NOTES
Defined terms
  non-metropolitan district: s 270(2)

Constitution and membership of Greater London Council and London borough councils

8(1) Sections 2 to 7 above shall not apply to London borough councils but, subject to subsection (2) below, the provisions of Schedule 2 to this Act shall have effect in relation to them instead.

(2)-(3) *Repealed*

Parishes

Parish meetings and councils

9(1) For every parish there shall be a parish meeting for the purpose of discussing parish affairs and exercising any functions conferred on such meetings by any enactment and, subject to the provisions of this Act or any instrument made thereunder, for every parish or group of parishes having a parish council before 1st April 1974 there shall continue to be a parish council.

(2)-(3) *Repealed*

(4) Subject to any order under section 10 or 11 below Part II of the Local Government Act 1992 or section 86 of the Local Government and Public Involvement in Health Act 2007, there shall be a separate parish council for
   (a) every parish which immediately before the passing of this Act was a borough included in a rural district;
   (b) every parish which immediately before the passing of this Act was coextensive with a rural district;
   (c) every parish established by paragraph 1 of Part IV of Schedule 1 to this Act;
   (d) every parish to which part of another parish is added by paragraph 2 of the said Part IV and which immediately before the passing of this Act had no parish council; and
   (e) every parish constituted under Part V of Schedule 1 to this Act.

(5) *Repealed*

(6) An order shall not be made under section 86 of the Local Government and Public Involvement in Health Act 2007 establishing a separate parish council for a parish grouped under a common parish council unless by that order or an order under section 11(4) below the parish is separated from the group or the group is dissolved, and where the group is not dissolved, the order under section 86 of the 2007 Act shall make such provision as appears to the district council to be necessary for the alteration of the parish council of the group.

Power to dissolve parish councils in small parishes

10(1) Where the population of a parish having a separate parish council includes not more than 150 local government electors, the parish meeting may apply to the district council or London borough council for the dissolution of the parish council, and thereupon the district council or London borough council may by order dissolve the parish council.

(2) Where an application under this section by a parish meeting is rejected, another such application may not be presented by that meeting within two years from the making of the previous application.

NOTES
Defined terms
   local government elector: s 270(1)

Orders for grouping parishes, dissolving groups and separating parishes from groups

11(1) The parish meeting of a parish may apply to the district council or London borough council for an order grouping the parish with some neighbouring parish or parishes in the same district or London borough under a common parish council or by adding the parish to an existing group of such parishes under such a council, and the district council or London borough council may thereupon make an order accordingly, but subject to subsection (2) below.

(2) Parishes shall not be grouped without the consent of the parish meeting of each of the parishes.

(3) A grouping order shall make the necessary provision
   (a) for the name of the group;

(b)   the electoral arrangements that are to apply to the council;

(c)   for the application to the parishes included in the group of all or any of the provisions of sections 298 to 303 of the Charities Act 2011 (parochial charities) and of any of the provisions of this Act with respect to the custody of parish documents, so as to preserve the separate rights of each parish;

(d)   for the dissolution of the separate parish council of any parish included in the group,

and the order may provide for the consent of the parish meeting of a parish being required to any particular act of the parish council and for any necessary adaptations of this Act to the group of parishes or to the parish meetings of the parishes in the group.

(3A)   In this section "electoral arrangements", in relation to a council, means all of the following

(a)   the year in which ordinary elections of councillors are to be held;

(b)   the number of councillors to be elected to the council by each parish;

(c)   the division (or not) of any of the parishes, into wards for the purpose of electing councillors;

(d)   the number and boundaries of any such wards;

(e)   the number of councillors to be elected for any such ward;

(f)   the name of any such ward.

(4)   The district council or London borough council may on the application of the council of a group of parishes or of the parish meeting of any parish included in a group of parishes make an order dissolving the group or separating one or more of those parishes from the group, and an order so made shall make such provision as appears to the district council or London borough council to be necessary for the election of a parish council for any of the parishes in the group, where it is dissolved, and for any of the parishes separated from the group, where it is not.

(5)   Parishes grouped under a common parish council before 1st April 1974 and situated in different districts on and after that date shall, notwithstanding that they are so situated, continue to be grouped under that council

(a)   unless an order is made under subsection (4) above or Part II of the Local Government Act 1992 or section 86 of the Local Government and Public Involvement in Health Act 2007 dissolving the group; or

(b)   except so far as such an order separates one or more of the parishes from the group;

and any order under subsection (4) above or section 86 of the Local Government and Public Involvement in Health Act 2007 in relation to any parishes so situated shall be made by the district councils concerned acting jointly.

NOTES

Defined terms

   grouped: s 270(1)

   grouping order: s 270(1)

Grouping: alternative styles

11A(1)   An order under section 11(1) which forms a new group may make the provision set out in subsection (3).

(2)   But the order must make that provision in either of these cases

(a)   if at least one of the parishes which is to be grouped does not have an alternative style, and at least one of them does have an alternative style;

(b)   if at least one of the parishes which is to be grouped has an alternative style, and at least one of them has a different alternative style.

(3)   The provision referred to in subsections (1) and (2) is

(a)   provision that each of the parishes in the group shall have an alternative style, or

(b)   provision that each of the parishes in the group which has an alternative style shall cease to have an alternative style.

(4)   Provision made by virtue of subsection (3)(a)

   (a)   must provide for each of the parishes to have the same alternative style;

   (b)   may provide for each of the parishes to have an alternative style which any of them already has;

   (c)   has the effect that each parish in the new group shall cease to have any different alternative style which it had before the provision was made.

(5)   An order under section 11(1) which adds one or more parishes to an existing group must make the provision set out in subsection (6) if

   (a)   the parishes in the group do not have an alternative style, and

   (b)   at least one of the parishes which is to be added has an alternative style.

(6)   The provision referred to in subsection (5) is provision that each added parish which has an alternative style shall cease to have an alternative style.

(7)   An order under section 11(1) which adds one or more parishes to an existing group must make the provision set out in subsection (8) if

   (a)   the parishes in the group have an alternative style, and

   (b)   at least one of the parishes which is to be added

      (i)   has a different alternative style, or

      (ii)   does not have any of the alternative styles.

(8)   The provision referred to in subsection (7) is provision that each added parish shall (if it does not already have the style) have the same alternative style as the parishes already in the group.

(9)   If an order makes provision under subsection (1) or (2) for parishes to have an alternative style, the group shall have the appropriate one of the following styles

   (a)   "group of communities";

   (b)   "group of neighbourhoods";

   (c)   "group of villages".

(10)   As soon as practicable after making an order which includes any provision under this section, the council which makes the order must give notice of the change of style to all of the following

   (a)   the Secretary of State;

   (b)   the Local Government Boundary Commission for England;

   (c)   the Office of National Statistics;

   (d)   the Director General of the Ordnance Survey;

   (e)   any district council or county council within whose area the parish lies.

NOTES

Defined terms
  grouped: s 270(1)
  grouping order: s 270(1)

De-grouping: alternative styles

11B(1)   This section applies if

   (a)   the parishes in a group of parishes have an alternative style, and

   (b)   an order under section 11(4) dissolves the group or separates one or more parishes from the group.

(2)   The order under section 11(4) must provide for each de-grouped parish to continue to have the alternative style.

(3)   In subsection (2) "de-grouped parish" means

   (a)   in the case of dissolution of the group, each parish in the group;

   (b)   in the case of separation of one or more parishes from the group, each parish that is separated.

Provision supplementary to sections 9 to 11

12(1)   An order made by a district council or district councils or by a London borough council under section 10 or 11 above may contain such incidental, consequential, transitional or supplementary provision as may appear to the district council or district councils or the London borough council to be necessary or proper for the purposes or in consequence of the order or for giving full effect thereto, and may include provision with respect to the transfer and management or custody of property (whether real or personal) and the transfer of rights and liabilities.

(2)   When any such order is made, section 16 of the Local Government and Public Involvement in Health Act 2007 (agreements about incidental matters) shall apply as if
   (i)   the reference in subsection (1) to an order under section 7 or 10 of that Act were to an order under section 10 or 11 of this Act; and
   (ii)   the reference in subsection (5)(b) to any order or regulations under Chapter 1 of Part 1 of that Act were to an order under section 10 or 11 of this Act.

(3)   Two copies of every order under section 10 or 11 above shall be sent to the Secretary of State.

Parishes: alternative styles

12A(1)   This section applies to a parish which is not grouped with any other parish.

(2)   The appropriate parish authority may resolve that the parish shall have one of the alternative styles.

(3)   If the parish has an alternative style, the appropriate parish authority may resolve that the parish shall cease to have that style.

(4)   A single resolution may provide for a parish
   (a)   to cease to have an alternative style, and
   (b)   to have another of the alternative styles instead.

(5)   As soon as practicable after passing a resolution under this section, the appropriate parish authority must give notice of the change of style to all of the following
   (a)   the Secretary of State;
   (b)   the Local Government Boundary Commission for England;
   (c)   the Office of National Statistics;
   (d)   the Director General of the Ordnance Survey;
   (e)   any district council, county council or London borough council within whose area the parish lies.

(6)   In this section "appropriate parish authority" means
   (a)   the parish council, or
   (b)   if the parish does not have a parish council, the parish meeting.

Groups of parishes: alternative styles

12B(1)   This section applies to a group of parishes.

(2)   The common parish council of the group may resolve that each of the grouped parishes shall have the same alternative style.

(3) If each of the grouped parishes has an alternative style, the common parish council of the group may resolve that each of the grouped parishes shall cease to have that style.

(4) A single resolution may provide for each of the grouped parishes
    (a) to cease to have an alternative style, and
    (b) to have the same one of the other alternative styles instead.

(5) If the common parish council passes a resolution under this section for each of the grouped parishes to have an alternative style, the group of parishes shall have the appropriate one of the following styles
    (a) "group of communities";
    (b) "group of neighbourhoods";
    (c) "group of villages".

(6) As soon as practicable after passing a resolution under this section, the common parish council of a group must give notice of the change of style to all of the following
    (a) the Secretary of State;
    (b) the Local Government Boundary Commission for England;
    (c) the Office of National Statistics;
    (d) the Director General of the Ordnance Survey;
    (e) any district council, county council or London borough council within whose area the group lies.

NOTES

Defined terms
    alternative style: s 17A(1), (2)
    grouped: s 270(1)

Constitution of parish meeting, etc

13(1) The parish meeting of a parish shall consist of the local government electors for the parish.

(2) Any act of a parish meeting may be signified by an instrument signed by the person presiding and two other local government electors present at the meeting, or, if an instrument under seal is required, by an instrument signed by those persons and sealed with the seal of the parish council in the case of a parish having a separate parish council or the parish trustees in any other case, if that council or those trustees have a seal, or, if they do not, with the seals of those persons.

(3) In a parish not having a separate parish council the chairman of the parish meeting and the proper officer of the district council shall be a body corporate by the name of "the Parish Trustees" with the addition of the name of the parish.

(4) The parish trustees of a parish shall act in accordance with any directions given by the parish meeting.

(5) Notwithstanding anything in any rule of law the parish trustees need not have a common seal, but where they have no seal any act of theirs which requires to be signified by an instrument under seal may be signified by an instrument signed and sealed by the persons who are the parish trustees.

(5A) If the parish has the style of community
    (a) the parish meeting shall have the style of "community meeting";
    (b) the parish trustees shall be known by the name of "The Community Trustees" with the addition of the name of the community.

(5B) If the parish has the style of neighbourhood
    (a) the parish meeting shall have the style of "neighbourhood meeting";
    (b) the parish trustees shall be known by the name of "The Neighbourhood Trustees" with the addition of the name of the neighbourhood.

(5C)   If the parish has the style of village
      (a)   the parish meeting shall have the style of "village meeting";
      (b)   the parish trustees shall be known by the name of "The Village Trustees" with the addition of the name of the village.

NOTES

Defined terms
  has the style of community: s 17A(1)-(3)
  has the style of neighbourhood: s 17A(1)-(3)
  has the style of village: s 17A(1)-(3)

local government elector: s 270(1)
proper officer: s 270(3)

Constitution and powers of parish council

14(1)   A parish council shall consist of the chairman and parish councillors and shall have all such functions as are vested in the council by this Act or otherwise.

(2)   The parish council shall be a body corporate by the name "The Parish Council" with the addition of the name of the particular parish.

(2A)   If the parish has the style of community, the council shall be known by the name "The Community Council" with the addition of the name of the community.

(2B)   If the parish has the style of neighbourhood, the council shall be known by the name "The Neighbourhood Council" with the addition of the name of the neighbourhood.

(2C)   If the parish has the style of village, the council shall be known by the name "The Village Council" with the addition of the name of the village.

(2D)   If parishes are grouped under a common parish council
      (a)   subsection (2), (2A), (2B) or (2C) (as appropriate) applies to that council as the subsection would apply in the case of the council of an individual parish; but
      (b)   the names of all of the parishes, communities, neighbourhoods or villages in the group are to be included in the name of the common council.

(3)   Notwithstanding anything in any rule of law, a parish council need not have a common seal, but where a parish council have no seal any act of theirs which is required to be signified by an instrument under seal may be signified by an instrument signed and sealed by two members of the council.

NOTES

Defined terms
  grouped: s 270(1)
  has the style of community: s 17A(1)-(3)
  has the style of neighbourhood: s 17A(1)-(3)

has the style of village: s 17A(1)-(3)

Chairman and vice-chairman of parish council or meeting

15(1)   The chairman of a parish council shall be elected annually by the council from among the elected councillors.

(2)   The election of a chairman shall be the first business transacted at the annual meeting of the parish council and if, apart from subsection (8) below, the person presiding at the meeting would have ceased to be a member of the parish council, he shall not be entitled to vote in the election except in accordance with subsection (3) below.

(3)   In the case of an equality of votes in the election of a chairman the person presiding at the meeting shall give a casting vote in addition to any other vote he may have.

(4)   The chairman shall, unless he resigns or becomes disqualified, continue in office until his successor becomes entitled to act as chairman.

(5)   A parish council may pay the chairman for the purpose of enabling him to meet the expenses of his office such allowance as the council think reasonable.

(6)   The parish council may appoint *a member* one of the elected members of the council to be vice-chairman of the council.

(7)   The vice-chairman shall, unless he resigns or becomes disqualified, hold office until immediately after the election of a chairman at the next annual meeting of the council.

(8)   During their term of office the chairman and vice-chairman shall continue to be members of the council notwithstanding the provisions of this Act relating to the retirement of parish councillors.

(9)   Subject to any standing orders made by the parish council, anything authorised or required to be done by, to or before the chairman may be done by, to or before the vice-chairman.

(10)   In a parish not having a separate parish council, the parish meeting shall, subject to any provisions of a grouping order, at their annual assembly elect a chairman for the year who shall continue in office until his successor is elected.

(11)   If the parish has the style of community, the chairman and vice-chairman shall (respectively) have the style
    (a) "chairman of the community council";
    (b) "vice-chairman of the community council".

(12)   If the parish has the style of neighbourhood, the chairman and vice-chairman shall (respectively) have the style
    (a) "chairman of the neighbourhood council";
    (b) "vice-chairman of the neighbourhood council".

(13)   If the parish has the style of village, the chairman and vice-chairman shall (respectively) have the style
    (a) "chairman of the village council";
    (b) "vice-chairman of the village council".

(14)   If parishes which have an alternative style are grouped under a common parish council, subsection (11), (12) or (13) (as appropriate) applies to the chairman and vicechairman of that council as the subsection would apply in the case of the council of an individual parish.

NOTES

Defined terms
  grouped: s 270(1)
  grouping order: s 270(1)
  has the style of community: s 17A(1)-(3)

has the style of neighbourhood: s 17A(1)-(3)
has the style of village: s 17A(1)-(3)

Parish councillors

16(1) The number of elected parish councillors for each parish council shall not be less than five.

(2)   Parish councillors shall be elected by the local government electors for the parish in accordance with this Act and Part I of the Representation of the People Act 1983 and relevant electoral arrangements.

(2A)   In their application to the election of parish councillors, this Act and Part 1 of the Representation of the People Act 1983 (c 2) are subject to the relevant electoral arrangements that apply to the election.

(2B)   For the purposes of this section "relevant electoral arrangements" means
    (a) any arrangements about the election of councillors that are made in, or applicable by virtue of, provision made by virtue of section 245(6)(b) of the Local Government and Public Involvement in Health Act 2007 (transitional, saving or transitory provision), and

(b) any electoral arrangements applicable to the council by virtue of an order under section 7 or 10 or an order under section 86 of the Local Government and Public Involvement in Health Act 2007.

(3) Subject to any provision included in an order by virtue of section 67 below and to the provisions of paragraphs 12 and 13 of Schedule 3 to this Act, the ordinary elections of parish councillors shall take place in 1976, 1979 and every fourth year thereafter, their term of office shall be three years in the case of those elected at the ordinary elections in 1976 and four years in the case of those elected at ordinary elections held thereafter, and the whole number of parish councillors shall retire together in every ordinary year of election of such councillors on the fourth day after the ordinary day of election of such councillors, and the newly elected councillors shall come into office on the day on which their predecessors retire.

(4) Where a parish is not divided into parish wards there shall be one election of parish councillors for the whole parish.

(5) Where a parish is divided into parish wards there shall be a separate election of parish councillors for each ward.

(6) If the parish has the style of community, the councillors shall have the style of "councillors of the community council".

(7) If the parish has the style of neighbourhood, the councillors shall have the style of "councillors of the neighbourhood council".

(8) If the parish has the style of village, the councillors shall have the style of "councillors of the village council".

(9) If parishes which have an alternative style are grouped under a common parish council, subsection (6), (7) or (8) (as appropriate) applies to the councillors of that council as the subsection would apply in the case of the council of an individual parish.

NOTES

Defined terms
alternative style: s 17A(1), (2)
grouped: s 270(1)
has the style of community: s 17A(1)-(3)
has the style of neighbourhood: s 17A(1)-(3)

has the style of village: s 17A(1)-(3)
local government elector: s 270(1)

Appointed councillors

16A(1) A parish council may appoint persons to be councillors of the council.

(2) The Secretary of State may by regulations make provision about
(a) the appointment of persons under this section;
(b) the holding of office after appointment under this section.

(3) The regulations may, in particular, make provision about any of the following matters
(a) persons who may be appointed;
(b) the number of persons who may be appointed;
(c) the term of office of persons appointed;
(d) the right of persons appointed to participate in decisionmaking by the council (including voting);
(e) purposes for which a person appointed is to be treated as an elected councillor;
(f) the filling of vacancies.

(4) In exercising a function under or by virtue of this section a parish council must have regard to any guidance issued by the Secretary of State about the exercise of that function.

(5) A statutory instrument containing regulations under this section is subject to annulment in pursuance of a resolution of either House of Parliament.

17 *Repealed*

Alternative styles: supplementary

17A(1) This section applies for the purposes of sections 9 to 16A.

(2) "Alternative style" means one of the following styles
- (a) "community";
- (b) "neighbourhood";
- (c) "village".

(3) References to a parish having an alternative style, or a particular alternative style, are references to the parish having that style by virtue of
- (a) a relevant order, or
- (b) a resolution under section 12A or 12B.

(4) The provisions of a relevant order which provide for a parish to have, or to cease to have, an alternative style are subject to any resolution under section 12A or 12B relating to that parish.

(5) A resolution under section 12A or 12B relating to a parish is subject to any provisions of a relevant order which provide for a parish to have, or to cease to have, an alternative style.

(6) A parish shall cease to have an alternative style if the parish begins to have the status of a town by virtue of section 245(6).

(7) In this section "relevant order" means an order under
- (a) section 11 of this Act, or
- (b) section 86 of the Local Government and Public Involvement in Health Act 2007.

Miscellaneous

Establishment of new authorities in England

18 Schedule 3 to this Act shall have effect with respect to the division of non-metropolitan counties into districts, the establishment of the new local authorities in England, the suspension of elections of members of existing local authorities there and related matters.

NOTES
Defined terms
   district: s 270(1)
   England: s 269
   existing: s 270(1)
   local authority: s 270(1)

   new: s 270(1)
   non-metropolitan county: s 270(2)

Extent of Part I

19 This Part of this Act shall extend to England only.

NOTES
Defined terms
   England: s 269

PART II
LOCAL GOVERNMENT AREAS AND AUTHORITIES IN WALES

New local government areas

New principal local government areas in Wales

20(1) For the administration of local government on and after 1st April 1996, the local government areas in Wales shall be

Local Government Act 1972

    (a) the new principal areas; and

    (b) the communities.

(2) The new principal areas (determined by reference to areas which, immediately before the passing of the Local Government (Wales) Act 1994, are local government areas) are set out in Parts I and II of Schedule 4 to this Act.

(3) Each of the new principal areas shall have the name given to it in Schedule 4.

(4) The new principal areas set out in Part I of Schedule 4 shall be counties and those set out in Part II of that Schedule shall be county boroughs.

(5) In this Act "principal area", in relation to Wales, means a county or county borough.

(6) The counties which were created by this Act, as originally enacted, as counties in Wales, and the districts within them, shall cease to exist on 1st April 1996 except that the preserved counties shall continue in existence (with, in some cases, modified boundaries) for certain purposes.

(7) The councils of the counties and districts mentioned in subsection (6) above shall cease to exist on 1st April 1996.

(8) The areas of the preserved counties are set out in Part III of Schedule 4 and are determined by reference to local government areas in existence immediately before the passing of the Local Government (Wales) Act 1994.

(9) The Secretary of State may by order change the name by which any of the preserved counties is for the time being known.

(10) Any such order shall be subject to annulment in pursuance of a resolution of either House of Parliament.

(11) The Welsh name of each of the new principal areas is shown in Schedule 4 immediately after its English name.

NOTES

Defined terms   Wales: s 269
  local government area: s 270(1)
  new: s 270(1)
  preserved county: s 270(1)

Principal councils

Constitution of principal councils in Wales

21(1) For every principal area in Wales there shall be a council consisting of a chairman and councillors.

(1A) Where a council falling within subsection (1) are operating executive arrangements which involve a mayor and cabinet executive, the council shall consist of an elected mayor, a chairman and councillors.

(1B) In such a case, a reference in this Act to a member of a council is a reference to
    (a) the elected mayor of the council,
    (b) the chairman of the council, or
    (c) a councillor of the council.

(2) Each such council shall be a body corporate and shall have the functions given to them by this Act or otherwise.

(3) Each council for a county in Wales shall have the name of the county with the addition
    (a) in the case of their English name, of the words "County Council" or the word "Council" (as in "Cardiganshire County Council" or "Cardiganshire Council"); and
    (b) in the case of their Welsh name, of the word "Cyngor" (as in "Cyngor Sir Aberteifi").

(4)   Each council for a county borough in Wales shall have the name of the county borough with the addition

    (a)   in the case of their English name, of the words "County Borough Council" or the word "Council" (as in "Caerphilly County Borough Council" or "Caerphilly Council"); and

    (b)   in the case of their Welsh name, of the words "Cyngor Bwrdeistref Sirol" or the word "Cyngor" (as in "Cyngor Bwrdeistref Sirol Caerffili" or "Cyngor Caerffili").

(5)   In the case of Abertawe, Caerdydd and Powys subsection (3)(b) above shall have effect as if it required the addition of the words "Cyngor Sir".

NOTES

Defined terms
  elected mayor: s 270(1)
  executive arrangements: s 270(1)
  mayor and cabinet executive: s 270(1)

principal area: s 270(1)
Wales: s 269

Term of office and retirement of councillors

25(1)   Councillors for a principal area shall be elected by the local government electors for that area in accordance with this Act and Part I of the Representation of the People Act 1983.

(2)   For the purpose of the election of councillors, every principal area in Wales shall be divided into electoral divisions, each returning such number of councillors as may be provided by an order under paragraph 2 of Schedule 5 to this Act or under or by virtue of the provisions of Part IV of this Act or Part 3 of the Local Government (Democracy) (Wales) Act 2013 (anaw 4).

(3)   There shall be a separate election for each electoral division.

NOTES

Defined terms
  local government elector: s 270(1)
  principal area: s 270(1)

Wales: s 269

Elections of councillors

26(1)   The ordinary elections of councillors of the new principal councils shall take place in 2017 and in every fourth year after 2017.

(2)   The term of office of every such councillor shall be four years.

(3)   On the fourth day after any such ordinary election

    (a)   the persons who were councillors immediately before the election shall retire; and

    (b)   the newly elected councillors shall assume office.

NOTES

Defined terms
  new: s 270(1)
  principal council: s 270(1)

27-34   *Not reproduced*

Community councillors

35(1)   Community councillors shall be elected by the local government electors for the community in accordance with this Act and Part I of the Representation of the People Act 1983.

(2)   There shall be ordinary elections of community councillors in 2017 and in every fourth year thereafter.

(2A)   The term of office of the community councillors shall be four years.

(2B)   On the fourth day after any such ordinary election

      (a)   the persons who were councillors immediately before the election shall retire; and

      (b)   the newly elected councillors shall assume office.

(3)   Where a community is not divided into community wards there shall be one election of community councillors for the whole community.

(4)   Where a community is divided into community wards there shall be a separate election of community councillors for each ward.

NOTES
Defined terms
   local government elector: s 270(1)

Extent of Part II

38   This Part of this Act shall extend to Wales only.

NOTES
Defined terms
   Wales: s 269

....

PART V
GENERAL PROVISIONS AS TO MEMBERS AND PROCEEDINGS OF LOCAL AUTHORITIES

Qualifications and disqualifications

Qualifications for election and holding office as member of local authority

79(1)   A person shall, unless disqualified by virtue of this Act or any other enactment, be qualified to be elected and to be a member of a local authority if he is a qualifying Commonwealth citizen or a citizen of the Republic of Ireland or a relevant citizen of the Union and on the relevant day he has attained the age of eighteen years and

      (a)   on that day he is and thereafter he continues to be a local government elector for the area of the authority; or

      (b)   he has during the whole of the twelve months preceding that day occupied as owner or tenant any land or other premises in that area; or

      (c)   his principal or only place of work during that twelve months has been in that area; or

      (d)   he has during the whole of those twelve months resided in that area; or

      (e)   in the case of a member of a parish or community council he has during the whole of those twelve months resided either in the parish or community or within three miles of it.

(2A)   In this section the expression "citizen of the Union" shall be construed in accordance with Article 20(1) of the Treaty on the Functioning of the European Union, and "relevant citizen of the Union" means such a citizen who is not a qualifying Commonwealth citizen or a citizen of the Republic of Ireland.

(2B)   For the purposes of this section, a person is a qualifying Commonwealth citizen if he is a Commonwealth citizen who either

      (a)   is not a person who requires leave under the Immigration Act 1971 to enter or remain in the United Kingdom, or

      (b)   is such a person but for the time being has (or is, by virtue of any enactment, to be treated as having) indefinite leave to remain within the meaning of that Act.

(2C)   But a person is not a qualifying Commonwealth citizen by virtue of subsection (2B)(a) if he does not require leave to enter or remain in the United Kingdom by virtue only of section 8 of the Immigration Act 1971 (exceptions to requirement for leave in special cases).

(2) In this section "relevant day", in relation to any candidate, means

    (a) except in the case of an election not preceded by the nomination of candidates, the day on which he is nominated as a candidate and also, if there is a poll, the day of election; and

    (b) in the said excepted case, the day of election.

(3) *Repealed*

NOTES

Defined terms
  land: s 270(1)
  local authority: s 270(1)

local government elector: s 270(1)

Disqualifications for election and holding office as member of local authority

80(1) Subject to the provisions of section 81 below, a person shall be disqualified for being elected or being a member of a local authority if he

    (a) holds any paid office or employment (other than the office of chairman, vice-chairman or deputy chairman , deputy chairman, presiding member or deputy presiding member or, in the case of a local authority which are operating executive arrangements which involve a leader and cabinet executive, the office of executive leader or member of the executive) appointments or elections to which are or may be made or confirmed by the local authority or any committee or subcommittee of the authority or by a joint committee or National Park authority on which the authority are represented or by any person holding any such office or employment; or

    (b) is the subject of a bankruptcy restrictions order or an interim bankruptcy restrictions order, or a debt relief restrictions order or interim debt relief restrictions order under Schedule 4ZB of the Insolvency Act 1986; or

    (c) *Repealed*

    (d) has within five years before the day of election or since his election been convicted in the United Kingdom, the Channel Islands or the Isle of Man of any offence and has had passed on him a sentence of imprisonment (whether suspended or not) for a period of not less than three months without the option of a fine; or

    (e) is disqualified for being elected or for being a member of that authority under Part III of the Representation of the People Act 1983 .

(2) Subject to the provisions of section 81 below, a paid officer of a local authority who is employed under the direction of

    (a) a committee or subcommittee of the authority any member of which is appointed on the nomination of some other local authority; or

    (b) a joint board, joint authority, economic prosperity board, combined authority or joint committee on which the authority are represented and any member of which is so appointed;

shall be disqualified for being elected or being a member of that other local authority.

(2AA) A paid member of staff of the Greater London Authority who is employed under the direction of a joint committee the membership of which includes

    (a) one or more persons appointed on the nomination of the Authority acting by the Mayor, and

    (b) one or more members of one or more London borough councils appointed to the committee on the nomination of those councils,

shall be disqualified for being elected or being a member of any of those London borough councils.

(2AB) A person who is employed by or under the direction of a strategic planning panel is disqualified for being elected or being a member of a local authority which is a constituent local planning authority in relation to that panel (within the meaning of paragraph 3(3) of Schedule 2A to the Planning and Compulsory Purchase Act 2004).

(2A) Subsection (2) above shall have effect as if the reference to a joint board included a reference to a National Park authority.

(2B) For the purposes of this section a local authority shall be treated as represented on a National Park authority if it is entitled to make any appointment of a local authority member of the National Park authority.

(3) Subsection (1)(a) shall have effect in relation to a teacher in a school maintained by the local authority who does not hold an employment falling within that provision as it has effect in relation to a teacher in such a school who holds such an employment.

(4) *Repealed*

(5) For the purposes of subsection (1) (d) above, the ordinary date on which the period allowed for making an appeal or application with respect to the conviction expires or, if such an appeal or application is made, the date on which the appeal or application is finally disposed of or abandoned or fails by reason of the non-prosecution thereof shall be deemed to be the date of the conviction,

(6) *Repealed*

NOTES
Defined terms
chairman of a council in the application of this section to a London borough: s 270(4)(a)
combined authority: s 270(1)
economic prosperity board: s 270(1)
executive: s 270(1)
executive arrangements: s 270(1)
executive leader: s 270(1)
joint authority: s 270(1)
leader and cabinet executive: s 270(1)
local authority: s 270(1)
vice-chairman of a council in the application of this section to a London borough: s 270(4)(b)

Exceptions to provisions of section 80

1(1)-(3) *Repealed*

(4) Section 80(2) and (3) above shall not operate so as to disqualify

　　(a) any person by reason of his being a teacher, or otherwise employed, in a school, or other educational institution maintained or assisted by a county council for being a member of a district council by reason that the district council nominates members of the education committee of the county council; or

　　(b) *Repealed*

Validity of acts done by unqualified persons

82(1) The acts and proceedings of any person elected to an office under this Act or elected or appointed to an office under Part IV of the Local Government Act 1985 or elected as elected mayor or executive leader and acting in that office shall, notwithstanding his disqualification or want of qualification, be as valid and effectual as if he had been qualified.

(2) Subsection (1) above shall have effect, in relation to the Broads Authority, as if the references to this Act included a reference to the Norfolk and Suffolk Broads Act 1988.

NOTES
Defined terms
elected mayor: s 270(1)
executive leader: s 270(1)

Acceptance, resignation and vacation of office, and casual vacancies

Declaration of acceptance of office

83(1)   The person elected to any of the following offices, that is to say, the office of chairman, vicechairman, presiding member, deputy presiding member, councillor or elected mayor of the council of a county, county borough, district or London borough shall not, unless he has made a declaration of acceptance of office in a form prescribed by an order made by the Secretary of State, and the declaration has within two months from the day of the election been delivered to the proper officer of the council, act in the office except for the purpose of taking such a declaration.

(2)   If such a declaration is not made and delivered to the proper officer within the appointed time, the office of the person elected shall at the expiration of that time become vacant.

(3)   The declaration shall be made before either
   (a)   two members of the council to which the declarant is elected; or
   (aa) an elected mayor of the council to which the declarant is elected; or
   (b)   the proper officer of the council; or
   (c)   a justice of the peace or magistrate in the United Kingdom, the Channel Isles or the Isle of Man; or
   (d)   a commissioner appointed to administer oaths in the Senior Courts.

(4)   A person elected to the office of chairman of a parish or community council or parish or community councillor shall
   (a)   in the case of the chairman, at the meeting at which he is elected;
   (b)   in the case of a councillor, before or at the first meeting of the parish or community council after his election; or
   (c)   in either case if the council at that meeting so permit, before or at a later meeting fixed by the council;
   make in the presence of a member of the council or of the proper officer of the council and deliver to the council a declaration of acceptance of office in a form prescribed by an order made by the Secretary of State, and if he fails to do so his office shall thereupon become vacant.

(5)   Any person before whom a declaration is authorised to be made under this section may take the declaration.

NOTES

Subordinate legislation
Local Elections (Declaration of Acceptance of Office) (Welsh Forms) Order 1991, SI 1991/1169.
Local Elections (Declaration of Acceptance of Office) (Wales) Order 2004, SI 2004/1508
Local Elections (Declaration of Acceptance of Office) Order 2012, SI 2012/1465

Defined terms
chairman of a council in the application of this section

to a London borough: s 270(4)(a)
county: s 270(1)
district: s 270(1)
elected mayor: s 270(1)
proper officer: s 270(3), (4)(c)
vice-chairman of a council in the application of this section to a London borough: s 270(4)(b)

Resignation

84(1)   A person elected to any office under this Act or elected as an elected mayor may at any time resign his office by written notice delivered
   (a)   except in a case falling within paragraph (b), (c) or (d) below, to the proper officer of the council;
   (b)   in the case of a person elected to a corporate office in a London borough, to the proper officer of the borough;
   (c)   in the case of a parish or community councillor, to the chairman of the parish or community council;

(d) in the case of a chairman of a parish or community council or of a parish meeting, to the council or the meeting, as the case may be;

and his resignation shall take effect upon the receipt of the notice by the person or body to whom it is required to be delivered.

(2) A person elected or appointed to an office under Part IV of the Local Government Act 1985 may at any time resign his office by written notice delivered to the proper officer of the authority of which he is a member and his resignation shall take effect upon the receipt of the notice by that officer.

NOTES
Defined terms
   elected mayor: s 270(1)
   proper officer: s 270(3), (4)(c)

Vacation of office by failure to attend meetings

85(1) Subject to subsections (2) and (3) below, if a member of a local authority fails throughout a period of six consecutive months from the date of his last attendance to attend any meeting of the authority, he shall, unless the failure was due to some reason approved by the authority before the expiry of that period, cease to be a member of the authority.

(2) Attendance as a member at a meeting of any committee or subcommittee of the authority, or at a meeting of any joint committee, joint board or other body by whom for the time being any of the functions of the authority are being discharged, or who were appointed to advise the authority on any matter relating to the discharge of their functions, and attendance as representative of the authority at a meeting of any body of persons, shall be deemed for the purposes of subsection (1) above to be attendance at a meeting of the authority.

(2A) Subject to subsections (2B) and (3), if a member of a local authority which are operating executive arrangements, who is also a member of the executive of that local authority, fails throughout a period of six consecutive months from the date of his last attendance to attend any meeting of the executive, he shall, unless the failure was due to some reason approved by the local authority before the expiry of that period, cease to be a member of the local authority.

(2B) For the purposes of this section

(a) the discharge by a member, acting alone, of any function which is the responsibility of the executive; and

(b) in respect of a mayor and cabinet executive or leader and cabinet executive, attendance as a member at a meeting of a committee of the executive,

shall each be deemed to be attendance at a meeting of the executive.

(3) A member of any branch of Her Majesty's naval, military or air forces when employed during war or any emergency on any naval, military or air force service, and a person whose employment in the service of Her Majesty in connection with war or any emergency is such as, in the opinion of the Secretary of State, to entitle him to relief from disqualification on account of absence, shall not cease to be a member of a local authority by reason only of a failure to attend meetings of the local authority or of a failure to attend meetings of the executive if the failure is due to that employment.

(3A) Any period during which a member of a local authority is suspended or partially suspended under section 66, 73, 78, or 79 of the Local Government Act 2000 shall be disregarded for the purpose of calculating the period of six consecutive months under subsection (1) or (2A) above (and, accordingly, a period during which a member fails to attend meetings of the authority or, as the case may be, meetings of the executive that falls immediately before, and another such period that falls immediately after, a period of suspension or partial suspension shall be treated as consecutive).

(3B) Subsections (3C) and (3D) apply for the purpose of calculating the period of six consecutive months under subsection (1) or (2A).

(3C) Any period during which a member of a local authority in Wales is exercising a right to absence under Part 2 of the Local Government (Wales) Measure 2011 is to be disregarded.

(3D) The following two periods are to be treated as consecutive

    (a) the period during which a member of a local authority in Wales fails to attend meetings of the authority or, as the case may be, meetings of the executive that falls immediately before the period described in subsection (3C), and

    (b) the period that falls immediately after the period described in subsection (3C).

(4) In this section "local authority" includes a joint authority, an economic prosperity board and a combined authority .

NOTES

Defined terms
  combined authority: s 270(1)
  economic prosperity board: s 270(1)
  executive: s 270(1)
  executive arrangements: s 270(1)
  joint authority: s 270(1)
  leader and cabinet executive: s 270(1)

local authority: s 270(1) (and sub-s (4) of this section)
mayor and cabinet executive: s 270(1)
member of a local authority in the application of this section to London: s 270(4)(a)
Wales: s 269

Declaration by local authority of vacancy in office in certain cases

86(1) Where a member of a local authority

    (a) ceases to be qualified to be a member of the authority; or

    (b) becomes disqualified for being a member of the authority otherwise than under section 79 of the Local Government Act 2000 or section 34 of the Localism Act 2011 or by virtue of a conviction or a breach of any provision of Part II of the Representation of the People Act 1983 ; or

    (c) ceases to be a member of the authority by reason of failure to attend meetings of the authority;

the authority shall, except in any case in which a declaration has been made by the High Court under this Part of this Act, forthwith declare his office to be vacant.

(2) In this section "local authority" includes a joint authority, an economic prosperity board and a combined authority.

NOTES

Defined terms
  combined authority: s 270(1)
  economic prosperity board: s 270(1)
  joint authority: s 270(1)
  local authority: s 270(1) (and sub-s (2) of this section)

member of a local authority in the application of this section to London: s 270(4)(a)

Date of casual vacancies

87(1) For the purpose of filling a casual vacancy in any office for which an election is held under this Act, the date on which the vacancy is to be deemed to have occurred shall be

    (a) in the case of non-acceptance of office by any person who is required to make and deliver a declaration of acceptance of office, on the expiration of the period appointed under this Part of this Act for the delivery of the declaration;

    (b) in the case of resignation, upon the receipt of the notice of resignation by the person or body to whom the notice is required to be delivered;

    (c) in the case of death, on the date of death;

    (d) in the case of a disqualification by virtue of a conviction, on the expiration of the ordinary period allowed for making an appeal or application with respect to the conviction or, if an appeal or application is made, on the date on which that appeal or application is finally disposed of or abandoned or fails by reason of nonprosecution thereof;

(e) in the case of an election being declared void on an election petition, on the date of the report or certificate of the election court;

(ee) in the case of a disqualification under section 79 of the Local Government Act 2000 or section 34 of the Localism Act 2011 or, on the expiration of the ordinary period allowed for making an appeal or application with respect to the relevant decision or order under that section or, if an appeal or application is made, on the date on which that appeal or application is finally disposed of or abandoned or fails by reason of nonprosecution thereof;

(f) in the case of a person ceasing to be qualified to be a member of a local authority, or becoming disqualified, for any reason other than one mentioned in paragraphs (a) to (ee) above, or ceasing to be a member of a local authority by reason of failure to attend meetings, on the date on which his office is declared to have been vacated either by the High Court or by the local authority, as the case may be; and

(g) *Repealed*

(2) Public notice of a casual vacancy in any such office as is referred to in subsection (1) above shall be given by the local authority in which the office exists; and the steps required to be taken to give public notice in accordance with section 232 below shall be taken

(a) in a case where the local authority declare the office to be vacant, immediately after the declaration; and

(b) in any other case, as soon as practicable after the date on which, by virtue of subsection (1) above, the vacancy is deemed to have occurred.

(3) *Repealed*

NOTES
Defined terms
local authority: s 270(1)
member of a local authority in the application of this

section to London: s 270(4)(a)

Filling of casual vacancy in case of chairman, etc

88(1) On a casual vacancy occurring in the office of chairman of any council , an election to fill the vacancy shall be held not later than the next ordinary meeting of the council held after the date on which the vacancy occurs, or if that meeting is held within fourteen days after that date, then not later than the next following ordinary meeting of the council, and shall be conducted in the same manner as an ordinary election.

(2) A meeting of the council for the election may be convened by the proper officer of the authority.

(2A) *Repealed*

(3) In a parish not having a separate parish council, a casual vacancy in the office of chairman of the parish meeting shall be filled by the parish meeting, and a parish meeting shall be convened for the purpose of filling the vacancy forthwith.

NOTES
Defined terms
chairman of the council in the application of this
section to a London borough: s 270(4)(a)

proper officer: s 270(3), (4)(c)

Filling of casual vacancies in case of councillors

89(1) Subject to the provisions of this section, on a casual vacancy occurring in the office of councillor for any principal area, an election to fill the vacancy shall be held

(a) in a case in which the High Court or the council have declared the office to be vacant, within thirty-five days (computed in accordance with section 243(4) below) from the date of the declaration;

(b) in any other case, within thirty-five days (so computed) after notice in writing of the vacancy has been given to the proper officer of the authority by two local government electors for the area.

(2) The day of election to fill a casual vacancy in any office mentioned in subsection (1) above shall be fixed by the returning officer

(3) Where a casual vacancy in any such office occurs within six months before the day on which the councillor whose office is vacant would regularly have retired, an election shall not be held under subsection (1) above unless on the occurrence of the vacancy (or in the case of a number of simultaneous vacancies, the occurrence of the vacancies) the total number of unfilled vacancies in the membership of the council exceeds one third of the whole number of members; and where an election under subsection (1) above is not held, the vacancy shall be filled at the next ordinary election.

(3A) *Repealed*

(4) Where more than one casual vacancy in the office of councillor of a district in which councillors are elected by thirds is filled at the same election, the person elected by the smallest number of votes shall be deemed to be elected in place of the councillor who would regularly have first retired, and the person elected by the next smallest number of votes shall be deemed to be elected in place of the councillor who would regularly have next retired and so with respect to the others; and if there has not been a contested election, or if any doubt arises, the order of retirement shall be determined by lot.

(5) Where an election to fill one or more casual vacancies in the office of councillor of any such district is combined with an ordinary election of councillors, the following provisions shall apply
  (a) where an election is contested
    (i) the persons who are elected by the smallest numbers of votes, or if any relevant votes are equal such persons as are determined by lot, shall be deemed elected to fill the casual vacancies;
    (ii) if the persons elected to fill the casual vacancies will hold office for different periods, the person elected by the smallest number of votes or, if the relevant votes are equal, such person as is determined by lot, shall hold office for the shorter period, and so with respect to the others;
  (b) where the election is not contested
    (i) those declared elected (if fewer than the vacancies to be filled) shall be deemed elected to fill the vacancies in which they will hold office for the longest periods;
    (ii) where there are two or more persons declared elected and they are to fill vacancies in which they will hold office for different periods, any retiring councillors elected shall be deemed elected to fill the vacancies in which they will hold office for the longest period, and the question which of the persons declared elected who are not retiring councillors is to be deemed elected to fill any of the vacancies not filled by retiring councillors shall be determined by lot.

(6) A casual vacancy among parish or community councillors shall be filled by election or by the parish or community council in accordance with rules made under section 36 of the Representation of the People Act 1983.

(7) Where under this section any question is required to be determined by lot
  (a) in the case of a contested election, the lot shall be drawn by the returning officer immediately after the question has arisen; and
  (b) in any other case, the lot shall be drawn at the next meeting of the council after the question has arisen, and the drawing shall be conducted under the direction of the person presiding at the meeting.

NOTES
Defined terms
  district: s 270(1)
  local government elector: s 270(1)
principal area: ss 20(5), 270(1)
proper officer: s 270(3), (4)(c)

Term of office of persons filling casual vacancies

90 A person elected or appointed under the foregoing provisions of this Act in England or Wales or under Part IV of the Local Government Act 1985 to fill any casual vacancy shall hold office until the date upon which the person in whose place he is elected or appointed would regularly have retired, and he shall then retire.

NOTES

Defined terms
England: s 269
Wales: s 269

Temporary appointment of members of parish and community councils

91(1) Where there are so many vacancies in the office of parish or community councillor that the parish or community council are unable to act, the district council or Welsh principal council may by order appoint persons to fill all or any of the vacancies until other councillors are elected and take up office.

(2) In the case of a common parish council under which are grouped, by virtue of section 11(5) above, parishes situated in different districts, the reference in subsection (1) above to the district council shall be construed as a reference to the council of the district in which there is the greater number of local government electors for the parishes in the group.

(3) Two copies of every order made under this section shall be sent to the Secretary of State.

NOTES

Defined terms
grouped: s 270(1)
local government elector: s 270(1)

principal council: s 270(1)

Proceedings for disqualification

Proceedings for disqualification

92(1) Proceedings against any person on the ground that he acted or claims to be entitled to act as a member of a local authority while disqualified for so acting within the meaning of this section may be instituted by, and only by, any local government elector for the area concerned
   (a) in the High Court or a magistrates' court if that person so acted;
   (b) in the High Court if that person claims to be entitled so to act;
   but proceedings under paragraph (a) above shall not be instituted against any person after the expiration of more than six months from the date on which he so acted.

(2) Where in proceedings instituted under this section it is proved that the defendant has acted as a member of a local authority while disqualified for so acting, then
   (a) if the proceedings are in the High Court, the High Court may
      (i) make a declaration to that effect and declare that the office in which the defendant has acted is vacant;
      (ii) grant an injunction restraining the defendant from so acting;
      (iii) order that the defendant shall forfeit to Her Majesty such sum as the court think fit, not exceeding £50 for each occasion on which he so acted while disqualified;
   (b) if the proceedings are in a magistrates' court, the magistrates' court may, subject to the provisions of this section, convict the defendant and impose on him a fine not exceeding level 3 on the standard scale for each occasion on which he so acted while disqualified.

(3) Where proceedings under this section are instituted in a magistrates' court, then
   (a) if the court is satisfied that the matter would be more properly dealt with in the High Court, it shall by order discontinue the proceedings;

(b) if the High Court, on application made to it by the defendant within fourteen days after service of the summons, is satisfied that the matter would be more properly dealt with in the High Court, it may make an order, which shall not be subject to any appeal, requiring the magistrates' court by order to discontinue the proceedings.

(4) Where in proceedings instituted under this section in the High Court it is proved that the defendant claims to act as a member of a local authority and is disqualified for so acting, the court may make a declaration to that effect and declare that the office in which the defendant claims to be entitled to act is vacant and grant an injunction restraining him from so acting.

(5) No proceedings shall be instituted against a person otherwise than under this section on the ground that he has, while disqualified for acting as a member of a local authority, so acted or claimed to be entitled so to act.

(6) For the purposes of this section a person shall be deemed to be disqualified for acting as a member of a local authority

(a) if he is not qualified to be, or is disqualified for being, a member of the authority; or

(b) if by reason of failure to make and deliver the declaration of acceptance of office within the period required, or by reason of resignation or failure to attend meetings of the local authority, he has ceased to be a member of the authority.

(7) In this section "local authority" includes a joint authority, an economic prosperity board and a combined authority ; and in relation to a joint authority, an economic prosperity board or a combined authority the reference in subsection (1) above to a local government elector for the area concerned shall be construed as a reference to a local government elector for any local government area in the area for which the authority is established.

(7A) *Repealed*

(7B) *Repealed*

(8) In relation to the Broads Authority, the reference in subsection (1) above to a local government elector for the area concerned shall be construed as a reference to a local government elector for the area of any of the local authorities mentioned in section 1(3)(a) of the Norfolk and Suffolk Broads Act 1988.

NOTES

Defined terms

combined authority: s 270(1)
economic prosperity board: s 270(1)
joint authority: s 270(1)
local authority: s 270(1) (and sub-ss (7), (7A) of this section)
local government area: s 270(1)

local government elector: s 270(1) (and sub-ss (7), (8) of this section)
member of a local authority in the application of this section to a London borough: s 270(4)(a)

Meaning of "England" and "Wales"

269 In this Act "Wales" means the combined area of the preserved counties and "England" does not include any area which is included in any of the preserved counties.

General provisions as to interpretation

270(1) In this Act, except where the context otherwise requires, the following expressions have the following meanings respectively, that is to say

"alternative arrangements" has the same meaning as in Part II of the Local Government Act 2000;

"appropriate Minister", in relation to the making of an order or regulation or the giving of a direction with respect to any matter, means the Minister in charge of any Government department concerned with that matter; but the validity of any order, regulation or direction purporting to be made or given by any Minister by virtue of a power conferred on the appropriate Minister by this Act shall not be affected by any question as to whether or not that Minister was the appropriate Minister for the purpose;

"bank holiday break" means any bank holiday not included in the Christmas break or the Easter break and the period beginning with the last week day before that bank holiday and ending with the next week day which is not a bank holiday;

"the Broads" has the same meaning as in the Norfolk and Suffolk Broads Act 1988;

"Christmas break" means the period beginning with the last week day before Christmas Day and ending with the first week day after Christmas Day which is not a bank holiday;

"the City" means the City of London;

"combined authority" means a combined authority established under section 103 of the Local Democracy, Economic Development and Construction Act 2009;

"Common Council" means the Common Council of the City;

"county" without more, means, in relation to England, a metropolitan county or a non-metropolitan county, but in the expressions "county council", "council of a county", "county councillor" and "councillor of a county" means, in relation to England, a non-metropolitan county only;

"district", without more, means, in relation to England, a metropolitan district or a non-metropolitan district;

"Easter break" means the period beginning with the Thursday before and ending with the Tuesday after Easter Day;

"economic prosperity board" means an economic prosperity board established under section 88 of the Local Democracy, Economic Development and Construction Act 2009;

"elected mayor" has

    (a) in relation to England, the same meaning as in Part 1A of the Local Government Act 2000, and

    (b) in relation to Wales, the same meaning as in Part II of the Local Government Act 2000;

"electoral area" means any area for which councillors are elected to any local authority;

"executive", "executive arrangements" and "executive leader" have

    (a) in relation to England, the same meaning as in Part 1A of the Local Government Act 2000, and

    (b) in relation to Wales, the same meaning as in Part II of the Local Government Act 2000;

"existing", in relation to a local government or other area or a local authority or other body, except in sections 1 and 20 above, means that area or body as it existed immediately before the passing of this Act;

"financial year" means the period of twelve months ending with 31st March in any year;

"grouped", in relation to a parish or community, means grouped by or by virtue of any provision of this Act or any previous corresponding enactment under a common parish or community council, and "grouping order" shall be construed accordingly;

"joint authority" means an authority established by Part IV of the Local Government Act 1985;

"land" includes any interest in land and any easement or right in, to or over land;

"leader and cabinet executive" means

    (a) in relation to England: a leader and cabinet executive (England);

    (b) in relation to Wales: a leader and cabinet executive (Wales);

"leader and cabinet executive (England)" has the same meaning as in Part 1A of the Local Government Act 2000;

"leader and cabinet executive (Wales)" has the same meaning as in Part 2 of the Local Government Act 2000;

"local authority" means a county council, a district council, a London borough council or a parish council but, in relation to Wales, means a county council, county borough council or community council;

"local government area" means

(a) in relation to England, a county, Greater London, a district, a London borough or a parish;

(b) in relation to Wales, a county, county borough or community;

"local government elector" means a person registered as a local government elector in the register of electors in accordance with the provisions of the Representation of the People Acts;

"local statutory provision" means a provision of a local Act (including an Act confirming a provisional order) or a provision of a public general Act passed with respect only to the whole or part of an existing local government area or a provision of an instrument made under any such local or public general Act or of an instrument in the nature of a local enactment made under any other Act;

"mayor and cabinet executive" *and* "mayor and council manager executive" has

(a) in relation to England, the same meaning as in Part 1A of the Local Government Act 2000, and

(b) in relation to Wales, the same meaning as in Part II of the Local Government Act 2000;

"new", in relation to any area or authority, means an area or authority established by or under this Act including one established by virtue of any provision of the Local Government (Wales) Act 1994;

"1933 Act" means the Local Government Act 1933;

"1963 Act" means the London Government Act 1963;

"open space" has the meaning assigned to it by section 336(1) of the Town and Country Planning Act 1990;

"prescribed" means prescribed by regulations made by the Secretary of State;

"preserved county" means any county created by this Act as a county in Wales, as it stood immediately before the passing of the Local Government (Wales) Act 1994 but subject to any provision of the Act of 1994, or any provision made under this Act, redrawing its boundaries;

"principal area" means a non-metropolitan county, a district or a London borough but, in relation to Wales, means a county or county borough;

"principal council" means a council elected for a principal area;

"public body" includes

(a) a local authority and a joint board on which, and a joint committee on which, a local authority or parish meeting are represented;

(b) any trustees, commissioners or other persons who, for public purposes and not for their own profit, act under any enactment or instrument for the improvement of any place, for the supply of water to any place, or for providing or maintaining a cemetery or market in any place; and

(c) any other authority having powers of levying or issuing a precept for any rate for public purposes;

and "district" means, in relation to a public body other than a local authority, the area for which the public body acts;

"specified papers", in relation to a parish or community, means the public books, writings and papers of the parish or community (including any photographic copies thereof) and all documents directed by law to be kept therewith;

"the Temples" means the Inner Temple and the Middle Temple;

(2)   In this Act and in any other enactment, whether passed before, at the same time as, or after this Act, the expression "non-metropolitan county" means any county other than a metropolitan county, and the expression "non-metropolitan district" means any district other than a metropolitan district.

(3)   Any reference in this Act to a proper officer and any reference which by virtue of this Act is to be construed as such a reference shall, in relation to any purpose and any local authority or other body or any area, be construed as a reference to an officer appointed for that purpose by that body or for that area, as the case may be.

(4)   In any provision of this Act which applies to a London borough, except Schedule 2 to this Act,

    (a)   any reference to the chairman of the council or of any class of councils comprising the council or to a member of a local authority shall be construed as or, as the case may be, as including a reference to the mayor of the borough;

    (b)   any reference to the vice-chairman of the council or any such class of councils shall be construed as a reference to the deputy mayor of the borough; and

    (c)   any reference to the proper officer of the council or any such class of councils shall be construed as a reference to the proper officer of the borough.

(4A) Where a London borough council are operating executive arrangements which involve a mayor and cabinet executive, subsection (4) above shall have effect with the omission of paragraphs (a) and (b).

(5)   In this Act, except where the context otherwise requires, references to any enactment shall be construed as references to that enactment as amended, extended or applied by or under any other enactment, including any enactment contained in this Act.

Local Government Act 2000

An Act to make provision with respect to the functions and procedures of local authorities and provision with respect to local authority elections; to make provision with respect to grants and housing benefit in respect of certain welfare services; to amend section 29 of the Children Act 1989; and for connected purposes.

28th July 2000

PART I
PROMOTION OF ECONOMIC, SOCIAL OR ENVIRONMENTAL WELLBEING ETC

PART 1A
ARRANGEMENTS WITH RESPECT TO LOCAL AUTHORITY GOVERNANCE IN ENGLAND

PART II
LOCAL AUTHORITIES IN WALES: ARRANGEMENTS WITH RESPECT TO EXECUTIVES ETC

PART I

PROMOTION OF ECONOMIC, SOCIAL OR ENVIRONMENTAL WELLBEING ETC

ARRANGEMENTS WITH RESPECT TO LOCAL AUTHORITY GOVERNANCE IN ENGLAND

9B-9L   *Not reproduced*

Referendums

Cases in which change is subject to approval in a referendum in accordance with sections 9MA and 9MB

9M(1)   A change in governance arrangements which a local authority proposes to make by resolution is subject to approval in a referendum in either of the following cases.

(2)   The first case is where
    (a)   the proposed change in governance arrangements is of a kind set out in
        (i) section 9K (change from one form of governance to another), or
        (ii)   section 9KA (change to a different form of executive), and
    (b)   the implementation of the local authority's existing form of governance or existing form of executive was approved in a referendum under this Chapter.

(3)   The second case is where the local authority resolves that a proposed change in governance arrangements is to be subject to approval in a referendum.

NOTES

Defined terms   local authority: s 9R(1)
   change in governance arrangements: s 9OA(2)
   executive: ss 9C, 9R(1)
   form of governance: s 9OA(4)

Referendum: proposals by local authority

9MA(1)   This section applies to a local authority which wishes to make a change in governance arrangements that is subject to approval in a referendum under section 9M.

(2)   The local authority must draw up proposals for the change.

(3)   The proposals must include
    (a)   a timetable with respect to the implementation of the proposals,
    (b)   details of any transitional arrangements which are necessary for the implementation of the proposals, and
    (c)   a statement that the change in governance arrangements is to be subject to approval in a referendum.

(4)   Subsections (5) and (6) apply where the proposed change in governance arrangements is of the kind set out in
    (a)   section 9K (change from one form of governance to another), or
    (b)   section 9KA (change to a different form of executive).

(5)   If the proposed change in governance arrangements would result in the local authority having executive arrangements, the proposals must state the extent to which the functions specified in regulations under section 9D(3)(b) are to be the responsibility of the executive which will be operated if the proposals are implemented.

(6)   The proposals (particularly any provision about timetables and transitional matters included in accordance with subsection (3)) must be such as to ensure that the proposed change can take effect (so far as required to) in accordance with section 9L(2).

(7)   After drawing up the proposals, the local authority must
    (a)   secure that copies of a document setting out the proposals are available at its principal office for inspection by members of the public at all reasonable times, and
    (b)   publish in one or more newspapers circulating in its area a notice which
        (i)   states that the authority has drawn up the proposals,

(ii)   describes the main features of the proposals,

(iii) states that copies of a document setting out the proposals are available at the authority's principal office for inspection by members of the public at such times as may be specified in the notice, and

(iv) specifies the address of the authority's principal office.

NOTES

Defined terms

change in governance arrangements: s 9OA(2)

executive: ss 9C, 9R(1)

executive arrangements: ss 9B(4), 9R(1)

local authority: s 9R(1)

Requirement to hold and give effect to referendum

9MB(1)   This section applies to a local authority which wishes to make a change in governance arrangements that is subject to approval in a referendum under section 9M.

(2)   The local authority must, after complying with section 9MA(7), hold a referendum on its proposals before taking any steps to implement them.

(3)   The local authority may not pass a resolution which makes the proposed change unless the result of the referendum is to approve the proposals.

(4)   Any such resolution must be passed within the period of 28 days beginning with the day when the referendum is held.

(5)   Any such resolution must be passed at a meeting which is specially convened for the purpose of deciding the resolution with notice of the object.

NOTES

Defined terms

change in governance arrangements: s 9OA(2)

local authority: s 9R(1)

Referendum following petition

9MC(1)   The Secretary of State may by regulations make provision for or in connection with requiring a local authority which receives a petition which complies with the provisions of the regulations to hold a referendum, in such circumstances as may be prescribed in the regulations, on whether the authority should have a relevant type of governance arrangement.

(2)   Regulations under subsection (1) may, in particular, include provision

(a) as to the form and content of petitions (including provision for petitions in electronic form),

(b) as to the minimum number of local government electors for a local authority's area who must support any petition presented to the authority during any period specified in the regulations,

(c) for or in connection with requiring an officer of a local authority to publish the number of local government electors for the authority's area who must support any petition presented to the authority,

(d) as to the way in which local government electors for a local authority's area are to support a petition (including provision enabling local government electors to support petitions by telephone or by electronic means),

(e) as to the action which may, may not or must be taken by a local authority in connection with any petition,

(f) as to the manner in which a petition is to be presented to a local authority,

(g) as to the verification of any petition,

(h) as to the date on which, or the time by which, a referendum must be held,

(i) as to the action which may, may not or must be taken by a local authority before or in connection with a referendum,

(j)   as to the action which may, may not or must be taken by a local authority after a referendum, and

(k)   for or in connection with enabling the Secretary of State, in the event of any failure by a local authority to take any action permitted or required by virtue of the regulations, to take that action.

(3)   Provision made by virtue of subsection (2) may, in particular, apply or reproduce (with or without modifications) any provisions of, or made under, this Chapter.

(4)   The number of local government electors mentioned in subsection (2)(b) is to be calculated at such times as may be provided by regulations under this section and (unless such regulations otherwise provide) is to be 5 per cent of the number of local government electors at each of those times.

(5)   This section is subject to section 9NA (effect of order requiring, and giving effect to, referendum on change to mayor and cabinet executive).

NOTES
Defined terms
    local authority: s 9R(1)
    local government elector: s 9R(1)

relevant type of governance arrangement: s 9OA(3)

Referendum following direction

9MD(1)   The Secretary of State may by regulations make provision for or in connection with enabling the Secretary of State, in such circumstances as may be prescribed in the regulations, to direct a local authority to hold a referendum on whether it should have a relevant type of governance arrangements specified in the direction.

(2)   Regulations under this section may, in particular, include provision
(a)   as to the date on which, or the time by which, a referendum must be held,
(b)   as to the action which may, may not or must be taken by a local authority before or in connection with a referendum,
(c)   as to the action which may, may not or must be taken by a local authority after a referendum, and
(d)   for or in connection with enabling the Secretary of State, in the event of any failure by a local authority to take any action permitted or required by virtue of the regulations, to take that action.

(3)   Provision made by virtue of subsection (2) may, in particular, apply or reproduce (with or without modifications) any provisions of, or made under, this Chapter.

(4)   This section is subject to section 9NA (effect of order requiring, and giving effect to, referendum on change to mayor and cabinet executive).

NOTES
Defined terms
    local authority: s 9R(1)
    relevant type of governance arrangement: s 9OA(3)

Referendum following order

9ME(1)   The Secretary of State may by order make provision requiring every local authority, or every local authority falling within a description of authority specified in the order, to hold a referendum on whether they should have a relevant type of governance arrangements specified in the order.

(2)   An order under this section may, in particular, include provision
(a)   as to the date on which, or the time by which, a referendum must be held,
(b)   as to the action which may, may not or must be taken by a local authority before or in connection with a referendum,
(c)   as to the action which may, may not or must be taken by a local authority after a referendum, and

(d) for or in connection with enabling the Secretary of State, in the event of any failure by a local authority to take any action permitted or required by virtue of the order, to take that action.

(3) Provision made by virtue of subsection (2) may, in particular, apply or reproduce (with or without modifications) any provisions of, or made under, this Chapter.

(4) This section is subject to section 9NA (effect of order requiring, and giving effect to, referendum on change to mayor and cabinet executive).

NOTES
Defined terms
  local authority: s 9R(1)
  relevant type of governance arrangement: s 9OA(3)

Further provision with respect to referendums

9MF(1) If a local authority holds a referendum under this Chapter ("Referendum A") it may not hold, or be required to hold, another referendum under this Chapter ("Referendum B") within the period of ten years beginning with the date of Referendum A, unless subsection (2) or (3) applies.

(2) This subsection applies if
  (a) Referendum A was held by the authority by virtue of an order under section 9N (power by order to require, and give effect to, referendum on change to mayor and cabinet executive), and
  (b) the proposal for the authority to operate a mayor and cabinet executive was rejected in Referendum A.

(3) This subsection applies if Referendum B is required to be held by virtue of an order made under section 9N.

(4) If the result of a referendum held by virtue of regulations, an order or a direction made under any provision of this Chapter is to approve the proposals to which the referendum relates, the local authority concerned must implement those proposals.

(5) If the result of a referendum held by virtue of regulations, an order or a direction made under any provision of this Chapter is to reject the proposals to which the referendum relates, the local authority concerned may not implement those proposals.

(6) Subsections (4) and (5) do not apply to a referendum held by virtue of section 9N (but see section 9N(2)(c)).

NOTES
Defined terms
  local authority: s 9R(1)
  mayor and cabinet executive: ss 9C(2), 9R(1)

Voting in and conduct of referendums

9MG(1) The persons entitled to vote in a referendum held by a local authority under this Chapter are those who on the day of the referendum
  (a) would be entitled to vote as electors at an election of councillors for an electoral area which is situated within the authority's area, and
  (b) are registered in the register of local government electors at an address within the authority's area.

(2) The Secretary of State or the Chancellor of the Duchy of Lancaster may by regulations make provision as to the conduct of referendums under this Chapter.

(3) The Secretary of State or the Chancellor of the Duchy of Lancaster may by regulations make provision for the combination of polls at referendums under this Chapter with polls at any elections.

(4) Regulations under subsection (2) or (3) may apply or incorporate, with or without modifications or exceptions, any provision of any enactment (whenever passed or made) relating to elections or referendums.

(5) Regulations under subsection (2) may, in particular, include provision
    (a) as to the question to be asked in a referendum,
    (b) as to the publicity to be given in connection with a referendum (including the publicity to be given with respect to the consequences of the referendum),
    (c) about the limitation of expenditure in connection with a referendum (and the creation of criminal offences in connection with the limitation of such expenditure),
    (d) as to the conduct of the authority, members of the authority and officers of the authority in relation to a referendum,
    (e) as to when, where and how voting in a referendum is to take place,
    (f) as to how the votes cast in a referendum are to be counted, and
    (g) for disregarding alterations in a register of electors.

(6) Before making any regulations under this section that include provision as to the question to be asked in a referendum, the Secretary of State or the Chancellor of the Duchy of Lancaster must consult the Electoral Commission.

NOTES

Subordinate Legislation
  Local Authorities (Conduct of Referendums) (England) Regulations 2012, SI 2012/323

enactment: s 9R(1)
local authority: s 9R(1)
local government elector: s 9R(1)

Defined terms
  electoral area: s 9R(1)

Requiring referendum on change to mayor and cabinet executive

9N(1) The Secretary of State may by order require a specified local authority to hold a referendum on whether the authority should operate a mayor and cabinet executive.

(2) An order under this section may include provision
    (a) as to the date on which, or the time by which, a referendum must be held,
    (b) as to the action which may, may not or must be taken by a local authority before or in connection with a referendum,
    (c) as to the effect of a referendum and the action which may, may not or must be taken by a local authority after a referendum,
    (d) for or in connection with enabling the Secretary of State, in the event of any failure by a local authority to take any action permitted or required by virtue of the order, to take that action.

(3) Provision made by virtue of subsection (2) may, in particular, apply or reproduce (with or without modifications) any provisions of, or made under, this Chapter.

(4) In this section "specified" means specified in an order made by the Secretary of State under this section.

NOTES

Defined terms
  local authority: s 9R(1)
  mayor and cabinet executive: ss 9C(2), 9R(1)

Effect of section 9N order

9NA(1) Subject as follows, the provisions of this Chapter listed in subsection (2) do not apply to a local authority in relation to whom an order under section 9N has been made (and has not been revoked) unless the proposal for the authority to operate a mayor and cabinet executive has been rejected in the referendum held under the order.

(2) Those provisions are

(a) section 9K (changing from one form of governance to another);
(b) section 9KA (executive arrangements: different form of executive);
(c) section 9MC (referendum following petition);
(d) section 9MD (referendum following direction);
(e) section 9ME (referendum following order).

NOTES
Defined terms
   local authority: s 9R(1)
   mayor and cabinet executive: ss 9C(2), 9R(1)

Variation of mayoral executive

9NB(1) This section applies to a change in governance arrangements of the kind set out in section 9KB (variation of executive arrangements) if the local authority is operating a mayor and cabinet executive.

(2) The local authority may not resolve to make a change in governance arrangements unless the elected mayor has given written consent to the proposed change.

NOTES
Defined terms   mayor and cabinet executive: ss 9C(2), 9R(1)
   change in governance arrangements: s 9OA(2)
   elected mayor: ss 9H(1), 9R(1)
   local authority: s 9R(1)

Miscellaneous

General

9O(1) A local authority may not
(a) cease to operate a form of governance, or
(b) vary executive arrangements,
other than in accordance with this Chapter.

(2) In making a change in governance arrangements, the local authority must comply with any directions given by the Secretary of State in connection with the making of such a change.

NOTES
Defined terms   local authority: s 9R(1)
   change in governance arrangements: s 9OA(2)
   executive arrangements: ss 9B(4), 9R(1)
   form of governance: s 9OA(4)

Interpretation

9OA(1) This section applies for the purposes of this Chapter.

(2) References to a change in governance arrangements are references to any change of a kind set out in sections 9K to 9KB.

(3) References to a relevant type of governance arrangement are references to
(a) a leader and cabinet executive (England);
(b) a mayor and cabinet executive;
(c) a committee system;
(d) any prescribed arrangements.

(4) References to a form of governance are references to
(a) executive arrangements;
(b) a committee system;
(c) any prescribed arrangements.

NOTES

Defined terms
   committee system: ss 9B(4), 9R(1)
   executive arrangements: ss 9B(4), 9R(1)
   leader and cabinet executive (England): ss 9C(3), 9R(1)

mayor and cabinet executive: ss 9C(2), 9R(1)
prescribed arrangements: ss 9B(4), 9R(1)

Interpretation

Interpretation of Part 1A

9R(1) In this Part, unless the context otherwise requires

"committee system" has the meaning given by section 9B,

"committee system local authority" has the meaning given by section 9J(3),

"elected mayor" has the meaning given by section 9H,

"electoral area" has the meaning given by section 203(1) of the Representation of the People Act 1983,

"enactment" includes an enactment contained in a local Act or comprised in subordinate legislation (within the meaning of the Interpretation Act 1978),

"executive", in relation to a local authority, is to be construed in accordance with section 9C,

"executive arrangements" has the meaning given by section 9B,

"executive leader" has the meaning given by section 9C(3)(a),

"first preference vote" has the meaning given by section 9HC,

"leader and cabinet executive (England)" has the meaning given by section 9C(3),

"local authority" means a county council in England, a district council or a London borough council,

"local government elector" has the meaning given by section 270(1) of the Local Government Act 1972,

"mayor and cabinet executive" has the meaning given by section 9C(2),

"ordinary day of election", in relation to a local authority, means the day of ordinary elections of councillors of the authority,

"the political balance requirements" means the provisions made by or under sections 15 to 17 of, and Schedule 1 to, the Local Government and Housing Act 1989,

"prescribed arrangements" has the meaning give by section 9B, and

"second preference vote" has the meaning given by section 9HC.

(2) In this Part "relevant election years", in relation to a local authority, means the years specified in the second column of the following table in relation to that type of authority.

Type of local authority	Relevant election years
Metropolitan district	2014 and every fourth year afterwards
County	2013 and every fourth year afterwards
London borough	2014 and every fourth year afterwards
Non-metropolitan district	2011 and every fourth year afterwards

(3) Any reference in this Part to the chairman of a local authority

  (a) is a reference to that person whether or not the person is entitled to another style, and

  (b) in the case of a London borough, is a reference to the person who (disregarding paragraphs 5B to 5I of Schedule 2 to the Local Government Act 1972) is referred to in Part 1 of that Schedule as the mayor of the borough.

(4) Any reference in this Part to the vicechairman of a local authority

  (a) is a reference to that person whether or not the person is entitled to another style, and

  (b) in the case of a London borough, is a reference to the person who (disregarding paragraphs 5B to 5I of Schedule 2 to the Local Government Act 1972) is referred to in Part 1 of that Schedule as the deputy mayor.

(5) Any reference in this Part to the discharge of any functions includes a reference to the doing of anything which is calculated to facilitate, or is conducive or incidental to, the discharge of those functions.

(6) Section 101 of the Local Government Act 1972 does not apply to the function of the passing of a resolution under any provision made by or under this Part.

(7) Any functions conferred on a local authority by virtue of this Part are not to be the responsibility of an executive of the authority under executive arrangements.

(8) Any directions given by the Secretary of State under any provision of this Part

    (a) may be varied or revoked by subsequent directions given by the Secretary of State under that provision, and

    (b) may make different provision for different cases, different local authorities or different descriptions of local authority.

PART II
LOCAL AUTHORITIES IN WALES: ARRANGEMENTS WITH RESPECT TO EXECUTIVES ETC

Referendums

Referendum following petition

34(1) The Welsh Ministers may by regulations make provision for or in connection with requiring a local authority which receive a petition which complies with the provisions of the regulations to hold a referendum, in such circumstances as may be prescribed in the regulations, on whether the authority should operate a relevant form of executive.

(1A) In this section "relevant form of executive" means executive arrangements involving a form of executive for which a referendum is required.

(2) The provision which may be made by regulations under subsection (1) includes provision

    (a) as to the form and content of petitions (including provision for petitions in electronic form),

    (b) as to the minimum number of local government electors for a local authority's area who must support any petition presented to the authority during any period specified in the regulations,

    (c) for or in connection with requiring an officer of a local authority to publish the number of local government electors for the authority's area who must support any petition presented to the authority,

    (d) as to the way in which local government electors for a local authority's area are to support a petition (including provision enabling local government electors to support petitions by telephone or by electronic means),

    (e) as to the action which may, may not or must be taken by a local authority in connection with any petition,

    (f) as to the manner in which a petition is to be presented to a local authority,

    (g) as to the verification of any petition,

    (h) as to the date on which, or the time by which, a referendum must be held,

    (i) as to the action which may, may not or must be taken by a local authority before or in connection with a referendum,

    (j) as to the action which may, may not or must be taken by a local authority after a referendum, and

    (k) for or in connection with enabling the Welsh Ministers, in the event of any failure by a local authority to take any action permitted or required by virtue of the regulations, to take that action.

(3)   The provision which may be made by virtue of subsection (2) includes provision which applies or reproduces (with or without modifications) any provisions of section 25, 27, 28, 29 or 33 or 29.

(4)   The number of local government electors mentioned in subsection (2)(b) is to be calculated at such times as may be provided by regulations under this section and (unless such regulations otherwise provide) is to be 5 per cent of the number of local government electors at each of those times.

(5)   Nothing in subsection (2), (3) or (4) affects the generality of the power under subsection (1).

NOTES
Subordinate Legislation
  Local Authorities (Referendums) (Petitions and Directions) (Wales) Regulations 2001, SI 2001/2292.

Referendum following direction

35(1)   The Welsh Ministers may by regulations make provision for or in connection with enabling them, in such circumstances as may be prescribed in the regulations, to direct a local authority to hold a referendum on whether they should operate executive arrangements involving an executive which takes such form permitted by or under section 11 as may be specified in the direction.

(2)   The provision which may be made by regulations under this section includes provision
       (a)   as to the date on which, or the time by which, a referendum must be held,
       (b)   as to the action which may, may not or must be taken by a local authority before or in connection with a referendum,
       (c)   as to the action which may, may not or must be taken by a local authority after a referendum, and
       (d)   for or in connection with enabling the Welsh Ministers, in the event of any failure by a local authority to take any action permitted or required by virtue of the regulations, to take that action.

(3)   The provision which may be made by virtue of subsection (2) includes provision which applies or reproduces (with or without modifications) any provisions of section 25, 27, 28, 29 or 33 or 29.

(4)   Nothing in subsection (2) or (3) affects the generality of the power under subsection (1).

NOTES
Subordinate legislation
  Local Authorities (Referendums) (Petitions and Directions) (Wales) Regulations 2001, SI 2001/2292

Referendum following order

36(1)   The Welsh Ministers may by order make provision requiring every local authority, or every local authority falling within any description of authority specified in the order, to hold a referendum on whether they should operate executive arrangements involving an executive which takes such form permitted by or under section 11 as may be specified in the order.

(2)   The provision which may be made by an order under this section includes provision
       (a)   as to the date on which, or the time by which, a referendum must be held,
       (b)   as to the action which may, may not or must be taken by a local authority before or in connection with a referendum,
       (c)   as to the action which may, may not or must be taken by a local authority after a referendum,

    (d) for or in connection with enabling the Welsh Ministers, in the event of any failure by a local authority to take any action permitted or required by virtue of the order, to take that action.

(3) The provision which may be made by virtue of subsection (2) includes provision which applies or reproduces (with or without modifications) any provisions of section 25, 27, 28, 29 or 33 or 29.

(4) Nothing in subsection (2) or (3) affects the generality of the power under subsection (1).

Elected mayors etc

Elected mayors etc

39(1) In this Part "elected mayor", in relation to a local authority, means an individual elected as mayor of the authority by the local government electors for the authority's area in accordance with the provisions made by or under this Part.

(2) *Repealed*

(3) An elected mayor of a local authority is to be entitled to the style of "mayor" or "maer".

(4) In this Part "elected executive member" means an individual elected as a member of a local authority executive by the local government electors for the authority's area in accordance with the provisions made by or under this Part, but not include an elected mayor.

(5A) A reference in any enactment (whenever passed or made) to
    (a) a member of a local authority, or
    (b) a councillor of a local authority,
does not include a reference to an elected mayor of the authority.

(5B) But subsection (5A) is subject to
    (a) regulations made by the Welsh Ministers under this paragraph which provide that an elected mayor is to be treated as member or councillor of a local authority for the purposes of an enactment (whenever passed or made), and
    (b) any other contrary intention that appears in any enactment (whenever passed or made).

(5C) Section 21(1A) of the Local Government Act 1972 is not to be taken to indicate any contrary intention for the purposes of subsection (5B)(b).

(5D) A statutory instrument containing regulations made under subsection (5B)(a) is subject to annulment in pursuance of a resolution of the National Assembly for Wales.

(6) *Repealed*

(7) The term of office of an elected mayor of a local authority is to be four years.

(8) This section is subject to regulations under section 41.

NOTES

Subordinate Legislation
Local Authorities (Elected Mayor and Mayor's Assistant) (England) Regulations 2002, SI 2002/975
Local Authorities (Elected Mayors) (England) Regulations 2004, SI 2004/1815
Local Authorities (Elected Mayors) (England) Regulations

2005, SI 2005/2121
Local Authorities (Elected Mayors) (England) Regulations 2008

Election as elected mayor and councillor

40(1) If the person who is returned at an election as the elected mayor of a local authority is also returned at an election held at the same time as a councillor of the authority, a vacancy shall arise in the office of councillor.

(2) If the person who is returned at an election ("the mayoral election") as the elected mayor of a local authority

(a)   is a councillor of the authority, and

(b)   was returned as such a councillor at an election held at an earlier time than the mayoral election,

a vacancy shall arise in the office of councillor.

(3)   Subject to subsection (4), a person who is the elected mayor of a local authority may not be a candidate in an election for the return of a councillor or councillors of the authority.

(4)   A person who is the elected mayor of a local authority may be a candidate in an election for the return of a councillor or councillors of the authority if the election is held at the same time as an election for the return of the elected mayor of the authority, but subsection (1) applies if he is a candidate in both such elections and he is returned both as the elected mayor and as a councillor.

Time of elections etc

41   The Welsh Ministers may by regulations make provision

(a)   as to the dates on which and years in which elections for the return of elected mayors or elected executive members may or must take place,

(b)   as to the intervals between elections for the return of elected mayors or elected executive members,

(c)   as to the term of office of elected mayors or elected executive members, and

(d)   as to the filling of vacancies in the office of elected mayor or elected executive member.

Voting at elections of elected mayors

42(1)   Each person entitled to vote as an elector at an election for the return of an elected mayor is to have the following vote or votes

(a)   one vote (referred to in this Part as a first preference vote) which may be given for the voter's first preference from among the candidates to be the elected mayor, and

(b)   if there are three or more candidates to be the elected mayor, one vote (referred to in this Part as a second preference vote) which may be given for the voter's second preference from among those candidates.

(2)   The elected mayor is to be returned under the simple majority system, unless there are three or more candidates.

(3)   If there are three or more candidates to be the elected mayor, the elected mayor is to be returned under the supplementary vote system in accordance with Schedule 2.

Entitlement to vote

43(1)   The persons entitled to vote as electors at an election for the return of an elected mayor or elected executive member are those who on the day of the poll

(a)   would be entitled to vote as electors at an election of councillors for an electoral area which is situated within the area of the local authority concerned, and

(b)   are registered in the register of local government electors at an address within the authority's area.

(2)   A person is not entitled as an elector to cast more than one first preference vote, or more than one second preference vote, at an election for the return of an elected mayor.

Power to make provision about elections

44(1)   The Secretary of State or the Chancellor of the Duchy of Lancaster may by regulations make provision as to

(a)   the conduct of elections for the return of elected mayors or elected executive members, and

(b)   the questioning of elections for the return of elected mayors or elected executive members and the consequences of irregularities.

(2)   The provision which may be made under subsection (1)(a) includes, in particular, provision
    (a)   about the registration of electors,
    (b)   for disregarding alterations in a register of electors,
    (c)   about the limitation of election expenses (and the creation of criminal offences in connection with the limitation of such expenses),
    (d)   for the combination of polls at elections for the return of elected mayors and other elections (including elections for the return of elected executive members), and
    (e)   for the combination of polls at elections for the return of elected executive members and other elections (including elections for the return of elected mayors).

(3)   Regulations under this section may
    (a)   apply or incorporate, with or without modifications or exceptions, any provision of, or made under, the Representation of the People Acts or any provision of any other enactment (whenever passed or made) relating to parliamentary elections or local government elections,
    (b)   modify any form contained in, or in regulations or rules made under, the Representation of the People Acts so far as may be necessary to enable it to be used both for the original purpose and in relation to elections for the return of elected mayors or elected executive members, and
    (c)   so far as may be necessary in consequence of any provision made by or under this Part or any regulations under this section, amend any provision of any enactment (whenever passed or made) relating to the registration of parliamentary electors or local government electors.

(3A)   Before making any regulations under this section, the Secretary of State or the Chancellor of the Duchy of Lancaster shall consult the Electoral Commission.

(3B)   In addition, the power of the Secretary of State or the Chancellor of the Duchy of Lancaster to make regulations under this section so far as relating to matters mentioned in subsection (2)(c) shall be exercisable only on, and in accordance with, a recommendation of the Electoral Commission, except where the Secretary of State or the Chancellor of the Duchy of Lancaster considers that it is expedient to exercise that power in consequence of changes in the value of money.

(4)   No return of an elected mayor or elected executive member at an election is to be questioned except by an election petition under the provisions of Part III of the Representation of the People Act 1983 as applied by or incorporated in regulations under this section.

NOTES

Subordinate Legislation
Representation of the People (Combination of Polls) (England and Wales) Regulations 2004, SI 2004/294.
Local Authorities (Mayoral Elections) (England and Wales) Regulations 2007, SI 2007/1024

Provisions with respect to referendums

Provisions with respect to referendums

45(1)   A local authority may not hold more than one referendum in any period of five years.

(2)   If the result of a referendum held by virtue of regulations or an order made under any provision of this Part is to approve the proposals to which the referendum relates, the local authority concerned must implement those proposals in accordance with any provision made by the regulations or order.

(3) If the result of a referendum held by virtue of regulations or an order made under any provision of this Part is to reject the proposals to which the referendum relates, the local authority concerned may not implement those proposals but must instead comply with any provision made by the regulations or order.

(4) The persons entitled to vote in a referendum held by a local authority are those who on the day of the referendum

    (a) would be entitled to vote as electors at an election of councillors for an electoral area which is situated within the authority's area, and

    (b) are registered in the register of local government electors at an address within the authority's area.

(5) The Welsh Ministers may by regulations make provision as to the conduct of referendums.

(6) The Welsh Ministers may by regulations make provision for the combination of polls at referendums with polls at any elections.

(7) Regulations under subsection (5) or (6) may apply or incorporate, with or without modifications or exceptions, any provision of any enactment (whenever passed or made) relating to elections or referendums.

(8) The provision which may be made under subsection (5) includes, in particular, provision

    (a) as to the question to be asked in a referendum,

    (b) as to the publicity to be given in connection with a referendum (including the publicity to be given with respect to the consequences of the referendum),

    (c) about the limitation of expenditure in connection with a referendum (and the creation of criminal offences in connection with the limitation of such expenditure),

    (d) as to the conduct of the authority, members of the authority and officers of the authority in relation to a referendum,

    (e) as to when, where and how voting in a referendum is to take place,

    (f) as to how the votes cast in a referendum are to be counted, and

    (g) for disregarding alterations in a register of electors.

(8A) Before making any regulations under this section, the Welsh Ministers shall consult the Electoral Commission, but this subsection does not apply to

    (a) provisions which specify the wording of the question to be asked in a referendum, or

    (b) provisions for matters mentioned in subsection (8)(c).

(8B) No regulations which specify the wording of the question to be asked in a referendum may be made under subsection (5) unless

    (a) before laying a draft of the regulations before the National Assembly for Wales, the Welsh Ministers consulted the Electoral Commission as to the intelligibility of that question, and

    (b) when so laying the draft, the Welsh Ministers also laid before the National Assembly for Wales a report stating any views as to the intelligibility of that question which were expressed by the Electoral Commission in response to that consultation.

(8C) Where any such regulations specify not only the question to be asked in a referendum but also any statement which is to precede that question on the ballot paper at the referendum, any reference in subsection (8B) to the intelligibility of that question is to be read as a reference to the intelligibility of that question and that statement taken together.

(8D) No regulations which make provision for the matters mentioned in subsection (8)(c) may be made under subsection (5) unless

(a) before laying a draft of the regulations before the National Assembly for Wales, the Welsh Ministers sought, and had regard to, the views of the Electoral Commission as to the provision to be made by the regulations as to those matters, and

(b) where the draft regulations laid before the National Assembly for Wales made provision as to those matters otherwise than in accordance with the views of the Electoral Commission, the Welsh Ministers, when so laying the draft, also laid before the Assembly a statement of their reasons for departing from the views of the Commission.

(9) In subsections (1), (4) to (6) and (8) to (8C) "referendum" means a referendum held under section 27 or by virtue of regulations or an order made under any provision of this Part or under section 40 of the Local Government (Wales) Measure 2011.

NOTES

Subordinate Legislation
Representation of the People (Combination of Polls) (England and Wales) Regulations 2004, SI 2004/294.
Local Authorities (Conduct of Referendums) (Wales)
Regulations 2008, SI 2008/1848

Amendments to the 1972 Act

Amendments to the 1972 Act

46 Schedule 3, which contains amendments to the Local Government Act 1972, has effect.

Power to make further provision

Power to make incidental, consequential provision etc

47(1) The Welsh Ministers may by order make such incidental, consequential, transitional or supplemental provision as they consider necessary or expedient for the purposes of, in consequence of, or for giving full effect to, any provision made by or under this Part.

(2) The provision which may be made under subsection (1) includes provision modifying any enactment (whenever passed or made).

(3) The power under subsection (2) to modify an enactment is a power
  (a) to apply that enactment with or without modifications,
  (b) to extend, disapply or amend that enactment, or
  (c) to repeal or revoke that enactment with or without savings.

(4) The provision which may be made under subsection (1) includes provision relating to changes in local authority governance arrangements.

(5) That includes
  (a) provision relating to the old governance arrangements, the new governance arrangements, or both kinds of governance arrangements,
  (b) provision as to the dates on which and years in which relevant elections may or must be held,
  (c) provision as to the intervals between relevant elections, and
  (d) provision as to the term of office of any member of any form of executive.

(6) In subsection (5) "relevant election" means
  (a) an election for the return of an elected mayor;
  (b) *Repealed*.

(7) Nothing in subsection (2), (3), (4) or (5) affects the generality of the power in subsection (1).

NOTES

Subordinate Legislation
Local Authorities (Executive Arrangements) (Modification of Enactments and Further Provisions) (Wales) Order 2002, SI 2002/803.
Local Authorities (Executive and Alternative Arrangements) (Modification of Enactments and Other Provisions) (Wales) Order 2002, SI 2002/808

Interpretation of Part II

48(1) In this Part, unless the context otherwise requires

"alternative arrangements" has the meaning given by section 32(1),

"elected executive member" has the meaning given by section 39(4),

"elected mayor" has the meaning given by section 39(1),

"electoral area" has the meaning given by section 203(1) of the Representation of the People Act 1983,

"enactment" includes an enactment contained in a local Act or comprised in subordinate legislation (within the meaning of the Interpretation Act 1978),

"executive", in relation to a local authority, is to be construed in accordance with section 11,

"executive arrangements" has the meaning given by section 10,

"executive leader" has the meaning given by section 11(3)(a),

"fallback proposals" and "outline fallback proposals" are to be construed in accordance with section 27(1) and (2),

"first preference vote" has the meaning given by section 42(1)(a),

"local authority" means a county council in Wales or a county borough council,

"local government elector" has the meaning given by section 270(1) of the Local Government Act 1972,

"overview and scrutiny committee" has the meaning given by section 21(1),

"the political balance requirements" means the provisions made by or under sections 15 to 17 of, and Schedule 1 to, the Local Government and Housing Act 1989,

"second preference vote" has the meaning given by section 42(1)(b).

(1A) *Repealed*

(2) Any reference in this Part to the chairman of a local authority
   (a) is a reference to that person whether or not he is entitled to another style.
   (b) *Repealed*.

(3) Any reference in this Part to the vicechairman of a local authority
   (a) is a reference to that person whether or not he is entitled to another style, and
   (b) *Repealed*.

(4) Any reference in this Part to the discharge of any functions includes a reference to the doing of anything which is calculated to facilitate, or is conducive or incidental to, the discharge of those functions.

(5) Section 101 of the Local Government Act 1972 does not apply to the function of the passing of a resolution under any provision made by or under this Part.

(6) Any functions conferred on a local authority by virtue of this Part are not to be the responsibility of an executive of the authority under executive arrangements.

(7) Any directions given by the Welsh Ministers under any provision of this Part
   (a) may be varied or revoked by subsequent directions given by them under that provision, and
   (b) may make different provision for different cases, local authorities or descriptions of local authority.

PART III
CONDUCT OF LOCAL GOVERNMENT MEMBERS AND EMPLOYEES

49-83 *Not reproduced*

PART IV
ELECTIONS

Meaning of "local authority" and "principal council" in Part IV

84(1)   In relation to England
"local authority" means a principal council or a parish council,
"principal council" means a county council, a district council or a London borough council.

(2)   In relation to Wales
"local authority" means a principal council or a community council,
"principal council" means a county council or a county borough council.

(3)   This section applies for the purposes of this Part.

Options for elections

85(1)   For the purposes of this Part the three options for the scheme for the ordinary elections of councillors of a principal council are those set out in this section.

(2)   The first option is for a scheme under which
(a)   the term of office of councillors is four years,
(b)   the elections are held in a given year and every fourth year after it,
(c)   all the councillors are elected in each year in which the elections are held, and
(d)   the councillors retire together.

(3)   The second option is for a scheme under which
(a)   the term of office of councillors is four years,
(b)   the elections are held in a given year and every second year after it,
(c)   one half (or as nearly as may be) of the councillors are elected in each year in which the elections are held, and
(d)   one half (or as nearly as may be) of the councillors retire in each year in which the elections are held.

(4)   The third option is for a scheme under which
(a)   the term of office of councillors is four years,
(b)   the elections are held in a given year and every year after it other than every third year after it,
(c)   one third (or as nearly as may be) of the councillors are elected in each year in which the elections are held, and
(d)   one third (or as nearly as may be) of the councillors retire in each year in which the elections are held.

NOTES
Defined terms
principal council: s 84

Power to specify a scheme for elections

86(A1)   The Secretary of State may by order make provision to secure that the scheme for the ordinary elections of councillors of any specified council in England is the scheme under the first option set out in section 85.

(1)   The Secretary of State may by order make provision to secure that the scheme for the ordinary elections of councillors of any specified council in Wales is the scheme under such of the options set out in section 85 as is specified in the order.

(2)   A council is specified if it is
(a)   a principal council (or one of the principal councils) specified by name in the order, or

(b)   a principal council falling within any description of principal council specified in the order.

(3)   An order may make provision in relation to a council if the scheme specified in the order is different from the scheme which prevails (whether by virtue of an earlier order under this section or otherwise) for the ordinary elections of its councillors.

(4)   An order may include provision specifying the years in which the ordinary elections are to be held.

(5)   In a case where the specified scheme is that under the second or third option, an order may include provision for identifying which councillors are to retire in a particular year, and such provision may include
(a)   provision for identifying the electoral divisions or wards affected,
(b)   provision for identifying the councillors affected within particular electoral divisions or wards.

(6)   Provision under subsection (5) may include
(a)   provision allowing the Secretary of State to direct councils to propose methods (complying with any guidance he may issue) for identifying electoral divisions, wards or councillors,
(b)   provision allowing him to give directions as to the methods to be adopted (whether those proposed or otherwise).

(7)   An order may include provision designed to secure the transition from a prevailing scheme to the one specified in the order, and such provision may include
(a)   provision to secure the retirement of existing councillors at times different from those applying under a prevailing scheme,
(b)   in a case where the specified scheme is that under the second or third option, provision for the initial election of all the councillors, for the retirement of some of them before the end of the normal term of four years, and for identifying which of them are so to retire.

NOTES

Subordinate Legislation
Local Authorities (Scheme for Elections of Specified Councils) (England) Order 2002, SI 2002/1962

Defined terms
principal council: s 84

Power to change years in which elections held

87(1)   The Secretary of State may by order make provision which changes the years in which the ordinary elections of councillors of any specified local authority are to be held but which does not change the scheme which prevails (whether by virtue of an order under section 86 or otherwise) for the ordinary elections of those councillors.

(2)   A local authority is specified if it is
(a)   a local authority (or one of the local authorities) specified by name in the order, or
(b)   a local authority falling within any class or description of local authority specified in the order.

(3)   An order may include provision to secure the retirement of existing councillors at times different from those at which they would otherwise retire.

NOTES

Subordinate Legislation
Local Government Elections (Wales) Order 2001, SI 2001/3540.
Local Authorities (Scheme for Elections of Specified Councils) (England) Order 2002, SI 2002/1962.

Defined terms
principal council: s 84

SCHEDULE 2
Election of Elected Mayor

Application

1   This Schedule applies where there are three or more candidates to be an elected mayor of a local authority.

Candidate with overall majority of first preference votes

2   If one of the candidates to be the elected mayor receives more than half of all the first preference votes given in the election that candidate is to be returned as the elected mayor.

No candidate with overall majority of first preference votes

3(1)   If none of the candidates to be the elected mayor receives more than half of all the first preference votes given in the election the following provisions of this paragraph are to have effect.

(2)   The two candidates who received the greatest number of first preference votes given in the election remain in the contest.

(3)   If, by reason of an equality of first preference votes, three or more candidates are qualified to remain in the contest by virtue of sub-paragraph (2), all of them remain in the contest.

(4)   The other candidates are eliminated from the contest.

(5)   The number of second preference votes given in the election for each of the candidates remaining in the contest by voters who did not give their first preference vote to any of those candidates is to be ascertained.

(6)   That number is to be added to the number of first preference votes given for that candidate, to give his total number of preference votes.

(7)   The person who is to be returned as the elected mayor is that one of the candidates remaining in the contest who has the greatest total number of preference votes.

(8)   If, by reason of an equality of total number of preference votes, two or more candidates remaining in the contest each have the greatest total number of preference votes, the returning officer is to decide by lots which of them is to be returned as the elected mayor.

PART V
MISCELLANEOUS

–104   *Not reproduced*

PART VI
SUPPLEMENTAL

–109   *Not reproduced*

Local Government Finance Act 1992

CHAPTER 4ZA
REFERENDUMS RELATING TO COUNCIL TAX INCREASES

Interpretation of Chapter

52ZA(1)   In this Chapter
    (a)   a reference to a billing authority is to a billing authority in England,
    (b)   a reference to a major precepting authority is to a major precepting authority in England, and
    (c)   a reference to a local precepting authority is to a local precepting authority in England.

  (2)   In this Chapter
    (a)   a reference to an authority is to an authority of a kind mentioned in subsection (1) above;
    (b)   a reference to a precepting authority is to an authority of a kind mentioned in subsection (1)(b) or (c) above.

  (3)   Section 52ZX below defines references in this Chapter to an authority's relevant basic amount of council tax.

NOTES
Defined terms
  billing authority: ss 1(2), 69(1)
  council tax: s 1(1)
  local precepting authority: ss 39(2), 69(1)

major precepting authority: ss 39(1), 69(1)

Determination of whether increase excessive

Duty to determine whether council tax excessive

52ZB(1)   A billing authority must determine whether its relevant basic amount of council tax for a financial year is excessive.

  (2)   Sections 52ZF to 52ZI below (duty to hold referendum etc in case of excessive council tax increase by billing authority) apply where the amount mentioned in subsection (1) above is excessive.

  (3)   A major precepting authority must determine whether its relevant basic amount of council tax for a financial year is excessive.

  (4)   Sections 52ZJ and 52ZK and 52ZN to 52ZP below (duty to hold referendum etc in case of excessive council tax increase by major precepting authority) apply where an amount mentioned in subsection (3) above is excessive.

  (5)   A local precepting authority must determine whether its relevant basic amount of council tax for a financial year is excessive.

  (6)   Sections 52ZL to 52ZP below (duty to hold referendum etc in case of excessive council tax increase by local precepting authority) apply where the amount mentioned in subsection (5) above is excessive.

  (7)   A determination under this section for a financial year must be made as soon as is reasonably practicable after principles under section 52ZC below for that year are approved by a resolution of the House of Commons under section 52ZD below.

NOTES
Defined terms
  billing authority: ss 1(2), 52ZA(1)(a), 69(1)
  financial year: ss 69(1), 116(1)
  local precepting authority: ss 39(2), 52ZA(1)(c), 69(1)

major precepting authority: ss 39(1), 52ZA(1)(b), 69(1)
relevant basic amount of council tax: ss 52ZA(3), 52ZX

Determination of whether increase is excessive

2ZC(1) The question whether an authority's relevant basic amount of council tax for a financial year ("the year under consideration") is excessive must be decided in accordance with a set of principles determined by the Secretary of State for the year.

(2) A set of principles
   (a) may contain one principle or two or more principles;
   (b) must constitute or include a comparison falling within subsection (3) below.

(3) A comparison falls within this subsection if it is between
   (a) the authority's relevant basic amount of council tax for the year under consideration, and
   (b) the authority's relevant basic amount of council tax for the financial year immediately preceding the year under consideration.

(4) If for the purposes of this section the Secretary of State determines categories of authority for the year under consideration
   (a) any principles determined for the year must be such that the same set is determined for all authorities (if more than one) falling within the same category;
   (b) as regards an authority which does not fall within any of the categories, the authority's relevant basic amount of council tax for the year is not capable of being excessive for the purposes of this Chapter.

(5) If the Secretary of State does not determine such categories, any principles determined for the year under consideration must be such that the same set is determined for all authorities.

(6) A principle that applies to the Greater London Authority and that constitutes or includes a comparison falling within subsection (3) above may only provide for
   (a) a comparison between unadjusted relevant basic amounts of council tax,
   (b) a comparison between adjusted relevant basic amounts of council tax, or
   (c) a comparison within paragraph (a) and a comparison within paragraph (b).

(7) In determining categories of authorities for the year under consideration the Secretary of State must take into account any information that the Secretary of State thinks is relevant.

NOTES
Defined terms
   an authority: s 52ZA(2)(a)
   financial year: ss 69(1), 116(1)

relevant basic amount of council tax: ss 52ZA(3), 52ZX

Approval of principles

2ZD(1) The principles for a financial year must be set out in a report which must be laid before the House of Commons.

(2) If a report for a financial year is not laid before the specified date or, if so laid, is not approved by resolution of the House of Commons on or before the specified date
   (a) no principles have effect for that year, and
   (b) accordingly, no authority's relevant basic amount of council tax for the year is capable of being excessive for the purposes of this Chapter.

(3) If the Secretary of State does not propose to determine a set of principles for a financial year, the Secretary of State must lay a report before the House of Commons before the specified date giving the Secretary of State's reasons for not doing so.

(4) In this section "the specified date", in relation to a financial year, means the date on which the local government finance report for the year under paragraph 5(1) of Schedule 7B to the 1988 Act is approved by resolution of the House of Commons.

NOTES

Defined terms
the 1988 Act: s 116(1)
an authority: s 52ZA(2)(a)
financial year: ss 69(1), 116(1)

relevant basic amount of council tax: ss 52ZA(3), 52ZX

Alternative notional amounts

52ZE(1) The Secretary of State may make a report specifying an alternative notional amount in relation to any year under consideration and any authority.

(2) An alternative notional amount is an amount which the Secretary of State thinks should be used as the basis of any comparison in applying section 52ZC above in place of the authority's relevant basic amount of council tax for the preceding year.

(3) A report under this section

(a) may relate to two or more authorities;

(b) may be amended by a subsequent report under this section;

(c) must contain such explanation as the Secretary of State thinks desirable of the need for the calculation of the alternative notional amount and the method for that calculation;

(d) must be laid before the House of Commons.

(4) Subsection (5) below applies if a report under this section for a financial year is approved by resolution of the House of Commons on or before the date on which the report under section 52ZD above for that year is approved by resolution of the House of Commons.

(5) Section 52ZC above has effect, as regards the year under consideration and any authority to which the report relates, as if the reference in subsection (3) of that section to the authority's relevant basic amount of council tax for the financial year immediately preceding the year under consideration were a reference to the alternative notional amount for that year.

(6) In this section "year under consideration" has the same meaning as in section 52ZC above.

NOTES

Defined terms
an authority: s 52ZA(2)(a)
financial year: ss 69(1), 116(1)

relevant basic amount of council tax: ss 52ZA(3), 52ZX

Excessive increase in council tax by billing authority

Billing authority's duty to make substitute calculations

52ZF(1) The billing authority must make substitute calculations for the financial year in compliance with this section; but those calculations do not have effect for the purposes of Chapter 3 above except in accordance with sections 52ZH and 52ZI below.

(2) Substitute calculations for a financial year comply with this section if

(a) they are made in accordance with sections 31A, 31B and 34 to 36 above, ignoring section 31A(11) above for this purpose,

(b) the relevant basic amount of council tax produced by applying section 52ZX below to the calculations is not excessive by reference to the principles determined by the Secretary of State under section 52ZC above for the year, and

(c) they are made in accordance with this section.

(3) In making the substitute calculations, the authority must

(a) use the amount determined in the previous calculation for the year under section 31A(3) above so far as relating to amounts which the authority estimates it will accrue in the year in respect of locally retained non-domestic rates, revenue support grant, special grant or (in the case of the Common Council only) police grant, and

(b)   use the amount determined in the previous calculation for the year for item T in section 31B(1) above and (where applicable) item TP in section 34(3) above.

(3A)   In this Chapter, "locally retained non-domestic rates", in relation to a billing authority or a major precepting authority, means amounts received by the authority under, or under regulations under, Schedule 7B to the Local Government Finance Act 1988, or under regulations under section 99(3) of that Act in connection with the operation of that Schedule.

(4)   *Repealed*

NOTES

Defined terms
billing authority: ss 1(2), 52ZA(1)(a), 69(1)
the Common Council: s 69(1)
financial year: ss 69(1), 116(1)

major precepting authority: ss 39(1), 52ZA(1)(b) 69(1)
relevant basic amount of council tax: ss 52ZA(3), 52ZX

Arrangements for referendum

2ZG(1)   The billing authority must make arrangements to hold a referendum in relation to the authority's relevant basic amount of council tax for the financial year in accordance with this section.

(2)   Subject as follows, the referendum is to be held on a date decided by the billing authority.

(3)   That date must be not later than
(a)   the first Thursday in May in the financial year, or
(b)   such other date in that year as the Secretary of State may specify by order.

(4)   An order under subsection (3) above must be made not later than
(a)   1 February in the financial year preceding the year mentioned in paragraph (b) of that subsection, or
(b)   in the case of an order affecting more than one financial year, 1 February in the financial year preceding the first of those years.

(5)   The persons entitled to vote in the referendum are those who, on the day of the referendum
(a)   would be entitled to vote as electors at an election for members for an electoral area of the billing authority, and
(b)   are registered in the register of local government electors at an address within the billing authority's area.

(5A)   As soon as is reasonably practicable after determining that it is required to hold a referendum in relation to its relevant basic amount of council tax for the financial year, the billing authority must notify that fact in writing to any body that has issued a levy or a special levy to it for the financial year.

(6)   In this section
"electoral area" means
(a)   where the billing authority is a district council, a London borough council or the Common Council of the City of London, a ward;
(b)   where the billing authority is a county council, an electoral division;
(c)   where the billing authority is the Council of the Isles of Scilly, a parish;
"register of local government electors" means the register of local government electors kept in accordance with the provisions of the Representation of the People Acts.

(7)   This section is subject to regulations under section 52ZQ below.

NOTES

Subordinate Legislation
Local Authority (Referendums Relating to Council Tax Increases) (Date of Referendum) (England) Order 2013, SI 2013/2862

Defined terms
billing authority: ss 1(2), 52ZA(1)(a), 69(1)
financial year: ss 69(1), 116(1)
levy: s 69(1)
relevant basic amount of council tax: ss 52ZA(3), 52ZX

special levy: s 69(1)

Effect of referendum

52ZH(1) The billing authority must inform the Secretary of State, and any body the authority was required to notify under section 52ZG(5A), of the result of the referendum.

(2) Subsection (3) below applies if the result is that the billing authority's relevant basic amount of council tax for the financial year is approved by a majority of persons voting in the referendum.

(3) The authority's calculations from which that amount was derived continue to have effect for that year for the purposes of this Act.

(4) Subsection (5) below applies if the result is that the billing authority's relevant basic amount of council tax for the financial year is not approved by a majority of persons voting in the referendum.

(5) The substitute calculations made in relation to the year under section 52ZF above have effect in relation to the authority and the financial year.

NOTES
Defined terms
billing authority: ss 1(2), 52ZA(1)(a), 69(1)
financial year: ss 69(1), 116(1)

relevant basic amount of council tax: ss 52ZA(3), 52ZX

Failure to hold referendum

52ZI(1) If the billing authority fails to hold a referendum in accordance with this Chapter, the substitute calculations made in relation to the year under section 52ZF above have effect in relation to the authority and the financial year.

(2) If the authority has not made those substitute calculations, during the period of restriction the authority has no power to transfer any amount from its collection fund to its general fund; and sections 97 and 98 of the 1988 Act have effect accordingly.

(3) In subsection (2) above "the period of restriction" means the period
   (a) beginning with the latest date on which the referendum could have been held, and
   (b) ending with the date (if any) when the billing authority makes the substitute calculations.

NOTES
Defined terms
the 1988 Act: s 116(1)
billing authority: ss 1(2), 52ZA(1)(a), 69(1)
a billing authority's general fund: s 69(2)(c)

financial year: ss 69(1), 116(1)

Excessive increase in council tax by precepting authority
Major precepting authority's duty to make substitute calculations

52ZJ(1) The major precepting authority must make substitute calculations for the financial year in compliance with this section.

(2) Substitute calculations made for a financial year by a major precepting authority other than the Greater London Authority comply with this section if
   (a) they are made in accordance with sections 42A, 42B and 45 to 48 above,
   (b) the relevant basic amount of council tax for the year produced by the calculations is not excessive by reference to the principles determined by the Secretary of State under section 52ZC above for the year, and
   (c) they are made in accordance with this section.

(3) Substitute calculations made for a financial year by the Greater London Authority comply with this section if

(a) they are made by applying the relevant London provisions and sections 47 and 48 above to the Authority's substitute consolidated council tax requirement for the year, and

(b) they are made in accordance with this section.

(4) In making the substitute calculations, a major precepting authority other than the Greater London Authority must

(a) use the amount determined in the previous calculation under section 42A(3) above so far as relating to amounts which the authority estimates it will accrue in the year in respect of locally retained non-domestic rates, revenue support grant, special grant or police grant, and

(b) use the amount determined in the previous calculation for item T in section 42B(1) above or (where applicable) item TP in section 45(3) above.

(5) *Repealed*

(6) In making the substitute calculations, the Greater London Authority must use any amount determined in the previous calculations for item T in section 88(2) of the Greater London Authority Act 1999 or for item TP2 in section 89(4) of that Act.

(7) In this Chapter
"the relevant London provisions" means sections 88 and (where applicable) 89 of the Greater London Authority Act 1999;
"the Authority's substitute consolidated council tax requirement", in relation to a financial year, means the Authority's substitute consolidated council tax requirement
(a) agreed under Schedule 6 to the Greater London Authority Act 1999, or
(b) set out in its substitute consolidated budget as agreed under that Schedule, as the case may be.

NOTES

Defined terms   relevant basic amount of council tax: ss 52ZA(3), 52ZX
financial year: ss 69(1), 116(1)
locally retained non-domestic rates: s 52ZF(3A)
major precepting authority: ss 39(1), 52ZA(1)(b), 69(1)

Major precepting authority's duty to notify appropriate billing authorities

52ZK(1) The major precepting authority must notify each appropriate billing authority
(a) that its relevant basic amount of council tax for a financial year is excessive, and
(b) that the billing authority is required to hold a referendum in accordance with this Chapter.

(1A) As soon as is reasonably practicable after determining that its relevant basic amount of council tax for the financial year is excessive, the major precepting authority must also notify the matters mentioned in subsection (1) in writing to any body that
(a) has issued a levy to it for the financial year, or
(b) in the case of the Greater London Authority, has issued a levy to any constituent body for the financial year.

(2) A notification under subsection (1) must include a precept in accordance with the following provisions; but that precept does not have effect for the purposes of Chapters 3 and 4 above except in accordance with sections 52ZO and 52ZP below.

(3) A precept issued to a billing authority under this section by a major precepting authority other than the Greater London Authority must state
(a) the amount which, in relation to the year and each category of dwellings in the billing authority's area, has been calculated by the precepting authority in accordance with sections 42A, 42B and 45 to 47 above as applied by section 52ZJ above, and

(b) the amount which has been calculated by the precepting authority in accordance with section 48 above as applied by section 52ZJ above as the amount payable by the billing authority for the year.

(4) Dwellings fall within different categories for the purposes of subsection (3) above according as different calculations have been made in relation to them as mentioned in paragraph (a) of that subsection.

(5) A precept issued to a billing authority under this section by the Greater London Authority must state

    (a) the amount which, in relation to the year and each category of dwellings in the billing authority's area, has been calculated by applying, in accordance with section 52ZJ above, the relevant London provisions and section 47 above to the Authority's substitute consolidated council tax requirement, and

    (b) the amount which has been calculated by the Authority in accordance with section 48 above as applied by section 52ZJ above as the amount payable by the billing authority for the year.

(6) Dwellings fall within different categories for the purposes of subsection (5) above according as different calculations have been made in relation to them as mentioned in paragraph (a) of that subsection.

(7) A major precepting authority must assume for the purposes of subsections (3) and (5) above that each of the valuation bands is shown in the billing authority's valuation list as applicable to one or more dwellings situated in its area or (as the case may be) each part of its area as respects which different calculations have been made.

(8) The Secretary of State must by regulations prescribe a date by which a notification under subsection (1) must be made.

(9) This section does not require the Greater London Authority to notify a billing authority to which this subsection applies unless the Authority's unadjusted relevant basic amount of council tax for the year is excessive.

(10) Subsection (9) above applies to a billing authority if the special item within the meaning of section 89(2) of the Greater London Authority Act 1999 does not apply to any part of the authority's area.

NOTES
Subordinate Legislation
  Local Authority (Referendums Relating to Council Tax Increases) Regulations 2012, SI 2012/460

Defined terms
  the Authority's substitute consolidated council tax requirement: s 52ZJ(7)
  billing authority: ss 1(2), 52ZA(1)(a), 69(1)

dwelling: ss 3, 69(1)
financial year: ss 69(1), 116(1)
levy: s 69(1)
major precepting authority: ss 39(1), 52ZA(1)(b), 69(1)
relevant basic amount of council tax: ss 52ZA(3), 52ZX
the relevant London provisions: s 52ZJ(7)

Local precepting authority's duty to make substitute calculations

52ZL(1) The local precepting authority must make substitute calculations for the financial year in compliance with this section.

(2) Substitute calculations for a financial year comply with this section if

    (a) they are made in accordance with section 49A above, and

    (b) the relevant basic amount of council tax produced by applying section 52ZX below to the calculations is not excessive by reference to the principles determined by the Secretary of State under section 52ZC above for the year.

NOTES
Defined terms
  financial year: ss 69(1), 116(1)
  local precepting authority: ss 39(2), 52ZA(1)(c), 69(1)

relevant basic amount of council tax: ss 52ZA(3), 52ZX

Local precepting authority's duty to notify appropriate billing authority

2ZM(1)   The local precepting authority must notify its appropriate billing authority
    (a)   that its relevant basic amount of council tax for a financial year is excessive, and
    (b)   that the billing authority is required to hold a referendum in accordance with this Chapter.

  (2)   A notification under this section must include a precept in accordance with subsection (3) below; but that precept does not have effect for the purposes of Chapters 3 and 4 above except in accordance with sections 52ZO and 52ZP below.

  (3)   The precept must state, as the amount payable by the billing authority for the year, the amount which has been calculated by the local precepting authority under section 49A above as applied by section 52ZL above.

  (4)   The Secretary of State must by regulations prescribe a date by which the notification must be made.

NOTES
Subordinate Legislation
  Local Authority (Referendums Relating to Council Tax Increases) Regulations 2012, SI 2012/460

financial year: ss 69(1), 116(1)
local precepting authority: ss 39(2), 52ZA(1)(c), 69(1)
relevant basic amount of council tax: ss 52ZA(3), 52ZX

Defined terms
  billing authority: ss 1(2), 52ZA(1)(a), 69(1)

Arrangements for referendum

2ZN(1)   A billing authority that is notified under section 52ZK or 52ZM above must make arrangements to hold a referendum in relation to the precepting authority's relevant basic amount of council tax for the financial year in accordance with this section.

  (2)   Where the referendum is one of two or more referendums required to be held in respect of the same calculation, it is to be held on
    (a)   the first Thursday in May in the financial year, or
    (b)   such other date as the Secretary of State may specify by order.

  (3)   Otherwise the referendum is to be held on a date decided by the billing authority; but this is subject to subsection (4) below.

  (4)   That date must be not later than
    (a)   the first Thursday in May in the financial year, or
    (b)   such other date in that year as the Secretary of State may specify by order.

  (5)   An order under subsection (2) or (4) above must be made not later than
    (a)   1 February in the financial year preceding the year mentioned in paragraph (b) of that subsection, or
    (b)   in the case of an order affecting more than one financial year, 1 February in the financial year preceding the first of those years.

  (6)   The persons entitled to vote in the referendum are those who, on the day of the referendum
    (a)   would be entitled to vote as electors at an election for members for an electoral area of the billing authority that falls wholly or partly within the precepting authority's area, and
    (b)   are registered in the register of local government electors at an address that is within both
      (i)   the precepting authority's area, and
      (ii)   the billing authority's area.

  (7)   Subject to subsection (8) below, the billing authority may recover from the precepting authority the expenses that are incurred by the billing authority in connection with the referendum.

(8)   The Secretary of State may by regulations make provision for cases in which
    (a)   subsection (7) above does not apply, or
    (b)   that subsection applies with modifications.

(9)   In this section
    "electoral area" means
        (a)   in relation to a district council, a London borough council or the Common Council of the City of London, a ward;
        (b)   in relation to a county council, an electoral division;
        (c)   in relation to the Council of the Isles of Scilly, a parish;
    "register of local government electors" means the register of local government electors kept in accordance with the provisions of the Representation of the People Acts.

(10)   This section is subject to regulations under section 52ZQ below.

NOTES

Subordinate Legislation
Local Authority (Referendums Relating to Council Tax Increases) Regulations 2012, SI 2012/460
Local Authority (Referendums Relating to Council Tax Increases) (Date of Referendum) (England) Order 2013, SI 2013/2862

Defined terms
billing authority: ss 1(2), 52ZA(1)(a), 69(1)
financial year: ss 69(1), 116(1)
precepting authority: s 52ZA(2)(b)
relevant basic amount of council tax: ss 52ZA(3), 52ZX

Effect of referendum

52ZO(1)   The precepting authority must inform the Secretary of State, and any body the authority was required to notify under section 52ZK(1A), of the result of the referendum or (as the case may be) each of them.

(2)   Subsection (3) below applies if
    (a)   in a case where one referendum is held in respect of the precepting authority's relevant basic amount of council tax for the financial year, that amount is approved by a majority of persons voting in the referendum, or
    (b)   in a case where two or more referendums are held in respect of that amount, that amount is approved by a majority of persons voting in all of those referendums taken together.

(3)   The precepting authority's calculations that include that amount or (as the case may be) from which that amount was derived continue to have effect for the year for the purposes of this Act.

(4)   Subsections (5) and (6) below apply if
    (a)   in a case where one referendum is held in respect of the precepting authority's relevant basic amount of council tax for a financial year, that amount is not approved by a majority of persons voting in the referendum, or
    (b)   in a case where two or more referendums are held in respect of that amount, that amount is not approved by a majority of persons voting in all of those referendums taken together.

(5)   Any precept issued to a billing authority under section 52ZK or 52ZM above as part of a notification that triggered the referendum has effect as a precept issued to that billing authority for the year for the purposes of Chapter 3 above.

(6)   Where the precept was issued to a billing authority by a local precepting authority under section 52ZM above, section 36A above has effect in relation to the billing authority as if it required the authority to make calculations in substitution on the basis of the precept (rather than permitting it to do so).

(7) In the case of a major precepting authority other than the Greater London Authority, section 30 above has effect by virtue of subsection (5) above in relation to that precept as if

    (a) references to amounts calculated under Chapter 4 above were to amounts calculated as mentioned in section 52ZJ(2) above, and

    (b) the reference to the amount stated in accordance with section 40 above were to the amount stated in accordance with section 52ZK(3)(b) above.

(8) In the case of the Greater London Authority, section 30 above has effect by virtue of subsection (5) above in relation to that precept as if

    (a) references that are to be read as amounts calculated under Chapter 1 of Part 3 of the Greater London Authority Act 1999 were to amounts calculated as mentioned in section 52ZJ(3) above, and

    (b) the reference to the amount stated in accordance with section 40 above were to the amount stated in accordance with 52ZK(5)(b) above.

(9) If the precepting authority has already issued a precept for the financial year (originally or by way of substitute) to the billing authority

    (a) subsections (3) and (4) of section 42 above apply to the precept within subsection (5) above as they apply to a precept issued in substitution under that section, but

    (b) the references in those subsections to the amount of the new precept are to be read as references to the amount stated in the precept within subsection (5) above in accordance with section 52ZK(3)(b) or (5)(b) above.

NOTES

Defined terms
billing authority: ss 1(2), 52ZA(1)(a), 69(1)
financial year: ss 69(1), 116(1)
local precepting authority: ss 39(2), 52ZA(1)(c), 69(1)
major precepting authority: ss 39(1), 52ZA(1)(b), 69(1)

precepting authority: s 52ZA(2)(b)
relevant basic amount of council tax: ss 52ZA(3), 52ZX

Failure to hold referendum

52ZP(1) This section applies if a billing authority that is required to be notified by a precepting authority under section 52ZK or 52ZM above fails to hold a referendum in accordance with this Chapter.

(2) Subsections (3) to (6) below apply if the precepting authority has failed to notify the billing authority in accordance with section 52ZK or 52ZM above.

(3) The precepting authority must issue a precept for the year to the billing authority in accordance with that section; and such a precept has effect for the purposes of Chapter 3 above.

(4) During the period of restriction no billing authority to which the precepting authority has power to issue a precept has power to pay anything in respect of a precept issued by the precepting authority for the year.

(5) In subsection (4) above "the period of restriction" means the period

    (a) beginning with the date on which the referendum would have been required to be held or (as the case may be) the latest date on which it could have been held if the notification had been made, and

    (b) ending with the date (if any) when the precepting authority complies with subsection (3) above.

(6) Where a precept under subsection (3) above is issued to a billing authority by a local precepting authority, section 36A above has effect in relation to the billing authority as if it required the authority to make calculations in substitution on the basis of the precept (rather than permitting it to do so).

(7) If the precepting authority has notified the billing authority in accordance with section 52ZK or 52ZM above, the precept issued to the billing authority under section 52ZK or

52ZM above as part of the notification has effect as a precept issued to that billing authority for the year for the purposes of Chapter 3 above.

(8) Where the precept was issued to a billing authority by a local precepting authority under section 52ZM above, section 36A above has effect in relation to the billing authority as if it required the authority to make calculations in substitution on the basis of the precept (rather than permitting it to do so).

(9) Subsections (7) to (9) of section 52ZO above apply to a precept within subsection (3) or (7) above as they apply to a precept within subsection (5) of that section.

NOTES

Defined terms
billing authority: ss 1(2), 52ZA(1)(a), 69(1)
local precepting authority: ss 39(2), 52ZA(1)(c), 69(1)

precepting authority: s 52ZA(2)(b)

Regulations about referendums

Regulations about referendums

52ZQ(1) The Secretary of State or the Chancellor of the Duchy of Lancaster may by regulations make provision as to the conduct of referendums under this Chapter.

(2) The Secretary of State or the Chancellor of the Duchy of Lancaster may by regulations make provision for
  (a) the combination of polls at two or more referendums under this Chapter;
  (b) the combination of polls at referendums under this Chapter with polls at any elections or any referendums held otherwise than under this Chapter.

(3) Regulations under this section may apply or incorporate, with or without modifications or exceptions, any provision of any enactment (whenever passed or made) relating to elections or referendums.

(4) The provision which may be made under this section includes, in particular, provision
  (a) as to the question to be asked in a referendum;
  (b) as to the publicity to be given in connection with a referendum (including the publicity to be given with respect to the consequences of the referendum and its result);
  (c) about the limitation of expenditure in connection with a referendum;
  (d) as to the conduct of the authority, members of the authority and officers of the authority in relation to a referendum (including provision modifying the effect of section 2 (prohibition of political publicity) of the Local Government Act 1986);
  (e) as to when, where and how voting in a referendum is to take place;
  (f) as to how the votes cast in a referendum are to be counted;
  (g) for disregarding alterations in a register of electors;
  (h) for the questioning of the result of a referendum by a court or tribunal.

(5) But where the regulations apply or incorporate (with or without modifications) any provision that creates an offence, the regulations may not impose a penalty greater than is provided for in respect of that offence.

(6) Before making any regulations under this section, the Secretary of State or the Chancellor of the Duchy of Lancaster must consult the Electoral Commission.

(7) No regulations under this section are to be made unless a draft of the regulations has been laid before and approved by resolution of each House of Parliament.

(8) In this section "enactment" includes an enactment contained in a local Act or comprised in subordinate legislation (within the meaning of the Interpretation Act 1978).

NOTES

Subordinate Legislation
Local Authorities (Conduct of Referendums) (Council Tax Increases) (England) Regulations 2012

Defined terms
an authority: s 52ZA(2)(a)

Direction that referendum provisions are not to apply

2ZR(1) The Secretary of State may give a direction under this section to an authority other than the Greater London Authority if it appears to the Secretary of State that, unless the authority's council tax calculations are such as to produce a relevant basic amount of council tax that is excessive by reference to the principles determined by the Secretary of State for the year

    (a) the authority will be unable to discharge its functions in an effective manner, or

    (b) the authority will be unable to meet its financial obligations.

(2) The Secretary of State may give a direction under this section to the Greater London Authority if it appears to the Secretary of State that, unless the Authority's council tax calculations are such as to produce a relevant basic amount of council tax that is excessive by reference to the principles determined by the Secretary of State for the year

    (a) one or more of the Authority's constituent bodies will be unable to discharge its functions in an effective manner, or

    (b) one or more of those bodies will be unable to meet its financial obligations.

(3) The effect of a direction under this section is that the referendum provisions do not apply for the financial year to, and no further step is to be taken for the financial year under the referendum provisions by

    (a) the authority to whom it is made, and

    (b) where that authority is a precepting authority, a billing authority as a result of any notification under section 52ZK or 52ZM above by the precepting authority.

(4) A direction under this section may be given to an authority other than the Greater London Authority

    (a) whether or not the authority has carried out its council tax calculations for the financial year, and

    (b) in the case of a billing authority, whether or not the authority has set an amount of council tax for the financial year under section 30 above.

(5) A direction under this section may be given to the Greater London Authority only if it has carried out its council tax calculations for the financial year.

(6) But a direction under this section may not be given to an authority if

    (a) a referendum has been held relating to the authority's relevant basic amount of council tax for the financial year, and

    (b) that amount has not been approved as mentioned in section 52ZH above (where the authority is a billing authority) or section 52ZO above (where the authority is a precepting authority).

(7) The following sections make further provision about the effect of a direction under this section

    (a) for a billing authority: section 52ZS below;

    (b) for a major precepting authority other than the Greater London Authority: section 52ZT below;

    (c) for the Greater London Authority: section 52ZU below;

    (d) for a local precepting authority: section 52ZV below.

(8) In this Part

    "constituent body" means

        (a) the Mayor of London,

        (b) the London Assembly, or

        (c) a functional body within the meaning of section 424 of the Greater London Authority Act 1999;

    "council tax calculations" means

        (a) in relation to a billing authority, calculations under sections 31A, 31B and 34 to 36 above,

(b) in relation to a major precepting authority other than the Greater London Authority, calculations under sections 42A, 42B and 45 to 48 above,

(c) in relation to the Greater London Authority, calculations under sections 85 to 90 of the Greater London Authority Act 1999 and sections 47 and 48 above, and

(d) in the case of a local precepting authority, calculations under section 49A above;

"the referendum provisions" means

(a) where the direction is given to a billing authority, sections 52ZB and 52ZF to 52ZI above,

(b) where the direction is given to a major precepting authority, sections 52ZB, 52ZJ, 52ZK and 52ZN to 52ZP above, and

(c) where the direction is given to a local precepting authority, sections 52ZB and 52ZL to 52ZP above.

NOTES

Defined terms
an authority: s 52ZA(2)(a)
billing authority: ss 1(2), 52ZA(1)(a), 69(1)
council tax: s 1(1)
financial year: ss 69(1), 116(1)
local precepting authority: ss 39(2), 52ZA(1)(c), 69(1)

major precepting authority: ss 39(1), 52ZA(1)(b), 69(1)
precepting authority: s 52ZA(2)(b)
relevant basic amount of council tax: ss 52ZA(3), 52ZX

Directions to billing authorities

52ZS(1) This section applies if the Secretary of State gives a direction under section 52ZR above to a billing authority.

(2) The direction must state the amount that is to be the amount of the billing authority's council tax requirement for the financial year.

(3) If the direction is given before the billing authority has carried out its council tax calculations for the financial year, that amount is to be treated for all purposes as the amount calculated by the billing authority under section 31A above.

(4) If the direction is given after the billing authority has carried out its council tax calculations for the financial year (whether or not it has set an amount of council tax for the year)

(a) those calculations are of no effect, and

(b) the authority must make substitute calculations for the year in accordance with section 36A above.

(5) For the purposes of those and any subsequent substitute calculations and the application of Chapter 3 above to them

(a) the amount stated in the direction as the amount of the billing authority's council tax requirement for the financial year is to be treated as the amount calculated by the billing authority under section 31A above, and

(b) subsections (2)(a) and (4) of section 36A above are to be ignored.

NOTES

Defined terms
billing authority: ss 1(2), 52ZA(1)(a), 69(1)
council tax: s 1(1)
council tax calculations: s 52ZR(8)

financial year: ss 69(1), 116(1)

Directions to major precepting authorities

52ZT(1) This section applies if the Secretary of State gives a direction under section 52ZR above to a major precepting authority other than the Greater London Authority.

(2) The direction must state the amount that is to be the amount of the major precepting authority's council tax requirement for the financial year.

(3)   If the direction is given before the major precepting authority has carried out its council tax calculations for the financial year, that amount is to be treated for all purposes as the amount calculated by the major precepting authority under section 42A above.

(4)   If the direction is given after the major precepting authority has carried out its council tax calculations for the financial year (whether or not it has issued a precept for the year)

    (a)   those calculations are of no effect, and

    (b)   the authority must make substitute calculations for the year in accordance with section 49 above.

(5)   For the purposes of those and any subsequent substitute calculations and the application of Chapters 3 and 4 above to them

    (a)   the amount stated in the direction as the amount of the major precepting authority's council tax requirement for the financial year is to be treated as the amount calculated by the billing authority under section 42A above, and

    (b)   subsection (2)(za) of section 49 above is to be ignored.

NOTES

Defined terms

  council tax: s 1(1)

  council tax calculations: s 52ZR(8)

  financial year: ss 69(1), 116(1)

major precepting authority: ss 39(1), 52ZA(1)(b), 69(1)

Directions to the Greater London Authority

52ZU(1)   This section applies if the Secretary of State gives a direction under section 52ZR above to the Greater London Authority.

(2)   The direction must specify the amount that is to be the component council tax requirement for the relevant constituent body for the year.

(3)   The Greater London Authority must make calculations in substitution in relation to the financial year under subsections (4) to (7) of section 85 of the Greater London Authority Act 1999 in relation to

    (a)   the relevant constituent body alone, or

    (b)   the relevant constituent body and one or more other constituent bodies.

(4)   Subsection (5) below applies if the result of the substitute calculations is such that

    (a)   there is an increase in the Greater London Authority's consolidated council tax requirement for the year, or

    (b)   there is no such increase, but the results of the calculations in substitution made in accordance with sections 85, 86 and 88 to 90 of and Schedule 7 to the Greater London Authority Act 1999 and sections 47 and 48 above would be different from the last relevant calculations in relation to the year.

(5)   The Greater London Authority must make calculations in substitution in accordance with the provisions mentioned in subsection (4)(b) above.

(6)   In subsection (4)(b) above "the last relevant calculations" means the last calculations made by the Greater London Authority in relation to the financial year in accordance with

    (a)   sections 85 to 90 of the Greater London Authority Act 1999 and sections 47 and 48 above, or

    (b)   sections 85, 86 and 88 to 90 of and Schedule 7 to that Act and sections 47 and 48 above.

(7)   None of the substitute calculations is to have any effect if

    (a)   the amount calculated under section 85(6) or (7) of the Greater London Authority Act 1999 for the relevant constituent body is not in compliance with the direction,

    (b)   there is an increase in the Greater London Authority's consolidated council tax requirement for the financial year (as last calculated) which exceeds the increase required to be made to the component council tax requirement for the relevant constituent body (as last calculated for the year) to comply with the direction, or

(c) in making the calculations under section 88(2) or 89(3) of that Act, the Authority fails to comply with subsection (8) below.

(8) In making substitute calculations under section 88(2) or 89(3) of the Greater London Authority Act 1999 the Greater London Authority must use any amount determined in the previous calculations for item T in section 88(2) of that Act or for item TP2 in section 89(4) of that Act.

(9) Subsections (7)(c) and (8) above do not apply if the previous calculations have been quashed because of a failure to comply with the appropriate Greater London provisions in making the calculations.

(10) For the purposes of subsection (9) above "the appropriate Greater London provisions" means

(a) in the case of calculations required to be made in accordance with sections 85 to 90 of the Greater London Authority Act 1999 and sections 47 and 48 above, those provisions, and

(b) in the case of calculations required to be made in accordance with sections 85, 86 and 88 to 90 of and Schedule 7 to that Act and sections 47 and 48 above, those provisions.

(11) Any substitute calculations under this section are to be made in accordance with Schedule 7 to the Greater London Authority Act 1999.

(12) In this Part

"component council tax requirement" has the meaning given by section 85(6) of the Greater London Authority Act 1999;

"consolidated council tax requirement" has the meaning given by section 85(8) of the Greater London Authority Act 1999;

"the relevant constituent body", in relation to a direction under section 52ZR above, means the constituent body by reference to which the direction was given (or, if there is more than one such body, each of them).

NOTES
Defined terms
constituent body: s 52ZR(8)
financial year: ss 69(1), 116(1)

Further provisions about directions

52ZW(1) An authority that is required to make substitute calculations for a financial year by virtue of any of sections 52ZS to 52ZU above

(a) must make the calculations, and

(b) in the case of a major precepting authority, must issue any precepts in substitution required in consequence under section 42 above,

before the end of the period mentioned in subsection (3) below.

(2) A local precepting authority to which section 52ZV(4) above applies must issue any precepts in substitution required in consequence under section 42 above before the end of the period mentioned in subsection (3) below.

(3) That period is

(a) the period of 35 days beginning with the day on which the authority receives the direction (where it is the Greater London Authority), or

(b) the period of 21 days beginning with the day on which the authority receives the direction (in any other case).

(4)   In the case of a billing authority, the authority has no power during the period of restriction to transfer any amount from its collection fund to its general fund; and sections 97 and 98 of the 1988 Act have effect accordingly.

(5)   In the case of a precepting authority, no authority to which it has power to issue a precept has power during the period of restriction to pay anything in respect of a precept issued by the precepting authority for the financial year.

(6)   For the purposes of subsections (4) and (5) above "the period of restriction" is the period
    (a)   beginning at the end of the period mentioned in subsection (3) above, and
    (b)   ending at the time (if any) when the authority complies with subsection (1) or (2) above (as the case may be).

(7)   The following provisions of this section apply to substitute calculations by the Greater London Authority other than those made pursuant to section 52ZU above.

(8)   Subject to variation or revocation, a direction under section 52ZR above has effect in relation to any substitute calculations made under any enactment by the Greater London Authority
    (a)   in accordance with sections 85, 86 and 88 to 90 of and Schedule 7 to the Greater London Authority Act 1999 and sections 47 and 48 above,
    (b)   in relation to the financial year to which the direction relates, and
    (c)   at any time after the direction is given.

(9)   Where a direction under section 52ZR above has effect in relation to any substitute calculations by virtue of subsection (8) above, none of the calculations have effect if the amount calculated under section 85(6) of the Greater London Authority Act 1999 for the relevant constituent body is not in compliance with the direction.

NOTES
Defined terms
  the 1988 Act: s 116(1)
  an authority: s 52ZA(2)(a)
  billing authority: ss 1(2), 52ZA(1)(a), 69(1)
  financial year: ss 69(1), 116(1)
  local precepting authority: ss 39(2), 52ZA(1)(c), 69(1)

  major precepting authority: ss 39(1), 52ZA(1)(b), 69(1)
  precepting authority: s 52ZA(2)(b)
  the relevant constituent body: s 52ZU(12)

Meaning of basic amount of council tax
Meaning of relevant basic amount of council tax

2ZX(1)   Any reference in this Chapter to a billing authority's relevant basic amount of council tax for a financial year is a reference to the amount that would be calculated by it in relation to the year under section 31B(1) above if section 31A above did not require or permit it to take into account the amount of any precepts
    (a)   issued to it for the year by local precepting authorities, or
    (b)   anticipated by it in pursuance of regulations under section 41 above.

(2)   In the case of a major precepting authority other than . . . the Greater London Authority, any reference in this Chapter to the authority's relevant basic amount of council tax for a financial year is a reference to the amount calculated by it in relation to the year under section 42B(1) above.

(3)   *Repealed*

(4)   In the case of a major precepting authority that is the Greater London Authority, any reference in this Chapter to the authority's relevant basic amount of council tax for a financial year is a reference to
    (a)   the amount calculated by it in relation to the year under section 88(2) of the Greater London Authority Act 1999 (referred to in this Chapter as the Greater London Authority's unadjusted relevant basic amount of council tax for the year), or

(b) any amount calculated by it in relation to the year under section 89(3) of that Act (referred to in this Chapter as the Greater London Authority's adjusted relevant basic amount of council tax for the year).

(5) Any reference in this Chapter to a local precepting authority's relevant basic amount of council tax for a financial year is a reference to the amount found by applying the formula R/T
where
R is the amount calculated by the authority under section 49A(4) above as its council tax requirement for the year;
T is the amount which is calculated by the billing authority to which the authority issues precepts ("the billing authority concerned") as its council tax base for the year for the part of its area comprising the authority's area and is notified by it to the authority within the prescribed period.

(6) Where the aggregate calculated by the authority for the year under subsection (2) of section 49A above does not exceed that so calculated under subsection (3) of that section, the amount for item R in subsection (5) above is to be nil.

(7) The Secretary of State must make regulations containing rules for making for any year the calculation required by item T in subsection (5) above; and the billing authority concerned must make the calculations for any year in accordance with the rules for the time being effective (as regards the year) under the regulations.

(8) Regulations prescribing a period for the purposes of item T in subsection (5) above may provide that, in any case where a billing authority fails to notify its calculation to the precepting authority concerned within that period, that item must be determined in the prescribed manner by such authority or authorities as may be prescribed.

(9) In the application of this section any calculation for which another has been substituted is to be disregarded.

NOTES
Subordinate Legislation
Local Authority (Referendums Relating to Council Tax Increases) Regulations 2012, SI 2012/460
Local Authorities (Calculation of Council Tax Base) (England) Regulations 2012, SI 2012/2914

council tax: s 1(1)
financial year: ss 69(1), 116(1)
local precepting authority: ss 39(2), 52ZA(1)(c), 69(1)
major precepting authority: ss 39(1), 52ZA(1)(b), 69(1)
prescribed: s 116(1)

Defined terms
billing authority: ss 1(2), 52ZA(1)(a), 69(1)

Information for purposes of Chapter 4ZA

52ZY(1) The Secretary of State may serve on an authority a notice requiring it to supply to the Secretary of State such information as is specified in the notice and required for the purposes of the performance of the Secretary of State's functions under this Chapter.

(2) The authority must supply the information required if it is in its possession or control, and must do so in such form and manner and at such time as the Secretary of State specifies in the notice.

(3) If an authority fails to comply with subsection (2) above, the Secretary of State may exercise the Secretary of State's functions on the basis of such assumptions and estimates as the Secretary of State thinks fit.

(4) In exercising those functions, the Secretary of State may also take into account any other available information, whatever its source and whether or not obtained under a provision contained in or made under this or any other Act.

NOTES
Defined terms
an authority: s 52ZA(2)(a)

Local Government and Housing Act 1989

PART I
LOCAL AUTHORITY MEMBERS, OFFICERS, STAFF AND COMMITTEES ETC

Political restriction of officers and staff

Disqualification and political restriction of certain officers and staff

1(1) A person shall be disqualified from becoming (whether by election or otherwise) or remaining a member of a local authority if he holds a politically restricted post under that local authority or any other local authority in Great Britain.

(2)(4) *Repealed*

(5) The terms of appointment or conditions of employment of every person holding a politically restricted post under a local authority (including persons appointed to such posts before the coming into force of this section) shall be deemed to incorporate such requirements for restricting his political activities as may be prescribed for the purposes of this subsection by regulations made by the Secretary of State.

(6) Regulations under subsection (5) above may contain such incidental provision and such supplemental, consequential and transitional provision in connection with their other provisions as the Secretary of State considers appropriate and, without prejudice to section 190(1) below, may contain such exceptions for persons appointed in pursuance of section 9 below as he thinks fit.

(7) So far as it has effect in relation to disqualification for election, this section has effect with respect to any election occurring not less than two months after the coming into force of this section and, so far as it relates to becoming in any other way a member of a local authority, this section has effect with respect to any action which, apart from this section, would result in a person becoming a member of the authority not less than two months after the coming into force of this section.

(8) If, immediately before the expiry of the period of two months referred to in subsection (7) above, a person who is a member of a local authority holds a politically restricted post under that or any other local authority, nothing in this section shall apply to him until the expiry of the period for which he was elected or for which he otherwise became a member of the authority.

(9) In this section a reference to a person holding a politically restricted post under a local authority includes a reference to every member of the staff of an elected local policing body, except for a deputy police and crime commissioner.

NOTES

Subordinate Legislation
Local Government Officers (Political Restrictions) Regulations 1990, SI 1990/851

Defined terms
local authority: s 21(1), (2)

Politically restricted posts

2(1) The following persons are to be regarded for the purposes of this Part as holding politically restricted posts under a local authority
    (a) the person designated under section 4 below as the head of the authority's paid service;
    (b) the statutory chief officers;
    (c) a non-statutory chief officer;
    (d) a deputy chief officer;
    (e) the monitoring officer designated under section 5 below;

    (f)   any person holding a post to which he was appointed in pursuance of section 9 below;

    (g)   any person not falling within paragraphs (a) to (f) above whose post is for the time being specified by the authority in a list maintained in accordance with subsection (2) below and any directions under section 3 or 3A below or with section 100G(2) of the Local Government Act 1972 or section 50G(2) of the Local Government (Scotland) Act 1973 (list of officers to whom powers are delegated); and

    (h)   the head of democratic services designated under section 8 of the Local Government (Wales) Measure 2011.

(2)   It shall be the duty of every local authority to prepare and maintain a list of such of the following posts under the authority, namely

    (a)   *Repealed*

    (b)   *Repealed*

    (c)   posts the duties of which appear to the authority to fall within subsection (3) below,

as are not posts for the time being exempted under section 3 or 3A below, posts for the time being listed under section 100G(2) of the Local Government Act 1972 or section 50G(2) of the Local Government (Scotland) Act 1973 or posts of a description specified in regulations made by the Secretary of State for the purposes of this subsection.

(3)   The duties of a post under a local authority fall within this subsection if they consist in or involve one or both of the following, that is to say

    (a)   giving advice on a regular basis to the authority themselves, to any committee or sub-committee of the authority or to any joint committee on which the authority are represented or, where the authority are operating executive arrangements, to the executive of the authority, to any committee of that executive, or to any member of that executive who is also a member of the authority;

    (b)   speaking on behalf of the authority on a regular basis to journalists or broadcasters.

(4)   It shall be the duty of every local authority to deposit the first list prepared under subsection (2) above with the proper officer before the expiry of the period of two months beginning with the coming into force of this section; and it shall also be their duty, on subsequently making any modifications of that list, to deposit a revised list with that officer.

(5)   It shall be the duty of every local authority in Scotland and Wales in performing their duties under this section to have regard to such general advice as may be given by virtue of subsection (1)(b) of section 3 below by a person appointed under that subsection.

(5A)   It shall be the duty of every local authority in England in performing their duties under this section to have regard to such general advice as may be given by virtue of section 3B below by the Secretary of State.

(6)   In this section "the statutory chief officers" means

    (za) the director of children's services appointed under section 18 of the Children Act 2004 and the director of adult social services appointed under section 6(A1) of the Local Authority Social Services Act 1970 (in the case of a local authority in England);

    (zb) the director of public health appointed under section 73A(1) of the National Health Service Act 2006;

    (a)   the chief education officer appointed under section 532 of the Education Act 1996 (in the case of a local authority in Wales);

    (b)   the chief officer of a fire brigade maintained under the Fire Services Act 1947 and appointed under regulations made under section 18(1)(a) of that Act;

    (c)   the director of social services (in the case of a local authority in Wales) or chief social work officer appointed under section 6 of the Local Authority Social Services Act 1970 or section 3 of the Social Work (Scotland) Act 1968; and

(d) the officer having responsibility, for the purposes of section 151 of the Local Government Act 1972, section 73 of the Local Government Act 1985, section 112 of the Local Government Finance Act 1988, section 127(2) of the Greater London Authority Act 1999 or section 6 below or for the purposes of section 95 of the Local Government (Scotland) Act 1973, for the administration of the authority's financial affairs.

(7) In this section "non-statutory chief officer" means, subject to the following provisions of this section

    (a) a person for whom the head of the authority's paid service is directly responsible;

    (b) a person who, as respects all or most of the duties of his post, is required to report directly or is directly accountable to the head of the authority's paid service; and

    (c) any person who, as respects all or most of the duties of his post, is required to report directly or is directly accountable to the local authority themselves or any committee or subcommittee of the authority.

(8) In this section "deputy chief officer" means, subject to the following provisions of this section, a person who, as respects all or most of the duties of his post, is required to report directly or is directly accountable to one or more of the statutory or non-statutory chief officers.

(9) A person whose duties are solely secretarial or clerical or are otherwise in the nature of support services shall not be regarded as a non-statutory chief officer or a deputy chief officer for the purposes of this Part.

(10) Nothing in this section shall have the effect of requiring any person to be regarded as holding a politically restricted post by reason of his holding

    (a) the post of head teacher or principal of a school, college or other educational institution or establishment which, in England and Wales, is maintained or assisted by a local authority or, in Scotland, is under the management of or is assisted by an education authority; or

    (b) any other post as a teacher or lecturer in any such school, college, institution or establishment,

or of requiring any such post to be included in any list prepared and maintained under this section.

(11) Regulations under this section may contain such incidental provision and such supplemental, consequential and transitional provision in connection with their other provisions as the Secretary of State considers appropriate.

NOTES

Defined terms
executive: s 21(3)
executive arrangements: s 21(3)
local authority: s 21(1), (2)

proper officer: s 21(3)

Grant and supervision of exemptions from political restriction: Scotland and Wales

3(1) It shall be the duty of the Scottish Ministers to appoint in relation to Scotland, and the duty of the Welsh Ministers to appoint in relation to Wales, a person

    (a) to carry out the functions in relation to political restriction which are conferred by subsections (2) to (7) below; and

    (b) to give such general advice with respect to the determination of questions arising by virtue of section 2(3) above as that person considers appropriate after consulting such representatives of local government and such organisations appearing to him to represent employees in local government as he considers appropriate.

(2) A person appointed under subsection (1) above

    (a) shall consider any application for exemption from political restriction which is made to him, in respect of any post under a local authority, by the holder for the time being of that post; and

    (b) may, on the application of any person or otherwise, give directions to a local authority requiring it to include a post in the list maintained by the authority under section 2(2) above.

(3)   An application shall not be made by virtue of subsection (2)(a) above in respect of a post under a local authority except where

    (a) the authority have specified or are proposing to specify the post in the list maintained by the authority under subsection (2) of section 2 above;

    (b) *Repealed*

(4)   If, on an application made by virtue of subsection (2)(a) above in respect of any post under a local authority, the person to whom the application is made is satisfied that the duties of the post do not fall within section 2(3) above, that person shall direct

    (a) that, for so long as the direction has effect in accordance with its terms, the post is not to be regarded as a politically restricted post; and

    (b) that, accordingly, the post is not to be specified in the list maintained by that authority under section 2(2) above or, as the case may be, is to be removed from that list.

(5)   A person appointed under subsection (1) above shall not give a direction under subsection (2)(b) above in respect of any post under a local authority except where he is satisfied that the post

    (a) is a post the duties of which fall within section 2(3) above; and

    (b) is neither included in any list maintained by the authority in accordance with section 2(2) above, section 100G(2) of the Local Government Act 1972 or section 50G(2) of the Local Government (Scotland) Act 1973 nor of a description specified in any regulations under section 2(2) above.

(6)   It shall be the duty of a local authority

    (a) to give a person appointed under subsection (1) above all such information as that person may reasonably require for the purpose of carrying out his functions under this section;

    (b) to comply with any direction under this section with respect to the list maintained by the authority; and

    (c) on being given a direction by virtue of subsection (2)(b) above, to notify the terms of the direction to the holder for the time being of the post to which the direction relates.

(7)   It shall be the duty of a person appointed under subsection (1) above, in carrying out his functions under this section, to give priority, according to the time available before the election, to any application made by virtue of subsection (2)(a) above by a person who certifies that it is made for the purpose of enabling him to be a candidate in a forthcoming election.

(8)   The Secretary of State may

    (a) *Repealed*

    (b) provide for the appointment of such members of staff to assist any person appointed under subsection (1), and to act on that person's behalf, as the Secretary of State may with the consent of the Treasury determine;

    (c) pay to or in respect of a person appointed under that subsection and members of such a person's staff such remuneration and such other sums by way of, or towards, the payment of pensions, allowances and gratuities as the Secretary of State may so determine; and

    (d) provide for a person appointed under that subsection and such a persons' staff to hold office on such other terms as the Secretary of State may so determine.

Grant and supervision of exemptions from political restriction: England

3A(1) The head of paid service of a local authority in England

    (a) must consider any application for exemption from political restriction which is made to the head of paid service, in respect of any post under the authority, by the holder for the time being of that post; and

    (b) may, on the application of any person or otherwise, give directions to the authority requiring it to include a post in the list maintained by the authority under section 2(2).

  (2) An application may not be made under subsection (1)(a) unless

    (a) the authority have specified or are proposing to specify the post in the list maintained by them under section 2(2);

    (b) *Repealed*

  (3) If, on an application under subsection (1)(a) in respect of any post, the head of paid service is satisfied that the duties of the post do not fall within section 2(3), the head of paid service must direct

    (a) that, for so long as the direction has effect in accordance with its terms, the post is not to be regarded as a politically restricted post; and

    (b) that accordingly the post is not to be specified in the list maintained by the authority under section 2(2) or (as the case may be) is to be removed from that list.

  (4) A local authority's head of paid service may not give a direction under subsection (1)(b) in respect of any post unless the head of paid service is satisfied that

    (a) the duties of the post fall within section 2(3); and

    (b) the post is neither

      (i) in any list maintained by the authority in accordance with section 2(2) above or section 100G(2) of the Local Government Act 1972; nor

      (ii) of a description specified in any regulations under section 2(2) above.

  (5) *Repealed*

  (6) Every local authority in England must

    (a) give its head of paid service all such information as the head of paid service may reasonably require for the purpose of carrying out functions under this section;

    (b) comply with any direction under this section with respect to the list maintained by the authority; and

    (c) on being given a direction under subsection (1)(b), notify the terms of the direction to the person who holds the post to which the direction relates.

  (7) In carrying out functions under this section a local authority's head of paid service must give priority, according to the time available before the election, to any application under subsection (1)(a) from a person who certifies that the application is made for the purpose of enabling him to be a candidate in a forthcoming election.

  (7A) In carrying out functions under this section a local authority's head of paid service must consult the monitoring officer of that authority (unless they are the same person).

  (7B) The Secretary of State may by regulations make provision about the application of this section to a local authority that is not required to designate one of its officers as the head of its paid service.

  (7C) Regulations under subsection (7B) may apply any provisions of this section (with or without modifications) to an authority to which they apply.

  (8) *Repealed*

(9)   *Repealed*

(10) *Repealed*

NOTES

Subordinate Legislation
   Local Authorities (Exemption from Political Restrictions)
   (Designation) Regulations 2012, SI 2012/1644

local authority: s 21(1), (2)
the monitoring officer: s 5(1)
officer: s 21(4)

Defined terms

General advice as to politically restricted posts: England

3B(1)   The Secretary of State may in relation to England give such general advice with respect to the determination of questions arising by virtue of section 2(3) as he considers appropriate.

(2)   Before giving general advice under this section the Secretary of State must consult such representatives of local government and such organisations appearing to him to represent employees in local government as he considers appropriate.

Duties of particular officers

Designation and reports of head of paid service

4(1)   It shall be the duty of every relevant authority
   (a)   to designate one of their officers as the head of their paid service; and
   (b)   to provide that officer with such staff, accommodation and other resources as are, in his opinion, sufficient to allow his duties under this section to be performed.

(1A)   In the case of an elected local policing body, the body's chief executive is to be taken to have been designated as the head of the body's paid service (and, accordingly, subsection (1)(a) does not apply; but references to persons designated under this section include references to the body's chief executive).

(2)   It shall be the duty of the head of a relevant authority's paid service, where he considers it appropriate to do so in respect of any proposals of his with respect to any of the matters specified in subsection (3) below, to prepare a report to the authority setting out his proposals.

(3)   Those matters are
   (a)   the manner in which the discharge by the authority of their different functions is co-ordinated;
   (b)   the number and grades of staff required by the authority for the discharge of their functions;
   (c)   the organisation of the authority's staff; and
   (d)   the appointment and proper management of the authority's staff.

(4)   It shall be the duty of the head of a relevant authority's paid service, as soon as practicable after he has prepared a report under this section, to arrange for a copy of it to be sent
   (a)   in the case of an elected local policing body, to the body and to the police and crime panel for the body's police area; and
   (b)   in any other case, to each member of the authority.

(5)   It shall be the duty of a relevant authority (other than an elected local policing body) to consider any report under this section by the head of their paid service at a meeting held not more than three months after copies of the report are first sent to members of the authority; and nothing in section 101 of the Local Government Act 1972 or in section 56 of the Local Government (Scotland) Act 1973 (delegation) shall apply to the duty imposed by virtue of this subsection.

(5A) It shall be the duty of an elected local policing body to consider any report under this section by the head of the body's paid service, and to do so no later than three months after the body is sent a copy of the report.

(6) In this section "relevant authority"

    (a) in relation to England and Wales, means a local authority of any of the descriptions specified in paragraphs (a) to (e), (ja) and (jb) of section 21(1) below and an elected local policing body; and

    (b) in relation to Scotland, means a council constituted under section 2 of the Local Government etc (Scotland) Act 1994.

(7) This section shall come into force at the expiry of the period of two months beginning on the day this Act is passed.

NOTES

Defined terms
    local authority: s 21(1), (2)
    officer: s 21(4)

Designation and reports of monitoring officer

5(1) It shall be the duty of every relevant authority

    (a) to designate one of their officers (to be known as "the monitoring officer") as the officer responsible for performing the duties imposed by this section and, where relevant, section 5A below; and

    (b) to provide that officer with such staff, accommodation and other resources as are, in his opinion, sufficient to allow those duties and, where relevant, the duties under section 5A below to be performed;

and subject to subsection (1A) below the officer so designated may be the head of the authority's paid service but shall not be their chief finance officer.

(1A) The officer designated under subsection (1) above by a relevant authority to which this subsection applies may not be the head of that authority's paid service.

(1B) Subsection (1A) above applies to the following relevant authorities in England and Wales

    (a) a county council,

    (b) a county borough council,

    (c) a district council,

    (d) a London borough council,

    (e) the Greater London Authority, and

    (f) the Common Council of the City of London in its capacity as a local authority, police authority or port health authority.

(1C) In the case of an elected local policing body, the body's chief executive is to be taken to have been designated as the monitoring officer (and, accordingly, subsection (1)(a) does not apply; but references to persons designated under this section include references to the body's chief executive).

(2) Subject to subsection (2B), it shall be the duty of a relevant authority's monitoring officer, if it at any time appears to him that any proposal, decision or omission by the authority, by any committee, or subcommittee of the authority, by any person holding any office or employment under the authority or by any joint committee on which the authority are represented constitutes, has given rise to or is likely to or would give rise to

    (a) a contravention by the authority, by any committee, or subcommittee of the authority, by any person holding any office or employment under the authority or by any such joint committee of any enactment or rule of law or of any code of practice made or approved by or under any enactment; or

    (aa) any such maladministration or failure as is mentioned in Part 3 of the Local Government Act 1974 (Local Commissioners), or

(b) any such maladministration or injustice as is mentioned in Part II of the Local Government (Scotland) Act 1975 (which makes corresponding provision for Scotland); or

(c) a matter which the Public Services Ombudsman for Wales would be entitled to investigate under the Public Services Ombudsman (Wales) Act 2005,

to prepare a report to the authority with respect to that proposal, decision or omission.

(2A) No duty shall arise by virtue of subsection (2)(b) above unless a Local Commissioner (within the meaning of the Local Government Act 1974) has conducted an investigation under Part III of that Act in relation to the proposal, decision or omission concerned.

(2AA) No duty shall arise by virtue of subsection (2)(c) above unless the Public Services Ombudsman for Wales has conducted an investigation under the Public Services Ombudsman (Wales) Act 2005 in relation to the proposal, decision or omission concerned.

(2B) Where a relevant authority are operating executive arrangements, the monitoring officer of the relevant authority shall not make a report under subsection (2) in respect of any proposal, decision or omission unless it is a proposal, decision or omission made otherwise than by or on behalf of the relevant authority's executive.

(3) It shall be the duty of a relevant authority's monitoring officer
  (a) in preparing a report under this section to consult so far as practicable with the person who is for the time being designated as the head of the authority's paid service under section 4 above and with their chief finance officer; and
  (b) as soon as practicable after such a report has been prepared by him or his deputy, to arrange for a copy of it to be sent
    (a) in the case of an elected local policing body, to the body and to the police and crime panel for the body's police area; and
    (b) in any other case, to each member of the authority and, in a case where the relevant authority have a mayor and council manager executive, to the council manager of the authority.

(3A) The references in subsection (2) above, in relation to a relevant authority in England, to a committee or subcommittee of the authority and to a joint committee on which they are represented shall be taken to include references to
  (a) any inshore fisheries and conservation authority ("IFC authority") the members of which include persons who are members of the relevant authority, and
  (b) any subcommittee appointed by such an authority;
but in relation to any such IFC authority or subcommittee the reference in subsection (3)(b) above to each member of the authority shall have effect as a reference to each member of the IFC authority or, as the case may be, of the IFC authority which appointed the subcommittee.

(4) *Repealed*

(5) It shall be the duty of a relevant authority and of any IFC authority falling within paragraph (a) of subsection (3A) above
  (a) to consider any report under this section by a monitoring officer or his deputy
    (i) in the case of an elected local policing body, no later than three months after the body is sent a copy of the report; and
    (ii) in any other case, at a meeting held not more than twentyone days after copies of the report are first sent to members of the authority; and
  (b) without prejudice to any duty imposed by virtue of section 115 of the Local Government Finance Act 1988 (duties in respect of conduct involving contraventions of financial obligations) or otherwise, to ensure that no step is taken for giving effect to any proposal or decision to which such a report relates at any time while the implementation of the proposal or decision is suspended in consequence of the report;

and nothing in section 101 of the Local Government Act 1972 or in section 56 of the Local Government (Scotland) Act 1973 (delegation) shall apply to the duty imposed by virtue of paragraph (a) above.

(6) For the purposes of paragraph (b) of subsection (5) above the implementation of a proposal or decision to which a report under this section relates shall be suspended in consequence of the report until the end of the first business day after the day on which consideration of that report under paragraph (a) of that subsection is concluded.

(7) The duties of a relevant authority's monitoring officer under this section shall be performed by him personally or, where he is unable to act owing to absence or illness, personally by such member of his staff as he has for the time being nominated as his deputy for the purposes of this section.

(7A) Subsection (7) above shall have effect subject to section 82A of the Local Government Act 2000 (monitoring officers: delegation of functions under Part 3 of that Act).

(8) In this section and in section 5A

"business day", in relation to a relevant authority, means any day which is not a Saturday or Sunday, Christmas Day, Good Friday or any day which is a bank holiday under the Banking and Financial Dealings Act 1971 in the part of Great Britain where the area of the authority is situated;

"chief finance officer", in relation to a relevant authority, means the officer having responsibility, for the purposes of section 151 of the Local Government Act 1972, section 73 of the Local Government Act 1985, section 112 of the Local Government Finance Act 1988, section 127(2) of the Greater London Authority Act 1999, Schedule 1 to the Police Reform and Social Responsibility Act 2011 or section 6 below or for the purposes of section 95 of the Local Government (Scotland) Act 1973, for the administration of the authority's financial affairs;

"inshore fisheries and conservation authority" means the authority for an inshore fisheries and conservation district established under section 149 of the Marine and Coastal Access Act 2009;

"relevant authority"

(a) in relation to England and Wales, means a local authority of any of the descriptions specified in paragraphs (a) to (k) of section 21(1) below and an elected local policing body; and

(b) in relation to Scotland, means a local authority.

(8A) Any reference in this section to the duties of a monitoring officer imposed by this section, or to the duties of a monitoring officer under this section, shall include a reference to the functions which are conferred on a monitoring officer by virtue of Part III of the Local Government Act 2000.

(8B) Any reference in this section to the duties of a monitoring officer imposed by this section, or to the duties of a monitoring officer under this section, shall include a reference to duties conferred on a monitoring officer by paragraph 38B of Schedule 12 to the Local Government Act 1972 (duties of monitoring officer for principal council in Wales in relation to polls consequent on community meetings).

(9) This section shall come into force at the expiry of the period of two months beginning on the day this Act is passed.

NOTES

Defined terms
contravention: s 21(3)
executive: s 21(3)
executive arrangements: s 21(3)

local authority: s 21(1), (2)
officer: s 21(4)

Reports of monitoring officerlocal authorities operating executive arrangements

5A(1)   Where a relevant authority are operating executive arrangements, the monitoring officer of that authority shall be responsible for performing the duties imposed by this section.

(2)   It shall be the duty of the monitoring officer of a relevant authority that is referred to in subsection (1) above, if at any time it appears to him that any proposal, decision or omission, in the course of the discharge of functions of the relevant authority, by or on behalf of the relevant authority's executive, constitutes, has given rise to or is likely to or would give rise to any of the events referred to in subsection (3), to prepare a report to the executive of the authority with respect to that proposal, decision or omission.

(3)   The events referred to for the purposes of subsection (2) are
   (a)   a contravention, by the relevant authority's executive or any person on behalf of the executive, of any enactment or rule of law; or
   (b)   any such maladministration or failure as is mentioned in Part III of the Local Government Act 1974 (Local Commissioners); or
   (c)   a matter which the Public Services Ombudsman for Wales would be entitled to investigate under the Public Services Ombudsman (Wales) Act 2005.

(4)   No duty shall arise by virtue of subsection (3)(b) above unless a Local Commissioner (within the meaning of the Local Government Act 1974) has conducted an investigation under Part III of that Act in relation to the proposal, decision or omission concerned.

(4A)   No duty shall arise by virtue of subsection (3)(c) above unless the Public Services Ombudsman for Wales has conducted an investigation under the Public Services Ombudsman (Wales) Act 2005 in relation to the proposal, decision or omission concerned.

(5)   It shall be the duty of an authority's monitoring officer
   (a)   in preparing a report under subsection (2) to consult so far as practicable with the person who is for the time being designated as the head of the authority's paid service under section 4 above and with their chief finance officer; and
   (b)   as soon as practicable after such a report has been prepared by him or his deputy, to arrange for a copy of it to be sent to each member of the authority and, where the authority has a mayor and council manager executive, the council manager.

(6)   It shall be the duty of the authority's executive
   (a)   to consider any report under this section by a monitoring officer or his deputy at a meeting held not more than twenty-one days after copies of the report are first sent to members of the executive; and
   (b)   without prejudice to any duty imposed by virtue of section 115B of the Local Government Finance Act 1988 (duties of executive as regards reports) or otherwise, to ensure that no step is taken for giving effect to any proposal or decision to which such a report relates at any time while the implementation of the proposal or decision is suspended in consequence of the report.

(7)   For the purposes of paragraph (b) of subsection (6) above the implementation of a proposal or decision to which a report under this section, by a monitoring officer or his deputy, relates shall be suspended in consequence of the report until the end of the first business day after the day on which consideration of that report under paragraph (a) of that subsection is concluded.

(8)   As soon as practicable after the executive has concluded its consideration of the report of the monitoring officer or his deputy, the executive shall prepare a report which specifies
   (a)   what action (if any) the executive has taken in response to the report of the monitoring officer or his deputy;
   (b)   what action (if any) the executive proposes to take in response to that report and when it proposes to take that action; and
   (c)   the reasons for taking the action specified in the executive's report or, as the case may be, for taking no action.

(9) As soon as practicable after the executive has prepared a report under subsection (8), the executive shall arrange for a copy of it to be sent to each member of the authority and the authority's monitoring officer.

(10) The duties of an authority's monitoring officer under this section shall be performed by him personally or, where he is unable to act owing to absence or illness, personally by such member of his staff as he has for the time being nominated as his deputy for the purposes of this section.

NOTES

Defined terms
   business day: s 5(8)
   chief finance officer: s 5(8)
   contravention: s 21(3)
   executive: s 21(3)

   executive arrangements: s 21(3)
   the monitoring officer: s 5(1)
   relevant authority: s 5(8)

6-8 *Not reproduced*

Assistants for political groups

9(1) Nothing in section 7(1) above or in any enactment, standing order or rule of law by virtue of which it is unlawful for a relevant authority or any committee or subcommittee of such an authority to have regard to any person's political activities or affiliations in determining whether he should be appointed to any paid office or employment under the authority shall apply to the appointment of a person in pursuance of this section.

(2) An appointment is an appointment in pursuance of this section if
   (a) the appointment is made for the purpose of providing assistance, in the discharge of any of their functions as members of a relevant authority, to the members of any political group to which members of the authority belong;
   (b) the terms of the appointment comply with subsection (3) below;
   (c) the appointment is to one of not more than three posts which a relevant authority have decided to create for the purposes of this section; and
   (d) each of those posts falls, under the standing orders of the authority, to be filled from time to time in accordance with the wishes of a political group to which the post has been allocated under those standing orders.

(3) The terms on which any person is appointed to or holds any appointment in pursuance of this section must be such as secure that the annual rate of remuneration for the post is less than the relevant amount and that the appointment terminates at or before the end of
   (a) in the case of a post under an authority in England and Wales, the day in the appropriate year on which the authority hold the meeting which they are required to hold in pursuance of paragraph 1 of Part I of Schedule 12 to the Local Government Act 1972 (annual meeting of principal councils); and
   (b) in the case of a post under an authority in Scotland, the first day after the appointment on which a meeting is held in pursuance of the requirement under paragraph 1 of Schedule 7 to the Local Government (Scotland) Act 1973 that a meeting is held within twenty-one days from the date of an election.

(4) For the purposes of subsection (3) above the annual rate of remuneration for a post under a relevant authority is less than the relevant amount if the annual rate of remuneration in respect of the post
   (a) is less than £13,500 or such higher amount as the Secretary of State may by order made by statutory instrument specify; and
   (b) where that post is a part time post, would be less than that amount if it were a full time post and carried remuneration at the same rate;
and a statutory instrument containing an order under this subsection shall be subject to annulment in pursuance of a resolution of either House of Parliament.

(4A)   An order made under subsection (4)(a) above in relation to England or Wales may, instead of specifying an amount, specify a point on a relevant scale specified by the order.

(4B)   A "relevant scale" is a scale consisting of points and of amounts corresponding to those points.

(4C)   In relation to any time while an order made by virtue of subsection (4A) above is in force, the amount that at that time corresponds to the point specified by the order is to be treated for the purposes of subsection (4)(a) above as specified by the order.

(5)   The standing orders of a relevant authority the members of which are divided into different political groups shall, for the purposes of subsection (2)(d) above

    (a)   prohibit the making of an appointment to any post allocated to a political group until the authority have allocated a post to each of the groups which qualify for one;

    (b)   prohibit the allocation of a post to a political group which does not qualify for one; and

    (c)   prohibit the allocation of more than one post to any one political group.

(6)   Subject to subsection (7) below, where the members of a relevant authority are divided into different political groups, a group shall qualify for a post if

    (a)   the membership of that group comprises at least one‑tenth of the membership of the authority;

    (b)   the number of the other groups (if any) which are larger than that group does not exceed two; and

    (c)   where the number of the other groups which are the same size as or larger than that group exceeds two, the authority have determined that that group should be a group to which a post is allocated;

and it shall be the duty of a relevant authority, before making any allocation for the purposes of this section in a case in which there are groups which would qualify for posts if paragraph (c) above were disregarded, to make such determinations under that paragraph as secure that there are no more nor less than three groups which do qualify for a post.

(7)   Where the members of a relevant authority are divided into political groups only one of which has a membership that comprises one‑tenth or more of the membership of the authority

    (a)   the groups qualifying for a post shall be that group and one other group; and

    (b)   the other group shall be the one with the next largest membership or, in a case in which there is more than one group with the next largest membership, such one of those groups as may be determined by the authority;

and, in such a case, it shall be the duty of the authority to determine which of the groups with the next largest membership is to qualify for a post before making any allocation for the purposes of this section to the group with the largest membership.

(8)   Neither a relevant authority nor any committee or subcommittee of a relevant authority shall exercise any power under

    (a)   section 101 of the Local Government Act 1972 (delegation); or

    (b)   section 56 of the Local Government (Scotland) Act 1973 (which makes corresponding provision for Scotland); or

    (c)   Part II of the Local Government Act 2000 (arrangements with respect to executives etc),

so as to arrange for the discharge of any of the authority's functions by any person who holds a post under the authority to which he was appointed in pursuance of this section.

(8A)   Neither an executive, a committee of an executive or a member of an executive, of a relevant authority, shall exercise any power under

    (a)   sections 14 to 18 of the Local Government Act 2000 (discharge of functions); or

    (b) section 101(5) of the Local Government Act 1972 (arrangements for the discharge of functions by local authorities),

so as to arrange for the discharge of any of the authority's functions by any person who holds a post under the authority to which he was appointed in pursuance of this section.

(8B) An area committee of a relevant authority shall not exercise any power under arrangements made under regulations made under section 18 of the Local Government Act 2000 (discharge of functions by area committees) so as to arrange for the discharge of any of the authority's functions by any person who holds a post under the authority to which he was appointed in pursuance of this section.

(9) No person holding any office or employment under a relevant authority shall be required to work under the direction of a person holding a post to which he was appointed in pursuance of this section except for the purpose of providing that person, or the political group to which his post is allocated, with secretarial or clerical services.

(10) Without prejudice to section 8 above, the Secretary of State may, for the purposes of this section and any standing orders relating to appointments in pursuance of this section, by regulations make provision

    (a) as to the circumstances in which the members of a relevant authority are to be treated as divided into different political groups;

    (b) as to the persons who are to be treated as members of such a group and as to when a person is to be treated as having ceased to be a member of such a group;

    (c) requiring the question whether a person is or is not a member of a political group to be determined in such manner as may be provided for by or under the regulations;

    (d) requiring a relevant authority from time to time to review allocations made for the purposes of this section;

    (e) specifying the manner in which, and times at which, the wishes of a political group are to be expressed and the consequences of a failure by such a group to express its wishes;

and regulations under this section may contain such incidental provision and such supplemental, consequential and transitional provision in connection with their other provisions as the Secretary of State considers appropriate.

(11) In this section

"appropriate year", in relation to a post held by any person under a relevant authority, means

    (a) where the authority is subject to whole council elections by virtue of Chapter 1 of Part 2 of the Local Government and Public Involvement in Health Act 2007, the period of twelve months beginning with the first such election to be held after that person is appointed to that post; and

    (b) in any other case, the period of twelve months beginning with the third anniversary of that person's appointment to that post;

"area committee" has the same meaning as in section 18 of the Local Government Act 2000;

"membership", in relation to a relevant authority, means the number of persons who are for the time being members of the authority;

"relevant authority"

    (a) in relation to England and Wales, means the council of any county, county borough, district or London borough; and

    (b) in relation to Scotland, means a council constituted under section 2 of the Local Government etc (Scotland) Act 1994.

NOTES

Subordinate Legislation
Local Government (Committees and Political Groups) Regulations 1990, SI 1990/1553

Local Government (Assistants for Political Groups) (Remuneration) Order 1995, SI 1995/2456
Local Government (Assistants for Political Groups)

Defined terms
   executive: s 21(3)

11-12   *Not reproduced*

Voting rights of members of certain committees

Voting rights of members of certain committees: England and Wales

13(1)   Subject to the following provisions of this section, a person who

   (a)   is a member of a committee appointed under a power to which this section applies by a relevant authority and is not a member of that authority;

   (b)   is a member of a joint committee appointed under such a power by two or more relevant authorities and is not a member of any of those authorities; or

   (c)   is a member of a subcommittee appointed under such a power by such a committee as is mentioned in paragraph (a) or (b) above and is not a member of the relevant authority, or one of the relevant authorities, which appointed that committee,

   shall for all purposes be treated as a nonvoting member of that committee, joint committee or, as the case may be, subcommittee.

(2)   The powers to which this section applies are

   (a)   the powers conferred on any relevant authority by subsection (1) of section 102 of the Local Government Act 1972 (ordinary committees, joint committees and subcommittees);

   (b)   *Repealed*

   (c)   *Repealed*

(3)   Nothing in subsection (1) above shall require a person to be treated as a nonvoting member of a committee or subcommittee falling within subsection (4) below; but, except

   (a)   in the case of a subcommittee appointed by a committee falling within paragraph (e) of that subsection; and

   (b)   in such cases as may be prescribed by regulations made by the Secretary of State,

   a person who is a member of a subcommittee falling within that subsection shall for all purposes be treated as a nonvoting member of that subcommittee unless he is a member of the committee which appointed the subcommittee.

(4)   A committee or subcommittee falls within this subsection if it is

   (a)   *Repealed*

   (b)   *Repealed*

   (c)   a committee established in accordance with any regulations made by virtue of section 7 of the Superannuation Act 1972 (regulations making provision for the superannuation of persons employed in local government service etc);

   (d)   *Repealed*

   (e)   a committee appointed under section 102(4) of the Local Government Act 1972 (appointment of advisory committees by local authorities);

   (f)   a committee constituted in accordance with Part I of Schedule 33 to the Education Act 1996 (constitution of appeal committees for admissions appeals etc);

   (fa)   an inshore fisheries and conservation authority for a district established under section 149 of the Marine and Coastal Access Act 2009;

   (fb)   a committee of a relevant authority which is the scheme manager (or scheme manager and pension board) of a scheme under section 1 of the Public Service Pensions Act 2013;

      (g) a committee established exclusively for the purpose of discharging such functions of a relevant authority as may be prescribed by regulations made by the Secretary of State;

      (h) a subcommittee appointed by a committee falling within any of paragraphs (b) to (g) above or such a subcommittee as is so prescribed.

(5) Nothing in this section shall prevent the appointment of a person who is not a member of a local authority as a voting member of

      (a) any committee or subcommittee appointed by the local authority wholly or partly for the purpose of discharging any education functions of the authority,

      (b) any joint committee appointed by two or more local authorities wholly or partly for the purpose of discharging any education functions of the authorities, or

      (c) any subcommittee appointed by any such committee or joint committee wholly or partly for the purpose of discharging any of that committee's functions with respect to education,

where that appointment is required either by directions given by the Secretary of State under section 499 of the Education Act 1996 (power of Secretary of State to direct appointment of members of committees) or pursuant to regulations under subsection (6) of that section.

(5A) Nothing in this section shall prevent the appointment of a council manager of a local authority, or one other officer of that local authority in his place, as a voting member of a joint committee, or a subcommittee of such a committee, where

      (a) that local authority have a mayor and council manager executive; and

      (b) the joint committee or the subcommittee has been appointed for the purpose of discharging functions which, as respects that local authority, are the responsibility of that executive.

(6) *Repealed*

(7) Where a person is treated by virtue of this section as a nonvoting member of any committee, joint committee or subcommittee, he shall not be entitled to vote at any meeting of the committee, joint committee or subcommittee on any question which falls to be decided at that meeting; and the reference in subsection (5) above to a voting member, in relation to any committee, joint committee or subcommittee appointed for the purpose mentioned in that subsection, is a reference to a person who is entitled to vote at any meeting of that committee or subcommittee on any question which falls to be decided at that meeting.

(8) *Repealed*

(9) In this section

    "council manager", "executive" and "mayor and council manager executive" have the same meaning as in Part II of the Local Government Act 2000 (arrangements with respect to executives etc);

    "education functions" has the meaning given by section 579(1) of the Education Act 1996; and

    "relevant authority" means a local authority of any of the descriptions specified in paragraphs (a) to (f) or (h) to (jb) , (h) to (jb) or (n) of section 21(1) below or any parish or community council;

and references in this section to voting include references to making use of a casting vote.

NOTES

Subordinate Legislation
Local Government (Committees and Political Groups) Regulations 1990, SI 1990/1553
Parish and Community Councils (Committees) Regulations 1990, SI 1990/2476

Defined terms
local authority: s 21(1), (2)

Voting rights of members of certain committees: Scotland

14(1) Subject to the following provisions of this section, a person who

    (a) is a member of a committee appointed under subsection (1) of section 57 of the Local Government (Scotland) Act 1973 by a relevant authority and is not a member of that authority;

    (b) is a member of a joint committee appointed under that subsection by two or more relevant authorities and is not a member of any of those authorities; or

    (c) is a member of a subcommittee appointed under that subsection by such a committee as is mentioned in paragraph (a) or (b) above and is not a member of the relevant authority, or one of the relevant authorities, which appointed that committee,

shall for all purposes be treated as a nonvoting member of that committee, joint committee or, as the case may be, subcommittee.

(2)-(3) *Repealed*

(4) Nothing in subsection (1) above shall require a person to be treated as a nonvoting member of a committee or subcommittee falling within subsection (5) below; but, except

    (a) in the case of a subcommittee appointed by a committee falling within paragraph (b) of that subsection; and

    (b) in such cases as may be prescribed by regulations made by the Secretary of State,

a person who is a member of a subcommittee falling within that subsection shall for all purposes be treated as a nonvoting member of that subcommittee unless he is a member of the committee which appointed the subcommittee.

(5) A committee or subcommittee falls within this subsection if it is

    (a) a committee established in accordance with any regulations made by virtue of section 7 of the Superannuation Act 1972 (regulations making provision for the superannuation of persons employed in local government service etc);

    (b) a committee appointed under section 57(4) of the Local Government (Scotland) Act 1973 (appointment of advisory committees by local authorities);

    (c) a committee constituted in accordance with Schedule A1 to the Education (Scotland) Act 1980 (appeal committees for hearing placing and other appeals);

    (d) *Repealed*

    (e) a committee established exclusively for the purpose of discharging such functions of a relevant authority as may be prescribed by regulations made by the Secretary of State;

    (f) a subcommittee appointed by a committee falling within any of paragraphs (a) to (c) or (e) above or such a subcommittee as is so prescribed.

(6) Nothing in this section shall prevent the appointment as a voting member of

    (a) a committee such as is mentioned in subsection (1) of section 124 of the Local Government (Scotland) Act 1973 (committees appointed by education authority); or

    (b) a joint committee of two or more authorities whose purposes include either of those mentioned in paragraphs (a) and (b) of that subsection; or

    (c) any subcommittee of such a committee or joint committee,

of a person such as is mentioned in subsection (4) of the said section 124.

(7) Where a person is treated by virtue of this section as a nonvoting member of any committee, joint committee or subcommittee, he shall not be entitled to vote at any meeting of the committee, joint committee or subcommittee on any question which falls to be decided at that meeting; and the reference in subsection (6) above to a voting member, in relation to any such committee, joint committee or subcommittee as is mentioned in that subsection, is a reference to a person who is entitled to vote at any meeting of that committee, joint committee or subcommittee on any question which falls to be decided at that meeting.

(8)   *Repealed*

(9)   In this section "relevant authority" means a council constituted under section 2 of the Local Government etc (Scotland) Act 1994; and references in this section to voting include references to making use of a casting vote.

15-20   *Not reproduced*

Interpretation of Part I

Interpretation of Part I

21(1)   Any reference in this Part to a local authority is, in relation to England and Wales, a reference to a body of one of the following descriptions

    (a)   a county council;

    (aa) a county borough council;

    (b)   a district council;

    (c)   a London borough council;

    (d)   the Common Council of the City of London in its capacity as a local authority, police authority or port health authority;

    (e)   the Council of the Isles of Scilly;

    (f)   a fire and rescue authority constituted by a scheme under section 2 of the Fire and Rescue Services Act 2004 or a scheme to which section 4 of that Act applies;

    (g)   *Repealed*

    (ga) *Repealed*

    (h)   an authority established under section 10 of the Local Government Act 1985 (waste disposal authorities);

    (i)   a joint authority established by Part IV of that Act (fire and rescue services and transport) or the London Fire and Emergency Planning Authority;

    (j)   any body established pursuant to an order under section 67 of that Act (successors to residuary bodies);

    (ja) an economic prosperity board established under section 88 of the Local Democracy, Economic Development and Construction Act 2009;

    (jb) a combined authority established under section 103 of that Act

    (k)   the Broads Authority;

    (l)   any joint board the constituent members of which consist of any of the bodies specified above;

    (m)   *Repealed*; and

    (n)   a joint planning board constituted for an area in Wales outside a National Park by an order under section 2(1B) of the Town and Country Planning Act 1990.

(2)   Any reference in this Part to a local authority is, in relation to Scotland, a reference to a council constituted under section 2 of the Local Government etc (Scotland) Act 1994 or a joint board within the meaning of section 235(1) of the Local Government (Scotland) Act 1973.

(3)   In this Part

    "contravention" includes a failure to comply;

    "council manager", "executive", "executive arrangements" and "mayor and council manager executive" have the same meaning as in Part II of the Local Government Act 2000;

    "modifications" includes additions, alterations and omissions;

    "proper officer"

        (a)   in relation to a local authority in England and Wales, has the same meaning as in the Local Government Act 1972; and

    (b) in relation to a local authority in Scotland, has the same meaning as in the Local Government (Scotland) Act 1973; and

"subordinate legislation" has the same meaning as in the Interpretation Act 1978.

(4) References in this Part to an officer of a local authority or to a paid office under a local authority do not include references to, or to the office of, the chairman or vice-chairman of the authority (whether referred to as such, as mayor, Lord Mayor, deputy mayor, as Lord Provost or otherwise) or a member of any executive of the authority (other than a council manager).

Local Government and Public Involvement in Health Act 2007

An Act to make provision with respect to local government and the functions and procedures of local authorities and certain other authorities; to make provision with respect to persons with functions of inspection and audit in relation to local government; to establish the Valuation Tribunal for England; to make provision in connection with local involvement networks; to abolish Patients' Forums and the Commission for Patient and Public Involvement in Health; to make provision with respect to local consultation in connection with health services; and for connected purposes.

30th October 2007

PART 1
STRUCTURAL AND BOUNDARY CHANGE IN ENGLAND

CHAPTER 1
STRUCTURAL AND BOUNDARY CHANGE

CHAPTER 2
CONTROL OF DISPOSALS ETC

PART 2
ELECTORAL ARRANGEMENTS

CHAPTER 1
POWER OF DISTRICT COUNCILS IN ENGLAND TO CHANGE ELECTORAL SCHEME

PART 1
STRUCTURAL AND BOUNDARY CHANGE IN ENGLAND

CHAPTER 1
STRUCTURAL AND BOUNDARY CHANGE

Change from two tiers to single tier of local government

"Principal authority" and "single tier of local government"

1(1)　For the purposes of this Chapter, each of the following is a "principal authority"
    (a)　a county council in England;
    (b)　a district council in England.

(2)　For the purposes of this Chapter there is "a single tier of local government" for an area if
    (a)　there is a county council and no district councils for that area; or
    (b)　there is a district council and no county council for that area.

(3)　For the purposes of subsection (2)(b) there is a county council "for" an area which is a district if there is a county council which has in relation to that area the functions of a county council.

Invitations and directions for proposals for single tier of local government

2(1)　The Secretary of State may invite or direct any principal authority to make one of the following proposals
    (a)　a Type A proposal;
    (b)　a Type B proposal;
    (c)　a Type C proposal;
    (d)　a combined proposal.

(2)　A Type A proposal is a proposal that there should be a single tier of local government for the area which is the county concerned.

(3)　A Type B proposal is a proposal that there should be a single tier of local government for an area which
    (a)　is currently a district, or two or more districts, in the county concerned; and
    (b)　is specified in the proposal.

(4)　A Type C proposal is a proposal that there should be a single tier of local government for an area specified in the proposal which currently consists of
    (a)　the county concerned or one or more districts in the county concerned; and
    (b)　one or more relevant adjoining areas.

(5)　A combined proposal is a proposal that consists of
    (a)　two or more Type B proposals,
    (b)　two or more Type C proposals, or
    (c)　one or more Type B proposals and one or more Type C proposals,
but a proposal is not a combined proposal if it includes any Type B or C proposals that are alternatives.

(6)　In this section "the county concerned" means
    (a)　in relation to a principal authority which is the council for a county, that county;
    (b)　in relation to a principal authority which is the council for a district, the county in which the district is.

(7)　In this section a "relevant adjoining area" means an area which adjoins the county concerned and is currently a county in England, a district in England, or two or more such counties or districts.

(8)　An invitation or direction may either

   (a) be such that the authority may choose whether to make a Type A, Type B, Type C or combined proposal; or

   (b) specify which one of those kinds of proposal is invited (or, in the case of a direction, required).

(9)   Subsection (1) is subject to section 3(1).

NOTES

Defined terms
   principal authority: ss 1(1), 23(1)
   a single tier of local government: s 1(2)

Invitations, directions and proposals: supplementary

3(1)   A direction under section 2

   (a) may not be given after 25 January 2008; and

   (b) may be given on or before that date only where the Secretary of State believes that giving the direction would be in the interests of effective and convenient local government.

(2)   A direction under section 2 may specify a date by which a proposal must be made.

(3)   An invitation under section 2 may specify a date by which a proposal may be made.

(4)   A proposal made by virtue of section 2 may not specify an area as one for which there should be a single tier of local government unless the whole or any part of that area is currently a two-tier area (as defined by section 23(2)).

(5)   In responding to an invitation under section 2, or complying with a direction under that section, an authority must have regard to any guidance from the Secretary of State as to

   (a) what a proposal should seek to achieve;

   (b) matters that should be taken into account in formulating a proposal.

(6)   Where invitations or directions under section 2 are given to more than one authority, any authority that has received an invitation or direction may respond to the invitation, or comply with the direction, either by

   (a) making its own proposal in accordance with the invitation or direction; or

   (b) making a proposal, in accordance with the invitation or direction, jointly with any of the other authorities.

(7)   An invitation or direction under section 2 may be varied or revoked.

(8)   But a direction under section 2 may not be varied after 25 January 2008 if

   (a) the direction as originally given required the making of a Type A or Type B proposal; and

   (b) the direction as varied would require or permit the making of a Type C or combined proposal.

NOTES

Defined terms
   combined proposal: ss 2(5), 23(1)   Type B proposal: ss 2(3), 23(1)
   in response to: s 23(3)   Type C proposal: ss 2(4), 23(1)
   a single tier of local government: s 1(2)
   Type A proposal: ss 2(2), 23(1)

Request for Local Government Boundary Commission's advice

4(1)   This section applies where the Secretary of State receives a proposal in response to an invitation or direction under section 2.

(2)   The Secretary of State may request the Local Government Boundary Commission to advise, no later than a date specified in the request, on any matter that

   (a) relates to the proposal; and

   (b) is specified in the request.

(3)   The Secretary of State may at any time substitute a later date for the date specified in a request under subsection (2) (or for any date previously substituted under this subsection).

NOTES
Defined terms
  in response to: s 23(3)
  the Local Government Boundary Commission: s 23(1)

Local Government Boundary Commission's powers

5(1)   This section applies where the Local Government Boundary Commission receive a request for advice under section 4.

(2)   The Local Government Boundary Commission may provide the advice requested.

(3)   Where they provide that advice, the Local Government Boundary Commission may also do any of the following that they think appropriate
(a)   recommend that the Secretary of State implements the proposal without modification;
(b)   recommend that he does not implement it;
(c)   make an alternative proposal to him.

(4)   In subsection (3)(a) "the proposal" means the Type A, Type B, Type C or combined proposal to which the request for advice related.

(5)   In subsection (3)(c) "an alternative proposal" means
(a)   a proposal that there should be a single tier of local government for an area that
(i)   is, or includes, the whole or part of the county concerned; and
(ii)   is specified in the alternative proposal; or
(b)   a proposal consisting of two or more proposals that are within paragraph (a) (and are not alternatives to one another).

(6)   In this section "the county concerned" means
(a)   the county that, under section 2(6), is the county concerned in relation to the authority which made the proposal referred to in subsection (4) above; or
(b)   where that proposal was made by more than one authority, any county that (under section 2(6)) is the county concerned in relation to any of the authorities which made that proposal.

(7)   The area specified in an alternative proposal under this section may not extend into any area that is currently outside all local government areas.

NOTES
Defined terms
  combined proposal: ss 2(5), 23(1)
  local government area: s 23(1)
  the Local Government Boundary Commission: s 23(1)
  a single tier of local government: s 1(2)

Type A proposal: ss 2(2), 23(1)
Type B proposal: ss 2(3), 23(1)
Type C proposal: ss 2(4), 23(1)

Local Government Boundary Commission's procedure

6(1)   A local authority must if requested by the Local Government Boundary Commission to do so provide the Commission, by such date as the Commission may specify, with any information that the Commission may reasonably require in connection with any of their functions under section 5.

(2)   In making a recommendation or alternative proposal under section 5 the Local Government Boundary Commission must have regard to any guidance from the Secretary of State about the exercise of the Commission's functions under that section.

(3)   Any recommendation or alternative proposal under section 5 must be made no later than the relevant date.

(4) Before making an alternative proposal under section 5(3)(c) the Local Government Boundary Commission must
    (a) publish a draft of the proposal; and
    (b) take such steps as they consider sufficient to secure that persons who may be interested are informed of
        (i) the draft proposal; and
        (ii) the period within which representations about it may be made to the Commission.

(5) The Local Government Boundary Commission
    (a) must take into account any representations made to them within that period; and
    (b) if they make any proposal to the Secretary of State, must inform any person who made such representations
        (i) of the proposal made; and
        (ii) that representations about the proposal may be made to the Secretary of State until the end of the relevant period.

(6) In subsection (5)(b) "the relevant period" means four weeks beginning with the relevant date.

(7) In this section and section 7 "the relevant date" means the date specified in the request under section 4(2) (or, if a later date is substituted under section 4(3), the date substituted (or last substituted) under that provision).

NOTES
Defined terms
  local authority: s 23(1)
  the Local Government Boundary Commission: s 23(1)

Implementation of proposals by order

7(1) Where the Secretary of State has received a proposal in response to an invitation or direction under section 2, he may
    (a) by order implement the proposal, with or without modification;
    (b) if he has received an alternative proposal from the Local Government Boundary Commission under section 5, by order implement that alternative proposal with or without modification; or
    (c) decide to take no action.

(2) But where the Secretary of State has made a request under section 4 in relation to the proposal received in response to the invitation or direction, he may not make an order or decision under this section before the end of six weeks beginning with the relevant date (as defined by section 6(7)).

(3) The Secretary of State may not in any case make an order under subsection (1)(a) implementing a proposal unless he has consulted the following about the proposal
    (a) every authority affected by the proposal (except the authority or authorities which made it); and
    (b) such other persons as he considers appropriate.

(4) For the purposes of this section an authority is "affected by" a proposal if it is a principal authority for an area which is, or any part of which is, in an area that the proposal suggests should have a single tier of local government.

(5) Subsection (3) does not apply if the proposal was made jointly by every authority affected by it, and in that case the Secretary of State may before making an order under subsection (1)(a) (or deciding not to) consult such other persons as he considers appropriate.

(6) In any case where he has received an alternative proposal from the Local Government Boundary Commission under section 5, the Secretary of State may request the

Commission to provide him with information or advice on any matter relating to the proposal.

(7) Where they receive such a request the Local Government Boundary Commission may provide the information or advice requested.

NOTES

Subordinate Legislation

Local Government (Structural Changes) (Areas and Membership of Public Bodies in Bedfordshire and Cheshire) Order 2009, SI 2009/119.
Local Government (Structural Changes) (Miscellaneous Amendments and Other Provision) Order 2009, SI 2009/837.

Defined terms

in response to: s 23(3)
the Local Government Boundary Commission: s 23(1)
principal authority: ss 1(1), 23(1)
a single tier of local government: s 1(2)

Boundary change

Review by Local Government Boundary Commission of local government areas

8(1) The Local Government Boundary Commission may, either on their own initiative or at the request of the Secretary of State or a local authority, conduct a review of one or more local government areas.

(2) Where they have conducted a review under this section the Local Government Boundary Commission may (subject to subsection (4)) recommend to the Secretary of State such boundary change as in consequence of the review seems to them desirable.

(3) For the purposes of this section "boundary change" means any of the following or any combination of the following
   (a) the alteration of a local government area boundary;
   (b) the abolition of a local government area;
   (c) the constitution of a new local government area.

(4) None of the following may be recommended under this section
   (a) a change consisting of the alteration of the boundary of a single-tier area and consequent abolition of an area that is currently two-tier;
   (b) a change consisting of the alteration of the boundary of a two-tier area and consequent abolition of an area that is currently single-tier;
   (c) a change consisting of the constitution of a new local government area and consequent abolition of an existing local government area, where the new local government area would include
      (i) the whole or part of any area that is currently single-tier; and
      (ii) the whole or part of any area that is currently two-tier;
   (d) a change consisting of the alteration of a local government area, or constitution of a new local government area, where the altered or new area would extend into an area that is currently outside all local government areas;
   (e) a change whose effect would be that England (excluding the Isles of Scilly, the City of London, the Inner Temple and the Middle Temple) is no longer divided into areas each of which is
      (i) a county divided into districts, or comprising one district; or
      (ii) a London borough.

(5) Where the Local Government Boundary Commission have conducted a review under this section and consider that no boundary change is desirable, they may recommend to the Secretary of State that no boundary change should be made.

(6) In considering whether (and, if so, what) boundary change is desirable, the Local Government Boundary Commission must have regard to
   (a) the need to secure effective and convenient local government; and
   (b) the need to reflect the identities and interests of local communities.

(6A) Where under subsection (2) the Local Government Boundary Commission recommend that a boundary change should be made in relation to any local government area, the Commission must recommend to the Secretary of State whether, in consequence, a change should be made to
    (a) the electoral arrangements of the area of a local authority;
    (b) the electoral arrangements of the area of a parish council.

(6B) In subsection (6A)(a) "electoral arrangements", in relation to the area of a local authority means
    (a) the total number of members of the local authority ("councillors");
    (b) the number and boundaries of electoral areas for the purposes of the election of councillors;
    (c) the number of councillors to be returned by any electoral area in that area; and
    (d) the name of any electoral area.

(6C) In subsection (6A)(b) "electoral arrangements", in relation to the area of a parish council means
    (a) the total number of members of the parish council ("parish councillors");
    (b) arrangements for the division of the parish or (in the case of a common parish council) any of the parishes into wards for the purposes of the election of parish councillors;
    (c) the number and boundaries of any wards;
    (d) the number of parish councillors to be returned by any ward or, in the case of a common parish council, by each parish; and
    (e) the name of any ward.

(6D) Schedule 2 to the Local Democracy, Economic Development and Construction Act 2009 applies in relation to the making of recommendations under subsection (6A).

(6E) Where under subsection (2) the Local Government Boundary Commission recommend that a boundary change should be made in relation to the area of a London borough council, the Commission must recommend to the Secretary of State whether, in consequence, a change should be made to the area of any constituency for the London Assembly in order to comply with the rules set out in paragraph 7 of Schedule 1 to the Greater London Authority Act 1999.

(7) In exercising a function under this section, a local authority or the Local Government Boundary Commission must have regard to any guidance from the Secretary of State about the exercise of that function.

(8) A local authority must if requested by the Local Government Boundary Commission to do so provide the Commission, by such date as the Commission may specify, with any information that the Commission may reasonably require in connection with any of their functions under this section.

NOTES

Defined terms
  local authority: s 23(1)
  local government area: s 23(1)
  the Local Government Boundary Commission: s 23(1)

single-tier: s 23(1), (2)
two-tier: s 23(1), (2)

Local Government Boundary Commission's review: consultation etc

9(1) This section applies where the Boundary Committee conduct a review under section 8.

(2) In conducting the review the Local Government Boundary Commission must consult
    (a) the council of any local government area to which the review relates; and
    (b) such other local authorities, parish councils and other persons as appear to them to have an interest.

(3) Before making any recommendation to the Secretary of State the Local Government Boundary Commission must

(a) publish a draft of the recommendation; and

(b) take such steps as they consider sufficient to secure that persons who may be interested are informed of

(i) the draft recommendation; and

(ii) the period within which representations about it may be made to the Commission.

(4) The Local Government Boundary Commission

(a) must take into account any representations made to them within that period; and

(b) if they make any recommendation to the Secretary of State, must inform any person who made such representations

(i) of the recommendation made; and

(ii) that representations about the recommendation may be made to the Secretary of State until the end of four weeks beginning with the recommendation date.

(5) In this section and section 10 "the recommendation date" means the date the recommendation was sent by the Local Government Boundary Commission to the Secretary of State.

NOTES

Defined terms
local authority: s 23(1)
local government area: s 23(1)
the Local Government Boundary Commission: s 23(1)

Implementation of recommendations by order

10(1) Where the Local Government Boundary Commission make a recommendation to the Secretary of State under section 8(2), the Secretary of State may do any of the following

(a) by order implement the recommendation, with or without modification;

(b) decide to take no action with respect to the recommendation;

(c) make a request under section 8 for a further review.

(2) Where the Local Government Boundary Commission make a recommendation to the Secretary of State under section 8(5) the Secretary of State may

(a) make a request under section 8 for a further review; or

(b) decide not to make such a request.

(2A) Subsections (2B) to (2D) apply where the Local Government Boundary Commission make a recommendation to the Secretary of State under section 8(6A) or (6E) in consequence of a recommendation under section 8(2).

(2B) Where under subsection (1)(a) the Secretary of State implements the recommendation under section 8(2) without modification, the Secretary of State must by order implement the recommendation under section 8(6A) or (6E).

(2C) Where pursuant to subsection (1)(a) the Secretary of State proposes to implement the recommendation under section 8(2) with modification, the Secretary of State must request the Local Government Boundary Commission to recommend whether a modification is needed to their recommendation under section 8(6A) or (6E).

(2D) Where under section (1)(a) the Secretary of State implements a recommendation under section 8(2) with modification

(a) if the Local Government Boundary Commission have recommended under subsection (2C) that a modification is needed to their recommendation under section 8(6A) or (6E), the Secretary of State must by order implement the recommendation under section 8(6A) or (6E) with that modification;

(b) if the Local Government Boundary Commission have recommended under subsection (2C) that no modification is needed to the recommendation under section 8(6A) or (6E), the Secretary of State must by order implement that recommendation.

(3) The Secretary of State may not do as mentioned in paragraph (a), (b) or (c) of subsection (1) or paragraph (a) or (b) of subsection (2) before the end of six weeks beginning with the recommendation date (as defined by section 9(5)).

(4) Before doing as mentioned in any of those paragraphs the Secretary of State may request the Local Government Boundary Commission to provide him with information or advice on any matter relating to the recommendation.

(5) Where they receive such a request the Local Government Boundary Commission may provide the information or advice requested.

NOTES

Defined terms
the Local Government Boundary Commission: s 23(1)

Implementation of changes

Implementation orders: provision that may be included

11(1) An order under section 7 or 10 may in particular include provision, for the purpose of implementing a proposal or recommendation or in connection with the implementation of a proposal or recommendation, for or with respect to
(a) any of the matters mentioned in subsection (3);
(b) any of the matters mentioned in subsection (4) (incidental, consequential etc matters).

(2) In subsection (1) "implementing" includes implementing with modifications and "implementation" is to be read accordingly.

(3) The matters referred to in subsection (1)(a) are
(a) the constitution of a new local government area;
(b) the abolition of any existing local government area;
(c) the boundary of any local government area;
(d) whether a county or district is to be metropolitan or non-metropolitan;
(e) the establishment, as a county council, district council or London borough council, of an authority for any local government area;
(f) the winding up and dissolution of an existing local authority;
(g) the transfer to a county council of the functions, in relation to an area, of district councils;
(h) the transfer to a district council of the functions, in relation to an area, of a county council;
(i) electoral matters within the meaning of section 12.

(4) The matters referred to in subsection (1)(b) are
(a) the name of any local government area;
(b) the name of any local authority;
(c) the boundary of any parish;
(d) *Repealed*
(e) the establishment or membership of public bodies in any area affected by the order and the election of members of such bodies;
(f) the abolition or establishment, or the restriction or extension, of the jurisdiction of any public body in or over any part of any area affected by the order;
(g) the boundary of any police area in England.

(5) For the purposes of subsection (3)(e)

    (a) the "establishment" of an authority as a council for a county includes an existing district council's becoming the county council for the county;

    (b) the "establishment" of an authority as a council for a district includes an existing county council's becoming the district council for the district.

(6) The power of the Secretary of State under section 7(1)(a) to implement a proposal with modifications includes power to make provision whose effect is that there will be a single tier of local government for an area ("the area concerned") that

    (a) includes all or part of an area specified in the proposal as one for which there should be a single tier of local government; but

    (b) is not an area that could itself have been so specified.

(7) But subsection (6) does not authorise the area concerned to extend into any area that is currently outside all local government areas.

NOTES

Subordinate Legislation

Local Government (Structural Changes) (Areas and Membership of Public Bodies in Bedfordshire and Cheshire) Order 2009, SI 2009/119.

Local Government (Structural Changes) (Miscellaneous Amendments and Other Provision) Order 2009, SI 2009/837.

Defined terms

local authority: s 23(1)

local government area: s 23(1)

public body: s 23(1)

a single tier of local government: s 1(2)

Provision relating to membership etc of authorities

12(1) In section 11(3) "electoral matters" means any of the following

    (a) the total number of members of any local authority or parish council ("councillors");

    (b) the number and boundaries of electoral areas for the purposes of the election of councillors;

    (c) the number of councillors to be returned by any electoral area;

    (d) the name of any electoral area;

    (e) the election of councillors for any electoral areas;

    (f) the order of retirement of councillors;

    (g) the election of a mayor of a local authority;

    (h) the election of an executive of a local authority;

    (i) the appointment by the Secretary of State of members of an existing local authority to be members of a new local authority for a transitional period;

    (j) the appointment for a transitional period of an executive of a new local authority;

    (k) the functions of a new local authority, and the discharge of those functions, during a transitional period;

    (l) the ordinary year of election for a parish council.

(2) In subsection (1)(i) to (k)

    "a new local authority" means a local authority established by the order;

    "a transitional period" means a period before the coming into office of members of the authority elected at the first election after the establishment of the authority.

(3) In subsection (2) "established" and "establishment" are to be read in accordance with section 11(5).

(4) An order under section 7 or 10 may provide for an electoral division of a non-metropolitan county to return more than one councillor, and in such a case section 6(2)(a) of the Local Government Act 1972 (c 70) does not apply.

(5) As soon as practicable after the making of an order under section 7 or 10, the Local Government Boundary Commission must consider whether to exercise its power under

section 56(2) of the Local Democracy, Economic Development and Construction Act 2009 (electoral reviews).

(6)   *Repealed*

NOTES
Defined terms
  local authority: s 23(1)
  the Local Government Boundary Commission: s 23(1)

Implementation orders: further provision

13(1)   The power to make an order under section 7 or 10 includes (as well as power to make any provision authorised by section 11(1)(b)) power to make any other incidental, consequential, transitional or supplementary provision.

(2)   Subsection (1) is to be read with section 15.

(3)   Any incidental, consequential, transitional or supplementary provision included in an order under section 7 or 10 may relate either to other provisions of the order or to a previous order under section 7 or 10 (and the reference in section 12(2) to "the order" accordingly includes a previous order under section 7 or 10).

(4)   The Secretary of State must exercise his powers under section 11(4)(g) in such a way as to ensure that none of the following is divided between two or more police areas
   (a)   a county in which there are no district councils;
   (b)   a district;
   (c)   a London borough.

PART 2
ELECTORAL ARRANGEMENTS

CHAPTER 1
POWER OF DISTRICT COUNCILS IN ENGLAND TO CHANGE ELECTORAL SCHEME

Introductory

Schemes for elections

31   For the purposes of this Chapter
   (a)   a council is "subject to a scheme for whole-council elections" if all of its councillors are to be elected in each year in which it holds ordinary elections of councillors;
   (b)   a council is "subject to a scheme for elections by halves" if one-half (or as nearly as may be) of its councillors are to be elected in each year in which it holds ordinary elections of councillors;
   (c)   a council is "subject to a scheme for elections by thirds" if one-third (or as nearly as may be) of its councillors are to be elected in each year in which it holds ordinary elections of councillors.

Minimum period between resolutions to change electoral schemes

31A   If a council passes a resolution under section 32, 37 or 39 ("the earlier resolution") it may not pass another resolution under any of those sections before the end of five years beginning with the day on which the earlier resolution is passed.

Power of district councils to change to whole-council elections

Resolution for whole-council elections

32(1) A district council in England that is subject to a scheme for elections by halves or by thirds may resolve that it is to be subject instead to the scheme for whole-council elections under section 34.

(2) A resolution under this section is referred to in this Chapter as a "resolution for whole-council elections".

NOTES
Defined terms   subject to a scheme for whole-council elections: s 31(a)
 subject to a scheme for elections by halves: s 31(b)
 subject to a scheme for elections by thirds: s 31(c)

Resolution for whole-council elections: requirements

33(1) A council must comply with this section in passing a resolution for whole-council elections.

(2) The council must not pass the resolution unless it has taken reasonable steps to consult such persons as it thinks appropriate on the proposed change.

(3) The resolution must be passed
    (a) at a meeting which is specially convened for the purpose of deciding the resolution with notice of the object, and
    (b) by a majority of at least two thirds of the members voting on it.

(3A) The resolution must specify the year for the first ordinary elections of the council at which all councillors are to be elected.

(3B) In the case of a district council for a district in a county for which there is a county council, the year specified under subsection (3A) may not be a county-council-elections year; and here "county-council-elections year" means 2013 and every fourth year afterwards.

(4) *Repealed*

(5) In subsection (3) the reference to the members of the council includes, in a case where the council are operating a mayor and cabinet executive, the elected mayor of the council.

(6) *Repealed*

(7) *Repealed*

NOTES
Defined terms
 resolution for whole-council elections: s 32(2)

Scheme for whole-council elections

34(1) On passing a resolution for whole-council elections, a council becomes subject to the following electoral scheme.

(2) Ordinary elections of the councillors of the council are to be held in
    (a) the year specified under section 33(3A) in the resolution, and
    (b) every fourth year afterwards.

(3) All councillors are to be elected in each year in which ordinary elections are held.

(4) On the fourth day after ordinary elections are held
    (a) the councillors elected in those elections are to come into office, and
    (b) the sitting councillors are to retire.

(4A) Ordinary elections of councillors of the council under the previous electoral scheme are to be held in accordance with that scheme in any year that
    (a) is earlier than the year specified under section 33(3A) in the resolution for whole-council elections, and

(b) is a year in which, under the previous electoral scheme, ordinary elections of councillors of the council are due to be held.

(4B) In subsection (4A) "the previous electoral scheme" means the scheme for the ordinary elections of councillors of the council that applied to it immediately before it passed the resolution for whole-council elections.

(5) Repealed

(6) Repealed

NOTES
Defined terms
  resolution for whole-council elections: s 32(2)

Publicity

35(1) A council must comply with this section as soon as practicable after passing a resolution for whole-council elections.

(2) The council must produce an explanatory document.

(3) The council must make the explanatory document
  (a) available for public inspection at the council's principal office at all reasonable times, and
  (b) available to the public by such other means as the council thinks appropriate.

(4) The council must publicise these matters
  (a) that the council has become subject to the scheme for whole-council elections under section 34;
  (b) when elections will first take place in accordance with the scheme;
  (c) how the explanatory document is available in accordance with subsection (3);
  (d) the address of the council's principal office.

(5) It is for the council to decide how those matters are to be publicised.

(6) An explanatory document is a document which sets out details of the new electoral scheme as it applies to the council.

NOTES
Defined terms
  resolution for whole-council elections: s 32(2)

Notice to Local Government Boundary Commission for England

36(1) A council must comply with this section as soon as practicable after passing a resolution for whole-council elections.

(2) The council must give the Local Government Boundary Commission notice that it has passed the resolution.

(3) In this Chapter, "Local Government Boundary Commission" means the Local Government Boundary Commission for England.

NOTES
Defined terms
  resolution for whole-council elections: s 32(2)

Power of district councils to revert to partial-council elections

Resolution for elections by halves

37(1) A non-metropolitan district council in England that
  (a) was formerly subject to a scheme for elections by halves, but
  (b) is for the time being subject to a scheme for whole-council elections,

may resolve that it is to revert to being subject to a scheme for elections by halves.

(2)   For the purposes of this section, a council that is subject to a scheme for whole-council elections was "formerly subject" to a scheme for elections by halves if it was subject to such a scheme at any time in the period beginning with

    (a)   1 April 1974, or

    (b)   if later, the date on which the council was created.

(3)   A resolution under this section is referred to in this Chapter as a "resolution for elections by halves".

NOTES
Defined terms
    subject to a scheme for elections by halves: s 31(b)
    subject to a scheme for whole-council elections: s 31(a)

Resolution for elections by halves: requirements

38(1)   A council must comply with this section in passing a resolution for elections by halves.

(2)   The council must not pass the resolution unless it has taken reasonable steps to consult such persons as it thinks appropriate on the proposed change.

(3)   The resolution must be passed

    (a)   at a meeting which is specially convened for the purpose of deciding the resolution with notice of the object, and

    (b)   by a majority of at least two thirds of the members voting on it.

(4)   *Repealed*

(5)   In subsection (3) the reference to the members of the council includes, in a case where the council are operating a mayor and cabinet executive, the elected mayor of the council.

(6)   *Repealed*

(7)   *Repealed*

NOTES
Defined terms
    resolution for elections by halves: s 37(3)

Resolution for elections by thirds

39(1)   A district council in England that

    (a)   was formerly subject to a scheme for elections by thirds, but

    (b)   is for the time being subject to a scheme for whole-council elections,

may resolve that it is to revert to being subject to a scheme for elections by thirds.

(2)   For the purposes of this section, a council that is subject to a scheme for whole-council elections was "formerly subject" to a scheme for elections by thirds if it was subject to such a scheme at any time in the period beginning with

    (a)   1 April 1974, or

    (b)   if later, the date on which the council was created.

(3)   A resolution under this section is referred to in this Chapter as a "resolution for elections by thirds".

NOTES
Defined terms
    subject to a scheme for elections by thirds: s 31(c)
    subject to a scheme for whole-council elections: s 31(a)

Resolution for elections by thirds: requirements

40(1)   A council must comply with this section in passing a resolution for elections by thirds.

(2) The council must not pass the resolution unless it has taken reasonable steps to consult such persons as it thinks appropriate on the proposed change.

(3) The resolution must be passed
 (a) at a meeting which is specially convened for the purpose of deciding the resolution with notice of the object, and
 (b) by a majority of at least two thirds of the members voting on it.

(4) *Repealed*

(5) In subsection (3) the reference to the members of the council includes, in a case where the council are operating a mayor and cabinet executive, the elected mayor of the council.

(6) *Repealed*

(7) *Repealed*

NOTES
Defined terms
  resolution for elections by thirds: s 39(3)

Publicity for resolution

41(1) A council must comply with this section as soon as practicable after passing a resolution for elections by halves or a resolution for elections by thirds.

(2) The council must produce an explanatory document.

(3) The council must make the explanatory document
 (a) available for public inspection at the council's principal office at all reasonable times, and
 (b) available to the public by such other means as the council thinks appropriate.

(4) The council must publicise these matters
 (a) that the council has resolved to become subject to the new electoral scheme;
 (b) that the Local Government Boundary Commission is to make provision by order about the operation of, and transition to, the new electoral scheme;
 (c) how the explanatory document is available in accordance with subsection (3);
 (d) the address of the council's principal office.

(5) It is for the council to decide how these matters are to be publicised.

(6) An explanatory document is a document which sets out details of the new electoral scheme (so far as the details are known at the time the document is prepared).

NOTES
Defined terms   resolution for elections by thirds: s 39(3)
  Local Government Boundary Commission: s 36(3)
  resolution for elections by halves: s 37(3)

Notice to Local Government Boundary Commission

42(1) A council must comply with this section as soon as practicable after passing a resolution for elections by halves or a resolution for elections by thirds.

(2) The council must give the Local Government Boundary Commission notice that it has passed the resolution.

NOTES
Defined terms   resolution for elections by thirds: s 39(3)
  Local Government Boundary Commission: s 36(3)
  resolution for elections by halves: s 37(3)

Local Government Boundary Commission to consider whether electoral review is necessary

43(1) This section applies if the Local Government Boundary Commission receive notice under section 42 that a council has passed a resolution for elections by halves or a resolution for elections by thirds.

(2) As soon as practicable after receiving the notice, the Local Government Boundary Commission must consider whether to exercise its power under section 56(2) of the Local Democracy, Economic Development and Construction Act 2009 to conduct a review of the district in question (or any part of it).

(3) As soon as practicable after deciding whether or not to conduct such a review, the Local Government Boundary Commission must give the council notice of the decision.

NOTES
Defined terms
  Local Government Boundary Commission: s 36(3)
  resolution for elections by halves: s 37(3)

resolution for elections by thirds: s 39(3)

Local Government Boundary Commission to make order for new electoral scheme

44(1) Where the Local Government Boundary Commission receive notice under section 42 that a council has passed a resolution, they must
    (a) in the case of a resolution for elections by halves, make an order for elections by halves in relation to the council (see sections 45 and 46);
    (b) in the case of a resolution for elections by thirds, make an order for elections by thirds in relation to the council (see sections 47 and 48).

(2) But the Local Government Boundary Commission must not make the order
    (a) before it has decided whether or not conduct an electoral review (see section 43(2)), and
    (b) if it has decided to conduct such a review, before the review is concluded.

NOTES
Defined terms
  Local Government Boundary Commission: s 36(3)
  resolution for elections by halves: s 37(3)

resolution for elections by thirds: s 39(3)

Order for elections by halves: years in which elections are to be held

45(1) An order for elections by halves in relation to a council must secure that the ordinary elections of councillors of the council are held in years determined in accordance with this section.

(2) Ordinary elections of the councillors of the council are to be held in
    (a) the first relevant year after the year in which the Local Government Boundary Commission makes the order, and
    (b) each subsequent year for elections by halves.

(3) In this section
    "relevant year" means 2011 and every fourth year afterwards;
    "year for elections by halves" means 2012 and every second year afterwards.

NOTES
Defined terms
  Local Government Boundary Commission: s 36(3)

Orders for elections by halves: councillors to be elected at ordinary elections

46(1) An order for elections by halves in relation to a council must make provision for the election and retirement of councillors in accordance with this section.

(2) In the case of the ordinary elections held in the year determined in accordance with section 45(2)(a)
    (a) all of the councillors are to be elected;

     (b) on the fourth day after the elections are held

        (i)   the councillors elected in those elections are to come into office, and

        (ii) all of the sitting councillors are to retire.

  (3) In the case of ordinary elections held subsequently

     (a) one half (or as nearly as may be) of the councillors are to be elected;

     (b) on the fourth day after the elections are held

        (i)   the councillors elected in those elections are to come into office, and

        (ii) the specified sitting councillors are to retire.

  (4) The order must include provision for identifying which councillors are to retire in each year in which ordinary elections are to be held (other than the first), including provision for identifying

     (a) the wards affected;

     (b) the councillors affected within particular wards.

  (5) In this section "specified sitting councillors", in relation to ordinary elections, means the sitting councillors who are to retire in the year of those elections by virtue of the order.

Order for elections by thirds: years in which elections are to be held

47(1) An order for elections by thirds in relation to a council must secure that the ordinary elections of councillors of the council are held in years determined in accordance with this section.

  (2) Ordinary elections of the councillors of the council are to be held in

     (a) the first relevant year after the year in which the Electoral Commission make Local Government Boundary Commission makes the order, and

     (b) each subsequent year, unless it is a fallow year.

  (3) In this section

     "fallow year" means 2013 and every fourth year afterwards;

     "relevant year" means

        (a) in relation to a metropolitan district council: 2014 and every fourth year afterwards;

        (b) in relation to a non-metropolitan district council: 2011 and every fourth year afterwards.

NOTES

Defined terms

  Local Government Boundary Commission: s 36(3)

Order for elections by thirds: councillors to be elected at ordinary elections

48(1) An order for elections by thirds in relation to a council must make provision for the election and retirement of councillors in accordance with this section.

  (2) In the case of the ordinary elections held in the year determined in accordance with section 47(2)(a)

     (a) all of the councillors are to be elected;

     (b) on the fourth day after the elections are held

        (i)   the councillors elected in those elections are to come into office, and

        (ii) all of the sitting councillors are to retire.

  (3) In the case of ordinary elections held subsequently

     (a) one third (or as nearly as may be) of the councillors are to be elected;

     (b) on the fourth day after the elections are held

        (i)   the councillors elected in those elections are to come into office, and

        (ii) the specified sitting councillors are to retire.

(4) The order must include provision for identifying which councillors are to retire in each year in which ordinary elections are to be held (other than the first), including provision for identifying
   (a) the wards affected;
   (b) the councillors affected within particular wards.

(5) In this section "specified sitting councillors", in relation to ordinary elections, means the sitting councillors who are to retire in the year of those elections by virtue of the order.

Order for elections by halves or elections by thirds: transitional provision

49(1) An order under section 44 (order for elections by halves or for elections by thirds) may include provision about the transition to the council's new electoral scheme.

(2) Provision made by virtue of this section may, in particular, include provision for the retirement of some councillors after their initial election at times different from those otherwise applying, and for identifying which of them are so to retire.

Power of Local Government Boundary Commission to make incidental etc provision

50 The Local Government Boundary Commission may by order make incidental, consequential, transitional or supplemental provision in connection with provision made by order under section 44 (order for elections by halves or for elections by thirds).

NOTES
Defined terms
   Local Government Boundary Commission: s 36(3)

Position if Local Government Boundary Commission act under existing powers

51 In a case in which
   (a) the Local Government Boundary Commission decides to conduct an electoral review (see section 43(2)), and
   (b) pursuant to that review the Commission makes recommendations for electoral changes,
nothing in this Chapter requires the Commission to make any provision in relation to matters dealt with, or to be dealt with, by the Commission in an order under section 59 of the Local Democracy, Economic Development and Construction Act 2009 giving effect to those recommendations.

NOTES
Defined terms
   Local Government Boundary Commission: s 36(3)

Publicity for order by Local Government Boundary Commission

52(1) A council must comply with this section as soon as practicable after the Local Government Boundary Commission has made an order under section 44 (order for elections by halves or for elections by thirds) in relation to it.

(2) The council must produce an explanatory document.

(3) The council must make the explanatory document
   (a) available for public inspection at the council's principal office at all reasonable times, and
   (b) available to the public by such other means as the council thinks appropriate.

(4) The council must publicise these matters
   (a) that the council has become subject to the new electoral scheme;
   (b) how the explanatory document is available in accordance with subsection (3);
   (c) the address of the council's principal office.

(5)   It is for the council to decide how these matters are to be publicised.

(6)   An explanatory document is a document which sets out details of the new electoral scheme.

NOTES

Defined terms
    Local Government Boundary Commission: s 36(3)

Power of district councils to alter years of ordinary elections of parish councillors

Power of council to alter years of ordinary elections of parish councillors

53(1)   This section applies if a council passes a resolution under this Chapter.

(2)   The council may by order make provision that changes the years in which the ordinary elections of parish councillors for any parish situated in the council's area are to be held.

(3)   The power may only be exercised so as to secure that those elections are to be held in years in which ordinary elections of district councillors for a ward in which any part of the parish is situated are to be held.

(4)   The order may include transitional provision
    (a)   for the retirement of existing parish councillors at times different from those otherwise applying;
    (b)   for the retirement of some parish councillors after their initial election after the order comes into force at times different from those otherwise applying.

Amendment of existing provisions about schemes for ordinary elections

Amendment of existing provisions about schemes for ordinary elections

54   *Amends various legislation: not reproduced here*

CHAPTER 2
MISCELLANEOUS

55-57   *Repealed*

Electoral areas in England

Metropolitan districts: councillors per ward

58   *Amends the Local Government Act 1972: not reproduced here*

Change of name of electoral area

59(1)   A local authority may, by resolution, change the name of any of the authority's electoral areas.

(2)   A local authority must comply with subsections (3) to (5) in passing a resolution to change the name of an electoral area.

(3)   The local authority must not pass the resolution unless it has taken reasonable steps to consult such persons as it considers appropriate on the proposed name.

(4)   The resolution must be passed
    (a)   at a meeting which is specially convened for the purpose of deciding the resolution with notice of the object, and
    (b)   by a majority of at least two thirds of the members voting on it.

(5) If the name of the electoral area is protected, the resolution may not be passed unless the Local Government Boundary Commission has first agreed to the proposed change.

(6) As soon as practicable after a resolution is passed, the local authority must give notice of the change of name to all of the following
    (a) the Local Government Boundary Commission;
    (b) the Boundary Commission for England;
    (c) the Office of National Statistics;
    (d) the Director General of the Ordnance Survey;
    (e) if the local authority is a county council, the district council (if any) within whose area the electoral area lies;
    (f) if the local authority is a district council, the county council (if any) within whose area the electoral area lies.

(7) The change of name does not take effect until the Local Government Boundary Commission have been given notice of the change.

(8) For the purposes of this section the name of an electoral area is "protected" if
    (a) the name was given to the electoral area by or in pursuance of an order under section 17 of the Local Government Act 1992 (c 19), section 59 of the Local Democracy, Economic Development and Construction Act 2009 or section 14 of the Local Government and Rating Act 1997 (c 29), and
    (b) that order was made during the period of five years ending with the day on which a resolution to change the name is to be passed.

(9) In subsection (4) the reference to the members of the council includes, in a case where the council are operating a mayor and cabinet executive, the elected mayor of the council.

(10) In this section
    "electoral area", in relation to a local authority, means any area for which councillors are elected to the authority;
    "local authority" means
        (a) a county council in England;
        (b) a district council in England; or
        (c) a London borough council.

Election dates

Power to change date of local elections to date of European Parliamentary general election

60   *Amends the Representation of the People Act 1983: not reproduced here*

Lords Spiritual (Women) Act 2015

An Act to make time-limited provision for vacancies among the Lords Spiritual to be filled by bishops who are women.

BE IT ENACTED by the Queen's most Excellent Majesty, by and with the advice and consent of the Lords Spiritual and Temporal, and Commons, in this present Parliament assembled, and by the authority of the same, as follows:

1   Vacancies among the Lords Spiritual
2   Commencement, extent and short title

Vacancies among the Lords Spiritual

1(1)   This section applies where

     (a)   a vacancy arises among the Lords Spiritual in the House of Lords in the 10 years beginning with the day on which this Act comes into force,

     (b)   at the time the vacancy arises there is at least one eligible bishop who is a woman, and

     (c)   the person who would otherwise be entitled to fill the vacancy under section 5 of the Bishoprics Act 1878 is a man.

   (2)   If at the time the vacancy arises there is only one eligible bishop who is a woman, the vacancy is to be filled by the issue of writs of summons to her.

   (3)   If at the time the vacancy arises there are two or more eligible bishops who are women, the vacancy is to be filled by the issue of writs of summons to the one whose election as a bishop of a diocese in England was confirmed first.

   (4)   In this section "eligible bishop" means a bishop of a diocese in England who is not yet entitled in that capacity to the issue of writs of summons.

   (5)   The reference in subsection (1) to a vacancy does not include a vacancy arising by the avoidance of the see of Canterbury, York, London, Durham or Winchester.

Commencement, extent and short title

2(1)   This Act comes into force on the day Parliament first meets following the first parliamentary general election after this Act is passed.

   (2)   This Act extends to England and Wales, Scotland and Northern Ireland.

   (3)   This Act may be cited as the Lords Spiritual (Women) Act 2015.

Mental Health (Discrimination) Act 2013

1 Members of Parliament etc

(1) Section 141 of the Mental Health Act 1983 (disqualification of MPs and members of devolved bodies on grounds of mental illness) is repealed.

(2) Any rule of the common law which disqualifies a person from membership of the House of Commons on grounds of mental illness is abolished.

(3) The Schedule (which includes amendments and repeals consequential on subsection (1)) has effect.

Northern Ireland Act 1998

An Act to make new provision for the government of Northern Ireland for the purpose of implementing the agreement reached at multiparty talks on Northern Ireland set out in Command Paper 3883.

19th November 1998

PART I
PRELIMINARY

Status of Northern Ireland

1(1)   It is hereby declared that Northern Ireland in its entirety remains part of the United Kingdom and shall not cease to be so without the consent of a majority of the people of Northern Ireland voting in a poll held for the purposes of this section in accordance with Schedule 1.

(2)   But if the wish expressed by a majority in such a poll is that Northern Ireland should cease to be part of the United Kingdom and form part of a united Ireland, the Secretary of State shall lay before Parliament such proposals to give effect to that wish as may be agreed between Her Majesty's Government in the United Kingdom and the Government of Ireland.

Previous enactments

2   The Government of Ireland Act 1920 is repealed; and this Act shall have effect notwithstanding any other previous enactment.

NOTES
Defined terms
   enactment: s 98(1)

Devolution order

3(1)   If it appears to the Secretary of State that sufficient progress has been made in implementing the Belfast Agreement, he shall lay before Parliament the draft of an Order in Council appointing a day for the commencement of Parts II and III ("the appointed day").

(2)   If the draft Order laid before Parliament under subsection (1) is approved by resolution of each House of Parliament, the Secretary of State shall submit it to Her Majesty in Council and Her Majesty in Council may make the Order.

NOTES
Defined terms
   the Belfast Agreement: s 98(1)

Transferred, excepted and reserved matters

4(1)   In this Act

"excepted matter" means any matter falling within a description specified in Schedule 2;

"reserved matter" means any matter falling within a description specified in Schedule 3;

"transferred matter" means any matter which is not an excepted or reserved matter.

(2)   If at any time after the appointed day it appears to the Secretary of State

(a)   that any reserved matter should become a transferred matter; or

(b)   that any transferred matter should become a reserved matter,

he may, subject to subsections (2A) to (3D), lay before Parliament the draft of an Order in Council amending Schedule 3 so that the matter ceases to be or, as the case may be, becomes a reserved matter with effect from such date as may be specified in the Order.

(2A)   The Secretary of State shall not lay before Parliament under subsection (2) the draft of an Order amending Schedule 3 so that a policing and justice matter ceases to be a reserved matter unless

(a)   a motion for a resolution praying that the matter should cease to be a reserved matter is tabled by the First Minister and the deputy First Minister acting jointly; and

(b)   the resolution is passed by the Assembly with the support of a majority of the members voting on the motion, a majority of the designated Nationalists voting and a majority of the designated Unionists voting.

(3)   The Secretary of State shall not lay before Parliament under subsection (2) the draft of any other Order unless the Assembly has passed with crosscommunity support a resolution praying that the matter concerned should cease to be or, as the case may be, should become a reserved matter.

(3A)   The Secretary of State shall not lay before Parliament under subsection (2) the draft of an Order amending paragraph 16 of Schedule 3 (Civil Service Commissioners for Northern Ireland) unless the Secretary of State has, at least three months before laying the draft, laid a report before Parliament.

(3B)   The report under subsection (3A) must set out the Secretary of State's view of the effect (if any) that the Order would have on

(a)   the independence of the Civil Service Commissioners for Northern Ireland;

(b)   the application of the principle that persons should be selected for appointment to the Northern Ireland Civil Service on merit on the basis of fair and open competition; and

(c)   the impartiality of the Northern Ireland Civil Service.

(3C)   The Secretary of State shall not lay before Parliament under subsection (2) the draft of an Order amending paragraph 42(aa) of Schedule 3 (Northern Ireland Human Rights Commission) unless the Secretary of State has, at least three months before laying the draft, laid a report before Parliament.

(3D)   The report under subsection (3C) must set out the Secretary of State's view of the effect (if any) that the Order would have on

(a)   the independence of the Northern Ireland Human Rights Commission;

(b)   the application of internationally accepted principles relating to national human rights institutions; and

(c)   the relationship between the Northern Ireland Human Rights Commission and the Assembly.

(4)   If the draft of an Order laid before Parliament under subsection (2) is approved by resolution of each House of Parliament, the Secretary of State shall submit it to Her Majesty in Council and Her Majesty in Council may make the Order.

(5) In this Act

"the Assembly" means the New Northern Ireland Assembly, which after the appointed day shall be known as the Northern Ireland Assembly;

"cross-community support", in relation to a vote on any matter, means

(a) the support of a majority of the members voting, a majority of the designated Nationalists voting and a majority of the designated Unionists voting; or

(b) the support of 60 per cent of the members voting, 40 per cent of the designated Nationalists voting and 40 per cent of the designated Unionists voting;

"designated Nationalist" means a member designated as a Nationalist in accordance with standing orders of the Assembly and "designated Unionist" shall be construed accordingly.

(5A) Standing orders of the Assembly shall provide that a member of the Assembly designated in accordance with the standing orders as a Nationalist, as a Unionist or as Other may change his designation only if

(a) (being a member of a political party) he becomes a member of a different political party or he ceases to be a member of any political party;

(b) (not being a member of any political party) he becomes a member of a political party.

(6) In this section "policing and justice matter" means a matter falling within a description specified in

(a) any of paragraphs 9 to 12, 14A to 15A and 17 of Schedule 3; or

(b) any other provision of that Schedule designated for this purpose by an order made by the Secretary of State.

NOTES

Subordinate Legislation
Northern Ireland Act 1998 (Amendment of Schedule 3) Order 2010, SI 2010/977

Defined terms
the appointed day: ss 3(1), 98(1)

PART IV
THE NORTHERN IRELAND ASSEMBLY

Elections etc

Dates of elections and dissolutions

31(1) Subject to subsections (2) to (3), the date of the poll for the election of each Assembly shall be the first Thursday in May in the fifth calendar year following that in which its predecessor was elected; and the predecessor shall be dissolved at the beginning of the minimum period which ends with that date.

(2) The date of the poll for the election of the Assembly next following the Assembly elected at the poll on 26 November 2003 shall be 7 March 2007; and the Assembly elected on 26 November 2003 shall be dissolved on 30 January 2007.

(3) The Secretary of State may at any time by order direct that the date of the poll for the election of the next Assembly shall, instead of being that specified in subsection (1)..., be a date specified in the order being a date falling not more than two months before or after the date specified in that subsection.

(4) An Assembly elected under this section or section 32 shall meet within the period of eight days beginning with the day of the poll at which it is elected.

(5) For the purposes of subsection (4), a Saturday, a Sunday, Christmas Day, Good Friday and any day which is a bank holiday in Northern Ireland shall be disregarded, as shall any day on which section 1 of the Northern Ireland Act 2000 is in force.

(6)   In this section "minimum period" means a period determined in accordance with an order of the Secretary of State.

NOTES

Subordinate Legislation
Northern Ireland Assembly (Minimum Period) Order 2010, SI 2010/2944

Defined terms
the Assembly: ss 4(5), 98(1)

Extraordinary elections

32(1)   If the Assembly passes a resolution that it should be dissolved the Secretary of State shall propose a date for the poll for the election of the next Assembly.

(2)   A resolution under subsection (1) shall not be passed without the support of a number of members of the Assembly which equals or exceeds two thirds of the total number of seats in the Assembly.

(3)   If

(a)   the period mentioned in section 16A(3) ends without the offices of First Minister and deputy First Minister and the Ministerial offices to be held by Northern Ireland Ministers having been filled; or

(b)   the period mentioned in section 16B(3) ends without the offices of First Minister and deputy First Minister having been filled,

the Secretary of State shall propose a date for the poll for the election of the next Assembly.

(4)   If the Secretary of State proposes a date under subsection (1) or (3), Her Majesty may by Order in Council

(a)   direct that the date of the poll for the election of the next Assembly shall, instead of being determined in accordance with section 31, be the date proposed; and

(b)   provide for the Assembly to be dissolved on a date specified in the Order.

NOTES

Subordinate Legislation
Northern Ireland (Date of Next Assembly Poll) Order 2001, SI 2001/3959

Defined terms
the Assembly: ss 4(5), 98(1)

Constituencies and numbers of members

33(1)   The members of the Assembly shall be returned for the parliamentary constituencies in Northern Ireland.

(2)   Each constituency shall return six members.

(3)   An Order in Council under the Parliamentary Constituencies Act 1986 changing a parliamentary constituency in Northern Ireland shall have effect for the purposes of this Act in relation to

(a)   the first election under section 31 or 32 which takes place after the Order comes into force; and

(b)   later elections under that section and by-elections.

NOTES

Defined terms
the Assembly: ss 4(5), 98(1)
Northern Ireland: s 98(1)

Elections and franchise

34(1)   This section applies to elections of members of the Assembly, including by-elections.

(2)   Each vote in the poll at an election shall be a single transferable vote.

(3)   A single transferable vote is a vote

(a) capable of being given so as to indicate the voter's order of preference for the candidates for election as members for the constituency; and

(b) capable of being transferred to the next choice when the vote is not needed to give a prior choice the necessary quota of votes or when a prior choice is eliminated from the list of candidates because of a deficiency in the number of votes given for him.

(4) The Secretary of State may by order make provision about elections or any matter relating to them.

(5) In particular, an order under subsection (4) may make

(a) provision as to the persons entitled to vote at an election and the registration of such persons;

(b) provision for securing that no person stands as a candidate for more than one constituency at a general election;

(c) provision for determining the date of the poll at a by-election;

(d) provision about deposits.

(6) An order under subsection (4) may apply (with or without modifications) any provision of, or made under, any enactment.

(7) An order under subsection (4) may make different provision for different areas about the conduct of elections, including different provision about the registration of persons entitled to vote at an election.

NOTES

Subordinate Legislation
Northern Ireland Assembly (Elections) Order 2001, SI 2001/2599
Northern Ireland Assembly (Elections) (Forms) Order 2015, SI 2015/222

Defined terms
the Assembly: ss 4(5), 98(1)
enactment: s 98(1)

Vacancies

35(1) The Secretary of State may by order make provision for the filling of vacancies occurring in the Assembly's membership.

(2) Such provision may be made by reference to by-elections or substitutes or such other method of filling vacancies as the Secretary of State thinks fit.

(3) If a seat becomes vacant, the Presiding Officer shall as soon as reasonably practicable inform the Chief Electoral Officer for Northern Ireland.

(4) The validity of any proceedings of the Assembly is not affected by any vacancy in its membership.

(5) An order under subsection (1) may apply (with or without modifications) any provision of, or made under, any enactment.

NOTES

Subordinate Legislation
Northern Ireland Assembly (Elections) Order 2001, SI 2001/2599

Defined terms
the Assembly: ss 4(5), 98(1)
enactment: s 98(1)

Disqualification

Disqualification

36(1) The Northern Ireland Assembly Disqualification Act 1975 shall have effect as if any reference to the Assembly established under section 1 of the Northern Ireland Assembly Act 1973 were a reference to the Assembly.

(2) No recommendation shall be made to Her Majesty to make an Order in Council under section 3(1) of the Northern Ireland Assembly Disqualification Act 1975 (power to amend Schedule 1) without the consent of the Secretary of State.

(3) A person who is Her Majesty's LordLieutenant or Lieutenant for a county or county borough in Northern Ireland is disqualified for membership of the Assembly for a constituency comprising the whole or part of the county or county borough.

(4) A person is disqualified for membership of the Assembly if he is disqualified for membership of the House of Commons otherwise than under the House of Commons Disqualification Act 1975.

(5) *Repealed*

(6) A person is not disqualified for membership of the Assembly by virtue of subsection (4) by reason only that
    (a) he is a peer; or
    (b) he is a Lord Spiritual.

(7) A person is not disqualified for membership of the Assembly by virtue of subsection (4) by reason only that he is disqualified under section 3 of the Act of Settlement (certain persons born out of the Kingdom) if he is a citizen of the European Union.

NOTES
Defined terms
the Assembly: ss 4(5), 98(1)

Effect of disqualification and provision for relief

37(1) Subject to any order made by the Assembly under this section
    (a) if any person disqualified by virtue of section 36 is returned as a member of the Assembly, his return shall be void; and
    (b) if any person being a member of the Assembly becomes disqualified by virtue of that section, his seat shall be vacated.

(2) If, in a case which falls or is alleged to fall within subsection (1) otherwise than by virtue of section 36(4), it appears to the Assembly
    (a) that the grounds of disqualification or alleged disqualification which subsisted or arose at the material time have been removed; and
    (b) that it is otherwise proper so to do,
the Assembly may by order direct that any such disqualification incurred on those grounds at that time shall be disregarded for the purposes of this section.

(3) No order under subsection (2) shall affect the proceedings on any election petition or any determination of an election court.

(4) Subsection (1)(b) has effect subject to section 427 of the Insolvency Act 1986 (bankruptcy etc); and where, in consequence of that section, the seat of a disqualified member of the Assembly has not been vacated
    (a) he shall not participate in any proceedings of the Assembly; and
    (b) any of his other rights and privileges as a member of the Assembly may be withdrawn by a resolution of the Assembly.

(5) The validity of any proceedings of the Assembly is not affected by the disqualification of any person from being a member of the Assembly or from being a member for the constituency for which he purports to sit.

NOTES
Amendments to come into force
In (1)(a) insert "the Northern Ireland Assembly Disqualification Act 1975 or" before "section 36."
In 1(b) insert "that Act or" before "any section"fs

Defined terms
the Assembly: ss 4(5), 98(1)

Disqualification: judicial proceedings

38(1)   Any person who claims that a person purporting to be a member of the Assembly
    (a)   is disqualified; or
    (b)   was disqualified when, or at any time since, he was returned,
may apply to the High Court of Justice in Northern Ireland for a declaration to that effect.

(2)   On an application
    (a)   the person in respect of whom the application is made shall be the respondent;
    (b)   the applicant shall give such security for costs, not exceeding £5,000, as the court may direct; and
    (c)   the decision of the court shall be final.

(3)   A declaration made in accordance with this section shall be certified in writing to the Secretary of State by the court.

(4)   No such declaration shall be made in respect of a person on any grounds if an order has been made by the Assembly under subsection (2) of section 37 directing that any disqualification incurred by him on those grounds shall be disregarded for the purposes of that section.

(5)   No declaration shall be made in respect of any person on grounds which subsisted when he was elected if an election petition is pending or has been tried in which his disqualification on those grounds is or was in issue.

(6)   The Secretary of State may by order substitute for the amount specified in subsection (2)(b) such other amount as may be specified in the order.

NOTES

Defined terms
   the Assembly: ss 4(5), 98(1)

Interpretation

98(1)   In this Act
    "the appointed day" has the meaning given by section 3(1);
    "the Assembly" has the meaning given by section 4(5);
    "the Belfast Agreement" means the agreement reached at multiparty talks on Northern Ireland set out in Command Paper 3883;
    "EU law" means
      (a)   all rights, powers, liabilities, obligations and restrictions created or arising by or under the EU Treaties; and
      (b)   all remedies and procedures provided for by or under those Treaties;
    "the Convention rights" has the same meaning as in the Human Rights Act 1998;
    "crosscommunity support" has the meaning given by section 4(5);
    "designated Nationalist" and "designated Unionist" have the meanings given by section 4(5);
    "document" includes anything in which information is recorded in any form;
    "enactment" includes any provision of this Act and any provision of, or of any instrument made under, Northern Ireland legislation;
    "excepted matter" has the meaning given by section 4(1);
    "financial year", unless the context otherwise requires, means a year ending with 31st March;
    "functions" includes powers and duties, and "confer", in relation to functions, includes impose;
    "international obligations" means any international obligations of the United Kingdom other than obligations to observe and implement EU law or the Convention rights;
    "Minister", unless the context otherwise requires, has the meaning given by section 7(3);
    "Minister of the Crown" includes the Treasury;

"modify", in relation to an enactment, includes amend or repeal;

"Northern Ireland" includes so much of the internal waters and territorial sea of the United Kingdom as are adjacent to Northern Ireland;

"Northern Ireland legislation" means

    (a) Acts of the Parliament of Ireland;

    (b) Acts of the Parliament of Northern Ireland;

    (c) Orders in Council under section 1(3) of the Northern Ireland (Temporary Provisions) Act 1972;

    (d) Measures of the Northern Ireland Assembly established under section 1 of the Northern Ireland Assembly Act 1973;

    (e) Orders in Council under Schedule 1 to the Northern Ireland Act 1974;

    (f) Acts of the Assembly; and

    (g) Orders in Council under section 85;

"the Northern Ireland zone" means the sea within British fishery limits which is adjacent to Northern Ireland;

"the pledge of office" has the meaning given by section 16C(14);

"political opinion" and "religious belief" shall be construed in accordance with Article 2(3) and (4) of the Fair Employment and Treatment (Northern Ireland) Order 1998;

"proceedings", in relation to the Assembly, includes proceedings of any committee;

"property" includes rights and interests of any description;

"reserved matter" has the meaning given by section 4(1);

"the St Andrews Agreement" means the agreement reached on 13 October 2006 at multiparty talks on Northern Ireland held at St Andrews;

"subordinate legislation" has the same meaning as in the Interpretation Act 1978 and also includes an instrument made under Northern Ireland legislation;

"transferred matter" has the meaning given by section 4(1).

(2)   For the purposes of this Act, a provision of any enactment, Bill or subordinate legislation deals with the matter, or each of the matters, which it affects otherwise than incidentally.

(3)   For the purposes of this Act, a provision of any Act or Bill which modifies a provision of

    (a) the Agricultural Wages (Regulation) (Northern Ireland) Order 1977;

    (b) the Employment Rights (Northern Ireland) Order 1996; or

    (c) the Industrial Tribunals (Northern Ireland) Order 1996,

which is amended or applied by or under the National Minimum Wage Act 1998 shall not be treated as dealing with a matter falling within the subject-matter of that Act if the modification affects the national minimum wage and other employment matters in the same way.

(4)   For the purposes of this Act, a provision of an Act of the Assembly or of subordinate legislation discriminates against any person or class of persons if it treats that person or that class less favourably in any circumstances than other persons are treated in those circumstances by the law for the time being in force in Northern Ireland.

(5)   For those purposes a person discriminates against another person or a class of persons if he treats that other person or that class less favourably in any circumstances than he treats or would treat other persons in those circumstances.

(6)   No provision of an Act of the Assembly or of subordinate legislation, and no making, confirmation or approval of a provision of subordinate legislation, shall be treated for the purposes of this Act as discriminating if the provision has the effect of safeguarding national security or protecting public safety or public order.

(7)   No other act done by any person shall be treated for the purposes of this Act as discriminating if

    (a) the act is done for the purpose of safeguarding national security or protecting public safety or public order; and

    (b) the doing of the act is justified by that purpose.

(8) Her Majesty may by Order in Council determine, or make provision for determining, for such purposes of this Act as may be specified, any boundary between
  (a) the waters or parts of the sea which are to be treated as adjacent to Northern Ireland; and
  (b) those which are not,
and may make different determinations or provisions for different purposes.

(9) No recommendation shall be made to Her Majesty to make an Order in Council under subsection (8) unless a draft of the Order has been laid before and approved by resolution of each House of Parliament.

SCHEDULE 1
POLLS FOR THE PURPOSES OF SECTION 1

Section 1(1)

1 The Secretary of State may by order direct the holding of a poll for the purposes of section 1 on a date specified in the order.

2 Subject to paragraph 3, the Secretary of State shall exercise the power under paragraph 1 if at any time it appears likely to him that a majority of those voting would express a wish that Northern Ireland should cease to be part of the United Kingdom and form part of a united Ireland.

3 The Secretary of State shall not make an order under paragraph 1 earlier than seven years after the holding of a previous poll under this Schedule.

4(1) An order under this Schedule directing the holding of a poll shall specify
  (a) the persons entitled to vote; and
  (b) the question or questions to be asked.

(2) An order
  (a) may include any other provision about the poll which the Secretary of State thinks expedient (including the creation of criminal offences); and
  (b) may apply (with or without modification) any provision of, or made under, any enactment.

Northern Ireland Assembly Disqualification Act 1975

An Act to consolidate certain enactments relating to disqualification for membership of the Northern Ireland Assembly

8th May 1975

Disqualification of holders of certain offices and places

(1)   Subject to the provisions of this Act, a person is disqualified for membership of the Northern Ireland Assembly who for the time being

(za) is a member of the House of Commons;

(a)   holds any of the judicial offices specified in Part 1 of Schedule 1 to this Act;

(b)   is employed in the civil service of the Crown, whether in an established capacity or not, and whether for the whole or part of his time;

(c)   is a member of any of the regular armed forces of the Crown . . .;

(d)   is a member of any police force maintained by a local policing body or a police authority;

(da) is a member of the Dáil Éireann (House of Representatives of Ireland);

(e)   is a member of the legislature of any country or territory outside the Commonwealth (other than Ireland); or

(f) holds any office described in Part 2 or 3 of Schedule 1.

(2)   In this section

"civil service of the Crown" includes the civil service of Northern Ireland, the Northern Ireland Court Service, Her Majesty's Diplomatic Service and Her Majesty's Overseas Civil Service;

"police authority" means any police authority within the meaning of the Police Act 1996 (c 16), the Scottish Police Authority (c 77), or the Northern Ireland Policing Board; and "member" in relation to a police force means a person employed as a fulltime constable;

"regular armed forces of the Crown" means the Royal Navy, the Royal Marines, the regular army (as defined by section 374 of the Armed Forces Act 2006) or the Royal Air Force.

(3)   Except as provided by this Act, a person shall not be disqualified for membership of the Northern Ireland Assembly by reason of his holding an office or place of profit under the Crown or any other office or place; and a person shall not be disqualified for appointment to or for holding any office or place by reason of his being a member of the Assembly.

Members of the House of Commons

1A (1)   A person returned at an election as a member of the Northern Ireland Assembly is not disqualified under section 1(1)(za) at any time in the period of 8 days beginning with the day the person is so returned.

(2) Subsection (3) applies where a person
    (a) is returned at an election as a member of the Northern Ireland Assembly,
    (b) on being so returned is a candidate for election to the House of Commons, and
    (c) is subsequently returned at that election as a member of that House.

(3) The person is not disqualified under section 1(1)(za) at any time in the period of 8 days beginning with the day the person is returned as a member of the House of Commons.

(4) A person is a "candidate for election to the House of Commons" if the person's nomination paper for election as a member of the House of Commons has been delivered to the returning officer under rule 6 of Schedule 1 to the Representation of the People Act 1983 (parliamentary election rules).

Members of the Dáil Éireann

1B A person returned at an election as a member of the Northern Ireland Assembly is not disqualified under section 1(1)(db) at any time in the period of 8 days beginning with the day the person is so returned.

Reserve and auxiliary forces, etc

2(1) Notwithstanding section 1(1)(c) above
    (a) a person who is an officer on the retired or emergency list of any of the regular armed forces of the Crown, or who holds an emergency commission in any of those forces, or belongs to any reserve of officers of any of those forces, is not disqualified as a member of those forces; and
    (b) a naval, army, marine or air force pensioner, or former soldier, who is recalled for service for which he is liable as such is not disqualified as a member of the regular armed forces of the Crown.

(2) A person is not disqualified under section 1(1)(c) above by reason of his being an Admiral of the Fleet, a Field Marshal or a Marshal of the Royal Air Force, if he does not for the time being hold an appointment in the naval, military or air force service of the Crown.

(3) A person is not disqualified under section 1(1)(b) above by reason of his being a member of the Royal Observer Corps unless he is employed as such for the whole of his time.

Power to amend Schedule 1

3(1) If at any time it is resolved by the Northern Ireland Assembly that Schedule 1 to this Act be amended, whether by the addition or omission of any office or the removal of any office from one Part of the Schedule to another, or by altering the description of any office specified therein, Her Majesty may by Order in Council amend that Schedule accordingly.

(2) A copy of this Act as from time to time amended by Order in Council under this section or by or under any other enactment shall be prepared and certified by the Clerk of the Parliaments and deposited with the rolls of Parliament; and all copies of this Act thereafter to be printed by Her Majesty's printer shall be printed in accordance with the copy so certified.

Relaxation of obligation to accept office

4(1) No person being a member of the Northern Ireland Assembly, or for the time being nominated as a candidate for election to the Assembly, shall be required to accept any office or place by virtue of which he would be disqualified by this Act for membership of the Assembly.

(2)   This section does not affect any obligation to serve in the armed forces of the Crown, whether imposed by an enactment or otherwise.

5   *Repealed*

Short title

5   This Act may be cited as the Northern Ireland Assembly Disqualification Act 1975.

SCHEDULE 1

OFFICES DISQUALIFYING FOR MEMBERSHIP

Part I
Judicial Offices

Judge of the Supreme Court.
Judge of the High Court of Justice or Court of Appeal.
Judge of the Court of Session.
Judge of the High Court of Justice or Court of Appeal in Northern Ireland.
Judge of the Court Martial Appeal Court.
Chairman of the Scottish Land Court.
Circuit Judge.
Sheriff principal, sheriff, summary sheriff, temporary sheriff principal, parttime sheriff or parttime summary sheriff in Scotland.
County Court Judge or deputy County Court Judge in Northern Ireland.
District Judge (Magistrates' Courts) (but not Deputy District Judge Magistrates' Courts).
Resident Magistrate appointed under the Magistrates' Courts Act (Northern Ireland) 1964 (c 21 (NI)).
Chief or other Child Support Commissioner for Northern Ireland (excluding a person appointed under paragraph 4 of Schedule 4 to the Child Support Act 1991 (c 48)).
Chief or other Social Security Commissioner (not including a deputy Commissioner).
Chief or other Social Security Commissioner for Northern Ireland (not including a deputy Commissioner).
Umpire or Deputy Umpire appointed under Schedule 2 to the Reserve Forces (Safeguard of Employment) Act 1985 (c 17) for the purposes of section 9 of that Act.

Part II
Bodies of which All Members are Disqualified

The Administrative Justice and Tribunals Council.
The Advisory Board for the Research Councils.
The Agrément Board.
The Agriculture and Horticulture Development Board.
The Agrifood and Biosciences Institute.
The Appointments Commission.
An Arbitration Tribunal established under Schedule 3 to the Industry Act 1975 (c 68) .
The British Railways Board.
The British Waterways Board.
The Cable Authority.
The Care Council for Wales.
The Care Quality Commission and the Healthwatch England committee.
The Channel Four Television Corporation.
The Charity Commission.
The Charity Commission for Northern Ireland.

The Charity Tribunal for Northern Ireland.

The Civil Aviation Authority.

The Civil Service Commission.

The Coal Authority.

The Commission for Equality and Human Rights.

The Commission for Health Improvement.

The Commission on Human Medicines.

The Commission for Local Administration in England.

The Commission for Local Administration in Wales.

The Committee on Climate Change.

The Competition Appeal Tribunal.

The Competition and Markets Authority.

The Competition Service.

The Consumer Council for Water, and each regional committee of the Council established under section 27A of the Water Industry Act 1991.

The Copyright Tribunal.

The Criminal Cases Review Commission.

The Crown Agents Holding and Realisation Board.

The Crown Estate Commissioners.

A development corporation established under Part III of the Strategic Investment and Regeneration of Sites (Northern Ireland) Order 2003.

The Disability Living Allowance Advisory Board for Northern Ireland.

The Disclosure and Barring Service.

The Electoral Commission.

Enterprise Ulster.

The Environment Agency.

The Equality Commission for Northern Ireland.

The Fair Employment Tribunal for Northern Ireland.

The First-tier Tribunal.

The Food Standards Agency.

The Foreign Compensation Commission.

The Gambling Commission.

Gangmasters Licensing Authority.

The Health and Care Professions Council.

The Health and Safety Executive for Northern Ireland.

The Health and Social Care Information Centre.

The Homes and Communities Agency.

The Human Fertilisation and Embryology Authority.

The Human Tissue Authority.

The Independent Commission for Police Complaints for Northern Ireland.

The Independent Parliamentary Standards Authority.

The Independent Police Complaints Commission.

An Industrial Court.

The Industrial Estates Corporations constituted in accordance with the Local Employment Act 1972 (c 5).

The Industrial Injuries Advisory Council.

Invest Northern Ireland.

The Juvenile Justice Board.

The Labour Relations Agency.

The Laganside Corporation.

The Lands Tribunal for Northern Ireland.

The Lands Tribunal for Scotland.

The Law Commission.

The Legal Services Board.

The Legal Services Commission.

The Livestock and Meat Commission for Northern Ireland.

The Low Pay Commission appointed under section 8(9) of the National Minimum Wage Act 1998 (c 39).

The Mental Health Commission for Northern Ireland.

The Mental Health Review Tribunal for Northern Ireland constituted under the Mental Health Act (Northern Ireland) 1961 (c 15 (NI)).

The Metrication Board.

The Ministry of Defence (Army Department) Teachers Selection Board.

The National Audit Office.

A National Broadcasting Council.

The National Institute for Health and Care Excellence.

The National Research Development Corporation.

A New Town Commission established under the New Towns Act (Northern Ireland) 1965 (c 13 (NI)).

The Northern Ireland Authority for Utility Regulation.

The Northern Ireland Fire and Rescue Service Board.

The Northern Ireland Health and Personal Social Services Regulation and Improvement Authority.

The Northern Ireland Housing Executive.

The Northern Ireland Judicial Appointments Commission.

The Northern Ireland Law Commission.

The Northern Ireland Practice and Education Council for Nursing and Midwifery.

The Northern Ireland Social Care Council.

The Northern Ireland Valuation Tribunal

The Nuclear Decommissioning Authority.

The Office for Budget Responsibility.

The Office of Communications.

The Office for Legal Complaints.

The Office for Nuclear Regulation.

The Office for Standards in Education, Children's Services and Skills.

The Oil and Pipelines Agency.

A Panel of Chairmen of Reinstatement Committees constituted under Schedule 2 to the Reserve Forces (Safeguard of Employment) Act 1985 (c 17) for the purposes of section 8 of that Act.

The Panel of Official Arbitrators constituted for the purposes of the Acquisition of Land (Assessment of Compensation) Act 1919 (c 57).

The Parades Commission for Northern Ireland.

A Pensions Appeal Tribunal.

The Board of the Pension Protection Fund.

The Pensions Regulator.

The Planning Appeals Commission in Northern Ireland.

The Probation Board for Northern Ireland.

The Professional Standards Authority for Health and Social Care.

A Rural Development Board in Northern Ireland.

The Scottish Committee of the Administrative Justice and Tribunals Council.

The Scottish Environment Protection Agency.

The Scottish Land Court.

The Scottish Law Commission.

The Sea Fish Industry Authority.

The Sea Fish Licence Tribunal.

The Security Industry Authority.

Seirbheis nam Meadhanan Gàidhlig.

The Single Source Regulations Office.

The Social Mobility and Child Poverty Commission.

The Social Security Advisory Committee.

The Sports Grounds Safety Authority.

The Staff Commission for Wales (Comisiwn Staff Cymru).

The Statistics Board.

The Strategic Rail Authority.

The Transport Tribunal.

A tribunal established under Article 3 of the Industrial Tribunals (Northern Ireland) Order 1996 (SI 1996/1921 (NI 18)) including any panel constituted for the purpose of such tribunal.

The Tribunal established under section 91 of the Northern Ireland Act 1998 (c 47).

The Tribunal established under section 65 of the Regulation of Investigatory Powers Act 2000 (c 23).

The trustee corporation established by section 75 of the Pensions Act 2008.

The United Kingdom Atomic Energy Authority.

The University Grants Committee.

The Upper Tribunal.

The Water Appeals Commission for Northern Ireland.

The Water Services Regulation Authority.

The Welsh Committee of the Administrative Justice and Tribunals Council.

Part III
Other Disqualifying Offices

Additional Commissioner of the Equality Commission for Northern Ireland.

Adjudicating medical practitioner or specially qualified adjudicating medical practitioner.

Agent for Northern Ireland in Great Britain.

Ambassador representing Her Majesty's Government in the United Kingdom.

Appeal Officer for Community Interest Companies.

Arbitrator or other person appointed to hear a dispute under the Drainage (Northern Ireland) Order 1973 (SI 1973/69 (NI 1)).

Assembly Ombudsman for Northern Ireland.

Assistant Electoral Commissioners.

Attorney General for Northern Ireland.

Boundary Commissioner or Assistant Boundary Commissioner appointed under Schedule 1 to the Parliamentary Constituencies Act 1986 (c 56).

Certification Officer for Northern Ireland.

Chair or any member, not also being an employee, of the Patient and Client Council established under section 16 of the Health and Social Care (Reform) Act (Northern Ireland) 2009.

Chair or any member, not also being an employee, of the Regional Health and Social Care Board established under section 7 of the Health and Social Care (Reform) Act (Northern Ireland) 2009.

Chair or any member, not also being an employee, of the Regional Agency for Public Health and Social Wellbeing established under section 12 of the Health and Social Care (Reform) Act (Northern Ireland) 2009.

Chair or any member, not also being an employee, of the Regional Business Services Organisation established under section 14 of the Health and Social Care (Reform) Act (Northern Ireland) 2009.

Chair of the Safeguarding Board for Northern Ireland.

Chair or other member of Monitor.

Chairman of the Advisory Committee on Distinction Awards in Northern Ireland.

Chairman or vice-chairman of the Arts Council of Northern Ireland.

Chairman, or member in receipt of remuneration, of the Big Lottery Fund.

Chairman of the Board of Trustees of the National Museums and Galleries of Northern Ireland.

Chairman or Director General of the British Council.

Chairman of the Fisheries Conservancy Board for Northern Ireland.

Chairman and deputy chairman of the General Consumer Council for Northern Ireland.

Chairman or nonexecutive director of a Health and Social Services trust established under the Health and Personal Social Services (Northern Ireland) Order 1991 (SI 1991/194 (NI 1)).

Chairman of the Local Government Staff Commission for Northern Ireland.

Paid Chairman of an industrial training board constituted under the Industrial Training (Northern Ireland) Order 1984 (SI 1984/1159 (NI 9)) or of a committee appointed under that Order.

Chairman of the Northern Ireland Tourist Board.

Chairman or director of the Northern Ireland Transport Holding Company, or of any company which is a subsidiary of that Company.

Chairman, or member in receipt of remuneration, of the Olympic Lottery Distributor.

Any Chairman of the Plant Varieties and Seeds Tribunal.

Chairman of the Scottish Legal Aid Board.

Chairman of the Staff Commission for Education and Library Boards in Northern Ireland.

Chief Electoral Officer or Deputy Electoral Officer for Northern Ireland.

Chief Inspector of Criminal Justice in Northern Ireland.

Chief Land Registrar.

The Chief Ombudsman or an assistant ombudsman appointed under section 122 of the Legal Services Act 2007 (Chief Ombudsman and assistant ombudsmen appointed for the purposes of the ombudsman scheme).

The Chief Regulator of Qualifications and Examinations, the chair of the Office of Qualifications and Examinations Regulation and any member of the Office of Qualifications and Examinations Regulation in receipt of remuneration.

Children's Commissioner.

Children's Commissioner for Wales.

Civil Service Commissioner for Northern Ireland.

Clerk of the Crown and Peace in Northern Ireland.

Clerk or deputy clerk of a district council in Northern Ireland.

Clerk or Assistant Clerk of Petty Sessions in Northern Ireland.

Commissioner for Children and Young People for Northern Ireland.

Commissioner for Older People for Northern Ireland

Commissioner for Older People in Wales

Commissioner for Parliamentary Investigations.

Commissioner for the Retention and Use of Biometric Material.

Commissioner for Victims and Survivors for Northern Ireland

Commissioner or Assistant Commissioner appointed under section 50(1) or (2) of, or Schedule 4 to, the Local Government Act (Northern Ireland) 1972 (c 9 (NI)).

Commissioner of the City of London Police.

Commissioner appointed under section 67(1) of the Police (Northern Ireland) Act 2000 (c 32).

Compliance Officer for the Independent Parliamentary Standards Authority.

Comptroller and AuditorGeneral for Northern Ireland.

Coroner or deputy coroner appointed for any district in Northern Ireland.

Senior coroner, area coroner or assistant coroner appointed under Part 1 of the Coroners and Justice Act 2009.

Coroner for Treasure.

Deputy Chief Coroner appointed by the Lord Chancellor under that Part who is not also a senior coroner.

Correspondent appointed by the Commissioners of Customs and Excise.

Crown Solicitor for Northern Ireland.

Deputy Electoral Commissioners.

Director of the British Sugar Corporation Limited appointed by the Ministers as defined by section 17 of the Sugar Act 1956 (c 48).

Director of Cable and Wireless Limited nominated by a Minister of the Crown or government department.

Director of any of the following

(a) a company which for the time being holds a licence under Chapter I of Part I of the Transport Act 2000 (c 38) (a licence company);

(b) a company of which a licence company is a subsidiary (within the meaning given by section 1159 of the Companies Act 2006);

(c) a company which is a subsidiary (within the meaning so given) of a licence company.

Director of the Commonwealth Development Corporation nominated or appointed by the Secretary of State.

Director of a company appointed as a water or sewerage undertaker under the Water and Sewerage Services (Northern Ireland) Order 2006, being a director nominated or appointed by a Northern Ireland department or by a person acting on behalf of a Northern Ireland department.

Director of a company for the time being holding an appointment under Chapter I of Part II of the Water Industry Act 1991 (c 56) or of such a company's holding company, being a director nominated or appointed by a Minister of the Crown or by a person acting on behalf of the Crown.

Director of Harland and Wolff Limited.

Director of a Local Healthwatch organisation.

Director of Short Brothers Limited.

Director appointed at a salary of the National Building Agency.

Director of any of the following, being a director appointed or nominated by a Minister of the Crown or by a person acting on behalf of the Crown

(a) a Post Office company,

(b) a Royal Mail company,

(c) the original holding company, and

(d) a parent company of a company within any of paragraphs (a) to (c).

Expressions used in paragraphs (a) to (d) have the same meaning as in Part 1 of the Postal Services Act 2011.

Director of a publicly controlled company (within the meaning of Chapter 2 of Part 1 of the Energy Act 2004) to which transfers have been made in accordance with provisions of nuclear transfer schemes authorised by that Chapter.

Director of a publicly owned successor company (within the meaning of the Atomic Energy Authority Act 1995 (c 37)).

Director, or Deputy Director, of Public Prosecutions for Northern Ireland.

Director of SB (Realisations) Limited nominated or appointed by a Minister of the Crown or government department.

Director or receiver appointed by the Department or Ministry of Finance for Northern Ireland of any company.

Director of the successor company (within the meaning of Part V of the Airports (Northern Ireland) Order 1994 (SI 1994/426 (NI 1))), being a director nominated or appointed by a Northern Ireland department or by a person acting on behalf of a Northern Ireland department.

Director of the successor company (within the meaning of the British Technology Group Act 1991 (c 66)) being a director nominated or appointed by a Minister of the Crown or by a person acting on behalf of the Crown.

Director of the successor company (within the meaning of the Crown Agents Act 1995 (c 24)) being a director nominated or appointed by a Minister of the Crown or by a person acting on behalf of the Crown.

Director of the successor company (within the meaning of Part II of the Electricity Act 1989 (c 29)), being a director nominated or appointed by a Minister of the Crown or by a person acting on behalf of the Crown.

Director of a successor company (within the meaning of Part III of the Electricity (Northern Ireland) Order 1992 (SI 1992/231 (NI 1))), being a director nominated or appointed by a Northern Ireland department or by a person acting on behalf of a Northern Ireland department.

Director of the successor company (within the meaning of the Gas Act 1986 (c 44)), being a director nominated or appointed by a Minister of the Crown or by a person acting on behalf of the Crown.

Director of the Holding Company referred to in the Transport Act 1962 (c 46).

Director General of Electricity Supply for Northern Ireland.

Director General of Gas for Northern Ireland.

Employee of the National Audit Office.

Examiner or member of a board of interviewers appointed by the Civil Service Commissioners.

Examiner for entrance examination to, or member of a board of interviewers for entrance to, the civil service of Northern Ireland.

Governor of the British Broadcasting Corporation.

Governor, Deputy Governor or nonexecutive director of the Bank of England.

Governor, Lieutenant Governor and Secretary, or Captain of Invalids of Chelsea Hospital.

Governor, Medical Officer or other officer or member of the staff of a prison to which the Prison Act (Northern Ireland) 1953 (c 18 (NI)) applies.

Health Service Commissioner for England.

Health Service Commissioner for Wales.

Her Majesty's Chief Inspector of Education and Training in Wales or Prif Arolygydd Ei Mawrhydi dros Addysg a Hyfforddiant yng Nghymru.

High Commissioner representing Her Majesty's Government in the United Kingdom.

The Immigration Services Commissioner.

The Deputy Immigration Services Commissioner.

Independent Antislavery Commissioner.

Independent Assessor of Military Complaints Procedures in Northern Ireland.

Independent person appointed under section 7(3) or section 8(4) of the Caravans Act (Northern Ireland) 1963 (c 17 (NI)).

The Information Commissioner.

Investigating Commissioner of, or member of a decisionmaking committee of, the Commission for Equality and Human Rights.

Judge Advocate General, Vice Judge Advocate General, or Assistant Judge Advocate General.

Juries Officer.

Lay observers appointed under Article 42 of the Solicitors (Northern Ireland) Order 1976 (SI 1976/582 (NI 12)).

The Legal Services Ombudsman.

Member of an Agricultural Marketing Board appointed by the Minister under Schedule 2 to the Agricultural Marketing Act 1958 (c 47).

Member of staff of the Children's Commissioner.

Member of staff of the Commissioner for Older People in Wales

Member of the Determinations Panel established by the Pensions Regulator under section 9 of the Pensions Act 2004.

Member of the staff of the Electoral Commission.

Member of the Financial Policy Committee of the Bank of England appointed under section 9B(1)(d) or (e) of the Bank of England Act 1998.

Member of the governing body of the Financial Conduct Authority.

Member of the governing body of the Prudential Regulation Authority.

Member appointed by the Minister of Agriculture, Fisheries and Food . . . of an agricultural wages committee established under the Agricultural Wages Act 1948 (c 47) or chairman of such a committee.

Member of the Monetary Policy Committee of the Bank of England appointed under section 13(2)(b) or (c) of the Bank of England Act 1998 (c 11).

Any member, in receipt of remuneration, of a panel of persons who may be selected to act as members of the Pensions Regulator Tribunal.

Any member of the Residuary Body for Wales (Corff Gweddilliol Cymru) in receipt of remuneration.

Member appointed by the Secretary of State of the Scottish Agricultural Wages Board.

Member of a panel of persons appointed under Article 7 of the Social Security (Northern Ireland) Order 1998 (SI 1998/1506 (NI 10)).

Member appointed by the Head of the Department of Agriculture of an Agricultural Marketing Board constituted under Part II of the Agricultural Marketing (Northern Ireland) Order 1982 (SI 1982/1080 (NI 12)).

Member appointed by the Head of the Department or Minister of Agriculture for Northern Ireland of the Agricultural Wages Board for Northern Ireland.

Member of the staff of the Children's Commissioner for Wales.

Member of the staff of the Northern Ireland Audit Office.

Member of staff of the Office for Nuclear Regulation (within the meaning of Part 3 of the Energy Act 2013).

Member of a panel of valuers appointed at an annual salary under section 4 of the Inland Revenue Regulation Act 1890 (c 21).

Member of the staff of the Disclosure and Barring Service.

Any member of the staff of the State Pathologist's Department.

Northern Ireland Commissioner for Complaints.

Northern Ireland Human Rights Commissioner.

Northern Ireland Judicial Appointments Ombudsman.

Officer or other member of the County Court service within the meaning of the County Courts Act (Northern Ireland) 1959 (c 25 (NI)).

Officer or servant of the Crown Estate Commissioners.

Officer of the Senior Courts being the holder of any office listed in any Part of Schedule 2 to the Senior Courts Act 1981 (c 54) or a district registrar, or assistant district registrar, of the High Court.

Ombudsman for the Board of the Pension Protection Fund and any deputy to that Ombudsman appointed under section 210 of the Pensions Act 2004.

Parliamentary Commissioner for Administration.

Parole Commissioner for Northern Ireland

Pensions Ombudsman and any deputy to that Ombudsman appointed under section 145A of the Pension Schemes Act 1993.

Person on the list of those eligible to sit as members of a Gender Recognition Panel.

The Police Ombudsman for Northern Ireland.

President of appeal tribunals (within the meaning of Chapter I of Part II of the Social Security (Northern Ireland) Order 1998 (SI 1998/1506 (NI 10)) appointed under Article 6 of that Order.

Receiver for the Metropolitan Police District.

Registrar or Assistant Registrar appointed under section 6 or section 7 of the County Courts Act 1984 (c 28).

Registrar of the Privy Council.

Regulator of Community Interest Companies.

Scottish Public Services Ombudsman.

Sentence Review Commissioner.

Standing Counsel to any department of Her Majesty's Government in the United Kingdom.

Statutory officer appointed under section 70 of the Judicature (Northern Ireland) Act 1978 (c 23).

Substitution Officer of the Royal Air Force.

Technical Adviser to the Commissioners of Customs and Excise.

Traffic Director for London.

SCHEDULE 2

Repealed

SCHEDULE 3

Repealed

Parliament (Qualification of Women) Act 1918

An Act to amend the Law with respect to the Capacity of Women to sit in Parliament

21st November 1918

1   Capacity of women to be members of Parliament
2   Short title

1 Capacity of women to be members of Parliament

A woman shall not be disqualified by sex or marriage for being elected to or sitting or voting as a Member of the Commons House of Parliament.

2 Short title

This Act may be cited as the Parliament (Qualification of Women) Act 1918.

Parliamentary Constituencies Act 1986

An Act to consolidate the House of Commons (Redistribution of Seats) Acts 1949 to 1979 and certain related enactments

7th November 1986

Parliamentary constituencies

1(1)   There shall for the purpose of parliamentary elections be the county and borough constituencies (or in Scotland the county and burgh constituencies), each returning a single member, which are described in Orders in Council made under this Act.

(2)   In this Act and, except where the context otherwise requires, in any Act passed after the Representation of the People Act 1948, "constituency" means an area having separate representation in the House of Commons.

The Boundary Commissions

2(1)   For the purpose of the continuous review of the distribution of seats at parliamentary elections, there shall continue to be four permanent Boundary Commissions, namely a Boundary Commission for England, a Boundary Commission for Scotland, a Boundary Commission for Wales and a Boundary Commission for Northern Ireland.

(2)   Schedule 1 to this Act shall have effect with respect to the constitution of, and other matters relating to, the Boundary Commissions.

Reports of the Commissions

3(1)   Each Boundary Commission shall keep under review the representation in the House of Commons of the part of the United Kingdom with which they are concerned and shall, in accordance with subsection (2) below, submit to the Secretary of State reports with respect to the whole of that part of the United Kingdom, either
   (a)   showing the constituencies into which they recommend that it should be divided in order to give effect to the rules set out in Schedule 2 to this Act (read with paragraph 7 of that Schedule), or
   (b)   stating that, in the opinion of the Commission, no alteration is required to be made in respect of that part of the United Kingdom in order to give effect to the said rules . . ..

(2)   A Boundary Commission shall submit reports under subsection (1) above periodically
   (a)   before 1st October 2018 but not before 1st September 2018, and

      (b)   before 1st October of every fifth year after that.

(2A)   A failure by a Boundary Commission to submit a report within the time limit which is appropriate to that report shall not be regarded as invalidating the report for the purposes of any enactment.

(2B)   In relation to any report which a Boundary Commission are required by subsection (2) above to submit before a particular date but have not yet submitted (a "pending boundary report"), the Commission shall submit to the Speaker of the House of Commons

      (a)   during the January that begins one year and nine months before that date, and

      (b)   during each subsequent January,

a report setting out what progress they have made with the preparation of the pending boundary report, with particular reference to the requirement in subsection (2) above.

(2C)   On receiving a report under subsection (2B) above, the Speaker shall lay it before Parliament.

(3)   *Repealed*

(4)   A report of a Boundary Commission under this Act showing the constituencies into which they recommend that any area should be divided shall state, as respects each constituency, the name by which they recommend that it should be known, and whether they recommend that it should be a county constituency or a borough constituency (or in Scotland a county constituency or a burgh constituency).

(5)   As soon as may be after the submission of a report under subsection (1) above, the Secretary of State shall lay the report before Parliament.

(5A)   As soon as may be after the submission of all four reports under subsection (1) above that are required by subsection (2) above to be submitted before a particular date, the Secretary of State shall lay before Parliament the draft of an Order in Council for giving effect to the recommendations contained in them.

(5B)   Where

      (a)   a Boundary Commission have submitted a report under subsection (1) above (but no draft under subsection (5A) above has yet been laid in relation to the report),

      (b)   the Commission notify the Secretary of State that the recommendations contained in the report are to have effect with specified modifications, and

      (c)   the Commission submit to the Secretary of State a statement of the reasons for those modifications,

the draft under subsection (5A) above shall give effect to the recommendations with those modifications.

(5C)   Subsections (5A) and (5B) above do not apply where each of the reports mentioned in subsection (5) above states that no alteration is required to be made in respect of the part of the United Kingdom with which the Commission in question are concerned.

(6)   Schedule 2 to this Act which contains the rules referred to above and related provisions shall have effect.

(7)   For the purposes of the application of the rules in paragraph 4 of Schedule 2 to this Act (relationship between constituencies and certain local government boundaries) a report of a Boundary Commission under subsection (1) above shall take the tenth anniversary of the date of the submission of the most recent report of the Commission under subsection (1) above; but nothing in this subsection shall prevent a Boundary Commission publishing proposed recommendations which take account of boundaries which at the time of publication are prospective only.

(8)   *Repealed*

3A *Repealed*

Orders in Council

4(1)   The draft of any Order in Council laid before Parliament by the Secretary of State under this Act for giving effect, whether with or without modifications, to the recommendations contained in the report of a Boundary Commission may make provision for any matters which appear to him to be incidental to, or consequential on, the recommendations.

(2)   Where any such draft gives effect to any such recommendations with modifications, the Secretary of State shall lay before Parliament together with the draft the statement submitted under section 3(5B)(c) above of the reasons for the modifications.

(3)   If any such draft is approved by resolution of each House of Parliament, the Secretary of State shall submit it to Her Majesty in Council.

(4)   If a motion for the approval of any such draft is rejected by either House of Parliament or withdrawn by leave of the House, the Secretary of State may amend the draft and lay the amended draft before Parliament, and if the draft as so amended is approved by resolution of each House of Parliament, the Secretary of State shall submit it to Her Majesty in Council.

(5)   Where the draft of an Order in Council is submitted to Her Majesty in Council under this Act, Her Majesty in Council may make an Order in terms of the draft which (subject to subsection (6) below) shall come into force on such date as may be specified in the Order and shall have effect notwithstanding anything in any enactment.

(6)   The coming into force of any such Order shall not affect any parliamentary election or the constitution of the House of Commons until the dissolution of the Parliament then in being.

(7)   The validity of any Order in Council purporting to be made under this Act and reciting that a draft of the Order has been approved by resolution of each House of Parliament shall not be called in question in any legal proceedings whatsoever.

NOTES
Subordinate Legislation
Parliamentary Constituencies (Northern Ireland) Order 1995, SI 1995/2992.
Parliamentary Constituencies (Scotland) Order 2005, SI 2005/250.
Parliamentary Constituencies and Assembly Electoral Regions (Wales) Order 2006, SI 2006/1041.
Parliamentary Constituencies (England) Order 2007, SI 2007/1681.
Parliamentary Constituencies (Northern Ireland) Order 2008, SI 2008/1486.

Publicity and consultation

5(1)   Once a Boundary Commission have decided what constituencies they propose to recommend in a report under section 3(1)(a) above
      (a)   the Commission shall take such steps as they think fit to inform people in each of the proposed constituencies
            (i)   what the proposals are,
            (ii)   that a copy of the proposals is open to inspection at a specified place within the proposed constituency, and
            (iii) that written representations with respect to the proposals may be made to the Commission during a specified period of 12 weeks ("the initial consultation period");
      (b)   the Commission shall cause public hearings to be held during the period beginning with the fifth week of the initial consultation period and ending with the tenth week of it.

(2) Subsection (1)(a)(ii) above does not apply to a constituency with respect to which no alteration is proposed.

(3) Schedule 2A to this Act, which makes further provision about public hearings under subsection (1)(b) above, has effect.

(4) After the end of the initial consultation period the Commission
   (a) shall publish, in such manner as they think fit, representations made as mentioned in subsection (1)(a) above and records of public hearings held under subsection (1)(b) above;
   (b) shall take such steps as they think fit to inform people in the proposed constituencies that further written representations with respect to the things published under paragraph (a) above may be made to the Commission during a specified period of four weeks ("the secondary consultation period").

(5) If after the end of the secondary consultation period the Commission are minded to revise their original proposals so as to recommend different constituencies, they shall take such steps as they see fit to inform people in each of those revised proposed constituencies
   (a) what the revised proposals are,
   (b) that a copy of the revised proposals is open to inspection at a specified place within the revised proposed constituency, and
   (c) that written representations with respect to the revised proposals may be made to the Commission during a specified period of eight weeks.

(6) Subsection (5) above does not apply to any proposals to make further revisions.

(7) Steps taken under subsection (4) or (5) above need not be of the same kind as those taken under subsection (1) above.

(8) A Boundary Commission shall take into consideration
   (a) written representations duly made to them as mentioned in subsection (1)(a), (4)(b) or (5)(c) above, and
   (b) representations made at public hearings under subsection (1)(b) above.

(9) Except as provided by this section and Schedule 2A to this Act, a Boundary Commission shall not cause any public hearing or inquiry to be held for the purposes of a report under this Act.

(10) Where a Boundary Commission publish
   (a) general information about how they propose to carry out their functions (including, in the case of the Boundary Commission for England, information about the extent (if any) to which they propose to take into account the boundaries mentioned in rule 5(2) of Schedule 2 to this Act), or
   (b) anything else to which subsection (1), (4) or (5) above does not apply,
   it is for the Commission to determine whether to invite representations and, if they decide to do so, the procedure that is to apply.

6 *Repealed*

6A *Repealed*

Functions of the Chancellor of the Duchy of Lancaster

6B See the Chancellor of the Duchy of Lancaster Order 2015, by virtue of which functions of the Secretary of State under this Act are exercisable concurrently with the Chancellor of the Duchy of Lancaster.

Consequential amendments

7   Schedule 3 to this Act shall have effect.

Repeals and revocation

8(1)   The enactments specified in Schedule 4 to this Act are hereby repealed to the extent specified in the third column of that Schedule.

(2)   *Repealed*

(3)   *Repealed*

Citation, commencement and extent

9(1)   This Act may be cited as the Parliamentary Constituencies Act 1986, and shall be included among the Acts which may be cited as the Representation of the People Acts.

(2)   This Act shall come into force at the end of the period of three months beginning with the day on which it is passed.

(3)   This Act extends to Northern Ireland.

SCHEDULE 1

THE BOUNDARY COMMISSIONS

Section 2

Constitution

1   The Speaker of the House of Commons shall be the chairman of each of the four Commissions.

2   Each of the four Commissions shall consist of the chairman, a deputy chairman and two other members appointed by the Secretary of State.

3   The deputy chairman
   (a)   in the case of the Commission for England shall be a judge of the High Court appointed by the Lord Chancellor,
   (b)   in the case of the Commission for Scotland shall be a judge of the Court of Session appointed by the Lord President of the Court of Session,
   (c)   in the case of the Commission for Wales shall be a judge of the High Court appointed by the Lord Chancellor,
   (d)   in the case of the Commission for Northern Ireland shall be a judge of the High Court in Northern Ireland appointed by the Lord Chief Justice of Northern Ireland.

4   A member of any Commission (other than the chairman) shall hold his appointment for such term and on such conditions as may be determined before his appointment by the person appointing him.

4A   In the case of a member of a Commission other than the chairman or deputy chairman, the conditions referred to in paragraph 4 above may include such provisions with respect to remuneration as the Secretary of State may determine with the approval of the Treasury.

Officers

5 The officers of each Commission shall include, as assessors, the following persons
  (a) in the case of the Commission for England, the Statistics Board and the Director General of Ordnance Survey,
  (b) in the case of the Commission for Scotland, the Registrar General of Births, Deaths and Marriages for Scotland and the Director General of Ordnance Survey,
  (c) in the case of the Commission for Wales, the Statistics Board and the Director General of Ordnance Survey,
  (d) in the case of the Commission for Northern Ireland, the Registrar General of Births and Deaths in Northern Ireland, the Commissioner of Valuation for Northern Ireland, the Chief Electoral Officer for Northern Ireland and the Chief Survey Officer of Land and Property Services.

6(1) The Secretary of State may, at the request of any Commission, appoint one or more assistant Commissioners to assist the Commission in the discharge of their functions.

(2) Any such assistant Commissioner shall be appointed either for a certain term or for the purposes of a particular matter, and on such conditions as to remuneration and otherwise as may be determined before his appointment by the Secretary of State with the approval of the Treasury.

7 The Secretary of State shall appoint a secretary to each of the Commissions, and may appoint such other officers of any Commission as he may determine with the approval of the Treasury, and the term and conditions of any such appointment shall be such as may be so determined.

Expenses

8 The expenses of each Commission, including the remuneration and travelling and other expenses of the members, assistant Commissioners, secretary and other officers, shall be paid out of money by Parliament.

Proceedings and instruments

9 A Commission shall have power to act notwithstanding a vacancy among their members, and at any meeting of a Commission two, or such greater number as the Commission may determine, shall be the quorum.

10 For the purpose of considering any matter of common concern, the Commissions, or any two or three of them, may hold joint meetings.

11 Subject to the provisions of this Act, each of the Commissions shall have power to regulate their own procedure.

12 Every document purporting to be an instrument made or issued by a Commission and to be signed by the secretary or any person authorised to act in that behalf, shall be received in evidence and shall, until the contrary is proved, be deemed to be an instrument made or issued by the Commission.

SCHEDULE 2
RULES FOR DISTRIBUTION OF SEATS
Number of constituencies

1   The number of constituencies in the United Kingdom shall be 600.

Electorate per constituency

2(1)   The electorate of any constituency shall be
    (a)   no less than 95% of the United Kingdom electoral quota, and
    (b)   no more than 105% of that quota.

(2)   This rule is subject to rules 4(2), 6(3) and 7.

(3)   In this Schedule the "United Kingdom electoral quota" means
    U / 596
    where U is the electorate of the United Kingdom minus the electorate of the constituencies mentioned in rule 6.

Allocation of constituencies to parts of the United Kingdom

3(1)   Each constituency shall be wholly in one of the four parts of the United Kingdom (England, Wales, Scotland and Northern Ireland).

(2)   The number of constituencies in each part of the United Kingdom shall be determined in accordance with the allocation method set out in rule 8.

Area of constituencies

4(1)   A constituency shall not have an area of more than 13,000 square kilometres.

(2)   A constituency does not have to comply with rule 2(1)(a) if
    (a)   it has an area of more than 12,000 square kilometres, and
    (b)   the Boundary Commission concerned are satisfied that it is not reasonably possible for the constituency to comply with that rule.

Factors

5(1)   A Boundary Commission may take into account, if and to such extent as they think fit
    (a)   special geographical considerations, including in particular the size, shape and accessibility of a constituency;
    (b)   local government boundaries as they exist on the most recent ordinary councilelection day before the review date;
    (c)   boundaries of existing constituencies;
    (d)   any local ties that would be broken by changes in constituencies;
    (e)   the inconveniences attendant on such changes.

(2)   The Boundary Commission for England may take into account, if and to such extent as they think fit, boundaries of the electoral regions specified in Schedule 1 to the European Parliamentary Elections Act 2002 (ignoring paragraph 2(2) of that Schedule and the references to Gibraltar) as it has effect on the most recent ordinary councilelection day before the review date.

(3)   This rule has effect subject to rules 2 and 4.

Protected constituencies

6(1)   There shall be two constituencies in the Isle of Wight.

(2)   There shall continue to be
    (a)   a constituency named Orkney and Shetland, comprising the areas of the Orkney Islands Council and the Shetland Islands Council;
    (b)   a constituency named Na hEileanan an Iar, comprising the area of Comhairle nan Eilean Siar.

(3)   Rule 2 does not apply to these constituencies.

Northern Ireland

7(1)   In relation to Northern Ireland, sub-paragraph (2) below applies in place of rule 2 where
    (a)   the difference between
        (i)   the electorate of Northern Ireland, and
        (ii)   the United Kingdom electoral quota multiplied by the number of seats in Northern Ireland (determined under rule 8),
    exceeds one third of the United Kingdom electoral quota, and
    (b)   the Boundary Commission for Northern Ireland consider that having to apply rule 2 would unreasonably impair
        (i)   their ability to take into account the factors set out in rule 5(1), or
        (ii)   their ability to comply with section 3(2) of this Act.

(2)   The electorate of any constituency shall be
    (a)   no less than whichever is the lesser of
        $N - A$
        and 95% of the United Kingdom electoral quota, and
    (b)   no more than whichever is the greater of
        $N + A$
        and 105% of the United Kingdom electoral quota,
    where
        N is the electorate of Northern Ireland divided by the number of seats in Northern Ireland (determined under rule 8), and
        A is 5% of the United Kingdom electoral quota.

The allocation method

8(1)   The allocation method referred to in rule 3(2) is as follows.

(2)   The first constituency shall be allocated to the part of the United Kingdom with the greatest electorate.

(3)   The second and subsequent constituencies shall be allocated in the same way, except that the electorate of a part of the United Kingdom to which one or more constituencies have already been allocated is to be divided by
    $2C + 1$
    where C is the number of constituencies already allocated to that part.

(4)   Where the figure given by sub-paragraph (3) above is the same for two or more parts of the United Kingdom, the part to which a constituency is to be allocated shall be the one with the smaller or smallest actual electorate.

(5)   This rule does not apply to the constituencies mentioned in rule 6, and accordingly
    (a)   the electorate of England shall be treated for the purposes of this rule as reduced by the electorate of the constituencies mentioned in rule 6(1);
    (b)   the electorate of Scotland shall be treated for the purposes of this rule as reduced by the electorate of the constituencies mentioned in rule 6(2).

Interpretation

9(1)   This rule has effect for the purposes of this Schedule.

(2)   The "electorate" of the United Kingdom, or of a part of the United Kingdom or a constituency, is the total number of persons whose names appear on the relevant version of a register of parliamentary electors in respect of addresses in the United Kingdom, or in that part or that constituency.

For this purpose the relevant version of a register is the version that is required by virtue of subsection (1) of section 13 of the Representation of the People Act 1983 to be published no later than the review date, or would be so required but for
- (a) any power under that section to prescribe a later date, or
- (b) subsection (1A) of that section.

(3) "Local government boundaries" are
- (a) in England, the boundaries of counties and their electoral divisions, districts and their wards, London boroughs and their wards and the City of London,
- (b) in Wales, the boundaries of counties, county boroughs, electoral divisions, communities and community wards,
- (c) in Scotland, the boundaries of local government areas and the electoral wards into which they are divided under section 1 of the Local Governance (Scotland) Act 2004, and
- (d) in Northern Ireland, the boundaries of wards.

(4) "Ordinary council-election day" is
- (a) in relation to England and Wales, the ordinary day of election of councillors for local government areas;
- (b) in relation to Scotland, the day on which the poll is held at ordinary elections of councillors for local government areas;
- (c) in relation to Northern Ireland, the day of an election for any district council (other than an election to fill a casual vacancy).

(5) The "review date", in relation to a report under section 3(1) of this Act that a Boundary Commission is required (by section 3(2)) to submit before a particular date, is two years and ten months before that date.

(6) "The United Kingdom electoral quota" has the meaning given by rule 2(3).

(7) A reference in rule 6 to an area is to the area as it existed on the coming into force of Part 2 of the Parliamentary Voting System and Constituencies Act 2011.

SCHEDULE 2A
PUBLIC HEARINGS ABOUT BOUNDARY COMMISSION PROPOSALS

Purpose of hearings

1 The purpose of a public hearing is to enable representations to be made about any of the proposals with which the hearing is concerned.

Number of hearings

2(1) In relation to any particular report under section 3(1)(a) of this Act
- (a) the Boundary Commission for England shall cause at least two and no more than five public hearings to be held in each English region;
- (b) the Boundary Commission for Scotland shall cause at least two and no more than five public hearings to be held in Scotland;
- (c) the Boundary Commission for Wales shall cause at least two and no more than five public hearings to be held in Wales;
- (d) the Boundary Commission for Northern Ireland shall cause at least two and no more than five public hearings to be held in Northern Ireland.

(2) The public hearings in an English region shall be concerned with proposals for that region, and shall between them cover the whole region.

(3) The public hearings in Scotland shall be concerned with proposals for Scotland, and shall between them cover the whole of Scotland.

(4) The public hearings in Wales shall be concerned with proposals for Wales, and shall between them cover the whole of Wales.

(5) The public hearings in Northern Ireland shall be concerned with proposals for Northern Ireland, and shall between them cover the whole of Northern Ireland.

Chair of hearing

3 For each public hearing the Boundary Commission concerned shall appoint a person to chair the hearing.

Length of hearings

4 A public hearing shall be completed within two days.

Procedure at hearings

5 It is for the chair of each public hearing to determine the procedure that is to govern that hearing.

6 The chair shall make arrangements for a public hearing to begin with an explanation of
   (a) the proposals with which the hearing is concerned;
   (b) how written representations about the proposals may be made (as mentioned in section 5(1)(a), (4)(b) or (5)(c) of this Act).

7(1) The chair of a public hearing must allow representations to be made
   (a) by each qualifying party;
   (b) by any other persons (whether individuals or organisations) considered by the chair to have an interest in any of the proposals with which the hearing is concerned.
   Paragraph (b) above has effect subject to sub-paragraph (3)(b) below.

(2) The chair may restrict the amount of time allowed for representations
   (a) by qualifying parties, and
   (b) by other persons,
   and need not allow the same amount to each.

(3) The chair may determine
   (a) the order in which representations are made, and
   (b) if necessary because of shortage of time, which of those wishing to make representations are not allowed to do so,
   in whatever way the chair decides.

8(1) The chair may put questions, or allow questions to be put, to a person present at the hearing.

(2) If questions are allowed to be put, the chair may regulate the manner of questioning or restrict the number of questions a person may ask.

Interpretation

9 In this Schedule
   "the chair" means the person appointed under paragraph 3 above;
   "English region" means an electoral region specified in Schedule 1 to the European Parliamentary Elections Act 2002 (ignoring paragraph 2(2) of that Schedule and the references to Gibraltar) as it has effect on the day referred to in rule 5(2) of Schedule 2 to this Act;

"public hearing" means a hearing under section 5(1)(b) of this Act;

"qualifying party" means a party that is registered under Part 2 of the Political Parties, Elections and Referendums Act 2000 and either

(a) has at least one Member of the House of Commons representing a constituency in the region, or (as the case may be) the part of the United Kingdom, in which the hearing is held, or

(b) received at least 10% of the votes cast in that region or part in the most recent parliamentary general election.

Police Reform and Social Responsibility Act 2011

An Act to make provision about the administration and governance of police forces; about the licensing of, and for the imposition of a late night levy in relation to, the sale and supply of alcohol, and for the repeal of provisions about alcohol disorder zones; for the repeal of sections 132 to 138 of the Serious Organised Crime and Police Act 2005 and for the prohibition of certain activities in Parliament Square; to enable provision in local authority byelaws to include powers of seizure and forfeiture; about the control of dangerous or otherwise harmful drugs; to restrict the issue of arrest warrants for certain extraterritorial offences; and for connected purposes.

15th September 2011

PART 1
POLICE REFORM
Chapter 1
Police Areas Outside London

___

PART 1
POLICE REFORM

Chapter 1
Police Areas Outside London

Police and crime commissioners

1(1)   There is to be a police and crime commissioner for each police area listed in Schedule 1 to the Police Act 1996 (police areas outside London).

(2)   A police and crime commissioner is a corporation sole.

(3)   The name of the police and crime commissioner for a police area is "the Police and Crime Commissioner for" with the addition of the name of the police area.

(4)   The police and crime commissioner for a police area is to be elected, and hold office, in accordance with Chapter 6.

(5)   A police and crime commissioner has
   (a)   the functions conferred by this section,
   (b)   the functions relating to community safety and crime prevention conferred by Chapter 3, and
   (c)   the other functions conferred by this Act and other enactments.

(6)   The police and crime commissioner for a police area must
   (a)   secure the maintenance of the police force for that area, and
   (b)   secure that the police force is efficient and effective.

(7)   The police and crime commissioner for a police area must hold the relevant chief constable to account for the exercise of

(a)   the functions of the chief constable, and

(b)   the functions of persons under the direction and control of the chief constable.

(8)   The police and crime commissioner must, in particular, hold the chief constable to account for

    (a)   the exercise of the duty under section 8(2) (duty to have regard to police and crime plan);

    (b)   the exercise of the duty under section 37A(2) of the Police Act 1996 (duty to have regard to strategic policing requirement);

    (c)   the exercise of the duty under section 39A(7) of the Police Act 1996 (duty to have regard to codes of practice issued by Secretary of State);

    (d)   the effectiveness and efficiency of the chief constable's arrangements for co-operating with other persons in the exercise of the chief constable's functions (whether under section 22A of the Police Act 1996 or otherwise);

    (e)   the effectiveness and efficiency of the chief constable's arrangements under section 34 (engagement with local people);

    (f)   the extent to which the chief constable has complied with section 35 (value for money);

    (g)   the exercise of duties relating to equality and diversity that are imposed on the chief constable by any enactment;

    (h)   the exercise of duties in relation to the safeguarding of children and the promotion of child welfare that are imposed on the chief constable by sections 10 and 11 of the Children Act 2004.

(9)   The police authorities established for police areas under section 3 of the Police Act 1996 are abolished.

(10)   Schedule 1 (police and crime commissioners) has effect.

2-49   *Not reproduced*

Chapter 6
Police and Crime Commissioners: Elections and Vacancies

Holding of elections

Ordinary elections

50(1)   An election of police and crime commissioners for all police areas (an "ordinary election") is to be held

    (a)   in 2012;

    (b)   in each subsequent fourth year.

(2)   The poll at the ordinary election of police and crime commissioners in 2012 is to be held on 15 November 2012.

(3)   The poll at an ordinary election of police and crime commissioners in any year after 2012 is to be held on the ordinary day of election in the year of the election.

(4)   But, if the Secretary of State or the Chancellor of the Duchy of Lancaster so specifies in an order, the poll at an ordinary election of police and crime commissioners in any year after 2012 is to be held on such day in the year of the election as may be specified in the order.

(5)   An order under subsection (4)

    (a)   may not specify, as the day of a poll, a day which is before the ordinary day of election in the year of the election;

    (b)   may not be made within the period of six months ending with the ordinary day of election in relation to England, or (if earlier) the ordinary day of election in relation to Wales, in the year of the election (or the first of the elections) to which the order relates.

(6) In this section, "the ordinary day of election" in any year means

    (a) in relation to England, the day which is the ordinary day of election in that year of councillors for counties in England and districts (see sections 37 and 37A of the Representation of the People Act 1983), and

    (b) in relation to Wales, the day which is the ordinary day of election in that year of councillors for counties in Wales and county boroughs (see sections 37 and 37B of that Act).

(7) The term of office of a person elected as a police and crime commissioner at an ordinary election

    (a) begins with the seventh day after the day of the poll at the election, and

    (b) ends with the sixth day after the day of the poll at the next ordinary election of police and crime commissioners.

(8) Subsection (7) is subject to any provision of or made under this or any other Act relating to the appointment or election of police and crime commissioners or their ceasing to hold office.

NOTES

Defined terms

    police area: s 102(1)

Election to fill vacancy in office of commissioner

51(1) This section applies where a vacancy occurs in the office of police and crime commissioner for a police area.

(2) An election must be held to fill the vacancy.

(3) The police area returning officer must fix the date of the poll at the election.

(4) The date fixed must be not more than 35 days after the relevant event (computed in accordance with section 73).

(5) For the purposes of subsection (4), "the relevant event" means

    (a) in a case where the High Court or the appropriate officer has declared the office to be vacant, the making of that declaration;

    (b) in any other case, the giving of notice of the vacancy to the appropriate officer by two or more relevant electors.

(6) For this purpose "relevant elector" means a person who is registered in a register of local government electors in respect of an address within the police area.

(7) If the vacancy occurs within the period of six months ending with the day of the poll at the next ordinary election of police and crime commissioners

    (a) no election is to be held under subsection (2) in respect of the vacancy, and

    (b) accordingly, the office is to be left unfilled until that ordinary election.

(8) The term of office of a person elected as a police and crime commissioner for a police area at an election to fill a vacancy in the office

    (a) begins immediately the person is declared to be elected as police and crime commissioner for the area;

    (b) ends at the time when it would have ended had the person been elected at the most recent ordinary election of police and crime commissioners.

(9) In the case of a vacancy occurring in consequence of the failure of, or other irregularity in relation to, an election, subsections (3) and (4) have effect subject to any provision made by an order under section 58.

Persons entitled to vote

52(1) A person is entitled to vote as an elector at an election of a police and crime commissioner for a police area if on the date of the poll
   (a) the person would be entitled to vote as an elector at a local government election in an electoral area wholly or partly comprised in the police area, and
   (b) the address in respect of which the person is registered in the register of local government electors for that electoral area is within the police area.

   (2) A person is not entitled to vote as an elector more than once in the same police area at any election of a police and crime commissioner.

Public awareness about elections: role of Electoral Commission

53   The Electoral Commission must, in relation to
   (a) each ordinary election of police and crime commissioners under section 50,
   (b) each election to fill a vacancy in the office of police and crime commissioner for a police area under section 51,
   take such steps as it considers appropriate to raise public awareness about the election and how to vote in it.

Conduct of elections

Returning officers etc

54(1) The returning officer for an election of a police and crime commissioner for a police area ("the police area returning officer") is to be a person who
   (a) is an acting returning officer by virtue of section 28(1) of the Representation of the People Act 1983 (acting returning officer for parliamentary election) for a constituency falling wholly or partly within the police area, and
   (b) is designated for the purposes of this subsection by order of the Secretary of State or the Chancellor of the Duchy of Lancaster.

   (2) The Secretary of State or the Chancellor of the Duchy of Lancaster may by regulations confer functions
   (a) on police area returning officers, and
   (b) on local returning officers.

   (3) Regulations under subsection (2) may apply or incorporate, with or without modifications or exceptions, any relevant provision.

   (4) Each relevant local authority must place the services of its officers at the disposal of any person on whom functions are conferred under subsection (2) in relation to the police area for the purpose of assisting that person in the discharge of those functions.

(5) In this section
"local authority" means
(a) a district council,
(b) a county council in England for a county in which there are no district councils,
(c) the Council of the Isles of Scilly,
(d) a county council or county borough council in Wales;
"local election" means an election of members of a local authority;
"local returning officer" means a person who, by virtue of section 35 of the Representation of the People Act 1983, is a returning officer for any local elections;
"relevant local authority", in relation to a police area, means a local authority whose area falls wholly or partly within the police area;
"relevant provision" means any provision (whenever passed or made) of, or made under, any of the following
(a) the Representation of the People Acts,
(b) the Local Government Act 1972,
(c) the Local Government Act 2000,
(d) the Political Parties, Elections and Referendums Act 2000,
(e) the European Parliamentary Elections Act 2002,
(f) the Government of Wales Act 2006, and
(g) any other enactment relating to parliamentary elections, European Parliamentary elections or local government elections.

NOTES

Subordinate Legislation
Police and Crime Commissioner Elections (Designation of Police Area Returning Officers) (No 2) Order 2012, SI 2012/2085
Police and Crime Commissioner Elections (Designation of Police Area Returning Officers) Order 2015, SI 2015/2031
Police and Crime Commissioner Elections (Functions of Returning Officers) Regulations 2012, SI 2012/1918

Defined terms
local government election: s 76
police area: s 102(1)

Returning officers: expenditure

55(1) A returning officer may recover charges in respect of services rendered, or expenses incurred, by the officer for or in connection with an election of a police and crime commissioner if
(a) the services were necessarily rendered, or the expenses were necessarily incurred, for the efficient and effective conduct of the election, and
(b) the total of the officer's charges does not exceed the amount ("the overall maximum recoverable amount") specified in, or determined in accordance with, an order made by the Minister, with the consent of the Treasury, for the purposes of this subsection.

(2) An order under subsection (1) may specify, or make provision for determining in accordance with the order, a maximum recoverable amount for services or expenses of any specified description.

(3) Subject to subsection (4), the returning officer may not recover more than the specified maximum recoverable amount in respect of any specified services or expenses.

(4) In a particular case the Minister may authorise the payment of
(a) more than the overall maximum recoverable amount, or
(b) more than the specified maximum recoverable amount for any specified services or expenses,
if the Minister is satisfied that the conditions in subsection (5) are met.

(5) Those conditions are

    (a)   that it was reasonable for the returning officer concerned to render the services or incur the expenses, and

    (b)   that the charges in question are reasonable.

(6)   The amount of any charges recoverable in accordance with this section is to be paid by the Minister on an account being submitted to the Minister.

(7)   But the Minister may, before payment, apply for the account to be taxed under section 56.

(8)   Where the superannuation contributions required to be paid by a local authority in respect of any person are increased by any fee paid under this section as part of a returning officer's charges at an election of a police and crime commissioner, then on an account being submitted to the Minister a sum equal to the increase must be paid to the authority by the Minister.

(9)   On the request of a returning officer for an advance on account of the officer's charges, the Minister may make such an advance on such terms as the Minister thinks fit.

(10)   The Minister may by regulations make provision as to

    (a)   the time when, and

    (b)   the manner and form in which,

accounts are to be rendered to the Minister for the purposes of the payment of a returning officer's charges.

(11)   Any sums required by the Minister for making payments under this section are to be charged on, and paid out of, the Consolidated Fund.

(12)   In this section

    "local authority" has the same meaning as in section 54;

    "local returning officer" has the same meaning as in that section;

    "the Minister" means the Secretary of State or the Chancellor of the Duchy of Lancaster;

    "returning officer" means

        (a)   a police area returning officer, or

        (b)   a local returning officer on whom functions are conferred under subsection (2) of section 54;

    "specified" means specified in, or determined in accordance with, an order under subsection (1).

NOTES

Subordinate Legislation

Police and Crime Commissioner Elections (Returning Officers' Accounts) Regulations 2012, SI 2012/2088

Police and Crime Commissioner Elections (Local Returning Officers' and Police Area Returning Officers' Charges) Order 2012, SI 2012/2378

Defined terms

local authority: s 54(5)

local returning officer: s 54(5)

police area returning officer: ss 54, 76

Taxation of returning officer's account

56(1)   Any application under section 55(7) for a returning officer's account to be taxed is to be made to the county court.

(2)   On any such application the court has jurisdiction

    (a)   to tax the account

        (i) in such manner, and

        (ii)   at such time and place,

    as the court thinks fit, and

    (b)   finally to determine the amount payable to the returning officer.

(3) On any such application the returning officer may apply to the court to examine any claim made by any person against the officer in respect of matters charged in the account.

(4) Where an application is made in respect of a claim under subsection (3)
    (a) notice of the application must be given to the claimant;
    (b) the court must give the claimant an opportunity to be heard and to tender any evidence;
    (c) the court may allow or disallow the claim, with or without costs;
    (d) the determination of the court is final for all purposes and as against all persons.

(5) In this section "returning officer" has the same meaning as in section 55.

NOTES

Defined terms
    returning officer: s 55(12)

Voting at elections of police and crime commissioners

57(1) This section applies to any election under this Chapter of a police and crime commissioner for a police area.

(2) The commissioner is to be returned under the simple majority system, unless there are three or more candidates.

(3) If there are three or more candidates
    (a) the commissioner is to be returned under the supplementary vote system, and
    (b) any vote in the election is a supplementary vote.

(4) Schedule 9 (the supplementary vote system) has effect.

(5) In subsection (3), "supplementary vote" means a vote capable of being given to indicate first and second preferences from among the candidates.

NOTES

Defined terms
    police area: s 102(1)

Power to make provision about elections etc

58(1) The Secretary of State or the Chancellor of the Duchy of Lancaster may by order make provision as to
    (a) the conduct of elections of persons to be police and crime commissioners;
    (b) the questioning of such an election and the consequences of irregularities.

(2) The provision which may be made under subsection (1)(a) includes, in particular, provision
    (a) about registration of electors;
    (b) for disregarding alterations in a register of electors;
    (c) about the registration or other recognition of political parties and other persons incurring expenditure in relation to elections of police and crime commissioners;
    (d) about funding and expenditure, in relation to elections of police and crime commissioners, of candidates, political parties and other persons incurring such expenditure;
    (e) for the combination of polls at elections of police and crime commissioners and other polls;
    (f) for any election held in consequence of any irregularity at an ordinary election to be treated as held at an ordinary election for any of the purposes of this Act.

(3) An order under subsection (1) may

    (a) apply or incorporate, with or without modifications or exceptions, any relevant provision;

    (b) modify any form contained in any relevant provision so far as may be necessary to enable it to be used both for the original purpose and in relation to elections for police and crime commissioners;

    (c) include provision creating criminal offences.

(4) Provision within paragraph (d) of subsection (2) includes, in particular

    (a) provision prohibiting, or imposing limitations on, funding or expenditure of any kind mentioned in that paragraph, and

    (b) provision for treating funding or expenditure of any such kind which does not relate exclusively to an election of police and crime commissioners as being (or not being), wholly or partly, funding or expenditure in relation to which

        (i) any provision within paragraph (a) applies, or

        (ii) any relevant provision applies.

(5) The Secretary of State or the Chancellor of the Duchy of Lancaster may by order make modifications of any relevant provision that are consequential on any provision of

    (a) section 1(4),

    (b) this Chapter,

    (c) an order under subsection (1), or

    (d) regulations under section 54.

(6) Provision that may be made under subsection (5) includes, in particular, provision modifying any relevant provision so as to apply (with or without modifications)

    (a) in relation to elections for police and crime commissioners as it applies in relation to other elections;

    (b) in relation to police and crime commissioners as it applies in relation to persons elected at other elections.

(7) In this section

"relevant provision" means any provision (whenever passed or made) of, or made under, any of the following

    (a) the Representation of the People Acts,

    (b) the Local Government Act 1972,

    (c) the Local Government Act 2000,

    (d) the Political Parties, Elections and Referendums Act 2000,

    (e) the European Parliamentary Elections Act 2002,

    (f) the Government of Wales Act 2006, and

    (g) any other enactment relating to parliamentary elections, European Parliamentary elections or local government elections;

"modify" includes amend, repeal or revoke (and related terms are to be read accordingly).

NOTES

Subordinate Legislation

Police and Crime Commissioner Elections Order 2012, SI 2012/1917

Police and Crime Commissioner Elections (Welsh Forms) Order 2012, SI 2012/2768

Police and Crime Commissioner Elections Order 2015, SI 2015/665

Defined terms

elector: s 76

local government election: s 76

ordinary election: ss 50, 76

Vacancy in office of police and crime commissioner

Date of vacancy in office of commissioner

59(1) For the purposes of this Chapter, a vacancy in the office of police and crime commissioner for a police area is to be regarded as occurring

(a) in the case of a vacancy in consequence of the failure of, or other irregularity in relation to, an election, at the time specified in an order under section 58;

(b) in the case of resignation, on receipt of the notice of resignation by the appropriate officer;

(c) in the case of death, on the date of death;

(d) in any case within subsection (2), on the date on which the office of police and crime commissioner for the police area is declared to have been vacated by the High Court or by the appropriate officer, as the case may be.

(2) The cases referred to in subsection (1)(d) are

(a) where the person elected as police and crime commissioner fails to make and deliver a declaration of acceptance of office in accordance with section 70;

(b) where a vacancy arises under section 63 (incapacity of commissioner: acting commissioner acting for 6 months);

(c) where a person becomes disqualified

(i) from being a police and crime commissioner, or

(ii) from being the police and crime commissioner for the police area.

(3) The appropriate officer must give public notice of a vacancy in the office of police and crime commissioner for a police area.

(4) The appropriate officer must give notice of a vacancy in the office of police and crime commissioner for a police area to the police area returning officer.

(5) Any notice under subsection (3) or (4) must be given as soon as practicable after the date on which the vacancy is to be regarded under this section as occurring.

NOTES

Defined terms
   appropriate officer: ss 75, 76
   police area: s 102(1)

police area returning officer: ss 54, 76

Declaration of vacancy in certain cases

60(1) Subsection (2) applies where

(a) a police and crime commissioner for a police area becomes disqualified (whether by virtue of this or any other Act)

(i) from being a police and crime commissioner, or

(ii) from being the police and crime commissioner for the police area,

(b) the person elected as police and crime commissioner for a police area fails to make and deliver a declaration of acceptance of office in accordance with section 70, or

(c) a vacancy arises under section 63 (incapacity of commissioner: acting commissioner acting for 6 months).

(2) The appropriate officer must forthwith declare the office of police and crime commissioner for that police area to be vacant, unless

(a) it has been declared vacant by the High Court, or

(b) an application has been made to the High Court for a declaration under section 71 and the grounds in issue include any ground on which the appropriate officer would (but for this paragraph) make the declaration.

NOTES

Defined terms
   appropriate officer: ss 75, 76
   police area: s 102(1)

Resignation of commissioner

61(1) A police and crime commissioner may at any time resign office by giving notice to the appropriate officer.

(2) Any such resignation takes effect on the officer's receipt of the notice.

NOTES
Defined terms
appropriate officer: ss 75, 76

Vacancy or incapacity

Appointment of acting commissioner

62(1) The police and crime panel for a police area must appoint a person to act as police and crime commissioner for that area (the "acting commissioner") if

    (a) no person holds the office of police and crime commissioner for that area,

    (b) the police and crime commissioner for that area is incapacitated, or

    (c) the police and crime commissioner for that area is suspended in accordance with section 30.

(2) The police and crime panel may appoint a person as acting commissioner only if the person is a member of the police and crime commissioner's staff at the time of the appointment.

(3) In appointing a person as acting commissioner in a case where the police and crime commissioner is incapacitated, the police and crime panel must have regard to any representations made by the commissioner in relation to the appointment.

(4) All the functions of a police and crime commissioner are exercisable by an acting commissioner, apart from issuing or varying a police and crime plan under section 5.

(5) Any property or rights vested in the police and crime commissioner may be dealt with by the acting commissioner as if vested in the acting commissioner.

(6) The appointment of an acting commissioner ceases to have effect upon the occurrence of the earliest of these events

    (a) the election of a person as police and crime commissioner;

    (b) the termination by the police and crime panel, or by the acting commissioner, of the appointment of the acting commissioner;

    (c) in a case where the acting commissioner is appointed because the police and crime commissioner is incapacitated, the commissioner ceasing to be incapacitated;

    (d) in a case where the acting commissioner is appointed because the police and crime commissioner is suspended, the commissioner ceasing to be suspended.

(7) In a case where

    (a) the acting commissioner is appointed because the police and crime commissioner is incapacitated or suspended, and

    (b) a vacancy subsequently occurs in the office of police and crime commissioner,

the occurrence of that vacancy does not affect the appointment of the acting commissioner (and accordingly subsection (6)(c) or (d) does not apply).

(8) For the purposes of this section

    (a) a police and crime commissioner is incapacitated if the commissioner is unable to exercise the functions of commissioner, except where the commissioner is unable to exercise those functions only because the commissioner has yet to give a declaration of office under section 70; and

    (b) it is for the police and crime panel for a police area to determine whether or not the police and crime commissioner for that area is incapacitated.

(9) Subject to subsection (4), a reference in any enactment to a police and crime commissioner includes a reference to an acting commissioner.

NOTES

Defined terms
police and crime panel: s 102(1)
police and crime plan: ss 7, 102(1)
police area: s 102(1)

staff: s 102(3

Vacancy where acting commissioner acts for 6 months

63(1) Subsection (2) applies where
  (a) an acting commissioner is appointed under section 62 to act for the police and crime commissioner for a police area because the police and crime commissioner is incapacitated, and
  (b) the police and crime commissioner does not cease to be incapacitated during the period of 6 months beginning with the day on which the acting commissioner is appointed.

(2) At the end of that 6 month period
  (a) the police and crime commissioner ceases to be police and crime commissioner, and
  (b) accordingly, the office of police and crime commissioner for that police area becomes vacant.

NOTES

Defined terms
police area: s 102(1)

Disqualification

Disqualification from election as police and crime commissioner

64(1) A person is disqualified from being elected to the office of police and crime commissioner for a police area at any election unless
  (a) the person has attained the age of 18 when nominated as a candidate at the election, and
  (b) on each relevant day, the person is registered in the register of local government electors for an electoral area in respect of an address in the police area.

(2) In this section "relevant day", in relation to a person who is a candidate at an election, means
  (a) the day on which the person is nominated as a candidate at the election;
  (b) the day of the poll at the election.

(3) A person is disqualified from being elected to the office of police and crime commissioner for a police area at an ordinary election if the person has been nominated as a candidate for election as police and crime commissioner for any other police area at that election.

(4) A person is disqualified from being elected to the office of police and crime commissioner for a police area at an election other than an ordinary election if
  (a) the person is police and crime commissioner for any other police area, or
  (b) the person has been nominated as a candidate for election as police and crime commissioner for any other police area for which an election is held on the same day.

NOTES

Defined terms

electoral area: s 76

local government elector: s 76
ordinary election: ss 50, 76
police area: s 102(1)

Disqualification from election or holding office as police and crime commissioner: police grounds

65(1) A person is disqualified from being elected as, or being, a police and crime commissioner if the person

(a) is disqualified from being a member of the House of Commons under section 1(1)(d) of the House of Commons Disqualification Act 1975 (members of police forces for police areas in the United Kingdom);

(b) is a member of

(i) the British Transport Police Force;

(ii) the Civil Nuclear Constabulary;

(c) is a special constable appointed

(i) under section 27 of the Police Act 1996 for a police area or the City of London police area;

(ii) under section 25 of the Railways and Transport Safety Act 2003 (British Transport Police Force);

(d) is a member of staff of the chief officer of police of any police force maintained for a police area;

(e) is a member of staff of

(i) a police and crime commissioner;

(ii) the Mayor's Office for Policing and Crime;

(f) is the Mayor of London;

(g) is a member of the Common Council of the City of London or a member of staff of that Council in its capacity as a police authority;

(h) is a member (including a member who is chairman or chief executive), or member of staff, of

(i) the British Transport Police Authority;

(ii) the Civil Nuclear Police Authority;

(iii) the Independent Police Complaints Commission;

(iv) the Serious Organised Crime Agency;

(i) holds any employment in an entity which is under the control of

(i) a local policing body;

(ii) any body mentioned in paragraph (h);

(iii) the chief officer of police for any police force maintained for a police area or the City of London police area;

(iv) the chief officer of police for any police force mentioned in paragraph (b).

(2) In this section, "member of staff", in relation to any person ("A"), includes a person ("B") who works for A

(a) under a contract of employment,

(b) under a contract for services, or

(c) in accordance with arrangements made between B's employer and A;

and for this purpose B works for A if B provides services for A under the direction and control of A.

(3) In subsection (1)(i), the reference to an entity under the control of a local policing body or other body or a chief officer of police is to be construed in accordance with regulations made by the Secretary of State or the Chancellor of the Duchy of Lancaster.

(4) In its application in relation to the first election of a police and crime commissioner to be held for a police area, this section applies as if

(a) for paragraphs (d) to (g) of subsection (1) there were substituted

"(d) any member, or member of staff, of a police authority within the meaning of the Police Act 1996 (see section 101 of that Act);", and
(b) for paragraph (i)(i) of that subsection there were substituted
"(i) a police authority within the meaning of the Police Act 1996."

NOTES

Subordinate Legislation
Police and Crime Commissioner (Disqualification) (Supplementary Provisions) Regulations 2012, SI 2012/2087

Defined terms
chief officer of police: s 102(1)
police area: s 102(1)
staff: s 102(3), (5)

Disqualification from election or holding office as police and crime commissioner: other grounds

66(1) A person is disqualified from being elected as, or being, a police and crime commissioner unless the person satisfies the citizenship condition (see section 68).

(2) A person is disqualified from being elected as, or being, a police and crime commissioner if the person

(a) is disqualified from being a member of the House of Commons under section 1(1)(a) to (c) of the House of Commons Disqualification Act 1975 (judges, civil servants, members of the armed forces), or

(b) is a member of the legislature of any country or territory outside the United Kingdom.

(3) A person is disqualified from being elected as, or being, a police and crime commissioner if

(a) the person is the subject of

(i) a debt relief restrictions order under paragraph 1 of Schedule 4ZB to the Insolvency Act 1986;

(ii) an interim debt relief restrictions order under paragraph 5 of that Schedule;

(iii) a bankruptcy restrictions order under paragraph 1 of Schedule 4A to that Act;

(iv) a bankruptcy restrictions interim order under paragraph 5 of that Schedule;

(b) a debt relief restrictions undertaking has effect in respect of the person under paragraph 7 of Schedule 4ZB to that Act;

(c) the person has been convicted in the United Kingdom, the Channel Islands, or the Isle of Man, of any imprisonable offence (whether or not sentenced to a term of imprisonment in respect of the offence); or

(d) the person is incapable of being elected as a member of the House of Commons, or is required to vacate a seat in the House of Commons, under Part 3 of the Representation of the People Act 1983 (consequences of corrupt or illegal practices).

(4) For the purpose of subsection (3)(c)

(a) "imprisonable offence" means an offence

(i) for which a person who has attained the age of 18 years may be sentenced to a term of imprisonment, or

(ii) for which, in the case of such a person, the sentence is fixed by law as life imprisonment;

(b) a person is to be treated as having been convicted

(i) on the expiry of the ordinary period allowed for an appeal or application in respect of the conviction, or

(ii) if an appeal or application is made in respect of the conviction, when the appeal or application is finally disposed of or abandoned or fails by reason of non-prosecution.

(5)   A person is disqualified from being elected as, or being, police and crime commissioner for a police area if the person

    (a)   is a member of staff of a relevant council, or

    (b)   holds any employment in an entity which is under the control of a relevant council within subsection (7)(a), (b), (c) or (f).

(6)   For this purpose

"member of staff" has the same meaning as in section 65;

"relevant council", in relation to a police area, means a council within subsection (7) for an area which, or any part of which, lies within the police area.

(7)   Those councils are

    (a)   a county council;

    (b)   a county borough council;

    (c)   a district council;

    (d)   a parish council;

    (e)   a community council;

    (f)   the Council of the Isles of Scilly.

(8)   In subsection (5)(b), the reference to an entity under the control of a relevant council is to be construed in accordance with regulations made by the Secretary of State or the Chancellor of the Duchy of Lancaster.

(9)   Nothing in subsection (5) is to be taken to disqualify a person by virtue of being a teacher, or otherwise employed, in a school or other educational institution maintained or assisted by a relevant council.

NOTES

Subordinate Legislation
Police and Crime Commissioner (Disqualification) (Supplementary Provisions) Regulations 2012, SI 2012/2087

Defined terms
member of staff: s 65(2)
police area: s 102(1)

Disqualification of person holding office as police and crime commissioner

67   A person becomes disqualified from being a police and crime commissioner upon becoming a member of

    (a)   the House of Commons;

    (b)   the Scottish Parliament;

    (c)   the National Assembly for Wales;

    (d)   the Northern Ireland Assembly;

    (e)   the European Parliament.

Citizenship condition

68(1)   This section applies for the purposes of section 66.

(2)   A person satisfies the citizenship condition if the person is

    (a)   a qualifying Commonwealth citizen,

    (b)   a citizen of the Republic of Ireland, or

    (c)   a citizen of the Union.

(3)   For the purposes of this section, a person is a qualifying Commonwealth citizen if the person is a Commonwealth citizen and

    (a)   is not a person who requires leave under the Immigration Act 1971 to enter or remain in the United Kingdom, or

    (b)   is a person who requires such leave but for the time being has (or is, by virtue of any enactment, to be treated as having) indefinite leave to remain within the meaning of that Act.

(4) But a person who does not require leave to enter or remain in the United Kingdom by virtue only of section 8 of the Immigration Act 1971 (exceptions to requirement for leave in special cases) is not a qualifying Commonwealth citizen by virtue of subsection (3)(a).

(5) In this section the expression "citizen of the Union" is to be construed in accordance with Article 20(1) of the Treaty on the Functioning of the European Union.

Validity of acts

69 The acts of a person elected as police and crime commissioner for a police area under this Chapter who acts in that office are, despite any disqualification
  (a) from being, or being elected as, a police and crime commissioner, or
  (b) from being, or being elected as police and crime commissioner for that area,
as valid and effectual as if the person had not been so disqualified.

NOTES
Defined terms
  police area: s 102(1)

Elections: further provision
Declaration of acceptance of office of police and crime commissioner

70(1) A person elected to the office of police and crime commissioner for any police area may not act in that office unless the person has
  (a) made a declaration of acceptance of the office in a form specified in an order made by the Secretary of State or the Chancellor of the Duchy of Lancaster, and
  (b) delivered the declaration to the appropriate officer,
in each case, when not ineligible by virtue of subsection (5).

(2) If the person fails to make and deliver a declaration in accordance with subsection (1) within the period of two months beginning with the day after the election, the office of police and crime commissioner for that area becomes vacant at the end of the period.

(3) Any declaration made under this section must be made before
  (a) the appropriate officer;
  (b) a justice of the peace or magistrate in the United Kingdom, the Channel Islands or the Isle of Man, or
  (c) a commissioner appointed to administer oaths in the Senior Courts.

(4) Any person before whom a declaration is authorised to be made under this section may take the declaration.

(5) A person is ineligible to make or give a declaration of acceptance of office under this section in respect of the office of police and crime commissioner for a police area at any time when the person is a member of
  (a) the House of Commons;
  (b) the Scottish Parliament;
  (c) the National Assembly for Wales;
  (d) the Northern Ireland Assembly;
  (e) the European Parliament.

(6) No salary, and no payment towards the provision of superannuation benefits, is to be paid under this Act to or in respect of a police and crime commissioner until the commissioner has complied with the requirements of subsection (1).

(7) Subsection (6) does not affect any entitlement of a police and crime commissioner to payments in respect of the period before the commissioner complies with the

requirements of subsection (1) once the commissioner has complied with those requirements.

NOTES
Subordinate Legislation
  Police and Crime Commissioner Elections (Declaration of Acceptance of Office) Order 2012, SI 2012/2553

Defined terms
  appropriate officer: ss 75, 76
  police area: s 102(1)

Judicial proceedings as to disqualification or vacancy

71(1) Any person who claims that a person purporting to be a police and crime commissioner for a police area is, or at any time since being elected has been, disqualified
  (a) from being a police and crime commissioner; or
  (b) from being police and crime commissioner for the police area,
  may apply to the High Court for a declaration to that effect, and that accordingly the office of police and crime commissioner for the area is vacant.

(2) An application under subsection (1) in respect of any person may be made whether the grounds on which it is made are alleged to have subsisted at the time when the person was elected or to have arisen subsequently.

(3) No declaration may be made under this section in respect of any person on grounds which subsisted when the person was elected, if an election petition under an order under section 58 is pending or has been tried in which the person's disqualification on those grounds is or was in issue.

(4) Any person who claims that a person purporting to be a police and crime commissioner for a police area has ceased to be the police and crime commissioner for the police area by virtue of
  (a) section 63, or
  (b) section 70,
  may apply to the High Court for a declaration to that effect.

(5) On an application under this section
  (a) the person in respect of whom the application is made is to be the respondent, and
  (b) the applicant must give such security for the costs of the proceedings as the court may direct.

(6) The amount of the security may not exceed £5,000 or such other sum as the Secretary of State or the Chancellor of the Duchy of Lancaster may specify by order.

(7) The decision of the court on an application under this section is final.

NOTES
Defined terms
  police area: s 102(1)

Amendment of police areas: term of office of commissioner

72(1) Subsection (2) applies where a person becomes police and crime commissioner for a resulting police area by virtue of, or of an election required to be held by, a police area alteration order.

(2) The person's term of office as police and crime commissioner ends at the time when it would end had the person been elected as police and crime commissioner at the previous ordinary election of commissioners in England or, as the case may be, Wales.

(3) In this section

"police area alteration order" means

    (a) an order under section 32 of the Police Act 1996 (power to alter police areas by order);

    (b) an order under section 10 of the Local Government and Public Involvement in Health Act 2007 (implementation of Boundary Committee for England review of local government areas) which alters the boundary of any police area in England;

    (c) an order under section 45 of the Local Government (Democracy) (Wales) Act 2013 (anaw 4) (recommendations for changes to police areas) which alters the boundary of any police area in Wales;

"resulting police area", in relation to a police area alteration order, means a police area existing immediately after the order comes into force

    (a) which is created by the order, or

    (b) any part of whose boundary results from the order.

(4) References in this section to the coming into force of a police area alteration order are references to the changes in police areas made by the order taking effect.

NOTES
Defined terms
  ordinary election: ss 50, 76
  police area: s 102(1)

Computation of time and timing of elections etc

73(1) Subsection (2) applies where the day, or the last day, on which anything is required or permitted to be done by or under section 50, 51 or 70 is not a business day.

(2) The requirement or permission is deemed to relate instead to the first business day after that day.

(3) Where under subsection (2) the day of an election is postponed, the day to which it is postponed is to be treated as the day of election for the purpose of

    (a) any provision of, or made under, this Act, or

    (b) any relevant provision (within the meaning of section 58).

(4) Any day which is not a business day is to be disregarded in computing any period of time for the purpose of section 51.

(5) In this section, "business day" means a day other than
    a Saturday,
    a Sunday,
    Christmas Eve,
    Christmas Day,
    Good Friday,
    a bank holiday, or
    a day appointed for public thanksgiving or mourning.

Elections: consequential amendments

74 Schedule 10 (consequential amendments relating to elections of persons as police and crime commissioners) has effect.

The appropriate officer

75(1) For each police area, other than the metropolitan police district, the Secretary of State or the Chancellor of the Duchy of Lancaster must by order designate a local authority.

(2) In this Chapter, the "appropriate officer", in relation to any such police area, means the head of paid service of the local authority designated for that police area.

(3) In this section

"local authority" means

(a) a district council,

(b) a county council in England for a county in which there are no district councils,

(c) the Council of the Isles of Scilly,

(d) a county council or county borough council in Wales;

"head of paid service", in relation to a council, means the person designated by the council under section 4(1)(a) of the Local Government Act 1989.

NOTES

Subordinate Legislation

Police and Crime Commissioner Elections (Designation of Local Authorities) (No 2) Order 2012, SI 2012/2084

Police and Crime Commissioner Elections (Designation of Local Authorities) Order 2015, SI 2015/2028

Defined terms

police area: s 102(1)

Interpretation of Chapter 6

76 In this Chapter, the following terms have the following meanings, unless the context otherwise requires

"appropriate officer" has the meaning given by section 75;

"elector"

(a) in relation to an election of a police and crime commissioner, means a person entitled to vote at the election;

(b) in relation to a local government election, has the same meaning as in the Representation of the People Act 1983 (see section 202 of that Act);

"electoral area" has the same meaning as in that Act as it applies in relation to England and Wales (see section 203 of that Act);

"local government election" has the same meaning as in that Act as it applies in relation to England and Wales (see section 203 of that Act);

"local government elector" means a person registered as a local government elector in the register of electors in accordance with the provisions of the Representation of the People Acts;

"ordinary election" has the meaning given in section 50;

"police area returning officer" has the meaning given by section 54.

Interpretation of Part 1

102(1) In this Part (unless otherwise specified)

"chief executive" means

(a) in relation to a police and crime commissioner, the chief executive appointed by the commissioner under Schedule 1;

(b) in relation to the Mayor's Office for Policing and Crime, the chief executive appointed by the Office under Schedule 3;

"chief finance officer" means

(a) in relation to a police and crime commissioner, the chief finance officer appointed by the commissioner under Schedule 1;

(b) in relation to the chief constable of a police force to which Chapter 1 applies, the chief finance officer appointed by the chief constable under Schedule 2;

(c) in relation to the Mayor's Office for Policing and Crime, the chief finance officer appointed by the Office under Schedule 3;

(d) in relation to the Commissioner of Police of the Metropolis, the chief finance officer appointed by the Commissioner under Schedule 4;

"chief officer of police" means

(a) in relation to a police force maintained under section 2 of the Police Act 1996, the chief constable of that force;

(b) in relation to the metropolitan police force, the Commissioner of Police of the Metropolis;

"crime and disorder reduction" has the meaning given in section 101;

"elected local policing body" means

(a) in relation to a police area listed in Schedule 1 to the Police Act 1996, the police and crime commissioner for the area;

(b) in relation to the metropolitan police district, the Mayor's Office for Policing and Crime;

"national or international functions" means functions relating to

(a) the protection of prominent persons or their residences,

(b) national security,

(c) counterterrorism, or

(d) the provision of services for any other national or international purpose;

"police and crime panel" means

(a) in relation to a police area listed in Schedule 1 to the Police Act 1996, the police and crime panel referred to in subsection (1) of section 28;

(b) in relation to the metropolitan police district, the committee established under section 32;

"police and crime plan" has the meaning given in section 7;

"police area" means

(a) a police area listed in Schedule 1 to the Police Act 1996 (police areas outside London), and

(b) the metropolitan police district;

"relevant chief officer of police", in relation to

(a) a police area,

(b) the police force for a police area,

(c) the elected local policing body for a police area, or

(d) the police and crime panel for a police area,

means the chief officer of police of the police force for that area;

"relevant elected local policing body", in relation to

(a) a police area,

(b) the police force for a police area,

(c) the chief officer of police of the police force for a police area, or

(d) the police and crime panel for a police area,

means the elected local policing body for that area;

"relevant police and crime panel", in relation to

(a) a police area,

(b) the police force for a police area,

(c) the chief officer of police of the police force for a police area, or

(d) the elected local policing body for a police area,

means the police and crime panel for that area;

"relevant police force", in relation to

(a) a police area,

(b) a chief officer of police of the police force for a police area,

(c) the elected local policing body for a police area, or

(d) the police and crime panel for a police area,

means the police force for that area.

(2) References in this Part to a police and crime commissioner's area are references to the police area for which the commissioner is established.

(3) References in this Part to a police and crime commissioner's staff are references to the following persons appointed under Schedule 1

(a) the commissioner's chief executive;

(b) the commissioner's chief finance officer; and

(c) other staff;

and to the person (if any) appointed as the deputy police and crime commissioner under section 18.

(4) References in this Part to a police force's civilian staff are (except in the case of the metropolitan police force) references to

    (a) the chief finance officer appointed by the chief constable of the force under paragraph 4 of Schedule 2, and

    (b) the other staff appointed by that chief constable under that Schedule.

(5) References in this Part to the staff of the Mayor's Office for Policing and Crime are references to

    (a) the Office's chief finance officer appointed under section 127(2) of the Greater London Authority Act 1999;

    (b) the Office's chief executive appointed under Schedule 3;

    (c) other staff appointed under Schedule 3; and

    (d) the person (if any) appointed under section 19 as the Deputy Mayor for Policing and Crime (subject to paragraph 4(4) of Schedule 3 (Deputy Mayor an Assembly member)).

(6) References in this Part to the metropolitan police force's civilian staff are references to

    (a) the chief finance officer appointed by the Commissioner of Police of the Metropolis under paragraph 1 of Schedule 4, and

    (b) the other staff appointed by the Commissioner under that Schedule.

SCHEDULE 9
Supplementary Vote System

Section 57

Application

1 This Schedule applies to an election under Chapter 6 of Part 1 of a police and crime commissioner for a police area at which there are three or more candidates.

First preference vote and second preference vote

2 In this Schedule

"first preference vote" means a vote to the extent that it is given so as to indicate a first preference from among the candidates to be the police and crime commissioner;

"second preference vote" means a vote to the extent that it is given so as to indicate a second preference from among the candidates to be the police and crime commissioner.

Candidate with overall majority of first preference votes

3 If one of the candidates to be the police and crime commissioner receives more than half of all the first preference votes given in the police area, that candidate is to be returned as the police and crime commissioner.

No candidate with overall majority of first preference votes

4(1) If none of the candidates to be the police and crime commissioner receives more than half of all the first preference votes given in the police area, the following provisions of this paragraph apply.

(2) The two candidates who received the greatest number of first preference votes given in the police area remain in the contest.

(3) If, by reason of an equality of first preference votes, three or more candidates are qualified to remain in the contest by virtue of sub-paragraph (2), all of them remain in the contest.

(4) The other candidates are eliminated from the contest.

(5) The number of second preference votes given in the police area for each of the candidates remaining in the contest by votes which did not give a first preference vote to any of those candidates must be ascertained.

(6) That number must be added to the number of first preference votes given for that candidate, to give the total number of preference votes for that candidate.

(7) The person who is to be returned as the police and crime commissioner for the police area is that one of the candidates remaining in the contest who has the greatest total number of preference votes.

(8) If, by reason of an equality of total number of preference votes, two or more candidates remaining in the contest each have the greatest total number of preference votes, the police area returning officer must decide by lots which of them is to be returned as the police and crime commissioner.

Political Parties, Elections and Referendums Act 2000[1]

An Act to establish an Electoral Commission; to make provision about the registration and finances of political parties; to make provision about donations and expenditure for political purposes; to make provision about election and referendum campaigns and the conduct of referendums; to make provision about election petitions and other legal proceedings in connection with elections; to reduce the qualifying periods set out in sections 1 and 3 of the Representation of the People Act 1985; to make pre-consolidation amendments relating to European Parliamentary Elections; and for connected purposes.

30th November 2000

PART I
THE ELECTORAL COMMISSION

The operation of prospective amendments, some of which have been noted, should always be checked.

PART II
REGISTRATION OF POLITICAL PARTIES

PART III
ACCOUNTING REQUIREMENTS FOR REGISTERED PARTIES

PART IV
CONTROL OF DONATIONS TO REGISTERED PARTIES AND THEIR MEMBERS ETC

Chapter I
Donations to Registered Parties

Chapter II
Restrictions on Donations to Registered Parties

Permissible donations

Forfeiture of certain donations

Evasion of restrictions on donations

Chapter III
Reporting of Donations to Registered Parties

Reports to be made by registered parties

Extension of reporting requirements

Register of donations

Chapter IV

PART V
CONTROL OF CAMPAIGN EXPENDITURE

Preliminary

PART VI
CONTROLS RELATING TO THIRD PARTY NATIONAL ELECTION CAMPAIGNS

Chapter I
Preliminary

Controlled expenditure by third parties

Chapter II
Financial Controls

General restrictions relating to controlled expenditure by recognised third parties

PART VII
REFERENDUMS

Chapter I
Preliminary

Chapter II
Financial Controls

162   Interpretation: exempt trust donations
163   Short title, commencement, transitional provisions and extent

SCHEDULES

PART I
THE ELECTORAL COMMISSION

Establishment of Electoral Commission and bodies with related functions

Establishment of the Electoral Commission

1 (1)   There shall be a body corporate to be known as the Electoral Commission or, in Welsh, Comisiwn Etholiadol (in this Act referred to as "the Commission").

   (2)   The Commission shall consist of members to be known as Electoral Commissioners.

   (3)   There shall be nine or ten Electoral Commissioners.

   (4)   The Electoral Commissioners shall be appointed by Her Majesty (in accordance with section 3).

(5) Her Majesty shall (in accordance with section 3 but subject to section 3A(6)) appoint one of the Electoral Commissioners to be the chairman of the Commission.

(6) Schedule 1, which makes further provision in relation to the Commission, shall have effect.

Speaker's Committee

2 (1) There shall be a Committee (to be known as "the Speaker's Committee") to perform the functions conferred on the Committee by this Act.

(2) The Speaker's Committee shall consist of the Speaker of the House of Commons, who shall be the chairman of the Committee, and the following other members, namely
    (a) the Member of the House of Commons who is for the time being the Chairman of the Home Affairs Select Committee of the House of Commons;
    (b) the Chancellor of the Duchy of Lancaster;
    (c) a Member of the House of Commons who is a Minister of the Crown with responsibilities in relation to local government; and
    (d) five Members of the House of Commons who are not Ministers of the Crown.

(3) The member of the Committee mentioned in subsection (2)(c) shall be appointed to membership of the Committee by the Prime Minister.

(4) The members of the Committee mentioned in subsection (2)(d) shall be appointed to membership of the Committee by the Speaker of the House of Commons.

(5) Schedule 2, which makes further provision in relation to the Speaker's Committee, shall have effect.

(6) In this section and that Schedule, references to the Home Affairs Select Committee shall
    (a) if the name of that Committee is changed, be taken (subject to paragraph (b)) to be references to the Committee by its new name;
    (b) if the functions of that Committee at the passing of this Act with respect to electoral matters (or functions substantially corresponding thereto) become functions of a different committee of the House of Commons, be taken to be references to the committee by whom the functions are for the time being exercisable.

Appointment of Electoral Commissioners and Commission chairman

3 (1) The powers of Her Majesty under section 1(4) and (5) shall be exercisable on an Address from the House of Commons.

(2) A motion for such an Address may be made only if
    (a) the Speaker of the House of Commons agrees that the motion may be made;
    (b) the motion has been the subject of consultation with the registered leader of each registered party to which two or more Members of the House of Commons then belong; and
    (c) each person whose appointment is proposed in the motion has been selected in accordance with a procedure put in place and overseen by the Speaker's Committee.

(3) Such an Address shall specify the period (not exceeding 10 years) for which each proposed Electoral Commissioner to whom the Address relates is to hold office as such Commissioner or (as the case may be) the period for which the proposed chairman of the Commission is to hold office as such chairman.

(4) Subject to subsection (4A), a person may not be appointed as an Electoral Commissioner if the person

    (a) is a member of a registered party;

    (b) is an officer or employee of a registered party or of any accounting unit of such a party;

    (c) holds a relevant elective office (within the meaning of Schedule 7); or

    (d) has at any time within the last five years

        (i)   been such an officer or employee as is mentioned in paragraph (b), or

        (ii) held such an office as is mentioned in paragraph (c), or

        (iii) been named as a donor in the register of donations reported under Chapter III or V of Part IV, or

        (iv) been named as a participant in the register of recordable transactions reported under Part 4A.

(4A) Paragraphs (a) and (d) of subsection (4) do not apply to the appointment of a person as a nominated Commissioner (within the meaning of section 3A).

(5) An Electoral Commissioner, or the chairman of the Commission, may be reappointed (or further reappointed).

(5A) In the case of a reappointment (or further reappointment) of an Electoral Commissioner, the reference in subsection (2)(c) to being selected in accordance with a procedure put in place and overseen by the Speaker's Committee is to be read as including a reference to being recommended for reappointment (or further reappointment) by that Committee.

(6) In subsection (2)(b) the reference to Members of the House of Commons does not include any Member of that House who at the time in question

    (a) has not made and subscribed the oath required by the Parliamentary Oaths Act 1866 (or the corresponding affirmation); or

    (b) is disqualified from sitting and voting in that House.

(7) In this section "registered party"

    (a) includes (in relation to times before the appointed day for the purposes of Part II of this Act) a party registered under the Registration of Political Parties Act 1998; and

    (b) in subsection (4)(b) also includes (in relation to times before 1st April 1999) any political party.

NOTES

Defined terms
  accounting unit: ss 26(11), 160(1)
  the Commission: s 160(1)

registered party: s 160(1) (and sub-s (7))

Four Electoral Commissioners to be persons put forward by parties

3A (1) Four of the Electoral Commissioners shall each be a person whom the registered leader of a qualifying party put forward to be considered for appointment as an Electoral Commissioner (a "nominated Commissioner").

(2) In subsection (1) "qualifying party" means a registered party with two or more Members of the House of Commons at the time of the person's appointment.

(3) Three of the nominated Commissioners shall each be a person put forward by the registered leader of one of the three largest nominating parties at the time of the person's appointment.

(4) In subsection (3) "nominating party" means a party whose registered leader

    (a) has put forward three persons to be considered for appointment as a nominated Commissioner, or

    (b) previously put forward persons one of whom was appointed as a nominated Commissioner and is expected to continue to hold office.

(5) No appointment may be made that would result in two or more nominated Commissioners being persons put forward by the leader of the same party (and nothing in this section has effect so as to require that result).

(6) A nominated Commissioner may not be appointed as the chairman of the Commission.

(7) For the purposes of this section, the relative size of any two or more registered parties shall be determined according to the number of Members of the House of Commons belonging to each party at the time in question (or, in the case of two parties with the same number of Members, according to the total number of votes cast for persons standing for election in the name of each of those parties at the most recent parliamentary general election).

(8) A reference in this section to a Member of the House of Commons does not include any Member of that House who at the time in question

    (a) has not made and subscribed the oath required by the Parliamentary Oaths Act 1866 (or the corresponding affirmation), or

    (b) is disqualified from sitting and voting in that House.

NOTES

Defined terms

  registered party: s 160(1)

Parliamentary Parties Panel

4 (1) There shall be a panel (to be known as "the Parliamentary Parties Panel") which consists of representatives of qualifying parties appointed in accordance with this section.

(2) The function of the panel shall be to submit representations or information to the Commission about such matters affecting political parties as the panel think fit.

(3) Where the panel submit any such representations or information to the Commission, the Commission shall

    (a) consider the representations or information, and

    (b) decide whether, and (if so) to what extent, they should act on the representations or information.

(4) Each qualifying party shall be entitled to be represented on the panel by a person appointed to the panel by the treasurer of the party.

(5) Subject to subsection (6), a person so appointed shall be a member of the panel for such period as the treasurer of the party may determine when making the appointment.

(6) A person so appointed shall cease to be a member of the panel if at any time

    (a) his appointment is terminated for any reason by the treasurer of the party, or

    (b) the party ceases to be a qualifying party.

(7) The panel may determine their own procedure.

(8) The validity of any proceedings of the panel shall not be affected by any failure by the treasurer of a qualifying party to make any appointment in accordance with this section.

(9) In this section "qualifying party" means a registered party

    (a) to which two or more Members of the House of Commons for the time being belong, who have made and subscribed to the oath required by the Parliamentary Oaths Act 1866 (or the corresponding affirmation) and are not disqualified from sitting or voting in the House; or

    (b) to which two or more such Members belonged immediately after the most recent parliamentary general election.

Commission's general functions

Reports on elections and referendums , referendums etc

5 (1)   The Commission shall, after

      (a)   each election to which this section applies, and

      (b)   each referendum to which Part VII applies,

   prepare and publish (in such manner as the Commission may determine) a report on the administration of the election or referendum.

   (2)   The elections to which this section applies are the following, namely

      (a)   a parliamentary general election;

      (b)   a European Parliamentary general election;

      (c)   a Scottish Parliamentary general election;

      (d)   a National Assembly for Wales general election;

      (e)   a Northern Ireland Assembly general election;

      (f)   an ordinary election of police and crime commissioners.

(2A)   After

      (a)   a parliamentary by-election,

      (b)   an election held under section 9 of the Scotland Act 1998 (election for the Scottish Parliament in the case of a constituency vacancy),

      (c)   an election held under section 10 of the Government of Wales Act 2006 (election for the National Assembly for Wales in the case of a constituency vacancy), or

      (d)   an election held under section 51 of the Police Reform and Social Responsibility Act 2011 (election to fill vacancy in office of police and crime commissioner),

   the Commission may prepare and publish (in such manner as the Commission may determine) a report on the administration of the election.

(2B)   After an ordinary election of councillors for local government areas in Scotland, the Commission must prepare and publish (in such manner as the Commission may determine) a report on the administration of the election.

   (3)   After a poll held under section 64 of the Government of Wales Act 2006 the Commission shall, if requested to do so by the Welsh Ministers, at their expense prepare and publish (in such manner as the Commission may determine) a report on the administration of the poll.

   (4)   After the end of a recall petition period (within the meaning of Schedule 3 to the Recall of MPs Act 2015), the Commission must prepare and publish (in such manner as the Commission may determine) a report on the actions taken, or not taken, under or by virtue of that Act in relation to the recall petition in question after the giving of the Speaker's notice under section 5 of that Act in relation to that petition.

Reviews of electoral and political matters

6 (1)   The Commission shall keep under review, and from time to time submit reports to the Secretary of State on, the following matters, namely

(a) such matters relating to elections to which this section applies as the Commission may determine from time to time;

(b) such matters relating to referendums to which this section applies as the Commission may so determine;

(ba) such matters relating to recall petitions as the Commission may so determine;

(c) the redistribution of seats at parliamentary elections;

(d) if any functions are transferred by an order under section 18(1), 19(1) or 20(1), the matters in relation to which those functions are exercisable;

(e) the registration of political parties and the regulation of their income and expenditure;

(f) political advertising in the broadcast and other electronic media;

(g) the law relating to the matters mentioned in each of paragraphs (a) to (f).

(2) At the request of the Secretary of State, and within such time as the Secretary of State may specify, the Commission shall

(a) review, and

(b) submit a report to the Secretary of State on,

such matter or matters (whether or not falling within subsection (1)) as the Secretary of State may specify.

(3) The Commission shall not, however, carry out any review (or make any report) under this section with respect to any of the following matters, namely

(a) the funding of political parties under section 97 of the Scotland Act 1998 or for the purpose of assisting members of the Northern Ireland Assembly connected with such parties to perform their Assembly duties or the funding of political groups under section 24 of the Government of Wales Act 2006;

(b) the conduct of referendums held in pursuance of any provision made by or under an Act of the Scottish Parliament or the Northern Ireland Assembly or the conduct of any poll under section 64 of the Government of Wales Act 2006;

(ba) how a member of the House of Commons becomes subject to a recall petition process under sections 1 to 5 of the Recall of MPs Act 2015;

(c) the law relating to the matters mentioned in each of paragraphs (a) and (b) to (ba).

(4) Where any review carried out under this section relates to elections or referendums, referendums or recall petitions in Northern Ireland, the Commission shall consult the Chief Electoral Officer for Northern Ireland with respect to such elections or referendums, referendums or recall petitions.

(5) Each report made by the Commission under this section shall be published by them in such manner as they may determine.

(6) The elections and referendums to which this section applies are

(a) in the case of elections

(i) the elections mentioned in section 5(2),

(ii) local government elections in England or Wales, and

(iii) local elections in Northern Ireland; and

(b) in the case of referendums, referendums to which Part VII applies and those under Part II of the Local Government Act 2000.

NOTES

Prospective operation
  Sub-s s(1)(ba) and (3)(ba) not yet in operation

Defined terms
  the Commission: s 160(1)
  functions: s 160(1)

local election: s 160(1)
local government election: s 160(1)
the Secretary of State: s 159A

Attendance of representatives of Commission at elections etc

6A (1) A representative of the Commission may attend
    (a) proceedings relating to an election specified in subsection (5) which are the responsibility of the returning officer for the election;
    (b) proceedings relating to a referendum to which Part 7 applies which are the responsibility of the relevant counting officer;
    (c) proceedings relating to a recall petition which are the responsibility of the petition officer in relation to the petition.

(2) The right conferred on a representative of the Commission by this section is subject to any enactment which regulates attendance at the proceedings in question.

(3) In this section, "representative of the Commission" means any of the following
    (a) a member of the Commission;
    (b) a member of staff of the Commission;
    (c) a person appointed by the Commission for the purposes of this section.

(4) A reference to the relevant counting officer must be construed
    (a) if the area to which the proceedings relates is in Great Britain, in accordance with section 128(3);
    (b) if the area to which the proceedings relates is Northern Ireland, as a reference to the Chief Electoral Officer for Northern Ireland.

(5) The elections specified in this subsection are
    (a) an election mentioned in section 5(2);
    (b) a parliamentary by-election;
    (c) an election under section 9 of the Scotland Act 1998 (constituency vacancies);
    (d) an election under section 10 of the Government of Wales Act 2006 (constituency vacancies);
    (da) an election under section 51 of the Police Reform and Social Responsibility Act 2011 (election to fill vacancy in office of police and crime commissioner);
    (e) a local government election in England or Wales;
    (ea) a local government election in Scotland;
    (f) a local election in Northern Ireland.

NOTES
Prospective operation
  Sub-s (1)(c) not yet in operation

Defined terms
  the Commission: s 160(1)

local election (in Northern Ireland): s 160(1)
local government election: s 160(1)

Observation of working practices by representatives of Commission

6B (1) A representative of the Commission may observe the working practices of any of the following
    (a) an electoral registration officer;
    (b) a returning officer;
    (c) a relevant counting officer;
    (d) any person acting under the direction of a person mentioned in paragraphs (a) to (c).

(2) In this section
    (a) "relevant counting officer", and
    (b) "representative of the Commission",
  must be construed in accordance with section 6A.

(3) *Repealed*

NOTES

Defined terms
the Commission: s 160(1)
relevant counting officer: s 6A(4)

Accredited observers: individuals

6C (1)   A person who is aged 16 or over may apply to the Commission to be an accredited observer at any of the following proceedings relating to an election specified in subsection (5) of section 6A or a referendum to which Part 7 applies

    (a)   proceedings at the issue or receipt of postal ballot papers;

    (b)   proceedings at the poll;

    (c)   proceedings at the counting of votes.

(2)   If the Commission grant the application, the accredited observer may attend the proceedings in question.

(3)   An application under subsection (1) must be made in the manner specified in the code of practice issued under section 6F or, in relation to a local government election in Scotland, section 6G.

(4)   The Commission may at any time revoke the grant of an application under subsection (1).

(5)   If the Commission

    (a)   refuse an application under subsection (1), or

    (b)   revoke the grant of any such application,

    they must give their decision in writing and must at the same time give reasons in writing for the refusal or revocation.

(6)   The right conferred on an accredited observer by this section is subject to any enactment which regulates attendance at the proceedings in question.

NOTES
Defined terms
the Commission: s 160(1)

Accredited observers: organisations

6D (1)   An organisation may apply to the Commission to be accredited for the purpose of nominating observers at any of the following proceedings relating to an election specified in subsection (5) of section 6A or a referendum to which Part 7 applies

    (a)   proceedings at the issue or receipt of postal ballot papers;

    (b)   proceedings at the poll;

    (c)   proceedings at the counting of votes.

(2)   If the Commission grant the application the organisation may nominate members who may attend the proceedings in question.

(3)   The Commission, in granting an application under this section, may specify a limit on the number of observers nominated by the organisation who may attend, at the same time, specified proceedings by virtue of this section.

(4)   An application under subsection (1) must be made in the manner specified in the code of practice issued under section 6F or, in relation to a local government election in Scotland, section 6G.

(5)   The Commission may at any time revoke the grant of an application under subsection (1).

(6)   If the Commission

    (a)   refuse an application under subsection (1), or

    (b)   revoke the grant of any such application,

they must give their decision in writing and must at the same time give reasons in writing for the refusal or revocation.

(7) The right conferred by this section is subject to any enactment which regulates attendance at the proceedings in question.

NOTES
Defined terms
the Commission: s 160(1)

Attendance and conduct of observers

6E (1) A relevant officer may limit the number of persons who may be present at any proceedings at the same time in pursuance of section 6C or 6D.

(2) If a person who is entitled to attend any proceedings by virtue of section 6C or 6D misconducts himself while attending the proceedings, the relevant officer may cancel the person's entitlement.

(3) Subsection (2) does not affect any power a relevant officer has by virtue of any enactment or rule of law to remove a person from any place.

(4) A relevant officer is
   (a) in the case of proceedings at a polling station, the presiding officer;
   (b) in the case of any other proceedings at an election, the returning officer;
   (c) in the case of any other proceedings at a referendum, the relevant counting officer (within the meaning of section 6A);
   (d) such other person as a person mentioned in paragraph (a), (b) or (c) authorises for the purposes of the proceedings mentioned in that paragraph.

NOTES
Defined terms
relevant counting officer: s 6A(4)

Code of practice on attendance of observers at elections etc

6F (1) The Commission must prepare a code of practice on the attendance of
   (a) representatives of the Commission,
   (b) accredited observers, and
   (c) nominated members of accredited organisations,
at elections specified in subsection (5) of section 6A (other than a local government election in Scotland) and referendums to which Part 7 applies.

(1A) The code must also cover the attendance of representatives of the Commission at proceedings relating to a recall petition which are the responsibility of the petition officer in relation to the petition.

(2) The code must in particular
   (a) specify the manner in which applications under sections 6C(1) and 6D(1) are to be made to the Commission;
   (b) specify the criteria to be taken into account by the Commission in determining such applications;
   (c) give guidance to relevant officers (within the meaning of section 6E) as to the exercise of the power conferred by subsection (1) of that section;
   (d) give guidance to such officers as to the exercise of the power mentioned in subsection (2) of that section as it relates to a person having the permission mentioned in subsection (1) of that section;
   (e) give guidance to such officers as to the exercise of any power under any enactment to control the number of persons present at any proceedings

relating to an election or referendum as it relates to a person having such permission;

    (f)   give guidance to representatives of the Commission, accredited observers and nominated members of accredited organisations on the exercise of the rights conferred by sections 6A, 6B, 6C and 6D.

(3)   The code may make different provision for different purposes.

(4)   Before preparing the code, the Commission must consult the Secretary of State.

(5)   The Commission must lay the code before each House of Parliament.

(6)   The Commission must publish the code (in such manner as the Commission may determine).

(7)   The following persons must have regard to the code in exercising any function conferred by section 6A, 6B, 6C, 6D or 6E
    (a)   the Commission;
    (b)   representatives of the Commission;
    (c)   relevant officers (within the meaning of section 6E);
    (d)   relevant counting officers.

(8)   The Commission may at any time revise the code.

(9)   Subsections (4) to (7) apply in relation to a revision of the code as they apply in relation to the code.

(10)   In this section and section 6G
    (a)   "accredited observer" must be construed in accordance with section 6C;
    (b)   "accredited organisation" must be construed in accordance with section 6D, and "nominated member" must be construed accordingly;
    (c)   "relevant counting officer" must be construed in accordance with section 6A;
    (d)   "representative of the Commission" has the same meaning as in section 6A.

NOTES

Prospective operation
  Sub-s (1A) not yet in operation

Defined terms
  the Commission: s 160(1)
  relevant counting officer: s 6A(4) (by virtue of sub-s (10)(c))

relevant officer: s 6E(4)
representative of the Commission: s 6A(3) (by virtue of sub-s (10)(d))

Code of practice on attendance of observers at local government elections in Scotland

6G (1)   The Commission must prepare a code of practice on the attendance of
    (a)   representatives of the Commission;
    (b)   accredited observers; and
    (c)   nominated members of accredited organisations,
  at local government elections in Scotland.

(2)   The code must in particular
    (a)   specify the manner in which applications under section 6C(1) and 6D(1) are to be made to the Commission;
    (b)   specify the criteria to be taken into account by the Commission in determining such applications;
    (c)   give guidance to relevant officers (within the meaning of section 6E) as to the exercise of the power conferred by subsection (1) of that section;
    (d)   give guidance to such officers as to the exercise of the power mentioned in subsection (2) of that section as it relates to a person having the permission mentioned in subsection (1) of that section;

(e) give guidance to such officers as to the exercise of any power under any enactment to control the number of persons present at any proceedings relating to an election as it relates to a person having such permission;

(f) give guidance to representatives of the Commission, accredited observers and nominated members of accredited organisations on the exercise of the rights conferred by sections 6A, 6B, 6C and 6D.

(3) The code may make different provision for different purposes.

(4) Before preparing the code, the Commission must consult the Scottish Ministers.

(5) The Commission must lay the code before the Scottish Parliament.

(6) The Commission must publish the code (in such matter as they may determine).

(7) The following persons must have regard to the code in exercising any function conferred by section 6A, 6B, 6C, 6D or 6E
   (a) the Commission;
   (b) representatives of the Commission;
   (c) relevant officers (within the meaning of section 6E).

(8) The Commission may at any time revise the code.

(9) Subsections (4) to (7) apply in relation to a revision of the code as they apply in relation to the code.

Commission to be consulted on changes to electoral law

7 (1) Before making an instrument to which this section applies, the authority making the instrument shall consult the Commission.

(2) This section applies to an instrument containing
   (a) regulations under the European Parliamentary Elections Act 2002;
   (b) an order under section 6(2)(b) or (3)(b) of that Act (designations of regional returning officers);
   (c) an order under section 24(1)(c), (cc) or (e), 25(1)(b), 28(1)(b) or 35(2B) of the Representation of the People Act 1983 (designations of returning officers and acting returning officers);
   (d) rules under section 36 of that Act (local government elections in England and Wales);
   (e) regulations under that Act ("the 1983 Act"), or under the Representation of the People Act 1985, in relation to which section 201(2) of the 1983 Act (regulations which may not be made unless a draft of them has been laid before and approved by a resolution of each House of Parliament) has effect;
   (ea) regulations made by virtue of paragraph 7F of Schedule 4 to the Representation of the People Act 2000 (regulations made by the Scottish Ministers about notification of rejected postal votes in relation to local government elections in Scotland);
   (f) an order under section 13 or 64(3) of the Government of Wales Act 2006 (conduct of elections to the National Assembly for Wales and of polls held by Welsh Ministers);
   (g) an order under section 12(1) or (6) or regulations under section 12A(1) of the Scotland Act 1998 (conduct of elections to the Scottish Parliament);
   (h) an order under section 34(4) of the Northern Ireland Act 1998 (conduct of elections to the Northern Ireland Assembly);
   (ha) an order under subsection (1)(b) of section 54 of the Police Reform and Social Responsibility Act 2011 (designations of returning officers for elections of persons as police and crime commissioners in England and Wales);

(hb) regulations under subsection (2) of that section (functions of returning officers and local returning officers for such elections);

(hc) an order under section 58 of that Act (conduct of elections of persons as police and crime commissioners in England and Wales);

(i) an order under section 17A(3) of the Greater London Authority Act 1999 (free delivery of election addresses at elections to the Greater London Authority);

(j) an order under section 3(1) of the Local Governance (Scotland) Act 2004;

(k) regulations under section 9(5) or 18 of the Recall of MPs Act 2015 (wording of the recall petition signing sheet and the conduct of a recall petition etc).

(3) No draft Order shall be laid before Parliament under section 84(4) of the Northern Ireland Act 1998 (power to make provision with respect to elections in Northern Ireland) except after consultation with the Commission.

NOTES

Subordinate Legislation
District Electoral Areas Commissioner (Northern Ireland)
  Order 2012, SI 2012/3074

Defined terms
  the Commission: s 160(1)

Powers with respect to elections exercisable only on Commission recommendation

8 (1) The function of giving directions under section 52(1) of the Representation of the People Act 1983 (directions as to discharge of registration duties) shall be exercisable only on, and in accordance with, a recommendation of the Commission.

(2) A function to which this subsection applies shall, unless the person on whom the function is conferred considers that the exercise of the function is expedient in consequence of changes in the value of money, be exercisable only on, and in accordance with, a recommendation of the Commission.

(3) Subsection (2) applies to the following functions, namely

(a) the making of orders under section 76(2A) of that Act (limitation of expenses in connection with elections to the Greater London Authority);

(b) the making of orders under section 13 of the Government of Wales Act 2006 or section 12 of the Scotland Act 1998 so far as relating to the matters mentioned in subsection (2)(c) of the section (limitation of expenses in connection with elections to the National Assembly for Wales or Scottish Parliament);

(c) the making of regulations under section 7(2)(a) of the European Parliamentary Elections Act 2002 (limitation of expenses in connection with elections to the European Parliament);

(d) the making of orders under section 58 of the Police Reform and Social Responsibility Act 2011 so far as relating to the matters mentioned in subsection (2)(d) of that section (funding and expenditure of candidates, political parties and other persons in connection with elections of persons as police and crime commissioners in England and Wales).

NOTES

Prospective operation
  Sub-s (3)(d) not yet in operation

the Commission: s 160(1)
functions: s 160(1)

Defined terms

Involvement of Commission in changes in electoral procedures

9 (1) The Commission

(a) may participate with any relevant local authority in the joint submission of proposals falling within section 10(1) of the Representation of the People Act 2000 (pilot schemes); and

(b) shall have such other functions in relation to
  (i)   orders and schemes under section 10 of that Act, and
  (ii) orders under section 11 of that Act (revision of procedures in the light of pilot schemes),
  as are conferred on the Commission by those sections.

(2) Where any scheme under section 10 of that Act falls to be implemented following the approval by the Secretary of State of proposals jointly submitted by the Commission and a relevant local authority as mentioned in subsection (1)(a) above, the Commission may, in connection with the implementation of the scheme, provide that authority with such assistance (except financial assistance) as the Commission think fit.

(3) In this section "relevant local authority" has the same meaning as in section 10 of that Act.

NOTES

Defined terms
  the Commission: s 160(1)
  functions: s 160(1)

Setting of performance standards

9A (1) The Commission may from time to time
  (a)   determine standards of performance for relevant officers, and
  (b)   publish, in such form and in such manner as they consider appropriate, the standards so determined.

(2) The standards of performance are such standards as the Commission think ought to be achieved by
  (a)   electoral registration officers in the performance of their functions;
  (b)   returning officers in the administration of the elections specified in subsection (6);
  (c)   counting officers in the administration of the referendums specified in subsection (7).

(3) Before determining standards under subsection (1), the Commission must consult
  (a)   the Secretary of State, and
  (b)   any other person they think appropriate.

(4) The Commission may determine different standards for different descriptions of relevant officers.

(5) When the Commission publish standards under subsection (1) they must send a copy of the published standards to the Secretary of State who must lay a copy of the published standards before each House of Parliament.

(6) The elections specified in this subsection are
  (a)   an election mentioned in section 5(2);
  (b)   a parliamentary by-election;
  (c)   an election under section 9 of the Scotland Act 1998 (constituency vacancies);
  (d)   an election under section 10 of the Government of Wales Act 2006 (constituency vacancies);
  (da) an election under section 51 of the Police Reform and Social Responsibility Act 2011 (election to fill vacancy in office of police and crime commissioner);
  (e)   a local government election in England or Wales
  (f)   a local government election in Scotland.

(7) The referendums specified in this subsection are
  (a)   a referendum to which Part 7 applies;

(b) a referendum under Part 2 of the Local Government Act 2000.

(8) For the purposes of this section and sections 9B and 9C, the relevant officers are
    (a) electoral registration officers;
    (b) in relation to elections within subsection (6), returning officers;
    (c) in relation to referendums within subsection (7), counting officers.

NOTES
Defined terms
  the Commission: s 160(1)
  functions: s 160(1)
                         local government election: s 160(1)

Returns and reports on performance standards

9B (1) The Commission may from time to time issue directions to relevant officers to provide the Commission with such reports regarding their level of performance against the standards determined under section 9A(1) as may be specified in the direction.

(2) A direction under subsection (1)
    (a) must specify the relevant officer or officers to whom it is issued (and may specify a description or descriptions of relevant officers),
    (b) may require the report or reports to relate to such elections or referendums (or both) as may be specified in the direction, and
    (c) may require the report or reports to be provided in a form specified in the direction.

(3) A report provided to the Commission in pursuance of subsection (1) may be published by the relevant officer to whom it relates.

(4) The Commission shall from time to time prepare and publish (in such manner as the Commission may determine) assessments of the level of performance by relevant officers against the standards determined under section 9A(1).

(5) An assessment under subsection (4)
    (a) must specify the relevant officer or officers to whom it relates;
    (b) must specify the period to which it relates;
    (c) may specify the elections or referendums (or both) to which it relates.

(6) The Commission must not prepare an assessment under subsection (4) unless they have received reports in pursuance of subsection (1) from the relevant officer or officers for the matters to which the assessment relates.

(7) Before publishing an assessment under subsection (4), the Commission shall
    (a) provide to each relevant officer a copy of those parts of the assessment which relate to him;
    (b) have regard to any comments made by him regarding the factual accuracy of the assessment.

NOTES
Defined terms
  the Commission: s 160(1)
  relevant officers: s 9A(8)

Provision of information about expenditure on elections etc

9C (1) The Commission may by notice in writing direct a relevant officer to provide the Commission with such expenditure information as may be specified in the direction.

(2) Expenditure information is information relating to
    (a) in the case of an electoral registration officer, expenditure in connection with the performance of his functions;

(b)   in the case of a returning officer, expenditure in connection with the election or elections specified in section 9A(6) for which he is appointed or otherwise holds office;

(c)   in the case of a counting officer, expenditure in connection with the referendum or referendums specified in section 9A(7) for which he is appointed.

(3)   A direction under subsection (1)

(a)   may require the information to relate to such elections or (as the case may be) referendums as may be specified in the direction;

(b)   may require the information to be provided in a form specified in the direction;

(c)   may specify the time within which the information must be provided.

(4)   This section does not affect any other power of the Commission to request information.

NOTES

Defined terms
  the Commission: s 160(1)
  relevant officers: s 9A(8)

Giving of advice and assistance

10 (1)   The Commission may, at the request of any relevant body, provide the body with advice and assistance as respects any matter in which the Commission have skill and experience.

(2)   The assistance which may be so provided includes (in particular) the secondment of members of the Commission's staff.

(3)   The Commission may also

(a)   provide advice and assistance to

(i)   registration officers,

(ii)   returning officers at relevant elections,

(iii)   registered parties,

(iv)   recognised third parties within the meaning of Part VI, and

(v)   permitted participants within the meaning of Part VII;

(vi)   petition officers in relation to recall petitions, and

(vii) accredited campaigners within the meaning of Schedule 3 to the Recall of MPs Act 2015 (see Part 5 of that Schedule);

(b)   provide advice and assistance to other persons which is incidental to, or otherwise connected with, the discharge by the Commission of their functions.

(4)   The Commission

(a)   may make charges for advice or assistance provided by them under subsection (1); but

(b)   may not make charges for advice and assistance provided under subsection (3).

(5)   Nothing in this section authorises the Commission to provide any form of financial assistance.

(6)   In this section "relevant body" means

(a)   the Scottish Parliament;

(b)   the Scottish Executive;

(c)   the National Assembly for Wales;

(ca)   the National Assembly for Wales Commission;

(caa) the Welsh Ministers;

(d)   the Northern Ireland Assembly;

(e)   the Executive Committee of the Northern Ireland Assembly;

(f)   any of the following local authorities

(i)   in England, the council of a county, district or London borough,

(ii)   in Wales, the council of a county or county borough, and

(iii) in Scotland, a council constituted under section 2 of the Local Government etc (Scotland) Act 1994;

(g)   a national or regional parliament or government in a country other than the United Kingdom;

(h)   a body in any such other country having functions corresponding to any of the functions of the Commission;

(i)   an organisation of which two or more countries (or their governments) are members or a subordinate body of such an organisation.

(7)   In this section "relevant election" means any election falling within section 22(5).

(8)   *Repealed*

(9)   *Repealed*

(10) *Repealed*

NOTES

Prospective operation
  Sub-s (3)(vi) and (vii) not yet in operation

Defined terms
  the Commission: s 160(1)

functions: s 160(1)
registered party: s 160(1)

Broadcasters to have regard to Commission's views on party political broadcasts

11 (1) *Repealed*

(2)   *Repealed*

(3)   The British Broadcasting Corporation shall have regard, in determining its policy with respect to party political broadcasts, to any views expressed by the Electoral Commission for the purposes of this subsection.

Policy development grants

12(1)   For the purposes of this section

(a)   "a policy development grant" is a grant to a represented registered party to assist the party with the development of policies for inclusion in any manifesto on the basis of which

(i)   candidates authorised to stand by the party will seek to be elected at an election which is a relevant election for the purposes of Part II, or

(ii) the party itself will seek to be so elected (in the case of such an election for which the party itself may be nominated); and

(b)   a registered party is "represented" if there are at least two Members of the House of Commons belonging to the party who

(i)   have made and subscribed the oath required by the Parliamentary Oaths Act 1866 (or the corresponding affirmation), and

(ii) are not disqualified from sitting or voting in that House.

(2)   The Commission shall submit recommendations to the Secretary of State for the terms of a scheme for the making by the Commission of policy development grants.

(3)   Where the Secretary of State receives recommendations under subsection (2), he shall make an order setting out such a scheme in terms which, with any modifications he considers appropriate, give effect to the recommendations.

(4)   The scheme shall, in particular, specify or provide for the determination of

(a)   the parties eligible for policy development grants, and

    (b) how any money provided to the Commission for the making of policy development grants is to be allocated between the parties eligible for such grants.

(5) The Commission shall keep under review the terms of any scheme under this section and shall make recommendations to the Secretary of State for any variations to the scheme which they consider appropriate.

(6) Where the Secretary of State receives recommendations under subsection (5), he shall make an order giving effect, with any modifications he considers appropriate, to the recommendations.

(7) Where any such modifications as are mentioned in subsection (3) or (6) would result in an order under that subsection giving effect with modifications to any recommendations of the Commission in respect of either of the matters mentioned in subsection (4), the order shall not be made without the agreement of the Commission to the modifications so far as relating to those matters.

(8) The Commission shall make such grants as are provided for under any scheme under this section, and any such grants may be made subject to such conditions as (consistently with the terms of the scheme) the Commission consider appropriate; but nothing in such a scheme shall have effect to authorise the Commission to make in any financial year more than £2 million in policy development grants.

(9) The Secretary of State may by order made with the consent of the Treasury vary the sum for the time being specified in subsection (8).

NOTES

Subordinate Legislation
Elections (Policy Development Grants Scheme) Order
  2006, SI 2006/602

Defined terms
  the Commission: s 160(1)
  conditions: s 160(5)

financial year: s 21
modifications: s 160(1)
a person standing for election in the name of a
  registered party: s 22(6)
registered party: s 160(1)

Education about electoral and democratic systems

13 (1) The Commission shall promote public awareness of
    (a) current electoral systems in the United Kingdom and any pending such systems, together with such matters connected with any such existing or pending systems as the Commission may determine;
    (b) *Repealed*
    (c) *Repealed*

(1A) Subsection (1) applies to the promotion of public awareness in Gibraltar with the following modifications
    (a) in paragraph (a), for "in the United Kingdom" there is substituted "for elections to the European Parliament in the United Kingdom and Gibraltar";
    (b) *Repealed*

(2) For the purposes of subsection (1) any system such as is mentioned in paragraph (a) of that subsection is pending at a time when arrangements for giving effect to it have been made by any enactment but the arrangements are not yet in force.

(3) *Repealed*

(4) The Commission shall perform their functions under subsection (1) in such manner as they think fit but may, in particular, do so by
    (a) carrying out programmes of education or information to promote public awareness of any of the matters mentioned in subsection (1); or

(b) making grants to other persons or bodies for the purpose of enabling them to carry out such programmes.

(5) Any grant under subsection (4)(b) may be made subject to such conditions as the Commission consider appropriate.

(6) The total expenditure incurred in any financial year by the Commission in performing their functions under subsection (1) (whether by making grants or otherwise) shall not exceed such sum as is for the time being specified for the purposes of this subsection by an order made by the Secretary of State with the consent of the Treasury.

(7) *Repealed*

(8) Subsection (6) shall not apply to the expenditure incurred by the Commission in performing their functions exercisable in relation to local government elections in Scotland.

(9) *Repealed*

(10) *Repealed*

(11) *Repealed*

(12) Subsection (6) shall not apply to the expenditure incurred by the Commission to the extent that it is, or is to be, met under paragraph 6 of Schedule 2 to the Government of Wales Act 2006.

NOTES

Subordinate Legislation
Electoral Commission (Limit on Public Awareness Expenditure) Order 2014, SI 2014/510

Defined terms
body: s 160(1)
the Commission: s 160(1)

conditions: s 160(5)
financial year: s 21
functions: s 160(1)
local government election: s 160(1)
modifications: s 160(1)

Reimbursement of costs by Scottish Ministers etc

13A (1) The Scottish Ministers must reimburse the Commission for any expenditure incurred by them which is attributable to the exercise of the functions mentioned in subsection (2).

(2) The functions are the Commission's functions under this Part in relation to local government elections in Scotland.

(3) The total expenditure incurred in any financial year by the Commission in performing the functions mentioned in subsection (2) must not exceed such sum as is for the time being specified by an order made by the Scottish Ministers.

(4) The power to make an order under subsection (3) is exercisable by statutory instrument subject to annulment in pursuance of a resolution of the Scottish Parliament.

14-20A *Repealed*

Interpretation of Part I

21 (1) In this Part "financial year", in relation to the Commission, means a period of 12 months ending with 31st March; but the first financial year of the Commission is the period beginning with the date of the establishment of the Commission and ending with the next 31st March.

(2) In this Part, "petition officer" and "recall petition" have the same meaning as in the Recall of MPs Act 2015 (see section 22 of that Act).

NOTES
Prospective operation
  Sub-s (2) not yet in operation

Defined terms
  the Commission: s 160(1)

PART II
REGISTRATION OF POLITICAL PARTIES

Requirement for registration

Parties to be registered in order to field candidates at elections

22 (1) Subject to subsection (4), no nomination may be made in relation to a relevant election unless the nomination is in respect of

    (a) a person who stands for election in the name of a qualifying registered party; or

    (b) a person who does not purport to represent any party; or

    (c) a qualifying registered party, where the election is one for which registered parties may be nominated.

(2) For the purposes of subsection (1) a party (other than a minor party) is a "qualifying registered party" in relation to a relevant election if

    (a) the constituency, police area, local government area or electoral region in which the election is held

        (i) is in England, Scotland or Wales, or

        (ii) is the electoral region of Scotland or Wales,

    and the party was, on the last day for publication of notice of the election on the day ("the relevant day") which is two days before the last day for the delivery of nomination papers at that election, registered in respect of that part of Great Britain in the Great Britain register maintained by the Commission under section 23, or

    (b) the constituency, district electoral area or electoral region in which the election is held

        (i) is in Northern Ireland, or

        (ii) is the electoral region of Northern Ireland,

    and the party was, on that day on the relevant day, registered in the Northern Ireland register maintained by the Commission under that section.

(2A) For the purposes of subsection (2) any day falling within rule 2(1) of the parliamentary elections rules in Schedule 1 to the Representation of the People Act 1983 (subject to rule 2(2A)) shall be disregarded.

(3) For the purposes of subsection (1) a person does not purport to represent any party if either

    (a) the description of the candidate given in his nomination paper, is

        (i) "Independent", or

        (ii) where the candidate is the Speaker of the House of Commons seeking reelection, "The Speaker seeking reelection"; or

    (b) no description of the candidate is given in his nomination paper.

(4) Subsection (1) does not apply in relation to any parish or community election.

(5) The following elections are relevant elections for the purposes of this Part

    (a) parliamentary elections,

    (b) elections to the European Parliament,

    (c) elections to the Scottish Parliament,

(d)   elections to the National Assembly for Wales,

(e)   elections to the Northern Ireland Assembly,

(ea) elections of police and crime commissioners,

(f)   local government elections, and

(g)   local elections in Northern Ireland.

(6)   For the purposes of this Act a person stands for election in the name of a registered party if his nomination paper includes a description authorised by a certificate issued by or on behalf of the registered nominating officer of the party.

NOTES

Defined terms
  the Commission: s 160(1)
  the Great Britain register: ss 23(2)(a), 160(1)
  local election: s 160(1)
  local government election: s 160(1)
  minor party: s 160(1)

  the Northern Ireland register: ss 23(2)(b), 160(1)
  parish or community election: s 40(1)
  party: s 40(1)
  registered: s 40(1)

The registers of political parties

The new registers

23 (1)   In place of the register of political parties maintained by the registrar of companies under the Registration of Political Parties Act 1998, there shall be the new registers of political parties mentioned in subsection (2) which

(a)   shall be maintained by the Commission, and

(b)   (subject to the provisions of this section) shall be so maintained in such form as the Commission may determine.

(2)   The new registers of political parties are

(a)   a register of parties that intend to contest relevant elections in one or more of England, Scotland and Wales (referred to in this Act as "the Great Britain register"); and

(b)   a register of parties that intend to contest relevant elections in Northern Ireland (referred to in this Act as "the Northern Ireland register").

(3)   Each party registered in the Great Britain register shall be so registered in respect of one or more of England, Scotland and Wales; and the entry for each party so registered shall be marked so as to indicate

(a)   the part or parts of Great Britain in respect of which it is registered; and

(b)   if the party is a minor party, that it is such a party.

(4)   A party may be registered under this Part in both of the new registers, but where a party is so registered

(a)   the party as registered in the Great Britain register, and

(b)   the party as registered in the Northern Ireland register,

shall constitute two separate registered parties.

(5)   In such a case

(a)   the party shall for the purposes of this Act be so organised and administered as to secure that the financial affairs of the party in Great Britain are conducted separately from those of the party in Northern Ireland;

(b)   the financial affairs of the party in Great Britain or (as the case may be) Northern Ireland, shall accordingly constitute for those purposes the financial affairs of the party as registered in the Great Britain register or (as the case may be) the Northern Ireland register; and

(c)   any application for the registration of a party in accordance with subsection (4) shall similarly be made and determined by reference to the party's organisation and activities in Great Britain and Northern Ireland respectively.

(6)   The Secretary of State may by order make provision for the transfer to the Commission of any property, rights and liabilities to which the registrar of companies is entitled or subject in connection with his functions under the Registration of Political Parties Act 1998; and an order under this subsection may in particular provide for the order to have effect despite any provision (of whatever nature) which would prevent or restrict the transfer of the property, rights or liabilities otherwise than by the order.

NOTES

Defined terms
  the Commission: s 160(1)
  functions: s 160(1)
  minor party: s 160(1)
  party: s 40(1)
  property: s 160(1)
  registered: s 40(1)

registered party contests an election: s 40(2)
the registrar of companies: s 40(1)
relevant election: ss 22(5), 40(1)
the Secretary of State: s 159A

Preliminary requirements

Officeholders to be registered

24 (1)   For each registered party there shall be
    (a)   a person registered as the party's leader;
    (b)   a person registered as the party's nominating officer; and
    (c)   a person registered as the party's treasurer;
    but the person registered as leader may also be registered as nominating officer or treasurer (or both).

(2)   The person registered as a party's leader must be
    (a)   the overall leader of the party; or
    (b)   where there is no overall leader of the party, a person who is the leader of the party for some particular purpose.

(3)   The person registered as a party's nominating officer must have responsibility for the arrangements for
    (a)   the submission by representatives of the party of lists of candidates for the purpose of elections;
    (b)   the issuing of such certificates as are mentioned in section 22(6); and
    (c)   the approval of descriptions and emblems used on nomination and ballot papers at elections.

(4)   The person registered as a party's treasurer shall be responsible for compliance on the part of the party
    (a)   with the provisions of Parts 3, 4 and 4A (accounting requirements and control of donations, loans and certain other transactions), and
    (b)   unless a person is registered as the party's campaigns officer in accordance with section 25, with the provisions of Parts V to VII (campaign expenditure, third party expenditure and referendums) and Schedules 3 to 5 to the Recall of MPs Act 2015 (financial controls on recall petitions) as well.

(5)   In the case of a party with accounting units the person registered as the party's treasurer shall, in relation to the provisions of Part III, be responsible for compliance on the part of the party's central organisation (rather than of the party).

(6)   Where
    (a)   the person registered as a party's treasurer dies, or

(b) his appointment as treasurer terminates for any other reason,

then, until such time as another person is registered as the party's treasurer in pursuance of an application under section 31(3)(a), the appropriate person shall be treated for all purposes of this Act (except subsection (8)) as if he were registered also as its treasurer.

(7) In subsection (6) "the appropriate person" means
    (a) the person registered as the party's leader; or
    (b) if that person is also registered as its treasurer but not as its nominating officer, the person registered as its nominating officer; or
    (c) if that person is also registered both as its treasurer and as its nominating officer, any other officer of the party registered in accordance with Schedule 4.

(8) A person commits an offence if
    (a) he is registered as treasurer of a registered party, and
    (b) he has been convicted, at any time within the period of five years ending with the date of registration, of any offence under this Act or of any other offence committed in connection with a relevant election, an election to the House of Assembly of Gibraltar or a , a referendum within the meaning of Part VII or a recall petition within the meaning of the Recall of MPs Act 2015 (see section 1(2) of that Act).

(9) Where a person registered as treasurer of a registered party is convicted of an offence falling within subsection (8)(b), his appointment as treasurer of the party shall terminate on the date of the conviction.

(10) In connection with the registration of a party in both the Great Britain register and the Northern Ireland register in accordance with section 23(4)
    (a) a person may be registered in the Northern Ireland register as leader of the separate party registered in that register if (although not such a leader of the party as is mentioned in subsection (2) above) he is leader of the party in Northern Ireland; and
    (b) references to a person's responsibilities in subsection (3) or (4) above shall be read as references to the responsibilities that he will have with respect to the separate party registered in the Great Britain register or the Northern Ireland register, as appropriate.

NOTES

Prospective operation
Sub-s (4)(b) not yet in operation

Defined terms
central organisation: ss 26(11), 160(1)
the Great Britain register: ss 23(2)(a), 160(1)
the Northern Ireland register: ss 23(2)(b), 160(1)

party: s 40(1)
party with accounting units: ss 26(11), 160(1)
registered: s 40(1)
relevant election: s 22(5)

Parties with campaigns officers

25 (1) In the case of any registered party a person
    (a) may be registered as the party's campaigns officer, and
    (b) may be so registered whether or not he is also registered as the party's leader or nominating officer (or both).

(2) The person registered as a party's campaign officer shall be responsible for compliance on the part of the party with the provisions of Parts V to VII and Schedules 3 to 5 to the Recall of MPs Act 2015 (financial controls on recall petitions).

(3) So long as a party is registered as a party with a campaigns officer, section 24(6), (8) and (9) shall apply in relation to a person registered as the party's campaigns officer as they apply in relation to a person registered as treasurer of the party, except that in

section 24(6) the reference to the appropriate person shall be read as a reference to the person registered as treasurer of the party.

(4) The person registered as a party's campaigns officer may appoint, on such terms as he may determine, one or more deputy campaigns officers of the party for the purposes of Part V, but not more than 12 persons may hold such appointments at the same time.

(5) For the purposes of this section
  (a) the provisions of section 74(2) to (10) shall apply in relation to a party's campaigns officer and the appointment of a person as deputy campaigns officer as they apply in relation to a party's treasurer and the appointment of a person as deputy treasurer, and
  (b) any reference in those provisions to a treasurer or (as the case may be) deputy treasurer shall accordingly be read as a reference to a campaigns officer or (as the case may be) deputy campaigns officer.

(6) In relation to any time when a party is (or was) registered as a party with a campaigns officer
  (a) the provisions of Part V (other than section 74) and Parts VI and VII shall apply as if any reference to the treasurer of the party were a reference to the registered campaigns officer, and any reference to a deputy treasurer of the party were a reference to a deputy campaigns officer of the party; and
  (b) the provisions of Part X (enforcement) shall apply in connection with matters relevant for the purposes of Parts V to VII as if any reference to a person who is or has been the treasurer of the party were a reference to a person who is or has been the registered campaigns officer.

(7) In relation to any time when a party is (or was) registered as a party with a campaigns officer, the provisions of Schedules 3 to 5 to the Recall of MPs Act 2015 shall apply as if any reference to the treasurer of the party were a reference to the registered campaigns officer.

NOTES
Defined terms
  party: s 40(1)
  registered: s 40(1)

Financial structure of registered party: adoption of scheme

26 (1) A party may not be registered unless it has adopted a scheme which
  (a) sets out the arrangements for regulating the financial affairs of the party for the purposes of this Act; and
  (b) has been approved in writing by the Commission.

(2) The scheme must in particular determine for the purposes of this Act whether the party is to be taken to consist of
  (a) a single organisation with no division of responsibility for the financial affairs and transactions of the party for the purposes of Part III (accounting requirements), or
  (b) a central organisation and one or more separate accounting units, that is to say constituent or affiliated organisations each of which is to be responsible for its own financial affairs and transactions for the purposes of that Part.

(3) In the latter case the scheme must
  (a) identify, by reference to organisations mentioned in the party's constitution, those which are to constitute the central organisation and the accounting units respectively; and
  (b) give the name of each of those organisations.

(4) The scheme must in every case include such other information as may be prescribed by regulations made by the Commission.

(5) Where a draft scheme is submitted by a party for the Commission's approval, the Commission may either
   (a) approve the scheme, or
   (b) give the party a notice requesting it to submit a revised scheme to them,
as they think fit.

(6) If under subsection (5) the Commission request a party to submit a revised scheme, they may specify either or both of the following, namely
   (a) any matters which they consider should be dealt with in the revised scheme; and
   (b) any modifications which they consider should be incorporated in it.

(7) A registered party may at any time notify the Commission that it wishes to replace the scheme for the time being approved in relation to it under this section with a further scheme complying with subsections (1) to (4); and where it so notifies the Commission
   (a) it shall submit for the Commission's approval a draft of the replacement scheme;
   (b) subsections (5) and (6) shall apply in connection with the approval by the Commission of that scheme; and
   (c) once that scheme has been approved in writing by the Commission it shall have effect as the party's scheme under this section.

(8) For the purposes of this section none of the following shall be taken to be a constituent or affiliated organisation in relation to a party
   (a) a trade union within the meaning of the Trade Union and Labour Relations (Consolidation) Act 1992 or the Industrial Relations (Northern Ireland) Order 1992;
   (b) a friendly society registered under the Friendly Societies Act 1974, a registered society within the meaning of the Co-operative and Community Benefit Societies Act 2014 or a society registered (or deemed to be registered) under the Industrial and Provident Societies Act (Northern Ireland) 1969;
   (c) any other organisation specified, or of a description specified, in an order made by the Secretary of State on the recommendation of the Commission.

(9) In this section "constitution", in relation to a party, means the document or documents (of whatever name) by which the structure and organisation of the party is determined.

(10) In connection with the registration of a party in both the Great Britain register and the Northern Ireland register, subsection (1)(a) and the other provisions of this section apply (in accordance with section 23(5)) separately in relation to the party in Great Britain and the party in Northern Ireland, and in that connection
   (a) any reference in this section to a constituent or affiliated organisation in relation to the party shall be read as a reference to a constituent or affiliated organisation in relation to the party in Great Britain or the party in Northern Ireland, as appropriate; and
   (b) any reference in this Part to the party's constitution shall be read as a reference to the party's constitution so far as relating to the party in Great Britain or the party in Northern Ireland, as appropriate;
and the party's scheme must show that the financial affairs of the party in Great Britain will be conducted separately from those of the party in Northern Ireland.

(11) For the purposes of this Act
   (a) "accounting unit" means a constituent or affiliated organisation falling within paragraph (b) of subsection (2);

(b) a registered party is a "party with accounting units" if the party's scheme under this section identifies the party as being one falling within that paragraph; and

(c) in the case of such a party, the "central organisation" of the party is the central organisation referred to in that paragraph.

NOTES

Subordinate Legislation
Registered Parties (Non-constituent and Non-affiliated Organisations) Order 2000, SI 2000/3183.

Defined terms
the Commission: s 160(1)
document: s 160(1)
the Great Britain register: ss 23(2)(a), 160(1)

modifications: s 160(1)
the Northern Ireland register: ss 23(2)(b), 160(1)
organisation: s 160(1)
party: s 40(1)
registered: s 40(1)
the Secretary of State: s 159A

Financial structure of registered party: accounting units

27 (1) This section applies where a registered party is a party with accounting units.

(2) For each accounting unit there shall be

(a) a person registered as the treasurer of the unit who shall be responsible for compliance on the part of the unit with the provisions of Parts 3, 4 and 4A so far as relating to it; and

(b) another person who is an officer of the unit registered for the purposes of subsection (3).

(3) Section 24(6), (8) and (9) shall apply in relation to a person registered as treasurer of an accounting unit as they apply in relation to a person registered as treasurer of the party, except that in section 24(6) the reference to the appropriate person shall be read as a reference to the officer of the unit who is registered for the purposes of this subsection.

NOTES

Defined terms
accounting unit: ss 26(11), 160(1)
party: s 40(1)
party with accounting units: ss 26(11), 160(1)

registered: s 40(1)

Registration

Registration of parties

28 (1) A party may apply to be registered under this Part by sending to the Commission an application which

(a) complies with the requirements of Part I of Schedule 4, and

(b) is accompanied by a declaration falling within subsection (2).

(2) The declarations falling within this subsection are

(a) a declaration that the party

(i) intends to contest one or more relevant elections in Great Britain and one or more such elections in Northern Ireland, and

(ii) is accordingly applying to be registered (as two such separate parties as are mentioned in section 23(4)) in both the Great Britain register and the Northern Ireland register;

(b) a declaration that the party

(i) intends to contest one or more relevant elections (which will not be confined to one or more parish or community elections) in Great Britain only, and

(ii) is accordingly applying to be registered in the Great Britain register only;

    (c) a declaration that the party
        (i)   intends to contest one or more relevant elections in Northern Ireland only, and
        (ii) is accordingly applying to be registered in the Northern Ireland register only;
    (d) a declaration that the party
        (i)   intends only to contest one or more parish or community elections, and
        (ii) is accordingly applying to be registered in the Great Britain register only.

(3)   A declaration falling within paragraph (a), (b) or (d) of subsection (2) must specify the part or parts of Great Britain in respect of which the party is applying to be registered in the Great Britain register.

(3A) A declaration under subsection (2)(a) or (b) which specifies that the party is applying to be registered in respect of England may include a statement that the party intends to contest one or more elections to the European Parliament in the combined region.

(4)   Where a party sends an application to the Commission in accordance with subsection (1), the Commission shall grant the application unless in their opinion the party proposes a registered name which
    (a) would either
        (i)   be the same as that of a party which is already registered in the register in which that party is applying to be registered, or
        (ii) be likely to result in electors confusing that party with a party which is already registered in respect of the relevant part of the United Kingdom,
    (b) comprises more than six words,
    (c) is obscene or offensive,
    (d) includes words the publication of which would be likely to amount to the commission of an offence,
    (da) would be likely, were it to appear on a ballot paper issued at an election
        (i)   to result in an elector being misled as to the effect of his vote, or
        (ii) to contradict, or hinder an elector's understanding of, any directions for his guidance in voting given on the ballot paper or elsewhere,
    (e) includes any script other than Roman script, or
    (f) includes any word or expression prohibited by order made by the Secretary of State after consulting the Commission,
    or it appears to the Commission that the party has failed to adopt a scheme approved under section 26.

(5)   In subsection (4)(a) "already registered in respect of the relevant part of the United Kingdom" means
    (a) in connection with registration of the applicant party in the Great Britain register, already registered in respect of any part of Great Britain in respect of which that party is applying to be registered;
    (b) in connection with registration of the applicant party in the Northern Ireland register, already registered in that register.

(6)   An order under subsection (4)(f) may except the use of a word or expression from the prohibition in specified circumstances.

(7)   If
    (a) at any time two or more applications for registration are pending each of which would (in the absence of the other or others) fall to be granted by the Commission, but
    (b) the registered names proposed by the applicant parties are such that, if one of those names was already registered in pursuance of the application in question,

the Commission would be required to refuse the other application or applications by virtue of subsection (4)(a),

the Commission shall determine by reference to the history of each of the applicant parties which of them has, in the Commission's opinion, the greater or greatest claim to the name proposed by it, and shall then grant the application by that party and refuse the other application or applications.

(8) Where the Commission grant an application by a party under this section, they shall include in the party's entry in the register

    (a) the particulars, apart from home addresses, given in the application in accordance with paragraphs 2 to 4, 5(2) and 6 of Schedule 4;

    (b) the date of registration;

    (c) any statement made under subsection (3A); and

    (d) if the party

        (i) is established in Gibraltar (in this Act referred to as a "Gibraltar party"); and

        (ii) has made a statement under subsection (3A), a notice that it is a Gibraltar party.

(9) Where the Commission refuse an application by a party under this section, they shall notify the party of their reasons for refusing the application.

(10) In this Part "the register" means

    (a) in relation to a party registered in the Great Britain register, the Great Britain register, and

    (b) in relation to a party registered in the Northern Ireland register, the Northern Ireland register.

NOTES

Defined terms
combined region: s 160(1)
the Commission: s 160(1)
the Great Britain register: ss 23(2)(a), 160(1)
the Northern Ireland register: ss 23(2)(b), 160(1)
parish or community election: s 40(1)
party: s 40(1)

registered: s 40(1)
registered party contests an election: s 40(2)
registration: s 40(1)
relevant election: s 22(5)
the Secretary of State: s 159A

Descriptions

28A(1) A party's application under section 28 may include a request for the registration of up to 12 descriptions to be used on nomination papers or ballot papers.

(2) Where a request is made by a party under this section in relation to a description, the Commission shall register the description as a description of the party unless it is of more than six words in length or in their opinion it

    (a) would be the same as the name of a party or the registered description of a party which (in either case) is already registered in the register in which that party is applying to be registered,

    (b) would be likely to result in electors confusing that party with another party which is already registered in respect of the relevant part of the United Kingdom,

    (c) is obscene or offensive,

    (d) is of such a character that its publication would be likely to amount to the commission of an offence,

    (e) would be likely, were it to appear on a ballot paper issued at an election

        (i) to result in an elector being misled as to the effect of his vote, or

        (ii) to contradict, or hinder an elector's understanding of, any directions for his guidance in voting given on the ballot paper or elsewhere,

    (f) includes any script other than Roman script, or

(g) includes a word or expression prohibited by order made by the Secretary of State.

(3) In subsection (2)(b) "already registered in respect of the relevant part of the United Kingdom" has the meaning given by section 28(5).

(4) An order under subsection (2)(g) may except the use of a word or expression from the prohibition in specified circumstances.

(5) In the application of subsection (2) above to a party which has made a declaration falling within section 28(2) which specifies Wales as a part of Great Britain in respect of which it is applying to be registered, for "it is of more than six words in length" substitute "its length exceeds six words in either English or Welsh or, if the description is also expressed in the other of those languages, six words in that other language".

(6) The Secretary of State may, by order, substitute for the number "12" in subsection (1) such other number as he thinks appropriate.

(7) An order under subsection (2)(g) or (6) must not be made unless the Secretary of State first consults the Commission.

NOTES

Defined terms
the Commission: s 160(1)
party: s 40(1)
the register: ss 28(10), 40(1)
registered: s 40(1)

registration: s 40(1)
the Secretary of State: s 159A

Joint descriptions

28B (1) Two or more parties which are registered under section 28 above in the same register may apply to the Commission to register a description for use by a candidate standing in the name of both or all of the parties jointly.

(2) The following provisions of section 28A apply to an application under this section as they apply to an application under that section
   (a) subsections (2) to (5);
   (b) subsection (7), so far as it relates to subsection (2)(g).

(3) Subsections (1)(bb), (4A) to (4D) and (6A) of section 30 apply to a description mentioned in subsection (1) above as they apply to a description to which section 28A applies; and for the purposes of such application
   (a) any reference to a party in section 30 (except in relation to an application to remove a description under subsection (1)(bb) of that section) must be construed as a reference to the parties mentioned in subsection (1) above acting jointly,
   (b) section 30(4A)(a) must be taken to read "the parties already have a description registered in pursuance of section 28B above", and
   (c) the requirement in paragraph 9 of Schedule 4 for an application under section 30 to be signed by the responsible officer of a party must be taken to be a requirement for the application to be signed by a responsible officer of each party which joins in the application.

NOTES

Defined terms
the Commission: s 160(1)
party: s 40(1)
the register: ss 28(10), 40(1)

registered: s 40(1)

Emblems

29 (1)   A party's application under section 28 may include a request for the registration of up to three emblems to be used by the party on ballot papers.

(2)   Where a request is made by a party under this section in relation to an emblem, the Commission shall register the emblem as an emblem of the party unless in their opinion it

    (a)   would either

        (i)   be the same as a registered emblem of a party which is already registered in the register in which that party is applying to be registered, or

        (ii)   be likely to be confused by voters with a registered emblem of a party which is already registered in respect of the relevant part of the United Kingdom,

    (b)   is obscene or offensive,

    (c)   is of such a character that its publication would be likely to amount to the commission of an offence,

    (ca)   would be likely, were it to appear on a ballot paper issued at an election

        (i)   to result in an elector being misled as to the effect of his vote, or

        (ii)   to contradict, or hinder an elector's understanding of, any directions for his guidance in voting given on the ballot paper or elsewhere, or

    (d)   includes a word or expression prohibited by virtue of section 28(4)(f).

(3)   In subsection (2)(a) "already registered in respect of the relevant part of the United Kingdom" has the meaning given by section 28(5).

(4)   A registered emblem shall be a black and white representation of the emblem shown in the application.

(5)   Where the Commission refuse a request made by a party under this section in relation to an emblem, they shall notify the party of their reasons for refusing the request.

NOTES

Defined terms
  the Commission: s 160(1)
  party: s 40(1)
  the register: ss 28(10), 40(1)

registered: s 40(1)
registration: s 40(1)

Changes to the register

30 (1)   A party may apply to the Commission to have its entry in the register altered by

    (a)   changing its registered name,

    (b)   (if registered in the Great Britain register) changing the part or parts of Great Britain in respect of which it is registered,

    (ba)   (if registered in the Great Britain register in respect of England) the addition or removal of a statement that the party intends to contest one or more elections to the European Parliament in the combined region,

    (bb)   the addition, alteration, substitution or removal of a description,

    (c)   the addition, substitution or removal of an emblem,

    (d)   the addition or removal of a statement that a party is registered as a party with a campaigns officer, or

    (e)   the addition of information prescribed under paragraph 6 of Schedule 4 since

        (i)   the time when the party applied for registration, or

        (ii)   if a notification has been previously given under section 32 in relation to the party, the time when the last such notification was given.

(2)   Subject to subsections (3) to (6A), the Commission shall grant an application under this section.

(2A)   If the party

    (a)   is a Gibraltar party; and

    (b) the Commission grants an application to have its entry in the register altered by the addition of a statement that it intends to contest one or more elections to the European Parliament in the combined region,

the Commission shall include in the party's entry in the register a notice that it is a Gibraltar party.

(3)   The Commission shall refuse an application to change a party's registered name if, in their opinion, any of paragraphs (a) to (f) of section 28(4) apply to the new name.

(4)   The Commission shall refuse an application to change the part or parts of Great Britain in respect of which a party is registered if, in their opinion, the change would be likely to result in

    (a)   such confusion in relation to the party's registered name as is mentioned in paragraph (a) of section 28(4), or

    (aa) such confusion in relation to a registered description of the party as is mentioned in paragraph (b) of section 28A(2), or

    (b)   such confusion in relation to a registered emblem of the party as is mentioned in paragraph (a) of section 29(2).

(4A) The Commission shall refuse an application to add a description if

    (a)   the party already has 12 descriptions (or such other maximum number of descriptions as is substituted by order under section 28A(6)),

    (b)   the length of the description exceeds six words, or

    (c)   in the Commission's opinion, any of paragraphs (a) to (g) of section 28A(2) apply to the description.

(4B) The Commission shall refuse an application to alter a description if the effect of the alteration

    (a)   is that the length of the description as altered will exceed six words, or

    (b)   in their opinion, is that any of paragraphs (a) to (g) of section 28A(2) will apply to the description as altered.

(4C) The Commission shall refuse to substitute a description if

    (a)   the length of the new description will exceed six words, or

    (b)   in their opinion any of paragraphs (a) to (g) of section 28A(2) apply to the new description.

(4D) In the application of subsection (4A)(b), (4B)(a) or (4C)(a) above to a party which has made a declaration falling within section 28(2) which specifies Wales as a part of Great Britain in respect of which it is registered, for "six words" substitute "six words in either English or Welsh or, if the description is also expressed in the other of those languages, six words in that other language".

(5)   The Commission shall refuse an application to add an emblem if

    (a)   the party already has three registered emblems, or

    (b)   in the Commission's opinion, any of paragraphs (a) to (d) of section 29(2) apply to the emblem.

(6)   The Commission shall refuse to substitute an emblem if in their opinion any of paragraphs (a) to (d) of section 29(2) apply to the new emblem.

(6A) If an application under this section for the substitution or removal of a description is granted at any time between

    (a)   the date of publication of the notice of election at an election in which there are one or more candidates standing in the name of the party, and

    (b)   the poll at the election,

the change does not take effect until the day following the poll.

(7)   For the purposes of subsection (3), (4A), (4B), (4C), (5) or (6)

    (a)   section 28(4)(a) and section 28(5), or

(aa) section 28A(2)(a) and section 28(5) as it applies by virtue of section 28A(3), or

(ab) section 28A(2)(a) as it applies by virtue of section 28B(2), or

(b) section 29(2)(a) and section 28(5) (as it applies by virtue of section 29(3)),

as the case may be, shall each have effect as if the words "applying to be" were omitted.

(8) Where the Commission refuse an application by a party under this section, they shall notify the party of their reasons for refusing the application.

(9) Part II of Schedule 4 applies to applications under this section.

NOTES

Defined terms
combined region: s 160(1)
the Commission: s 160(1)
Gibraltar party: ss 28(8)(d), 160(1)
the Great Britain register: ss 23(2)(a), 160(1)
party: s 40(1)

the register: ss 28(10), 40(1)
registered: s 40(1)
registration: s 40(1)

Notification of changes in party's officers etc

31 (1) If at any time any particulars in a party's entry in the register which relate to any relevant matter cease to be accurate, the person registered as treasurer of the party must give the Commission a notification under this section.

(2) For the purposes of this section "relevant matter" means any of the following
   (a) the name of any registered officer of the party;
   (b) the home address of any such officer;
   (c) the address of the party's headquarters (or, if it has no headquarters, the address to which communications to the party may be sent);
   (d) the name of the treasurer of any accounting unit of the party or of any officer of such a unit registered for the purposes of section 27(3);
   (e) the name of any accounting unit of the party;
   (f) the address of the headquarters of any accounting unit of the party (or, if it has no headquarters, the address to which communications to the accounting unit may be sent).

(3) A notification under this section (other than under subsection (3A)) must specify the relevant matter in respect of which the registered particulars have ceased to be accurate, and
   (a) if that matter is specified in subsection (2)(a) or (d)
      (i) specify the name of the officer replacing the person currently registered as holder of the office in question, and
      (ii) (if that person is so registered as an officer of the party) include an application for the registration of the replacement officer which complies with Part III of Schedule 4; and
   (b) otherwise, specify accurate particulars in respect of that matter.

(3A) If a party's entry in the register includes a statement that it intends to contest one or more elections to the European Parliament in the combined region and the statement ceases to be accurate, the person registered as the treasurer of the party must give the Commission a notification to that effect under this section.

(4) A notification under this section must be given to the Commission
   (a) where subsection (1) applies by reason of the death or the termination for any other reason of the appointment of any registered officer of the party, within the period of 14 days beginning with the date of his death or the termination of his appointment;
   (b) where that subsection applies by reason of any other change in circumstances, within the period of 28 days beginning with the date when the change occurs;

(c) where subsection (3A) applies, within the period of 14 days beginning with the date when the statement ceases to be accurate.

(5) Where the Commission receive a notification under this section, they shall cause any change required as a consequence of the notification to be made in the party's entry in the register as soon as is reasonably practicable.

(6) In the case of a party with accounting units any reference to the party in subsection (2)(c) shall be read as a reference to the central organisation.

(7) For the purposes of this section any particulars held by the Commission in respect of the home address of any registered officer of the party shall be taken to be particulars contained in the party's entry in the register.

NOTES

Defined terms
accounting unit: ss 26(11), 160(1)
central organisation: ss 26(11), 160(1)
combined region: s 160(1)
the Commission: s 160(1)
party: s 40(1)

party with accounting units: ss 26(11), 160(1)
the register: ss 28(10), 40(1)
registered: s 40(1)
registration: s 40(1)

Confirmation of registered particulars etc

32 (1) The person registered as treasurer of a party must, within the specified period, give a notification under this section to the Commission.

(1A) In subsection (1), "the specified period" means the period

(a) beginning on the first day of the period within which the statement of accounts for any financial year of the party is required to be delivered to the Commission by virtue of section 45, and

(b) ending six months after the last day of that period.

(2) A notification under this section must

(a) state that the particulars in the party's entry in the register remain accurate and include any information prescribed under paragraph 6 of Schedule 4 since the relevant time, or

(b) so far as necessary to secure that such particulars will both be accurate and include any information so prescribed, contain one or more of the following, namely

(i) an application under section 30,

(ii) a notification under section 31, or

(iii) any information so prescribed.

(3) A notification under this section must also give particulars of any change occurring in the party's constitution (within the meaning of section 26) since the relevant time.

(4) In subsections (2) and (3) "the relevant time" means

(a) the time when the party applied for registration, or

(b) if a notification has been previously given under this section in relation to the party, the time when the last such notification was given.

(5) A notification under this section must be accompanied by any fee prescribed by order made by the Secretary of State.

(6) For the purposes of this section any particulars held by the Commission in respect of the home address of any registered officer of the party shall be taken to be particulars contained in the party's entry in the register.

NOTES

Subordinate Legislation
Registration of Political Parties (Fees) Order 2001, SI 2001/83

Defined terms
the Commission: s 160(1)
financial year: ss 40(1), 41(6)

party: s 40(1)
the register: ss 28(10), 40(1)
registered: s 40(1)
registration: s 40(1)

the Secretary of State: s 159A

Party ceasing to be registered

33 (1) Once a party is registered its entry may only be removed from the register in accordance with subsection (2) or (2A).

(2) Where
    (a) a party applies to have its entry removed from the register, and
    (b) the application includes a declaration on behalf of the party that it does not intend to have any candidates at any relevant election,
the Commission shall remove the party's entry from the register.

(2A) Where the Commission does not receive a notification required by virtue of section 32(1) or 34(3) on or before the specified day, the Commission shall remove the party's entry from the register.

(2B) In subsection (2A) "the specified day" means
    (a) in relation to a notification required by virtue of section 32(1), the last day of the specified period for the purposes of that subsection;
    (b) in relation to a notification required by virtue of section 34(3), the day which falls six months after the relevant anniversary of the party's inclusion in the register.

(2C) In subsection (2B)(b), "relevant anniversary" means the anniversary in relation to which the notification is required to be given by virtue of section 34(3).

(3) On the removal of a party's entry from the register by virtue of subsection (2) or (2A) the party shall cease to be a registered party.

(4) However, until the relevant time
    (a) the Commission shall, when considering applications made by other parties under this Part, treat the entry as if it were still contained in the register, and
    (b) the requirements of Parts III to V shall continue to apply to the party as if it were still registered.

(4A) In subsection (4), "the relevant time" means
    (a) if
      (i) the party's entry is removed by virtue of subsection (2), and
      (ii) its gross income or total expenditure in its financial year preceding the year in which the entry is removed is £25,000 or more,
    the end of the financial year of the party which follows that in which the entry is removed;
    (b) otherwise, the end of the financial year of the party in which the entry is removed.

(5) Part IV of Schedule 4 applies to applications under subsection (2).

NOTES
Defined terms
  the Commission: s 160(1)
  financial year: ss 40(1), 41(6)
  party: s 40(1)
  the register: ss 28(10), 40(1)

  registered: s 40(1)
  relevant election: s 22(5)

Registration of minor parties

34 (1) This section applies to any party registered in the Great Britain register in pursuance of a declaration falling within section 28(2)(d) (referred to in this Act as a "minor party").

(2) The following provisions do not apply to a minor party
    (a) any provisions of this Part so far as relating to the registration of a treasurer or campaigns officer for a registered party or otherwise referring to a registered treasurer or campaigns officer (or any deputy campaigns officer);
    (b) sections 26 and 27; and
    (c) section 36;
but this is subject to subsection (8)(a).

(3) The registered leader of a minor party must, in the case of each anniversary of the party's inclusion in the register, give a notification under this subsection to the Commission within the period beginning one month before the anniversary and ending six months after it.

(4) A notification under subsection (3) must
    (a) state that the particulars in the party's entry in the register remain accurate and include any information prescribed under paragraph 6 of Schedule 4 since the relevant time, or
    (b) so far as necessary to secure that such particulars will both be accurate and include any information so prescribed, contain one or more of the following, namely
        (i) an application under section 30,
        (ii) a notification under section 31, or
        (iii) any information so prescribed.

(5) In subsection (4) "the relevant time" means
    (a) the time when the party applied for registration, or
    (b) if a notification has previously been given under subsection (3) in relation to the party, the time when the last such notification was given;
and for the purposes of subsection (4) any particulars held by the Commission in respect of the home address of any registered officer of the party shall be taken to be particulars contained in the party's entry in the register.

(6) A notification under subsection (3) must be accompanied by any fee prescribed by order made by the Secretary of State.

(7) In addition to being able to make an application under section 30, a minor party may apply to the Commission to have
    (a) the declaration mentioned in subsection (1) above cancelled, and
    (b) the party's existing entry in the Great Britain register replaced by such entry or entries (in that or the Northern Ireland register) as accord with a fresh declaration sent by the party to the Commission and falling within section 28(2)(a), (b) or (c).

(8) Where a minor party makes an application under subsection (7)
    (a) the provisions mentioned in subsection (2)(a) and (b) shall apply to the party;
    (b) the party must provide the Commission with such information as
        (i) would, by virtue of Schedule 4, be required to be provided in connection with an application by the party under section 28 to be registered in accordance with the fresh declaration mentioned in subsection (7)(b), and
        (ii) has not already been provided in connection with its existing registration as a minor party; and
    (c) the following provisions, namely
        (i) sections 28(4) to (8), 28A and 29, and
        (ii) paragraphs 1(2) and 7 of Schedule 4,
shall apply, with any necessary modifications, in relation to the party's application as if it were such an application under section 28 as is mentioned in paragraph (b)(I).

NOTES

Defined terms
  the Commission: s 160(1)
  the Great Britain register: ss 23(2)(a), 160(1)
  modifications: s 160(1)
  the Northern Ireland register: ss 23(2)(b), 160(1)
  party: s 40(1)

  the register: ss 28(10), 40(1)
  registered: s 40(1)
  registration: s 40(1)
  the Secretary of State: s 159A

Request by Secretary of State

35 On receipt of a request made by the Secretary of State, the Commission shall send a copy of the Great Britain or Northern Ireland register, or any parts of it specified in the request, to

  (a) the Secretary of State; or

  (b) any other person so specified.

NOTES

Defined terms
  the Commission: s 160(1)
  the Great Britain register: ss 23(2)(a), 160(1)
  the Northern Ireland register: ss 23(2)(b), 160(1)

  the Secretary of State: s 159A

Assistance by Commission for existing registered parties

36 (1) The Commission may, in accordance with a scheme prepared by them for the purposes of this section, provide assistance for existing parties with a view to helping them to meet, or to reducing, the expenses falling to be initially incurred by them in order to comply with Parts III and IV.

(2) The assistance which may be so provided to an existing party may take the form of

  (a) a grant to the party, or

  (b) the provision of non-financial benefits to the party (such as the provision of computer software free of charge),

or both, as the scheme may determine.

(3) The scheme may provide for an existing party's entitlement to assistance under this section to depend on the Commission's being satisfied that the expenses falling to be incurred by the party as mentioned in subsection (1) exceed an amount specified in the scheme.

(4) Any grant under this section may be made subject to such conditions as the Commission consider appropriate.

(5) The total expenditure incurred by the Commission in providing assistance under this section (whether by grants or otherwise) shall not exceed £700,000.

(6) The Commission shall publish the scheme in such manner as they consider appropriate.

(7) In this section "existing party" means any party registered under the Registration of Political Parties Act 1998 at the commencement of this section.

NOTES

Defined terms
  the Commission: s 160(1)
  conditions: s 160(5)

  party: s 40(1)

Supplemental

Party political broadcasts

37 (1) A broadcaster shall not include in its broadcasting services any party political broadcast made on behalf of a party which is not a registered party.

(2) In this Act "broadcaster" means
    (a) the holder of a licence under the Broadcasting Act 1990 or 1996,
    (b) the British Broadcasting Corporation, or
    (c) Sianel Pedwar Cymru.

(3) The reference in subsection (1) to a broadcaster includes a reference to the Gibraltar Broadcasting Corporation, but only as respects party political broadcasts relating to elections to the European Parliament.

NOTES
Defined terms
    party: s 40(1)
    registered: s 40(1)

Amendment of parliamentary elections rules

38 (1) The rules set out in Schedule 1 to the Representation of the People Act 1983 (the parliamentary elections rules) shall be amended as follows.

(2) In rule 6 (nomination of candidates), for paragraph (3) there shall be substituted

"(3) The description, if any, must consist of either
    (a) a description (of not more than 6 words in length) which is authorised as mentioned in rule 6A(1) below; or
    (b) the word "Independent" or, where the candidate is the Speaker of the House of Commons seeking reelection, the words "The Speaker seeking reelection"."

(3) In rule 6A (nomination papers: name of registered political party)
    (a) in paragraph (1), after "unless" there shall be inserted "the party is a qualifying party in relation to the constituency and"; and
    (b) for paragraph (3) there shall be substituted

"(3) For the purposes of the application of this rule in relation to an election
    (a) "registered political party" means a party which was registered under Part II of the Political Parties, Elections and Referendums Act 2000 at the time by which the notice of the election is required to be published by virtue of rule 1 ("the relevant time");
    (b) a registered political party is a qualifying party in relation to a constituency if
        (i) the constituency is in England, Scotland or Wales and the party was at the relevant time registered in respect of that part of Great Britain in the Great Britain register maintained under that Part of that Act, or
        (ii) the constituency is in Northern Ireland and the party was at the relevant time registered in the Northern Ireland register maintained under that Part of that Act."

(4) In the Appendix of Forms, in the form of nomination paper, for "Merchant" there shall be substituted "Independent".

False statements: offence

39 A person commits an offence if
    (a) he knowingly or recklessly makes a statement to the Commission which is false in any material particular, and

(b) the statement is made, or purports to be made, on behalf of a party for any purpose of this Part of this Act.

NOTES
Defined terms
    the Commission: s 160(1)
    party: s 40(1)

Interpretation of Part II

40 (1)   In this Part

"the appointed day" means the day appointed under section 163(2) for the coming into force of section 23;

"financial year", in relation to a registered party, shall be construed in accordance with section 41(6);

"parish or community election" means an election of councillors for a parish in England or a community in Wales;

"party" includes any organisation or person;

"the register" shall be construed in accordance with section 28(10);

"registered" (unless the context otherwise requires) means registered under this Part (whether in the Great Britain or the Northern Ireland register), and other references to registration shall be construed accordingly;

"the registrar of companies" means the registrar or other officer who performs the duty of registering companies under the Companies Act 1985;

"relevant election" shall be construed in accordance with section 22(5).

(2)   For the purposes of this Part a registered party contests an election

(a)   by one or more candidates standing for election in the party's name at the election, or

(b)   by the party itself standing nominated at the election.

(3)   The combined region is to be regarded as part of England for the purposes of

(a)   the references to England in sections 22(2)(a), 23(2)(a) and (3), 28(3A) and 30(1)(ba);

(b)   the references to Great Britain (other than in the expression "Great Britain register") in sections 23(5)(c) and 28(2)(a) and (b); and

(c)   any reference in this Part to a part or parts of Great Britain or to a part or parts of the United Kingdom (other than a reference by name to a particular part).

NOTES
Defined terms
    combined region: s 160(1)
    organisation: s 160(1)
    a person standing for election in the name of a

registered party: s 22(6)

PART III
ACCOUNTING REQUIREMENTS FOR REGISTERED PARTIES

Accounting records

Duty to keep accounting records

41 (1)   The treasurer of a registered party must ensure that accounting records are kept with respect to the party which are sufficient to show and explain the party's transactions.

(2)   The accounting records must be such as to

(a)   disclose at any time, with reasonable accuracy, the financial position of the party at that time; and

(b) enable the treasurer to ensure that any statement of accounts prepared by him under section 42 complies with the requirements of regulations under subsection (2)(a) of that section.

(3) The accounting records must in particular contain
  (a) entries showing from day to day all sums of money received and expended by the party, and the matters in respect of which the receipt and expenditure take place; and
  (b) a record of the assets and liabilities of the party.

(4) The treasurer must ensure that any accounting records made for the purposes of this section in respect of the party are preserved for at least six years from the end of the financial year of the party in which they are made.

(5) Where a party ceases to be registered within the period of six years mentioned in subsection (4) as it applies to any accounting records, the obligation to ensure that those records are preserved in accordance with that subsection shall continue to be discharged by the last treasurer of the party unless
  (a) the Commission consent in writing to the records being destroyed, or
  (b) the Commission direct in writing that the records may be otherwise disposed of and the records are disposed of in accordance with the direction.

(6) In this Part "financial year", in relation to a registered party, means such period as may be determined by the Commission under subsection (7), whether in relation to
  (a) registered parties generally,
  (b) any description of registered parties which includes the party, or
  (c) the party itself.

(7) The Commission may determine that the period which is to be a financial year of a registered party shall be
  (a) a period of twelve months specified by the Commission, or
  (b) a shorter period specified by them for any transitional purposes;
  and different determinations may be made under this subsection in respect of financial years beginning on different dates.

(8) The Commission shall notify registered parties of any determination under subsection (7) which affects them.

(9) Nothing in this Part applies in relation to a minor party.

NOTES
Defined terms
  the Commission: s 160(1)
  minor party: s 160(1)
  record: s 160(1)

registered party: s 160(1)
treasurer: s 160(1)

Statements of accounts

Annual statements of accounts

42 (1) The treasurer of a registered party shall prepare a statement of accounts in respect of each financial year of the party.

(2) A statement of accounts under this section must
  (a) comply with such requirements as to its form and contents as may be prescribed by regulations made by the Commission; and
  (b) be approved
    (i) by the management committee of the party, if there is one, and
    (ii) otherwise by the registered leader of the party.

(3) Regulations under subsection (2)(a) may in particular
  (a) require any such statement to be prepared in accordance with such methods and principles as are specified or referred to in the regulations;
  (b) specify information which is to be provided by way of notes to the accounts.

(4) Without prejudice to the generality of paragraph 22(7) of Schedule 1 (power to make different provision for different cases), regulations under subsection (2)(a) may impose different requirements
  (a) according to which of the following bands the gross income or total expenditure of a party falls within
    (i) not exceeding £25,000;
    (ii) exceeding £25,000 but not £100,000;
    (iii) exceeding £100,000 but not £250,000;
    (iv) exceeding £250,000;
  (b) in respect of (on the one hand) parties registered in the Great Britain register and (on the other) those registered in the Northern Ireland register.

(4A) The Secretary of State may by order amend subsection (4)(a) by varying the number of bands set out in it.

(4B) The Secretary of State may not make an order under subsection (4A) except to give effect to a recommendation of the Commission.

(5) *Repealed*

(6) The treasurer of a registered party shall ensure that any statement of accounts prepared under this section in respect of the party is preserved for at least six years from the end of the financial year to which the statement relates.

(7) Subsection (5) of section 41 shall apply in relation to the preservation of any such statement as it applies in relation to the preservation of any accounting records (the references to subsection (4) of that section being read as references to subsection (6) above).

(8) In this Part "gross income" means gross recorded income from all sources.

NOTES
Defined terms
  the Commission: s 160(1)
  financial year: s 41(6)
  the Great Britain register: ss 23(2)(a), 160(1)
  the Northern Ireland register: ss 23(2)(b), 160(1)

registered party: s 160(1)
the Secretary of State: s 159A
treasurer: s 160(1)

Annual audits

43 (1) Where a registered party's gross income or total expenditure in any financial year exceeds £250,000, the accounts of the party for that year must be audited by a qualified auditor.

  (2) Where
    (a) a registered party's gross income or total expenditure in any financial year does not exceed £250,000, but
    (b) the Commission consider it desirable that the accounts of the party for that year should be audited,
  the Commission may (at any time) give the treasurer of the party a direction requiring those accounts to be audited by a qualified auditor.

  (3) An audit under this section must be carried out
    (a) by the end of the period of six months from the end of the financial year in question, if the audit is required by subsection (1), or
    (b) by the later of

      (i)   the end of the period of six months from the end of the financial year in question, and

      (ii) the end of the period of three months from the date of the direction under subsection (2),

if the audit is required by such a direction.

(4) If it appears to the Commission that any accounts required to be audited by virtue of

     (a) subsection (1), or

     (b) a direction under subsection (2),

have not been duly audited by the time mentioned in subsection (3)(a) or (b) (as the case may be), the Commission may appoint a qualified auditor to audit those accounts.

(5) The expenses of any audit carried out by an auditor appointed by the Commission, including the auditor's remuneration, may be recovered by the Commission from the funds of the party concerned as a debt due to the Commission.

(6) The Commission may by regulations make provision with respect to

     (a) the appointment of auditors to carry out audits under this section;

     (b) the duties of auditors so appointed; and

     (c) the removal or resignation of such auditors and matters connected with their removal or resignation.

(7) Regulations under subsection (6)(c) may make provision requiring such person as is specified in the regulations to deliver to the Commission, in a case where such an auditor is removed or resigns, a copy of such document relating to the auditor's removal or resignation as is so specified; and any such person commits an offence if he fails to comply with any such requirement.

(8) Subsection (6)(a) does not apply in relation to the appointment of auditors by the Commission under subsection (4).

NOTES

Defined terms

  the Commission: s 160(1)

  document: s 160(1)

  financial year: s 41(6)

  gross income: s 42(8)

  qualified auditor: s 160(1), (2)

  registered party: s 160(1)

  treasurer: s 160(1)

Supplementary provisions about auditors

44 (1) An auditor appointed to carry out an audit under section 43

     (a) has a right of access at all reasonable times to the party's books, documents and other records; and

     (b) is entitled to require from the treasurer or any other officer of the party, or from any former treasurer or officer of the party, such information and explanations as he thinks necessary for the performance of his duty as auditor.

(2) If any person fails to provide an auditor with any access, information or explanation to which the auditor is entitled by virtue of subsection (1), the Commission may give that person such written directions as they consider appropriate for securing that the default is made good.

(3) A person guilty of disobedience to any directions of the Commission under subsection (2) may, on the application of the Commission to the High Court or the Court of Session, be dealt with as for disobedience to an order of that Court.

(4) A person commits an offence if he knowingly or recklessly makes to an auditor appointed to carry out an audit under section 43 a statement (whether written or oral) which

    (a) conveys or purports to convey any information or explanation to which the auditor is entitled by virtue of subsection (1), and

    (b) is misleading, false or deceptive in a material particular.

(5) In the application of this section to Gibraltar, the reference to the High Court shall have effect as if it were a reference to the Gibraltar court.

NOTES

Defined terms
  the Commission: s 160(1)
  document: s 160(1)
  Gibraltar court: s 160(1)

record: s 160(1)
treasurer: s 160(1)

Delivery of statements of accounts etc to Commission

45 (1) The treasurer of a registered party shall, if the party's accounts for a financial year are not required to be audited by virtue of section 43(1) or (2), within 4 months of the end of that financial year deliver to the Commission

    (a) the statement of accounts prepared for that year under section 42; and

    (b) the notification required to be sent with that statement by virtue of section 32(1).

(2) If a registered party's accounts for a financial year are required to be audited by virtue of section 43(1) or (2), the treasurer of the party shall, no later than 7 days after the end of the period allowed under section 43(3) for the audit of the accounts, deliver to the Commission

    (a) the documents mentioned in paragraphs (a) and (b) of subsection (1); and

    (b) a copy of the auditor's report (unless the auditor was appointed by the Commission under section 43(4)).

(3) If for any special reason the Commission think it fit to do so they may, on an application made to them before the end of the period otherwise allowed under this section for delivering a party's documents within subsection (1) or (2) for any financial year, by notice extend that period by a further period specified in the notice.

(4) Any documents delivered to the Commission under this section shall be kept by the Commission for such period as they think fit.

NOTES

Defined terms
  the Commission: s 160(1)
  document: s 160(1)
  financial year: s 41(6)

registered party: s 160(1)
treasurer: s 160(1)

Public inspection of parties' statements of accounts

46 Where the Commission receive any statement of accounts under section 45, they shall

    (a) as soon as reasonably practicable after receiving the statement, make a copy of the statement available for public inspection; and

    (b) keep any such copy available for public inspection for the period for which the statement is kept by them or, if they so determine, during such shorter period as they may specify.

NOTES

Defined terms
  the Commission: s 160(1)

Criminal penalty for failure to submit proper statement of accounts

47 (1) If in the case of a registered party

    (a)   any requirements of regulations under section 42(2)(a) are, without reasonable excuse, not complied with in relation to any statement of accounts delivered to the Commission under section 45, or

    (b)   any statement of accounts, notification or auditor's report required to be delivered to the Commission under that section is, without reasonable excuse, not delivered to them before the end of the relevant period,

the person who was the treasurer of the party immediately before the end of that period is guilty of an offence.

(2)   *Repealed*

(3)   *Repealed*

(4)   In this section "the relevant period" means the period allowed by section 45(1) or (2) for delivering the statement, notification or report to the Commission or, if that period has been extended (or further extended) under section 45(3), that period as so extended.

NOTES

Defined terms
   the Commission: s 160(1)
   registered party: s 160(1)

treasurer: s 160(1)

Revision of statements of accounts

Revision of defective statements of accounts

48 (1)   If it appears to the treasurer of a registered party that any statement of accounts for any financial year of the party has not complied with any requirements of regulations under section 42(2)(a) ("the prescribed requirements"), he may prepare a revised statement of accounts.

(2)   Where that statement of accounts has been delivered to the Commission, the revisions shall be confined to

    (a)   the correction of those respects in which the statement did not comply with the prescribed requirements, and

    (b)   the making of any necessary consequential alterations.

(3)   If it appears to the Commission that there is, or may be, a question whether any statement of accounts delivered to them under section 45 complies with the prescribed requirements, they may give notice to the treasurer of the party in question indicating the respects in which it appears to them that such a question arises or may arise.

(4)   The notice shall specify a period of not less than one month for the treasurer to give the Commission an explanation of the statement of accounts or prepare a revised statement.

(5)   If at the end of the specified period, or such longer period as the Commission may allow, it appears to the Commission

    (a)   that no satisfactory explanation of the statement of accounts has been given, and

    (b)   that the statement has not been revised so as to comply with the prescribed requirements,

they may, if they think fit, make an application to the court under subsection (6).

(6)   The Commission may under this subsection make an application to the court

    (a)   for a declaration or declarator that the statement of accounts does not comply with the prescribed requirements, and

(b) for an order requiring the treasurer of the party to prepare a revised statement of accounts.

(7) If the court orders the preparation of revised accounts, it may
    (a) give such directions as it thinks fit;
    (b) order that all or part of the costs (or in Scotland expenses) of and incidental to the application are to be borne by the registered leader and the treasurer of the party.

(8) Where the court makes an order under paragraph (b) of subsection (7) it shall have regard to whether the officers mentioned in that paragraph knew or ought to have known that the statement did not comply with the prescribed requirements, and it may
    (a) order the payment of different amounts by different officers;
    (b) exclude one of the officers from the order; or
    (c) exclude both officers from the order and instead order the payment of all or part of the costs (or expenses) mentioned in that paragraph out of the funds of the party.

(9) The Commission may by regulations make provision with respect to the application of provisions of this Part in relation to the preparation and auditing of revised statements of accounts, and their delivery to the Commission, and may in particular make provision
    (a) for any matter for which provision may be made by regulations under section 43(6);
    (b) for disapplying, to such extent or in such circumstances (or both) as regulations under this subsection may specify, any of the provisions of section 47(1).

(10) Section 46 applies in relation to any revised statement of accounts received by the Commission in accordance with regulations under subsection (9) as it applies in relation to any statement of accounts received by them under section 45.

(11) The provisions of this section apply equally to statements of accounts that have already been revised, in which case the references to revised statements of accounts shall be read as references to further revised statements.

(12) In this section "the court"
    (a) in relation to England and Wales means the county court and, in Northern Ireland, means a county court;
    (b) in relation to Scotland, means the sheriff;
    (c) in relation to Gibraltar, means the Gibraltar court.

NOTES

Defined terms
  the Commission: s 160(1)
  financial year: s 41(6)
  Gibraltar court: s 160(1)

registered party: s 160(1)
treasurer: s 160(1)

Parties with accounting units

Division of responsibilities in case of party with accounting units

49 Where a registered party is a party with accounting units, sections 41 to 48 have effect in accordance with Schedule 5, which makes provision for securing that
    (a) financial matters relating to the party exclusive of those relating to any accounting unit, and
    (b) financial matters relating to any such unit,

are dealt with separately for the purposes of this Part.

NOTES

Defined terms   registered party: s 160(1)
    accounting unit: ss 26(11), 160(1)
    party with accounting units: ss 26(11), 160(1)

PART IV

CONTROL OF DONATIONS TO REGISTERED PARTIES AND THEIR MEMBERS ETC

Chapter I
Donations to Registered Parties

Donations for purposes of Part IV

50 (1)   The following provisions have effect for the purposes of this Part.

  (2)   "Donation", in relation to a registered party, means (subject to section 52)

     (a)   any gift to the party of money or other property;

     (b)   any sponsorship provided in relation to the party (as defined by section 51);

     (c)   any subscription or other fee paid for affiliation to, or membership of, the party;

     (d)   any money spent (otherwise than by or on behalf of the party) in paying any expenses incurred directly or indirectly by the party;

     (e)   *Repealed*

     (f)   the provision otherwise than on commercial terms of any property, services or facilities for the use or benefit of the party (including the services of any person).

  (3)   Where

     (a)   any money or other property is transferred to a registered party pursuant to any transaction or arrangement involving the provision by or on behalf of the party of any property, services or facilities or other consideration of monetary value, and

     (b)   the total value in monetary terms of the consideration so provided by or on behalf of the party is less than the value of the money or (as the case may be) the market value of the property transferred,

    the transfer of the money or property shall (subject to subsection (5)) constitute a gift to the party for the purposes of subsection (2)(a).

  (4)   In determining

     (a)   *Repealed*

     (b)   for the purposes of subsection (2)(f), whether any property, services or facilities provided for the use or benefit of a registered party is or are so provided otherwise than on such terms,

    regard shall be had to the total value in monetary terms of the consideration provided by or on behalf of the party in respect of the provision of the property, services or facilities.

  (5)   Where (apart from this subsection) anything would be a donation both by virtue of subsection (2)(b) and by virtue of any other provision of this section, subsection (2)(b) (together with section 51) shall apply in relation to it to the exclusion of the other provision of this section.

  (6)   Anything given or transferred to any officer, member, trustee or agent of a registered party in his capacity as such (and not for his own use or benefit) is to be regarded as given or transferred to the party (and references to donations received by a party accordingly include donations so given or transferred).

(7)   Except so far as a contrary intention appears, references to a registered party in the context of

(a)   the making of donations to, or the receipt or acceptance of donations by, a registered party, or

(b)   any provision having effect for or in connection with determining what constitutes a donation to such a party,

shall, in the case of a party with accounting units, be construed as references to the central organisation of the party or any of its accounting units.

(8)   In this section

(a)   any reference to anything being given or transferred to a party or any person is a reference to its being so given or transferred either directly or indirectly through any third person;

(b)   "gift" includes bequest.

(9)   Nothing in this Part applies in relation to donations received by a minor party.

NOTES

Defined terms
  accounting units: s 26(11)
  bequest: s 160(1)
  central organisation: ss 26(11), 160(1)
  market value: s 160(1)
  minor party: s 160(1)

party with accounting units: ss 26(11), 160(1)
property: s 160(1)
registered party: s 160(1) (and sub-s (7) of this section)

Sponsorship

51 (1)   For the purposes of this Part sponsorship is provided in relation to a registered party if

(a)   any money or other property is transferred to the party or to any person for the benefit of the party, and

(b)   the purpose (or one of the purposes) of the transfer is (or must, having regard to all the circumstances, reasonably be assumed to be)

(i)   to help the party with meeting, or to meet, to any extent any defined expenses incurred or to be incurred by or on behalf of the party, or

(ii)   to secure that to any extent any such expenses are not so incurred.

(2)   In subsection (1) "defined expenses" means expenses in connection with

(a)   any conference, meeting or other event organised by or on behalf of the party;

(b)   the preparation, production or dissemination of any publication by or on behalf of the party; or

(c)   any study or research organised by or on behalf of the party.

(3)   The following do not, however, constitute sponsorship by virtue of subsection (1)

(a)   the making of any payment in respect of

(i)   any charge for admission to any conference, meeting or other event, or

(ii)   the purchase price of, or any other charge for access to, any publication;

(b)   the making of any payment in respect of the inclusion of an advertisement in any publication where the payment is made at the commercial rate payable for the inclusion of such an advertisement in any such publication;

and subsection (1) also has effect subject to section 52(3).

(4)   The Secretary of State may by order made on the recommendation of the Commission amend subsection (2) or (3).

(5)   In this section "publication" means a publication made available in whatever form and by whatever means (whether or not to the public at large or any section of the public).

NOTES

Defined terms
  the Commission: s 160(1)
  property: s 160(1)

registered party: ss 50(7), 160(1)
the Secretary of State: s 159A

Payments, services etc not to be regarded as donations

52 (1) For the purposes of this Part none of the following shall be regarded as a donation
    (a) *Repealed*
    (b) any grant under section 170 of the Criminal Justice and Public Order Act 1994 (security costs at party conferences);
    (c) any payment made by or on behalf of the European Parliament for the purpose of assisting members of the Parliament to perform their functions as such members;
    (d) the transmission by a broadcaster, free of charge, of a party political broadcast or a referendum campaign broadcast (within the meaning of section 127);
    (e) any other facilities provided in pursuance of any right conferred on candidates or a party at an election or a referendum by any enactment;
    (f) the provision of assistance by a person appointed under section 9 of the Local Government and Housing Act 1989;
    (g) the provision by any individual of his own services which he provides voluntarily in his own time and free of charge;
    (h) any interest accruing to a registered party in respect of any donation which is dealt with by the party in accordance with section 56(2)(a) or (b).

  (2) For the purposes of this Part there shall be disregarded
    (a) any donation which (in accordance with any enactment) falls to be included in a return as to election expenses in respect of a candidate or candidates at a particular election; and
    (b) any donation whose value (as determined in accordance with section 53) is not more than £500.

  (3) Nothing in section 50 or 51 shall have the result that a payment made in respect of the hire of a stand at a party conference organised by or on behalf of a registered party is to constitute a donation to the party for the purposes of this Part if or to the extent that the payment does not exceed such of the maximum rates which the Commission determine to be reasonable for the hire of stands at party conferences as is applicable to the hire of the stand in question.

  (4) The reference in subsection (1)(d) to the transmission by a broadcaster of a party political broadcast includes a reference to the transmission by the Gibraltar Broadcasting Corporation of such a broadcast.

NOTES

Defined terms
broadcaster: s 37(2)
the Commission: s 160(1)
donation: ss 50, 161
enactment: s 160(1)

functions: s 160(1)
registered party: ss 50(7), 160(1)

Value of donations

53 (1) The value of any donation falling within section 50(2)(a) (other than money) shall be taken to be the market value of the property in question.

  (2) Where, however, section 50(2)(a) applies by virtue of section 50(3), the value of the donation shall be taken to be the difference between
    (a) the value of the money, or the market value of the property, in question, and
    (b) the total value in monetary terms of the consideration provided by or on behalf of the party.

  (3) The value of any donation falling within section 50(2)(b) shall be taken to be the value of the money, or (as the case may be) the market value of the property, transferred as mentioned in section 51(1); and accordingly any value in monetary terms of any

benefit conferred on the person providing the sponsorship in question shall be disregarded.

(4) The value of any donation falling within section 50(2)(f) shall be taken to be the amount representing the difference between

    (a) the total value in monetary terms of the consideration that would have had to be provided by or on behalf of the party in respect of the provision of the property, services or facilities if

        (i) *Repealed*

        (ii) the property, services or facilities had been provided,

    on commercial terms, and

    (b) the total value in monetary terms of the consideration (if any) actually so provided by or on behalf of the party.

(5) Subsection (6) applies where a donation such as is mentioned in subsection (3) confers an enduring benefit on the party during the whole or part of

    (a) any period for which a report is to be prepared under this Part, or

    (b) two or more such periods.

(6) In such a case, the amount to be recorded in any such report shall be so much of the total value of the donation (as determined in accordance with subsection (3)) as accrues during the whole or part of the period to which the report relates.

NOTES

Defined terms

    donation: ss 50, 161

    market value: s 160(1)

property: s 160(1)

Chapter II
Restrictions on Donations to Registered Parties

Permissible donations

Permissible donors

54 (1) A donation received by a registered party must not be accepted by the party if

    (a) the person by whom the donation would be made is not, at the time of its receipt by the party, a permissible donor; or

    (aa) any declaration required to be made in respect of the donation by section 54A or 54B has not been received by the party; or

    (b) the party is (whether because the donation is given anonymously or by reason of any deception or concealment or otherwise) unable to ascertain the identity of that person the person offering the donation.

(2) For the purposes of this Part the following are permissible donors

    (a) an individual registered in an electoral register who is registered in an electoral register and (subject to subsection (2ZB)) satisfies the condition set out in subsection (2ZA);

    (b) a company

        (i) registered under the Companies Act 2006, and

        (ii) incorporated within the United Kingdom or another member State,

  which carries on business in the United Kingdom;

    (c) a registered party, other than a Gibraltar party whose entry in the register includes a statement that it intends to contest one or more elections to the European Parliament in the combined region;

    (d) a trade union entered in the list kept under the Trade Union and Labour Relations (Consolidation) Act 1992 or the Industrial Relations (Northern Ireland) Order 1992;

    (e) a building society (within the meaning of the Building Societies Act 1986);

    (f) a limited liability partnership registered under the Limited Liability Partnerships Act 2000 which carries on business in the United Kingdom;

    (g) a friendly society registered under the Friendly Societies Act 1974, a registered society within the meaning of the Co-operative and Community Benefit Societies Act 2014 or a society registered (or deemed to be registered) under the Industrial and Provident Societies Act (Northern Ireland) 1969; and

    (h) any unincorporated association of two or more persons which does not fall within any of the preceding paragraphs but which carries on business or other activities wholly or mainly in the United Kingdom and whose main office is there.

(2ZA) The condition referred to in subsection (2)(a) is that the individual's liability to income tax for the current tax year (including eligibility to make any claim) falls to be determined (or would fall to be determined) on the basis that the individual is resident, ordinarily resident and domiciled in the United Kingdom in that year.

        In this subsection "tax year" has the meaning given by section 4 of the Income Tax Act 2007.

(2ZB) The condition set out in subsection (2ZA) applies in relation to a donation only if

    (a) it is a donation of more than £7,500, or

    (b) when the donation is added to any other relevant benefit or benefits accruing in the same calendar year as the donation, the aggregate amount of the benefits is more than £7,500.

(2ZC) For the purposes of subsection (2ZB)(b) "relevant benefit" and "accruing" have the meaning given by section 62(3A).

(2A) As respects a registered party whose entry in the register includes a statement that it intends to contest one or more elections to the European Parliament in the combined region, the following are also permissible donors for the purposes of this Part

    (a) a Gibraltar elector;

    (b) a company

        (i) registered under the Companies Act; and

        (ii) incorporated within Gibraltar, the United Kingdom or another member State, which carries on business in Gibraltar;

    (c) a Gibraltar party whose entry in the register includes a statement that it intends to contest one or more elections to the European Parliament in the combined region;

    (d) a trade union within the meaning of the Trade Union and Trade Disputes Act;

    (e) a building society within the meaning of the Banking (Extension to Building Societies) Act;

    (f) a limited liability partnership registered under the Limited Partnerships Ordinance, which carries on business in Gibraltar; and

    (g) any unincorporated association of two or more persons which does not fall within any of the preceding paragraphs but which carries on business or other activities wholly or mainly in Gibraltar and whose main office is there,

but, in the case of a party other than a Gibraltar party, only where the donation is received by the party within the period of four months ending with the date of the poll for an election to the European Parliament in the combined region.

(3) In relation to a donation in the form of a bequest subsection (2)(a) shall be read as referring to an individual who was, at any time within the period of five years ending with the date of his death, registered in an electoral register.

(3A)   In relation to a donation in the form of a bequest subsection (2A)(a) shall be read as referring to an individual who was, at any time within the period of five years ending with the date of his death, a Gibraltar elector.

(4)   Where any person ("the principal donor") causes an amount ("the principal donation") to be received by a registered party by way of a donation

    (a)   on behalf of himself and one or more other persons, or

    (b)   on behalf of two or more other persons,

then for the purposes of this Part each individual contribution by a person falling within paragraph (a) or (b) of more than £500 shall be treated as if it were a separate donation received from that person.

(5)   In relation to each such separate donation, the principal donor must ensure that, at the time when the principal donation is received by the party, the party is given

    (a)   (except in the case of a donation which the principal donor is treated as making) all such details in respect of the person treated as making the donation as are required by virtue of paragraph 2 or 2A of Schedule 6 to be given in respect of the donor of a recordable donation; and

    (b)   (in any case) all such details in respect of the donation as are required by virtue of paragraph 4 of Schedule 6 to be given in respect of a recordable donation.

(6)   Where

    (a)   any person ("the agent") causes an amount to be received by a registered party by way of a donation on behalf of another person ("the donor"), and

    (b)   the amount of that donation is more than £500,

the agent must ensure that, at the time when the donation is received by the party, the party is given all such details in respect of the donor as are required by virtue of paragraph 2 or 2A of Schedule 6 to be given in respect of the donor of a recordable donation.

(7)   A person commits an offence if, without reasonable excuse, he fails to comply with subsection (5) or (6).

(8)   In this section "electoral register" means any of the following

    (a)   a register of parliamentary or local government electors maintained under section 9 of the Representation of the People Act 1983;

    (b)   a register of relevant citizens of the European Union prepared under the European Parliamentary Elections (Franchise of Relevant Citizens of the Union) Regulations 2001; or

    (c)   a register of peers prepared under regulations under section 3 of the Representation of the People Act 1985.

NOTES

Prospective operation
  Sub-ss (1)(aa), (2ZA)-(2ZC) not yet in operation

Defined terms
  Banking (Extension to Building Societies) Act: s 160(6)
  bequest: s 160(1)
  business: s 160(1)
  combined region: s 160(1)
  Companies Act: s 160(6)

donation: ss 50, 161
Gibraltar elector: s 160(1)
Gibraltar party: ss 28(8)(d), 160(1)
Limited Partnerships Ordinance: cf s 160(6)
registered party: ss 50(7), 160(1)
Trade Union and Trade Disputes Act: s 160(6)

Declaration as to source of donation

54A (1)   Where a person (P) causes an amount exceeding £7,500 to be received by a registered party by way of a donation, a written declaration must be given to the party

    (a)   by P, if P is an individual, or

    (b)   if not, by an individual authorised by P to make the declaration, stating, to the best of the individual's knowledge and belief, whether or not subsection (2) applies to the donation.

(2) This subsection applies to the donation if
- (a) a person other than P has provided, or is expected to provide, money or any other benefit to P with a view to, or otherwise in connection with, the making of the donation, and
- (b) the money, or the value of the benefit, is more than £7,500.

(3) Where a declaration under this section contains a statement to the effect that subsection (2) applies to the donation, it must also
- (a) state whether or not, in the opinion of the person making the declaration
  - (i) subsection (4) of section 54 applies to the donation;
  - (ii) subsection (6) of that section applies to it;
- (b) if the person's opinion is that neither of those subsections applies to the donation, give the person's reasons for that opinion.

(4) A declaration under this section must also state the full name and address of the person by whom it is made and, where subsection (1)(b) applies
- (a) state that the person is authorised by P to make the declaration;
- (b) describe the person's role or position in relation to P.

(5) A person who knowingly or recklessly makes a false declaration under this section commits an offence.

(6) Regulations made by the Secretary of State may make provision as to how the value of a benefit is to be calculated for the purposes of subsection (2).

NOTES

Prospective operation
   This section not yet in operation

registered party: ss 50(7), 160(1)
Secretary of State: s 159A

Defined terms
   donation: ss 50, 161

Declaration as to whether residence etc condition satisfied

54B (1) An individual making to a registered party a donation in relation to which the condition set out in section 54(2ZA) applies must give to the party a written declaration stating whether or not the individual satisfies that condition.

(2) A declaration under this section must also state the individual's full name and address.

(3) A person who knowingly or recklessly makes a false declaration under this section commits an offence.

(4) The Secretary of State may by regulations make provision requiring a declaration under this section to be retained for a specified period.

(5) The requirement in subsection (1) does not apply where, by reason of section 71B(1)(a), the individual by whom the donation would be made is a permissible donor in relation to the donation at the time of its receipt by the party.

NOTES

Prospective operation
   This section not yet in operation

permissible donor: s 54(2)
registered party: ss 50(7), 160(1)
Secretary of State: s 159A

Defined terms
   donation: ss 50, 161

Payments etc which are (or are not) to be treated as donations by permissible donors

55 (1) The following provisions have effect for the purposes of this Part.

(2) Any payment out of public funds received by a registered party shall (subject to section 52(1)(b)) be regarded as a donation received by the party from a permissible donor.

But such a payment shall not be regarded as a donation for the purposes of section 54A or 54B or paragraph 6A or 6B of Schedule 7.

(3) Any donation received by a registered party shall (if it would not otherwise fall to be so regarded) be regarded as a donation received by the party from a permissible donor if and to the extent that

    (a) the purpose of the donation is to meet qualifying costs incurred or to be incurred in connection with a visit by any member or officer of the party to a country or territory outside the United Kingdom, and

    (b) the amount of the donation does not exceed a reasonable amount in respect of such costs.

(4) In subsection (3) "qualifying costs", in relation to any member or officer of the party, means costs relating to that person in respect of

    (a) travelling between the United Kingdom and the country or territory in question, or

    (b) travelling, accommodation or subsistence while within that country or territory.

(5) Any exempt trust donation received by a registered party shall be regarded as a donation received by the party from a permissible donor.

(5A) Any exempt Gibraltar trust donation received by a registered party shall be regarded as a donation received by the party from a permissible donor if

    (a) at the time the donation is received by the party, its entry in the register includes a statement that it intends to contest one or more elections to the European Parliament in the combined region; and

    (b) in the case of a party other than a Gibraltar party, the donation is received by the party within the period of four months ending with the date of the poll for an election to the European Parliament in the combined region.

(6) But any donation received by a registered party from a trustee of any property (in his capacity as such) which is not

    (a) an exempt trust donation, or

    (aa) an exempt Gibraltar trust donation regarded by virtue of subsection (5A) as received from a permissible donor, or

    (b) a donation transmitted by the trustee to the party on behalf of beneficiaries under the trust who are

        (i) persons who at the time of its receipt by the party are permissible donors, or

        (ii) the members of an unincorporated association which at that time is a permissible donor,

shall be regarded as a donation received by the party from a person who is not a permissible donor.

NOTES

Prospective operation
Last sentence in sub-s (2) not yet in operation

Defined terms
combined region: s 160(1)
donation: ss 50, 161
exempt Gibraltar trust donation: ss 160(1), 162
exempt trust donation: ss 160(1), 162

Gibraltar party: ss 28(8)(d), 160(1)
payments out of public funds: s 160(4)
permissible donor: s 54(2)
property: s 160(1)
registered party: ss 50(7), 160(1)

Acceptance or return of donations: general

56 (1) Where

(a) a donation is received by a registered party, and

(b) it is not immediately decided that the party should (for whatever reason) refuse the donation,

all reasonable steps must be taken forthwith by or on behalf of the party to verify (or, so far as any of the following is not apparent, ascertain) the identity of the donor, whether he is a permissible donor, and (if that appears to be the case) all such details in respect of him as are required by virtue of paragraph 2 or 2A of Schedule 6 to be given in respect of the donor of a recordable donation.

(1A) In so far as subsection (1) requires steps to be taken to verify or ascertain whether an individual satisfies the condition set out in section 54(2ZA), the requirement is treated as having being complied with if

(a) the individual has given to the party a declaration under section 54B stating that the individual satisfies that condition, and

(b) the party had no reasonable grounds for thinking that the statement was incorrect.

(2) If a registered party receives a donation which it is prohibited from accepting by virtue of section 54(1), or which it is decided that the party should for any other reason refuse, then

(a) unless the donation falls within section 54(1)(aa) or (b), the donation, or a payment of an equivalent amount, must be sent back to the person who made the donation or any person appearing to be acting on his behalf,

(aa) if the donation falls within section 54(1)(aa) (but not section 54(1)(b)), the donation, or a payment of an equivalent amount, must be sent back to the person appearing to be the donor,

(b) if the donation falls within section 54(1)(b), the required steps (as defined by section 57(1)) must be taken in relation to the donation,

within the period of 30 days beginning with the date when the donation is received by the party.

(3) Where

(a) subsection (2)(a) applies in relation to a donation, and

(b) the donation is not dealt with in accordance with that provision,

the party and the treasurer of the party are each guilty of an offence.

(3A) Where a party or its treasurer is charged with an offence under subsection (3), it shall be a defence to prove that

(a) all reasonable steps were taken by or on behalf of the party to verify (or ascertain) whether the donor was a permissible donor, and

(b) as a result, the treasurer believed the donor to be a permissible donor.

(3B) Where

(a) subsection (2)(aa) applies in relation to a donation, and

(b) the donation is not dealt with in accordance with that provision,

the party and the treasurer of the party are each guilty of an offence.

(4) Where

(a) subsection (2)(b) applies in relation to a donation, and

(b) the donation is not dealt with in accordance with that provision,

the treasurer of the party is guilty of an offence.

(5) For the purposes of this Part a donation received by a registered party shall be taken to have been accepted by the party unless

(a) the steps mentioned in paragraph (a), (aa) or (b) of subsection (2) are taken in relation to the donation within the period of 30 days mentioned in that subsection; and

(b) a record can be produced of the receipt of the donation and

(i)   of the return of the donation, or the equivalent amount, as mentioned in subsection (2)(a) or (aa), or

(ii)   of the required steps being taken in relation to the donation as mentioned in subsection (2)(b),

as the case may be.

(6) Where a donation is received by a registered party in the form of an amount paid into any account held by the party with a financial institution, it shall be taken for the purposes of this Part to have been received by the party at the time when the party is notified in the usual way of the payment into the account.

NOTES

Prospective operation
    Sub-ss (1A), (2)(aa) and (3B) not yet in operation

Defined terms
    donation: ss 50, 161
    permissible donor: s 54(2)

record: s 160(1)
recordable donation: Sch 6, para 1
registered party: ss 50(7), 160(1)
treasurer: s 160(1)

Return of donations where donor unidentifiable

57 (1)   For the purposes of section 56(2)(b) the required steps are as follows

(a)   if the donation mentioned in that provision was transmitted by a person other than the donor, and the identity of that person is apparent, to return the donation to that person;

(b)   if paragraph (a) does not apply but it is apparent that the donor has, in connection with the donation, used any facility provided by an identifiable financial institution, to return the donation to that institution; and

(c)   in any other case, to send the donation to the Commission.

(2) In subsection (1) any reference to returning or sending a donation to any person or body includes a reference to sending a payment of an equivalent amount to that person or body.

(3) Any amount sent to the Commission in pursuance of subsection (1)(c) shall be paid by them into the Consolidated Fund.

NOTES

Defined terms
    body: s 160(1)
    the Commission: s 160(1)

donation: ss 50, 161

57A   *Repealed*

Forfeiture of certain donations

Forfeiture of donations made by impermissible or unidentifiable donors

58 (1)   This section applies to any donation received by a registered party

(a)   which, by virtue of section 54(1)(a), (aa) or (b), the party are prohibited from accepting, but

(b)   which has been accepted by the party.

(2) The court may, on an application made by the Commission, order the forfeiture by the party of an amount equal to the value of the donation.

(3) The standard of proof in proceedings on an application under this section shall be that applicable to civil proceedings.

(4) An order may be made under this section whether or not proceedings are brought against any person for an offence connected with the donation.

(5)   In this section "the court" means

    (a)   in relation to England and Wales, a magistrates' court;

    (b)   in relation to Scotland, the sheriff;

    (c)   in relation to Northern Ireland, a court of summary jurisdiction;

    (d)   in relation to Gibraltar, the Gibraltar court;

and proceedings on an application under this section to the sheriff shall be civil proceedings.

NOTES

Defined terms
the Commission: s 160(1)
donation: ss 50, 161
Gibraltar court: s 160(1)

registered party: ss 50(7), 160(1)

Appeal against order under section 58

59 (1)   Subsection (2) applies where an order ("the forfeiture order") is made under section 58 by a magistrates' court or a court of summary jurisdiction in Northern Ireland.

  (2)   The registered party may, before the end of the period of 30 days beginning with the date on which the forfeiture order is made, appeal to the Crown Court or, in Northern Ireland, to a county court.

(2A)   In the application of subsections (1) and (2) to Gibraltar, the references to a magistrates' court and the Crown court shall have effect as if they were references to the Gibraltar court.

  (3)   An appeal under subsection (2) shall be by way of a rehearing; and the court hearing such an appeal may make such order as it considers appropriate.

  (4)   Subsections (3) and (4) of section 58 apply in relation to a rehearing on an appeal under subsection (2) as they apply in relation to proceedings under that section.

  (5)   Where an order is made under section 58 by the sheriff, the registered party may appeal against the order to the Court of Session.

NOTES

Defined terms
Gibraltar court: s 160(1)
registered party: ss 50(7), 160(1)

Supplementary provisions about orders under section 58

60 (1)   In relation to courts in any part of the United Kingdom, provision may be made by rules of court

    (a)   with respect to applications or appeals to any court under section 58 or 59,

    (b)   for the giving of notice of such applications or appeals to persons affected,

    (c)   for the joinder, or in Scotland sisting, of such persons as parties,

and generally with respect to the procedure under those sections before any court.

  (2)   Subsection (1) is without prejudice to the generality of any existing power to make rules.

  (3)   Any amount forfeited by an order under section 58 or 59 shall be paid into the Consolidated Fund.

  (4)   Subsection (3) does not apply

    (a)   where an appeal is made under section 59(2) or (5), before the appeal is determined or otherwise disposed of; and

    (b)   in any other case

  (i) where the forfeiture was ordered by a magistrates' court or a court of summary jurisdiction in Northern Ireland or the Gibraltar court, before the end of the period of 30 days mentioned in section 59(2); or

  (ii) where the forfeiture was ordered by the sheriff, before the end of any period within which, in accordance with rules of court, an appeal under section 59(5) must be made.

(5) In the case of a registered party which is not a body corporate

  (a) proceedings under section 58 or 59 shall be brought against or by the party in its own name (and not in that of any of its members);

  (b) for the purposes of any such proceedings any rules of court relating to the service of documents apply as if the party were a body corporate; and

  (c) any amount forfeited by an order under section 58 or 59 shall be paid out of the funds of the party.

NOTES

Defined terms
document: s 160(1)
Gibraltar court: s 160(1)

registered party: ss 50(7), 160(1)

Evasion of restrictions on donations

Offences concerned with evasion of restrictions on donations

61 (1) A person commits an offence if he

  (a) knowingly enters into, or

  (b) knowingly does any act in furtherance of,

any arrangement which facilitates or is likely to facilitate, whether by means of any concealment or disguise or otherwise, the making of donations to a registered party by any person or body other than a permissible donor.

(2) A person commits an offence if

  (a) he knowingly gives the treasurer of a registered party any information relating to

  (i) the amount of any donation made to the party, or

  (ii) the person or body making such a donation,

which is false in a material particular; or

  (b) with intent to deceive, he withholds from the treasurer of a registered party any material information relating to a matter within paragraph (a)(i) or (ii).

NOTES

Defined terms
body: s 160(1)
donation: ss 50, 161
registered party: ss 50(7), 160(1)

treasurer: s 160(1)

Chapter III
Reporting of Donations to Registered Parties

Reports to be made by registered parties

Quarterly donation reports

62 (1) The treasurer of a registered party shall, in the case of each year, prepare a report under this subsection in respect of each of the following periods

  (a) January to March;

      (b) April to June;

      (c) July to September;

      (d) October to December.

(2)   In this section

    "donation report" means a report prepared under subsection (1);

    "reporting period", in relation to such a report, means the period mentioned in any of paragraphs (a) to (d) of that subsection to which the report relates.

(3)   The donation reports for any year shall, in the case of each permissible donor from whom any donation is accepted by the party during that year, comply with the following provisions of this section so far as they require any such donation to be recorded in a donation report; and in those provisions any such donation is referred to, in relation to the donor and that year, as a "relevant donation".

(3A) "Relevant benefit", in relation to any person and any year, means

      (a) a relevant donation accepted by the party from that person as a donor, or

      (b) a relevant transaction within the meaning of section 71M(3) entered into by the party and that person as a participant,

    and a relevant benefit accrues when it is accepted (if it is a donation) or entered into (if it is a transaction).

(4)   Where no previous relevant benefit or benefits has or have been required to be recorded under this subsection or section 71M(4), a relevant donation must be recorded

      (a) if it is a donation of more than £7,500, or

      (b) if, when it is added to any other relevant benefit or benefits, the aggregate amount of the benefits is more than £7,500.

(5)   A donation to which subsection (4) applies must

      (a) (if within paragraph (a) of that subsection) be recorded in the donation report for the reporting period in which it is accepted, or

      (b) (if within paragraph (b) of that subsection) be recorded (together with any other relevant donation or donations included in the aggregate amount mentioned in that paragraph) in the donation report for the reporting period in which the benefit which causes that aggregate amount to be more than £7,500 accrues.

(6)   Where any previous relevant benefit or benefits has or have been required to be recorded under subsection (4) or section 71M(4), a relevant donation must be recorded at the point when there has or have been accepted

      (a) since the benefit or benefits required to be recorded under that provision, or

      (b) if any relevant benefit or benefits has or have previously been required to be recorded under this subsection or section 71M(6), since the benefit or benefits last required to be so recorded,

    any relevant donation falling within subsection (6A).

(6A) A relevant donation falls within this subsection

      (a) if it is a donation of more than £1,500, or

      (b) if, when it is added to any other relevant benefit or benefits accruing since the time mentioned in subsection (6)(a) or (b), the aggregate amount of the benefits is more than £1,500.

(7)   A donation to which subsection (6) applies on any occasion must

      (a) if it is the only benefit required to be recorded on that occasion, be recorded in the donation report for the reporting period in which it is accepted, or

      (b) in any other case be recorded (together with any other relevant donation or donations included in the aggregate amount mentioned in subsection (6A)) in the donation report for the reporting period in which the benefit which causes that aggregate amount to be more than £1,500 accrues.

(8)   For the purposes of subsections (4) to (7) as they apply in relation to any year
    (a)   each payment to which section 55(2) applies and which is accepted by the party during that year shall be treated as a relevant donation in relation to that year, and
    (b)   each payment to which section 55(3) applies and which is received from a particular donor and accepted by the party during that year shall be treated as a relevant donation in relation to the donor and that year;
and the donation reports for the year shall accordingly comply with subsections (4) to (7) so far as they operate, by virtue of paragraph (a) or (b) above, to require any relevant donation falling within that paragraph to be recorded in a donation report.

(9)   A donation report must also record every donation falling within section 54(1)(a), (aa) or (b) and dealt with during the reporting period in accordance with section 56(2).

(10)   If during any reporting period
    (a)   no donations have been accepted by the party which, by virtue of the preceding provisions of this section, are required to be recorded in the donation report for that period, and
    (b)   no donations have been dealt with as mentioned in subsection (9),
the report shall contain a statement to that effect.

(11)   Where a registered party is a party with accounting units, subsections (3) to (10) shall apply separately in relation to the central organisation of the party and each of its accounting units
    (a)   as if any reference to the party were a reference to the central organisation or (as the case may be) to such an accounting unit; but
    (b)   with the substitution, in relation to such an accounting unit, of "£1,500" for "£7,500" in each place where it occurs in subsections (4) and (5).

(12)   However, for the purposes of subsections (3) to (7) in their application in relation to the central organisation and any year by virtue of subsection (11), any donation
    (a)   which is accepted from a permissible donor by any of the accounting units during that year, but
    (b)   which is not required to be recorded under subsection (4) or (6) (as they apply by virtue of subsection (11)) as a donation accepted by the accounting unit,
shall be treated as a donation accepted from the donor during that year by the central organisation.

(13)   Schedule 6 has effect with respect to the information to be given in donation reports.

NOTES

Defined terms
    accounting unit: ss 26(11), 160(1)
    central organisation: ss 26(11), 160(1)
    donation: ss 50, 161
    party with accounting units: ss 26(11), 160(1)

    registered party: ss 50(7), 160(1)
    treasurer: s 160(1)

Exemption from requirement to prepare quarterly reports

62A (1)   This section applies if each of four consecutive donation reports prepared by the treasurer of a registered party in pursuance of subsection (1) of section 62 contains
    (a)   in the case of a party without accounting units, a statement under subsection (10) of that section, or
    (b)   in the case of a party with accounting units, statements under subsection (10) of that section in relation to the central organisation of the party and each of its accounting units.

(2)   The treasurer is not required to prepare any further donation reports in pursuance of subsection (1) of that section until a recordable donation

(a) is accepted by the registered party, or

(b) is dealt with by the registered party in accordance with section 56(2).

(3) A recordable donation is a donation which is required to be recorded by virtue of any of subsections (4) to (9) of section 62 (including those subsections as applied by subsection (11) of that section).

(4) If a recordable donation is accepted or (as the case may be) dealt with in accordance with section 56(2), nothing in this section affects the operation of section 62 in relation to

(a) the reporting period in which the recordable donation is so accepted or dealt with, or

(b) any subsequent reporting period which falls before the time (if any) when this section again applies in relation to the party.

(5) In this section, "donation report" and "reporting period" have the same meaning as in section 62.

NOTES

Defined terms
accounting units: s 26(10)
central organisation: ss 26(11), 160(1)
donation: ss 50, 161
party with accounting units: ss 26(11), 160(1)

registered party: ss 50(7), 160(1)
treasurer: s 160(1)

Weekly donation reports during general election periods

63 (1) Subject to section 64, the treasurer of a registered party shall, in the case of any general election period, prepare a report under this section in respect of each of the following periods

(a) the period of seven days beginning with the first day of the general election period;

(b) each succeeding period of seven days falling within the general election period; and

(c) any final period of less than seven days falling within that period.

(2) In this section
"weekly report" means a report prepared under subsection (1);
"reporting period", in relation to such a report, means the period mentioned in any of paragraphs (a) to (c) of that subsection to which the report relates.

(3) The weekly report for any reporting period shall record each donation of more than £7,500 received during that period

(a) by the party (if it is not a party with accounting units); or

(b) by the central organisation of the party (if it is a party with accounting units).

(4) If during any reporting period no donations falling within subsection (3) have been received as mentioned in that subsection, the weekly report for that period shall contain a statement to that effect.

(5) Schedule 6 has effect with respect to the information to be given in weekly reports.

(6) In this section and section 64 "general election period" means the period

(a) beginning with the date on which Parliament is dissolved by section 3(1) of the Fixed-term Parliaments Act 2011 for a parliamentary general election, and

(b) ending with the date of the poll.

NOTES

Defined terms
accounting unit: ss 26(11), 160(1)
central organisation: ss 26(11), 160(1)
donation: ss 50, 161

party with accounting units: ss 26(11), 160(1)
registered party: ss 50(7), 160(1)
treasurer: s 160(1)

Exemptions from section 63

64 (1)   Section 63(1) shall not apply in relation to a registered party in respect of a general election period if the party has made an exemption declaration which covers the general election in question.

   (2)   A registered party shall be taken to have made an exemption declaration which covers a particular general election if a declaration that the party does not intend to have any candidates at that election
      (a)   is signed by the responsible officers of the party; and
      (b)   is sent to the Commission within the period of seven days beginning with the date mentioned in section 63(6)(a).

   (3)   A registered party shall also be taken to have made an exemption declaration which covers a particular general election if the party's application for registration was accompanied by a declaration that the party was not intending to have candidates at parliamentary elections and either
      (a)   the poll for the general election in question takes place within the period of twelve months beginning with the date of its registration; or
      (b)   the declaration has been confirmed in the party's most recent notification given to the Commission under section 32 and the poll for the general election in question takes place within the period of twelve months beginning with the date when that notification was so given.

   (4)   An exemption declaration shall, however, not cover a particular general election if the party in question withdraws its declaration by a notice
      (a)   signed by the responsible officers of the party, and
      (b)   sent to the Commission,
   before the beginning of the general election period.

   (5)   Where
      (a)   a registered party has made an exemption declaration which (apart from this subsection) would cover a particular general election, but
      (b)   the party has one or more candidates at that election,
         the exemption declaration shall be treated as if it had been withdrawn at the beginning of the general election period (and the requirements of section 63 shall accordingly apply retrospectively as from the beginning of that period).

   (6)   Subsection (3) shall apply to a party registered immediately before the date on which this section comes into force as if it referred to a declaration in the terms mentioned in that subsection having been
      (a)   signed by the responsible officers of the party, and
      (b)   sent to the Commission within the period of six weeks beginning with that date.

   (7)   For the purposes of this section "the responsible officers" are
      (a)   the registered leader;
      (b)   the registered nominating officer; and
      (c)   where the leader and the nominating officer are the same person, any other registered officer.

   (8)   If any responsible officer is unable to sign a declaration or notice for the purposes of any provision of this section
      (a)   the holder of some other office in the party may sign in his place, and
      (b)   the declaration or notice must include a statement of the reason why the responsible officer is unable to sign and a declaration that the holder of the other office is authorised to sign in his place.

   (9)   For the purposes of this section and section 65 a registered party shall be taken to have a candidate at a general election if any statement published, in connection with the

election, under rule 14 of the rules set out in Schedule 1 to the Representation of the People Act 1983 (parliamentary election rules) contains the name of a candidate standing in the name of the party.

NOTES

Submission of donation reports to Commission

65 (1)   A donation report under section 62 shall be delivered to the Commission by the treasurer of the party in question within the period of 30 days beginning with the end of the reporting period to which it relates.

(2)   A donation report under section 63 shall be delivered to the Commission by the treasurer of the party in question

    (a)   within the period of 7 days beginning with the end of the reporting period to which it relates; or

    (b)   (if that is not possible in the case of any party to which section 63(1) applies by virtue of section 64(5)) within the period of 7 days beginning with the first day on which the party has a candidate at the election in question.

(2A)   If a donation report under section 62 or 63 states that the registered party has seen evidence of such description as is prescribed by the Secretary of State in regulations that an individual donor has an anonymous entry in an electoral register (within the meaning of the Representation of the People Act 1983), the report must be accompanied by a copy of the evidence.

(3)   The treasurer of a registered party commits an offence if, without reasonable excuse, he fails to comply with the requirements of subsection (1) or (2) in relation to a donation report.

(4)   The treasurer of a registered party also commits an offence if, without reasonable excuse, he delivers a donation report to the Commission which does not comply with any requirements of this Part as regards the information to be given in such a report.

(5)   *Repealed*

(6)   Where the court is satisfied, on an application made by the Commission, that any failure to comply with any such requirements in relation to any donation to a registered party was attributable to an intention on the part of any person to conceal the existence or true amount of the donation, the court may order the forfeiture by the party of an amount equal to the value of the donation.

(7)   The following provisions, namely

    (a)   subsections (3) to (5) of section 58, and

    (b)   sections 59 and 60,

shall apply for the purposes, or in connection with the operation, of subsection (6) above as they apply for the purposes, or in connection with the operation, of section 58.

(8)   Section 64(9) applies for the purposes of this section.

NOTES

Declaration by treasurer in donation report

66 (1) Each donation report under section 62 or 63 must, when delivered to the Commission, be accompanied by a declaration made by the treasurer which complies with subsection (2), (3) or (4).

(2) In the case of a report under section 62 (other than one making a nil return), the declaration must state that, to the best of the treasurer's knowledge and belief
   (a) all the donations recorded in the report as having been accepted by the party are from permissible donors, and
   (b) during the reporting period
      (i) no other donations required to be recorded in the report have been accepted by the party, and
      (ii) no donation from any person or body other than a permissible donor has been accepted by the party.

(3) For the purposes of subsection (2) a return under section 62 makes a nil return if it contains such a statement as is mentioned in subsection (10) of that section; and in the case of such a report the declaration must state that, to the best of the treasurer's knowledge and belief
   (a) that statement is accurate; and
   (b) during the reporting period no donation from any person or body other than a permissible donor has been accepted by the party.

(4) In the case of a report under section 63, the declaration must state that, to the best of the treasurer's knowledge and belief, no donations have been received by the party, or (if section 63(3)(b) applies) by its central organisation, during the reporting period which
   (a) are required to be recorded in the report, but
   (b) are not so recorded.

(5) A person commits an offence if he knowingly or recklessly makes a false declaration under this section.

NOTES

Defined terms
   body: s 160(1)
   central organisation: ss 26(11), 160(1)
   the Commission: s 160(1)

donation: ss 50, 161
treasurer: s 160(1)

Extension of reporting requirements

Weekly donation reports in connection with elections other than general elections

67 (1) The Secretary of State may, after consulting the Commission and all registered parties, by order make provision for
   (a) sections 63 and 64, together with Schedule 6,
   (b) sections 65 and 66, and
   (c) an order under paragraph 16 of Schedule 19C so far as applying in relation to section 65(1) or (2),
to apply in relation to the specified election period in the case of one or more relevant elections with such modifications as are specified in the order.

(2) In this section
   (a) "specified election period", in relation to a relevant election, means such period ending with the date of the poll for the election as may be specified in an order under subsection (1);
   (b) "relevant election" means

(i)   an election to the European Parliament;

(ii)   an election to the Scottish Parliament;

(iii)   an election to the National Assembly for Wales;

(iv)   an election to the Northern Ireland Assembly; or

(v)   an election of a police and crime commissioner.

NOTES

Defined terms   the Secretary of State: s 159A

    the Commission: s 160(1)

    modifications: s 160(1)

    registered party: ss 50(7), 160(1)

68   *Repealed*

Register of donations

Register of recordable donations

69 (1)   The Commission shall maintain a register of all donations reported to them under this Chapter.

  (2)   The register shall be maintained by the Commission in such form as they may determine and shall contain the following details in the case of each such donation

        (a)   the amount or value of the donation;

        (aa) whether the donation is in the form of sponsorship (within the meaning of section 51);

        (b)   (subject to subsection (4)) such other details as have been given in relation to the donation in pursuance of paragraph 2, 2A, 3, 3A, 6 or 7(a) or (c) of Schedule 6; and

        (c)   the relevant date for the donation within the meaning of paragraph 5 of that Schedule, and (in the case of a donation falling within sub-paragraph (2) of that paragraph) the details given in pursuance of that sub-paragraph.

  (3)   *Repealed*

  (4)   The details required by virtue of subsection (2) do not include, in the case of any donation by an individual, the donor's address.

  (5)   Where any donation or donations is or are reported to the Commission under this Chapter, they shall cause the details mentioned in subsection (2) to be entered in the register in respect of the donation or donations as soon as is reasonably practicable.

NOTES

Defined terms

    the Commission: s 160(1)

    donation: ss 50, 161

Chapter IV

70   *Repealed*

Chapter V
Control of Donations to Individuals and Members Associations

Control of donations to individuals and members associations

71 Schedule 7, which makes provision for controlling donations to individual members of registered parties, associations of such members, and certain elected office holders, shall have effect.

Chapter VI
Special Provision in Connection with Northern Ireland

Introduction

71A (1) The following provisions have effect for the interpretation of this Chapter.

(2) "Northern Ireland recipient" means
   (a) a party registered in the Northern Ireland register, or
   (b) a regulated donee who is
      (i) an individual ordinarily resident in Northern Ireland, or
      (ii) a members association wholly or mainly consisting of members of a Northern Ireland party.

(3) "Regulated donee" and "members association" have the same meaning as in Schedule 7.

(4) "Prescribed" means prescribed by an order made by the Secretary of State after consulting the Commission.

NOTES

Defined terms
  the Commission: s 160(1)
  members association: Sch 7, Pt 1, para 1(6) (by virtue of sub-s (3) of this section)
  the Northern Ireland register: ss 23(2)(b), 160(1)
  registered party: ss 50(7), 160(1)

regulated donee: Sch 7, Pt 1, para 1(7) (by virtue of sub-s (3) of this section)
the Secretary of State: s 159A

Extension of categories of permissible donors in relation to Northern Ireland recipients

71B (1) In relation to a donation to a Northern Ireland recipient, section 54(2) has effect as if the following were also permissible donors
   (a) an Irish citizen in relation to whom any prescribed conditions are met;
   (b) a body which is of a prescribed description or category and in relation to which any prescribed conditions are met.

(2) A description or category of body must not be prescribed for the purposes of subsection (1)(b) unless the Secretary of State is satisfied that a body of that description or category would be entitled under Irish law to donate to an Irish political party.

(3) In relation to a donation in the form of a bequest subsection (1)(a) is to be read as referring to an individual
   (a) who at any time within the period of five years ending with the date of his death was an Irish citizen, and
   (b) in relation to whom, at the time of his death, any prescribed conditions were met.

NOTES
Subordinate Legislation

(Northern Ireland Political Parties) Order 2007, SI 2007/2501

terms
> bequest: s 160(1)
> body: s 160(1)
> donation: ss 50, 161
> Northern Ireland recipient: s 71A(1), (2)
> permissible donor: s 54(2)
> prescribed: s 71A(1), (4)
> the Secretary of State: s 159A

Northern Ireland recipients not permissible donors in relation to Great Britain

71C (1)   In relation to a donation received by
    (a)   a registered party which is registered in the Great Britain register, or
    (b)   a regulated donee resident or carrying on activities in Great Britain,
    section 54(2) has effect as if it did not include a party registered in the Northern Ireland register.

  (2)   The reference in subsection (1)(b) to Great Britain includes the combined region.

NOTES

Defined terms
> combined region: s 160(1)
> donation: ss 50, 161
> the Great Britain register: ss 23(2)(a), 160(1)
> the Northern Ireland register: ss 23(2)(b), 160(1)

registered party: ss 50(7), 160(1)
regulated donee: Sch 7, Pt 1, para 1(7) (by virtue of s 71A(1), (3))

PART IVA
REGULATION OF LOANS AND RELATED TRANSACTIONS

Chapter 1

Regulated transactions

71F (1)   In this Part, a reference to a regulated transaction must be construed in accordance with this section.

  (2)   An agreement between a registered party and another person by which the other person makes a loan of money to the party is a regulated transaction.

  (3)   An agreement between a registered party and another person by which the other person provides a credit facility to the party is a regulated transaction.

  (4)   Where
    (a)   a registered party and another person (A) enter into a regulated transaction of a description mentioned in subsection (2) or (3) or a transaction under which any property, services or facilities are provided for the use or benefit of the party (including the services of any person), and
    (b)   A also enters into an arrangement whereby another person (B) gives any form of security (whether real or personal) for a sum owed to A by the party under the transaction mentioned in paragraph (a),
    the arrangement is a regulated transaction.

  (5)   An agreement or arrangement is also a regulated transaction if
    (a)   the terms of the agreement or arrangement as first entered into do not constitute a regulated transaction by virtue of subsection (2), (3) or (4), but

(b) the terms are subsequently varied in such a way that the agreement or arrangement becomes a regulated transaction.

(6) References in subsections (2) and (3) to a registered party include references to an officer, member, trustee or agent of the party if he makes the agreement as such.

(7) References in subsection (4) to a registered party include references to an officer, member, trustee or agent of the party if the property, services or facilities are provided to him, or the sum is owed by him, as such.

(8) Except so far as the contrary intention appears, references to a registered party in the context of

(a) the making of a loan to a registered party,

(b) the provision of a credit facility to a registered party, or

(c) a sum being owed by a registered party,

must, in the case of a party with accounting units, be construed as references to the central organisation of the party or any of its accounting units.

(9) A reference to a connected transaction is a reference to the transaction mentioned in subsection (4)(b).

(10) In this section a reference to anything being done by or in relation to a party or a person includes a reference to its being done directly or indirectly through a third person.

(11) A credit facility is an agreement whereby a registered party is enabled to receive from time to time from another party to the agreement a loan of money not exceeding such amount (taking account of any repayments made by the registered party) as is specified in or determined in accordance with the agreement.

(12) An agreement or arrangement is not a regulated transaction

(a) to the extent that, in accordance with any enactment, a payment made in pursuance of the agreement or arrangement falls to be included in a return as to election expenses in respect of a candidate or candidates at a particular election, or

(b) if its value is not more than £500.

(13) The Secretary of State may, by order, specify circumstances or any description of circumstances in which an agreement or arrangement falling within any of subsections (2) to (5) is not a regulated transaction.

NOTES

Defined terms
accounting units: s 26(11)
central organisation: ss 26(11), 160(1)
enactment: s 160(1)
party with accounting units: ss 26(11), 160(1)

registered party: s 160(1) (and note sub-ss (6)-(8) of this section)
the Secretary of State: s 159A

Valuation of regulated transaction

71G (1) The value of a regulated transaction which is a loan is the value of the total amount to be lent under the loan agreement.

(2) The value of a regulated transaction which is a credit facility is the maximum amount which may be borrowed under the agreement for the facility.

(3) The value of a regulated transaction which is an arrangement by which any form of security is given is the contingent liability under the security provided.

(4) For the purposes of subsections (1) and (2), no account is to be taken of the effect of any provision contained in a loan agreement or an agreement for a credit facility at the time it is entered into which enables outstanding interest to be added to any sum for

the time being owed in respect of the loan or credit facility, whether or not any such interest has been so added.

NOTES

Defined terms
    credit facility: ss 71F(11), 71X(1)
    regulated transaction: ss 71F, 71X(1)

Prohibition on increase in value of Gibraltar regulated transaction following European parliamentary election

1GA(1) This section applies to a Gibraltar regulated transaction which is entered into within the permitted period and which does not fall to be dealt with by section 71HA.

(2) A registered party which is not a Gibraltar party shall not, whether during the permitted period or otherwise, enter into an arrangement with any person which has the effect, on or after the date of the poll for an election to the European Parliament in the combined region, of increasing the value of a transaction to which this section applies or which enables that value to be increased.

(3) Where such a party enters into an arrangement contrary to subsection (2), the related transaction is to be treated for the purposes of this Part (other than this section) as if it was entered into with a participant who is not an authorised participant within the meaning of section 71H(3A).

(4) This section does not apply to an arrangement entered into before the commencement of the European Parliamentary Elections (Loans and Related Transactions and Miscellaneous Provisions) (United Kingdom and Gibraltar) Order 2009.

NOTES

Defined terms
    combined region: s 160(1)
    Gibraltar party: ss 28(8)(d), 160(1)
    Gibraltar regulated transaction: s 71X(1)

    permitted period: s 71X(1)
    registered party: s 160(1)

Authorised participants

71H (1) A registered party must not
    (a) be a party to a regulated transaction to which any of the other parties is not an authorised participant;
    (b) derive a benefit in consequence of a connected transaction if any of the parties to that transaction is not an authorised participant.

(2) This section does not apply to a regulated transaction if it was entered into before the commencement of section 61 of the Electoral Administration Act 2006.

(3) In this Part, an authorised participant is a person who is a permissible donor within the meaning of section 54(2).

(3ZA) For the purposes of subsection (3), any reference to a donation in section 54(2ZB) is to be read as a reference to a regulated transaction.

(3A) As respects a registered party whose entry in the register includes a statement that it intends to contest one or more elections to the European Parliament in the combined region, "authorised participant" means a person who is a permissible donor under section 54(2A).

(3B) In its application for the purposes of this Part by virtue of subsection (3A), section 54(2A) has effect as if for "the donation is received" there were substituted "the regulated transaction" is entered into.

(4) The Secretary of State may, by order, specify circumstances or any description of circumstances in which a person who is not a permissible donor is to be treated as an authorised participant.

NOTES

Prospective operation
Sub-s (3ZA) not yet in operation

Defined terms
combined region: s 160(1)

connected transaction: ss 71F(9), 71X(1)
registered party: ss 71F(6)-(8), 160(1)
regulated transaction: ss 71F, 71X(1)

Declaration that residence etc condition is satisfied

1HZA (1) A registered party must not be a party to a regulated transaction to which this section applies unless the registered party has received a written declaration from each of the other parties to the transaction who is an individual stating that the individual satisfies the condition set out in section 54(2ZA).

(2) This section applies to a regulated transaction
 (a) if the value of the transaction is more than £7,500, or
 (b) if the aggregate amount of it and any other relevant benefit or benefits accruing in the same calendar year as the transaction is more than £7,500.

(3) For the purposes of subsection (2)(b) "relevant benefit" and "accruing" have the meaning given by section 71M(3).

(4) A declaration under this section must also state the individual's full name and address.

(5) A person who knowingly or recklessly makes a false declaration under this section commits an offence.

(6) The Secretary of State may by regulations make provision requiring a declaration under this section to be retained for a specified period.

(7) The reference in subsection (1) to each of the other parties to the transaction does not include any individual who, at the time the transaction is entered into, is an authorised participant in relation to it by reason of section 71Z1(1)(a).

NOTES

Prospective operation
Not yet in operation

Defined terms
authorised participant: ss 71H, 71X(1)

registered party: ss 71F(6)-(8), 160(1)
regulated transaction: ss 71F, 71X(1)
the Secretary of State: s 159A

Financial limit on Gibraltar donations and Gibraltar regulated transactions

71HA (1) This section applies where the permitted maximum is exceeded by the aggregate value of
 (a) Gibraltar donations which are received and accepted;
 (b) Gibraltar regulated transactions which are entered into;
 within the permitted period by a registered party which is not a Gibraltar party.

(2) Such of the Gibraltar donations and Gibraltar regulated transactions as fall within subsection (3) are to be treated for the purposes of Part 4 and this Part as if
 (a) they were received or entered into, as the case may be, at the end of the period of three months after the end of the permitted period;
 (b) in the case of a Gibraltar donation, it was received from a person who was not a permissible donor at the time;
 (c) in the case of a Gibraltar regulated transaction, it was entered into with a person who was not an authorised participant at the time.

(3) A Gibraltar donation or Gibraltar regulated transaction falls within this subsection if

(a) in a case where it is the first of the Gibraltar donations received or is the only one, the value of the donation alone exceeds the permitted maximum;

(b) in a case where it is the first of the Gibraltar regulated transactions entered into or is the only one, the value of the transaction alone exceeds the permitted maximum; or

(c) otherwise, the aggregate value of that donation or regulated transaction and such of the Gibraltar donations and Gibraltar regulated transactions previously received or entered into, as the case may be, exceeds the permitted maximum.

(4) But

(a) in a case within subsection (3)(a), only so much of the donation as exceeds the permitted maximum is a donation falling within subsection (3); and

(b) in a case within subsection (3)(c) in which the aggregate value of the Gibraltar donations and Gibraltar regulated transactions previously received or entered into, as the case may be, does not exceed the permitted maximum, only so much of the donation as exceeds the difference between that aggregate value and the permitted maximum is a donation falling within subsection (3).

(5) In this section "permitted maximum" means an amount equal to the limit imposed by paragraph 4(2) of Schedule 9 on campaign expenditure incurred by or on behalf of a registered party which is not a Gibraltar party and which stands for election at an election to the European Parliament in the combined region.

NOTES

Defined terms
authorised participant: ss 71H, 71X(1)
combined region: s 160(1)
Gibraltar donation: s 71X(1)
Gibraltar party: ss 28(8)(d), 160(1)
Gibraltar regulated transaction: s 71X(1)

permitted period: s 71X(1)
permissible donor: s 54(2) (by virtue of s 71H(3))
registered party: ss 71F(6)-(8), 160(1)

Regulated transaction involving unauthorised participant

71I (1) This section applies if a registered party is a party to a regulated transaction in which another participant is not an authorised participant.

(2) The transaction is void.

(3) Despite subsection (2)

(a) any money received by the registered party by virtue of the transaction must be repaid by the treasurer of the party to the person from whom it was received, along with interest at such rate as is determined in accordance with an order made by the Secretary of State;

(b) that person is entitled to recover the money, along with such interest.

(4) If

(a) the money is not (for whatever reason) repaid as mentioned in subsection (3)(a), or

(b) the person entitled to recover the money refuses or fails to do so,

the Commission may apply to the court to make such order as it thinks fit to restore (so far as is possible) the parties to the transaction to the position they would have been in if the transaction had not been entered into.

(5) An order under subsection (4) may in particular

(a) where the transaction is a loan or credit facility, require that any amount owed by the registered party be repaid (and that no further sums be advanced under it);

(b) where any form of security is given for a sum owed under the transaction, require that security to be discharged.

(6) In the case of a regulated transaction where a party other than a registered party
    (a) at the time the registered party enters into the transaction, is an authorised participant, but
    (b) subsequently, for whatever reason, ceases to be an authorised participant,
the transaction is void and subsections (3) to (5) apply with effect from the time when the other party ceased to be an authorised participant.

(7) This section does not apply to a regulated transaction if it was entered into before the commencement of section 61 of the Electoral Administration Act 2006.

NOTES

Defined terms
    authorised participant: ss 71H, 71X(1)
    the Commission: s 160(1)
    registered party: ss 71F(6)-(8), 160(1)
    regulated transaction: ss 71F, 71X(1)

the Secretary of State: s 159A
treasurer: s 160(1)

Guarantees and securities: unauthorised participants

71J (1) This section applies if
    (a) a registered party and another person (A) enter into a transaction of a description mentioned in section 71F(4)(a),
    (b) A is party to a regulated transaction of a description mentioned in section 71F(4)(b) ("the connected transaction") with another person (B), and
    (c) B is not an authorised participant.

(2) Section 71I(2) to (5) applies to the transaction mentioned in subsection (1)(a).

(3) The connected transaction is void.

(4) Subsection (5) applies if (but only if) A is unable to recover from the party the whole of the money mentioned in section 71I(3)(a) (as applied by subsection (2) above), along with such interest as is there mentioned.

(5) Despite subsection (3), A is entitled to recover from B any part of that money (and such interest) that is not recovered from the party.

(6) Subsection (5) does not entitle A to recover more than the contingent liability under the security provided by virtue of the connected transaction.

(7) In the case of a connected transaction where B
    (a) at the time A enters into the transaction, is an authorised participant, but
    (b) subsequently, for whatever reason, ceases to be an authorised participant,
subsections (2) to (6) apply with effect from the time when B ceased to be an authorised participant.

(8) This section does not apply to a regulated transaction if it was entered into before the commencement of section 61 of the Electoral Administration Act 2006.

(9) If the transaction mentioned in section 71F(4)(a) is not a regulated transaction of a description mentioned in section 71F(2) or (3), references in this section and section 71I(2) to (5) (as applied by subsection (2) above) to the repayment or recovery of money must be construed as references to (as the case may be)
    (a) the return or recovery of any property provided under the transaction,
    (b) to the extent that such property is incapable of being returned or recovered or its market value has diminished since the time the transaction was entered into, the repayment or recovery of the market value at that time, or
    (c) the market value (at that time) of any facilities or services provided under the transaction.

NOTES

Defined terms

authorised participant: ss 71H, 71X(1)

connected transaction: ss 71F(9), 71X(1)
registered party: ss 71F(6)-(8), 160(1)
regulated transaction: ss 71F, 71X(1)

Transfer to unauthorised participant invalid

71K   If an authorised participant purports to transfer his interest in a regulated transaction to a person who is not an authorised participant the purported transfer is of no effect.

NOTES
Defined terms
authorised participant: ss 71H, 71X(1)
regulated transaction: ss 71F, 71X(1)

Offences relating to regulated transactions

71L (1)   A registered party commits an offence if
    (a)   it enters into a regulated transaction of a description mentioned in section 71F(2) or (3) in which another participant is not an authorised participant, and
    (b)   an officer of the party knew or ought reasonably to have known of the matters mentioned in paragraph (a).

  (2)   A person commits an offence if
    (a)   he is the treasurer of a registered party,
    (b)   the party enters into a regulated transaction of a description mentioned in section 71F(2) or (3) in which another participant is not an authorised participant, and
    (c)   he knew or ought reasonably to have known of the matters mentioned in paragraph (b).

  (3)   A registered party commits an offence if
    (a)   it enters into a regulated transaction of a description mentioned in section 71F(2) or (3) in which another participant is not an authorised participant,
    (b)   no officer of the party knew or ought reasonably to have known that the other participant is not an authorised participant, and
    (c)   as soon as practicable after knowledge of the matters mentioned in paragraph (a) comes to the treasurer of the party he fails to take all reasonable steps to repay any money which the party has received by virtue of the transaction.

  (4)   A person who is the treasurer of a registered party commits an offence if
    (a)   the party enters into a regulated transaction of a description mentioned in section 71F(2) or (3) in which another participant is not an authorised participant,
    (b)   subsection (2)(c) does not apply to him, and
    (c)   as soon as practicable after knowledge of the matters mentioned in paragraph (a) comes to him he fails to take all reasonable steps to repay any money which the party has received by virtue of the transaction.

  (5)   A registered party commits an offence if
    (a)   it benefits from or falls to benefit in consequence of a connected transaction to which any of the parties is not an authorised participant, and
    (b)   an officer of the party knew or ought reasonably to have known of the matters mentioned in paragraph (a).

  (6)   A person commits an offence if
    (a)   he is the treasurer of a registered party,
    (b)   the party benefits from or falls to benefit in consequence of a connected transaction to which any of the parties is not an authorised participant, and
    (c)   he knew or ought reasonably to have known of the matters mentioned in paragraph (b).

(7) A registered party commits an offence if
    (a) it is a party to a transaction of a description mentioned in section 71F(4)(a),
    (b) it benefits from or falls to benefit in consequence of a connected transaction to which any of the parties is not an authorised participant,
    (c) no officer of the party knew or ought reasonably to have known of the matters mentioned in paragraphs (a) and (b), and
    (d) as soon as practicable after knowledge of the matters mentioned in paragraphs (a) and (b) comes to the treasurer of the party he fails to take all reasonable steps to pay to any person who has provided the party with any benefit in consequence of the connected transaction the value of the benefit.

(8) A person who is the treasurer of a registered party commits an offence if
    (a) the party is a party to a transaction of a description mentioned in section 71F(4)(a),
    (b) the party benefits from or falls to benefit in consequence of a connected transaction to which any of the parties is not an authorised participant,
    (c) subsection (6)(c) does not apply to him, and
    (d) as soon as practicable after knowledge of the matters mentioned in paragraphs (a) and (b) comes to him he fails to take all reasonable steps to pay to any person who has provided the party with any benefit in consequence of the connected transaction the value of the benefit.

(9) A person commits an offence if he
    (a) knowingly enters into, or
    (b) knowingly does any act in furtherance of,
any arrangement which facilitates or is likely to facilitate, whether by means of concealment or disguise or otherwise, the participation by a registered party in a regulated transaction with a person other than an authorised participant.

(9A) An offence cannot be committed under subsection (1), (2), (5) or (6) on the basis that a person (P) ought reasonably to have known that a particular individual does not satisfy the condition set out in section 54(2ZA) (and is therefore not an authorised participant) if
    (a) the individual has given a declaration under section 71HZA stating that the individual satisfies that condition, and
    (b) P had no reasonable grounds for thinking that the statement was incorrect.

(10) It is a defence for a person charged with an offence under subsection (2) to prove that he took all reasonable steps to prevent the registered party entering the transaction.

(11) It is a defence for a person charged with an offence under subsection (6) to prove that he took all reasonable steps to prevent the registered party benefiting in consequence of the connected transaction.

(12) A reference to a registered party entering into a regulated transaction includes a reference to any circumstances in which the terms of a regulated transaction are varied so as to increase the amount of money to which the party is entitled in consequence of the transaction.

(13) A reference to a registered party entering into a transaction in which another participant is not an authorised participant includes a reference to any circumstances in which another party to the transaction who is an authorised participant ceases (for whatever reason) to be an authorised participant.

(14) This section does not apply to a transaction which is entered into before the commencement of section 61 of the Electoral Administration Act 2006.

NOTES

Prospective operation   Sub-s (9A) not yet in operation

regulated transaction: ss 71F, 71X(1)
treasurer: s 160(1)

Defined terms
  authorised participant: ss 71H, 71X(1)
  connected transaction: ss 71F(9), 71X(1)
  registered party: ss 71F(6)-(8), 160(1)

Quarterly reports of regulated transactions

71M (1)   The treasurer of a registered party must, in the case of each year, prepare a report under this subsection in respect of each of the following periods

   (a)   January to March;
   (b)   April to June;
   (c)   July to September;
   (d)   October to December.

(2)   The reports prepared under subsection (1) for any year must, in the case of each authorised participant who enters into or is party to a regulated transaction with the party in that year, comply with

   (a)   the following provisions of this section so far as they require any such transaction to be recorded in such a report;
   (b)   section 71N so far as it requires any changes in relation to any such transaction to be so recorded.

(3)   In this section
   "transaction report" means a report prepared under subsection (1);
   "reporting period", in relation to such a report, means the period mentioned in any of paragraphs (a) to (d) of that subsection to which the report relates;
   "relevant transaction", in relation to an authorised participant and a year, means a regulated transaction entered into by the participant and the registered party in that year;
   "relevant benefit", in relation to any person and any year, means

   (a)   a relevant donation within the meaning of section 62(3) accepted by the party from that person as a donor, or
   (b)   a relevant transaction entered into by the party and that person as a participant,

   and a relevant benefit accrues when it is accepted (if it is a donation) or entered into (if it is a transaction).

(4)   Where no previous relevant benefit or benefits has or have been required to be recorded under this subsection or section 62(4), a relevant transaction must be recorded

   (a)   if the value of the transaction is more than £7,500, or
   (b)   if the aggregate amount of it and any other relevant benefit or benefits is more than £7,500.

(5)   A transaction to which subsection (4) applies must

   (a)   if it falls within paragraph (a) of that subsection, be recorded in the transaction report for the reporting period in which the transaction is entered into, or
   (b)   if it falls within paragraph (b) of that subsection, be recorded (together with any other relevant transaction or transactions included in the aggregate amount mentioned in that paragraph) in the transaction report for the reporting period in which the benefit which causes that aggregate to be more than £7,500 accrues.

(6)   Where any previous relevant benefit or benefits has or have been required to be recorded under subsection (4) or section 62(4), a relevant transaction must be recorded at the point when a relevant transaction falling within subsection (7) has been entered into

    (a)   since the benefit or benefits required to be recorded under that provision, or

    (b)   if any relevant benefit or benefits has or have previously been required to be recorded under this subsection or section 62(6), since the benefit or benefits last required to be so recorded.

(7)   A relevant transaction falls within this subsection

    (a)   if the value of the transaction is more than £1,500, or

    (b)   if, when it is added to any other relevant benefit or benefits accruing since the time mentioned in subsection (6)(a) or (b), the aggregate amount of the benefits is more than £1,500.

(8)   A transaction to which subsection (6) applies on any occasion must

    (a)   if it is the only benefit required to be recorded on that occasion, be recorded in the transaction report for the reporting period in which it is entered into, or

    (b)   in any other case, be recorded (together with any other relevant transaction or transactions included in the aggregate amount mentioned in subsection (7)) in the transaction report for the reporting period in which the benefit which causes that aggregate amount to be more than £1,500 accrues.

(9)   A transaction report must also record any regulated transaction which is entered into by the party and a person who is not an authorised participant and is dealt with during the reporting period in accordance with section 71I or 71J.

(10)   If during any reporting period no transactions have been entered into by the party which, by virtue of the preceding provisions of this section, are required to be recorded in the transaction report for that period, the report must contain a statement to that effect.

(11)   Where a registered party is a party with accounting units, subsections (2) to (10) apply separately in relation to the central organisation of the party and each of its accounting units

    (a)   as if any reference to the party were a reference to the central organisation or (as the case may be) to such an accounting unit; but

    (b)   with the substitution, in relation to such an accounting unit, of "£1,500" for "£7,500" in each place where it occurs in subsections (4) and (5).

(12)   However, for the purposes of subsections (2) to (9) in their application to the central organisation and any year by virtue of subsection (11), any transaction

    (a)   which is entered into by an authorised participant and any of the accounting units during that year, but

    (b)   which is not required to be recorded under subsection (4) or (6) (as they apply by virtue of subsection (11)) as a transaction entered into by the accounting unit,

must be treated as a transaction entered into by the authorised participant and the central organisation.

(13)   Schedule 6A has effect with respect to the information to be given in transaction reports.

NOTES

Defined terms
accounting units: ss 26(11), 160(1)
authorised participant: ss 71H, 71X(1)
central organisation: ss 26(11), 160(1)
party with accounting units: ss 26(11), 160(1)

registered party: ss 71F(6)-(8), 71X(2), 160(1)
regulated transaction: ss 71F, 71X(1)
treasurer: s 160(1)

Changes to be recorded in quarterly reports

71N (1)   If during any reporting period, in the case of any recorded transaction

(a) another authorised participant becomes party to the transaction (whether in place of or in addition to any existing participant),

(b) there is any change in the details given in relation to the transaction in pursuance of paragraph 5, 6 or 7 of Schedule 6A, or

(c) the transaction comes to an end,

the change must be recorded in the transaction report for that period.

(2) For the purposes of subsection (1)(c), a loan comes to an end if

(a) the whole debt (or all the remaining debt) is repaid;

(b) the creditor releases the whole debt (or all the remaining debt);

and in such a case the transaction report must state how the loan has come to an end.

(3) A transaction report must also record any change by which a person who is not an authorised participant becomes party to the transaction (whether in place of or in addition to any existing participant) and in consequence of which the transaction is dealt with in accordance with section 71I or 71J.

(4) If during any reporting period there have been no changes (as mentioned in subsection (1) or (3)) to any recorded transaction, the report must contain a statement to that effect.

(5) A recorded transaction, in relation to a reporting period, is a regulated transaction which is or has been recorded in a transaction report for that or a previous reporting period.

(6) Where a registered party is a party with accounting units, subsections (1) to (5) apply separately in relation to the central organisation of the party and each of its accounting units; and the reference in subsection (5) to a transaction report for a previous reporting period is a reference to a report prepared in relation the central organisation or accounting unit, as the case may be.

(7) In this section, "reporting period" and "transaction report" have the meanings given in section 71M.

NOTES

Defined terms
accounting units: s 26(11)
authorised participant: ss 71H, 71X(1)
central organisation: ss 26(11), 160(1)
party with accounting units: ss 26(11), 160(1)
registered party: ss 71F(6)-(8), 71X(2), 160(1)

regulated transaction: ss 71F, 71X(1)
reporting period: s 71M(3)
transaction report: s 71M(3)

Existing transactions

10 (1) This section applies in relation to the first report prepared under section 71M(1) by the treasurer of a party which, at the date on which that section comes into force, is a registered party.

(2) Sections 71M and 71N have effect, in the case of a person (whether or not an authorised participant) who is a party to an existing transaction, as if

(a) that transaction had been entered into in the reporting period to which the report relates;

(b) any change (as mentioned in section 71N(1) or (3)) to the transaction had occurred during that period;

(c) references in section 71M to a relevant benefit did not include references to a relevant donation.

(3) An existing transaction is a regulated transaction which, at the date on which section 71M comes into force, has not come to an end for the purposes of section 71N(1)(c).

(4) The date referred to in subsection (3) for the purposes of Gibraltar is the commencement date of the European Parliamentary Elections (Loans and Related

Transactions and Miscellaneous Provisions) (united Kingdom and Gibraltar) Order 2009.

Exemption from requirement to prepare quarterly reports

71P (1) This section applies if each of four consecutive transaction reports prepared by the treasurer of a registered party in pursuance of subsection (1) of section 71M contains

    (a) in the case of a party without accounting units, a statement under subsection (10) of that section and a statement under subsection (4) of section 71N, or

    (b) in the case of a party with accounting units, statements under each of those subsections in relation to the central organisation of the party and each of its accounting units.

(2) The treasurer is not required to prepare any further transaction reports in pursuance of subsection (1) of section 71M until

    (a) a recordable transaction is entered into by the registered party, or

    (b) a recordable change is made to a recorded transaction.

(3) A recordable transaction is a transaction which is required to be recorded by virtue of any of subsections (4) to (9) of section 71M (including those subsections as applied by subsection (11) of that section).

(4) A recordable change is a change which is required to be recorded by virtue of subsection (1) of section 71N (including that subsection as applied by subsection (6) of that section).

(5) If a recordable transaction is entered into or a recordable change is made, nothing in this section affects the operation of section 71M or 71N in relation to

    (a) the reporting period in which the recordable transaction is entered into or the recordable change is made, or

    (b) any subsequent reporting period which falls before the time (if any) when this section again applies in relation to the party.

(6) In this section
"transaction report" and "reporting period" have the same meaning as in section 71M;
"recorded transaction" has the same meaning as in section 71N.

Weekly transaction reports during general election periods

71Q (1) Subject to section 71R, the treasurer of a registered party must, in the case of any general election period, prepare a report under this subsection in respect of each of the following periods

    (a) the period of seven days beginning with the first day of the general election period,

    (b) each succeeding period of seven days falling within the general election period, and

    (c) any final period of less than seven days falling within that period.

(2)　In this section

"weekly report" means a report prepared under subsection (1);

"reporting period", in relation to such a report, means the period mentioned in any of paragraphs (a) to (c) of that subsection to which the report relates.

(3)　The weekly report for any reporting period must record each regulated transaction which has a value of more than £7,500 entered into during that period

(a)　by the party (if it is not a party with accounting units), or

(b)　by the central organisation of the party (if it is a party with accounting units).

(4)　If during any reporting period no transactions falling within subsection (3) have been entered into as mentioned in that subsection, the weekly report for that period must contain a statement to that effect.

(5)　Schedule 6A has effect with respect to the information to be given in weekly reports.

(6)　The weekly report for any reporting period must also record any change (as mentioned in section 71N(1) or (3)) during that period to a regulated transaction recorded

(a)　by the party (if it is not a party with accounting units), or

(b)　by the central organisation of the party (if it is a party with accounting units).

(7)　For the purposes of subsection (6), a transaction is recorded by a party or the central organisation of a party if it is or has been recorded in

(a)　a transaction report prepared under section 71M(1), or

(b)　a weekly report prepared for that or a previous reporting period falling within the general election period.

(8)　If during any reporting period there have been no changes falling within subsection (6), the weekly report for that period must contain a statement to that effect.

(9)　In this section and section 71R "general election period" has the meaning given in section 63.

NOTES

Defined terms
accounting units: s 26(11)
central organisation: ss 26(11), 160(1)
general election period: s 63(6) (by virtue of sub-s (9) of this section)
party with accounting units: ss 26(11), 160(1)

registered party: ss 71F(6)-(8), 71X(2), 160(1)
regulated transaction: ss 71F, 71X(1)
treasurer: s 160(1)

Exemptions from section 71Q

71R (1)　Section 71Q(1) does not apply in relation to a registered party in respect of a general election period if the party has made an exemption declaration under section 64 which covers the general election in question.

(1A)　Section 71Q does not apply in relation to a Gibraltar party.

(2)　In its application (in accordance with subsection (1)) in relation to section 71Q, section 64 is to be read subject to the following modifications

(a)　the reference in subsection (5) to section 63 is to be read as a reference to section 71Q;

(b)　subsection (6) is omitted.

NOTES

Defined terms
general election period: s 63(6) (by virtue of s 71Q(9))
Gibraltar party: ss 28(8)(d), 160(1)

registered party: ss 71F(6)-(8), 71X(2), 160(1)

Submission of transaction reports to Commission

71S (1) A transaction report under section 71M must be delivered to the Commission by the treasurer of the party in question within the period of 30 days beginning with the end of the reporting period to which it relates.

(2) A transaction report under section 71Q must be delivered to the Commission by the treasurer of the party in question

(a) within the period of 7 days beginning with the end of the reporting period to which it relates, or

(b) if that is not possible in the case of any party to which section 71Q applies by virtue of section 64(5) (as applied by section 71R), within the period of 7 days beginning with the first day on which the party has a candidate at the election in question.

(3) If a transaction report under section 71M or 71Q states that the registered party has seen evidence of such description as is prescribed by the Secretary of State in regulations that an individual participant has an anonymous entry in the electoral register (within the meaning of the Representation of the People Act 1983 or corresponding provisions forming part of the law of Gibraltar), the report must be accompanied by a copy of the evidence.

(4) The treasurer of a registered party commits an offence if, without reasonable excuse, he fails to comply with the requirements of subsection (1) or (2) in relation to a transaction report.

(5) The treasurer of a registered party also commits an offence if, without reasonable excuse, he delivers a transaction report to the Commission which does not comply with any requirements of this Part as regards the recording of transactions, or changes to transactions, in such a report.

(6) *Repealed*

(7) Where the court is satisfied, on an application made by the Commission, that any failure to comply with any such requirements in relation to

(a) any transaction entered into by a registered party, or

(b) any change made to a transaction to which the registered party is a party,

was attributable to an intention on the part of any person to conceal the existence or true value of the transaction, the court may make such order as it thinks fit to restore (so far as is possible) the parties to the transaction to the position they would have been in if the transaction had not been entered into.

(8) An order under subsection (7) may in particular

(a) where the transaction is a loan or credit facility, require that any amount owed by the registered party be repaid (and that no further sums be advanced under it);

(b) where any form of security is given for a sum owed under the transaction, or the transaction is an arrangement by which any form of security is given, require that the security be discharged.

(9) The reference in subsection (2) to a party having a candidate at an election must be construed in accordance with section 64(9).

NOTES

Defined terms
the Commission: s 160(1)
credit facility: ss 71F(11), 71X(1)
registered party: ss 71F(6)-(8), 71X(2), 160(1)
reporting period: ss 71M(3), 71Q(2)

the Secretary of State: s 159A
transaction report: s 71M(3)
treasurer: s 160(1)

Declaration by treasurer in transaction report

71T (1) Each transaction report under section 71M or 71Q must, when delivered to the Commission, be accompanied by a declaration made by the treasurer which complies with subsection (2), (3) or (4).

(2) In the case of a report under section 71M (other than one making a nil return), the declaration must state that, to the best of the treasurer's knowledge and belief

(a) all the transactions recorded in the report were entered into by the party with authorised participants,

(b) during the reporting period no transaction has been entered into by the party which is required to be recorded in the report but is not so recorded,

(c) during the reporting period no change has been made to a regulated transaction which is required to be recorded in the report but is not so recorded, and

(d) during the reporting period the party has not entered into any regulated transaction with a person or body other than an authorised participant.

(3) For the purposes of subsection (2) a return under section 71M makes a nil return if it contains such a statement as is mentioned in subsection (10) of that section and a statement as is mentioned in subsection (4) of section 71N; and in the case of such a report the declaration must state that, to the best of the treasurer's knowledge and belief

(a) those statements are accurate, and

(b) during the reporting period the party has not entered into any regulated transaction with a person or body other than an authorised participant.

(4) In the case of a report under section 71Q, the declaration must state that, to the best of the treasurer's knowledge and belief

(a) no transaction has been entered into by the party, or (if section 71Q(3)(b) applies) by its central organisation, during the reporting period which is required to be recorded in the report but is not so recorded, and

(b) no change has been made to a regulated transaction during the reporting period which is required to be recorded in the report but is not so recorded.

(5) A person commits an offence if he knowingly or recklessly makes a false declaration under this section.

NOTES

Defined terms
authorised participant: ss 71H, 71X(1)
body: s 160(1)
central organisation: ss 26(11), 160(1)
the Commission: s 160(1)
regulated transaction: ss 71F, 71X(1)

reporting period: s 71M(3)
transaction report: s 71M(3)
treasurer: s 160(1)

Weekly donation reports in connection with elections other than general elections

71U (1) The Secretary of State may, after consulting the Commission and all registered parties, by order make provision for

(a) sections 71Q and 71R, together with Schedule 6A,

(b) sections 71S and 71T, and

(c) an order under paragraph 16 of Schedule 19C so far as applying in relation to section 71S(1) or (2),

to apply in relation to the specified election period in the case of one or more relevant elections with such modifications as are specified in the order.

(2) In this section "specified election period" and "relevant election" have the meanings given in section 67.

(3) An order applying the provisions mentioned in subsection (1)(a) may disapply section 71R(1A) (which excludes Gibraltar parties from the operation of section 71Q).

NOTES

Defined terms
the Commission: s 160(1)
Gibraltar party: ss 28(8)(d), 160(1)
modifications: s 160(1)
registered party: ss 71F(6)-(8), 71X(2), 160(1)
relevant election: s 67(2)(b) (by virtue of sub-s (2) of

this section)
the Secretary of State: s 159A
specified election period: s 67(2)(a) (by virtue of sub-s (2) of this section)

Register of recordable transactions

71V (1) The Commission must maintain a register of all transactions (and all changes) reported to them under this Part.

(2) The register must be maintained by the Commission in such form as they may determine and must contain the following details in the case of each such transaction

    (a) the value of the transaction;

    (b) (subject to subsection (3)) such other details as have been given in relation to the transaction in pursuance of any of paragraphs 2 to 7 of Schedule 6A;

    (c) the relevant date for the transaction within the meaning of paragraph 8 of that Schedule.

(3) The details required by virtue of subsection (2) do not include, in the case of any transaction entered into by an authorised participant who is an individual, the individual's address.

(4) Where

    (a) any transaction or transactions is or are reported to the Commission under this Part, or

    (b) any change or changes is or are so reported to them,

they must cause the details mentioned in subsection (2) to be entered or, as the case may be, changed in the register in respect of the transaction or transactions as soon as is reasonably practicable.

NOTES

Defined terms
authorised participant: ss 71H, 71X(1)
the Commission: s 160(1)

Proceedings under sections 71I and 71S

71W (1) This section has effect in relation to proceedings on applications under sections 71I(4) and 71S(7).

(2) The court is

    (a) in England and Wales, the county court;

    (b) in Scotland, the sheriff, and the proceedings are civil proceedings;

    (c) in Northern Ireland, the county court;

    (d) in Gibraltar, the Gibraltar Court.

(3) The standard of proof is that applicable to civil proceedings.

(4) An order may be made whether or not proceedings are brought against any person for an offence under section 71L, 71S or 71T.

(5) An appeal against an order made by the sheriff may be made to the Court of Session.

(6) Rules of court in any part of the United Kingdom may make provision

    (a) with respect to applications or appeals from proceedings on such applications;

    (b) for the giving of notice of such applications or appeals to persons affected;

(c) for the joinder, or in Scotland sisting, of such persons as parties;

(d) generally with respect to procedure in such applications or appeals.

(7) Subsection (6) does not affect any existing power to make rules.

NOTES
Defined terms
  Gibraltar court: s 160(1)

Construction of Part 4A

71X (1) In this Part—

  "authorised participant" must be construed in accordance with section 71H;

  "connected transaction" has the meaning given by section 71F(9);

  "credit facility" has the meaning given by section 71F(11);

  "Gibraltar donation" means a donation—

  (a) which is received from a permissible donor falling within subsection (2A) (but not subsection (2)) of section 54; or

  (b) which is an exempt Gibraltar trust donation regarded by virtue of section 55(5A) as received from a permissible donor.

  "Gibraltar regulated transaction" means a regulated transaction which is entered into with an authorised participant who, by virtue of section 71H(3A), is listed in section 54(2A) (but not subsection (2));

  "permitted period" means the period of four months ending with the date of the poll for an election to the European Parliament in the combined region;

  "regulated transaction" must be construed in accordance with section 71F.

(2) For the purposes of any provision relating to the reporting of transactions, anything required to be done by a registered party in consequence of its being a party to a regulated transaction must also be done by it, if it is a party to a transaction of a description mentioned in section 71F(4)(a), as if it were a party to the connected transaction.

NOTES
Defined terms   registered party: ss 71F(6)–(8), 160(1)
  combined region: s 160(1)
  exempt Gibraltar trust donation: ss 160(1), 162
  permissible donor: s 54(2) (by virtue of s 71H(3))

Control of loans etc: individuals and members associations

71Y Schedule 7A, which makes provisions for controlling loans and certain other transactions to individual members of registered parties, associations of such members, and certain elected office holders, shall have effect.

NOTES
Defined terms
  registered party: s 160(1)

Chapter 2
Special Provision in Connection with Northern Ireland

Introduction

71Z (1) The following provisions have effect for the interpretation of this Chapter.

(2) "Northern Ireland participant" means—

  (a) a party registered in the Northern Ireland register, or

  (b) a regulated participant who is—

      (i)   an individual ordinarily resident in Northern Ireland, or

      (ii) a members association wholly or mainly consisting of members of a Northern Ireland party.

(3)   "Regulated participant" and "members association" have the same meaning as in Schedule 7A.

(4)   "Prescribed" means prescribed by an order made by the Secretary of State after consulting the Commission.

NOTES

Defined terms

the Commission: s 160(1)

members association: Sch 7A, Pt I, para 1(7) (by virtue of sub-s (3) of this section and Sch 7, para 1(6))

the Northern Ireland register: ss 23(2)(b), 160(1)

regulated participant: Sch 7A, para 1 (by virtue of sub-s (3) of this section)

the Secretary of State: s 159A

Extension of categories of authorised participants in relation to Northern Ireland participants

71Z1 (1)   In relation to a regulated transaction or controlled transaction involving a Northern Ireland participant, section 71H(3) and paragraph 4(3) of Schedule 7A have effect as if the following were also authorised participants

      (a) an Irish citizen in relation to whom any prescribed conditions are met;

      (b) a body which is of a prescribed description or category and in relation to which any prescribed conditions are met.

(2)   A description or category of body must not be prescribed for the purposes of subsection (1)(b) unless the Secretary of State is satisfied that a body of that description or category would be entitled under Irish law to enter into a transaction which corresponds to a regulated or controlled transaction in relation to an Irish political party.

NOTES

Defined terms

authorised participant: ss 71H, 71X(1)

body: s 160(1)

Northern Ireland participant: s 71Z(2)

prescribed: s 71Z(4)

regulated transaction: ss 71F, 71X(1)

the Secretary of State: s 159A

Northern Ireland participants are not authorised participants in relation to Great Britain

71Z2 (1)   In relation to a regulated transaction or controlled transaction to which

      (a) a registered party which is registered in the Great Britain register, or

      (b) a regulated participant resident or carrying on activities in Great Britain,

      is a party, section 71H(3) and paragraph 4(3) of Schedule 7A, have effect as if a party registered in the Northern Ireland register is not an authorised participant.

(2)   The reference in subsection (1)(b) to Great Britain includes the combined region.

NOTES

Defined terms

authorised participant: ss 71H, 71X(1)

combined region: s 160(1)

the Great Britain register: ss 23(2)(a), 160(1)

the Northern Ireland register: ss 23(2)(b), 160(1)

registered party: s 160(1)

regulated participant: Sch 7A, para 1 (by virtue of s 71Z(3))

regulated transaction: ss 71F, 71X(1)

PART V
CONTROL OF CAMPAIGN EXPENDITURE

Preliminary

Campaign expenditure

72 (1)   The following provisions have effect for the purposes of this Part.

(2)   "Campaign expenditure", in relation to a registered party, means (subject to subsection (7)) expenses incurred by or on behalf of the party which are expenses falling within Part I of Schedule 8 and so incurred for election purposes.

(3)   "Election campaign", in relation to a registered party, means a campaign conducted by the party for election purposes.

(4)   "For election purposes", in relation to a registered party, means for the purpose of or in connection with
   (a)   promoting or procuring electoral success for the party at any relevant election, that is to say, the return at any such election of candidates
      (i)   standing in the name of the party, or
      (ii)   included in a list of candidates submitted by the party in connection with the election; or
   (b)   otherwise enhancing the standing
      (i)   of the party, or
      (ii)   of any such candidates,
   with the electorate in connection with future relevant elections (whether imminent or otherwise).

(5)   For the purposes of subsection (4)
   (a)   the reference to doing any of the things mentioned in paragraph (a) or (as the case may be) paragraph (b) of that subsection includes doing so by prejudicing the electoral prospects at the election of other parties or candidates or (as the case may be) by prejudicing the standing with the electorate of other parties or candidates;
   (b)   a course of conduct may constitute the doing of one of those things even though it does not involve any express mention being made of the name of any party or candidate; and
   (c)   it is immaterial that any candidates standing in the name of the party also stand in the name of one or more other registered parties.

(6)   "Relevant election" has the same meaning as in Part II.

(7)   "Campaign expenditure" does not include anything which (in accordance with any enactment) falls to be included in
   (a)   a return as to election expenses in respect of a candidate or candidates at a particular election, or
   (b)   a recall petition return within the meaning of Schedule 5 to the Recall of MPs Act 2015 (see paragraph 1 of that Schedule).

(8)   Where a registered party is a party with accounting units
   (a)   expenses incurred or to be incurred by or on behalf of any accounting unit of the party shall be regarded as expenses incurred or to be incurred by or on behalf of the party, and
   (b)   references to campaign expenditure incurred or to be incurred by or on behalf of a registered party accordingly extend, in relation to the party, to expenses which constitute such expenditure by virtue of paragraph (a).

(9)   In this section "candidates" includes future candidates, whether identifiable or not.

(10)   Nothing in this Part applies in relation to expenses incurred or to be incurred by or on behalf of a minor party.

NOTES

Prospective operation
   Sub-s (7)(b) not yet in operation   *Defined terms*

accounting unit: ss 26(11), 160(1)   registered party: s 22(6)
enactment: s 160(1)   registered party: s 160(1)
minor party: s 160(1)
party with accounting units: ss 26(11), 160(1)
a person standing for election in the name of a

Notional campaign expenditure

73 (1)   This section applies where, in the case of a registered party

    (a) either

        (i) property is transferred to the party free of charge or at a discount of more than 10 per cent of its market value, or

        (ii) property, services or facilities is or are provided for the use or benefit of the party free of charge or at a discount of more than 10 per cent of the commercial rate for the use of the property or for the provision of the services or facilities, and

    (b) the property, services or facilities is or are made use of by or on behalf of the party in circumstances such that, if any expenses were to be (or are) actually incurred by or on behalf of the party in respect of that use, they would be (or are) campaign expenditure incurred by or on behalf of the party.

  (2)   Where this section applies, an amount of campaign expenditure determined in accordance with this section ("the appropriate amount") shall be treated, for the purposes of this Part, as incurred by the party during the period for which the property, services or facilities is or are made use of as mentioned in subsection (1)(b).

      This subsection has effect subject to subsection (9).

  (3)   Where subsection (1)(a)(i) applies, the appropriate amount is such proportion of either

    (a) the market value of the property (where the property is transferred free of charge), or

    (b) the difference between the market value of the property and the amount of expenses actually incurred by or on behalf of the party in respect of the property (where the property is transferred at a discount),

      as is reasonably attributable to the use made of the property as mentioned in subsection (1)(b).

  (4)   Where subsection (1)(a)(ii) applies, the appropriate amount is such proportion of either

    (a) the commercial rate for the use of the property or the provision of the services or facilities (where the property, services or facilities is or are provided free of charge), or

    (b) the difference between that commercial rate and the amount of expenses actually incurred by or on behalf of the party in respect of the use of the property or the provision of the services or facilities (where the property, services or facilities is or are provided at a discount),

      as is reasonably attributable to the use made of the property, services or facilities as mentioned in subsection (1)(b).

  (5)   Where the services of an employee are made available by his employer for the use or benefit of a registered party, then for the purposes of this section the amount which is to be taken as constituting the commercial rate for the provision of those services shall be the amount of the remuneration or allowances payable to the employee by his employer in respect of the period for which his services are made available (but shall not include any amount in respect of contributions or other payments for which the employer is liable in respect of the employee).

  (6)   Where an amount of campaign expenditure is treated, by virtue of subsection (2), as incurred by or on behalf of a party during any period the whole or part of which falls

within any period which is, in relation to the party, a relevant campaign period for the purposes of section 80, then

- (a) the amount mentioned in subsection (7) shall be treated as incurred by or on behalf of the party during the relevant campaign period, and
- (b) the treasurer or a deputy treasurer appointed under section 74 shall make a declaration of that amount,

unless that amount is not more than £200.

(7) The amount referred to in subsection (6) is such proportion of the appropriate amount (determined in accordance with subsection (3) or (4)) as reasonably represents the use made of the property, services or facilities as mentioned in subsection (1)(b) during the relevant campaign period.

(8) A person commits an offence if he knowingly or recklessly makes a false declaration under subsection (6).

(9) No amount of campaign expenditure shall be regarded as incurred by virtue of subsection (2) in respect of
- (a) the transmission by a broadcaster of a party political broadcast;
- (b) any facilities provided in accordance with any right conferred on candidates or a party at an election by any enactment; or
- (c) the provision by any individual of his own services which he provides voluntarily in his own time and free of charge.

(10) In subsections (1), (3), (4) and (5) any reference to anything done by or in relation to a registered party includes a reference to anything done by or in relation to any accounting unit of the party; and section 50(6) and (8)(a) shall apply with any necessary modifications for the purpose of determining, for the purposes of subsection (1), whether property is transferred to a registered party or to any such unit.

(11) The reference in subsection (9)(a) to a broadcaster includes a reference to the Gibraltar Broadcasting Corporation.

NOTES

Defined terms
accounting unit: ss 26(11), 160(1)
broadcaster: ss 37(2), 160(1)
campaign expenditure: s 72(2), (7), (8)
enactment: s 160(1)
market value: s 160(1)
modifications: s 160(1)

party with accounting units: ss 26(11), 160(1)
property: s 160(1)
registered party: s 160(1)
treasurer: s 160(1)

Officers of registered party with responsibility for campaign expenditure

74 (1) The treasurer of a registered party may appoint, on such terms as he may determine, one or more deputy treasurers of the party for the purposes of this Part, but not more than 12 persons may hold such appointments at the same time.

(2) The appointment of a person as deputy treasurer of a party is effective for those purposes once the treasurer has given the Commission a notification of the appointment which
- (a) contains the name of the person so appointed and the address of his office; and
- (b) is accompanied by a declaration of acceptance of office signed by that person.

(3) A person is not, however, eligible to be appointed as deputy treasurer of a registered party if, at any time within the last five years, he has been convicted of any offence under this Act or of any other offence committed in connection with a relevant election within the meaning of Part II, an election to the House of Assembly of Gibraltar or a , a referendum within the meaning of Part VII or a recall petition within the meaning of the Recall of MPs Act 2015 (see section 1(2) of that Act).

(4)   A person commits an offence if he accepts the office of deputy treasurer of a registered party when, by virtue of subsection (3), he is not eligible to be so appointed.

(5)   Where a deputy treasurer of a registered party is convicted of an offence falling within subsection (3), his appointment as deputy treasurer shall terminate on the date of the conviction.

(6)   If, where the appointment of any deputy treasurer of a registered party has been notified to the Commission under subsection (2)

    (a)   the deputy treasurer dies or his appointment terminates for any other reason, or

    (b)   any change occurs in the address of his office,

the treasurer of the party must notify the Commission of that fact within the appropriate period.

(7)   In subsection (6) "the appropriate period" means

    (a)   the period of 14 days beginning with the date of the deputy treasurer's death or the termination of his appointment, or

    (b)   the period of 28 days beginning with the date when the change of address occurs,

as the case may be.

(8)   The name of any deputy treasurer of a registered party and the address of his office, as notified to the Commission in accordance with this section, shall be included in the party's entry in the Great Britain or Northern Ireland register.

(9)   Where the Commission receive a notification under subsection (6), they shall cause any change required as a consequence of the notification to be made in any such entry as soon as is reasonably practicable.

(10)   For the purposes of this Part

    (a)   the address of the treasurer of a registered party shall be regarded as being the registered address of the party; and

    (b)   the address of any deputy treasurer of such a party shall be regarded as being the address for the time being registered in relation to him in accordance with subsection (8).

NOTES

Prospective operation
  Last part of sub-s (3) not yet in operation

Defined terms
  the Commission: s 160(1)
  the Great Britain register: ss 23(2)(a), 160(1)

the Northern Ireland register: ss 23(2)(b), 160(1)
registered party: s 160(1)
treasurer: s 160(1)

General restrictions relating to campaign expenditure

Restriction on incurring campaign expenditure

75 (1)   No campaign expenditure shall be incurred by or on behalf of a registered party unless it is incurred with the authority of

    (a)   the treasurer of the party,

    (b)   a deputy treasurer of the party, or

    (c)   a person authorised in writing by the treasurer or a deputy treasurer.

(2)   A person commits an offence if, without reasonable excuse, he incurs any expenses in contravention of subsection (1).

(3)   Where any expenses are incurred in contravention of subsection (1), the expenses shall not count for the purposes of sections 79 to 83 or Schedule 9 as campaign expenditure incurred by or on behalf of the party.

NOTES
Defined terms   treasurer: s 160(1)
  campaign expenditure: s 72(2), (7), (8)
  registered party: s 160(1)

Restriction on payments in respect of campaign expenditure

76 (1)   No payment (of whatever nature) may be made in respect of any campaign expenditure incurred or to be incurred by or on behalf of a registered party unless it is made by
    (a)   the treasurer of the party,
    (b)   a deputy treasurer of the party, or
    (c)   a person authorised in writing by the treasurer or a deputy treasurer.

(2)   Any payment made in respect of any such expenditure by a person within any of paragraphs (a) to (c) of subsection (1) must be supported by an invoice or a receipt unless it is not more than £200.

(3)   Where a person within paragraph (b) or (c) of subsection (1) makes a payment to which subsection (2) applies, he must deliver to the treasurer
    (a)   notification that he has made the payment, and
    (b)   the supporting invoice or receipt,
as soon as possible after making the payment.

(4)   A person commits an offence if, without reasonable excuse
    (a)   he makes any payment in contravention of subsection (1), or
    (b)   he contravenes subsection (3).

NOTES
Defined terms   treasurer: s 160(1)
  campaign expenditure: s 72(2), (7), (8)
  contravention: s 160(1)
  registered party: s 160(1)

Restriction on making claims in respect of campaign expenditure

77 (1)   A claim for payment in respect of campaign expenditure incurred by or on behalf of a registered party during any period which is, in relation to the party, a relevant campaign period (within the meaning of section 80) shall not be payable if the claim is not sent to
    (a)   the treasurer or a deputy treasurer of the party, or
    (b)   any other person authorised under section 75 to incur the expenditure,
not later than 30 days after the end of the relevant campaign period.

(2)   Any claim sent in accordance with subsection (1) shall be paid not later than 60 days after the end of the relevant campaign period.

(3)   A person commits an offence if, without reasonable excuse
    (a)   he pays any claim which by virtue of subsection (1) is not payable, or
    (b)   he makes any payment in respect of a claim after the end of the period allowed under subsection (2).

(4)   In the case of any claim to which subsection (1) applies
    (a)   the person making the claim, or
    (b)   the person with whose authority the expenditure in question was incurred,
may apply in England and Wales to the High Court or the county court or, in Northern Ireland, to the High Court or a county court or, in Scotland, to the Court of Session or

the sheriff for leave for the claim to be paid although sent in after the end of the period mentioned in that subsection; and the court, if satisfied that for any special reason it is appropriate to do so, may by order grant the leave.

(5)   Nothing in subsection (1) or (2) shall apply in relation to any sum paid in pursuance of the order of leave.

(6)   Subsection (2) is without prejudice to any rights of a creditor of a registered party to obtain payment before the end of the period allowed under that subsection.

(7)   The jurisdiction conferred by subsection (4) on the Court of Session or the sheriff may be exercised in such manner as is prescribed by Act of Sederunt; and any order made by the sheriff by virtue of that subsection may be appealed to the Court of Session.

(8)   Article 60 of the County Courts (Northern Ireland) Order 1980 (appeals from county courts) shall apply in relation to any order of a county court in Northern Ireland made by virtue of subsection (4) as it applies in relation to any such decree of a county court as is mentioned in paragraph (1) of that Article.

(9)   Where, in the case of any campaign expenditure, the period allowed under subsection (1) or (2) would (apart from this subsection) end on
    (a)   a Saturday or Sunday or Christmas Eve, Christmas Day, or Good Friday,
    (b)   a bank holiday, or
    (c)   a day appointed for public thanksgiving or mourning,
the period instead ends on the first day following that day which is not one of those days.

(10)   In subsection (9)(b) "bank holiday" means a day within subsection (11) or a day which under the Banking and Financial Dealings Act 1971 is a bank holiday in any part of the United Kingdom
    (a)   in which is situated the office of the treasurer, deputy treasurer or (as the case may be) other authorised person to whom the claim is sent pursuant to subsection (1); or
    (b)   in which the person providing the property, services or facilities to which the expenditure relates conducts his business; or
    (c)   (if he conducts his business in more than one part of the United Kingdom) in which is situated the office from which dealings relating to the expenditure were conducted.

(11)   A day is within this subsection if under the law of Gibraltar it is a bank holiday or a public holiday and
    (a)   the office of the treasurer, deputy treasurer or (as the case may be) other authorised person to whom the claim is sent pursuant to subsection (1) is situated in Gibraltar; or
    (b)   the person providing the property, services or facilities to which the expenditure relates conducts his business in Gibraltar; or
    (c)   (if he conducts his business in one or more parts of the United Kingdom and Gibraltar) the office from which dealings relating to the expenditure were conducted is situated in Gibraltar.

(12)   In its application to Gibraltar, subsection (4) has effect as if for the words between "apply" and "leave" there were substituted "to the Gibraltar court for".

NOTES
Defined terms
  business: s 160(1)
  campaign expenditure: s 72(2), (7), (8)
  Gibraltar court: s 160(1)
  property: s 160(1)
  registered party: s 160(1)
  treasurer: s 160(1)

Disputed claims

78 (1)   This section applies where

    (a)   a claim for payment in respect of campaign expenditure incurred by or on behalf of a registered party as mentioned in section 77(1) is sent to

        (i)   the treasurer of the party, or

        (ii)   any other person with whose authority it is alleged that the expenditure was incurred,

      within the period allowed under that provision; and

    (b)   the treasurer or other person to whom the claim is sent fails or refuses to pay the claim within the period allowed under section 77(2);

    and the claim is referred to in this section as "the disputed claim".

(2)   The person by whom the disputed claim is made may bring an action for the disputed claim, and nothing in section 77(2) shall apply in relation to any sum paid in pursuance of any judgment or order made by a court in the proceedings.

(3)   Subsections (4) to (8) of section 77 shall apply in relation to an application made by the person mentioned in subsection (1)(b) above for leave to pay the disputed claim as they apply in relation to an application for leave to pay a claim (whether it is disputed or otherwise) which is sent in after the period allowed under section 77(1).

NOTES

Defined terms
  campaign expenditure: s 72(2), (7), (8)
  registered party: s 160(1)

treasurer: s 160(1)

Financial limits

Limits on campaign expenditure

79 (1)   Schedule 9 has effect for imposing limits on campaign expenditure incurred by or on behalf of registered parties in England, Scotland, Wales or Northern Ireland during the periods specified in that Schedule.

(2)   Where, during the period in relation to which any such limit applies in relation to a registered party, any campaign expenditure is incurred by or on behalf of the party in excess of that limit

    (a)   the treasurer or any deputy treasurer of the party is guilty of an offence if

        (i)   he authorised the expenditure to be incurred by or on behalf of the party, and

        (ii)   he knew or ought reasonably to have known that the expenditure would be incurred in excess of that limit; and

    (b)   the party is also guilty of an offence.

(3)   It shall be a defence for any person or registered party charged with an offence under subsection (2) to show

    (a)   that any code of practice for the time being issued under paragraph 3 of Schedule 8 was complied with in determining the items and amounts of campaign expenditure to be entered in the relevant return under section 80, and

    (b)   that the limit would not have been exceeded on the basis of the items and amounts entered in that return.

(3A)   See section 94F (expenditure by or on behalf of recognised third party targeted at a registered party) for

    (a)   provision under which expenditure incurred by or on behalf of a third party may count towards the limit mentioned in subsection (2), and

(b) provision modifying subsection (2)(a)(i) in its application to such expenditure.

(4) Where

   (a) at any time before the beginning of any relevant campaign period (within the meaning of section 80), any expenses within section 72(2) are incurred by or on behalf of a registered party in respect of any property, services or facilities, but

   (b) the property, services or facilities is or are made use of by or on behalf of the party during the relevant campaign period in circumstances such that, had any expenses been incurred in respect of that use during that period, they would by virtue of section 72(2) have constituted campaign expenditure incurred by or on behalf of the party during that period,

the appropriate proportion of the expenses mentioned in paragraph (a) shall be treated for the purposes of this section, sections 80 to 83 and Schedule 9 as campaign expenditure incurred by or on behalf of the party during that period.

(5) For the purposes of subsection (4) the appropriate proportion of the expenses mentioned in paragraph (a) of that subsection is such proportion of those expenses as is reasonably attributable to the use made of the property, services or facilities as mentioned in paragraph (b).

NOTES

Defined terms
  campaign expenditure: s 72(2), (7), (8)
  property: s 160(1)
  registered party: s 160(1)

treasurer: s 160(1)

Returns

Returns as to campaign expenditure

80 (1) For the purposes of this section

   (a) "the relevant campaign period", in relation to any limit imposed by Schedule 9, is the period in relation to which the limit is so imposed; and

   (b) a part of the United Kingdom is a "relevant" part, in relation to any limit imposed by Schedule 9, if the limit applies to campaign expenditure which (within the meaning of that Schedule) is incurred in that part.

(2) Where

   (a) any limit imposed by Schedule 9 applies to campaign expenditure incurred by or on behalf of a registered party during the relevant campaign period, and

   (b) that period ends,

the treasurer of the party shall prepare a return under this section in respect of campaign expenditure incurred by or on behalf of the party during that period in any relevant part or parts of the United Kingdom.

(3) A return under this section must specify the poll for the relevant election (or, as the case may be, the polls for the relevant elections) that took place during the relevant campaign period, and must contain

   (a) a statement of all payments made in respect of campaign expenditure incurred by or on behalf of the party during the relevant campaign period in the relevant part or parts of the United Kingdom;

   (b) a statement of all disputed claims (within the meaning of section 78) of which the treasurer is aware; and

   (c) a statement of all the unpaid claims (if any) of which the treasurer is aware in respect of which an application has been made, or is about to be made, to a court under section 77(4).

(4) A return under this section must be accompanied by

(a)   all invoices or receipts relating to the payments mentioned in subsection (3)(a);

(b)   in the case of any campaign expenditure treated as incurred by the party by virtue of section 73, any declaration falling to be made with respect to that expenditure in accordance with section 73(6); and

(c)   in the case of any campaign expenditure treated as incurred by the party by virtue of section 94F(2) (expenditure by or on behalf of recognised third party targeted at a registered party), any declaration falling to be made with respect to that expenditure in accordance with section 94F(5).

(5)   Where, however, any payments or claims falling to be dealt with in a return by virtue of subsection (3) have already been dealt with in an earlier return under this section

(a)   it shall be sufficient for the later return to deal with those payments or claims by specifying overall amounts in respect of them; and

(b)   the requirement imposed by subsection (4) does not apply to any invoices, receipts or declarations which accompanied the earlier return and are specified as such in the later return.

(6)   The Commission may by regulations prescribe a form of return which may be used for the purposes of this section.

NOTES

Defined terms
   campaign expenditure: s 72(2), (7), (8)
   the Commission: s 160(1)
   registered party: s 160(1)

treasurer: s 160(1)

Auditor's report on return

81 (1)   Where during a relevant campaign period the campaign expenditure incurred by or on behalf of a registered party in the relevant part or parts of the United Kingdom exceeds £250,000, a report must be prepared by a qualified auditor on the return prepared under section 80 in respect of that expenditure.

(2)   The following provisions, namely

(a)   section 43(6) and (7), and

(b)   section 44,

shall apply in relation to the appointment of an auditor to prepare a report under subsection (1) or (as the case may be) an auditor so appointed as they apply in relation to the appointment of an auditor to carry out an audit under section 43 or (as the case may be) an auditor so appointed.

(3)   Subsection (1) of section 80 applies for the purposes of this section as it applies for the purposes of section 80.

NOTES

Defined terms
   campaign expenditure: s 72(2), (7), (8)
   qualified auditor: s 160(1), (2)
   registered party: s 160(1)
   relevant part of the United Kingdom: s 80(1) (by virtue

of sub-s (3) of this section)
the relevant campaign period: s 80(1) (by virtue of
sub-s (3) of this section)

Delivery of returns to the Commission

82 (1)   Where

(a)   any return falls to be prepared under section 80, and

(b)   an auditor's report on it falls to be prepared under section 81(1),

the treasurer of the party shall deliver the return to the Commission, together with a copy of the auditor's report, within six months of the end of the relevant campaign period.

(2)   In the case of any other return falling to be prepared under section 80, the treasurer of the party shall deliver the return to the Commission within three months of the end of the relevant campaign period.

(3)   Where, after the date on which a return is delivered to the Commission under this section, leave is given by a court under section 77(4) for any claim to be paid, the treasurer of the party in question shall, within seven days after the payment, deliver to the Commission a return of any sums paid in pursuance of the leave accompanied by a copy of the order of the court giving the leave.

(4)   The treasurer of a registered party commits an offence if, without reasonable excuse, he
    (a)   fails to comply with the requirements of subsection (1) or (2) in relation to any return or report to which that subsection applies;
    (b)   delivers a return which does not comply with the requirements of section 80(3) or (4); or
    (c)   fails to comply with the requirements of subsection (3) in relation to a return under that subsection.

NOTES
Defined terms   treasurer: s 160(1)
  the Commission: s 160(1)
  registered party: s 160(1)
  the relevant campaign period: s 80(1)

Declaration by treasurer as to return under section 80

83 (1)   Each return under section 80 must, when delivered to the Commission, be accompanied by a declaration which complies with subsection (2) and is signed by the treasurer.

(2)   The declaration must state
    (a)   that the treasurer has examined the return in question; and
    (b)   that to the best of his knowledge and belief
        (i)   it is a complete and correct return as required by law, and
        (ii)   all expenses shown in it as paid have been paid by him or a deputy treasurer of the party or a person authorised under section 76.

(3)   A person commits an offence if
    (a)   he knowingly or recklessly makes a false declaration under this section; or
    (b)   subsection (1) is contravened at a time when he is treasurer of the registered party to which the return relates.

NOTES
Defined terms   treasurer: s 160(1)
  the Commission: s 160(1)
  contravention: s 160(1)
  registered party: s 160(1)

Public inspection of returns under section 80

84 (1)   Where the Commission receive any return under section 80, they shall
    (a)   as soon as reasonably practicable after receiving the return, make a copy of the return, and of any documents accompanying it, available for public inspection; and
    (b)   keep any such copy available for public inspection for the period for which the return or other document is kept by them.

(2)   At the end of the period of two years beginning with the date when any return or other document mentioned in subsection (1) is received by the Commission

    (a)   they may cause the return or other document to be destroyed; but

    (b)   if requested to do so by the treasurer of the party concerned, they shall arrange for the return or other document to be returned to the treasurer.

NOTES

Defined terms   treasurer: s 160(1)

   the Commission: s 160(1)

   document: s 160(1)

PART VI
CONTROLS RELATING TO THIRD PARTY NATIONAL ELECTION CAMPAIGNS

Chapter I
Preliminary

Controlled expenditure by third parties

85 (1)   The following provisions have effect for the purposes of this Part.

  (2)   "Controlled expenditure", in relation to a third party, means (subject to section 87) expenses incurred by or on behalf of the third party where

    (a)   the expenses fall within Part 1 of Schedule 8A, and

    (b)   the expenditure can reasonably be regarded as intended to promote or procure electoral success at any relevant election for

       (i)   one or more particular registered parties,

       (ii)   one or more registered parties who advocate (or do not advocate) particular policies or who otherwise fall within a particular category of such parties, or

       (iii)   candidates who hold (or do not hold) particular opinions or who advocate (or do not advocate) particular policies or who otherwise fall within a particular category of candidates.

  (3)   *Repealed*

  (4)   For the purposes of subsection (2)(b)

    (a)   the reference to electoral success at any relevant election is a reference

       (i)   in relation to a registered party, to the return at any such election of candidates standing in the name of the party or included in a list of candidates submitted by the party in connection with the election, and

       (ii)   in relation to candidates, to their return at any such election; and

    (b)   the reference to doing any of the things mentioned in that provision includes doing so by prejudicing the electoral prospects at the election of other parties or candidates; and

    (c)   a course of conduct may constitute the doing of one of those things even though it does not involve any express mention being made of the name of any party or candidate.

 (4A)   In determining whether expenditure can reasonably be regarded as intended to promote or procure electoral success as mentioned in subsection (2)(b), it is immaterial that it can reasonably be regarded as intended to achieve any other purpose as well.

  (5)   "Recognised third party" means a third party for the time being recognised under section 88 for the purposes of this Part.

(5A) "Recognised Gibraltar third party" means a recognised third party falling within paragraph (d) or (e) (but not paragraph (a), (b) or (c)) of section 88(2).

(6) "Relevant election" has the same meaning as in Part II.

(7) "Responsible person", in relation to a recognised third party, means

    (a) if the third party is an individual, that individual;

    (b) if the third party is a registered party

        (i) the treasurer of the party, or

        (ii) in the case of a minor party, the person for the time being notified to the Commission by the party in accordance with section 88(3)(b)(iii); and

    (c) otherwise, the person or officer for the time being notified to the Commission by the third party in accordance with section 88(3)(c)(ii) or (d)(ii).

(8) "Third party", in relation to any relevant election, means

    (a) any person or body other than a registered party; or

    (b) subject to subsection (9), any registered party.

(9) In connection with the application of subsection (2) in relation to expenses incurred by or on behalf of a third party which is a registered party, any reference in that subsection to a registered party or registered parties or to any candidates does not include

    (a) the party itself, or

    (b) any candidates standing in the name of the party at any relevant election or included in any list submitted by the party in connection with any such election, as the case may be.

(10) In this section "candidates" includes future candidates, whether identifiable or not.

NOTES

Defined terms
  body: s 160(1)
  the Commission: s 160(1)
  minor party: s 160(1)
  a person standing for election in the name of a

registered party: s 22(6)
registered party: s 160(1)
treasurer: s 160(1)

Notional controlled expenditure

86 (1) This section applies where, in the case of a third party

    (a) either

        (i) property is transferred to the third party free of charge or at a discount of more than 10 per cent of its market value, or

        (ii) property, services or facilities is or are provided for the use or benefit of the third party free of charge or at a discount of more than 10 per cent of the commercial rate for the use of the property or for the provision of the services or facilities, and

    (b) the property, services or facilities is or are made use of by or on behalf of the third party in circumstances such that, if any expenses were to be (or are) actually incurred by or on behalf of the third party in respect of that use, they would be (or are) controlled expenditure incurred by or on behalf of the third party.

(2) Where this section applies, an amount of controlled expenditure determined in accordance with this section ("the appropriate amount") shall be treated, for the purposes of this Part, as incurred by the third party during the period for which the property, services or facilities is or are made use of as mentioned in subsection (1)(b). This subsection has effect subject to section 87.

(3) Where subsection (1)(a)(i) applies, the appropriate amount is such proportion of either

     (a) the market value of the property (where the property is transferred free of charge), or

     (b) the difference between the market value of the property and the amount of expenses actually incurred by or on behalf of the third party in respect of the property (where the property is transferred at a discount),

as is reasonably attributable to the use made of the property as mentioned in subsection (1)(b).

(4) Where subsection (1)(a)(ii) applies, the appropriate amount is such proportion of either

     (a) the commercial rate for the use of the property or the provision of the services or facilities (where the property, services or facilities is or are provided free of charge), or

     (b) the difference between that commercial rate and the amount of expenses actually incurred by or on behalf of the third party in respect of the use of the property or the provision of the services or facilities (where the property, services or facilities is or are provided at a discount),

as is reasonably attributable to the use made of the property, services or facilities as mentioned in subsection (1)(b).

(5) Where the services of an employee are made available by his employer for the use or benefit of a third party, then for the purposes of this section the amount which is to be taken as constituting the commercial rate for the provision of those services shall be the amount of the remuneration and allowances payable to the employee by his employer in respect of the period for which his services are so made available (but shall not include any amount in respect of any contributions or other payments for which the employer is liable in respect of the employee).

(6) Where an amount of controlled expenditure is treated, by virtue of subsection (2), as incurred by or on behalf of a third party during any period the whole or part of which falls within any period which is a regulated period (as defined by section 94(10)(a)), then

     (a) the amount mentioned in subsection (7) shall be treated as incurred by or on behalf of the third party during the regulated period, and

     (b) if a return falls to be prepared under section 96 in respect of controlled expenditure incurred by or on behalf of the third party during that period, the responsible person shall make a declaration of that amount,

unless that amount is not more than £200.

(7) The amount referred to in subsection (6) is such proportion of the appropriate amount (determined in accordance with subsection (3) or (4)) as reasonably represents the use made of the property, services or facilities as mentioned in subsection (1)(b) during the regulated period.

(8) A person commits an offence if he knowingly or recklessly makes a false declaration under subsection (6).

(9) Paragraph 2(5) and (6)(a) of Schedule 11 shall apply with any necessary modifications for the purpose of determining, for the purposes of subsection (1), whether property is transferred to a third party.

NOTES

Defined terms
controlled expenditure: s 85(2)
market value: s 160(1)
modifications: s 160(1)
property: s 160(1)

responsible person: s 85(7)
third party: s 85(8), (9)

Expenditure by third parties which is not controlled expenditure

87 (1) No amount of controlled expenditure shall be regarded as incurred by a third party by virtue of section 85 or 86 in respect of

(a) *Repealed*

(b) any property, services or facilities to the extent that the property, services or facilities is or are used in circumstances in which

(i) an amount of campaign expenditure is to be regarded as incurred by or on behalf of a registered party for the purposes of Part V, or

(ii) an amount of expenses falls (in accordance with any enactment) to be included in a return as to election expenses in respect of a candidate or candidates at a particular election, or

(iii) an amount of expenses falls to be included in a recall petition return within the meaning of Schedule 5 to the Recall of MPs Act 2015 (see paragraph 1 of that Schedule),

in respect of that use.

(2) *Repealed*

(3) The reference in subsection (1)(b)(i) to circumstances in which an amount of campaign expenditure is to be regarded as incurred by or on behalf of a registered party for the purposes of Part 5 does not include circumstances in which an amount of campaign expenditure is treated as incurred by a registered party under section 94F(2).

NOTES

Prospective operation
Sub-s (1)(b)(iii) not yet in operation

Defined terms
controlled expenditure: s 85(2)
enactment: s 160(1)

property: s 160(1)
registered party: s 160(1)
third party: s 85(8), (9)

Recognised third parties

Third parties recognised for the purposes of this Part

88 (1) A third party is recognised for the purposes of this Part if

(a) the third party has given the Commission a notification under this subsection which complies with subsection (3), and

(b) that notification is for the time being in force.

(2) A third party may only give a notification under subsection (1) if the third party is

(a) an individual resident in the United Kingdom or registered in an electoral register (as defined by section 54(8)) who is not the responsible person in relation to another third party,

(b) a registered party other than a Gibraltar party whose entry in the register includes a statement that it intends to contest one or more elections to the European Parliament in the combined region, or

(c) a body falling within any of paragraphs (b) and (d) to (h) of section 54(2),

(ca) a body incorporated by Royal Charter which does not fall within any of those paragraphs of section 54(2),

(cb) a charitable incorporated organisation within the meaning of Part 11 of the Charities Act 2011 or within the meaning of the Charities Act (Northern Ireland) 2008,

(cc) a Scottish charitable incorporated organisation within the meaning of Chapter 7 of Part 1 of the Charities and Trustee Investment (Scotland) Act 2005 (asp 10),

(cd) a partnership constituted under the law of Scotland which carries on business in the United Kingdom,

      (d)   an individual who is resident in Gibraltar or is a Gibraltar elector, or

      (e)   a body falling within any of paragraphs (b) to (g) of section 54(2A).

(3)   A notification under subsection (1) must

      (a)   if given by an individual, state

           (i)   his full name, and

           (ii)   his home address in the United Kingdom, or (if he has no such address in the United Kingdom) his home address elsewhere,

           (iii)   (if he is a Gibraltar elector who is not resident in Gibraltar and the first version of the Gibraltar register has not been published) that he is registered in the register of electors used for House of Assembly elections,

      and be signed by him;

      (b)   if given by a registered party, state

           (i)   the party's registered name,

           (ii)   the address of its registered headquarters, and

           (iii)   (in the case of a minor party) the name of the person who will be responsible for compliance on the part of the party with the provisions of Chapter II,

      and be signed by the responsible officers of the party (within the meaning of section 64); and

      (c)   if given by a body falling within any of paragraphs (b) and (d) to (h) of section 54(2) or any of paragraphs (b) and (d) to (g) of section 54(2A), state

           (i)   all such details in respect of the body as are required by virtue of any of sub-paragraphs (4) and (6) to (10) of paragraph 2 of Schedule 6 to be given in respect of such a body as the donor of a recordable donation,

           (ia)   in the case of a body falling within any of paragraphs (b) and (d) to (h) of section 54(2), the names of the relevant participators in relation to the body (see subsection (3B)), and

           (ii)   the name of the person or officer who will be responsible for compliance on the part of the body with the provisions of Chapter II,

      and be signed by the body's secretary or a person who acts in a similar capacity in relation to the body;

      (d)   if given by a body falling within any of paragraphs (ca) to (cd) of subsection (2), state

           (i)   the relevant details in relation to the body (see subsection (3C)), and

           (ii)   the name of the person or officer who will be responsible for compliance on the part of the body with the provisions of Chapter 2,

      and be signed by the body's secretary or a person who acts in a similar capacity in relation to the body.

(3A)   A notification given by a third party does not comply with the requirement in subsection (3)(b)(iii), (c)(ii) or (d)(ii) (to state the name of the person who will be responsible for compliance) if the person whose name is stated is

      (a)   the responsible person in relation to another third party,

      (b)   an individual who gives a notification under subsection (1) at the same time, or

      (c)   the person whose name is stated, in purported compliance with the requirement in subsection (3)(b)(iii), (c)(ii) or (d)(ii), in a notification given at the same time by another third party.

      In this subsection "the person", in relation to a notification to which subsection (3)(c) or (d) applies, is to be read as "the person or officer".

(3B)   For the purposes of subsection (3)(c), the "relevant participators" in relation to a body are

      (a)   in the case of a body falling with section 54(2)(b) (companies), the body's directors;

(b) in the case of a body falling within section 54(2)(d) (trade unions), the body's officers (within the meaning of the Trade Union and Labour Relations (Consolidation) Act 1992: see section 119 of that Act);

(c) in the case of a body falling within section 54(2)(e) (building societies), the body's directors;

(d) in the case of a body falling within section 54(2)(f) (limited liability partnerships), the body's members;

(e) in the case of a body falling within section 54(2)(g) (friendly societies etc)

    (i) where the body is a friendly society, the members of the body's committee of management;

    (ii) otherwise, the members of the body's committee of management or other directing body;

(f) in the case of a body falling within section 54(2)(h) (unincorporated associations)

    (i) where the body has more than 15 members and has officers or a governing body, those officers or the members of that governing body;

    (ii) otherwise, the body's members.

(3C) For the purposes of subsection (3)(d), the "relevant details" in relation to a body are

(a) in the case of a body falling within subsection (2)(ca) (body incorporated by Royal Charter)

    (i) the name of the body,

    (ii) the address of its main office in the United Kingdom, and

    (iii) the names of its officers or the members of its governing body;

(b) in the case of a body falling within subsection (2)(cb) or (cc) (charitable incorporated organisation)

    (i) the name of the body,

    (ii) the address of its principal office, and

    (iii) the names of its charity trustees within the meaning of the Charities Act 2011, the Charities Act (Northern Ireland) 2008 or the Charities and Trustee Investment (Scotland) Act 2005 (asp 10);

(c) in the case of a body falling within subsection (2)(cd) (Scottish partnership)

    (i) the name of the body,

    (ii) the address of its main office in the United Kingdom, and

    (iii) the names of the partners.

(4) Subject to the following provisions of this section, a notification under subsection (1) ("the original notification")

(a) shall be in force as from the date on which it is received by the Commission, but

(b) shall, subject to subsection (5), lapse at the end of the period of three months beginning with any anniversary of that date unless the third party notifies the Commission that the third party wishes the original notification to continue in force.

(5) Where

(a) the original notification would apart from this subsection lapse under subsection (4)(b) at the end of any such period of three months as is mentioned in that provision, but

(b) the end of that period falls within any regulated period at the end of which a return will fall to be prepared under section 96 in respect of controlled expenditure incurred by or on behalf of the third party during the regulated period,

the original notification shall be treated, for all purposes connected with controlled expenditure so incurred during the regulated period, as lapsing at the end of that period instead.

(6) A notification under subsection (4)(b) ("the renewal notification") must either
  (a) confirm that all the statements contained in the original notification, as it has effect for the time being, are accurate; or
  (b) indicate that any statement contained in that notification, as it so has effect, is replaced by some other statement conforming with subsection (3).

(7) A notification under subsection (4)(b) must be received by the Commission during the period beginning one month before the relevant anniversary for the purposes of that provision and ending three months after it.

(8) A third party may, at any time after giving the original notification, give the Commission a notification ("a notification of alteration") indicating that any statement contained in the original notification, as it has effect for the time being, is replaced by some other statement
  (a) contained in the notification of alteration, and
  (b) conforming with subsection (3).

NOTES
Defined terms
  body: s 160(1)
  combined region: s 160(1)
  the Commission: s 160(1)
  controlled expenditure: s 85(2)
  Gibraltar elector: s 160(1)
  Gibraltar party: ss 28(8)(d), 160(1)
  Gibraltar register: s 160(1)

  minor party: s 160(1)
  recordable donation: Sch 6, para 1
  registered party: s 160(1)
  responsible person: s 85(7)
  third party: s 85(8), (9)

Register of notifications for purposes of section 88

89 (1) The Commission shall maintain a register of all notifications given to them under section 88(1) which are for the time being in force.

(2) The register shall be maintained by the Commission in such form as they may determine and shall contain, in the case of each such notification, all the information contained in the notification as it has effect for the time being in accordance with section 88.

(3) Where any notification is given to the Commission under section 88, they shall cause all the information contained in the notification, or (as the case may be) any new information contained in it, to be entered in the register as soon as is reasonably practicable.

(4) The information to be entered in the register in respect of a third party who is an individual shall, however, not include his home address.

NOTES
Defined terms
  the Commission: s 160(1)
  third party: s 85(8), (9)

Chapter II
Financial Controls

General restrictions relating to controlled expenditure by recognised third parties
Restriction on incurring controlled expenditure

90 (1) No amount of controlled expenditure shall be incurred by or on behalf of a recognised third party unless it is incurred with the authority of
  (a) the responsible person; or

    (b)   a person authorised in writing by the responsible person.

(2)   A person commits an offence if, without reasonable excuse, he incurs any expenses in contravention of subsection (1).

(3)   Where, in the case of a recognised third party that is a registered party, any expenses are incurred in contravention of subsection (1), the expenses shall not count for the purposes of sections 94 to 99A or Schedule 10 as controlled expenditure incurred by or on behalf of the recognised third party.

(4)   This section does not apply in relation to a recognised Gibraltar third party except in relation to controlled expenditure incurred by or on behalf of that party during the period of four months ending with the date of the poll for a general election to the European Parliament.

NOTES

Defined terms
  contravention: s 160(1)
  controlled expenditure: s 85(2)
  recognised Gibraltar third party: s 85(5A)
  recognised third party: s 85(5)

registered party: s 160(1)
responsible person: s 85(7)

Restriction on payments in respect of controlled expenditure

91 (1)   No payment (of whatever nature) may be made in respect of any controlled expenditure incurred or to be incurred by or on behalf of a recognised third party unless it is made by
    (a)   the responsible person, or
    (b)   a person authorised in writing by the responsible person.

(2)   Any payment made in respect of any such expenditure by a person within paragraph (a) or (b) of subsection (1) must be supported by an invoice or a receipt unless it is not more than £200.

(3)   Where a person within paragraph (b) of subsection (1) makes a payment to which subsection (2) applies, he must deliver to the responsible person
    (a)   notification that he has made the payment, and
    (b)   the supporting invoice or receipt,
as soon as possible after making the payment.

(4)   A person commits an offence if, without reasonable excuse
    (a)   he makes any payment in contravention of subsection (1), or
    (b)   he contravenes subsection (3).

(5)   This section does not apply in relation to a recognised Gibraltar third party except in relation to controlled expenditure incurred or to be incurred by or on behalf of that party during the period of four months ending with the date of the poll for a general election to the European Parliament.

NOTES

Defined terms
  contravention: s 160(1)
  controlled expenditure: s 85(2)
  recognised Gibraltar third party: s 85(5A)

recognised third party: s 85(5)
responsible person: s 85(7)

Restriction on making claims in respect of controlled expenditure

92 (1)   A claim for payment in respect of controlled expenditure incurred by or on behalf of a recognised third party during any period which is a regulated period (as defined by section 94(10)(a)) shall not be payable if the claim is not sent to
    (a)   the responsible person, or
    (b)   any other person authorised under section 90 to incur the expenditure,

not later than 30 days after the end of the regulated period.

(2) Any claim sent in accordance with subsection (1) shall be paid not later than 60 days after the end of the regulated period.

(3) A person commits an offence if, without reasonable excuse

    (a) he pays any claim which by virtue of subsection (1) is not payable, or

    (b) he makes any payment in respect of a claim after the end of the period allowed under subsection (2).

(4) In the case of any claim to which subsection (1) applies

    (a) the person making the claim, or

    (b) the person with whose authority the expenditure in question was incurred,

may apply in England and Wales to the High Court or the county court or, in Northern Ireland, to the High Court or a county court or, in Scotland, to the Court of Session or the sheriff for leave for the claim to be paid although sent in after the end of the period mentioned in that subsection; and the court, if satisfied that for any special reason it is appropriate to do so, may by order grant the leave.

(5) Nothing in subsection (1) or (2) shall apply in relation to any sum paid in pursuance of the order of leave.

(6) Subsection (2) is without prejudice to any rights of a creditor of a recognised third party to obtain payment before the end of the period allowed under that subsection.

(7) Subsections (7) to (11) of section 77 shall apply for the purposes of this section as if

    (a) any reference to subsection (1), (2) or (4) of that section were a reference to subsection (1), (2) or (4) above;

    (b) any reference to campaign expenditure were a reference to controlled expenditure; and

    (c) any reference to the treasurer or deputy treasurer of the registered party were a reference to the responsible person in relation to the recognised third party.

(8) In its application to Gibraltar, subsection (4) has effect as if for the words between "apply" and "leave" there were substituted "to the Gibraltar court for".

NOTES

Defined terms
  controlled expenditure: s 85(2)
  Gibraltar court: s 160(1)
  recognised third party: s 85(5)

responsible person: s 85(7)

Disputed claims

93 (1) This section applies where

    (a) a claim for payment in respect of controlled expenditure incurred by or on behalf of a recognised third party as mentioned in section 92(1) is sent to

      (i) the responsible person, or

      (ii) any other person with whose authority it is alleged that the expenditure was incurred,

    within the period allowed under that provision; and

    (b) the responsible person or other person to whom the claim is sent fails or refuses to pay the claim within the period allowed under section 92(2);

    and the claim is referred to in this section as "the disputed claim".

(2) The person by whom the disputed claim is made may bring an action for the disputed claim, and nothing in section 92(2) shall apply in relation to any sum paid in pursuance of any judgment or order made by a court in the proceedings.

(3) For the purposes of this section

(a) subsections (4) and (5) of section 92 shall apply in relation to an application made by the person mentioned in subsection (1)(b) above for leave to pay the disputed claim as they apply in relation to an application for leave to pay a claim (whether it is disputed or otherwise) which is sent in after the period allowed under section 92(1); and

(b) subsections (7) and (8) of section 77 shall apply as if any reference to subsection (4) of that section were a reference to section 92(4) as applied by paragraph (a) above.

NOTES

Defined terms
 controlled expenditure: s 85(2)
 recognised third party: s 85(5)
 responsible person: s 85(7)

Limits on controlled expenditure by third parties

94 (1) Schedule 10 has effect for imposing limits on controlled expenditure incurred by or on behalf of recognised third parties in England, Scotland, Wales or Northern Ireland, or in particular parliamentary constituencies, during the periods specified in that Schedule.

(2) Where during a regulated period any controlled expenditure is incurred in a relevant part of the United Kingdom or a parliamentary constituency by or on behalf of a recognised third party in excess of the limit imposed by Schedule 10 in relation to that period and part of the United Kingdom or parliamentary constituency, then

(a) if the third party is not an individual

(i) the responsible person is guilty of an offence if he authorised the expenditure to be incurred by or on behalf of the third party and he knew or ought reasonably to have known that the expenditure would be incurred in excess of that limit, and

(ii) the third party is also guilty of an offence;

(b) if the third party is an individual, he is guilty of an offence if he knew or ought reasonably to have known that the expenditure would be incurred in excess of that limit.

(3) Subsection (4) applies where

(a) either

(i) during a regulated period, any controlled expenditure is incurred in a part of the United Kingdom by or on behalf of a third party in excess of the limit for that part of the United Kingdom mentioned in subsection (5), or

(ii) during a regulated period in relation to which any limit is imposed by paragraph 3, 9, 10 or 11 of Schedule 10 (periods involving parliamentary general elections), any controlled expenditure is incurred in a particular parliamentary constituency by or on behalf of a third party in excess of the limit mentioned in subsection (5ZA), and

(b) the third party is not a recognised third party.

(3A) For provision requiring certain controlled expenditure to be disregarded in determining for the purposes of subsection (3)(a) whether a limit is exceeded, see section 94B(3) (arrangements between third parties notified to the Commission).

(4) In the case mentioned in subsection (3)

(a) if the third party is not an individual

(i) any person who authorised the expenditure to be incurred by or on behalf of the third party is guilty of an offence if he knew or ought reasonably to have known that the expenditure would be incurred in excess of that limit, and

(ii) the third party is also guilty of an offence;

(b) if the third party is an individual, he is guilty of an offence if he knew or ought reasonably to have known that the expenditure would be incurred in excess of that limit.

(4A) It is a defence for any person or third party charged with an offence under subsection (2) or (4) to show

(a) that any code of practice for the time being issued under paragraph 3 of Schedule 8A was complied with in determining whether any expenditure is controlled expenditure for the purposes of this Part, and

(b) that the offence would not have been committed on the basis of the controlled expenditure as determined in accordance with the code.

(5) The limits referred to in subsection (3)(a)(i) are as follows

(a) £20,000 for England; and

(b) £10,000 for each of Scotland, Wales and Northern Ireland.

(5ZA) The limit referred to in subsection (3)(a)(ii) is 0.05% of the total of the maximum campaign expenditure limits in England, Scotland, Wales and Northern Ireland.

(5A) Subsections (3) to (5ZA) and section 94B(3) to (7) apply to a recognised Gibraltar third party as they apply to a third party that is not a recognised third party, subject to the following modification namely that for the purposes of those provisions any expenditure incurred by or on behalf of the recognised Gibraltar third party during the period of four months ending with the date of the poll for a general election to the European Parliament is to be disregarded.

(6) Where

(a) during a regulated period any controlled expenditure is incurred in a particular part of the United Kingdom or a particular parliamentary constituency by or on behalf of a third party, and

(b) the expenditure is so incurred in pursuance of a plan or other arrangement whereby controlled expenditure is to be incurred by or on behalf of

(i) that third party, and

(ii) one or more other third parties,

respectively and the expenditure can reasonably be regarded as intended to achieve a common purpose falling within section 85(2)(b),

the expenditure mentioned in paragraph (a) shall be treated for the purposes of this section, sections 94D to 94H and Schedule 10 as having also been incurred, during the period and in the part of the United Kingdom or parliamentary constituency concerned, by or on behalf of the other third party (or, as the case may be, each of the other third parties) mentioned in paragraph (b)(ii).

(7) Subsection (6) applies whether or not any of the third parties in question is a recognised third party.

(8) Where

(a) at any time before the beginning of any regulated period any expenses within section 85(2) are incurred by or on behalf of a third party in respect of any property, services or facilities, but

(b) the property, services or facilities is or are made use of by or on behalf of the third party during the regulated period in circumstances such that, had any expenses been incurred in respect of that use during that period, they would by virtue of section 85(2) have constituted controlled expenditure incurred by or on behalf of the third party during that period,

the appropriate proportion of the expenses mentioned in paragraph (a) shall be treated for the purposes of this section, sections 94A and 94B, sections 94D to 94H, sections 96 to 99A and Schedule 10 as controlled expenditure incurred by or on behalf of the third party during that period.

(9) For the purposes of subsection (8) the appropriate proportion of the expenses mentioned in paragraph (a) of that subsection is such proportion of those expenses as is reasonably attributable to the use made of the property, services or facilities as mentioned in paragraph (b).

(10) For the purposes of this section, sections 94A and 94B, sections 94D to 94H, sections 96 to 99A and Schedule 10

    (a) a "regulated period" is (subject to subsection (11)) a period in relation to which any limit is imposed by Schedule 10;

    (b) any reference to controlled expenditure incurred by or on behalf of a recognised third party during a regulated period includes any controlled expenditure so incurred during that period at any time before the third party became a recognised third party;

    (c) a part of the United Kingdom is a "relevant part" if any limit imposed by Schedule 10 applies to controlled expenditure which is incurred in that part;

    (d) any reference to controlled expenditure being incurred in a part of the United Kingdom shall be construed in accordance with paragraph 2 of that Schedule;

    (e) the "maximum campaign expenditure limit" in a part of the United Kingdom is the limit imposed by paragraph 3 of Schedule 9 in relation to campaign expenditure incurred in the relevant period (within the meaning of that paragraph) by or on behalf of a registered party which contests all the constituencies in that part (and to which sub-paragraph (6) of that paragraph does not apply);

    (f) any reference to controlled expenditure being incurred in a parliamentary constituency shall be construed in accordance with paragraph 2A of Schedule 10.

(11) As respects a recognised Gibraltar third party, the periods in relation to which paragraphs 3 and 5 to 11 of Schedule 10 impose limits

    (a) are regulated periods for the purposes of this section and sections 94A and 94B, but

    (b) are not regulated periods for the purposes of sections 92, 93 and 96 to 99A.

NOTES

Defined terms
  controlled expenditure: s 85(2)
  election material: s 85(3), (4)
  property: s 160(1)
  recognised Gibraltar third party: s 85(5A)

  recognised third party: s 85(5)
  responsible person: s 85(7)
  third party: s 85(8), (9)

Arrangements between third parties notified to the Commission

94A (1) A recognised third party may, at any time before the end of a regulated period, send a notice to the Commission

    (a) stating that it is party to an arrangement of the kind mentioned in section 94(6),

    (b) undertaking to be a lead campaigner in relation to the arrangement, and

    (c) identifying one or more other third parties that are parties to the arrangement and have undertaken to be minor campaigners in relation to it.

(2) A recognised third party that has sent a notice under subsection (1) may, at any time before the end of the regulated period, send one or more supplementary notices to the Commission identifying additional third parties that are parties to the arrangement and have undertaken to be minor campaigners in relation to it.

(3) As from the date of receipt by the Commission of

    (a) a notice under subsection (1), the recognised third party that sent the notice becomes "a lead campaigner" in relation to the arrangement;

(b) a notice under subsection (1) or (2), a third party identified in the notice becomes "a minor campaigner" in relation to the arrangement.

(4) A notice under subsection (1) or (2) may not
  (a) identify as a minor campaigner a third party that is a lead campaigner in relation to the same arrangement, or
  (b) be sent by a recognised Gibraltar third party.

(5) The Commission must, as soon as reasonably practicable after receiving
  (a) a notice under subsection (1), enter in the register maintained under section 89 (register of notifications) the fact that the recognised third party that sent the notice is a lead campaigner in relation to the arrangement;
  (b) a notice under subsection (1) or (2), enter in that register the name of each third party identified in the notice and the fact that it is a minor campaigner in relation to the arrangement.

(6) For provision about the effect of sending a notice under this section, see section 94B.

NOTES

Defined terms
  the Commission: s 160(1)
  recognised Gibraltar third party: s 85(5A)
  recognised third party: s 85(5)

regulated period: s 94(10), (11)

Effect where arrangements are notified under section 94A

94B (1) Subsection (2) applies where controlled expenditure is incurred during a regulated period in a part of the United Kingdom
  (a) by or on behalf of a minor campaigner in relation to an arrangement, and
  (b) in pursuance of the arrangement.

(2) The expenditure is treated for the purposes of sections 96 to 99A (returns as to controlled expenditure) as having also been incurred, during the period and in the part of the United Kingdom concerned, by or on behalf of any lead campaigner in relation to the arrangement who sent a notice under section 94A(1) or (2) identifying the minor campaigner.

(3) In determining for the purposes of section 94(3)(a) whether a limit is exceeded by a third party during a regulated period, controlled expenditure incurred by or on behalf of the third party is to be disregarded if
  (a) conditions A and B are met in relation to the expenditure, and
  (b) condition C is met.

(4) Condition A is that the expenditure
  (a) is incurred in pursuance of an arrangement that has been notified to the Commission under section 94A(1), and
  (b) is, by virtue of section 94(6), treated for the purposes of section 94 and Schedule 10 as incurred by or on behalf of the third party.

(5) Condition B is that the third party is, at the time the expenditure is incurred, a minor campaigner in relation to the arrangement.

(6) Condition C is that
  (a) the total of the controlled expenditure incurred during the regulated period in any part of the United Kingdom by or on behalf of the third party, disregarding any expenditure in relation to which conditions A and B are met, does not exceed the limit for that part mentioned in section 94(5), and
  (b) in the case of a regulated period in relation to which any limit is imposed by paragraph 3, 9 10 or 11 of Schedule 10 (periods involving parliamentary general elections), the total of the controlled expenditure incurred during the regulated period in any particular constituency by or on behalf of the third party,

disregarding any expenditure in relation to which conditions A and B are met, does not exceed the limit mentioned in section 94(5ZA).

(7) References in subsection (6) to controlled expenditure incurred by or on behalf of the third party include controlled expenditure that is, by virtue of section 94(6), treated for the purposes of section 94 and Schedule 10 as so incurred.

NOTES

Defined terms
the Commission: s 160(1)
controlled expenditure: s 85(2)
regulated period: s 94(10), (11)

third party: s 85(8), (9)

Financial limits on targeted controlled expenditure

Overview of sections 94D to 94H

94C (1) Sections 94D to 94H impose limits on, and make other provision relating to, controlled expenditure incurred by or on behalf of a recognised third party where the expenditure is targeted at a particular registered party.

(2) Section 94D defines when controlled expenditure is regarded as targeted at a particular registered party, specifies the limits and specifies the periods over which the limits operate.

(3) Section 94E makes provision about the consequences where controlled expenditure targeted at a registered party is incurred by or on behalf of a recognised third party in excess of a limit without authorisation from the registered party.

(4) Section 94F makes provision about the consequences where controlled expenditure targeted at a registered party is incurred by or on behalf of a recognised third party in excess of a limit with authorisation from the registered party.

(5) Section 94G makes provision about how a registered party may give or withdraw authorisation (including provision enabling the registered party to specify a cap on the amount of expenditure authorised).

(6) Section 94H makes provision about the meaning of references to expenditure that "exceeds" a targeted expenditure limit or cap.

NOTES

Defined terms
controlled expenditure: s 85(2)
recognised third party: s 85(5)

registered party: s 160(1)

Meaning of "targeted", "targeted expenditure limit" etc

94D (1) Controlled expenditure is "targeted" at a particular registered party if it can reasonably be regarded as
    (a) intended to benefit that party or any of its candidates, and
    (b) not intended to benefit any other registered party or any of its candidates.

(2) A limit (a "targeted expenditure limit") applies to controlled expenditure that
    (a) is incurred during a qualifying regulated period in England, Scotland, Wales or Northern Ireland, and
    (b) is targeted at a particular registered party.

(3) A "qualifying regulated period" is a period in relation to which limits are imposed by paragraph 3, 9, 10 or 11 of Schedule 10 (periods involving parliamentary general elections).

(4) The targeted expenditure limit applying to controlled expenditure incurred during a qualifying regulated period in a part of the United Kingdom is

(a) for the period in relation to which limits are imposed by paragraph 3(2) of Schedule 10, 0.2% of the maximum campaign expenditure limit in that part of the United Kingdom, and

(b) for any other qualifying regulated period, the relevant proportion of the limit determined in accordance with paragraph (a).

(5) In subsection (4)(b) "the relevant proportion" means

A / B

where

A is the number of days in the period mentioned in subsection (4)(b);

B is the number of days in the period mentioned in subsection (4)(a).

(6) This section applies for the purposes of sections 94E to 94H.

NOTES

Defined terms   registered party: s 160(1)

   controlled expenditure: s 85(2)

   maximum campaign expenditure limit: s 94(10)

Unauthorised expenditure in excess of targeted expenditure limit

94E (1) This section applies if

(a) controlled expenditure which is targeted at a particular registered party ("the registered party") is incurred by or on behalf of a recognised third party ("the third party"),

(b) the expenditure exceeds a targeted expenditure limit (to any extent), and

(c) at the time the expenditure is incurred

    (i) the third party is not authorised by the registered party to incur expenditure targeted at it, or

    (ii) the third party is so authorised, but the expenditure exceeds a cap specified in the authorisation (to any extent).

(2) If the third party is not an individual

(a) the responsible person is guilty of an offence if the person authorised the expenditure to be incurred by or on behalf of the third party and the person knew or ought reasonably to have known that the expenditure would be incurred in excess of the targeted expenditure limit, and

(b) the third party is also guilty of an offence.

(3) If the third party is an individual, the third party is guilty of an offence if the third party knew or ought reasonably to have known that the expenditure would be incurred in excess of the targeted expenditure limit.

(4) It is a defence for a third party charged with an offence under subsection (2) or (3) to show

(a) that any code of practice for the time being issued under paragraph 3 of Schedule 8A was complied with in determining whether any expenditure is controlled expenditure for the purposes of this Part, and

(b) that the offence would not have been committed on the basis of the controlled expenditure as determined in accordance with the code.

NOTES

Defined terms   targeted expenditure limit: s 94D(2)

   controlled expenditure: s 85(2)   third party: s 85(8), (9)

   exceeds (a targeted expenditure limit or cap): s 94H

   recognised third party: s 85(5)

   registered party: s 160(1)

Authorised expenditure in excess of targeted expenditure limit

94F (1)   This section applies if

(a) controlled expenditure which is targeted at a particular registered party ("the registered party") is incurred by or on behalf of a recognised third party ("the third party"),

(b) the expenditure exceeds a targeted expenditure limit (to any extent),

(c) at the time the expenditure is incurred the third party is authorised by the registered party to incur expenditure targeted at it, and

(d) if the registered party specified a cap in the authorisation, the expenditure, or any part of it, does not exceed the cap.

(2) The authorised amount is treated for the purposes of section 79(2) (limits on campaign expenditure) as if

   (a) it were campaign expenditure within the meaning of Part 5, and

   (b) it was incurred by the registered party at the same time as the controlled expenditure mentioned in subsection (1)(a) was in fact incurred by or on behalf of the third party.

(3) For the purposes of this section, "the authorised amount" is the amount of the controlled expenditure incurred as mentioned in subsection (1)(a) less

   (a) such amount, if any, of that expenditure as does not exceed the targeted expenditure limit, and

   (b) such amount, if any, of that expenditure as exceeds a cap specified by the registered party in its authorisation of the third party.

(4) In determining whether, by virtue of subsection (2), the incurring of controlled expenditure by or on behalf of the third party constitutes an offence under section 79(2) by the treasurer or any deputy treasurer of the registered party, section 79(2)(a)(i) is treated as if the reference in that provision to the authorisation of the expenditure were to the signing of the authorisation under section 94G.

(5) The treasurer or a deputy treasurer of the registered party must make a declaration of

   (a) the amount of the controlled expenditure incurred as mentioned in subsection (1)(a), and

   (b) the authorised amount.

(6) A person commits an offence if the person knowingly or recklessly makes a false declaration under subsection (5).

NOTES

Defined terms
controlled expenditure: s 85(2)
exceeds (a targeted expenditure limit or cap): s 94H
recognised third party: s 85(5)
registered party: s 160(1)

targeted expenditure limit: s 94D(2)
treasurer: s 160(1)

Authorisation

94G (1) A registered party may authorise a recognised third party to incur controlled expenditure in England, Scotland, Wales or Northern Ireland that is targeted at the registered party.

(2) An authorisation

   (a) must be in writing,

   (b) must be signed by a relevant officer,

   (c) must specify the part of the United Kingdom to which it relates, and

   (d) may specify a cap on the amount of expenditure authorised.

(3) An authorisation is of no effect until a copy of it has been given to the Commission by the registered party.

(4)   The Commission must, as soon as is reasonably practicable after receiving a copy of an authorisation, enter in the register maintained under section 89 (register of notifications)

    (a)   the fact that the registered party has given the authorisation, and

    (b)   the information specified in it.

(5)   A registered party may at any time withdraw an authorisation already given.

(6)   A withdrawal of an authorisation

    (a)   must be in writing, and

    (b)   must be signed by a relevant officer.

(7)   A withdrawal of an authorisation is of no effect until a copy of it has been given to the Commission by the registered party.

(8)   The Commission must, as soon as is reasonably practicable after receiving a copy of a withdrawal of an authorisation, update the register maintained under section 89.

(9)   For the purposes of this section "relevant officer", in relation to a registered party, means

    (a)   the treasurer of the party, or

    (b)   a deputy treasurer of the party.

NOTES

Defined terms
  the Commission: s 160(1)
  recognised third party: s 85(5)
  registered party: s 160(1)

treasurer: s 160(1)

Expenditure that "exceeds" a targeted expenditure limit or cap

94H (1)   Controlled expenditure incurred by or on behalf of a recognised third party during a qualifying regulated period in any part of the United Kingdom that is targeted at a particular registered party "exceeds"

    (a)   a targeted expenditure limit, or

    (b)   a cap specified by the registered party in its authorisation of the third party,

if and to the extent that the relevant cumulative total is in excess of that limit or cap.

(2)   For this purpose "the relevant cumulative total" is the total of

    (a)   the controlled expenditure incurred as mentioned in subsection (1), and

    (b)   the total of any controlled expenditure targeted at the same registered party which has already been incurred by or on behalf of the third party during the qualifying regulated period in that part of the United Kingdom.

NOTES

Defined terms
  controlled expenditure: s 85(2)
  controlled expenditure being incurred in a part of the
  United Kingdom: s 94(10)
  recognised third party: s 85(5)

registered party: s 160(1)
targeted expenditure limit: s 94D(2)

Donations to recognised third parties

Control of donations to recognised third parties

95   Schedule 11 has effect for controlling donations to recognised third parties which either are not registered parties or are minor parties.

NOTES

Defined terms
  minor party: s 160(1)

recognised third party: s 85(5)
registered party: s 160(1)

Quarterly and weekly reports of donations to recognised third parties

Quarterly donation reports

95A (1) The responsible person in relation to a recognised third party must, in respect of each reporting period that falls within a pre-dissolution period, prepare a report about reportable donations ("a quarterly report").

  (2) The reporting periods are

   (a) the period of 3 months beginning with the first day of the pre-dissolution period,

   (b) each succeeding period of 3 months falling within the pre-dissolution period, and

   (c) any final period of less than 3 months falling within that period.

  (3) A "pre-dissolution period" means a period

   (a) beginning with the first day of a qualifying regulated period, and

   (b) ending with the day before the day (or the last day) during that qualifying regulated period on which Parliament is dissolved.

  (4) A "qualifying regulated period" is a period in relation to which any limit is imposed by paragraph 3, 9, 10 or 11 of Schedule 10 (periods involving parliamentary general elections) other than a period including the date of the poll for an early parliamentary general election.

  (5) An "early parliamentary general election" is a parliamentary general election the date of the poll for which is appointed under section 2(7) of the Fixed-term Parliaments Act 2011.

  (6) A quarterly report must comply with the requirements of Schedule 11A.

  (7) A "reportable donation" means a relevant donation (within the meaning of Schedule 11) which

   (a) is received by the recognised third party in respect of the relevant election or elections the poll or polls for which take place during the qualifying regulated period, and

   (b) is accepted, or is dealt with in accordance with section 56(2) (as applied by paragraph 7 of Schedule 11), by the recognised third party during the reporting period.

  (8) A quarterly report must be delivered to the Commission by the responsible person within the period of 30 days beginning with the end of the reporting period to which it relates.

  (9) The report must be accompanied by a declaration signed by the responsible person stating that, to the best of that person's knowledge and belief

   (a) all reportable donations (if any) recorded in the report as having been accepted by the recognised third party are from permissible donors, and

   (b) there are no reportable donations which are required to be recorded in the report in accordance with Schedule 11A which are not so recorded.

  (10) This section does not require the preparation of a quarterly report in respect of a reporting period if no reportable donations are accepted, or dealt with, as described in subsection (7)(b), by the recognised third party during that period.

  (11) This section does not apply in relation to

   (a) a recognised third party which is a registered party other than a minor party, or

   (b) a recognised Gibraltar third party.

NOTES

Defined terms
  the Commission: s 160(1)
  recognised Gibraltar third party: s 85(5A)
  recognised third party: s 85(5)

registered party: s 160(1)
responsible person: s 85(7)

Weekly donation reports during general election periods

95B (1) The responsible person in relation to a recognised third party must, in respect of each reporting period that falls within a general election period, prepare a report about substantial donations ("a weekly report").

(2) The reporting periods are
    (a) the period of 7 days beginning with the first day of the general election period,
    (b) each succeeding period of 7 days falling within the general election period, and
    (c) any final period of less than 7 days falling within that period.

(3) A "general election period" means the period
    (a) beginning with the day on which Parliament is dissolved for a parliamentary general election, and
    (b) ending with the date during a qualifying regulated period which is the date of the poll for that election.

(4) A weekly report must comply with the requirements of Schedule 11A.

(5) A "substantial donation" means a relevant donation of a substantial value which is received by the recognised third party during the reporting period in respect of the relevant election or elections the poll or polls for which take place during the qualifying regulated period.

(6) A relevant donation is "of a substantial value" if its value (as determined in accordance with paragraph 5 of Schedule 11) is more than £7,500.

(7) A weekly report must be delivered to the Commission by the responsible person within the period of 7 days beginning with the end of the reporting period to which it relates.

(8) The report must be accompanied by a declaration signed by the responsible person stating that, to the best of that person's knowledge and belief, no substantial donations have been received by the recognised third party during the reporting period which are required to be recorded in the report in accordance with Schedule 11A and are not so recorded.

(9) This section does not require the preparation of a weekly report in respect of a reporting period if no substantial donations are received by the recognised third party during that period.

(10) In this section
    "qualifying regulated period" means a period in relation to which any limit is imposed by paragraph 3, 9, 10 or 11 of Schedule 10 (periods involving parliamentary general elections);
    "relevant donation" has the same meaning as in Schedule 11.

(11) This section does not apply in relation to
    (a) a recognised third party which is a registered party other than a minor party, or
    (b) a recognised Gibraltar third party.

NOTES

Defined terms
  the Commission: s 160(1)
  minor party: s 160(1)
  recognised Gibraltar third party: s 85(5A)
  recognised third party: s 85(5)

registered party: s 160(1)
responsible person: s 85(7)

Related offences

95C (1)   The responsible person in relation to a recognised third party commits an offence if, without reasonable excuse, the responsible person

(a)   fails to deliver a quarterly or weekly report in accordance with section 95A(8) or 95B(7),

(b)   delivers a quarterly or weekly report to the Commission without the accompanying declaration required under section 95A(9) or 95B(8), or

(c)   delivers a quarterly or weekly report to the Commission which does not comply with the requirements of Schedule 11A.

(2)   The responsible person in relation to a recognised third party commits an offence if the person knowingly or recklessly makes a false declaration under section 95A(9) or 95B(8).

NOTES

Defined terms

the Commission: s 160(1)

recognised third party: s 85(5)

responsible person: s 85(7)

Forfeiture

95D (1)   The court may, on an application made by the Commission, order the forfeiture by a recognised third party of an amount equal to the value of a relevant donation where the court is satisfied that

(a)   a failure by the responsible person to deliver a quarterly or weekly report in accordance with section 95A(8) or 95B(7), or

(b)   the delivery by the responsible person of a quarterly or weekly report which fails to comply with a requirement of Schedule 11A,

was attributable to an intention on the part of any person to conceal the existence or true amount of the donation.

(2)   The standard of proof in proceedings on an application under this section is that applicable to civil proceedings.

(3)   A forfeiture order may be made under this section whether or not proceedings are brought against any person for an offence connected with the donation.

(4)   In this section "the court" means

(a)   in relation to England and Wales, a magistrates' court;

(b)   in relation to Scotland, the sheriff;

(c)   in relation to Northern Ireland, a court of summary jurisdiction.

(5)   Proceedings on an application under this section to the sheriff are civil proceedings.

(6)   Sections 59 and 60 (appeals etc against forfeiture orders) apply for the purposes, or in connection with the operation, of this section in relation to a recognised third party as they apply for the purposes, or in connection with the operation, of section 58 in relation to a registered party.

(7)   In this section "relevant donation" has the same meaning as in Schedule 11.

NOTES

Defined terms

the Commission: s 160(1)

recognised third party: s 85(5)

registered party: s 160(1)

responsible person: s 85(7)

Sections 95A to 95D: supplementary

95E (1)   This section applies where the requirements in section 95A or 95B to prepare quarterly or weekly reports in the case of a pre-dissolution period or a general election period have effect in relation to a recognised third party.

   (2)   If the third party's notification under section 88(1) lapses during the pre-dissolution period or the general election period, the requirements in section 95A or 95B (as the case may be) continue to have effect in relation to the third party

   (a)   in respect of the reporting period in which the notification lapses, and

   (b)   in respect of each reporting period (if any) which preceded that period and which falls within the pre-dissolution period or the general election period.

   (3)   If the third party's notification under section 88(1) lapses at or after the end of the pre-dissolution period or the general election period, the requirements in section 95A or 95B (as the case may be) continue to have effect in relation to the third party in the case of that period.

   (4)   In a case where subsection (2) or (3) applies, references in sections 95A to 95D to the responsible person are to be read, for the purposes of, or in connection with, the discharge of obligations of the responsible person under those sections, as references to the person who was the responsible person in relation to the recognised third party immediately before the notification lapsed.

   (5)   In this section

   (a)   "pre-dissolution period" and "reporting period", in relation to a quarterly report, have the same meaning as in section 95A, and

   (b)   "general election period" and "reporting period", in relation to a weekly report, have the same meaning as in section 95B.

NOTES

Defined terms
   recognised third party: s 85(5)
   responsible person: s 85(7)

Public inspection of reports

95F (1)   Where the Commission receive a quarterly or weekly report under section 95A or 95B, they must

   (a)   as soon as reasonably practicable after receiving the report, make a copy of the report, and of any documents accompanying it, available for public inspection, and

   (b)   keep any such copy available for public inspection for the period for which the report or other document is kept by them.

   (2)   The Commission must secure that the copy of the report made available for public inspection does not include, in the case of any donation by an individual, the donor's address.

   (3)   At the end of the period of 2 years beginning with the date when any report or other document mentioned in subsection (1) is received by the Commission

   (a)   they may cause the report or other document to be destroyed, but

   (b)   if requested to do so by the responsible person in relation to the third party concerned, they must arrange for the report or other document to be returned to that person.

NOTES

Defined terms
   the Commission: s 160(1)
   responsible person: s 85(7)

third party: s 85(8), (9)

Returns

Returns as to controlled expenditure

96 (1) Subsection (1A) applies where

    (a) during a regulated period, any controlled expenditure is incurred by or on behalf of a recognised third party in a relevant part of the United Kingdom, and

    (b) the incurring of that expenditure would, if the third party had not been recognised, have been an offence under section 94(4) (whether because it was incurred in excess of a limit mentioned in section 94(5) or 94(5ZA)).

(1A) The responsible person must prepare a return in respect of the controlled expenditure incurred by or on behalf of the third party during that period in each relevant part of the United Kingdom.

(2) A return under this section must specify the poll for the relevant election (or, as the case may be, the polls for the relevant elections) that took place during the regulated period in question, and must contain

    (a) a statement of all payments made in respect of controlled expenditure incurred by or on behalf of the third party during that period in the relevant part or parts of the United Kingdom;

    (aa) a statement listing each constituency (if any) in which the controlled expenditure incurred by or on behalf of the third party during that period exceeded 0.04% of the total of the maximum campaign expenditure limits in England, Scotland, Wales and Northern Ireland;

    (ab) a statement showing, for each constituency listed under paragraph (aa), all payments made in respect of controlled expenditure incurred by or on behalf of the third party during that period in that constituency;

    (b) a statement of all disputed claims (within the meaning of section 93) of which the responsible person is aware;

    (c) a statement of all the unpaid claims (if any) of which the responsible person is aware in respect of which an application has been made, or is about to be made, to a court under section 92(4); and

    (d) in a case where the third party either is not a registered party or is a minor party, a statement of relevant donations received by the third party in respect of the relevant election or elections which complies with the requirements of paragraphs 10 and 11 of Schedule 11.

(3) A return under this section must be accompanied by

    (a) all invoices or receipts relating to the payments mentioned in subsection (2)(a) or (ab); and

    (b) in the case of any controlled expenditure treated as incurred by the third party by virtue of section 86, any declaration falling to be made with respect to that expenditure in accordance with section 86(6).

(4) Where, however, any payments or claims falling to be dealt with in a return by virtue of subsection (2) have already been dealt with in an earlier return under this section

    (a) it shall be sufficient for the later return to deal with those payments or claims by specifying overall amounts in respect of them; and

    (b) the requirement imposed by subsection (3) does not apply to any invoices, receipts or declarations which accompanied the earlier return and are specified as such in the later return.

(5) Subsections (2) to (4) do not apply to any controlled expenditure incurred at any time before the third party became a recognised third party, but the return must be accompanied by a declaration made by the responsible person of the total amount of such expenditure incurred at any such time.

(6) The Commission may by regulations prescribe a form of return which may be used for the purposes of this section.

(7) Where subsection (1A) applies in relation to a recognised third party and any regulated period

    (a) the requirements as to the preparation of a return under this section in respect of controlled expenditure shall have effect in relation to the third party despite the third party ceasing to be a recognised third party at or after the end of the regulated period by virtue of the lapse of the third party's notification under section 88(1); and

    (b) for the purposes of, or in connection with, the discharge of obligations of the responsible person under this section and sections 98 and 99 in relation to any such return, references to the responsible person shall be read as references to the person who was the responsible person in relation to the third party immediately before that notification lapsed.

(8) In this section "relevant donation" has the same meaning as in Schedule 11.

NOTES

Defined terms

the Commission: s 160(1)	registered party: s 160(1)
controlled expenditure: s 85(2)	regulated period: s 94(10), (11)
controlled expenditure being incurred in a part of the United Kingdom: s 94(10)	relevant election: s 85(6)
	relevant part of the United Kingdom: s 94(10)
controlled expenditure incurred by or on behalf of a recognised third party during a regulated period: s 94(10)	responsible person: s 85(7)
	third party: s 85(8), (9)
minor party: s 160(1)	
recognised third party: s 85(5)	

Statement of accounts

96A (1) Where

    (a) a return falls to be prepared under section 96 in respect of controlled expenditure incurred by or on behalf of a recognised third party during a regulated period, and

    (b) the period is one in relation to which any limit is imposed by paragraph 3, 9, 10 or 11 of Schedule 10 (periods involving parliamentary general elections),

the responsible person must, subject to subsections (8) and (9), also prepare a statement of accounts in respect of the regulated period.

(2) A statement of accounts under this section must include

    (a) a statement of the income and expenditure of the third party for the regulated period, and

    (b) a statement of its assets and liabilities at the end of that period.

(3) A statement of accounts under this section must comply with such requirements as to the form and contents of the statement as may be prescribed by regulations made by the Commission.

(4) Regulations under subsection (3) may in particular

    (a) require any statement of accounts to be prepared in accordance with such methods and principles as are specified or referred to in the regulations;

    (b) specify information which is to be provided by way of notes to the accounts.

(5) Without prejudice to the generality of paragraph 22(7) of Schedule 1 (power to make different provision for different cases), regulations under subsection (3) may impose different requirements according to which of the following bands the gross income or total expenditure of a third party falls within

    (a) not exceeding £25,000;

    (b) exceeding £25,000 but not £100,000;

    (c) exceeding £100,000 but not £250,000;

    (d) exceeding £250,000.

(6)   The Secretary of State may by order amend subsection (5) by varying the number of bands set out in it.

(7)   The Secretary of State may not make an order under subsection (6) except to give effect to a recommendation of the Commission.

(8)   This section does not apply if the third party is an individual.

(9)   This section does not apply to a third party in relation to a regulated period if the Commission are satisfied

    (a)   that a statement or statements prepared or to be prepared by the third party under any enactment contains or will contain the information required by subsection (2) or equivalent information, and

    (b)   that the Commission are, or will be, able to inspect that statement or those statements.

(10)   Equivalent information is

    (a)   a statement or statements of the income and expenditure for a period or periods other than the regulated period, or

    (b)   a statement or statements of assets and liabilities at a date or dates other than the end of that period,

but which in the Commission's opinion gives a sufficient indication of the third party's accounts for, or at the end of, the regulated period.

(11)   Where section 96(7) (lapse of notification) applies to the preparation of a return

    (a)   the reference to the responsible person in subsection (1) of this section is to be read as a reference to the person described in section 96(7)(b), and

    (b)   for the purposes of, or in connection with, the discharge of obligations of the responsible person under sections 98 and 99A in relation to a statement of accounts under this section, references to the responsible person are to be read as references to that person.

(12)   In this section and section 97 "gross income" means gross recorded income from all sources.

NOTES

Defined terms
    the Commission: s 160(1)
    controlled expenditure: s 85(2)
    recognised third party: s 85(5)
    regulated period: s 94(10), (11)

    responsible person: s 85(7)
    the Secretary of State: s 159A
    third party: s 85(8), (9)

Auditor's report on return or statement of accounts

97 (1)   Where during any regulated period the controlled expenditure incurred by or on behalf of a recognised third party in the relevant part or parts of the United Kingdom exceeds £250,000, a report must be prepared by a qualified auditor on the return prepared under section 96 in respect of that expenditure.

(1A)   A report must be prepared by a qualified auditor on any statement of accounts prepared under section 96A in respect of a regulated period, if

    (a)   a report falls to be prepared under subsection (1) on the return mentioned in section 96A(1)(a), or

    (b)   during the regulated period the gross income or total expenditure of the third party exceeds £250,000.

(2)   The following provisions, namely

    (a)   section 43(6) and (7), and

    (b)   section 44,

shall apply in relation to the appointment of an auditor to prepare a report under subsection (1) or (1A) or (as the case may be) an auditor so appointed as they apply in relation to the appointment of an auditor to carry out an audit under section 43 or (as the case may be) an auditor so appointed.

NOTES

Defined terms
controlled expenditure: s 85(2)
controlled expenditure being incurred in a part of the United Kingdom: s 94(10)
controlled expenditure incurred by or on behalf of a recognised third party during a regulated period: s 94(10)

qualified auditor: s 160(1), (2)
recognised third party: s 85(5)
regulated period: s 94(10), (11)
relevant part of the United Kingdom: s 94(10)

Delivery of returns to the Commission

98 (1)   Where

(a) any return falls to be prepared under section 96 in respect of controlled expenditure incurred by or on behalf of a recognised third party during a regulated period, and

(b) an auditor's report on it falls to be prepared under section 97(1),

the responsible person shall deliver the return to the Commission, together with a copy of the auditor's report, within six months of the end of that period.

(2)   In the case of any other return falling to be prepared under section 96 in respect of controlled expenditure incurred by or on behalf of a recognised third party during a regulated period, the responsible person shall deliver the return to the Commission within three months of the end of that period.

(2A)   Where a statement of accounts falls to be prepared under section 96A, the responsible person must deliver

(a) the statement, and

(b) if an auditor's report on the statement falls to be prepared under section 97(1A), that report,

to the Commission before the end of the period of 6 months beginning with the end of the period under subsection (1) or (2) for the delivery of the relevant section 96 return.

(2B)   "The relevant section 96 return" means the return mentioned in section 96A(1)(a) which gives rise to the duty to prepare the statement of accounts.

(3)   Where, after the date on which a return is delivered to the Commission under this section, leave is given by a court under section 92(4) for any claim to be paid, the responsible person shall, within seven days after the payment, deliver to the Commission a return of any sums paid in pursuance of the leave accompanied by a copy of the order of the court giving the leave.

(4)   The responsible person in the case of a recognised third party commits an offence if, without reasonable excuse, he

(a) fails to comply with the requirements of subsection (1) or (2) in relation to any return or report to which that subsection applies; or

(aa) fails to comply with the requirements of subsection (2A) in relation to any statement or report to which that subsection applies; or

(b) delivers a return which does not comply with the requirements of section 96(2) or (3); or

(ba) delivers a statement which does not comply with the requirements of section 96A(2) or (3); or

(c) fails to comply with the requirements of subsection (3) in relation to a return under that subsection.

NOTES

Defined terms
the Commission: s 160(1)
controlled expenditure: s 85(2)
controlled expenditure incurred by or on behalf of a
recognised third party during a regulated period: s 94(10)

recognised third party: s 85(5)
regulated period: s 94(10), (11)
responsible person: s 85(7)

Declaration by responsible person as to return under section 96

99 (1) Each return prepared under section 96 in respect of controlled expenditure incurred by or on behalf of a recognised third party during a regulated period must, when delivered to the Commission, be accompanied by a declaration which complies with subsections (2) and (3) and is signed by the responsible person.

(2) The declaration must state
    (a) that the responsible person has examined the return in question;
    (b) that to the best of his knowledge and belief
        (i) it is a complete and correct return as required by law, and
        (ii) all expenses shown in it as paid have been paid by him or a person authorised by him.

(2A) Subsection (2)(b)(ii) does not apply to expenses that are treated as incurred by or on behalf of the recognised third party by virtue of section 94B(2) (arrangements between third parties notified to the Commission).

(3) The declaration must also state, in a case where the third party either is not a registered party or is a minor party, that
    (a) all relevant donations recorded in the return as having been accepted by the third party are from permissible donors, and
    (b) no other relevant donations have been accepted by the third party in respect of the relevant election or elections which took place during the regulated period.

(4) A person commits an offence if
    (a) he knowingly or recklessly makes a false declaration under this section; or
    (b) subsection (1) is contravened at a time when he is the responsible person in the case of the recognised third party to which the return relates.

(5) In this section "relevant donation" has the same meaning as in Schedule 11.

NOTES
Defined terms
the Commission: s 160(1)
contravention: s 160(1)
controlled expenditure: s 85(2)
controlled expenditure incurred by or on behalf of a
recognised third party during a regulated period: s 94(10)
minor party: s 160(1)
recognised third party: s 85(5)

registered party: s 160(1)
regulated period: s 94(10), (11)
relevant election: s 85(6)
responsible person: s 85(7)
third party: s 85(8), (9)

Declaration by responsible person as to statement of accounts under section 96A

99A (1) Each statement of accounts prepared under section 96A must, when delivered to the Commission, be accompanied by a declaration which complies with subsection (2) and is signed by the responsible person.

(2) The declaration must state
    (a) that the responsible person has examined the statement in question; and
    (b) that to the best of that person's knowledge and belief it is a complete and correct statement of accounts as required by law.

(3) A person commits an offence if
    (a) that person knowingly or recklessly makes a false declaration under this section; or

(b) subsection (1) is contravened without reasonable excuse at a time when that person is the responsible person in the case of the recognised third party to which the statement of accounts relates.

NOTES

Defined terms
the Commission: s 160(1)
recognised third party: s 85(5)

responsible person: s 85(7)

Public inspection of returns under section 96

100 (1)   Where the Commission receive any return under section 96, they shall
(a)   as soon as reasonably practicable after receiving the return, make a copy of the return, and of any documents accompanying it, available for public inspection; and
(b)   keep any such copy available for public inspection for the period for which the return or other document is kept by them.

(2)   If the return contains a statement of relevant donations in accordance with section 96(2)(d), the Commission shall secure that the copy of the statement made available for public inspection does not include, in the case of any donation by an individual, the donor's address.

(3)   At the end of the period of two years beginning with the date when any return or other document mentioned in subsection (1) is received by the Commission
(a)   they may cause the return or other document to be destroyed; but
(b)   if requested to do so by the responsible person in the case of the third party concerned, they shall arrange for the return or other document to be returned to that person.

(4)   Where a statement of accounts is delivered under section 98(2A), this section applies as if the statement and any documents accompanying it
(a)   were documents accompanying the relevant section 96 return, and
(b)   (for the purposes of subsection (3)) were received by the Commission when the return was received.

(5)   In subsection (4)(a), "the relevant section 96 return" has the meaning given by section 98(2B).

NOTES

Defined terms
the Commission: s 160(1)
document: s 160(1)
responsible person: s 85(7)

third party: s 85(8), (9)

PART VII
REFERENDUMS

Chapter I
Preliminary

Referendums to which this Part applies

Referendums to which this Part applies

101 (1)   Subject to the following provisions of this section, this Part applies to any referendum held throughout

(a)   the United Kingdom;

(b)   one or more of England, Scotland, Wales and Northern Ireland; or

(c)   any region in England specified in Schedule 1 to the Regional Development Agencies Act 1998.

(2)   In this Part

(a)   "referendum" means a referendum or other poll held, in pursuance of any provision made by or under an Act of Parliament, on one or more questions specified in or in accordance with any such provision;

(b)   "question" includes proposition (and "answer" accordingly includes response).

(3)   A poll held under section 64 of the Government of Wales Act 2006 is not, however, to be taken to be a referendum falling within subsection (2).

(4)   If the Secretary of State by order so provides

(a)   subsection (2) shall apply to any specified Bill which has been introduced into Parliament before the making of the order as if it were an Act; and

(b)   any specified provisions of this Part shall apply, subject to any specified modifications, in relation to any specified referendum for which provision is made by the Bill.

(5)   In subsection (4) "specified" means specified in the order under that subsection.

NOTES
Defined terms
modifications: s 160(1)
the Secretary of State: s 159A

Referendum period

102 (1)   For the purposes of this Part the referendum period for any referendum to which this Part applies shall be determined in accordance with this section.

(2)   In the case of a referendum held in accordance with Schedule 1 to the Northern Ireland Act 1998, the referendum period

(a)   begins with the date when the draft of an order under that Schedule is laid before Parliament for approval by each House in accordance with section 96(2) of that Act; and

(b)   ends with the date of the poll.

(3)   In the case of a referendum held in pursuance of any provision made by or under any other Act, the referendum period shall (subject to subsections (4) and (5)) be such period as is provided for by or under that Act.

(4)   In the case of a referendum to which an order under section 101(4) applies, the referendum period shall be such period (not exceeding six months) as may be specified in the order.

(5)   If (apart from this subsection) the referendum period in a case within subsection (4) would end after the date of the poll, it shall instead end on that date.

NOTES
Defined terms
referendum: s 101(2)-(5)

Date of poll

103 (1)   Where the date of the poll in the case of any referendum to which this Part applies falls to be fixed under any provision made by or under any Act, the date so fixed shall not be earlier than 28 days after the end of the period of 14 days mentioned in section 109(3).

(2) If an order under section 109(6) applies to the referendum, subsection (1) shall be read as referring to the period which by virtue of the order is to apply instead of that period of 14 days.

NOTES
Defined terms
    referendum: s 101(2)-(5)

Referendum questions

104 (1) Subsection (2) applies where a Bill is introduced into Parliament which
    (a) provides for the holding of a poll that would be a referendum to which this Part applies, and
    (b) specifies the wording of the referendum question.

(2) The Commission shall consider the wording of the referendum question, and shall publish a statement of any views of the Commission as to the intelligibility of that question
    (a) as soon as reasonably practicable after the Bill is introduced, and
    (b) in such manner as they may determine.

(3) Subsections (4) and (5) apply where the wording of the referendum question in the case of any poll that would be a referendum to which this Part applies falls to be specified in subordinate legislation within the meaning of the Interpretation Act 1978.

(4) If a draft of the instrument in question is to be laid before Parliament for approval by each House, the Secretary of State
    (a) shall consult the Commission on the wording of the referendum question before any such draft is so laid, and
    (b) shall, at the time when any such draft is so laid, lay before each House a report stating any views as to the intelligibility of that question which the Commission have expressed in response to that consultation.

(5) If the instrument in question is to be subject to annulment in pursuance of a resolution of either House of Parliament, the Secretary of State
    (a) shall consult the Commission on the wording of the referendum question before making the instrument; and
    (b) shall, at the time when the instrument is laid before Parliament, lay before each House a report stating any views as to the intelligibility of that question which the Commission have expressed in response to that consultation.

(6) Where any Bill, draft instrument or instrument to which subsection (2), (4) or (5) applies specifies not only the referendum question but also any statement which is to precede that question on the ballot paper at the referendum, any reference in that subsection to the referendum question shall be read as a reference to that question and that statement taken together.

(7) In this section "the referendum question" means the question or questions to be included in the ballot paper at the referendum.

NOTES
Defined terms   the Secretary of State: s 159A
    the Commission: s 160(1)
    question: s 101(2)(b)
    referendum: s 101(2)-(5)

Permitted participants

105 (1) In this Part "permitted participant", in relation to a particular referendum to which this Part applies, means

(a)   a registered party by whom a declaration has been made under section 106 in relation to the referendum; or

(b)   any of the following by whom a notification has been given under section 106 in relation to the referendum, namely

(i)   any individual resident in the United Kingdom or registered in an electoral register (as defined by section 54(8)), or

(ii)   any body falling within any of paragraphs (b) and (d) to (h) of section 54(2).

(2)   In this Part "responsible person" means

(a)   if the permitted participant is a registered party

(i)   the treasurer of the party, or

(ii)   in the case of a minor party, the person for the time being notified to the Commission by the party in accordance with section 106(2)(b);

(b)   if the permitted participant is an individual, that individual; and

(c)   otherwise, the person or officer for the time being notified to the Commission by the permitted participant in accordance with section 106(4)(b)(ii).

NOTES

Defined terms

body: s 160(1)
the Commission: s 160(1)
minor party: s 160(1)
referendum: s 101(2)-(5)

registered party: s 160(1)
treasurer: s 160(1)

Declarations and notifications for purposes of section 105

106 (1)   For the purposes of section 105(1) a registered party makes a declaration to the Commission under this section if the party makes a declaration to the Commission which identifies

(a)   the referendum to which it relates, and

(b)   the outcome or outcomes for which the party proposes to campaign.

(2)   A declaration under this section

(a)   must be signed by the responsible officers of the party (within the meaning of section 64); and

(b)   if made by a minor party, must be accompanied by a notification which states the name of the person who will be responsible for compliance on the part of the party with the provisions of Chapter II.

(3)   For the purposes of section 105(1) an individual or body gives a notification to the Commission under this section if he or it gives the Commission a notification which identifies

(a)   the referendum to which it relates, and

(b)   the outcome or outcomes for which the giver of the notification proposes to campaign.

(4)   A notification under this section must

(a)   if given by an individual, state

(i)   his full name, and

(ii)   his home address in the United Kingdom, or (if he has no such address in the United Kingdom) his home address elsewhere,

and be signed by him;

(b)   if given by a body falling within any of paragraphs (b) and (d) to (h) of section 54(2), state

(i)   all such details in respect of the body as are required by virtue of any of sub-paragraphs (4) and (6) to (10) of paragraph 2 of Schedule 6 to be given in respect of such a body as the donor of a recordable donation, and

(ii) the name of the person or officer who will be responsible for compliance on the part of the body with the provisions of Chapter II,

and be signed by the body's secretary or a person who acts in a similar capacity in relation to the body.

(5) If at any time before the end of the compliance period any of the statements which, in accordance with any provision of subsection (4), are contained in a notification under this section (as it has effect for the time being) ceases to be accurate, the permitted participant by whom the notification was given shall give the Commission a notification ("a notification of alteration") indicating that that statement is replaced by some other statement

(a) contained in the notification of alteration, and

(b) conforming with that provision of subsection (4).

(6) For the purposes of subsection (5)

(a) "the compliance period" is the period during which any provisions of Chapter II remain to be complied with on the part of the permitted participant; and

(b) any reference to subsection (4) shall be read, in relation to a notification under subsection (2), as a reference to subsection (2).

(7) In this section and sections 108 and 109 "outcome", in the case of a referendum, means a particular outcome in relation to any question asked in the referendum.

NOTES

Defined terms

body: s 160(1)
the Commission: s 160(1)
minor party: s 160(1)
permitted participant: s 105(1)
question: s 101(2)(b)

recordable donation: Sch 6, para 1
referendum: s 101(2)-(5)
registered party: s 160(1)

Register of declarations and notifications for purposes of section 105

107 (1) The Commission shall maintain a register of

(a) all declarations made to them under section 106; and

(b) all notifications given to them under that section.

(2) The register shall be maintained by the Commission in such form as they may determine and shall contain, in the case of each such declaration or notification, all of the information supplied to the Commission in connection with it in pursuance of section 106.

(3) Where any declaration or notification is made or given to the Commission under section 106, they shall cause

(a) the information mentioned in subsection (2) to be entered in the register, or

(b) in the case of a notification under section 106(5), any change required as a consequence of the notification to be made in the register,

as soon as is reasonably practicable.

(4) The information to be entered in the register in respect of a permitted participant who is an individual shall, however, not include his home address.

NOTES

Defined terms

the Commission: s 160(1)
permitted participant: s 105(1)

Assistance for designated organisations

Designation of organisations to whom assistance is available

108 (1) The Commission may, in respect of any referendum to which this Part applies, designate permitted participants as organisations to whom assistance is available in accordance with section 110.

(2) Where there are only two possible outcomes in the case of a referendum to which this Part applies, the Commission

    (a) may, in relation to each of those outcomes, designate one permitted participant as representing those campaigning for the outcome in question; but

    (b) otherwise shall not make any designation in respect of the referendum.

(3) Where there are more than two possible outcomes in the case of a referendum to which this Part applies, the Secretary of State may, after consulting the Commission, by order specify the possible outcomes in relation to which permitted participants may be designated in accordance with subsection (4).

(4) In such a case the Commission

    (a) may, in relation to each of two or more outcomes specified in any such order, designate one permitted participant as representing those campaigning for the outcome in question; but

    (b) otherwise shall not make any designation in respect of the referendum.

NOTES

Defined terms
the Commission: s 160(1)
organisation: s 160(1)
outcome: s 106(7)
permitted participant: s 105(1)

referendum: s 101(2)-(5)
the Secretary of State: s 159A

Applications for designation under section 108

109 (1) A permitted participant seeking to be designated under section 108 must make an application for the purpose to the Commission.

(2) An application for designation must

    (a) be accompanied by information or statements designed to show that the applicant adequately represents those campaigning for the outcome at the referendum in relation to which the applicant seeks to be designated; and

    (b) be made within the period of 28 days beginning with the first day of the referendum period.

(3) Where an application for designation has been made to the Commission in accordance with this section, the application must be determined by the Commission within the period of 14 days beginning with the day after the end of the period of 28 days mentioned in subsection (2)(b).

(4) If there is only one application in relation to a particular outcome at the referendum, the Commission shall designate the applicant unless

    (a) they are not satisfied that the applicant adequately represents those campaigning for that outcome; or

    (b) they are prevented from making any designation by virtue of section 108(2)(b) or (4)(b).

(5) If there is more than one application in relation to a particular outcome at the referendum, the Commission shall designate whichever of the applicants appears to them to represent to the greatest extent those campaigning for that outcome unless

    (a) they are not satisfied that any of the applicants adequately represents those campaigning for that outcome; or

    (b) they are prevented from making any designation by virtue of section 108(2)(b) or (4)(b).

(6) The Secretary of State may, in the case of any referendum to which this Part applies, by order provide for this section to have effect as if each, or either, of the periods of 28 and 14 days referred to in subsections (2) and (3) was instead such shorter or longer period as is specified in the order.

(7) In this section, in relation to a referendum, any reference to designation is to designation in respect of the referendum under section 108.

NOTES

Subordinate Legislation
National Assembly for Wales Referendum (Assembly Act
    Provisions) (Limit on Referendum Expenses Etc) Order
    2010, SI 2010/2985

outcome: s 106(7)
permitted participant: s 105(1)
referendum: s 101(2)-(5)
the Secretary of State: s 159A

Defined terms
    the Commission: s 160(1)

Assistance available to designated organisations

110 (1) Where the Commission have made any designations under section 108 in respect of a referendum, assistance shall be available to the designated organisations in accordance with this section.

(2) The Commission shall make to each designated organisation a grant of the same amount, which shall be an amount not exceeding £600,000 determined by the Commission.

(3) A grant under subsection (2) may be made subject to such conditions as the Commission consider appropriate.

(4) Each designated organisation (or, as the case may be, persons authorised by the organisation) shall have the rights conferred by or by virtue of Schedule 12, which makes provision as to
  (a) the sending of referendum addresses free of charge;
  (b) the use of rooms free of charge for holding public meetings; and
  (c) referendum campaign broadcasts.

(5) In this section and Schedule 12 "designated organisation", in relation to a referendum, means a person or body designated by the Commission under section 108 in respect of that referendum.

NOTES

Defined terms
    body: s 160(1)
    the Commission: s 160(1)
    conditions: s 160(5)

referendum: s 101(2)-(5)

Chapter II
Financial Controls

Referendum expenses

Referendum expenses

111 (1) The following provisions have effect for the purposes of this Part.

(2) "Referendum expenses", in relation to a referendum to which this Part applies, means expenses incurred by or on behalf of any individual or body which are expenses falling within Part I of Schedule 13 and incurred for referendum purposes.

(3) "For referendum purposes" means

(a) in connection with the conduct or management of any campaign conducted with a view to promoting or procuring a particular outcome in relation to any question asked in the referendum, or

(b) otherwise in connection with promoting or procuring any such outcome.

(4) "Referendum campaign" means a campaign such as is mentioned in subsection (3)(a); and "campaign organiser", in relation to referendum expenses, means the individual or body by whom or on whose behalf the expenses are incurred.

NOTES

Defined terms   referendum: s 101(2)-(5)
  body: s 160(1)
    question: s 101(2)(b)

Notional referendum expenses

112 (1) This section applies where, in the case of any individual or body

    (a) either

        (i) property is transferred to the individual or body free of charge or at a discount of more than 10 per cent of its market value, or

        (ii) property, services or facilities is or are provided for the use or benefit of the individual or body free of charge or at a discount of more than 10 per cent of the commercial rate for the use of the property or for the provision of the services or facilities, and

    (b) the property, services or facilities is or are made use of by or on behalf of the individual or body in circumstances such that, if any expenses were to be (or are) actually incurred by or on behalf of the individual or body in respect of that use, they would be (or are) referendum expenses incurred by or on behalf of the individual or body.

(2) Where this section applies, an amount of referendum expenses determined in accordance with this section ("the appropriate amount") shall be treated, for the purposes of this Part, as incurred by the individual or body during the period for which the property, services or facilities is or are made use of as mentioned in subsection (1)(b).

This subsection has effect subject to subsection (9).

(3) Where subsection (1)(a)(i) applies, the appropriate amount is such proportion of either

    (a) the market value of the property (where the property is transferred free of charge), or

    (b) the difference between the market value of the property and the amount of expenses actually incurred by or on behalf of the individual or body in respect of the property (where the property is transferred at a discount),

as is reasonably attributable to the use made of the property as mentioned in subsection (1)(b).

(4) Where subsection (1)(a)(ii) applies, the appropriate amount is such proportion of either

    (a) the commercial rate for the use of the property or the provision of the services or facilities (where the property, services or facilities is or are provided free of charge), or

    (b) the difference between that commercial rate and the amount of expenses actually incurred by or on behalf of the individual or body in respect of the use of the property or the provision of the services or facilities (where the property, services or facilities is or are provided at a discount),

as is reasonably attributable to the use made of the property, services or facilities as mentioned in subsection (1)(b).

(5) Where the services of an employee are made available by his employer for the use or benefit of an individual or body, then for the purposes of this section the amount which is to be taken as constituting the commercial rate for the provision of those services shall be the amount of the remuneration or allowances payable to the employee by his employer in respect of the period for which his services are made available (but shall not include any amount in respect of contributions or other payments for which the employer is liable in respect of the employee).

(6) Where an amount of referendum expenses is treated, by virtue of subsection (2), as incurred by or on behalf of an individual or body during any period the whole or part of which falls within the period which is, in relation to the referendum to which the expenses relate, the referendum period then

    (a) the amount mentioned in subsection (7) shall be treated as incurred by or on behalf of the individual or body during the referendum period, and

    (b) if a return falls to be prepared under section 120 in respect of referendum expenses incurred by or on behalf of the individual or body during that period, the responsible person shall make a declaration of that amount,

    unless that amount is not more than £200.

(7) The amount referred to in subsection (6) is such proportion of the appropriate amount (determined in accordance with subsection (3) or (4)) as reasonably represents the use made of the property, services or facilities as mentioned in subsection (1)(b) during the referendum period.

(8) A person commits an offence if he knowingly or recklessly makes a false declaration under subsection (6).

(9) No amount of referendum expenses shall be regarded as incurred by virtue of subsection (2) in respect of

    (a) the transmission by a broadcaster of a referendum campaign broadcast (within the meaning of section 127);

    (b) the provision of any rights conferred on a designated organisation (or persons authorised by such an organisation) by virtue of section 110(4) and Schedule 12; or

    (c) the provision by any individual of his own services which he provides voluntarily in his own time and free of charge.

(10) Paragraph 2(5) and (6)(a) of Schedule 15 shall apply with any necessary modifications for the purpose of determining, for the purposes of subsection (1), whether property is transferred to an individual or body.

NOTES

Defined terms
  body: s 160(1)
  broadcaster: s 37(2)
  market value: s 160(1)
  modifications: s 160(1)
  property: s 160(1)

referendum: s 101(2)-(5)
referendum expenses: s 111(2)
responsible person: s 105(2)

General restrictions relating to referendum expenses incurred by permitted participants

Restriction on incurring referendum expenses

113 (1) No amount of referendum expenses shall be incurred by or on behalf of a permitted participant unless it is incurred with the authority of

    (a) the responsible person; or

    (b) a person authorised in writing by the responsible person.

(2)   A person commits an offence if, without reasonable excuse, he incurs any expenses in contravention of subsection (1).

(3)   Where, in the case of a permitted participant that is a registered party, any expenses are incurred in contravention of subsection (1), the expenses shall not count for the purposes of sections 117 to 123 or Schedule 14 as referendum expenses incurred by or on behalf of the permitted participant.

NOTES

Defined terms
   contravention: s 160(1)
   permitted participant: s 105(1)
   referendum expenses: s 111(2)

   registered party: s 160(1)
   responsible person: s 105(2)

Restriction on payments in respect of referendum expenses

114 (1)   No payment (of whatever nature) may be made in respect of any referendum expenses incurred or to be incurred by or on behalf of a permitted participant unless it is made by
    (a)   the responsible person, or
    (b)   a person authorised in writing by the responsible person.

(2)   Any payment made in respect of any such expenses by a person within paragraph (a) or (b) of subsection (1) must be supported by an invoice or a receipt unless it is not more than £200.

(3)   Where a person within paragraph (b) of subsection (1) makes a payment to which subsection (2) applies, he must deliver to the responsible person
    (a)   notification that he has made the payment, and
    (b)   the supporting invoice or receipt,
as soon as possible after making the payment.

(4)   A person commits an offence if, without reasonable excuse,
    (a)   he makes any payment in contravention of subsection (1), or
    (b)   he contravenes subsection (3).

NOTES

Defined terms
   contravention: s 160(1)
   permitted participant: s 105(1)
   referendum expenses: s 111(2)

   responsible person: s 105(2)

Restriction on making claims in respect of referendum expenses

115 (1)   A claim for payment in respect of referendum expenses incurred by or on behalf of a permitted participant during a referendum period shall not be payable if the claim is not sent to
    (a)   the responsible person, or
    (b)   any other person authorised under section 113 to incur the expenses,
not later than 30 days after the end of the referendum period.

(2)   Any claim sent in accordance with subsection (1) shall be paid not later than 60 days after the end of the referendum period.

(3)   A person commits an offence if, without reasonable excuse,
    (a)   he pays any claim which by virtue of subsection (1) is not payable, or
    (b)   he makes any payment in respect of a claim after the end of the period allowed under subsection (2).

(4)   In the case of any claim to which subsection (1) applies
    (a)   the person making the claim, or
    (b)   the person with whose authority the expenses in question were incurred,

may apply in England and Wales to the High Court or the county court or, in Northern Ireland, to the High Court or a county court or, in Scotland, to the Court of Session or the sheriff for leave for the claim to be paid although sent in after the end of the period mentioned in that subsection; and the court, if satisfied that for any special reason it is appropriate to do so, may by order grant the leave.

(5) Nothing in subsection (1) or (2) shall apply in relation to any sum paid in pursuance of the order of leave.

(6) Subsection (2) is without prejudice to any rights of a creditor of a permitted participant to obtain payment before the end of the period allowed under that subsection.

(7) Subsections (7) to (10) of section 77 shall apply for the purposes of this section as if

   (a) any reference to subsection (1), (2) or (4) of that section were a reference to subsection (1), (2) or (4) above; and

   (b) any reference to campaign expenditure were a reference to referendum expenses; and

   (c) any reference to the treasurer or deputy treasurer of the registered party were a reference to the responsible person in relation to the permitted participant.

NOTES

Defined terms
  permitted participant: s 105(1)
  referendum expenses: s 111(2)

responsible person: s 105(2)

Disputed claims

116 (1) This section applies where

   (a) a claim for payment in respect of referendum expenses incurred by or on behalf of a permitted participant as mentioned in section 115(1) is sent to

     (i) the responsible person, or

     (ii) any other person with whose authority it is alleged that the expenditure was incurred,

   within the period allowed under that provision; and

   (b) the responsible person or other person to whom the claim is sent fails or refuses to pay the claim within the period allowed under section 115(2);

   and the claim is referred to in this section as "the disputed claim".

(2) The person by whom the disputed claim is made may bring an action for the disputed claim, and nothing in section 115(2) shall apply in relation to any sum paid in pursuance of any judgment or order made by a court in the proceedings.

(3) For the purposes of this section

   (a) subsections (4) and (5) of section 115 shall apply in relation to an application made by the person mentioned in subsection (1)(b) above for leave to pay the disputed claim as they apply in relation to an application for leave to pay a claim (whether it is disputed or otherwise) which is sent in after the period allowed under section 115(1); and

   (b) subsections (7) and (8) of section 77 shall apply as if any reference to subsection (4) of that section were a reference to section 115(4) as applied by paragraph (a) above.

NOTES

Defined terms
  permitted participant: s 105(1)
  referendum expenses: s 111(2)

responsible person: s 105(2)

Financial limits

General restriction on referendum expenses

117 (1)   The total referendum expenses incurred by or on behalf of any individual or body during the referendum period in the case of a particular referendum to which this Part applies must not exceed £10,000 unless the individual or body is a permitted participant.

(2)   Where

    (a)   during the referendum period any referendum expenses are incurred by or on behalf of any individual in excess of the limit imposed by subsection (1), and

    (b)   he is not a permitted participant,

he is guilty of an offence if he knew, or ought reasonably to have known, that the expenses were being incurred in excess of that limit.

(3)   Where

    (a)   during the referendum period any referendum expenses are incurred by or on behalf of any body in excess of the limit imposed by subsection (1), and

    (b)   the body is not a permitted participant,

any person who authorised the expenses to be incurred by or on behalf of the body is guilty of an offence if he knew, or ought reasonably to have known, that the expenses would be incurred in excess of that limit.

(4)   Where subsection (3)(a) and (b) apply, the body in question is also guilty of an offence.

(5)   Where

    (a)   at any time before the beginning of any referendum period, any expenses within section 111(2) are incurred by or on behalf of an individual or body in respect of any property, services or facilities, but

    (b)   the property, services or facilities is or are made use of by or on behalf of the individual or body during the referendum period in circumstances such that, had any expenses been incurred in respect of that use during that period, they would by virtue of section 111(2) have constituted referendum expenses incurred by or on behalf of the individual or body during that period,

the appropriate proportion of the expenses mentioned in paragraph (a) shall be treated for the purposes of this section as referendum expenses incurred by or on behalf of the individual or body during that period.

(6)   For the purposes of subsection (5) the appropriate proportion of the expenses mentioned in paragraph (a) of that subsection is such proportion of those expenses as is reasonably attributable to the use made of the property, services or facilities as mentioned in paragraph (b).

NOTES
Defined terms
body: s 160(1)
permitted participant: s 105(1)
property: s 160(1)

referendum: s 101(2)-(5)
referendum expenses: s 111(2)

Special restrictions on referendum expenses by permitted participants

118 (1)   Schedule 14 has effect for imposing, in connection with a referendum to which this Part applies, limits on referendum expenses incurred by or on behalf of permitted participants during the referendum period in the case of that referendum.

(2)   Where any referendum expenses are incurred by or on behalf of a permitted participant during any such period in excess of any limit imposed by Schedule 14, then

    (a)   if the permitted participant is a registered party falling within section 105(1)(a)

      (i)   the responsible person or any deputy treasurer of the party is guilty of an offence if he authorised the expenses to be incurred by or on behalf of the party and he knew or ought reasonably to have known that the expenses would be incurred in excess of that limit, and

    (ii)   the party is also guilty of an offence;

  (b) if the permitted participant is an individual falling within section 105(1)(b), that individual is guilty of an offence if he knew or ought reasonably to have known that the expenses would be incurred in excess of that limit;

  (c) if the permitted participant is a body falling within section 105(1)(b)

    (i)   the responsible person is guilty of an offence if he authorised the expenses to be incurred by or on behalf of the body and he knew or ought reasonably to have known that the expenses would be incurred in excess of that limit, and

    (ii) the body is also guilty of an offence.

(3) It shall be a defence for a permitted participant or other person charged with an offence under subsection (2) to show

  (a) that any code of practice for the time being issued under paragraph 3 of Schedule 13 was complied with in determining the items and amounts of referendum expenses to be entered in the relevant return under section 120, and

  (b) that the limit would not have been exceeded on the basis of the items and amounts entered in that return.

(4) Section 117(5) and (6) shall apply, for the purposes of this section, sections 120 to 123 and Schedule 14, in relation to an individual or body that has become a permitted participant as they apply for the purposes of section 117 in relation to an individual or body that is not a permitted participant.

(5) For the purposes of this section and sections 120 to 123 and Schedule 14, any reference to referendum expenses incurred by or on behalf of a permitted participant during the referendum period includes any referendum expenses so incurred at any time before the individual or body became a permitted participant.

NOTES

Defined terms
  body: s 160(1)
  permitted participant: s 105(1)
  referendum: s 101(2)-(5)
  referendum expenses: s 111(2)

registered party: s 160(1)
responsible person: s 105(2)
treasurer: s 160(1)

Donations to permitted participants

Control of donations to permitted participants

119 Schedule 15 has effect for controlling donations to permitted participants that either are not registered parties or are minor parties.

NOTES

Defined terms
  minor party: s 160(1)
  permitted party: s 105(1)

registered party: s 160(1)

Returns

Returns as to referendum expenses

120 (1) Where

  (a) any referendum expenses are incurred by or on behalf of a permitted participant during any referendum period (within the meaning of section 102), and

(b) that period ends,

the responsible person shall make a return under this section in respect of the referendum expenses incurred by or on behalf of the permitted participant during that period.

(2) A return under this section must specify the referendum to which the expenditure relates and must contain

    (a) a statement of all payments made in respect of referendum expenses incurred by or on behalf of the permitted participant during the referendum period in question;

    (b) a statement of all disputed claims (within the meaning of section 116);

    (c) a statement of all the unpaid claims (if any) of which the responsible person is aware in respect of which an application has been made, or is about to be made, to a court under section 115(4); and

    (d) in a case where the permitted participant either is not a registered party or is a minor party, a statement of relevant donations received in respect of the referendum which complies with the requirements of paragraphs 10 and 11 of Schedule 15.

(3) A return under this section must be accompanied by

    (a) all invoices or receipts relating to the payments mentioned in subsection (2)(a); and

    (b) in the case of any referendum expenses treated as incurred by virtue of section 112, any declaration falling to be made with respect to those expenses in accordance with section 112(6).

(4) Subsections (2) and (3) do not apply to any referendum expenses incurred at any time before the individual or body became a permitted participant, but the return must be accompanied by a declaration made by the responsible person of the total amount of such expenses incurred at any such time.

(5) The Commission may by regulations prescribe a form of return which may be used for the purposes of this section.

(6) In this section "relevant donation" has the same meaning as in Schedule 15.

NOTES

Defined terms

body: s 160(1)

the Commission: s 160(1)

minor party: s 160(1)

permitted participant: s 105(1)

referendum: s 101(2)-(5)

referendum expenses: s 111(2)

registered party: s 160(1)

responsible person: s 105(2)

Auditor's report on return

121 (1) Where during any referendum period the referendum expenses incurred by or on behalf of a permitted participant exceed £250,000, a report must be prepared by a qualified auditor on the return prepared under section 120 in respect of those expenses.

(2) The following provisions, namely

    (a) section 43(6) and (7), and

    (b) section 44,

shall apply in relation to the appointment of an auditor to prepare a report under subsection (1) or (as the case may be) an auditor so appointed as they apply in relation to the appointment of an auditor to carry out an audit under section 43 or (as the case may be) an auditor so appointed.

NOTES

Defined terms   referendum expenses: s 111(2)
    permitted participant: s 105(1)
    qualified auditor: s 160(1), (2)

Delivery of returns to Commission

122 (1)   Where

       (a)   any return falls to be prepared under section 120 in respect of referendum expenses incurred by or on behalf of a permitted participant, and

       (b)   an auditor's report on it falls to be prepared under section 121(1),

the responsible person shall deliver the return to the Commission, together with a copy of the auditor's report, within six months of the end of the relevant referendum period.

   (2)   In the case of any other return falling to be prepared under section 120, the responsible person shall deliver the return to the Commission within three months of the end of the relevant referendum period.

   (3)   Where after the date on which a return is delivered to the Commission under this section, leave is given by a court under section 115(4) for any claim to be paid, the responsible person shall, within seven days after the payment, deliver to the Commission a return of any sums paid in pursuance of the leave accompanied by a copy of the court order giving the leave.

   (4)   The responsible person commits an offence if, without reasonable excuse, he

       (a)   fails to comply with the requirements of subsection (1) or (2) in relation to a return under section 120;

       (b)   delivers a return which does not comply with the requirements of section 120(2) or (3); or

       (c)   fails to comply with the requirements of subsection (3) in relation to a return under that subsection.

NOTES

Defined terms   responsible person: s 105(2)
    the Commission: s 160(1)
    permitted participant: s 105(1)
    referendum expenses: s 111(2)

Declaration of responsible person as to return under section 120

123 (1)   Each return prepared under section 120 in respect of referendum expenses incurred by or on behalf of a permitted participant must be accompanied by a declaration which complies with subsection (2) and is signed by the responsible person.

   (2)   The declaration must state

       (a)   that the responsible person has examined the return in question;

       (b)   that to the best of his knowledge and belief

          (i)   it is a complete and correct return as required by law, and

          (ii)   all expenses shown in it as paid have been paid by him or a person authorised by him.

   (3)   The declaration must also state, in a case where the permitted participant either is not a registered party or is a minor party, that

       (a)   all relevant donations recorded in the return as having been accepted by the permitted participant are from permissible donors, and

       (b)   no other relevant donations have been accepted by the permitted participant.

   (4)   A person commits an offence if

       (a)   he knowingly or recklessly makes a false declaration under this section; or

       (b)   subsection (1) is contravened at a time when he is the responsible person in the case of the permitted participant to which the return relates.

(5)   In this section "relevant donation" has the same meaning as in Schedule 15.

NOTES

Defined terms
   minor party: s 160(1)
   permitted participant: s 105(1)
   referendum expenses: s 111(2)

registered party: s 160(1)
responsible person: s 105(2)

Public inspection of returns under section 120

124 (1)   Where the Commission receive any return under section 120 they shall

    (a)   as soon as reasonably practicable after receiving the return, make a copy of the return and of the documents accompanying it available for public inspection; and

    (b)   keep any such copy available for public inspection for the period for which the return or other document is kept by them.

(2)   If the return contains a statement of relevant donations in accordance with section 120(2)(d), the Commission shall secure that the copy of the statement made available for public inspection does not include, in the case of any donation by an individual, the donor's address.

(3)   At the end of the period of two years beginning with the date when any return or other document mentioned in subsection (1) is received by the Commission

    (a)   they may cause the return or other document to be destroyed; but

    (b)   if requested to do so by the responsible person in the case of the permitted participant concerned, they shall arrange for the return or other document to be returned to that person.

NOTES

Defined terms
   the Commission: s 160(1)
   document: s 160(1)
   permitted participant: s 105(1)

responsible person: s 105(2)

Chapter III
Controls on Publications

Restriction on publication etc of promotional material by central and local government etc

125 (1)   This section applies to any material which

    (a)   provides general information about a referendum to which this Part applies;

    (b)   deals with any of the issues raised by any question on which such a referendum is being held;

    (c)   puts any arguments for or against any particular answer to any such question; or

    (d)   is designed to encourage voting at such a referendum.

(2)   Subject to subsection (3), no material to which this section applies shall be published during the relevant period by or on behalf of

    (a)   any Minister of the Crown, government department or local authority; or

    (b)   any other person or body whose expenses are defrayed wholly or mainly out of public funds or by any local authority.

(3)   Subsection (2) does not apply to

    (a)   material made available to persons in response to specific requests for information or to persons specifically seeking access to it;

(b) anything done by or on behalf of the Commission or a person or body designated under section 108 (designation of organisations to whom assistance is available);

(c) the publication of information relating to the holding of the poll; or

(d) the issue of press notices;

and subsection (2)(b) shall not be taken as applying to the British Broadcasting Corporation or Sianel Pedwar Cymru.

(4) In this section

(a) "publish" means make available to the public at large, or any section of the public, in whatever form and by whatever means (and "publication" shall be construed accordingly);

(b) "the relevant period", in relation to a referendum, means the period of 28 days ending with the date of the poll.

NOTES

Details to appear on referendum material

126 (1) No material wholly or mainly relating to a referendum to which this Part applies shall be published during the referendum period unless

(a) in the case of material which is, or is contained in, such a printed document as is mentioned in subsection (3), (4) or (5), the requirements of that subsection are complied with; or

(b) in the case of any other material, any requirements falling to be complied with in relation to the material by virtue of regulations under subsection (6) are complied with.

(2) For the purposes of subsections (3) to (5) the following details are "the relevant details" in the case of any material falling within subsection (1)(a), namely

(a) the name and address of the printer of the document;

(b) the name and address of the promoter of the material; and

(c) the name and address of any person on behalf of whom the material is being published (and who is not the promoter).

(3) Where the material is a document consisting (or consisting principally) of a single side of printed matter, the relevant details must appear on the face of the document.

(4) Where the material is a printed document other than one to which subsection (3) applies, the relevant details must appear either on the first or the last page of the document.

(5) Where the material is an advertisement contained in a newspaper or periodical

(a) the name and address of the printer of the newspaper or periodical must appear either on its first or last page; and

(b) the relevant details specified in subsection (2)(b) and (c) must be included in the advertisement.

(6) The Secretary of State may, after consulting the Commission, by regulations make provision for and in connection with the imposition of requirements as to the inclusion in material falling within subsection (1)(b) of the following details, namely

(a) the name and address of the promoter of the material; and

(b) the name and address of any person on behalf of whom the material is being published (and who is not the promoter).

(7) Regulations under subsection (6) may in particular specify

    (a) the manner and form in which such details must be included in any such material for the purpose of complying with any such requirement;

    (b) circumstances in which

        (i) any such requirement does not have to be complied with by a person of any description specified in the regulations, or

        (ii) a breach of any such requirement by a person of any description so specified is not to result in the commission of an offence under this section by that person or by a person of any other such description;

    (c) circumstances in which material is, or is not, to be taken for the purposes of the regulations to be published or (as the case may be) published by a person of any description so specified.

(8) Where during the referendum period any material falling within subsection (1)(a) is published in contravention of subsection (1), then (subject to subsection (10))

    (a) the promoter of the material,

    (b) any other person by whom the material is so published, and

    (c) the printer of the document,

shall be guilty of an offence.

(9) Where during the referendum period any material falling within subsection (1)(b) is published in contravention of subsection (1), then (subject to regulations made by virtue of subsection (7)(b) and to subsection (10))

    (a) the promoter of the material, and

    (b) any other person by whom the material is so published,

shall be guilty of an offence.

(10) It shall be a defence for a person charged with an offence under this section to prove

    (a) that the contravention of subsection (1) arose from circumstances beyond his control; and

    (b) that he took all reasonable steps, and exercised all due diligence, to ensure that that contravention would not arise.

(10A) Subsection (1) does not apply to any material published for the purposes of a referendum if the publication is required under or by virtue of any enactment.

(11) In this section

"print" means print by whatever means, and "printer" shall be construed accordingly;

"the promoter", in relation to any material falling within subsection (1), means the person causing the material to be published;

"publish" means make available to the public at large, or any section of the public, in whatever form and by whatever means.

NOTES

Defined terms

the Commission: s 160(1)

contravention: s 160(1)

document: s 160(1)

enactment: s 160(1)

referendum: s 101(2)-(5)

the Secretary of State: s 159A

Referendum campaign broadcasts

127 (1) A broadcaster shall not include in its broadcasting services any referendum campaign broadcast made on behalf of any person or body other than one designated in respect of the referendum in question under section 108.

(2) In this section "referendum campaign broadcast" means any broadcast whose purpose (or main purpose) is or may reasonably be assumed to be

(a) to further any campaign conducted with a view to promoting or procuring a particular outcome in relation to any question asked in a referendum to which this Part applies, or

(b) otherwise to promote or procure any such outcome.

NOTES

Defined terms
body: s 160(1)
broadcaster: s 37
question: s 101(2)(b)

referendum: s 101(2)-(5)
referendum campaign: s 111(4)

Chapter IV
Conduct of Referendums

Chief Counting Officers, and counting officers, for referendums

128 (1) This section has effect in relation to any referendum to which this Part applies.

(2) There shall be a Chief Counting Officer for the referendum, who (subject to subsection (8)) shall be
    (a) the chairman of the Commission, or
    (b) if the chairman of the Commission appoints some other person to act as Chief Counting Officer for the referendum, the person so appointed.

(3) The Chief Counting Officer for the referendum shall appoint a counting officer for each relevant area in Great Britain.

(4) The local authority in the case of each such area shall place the services of their officers at the disposal of the counting officer for the area for the purpose of assisting him in the discharge of his functions.

(5) Each counting officer shall, as respects the votes cast in the area for which he is appointed, certify
    (a) the number of ballot papers counted by him, and
    (b) the number of votes cast in favour of each answer to a question asked in the referendum.

(6) The Chief Counting Officer shall certify
    (a) the total number of ballot papers counted, and
    (b) the total number of votes cast in favour of each answer to a question asked in the referendum,
in the whole of the referendum area.

(7) Where two or more forms of ballot paper are used in the referendum, a separate number shall be certified under subsection (5)(a) or (6)(a) in relation to each form of ballot paper so used.

(8) Where the referendum is held in Northern Ireland, the Chief Electoral Officer for Northern Ireland
    (a) shall be the Chief Counting Officer for the referendum if it is held only in Northern Ireland, and
    (b) in any other case shall be treated, for the purposes of subsection (5), as if he were a counting officer appointed under this section for the whole of Northern Ireland.

(9) In this section
    (a) "relevant area in Great Britain" means any of the following
      (i) a district in England or a London borough,

(ii) the City of London (including the Inner and Middle Temples), the Isle of Wight or the Isles of Scilly,

(iii) a local government area in Scotland, or

(iv) a county or county borough in Wales,

where it is comprised in the referendum area;

(b) "the local authority"

(i) in the case of an area falling within paragraph (a)(i), (iii) or (iv), means the council for that area, and

(ii) in the case of an area falling within paragraph (a)(ii), means the Common Council of the City of London, the Council of the Isle of Wight or the Council of the Isles of Scilly, as the case may be;

(c) "the referendum area" means the parts or part of the United Kingdom, or (as the case may be) the region in England, throughout which the referendum is held as mentioned in section 101(1).

NOTES

Defined terms
  answer: s 101(2)(b)
  the Commission: s 160(1)
  functions: s 160(1)

  question: s 101(2)(b)
  referendum: s 101(2)-(5)

Orders regulating conduct of referendums

129 (1) The Secretary of State may by order make such provision as he considers expedient for or in connection with regulating the conduct of referendums to which this Part applies.

(2) An order under this section may, in particular
(a) make provision for the creation of offences;
(b) apply (with or without modification) any provision of any enactment;
and different provision may be made under this section in relation to different parts of the United Kingdom.

(3) An order under this section shall not apply in relation to any referendum in relation to which specific provision is made by any other enactment for or in connection with regulating any matters relating to the conduct of the referendum, except to such extent (if any) as may be provided by that enactment.

(4) Before making an order under this section the Secretary of State shall consult the Commission.

NOTES

Subordinate Legislation
Regional Assembly and Local Government Referendums
  Order 2004, SI 2004/1962.

Defined terms
  the Commission: s 160(1)

enactment: s 160(1)
modifications: s 160(1)
referendum: s 101(2)-(5)
the Secretary of State: s 159A

PART VIII
ELECTION CAMPAIGNS AND PROCEEDINGS

Control of donations to candidates

130 (1) The Representation of the People Act 1983 shall be amended as follows.

(2) After section 71 there shall be inserted
Not reproduced

143 (1)   No election material shall be published unless
    (a) in the case of material which is, or is contained in, such a printed document as is mentioned in subsection (3), (4) or (5), the requirements of that subsection are complied with; or
    (b) in the case of any other material, any requirements falling to be complied with in relation to the material by virtue of regulations under subsection (6) are complied with.

(2)   For the purposes of subsections (3) to (5) the following details are "the relevant details" in the case of any material falling within subsection (1)(a), namely
    (a) the name and address of the printer of the document;
    (b) the name and address of the promoter of the material; and
    (c) the name and address of any person on behalf of whom the material is being published (and who is not the promoter).

(2A)   For the purposes of subsection (2)(c), election material to which subsection (2B) applies
    (a) is not to be regarded as being published on behalf of a candidate merely because it can be regarded as promoting or procuring his electoral success, but
    (b) may be regarded as being published on behalf of the party mentioned in subsection (2B).

(2B)   This subsection applies to election material which can be reasonably regarded as promoting or procuring the electoral success of two or more candidates standing in the name of a party or included in a list of candidates submitted by the party in connection with the election.

(3)   Where the material is a document consisting (or consisting principally) of a single side of printed matter, the relevant details must appear on the face of the document.

(4)   Where the material is a printed document other than one to which subsection (3) applies, the relevant details must appear either on the first or the last page of the document.

(5)   Where the material is an advertisement contained in a newspaper or periodical
    (a) the name and address of the printer of the newspaper or periodical must appear either on its first or last page; and
    (b) the relevant details specified in subsection (2)(b) and (c) must be included in the advertisement.

(6)   The Secretary of State may, after consulting the Commission, by regulations make provision for and in connection with the imposition of requirements as to the inclusion in material falling within subsection (1)(b) of the following details, namely
    (a) the name and address of the promoter of the material; and
    (b) the name and address of any person on behalf of whom the material is being published (and who is not the promoter).

(7)   Regulations under subsection (6) may in particular specify
    (a) the manner and form in which such details must be included in any such material for the purpose of complying with any such requirement;
    (b) circumstances in which
        (i) any such requirement does not have to be complied with by a person of any description specified in the regulations, or
        (ii) a breach of any such requirement by a person of any description so specified is not to result in the commission of an offence under this section by that person or by a person of any other such description;

(c) circumstances in which material is, or is not, to be taken for the purposes of the regulations to be published or (as the case may be) published by a person of any description so specified.

(8) Where any material falling within subsection (1)(a) is published in contravention of subsection (1), then (subject to subsection (10))

(a) the promoter of the material,

(b) any other person by whom the material is so published, and

(c) the printer of the document,

shall be guilty of an offence.

(9) Where any material falling within subsection (1)(b) is published in contravention of subsection (1), then (subject to regulations made by virtue of subsection (7)(b) and to subsection (10))

(a) the promoter of the material, and

(b) any other person by whom the material is so published,

shall be guilty of an offence.

(10) It shall be a defence for a person charged with an offence under this section to prove

(a) that the contravention of subsection (1) arose from circumstances beyond his control; and

(b) that he took all reasonable steps, and exercised all due diligence, to ensure that that contravention would not arise.

(11) In this section

"election material" has the meaning given by section 143A;

"print" means print by whatever means, and "printer" shall be construed accordingly;

"the promoter", in relation to any election material, means the person causing the material to be published;

"publish" means make available to the public at large, or any section of the public, in whatever form and by whatever means.

NOTES

Meaning of "election material"

43A (1) "Election material" means material which can reasonably be regarded as intended to promote or procure electoral success at any relevant election for

(a) one or more particular registered parties,

(b) one or more registered parties who advocate (or do not advocate) particular policies or who otherwise fall within a particular category of such parties, or

(c) candidates who hold (or do not hold) particular opinions or who advocate (or do not advocate) particular policies or who otherwise fall within a particular category of candidates.

(2) For the purposes of subsection (1)

(a) the reference to electoral success at any relevant election is a reference

(i) in relation to a registered party, to the return at any such election of candidates standing in the name of the party or included in a list of candidates submitted by the party in connection with the election, and

(ii) in relation to candidates, to their return at any such election,

(b) the reference to doing any of the things mentioned in that subsection includes doing so by prejudicing the electoral prospects at the election of other parties or candidates, and

(c) a course of conduct may constitute the doing of one of those things even though it does not involve any express mention being made of the name of any party or candidate.

(3) In determining whether material can reasonably be regarded as intended to promote or procure electoral success as mentioned in subsection (1), it is immaterial that it can reasonably be regarded as intended to achieve any other purpose as well.

(4) In this section
"candidate" includes a future candidate, whether identifiable or not;
"relevant election" has the same meaning as in Part 2 (see section 22(5)).

NOTES

Defined terms
registered party: s 160(1)

Broadcasting during election period

Broadcasting of local items during election period

144   *Not reproduced*

Enforcement of Act

Duties of Commission with respect to compliance with controls imposed by the Act etc

145 (1) The Commission must monitor, and take all reasonable steps to secure, compliance with
  (a) the restrictions and other requirements imposed by or by virtue of
    (i) sections 24, 31 and 34,
    (ii) Parts 3 to 7, and
    (iii) sections 143 and 148; and
  (b) the restrictions and other requirements imposed by other enactments in relation to
    (i) election expenses incurred by or on behalf of candidates at elections, or
    (ii) donations to such candidates or their election agents.

(2) Subsection (1)(b) does not apply in relation to local government elections in Scotland unless and to the extent that the Scottish Ministers by order so provide.

(3) For the purposes of subsection (2), the reference in subsection (1)(b) to any enactment shall include a reference to any enactment comprised in or in an instrument made under an Act of the Scottish Parliament.

(4) Section 156(5) shall apply to an order made by the Scottish Ministers under subsection (2) as it applies to an order made by the Secretary of State under this Act and the reference in that section to enactments shall include a reference to any enactment comprised in or in an instrument made under an Act of the Scottish Parliament.

(5) The power of the Scottish Ministers to make an order under subsection (2) shall be exercisable by statutory instrument subject to annulment in pursuance of a resolution of the Scottish Parliament.

(6) The Scottish Ministers shall reimburse the Commission for any expenditure incurred by them which is attributable to the exercise of any function conferred by virtue of an order made under subsection (2).

(6A) The Commission may prepare and publish guidance setting out, in relation to any requirement referred to in subsection (1), their opinion on any of the following matters
  (a) what it is necessary, or is sufficient, to do (or avoid doing) in order to comply with the requirement;

(b) what it is desirable to do (or avoid doing) in view of the purpose of the requirement.

(6B) Each report by the Commission under paragraph 20 of Schedule 1 shall set out the steps the Commission have taken during the year in question to secure compliance with the restrictions and other requirements mentioned in subsection (1).

(7) In this section, section 148 and Schedule 19B
"election" means a relevant election for the purposes of Part II;
"election agent" includes a sub-agent.

NOTES

Defined terms
the Commission: s 160(1)
enactment: s 160(1)
function: s 160(1)

local government election: s 160(1)
Secretary of State: s 159A

Investigatory powers of Commission

146   Schedule 19B makes provision about the investigatory powers of the Commission.

NOTES

Defined terms
the Commission: s 160(1)

Civil sanctions

147   Schedule 19C makes provision for civil sanctions in relation to
(a) the commission of offences under this Act;
(b) the contravention of restrictions or requirements imposed by or by virtue of this Act.

NOTES

Defined terms
contravention: s 160(1)

General offences

148 (1) A person commits an offence if he
(a) alters, suppresses, conceals or destroys, or
(b) causes or permits the alteration, suppression, concealment or destruction of,
any book, record or other document which is or is liable to be required to be produced for inspection under paragraph 1 or 3 of Schedule 19B, and does so with the intention of falsifying the document or enabling any person to evade any of the provisions of this Act.

(2) Where the relevant person in the case of a supervised organisation, or a person acting on his behalf, requests a person holding an office in any such organisation ("the officeholder") to supply the relevant person with any information which he reasonably requires for the purposes of any of the provisions of this Act, the officeholder commits an offence if
(a) without reasonable excuse, he fails to supply the relevant person with that information as soon as is reasonably practicable, or
(b) in purporting to comply with the request, he knowingly supplies the relevant person with any information which is false in a material particular.

(3) A person commits an offence if, with intent to deceive, he withholds
(a) from the relevant person in the case of a supervised organisation, or
(b) from a supervised individual,
any information required by the relevant person or that individual for the purposes of any of the provisions of this Act.

(4) In subsections (1) to (3) any reference to a supervised organisation or individual includes a reference to a former supervised organisation or individual.

(5) Subsections (1) and (3) shall apply in relation to a person who is (or has been)
    (a) a candidate at an election (other than a local government election in Scotland), or
    (b) the election agent for such a candidate,

as they apply in relation to a supervised individual (or a former supervised individual), except that in their application in relation to any such person any reference to any of the provisions of this Act includes a reference to any other enactment imposing any restriction or other requirement falling within section 145(1)(b).

(6) In this section
    (a) "supervised individual" means an individual who is a regulated donee, regulated participant, a recognised third party or a permitted participant;
    (b) "supervised organisation" means
        (i) a registered party or (in the case of such a party with accounting units) the central organisation of the party or any of its accounting units,
        (ii) a regulated donee which is a members association,
        (iia) a regulated participant which is a members association,
        (iii) a recognised third party other than an individual, or
        (iv) a permitted participant other than an individual;
    (c) "relevant person" means a person who is (or has been)
        (i) in relation to a registered party (other than a minor party) or the central organisation of such a party, the treasurer of the party,
        (ii) in relation to any accounting unit of such a party, the registered treasurer of the unit,
        (iii) in relation to a regulated donee which is a members association, the responsible person for the purposes of Schedule 7,
        (iiia) in relation to a regulated participant which is a members association, the person responsible for the purposes of Schedule 7A,
        (iv) in relation to a recognised third party, the responsible person for the purposes of Part VI,
        (v) in relation to a permitted participant, the responsible person for the purposes of Part VII;
    (d) "regulated donee" and "members association" have the same meaning as in Schedule 7;
    (da) "regulated participant" has the same meaning as in Schedule 7A;
    (e) "recognised third party" and "permitted participant" have the same meaning as in Parts VI and VII respectively.

NOTES
Defined terms
accounting unit: s 26(11)
central organisation: ss 26(11), 160(1)
document: s 160(1)
election: s 145(7)
election agent: s 145(7)
enactment: s 160(1)
local government election: s 160(1)
minor party: s 160(1)
party with accounting units: ss 26(11), 160(1)
record: s 160(1)
registered party: s 160(1)
treasurer: s 160(1)

Inspection of registers etc

Inspection of Commission's registers etc

149 (1) This section applies to any register kept by the Commission under
    (a) section 23;

(b)   section 69;
(ba) section 71V;
(c)   section 89;
(d)   section 107;
(e)   paragraph 19 of Schedule 7;
(f)   paragraph 7 of Schedule 19A.

(2)   The Commission shall make a copy of the register available for public inspection during ordinary office hours, either at the Commission's offices or at some convenient place appointed by them.

(3)   The Commission may make other arrangements for members of the public to have access to the contents of the register.

(4)   If requested to do so by any person, the Commission shall supply him with a copy of the register or any part of it.

(5)   The Commission may charge such reasonable fee as they may determine in respect of
(a)   any inspection or access allowed under subsection (2) or (3); or
(b)   any copy supplied under subsection (4).

(6)   Subsections (2) to (5) shall apply in relation to any document a copy of which the Commission are for the time being required to make available for public inspection by virtue of
(a)   section 46,
(b)   section 84,
(ba) section 95F,
(c)   section 100, or
(d)   section 124,
as they apply in relation to any register falling within subsection (1).

(7)   Where any register falling within subsection (1) or any document falling within subsection (6) is held by the Commission in electronic form, any copy
(a)   made available for public inspection under subsection (2), or
(b)   supplied under subsection (4),
must be made available, or (as the case may be) supplied, in a legible form.

NOTES

Defined terms
   the Commission: s 160(1)
   document: s 160(1)

Provisions relating to offences

Punishment of offences

150 (1)   Schedule 20 makes provision for the punishment of offences under this Act.

(2)   In relation to an offence under any provision specified in the first column of that Schedule, the second column shows
(a)   whether the offence is punishable on summary conviction only or is punishable either on summary conviction or on conviction on indictment; and
(b)   the maximum punishment (or, in the case of a fine on a conviction on indictment, the punishment) which may be imposed by way of fine or imprisonment on a person convicted of the offence in the way specified;
and, where that column shows two alternative penalties that may be imposed on a person convicted in the way specified, as a further alternative both of those penalties may be imposed on him.

(3)   In the second column of that Schedule

(a) "Level 5" means a fine not exceeding level 5 on the standard scale;

(b) "statutory maximum" means a fine not exceeding the statutory maximum; and

(c) any reference to 51 weeks, 1 year or 6 months is a reference to a term of imprisonment not exceeding 51 weeks, 1 year or 6 months (as the case may be).

(4) In the application of this section to Gibraltar

(a) the reference to the standard scale shall have effect as if it were a reference to the standard scale pursuant to section 189 of, and Schedule 6 to, the Criminal Procedure Ordinance; and

(b) the reference to the statutory maximum shall have effect as if it were a reference to level 5 on that scale.

(5) In the application of Schedule 20 to England and Wales in relation to an offence committed before the commencement of section 281(5) of the Criminal Justice Act 2003 (alteration of penalties for summary offences), a reference to 51 weeks is to be read as a reference to 6 months.

NOTES
Defined terms
Criminal Procedure Ordinance: cf s 160(6)

Summary proceedings

151 (1) Summary proceedings for any offence under this Act may, without prejudice to any jurisdiction exercisable apart from this subsection, be taken against any body, including an unincorporated association, at any place at which it has a place of business, and against an individual at any place at which he is for the time being.

(2) Despite anything in section 127(1) of the Magistrates' Courts Act 1980, any information relating to an offence under this Act which is triable by a magistrates' court in England and Wales may be so tried if it is laid at any time within three years after the commission of the offence and within six months after the relevant date.

(3) Despite anything in section 136 of the Criminal Procedure (Scotland) Act 1995, summary proceedings for such an offence may be commenced in Scotland at any time within three years after the commission of the offence and within six months after the relevant date; and subsection (3) of that section shall apply for the purposes of this subsection as it applies for the purposes of that section.

(4) Despite anything in Article 19(1) of the Magistrates' Courts (Northern Ireland) Order 1981, a complaint relating to such an offence which is triable by a court of summary jurisdiction in Northern Ireland may be so tried if it is made at any time within three years after the commission of the offence and within six months after the relevant date.

(4A) Despite anything in section 117 of the Criminal Procedure Ordinance, any information or complaint relating to such an offence which is triable by a magistrates' court in Gibraltar may be so tried if it is laid or made at any time within three years after the commission of the offence and within six months after the relevant date.

(5) In this section "the relevant date" means the date on which evidence sufficient in the opinion of the prosecutor to justify proceedings comes to his knowledge.

(6) For the purposes of subsection (5) a certificate of any prosecutor as to the date on which such evidence as is there mentioned came to his knowledge shall be conclusive evidence of that fact.

NOTES
Defined terms
body: s 160(1)
Criminal Procedure Ordinance: cf s 160(6)

Offences committed by bodies corporate

152 (1)   Where an offence under this Act committed by a body corporate is proved to have been committed with the consent or connivance of, or to be attributable to any neglect on the part of

    (a)   any director, manager, secretary or other similar officer of the body corporate, or

    (b)   any person who was purporting to act in any such capacity,

he, as well as the body corporate, shall be guilty of that offence and be liable to be proceeded against and punished accordingly.

(2)   Where the affairs of a body corporate are managed by its members, subsection (1) shall apply in relation to the acts and defaults of a member in connection with his functions of management as if he were a director of the body corporate.

Offences committed by unincorporated associations

153 (1)   Proceedings for an offence alleged to have been committed under this Act by an unincorporated association shall be brought against the association in its own name (and not in that of any of its members) and, for the purposes of any such proceedings, any rules of court relating to the service of documents shall have effect as if the association were a corporation.

(2)   A fine imposed on an unincorporated association on its conviction of an offence under this Act shall be paid out of the funds of the association.

(3)   Section 33 of the Criminal Justice Act 1925 and Schedule 3 to the Magistrates' Courts Act 1980 (procedure on charge of offence against a corporation) shall have effect in a case in which an unincorporated association is charged in England or Wales with an offence under this Act in like manner as they have effect in the case of a corporation so charged.

(4)   In relation to any proceedings on indictment in Scotland for an offence alleged to have been committed under this Act by an unincorporated association, section 70 of the Criminal Procedure (Scotland) Act 1995 (proceedings on indictment against bodies corporate) shall have effect as if the association were a body corporate.

(5)   Section 18 of the Criminal Justice Act (Northern Ireland) 1945 and Schedule 4 to the Magistrates' Courts (Northern Ireland) Order 1981 (procedure on charge of offence against a corporation) shall have effect in a case in which an unincorporated association is charged in Northern Ireland with an offence under this Act in like manner as they have effect in the case of a corporation so charged.

(5A)   Sections 124 and 144 of, and Schedule 4 to, the Criminal Procedure Ordinance shall have effect in a case in which an unincorporated association is charged in Gibraltar with an offence under this Act in like manner as they have effect in the case of a corporation so charged.

(6)   Where a partnership is guilty of an offence under this Act and the offence is proved to have been committed with the consent or connivance of, or to be attributable to any neglect on the part of, any partner, he as well as the partnership shall be guilty of that offence and be liable to be proceeded against and punished accordingly.

(7)   Where any other unincorporated association is guilty of an offence under this Act and the offence is proved to have been committed with the consent or connivance of, or to be attributable to any neglect on the part of

    (a)   any officer of the association, or

    (b)   any member of the committee or other similar governing body of the association, he, as well as the association, shall be guilty of that offence and be liable to be proceeded against and punished accordingly.

NOTES
Defined terms
 Criminal Procedure Ordinance: cf s 160(6)
 document: s 160(1)

Duty of court to report convictions to Commission

154 The court by or before which a person is convicted of
    (a) an offence under this Act, or
    (b) an offence committed in connection with a relevant election (within the meaning of Part II),
shall notify the Commission of his conviction as soon as is practicable.

NOTES
Defined terms
 the Commission: s 160(1)

Variation of specified sums

Power to vary specified sums or percentages

155 (1) The Secretary of State may by order vary any sum for the time being specified in any provision of this Act (other than the sum specified in section 12(8) or 36(5)).

  (2) The Secretary of State may make such an order either
    (a) where he considers it expedient to do so in consequence of changes in the value of money, or
    (b) where the order gives effect to a recommendation of the Commission.

  (3) Subsection (4) applies in relation to the sums specified in
    (a) Part 4;
    (b) Part 4A;
    (c) Schedule 11;
    (ca) section 95B(6);
    (cb) Schedule 11A;
    (d) Schedule 15;
    (e) Schedule 19A.

  (4) In each Parliament, other than a Parliament that is dissolved less than two years after the date of its first sitting, the Secretary of State must either
    (a) make an order in pursuance of subsection (2)(a), or
    (b) lay before Parliament a statement setting out the Secretary of State's reasons for not doing so.

  (5) The Secretary of State may by order vary any percentage for the time being specified in
    (a) section 94(5ZA), 94D(4) or 96(2)(aa), or
    (b) paragraph 3(2) or (2A) of Schedule 10.

  (6) The Secretary of State may make an order under subsection (5) only if it gives effect to a recommendation of the Commission.

NOTES
Defined terms
 the Commission: s 160(1)
 the Secretary of State: s 159A

Supplementary

Orders and regulations

156 (1) Any power of the Secretary of State to make any order or regulations under this Act shall be exercised by statutory instrument.

(2) Subject to subsections (3) to (4A), a statutory instrument containing any order or regulations made under this Act by the Secretary of State shall be subject to annulment in pursuance of a resolution of either House of Parliament.

(3) Subsection (2) does not apply to
   (a) any order under section 163(2) or paragraph 14(7) of Schedule 1; or
   (b) any order made in pursuance of section 155(2)(a).

(4) Subsection (2) also does not apply to any order under
   (a) *Repealed*
   (b) section 51(4),
   (c) section 67(1),
   (ca) any provision of Chapter 6 of Part 4;
   (d) *Repealed*
   (da) section 71F(13),
   (db) section 71H(4),
   (dc) section 71U(1),
   (dd) any provision of Chapter 2 of Part 4A,
   (e) section 101(4),
   (f) section 108(3),
   (g) section 109(6),
   (h) section 129,
   (ha) paragraph 9 of Schedule 6A,
   (i) paragraph 3(4) of Schedule 7,
   (ia) paragraph 2(9) or 4(4) of Schedule 7A,
   (j) paragraph 4 of Schedule 8,
   (ja) paragraph 4 of Schedule 8A,
   (k) paragraph 3(4) of Schedule 11,
   (l) paragraph 4 of Schedule 13,
   (m) paragraph 2 of Schedule 14, or
   (n) paragraph 3(4) of Schedule 15;

and no such order shall be made (whether alone or with other provisions) unless a draft of the statutory instrument containing the order has been laid before, and approved by a resolution of, each House of Parliament.

(4A) An order under paragraph 16 of Schedule 19C that contains
   (a) provision made by virtue of paragraph 1(1), (2), (3), (4) or (5), paragraph 5(1), (2), (3) or (4), paragraph 10(2)(b) or (3)(b) or paragraph 15(1)(a) of that Schedule, or
   (b) provision amending an Act,

shall not be made unless a draft of the statutory instrument containing the order has been laid before, and approved by a resolution of, each House of Parliament; and subsection (2) does not apply to such an order.

(5) Any order or regulations made by the Secretary of State under this Act may
   (a) contain such consequential, incidental, supplementary or transitional provisions or savings (including provisions amending, repealing or revoking enactments) as the Secretary of State considers appropriate; and
   (b) make different provision for different cases.

(6) Nothing in this Act shall be read as affecting the generality of subsection (5) (including that subsection as applied by section 19(9)).

(7) Paragraphs 21 to 23 of Schedule 1 contain provisions relating to regulations made by the Commission.

NOTES
Defined terms
   the Commission: s 160(1)
   enactment: s 160(1)

                        Secretary of State: s 159A

Documents for purposes of the Act

157 (1)   Any application, notice or notification required or authorised to be made or given under this Act must be in writing.

   (2)   Any document required or authorised to be given or sent under this Act may be sent by post.

NOTES
Defined terms
   document: s 160(1)

Minor and consequential amendments and repeals

158 (1)   The minor and consequential amendments specified in Schedule 21 shall have effect.

   (2)   The enactments specified in Schedule 22 are repealed to the extent specified.

   (3)   However, none of the repeals
      (a)   of provisions of Part II (other than those relating to sections 72, 73, 79, 81, 82, 101 to 105, and 108 and Schedule 3) or III of the Representation of the People Act 1983 (election campaigns and legal proceedings in respect of elections), or
      (b)   of provisions amending any of those provisions,
   have effect in relation to local government elections in Scotland.

NOTES
Defined terms
   local government election: s 160(1)

Financial provisions

159 (1)   There shall be paid out of money provided by Parliament
      (a)   any expenses incurred by the Secretary of State in consequence of this Act; and
      (b)   any increase attributable to this Act in the sums which under any other Act are payable out of money so provided.

   (2)   There shall be charged on and paid out of the Consolidated Fund any increase attributable to this Act in the sums to be charged on and paid out of that Fund under any other Act.

NOTES
Defined terms
   Secretary of State: s 159A

Functions of the Chancellor of the Duchy of Lancaster

159A   In this Act, except
      (a)   sections 9,18(2) and (4), Chapter 6 of Part 4 and Chapter 2 of Part 4A, and
      (b)   paragraph 7 of Schedule 9,
      "the Secretary of State" means the Secretary of State or the Chancellor of the Duchy of Lancaster.

General interpretation

160 (1)   In this Act
   "accounting unit" and "party with accounting units" shall be construed in accordance with section 26(11);

"bequest" includes any form of testamentary disposition;

"body", without more, means a body corporate or any combination of persons or other unincorporated association;

"broadcaster" has the meaning given by section 37(2);

"business" includes every trade, profession and occupation;

"central organisation", in relation to a registered party, shall be construed in accordance with section 26(11);

"combined region" means the electoral region which includes Gibraltar, namely the South West electoral region;

"the Commission" means the Electoral Commission;

"contravention" includes a failure to comply, and cognate expressions shall be construed accordingly;

"document" means a document in whatever form it is kept;

"enactment" includes

    (a) any provision of an Act (including this Act),

    (b) any provision of or of any instrument made under Northern Ireland legislation, and

    (c) any provision of subordinate legislation (within the meaning of the Interpretation Act 1978);

"exempt Gibraltar trust donation" has the meaning given by section 162;

"exempt trust donation" has the meaning given by section 162;

"functions" includes powers and duties;

"Gibraltar court" as respects any purpose, means the court determined by or under the law of Gibraltar to be the court for that purpose;

"Gibraltar elector" means an individual

    (a) who is registered in the Gibraltar register, or

    (b) if the first version of that register has not been published

        (i) who is registered in the register of electors used for House of Assembly elections, or

        (ii) who is resident in Gibraltar, aged 16 or over and is a Commonwealth citizen or a citizen of the European Union (other than a Commonwealth citizen);

"Gibraltar party" has the meaning given by section 28(8)(d);

"Gibraltar register" has the meaning given by section 14 of the European Parliament (Representation) Act 2003;

"the Great Britain register" and "the Northern Ireland register" mean the registers of political parties referred to in section 23(2)(a) and (b) respectively;

"local election", in relation to Northern Ireland, means a local election within the meaning of the Electoral Law Act (Northern Ireland) 1962;

"local government election" means a local government election within the meaning of section 191, 203 or 204 of the Representation of the People Act 1983 or an election under Part II of the Local Government Act 2000 for the return of an elected mayor;

"market value", in relation to any property, means the price which might reasonably be expected to be paid for the property on a sale in the open market;

"minor party" means (in accordance with section 34(1)) a party registered in the Great Britain register in pursuance of a declaration falling within section 28(2)(d);

"modifications" includes additions, omissions and amendments, and "modify" shall be construed accordingly;

"organisation" includes any body corporate and any combination of persons or other unincorporated association;

"property" includes any description of property, and references to the provision of property accordingly include the supply of goods;

"qualified auditor" means (subject to subsection (2))

    (a) a person who is eligible for appointment as a statutory auditor under Part 42 of the Companies Act 2006; or

    (b) in the case of a Gibraltar party, a person who is, in accordance with section 6 of the Auditors Approval and Registration Ordinance 1998, eligible for appointment as a company auditor

"record" means a record in whatever form it is kept;

"registered party" means a party registered under Part II of this Act;

"restriction" includes prohibition;

"treasurer", in relation to a registered party, means registered treasurer.

(2) A person is not a qualified auditor in relation to any registered party or any other body or individual if he is

    (a) a member of the party or body or the individual himself, or

    (b) an officer or employee of the party, body or individual.

For this purpose "officer or employee" does not include an auditor.

(3) References in this Act to a person standing for election in the name of a registered party shall be construed in accordance with section 22(6).

(4) References in this Act (in whatever terms) to payments out of public funds are references to any of the following, namely

    (a) payments out of

        (i) the Consolidated Fund of the United Kingdom, the Scottish Consolidated Fund, the Welsh Consolidated Fund or the Consolidated Fund of Northern Ireland, or

        (ii) money provided by Parliament or appropriated by Act of the Northern Ireland Assembly;

    (b) payments by

        (i) any Minister of the Crown, the Scottish Ministers, the Welsh Ministers or any Minister within the meaning of the Northern Ireland Act 1998,

        (ii) any government department (including a Northern Ireland department), the Welsh Assembly Government or any part of the Scottish Administration,

        (iii) *Repealed*

    (c) payments by the Scottish Parliamentary Corporate Body, the National Assembly for Wales Commission or the Northern Ireland Assembly Commission; and

    (d) payments by the Electoral Commission;

and references in this Act (in whatever terms) to expenses met, or things provided, out of public funds are references to expenses met, or things provided, by means of any such payments.

(5) References in this Act to conditions, in the context of grants being made subject to conditions, include conditions requiring repayment of the grants in specified circumstances.

(6) References in this Act to a named Act are to the Gibraltar Act of that name.

Interpretation: donations

161 (1) This section has effect for the purposes of the provisions of this Act relating to donations.

(2) Where any provision of this Act refers to a donation for the purpose of meeting a particular kind of expenses incurred by or on behalf of a person of a particular description

    (a) the reference includes a reference to a donation for the purpose of securing that any such expenses are not so incurred; and

    (b) a donation shall be taken to be a donation for either of those purposes if, having regard to all the circumstances, it must be reasonably assumed to be such a donation.

(3) Subsections (4) and (5) apply to any provision of this Act which provides, in relation to a person of a particular description ("the donee"), that money spent (otherwise than by or on behalf of the donee) in paying any expenses incurred directly or indirectly by the donee is to constitute a donation to the donee.

(4) The reference in any such provision to money so spent is a reference to money so spent by a person, other than the donee, out of his own resources (with no right to reimbursement out of the resources of the donee).

(5) Where by virtue of any such provision any amount of money so spent constitutes a donation to the donee, the donee shall be treated as receiving an equivalent amount on the date on which the money is paid to the creditor in respect of the expenses in question.

(6) For the purposes of this Act it is immaterial whether a donation received by a registered party or a person of any other description is so received in the United Kingdom or elsewhere.

NOTES

Defined terms
   registered party: s 160(1)

Interpretation: exempt trust donations

162 (1) For the purposes of this Act
   (a) "exempt trust donation" means a donation to which subsection (2) or (3) applies, other than one falling within subsection (5);
   (b) "exempt Gibraltar trust donation" means a donation to which subsection (3A) applies, other than one falling within subsection (5).

(2) This subsection applies to any donation received from a trustee of any property in accordance with the terms of a trust
   (a) which was created before 27th July 1999,
   (b) to which no property has been transferred on or after that date, and
   (c) whose terms have not been varied on or after that date,
   provided that, at or before the time of the receipt of the donation, the trustee gives the recipient of the donation the full name of the person who created the trust and of every other person by whom, or under whose will, property was transferred to the trust before that date.

(3) This subsection applies to any donation received from a trustee of any property in accordance with the terms of a trust
   (a) which was created by
      (i) a person who was a permissible donor falling within section 54(2) at the time when the trust was created, or
      (ii) the will of a person falling within section 54(3), and
   (b) to which no property has been transferred otherwise than
      (i) by a person who was a permissible donor falling within section 54(2) at the time of the transfer, or
      (ii) under the will of a person falling within section 54(3),
   provided that, at or before the time of the receipt of the donation, the trustee gives the recipient of the donation the relevant information.

(3A) This subsection applies to any donation received from a trustee of any property in accordance with the terms of a trust
   (a) which was created by
      (i) a person falling within section 54(2A)(a) to (g) at the time when the trust was created, or

      (ii)   the will of a person falling within section 54(3A), and

   (b)   to which no property has been transferred other than

      (i)   by a person falling within section 54(2A)(a) to (g) at the time of the transfer, or

      (ii)   under the will of a person falling within section 54(3A),

provided that, at or before the time of the receipt of the donation, the trustee gives the recipient of the donation the relevant information.

(4)   For the purposes of subsections (3) and (3A) "the relevant information" means the information which is required by virtue of paragraph 2 of Schedule 6 to be given in respect of a recordable donation to which that subsection applies.

(5)   A donation falls within this subsection if it is received from a trustee of any property pursuant to the exercise of any discretion vested by a trust in him or any other person.

(6)   In this section

   (a)   "donation" means a donation for the purposes of the provisions of this Act in which the relevant reference to an exempt trust donation or exempt Gibraltar trust donation occurs;

   (b)   "property", in the context of the transfer of property to a trust, does not include any income of the trust;

   (c)   "trust" includes a trust created by a will; and

   (d)   any reference to a donation received from a trustee is a reference to a donation received from a trustee in his capacity as such, other than a donation transmitted on behalf of a beneficiary under a trust.

NOTES

Defined terms
   property: s 160(1) (and sub-s (6)(b) of this section)
   recordable donation: Sch 6, para 1

Short title, commencement, transitional provisions and extent

163 (1)   This Act may be cited as the Political Parties, Elections and Referendums Act 2000.

(2)   Subject to subsections (3) and (4), this Act does not come into force until such day as the Secretary of State may by order appoint; and different days may be so appointed for different purposes.

(3)   The following provisions come into force on the day on which this Act is passed

   (a)   sections 1 to 3 and Schedules 1 and 2,

   (b)   sections 156, 159 and 160, and paragraph 12(1) and (4) of Schedule 21,

   (c)   this section, and Part II of Schedule 23, and

   (d)   any other provision so far as it confers power to make an order or regulations.

(4)   The following provisions come into force at the end of the period of two weeks beginning with the day on which this Act is passed

   (a)   section 36,

   (b)   Part I of Schedule 23, and

   (c)   any provision of Part II of this Act so far as necessary for the purposes of the operation of any provision of Part I of that Schedule.

(5)   An order under subsection (2) may contain such transitional provisions and savings (including provisions modifying enactments) as the Secretary of State considers appropriate.

(6)   Such an order may, in particular, make provision as respects the operation of any financial limit imposed by any provision of this Act in cases where a period in relation to which any such limit is imposed would otherwise begin at a time before the commencement of that provision of this Act.

(7) The transitional provisions contained in Schedule 23 shall have effect.

(8) Subject to subsections (9) and (10), this Act extends to the whole of the United Kingdom.

(9) Part IX and paragraphs 2 and 3 of Schedule 12 and paragraphs 12 and 13 of Schedule 23 extend to England, Wales and Scotland.

(10) Subject to any express limitation contained in this Act, the extent of any amendment or repeal made by this Act is the same as that of the enactment amended or repealed.

(11) The following provisions of this Act extend to Gibraltar
   (a) Part 1 (The Electoral Commission), except sections 9, 12 and 14 to 20;
   (b) Part 2 (Registration of Political Parties), except sections 36 and 38;
   (c) Part 3 (Accounting requirements for registered parties);
   (d) Part 4 (Control of donations to registered parties and their members etc);
   (da) Part 4A (Regulation of Loans and Related Transactions);
   (e) Part 5 (Control of campaign expenditure);
   (f) Part 6 (Controls relating to third party national election campaigns); and
   (g) Part 10 (Miscellaneous and general), except sections 141, 142, 144 and 158.

NOTES
Defined terms
   enactment: s 160(1)
   Secretary of State: s 159A

SCHEDULE 1
THE ELECTORAL COMMISSION

Section 1

Status of Commission and their property

1 (1) The Commission shall not be regarded
   (a) as the servant or agent of the Crown, or
   (b) as enjoying any status, immunity or privilege of the Crown.

(2) The property of the Commission shall not be regarded as property of, or property held on behalf of, the Crown.

Powers

2 The Commission may do anything (except borrow money) which is calculated to facilitate, or is incidental or conducive to, the carrying out of any of their functions.

Term of office etc of Electoral Commissioners

3 (1) Subject to the provisions of this paragraph, an Electoral Commissioner shall hold office as such Commissioner
   (a) for the period for which he is appointed, and
   (b) otherwise in accordance with the terms of his appointment.

(2) The period for which an Electoral Commissioner is appointed shall be the period specified in relation to him in the address pursuant to which he is appointed.

(3) Subject to sub-paragraph (3A), an Electoral Commissioner shall cease to hold office on the occurrence of any of the following events

(a) he consents to being nominated as a candidate at a relevant election (within the meaning of Part II) or to being included in a registered party's list of candidates at such an election;

(b) he takes up any office or employment in or with
  (i) a registered party or any accounting unit of such a party,
  (ii) a recognised third party (within the meaning of Part VI), or
  (iii) a permitted participant (within the meaning of Part VII), or
  (iv) an accredited campaigner within the meaning of Schedule 3 to the Recall of MPs Act 2015 (see Part 5 of that Schedule);

(c) he is named as a donor in
  (i) the register of donations reported under Chapter 3 or 5 of Part 4,
  (ii) any quarterly or weekly report delivered to the Commission under section 95A or 95B, or
  (iii) any statement of donations included in a return delivered to the Commission under section 98 or 122 or in a recall petition return delivered to a petition officer under paragraph 6 of Schedule 5 to the Recall of MPs Act 2015;

(ca) he is named as a participant in the register of recordable transactions reported under Part 4A;

(d) he becomes a member of a registered party.

(3A) Paragraph (d) of sub-paragraph (3) does not apply to a nominated Commissioner (within the meaning of section 3A).

(4) An Electoral Commissioner may be removed from office by Her Majesty in pursuance of an Address from the House of Commons.

(5) No motion shall be made for such an Address unless the Speaker's Committee have presented a report to the House of Commons stating that the Committee are satisfied that one or more of the following grounds is made out in the case of the Electoral Commissioner in question

(a) he has failed to discharge the functions of his office for a continuous period of at least 3 months;

(b) he has failed to comply with the terms of his appointment;

(c) he has been convicted of a criminal offence;

(d) he is an undischarged bankrupt or his estate has been sequestrated in Scotland and he has not been discharged;

(da) a moratorium period under a debt relief order applies in relation to him (under Part 7A of the Insolvency Act 1986);

(e) he has made an arrangement or composition contract with, or has granted a trust deed for, his creditors;

(f) he is otherwise unfit to hold his office or unable to carry out its functions.

(6) A motion for such an Address shall not be made on the ground mentioned in sub-paragraph (5)(a) if more than 3 months have elapsed since the end of the period in question.

(7) An Electoral Commissioner may be relieved of his office by Her Majesty at his own request.

(8) In this paragraph "registered party" includes, in relation to times before the appointed day for the purposes of Part II of this Act, a party registered under the Registration of Political Parties Act 1998.

(9) In this paragraph, sub-paragraph (5)(da) does not extend to Gibraltar.

Term of office etc of Commission chairman

4 (1)   Subject to the provisions of this paragraph, the chairman of the Commission shall hold office as such chairman
    (a)   for the period for which he is appointed, and
    (b)   otherwise in accordance with the terms of his appointment.

  (2)   The period for which a person is appointed as chairman of the Commission shall be the period specified in relation to him in the address pursuant to which he is appointed.

  (3)   The chairman of the Commission may be relieved of his office of chairman by Her Majesty at his own request.

  (4)   If the chairman of the Commission ceases to be an Electoral Commissioner, he also ceases to be chairman.

Electoral Commissioners: salary etc

5 (1)   There shall be paid to an Electoral Commissioner such remuneration, and any such allowances or expenses, as may be specified in a resolution of the House of Commons.

  (2)   If a resolution of the House of Commons so provides in the case of any person who is an Electoral Commissioner or former Electoral Commissioner
    (a)   such amounts shall be paid towards the provision of superannuation benefits for or in respect of him as may be specified in the resolution;
    (b)   (in the case of a former Electoral Commissioner) such pension shall be paid to or in respect of him as may be so specified.

  (3)   A resolution for the purposes of this paragraph may
    (a)   specify the amounts to be paid;
    (b)   provide that the amounts to be paid shall be the same as, or calculated on the same basis as, those payable to or in respect of a person employed in a specified office under, or in a specified capacity in the service of, the Crown;
    (c)   specify the amounts to be paid and provide for them to be increased by reference to such variables as may be specified in the resolution;
    (d)   have the effect of making different provision for different Electoral Commissioners or former Electoral Commissioners.

  (4)   A resolution for the purposes of this paragraph may take effect from the date on which it is passed or from any earlier or later date specified in the resolution.

  (5)   Any amount payable under this paragraph (other than by way of expenses) shall be charged on and issued out of the Consolidated Fund.

  (6)   Any amount payable under this paragraph by way of expenses shall be paid by the Commission.

  (7)   In this paragraph "pension" includes allowance and gratuity .

  6   *Repealed*

Assistant Electoral Commissioners

7 (1)   The Commission may appoint one or more Assistant Electoral Commissioners to inquire into, and report to the Commission on, such matters as the Commission or a Boundary Committee think fit.

  (2)   A person may not be appointed as an Assistant Electoral Commissioner if he is prevented by section 3(4) (read without regard to section 3(4A)) from being appointed as an Electoral Commissioner.

  (3)   An Assistant Electoral Commissioner shall

    (a) be appointed either for a fixed term or for the purposes of a particular inquiry; and

    (b) (subject to sub-paragraph (4)) hold and vacate office in accordance with the terms of his appointment.

(4) An Assistant Electoral Commissioner shall cease to hold office on the occurrence of such an event as is mentioned in any of paragraphs (a) to (d) of paragraph 3(3).

(5) The Commission shall pay an Assistant Electoral Commissioner such remuneration, and any such allowances or expenses, as may be provided for by or under the terms of his appointment.

Committees

8 (1) The Commission may establish any committees which the Commission consider appropriate.

(2) Any committee of the Commission established under sub-paragraph (1) may establish one or more subcommittees.

(3) A person shall not be a member of a committee or subcommittee established under this paragraph unless he is an Electoral Commissioner.

Delegation to committees

9 (1) The Commission may delegate functions of the Commission (to such extent as the Commission may determine) to any committee of the Commission established under paragraph 8(1).

(2) *Repealed*

(3) A committee of the Commission established under paragraph 8(1) may delegate functions of the committee (to such extent as the committee may determine) to any subcommittee of the committee.

Procedure and proceedings

10 (1) The Commission shall regulate their own procedure, and the procedure of their committees and subcommittees, including the quorum for meetings.

(2) The validity of any proceedings of the Commission, or of any of their committees or subcommittees, shall not be affected by

    (a) any vacancy among the members of the Commission, or of the committee or subcommittee, or

    (b) any defect in the appointments of any such member.

Staff

11 (1) The Commission

    (a) shall appoint a chief executive, and

    (b) may appoint such other staff as the Commission consider necessary to assist them and their committees in the performance of their functions.

(2) *Repealed*

(3) Subject to paragraph 11A(4), the staff of the Commission shall be appointed on such terms and conditions as the Commission may determine; and the Commission shall pay their staff such remuneration as may be provided for by or under their terms of appointment.

(4) *Repealed*

(5)   In determining the terms and conditions of staff under sub-paragraph (3) above, the Commission shall have regard to the desirability of keeping the remuneration and other terms and conditions of employment of its staff broadly in line with those applying to persons employed in the civil service of the State.

(6)   Service as an officer or employee of the Commission shall be included in the kinds of employment to which a scheme under section 1 of the Superannuation Act 1972 can apply; and, accordingly, in Schedule 1 to that Act (which lists the kinds of employment to which a scheme can apply), the following entry shall be inserted at the end of the list of   "Royal Commissions and other Commissions"
      "Electoral Commission".

(7)   The Commission shall pay to the Minister for the Civil Service, at such times as he may direct, such sums as he may determine in respect of any increase attributable to sub-paragraph (6) in the sums payable out of money provided by Parliament under the Superannuation Act 1972.

(8)   No member of the staff of the Commission shall be regarded
      (a)   as the servant or agent of the Crown, or
      (b)   as enjoying any status, immunity or privilege of the Crown.

(9)   The Secretary of State may appoint a person to be the Commission's chief executive until such time as the first person to be appointed by the Commission as their chief executive takes up office; and until such time as the Commission have appointed their own staff the Secretary of State may appoint persons to serve as members of the Commission's staff.

(10)   Until such time as the Commission may determine, the Commission's chief executive appointed under sub-paragraph (9) may incur expenditure and do other things in the name and on behalf of the Commission, whether or not the membership of the Commission has yet to be constituted in accordance with section 1.

(11)   The power conferred by sub-paragraph (10) shall be exercisable by that person subject to and in accordance with any directions given to him by the Secretary of State.

Political restrictions on staff

11A (1)   A person may not be appointed as a member of the staff of the Commission if the person
         (a)   is an officer or employee of a registered party or of any accounting unit of such a party;
         (b)   holds a relevant elective office (within the meaning of Schedule 7);
         (c)   has at any time within the relevant period (see sub-paragraph (2))
               (i)   been such an officer or employee as is mentioned in paragraph (a), or
               (ii)   held such an office as is mentioned in paragraph (b), or
               (iii) been named as a donor in the register of donations reported under Chapter 3 or 5 of Part 4, or
               (iv)   been named as a participant in the register of recordable transactions reported under Part 4A.

   (2)   The relevant period is
         (a)   in relation to appointment as chief executive of the Commission, the last five years;
         (b)   in relation to appointment to a post on the staff of the Commission that is designated by a notice in force under paragraph 11B, the period (immediately preceding the appointment) specified by the notice;
         (c)   in relation to appointment as any other member of the staff of the Commission, the last 12 months.

(3) A member of a registered party may not be appointed as chief executive of the Commission.

(4) The appointment of any member of the staff of the Commission shall terminate
    (a) in the case of the chief executive, on the occurrence of such an event as is mentioned in any of paragraphs (a) to (d) of paragraph 3(3);
    (b) in any other case, on the occurrence of such an event as is mentioned in any of paragraphs (a) to (ca) of paragraph 3(3).

11B (1) The chief executive of the Commission may by giving notice to the Speaker's Committee
    (a) designate a particular post on the staff of the Commission, and
    (b) specify as the relevant period for that post, for the purposes of paragraph 11A(2)(b), a period of two years or more,
if the chief executive reasonably believes that it is necessary to do so in order to maintain public confidence in the effectiveness of the Commission in carrying out any of its functions.

(2) The period specified under sub-paragraph (1)(b) may not be more than five years.

(3) In deciding what that period should be, the chief executive of the Commission shall take into account
    (a) the level of seniority of the post;
    (b) how likely it is that any holder of the post will be required to deal with politically sensitive matters.

(4) Each notice under sub-paragraph (1) must relate to only one post.

(5) A notice under sub-paragraph (1)
    (a) has effect from the day on which it is received by the Speaker's Committee, and
    (b) (subject to sub-paragraphs (6) and (7)) expires at the end of the period of three years beginning with that day.

(6) Sub-paragraph (5)(b) does not prevent a further notice being given under sub-paragraph (1) in relation to the post in question, either
    (a) before the previous notice would have expired, or
    (b) at any time after the expiry of the previous notice.
A further notice received by the Speaker's Committee before the previous notice would have expired supersedes the previous notice.

(7) If the chief executive of the Commission gives notice (a "cancellation notice") to the Speaker's Committee cancelling a notice under sub-paragraph (1), the notice under that sub-paragraph ceases to have effect
    (a) on the day on which the cancellation notice is received by the Speaker's Committee, or
    (b) (if later) on such date as may be specified in the cancellation notice.

(8) Before giving a notice under this paragraph the chief executive of the Commission shall consult the Speaker's Committee.

(9) The Commission shall publish, in such manner as they consider appropriate, information setting out the effect of all notices under sub-paragraph (1) that are in force at any particular time.

Delegation to staff

12 Each of the following
    (a) the Commission,
    (b) any committee of the Commission,

(c)   any subcommittee of such a committee, and

(d)   the Commission's chief executive,

may delegate functions of theirs or his (to such extent as they or he may determine) to the Commission's staff (either generally or otherwise).

Delegation and contracting out of superannuation functions

13 (1)   Section 1(2) of the Superannuation Act 1972 (delegation of functions relating to civil service superannuation schemes by Minister for the Civil Service to another officer of the Crown etc) shall have effect as if the reference to an officer of the Crown other than a Minister included the Commission's chief executive.

(2)   Any administration function conferred on the Commission's chief executive under section 1(2) of the Superannuation Act 1972 (as it has effect in accordance with sub-paragraph (1)) may be exercised by (or by employees of) such person as may be authorised in that behalf by the Commission's chief executive.

(3)   For the purposes of this paragraph an "administration function" is a function of administering schemes

(a)   made under section 1 of the Superannuation Act 1972, and

(b)   from time to time in force.

(4)   An authorisation given by virtue of sub-paragraph (2) may authorise the exercise of an administration function

(a)   either wholly or to such extent as may be specified in the authorisation;

(b)   either generally or in such cases as may be so specified; and

(c)   either unconditionally or subject to the fulfilment of such conditions as may be so specified.

(5)   An authorisation given by virtue of sub-paragraph (2)

(a)   shall be treated for all purposes as if it were given by virtue of an order under section 69 of the Deregulation and Contracting Out Act 1994 (contracting out of functions of Ministers and officeholders);

(b)   may be revoked at any time by the Commission (as well as by the chief executive).

Financing of Commission

14 (1)   The expenditure of the Commission, so far as it cannot be met out of income received by the Commission, shall be met, in accordance with this paragraph, out of money provided by Parliament (except so far as it is

(a)   reimbursed by the Secretary of State under section 18(9) or the Scottish Ministers in pursuance of section 13A, 19(11) or 145(6);

(b)   met by the Welsh Ministers in pursuance of section 5(3) or 20(12); or

(c)   met by the National Assembly for Wales Commission under Schedule 2 paragraph 6 to the Government of Wales Act 2006.

(2)   For each financial year (other than the Commission's first financial year) the Commission shall prepare, and submit to the Speaker's Committee, an estimate of the Commission's income and expenditure.

(3)   The Speaker's Committee shall

(a)   examine each such estimate submitted to them; and

(b)   decide whether they are satisfied that the estimated level of income and expenditure is consistent with the economical, efficient and effective discharge by the Commission of their functions; and

(c)   if they are not so satisfied, shall make such modifications to the estimate as they consider appropriate for the purpose of achieving such consistency.

(4) Before deciding whether they are so satisfied or making any such modifications, the Speaker's Committee shall

    (a) have regard to the most recent report made to them by the Comptroller and Auditor General under paragraph 16 and to any recommendations contained in that report; and

    (b) consult the Treasury and have regard to any advice which the Treasury may give.

(5) The Speaker's Committee shall, after concluding their examination and making their modifications (if any) to the estimate, lay the estimate before the House of Commons.

(6) If the Speaker's Committee, in the discharge of their functions under this paragraph

    (a) do not follow any recommendation contained in the report of the Comptroller and Auditor General,

    (b) do not follow any advice given to them by the Treasury, or

    (c) make any modification to the estimate,

they shall include in the next report which they make to the House of Commons under paragraph 1 of Schedule 2 a statement of their reasons for so doing.

(7) The Secretary of State may by order provide for the transfer to the Commission of such property, rights and liabilities

    (a) to which he is entitled or subject, and

    (b) which are specified in the order,

as he considers appropriate in connection with the establishment of the Commission.

(8) Such an order may in particular provide for the order to have effect despite any provision (of whatever nature) which would prevent or restrict the transfer of any such property, rights or liabilities otherwise than by the order.

Five year plan

15 (1) When the Commission submit to the Speaker's Committee such an estimate as is mentioned in paragraph 14 in respect of the first financial year to begin after the day on which Parliament meets for the first time following a parliamentary general election, the Commission shall also submit to the Committee a plan prepared by the Commission setting out the Commission's

    (a) aims and objectives for the period of five years beginning with the financial year to which the estimate relates, and

    (b) estimated requirements for resources during that five-year period.

(1A) The Speaker's Committee may require the Commission to submit a plan under sub-paragraph (1) when the Commission submit such an estimate as is mentioned in paragraph 14 in respect of a financial year other than one mentioned in that sub-paragraph.

(2) The Speaker's Committee shall

    (a) examine each plan submitted to them;

    (b) decide whether they are satisfied that the plan is consistent with the economical, efficient and effective discharge by the Commission of their functions; and

    (c) if they are not so satisfied, shall make such modifications to the plan as they consider appropriate for the purpose of achieving such consistency.

(3) Before deciding whether they are so satisfied or making any such modifications, the Speaker's Committee shall

    (a) have regard to the most recent report made to them by the Comptroller and Auditor General under paragraph 16 and to any recommendations contained in that report; and

(b)   consult the Treasury and have regard to any advice which the Treasury may give.

(4)   The Speaker's Committee shall, after concluding their examination and making their modifications (if any) to the plan, lay the plan before the House of Commons.

(5)   If the Speaker's Committee, in the discharge of their functions under this paragraph

    (a)   do not follow any recommendation contained in the report of the Comptroller and Auditor General,

    (b)   do not follow any advice given to them by the Treasury, or

    (c)   make any modification to the plan,

they shall include in the next report which they make to the House of Commons under paragraph 1 of Schedule 2 a statement of their reasons for so doing.

Annual Examination of Commission by Comptroller and Auditor General

16 (1)   For the purpose of assisting the Speaker's Committee to discharge their functions under paragraphs 14 and 15 in respect of any year when both an estimate under paragraph 14 and a five-year plan under paragraph 15 are submitted to them, the Comptroller and Auditor General shall in each year before the Committee consider the estimate and plan

    (a)   carry out an examination into the economy, efficiency or effectiveness (or, if he so determines, any combination thereof) with which the Commission have used their resources in discharging their functions (or, if he so determines, any particular functions of theirs);

    (b)   report to the Speaker's Committee the results of the examination; and

    (c)   include in his report such recommendations as he considers appropriate in the light of the examination.

(2)   Section 8 of the National Audit Act 1983 (right to obtain documents and information) shall apply in relation to any examination under this paragraph as it applies in relation to an examination under section 6 of that Act.

Accounts

17 (1)   The Commission shall keep proper accounting records.

(2)   The Commission shall, for each financial year, prepare accounts in accordance with directions given to the Commission by the Treasury.

(3)   The directions which the Treasury may give under sub-paragraph (2) include, in particular, directions as to

    (a)   the information to be contained in the accounts and the manner in which it is to be presented,

    (b)   the methods and principles in accordance with which the accounts are to be prepared, and

    (c)   the additional information (if any) that is to accompany the accounts.

Audit

18 (1)   The accounts prepared by the Commission for any financial year shall be submitted by the Commission to

    (a)   the Comptroller and Auditor General, and

    (b)   the Speaker's Committee,

as soon after the end of the financial year as may be practicable.

(2)   The Comptroller and Auditor General shall

    (a)   examine and certify any accounts submitted to him under this paragraph, and

(b) lay before each House of Parliament a copy of the accounts as certified by him together with his report on them.

Accounting officer

19 (1) The Speaker's Committee shall designate a member of the Commission's staff to be the Commission's accounting officer.

(2) The Commission's accounting officer shall have, in relation to the Commission's accounts and finances, the responsibilities that are from time to time specified by the Speaker's Committee.

(3) In this paragraph references to responsibilities include in particular
   (a) responsibilities in relation to the signing of accounts;
   (b) responsibilities for the propriety and regularity of the Commission's finances; and
   (c) responsibilities for the economy, efficiency and effectiveness with which the Commission's resources are used.

(4) The responsibilities which may be specified under this paragraph include responsibilities owed to the Commission, the Speaker's Committee or the House of Commons or its Committee of Public Accounts.

(5) In this paragraph any reference to the Public Accounts Committee of the House of Commons shall, if
   (a) the name of the Committee is changed, or
   (b) the functions of the Committee at the passing of this Act (or functions substantially corresponding thereto) become functions of a different committee of the House of Commons,
   be taken to be references to the Committee by its new name or (as the case may be) to the committee by whom the functions are for the time being exercisable.

(6) The Secretary of State may designate any member of the Commission's staff or other person to be the Commission's accounting officer until such time as the first designation made under sub-paragraph (1) takes effect.

Reports

20 (1) The Commission shall, as soon after the end of each financial year as may be practicable, prepare and lay before each House of Parliament a report about the performance of the Commission's functions during that financial year.

(2) The Commission shall, on so laying such a report, publish the report in such manner as they determine.

(3) The functions referred to in sub-paragraph (1) do not include the Commission's functions under Part 1 in relation to local government elections in Scotland.

20A (1) The Commission must, as soon after the end of each financial year as may be practicable, prepare and lay before the Scottish Parliament a report about the performance of the functions mentioned in sub-paragraph (3) during that financial year.

(2) On laying the report, the Commission must publish the report in such manner as they may determine.

(3) The functions are the Commission's functions under Part 1 in relation to local government elections in Scotland.

Notification of Commission regulations

21 (1) If the Commission make any regulations, they must give a copy to the Secretary of State without delay.

(2) If the Commission alter or revoke any regulations, they must give notice to the Secretary of State without delay.

(3) Notice of an alteration must include details of the alteration.

Regulation making instruments

22 (1) Any power conferred on the Commission to make regulations is exercisable in writing.

(2) An instrument by which regulations are made by the Commission ("a regulation-making instrument") must specify the provision under which the regulations are made.

(3) To the extent to which a regulation-making instrument does not comply with sub-paragraph (2), it is void.

(4) Immediately after a regulation-making instrument is made, it must be printed and made available to the public.

(5) The Commission may charge a reasonable fee for providing a person with a copy of a regulation-making instrument.

(6) A person is not to be taken to have contravened any regulation made by the Commission if he shows that at the time of the alleged contravention the regulation-making instrument concerned had not been made available in accordance with this paragraph.

(7) Any power of the Commission to make regulations includes power to make different provision for different cases.

Verification of regulations

23 (1) The production of a printed copy of a regulation-making instrument purporting to be made by the Commission
   (a) on which is endorsed a certificate signed by a member of the Commission's staff authorised by the Commission for that purpose, and
   (b) which contains the required statements,
   is evidence (or in Scotland sufficient evidence) of the facts stated in the certificate.

(2) The required statements are
   (a) that the instrument was made by the Commission;
   (b) that the copy is a true copy of the instrument; and
   (c) that on a specified date the instrument was made available to the public in accordance with paragraph 22(4).

(3) A certificate purporting to be signed as mentioned in sub-paragraph (1) is to be taken to have been properly signed unless the contrary is shown.

(4) A person who wishes in any legal proceedings to rely on a regulation-making instrument may require the Commission to endorse a copy of the instrument with a certificate of the kind mentioned in sub-paragraph (1).

Documentary evidence

24 A document purporting to be
   (a) duly executed under the seal of the Commission, or
   (b) signed on behalf of the Commission,

shall be received in evidence and shall, unless the contrary is proved, be taken to be so executed or signed.

Interpretation

25　In this Schedule "delegate" includes further delegate.

NOTES

Defined terms

accounting unit: ss 26(11), 160(1)
the Commission: s 160(1)
donation: s 161
financial year: s 21
functions: s 160(1)
modifications: s 160(1)

party with accounting units: ss 26(11), 160(1)
property: s 160(1)
registered party: s 160(1) (and para 3(8) of this Schedule)
the Secretary of State: s 159A
the Speaker's Committee: s 2(1)

SCHEDULE 2
THE SPEAKER'S COMMITTEE

Section 2

Reports

1 (1)　The Speaker's Committee shall, at least once in each year, make to the House of Commons a report on the exercise by the Committee of their functions.

(2)　For the purposes of the law of defamation the publication of any matter by the Speaker's Committee in making such a report shall be absolutely privileged.

Term of office of Committee members

2 (1)　In this paragraph "appointed member" means a member of the Speaker's Committee other than
  (a)　the Speaker of the House of Commons;
  (b)　the member who is the Chairman of the Home Affairs Committee of the House of Commons; or
  (c)　the member who is the Chancellor of the Duchy of Lancaster.

(2)　An appointed member shall cease to be a member of the Speaker's Committee if
  (a)　he ceases to be a Member of the House of Commons; or
  (b)　another person is appointed to be a member of the Committee in his place.

(3)　An appointed member may resign from the Committee at any time by giving notice to the Speaker.

(4)　Subject to sub-paragraphs (2) and (3), an appointed member shall be a member of the Committee for the duration of the Parliament in which he is appointed.

(5)　An appointed member may be reappointed (or further reappointed) to membership of the Committee.

Committee proceedings

3 (1)　The Speaker's Committee may determine their own procedure.

(2)　The validity of any proceedings of the Committee shall not be affected by
  (a)　any vacancy among, or
  (b)　any defect in the appointment of any of,
the members of the Committee.

(3)   The Committee may appoint a member of the Committee to act as chairman at any meeting of the Committee in the absence of the Speaker.

NOTES

Defined terms
  the Speaker's Committee: s 2(1)

SCHEDULE 3

Repealed

SCHEDULE 4
APPLICATIONS UNDER PART II

Sections 28, 30, 31 and 33

Part I
Application for Registration

Introductory

1 (1)   Paragraphs 2 to 7 must be complied with in relation to an application under section 28.

(2)   Such an application must be accompanied by any fee prescribed by order made by the Secretary of State.

(3)   In the following provisions of this Part of this Schedule "an application" means an application under section 28.

Names

2 (1)   An application for registration in the Great Britain register must specify either
(a)   a name to be the party's registered name, or
(b)   a name in Welsh and a name in English to be the party's registered names.

(2)   If a name to be registered in that register is in a language other than English or Welsh, the application must include an English translation.

(3)   An application for registration in the Northern Ireland register must specify either
(a)   a name to be the party's registered name, or
(b)   a name in Irish and a name in English to be the party's registered names.

(4)   If a name to be registered in that register is in a language other than English or Irish, the application must include an English translation.

Headquarters

3 (1)   An application must specify
(a)   the address of the party's headquarters, or
(b)   if the party has no headquarters, an address to which communications to the party may be sent.

(2)   Where the party is a party with accounting units, any reference to the party in sub-paragraph (1) above is to be read as a reference to the central organisation.

Registered officers

4 (1)   An application must give the name and home address of each of the following
(a)   a person to be registered as the party's leader;

    (b) a person to be registered as the party's nominating officer;

    (c) a person to be registered as the party's treasurer.

(2) If the application is for the party to be registered as a party with a campaigns officer, the application must also give the name and home address of a person to be registered as the party's campaigns officer.

(3) If the person to be registered as the party's leader is (as mentioned in section 24(2)) the leader of the party for some particular purpose, the application must specify that purpose.

(4) If one person is named in an application as leader, nominating officer and treasurer, the application must also give the name and home address of the holder of some other specified office in the party.

Party organisation

5 (1) An application must be accompanied by

    (a) a copy of the party's constitution (within the meaning of section 26); and

    (b) a draft of the scheme which the party proposes to adopt for the purposes of section 26 if approved by the Commission under that section.

(2) Where the party is a party with accounting units, the application must state in relation to each accounting unit

    (a) the name of the accounting unit and of its treasurer and of the officer to be registered for the purposes of section 27(3), and

    (b) the address of its headquarters or, if it has no headquarters, an address to which communications to the accounting unit may be sent.

Additional information

6 An application must include any other information prescribed by regulations made by the Commission.

Signature

7 (1) An application must be signed

    (a) by the proposed registered leader or registered nominating officer,

    (b) by the proposed registered treasurer, and

    (c) (if the application is for the party to be registered as a party with a campaigns officer) by the proposed registered campaigns officer,

and must include a declaration by each person signing the application that he is authorised to sign it on behalf of the party.

(2) An application may be signed by the same person in his capacity as proposed registered leader or registered nominating officer and in his capacity as proposed registered treasurer or as proposed registered campaigns officer, but in that case it must be apparent from the application that he is signing it in both of those capacities.

NOTES

Defined terms

accounting unit: ss 26(11), 160(1)
central organisation: ss 26(11), 160(1)
the Commission: s 160(1)
the Great Britain register: ss 23(2)(a), 160(1)
the Northern Ireland register: ss 23(2)(b), 160(1)
party: s 40(1)

party with accounting units: ss 26(11), 160(1)
registered: s 40(1)
the Secretary of State: s 159A
treasurer: s 160(1)

Part II

Application for Alteration of Entry

Introductory

8 (1) Paragraph 9 and (if applicable) paragraph 10 must be complied with in relation to an application under section 30.

(2) Such an application must be accompanied by any fee prescribed by order made by the Secretary of State.

(3) In paragraphs 9 and 10 "an application" means an application under section 30.

Signature

9 (1) Subject to sub-paragraph (3), an application must be signed by the responsible officers of the party.

(2) For the purposes of this paragraph "the responsible officers" are
    (a) the registered leader;
    (b) the registered nominating officer;
    (c) the registered treasurer;
    (d) where the leader, the nominating officer and the treasurer are the same person, any other registered officer.

(3) If any responsible officer is unable to sign an application
    (a) the holder of some other office in the party may sign in his place, and
    (b) the application must include a statement of the reason why the responsible officer is unable to sign and a declaration that the holder of the other office is authorised to sign in his place.

Details of campaigns officer

10 If an application is for the addition of a statement that the party is registered as a party with a campaigns officer, the application must
    (a) give the name and home address of the person who is to be registered as the party's campaigns officer; and
    (b) be accompanied by a declaration of acceptance of office signed by that person.

NOTES

Defined terms
  party: s 40(1)
  registered: s 40(1)
  the Secretary of State: s 159A

treasurer: s 160(1)

Part III
Application for Registration of Replacement Officer

Introductory

11 (1) Paragraphs 12 and 13 must be complied with in relation to an application under section 31(3)(a).

(2) In paragraphs 12 and 13 "an application" means an application under section 31(3)(a).

Details of replacement etc officers

12 (1) If as a result of an application one person will be registered as leader, nominating officer and treasurer, the application must request the addition of the name of the holder of some other specified office in the party.

(2) If an application requests
   (a) the substitution of the name of a leader, nominating officer, treasurer or other officer, or
   (b) an addition in accordance with sub-paragraph (1),
the application must give the home address of the person whose name is to be substituted or added.

Signature

13 (1) Subject to sub-paragraph (3), an application must be signed by
   (a) each person (other than the person to be registered in pursuance of the application) who is one of the responsible officers of the party; and
   (b) the person who is to be so registered.

(2) For the purposes of this paragraph "the responsible officers" has the same meaning as in paragraph 9.

(3) If any such person as is mentioned in sub-paragraph (1)(a) is unable to sign an application
   (a) the holder of some other office in the party may sign in his place, and
   (b) the application must include a statement of the reason why the person in question is unable to sign and a declaration that the holder of the other office is authorised to sign in his place.

NOTES
Defined terms
   party: s 40(1)
   registered: s 40(1)

treasurer: s 160(1)

Part IV
Application for Removal of Entry

Signature

14 Paragraph 9 above shall apply in relation to an application under section 33 as it applies in relation to an application under section 30.

SCHEDULE 5
ACCOUNTING UNITS: APPLICATION OF ACCOUNTING REQUIREMENTS
Section 49

Introductory

1 (1) This Schedule provides for the application of sections 41 to 48 in a case where a registered party is a party with accounting units.

(2) For the purposes of this Schedule all or any of the following are financial matters relating to a party or (as the case may be) an accounting unit, namely
   (a) its transactions and financial position; and
   (b) its assets and liabilities.

(3) For the purposes of this Schedule, and any provision as applied by this Schedule, an accounting unit's financial year is the same as that of the party.

(4) In this Schedule "treasurer", in relation to an accounting unit, means the person specified in the Great Britain or Northern Ireland register as the unit's treasurer.

(5) If any question arises under this Schedule as to whether, in relation to any matter, anything falls to be done by the treasurer of a party or by the treasurer of an accounting unit, it shall be determined by the Commission.

Accounting records

2 (1) Section 41
  (a) shall not impose any duty on the treasurer of the party in relation to any financial matters relating to any accounting unit; but
  (b) shall apply with any necessary modifications to the treasurer of each such unit so as to make provision for or in connection with requiring the keeping and preservation of proper accounting records with respect to financial matters relating to the unit.

  (2) In its application in relation to an accounting unit, section 41(5) shall be read as if the reference to the last treasurer of the party were to the last treasurer of the unit.

Annual statements of accounts

3 (1) Section 42
  (a) shall not impose any duty on the treasurer of the party in relation to any financial matter relating to any accounting unit; but
  (b) shall apply with any necessary modifications to the treasurer of each such unit so as to make provision for or in connection with requiring the preparation, in respect of each financial year, of a statement of accounts relating to financial matters relating to the unit.

  (2) In its application in relation to any such statement of accounts, section 42(2)(b) shall be read as requiring approval
  (a) by the management committee of the unit, if there is one; and
  (b) otherwise by an officer of the unit other than its treasurer.

  (3) In its application in relation to a party with accounting units or (as the case may be) to any accounting unit, section 42(4)(a) shall be read as if the reference to the gross income or total expenditure of the party were
  (a) to the gross income or total expenditure of the party exclusive of any income or expenditure of any accounting unit, or
  (b) to the gross income or total expenditure of the unit,
  as the case may be.

Annual audits

4 (1) Section 43 shall apply in relation to any accounting unit and its treasurer as it applies in relation to the party and its treasurer.

  (2) In its application in relation to the party or (as the case may be) to any accounting unit, section 43(1) or (2) shall be read as if the reference to the gross income or total expenditure of the party were
  (a) to the gross income or total expenditure of the party exclusive of any income or expenditure of any accounting unit, or
  (b) to the gross income or total expenditure of the unit,
  as the case may be.

Supplementary provisions about auditors

5 (1) Section 44 shall apply in relation to any accounting unit and the treasurer, or any other officer, of any such unit as it applies in relation to the party and the treasurer, or any other officer, of the party.

(2) In sub-paragraph (1) any reference to a treasurer or other officer includes a former treasurer or other officer.

Submission of statements of accounts etc to Commission

6 (1) In the case of any accounting unit whose gross income or total expenditure in a financial year exceeds £25,000, section 45 shall (except so far as it relates to any notification under section 32) apply in relation to the accounting unit and the treasurer of the unit as it applies in relation to the party and the treasurer of the party.

(2) If the Commission in the case of any other accounting unit at any time so require by notice in relation to any financial year, the treasurer of the unit shall no later than the relevant date send the Commission

  (a) the statement of accounts prepared for that year in accordance with paragraph 3, and

  (b) if the unit's accounts for that year have been audited in accordance with paragraph 4, a copy of the auditor's report.

(3) In sub-paragraph (2) "the relevant date" means

  (a) if the unit's accounts for the financial year are not required to be audited in accordance with paragraph 4, the end of the period of three months from the end of that year or (if later) the end of the period of 30 days beginning with the day when the requirement under sub-paragraph (2) is imposed;

  (b) if the unit's accounts for that year are required to be so audited, the end of the period of six months from the end of that year or (if later) the end of the period of three months beginning with the date when the requirement under sub-paragraph (2) is imposed.

(4) If for any special reason the Commission think it fit to do so they may, on an application made to them before the end of the period otherwise allowed under this paragraph for sending a unit's documents within sub-paragraph (2) for any financial year, by notice extend that period by a further period specified in the notice.

(5) Any reference to section 45 in any of sections 46 to 48 (as they apply in accordance with this Schedule) shall be read as including a reference to sub-paragraph (2) above.

Public inspection of parties' statements of accounts

7 Section 46 shall apply in relation to any statement of accounts received by the Commission from an accounting unit as it applies in relation to a statement of accounts received by them from the party.

Criminal penalty for failure to submit proper statement of accounts etc

8 (1) Subject to sub-paragraph (2), section 47 shall apply in relation to any accounting unit and the treasurer of any such unit as it applies in relation to the party and the treasurer of the party.

(2) In a case where paragraph 6(2) applies

  (a) subsection (4) of section 47 shall not apply, and

  (b) the relevant period for the purposes of that section (as it applies in accordance with sub-paragraph (1) above) shall instead be the period allowed by paragraph 6(2) and (3) for sending the statement of accounts or auditor's report to the

Commission or, if that period has been extended under paragraph 6(4), that period as so extended.

Revision of statement of accounts

9 (1) Subject to sub-paragraph (2), section 48 shall apply in relation to any accounting unit and the treasurer of any such unit as it applies in relation to the party and the treasurer of the party.

(2) In its application in relation to any such unit

   (a) section 48(7) shall have effect with the omission of the reference to the registered leader of the party; and

   (b) section 48(8) shall accordingly have effect with the omission of paragraphs (a) and (b) and all references to the registered leader of the party.

NOTES

Defined terms

accounting unit: ss 26(11), 160(1)
the Commission: s 160(1)
document: s 160(1)
financial year: ss 40(1), 41(6)
the Great Britain register: ss 23(2)(a), 160(1)
gross income: s 42(8)
modifications: s 160(1)

the Northern Ireland register: ss 23(2)(b), 160(1)
party with accounting units: ss 26(11), 160(1)
record: s 160(1)
registered party: s 160(1)
treasurer: s 160(1)

SCHEDULE 6
DETAILS TO BE GIVEN IN DONATION REPORTS

Sections 62 and 63

Preliminary

1 (1) In this Schedule

   (a) "quarterly report" means a report required to be prepared by virtue of section 62;

   (b) "weekly report" means a report required to be prepared by virtue of section 63; and "recordable donation", in relation to a quarterly or weekly report, means a donation required to be recorded in that report.

(2) References in this Schedule to a registered party shall, in the case of a party with accounting units, be read as references to the central organisation of the party.

Declarations as to source of donation or as to whether residence etc condition satisfied

1A (1) In relation to each recordable donation in the case of which a declaration under section 54A has been given, a quarterly or weekly report must either

   (a) state that no reason was found to think that the declaration was untruthful or inaccurate, or

   (b) give details of any respects in which the declaration was found or suspected to be untruthful or inaccurate.

(2) In relation to each recordable donation in the case of which a declaration under section 54B has been given, a quarterly report must either

   (a) state that no reason was found for thinking that the declaration was incorrect, or

   (b) give details of any respects in which the declaration was found or suspected to be incorrect.

Identity of donors: quarterly reports

2 (1) In relation to each recordable donation (other than one to which paragraph 2A, 6 or 7 applies) a quarterly report must give the following information about the donor

    (a) the information required by any of sub-paragraphs (2) to (10), (12) and (13) below; and

    (b) such other information as may be required by regulations made by the Secretary of State after consulting the Commission;

or, in the case of a donation falling within sub-paragraph (11) below, the information required by that sub-paragraph.

(2) In the case of an individual the report must give his full name and

    (a) if his address is, at the date of receipt of the donation, shown in an electoral register (within the meaning of section 54) or the Gibraltar register, that address; and

    (b) otherwise, his home address (whether in the United Kingdom or elsewhere).

(2A) In the case of a donation from a Gibraltar elector, received on a date before the date of publication of the first version of the Gibraltar register

    (a) the reference in sub-paragraph (2)(a) to the Gibraltar register shall have effect as if it were a reference to the register of electors used for Gibraltar Parliament elections; and

    (b) where, on the date of receipt of the donation, the elector was not registered in the register of electors used for Gibraltar Parliament elections, the report must confirm that on that date he was aged 16 or over and was a Commonwealth citizen or a citizen of the European Union (other than a Commonwealth citizen).

(3) Sub-paragraph (2) does not apply in the case of a donation in the form of a bequest, and in such a case the report must state that the donation was received in pursuance of a bequest and give

    (a) the full name of the person who made the bequest; and

    (b) his address at the time of his death or, if he was not then registered in an electoral register (within the meaning of section 54) or the Gibraltar register at that address, the last address at which he was so registered during the period of five years ending with the date of his death.

(3A) In the application of sub-paragraph (3) to a bequest made by a person who was a Gibraltar elector

    (a) in relation to any time before the publication of the first version of the Gibraltar register, the reference in sub-paragraph (3)(b) to the Gibraltar register shall have effect as if it were a reference to the register of electors used for Gibraltar Parliament elections;

    (b) where the person who made the bequest

        (i) died before the end of the period of five years beginning with the date on which the first version of the Gibraltar register was published, and

        (ii) was not registered in the Gibraltar register or the register of electors used for Gibraltar Parliament elections during the period of five years ending with the date of his death,

    the reference in sub-paragraph (3)(b) to the last address at which he was registered during the period mentioned there shall have effect as if it were a reference to the address at which he was last resident in Gibraltar during that period; and

    (c) where sub-paragraph (b) above applies, the report must confirm that the person who made the bequest was aged 16 or over and was a Commonwealth citizen or a citizen of the European Union (other than a Commonwealth citizen) at any time during the period of five years ending with the date of his death when he was resident in Gibraltar.

(3B)   Sub-paragraph (2) applies in the case of a donation by a person who has an anonymous entry in an electoral register (within the meaning of the Representation of the People Act 1983), as if for paragraphs (a) and (b) there were substituted "state that the registered party has seen evidence of such description as is prescribed by the Secretary of State in regulations that the individual has an anonymous entry in an electoral register (within the meaning of the Representation of the People Act 1983)".

(3C)   Sub-paragraph (3) applies in the case of a donation in the form of a bequest by a person who either
    (a)   at the time of his death, or
    (b)   at any time in the period of five years ending with the date of his death,
had an anonymous entry in an electoral register (within the meaning of the Representation of the People Act 1983), as if for paragraph (b) there were substituted
"(b) a statement that the registered party has seen evidence of such description as is prescribed by the Secretary of State in regulations that the individual had
    (i)   at the time of his death, or
    (ii)   at any time in the period of five years ending with the date of his death,
an anonymous entry in an electoral register (within the meaning of the Representation of the People Act 1983)."

(4)   In the case of a company falling within section 54(2)(b) or 54(2A)(b) the report must give
    (a)   the company's registered name;
    (b)   the address of its registered office; and
    (c)   the number with which it is registered.

(5)   In the case of a registered party the report must give
    (a)   the party's registered name; and
    (b)   the address of its registered headquarters.

(6)   In the case of a trade union falling within section 54(2)(d) or 54(2A)(d) the report must give
    (a)   the name of the union, and
    (b)   the address of its head or main office,
as shown in the list kept under the Trade Union and Labour Relations (Consolidation) Act 1992 or the Industrial Relations (Northern Ireland) Order 1992 or as registered in accordance with the Trade Unions and Trade Disputes Act.

(7)   In the case of a building society within the meaning of the Building Societies Act 1986 or the Banking (Extension to Building Societies) Act, the report must give
    (a)   the name of the society; and
    (b)   the address of its principal office.

(8)   In the case of a limited liability partnership falling within section 54(2)(f) or 54(2A)(f), the report must give
    (a)   the partnership's registered name; and
    (b)   the address of its registered office.

(9)   In the case of a friendly or other registered society falling within section 54(2)(g) the report must give
    (a)   the name of the society, and
    (b)   the address of its registered office.

(10)   In the case of an unincorporated association falling within section 54(2)(h) or 54(2A)(g) the report must give
    (a)   the name of the association; and
    (b)   the address of its main office in the United Kingdom or Gibraltar.

(11) In the case of a payment to which section 55(2) applies the report must give the statutory or other provision under which it was made.

(12) In the case of a donation to which section 55(3) applies, the report must give the full name and address of the donor.

(13) In the case of a donation to which section 55(5) or 55(5A) applies, the report must state that the donation was received from a trustee, and

    (a) in the case of a donation falling within section 162(2), give

        (i) the date on which the trust was created, and

        (ii) the full name of the person who created the trust and of every other person by whom, or under whose will, property was transferred to the trust before 27th July 1999, and

    (b) in the case of a donation falling within section 162(3) or 162(3A), give in respect of

        (i) the person who created the trust, and,

        (ii) every other person by whom, or under whose will, property has been transferred to the trust,

the information which is required by any of sub-paragraphs (2) to (10) to be given in respect of the donor of a recordable donation.

(14) In this Act or the Representation of the People Act 1983 any reference (however expressed) to information about the donor of a donation which is framed by reference to this paragraph is, in relation to such a donation as is mentioned in paragraph (a) or (b) of sub-paragraph (13), a reference to information about every person specified in paragraph (a) or (b) of that sub-paragraph.

2A (1) In relation to each recordable donation that is an Irish donation a quarterly report must comply with the following requirements of this paragraph.

(2) "Irish donation" means a donation made in reliance on section 71B(1)(a) or (b) (extension of categories of permissible donors in relation to Northern Ireland recipients).

(3) The report must record the fact that the donation is an Irish donation.

(4) In the case of a donation by an Irish citizen the report must also

    (a) give the donor's full name, and

    (b) be accompanied by one of the following documents

        (i) a copy of the donor's Irish passport certified by the Department of Foreign Affairs of Ireland;

        (ii) a copy of the donor's certificate of nationality certified by the Department of Foreign Affairs of Ireland; or

        (iii) a copy of the donor's certificate of naturalisation certified by the Department of Foreign Affairs of Ireland,

but this sub-paragraph does not apply to a donation in the form of a bequest.

(5) In the case of a donation in the form of a bequest the report must also

    (a) state that the donation was received in pursuance of a bequest;

    (b) give the full name of the person who made the bequest; and

    (c) be accompanied by either one of the documents listed in sub-paragraph (4)(b)(i) to (iii) or a statement by the Department of Foreign Affairs of Ireland that documentation submitted to that Department following the death of the person who made the bequest would have been acceptable in support of an application for an Irish passport had it been submitted when he was alive.

(6) In the case of a donation by a company the report must also give

     (a) the company's registered name;

     (b) the address of its registered office; and

     (c) the number with which it is registered.

(7) In the case of a donation by a political party the report must also give

     (a) the party's registered name; and

     (b) the address of its registered headquarters.

(8) In the case of a donation by a trade union the report must also give

     (a) the name of the trade union; and

     (b) the address of its head or main office.

(9) In the case of a donation by a building society the report must also give

     (a) the name of the society; and

     (b) the address of its principal office.

(10) In the case of a donation by a limited liability partnership the report must also give

     (a) the partnership's registered name; and

     (b) the address of its registered office.

(11) In the case of a donation by a friendly society, a registered society within the meaning of the Co-operative and Community Benefit Societies Act 2014 or a society registered (or deemed to be registered) under the Industrial and Provident Societies Act (Northern Ireland) 1969, the report must also give

     (a) the name of the society; and

     (b) the address of its registered office.

(12) In the case of a donation by an unincorporated association the report must also

     (a) give the name of the association;

     (b) give the address of its main office in Ireland; and

     (c) be accompanied by a statement made by a solicitor currently practising in Ireland confirming the name and address of the association and the fact that it is an unincorporated association.

(13) In the case of a donation received in accordance with the terms of a trust the report must also

     (a) state that the donation was received from a trustee;

     (b) give the date on which the trust was created;

     (c) give the address of the trust's office; and

     (d) give, in relation to any settlor, the information that is required to be given under sub-paragraphs (4) to (12) of this paragraph.

(14) "Settlor" means

     (a) the person who created the trust; and

     (b) every other person by whom, or under whose will, property has been transferred into the trust.

(15) In the case of a trust created before 1st November 2007 sub-paragraph (13)(d)

     (a) does not require the report to give any information in relation to the person who created the trust apart from his name;

     (b) does not require the report to give any information in relation to any other person by whom, or under whose will, property has been transferred into the trust before 1st November 2007.

Identity of donors: weekly reports

3 (1) In relation to each recordable donation a weekly report must give all such details of the name and address of the donor as are for the time being known to the party.

(2) In the case of a donation by a person who has an anonymous entry in an electoral register (within the meaning of the Representation of the People Act 1983), instead of giving details of the address of the donor the party must state that it has seen evidence of such description as is prescribed by the Secretary of State in regulations that the person has such an entry.

(3) In the case of a donation in the form of a bequest by a person who either
    (a) at the time of his death, or
    (b) at any time in the period of five years ending at the date of his death,
had such an entry, instead of giving details of the address of the donor, the party must state that it has seen evidence of such description as is prescribed by the Secretary of State in regulations that the person had, at that time, such an entry.

(4) This paragraph does not apply in relation to a recordable donation that is an Irish donation (within the meaning given by paragraph 2A(2)).

3A In relation to each recordable donation that is an Irish donation (within the meaning given by paragraph 2A(2)) a weekly report must
    (a) record the fact that the donation is an Irish donation; and
    (b) give the name of the donor.

Value of donation

4 (1) In relation to each recordable donation a quarterly or weekly report must give the following details about the donation.

(2) If the donation was a donation of money (in cash or otherwise) the report must give the amount of the donation.

(3) Otherwise the report must give details of the nature of the donation and its value as determined in accordance with section 53.

Circumstances in which donation made

5 (1) In relation to each recordable donation a quarterly or weekly report must
    (a) give the relevant date for the donation; and
    (b) (in the case of a quarterly report)
      (i) state whether the donation was made to the registered party or any accounting unit of the party; or
      (ii) in the case of a donation to which section 62(12) applies, indicate that it is a donation which falls to be treated as made to the party by virtue of that provision.

(2) In the case of a donation to which section 55(3) applies, the report must in addition give
    (a) the date or dates on or between which the visit to which the donation relates took place, and
    (b) the destination and purpose of the visit.

(3) For the purposes of this paragraph as it applies to a quarterly report, the relevant date for a donation is
    (a) (if within section 62(4)(a) or (7)(a)) the date when the donation was accepted by the party or the accounting unit;
    (b) (if within section 62(4)(b) or (7)(b)) the date when the donation was accepted by the party or the accounting unit which caused the aggregate amount in question to be more than the limit specified in that provision;
    (c) (if within section 62(9)) the date when the donation was received.

(4)   For the purposes of this paragraph as it applies to a weekly report, the relevant date for a donation is the date when the donation was received by the party or its central organisation as mentioned in section 63(3).

Application of reporting requirement

5A   If the requirement to record the donation arises only because the value of the donation has, for the purposes of section 62(4) or (6), been aggregated with the value of any relevant transaction or transactions (within the meaning of section 71M), a quarterly report must contain a statement to that effect.

Donations from impermissible donors or without required declaration

6   In relation to each recordable donation to which section 54(1)(a) section 54(1)(a) or (aa) applies a quarterly report must
     (a)   give the name and address of the donor or the person appearing to be the donor;
     (b)   give the date when, and the manner in which, the donation was dealt with in accordance with section 56(2)(a) section 56(2)(a) or (aa);
     (c)   if the donation is a Gibraltar donation (within the meaning of section 57A), record that fact.

Donations from unidentifiable donors

7   In relation to each recordable donation to which section 54(1)(b) applies a quarterly report must give
     (a)   details of the manner in which it was made,
     (b)   details of any element of deception or concealment employed by the donor of which the registered party or any accounting unit of the party became aware and the means by which it was revealed; and
     (c)   the date when, and the manner in which, the donation was dealt with in accordance with section 56(2)(b).

Other details

8   A quarterly or weekly report must give such other information (if any) as is required by regulations made by the Commission.

NOTES

Prospective operation
Para (1A) not yet in operation

Defined terms
accounting unit: ss 26(11), 160(1)
Banking (Extension to Building Societies) Act: s 160(6)
bequest: s 160(1)
central organisation: ss 26(11), 160(1)
the Commission: s 160(1)
donation: ss 50, 161

Gibraltar elector: s 160(1)
Gibraltar register: s 160(1)
party with accounting units: ss 26(11), 160(1)
property: s 160(1)
registered party: ss 50(7), 160(1) (and note para 1(2) of this Schedule)
the Secretary of State: s 159A
Trade Union and Trade Disputes Act: s 160(6)

SCHEDULE 6A
DETAILS TO BE GIVEN IN TRANSACTION REPORTS

Preliminary

1 (1)   In this Schedule
     (a)   "quarterly report" means a report required to be prepared by virtue of section 71M;

(b) "weekly report" means a report required to be prepared by virtue of section 71Q;

and "recordable transaction", in relation to a quarterly or weekly report, means a transaction required to be recorded in that report.

(2) References in this Schedule to a registered party must, in the case of a party with accounting units, be read as references to the central organisation of the party.

Declaration as to whether residence etc condition satisfied

1A In relation to each recordable transaction in the case of which a declaration under section 71HZA has been given, a quarterly report must either
   (a) state that no reason was found to think that the declaration was incorrect, or
   (b) give details of any respects in which the declaration was found or suspected to be incorrect.

Identity of authorised participants: quarterly reports

2 (1) In relation to each recordable transaction (other than one to which paragraph 2A applies), a quarterly report must give the following information about each authorised participant (other than the registered party deriving the benefit of the transaction) that is required by any of sub-paragraphs (2) to (10).

(2) In the case of an individual the report must give his full name and
   (a) if his address is, at the date the transaction is entered into, shown in an electoral register (within the meaning of section 54) or the Gibraltar register, that address, and
   (b) otherwise, his home address (whether in the United Kingdom or elsewhere).

(3) Sub-paragraph (2) applies in the case of an individual who has an anonymous entry in an electoral register (within the meaning of the Representation of the People Act 1983) as if for paragraphs (a) and (b) there were substituted "state that the registered party has seen evidence of such description as is prescribed by the Secretary of State in regulations that the individual has an anonymous entry in an electoral register (within the meaning of the Representation of the People Act 1983 or corresponding provisions forming part of the law of Gibraltar)".

(4) In the case of a company falling within section 54(2)(b) or section 54(2A)(b) the report must give
   (a) the company's registered name,
   (b) the address of its registered office, and
   (c) the number with which it is registered.

(5) In the case of a registered party the report must give
   (a) the party's registered name, and
   (b) the address of its registered headquarters.

(6) In the case of trade union falling within section 54(2)(d) or section 54(2A)(d) the report must give
   (a) the name of the union, and
   (b) the address of its head or main office,
   as shown in the list kept under the Trade Union and Labour Relations (Consolidation) Act 1992 or the Industrial Relations (Northern Ireland) Order 1992 or as registered in accordance with the Trade Unions and Trade Disputes Act.

(7) In the case of a building society within the meaning of the Building Societies Act 1986 or which is an existing registered society within the meaning of the Banking (Extension to Building Societies) Act the report must give
   (a) the name of the society, and

      (b) the address of its principal office.

(8) In the case of a limited liability partnership falling within section 54(2)(f) or section 54(2A)(f) the report must give
     (a) the partnership's registered name, and
     (b) the address of its registered office.

(9) In the case of a friendly or other registered society falling within section 54(2)(g) the report must give
     (a) the name of the society, and
     (b) the address of its registered office.

(10) In the case of an unincorporated association falling within section 54(2)(h) or section 54(2A)(g) the report must give
     (a) the name of the association, and
     (b) the address of its main office in the United Kingdom or Gibraltar, as the case may be.

2A (1) In relation to each recordable transaction that is an Irish transaction a quarterly report must comply with the following requirements of this paragraph in relation to each authorised participant (other than the registered party deriving the benefit of the transaction).

(2) "Irish transaction" means a transaction which is entered into in reliance on section 71Z1(1)(a) or (b) (extension of categories of authorised participants in relation to Northern Ireland participants).

(3) The report must record the fact that the transaction is an Irish transaction.

(4) In the case of a participant who is an Irish citizen the report must also
     (a) give the participant's full name, and
     (b) be accompanied by one of the following documents
         (i) a copy of the participant's Irish passport certified by the Department of Foreign Affairs of Ireland;
        (ii) a copy of the participant's certificate of nationality certified by the Department of Foreign Affairs of Ireland; or
       (iii) a copy of the participant's certificate of naturalisation certified by the Department of Foreign Affairs of Ireland.

(5) In the case of a participant who is a company the report must also give
     (a) the company's registered name;
     (b) the address of its registered office; and
     (c) the number with which it is registered.

(6) In the case of a participant who is a political party the report must also give
     (a) the party's registered name; and
     (b) the address of its registered headquarters.

(7) In the case of a participant who is a trade union the report must also give
     (a) the name of the trade union; and
     (b) the address of its head or main office.

(8) In the case of a participant who is a building society the report must also give
     (a) the name of the society; and
     (b) the address of its principal office.

(9) In the case of a participant who is a limited liability partnership the report must also give
     (a) the partnership's registered name; and
     (b) the address of its registered office.

(10) In the case of a participant who is a friendly society, a registered society within the meaning of the Co-operative and Community Benefit Societies Act 2014 or a society registered (or deemed to be registered) under the Industrial and Provident Societies Act (Northern Ireland) 1969, the report must also give

    (a) the name of the society; and

    (b) the address of its registered office.

(11) In the case of a participant who is an unincorporated association the report must also

    (a) give the name of the association;

    (b) give the address of its main office in Ireland; and

    (c) be accompanied by a statement made by a firm of solicitors currently practising in Ireland confirming the name and address of the association and the fact that it is an unincorporated association.

Identity of authorised participants: weekly reports

3 (1) In relation to each recordable transaction, a weekly report must give all such details of the name and address of each authorised participant (other than the registered party deriving the benefit from the transaction) as are for the time being known to the party.

(2) In the case of a participant who is an individual having an anonymous entry in an electoral register (within the meaning of the Representation of the People Act 1983 or corresponding provisions forming part of the law of Gibraltar) instead of giving details of the address of the individual the party must state that it has seen evidence of such description as is prescribed by the Secretary of State in regulations that the individual has such an entry.

(3) This paragraph does not apply in relation to a recordable transaction that is an Irish transaction (within the meaning given by paragraph 2A(2)).

3A In relation to each recordable transaction that is an Irish transaction (within the meaning given by paragraph 2A(2)), a weekly report must

    (a) give all such details of the name of each authorised participant who is a party to the transaction (other than the registered party deriving the benefit from the transaction) as are for the time being known to the registered party; and

    (b) record the fact that the transaction is an Irish transaction.

Identity of unauthorised participants

4 (1) In relation to each recordable transaction to which a person who is not an authorised participant is a party, a quarterly or weekly report must give

    (a) the name and address of the person;

    (b) the date when, and the manner in which, the transaction was dealt with in accordance with subsections (3) to (5) of section 71I or those subsections as applied by section 71I(6) or 71J(2).

(2) This paragraph does not apply in relation to a recordable transaction that is an Irish transaction (within the meaning given by paragraph 2A(2)).

4A In relation to each recordable transaction that is an Irish transaction (within the meaning given by paragraph 2A(2)) to which a person who is not an authorised participant is a party, a quarterly or weekly report must

    (a) give the name of the person;

    (b) record the fact that the transaction is an Irish transaction; and

    (c) give the date when, and the manner in which, the transaction was dealt with in accordance with subsections (3) to (5) of section 71I or those subsections as applied by section 71I(6) or 71J(2).

Details of transaction

5 (1) In relation to each recordable transaction a report must give the following details about the transaction.

(2) A quarterly or weekly report must give the nature of the transaction (that is to say, whether it is a loan, a credit facility or an arrangement by which any form of security is given).

(3) A quarterly or weekly report must give the value of the transaction (determined in accordance with section 71G) or, in the case of a credit facility or security to which no limit is specified, a statement to that effect.

(4) A quarterly or weekly report must give the relevant date for the transaction (determined in accordance with paragraph 8).

(5) If the requirement to record the transaction arises only because the value of the transaction has, for the purposes of section 71M(4) or (7), been aggregated with the value of any relevant donation or donations (within the meaning of section 62), a quarterly report must contain a statement to that effect.

(6) A quarterly report must
    (a) state whether the transaction was entered into by the registered party or any accounting unit of the party, or
    (b) in the case of a transaction to which section 71M(12) applies, indicate that it is a transaction which falls to be treated as made to the party by virtue of that provision.

6 (1) In relation to each recordable transaction of a description mentioned in section 71F(2) or (3), a quarterly or weekly report must give the following details about the transaction.

(2) The report must give
    (a) the date when the loan is to be repaid or the facility is to end (or a statement that the loan or facility is indefinite), or
    (b) where that date is to be determined under the agreement, a statement of how it is to be so determined.

(3) The report must give
    (a) the rate of interest payable on the loan or on sums advanced under the facility (or a statement that no interest is payable), or
    (b) where that rate is to be determined under the agreement, a statement of how it is to be so determined.

(4) The report must state whether the agreement contains a provision which enables outstanding interest to be added to any sum for the time being owed in respect of the loan or credit facility.

(5) The report must state whether any form of security is given in respect of the loan or the sums advanced under the facility.

7 (1) In relation to each recordable transaction of a description mentioned in section 71F(4)(b), a quarterly or weekly report must give the following details about the transaction.

(2) The report must
    (a) if the transaction mentioned in section 71F(4)(a) is a regulated transaction, identify that transaction by reference to the transaction report in which it is recorded;

(b) in any other case, give a description of the principal features of that transaction.

(3) Where the security given consists in or includes rights over any property, the report must state the nature of that property.

(4) The report must

(a) if the person giving the security receives from the registered party any consideration for giving the security, give a statement of that consideration;

(b) in any other case, state that no such consideration is received.

8 (1) For the purposes of paragraph 5(4) as it applies to a quarterly report, the relevant date for a transaction is

(a) if the transaction is within section 71M(4)(a) or (7)(a), the date when the transaction was entered into by the party or the accounting unit;

(b) if the transaction is within section 71M(4)(b) or (7)(b), the date when the party or the accounting unit entered into the transaction which caused the aggregate amount in question to be more than the limit specified in that provision.

(2) For the purposes of paragraph 5(4) as it applies to a weekly report, the relevant date for a transaction is the date when the transaction was entered into by the party or its central organisation as mentioned in section 71Q(3).

Other details

9 (1) The Secretary of State may by order amend paragraphs 2 to 7 so as to vary the details which a quarterly or weekly report must give about a transaction.

(2) The Secretary of State must not make an order under sub-paragraph (1) unless he first consults the Commission.

NOTES

Prospective operation
 Para (1A) not yet in operation

Subordinate Legislation
Political Donations and Regulated Transactions (Anonymous Electors) Regulations 2014, SI 2014/1806

Defined terms
 accounting units: ss 26(11), 160(1)
 authorised participant: ss 71H, 71X(1)
 Banking (Extension to Building Societies) Act: s 160(6)

central organisation: ss 26(11), 160(1)
the Commission: s 160(1)
credit facility: ss 71F(11), 71X(1)
the Gibraltar register: s 160(1)
party with accounting units: ss 26(11), 160(1)
registered party: ss 71F(6)-(8), 71X(2), 160(1) (and note para 1(2) of this Schedule)
the Secretary of State: s 159A
Trade Union and Trade Disputes Act: s 160(6)

SCHEDULE 7
CONTROL OF DONATIONS TO INDIVIDUALS AND MEMBERS ASSOCIATIONS

Section 71

Part I
Introductory

Operation and interpretation of Schedule

1 (1) This Schedule has effect for controlling donations to

(a) members of registered parties;

(b) members associations; and

(c) holders of relevant elective offices.

(2) The following provisions have effect for the purposes of this Schedule.

(3) "Controlled donation"
  (a) in relation to a member of a registered party, means a donation received by that person which is
    (i)   offered to him, or
    (ii) where it has been accepted, retained by him,
    for his use or benefit in connection with any of his political activities as a member of the party;
  (b) in relation to a members association, means a donation received by the association which is
    (i)   offered to the association, or
    (ii) where it has been accepted, retained by the association,
    for its use or benefit in connection with any of its political activities;
  (c) in relation to a holder of a relevant elective office, means a donation received by that person which is
    (i)   offered to him, or
    (ii) where it has been accepted, retained by him,
    for his use or benefit (as the holder of such an office) in connection with any of his political activities.

(4) For the purposes of this Schedule the political activities of a party member or (as the case may be) of a members association include, in particular
  (a) promoting or procuring the election of any person to any position in, or to any committee of, the party in question;
  (b) promoting or procuring the selection of any person as the party's candidate for election to a relevant elective office; and
  (c) promoting or developing policies with a view to their adoption by the party;
  and in the application of paragraph (a) or (b) to a party member the reference to any person includes that member.

(5) "Donation" shall be construed in accordance with paragraphs 2 to 4; and (in the absence of any express indication) a donation shall be taken to have been offered to, or retained by, a person or organisation as mentioned in sub-paragraph (1)(a), (b) or (c) if, having regard to all the circumstances, it must reasonably be assumed to have been so offered or retained.

(6) "Members association" means any organisation whose membership consists wholly or mainly of members of a registered party, other than
  (a) a registered party falling within section 26(2)(a); or
  (b) an organisation falling within section 26(2)(b) (that is, the central organisation of a registered party or an accounting unit of such a party).

(7) "Regulated donee" means
  (a) a member of a registered party;
  (b) a members association; or
  (c) the holder of a relevant elective office, whether or not he is a member of a registered party.

(8) "Relevant elective office" means the office of
  (a) member of the House of Commons;
  (b) member of the European Parliament elected in the United Kingdom (including the combined region);
  (c) member of the Scottish Parliament;
  (d) member of the National Assembly for Wales;
  (e) member of the Northern Ireland Assembly;
  (ea) police and crime commissioner;
  (f) member of

(i) any local authority in any part of the United Kingdom, including the Common Council of the City of London but excluding a parish or community council, or

(ii) the Greater London Assembly; or

(g) Mayor of London or elected mayor within the meaning of Part II of the Local Government Act 2000.

(9) "The responsible person", in relation to a members association, means

    (a) the treasurer, if there is one, and

    (b) otherwise, the person who is the responsible person by virtue of a notice in force under paragraph 1A.

(10) *Repealed*

(11) *Repealed*

Appointment of responsible person by members association with no treasurer

1A (1) A members association which does not have a treasurer

    (a) may appoint an individual to be the responsible person in relation to the association by giving notice to the Commission;

    (b) shall do so within the period of 30 days beginning with the date on which the association

      (i) accepts a controlled donation which is a recordable donation for the purposes of paragraph 10, or

      (ii) receives a controlled donation falling within paragraph 6(1)(a) or (b),

    if a notice under this sub-paragraph is not in force on that date.

(2) A notice under sub-paragraph (1)

    (a) must be signed on behalf of the members association;

    (b) must contain a statement signed by the individual to be appointed as the responsible person confirming that the individual is willing to be appointed.

(3) A notice under sub-paragraph (1) must state

    (a) the name and address of the members association;

    (b) the full name of the individual to be appointed as the responsible person;

    (c) the individual's home address in the United Kingdom, or (if there is no such home address) the individual's home address elsewhere.

(4) Subject to the following provisions of this paragraph, a notice under sub-paragraph (1) ("the original notice")

    (a) shall be in force as from the date on which it is received by the Commission, but

    (b) shall lapse at the end of the period of 12 months beginning with that date unless the members association or the responsible person gives the Commission a notice (a "renewal notice") that they both wish the original notice to remain in force.

(5) A renewal notice

    (a) has the effect of extending the validity of the original notice for a further 12 months beginning with the time when it would otherwise have lapsed (whether under sub-paragraph (4)(b) or on the expiry of a previous extension under this sub-paragraph);

    (b) must be received by the Commission during the period of one month ending at that time.

(6) A renewal notice must either

    (a) confirm that all the statements contained in the original notice, as it has effect for the time being, are accurate; or

(b) indicate that any statement contained in that notice, as it so has effect, is replaced by some other statement conforming with the relevant provision of sub-paragraph (3).

A renewal notice must be signed on behalf of the members association and by the responsible person.

(7) The members association or the responsible person may, at any time after giving the original notice, give the Commission a notice (a "notice of alteration") indicating that any statement contained in the original notice, as it has effect for the time being, is replaced by some other statement

    (a) contained in the notice of alteration, and

    (b) conforming with the relevant provision of sub-paragraph (3).

A notice of alteration takes effect on the day on which it is received by the Commission or (if later) on such date as may be specified in the notice.

(8) A notice of alteration must be signed

    (a) on behalf of the members association, and

    (b) by the responsible person or, in the case of a notice substituting a different individual as the responsible person, by that individual.

(9) A notice under sub-paragraph (1) that has been in force for at least 12 months ceases to have effect on receipt by the Commission of a notice terminating it (a "notice of termination")

    (a) given by and signed on behalf of the members association, or

    (b) given and signed by the responsible person.

(10) On receipt of a notice of termination given by the members association or by the responsible person, the Commission must inform the other party as soon as is reasonably practicable (unless the notice was signed both on behalf of the members association and by the responsible person).

(11) A reference in this paragraph to a notice being signed on behalf of a members association is to the notice being signed by the secretary of the association or by a person who acts in a similar capacity in relation to the association.

(12) A notice under the Schedule 7A version of this paragraph also has effect as a notice under this paragraph.

The "Schedule 7A version" of this paragraph means this paragraph as it applies, in relation to controlled transactions, by virtue of paragraph 1(7A) of Schedule 7A.

Offence of failing to comply with paragraph 1A

1B   A members association commits an offence if

    (a) it is subject to the requirement in paragraph 1A(1)(b), and

    (b) without reasonable excuse it fails to comply with the requirement.

Donations: general rules

2 (1)   "Donation", in relation to a regulated donee, means (subject to paragraph 4)

    (a) any gift to the donee of money or other property;

    (b) any sponsorship provided in relation to the donee (as defined by paragraph 3);

    (c) any money spent (otherwise than by or on behalf of the donee) in paying any expenses incurred directly or indirectly by the donee;

    (d) *Repealed*

    (e) the provision otherwise than on commercial terms of any property, services or facilities for the use or benefit of the donee (including the services of any person);

    (f) (where the donee is a members association) any subscription or other fee paid for affiliation to, or membership of, the donee.

(2) Where

    (a) any money or other property is transferred to a regulated donee pursuant to any transaction or arrangement involving the provision by or on behalf of the donee of any property, services or facilities or other consideration of monetary value, and

    (b) the total value in monetary terms of the consideration so provided by or on behalf of the donee is less than the value of the money or (as the case may be) the market value of the property transferred,

the transfer of the money or property shall (subject to sub-paragraph (4)) constitute a gift to the donee for the purposes of sub-paragraph (1)(a).

(3) In determining

    (a) *Repealed*

    (b) for the purposes of sub-paragraph (1)(e) whether any property, services or facilities provided for the use or benefit of a regulated donee is or are so provided otherwise than on such terms,

regard shall be had to the total value in monetary terms of the consideration provided by or on behalf of the donee in respect of the provision of the property, services or facilities.

(4) Where (apart from this sub-paragraph) anything would be a donation both by virtue of sub-paragraph (1)(b) and by virtue of any other provision of this paragraph, sub-paragraph (1)(b) (together with paragraph 3) shall apply in relation to it to the exclusion of the other provision of this paragraph.

(5) Anything given or transferred to any officer, member, trustee or agent of a members association in his capacity as such (and not for his own use or benefit) is to be regarded as given or transferred to the association (and references to donations received by a regulated donee accordingly include, in the case of a members association, donations so given or transferred).

(6) In this paragraph

    (a) any reference to anything being given or transferred to a regulated donee or any other person is a reference to its being so given or transferred either directly or indirectly through any third person;

    (b) "gift" includes bequest.

Sponsorship

3 (1) For the purposes of this Schedule sponsorship is provided in relation to a regulated donee if

    (a) any money or other property is transferred to the donee or to any person for the benefit of the donee, and

    (b) the purpose (or one of the purposes) of the transfer is (or must, having regard to all the circumstances, reasonably be assumed to be)

        (i) to help the donee with meeting, or to meet, to any extent any defined expenses incurred or to be incurred by or on behalf of the donee, or

        (ii) to secure that to any extent any such expenses are not so incurred.

(2) In sub-paragraph (1) "defined expenses" means expenses in connection with

    (a) any conference, meeting or other event organised by or on behalf of the donee,

    (b) the preparation, production or dissemination of any publication by or on behalf of the donee, or

    (c) any study or research organised by or on behalf of the donee.

(3) The following do not, however, constitute sponsorship by virtue of sub-paragraph (1)

    (a) the making of any payment in respect of

        (i) any charge for admission to any conference, meeting or other event, or

        (ii)   the purchase price of, or any other charge for access to, any publication;

    (b) the making of any payment in respect of the inclusion of an advertisement in any publication where the payment is made at the commercial rate payable for the inclusion of such an advertisement in any such publication.

(4)   The Secretary of State may by order made on the recommendation of the Commission amend sub-paragraph (2) or (3).

(5)   In this paragraph "publication" means a publication made available in whatever form and by whatever means (whether or not to the public at large or any section of the public).

Payments etc not to be regarded as donations

4 (1)   None of the following shall be regarded as a donation
    (a) any facility provided in pursuance of any right conferred on candidates at an election by any enactment;
    (aa) remuneration allowed to an employee by his employer if the employee is a member of a local authority and the remuneration is in respect of time the employer permits the employee to take off during the employee's working hours for qualifying business
       (i)   of the authority,
       (ii) of any body to which the employee is appointed by, or is appointed following nomination by, the authority or a group of bodies that includes the authority, or
       (iii) of any other body if it is a public body;
    (b) the provision of assistance by a person appointed under section 9 of the Local Government and Housing Act 1989;
    (c) the provision by any individual of his own services which he provides voluntarily and in his own time;
    (d) any interest accruing to a regulated donee in respect of any donation which is dealt with by the donee in accordance with section 56(2)(a) or (b) (as applied by paragraph 8);
    (e) any money or other property, or any services or facilities, provided out of public funds for the personal security of a regulated donee who is an individual.

(2)   For the avoidance of doubt no remuneration or allowances paid to the holder of a relevant elective office in his capacity as such shall be regarded as a donation.

(3)   There shall also be disregarded
    (a) any donation which (in accordance with any enactment) falls to be included in a return as to election expenses in respect of a candidate or candidates at a particular election; and
    (b) any donation whose value (as determined in accordance with paragraph 5) is not more than £500.

(4)   In sub-paragraph (1)(aa)
   "employee" and "employer"
    (a) in relation to England and Wales, and Scotland, have the same meaning as in the Employment Rights Act 1996, and
    (b) in relation to Northern Ireland, have the same meaning as in the Employment Rights (Northern Ireland) Order 1996;
   "local authority" means a local authority in any part of the United Kingdom, including the Common Council of the City of London but excluding a parish or community council;
   "working hours" of an employee

(a) in relation to England and Wales, and Scotland, has the same meaning as in section 50 of the Employment Rights Act 1996, and

(b) in relation to Northern Ireland, has the same meaning as in Article 78 of the Employment Rights (Northern Ireland) Order 1996;

"qualifying business", in relation to a body, means

(a) the doing of anything for the purpose of the discharge of the functions of the body or of any of its committees or subcommittees, and

(b) where the body is a local authority operating executive arrangements within the meaning of Part 2 of the Local Government Act 2000 and arrangements exist for functions of any other body to be discharged by the authority's executive or any committee or member of the executive, the doing of anything for the purpose of the discharge of those functions.

Value of donations

5 (1) The value of any donation falling within paragraph 2(1)(a) (other than money) shall be taken to be the market value of the property in question.

(2) Where, however, paragraph 2(1)(a) applies by virtue of paragraph 2(2) the value of the donation shall be taken to be the difference between

(a) the value of the money, or the market value of the property, in question, and

(b) the total value in monetary terms of the consideration provided by or on behalf of the donee.

(3) The value of any donation falling within paragraph 2(1)(b) shall be taken to be the value of the money, or (as the case may be) the market value of the property, transferred as mentioned in paragraph 3(1); and accordingly any value in monetary terms of any benefit conferred on the person providing the sponsorship in question shall be disregarded.

(4) The value of any donation falling within paragraph 2(1)(e) shall be taken to be the amount representing the difference between

(a) the total value in monetary terms of the consideration that would have had to be provided by or on behalf of the donee in respect of the provision of the property, services or facilities if

(i) *Repealed*

(ii) the property, services or facilities had been provided, on commercial terms, and

(b) the total value in monetary terms of the consideration (if any) actually so provided by or on behalf of the donee.

(5) Where a donation such as is mentioned in sub-paragraph (4) confers an enduring benefit on the donee over a particular period, the value of the donation

(a) shall be determined at the time when it is made, but

(b) shall be so determined by reference to the total benefit accruing to the donee over that period.

NOTES

Defined terms

accounting unit: ss 26(11), 160(1)
bequest: s 160(1)
body: s 160(1)
central organisation: ss 26(11), 160(1)
combined region: s 160(1)
the Commission: s 160(1)
enactment: s 160(1)
functions: s 160(1)
market value: s 160(1)

organisation: s 160(1)
party with accounting units: ss 26(11), 160(1)
property: s 160(1)
provided out of public funds: s 160(4)
registered party: ss 50(7), 160(1)
the Secretary of State: s 159A
treasurer: s 160(1)

Part II
Controls on Donations

Prohibition on accepting donations from impermissible donors

6 (1)   A controlled donation received by a regulated donee must not be accepted by the donee if
    (a)   the person by whom the donation would be made is not, at the time of its receipt by the donee, a permissible donor, or
    (aa)   any declaration required to be made in respect of the donation by paragraph 6A or 6B has not been received by the donee, or
    (b)   the donee is (whether because the donation is given anonymously or by reason of any deception or concealment or otherwise) unable to ascertain the identity of that person the person offering the donation.

(2)   Where any person ("the principal donor") causes an amount ("the principal donation") to be received by a regulated donee by way of a donation
    (a)   on behalf of himself and one or more other persons, or
    (b)   on behalf of two or more other persons,
then for the purposes of this Schedule each individual contribution by a person falling within paragraph (a) or (b) of more than £500 shall be treated as if it were a separate donation received from that person.

(3)   In relation to each such separate donation, the principal donor must ensure that, at the time when the principal donation is received by the regulated donee, the responsible person is given
    (a)   (except in the case of a donation which the principal donor is treated as making) all such details in respect of the person treated as making the donation as are required by virtue of paragraph 2 or 2A of Schedule 6 to be given in respect of the donor of a recordable donation to a registered party; and
    (b)   (in any case) all such details in respect of the donation as are required by virtue of paragraph 4 of Schedule 6 to be given in respect of a recordable donation to a registered party.

(4)   Where
    (a)   any person ("the agent") causes an amount to be received by a regulated donee by way of a donation on behalf of another person ("the donor"), and
    (b)   the amount of the donation is more than £500,
the agent must ensure that, at the time when the donation is received by the regulated donee, the responsible person is given all such details in respect of the donor as are required by virtue of paragraph 2 or 2A of Schedule 6 to be given in respect of the donor of a recordable donation to a registered party.

(5)   A person commits an offence if, without reasonable excuse, he fails to comply with sub-paragraph (3) or (4).

Declaration as to source of donation

6A (1)   Where a person (P) causes an amount exceeding £7,500 to be received by a regulated donee by way of a donation, a written declaration must be given to the donee
    (a)   by P, if P is an individual, or
    (b)   if not, by an individual authorised by P to make the declaration,
stating, to the best of the individual's knowledge and belief, whether or not sub-paragraph (2) applies to the donation.

(2)   This sub-paragraph applies to the donation if

    (a) a person other than P has provided, or is expected to provide, money or any other benefit to P with a view to, or otherwise in connection with, the making of the donation, and

    (b) the money, or the value of the benefit, is more than £7,500.

(3) Where a declaration under this paragraph contains a statement to the effect that sub-paragraph (2) applies to the donation, it must also

    (a) state whether or not, in the opinion of the person making the declaration

       (i) sub-paragraph (2) of paragraph 6 applies to the donation;

      (ii) sub-paragraph (4) of that paragraph applies to it;

    (b) if the person's opinion is that neither of those sub-paragraphs applies to the donation, give the person's reasons for that opinion.

(4) The declaration must also state the full name and address of the person by whom it is made and, where sub-paragraph (1)(b) applies

    (a) state that the person is authorised by P to make the declaration;

    (b) describe the person's role or position in relation to P.

(5) A person who knowingly or recklessly makes a false declaration under this paragraph commits an offence.

(6) Regulations made by the Secretary of State may make provision as to how the value of a benefit is to be calculated for the purposes of sub-paragraph (2).

Declaration as to whether residence etc condition satisfied

6B (1) An individual making to a regulated donee a donation in relation to which the condition set out in section 54(2ZA) applies must give to the donee a written declaration stating whether or not the individual satisfies that condition.

(2) A declaration under this paragraph must also state the individual's full name and address.

(3) A person who knowingly or recklessly makes a false declaration under this paragraph commits an offence.

(4) The Secretary of State may by regulations make provision requiring a declaration under this paragraph to be retained for a specified period.

(5) The requirement in sub-paragraph (1) does not apply where, by reason of section 71B(1)(a), the individual by whom the donation would be made is a permissible donor in relation to the donation at the time of its receipt by the donee.

Payments etc which are (or are not) to be treated as donations by permissible donors

7 (1) The following provisions have effect for the purposes of this Schedule.

(1A) A person falling within section 54(2A)(a) to (g) is a permissible donor if

    (a) the controlled donation is received by

       (i) a member of a registered party; or

      (ii) a members association whose membership consists wholly or mainly of members of a registered party,

    and the party is a Gibraltar party whose entry in the register includes a statement that it intends to contest one or more elections to the European Parliament in the combined region; or

    (b) the controlled donation is received by a member of the European Parliament elected in the combined region.

(2) Any payment out of public funds received by a regulated donee which is a members association, for its use and benefit in connection with any of its political activities, shall

be regarded as a controlled donation received by the association from a permissible donor.

(3) Any donation received by a regulated donee shall (if it would not otherwise fall to be so regarded) be regarded as a controlled donation received by the donee from a permissible donor if and to the extent that

    (a) the purpose of the donation is to meet qualifying costs incurred or to be incurred in connection with any visit

        (i) by the donee in connection with any of the donee's political activities, or

        (ii) in the case of a members association, by any member or officer of the association in connection with any of its political activities,

    to a country or territory outside the United Kingdom, and

    (b) the amount of the donation does not exceed a reasonable amount in respect of such costs.

(4) In sub-paragraph (3) "qualifying costs", in relation to the donee or (as the case may be) any member or officer of the donee, means costs relating to that person in respect of

    (a) travelling between the United Kingdom and the country or territory in question; or

    (b) travelling, accommodation or subsistence while within that country or territory.

(5) Any controlled donation received by a regulated donee which is an exempt trust donation shall be regarded as a controlled donation received by the donee from a permissible donor.

(5A) Any controlled donation received by a regulated donee which is an exempt Gibraltar trust donation shall be regarded as a controlled donation received by the donee from a permissible donor if

    (a) the donation is received by

        (i) a member of a registered party; or

        (ii) a members association whose membership consists wholly or mainly of members of a registered party,

    and the party is a Gibraltar party whose entry in the register includes a statement that it intends to contest one or more elections to the European Parliament in the combined region; or

    (b) the donation is received by a member of the European Parliament elected in the combined region.

(6) But any controlled donation received by a regulated donee from a trustee of any property (in his capacity as such) which is not

    (a) an exempt trust donation, or

    (aa) an exempt Gibraltar trust donation regarded by virtue of sub-paragraph (5A) as received from a permissible donor, or

    (b) a controlled donation transmitted by the trustee to the donee on behalf of beneficiaries under the trust who are

        (i) persons who at the time of its receipt by the donee are permissible donors falling within section 54(2) or permissible donors by virtue of sub-paragraph (1A), or

        (ii) the members of an unincorporated association which at that time is a permissible donor,

    shall be regarded as a controlled donation received by the donee from a person who is not a permissible donor.

Acceptance or return of donations

8 (1) Sections 56 to 60 shall apply for the purposes of this Schedule in relation to a regulated donee and any controlled donation received by a regulated donee as they apply for the

purposes of this Part in relation to a registered party and any donation received by a registered party.

(1A) In its application in accordance with sub-paragraph (1), section 56(1A)(a) shall have effect as if the reference to a declaration under section 54B were construed as a reference to a declaration under paragraph 6B above.

(2) In its application in accordance with sub-paragraph (1), section 56(3) and (4) section 56(3), (3B) and (4) shall each have effect as if the reference to the treasurer of the party were construed

    (a) in relation to a regulated donee other than a members association, as a reference to the donee; and

    (b) in relation to a members association, as a reference to the responsible person.

Evasion of restrictions on donations

9   Section 61 shall apply for the purposes of this Schedule as if

    (a) any reference to donations were to controlled donations;

    (b) any reference to a registered party were to a regulated donee; and

    (c) any reference to the treasurer of such a party were construed as mentioned in paragraph 8(2)(a) or (b).

NOTES

Prospective operation
  Paras 6(1)(aa), 6A, 6B not yet in operation

Defined terms
  combined region: s 160(1)
  controlled donation: Sch 7, Pt I, para 1(2), (3)
  donation: Sch 7, Pt 1, paras 1(2), (5), 2-4
  exempt Gibraltar trust donation: s 162
  exempt trust donation: s 162
  Gibraltar party: ss 28(8)(d), 160(1)

members association: Sch 7, Pt I, para 1(2), (6)
political activities: Sch 7, Pt I, para 1(2), (4)
property: s 160(1)
provided out of public funds: s 160(4)
recordable donation: Sch 6, para 1
registered party: ss 50(7), 160(1)
regulated donee: Sch 7, Pt I, para 1(2), (7)
the responsible person: Sch 7, Pt I, para 1(2), (9)

Part III
Reporting of Donations by Regulated Donees

Donation reports: donations from permissible donors etc

10 (1)   A regulated donee must prepare a report under this paragraph in respect of each controlled donation accepted by the donee which is a recordable donation each controlled donation which is a recordable donation and either

    (a) has been accepted by the donee, or

    (b) has not been accepted by the donee but is a donation in the case of which a declaration under paragraph 6A or 6B has been given.

(1A) For the purposes of this paragraph a controlled donation is a recordable donation

    (a) if it is a donation of more than £7,500 (where the donee is a members association) or £1,500 (in any other case);

    (b) if, when it is added to any other controlled benefit or benefits accruing to the donee

      (i) from the same person and in the same calendar year, and

      (ii) in respect of which no report has been previously made under this paragraph,

    the aggregate amount of the benefits is more than £7,500 (where the donee is a members association) or £1,500 (in any other case).

(1B) A controlled benefit is

    (a) a controlled donation;

(b) a controlled transaction within the meaning of paragraph 2 of Schedule 7A.

(1C) A controlled benefit which is a controlled donation accrues
    (a) from the permissible donor who made it, and
    (b) when it is accepted by the donee.

(1D) A controlled benefit which is a controlled transaction accrues
    (a) from any authorised participant (within the meaning of paragraph 4(3) of Schedule 7A) who is a party to it, and
    (b) when it is entered into;
and paragraph 9(6) of Schedule 7A applies for the purposes of paragraph (b) above.

(2) A regulated donee must deliver the report prepared by virtue of sub-paragraph (1) to the Commission within the period of 30 days beginning with
    (a) if sub-paragraph (1A)(a) applies, the date of acceptance of the donation;
    (b) if sub-paragraph (1A)(b) applies, the date on which the benefit which causes the aggregate amount to exceed £7,500 or (as the case may be) £1,000 £1,500 accrues.

(3) Each report prepared by virtue of sub-paragraph (1) must
    (a) give the name and address of the donee; and
    (b) if he is the holder of a relevant elective office, specify the office in question.

(4) Each such report must also give
    (a) such information as is required to be given, in the case of a report prepared by virtue of section 62 by virtue of paragraphs 2 , 2A and 4 , by virtue of paragraphs 1A, 2, 2A and 4 of Schedule 6;
    (b) the date when the donation was accepted by the donee, and
    (c) such other information as is required by regulations made by the Commission.

(4A) In the case of a donation made by an individual who has an anonymous entry in an electoral register (within the meaning of the Representation of the People Act 1983), if the report states that the donee has seen evidence of such description as is prescribed by the Secretary of State in regulations that the individual has such an anonymous entry, the report must be accompanied by a copy of the evidence.

(5) In the application of paragraphs 2 , 2A and 4 paragraphs 1A, 2, 2A and 4 of Schedule 6 in accordance with sub-paragraph (4) above
    (a) any reference to a recordable donation within the meaning of that Schedule shall be construed as a reference to a recordable donation within the meaning of this paragraph;
    (aa) any reference to section 54A shall be read as a reference to paragraph 6A above, and any reference to section 54B shall be read as a reference to paragraph 6B above;
    (b) any reference to section 55(2) or to section 55(3) shall be construed as a reference to paragraph 7(2) above or to paragraph 7(3) above respectively; and
    (c) any reference to section 53 shall be construed as a reference to paragraph 5 above.

(6) In the case of a controlled benefit which is a donation to which paragraph 7(2) applies, sub-paragraph (1A)(b) above shall have effect as if for "from the same person" there were substituted "in circumstances falling within paragraph 7(2)".

(7) In the case of a controlled benefit which is a donation to which paragraph 7(3) applies
    (a) sub-paragraph (1A)(b) above shall have effect as if for "from the same person" there were substituted "in circumstances falling within paragraph 7(3) by the same donor"; and
    (b) any report prepared by virtue of sub-paragraph (1) above in respect of the donation must give

(i)   the date or dates on or between which the visit to which the donation relates took place, and

(ii) the destination and purpose of the visit.

(8) This paragraph does not apply to a donation received by a holder of a relevant elective office unless he is not a member of a registered party and is either

(a) a member of the Scottish Parliament, or

(b) a member of a local authority in Scotland.

(9) For the purposes of sub-paragraph (8), it is immaterial whether the donation is made to the holder of the relevant elective office in that capacity or in his capacity as a member of a registered party.

Donation reports: donations from impermissible or unidentifiable donors or without required declaration

11 (1) A regulated donee shall

(a) prepare a report under this paragraph in respect of each controlled donation received by the donee and falling within paragraph 6(1)(a), (aa) or (b); and

(b) deliver the report to the Commission within the period of 30 days beginning with the date when the donation was dealt with in accordance with section 56(2)(a), (aa) or (b).

(2) Each such report must

(a) give the name and address of the donee; and

(b) if he is the holder of a relevant elective office, specify the office in question.

(3) Each such report in respect of a donation falling within paragraph 6(1)(a) or (aa) must also give

(a) the name and address of the person appearing to be the donor;

(b) the amount of the donation (if a donation of money, in cash or otherwise) or (in any other case) the nature of the donation and its value as determined in accordance with paragraph 5;

(c) the date when the donation was received and the date when, and the manner in which, it was dealt with in accordance with section 56(2)(a) or (aa); and

(d) such other information as is required by regulations made by the Commission.

(4) Each such report in respect of a donation falling within paragraph 6(1)(b) must also give

(a) details of the manner in which it was made;

(b) the amount of the donation (if a donation of money, in cash or otherwise) or (in any other case) the nature of the donation and its value as determined in accordance with paragraph 5;

(c) the date when the donation was received, and the date when, and the manner in which, it was dealt with in accordance with section 56(2)(b); and

(d) such other information as is required by regulations made by the Commission.

(5) In this paragraph any reference to any provision of section 56 is a reference to that provision as applied by paragraph 8.

Offence of failing to deliver donation report

12 (1) Where a report required to be delivered to the Commission under paragraph 10(1) or 11(1) is, without reasonable excuse not delivered by the end of the period of 30 days mentioned in paragraph 10(2) or 11(1)

(a) in the case of a regulated donee other than a members association, the regulated donee is guilty of an offence;

(b) in the case of a members association, the association and the responsible person are guilty of an offence.

(2) If such a report is delivered to the Commission which, without reasonable excuse, does not comply with any requirements of paragraph 10 or 11 as regards the information to be given in such a report

    (a) in the case of a regulated donee other than a members association, the regulated donee is guilty of an offence;

    (b) in the case of a members association, the association and the responsible person are guilty of an offence.

(3) *Repealed*

(4) Where the court is satisfied, on an application made by the Commission, that any failure to comply with any such requirements in relation to any donation to the regulated donee was attributable to an intention on the part of any person to conceal the existence or true amount of the donation, the court may order the forfeiture by the donee of an amount equal to the value of the donation.

(5) The following provisions, namely

    (a) subsections (3) to (5) of section 58, and

    (b) sections 59 and 60,

shall apply for the purposes, or in connection with the operation, of sub-paragraph (4) in relation to a regulated donee as they apply for the purposes, or in connection with the operation, of section 58 in relation to a registered party.

Declaration in donation report

13 (1) Each report under paragraph 10 or 11 must, when delivered to the Commission, be accompanied by a declaration made by

    (a) the regulated donee, or

    (b) (if a members association) the responsible person,

which complies with sub-paragraph (2) or (3).

(2) In the case of a report under paragraph 10, the declaration must state that, to the best of the declarant's knowledge and belief, any donation recorded in the report as having been accepted by the donee was from a permissible donor.

(3) In the case of a report under paragraph 11, the declaration must state that, to the best of the declarant's knowledge and belief, the donation recorded in the report as having been received by the donee, or a payment of an equivalent amount, has been returned to the donor or otherwise dealt with in accordance with the provisions of Chapter II of Part IV of this Act.

(4) A person commits an offence if he knowingly or recklessly makes a false declaration under this paragraph.

NOTES

Prospective operation
Parts of para 10 not yet in operation

Defined terms
the Commission: s 160(1)
controlled donation: Sch 7, Pt I, para 1(2), (3) (and see also para 10(1A) of this Part of this Schedule)
donation: Sch 7, Pt I, para 1(2), (5), 2-4
members association: Sch 7, Pt I, para 1(2), (6)

recordable donation: Sch 6, para 1
registered party: ss 50(7), 160(1)
regulated donee: Sch 7, Pt I, para 1(2), (7)
relevant elective office: Sch 7, Pt I, para 1(2), (8)
the responsible person: Sch 7, Pt I, para 1(2), (9)
the Secretary of State: s 159A

Part V
Register of Donations

Register of recordable donations

15 (1)   Section 69 shall apply in relation to donations reported to the Commission under this Schedule ("relevant donations") as it applies to donations reported to them under Chapter III of Part IV of this Act.

  (2)   But in its application in accordance with sub-paragraph (1), section 69 shall have effect with the modifications set out in sub-paragraph (3).

  (3)   Those modifications are as follows

      (a)   subsection (2) shall have effect in relation to a relevant donation as if (instead of requiring the register to contain the details mentioned in paragraphs (a) to (c) of that subsection) it required the register to contain such details as have been given in relation to the donation in pursuance of paragraph 10(3), 10(4), 11(2), 11(3) or 11(4); and

      (b)   *Repealed.*

Donations to holders of certain elective offices

15A (1)   This paragraph applies in relation to donations received by a holder of a relevant elective office, other than a police and crime commissioner if

      (a)   the relevant body has in place arrangements requiring the holder of the office to report such donations, and

      (b)   the Commission think that the arrangements correspond to the requirements of paragraph 10.

  (2)   The Commission must make such arrangements as they think appropriate corresponding to section 69 as modified in pursuance of paragraph 15(3) to maintain a register of such information as they receive relating to such donations.

  (3)   In sub-paragraph (1)(a) a relevant body is

      (a)   if the holder of a relevant elective office is a member of a body mentioned in paragraphs (a) to (f) of paragraph 1(8), that body;

      (b)   if the holder of a relevant elective office is the Mayor of London, the London Assembly;

      (c)   if the holder of a relevant elective office is an elected mayor within the meaning of Part 2 of the Local Government Act 2000, the local authority of which he is the mayor.

NOTES

Defined terms
  body: s 160(1)
  the Commission: s 160(1)
  donation: Sch 7, Pt I, paras 1(2), (5), 2-4

modifications: s 160(1)
relevant elective office: Sch 7, Pt I, para 1(2), (8)

Part VI

Repealed

Part VII
Compliance Officers

Functions and liabilities of compliance officers

17 (1)   A regulated donee who is the holder of a relevant elective office (the "officeholder") may, by giving a notice to the Commission which complies with paragraph 18(1), appoint an individual as compliance officer for the officeholder.

  (2)   Where a notice under this paragraph is for the time being in force

    (a) any duty imposed on the officeholder by virtue of paragraph 8, or under paragraph 10, 11 or 13, may be discharged either by the officeholder or by the compliance officer;

    (b) section 56(3), (3B) and (4) as applied by paragraph 8, and paragraph 12(1) and (2), apply to the compliance officer as well as the officeholder (so that either or both of them may be charged with any offence under those provisions);

    (c) if the compliance officer makes a declaration under paragraph 13, paragraph 13(4) applies to the compliance officer instead of the officeholder.

(3)   The compliance officer for an officeholder cannot be guilty of an offence under paragraph 12(1) or (2) in respect of any controlled donation received by the officeholder at a time when the notice under this paragraph was not in force.

(4)   A person commits an offence if, at a time when a notice under this paragraph is in force in relation to an officeholder, the person knowingly gives the compliance officer any information relating to

    (a) the amount of any controlled donation made to the officeholder, or

    (b) the person or body making such a donation,

which is false in a material particular.

Notices of appointment, renewal, alteration and termination

18 (1) A notice under paragraph 17

    (a) must be signed by the officeholder, and

    (b) must contain a statement signed by the individual to be appointed as compliance officer confirming that the individual is willing to be appointed.

(2)   A notice under paragraph 17 must state

    (a) the full name of the officeholder,

    (b) the relevant elected office that the person holds,

    (c) the officeholder's home address in the United Kingdom, or (if there is no such home address) the officeholder's home address elsewhere, and

    (d) if the officeholder is a member of a registered party, the party's registered name and the address of its registered headquarters.

(3)   A notice under paragraph 17 must also state

    (a) the full name of the individual to be appointed as compliance officer,

    (b) if the individual holds a relevant elected office, what that office is,

    (c) the individual's home address in the United Kingdom, or (if there is no such home address) the individual's home address elsewhere, and

    (d) if the individual is a member of a registered party, the party's registered name and the address of its registered headquarters.

(4)   Subject to the following provisions of this paragraph, a notice under paragraph 17 ("the original notice")

    (a) shall be in force as from the date on which it is received by the Commission, but

    (b) shall lapse at the end of the period of 12 months beginning with that date unless the officeholder or the compliance officer gives the Commission a notice (a "renewal notice") that they both wish the original notice to remain in force.

(5)   A renewal notice

    (a) has the effect of extending the validity of the original notice for a further 12 months beginning with the time when it would otherwise have lapsed (whether under sub-paragraph (4)(b) or on the expiry of a previous extension under this sub-paragraph);

    (b) must be received by the Commission during the period of one month ending at that time.

(6)   A renewal notice must either

(a) confirm that all the statements contained in the original notice, as it has effect for the time being, are accurate; or

(b) indicate that any statement contained in that notice, as it so has effect, is replaced by some other statement conforming with the relevant provision of sub-paragraph (2) or (3).

A renewal notice must be signed by the officeholder and the compliance officer.

(7) The officeholder or the compliance officer may, at any time after giving the original notice, give the Commission a notice (a "notice of alteration") indicating that any statement contained in the original notice, as it has effect for the time being, is replaced by some other statement

(a) contained in the notice of alteration, and

(b) conforming with the relevant provision of sub-paragraph (2) or (3).

A notice of alteration takes effect on the day on which it is received by the Commission or (if later) on such date as may be specified in the notice.

(8) A notice of alteration must be signed

(a) by the officeholder, and

(b) by the compliance officer or, in the case of a notice substituting a different individual as the compliance officer, by that individual.

(9) A notice under paragraph 17 ceases to have effect on receipt by the Commission of a notice terminating it (a "notice of termination") given and signed by the officeholder or by the compliance officer.

(10) On receipt of a notice of termination given by the officeholder or by the compliance officer, the Commission must inform the other party as soon as is reasonably practicable (unless the notice was signed both by the officeholder and by the compliance officer).

Register of compliance officers

19 (1) The Commission shall maintain a register of all notices given to them under paragraph 17 which are for the time being in force.

(2) The register shall be maintained by the Commission in such form as they may determine and shall contain, in the case of each such notice, all the information contained in the notice as it has effect for the time being in accordance with paragraph 18.

(3) Where any notice is given to the Commission under paragraph 17 or sub-paragraph (4)(b) or (7) of paragraph 18, they shall cause all the information contained in the notice, or (as the case may be) any new information contained in it, to be entered in the register as soon as is reasonably practicable.

(4) The information to be entered in the register in respect of any individual shall, however, not include the individual's home address.

NOTES

Defined terms
body: s 160(1)
the Commission: s 160(1)
controlled donation: Sch 7, Pt 1, para 1(2), (3)
registered party: s 160(1)

regulated donee: Sch 7, Pt 1, para 1(2), (7)
relevant elective office: Sch 7, Pt 1, para 1(2), (8)

SCHEDULE 7A
CONTROL OF LOANS ETC TO INDIVIDUALS AND MEMBERS ASSOCIATIONS

Operation and construction of Schedule

1 (1) This Schedule has effect for controlling loans and certain other transactions where one of the parties to the transaction is
    (a) a member of a registered party,
    (b) a members association, or
    (c) the holder of a relevant elective office.

(2) The following provisions have effect for the purposes of this Schedule.

(3) References to a controlled transaction must be construed in accordance with paragraph 2.

(4) A reference to a connected transaction is a reference to a controlled transaction falling within paragraph 2(3)(b).

(5) A regulated participant is
    (a) a member of a registered party;
    (b) a members association;
    (c) the holder of a relevant elective office, whether or not he is a member of a registered party.

(6) A credit facility is an agreement whereby a regulated participant is enabled to receive from time to time from another party to the agreement a loan of money not exceeding such amount (taking account of any repayments made by the regulated participant) as is specified in or determined in accordance with the agreement.

(7) References to each of the following must be construed in accordance with Schedule 7
    (a) the political activities of a party member or a members association;
    (b) members association;
    (c) relevant elective office;
    (d) the responsible person (in relation to a members association).

(7A) Paragraphs 1A and 1B of Schedule 7 apply for the purposes of this Schedule, in relation to controlled transactions, as they apply for the purposes of that Schedule in relation to controlled donations.

(7B) Paragraph 1A(1)(b) of Schedule 7, as it applies by virtue of sub-paragraph (7A) above, has effect as if for sub-paragraphs (i) and (ii) there were substituted
    "(i) enters into a controlled transaction which is a recordable transaction for the purposes of paragraph 9 of Schedule 7A, or
    (ii) enters into a controlled transaction falling within paragraph 5 or 6(1)(b) of that Schedule,".

(7C) A notice under paragraph 1A of Schedule 7 also has effect as a notice under the Schedule 7A version of that paragraph.
The "Schedule 7A version" of paragraph 1A of Schedule 7 means that paragraph as it applies, in relation to controlled transactions, by virtue of sub-paragraph (7A) above.

(8) This Schedule does not have effect in relation to
    (a) a member of the Scottish Parliament, or
    (b) a member of a local authority in Scotland,
if he is not also a member of a registered party.

Controlled transaction

2 (1) An agreement between a regulated participant and another person by which the other person makes a loan of money to the regulated participant is a controlled transaction if the use condition is satisfied.

(2) An agreement between a regulated participant and another person by which the other person provides a credit facility to the regulated participant is a controlled transaction if the use condition is satisfied.

(3) Where

    (a) a regulated participant and another person (A) enter into a controlled transaction of a description mentioned in sub-paragraph (1) or (2) or a transaction under which any property, services or facilities are provided for the use or benefit of the regulated participant (including the services of any person),

    (b) A also enters into an arrangement where a third person gives any form of security (whether real or personal) for a sum owed to A by the regulated participant under the transaction mentioned in paragraph (a), and

    (c) the use condition is satisfied,

the arrangement is a controlled transaction.

(4) An agreement or arrangement is not a controlled transaction

    (a) to the extent that in accordance with any enactment a payment made in pursuance of the agreement or arrangement falls to be included in a return as to election expenses in respect of a candidate or candidates at a particular election, or

    (b) if its value is not more than £500.

(5) Anything given or transferred to an officer, member, trustee or agent of a members association in his capacity as such (and not for his own use or benefit) is to be regarded as given or transferred to the association (and references to money or any other benefit received by a regulated participant accordingly include, in the case of a members association, money or any other benefit so given or transferred).

(6) The use condition is that the regulated participant intends at the time he enters into a transaction mentioned in sub-paragraph (1), (2) or (3)(a) to use any money or benefit obtained in consequence of the transaction in connection with relevant political activities.

(7) For the purposes of sub-paragraph (6), it is immaterial that only part of the money or benefit is intended to be used in connection with relevant political activities.

(8) Relevant political activities are

    (a) if the regulated participant is a member of a registered party, any of his political activities as a member of the party;

    (b) if the regulated participant is a members association, any of its political activities;

    (c) if the regulated participant is a holder of a relevant elective office, any of his political activities.

(9) The Secretary of State may, by order, specify circumstances or any description of circumstances in which an agreement or arrangement falling within any of sub-paragraphs (1) to (3) is not a controlled transaction.

Valuation of controlled transactions

3 (1) The value of a controlled transaction which is a loan is the value of the total amount to be lent under the loan agreement.

(2) The value of a controlled transaction which is a credit facility is the maximum amount which may be borrowed under the agreement for the facility.

(3) The value of a controlled transaction which is an arrangement by which any form of security is given is the contingent liability under the security provided.

(4) For the purposes of sub-paragraphs (1) and (2), no account is to be taken of the effect of any provision contained in a loan agreement or an agreement for a credit facility at the time it is entered into which enables outstanding interest to be added to any sum for the time being owed in respect of the loan or credit facility, whether or not any such interest has been so added.

Authorised participants

4 (1) A regulated participant must not
   (a) be a party to a controlled transaction to which any of the other parties is not an authorised participant;
   (b) derive a benefit in consequence of a connected transaction if any of the parties to that transaction is not an authorised participant.

(2) This paragraph does not apply to a controlled transaction if it was entered into before the commencement of section 61 of the Electoral Administration Act 2006.

(3) In this Schedule, an authorised participant is a person who is a permissible donor within the meaning of section 54(2).

(3A) A person who is a permissible donor within the meaning of section 54(2A) is also an authorised participant if
   (a) the regulated transaction is entered into by
      (i) a member of a registered party; or
      (ii) a members association whose membership consists wholly or mainly of members of a registered party,
   and the party is a Gibraltar party whose entry in the register includes a statement that it intends to contest one or more elections to the European Parliament in the combined region; or
   (b) the regulated transaction is entered into by a member of the European Parliament elected in the combined region.

(3B) In its application for the purposes of this Part by virtue of subsection (3A), section 54(2A) has effect as if for "the donation is received" there were substituted "the regulated transaction" is entered into.

(4) The Secretary of State may, by order, specify circumstances or any description of circumstances in which a person who is not a permissible donor is to be treated as an authorised participant.

Declaration that residence etc condition satisfied

4A (1) A regulated participant must not be a party to a controlled transaction to which this paragraph applies unless the regulated participant has received a written declaration from each of the other parties to the transaction who is an individual stating that the individual satisfies the condition set out in section 54(2ZA).

(2) This paragraph applies to a controlled transaction
   (a) if the value of the transaction is more than £7,500, or
   (b) if the aggregate amount of it and any other relevant benefit or benefits accruing in the same calendar year as the transaction is more than £7,500.

(3) For the purposes of sub-paragraph (2) "relevant benefit" and "accruing" have the meaning given by section 71M(3).

(4) A declaration under this paragraph must also state the full name and address of the person by whom it is made.

(5) A person who knowingly or recklessly makes a false declaration under this paragraph commits an offence.

(6) The Secretary of State may by regulations make provision requiring a declaration under this paragraph to be retained for a specified period.

(7) The reference in sub-paragraph (1) to each of the other parties to the transaction does not include any individual who, at the time the transaction is entered into, is an authorised participant in relation to it by reason of section 71Z1(1)(a).

Controlled transaction involving unauthorised participant

5 (1) This paragraph applies if a regulated participant is a party to a controlled transaction in which another participant is not an authorised participant.

(2) The transaction is void.

(3) Despite sub-paragraph (2)
   (a) any money received by the regulated participant by virtue of the transaction must be repaid by the regulated participant to the person from whom it was received, along with interest at such rate as is determined in accordance with an order made by the Secretary of State;
   (b) that person is entitled to recover the money, along with such interest.

(4) If
   (a) the money is not (for whatever reason) repaid as mentioned in sub-paragraph (3)(a), or
   (b) the person entitled to recover the money refuses or fails to do so,
   the Commission may apply to the court to make such order as it thinks fit to restore (so far as is possible) the parties to the transaction to the position they would have been in if the transaction had not been entered into.

(5) In the case of a controlled transaction where a party other than a regulated participant
   (a) at the time the regulated participant enters into the transaction, is an authorised participant, but
   (b) subsequently, for whatever reason, ceases to be an authorised participant,
   the transaction is void and sub-paragraphs (3) and (4) apply with effect from the time when the other party ceased to be an authorised participant.

(6) This paragraph does not apply to a controlled transaction if it was entered into before the commencement of section 61 of the Electoral Administration Act 2006.

Guarantees and securities: unauthorised participants

6 (1) This paragraph applies if
   (a) a regulated participant and another person (A) enter into a transaction of a description mentioned in paragraph 2(3)(a),
   (b) A is party to a controlled transaction of a description mentioned in paragraph 2(3)(b) ("the connected transaction") with another person (B), and
   (c) B is not an authorised participant.

(2) Paragraph 5(2) to (4) applies to the transaction mentioned in sub-paragraph (1)(a).

(3) The connected transaction is void.

(4) Sub-paragraph (5) applies if (but only if) A is unable to recover from the regulated participant the whole of the money mentioned in paragraph 5(3)(a) (as applied by sub-paragraph (2) above), along with such interest as is there mentioned.

(5) Despite sub-paragraph (3), A is entitled to recover from B any part of that money (and such interest) that is not recovered from the regulated participant.

(6) Sub-paragraph (5) does not entitle A to recover more than the contingent liability under the security provided by virtue of the connected transaction.

(7) In the case of a connected transaction where B
    (a) at the time A enters into the transaction, is an authorised participant, but
    (b) subsequently, for whatever reason, ceases to be an authorised participant,
sub-paragraphs (2) to (6) apply with effect from the time when B ceased to be an authorised participant.

(8) This paragraph does not apply to a regulated transaction if it was entered into before the commencement of section 61 of the Electoral Administration Act 2006.

(9) If the transaction mentioned in paragraph 2(3)(a) is not a controlled transaction of a description mentioned in paragraph 2(1) or (2), references in this paragraph and paragraph 5(2) to (4) (as applied by sub-paragraph (2) above) to the repayment or recovery of money must be construed as references to (as the case may be)
    (a) the return or recovery of any property provided under the transaction,
    (b) to the extent that such is incapable of being returned or recovered or its market value has diminished since the time the transaction was entered into, the repayment or recovery of the market value at that time, or
    (c) the market value (at that time) of any facilities or services provided under the transaction.

Transfer to unauthorised participant invalid

7 If an authorised participant purports to transfer his interest in a controlled transaction to a person who is not an authorised participant the purported transfer is of no effect.

Offences

8 (1) An individual who is a regulated participant commits an offence if
    (a) he enters into a controlled transaction of a description mentioned in paragraph 2(1) or (2) in which another participant is not an authorised participant, and
    (b) he knew or ought reasonably to have known that the other participant was not an authorised participant.

(2) A responsible person of a members association commits an offence if
    (a) the association enters into a controlled transaction of a description mentioned in paragraph 2(1) or (2) in which another participant is not an authorised participant, and
    (b) he knew or ought reasonably to have known of the matters mentioned in paragraph (a).

(3) An individual who is a regulated participant commits an offence if
    (a) he enters into a controlled transaction of a description mentioned in paragraph 2(1) or (2) in which another participant is not an authorised participant,
    (b) sub-paragraph (1)(b) does not apply to him, and
    (c) as soon as practicable after knowledge that the other participant is not an authorised participant comes to him he fails to take all reasonable steps to repay any money which he has received by virtue of the transaction.

(4) A responsible person of a members association commits an offence if
    (a) the association enters into a controlled transaction of a description mentioned in paragraph 2(1) or (2) in which another participant is not an authorised participant,

      (b)   sub-paragraph (2)(b) does not apply to him, and

      (c)   as soon as practicable after knowledge of the matters mentioned in paragraph (a) comes to him he fails to take all reasonable steps to repay any money which the association has received by virtue of the transaction.

(5)   An individual who is a regulated participant commits an offence if

      (a)   he benefits from or falls to benefit in consequence of a connected transaction to which any of the parties is not an authorised participant, and

      (b)   he knew or ought reasonably to have known that one of the other parties was not an authorised participant.

(6)   A responsible person of a members association commits an offence if

      (a)   the association benefits from or falls to benefit in consequence of a connected transaction to which any of the parties is not an authorised participant, and

      (b)   he knew or ought reasonably to have known of the matters mentioned in paragraph (a).

(7)   An individual who is a regulated participant commits an offence if

      (a)   he is a party to a transaction of a description mentioned in paragraph 2(3)(a),

      (b)   he benefits from or falls to benefit in consequence of a connected transaction to which any of the parties is not an authorised participant,

      (c)   sub-paragraph (5)(b) does not apply to him, and

      (d)   as soon as practicable after knowledge comes to him that one of the parties to the connected transaction is not an authorised participant he fails to take all reasonable steps to repay to any person who has provided him with any benefit in consequence of the connected transaction the value of the benefit.

(8)   A responsible person of a members association commits an offence if

      (a)   the association is a party to a transaction of a description mentioned in paragraph 2(3)(a),

      (b)   the association benefits from or falls to benefit in consequence of a connected transaction to which any of the parties is not an authorised participant,

      (c)   sub-paragraph (6)(b) does not apply to him, and

      (d)   as soon as practicable after knowledge comes to him that one of the parties to the connected transaction is not an authorised participant he fails to take all reasonable steps to repay to any person who has provided the association with any benefit in consequence of the connected transaction the value of the benefit.

(9)   A person commits an offence if he

      (a)   knowingly enters into, or

      (b)   knowingly does any act in furtherance of,

any arrangement which facilitates or is likely to facilitate, whether by means of concealment or disguise or otherwise, the participation by a regulated participant in a controlled transaction with a person other than an authorised participant.

(9A)   A person (P) cannot commit an offence under sub-paragraph (1), (2), (5) or (6) on the basis that P ought reasonably to have known that a particular individual does not satisfy the condition set out in section 54(2ZA) (and is therefore not an authorised participant) if

      (a)   the individual has given a declaration under paragraph 4A stating that the individual satisfies that condition, and

      (b)   P had no reasonable grounds for thinking that the statement was incorrect.

(10)   It is a defence for a person charged with an offence under sub-paragraph (2) to prove that he took all reasonable steps to prevent the members association entering into the transaction.

(11) It is a defence for a person charged with an offence under sub-paragraph (6) to prove that he took all reasonable steps to prevent the members association benefiting in consequence of the connected transaction.

(12) A reference to a regulated participant entering into a controlled transaction includes a reference to any circumstances in which the terms of a controlled transaction are varied so as to increase the amount of money to which the regulated participant is entitled in consequence of the transaction.

(13) A reference to a regulated participant entering into a transaction in which another participant is not an authorised participant includes a reference to any circumstances in which another party to the transaction who is an authorised participant ceases (for whatever reason) to be an authorised participant.

(14) This paragraph does not apply to a transaction which is entered into before the commencement of section 61 of the Electoral Administration Act 2006.

Transaction reports: transactions with authorised participants

9 (1) A regulated participant must prepare a report under this paragraph in respect of each controlled transaction entered into by him which is a recordable transaction.

(2) For the purposes of this paragraph a controlled transaction is a recordable transaction
   (a) if the value of the transaction is more than £7,500 (where the regulated participant is a members association) or £1,500 (in any other case), or
   (b) if the aggregate value of it and any other controlled benefit or benefits accruing to the regulated participant
      (i) from the same person and in the same calendar year, and
      (ii) in respect of which no report has been previously made under this paragraph,
   is more than £7,500 (where the regulated participant is a members association) or £1,500 (in any other case).

(3) A controlled benefit is
   (a) a controlled donation within the meaning of paragraph 1(3) of Schedule 7;
   (b) a controlled transaction.

(4) A controlled benefit which is a controlled donation accrues
   (a) from the permissible donor (within the meaning of section 54(2) or (2A)) who made it, and
   (b) when it is accepted by the donee.

(5) A controlled benefit which is a controlled transaction accrues
   (a) from any authorised participant who is a party to it, and
   (b) when it is entered into.

(6) For the purposes of this paragraph, if
   (a) the value of a controlled transaction as first entered into is such that it is not a recordable transaction, but
   (b) the terms of the transaction are subsequently varied in such a way that it becomes a recordable transaction,
   the regulated participant must be treated as having entered into a recordable transaction on the date when the variation takes effect.

(7) A regulated participant must deliver the report prepared in accordance with sub-paragraph (1) to the Commission within the period of 30 days beginning with
   (a) if sub-paragraph (2)(a) applies, the date on which the transaction is entered into;

(b) if sub-paragraph (2)(b) applies, the date on which the benefit which causes the aggregate amount to exceed £7,500 or (as the case may be) £1,500 accrues.

(8) Each report prepared in accordance with sub-paragraph (1) must
   (a) give the name and address of the regulated participant, and
   (b) if he is the holder of a relevant elective office, specify the office in question.

(9) Each such report must also give
   (a) such information as is required to be given, in the case of a report prepared in accordance with section 71M, by virtue of paragraphs 2 paragraphs 1A, 2, 2A and 5(2) and (3) of Schedule 6A;
   (b) in relation to a controlled transaction of a description mentioned in paragraph 2(1) or (2) above, such information as is required to be given, in the case of a report prepared in accordance with that section, by virtue of paragraph 6 of that Schedule;
   (c) in relation to a controlled transaction of a description mentioned in paragraph 2(3)(b) above, such information as is required to be given, in the case of a report prepared in accordance with that section, by virtue of paragraph 7 of that Schedule;
   (d) the date on which the transaction is entered into;
   (e) such other information as is required by regulations made by the Commission.

(10) In the application of paragraphs 2 paragraphs 1A, 2, 2A, 5(2) and (3), 6 and 7 of Schedule 6A in accordance with sub-paragraph (9) above
   (a) any reference to a recordable transaction within the meaning of that Schedule must be construed as a reference to a recordable transaction within the meaning of this paragraph;
   (b) any reference to section 71G or section 71F(4)(a) must be construed as a reference to paragraph 3 above or paragraph 2(3)(a) above;
   (ba) any reference to section 71HZA must be construed as a reference to paragraph 4A above;
   (c) any reference to a regulated transaction or a registered party within the meaning of that Schedule must be construed as a reference to a controlled transaction or a regulated participant within the meaning of this paragraph;
   (d) any reference to a transaction report within the meaning of that Schedule must be construed as a reference to a report under this paragraph.

Transaction reports: transactions with unauthorised participants

10 (1) A regulated participant must
   (a) prepare a report under this paragraph in respect of each controlled transaction entered into by him and falling within paragraph 5 or 6(1)(b), and
   (b) deliver the report to the Commission within the period of 30 days beginning with the date when the transaction was dealt with in accordance with that paragraph.

(2) Each such report must
   (a) give the name and address of the regulated participant;
   (b) if he is the holder of a relevant elective office, specify the office in question.

(3) Subject to sub-paragraph (5), each such report in respect of a transaction falling within paragraph 5 must also give
   (a) the name and address of the unauthorised participant;
   (b) the nature of the transaction (that is to say, whether it is a loan or a credit facility);
   (c) the value of the transaction or, in the case of a credit facility to which no limit is specified, a statement to that effect;

    (d) the date on which the transaction was entered into and the date when, and manner in which, it was dealt with in accordance with paragraph 5;

    (e) such other information as is required by regulations made by the Commission.

(4) Subject to sub-paragraph (5), each such report in respect of a transaction falling within paragraph 6(1)(b) must also give

    (a) the name and address of the unauthorised participant;

    (b) the value of the transaction or, in the case of a security to which no limit is specified, a statement to that effect;

    (c) a description of the principal features of the transaction mentioned in paragraph 6(1)(a);

    (d) where the security given consists in or includes rights over any property, the nature of that property;

    (e) the date on which the transaction was entered into and the date when, and manner in which, it was dealt with in accordance with paragraph 6;

    (f) such other information as is required by regulations made by the Commission.

(5) In relation to a transaction falling within paragraph 5 or 6(1)(b) which is an Irish transaction within the meaning of paragraph 2A(2) of Schedule 6A, each such report must record the fact that the transaction is an Irish transaction.

Transaction reports: changes to recorded transactions

11 (1) A regulated participant must

    (a) prepare a report under this paragraph in respect of each change to a recorded transaction; and

    (b) deliver the report to the Commission within the period of 30 days beginning with the date on which the change takes effect.

(2) A recorded transaction is a transaction recorded in a report under paragraph 9.

(3) There is a change to a recorded transaction if

    (a) another authorised participant becomes party to the transaction (whether in place of or in addition to any existing participant),

    (b) there is any change in the details given in relation to the transaction in pursuance of paragraph 9(9), or

    (c) the transaction comes to an end.

(4) For the purposes of sub-paragraph (3)(c), a loan comes to an end if

    (a) the whole debt (or all the remaining debt) is repaid;

    (b) the creditor releases the whole debt (or all the remaining debt).

(5) There is also a change to a recorded transaction if a person who is not an authorised participant becomes party to the transaction (whether in place of or in addition to any existing participant).

(6) Each report prepared in accordance with sub-paragraph (1) must

    (a) give the name and address of the regulated participant; and

    (b) if he is the holder of a relevant elective office, specify the office in question.

(7) Each such report must also give

    (a) details of the change;

    (b) the date on which the change takes effect;

    (c) in the case of a change falling within sub-paragraph (5), the date when and the manner in which the transaction was dealt with in accordance with paragraph 5 or 6;

    (d) such other information as is required by regulations made by the Commission.

Offence of failing to deliver transaction report

12 (1) Where a report required to be delivered to the Commission under paragraph 9(1), 10(1) or 11(1) is, without reasonable excuse, not delivered by the end of the period of 30 days mentioned in paragraph 9(7), 10(1) or 11(1)

   (a) in the case of a regulated participant other than a members association, the regulated participant is guilty of an offence;

   (b) in the case of a members association, the association and the responsible person are guilty of an offence.

(2) If such a report is delivered to the Commission which, without reasonable excuse, does not comply with any requirements of paragraph 9, 10 or 11 as regards the information to be given in such a report

   (a) in the case of a regulated participant other than a members association, the regulated participant is guilty of an offence;

   (b) in the case of a members association, the association and the responsible person are guilty of an offence.

(3) *Repealed*

(4) Where the court is satisfied, on an application made by the Commission, that any failure to comply with any such requirements in relation to any transaction entered into by a regulated participant was attributable to an intention on the part of any person to conceal the existence or true value of the transaction, the court may make such order as it thinks fit to restore (so far as is possible) the parties to the transaction to the position they would have been in if the transaction had not been entered into.

(5) An order under sub-paragraph (4) may in particular

   (a) where the transaction is a loan or credit facility, require that any amount owed by the regulated participant be repaid (and that no further sums be advanced under it);

   (b) where any form of security is given for a sum owed under the transaction, or the transaction is an arrangement by which any form of security is given, require that the security be discharged.

Declaration in transaction report

13 (1) Each report under paragraph 9 or 10 must, when delivered to the Commission, be accompanied by a declaration made by

   (a) the regulated participant, or

   (b) (if a members association) the responsible person,

which complies with sub-paragraph (2) or (3).

(2) In the case of a report under paragraph 9, the declaration must state that, to the best of the declarant's knowledge and belief, any transaction recorded in the report as having been entered into by the regulated participant was entered into with an authorised participant.

(3) In the case of a report under paragraph 10, the declaration must state that, to the best of the declarant's knowledge and belief, the transaction recorded in the report as having been entered into by the regulated participant has been dealt with in accordance with paragraph 5 or 6.

(4) A person commits an offence if he knowingly or recklessly makes a false declaration under this paragraph.

Existing transactions

14 (1) Paragraphs 9 to 11 have effect in relation to existing transactions as they have effect in relation to transactions entered into after the date on which those paragraphs come into force, except that

    (a) references in paragraph 9 to a controlled benefit do not include references to a controlled donation;

    (b) in paragraph 9(2)(b)(i) the words "and in the same calendar year" are omitted;

    (c) the requirement in paragraph 9(7), 10(1)(b) or 11(1)(b) is a requirement to deliver the report within the period of 60 days beginning with the date on which that provision comes into force.

  (2) An existing transaction is a controlled transaction which, at the date on which paragraphs 9 to 11 come into force, has not come to an end for the purposes of paragraph 11(3)(c).

Register of recordable transactions

15 (1) Section 71V applies in relation to transactions reported to the Commission under this Schedule ("relevant transactions") as it applies to transactions reported to them under Part 4A of this Act.

  (2) But in its application in accordance with sub-paragraph (1), section 71V(2) has effect in relation to a relevant transaction as if (instead of requiring the register to contain the details mentioned in paragraphs (a) to (c) of that subsection) it required the register to contain such details as have been given in relation to the transaction in pursuance of paragraph 9(8) and (9), 10(2), (3) and (4) 10(2) to (5) or 11(6) and (7).

16 (1) Paragraph 9 does not apply to holders of a relevant elective office.

  (2) Sub-paragraph (3) applies in relation to transactions in which a holder of a relevant elective office is a participant if

    (a) the relevant body has in place arrangements requiring the holder of the office to report such transactions, and

    (b) the Commission think that the arrangements correspond to the requirements of paragraph 9.

  (3) The Commission must make such arrangements as they think appropriate corresponding to section 71V (subject to such modifications as may be prescribed by the Secretary of State in regulations) to maintain a register of such information as they receive relating to such transactions.

  (4) In sub-paragraph (2)(a) a relevant body is

    (a) if the holder of a relevant elective office is a member of a body mentioned in paragraphs (a) to (f) of paragraph 1(8) of Schedule 7, that body;

    (b) if the holder of a relevant elective office is the Mayor of London, the London Assembly;

    (c) if the holder of a relevant elective office is an elected mayor within the meaning of Part 2 of the Local Government Act 2000, the local authority of which he is the mayor.

  (5) For the purposes of sub-paragraph (1) it is immaterial whether the transaction is entered into by the holder of the office in that capacity or in his capacity as a member of a registered party.

Proceedings under paragraphs 5 and 12

17 (1) This paragraph has effect in relation to proceedings on applications under paragraphs 5(4) and 12(4).

(2)   The court is

    (a)   in England and Wales, the county court;

    (b)   in Scotland, the sheriff, and the proceedings are civil proceedings;

    (c)   in Northern Ireland, the county court;

    (d)   in Gibraltar, the Gibraltar Court.

(3)   The standard of proof is that applicable to civil proceedings.

(4)   An order may be made whether or not proceedings are brought against any person for an offence under paragraph 8 or 12(1) or (2).

(5)   An appeal against an order made by the sheriff may be made to the Court of Session.

(6)   Rules of court in any part of the United Kingdom may make provision

    (a)   with respect to applications or appeals from proceedings on such applications;

    (b)   for the giving of notice of such applications or appeals to persons affected;

    (c)   for the joinder, or in Scotland sisting, of such persons as parties;

    (d)   generally with respect to procedure in such applications or appeals.

(7)   Sub-paragraph (6) does not affect any existing power to make rules.

Compliance officers

18 (1)   This paragraph applies where a regulated participant who is the holder of a relevant elective office (the "officeholder") has given a notice to the Commission under paragraph 17 of Schedule 7 appointing an individual as compliance officer for the officeholder.

(2)   Where the notice is for the time being in force

    (a)   any duty imposed on the officeholder under paragraph 9, 10, 11 or 13 may be discharged either by the officeholder or by the compliance officer;

    (b)   paragraph 12(1) and (2) applies to the compliance officer as well as the officeholder (so that either or both of them may be charged with an offence under paragraph 12(1) or (2));

    (c)   if the compliance officer makes a declaration under paragraph 13, paragraph 13(4) applies to the compliance officer instead of the officeholder.

(3)   The compliance officer for an officeholder cannot be guilty of an offence under paragraph 12(1) or (2) in respect of any controlled transaction entered into by the officeholder at a time when the notice was not in force.

NOTES

Prospective operation
  Para (4A) not yet in operation

Defined terms
  combined region: s 160(1)
  the Commission: s 160(1)
  enactment: s 160(1)
  Gibraltar court: s 160(1)
  Gibraltar party: ss 28(8)(d), 160(1)
  market value: s 160(1)
  members association: Sch 7, Pt I, para 1(2), (6) (by virtue of para 1(7) of this Schedule)
  modifications: s 160(1)

political activities of a party member or a members association: Sch 7, Pt I, para 1(2), (4) (by virtue of para 1(7) of this Schedule)
property: s 160(1)
registered party: s 160(1)
relevant elective office: Sch 7, Pt I, para 1(2), (8) (by virtue of para 1(7) of this Schedule)
the responsible person: Sch 7, Pt 1, para 1(2), (9) (by virtue of para 1(7) of this Schedule), as modified by para 1(7)(d)
the Secretary of State: s 159A

SCHEDULE 8
CAMPAIGN EXPENDITURE: QUALIFYING EXPENSES

Section 72

Part I

Qualifying Expenses

Expenses qualifying where incurred for election purposes

1 For the purposes of section 72(2) the expenses falling within this Part of this Schedule are expenses incurred in respect of any of the matters set out in the following list.

List of Matters

(1) Party political broadcasts.

Expenses in respect of such broadcasts include agency fees, design costs and other costs in connection with preparing or producing such broadcasts.

(2) Advertising of any nature (whatever the medium used).

Expenses in respect of such advertising include agency fees, design costs and other costs in connection with preparing, producing, distributing or otherwise disseminating such advertising or anything incorporating such advertising and intended to be distributed for the purpose of disseminating it.

(3) Unsolicited material addressed to electors (whether addressed to them by name or intended for delivery to households within any particular area or areas).

Expenses in respect of such material include design costs and other costs in connection with preparing, producing or distributing such material (including the cost of postage).

(4) Any manifesto or other document setting out the party's policies.

Expenses in respect of such a document include design costs and other costs in connection with preparing or producing or distributing or otherwise disseminating any such document.

(5) Market research or canvassing conducted for the purpose of ascertaining polling intentions.

(6) The provision of any services or facilities in connection with press conferences or other dealings with the media.

(7) Transport (by any means) of persons to any place or places with a view to obtaining publicity in connection with an election campaign.

Expenses in respect of the transport of such persons include the costs of hiring a particular means of transport for the whole or part of the period during which the election campaign is being conducted.

(8) Rallies and other events, including public meetings (but not annual or other party conferences) organised so as to obtain publicity in connection with an election campaign or for other purposes connected with an election campaign.

Expenses in respect of such events include costs incurred in connection with the attendance of persons at such events, the hire of premises for the purposes of such events or the provision of goods, services or facilities at them.

Exclusions

2 (1) Nothing in paragraph 1 shall be taken as extending to

(a) any expenses in respect of newsletters or similar publications issued by or on behalf of the party with a view to giving electors in a particular electoral area information about the opinions or activities of, or other personal information relating to, their elected representatives or existing or prospective candidates;

(b) any expenses incurred in respect of unsolicited material addressed to party members;

(c) any expenses in respect of any property, services or facilities so far as those expenses fall to be met out of public funds;

(d) any expenses incurred in respect of the remuneration or allowances payable to any member of the staff (whether permanent or otherwise) of the party; or

(e) any expenses incurred in respect of an individual by way of travelling expenses (by any means of transport) or in providing for his accommodation or other personal needs to the extent that the expenses are paid by the individual from his own resources and are not reimbursed to him.

(2) Sub-paragraph (1)(a) does not apply in relation to any expenses which are incurred

(a) in respect of newsletters or similar publications issued by or on behalf of a party with a view to giving electors in a particular electoral area information about the opinions or activities of, or other personal information relating to, a member of the European Parliament elected in Great Britain (including the combined region) or existing or prospective candidates for such election; and

(b) within the period of four months ending with the date of the poll for an election to the European Parliament.

NOTES

Defined terms
combined region: s 160(1)
document: s 160(1)
election campaign: s 72(3)

expenses met out of public funds: s 160(4)
property: s 160(1)

Part II
Supplemental

Guidance by Commission

3 (1) The Commission may prepare, and from time to time revise, a code of practice giving guidance as to the kinds of expenses which do, or do not, fall within Part I of this Schedule.

(2) Once the Commission have prepared a draft code under this paragraph, they shall submit it to the Secretary of State for his approval.

(3) The Secretary of State may approve a draft code either without modification or with such modifications as he may determine.

(4) Once the Secretary of State has approved a draft code he shall lay a copy of the draft, whether

(a) in its original form, or

(b) in a form which incorporates any modifications determined under sub-paragraph (3),

before each House of Parliament.

(5) If the draft incorporates any such modifications, the Secretary of State shall at the same time lay before each House a statement of his reasons for making them.

(6) If, within the 40day period, either House resolves not to approve the draft, the Secretary of State shall take no further steps in relation to the draft code.

(7) If no such resolution is made within the 40day period

(a) the Secretary of State shall issue the code in the form of the draft laid before Parliament, and

(b) the code shall come into force on such date as the Secretary of State may by order appoint;

and the Commission shall arrange for it to be published in such manner as they consider appropriate.

(8) Sub-paragraph (6) does not prevent a new draft code from being laid before Parliament.

(9) In this paragraph "40 day period", in relation to a draft code, means
   (a) if the draft is laid before one House on a day later than the day on which it is laid before the other House, the period of 40 days beginning with the later of the two days, and
   (b) in any other case, the period of 40 days beginning with the day on which the draft is laid before each House,

no account being taken of any period during which Parliament is dissolved or prorogued or during which both Houses are adjourned for more than four days.

(10) In this paragraph references to a draft code include a draft revised code.

Power to amend Part I

4 (1) The Secretary of State may by order make such amendments of Part I of this Schedule as he considers appropriate.

(2) The Secretary of State may make such an order either
   (a) where the order gives effect to a recommendation of the Commission; or
   (b) after consultation with the Commission.

NOTES

Defined terms   the Secretary of State: s 159A
   the Commission: s 160(1)
   modifications: s 160(1)

SCHEDULE 8A
CONTROLLED EXPENDITURE: QUALIFYING EXPENSES

Section 85

Part 1
Qualifying Expenses

1   For the purposes of section 85(2) the expenses falling within this Part of this Schedule are expenses incurred in respect of any of the matters set out in the following list.

List of matters

(1) The production or publication of material which is made available to the public at large or any section of the public (in whatever form and by whatever means).

(2) Canvassing, or market research seeking views or information from, members of the public.

(3) Press conferences, or other media events, organised by or on behalf of the third party.

(4) Transport (by any means) of persons to any place or places with a view to obtaining publicity.

(5) Public rallies or other public events, other than
   (a) annual conferences of the third party, or
   (b) any public procession or protest meeting, within the meaning of the Public Processions (Northern Ireland) Act 1998, in respect of which notice is given in accordance with section 6 or 7 of that Act (advance notice of public processions or related protest meetings).

   Expenses in respect of such events include costs incurred in connection with the attendance of persons at such events, the hire of premises for the purposes of such events or the provision of goods, services or facilities at them.

But expenses in respect of such events do not include costs incurred in providing for the protection of persons or property.

2 (1) Nothing in paragraph 1 extends to

    (a) expenses incurred in respect of the publication of any matter relating to an election, other than an advertisement, in

        (i) a newspaper or periodical,

        (ii) a broadcast made by the British Broadcasting Corporation, by Sianel Pedwar Cymru or by the Gibraltar Broadcasting Corporation, or

        (iii) a programme included in any service licensed under Part 1 or 3 of the Broadcasting Act 1990 or Part 1 or 2 of the Broadcasting Act 1996;

    (b) expenses incurred in respect of, or in consequence of, the translation of anything from English into Welsh or from Welsh into English;

    (c) reasonable personal expenses incurred by an individual in travelling or in providing for the individual's accommodation or other personal needs;

    (d) reasonable expenses incurred that are reasonably attributable to an individual's disability;

    (e) expenses incurred in respect of the provision by any individual of the individual's own services which the individual provides voluntarily in the individual's own time and free of charge.

(2) In sub-paragraph (1)(d), "disability" has the same meaning as in the Equality Act 2010 (see section 6 of that Act).

NOTES

Defined terms
   third party: s 85(8), (9)

Part 2
Supplemental

Guidance by the Commission

3 (1) The Commission may prepare, and from time to time revise, a code of practice giving guidance as to the kinds of expenses which do, or do not, fall within Part 1 of this Schedule.

(2) Once the Commission have prepared a draft code under this paragraph, they shall submit it to the Secretary of State for his approval.

(3) The Secretary of State may approve a draft code either without modification or with such modifications as he may determine.

(4) Once the Secretary of State has approved a draft code he shall lay a copy of the draft, whether

    (a) in its original form, or

    (b) in a form which incorporates any modifications determined under sub-paragraph (3),

before each House of Parliament.

(5) If the draft incorporates any such modifications, the Secretary of State shall at the same time lay before each House a statement of his reasons for making them.

(6) If, within the 40day period, either House resolves not to approve the draft, the Secretary of State shall take no further steps in relation to the draft code.

(7) If no such resolution is made within the 40day period

(a) the Secretary of State shall issue the code in the form of the draft laid before Parliament, and

(b) the code shall come into force on such date as the Secretary of State may by order appoint,

and the Commission shall arrange for it to be published in such manner as they consider appropriate.

(8) Sub-paragraph (6) does not prevent a new draft code from being laid before Parliament.

(9) In this paragraph "40-day period", in relation to a draft code, means

(a) if the draft is laid before one House on a day later than the day on which it is laid before the other House, the period of 40 days beginning with the later of the two days, and

(b) in any other case, the period of 40 days beginning with the day on which the draft is laid before each House,

no account being taken of any period during which Parliament is dissolved or prorogued or during which both Houses are adjourned for more than four days.

(10) In this paragraph references to a draft code include a draft revised code.

Power to amend Part 1

4 (1) The Secretary of State may by order make such amendments of Part 1 of this Schedule as he considers appropriate.

(2) The Secretary of State may make such an order either

(a) where the order gives effect to a recommendation of the Commission, or

(b) after consultation with the Commission.

NOTES

Defined terms
  the Commission: s 160(1)
  the Secretary of State: s 159A

SCHEDULE 9
LIMITS ON CAMPAIGN EXPENDITURE

Section 79

Part I
Introductory

Interpretation

1 (1) In this Schedule

(a) "an ordinary general election to the Scottish Parliament" means an election held under section 2 of the Scotland Act 1998;

(b) "an extraordinary general election to the Scottish Parliament" means an election held under section 3 of the Scotland Act 1998;

(c) "an ordinary general election to the National Assembly for Wales" means an election held under section 3 of the Government of Wales Act 2006;

(ca) "an extraordinary general election to the National Assembly for Wales" means an election held under section 5 of the Government of Wales Act 2006;

(d) "an ordinary general election to the Northern Ireland Assembly" means an election held under section 31 of the Northern Ireland Act 1998; and

(e) "an extraordinary general election to the Northern Ireland Assembly" means an election held under section 32 of the Northern Ireland Act 1998.

(2) For the purposes of this Schedule a registered party

    (a) contests a constituency if any candidate stands for election for that constituency in the name of the party; and

    (b) contests any region if the party is included in the statement of parties and candidates nominated for that region.

(3) For the purposes of this Schedule a parliamentary general election is pending during the period

    (a) beginning with the date on which Parliament is dissolved by section 3(1) of the Fixed-term Parliaments Act 2011 for a parliamentary general election, and

    (b) ending with the date of the poll for that election.

Attribution of expenditure to different parts of the United Kingdom

2 (1) For the purposes of this Schedule

    (a) campaign expenditure incurred by or on behalf of a party registered in the Great Britain register shall (subject to the following provisions of this paragraph) be attributed to each of England, Scotland and Wales in proportion to the number of parliamentary constituencies for the time being situated in that part of Great Britain; and

    (b) campaign expenditure incurred by or on behalf of a party registered in the Northern Ireland register shall be attributed solely to Northern Ireland.

(2) Campaign expenditure whose effects are wholly or substantially confined to any particular parts or part of Great Britain

    (a) shall be attributed to those parts in proportion to the number of parliamentary constituencies for the time being situated in those parts, or

    (b) shall be attributed solely to that part,

as the case may be.

(3) For the purposes of sub-paragraph (2) the effects of campaign expenditure are wholly or substantially confined to any particular parts or part of Great Britain if they have no significant effects in any other part or parts (so that, for example, expenditure on an advertisement in a newspaper circulating in Wales is to be attributed solely to Wales if the newspaper does not circulate to any significant extent in any other part of Great Britain).

(3A) As respects campaign expenditure incurred in the period of four months ending with the date of the poll for an election to the European Parliament in the combined region, that region is to be regarded as part of England for the purposes of the references in sub-paragraphs (2) and (3) to a part or parts of Great Britain.

(4) References in this Schedule to campaign expenditure "in" a particular part of the United Kingdom are accordingly to campaign expenditure which is to be attributed to that part in accordance with this paragraph.

NOTES

Defined terms

    campaign expenditure: s 72(2), (7), (8)

    combined region: s 160(1)

    the Great Britain register: ss 23(2)(a), 160(1)

    the Northern Ireland register: ss 23(2)(b), 160(1)

a person standing for election in the name of a registered party: s 22(6)

registered party: s 160(1)

Part II
General Limits

Parliamentary general elections

3 (1)   This paragraph imposes limits in relation to campaign expenditure incurred by or on behalf of a registered party which contests one or more constituencies at a parliamentary general election.

(2)   Where a registered party contests one or more constituencies in England, Scotland or Wales, the limit applying to campaign expenditure which is incurred by or on behalf of the party in the relevant period in that part of Great Britain is
    (a)   £30,000 multiplied by the number of constituencies contested by the party in that part of Great Britain; or
    (b)   if greater, the appropriate amount specified in sub-paragraph (3).

(3)   The appropriate amount is
    (a)   in relation to England, £810,000;
    (b)   in relation to Scotland, £120,000; and
    (c)   in relation to Wales, £60,000.

(4)   Where a registered party contests one or more constituencies in Northern Ireland, the limit applying to campaign expenditure which is incurred by or on behalf of the party in the relevant period in Northern Ireland is £30,000 multiplied by the number of constituencies contested by the party there.

(5)   Sub-paragraph (6) applies to a registered party in a case where at the election a candidate stands for election in any constituency in the name of that party and one or more other registered parties.

(6)   In such a case, the amount applying to the party in respect of the constituency under sub-paragraph (2)(a) or (4) (as the case may be) shall, instead of being the amount specified in that provision, be that amount divided by the number of registered parties in whose name the candidate stands for election as mentioned in sub-paragraph (5).

(7)   For the purposes of this paragraph the relevant period is
    (a)   (subject to paragraph (b)) the period of 365 days ending with the date of the poll for the election;
    (b)   where the election ("the election in question") follows another parliamentary general election held less than 365 days previously, the period
        (i)   beginning with the day after the date of the poll for the earlier election, and
        (ii)   ending with the date of the poll for the election in question.

General elections to European Parliament

4 (1)   This paragraph imposes limits in relation to campaign expenditure incurred by or on behalf of a registered party which stands for election or (as the case may be) in whose name candidates stand for election at a general election to the European Parliament.

(2)   Where at the election a registered party stands for election in only one electoral region in England (including the combined region), the limit applying to campaign expenditure which is incurred by or on behalf of the party in the relevant period in England is £45,000 multiplied by the number of MEPs to be returned for that region at the election.

(3)   Where at the election a registered party stands for election in two or more electoral regions in England (including the combined region), the limit applying to campaign expenditure incurred by or on behalf of the party in the relevant period in England is £45,000 multiplied by the total number of MEPs to be returned for those regions, taken together.

(4)   Where at the election
    (a)   a registered party stands for election in Scotland or Wales, or

(b) one or more candidates stand for election in Northern Ireland in the name of a registered party,

the limit applying to campaign expenditure which is incurred by or on behalf of the party in the relevant period in that part of the United Kingdom is £45,000 multiplied by the number of MEPs to be returned for that part of the United Kingdom at the election.

(5) For the purposes of this paragraph the relevant period is the period of four months ending with the date of the poll for the election.

General elections to Scottish Parliament

5 (1) This paragraph imposes limits in relation to campaign expenditure incurred by or on behalf of a registered party which contests one or more constituencies or regions at an ordinary or extraordinary general election to the Scottish Parliament.

(2) The limit applying to campaign expenditure which is incurred by or on behalf of a registered party in the relevant period in Scotland is
(a) £12,000 for each constituency contested by the party; plus
(b) £80,000 for each region contested by the party.

(2A) Sub-paragraph (2B) applies to a registered party in a case where at the election a candidate stands for election in any constituency in the name of that party and one or more other registered parties.

(2B) In such a case, the amount applying to the party in respect of the constituency under sub-paragraph (2)(a) shall, instead of being the amount specified in that sub-paragraph, be that amount divided by the number of registered parties in whose name the candidate stands for election as mentioned in sub-paragraph (2A).

(3) In the case of an ordinary general election, "the relevant period" for the purposes of this paragraph is the period beginning with the appropriate date (as defined by sub-paragraph (4)) and ending with the date of the poll.

(4) In sub-paragraph (3) "the appropriate date" means the date which falls four months before the date of the poll where
(a) the date of the poll is that determined by section 2(2) of the Scotland Act 1998; or
(b) no less than five months before the day on which the poll would have taken place under section 2(2) of that Act, the date of the poll is brought forward under section 2(5) of that Act; or
(c) no less than four months before the day on which the poll would have taken place under section 2(2) of that Act, the date of the poll is postponed under section 2(5) of that Act;

but where the date of the poll is brought forward or postponed otherwise than as mentioned in paragraph (b) or (c) above "the appropriate date" means the date which falls four months before the date when the poll would have taken place under section 2(2) of the Act.

(5) In the case of an extraordinary general election, "the relevant period" for the purposes of this paragraph is the period beginning with the date when the Presiding Officer proposes a day for the poll for the election under section 3(1) of the Scotland Act 1998 and ending with the date of the poll for the election.

General elections to the National Assembly for Wales

6 (1) This paragraph imposes limits in relation to campaign expenditure incurred by or on behalf of a registered party which contests one or more constituencies or regions at an ordinary or extra ordinary general election to the National Assembly for Wales.

(2)   The limit applying to campaign expenditure which is incurred by or on behalf of a registered party in the relevant period in Wales is
  (a)   £10,000 for each constituency contested by the party; plus
  (b)   £40,000 for each region contested by the party.

(2A)   Sub-paragraph (2B) applies to a registered party in a case where at the election a candidate stands for election in any constituency in the name of that party and one or more other registered parties.

(2B)   In such a case, the amount applying to the party in respect of the constituency under sub-paragraph (2)(a) shall, instead of being the amount specified in that sub-paragraph, be that amount divided by the number of registered parties in whose name the candidate stands for election as mentioned in sub-paragraph (2A).

(3)   In the case of an ordinary general election "the relevant period" is the period beginning with the appropriate date (as defined by sub-paragraph (4)) and ending with the date of the poll.

(4)   In sub-paragraph (3) "the appropriate date" is the date which falls four months before the date of the poll where
  (a)   the date of the poll is that determined by section 3(1) of the Government of Wales Act 2006;
  (b)   no less than five months before the day on which the poll would have taken place under section 3(1) of that Act, the date of the poll is brought forward under section 4(1) of that Act; or
  (c)   no less than four months before the day on which the poll would have taken place under section 3(1) of that Act, the date of the poll is postponed under section 4(1) of that Act;
but where the date of the poll is brought forward or postponed otherwise than as mentioned in paragraph (b) or (c) above "the appropriate date" means the date which falls four months before the date when the poll would have taken place under section 3(1) of that Act.

(5)   In the case of an extraordinary general election, "the relevant period" for the purposes of this paragraph is the period beginning with the date when the Secretary of State proposes a date for the poll for the election under section 5(1) of the Government of Wales Act 2006 and ending with the date of the poll for the election.

General elections to Northern Ireland Assembly

7 (1)   This paragraph imposes limits in relation to campaign expenditure incurred by or on behalf of a registered party which contests one or more constituencies at an ordinary or extraordinary general election to the Northern Ireland Assembly.

(2)   The limit applying to campaign expenditure which is incurred by or on behalf of a registered party in the relevant period in Northern Ireland is £17,000 for each constituency contested by the party.

(2A)   Sub-paragraph (2B) applies to a registered party in a case where at the election a candidate stands for election in any constituency in the name of that party and one or more other registered parties.

(2B)   In such a case, the amount applying to the party in respect of the constituency under sub-paragraph (2) shall, instead of being the amount specified in that sub-paragraph, be that amount divided by the number of registered parties in whose name the candidate stands for election as mentioned in sub-paragraph (2A).

(3) In the case of an ordinary general election, "the relevant period" for the purposes of this paragraph is the period beginning with the appropriate date (as defined by sub-paragraph (4)) and ending with the date of the poll.

(4) In sub-paragraph (3) "the appropriate date" means the date which falls four months before the date of the poll where

  (a) the date of the poll is that determined by section 31(1) and (2) of the Northern Ireland Act 1998;

  (b) no less than five months before the day on which the poll would have taken place under section 31(1) and (2) of that Act, the date of the poll is brought forward under section 31(3) of that Act; or

  (c) no less than four months before the day on which the poll would have taken place under section 31(1) and (2) of that Act, the date of the poll is postponed under section 31(3) of that Act;

but where the date of the poll is brought forward or postponed otherwise than as mentioned in paragraph (b) or (c) above "the appropriate date" means the date which falls four months before the date when the poll would have taken place under section 31(1) and (2) of that Act.

(5) In the case of an extraordinary general election, "the relevant period" for the purposes of this paragraph is the period beginning with the date when the Secretary of State proposes a date for the poll for the election under section 32(1) or (3) of the Northern Ireland Act 1998 and ending with the date of the poll for the election.

NOTES

Defined terms

campaign expenditure: s 72(2), (7), (8)
combined region: s 160(1)
contests a constituency: Sch 9, Pt I, para 1(2)(a)
contests any region: Sch 9, Pt I, para 1(2)(b)
extraordinary election to the National Assembly for Wales: Sch 9, Pt I, para 1(1)(ca)
extraordinary general election to the Northern Ireland Assembly: Sch 9, Pt I, para 1(1)(e)
extraordinary general election to the Scottish Parliament: Sch 9, Pt I, para 1(1)(b)
ordinary election to the National Assembly for Wales:

Sch 9, Pt I, para 1(1)(c)
ordinary general election to the Northern Ireland Assembly: Sch 9, Pt I, para 1(1)(d)
ordinary general election to the Scottish Parliament: Sch 9, Pt I, para 1(1)(a)
a person standing for election in the name of a registered party: s 22(6)
registered party: s 160(1)
Secretary of State: s 159A

Part III
Limits Applying in Special Circumstances

Combination of elections to European Parliament and to devolved legislature

8 (1) This paragraph applies where (apart from this paragraph)

  (a) separate limits would apply as follows to campaign expenditure incurred by or on behalf of a registered party in Scotland, Wales or Northern Ireland (as the case may be), namely

    (i) under paragraph 4 in relation to a general election to the European Parliament; and

    (ii) under paragraph 5, 6 or 7 in relation to an election within that paragraph; and

  (b) any part of the period which would be the relevant period for the purposes of paragraph 4 falls within any part of the period which would be the relevant period for the purposes of paragraph 5, 6 or 7.

(2) In such a case

  (a) neither paragraph 4 nor paragraph 5, 6 or 7 (as the case may be) shall apply, in connection with either of those elections, to campaign expenditure incurred by or on behalf of the party in Scotland, Wales or Northern Ireland (as the case may be); and

    (b)   the limit imposed by this paragraph shall apply to it instead.

(3)   The limit applying to campaign expenditure which is incurred by or on behalf of the party in the relevant period for the purposes of this paragraph in Scotland, Wales or Northern Ireland (as the case may be) is the aggregate of

    (a)   the limit which by virtue of paragraph 4 would (apart from this paragraph) apply to such expenditure incurred in that part of the United Kingdom during the relevant period for the purposes of that paragraph; and

    (b)   the limit which by virtue of paragraph 5, 6 or 7 would (apart from this paragraph) apply to such expenditure incurred in that part of the United Kingdom during the relevant period for the purposes of that paragraph.

(4)   For the purposes of this paragraph "the relevant period" is the period which

    (a)   begins with whichever is the earlier of the dates on which the periods mentioned in sub-paragraph (1) begin, and

    (b)   ends with whichever is the later of the dates on which those periods end.

Combined limits where parliamentary election pending

9 (1)   This paragraph applies where

    (a)   separate limits would (apart from this paragraph) apply as follows to campaign expenditure incurred by or on behalf of a registered party in England, Scotland, Wales or Northern Ireland (as the case may be), namely

        (i)   under paragraph 3 in relation to a parliamentary general election; and

        (ii) under paragraph 4, 5, 6, 7 or 8 in relation to an election or elections within that paragraph; and

    (b)   the parliamentary general election is pending during any part of the period in relation to which the limit imposed by paragraph 4, 5, 6, 7 or 8 would (apart from this paragraph) apply.

(2)   In such a case

    (a)   neither paragraph 3, nor paragraph 4, 5, 6, 7 or 8 (as the case may be) shall apply to the expenditure mentioned in sub-paragraph (1)(a); and

    (b)   the limit or limits imposed by this paragraph shall apply to it instead.

(3)   Subject to sub-paragraphs (5) to (7), the limit applying to campaign expenditure which is incurred by or on behalf of the registered party in the relevant period for the purposes of this sub-paragraph in England, Scotland, Wales or Northern Ireland (as the case may be) is the aggregate of

    (a)   the limit which by virtue of paragraph 3 would (apart from this paragraph) apply to such expenditure incurred in that part of the United Kingdom during the relevant period for the purposes of that paragraph; and

    (b)   the limit which by virtue of paragraph 4, 5, 6, 7 or 8 would (apart from this paragraph) apply to such expenditure incurred in that part of the United Kingdom during the relevant period for the purposes of that paragraph.

(4)   For the purposes of sub-paragraph (3) "the relevant period" is

    (a)   where the parliamentary general election takes place at the same time as, or later than

        (i)   the election in relation to which paragraph 4, 5, 6 or 7 would otherwise apply, or

        (ii) (as the case may be) the later of the elections in relation to which paragraph 8 would otherwise apply,

the period which for the purposes of paragraph 3 is the relevant period in relation to the parliamentary general election;

    (b) where the parliamentary general election takes place earlier than the election mentioned in paragraph (a)(i) or (ii), the period which

        (i) begins at the beginning of the period mentioned in paragraph (a), and

        (ii) ends with the date of the poll for the later, or (where paragraph 8 would otherwise apply) the last, of the elections.

(5) Where sub-paragraph (1)(a)(i) is applicable in the case of each of two parliamentary general elections which are pending during different parts of any such period as is mentioned in sub-paragraph (1)(b), the limits applying to campaign expenditure which is incurred by or on behalf of the registered party in the relevant periods in England, Scotland, Wales or Northern Ireland (as the case may be) are as follows

    (a) in the case of expenditure incurred in the first relevant period, the limit is the aggregate of

        (i) the limit which by virtue of paragraph 3 would (apart from this paragraph) apply, in connection with the first of the parliamentary general elections to take place, to such expenditure incurred in that part of the United Kingdom during the relevant period for the purposes of that paragraph, and

        (ii) the limit mentioned in sub-paragraph (3)(b) above; and

    (b) in the case of expenditure incurred in the second relevant period, the limit is the limit which by virtue of paragraph 3 would (apart from this paragraph) apply, in connection with the second parliamentary general election to take place, to such expenditure incurred in that part of the United Kingdom during the relevant period for the purposes of that paragraph.

(6) For the purposes of sub-paragraph (5) "the first relevant period" is the period which

    (a) begins at the beginning of the period which would, apart from this paragraph, apply for the purposes of paragraph 3 to the first of the parliamentary general elections to take place; and

    (b) ends with the date on which Parliament is dissolved by section 3(1) of the Fixed-term Parliaments Act 2011 for the second of the parliamentary general elections to take place.

(7) For the purposes of sub-paragraph (5) "the second relevant period" is the period which

    (a) begins on the day after the date mentioned in sub-paragraph (6)(b) above; and

    (b) ends with whichever is the later of the following, namely

        (i) the date of the poll for the second parliamentary general election to take place; and

        (ii) the date of the poll for the election in relation to which paragraph 4, 5, 6 or 7 would otherwise apply or, as the case may be, the date of the poll for the later of the elections in relation to which paragraph 8 would otherwise apply.

Combination of limit under paragraph 9 and other limit

10 (1) This paragraph applies where

    (a) a limit under paragraph 9 would (apart from this paragraph) apply to campaign expenditure incurred by or on behalf of a registered party in England, Scotland, Wales or Northern Ireland (as the case may be) in relation to a period that would either be

        (i) a relevant period for the purposes of paragraph 9(3), or

        (ii) a first relevant period for the purposes of paragraph 9(5); and

    (b) another limit under paragraph 4, 5, 6, 7 or 8 applies to campaign expenditure incurred by or on behalf of the party in that part of the United Kingdom in relation to a period ("the other campaign period") which is not a period during which the parliamentary general election is pending but which either

        (i) falls wholly within, or

      (ii)   ends at any time falling within,

the period mentioned in paragraph (a).

(2)   In such a case

    (a)   the limit imposed by paragraph 9 shall not apply in relation to the period mentioned in sub-paragraph (1)(a); and

    (b)   instead the limit imposed by this paragraph shall apply in relation to the period which is the combined period for the purposes of this paragraph.

(3)   The limit applying to campaign expenditure which is incurred by or on behalf of the party during the combined period in England, Scotland, Wales or Northern Ireland (as the case may be) is the aggregate of

    (a)   the limit which by virtue of paragraph 9 would (apart from this paragraph) apply to such expenditure incurred in that part of the United Kingdom during the period mentioned in sub-paragraph (1)(a); and

    (b)   the limit applying, by virtue of paragraph 4, 5, 6, 7 or 8 (as the case may be), to such expenditure incurred in that part of the United Kingdom during the relevant period for the purposes of that paragraph.

(4)   For the purposes of this paragraph "the combined period" is the period which begins with whichever is the earlier of the following, namely

    (a)   the beginning of the period which is the relevant period for the purposes of paragraph 4, 5, 6, 7 or 8 (as the case may be), and

    (b)   the beginning of the period mentioned in sub-paragraph (1)(a),

and ends at the end of the period mentioned in sub-paragraph (1)(a).

(5)   Nothing in this paragraph affects the application of any limit imposed by virtue of paragraph 4, 5, 6, 7 or 8 in relation to any period which is a relevant period for the purposes of that paragraph.

Combination of parliamentary general election and other election, or elections, falling within paragraphs 4 to 8

11 (1)   This paragraph applies where

    (a)   a limit under paragraph 3 would (apart from this paragraph) apply to campaign expenditure incurred by or on behalf of a registered party in England, Scotland, Wales or Northern Ireland (as the case may be);

    (b)   another limit under paragraph 4, 5, 6, 7 or 8 applies to campaign expenditure incurred by or on behalf of the party in that part of the United Kingdom in relation to any period ("the other campaign period") which either

        (i)   falls wholly within, or

        (ii)   ends at any time falling within,

the period which would (apart from this paragraph) be the relevant period for the purposes of paragraph 3 in relation to the parliamentary general election; and

    (c)   paragraph 9 does not apply in connection with that expenditure.

(2)   In such a case

    (a)   the limit imposed by paragraph 3 shall not apply in relation to the relevant period for the purposes of that paragraph, and

    (b)   instead the limit imposed by this paragraph shall apply in relation to the period which is the combined period for the purposes of this paragraph.

(3)   The limit applying to campaign expenditure which is incurred by or on behalf of the party in the combined period in England, Scotland, Wales or Northern Ireland, as the case may be, is the aggregate of

    (a)   the limit which by virtue of paragraph 3 would (apart from this paragraph) apply to such expenditure incurred in that part of the United Kingdom during the relevant period for the purposes of that paragraph; and

      (b) the limit applying by virtue of paragraph 4, 5, 6, 7 or 8 (as the case may be) to such expenditure incurred in that part of the United Kingdom during the relevant period for the purposes of that paragraph.

(4) Where two or more periods ("the other campaign periods") which are relevant periods for the purposes of any of paragraphs 4, 5, 7 or 8

      (a) fall wholly within, or

      (b) end at any time falling within,

the period which would (apart from this paragraph) be the relevant period for the purposes of paragraph 3 in relation to the parliamentary general election, sub-paragraph (3)(b) shall operate in relation to each of the limits applying in relation to those periods so as to produce two or more amounts to be added to the amount referred to in sub-paragraph (3)(a).

(5) For the purposes of this paragraph "the combined period" is the period which begins with whichever is the earlier of the following, namely

      (a) the beginning of

          (i) the period which is the relevant period for the purposes of paragraph 4, 5, 6, 7 or 8 (as the case may be), or

          (ii) where sub-paragraph (4) applies, whichever of the relevant periods for the purposes of any of paragraphs 4, 5, 7 or 8 is the first to begin, and

      (b) the beginning of the period which would (apart from this paragraph) be the relevant period for the purposes of paragraph 3 in relation to the parliamentary general election,

and ends with the date of the poll for the parliamentary general election.

(6) Nothing in this paragraph affects the application of any limit imposed by virtue of paragraph 4, 5, 6, 7 or 8 in relation to any period which is a relevant period for the purposes of that paragraph.

NOTES

Defined terms

  campaign expenditure: s 72(2), (7), (8)

  parliamentary general election is pending: Sch 9, Pt I, para 1(3)

registered party: s 160(1)

SCHEDULE 10
LIMITS ON CONTROLLED EXPENDITURE

Section 94

Part I
Introductory

Interpretation

1 (1) In this Schedule

      (a) "an ordinary general election to the Scottish Parliament" means an election held under section 2 of the Scotland Act 1998;

      (b) "an extraordinary general election to the Scottish Parliament" means an election held under section 3 of the Scotland Act 1998;

      (c) "an ordinary general election to the National Assembly for Wales" means an election under section 3 of the Government of Wales Act 2006;

      (ca) "an extraordinary general election to the National Assembly for Wales" means an election under section 5 of the Government of Wales Act 2006;

      (d) "an ordinary general election to the Northern Ireland Assembly" means an election held under section 31 of the Northern Ireland Act 1998; and

(e) "an extraordinary general election to the Northern Ireland Assembly" means an election held under section 32 of the Northern Ireland Act 1998.

(2) For the purposes of this Schedule a parliamentary general election is pending during the period
  (a) beginning with the date on which Parliament is dissolved by section 3(1) of the Fixed-term Parliaments Act 2011 for a parliamentary general election, and
  (b) ending with the date of the poll for that election.

(3) Paragraphs 3 and 5 to 11 do not apply in relation to a recognised Gibraltar third party.

Attribution of expenditure to different parts of the United Kingdom

2 (1) For the purposes of this Schedule controlled expenditure incurred by or on behalf of any recognised third party shall (subject to the following provisions of this paragraph) be attributed to each of England, Scotland, Wales and Northern Ireland in proportion to the number of parliamentary constituencies for the time being situated in that part of the United Kingdom.

(2) Controlled expenditure whose effects are wholly or substantially confined to any particular parts or part of the United Kingdom
  (a) shall be attributed to those parts in proportion to the number of parliamentary constituencies for the time being situated in those parts, or
  (b) shall be attributed solely to that part,
  as the case may be.

(3) For the purposes of sub-paragraph (2) the effects of controlled expenditure are wholly or substantially confined to any particular parts or part of the United Kingdom if they have no significant effects in any other part or parts (so that, for example, expenditure on an advertisement in a newspaper circulating in Wales is to be attributed solely to Wales if the newspaper does not circulate to any significant extent in any other part of the United Kingdom).

(3A) As respects controlled expenditure incurred in the period of four months ending with the date of the poll for an election to the European Parliament in the combined region, that region is to be regarded as part of England for the purposes of the references in sub-paragraphs (2) and (3) to a part or parts of the United Kingdom.

(4) References in this Schedule to controlled expenditure "in" a particular part of the United Kingdom are accordingly to controlled expenditure which is to be attributed to that part in accordance with this paragraph.

Attribution of expenditure to different parliamentary constituencies

2A (1) For the purposes of this Schedule controlled expenditure incurred by or on behalf of any recognised third party shall (subject to the following provisions of this paragraph) be attributed to each parliamentary constituency in equal proportions.

(2) Controlled expenditure whose effects are wholly or substantially confined to any particular constituencies or constituency
  (a) shall be attributed to those constituencies in equal proportions, or
  (b) shall be attributed solely to that constituency,
  as the case may be.

(3) For the purposes of sub-paragraph (2), the effects of controlled expenditure are wholly or substantially confined to any particular constituencies or constituency if they have no significant effects in any other constituency or constituencies.

(4) References in this Schedule to controlled expenditure "in" a particular constituency are accordingly to controlled expenditure which is to be attributed to that constituency in accordance with this paragraph.

NOTES

Defined terms
  combined region: s 160(1)
  controlled expenditure: s 85(2)
  recognised Gibraltar third party: s 85(5A)

  recognised third party: s 85(5)

Part II
General Limits

Parliamentary general elections

3 (1) This paragraph imposes limits in relation to a parliamentary general election.

(2) The limit applying to controlled expenditure which is incurred by or on behalf of a recognised third party in the relevant period in each of England, Scotland, Wales and Northern Ireland is
  (a) in relation to England, 2% of the maximum campaign expenditure limit in England;
  (b) in relation to Scotland, £20,000 plus 2% of the maximum campaign expenditure limit in Scotland;
  (c) in relation to Wales, £20,000 plus 2% of the maximum campaign expenditure limit in Wales;
  (d) in relation to Northern Ireland, £20,000 plus 2% of the maximum campaign expenditure limit in Northern Ireland.

(2A) The limit applying to controlled expenditure which is incurred by or on behalf of a recognised third party in the relevant period in any particular parliamentary constituency is 0.05% of the total of the maximum campaign expenditure limits in England, Scotland, Wales and Northern Ireland.

(3) For the purposes of this paragraph the relevant period is
  (a) (subject to paragraph (b)) the period of 365 days ending with the date of the poll for the election;
  (b) where the election ("the election in question") follows another parliamentary general election held less than 365 days previously, the period
    (i) beginning with the day after the date of the poll for the earlier election, and
    (ii) ending with the date of the poll for the election in question.

General elections to European Parliament

4 (1) This paragraph imposes limits in relation to a general election to the European Parliament.

(2) The limit applying to controlled expenditure which is incurred by or on behalf of a recognised third party in the relevant period in each of England, Scotland, Wales and Northern Ireland is
  (a) in relation to England, £159,750;
  (b) in relation to Scotland, £18,000;
  (c) in relation to Wales, £11,259; and
  (d) in relation to Northern Ireland, £6,750.

(2A) As respects a recognised Gibraltar third party, sub-paragraph (2) shall have effect as if for paragraphs (a) to (d) there were substituted
  "(a) in relation to England, £16,000; and

701

    (b) in relation to Scotland, Wales or Northern Ireland, £5,000".

(3)   For the purposes of this paragraph the relevant period is the period of four months ending with the date of the poll for the election.

General elections to Scottish Parliament

5 (1)   This paragraph imposes limits in relation to an ordinary or extraordinary general election to the Scottish Parliament.

(2)   The limit applying to controlled expenditure which is incurred by or on behalf of a recognised third party in the relevant period in Scotland is £75,800.

(3)   In the case of an ordinary general election, "the relevant period" for the purposes of this paragraph is the period beginning with the appropriate date (as defined by sub-paragraph (4)) and ending with the date of the poll.

(4)   In sub-paragraph (3) "the appropriate date" means the date which falls four months before the date of the poll where

    (a) the date of the poll is that determined by section 2(2) of the Scotland Act 1998; or

    (b) no less than five months before the day on which the poll would have taken place under section 2(2) of that Act, the date of the poll is brought forward under section 2(5) of that Act; or

    (c) no less than four months before the day on which the poll would have taken place under section 2(2) of that Act, the date of the poll is postponed under section 2(5) of that Act;

but where the date of the poll is brought forward or postponed otherwise than as mentioned in paragraph (b) or (c) above "the appropriate date" means the date which falls four months before the date when the poll would have taken place under section 2(2) of the Act.

(5)   In the case of an extraordinary general election, "the relevant period" for the purposes of this paragraph is the period beginning with the date when the Presiding Officer proposes a day for the poll for the election under section 3(1) of the Scotland Act 1998 and ending with the date of the poll for the election.

General elections to the National Assembly for Wales

6 (1)   This paragraph imposes limits in relation to an ordinary general election to the National Assembly for Wales.

(2)   The limit applying to controlled expenditure which is incurred by or on behalf of a recognised third party in the relevant period in Wales is £30,000.

(3)   In the case of an ordinary general election "the relevant period" is the period beginning with the appropriate date (as defined by sub-paragraph (4)) and ending with the date of the poll.

(4)   In sub-paragraph (3) "the appropriate date" is the date which falls four months before the date of the poll where

    (a) the date of the poll is that determined by section 3(1) of the Government of Wales Act 2006;

    (b) no less than five months before the day on which the poll would have taken place under section 3(1) of that Act, the date of the poll is brought forward under section 4(1) of that Act; or

    (c) no less than four months before the day on which the poll would have taken place under section 3(1) of that Act, the date of the poll is postponed under section 4(1) of that Act;

but where the date of the poll is brought forward or postponed otherwise than as mentioned in paragraph (b) or (c) above "the appropriate date" means the date which falls four months before the date when the poll would have taken place under section 3(1) of that Act.

(5) In the case of an extraordinary general election, "the relevant period" for the purposes of this paragraph is the period beginning with the date when the Secretary of State proposes a date for the poll for the election under section 5(1) of the Government of Wales Act 2006 and ending with the date of the poll for the election.

General elections to Northern Ireland Assembly

7 (1) This paragraph imposes limits in relation to an ordinary or extraordinary general election to the Northern Ireland Assembly.

(2) The limit applying to controlled expenditure which is incurred by or on behalf of a recognised third party in the relevant period in Northern Ireland is £15,300.

(3) In the case of an ordinary general election, "the relevant period" for the purposes of this paragraph is the period beginning with the appropriate date (as defined by sub-paragraph (4)) and ending with the date of the poll.

(4) In sub-paragraph (3) "the appropriate date" means the date which falls four months before the date of the poll where

(a) the date of the poll is that determined by section 31(1) and (2) of the Northern Ireland Act 1998; or

(b) no less than five months before the day on which the poll would have taken place under section 31(1) and (2) of that Act, the date of the poll is brought forward under section 31(3) of that Act; or

(c) no less than four months before the day on which the poll would have taken place under section 31(1) and (2) of that Act, the date of the poll is postponed under section 31(3) of that Act;

but where the date of the poll is brought forward or postponed otherwise than as mentioned in paragraph (b) or (c) above "the appropriate date" means the date which falls four months before the date when the poll would have taken place under section 31(1) and (2) of that Act.

(5) In the case of an extraordinary general election, "the relevant period" for the purposes of this paragraph is the period beginning with the date when the Secretary of State proposes a date for the poll for the election under section 32(1) or (3) of the Northern Ireland Act 1998 and ending with the date of the poll for the election.

NOTES

Defined terms
controlled expenditure: s 85(2)
an extraordinary election to the National Assembly for Wales: Sch 10, Pt I, para 1(1)(ca)
an extraordinary general election to the Northern Ireland Assembly: Sch 10, Pt I, para 1(1)(e)
an extraordinary general election to the Scottish Parliament: Sch 10, Pt I, para 1(1)(b)
an ordinary election to the National Assembly for Wales: Sch 10, Pt I, para 1(1)(c)

an ordinary general election to the Northern Ireland Assembly: Sch 10, Pt I, para 1(1)(d)
an ordinary general election to the Scottish Parliament: Sch 10, Pt I, para 1(1)(a)
recognised Gibraltar third party: s 85(5A)
recognised third party: s 85(5)
the Secretary of State: s 159A

Part III
Limits Applying In Special Circumstances

Combination of elections to European Parliament and to devolved legislature

8 (1)   This paragraph imposes, in the circumstances mentioned in sub-paragraph (2), a limit in relation to

(a)   a general election to the European Parliament; and

(b)   an election to which paragraph 5, 6 or 7 would (apart from this paragraph) apply.

(2)   Where any part of the period which is the relevant period for the purposes of paragraph 4 in relation to a general election to the European Parliament falls within any period which is the relevant period for the purposes of any of paragraphs 5 to 7 in relation to an election to the legislature mentioned in that paragraph

(a)   neither paragraph 4 nor paragraph 5, 6 or 7 (as the case may be) shall apply, in connection with either of those elections, to controlled expenditure incurred by or on behalf of a recognised third party in the part of the United Kingdom mentioned in paragraph 5(2), 6(2) or 7(2) (as the case may be); and

(b)   the limit imposed by this paragraph shall apply to it instead.

(3)   The limit applying to controlled expenditure which is incurred by or on behalf of a recognised third party in the relevant period for the purposes of this paragraph in Scotland, Wales or Northern Ireland (as the case may be) is the aggregate of

(a)   the limit which by virtue of paragraph 4 would (apart from this paragraph) apply to such expenditure incurred in that part of the United Kingdom during the relevant period for the purposes of that paragraph; and

(b)   the limit which by virtue of paragraph 5, 6 or 7 would (apart from this paragraph) apply to such expenditure incurred in that part of the United Kingdom during the relevant period for the purposes of that paragraph.

(4)   For the purposes of this paragraph "the relevant period" is the period which

(a)   begins with whichever is the earlier of the dates on which the periods mentioned in sub-paragraph (2) begin, and

(b)   ends with whichever is the later of the dates on which those periods end.

Combined limits where parliamentary election pending

9 (1)   This paragraph imposes

(a)   in the circumstances mentioned in sub-paragraph (2), limits in relation to

(i)   such a pending parliamentary general election as is mentioned in that sub-paragraph, and

(ii)   an election, or elections, in relation to which the limit imposed by any of paragraphs 4 to 8 would otherwise apply as mentioned in that sub-paragraph; and

(b)   in the circumstances mentioned in sub-paragraph (5), limits in relation to

(i)   two such pending parliamentary elections as are mentioned in that sub-paragraph, and

(ii)   an election, or elections, in relation to which the limit imposed by any of paragraphs 4 to 8 would otherwise apply as mentioned in sub-paragraph (2).

(2)   Where a parliamentary general election is pending during any part of the period in relation to which a limit imposed by any of paragraphs 4 to 8 would otherwise apply to controlled expenditure incurred by or on behalf of a recognised third party in a particular part of the United Kingdom

(a)   neither that paragraph, nor paragraph 3, shall apply in relation to such expenditure; and

(b)   the limits imposed by this paragraph shall apply to it instead.

(3)   Subject to sub-paragraphs (5) to (7), the limit applying to controlled expenditure which is incurred by or on behalf of the recognised third party in the relevant period for the purposes of this sub-paragraph in England, Scotland, Wales or Northern Ireland (as the case may be) is the aggregate of

    (a)   the limit which by virtue of paragraph 3 would (apart from this paragraph) apply to such expenditure incurred in that part of the United Kingdom during the relevant period for the purposes of that paragraph; and

    (b)   the limit which by virtue of paragraph 4, 5, 6, 7 or 8 would (apart from this paragraph) apply to such expenditure incurred in that part of the United Kingdom during the relevant period for the purposes of that paragraph.

(3A)   Subject to sub-paragraphs (5) to (7), the limit applying to controlled expenditure which is incurred by or on behalf of the recognised third party in the relevant period in any particular parliamentary constituency is the relevant proportion of the limit mentioned in paragraph 3(2A).

(3B)   For this purpose "the relevant proportion" means
A / B
where
A is the number of days in the relevant period;
B is the number of days in the period which is the relevant period for the purposes of paragraph 3.

(4)   For the purposes of sub-paragraphs (3) to (3B) "the relevant period" is

    (a)   where the parliamentary general election takes place at the same time as, or later than

       (i)   the election in relation to which paragraph 4, 5, 6 or 7 would otherwise apply, or

       (ii)   (as the case may be) the later of the elections in relation to which paragraph 8 would otherwise apply,

the period which for the purposes of paragraph 3 is the relevant period in relation to the parliamentary general election;

    (b)   where the parliamentary general election takes place earlier than the election mentioned in paragraph (a)(i) or (ii), the period which

       (i)   begins at the beginning of the period mentioned in paragraph (a), and

      (ii)   ends with the date of the poll for the later, or (where paragraph 8 would otherwise apply) the last, of the elections.

(5)   Where two parliamentary general elections are pending during different parts of any such period as is mentioned in sub-paragraph (2), the limits applying to controlled expenditure which is incurred by or on behalf of the recognised third party in the relevant periods in England, Scotland, Wales or Northern Ireland (as the case may be) are as follows

    (a)   in the case of expenditure incurred in the first relevant period, the limit is the aggregate of

       (i)   the limit which by virtue of paragraph 3 would (apart from this paragraph) apply, in connection with the first of the parliamentary general elections to take place, to such expenditure incurred in that part of the United Kingdom during the relevant period for the purposes of that paragraph, and

      (ii)   the limit mentioned in sub-paragraph (3)(b) above; and

    (b)   in the case of expenditure incurred in the second relevant period, the limit is the limit which by virtue of paragraph 3 would (apart from this paragraph) apply, in connection with the second parliamentary general election to take place, to such expenditure incurred in that part of the United Kingdom during the relevant period for the purposes of that paragraph.

(5A)   Where two parliamentary general elections are pending during different parts of any such period as is mentioned in sub-paragraph (2)

    (a)   the limit applying to controlled expenditure which is incurred by or on behalf of the recognised third party in the first relevant period in any particular parliamentary constituency is the relevant proportion of the limit mentioned in paragraph 3(2A), and

    (b)   the limit applying to controlled expenditure which is incurred by or on behalf of the recognised third party in the second relevant period in any particular parliamentary constituency is the relevant proportion of the limit mentioned in paragraph 3(2A).

(5B)   For these purposes "the relevant proportion" means

A / B

where

A is the number of days in the first relevant period or (as the case may be) the second relevant period;

B is the number of days in the period which is the relevant period for the purposes of paragraph 3.

(6)   For the purposes of sub-paragraphs (5) to (5B) "the first relevant period" is the period which

    (a)   begins at the beginning of the period which would, apart from this paragraph, apply for the purposes of paragraph 3 to the first of the parliamentary general elections to take place; and

    (b)   ends with the date on which Parliament is dissolved by section 3(1) of the Fixed-term Parliaments Act 2011 for the second of the parliamentary general elections to take place.

(7)   For the purposes of sub-paragraphs (5) to (5B) "the second relevant period" is the period which

    (a)   begins on the day after the date mentioned in sub-paragraph (6)(b) above; and

    (b)   ends with whichever is the later of the following, namely

        (i)   the date of the poll for the second parliamentary general election to take place; and

        (ii)   the date of the poll for the election in relation to which paragraph 4, 5, 6 or 7 would otherwise apply or, as the case may be, the date of the poll for the later of the elections in relation to which paragraph 8 would otherwise apply.

Combination of limit under paragraph 9 and other limit

10 (1)   This paragraph imposes limits where

    (a)   paragraph 9 would (apart from this paragraph) impose limits on controlled expenditure in relation to a period that would either be

        (i)   a relevant period for the purposes of paragraph 9(3) to (3B), or

        (ii)   a first relevant period for the purposes of paragraph 9(5) to (5B); and

    (b)   any period ("the other controlled period") which is the relevant period for the purposes of any of paragraphs 4 to 8, but is not a period during which the parliamentary general election is pending, either

        (i)   falls wholly within, or

        (ii)   ends at any time falling within,

    the period mentioned in paragraph (a).

(2)   In such a case

    (a)   the limits imposed by paragraph 9 shall not apply in relation to the period mentioned in sub-paragraph (1)(a); and

(b) instead the limits imposed by this paragraph shall apply in relation to the period which is the combined period for the purposes of this paragraph.

(3) The limit applying to controlled expenditure which is incurred by or on behalf of a recognised third party during the combined period in England, Scotland, Wales or Northern Ireland (as the case may be) is the aggregate of

    (a) the limit which by virtue of paragraph 9 would (apart from this paragraph) apply to such expenditure incurred in that part of the United Kingdom during the period mentioned in sub-paragraph (1)(a); and

    (b) the limit applying, by virtue of paragraph 4, 5, 6, 7 or 8 (as the case may be), to such expenditure incurred in that part of the United Kingdom during the relevant period for the purposes of that paragraph.

(3A) The limit applying to controlled expenditure which is incurred by or on behalf of the recognised third party during the combined period in any particular parliamentary constituency is the relevant proportion of the limit mentioned in paragraph 3(2A).

(3B) For this purpose "the relevant proportion" means

A / B

where

A is the number of days in the combined period;

B is the number of days in the period which is the relevant period for the purposes of paragraph 3.

(4) For the purposes of this paragraph "the combined period" is the period which begins with whichever is the earlier of the following, namely

    (a) the beginning of the period which is the relevant period for the purposes of paragraph 4, 5, 6, 7 or 8 (as the case may be), and

    (b) the beginning of the period mentioned in sub-paragraph (1)(a),

and ends at the end of the period mentioned in sub-paragraph (1)(a).

(5) Nothing in this paragraph affects the application of any limit imposed by virtue of paragraph 4, 5, 6, 7 or 8 in relation to any period which is a relevant period for the purposes of that paragraph.

Combination of parliamentary general election and other election, or elections, falling within paragraphs 4 to 8

11 (1) This paragraph imposes limits where

    (a) any period ("the other controlled period") which is the relevant period for the purposes of any of paragraphs 4 to 8 either

        (i) falls wholly within, or

        (ii) ends at any time falling within,

the period which would (apart from this paragraph) be the relevant period for the purposes of paragraph 3 in relation to a parliamentary general election; and

    (b) paragraph 9 does not apply in connection with those elections.

(2) In such a case

    (a) the limits imposed by paragraph 3 shall not apply in relation to the relevant period for the purposes of that paragraph, and

    (b) instead the limits imposed by this paragraph shall apply in relation to the period which is the combined period for the purposes of this paragraph.

(3) The limit applying to controlled expenditure which is incurred by or on behalf of a recognised third party in the combined period in England, Scotland, Wales or Northern Ireland, as the case may be, is the aggregate of

(a) the limit which by virtue of paragraph 3 would (apart from this paragraph) apply to such expenditure incurred in that part of the United Kingdom during the relevant period for the purposes of that paragraph; and

(b) the limit applying by virtue of paragraph 4, 5, 6, 7 or 8 (as the case may be) to such expenditure incurred in that part of the United Kingdom during the relevant period for the purposes of that paragraph.

(4) Where two or more periods ("the other controlled periods") which are relevant periods for the purposes of any of paragraphs 4, 5, 7 or 8

(a) fall wholly within, or

(b) end at any time falling within,

the period which would (apart from this paragraph) be the relevant period for the purposes of paragraph 3 in relation to the parliamentary general election, sub-paragraph (3)(b) shall operate in relation to each of the limits applying in relation to those periods so as to produce two or more amounts to be added to the amount referred to in sub-paragraph (3)(a).

(4A) The limit applying to controlled expenditure which is incurred by or on behalf of the recognised third party during the combined period in any particular parliamentary constituency is the relevant proportion of the limit mentioned in paragraph 3(2A).

(4B) For this purpose "the relevant proportion" means

A / B

where

A is the number of days in the combined period;

B is the number of days in the period which is the relevant period for the purposes of paragraph 3.

(5) For the purposes of this paragraph "the combined period" is the period which begins with whichever is the earlier of the following, namely

(a) the beginning of

(i) the period which is the relevant period for the purposes of paragraph 4, 5, 6, 7 or 8 (as the case may be), or

(ii) where sub-paragraph (4) applies, whichever of the relevant periods for the purposes of paragraph 4, 5, 7 or 8 is the first to begin, and

(b) the beginning of the period which would (apart from this paragraph) be the relevant period for the purposes of paragraph 3 in relation to the parliamentary general election,

and ends with the date of the poll for the parliamentary general election.

(6) Nothing in this paragraph affects the application of any limit imposed by virtue of paragraph 4, 5, 6, 7 or 8 in relation to any period which is a relevant period for the purposes of that paragraph.

NOTES

Defined terms
controlled expenditure: s 85(2)
pending parliamentary election: Sch 10, Pt 1, para 1(2)

recognised third party: s 85(5)

SCHEDULE 11
CONTROL OF DONATIONS TO RECOGNISED THIRD PARTIES

Section 95

Part I
Introductory

Operation and interpretation of Schedule

1 (1)   This Schedule has effect for controlling donations to recognised third parties which either are not registered parties or are minor parties.

(2)   The following provisions have effect for the purposes of this Schedule.

(3)   In accordance with sub-paragraph (1), "recognised third party" does not include a recognised third party which is a registered party other than a minor party.

(4)   "Relevant donation", in relation to a recognised third party, means a donation to the recognised third party for the purpose of meeting controlled expenditure incurred by or on behalf of that third party.

(5)   "Donation" shall be construed in accordance with paragraphs 2 to 4.

(6)   References to a permissible donor falling within section 54(2) do not include a registered party.

Donations: general rules

2 (1)   "Donation", in relation to a recognised third party, means (subject to paragraph 4)
   (a)   any gift to the recognised third party of money or other property;
   (b)   any sponsorship provided in relation to the recognised third party (as defined by paragraph 3);
   (c)   any money spent (otherwise than by or on behalf of the recognised third party) in paying any controlled expenditure incurred by or on behalf of the recognised third party;
   (d)   any money lent to the recognised third party otherwise than on commercial terms;
   (e)   the provision otherwise than on commercial terms of any property, services or facilities for the use or benefit of the recognised third party (including the services of any person); and
   (f) in the case of a recognised third party, other than an individual, any subscription or other fee paid for affiliation to, or membership of, the third party.

(2)   Where
   (a)   any money or other property is transferred to a recognised third party pursuant to any transaction or arrangement involving the provision by or on behalf of the recognised third party of any property, services or facilities or other consideration of monetary value, and
   (b)   the total value in monetary terms of the consideration so provided by or on behalf of the recognised third party is less than the value of the money or (as the case may be) the market value of the property transferred,
   the transfer of the money or property shall (subject to sub-paragraph (4)) constitute a gift to the recognised third party for the purposes of sub-paragraph (1)(a).

(3)   In determining
   (a)   for the purposes of sub-paragraph (1)(d) whether any money lent to a recognised third party is so lent otherwise than on commercial terms, or

709

(b) for the purposes of sub-paragraph (1)(e) whether any property, services or facilities provided for the use or benefit of a recognised third party is or are so provided otherwise than on such terms,

regard shall be had to the total value in monetary terms of the consideration provided by or on behalf of the recognised third party in respect of the loan or the provision of the property, services or facilities.

(4) Where (apart from this sub-paragraph) anything would be a donation both by virtue of sub-paragraph (1)(b) and by virtue of any other provision of this paragraph, sub-paragraph (1)(b) (together with paragraph 3) shall apply in relation to it to the exclusion of the other provision of this paragraph.

(5) Anything given or transferred to any officer, member, trustee or agent of a recognised third party in his capacity as such (and not for his own use or benefit) is to be regarded as given or transferred to the recognised third party (and references to donations received by a recognised third party accordingly include donations so given or transferred).

(6) In this paragraph
  (a) any reference to anything being given or transferred to a recognised third party includes a reference to its being given or transferred either directly or indirectly through any third person;
  (b) "gift" includes bequest.

Sponsorship

3 (1) For the purposes of this Schedule sponsorship is provided in relation to a recognised third party if
  (a) any money or other property is transferred to the recognised third party or to any person for the benefit of the recognised third party, and
  (b) the purpose (or one of the purposes) of the transfer is (or must, having regard to all the circumstances, reasonably be assumed to be)
    (i) to help the recognised third party with meeting, or to meet, to any extent any defined expenses incurred or to be incurred by or on behalf of the recognised third party, or
    (ii) to secure that to any extent any such expenses are not so incurred.

(2) In sub-paragraph (1) "defined expenses" means expenses in connection with
  (a) any conference, meeting or other event organised by or on behalf of the recognised third party,
  (b) the preparation, production or dissemination of any publication by or on behalf of the recognised third party, or
  (c) any study or research organised by or on behalf of the recognised third party.

(3) The following do not, however, constitute sponsorship by virtue of sub-paragraph (1)
  (a) the making of any payment in respect of
    (i) any charge for admission to any conference, meeting or other event, or
    (ii) the purchase price of, or any other charge for access to, any publication;
  (b) the making of any payment in respect of the inclusion of an advertisement in any publication where the payment is made at the commercial rate payable for the inclusion of such an advertisement in any such publication.

(4) The Secretary of State may by order made on the recommendation of the Commission amend sub-paragraph (2) or (3).

(5) In this paragraph "publication" means a publication made available in whatever form and by whatever means (whether or not to the public at large or any section of the public).

Payments etc not to be regarded as donations

4 (1) None of the following shall be regarded as a donation

    (a) the provision by an individual of his own services which he provides voluntarily in his own time and free of charge;

    (b) any interest accruing to a recognised third party in respect of any donation which is dealt with by the responsible person in accordance with section 56(2)(a) or (b) (as applied by paragraph 7).

  (2) Any donation whose value (as determined in accordance with paragraph 5) is not more than £500 shall be disregarded.

  (3) Any payment out of public funds shall not be regarded as a donation for the purposes of paragraph 6A or 6B.

Value of donations

5 (1) The value of any donation falling within paragraph 2(1)(a) (other than money) shall be taken to be the market value of the property in question.

  (2) Where, however, paragraph 2(1)(a) applies by virtue of paragraph 2(2), the value of the donation shall be taken to be the difference between

    (a) the value of the money, or the market value of the property, in question, and

    (b) the total value in monetary terms of the consideration provided by or on behalf of the recognised third party.

  (3) The value of any donation falling within paragraph 2(1)(b) shall be taken to be the value of the money, or (as the case may be) the market value of the property, transferred as mentioned in paragraph 3(1); and accordingly any value in monetary terms of any benefit conferred on the person providing the sponsorship in question shall be disregarded.

  (4) The value of any donation falling within paragraph 2(1)(d) or (e) shall be taken to be the amount representing the difference between

    (a) the total value in monetary terms of the consideration that would have had to be provided by or on behalf of the recognised third party in respect of the loan or the provision of the property, services or facilities if

      (i) the loan had been made, or

      (ii) the property, services or facilities had been provided,

    on commercial terms, and

    (b) the total value in monetary terms of the consideration (if any) actually so provided by or on behalf of the recognised third party.

  (5) Where a donation such as is mentioned in sub-paragraph (4) confers an enduring benefit on the donee over a particular period, the value of the donation

    (a) shall be determined at the time when it is made, but

    (b) shall be so determined by reference to the total benefit accruing to the donee over that period.

NOTES

Defined terms

bequest: s 160(1)
the Commission: s 160(1)
controlled expenditure: s 85(2)
market value: s 160(1)
minor party: s 160(1)
property: s 160(1)

recognised third party: s 85(5) (and para 1(3) of this Schedule)
registered party: s 160(1)
responsible person: s 85(7)
the Secretary of State: s 159A

Part II
Controls on Donations

Prohibition on accepting donations from impermissible donors

6 (1)   A relevant donation received by a recognised third party must not be accepted if

    (a)   the person by whom the donation would be made is not, at the time of its receipt by the recognised third party, a permissible donor falling within section 54(2); or

    (aa)   in the case of a donation of an amount exceeding £7,500, the recognised third party has not been given a declaration as required by paragraph 6A; or

    (aa)   any declaration required to be made in respect of the donation by paragraph 6A or 6B has not been received by the recognised third party; or

    (b)   the recognised third party is (whether because the donation is given anonymously or by reason of any deception or concealment or otherwise) unable to ascertain the identity of the person offering the donation.

(1A)   In the case of a relevant donation received by a recognised Gibraltar third party sub-paragraph (1) shall have effect as if in sub-paragraph (a) after "54(2)" there were inserted "or a person falling within any of paragraphs (a), (b) and (d) to (g) of section 54(2A).

(2)   For the purposes of this Schedule, any relevant donation received by a recognised third party which is an exempt trust donation shall be regarded as a relevant donation received by the recognised third party from a permissible donor.

(2A)   For the purposes of this Schedule any relevant donation received by a recognised Gibraltar third party which is an exempt Gibraltar trust donation shall be regarded as a relevant donation received by the third party from a person falling within any of paragraphs (a), (b) and (d) to (g) of section 54(2A).

(3)   But, for the purposes of this Schedule, any relevant donation received by a recognised third party from a trustee of any property (in his capacity as such) which is not

    (a)   an exempt trust donation, or

    (b)   a relevant donation transmitted by the trustee to the recognised third party on behalf of beneficiaries under the trust who are

      (i)   persons who at the time of its receipt by the recognised third party are permissible donors falling within section 54(2), or

      (ii)   the members of an unincorporated association which at that time is such a permissible donor,

shall be regarded as a relevant donation received by the recognised third party from a person who is not such a permissible donor.

(3A)   As respects any relevant donation received by a recognised Gibraltar third party, sub-paragraph (3) shall have effect as if

    (a)   after sub-paragraph (a) there were inserted

    "(aa)   an exempt Gibraltar trust donation,";

    (b)   in sub-paragraph (b)(i) after "54(2)" there were inserted "or persons falling within any of paragraphs (a), (b) and (d) to (g) of section 54(2A)";

    (c)   in sub-paragraph (b)(ii) after "donor" there were inserted "or falls within section 54(2A)(g)"; and

    (d)   at the end there were inserted "and is not a person falling within any of paragraphs (a), (b) and (d) to (g) of section 54(2A)".

(4)   Where any person ("the principal donor") causes an amount ("the principal donation") to be received by a recognised third party by way of a relevant donation

    (a)   on behalf of himself and one or more other persons, or

    (b)   on behalf of two or more other persons,

then for the purposes of this Schedule each individual contribution by a person falling within paragraph (a) or (b) of more than £500 shall be treated as if it were a separate donation received from that person.

(5) In relation to each such separate donation, the principal donor must ensure that, at the time when the principal donation is received by the recognised third party, the responsible person is given

    (a) (except in the case of a donation which the principal donor is treated as making) all such details in respect of the person treated as making the donation as are required by virtue of paragraph 10(1)(c) to be given in respect of the donor of a donation to which that paragraph applies; and

    (b) (in any case) all such details in respect of the donation as are required by virtue of paragraph 10(1)(a).

(6) Where

    (a) any person ("the agent") causes an amount to be received by a recognised third party by way of a donation on behalf of another person ("the donor"), and

    (b) the amount of the donation is more than £500,

the agent must ensure that, at the time when the donation is received by the recognised third party, the responsible person is given all such details in respect of the donor as are required by virtue of paragraph 10(1)(c) to be given in respect of the donor of a donation to which that paragraph applies.

(7) A person commits an offence if, without reasonable excuse, he fails to comply with sub-paragraph (5) or (6).

Declaration as to source of donation

6A (1) Where a person (P) causes an amount exceeding £7,500 to be received by a recognised third party by way of a donation, a written declaration must be given to the recognised third party

    (a) by P, if P is an individual, or

    (b) if not, by an individual authorised by P to make the declaration,

stating, to the best of the individual's knowledge and belief, whether or not sub-paragraph (2) applies to the donation.

(2) This sub-paragraph applies to the donation if

    (a) a person other than P has provided, or is expected to provide, money or any other benefit to P with a view to, or otherwise in connection with, the making of the donation, and

    (b) the money, or the value of the benefit, is more than £7,500.

(3) Where a declaration under this paragraph contains a statement to the effect that sub-paragraph (2) applies to the donation, it must also

    (a) state whether or not, in the opinion of the person making the declaration

        (i) sub-paragraph (4) of paragraph 6 applies to the donation;

        (ii) sub-paragraph (6) of that paragraph applies to it;

    (b) if the person's opinion is that neither of those sub-paragraphs applies to the donation, give the person's reasons for that opinion.

(4) The declaration must also state the full name and address of the person by whom it is made and, where sub-paragraph (1)(b) applies

    (a) state that the person is authorised by P to make the declaration;

    (b) describe the person's role or position in relation to P.

(5) A person who knowingly or recklessly makes a false declaration under this paragraph commits an offence.

(6) Regulations made by the Secretary of State may make provision as to how the value of a benefit is to be calculated for the purposes of sub-paragraph (2).

Declaration as to whether residence etc condition satisfied

6B (1) An individual making to a recognised third party a donation in relation to which the condition set out in section 54(2ZA) applies must give to the recognised third party a written declaration stating whether or not the individual satisfies that condition.

(2) A declaration under this paragraph must also state the full name and address of the person by whom it is made.

(3) A person who knowingly or recklessly makes a false declaration under this paragraph commits an offence.

(4) The Secretary of State may by regulations make provision requiring a declaration under this paragraph to be retained for a specified period.

Acceptance or return of donations

7 (1) Sections 56 to 60 shall apply for the purposes of this Schedule in relation to a recognised third party and any relevant donation received by a recognised third party as they apply in relation to a registered party and any donation received by a registered party.

(2) In the application of sections 56 to 60 in accordance with sub-paragraph (1)

    (a) section 56(1) shall have effect as if the reference to the particulars relating to a donor which would be required to be included in a donation report by virtue of paragraph 2 of Schedule 6 (if the donation were a recordable donation within the meaning of that Schedule) were construed as a reference to the particulars which are required to be included in a return by virtue of paragraph 10(1)(c) (in relation to a donation to which that paragraph applies); and

    (aa) section 56(1A)(a) shall have effect as if the reference to a declaration under section 54B were construed as a reference to a declaration under paragraph 6B above; and

    (b) section 56(3) and (4) section 56(3), (3B) and (4) shall each have effect as if any reference to the treasurer of the party were construed as a reference to the responsible person.

Evasion of restrictions on donations

8 Section 61 shall apply for the purposes of this Schedule as if

    (a) any reference to donations were to relevant donations;

    (b) any reference to a registered party were a reference to a recognised third party; and

    (c) any reference to the treasurer of a registered party were, in relation to a recognised third party, a reference to the responsible person.

NOTES

Defined terms

donation: Sch 11, Pt I, paras 1(5), 2-4
exempt Gibraltar trust donation: s 162
exempt trust donation: s 162
permissible donor falling within section 54(2): Sch 11, Pt I, para 1(6)
property: s 160(1)
recognised Gibraltar third party: s 85(5A)

recognised third party: s 85(5), Sch 11, Pt I, para 1(3)
registered party: s 160(1)
relevant donation: Sch 11, Pt I, para 1(4)
responsible person: s 85(7)
treasurer: s 160(1)

Part III
Reporting of Donations in Section 96 Return

Statement of relevant donations

9   The recognised third party must include in any return required to be prepared under section 96 a statement of relevant donations received in respect of the relevant election or elections (within the meaning of that section) which complies with ~~paragraphs 10 and 11~~ paragraphs 9A to 11.

Declarations under paragraph 6A or 6B

9A (1) In relation to each relevant donation falling within paragraph 10(2) in the case of which a declaration under paragraph 6A has been given, the statement must either

   (a) state that no reason was found to think that the declaration was untruthful or inaccurate, or

   (b) give details of any respects in which the declaration was found or suspected to be untruthful or inaccurate.

   (2) In relation to each relevant donation falling with paragraph 10(2) in the case of which a declaration under paragraph 6B has been given, the statement must either

   (a) state that no reason was found for thinking that the declaration was incorrect, or

   (b) give details of any respects in which the declaration was found or suspected to be incorrect.

Donations from permissible donors

10 (1) The statement must record, in relation to each relevant donation falling within sub-paragraph (2) which is accepted by the recognised third party

   (a) the amount of the donation (if a donation of money, in cash or otherwise) or (in any other case) the nature of the donation and its value as determined in accordance with paragraph 5;

   (b) the date when the donation was accepted by the recognised third party; and

   (c) the information about the donor which is, in connection with recordable donations to registered parties, required to be recorded in donation reports by virtue of paragraph 2 of Schedule 6.

   (2) Sub-paragraph (1) applies to a relevant donation where

   (a) the value of the donation is more than £7,500, or

   (b) the value of the donation, when added to the value of any other donation or donations made by the same donor (whether or not falling within paragraph (a)), is more than that amount.

   (3) The statement must also record

   (a) the total value of any relevant donations, other than those falling within sub-paragraph (2), which are accepted by the recognised third party; and

   (b) such other information as may be required by regulations made by the Commission.

   (4) In the case of a donation made by an individual who has an anonymous entry in an electoral register (within the meaning of the Representation of the People Act 1983) if the statement states that the recognised third party has seen evidence of such description as is prescribed by the Secretary of State in regulations that the individual has such an anonymous entry, the statement must be accompanied by a copy of the evidence.

Donations from impermissible donors impermissible or unidentifiable donors or without required declaration

11 (1) This paragraph applies to relevant donations falling within paragraph 6(1)(a) or (b) paragraph 6(1)(a), (aa) or (b).

   (2) Where paragraph 6(1)(a) paragraph 6(1)(a) or (aa) applies, the statement must record

   (a) the name and address of the donor or the person appearing to be the donor;

   (b) the amount of the donation (if a donation of money, in cash or otherwise) or (in any other case) the nature of the donation and its value as determined in accordance with paragraph 5;

   (c) the date when the donation was received, and the date when, and the manner in which, it was dealt with in accordance with section 56(2)(a) section 56(2)(a) or (aa); and

   (d) such other information as is required by regulations made by the Commission.

   (3) Where paragraph 6(1)(b) applies, the statement must record

   (a) details of the manner in which the donation was made;

   (b) the amount of the donation (if a donation of money, in cash or otherwise) or (in any other case) the nature of the donation and its value as determined in accordance with paragraph 5;

   (c) the date when the donation was received, and the date when, and the manner in which, it was dealt with in accordance with section 56(2)(b); and

   (d) such other information as is required by regulations made by the Commission.

   (4) In this paragraph any reference to any provision of section 56 is a reference to that provision as applied by paragraph 7.

NOTES

Subordinate Legislation
Political Donations and Regulated Transactions (Anonymous Electors) Regulations 2014, SI 2014/1806.

Defined terms
   the Commission: s 160(1)
   donation: Sch 11, Pt I, paras 1(5), 2-4

recognised third party: s 85(5), Sch 11, Pt I, para 1(3)
registered party: s 160(1)
relevant donation: Sch 11, Pt 1, para 1(4)
the Secretary of State: s 159A

SCHEDULE 11A
REQUIREMENTS OF QUARTERLY AND WEEKLY DONATION REPORTS

Part 1

Preliminary

1 (1) In this Schedule

   (a) "quarterly report" means a report required to be prepared under section 95A;

   (b) "reportable donation", in relation to a quarterly report, has the same meaning as in that section;

   (c) "weekly report" means a report required to be prepared under section 95B;

   (d) "substantial donation", in relation to a weekly report, has the same meaning as in that section;

   (e) "reporting period", in relation to a report, means the reporting period within the meaning of section 95A or 95B in respect of which the report is made.

   (2) References in this Schedule to the value of a donation are to its value as determined in accordance with paragraph 5 of Schedule 11.

(3)   References in this Schedule to section 56 are to that section as applied by paragraph 7 of Schedule 11.

Part 2
Quarterly Reports

Requirements of quarterly reports

2 (1)   A quarterly report in respect of a reporting period
    (a)   must contain the statement mentioned in paragraph 3 (reportable donations accepted during reporting period), and
    (b)   must contain the statement mentioned in paragraph 5 (reportable donations from impermissible or unidentifiable donors dealt with during reporting period).

(2)   Where, because of the application of paragraph 2(3B) of Schedule 6 by virtue of paragraph 3(2)(a), the information required in the statement mentioned in paragraph 3 is a statement that the recognised third party has seen certain evidence that an individual has an anonymous entry in an electoral register (within the meaning of the Representation of the People Act 1983), the quarterly report must be accompanied by that evidence.

Statement relating to reportable donations accepted during reporting period

3 (1)   The statement required by paragraph 2(1)(a) to be contained in a quarterly report is a statement recording
    (a)   the appropriate details in relation to each reportable donation accepted by the recognised third party during the reporting period which is of a substantial value in the context of that period,
    (b)   the total value of all other reportable donations which are accepted by the recognised third party during the reporting period, and
    (c)   such other information as may be required by regulations made by the Commission.

(2)   In relation to a reportable donation of the kind mentioned in sub-paragraph (1)(a), the "appropriate details" means
    (a)   the information about the donor which is, in connection with recordable donations to registered parties, required to be recorded in donation reports by virtue of paragraph 2 of Schedule 6,
    (b)   where the donation is of money, the amount of the donation,
    (c)   where the donation is not of money, the nature of the donation and its value,
    (d)   the date the donation was accepted by the recognised third party, and
    (e)   such other information as may be required by regulations made by the Commission.

4 (1)   For the purposes of paragraph 3(1)(a), a reportable donation is of a substantial value in the context of a reporting period ("the reporting period") if
    (a)   in a case where there are no reportable donations made by the donor which have been recordable in any previous relevant quarterly report, condition A is met;
    (b)   in any other case, condition B is met.

(2)   Condition A is met if
    (a)   the value of the donation is more than £7,500, or

(b) its value, when added to the value of all other reportable donations (if any) made by the same donor which are accepted by the recognised third party in the relevant pre-dissolution period, is more than £7,500.

(3) Condition B is met if
  (a) the value of the donation is more than £1,500, or
  (b) its value, when added to the value of all other reportable donations (if any) made by the same donor which fall within sub-paragraph (4), is more than £1,500.

(4) A reportable donation falls within this sub-paragraph if
  (a) it is accepted by the recognised third party in the relevant pre-dissolution period, and
  (b) it was not recordable in any previous relevant quarterly report.

(5) If a reportable donation which is aggregated under sub-paragraph (2)(b) or (3)(b) was accepted by the recognised third party in a previous reporting period, the donation is to be treated for the purposes of paragraph 3(1)(a) as accepted by the third party during the reporting period.

(6) For the purposes of this paragraph a donation is "recordable in any previous relevant quarterly report" if details of the donation were required to be recorded under paragraph 3(1)(a) in any previous quarterly report in relation to the recognised third party in the case of the relevant pre-dissolution period.

(7) In this paragraph, "the relevant pre-dissolution period" means the pre-dissolution period (within the meaning of section 95A) within which the reporting period falls.

Statement of reportable donations dealt with during reporting period

5 (1) The statement required by paragraph 2(1)(b) to be contained in a quarterly report is a statement recording the appropriate details in relation to each reportable donation which
  (a) the recognised third party is prohibited from accepting by virtue of
    (i) paragraph 6(1)(a) of Schedule 11, or
    (ii) paragraph 6(1)(b) of that Schedule, and
  (b) is dealt with by the recognised third party during the reporting period in accordance with section 56(2).

(2) In relation to a reportable donation of the kind mentioned in sub-paragraph (1)(a)(i), the "appropriate details" means
  (a) the name and address of the donor,
  (b) where the donation is of money, the amount of the donation,
  (c) where the donation is not of money, the nature of the donation and its value,
  (d) the date the donation was received by the recognised third party,
  (e) the date and manner in which the donation was dealt with in accordance with section 56(2)(a), and
  (f) such other information as may be required by regulations made by the Commission.

(3) In relation to a reportable donation of the kind mentioned in sub-paragraph (1)(a)(ii), the "appropriate details" means
  (a) details of the manner in which the donation was made,
  (b) where the donation is of money, the amount of the donation,
  (c) where the donation is not of money, the nature of the donation and its value,
  (d) the date the donation was received by the recognised third party,
  (e) the date and manner in which the donation was dealt with in accordance with section 56(2)(b), and

(f) such other information as may be required by regulations made by the Commission.

Supplementary

6   Where reference is made in this Part to a donation being accepted, or dealt with in accordance with section 56(2), by a recognised third party during a reporting period, it is irrelevant whether the donation was also received by that party in that period.

NOTES
Defined terms
the Commission: s 160(1)
quarterly report: Sch 11A, Pt 1 para 1(1)
recognised third party: s 85(5)
registered party: s 160(1)

reportable donation: Sch 11A, Pt 1 para 1(1)
reporting period: Sch 11A, Pt 1 para 1(1)
value of the donation: Sch 11A, Pt 1 para 1(2)

Part 3
Weekly Reports

7 (1)   A weekly report in respect of a reporting period must contain a statement recording the appropriate details in relation to each substantial donation received by the recognised third party during that period.

(2)   The "appropriate details" means
(a)   the information about the donor which is, in connection with recordable donations to registered parties, required to be recorded in donation reports by virtue of paragraph 3 of Schedule 6,
(b)   where the donation is of money, the amount of the donation,
(c)   where the donation is not of money, the nature of the donation and its value,
(d)   the date the donation was received by the recognised third party, and
(e)   such other information as may be required by regulations made by the Commission.

NOTES
Defined terms
the Commission: s 160(1)
recognised third party: s 85(5)
registered party: s 160(1)
reporting period: Sch 11A, Pt 1 para 1(1)

substantial donation: Sch 11A, Pt 1 para 1(1)
weekly report: Sch 11A, Pt 1 para 1(1)

SCHEDULE 12
ASSISTANCE AVAILABLE TO DESIGNATED ORGANISATIONS

Section 110

Right to send referendum address post free

1 (1)   A designated organisation is, subject to such reasonable terms and conditions as the universal service provider concerned may specify, entitled to send free of any charge for postage which would otherwise be made by a universal service provider either
(a)   one unaddressed postal communication, containing matter relating to the referendum only and not exceeding 60 grammes in weight, to each place in the referendum area which, in accordance with those terms and conditions, constitutes a delivery point for the purposes of this sub-paragraph; or
(b)   one such postal communication addressed to each person entitled to vote at the referendum.

(2) A designated organisation is also, subject to any such terms and conditions, entitled to send free of any such charge for postage to each person entered in the list of proxies for the referendum one such postal communication for each appointment in respect of which that person is so entered.

(3) Section 200A of the Representation of the People Act 1983 (remuneration of universal service provider for free postal services rendered in relation to parliamentary elections) shall apply in relation to a postal service rendered by a universal service provider in pursuance of this paragraph as it applies in relation to a postal service rendered by such a provider in pursuance of that Act.

(4) In this paragraph
"the referendum area" means the area throughout which the referendum is being held;
"universal service provider" has the same meaning as in Part 3 of the Postal Services Act 2011.

(5) If this paragraph comes into force at a time when the amendments made to section 91 of the Representation of the People Act 1983 by the Postal Services Act 2000 have not come into force, then until such time as those amendments come into force, this paragraph shall have effect subject to such modifications as may be specified in the order under section 163 of this Act which brings this paragraph into force.

Right to use rooms for holding public meetings

2 (1) Subject to the provisions of this paragraph, persons authorised by a designated organisation are entitled for the purpose of holding public meetings in furtherance of the organisation's referendum campaign to the use free of charge, at reasonable times during the relevant period, of
  (a) a suitable room in the premises of a school to which this paragraph applies in accordance with sub-paragraph (2);
  (b) any meeting room to which this paragraph applies in accordance with sub-paragraph (3).
For this purpose "the relevant period" means the period of 28 days ending with the day before the date of the poll.

(2) This paragraph applies
  (a) in England and Wales, to community, foundation and voluntary schools whose premises are situated in the referendum area, and
  (b) in Scotland, to any school whose premises are so situated, other than an independent school within the meaning of the Education (Scotland) Act 1980.

(3) This paragraph applies to meeting rooms situated in the referendum area the expense of maintaining which is payable wholly or mainly out of public funds or by any local authority, or by a body whose expenses are so payable.

(4) Where a room is used for a meeting in pursuance of the rights conferred by this paragraph, the person by whom or on whose behalf the meeting is convened
  (a) shall defray any expenses incurred in preparing, warming, lighting and cleaning the room and providing attendance for the meeting and restoring the room to its usual condition after the meeting; and
  (b) shall defray any damage done to the room or the premises in which it is situated, or to the furniture, fittings or apparatus in the room or premises.

(5) A person is not entitled to exercise the rights conferred by this paragraph except on reasonable notice; and this paragraph does not authorise any interference with the hours during which a room in school premises is used for educational purposes, or any interference with the use of a meeting room either for the purposes of the person maintaining it or under a prior agreement for its letting for any purpose.

(6)   For the purposes of this paragraph (except those of paragraph (b) of sub-paragraph (4)), the premises of a school shall not be taken to include any private dwelling, and in this paragraph

"dwelling" includes any part of a building where that part is occupied separately as a dwelling;

"meeting room" means any room which it is the practice to let for public meetings; and "room" includes a hall, gallery or gymnasium.

(7)   In this paragraph "the referendum area" means the area throughout which the referendum is being held.

(8)   Neither this paragraph, nor paragraph 3, applies to Northern Ireland.

Supplementary provisions about use of rooms for public meetings

3 (1)   This paragraph has effect with respect to the rights conferred by paragraph 2 and the arrangements to be made for their exercise.

(2)   Any arrangements for the use of a room in school premises shall be made
    (a)   with the local authority (or, in Scotland, education authority) maintaining the school, or
    (b)   in the case of a room in the premises of a foundation or voluntary aided school, with the governing body of the school.

(3)   Any question as to the rooms in school premises which a person authorised by a designated organisation is entitled to use, or as to the times at which he is entitled to use them, or as to the notice which is reasonable, shall be determined by the Secretary of State.

(4)   Any person authorised by a designated organisation is entitled at all reasonable hours to inspect
    (a)   any lists prepared in pursuance of paragraph 4 or 6 of Schedule 5 to the Representation of the People Act 1983 (use of rooms for parliamentary election meetings), or
    (b)   a copy of any such lists,
in connection with exercising the rights conferred by paragraph 2.

(5)   In this paragraph "local authority" has the meaning given by section 579(1) of the Education Act 1996.

Referendum campaign broadcasts

4 (1)-(5)   *Repealed*

(6)   The British Broadcasting Corporation shall have regard, in determining its policy with respect to referendum campaign broadcasts by designated organisations, to any views expressed by the Electoral Commission for the purposes of this sub-paragraph.

(7)   In this paragraph

"referendum campaign broadcast" has the same meaning as in section 127.

NOTES
Defined terms
  body: s 160(1)
  designated organisation: s 110(5)
  expenses met out of public funds: s 160(4)
  modifications: s 160(1)

referendum: s 101(2)-(5)
referendum campaign: s 111(4)
the Secretary of State: s 159A

SCHEDULE 13

REFERENDUM EXPENSES: QUALIFYING EXPENSES

Part I
Qualifying Expenses

Expenses qualifying where incurred for referendum purposes

1   For the purposes of section 111(2) the expenses falling within this Part of this Schedule are expenses incurred in respect of any of the matters set out in the following list.
List of Matters

     (1)   Referendum campaign broadcasts.
         Expenses in respect of such broadcasts include agency fees, design costs and other costs in connection with preparing or producing such broadcasts.

     (2)   Advertising of any nature (whatever the medium used).
         Expenses in respect of such advertising include agency fees, design costs and other costs in connection with preparing, producing, distributing or otherwise disseminating such advertising or anything incorporating such advertising and intended to be distributed for the purpose of disseminating it.

     (3)   Unsolicited material addressed to electors (whether addressed to them by name or intended for delivery to households within any particular area or areas).
         Expenses in respect of such material include design costs and other costs in connection with preparing, producing or distributing such material (including the cost of postage).

     (4)   Any material to which section 125 applies.
         Expenses in respect of such material include design costs and other costs in connection with preparing or producing or distributing or otherwise disseminating such material.

     (5)   Market research or canvassing conducted for the purpose of ascertaining polling intentions.

     (6)   The provision of any services or facilities in connection with press conferences or other dealings with the media.

     (7)   Transport (by any means) of persons to any place or places with a view to obtaining publicity in connection with a referendum campaign.
         Expenses in respect of the transport of such persons include the costs of hiring a particular means of transport for the whole or part of the period during which the campaign is being conducted.

     (8)   Rallies and other events, including public meetings (but not annual or other party conferences) organised so as to obtain publicity in connection with a referendum campaign or for other purposes connected with a referendum campaign.
         Expenses in respect of such events include costs incurred in connection with the attendance of persons at such events, the hire of premises for the purposes of such events or the provision of goods, services or facilities at them.

Exclusions

2   Nothing in paragraph 1 shall be taken as extending to
     (a)   any expenses in respect of any property, services or facilities so far as those expenses fall to be met out of public funds;
     (b)   any expenses incurred in respect of the remuneration or allowances payable to any member of the staff (whether permanent or otherwise) of the campaign organiser; or

(c) any expenses incurred in respect of an individual by way of travelling expenses (by any means of transport) or in providing for his accommodation or other personal needs to the extent that the expenses are paid by the individual from his own resources and are not reimbursed to him.

NOTES

Defined terms

campaign organiser: s 111(4)
expenses met out of public funds: s 160(4)
property: s 160(1)

referendum: s 101(2)-(5)
referendum campaign: s 111(4)

Part II
Supplemental

Guidance by Commission

3 (1) The Commission may prepare, and from time to time revise, a code of practice giving guidance as to the kinds of expenses which do, or do not, fall within Part I of this Schedule.

(2) Once the Commission have prepared a draft code under this paragraph, they shall submit it to the Secretary of State for his approval.

(3) The Secretary of State may approve a draft code either without modification or with such modifications as he may determine.

(4) Once the Secretary of State has approved a draft code he shall lay a copy of the draft, whether

    (a) in its original form, or

    (b) in a form which incorporates any modifications determined under sub-paragraph (3),

before each House of Parliament.

(5) If the draft incorporates any such modifications, the Secretary of State shall at the same time lay before each House a statement of his reasons for making them.

(6) If, within the 40day period, either House resolves not to approve the draft, the Secretary of State shall take no further steps in relation to the draft code.

(7) If no such resolution is made within the 40day period

    (a) the Secretary of State shall issue the code in the form of the draft laid before Parliament, and

    (b) the code shall come into force on such date as the Secretary of State may by order appoint;

and the Commission shall arrange for it to be published in such manner as they consider appropriate.

(8) Sub-paragraph (6) does not prevent a new draft code from being laid before Parliament.

(9) In this paragraph "40day period", in relation to a draft code, means

    (a) if the draft is laid before one House on a day later than the day on which it is laid before the other House, the period of 40 days beginning with the later of the two days, and

    (b) in any other case, the period of 40 days beginning with the day on which the draft is laid before each House,

no account being taken of any period during which Parliament is dissolved or prorogued or during which both Houses are adjourned for more than four days.

(10) In this paragraph references to a draft code include a draft revised code.

Power to amend Part I

4 (1)   The Secretary of State may by order make such amendments of Part I of this Schedule as he considers appropriate.

   (2)   The Secretary of State may make such an order either
       (a)   where the order gives effect to a recommendation of the Commission; or
       (b)   after consultation with the Commission.

NOTES

Defined terms   the Secretary of State: s 159A
   the Commission: s 160(1)
   modifications: s 160(1)

SCHEDULE 14
LIMITS ON REFERENDUM EXPENSES BY PERMITTED PARTICIPANTS

Section 118

Limits in relation to referendums held throughout United Kingdom

1 (1)   This paragraph imposes limits in relation to a referendum falling within section 101(1)(a).

   (2)   The limit on referendum expenses incurred by or on behalf of a permitted participant during the referendum period in the case of such a referendum is
       (a)   £5 million in the case of a person or body designated under section 108;
       (b)   in the case of a registered party falling within section 105(1)(a) but not designated under section 108
           (i)   £5 million, if the party's relevant percentage exceeds 30 per cent,
           (ii)   £4 million, if the party's relevant percentage is more than 20 per cent but not more than 30 per cent,
           (iii) £3 million, if the party's relevant percentage is more than 10 per cent but not more than 20 per cent,
           (iv)   £2 million, if the party's relevant percentage is more than 5 per cent but not more than 10 per cent,
           (v)   £500,000, if the party's relevant percentage is not more than 5 per cent or if it has no relevant percentage; and
       (c)   £500,000 in the case of a person or body falling within section 105(1)(b) but not designated under section 108.

   (3)   For the purposes of this paragraph
       (a)   a registered party has a relevant percentage in relation to a referendum to which this paragraph applies if, at the last parliamentary general election taking place before the referendum, votes were cast for one or more candidates at the election authorised to use the party's registered name; and
       (b)   the amount of its relevant percentage is equal to the percentage of the total number of votes cast for all candidates at that election which is represented by the total number of votes cast for the candidate or candidates mentioned in paragraph (a).

   (4)   Where at any such general election a candidate was authorised to use the registered name of more than one registered party, then for the purposes of sub-paragraph (3)(b) as it applies in relation to each of those parties, the number of votes cast for the candidate shall be taken to be the total number cast for him divided by the number of parties.

(5) In this paragraph any reference to a parliamentary general election is to one taking place after the passing of this Act.

Limits in relation to referendums held in particular parts of United Kingdom

2 (1) This paragraph imposes limits in relation to a referendum to which this Part applies, other than one falling within section 101(1)(a).

(2) The limit on referendum expenses incurred by or on behalf of a permitted participant during the referendum period in the case of such a referendum is such amount as the Secretary of State may by order prescribe.

(3) Different amounts may be so prescribed for different referendums or different categories of permitted participants.

(4) Before making an order under this paragraph the Secretary of State shall seek, and have regard to, the views of the Commission.

(5) Where the Secretary of State proposes to make such an order otherwise than in accordance with the views of the Commission, he shall on laying a draft of a statutory instrument containing the order before each House of Parliament also lay before each House a statement of his reasons for departing from the views of the Commission.

NOTES

Defined terms
  body: s 160(1)
  the Commission: s 160(1)
  permitted participant: s 105(1)
  referendum: s 101(2)-(5)

referendum expenses: s 111(2)
registered party: s 160(1)
the Secretary of State: s 159A

SCHEDULE 15
CONTROL OF DONATIONS TO PERMITTED PARTICIPANTS

Section 119

Part I
Introductory

Operation and interpretation of Schedule

1 (1) This Schedule has effect for controlling donations to permitted participants that either are not registered parties or are minor parties.

(2) The following provisions have effect for the purposes of this Schedule.

(3) In accordance with sub-paragraph (1) "permitted participant" does not include a permitted participant which is a registered party other than a minor party.

(4) "Relevant donation", in relation to a permitted participant at a referendum, means a donation to the permitted participant for the purpose of meeting referendum expenses incurred by or on behalf of the permitted participant.

(5) "Donation" shall be construed in accordance with paragraphs 2 to 4.

(6) In relation to donations received by a permitted participant other than a designated organisation, references to a permissible donor falling within section 54(2) do not include a registered party.

In this sub-paragraph "designated organisation" has the meaning given by section 110(5).

Donations: general rules

2 (1) "Donation", in relation to a permitted participant, means (subject to paragraph 4)

    (a)   any gift to the permitted participant of money or other property;

    (b)   any sponsorship provided in relation to the permitted participant (as defined by paragraph 3);

    (c)   any money spent (otherwise than by or on behalf of the permitted participant) in paying any referendum expenses incurred by or on behalf of the permitted participant;

    (d)   any money lent to the permitted participant otherwise than on commercial terms;

    (e)   the provision otherwise than on commercial terms of any property, services or facilities for the use or benefit of the permitted participant (including the services of any person);

    (f)   in the case of a permitted participant other than an individual, any subscription or other fee paid for affiliation to, or membership of, the permitted participant.

(2)   Where

    (a)   any money or other property is transferred to a permitted participant pursuant to any transaction or arrangement involving the provision by or on behalf of the permitted participant of any property, services or facilities or other consideration of monetary value, and

    (b)   the total value in monetary terms of the consideration so provided by or on behalf of the permitted participant is less than the value of the money or (as the case may be) the market value of the property transferred,

the transfer of the money or property shall (subject to sub-paragraph (4)) constitute a gift to the permitted participant for the purposes of sub-paragraph (1)(a).

(3)   In determining

    (a)   for the purposes of sub-paragraph (1)(d) whether any money lent to a permitted participant is so lent otherwise than on commercial terms, or

    (b)   for the purposes of sub-paragraph (1)(e) whether any property, services or facilities provided for the use or benefit of a permitted participant is or are so provided otherwise than on such terms,

regard shall be had to the total value in monetary terms of the consideration provided by or on behalf of the permitted participant in respect of the loan or the provision of the property, services or facilities.

(4)   Where (apart from this sub-paragraph) anything would be a donation both by virtue of sub-paragraph (1)(b) and by virtue of any other provision of this paragraph, sub-paragraph (1)(b) (together with paragraph 3) shall apply in relation to it to the exclusion of the other provision of this paragraph.

(5)   Anything given or transferred to any officer, member, trustee or agent of a permitted participant in his capacity as such (and not for his own use or benefit) is to be regarded as given or transferred to the permitted participant (and references to donations received by a permitted participant accordingly include donations so given or transferred).

(6)   In this paragraph

    (a)   any reference to anything being given or transferred to a permitted participant or any other person is a reference to its being given or transferred either directly or indirectly through any third person;

    (b)   "gift" includes bequest.

Sponsorship

3 (1)   For the purposes of this Schedule sponsorship is provided in relation to a permitted participant if

(a) any money or other property is transferred to the permitted participant or to any person for the benefit of the permitted participant, and

(b) the purpose (or one of the purposes) of the transfer is (or must, having regard to all the circumstances, reasonably be assumed to be)

    (i) to help the permitted participant with meeting, or to meet, to any extent any defined expenses incurred or to be incurred by or on behalf of the permitted participant, or

    (ii) to secure that to any extent any such expenses are not so incurred.

(2) In sub-paragraph (1) "defined expenses" means expenses in connection with

    (a) any conference, meeting or other event organised by or on behalf of the permitted participant,

    (b) the preparation, production or dissemination of any publication by or on behalf of the permitted participant, or

    (c) any study or research organised by or on behalf of the permitted participant.

(3) The following do not, however, constitute sponsorship by virtue of sub-paragraph (1)

    (a) the making of any payment in respect of

        (i) any charge for admission to any conference, meeting or other event, or

        (ii) the purchase price of, or any other charge for access to, any publication;

    (b) the making of any payment in respect of the inclusion of an advertisement in any publication where the payment is made at the commercial rate payable for the inclusion of such an advertisement in any such publication.

(4) The Secretary of State may by order made on the recommendation of the Commission amend sub-paragraph (2) or (3).

(5) In this paragraph "publication" means a publication made available in whatever form and by whatever means (whether or not to the public at large or any section of the public).

Payments etc not to be regarded as donations

4 (1) None of the following shall be regarded as a donation

    (a) any grant provided out of public funds, other than a grant provided to a designated organisation by virtue of section 110(2);

    (b) the provision of any rights conferred on a designated organisation (or persons authorised by a designated organisation) by virtue of section 110(4) and Schedule 12;

    (c) the provision by an individual of his own services which he provides voluntarily in his own time and free of charge; or

    (d) any interest accruing to a permitted participant in respect of any donation which is dealt with by the permitted participant in accordance with section 56(2)(a) or (b) (as applied by paragraph 7).

(2) Any donation whose value (as determined in accordance with paragraph 5) is not more than £500 shall be disregarded.

(3) Any payment out of public funds shall not be regarded as a donation for the purposes of paragraph 6A or 6B.

(4) For all other purposes of this Schedule, such a payment shall not be regarded as a donation unless it is a grant provided to a designated organisation by virtue of section 110(2).

Value of donations

5 (1) The value of any donation falling within paragraph 2(1)(a) (other than money) shall be taken to be the market value of the property in question.

(2) Where, however, paragraph 2(1)(a) applies by virtue of paragraph 2(2), the value of the donation shall be taken to be the difference between
    (a) the value of the money, or the market value of the property, in question, and
    (b) the total value in monetary terms of the consideration provided by or on behalf of the permitted participant.

(3) The value of any donation falling within paragraph 2(1)(b) shall be taken to be the value of the money, or (as the case may be) the market value of the property, transferred as mentioned in paragraph 3(1); and accordingly any value in monetary terms of any benefit conferred on the person providing the sponsorship in question shall be disregarded.

(4) The value of any donation falling within paragraph 2(1)(d) or (e) shall be taken to be the amount representing the difference between
    (a) the total value in monetary terms of the consideration that would have had to be provided by or on behalf of the permitted participant in respect of the loan or the provision of the property, services or facilities if
        (i)   the loan had been made, or
        (ii) the property, services or facilities had been provided,
    on commercial terms, and
    (b) the total value in monetary terms of the consideration (if any) actually so provided by or on behalf of the permitted participant.

(5) Where a donation such as is mentioned in sub-paragraph (4) confers an enduring benefit on the donee over a particular period, the value of the donation
    (a) shall be determined at the time when it is made, but
    (b) shall be so determined by reference to the total benefit accruing to the donee over that period.

NOTES

Defined terms

bequest: s 160(1)
the Commission: s 160(1)
market value: s 160(1)
minor party: s 160(1)
permitted participant: s 105(1)
property: s 160(1)

provided out of public funds: s 160(4)
referendum: s 101(2)-(5)
referendum expenses: s 111(2)
registered party: s 160(1)
the Secretary of State: s 159A

Part II
Controls on Donations

Prohibition on accepting donations from impermissible donors

6 (1) A relevant donation received by a permitted participant must not be accepted by the permitted participant if
    (a) the person by whom the donation would be made is not, at the time of its receipt by the permitted participant, a permissible donor falling within section 54(2), or
    (aa) in the case of a donation of an amount exceeding £7,500, the permitted participant has not been given a declaration as required by paragraph 6A, or
    (aa) any declaration required to be made in respect of the donation by paragraph 6A or 6B has not been received by the permitted participant, or

(b) the permitted participant is (whether because the donation is given anonymously or by reason of any deception or concealment or otherwise) unable to ascertain the identity of the person offering the donation.

(2) For the purposes of this Schedule any payment received by a designated organisation by virtue of section 110(2) shall be regarded as a donation received by the organisation from a permissible donor falling within section 54(2).

(3) For the purposes of this Schedule, any relevant donation received by a permitted participant which is an exempt trust donation shall be regarded as a relevant donation received by the permitted participant from a permissible donor.

(4) But, for the purposes of this Schedule, any relevant donation received by a permitted participant from a trustee of any property (in his capacity as such) which is not
   (a) an exempt trust donation, or
   (b) a relevant donation transmitted by the trustee to the permitted participant on behalf of beneficiaries under the trust who are
      (i) persons who at the time of its receipt by the permitted participant are permissible donors falling within section 54(2), or
      (ii) the members of an unincorporated association which at that time is such a permissible donor,
shall be regarded as a relevant donation received by the permitted participant from a person who is not such a permissible donor.

(5) Where any person ("the principal donor") causes an amount ("the principal donation") to be received by a permitted participant by way of a relevant donation
   (a) on behalf of himself and one or more other persons, or
   (b) on behalf of two or more other persons,
then for the purposes of this Schedule each individual contribution by a person falling within paragraph (a) or (b) of more than £500 shall be treated as if it were a separate donation received from that person.

(6) In relation to each such separate donation, the principal donor must ensure that, at the time when the principal donation is received by the permitted participant, the responsible person is given
   (a) (except in the case of a donation which the principal donor is treated as making) all such details in respect of the person treated as making the donation as are required by virtue of paragraph 10(1)(c) to be given in respect of the donor of a donation to which that paragraph applies; and
   (b) (in any case) all such details in respect of the donation as are required by virtue of paragraph 10(1)(a).

(7) Where
   (a) any person ("the agent") causes an amount to be received by a permitted participant by way of a donation on behalf of another person ("the donor"), and
   (b) the amount of the donation is more than £500,
the agent must ensure that, at the time when the donation is received by the permitted participant, the responsible person is given all such details in respect of the donor as are required by virtue of paragraph 10(1)(c) to be given in respect of the donor of a donation to which that paragraph applies.

(8) A person commits an offence if, without reasonable excuse, he fails to comply with sub-paragraph (6) or (7).

Declaration as to source of donation

6A (1) Where a person (P) causes an amount exceeding £7,500 to be received by a permitted participant by way of a donation, a written declaration must be given to the permitted participant

    (a) by P, if P is an individual, or

    (b) if not, by an individual authorised by P to make the declaration,

stating, to the best of the individual's knowledge and belief, whether or not sub-paragraph (2) applies to the donation.

  (2) This sub-paragraph applies to the donation if

    (a) a person other than P has provided, or is expected to provide, money or any other benefit to P with a view to, or otherwise in connection with, the making of the donation, and

    (b) the money, or the value of the benefit, is more than £7,500.

  (3) Where a declaration under this paragraph contains a statement to the effect that sub-paragraph (2) applies to the donation, it must also

    (a) state whether or not, in the opinion of the person making the declaration

      (i) sub-paragraph (5) of paragraph 6 applies to the donation;

      (ii) sub-paragraph (7) of that paragraph applies to it;

    (b) if the person's opinion is that neither of those sub-paragraphs applies to the donation, give the person's reasons for that opinion.

  (4) The declaration must also state the full name and address of the person by whom it is made and, where sub-paragraph (1)(b) applies

    (a) state that the person is authorised by P to make the declaration;

    (b) describe the person's role or position in relation to P.

  (5) A person who knowingly or recklessly makes a false declaration under this paragraph commits an offence.

  (6) Regulations made by the Secretary of State may make provision as to how the value of a benefit is to be calculated for the purposes of sub-paragraph (2).

Declaration as to whether residence etc condition satisfied

6B (1) An individual making to a permitted participant a donation in relation to which the condition set out in section 54(2ZA) applies must give to the permitted participant a declaration stating whether or not the individual satisfies that condition.

  (2) A declaration under this paragraph must also state the individual's full name and address.

  (3) A person who knowingly or recklessly makes a false declaration under this paragraph commits an offence.

  (4) The Secretary of State may by regulations make provision requiring a declaration under this paragraph to be retained for a specified period.

Acceptance or return of donations

7 (1) Sections 56 to 60 shall apply for the purposes of this Schedule in relation to a permitted participant and any relevant donation received by a permitted participant as they apply in relation to a registered party and a donation received by a registered party.

  (2) In the application of sections 56 to 60 in accordance with sub-paragraph (1)

    (a) section 56(1) shall have effect as if the reference to the particulars relating to a donor which would be required to be included in a donation report by virtue of paragraph 2 of Schedule 6 (if the donation were a recordable donation within the meaning of that Schedule) were construed as a reference to the particulars which are required to be included in a return by virtue of paragraph 10(1)(c) (in relation to a donation to which that paragraph applies); and

(aa) section 56(1A)(a) shall have effect as if the reference to a declaration under section 54B were construed as a reference to a declaration under paragraph 6B above; and

(b) ~~section 56(3) and (4)~~ section 56(3), (3B) and (4) shall each have effect as if any reference to the treasurer of a registered party were construed as a reference to the responsible person in relation to the permitted participant.

Evasion of restrictions on donations

8   Section 61 shall apply for the purposes of this Schedule as if
(a) any reference to donations were to relevant donations;
(b) any reference to a registered party were a reference to a permitted participant; and
(c) any reference to the treasurer of such a party were, in relation to a permitted participant, a reference to the responsible person.

NOTES

Defined terms
donation: Sch 15, Pt I, paras 1(2), (5), 2–4
exempt trust donation: s 162
permissible donor falling within section 54(2): Sch 15, Pt I, para 1(2), (6)
permitted participant: s 105(1), Sch 15, Pt I, para 1(2), (3)
property: s 160(1)

registered party: s 160(1)
relevant donation: Sch 15, Pt I, para 1(2), (4)
responsible person: s 105(2)
treasurer: s 160(1)

Part III
Reporting of Donations

Statement of relevant donations

9   The responsible person in relation to a permitted participant must include in any return required to be prepared under section 120 a statement of relevant donations which complies with ~~paragraphs 10 and 11~~ paragraphs 9A to 11.

Declarations under paragraph 6A or 6B

9A (1) In relation to each relevant donation falling within paragraph 10(2) in the case of which a declaration under paragraph 6A has been given, the statement must either
(a) state that no reason was found to think that the declaration was untruthful or inaccurate, or
(b) give details of any respects in which the declaration was found or suspected to be untruthful or inaccurate.

(2) In relation to each relevant donation falling with paragraph 10(2) in the case of which a declaration under paragraph 6B has been given, the statement must either
(a) state that no reason was found for thinking that the declaration was incorrect, or
(b) give details of any respects in which the declaration was found or suspected to be incorrect.

Donations from permissible donors

10 (1) The statement must record, in relation to each relevant donation falling within sub-paragraph (2) which is accepted by the permitted participant

(a) the amount of the donation (if a donation of money, in cash or otherwise) or (in any other case) the nature of the donation and its value as determined in accordance with paragraph 5;

(b) the date when the donation was accepted by the permitted participant; and

(c) the information about the donor which is, in connection with recordable donations to registered parties, required to be recorded in donation reports by virtue of paragraph 2 of Schedule 6.

(2) Sub-paragraph (1) applies to a relevant donation where
(a) the value of the donation is more than £7,500, or
(b) the value of the donation, when added to the value of any other donation or donations made by the same donor (whether or not falling within paragraph (a)), is more than that amount.

(3) The statement must also record
(a) the total value of any relevant donations, other than those falling within sub-paragraph (2), which are accepted by the permitted participant; and
(b) such other information as may be required by regulations made by the Commission.

(4) In the case of a donation made by an individual who has an anonymous entry in an electoral register (within the meaning of the Representation of the People Act 1983) if the statement states that the permitted participant has seen evidence of such description as is prescribed by the Secretary of State in regulations that the individual has such an anonymous entry, the statement must be accompanied by a copy of the evidence.

Donations from impermissible or unidentifiable donors or without required declaration

11 (1) This paragraph applies to relevant donations falling within paragraph 6(1)(a) or (b) paragraph 6(1)(a), (aa) or (b).

(2) Where paragraph 6(1)(a) paragraph 6(1)(a) or (aa) applies, the statement must record
(a) the name and address of the donor or the person appearing to be the donor;
(b) the amount of the donation (if a donation of money, in cash or otherwise) or (in any other case) the nature of the donation and its value as determined in accordance with paragraph 5;
(c) the date when the donation was received, and the date when, and the manner in which, it was dealt with in accordance with section 56(2)(a) section 56(2)(a) or (aa); and
(d) such other information as is required by regulations made by the Commission.

(3) Where paragraph 6(1)(b) applies the statement must record
(a) details of the manner in which the donation was made;
(b) the amount of the donation (if a donation of money, in cash or otherwise) or (in any other case) the nature of the donation and its value as determined in accordance with paragraph 5;
(c) the date when the donation was received, and the date when, and the manner in which, it was dealt with in accordance with section 56(2)(b); and
(d) such other information as is required by regulations made by the Commission.

(4) In this paragraph any reference to any provision of section 56 is a reference to that provision as applied by paragraph 7.

NOTES

Defined terms
the Commission: s 160(1)
donation: Sch 15, Pt I, paras 1(2), (5), 2-4
permitted participant: s 105(1) and Sch 15, Pt I, para

1(2), (3
registered party: s 160(1)
relevant donations: Sch 15, Pt I para 1(2), (4)
responsible person: s 105(2)

SCHEDULE 16
CONTROL OF DONATIONS TO CANDIDATES: NEW SCHEDULE 2A TO THE REPRESENTATION OF THE PEOPLE ACT 1983

Not reproduced

SCHEDULE 17
AMENDMENTS RELATING TO ELECTION PETITIONS

Not reproduced

SCHEDULE 18

Not reproduced

SCHEDULE 19

Repealed

SCHEDULE 19A
REPORTS OF GIFTS RECEIVED BY UNINCORPORATED ASSOCIATIONS MAKING POLITICAL CONTRIBUTIONS

Section 140A

Requirement to notify Commission of political contributions over £25,000

1 (1) Where in any calendar year an unincorporated association falling within section 54(2)(h)

   (a) makes a political contribution of more than £25,000, not having previously made any political contributions in that year, or

   (b) makes a political contribution which takes the total amount of such contributions made by it in that year above £25,000,

   the association must notify the Commission accordingly within the period of 30 days beginning with the date on which the contribution was made.

(2) An unincorporated association makes a "political contribution" in any of the following cases

   (a) it makes a donation (within the meaning of Part 4) to a registered party;

   (b) it makes a loan of money to a registered party, or discharges (to any extent) a liability of a registered party, in pursuance of a regulated transaction (within the meaning of Part 4A);

   (c) it makes a donation (within the meaning of Schedule 7) to a regulated donee;

   (d) it makes a loan of money to a regulated donee, or discharges (to any extent) a liability of a regulated donee, in pursuance of a controlled transaction (within the meaning of Schedule 7A);

   (e) it makes a donation (within the meaning of Schedule 11) to a recognised third party;

   (f) it makes a donation (within the meaning of Schedule 15) to a permitted participant;

733

(g) it makes a relevant donation within the meaning of Schedule 4 to the Recall of MPs Act 2015 (see Part 1 of that Schedule) to an accredited campaigner.

(3) For the purposes of sub-paragraph (1)(b) a contribution is not counted towards the total unless it is a contribution of more than £500.

(4) In this paragraph
"accredited campaigner" has the same meaning as in Schedule 3 to the Recall of MPs Act 2015 (see Part 5 of that Schedule);
"permitted participant" has the meaning given in section 105 except that it does not include a registered party other than a minor party;
"recognised third party" has the meaning given in section 85;
"regulated donee" has the meaning given in Part 1 of Schedule 7.

(5) For the purposes of this paragraph
  (a) the value of a donation to a registered party shall be determined in accordance with section 53;
  (b) the value of a donation to a regulated donee shall be determined in accordance with paragraph 5 of Schedule 7;
  (c) the value of a donation to a recognised third party shall be determined in accordance with paragraph 5 of Schedule 11;
  (d) the value of a donation to a permitted participant shall be determined in accordance with paragraph 5 of Schedule 15;
  (e) the value of a contribution within sub-paragraph (2)(b) or (d) is the amount of money lent or liability discharged;
  (f) the value of a donation to an accredited campaigner shall be determined in accordance with paragraph 5 of Schedule 4 to the Recall of MPs Act 2015.

(6) Where a donation, or a sum of money lent, is sent on one day and received on another, the donation or loan is treated for the purposes of this paragraph as made on the earlier of those days.

Requirement to report gifts received to Commission

2 (1) This paragraph applies where the making of a political contribution by an unincorporated association causes the association to be subject to the notification requirement in paragraph 1; and in this paragraph
"the contribution date" means the date on which that contribution was made;
"quarter" means a period of three months ending on 31st March, 30th June, 30th September or 31st December.

(2) Within the period of 60 days beginning with the contribution date, the unincorporated association must make a report to the Commission
  (a) specifying every gift of more than £7,500 received by the association in the period
    (i)   beginning at the start of the calendar year preceding the year in which the contribution date falls, and
    (ii) ending with the contribution date, or
  (b) (if it is the case) stating that the association received no such gifts in the period mentioned in paragraph (a).

(3) Within the period of 30 days following the end of the first quarter to begin after the contribution date, the unincorporated association must make a report to the Commission
  (a) specifying every gift of more than £7,500 received by the association in the period
    (i)   beginning with the day after the contribution date, and
    (ii) ending with the end of the quarter, or

    (b) (if it is the case) stating that the association received no such gifts in the period mentioned in paragraph (a).

(4) In relation to each subsequent quarter ending in the calendar year in which the contribution date falls or in the following calendar year, the unincorporated association must within the period of 30 days following the end of the quarter make a report to the Commission

    (a) specifying every gift of more than £7,500 received by the association in the quarter, or

    (b) (if it is the case) stating that the association received no such gifts in the quarter.

(5) Where

    (a) an unincorporated association receives two or more gifts of more than £500 from the same person in the same calendar year, and

    (b) those gifts amount to more than £7,500 in total,

the association is treated for the purposes of this paragraph as receiving a gift of more than £7,500 on the day on which it receives the gift that takes the total amount of gifts from that person in that year above £7,500.

(6) Where

    (a) an unincorporated association receives (or is treated by sub-paragraph (5) as receiving) a gift of more than £7,500 from a particular person, and

    (b) later in the same calendar year the association receives a gift of more than £1,500 from the same person,

that subsequent gift is treated for the purposes of this paragraph in the same way as a gift of more than £7,500.

(7) A reference in this paragraph to a gift of more than a certain amount is to be read, in the case of a gift in a form other than money, as a reference to a gift with a value of more than that amount.

(8) Nothing in this paragraph requires an unincorporated association to report to the Commission

    (a) any gift that it has already reported to them under this paragraph, or

    (b) in the case of an association that at the relevant time was a members association within the meaning of Schedule 7, any gift that it is required to report to them under Part 3 of that Schedule.

Information to be included in reports under paragraph 2

3 (1) A report under paragraph 2 must give the following information in relation to each gift that is required to be specified

    (a) the date on which it was received;

    (b) the form that it took;

    (c) the amount or value of it;

    (d) whatever details the unincorporated association knows of the name and address of the person by whom the gift was made.

(2) Where paragraph 2(5) applies, each of the gifts of more than £500 mentioned in that provision is required to be specified separately for the purposes of sub-paragraph (1).

(3) Where a person ("P") makes a gift indirectly through one or more intermediaries, the reference in sub-paragraph (1)(d) to the person by whom the gift was made is to be read as a reference to P and each of the intermediaries.

Declaration by authorised individual

4   A notification under paragraph 1 or a report under paragraph 2 must contain a declaration, made by an individual authorised to do so by the unincorporated association concerned, that to the best of the individual's knowledge and belief
    (a) everything stated in the notification or report is accurate, and
    (b) the notification or report contains everything that it is required to contain by this Schedule.

Additional matters to be included in notifications and reports

5   A notification under paragraph 1 or a report under paragraph 2 must (as well as containing the things that paragraphs 1 and 4 or paragraphs 3 and 4 require it to contain)
    (a) state the name of the unincorporated association by which it is given;
    (b) state the address of the association's main office in the United Kingdom;
    (c) state the full name and address of the individual making the declaration under paragraph 4;
    (d) state that the individual is authorised by the unincorporated association to make the declaration;
    (e) describe the individual's role or position in relation to the association.

Offences

6 (1) An unincorporated association commits an offence if it
    (a) is required by paragraph 1 to give a notification to the Commission, or
    (b) is required by paragraph 2 to make a report to the Commission,
and fails without reasonable excuse to do so within the permitted period.

(2) An unincorporated association commits an offence if, without reasonable excuse, it
    (a) gives a notification to the Commission under paragraph 1, or
    (b) makes a report to the Commission under paragraph 2,
which fails to comply with any requirement of this Schedule applying to the notification or report.

(3) An individual who knowingly or recklessly makes a false declaration under paragraph 4 commits an offence.

(4) For the purposes of sub-paragraph (1) the "permitted period" is
    (a) in relation to a notification under paragraph 1, the period of 30 days mentioned in paragraph 1(1);
    (b) in relation to a notice under sub-paragraph (2) of paragraph 2, the period of 60 days mentioned in that sub-paragraph;
    (c) in relation to a notice under sub-paragraph (3) of paragraph 2, the period of 30 days mentioned in that sub-paragraph;
    (d) in relation to a notice under sub-paragraph (4) of paragraph 2, the period of 30 days mentioned in that sub-paragraph.

Register of recordable gifts to unincorporated associations

7 (1) The Commission shall maintain a register of all notifications made to them under paragraph 1 and all gifts reported to them under paragraph 2.

(2) The register shall be maintained by the Commission in such form as they may determine and shall contain the following details
    (a) in the case of each notification under paragraph 1
        (i)   the name of the unincorporated association by which the notification was given;
        (ii) the address of the association's main office in the United Kingdom;
        (iii) the date on which the notification was given;

    (b) in the case of each gift reported under paragraph 2
       (i)   the name of the unincorporated association by which the report was given;
       (ii) the address of the association's main office in the United Kingdom;
       (iii) (subject to sub-paragraph (4) and paragraph 8) the information provided under paragraph 3.

(3)   Where the Commission are given any notification under paragraph 1 or any report under paragraph 2, they shall cause the details mentioned in sub-paragraph (2)(a) (in respect of a notification) or sub-paragraph (2)(b) (in respect of a report) to be entered in the register as soon as is reasonably practicable.

(4)   The information to be entered in the register in respect of any individual shall not include the individual's home address.

8 (1) This paragraph applies where
    (a) an unincorporated association receives a gift in respect of which an entry falls to be made in the register under paragraph 7, and
    (b) at the time when the gift is received there is no entry in the register in respect of that unincorporated association.

(2)   The Commission shall not include in the register any information that would or might identify a person as someone by or through whom the gift was made unless
    (a) they have given to the person a notice stating that they propose to include such information, and inviting representations on the matter, and
    (b) they decide, having considered any representations made by the person, that it is reasonable to include such information in the register.

(3)   The Commission shall make reasonable efforts to give a notice under sub-paragraph (2)(a) in any case where, if a notice is not given, sub-paragraph (2) prevents information from being included in the register.

(4)   The Commission shall not make a decision on the matter referred to in sub-paragraph (2)(b) until after the period of 45 days beginning with the date on which they gave the notice under sub-paragraph (2)(a), unless representations from the person concerned are received before the end of that period.

(5)   Once they have made a decision on that matter the Commission shall give notification of it to the person concerned.

Meaning of "gift", etc

9 (1) In this Schedule "gift" includes bequest.

(2)   Anything given or transferred to any officer, member, trustee or agent of an unincorporated association in that person's capacity as such (and not for the person's own use or benefit) is to be regarded for the purposes of this Schedule as given or transferred to the association (and references to gifts received by an unincorporated association are to be read accordingly).

(3)   Regulations made by the Secretary of State may
    (a) make provision as to things that are, or are not, to be regarded as gifts to unincorporated associations for the purposes of this Schedule;
    (b) make provision as to how the value of a gift to an unincorporated association is to be calculated for the purposes of this Schedule.

(4)   Provision made under sub-paragraph (3)(a) may, in particular, provide for a person to be treated as making a gift where that person
    (a) pays expenses incurred by another;
    (b) lends money to another otherwise than on commercial terms;

(c)   provides any property, services or facilities for the use or benefit of another otherwise than on commercial terms;

(d)   transfers any money or other property for a consideration that is worth less than what is transferred (or for no consideration).

NOTES

Defined terms
  bequest: s 160(1)
  the Commission: s 160(1)
  controlled transaction: Sch 7A, para 2 (by virtue of
  para 1(2)(d) of this Schedule)
  donation: s 50, Sch 7, Pt I, paras 1(5), 2-4, Sch 11, Pt I,
  paras 1(5), 2-4, Sch 15, Pt I, paras 1(5), 2-4 (by virtue of
  para 1(2)(a), (c), (e), (f) of this Schedule)
  minor party: s 160(1)

property: s 160(1)
registered party: s 160(1)
regulated donee: Sch 7, Pt 1, para 1(7) (by virtue of
para 1(4) of this Schedule)
regulated transaction: s 71F (by virtue of para 1(2)(b))
the Secretary of State: s 159A

SCHEDULE 19B

INVESTIGATORY POWERS OF COMMISSION

Section 146

Power to require disclosure

1 (1)   This paragraph applies to the following organisations and individuals

(a)   a registered party or, in the case of a registered party with accounting units
   (i)   the central organisation of the party;
   (ii)   an accounting unit of the party;
(b)   a recognised third party (within the meaning of Part 6);
(c)   a permitted participant (within the meaning of Part 7);
(d)   a regulated donee (within the meaning of Schedule 7);
(e)   a regulated participant (within the meaning of Schedule 7A);
(f)   a candidate at an election (other than a local government election in Scotland);
(g)   the election agent for such a candidate;
(h)   an organisation or individual formerly falling within any of paragraphs (a) to (g).

(2)   The Commission may give a disclosure notice to a person who

(a)   is the treasurer or another officer of an organisation to which this paragraph applies, or has been at any time in the period of five years ending with the day on which the notice is given; or
(b)   is an individual to whom this paragraph applies.

(3)   A disclosure notice is a notice requiring the person to whom it is given

(a)   to produce, for inspection by the Commission or a person authorised by the Commission, any documents which
   (i)   relate to the income and expenditure of the organisation or individual in question, and
   (ii)   are reasonably required by the Commission for the purposes of carrying out their functions; or
(b)   to provide the Commission, or a person authorised by the Commission, with any information or explanation which relates to that income and expenditure and is reasonably required by the Commission for those purposes.

(4)   A person to whom a disclosure notice is given shall comply with it within such reasonable time as is specified in the notice.

Inspection warrants

2 (1)   This paragraph applies to the following organisations and individuals

    (a) a registered party or, in the case of a registered party with accounting units
       (i)   the central organisation of the party;
       (ii) an accounting unit of the party;
    (b) a recognised third party (within the meaning of Part 6);
    (c) a permitted participant (within the meaning of Part 7);
    (d) a members association (within the meaning of Schedule 7).

(2) A justice of the peace may issue an inspection warrant in relation to premises occupied by any such organisation or individual if satisfied, on information on oath given by or on behalf of the Commission, that
    (a) there are reasonable grounds for believing that on those premises there are documents relating to the income and expenditure of the organisation or individual,
    (b) the Commission need to inspect the documents for the purposes of carrying out functions of the Commission other than investigatory functions, and
    (c) permission to inspect the documents on the premises has been requested by the Commission and has been unreasonably refused.

(3) An inspection warrant is a warrant authorising a member of the Commission's staff
    (a) at any reasonable time to enter the premises specified in the warrant, and
    (b) having entered the premises, to inspect any documents within sub-paragraph (2)(a).

(4) An inspection warrant also authorises the person who executes the warrant to be accompanied by any other persons who the Commission consider are needed to assist in executing it.

(5) The person executing an inspection warrant must, if required to do so, produce
    (a) the warrant, and
    (b) documentary evidence that the person is a member of the Commission's staff,
for inspection by the occupier of the premises that are specified in the warrant or by anyone acting on the occupier's behalf.

(6) An inspection warrant continues in force until the end of the period of one month beginning with the day on which it is issued.

(7) An inspection warrant may not be used for the purposes of carrying out investigatory functions.

(8) In this paragraph "investigatory functions" means functions of investigating suspected offences under this Act or suspected contraventions of restrictions or requirements imposed by or by virtue of this Act.

(9) In the application of this paragraph to Scotland
    (a) a reference to a justice of the peace is to be read as a reference to a justice of the peace or a sheriff;
    (b) a reference to information on oath is to be read as a reference to evidence on oath.

Powers in relation to suspected offences or contraventions

3 (1) This paragraph applies where the Commission have reasonable grounds to suspect that
    (a) a person has committed an offence under this Act, or
    (b) a person has contravened (otherwise than by committing an offence) any restriction or other requirement imposed by or by virtue of this Act.
In this paragraph "the suspected offence or contravention" means the offence or contravention referred to above.

(2) The Commission may by notice require any person (including an organisation to which, or an individual to whom, paragraph 1 applies)

    (a) to produce, for inspection by the Commission or a person authorised by the Commission, any documents that they reasonably require for the purposes of investigating the suspected offence or contravention;

    (b) to provide the Commission, or a person authorised by the Commission, with any information or explanation that they reasonably require for those purposes.

(3) A person to whom a notice is given under sub-paragraph (2) shall comply with it within such reasonable time as is specified in the notice.

(4) A person authorised by the Commission ("the investigator") may require

    (a) the person mentioned in sub-paragraph (1), if that person is an individual, or

    (b) an individual who the investigator reasonably believes has relevant information,

to attend before the investigator at a specified time and place and answer any questions that the investigator reasonably considers to be relevant.

(5) In sub-paragraph (4) "relevant" means relevant to an investigation by the Commission of the suspected offence or contravention.

Court order for delivery of documents or provision of information etc

4 (1) This paragraph applies where the Commission have given a notice under paragraph 3 requiring documents to be produced.

(2) The High Court or (in Scotland) the Court of Session may make a document-disclosure order against a person ("the respondent") if satisfied on an application by the Commission that

    (a) there are reasonable grounds to suspect that a person (whether or not the respondent) has committed an offence under this Act or has contravened (otherwise than by committing an offence) any restriction or other requirement imposed by or by virtue of this Act, and

    (b) there are documents referred to in the notice under paragraph 3 which

        (i) have not been produced as required by the notice (either within the time specified in the notice for compliance or subsequently),

        (ii) are reasonably required by the Commission for the purposes of investigating the offence or contravention referred to in paragraph (a), and

        (iii) are in the custody or under the control of the respondent.

(3) A document disclosure order is an order requiring the respondent to deliver to the Commission, within such time as is specified in the order, such documents falling within sub-paragraph (2)(b) as are identified in the order (either specifically or by reference to any category or description of document).

(4) For the purposes of sub-paragraph (2)(b)(iii) a document is under a person's control if it is in the person's possession or if the person has a right to possession of it.

(5) A person who fails to comply with a document disclosure order may not, in respect of that failure, be both punished for contempt of court and convicted of an offence under paragraph 13(1).

5 (1) This paragraph applies where the Commission have given a notice under paragraph 3 requiring any information or explanation to be provided.

(2) The High Court or (in Scotland) the Court of Session may make an information disclosure order against a person ("the respondent") if satisfied on an application by the Commission that

(a) there are reasonable grounds to suspect that a person (whether or not the respondent) has committed an offence under this Act or has contravened (otherwise than by committing an offence) any restriction or other requirement imposed by or by virtue of this Act, and

(b) there is any information or explanation referred to in the notice under paragraph 3 which

    (i) has not been provided as required by the notice (either within the time specified in the notice for compliance or subsequently),

    (ii) is reasonably required by the Commission for the purposes of investigating the offence or contravention referred to in paragraph (a), and

    (iii) the respondent is able to provide.

(3) An information disclosure order is an order requiring the respondent to provide to the Commission, within such time as is specified in the order, such information or explanation falling within sub-paragraph (2)(b) as is identified in the order.

(4) A person who fails to comply with an information disclosure order may not, in respect of that failure, be both punished for contempt of court and convicted of an offence under paragraph 13(1).

Retention of documents delivered under paragraph 4

6 (1) The Commission may retain any documents delivered to them in compliance with an order under paragraph 4 for a period of three months (or for longer if any of following sub-paragraphs applies).
In this paragraph "the documents" and "the three-month period" mean the documents and the period mentioned above.

(2) If within the three-month period proceedings to which the documents are relevant are commenced against any person for any criminal offence, the documents may be retained until the conclusion of those proceedings.

(3) If within the three-month period the Commission serve a notice under paragraph 2(1) of Schedule 19C of a proposal to impose a fixed monetary penalty on any person and the documents are relevant to the decision to serve the notice, the documents may be retained

(a) until liability for the penalty is discharged as mentioned in paragraph 2(2) of that Schedule (if it is);

(b) until the Commission decide not to impose a fixed monetary penalty (if that is what they decide);

(c) until the end of the period given by sub-paragraph (5) (if they do impose a fixed monetary penalty).

(4) If within the three-month period the Commission serve a notice under paragraph 6(1) of Schedule 19C of a proposal to impose a discretionary requirement on any person and the documents are relevant to the decision to serve the notice, the documents may be retained

(a) until the Commission decide not to impose a discretionary requirement (if that is what they decide);

(b) until the end of the period given by sub-paragraph (5) (if they do impose a discretionary requirement).

(5) If within the three-month period

(a) a notice is served imposing a fixed monetary penalty on any person under paragraph 2(4) of Schedule 19C and the documents are relevant to the decision to impose the penalty, or

     (b) a notice is served imposing a discretionary requirement on any person under paragraph 6(5) of that Schedule and the documents are relevant to the decision to impose the requirement,

the documents may be retained until the end of the period allowed for bringing an appeal against that decision or (if an appeal is brought) until the conclusion of proceedings on the appeal.

(6) If within the three-month period

     (a) a stop notice is served on any person under paragraph 10 of Schedule 19C, and

     (b) the documents are relevant to the decision to serve the notice,

the documents may be retained until the end of the period allowed for bringing an appeal against that decision or (if an appeal is brought) until the conclusion of proceedings on the appeal.

(7) If within the three-month period or the period given by sub-paragraph (6) (or, if applicable, by sub-paragraph (4) or (5)(b))

     (a) the Commission, having served a stop notice on any person under paragraph 10 of Schedule 19C, decide not to issue a completion certificate under paragraph 12 of that Schedule in relation to the stop notice, and

     (b) the documents are relevant to the decision not to issue the certificate,

the documents may be retained until the end of the period allowed for bringing an appeal against that decision or (if an appeal is brought) until the conclusion of proceedings on the appeal.

Power to make copies and records

7   The Commission or a person authorised by the Commission

     (a) may make copies of, or make records of any information contained in

        (i)   any documents produced or inspected under this Schedule;

        (ii) any documents delivered to them in compliance with an order under paragraph 4;

     (b) may make copies or records of any information or explanation provided under this Schedule.

Authorisation to be in writing

8   An authorisation of a person by the Commission under this Schedule must be in writing.

Meaning of "documents"

9   In this Schedule "documents" includes any books or records.

Documents in electronic form

10 (1) In the case of documents kept in electronic form

     (a) a power of the Commission under this Schedule to require documents to be produced for inspection includes power to require a copy of the documents to be made available for inspection in legible form;

     (b) a power of a person ("the inspector") under this Schedule to inspect documents includes power to require any person on the premises in question to give any assistance that the inspector reasonably requires to enable the inspector

        (i)   to inspect and make copies of the documents in legible form or to make records of information contained in them, or

        (ii) to inspect and check the operation of any computer, and any associated apparatus or material, that is or has been in use in connection with the keeping of the documents.

(2) Paragraph 7(a) applies in relation to any copy made available as mentioned in sub-paragraph (1)(a) above.

Legal professional privilege

11 Nothing in this Schedule requires a person to produce or provide, or authorises a person to inspect or take possession of, anything in respect of which a claim to legal professional privilege (in Scotland, to confidentiality of communications) could be maintained in legal proceedings.

Admissibility of statements

12 (1) A statement made by a person ("P") in compliance with a requirement imposed under this Schedule is admissible in evidence in any proceedings (as long as it also complies with any requirements governing the admissibility of evidence in the circumstances in question).

(2) But in criminal proceedings in which P is charged with an offence other than one to which sub-paragraph (3) applies or in proceedings within sub-paragraph (4) to which both the Commission and P are parties

(a) no evidence relating to the statement is admissible against P, and

(b) no question relating to the statement may be asked on behalf of the prosecution or (as the case may be) the Commission in cross-examination of P,

unless evidence relating to it is adduced, or a question relating to it is asked, in the proceedings by or on behalf of P.

(3) This sub-paragraph applies to

(a) an offence under paragraph 13(3);

(b) an offence under section 5 of the Perjury Act 1911 (false statements made otherwise than on oath);

(c) an offence under section 44(2) of the Criminal Law (Consolidation) (Scotland) Act 1995 (false statements made otherwise than on oath);

(d) an offence under Article 10 of the Perjury (Northern Ireland) Order 1979 (false statements made otherwise than on oath).

(4) Proceedings are within this sub-paragraph if they arise out of the exercise by the Commission of any of their powers under Schedule 19C other than powers in relation to an offence under paragraph 13(3) below.

Offences

13 (1) A person who fails, without reasonable excuse, to comply with any requirement imposed under or by virtue of this Schedule commits an offence.

(2) A person who intentionally obstructs a person authorised by or by virtue of this Schedule in the carrying out of that person's functions under the authorisation commits an offence.

(3) A person who knowingly or recklessly provides false information in purported compliance with a requirement imposed under or by virtue of this Schedule commits an offence.

Guidance by Commission

14 (1) The Commission shall prepare and publish guidance as to

(a) the circumstances in which the Commission are likely to give a notice under paragraph 1 or 3(2);

(b)   the consequences (including criminal sanctions) that may result from a failure to comply with such a notice;

(c)   the circumstances in which the Commission are likely to apply for a warrant under paragraph 2;

(d)   the procedures to be followed in connection with questioning under paragraph 3(4);

(e)   the circumstances in which the Commission are likely to apply for an order under paragraph 4 or 5;

(f)   the principles and practices to be applied in connection with the exercise of powers under paragraphs 6 and 7;

(g)   any other matters concerning the exercise of powers under this Schedule about which the Commission consider that guidance would be useful.

(2)   Where appropriate, the Commission shall revise guidance published under this paragraph and publish the revised guidance.

(3)   The Commission shall consult such persons as they consider appropriate before publishing guidance or revised guidance under this paragraph.

(4)   The Commission shall have regard to the guidance or revised guidance published under this paragraph in exercising their functions.

Information about use of investigatory powers in Commission's annual report

15 (1)   Each report by the Commission under paragraph 20 of Schedule 1 shall contain information about the use made by the Commission of their powers under this Schedule during the year in question.

(2)   The report shall, in particular, specify

(a)   the cases in which a notice was given under paragraph 1 or 3(2);

(b)   the cases in which premises were entered under a warrant issued under paragraph 2;

(c)   the cases in which a requirement was imposed under paragraph 3(4);

(d)   the cases in which an order under paragraph 4 or 5
(i)   was applied for;
(ii)   was made.

(3)   This paragraph does not require the Commission to include in a report any information that, in their opinion, it would be inappropriate to include on the ground that to do so

(a)   would or might be unlawful, or

(b)   might adversely affect any current investigation or proceedings.

NOTES

Defined terms

accounting units: ss 26(11), 160(1)
central organisation: ss 26(11), 160(1)
the Commission: s 160(1)
contravention: s 160(1)
document: s 160(1)
functions: s 160(1)
local government election: s 160(1)
members association: Sch 7, para 1(6)
organisation: s 160(1)

party with accounting units: ss 26(11), 160(1)
permitted participant: s 105(1)
recognised third party: ss 85(5), 88
registered party: s 160(1)
regulated donee: Sch 7, Pt 1, para 1(7)
regulated participant: Sch 7A, para 1(5)
treasurer: s 160(1)

Schedule 19C
Civil Sanctions

Section 147

Part 1
Fixed Monetary Penalties

Imposition of fixed monetary penalties

1 (1) The Commission may by notice impose a fixed monetary penalty on a person if satisfied beyond reasonable doubt that the person
  (a) has committed a prescribed offence under this Act, or
  (b) has (otherwise than by committing an offence under this Act) contravened a prescribed restriction or requirement imposed by or by virtue of this Act.

(2) The Commission may by notice impose a fixed monetary penalty on a registered party if satisfied beyond reasonable doubt that a person holding an office within that party
  (a) has committed a prescribed offence under this Act, or
  (b) has (otherwise than by committing an offence under this Act) contravened a prescribed restriction or requirement imposed by or by virtue of this Act.

(3) The Commission may by notice impose a fixed monetary penalty on a recognised third party if satisfied beyond reasonable doubt that the responsible person
  (a) has committed a prescribed offence under this Act, or
  (b) has (otherwise than by committing an offence under this Act) contravened a prescribed restriction or requirement imposed by or by virtue of this Act.

(4) The Commission may by notice impose a fixed monetary penalty on a permitted participant if satisfied beyond reasonable doubt that the responsible person
  (a) has committed a prescribed offence under this Act, or
  (b) has (otherwise than by committing an offence under this Act) contravened a prescribed restriction or requirement imposed by or by virtue of this Act.

(5) For the purposes of this Schedule a "fixed monetary penalty" is a requirement to pay to the Commission a penalty of a prescribed amount.

(6) In the case of a fixed monetary penalty imposed under sub-paragraph (1)(a), (2)(a), (3)(a) or (4)(a), where the offence in question is
  (a) triable summarily (whether or not it is also triable on indictment), and
  (b) punishable on summary conviction by a fine (whether or not it is also punishable by a term of imprisonment),
the amount of the penalty may not exceed the maximum amount (if any) of that fine.

Representations and appeals etc

2 (1) Where the Commission propose to impose a fixed monetary penalty on a person, they shall serve on the person a notice of what is proposed.

(2) A notice under sub-paragraph (1) must offer the person the opportunity to discharge the person's liability for the fixed monetary penalty by payment of a prescribed sum (which must be less than or equal to the amount of the penalty).
The following provisions of this paragraph apply if the person does not do so.

(3) The person may make written representations and objections to the Commission in relation to the proposed imposition of the fixed monetary penalty.

(4) After the end of the period for making such representations and objections (see paragraph 3(2)) the Commission shall decide whether to impose the fixed monetary penalty.
If they decide to do so they shall serve on the person a notice imposing the penalty.

(5) The Commission may not impose a fixed monetary penalty on a person
 (a) if, taking into account (in particular) any matter raised by the person, the Commission are no longer satisfied as mentioned in paragraph 1(1), (2), (3) or (4) (as applicable);
 (b) in such other circumstances as may be prescribed.

(6) A person on whom a fixed monetary penalty is imposed may appeal against the decision to impose the penalty on the ground that
 (a) it was based on an error of fact,
 (b) it was wrong in law, or
 (c) it was unreasonable,
 or on such other grounds as may be prescribed.

(7) An appeal under sub-paragraph (6) is to (in England and Wales) the county court or (in Northern Ireland) a county court or (in Scotland) the sheriff.

Information to be included in notices under paragraph 2

3 (1) A notice under paragraph 2(1) must include information as to
 (a) the grounds for the proposal to impose the fixed monetary penalty;
 (b) the effect of payment of the sum referred to in paragraph 2(2);
 (c) the right to make representations and objections;
 (d) the circumstances in which the Commission may not impose the fixed monetary penalty.

(2) Such a notice must also specify
 (a) the period within which liability for the fixed monetary penalty may be discharged, and
 (b) the period within which representations and objections may be made.
 Neither period may be more than 28 days beginning with the day on which the notice is received.

(3) A notice under paragraph 2(4) must include information as to
 (a) the grounds for imposing the fixed monetary penalty;
 (b) how payment may be made;
 (c) the period within which payment may be made;
 (d) any early payment discounts or late payment penalties;
 (e) rights of appeal;
 (f) the consequences of nonpayment.

Fixed monetary penalties: criminal proceedings and conviction

4 (1) Where a notice under paragraph 2(1) is served on a person
 (a) no criminal proceedings for an offence under this Act may be instituted against the person in respect of the act or omission to which the notice relates before the end of the period within which the person's liability may be discharged as mentioned in paragraph 2(2) (see paragraph 3(2));
 (b) if the liability is so discharged, the person may not at any time be convicted of an offence under this Act in relation to that act or omission.

(2) A person on whom a fixed monetary penalty is imposed may not at any time be convicted of an offence under this Act in respect of the act or omission giving rise to the penalty.

NOTES

Defined terms
the Commission: s 160(1)
contravention: s 160(1)
permitted participant: s 105(1), Sch 19C, Pt 7, para 29

prescribed: Sch 19C, Pt 7, para 29
recognised third party: s 85(5), Sch 19C, Pt 7, para 29
registered party: s 160(1)
responsible person: ss 85(7), 105(2), Sch 19C, Pt 7,

Part 2
Discretionary Requirements

Imposition of discretionary requirements

5 (1) The Commission may impose one or more discretionary requirements on a person if satisfied beyond reasonable doubt that the person
    (a) has committed a prescribed offence under this Act, or
    (b) has (otherwise than by committing an offence under this Act) contravened a prescribed restriction or requirement imposed by or by virtue of this Act.

(2) The Commission may impose one or more discretionary requirements on a registered party if satisfied beyond reasonable doubt that a person holding an office within that party
    (a) has committed a prescribed offence under this Act, or
    (b) has (otherwise than by committing an offence under this Act) contravened a prescribed restriction or requirement imposed by or by virtue of this Act.

(3) The Commission may impose one or more discretionary requirements on a recognised third party if satisfied beyond reasonable doubt that the responsible person
    (a) has committed a prescribed offence under this Act, or
    (b) has (otherwise than by committing an offence under this Act) contravened a prescribed restriction or requirement imposed by or by virtue of this Act.

(4) The Commission may impose one or more discretionary requirements on a permitted participant if satisfied beyond reasonable doubt that the responsible person
    (a) has committed a prescribed offence under this Act, or
    (b) has (otherwise than by committing an offence under this Act) contravened a prescribed restriction or requirement imposed by or by virtue of this Act.

(5) For the purposes of this Schedule a "discretionary requirement" is
    (a) a requirement to pay a monetary penalty to the Commission of such amount as the Commission may determine,
    (b) a requirement to take such steps as the Commission may specify, within such period as they may specify, to secure that the offence or contravention does not continue or recur, or
    (c) a requirement to take such steps as the Commission may specify, within such period as they may specify, to secure that the position is, so far as possible, restored to what it would have been if the offence or contravention had not happened.

(6) Discretionary requirements may not be imposed on the same person on more than one occasion in relation to the same act or omission.

(7) In this Schedule
"variable monetary penalty" means such a requirement as is referred to in sub-paragraph (5)(a);
"non-monetary discretionary requirement" means such a requirement as is referred to in sub-paragraph (5)(b) or (c).

(8) In the case of a variable monetary penalty imposed under sub-paragraph (1)(a), (2)(a), (3)(a) or (4)(a), where the offence in question is
    (a) triable summarily only, and
    (b) punishable on summary conviction by a fine (whether or not it is also punishable by a term of imprisonment),
the amount of the penalty may not exceed the maximum amount of that fine.

Representations and appeals etc

6 (1) Where the Commission propose to impose a discretionary requirement on a person, they shall serve on the person a notice of what is proposed.

(2) A person served with a notice under sub-paragraph (1) may make written representations and objections to the Commission in relation to the proposed imposition of the discretionary requirement.

(3) After the end of the period for making such representations and objections (see paragraph 7(2)) the Commission shall decide whether
    (a) to impose the discretionary requirement, with or without modifications, or
    (b) to impose any other discretionary requirement that the Commission have power to impose under paragraph 5.

(4) The Commission may not impose a discretionary requirement on a person
    (a) if, taking into account (in particular) any matter raised by the person, the Commission are no longer satisfied as mentioned in paragraph 5(1), (2), (3) or (4) (as applicable);
    (b) in such other circumstances as may be prescribed.

(5) Where the Commission decide to impose a discretionary requirement on a person, they shall serve on the person a notice specifying what the requirement is.

(6) A person on whom a discretionary requirement is imposed may appeal against the decision to impose the requirement on the ground
    (a) that the decision was based on an error of fact,
    (b) that the decision was wrong in law,
    (c) in the case of a variable monetary penalty, that the amount of the penalty is unreasonable,
    (d) in the case of a non-monetary discretionary requirement, that the nature of the requirement is unreasonable, or
    (e) that the decision is unreasonable for any other reason,
    or on such other grounds as may be prescribed.

(7) An appeal under sub-paragraph (6) is to (in England and Wales) the county court or (in Northern Ireland) a county court or (in Scotland) the sheriff.

Information to be included in notices under paragraph 6

7 (1) A notice under paragraph 6(1) must include information as to
    (a) the grounds for the proposal to impose the discretionary requirement;
    (b) the right to make representations and objections;
    (c) the circumstances in which the Commission may not impose the discretionary requirement.

(2) Such a notice must also specify the period within which representations and objections may be made.
    That period may not be less than 28 days beginning with the day on which the notice is received.

(3) A notice under paragraph 6(5) must include information as to
    (a) the grounds for imposing the discretionary requirement;
    (b) where the discretionary requirement is a variable monetary penalty
        (i) how payment may be made,
        (ii) the period within which payment must be made, and
        (iii) any early payment discounts or late payment penalties;
    (c) rights of appeal;
    (d) the consequences of non-compliance.

Discretionary requirements: criminal conviction

8 (1) A person on whom a discretionary requirement is imposed may not at any time be convicted of an offence under this Act in respect of the act or omission giving rise to the requirement.

(2) Sub-paragraph (1) does not apply where
  (a) a non-monetary discretionary requirement is imposed on the person,
  (b) no variable monetary penalty is imposed on the person, and
  (c) the person fails to comply with the non-monetary discretionary requirement.

Failure to comply with discretionary requirements

9 (1) The Commission may by notice impose a monetary penalty (a "non-compliance penalty") on a person for failing to comply with a non-monetary discretionary requirement imposed on the person.

(2) Subject to any prescribed criteria, or any prescribed maximum or minimum amounts, the amount of a non-compliance penalty is to be such as the Commission may determine.

(3) A person served with a notice imposing a non-compliance penalty may appeal against the notice on the ground that the decision to serve the notice
  (a) was based on an error of fact,
  (b) was wrong in law, or
  (c) was unfair or unreasonable for any reason (for example because the amount is unreasonable),
  or on such other grounds as may be prescribed.

(4) An appeal under sub-paragraph (3) is to (in England and Wales) the county court or (in Northern Ireland) a county court or (in Scotland) the sheriff.

NOTES

Defined terms
  the Commission: s 160(1)
  contravention: s 160(1)
  modifications: s 160(1)
  permitted participant: s 105(1), Sch 19C, Pt 7, para 29
  prescribed: Sch 19C, Pt 7, para 29

recognised third party: s 85(5), Sch 19C, Pt 7, para 29
registered party: s 160(1)
responsible person: ss 85(1), 105(2), Sch 19C, Pt 7, para 29

Part 3
Stop Notices

Imposition of stop notices

10 (1) Where sub-paragraph (2) or (3) applies, the Commission may serve on a person a notice (a "stop notice") prohibiting the person from carrying on an activity specified in the notice until the person has taken the steps specified in the notice.

(2) This sub-paragraph applies where
  (a) the person is carrying on the activity,
  (b) the Commission reasonably believe that the activity as carried on by the person involves or is likely to involve the person
    (i) committing a prescribed offence under this Act, or
    (ii) contravening (otherwise than by committing an offence under this Act) a prescribed restriction or requirement imposed by or by virtue of this Act, and
  (c) the Commission reasonably believe that the activity as carried on by the person is seriously damaging public confidence in the effectiveness of the controls in

this Act on the income and expenditure of registered parties and others, or presents a significant risk of doing so.

(3) This sub-paragraph applies where

    (a) the person is likely to carry on the activity,

    (b) the Commission reasonably believe that the activity as carried on by the person will involve or will be likely to involve the person

        (i) committing a prescribed offence under this Act, or

        (ii) contravening (otherwise than by committing an offence under this Act) a prescribed restriction or requirement imposed by or by virtue of this Act, and

    (c) the Commission reasonably believe that the activity as likely to be carried on by the person will seriously damage public confidence in the effectiveness of the controls mentioned in sub-paragraph (2)(c), or will present a significant risk of doing so.

(4) The steps referred to in sub-paragraph (1) must be steps to secure that the activity is carried on or (as the case may be) will be carried on in a way that does not involve the person acting as mentioned in sub-paragraph (2)(b) or (3)(b).

Information to be included in stop notices

11 A stop notice must include information as to

    (a) the grounds for serving the notice;

    (b) rights of appeal;

    (c) the consequences of not complying with the notice.

Completion certificates

12 (1) Where, after the service of a stop notice on a person, the Commission are satisfied that the person has taken the steps specified in the notice, they shall issue a certificate to that effect (a "completion certificate").

(2) A stop notice ceases to have effect on the issue of a completion certificate relating to that notice.

(3) A person on whom a stop notice is served may at any time apply for a completion certificate.

The Commission shall make a decision whether to issue a completion certificate within 14 days of the day on which they receive such an application.

Appeals etc

13 (1) A person served with a stop notice may appeal against the decision to serve it on the ground that

    (a) the decision was based on an error of fact,

    (b) the decision was wrong in law,

    (c) the decision was unreasonable,

    (d) any step specified in the notice is unreasonable, or

    (e) the person has not acted as mentioned in paragraph 10(2)(b) or (3)(b) and would not have done so even if the stop notice had not been served,

or on such other grounds as may be prescribed.

(2) A person served with a stop notice may appeal against a decision not to issue a completion certificate on the ground that the decision

    (a) was based on an error of fact,

    (b) was wrong in law, or

    (c) was unfair or unreasonable,

or an such other grounds as may be prescribed.

(3) An appeal under sub-paragraph (1) or (2) is to (in England and Wales) the county court or (in Northern Ireland) a county court or (in Scotland) the sheriff.

Failure to comply with stop notice

14 A person served with a stop notice who does not comply with it is guilty of an offence.

NOTES

Defined terms
the Commission: s 160(1)
contravention: s 160(1)
registered party: s 160(1)

prescribed: Sch 19C, Pt 7, para 29

Part 4
Enforcement Undertakings

Enforcement Undertakings

15 (1) This paragraph applies where
    (a) the Commission have reasonable grounds to suspect that a person
        (i) has committed a prescribed offence under this Act, or
        (ii) has (otherwise than by committing an offence under this Act) contravened a prescribed restriction or requirement imposed by or by virtue of this Act,
    (b) the person offers an undertaking (an "enforcement undertaking") to take such action, within such period, as is specified in the undertaking,
    (c) the action so specified is
        (i) action to secure that the offence or contravention does not continue or recur,
        (ii) action to secure that the position is, so far as possible, restored to what it would have been if the offence or contravention had not happened, or
        (iii) action of a prescribed description, and
    (d) the Commission accept the undertaking.

(2) Unless the person has failed to comply with the undertaking or any part of it
    (a) the person may not at any time be convicted of an offence under this Act in respect of the act or omission to which the undertaking relates;
    (b) the Commission may not impose on the person any fixed monetary penalty that they would otherwise have power to impose by virtue of paragraph 1 in respect of that act or omission;
    (c) the Commission may not impose on the person any discretionary requirement that they would otherwise have power to impose by virtue of paragraph 5 in respect of that act or omission.

NOTES

Defined terms
the Commission: s 160(1)
contravention: s 160(1)
discretionary requirement: Sch 19C, Pt 2, para 5(5), Pt 7, para 29

fixed monetary penalty: Sch 19C, Pt 1, para 1(5), Pt 7, para 29
prescribed: Sch 19C, Pt 7, para 29

Part 5
Power to Make Supplementary Provision etc by Order

Supplementary orders: general

16 (1) The Secretary of State may by order (a "supplementary order")

(a) make provision (including transitional provision) supplementing that made by this Schedule;

(b) make provision that is consequential on or incidental to that made by this Schedule.

(2) The following provisions of this Part are not to be read as limiting the power conferred by sub-paragraph (1).

(3) A supplementary order may make provision amending, repealing or revoking an enactment (whenever passed or made).

Consultation

17 (1) Before making a supplementary order the Secretary of State shall consult the Commission and such other persons (if any) as the Secretary of State considers appropriate.

(2) If, as a result of any consultation required by sub-paragraph (1), it appears to the Secretary of State that it is appropriate substantially to change the whole or any part of the proposals, the Secretary of State shall undertake such further consultation with respect to the changes as the Secretary of State considers appropriate.

(3) If, before the day on which this Schedule comes into effect, any consultation was undertaken which, had it been undertaken after that day, would to any extent have satisfied the requirements of this paragraph, those requirements may to that extent be taken to have been satisfied.

Monetary penalties

18 (1) A supplementary order may make any of the following provision in relation to the power of the Commission to require a person to pay a fixed monetary penalty, a variable monetary penalty or a non-compliance penalty

(a) provision for early payment discounts;

(b) provision for the payment of interest or other financial penalties for late payment;

(c) provision for enforcement.

(2) Provision made by virtue of sub-paragraph (1)(b) must secure that the interest or other financial penalties for late payment do not in total exceed the amount of the penalty itself.

(3) Provision made by virtue of sub-paragraph (1)(c) may include

(a) provision for the Commission to recover the penalty, and any interest or other financial penalty for late payment, as a civil debt;

(b) provision for the penalty, and any interest or other financial penalty for late payment, to be recoverable, on the order of a court, as if payable under a court order.

(4) In relation to the power of the Commission to require a person to pay a fixed monetary penalty, a variable monetary penalty or a non-compliance penalty for failing to comply with a requirement or undertaking by the end of a particular period, a supplementary order may

(a) make provision under which the amount of the penalty is determined by reference to the length of time between the end of that period and the time of compliance;

(b) make provision for successive penalties to be payable in a case of continued failure to comply.

Enforcement undertakings

19 A supplementary order may make any of the following provision in relation to an enforcement undertaking

   (a) provision as to the procedure for entering into an undertaking;

   (b) provision as to the terms of an undertaking;

   (c) provision as to publication of an undertaking by the Commission;

   (d) provision as to variation of an undertaking;

   (e) provision as to circumstances in which a person may be regarded as having complied with an undertaking;

   (f) provision as to monitoring by the Commission of compliance with an undertaking;

   (g) provision as to certification by the Commission that an undertaking has been complied with;

   (h) provision for appeals against refusal to give such certification;

   (i) in a case where a person has given inaccurate, misleading or incomplete information in relation to an undertaking, provision for the person to be regarded as not having complied with it;

   (j) in a case where a person has complied partly but not fully with an undertaking, provision for that part compliance to be taken into account in the imposition of any criminal or other sanction on the person.

Extension of time for taking criminal proceedings

20 For the purposes of enabling criminal proceedings to be instituted against a person in respect of an offence under this Act

   (a) in the case referred to in paragraph 8(2), or

   (b) in a case where there has been a breach of an enforcement undertaking or any part of an enforcement undertaking,

a supplementary order may make provision extending any period within which such proceedings may be instituted.

Appeals

21 (1) A supplementary order may make any of the following provision in relation to an appeal in respect of the imposition of a requirement, or the service of a notice, under this Schedule

   (a) provision suspending the requirement or notice pending determination of the appeal;

   (b) provision as to the powers of the court to which the appeal is made;

   (c) provision as to how a sum payable in pursuance of a decision of that court is to be recoverable.

  (2) Provision made by virtue of sub-paragraph (1)(b) may in particular include provision conferring on the court to which the appeal is made

   (a) power to withdraw the requirement or notice;

   (b) power to confirm the requirement or notice;

   (c) power to take such steps as the Commission could take in relation to the act or omission giving rise to the requirement or notice;

   (d) power to remit the decision whether to confirm the requirement or notice, or any matter relating to that decision, to the Commission;

   (e) power to award costs or (in the case of a court in Scotland) expenses.

NOTES

Subordinate Legislation

Political Parties, Elections and Referendums (Civil Sanctions) Order 2010, SI 2010/2860.

Defined terms

the Commission: s 160(1)

Part 6
General and Supplemental

Combination of sanctions

22 (1)   The Commission may not serve on a person a notice under paragraph 2(1) (notice of proposed fixed monetary penalty) in relation to any act or omission in relation to which

(a)   a discretionary requirement has been imposed on that person, or

(b)   a stop notice has been served on that person.

(2)   The Commission may not serve on a person a notice under paragraph 6(1) (notice of proposed discretionary requirement), or serve a stop notice on a person, in relation to any act or omission in relation to which

(a)   a fixed monetary penalty has been imposed on that person, or

(b)   the person's liability for a fixed monetary penalty has been discharged as mentioned in paragraph 2(2).

Use of statements made compulsorily

23 (1)   The Commission must not take into account a statement made by a person in compliance with a requirement imposed under Schedule 19B in deciding whether

(a)   to impose a fixed monetary penalty on the person;

(b)   to impose a discretionary requirement on the person;

(c)   to serve a stop notice on the person.

(2)   Sub-paragraph (1)(a) or (b) does not apply to a penalty or requirement imposed in respect of an offence under paragraph 13(3) of Schedule 19B (providing false information in purported compliance with a requirement under that Schedule).

Unincorporated associations

24   Any amount that is payable under this Schedule by an unincorporated association shall be paid out of the funds of the association.

Guidance as to enforcement

25 (1)   The Commission shall prepare and publish guidance as to

(a)   the sanctions (including criminal sanctions) that may be imposed on a person who

(i)   commits an offence under this Act, or

(ii)   contravenes a restriction or requirement that is prescribed for the purposes of paragraph 1, 5, 10 or 15;

(b)   the action that the Commission may take in relation to such a person (whether by virtue of this Schedule or otherwise);

(c)   the circumstances in which the Commission are likely to take any such action.

(2)   The guidance must include guidance about the Commission's use of the power to impose a fixed monetary penalty, with information as to

(a)   the circumstances in which such a penalty may not be imposed;

(b)   the amount of such a penalty;

    (c)   how liability for such a penalty may be discharged and the effect of discharge;

    (d)   rights to make representations and objections and rights of appeal in relation to such a penalty.

(3)   The guidance must include guidance about the Commission's use of the power to impose a discretionary requirement, with information as to

    (a)   the circumstances in which such a requirement may not be imposed;

    (b)   rights to make representations and objections and rights of appeal in relation to such a requirement;

    (c)   in the case of a variable monetary penalty, the matters likely to be taken into account by the Commission in determining the amount of the penalty (including, where relevant, any discounts for voluntary reporting of non-compliance).

(4)   The guidance must include guidance about the Commission's use of the power to serve a stop notice, with information as to

    (a)   the circumstances in which such a notice may not be served;

    (b)   rights of appeal in relation to such a notice.

(5)   The guidance must include guidance about the Commission's use of the power to accept an enforcement undertaking.

(6)   Where appropriate, the Commission shall revise guidance published under this paragraph and publish the revised guidance.

(7)   The Commission shall consult such persons as they consider appropriate before publishing guidance or revised guidance under this paragraph.

(8)   The Commission shall have regard to the guidance or revised guidance published under this paragraph in exercising their functions.

Payment of penalties etc into Consolidated Fund

26   Where, in pursuance of any provision contained in or made under this Schedule, the Commission receive

    (a)   a fixed monetary penalty, a variable monetary penalty or a non-compliance penalty,

    (b)   any interest or other financial penalty for late payment of such a penalty, or

    (c)   a sum paid as mentioned in paragraph 2(2) (in discharge of liability for a fixed monetary penalty),

they shall pay it into the Consolidated Fund.

Reports on use of civil sanctions

27 (1)   Each report by the Commission under paragraph 20 of Schedule 1 shall contain information about the use made by the Commission of their powers under this Schedule during the year in question.

(2)   The report shall, in particular, specify

    (a)   the cases in which a fixed monetary penalty or discretionary requirement was imposed or a stop notice served (other than cases in which the penalty, requirement or notice was overturned on appeal);

    (b)   the cases in which liability for a fixed monetary penalty was discharged as mentioned in paragraph 2(2);

    (c)   the cases in which an enforcement undertaking was accepted.

(3)   This paragraph does not require the Commission to include in a report any information that, in their opinion, it would be inappropriate to include on the ground that to do so

    (a)   would or might be unlawful, or

(b) might adversely affect any current investigation or proceedings.

Disclosure of information

28 (1) Information held by or on behalf of
    (a) the Crown Prosecution Service,
    (b) a member of a police force in England and Wales,
    (c) a Procurator Fiscal,
    (d) a constable of the Police Service of Scotland,
    (e) the Public Prosecution Service for Northern Ireland, or
    (f) a member of the Police Service of Northern Ireland,
may be disclosed to the Commission for the purpose of the exercise by the Commission of any powers conferred on them under or by virtue of this Schedule.

(2) It is immaterial for the purposes of sub-paragraph (1) whether the information was obtained before or after the coming into effect of this Schedule.

(3) A disclosure under this paragraph is not to be taken to breach any restriction on the disclosure of information (however imposed).

(4) Nothing in this paragraph authorises the making of a disclosure in contravention of
    (a) the Data Protection Act 1998, or
    (b) Part 1 of the Regulation of Investigatory Powers Act 2000.

(5) This paragraph does not affect a power to disclose that exists apart from this paragraph.

NOTES

Defined terms
the Commission: s 160(1)
contravention: s 160(1)
discretionary requirement: Sch 19C, Pt 2, para 5(5), Pt 7, para 29
enforcement undertaking: Sch 19C, Pt 4, para 15(1)(b), Pt 7, para 29
fixed monetary penalty: Sch 19C, Pt 1, para 1(5), Pt 7, para 29

functions: s 160(1)
non-compliance penalty: Sch 19C, Pt 2, para 9(1), Pt 7, para 29
prescribed: Sch 19C, Pt 7, para 29
stop notice: Sch 19C, Pt 3, para 10(1), Pt 7, para 29
variable monetary penalty: Sch 19C, Pt 2, para 5(7), Pt 7, para 29

Part 7
Interpretation

Interpretation of Schedule

29 In this Schedule
"completion certificate" has the meaning given in paragraph 12(1);
"discretionary requirement" has the meaning given in paragraph 5(5);
"enforcement undertaking" has the meaning given in paragraph 15(1)(b);
"fixed monetary penalty" has the meaning given in paragraph 1(5);
"non-compliance penalty" has the meaning given in paragraph 9(1);
"non-monetary discretionary requirement" has the meaning given in paragraph 5(7);
"permitted participant" has the meaning given in section 105(1);
"prescribed" means prescribed in a supplementary order;
"recognised third party" has the meaning given in section 85(5);
"responsible person"
    (a) in relation to a recognised third party, has the meaning given in section 85(7);
    (b) in relation to a permitted participant, has the meaning given in section 105(2);
"stop notice" has the meaning given in paragraph 10(1);
"supplementary order" has the meaning given in paragraph 16(1);
"variable monetary penalty" has the meaning given in paragraph 5(7).

SCHEDULE 20
PENALTIES

Section 150

Provision creating offence	Penalty
Section 24(8) (registration as treasurer where convicted of certain offences)	On summary conviction: Level 5
Section 39 (false statements)	On summary conviction: Level 5
Section 43(7) (failure to deliver statement relating to auditor's resignation etc)	On summary conviction: statutory maximum or 6 months On indictment: fine or 1 year
Section 44(4) (making false statement to auditor)	On summary conviction: statutory maximum or 6 months On indictment: fine or 1 year
Section 47(1)(a) (failure to deliver proper statement of accounts)	On summary conviction: Level 5
Section 47(1)(b) (failure to deliver accounts within time limits)	On summary conviction: Level 5
Section 54(7) (failure to provide information about donors)	On summary conviction: statutory maximum or 6 months On indictment: fine or 1 year
Section 54A(5) (making a false declaration as to source of donation)	On summary conviction in England and Wales or Scotland: statutory maximum or 12 months On summary conviction in Northern Ireland: statutory maximum or 6 months On indictment: fine or 1 year
Section 54B(3) (making a false declaration as to whether residence etc condition satisfied)	On summary conviction in England and Wales or Scotland: statutory maximum or 12 months On summary conviction in Northern Ireland: statutory maximum or 6 months On indictment: fine or 1 year
Section 56*(3) or (4)* (3), (3B) or (4) (failure to return donations)	On summary conviction: statutory maximum or 6 months On indictment: fine or 1 year
Section 61(1) (facilitating the making of donations by impermissible donors)	On summary conviction: statutory maximum or 6 months On indictment: fine or 1 year
Section 61(2)(a) (knowingly giving treasurer false	On summary conviction: statutory

Provision creating offence	Penalty
information about donations)	maximum or 6 months
	On indictment: fine or 1 year
Section 61(2)(b) (withholding information about donations from treasurer with intent to deceive)	On summary conviction: statutory maximum or 6 months
	On indictment: fine or 1 year
Section 65(3) (failure to deliver donation reports to Commission within time limits)	On summary conviction: Level 5
Section 65(4) (failure to comply with requirements for recording donations in donation report)	On summary conviction: statutory maximum or 6 months
	On indictment: fine or 1 year
Section 66(5) (making a false declaration about donation report)	On summary conviction: statutory maximum or 6 months
	On indictment: fine or 1 year
Section 71HZA(5) (making a false declaration as to whether residence etc condition satisfied)	On summary conviction in England and Wales or Scotland: statutory maximum or 12 months
	On summary conviction in Northern Ireland: statutory maximum or 6 months
	On indictment: fine or 1 year
Section 71L(1) (registered party entering into regulated transaction with unauthorised participant)	On summary conviction: statutory maximum
	On indictment: fine
Section 71L(2) (treasurer of party entering into regulated transaction with unauthorised participant)	On summary conviction: statutory maximum or 12 months
	On indictment: fine or 1 year
Section 71L(3) (party liable if treasurer fails to repay money obtained under regulated transaction with unauthorised participant)	On summary conviction: statutory maximum
	On indictment: fine
Section 71L(4) (treasurer failing to repay money obtained under regulated transaction with unauthorised participant)	On summary conviction: statutory maximum or 12 months
	On indictment: fine or 1 year
Section 71L(5) (party benefiting from connected transaction to which an unauthorised participant is a party)	On summary conviction: statutory maximum
	On indictment: fine
Section 71L(6) (treasurer of registered party which	On summary conviction: statutory

Provision creating offence	Penalty
benefits from connected transaction to which an unauthorised participant is a party)	maximum or 12 months
	On indictment: fine or 1 year
Section 71L(7) (party liable if treasurer fails to repay benefit obtained in consequence of security given by unauthorised participant)	On summary conviction: statutory maximum
	On indictment: fine
Section 71L(8) (treasurer failing to repay benefit obtained in consequence of security given by unauthorised participant)	On summary conviction: statutory maximum or 12 months
	On indictment: fine or 1 year
Section 71L(9) (facilitating a regulated transaction involving unauthorised participant)	On summary conviction: statutory maximum or 12 months
	On indictment: fine or 1 year
Section 71S(4) (failure to deliver transaction reports to Commission within time limits)	On summary conviction: Level 5
Section 71S(5) (failure to comply with requirements for recording transactions in transaction report)	On summary conviction: statutory maximum or 12 months
	On indictment: fine or 1 year
Section 71T(5) (making a false declaration about transaction report)	On summary conviction: statutory maximum or 12 months
	On indictment: fine or 1 year
Section 73(8) (making a false declaration about value of property etc)	On summary conviction: statutory maximum or 6 months
	On indictment: fine or 1 year
Section 74(4) (acceptance by ineligible person of office of deputy treasurer)	On summary conviction: Level 5
Section 75(2) (incurring campaign expenditure without authority)	On summary conviction: Level 5
Section 76(4)(a) (making payments in respect of campaign expenditure without authority)	On summary conviction: Level 5
Section 76(4)(b) (failure to notify treasurer of payments in respect of campaign expenditure)	On summary conviction: Level 5
Section 77(3)(a) (paying claim in respect of campaign expenditure where failure to comply with procedure)	On summary conviction: Level 5
Section 77(3)(b) (paying claim in respect of campaign expenditure outside specified time period)	On summary conviction: Level 5
Section 79(2) (exceeding limits on campaign expenditure)	On summary conviction: statutory maximum

Provision creating offence	Penalty
	On indictment: fine
Section 82(4)(a) (failure of treasurer to deliver return and auditor's report to Commission)	On summary conviction: Level 5
Section 82(4)(b) (failure to comply with requirements for returns)	On summary conviction: statutory maximum or 6 months
	On indictment: fine or 1 year
Section 82(4)(c) (failure of treasurer to deliver return and court order to Commission)	On summary conviction: Level 5
Section 83(3)(a) (making a false declaration to Commission when delivering return)	On summary conviction: statutory maximum or 6 months
	On indictment: fine or 1 year
Section 83(3)(b) (failure to deliver signed declaration with return to Commission)	On summary conviction: statutory maximum or 6 months
	On indictment: fine or 1 year
Section 86(8) (making false declaration about value of property etc)	On summary conviction: statutory maximum or 6 months
	On indictment: fine or 1 year
Section 90(2) (incurring controlled expenditure without authority)	On summary conviction: Level 5
Section 91(4)(a) (making payments in respect of controlled expenditure without authority)	On summary conviction: Level 5
Section 91(4)(b) (failure to notify responsible person of payments in respect of controlled expenditure)	On summary conviction: Level 5
Section 92(3)(a) (paying claim in respect of controlled expenditure where failure to comply with procedure)	On summary conviction: Level 5
Section 92(3)(b) (paying claim in respect of controlled expenditure outside specified time period)	On summary conviction: Level 5
Section 94(2) or (4) (exceeding limits on controlled expenditure)	On summary conviction: statutory maximum
	On indictment: fine
Section 94E(2) or (3) (exceeding limits on targeted controlled expenditure when not authorised)	On summary conviction: statutory maximum
	On indictment: fine
Section 94F(6) (making false declaration about amount of expenditure incurred by or on behalf of third party and targeted at the registered party)	On summary conviction: statutory maximum or 6 months
	On indictment: fine or 1 year
Section 95C(1)(a) (failure of responsible person to deliver quarterly or weekly report to Commission)	On summary conviction: Level 5

Provision creating offence	Penalty
Section 95C(1)(b) (failure to deliver signed declaration with quarterly or weekly report to the Commission)	On summary conviction: statutory maximum or 6 months On indictment: fine or 1 year
Section 95C(1)(c) (failure to comply with requirements for quarterly or weekly reports)	On summary conviction: statutory maximum or 6 months On indictment: fine or 1 year
Section 95C(2) (making a false declaration to Commission when delivering quarterly or weekly report)	On summary conviction: statutory maximum or 6 months On indictment: fine or 1 year
Section 98(4)(a) (failure of responsible person to deliver return and auditor's report to Commission)	On summary conviction: Level 5
Section 98(4)(aa) (failure of responsible person to deliver statement of accounts and auditor's report to Commission)	On summary conviction: Level 5
Section 98(4)(b) (failure to comply with requirements for returns)	On summary conviction: statutory maximum or 6 months On indictment: fine or 1 year
Section 98(4)(ba) (failure to comply with requirements for statements of accounts)	On summary conviction: statutory maximum or 6 months On indictment: fine or 1 year
Section 98(4)(c) (failure to deliver return and court order to Commission)	On summary conviction: Level 5
Section 99(4)(a) (making a false declaration to Commission when delivering return)	On summary conviction: statutory maximum or 6 months On indictment: fine or 1 year
Section 99(4)(b) (failure to deliver signed declaration with return to Commission)	On summary conviction: statutory maximum or 6 months On indictment: fine or 1 year
Section 99A(3)(a) (making a false declaration to Commission when delivering statement of accounts)	On summary conviction: statutory maximum or 6 months On indictment: fine or 1 year
Section 99A(3)(b) (failure to deliver signed declaration with statement of accounts to Commission)	On summary conviction: statutory maximum or 6 months On indictment: fine or 1 year
Section 112(8) (making a false declaration about value of property etc)	On summary conviction: statutory maximum or 6 months On indictment: fine or 1 year

Provision creating offence	Penalty
Section 113(2) (incurring referendum expenses without authority)	On summary conviction: Level 5
Section 114(4)(a) (making payments in respect of referendum expenses without authority)	On summary conviction: Level 5
Section 114(4)(b) (failure to notify responsible person of payments in respect of referendum expenses)	On summary conviction: Level 5
Section 115(3)(a) (paying claim in respect of referendum expenses where failure to comply with procedure)	On summary conviction: Level 5
Section 115(3)(b) (paying claim in respect of referendum expenses outside specified time period)	On summary conviction: Level 5
Section 117(2) (individual (other than permitted participant) exceeding limits on referendum expenses)	On summary conviction: statutory maximum or 6 months On indictment: fine or 1 year
Section 117(3) or (4) (body (other than permitted participant) exceeding limits on referendum expenses)	On summary conviction: statutory maximum or 6 months On indictment: fine or 1 year
Section 118(2) (permitted participant exceeding limits on referendum expenses)	On summary conviction: statutory maximum On indictment: fine
Section 122(4)(a) (failure to deliver return and auditor's report to Commission)	On summary conviction: Level 5
Section 122(4)(b) (failure to comply with requirements for returns)	On summary conviction: statutory maximum or 6 months On indictment: fine or 1 year
Section 122(4)(c) (failure to deliver return and court order to Commission)	On summary conviction: Level 5
Section 123(4)(a) (making a false declaration to Commission when delivering return)	On summary conviction: statutory maximum or 6 months On indictment: fine or 1 year
Section 123(4)(b) (failure to deliver signed declaration with return to Commission)	On summary conviction: statutory maximum or 6 months On indictment : fine or 1 year
Section 126(8) or (9) (printing or publishing referendum material without details of printer or publisher)	On summary conviction: Level 5
Section 143(8) or (9) (printing or publishing election material without details of printer or publisher)	On summary conviction: Level 5

Provision creating offence	Penalty
Section 148(1) (alteration of documents etc)	On summary conviction: statutory maximum or 6 months
	On indictment: fine or 1 year
Section 148(2)(a) (failure to supply relevant person with information)	On summary conviction: Level 5
Section 148(2)(b) (supplying relevant person with false information)	On summary conviction: statutory maximum or 6 months
	On indictment: fine or 1 year
Section 148(3) (withholding information from relevant person with intent to deceive)	On summary conviction: statutory maximum or 6 months
	On indictment: fine or 1 year
Paragraph 1B of Schedule 7 (failure by members association to comply with requirement to appoint responsible person)	On summary conviction: Level 5
Paragraph 6A(5) of Schedule 7 (making a false declaration as to source of donation)	On summary conviction in England and Wales or Scotland: statutory maximum or 12 months
	On summary conviction in Northern Ireland: statutory maximum or 6 months
	On indictment: fine or 1 year
Paragraph 6B(3) of Schedule 7 (making a false declaration as to whether residence etc condition satisfied)	On summary conviction in England and Wales or Scotland: statutory maximum or 12 months
	On summary conviction in Northern Ireland: statutory maximum or 6 months
	On indictment: fine or 1 year
Paragraph 6(5) of Schedule 7 (failure to provide information about donors)	On summary conviction: statutory maximum or 6 months
	On indictment: fine or 1 year
Paragraph 12(1) of Schedule 7 (failure to deliver donation report to Commission within time limit)	On summary conviction: Level 5
Paragraph 12(2) of Schedule 7 (failure to comply with requirements for recording donations in donation reports)	On summary conviction: statutory maximum or 6 months
	On indictment: fine or 1 year
Paragraph 13(4) of Schedule 7 (making a false declaration about donation report)	On summary conviction: statutory maximum or 6 months
	On indictment: fine or 1 year
Paragraph 17(4) of Schedule 7 (knowingly giving	On summary conviction in England and

Provision creating offence	Penalty
compliance officer false information about donations)	Wales or Scotland: statutory maximum or 12 months
	On summary conviction in Northern Ireland: statutory maximum or 6 months
	On indictment: fine or 1 year
Paragraph 4A(5) of Schedule 7A (making a false declaration as to whether residence etc condition satisfied)	On summary conviction in England and Wales or Scotland: statutory maximum or 12 months
	On summary conviction in Northern Ireland: statutory maximum or 6 months
	On indictment: fine or 1 year
Paragraph 8(1) of Schedule 7A (individual regulated participant knowingly enters controlled transaction with unauthorised participant)	On summary conviction: statutory maximum or 12 months
	On indictment: fine or 1 year
Paragraph 8(2) of Schedule 7A (responsible person of members association which enters controlled transaction with unauthorised participant)	On summary conviction: statutory maximum or 12 months
	On indictment: fine or 1 year
Paragraph 8(3) of Schedule 7A (individual regulated participant failing to repay money obtained under controlled transaction with unauthorised participant)	On summary conviction: statutory maximum or 12 months
	On indictment: fine or 1 year
Paragraph 8(4) of Schedule 7A (responsible person failing to repay money obtained by members association under controlled transaction with unauthorised participant)	On summary conviction: statutory maximum or 12 months
	On indictment: fine or 1 year
Paragraph 8(5) of Schedule 7A (individual regulated participant knowingly benefits from connected transaction involving unauthorised participant)	On summary conviction: statutory maximum or 12 months
	On indictment: fine or 1 year
Paragraph 8(6) of Schedule 7A (responsible person of members association which knowingly benefits from connected transaction involving unauthorised participant)	On summary conviction: statutory maximum or 12 months
	On indictment: fine or 1 year
Paragraph 8(7) of Schedule 7A (individual regulated participant failing to repay value of benefit obtained in consequence of connected transaction	On summary conviction: statutory maximum or 12 months

Provision creating offence	Penalty
involving unauthorised participant)	On indictment: fine or 1 year
Paragraph 8(8) of Schedule 7A (responsible person failing to repay value of benefit obtained by members association in consequence of connected transaction involving unauthorised participant)	On summary conviction: statutory maximum or 12 months
	On indictment: fine or 1 year
Paragraph 8(9) of Schedule 7A (facilitating controlled transaction involving unauthorised participant)	On summary conviction: statutory maximum or 12 months
	On indictment: fine or 1 year
Paragraph 12(1) of Schedule 7A (failure to deliver transaction report to Commission within time limit)	On summary conviction: Level 5
Paragraph 12(2) of Schedule 7A (failure to comply with requirements for recording transactions on transaction reports)	On summary conviction: statutory maximum or 12 months
	On indictment: fine or 1 year
Paragraph 13(4) of Schedule 7A (making a false declaration about a transaction report)	On summary conviction: statutory maximum or 12 months
	On indictment: fine or 1 year
Paragraph 6(7) of Schedule 11 (failure to provide information about donors)	On summary conviction: statutory maximum or 6 months
	On indictment: fine or 1 year
Paragraph 6A(5) of Schedule 11 (making a false declaration as to source of donation)	On summary conviction in England and Wales or Scotland: statutory maximum or 12 months
	On summary conviction in Northern Ireland: statutory maximum or 6 months
	On indictment: fine or 1 year
Paragraph 6B(3) of Schedule 11 (making a false declaration as to whether residence etc condition satisfied)	On summary conviction in England and Wales or Scotland: statutory maximum or 12 months
	On summary conviction in Northern Ireland: statutory maximum or 6 months
	On indictment: fine or 1 year
Paragraph 6(8) of Schedule 15 (failure to provide information about donors)	On summary conviction: statutory maximum or 6 months
	On indictment: fine or 1 year
Paragraph 6A(5) of Schedule 15 (making a false	On summary conviction in England and

Provision creating offence	Penalty
declaration as to source of donation)	Wales or Scotland: statutory maximum or 12 months
	On summary conviction in Northern Ireland: statutory maximum or 6 months
	On indictment: fine or 1 year
Paragraph 6B(3) of Schedule 15 (making a false declaration as to whether residence etc condition satisfied)	On summary conviction in England and Wales or Scotland: statutory maximum or 12 months
	On summary conviction in Northern Ireland: statutory maximum or 6 months
	On indictment: fine or 1 year
Paragraph 6(1) of Schedule 19A (failure to give notification or report within specified period)	On summary conviction: Level 5
Paragraph 6(2) of Schedule 19A (giving notification or report that fails to comply with requirements of that Schedule)	On summary conviction in England and Wales or Scotland: statutory maximum or 12 months
	On summary conviction in Northern Ireland: statutory maximum or 6 months
	On indictment: fine or 1 year
Paragraph 6(3) of Schedule 19A (making false declaration in notification or report)	On summary conviction in England and Wales or Scotland: statutory maximum or 12 months
	On summary conviction in Northern Ireland: statutory maximum or 6 months
	On indictment: fine or 1 year
Paragraph 13(1) of Schedule 19B (failure to comply with investigation requirement)	On summary conviction: Level 5
Paragraph 13(2) of Schedule 19B (intentional obstruction of person exercising investigatory power)	On summary conviction: Level 5
Paragraph 13(3) of Schedule 19B (providing false information in purported compliance with investigation requirement)	On summary conviction in England and Wales or Scotland: statutory maximum or 12 months
	On summary conviction in Northern Ireland: statutory maximum or 6 months
	On indictment: fine or 1 year
Paragraph 14 of Schedule 19C (failure to comply with stop notice)	On summary conviction in England and Wales: fine or 12 months *or* On

Provision creating offence	Penalty
	summary conviction in Scotland: £20,000 or 12 months
	On summary conviction in Northern Ireland: £20,000 or 6 months
	On indictment: fine or 2 years

SCHEDULE 21

Not reproduced

SCHEDULE 22
REPEALS

Not reproduced

SCHEDULE 23
TRANSITIONAL PROVISIONS

Not reproduced

Public Order Act 1936

An Act to prohibit the wearing of uniforms in connection with political objects and the maintenance by private persons of associations of military or similar character; and to make further provision for the preservation of public order on the occasion of public processions and meetings and in public places

18th December 1936

Prohibition of uniforms in connection with political objects

1(1)   Subject as hereinafter provided, any person who in any public place or at any public meeting wears uniform signifying his association with any political organisation or with the promotion of any political object shall be guilty of an offence:
Provided that, if the chief officer of police is satisfied that the wearing of any such uniform as aforesaid on any ceremonial, anniversary, or other special occasion will not be likely to involve risk of public disorder, he may, with the consent of a Secretary of State, by order permit the wearing of such uniform on that occasion either absolutely or subject to such conditions as may be specified in the order.

(2)   Where any person is charged before any court with an offence under this section, no further proceedings in respect thereof shall be taken against him without the consent of the Attorney-General except such as are authorised by section 6 of the Prosecution of Offences Act 1979) so, however, that if that person is remanded in custody he shall, after the expiration of a period of eight days from the date on which he was so remanded, be entitled to be released on bail without sureties unless within that period the Attorney-General has consented to such further proceedings as aforesaid.

NOTES

Defined terms   public place: s 9(1)
    meeting: s 9(1)
    public meeting: s 9(1)

Prohibition of quasi-military organisations

2(1)   If the members or adherents of any association of persons, whether incorporated or not, are
       (a) organised or trained or equipped for the purpose of enabling them to be employed in usurping the functions of the police or of the armed forces of the Crown; or
       (b) organised and trained or organised and equipped either for the purpose of enabling them to be employed for the use or display of physical force in promoting any political object, or in such manner as to arouse reasonable apprehension that they are organised and either trained or equipped for that purpose;

then any person who takes part in the control or management of the association, or in so organising or training as aforesaid any members or adherents thereof, shall be guilty of an offence under this section:

Provided that in any proceedings against a person charged with the offence of taking part in the control or management of such an association as aforesaid it shall be a defence to that charge to prove that he neither consented to nor connived at the organisation, training, or equipment of members or adherents of the association in contravention of the provisions of this section.

(2) No prosecution shall be instituted under this section without the consent of the Attorney-General.

(3) If upon application being made by the Attorney-General it appears to the High Court that any association is an association of which members or adherents are organised, trained, or equipped in contravention of the provisions of this section, the Court may make such order as appears necessary to prevent any disposition without the leave of the Court of property held by or for the association and in accordance with rules of court may direct an inquiry and report to be made as to any such property as aforesaid and as to the affairs of the association and make such further orders as appear to the Court to be just and equitable for the application of such property in or towards the discharge of the liabilities of the association lawfully incurred before the date of the application or since that date with the approval of the Court, in or towards the repayment of moneys to persons who became subscribers or contributors to the association in good faith and without knowledge of any such contravention as aforesaid, and in or towards any costs incurred in connection with any such inquiry and report as aforesaid or in winding-up or dissolving the association, and may order that any property which is not directed by the Court to be so applied as aforesaid shall be forfeited to the Crown.

(4) In any criminal or civil proceedings under this section proof of things done or of words written, spoken or published (whether or not in the presence of any party to the proceedings) by any person taking part in the control or management of an association or in organising, training or equipping members or adherents of an association shall be admissible as evidence of the purposes for which, or the manner in which, members or adherents of the association (whether those persons or others) were organised, or trained, or equipped.

(5) If a judge of the High Court is satisfied by information on oath that there is reasonable ground for suspecting that an offence under this section has been committed, and that evidence of the commission thereof is to be found at any premises or place specified in the information, he may, on an application made by an officer of police of a rank not lower than that of inspector, grant a search warrant authorising any such officer as aforesaid named in the warrant together with any other persons named in the warrant and any other officers of police to enter the premises or place at any time within *one month* three months from the date of the warrant, if necessary by force, and to search the premises or place and every person found therein, and to seize anything found on the premises or place or on any such person which the officer has reasonable ground for suspecting to be evidence of the commission of such an offence as aforesaid:

Provided that no woman shall, in pursuance of a warrant issued under this subsection, be searched except by a woman.

(6) Nothing in this section shall be construed as prohibiting the employment of a reasonable number of persons as stewards to assist in the preservation of order at any public meeting held upon private premises, or the making of arrangements for that purpose or the instruction of the persons to be so employed in their lawful duties as such stewards, or their being furnished with badges or other distinguishing signs.

NOTES
Defined terms
    meeting: s 9(1)
    private premises: s 9(1)

public meeting: s 9(1)

Enforcement

7(1)   Any person who commits an offence under section two of this Act shall be liable on summary conviction to imprisonment for a term not exceeding six months or to a fine not exceeding the prescribed sum, or to both such imprisonment and fine, or, on conviction on indictment, to imprisonment for a term not exceeding two years or to a fine of any amount or to both such imprisonment and fine.

(2)   Any person guilty of any offence under this Act other than an offence under section 2 shall be liable on summary conviction to imprisonment for a term not exceeding three months or to a fine not exceeding level 4 on the standard scale, or to both such imprisonment and fine.

(3)   *Repealed*

Application to Scotland

8   This Act shall apply to Scotland subject to the following modifications:

(1)   Subsection (2) of section one and subsection (2) of section two of this Act shall not apply.

(2)   In subsection (3) of section two the Lord Advocate shall be substituted for the Attorney-General and the Court of Session shall be substituted for the High Court.

(3)   Subsection (5) of section two shall have effect as if for any reference to a judge of the High Court there were substituted a reference to the sheriff and any application for a search warrant under the said subsection shall be made by the procurator fiscal instead of such officer as is therein mentioned.

(4)   The power conferred on the sheriff by subsection (5) of section two, as modified by the last foregoing paragraph, shall not be exercisable by an honorary sheriff.

(5)   *Repealed*

(6)   *Repealed*

Interpretation, etc

9(1)   In this Act the following expressions have the meanings hereby respectively assigned to them, that is to say:

    "Meeting" means a meeting held for the purpose of the discussion of matters of public interest or for the purpose of the expression of views on such matters;

    "Private premises" means premises to which the public have access (whether on payment or otherwise) only by permission of the owner, occupier, or lessee of the premises;

    "Public meeting" includes any meeting in a public place and any meeting which the public or any section thereof are permitted to attend, whether on payment or otherwise;

    "Public place" includes any highway and any other premises or place to which at the material time the public have or are permitted to have access, whether on payment or otherwise;

    "Recognised corps" means a rifle club, miniature rifle club or cadet corps approved by a Secretary of State under the Firearms Acts 1920 to 1936, for the purposes of those Acts.

(2)   *Repealed*

(3) Any order made under this Act by a chief officer of police may be revoked or varied by a subsequent order made in like manner.

(4) The powers conferred by this Act on any chief officer of police may, in the event of a vacancy in the office or in the event of the chief officer of police being unable to act owing to illness or absence, be exercised by the person duly authorised in accordance with directions given by a Secretary of State to exercise those powers on behalf of the chief officer of police.

Recall of MPs Act 2015

An Act to make provision about the recall of members of the House of Commons; and for connected purposes.

26th March 2015

How an MP becomes subject to a recall petition process

772

How an MP becomes subject to a recall petition process

1(1)   An MP becomes subject to a recall petition process if
    (a)   the first, second or third recall condition has been met in relation to the MP, and
    (b)   the Speaker gives notice of that fact under section 5.

(2)   In this Act "recall petition" means a petition calling
    (a)   for an MP to lose his or her seat in the House of Commons, and
    (b)   for a by-election to be held to decide who should be the MP for the constituency in question.

(3)   The first recall condition is that
    (a)   the MP has, after becoming an MP, been convicted in the United Kingdom of an offence and sentenced or ordered to be imprisoned or detained, and
    (b)   the appeal period expires without the conviction, sentence or order having being overturned on appeal.
    Sections 2 to 4 contain more about the first recall condition.

(4)   The second recall condition is that, following on from a report from the Committee on Standards in relation to the MP, the House of Commons orders the suspension of the MP from the service of the House for a specified period of the requisite length.

(5)   A specified period is "of the requisite length" for the purposes of subsection (4) if
    (a)   where the period is expressed as a number of sitting days, the period specified is of at least 10 sitting days, or
    (b)   in any other case, the period specified (however expressed) is a period of at least 14 days.

(6)   For the purposes of subsection (4) it does not matter
    (a)   when the period of suspension starts, and
    (b)   where that period is expressed as a number of sitting days, what provision (if any) is made by the House regarding what does, or does not, count as a sitting day for the purpose of calculating that period.

(7)   The reference in subsection (4) to the Committee on Standards is to any committee of the House of Commons concerned with the standards of conduct of individual members of that House.

(8)   Any question arising under subsection (7) is to be determined by the Speaker.

(9)   The third recall condition is that
    (a)   the MP has, after becoming an MP, been convicted of an offence under section 10 of the Parliamentary Standards Act 2009 (offence of providing false or misleading information for allowances claims), and
    (b)   the appeal period expires without the conviction having been overturned on appeal.
    Sections 2 to 4 contain more about the third recall condition.

(10)   The provision made by or under this Act does not affect other ways in which an MP's seat may be vacated, whether
    (a)   by the MP's disqualification for example, under the Representation of the People Act 1981 (disqualification of certain offenders), or
    (b)   by the MP's death or otherwise.

(11)   The loss by an MP of his or her seat under this Act as a result of a recall petition does not prevent him or her standing in the resulting by-election.

NOTES

Defined terms
  MP: s 22(1)

overturned on appeal: s 22(1)
the Speaker: s 22(1)

The first and third recall conditions: further provision

2(1)   In section 1(3) and (9) (the first and third recall conditions)

   (a)   the reference to an offence includes an offence committed before the MP became an MP and an offence committed before the day on which section 1 comes into force, but

   (b)   the reference to an MP being convicted of an offence is only to an MP being convicted of an offence on or after the day on which section 1 comes into force.

   (2)   The reference in section 1(3) to an offence does not include an offence mentioned in section 1(9).

   (3)   The reference in section 1(3) to an MP being sentenced or ordered

   (a)   includes the MP being sentenced or ordered where the sentence or order is suspended,

   (b)   does not include the MP being remanded in custody, and

   (c)   does not include the MP being authorised to be detained under mental health legislation if there is no sentence or order for imprisonment or detention other than under that legislation.

   (4)   "Mental health legislation" means

   (a)   the Mental Health Act 1983,

   (b)   Part 6 or section 200(2)(b) of the Criminal Procedure (Scotland) Act 1995, or

   (c)   the Mental Health (Northern Ireland) Order 1986 (SI 1986/595 (N.I. 4)).

   (5)   For the purposes of this Act the time at which a person becomes an MP is the beginning of the day after

   (a)   the polling day for the parliamentary election at which the person is elected as an MP, or

   (b)   where the person has been elected as an MP more than once, the polling day for the parliamentary election at which the person was last so elected.

NOTES
Defined terms
   MP: s 22(1)

The first and third recall conditions: expiry of appeal period

3(1)   For the purposes of section 1(3) and (9) (the first and third recall conditions), the appeal period expires at the earliest time at which

   (a)   it is no longer possible for there to be a relevant appeal, and

   (b)   all relevant appeals have been determined or otherwise disposed of.

   (2)   "Relevant appeal", in relation to the first recall condition, means

   (a)   an appeal that

   (i)   is in respect of the conviction, sentence or order mentioned in section 1(3), and

   (ii)   is brought within the usual period, or

   (b)   an appeal that

   (i)   is in respect of the determination of an appeal that was itself a relevant appeal, and

   (ii)   is brought within the period of 28 days beginning with the date of that determination or, if it ends earlier, the usual period.

   (3)   "Relevant appeal", in relation to the third recall condition, means

   (a)   an appeal that

   (i)   is in respect of the conviction mentioned in section 1(9) or of any sentence or order imposed in relation to that conviction, and

   (ii)   is brought within the usual period, or

(b) an appeal that
  (i)   is in respect of the determination of an appeal that was itself a relevant appeal, and
  (ii) is brought within the period of 28 days beginning with the date of that determination or, if it ends earlier, the usual period.

(4) References in this section to an appeal being brought within the usual period are to the appeal being brought within the period allowed for bringing an appeal of the kind in question, disregarding the possibility of an appeal out of time with permission.

(5) References in this section to an appeal
  (a) are to an appeal to a court in the United Kingdom;
  (b) include an application (and accordingly references to an appeal being brought include an application being made);
  (c) include an appeal under paragraph 13(a) of Schedule 6 to the Scotland Act 1998, paragraph 31(a) of Schedule 10 to the Northern Ireland Act 1998 or paragraph 21(a) of Schedule 9 to the Government of Wales Act 2006 (appeal against a determination, in proceedings in Scotland, of a Scottish, Northern Irish or Welsh devolution issue), or an appeal under section 288AA of the Criminal Procedure (Scotland) Act 1995 (appeal on compatibility issues);
  (d) do not include a reference under Part 2 of the Criminal Appeal Act 1995 (the Criminal Cases Review Commission) or Part 10A of the Criminal Procedure (Scotland) Act 1995 (the Scottish Criminal Cases Review Commission), or a petition to the nobile officium.

(6) References in this section to the determination of an appeal are, where the court to which the appeal is brought remits the matter to another court, to the disposal of the proceedings by that other court.

The first and third recall conditions: courts to notify the Speaker

4(1) This section applies if an MP, after becoming an MP
  (a) is convicted in the United Kingdom of an offence and sentenced or ordered to be imprisoned or detained within the meaning of section 1(3) (see section 2), or
  (b) is convicted of an offence mentioned in section 1(9) within the meaning of that provision (see section 2).

(2) The court that imposes the sentence or order in relation to the conviction must notify the Speaker
  (a) of the conviction and of the sentence or order, and
  (b) whether an appeal may be brought in respect of the conviction, sentence or order.

(3) Subsections (4) to (6) apply in a case in which an appeal is brought in respect of the conviction, sentence or order (including from a court that determines or otherwise disposes of such an appeal).

(4) The court to which the appeal is brought must notify the Speaker that an appeal has been brought in respect of the conviction, sentence or order.

(5) Where the appeal is determined or otherwise disposed of, the relevant court must notify the Speaker
  (a) that the appeal has been determined or otherwise disposed of,
  (b) that
    (i)   in a case within subsection (1)(a), the conviction, sentence or order has, or has not, been overturned on appeal;
    (ii) in a case within subsection (1)(b), the conviction has, or has not, been overturned on appeal, and

(c) whether any further appeal may be brought in respect of the conviction, sentence or order.

(6) "The relevant court" means

    (a) the court to which the appeal is brought, or

    (b) if that court remits the matter to another court, that other court.

(7) Section 3(5) and (6) (interpretation of references to an appeal and to the determination of an appeal) apply in relation to this section as they apply in relation to section 3, except that references in this section to an appeal do include a petition to the nobile officium.

(8) A court is not required under this section to notify the Speaker if, at any time since the application of the section, the MP's seat has been vacated (whether by the MP's disqualification or death, or otherwise).

NOTES

Defined terms

  appeal: s 3(6) (by virtue of sub-s (7))

  determination of an appeal: s 3(7) (by virtue of sub-s (7))

  duty to notify: s 22(5)

  MP: s 22(1)

  overturned on appeal: s 22(1)

  the Speaker: s 22(1)

  time at which a person becomes an MP: s 2(5)

Speaker's notice that first, second or third recall condition has been met

5(1) As soon as reasonably practicable after becoming aware that the first, second or third recall condition has been met in relation to an MP, the Speaker must give notice of that fact to the petition officer for the MP's constituency.

(2) But subsection (1) does not apply if it would require the Speaker to give notice at a time

    (a) within the period of 6 months ending with the polling day for the next parliamentary general election,

    (b) when the MP is already subject to a recall petition process, or

    (c) when the MP's seat has already been vacated (whether by the MP's disqualification or death, or otherwise).

(3) For the purposes of subsection (2)(a), the possibility that, after the time mentioned in that subsection, the polling day for a parliamentary general election will be altered by virtue of section 1(5) or 2(7) of the Fixedterm Parliaments Act 2011 is to be disregarded.

(4) For the purposes of subsection (2)(b), an MP is "subject to a recall petition process" during the period beginning with the giving of a notice under this section in relation to the MP and ending with

    (a) the receipt by the petition officer of a notice under section 13(6) (early termination of recall petition process) in relation to the recall petition in question, or

    (b) the giving by the petition officer of a notice under section 14(2)(b) (determination of whether recall petition successful) of the outcome of that recall petition.

(5) A notice under this section

    (a) must specify the day on which it is given,

    (b) must specify which of the recall conditions has been met in relation to the MP, and

    (c) in a case in which the first recall condition has been met, must specify the offence of which the MP has been convicted.

(6) For the purposes of this Act, a notice under this section

    (a) is to be treated as given on the day specified in it under subsection (5)(a), and

(b) is to be treated as received by the petition officer on the first working day after the day on which it is given.

(7) References in this Act to a "Speaker's notice" are to a notice under this section.

NOTES

Defined terms
  duty to notify: s 22(5)
  MP: s 22(1)
  petition officer: ss 6(2), 22(1)
  recall petition: ss 1(2), 22(1)

the Speaker: s 22(1)
working day: s 22(1)

Conduct of the Recall Petition Process

Petition officers

6(1) There is to be a petition officer in relation to a recall petition for each constituency as determined as follows

Location of constituency	Identity of petition officer
England or Wales	The person who is the acting returning officer in relation to the constituency by virtue of section 28 of the Representation of the People Act 1983 (discharge of returning officer's functions in England and Wales).
Scotland	The person who is the returning officer in relation to the constituency by virtue of section 25 of that Act (returning officers: Scotland).
Northern Ireland	The Chief Electoral Officer for Northern Ireland.

(2) References in this Act to a petition officer are to a petition officer under this section.

(3) Schedule 1 contains more about petition officers.

NOTES

Defined terms
  recall petition: ss 1(2), 22(1)

Where and from when the recall petition may be signed

7(1) Where the petition officer for a constituency receives a Speaker's notice, the officer must, as soon as reasonably practicable, designate
  (a) a place, or places, at which a recall petition is to be made available for signing, and
  (b) a day from which the petition is to be made available for signing.

(2) A maximum of 10 places may be designated under subsection (1)(a).

(3) The petition officer must, in determining which place or places to designate under subsection (1)(a), seek to ensure
  (a) that all persons entitled to sign the recall petition have such reasonable facilities for signing it as are practicable in the circumstances, and
  (b) that, so far as is reasonable and practicable, every place designated is accessible to disabled persons.

(4) The petition officer must designate under subsection (1)(b)
  (a) the day which is the 10th working day after the day on which the officer received the Speaker's notice, or
  (b) if it is not reasonably practicable to designate that day, the first subsequent working day that it is reasonably practicable to designate.

(5)   In this Act
"the designated place or places" means the place or places designated under subsection (1)(a);
"the designated day" means the day designated under subsection (1)(b).

Notice of petition to be sent to registered electors

8(1)   As soon as reasonably practicable after determining the designated place or places and the designated day under section 7, the petition officer must send a notice of petition in accordance with regulations under section 18
  (a)   to such descriptions of persons registered in the register of parliamentary electors for the constituency as are to be specified in such regulations, and
  (b)   to such other descriptions of persons as may be specified in such regulations.

(2)   Regulations under section 18 must require the notice to contain information relating to the recall condition which has been met in relation to the MP.

Recall petition to be made available for signing

9(1)   The petition officer must ensure that the recall petition is made available for signing throughout the signing period at the designated place or places, and by post, in accordance with regulations under section 18.

(2)   In this Act "the signing period" means the period of 6 weeks beginning with the designated day.

(3)   The recall petition is made available for signing at the designated place or places, or by post, by a separate petition signing sheet being available for signing by each person entitled to sign the petition at that place, or by post, in accordance with regulations under section 18.

(4)   The wording of a petition signing sheet must include the following
"By signing in the box below, you are signing a petition for *name of the MP,* the MP for *name of constituency,* to lose *his/her* seat in the House of Commons, and for a by-election to be held to decide who should be the MP for that constituency. The loss of *his/her* seat does not prevent the MP standing in this by-election.
If at least 10% of eligible registered electors in the constituency sign the petition, the MP will lose *his/her* seat in the House of Commons and a by-election will be held for the constituency. If less than 10% of eligible registered electors in the constituency sign the petition, the MP will not lose *his/her* seat as a result of the petition and therefore no by-election will be held."

(5)   The Minister may by regulations amend subsection (4).

(6)   Regulations under subsection (5) are subject to affirmative resolution procedure.

petition officer: ss 6(2), 22(1)
recall petition: ss 1(2), 22(1)
signing of a recall petition: ss 11(4), 22(4)

Persons entitled to sign a recall petition

10(1)   A person is entitled to sign a recall petition on a day during the signing period if, on that day

(a)   the person is registered in the register of parliamentary electors for the constituency,

(b)   the person is aged 18 or over, or the date of his or her 18th birthday is before the end of the signing period, and

(c)   the person would be entitled to vote as an elector at a parliamentary election in the constituency.

(2)   Any alteration made to the register of parliamentary electors for the constituency which takes effect

(a)   after the day on which the Speaker's notice is given, and

(b)   on or before the cut-off day,

does not have effect for the purposes of subsection (1)(a) if it results from a late application for registration.

(3)   Any alteration made to the register of parliamentary electors for the constituency which takes effect after the cut-off day does not have effect for the purposes of subsection (1)(a) unless it takes effect under section 13BC(6) of the Representation of the People Act 1983 (alterations for court orders or errors).

(4)   For the purposes of this Act

(a)   "the cut-off day" means the 3rd working day before the beginning of the signing period, and

(b)   "late application for registration" means an application for registration that

(i)   is made after the day on which the Speaker's notice is given, or

(ii)   is treated as made by virtue of section 10A(2) of the Representation of the People Act 1983 (return of canvass form treated as application for registration) in respect of a form returned after that day.

(5)   For the purposes of subsection (1)(c), section 1(1)(a) and (d) of the Representation of the People Act 1983 (requirement to be registered and of voting age) are to be disregarded.

(6)   Schedule 2 inserts section 13BC of the Representation of the People Act 1983 and makes other amendments relating to the alteration of registers of parliamentary electors.

NOTES

Defined terms
  recall petition: ss 1(2), 22(1)
  register of parliamentary electors: s 22(2), (3)
  signing of a recall petition: ss 11(4), 22(4)
  the signing period: ss 9(2), 22(1)

Speaker's notice: ss 5(7), 22(1)
working day: s 22(1)

How entitlement to sign a recall petition is to be exercised

11(1)   A person who is entitled to sign a recall petition may sign it

(a)   in person,

(b)   by post, or

(c)   by proxy,

subject to meeting the requirements of regulations under section 18 about signing it by that method.

(2)   A person who is entitled to sign a recall petition may sign it only once.

(3) Once a recall petition has been signed, the signature cannot be withdrawn.

(4) Unless stated otherwise, references in this Act (however expressed) to the signing of a recall petition by a person are to the person signing it by any of the methods mentioned in subsection (1) otherwise than as a proxy for another person.

NOTES
Defined terms
  recall petition: ss 1(2), 22(1)

Double signing

12(1) A person commits an offence if the person signs the same recall petition, otherwise than by proxy, more than once.

(2) A person commits an offence if the person signs a recall petition in person or by post knowing that a person appointed to sign the petition as his or her proxy
  (a) has already signed the petition in person as his or her proxy, or
  (b) in accordance with provision made by regulations under section 18, is entitled to sign the petition as his or her proxy by post.

(3) A person commits an offence if the person signs the same recall petition as proxy for the same person more than once.

(4) A person commits an offence if the person signs a recall petition as proxy for another person knowing that the other person has already signed the petition in person or by post.

(5) An offence under this section is treated
  (a) for the purposes of section 169 of the Representation of the People Act 1983 (mode of prosecution and penalty for illegal practices) as an illegal practice,
  (b) for the purposes of section 173 of that Act (incapacities on conviction of corrupt or illegal practice) as an illegal practice under section 61 of that Act (other voting offences),
  (c) for the purposes of section 178 of that Act (prosecution of offences committed outside the United Kingdom) as an offence under that Act, and
  (d) for the purposes of section 112 of the Electoral Law Act (Northern Ireland) 1962 (c 14 (N.I.)) (incapacities on conviction of corrupt or illegal practice) as an illegal practice under paragraph 12A of Schedule 9 to that Act (other voting offences).

(6) The court before which a person is convicted of an offence under this section may, if it thinks it just in the special circumstances of the case, mitigate or entirely remit any incapacity imposed by virtue of
  (a) section 173 of the Representation of the People Act 1983, or
  (b) section 112 of the Electoral Law Act (Northern Ireland) 1962.

Early Termination of Recall Petition Process

NOTES
Defined terms
  recall petition: ss 1(2), 22(1)
  signing of a recall petition: ss 11(4), 22(4)

Early termination of recall petition process

13(1) This section applies where any of the following conditions is met at any time after the Speaker's notice is given but before notice of the outcome of the recall petition has been given under section 14(2)(b).

(2) The first condition is that

(a) the polling day for the next parliamentary general election is brought forward by virtue of section 2(7) of the Fixedterm Parliaments Act 2011, and

(b) the new day is within the period of 6 months beginning with the day on which the Speaker's notice was given.

(3) The second condition is that the MP's seat is vacated (whether by the MP's disqualification or death, or otherwise).

(4) The third condition is that, in a case in which the first recall condition was met in relation to the MP, the conviction, sentence or order in question is overturned on appeal.

(5) The fourth condition is that, in a case in which the third recall condition was met in relation to the MP, the conviction in question is overturned on appeal.

(6) As soon as reasonably practicable after becoming aware that this section applies, the Speaker must notify the petition officer that the section applies, specifying which of the conditions above has been met.

(7) On the petition officer receiving a notice under subsection (6)

(a) sections 7 to 11 cease to apply in relation to the recall petition, and

(b) no further action is to be taken under or by virtue of this Act in relation to the process relating to the signing of the recall petition except

(i) the action required under subsection (8), and

(ii) any action which may be required or permitted by regulations under section 18 in relation to the termination of that process.

(8) As soon as reasonably practicable after receiving a notice under subsection (6), the petition officer must

(a) take such steps as the officer considers necessary to terminate the process relating to the signing of the recall petition, and

(b) give a public notice of the termination of that process in accordance with regulations under section 18.

(9) The Speaker must lay before the House of Commons any notice given under subsection (6).

NOTES

Defined terms
duty to notify: s 22(5)
MP: s 22(1)
overturned on appeal: s 22(1)
petition officer: ss 6(2), 22(1)
recall petition: ss 1(2), 22(1)

signing of a recall petition: ss 11(4), 22(4)
the Speaker: s 22(1)
Speaker's notice: ss 5(7), 22(1)

Outcome of Recall Petition

Determination of whether recall petition successful

14(1) This section applies unless the petition officer has received a notice under section 13(6) (early termination of recall petition process).

(2) As soon as reasonably practicable after the end of the signing period, the petition officer must

(a) determine whether the recall petition was successful,

(b) notify the Speaker that the recall petition was successful or unsuccessful, as the case may be, and

(c) having done that, give a public notice of the outcome of the recall petition in accordance with regulations under section 18.

(3)　For the purposes of this Act, a recall petition is successful if the number of persons who validly sign the petition is at least 10% of the number of eligible registered electors.

　　"The number of eligible registered electors" is the number of persons registered in the register of parliamentary electors for the constituency on the last day of the signing period excluding those who, according to their entry in the register, are aged under 18 on that day.

(4)　Any alteration made to the register of parliamentary electors for the constituency which takes effect

　　(a)　after the day on which the Speaker's notice is given, and

　　(b)　on or before the cut-off day,

does not have effect for the purposes of subsection (3) if it results from a late application for registration.

(5)　Any alteration made to the register of parliamentary electors for the constituency which takes effect after the cut-off day does not have effect for the purposes of subsection (3) unless it takes effect under section 13BC(6) of the Representation of the People Act 1983 (alterations for court orders or errors).

(6)　For the purposes of subsection (3), a person validly signs a recall petition if

　　(a)　the person signs the petition on a day during the signing period on which the person is entitled to do so under section 10,

　　(b)　the person has not previously signed the petition,

　　(c)　each condition (if any) imposed by regulations under section 18 of the kind mentioned in section 18(3)(d)(i) (conditions for the exercise of entitlement to sign) applicable to the method of signing used is met,

　　(d)　the person's signing of the petition is not invalid for the purposes of this Act under regulations under section 18 of the kind mentioned in section 18(3)(d)(iv), and

　　(e)　the person is not within subsection (7).

(7)　A person is within this subsection if, on the last day of the signing period, the person is not registered in the register of parliamentary electors for the constituency because the person's entry has been removed by an alteration taking effect under section 13BC(6) of the Representation of the People Act 1983.

(8)　The Speaker must lay before the House of Commons any notice received under subsection (2)(b).

NOTES

Defined terms
　the cut-off day: ss 10(4)(a), 22(1)
　duty to notify: s 22(5)
　late application for registration: ss 10(4)(b), 22(1)
　petition officer: ss 6(2), 22(1)
　recall petition: ss 1(2), 22(1)
　register of parliamentary electors: s 22(2), (3)

　signing of a recall petition: ss 11(4), 22(4)
　the signing period: ss 9(2), 22(1)
　the Speaker: s 22(1)
　Speaker's notice: ss 5(7), 22(1)

Effect of successful petition

15(1)　If the petition officer notifies the Speaker under section 14(2)(b) that the recall petition was successful, the MP's seat becomes vacant on the giving of that notice.

(2)　That does not apply if the seat has already been vacated (whether by the MP's disqualification or death, or otherwise).

(3)　Subsection (1) is subject to regulations under section 18 about the questioning of the outcome of the recall petition.

NOTES

Defined terms　　　　　　　　　　　　　　　　MP: s 22(1)

petition officer: ss 6(2), 22(1)
recall petition: ss 1(2), 22(1)
the Speaker: s 22(1)

Financial Controls

Expenses, donations and reporting

16(1)   Schedule 3 regulates expenditure in relation to recall petitions.

(2)   Schedule 4 regulates donations in relation to recall petitions.

(3)   Schedule 5 imposes reporting requirements in connection with the financial control of recall petitions.

(4)   The Minister may by regulations amend Schedule 4 or 5 to make provision corresponding or similar to any of the modifications to Schedule 15 to PPERA 2000 (control of donations to permitted participants) made by or under the Political Parties and Elections Act 2009 (other than section 20 of that Act).

(5)   Regulations under subsection (4) are subject to affirmative resolution procedure.

NOTES
Defined terms   recall petition: ss 1(2), 22(1)
   the Minister: s 22(1)
   PPERA 2000: s 22(1)

Loans

17   *Amends the Electoral Administration Act 2006: not reproduced here.*

Final Provisions

Power to make further provision about conduct of a recall petition etc

18(1)   The Minister may by regulations

    (a)   make further provision about the conduct of a recall petition;

    (b)   make provision about the questioning of the outcome of a recall petition and the consequences of irregularities;

    (c)   make further provision about the giving, sending, delivery or receipt of notices or other documents under this Act.

(2)   Regulations under subsection (1) may

    (a)   apply or incorporate any provision of electoral legislation (with or without modifications or exceptions);

    (b)   amend any form contained in a provision of electoral legislation for use in relation to recall petitions;

    (c)   make provision conferring a discretion on any person;

    (d)   make provision creating a criminal offence;

    (e)   make further provision about criminal offences under this Act.

(3)   The provision that may be made under subsection (1)(a) includes, in particular

    (a)   provision about the notice of petition under section 8, the petition signing sheet under section 9 or the public notice required under section 13(8)(b) or 14(2)(c);

    (b)   provision permitting or requiring the petition officer not to make the recall petition available for signing at the designated place or places at particular times of the day or on particular days;

    (c)   provision allocating persons registered in the register of parliamentary electors for a constituency to a particular designated place and limiting the availability of the petition for signing at that place to signing by persons so allocated who are entitled to sign it;

(d) provision about signing a recall petition in person, by post or by proxy, and in particular

    (i) provision under which an entitlement to sign a recall petition in person, by post or by proxy may be exercised only where conditions specified in the regulations are met;

    (ii) provision about what a person must do in order to be regarded as having signed a recall petition for the purposes of this Act;

    (iii) provision about when a person who signs a recall petition by post is treated as signing it for the purposes of this Act;

    (iv) provision about when a person's signing of a recall petition is invalid for the purposes of this Act;

(e) provision permitting or requiring the petition officer, in determining under section 14(2)(a) whether a recall petition was successful, to treat a person who signed the petition as having validly signed it for the purposes of section 14(3);

(f) provision about access to, or the supply of copies of, the register of parliamentary electors for a constituency or documents produced in relation to a recall petition;

(g) provision about the retention or disposal of documents or other information in relation to a recall petition;

(h) further provision about the regulation of campaigning in relation to a recall petition.

(4) Provision made as mentioned in subsection (3)(e) does not affect

(a) the question of whether, for the purposes of provision made under subsection (1)(b), a person validly signed a recall petition for the purposes of section 14(3) (determination of whether recall petition successful), or

(b) liability to any penalty arising from a person signing a recall petition but failing to validly sign it for the purposes of section 14(3).

(5) The outcome of a recall petition may be questioned only in accordance with provision made under subsection (1)(b).

(6) The provision that may be made under subsection (1)(c) includes

(a) provision about how a notice or other document authorised or required under this Act to be given, sent or delivered is given, sent or delivered;

(b) provision about the circumstances in which, and the time at which, a notice or other document is (or is to be treated as having been) given, sent, delivered or received.

(7) For the purposes of this section, "a provision of electoral legislation" means

(a) a provision of, or made under, the Representation of the People Acts, or

(b) a provision of other legislation which is a provision relating to elections.

(8) Regulations under this section are subject to affirmative resolution procedure.

NOTES

Defined terms
the designated place or places: ss 7(5), 22(1)
legislation: s 22(1)
the Minister: s 22(1)
modifications: s 22(1)
petition officer: ss 6(2), 22(1)

recall petition: ss 1(2), 22(1)
register of parliamentary electors: s 22(2), (3)
signing of a recall petition: ss 11(4), 22(4)

Performance of the Speaker's functions by others

19(1) If a relevant circumstance arises, the functions of the Speaker under or by virtue of this Act ("the Speaker's functions") are to be performed by the Chairman of Ways and Means or a Deputy Chairman of Ways and Means.

(2) For the purposes of this section, a "relevant circumstance" arises if

    (a) the Speaker is unable to perform the Speaker's functions because of absence, illness or for any other reason,

    (b) the first, second or third recall condition has been met in relation to the Speaker, or

    (c) there is a vacancy in the office of the Speaker.

NOTES

Defined terms
  the Speaker: s 22(1)

Minor and consequential amendments

20 Schedule 6 contains minor and consequential amendments.

Regulations

21(1) Regulations under this Act are to be made by statutory instrument.

(2) But that does not apply to regulations under

    (a) paragraph 3(9) of Schedule 1 (regulations made by the Minister about petition officer's accounts), or

    (b) paragraph 1(4) of Schedule 5 (regulations made by the Electoral Commission about the form of a recall petition return).

(3) Regulations under this Act may

    (a) make consequential, supplementary, incidental, transitional or saving provision;

    (b) make different provision for different purposes or areas.

(4) The power under subsection (3)(a) includes, in the case of regulations under section 18 (power to make further provision about conduct of a recall petition etc), the power to amend legislation.

(5) Section 26 of the Welsh Language Act 1993 (power to prescribe Welsh version) applies in relation to regulations under this Act as it applies in relation to Acts of Parliament.

(6) Where regulations under this Act

    (a) are subject to "affirmative resolution procedure" they must not be made unless a draft of the statutory instrument containing them has been laid before, and approved by a resolution of, each House of Parliament;

    (b) are subject to "negative resolution procedure" the statutory instrument containing them is subject to annulment in pursuance of a resolution of either House of Parliament.

(7) Provision that may be made by regulations under this Act for which no Parliamentary procedure is required may be included in regulations subject to affirmative or negative resolution procedure.

(8) Provision that may be made by regulations under this Act subject to negative resolution procedure may be included in regulations subject to affirmative resolution procedure.

(9) This section (apart from subsection (7)) does not apply to regulations under section 24 (commencement).

NOTES

Defined terms
   legislation: s 22(1)

Interpretation

22(1)   In this Act

      "the cut-off day" has the meaning given by section 10(4)(a);

      "the designated day" has the meaning given by section 7(5);

      "the designated place or places" has the meaning given by section 7(5);

      "late application for registration" has the meaning given by section 10(4)(b);

      "legislation" means

         (a)   an Act of Parliament,

         (b)   an Act of the Scottish Parliament,

         (c)   an Act or Measure of the National Assembly for Wales,

         (d)   Northern Ireland legislation, or

         (e)   an instrument made under legislation as mentioned in any of paragraphs (a) to (d) above;

      "the Minister" means the Chancellor of the Duchy of Lancaster or the Secretary of State;

      "modifications" includes additions, omissions and amendments;

      "MP" means member of the House of Commons (and see section 2(5) regarding the time at which a person becomes an MP);

      "overturned on appeal" means

         (a)   in relation to a conviction, that there is no longer a conviction for the purposes of section 1(3) or (9) (as the case may be), and

         (b)   in relation to a sentence or order

            (i)   varied so that it is no longer a sentence or order that the MP be imprisoned or detained within the meaning of section 1(3), or

            (ii)   replaced with another sentence or order that is not a sentence or order that the MP be imprisoned or detained within the meaning of that provision;

      "petition officer" has the meaning given by section 6(2);

      "PPERA 2000" means the Political Parties, Elections and Referendums Act 2000;

      "recall petition" has the meaning given by section 1(2);

      "the signing period" has the meaning given by section 9(2);

      "the Speaker" means the Speaker of the House of Commons;

      "Speaker's notice" has the meaning given by section 5(7) (and see section 5(6) regarding when it is given and received);

      "working day" means a day that is not

         (a)   a Saturday or Sunday,

         (b)   Christmas Eve, Christmas Day or Good Friday, or

         (c)   a bank holiday or a day appointed for public thanksgiving or mourning,

      and for that purpose "bank holiday" means a day that is a bank holiday in the part of the United Kingdom in which the MP's constituency is situated.

  (2)   References in this Act to the register of parliamentary electors for a constituency are to the register of parliamentary electors for the constituency maintained under section 9 of the Representation of the People Act 1983.

  (3)   Where under that section two or more registration officers maintain registers of parliamentary electors in respect of different parts of the same constituency, then in relation to that constituency

         (a)   references in this Act (other than in section 14(3) and (7)) to the register of parliamentary electors for the constituency are to be read as references to one of those registers in respect of a part of the constituency,

    (b) the reference in section 14(3) to "the number of persons registered in the register of parliamentary electors for the constituency on the last day of the signing period excluding those who, according to their entry in the register, are aged under 18 on that day" is to be read as a reference to the number given by

        (i) determining, in the case of each of those registers in respect of a part of the constituency, the number of persons registered in that register on that day excluding those who, according to their entry in that register, are aged under 18 on that day, and

        (ii) then adding together the numbers so determined, and

    (c) the reference in section 14(7) to a person who is not registered in the register of parliamentary electors for the constituency is to be read as a reference to a person who is not registered in any of those registers.

(4) References in this Act (however expressed) to the signing of a recall petition by a person are to be read in accordance with section 11(4).

(5) A duty under this Act to notify (however expressed) is a duty to give notice in writing.

Extent

23(1) An amendment or repeal by this Act has the same extent as the provision of legislation to which it relates.

(2) Subject to that, this Act extends to England and Wales, Scotland and Northern Ireland.

NOTES
Defined terms
  legislation: s 22(1)

Commencement

24(1) The following provisions come into force on the day on which this Act is passed

    (a) section 9(5) and (6) (power by regulations to amend section 9(4) (wording of petition signing sheet));

    (b) section 16(4) and (5) (power by regulations to amend Schedule 4 or 5);

    (c) section 17 (amendments to the Electoral Administration Act 2006 conferring power by order to make provision about loans);

    (d) section 18 (power to make further provision about conduct of a recall petition etc);

    (e) section 21 (regulations);

    (f) sections 22 and 23 (interpretation and extent);

    (g) this section;

    (h) section 25 (short title).

(2) The following provisions (which contain other regulationmaking powers and related provision) also come into force on the day on which this Act is passed

    (a) section 6(3) and paragraph 3 of Schedule 1, for the purposes of making regulations under that paragraph;

    (b) section 8 so far as relating to the making of regulations under section 18;

    (c) section 10(6) and paragraphs 1 and 7 of Schedule 2, for the purposes of making regulations under section 13BC of the Representation of the People Act 1983 (as inserted by paragraph 7);

    (d) paragraphs 16, 23 and 24 of Schedule 3 (and section 16(1) so far as relating to those paragraphs);

    (e) paragraphs 3(4) to (6) and 8 of Schedule 4 (and section 16(2) so far as relating to those provisions of that Schedule);

    (f) section 16(3) and paragraphs 1, 3, 4 and 9 of Schedule 5, for the purposes of making regulations under those paragraphs;

(g) paragraph 3(6) of Schedule 6 (which amends section 7(2) of PPERA 2000) (and paragraphs 2 and 3(1) of that Schedule, and section 20, so far as relating to paragraph 3(6)).

(3) The remaining provisions of this Act come into force on such day as the Minister may by regulations made by statutory instrument appoint.

(4) Those regulations
   (a) may appoint different days for different purposes;
   (b) may make transitional, transitory or saving provision.

NOTES
Defined terms
   the Minister: s 22(1)

Short title

25 This Act may be cited as the Recall of MPs Act 2015.

SCHEDULE 1
PETITION OFFICERS

Section 6

Petition officer's general duty

1 It is the petition officer's general duty to do anything necessary for effectually conducting a recall petition in accordance with this Act and regulations made under it.

Performance of petition officer's functions: delegation, assistance etc

2(1) Sub-paragraphs (2) and (3) apply in relation to a petition officer for a constituency in England, Wales or Scotland.

(2) The petition officer may appoint one or more deputies to perform any or all of the officer's functions under or by virtue of this Act.

(3) Each local authority whose area falls wholly or partly within the constituency must place the services of its officers at the disposal of the petition officer for the purpose of assisting the petition officer in the performance of the officer's functions under or by virtue of this Act.

(4) "Local authority" means
   (a) a district council,
   (b) a county council in England for a county in which there are no district councils,
   (c) a London borough council,
   (d) the Common Council of the City of London,
   (e) the Council of the Isles of Scilly,
   (f) a county council or county borough council in Wales, or
   (g) a council constituted under section 2 of the Local Government etc (Scotland) Act 1994 (c 39).

(5) Sections 14(5) and 14A(2) and (3) of the Electoral Law Act (Northern Ireland) 1962 (c 14 (NI)) (appointment of temporary deputy, delegation to assistants and involvement of officers of local authorities) have effect in relation to the Chief Electoral Officer for Northern Ireland in his or her capacity as a petition officer in relation to a recall petition.

Expenditure

3(1) A petition officer may recover from the Minister charges in respect of services rendered, or expenses incurred, by the officer for or in connection with the performance of the officer's functions under or by virtue of this Act if

  (a) the services were necessarily rendered, or the expenses were necessarily incurred, for the efficient and effective performance of those functions, and

  (b) the total of the officer's charges does not exceed the amount ("the overall maximum recoverable amount") specified in, or determined in accordance with, regulations made by the Minister, with the consent of the Treasury, for the purposes of this sub-paragraph.

(2) Regulations under sub-paragraph (1) may specify, or make provision for determining in accordance with the regulations, a maximum recoverable amount for services or expenses of any specified description.

(3) The petition officer may not recover more than the specified maximum recoverable amount in respect of any specified services or expenses.

(4) But in a particular case the Minister may, if satisfied that the conditions in sub-paragraph (5) are met, and with the consent of the Treasury, authorise the payment of

  (a) more than the overall maximum recoverable amount, or

  (b) more than the specified maximum recoverable amount for any specified services or expenses.

(5) Those conditions are

  (a) that it was reasonable for the petition officer to render the services or incur the expenses, and

  (b) that the charges in question are reasonable.

(6) The amount of any charges recoverable in accordance with this paragraph is to be paid by the Minister on an account being submitted to the Minister.

(7) But the Minister may, before payment, apply for the account to be taxed under paragraph 4.

(8) On the request of a petition officer for an advance on account of the officer's charges, the Minister may make an advance on such terms as the Minister thinks fit.

(9) The Minister may by regulations make provision as to

  (a) the time when accounts are to be rendered to the Minister for the purposes of the payment of a petition officer's charges, and

  (b) the manner and form in which such accounts are to be so rendered.

(10) Any sums required by the Minister for making payments under this paragraph are to be charged on, and paid out of, the Consolidated Fund.

(11) In sub-paragraphs (2) to (4), "specified" means specified in, or determined in accordance with, regulations under sub-paragraph (1).

Taxation of petition officer's account

4(1) An application under paragraph 3(7) for a petition officer's account to be taxed ("a taxation application") is made

  (a) in the case of a petition officer for a constituency in England or Wales, to the county court,

  (b) in the case of a petition officer for a constituency in Scotland, to the Auditor of the Court of Session ("the Auditor"), and

  (c) in the case of a petition officer for a constituency in Northern Ireland, to the county court that has jurisdiction where the headquarters of the Chief Electoral Officer for Northern Ireland are situated.

(2) On a taxation application the court or Auditor has jurisdiction

(a) to tax the account in such manner, and at such time and place, as the court or Auditor thinks fit, and

(b) finally to determine the amount payable to the petition officer.

(3) On a taxation application the petition officer may apply to the court or Auditor to examine any claim made by any person ("the claimant") against the officer in respect of matters charged in the account.

(4) Where such an application is made in respect of a claim

(a) notice of the application must be given to the claimant;

(b) the court or Auditor must give the claimant an opportunity to be heard and to tender any evidence;

(c) the court or Auditor may allow, disallow or reduce the claim, with or without costs;

(d) the determination of the court or Auditor is final for all purposes and as against all persons.

NOTES

Defined terms
the Minister: s 22(1)
petition officer: ss 6(2), 22(1)

recall petition: ss 1(2), 22(1)

SCHEDULE 2
ALTERATION OF REGISTERS OF PARLIAMENTARY ELECTORS

Section 10

Amends Representation of the People Act 1983: not reproduced here

SCHEDULE 3
REGULATION OF EXPENDITURE

Section 16

Part 1
Introduction

Overview

1(1) This Schedule regulates expenditure in relation to recall petitions.

(2) Part 2 limits the amount of petition expenses that may be incurred during the recall petition period

(a) by or on behalf of persons who are not accredited campaigners, and

(b) by or on behalf of accredited campaigners.

(3) Part 3 imposes further controls on the petition expenses of accredited campaigners.

(4) Part 4 defines "petition expense".

(5) Part 5 defines "accredited campaigner" and identifies the responsible person in relation to an accredited campaigner.

(6) Part 6 contains supplementary provision, including

(a) provision about offences under this Schedule which are a corrupt or illegal practice, and

(b) provision applying the definitions of "registered party", "minor party" and certain other expressions used in PPERA 2000.

(7)   In this Schedule, "the recall petition period", in relation to a recall petition, means the period

    (a)   beginning with the day after that on which the Speaker's notice is given, and

    (b)   ending with the day on which the petition officer

        (i)   receives a notice under section 13(6) (early termination of recall petition process), or

        (ii)   gives a notice under section 14(2)(b) (determination of whether recall petition successful).

NOTES

Defined terms
  accredited campaigner: Sch 3, Pt 5
  petition expense: Sch 3, Pt 4
  petition officer: ss 6(2), 22(1)
  PPERA 2000: s 22(1)

  recall petition: ss 1(2), 22(1)
  Speaker's notice: ss 5(7), 22(1)

Part 2
Limits on Expenditure

Limit on petition expenditure: persons other than accredited campaigners

2(1)   The total petition expenses incurred during the recall petition period by or on behalf of a person who is not an accredited campaigner must not exceed £500.

  (2)   The following provisions of this paragraph apply where

    (a)   at any time during the recall petition period any petition expenses are incurred by or on behalf of a person ("P") in excess of the limit imposed by sub-paragraph (1), and

    (b)   P is not at that time an accredited campaigner.

  (3)   Where P is an individual, P commits an offence if P knew or ought reasonably to have known that the expenses would be incurred in excess of that limit.

  (4)   Where P is a body

    (a)   P commits an offence, and

    (b)   any person who authorised the expenses to be incurred by or on behalf of P commits an offence if the person knew or ought reasonably to have known that the expenses would be incurred in excess of that limit.

  (5)   An offence under this paragraph is a corrupt practice.

Limit on petition expenditure: accredited campaigners

3(1)   The total petition expenses incurred during the recall petition period by or on behalf of an accredited campaigner must not exceed £10,000.

  (2)   The following provisions of this paragraph apply where

    (a)   at any time during the recall petition period any petition expenses are incurred by or on behalf of a person ("P") in excess of the limit imposed by sub-paragraph (1), and

    (b)   P is at that time an accredited campaigner.

  (3)   Where P is an individual

    (a)   P commits an offence if P knew or ought reasonably to have known that the expenses would be incurred in excess of that limit, and

    (b)   where the responsible person is a different individual, the responsible person commits an offence if he or she

        (i)   authorised the expenses to be incurred by or on behalf of P, and

          (ii)   knew or ought reasonably to have known that the expenses would be incurred in excess of that limit.

(4)   Where P is a registered party or is a body that is not a registered party
      (a)   P commits an offence, and
      (b)   the responsible person commits an offence if he or she
          (i)   authorised the expenses to be incurred by or on behalf of P, and
          (ii)   knew or ought reasonably to have known that the expenses would be incurred in excess of that limit.

(5)   In proceedings for an offence under this paragraph it is a defence to show that
      (a)   any code of practice for the time being in force under paragraph 16 (guidance as to meaning of "petition expense") was complied with in determining the items and amounts of petition expenses to be entered in the relevant return under paragraph 1 of Schedule 5 (reporting requirements), and
      (b)   the limit imposed by sub-paragraph (1) would not have been exceeded on the basis of the items and amounts entered in that return.

(6)   A person is taken to have shown the matters specified in sub-paragraph (5) if
      (a)   sufficient evidence of those matters is adduced to raise an issue with respect to them, and
      (b)   the contrary is not proved beyond reasonable doubt.

(7)   An offence under this paragraph is an illegal practice.

Expenses incurred by persons acting in concert

4(1)   This paragraph applies where petition expenses are incurred by or on behalf of a person in pursuance of a relevant plan.

(2)   "Relevant plan" means a plan or other arrangement by which
      (a)   petition expenses are to be incurred by or on behalf of the person mentioned in sub-paragraph (1), and
      (b)   petition expenses are to be incurred by or on behalf of one or more other persons,
with a view to, or otherwise in connection with, promoting or procuring the success or failure of the recall petition.

(3)   The expenses mentioned in sub-paragraph (1) are treated for the purposes of this Part of this Schedule (apart from this paragraph) as also having been incurred by or on behalf of the other person (or, as the case may be, each of the other persons) mentioned in sub-paragraph (2)(b).

Expenses incurred before the recall petition period

5(1)   This paragraph applies where
      (a)   before the beginning of the recall petition period, a petition expense is incurred by or on behalf of a person in respect of property, services or facilities, and
      (b)   the property, services or facilities is or are made use of by or on behalf of the person during the recall petition period with a view to, or otherwise in connection with, promoting or procuring the success or failure of the recall petition.

(2)   The appropriate proportion of the petition expense is treated for the purposes of this Part of this Schedule as incurred during the recall petition period by or on behalf of the person.

(3)   The "appropriate proportion" of the expense is such proportion of it as is reasonably attributable to the use made of the property, services or facilities as mentioned in sub-paragraph (1)(b).

Notional petition expenses

6(1)   This paragraph applies where the following two conditions are met in relation to a person ("P").

(2)   The first condition is that

(a)   property is transferred to P free of charge or at a discount of more than 10% of the market value of the property, or

(b)   property, services or facilities is or are provided for the use or benefit of P free of charge or at a discount of more than 10% of the commercial rate for the use of the property or for the provision of the services or facilities.

(3)   The second condition is that the property, services or facilities is or are made use of by or on behalf of P

(a)   for a period any part of which falls within the recall petition period, and

(b)   in circumstances such that, if any expenses were to be (or are) actually incurred by or on behalf of P in respect of that use, they would be (or are) petition expenses by virtue of Part 4 of this Schedule.

(4)   Where this paragraph applies

(a)   an amount of expenses determined in accordance with the following provisions of this paragraph ("the gross notional amount") is treated for the purposes of this Part of this Schedule as incurred by P, and

(b)   the appropriate proportion of the gross notional amount is treated for the purposes of this Part of this Schedule as petition expenses incurred by P during the recall petition period.

(5)   The "appropriate proportion" of the gross notional amount is such proportion of that amount as is reasonably attributable to the use made of the property, services or facilities as mentioned in sub-paragraph (3) during the recall petition period.

(6)   Where sub-paragraph (2)(a) applies, the gross notional amount is such proportion of either

(a)   the market value of the property (where the property is transferred free of charge), or

(b)   the difference between the market value of the property and the amount of expenses actually incurred by or on behalf of P in respect of the property (where the property is transferred at a discount),

as is reasonably attributable to the use made of the property as mentioned in sub-paragraph (3) during the recall petition period.

(7)   Where sub-paragraph (2)(b) applies, the gross notional amount is such proportion of either

(a)   the commercial rate for the use of the property or the provision of the services or facilities (where the property, services or facilities is or are provided free of charge), or

(b)   the difference between that commercial rate and the amount of expenses actually incurred by or on behalf of P in respect of the use of the property or the provision of the services or facilities (where the property, services or facilities is or are provided at a discount),

as is reasonably attributable to the use made of the property, services or facilities as mentioned in sub-paragraph (3) during the recall petition period.

(8)   Where the services of an employee are made available by his or her employer for the use or benefit of a person, then for the purposes of this paragraph the amount that is to be taken as constituting the commercial rate for the provision of those services is

(a) the amount of the remuneration and allowances payable to the employee by the employer in respect of the period for which the employee's services are made available, but

(b) excluding from the amount mentioned in paragraph (a) any amount in respect of contributions or other payments for which the employer is liable in respect of the employee.

(9) Sub-paragraph (4)(b) does not apply if it would (apart from this sub-paragraph) treat an amount of £50 or less as petition expenses incurred by P during the recall petition period.

(10) In this paragraph a reference to property being transferred to P, or to property, services or facilities being provided for the use or benefit of P, includes

(a) property being transferred to, or property, services or facilities being provided for the use or benefit of, any officer, member, trustee or agent of P in his or her capacity as such, and

(b) property being transferred, or property, services or facilities being provided, indirectly through a third person.

Petition expenses incurred before becoming an accredited campaigner

7 A reference in this Part of this Schedule to a petition expense incurred during the recall petition period by or on behalf of an accredited campaigner includes

(a) any petition expense incurred during that period by or on behalf of a person who is not an accredited campaigner in relation to the recall petition in question at the time the expense is incurred but who subsequently becomes such an accredited campaigner, and

(b) any petition expense treated by virtue of paragraph 5 or 6 as incurred during that period by or on behalf of a person where that person becomes an accredited campaigner in relation to the recall petition in question during that period.

NOTES

Defined terms
  accredited campaigner: Sch 3, Pt 5
  market value: Sch 3, Pt 6
  petition expense: Sch 3, Pt 4
  property: Sch 3, Pt 6

recall petition period: Sch 3, Pt 1
registered party: Sch 3, Pt 6

Part 3
Petition Expenses of Accredited Campaigners: General Controls

Restriction on incurring petition expenses

8(1) No petition expenses are to be incurred by or on behalf of an accredited campaigner unless they are incurred with the authority of

(a) the responsible person, or

(b) a person authorised in writing by the responsible person to incur the expenses.

(2) A person commits an offence if, without reasonable excuse, the person incurs an expense in contravention of sub-paragraph (1).

(3) An offence under this paragraph is a corrupt practice.

Restriction on payments in respect of petition expenses

9(1) No payment may be made in respect of petition expenses incurred, or to be incurred, by or on behalf of an accredited campaigner unless it is made by

    (a) the responsible person, or

    (b) a person authorised in writing by the responsible person to make the payment.

(2) Any payment of £20 or more made in respect of such expenses by a person within sub-paragraph (1)(a) or (b) must be supported by an invoice or receipt.

(3) Where a person within sub-paragraph (1)(b) ("P") makes a payment required by sub-paragraph (2) to be supported by an invoice or receipt, P must, as soon as reasonably practicable after making the payment, deliver to the responsible person

    (a) notification that P has made the payment, and

    (b) the supporting invoice or receipt.

(4) A person commits an offence if, without reasonable excuse, the person

    (a) makes a payment in contravention of sub-paragraph (1), or

    (b) contravenes sub-paragraph (3).

(5) An offence under this paragraph is an illegal practice.

Restrictions on payment of claims in respect of petition expenses

10(1) A relevant claim is not payable unless it

    (a) is sent to the responsible person or to a person authorised under paragraph 8 to incur the expenses, and

    (b) is sent before the end of the period of 21 days beginning with the first day after the recall petition period.

(2) A relevant claim must be paid before the end of the period of 28 days beginning with the first day after the recall petition period.

(3) In this Part of this Schedule "relevant claim" means a claim for payment in respect of petition expenses incurred during the recall petition period by or on behalf of an accredited campaigner.

(4) A person commits an offence if, without reasonable excuse, the person

    (a) makes a payment in respect of a relevant claim which by virtue of sub-paragraph (1) is not payable, or

    (b) makes a payment in respect of a relevant claim after the end of the period allowed under sub-paragraph (2).

(5) An offence under this paragraph is an illegal practice.

(6) Where the period allowed under sub-paragraph (1)(b) or (2) would, apart from this sub-paragraph, end on a day that is not a qualifying day, the period instead ends on the first subsequent day that is a qualifying day.

(7) "Qualifying day" means a day that is not

    (a) a Saturday or Sunday,

    (b) Christmas Eve, Christmas Day or Good Friday, or

    (c) a bank holiday or a day appointed for public thanksgiving or mourning.

(8) For this purpose "bank holiday" means a bank holiday in

    (a) the part of the United Kingdom in which is situated the office of the person to whom the claim is sent pursuant to sub-paragraph (1), or

    (b) the part of the United Kingdom in which the person providing the property, services or facilities to which the expenses in question relate conducts business (or, if that person conducts business in more than one part of the United Kingdom, the part of the United Kingdom in which is situated the office from which dealings relating to the expenses were conducted).

(9)   Sub-paragraph (2) does not
    (a)   affect any right of a creditor of an accredited campaigner to obtain payment before the end of the period allowed under that sub-paragraph, or
    (b)   impose an obligation to pay a relevant claim that is not payable apart from that sub-paragraph.

Payment of claims in respect of petition expenses: application for leave to pay late claims

11(1)   An application may be made to the appropriate court for leave for a relevant claim to be paid although sent to a person mentioned in paragraph 10(1)(a) after the end of the period allowed under paragraph 10(1)(b); and the appropriate court, if satisfied that for any special reason it is appropriate to do so, may by order grant the leave.

(2)   An application under sub-paragraph (1) may be made by
    (a)   the person making the claim, or
    (b)   the person with whose authority the expenses in question were incurred.

(3)   In this paragraph "appropriate court" means
    (a)   in England and Wales, the High Court or the county court,
    (b)   in Scotland, the Court of Session or the sheriff, or
    (c)   in Northern Ireland, the High Court or a county court.

(4)   Paragraph 10(1) and (2) do not apply in relation to any sum paid in pursuance of the order of leave.

(5)   The jurisdiction conferred by this paragraph on the Court of Session or the sheriff may be exercised in such manner as is prescribed by Act of Sederunt; and any order made by the sheriff by virtue of this paragraph may be appealed to the Court of Session.

(6)   Article 60 of the County Courts (Northern Ireland) Order 1980 (SI 1980/397 (N.I. 3)) (appeals from county courts) applies in relation to an order of a county court in Northern Ireland made by virtue of this paragraph as it applies in relation to any such decree of a county court as is mentioned in paragraph (1) of that Article.

Disputed claims

12(1)   A person who makes a disputed claim may bring an action for it; and paragraph 10(2) does not apply in relation to any sum paid in pursuance of a judgment or order made by a court in the proceedings.

(2)   In this paragraph "disputed claim" means a relevant claim that
    (a)   is sent as mentioned in paragraph 10(1)(a) and (b), but
    (b)   is not paid before the end of the period allowed under paragraph 10(2).

(3)   A person to whom a disputed claim is sent may make an application to the appropriate court for leave for it to be paid after the end of the period allowed under paragraph 10(2); and the appropriate court, if satisfied that for any special reason it is appropriate to do so, may by order grant the leave.

(4)   In this paragraph "appropriate court" has the same meaning as in paragraph 11.

(5)   Paragraph 10(2) does not apply in relation to any sum paid in pursuance of an order of leave granted under sub-paragraph (3).

(6)   The jurisdiction conferred by sub-paragraph (3) on the Court of Session or the sheriff may be exercised in such manner as is prescribed by Act of Sederunt; and any order made by the sheriff by virtue of that sub-paragraph may be appealed to the Court of Session.

(7)   Article 60 of the County Courts (Northern Ireland) Order 1980 (SI 1980/397 (NI 3)) (appeals from county courts) applies in relation to an order of a county court in Northern Ireland made by virtue of sub-paragraph (3) as it applies in relation to any such decree of a county court as is mentioned in paragraph (1) of that Article.

NOTES

Defined terms
  bank holiday: s 22(1) (and see para 10(8))
  business: Sch 3, Pt 6
  accredited campaigner: Sch 3, Pt 5
  petition expense: Sch 3, Pt 4

property: Sch 3, Pt 6
recall petition period: Sch 3, Pt 1

Part 4
Meaning of "Petition Expense"

Meaning of "petition expense"

13(1)   For the purposes of this Schedule an expense is a "petition expense" if

(a)   it is incurred with a view to, or otherwise in connection with, promoting or procuring the success or failure of a recall petition,

(b)   it is incurred in respect of a matter listed in paragraph 14,

(c)   it is not incurred in respect of a matter listed in paragraph 15, and

(d)   it is not a relevant personal expense of an individual ("P") that is paid by P from P's own resources and is not reimbursed to P.

(2)   For the purposes of sub-paragraph (1)(d) an expense is a "relevant personal expense" of P if it is incurred in respect of

(a)   transport for P (by any means),

(b)   accommodation for P, or

(c)   other personal needs of P.

List of matters

14(1)   The matters referred to in paragraph 13(1)(b) are as follows.

(2)   Advertising of any nature (whatever the medium used).
Expenses incurred in respect of this matter include design costs and other costs in connection with preparing, producing or distributing such material (including the cost of postage).

(3)   Unsolicited material addressed to persons entitled to sign the recall petition (whether addressed to them by name or intended for delivery to households within any particular area).

(4)   Transport (by any means) of persons to any place.

(5)   Public meetings (of any kind).
Expenses incurred in respect of this matter include costs incurred in connection with the attendance of persons at such meetings, the hire of premises for the purposes of such meetings or the provision of goods, services or facilities at them.

(6)   The services of a responsible person in relation to an accredited campaigner, or of any other person engaged in connection with promoting or procuring the success or failure of the recall petition.

(7)   Accommodation and administrative costs.

General exclusions

15(1)   The matters referred to in paragraph 13(1)(c) are as follows.

(2) The publication of any matter, other than an advertisement, relating to the recall petition in

    (a) a newspaper or periodical,

    (b) a broadcast made by the British Broadcasting Corporation or by Sianel Pedwar Cymru, or

    (c) a programme included in any service licensed under Part 1 or 3 of the Broadcasting Act 1990 or Part 1 or 2 of the Broadcasting Act 1996.

(3) The provision by an individual of his or her own services where the services are provided voluntarily in his or her own time and free of charge.

(4) The provision by an individual of accommodation which is his or her sole or main residence if the provision is made free of charge.

(5) The provision by an individual of transport if the means of transport was acquired by him or her principally for his or her personal use and the provision is made free of charge.

(6) The provision by an individual of computing or printing equipment if the equipment was acquired by him or her principally for his or her personal use and the provision is made free of charge.

Guidance

16(1) The Electoral Commission ("the Commission") may prepare, and from time to time revise, a code of practice giving

    (a) guidance as to the cases or circumstances in which expenses are, or are not, within paragraph 13(1)(a);

    (b) guidance as to the matters which are, or are not, within paragraph 14 or 15.

(2) Once the Commission have prepared a draft code under this paragraph, they must submit it to the Minister for approval.

(3) The Minister may approve a draft code either without modification or with such modifications as the Minister may determine.

(4) Once the Minister has approved a draft code, the Minister must lay before Parliament

    (a) a copy of the draft, incorporating any modifications determined under sub-paragraph (3), and

    (b) if the draft incorporates any such modifications, a statement of the Minister's reasons for making them.

(5) If, within the 40day period, either House of Parliament resolves not to approve the draft, neither the Minister nor the Commission are to take any further step in relation to the draft code.

(6) If no such resolution is made within the 40day period

    (a) the Commission must arrange for the code to be published, in such manner as they think appropriate, and

    (b) the code comes into force on such date as the Minister may by regulations appoint.

(7) Sub-paragraph (5) does not prevent a new draft code from being laid before Parliament.

(8) In this paragraph "the 40day period", in relation to a draft code, means

    (a) if the draft is laid before the two Houses of Parliament on different days, the period of 40 days beginning with the later of the two days, and

    (b) in any other case, the period of 40 days beginning with the day on which the draft is laid before each House.

For that purpose, no account is to be taken of any period during which Parliament is dissolved or prorogued or during which both Houses are adjourned for more than 4 days.

(9)   In this paragraph references to a draft code include a revised draft code.

NOTES
Defined terms
   accredited campaigner: Sch 3, Pt 5
   the Minister: s 22(1)
   modifications: s 22(1)

recall petition: ss 1(2), 22(1)

Part 5
Accredited Campaigners and Responsible Persons

Meaning of "accredited campaigner"

17(1)   In this Schedule "accredited campaigner" means a person ("P") who
   (a)   is eligible to be an accredited campaigner (see paragraph 18),
   (b)   has delivered to the petition officer an accreditation notice (see paragraph 19), and
   (c)   has delivered to the petition officer a statement, signed by the individual named under paragraph 19(1)(d), confirming that he or she is willing to exercise the functions conferred by or by virtue of this Act on the responsible person in relation to P.

(2)   Sub-paragraph (1)(c) does not apply where
   (a)   P is a registered party but is not a minor party, or
   (b)   P is the individual named under paragraph 19(1)(d).

Eligibility to be an accredited campaigner

18(1)   A person is eligible to be an accredited campaigner if the person is any of the following
   (a)   a registered party;
   (b)   an individual who is resident in the United Kingdom;
   (c)   an individual who is registered in an electoral register;
   (d)   a company incorporated in the United Kingdom or another member State that is registered under the Companies Act 2006 and carries on business in the United Kingdom;
   (e)   a trade union entered in the list kept under the Trade Union and Labour Relations (Consolidation) Act 1992 or the Industrial Relations (Northern Ireland) Order 1992 (SI 1992/807 (N.I. 5));
   (f)   a building society (within the meaning of the Building Societies Act 1986);
   (g)   a limited liability partnership, registered under the Limited Liability Partnerships Act 2000, that carries on business in the United Kingdom;
   (h)   a friendly society registered under the Friendly Societies Act 1974, a registered society within the meaning of the Co-operative and Community Benefit Societies Act 2014 or a society registered (or deemed to be registered) under the Industrial and Provident Societies Act (Northern Ireland) 1969 (c 24 (N.I.));
   (i)   an unincorporated association of two or more persons that is not within any of the preceding paragraphs but carries on business or other activities wholly or mainly in the United Kingdom and whose main office is there.

(2)   In this paragraph "an electoral register" means
   (a)   a register of parliamentary or local government electors maintained under section 9 of the Representation of the People Act 1983,

(b) a register of relevant citizens of the European Union prepared under the European Parliamentary Elections (Franchise of Relevant Citizens of the Union) Regulations 2001 (SI 2001/1184), or

(c) a register of peers prepared under regulations under section 3 of the Representation of the People Act 1985.

Accreditation notice

19(1) In this Part of this Schedule, "accreditation notice", in relation to a person ("P") who is eligible to be an accredited campaigner, means a notice

    (a) identifying the recall petition to which it relates,

    (b) stating whether P proposes to campaign for the success or failure of the petition,

    (c) giving such further information as is required under sub-paragraph (3) in relation to P,

    (d) naming an individual who is to exercise the functions conferred by or by virtue of this Act on the responsible person in relation to P, and

    (e) signed by a person authorised under sub-paragraph (4) to sign it in relation to P.

(2) Sub-paragraph (1)(d)

    (a) does not apply where P is a registered party but is not a minor party (see paragraph 21(1));

    (b) may be complied with, where P is an individual, by naming P or another individual;

    (c) may be complied with by naming the holder of an office.

(3) The further information mentioned in sub-paragraph (1)(c) is as set out in the following table

Where P is....	The further information required is...
a registered party	(a) the party's registered name, and
	(b) the address of the party's headquarters or, if it has no headquarters, the address to which communications to the party may be sent
an individual	(a) the individual's full name, and
	(b) the individual's home address in the United Kingdom or, if he or she has no home address in the United Kingdom, his or her home address elsewhere
a company within paragraph 18(1)(d)	(a) the company's registered name,
	(b) the address of its registered office, and
	(c) its registered number
a trade union within paragraph 18(1)(e)	(a) the name of the union as shown in the list kept under the Trade Union and Labour Relations (Consolidation) Act 1992 or the Industrial Relations (Northern Ireland) Order 1992 (SI 1992/807 (N.I. 5)), and
	(b) the address of its head or main office, as shown in that list
a building society within paragraph 18(1)(f)	(a) the name of the society, and
	(b) the address of its principal office
a limited liability partnership within paragraph 18(1)(g)	(a) the partnership's registered name, and
	(b) the address of its registered office
a friendly or other society within paragraph	(a) the name of the society, and
	(b) the address of its registered office

| 18(1)(h)
an unincorporated association within paragraph 18(1)(i) | (a) the name of the association, and
(b) the address of its main office in the United Kingdom |

(4) The persons authorised for the purposes of sub-paragraph (1)(e) to sign an accreditation notice are
  (a) where P is an individual, P;
  (b) where P is a registered party, the responsible officers of the party (within the meaning of section 64 of PPERA 2000);
  (c) where P is a body other than a registered party, the body's secretary or a person who acts in a similar capacity in relation to the body.

Notice of alteration

20(1) This paragraph applies if, at any time before the end of the compliance period, any information which in accordance with this Schedule is contained in an accreditation notice ceases to be accurate.

(2) The accredited campaigner must, as soon as reasonably practicable after becoming aware of the inaccuracy, deliver a notice ("a notice of alteration") to the petition officer
  (a) indicating that the accreditation notice has become inaccurate, and
  (b) containing a corrected version of the accreditation notice.

(3) References in sub-paragraphs (1) and (2) to an accreditation notice include a corrected version of an accreditation notice.

(4) The accredited campaigner commits an offence if the accredited campaigner fails to deliver a notice of alteration in accordance with sub-paragraph (2).

(5) A person guilty of an offence under this paragraph is liable on summary conviction
  (a) in England and Wales, to a fine,
  (b) in Scotland, to a fine not exceeding level 5 on the standard scale, and
  (c) in Northern Ireland, to a fine not exceeding level 5 on the standard scale.

(6) Where a notice of alteration names a new individual who is to exercise the functions conferred by or by virtue of this Act on the responsible person in relation to the accredited campaigner, it must be accompanied by a statement, signed by that individual, confirming that he or she is willing to exercise those functions.

(7) Sub-paragraph (6) does not apply where the new individual named in the notice of alteration is the accredited campaigner.

(8) In this paragraph "the compliance period" means the period during which any provision of
  (a) this Schedule (apart from this paragraph),
  (b) Schedule 4 (control of donations to accredited campaigners),
  (c) Schedule 5 (recall petition returns), or
  (d) any order under section 62 of the Electoral Administration Act 2006 (loans),
  remains to be complied with on the part of the accredited campaigner.

(9) In sub-paragraph (5)(a), the reference to a fine is to be read as a reference to a fine not exceeding level 5 on the standard scale in relation to an offence committed before section 85(1) of the Legal Aid, Sentencing and Punishment of Offenders Act 2012 comes into force.

The responsible person

21(1) If the accredited campaigner is a registered party but is not a minor party, the responsible person in relation to the accredited campaigner is the treasurer of the party.

(2) In any other case, the responsible person in relation to the accredited campaigner is
    (a) the individual named in the accreditation notice as the person who is to exercise the functions conferred by or by virtue of this Act on the responsible person in relation to the accredited campaigner, or
    (b) if a notice of alteration has been delivered which names a new individual who is to exercise those functions, the individual named in that notice.

(3) But where the individual named as mentioned in sub-paragraph (2)(a) or (b) is not the accredited campaigner, that named individual is the responsible person in relation to the accredited campaigner only if
    (a) in a case within sub-paragraph (2)(a), the accreditation notice is accompanied by the statement required by paragraph 17(1)(c), or
    (b) in a case within sub-paragraph (2)(b), the notice of alteration is accompanied by the statement required by paragraph 20(6).

Duty of petition officer to publish information about accredited campaigners

22(1) The petition officer must, as soon as reasonably practicable after receiving an accreditation notice under paragraph 17 or a corrected version of an accreditation notice under paragraph 20, make the information contained in it available to the public in any way the officer thinks fit.

(2) But the petition officer must not make available to the public the home address of an accredited campaigner who is an individual.

NOTES

Defined terms
  petition expense: Sch 3, Pt 4
  PPERA 2000: s 22(1)
  register of parliamentary electors: s 22(2), (3)

registered party: Sch 3, Pt 6
treasurer of a registered party: Sch 3, Pt 6

Part 6

Final Provisions

Power to alter meaning of "petition expense"

23(1) The Minister may by regulations amend paragraph 14 or 15.

(2) Before making regulations under this paragraph the Minister must consult the Electoral Commission.

(3) Regulations under this paragraph are subject to affirmative resolution procedure.

Power to alter certain financial limits

24(1) The Minister may by regulations amend any of the following provisions so as to substitute a different amount for the amount for the time being mentioned in the provision
    (a) paragraph 2(1) (limit on petition expenditure for person other than an accredited campaigner);
    (b) paragraph 3(1) (limit on petition expenditure for accredited campaigner);
    (c) paragraph 6(9) (amount at or below which notional petition expense is to be disregarded);

(d) paragraph 9(2) (amount at or above which petition expense of accredited campaigner must be supported by invoice or receipt).

(2) Before making regulations under this paragraph the Minister must consult the Electoral Commission.

(3) Regulations under this paragraph are subject to affirmative resolution procedure.

(4) Sub-paragraphs (2) and (3) do not apply where the Minister considers that the substitution is expedient in consequence of changes in the value of money.

Corrupt and illegal practices

25(1) An offence that is a corrupt practice under this Schedule is treated

   (a) for the purposes of section 168 of the Representation of the People Act 1983 (mode of prosecution and penalty for corrupt practices) as a corrupt practice,

   (b) for the purposes of section 173 of that Act (incapacities on conviction of corrupt or illegal practice) as a corrupt practice,

   (c) for the purposes of section 173A of that Act (incapacity to hold public or judicial office in Scotland) as a corrupt practice,

   (d) for the purposes of section 178 of that Act (prosecution of offences committed outside the United Kingdom) as an offence under that Act,

   (e) for the purposes of section 179 of that Act (offences by associations) as a corrupt practice, and

   (f) for the purposes of section 112 of the Electoral Law Act (Northern Ireland) 1962 (c 14 (N.I.)) (incapacities on conviction of corrupt or illegal practice) as a corrupt practice.

(2) An offence that is an illegal practice under this Schedule is treated

   (a) for the purposes of section 169 of the Representation of the People Act 1983 (mode of prosecution and penalty for illegal practices) as an illegal practice,

   (b) for the purposes of section 173 of that Act (incapacities on conviction of corrupt or illegal practice) as an illegal practice,

   (c) for the purposes of section 178 of that Act (prosecution of offences committed outside the United Kingdom) as an offence under that Act,

   (d) for the purposes of section 179 of that Act (offences by associations) as an illegal practice, and

   (e) for the purposes of section 112 of the Electoral Law Act (Northern Ireland) 1962 (incapacities on conviction of corrupt or illegal practice) as an illegal practice.

Application of defined terms in PPERA 2000

26(1) In this Schedule, the following expressions have the same meaning as in PPERA 2000: "business"; "market value"; "minor party"; "property"; "registered party"; "treasurer" (see section 160(1) of that Act).

(2) In the case of references to the treasurer of a registered party, see section 25(7) of that Act (which is inserted by paragraph 4(3) of Schedule 6 to this Act).

NOTES
Defined terms
   the Minister: s 22(1)
   PPERA 2000: s 22(1)

SCHEDULE 4
Control of Donations to Accredited Campaigners

Section 16

Part 1
Introduction and Interpretation

Operation of Schedule and meaning of "accredited campaigner" and "relevant donation" etc

1(1)   This Schedule has effect for controlling relevant donations to accredited campaigners who

      (a)   are not registered parties, or

      (b)   are registered parties but are minor parties.

(2)   In this Schedule, "accredited campaigner" has the same meaning as in Schedule 3 (see Part 5 of that Schedule) but does not include an accredited campaigner that is a registered party unless it is a minor party.

(3)   In this Schedule, "relevant donation", in relation to an accredited campaigner, means a donation to the accredited campaigner for

      (a)   the purpose of meeting petition expenses incurred by or on behalf of the accredited campaigner, or

      (b)   the purpose of securing that petition expenses are not so incurred.

(4)   A donation is to be taken to be for the purpose mentioned in sub-paragraph (3)(a) or (b) if, having regard to all the circumstances, it must reasonably be assumed to be for that purpose.

(5)   For the meaning of "donation" see paragraphs 2 to 4.

(6)   In this Schedule

      "minor party" and "registered party" have the same meaning as in PPERA 2000 (see section 160(1) of that Act);

      "petition expense" has the same meaning as in Schedule 3 (see Part 4 of that Schedule);

      "responsible person" means the person determined in accordance with paragraph 21 of that Schedule.

Donations: general rules

2(1)   In this Schedule, "donation", in relation to an accredited campaigner, means

      (a)   a gift to the accredited campaigner of money or other property,

      (b)   sponsorship provided in relation to the accredited campaigner (see paragraph 3),

      (c)   money spent by a person other than the accredited campaigner in paying petition expenses where

          (i)   the petition expenses were incurred by or on behalf of the accredited campaigner, and

          (ii)   the payments are out of the person's own resources (with no right to reimbursement by the accredited campaigner),

      (d)   money lent to the accredited campaigner otherwise than on commercial terms,

      (e)   the provision, otherwise than on commercial terms, of property, services or facilities for the use or benefit of the accredited campaigner (including the services of a person), or

      (f)   in the case of an accredited campaigner other than an individual, a subscription or other fee paid for affiliation to, or membership of, the accredited campaigner.

      But this sub-paragraph is subject to the exceptions in paragraph 4.

(2)   In sub-paragraph (1)(a), "gift" includes a transfer of money or other property where

(a) the transfer is in pursuance of a transaction or arrangement involving the provision by or on behalf of the accredited campaigner of any property, services or facilities or other consideration of monetary value, and

(b) the total value in monetary terms of the consideration so provided is less than the value of the money, or the market value of the property, transferred.

(3) Where, by virtue of sub-paragraph (1)(c), money spent constitutes a donation to an accredited campaigner, the accredited campaigner is treated as receiving an equivalent amount on the date on which the money is paid to the creditor in respect of the expenses in question.

(4) In determining

(a) for the purposes of sub-paragraph (1)(d) whether money lent to an accredited campaigner is lent otherwise than on commercial terms, or

(b) for the purposes of sub-paragraph (1)(e) whether property, services or facilities provided for the use or benefit of an accredited campaigner is or are provided otherwise than on commercial terms,

regard is to be had to the total value in monetary terms of the consideration provided by or on behalf of the accredited campaigner in respect of the loan or the provision of the property, services or facilities.

(5) Where, apart from this sub-paragraph, anything would be a donation

(a) by virtue of sub-paragraph (1)(b), and

(b) by virtue of any other provision of this paragraph,

sub-paragraph (1)(b) applies in relation to it to the exclusion of the other provision of this paragraph.

(6) A reference in this Schedule

(a) to property being transferred to the accredited campaigner includes property being transferred to any officer, member, trustee or agent of the accredited campaigner in his or her capacity as such, or

(b) to property, services or facilities being provided for the use or benefit of the accredited campaigner, includes property, services or facilities being provided for the use or benefit of any officer, member, trustee or agent of the accredited campaigner in his or her capacity as such.

(7) In this paragraph

(a) references to a thing being given or transferred include its being given or transferred indirectly through a third person, and

(b) "gift" includes bequest.

(8) For the purposes of this Schedule it is immaterial whether a donation is made or received in the United Kingdom or elsewhere.

Sponsorship

3(1) For the purposes of this Schedule sponsorship is provided in relation to an accredited campaigner if

(a) money or other property is transferred to the accredited campaigner or to any person for the benefit of the accredited campaigner, and

(b) the purpose (or one of the purposes) of the transfer is (or, having regard to all the circumstances, must reasonably be assumed to be)

(i) to help the accredited campaigner with meeting, or to meet, to any extent, defined expenses incurred or to be incurred by or on behalf of the accredited campaigner, or

(ii) to secure that, to any extent, defined expenses are not incurred by or on behalf of the accredited campaigner.

(2)   "Defined expenses" means expenses in connection with

   (a)   a conference, meeting or other event organised by or on behalf of the accredited campaigner,

   (b)   the preparation, production or dissemination of any publication by or on behalf of the accredited campaigner, or

   (c)   study or research organised by or on behalf of the accredited campaigner.

(3)   But the following do not constitute sponsorship for the purposes of this Schedule

   (a)   the making of a payment in respect of a charge for admission to a conference, meeting or other event;

   (b)   the making of a payment in respect of the purchase price of, or any other charge for access to, any publication;

   (c)   the making of a payment in respect of the inclusion of an advertisement in any publication where the payment is made at a commercial rate.

(4)   The Minister may by regulations amend sub-paragraph (2) or (3).

(5)   Before making regulations under this paragraph the Minister must consult the Electoral Commission.

(6)   Regulations under this paragraph are subject to affirmative resolution procedure.

(7)   In this paragraph "publication" means a publication made available in any form and by any means (whether or not to the public or any section of the public).

Payments etc not to be regarded as donations

4(1)   In this Schedule "donation" does not include

   (a)   a donation as described in paragraph 2(1)(a) to (f)

      (i)   whose amount, where the donation is of money, is £500 or less, or

      (ii)   whose value (as determined in accordance with paragraph 5), where the donation is not of money, is £500 or less,

   (b)   the provision by an individual of his or her own services where the services are provided voluntarily in his or her own time and free of charge,

   (c)   interest accruing to an accredited campaigner in respect of a donation which is dealt with by the accredited campaigner in accordance with paragraph 14(2) or 15(2) (duty to return donations from impermissible or unidentifiable donors), or

   (d)   a grant provided out of public funds.

(2)   "Provided out of public funds" has the same meaning as in PPERA 2000 (see section 160(4) of that Act).

Value of donations

5(1)   This paragraph has effect for the purposes of this Schedule.

(2)   The value of a donation within paragraph 2(1)(a) is the value of the money or the market value of the property.

(3)   But where that provision applies by virtue of paragraph 2(2), the value of the donation is the difference between

   (a)   the value of the money, or the market value of the property, and

   (b)   the total value in monetary terms of the consideration provided by or on behalf of the accredited campaigner.

(4)   The value of a donation within paragraph 2(1)(b) is

   (a)   the value of the money transferred as mentioned in paragraph 3(1), or

   (b)   the market value of the property so transferred;

and accordingly the value in monetary terms of any benefit conferred on the person providing the sponsorship in question is to be disregarded.

(5)   The value of a donation within paragraph 2(1)(d) is the difference between
  (a)   the total value in monetary terms of the consideration that would have had to be provided by or on behalf of the accredited campaigner in respect of the loan if the loan had been made on commercial terms, and
  (b)   the total value in monetary terms of the consideration (if any) actually provided by or on behalf of the accredited campaigner in respect of the loan.

(6)   The value of a donation within paragraph 2(1)(e) is the difference between
  (a)   the total value in monetary terms of the consideration that would have had to be provided by or on behalf of the accredited campaigner in respect of the provision of the property, services or facilities if the property, services or facilities had been provided on commercial terms, and
  (b)   the total value in monetary terms of the consideration (if any) actually provided by or on behalf of the accredited campaigner in respect of the provision of the property, services or facilities.

(7)   Where a donation within paragraph 2(1)(d) or (e) confers an enduring benefit on the donee over a particular period, the value of the donation
  (a)   is to be determined at the time the donation is received, and
  (b)   must be determined by reference to the total benefit accruing to the donee over that period.

Meaning of "permissible donor"

6(1)   In this Schedule "permissible donor" means
  (a)   a registered party (other than a Gibraltar party whose entry in the register includes a statement that it intends to contest one or more elections to the European Parliament in the combined region),
  (b)   an individual who is registered in an electoral register,
  (c)   a company incorporated in the United Kingdom or another member State that is registered under the Companies Act 2006 and carries on business in the United Kingdom,
  (d)   a trade union entered in the list kept under the Trade Union and Labour Relations (Consolidation) Act 1992 or the Industrial Relations (Northern Ireland) Order 1992 (SI 1992/807 (N.I. 5)),
  (e)   a building society (within the meaning of the Building Societies Act 1986),
  (f)   a limited liability partnership, registered under the Limited Liability Partnerships Act 2000, that carries on business in the United Kingdom,
  (g)   a friendly society registered under the Friendly Societies Act 1974, a registered society within the meaning of the Co-operative and Community Benefit Societies Act 2014 or a society registered (or deemed to be registered) under the Industrial and Provident Societies Act (Northern Ireland) 1969 (c 24 (N.I.)), or
  (h)   an unincorporated association of two or more persons that is not within any of the preceding paragraphs but carries on business or other activities wholly or mainly in the United Kingdom and whose main office is there.

(2)   But "permissible donor" does not include, in relation to a recall petition in respect of an MP for a constituency in Great Britain, a party registered in the Northern Ireland register maintained by the Electoral Commission under Part 2 of PPERA 2000 (registration of political parties).

(3)   In relation to a donation in the form of a bequest, sub-paragraph (1)(b) has effect as if it referred to an individual who was, at any time within the period of 5 years ending with the date of his or her death, registered in an electoral register.

(4)   In this paragraph "an electoral register" means

(a) a register of parliamentary or local government electors maintained under section 9 of the Representation of the People Act 1983,

(b) a register of relevant citizens of the European Union prepared under the European Parliamentary Elections (Franchise of Relevant Citizens of the Union) Regulations 2001 (SI 2001/1184), or

(c) a register of peers prepared under regulations under section 3 of the Representation of the People Act 1985.

Return of donations

7   References in this Schedule to returning a donation (however expressed) include returning an equivalent amount or, where the donation is not of money, returning an amount equivalent to the value of the donation.

Power to alter certain financial limits

8(1)   The Minister may by regulations amend any of the following provisions so as to substitute a different amount for the amount for the time being mentioned in the provision

    (a) paragraph 4(1)(a)(i) or (ii) (amount at or below which donation is to be disregarded);

    (b) paragraph 12(2) (amount above which donations made on behalf of other persons are treated as separate donations).

(2)   Before making regulations under this paragraph the Minister must consult the Electoral Commission.

(3)   Regulations under this paragraph are subject to affirmative resolution procedure.

(4)   Sub-paragraphs (2) and (3) do not apply where the Minister considers that the substitution is expedient in consequence of changes in the value of money.

NOTES

Defined terms	the Minister: s 22(1)
bequest: Sch 4, Pt 2	PPERA 2000: s 22(1)
business: Sch 4, Pt 2	property: Sch 4, Pt 2
combined region: Sch 4, Pt 2	register of parliamentary electors: s 22(2), (3)
Gibraltar party: Sch 4, Pt 2	
market value: Sch 4, Pt 2	

Part 2
Control of Donations

Prohibition on accepting donations from impermissible or unidentifiable donors

9   A relevant donation received by an accredited campaigner must not be accepted by the accredited campaigner if

    (a) the donor is not, at the time of its receipt, a permissible donor, or

    (b) the accredited campaigner is unable to ascertain the identity of the donor (whether because the donation is given anonymously or by reason of any deception or concealment or otherwise).

Donations treated as received or not received from permissible donors

10(1)   For the purposes of this Schedule

    (a) a relevant donation received by an accredited campaigner which is an exempt trust donation is treated as a relevant donation received from a permissible donor;

(b) any other relevant donation received by an accredited campaigner from a trustee of any property (in the trustee's capacity as such) is treated as a relevant donation received otherwise than from a permissible donor.

(2) Sub-paragraph (1)(b) does not apply to a relevant donation transmitted by the trustee to the accredited campaigner on behalf of beneficiaries under the trust all of whom are

(a) persons who are, at the time of its receipt, permissible donors, or

(b) members of an unincorporated association which is, at that time, a permissible donor.

Meaning of "exempt trust donation" in paragraph 10

11(1) In paragraph 10 "exempt trust donation" means a donation that

(a) meets condition A or B, and

(b) is not received from a trustee of any property pursuant to the exercise of any discretion vested by a trust in the trustee or any other person.

(2) Condition A is that

(a) the donation is received from a trustee of any property in accordance with the terms of a relevant trust, and

(b) at or before the time of the receipt of the donation, the trustee gives the recipient of the donation the full name of the person who created the trust and of every other person by whom, or under whose will, property was transferred to the trust before that date.

(3) "Relevant trust" means a trust

(a) which was created before 27th July 1999,

(b) to which no property has been transferred on or after that date, and

(c) whose terms have not been varied on or after that date.

(4) Condition B is that

(a) the donation is received from a trustee of any property in accordance with the terms of a qualifying trust, and

(b) at or before the time of the receipt of the donation, the trustee gives the recipient of the donation all such details in respect of the donor as are required by paragraph 3(1)(a)(iii) of Schedule 5 (recall petition returns).

(5) "Qualifying trust" means a trust

(a) which was created by

(i) a person who was a permissible donor at the time the trust was created, or

(ii) in the case of a donation in the form of a bequest, the will of an individual within paragraph 6(3), and

(b) to which no property has been transferred otherwise than

(i) by a person who was a permissible donor at the time of the transfer, or

(ii) in the case of a donation in the form of a bequest, under the will of an individual within paragraph 6(3).

(6) In this paragraph

(a) "property", in the context of the transfer of property to a trust, does not include income of the trust;

(b) "trust" includes a trust created by a will;

(c) a reference to a donation received from a trustee

(i) is a reference to a donation received from the trustee in the trustee's capacity as such, but

(ii) does not include a donation transmitted on behalf of a beneficiary under a trust.

Donations made on behalf of other persons

12(1)   Sub-paragraphs (2) and (3) apply where
      (a)   a person ("the agent") causes an amount ("the relevant amount") to be received by an accredited campaigner
          (i)   on behalf of the agent and one or more other persons, or
          (ii)   on behalf of two or more other persons, and
      (b)   the agent acts as mentioned in paragraph (a) for the purpose of
          (i)   meeting petition expenses incurred by or on behalf of the accredited campaigner, or
          (ii)   securing that petition expenses are not so incurred.

  (2)   For the purposes of this Schedule each individual contribution by a person within sub-paragraph (1)(a)(i) or (ii) of more than £500 is treated as if it were a separate donation received from that person.

  (3)   In relation to each such separate donation, the agent must ensure that, at the time when the relevant amount is received by the accredited campaigner, the responsible person is given
      (a)   all such details in respect of the donation as are required by paragraph 3(1)(a)(i) of Schedule 5 (recall petition returns), and
      (b)   except in the case of a donation which the agent is treated as making, all such details in respect of the donor as are required by paragraph 3(1)(a)(iii) of that Schedule.

  (4)   Sub-paragraph (5) applies where a person ("the agent") causes an amount to be received by an accredited campaigner by way of a relevant donation on behalf of one other person ("the donor").

  (5)   The agent must ensure that, at the time when the donation is received by the accredited campaigner, the responsible person is given all such details in respect of the donor as are required by paragraph 3(1)(a)(iii) of Schedule 5.

  (6)   A person commits an offence if, without reasonable excuse, the person fails to comply with sub-paragraph (3) or (5).

  (7)   A person guilty of an offence under this paragraph is liable
      (a)   on conviction on indictment, to imprisonment for a term not exceeding 12 months or a fine (or both), and
      (b)   on summary conviction
          (i)   in England and Wales, to imprisonment for a term not exceeding 12 months or a fine (or both),
          (ii)   in Scotland, to imprisonment for a term not exceeding 12 months or a fine not exceeding the statutory maximum (or both), and
          (iii)   in Northern Ireland, to imprisonment for a term not exceeding 6 months or a fine not exceeding the statutory maximum (or both).

Duty to verify identity of donor

13(1)   This paragraph applies where
      (a)   a relevant donation is received by an accredited campaigner, and
      (b)   it is not immediately decided that the accredited campaigner should (for whatever reason) refuse the donation.

  (2)   All reasonable steps must be taken immediately by or on behalf of the accredited campaigner to verify (or, so far as any of the following is not apparent, ascertain)
      (a)   the identity of the donor,
      (b)   whether the donor is a permissible donor, and

(c) if it appears that the donor is a permissible donor, all such details in respect of the donor as are required by paragraph 3(1)(a)(iii) of Schedule 5 (recall petition returns).

Duty to return donations from impermissible donors

14(1) This paragraph applies where an accredited campaigner receives a relevant donation which the accredited campaigner is prohibited from accepting by virtue of paragraph 9(a) (impermissible donor) but not by virtue of paragraph 9(b) (unidentifiable donor).

(2) The donation must, before the end of the period of 30 days beginning with the day on which the donation is received, be returned to
(a) the donor, or
(b) any person appearing to be acting on that person's behalf.

(3) If sub-paragraph (2) is not complied with, an offence is committed by
(a) the accredited campaigner, and
(b) the responsible person.

(4) It is a defence for a person charged with an offence under this paragraph to show that
(a) all reasonable steps were taken by or on behalf of the accredited campaigner to verify (or ascertain) whether the donor was a permissible donor, and
(b) as a result, the relevant person believed the donor to be a permissible donor.

(5) "The relevant person" means
(a) where the person charged with the offence is an individual, that individual, and
(b) otherwise, the responsible person.

(6) A person guilty of an offence under this paragraph is liable
(a) on conviction on indictment, to imprisonment for a term not exceeding 12 months or a fine (or both), and
(b) on summary conviction
(i) in England and Wales, to imprisonment for a term not exceeding 12 months or a fine (or both),
(ii) in Scotland, to imprisonment for a term not exceeding 12 months or a fine not exceeding the statutory maximum (or both), and
(iii) in Northern Ireland, to imprisonment for a term not exceeding 6 months or a fine not exceeding the statutory maximum (or both).

Duty to return donations from unidentifiable donors

15(1) This paragraph applies where an accredited campaigner receives a relevant donation which the accredited campaigner is prohibited from accepting by virtue of paragraph 9(b) (unidentifiable donor).

(2) The donation must be returned to the appropriate person before the end of the period of 30 days beginning with the day on which the donation is received.

(3) "The appropriate person" means
(a) where the donation was transmitted by a person other than the donor, and the identity of that person is apparent, that person,
(b) where the identity of the person by whom the donation was transmitted is not apparent, but it is apparent that the donor has, in connection with the donation, used any facility provided by an identifiable financial institution, that institution, and
(c) in any other case, the Electoral Commission.

(4) If sub-paragraph (2) is not complied with an offence is committed by
(a) the accredited campaigner, and
(b) the responsible person.

(5) A person guilty of an offence under this paragraph is liable
    (a) on conviction on indictment, to imprisonment for a term not exceeding 12 months or a fine (or both), and
    (b) on summary conviction
        (i) in England and Wales, to imprisonment for a term not exceeding 12 months or a fine (or both),
        (ii) in Scotland, to imprisonment for a term not exceeding 12 months or a fine not exceeding the statutory maximum (or both), and
        (iii) in Northern Ireland, to imprisonment for a term not exceeding 6 months or a fine not exceeding the statutory maximum (or both).

(6) The Electoral Commission must pay into the Consolidated Fund any amount received by virtue of this paragraph.

Circumstances in which donations treated as accepted or received

16(1) A relevant donation received by an accredited campaigner that is not accepted before the end of the period of 30 days beginning with the day on which it is received is treated for the purposes of this Act as accepted by the accredited campaigner at the end of that period.

(2) Sub-paragraph (1) does not apply where
    (a) paragraph 14(2) or 15(2) (return of donations from impermissible or unidentifiable donors) has been complied with in relation to the donation, and
    (b) a record can be produced of the receipt of the donation, and of the donation being returned as required by paragraph 14(2) or 15(2).

(3) Where a relevant donation is received by an accredited campaigner in the form of an amount paid into an account held by the accredited campaigner with a financial institution, it is treated for the purposes of this Act as received at the time the accredited campaigner is notified in the usual way of the payment into the account.

Forfeiture of donations made by impermissible or unidentifiable donors

17(1) This paragraph applies where an accredited campaigner accepts a relevant donation in contravention of paragraph 9.

(2) The court may, on an application made by the Electoral Commission, order the forfeiture by the accredited campaigner of an amount equal to
    (a) the amount of the donation, where it is of money, or
    (b) the value of the donation, where it is not of money.

(3) The standard of proof in proceedings on an application under this paragraph is that applicable to civil proceedings.

(4) An order may be made under this paragraph whether or not proceedings are brought against any person for an offence connected with the donation.

(5) In this paragraph "the court" means
    (a) in relation to England and Wales, a magistrates' court;
    (b) in relation to Scotland, the sheriff;
    (c) in relation to Northern Ireland, a court of summary jurisdiction.

(6) Proceedings on an application under this paragraph to the sheriff are civil proceedings.

Appeal against order under paragraph 17

18(1) Sub-paragraphs (2) to (5) apply where an order is made under paragraph 17 by
    (a) a magistrates' court, or
    (b) a court of summary jurisdiction in Northern Ireland.

(2) The accredited campaigner may, before the end of the period of 30 days beginning with the day on which the order is made, appeal to the Crown Court or, in Northern Ireland, to a county court.

(3) An appeal under sub-paragraph (2) is by way of a rehearing.

(4) The standard of proof in proceedings on an appeal under sub-paragraph (2) is that applicable to civil proceedings.

(5) The court on hearing an appeal under sub-paragraph (2)
  (a) may make such order as it considers appropriate, and
  (b) may make an order whether or not proceedings are brought against any person for an offence connected with the donation.

(6) Where an order is made under paragraph 17 by the sheriff, the accredited campaigner may appeal against the order to the Court of Session.

Supplementary provision about orders under paragraph 17 or 18

19(1) Provision may be made by rules of court
  (a) with respect to applications or appeals under paragraph 17 or 18 to any court,
  (b) for the giving of notice of such applications or appeals to persons affected,
  (c) for the joinder, or in Scotland sisting, of such persons as parties, or
  (d) otherwise in respect of the procedure under those paragraphs before any court.

(2) Sub-paragraph (1) is without prejudice to the generality of any other power to make rules of court.

(3) Any amount forfeited in compliance with an order under paragraph 17 or 18 must be paid into the Consolidated Fund.

(4) Sub-paragraph (3) does not apply
  (a) where the forfeiture was ordered under paragraph 17 by a magistrates' court or a court of summary jurisdiction in Northern Ireland, before the end of the period of 30 days beginning with the day on which the order is made;
  (b) where the forfeiture was ordered by the sheriff under paragraph 17, before the end of any period within which, in accordance with rules of court, any appeal under paragraph 18(6) must be made;
  (c) where an appeal is made under paragraph 18, before the appeal is determined or otherwise disposed of.

(5) Where the accredited campaigner is an unincorporated body
  (a) proceedings under paragraph 17 or 18 are to be brought against or by the body in its own name (and not in that of any of its members),
  (b) for the purposes of any such proceedings, any rules of court relating to the service of documents apply as if the body were a body corporate, and
  (c) any amount forfeited in accordance with an order under paragraph 17 or 18 is to be paid out of the funds of the body.

Evasion of restrictions on donations

20(1) A person commits an offence if the person
  (a) knowingly enters into an evasion arrangement, or
  (b) knowingly does any act in furtherance of an evasion arrangement.

(2) "An evasion arrangement" is any arrangement which facilitates or is likely to facilitate, whether by means of any concealment or disguise or otherwise, the making of relevant donations to an accredited campaigner by any person other than a permissible donor.

(3) A person commits an offence if the person knowingly gives the responsible person in relation to an accredited campaigner

(a) information relating to the amount or value of any relevant donation made to the accredited campaigner which is false in a material particular, or

(b) information relating to the person making such a donation which is false in a material particular.

(4) A person commits an offence if the person, with intent to deceive, withholds from the responsible person in relation to an accredited campaigner

(a) material information relating to the amount or value of any relevant donation made to the accredited campaigner, or

(b) material information relating to the person making such a donation.

(5) A person guilty of an offence under this paragraph is liable

(a) on conviction on indictment, to imprisonment for a term not exceeding 12 months or a fine (or both), and

(b) on summary conviction

(i) in England and Wales, to imprisonment for a term not exceeding 12 months or a fine (or both),

(ii) in Scotland, to imprisonment for a term not exceeding 12 months or a fine not exceeding the statutory maximum (or both), and

(iii) in Northern Ireland, to imprisonment for a term not exceeding 6 months or a fine not exceeding the statutory maximum (or both).

Further provision about offences under this Schedule

21(1) The following provisions of PPERA 2000 apply in relation to offences under this Schedule as they apply in relation to offences under that Act

(a) section 151 (summary proceedings);

(b) section 152 (offences committed by bodies corporate);

(c) section 153 (offences committed by unincorporated associations);

(d) section 154 (court to report convictions to Electoral Commission).

(2) In paragraphs 12(7)(b)(i), 14(6)(b)(i), 15(5)(b)(i) and 20(5)(b)(i)

(a) the reference to 12 months is to be read as a reference to 6 months in relation to an offence committed before section 154(1) of the Criminal Justice Act 2003 comes into force, and

(b) the reference to a fine is to be read as a reference to a fine not exceeding the statutory maximum in relation to an offence committed before section 85(1) of the Legal Aid, Sentencing and Punishment of Offenders Act 2012 comes into force.

Application of defined terms in PPERA 2000

22 In this Schedule, the following expressions have the same meaning as in PPERA 2000: "bequest"; "business"; "combined region"; "Gibraltar party"; "market value"; "property" (see section 160(1) of that Act).

NOTES

Defined terms
accredited campaigner: Sch 4, Pt 1
donation: Sch 4, Pt 1
permissible donor: Sch 4, Pt 1
petition expense: Sch 4, Pt 1

PPERA 2000: s 22(1)
relevant donation: Sch 4, Pt 1

SCHEDULE 5
Recall Petition Returns

Section 16

Recall petition returns

1(1) The responsible person in relation to an accredited campaigner must make a return, referred to in this Schedule as a "recall petition return".

(2) The recall petition return must specify the recall petition to which it relates and

(a) must contain the statements, and be accompanied by the documents, mentioned in paragraph 2 (statements and accompanying documents relating to petition expenses),

(b) must, in the case of an accredited campaigner to whom this paragraph applies

(i) contain the statement mentioned in paragraph 3(1),

(ii) be accompanied, where paragraph 3(2) applies, by the documents required by that provision, and

(iii) contain the statement mentioned in paragraph 4, and

(c) must be accompanied by the declaration required by paragraph 5 (declaration of responsible person).

(3) Sub-paragraph (2)(b) applies to an accredited campaigner who

(a) is not a registered party, or

(b) is a registered party but is a minor party.

(4) The Electoral Commission may by regulations prescribe a form of return which may be used for the purposes of this Schedule.

(5) In this Schedule

"accredited campaigner" has the same meaning as in Schedule 3 (see Part 5 of that Schedule);

"minor party" and "registered party" have the same meaning as in PPERA 2000 (see section 160(1) of that Act);

"petition expense" has the same meaning as in Schedule 3 (see Part 4 of that Schedule);

"the recall petition period" has the same meaning as in Schedule 3 (see paragraph 1(7) of that Schedule);

"relevant donation" has the same meaning as in Schedule 4 (see Part 1 of that Schedule);

"responsible person" means the person determined in accordance with paragraph 21 of Schedule 3.

Statements and accompanying documents relating to petition expenses

2(1) The statements required by paragraph 1(2)(a) to be contained in the recall petition return are

(a) a statement of all payments made in respect of petition expenses incurred by or on behalf of the accredited campaigner during the recall petition period, or a statement that there were no such payments,

(b) a statement of all unpaid claims in respect of which the responsible person is aware that an application has been made, or is about to be made, to a court under paragraph 11 of Schedule 3 (application for leave to pay out of time), or a statement that the responsible person is not aware of any such claims, and

(c) a statement of all disputed claims (within the meaning of paragraph 12 of that Schedule), or a statement that there were no such claims.

(2) Sub-paragraph (1) does not apply to payments made in respect of preaccreditation expenses or to claims for the payment of such expenses.

(3) The documents required by paragraph 1(2)(a) to accompany the recall petition return are

    (a) an invoice or receipt in respect of each payment (if any) that is

        (i) included in the statement under sub-paragraph (1)(a), and

        (ii) required by paragraph 9(2) of Schedule 3 to be supported by an invoice or receipt,

    (b) a declaration made by the responsible person of all amounts treated under paragraph 4 of that Schedule (expenses incurred by persons acting in concert) as petition expenses incurred by or on behalf of the accredited campaigner during the recall petition period, or a declaration that there were no such amounts,

    (c) a declaration made by the responsible person of all amounts treated under paragraph 6(4)(b) of that Schedule (notional petition expenses) as petition expenses incurred by the accredited campaigner during the recall petition period, or a declaration that there were no such amounts, and

    (d) a declaration made by the responsible person of the total amount of preaccreditation expenses, or a declaration that there were no such expenses.

(4) In this paragraph "pre-accreditation expenses" means

    (a) petition expenses treated as incurred by or on behalf of the accredited campaigner during the recall petition period by virtue of paragraph 5 of Schedule 3 (expenses incurred before recall petition period), and

    (b) petition expenses of the kind referred to in paragraph 7(a) of that Schedule (expenses incurred during recall petition period but before accreditation).

Statement and accompanying documents relating to relevant donations accepted

3(1) The statement required by paragraph 1(2)(b)(i) to be contained in the recall petition return is

    (a) a statement recording, in relation to each relevant donation accepted by the accredited campaigner

        (i) the amount of the donation or, where the donation is not of money, the nature of the donation and its value (as determined in accordance with paragraph 5 of Schedule 4),

        (ii) the date the donation was accepted by the accredited campaigner,

        (iii) the information about the donor which is, in connection with recordable donations to registered parties, required to be recorded in donation reports by virtue of paragraph 2 of Schedule 6 to PPERA 2000 (reading references in sub-paragraphs (3B) and (3C) to the registered party as references to the accredited campaigner), and

        (iv) such other information as may be required by regulations made by the Minister, or

    (b) a statement recording that no relevant donations were accepted by the accredited campaigner.

(2) If the information recorded under sub-paragraph (1)(a)(iii) includes a statement of the kind mentioned in paragraph 2(3B) or (3C) of Schedule 6 to PPERA 2000 (statement that accredited campaigner has seen evidence of anonymous entry in electoral register), the return must be accompanied by a copy of the evidence referred to in the statement.

(3) Before making regulations under this paragraph the Minister must consult the Electoral Commission.

(4) Regulations under this paragraph are subject to negative resolution procedure.

Statement relating to relevant donations received from impermissible or unidentifiable donors

4(1) The statement required by paragraph 1(2)(b)(iii) to be contained in the recall petition return is a statement

    (a) recording the appropriate details in relation to each relevant donation that the accredited campaigner received but was prohibited from accepting by virtue of paragraph 9(a) of Schedule 4 (impermissible donor), or recording that no relevant donations of that kind were received, and

    (b) recording the appropriate details in relation to each relevant donation that the accredited campaigner received but was prohibited from accepting by virtue of paragraph 9(b) of that Schedule (unidentifiable donor), or recording that no relevant donations of that kind were received.

(2) In relation to a relevant donation of the kind mentioned in sub-paragraph (1)(a), "the appropriate details" means

    (a) the name and address of the donor,

    (b) where the donation is of money, the amount of the donation,

    (c) where the donation is not of money, the nature of the donation and its value (as determined in accordance with paragraph 5 of Schedule 4),

    (d) the date the donation was received by the accredited campaigner,

    (e) the date and manner in which the donation was returned in accordance with paragraph 14(2) of Schedule 4, and

    (f) such other information as may be required by regulations made by the Minister.

(3) In relation to a relevant donation of the kind mentioned in sub-paragraph (1)(b), "the appropriate details" means

    (a) details of the manner in which the donation was made,

    (b) where the donation is of money, the amount of the donation,

    (c) where the donation is not of money, the nature of the donation and its value (as determined in accordance with paragraph 5 of Schedule 4),

    (d) the date the donation was received by the accredited campaigner,

    (e) the date and manner in which the donation was returned in accordance with paragraph 15(2) of Schedule 4, and

    (f) such other information as may be required by regulations made by the Minister.

(4) Before making regulations under this paragraph the Minister must consult the Electoral Commission.

(5) Regulations under this paragraph are subject to negative resolution procedure.

Declaration of responsible person as to return

5(1) The responsible person must make the following declaration

    (a) that the responsible person has examined the recall petition return, and

    (b) that to the best of the responsible person's knowledge and belief

        (i) it is a complete and correct return as required by law, and

        (ii) all expenses shown in it as paid have been paid by the responsible person or a person authorised by the responsible person to make the payment.

(2) In the case of an accredited campaigner to whom this sub-paragraph applies, the declaration must also state

    (a) that all relevant donations recorded in the return as having been accepted by the accredited campaigner are from permissible donors (within the meaning of Schedule 4: see paragraph 6 of that Schedule), and

      (b) that no other relevant donations have been accepted by the accredited campaigner.

(3)   Sub-paragraph (2) applies to an accredited campaigner who
      (a) is not a registered party, or
      (b) is a registered party but is a minor party.

(4)   The declaration must be signed by the responsible person.

Delivery of return etc to petition officer and supplementary returns

6(1)   The responsible person must, within 30 days of the end of the recall petition period, deliver to the petition officer
      (a) the recall petition return, and
      (b) all documents required by this Schedule to accompany the return.

(2)   Where, after the date on which the return is delivered to the petition officer, leave is granted by a court under paragraph 11 of Schedule 3 (leave for payment of late claim), the responsible person must, within 7 days of any payment made in pursuance of the order of leave, deliver to the petition officer a supplementary return.

(3)   The supplementary return
      (a) must state the amount of the payment, and
      (b) must be accompanied by a copy of the court order granting the leave.

Offences relating to return

7(1)   The responsible person commits an offence if, without reasonable excuse, he or she
      (a) fails to deliver a recall petition return in accordance with paragraph 6(1)(a),
      (b) delivers a recall petition return to the petition officer that does not contain a statement required by paragraph 1(2)(a) or (b),
      (c) fails to deliver a document, other than a declaration under paragraph 5, in accordance with paragraph 6(1)(b),
      (d) fails to deliver a supplementary return in accordance with paragraph 6(2), or
      (e) delivers a supplementary return to the petition officer that does not comply with paragraph 6(3).

(2)   An offence under sub-paragraph (1) is an illegal practice.

(3)   The responsible person commits an offence if without reasonable excuse, he or she fails to deliver a declaration under paragraph 5 in accordance with paragraph 6(1)(b).

(4)   The responsible person commits an offence if he or she delivers a declaration under paragraph 2(3)(b), (c) or (d) or 5 to the petition officer where
      (a) the declaration is false, and
      (b) at the time the responsible person made the declaration, he or she knew that it was false, or was reckless as to whether it was false.

(5)   An offence under sub-paragraph (3) or (4) is a corrupt practice.

(6)   Paragraph 25 of Schedule 3 (which is about offences under that Schedule which are corrupt or illegal practices) applies to an offence under this paragraph as it applies to an offence under that Schedule.

Onward delivery of returns to Electoral Commission

8(1)   The petition officer must deliver to the Electoral Commission
      (a) a copy of a recall petition return received by the officer;
      (b) a copy of a declaration, or other document, received by the officer accompanying a recall petition return;
      (c) a copy of a supplementary return received by the officer;

(d) a copy of a document accompanying such a return and received by the officer in accordance with paragraph 6(3)(b).

(2) Delivery under sub-paragraph (1) must be as soon as reasonably practicable after the officer receives the document in question.

Inspection of returns and accompanying documents

9(1) The petition officer must
    (a) as soon as reasonably practicable after receiving
        (i) a recall petition return,
        (ii) a supplementary return, or
        (iii) a declaration,
    make the return or declaration available for public inspection at the officer's office or other convenient place chosen by the officer;
    (b) continue to make the return or declaration available for inspection at such a place for the period of 2 years beginning with the date on which the return is received;
    (c) supply a copy of the return or declaration, or of any other document accompanying the return in accordance with this Schedule, to any person who
        (i) requests it within that period of 2 years, and
        (ii) pays such fee as may be prescribed in regulations made by the Minister.

(2) Where sub-paragraph (1) applies in relation to a recall petition return that contains a statement mentioned in paragraph 3 or 4 that includes the home address of a donor who is an individual, the duties imposed by sub-paragraph (1) apply in relation to a copy of the statement that does not include the donor's home address.

(3) The petition officer must, within 40 days of the end of the recall petition period
    (a) notify the responsible person in relation to each accredited campaigner of the relevant information, and
    (b) publish the relevant information in such manner as the petition officer thinks fit.

(4) "The relevant information" means the place at which, and times at which, recall petition returns, supplementary returns (if any) and declarations are to be made available for public inspection under sub-paragraph (1).

(5) After the expiry of the 2 year period mentioned in sub-paragraph (1)(b), the petition officer must
    (a) cause the recall petition return (or, as the case may be, the supplementary return), and any declaration or other document accompanying the return, to be destroyed, or
    (b) if the responsible person in relation to the accredited campaigner in question so requests, cause the return and those documents (or any of them) to be returned to the responsible person.

(6) Regulations under this paragraph are subject to affirmative resolution procedure.

(7) References in this paragraph to a declaration are to a declaration under paragraph 2(3)(b), (c) or (d) or 5.

Application of certain provisions of Schedule 3

10 The following provisions of Schedule 3 (regulation of expenditure) apply for the purposes of this Schedule as they apply for the purposes of Part 2 of that Schedule
    (a) paragraph 4 (expenses incurred by persons acting in concert);
    (b) paragraph 5 (expenses incurred before the recall petition period);
    (c) paragraph 6 (notional petition expenses);
    (d) paragraph 7 (expenses incurred before becoming an accredited campaigner).

SCHEDULE 6
Minor and Consequential Amendments

Section 20

Not reproduced here

Recess Elections Act 1975

An Act to consolidate the enactments relating to the issue of warrants for by-elections when the House of Commons is in recess, and to repeal, as unnecessary, section 106(2) of the Bankruptcy Act 1914

12th November 1975

1   Issue of warrants by Speaker for making out writs
2   Restrictions on Speaker's Powers
3   Acceptance of office
4   Appointment of Members to exercise Speaker's powers
5   Citation etc

1   Issue of warrants by Speaker for making out writs

(1)   During any recess of the House of Commons, whether by prorogation or adjournment, it shall be the duty of the Speaker, subject to the provisions of this Act, upon receipt of a certificate of vacancy to issue his warrant to the Clerk of the Crown in Chancery to make out a new writ for electing a Member of the House in place of a Member whose seat has become vacant

     (a)   because he has died or become disqualified as a peer for membership of the House of Commons, either during the recess or before it;

     (b)   because he has accepted a disqualifying office during the recess; or

     (c)   because of his bankruptcy.

(2)   In this Act
"certificate of vacancy" means

     (a)   where the seat has become vacant because the Member has died, become disqualified as a peer for membership of the House of Commons or accepted a disqualifying office, a certificate under the hands of two Members of the House of Commons in the form set out in Schedule 1 to this Act, or to the like effect; and

     (b)   where the seat has become vacant because of a Member's bankruptcy, a certificate under section 427(6)(a) of the Insolvency Act 1986;

""disqualifying office" means any office, other than the office of steward or bailiff of Her Majesty's three Chiltern Hundreds of Stoke, Desborough and Burnham or of the Manor of Northstead, which disqualifies its holder for membership of the House of Commons;

2   Restrictions on Speaker's Powers

(1)   The Speaker shall cause notice of his receipt of a certificate of vacancy to be inserted in the London Gazette.

(2)   The Speaker shall not issue a warrant under section 1 above until six days after the insertion of the notice.

(3)   The Speaker shall not issue such a warrant unless he has received the certificate of vacancy so long before the date of the next meeting of the House of Commons for the despatch of business that the writ for the by-election may be issued before that date.

(4)   Except where a seat has become vacant because of a Member's bankruptcy, the Speaker shall not issue such a warrant

     (a)   unless the return of the writ for the election of the Member whose seat has become vacant has been brought into the office of the Clerk of the Crown in

Chancery fifteen days at least before the end of the last sitting of the House of Commons before the Speaker's receipt of the certificate of vacancy; or

(b)   if a petition against the election of the Member whose seat has become vacant was pending when Parliament was prorogued or the House of Commons was adjourned.

NOTES
Defined terms
   certificate of vacancy: s 1(2)

3 Acceptance of office

(1)   A Member of the House of Commons who accepts a disqualifying office shall forthwith give written notice of his acceptance to the Speaker; and the notice may be given by signing a certificate of vacancy.

(2)   Where a seat becomes vacant on a Member's acceptance of a disqualifying office, the Speaker shall not issue a warrant under section 1 above unless the certificate of vacancy is accompanied by a copy of the issue of the London, Edinburgh or Belfast Gazette in which the Member's appointment to that office was gazetted.

NOTES
Defined terms
   certificate of vacancy: s 1(2)
   disqualifying office: s 1(2)

4 Appointment of Members to exercise Speaker's powers

(1)   It shall be the duty of the Speaker, within a convenient time after taking office, by instrument in writing under his hand and seal, to appoint not more than seven nor less than three Members of the House of Commons to exercise the powers given to the Speaker by this Act at any time when there is no Speaker or the Speaker is out of the United Kingdom; and if the number of persons appointed is reduced to less than three, he may appoint one or more further Members.

(2)   An appointment shall remain in force until the dissolution of the Parliament in which it is made.

(3)   An appointment shall be entered in the journals of the House of Commons and be published once in the London Gazette, and the instrument of appointment shall be preserved by the Clerk of the House of Commons, and a duplicate filed in the office of the Clerk of the Crown in Chancery.

(4)   The powers of the Speaker may be exercised by any one of the Members appointed under this section, but when notice of the issue of a warrant is brought to the publisher of the Gazette and is signed by a Member so appointed, the publisher shall give a receipt for it, specifying the day and hour when it was received, and if more than one notice is brought to him relevant to the same election, he shall insert in the Gazette only the notice first received.

5 Citation etc

(1)   This Act may be cited as the Recess Elections Act 1975.

(2)-(7)   ....

(8)   It is hereby declared that this Act extends to Northern Ireland.

SCHEDULE 1
Certificate of Vacancy
Section 1

We, whose names are underwritten, being two Members of the House of Commons, do hereby certify

(that .. ..Member of Parliament for .. ..died on .. ..19 .. ..;)

(that .. ..Member of Parliament for .. ..has become disqualified as a peer for membership of the House of Commons;)

(that .. ..Member of Parliament for .. ..has accepted the office of .. .., and that his appointment to that office has been gazetted in the issue of the .. ..Gazette dated .. ..19 .. ..;)

and we give you this notice to the intent that you may issue your warrant to the Clerk of the Crown in Chancery to make out a new writ for the election of a Member to serve as Member of Parliament for .. ..in place of him.

To the Speaker of the House of Commons.

NOTE. If there is no Speaker, or if the Speaker is out of the United Kingdom, this certificate may be addressed to any one of the persons appointed under section 4 of the Recess Elections Act 1975 to exercise the Speaker's powers under that Act.

SCHEDULE 2

Repealed

Representation of the People Act 1981

An Act to disqualify certain persons for election to the House of Commons; to make changes in the timetable for parliamentary elections; and for connected purposes

2nd July 1981

Disqualification of certain offenders for membership of the House of Commons

1   A person found guilty of one or more offences (whether before or after the passing of this Act and whether in the United Kingdom or elsewhere), and sentenced or ordered to be imprisoned or detained indefinitely or for more than one year, shall be disqualified for membership of the House of Commons while detained anywhere in the British Islands or the Republic of Ireland in pursuance of the sentence or order or while unlawfully at large at a time when he would otherwise be so detained.

Effects of disqualification

2(1)   If a person disqualified by this Act for membership of the House of Commons is elected to that House his election shall be void; and if such a person is nominated for election as a member of that House his nomination shall be void.

(2)   If a member of the House of Commons becomes disqualified by this Act for membership of that House his seat shall be vacated.

3 *Repealed*

Citation

4.   This Act may be cited as the Representation of the People Act 1981 and shall be included among the Acts which may be cited together as the Representation of the People Acts.

Representation of the People Act 1983

An Act to consolidate the Representation of the People Acts of 1949, 1969, 1977, 1978 and 1980, the Electoral Registers Acts of 1949 and 1953, the Elections (Welsh Forms) Act 1964, Part III of the Local Government Act 1972, sections 6 to 10 of the Local Government (Scotland) Act 1973, the Representation of the People (Armed Forces) Act 1976, the Returning Officers (Scotland) Act 1977, section 3 of the Representation of the People Act 1981, section 62 of and Schedule 2 to the Mental Health (Amendment) Act 1982, and connected provisions; and to repeal as obsolete the Representation of the People Act 1979 and other enactments related to the Representation of the People Acts

8th February 1983

BE IT ENACTED by the Queen's most Excellent Majesty, by and with the advice and consent of the Lords Spiritual and Temporal, and Commons, in this present Parliament assembled, and by the authority of the same, as follows:-

PART I
PARLIAMENTARY AND LOCAL GOVERNMENT FRANCHISE AND ITS EXERCISE

828

PART IV
SPECIAL PROVISIONS AS TO OTHER LOCAL ELECTIONS

PART V
GENERAL AND SUPPLEMENTAL

PART I

PARLIAMENTARY AND LOCAL GOVERNMENT FRANCHISE AND ITS EXERCISE

Parliamentary and local government franchise

Parliamentary electors

1(1) A person is entitled to vote as an elector at a parliamentary election in any constituency if on the date of the poll he—

    (a) is registered in the register of parliamentary electors for that constituency;

    (b) is not subject to any legal incapacity to vote (age apart);

    (c) is either a Commonwealth citizen or a citizen of the Republic of Ireland; and

    (d)   is of voting age (that is, 18 years or over).

(2)   A person is not entitled to vote as an elector—

    (a)   more than once in the same constituency at any parliamentary election; or

    (b)   in more than one constituency at a general election.

NOTES

Derivation
  RPA 1949 s 1
  RPA 1969 s 1

Defined terms
  age: s 202(2)
  constituency: Parliamentary Constituencies Act 1986

s 1(2)
elector: s 202(1)
legal incapacity: s 202(1)
parliamentary election: Interpretation Act 1978 Sch 1
vote: s 202(1)

Local government electors

2(1)   A person is entitled to vote as an elector at a local government election in any electoral area if on the date of the poll he—

    (a)   is registered in the register of local government electors for that area;

    (b)   is not subject to any legal incapacity to vote (age apart);

    (c)   is a Commonwealth citizen, a citizen of the Republic of Ireland or a relevant citizen of the Union; and

    (d)   is of voting age (that is, 18 years or over, except in Scotland (see subsection (1A))).

(1A)   In Scotland, voting age is 16 years or over.

(2)   A person is not entitled to vote as an elector—

    (a)   more than once in the same electoral area at any local government election; or

    (b)   in more than one electoral area at an ordinary election for a local government area which is not a single electoral area.

NOTES

Derivation
  RPA 1949 s 2
  RPA 1969 s 1

Defined terms
  age: s 202(2)
  elector: s 202(1)
  electoral area (E&W): ss 191(1), 203(1)
  electoral area (S): s 204(1)

legal incapacity: s 202(1)
local government area (E&W): ss 191(1), 203(1)
local government area (S): s 204(1)
local government election (E&W): ss 191(1), 203(1), (1A)
local government election (S): s 204(1)
relevant citizen of the Union: s 202(1)
vote: s 202(1)

Disfranchisement of offenders in prison etc

3(1)   A convicted person during the time that he is detained in a penal institution in pursuance of his sentence or unlawfully at large when he would otherwise be so detained is legally incapable of voting at any parliamentary or local government election.

(2)   For this purpose—

    (a)   "convicted person" means any person found guilty of an offence (whether under the law of the United Kingdom or not), including a person found guilty by a court of a service offence within the meaning of the Armed Forces Act 2006, but not including a person dealt with by committal or other summary process for contempt of court; and

    (b)   "penal institution" means an institution to which the Prison Act 1952, the Prisons (Scotland) Act 1952 or the Prison Act (Northern Ireland) 1953 applies; and

    (c)   a person detained for default in complying with his sentence shall not be treated as detained in pursuance of the sentence, whether or not the sentence provided for detention in the event of default, but a person detained by virtue of a conditional pardon in respect of an offence shall be treated as detained in pursuance of his sentence for the offence.

(3) It is immaterial for the purposes of this section whether a conviction or sentence was before or after the passing of this Act.

NOTES

Derivation
  RPA 1969 s 4

local government election (S): s 204(1)
United Kingdom: Interpretation Act 1978 Sch 1

Defined terms
  local government election (E&W): ss 191(1), 203(1), (1A)

Disfranchisement of offenders detained in mental hospitals

3A(1) A person to whom this section applies is, during the time that he is—
  (a) detained at any place in pursuance of the order or direction by virtue of which this section applies to him, or
  (b) unlawfully at large when he would otherwise be so detained,
  legally incapable of voting at any parliamentary or local government election.

(2) As respects England and Wales, this section applies to the following persons—
  (a) any person in respect of whom—
    (i) an order has been made under section 37, 38, 44 or 51(5) of the Mental Health Act 1983, or
    (ii) a direction has been given under section 45A, 46 or 47 of that Act;
  (b) any person in respect of whom an order has been made under section 5(2)(a) of the Criminal Procedure (Insanity) Act 1964; and
  (c) any person in respect of whom the Court of Appeal has made an order under—
    (i) section 6(2)(a) of the Criminal Appeal Act 1968, or
    (ii) section 14(2)(a) of that Act.

(3) As respects Scotland, this section applies to the following persons—
  (a) any person in respect of whom an order has been made under section 53, 54, 57(2)(a) or (b), 57A(2) or 58 of the Criminal Procedure (Scotland) Act 1995; and
  (b) any person in respect of whom a direction has been given under section 136 of the Mental Health (Care and Treatment) (Scotland) Act 2003 or section 59A of that Act of 1995.

(4) As respects Northern Ireland, this section applies to the following persons—
  (a) any person in respect of whom—
    (i) an order has been made under Article 44, 45, 50A(2)(a) or 57(5) of the Mental Health (Northern Ireland) Order 1986, or
    (ii) a direction has been given under Article 52 or 53 of that Order; and
  (b) any person in respect of whom the Court of Appeal has made an order under—
    (i) section 11(1)(b) or (2)(b) of the Criminal Appeal (Northern Ireland) Act 1980, or
    (ii) section 13(5A) of that Act.

(5) The reference in subsection (2)(a)(i) to an order under section 37 or 38 of the Mental Health Act 1983 includes such an order made by virtue of Schedule 4 to the Armed Forces Act 2006 (including as applied by section 16(2) of the Court Martial Appeals Act 1968).

(6) In this section any reference to a person in respect of whom any order or direction falling within subsection (2), (3) or (4) has been made or given includes a reference to a person in respect of whom any such order or direction is, by virtue of any enactment,

to be treated as having been made or given in connection with his transfer to a place in the part of the United Kingdom mentioned in that subsection.

(7) Any reference in any of subsections (2) to (4) above to a provision of any Act or Order includes a reference to any earlier provision (whether of that Act or Order as originally enacted or made or as previously amended, or otherwise) to the like effect.

NOTES

Derivation
RPA 2000 s 2

Defined terms
court of appeal: Interpretation Act 1978 Sch 1
enactment: Interpretation Act 1978 Sch 1
enactment (NI): s 205
England: Interpretation Act 1978 Sch 1

local government election (E&W): ss 191(1), 203(1), (1A)
local government election (S): s 204(1)
United Kingdom: Interpretation Act 1978 Sch 1
vote: s 202(1)
Wales: Interpretation Act 1978 Sch 1

Entitlement to registration

Entitlement to be registered as parliamentary or local government elector

4(1) A person is entitled to be registered in the register of parliamentary electors for any constituency or part of a constituency if on the relevant date he—
(a) is resident in the constituency or that part of it;
(b) is not subject to any legal incapacity to vote (age apart);
(c) is either a qualifying Commonwealth citizen or a citizen of the Republic of Ireland; and
(d) is of voting age.

(2) *Repealed*

(3) A person is entitled to be registered in the register of local government electors for any electoral area if on the relevant date he—
(a) is resident in that area;
(b) is not subject to any legal incapacity to vote (age apart);
(c) is a qualifying Commonwealth citizen, a citizen of the Republic of Ireland or a relevant citizen of the Union; and
(d) is of voting age.

(4) The preceding provisions have effect—
(a) subject to—
(i) any enactment imposing a disqualification for registration as a parliamentary, or (as the case may be) local government, elector; and
(ii) compliance with any prescribed requirements; and
(b) (as respects registration as a parliamentary elector) without prejudice to section 2(1) of the Representation of the People Act 1985 (registration of British citizens overseas).

(5) A person otherwise qualified is (despite subsection (1)(d) or (3)(d), as the case may be) entitled to be registered in a register of parliamentary electors or local government electors if he will attain voting age before the end of the period of 12 months beginning with the 1st December next following the relevant date, but—
(a) his entry in the register shall give the date on which he will attain that age; and
(b) until the date given in the entry he shall not by virtue of the entry be treated as an elector for any purposes other than those of an election the date of the poll for which is the date so given or any later date.

(5A) If a person entitled to be registered by virtue of subsection (5) above has an anonymous entry in the register, the references in paragraphs (a) and (b) of that subsection to his entry in the register are to be read as references to his entry in the record of anonymous entries prepared in pursuance of paragraph 8A of Schedule 2 below.

(6) In this section—

"qualifying Commonwealth citizen" means a Commonwealth citizen who either—

    (a) is not a person who requires leave under the Immigration Act 1971 to enter or remain in the United Kingdom, or

    (b) is such a person but for the time being has (or is, by virtue of any enactment, to be treated as having) any description of such leave;

"the relevant date", in relation to a person, means—

    (a) the date on which an application for registration is made (or, by virtue of section 10A(2) below, is treated as having been made) by him;

    (b) in the case of a person applying for registration in pursuance of a declaration of local connection or a service declaration, the date on which the declaration was made.

NOTES

Derivation
Electoral Registers Act 1949 s 1
RPA 2000 s 1(2)

Extension of application
Local and European Parliamentary Elections (Registration of Citizens of Accession States) Regulations 2003, SI 2003/1557, reg 2(1), (2), (3)(a).

Defined terms
age: s 202(2)
constituency: Parliamentary Constituencies Act 1986 s 1(2)

election: s 202(1)
elector: s 202(1)
electoral area (E&W): ss 191(1), 203(1)
electoral area (S): s 204(1)
enactment: Interpretation Act 1978 Sch 1
enactment (NI): s 205
legal incapacity: s 202(1)
prescribed: s 202(1)
relevant citizen of the Union: s 202(1)
United Kingdom: Interpretation Act 1978 Sch 1
vote: s 202(1)

Residence: general

5(1) This section applies where the question whether a person is resident at a particular address on the relevant date for the purposes of section 4 above falls to be determined for the purposes of that section.

(2) Regard shall be had, in particular, to the purpose and other circumstances, as well as to the fact, of his presence at, or absence from, the address on that date.

For example, where at a particular time a person is staying at any place otherwise than on a permanent basis, he may in all the circumstances be taken to be at that time—

    (a) resident there if he has no home elsewhere, or

    (b) not resident there if he does have a home elsewhere.

(3) For the purpose of determining whether a person is resident in a dwelling on the relevant date for the purposes of section 4 above, his residence in the dwelling shall not be taken to have been interrupted by reason of his absence in the performance of any duty arising from or incidental to any office, service or employment held or undertaken by him if—

    (a) he intends to resume actual residence within six months of giving up such residence, and will not be prevented from doing so by the performance of that duty; or

    (b) the dwelling serves as a permanent place of residence (whether for himself or for himself and other persons) and he would be in actual residence there but for his absence in the performance of that duty.

(4) For the purposes of subsection (3) above any temporary period of unemployment shall be disregarded.

(5) Subsection (3) above shall apply in relation to a person's absence by reason of his attendance on a course provided by an educational institution as it applies in relation to a person's absence in the performance of any duty such as is mentioned in that subsection.

(6) Subject to sections 7 and 7A below, a person who is detained at any place in legal custody shall not, by reason of his presence there, be treated for the purposes of section 4 above as resident there.

NOTES

Derivation
RPA 1949 s 4
RPA 2000 s 3

Defined terms
dwelling: s 202(1)

Residence: merchant seamen

6 At any time when a merchant seaman is not resident in the United Kingdom and would have been resident there but for the nature of his occupation, he shall be entitled to be treated for the purposes of section 4 above as resident—
   (a) at any place at which he would have been resident but for the nature of his occupation; or
   (b) at any hostel or club providing accommodation for merchant seamen at which he commonly stays in the course of his occupation.

For this purpose "merchant seaman" means any person not having a service qualification whose employment or the greater part of it is carried out on board seagoing ships, and includes any such person while temporarily without employment.

NOTES

Derivation
RPA 1969 s 3

Defined terms
resident: s 5

service qualification: s 14
United Kingdom: Interpretation Act 1978 Sch 1

Residence: patients in mental hospitals who are not detained offenders or on remand

7(1) This section applies to a person who—
   (a) is a patient in a mental hospital (whether or not he is liable to be detained there), but
   (b) is not a person to whom section 3A above or section 7A below applies.

(2) A person to whom this section applies shall (subject to subsection (5) below) be regarded for the purposes of section 4 above as resident at the mental hospital in question if the length of the period which he is likely to spend at the hospital is sufficient for him to be regarded as being resident there for the purposes of electoral registration.

(3) A person registered in a register of electors in pursuance of an application for registration made by virtue of subsection (2) above is entitled to remain so registered until—
   (a) the end of the period of 12 months beginning with the date when the entry in the register first takes effect, or
   (aa) the registration officer determines in accordance with regulations that the person was not entitled to be registered, or
   (ab) the registration officer determines in accordance with regulations that the person was registered as the result of an application under section 10ZC made by some other person or that the person's entry has been altered as the result of an application under section 10ZD made by some other person, or

(b) another entry made in respect of him in any register of electors takes effect (whether or not in pursuance of an application made by virtue of subsection (2)),

whichever first occurs.

(4) Where the entitlement of such a person to remain so registered terminates by virtue of subsection (3) above, the registration officer concerned shall remove that person's entry from the register, unless he is entitled to remain registered in pursuance of a further application made by virtue of subsection (2).

(5) Subsection (2) above shall not be taken as precluding the registration of a person to whom this section applies—

(a) by virtue of his residence at some place other than the mental hospital in which he is a patient, or

(b) in pursuance of a declaration of local connection.

(6) In this section "mental hospital" means any establishment (or part of an establishment) maintained wholly or mainly for the reception and treatment of persons suffering from any form of mental disorder; and for this purpose "mental disorder"—

(a) in relation to England or Wales, has the same meaning as in the Mental Health Act 1983,

(b) in relation to Scotland, has the same meaning as in the Mental Health (Care and Treatment) (Scotland) Act 2003, and

(c) in relation to Northern Ireland, has the same meaning as in the Mental Health (Northern Ireland) Order 1986.

NOTES

Derivation
RPA s 4(3)
RPA 2000 s 4

Subordinate Legislation
Representation of the People (England and Wales) (Amendment) (No 2) Regulations 2006, SI 2006/2910.
Representation of the People (Scotland) (Amendment) Regulations 2007, SI 2007/925.
Representation of the People (Northern Ireland)

Regulations 2008, SI 2008/1741.

Defined terms
England: Interpretation Act 1978 Sch 1
register of electors: see s 9
registration officer: s 8(1)
resident: s 5
Wales: Interpretation Act 1978 Sch 1

Residence: persons remanded in custody etc

7A(1) This section applies to a person who is detained at any place pursuant to a relevant order or direction and is so detained otherwise than after—

(a) being convicted of any offence, or

(b) a finding in criminal proceedings that he did the act or made the omission charged.

(2) A person to whom this section applies shall (subject to subsection (5) below) be regarded for the purposes of section 4 above as resident at the place at which he is detained if the length of the period which he is likely to spend at that place is sufficient for him to be regarded as being resident there for the purposes of electoral registration.

(3) A person registered in a register of electors in pursuance of an application for registration made by virtue of subsection (2) above is entitled to remain so registered until—

(a) the end of the period of 12 months beginning with the date when the entry in the register first takes effect, or

(aa) the registration officer determines in accordance with regulations that the person was not entitled to be registered, or (ab) the registration officer determines in accordance with regulations that the person was registered as the result of an application under section 10ZC made by some other person or that the person's entry has been altered as the result of an application under section 10ZD made by some other person, or

(b) another entry made in respect of him in any register of electors takes effect (whether or not in pursuance of an application made by virtue of subsection (2)),

whichever first occurs.

(4) Where the entitlement of such a person to remain so registered terminates by virtue of subsection (3) above, the registration officer concerned shall remove that person's entry from the register, unless he is entitled to remain registered in pursuance of a further application made by virtue of subsection (2).

(5) Subsection (2) above shall not be taken as precluding the registration of a person to whom this section applies—

(a) by virtue of his residence at some place other than the place at which he is detained, or

(b) in pursuance of a declaration of local connection.

(6) In this section "a relevant order or direction" means—

(a) a remand or committal in custody;

(b) a remand to a hospital under section 35 or 36 of the Mental Health Act 1983 or Article 42 or 43 of the Mental Health (Northern Ireland) Order 1986;

(c) a direction for removal to a hospital under section 48 of that Act or Article 54 of that Order;

(d) an assessment order under section 52D or a treatment order under section 52M of the Criminal Procedure (Scotland) Act 1995; or

(e) a transfer for treatment direction under section 136 of the Mental Health (Care and Treatment) (Scotland) Act 2003 made in respect of a person to whom that section applies by virtue of article 13 of the Mental Health (Care and Treatment) (Scotland) Act 2003 (Consequential Provisions) Order 2005.

NOTES

Derivation
RPA 2000 s 5

Subordinate Legislation
Representation of the People (England and Wales) (Amendment) (No 2) Regulations 2006, SI 2006/2910.
Representation of the People (Scotland) (Amendment) Regulations 2007, SI 2007/925.

Representation of the People (Northern Ireland) Regulations 2008, SI 2008/1741.

Defined terms
register of electors: see s 9
registration officer: s 8(1)
Wales: Interpretation Act 1978 Sch 1

Notional residence: declarations of local connection

7B(1) A declaration under this section ("a declaration of local connection")—

(a) may be made only by a person to whom this section applies, but

(b) may be made by such a person despite the fact that by reason of his age he is not entitled to vote.

(2) This section applies to any person who on the date when he makes such a declaration is—

(a) a person to whom section 7 above applies and who would not be entitled to be registered by virtue of residence at any place other than the mental hospital (within the meaning of that section) at which he is a patient, or

(b) a person to whom section 7A applies and who would not be entitled to be registered by virtue of residence at any place other than the place at which he is detained as mentioned in subsection (1) of that section, or

(c) a person who does not fall within paragraph (a) or (b) above (and is not otherwise in legal custody) and who is not, for the purposes of section 4 above, resident at any address in the United Kingdom (a "homeless person").

(2A) In relation to the registration of local government electors in Scotland, this section also applies to a person who, on the date on which the person makes a declaration under subsection (1)—
    (a) is under the age of 16,
    (b) does not fall within any of paragraphs (a) to (c) of subsection (2), and
    (c) meets either of the requirements specified in subsection (2B).

(2B) The requirements are that—
    (a) the person is, or has been, a child looked after by a local authority, or
    (b) the person is being kept in secure accommodation.

(2C) For the purposes of subsection (2B)—
    (a) the reference to a child looked after by a local authority is to be construed in accordance with section 17(6) of the Children (Scotland) Act 1995 (duty of local authorities in relation to looked after children), and
    (b) "secure accommodation" means accommodation provided, for the purpose of restricting the liberty of children, in an establishment in Scotland (whether managed by a local authority, a voluntary organisation or any other person) that—
        (i) provides residential accommodation for children for the purposes of the Children's Hearings (Scotland) Act 2011, the Children (Scotland) Act 1995 or the Social Work (Scotland) Act 1968, and
        (ii) is approved in accordance with regulations made under section 78(2) of the Public Services Reform (Scotland) Act 2010 (regulations in relation to care services).

(3) A declaration of local connection shall state—
    (a) the name of the declarant and either—
        (i) an address to which correspondence for him from either the registration officer concerned or the returning officer can be delivered, or
        (ii) that he is willing to collect such correspondence periodically from the registration officer's office;
    (b) the date of the declaration;
    (c) that on the date of the declaration the declarant falls into one of the categories of persons to whom this section applies, specifying—
        (i) the category in question, and
        (ii) (in the case of a person falling within subsection (2)(a) or (b) above) the name and address of the mental hospital at which he is a patient or (as the case may be) of the place at which he is detained;
    (d) the required address (as defined by subsection (4) below);
    (e) that on the date of the declaration the declarant is a Commonwealth citizen or a citizen of the Republic of Ireland or (if the declaration is made for the purposes only of local government elections) a relevant citizen of the Union;
    (f) whether the declarant has on the date of the declaration attained the age of 18 years, and, if he has not, the date of his birth.

(4) For the purposes of this section "the required address" is—
    (a) in the case of a person falling within subsection (2)(a) or (b) above—
        (i) the address in the United Kingdom where he would be residing if he were not such a patient, or detained, as mentioned in that provision, or
        (ii) if he cannot give such an address, an address in the United Kingdom at which he has resided;

    (b) in the case of a homeless person, the address of, or which is nearest to, a place in the United Kingdom where he commonly spends a substantial part of his time (whether during the day or at night);

    (c) in the case of a person falling within subsection (2A), any address in Scotland at which the person has previously been resident.

(5) *Repealed*

(6) Where a declaration of local connection made by a homeless person is delivered to the registration officer concerned during the period—

    (a) beginning with the date when a vacancy occurs—

        (i) in the seat for the parliamentary constituency within which the required address falls, or

        (ii) in the seat for any Scottish Parliament constituency or National Assembly for Wales constituency within which it falls, and

    (b) ending on the final nomination day (within the meaning of section 13B below) for the parliamentary by-election, or (as the case may be) the election under section 9 of the Scotland Act 1998 or section 10 of the Government of Wales Act 2006, held in respect of that vacancy,

the declaration must state that, during the period of three months ending on the date of the declaration, the declarant has commonly been spending a substantial part of his time (whether during the day or at night) at, or near, the required address.

(7) No declaration of local connection shall be specially made by a person for the purposes of local government elections, and any such declaration made for the purposes of parliamentary elections shall have effect also for the purposes of local government elections; but—

    (a) a declaration of local connection may be made for the purposes only of local government elections by a person who is as a peer subject to a legal incapacity to vote at parliamentary elections or by a relevant citizen of the Union; and

    (b) where so made, shall be marked to show that it is available for local government elections only, but shall in all other respects be the same as other declarations of local connection.

(7A) Despite anything in subsection (7), in relation to Scotland, a relevant declaration made by a person has effect only for the purposes of the person's registration as a local government elector.

(7B) In subsection (7A), "relevant declaration" means—

    (a) a declaration of local connection made by virtue of subsection (2A),

    (b) any other declaration of local connection made by a person who, on the date on which the declaration is made, is—

        (i) under the age of 17, and

        (ii) not entitled to be registered in the register of parliamentary electors.

(7C) A relevant declaration referred to in subsection (7A) must be marked to show that it is available only for the purposes of registration as a local government elector, but otherwise is to be the same as other declarations of local connection.

(8) If a person—

    (a) makes a declaration of local connection stating more than one address under subsection (3)(d) above, or

    (b) makes more than one declaration of local connection bearing the same date and stating different addresses under that provision,

the declaration or declarations shall be void.

(9) A declaration of local connection may be cancelled at any time by the declarant.

(10) A declaration of local connection shall be of no effect unless it is received by the registration officer concerned within the period of three months beginning with the date of the declaration.

NOTES

Derivation
   RPA 2000 s 6

Extension of application
Local and European Parliamentary Elections (Registration of Citizens of Accession States) Regulations 2003, SI 2003/1557.

Defined terms
   age: s 202(2)
   citizen of the Union: s 202(1)

constituency: Parliamentary Constituencies Act 1986 s 1(2)
local government election (E&W): s 203(1), (1A)
local government election (S): s 204(1)
parliamentary election: Interpretation Act 1978 Sch 1
registration officer: s 8(1)
returning officer: see ss 24-27
United Kingdom: Interpretation Act 1978 Sch 1
vote: s 202(1)
Wales: Interpretation Act 1978 Sch 1

Effect of declaration of local connection

7C(1) Where a person's declaration of local connection is in force when he applies for registration, he shall be regarded for the purposes of section 4 above as—

   (a) resident on the date of the declaration at the address stated in it in accordance with section 7B(3)(d) above;

   (b) *Repealed*

(2) A person registered in a register of electors in pursuance of a declaration of local connection is entitled to remain so registered until—

   (a) the end of the period of 12 months beginning with the date when the entry in the register first takes effect,

   (aa) the registration officer determines in accordance with regulations that the person was not entitled to be registered,

   (ab) the registration officer determines in accordance with regulations that the person was registered as the result of an application under section 10ZC made by some other person or that the person's entry has been altered as the result of an application under section 10ZD made by some other person,

   (b) the declaration is cancelled under section 7B(9) above, or

   (c) another entry made in respect of him in any register of electors takes effect (whether or not in pursuance of a declaration of local connection),

   whichever first occurs.

(3) Where the entitlement of such a person to remain so registered terminates by virtue of subsection (2) above, the registration officer concerned shall remove that person's entry from the register, unless he is entitled to remain registered in pursuance of a further declaration of local connection.

(4) This section shall not be taken as precluding the registration of a person falling within section 7B(2)(a) or (b) above in pursuance of an application made by virtue of section 7(2) or 7A(2) above.

NOTES

Derivation
   RPA 2000 s 6

Subordinate Legislation
Representation of the People (England and Wales) (Amendment) (No 2) Regulations 2006, SI 2006/2910.
Representation of the People (Scotland) (Amendment) Regulations 2007, SI 2007/925.

Representation of the People (Northern Ireland) Regulations 2008, SI 2008/1741.

Defined terms
   register of electors: see s 9
   registration officer: s 8(1)

Registration of parliamentary and local government electors

Registration officers

8(1) For the registration of electors there shall be electoral registration officers (in this Act referred to as "registration officers").

(2) In England—

(a) the council of every district and London borough shall appoint an officer of the council to be registration officer for any constituency or part of a constituency coterminous with or situated in the district or borough, and

(b) in relation to any constituency part of which consists of some or all of the area of the City and the Inner and Middle Temples, the Common Council shall appoint an officer to be registration officer for that part of the constituency.

(2A) In Wales, the council of every county or county borough shall appoint an officer of the council to be registration officer for any constituency or part of a constituency coterminous with or situated in the area of the council.

(3) In Scotland, every local authority shall appoint an officer of the authority for their area or for any adjoining area, or an officer appointed by any combination of local authorities, to be registration officer for any constituency or part of a constituency which is situated within their area.

(4) In Northern Ireland, the Chief Electoral Officer for Northern Ireland is the registration officer for each constituency.

NOTES

Derivation
RPA 1949 s 6(1)
LGA 1972 ss 39, 270

Defined terms
constituency: Parliamentary Constituencies Act 1986 s 1(2)

local authority (S): s 204(1)
London borough: s 203(2) and Interpretation Act 1978 Sch 1
registration officer: s 8(1)
Wales: Interpretation Act 1978 Sch 1

Registers of electors

9(1) Each registration officer shall maintain—

(a) a register of parliamentary electors for each constituency or part of a constituency in the area for which he acts; and

(b) a register of local government electors for the local government areas or parts of local government areas included in the area for which he acts.

(2) Subject to any other provision of this Act, each register shall contain—

(a) the names of persons who appear to the registration officer to be entitled to be registered in it and in respect of whom a successful application for registration has been made;

(b) (subject to any prescribed exceptions) the qualifying addresses of the persons registered in it; and

(c) in relation to each such person, that person's electoral number.

(3) A person's electoral number is such number (with or without any letters) as is for the time being allocated by the registration officer to that person as his electoral number for the purposes of the register in question.

(4) Electoral numbers shall be allocated by a registration officer in such a way as to ensure, so far as is reasonably practicable, that in each separate part of a register the numbers run consecutively.

(5) The registers of parliamentary electors and of local government electors shall so far as practicable be combined, the entries of persons registered only as parliamentary electors or local government electors being marked to indicate that fact.

(6) *Repealed*

(7) Where under this section two or more registration officers maintain registers of parliamentary electors in respect of different parts of the same constituency, then in relation to that constituency any reference in this Act (whether express or implied) to the register of parliamentary electors for a constituency shall be read—

    (a) as a reference to one of those registers, or

    (b) in relation to one of those registration officers, as the register maintained by him,

as the context may require.

(8) In this Act—

    (a) any reference, in relation to a registration officer, to "his" registers is a reference to the registers maintained by him under this section; and

    (b) "qualifying address", in relation to a person registered in a register of electors, is the address in respect of which he is entitled to be so registered.

NOTES

Derivation
RPA 1949 s 7
RPA 1969 s 7

Application
This version applies to England, Scotland and Wales only

Derivation
RPA 1949 s 7
RPA 1969 s 7

Defined terms
constituency: Parliamentary Constituencies Act 1986 s 1(2)
local government area (E&W): ss 191(1), 203(1)
local government area (S): s 204(1)
prescribed: s 202(1)
registration officer: s 8(1)

(1) Each registration officer shall maintain—

    (a) a register of parliamentary electors for each constituency or part of a constituency in the area for which he acts; and

    (b) a register of local government electors for the local government areas or parts of local government areas included in the area for which he acts.

(2) Each register shall contain—

    (a) the names of the persons appearing to the registration officer to be entitled to be registered in it (subject to their complying with any prescribed requirements);

    (b) (subject to any prescribed exceptions) the qualifying addresses of the persons registered in it; and

    (c) in relation to each such person, that person's electoral number.

(3) A person's electoral number is such number (with or without any letters) as is for the time being allocated by the registration officer to that person as his electoral number for the purposes of the register in question.

(4) Electoral numbers shall be allocated by a registration officer in such a way as to ensure, so far as is reasonably practicable, that in each separate part of a register the numbers run consecutively.

(5) The registers of parliamentary electors and of local government electors shall so far as practicable be combined, the names of persons registered only as parliamentary electors or local government electors being marked to indicate that fact.

(6) A registration officer's duty under subsection (1) above includes the duty to take reasonable steps to obtain information required by him in connection with the performance of his duty under that subsection (without prejudice to any specific requirement of this Act or regulations under it).

(7) Where under this section two or more registration officers maintain registers of parliamentary electors in respect of different parts of the same constituency, then in relation to that constituency any reference in this Act (whether express or implied) to the register of parliamentary electors for a constituency shall be read—

   (a) as a reference to one of those registers, or

   (b) in relation to one of those registration officers, as the register maintained by him,

   as the context may require.

(8) In this Act—

   (a) any reference, in relation to a registration officer, to "his" registers is a reference to the registers maintained by him under this section; and

   (b) "qualifying address", in relation to a person registered in a register of electors, is the address in respect of which he is entitled to be so registered.

NOTES

Application
This version applies to Northern Ireland only

Derivation
RPA 1949 s 7
RPA 1969 s 7

Defined terms
constituency: Parliamentary Constituencies Act 1986 s 1(2)
local government area (E&W): ss 191(1), 203(1)
local government area (S): s 204(1)
prescribed: s 202(1)
registration officer: s 8(1)

Registration officers: duty to take necessary steps

9A(1) Each registration officer must take all steps that are necessary for the purpose of complying with his duty to maintain the registers under section 9 above and for the purpose of securing that, so far as is reasonably practicable, persons who are entitled to be registered in a register (and no others) are registered in it.

(2) The steps include—

   (a) sending more than once to any address the form to be used for the canvass under section 9D below;

   (b) making on one or more occasions house to house inquiries under subsection (5) of that section;

   (c) making contact by such other means as the registration officer thinks appropriate with persons who do not have an entry in a register;

   (d) inspecting any records held by any person which he is permitted to inspect under or by virtue of any enactment or rule of law;

   (e) providing training to persons under his direction or control in connection with the carrying out of the duty.

(3) Regulations made by the Secretary of State may amend subsection (2) by—

   (a) varying any of the paragraphs in that subsection;

   (b) inserting any paragraph;

   (c) repealing any paragraph.

NOTES

Derivation
Electoral Administration Act 2006 s 9

Defined terms
enactment: Interpretation Act 1978 Sch 1

enactment (NI): s 205
person: s 202(1)
registration officer: s 8(1)

Anonymous registration

9B(1) An application under this section (an application for an anonymous entry) may be made—

     (a) by any person, in conjunction with an application for registration under section 10ZC, or

     (b) by a person who already has an anonymous entry, for the purposes of remaining registered with such an entry (see section 9C(3)).

(1A) An application for an anonymous entry must be made in accordance with prescribed requirements and must be accompanied by—

     (a) a declaration made in accordance with prescribed requirements, and

     (b) such evidence in support as may be prescribed.

(2) A registration officer who receives an application for an anonymous entry must determine whether the safety test is satisfied (unless, in the case of an application under subsection (1)(a), the person's application for registration has been rejected otherwise than by virtue of this section).

(3) If the registration officer determines that the safety test is satisfied—

     (a) section 9(2) above does not apply in relation to the person; and

     (b) the person's entry in the register shall instead contain letters in the prescribed form and his electoral number.

(4) An entry containing the matters mentioned in subsection (3)(b) above is referred to in this Act as an anonymous entry.

(5) If an anonymous entry is made in respect of a person as the result of an application under subsection (1)(a), the registration officer shall remove any other entry in the register for that person.

(6) If a person makes an application under subsection (1)(a) and the registration officer determines that the safety test is not satisfied, no entry is to be made in the register as a result of the person's application under section 10ZC (whether an anonymous entry or otherwise).

(7) Subsection (6) above does not affect—

     (a) any other entry in the register for the person;

     (b) the determination of any further application for registration which is made by the person.

(8) Any communication sent by a registration officer or the returning officer for any election to a person who has an anonymous entry (A) must be sent in an envelope or other form of covering so as not to disclose to any other person that A has an anonymous entry.

(9) *Repealed*

(10) The safety test is satisfied if the safety of the applicant for an anonymous entry or that of any other person of the same household would be at risk if the register contains the name of the applicant or his qualifying address.

(11) In this section, "determines" means determines in accordance with regulations.

NOTES

Derivation
  Electoral Administration Act 2006 s 10

Subordinate Legislation
Representation of the People (Amendment) Regulations 2009, SI 2009/725.
Representation of the People (England and Wales) (Description of Electoral Registers and Amendment) Regulations 2013, SI 2013/3198.
Representation of the People (Northern Ireland)

(Amendment) Regulations 2014, SI 2014/1808.

Defined terms
  prescribed: s 202(1)
  register: s 9
  registration officer: s 8(1)
  returning officer: see ss 24-28

Removal of anonymous entry

9C(1) If a person has an anonymous entry in a register, his entitlement to remain registered terminates—

(a) at the end of the period of 12 months beginning with the date when the entry in the register first takes effect, or

(b) if the declaration made for the purposes of section 9B is cancelled at any time before the expiry of that 12 month period, at the time when the declaration is cancelled.

(2) Subsection (1) above does not affect the application of any other provision of this Act or of the Representation of the People Act 1985 which has the effect that the person's entitlement to registration terminates before the expiry of the 12 month period mentioned in subsection (1) or before the cancellation of the declaration made for the purposes of section 9B.

(3) If a person's entitlement to remain registered terminates by virtue of subsection (1) above, the registration officer concerned shall remove his entry from the register, unless he is entitled to remain registered with an anonymous entry in pursuance of a further application under section 9B.

NOTES

Derivation
Electoral Administration Act 2006 s 10

Subordinate Legislation
Representation of the People (Northern Ireland) (Amendment) Regulations 2014, SI 2014/1808.

Defined terms
anonymous entry: ss 9B(4), 202(1)
month: Interpretation Act 1978 Sch 1
registration officer: s 8(1)

Maintenance of registers: duty to conduct canvass in Great Britain

9D(1) Each registration officer in Great Britain must conduct an annual canvass in relation to the area for which the officer acts.

(2) The purpose of the canvass is to ascertain—

(a) the names and addresses of persons who are entitled to be registered in a register maintained by the officer but who are not registered;

(b) those persons who are registered in such a register but who are not entitled to be registered.

(3) The canvass is to be conducted in a manner to be set out in regulations.

(4) The regulations may confer functions on the Electoral Commission (for example, the Commission may be required to design a canvass form).

(5) A registration officer may make house to house inquiries for the purposes of the canvass, for example—

(a) to obtain information before sending out a canvass form,

(b) to supplement information provided on a canvass form, or

(c) to obtain information where no canvass form is returned.

(6) Nothing in this section applies in relation to—

(a) the registration of persons in respect of residence in penal institutions (within the meaning of section 3) or mental hospitals (within the meaning of section 7) or other places at which persons to whom section 7A applies may be detained,

(b) the registration of persons in pursuance of declarations of local connection, service declarations or overseas electors' declarations, or

(c) the registration of persons with anonymous entries in the register.

NOTES

Derivation
Electoral Registration and Administration Act 2013 s 4

Subordinate Legislation

Representation of the People (England and Wales) (Amendment) Regulations 2015, SI 2015/467

Representation of the People (Scotland) (Amendment) Regulations 2015, SI 2015/450

Defined terms
anonymous entry: ss 9B(4), 202(1)
Electoral Commission: see Political Parties, Elections and Referendums Act 2000 s 1
Great Britain: Union with Scotland Act 1706 art 1 and Interpretation Act 1978 s 22(1) and Sch 2 para 5
mental hospital: s 7
penal institutions: s 3
registration officer: s 8(1)

Maintenance of registers: invitations to register in Great Britain

9E(1)   A registration officer in Great Britain must give a person an invitation to apply for registration in a register maintained by the officer if—

    (a)   the officer is aware of the person's name and address,

    (b)   the person is not registered in the register, and

    (c)   the officer has reason to believe that the person may be entitled to be registered in the register.

(2)   Regulations may make provision about invitations under subsection (1), including—

    (a)   provision about the form and contents of invitations;

    (b)   provision about the giving of invitations (for example, provision about the manner in which they must be given or how often they must be given);

    (c)   provision requiring invitations to be accompanied by, or combined with, application forms or other documents (including partially completed application forms).

(3)   Regulations under subsection (2) may confer functions on the Electoral Commission (for example, the Commission may be required to design an invitation).

(4)   A registration officer who gives a person an invitation under subsection (1) may subsequently require the person to make an application for registration by a specified date.

(5)   A requirement under subsection (4) is of no effect if the person is not entitled to be registered.

(6)   Regulations—

    (a)   may make provision about requirements under subsection (4) (including provision for them to be cancelled in specified circumstances);

    (b)   may specify steps that a registration officer must take before imposing a requirement.

(7)   A registration officer may impose a civil penalty on a person who fails to comply with a requirement imposed by the officer under subsection (4).

(8)   For more about civil penalties under this section, see Schedule ZA1.

NOTES

Derivation
Electoral Registration and Administration Act 2013 s 5

Subordinate Legislation
Representation of the People (England and Wales) (Description of Electoral Registers and Amendment) Regulations 2013, SI 2013/3198.
Representation of the People (England and Wales) (Amendment) Regulations 2014, SI 2014/1234.
Representation of the People (Scotland) (Amendment) Regulations 2014, SI 2014/1250.

Defined terms
Electoral Commission: see Political Parties, Elections and Referendums Act 2000 s 1
Great Britain: Union with Scotland Act 1706 art 1 and Interpretation Act 1978 s 22(1) and Sch 2 para 5
registration officer: s 8(1)

Maintenance of registers: duty to conduct canvass

10(1)   *Repealed*

(1A) The Chief Electoral Officer for Northern Ireland must conduct a canvass in Northern Ireland in such years as are determined in accordance with section 10ZA.

(2) The canvass under subsection (1A) shall be conducted by reference to residence on 15th October in the year in which it is conducted.

(3) A canvass under this section shall not, however, be concerned with—

    (a) the registration of persons in respect of residence in penal institutions (within the meaning of section 3 above) or mental hospitals (within the meaning of section 7 above) or other places at which persons to whom section 7A above applies may be detained; or

    (b) the registration of persons in pursuance of—

        (i) declarations of local connection,

        (ii) service declarations, or

        (iii) overseas electors' declarations;

    (c) *Repealed*

(4) The form to be used for the purposes of a canvass under this section must be a form prescribed for those purposes.

(4A) Subject to subsection (4B) below, the information to be obtained by the use of such a form shall include—

    (a) the signature of each of the persons in relation to whom the form is completed;

    (b) the date of birth of each such person; and

    (c) in relation to each such person—

        (i) his national insurance number or a statement that he does not have one,

        (ii) *Repealed,* and

        (iii) any address in the United Kingdom in respect of which he is or has applied to be registered (other than the address in respect of which the form is completed),

and the power in subsection (4) above to prescribe a form includes power to give effect to the requirements of this subsection.

(4B) The Chief Electoral Officer for Northern Ireland may dispense with the requirement mentioned in subsection (4A)(a) above in relation to any person if he is satisfied that it is not reasonably practicable for that person to sign in a consistent and distinctive way because of blindness or any other disability of his or because he is unable to read.

(5) In connection with a canvass under this section the Chief Electoral Officer for Northern Ireland may, for the purpose of—

    (a) supplementing the information obtained by the use of any such form, or

    (b) where any such form has not been returned, obtaining any information designed to be obtained by the use of the form,

make such house to house inquiries as he thinks fit.

(6) On the conclusion of a canvass under this section the Chief Electoral Officer for Northern Ireland shall make such alterations in his registers as fall to be made in accordance with section 10A below as a result of the canvass.

(7) In this section "residence" means residence for the purposes of section 4 above.

NOTES

Derivation
RPA 1949, s 9(1)
RPA 2000 s 8

Subordinate Legislation
Representation of the People (Northern Ireland) (Amendment) Regulations 2013, SI 2013/1846.

Defined terms

declaration of local connection: see s 7B
his registers: s 9(8)
overseas elector's declaration: s 202(1) and RPA 1985 s 2
person: s 202(1)
prescribed: s 202(1)
registration officer: s 8(1)
service declaration: see s 15
United Kingdom: Interpretation Act 1978 Sch 1

Northern Ireland: timing of canvass

10ZA(1) A canvass under section 10(1A) must be conducted in—

    (a) the year 2010, unless the Secretary of State makes an order providing that the requirement in this paragraph does not apply;

    (b) every tenth year following 2010.

(2) A canvass under section 10(1A) must be conducted in an intervening year if—

    (a) on or before 15th April in that year, the Chief Electoral Officer for Northern Ireland has made a recommendation in favour of a canvass being conducted in that year for the purpose of meeting the relevant registration objectives, and

    (b) the Secretary of State, having considered the recommendation, has notified the Chief Electoral Officer that he is satisfied that the public interest requires a canvass to be conducted for that purpose.

(3) If no canvass under section 10(1A) is conducted before the end of 2015, a canvass must be conducted in 2016.

(4) "Intervening year" means a year other than—

    (a) 2010,

    (b) every tenth year following 2010, and

    (c) if no canvass under section 10(1A) is conducted before the end of 2015, 2016.

(5) The Secretary of State may not make an order under subsection (1)(a) unless—

    (a) on or before 15th April 2010, the Chief Electoral Officer for Northern Ireland has made a recommendation against a canvass being conducted in the year 2010 for the purpose of meeting the relevant registration objectives, and

    (b) the Secretary of State, having considered the recommendation, is satisfied that the public interest does not require a canvass to be conducted for that purpose.

(6) The power to make an order under subsection (1)(a) is exercisable by statutory instrument.

(7) No order is to be made under subsection (1)(a) unless a draft of the order has been laid before and approved by a resolution of each House of Parliament.

(8) "Recommendation" means a written recommendation to the Secretary of State.

NOTES

Derivation
Northern Ireland (Miscellaneous Provisions) Act 2006 s 3

Defined terms
relevant registration objectives: s 10ZB
written: Interpretation Act 1978 Sch 1

Subordinate Legislation
Representation of the People (Timing of the Canvass) (Northern Ireland) Order 2010, SI 2010/1152.

The relevant registration objectives (Northern Ireland)

10ZB(1) The relevant registration objectives are to secure, so far as reasonably practicable—

    (a) that every person who is entitled to be registered in a register is registered in it,

    (b) that no person who is not entitled to be registered in a register is registered in it, and

    (c) that none of the required information relating to any person registered in a register is false.

(2) But, in applying subsection (1), the registrations of the persons mentioned in section 10(3) (registrations with which a canvass is not concerned) must be disregarded.

(3) "Register" means a register maintained by the Chief Electoral Officer for Northern Ireland under section 9.

(4) "The required information" means the following (as appearing in the register or other records of the Chief Electoral Officer)—

(a) the person's name;
(b) the person's qualifying address;
(c) the person's date of birth;
(d) subject to subsections (5) and (6), the person's signature;
(e) the person's national insurance number or a statement that he does not have one.

(5) The required information does not include the person's signature if—

(a) the Chief Electoral Officer has dispensed with the requirement to provide a signature,
(b)

(6) *Repealed*

(7) "False", in relation to a signature, means that the signature is not the usual signature of, or was written by a person other than, the person whose signature it purports to be.

(8) *Repealed*

NOTES
Derivation
Northern Ireland (Miscellaneous Provisions) Act 2006 s 4

Defined terms
qualifying address: ss 9(8), 202(1)
written: Interpretation Act 1978 Sch 1

Registration of electors in Great Britain

10ZC(1) A registration officer in Great Britain must enter a person ("P") in a register maintained by the officer if—

(a) an application for registration is made by someone who appears to the officer to be P,
(b) any requirements imposed by or under this Act in relation to the application are met, and
(c) P appears to the officer to be entitled to be registered in the register.

(2) In determining an application under this section, the officer must consider any objection made in accordance with the prescribed requirements by another person whose name appears in the register.

(3) Regulations may make provision about the procedure for determining applications under this section.

NOTES
Derivation
Electoral Registration and Administration Act 2013 s 1

Subordinate Legislation
Representation of the People (England and Wales) (Description of Electoral Registers and Amendment) Regulations 2013, SI 2013/3198 (made under sub-ss (2), (3)).
Representation of the People (Scotland) (Amendment) Regulations 2014, SI 2014/1250 (made under sub-ss (2), (3)).
Representation of the People (England and Wales)

(Amendment) Regulations 2015, SI 2015/467 (made under sub-s (3)).
Representation of the People (Scotland) (Amendment) Regulations 2015, SI 2015/450 (made under sub-s (3)).

Defined terms
Great Britain: Union with Scotland Act 1706 art 1 and Interpretation Act 1978 s 22(1) and Sch 2 para 5
his registers: s 9(8)
registration officer: s 8(1)

Registration of electors in Great Britain: alterations

10ZD(1) A registration officer in Great Britain must alter the name or address in respect of which a person ("P") is registered in a register maintained by the officer if—

(a) an application for alteration is made by someone who appears to the officer to be P,

(b) any requirements imposed by or under this Act in relation to the application are met, and

(c) P appears to the officer to be entitled to be registered in the register in respect of the new name or the new address (as the case may be).

(2) In determining an application under this section, the officer must consider any objection made in accordance with the prescribed requirements by another person whose name appears in the register.

(3) Regulations may make provision about the procedure for determining applications under this section.

NOTES

Derivation
Electoral Registration and Administration Act 2013 s 1

Subordinate Legislation
Representation of the People (England and Wales) (Description of Electoral Registers and Amendment) Regulations 2013, SI 2013/3198).
Representation of the People (Scotland) (Amendment) Regulations 2014, SI 2014/1250.
Representation of the People (England and Wales)

(Amendment) Regulations 2015, SI 2015/467.
Representation of the People (Scotland) (Amendment) Regulations 2015, SI 2015/450.

Defined terms
Great Britain: Union with Scotland Act 1706 art 1 and Interpretation Act 1978 s 22(1) and Sch 2 para 5
his registers: s 9(8)
registration officer: s 8(1)

Removal of electors in Great Britain from register

0ZE(1) Where a person is entered in a register in respect of an address in Great Britain, the person is entitled to remain registered until the registration officer concerned determines that—

(a) the person was not entitled to be registered in respect of the address,

(b) the person has ceased to be resident at the address or has otherwise ceased to satisfy the conditions for registration set out in section 4, or

(c) the person was registered as the result of an application under section 10ZC made by some other person or the person's entry has been altered as the result of an application under section 10ZD made by some other person.

(2) Where a person's entitlement to remain registered terminates by virtue of subsection (1), the officer must remove the person's entry from the register.

(3) A registration officer may make house to house inquiries for the purpose of deciding whether or not to make a determination under subsection (1).

(4) Regulations may make provision about the procedure for making determinations under subsection (1), which may include provision requiring an officer to take prescribed steps before making a determination.

(5) A registration officer in Great Britain must consider whether to make a determination under subsection (1) if the officer—

(a) receives an objection to a person's registration in a register maintained by the officer, or

(b) otherwise becomes aware of information that causes the officer to suspect that a condition in subsection (1)(a) to (c) may be met in relation to a person's entry in such a register.

(6) Subsection (5)(a)—

(a) applies only if the objection to the person's registration is made in accordance with the prescribed requirements by someone whose name appears in the register, and

(b) does not apply if the person has an anonymous entry in the register.

(7) Nothing in this section applies in relation to the registration of persons in pursuance of—

    (a) applications for registration made by virtue of section 7(2) or 7A(2), or

    (b) declarations of local connection, service declarations or overseas electors' declarations.

(8) In this section "resident" means resident for the purposes of section 4.

NOTES

Derivation
Electoral Registration and Administration Act 2013 s 1

Subordinate Legislation
Representation of the People (England and Wales) (Description of Electoral Registers and Amendment) Regulations 2013, SI 2013/3198.
Representation of the People (Scotland) (Amendment) Regulations 2014, SI 2014/1250).

Defined terms
Great Britain: Union with Scotland Act 1706 art 1 and Interpretation Act 1978 s 22(1) and Sch 2 para 5
his registers: s 9(8)
registration officer: s 8(1)

Maintenance of the registers: registration of electors in Northern Ireland

10A(1) The Chief Electoral Officer for Northern Ireland shall determine all applications for registration which are—

    (a) made to him in accordance with the prescribed requirements, or

    (b) treated as made to him by virtue of subsection (2) below.

(1A) Subject to subsection (1B) below, an application for registration in respect of an address in Northern Ireland shall include—

    (a) the signature of each of the persons to whom the application relates;

    (b) the date of birth of each such person; and

    (c) in relation to each such person—

        (i) his national insurance number or a statement that he does not have one,

        (ii) *Repealed* and

        (iii) any other address in the United Kingdom in respect of which he is or has applied to be registered,

and the power in subsection (1) above to prescribe requirements includes power to give effect to the requirements of this subsection.

(1B) The Chief Electoral Officer for Northern Ireland may dispense with the requirement mentioned in subsection (1A)(a) above in relation to any person if he is satisfied that it is not reasonably practicable for that person to sign in a consistent and distinctive way because of blindness or any other disability of his or because he is unable to read.

(2) Where—

    (a) in connection with a canvass under section 10 above, the form completed in respect of any address specifies any person as a person who is entitled to be registered in a register, and

    (b) that person is not for the time being registered in the register in respect of that address,

he shall be treated as having made an application for registration in the register in respect of that address.

(2A) The application referred to in subsection (2) above shall be treated as made on the 15th October in the year in question.

(3) The Chief Electoral Officer for Northern Ireland shall also determine all objections to a person's registration in Northern Ireland made in accordance with the prescribed requirements by another person whose name appears in the register in question.

(3A) Subsection (3) above applies to an objection to a person's registration whether the objection is made before or after the person is registered in the register.

(3B) *Repealed*

(4) Subsections (1) and (3) above apply to applications and objections in Northern Ireland asking—
    (a) for the omission, insertion or alteration of a date as that on which a person will become of voting age and entitled to registration, or
    (b) for the alteration of the qualifying address in respect of which a person is registered,
    as they apply to applications for registration and objections to a person's registration respectively.

(5) Subject to subsection (5A) below, where a person ("the elector") is entered in a register in respect of any address in Northern Ireland, the elector is entitled to remain registered in the register in respect of that address until such time as the Chief Electoral Officer for Northern Ireland—
    (a) determines, on the conclusion of a canvass under section 10 above, that the elector was not resident at that address on the 15th October in question, or that because—
        (i) the form mentioned in section 10(4) above was not returned in respect of that address, or
        (ii) for any other reason, insufficient information was obtained as to whether the elector was resident at that address on that date,
        the Officer is unable to satisfy himself that the elector was then so resident at that address, or
    (b) determines that the elector was not entitled to be registered in respect of that address or that he has ceased to be resident at that address or has otherwise ceased to satisfy the conditions for registration set out in section 4 above.

(5A) A person's name is to be removed from the register in respect of any address if—
    (a) the form mentioned in section 10(4) above in respect of that address does not include all the information relating to him required by virtue of section 10(4A) above; or
    (b) the Chief Electoral Officer for Northern Ireland determines that he is not satisfied with the information relating to that person which was included in that form pursuant to that requirement.

(5B) The Chief Electoral Officer for Northern Ireland may, for the purpose of obtaining any information relevant to a determination under subsection (5)(b) above, make such house to house inquiries as he thinks fit.

(6) Where the entitlement of a person to remain registered in a register in respect of any address terminates by virtue of subsection (5) above, or his name is to be removed from it by virtue of subsection (5A) above, the Chief Electoral Officer for Northern Ireland shall remove that person's entry from the register once the officer has satisfied any prescribed requirements applying in relation to the removal of that entry.

(7) Subsection (6) above does not apply if, or to the extent that, regulations so provide in relation to any prescribed circumstances; and regulations may, in particular, authorise the Chief Electoral Officer for Northern Ireland to retain entries in his registers for the prescribed period if he thinks fit in cases where the form mentioned in section 10(4) above has not been returned in respect of any address.

(8) Nothing in subsection (5), (5A) or (6) applies in relation to the registration of persons in pursuance of—
    (a) applications for registration made by virtue of section 7(2) or 7A(2) above; or
    (b) declarations falling within section 10(3)(b) above.

(9) In this section—

"determines" means determines in accordance with regulations;
"resident" means resident for the purposes of section 4 above."

NOTES

Derivation
RPA 2000 s 8

Subordinate Legislation
Representation of the People (England and Wales) Regulations 2001, SI 2001/341.
Representation of the People (Scotland) Regulations 2001, SI 2001/497.
Representation of the People (Northern Ireland) Regulations 2008, SI 2008/1741.

Defined terms
United Kingdom: Interpretation Act 1978 Sch 1
his registers: s 9(8)
prescribed: s 202(1)
qualifying address: ss 9(8), 202(1)
registration officer: s 8(1)

11 *Repealed*

12 *Repealed*

Publication of registers

13(1) Each registration officer must for each year publish a revised version of his registers—

  (a) if there is a canvass in his area in that year, during the period starting with the end of the canvass in that year and ending with 1st December in that year or such later date as may be prescribed, or

  (b) if (in Northern Ireland) there is no canvass in that year, on 1st December in that year or by such later date as may be prescribed.

(1A) Subsection (1)(a) above has effect, in the case of a registration officer acting for an area in which (or in part of which) an election to which section 13B below applies is held during the period—

  (a) starting with 1st July in the year in question, and

  (b) ending with 1st December in that year,

  as if for "1st December in that year" there were substituted "1st February in the following year".

(2) The revised versions of the registers shall incorporate—

  (a) all the alterations which are required to be made in them as mentioned in section 10(6) above; and

  (b) any alterations which are required to be made by virtue of section 13A(3) or (3A) below.

(3) A registration officer may in addition, if he thinks fit, publish a revised version of either of his registers at any time between—

  (a) the time when the register was last published in accordance with subsection (1) above, and

  (b) the time when it is due to be next so published;

  and a registration officer proposing to publish a revised version of a register in accordance with this subsection must publish notice of his intention to do so by such time and in such manner as may be prescribed.

(4) When revising a register for publication under this section the registration officer shall make such changes affecting the electoral numbers of persons registered in the register as he considers necessary in order to comply with section 9(4) above.

(5) Where a revised version of a register is published at any time under this section, the register has effect in the form in which it is so published as from that time until the time when—

  (a) a revised version is next so published, or

    (b) if earlier, any alteration to the register takes effect under any of sections 13A to 13BA below.

(6) Any reference in this section or section 13A below to the publication of a revised version of the register is to its publication in accordance with regulations made in pursuance of paragraphs 10A and 10B(1)(a) of Schedule 2 to this Act.

NOTES

Derivation
  Electoral Registers Act 1949 s 1

Prospective amendment
  s 13(5)(b) replace "13BA" with "13BC", effected by Recall of MPs Act 2015 s 10(6)

Defined terms
  his registers: s 9(8)
  prescribed: s 202(1)
  registration officer: s 8(1)

Alteration of registers

13A(1) This section applies where, at any time ("the relevant time") after the publication of a revised version of a register by a registration officer under section 13 above, the registration officer—
    (za) is required by section 10ZC(1) to enter a person in the register;
    (zb) is required by section 10ZD(1) to alter a person's entry in the register;
    (a) on an application for registration in Northern Ireland being made by any person in accordance with the prescribed requirements, determines that that person is entitled to be so registered;
    (b) is required, by virtue of any provision of this Part of this Act, to remove a person's entry from the register;
    (c) is notified of any decision on an appeal by virtue of section 56 or 58 below which requires any such alteration in the register as is mentioned in subsection (4) of that section; or
    (d) determines that the register contains any clerical error or, in the case of a registration officer in Great Britain, determines that the register contains any information that is incorrect.

(2) In such a case the registration officer shall (subject to subsection (3) below) issue, in the prescribed manner, a notice specifying the appropriate alteration in the register; and—
    (a) the notice shall be so issued by him—
      (i) on the first day of the month which follows that in which the relevant time falls, or
      (ii) if that day is less than 14 days after that time, on the first day of the month immediately following that month; and
    (b) (subject to sections 13B(1) and 13BA(1) below) the alteration in question shall have effect as from the beginning of the day on which the notice is issued.

(2A) Subject to subsection (2B) below, an application for registration under subsection (1)(a) above in respect of an address in Northern Ireland shall include—
    (a) the signature of each of the persons to whom the application relates;
    (b) the date of birth of each such person; and
    (c) in relation to each such person—
      (i) his national insurance number or a statement that he does not have one,
      (ii) *Repealed* and
      (iii) any other address in the United Kingdom in respect of which he is or has applied to be registered,
and the power in subsection (1)(a) above to prescribe requirements includes power to give effect to the requirements of this subsection.

(2B) The Chief Electoral Officer for Northern Ireland may dispense with the requirement mentioned in subsection (2A)(a) above in relation to any person if he is satisfied that it is not reasonably practicable for that person to sign in a consistent and distinctive way because of any incapacity of his or because he is unable to read.

(3) Subsection (2) above does not require a registration officer to issue a notice under that subsection in a case where (apart from this subsection) that subsection would require the notice to be issued—

    (a) at the beginning of the month containing the date on which a revised version of the register is next due to be published in accordance with section 13(1) or (3) above, or

    (b) at the beginning of either of the two months preceding that containing the date on which a revised version of the register is next due to be published in accordance with section 13(1)(a) above,

and in such a case the alteration in question shall be made in that revised version of the register.

(3A) Subsection (2)(a)(ii) also does not require a registration officer in Great Britain to issue a notice under subsection (2) in a case where the month which follows that in which the relevant time falls is the month containing the date on which a revised version of the register is next due to be published in accordance with section 13(1)(a); and in such a case the alteration in question shall be made in that revised version of the register.

(4) Subsection (2) above also does not require a registration officer to issue a notice under that subsection in a case where section 13AB(2), 13B(3), (3B) or (3D), 13BA(3), (6) or (9) or 13BC(3) or (6) below requires him to issue a notice under that provision.

(5) No alteration affecting a published version of a register of electors shall be made otherwise than in accordance with this section, section 13AB, section 13B, section 13BA, or section 13BC below.

(6) For the purposes of subsection (1) above "determines" means determines in accordance with regulations; and section 119 below shall apply for the purposes of subsection (2)(a) above as if it were contained in Part II of this Act.

NOTES

Derivation
RPA 2000 s 8

Prospective amendment
Underlined words in (4) and (5) not yet in force, effected by Recall of MPs Act 2015 s 10(6)

Subordinate Legislation
Representation of the People (England and Wales) Regulations 2001, SI 2001/341.
Representation of the People (Scotland) Regulations 2001, SI 2001/497.
Representation of the People (Northern Ireland)

Regulations 2008, SI 2008/1741.

Defined terms
Great Britain: Union with Scotland Act 1706 art 1 and Interpretation Act 1978 s 22(1) and Sch 2 para 5
month: Interpretation Act 1978 Sch 1
prescribed: s 202(1)
publication of a revised version of the register: s 13(6)
register of electors: see s 9
registration officer: s 8(1)
Defined terms

Alteration of registers: interim publication dates

13AB(1) Subsections (2) and (3) apply in relation to an interim publication date where—

    (a) at any time before the interim publication date, section 13A applies to a registration officer (by virtue of section 13A(1)) in connection with a determination, requirement or decision within section 13A(1)(za), (zb), (b), (c) or (d),

    (b) in consequence of the determination, requirement or decision an entry relating to a person falls to be made in (or removed from) the register in respect of an address in the relevant election area, and

(c) no alteration made in consequence of the determination, requirement or decision has already taken effect, or is due to take effect, under a relevant provision on or before the interim publication date.

(2) On the interim publication date the registration officer must issue, in the prescribed manner, a notice specifying the appropriate alteration in the register.

(3) The alteration takes effect from the beginning of the interim publication date.

(4) There are two interim publication dates (in relation to a registration officer and an election to which this section applies).

(5) The first interim publication date is the last day on which nomination papers may be delivered to the returning officer for the purposes of the election.

(6) The second interim publication date is to be determined by the registration officer, but must be a day after the first interim publication date and before the appropriate publication date.

(7) In subsection (1)(c) "relevant provision" means—

    (a) in relation to the first interim publication date, section 13A(2) or 13BC(3) or (6);

    (b) in relation to the second interim publication date, section 13A(2) and subsection (3) as it applies in relation to the first interim publication date

    (b) in relation to the second interim publication date—

        (i) section 13A(2);

        (ii) section 13BC(3) or (6);

        (iii) subsection (3) of this section as it applies in relation to the first interim publication date.

(7A) In determining for the purposes of subsection (1)(c) whether an alteration made in consequence of the determination, requirement or decision is due to take effect under section 13BC(3) on or before the interim publication date, the reference to section 13AB in section 13BC(2) is to be disregarded.

(8) This section applies to—

    (a) parliamentary elections in England, Wales or Scotland;

    (b) elections in England, Wales or Scotland to the European Parliament;

    (c) elections to the Scottish Parliament;

    (d) elections to the National Assembly for Wales;

    (e) local government elections in England, Wales or Scotland;

    (f) elections of police and crime commissioners in England and Wales.

(9) Subsections (5) and (6) of section 13B apply for the purposes of this section as they apply for the purposes of that section.

(10) Subsection (2) does not require a registration officer to issue a notice under that subsection in a case where section 13BC(3) or (6) requires the officer to issue a notice under that provision at an earlier time.

NOTES

Derivation
Electoral Registration and Administration Act 2013 s 16

Subordinate Legislation
Representation of the People (England and Wales) (Description of Electoral Registers and Amendment) Regulations 2013, SI 2013/3198.
Representation of the People (Scotland) (Amendment) Regulations 2015, SI 2015/450 (made under sub-s (2)).

Defined terms
England: Interpretation Act 1978 Sch 1
local government election (E&W): ss 191(1), 203(1), (1A)
local government election (S): s 204(1)
parliamentary election: Interpretation Act 1978 Sch 1
registration officer: s 8(1)
returning officer: see ss 24-27
Wales: Interpretation Act 1978 Sch 1

Alteration of registers: pending elections

13B(1) If, by virtue of section 13A(2) above, an alteration in a published version of a register is to take effect after the fifth day before the date of the poll for an election to which this section applies, the alteration does not have effect for the purposes of the election.

(2) Subsection (3) below applies where—

    (a) at any time before the appropriate publication date in the case of an election to which this section applies, section 13A above applies to a registration officer, by virtue of subsection (1) of that section, in connection with a determination, requirement or decision falling within any of paragraphs (za), (zb), (b), (c) and (d) of that subsection;

    (b) in consequence of the determination, requirement or decision an entry relating to a person falls to be made in (or removed from) the register in respect of an address in the relevant election area; and

    (c) no alteration made in consequence of the determination, requirement or decision—

        (i) has already taken effect, or

        (ii) is due to take effect,

under subsection (2) of that section, or under section 13AB(3) or section 13BC(3) or (6), on or before the fifth day before the date of the poll.

(3) In such a case the registration officer shall issue, in the prescribed manner, a notice specifying the appropriate alteration in the register; and—

    (a) the notice shall be so issued by him on the appropriate publication date; and

    (b) the alteration shall take effect as from the beginning of that day.

(3ZA) In determining for the purposes of subsection (2)(c) whether an alteration made in consequence of the determination, requirement or decision is due to take effect under section 13BC(3) on or before the fifth day before the date of the poll, the reference to section 13B in section 13BC(2) is to be disregarded.

(3ZB) Subsection (3) does not require a registration officer to issue a notice under that subsection in a case where section 13BC(3) or (6) requires the officer to issue a notice under that provision at an earlier time.

(3A) Subsection (3B) below applies where—

    (a) at any time on or after the appropriate publication date in the case of an election to which this section applies but before the prescribed time on the day of the poll, section 13A above applies to a registration officer, by virtue of subsection (1) of that section, in connection with a notification mentioned in paragraph (c) of that subsection; and

    (b) in consequence of the notification—

        (i) an entry relating to that person falls to be made in the register in respect of an address in the relevant election area, or

        (ii) his entry in the register requires to be altered.

(3B) In such a case the registration officer shall issue, in the prescribed manner, a notice specifying the appropriate alteration in the register; and—

    (a) the notice shall be so issued by him when he receives the notification; and

    (b) the alteration shall take effect as from the beginning of the day on which the notice is issued.

(3C) Subsection (3D) below applies where—

    (a) at any time on or after the appropriate publication date in the case of an election to which this section applies but before the prescribed time on the day of the poll, section 13A above applies to a registration officer, by virtue of subsection (1) of that section, in connection with a determination falling within paragraph (d) of that subsection;

      (b)   the determination was made following a representation made by or on behalf of a person to the registration officer; and

      (c)   in consequence of the determination—

          (i)   an entry relating to that person falls to be made in the register in respect of an address in the relevant election area, or

          (ii) his entry in the register requires to be altered.

(3D)   In such a case the registration officer shall issue, in the prescribed manner, a notice specifying the appropriate alteration in the register; and—

      (a)   the notice shall be so issued by him when he makes the determination; and

      (b)   the alteration shall take effect as from the beginning of the day on which the notice is issued.

(3E)   In subsection (3C)(b) above, "representation" means a representation made in accordance with prescribed requirements to the effect that the register contains a clerical error.

(4)   This section applies to the following elections—

      (a)   parliamentary elections in England, Wales or Scotland,

      (b)   elections to the European Parliament in England, Wales or Scotland,

      (c)   elections to the Scottish Parliament,

      (d)   elections to the National Assembly for Wales,

      (e)   *Repealed*

      (f)   local government elections in England, Wales or Scotland, and

      (g)   elections of police and crime commissioners in England and Wales.

(5)   In this section—

     "the appropriate publication date", in relation to a registration officer and an election to which this section applies, means either the sixth or the fifth day before the date of the poll, as the registration officer may determine;

     "the final nomination day", in relation to such an election, means the last day on which nomination papers may be delivered to the returning officer for the purposes of the election;

     "the relevant election area", in relation to a registration officer and such an election, means—

      (a)   the area for which the registration officer acts, or

      (b)   if the election is held in only part of that area, the part of that area in question.

(6)   Section 119 below shall apply for the purposes of this section as if—

      (a)   it were contained in Part II of this Act; and

      (b)   each of the days referred to in this section were the day on which anything is required or permitted to be done by or in pursuance of that Part of this Act.

NOTES

Derivation
  RPA 2000 s 8

Prospective amendment
  Underlined words not yet in effect, amendment
  effected by Recall of MPs Act 2015 s 10(6)

Subordinate legislation
Representation of the People (England and Wales) (Amendment) (No 2) Regulations 2006, SI 2006/2910.
Representation of the People (Scotland) (Amendment) Regulations 2007, SI 2007/925.
European Parliamentary Elections (Amendment) Regulations 2009, SI 2009/186.

Defined terms
England: Interpretation Act 1978 Sch 1
local government election (E&W): s 203(1), (3)
local government election (S): s 204(1)
parliamentary election: Interpretation Act 1978 Sch 1
prescribed: s 202(1)
registration officer: s 8(1)
Wales: Interpretation Act 1978 Sch 1

Alteration of registers in Northern Ireland: pending elections

13BA(1) An alteration in a published version of a register of electors which takes effect under section 13A(2) or section 13BC(3) or (6) after the final nomination day in the case of an election to which this section applies is of no effect for the purposes of that election unless the alteration—

    (a) is made in consequence of a decision or determination falling within section 13A(1)(c) or (d), and

    (b) takes effect on or before the fifth day before the date of the poll.

  (2) Subsection (3) applies if—

    (a) at any time before the appropriate publication date in the case of an election to which this section applies, section 13A applies to the Chief Electoral Officer for Northern Ireland (by virtue of section 13A(1)) in connection with a determination or requirement falling within section 13A(1)(a) or (b), and

    (b) no alteration made in consequence of that determination or requirement—

      (i) has already taken effect, or

      (ii) is due to take effect,

  under section 13A(2), or section 13BC(3), on or before the final nomination day.

  (3) If, no later than the prescribed date, the Chief Electoral Officer is supplied with such additional material supporting the alteration as is prescribed, he must, on the appropriate publication date, issue a notice specifying the appropriate alteration in the register.

  (3A) In determining for the purposes of subsection (2)(b) whether an alteration made in consequence of the determination or requirement is due to take effect under section 13BC(3) on or before the final nomination day, the reference to section 13BA in section 13BC(2) is to be disregarded.

  (3B) Subsection (3) does not require the Chief Electoral Officer to issue a notice under that subsection in a case where section 13BC(3) requires the officer to issue a notice under that provision at an earlier time.

  (4) *Repealed*

  (5) Subsection (6) applies if—

    (a) at any time before the appropriate publication date in the case of an election to which this section applies, section 13A applies to the Chief Electoral Officer for Northern Ireland (by virtue of section 13A(1)) in connection with a decision or determination falling within section 13A(1)(c) or (d), and

    (b) no alteration made in consequence of that decision or determination—

      (i) has already taken effect, or

      (ii) is due to take effect,

  under section 13A(2), or section 13BC(3) or (6), on or before the fifth day before the date of the poll.

  (6) The Chief Electoral Officer must, on the appropriate publication date, issue a notice specifying the appropriate alteration in the register.

  (6A) In determining for the purposes of subsection (5)(b) whether an alteration made in consequence of the decision or determination is due to take effect under section 13BC(3) on or before the fifth day before the date of the poll, the reference to section 13BA in section 13BC(2) is to be disregarded.

  (6B) Subsection (6) does not require the Chief Electoral Officer to issue a notice under that subsection in a case where section 13BC(3) or (6) requires the officer to issue a notice under that provision at an earlier time.

  (7) Subsection (9) applies if—

(a) at any time on or after the appropriate publication date in the case of an election to which this section applies but before the prescribed time on the day of the poll, section 13A applies to the Chief Electoral Officer for Northern Ireland (by virtue of section 13A(1)), in connection with a notification mentioned in section 13A(1)(c), and

(b) in consequence of the notification—
  (i) an entry relating to that person falls to be made in the register in respect of an address in the relevant election area, or
  (ii) his entry in the register needs to be altered.

(8) Subsection (9) also applies if—
  (a) at any time on or after the appropriate publication date in the case of an election to which this section applies but before the prescribed time on the day of the poll, section 13A applies to the Chief Electoral Officer for Northern Ireland (by virtue of section 13A(1)), in connection with a determination falling within section 13A(1)(d),
  (b) the determination was made following a representation made by or on behalf of a person to the Chief Electoral Officer, and
  (c) in consequence of the determination—
    (i) an entry relating to that person falls to be made in the register in respect of an address in the relevant election area, or
    (ii) his entry in the register needs to be altered.

(9) The Chief Electoral Officer must, when—
  (a) he receives the notification referred to in subsection (7), or
  (b) he makes the determination referred to in subsection (8),
issue a notice specifying the appropriate alteration in the register.

(10) In subsection (8)(b), "representation" means a representation made in accordance with prescribed requirements to the effect that the register contains a clerical error.

(11) A notice under subsection (3), (6) or (9)—
  (a) is to be issued in the prescribed manner, and
  (b) takes effect from the beginning of the day on which it is issued.

(12) This section applies to—
  (a) parliamentary elections in Northern Ireland,
  (b) elections in Northern Ireland to the European Parliament, and
  (c) elections to the Northern Ireland Assembly.

(13) Subsections (5) and (6) of section 13B apply for the purposes of this section as they apply for the purposes of that section.

NOTES

Derivation
Northern Ireland (Miscellaneous Provisions) Act 2006 s 6

Subordinate legislation
Representation of the People (Northern Ireland) Regulations 2008, SI 2008/1741

Defined terms
the absent voter list: s 202(1)

the appropriate publication date: ss 13B(5) and 13BA(13)
elector: s 202(1)
the final nomination day: ss 13B(5) and 13BA(13)
parliamentary election: Interpretation Act 1978 Sch 1
prescribed: s 202(1)
register of electors: see s 9
the relevant election area: ss 13B(5) and 13BA(13)

13BB **Repealed**

Alteration of registers: recall petition

13BC(1) This section applies if—

(a) a Speaker's notice is given in relation to a recall petition in respect of an MP under the Recall of MPs Act 2015 ("the 2015 Act"), and

(b) a day is designated in relation to that petition under section 7(1)(b) of that Act (first day of the signing period).

(2) Subsection (3) applies where—

    (a) at any time before the cut-off day, section 13A applies to a registration officer, by virtue of subsection (1) of that section, in connection with—

        (i) a requirement or determination falling within paragraph (za) or (a) of that subsection in respect of a qualifying application for registration,

        (ii) a requirement falling within paragraph (zb) of that subsection in respect of an entry in the register resulting from a qualifying application for registration, or

        (iii) a requirement, decision or determination falling within any of paragraphs (b) to (d) of that subsection,

    (b) in consequence of the requirement, determination or decision, an entry relating to a person falls to be made or altered in, or removed from, the relevant register,

    (c) no alteration made in consequence of the requirement, determination or decision has already taken effect, or is due to take effect, under section 13A, 13AB, 13B or 13BA on or before the cut-off day, and

    (d) if the relevant register is for a constituency in Northern Ireland, the Chief Electoral Officer for Northern Ireland is supplied on or before the prescribed date with such additional material as is prescribed supporting the appropriate alteration in the register.

(3) In such a case—

    (a) the registration officer must issue, in the prescribed manner on the cut-off day, a notice specifying the appropriate alteration in the register, and

    (b) subject to sections 13B(1) and 13BA(1), the alteration is to take effect as from the beginning of the day on which the notice is issued.

(4) In determining for the purposes of subsection (2)(c) whether an alteration made in consequence of the requirement, determination or decision is due to take effect under section 13AB, 13B or 13BA on or before the cut-off day, the references to section 13BC(3) in section 13AB(7), 13B(2) and 13BA(2) and (5) are to be disregarded.

(5) Subsection (6) applies where—

    (a) at any time on or after the cut-off day but before the prescribed time on the last day of the signing period, section 13A applies to a registration officer, by virtue of subsection (1) of that section, in connection with—

        (i) a notification mentioned in paragraph (c) of that subsection, or

        (ii) a determination falling within paragraph (d) of that subsection, and

    (b) in consequence of the notification or determination, an entry relating to a person falls to be made or altered in, or removed from, the relevant register.

(6) In such a case—

    (a) the registration officer must issue, in the prescribed manner and on the appropriate day, a notice specifying the appropriate alteration in the register, and

    (b) subject to sections 13B(1) and 13BA(1), the alteration is to take effect as from the beginning of the day on which the notice is issued.

(7) "The appropriate day" means—

    (a) in a case falling within subsection (5)(a)(i), the day when the registration officer receives the notification referred to in that provision (or, if that is not a working day, the next working day);

(b) in a case falling within subsection (5)(a)(ii), the day when the registration officer makes the determination referred to in that provision (or, if that is not a working day, the next working day).

(8) If the petition officer in relation to the recall petition receives a notice under section 13(6) of the 2015 Act (early termination of recall petition process), this section ceases to apply in the case of that petition.

(9) But if, at the time when that notice is so received—

    (a) the registration officer is under a duty under subsection (3) or (6) of this section to issue a notice, but

    (b) has not yet issued the notice,

the registration officer remains under that duty to issue the notice at the time at which it would have been required to be issued if subsection (8) had not applied.

(10) In this section—

    (a) "the cut-off day" means the 3rd working day before the beginning of the signing period,

    (b) "qualifying application for registration" means an application for registration that—

        (i) is made on or before the day on which the Speaker's notice is given, or

        (ii) is treated as made by virtue of section 10A(2) (return of canvass form treated as application for registration) in respect of a form returned on or before that day,

    (c) "relevant register" means the register of parliamentary electors for the MP's constituency,

    (d) the following expressions have the same meaning as in the 2015 Act: "MP", "petition officer", "recall petition", "the signing period", "Speaker's notice" and "working day" (see section 22 of that Act), and

    (e) any reference to a notice given under the 2015 Act or the time at which such a notice is given has the same meaning as in that Act.

NOTES

Derivation
Recall of MPs Act 2015 s 10

s 1(2)
registration officer: s 8(1)

Defined terms
constituency: Parliamentary Constituencies Act 1986

Electoral identity card: Northern Ireland

13C(1) This section applies where a person makes an application in accordance with any prescribed requirements to the Chief Electoral Officer for Northern Ireland for an electoral identity card.

(2) Regulations may provide for—

    (a) the descriptions of person who may make such an application; and

    (b) the form in which such an application is to be made.

(3) The Chief Electoral Officer shall determine such an application and, if he is satisfied that the information given by the applicant is correct, he shall issue an electoral identity card to the applicant free of charge.

(4) The electoral identity card issued to an applicant shall—

    (a) state his full name and date of birth,

    (b) bear his photograph,

    (c) indicate when the card ceases to be current, and

    (d) include such other information and be in such form as the Chief Electoral Officer shall determine.

(5) For the purposes of subsection (4) above and rule 37(1E) in Schedule 1 to this Act (specified documents), an electoral identity card becomes current on the date of its issue and ceases to be so on the expiry of the period of 10 years beginning with that date.

(6) Any expenses properly incurred by the Chief Electoral Officer in the performance of his functions under this section shall be treated as registration expenses of his for the purposes of this Act.

(7) In this section "determine" means determine in accordance with regulations (if any).

NOTES

Derivation
Electoral Fraud (Northern Ireland) Act 2002 s 4

Subordinate legislation
Representation of the People (Northern Ireland) Regulations 2008, SI 2008/1741

Defined terms
prescribed: s 202(1)
registration expenses: s 54(1)

Scottish local government elections: false information in connection with applications for absent voting

13CA(1) A person who provides false information in connection with an application mentioned in subsection (2) below commits an offence.

(2) The application referred to in subsection (1) above is an application—
   (a) relating to a local government election in Scotland; and
   (b) to which any of the following provisions of Schedule 4 to the Representation of the People Act 2000 (c 2) applies, namely—
      (i) paragraph 3(1) or (2);
      (ii) paragraph 4(1) or (2);
      (iii) paragraph 7(4).

(3) In relation to a signature, "false information" for the purposes of subsection (1) above means a signature which—
   (a) is not the usual signature of; or
   (b) was written by a person other than,
the person whose signature it purports to be.

(4) A person does not commit an offence under subsection (1) above if the person did not know, and had no reason to suspect, that the information was false.

(5) Where sufficient evidence is adduced to raise an issue with respect to the defence under subsection (4) above, the court must assume that the defence is satisfied unless the prosecutor proves beyond reasonable doubt that it is not.

(6) A person guilty of an offence under subsection (1) above is liable on summary conviction to (either or both)—
   (a) imprisonment for a term not exceeding 6 months;
   (b) a fine not exceeding level 5 on the standard scale.

NOTES

Application
This provision applies to Scotland only

Derivation
Local Electoral Administration and Registration Services (Scotland) Act 2006 s 12

Defined terms

local government election (S): s 204(1)
standard scale: Interpretation Act 1978 Sch 1
summary conviction (NI only): Interpretation Act 1978 Sch 1
written: Interpretation Act 1978 Sch 1

Provision of false information

13D(1) A person who for any purpose connected with the registration of electors provides to a registration officer any false information is guilty of an offence.

(1A) A person who provides false information in connection with an application (other than an application relating only to a local government election in Scotland) to which any of the following provisions of Schedule 4 to the Representation of the People Act 2000 (applications relating to absent voting) applies is guilty of an offence—

    (a) paragraph 3(1) or (2);

    (b) paragraph 4(1) or (2);

    (c) paragraph 7(4).

(2) A person who provides false information to the Chief Electoral Officer for Northern Ireland for the purpose of obtaining the dispensation referred to in section 10(4B), 10A(1B) or 13A(2B) above is guilty of an offence.

(3) In relation to a signature, "false information" for the purposes of subsection (1) or (1A) means a signature which—

    (a) is not the usual signature of; or

    (b) was written by a person other than,

the person whose signature it purports to be.

(4) A person does not commit an offence under subsection (1) or (1A) above if he did not know, and had no reason to suspect, that the information was false.

(5) Where sufficient evidence is adduced to raise an issue with respect to the defence under subsection (4) above, the court shall assume that the defence is satisfied unless the prosecution proves beyond reasonable doubt that it is not.

(6) A person guilty of an offence under this section shall be liable on summary conviction to—

    (a) imprisonment for a term not exceeding 51 weeks; or

    (b) a fine not exceeding level 5 on the standard scale,

or to both.

(7) In the application of subsection (6)(a) to Scotland and Northern Ireland, the reference to 51 weeks must be taken to be a reference to six months.

(8) In relation to an offence committed before the commencement of section 281(5) of the Criminal Justice Act 2003, the reference in subsection (6)(a) to 51 weeks must be taken to be a reference to six months.

NOTES

Derivation

Electoral Fraud (Northern Ireland) Act 2002
Electoral Administration Act 2006 s 15

Defined terms

elector: s 202(1)
local government election (S): s 204(1)

registration officer: s 8(1)
standard scale: Interpretation Act 1978 Sch 1
summary conviction (NI only): Interpretation Act 1978 Sch 1
written: Interpretation Act 1978 Sch 1

Service qualifications and declarations for registration

Service qualification

14(1) A person has a service qualification for the purposes of this Act who—

    (a) is a member of the forces,

    (b) (not being such a member) is employed in the service of the Crown in a post outside the United Kingdom of any prescribed class or description,

    (c) is employed by the British Council in a post outside the United Kingdom,

    (d) is the spouse or civil partner of a member of the forces,

(e) is the spouse or civil partner of a person mentioned in paragraph (b) or paragraph (c) above and is residing outside the United Kingdom to be with his or her spouse or civil partner,

and where a person leaves the United Kingdom to take up employment or residence as mentioned above or returns to the United Kingdom at the end of such employment or residence, the employment or residence shall be deemed to begin from the time of leaving or to continue until the time of returning, as the case may be.

(1A) In relation to the registration of local government electors in Scotland, a person also has a service qualification for the purposes of this Act if—
    (a) the person is under the age of 18,
    (b) a parent or guardian of the person has a service qualification under any of paragraphs (a) to (e) of subsection (1), and
    (c) the person is residing at a particular place in order to be with that parent or guardian.

(2) *Repealed*

NOTES

Derivation
  RPA 1949 ss 4, 10

Defined terms
  age: s 202(2)
  civil partner: Interpretation Act 1978 Sch 1

member of the forces: s 59(1)
prescribed: s 202(1)
spouse: Marriage (Same Sex Couples) Act 2013 Sch 3 para 1

Service declaration

15(1) A service declaration shall be made only—
    (a) by a person who has a service qualification, or
    (b) subject to any prescribed conditions, by a person about to leave the United Kingdom in such circumstances as to acquire a service qualification,

and a service declaration may be made by such a person notwithstanding the fact that by reason of his age he is not yet entitled to vote.

(2) Where a person is registered in a register of electors in pursuance of a service declaration, the person is entitled to remain so registered until—
    (a) the end of the period of 12 months beginning with the date when the entry in the register first takes effect,
    (aa) the registration officer determines in accordance with regulations that the person was not entitled to be registered,
    (ab) the registration officer determines in accordance with regulations that the person was registered as the result of an application under section 10ZC made by some other person or that the person's entry has been altered as the result of an application under section 10ZD made by some other person,
    (b) the declaration is cancelled under subsection (7) below, or
    (c) another entry made in respect of him in any register of electors takes effect (whether or not in pursuance of a service declaration),
whichever first occurs.

(3) Where the entitlement of such a person to remain so registered terminates by virtue of subsection (2) above, the registration officer concerned shall remove that person's entry from the register, unless he is entitled to remain registered in pursuance of a further service declaration.

(4) *Repealed*

(5) No service declaration shall be specially made by a person for the purpose of local government elections, and any service declaration made for the purpose of

parliamentary elections shall have effect also for the purpose of local government elections; but—

    (a) a service declaration may be made for the purpose of local government elections only by a person who is as a peer subject to a legal incapacity to vote at parliamentary elections, or by a relevant citizen of the Union; and

    (b) where so made, shall be marked to show that it is available for local government elections only, but shall in all other respects be the same as other service declarations.

(6) If a person—

    (a) makes a service declaration declaring to more than one address, or

    (b) makes more than one service declaration bearing the same date and declaring to different addresses,

the declaration or declarations shall be void.

(7) A service declaration may at any time be cancelled by the declarant.

(8) A service declaration shall be of no effect unless it is received by the registration officer concerned within the period of three months beginning with the date of the declaration.

(9) The Secretary of State may by order provide that, in relation to the persons mentioned in section 14(1)(a) and (d), subsection (2)(a) above has effect as if for the period of 12 months there were substituted such other period (not exceeding five years) as he thinks appropriate.

(10) The power to make an order under subsection (9) is exercisable by statutory instrument, which may contain such incidental or consequential provision as the Secretary of State thinks appropriate.

(11) No order may be made under subsection (9) unless—

    (a) the Secretary of State first consults the Electoral Commission, and

    (b) a draft of the instrument containing the order is laid before, and approved by a resolution of, each House of Parliament.

(12) If the period substituted by an order under subsection (9) is longer than the period for the time being in force, the longer period has effect in relation to any person who immediately before the order was made was entitled to remain in a register by virtue of subsection (2).

NOTES

Derivation
RPA 1949 s 10

Extension of application
Local and European Parliamentary Elections (Registration of Citizens of Accession States) Regulations 2003, SI 2003/1557
Service Voters' Registration Period Order 2010, SI 2010/882

Subordinate legislation
Representation of the People (Amendment) Regulations 1990, SI 1990/520.
Representation of the People (England and Wales) (Amendment) (No 2) Regulations 2006, SI 2006/2910.
Representation of the People (Scotland) (Amendment) Regulations 2007, SI 2007/925.
Representation of the People (Northern Ireland)

Regulations 2008, SI 2008/1741.
Service Voters' Registration Period Order 2010, SI 2010/882

Defined terms
Electoral Commission: see Political Parties, Elections and Referendums Act 2000 s 1
legal incapacity: s 202(1)
local government election (E&W): ss 191(1), 203(1), (1A)
local government election (S): s 204(1)
parliamentary election: Interpretation Act 1978 Sch 1
prescribed: s 202(1)
register of electors: see s 9
registration officer: s 8(1)
relevant citizen of the Union: s 202(1)
vote: s 202(1)

Contents of service declaration

16(1) A service declaration shall state—

(a) the date of the declaration,

(b) that on that date the declarant is, or but for the circumstances entitling him to make the declaration would have been, residing in the United Kingdom,

(c) *Repealed*

(d) the address where the declarant is or, as the case may be, would have been residing in the United Kingdom or, if he cannot give any such address, an address at which he has resided in the United Kingdom,

(e) that on the date of the declaration the declarant is a Commonwealth citizen or a citizen of the Republic of Ireland or a relevant citizen of the Union,

(f) whether the declarant had on the date of the declaration attained the age of 18 years, and, if he had not, the date of his birth, and

(g) such particulars (if any) as may be prescribed of the declarant's identity and service qualifications,

and (except where the declarant is a member of the forces or the spouse or civil partner of such a member) shall be attested in the prescribed manner.

(2) In relation to the registration of local government electors in Scotland, a service declaration made by a person claiming to have a service qualification under section 14(1A) does not require to be attested.

NOTES

Derivation
RPA1949 s 10

Extension of application
Local and European Parliamentary Elections (Registration of Citizens of Accession States) Regulations 2003
Scottish Independence Referendum (Franchise) Act 2013, ss 6, 7A

Subordinate legislation
Representation of the People (Scotland) (Amendment No 2) Regulations 2014, SI 2014/3124

Representation of the People (England and Wales) (Amendment No 2) Regulations 2014, SI 2014/3161

Defined terms
age: s 202(2)
civil partner: Interpretation Act 1978 Sch 1
member of the forces: s 59(1)
prescribed: s 202(1)
spouse: Marriage (Same Sex Couples) Act 2013 Sch 3 para 1

Effect of service declaration

17(1) Where a person's service declaration is in force when he applies for registration, he shall be regarded for the purposes of section 4 above as—

(a) resident on the date of the declaration at the address specified in it in accordance with section 16(d) above;

(b) *Repealed* and

(c) until the contrary is proved, as being a Commonwealth citizen or a citizen of the Republic of Ireland or a relevant citizen of the Union of the age appearing from the declaration and as not being subject to any legal incapacity except as so appearing.

(2) Where a service declaration appearing to be properly made out and (where required) attested is transmitted to the registration officer in the proper manner, the declarant shall, until the contrary is proved, be treated for the purposes of registration as having had from the date of the declaration or such later date, if any, as appears from it, and as continuing to have, a service qualification.

(3) In relation to the registration of local government electors in Scotland, subsection (2) is subject to section 15(3A).

NOTES

Derivation
RPA 1949 s 10

Extension of application

Local and European Parliamentary Elections (Registration of Citizens of Accession States) Regulations 2003
Scottish Independence Referendum (Franchise) Act

2013, ss 6, 7A

registration officer: s 8(1)
relevant citizen of the Union: s 202(1)

Defined terms
  legal incapacity: s 202(1)

Place and manner of voting at parliamentary elections

Polling districts at parliamentary elections

18A(1) Every constituency is to be divided into polling districts.

(2) A relevant authority must—

(a) divide its area into polling districts for the purpose of parliamentary elections for so much of any constituency as is situated in its area, and

(b) keep the polling districts under review.

(3) The following rules apply—

(a) the authority must seek to ensure that all electors in a constituency in its area have such reasonable facilities for voting as are practicable in the circumstances;

(b) in England, each parish is to be a separate polling district;

(c) in Wales, each community is to be a separate polling district;

(d) in Scotland, each electoral ward (within the meaning of section 1 of the Local Governance (Scotland) Act 2004) is to be divided into two or more separate polling districts.

(4) Subsection (3)(b) to (d) does not apply if, in any case, there are special circumstances.

(5) If an alteration of polling districts in an area is made under this section—

(a) the registration officer who acts for the area must make such adaptations of his register of parliamentary electors as are necessary to take account of the alteration, and

(b) the alteration is effective on the date on which the registration officer publishes a notice stating that the adaptations have been made by him.

(6) This section does not apply to Northern Ireland.

NOTES

Derivation
  Electoral Administration Act 2006 s 16

Defined terms
  community: see Local Government Act 1972 s 27
  constituency: Parliamentary Constituencies Act 1986 s 1(2)
  elector: s 202(1)
  England: Interpretation Act 1978 Sch 1

parish: see Local Government Act 1972 s 14
parliamentary election: Interpretation Act 1978 Sch 1
registration officer: s 8(1)
relevant authority: s 18E(3)
voting: see "vote" s 202(1)
Wales: Interpretation Act 1978 Sch 1

Polling districts at parliamentary elections: Northern Ireland

18AA(1) Every constituency in Northern Ireland is to be divided into polling districts.

(2) The Secretary of State must—

(a) divide Northern Ireland into polling districts for the purpose of parliamentary elections, and

(b) keep the polling districts under review.

(3) The Secretary of State must seek to ensure that all electors in Northern Ireland have such reasonable facilities for voting as are practicable in the circumstances.

(4) Before dividing Northern Ireland into polling districts under subsection (2)(a) or completing a review under subsection (2)(b), the Secretary of State must consult—

(a) the Electoral Commission, and

(b) any other person the Secretary of State considers appropriate.

(5) If an alteration of polling districts is made under this section—

(a) the Chief Electoral Officer for Northern Ireland must make such adaptations of the registers of parliamentary electors maintained by that officer as are necessary to take account of the alteration, and

(b) the alteration is effective on the date on which the Chief Electoral Officer publishes a notice stating that the adaptations have been made.

NOTES

Derivation
Local Elections (Northern Ireland) Order 2013/3156 art 9(3)

Defined terms
Electoral Commission: see Political Parties, Elections and Referendums Act 2000 s 1

constituency: Parliamentary Constituencies Act 1986 s 1(2)
elector: s 202(1)
parliamentary election: Interpretation Act 1978 Sch 1
voting: see "vote" s 202(1)

Polling places at parliamentary elections

18B(1) A polling place is to be designated for each polling district in a constituency.

(2) But subsection (1) does not apply if the size or other circumstances of a polling district are such that the situation of the polling stations does not materially affect the convenience of the electors or any body of them.

(3) A relevant authority must—

(a) designate the polling places for the polling districts in its area, and

(b) keep the polling places in its area under review.

(4) The following rules apply—

(a) the authority must seek to ensure that all electors in a constituency in its area have such reasonable facilities for voting as are practicable in the circumstances;

(b) the authority must seek to ensure that so far as is reasonable and practicable every polling place for which it is responsible is accessible to electors who are disabled;

(c) the authority must have regard to the accessibility to disabled persons of potential polling stations in any place which it is considering designating as a polling place or the designation of which as a polling place it is reviewing;

(d) the polling place for a polling district must be an area in the district, unless special circumstances make it desirable to designate an area wholly or partly outside the district;

(e) the polling place for a polling district must be small enough to indicate to electors in different parts of the district how they will be able to reach the polling station.

(5) If no polling place is designated for a polling district the polling district is to be taken to be the polling place.

NOTES

Derivation
Electoral Administration Act 2006 s 16

Defined terms
constituency: Parliamentary Constituencies Act 1986

s 1(2)
elector: s 202(1)
voting: see "vote" s 202(1)

Review of polling districts and places

18C(1) A relevant authority must during each compulsory review period carry out and complete—

(a) a review under section 18A of all the polling districts in its area, and

(b) a review under section 18B of all the polling places in its area.

(2) The compulsory review periods are—

(a) the period of 16 months beginning with 1st October 2013, and

(b) the period of 16 months beginning with 1st October of every fifth year after that.

(3) Subsection (1) does not prevent a relevant authority carrying out a review of some or all of the polling districts or polling places in its area at other times.

(6) Schedule A1 has effect in relation to a review.

(7) This section does not apply to Northern Ireland.

NOTES

Derivation
Electoral Administration Act 2006 s 16

relevant authority: s 18E(3)

Defined terms

Review of polling places: Northern Ireland

18CA(1) The Chief Electoral Officer for Northern Ireland must, during each compulsory review year, carry out and complete a review under section 18B of all the polling places in Northern Ireland.

(2) The compulsory review years are 2014 and every fifth year after that.

(3) Subsection (1) does not prevent the Chief Electoral Officer carrying out a review under section 18B of some or all of the polling places in Northern Ireland at other times.

(4) Subsection (1) does not require the Chief Electoral Officer to carry out and complete a review of all the polling places in Northern Ireland during a compulsory review year if reviews under section 18B of all those polling places are completed during the previous year.

(5) Schedule A1, except paragraphs 2 and 3, has effect in relation to a review under section 18B of polling places in Northern Ireland.

NOTES

Derivation
Local Elections (Northern Ireland) Order 2013/3156 art 9(5)

Review of polling districts and places: representations to Electoral Commission

18D(1) This section applies if in relation to a constituency in the area of a relevant authority a relevant representation is made to the Electoral Commission by—

(a) an interested authority in England and Wales;

(b) not less than 30 electors in the constituency;

(c) a person (other than the returning officer) who has made representations under Schedule A1;

(d) a person who is not an elector in a constituency in the authority's area but who the Commission think has sufficient interest in the accessibility of disabled persons to polling places in the area or has particular expertise in relation to the access to premises or facilities of disabled persons.

(2) A relevant representation is a representation that a review under section 18A or 18B has not been conducted by a relevant authority so as to—

(a) meet the reasonable requirements of the electors in the constituency or any body of those electors, or

(b) take sufficient account of the accessibility to disabled persons of polling stations within a designated polling place.

(3) The returning officer for the constituency may make observations on representations made under this section.

(4) The Electoral Commission must consider such representations and observations and may, if they think fit—

    (a) direct the relevant authority to make any alterations to the polling places designated by the review which the Commission think necessary in the circumstances;

    (b) if the authority fails to make the alterations before the end of the period of two months starting on the day the direction is given, make the alterations themselves.

(5) Alterations made by the Electoral Commission under subsection (4) have effect as if they had been made by the relevant authority.

(6) An interested authority in relation to a constituency in England and Wales is—

    (a) in England, the council of a parish, or where there is no such council the parish meeting of a parish, which is wholly or partly situated within the constituency;

    (b) in Wales, the council of a community which is so situated.

(7) The reference in subsection (1)(b) to electors does not include persons who have an anonymous entry in the register of parliamentary electors or local government electors.

NOTES

Derivation
Electoral Administration Act 2006 s 16

Defined terms
anonymous entry: s 202(1)
community: see Local Government Act 1972 s 27
elector: ss 18D(7), 202(1)
Electoral Commission: see Political Parties, Elections and Referendums Act 2000 s 1
constituency: Parliamentary Constituencies Act 1986

s 1(2)
elector: s 202(1)
England: Interpretation Act 1978 Sch 1
parish: see Local Government Act 1972 s 14
person: s 202(1)
relevant authority: s 18E(3)
returning officer: see ss 24-27
Wales: Interpretation Act 1978 Sch 1

Sections 18A to 18D: supplemental

18E(1) This section applies for the purposes of sections 18A to 18D.

(2) No election is to be questioned by reason of—

    (a) any non-compliance with the provisions of those sections, or

    (b) any informality relative to polling districts or polling places.

(3) Each of the following is a relevant authority—

    (a) in relation to England, the council of a district or London borough;

    (b) in relation to Scotland, a local authority;

    (c) in relation to Wales, the council of a county or county borough;

    (d) in relation to Northern Ireland, the Chief Electoral Officer for Northern Ireland.

(4) *Repealed*

NOTES

Derivation
Electoral Administration Act 2006 s 16

Defined terms
election: s 202(1)
England: Interpretation Act 1978 Sch 1

local authority (S): s 204(1)
London borough: s 203(2) and Interpretation Act 1978 Sch 1
Wales: Interpretation Act 1978 Sch 1

19-22 *Repealed*

Rules for parliamentary elections

23(1) The proceedings at a parliamentary election shall be conducted in accordance with the parliamentary elections rules in Schedule 1 to this Act.

(2) It is the returning officer's general duty at a parliamentary election to do all such acts and things as may be necessary for effectually conducting the election in the manner provided by those parliamentary elections rules.

(3) No parliamentary election shall be declared invalid by reason of any act or omission by the returning officer or any other person in breach of his official duty in connection with the election or otherwise of the parliamentary elections rules if it appears to the tribunal having cognizance of the question that—

   (a) the election was so conducted as to be substantially in accordance with the law as to elections; and

   (b) the act or omission did not affect its result.

NOTES

Derivation
   RPA 1949 s 16

parliamentary election: Interpretation Act 1978 Sch 1
returning officer: see ss 24-27

Defined terms

Returning officers: England and Wales

24(1) In England and Wales, the returning officer for a parliamentary election is—

   (a) in the case of a county constituency in England which is coterminous with or wholly contained in a county as defined by section 38 of the Sheriffs Act 1887, the sheriff of the county;

   (aa) in the case of a county constituency in Wales which is coterminous with or wholly contained in a preserved county as defined by section 64 of the Local Government (Wales) Act 1994, the sheriff of the county;

   (b) in the case of a borough constituency in England which is coterminous with or wholly contained in a district, the chairman of the district council;

   (bb) in the case of a borough constituency in Wales which is coterminous with or wholly contained in a county or county borough, the chairman of the county or county borough council;

   (c) in the case of any other constituency in England wholly outside Greater London, such sheriff or chairman of a district council as may be designated in an order by the Secretary of State made by statutory instrument;

   (cc) in the case of any other constituency in Wales, such sheriff or chairman of a county or county borough council as may be designated in an order by the Secretary of State so made;

   (d) in the case of a constituency which is coterminous with or wholly contained in a London borough, the mayor of the borough;

   (dd) where a council of a London borough are operating executive arrangements which involve a mayor and cabinet executive, paragraph (d) shall have effect as if for the words "the mayor" there were substituted "the chairman;

   (e) in the case of a constituency wholly or partly in Greater London which is situated partly in one London borough and partly in a district or any other London borough, the mayor or the chairman of such London borough or the chairman of such district council as may be designated in an order by the Secretary of State made by statutory instrument.

   The City, the Inner Temple and the Middle Temple shall be treated for the purposes of this section as if together they formed a London borough.

(1A)   In subsection (1), "executive arrangements", "mayor and cabinet executive" and "mayor and council manager executive" have the same meaning as in Part II of the Local Government Act 2000.

(2)   A parliamentary election is not liable to be questioned by reason of a defect in the title, or want of title, of the person presiding at or conducting the election, if that person was then in actual possession of, or acting in, the office giving the right to preside at or conduct the election.

NOTES

Derivation
   LGA 1972 ss 40, 266

Subordinate legislation
Returning Officers (Parliamentary Constituencies) (Wales) Order 2007, SI 2007/171
Returning Officers (Parliamentary Constituencies) (England) Order 2007, SI 2007/2878

Defined terms
   the City: ss 202(1), 203(2)

constituency: Parliamentary Constituencies Act 1986 s 1(2)
election: s 202(1)
England: Interpretation Act 1978 Sch 1
London borough: s 203(2) and Interpretation Act 1978 Sch 1
parliamentary election: Interpretation Act 1978 Sch 1
Wales: Interpretation Act 1978 Sch 1

Returning officers: Scotland

25(1)   In Scotland, the returning officer for a parliamentary election is—
   (a)   in the case of a constituency wholly situated in one local government area, the person under section 41 below who is, or who may discharge the functions of, the returning officer at elections of councillors for the local authority for that area;
   (b)   in the case of a constituency situated in more than one local government area, such person mentioned above as the Secretary of State may by order direct.

(2)   Every local authority shall place at the disposal of the returning officer for a constituency wholly or partly situated in their area, for the purpose of assisting the returning officer in the discharge of any functions conferred on him in relation to a parliamentary election in that constituency, the services of officers employed by the authority.

(3)   *Repealed*

NOTES

Derivation
   RPA 1949 s 17

Defined terms
   constituency: Parliamentary Constituencies Act 1986
   s 1(2)

local authority (S): s 204(1)
local authority area: s 204(1)
local authority election: s 204(1)
parliamentary election: Interpretation Act 1978 Sch 1

Returning officer: Northern Ireland

26(1)   In Northern Ireland, the Chief Electoral Officer for Northern Ireland is the returning officer for each constituency.

(2)   Sections 14(5) and 14A(2) and (3) of the Electoral Law Act (Northern Ireland) 1962 (appointment of temporary deputy and delegation to assistants) shall have effect in relation to the Chief Electoral Officer in his capacity as returning officer.

NOTES

Derivation
Local Government Reorganisation (Consequential Provisions) (Northern Ireland) Order 1973 SI 1973/2095

Defined terms
constituency: Parliamentary Constituencies Act 1986 s 1(2)

Returning officers generally

27(1) It is for the returning officer as such to execute the writ for a parliamentary election, and the office of returning officer is a distinct office from that by virtue of which he becomes returning officer.

(2) Where a person takes any office by virtue of which he becomes returning officer, he (and not the outgoing holder of the office) shall complete the execution of any writ for a parliamentary election previously issued and not yet returned.

(3) A person is not subject to any incapacity to vote at a parliamentary election by reason of being or acting as returning officer at that election.

NOTES

Derivation
  RPA 1949 s 17

returning officer: see ss 24-26
vote: s 202(1)

Defined terms
  parliamentary election: Interpretation Act 1978 Sch 1

Discharge of returning officer's functions in England and Wales

28(1) In England and Wales the duties of the returning officer for a parliamentary election (except those mentioned in subsection (2) below) shall be discharged, as acting returning officer—
  (a) in the case of a constituency in England for which the chairman of a district council or the mayor or the chairman of a London borough is returning officer by virtue of section 24(1) above, by the registration officer appointed by that council;
  (aa) in the case of a constituency in Wales for which the chairman of a county or county borough council is returning officer by virtue of that section, by the registration officer appointed by that council;
  (b) in the case of any other constituency, by such registration officer as may be designated in an order made by statutory instrument by the Secretary of State.

(2) The duties excepted from subsection (1) above are—
  (a) any duty imposed on a returning officer under rule 3 of the parliamentary elections rules; and
  (b) any duty so imposed under rule 50 of those rules which the person (if any) who for the time being holds the office of returning officer reserves to himself and undertakes to perform in person.

(3) The returning officer shall give to the acting returning officer written notice of any duties which he reserves to himself under paragraph (b) of subsection (2) above, and that paragraph shall, in the case of any election, apply to the duties (if any) of which the notice is so given not later than the day following that on which the writ is received, and to no others.

(4) In the discharge of the duties imposed by subsection (1) an acting returning officer has all the powers, obligations, rights and liabilities of the returning officer under this Act, and this Act has effect accordingly.

(5) An acting returning officer has power to appoint deputies to discharge all or any of those duties, and a Welsh county council or county borough council or a district council or London borough council may assign officers to assist in carrying out all or any of those duties.

(6) Section 25 of the Sheriffs Act 1887 (death of sheriff) does not authorise the under-sheriff to discharge the duties of returning officer, and upon a sheriff's death the acting returning officer shall discharge all the sheriff's duties as returning officer until another sheriff is appointed and has made the declaration of office.

NOTES

Derivation
RPA 1949 s 18
LGA 1972 s 40

Subordinate legislation
Returning Officers (Parliamentary Constituencies) (Wales) Order 2007, SI 2007/171
Returning Officers (Parliamentary Constituencies) (England) Order 2007, SI 2007/2878

Defined terms
constituency: Parliamentary Constituencies Act 1986 s 1(2)
England: Interpretation Act 1978 Sch 1
London borough: s 203(2) and Interpretation Act 1978 Sch 1
parliamentary election: Interpretation Act 1978 Sch 1
parliamentary election rules: s 202(1)
registration officer: s 8(1)
returning officer: s 24
Wales: Interpretation Act 1978 Sch 1
written: Interpretation Act 1978 Sch 1

Payments by and to returning officer

29(1)   No consideration shall be given by or to a returning officer for the making out, receipt, delivery or return of the writ for a parliamentary election or, subject to the following provisions of this section, otherwise in connection with its execution.

(2)   Nothing in subsection (1) above shall be taken as applying to any inclusive salary payable to a returning officer in respect of the office by virtue of which he becomes returning officer.

(3)   Subject to section 29A, a returning officer shall be entitled to recover his charges in respect of services rendered, or expenses incurred, for or in connection with a parliamentary election if—

(a)   the services were necessarily rendered, or the expenses were necessarily incurred, for the efficient and effective conduct of the election; and

(b)   the total of his charges does not exceed the amount ("the overall maximum recoverable amount") specified in, or determined in accordance with, an order made by the Secretary of State for the purposes of this subsection.

(3A)   An order under subsection (3) may specify, or make provision for determining in accordance with the order, a maximum recoverable amount for services or expenses of any specified description and, subject to subsection (3B) below, the returning officer may not recover more than that amount in respect of any such services or expenses.

(3B)   The Secretary of State may, in a particular case, authorise the payment of—

(a)   more than the overall maximum recoverable amount, or

(b)   more than the specified maximum recoverable amount for any specified services or expenses,

if he is satisfied that the conditions in subsection (3C) are met.

(3C)   The conditions referred to in subsection (3B) are—

(a)   that it was reasonable for the returning officer concerned to render the services or incur the expenses, and

(b)   that the charges in question are reasonable.

(4C)   The power to make orders under subsection (3) above shall be exercised by statutory instrument; and any such order may make different provision for different cases, circumstances or areas and may contain such incidental, supplemental, saving or transitional provisions as the Secretary of State thinks fit.

(5)   The amount of any charges recoverable in accordance with this section shall be charged on and paid out of the Consolidated Fund on an account being submitted to the Secretary of State, but the Secretary of State may if he thinks fit before payment, apply for the account to be taxed under the provisions of section 30 below.

(6) Where the superannuation contributions required to be paid by a local authority in respect of any person are increased by any fee paid under this section as part of a returning officer's charges at a parliamentary election, then on an account being submitted to the Secretary of State a sum equal to the increase shall be charged on and paid out of the Consolidated Fund to the authority.

(7) On the returning officer's request for an advance on account of his charges, the Secretary of State may, on such terms as he thinks fit, make such an advance.

(8) Regulations may make provision as to the time when and the manner and form in which accounts are to be rendered to the Secretary of State for the purposes of the payment of a returning officer's charges.

(9) Any exercise by the Secretary of State of his functions under subsection (3) above shall require the consent of the Treasury.

NOTES

Derivation
RPA 1949 s 20
RPA 1969 s 20

Modified application
Representation of the People (Combination of Polls) (England and Wales) Regulations 2004, SI 2004/294
Scottish Parliament (Elections etc) Order 2007, SI 2007/937
Northern Ireland Assembly (Elections) Order 2001, SI 2001/2599
Scottish Parliament (Elections etc) Order 2010, SI 2010/2999
Parliamentary Voting Systems and Constituencies Act 2011

Subordinate legislation
Parliamentary Elections (Returning Officers' Charges)

Order 2015, SI 2015/479
Scottish Parliament (Returning Officers' Charges) (Revocation) Order 2015, SI 2015/761
Parliamentary Elections (Returning Officer's Charges) (Northern Ireland) Order 2015, SI 2015/885

Defined terms
election: s 202(1)
Electoral Commission: see Political Parties, Elections and Referendums Act 2000 s 1
local authority (E&W): s 203(1)
local authority (S): s 204(1)
parliamentary election: Interpretation Act 1978 Sch 1
returning officer: see ss 24-27

Inadequate performance of returning officer: reduction of charges

29A(1) This section applies to a service rendered by a returning officer for or in connection with a parliamentary election in Great Britain which, in the opinion of the Electoral Commission, was inadequately performed.

(2) The Commission may recommend to the Secretary of State that the returning officer is entitled under section 29(3) to no more than a specified amount (which may be nil) in respect of that service.

(3) In making a recommendation under subsection (2), the Commission must have regard to—

(a) any report prepared under section 5 of the Political Parties, Elections and Referendums Act 2000 on the administration of the parliamentary election concerned,

(b) any assessments of the level of performance of the returning officer in relation to that election under section 9B(4) of that Act,

(c) any representations made to the Commission by the returning officer in respect of the performance of the service, and

(d) any other information relating to the performance of the service by the returning officer that has been provided to the Commission.

(4) Where the Commission makes a recommendation under subsection (2), the returning officer is entitled under section 29(3) to no more than the amount (which may be nil) determined by the Secretary of State, having regard to the recommendation by the Commission.

NOTES

Derivation
    Electoral Registration and Administration Act 2013 s 18

Defined terms
    Electoral Commission: see Political Parties, Elections and Referendums Act 2000 s 1

Great Britain: Union with Scotland Act 1706 art 1 and Interpretation Act 1978 s 22(1) and Sch 2 para 5
parliamentary election: Interpretation Act 1978 Sch 1
returning officer: see ss 24-27

Taxation of returning officer's account

30(1)   An application for a returning officer's account to be taxed shall be made—

        (a) where the account relates to an election in a constituency in England or Wales or in Northern Ireland, to the county court,

        (b) where the account relates to an election in a constituency in Scotland, to the Auditor of the Court of Session,

    and in this section the expression "the court" means that court or Auditor.

  (2)   On any such application the court has jurisdiction to tax the account in such manner and at such time and place as the court thinks fit, and finally to determine the amount payable to the returning officer.

  (3)   On any such application the returning officer may apply to the court to examine any claim made by any person against him in respect of matters charged in the account; and the court, after notice given to the claimant and after giving him an opportunity to be heard and to tender any evidence, may allow or disallow or reduce the claim objected to with or without costs; and the determination of the court shall be final for all purposes and as against all persons.

  (4)   Any reference in this section to the county court shall be taken, in relation to Northern Ireland, as a reference to the county court having jurisdiction at the place for the delivery of nomination papers at the election in question.

NOTES

Derivation
    RPA 1949 s 20

Modified application
    Representation of the People (Combination of Polls) (England and Wales) Regulations 2004, SI 2004/294

Defined terms
    constituency: Parliamentary Constituencies Act 1986

s 1(2)
county court: Interpretation Act 1978 Sch 1
England: Interpretation Act 1978 Sch 1
returning officer: see ss 24-27
person: s 202(1)
Wales: Interpretation Act 1978 Sch 1

Place and manner of voting at local government elections

Polling districts and stations at local government elections

31(1)   For elections of county councillors in England the county council may divide an electoral division into polling districts, and may alter any polling district, and for elections of London borough or district councillors the London borough or district council may divide the London borough or district or any ward thereof into polling districts, and may alter any polling district.

 (1A)   For elections of county or county borough councillors in Wales, the county or county borough council may divide an electoral division into polling districts and may alter any polling district.

 (1B)   For any Authority elections, a London borough council or the Common Council may divide their area into polling districts and may alter any polling district.

For the purposes of this subsection the Inner Temple and the Middle Temple shall be treated as forming part of the City.

(2) In Scotland, for elections of local authority councillors the local authority may divide an electoral ward into polling districts and may alter any polling district; but in the absence of special circumstances those polling districts shall be those which were last designated for the purpose of parliamentary elections under section 18A above.

(3) Any power to constitute polling districts for the purpose of local government elections shall be exercised so that electors from any parliamentary polling district wholly or partly within the electoral area can, in the absence of special circumstances, be allotted to a polling station within the parliamentary polling place for that district unless the parliamentary polling place is outside the electoral area.

(4)-(7) *Repealed*

NOTES

Derivation
RPA 1949 s 22
London Government Act 1963 s 8

Modified application
Local Authorities (Mayoral Elections) (England and Wales) Regulations 2007, SI 2007/1024
Local Authorities (Conduct of Referendums) (Wales) Regulations 2008, SI 2008/1848
Local Authorities (Conduct of Referendums) (England) Regulations 2012, SI 2012/323
Local Authorities (Conduct of Referendums) (Council Tax Increases) (England) Regulations 2012, SI 2012/444
Neighbourhood Planning (Referendums) Regulations 2012, SI 2012/2031

Defined terms
Authority election: s 203(1)
the City: ss 202(1), 203(2)
Common Council: s 202(1)
elector: s 202(1)
electoral area: s 202(1)
England: Interpretation Act 1978 Sch 1
local authority (S): s 204(1)
local government area (E&W): ss 191(1), 203(1)
local government area (S): s 204(1), (1A)
local government election (S): s 204(1)
London borough: s 203(2) and Interpretation Act 1978 Sch 1
parliamentary election: Interpretation Act 1978 Sch 1
Wales: Interpretation Act 1978 Sch 1

32 *Repealed*

33 *Repealed*

34 *Repealed*

Conduct of local government elections in England and Wales

Returning officers: local elections in England and Wales

35(1) In England every non-metropolitan county council shall appoint an officer of the council to be the returning officer for elections of councillors of the county and every district council shall appoint an officer of the council to be the returning officer for the elections of councillors of the district and an officer of the council to be the returning officer for elections of councillors of parishes within the district.

(1A) In Wales, the council of every county or county borough shall appoint—
  (a) an officer of the council to be the returning officer for elections of councillors of the county or county borough; and
  (b) an officer of the council to be the returning officer for elections of councillors of communities within the county or county borough.

(2) *Repealed*

(2A) Subsections (2B) and (2C) below have effect in relation to the Greater London Authority.

(2B)   The returning officer at an election of a constituency member of the London Assembly shall be such a person, or a person of such a description, as may be designated by the Secretary of State in an order made by statutory instrument.

(2C)   The returning officer—
   (a)   at any election of the Mayor of London,
   (b)   at the election of the London members of the London Assembly at an ordinary election, and
   (c)   for the purposes of section 11 of the 1999 Act (return of London members of the London Assembly otherwise than at an election),

shall be the proper officer of the Greater London Authority.

(3)   The returning officer at an election of London borough councillors shall be the proper officer of the borough.

(3A)   *Repealed*

(4)   The returning officer at any election mentioned in subsections (1) to (3) above may by writing under his hand appoint one or more persons to discharge all or any of his functions.

(5)   A local government election in England and Wales is not liable to be questioned by reason of a defect in the title, or want of title, of the person presiding at or conducting the election, if that person was then in actual possession of, or acting in, the office giving the right to preside at or conduct the election.

(6)   The council for any London borough shall place the services of its officers at the disposal of any person acting as the returning officer at an Authority election for an electoral area situated wholly or partly in the borough.

NOTES

Derivation
   LGA 1972 s 41

Modified application
Regional Assembly and Local Government Referendums Order 2004, SI 2004/1962
Local Authorities (Mayoral Elections) (England and Wales) Regulations 2007
Local Authorities (Conduct of Referendums) (Wales) Regulations 2008, SI 2008/1848
Local Authorities (Conduct of Referendums) (England) Regulations 2012, SI 2012/323
Local Authorities (Conduct of Referendums) (Council Tax Increases) (England) Regulations 2012, SI 2012/444
Neighbourhood Planning (Referendums) Regulations 2012, SI 2012/2031

Defined terms
   the 1999 Act: s 203(1)
   Assembly constituency: s 203(1)
   Authority election: s 203(1)

constituency: Parliamentary Constituencies Act 1986 s 1(2)
election: s 202(1)
election of a constituency member of the London Assembly: s 203(1)
election of the Mayor of London: s 203(1)
electoral area (E&W): ss 191(1), 203(1)
electoral area (S): s 204(1)
England: Interpretation Act 1978 Sch 1
local government election (E&W): ss 191(1), 203(1), (1A)
London borough: s 203(2) and Interpretation Act 1978 Sch 1
London member: s 203(1)
parish councillors: see Local Government Act 1972 s 16
proper officer: s 202(1)
returning officer: see ss 24, 27
Wales: Interpretation Act 1978 Sch 1
writing: Interpretation Act 1978 Sch 1

Local elections in England and Wales

36(1)   Elections of councillors for local government areas in England and Wales shall be conducted in accordance with rules made by the Secretary of State.

(2)   Rules made under this section shall apply the parliamentary elections rules in Schedule 1 to this Act, subject to such adaptations, alterations and exceptions as seem appropriate to the Secretary of State.

(2A)   As regards the Greater London Authority—
   (a)   Authority elections, and

        (b) the return of London members of the London Assembly otherwise than at an election,

shall be conducted in accordance with rules made under this subsection by the Secretary of State.

Rules made under this subsection need not comply with the requirements of subsection (2) above.

(2B) As regards lists of candidates submitted under paragraph 5 of Schedule 2 to the 1999 Act (election of London members), the provision that may be made by rules under subsection (2A) above includes provision for or in connection with any of the following—

        (a) the inclusion, withdrawal, addition or removal of persons;

        (b) cases where a person included in such a list is or becomes, or seeks to become, an individual candidate to be a London member of the London Assembly.

(3) Where the polls at—

        (a) the ordinary election of district councillors for any district ward or an election to fill a casual vacancy occurring in the office of such a councillor, and

        (b) the ordinary election of parish councillors for any parish or an election to fill a casual vacancy occurring in the office of such a councillor,

are to be taken on the same day and the elections are for related electoral areas, the polls at those elections shall be taken together.

(3AB) Where the polls at—

        (a) the ordinary election of councillors for any electoral division of a Welsh county or county borough or an election to fill a casual vacancy occurring in the office of such a councillor, and

        (b) the ordinary election of community councillors for any community or an election to fill a casual vacancy occurring in the office of such a councillor,

are to be taken on the same day and the elections are for related electoral areas, the polls at those elections shall be taken together.

(3AC) Where the polls at—

        (a) the ordinary election of councillors for any electoral division of a county in England in which there are no district councils or an election to fill a casual vacancy occurring in the office of such a councillor, and

        (b) the ordinary election of parish councillors for any parish or an election to fill a casual vacancy occurring in the office of such a councillor,

are to be taken on the same day and the elections are for related electoral areas, the polls at those elections shall be taken together.

(3A) For the purposes of this section electoral areas are related if they are coterminous or if one is situated within the other.

(3AA) *Repealed*

(3B) Where the polls at any elections are combined under this section the cost of taking the combined polls (excluding any cost solely attributable to one election) and any cost attributable to their combination shall be apportioned equally among the elections.

(3C) The Secretary of State may by regulations make such provision as he thinks fit in connection with the combining of polls at any elections under this section including provision modifying the Representation of the People Acts in relation to such elections.

(4) All expenditure properly incurred by a returning officer in relation to the holding of an election of a councillor for a principal area (that is, a county, a county borough a district or a London borough) shall, in so far as it does not, in cases where there is a scale fixed for the purposes of this section by the council for that area, exceed that scale, be paid by that council.

(4A) *Repealed*

(4B) All expenditure properly incurred by a returning officer in relation to the holding of an Authority election shall, in so far as it does not, in cases where there is a scale fixed for the purposes of this section by the Greater London Authority, exceed that scale, be paid by the Greater London Authority.

(5) All expenditure properly incurred by a returning officer in relation to the holding of an election of a parish councillor shall, in so far as it does not, in cases where there is a scale fixed for the purposes of this section by the council of the district in which the parish is situated, exceed that scale, be paid by the district council, but any expenditure so incurred shall, if the district council so require, be repaid to that council by the council of the parish for which the election is held.

(5A) All the expenditure properly incurred by a returning officer in relation to the holding of an election of a community councillor shall, in so far as it does not, in cases where there is a scale fixed for the purposes of this section by the council of the county or county borough in which the community is situated ("the principal council"), exceed that scale, be paid by the principal council; and if the principal council so require, any expenditure so incurred shall be repaid to them by the community council.

(6) Before a poll is taken at an election of a councillor for any local government area in England and Wales the council of that area or, in the case of an election of a parish or community councillor, the council who appointed the returning officer shall, at the request of the returning officer or of any person acting as returning officer, advance to him such reasonable sum in respect of his expenses at the election as he may require.

(6A) Subsection (6) above shall apply in relation to an Authority election as it applies in relation to an election of a councillor for any local government area in England and Wales, but taking the reference to the council of the area as a reference to the Greater London Authority.

(7) Rules made under this section shall be—
   (a) made by statutory instrument;
   (b) subject to annulment in pursuance of a resolution of either House of Parliament.

NOTES

Derivation
LGA 1972 s 42

Modified application
Representation of the People (Combination of Polls) (England and Wales) Regulations 2004, SI 2004/294
Local Authorities (Mayoral Elections) (England and Wales) Regulations 2007, SI 2007/1024
Local Authorities (Conduct of Referendums) (Wales) Regulations 2008, SI 2008/1848
Local Authorities (Conduct of Referendums) (England) Regulations 2012, SI 2012/323
Local Authorities (Conduct of Referendums) (Council Tax Increases) (England) Regulations 2012, SI 2012/444
Neighbourhood Planning (Referendums) Regulations 2012, SI 2012/2031
National Assembly for Wales (Representation of the People) Order 2007, SI 2007/236

Subordinate legislation
Parish and Community Meetings (Polls) Rules 1987, SI 1987/1
Representation of the People (England and Wales) Regulations 2001, SI 2001/341
Representation of the People (Combination of Polls) (England and Wales) Regulations 2004, SI 2004/294
Local Elections (Principal Areas) (England and Wales) Rules 2006, SI 2006/3304

Local Elections (Parishes and Communities) (England and Wales) Rules 2006, SI 2006/3305
Greater London Authority Elections Rules 2007, SI 2007/3541

Defined terms
the 1999 Act: s 203(1)
Authority election: s 203(1)
community councillors: see Local Government Act 1972 s 35
election: s 202(1)
election of the Mayor of London: s 203(1)
electoral area (E&W): ss 191(1), 203(1)
electoral area (S): s 204(1)
England: Interpretation Act 1978 Sch 1
local government area (E&W): ss 191(1), 203(1)
local government area (S): s 204(1)
London borough: s 203(2) and Interpretation Act 1978 Sch 1
London member: s 203(1)
parish councillors: see Local Government Act 1972 s 16
parliamentary election rules: s 203(1)
proper officer: s 202(1)
returning officer: see ss 24-27
Wales: Interpretation Act 1978 Sch 1

Ordinary day of local elections in England and Wales

37(1)   In every year the ordinary day of election of councillors is the same for all local government areas in England and Wales and is—

    (a)   the first Thursday in May;

    (b)   such other day as may be fixed by the Secretary of State by order made not later than 1st February in the year preceding the year (or, in the case of an order affecting more than one year, the first year) in which the order is to take effect.

(2)   As respects Authority elections, the power conferred by subsection (1)(b) above shall include power to make an order fixing a day other than the first Thursday in May as the day on which the poll is to be held at an ordinary election other than the first.

(2A)   Subsection (1) is subject to any order under—

    (a)   section 37A (local government areas in England), or

    (b)   section 37B (local government areas in Wales).

(3)   The power to make an order under this section is exercisable by statutory instrument.

NOTES

Derivation
    LGA 1972 ss 43, 266

local government area (E&W): ss 191(1), 203(1)
local government area (S): s 204(1)
Wales: Interpretation Act 1978 Sch 1

Defined terms
    Authority election: s 203(1)
    England: Interpretation Act 1978 Sch 1

Power to change date of local elections to date of European Parliamentary general election: England

37A(1)   The Secretary of State may by order provide that in a year in which a European Parliamentary general election is to be held—

    (a)   the ordinary day of election of councillors for counties in England, districts and London boroughs,

    (b)   the ordinary day of election of councillors for parishes, and

    (c)   as respects Authority elections, the day on which the poll is to be held at an ordinary election,

shall be changed so as to be the same as the date of the poll at the European Parliamentary general election.

(2)   An order under subsection (1) may make provision under all of paragraphs (a) to (c) or under one or more of those paragraphs.

(3)   An order under subsection (1) must relate to a single year and must be made at least six months before—

    (a)   the local election day in that year, or

    (b)   if earlier, the date of the poll at the European Parliamentary general election in that year.

(4)   For this purpose "the local election day" in a particular year is—

    (a)   the first Thursday in May, or

    (b)   if an order has been made under section 37(1)(b) (power to change date of council and Assembly elections) in relation to that year, the day specified in the order.

(5)   Before making an order under this section, the Secretary of State must consult—

    (a)   the Electoral Commission, and

    (b)   such other persons as he considers appropriate.

(6)   An order under subsection (1) may make incidental, supplementary or consequential provision or savings.

(7) Where the Welsh Ministers make an order under section 37B, the Secretary of State may by order make such consequential provision in relation to elections in England as he thinks fit.

(8) The powers under subsections (6) and (7) include power to make—
  (a) different provision for different purposes;
  (b) provision disapplying or modifying the application of an enactment or an instrument made under an enactment.

(9) An order under this section must be made by statutory instrument.

(10) A statutory instrument containing an order made under this section may not be made unless a draft of the instrument has been laid before and approved by a resolution of each House of Parliament.

NOTES

Derivation
Local Government and Public Involvement in Health Act 2007 s 60

Defined terms
Authority election: s 203(1)
Electoral Commission: see Political Parties, Elections and Referendums Act 2000 s 1

enactment: Interpretation Act 1978 Sch 1
enactment (NI): s 205
England: Interpretation Act 1978 Sch 1
parish councillors: see Local Government Act 1972 s 16
person: s 202(1)

Power to change date of local elections to date of European Parliamentary general election: Wales

37B(1) The Welsh Ministers may by order provide that, in a year in which a European Parliamentary general election is to be held, the ordinary day of election of councillors for—
  (a) counties in Wales and county boroughs, and
  (b) communities,
shall be changed so as to be the same as the date of the poll at the European Parliamentary general election.

(2) An order under subsection (1) may make provision under paragraphs (a) and (b) or under one of those paragraphs.

(3) An order under subsection (1) must relate to a single year and must be made at least six months before—
  (a) the local election day in that year, or
  (b) if earlier, the date of the poll at the European Parliamentary general election in that year.

(4) For this purpose "the local election day" in a particular year is—
  (a) the first Thursday in May, or
  (b) if an order has been made under section 37(1)(b) (power to change date of council and Assembly elections) in relation to that year, the day specified in the order.

(5) Before making an order under this section, the Welsh Ministers must consult—
  (a) the Electoral Commission, and
  (b) such other persons as they consider appropriate.

(6) An order under subsection (1) may make incidental, supplementary or consequential provision or savings.

(7) Where the Secretary of State makes an order under section 37A, the Welsh Ministers may by order make such consequential provision in relation to elections in Wales as they think fit.

(8)   The powers under subsections (6) and (7) include power to make—
    (a)   different provision for different purposes;
    (b)   provision disapplying or modifying the application of an enactment or an instrument made under an enactment.

(9)   An order under this section must be made by statutory instrument.

(10)   A statutory instrument containing an order made under this section may not be made unless a draft of the instrument has been laid before and approved by a resolution of the National Assembly for Wales.

NOTES

Derivation
Local Government and Public Involvement in Health Act 2007 s 60

Defined terms
Electoral Commission: see Political Parties, Elections and Referendums Act 2000 s 1

enactment: Interpretation Act 1978 Sch 1
enactment (NI): s 205
person: s 202(1)
Wales: Interpretation Act 1978 Sch 1

38   *Repealed*

Local elections void etc in England and Wales

39(1)   If in England and Wales at a local government election, other than an election for the return of the London members of the London Assembly,—
    (a)   the poll is countermanded or abandoned for any reason, or
    (b)   no person is or remains, or an insufficient number of persons are or remain, validly nominated to fill the vacancy or vacancies in respect of which the election is held,
the returning officer shall order an election to fill any vacancy which remains unfilled to be held on a day appointed by him.
That day shall be within the period of 35 days (computed according to section 40 below) beginning with the day fixed as the day of election for the first-mentioned election.

(1A)   *Repealed*

(2)   If for any other reason an election to an office under the Local Government Act 1972 or the 1999 Act, other than that of chairman of a parish or community council or parish meeting or parish or community councillor, is not held on the appointed day or within the appointed time, or fails either wholly or in part or becomes void, the High Court may order an election to be held on a day appointed by the court.

(3)   The High Court may order that the costs incurred by any person in connection with proceedings under subsection (2) above shall be paid by the local authority concerned.

(4)   In a case not falling within subsection (1) above—
    (a)   if any difficulty arises with respect to an election of parish or community councillors or of an individual parish or community councillor, or to the first meeting of a parish or community council after an ordinary election of parish or community councillors, or
    (b)   if a parish or community council is not properly constituted because an election is not held or is defective or for any other reason,
the district council or Welsh county or county borough council—
      (i)   may by order make any appointment or do anything which appears to them necessary or expedient for the proper holding of such an election or meeting and properly constituting the council, and

(ii) may, if it appears to them necessary, direct the holding of an election or meeting and fix the date for it.

(5) Where an election is ordered to be held under this section—

(a) rules under section 36 above relating to the notice to be given of an election and the manner in which an election is to be conducted apply in relation to the election so ordered to be held as they applied or would have applied in relation to the election which has not been duly held or has failed or become void;

(b) no fresh nomination is necessary in the case of a candidate who remains validly nominated for that election.

(6) An order made—

(a) under this section may include such modifications of the provisions of—

(i) this Part of this Act (and the rules under section 36), and

(ii) the Local Government Act 1972 or the 1999 Act,

as appear to the High Court, or, as the case may be, the district council or Welsh county or county borough council, necessary or expedient for carrying the order into effect;

(b) by a council under subsection (4) above with respect to an election of parish or community councillors may modify the provisions of—

(i) this Act (and the rules with respect to such elections under section 36); and

(ii) any other enactment relating to such elections.

(7) In the case of a common parish council under which are grouped, by virtue of section 11(5) of the Local Government Act 1972 (grouping of parishes), parishes situated in different districts, references in subsections (4) and (6) above to the district council shall be construed as references to the council of the district in which there is the greater number of local government electors for the parishes in the group.

(8) *Repealed*

(9) If a municipal election in a London borough is not held on the appointed day or within the appointed time or becomes void, the municipal corporation shall not thereby be dissolved or be disabled from acting.

NOTES

Derivation
LGA 1972 s 44
RPA 1949 s 36

Defined terms
the 1999 Act: s 203(1)
community council: see Local Government Act 1972 s 27
election: s 202(1)
elector: s 203(1)
enactment: Interpretation Act 1978 Sch 1
enactment (NI): s 205
England: Interpretation Act 1978 Sch 1
High Court (E,W&NI): Interpretation Act 1978 Sch 1
High Court (S): s 204(3)

local authority (E&W): s 203(1)
local authority (S): s 204(1)
local government area (E&W): ss 191(1), 203(1)
local government area (S): s 204(1)
local government election (E&W): ss 191(1), 203(1), (1A)
London borough: s 203(2) and Interpretation Act 1978 Sch 1
London member: s 203(1)
parish councillors: see Local Government Act 1972 s 16
returning officer: see ss 24, 27
Wales: Interpretation Act 1978 Sch 1

Timing as to local elections in England and Wales

40(1) When the day on which anything is required to be done by section 37 or section 39 above or section 3 of the 1999 Act is a Saturday, Sunday, Christmas Eve, Christmas Day, Good Friday, bank holiday or a day appointed for public thanksgiving or mourning, the requirement shall be deemed to relate to the first day thereafter which is not one of the days specified above.

(2) Where under subsection (1) above the day of election is postponed, the day to which it is postponed shall be treated for the purposes of this Act and the Local Government Act 1972 and (in the case of an Authority election) the 1999 Act as the day of election.

(3) In computing any period of time for the purpose of any rules under section 36 above or for the purposes of section 39 any day specified in subsection (1) shall be disregarded; but where between the giving of a notice of election and the completion of the poll a day is declared to be a bank holiday or day of public thanksgiving or mourning, the foregoing provision, so far as it relates to any such rules, shall not operate to invalidate any act which would have been valid apart from that provision.

This subsection, so far as it relates to any such rules, has effect subject to the provisions of those rules.

NOTES

Derivation
LGA 1972 s 243

Defined terms
the 1999 Act: s 203(1)

bank holiday: Banking and Financial Dealing Act 1971
England: Interpretation Act 1978 Sch 1
Wales: Interpretation Act 1978 Sch 1

Conduct of local government elections in Scotland

Returning officers: local elections in Scotland

41(1) Every local authority in Scotland shall appoint an officer of the authority to be the returning officer for each election of councillors for the authority, and if the person so appointed dies, resigns or is for any other reason unable to act, the authority may appoint another person to be returning officer at that election.

(2) A returning officer in Scotland appointed under this Act may by writing under his hand appoint one or more persons to discharge all or any of his functions.

(3) A local government election in Scotland is not liable to be questioned by reason of a defect in the title, or want of title, of the person presiding at or conducting the election, if that person was then in actual possession of, or acting in, the office giving the right to preside at or conduct the election.

NOTES

Derivation
Local Government (Scotland) Act 1973 s 6

Defined terms
election: s 202(1)
local authority (S): s 204(1)

local government election (S): s 204(1)
returning officer: see ss 25, 27
writing: Interpretation Act 1978 Sch 1

Local elections in Scotland

(1)-(4) *Repealed*

(5) All expenditure properly incurred by a returning officer in relation to the holding of an election of a councillor to a local authority shall be paid by the council of that authority, but only (in cases where there is a scale fixed for the purposes of this section by that council) in so far as it does not exceed that scale.

(6) Before a poll is taken at an election for a councillor for a local government area in Scotland, the council for that area shall, at the request of the returning officer or of any person acting as returning officer, advance to him such reasonable sum in respect of his expenses at the election as he may require.

(7) *Repealed*

NOTES

Derivation
Local Government (Scotland) Act 1973 s 7

Defined terms
election: s 202(1)
local authority (S): s 204(1)

local government area (S): s 204(1)   returning officer: see ss 25, 27

Day of ordinary local elections in Scotland, and other timing provisions

43(1)   In every year in which ordinary elections of councillors for local government areas in Scotland are held, the day on which the poll is held at an election is—

    (a)   the first Thursday in May; or

    (b)   such other day as may be fixed by the Secretary of State by order made by statutory instrument not later than 1st February in the year preceding the year or, in the case of an order affecting more than one year, the first year in which the order is to take effect.

(1A)   An order made under subsection (1)(b) above shall be subject to annulment in pursuance of a resolution of either House of Parliament.

(1B)   Despite subsection (1) above—

    (a)   *Repealed*

    (b)   if an extraordinary general election is, under section 3(2) of the Scotland Act 1998 (c 46) ("the 1998 Act") (which enables the holding of such an election), to be held on a day occurring within the relevant period, the Scottish Ministers may, by order, provide that the poll at the ordinary local election to be held that year shall be held on that day;

(1C)   In subsection (1B) above—

"extraordinary general election" means a general election for membership of the Scottish Parliament held under section 3 of the 1998 Act;

"ordinary local election" means an ordinary election of councillors for local government areas in Scotland held in accordance with section 5 of the 1994 Act and this Act;

"relevant period" means the period beginning with 11th March in a year in which an ordinary local election falls to be held and ending with the day which immediately precedes the first Thursday in May in that year,

and references to the time when a local election falls or does not fall to be held are to be construed in accordance with section 5(1A) or (1B) of the 1994 Act.

(1D)   An order under subsection (1B) above shall be made by statutory instrument.

(2)   Where—

    (a)   the day or the last day on which anything is required or permitted to be done by any rules under section 42 above, or

    (b)   the day on which anything is required to be done under subsection (1) or (1B) above or section 45(1) below,

is a Saturday, Sunday, Christmas Eve, Christmas Day, New Year's Day, Maundy Thursday, Good Friday, bank holiday, or a public holiday, or a day appointed for public thanksgiving or mourning, the requirement or permission shall be deemed to relate to the first day thereafter which is not one of the days before mentioned, but, save as aforesaid or as otherwise expressly provided in this Act or by the Local Government etc (Scotland) Act 1994, in reckoning a number of days for the purposes of this Part of this Act in so far as it relates to the conduct of local government elections in Scotland, the days before specified shall not be excluded.

(3)   Where the day on which the poll is held at an election is postponed under subsection (2) above, the day on which the poll is held shall be treated as the day of election for all purposes of this Act or that Act of 1994 relating to that election.

(4)   Where a day is declared to be a bank holiday or day of public thanksgiving or mourning, nothing in subsection (3) above affects the validity of any act done in relation to an election before or on the date of the declaration.

NOTES

Derivation
    Local Government (Scotland) Act 1973 s 8

Defined terms
    bank holiday: Banking and Financial Dealing Act 1971

election: s 202(1)
local authority area: s 204(1)
local government election (S): s 204(1)

44   Repealed

Non-election of local authority etc in Scotland

45(1)   If in Scotland—

    (a)   for any reason a local authority or members of a local authority are not elected in accordance with the provisions of this Act and the Local Government (Scotland) Act 1973, and the case is not otherwise provided for, or

    (b)   there is for any reason no legally constituted local authority for any area, or

    (c)   the number of members of a local authority then in office is less than the quorum ascertained in accordance with the provisions of Schedule 7 to that Act of 1973 (meetings and proceedings of local authorities),

the Secretary of State may direct the holding of an election for filling such vacancies as exist, and the election shall be held as soon as practicable after that, on a date to be fixed by him.

(2)   The Secretary of State may in that direction—

    (a)   make such provision as appears to him expedient for authorising any person to act in place of a local authority pending the election of members of the authority by an election under subsection (1) above; and

    (b)   make such incidental, consequential, transitional or supplemental provision as appears to him to be necessary or proper.

NOTES

Derivation
    Local Government (Scotland) Act 1973 s 10

Defined terms
    election: s 202(1)
    local authority (S): s 204(1)

Supplemental provisions as to local government elections

Further provision as to local election voting

46(1)   At a local government election for any electoral area no person shall as an elector and no person shall as proxy for any one elector—

    (a)   give more than one vote for any one candidate; or

    (b)   give more votes in all than the total number of councillors to be elected for the electoral area

but this subsection does not apply in relation to Authority elections (where the votes allowed to be given are as specified in the applicable provisions of section 4, 10 or 16 of the 1999 Act).

(2)   No person is subject to any incapacity to vote at a local government election by reason of his being or acting as returning officer at that election.

NOTES

Derivation
    RPA 1949 s 33

Defined terms
    the 1999 Act: s 203(1)

Authority election: s 203(1)
elector: s 202(1)
electoral area (E&W): ss 191(1), 203(1)
electoral area (S): s 204(1)
local government election (E&W): ss 191(1), 203(1), (1A)

local government election (S): s 204(1)
returning officer: see ss 24-27
vote: s 202(1)

Loan of equipment for local elections

47(1)   Any ballot boxes, fittings and compartments provided for parliamentary elections out of moneys provided by Parliament, may, on request, be lent to the returning officer at a local government election on such terms and conditions as the Secretary of State may determine.

(2)   Any ballot boxes, fittings and compartments provided by or belonging to—
   (a)   a local authority within the meaning of the Local Government Act 1972, or
   (b)   a local authority within the meaning of the Local Government (Scotland) Act 1973,
as the case may be, shall, on request, and if not required for immediate use by that authority, be lent to the returning officer at an election held under those Acts on such terms and conditions as may be agreed.

NOTES

Derivation
   RPA 1949 s 35

Prospective amendment
   In sub-s (1), replace "Secretary of State" with "Electoral Commission": Political Parties, Elections and Referendums Act 2000 s163

Defined terms
   Electoral Commission: see Political Parties, Elections and Referendums Act 2000 s 1
   local government election (E&W): ss 191(1), 203(1), (1A)
   local government election (S): s 204(1)
   returning officer: see ss 24-27
   parliamentary election: Interpretation Act 1978 Sch 1

Validity of local elections, and legal costs

48(1)   No local government election shall be declared invalid by reason of any act or omission of the returning officer or any other person in breach of his official duty in connection with the election or otherwise of rules under section 36 or section 42 above if it appears to the tribunal having cognizance of the question that—
   (a)   the election was so conducted as to be substantially in accordance with the law as to elections; and
   (b)   the act or omission did not affect its result.

(2)   A local government election, unless questioned by an election petition within the period fixed by law for those proceedings, shall be deemed to have been to all intents a good and valid election.

(3)   The council which is required to pay the expenses properly incurred by a returning officer in relation to any local government election may treat those expenses as including all costs properly incurred by the returning officer in connection with or in contemplation of any legal proceedings arising out of the election (including any criminal proceedings against the returning officer), whether or not the proceedings are in fact instituted.

(3A)   In the application of subsection (3) above in relation to an Authority election, the Greater London Authority shall be treated as the council which is required to pay the expenses properly incurred by the returning officer.

(4)   In Scotland the election of a member of a local authority shall not be affected by reason only of any nullity or irregularity in the election of any other member of the authority.

NOTES

Derivation
   RPA 1949 s 37
   RPA 1969 s 19

Defined terms
   Authority election: s 2013(1)

election: s 202(1)
election petition: s 202(1)
local authority (S): s 204(1)
local government election (E&W): ss 191(1), 203(1), (1A)

local government election (S): s 204(1)
returning officer: see ss 24-27

Supplemental provisions as to parliamentary and local government elections

Effect of registers

(1)-(3) *Repealed*

(4) Any entry in the register of parliamentary or local government electors, if it gives a date as that on which the person named will attain voting age, shall for any purpose of this Part relating to him as elector be conclusive that until the date given in the entry he is not of voting age nor entitled to be treated as an elector except for the purposes of an election at which the day fixed for the poll is that or a later date.

(4A) Subsection (4) applies to an entry in the record of anonymous entries as it applies to an entry in the register of parliamentary or local government electors.

(5) A person registered as a parliamentary or local government elector, or entered in the list of proxies, shall not be excluded from voting on any of the following grounds: but this shall not prevent the rejection of the vote on a scrutiny, or affect his liability to any penalty for voting.
The grounds are—
(a) that he is not of voting age;
(b) that he is not or was not at any particular time—
(i) a Commonwealth citizen;
(ii) a citizen of the Republic of Ireland;
(iii) in the case of a person registered as a parliamentary elector in pursuance of an overseas elector's declaration, a British citizen;
(iv) in the case of a person registered as a local government elector or entered in the list of proxies by virtue of being a relevant citizen of the Union, a relevant citizen of the Union;
(c) that he is or was at any particular time otherwise subject to any other legal incapacity to vote.

(6) *Repealed*

NOTES

Derivation
RPA 1949 s 39

Defined terms
elector: s 202(1)
legal incapacity: s 202(1)
the list of proxies: s 202(1)

overseas elector's declaration: s 202(1)
relevant citizen of the Union: s 202(1)
vote: s 202(1)
voting: see "vote" s 202(1)

Effect of misdescription

50 No misnomer or inaccurate description of any person or place named—
(a) in the register of parliamentary electors, or
(b) in the register of local government electors, or
(c) in any list, record, proxy paper, nomination paper, ballot paper, notice or other document required for the purposes of this Part of this Act, and the parliamentary elections rules,
affects the full operation of the document with respect to that person or place in any case where the description of the person or place is such as to be commonly understood.

NOTES
Derivation
   RPA s 39

Defined terms

elector: s 202(1)
parliamentary elections rules: s 202(1)

51   *Repealed*

Discharge of registration duties

52(1)   A registration officer shall comply with any general or special directions which may be given by the Secretary of State with respect to the arrangements to be made by the registration officer for carrying out his functions under this Act.

(1A)   Without prejudice to the generality of subsection (1) above, the directions which may be given under subsection (1) include directions requiring a registration officer to maintain his registers in a specified electronic form; and any such directions may in particular specify—

   (a)   the software which is to be used in connection with the maintenance of the registers in that form;

   (b)   the standards in accordance with which that software is to be maintained and updated;

   (c)   how information required (by or under any enactment) to be included in the registers is to be recorded and stored in that form.

(2)   Any of the duties and powers of a registration officer may be performed and exercised by any deputy for the time being approved by the council which appointed the registration officer, and the provisions of this Act apply to any such deputy so far as respects any duties or powers to be performed or exercised by him as they apply to the registration officer.

(3)   In England and Wales, any acts authorised or required to be done by or with respect to the registration officer may, in the event of his incapacity to act or of a vacancy, be done by or with respect to the proper officer of the council by whom the registration officer was appointed.

(4)   It shall be the duty—

   (a)   in England, of a district council or London borough council,

   (aa)   in Wales, of a county or county borough council, and

   (b)   in Scotland, of every local authority,

to assign such officers to assist the registration officer as may be required for carrying out his functions under this Act.

(5)   Subsection (2) above does not apply in Northern Ireland but sections 14(5) and 14A(2) and (3) of the Electoral Law Act (Northern Ireland) 1962 (appointment of temporary deputy and delegation to assistants) shall have effect in relation to the Chief Electoral Officer for Northern Ireland in his capacity as registration officer.

NOTES
Derivation
   RPA s 52

Defined terms
   enactment: Interpretation Act 1978 Sch 1
   enactment (NI): s 205
   England: Interpretation Act 1978 Sch 1
   his registers: s 9(8)

local authority (S): s 204(1)
London borough: s 203(2) and Interpretation Act 1978 Sch 1
proper officer: s 202(1)
registration officer: s 8(1)
Wales: Interpretation Act 1978 Sch 1

Power to make regulations as to registration etc

53(1)   Provision may be made by regulations—

   (a) with respect to the form of the register of electors and of any special lists or records required by this Act in connection with the register or with any election;

   (b) with respect to—

      (i) the procedure to be followed in the preparation of the register and the place and manner of its publication, and

      (ii) the procedure to be followed in the preparation of any such special lists or records, and the time, place and manner of their publication; and

   (c) generally with respect to any matters incidental to the provisions of this Act so far as those provisions relate to the registration of electors or to voting by post or proxy.

(2) *Repealed*

(3) Without prejudice to the generality of subsection (1) above, regulations made with respect to the matters mentioned in that subsection may contain any such provisions as are mentioned in Schedule 2 to this Act.

(4) Provision may also be made by regulations—

   (a) for the supply of any such record or special list as is mentioned in subsection (1) above to such persons as are prescribed;

   (b) with respect to any conditions subject to which the supply is made;

   (c) making it an offence (punishable on summary conviction by a fine not exceeding level 5 on the standard scale) for a person to fail to comply with any such condition.

(5) Before making regulations containing provision under paragraph 1A of Schedule 2, or paragraph 13(1ZB) of that Schedule so far as relating to that paragraph, the Secretary of State must consult—

   (a) the Electoral Commission,

   (b) the Information Commissioner, and

   (c) any other person the Secretary of State thinks appropriate.

(6) The Secretary of State may require the Electoral Commission to—

   (a) prepare a report on specified matters relating to the operation of any provision made under paragraph 1A of Schedule 2, and

   (b) give the Secretary of State a copy of the report by no later than a specified date.

(7) The Secretary of State must publish a copy of the report.

(8) A registration officer must comply with any request made by the Electoral Commission for information that it reasonably requires in connection with the preparation of a report under subsection (6).

NOTES

Derivation
  RPA 1949 s 42

Subordinate legislation
Representation of the People (Amendment) Regulations 1990, SI 1990/520
Representation of the People (England and Wales) Regulations 2001, SI 2001/341
Representation of the People (Scotland) Regulations 2001, SI 2001/497
Representation of the People (Northern Ireland) Regulations 2008, SI 2008/1741
Representation of the People (Postal Voting for Local Government Elections) (Scotland) Regulations 2007, SSI 2007/263
Representation of the People (Electoral Registration Data Schemes) Regulations 2011, SI 2011/1467
Electoral Registration (Disclosure of Electoral Registers) Regulations 2013, SI 2013/760

Representation of the People (Provision of Information Regarding Proxies) Regulations 2013, SI 2013/3199
Representation of the People (Supply of Information) Regulations 2014, SI 2014/2764
Parliamentary Elections (Forms) (Northern Ireland) Regulations 2015, SI 2015/221

Defined terms
  election: s 202(1)
  elector: s 202(1)
  Electoral Commission: see Political Parties, Elections and Referendums Act 2000 s 1
  register of electors: see s 9
  standard scale: Interpretation Act 1978 Sch 1
  summary conviction (NI only): Interpretation Act 1978 Sch 1
  voting: see "vote" s 202(1)

Payment of expenses of registration

54(1) Any expenses properly incurred by a registration officer in the performance of his functions under this Act or the Electoral Registration and Administration Act 2013 (in this Act referred to as "registration expenses") shall (except in Northern Ireland) be paid by the local authority by whom the registration officer was appointed.

(2) The registration expenses of the Chief Electoral Officer for Northern Ireland shall be paid out of moneys provided by Parliament.

(3) Any fees paid to the registration officer under this Act—
  (a) shall be accounted for by him and paid to the local authority by whom he was appointed;
  (b) in the case of the Chief Electoral Officer for Northern Ireland, shall be accounted for by him to the Secretary of State and paid into the Consolidated Fund.

(4) On the request of a registration officer for an advance on account of registration expenses—
  (a) the local authority by whom the registration officer was appointed may, if they think fit, make such an advance to him of such an amount and subject to such conditions as they may approve; or
  (b) in the case of the Chief Electoral Officer for Northern Ireland, the Secretary of State may, if he thinks fit, make such an advance to him of such an amount and subject to such conditions as the Secretary of State may approve.

(5) Any registration expenses or contributions to them paid by the Common Council shall be paid out of the general rate and any sums paid to the Common Council under this section shall be placed to the credit of that rate.

NOTES

Derivation
  RPA 1949 s 43

local authority (E&W): s 203(1)
local authority (S): s 204(1)
registration officer: s 8(1)

Defined terms
  the Common Council: s 202(1)

55 *Repealed*

Registration appeals: England and Wales

56(1) An appeal lies to the county court—
  (a) from any decision of a registration officer not to register a person following an application under section 10ZC,
  (aza) from any decision of a registration officer to register a person following an application under section 10ZC in a case where an objection has been made under that section,
  (azb) from any decision of a registration officer not to alter a register following an application under section 10ZD,
  (azc) from any decision of a registration officer to alter a register following an application under section 10ZD in a case where an objection has been made under that section,
  (azd) from any decision of a registration officer under section 10ZE, or any other provision of this Act, as a result of which a person's entitlement to remain registered terminates,
  (aa) from any decision of a registration officer not to make a determination under section 10ZE(1) following an objection under section 10ZE(5)(a),
  (ab) from a determination of the registration officer under section 9B(2) above,

(b) from any decision under this Act of the registration officer disallowing a person's application to vote by proxy or by post as elector or to vote by post as proxy, in any case where the application is not made for a particular election only,

(c)-(d) *Repealed*

but an appeal does not lie where the person desiring to appeal has not availed himself of a prescribed right to be heard by or make representations to the registration officer on the matter which is the subject of the appeal, or has not given the prescribed notice of appeal within the prescribed time.

(2) No appeal lies from the decision of the Court of Appeal on appeal from a decision of the county court under this section.

(3) An appeal to the county court or Court of Appeal by virtue of this section which is pending when notice of an election is given shall not prejudice the operation as respects the election of the decision appealed against, and anything done in pursuance of the decision shall be as good as if no such appeal had been brought and shall not be affected by the decision of the appeal.

(4) Notice shall be sent to the registration officer in manner provided by rules of court of the decision of the county court or of the Court of Appeal on any appeal by virtue of this section, and the registration officer shall, in accordance with sections 13A, 13AB *and 13B* , 13B and 13BC above, make such alterations in the register as may be required to give effect to the decision.

(4A) Where, as a result of the decision on an appeal, an alteration in the register made in pursuance of subsection (4) above takes effect under section 13(5), 13A(2), 13AB(3) or 13B(3) above on or before the last day on which nomination papers nominating candidates at an election may be delivered to the returning officer 13B(3) or *(3B)* or 13BC(3) or (6) above on or before the date of the poll, subsection (3) above does not apply to that appeal as respects that election.

(5) The registration officer shall undertake such duties in connection with appeals brought by virtue of this section as may be prescribed and shall on any such appeal be deemed to be a party to the proceedings, and the registration expenses payable to a registration officer shall include any expenses properly incurred by him by virtue of this subsection.

(6) *Repealed*

NOTES

Derivation
  RPA s 45

Prospective amendments
  Underlined words in (4A) are not yet in force: Recall of MPs Act 2015 s 10(6)

Defined terms
  county court: Interpretation Act 1978 Sch 1
  court of appeal: Interpretation Act 1978 Sch 1
  election: s 202(1)

elector: s 202(1)
England: Interpretation Act 1978 Sch 1
prescribed: s 202(1)
registration expenses: s 54(1)
registration officer: s 8(1)
returning officer: see ss 24-27
rules of court: Interpretation Act 1978 Sch 1
vote: s 202(1)
Wales: Interpretation Act 1978 Sch 1

Registration appeals: Scotland

57(1) Section 56 above applies to Scotland subject to the following modifications—

(a) subsection (2) shall be omitted;

(b) an appeal lies on any point of law from any decision of the sheriff under this section to the court of three judges constituted under subsection (2) below; and

(c) for any reference to the Court of Appeal there shall be substituted a reference to that court of three judges.

(2) The court for hearing appeals under paragraph (b) of subsection (1) above shall consist of three judges of the Court of Session who shall be appointed by the Court of Session by act of sederunt and of whom one judge shall be appointed from each division of the Inner House and one from the Lords Ordinary in the Outer House; and the Principal Clerk of Session shall be clerk of the court.

(3) The Court of Session may by act of sederunt fill any vacancy in the court of three judges, and regulate its sittings and forms of process so as to carry out the provisions of this Act; and acts of sederunt under this section may be made, and the court of three judges may sit, either during the sitting of the Court of Session or in vacation or recess.

NOTES

Derivation
  RPA 1949 s 45

Defined terms
  court of appeal: Interpretation Act 1978 Sch 1
  sheriff: Interpretation Act 1978

Subordinate legislation
  Act of Sederunt (Registration Appeal Court) 2013 SSI 2013/236

Registration appeals: Northern Ireland

58(1) An appeal lies to the county court—
    (a) from any decision under this Act of the Chief Electoral Officer for Northern Ireland on any application for registration or objection to a person's registration made to and considered by him;
    (b) from any decision under this Act of the Chief Electoral Officer (other than on an application for registration or objection to a person's registration) that a person registered in respect of any address was not entitled to be registered in respect of that address or that he has ceased to be resident at that address or has otherwise ceased to satisfy the conditions for registration set out in section 4;
    (ba) from a determination of the Chief Electoral Officer under section 9B(2) or section 9C(1B);
    (c) from any decision under this Act of the Chief Electoral Officer disallowing a person's application to vote by proxy or by post as elector or to vote by post as proxy, in any case where the application is not made for a particular election only.

(2) But an appeal does not lie where the person desiring to appeal—
    (a) has not availed himself of a prescribed right to be heard by or make representations to the Chief Electoral Officer on the matter which is the subject of the appeal, or
    (b) has not given the prescribed notice of appeal within the prescribed time.

(3) An appeal to the county court or Court of Appeal by virtue of this section which is pending when notice of an election is given does not prejudice the operation as respects the election of the decision appealed against, and anything done in pursuance of the decision—
    (a) is as good as if no such appeal had been brought, and
    (b) is not affected by the decision of the appeal.

(4) The Chief Electoral Officer must, in accordance with sections 13A, 13BA and 13BC, make such alterations in the register as may be required to give effect to the decision.

(5) Where, as a result of the decision on an appeal, an alteration in the register made in pursuance of subsection (4) takes effect under section 13(5), 13A(2), 13BA(6) or (9) or 13BC(3) or (6) on or before the date of the poll, subsection (3) does not apply to that appeal as respects that election.

(6) The Chief Electoral Officer—

    (a)   must undertake such duties in connection with appeals brought by virtue of this section as may be prescribed, and

    (b)   on any appeal is deemed to be a party to the proceedings;

and the registration expenses payable to him include any expenses properly incurred by virtue of this subsection.

(7)   Section 21(1) of the Interpretation Act (Northern Ireland) 1954 (rules regulating procedure of courts etc) applies as if the jurisdiction conferred by subsection (1) were conferred by any enactment within the meaning of that Act.

NOTES

Derivation
  RPA 1949 s 45

Prospective amendments
  Underlined words in (4) and (5) not yet in effect:
  Recall of MPs Act 2015 s 10(6)

county court: Interpretation Act 1978 Sch 1
court of appeal: Interpretation Act 1978 Sch 1
enactment: Interpretation Act 1978 Sch 1
enactment (NI): s 205
vote: s 202(1)

Defined terms

Supplemental provisions as to members of forces and service voters

59(1)   In this Part of this Act, the expression "member of the forces"—

    (a)   means a person serving on full pay as a member of any of the naval, military or air forces of the Crown raised in the United Kingdom; but

    (b)   does not include—

        (i)   a person serving only as a member of a reserve or auxiliary force except in so far as regulations provide that it shall include persons so serving during a period of emergency or

        (ii)   a member of the regular army whose terms of service are such that, except for the purpose of training, he is required to serve only in Northern Ireland.

(2)   Where a person—

    (a)   is not a member of the forces as defined by subsection (1) above, but

    (b)   is, in the performance of his duty as a member of any of Her Majesty's reserve or auxiliary forces, absent on the relevant date for the purposes of section 4 above from an address at which he has been residing,

any question arising under section 5(3) above whether his residence at that address has been interrupted on that date by his absence in the performance of that duty shall be determined as if the performance of it did not prevent his resuming actual residence at any time after that date.

(3)   Arrangements must be made by the appropriate government department for securing that every person having a service qualification by virtue of paragraph (a) or (b) of section 14(1) above has (so far as circumstances permit) an effective opportunity of exercising from time to time as occasion may require the rights conferred on him by this Act in relation to—

    (a)   registration in a register of electors (and in particular in relation to the making and cancellation of service declarations);

    (b)   the making and cancellation of appointments of a proxy;

    (c)   voting in person, by post or by proxy.

(3A)   Arrangements must be made by the appropriate government department for securing that every such person receives such instructions as to the effect of this Act and any regulations made under it, and such other assistance, as may be reasonably sufficient in connection with the exercise by that person and any spouse or civil partner of that person of any rights conferred on them as mentioned above.

(3B)   In subsections (3) and (3A) "the appropriate government department" means, in relation to members of the forces, the Ministry of Defence, and in relation to any other person means the government department under which he is employed in the employment giving the service qualification.

(3C)   The Ministry of Defence must maintain, in relation to each member of the forces who provides information relating to his registration as an elector, a record of such information.

(3D)   The Ministry of Defence must make arrangements to enable each member of the forces to update annually the information recorded under subsection (3C).

(4)   In relation to persons having a service qualification by virtue of paragraph (c) of section 14(1), the British Council shall be under a corresponding obligation to that imposed by subsections (3) and (3A) above on the appropriate government department.

NOTES

Derivation
RPA 1949 s 46

Defined terms
civil partner: Interpretation Act 1978 Sch 1
register of electors: see s 9

spouse: Marriage (Same Sex Couples) Act 2013 Sch 3 para 1
voting: see "vote" s 202(1)

Offences

Personation

60(1)   A person shall be guilty of a corrupt practice if he commits, or aids, abets, counsels or procures the commission of, the offence of personation.

(2)   A person shall be deemed to be guilty of personation at a parliamentary or local government election if he—

(a)   votes in person or by post as some other person, whether as an elector or as proxy, and whether that other person is living or dead or is a fictitious person; or

(b)   votes in person or by post as proxy—

(i)   for a person whom he knows or has reasonable grounds for supposing to be dead or to be a fictitious person; or

(ii)   when he knows or has reasonable grounds for supposing that his appointment as proxy is no longer in force.

(3)   For the purposes of this section, a person who has applied for a ballot paper for the purpose of voting in person or who has marked, whether validly or not, and returned a ballot paper issued for the purpose of voting by post, shall be deemed to have voted.

NOTES

Derivation
RPA 1949 s 47

Defined terms
elector: s 202(1)
local government election (E&W): ss 191(1), 203(1), (1A)

local government election (S): s 204(1)
person: s 202(1)
vote: s 202(1)
voting: see "vote" s 202(1)

Other voting offences

61(1)   A person shall be guilty of an offence if—

(a)   he votes in person or by post, whether as an elector or as proxy, or applies to vote by proxy or by post as elector, at a parliamentary or local government election, or at parliamentary or local government elections, knowing that he is subject to a legal incapacity to vote at the election or, as the case may be, at elections of that kind; or

    (b) he applies for the appointment of a proxy to vote for him at any parliamentary or local government election or at parliamentary or local government elections knowing that he is or the person to be appointed is subject to a legal incapacity to vote at the election or, as the case may be, at elections of that kind; or

    (c) he votes, whether in person or by post, as proxy for some other person at a parliamentary or local government election, knowing that that person is subject to a legal incapacity to vote.

For the purposes of this subsection references to a person being subject to a legal incapacity to vote do not, in relation to things done before polling day at the election or first election at or for which they are done, include his being below voting age if he will be of voting age on that day.

(2)   A person shall be guilty of an offence if—

    (a) he votes as elector otherwise than by proxy either—

        (i) more than once in the same constituency at any parliamentary election, or more than once in the same electoral area at any local government election; or

        (ii) in more than one constituency at a general election, or in more than one electoral area at an ordinary election of councillors for a local government area which is not a single electoral area; or

        (ii) in any constituency at a general election, or in any electoral area at such an ordinary election as mentioned above, when there is in force an appointment of a person to vote as his proxy at the election in some other constituency or electoral area; or

    (b) he votes as elector in person at a parliamentary or local government election at which he is entitled to vote by post; or

    (c) he votes as elector in person at a parliamentary or local government election, knowing that a person appointed to vote as his proxy at the election either has already voted in person at the election or is entitled to vote by post at the election; or

    (d) he applies for a person to be appointed as his proxy to vote for him at parliamentary elections in any constituency without applying for the cancellation of a previous appointment of a third person then in force in respect of that or another constituency or without withdrawing a pending application for such an appointment in respect of that or another constituency.

(2A)   In the case of Authority elections, paragraph (a) of subsection (2) above shall not have effect; but a person shall be guilty of an offence under this subsection if he votes as an elector otherwise than by proxy—

    (a) more than once at the same election of the Mayor of London;

    (b) more than once at the same election of the London members of the London Assembly at an ordinary election;

    (c) more than once in the same Assembly constituency at the same election of a constituency member of the London Assembly;

    (d) in more than one Assembly constituency at the same ordinary election; or

    (e) in any Assembly constituency at an ordinary election, or an election of the Mayor of London held under section 16 of the 1999 Act, when there is in force an appointment of a person to vote as his proxy at the election in some other Assembly constituency.

(3)   A person shall be guilty of an offence if—

    (a) he votes as proxy for the same elector either—

        (i) more than once in the same constituency at any parliamentary election, or more than once in the same electoral area at any local government election; or

      (ii) in more than one constituency at a general election, or in more than one electoral area at an ordinary election of councillors for a local government area which is not a single electoral area; or

    (b) he votes in person as proxy for an elector at a parliamentary or local government election at which he is entitled to vote by post as proxy for that elector; or

    (c) *Repealed*

    (d) he votes in person as proxy for an elector at a parliamentary or local government election knowing that the elector has already voted in person at the election.

(3A) In the case of Authority elections, paragraph (a) of subsection (3) above shall not have effect; but a person shall be guilty of an offence under this subsection if he votes as proxy for the same elector—

    (a) more than once at the same election of the Mayor of London;

    (b) more than once at the same election of the London members of the London Assembly at an ordinary election;

    (c) more than once in the same Assembly constituency at the same election of a constituency member of the London Assembly; or

    (d) in more than one Assembly constituency at the same ordinary election.

(4) A person shall also be guilty of an offence if he votes at a parliamentary election in any constituency or at a local government election in any electoral area as proxy for more than two persons of whom he is not the spouse, civil partner, parent, grandparent, brother, sister, child or grandchild.

(5) A person shall also be guilty of an offence if he knowingly induces or procures some other person to do an act which is, or but for that other person's want of knowledge would be, an offence by that other person under the foregoing subsections of this section.

(6) For the purposes of this section a person who has applied for a ballot paper for the purpose of voting in person, or who has marked, whether validly or not, and returned a ballot paper issued for the purpose of voting by post, shall be deemed to have voted, but for the purpose of determining whether an application for a ballot paper constitutes an offence under subsection (4) above, a previous application made in circumstances which entitle the applicant only to mark a tendered ballot paper shall, if he does not exercise that right, be disregarded.

(6A) A person is not guilty of an offence under subsection (2)(b) or (3)(b) above only by reason of his having marked a tendered ballot paper in pursuance of rule 40(1ZC) or (1ZE) of the parliamentary elections rules.

(6B) A person is not guilty of an offence under subsection (2)(b) or (3)(b) above by reason only of having marked or tendered a ballot paper at a local government election in Scotland in pursuance of any provision—

    (a) made under section 3(1) of the Local Governance (Scotland) Act 2004 (asp 9) as to the conduct of elections of councillors; and

    (b) which entitles him to do so despite the fact that he is or may be entitled to vote by post at the election.

(7) An offence under this section shall be an illegal practice, but—

    (a) the court before whom a person is convicted of any such offence may, if they think it just in the special circumstances of the case, mitigate or entirely remit any incapacity imposed by virtue of section 173 below; and

    (b) a candidate shall not be liable, nor shall his election be avoided, for an illegal practice under this section of any agent of his other than an offence under subsection (5) above.

NOTES

Derivation
  RPA 1949 s 48

Modified operation
  Modified, as to Northern Ireland, by the Elections (Northern Ireland) Act 1985 ss 2(5), 7(4)

Defined terms
  the 1999 Act: s 203(1)
  Assembly constituency: s 203(1)
  Authority election: s 203(1)
  child: cf Family Law Reform Act 1987 s 1
  civil partner: Interpretation Act 1978 Sch 1
  constituency: Parliamentary Constituencies Act 1986 s 1(2)
  election: s 202(1)
  election of a constituency member of the London Assembly: s 203(1)

election of the Mayor of London: s 203(1)
elector: s 202(1)
electoral area (E&W): ss 191(1), 203(1)
electoral area (S): s 204(1)
legal incapacity: s 202(1)
local government area (E&W): ss 191(1), 203(1)
local government area (S): s 204(1)
local government election (E&W): ss 191(1), 203(1), (1A)
local government election (S): s 204(1)
London member: s 203(1)
parliamentary election: Interpretation Act 1978 Sch 1
person: s 202(1)
spouse: Marriage (Same Sex Couples) Act 2013 Sch 3 para 1
vote: s 202(1)
voting: see "vote" s 202(1)

Offences as to declarations

62(1)   A person who—

    (a)   makes a declaration of local connection or a service declaration—

        (i)   when he is not authorised to do so by section 7B(1) or section 15(1) above, or

        (ii)   except as permitted by this Act, when he knows that he is subject to a legal incapacity to vote, or

        (iii)   when he knows that it contains a statement which is false, or

    (b)   attests a service declaration when he knows—

        (i)   that he is not authorised to do so, or

        (ii)   that it contains a false statement as to any particulars required by regulations under section 16 above,

    shall be guilty of an offence and liable on summary conviction to a fine not exceeding level 5 on the standard scale.

(1A)   A person who makes a declaration under section 9B(1A)(a) above—

    (a)   except as permitted by this Act, when he knows that he is subject to a legal incapacity to vote, or

    (b)   when he knows that it contains a statement which is false,

    shall be guilty of an offence and liable on summary conviction to a fine not exceeding level 5 on the standard scale.

(2)   Where the declaration is available only for local government elections the references in subsections (1) and (1A) above to a legal incapacity to vote refer to a legal incapacity to vote at local government elections.

NOTES

Derivation
  RPA 1949 s 49

Defined terms
  legal incapacity: s 202(1)
  local government election (E&W): ss 191(1), 203(1), (1A)
  local government election (S): s 204(1)

standard scale: Interpretation Act 1978 Sch 1
summary conviction (NI only): Interpretation Act 1978 Sch 1
vote: s 202(1)

Offences relating to applications for postal and proxy votes

62A(1)   A person commits an offence if he—

    (a)   engages in an act specified in subsection (2) at a parliamentary or local government election, and

(b) intends, by doing so, to deprive another of an opportunity to vote or to make for himself or another a gain of a vote to which he or the other is not otherwise entitled or a gain of money or property.

(2) These are the acts—

    (a) applying for a postal or proxy vote as some other person (whether that other person is living or dead or is a fictitious person);

    (b) otherwise making a false statement in, or in connection with, an application for a postal or proxy vote;

    (c) inducing the registration officer or returning officer to send a postal ballot paper or any communication relating to a postal or proxy vote to an address which has not been agreed to by the person entitled to the vote;

    (d) causing a communication relating to a postal or proxy vote or containing a postal ballot paper not to be delivered to the intended recipient.

(3) In subsection (1)(b), property includes any description of property.

(4) In subsection (2) a reference to a postal vote or a postal ballot paper includes a reference to a proxy postal vote or a proxy postal ballot paper (as the case may be).

(5) A person who commits an offence under subsection (1) or who aids, abets, counsels or procures the commission of such an offence is guilty of a corrupt practice.

(6) This section does not apply to anything done at a local government election in Scotland.

NOTES

Derivation
  Electoral Administration Act 2006 s 40

registration officer: s 8(1)
returning officer: see ss 24-27
vote: s 202(1)

Defined terms
  local government election (E&W): ss 191(1), 203(1), (1A)
  local government election (S): s 204(1)

Scottish local government elections: offences relating to applications for postal and proxy votes

62B(1) This section applies in relation to a local government election in Scotland.

(2) A person commits an offence if he—

    (a) engages in any of the acts specified in subsection (3) below at the election; and

    (b) intends, by doing so, to deprive another of an opportunity to vote or to make for himself or another a gain of a vote to which he or the other is not otherwise entitled or a gain of money or property.

(3) The acts referred to in subsection (2)(a) above are—

    (a) applying for a postal or proxy vote as some other person (whether that other person is living or dead or is a fictitious person);

    (b) otherwise making a false statement in, or in connection with, an application for a postal or proxy vote;

    (c) inducing the registration officer or returning officer to send a postal ballot paper or any communication relating to a postal or proxy vote to an address which has not been agreed to by the person entitled to the vote;

    (d) causing a communication relating to a postal or proxy vote or containing a postal ballot paper not to be delivered to the intended recipient.

(4) In subsection (2)(b) above, property includes any description of property.

(5) In subsection (3) above a reference to a postal vote or a postal ballot paper includes a reference to a proxy postal vote or a proxy postal ballot paper (as the case may be).

(6) A person who commits an offence under subsection (2) above or who aids, abets, counsels or procures the commission of such an offence is guilty of a corrupt practice.

(7) This subsection and subsection (6) extend to the whole of the United Kingdom, but otherwise this section extends only to Scotland.

NOTES

Derivation
Local Electoral Administration and Registration Services (Scotland) Act 2006

Defined terms
election: s 202(1)
local government election: s 204(1)

person: s 202(1)
registration officer: s 8(1)
returning officer: see ss 24-27
United Kingdom: Interpretation Act 1978 Sch 1
vote: s 202(1)

Breach of official duty

63(1) If a person to whom this section applies is, without reasonable cause, guilty of any act or omission in breach of his official duty, he shall be liable on summary conviction to a fine not exceeding level 5 on the standard scale.

(2) No person to whom this section applies shall be liable for breach of his official duty to any penalty at common law and no action for damages shall lie in respect of the breach by such a person of his official duty.

(3) The persons to whom this section applies are—
   (a) the Clerk of the Crown (or, in Northern Ireland, the Clerk of the Crown for Northern Ireland),
   (b) any registration officer, returning officer or presiding officer,
   (ba) a CORE keeper (within the meaning of Part 1 of the Electoral Administration Act 2006),
   (c) any other person whose duty it is to be responsible after a parliamentary or local government election for the used ballot papers and other documents (including returns and declarations as to expenses),
   (d) any official designated by a universal postal service provider, and
   (e) any deputy of a person mentioned in any of paragraphs (a) to (d) above or any person appointed to assist or in the course of his employment assisting a person so mentioned in connection with his official duties;
   and "official duty" shall for the purposes of this section be construed accordingly, but shall not include duties imposed otherwise than by the law relating to parliamentary or local government elections or the registration of parliamentary or local government electors.

(4) Where—
   (a) a returning officer for an election to which section 46 of the Electoral Administration Act 2006 applies is guilty of an act or omission in breach of his official duty, but
   (b) he remedies that act or omission in full by taking steps under subsection (1) of that section,
   he shall not be guilty of an offence under subsection (1) above.

(5) Subsection (4) does not affect any conviction which takes place, or any penalty which is imposed, before the date on which the act or omission is remedied in full.

NOTES

Derivation
RPA 1949 s 50

Defined terms
Clerk of the Crown: s 202(1)
election: s 202(1)

elector: s 202(1)
local government election (E&W): ss 191(1), 203(1), (1A)
local government election (S): s 204(1)
registration officer: s 8(1)
returning officer: see ss 24-27
standard scale: Interpretation Act 1978 Sch 1

summary conviction (NI only): Interpretation Act 1978
Sch 1

Tampering with nomination papers, ballot papers etc

65(1)   A person shall be guilty of an offence, if, at a parliamentary or local government election, he—

(a)   fraudulently defaces or fraudulently destroys any nomination paper; or

(b)   fraudulently defaces or fraudulently destroys any ballot paper, or the official mark on any ballot paper, or any postal voting statement or declaration of identity or official envelope used in connection with voting by post; or

(c)   without due authority supplies any ballot paper to any person; or

(d)   fraudulently puts into any ballot box any paper other than the ballot paper which he is authorised by law to put in; or

(e)   fraudulently takes out of the polling station any ballot paper; or

(f)   without due authority destroys, takes, opens or otherwise interferes with any ballot box or packet of ballot papers then in use for the purposes of the election; or

(g)   fraudulently or without due authority, as the case may be, attempts to do any of the foregoing acts.

(2)   In Scotland, a person shall be guilty of an offence if—

(a)   at a parliamentary or local government election, he forges any nomination paper, delivers to the returning officer any nomination paper knowing it to be forged, or forges or counterfeits any ballot paper or the official mark on any ballot paper; or

(b)   at a local government election, he signs any nomination paper as candidate or in any other capacity certifies the truth of any statement contained in it, knowing such statement to be false; or

(c)   he fraudulently or without due authority, as the case may be, attempts to do any of the foregoing acts.

(3)   If a returning officer, a presiding officer or a clerk appointed to assist in taking the poll, counting the votes or assisting at the proceedings in connection with the issue or receipt of postal ballot papers is guilty of an offence under this section, he shall be liable—

(a)   on conviction on indictment to a fine, or to imprisonment for a term not exceeding 2 years, or to both;

(b)   on summary conviction, to a fine not exceeding the statutory maximum, or to imprisonment for a term not exceeding 6 months, or to both.

(4)   If any other person is guilty of an offence under this section, he shall be liable on summary conviction to a fine not exceeding level 5 on the standard scale, or to imprisonment for a term not exceeding 6 months, or to both.

NOTES

Derivation
RPA 1949 s 52

Defined terms
election: s 202(1)
local government election (E&W): ss 191(1), 203(1), (1A)
local government election (S): s 204(1)
returning officer: see ss 24-27

standard scale: Interpretation Act 1978 Sch 1
statutory maximum: Interpretation Act 1978 Sch 1
summary conviction (NI only): Interpretation Act 1978 Sch 1
vote: s 202(1)
voting: see "vote" s 202(1)

False statements in nomination papers etc

65A(1)   A person is guilty of a corrupt practice if, in the case of any relevant election, he causes or permits to be included in a document delivered or otherwise furnished to a returning officer for use in connection with the election—

   (a)   a statement of the name or home address of a candidate at the election which he knows to be false in any particular; or

   (aa)   (where the election is a parliamentary election) a statement under rule 6(5)(b) of Schedule 1 to this Act which he knows to be false in any particular; or

   (b)   anything which purports to be the signature of an elector who proposes, seconds or assents to, the nomination of such a candidate but which he knows—

      (i)   was not written by the elector by whom it purports to have been written, or

      (ii)   if written by that elector, was not written by him for the purpose of signifying that he was proposing, seconding, or (as the case may be) assenting to, that candidate's nomination; or

   (c)   a certificate authorising for the purposes of rule 6A of the parliamentary elections rules the use by a candidate of a description if he knows that the candidate is standing at an election in another constituency in which the poll is to be held on the same day as the poll at the election to which the certificate relates.

(1A)   A person is guilty of a corrupt practice if, in the case of any relevant election, he makes in any document in which he gives his consent to his nomination as a candidate—

   (a)   a statement of his date of birth,

   (b)   a statement as to his qualification for being elected at that election, or

   (c)   a statement that he is not a candidate at an election for any other constituency the poll for which is to be held on the same day as the poll at the election to which the consent relates,

   which he knows to be false in any particular.

(1B)   For the purposes of subsection (1A), a statement as to a candidate's qualification is a statement—

   (a)   that he is qualified for being elected,

   (b)   that he will be qualified for being elected, or

   (c)   that to the best of his knowledge and belief he is not disqualified for being elected.

(2)   In this section "relevant election" means—

   (a)   any parliamentary election, or

   (b)   except for the purposes of subsections (1)(c) and (1A)(c), any local government election in England or Wales.

NOTES

Derivation
   RPA 2000 s 15

Defined terms
   constituency: Parliamentary Constituencies Act 1986 s 1(2)
   elector: s 202(1)
   England: Interpretation Act 1978 Sch 1

local government election (E&W): ss 191(1), 203(1), (1A)
parliamentary election: Interpretation Act 1978 Sch 1
returning officer: see ss 24-27
Wales: Interpretation Act 1978 Sch 1
written: Interpretation Act 1978 Sch 1

Scottish local government elections: false information in nomination papers etc

65B(1)   This section applies in relation to a local government election in Scotland.

(2)   A person is guilty of a corrupt practice if he causes or permits to be included in a document delivered or otherwise furnished to a returning officer for use in connection with the election—

(a) a statement of the name or home address of a candidate at the election which he knows to be false in any particular; or

(b) anything which purports to be the signature of an elector who proposes, seconds or assents to the nomination of such a candidate but which he knows—

    (i) was not written by the elector by whom it purports to have been written; or

    (ii) if written by that elector, was not written by him for the purpose of signifying that he was proposing, seconding or, as the case may be, assenting to that candidate's nomination.

(3) A person is guilty of a corrupt practice if he makes in any document in which he gives his consent to his nomination as a candidate at the election—

(a) a statement of his date of birth; or

(b) a statement as to his qualification for being elected at the election,

which he knows to be false in any particular.

(4) For the purposes of subsection (3) above, a statement as to a candidate's qualification is a statement—

(a) that he is qualified for being elected;

(b) that he will be qualified for being elected; or

(c) that to the best of his knowledge and belief he is not disqualified for being elected.

NOTES

Derivation
Local Electoral Administration and Registration Services (Scotland) Act 2006 s 13

Defined terms
elector: s 202(1)

local government election (S): s 204(1)
person: s 202(1)
returning officer: see ss 24-27
written: Interpretation Act 1978 Sch 1

Requirement of secrecy

66(1) The following persons—

(a) every returning officer and every presiding officer or clerk attending at a polling station,

(b) every candidate or election agent or polling agent so attending,

(c) every person so attending by virtue of any of sections 6A to 6D of the Political Parties, Elections and Referendums Act 2000,

(d) *Repealed*

shall maintain and aid in maintaining the secrecy of voting and shall not, except for some purpose authorised by law, communicate to any person before the poll is closed any information as to—

    (i) the name of any elector or proxy for an elector who has or has not applied for a ballot paper or voted at a polling station;

    (ii) the number on the register of electors of any elector who, or whose proxy, has or has not applied for a ballot paper or voted at a polling station; or

    (iii) the official mark.

(2) Every person attending at the counting of the votes shall maintain and aid in maintaining the secrecy of voting and shall not—

(a) ascertain or attempt to ascertain at the counting of the votes the number or other unique identifying mark on the back of any ballot paper;

(b) communicate any information obtained at the counting of the votes as to the candidate for whom any vote is given on any particular ballot paper.

(3) No person shall—

(a) interfere with or attempt to interfere with a voter when recording his vote;

      (b) otherwise obtain or attempt to obtain in a polling station information as to the candidate for whom a voter in that station is about to vote or has voted;

      (c) communicate at any time to any person any information obtained in a polling station as to the candidate for whom a voter in that station is about to vote or has voted, or as to the number or other unique identifying mark on the back of the ballot paper given to a voter at that station;

      (d) directly or indirectly induce a voter to display his ballot paper after he has marked it so as to make known to any person the name of the candidate for whom he has or has not voted.

(4) Every person attending the proceedings in connection with the issue or the receipt of ballot papers for persons voting by post shall maintain and aid in maintaining the secrecy of the voting and shall not—

      (a) except for some purpose authorised by law, communicate, before the poll is closed, to any person any information obtained at those proceedings as to the official mark; or

      (b) except for some purpose authorised by law, communicate to any person at any time any information obtained at those proceedings as to the number or other unique identifying mark on the back of the ballot paper sent to any person; or

      (c) except for some purpose authorised by law, attempt to ascertain at the proceedings in connection with the receipt of ballot papers the number or other unique identifying mark on the back of any ballot paper; or

      (d) attempt to ascertain at the proceedings in connection with the receipt of the ballot papers the candidate for whom any vote is given in any particular ballot paper or communicate any information with respect thereto obtained at those proceedings.

(5) No person having undertaken to assist a blind voter to vote shall communicate at any time to any person any information as to the candidate for whom that voter intends to vote or has voted, or as to the number or other unique identifying mark on the back of the ballot paper given for the use of that voter.

(6) If a person acts in contravention of this section he shall be liable on summary conviction to a fine not exceeding level 5 on the standard scale or to imprisonment for a term not exceeding 6 months.

(7) In their application in relation to an election of the London members of the London Assembly at an ordinary election, the preceding provisions of this section shall have effect with the insertion, after the words "the candidate for whom", in each place where they occur, of ", or the registered political party towards the return of whose candidates,".

(8) In relation to an election of the London members of the London Assembly at an ordinary election, any reference in this section to the return of a registered political party's candidates is a reference to the return of candidates included in the list of candidates submitted by the registered political party for the purposes of the election.

NOTES

Derivation
RPA 1949 s 53

Defined terms
election: s 202(1)
election agent: see s 67
elector: s 202(1)
London member: s 203(1)
person: s 202(1)
registered political party: s 202(1)
registered political party submitting a list of

candidates to be London members: s 203(1B)
register of electors: see s 9
returning officer: see ss 24-27
standard scale: Interpretation Act 1978 Sch 1
summary conviction (NI only): Interpretation Act 1978 Sch 1
vote: s 202(1)
voter: s 202(1)
voting: see "vote" s 202(1)

Prohibition on publication of exit polls

66A(1)   No person shall, in the case of an election to which this section applies, publish before the poll is closed—

   (a)   any statement relating to the way in which voters have voted at the election where that statement is (or might reasonably be taken to be) based on information given by voters after they have voted, or

   (b)   any forecast as to the result of the election which is (or might reasonably be taken to be) based on information so given.

   (2)   This section applies to—

   (a)   any parliamentary election; and

   (b)   any local government election in England or Wales.

   (3)   If a person acts in contravention of subsection (1) above, he shall be liable on summary conviction to a fine not exceeding level 5 on the standard scale or to imprisonment for a term not exceeding six months.

   (4)   In this section—

   "forecast" includes estimate;

   "publish" means make available to the public at large, or any section of the public, in whatever form and by whatever means;

   and any reference to the result of an election is a reference to the result of the election either as a whole or so far as any particular candidate or candidates at the election is or are concerned.

NOTES

Derivation
RPA 2000 s 15(1)

Defined terms
England: Interpretation Act 1978 Sch 1
local government election (E&W): ss 191(1), 203(1), (1A)
parliamentary election: Interpretation Act 1978 Sch 1
standard scale: Interpretation Act 1978 Sch 1

summary conviction (NI only): Interpretation Act 1978 Sch 1
vote: s 202(1)
voter: s 202(1)
Wales: Interpretation Act 1978 Sch 1

Failure to comply with conditions relating to supply etc of certain documents

66B(1)   A person is guilty of an offence—

   (a)   if he fails to comply with any conditions imposed in pursuance of regulations under rule 57 of the parliamentary elections rules, or

   (b)   if he is an appropriate supervisor of a person (P) who fails to comply with such a condition and he failed to take appropriate steps.

   (2)   P is not guilty of an offence under subsection (1) if—

   (a)   he has an appropriate supervisor, and

   (b)   he has complied with all the requirements imposed on him by his appropriate supervisor.

   (3)   A person who is not P or an appropriate supervisor is not guilty of an offence under subsection (1) if he takes all reasonable steps to ensure that he complies with the conditions.

   (4)   In subsections (1)(b) and (2)—

   (a)   an appropriate supervisor is a person who is a director of a company or concerned in the management of an organisation in which P is employed or under whose direction or control P is;

   (b)   appropriate steps are such steps as it was reasonable for the appropriate supervisor to take to secure the operation of procedures designed to prevent, so far as reasonably practicable, the occurrence of a failure to comply with the conditions.

(5)   A person guilty of an offence as mentioned in subsection (1) is liable on summary conviction to a fine not exceeding level 5 on the standard scale.

NOTES

Derivation
  Electoral Administration Act 2006

standard scale: Interpretation Act 1978 Sch 1
summary conviction (NI only): Interpretation Act 1978 Sch 1

Defined terms
  parliamentary election rules: s 202(1)

PART II

THE ELECTION CAMPAIGN

The election agent

Appointment of election agent

67(1)   Not later than the latest time for the delivery of notices of withdrawals for an election, a person shall be named by or on behalf of each candidate as the candidate's election agent, and the name and address of the candidate's election agent shall be declared in writing by the candidate or some other person on his behalf to the appropriate officer not later than that time.

(1A)   Where a registered political party submits a list of candidates to be London members of the London Assembly at an ordinary election, the requirements of subsection (1) above in relation to those candidates are that not later than the time there mentioned—

(a)   a person shall be named by or on behalf of the party as the election agent of all of those candidates; and

(b)   the declaration required by that subsection shall be made by or on behalf of the party.

(2)   A candidate may name himself as election agent, and upon doing so shall, so far as circumstances admit, be subject to the provisions of this Act both as a candidate and as an election agent, and, except where the context otherwise requires, any reference in this Act to an election agent shall be construed to refer to the candidate acting in his capacity of election agent.

(2A)   Where a registered political party submits a list of candidates to be London members of the London Assembly at an ordinary election, a candidate included in the list—

(a)   must not under subsection (2) above name himself as his own election agent, but

(b)   may be named by or on behalf of the party as the election agent of all the candidates included in the list,

and the provisions which have effect by virtue of subsection (2) above in relation to a candidate upon his naming himself as election agent shall also have effect in relation to a candidate upon his being named as election agent by virtue of paragraph (b) above.

(3)   Subject to subsection (3A) below, one election agent only shall be appointed for each candidate, but the appointment, whether the election agent appointed be the candidate himself or not, may be revoked.

(3A)   Where a registered political party submits a list of candidates to be London members of the London Assembly at an ordinary election—

(a) the same person must be appointed as election agent for all the candidates included in the list; and

(b) any such appointment may only be revoked by or on behalf of the party and in respect of all the candidates.

(4) If whether before, during or after the election the appointment (or deemed appointment) of an election agent is revoked or an election agent dies, another election agent shall be appointed forthwith and his name and address declared in writing to the appropriate officer.

(5) The declaration as a candidate's election agent of a person other than the candidate shall be of no effect under this section unless it is made and signed by that person or is accompanied by a written declaration of acceptance signed by him.

(5A) Where a registered political party submits a list of candidates to be London members of the London Assembly at an ordinary election, subsection (5) above shall apply in relation to the candidates included in that list as if the reference to a person other than the candidate were a reference to a person other than the candidate whose name appears highest on the list.

(6) Upon the name and address of an election agent being declared to the appropriate officer, the appropriate officer shall forthwith give public notice of that name and address.

(7) In this Part of this Act the expression "appropriate officer" means—

(a) in relation to a parliamentary election, the returning officer;

(aa) in relation to an Authority election, the returning officer for that election (as determined under subsection (2B) of section 35 or, as the case may be, paragraph (a) or (b) of subsection (2C) of that section);

(b) in relation to any other local government election, the proper officer of the authority for which the election is held.

NOTES

Derivation
RPA 1949 s 55
RPA 1969 s 11

Defined terms
Authority election: s 203(1)
candidate: s 118A
election: s 202(1)
local government election (E&W): ss 191(1), 203(1), (1A)
local government election (S): s 204(1)
London member: s 203(1)

notice: s 200
parliamentary election: Interpretation Act 1978 Sch 1
proper officer: s 202(1)
registered political party: s 202(1)
registered political party submitting a list of candidates to be London members: s 203(1B)
returning officer: see ss 24-27
writing: Interpretation Act 1978 Sch 1

Nomination of sub-agent at parliamentary or Authority elections

68(1) In the case of

(a) a parliamentary election for a county constituency, or

(b) an Authority election, an election agent for a candidate may appoint to act in any part of the constituency or electoral area one, but not more than one, deputy election agent (in this Act referred to as a sub-agent).

(2) As regards matters in a part of the constituency or electoral area for which there is a sub-agent the election agent may act by the sub-agent and—

(a) anything done for the purposes of this Act by or to the sub-agent in his part of the constituency or electoral area shall be deemed to be done by or to the election agent; and

(b) any act or default of a sub-agent which, if he were the election agent, would be an illegal practice or other offence against this Act shall be an illegal practice and offence against this Act committed by the sub-agent, and the sub-agent shall be liable to punishment accordingly; and

(c) the candidate shall suffer the like incapacity as if that act or default had been the election agent's act or default.

(3) Not later than the second day before the day of the poll the election agent shall declare in writing the name and address of every sub-agent to the appropriate officer, and the appropriate officer shall forthwith give public notice of the name and address of every sub-agent so declared.

(4A) Where a registered political party submits a list of candidates to be London members of the London Assembly at an ordinary election—

(a) the election agent for those candidates must, if he appoints a sub-agent for any part of the electoral area in the case of any of those candidates, appoint the same person as sub-agent for that part of the electoral area in the case of all of the candidates; and

(b) any such appointment may only be revoked in respect of all of the candidates.

(4) The appointment of a sub-agent—

(a) shall not be vacated by the election agent who appointed him ceasing to be election agent, but

(b) may be revoked by whoever is for the time being the candidate's election agent, and in the event of the revocation of the appointment or of the death of a sub-agent another sub-agent may be appointed, and his name and address shall be forthwith declared in writing to the appropriate officer, who shall forthwith give public notice of the name and address so declared.

(5) The declaration to be made to the appropriate officer, and the notice to be given by him, under subsection (3) or subsection (4) above shall specify the part of the constituency or electoral area within which any sub-agent is appointed to act.

NOTES

Derivation
RPA 1949 s 56
RPA 1969 s 11

Defined terms
appropriate officer: ss 67(7), 118
Authority election: s 203(1)
candidate: s 118A
constituency: Parliamentary Constituencies Act 1986 s 1(2)
election: s 202(1)
election agent: see s 67

electoral area (E&W): ss 191(1), 203(1)
electoral area (S): s 204(1)
London member: s 203(1)
notice: s 200
parliamentary election: Interpretation Act 1978 Sch 1
registered political party: s 202(1)
registered political party submitting a list of candidates to be London members: s 203(1B)
writing: Interpretation Act 1978 Sch 1

Office of election agent and sub-agent

69(1) Every election agent and every sub-agent shall have an office to which all claims, notices, legal process and other documents may be sent, and the address of the office shall be—

(a) declared to the appropriate officer at the same time as the appointment of the agent is declared to him; and

(b) stated in the public notice of the name of the agent.

(2) The office—

(a) of the election agent for a parliamentary election shall be within the constituency or an adjoining constituency or in a Welsh county or county borough, or London borough or district, which is partly comprised in or adjoins the constituency, and that of a sub-agent shall be in the area within which he is appointed to act; and

    (b) of an election agent for a local government election shall be within the local government area or in the constituency or one of the constituencies in which the area is comprised or in a Welsh county or county borough, or London borough or district, which adjoins it, and that of a sub-agent shall be in the area within which he is appointed to act.

(3) Any claim, notice, legal process or other document delivered at the office of the election agent or sub-agent and addressed to him, shall be deemed to have been served on him and every election agent or sub-agent may in respect of any matter connected with the election in which he is acting be sued in any court having jurisdiction at the place where his office is situated.

NOTES

Derivation
  RPA 1949 s 57
  RPA 1969 s 11

Defined terms
  appropriate officer: ss 67(7), 118
  constituency: Parliamentary Constituencies Act 1986 s
  London borough: s 203(2) and Interpretation Act 1978 Sch 1 1(2)
  election agent: see s 67

legal process: s 202(1)
local government area (E&W): ss 191(1), 203(1)
local government area (S): s 204(1)
local government election (E&W): ss 191(1), 203(1), (1A)
local government election (S): s 204(1)
London borough: s 203(2) and Interpretation Act 1978 Sch 1
parliamentary election: Interpretation Act 1978 Sch 1
sub-agent: ss 68(1), 202(1)

Effect of default in election agent's appointment

70(1) If no person's name and address is given as required by section 67 above as the election agent of a candidate who remains validly nominated at the latest time for delivery of notices of withdrawals, the candidate shall be deemed at that time to have named himself as election agent and to have revoked any appointment of another person as his election agent.

(2) If—
    (a) the person whose name and address have been so given as those of the candidate's election agent (not being the candidate himself) dies, and
    (b) a new appointment is not made on the day of the death or on the following day,
  the candidate shall be deemed to have appointed himself as from the time of death.

(3) If the appointment of a candidate's election agent is revoked without a new appointment being made, the candidate himself shall be deemed to have been appointed (or re-appointed) election agent.

(3A) The deemed appointment of a candidate as his own election agent may be revoked as if it were an actual appointment.

(4) Where a candidate is by virtue of this section to be treated as his own election agent, he shall be deemed to have his office—
    (a) at his address as given in the statement as to persons nominated (or where, in the case of a parliamentary election, the address is not given on that statement, the address as given under rule 6(4) of Schedule 1 to this Act); or
    (b) if that address is outside the permitted area for the office, at the qualifying address of the person (or first person) named in that statement as his proposer.

(5) Where in a local government election in Scotland a candidate is by virtue of this section to be treated as his own election agent, he shall be deemed to have his office—
    (a) at his address as given in his nomination paper or papers, or
    (b) if that address is outside the permitted area for the office, at the address of the person named as the proposer of the candidate in the nomination paper first delivered in which the address of the proposer is in the local government area.

(6) The appropriate officer on being satisfied that a candidate is by virtue of this section to be treated as his own election agent, shall forthwith proceed to publish the like notice as if the name and address of the candidate and the address of his office had been duly given to him under sections 67 and 69 above.

(7) In the case of a parliamentary election, subsection (6) above applies whether or not a statement has been made under rule 6(5) of Schedule 1 to this Act requiring the candidate's home address not to be made public.

NOTES

Derivation
RPA 1949 s 58

Defined terms
appropriate officer: ss 67(7), 118
candidate: s 118A
election agent: see s 67
local government area (E&W): ss 191(1), 203(1)

local government area (S): s 204(1)
local government election: ss 191(1), 203(1), (1A)
local government election (S): s 204(1)
notice: s 200
parliamentary election: Interpretation Act 1978 Sch 1
qualifying address: ss 9(8), 202(1)

Application of s 70 in relation to election of London members of the London Assembly

70A(1) Where a registered political party submits a list of candidates to be London members of the London Assembly at election of London an ordinary election—
    (a) section 70 shall not apply in relation to those candidates, but
    (b) the following provisions of this section shall have effect in place of that section.

(2) If no person's name and address is given as required by virtue of section 67(1A) as the election agent of all of the candidates included in the list who remain validly nominated at the latest time for delivery of notices of withdrawals—
    (a) the candidate whose name appears highest on the list shall be deemed at that time to have been named on behalf of the party as election agent for all of the candidates; and
    (b) any appointment of another person as election agent for those candidates shall be deemed to have been revoked.

(3) If—
    (a) the person whose name and address have been so given as those of the election agent for the candidates dies, and
    (b) a new appointment is not made on the day of the death or on the following day,
the candidate whose name appears highest on the list shall be deemed to have been named on behalf of the party as election agent for all of the candidates as from the time of death.

(4) If the appointment of the election agent for the candidates is revoked without a new appointment being made, the candidate whose name appears highest on the list shall be deemed to have been appointed (or re-appointed) election agent.

(5) The deemed appointment of a candidate as election agent may be revoked as if it were an actual appointment.

(6) Where a candidate included in the list is by virtue of this section to be treated as election agent, he shall be deemed to have his office—
    (a) at his address as given in the statement as to persons nominated; or
    (b) if that address is outside the permitted area for the office, at the qualifying address of the person (or first person) named in that statement as his proposer.

(7) The appropriate officer, on being satisfied that a candidate is by virtue of this section to be treated as election agent, shall forthwith proceed to publish the like notice as if the name and address of the candidate and the address of his office had been duly given to him under sections 67 and 69.

NOTES

Derivation
Greater London Authority Act 1999 s 17

Defined terms
appropriate officer: ss 67(7), 118
candidate: s 118A
election agent: see s 67
London member: s 203(1)

notice: s 200
qualifying address: ss 9(8), 202(1)
registered political party: s 202(1)
registered political party submitting a list of candidates to be London members: s 203(1B)

Elections where election agent not required

71   A candidate—
    (a)   at an election in England of parish councillors, or in Wales of community councillors, or
    (b)   at any election under the local government Act which is not a local government election,
need not have an election agent, and accordingly the foregoing provisions of this Part of this Act do not apply to those elections.

NOTES

Derivation
RPA 1949 s 59

Defined terms
community councillors: see Local Government Act 1972 s 35
election: s 202(1)
election under the local government act (E&W): ss 191(1), 203(1A)

England: Interpretation Act 1978 Sch 1
local government Act (E&W): s 203(1)
local government Act (S): s 204(1)
local government election (E&W): ss 191(1), 203(1), (1A)
local government election (S): s 204(1)
parish councillors: see Local Government Act 1972 s 16
Wales: Interpretation Act 1978 Sch 1

Donations to candidates

Control of donations to candidates

71A(1)   In the case of any candidate at an election, any money or other property provided (whether as a gift or loan)—
    (a)   by any person other than the candidate or his election agent, and
    (b)   for the purpose of meeting election expenses incurred by or on behalf of the candidate,
must be provided to the candidate or his election agent.

(2)   Subsection (1) above does not apply to any money or other property so provided for the purpose of meeting any such expenses which may be lawfully paid by a person other than the candidate, his election agent or any sub-agent (in the case of an election where sub-agents may be appointed).

(3)   A person who provides any money or other property in contravention of subsection (1) above shall be guilty of an illegal practice.

(4)   Schedule 2A to this Act shall have effect for the purpose of controlling donations to candidates.

(5)   In this section and that Schedule "property" includes any description of property, and references to the provision of property accordingly include the supply of goods.

NOTES

Derivation
Political Parties, Elections and Referendums Act 2000 s 130

Defined terms
candidate: s 118A

election: s 202(1)
election agent: see s 67
election expenses: ss 90ZA, 90C, 90D, 118, Sch 4A
person: s 202(1)
sub-agent: ss 68(1), 202(1)

Election expenses

72   *Repealed*

Payment of expenses through election agent

73(1) Subject to subsection (5) below, no payment (of whatever nature) shall be made by—
  (a) a candidate at an election, or
  (b) any other person,
  in respect of election expenses incurred by or on behalf of the candidate unless it is made by or through the candidate's election agent.

  (2) Every payment made by an election agent in respect of any election expenses shall, except where less than £20, be vouched for by a bill stating the particulars or by a receipt.

  (3) The references in the foregoing provisions of this section to an election agent shall, in relation to a parliamentary or Authority election where sub-agents are allowed, be taken as references to the election agent acting by himself or a sub-agent.

  (4) *Repealed*

  (5) This section does not apply to—
  (a) any expenses which are, in accordance with section 74(1) or (1B), 78(5) or 79(2) below, paid by the candidate;
  (b) any expenses which are paid in accordance with section 74(3) below by a person authorised as mentioned in that provision;
  (c) any expenses included in a declaration made by the election agent under section 74A below; or
  (d) any expenses which are to be regarded as incurred by or on behalf of the candidate by virtue of section 90ZA(5) below.

  (6) A person who makes any payment (of whatever nature) in contravention of subsection (1) above shall be guilty of an illegal practice.

NOTES

Derivation
RPA 1949 s 61

Defined terms
Authority election: s 203(1)
candidate: s 118A
election: s 202(1)

election agent: see s 67
election expenses: ss 90ZA, 90C, 90D, 118, Sch 4A
person: s 202(1)
sub-agent: ss 68(1), 202(1)

Expenses which may be paid otherwise than by election agent

74(1) The candidate at an election may pay any personal expenses incurred by him on account of or in connection with or incidental to the election, but
  (a) the amount which a candidate at a parliamentary election may pay shall not exceed £600,
  (b) the amount which a candidate at an election of the Mayor of London may pay shall not exceed £5,000,
  (c) the amount which a candidate at an election of a constituency member of the London Assembly may pay shall not exceed £600, and
  (d) the amount which a candidate to be a London member of the London Assembly at an ordinary election may pay shall not exceed £900,
  and, where paragraph (a), (b), (c) or (d) above applies, any further personal expenses so incurred by him shall be paid by his election agent.

  (1A) In the application of subsection (1) above in relation to a person who is a candidate in two or more Authority elections those elections shall be treated—

(a) if one of them is an election of the Mayor of London, as if they together constituted a single election falling within paragraph (b) of that subsection, and

(b) in any other case, as if they together constituted a single election falling within paragraph (d) of that subsection.

(1B) The candidate at an election may also pay any election expenses (other than expenses falling within subsection (1) above) which were incurred by him or on his behalf and in respect of which payment falls to be made before the date on which he appoints (or is deemed to have appointed) an election agent.

(2) The candidate shall send to his election agent within the time limited by this Act for sending in claims a written statement of the amount of expenses paid as mentioned in subsection (1) or (1B) above by the candidate.

(3) Any person may, if so authorised in writing by the candidate's election agent, pay any necessary expenses for stationery, postage, telegrams (or any similar means of communication) and other petty expenses, to a total amount not exceeding that named in the authority, but any excess above the total amount so named shall be paid by the election agent.

(4) A statement of the particulars of payments made by any person so authorised shall be sent to the election agent within the time limited by this Act for sending in claims, and shall be vouched for by a bill containing that person's receipt.

(5) Sections 78 and 79 below do not apply to expenses which, in accordance with any provision of this section, are paid otherwise than by the candidate's election agent.

NOTES

Derivation
RPA 1949 s 62

Defined terms
Authority election: s 203(1)
candidate: s 118A
constituency: Parliamentary Constituencies Act 1986 s 1(2)
election: s 202(1)
election agent: see s 67

election expenses: ss 90ZA, 90C, 90D, 118, Sch 4A
election of a constituency member of the London Assembly: s 203(1)
election of the Mayor of London: s 203(1)
London member: s 203(1)
parliamentary election: Interpretation Act 1978 Sch 1
personal expenses: s 118
writing: Interpretation Act 1978 Sch 1

Expenses incurred otherwise than for election purposes

74A(1) Neither section 73 above nor sections 78 and 79 below shall apply to election expenses—

(a) which are incurred by or on behalf of a candidate otherwise than for the purposes of the candidate's election, but

(b) which by virtue of section 90ZA(1) below fall to be regarded as election expenses by reason of the property, services or facilities in respect of which they were incurred being used for the purposes of the candidate's election.

(2) The candidate's election agent shall make a declaration of the amount (determined in accordance with section 90B below) of any election expenses falling within subsection (1) above.

(3) In this section "for the purposes of the candidate's election" has the same meaning as in sections 90ZA and 90C below.

NOTES

Derivation
Political Parties, Elections and Referendums Act 2000 s 138

Defined terms
candidate: s 118A
election agent: see s 67
election expenses: ss 90ZA, 90C, 90D, Sch 4A

Prohibition of expenses not authorised by election agent

75(1)   No expenses shall, with a view to promoting or procuring the election of a candidate (or, in the case of an election of the London members of the London Assembly at an ordinary election, a registered political party or candidates of that party) at an election, be incurred after he becomes a candidate at that election by any person other than the candidate, his election agent and persons authorised in writing by the election agent on account—

    (a)   of holding public meetings or organising any public display; or

    (b)   of issuing advertisements, circulars or publications; or

    (c)   of otherwise presenting to the electors the candidate or his views or the extent or nature of his backing or disparaging another candidate; or

    (d)   in the case of an election of the London members of the London Assembly at an ordinary election, of otherwise presenting to the electors the candidate's registered political party (if any) or the views of that party or the extent or nature of that party's backing or disparaging any other registered political party,

(1ZZA)   Paragraph (c) or (d) of subsection (1) above does not restrict the publication of any matter relating to the election in—

    (a)   a newspaper or other periodical,

    (b)   a broadcast made by the British Broadcasting Corporation or by Sianel Pedwar Cymru, or

    (c)   a programme included in any service licensed under Part 1 or 3 of the Broadcasting Act 1990 or Part 1 or 2 of the Broadcasting Act 1996.

(1ZZB)   Subsection (1) above does not apply to any expenses incurred by any person—

    (a)   which do not exceed in the aggregate the permitted sum (and are not incurred by that person as part of a concerted plan of action), or

    (b)   in travelling or in living away from home or similar personal expenses.

(1ZA)   For the purposes of subsection (1ZZB)(a) above, "the permitted sum" means—

    (a)   in respect of a candidate at a parliamentary election, £700;

    (b)   in respect of a candidate at a local government election, £50 together with an additional 0.5p for every entry in the register of local government electors for the electoral area in question as it has effect on the last day for publication of notice of the election;

and expenses shall be regarded as incurred by a person "as part of a concerted plan of action" if they are incurred by that person in pursuance of any plan or other arrangement whereby that person and one or more other persons are to incur, with a view to promoting or procuring the election of the same candidate, expenses which (disregarding subsection (1ZZB)(a)) fall within subsection (1) above.

(1A)   In the application of subsection (1) above in relation to an election of the London members of the London Assembly at an ordinary election, any reference to the candidate includes a reference to all or any of the candidates of a registered political party; and in the application of subsection (1ZA) above in relation to such an election the reference to the same candidate includes a reference to all or any of the candidates of the same registered political party.

(1B)   *Repealed*

(1C)   *Repealed*

(2)   Where a person incurs any expenses required by this section to be authorised by the election agent—

    (a)   that person shall within 21 days after the day on which the result of the election is declared deliver to the appropriate officer a return of the amount of those expenses, stating the election at which and the candidate in whose support they were incurred, and

(b) the return shall be accompanied by a declaration made by that person (or in the case of an association or body of persons, by a director, general manager, secretary or other similar officer of the association or body) verifying the return and giving particulars of the matters for which the expenses were incurred,

but this subsection does not apply to any person engaged or employed for payment or promise of payment by the candidate or his election agent.

(3) The return and declaration under the foregoing provisions of this section shall be in the prescribed form, and the authority received from the election agent shall be annexed to and deemed to form part of the return.

(4) A copy of every return and declaration made under subsection (2) above in relation to a parliamentary election in England, Wales or Northern Ireland must be sent to the relevant officer within 21 days after the day on which the result of the election is declared by the person making the return or declaration.

(4A) The relevant officer is—
  (a) in relation to England and Wales, the returning officer;
  (b) in relation to Northern Ireland, the Clerk of the Crown for Northern Ireland.

(4B) The returning officer must forward to the relevant registration officer (within the meaning of rule 55 of the parliamentary elections rules) every document sent to him in pursuance of subsection (4) above.

(4C) Rule 57 of those rules applies to any documents sent under this section to—
  (a) the relevant registration officer, or
  (b) the Clerk of the Crown for Northern Ireland.

(5) If a person—
  (a) incurs, or aids, abets, counsels or procures any other person to incur, any expenses in contravention of this section, or
  (b) knowingly makes the declaration required by subsection (2) falsely,

he shall be guilty of a corrupt practice; and if a person fails to deliver or send any declaration or return or a copy of it as required by this section he shall be guilty of an illegal practice, but—

  (i) the court before whom a person is convicted under this subsection may, if they think it just in the special circumstances of the case, mitigate or entirely remit any incapacity imposed by virtue of section 173 below; and
  (ii) a candidate shall not be liable, nor shall his election be avoided, for a corrupt or illegal practice under this subsection committed by an agent without his consent or connivance.

(6) Where any act or omission of an association or body of persons, corporate or unincorporate, is an offence declared to be a corrupt or illegal practice by this section, any person who at the time of the act or omission was a director, general manager, secretary or other similar officer of the association or body, or was purporting to act in any such capacity, shall be deemed to be guilty of that offence, unless he proves—

  (a) that the act or omission took place without his consent or connivance; and
  (b) that he exercised all such diligence to prevent the commission of the offence as he ought to have exercised having regard to the nature of his functions in that capacity and to all the circumstances.

(7) For the purposes of this section, in the case of an election of the London members of the London Assembly at an ordinary election, a candidate's registered political party is the registered political party (if any) which submitted for the purposes of that election a list of candidates on which the candidate in question is included.

(8) For the purposes of subsection (1), expenditure incurred before the date when a person becomes a candidate at the election is to be treated as having been incurred after that date if it is incurred in connection with any thing which is used or takes place after that date.

(11) This section does not apply in relation to a local government election in Scotland.

NOTES

Derivation
   RPA 1949 s 63

Subordinate legislation
   Greater London Authority Elections (Expenses) Order 2000 SI 2000/789

Defined terms
   appropriate officer: ss 67(7), 118
   candidate: s 118A
   Clerk of the Crown: s 202(1)
   constituency: Parliamentary Constituencies Act 1986 s 1(2)
   corrupt practice: see ss 60(1), 62A(5), 62B(2), (3), 65A(1), (2), 65B(2), (3), 75(5), 75ZB(4), 75A(7), 82(6), 113(1), 114(1), 115(1), Sch 1 rule 6A(2), Sch 4 para 5
   election: s 202(1)
   election agent: see s 67

elector: s 202(1)
electoral area (E&W): ss 191(1), 203(1)
electoral area (S): s 204(1)
England: Interpretation Act 1978 Sch 1
local government election (E&W): ss 191(1), 203(1), (1A)
local government election (S): s 204(1)
London member: s 203(1)
parliamentary election: Interpretation Act 1978 Sch 1
parliamentary election rules: s 202(1)
personal expenses: s 118
prescribed: s 202(1)
promoting or procuring a candidate's election: s 90ZA(6)
registered political party: s 202(1)
returning officer: see ss 24-27
Wales: Interpretation Act 1978 Sch 1
writing: Interpretation Act 1978 Sch 1

Return of permitted expenditure: power to require return

5ZA(1) The returning officer or the Electoral Commission may, at any time during the period of 6 months beginning with the date of the poll at a parliamentary election, request a relevant person to deliver to the officer or Commission a return of permitted expenditure in relation to a candidate at the election who is specified in the request.

(2) "Relevant person" means a person who—
   (a) is not required to deliver a return under section 75(2) in relation to the candidate, and
   (b) is not the candidate, the candidate's election agent, or a person engaged or employed for payment or promise of payment by the candidate or the candidate's election agent.

(3) "Return of permitted expenditure" means a return—
   (a) showing all permitted expenses incurred by the person in relation to the candidate, or
   (b) stating that the person incurred no such expenses or that the total such expenses incurred by the person was £200 or less.

(4) "Permitted expense", in relation to a candidate, means an expense incurred by the person in respect of the candidate which, if the person had been required to deliver a return under section 75(2) in relation to the candidate, would have been required to be included in that return.

NOTES

Derivation
   Transparency of Lobbying, Non-Party Campaigning and Trade Union Administration Act 2014 s 36

Defined terms
   candidate: s 118A
   Electoral Commission: see Political Parties, Elections

and Referendums Act 2000 s 1
election agent: see s 67
parliamentary election: Interpretation Act 1978 Sch 1
returning officer: see ss 24-27

Return of permitted expenditure: compliance and sanctions

75ZB(1) A person must comply with a request under section 75ZA(1) within the period of 21 days beginning with the day on which the request is received.

(2) A return of permitted expenditure must be accompanied by a declaration made by the person (or in the case of an association or body of persons, by a director, general manager, secretary or other similar officer of the association or body)—

(a) verifying the return, and

(b) in the case of a return of the kind mentioned in section 75ZA(3)(a), giving particulars of the matters for which the expenses were incurred.

(3) A person who fails to deliver a return or declaration in accordance with this section is guilty of an illegal practice.

(4) A person who knowingly makes a false declaration under subsection (2) is guilty of a corrupt practice.

(5) The court before whom a person is convicted under subsection (3) or (4) may, if they think it just in the special circumstances of the case, mitigate or entirely remit any incapacity imposed by virtue of section 173.

(6) Where any act or omission of an association or body of persons, corporate or unincorporate, is an offence declared to be a corrupt or illegal practice by this section, any person who at the time of the act or omission was a director, general manager, secretary or other similar officer of the association or body, or was purporting to act in any such capacity, shall be deemed to be guilty of that offence, unless he proves—

(a) that the act or omission took place without his consent or connivance, and

(b) that he exercised all such diligence to prevent the commission of the offence as he ought to have exercised having regard to the nature of his functions in that capacity and to all the circumstances.

NOTES

Derivation
Transparency of Lobbying, Non-Party Campaigning and Trade Union Administration Act 2014 s 36

65A(1), (2), 65B(2), (3), 75(5), 75ZB(4), 75A(7), 82(6), 113(1), 114(1), 115(1), Sch 1 rule 6A(2), Sch 4 para 5
person: s 202(1)

Defined terms
corrupt practice: see ss 60(1), 62A(5), 62B(2), (3),

Scottish local government elections: prohibition of expenses not authorised by election agent

75A(1) This section applies in relation to a local government election in Scotland.

(2) No person other than a candidate at the election, his election agent or a person authorised in writing by the election agent shall, with a view to promoting or procuring the election of the candidate, incur any expenses on account of—

(a) holding public meetings or organising any public display;

(b) issuing advertisements, circulars or publications; or

(c) otherwise presenting to the electors the candidate or his views or the extent or nature of his backing or disparaging another candidate.

(3) Subsection (2)(c) above does not restrict the publication of any matter relating to the election in—

(a) a newspaper or other periodical;

(b) a broadcast made by the British Broadcasting Corporation; or

(c) a programme included in any service licensed under Part 1 or 3 of the Broadcasting Act 1990 (c 42) or Part 1 or 2 of the Broadcasting Act 1996 (c 55).

(4) Subsection (2) does not apply to expenses incurred by any person—

(a) which do not exceed in the aggregate the permitted sum (and are not incurred by that person as part of a concerted plan of action); or

(b)   in travelling or in living away from home or similar personal expenses.

(5)   For the purposes of subsection (4)(a) above—

    (a)   "the permitted sum" means, in respect of each candidate, £50 together with an additional 0.5p for every entry in the register of local government electors for the electoral area in question as it has effect on the last day for publication of notice of the election; and

    (b)   expenses are to be regarded as incurred by a person "as part of a concerted plan of action" if they are incurred by that person in pursuance of any plan or other arrangement whereby that person and one or more other persons are to incur, with a view to promoting or procuring the election of the same candidate, expenses which (disregarding subsection (4)(a)) fall within subsection (2) above.

(6)   Where a person incurs any expenses required by subsection (2) above to be authorised by the election agent, that person shall, within 21 days after the day on which the result of the election is declared, deliver to the appropriate officer—

    (a)   a return of the amount of the expenses, stating the election at which, and the candidate in whose support they were incurred;

    (b)   a declaration by that person (or in the case of an association or body of persons, by a director, general manager, secretary or other similar officer of the association or body) verifying the return and giving particulars of the matters for which the expenses were incurred; and

    (c)   the authority received from the election agent (which, for the purposes of this section, is to be treated as forming part of the return).

(7)   A person is guilty of a corrupt practice if he—

    (a)   incurs, or aids, abets, counsels or procures any other persons to incur, any expenses in contravention of subsection (2) above; or

    (b)   makes a declaration required by subsection (6)(b) above which he knows to be false.

(8)   A person is guilty of an illegal practice if he fails to deliver any return or declaration as required by subsection (6) above.

(9)   The court by or before which a person is convicted of a corrupt or illegal practice under subsection (7) or (8) above may, if the court thinks it just in the special circumstances of the case, mitigate or entirely remit any incapacity incurred under section 173 or 173A of this Act by virtue of the conviction.

(10)   A candidate is not liable for, and his election is not void by reason of, a corrupt or illegal practice under subsection (7) or (8) above committed by an agent without his consent or connivance.

(11)   Where any act or omission of an association or body of persons (whether corporate or unincorporate) is a corrupt or illegal practice under this section, any person who at the time of the act or omission was a director, general manager, secretary or other similar officer of the association or body, or was purporting to act in any such capacity, is also guilty of the corrupt or illegal practice, unless the person proves—

    (a)   that the act or omission took place without his consent or connivance; and

    (b)   that he exercised all such diligence to prevent the commission of the offence as he ought to have exercised having regard to the nature of his functions in that capacity and to all the circumstances.

NOTES

Derivation

Local Electoral Administration and Registration Services (Scotland) Act 2006 s 16

Defined terms

appropriate officer: ss 67(7), 118

candidate: s 118

corrupt practice: see ss 60(1), 62A(5), 62B(2), (3), 65A(1), (2), 65B(2), (3), 75(5), 75ZB(4), 75A(7), 82(6), 113(1), 114(1), 115(1), Sch 1 rule 6A(2), Sch 4 para 5

election agent: see s 67

local government election (S): s 204(1)

writing: Interpretation Act 1978 Sch 1

Limitation of election expenses

76(1) The election expenses incurred by or on behalf of a candidate at an election must not in the aggregate exceed the maximum amount specified in subsection (2) below or, in the case of any of the Authority elections mentioned in subsection (2A)(a) to (c) below, the maximum amount prescribed by order under that subsection.

(1A) Where a registered political party submits a list of candidates to be London members of the London Assembly at an ordinary election, any election expenses incurred by or on behalf of any of those candidates must not in the aggregate exceed the maximum amount prescribed by order under subsection (2A)(d).

(1B) Where any election expenses are incurred in excess of a maximum amount specified in subsection (2) below or prescribed by order under subsection (2A) below, any candidate or election agent who—

(a) incurred, or authorised the incurring of, the election expenses, and

(b) knew or ought reasonably to have known that the expenses would be incurred in excess of that maximum amount,

shall be guilty of an illegal practice.

(2) That maximum amount is—

(a) for a candidate at a parliamentary general election, being an election—

(i) in a county constituency, £8,700 together with an additional 9p for every entry in the register of electors; and

(ii) in a borough constituency, £8,700 together with an additional 6p for every entry in the register of electors;

(aa) for a candidate at a parliamentary by-election, £100,000;

(b) for a candidate at a local government election other than an Authority election—

(i) *Repealed*

(ii) at any other local government election, £740 together with an additional 6p for every entry in the register of electors.

(2A) As respects Authority elections, each of the following, that is to say—

(a) the maximum amount for a candidate in an election of the Mayor of London,

(b) the maximum amount for a candidate in an election of a constituency member of the London Assembly,

(c) the maximum amount for an individual candidate in an election of the London members of the London Assembly at an ordinary election,

(d) the maximum amount for the purposes of subsection (1A) above,

shall be such as the Secretary of State may prescribe in an order made by statutory instrument.

(2B) An order under subsection (2A) above shall not be made unless a draft of the order has been laid before, and approved by a resolution of, each House of Parliament.

(3) *Repealed*

(4) In subsection (2) above "the register of electors" means the register of parliamentary electors, or (as the case may be) local government electors, for the constituency or electoral area in question as it has effect on the last day for publication of notice of the election.

(5) The maximum amount mentioned above for a candidate at a parliamentary election or an Authority election (including the maximum amount for the purposes of subsection

(1A) above) or a local government election in England or Wales is not required to cover the candidate's personal expenses.

(6)   Where at an election a poll is countermanded or abandoned by reason of a candidate's death, the maximum amount of election expenses shall, for any of the other candidates who then remain validly nominated, be twice or, if there has been a previous increase under this subsection, three times what it would have been but for any increase under this subsection; but the maximum amount shall not be affected for any candidate by the change in the timing of the election or of any step in the proceedings at the election.

NOTES

Derivation
   RPA 1949 s 64

Subordinate legislation
   Greater London Authority Elections (Expenses) Order 2000 SI 2000/789

Defined terms
   Authority election: s 203(1)
   borough constituency (S): 204(2)
   candidate: s 118A
   constituency: Parliamentary Constituencies Act 1986 s 1(2)
   election: s 202(1)
   election agent: see s 67
   election expenses: ss 90ZA, 90C, 90D, 118, Sch 4A
   election of a constituency member of the London

Assembly: s 203(1)
election of the Mayor of London: s 203(1)
electoral area (E&W): ss 191(1), 203(1)
electoral area (S): s 204(1)
England: Interpretation Act 1978 Sch 1
local government election (E&W): ss 191(1), 203(1), (1A)
local government election (S): s 204(1)
London member: s 203(1)
parliamentary election: Interpretation Act 1978 Sch 1
personal expenses: s 118
register of electors: see s 9
registered political party: s 202(1)
registered political party submitting a list of candidates to be London members: s 203(1B)
Wales: Interpretation Act 1978 Sch 1

Limitation of pre-candidacy election expenses for certain general elections

ZA(1)   This section applies where—

(a)   a Parliament is not dissolved until after the period of 55 months beginning with the day on which that Parliament first met ("the 55-month period"),

(b)   election expenses are incurred by or on behalf of a candidate at the parliamentary general election which follows the dissolution, and

(c)   the expenses are incurred in respect of a matter which is used during the period beginning immediately after the 55-month period and ending with the day on which the person becomes a candidate at that election.

For the purposes of this section, section 90ZA(1) has effect with the omission of the words "after the date when he becomes a candidate at the election".

(2)   Election expenses incurred as mentioned in subsection (1) must not in the aggregate exceed the permitted amount, which is the relevant percentage of the following sum—

(a)   for a candidate at an election in a county constituency, £30,700 plus 9p for every entry in the register of electors;

(b)   for a candidate at an election in a borough constituency, £30,700 plus 6p for every entry in the register of electors.

(3)   The relevant percentage is—

(a)   100% where the dissolution was during or after the 60th month of the Parliament;

(b)   90% where the dissolution was during its 59th month;

(c)   80% where the dissolution was during its 58th month;

(d)   70% where the dissolution was during its 57th month;

(e)   60% where the dissolution was during its 56th month.

For the purposes of this subsection, the "56th month" of a Parliament is the month beginning immediately after the 55-month period; and so on.

(4) In subsection (2) above "the register of electors" means the register of parliamentary electors for the constituency in question as it has effect on the last day for publication of notice of the election.

(5) Where election expenses are incurred as mentioned in subsection (1) in excess of the permitted amount, any candidate or election agent who—

    (a) incurred, or authorised the incurring of, the election expenses, and

    (b) knew or ought reasonably to have known that the expenses would be incurred in excess of that amount,

shall be guilty of an illegal practice.

(6) The candidate's personal expenses do not count towards the permitted amount.

NOTES

Derivation
Political Parties and Elections Act 2009

Defined terms
borough constituency (S): 204(2)
candidate: s 118A
constituency: Parliamentary Constituencies Act 1986 s 1(2)

election: s 202(1)
election agent: see s 67
election expenses: ss 90ZA, 90C, 90D, 118
month: Interpretation Act 1978 sch 1
personal expenses: s 118
register of electors: see s 9

Power to vary provisions about election expenses

76A(1) The Secretary of State may by order made by statutory instrument vary any of the sums to which this section applies—

    (a) where he considers that the variation is expedient in consequence of changes in the value of money, or

    (b) in order to give effect to a recommendation of the Electoral Commission.

(2) This section applies to any of the sums for the time being specified in—

    (a) section 73(2) above;

    (b) section 74(1)(a), (b), (c) or (d) above;

    (c) section 75(1ZA) above;

    (ca) section 75A(5) above; or

    (d) section 76(2) above;

    (e) section 76ZA(2) above.

(3) An order under subsection (1)(b) above shall be subject to annulment in pursuance of a resolution of either House of Parliament.

NOTES

Derivation
RPA 1985 s 14

Subordinate legislation
Representation of the People (Variation of Limits of Candidates' Election Expenses) Order 2014 SI 2014/1870
Representation of the People (Variation of Limits of Candidates' Local Government Election Expenses)

(Scotland) Order 2005, SSI 2005/102

Defined terms
Electoral Commission: see Political Parties, Elections and Referendums Act 2000 s 1

Expenses limit for joint candidates at local election

77(1) Where there are two or more joint candidates at a local government election other than an Authority election the maximum amount mentioned in section 76 above shall, for each of those joint candidates, be reduced by a quarter or, if there are more than two joint candidates, by one-third.

(2) Where two or more candidates appoint the same election agent, or by themselves or any agent or agents—

    (a) employ or use the services of the same clerks or messengers at the election, or

> (b)   hire or use the same committee rooms for the election, or
>
> (c)   publish a joint address, circular or notice at the election,

those candidates shall for the purposes of this section be deemed to be joint candidates; but—

> (i)   the employment and use of the same clerk, messenger or committee room, if accidental or casual, or of a trivial and unimportant character, shall not be deemed of itself to constitute persons joint candidates;
>
> (ii)   nothing in this subsection shall prevent candidates from ceasing to be joint candidates.

(3)   Where—

> (a)   any excess of expenses above the maximum allowed for one of two or more joint candidates has arisen owing to his having ceased to be a joint candidate, or to his having become a joint candidate after having begun to conduct his election as a separate candidate,
>
> (b)   the change was made in good faith,
>
> (c)   the excess is not more than under the circumstances is reasonable, and
>
> (d)   the total election expenses of the candidate do not exceed the maximum amount allowed for a separate candidate,

the excess shall be deemed to have arisen from a reasonable cause for the purposes of section 167 below.

NOTES

Derivation
  RPA 1949 s 65

Defined terms
  Authority election: s 203(1)
  candidate: s 118A
  committee room: s 118

election agent: see s 67
election expenses: ss 90ZA, 90C, 90D, 118
local government election (E&W): ss 191(1), 203(1), (1A)
local government election (S): s 204(1)

Time for sending in and paying claims

78(1)   Every claim against a candidate or his election agent in respect of election expenses which is not sent in to the election agent not later than 21 days after the day on which the result of the election is declared shall be barred and not paid.

(2)   All election expenses shall be paid not later than 28 days after that day.

(3)   An election agent who pays a claim in contravention of subsection (1) or makes a payment in contravention of subsection (2) above shall be guilty of an illegal practice; but where the election court reports that it has been proved to the court by the candidate that any payment was made by an election agent without the sanction or connivance of the candidate—

> (a)   the candidate's election shall not be void, nor
>
> (b)   shall he be subject to any incapacity under this Act by reason only of that payment having been made in contravention of this section.

(4)   The claimant or the candidate or his election agent may apply to the High Court or to the county court for leave to pay a claim for any election expenses, although sent in after that period of 21 days or although sent in to the candidate and not to the election agent, and the court on cause shown to their satisfaction may by order grant the leave. In relation to an application in respect of expenses for a local government election in Scotland the reference in this subsection to the High Court shall be omitted.

(5)   Any sum specified in the order of leave may be paid by the candidate or his election agent and when paid in pursuance of the leave shall not be deemed to be in contravention of subsection (2) above.

(6)   *Repealed*

(7) Article 60 of the County Courts (Northern Ireland) Order 1980 (appeals from county courts) shall apply in relation to any order of a county court in Northern Ireland made by virtue of subsection (4) above as it applies in relation to any such decree of a county court as is mentioned in paragraph (1) of that Article.

NOTES

Derivation
  RPA 1949 s 66

Defined terms
  candidate: s 118A
  county court: Interpretation Act 1978 Sch 1
  election: s 202(1)
  election agent: see s 67

election court: s 202(1)
election expenses: ss 90ZA, 90C, 90D, 118
High Court (E,W & NI): Interpretation Act 1978 Sch 1
High Court (S): s 204(3)
local government election (S): s 204(1)
report (S): s 204(7)

Disputed claims

79(1) If the election agent disputes any claim sent in to him within the period of 21 days mentioned in section 78 above or refuses or fails to pay the claim within the period of 28 days so mentioned, the claim shall be deemed to be a disputed claim.

(2) The claimant may, if he thinks fit, bring an action for a disputed claim in any competent court, and any sum paid by the candidate or his agent in pursuance of the judgment or order of the court shall not be deemed to be in contravention of section 73(1) above or of section 78(2).

(3) *Repealed*

(4) Subsections (4) to (7) of section 78 apply in relation to a disputed claim as they apply in relation to a claim for election expenses sent in after that period of 21 days.

NOTES

Derivation
  RPA 1949 s 67

Defined terms
  candidate: s 118A

disputed claim: s 118
election agent: see s 67
election expenses: ss 90ZA, 90C, 90D, 118

Election agent's claim

80 So far as circumstances admit, this Act applies to an election agent's claim for his remuneration and to its payment in like manner as if he were any other creditor, and if any difference arises about the amount of the claim, the claim shall be a disputed claim within the meaning of this Act and be dealt with accordingly.

NOTES

Derivation
  RPA 1949 s 68

Defined terms

disputed claim: s 118
election agent: see s 67

Return as to election expenses

81(1) Within 35 days after the day on which the result of the election is declared, the election agent of every candidate at the election shall deliver to the appropriate officer a true return containing as respects that candidate—

  (a) a statement of all election expenses incurred by or on behalf of the candidate; and

  (b) a statement of all payments made by the election agent together with all bills or receipts relating to the payments.

(1A) Subsection (1) above—

    (a) in its application in relation to an election of the Mayor of London, shall have effect with the substitution for "35 days" of "70 days"; and

    (b) in its application in relation to the election of the London members of the London Assembly at an ordinary election, shall have effect with the substitution for "35 days after the day on which the result of the election is declared" of "70 days after the day on which the last of the successful candidates at the election is declared to be returned.

(2) A return under this section must—

    (a) specify the poll by virtue of which the return is required;

    (b) specify the name of the candidate to whom the return relates and of the candidate's election agent; and

    (c) deal under a separate heading with any expenses in respect of which a return is required by virtue of section 75(2) or 75A(6) above.

(3) *Repealed*

(3A) The return shall also contain as respects that candidate—

    (a) a statement relating to such other expenses in connection with which provision is made by this Part as the Electoral Commission provide in regulations;

    (b) a statement relating to such claims (whether paid, unpaid or disputed) in connection with such election expenses or such other expenses mentioned in paragraph (a) as the Electoral Commission so provide;

    (c) a statement relating to such other matters as is prescribed

(4) *Repealed*

(4A) In relation to a local government election in Scotland, the return shall also contain as respects that candidate—

    (a) a statement relating to such expenses as the Scottish Ministers may by regulations prescribe, being expenses (other than election expenses) in connection with which provision is made by this Part;

    (b) a statement relating to such claims as the Scottish Ministers may so prescribe, being claims (whether paid, unpaid or disputed) in connection with election expenses or expenses prescribed under paragraph (a);

    (c) a statement relating to such other matters as the Scottish Ministers may so prescribe.

(4B) No regulations shall be made by the Scottish Ministers under subsection (4A) above unless a draft of the instrument containing the regulations has been laid before and approved by a resolution of the Scottish Parliament.

(5) Where after the date at which the return as to election expenses is delivered, leave is given by the court under section 78(4) above for any claim to be paid, the candidate or his election agent shall, within seven days after its payment, deliver to the appropriate officer a return of the sums paid in pursuance of the leave, accompanied by a copy of the order of the court giving the leave, and in default he shall be deemed to have failed to comply with the requirements of this section without such authorised excuse as is mentioned in section 86 below.

(6) Where a registered political party submits a list of two or more candidates to be London members of the London Assembly at an ordinary election, the preceding provisions of this section shall have effect in relation to those candidates and their election agent with the following modifications.

(7) The return which the election agent is required to deliver under subsection (1) above—

    (a) shall be in respect of all those candidates.

    (b) *Repealed*

(8) If any payments made by the election agent were in respect of two or more candidates, the return shall deal under a separate heading or subsection with all such payments, and the expenses to which they relate, in respect of those candidates.

(9) The statements which the return is required to contain by virtue of subsection (3A) above in respect of the matters there mentioned shall be a separate statement as respects each of the candidates in question.

(10) If and to the extent that any such matter is referable to two or more candidates together, the return shall contain a separate statement of that matter as respects those candidates.

(10A) The Electoral Commission may, by regulations, prescribe a form of return which may be used for the purposes of making any (or any description of) return required by this section.

(10B) In the application of subsection (10A) in relation to a local government election in Scotland, the reference to the Electoral Commission is to be read as if it were a reference to the Scottish Ministers.

(11) *Repealed*

NOTES

Derivation
  RPA 1949 s 69

Defined terms
  appropriate officer: ss 67(7), 118
  candidate: s 118A
  election: s 202(1)
  election agent: see s 67
  election expenses: ss 90ZA, 90C, 90D, 118
  election of the Mayor of London: s 203(1)
  Electoral Commission: see Political Parties, Elections

and Referendums Act 2000 s 1
local government election (S): s 204(1)
London member: s 203(1)
payment: s 118
prescribed: s 202(1)
registered political party: s 202(1)
registered political party submitting a list of candidates to be London members: s 203(1B)

Declarations as to election expenses

82(1) The return delivered under section 81(1) above shall be accompanied by a declaration made by the election agent in the appropriate form.

(2) At the same time that the election agent delivers that return, or within seven days afterwards, the candidate shall deliver to the appropriate officer a declaration made by him in the appropriate form.

(2A) For the purposes of subsections (1) and (2) above, "the appropriate form"—
  (a) in the case of the election agent for the candidates on a list submitted under paragraph 5 of Schedule 2 to the 1999 Act (election of London members) by a registered political party, is the form set out for the purpose in rules under section 36(2A) above;
  (b) in the case of any of the candidates included in such a list, is the form set out for the purpose in those rules; and
  (c) in any other case, is the form in Schedule 3 to this Act.

(3) Where the candidate is out of the United Kingdom when the return is so delivered—
  (a) the declaration required by subsection (2) above may be made by him within 14 days after his return to the United Kingdom, and
  (b) in that case, the declaration shall be forthwith delivered to the appropriate officer,
but the delay authorised by this provision in making the declaration shall not exonerate the election agent from complying with the provisions of this Act relating to the return and declaration as to election expenses.

(4) *Repealed*

(5) Where the candidate is his own election agent, the declaration by an election agent as to election expenses need not be made and the declaration by the candidate as to election expenses shall be modified as specified in the form in Schedule 3.

(5A) Where one of the candidates included in a list submitted under paragraph 5 of Schedule 2 to the 1999 Act (election of London members) by a registered political party is the election agent for those candidates, the declarations required by subsections (1) and (2) above shall instead be modified as specified in the form set out in the rules under section 36(2A) above.

(6) If a candidate or election agent knowingly makes the declaration required by this section falsely, he shall be guilty of a corrupt practice.

NOTES

Derivation
RPA 1949 s 70

Defined terms
the 1999 Act: s 203(1)
appropriate officer: ss 67(7), 118
candidate: s 118A

declaration as to election expenses: s 118
election agent: see s 67
registered political party: s 202(1)
return as to election expenses: s 118

Where no return and declarations needed at parliamentary elections

83 Notwithstanding anything in sections 81 and 82 above, no return or declaration as to election expenses shall be required in the case of a person—
   (a) who is a candidate at a parliamentary election, but is so only because he has been declared by others to be a candidate; and
   (b) who has not consented to the declaration or taken any part as a candidate in the election.

NOTES

Derivation
RPA 1949 s 71

Defined terms
candidate: s 118A

declaration as to election expenses: s 118
parliamentary election: Interpretation Act 1978 Sch 1
return as to election expenses: s 118

Penalty for failure as respects return or declarations

84 Subject to the provisions of section 86 below, if a candidate or election agent fails to comply with the requirements of section 81 or section 82 above he shall be guilty of an illegal practice.

NOTES

Derivation
RPA 1949 s 72

Defined terms

candidate: s 118A
election agent: see s 67

Penalty for sitting or voting where no return and declarations transmitted

85(1) If, in the case of any candidate, the return and declarations as to election expenses are not delivered before the expiry of the time limited for the purpose, that candidate shall not, after the expiry of that time, sit or vote in the House of Commons as member for the constituency for which the election was held until—
   (a) either that return and those declarations have been delivered, or
   (b) the date of the allowance of an authorised excuse for the failure to deliver that return and those declarations,
and if he sits or votes in contravention of this subsection he shall forfeit £100 for every day on which he so sits or votes.

(2)   In the application of subsection (1) above to a candidate at a local government election—

(a)   the reference to sitting or voting in the House of Commons for the constituency for which the election was held shall be taken as a reference to sitting or voting in the council for the local government area for which the election was held; and

(b)   £50 shall be substituted for £100 and, instead of civil proceedings for a penalty, summary proceedings may be instituted under the Magistrates' Courts Act 1980, or, in Scotland, in the sheriff court, and the person charged shall be liable on conviction to a fine not exceeding the amount of the penalty which would be recoverable in civil proceedings.

(2A) As respects Authority elections—

(a)   subsections (1) and (2) above shall not apply in relation to a candidate in an election of the Mayor of London (for which separate provision is made by section 85A below);

(b)   in the case of any other Authority election, the reference in subsection (2)(a) above to the council for the local government area for which the election was held shall be taken as a reference to the London Assembly; and

(c)   in the case of a candidate included in a list submitted under paragraph 5 of Schedule 2 to the 1999 Act (election of London members) by a registered political party, the references in subsection (1) above to the returns and declarations in respect of election expenses shall be taken as references to the declaration as to election expenses by the candidate.

(3)   Civil proceedings for a penalty under this section shall be commenced within the period of one year beginning with the day in respect of which the penalty is alleged to have been incurred.

(4)   For the purposes of subsection (3) above—

(a)   where the service or execution of legal process on or against the alleged offender is prevented by the absconding or concealment or act of the alleged offender, the issue of legal process shall be deemed to be a commencement of a proceeding; but,

(b)   where paragraph (a) does not apply, the service or execution of legal process on or against the alleged offender, and not its issue, shall be deemed to be the commencement of the proceeding.

(5)   Subsections (3) and (4) above do not apply in Scotland.

NOTES

Derivation
RPA 1949 s 71

Defined terms
the 1999 Act: s 203(1)
Authority election: s 203(1)
candidate: s 118A
constituency: Parliamentary Constituencies Act 1986 s 1(2)
date of the allowance of an authorised excuse: s 118
declaration as to election expenses: s 118
election: s 202(1)
election expenses: ss 90ZA, 90C, 90D, 118

election of the Mayor of London: s 203(1)
legal process: s 202(1)
local government area (E&W): ss 191(1), 203(1)
local government area (S): s 204(1)
local government election (E&W): s 203(1), (1A)
local government election (S): s 204(1)
registered political party: s 202(1)
return as to election expenses: s 118
sheriff (S): Interpretation Act 1978
vote: s 202(1)
voting: see "vote" s 202(1)

Disqualification where no return and declarations transmitted after election of Mayor of London

85A(1)   If, in the case of any candidate at an election of the Mayor of London, the return and declarations as to election expenses are not delivered before the expiry of the time limited for the purpose, the candidate shall, as respects that election, be disqualified from being elected or being the Mayor of London.

(2) Any application under section 86 below by such a candidate for relief in respect of a failure to deliver the return and declarations as to election expenses must be made within the period of 6 weeks following the day on which the time limited for their delivery expires.

(3) A disqualification under subsection (1) above shall not take effect unless or until—

    (a) the period specified in subsection (2) above for making an application for relief under section 86 below expires without such an application having been made; or

    (b) if such an application is made, the application—

        (i) is finally disposed of without relief being granted; or

        (ii) is abandoned or fails by reason of non-prosecution.

NOTES

Derivation
Greater London Authority Act 1999 s 17

declaration as to election expenses: s 118
election of the Mayor of London: s 203(1)
return as to election expenses: s 118

Defined terms
candidate: s 118A

Authorised excuses for failures as to return and declarations

86(1) A candidate or his election agent may apply for relief under this section to—

    (a) the High Court, except in relation to a local government election in Scotland;

    (b) an election court; or

    (c) the county court.

(1A) Where a person makes an application under this section he shall notify the Director of Public Prosecutions of the application and the Director or his assistant or any barrister, advocate, solicitor or authorised person duly appointed as the Director's representative may attend the hearing of the application and make representations at the hearing in respect of it.

(1B) In subsection (1A) "authorised person" means a person (other than a barrister or solicitor) who, for the purposes of the Legal Services Act 2007, is an authorised person in relation to an activity which constitutes the exercise of a right of audience (within the meaning of that Act).

(2) Relief under this section may be granted—

    (a) to a candidate, in respect of any failure to deliver the return and declarations as to election expenses, or any part of them, or in respect of any error or false statement in them; or

    (b) to an election agent, in respect of the failure to deliver the return and declarations which he was required to deliver, or any part of them, or in respect of any error or false statement in them.

(3) The application for relief may be made on the ground that the failure, error or false statement arose—

    (a) by reason of the applicant's illness; or

    (b) where the applicant is the candidate, by reason of the absence, death, illness or misconduct of his election agent or sub-agent or of any clerk or officer of such agent; or

    (c) where the applicant is the election agent, by reason of the death or illness of any prior election agent of the candidate, or of the absence, death, illness or misconduct of any sub-agent, clerk or officer of any election agent of the candidate; or

(d) by reason of inadvertence or any reasonable cause of a like nature,
and not by reason of any want of good faith on the applicant's part.

(4) The court may—
  (a) after such notice of the application in the constituency or local government area, as the case may be, as it considers fit, and
  (b) on production of such evidence of the grounds stated in the application and of the good faith of the application, and otherwise, as it considers fit,

make such order for allowing an authorised excuse for the failure, error or false statement as it considers just.

(5) Where it is proved to the court by the candidate—
  (a) that any act or omission of the election agent in relation to the return and declarations was without the sanction or connivance of the candidate, and
  (b) that the candidate took all reasonable means for preventing the act or omission,

the court shall relieve the candidate from the consequences of the act or omission of his election agent.

(6) An order under subsection (4) above may make the allowance conditional on the making of the return and declaration in a modified form or within an extended time, and upon the compliance with such other terms as to the court seem best calculated for carrying into effect the objects of this Part of this Act.

(7) An order under subsection (4) shall relieve the applicant for the order from any liability or consequences under this Act in respect of the matter excused by the order.

(8) The date of the order, or if conditions and terms are to be complied with, the date at which the applicant fully complies with them, is referred to in this Act as the date of the allowance of the excuse.

(9) *Repealed*

(10) Article 60 of the County Courts (Northern Ireland) Order 1980 (appeals from county courts) shall apply in relation to any order of a county court in Northern Ireland made by virtue of this section as it applies in relation to any such decree of a county court as is mentioned in paragraph (1) of that Article.

NOTES

Derivation
RPA 1949 s 74

Defined terms
candidate: s 118A
constituency: Parliamentary Constituencies Act 1986 s 1(2)
county court: Interpretation Act 1978 Sch 1
date of the allowance of the excuse: s 118
declaration as to election expenses: s 118
Director of Public Prosecutions (S): s 204(5)
Director of Public Prosecutions (NI): s 205(1)
election: s 202(1)

election agent: see s 67
election court: s 202(1)
election expenses: ss 90ZA, 90C, 90D, 118
High Court (E,W & NI): Interpretation Act 1978 Sch 1
local government area (E&W): ss 191(1), 203(1)
local government area (S): s 204(1)
local government election (S): s 204(1)
person: s 202(1)
return as to election expenses: s 118
sub-agent: ss 68(1), 202(1)

Court's power to require information from election agent or sub-agent

87(1) Where on an application under section 86 above it appears to the court that any person who is or has been an election agent or sub-agent has refused or failed to make such return, or to supply such particulars, as will enable the candidate and his election agent respectively to comply with the provisions of this Act as to the return or declarations as to election expenses, the court, before making an order under that section, shall order that person to attend before the court.

(2)   The court shall on the attendance of that person, unless he shows cause to the contrary, order him—

    (a)   to make the return and declaration, or

    (b)   to deliver a statement of the particulars required to be contained in the return, as the court considers just, within such time, to such person and in such manner as it may direct, or may order him to be examined with respect to the particulars.

(3)   If a person fails to comply with any order of the court under this section, the court may order him to pay a fine not exceeding the amount of the maximum fine to which he would be liable if at the time the order is made he were convicted of a summary offence on conviction of which he was liable to a fine of level 5 on the standard scale.

NOTES

Derivation
RPA 1949 s 75

Defined terms
candidate: s 118A
declaration as to election expenses: s 118
election agent: see s 67
election expenses: s 118

return as to election expenses: s 118
standard scale: Interpretation Act 1978 Sch 1
sub-agent: ss 68(1), 202(1)
summary offence (E&W only): Interpretation Act 1978 Sch 1

Duty of appropriate officer to forward returns and declarations to Electoral Commission

7A(1)   Where the appropriate officer receives any return or declaration under section 75, 81 or 82 above in respect of—

    (a)   a parliamentary election, or

    (b)   an election of the Mayor of London,

    he shall as soon as reasonably practicable after receiving the return or declaration deliver a copy of it to the Electoral Commission and, if so requested by the Commission, he shall also deliver to them a copy of any accompanying documents.

(2)   Where the appropriate officer receives any return or declaration under section 75, 81 or 82 in respect of any election other than one mentioned in subsection (1) above, he shall, if so requested by the Electoral Commission, deliver to them a copy of the return and any accompanying documents.

NOTES

Derivation
Political Parties, Elections and Referendums Act 2000
s 138

Defined terms
appropriate officer: ss 67(7), 118

election of the Mayor of London: s 203(1)
Electoral Commission: see Political Parties, Elections and Referendums Act 2000 s 1
parliamentary election: Interpretation Act 1978 Sch 1

Publication of time and place for inspection of returns and declarations

88   At a parliamentary election or an Authority election—

    (a)   the returning officer shall, within 10 days after the end of the time allowed for delivering to him returns as to election expenses, publish in not less than two newspapers circulating in the constituency or electoral area for which the election was held, and shall send to each of the election agents, a notice of the time and place at which the returns and declarations (including the accompanying documents) can be inspected; but

    (b)   if any return or declaration has not been received by the returning officer before the notice is despatched for publication, the notice shall so state, and a like notice about that return or declaration, if afterwards received, shall within 10 days after the receipt be published in like manner and sent to each of the election agents other than the agent who is in default or is agent for the candidate in default.

NOTES

Derivation
RPA 1969 s 8(5)

Defined terms
Authority election: s 203(1)
candidate: s 118A
constituency: Parliamentary Constituencies Act 1986
s 1(2)
declaration as to election expenses: s 118
election: s 202(1)

electoral area (E&W): ss 191(1), 203(1)
electoral area (S): s 204(1)
election agent: see s 67
election expenses s 118
notice: s 200
parliamentary election: Interpretation Act 1978 Sch 1
return as to election expenses: s 118
returning officer: see ss 24-27

Inspection of returns and declarations

89(1) Where the appropriate officer receives any return or declaration under section 75, 75A, 81 or 82 above he shall—

(a) as soon as reasonably practicable after receiving the return or declaration make a copy of it, and any accompanying documents, available for public inspection at his office, or some other convenient place chosen by him, for a period of two years beginning with the date when the return is received by him;

(b) if requested to do so by any person, and on payment of the prescribed fee, supply that person with a copy of the return or declaration and any accompanying documents.

(1A) If any such return contains a statement of donations in accordance with paragraph 10 of Schedule 2A to this Act, the appropriate officer shall secure that the copy of the statement made available for public inspection under subsection (1)(a) above or (as the case may be) supplied under subsection (1)(b) above does not include, in the case of any donation by an individual, the donor's address.

(2) After the expiry of those two years the appropriate officer—

(a) may cause those returns and declarations (including the accompanying documents) to be destroyed, or

(b) if the candidate or his election agent so require, shall return them to the candidate.

(3) Any returns or declarations delivered under section 75 or 75A shall be returned not to the candidate (if he or his election agent so require) but to the person delivering them, if he so requires.

NOTES

Derivation
RPA 1949 s 77

Subordinate legislation
Representation of the People (Amendment) Regulations 1990, SI 1990/520
Representation of the People (Northern Ireland) Regulations 2008, SI 2008/1741

Defined terms
appropriate officer: ss 67(7), 118
candidate: s 118A
election agent: see s 67
person: s 202(1)
prescribed: s 202(1)

Election expenses at elections where election agent not required

90(1) In relation to an election of parish councillors in England or of community councillors in Wales—

(a) section 76(1B) above and sections 90ZA(4) and 90C below have effect as if for the references to an election agent there were substituted references to any agent of the candidate;

(b) sections 71A to 75 and 78 to 89 above, and Schedule 2A to this Act, do not apply, and instead the provisions of Schedule 4 to this Act have effect but the form of declaration as to election expenses shall be that prescribed by rules under section 36 above relating to the election of parish or, as the case may be, community councillors, or a form to the like effect;

(c) section 76A(2) has effect as if it referred, in substitution for the provisions set out in paragraphs (a) to (c) of that subsection, to paragraph 3 of Schedule 4 to this Act.

(2) At an election under the local government Act which is not a local government election, sections 71A to 89 do not apply, and if a candidate at that election or any person on behalf of a candidate at that election knowingly pays any sum or incurs any expense, whether before, during or after that election, on account of or in respect of the conduct or management of the election he shall be guilty of an illegal practice.

NOTES

Derivation
RPA 1949 s 78
LGA 1972 s 42

Defined terms
candidate: s 118A
community councillors: see Local Government Act 1972 s 35
declaration as to election expenses: s 118
election: s 202(1)
election agent: see s 67
election expenses: s 118

election under the local government act (E&W): ss 191(1), 203(1A)
England: Interpretation Act 1978 Sch 1
local government Act (E&W): s 203(1)
local government Act (S): s 204(1)
local government election (E&W): ss 191(1), 203(1), (1A)
local government election (S): s 204(1)
parish councillors: see Local Government Act 1972 s 16
Wales: Interpretation Act 1978 Sch 1

Meaning of "election expenses"

90ZA(1) In this Part of this Act "election expenses" in relation to a candidate at an election means (subject to subsection (2) below and section 90C below) any expenses incurred at any time in respect of any matter specified in Part 1 of Schedule 4A which is used for the purposes of the candidate's election after the date when he becomes a candidate at the election.

(2) No election expenses are to be regarded as incurred by virtue of subsection (1) above or section 90C below in respect of any matter specified in Part 2 of Schedule 4A.

(3) In this section and in section 90C below, "for the purposes of the candidate's election" means with a view to, or otherwise in connection with, promoting or procuring the candidate's election at the election.

(4) For the purposes of this Part of this Act, election expenses are incurred by or on behalf of a candidate at an election if they are incurred—
(a) by the candidate or his election agent, or
(b) by any person authorised by the candidate or his election agent to incur expenses.

(5) A reference in this Part of this Act to a candidate at an election, in relation to election expenses, includes (where the context allows) a reference to a person who becomes a candidate at the election after the expenses are incurred.

(6) In this Part and in Part 3 of this Act, any reference (in whatever terms) to promoting or procuring a candidate's election at an election includes doing so by prejudicing the electoral prospects of another candidate at the election.

(7) Schedule 4A has effect.

(8) This section does not apply to a local government election in Scotland.

NOTES

Derivation
Electoral Administration Act 2006 s 27

Defined terms

candidate: s 118A
election: s 202(1)
election agent: see s 67
local government election (S): s 204(1)

person: s 202(1)

Scottish local government elections: meaning of "election expenses"

90ZB(1) This section applies in relation to a local government election in Scotland.

(2) In this Part of this Act, "election expenses", in relation to a candidate at such an election, means any expenses incurred at any time in respect of any matter specified in Part 1 of Schedule 4B which is used for the purposes of the candidate's election.

(3) For the purposes of subsection (2) above, it is immaterial whether any such matter is so used before or after the date when the candidate becomes a candidate at the election.

(4) No election expenses are to be regarded as incurred by virtue of subsection (2) above or section 90C below in respect of any matter specified in Part 2 of Schedule 4B.

(5) In this section and in section 90C below, "for the purposes of the candidate's election" means with a view to, or otherwise in connection with, promoting or procuring the candidate's election at the election.

(6) For the purposes of this Part of this Act so far as applying to a local government election in Scotland, election expenses are incurred by or on behalf of a candidate at the election if they are incurred—
    (a) by the candidate or his election agent; or
    (b) by any person authorised by the candidate or his election agent to incur expenses.

(7) In this Part of this Act so far as applying to a local government election in Scotland, any reference to election expenses incurred by or on behalf of a candidate at the election includes expenses—
    (a) which are incurred as mentioned in subsection (2) above before the date when he becomes a candidate at the election; but
    (b) which by virtue of that subsection and subsection (3) above fall to be regarded as election expenses.

(8) In this Part and in Part 3 of this Act so far as applying to a local government election in Scotland, any reference (in whatever terms) to promoting or procuring a candidate's election at an election includes doing so by prejudicing the electoral prospects of another candidate at the election.

NOTES
Application
This provision applies to Scotland only

Derivation
Local Electoral Administration and Registration Services (Scotland) Act 2006 s 17(1)

Defined terms
candidate: s 118
election expenses: s 118
local government election (S): s 204(1)

Property, goods, services etc provided free of charge or at a discount

90C(1) This section applies where, in the case of a candidate at an election—
    (a) either—
        (i) property or goods is or are transferred to the candidate or his election agent free of charge or at a discount of more than 10 per cent of the market value of the property or goods, or
        (ii) property, goods, services or facilities is or are provided for the use or benefit of the candidate free of charge or at a discount of more than 10 per

cent of the commercial rate for the use of the property or for the provision of the goods, services or facilities, and

    (b)   the property, goods, services or facilities is or are made use of by or on behalf of the candidate in circumstances such that, if any expenses were to be (or are) actually incurred by or on behalf of the candidate in respect of that use, they would be (or are) election expenses incurred by or on behalf of the candidate.

(2)   Where this section applies—

    (a)   an amount of election expenses determined in accordance with this section ("the appropriate amount") shall be treated, for the purposes of this Part of this Act, as incurred by the candidate, and

    (b)   the candidate's election agent shall make a declaration of that amount,

unless that amount is not more than £50.

This subsection has effect subject to Part 2 of Schedule 4A to this Act.

(3)   Where subsection (1)(a)(i) above applies, the appropriate amount is such proportion of either—

    (a)   the market value of the property or goods (where the property or goods is or are transferred free of charge), or

    (b)   the difference between the market value of the property or goods and the amount of expenses actually incurred by or on behalf of the candidate in respect of the property or goods (where the property or goods is or are transferred at a discount),

as is reasonably attributable to the use made of the property or goods as mentioned in subsection (1)(b) above.

(4)   Where subsection (1)(a)(ii) above applies, the appropriate amount is such proportion of either—

    (a)   the commercial rate for the use of the property or the provision of the goods, services or facilities (where the property, goods, services or facilities is or are provided free of charge), or

    (b)   the difference between that commercial rate and the amount of expenses actually incurred by or on behalf of the candidate in respect of the use of the property or the provision of the services or facilities (where the property, goods, services or facilities is or are provided at a discount),

as is reasonably attributable to the use made of the property, goods, services or facilities as mentioned in subsection (1)(b) above.

(5)   Where the services of an employee are made available by his employer for the use or benefit of a candidate, then for the purposes of this section the commercial rate for the provision of those services shall be the amount of the remuneration and allowances payable to the employee by his employer in respect of the period for which his services are so made available (but shall not include any amount in respect of any contributions or other payments for which the employer is liable in respect of the employee).

(6)   In this section "market value", in relation to any property or goods, means the price which might reasonably be expected to be paid for the property or goods on a sale in the open market; and paragraph 2(6)(a) of Schedule 2A to this Act shall apply with any necessary modifications for the purpose of determining, for the purposes of subsection (1) above, whether property or goods is or are transferred to a candidate or his election agent.

NOTES

Derivation

Political Parties, Elections and Referendums Act 2000 s 134

Defined terms

candidate: s 118A

election: s 202(1)
election agent: see s 67
election expenses: s 118

Modification of sections 90ZA and 90C

90D(1)   Sections 90ZA and 90C above shall have effect, in their application in relation to candidates at an election of London members of the London Assembly at an ordinary election, subject to the following modifications.

(2)   In relation to any such candidates included in a list of candidates submitted by a registered political party in connection with the election—
    (a)   references to anything done by or on behalf of, or in relation to, a candidate at the election shall be construed as a reference to any such thing done by or on behalf of, or in relation to, all or any of the candidates on the list; and
    (b)   "for the purposes of the candidate's election" shall (instead of having the meaning given by section 90ZA(3) above) be construed as meaning with a view to, or otherwise in connection with promoting or procuring electoral success for the party, that is to say, the return at the election of all or any of the candidates on the list.

(3)   Section 90ZA above shall have effect with the substitution of the following subsection for subsection (6)—
    "(6) In this Part, and in Part III of this Act, any reference (in whatever form) to promoting or procuring a candidate's election at an election, or to promoting or procuring electoral success for a party, includes doing so by prejudicing the electoral prospects of other candidates or parties at the election."

NOTES
Derivation
    Political Parties, Elections and Referendums Act 2000
    s 134

election: s 202(1)
London member: s 203(1)
registered political party: s 202(1)

Defined terms
    candidate: s 118A

Publicity at parliamentary elections

Candidate's right to send election address post free

91(1)   A candidate at a parliamentary election is, subject to such reasonable terms and conditions as the universal postal service provider concerned may specify, entitled to send free of any charge for postage which would otherwise be made by a universal postal service provider either—
    (a)   one unaddressed postal communication, containing matter relating to the election only and not exceeding 60 grammes in weight, to each place in the constituency which, in accordance with those terms and conditions, constitutes a delivery point for the purposes of this subsection; or
    (b)   one such postal communication addressed to each elector.

(2)   He is also, subject as mentioned above, entitled to send free of any such charge for postage as mentioned above to each person entered in the list of proxies for the election one such communication as mentioned above for each appointment in respect of which that person is so entered.

(2A)   The candidate may require the returning officer to make arrangements with the universal postal service provider for communications under subsection (1)(b) to be sent to persons who have anonymous entries in the register.

(2B)   Arrangements under subsection (2A) shall be such as to ensure that it is not disclosed to any other person that the addressee of such a communication has an anonymous entry.

(3)   A person shall not be deemed to be a candidate for the purposes of this section unless he is shown as standing nominated in the statement of persons nominated, but until the publication of that statement any person who declares himself to be a candidate shall be entitled to exercise the right of free postage conferred by this section if he gives such security as may be required by the universal postal service provider concerned for the payment of postage should he not be shown as standing nominated as mentioned above.

(4)   For the purposes of this section "elector"—
    (a)   means a person who is registered in the register of parliamentary electors for the constituency on the last day for publication of notice of the election; and
    (b)   includes a person then shown in that register (or, in the case of a person who has an anonymous entry in the register, in the record of anonymous entries) as below voting age if (but only if) it appears from the register (or from the record) that he will be of voting age on the day fixed for the poll.

(5)   *Repealed*

NOTES

Derivation
RPA 1949 s 79

Defined terms
anonymous entry: s 202(1)
 constituency: Parliamentary Constituencies Act 1986
 s 1(2)
candidate: s 118A (and sub-s (3) of this section)

the list of proxies: s 202(1)
parliamentary election: Interpretation Act 1978 Sch 1
record of anonymous entries: s 202(1)
returning officer: see ss 24–27
universal postal service provider: s 202(1)

Broadcasting from outside United Kingdom

92(1)   No person shall, with intent to influence persons to give or refrain from giving their votes at a parliamentary or local government election, include, or aid, abet, counsel or procure the inclusion of, any matter relating to the election in any programmes service (within the meaning of the Broadcasting Act 1990) provided from a place outside the United Kingdom otherwise than in pursuance of arrangements made with—
    (a)   the British Broadcasting Corporation;
    (b)   Sianel Pedwar Cymru; or
    (c)   the holder of any licence granted by the Office of Communications,
    for the reception and re-transmission of that matter by that body or the holder of that licence.

(2)   An offence under this section shall be an illegal practice, but the court before whom a person is convicted of an offence under this section may, if they think it just in the special circumstances of the case, mitigate or entirely remit any incapacity imposed by virtue of section 173 below.

(3)   Where any act or omission of an association or body of persons, corporate or unincorporate, is an illegal practice under this section, any person who at the time of the act or omission was a director, general manager, secretary or other similar officer of the association or body, or was purporting to act in any such capacity, shall be deemed to be guilty of the illegal practice, unless he proves—
    (a)   that the act or omission took place without his consent or connivance; and
    (b)   that he exercised all such diligence to prevent the commission of the illegal practice as he ought to have exercised having regard to the nature of his functions in that capacity and to all the circumstances.

NOTES
Derivation
RPA 1949 s 80

Defined terms
election: s 202(1)
local government election (E&W): ss 191(1), 203(1), (1A)

local government election (S): s 204(1)
person: s 202(1)
programme service: Broadcasting Act 1990 s 201
vote: s 202(1)

Broadcasting of local items during election period

93(1) Each broadcasting authority shall adopt a code of practice with respect to the participation of candidates at a parliamentary or local government election in items about the constituency or electoral area in question which are included in relevant services during the election period.

(2) The code for the time being adopted by a broadcasting authority under this section shall be either—
(a) a code drawn up by that authority, whether on their own or jointly with one or more other broadcasting authorities, or
(b) a code drawn up by one or more other such authorities;
and a broadcasting authority shall from time to time consider whether the code for the time being so adopted by them should be replaced by a further code falling within paragraph (a) or (b).

(3) Before drawing up a code under this section a broadcasting authority shall have regard to any views expressed by the Electoral Commission for the purposes of this subsection; and any such code may make different provision for different cases.

(4) The Office of Communications shall do all that they can to secure that the code for the time being adopted by them under this section is observed in the provision of relevant services; and the British Broadcasting Corporation and Sianel Pedwar Cymru shall each observe in the provision of relevant services the code so adopted by them.

(5) For the purposes of subsection (1) "the election period", in relation to an election, means the period beginning—
(a) (if a parliamentary general election) with the date of the dissolution of Parliament,
(b) (if a parliamentary by-election) with the date of the issue of the writ for the election or any earlier date on which a certificate of the vacancy is notified in the London Gazette in accordance with the Recess Elections Act 1975, or
(c) (if a local government election) with the last date for publication of notice of the election,
and ending with the close of the poll.

(6) In this section—
"broadcasting authority" means the British Broadcasting Corporation, the Office of Communications or Sianel Pedwar Cymru;
"candidate", in relation to an election, means a candidate standing nominated at the election or included in a list of candidates submitted in connection with it;
"relevant services"—
(a) in relation to the British Broadcasting Corporation or Sianel Pedwar Cymru, means services broadcast by that body;
(b) in relation to the Office of Communications, means services licensed under Part 1 or 3 of the Broadcasting Act 1990 or Part 1 or 2 of the Broadcasting Act 1996.

NOTES
Derivation
Political Parties, Elections and Referendums Act 2000

s 144

Defined terms
  candidate: s 118A
  constituency: Parliamentary Constituencies Act 1986
  s 1(2)
  election: s 202(1)
  electoral area (E&W): ss 191(1), 203(1)
  electoral area (S): s 204(1)

Electoral Commission: see Political Parties, Elections
and Referendums Act 2000 s 1
local government election (E&W): s 203(1), (1A)
local government election (S): s 204(1)

Imitation poll cards

94(1) No person shall for the purpose of promoting or procuring the election of any candidate at a parliamentary election or a local government election to which this section applies issue any poll card or document so closely resembling an official poll card as to be calculated to deceive, and subsections (2) and (3) of section 92 above apply as if an offence under this section were an offence under that section.

(2) This section applies to any local government election in relation to which rules made under section 36 or, in Scotland, section 42 above require an official poll card to be sent to electors in a form prescribed by the rules.

NOTES
Derivation
  RPA 1949 s 81

Defined terms
  candidate: s 118A
  election: s 202(1)
  local government election (E&W): ss 191(1), 203(1), (1A)

local government election (S): s 204(1)
parliamentary election: Interpretation Act 1978 Sch 1
person: s 202(1)
promoting or procuring a candidate's election: s
90ZA(6)

Election meetings

Schools and rooms for parliamentary election meetings

95(1) Subject to the provisions of this section, a candidate at a parliamentary election is entitled for the purpose of holding public meetings in furtherance of his candidature to the use free of charge at reasonable times between the receipt of the writ and the day preceding the date of the poll of—
  (a) a suitable room in the premises of a school to which this section applies;
  (b) any meeting room to which this section applies.

(2) This section applies—
  (a) in England and Wales, to community, foundation and voluntary schools of which the premises are situated in the constituency or an adjoining constituency, and
  (b) in Scotland, to any school of which the premises are so situated, not being an independent school within the meaning of the Education (Scotland) Act 1980,
  but a candidate is not entitled under this section to the use of a room in school premises outside the constituency if there is a suitable room in other premises in the constituency which are reasonably accessible from the same parts of the constituency as those outside and are premises of a school to which this section applies.

(3) This section applies to meeting rooms situated in the constituency, the expense of maintaining which is payable wholly or mainly out of public funds or out of any rate, or by a body whose expenses are so payable.

(4) Where a room is used for a meeting in pursuance of the rights conferred by this section, the person by whom or on whose behalf the meeting is convened—
  (a) shall defray any expenses incurred in preparing, warming, lighting and cleaning the room and providing attendance for the meeting and restoring the room to its usual condition after the meeting; and

(b) shall defray any damage done to the room or the premises in which it is situated, or to the furniture, fittings or apparatus in the room or premises.

(5) A candidate is not entitled to exercise the rights conferred by this section except on reasonable notice; and this section does not authorise any interference with the hours during which a room in school premises is used for educational purposes, or any interference with the use of a meeting room either for the purposes of the person maintaining it or under a prior agreement for its letting for any purpose.

(6) The provisions of Schedule 5 to this Act have effect with respect to the rights conferred by this section and the arrangements to be made for their exercise.

(7) For the purposes of this section (except those of paragraph (b) of subsection (4) above), the premises of a school shall not be taken to include any private dwelling, and in this section—

(a) the expression "meeting room" means any room which it is the practice to let for public meetings; and

(b) the expression "room" includes a hall, gallery or gymnasium.

(8) This section does not apply to Northern Ireland.

NOTES

Derivation
  RPA 1949 s 83

Defined terms
  candidate: s 118A
  constituency: Parliamentary Constituencies Act 1986

s 1(2)
dwelling: s 202(1)
election: s 202(1)
England: Interpretation Act 1978 Sch 1
parliamentary election: Interpretation Act 1978 Sch 1
Wales: Interpretation Act 1978 Sch 1

Schools and rooms for local election meetings

96(1) Subject to the provisions of this section, a candidate at a local government election is entitled for the purpose of holding public meetings to promote or procure the giving of votes at that election—

(i) for himself, or

(ii) if he is a candidate included in a list of candidates submitted by a registered political party at an election of the London members of the London Assembly at an ordinary election, towards the return of candidates on that list,

to the use free of charge at reasonable times between the last day on which notice of the election may be published in accordance with rules made under section 36 or, in Scotland, section 42 above and the day preceding the day of election of—

(a) a suitable room in the premises of a school to which this section applies; or

(b) a meeting room to which this section applies.

(2) This section applies—

(a) in England and Wales, to a community, foundation or voluntary school situated in the electoral area for which the candidate is standing (or, if there is no such school in the area, in any such school in an adjacent electoral area) or in a parish or community, as the case may be, in part comprised in that electoral area; and

(b) in Scotland, to any school (not being an independent school within the meaning of the Education (Scotland) Act 1980) situated in the electoral area for which the candidate is standing (or, if there is no such school in the area, in any such school in an adjacent electoral area).

(3) This section applies—

(a) in England and Wales, to any meeting room situated in the electoral area for which the candidate is standing or in a parish or community, as the case may be, in part comprised in that electoral area, the expense of maintaining which is payable wholly or mainly out of public funds or out of any rate, or by a body whose expenses are so payable;

    (b) in Scotland, to any meeting room the expense of maintaining which is payable by a local authority.

(4) Subsections (4), (5) and (7) of section 95 above and paragraph 1(1) of Schedule 5 to this Act shall apply for the purposes of this section as they apply for the purposes of that section, and any person stating himself to be, or to be authorised by, a candidate at a local government election in respect of an electoral area which falls (or partly falls) within a constituency, or his election agent, shall be entitled to inspect the lists prepared under Schedule 5 to this Act in relation to the constituency or a copy of them at all reasonable hours during the period beginning with the day on which notice of the election is published and ending with the day preceding the day of election.

NOTES

Derivation
  RPA 1949 s 83

Defined terms
  candidate: s 118A
  community: see Local Government Act 1972 s 27
  constituency: Parliamentary Constituencies Act 1986
  s 1(2)
  election: s 202(1)
  election agent: see s 67
  electoral area (E&W): ss 191(1), 203(1)
  electoral area (S): s 204(1)
  England: Interpretation Act 1978 Sch 1

local authority (S): s 204(1)
local government election (E&W): s 203(1), (1A)
local government election (S): s 204(1)
London member: s 203(1)
meeting room: ss 95(7), 96(4)
parish: see Local Government Act 1972 s 14
registered political party: s 202(1)
registered political party submitting a list of candidates to be London members: s 203(1B)
room: ss 95(7), 96(4)
vote: s 202(1)
Wales: Interpretation Act 1978 Sch 1

Disturbances at election meetings

97(1) A person who at a lawful public meeting to which this section applies acts, or incites others to act, in a disorderly manner for the purpose of preventing the transaction of the business for which the meeting was called together shall be guilty of an illegal practice.

(2) This section applies to—

    (a) a political meeting held in any constituency between the date of the issue of a writ for the return of a member of Parliament for the constituency and the date at which a return to the writ is made;

    (b) a meeting held with reference to a local government election in the electoral area for that election in the period beginning with the last date on which notice of the election may be published in accordance with rules made under section 36 or, in Scotland, section 42 above and ending with the day of election.

(3) If a constable reasonably suspects any person of committing an offence under subsection (1) above, he may if requested so to do by the chairman of the meeting require that person to declare to him immediately his name and address and, if that person refuses or fails so to declare his name and address or gives a false name and address, he shall be liable on summary conviction to a fine not exceeding level 1 on the standard scale,
  This subsection does not apply in Northern Ireland.

NOTES

Derivation
  RPA 1949 s 84

Defined terms
  constituency: Parliamentary Constituencies Act 1986
  s 1(2)
  electoral area (E&W): ss 191(1), 203(1)

electoral area (S): s 204(1)
local government election (E&W): ss 191(1), 203(1), (1A)
local government election (S): s 204(1)
standard scale: Interpretation Act 1978 Sch 1
summary conviction (NI only): Interpretation Act 1978
Sch 1

98   *Repealed*

Agency by election officials and canvassing by police officers

Officials not to act for candidates

99(1)   If—

- (a)   any returning officer at a parliamentary or local government election, or
- (b)   any officer or clerk appointed under the parliamentary elections rules, or the rules under section 36 or section 42 above, as the case may be, or
- (c)   any partner or clerk of any such person,

acts as a candidate's agent in the conduct or management of the election, he shall be guilty of an offence, but nothing in this subsection prevents a candidate from acting as his own election agent.

(2)   A person guilty of an offence under this section shall be liable on summary conviction to a fine not exceeding level 4 on the standard scale.

NOTES

Derivation
  RPA 1949 s 86

Defined terms
  candidate: s 118A
  election: s 202(1)
  election agent: see s 67
  local government election (E&W): ss 191(1), 203(1), (1A)

local government election (S): s 204(1)
parliamentary election: Interpretation Act 1978 Sch 1
parliamentary elections rules: s 202(1)
returning officer: see ss 24-27
standard scale: Interpretation Act 1978 Sch 1
summary conviction (NI only): Interpretation Act 1978 Sch 1

Illegal canvassing by police officers

100(1)   No member of a police force shall by word, message, writing or in any other manner, endeavour to persuade any person to give, or dissuade any person from giving, his vote, whether as an elector or as proxy—

- (a)   at any parliamentary election for a constituency, or
- (b)   at any local government election for any electoral area,

wholly or partly within the police area.

(2)   A person acting in contravention of subsection (1) above shall be liable on summary conviction to a fine not exceeding level 3 on the standard scale, but nothing in that subsection shall subject a member of a police force to any penalty for anything done in the discharge of his duty as a member of the force.

(3)   In this section references to a member of a police force and to a police area are to be taken in relation to Northern Ireland as references to a member of the Police Service of Northern Ireland and to Northern Ireland.

NOTES

Derivation
  RPA 1949 s 87

Defined terms
  constituency: Parliamentary Constituencies Act 1986 s 1(2)
  election: s 202(1)
  elector: s 202(1)
  electoral area (E&W): ss 191(1), 203(1)

electoral area (S): s 204(1)
local government election (E&W): ss 191(1), 203(1), (1A)
local government election (S): s 204(1)
parliamentary election: Interpretation Act 1978 Sch 1
standard scale: Interpretation Act 1978 Sch 1
summary conviction (NI only): Interpretation Act 1978 Sch 1
vote: s 202(1)
writing: Interpretation Act 1978 Sch 1

Conveyance of voters to and from poll

101   *Repealed*

102   *Repealed*

103   *Repealed*

104   *Repealed*

105   *Repealed*

Other illegal practices, payments, employments or hirings

False statements as to candidates

106(1)   A person who, or any director of any body or association corporate which—

    (a)   before or during an election,

    (b)   for the purpose of affecting the return of any candidate at the election,

makes or publishes any false statement of fact in relation to the candidate's personal character or conduct shall be guilty of an illegal practice, unless he can show that he had reasonable grounds for believing, and did believe, the statement to be true.

  (2)   A candidate shall not be liable nor shall his election be avoided for any illegal practice under subsection (1) above committed by his agent other than his election agent unless—

    (a)   it can be shown that the candidate or his election agent has authorised or consented to the committing of the illegal practice by the other agent or has paid for the circulation of the false statement constituting the illegal practice; or

    (b)   an election court find and report that the election of the candidate was procured or materially assisted in consequence of the making or publishing of such false statements.

  (3)   A person making or publishing any false statement of fact as mentioned above may be restrained by interim or perpetual injunction by the High Court or the county court from any repetition of that false statement or of a false statement of a similar character in relation to the candidate and, for the purpose of granting an interim injunction, prima facie proof of the falsity of the statement shall be sufficient.

  (4)   *Repealed*

  (5)   Any person who, before or during an election, knowingly publishes a false statement of a candidate's withdrawal at the election for the purpose of promoting or procuring the election of another candidate shall be guilty of an illegal practice.

  (6)   A candidate shall not be liable, nor shall his election be avoided, for an illegal practice under subsection (5) above committed by his agent other than his election agent.

  (7)   In the application of this section to an election where a candidate is not required to have an election agent, references to an election agent shall be omitted and the reference in subsection (6) above to an illegal practice committed by an agent of the candidate shall be taken as a reference to an illegal practice committed without the candidate's knowledge and consent.

  (8)   *Repealed*

  (9)   Article 60 of the County Courts (Northern Ireland) Order 1980 (appeals from county courts) shall apply in relation to any order of a county court in Northern Ireland made by virtue of subsection (3) above as it applies in relation to any such decree of a county court as is mentioned in paragraph (1) of that Article.

NOTES

Derivation
RPA 1949 s 91

Defined terms
candidate: s 118A
county court: Interpretation Act 1978 Sch 1

election: s 202(1)
election agent: see s 67
election court: s 202(1)
High Court (E, W & NI): Interpretation Act 1978 Sch 1
High Court (S): s 204(3)
injunction (S): s 204(6)

person: s 202(1)   report (S): s 204(7)
promoting or procuring a candidate's election: s 90ZA(6)

Corrupt withdrawal from candidature

107   Any person who corruptly induces or procures any other person to withdraw from being a candidate at an election, in consideration of any payment or promise of payment, and any person withdrawing in pursuance of the inducement or procurement, shall be guilty of an illegal payment.

NOTES

Derivation
RPA 1949 s 92

Defined terms

candidate: s 118A
election: s 202(1)
payment: s 118
person: s 202(1)

108   *Repealed*

Payments for exhibition of election notices

109(1)   No payment or contract for payment shall for the purpose of promoting or procuring the election of a candidate at an election be made to an elector or his proxy on account of the exhibition of, or the use of any house, land, building or premises for the exhibition of, any address, bill or notice, unless—

    (a)   it is the ordinary business of the elector or proxy as an advertising agent to exhibit for payment bills and advertisements; and

    (b)   the payment or contract is made in the ordinary course of that business.

(2)   If any payment or contract for payment is knowingly made in contravention of this section either before, during or after an election—

    (a)   the person making the payment or contract, and

    (b)   if he knew it to be in contravention of this Act, any person receiving the or being a party to the contract,

shall be guilty of an illegal practice.

NOTES

Derivation
RPA 1949 s 94

Defined terms
candidate: s 118A
election: s 202(1)
elector: s 202(1)

land: Interpretation Act 1978 Sch 1
payment: s 118
person: s 202(1)
promoting or procuring a candidate's election: s 90ZA(6)

Details to appear on election publications

110(1)   This section applies to any material which can reasonably be regarded as intended to promote or procure the election of a candidate at an election (whether or not it can be so regarded as intended to achieve any other purpose as well).

(2)   No material to which this section applies shall be published unless—

    (a)   in the case of material which is, or is contained in, such a document as is mentioned in subsection (4), (5) or (6) below, the requirements of that subsection are complied with; or

    (b)   in the case of any other material, any requirements failing to be complied with in relation to the material by virtue of regulations under subsection (7) below are complied with.

(3)   For the purposes of subsections (4) to (6) below the following details are "the relevant details" in the case of any material falling within subsection (2)(a) above, namely—

    (a)   the name and address of the printer of the document;

    (b)   the name and address of the promoter of the material; and

    (c)   the name and address of any person on behalf of whom the material is being published (and who is not the promoter).

(4)   Where the material is a document consisting (or consisting principally) of a single side of printed matter, the relevant details must appear on the face of the document.

(5)   Where the material is a printed document other than one to which subsection (4) above applies, the relevant details must appear either on the first or the last page of the document.

(6)   Where the material is an advertisement contained in a newspaper or periodical—

    (a)   the name and address of the printer of the newspaper or periodical must appear either on its first or last page; and

    (b)   the relevant details specified in subsection (3)(b) and (c) above must be included in the advertisement.

(7)   The Secretary of State may, after consulting the Electoral Commission, by regulations make provision for and in connection with the imposition of requirements as to the inclusion in material falling within subsection (2)(b) above of the following details, namely—

    (a)   the name and address of the promoter of the material; and

    (b)   the name and address of any person on behalf of whom the material is being published (and who is not the promoter).

(8)   Regulations under subsection (7) above may in particular specify—

    (a)   the manner and form in which such details must be included in any such material for the purpose of complying with any such requirement;

    (b)   circumstances in which—

        (i)   any such requirement does not have to be complied with by a person of any description specified in the regulations, or

        (ii)   a breach of any such requirement by a person of any description so specified is not to result in the commission of an offence under this section by that person or by a person of any other such description;

    (c)   circumstances in which material is, or is not, to be taken for the purposes of the regulations to be published or (as the case may be) published by a person of any description so specified.

(9)   Where any material falling within subsection (2)(a) above is published in contravention of subsection (2), then (subject to subsections (11) and (12) below)—

    (a)   the promoter of the material,

    (b)   any other person by whom the material is so published, and

    (c)   the printer of the document,

shall be guilty of an offence and liable on summary conviction to a fine not exceeding level 5 on the standard scale.

(10)   Where any material falling within subsection (2)(b) above is published in contravention of subsection (2), then (subject to regulations made by virtue of subsection (8)(b) above and to subsections (11) and (12) below)—

    (a)   the promoter of the material, and

    (b)   any other person by whom the material is so published,

shall be guilty of an offence and liable on summary conviction to a fine not exceeding level 5 on the standard scale.

(11)   It shall be a defence for a person charged with an offence under this section to prove—

    (a)   that the contravention of subsection (2) above arose from circumstances beyond his control; and

    (b)   that he took all reasonable steps, and exercised all due diligence, to ensure that that contravention would not arise.

(12) Where a candidate or his election agent would (apart from this subsection) be guilty of an offence under subsection (9) or (10) above, he shall instead be guilty of an illegal practice.

(13) In this section—

"print" means print by whatever means, and "printer" shall be construed accordingly;

"the promoter", in relation to any material to which this section applies, means the person causing the material to be published;

"publish" means make available to the public at large, or any section of the public, in whatever form and by whatever means.

(14) For the purpose of determining whether any material is material such as is mentioned in subsection (1) above, it is immaterial that it does not expressly mention the name of any candidate.

NOTES

Application
This does not apply to local government elections in Scotland

Derivation
RPA 1949 s 95

Defined terms
candidate: s 118A
election: s 202(1)
election agent: see s 67

Electoral Commission: see Political Parties, Elections and Referendums Act 2000 s 1
promoting or procuring a candidate's election: s 90ZA(6)
standard scale: Interpretation Act 1978 Sch 1
summary conviction (NI only): Interpretation Act 1978 Sch 1

Scottish local government elections: details to appear on election publications

110A(1) This section applies to any material which can reasonably be regarded as intended to promote or procure the election of a candidate at a local government election in Scotland (whether or not it can be so regarded as intended to achieve any other purpose as well).

(2) No material to which this section applies is to be published unless—

(a) in the case of material which is, or is contained in, such a document as is mentioned in subsection (4), (5) or (6) below, the requirements of that subsection are complied with; or

(b) in the case of any other material, any requirements falling to be complied with in relation to the material by virtue of regulations under subsection (7) below are complied with.

(3) For the purposes of subsections (4) to (6) below the following details are "the relevant details" in the case of any material falling within subsection (2)(a) above, namely—

(a) the name and address of the printer of the document;

(b) the name and address of the promoter of the material; and

(c) the name and address of any person on whose behalf the material is being published (and who is not the promoter).

(4) Where the material is a document consisting (or consisting principally) of a single side of printed matter, the relevant details must appear on the face of the document.

(5) Where the material is a printed document other than one to which subsection (4) above applies, the relevant details must appear on either the first or the last page of the document.

(6) Where the material is an advertisement contained in a newspaper or periodical—

(a) the name and address of the printer of the newspaper or periodical must appear on either its first or last page; and

(b) the relevant details specified in subsection (3)(b) and (c) above must be included in the advertisement.

(7) The Scottish Ministers may by regulations make provision for and in connection with the imposition of requirements as to the inclusion in material falling within subsection (2)(b) above of the following details, namely—

    (a) the name and address of the promoter of the material; and

    (b) the name and address of any person on whose behalf the material is being published (and who is not the promoter).

(8) Regulations under subsection (7) above may, in particular, specify—

    (a) the manner and form in which such details are to be included in any such material for the purpose of complying with any such requirement;

    (b) circumstances in which—

        (i) any such requirement does not have to be complied with by a person of any description specified in the regulations; or

        (ii) a breach of any such requirement by a person of any description so specified is not to result in the commission of an offence under this section by that person or by a person of any other such description;

    (c) circumstances in which material is, or is not, to be taken for the purposes of the regulations to be published or (as the case may be) published by a person of any description so specified.

(9) Regulations under subsection (7) may contain such incidental, supplemental, saving or transitional provision as the Scottish Ministers think fit.

(10) A statutory instrument containing regulations under subsection (7) above is subject to annulment in pursuance of a resolution of the Scottish Parliament.

(11) Where any material falling within subsection (2)(a) above is published in contravention of subsection (2), then (subject to subsections (13) and (14) below)—

    (a) the promoter of the material;

    (b) any other person by whom the material is so published; and

    (c) the printer of the document,

shall be guilty of an offence and liable on summary conviction to a fine not exceeding level 5 on the standard scale.

(12) Where any material falling within subsection (2)(b) above is published in contravention of subsection (2), then (subject to regulations made by virtue of subsection (8)(b) above and to subsections (13) and (14) below)—

    (a) the promoter of the material; and

    (b) any other person by whom the material is so published,

shall be guilty of an offence and liable on summary conviction to a fine not exceeding level 5 on the standard scale.

(13) It shall be a defence for a person charged with an offence under this section to prove—

    (a) that the contravention of subsection (2) above arose from circumstances beyond his control; and

    (b) that he took all reasonable steps, and exercised all due diligence, to ensure that that contravention would not arise.

(14) Where a candidate or his election agent would (apart from this subsection) be guilty of an offence under subsection (11) or (12) above, he shall instead be guilty of an illegal practice.

(15) In this section—

    "print" means print by whatever means, and "printer" shall be construed accordingly;

"the promoter", in relation to any material to which this section applies, means the person causing the material to be published;

"publish" means make available to the public at large, or any section of the public, in whatever form and by whatever means.

(16) For the purpose of determining whether any material is material such as is mentioned in subsection (1) above, it is immaterial that it does not expressly mention the name of any candidate.

NOTES
Derivation
Local Electoral Administration and Registration Services (Scotland) Act 2006 s 29

Defined terms
candidate: s 118A
election: s 202(1)
election agent: see s 67
local government election (S): s 204(1)

person: s 202(1)
promoting or procuring a candidate's election: s 90ZA(6)
standard scale: Interpretation Act 1978 Sch 1
summary conviction (NI only): Interpretation Act 1978 Sch 1

Prohibition of paid canvassers

111 If a person is, either before, during or after an election, engaged or employed for payment or promise of payment as a canvasser for the purpose of promoting or procuring a candidate's election—

(a) the person so engaging or employing him, and

(b) the person so engaged or employed,

shall be guilty of illegal employment.

NOTES
Derivation
RPA 1949 s 96

Defined terms
candidate: s 118A
election: s 202(1)

payment: s 118
person: s 202(1)
promoting or procuring a candidate's election: s 90ZA(6)

Providing money for illegal purposes

112 Where a person knowingly provides money—

(a) for any payment which is contrary to the provisions of this Act, or

(b) for any expenses incurred in excess of the maximum amount allowed by this Act, or

(c) for replacing any money expended in any such payment or expenses,

except where the payment or the incurring of the expenses may have been previously allowed in pursuance of section 167 below to be an exception, that person shall be guilty of an illegal payment.

NOTES
Derivation
RPA 1949 s 98

Defined terms
money: s 118

payment: s 118
person: s 202(1)

Bribery, treating and undue influence

Bribery

113 (1) A person shall be guilty of a corrupt practice if he is guilty of bribery.

(2) A person shall be guilty of bribery if he, directly or indirectly, by himself or by any other person on his behalf—

   (a) gives any money or procures any office to or for any voter or to or for any other person on behalf of any voter or to or for any other person in order to induce any voter to vote or refrain from voting, or

   (b) corruptly does any such act as mentioned above on account of any voter having voted or refrained from voting, or

   (c) makes any such gift or procurement as mentioned above to or for any person in order to induce that person to procure, or endeavour to procure, the return of any person at an election or the vote of any voter,

or if upon or in consequence of any such gift or procurement as mentioned above he procures or engages, promises or endeavours to procure the return of any person at an election or the vote of any voter.

For the purposes of this subsection—

   (i) references to giving money include references to giving, lending, agreeing to give or lend, offering, promising, or promising to procure or endeavour to procure any money or valuable consideration; and

   (ii) references to procuring any office include references to giving, procuring, agreeing to give or procure, offering, promising, or promising to procure or to endeavour to procure any office, place or employment; and

   (iii) references to procuring the return of any person at an election include, in the case of an election of the London members of the London Assembly at an ordinary election, references to procuring the return of candidates on a list of candidates submitted by a registered political party for the purposes of that election.

(3) A person shall be guilty of bribery if he advances or pays or causes to be paid any money to or for the use of any other person with the intent that that money or any part of it shall be expended in bribery at any election or knowingly pays or causes to be paid any money to any person in discharge or repayment of any money wholly or in part expended in bribery at any election.

(4) The foregoing provisions of this section shall not extend or be construed to extend to any money paid or agreed to be paid for or on account of any legal expenses incurred in good faith at or concerning an election.

(5) A voter shall be guilty of bribery if before or during an election he directly or indirectly by himself or by any other person on his behalf receives, agrees, or contracts for any money, gift, loan or valuable consideration, office, place or employment for himself or for any other person for voting or agreeing to vote or for refraining or agreeing to refrain from voting.

(6) A person shall be guilty of bribery if after an election he directly or indirectly by himself or by any other person on his behalf receives any money or valuable consideration on account of any person having voted or refrained from voting or having induced any other person to vote or refrain from voting.

(7) In this section the expression

   "voter" includes any person who has or claims to have a right to vote;.

NOTES

Derivation
RPA 1949 s 99

Defined terms
election: s 202(1)
London member: s 203(1)
payment: s 185

person: s 202(1)
registered political party: s 202(1)
registered political party submitting a list of candidates to be London members: s 203(1B)
vote: s 202(1)
voter: s 202(1)
voting: see "vote" s 202(1)

Treating

114(1) A person shall be guilty of a corrupt practice if he is guilty of treating.

(2) A person shall be guilty of treating if he corruptly, by himself or by any other person, either before, during or after an election, directly or indirectly gives or provides, or pays wholly or in part the expense of giving or providing, any meat, drink, entertainment or provision to or for any person—

(a) for the purpose of corruptly influencing that person or any other person to vote or refrain from voting; or

(b) on account of that person or any other person having voted or refrained from voting, or being about to vote or refrain from voting.

(3) Every elector or his proxy who corruptly accepts or takes any such meat, drink, entertainment or provision shall also be guilty of treating.

NOTES

Derivation
RPA 1983 s 100

Defined terms
election: s 202(1)
elector: s 202(1)

person: s 202(1)
vote: s 202(1)
voting: see "vote" s 202(1)

Undue influence

115(1) A person shall be guilty of a corrupt practice if he is guilty of undue influence.

(2) A person shall be guilty of undue influence—

(a) if he, directly or indirectly, by himself or by any other person on his behalf, makes use of or threatens to make use of any force, violence or restraint, or inflicts or threatens to inflict, by himself or by any other person, any temporal or spiritual injury, damage, harm or loss upon or against any person in order to induce or compel that person to vote or refrain from voting, or on account of that person having voted or refrained from voting; or

(b) if, by abduction, duress or any fraudulent device or contrivance, he impedes or prevents, or intends to impede or prevent, the free exercise of the franchise of an elector or proxy for an elector, or so compels, induces or prevails upon, or intends so to compel, induce or prevail upon, an elector or proxy for an elector either to vote or to refrain from voting.

NOTES

Derivation
RPA 1983 s 101

Defined terms
elector: s 202(1)

person: s 202(1)
vote: s 202(1)
voting: see "vote" s 202(1)

Supplemental

Rights of creditors

116 The provisions of this Part of this Act prohibiting—

(a) payments and contracts for payments,

(b) the payment or incurring of election expenses in excess of the maximum amount allowed by this Act; or

(c) the incurring of expenses not authorised by the election agent,

do not affect the right of any creditor, who, when the contract was made or the expense was incurred, was ignorant of that contract or expense being in contravention of this Act.

NOTES

Derivation
  RPA 1949 s 105

Defined terms
  election agent: see s 67

election expenses: ss 90ZA, 90C, 90D, 118
payment: s 118

Savings as to parliamentary elections

117(1) Where a person has been declared by others to be a candidate at a parliamentary election without his consent, nothing in this Part of this Act shall be construed to impose any liability on that person, unless he has afterwards given his assent to the declaration or has been nominated.

(2) Nothing in this Part makes it illegal for an employer to permit parliamentary electors or their proxies to absent themselves from his employment for a reasonable time for the purpose of voting at the poll at a parliamentary election without having any deduction from their salaries or wages on account of their absence, if the permission—

(a) is (so far as practicable without injury to the employer's business) given equally to all persons alike who are at the time in his employment, and

(b) is not given with a view to inducing any person to record his vote for any particular candidate at the election, and

(c) is not refused to any person for the purpose of preventing him from recording his vote for any particular candidate at the election,

but this subsection shall not be construed as making illegal any act which would not be illegal apart from this subsection.

NOTES

Derivation
  RPA 1949 s 104

Defined terms
  candidate: s 118A
  election: s 202(1)

elector: s 202(1)
parliamentary election: Interpretation Act 1978 Sch 1
vote: s 202(1)
voting: see "vote" s 202(1)

Interpretation of Part II

118 In this Part of this Act, unless the context otherwise requires—

"appropriate officer" has the meaning given by section 67(7) above;

For local government elections in Scotland only, the following definition of candidate applies:-

"candidate"—

(a) in relation to a parliamentary election, means a person who is elected to serve in Parliament at the election or a person who is nominated as a candidate at the election, or is declared by himself or by others to be a candidate on or after the day of the issue of the writ for the election, or after the dissolution or vacancy in consequence of which the writ was issued;

(b) in relation to an election under the local government Act, means a person elected or having been nominated or having declared himself a candidate for election, to the office to be filled at the election;

Otherwise, the following definition of candidate applies:-

"candidate" shall be construed in accordance with section 118A below;

"committee room" does not include any house or room occupied by a candidate as a dwelling, by reason only of the candidate transacting business there with his agents in relation to the election, and no room or building shall be deemed to be a committee room by reason only of the candidate or any agent of the candidate addressing in it electors, committee members or others;

"date of the allowance of an authorised excuse" has the meaning given by section 86(8) above, or paragraph 7 of Schedule 4 to this Act, as the case may be;

"declaration as to election expenses" means a declaration made under section 82 above, or, as the case may be, paragraph 3 of Schedule 4 to this Act;

"disputed claim" has the meaning given by section 79(1) above as extended by section 80 above.

"election expenses", in relation to an election, shall be construed in accordance with sections 90A sections 90ZA to 90D above;

"money" and "pecuniary reward" shall (except in sections 71A, 113 and 114 above and Schedule 2A to this Act) be deemed to include—

    (a) any office, place or employment, and

    (b) any valuable security or other equivalent of money, and

    (c) any valuable consideration,

and expressions referring to money shall be construed accordingly;

"payment" includes any pecuniary or other reward;

"personal expenses" as used with respect to the expenditure of any candidate in relation to any election includes the reasonable travelling expenses of the candidate, and the reasonable expenses of his living at hotels or elsewhere for the purposes of and in relation to the election;

"return as to election expenses" means a return (including the bills and receipts to be delivered with it) to be made under section 81(1) above, or, as the case may be, paragraph 3 of Schedule 4 to this Act.

NOTES

Derivation
RPA s 103

Defined terms
election: s 202(1)

local government Act (E&W): s 203(1)
local government Act (S): s 204(1)
parliamentary election: Interpretation Act 1978 Sch 1

Meaning of candidate

118A(1)   References to a candidate in this Part of this Act shall be construed in accordance with this section (except where the context otherwise requires).

    (2)   A person becomes a candidate at a parliamentary election—

        (a) on the date of—

            (i)   the dissolution of Parliament, or

            (ii) in the case of a by-election, the occurrence of the vacancy,

in consequence of which the writ for the election is issued if on or before that date he is declared by himself or by others to be a candidate at the election, and

        (b) otherwise, on the day on which he is so declared by himself or by others or on which he is nominated as a candidate at the election (whichever is the earlier).

    (3)   A person becomes a candidate at an election under the local government Act—

        (a) on the last day for publication of notice of the election if on or before that day he is declared by himself or by others to be a candidate at the election, and

        (b) otherwise, on the day on which he is so declared by himself or by others or on which he is nominated as a candidate at the election (whichever is the earlier),

or, in the case of a person included in a list of candidates submitted by a registered political party in connection with an election of the London members of the London Assembly at an ordinary election, on the day on which the list is submitted by the party.

NOTES

Application
This does not apply to local government elections in Scotland

Derivation
Political Parties, Elections and Referendums Act 2000

s 135

London member: s 203(1)
parliamentary election: Interpretation Act 1978 Sch 1
registered political party: s 202(1)
registered political party submitting a list of
candidates to be London members: s 203(1B)

Defined terms
election under the local government act (E&W): ss
191(1), 203(1A)
local government Act (E&W): s 203(1)
local government Act (S): s 204(1)

Computation of time for purposes of Part II

119(1)   Where the day or last day on which anything is required or permitted to be done by or in pursuance of this Part of this Act is any of the days mentioned in subsection (2) below—

(a)   the requirement or permission shall be deemed to relate to the first day thereafter which is not one of those days; and

(b)   in computing any period of not more than 7 days for the purposes of this Part any of the days so mentioned shall be disregarded.

(2)   The days referred to in subsection (1) above are Saturday, Sunday, Christmas Eve, Christmas Day, Good Friday, a bank holiday or a day appointed for public thanksgiving or mourning (but, in relation to a parliamentary general election, excluding any day to which rule 2 of the parliamentary elections rules does not apply by virtue of rule 2(2A)).

(3)   In this section "bank holiday", in relation to any election, means a day which is a bank holiday in the part of the United Kingdom in which the constituency or, as the case may be, electoral area is situated.

NOTES

Derivation
RPA 1949 s 106

Defined terms
bank holiday: Banking and Financial Dealing Act 1971
constituency: Parliamentary Constituencies Act 1986

s 1(2)
electoral area (E&W): ss 191(1), 203(1)
electoral area (S): s 204(1)
parliamentary elections rules: s 202(1)

PART III
LEGAL PROCEEDINGS

Questioning of a parliamentary election

Method of questioning parliamentary election

120(1)   No parliamentary election and no return to Parliament shall be questioned except by a petition complaining of an undue election or undue return ("a parliamentary election petition") presented in accordance with this Part of this Act.

(2)   A petition complaining of no return shall be deemed to be a parliamentary election petition and the High Court—

(a)   may make such order on the petition as they think expedient for compelling a return to be made; or

(b)   may allow the petition to be heard by an election court as provided with respect to ordinary election petitions.

NOTES

Derivation
RPA 1949 s 107

Defined terms
election court: s 202(1)

election petition: s 202(1)
High Court (E,W & NI): Interpretation Act 1978 Sch 1
parliamentary election: Interpretation Act 1978 Sch 1

Presentation and service of parliamentary election petition

121(1) A parliamentary election petition may be presented by one or more of the following persons—

    (a) a person who voted as an elector at the election or who had a right so to vote; or

    (b) a person claiming to have had a right to be elected or returned at the election; or

    (c) a person alleging himself to have been a candidate at the election.

(1A) The reference in subsection (1)(a) to a person who voted as an elector at an election or who had the right so to vote does not include a person who had an anonymous entry in the register of electors.

(2) The member whose election or return is complained of is hereinafter referred to as the respondent, but if the petition complains of the conduct of a returning officer, the returning officer shall for the purposes of this Part of this Act be deemed to be a respondent.

(3) The petition shall be in the prescribed form, state the prescribed matters and be signed by the petitioner, or all the petitioners if more than one, and shall be presented to the High Court, or to the Court of Session, or to the High Court of Northern Ireland depending on whether the constituency to which it relates is in England and Wales, or Scotland or Northern Ireland.

(4) The petition shall be presented by delivering it to the prescribed officer or otherwise dealing with it in the prescribed manner; and the prescribed officer shall send a copy of it to the returning officer of the constituency to which the petition relates, who shall forthwith publish it in that constituency.

(5) The petition shall be served in such manner as may be prescribed.

NOTES

Derivation
  RPA 1949 s 108

Defined terms
  anonymous entry: s 202(1)
  candidate: ss 118A, 185
  elector: s 202(1)
  England: Interpretation Act 1978 Sch 1
  constituency: Parliamentary Constituencies Act 1986

s 1(2)
High Court (E, W & NI): Interpretation Act 1978 Sch 1
High Court (S): s 204(3)
a parliamentary election petition: ss 120, 202(1)
prescribed: s 185
register of electors: see s 9
returning officer: see ss 24-27
vote: s 202(1)
Wales: Interpretation Act 1978 Sch 1

Time for presentation or amendment of parliamentary election petition

122(1) Subject to the provisions of this section, a parliamentary election petition shall be presented within 21 days after the return has been made to the Clerk of the Crown, or to the Clerk of the Crown for Northern Ireland, as the case may be, of the member to whose election the petition relates.

(2) If the petition questions the election or return upon an allegation of corrupt practices and specifically alleges a payment of money or other reward to have been made by the member or on his account or with his privity since the time of that return in pursuance or in furtherance of the alleged corrupt practice, it may be presented within 28 days after the date of the payment.

(3) A petition questioning the election or return upon an allegation of an illegal practice may, so far as respects that illegal practice, be presented—

    (a) within 21 days after the day specified in subsection (4) below; or

    (b) if specifically alleging a payment of money or some other act to have been made or done since the day so specified by the member to whose election the petition relates or an agent of his, or with the privity of that member or his election agent, in pursuance or in furtherance of the alleged illegal practice, within 28 days after the date of the payment or other act.

(4) The day referred to in subsection (3) above is the tenth day after the end of the time allowed for delivering to the returning officer returns as to election expenses at the election or, if later—

    (a) that on which the returning officer receives the return and declarations as to election expenses by that member and his election agent; or

    (b) where the return and declarations are received on different days, the last of those days; or

    (c) where there is an authorised excuse for failing to make the return and declarations, the date of the allowance of the excuse, or if there was a failure as regards two or more of them, and the excuse was allowed at different times, the date of the allowance of the last excuse.

(5) An election petition presented within the time limited by subsection (1) or subsection (2) above may, for the purpose of questioning the election or return upon an allegation of an illegal practice, be amended with the leave of the High Court within the time within which a petition questioning the election upon the allegation of that illegal practice could be presented under subsection (3).

(6) Subsections (3), (4) and (5) above apply—

    (a) notwithstanding that the act constituting the alleged illegal practice amounted to a corrupt practice; and

    (b) to a corrupt practice under section 75 above, as if it were an illegal practice.

(7) For the purposes of this section, an allegation that an election is avoided under section 164 below shall be deemed to be an allegation of corrupt practices, notwithstanding that the offences alleged are or include offences other than corrupt practices.

(8) *Repealed*

NOTES

Derivation
RPA 1949 s 109

Defined terms
Clerk of the Crown: s 202(1)
corrupt practice: see ss 60(1), 62A(5), 62B(2), (3), 65A(1), (2), 65B(2), (3), 75(5), 75ZB(4), 75A(7), 82(6), 113(1), 114(1), 115(1), Sch 1 rule 6A(2), Sch 4 para 5
date of the allowance of the excuse: ss 86(8), 118
declaration as to election expenses: s 185
election agent: see s 67
High Court (E, W & NI): Interpretation Act 1978 Sch 1

High Court (S): s 204(3)
illegal practice: ss 61(7), 68(2, 71A(3), 73(6), 75(5), 75ZB(3), 75A(8), (11), 76(1B), 76ZA(5), 78(3), 84, 90(2), 92(2), (3), 97(1), 106(1), (5), 109(2), 110(12), 110A(14), 175(2), 189(1), Sch 4 paras 1(2), 5
money: s 185
a parliamentary election petition: ss 120, 202(1)
payment: s 185
return as to election expenses: s 185
returning officer: see ss 24-27

Constitution of election court and place of trial

123(1) A parliamentary election petition shall be tried by—

    (a) two judges on the rota for the trial of parliamentary election petitions, and the judges for the time being on that rota shall, unless they otherwise agree, try the election petitions standing for trial according to their seniority,

    (b) in Northern Ireland, the two judges of the High Court or the Court of Appeal for the time being selected under section 108 of the Judicature (Northern Ireland) Act 1978,

and the judges presiding at the trial of a parliamentary election petition are hereinafter referred to as the election court.

(2) The election court has, subject to the provisions of this Act, the same powers, jurisdiction and authority as a judge of the High Court (or, in Scotland, a judge of the

Court of Session presiding at the trial of a civil cause without a jury) and shall be a court of record.

(3) The place of trial shall be within the constituency for which the election was held, but—

(a) the High Court may, on being satisfied that special circumstances exist rendering it desirable that the petition should be tried elsewhere, appoint some other convenient place for the trial; and

(b) if that constituency is wholly or partly in Greater London, the petition may be heard at such place within Greater London as the High Court may appoint.

(4) The election court may adjourn the trial from one place to another within the constituency.

NOTES

Derivation
　RPA 1949 s 110

Defined terms
　constituency: Parliamentary Constituencies Act 1986
　s 1(2)

court of appeal: Interpretation Act 1978 Sch 1
High Court (E, W & NI): Interpretation Act 1978 Sch 1
High Court (S): s 204(3)
a parliamentary election petition: ss 120, 202(1)

Judges' expenses and reception: England and Wales and Northern Ireland

124 In relation to the trial of a parliamentary election petition—

(a) in England and Wales and Northern Ireland, the travelling and other expenses of the judges and all expenses properly incurred in providing them with necessary accommodation and with a proper court shall be defrayed by the Treasury out of moneys provided by Parliament;

(b) *Repealed*

NOTES

Derivation
　RPA 1949 s 111

Defined terms
　England: Interpretation Act 1978 Sch 1
　money: s 185
　a parliamentary election petition: ss 120, 202(1)
　Wales: Interpretation Act 1978 Sch 1

Judges' expenses and reception: Scotland

125 In relation to the trial of a parliamentary election petition in Scotland—

(a) *Repealed*

(b) the travelling and other expenses of the judges, and of the officer or officers in attendance on them, and all expenses properly incurred in providing the judges with a proper court shall be defrayed by the Treasury out of moneys provided by Parliament.

NOTES

Derivation
　RPA 1949 s 111

Defined terms
　money: s 185
　a parliamentary election petition: ss 120, 202(1)

Attendance of House of Commons shorthand writer

126(1) The shorthand writer of the House of Commons or his deputy shall attend the trial and shall be sworn by one of the judges of the election court faithfully and truly to take down the evidence given at the trial and from time to time as occasion requires to transcribe that evidence or cause it to be transcribed.

(2) The shorthand writer shall take down the evidence and from time to time transcribe it or cause it to be transcribed and a copy of the evidence shall accompany the certificate given by the election court to the Speaker.

(3) In Scotland the expenses of the shorthand writer shall be deemed to be part of the expenses incurred under section 125 above.

NOTES

Derivation
  RPA 1949 s 111

Defined terms
  election court: ss 123(1), 202(1)
  Speaker: s 185

Questioning of a local election

Method of questioning local election

127 An election under the local government Act may be questioned on the ground that the person whose election is questioned—
  (a) was at the time of the election disqualified, or
  (b) was not duly elected,
or on the ground that the election was avoided by corrupt or illegal practices or on the grounds provided by section 164 or section 165 below, and shall not be questioned on any of those grounds except by an election petition.

NOTES

Derivation
  RPA 1949 s 112

Defined terms
  corrupt practice: see ss 60(1), 62A(5), 62B(2), (3), 65A(1), (2), 65B(2), (3), 75(5), 75ZB(4), 75A(7), 82(6), 113(1), 114(1), 115(1), Sch 1 rule 6A(2), Sch 4 para 5
  election petition: s 202(1)
  election under the local government act (E&W): ss

191(1), 203(1A)
illegal practice: ss 61(7), 68(2, 71A(3), 73(6), 75(5), 75ZB(3), 75A(8), (11), 76(1B), 76ZA(5), 78(3), 84, 90(2), 92(2), (3), 97(1), 106(1), (5), 109(2), 110(12), 110A(14), 175(2), 189(1), Sch 4 paras 1(2), 5
local government Act (E&W): s 203(1)
local government Act (S): s 204(1)

Presentation of petition questioning local election

128(1) A petition questioning an election under the local government Act may be presented either by four or more persons who voted as electors at the election or had a right so to vote, or by a person alleging himself to have been a candidate at the election.

(1A) The reference in subsection (1) to a person who voted as an elector at an election or who had the right so to vote does not include a person who had an anonymous entry in the register of electors.

(1B) *Repealed*

(2) A person whose election is questioned by the petition, and any returning officer of whose conduct the petition complains, may be made a respondent to the petition.

(3) The petition shall be in the prescribed form signed by the petitioner and shall be presented in the prescribed manner—
  (a) in England and Wales, to the High Court;
  (b) in Scotland, to the sheriff principal of the sheriffdom in which the election took place or, where the election was in respect of a local authority whose area is situated within more than one sheriffdom, to the sheriffs principal of the sheriffdoms in which the area of the authority is situated.

(4) In England and Wales the prescribed officer shall send a copy of the petition to the proper officer of the authority for which the election was held, who shall forthwith publish it in the area of that authority.

NOTES

Derivation
RPA 1949 s 113

Defined terms
anonymous entry: s 202(1)
candidate: ss 118A, 185
election under the local government act (E&W): ss 191(1), 203(1A)
elector: s 202(1)
England: Interpretation Act 1978 Sch 1
High Court (E, W & NI): Interpretation Act 1978 Sch 1
High Court (S): s 204(3)

local authority (S): s 204(1)
local government Act (E&W): s 203(1)
local government Act (S): s 204(1)
prescribed: s 185
proper officer: s 202(1)
register of electors: see s 9
returning officer: see ss 24-27
sheriff (S): Interpretation Act 1978 Sch 1
vote: s 202(1)
Wales: Interpretation Act 1978 Sch 1

Time for presentation or amendment of petition questioning local election

129(1) Subject to the provisions of this section, a petition questioning an election under the local government Act shall be presented within 21 days after the day on which the election was held.

(2) If the petition complains of the election—
(a) on the ground of a corrupt practice, and
(b) specifically alleges that a payment of money or other reward has been made or promised since the election by a candidate elected at the election, or on his account or with his privity, in pursuance or furtherance of that corrupt practice,
it may be presented at any time within 28 days after the date of the alleged payment or promise, whether or not any other petition against that person has been previously presented or tried.

(3) If the petition complains of the election—
(a) on the ground of an illegal practice, and
(b) specifically alleges a payment of money or other act made or done since the election by the candidate elected at the election, or by an agent of the candidate or with the privity of the candidate or his election agent, in pursuance or in furtherance of that illegal practice,
it may be presented at any time within 28 days after the date of that payment or act, whether or not any other petition against that person has been previously presented or tried.

(4) If the petition complains of an election where election expenses are allowed on the ground of an illegal practice, it may be presented at any time within 14 days after the day specified in subsection (5) below.

(5) The day referred to in subsection (4) above is—
(a) that on which the appropriate officer receives the return and declarations as to election expenses by that candidate and his election agent; or
(b) where the return and declarations are received on different days, the last of those days; or
(c) where there is an authorised excuse for failing to make the return and declarations, the date of the allowance of the excuse, or if there was a failure as regards two or more of them and the excuse was allowed at different times, the date of the allowance of the last excuse.

(6) An election petition presented within the time limited by subsection (1) or subsection (2) above may for the purpose of complaining of the election upon an allegation of an illegal practice, be amended with the leave of the High Court within the time within

which a petition complaining of the election on the ground of that illegal practice could, under this section, be presented.

In the application of this subsection to an election of councillors in Scotland, the reference in this subsection to subsection (2) above shall be omitted and for the reference to the High Court there shall be substituted a reference to the election court or the sheriff.

(7) Subsections (3), (4), (5) and (6) above apply—

    (a) notwithstanding that the act constituting the alleged illegal practice amounted to a corrupt practice; and

    (b) to a corrupt practice under section 75 or 75A above as if it were an illegal practice.

(8) For the purposes of this section, an allegation that an election is avoided under section 164 below shall be deemed to be an allegation of corrupt practices, notwithstanding that the offences alleged are or include offences other than corrupt practices.

(9) In relation to an election where candidates are not required to have election agents there shall be omitted—

    (a) the references in subsection (3) and paragraph (a) of subsection (5) above to an election agent; and

    (b) paragraphs (b) and (c) of subsection (5).

NOTES

Derivation
RPA 1949 s 114

Defined terms
appropriate officer: ss 67(7), 185
candidate: ss 118A, 185
corrupt practice: see ss 60(1), 62A(5), 62B(2), (3), 65A(1), (2), 65B(2), (3), 75(5), 75ZB(4), 75A(7), 82(6), 113(1), 114(1), 115(1), Sch 1 rule 6A(2), Sch 4 para 5
date of the allowance of the excuse: ss 86(8), 118
declaration as to election expenses: s 185
election: s 202(1)
election agent: see s 67
election court: ss 123, 202(1)
election under the local government act (E&W): ss

191(1), 203(1A)
High Court (E, W & NI): Interpretation Act 1978 Sch 1
High Court (S): s 204(3)
illegal practice: ss 61(7), 68(2, 71A(3), 73(6), 75(5), 75ZB(3), 75A(8), (11), 76(1B), 76ZA(5), 78(3), 84, 90(2), 92(2), (3), 97(1), 106(1), (5), 109(2), 110(12), 110A(14), 175(2), 189(1), Sch 4 paras 1(2), 5
local government Act (E&W): s 203(1)
local government Act (S): s 204(1)
money: s 185
payment: s 185
return as to election expenses: s 185
sheriff (S): Interpretation Act 1978 Sch 1

Election court for local election in England and Wales, and place of trial

130(1) A petition questioning an election in England and Wales under the local government Act shall be tried by an election court consisting of a person qualified and appointed as provided by this section.

(2) A person shall not be qualified to constitute an election court—

    (a) unless he satisfies the judicial-appointment eligibility condition on a 7-year basis; or

    (b) if the court is for the trial of an election petition relating to any local government area in which he resides.

(3) The judges for the time being on the rota for the trial of parliamentary election petitions, or any two of those judges—

    (a) may annually appoint as many qualified persons, not exceeding five, as they may think necessary as commissioners for the trial of petitions questioning elections in England and Wales under the local government Act; and

    (b) shall from time to time assign the petitions to be tried by each commissioner.

(4) If the commissioner to whom the trial of a petition is assigned dies, or declines to act or becomes incapable of acting, those judges or two of them may assign the trial to be

conducted or continued by any other of the commissioners appointed under this section.

(5) The election court has for the purposes of the trial the same powers and privileges as a judge on the trial of a parliamentary election petition.

(6) The place of trial shall be within the area of the authority for which the election was held, except that the High Court may, on being satisfied that special circumstances exist rendering it desirable that the petition should be tried elsewhere, appoint some other convenient place for the trial.

(7) The election court may in its discretion adjourn the trial from one place to another within the local government area or place where it is held.

NOTES

Derivation
RPA 1949 s 115

Defined terms
election under the local government act (E&W): ss 191(1), 203(1A)
England: Interpretation Act 1978 Sch 1
High Court (E, W & NI): Interpretation Act 1978 Sch 1
High Court (S): s 204(3)

local government Act (E&W): s 203(1)
local government Act (S): s 204(1)
local government area (E&W): ss 191(1), 203(1)
local government area (S): s 204(1)
a parliamentary election petition: ss 120, 202(1)
Wales: Interpretation Act 1978 Sch 1

Accommodation of and attendance on court

131(1) The proper officer of the authority for which the election was held shall provide suitable accommodation for holding the election court constituted under section 130 above and any expenses incurred by him for the purposes of this section and section 132 below shall be paid by that authority.

(2) The election court so constituted may employ officers and clerks as prescribed, and all constables and bailiffs shall give their assistance to the court in the execution of its duties.

(3) A shorthand writer (whose expenses, according to a prescribed scale, shall be treated as part of the expenses incurred in receiving the election court) shall attend the trial before that court, and—
   (a) shall be sworn by the court faithfully and truly to take down the evidence given at the trial, and
   (b) shall take down such evidence at length,
and a transcript of the notes of the evidence taken down by him shall, if the election court so directs, accompany the court's certificate.

NOTES

Derivation
RPA 1949 s 116

Defined terms
election: s 202(1)

election court: ss 130, 202(1)
prescribed: s 185
proper officer: s 202(1)

Remuneration and allowances

132(1) The remuneration and allowances to be paid to the commissioner for his services in respect of that trial and to any officers, clerks or shorthand writers employed under section 131 above in relation to that trial shall be fixed by a scale made and varied by the judges on the rota for the trial of parliamentary election petitions, with the Treasury's approval.

(2) The remuneration and allowances shall be paid in the first instance by the Treasury and shall be repaid to the Treasury on their certificate by the authority for which the election was held.

NOTES

Derivation
RPA 1949 s 116

Defined terms
election: s 202(1)

parliamentary election petition: s 202(1)
Treasury: Interpretation Act 1978 Sch 1

Repayments under ss 131 and 132

133(1) The election court constituted under section 130 above may in its discretion order that—

    (a) the expenses referred to in section 131 above, incurred by the proper officer of the authority for receiving the court, or

    (b) the remuneration and allowances referred to in section 132 above,

shall be repaid, wholly or in part, to the proper officer of the authority or to the Treasury, as the case may be—

    (i) when, in the opinion of the election court, the petition is frivolous and vexatious, by the petitioner;

    (ii) when, in the opinion of the election court, the respondent has been personally guilty of corrupt practices at the election, by that respondent.

(2) The order so made for the repayment of any sum by a petitioner or respondent may be enforced as an order for payment of costs, but a deposit made or a security given under this Part of this Act shall not be applied for any such repayment until all costs and expenses payable by the petitioner or respondent to any party to the petition have been satisfied.

NOTES

Derivation
RPA 1949 s 116

Defined terms
corrupt practice: see ss 60(1), 62A(5), 62B(2), (3), 65A(1), (2), 65B(2), (3), 75(5), 75ZB(4), 75A(7), 82(6), 113(1), 114(1), 115(1), Sch 1 rule 6A(2), Sch 4 para 5

costs: s 185
election court: ss 130, 202(1)
proper officer: s 202(1)
Treasury: Interpretation Act 1978 Sch 1

Election court for local election in Scotland, and place of trial

134(1) An election petition questioning an election of councillors in Scotland, and all proceedings incidental to and consequent on it, except as otherwise provided, shall be tried—

    (a) by the sheriff principal of the sheriffdom within which the challenged election took place; or

    (b) where the election was in respect of a local authority whose area is situated within more than one sheriffdom, by the sheriffs principal of the sheriffdoms in which the area of the authority is situated; and where in such a case the sheriffs principal are unable to reach a unanimous decision, they shall state a case for the Court of Session and the Court may pronounce any deliverance which it would have been competent for the sheriffs principal to make.

(2) The election court has for the purposes of the trial the same powers and privileges as a judge on the trial of a parliamentary election petition, except that any fine or order of committal unless imposed or made by the Court of Session in consequence of a case stated under subsection (1) above may, on summary application by the person aggrieved, be discharged or varied by the Court of Session, or in vacation by the judge acting as vacation judge on such terms, if any, as the Court of Session or judge may think fit.

(3) The place of trial shall be such place within the sheriffdom or sheriffdoms in which the area of the local authority is situated as the election court may determine.

(4) The election court may in its discretion adjourn the trial from one place to another within that sheriffdom or those sheriffdoms.

(5) The travelling and other expenses of the sheriff principal incurred by him in the execution of his duties under this Part of this Act shall be paid by the authority for which the election was held, but the election court may order repayment of those expenses to that authority by the parties to the petition or any of them, in such proportion as shall to the court seem proper.

(6) A shorthand writer shall attend at the trial of the petition, and shall be sworn by the election court faithfully and truly to take down the evidence given at the trial, and he shall take down the evidence at length.

NOTES

Derivation
RPA 1949 s 117

Defined terms
election: s 202(1)
election court: ss 134, 202(1)
election petition: s 202(1)

local authority (S): s 204(1)
parliamentary election petition: s 202(1)
person: s 202(1)
sheriff (S): Interpretation Act 1978 Sch 1

Consequences of local election declared void

135(1) Where on a petition questioning an election under the local government Act—
(a) the election of any person has been declared void, and
(b) no other person has been declared elected in his place,
a new election shall be held to fill the vacancy in the same manner as on a casual vacancy.

(1A) Subsection (1) above shall not apply in the case of an election of the London members of the London Assembly at an ordinary election (for which separate provision is made by section 135A below).

(2) For the purposes of that election any duties to be performed by any officer shall, if he has been declared not elected, be performed by a deputy or other person who might have acted for him if he had been incapacitated by illness.

(3) This section does not apply to Scotland.

NOTES

Derivation
RPA s 118

Defined terms
election: s 202(1)
election under the local government act (E&W): ss

191(1), 203(1A)
local government Act (E&W): s 203(1)
local government Act (S): s 204(1)
London member: s 203(1)

Consequences of election or return of London members being declared void

135A(1) This section applies where the election court has made a determination under section 145 below at the conclusion of the trial of a petition questioning the election of the London members of the London Assembly at an ordinary election.

(2) Where, pursuant to section 145(6) below, the proper officer of the Greater London Authority receives the copy of the certificate of the election court's determination in relation to the election which was questioned, he shall send notice of the determination to the Greater London returning officer.

(3) If the election is not declared void but—

(a)   the return of a candidate at the election is declared void, and

(b)   no other person has been declared returned in his place,

the vacancy shall be filled (or, as the case may be, remain unfilled) as if it were a casual vacancy (see section 11 of the Greater London Authority Act 1999).

(4)   If the election is declared void, a new election shall be held in the same manner as at an ordinary election.

(5)   The date of the poll at the new election shall be fixed by the Greater London returning officer.

(6)   The date fixed shall be no later than three months after the receipt by the Greater London returning officer of the notice under subsection (2) above.

(7)   A new election shall not be held if the latest date which may be fixed for the poll falls within the period of three months preceding an ordinary election.

(8)   If the determination of the election court is that the election is void, the Greater London returning officer shall inform the returning officer for each Assembly constituency of—

(a)   the contents of the notice under subsection (2) above; and

(b)   the date fixed for the poll at the new election.

(9)   The results of the elections of the constituency members of the London Assembly at the last ordinary election shall have effect for the purposes of ascertaining the results of the new election.

NOTES

Derivation
Greater London Authority Act 1999 s 17

Defined terms
Assembly constituency: s 203(1)
candidate: ss 118A, 185

constituency: Parliamentary Constituencies Act 1986 s 1(2)
constituency member: s 203(1)

Procedure on all election petitions

Security for costs

136(1)   At the time of presenting an election petition or within three days afterwards the petitioner shall give security for all costs which may become payable by him to any witness summoned on his behalf or to any respondent.

(2)   The security shall be—

(a)   in the case of a parliamentary election petition, such amount not exceeding £5,000 as the High Court or a judge of the High Court, directs on an application made by the petitioner; and

(b)   in the case of a petition questioning an election under the local government Act, such amount not exceeding £2,500 as the High Court, or a judge of the High Court, directs on an application made by the petitioner,

and shall be given in the prescribed manner by recognisance entered into by any number of sureties not exceeding four or by a deposit of money, or partly in one way and partly in the other; but in Scotland—

(i)   the amount mentioned in paragraph (a) above shall be such amount not exceeding £5,000 as the Court of Session or a judge of the Court of Session directs and the amount mentioned in paragraph (b) above shall be such amount not exceeding £2,500 as the election court or the sheriff directs; and

(ii)   the persons finding caution for that amount may exceed four.

(3) Within the prescribed time after giving the security the petitioner shall serve on the respondent in the prescribed manner—

    (a) a notice of the presentation of the petition and of the amount and nature of the security, and

    (b) a copy of the petition.

(4) Within a further prescribed time,, the respondent may object in writing to any recognisance on the ground that any surety is insufficient or is dead or cannot be found or ascertained for want of a sufficient description in the recognisance, or that a person named in the recognisance has not duly acknowledged the recognisance.

(5) *Repealed*

(6) An objection to a recognisance shall be decided in the prescribed manner.

(7) If the objection is allowed, the petitioner may within a further prescribed time, remove it by a deposit in the prescribed manner of such sum of money as will, in the opinion of the court or officer having cognisance of the matter, make the security sufficient.

(8) If no security is given as required by this section or any objection is allowed and not removed as mentioned above, no further proceedings shall be had on the petition.

NOTES

Derivation
RPA 1949 s 119

Subordinate Legislation
Election Petition Rules 1960
European Parliamentary Election Petition Rules 1979

Defined terms
costs: s 185
election court: ss 123, 130, 134, 202(1)
election petition: s 202(1)
election under the local government act (E&W): ss 191(1), 203(1A)

High Court (E, W & NI): Interpretation Act 1978 Sch 1
High Court (S): s 204(3)
local government Act (E&W): s 203(1)
local government Act (S): s 204(1)
money: s 185
a parliamentary election petition: ss 120, 202(1)
prescribed: s 185
recognisance (S): s 204(6)
respondent: ss 121(2), 128(2)
sheriff (S): Interpretation Act 1978 Sch 1
writing: Interpretation Act 1978 Sch 1

Petition at issue

137 (1) The petition shall be at issue as from the relevant time, as defined by subsection (2) below.

(2) In this section "the relevant time" means-

    (a) where the petitioner gives the security for costs required by section 136 above by a deposit of money equal to the amount of the security so required, the time when the security is so given; and

    (b) in any other case, the time when-

        (i) the time prescribed for the making of objections under section 136(4) above expires, or

        (ii) if such an objection is made, that objection is disallowed or removed,

    whichever happens later.

NOTES

Application
This provision does not apply to local government elections in Scotland

Derivation
RPA 1949 s 120

Defined terms
costs: s 185
election petition: s 202(1)
money: s 185(1)

137 The petition shall be at issue—

    (a) on the expiry of the time limited for objections; or

(b) if an objection is made, on that objection being disallowed or removed, whichever happens last.

NOTES

Application
This provision applies only to local government elections in Scotland

Derivation
RPA 1949 s 120

Defined terms
election petition: s 202(1)

List of petitions

138(1) The prescribed officer shall—

    (a) as soon as may be, make out a list of all election petitions at issue presented to the court of which he is officer, placing them in the order in which they were presented, and

    (b) keep at his office a copy of the list, open to inspection in the prescribed manner,

and the petitions questioning elections under the local government Act shall be in a separate list.

(2) The petitions shall, so far as convenient, be tried in the order in which they stand in the list.

(3) In the case of a petition questioning an election under the local government Act, two or more candidates may be made respondents to the same petition, and their cases may be tried at the same time, but for the purposes of this Part of this Act the petition shall be deemed to be a separate petition against each respondent.

(4) Where more petitions than one are presented relating to the same election or to elections under the local government Act held at the same time for more than one electoral area in the same local government area, all those petitions shall be bracketed together in the election list and shall be dealt with as one petition, standing, unless the High Court otherwise direct, in the election list in the place where the last of them would have stood if it had been the only petition presented.

(5) Subsections (1), (2) and (4) above do not apply in relation to petitions questioning an election of councillors in Scotland but where two or more of those petitions are presented relating to the same election they shall be tried together.

NOTES

Derivation
RPA 1949 s 121

Defined terms
candidate: ss 118A, 185
election petition: s 202(1)
election under the local government act (E&W): ss 191(1), 203(1A)
electoral area (E&W): ss 191(1), 203(1)
electoral area (S): s 204(1)

High Court (E, W & NI): Interpretation Act 1978 Sch 1
High Court (S): s 204(3)
local government Act (E&W): s 203(1)
local government Act (S): s 204(1)
local government area (E&W): ss 191(1), 203(1)
local government area (S): s 204(1)
prescribed: s 185

Trial of petition

139(1) An election petition shall be tried in open court, without a jury, and notice of the time and place of trial shall be given in the prescribed manner, not less than, in the case of a parliamentary election petition, 14 days and in any other case, seven days, before the day of trial.

(2) The election court may in its discretion adjourn the trial from time to time, but the trial shall, so far as is practicable consistently with the interests of justice in respect of the trial, be continued from day to day on every lawful day until its conclusion.

(3)   The trial of a parliamentary election petition shall be proceeded with notwithstanding the acceptance by the respondent of an office vacating his seat in Parliament and notwithstanding the prorogation of Parliament; and the trial of a petition questioning an election under the local government Act shall be proceeded with notwithstanding that the respondent has ceased to hold the office his election to which is questioned by the petition.

(4)   On the trial of a petition, unless the court otherwise directs, any charge of a corrupt practice may be gone into, and evidence in relation to it received, before any proof has been given of agency on behalf of any candidate in respect of the corrupt practice.
In relation to an election in England and Wales under the local government Act, this subsection applies as if corrupt practices included illegal practices.

(5)   On the trial of a petition complaining of an undue election and claiming the seat or office for some person, the respondent may give evidence to prove that that person was not duly elected, in the same manner as if he had presented a petition against the election of that person.

(6)   If the petition relates to an election conducted under the parliamentary elections rules or the rules under section 36 or section 42 above and it appears that there is an equality of votes between any candidates at the election, and that the addition of a vote would entitle any of those candidates to be declared elected then—

   (a)   any decision under the provisions as to equality of votes in the parliamentary elections rules or the rules under section 36 or section 42, as the case may be, shall in so far as it determines the question between those candidates, be effective also for the purposes of the petition; and

   (b)   in so far as that question is not determined by such a decision, the court shall decide between them by lot and proceed as if the one on whom the lot then falls had received an additional vote.

NOTES

Derivation
RPA 1949 s 122

Defined terms
candidate: ss 118A, 185
corrupt practice: see ss 60(1), 62A(5), 62B(2), (3), 65A(1), (2), 65B(2), (3), 75(5), 75ZB(4), 75A(7), 82(6), 113(1), 114(1), 115(1), Sch 1 rule 6A(2), Sch 4 para 5
election court: ss 123, 130, 134, 202(1)
election petition: s 202(1)
election under the local government act (E&W): ss 191(1), 203(1A)
England: Interpretation Act 1978 Sch 1
illegal practice: ss 61(7), 68(2, 71A(3), 73(6), 75(5),

75ZB(3), 75A(8), (11), 76(1B), 76ZA(5), 78(3), 84, 90(2), 92(2), (3), 97(1), 106(1), (5), 109(2), 110(12), 110A(14), 175(2), 189(1), Sch 4 paras 1(2), 5
local government Act (E&W): s 203(1)
local government Act (S): s 204(1)
a parliamentary election petition: ss 120, 202(1)
parliamentary elections rules: s 202(1)
prescribed: s 185
respondent: ss 121(2), 128(2)
vote: s 202(1)
Wales: Interpretation Act 1978 Sch 1

Witnesses

140(1)   Witnesses shall be summoned and sworn in the same manner as nearly as circumstances admit as in an action tried in the High Court, but this subsection does not apply to Scotland in relation to an election of councillors.

(2)   On the trial a member of the election court may, by order signed by him, require any person who appears to him to have been concerned in the election to attend as a witness, and any person refusing to obey the order shall be guilty of contempt of court.

(3)   The election court may examine any person so required to attend or who is in court although he is not called and examined by any party to the petition.

(4)   A witness may, after his examination by the court, be cross-examined by or on behalf of the petitioner and respondent, or either of them.

(5) *Repealed*

(6) The Director of Public Prosecutions shall without any direction from the court cause any person appearing to him to be able to give material evidence as to the subject of the trial to attend the trial and shall, with the leave of the court, examine him as a witness.

(7) Subsection (6) above does not apply to Scotland, and in Scotland one of the deputes of the Lord Advocate or the procurator-fiscal of the district may, if the Lord Advocate so decides, and shall, if the election court so requests attend the trial of the petition as part of his official duty.

NOTES

Derivation
RPA 1949 s 123

Defined terms
Director of Public Prosecutions (S): s 204(5)
Director of Public Prosecutions (NI): s 205(1)
election: s 202(1)

election court: ss 123, 130, 134, 202(1)
High Court (E, W & NI): Interpretation Act 1978 Sch 1
High Court (S): s 204(3)
respondent: ss 121(2), 128(2)

Duty to answer relevant questions

141(1) A person called as a witness respecting an election before any election court shall not be excused from answering any question relating to any offence at or connected with the election—

    (a) on the ground that the answer to it may incriminate or tend to incriminate—

        (i) that person or that person's spouse or civil partner, or

        (ii) in Scotland, that person; or

    (b) on the ground of privilege.

(2) An answer by a person to a question put by or before any election court shall not, except in the case of any criminal proceeding for perjury in respect of the evidence, be in any proceeding, civil or criminal, admissible in evidence against—

    (a) that person or that person's spouse or civil partner; or

    (b) in Scotland, that person.

(3)-(4) *Repealed*

NOTES

Derivation
RPA s 123

Defined terms
civil partner: Interpretation Act 1978 Sch 1
election: s 202(1)

election court: ss 123, 130, 134, 202(1)
spouse: see Civil Partnership Act 2004 ss 84, 208 and Marriage (Same Sex Couples) Act 2013 Sch 3 para 1

142 *Repealed*

Expenses of witnesses

143(1) The reasonable expenses incurred by any person in appearing to give evidence at the trial of an election petition, according to the scale allowed to witnesses on the trial of civil actions, may be allowed to him by a certificate of the election court or of the prescribed officer.

(2) If the witness was called and examined by virtue of section 140(2) above, the expenses referred to in subsection (1) above shall be deemed part of the expenses of providing a court, but otherwise they shall be deemed costs of the petition.
This subsection does not apply to Scotland in relation to an election of councillors.

NOTES
Derivation
  RPA 1949 s 123

Defined terms
  costs: s 185

election court: ss 123, 130, 134, 202(1)
election petition: s 202(1)
prescribed: s 185

Conclusion of trial of parliamentary election petition

144(1) At the conclusion of the trial of a parliamentary election petition, the election court shall determine whether the member whose election or return is complained of, or any and what other person, was duly returned or elected or whether the election was void, and the determination so certified shall be final to all intents as to the matters at issue on the petition.

(2) The election court shall forthwith certify in writing the determination to the Speaker.

(3) If the judges constituting the election court—

  (a) differ as to whether the member whose election or return is complained of was duly elected or returned, they shall certify that difference and the member shall be deemed to be duly elected or returned;

  (b) determine that the member was not duly elected or returned but differ as to the rest of the determination, they shall certify that difference and the election shall be deemed to be void.

(4) Where any charge is made in the petition of any corrupt or illegal practice having been committed at the election the court shall, in addition to giving a certificate, and at the same time, make a report to the Speaker as required by sections 158 and 160 below and also stating whether corrupt or illegal practices have, or whether there is reason to believe that corrupt or illegal practices have, extensively prevailed at the election.

(5) The election court may at the same time make a special report to the Speaker as to matters arising in the course of the trial an account of which in the judgment of the court ought to be submitted to the House of Commons.

(6) Every report sent to the Speaker under this section shall be signed by both judges of the election court and if the judges differ as to the subject of the report, they shall certify that difference and make no report on the subject on which they so differ.

(7) The House of Commons, on being informed by the Speaker of a certificate and any report of an election court, shall order the certificate and report (if any) to be entered in their Journals and shall give the necessary direction—

  (a) for confirming or altering the return, or

  (b) for issuing a writ for a new election, or

  (c) for carrying the determination into execution as the circumstances may require, and where the court make a special report, the House of Commons may make such order in respect of that report as they think proper.

NOTES
Derivation
  RPA 1949 s 124

Defined terms
  corrupt practice: see ss 60(1), 62A(5), 62B(2), (3), 65A(1), (2), 65B(2), (3), 75(5), 75ZB(4), 75A(7), 82(6), 113(1), 114(1), 115(1), Sch 1 rule 6A(2), Sch 4 para 5
  election court: ss 123, 202(1)
  illegal practice: ss 61(7), 68(2, 71A(3), 73(6), 75(5),

75ZB(3), 75A(8), (11), 76(1B), 76ZA(5), 78(3), 84, 90(2), 92(2), (3), 97(1), 106(1), (5), 109(2), 110(12), 110A(14), 175(2), 189(1), Sch 4 paras 1(2), 5
a parliamentary election petition: ss 120, 202(1)
report (S): s 204(7)
Speaker: s 185
writing: Interpretation Act 1978 Sch 1

Conclusion of trial of local election petition

145(1) At the conclusion of the trial of a petition questioning an election under the local government Act, the election court shall determine whether the person whose election is complained of, or any and what other person, was duly elected, or whether the election was void, and the determination so certified shall be final to all intents as to the matters at issue on the petition.

(1A) In the application of subsection (1) above in relation to an election of the London members of the London Assembly at an ordinary election, for the words from "shall determine" to "void," there shall be substituted "shall determine whether—
    (a) the person or persons whose return is complained of were duly returned,
    (b) some other person or persons should have been declared to be returned, or
    (c) the election was void.

(2) The election court shall forthwith certify in writing the determination to the High Court.

(3) Where a charge is made in the petition of any corrupt or illegal practice having been committed at the election the court shall, in addition to giving a certificate, and at the same time, make a report in writing to the High Court as required by sections 158 and 160 below and also stating whether any corrupt practices have, or whether there is reason to believe that any corrupt practices have, extensively prevailed at the election in the area of the authority for which the election was held or in any electoral area of that authority's area.

(4) The election court may at the same time make a special report to the High Court as to matters arising in the course of the trial an account of which in the judgment of the court ought to be submitted to the High Court.

(5) A copy of any certificate or report made to the High Court shall be sent by the High Court to the Secretary of State.

(6) The High Court shall by the signatures of two or more of its judges certify a copy of the certificate mentioned in subsection (5) above to the proper officer of the authority for which the election was held.

(7) The foregoing provisions of this section, except subsection (1) above, do not apply to Scotland, but where in a petition questioning an election of councillors in Scotland a charge is made of any corrupt or illegal practice having been committed at the election, the court—
    (a) shall determine the matters mentioned in sections 158 and 160 below; and
    (b) shall also determine whether any corrupt practices have, or whether there is reason to believe that any corrupt practices have, extensively prevailed at the election and whether illegal practices, payments, employments or hirings committed in reference to the election for the purpose of promoting the election of a candidate at the election have or have not so extensively prevailed that they may be reasonably supposed to have affected the result of the election.

NOTES

Derivation
    RPA 1949 s 125

Defined terms
    corrupt practice: see ss 60(1), 62A(5), 62B(2), (3), 65A(1), (2), 65B(2), (3), 75(5), 75ZB(4), 75A(7), 82(6), 113(1), 114(1), 115(1), Sch 1 rule 6A(2), Sch 4 para 5
    election court: ss 130, 134, 202(1)
    election under the local government act (E&W): ss 191(1), 203(1A)
    electoral area (E&W): ss 191(1), 203(1)
    electoral area (S): s 204(1)

High Court (E, W & NI): Interpretation Act 1978 Sch 1
High Court (S): s 204(3)
illegal employment: s 111
illegal payment: ss 107, 112
illegal practice: ss 61(7), 68(2, 71A(3), 73(6), 75(5), 75ZB(3), 75A(8), (11), 76(1B), 76ZA(5), 78(3), 84, 90(2), 92(2), (3), 97(1), 106(1), (5), 109(2), 110(12), 110A(14), 175(2), 189(1), Sch 4 paras 1(2), 5
local government Act (E&W): s 203(1)
local government Act (S): s 204(1)
London member: s 203(1)
proper officer: s 202(1)

report (S): s 204(7)
writing: Interpretation Act 1978 Sch 1

Determination in respect of election of Mayor of London or constituency member of London Assembly

145A (1) This section applies where the election court makes a determination under section 145 above in respect of—

(a) the election of the Mayor of London, or

(b) the election of a constituency member of the London Assembly,

and the conditions in subsections (2) and (3) below are satisfied.

(2) The first condition is that the determination of the election court is—

(a) that the person whose election is complained of was not duly elected; or

(b) that the election was void.

(3) The second condition is that the return of that person at that election was taken into account for the purpose of deciding which persons were to be returned as London members of the London Assembly.

(4) Where this section applies, the validity of the return of the London members of the London Assembly shall not be affected by—

(a) the determination of the election court; or

(b) in a case falling within subsection (1)(b) above, the subsequent return of a person as the constituency member for the Assembly constituency concerned.

NOTES

Derivation
Greater London Authority Act 1999 s 17

Defined terms
Assembly constituency: s 203(1)
constituency: Parliamentary Constituencies Act 1986 s 1(2)

election court: ss 130, 202(1)
election of a constituency member of the London Assembly: s 203(1)
election of the Mayor of London: s 203(1)
London member: s 203(1)

Special case for determination of High Court

146(1) If, on the application of any party to a petition made in the prescribed manner to the High Court, it appears to the High Court that the case raised by the petition can be conveniently stated as a special case, the High Court may direct it to be stated accordingly and the special case shall be heard before the High Court.

(2) In the case of a parliamentary election petition, the High Court shall certify to the Speaker its decision on the special case.

(3) In the case of a petition questioning an election in England and Wales under the local government Act, a statement of the decision on the special case shall be sent by the High Court to the Secretary of State and the High Court shall by the signatures of two or more of its judges also certify that statement to the proper officer of the authority for which the election was held.

(4) If it appears to the election court on the trial of an election petition that any question of law as to the admissibility of evidence or otherwise requires further consideration by the High Court, the election court may postpone the granting of a certificate until the question has been determined by the High Court, and for this purpose may reserve the question by stating a case for the decision of the High Court.

In the application of this subsection to Northern Ireland the references to the High Court are to the Court of Appeal.

(5) In Scotland the decision of the Court of Session on a special case under subsection (1) above shall be final and in the case of a petition questioning an election of councillors

in Scotland, the application under subsection (1) for a direction for the statement of a case for the Court of Session shall be made to the election court.

NOTES

Derivation
  RPA 1949 s 126

Defined terms
  court of appeal: Interpretation Act 1978 Sch 1
  election court: ss 123, 130, 134, 202(1)
  election under the local government act (E&W): ss 191(1), 203(1A)
  England: Interpretation Act 1978 Sch 1
  High Court (E, W & NI): Interpretation Act 1978 Sch 1

High Court (S): s 204(3)
local government Act (E&W): s 203(1)
local government Act (S): s 204(1)
a parliamentary election petition: ss 120, 202(1)
prescribed: s 185
proper officer: s 202(1)
Speaker: s 185
Wales: Interpretation Act 1978 Sch 1

Withdrawal of petition

147(1) A petitioner shall not withdraw an election petition without the leave of the election court or High Court on special application, made in the prescribed manner and at the prescribed time and place.

In the application of this subsection to a petition questioning an election of councillors in Scotland there shall be omitted the reference to the High Court.

(2) The application shall not be made until the prescribed notice of the intention to make it has been given in the constituency or local government area to which the petition relates.

(3) Where there are more petitioners than one, the application shall not be made except with the consent of all the petitioners.

(4) If a petition is withdrawn the petitioner shall be liable to pay the costs of the respondent.

NOTES

Derivation
  RPA 1949 s 127

Defined terms
  constituency: Parliamentary Constituencies Act 1986 s 1(2)
  costs: s 185
  election court: ss 123, 130, 134, 202(1)
  election petition: s 202(1)

High Court (E, W & NI): Interpretation Act 1978 Sch 1
High Court (S): s 204(3)
local government area (E&W): ss 191(1), 203(1)
local government area (S): s 204(1)
prescribed: s 185
respondent: ss 121(2), 128(2)

Evidence required for withdrawal of petition

148 (1) Before leave for the withdrawal of an election petition is granted, there shall be produced affidavits—

(a) by all the parties to the petition and their solicitors, and

(b) if the election was an election at which candidates are required to have election agents, by the election agents of all of those parties who were candidates at the election,

but the High Court may on cause shown dispense with the affidavit of any particular person if it seems to the court on special grounds just so to do.

In the application of this subsection to an election of councillors in Scotland, the reference to the High Court is to an election court, but, if the election was a local government election, the sheriff may act instead of the election court.

(2) Each affidavit shall state that, to the best of the deponent's knowledge and belief—

(a) no agreement or terms of any kind whatsoever has or have been made, and

(b) no undertaking has been entered into, in relation to the withdrawal of the petition, but if any lawful agreement has been made with respect to the withdrawal of the petition, the affidavit shall set forth that agreement and shall make the foregoing statement subject to what appears from the affidavit.

(3) The affidavits of the applicant and his solicitor shall further state the ground on which the petition is sought to be withdrawn.

(4) Copies of those affidavits shall be delivered to the Director of Public Prosecutions a reasonable time before the application for the withdrawal is heard, and the court—

    (a) may hear the Director of Public Prosecutions or his assistant or other representative in opposition to the allowance of the withdrawal of the petition; and

    (b) shall have power to receive the evidence on oath of any person or persons whose evidence the Director of Public Prosecutions or his assistant, or other representative, may consider material.

In the application of this subsection to an election of councillors in Scotland the references to the Director of Public Prosecutions include references to the procurator-fiscal.

(5) Where more than one solicitor is concerned for the petitioner or respondent, whether as agent for another solicitor or otherwise, the affidavit shall be made by all such solicitors.

(6) Except in Scotland, the jurisdiction vested by subsection (1) above in the High Court in matters relating to parliamentary elections shall, subject to rules of court, be exercised—

    (a) by one of the judges for the time being on the rota for the trial of parliamentary election petitions,

    (b) in Northern Ireland, by one of the judges of the High Court or the Court of Appeal for the time being selected under section 108 of the Judicature (Northern Ireland) Act 1978,

sitting either in court or at chambers, or may be exercised by a master of the Supreme Court in manner directed by and subject to appeal to those judges.

NOTES

Application
This provision now applies only to local authority election petitions in Scotland, and as extended by SSI

Derivation
RPA 1949 s 128

Defined terms
affidavit: Interpretation Act 1978 Sch 1
court of appeal: Interpretation Act 1978 Sch 1
Director of Public Prosecutions (S): s 204(5)
Director of Public Prosecutions (NI): s 205(1)

election agent: see s 67
election court: ss 123, 130, 134, 202(1)
election petition: s 202(1)
local government election (S): s 204(1)
High Court (E, W & NI): Interpretation Act 1978 Sch 1
High Court (S): s 204(3)
oath: Interpretation Act 1978 Sch 1
rules of court: Interpretation Act 1978 Sch 1
sheriff (S): Interpretation Act 1978 Sch 1
Supreme Court: Interpretation Act 1978 Sch 1

Penalty for corrupt withdrawal and breach of s 148

149 If a person makes any agreement or terms, or enters into any undertaking, in relation to the withdrawal of an election petition, and such agreement, terms or undertaking—

    (a) is or are for the withdrawal of the election petition in consideration of any payment, or in consideration that the seat or office should at any time be vacated, or in consideration of the withdrawal of any other election petition, or

    (b) is or are (whether lawful or unlawful) not mentioned in the affidavits referred to in section 148 above,

he shall be liable—

    (i) on conviction on indictment, to imprisonment for a term not exceeding one year, or to a fine, or to both;

(ii) on summary conviction, to imprisonment for a term not exceeding 6 months, or to a fine not exceeding the statutory maximum, or to both.

NOTES

Application
This provision now applied only to local authority election petitions in Scotland, and as extended by SSI

Derivation
RPA 1949 s 129

Defined terms
election petition: s 202(1)
statutory maximum: Interpretation Act 1978 Sch 1
summary conviction (NI only): Interpretation Act 1978 Sch 1

Substitution of new petitioner

150 (1) On the hearing of the application for leave to withdraw, any person who might have been a petitioner in respect of the election may apply to the court to be substituted as a petitioner, and the court may, if they think fit, substitute him accordingly.

(2) If the proposed withdrawal is in the opinion of the court the result of any agreement, terms or undertaking prohibited by section 149 above or induced by any corrupt bargain or consideration, the court may by order direct—

(a) that the security given on behalf of the original petitioner shall remain as security for any costs that may be incurred by the substituted petitioner, and

(b) that, to the extent of the sum named in the security, the original petitioner and his sureties shall be liable to pay the costs of the substituted petitioner.

(3) If the court does not so direct, then security to the same amount as would be required in the case of a new petition, and subject to the like conditions, shall be given on behalf of the substituted petitioner before he proceeds with his petition and within the prescribed time after the order of substitution.

(4) Subject to the above provisions, a substituted petitioner shall, as nearly as may be, stand in the same position and be subject to the same liabilities as the original petitioner.

NOTES

Application
This provision now applied only to local authority election petitions in Scotland, and as extended by SSI

Derivation
RPA 1949 s 130

Defined terms
costs: s 185
election petition: s 202(1)

Report on withdrawal

151(1) In every case of the withdrawal—

(a) of a parliamentary election petition, the court giving leave for the withdrawal shall make a report to the Speaker as required by subsection (2) below; and

(b) by leave of the election court, of a petition questioning an election in England and Wales under the local government Act, that court shall make a report in writing to the High Court as so required.

(2) The report shall state whether in the court's opinion the withdrawal of the petition was—

(a) the result of any agreement, terms or undertaking, or

(b) in consideration of any payment, or in consideration that the seat or office should at any time be vacated or in consideration of the withdrawal of any other election petition or for any other consideration,

and, if so, shall state the circumstances attending the withdrawal.

NOTES

Application
This provision now applied only to local authority

election petitions in Scotland, and as extended by SSI.

Derivation
RPA 1949 s 131

Defined terms
election court: ss 123, 130, 134, 202(1)
election petition: s 202(1)

England: Interpretation Act 1978 Sch 1
High Court (E, W & NI): Interpretation Act 1978 Sch 1
High Court (S): s 204(3)
report (S): s 204(7)
writing: Interpretation Act 1978 Sch 1
Wales: Interpretation Act 1978 Sch 1

Abatement of petition

152 (1) An election petition shall be abated by the death of a sole petitioner or of the survivor of several petitioners.

(2) The abatement shall not affect the liability of the petitioner or any other person to the payment of costs previously incurred.

(3) On the abatement the prescribed notice of it shall be given in the constituency or local government area to which the petition relates; and within the prescribed time after the notice is given, any person who might have been a petitioner in respect of the election may apply to the election court or High Court in the prescribed manner and in the prescribed time and place to be substituted as a petitioner; and the court may, if it thinks fit, substitute him accordingly.

(4) Security shall be given on behalf of a petitioner so substituted, as in the case of a new petition.

(5) In the application of this section to an election of councillors in Scotland the reference in subsection (3) above to the High Court shall be omitted, and the sheriff may act instead of the election court.

NOTES

Application
This provision now applied only to local authority election petitions in Scotland, and as extended by SSI.

Derivation
RPA 1949 s 133

Defined terms
constituency: Parliamentary Constituencies Act 1986

s 1(2)
costs: s 185
election court: ss 123, 130, 134, 202(1)
election petition: s 202(1)
High Court (E, W & NI): Interpretation Act 1978 Sch 1
High Court (S): s 204(3)
sheriff (S): Interpretation Act 1978 Sch 1

Withdrawal and substitution of respondents before trial

153 (1) If before the trial of an election petition a respondent other than a returning officer—

(a) gives the prescribed notice that he does not intend to oppose the petition or dies, or

(b) where the petition questions a parliamentary election or return, is summoned to Parliament as a peer by a writ issued under the Great Seal of the United Kingdom or the House of Commons have resolved that his seat is vacant, or

(c) where the petition questions an election under the local government Act, resigns or otherwise ceases to hold the office to which the petition relates,

notice of any of those matters shall be given in the constituency or local government area to which the petition relates, and, within the prescribed time after the notice is given, any person who might have been a petitioner in respect of the election may apply to a member of the election court or to the High Court to be admitted as a respondent to oppose the petition, and shall be admitted accordingly, except that the number of persons so admitted shall not exceed three.

(2) The notice to be given under subsection (1) above in any local government area shall be such as may be prescribed.

(3)   A respondent who has given the prescribed notice that he does not intend to oppose the petition shall not be allowed to appear or act as a party against the petition in any proceedings on the petition, and if the petition relates to a parliamentary election he shall not sit or vote in the House of Commons until the House of Commons has been informed of the report on the petition.

(4)   Where a respondent to a parliamentary election petition has given that notice in the prescribed time and manner, the High Court or either of the judges constituting the election court shall report that fact to the Speaker.

(5)   In the application of this section to an election of councillors in Scotland, the reference to the High Court shall be omitted and the sheriff may act instead of the election court.

NOTES

Application
This provision now applied only to local authority election petitions in Scotland, and as extended by SSI.

Derivation
RPA 1949 s 134

Defined terms
constituency: Parliamentary Constituencies Act 1986 s 1(2)
election court: ss 123, 130, 134, 202(1)

election petition: s 202(1)
election under the local government act (E&W): ss 191(1), 203(1A)
High Court (E, W & NI): Interpretation Act 1978 Sch 1
High Court (S): s 204(3)
parliamentary election: Interpretation Act 1978 Sch 1
report (S): s 204(7)
returning officer: see ss 24-27
sheriff (S): Interpretation Act 1978 Sch 1
vote: s 202(1)

Costs of petition

154(1)   All costs of and incidental to the presentation of an election petition and the proceedings consequent on it, except such as are by this Act otherwise provided for, shall be defrayed by the parties to the petition in such manner and in such proportions as the election court or High Court may determine.

(2)   In particular—
   (a)   any costs which in the opinion of the election court or High Court have been caused by vexatious conduct, unfounded allegations or unfounded objections on the part either of the petitioner or of the respondent, and
   (b)   any needless expense incurred or caused on the part of the petitioner or respondent,
   may be ordered to be defrayed by the parties by whom it has been incurred or caused whether or not they are on the whole successful.

(3)   In the application of this section to Scotland, references to the High Court shall be omitted in relation to an election of councillors.

NOTES

Derivation
RPA 1949 s 135

Defined terms
costs: s 185

election court: ss 123, 130, 134, 202(1)
election petition: s 202(1)
High Court (E, W & NI): Interpretation Act 1978 Sch 1
High Court (S): s 204(3)
respondent: ss 121(2), 128(2)

Neglect or refusal to pay costs

155(1)   Subsection (2) below applies if a petitioner neglects or refuses—
   (a)   in the case of a parliamentary election petition, for six months after demand, and
   (b)   in the case of a petition questioning an election under the local government Act, for three months after demand,
   to pay to any person summoned as a witness on his behalf or to the respondent any sum certified to be due to that person or the respondent for his costs, and the neglect

or refusal is, within one year after the demand, proved to the satisfaction of the High Court, or, in Scotland, the election court.

(2) Where subsection (1) above applies, every person who under this Act entered into a recognisance relating to that petition shall be held to be in default of the recognisance, and—

    (a) the prescribed officer shall thereupon certify the recognisance to be forfeited, and

    (b) it shall be dealt with as if forfeited by the Crown Court, or, in Northern Ireland, under the Fines Act (Ireland) 1851, as the case may be,

but in Scotland the prescribed officer shall, where otherwise competent under the provisions of this subsection—

    (i) certify that the conditions contained in the bond of caution have not been fulfilled; and

    (ii) it shall then be competent for the party or parties interested to register that bond, and do diligence upon it as accords of law.

NOTES

Derivation
  RPA 1949 s 135

Defined terms
  costs: s 185
  Crown Court: Interpretation Act 1978 Sch 1
  election court: ss 123, 130, 134, 202(1)
  election under the local government act (E&W): ss 191(1), 203(1A)

High Court (E, W & NI): Interpretation Act 1978 Sch 1
High Court (S): s 204(3)
local government Act (E&W): s 203(1)
local government Act (S): s 204(1)
parliamentary election petition: s 120
recognisance (S): s 204(6)
respondent: ss 121(2), 128(2)

Further provision as to costs

156(1) Where upon the trial of an election petition it appears to the election court—

    (a) that a corrupt practice has not been proved to have been committed in reference to the election by or with the knowledge and consent of the respondent to the petition, and

    (b) that the respondent took all reasonable means to prevent corrupt practices being committed on his behalf,

the court may, subject to the provisions of subsection (5) below, make such order with respect to the whole or part of the costs of the petition as is mentioned in that subsection.

(2)-(4) *Repealed*

(5) If it appears to the court that any person or persons is or are proved, whether by providing money or otherwise, to have been extensively engaged in corrupt practices, or to have encouraged or promoted extensive corrupt practices in reference to the election, the court may, after giving that person or those persons an opportunity of being heard by counsel, a solicitor or an authorised person and examining and cross-examining witnesses to show cause why the order should not be made—

    (a) order the whole or part of the costs to be paid by that person, or those persons or any of them, and

    (b) order that if the costs cannot be recovered from one or more of those persons they shall be paid by some other of those persons or by either of the parties to the petition.

(5A) In subsection (5) "authorised person" means a person (other than counsel or a solicitor) who, for the purposes of the Legal Services Act 2007, is an authorised person in relation to an activity which constitutes the exercise of a right of audience (within the meaning of that Act).

(6) Where any person appears to the court to have been guilty of a corrupt or illegal practice, the court may, after giving that person an opportunity of making a statement to show why the order should not be made, order the whole or any part of the costs of or incidental to any proceeding before the court in relation to that offence or to that person to be paid by that person to such person or persons as the court may direct.

NOTES

Derivation
RPA 1949 s 136

Defined terms
corrupt practice: see ss 60(1), 62A(5), 62B(2), (3), 65A(1), (2), 65B(2), (3), 75(5), 75ZB(4), 75A(7), 82(6), 113(1), 114(1), 115(1), Sch 1 rule 6A(2), Sch 4 para 5
costs: s 185
election: s 202(1)
election court: ss 123, 130, 134, 202(1)

election petition: s 202(1)
illegal practice: ss 61(7), 68(2, 71A(3), 73(6), 75(5), 75ZB(3), 75A(8), (11), 76(1B), 76ZA(5), 78(3), 84, 90(2), 92(2), (3), 97(1), 106(1), (5), 109(2), 110(12), 110A(14), 175(2), 189(1), Sch 4 paras 1(2), 5
money: s 185
person: s 202(1)
respondent: ss 121(2), 128(2)

Appeals and jurisdiction

157(1) No appeal lies without the special leave of the High Court from the decision of the High Court on any question of law, whether on appeal or otherwise, under the foregoing provisions of this Part of this Act, and if leave to appeal is granted the decision of the Court of Appeal in the case shall be final and conclusive.

(2) Subject to the provisions of this Act and of the rules made under it, the principles, practice and rules on which committees of the House of Commons used to act in dealing with election petitions shall be observed, so far as may be, by the High Court and election court in the case of election petitions, and in particular the principles and rules with regard to—

(a) agency,

(b) evidence,

(c) a scrutiny, and

(d) declaring any person elected in place of any other person declared not to have been duly elected,

shall be observed, as far as may be, in the case of a petition questioning an election under the local government Act as in the case of a parliamentary election petition.

(3) The High Court has, subject to the provisions of this Act, the same powers, jurisdiction and authority with respect to an election petition and the proceedings on it as if the petition were an ordinary action within its jurisdiction.

(4) The duties to be performed in relation to parliamentary elections by the prescribed officer under this Part shall be performed by such one or more of the masters of the Senior Courts (Queen's Bench Division) as the Lord Chief Justice may determine.

(5) *Repealed*

(6) The duties to be performed in relation to elections under the local government Act by the prescribed officer under this Part shall be performed by the prescribed officer of the High Court.

(7) In the application of this section to Scotland, subsections (1) and (4) to (6) above and, in relation to elections of councillors, subsection (3) above, shall be omitted, but the duties to be performed in relation to parliamentary elections by the prescribed officer under this Part shall be performed by the Principal Clerk of Session.

(8) Subsection (1) above does not apply in Northern Ireland and, in the application of subsections (4) and (5) to Northern Ireland, the references to the Lord Chief Justice are references to the Lord Chief Justice of Northern Ireland and the reference to any

master of the Senior Courts (Queen's Bench Division) is a reference to an officer of the Court of Judicature of Northern Ireland.

NOTES

Derivation
  RPA 1949 s 137

Defined terms
  court of appeal: Interpretation Act 1978 Sch 1
  election court: ss 123, 130, 134, 202(1)
  election petition: s 202(1)
  election under the local government act (E&W): ss 191(1), 203(1A)

High Court (E, W & NI): Interpretation Act 1978 Sch 1
High Court (S): s 204(3)
local government Act (E&W): s 203(1)
local government Act (S): s 204(1)
a parliamentary election petition: ss 120, 202(1)
parliamentary election: Interpretation Act 1978 Sch 1
prescribed: s 185

Consequences of finding by election court of corrupt or illegal practice

Report as to candidate guilty of a corrupt or illegal practice

158(1) The report of an election court under section 144 or section 145 above shall state whether any corrupt or illegal practice has or has not been proved to have been committed by or with the knowledge and consent of any candidate at the election, and the nature of the corrupt or illegal practice.

(2) For the purposes of sections 159 and 160 below—
    (a) if it is reported that a corrupt practice other than treating or undue influence was committed with the knowledge and consent of a candidate, he shall be treated as having been reported personally guilty of that corrupt practice, and
    (b) if it is reported that an illegal practice was committed with the knowledge and consent of a candidate at a parliamentary election, he shall be treated as having been reported personally guilty of that illegal practice.

(3) The report shall also state whether any of the candidates has been guilty by his agents of any corrupt or illegal practice in reference to the election; but if a candidate is reported guilty by his agents of treating, undue influence or any illegal practice, and the court further reports that the candidate has proved to the court—
    (a) that no corrupt or illegal practice was committed at the election by the candidate or his election agent and the offences mentioned in the report were committed contrary to the orders and without the sanction or connivance of the candidate or his election agent, and
    (b) that the candidate and his election agent took all reasonable means for preventing the commission of corrupt and illegal practices at the election, and
    (c) that the offences mentioned in the report were of a trivial, unimportant and limited character, and
    (d) that in all other respects the election was free from any corrupt or illegal practice on the part of the candidate and of his agents,
then the candidate shall not be treated for the purposes of section 159 as having been reported guilty by his agents of the offences mentioned in the report.
In relation to an election where candidates are not required to have election agents, for paragraphs (a) and (b) above the following paragraphs shall be substituted—
    "(a) that no corrupt or illegal practice was committed at the election by candidate or with his knowledge or consent and the offences mentioned in the report were committed without the sanction or connivance of the candidate, and
    (b) that all reasonable means for preventing the commission of corrupt and illegal practices at the election were taken by and on behalf of the candidate, ".

NOTES

Derivation
RPA 1949 s 138

Defined terms
candidate: ss 118A, 185
corrupt practice: see ss 60(1), 62A(5), 62B(2), (3), 65A(1), (2), 65B(2), (3), 75(5), 75ZB(4), 75A(7), 82(6), 113(1), 114(1), 115(1), Sch 1 rule 6A(2), Sch 4 para 5
election: s 202(1)
election agent: see s 67
election court: ss 123, 130, 134, 202(1)

illegal practice: ss 61(7), 68(2, 71A(3), 73(6), 75(5), 75ZB(3), 75A(8), (11), 76(1B), 76ZA(5), 78(3), 84, 90(2), 92(2), (3), 97(1), 106(1), (5), 109(2), 110(12), 110A(14), 175(2), 189(1), Sch 4 paras 1(2), 5
parliamentary election: Interpretation Act 1978 Sch 1
report (S): s 204(7)
treating: s 114(2), (3)
undue influence; s 115(2)

Candidate reported guilty of corrupt or illegal practice

159(1)   If a candidate who has been elected is reported by an election court personally guilty or guilty by his agents of any corrupt or illegal practice his election shall be void.

(2)   *Repealed*

(3)   A candidate at a local government election in Scotland who is reported personally guilty or guilty by his agents of any corrupt or illegal practice shall also be incapable from the date of the report of holding the office of councillor of any local authority in Scotland—

   (a)   for ten years, if reported personally guilty of a corrupt practice,

   (b)   for three years, if reported guilty by his agents of a corrupt practice, or

   (c)   during the period for which the candidate was elected to serve or for which if elected he might have served, if reported personally guilty or guilty by his agents of an illegal practice,

and if at the date of the report he holds any such office, then the office shall be vacated as from that date.

(4)   The provisions of this section as to the consequences of the report that a candidate was guilty by his agents of a corrupt or illegal practice have effect subject to the express provisions of this Act relating to particular acts which are declared to be corrupt or illegal practices.

NOTES

Derivation
RPA 1949 s 139

Defined terms
candidate: ss 118A, 185
corrupt practice: see ss 60(1), 62A(5), 62B(2), (3), 65A(1), (2), 65B(2), (3), 75(5), 75ZB(4), 75A(7), 82(6), 113(1), 114(1), 115(1), Sch 1 rule 6A(2), Sch 4 para 5
election court: ss 123, 130, 134, 202(1)

illegal practice: ss 61(7), 68(2, 71A(3), 73(6), 75(5), 75ZB(3), 75A(8), (11), 76(1B), 76ZA(5), 78(3), 84, 90(2), 92(2), (3), 97(1), 106(1), (5), 109(2), 110(12), 110A(14), 175(2), 189(1), Sch 4 paras 1(2), 5
local authority (S): s 204(1)
local government election (S): s 204(1)
report (S): s 204(7)

Persons reported personally guilty of corrupt or illegal practices

160(1)   The report of the election court under section 144 or section 145 above shall state the names of all persons (if any) who have been proved at the trial to have been guilty of any corrupt or illegal practice, but in the case of someone—

   (a)   who is not a party to the petition, or

   (b)   who is not a candidate on behalf of whom the seat or office is claimed by the petition,

the election court shall first cause notice to be given to him, and if he appears in pursuance of the notice shall give him an opportunity of being heard by himself and of calling evidence in his defence to show why he should not be so reported.

(2)   *Repealed*

(3) The report shall be laid before the Director of Public Prosecutions.

(4) Subject to the provisions of subsection (4A) and section 174 below, a candidate or other person reported by an election court personally guilty of a corrupt or illegal practice—

    (a) shall during the relevant period specified in subsection (5) below be incapable of—

        (i) being registered as an elector or voting at any parliamentary election in the United Kingdom or at any local government election in Great Britain,

        (ii) being elected to the House of Commons, or

        (iii) holding any elective office; and

    (b) if already elected to a seat in the House of Commons, or holding any such office, shall vacate the seat or office as from the date of the report.

(4A) The incapacity imposed by subsection (4)(a)(i) above applies only to a candidate or other person reported personally guilty of a corrupt practice under section 60, 62A or 62B above or of an illegal practice under section 61 above.

(5) For the purposes of subsection (4) above the relevant period is the period beginning with the date of the report and ending—

    (a) in the case of a person reported personally guilty of a corrupt practice, five years after that date, or

    (b) in the case of a person reported personally guilty of an illegal practice, three years after that date.

(5A) Subject to the provisions of section 174 but in addition to any incapacity arising by virtue of subsection (4) above, a candidate or other person reported by an election court personally guilty of a corrupt practice—

    (a) shall for the period of five years beginning with the date of the report, be incapable of holding any public or judicial office in Scotland, and

    (b) if already holding such an office, shall vacate it as from that date.

(5B) *Repealed*

(6) Without prejudice to the generality of the provisions of section 205(2) below, nothing in subsection (4) or subsection (5) above affects matters relating to the Northern Ireland Assembly or local elections or holding office in Northern Ireland.

(7) The provisions of this section as to the consequences of the report that a candidate was guilty by his agents of a corrupt or illegal practice have effect subject to the express provisions of this Act relating to particular acts which are declared to be corrupt or illegal practices.

NOTES

Derivation
RPA 1949 s 140

Defined terms
candidate: ss 118A, 185
corrupt practice: see ss 60(1), 62A(5), 62B(2), (3), 65A(1), (2), 65B(2), (3), 75(5), 75ZB(4), 75A(7), 82(6), 113(1), 114(1), 115(1), Sch 1 rule 6A(2), Sch 4 para 5
Director of Public Prosecutions (S): s 204(5)
Director of Public Prosecutions (NI): s 205(1)
election court: ss 123, 130, 134, 202(1)
elective office: s 185
elector: s 202(1)
Great Britain: Union with Scotland Act 1706 art 1 and Interpretation Act 1978 s 22(1) and Sch 2 para 5

illegal practice: ss 61(7), 68(2, 71A(3), 73(6), 75(5), 75ZB(3), 75A(8), (11), 76(1B), 76ZA(5), 78(3), 84, 90(2), 92(2), (3), 97(1), 106(1), (5), 109(2), 110(12), 110A(14), 175(2), 189(1), Sch 4 paras 1(2), 5
judicial office: s 185
local government election (E&W): ss 191(1), 203(1), (1A)
local government election (S): s 204(1)
parliamentary election: Interpretation Act 1978 Sch 1
person: s 202(1)
public office: s 185
report (S): s 204(7)
vote: s 202(1)
voting: see "vote" s 202(1)

Director of Public Prosecutions' duty to report corrupt practice

Justice of the Peace

161 Where a justice of the peace is reported by an election court to have been guilty of any corrupt practice in reference to an election, the court shall report the case to the Lord Chancellor and the Lord Chief Justice or, in the case of a justice of the peace for any area in Scotland, to the Secretary of State with such evidence as may have been given of the corrupt practice.

NOTES

Derivation
  RPA 1949 s 141

Defined terms
  corrupt practice: see ss 60(1), 62A(5), 62B(2), (3), 65A(1), (2), 65B(2), (3), 75(5), 75ZB(4), 75A(7), 82(6),

113(1), 114(1), 115(1), Sch 1 rule 6A(2), Sch 4 para 5
election: s 202(1)
election court: ss 123, 130, 134, 202(1)
report (S): s 204(7)

Member of legal and certain other professions

162(1) Where a barrister, advocate, solicitor, authorised person or any person who belongs to any profession the admission to which is regulated by law is reported by an election court to have been guilty of any corrupt practice in reference to an election,—

    (a) the court shall bring the matter before the Inn of Court Faculty of Advocates, High Court, tribunal or other body having power to take cognizance of any misconduct of the person in his profession; and

    (b) the Inn of Court Faculty of Advocates, High Court, tribunal or other body may deal with him as if the corrupt practice were misconduct by him in his profession.

  (2) In subsection (1) "authorised person" means a person (other than a barrister or solicitor) who, for the purposes of the Legal Services Act 2007, is an authorised person in relation to an activity which constitutes a reserved legal activity (within the meaning of that Act).

NOTES

Derivation
  RPA 1949 s 141

Defined terms
  corrupt practice: see ss 60(1), 62A(5), 62B(2), (3), 65A(1), (2), 65B(2), (3), 75(5), 75ZB(4), 75A(7), 82(6), 113(1), 114(1), 115(1), Sch 1 rule 6A(2), Sch 4 para 5

election: s 202(1)
election court: ss 123, 130, 134, 202(1)
High Court (E, W & NI): Interpretation Act 1978 Sch 1
High Court (S): s 204(3)
report (S): s 204(7)

Holder of licence or certificate under Licensing Acts

163(1) If it appears to an election court that a person holding a licence or certificate under the Licensing Acts has knowingly permitted any bribery or treating in reference to any election to take place upon his licensed premises—

    (a) the court shall, after affording him such rights as are conferred on those about to be reported under section 160(1) above, report the fact; and

    (b) the court shall bring the report before the licensing authority from whom, or on whose certificate, that person obtained his licence, and the licensing authority shall cause the report to be entered in the proper register of licences.

  (2) The entry of the report in that register shall be taken into consideration by the licensing authority in determining whether they will or will not grant a renewal of the licence or certificate of the person reported and may be a ground, if the authority think fit, for refusing renewal.

NOTES

Derivation
   RPA 1949 s 141

Defined terms
   election: s 202(1)
   election court: ss 123, 130, 134, 202(1)

Licensing Acts: s 185
register of licences (S): s 204(8)
report (S): s 204(7)
treating: s 114(2), (3)

Further provision as to avoidance of elections and striking off votes

Avoidance of election for general corruption etc

164(1)   Where on an election petition it is shown that corrupt or illegal practices or illegal payments, employments or hirings committed in reference to the election for the purpose of promoting or procuring the election of any person at that election have so extensively prevailed that they may be reasonably supposed to have affected the result—

    (a)   his election, if he has been elected, shall be void, and

    (b)   he shall be incapable of being elected to fill the vacancy or any of the vacancies for which the election was held.

(2)   An election shall not be liable to be avoided otherwise than under this section by reason of general corruption, bribery, treating or intimidation.

(3)   An election under the local government Act may be questioned on the ground that it is avoided under this section.

NOTES

Derivation
   RPA 1949 s 142

Defined terms
   corrupt practice: see ss 60(1), 62A(5), 62B(2), (3), 65A(1), (2), 65B(2), (3), 75(5), 75ZB(4), 75A(7), 82(6), 113(1), 114(1), 115(1), Sch 1 rule 6A(2), Sch 4 para 5
   election: s 202(1)
   election petition: s 202(1)
   election under the local government act (E&W): ss 191(1), 203(1A)
   illegal employment: s 111

illegal payment: ss 107, 112
illegal practice: ss 61(7), 68(2, 71A(3), 73(6), 75(5), 75ZB(3), 75A(8), (11), 76(1B), 76ZA(5), 78(3), 84, 90(2), 92(2), (3), 97(1), 106(1), (5), 109(2), 110(12), 110A(14), 175(2), 189(1), Sch 4 paras 1(2), 5
local government Act (E&W): s 203(1)
local government Act (S): s 204(1)
promoting or procuring a candidate's election: s 90ZA(6)
treating: s 114(2), (3)

Avoidance of election for employing corrupt agent

165(1)   If at a parliamentary or local government election a candidate or his election agent personally engages as a canvasser or agent for the conduct or management of the election any person whom he knows or has reasonable grounds for supposing to be subject to an incapacity to vote at the election by reason—

    (a)   of his having been convicted or reported of any corrupt or illegal practice within the meaning of this Act or of the law relating to elections for the Northern Ireland Assembly,

    (b)   *Repealed*

the candidate shall be incapable of being elected to fill the vacancy or any of the vacancies for which the election is held.

(2)   A local government election may be questioned on the ground that the person whose election is questioned was, at the time of the election, by virtue of this section incapable of being elected.

(3)   A vote given for a person who, at the time of the election, was by virtue of this section incapable of being elected shall not, by reason of that incapacity, be deemed to be thrown away so as to entitle another candidate to be declared elected, unless given at a poll consequent on the decision of an election court that he was so incapable.

(4) In the case of an election of the Mayor of London, a vote deemed in accordance with subsection (3) above to be thrown away shall be so deemed only to the extent that it is a vote given so as to indicate that the person who was under the incapacity is the voter's first or second preference from among the candidates.

NOTES

Derivation
RPA 1949 s 143

Defined terms
candidate: ss 118A, 185
corrupt practice: see ss 60(1), 62A(5), 62B(2), (3), 65A(1), (2), 65B(2), (3), 75(5), 75ZB(4), 75A(7), 82(6), 113(1), 114(1), 115(1), Sch 1 rule 6A(2), Sch 4 para 5
election agent: see s 67
election court: ss 123, 130, 134, 202(1)
election of the Mayor of London: s 203(1)

illegal practice: ss 61(7), 68(2, 71A(3), 73(6), 75(5), 75ZB(3), 75A(8), (11), 76(1B), 76ZA(5), 78(3), 84, 90(2), 92(2), (3), 97(1), 106(1), (5), 109(2), 110(12), 110A(14), 175(2), 189(1), Sch 4 paras 1(2), 5
local government election (E&W): s 203(1), (1A)
local government election (S): s 204(1)
report (S): s 204(7)
reported of a corrupt or illegal practice (S): s 204(7)
vote: s 202(1)

Votes to be struck off for corrupt or illegal practices

166(1) Where, on a parliamentary election petition claiming the seat for any person, a candidate is proved to have been guilty by himself, or by any person on his behalf, of bribery, treating or undue influence in respect of any person who voted at the election there shall, on a scrutiny, be struck off from the number of votes appearing to have been given to the candidate one vote for every person who voted at the election and is proved to have been so bribed, treated or unduly influenced.

(2) If any person who is guilty of a corrupt or illegal practice or of illegal payment, employment or hiring at an election votes at the election, his vote shall be void.

(3) If any person who is subject under any enactment relating to corrupt or illegal practices to an incapacity to vote at a parliamentary election, local government election or an election under the Local Government (Scotland) etc Act 1994 (c 39) to any public office in Scotland votes at that election, his vote shall be void.

NOTES

Derivation
RPA 1949 s 166

Defined terms
candidate: ss 118A, 185
corrupt practice: see ss 60(1), 62A(5), 62B(2), (3), 65A(1), (2), 65B(2), (3), 75(5), 75ZB(4), 75A(7), 82(6), 113(1), 114(1), 115(1), Sch 1 rule 6A(2), Sch 4 para 5
election: s 202(1)
enactment: Interpretation Act 1978 Sch 1
enactment (NI): s 205
illegal employment: s 111
illegal payment: ss 107, 112
illegal practice: ss 61(7), 68(2, 71A(3), 73(6), 75(5),

75ZB(3), 75A(8), (11), 76(1B), 76ZA(5), 78(3), 84, 90(2), 92(2), (3), 97(1), 106(1), (5), 109(2), 110(12), 110A(14), 175(2), 189(1), Sch 4 paras 1(2), 5
local government election (E&W): ss 191(1), 203(1), (1A)
local government election (S): s 204(1)
parliamentary election: Interpretation Act 1978 Sch 1
a parliamentary election petition: ss 120, 202(1)
public office: s 185
treating: s 114(2), (3)
undue influence; s 115(2)
vote: s 202(1)

Power to except innocent act from being illegal practice, payment, employment or hiring

Application for relief

167(1) An application for relief under this section may be made to the High Court or an election court or else, if in respect of a payment made in contravention of section 78(1) or (2) above, or of paragraph 1 of Schedule 4 to this Act, to the county court.

(1A) Where a person makes an application under this section he shall notify the Director of Public Prosecutions of the application and the Director or his assistant or representative may attend the hearing of the application and make representations at the hearing in respect of it.

(2) If it is shown to the court by such evidence as to the court seems sufficient—

    (a) that any act or omission of any person would apart from this section by reason of being in contravention of this Act be an illegal practice, payment, employment or hiring,

    (b) that the act or omission arose from inadvertence or from accidental miscalculation or from some other reasonable cause of a like nature, and in any case did not arise from any want of good faith, and

    (c) that such notice of the application has been given in the constituency or, as the case may be, the area of the authority for which the election was held, as to the court seems fit,

and under the circumstances it seems to the court to be just that either that or any other person should not be subject to any of the consequences under this Act of the act or omission, the court may make an order allowing the act or omission to be an exception from the provisions of this Act making it an illegal practice, payment, employment or hiring and upon the making of the order no person shall be subject to any of the consequences under this Act of that act or omission.

(3) In relation to an election of councillors in Scotland, the references in subsection (1) to applications to the High Court or the county court shall be omitted.

(4) *Repealed*

(5) Article 60 of the County Courts (Northern Ireland) Order 1980 (appeals from county courts) shall apply in relation to any order of a county court in Northern Ireland made by virtue of this section as it applies in relation to any such decree of a county court as is mentioned in paragraph (1) of that Article.

NOTES

Derivation
  RPA 1949 s 145

Defined terms
  constituency: Parliamentary Constituencies Act 1986 s 1(2)
  county court: Interpretation Act 1978 Sch 1
  Director of Public Prosecutions (S): s 204(5)
  Director of Public Prosecutions (NI): s 205(1)
  election: s 202(1)
  election court: ss 123, 130, 134, 202(1)

High Court (E, W & NI): Interpretation Act 1978 Sch 1
High Court (S): s 204(3)
illegal employment: s 111
illegal payment: ss 107, 112
illegal practice: ss 61(7), 68(2, 71A(3), 73(6), 75(5), 75ZB(3), 75A(8), (11), 76(1B), 76ZA(5), 78(3), 84, 90(2), 92(2), (3), 97(1), 106(1), (5), 109(2), 110(12), 110A(14), 175(2), 189(1), Sch 4 paras 1(2), 5

Prosecutions for corrupt or illegal practices

Prosecutions for corrupt practices

168(1) A person who is guilty of a corrupt practice shall be liable—

    (a) on conviction on indictment—

        (i) in the case of a corrupt practice under section 60 or 62A above, to imprisonment for a term not exceeding two years, or to a fine, or to both,

        (ii) in any other case, to imprisonment for a term not exceeding one year, or to a fine, or to both;

    (b) on summary conviction, to imprisonment for a term not exceeding 6 months, or to a fine not exceeding the statutory maximum, or to both.

(2)-(6) *Repealed*

(7) If it appears to the court by which any person holding a licence or certificate under the Licensing Acts is convicted of the offence of bribery or treating that the offence was committed on his licensed premises—

(a) the court shall direct the conviction to be entered in the proper register of licences, and

(b) the entry shall be taken into consideration by the licensing authority in determining whether they will or will not grant a renewal of the licence or certificate, and may be a ground, if the authority think fit, for refusing its renewal.

NOTES

Derivation
RPA 1949 s 146

Defined terms
corrupt practice: see ss 60(1), 62A(5), 62B(2), (3), 65A(1), (2), 65B(2), (3), 75(5), 75ZB(4), 75A(7), 82(6), 113(1), 114(1), 115(1), Sch 1 rule 6A(2), Sch 4 para 5
Licensing Acts: s 185

person: s 202(1)
register of licences (S): s 204(8)
statutory maximum: Interpretation Act 1978 Sch 1
summary conviction (NI only): Interpretation Act 1978 Sch 1
treating: s 114(2), (3)

Prosecutions for illegal practices

169 A person guilty of an illegal practice shall on summary conviction be liable to a fine not exceeding level 5 on the standard scale; and on a prosecution for an illegal practice it shall be sufficient to allege that the person charged was guilty of an illegal practice.

NOTES

Derivation
RPA 1949 s 146

Defined terms
illegal practice: ss 61(7), 68(2, 71A(3), 73(6), 75(5), 75ZB(3), 75A(8), (11), 76(1B), 76ZA(5), 78(3), 84, 90(2), 92(2), (3), 97(1), 106(1), (5), 109(2), 110(12), 110A(14),

175(2), 189(1), Sch 4 paras 1(2), 5
person: s 202(1)
standard scale: Interpretation Act 1978 Sch 1
summary conviction (NI only): Interpretation Act 1978 Sch 1

Conviction of illegal practice on charge of corrupt practice etc

170 A person charged with a corrupt practice may, if the circumstances warrant such finding, be found guilty of an illegal practice (which offence shall for that purpose be an indictable offence), and a person charged with an illegal practice may be found guilty of that offence notwithstanding that the act constituting the offence amounted to a corrupt practice.

NOTES

Derivation
RPA 1949 s 148

Defined terms
corrupt practice: see ss 60(1), 62A(5), 62B(2), (3), 65A(1), (2), 65B(2), (3), 75(5), 75ZB(4), 75A(7), 82(6), 113(1), 114(1), 115(1), Sch 1 rule 6A(2), Sch 4 para 5
illegal practice: ss 61(7), 68(2, 71A(3), 73(6), 75(5),

75ZB(3), 75A(8), (11), 76(1B), 76ZA(5), 78(3), 84, 90(2), 92(2), (3), 97(1), 106(1), (5), 109(2), 110(12), 110A(14), 175(2), 189(1), Sch 4 paras 1(2), 5
indictable offence (E&W only): Interpretation Act 1978 Sch 1
person: s 202(1)

171 *Repealed*

172 *Repealed*

Incapacities on conviction of corrupt or illegal practice

173(1) Subject to subsection (2) below, a person convicted of a corrupt or illegal practice—

(a) shall, during the relevant period specified in subsection (3) below, be incapable of—

(i) being registered as an elector or voting at any parliamentary election in the United Kingdom or at any local government election in Great Britain, or

(ii) being elected to the House of Commons, or

(iii)   holding any elective office; and

(b)   if already elected to a seat in the House of Commons or holding any such office, shall vacate the seat or office subject to and in accordance with subsections (4) and (5) below.

(2)   The incapacity imposed by subsection (1)(a)(i) above applies only to a person convicted of a corrupt practice under section 60, 62A or 62B above or of an illegal practice under section 61 above.

(3)   For the purposes of subsection (1)(a) above the relevant period is the period beginning with the date of the conviction and ending—

(a)   in the case of a person convicted of a corrupt practice, five years after that date, or

(b)   in the case of a person convicted of an illegal practice, three years after that date,

except that if (at any time within that period of five or three years) a court determines on an appeal by that person against the conviction that it should not be upheld, the relevant period shall end at that time instead.

(4)   Where subsection (1)(b) applies to any person, he shall (subject to subsection (5) below) vacate the seat or office in question at the appropriate time for the purposes of this section, namely—

(a)   the end of the period which is the period prescribed by law within which notice of appeal may be given, or an application for leave to appeal may be made, by him in respect of the conviction, or

(b)   if (at any time within that period) that period is extended—

(i)   the end of the period as so extended, or

(ii)   the end of the period of three months beginning with the date of the conviction,

whichever is the earlier.

(5)   If (before the appropriate time mentioned in subsection (4) above) notice of appeal is given, or an application for leave to appeal is made, by such a person in respect of the conviction, he shall vacate the seat or office in question at the end of the period of three months beginning with the date of the conviction unless—

(a)   such an appeal is dismissed or abandoned at any earlier time (in which case he shall vacate the seat or office at that time), or

(b)   at any time within that period of three months the court determines on such an appeal that the conviction should not be upheld (in which case the seat or office shall not be vacated by him).

(6)   Where such a person vacates a seat or office in accordance with subsection (4) or (5) above, no subsequent determination of a court that his conviction should not be upheld shall entitle him to resume the seat or office.

(7)   If a person convicted of a corrupt or illegal practice has already been elected to a seat in the House of Commons or to any elective office, he shall (in addition to being subject to the incapacities mentioned in subsection (1)(a) above) be suspended from performing any of his functions as a Member of Parliament, or (as the case may be) any of the functions of that office, during the period of suspension specified in subsection (8) below.

(8)   For the purposes of subsection (7) above the period of suspension is the period beginning with the date of the conviction and ending with—

(a)   the date on which the seat or office is vacated in accordance with subsection (4) or (5) above, or

(b)   where subsection (5)(b) above applies, the date on which the court determines that the conviction should not be upheld.

(9) Any incapacities or other requirement applying to a person by virtue of subsection (1) or (7) above applies in addition to any punishment imposed under section 168 or 169 above; but each of those subsections has effect subject to section 174 below.

(10) Without prejudice to the generality of section 205(2) below, nothing in this section affects matters relating to the Northern Ireland Assembly or local elections or holding office in Northern Ireland.

NOTES

Derivation
Political Parties, Elections and Referendums Act 2000 s 136

Defined terms
corrupt practice: see ss 60(1), 62A(5), 62B(2), (3), 65A(1), (2), 65B(2), (3), 75(5), 75ZB(4), 75A(7), 82(6), 113(1), 114(1), 115(1), Sch 1 rule 6A(2), Sch 4 para 5
elective office: s 185
elector: s 202(1)
Great Britain: Union with Scotland Act 1706 art 1 and

Interpretation Act 1978 s 22(1) and Sch 2 para 5
illegal practice: ss 61(7), 68(2, 71A(3), 73(6), 75(5), 75ZB(3), 75A(8), (11), 76(1B), 76ZA(5), 78(3), 84, 90(2), 92(2), (3), 97(1), 106(1), (5), 109(2), 110(12), 110A(14), 175(2), 189(1), Sch 4 paras 1(2), 5
local government election (E&W): s 203(1), (1A)
local government election (S): s 204(1)
parliamentary election: Interpretation Act 1978 Sch 1
voting: see "vote" s 202(1)

Incapacity to hold public or judicial office in Scotland

73A(1) Subject to section 174 below, a person convicted of a corrupt practice—

    (a) shall for the period of five years beginning with the date of his conviction, be incapable of holding any public or judicial office in Scotland, and

    (b) if already holding such an office, shall vacate it as from that date.

(2) Subsection (1) above applies in addition to—

    (a) any incapacity or other requirement applying to the person by virtue of section 173 above, and

    (b) any punishment imposed on him under section 168 above.

(3) *Repealed*

NOTES

Derivation
Political Parties, Elections and Referendums Act 2000 s 136

Defined terms

corrupt practice: see ss 60(1), 62A(5), 62B(2), (3), 65A(1), (2), 65B(2), (3), 75(5), 75ZB(4), 75A(7), 82(6), 113(1), 114(1), 115(1), Sch 1 rule 6A(2), Sch 4 para 5
judicial office: s 185
public office: s 185

Mitigation and remission of incapacities

Mitigation and remission etc

174(1) Where—

    (a) any person is subject to any incapacity by virtue of the report of an election court, and

    (b) he or some other person in respect of whose acts the incapacity was imposed is on a prosecution acquitted of any of the matters in respect of which the incapacity was imposed,

the court may order that the incapacity shall thenceforth cease so far as it is imposed in respect of those matters.

(2) Where any person who is subject to any incapacity as mentioned above is on a prosecution convicted of any such matters as are mentioned above, no further incapacity shall be taken to be imposed by reason of the conviction, and the court shall have the like power (if any) to mitigate or remit for the future the incapacity so far as it is imposed by section 160 above in respect of the matters of which he is convicted, as if the incapacity had been imposed by reason of the conviction.

(3) A court exercising any of the powers conferred by subsections (1) and (2) above shall make an order declaring how far, if at all, the incapacities imposed by virtue of the relevant report remain unaffected by the exercise of that power, and that order shall be conclusive for all purposes.

(4) Where a person convicted of a corrupt or illegal practice is subsequently reported to have been guilty of that practice by an election court, no further incapacity shall be imposed on him under section 160 by reason of the report.

(5) Where any person is subject to any incapacity by virtue of a conviction or of the report of an election court, and any witness who gave evidence against that person upon the proceeding for the conviction or report is convicted of perjury in respect of that evidence, the incapacitated person may apply to the High Court, and the court, if satisfied that the conviction or report so far as respects that person was based upon perjury, may order that the incapacity shall thenceforth cease.

(6) *Repealed*

NOTES

Derivation
RPA 1949 a 152

Defined terms
corrupt practice: see ss 60(1), 62A(5), 62B(2), (3), 65A(1), (2), 65B(2), (3), 75(5), 75ZB(4), 75A(7), 82(6), 113(1), 114(1), 115(1), Sch 1 rule 6A(2), Sch 4 para 5
election court: ss 123, 130, 134, 202(1)
High Court (E, W & NI): Interpretation Act 1978 Sch 1

High Court (S): s 204(3)
illegal practice: ss 61(7), 68(2, 71A(3), 73(6), 75(5), 75ZB(3), 75A(8), (11), 76(1B), 76ZA(5), 78(3), 84, 90(2), 92(2), (3), 97(1), 106(1), (5), 109(2), 110(12), 110A(14), 175(2), 189(1), Sch 4 paras 1(2), 5
report (S): s 204(7)

Illegal payments, employments or hirings

Illegal payments etc

175(1) A person guilty of an offence of illegal payment or employment shall, on summary conviction, be liable to a fine not exceeding level 5 on the standard scale; and on a prosecution for such an offence it shall be sufficient to allege that the person charged was guilty of an illegal payment or employment as the case may be.

(2) A candidate or election agent who is personally guilty of an offence of illegal payment or employment shall be guilty of an illegal practice, and if an offence of illegal payment or employment is committed with the candidate's knowledge and consent at an election where candidates are not required to have election agents, the candidate shall be guilty of an illegal practice.

(3) Any person charged with an offence of illegal payment or employment may be found guilty of that offence, notwithstanding that the act constituting the offence amounted to a corrupt or illegal practice.

NOTES

Derivation
RPA 1949 s 153

Defined terms
candidate: ss 118A, 185
corrupt practice: see ss 60(1), 62A(5), 62B(2), (3), 65A(1), (2), 65B(2), (3), 75(5), 75ZB(4), 75A(7), 82(6), 113(1), 114(1), 115(1), Sch 1 rule 6A(2), Sch 4 para 5
election: s 202(1)
election agent: see s 67
illegal employment: s 111

illegal payment: ss 107, 112
illegal practice: ss 61(7), 68(2, 71A(3), 73(6), 75(5), 75ZB(3), 75A(8), (11), 76(1B), 76ZA(5), 78(3), 84, 90(2), 92(2), (3), 97(1), 106(1), (5), 109(2), 110(12), 110A(14), 175(2), 189(1), Sch 4 paras 1(2), 5
person: s 202(1)
standard scale: Interpretation Act 1978 Sch 1
summary conviction (NI only): Interpretation Act 1978 Sch 1

General provisions as to prosecutions

Time limit for prosecutions

176(1) A proceeding against a person in respect of any offence under any provision contained in or made under this Act shall be commenced within one year after the offence was committed, and the time so limited by this section shall, in the case of any proceedings under the Magistrates' Courts Act 1980 (or, in Northern Ireland, the Magistrates' Courts (Northern Ireland) Order 1981) for any such offence be substituted for any limitation of time contained in that Act or Order.

(2) For the purposes of this section—

    (a) in England and Wales, the laying of an information;

    (b) in Scotland, the granting of a warrant to apprehend or cite the accused (if, in relation to an offence alleged to have been committed within the United Kingdom, such warrant is executed without delay); and

    (c) in Northern Ireland, the making of a complaint, shall be deemed to be the commencement of a proceeding.

(2A) A magistrates' court in England and Wales may act under subsection (2B) if it is satisfied on an application by a constable or Crown Prosecutor—

    (a) that there are exceptional circumstances which justify the granting of the application, and

    (b) that there has been no undue delay in the investigation of the offence to which the application relates.

(2B) The magistrates' court may extend the time within which proceedings must be commenced in pursuance of subsection (1) above to not more than 24 months after the offence was committed.

(2C) If the magistrates' court acts under subsection (2B), it may also make an order under subsection (2D) if it is satisfied, on an application by a constable or Crown Prosecutor, that documents retained by the relevant registration officer in pursuance of rule 57 of the parliamentary elections rules may provide evidence relating to the offence.

(2D) An order under this subsection is an order—

    (a) directing the relevant registration officer not to cause the documents to be destroyed at the expiry of the period of one year mentioned in rule 57, and

    (b) extending the period for which he is required to retain them under that rule by such further period not exceeding 12 months as is specified in the order.

(2E) The making of an order under subsection (2D) does not affect any other power to require the retention of the documents.

(2F) An application under this section must be made not more than one year after the offence was committed.

(2G) Any party to—

    (a) an application under subsection (2A), or

    (b) an application under subsection (2C),

who is aggrieved by the refusal of the magistrates' court to act under subsection (2B) or to make an order under subsection (2D) (as the case may be) may appeal to the Crown Court.

(3) *Repealed*

NOTES

Derivation
    RPA 1949 s 154

Defined terms

Crown Court: Interpretation Act 1978 Sch 1
England: Interpretation Act 1978 Sch 1
Magistrates' court: Interpretation Act 1978 Sch 1
parliamentary elections rules: s 202(1)

person: s 202(1)
registration officer: s 8(1)
Wales: Interpretation Act 1978 Sch 1

Local election offence punishable summarily

177(1)   A prosecution for any offence punishable summarily committed in reference to an election under the local government Act—

    (a)   may be instituted before any magistrates' court in the county in which the local government area for which the election was held is situated or which it adjoins; and

    (b)   the offence shall be deemed for all purposes to have been committed within the jurisdiction of that court.

This section does not apply in Scotland.

(2)   *Repealed*

NOTES

Derivation
  RPA 1949 s 159

Defined terms
  election under the local government act (E&W): ss 191(1), 203(1A)

local government Act: s 202(1)
local government area (E&W): ss 191(1), 203(1)
local government area (S): s 204(1)
Magistrates' court: Interpretation Act 1978 Sch 1

Prosecution of offences committed outside the United Kingdom

178   Proceedings in respect of an offence under this Act alleged to have been committed outside the United Kingdom by a Commonwealth citizen or citizen of the Republic of Ireland may be taken, and the offence may for all incidental purposes be treated as having been committed, in any place in the United Kingdom.

NOTES

Derivation
  RPA 1949 s 155

Defined terms
  United Kingdom: Interpretation Act 1978 Sch 1

Offences by associations

179   Where—

    (a)   any corrupt or illegal practice or any illegal payment, employment or hiring, or

    (b)   any offence under section 110 or 110A above,

is committed by any association or body of persons, corporate or unincorporate, the members of the association or body who have taken part in the commission of the offence shall be liable to any fine or punishment imposed for that offence by this Act.

NOTES

Derivation
  RPA 1949 s 156

Defined terms
  corrupt practice: see ss 60(1), 62A(5), 62B(2), (3), 65A(1), (2), 65B(2), (3), 75(5), 75ZB(4), 75A(7), 82(6), 113(1), 114(1), 115(1), Sch 1 rule 6A(2), Sch 4 para 5
  illegal employment: s 111

illegal payment: ss 107, 112
illegal practice: ss 61(7), 68(2, 71A(3), 73(6), 75(5), 75ZB(3), 75A(8), (11), 76(1B), 76ZA(5), 78(3), 84, 90(2), 92(2), (3), 97(1), 106(1), (5), 109(2), 110(12), 110A(14), 175(2), 189(1), Sch 4 paras 1(2), 5

Evidence by certificate of holding of elections

180   On—

    (a)   any prosecution for a corrupt or illegal practice or for any illegal payment, employment or hiring, and

    (b)   any proceedings for a penalty under section 85 above or paragraph 4 of Schedule 4 to this Act, the certificate of the returning officer at an election—

>   (i)   that the election mentioned in the certificate was duly held, and

>   (ii) that the person named in the certificate was a candidate at the election,

shall be sufficient evidence of the facts stated in it.

NOTES

Derivation
RPA 1949 s 158

Defined terms
candidate: ss 118A, 185
corrupt practice: see ss 60(1), 62A(5), 62B(2), (3), 65A(1), (2), 65B(2), (3), 75(5), 75ZB(4), 75A(7), 82(6), 113(1), 114(1), 115(1), Sch 1 rule 6A(2), Sch 4 para 5
election: s 202(1)

illegal employment: s 111
illegal payment: ss 107, 112
illegal practice: ss 61(7), 68(2, 71A(3), 73(6), 75(5), 75ZB(3), 75A(8), (11), 76(1B), 76ZA(5), 78(3), 84, 90(2), 92(2), (3), 97(1), 106(1), (5), 109(2), 110(12), 110A(14), 175(2), 189(1), Sch 4 paras 1(2), 5
returning officer: see ss 24-27

Evidence by certificate of electoral registration

180A The certificate of a registration officer that any person is or is not, or was or was not at any particular time, duly registered in one of the officer's registers in respect of any address shall be sufficient evidence of the facts stated in it; and a document purporting to be such a certificate shall be received in evidence and presumed to be such a certificate unless the contrary is proved.

NOTES

Derivation
RPA 2000 Scj 1

Defined terms
registration officer: s 8(1)

Director of Public Prosecutions

181(1) Where information is given to the Director of Public Prosecutions that any offence under this Act has been committed, it is his duty to make such inquiries and institute such prosecutions as the circumstances of the case appear to him to require.

(2) The Director by himself or by his assistant or by his representative appointed under subsection (3) below may and, if the election court so requests him, shall attend the trial of every election petition.

(3) The Director may nominate a barrister, solicitor or authorised person to be his representative for the purposes of this Part of this Act

(3A) In subsection (3) "authorised person" means a person (other than a barrister or solicitor) who, for the purposes of the Legal Services Act 2007, is an authorised person in relation to an activity which constitutes the exercise of a right of audience (within the meaning of that Act).

(4) The Director in performing any duty under this Act shall act in accordance with regulations under the Prosecution of Offences Act 1979, and subject to them in accordance with the directions (if any) given to him by the Attorney General; and any assistant or representative of the Director in performing any duty under this Part shall act in accordance with those regulations and directions (if any) and with the directions given to him by the Director.

(5) There shall be allowed to the Director and his assistant or representative for the purposes of this Part (other than his general duties under subsection (1) above) such allowances for expenses as the Treasury may approve.

(6) The costs incurred in defraying the expenses of the Director incurred for those purposes (including the remuneration of his representative) shall, in the first instance, be paid by the Treasury, and shall be deemed to be expenses of the election court; but if for any reasonable cause it seems just to the court so to do, the court shall order all

or part of those costs to be repaid to the Treasury by the parties to the petition, or such of them as the court may direct.

(7) In the application of this section to Scotland, subsections (2) to (6) shall be omitted.

(8) In the application of this section to Northern Ireland, the reference to the Prosecution of Offences Act 1979 does not apply.

NOTES

Application
Sub-s (4) has been repealed in relation to England and Wales.

Derivation
RPA 1949 s 159

Defined terms
Attorney General (S): s 204(5)

Attorney General (NI): s 205(1)
costs: s 185
Director of Public Prosecutions (S): s 204(5)
Director of Public Prosecutions (NI): s 205(1)
election court: ss 123, 130, 134, 202(1)
election petition: s 202(1)

Supplemental

Rules of procedure

182(1) The authority having for the time being power to make rules of court for the Senior Courts may make rules for the purposes of Part II and this Part of this Act.

(2) In relation to the power conferred by subsection (1) above to make rules—
(a) that power shall be exercisable by statutory instrument, and be treated for the purposes of the Statutory Instruments Act 1946 as if conferred on a Minister of the Crown; and
(b) a statutory instrument containing rules under subsection (1) shall be subject to annulment in pursuance of a resolution of either House of Parliament.

(3) This section does not apply to Scotland, but the Court of Session has power to make acts of sederunt for the purposes of Part II and this Part.

(4) This section does not apply to Northern Ireland.

NOTES

Derivation
RPA 1949 s 160

Defined terms
rules of court: Interpretation Act 1978 Sch 1

Costs

183(1) The rules of the Senior Courts with respect to costs to be allowed in actions, causes and matters in the High Court shall in principle and so far as practicable apply to the costs of petition and other proceedings under Part II or this Part of this Act, and the taxing officer shall not allow any costs higher than would be allowed in any action, cause or matter in the High Court on a common fund basis.

(2) Where any costs or other sums are, under the order of an election court or otherwise under this Part, to be paid by any person, those costs or sums shall be due from that person to the person or persons to whom they are to be paid and, if payable to the Treasury, shall be a debt due to Her Majesty and in either case may be recovered accordingly.

(3) The above provisions of this section do not apply to Scotland, but those costs shall, subject to any regulations which the Court of Session may make by act of sederunt, be taxed as nearly as possible according to the same principles as expenses between solicitor and client are taxed in a cause in the Court of Session, or, when incurred in relation to an election of councillors, the sheriff court.

NOTES

Derivation
  RPA 1949 s 161

Defined terms
  costs: s 185
  election court: ss 123, 130, 134, 202(1)

High Court (E, W & NI): Interpretation Act 1978 Sch 1
High Court (S): s 204(3)
person: s 202(1)
sheriff (S): Interpretation Act 1978 Sch 1

Service of notices

184(1) Any notice, legal process or other document required to be served on any person with reference to any proceeding respecting an election for the purpose of causing him to appear before the High Court, the county court, or any election court, or otherwise or of giving him an opportunity of making a statement, or showing cause, or being heard by himself before any court for any purpose of this Part of this Act may be served—

  (a) by delivering it to that person, or by leaving it at, or sending it by post by a registered letter or by the recorded delivery service, to his last known place of abode in the constituency or, as the case may be, the area of the authority for which the election was held; or

  (b) if the proceeding is before any court in such other manner as the court may direct.

(2) In proving service by post under this section it shall be sufficient to prove that the letter was prepaid, properly addressed, and registered or recorded with the postal operator (within the meaning of Part 3 of the Postal Services Act 2011) concerned.

NOTES

Derivation
  RPA 1949 s 162

Defined terms
  county court: Interpretation Act 1978 Sch 1
  election: s 202(1)
  election court: ss 123, 130, 134, 202(1)
  High Court (E, W & NI): Interpretation Act 1978 Sch 1

High Court (S): s 204(3)
legal process: s 202(1)
person: s 202(1)
recorded delivery service: Recorded Delivery Service Act 1962
service by post: see Interpretation Act 1978 s 7

Interpretation of Part III

185 In this Part of this Act, unless the context otherwise requires—

  "appropriate officer" has the same meaning as in section 67(7) above;

  "candidate" has the same meaning as in Part II of this Act and the saving in section 117(1) above applies in relation to this Part as in relation to Part II;

  "costs" includes charges and expenses;

  "date of the allowance of an authorised excuse" has the meaning assigned to it by section 86(8) above or paragraph 7 of Schedule 4 to this Act, as the case may be;

  "declaration as to election expenses" means a declaration made under section 82 above or, as the case may be, paragraph 3 of Schedule 4 to this Act;

  "elective office" means any office to which a local government election is held in England or Wales;

  "judicial office" includes the office of justice of the peace;

  "Licensing Acts" means the Licensing (Northern Ireland) Order 1996 (as that Order may from time to time have effect);

  "money" and "pecuniary reward" shall be deemed to include—

    (a) any office, place or employment, and

    (b) any valuable security or other equivalent of money, and

    (c) any valuable consideration,

    and expressions referring to money shall be construed accordingly;

  "payment" includes any pecuniary or other reward;

"prescribed" means prescribed by rules of court, or, in Northern Ireland, such rules under section 55 of the Judicature (Northern Ireland) Act 1978;

"public office" in relation to Scotland means any office held in Scotland—

(a)   under the Crown, or

(b)   under the charter of a city or borough, or

(c)   under the Acts relating to local government or public health or public education,

whether the office is that—

(i)   of mayor, provost, chief magistrate, chairman, alderman, councillor, member of a board, commission or other local authority in any local government or other area; or

(ii)   of proper officer or other officer under a council, board, commission or other authority; or

(iii)   of any other office to which a person is elected or appointed under any such charter or enactment as is mentioned above, including any other municipal or parochial office;

"return as to election expenses" means a return made under section 81 above or, as the case may be, paragraph 3 of Schedule 4 to this Act;

"Speaker" includes Deputy Speaker and, where the office of Speaker is vacant, Clerk of the House of Commons, or any other officer for the time being performing the duties of Clerk of the House of Commons.

NOTES

Derivation
RPA 1949 s 163

Defined terms
enactment: Interpretation Act 1978 Sch 1
enactment (NI): s 205
England: Interpretation Act 1978 Sch 1
local authority (E&W): s 203(1)

local authority (S): s 204(1)
local government election (E&W): ss 191(1), 203(1), (1A)
proper officer: s 202(1)
rules of court: Interpretation Act 1978 Sch 1
Wales: Interpretation Act 1978 Sch 1

Computation of time for purposes of Part III

186   Section 119 above applies in computing any period of time for the purposes of this Part of this Act as for the purposes of Part II of this Act.

NOTES

Derivation
RPA 1949 s 164

PART IV

SPECIAL PROVISIONS AS TO OTHER LOCAL ELECTIONS

England and Wales, and Scotland

Application of Act to certain local elections

187(1)   The following provisions of this Act—

(a)   in Part I, sections 60, 62A and 66,

(b)   Parts II and III,

(c)   in this Part, section 189,

so far as they apply to an election in England and Wales of—

(i)   parish or community councillors, or

(ii)   the chairman of a parish or community council or a parish meeting, have effect subject to such adaptations, modifications and exceptions as may be made by rules under section 36 above, but nothing in this subsection affects the operation of section 96 or section 100 above.

(2) Sections 48(1) and (2) and 63 above have effect as if any reference in them to a local government election included a reference to any other election under the Local Government etc (Scotland) Act 1994 (c 39) or the Local Government (Scotland) Act 1973.

NOTES

Derivation
RPA 1949 s 165

Defined terms
community councillors: see Local Government Act 1972 s 35
election under the local government Act (E&W): s 203(1A)

local government election (S): s 204(1)
England: Interpretation Act 1978 Sch 1
parish councillors: see Local Government Act 1972 s 16
Wales: Interpretation Act 1978 Sch 1

188 *Repealed*

Voting offences at certain local elections

189(1) If a person—

    (a) votes, or induces or procures any person to vote, at an election under the local government Act which is not a local government election,

    (b) knowing that he or that person is prohibited by any enactment from voting at that election,

he shall be guilty of an illegal practice.

(2) A candidate shall not be liable nor shall his election be avoided for any illegal practice under subsection (1) above committed without his knowledge or consent.

NOTES

Derivation
RPA 1949 s 168

Defined terms
election under the local government act (E&W): ss 191(1), 203(1A)
enactment: Interpretation Act 1978 Sch 1

enactment (NI): s 205
local government election (E&W): ss 191(1), 203(1), (1A)
local government election (S): s 204(1)
vote: s 202(1)
voting: see "vote" s 202(1)

189A *Repealed*

190 *Repealed*

The City

Municipal elections in the City

191(1) For the purposes of—

    (a) sections 60, 61 and 62A in Part I of this Act,

    (b) the whole of Part II of this Act except sections 96 and 99,

    (c) the whole of Part III of this Act,

    (d) section 189 above and sections 193 to 198 below, and

    (e) the whole of Part V of this Act,

"local government election" and "election under the local government Act" include a municipal election in the City (that is, an election to the office of mayor, alderman, common councilman or sheriff and also the election of any officer elected by the mayor, aldermen and liverymen in common hall),

"corporate office" includes each of those offices,

"local government area" includes the City,

"clerk of the authority" means in relation to the City, the town clerk of the City,

"electoral area" means in relation to a ward election, the ward, and in relation to any other municipal election in the City, the City.

In relation to municipal elections in the City those enactments have effect subject to the modifications mentioned in sections 193 to 196 below.

(2) Schedule 6 to this Act has effect as regards the operation of Part II (ward elections) of the City of London (Various Powers) Act 1957 and the City of London (Ward Elections) Act 2002.

NOTES

Derivation
　RPA 1949 s 167

Defined terms
　the City: s 202(1)

enactment: Interpretation Act 1978 Sch 1
local government area (E&W): ss 191(1), 203(1)
local government area (S): s 204(1)

192　*Repealed*

Personation and other voting offences

193　In relation to municipal elections in the City—
　　　(a)　in sections 60, 61 and 62A above "vote" does not include voting otherwise than on a poll; and
　　　(b)　in section 61(2), paragraph (a)(ii) does not apply.

NOTES

Derivation
　RPA 1949 167

Defined terms
　the City: s 202(1)

municipal election in the City: s 191(1)
vote: s 202(1)
voting: see "vote" s 202(1)

Broadcasting

194　In relation to municipal elections in the City—
　　　(a)　neither section 92 nor section 93 above apply by virtue of section 191 above to municipal elections in the City other than ward elections; and
　　　(b)　for the purposes of section 93(1) a ward election shall be deemed to be pending during the period beginning—
　　　　　(i)　in the case of an annual election three weeks before the day fixed for the election, and
　　　　　(ii)　in other cases with the day on which the precept is issued,
and ending in all cases with the day of the poll (or, if no poll is taken, with the day fixed for the election).

NOTES

Derivation
　RPA 1969 s 9

Defined terms
　the City: s 202(1)
　municipal election in the City: s 191(1)

Disturbances at meetings

195　In relation to municipal elections in the City—
　　　(a)　in section 97 above the reference to the day of election shall be taken as a reference to the day fixed for the election and (where a poll is taken) any day after that up to and including the day of the poll; but

(b) in relation to a meeting held with reference to an election other than an annual election that section does not apply to an offence committed on or before the day on which the precept is issued.

NOTES
Derivation
RPA 1949 s 167

Defined terms
the City: s 202(1)
municipal election in the City: s 191(1)

Costs or expenses

196 In relation to municipal elections in the City, any costs or expenses directed to be paid under section 132 by the authority for which the election was held shall—
(a) if incurred in respect of a ward election, be paid out of the general rate; and
(b) in any other case, be paid by the chamberlain of the City out of the City's cash.

NOTES
Derivation
RPA 1949 s 167

Defined terms
the City: s 202(1)
municipal election in the City: s 191(1)

Candidate's expenses: ward, and liverymen in common hall, elections

197(1) For a candidate at a ward election in the City the maximum amount of election expenses is £266 together with an additional 5.2p for every elector (taken according to the enumeration of the ward list to be used at the election); but the provision made by section 76(6) above for increasing the maximum amount of election expenses in the event of a candidate's death applies to the maximum amount under this subsection.

(2) A candidate at an election by liverymen in common hall need not have an election agent, his maximum amount of election expenses is 28.3p for every elector on the common hall register to be used at the election, and section 90 above and Schedule 4 to this Act apply at such an election as they apply to an election of parish councillors, but the form of declaration as to election expenses shall be such as may be prescribed by Act of Common Council and in this subsection "common hall register" means the list prepared under section 4 of the City of London Ballot Act 1887.

(3) The Secretary of State may by order vary a maximum amount of the candidate's election expenses specified in subsection (1) or subsection (2) above where in his opinion there has been a change in the value of money since the last occasion on which that amount was fixed (whether by such an order or otherwise), and the variation shall be such as in his opinion is justified by that change.
The power to make an order under this subsection is exercisable by statutory instrument which shall be subject to annulment in pursuance of a resolution of either House of Parliament.

NOTES
Derivation
RPA 1949 s 167

Subordinate legislation
Representation of the People (Variation of Limits of Candidates' Election Expenses) (City of London) Order 2005, SI 2005/153
Defined terms

the City: s 202(1)
election agent: see s 67
elector: s 202(1)
parish councillors: see Local Government Act 1972 s 16

Effect of avoidance of election to corporate office

198   In relation to the City, where a candidate who has been elected to a corporate office
is—

    (a)   by a certificate of an election court, or

    (b)   by a decision of the High Court,

declared not to have been duly elected, acts done by him in execution of the office
before the time when the certificate or decision is certified to the clerk of the authority
for which the election was held shall not be invalidated by reason of that declaration.

NOTES

Derivation
  RPA 1949 s 118

Defined terms
  the City: s 202(1)
  clerk of the authority: s 191(1)

corporate office: s 191(1)
election court: ss 123, 130, 134, 202(1)
High Court (E, W & NI): Interpretation Act 1978 Sch 1
High Court (S): s 204(3)

PART V
GENERAL AND SUPPLEMENTAL

Supplemental

Functions of the Chancellor of the Duchy of Lancaster

199ZA   See the Chancellor of the Duchy of Lancaster Order 2015, by virtue of which functions
of the Secretary of State under this Act are exercisable concurrently with the
Chancellor of the Duchy of Lancaster.

199   *Repealed*

199A   *Repealed*

Translations etc of certain documents

199B(1)   Subsections (2) and (3) below apply to any document which under or by virtue of this
Act is required or authorised to be given to voters or displayed in any place for the
purposes of a parliamentary or local government election.

(2)   The person who is required or authorised to give or display the document must, as he
thinks appropriate, give or display or otherwise make available in such form as he
thinks appropriate—

    (a)   the document in Braille;

    (b)   the document in languages other than English;

    (c)   graphical representations of the information contained in the document;

    (d)   other means of making the information contained in the document accessible
to persons who might not otherwise have reasonable access to the information.

(3)   The person required or authorised to give or display the document must also, as he
thinks appropriate, make available the information contained in the document in such
audible form as he thinks appropriate.

(4)   Subsections (2) and (3) above do not apply to—

    (a)   the nomination paper;

    (b)   the ballot paper.

(5)   The returning officer at a parliamentary election or a local government election may
cause to be displayed at every polling station in the election an enlarged sample copy
of the ballot paper.

(6)   The sample copy mentioned in subsection (5) above—

(a) in the case of a parliamentary election or a local government election where only one candidate is to be elected, must have printed the words "VOTE FOR ONE CANDIDATE ONLY" both at the top and immediately below the list of candidates,

(b) in the case of a local government election where more than one candidate is to be elected, must have printed the words "VOTE FOR NO MORE THAN *here insert the maximum number of candidates to be elected* CANDIDATES" both at the top and immediately below the list of candidates, and

(c) in each case, below the second occurrence of those words, may include a translation of those words into such other languages as the returning officer thinks appropriate.

(7) The returning officer at a parliamentary election or a local government election must provide at every polling station in the election an enlarged hand-held sample copy of the ballot paper for the assistance of voters who are partially sighted.

(8) The sample copy mentioned in subsection (7) above must be clearly marked as a specimen provided only for the guidance of voters.

(9) In the application of subsection (2)(b) to Northern Ireland any question as to whether a person is to give or display or otherwise make available a document in a language other than English is to be decided by the returning officer.

(10) This section does not apply to a local government election in Scotland.

NOTES

Derivation
Electoral Administration Act 2006 s 36

returning officer: see ss 24-27
parliamentary election: Interpretation Act 1978 Sch 1
voter: s 202(1)

Defined terms
local government election (E&W): ss 191(1), 203(1), (1A)
local government election (S): s 204(1)

Scottish local government elections: translations etc of certain documents

199C(1) Subsections (2) and (3) below apply to any document which, under or by virtue of this Act, is required or authorised to be given to voters or displayed in any place for the purposes of a local government election in Scotland.

(2) The person who is required or authorised to give or display the document must, as he thinks appropriate, also give or display or otherwise make available in such form as he thinks appropriate—
(a) the document in Braille;
(b) the document in languages other than English;
(c) graphical representations of the information contained in the document;
(d) other means of making the information contained in the document accessible to persons who might not otherwise have reasonable access to the information.

(3) The person required or authorised to give or display the document must also, as he thinks appropriate, make available the information contained in the document in such audible form as he thinks appropriate.

(4) Subsections (2) and (3) above do not apply to—
(a) the nomination paper; or
(b) the ballot paper.

NOTES

Derivation
Local Electoral Administration and Registration Services (Scotland) Act 2006

Defined terms
local government election (S): s 204(1)

Public notices, and declarations

200(1) A public notice required by or under this Act to be given by a returning officer for a parliamentary election shall be given by posting the notice in some conspicuous place or places in the constituency and may also be given in such other manner as he thinks desirable for publicising it.

(1A) A public notice required by or under this Act to be given by the proper officer of a local authority at a local government election shall be given by posting the notice in some conspicuous place or places in the local government area and may also be given in such other manner as he thinks desirable for publicising it.

(2) Any person before whom a declaration is authorised to be made under this Act may take the declaration.

NOTES
Derivation
RPA 1949 s 200

Defined terms
constituency: Parliamentary Constituencies Act 1986 s 1(2)
local authority (E&W): s 203(1)
local authority (S): s 204(1)
local government area (E&W): ss 191(1), 203(1)

local government area (S): s 204(1)
local government election (E&W): s 203(1), (1A)
local government election (S): s 204(1)
parliamentary election: Interpretation Act 1978 Sch 1
proper officer: s 202(1)
returning officer: see ss 24-27

Remuneration for free postal services provided under Act

200A(1) This section applies where any postal services are provided without charge by a universal postal service provider in pursuance of this Act.

(2) The universal postal service provider shall be entitled to be remunerated for having provided the services at the rate fixed in relation to them by virtue of a scheme under section 89 of the Postal Services Act 2000.

(3) A sum which a universal postal service provider is entitled to receive by virtue of this section shall be charged on, and issued out of, the Consolidated Fund.

(4) In this section "postal services" has the meaning given by section 27 of the Postal Services Act 2011.

NOTES
Derivation
Postal Services Act 2000 Sch 8

Defined terms
universal postal service provider: s 202(1)

Regulations

201(1) Any power conferred by this Act to make regulations shall, except where this Act otherwise provides, be a power exercisable by the Secretary of State by statutory instrument.

(2) No regulations shall be made under this Act by the Secretary of State otherwise than under section 110(7) above or section 203(4) below unless a draft of the regulations has been laid before and approved by a resolution of each House of Parliament.

(2A) Any regulations under section 110(7) above shall be subject to annulment in pursuance of a resolution of either House of Parliament.

(2C) Regulations made for the purposes only of omitting a particular kind of evidence from the kinds of evidence that a person is or may be required to provide by virtue of regulations under paragraph 1(2A) or 3ZA(3) of Schedule 2 shall be subject to annulment in pursuance of a resolution of either House of Parliament (and subsection (2) does not apply to regulations made for those purposes only).

(3)   Any regulations under this Act may make different provision for different cases, circumstances or areas and may contain such incidental, supplemental, saving or transitional provisions as the Secretary of State, or the Electoral Commission (in the case of any regulations made by them), thinks fit.

NOTES

Derivation
  RPA 1949 s 171

Defined terms
  Electoral Commission: see Political Parties, Elections and Referendums Act 2000 s 1

Interpretation

General provisions as to interpretation

202(1)   In this Act, unless the context otherwise requires—

"anonymous entry", in relation to a register of electors, shall be construed in accordance with section 9B above and "the record of anonymous entries", means the record prepared in pursuance of regulations made by virtue of paragraph 8A of Schedule 2 to this Act;

"citizen of the Union" shall be construed in accordance with Article 8.1 of the Treaty establishing the European Community (as amended by Title II of the Treaty on European Union), and "relevant citizen of the Union" means such a citizen who is not a Commonwealth citizen or a citizen of the Republic of Ireland;

"the City" means the City of London;

"Clerk of the Crown" means Clerk of the Crown in Chancery;

"Common Council" means the Common Council of the City;

"disability", in relation to doing a thing, includes a short term inability to do it;

"dwelling" includes any part of a building where that part is occupied separately as a dwelling;

"election" means a parliamentary election, an Authority election or an election under the local government Act;

"election court" means—

(a)   in relation to a parliamentary election petition, the judges presiding at the trial;

(b)   in relation to a petition questioning an Authority election or an election under the local government Act, the court constituted under this Act for the trial of that petition;

"election petition" means a petition presented in pursuance of Part III of this Act;

"elector" in relation to an election, means any person who has for the time being an entry on the register to be used at that election, but does not include those shown in the register (or, in the case of a person who has an anonymous entry in the register, in the record of anonymous entries) as below voting age on the day fixed for the poll;

"legal incapacity" includes (in addition, where applicable, to any incapacity by virtue of any subsisting provision of the common law) any disqualification imposed by this Act or any other Act;

"legal process" means a claim form, application notice, writ, summons or other process;

"the list of proxies" has, in relation to any election, the meaning given by paragraph 5(3) of Schedule 4 to the Representation of the People Act 2000 or, as respects Northern Ireland, by section 7 of the Representation of the People Act 1985 "overseas elector's declaration" has the meaning given by section 2 of the Representation of the People Act 1985

"parliamentary election petition" means an election petition questioning a parliamentary election or return;

"the postal voters list" means—

(a) in relation to England and Wales and Scotland, the list of persons kept in pursuance of paragraph 5(2) of Schedule 4 to the Representation of the People Act 2000 (persons whose applications to vote by post have been granted);

(b) in relation to Northern Ireland, the list of persons kept in pursuance of section 7(4)(a) of the Representation of the People Act 1985 (persons whose applications to vote by post have been granted);

"the proxy postal voters list" means—

(a) in relation to England and Wales and Scotland, the list of persons kept in pursuance of paragraph 7(8) of Schedule 4 to the Representation of the People Act 2000 (persons whose applications to vote by post as proxy have been granted);

(b) in relation to Northern Ireland, the list of persons kept in pursuance of section 9(9) of the Representation of the People Act 1985 (persons whose applications to vote by post as proxy have been granted);

"parliamentary elections rules" means the parliamentary elections rules in Schedule 1 to this Act;

"person" includes (without prejudice to the provisions of the Interpretation Act 1978) an association corporate or unincorporate;

"prescribed" except in Part III of this Act means prescribed by regulations;

"proper officer"—

(a) in relation to the Greater London Authority, has the same meaning as in the 1999 Act (see section 424(2) of that Act);

(b) except as provided by paragraph (a) above, in England and Wales means a proper officer within the meaning of section 270(3) and (4) of the Local Government Act 1972;

"qualifying address" shall be construed in accordance with section 9(8) above;

"registered political party" means a party registered under Part II of the Political Parties, Elections and Referendums Act 2000;

"service voter" means a person who has made a service declaration and is registered or entitled to be registered in pursuance of it;

"sub-agent" has the meaning given by section 68(1) above;

"universal postal service provider" means a universal service provider (within the meaning of Part 3 of the Postal Services Act 2011);

"voter" means a person voting at an election and includes a person voting as proxy and, except in the parliamentary elections rules, and the rules under section 36 and 42 above, a person voting by proxy, and "vote" (whether noun or verb) shall be construed accordingly, except that in those rules any reference to an elector voting or an elector's vote shall include a reference to an elector voting by proxy or an elector's vote given by proxy.

(2) For the purposes of the Representation of the People Acts a person shall be deemed not to have attained a given age until the commencement of the relevant anniversary of the day of his birth.

NOTES

Derivation
RPA 1949 s 171

Defined terms
the 1999 Act: s 203(1)

Authority election: s 203(1)
election under the local government act (E&W): ss 191(1), 203(1A)
England: Interpretation Act 1978 Sch 1
local government Act (E&W): s 203(1)

local government Act (S): s 204(1)   Wales: Interpretation Act 1978 Sch 1
parliamentary election: Interpretation Act 1978 Sch 1
register of electors: see s 9

Local government provisions as to England and Wales

203(1) In this Act, unless the context otherwise requires, in relation to England and Wales—

"the 1999 Act" means the Greater London Authority Act 1999;

"Assembly constituency" has the same meaning as in the 1999 Act (see section 2(4) and (5) of that Act);

"Authority election" means—

(a) any election of the Mayor of London;

(b) any election of a constituency member of the London Assembly; or

(c) the election of the London members of the London Assembly at an ordinary election

"constituency member", in relation to the London Assembly, has the same meaning as in the 1999 Act;

"election of a constituency member of the London Assembly" means—

(a) any such election at an ordinary election; or

(b) an election under section 10 of the 1999 Act (election to fill a vacancy in an Assembly constituency);

"election of the Mayor of London" means—

(a) any such election at an ordinary election; or

(b) an election under section 16 of the 1999 Act (election to fill a vacancy in the office of Mayor of London);

"electoral area" means

(a) any electoral division or ward or, in the case of a parish or community in which there are no wards, the parish or community, for which the election of councillors is held under the local government Act;

(b) Greater London, in the case of—

(i) any election of the Mayor of London; or

(ii) the election of the London members of the London Assembly at an ordinary election;

(c) any Assembly constituency for which the election of a constituency member of the London Assembly is held;

"local authority" means the Greater London Authority, a county council, a county borough council,, a district council, a London borough council or a parish or community council;

"local government Act" means the Local Government Act 1972;

"local government area" means Greater London, a county, county borough, London borough district, parish or community;

"local government election" means

(a) the election of councillors for any electoral area; or

(b) any Authority election

"London member", in relation to the London Assembly, has the same meaning as in the 1999 Act.

(1A) In the application of this Act in relation to England and Wales, unless the context otherwise requires, any reference to—

(a) a local government election, or

(b) an election under the local government Act,

shall be taken to include a reference to an Authority election.

(1B) Any reference in this Act to a registered political party submitting a list of candidates to be London members of the London Assembly at an ordinary election shall be construed in accordance with section 4(5)(a) of, and Part II of Schedule 2 to, the 1999 Act; and related expressions shall be construed accordingly.

(2) The following provisions of this Act, namely—

  (a) Part I, so far as it has effect for the purposes of parliamentary elections, and

  (b) Parts I to III, so far as they have effect for the purposes of Authority elections,

shall (subject to any express provision contained in the Part or Parts in question) apply in relation to the City as if the City were a London borough and the Common Council were a London borough council.

For the purposes of this subsection the Inner Temple and the Middle Temple shall be treated as forming part of the City.

(3) The modifications made by subsection (2) above do not affect section 52(4) above.

(4) This Act applies in relation to the Isles of Scilly as if those isles were a county and as if the council of those isles were a county council, except that—

  (a) the council shall appoint an officer of the council to be registration officer for the isles and paragraph 1(1) of Schedule 2 shall apply as if the isles were a district and the council were a district council;

  (b) the provisions of Part I relating to the conduct of local government elections shall have effect in relation to those isles subject to such adaptations as the Secretary of State may by regulations prescribe.

(5) For the purposes of section 265 of the Local Government Act 1972 (application to Isles of Scilly) the provisions of this Act as to rules made by the Secretary of State under section 36 above shall be deemed to be contained in a public general Act relating to local government.

NOTES

Derivation
  RPA 1949 s 172

Defined terms
  the City: s 202(1)
  Common Council: s 202(1)
  community: see Local Government Act 1972 s 27
  England: Interpretation Act 1978 Sch 1

London borough: s 203(2) and Interpretation Act 1978 Sch 1
parish councillors: see Local Government Act 1972 s 16
parliamentary election: Interpretation Act 1978 Sch 1
registered political party : s 202(1)
Wales: Interpretation Act 1978 Sch 1

Scotland and Northern Ireland

General application to Scotland

204(1) This section has (in addition to any express application elsewhere in this Act) effect for the general application of this Act to Scotland, and accordingly—

  "electoral area", in relation to a local government election, means the electoral ward for which the election is held;

  "local authority" means a council constituted under section 2 of the Local Government etc (Scotland) Act 1994;

  "local government Act" means the Local Governance (Scotland) Act 2004 (asp 9);

  "local government area" means the area of a local authority; and

  "local government election" means an election of councillors by local government electors for an electoral area.

(2) For a reference to a borough constituency substitute a reference to a burgh constituency.

(3) For a reference to the High Court substitute a reference to the Court of Session and for a reference to the county court or a judge of that court substitute a reference to the sheriff.

(4) The power conferred by section 57 above on the Court of Session to make acts of sederunt for the appointment of judges to hear appeals under that section or to fill any vacancy among the judges so appointed is not required to be exercisable by statutory instrument.

(5) A reference to the Director of Public Prosecutions or the Attorney General refers to the Lord Advocate.

(6) For a reference to a plaintiff or defendant substitute respectively a reference to a pursuer or defender, for a reference to a recognisance substitute a reference to a bond of caution and for a reference to an injunction substitute a reference to an interdict.

(7) Any reference to the report of an election court shall, in relation to an election court trying a petition questioning an election of councillors in Scotland, be construed as a reference to a finding of the court, and the expression "reported of a corrupt or illegal practice" shall be construed accordingly.

(8) For a reference to the register of licences substitute a reference to the register kept in pursuance of section 20 of the Licensing (Scotland) Act 1976.

(9) Section 231 of the Local Government (Scotland) Act 1973 (application to sheriff in cases of difficulty) applies to the provisions of sections 41 to 45 above as that section applied to those provisions immediately before their repeal and re-enactment by this Act.

(10) Notwithstanding the repeal by this Act of sections 19 and 43 of the Representation of the People Act 1918, those sections shall continue to have such effect as they had immediately before that repeal in relation to regulation 16 of section 2 of the Universities Elections Amendment (Scotland) Act 1881.

NOTES

Derivation
RPA 1949 s 173

Defined terms
constituency: Parliamentary Constituencies Act 1986 s 1(2)
corrupt practice: see ss 60(1), 62A(5), 62B(2), (3), 65A(1), (2), 65B(2), (3), 75(5), 75ZB(4), 75A(7), 82(6), 113(1), 114(1), 115(1), Sch 1 rule 6A(2), Sch 4 para 5
county court: Interpretation Act 1978 Sch 1

election court: ss 123, 130, 134
High Court (E, W & NI): Interpretation Act 1978 Sch 1
illegal practice: ss 61(7), 68(2, 71A(3), 73(6), 75(5), 75ZB(3), 75A(8), (11), 76(1B), 76ZA(5), 78(3), 84, 90(2), 92(2), (3), 97(1), 106(1), (5), 109(2), 110(12), 110A(14), 175(2), 189(1), Sch 4 paras 1(2), 5
sheriff (S): Interpretation Act 1978 Sch 1

General application to Northern Ireland

205(1) This section has (in addition to any express application elsewhere in the Act) effect for the general application of this Act to Northern Ireland, and accordingly—

    (a) a reference to the Attorney General refers to the Attorney General for Northern Ireland;

    (aa) a reference to the Director of Public Prosecutions refers to the Director of Public Prosecutions for Northern Ireland;

    (b) subject to subsection (2) below, a reference to any enactment shall be construed as a reference to that enactment as it applies in Northern Ireland.

(2) Nothing in this Act affects the law relating to local government in Northern Ireland.

NOTES

Derivation
RPA 1949 s 174

Defined terms
enactment: Interpretation Act 1978 Sch 1

Operation

Transitional and saving provisions, amendments and repeals

206 In Schedule 7 to this Act—

    (a) Part I has effect as to its transitional and saving provisions, and

    (b) Part II has effect as to its provisions relating to the interpretation of other Acts,

and subject to that Schedule—

    (i) the enactments and order specified in Schedule 8 to this Act have effect subject to the amendments consequent on this Act specified in that Schedule; and

    (ii) the enactments and orders specified in Schedule 9 to this Act (of which those in Part I are obsolete) are repealed or revoked to the extent specified in the third column of that Schedule.

NOTES

Defined terms

enactment: Interpretation Act 1978 Sch 1
enactment (NI): s 205

Citation and commencement

207(1) This Act may be cited as the Representation of the People Act 1983, and is included among the Acts which may be cited as the Representation of the People Acts.

(2) This Act shall come into force on such day as the Secretary of State may by order made by statutory instrument appoint.

SCHEDULES

SCHEDULE ZA1
CIVIL PENALTIES UNDER SECTION 9E

Introduction

1 This Schedule is about civil penalties under section 9E.

Amount

2 The amount of a civil penalty is to be specified in regulations.

Procedure

3(1) The procedure for imposing a civil penalty on a person is to be set out in regulations.

(2) The regulations must, in particular, require the registration officer to give the person written notice specifying—

    (a) the amount of the penalty,

    (b) the reasons for imposing it, and

    (c) the date by which and manner in which it is to be paid.

4 Regulations may specify steps that a registration officer must take before imposing a civil penalty.

Reviews and appeals

5(1) Regulations may give a person on whom a civil penalty is imposed—

    (a) a right to request a review of the decision to impose the penalty;

    (b) a right to appeal against the decision to the First-tier Tribunal.

(2) Regulations under this paragraph may, in particular—

    (a) specify the grounds on which a person may request a review or appeal;

    (b) specify the time within which a person must request a review or appeal;

    (c) require a person to request a review before appealing;

    (d) make provision about the procedure for a review;

    (e) make further provision about reviews and appeals (including provision as to the powers available on a review or appeal).

Power to create exceptions

6   Regulations may specify circumstances in which—

    (a) a civil penalty may not be imposed, or

    (b) a civil penalty may be cancelled.

Accounts and record keeping

7   Regulations may impose duties on registration officers about the keeping of accounts and other records in connection with civil penalties.

Interest and enforcement etc

8   Regulations may—

    (a) allow interest to be charged on a civil penalty that is paid late;

    (b) allow an additional penalty to be imposed for late payment.

9   In this Schedule "civil penalty" includes any interest or additional penalty.

10   Regulations may make provision about the recovery of civil penalties by registration officers.

11   A civil penalty received by a registration officer is to be paid into the Consolidated Fund.

Power to make further provision

12   Regulations may make further provision about civil penalties.

NOTES

Defined terms

    registration officer: s 8(1)

    written: Interpretation Act 1978 Sch 1

SCHEDULE A1
REVIEW OF POLLING DISTRICTS AND POLLING PLACES

1   The relevant authority must publish notice of the holding of a review.

2   The authority must consult the returning officer for every parliamentary election held in a constituency which is wholly or partly in its area.

3(1)   Every such returning officer must make representations to the authority.

  (2)   The representations must include information as to the location of polling stations (existing or proposed) within polling places (existing or proposed).

  (3)   The representations must be published in such manner as is prescribed.

4(1)   The authority must seek representations from such persons as it thinks have particular expertise in relation to access to premises or facilities for persons who have different forms of disability.

(2) Such persons must have an opportunity—
    (a) to make representations;
    (b) to comment on the returning officer's representations.

5 Any elector in a constituency situated in whole or in part in the authority's area may make representations.

6 Representations made by any person in connection with a review of polling places may include proposals for specified alternative polling places.

7 On completion of a review the authority must—
    (a) give reasons for its decisions in the review;
    (b) publish such other information as is prescribed.

NOTES

Defined terms

constituency: Parliamentary Constituencies Act 1986 s 1(2)

disability: s 202(1)

elector: s 202(1)

parliamentary election: Interpretation Act 1978 Sch 1

person: s 202(1)

prescribed: s 202(1)

relevant authority: s 18E(3)

returning officer: see ss 24-27

SCHEDULE 1
PARLIAMENTARY ELECTIONS RULES

Section 23

PART I
PROVISIONS AS TO TIME

Timetable

1 The proceedings at the election shall be conducted in accordance with the following Table.

TIMETABLE

Proceeding	Time	
Issue of writ	In the case of a general election, as soon as practicable after the dissolution of Parliament by section 3(1) of the Fixed-term Parliaments Act 2011.	In the case of a by-election, as soon as practicable after the issue of the warrant for the writ.
Publication of notice of election.	In the case of a general election or by-election, not later than 4 in the afternoon on the second day after that on which the writ is received.	

Proceeding	Time	
Delivery of nomination papers.	In the case of a general election, between the hours of 10 in the morning and 4 in the afternoon on any day after the date of publication of the notice of election, but not later than the sixth day after the date of the dissolution of Parliament by section 3(1) of the Fixed-term Parliaments Act 2011.	In the case of a by-election, the same as in the case of a general election, except that the last day shall be a day fixed by the returning officer and shall be not earlier than the third day after the date of publication of the notice of election nor later than the seventh day after that on which the writ is received.
Delivery of notices of withdrawals of candidature.	Within the time for the delivery of nomination papers at the election.	
The making of objections to nomination papers.	In the case of a general election or a by-election, during the hours allowed for delivery of nomination papers on the last day for their delivery and the hour following; but— (a) no objection may be made in the afternoon of that last day except to a nomination paper delivered within 24 hours of the last time for its delivery, and in the case of a nomination paper so delivered no objection may be so made to the sufficiency or nature of the particulars of the candidate unless made at or immediately after the time of the delivery of the nomination paper; and (b) the foregoing provisions do not apply to objections made in pursuance of rule 15(2).	
Publication of statement of persons nominated.	In the case of a general election or a by-election, — (a) if no objections to nomination papers are made, at the close of the time for doing so, or (b) if any such objections are made, not before they are disposed of but not later than 24 hours after the last time for delivery of nomination papers.	
Polling.	In the case of a general election, between the hours of 7 in the morning and 10 at night on the day determined under section 1 of the Fixed-term Parliaments Act 2011 or appointed under section 2(7) of that Act.	In the case of a by-election, between the hours of 7 in the morning and 10 at night on the day fixed by the returning officer, which shall not be earlier than the 17th nor later than the 19th day after the last day for delivery of nomination papers.

NOTES
Defined terms
   returning officer: see ss 24-27

Computation of time
2(1) In computing any period of time for the purposes of the Timetable—
    (a) a Saturday or Sunday,
    (b) a Christmas Eve, Christmas Day, Good Friday or a bank holiday, or
    (c) a day appointed for public thanksgiving or mourning,

shall be disregarded.

(1A) In relation to a general election, any day within paragraph (1)(a) to (c) shall not be treated as a day for the purpose of any proceedings in the Timetable before the polling day.

(1B) In relation to a by-election, any day within paragraph (1)(a) to (c) shall not be treated as a day for the purpose of any proceedings in the Timetable up to the completion of the poll nor shall the returning officer be obliged to proceed with the counting of the votes on such a day.

(2) In this rule "bank holiday" means—
  (a) in relation to a general election, a day which is a bank holiday under the Banking and Financial Dealings Act 1971 in any part of the United Kingdom,
  (b) in relation to a by-election, a day which is a bank holiday under that Act in that part of the United Kingdom in which the constituency is situated,
  but at a general election sub-paragraph (b) and not sub-paragraph (a) of this paragraph applies in relation to any proceedings—
    (i) commenced afresh by reason of a candidate's death;
    (ii) *Repealed*

(2A) In relation to a general election, this rule does not apply to a day which is a bank holiday or a day appointed for public thanksgiving or mourning if—
  (a) the day was not fixed or appointed as such before the dissolution of Parliament by section 3(1) of the Fixed-term Parliaments Act 2011, or
  (b) the day is one that is treated as a working day by section 3(6) of that Act.
  But, in relation to any proceedings commenced afresh by reason of a candidate's death, this paragraph is to be ignored.

(3) *Repealed*

NOTES

Defined terms   vote: s 202(1)
  bank holiday: Banking and Financial Dealing Act 1971
  returning officer: see ss 24-27

PART II
STAGES COMMON TO CONTESTED AND UNCONTESTED ELECTIONS

Issue of writ and notice of election

Issue of writ

3(1) Writs for parliamentary elections shall continue to be sealed and issued in accordance with the existing practice of the office of the Clerk of the Crown.

(2) Each writ shall be in the form in the Appendix and shall be directed to the returning officer by the title of his office as returning officer (and not by his name) and conveyed to him.

(3) Her Majesty may by Order in Council—
  (a) specify the manner in which writs are to be conveyed, whether by post, by an officer appointed by the Lord Chancellor or, as regards Northern Ireland, the Secretary of State, or otherwise, and make different provision for different classes of writs; and
  (b) provide for the giving of receipts for writs by persons to whom they are delivered or who may receive them in the course of their conveyance.

(4) Delivery of the writ to a person for the time being authorised by law to act as deputy for the officer who by virtue of his office is returning officer shall be as good as delivery to the returning officer.

(5) An Order in Council under this rule—

(a) may require a returning officer to provide an address to which writs are to be conveyed and any change of that address; and

(b) may provide for recording those addresses; and

(c) may provide that the delivery of a writ to a person found in and for the time being in charge of a place so recorded as the office of a returning officer shall be as good as delivery to that returning officer.

(6) The person to whom the writ is delivered shall endorse the date of receipt on the writ in the form shown in the Appendix.

(7) A draft of an Order in Council under this rule shall be laid before Parliament, and any such Order may provide for any incidental or supplemental matter.

NOTES

Defined terms   returning officer: see ss 24–27
    Clerk of the Crown: s 202(1)
    parliamentary election: Interpretation Act 1978 Sch 1
    person: s 202(1)

Conveyance of writ to acting returning officer

4(1) For an election in a constituency in England and Wales the writ shall (notwithstanding anything in rule 3 above) be conveyed to the acting returning officer if the returning officer—

(a) has so requested by notice in the form prescribed by an Order in Council under rule 3 and received by the Clerk of the Crown one month or more before the issue of the writ; and

(b) has not revoked it by a further notice in the form so prescribed and received within such time as is mentioned above.

(2) A notice under this rule has effect in relation to all constituencies—

(a) of which the person giving it is returning officer at the time of giving it; or

(b) of which he or a successor in office becomes returning officer by virtue of that office.

(3) Where by virtue of this rule writs are conveyed to the acting returning officer paragraph (5) of rule 3 applies in relation to him as it applies in relation to a returning officer.

NOTES

Defined terms   returning officer: see ss 24–27
    Clerk of the Crown: s 202(1)   Wales: Interpretation Act 1978 Sch 1
    England: Interpretation Act 1978 Sch 1
    month: Interpretation Act 1978 Sch 1
    person: s 202(1)

Notice of election

5(1) The returning officer shall publish notice of the election in the form in the Appendix, stating—

(a) the place and times at which nomination papers are to be delivered, and

(b) the date of the poll in the event of a contest,

and the notice shall state that forms of nomination paper may be obtained at that place and those times.

(1A) The notice of election must also state the arrangements which apply for the payment of the deposit required by rule 9 below to be made by means of the electronic transfer of funds.

(2) The notice of election shall state the date by which (except in such circumstances as may be prescribed)—
    (a) applications to vote by post or by proxy, and
    (b) other applications and notices about postal or proxy voting,
must reach the registration officer in order that they may be effective for the election.

(3) *Repealed*

NOTES
Defined terms
  Clerk of the Crown: s 202(1)
  prescribed: s 202(1)
  registration officer: s 8(1)
  returning officer: see ss 24-27
  vote: s 202(1)

Nomination

Nomination of candidates

6(1) Each candidate shall be nominated by a separate nomination paper, in the form in the Appendix delivered—
    (a) by the candidate himself, or
    (b) by his proposer or seconder,
to the returning officer at the place fixed for the purpose, but the paper may be so delivered on the candidate's behalf by his election agent if the agent's name and address have been previously given to the returning officer as required by section 67 of this Act or are so given at the time the paper is delivered.

(2) The nomination paper shall state the candidate's—
    (a) full names, and
    (b) *Repealed*
    (c) if desired, description,
and the surname shall be placed first in the list of his names.

(2A) If a candidate commonly uses—
    (a) a surname which is different from any other surname he has, or
    (b) a forename which is different from any other forename he has,
the nomination paper may state the commonly used surname or forename in addition to the other name.

(3) The description, if any, must consist of either—
    (a) a description which is authorised as mentioned in rule 6A(1) or (1B) below; or
    (b) the word "Independent" or, where the candidate is the Speaker of the House of Commons seeking re-election, the words "The Speaker seeking re-election".

(4) The nomination paper must be accompanied by a form (in this Schedule referred to as the "home address form") which states the candidate's—
    (a) full names, and
    (b) home address in full.
Provision in paragraph (1) above about delivery of the nomination paper applies also to the home address form.

(5) The home address form—
    (a) may contain a statement made and signed by the candidate that he requires the home address not to be made public; and

(b) if it does so, must state the constituency within which that address is situated (or, if that address is outside the United Kingdom, the country within which it is situated).

NOTES

Defined terms
    election agent: see s 67
    returning officer: see ss 24-27

Nomination papers: name of registered political party

6A(1) A nomination paper may not include a description of a candidate which is likely to lead electors to associate the candidate with a registered political party unless the party is a qualifying party in relation to the constituency and the description is authorised by a certificate—

(a) issued by or on behalf of the registered nominating officer of the party, and

(b) received by the returning officer at some time during the period for delivery of nomination papers set out in the Table in rule 1.

(1A) In paragraph (1) above an authorised description may be either—

(a) the name of the party registered under section 28 of the Political Parties, Elections and Referendums Act 2000, or

(b) a description of the party registered under section 28A of that Act.

(1B) A nomination paper may not include a description of a candidate which is likely to lead electors to associate the candidate with two or more registered political parties unless the parties are each qualifying parties in relation to the constituency and the description is a registered description authorised by a certificate—

(a) issued by or on behalf of the registered nominating officer of each of the parties, and

(b) received by the returning officer at some time during the period for delivery of nomination papers set out in the Table in rule 1.

(1C) For the purposes of paragraph (1B), a description is a registered description if it is a description registered for use by the parties under section 28B of the Political Parties, Elections and Referendums Act 2000.

(2) A person shall be guilty of a corrupt practice if he fraudulently purports to be authorised to issue a certificate under paragraph (1) or (1B) on behalf of a registered political party's nominating officer.

(3) For the purposes of the application of this rule in relation to an election—

(a) "registered political party" means a party which was registered under Part II of the Political Parties, Elections and Referendums Act 2000 on the day ("the relevant day") which is two days before the last day for the delivery of nomination papers at the election;

(b) a registered political party is a qualifying party in relation to a constituency if—

(i) the constituency is in England, Scotland or Wales and the party was on the relevant day registered in respect of that part of Great Britain in the Great Britain register maintained under that Part of that Act, or

(ii) the constituency is in Northern Ireland and the party was on the relevant day registered in the Northern Ireland register maintained under that Part of that Act.

(4) For the purposes of paragraph (3)(a) any day falling within rule 2(1) (subject to rule 2(2A)) shall be disregarded.

NOTES

Defined terms
    elector: s 202(1)

England: Interpretation Act 1978 Sch 1
person: s 202(1)

registered political party: s 202(1)
returning officer: see ss 24-27
Wales: Interpretation Act 1978 Sch 1

Subscription of nomination paper

7(1) The nomination paper shall be subscribed by two electors as proposer and seconder, and by eight other electors as assenting to the nomination.

(2) Where a nomination paper bears the signatures of more than the required number of persons as proposing, seconding or assenting to the nomination of a candidate, the signature or signatures (up to the required number) appearing first on the paper in each category shall be taken into account to the exclusion of any others in that category.

(3) The nomination paper shall give the electoral number of each person subscribing it.

(4) The returning officer—
   (a) shall supply any elector with a form of nomination paper at the place and during the time for delivery of nomination papers, and
   (b) shall at any elector's request prepare a nomination paper for signature,
   but it is not necessary for a nomination to be on a form supplied by the returning officer.

(5) A person shall not subscribe more than one nomination paper at the same election and, if he does, his signature shall be inoperative on any paper other than the one first delivered, but he shall not be prevented from subscribing a nomination paper by reason only of his having subscribed that of a candidate who has died or withdrawn before delivery of the first mentioned paper.

(6) In this rule "elector"—
   (a) means a person who is registered in the register of parliamentary electors for the constituency on the last day for publication of notice of the election; and
   (b) includes a person then shown in that register as below voting age if (but only if) it appears from the register that he will be of voting age on the day fixed for the poll.

(7) But, in this rule, "elector" does not include a person who has an anonymous entry in the register.

NOTES
Defined terms
anonymous entry: ss 9B, 202(1)
returning officer: see ss 24-27

Consent to nomination

8(1) A person shall not be validly nominated unless his consent to nomination—
   (a) is given in writing on or within one month before the day fixed as the last day for the delivery of nomination papers,
   (b) is attested by one witness, and
   (c) is delivered at the place and within the time for the delivery of nomination papers,
   subject to paragraph (2) below.

(2) If the returning officer is satisfied that owing to the absence of a person from the United Kingdom it has not been reasonably practicable for his consent in writing to be given as mentioned above, a telegram (or any similar means of communication) consenting to his nomination and purporting to have been sent by him shall be deemed for the purposes of this rule to be consent in writing given by him on the day

on which it purports to have been sent, and attestation of his consent shall not be required.

(3) A candidate's consent given under this rule—

    (a) shall state the day, month and year of his birth; and

    (b) shall state—

        (i) that he is aware of the provisions of the House of Commons Disqualification Act 1975; and

        (ii) that to the best of his knowledge and belief he is not disqualified for membership of the House of Commons;

    (c) shall state that he is not a candidate at an election for any other constituency the poll for which is to be held on the same day as that for the election to which the consent relates.

NOTES

Defined terms
    month: Interpretation Act 1978 Sch 1
    returning officer: see ss 24–27

writing: Interpretation Act 1978 Sch 1

Deposit

9(1) A person shall not be validly nominated unless the sum of £500 is deposited by him or on his behalf with the returning officer at the place and during the time for delivery of nomination papers.

(2) The deposit may be made either—

    (a) by the deposit of any legal tender, or

    (b) by means of a banker's draft, or

    (c) with the returning officer's consent, in any other manner (including by means of a debit or credit card or the electronic transfer of funds),

but the returning officer may refuse to accept a deposit sought to be made by means of a banker's draft if he does not know that the drawer carries on business as a banker in the United Kingdom.

(3) Where the deposit is made on behalf of the candidate, the person making the deposit shall at the time he makes it give his name and address to the returning officer (unless they have previously been given to him under section 67 of this Act or rule 6(4) above).

NOTES

Defined terms
    person: s 202(1)
    returning officer: see ss 24–27

Place for delivery of nomination papers

10(1) The returning officer shall fix the place at which nomination papers are to be delivered to him, and shall attend there during the time for their delivery and for the making of objections to them.

(2) Except in Scotland, the place shall be in—

    (a) the constituency; or

    (b) the registration area which includes the constituency; or

    (c) unless the constituency is a borough constituency, in a district or Welsh county or county borough adjoining the constituency or registration area.

For the purposes of paragraph (b) above "registration area" means—

        (i) in England and Wales, the area of two or more constituencies which have the same registration officer;

        (ii) in Northern Ireland, the county borough of Belfast and each county.

(3) In Scotland the place shall be in—

    (a) the constituency; or

(b) the local government area or (if more than one) any of the local government areas in which the constituency is situated; or

(c) any local government area adjoining the local government area or local government areas (as the case may be) in which the constituency is situated.

NOTES

Defined terms

England: Interpretation Act 1978 Sch 1

local government area (E&W): ss 191(1), 203(1)

local government area (S): s 204(1)

returning officer: see ss 24-27

Wales: Interpretation Act 1978 Sch 1

Right to attend nomination

11(1) Except for the purpose of delivering a nomination paper or of assisting the returning officer, and subject to paragraph (4) below, no person is entitled to attend the proceedings during the time for delivery of nomination papers or for making objections to them unless he is—

(a) a person standing nominated as a candidate, or

(b) the election agent, proposer or seconder of such a person, or

(c) a person who is entitled to attend by virtue of section 6A or 6B of the Political Parties, Elections and Referendums Act 2000,

but where a candidate acts as his own election agent he may name one other person who shall be entitled to attend in place of his election agent.

(2) Where a person stands nominated by more than one nomination paper, only the persons subscribing as proposer and seconder—

(a) to such one of those papers as he may select, or

(b) in default of such a selection, to that one of those papers which is first delivered,

shall be entitled to attend as his proposer and seconder.

(3) The right to attend conferred by this rule includes the right—

(a) to inspect, and

(b) to object to the validity of,

any nomination paper and associated home address form.

(3A) Paragraph (3) does not apply to a person mentioned in paragraph (1)(c).

(4) One other person chosen by the candidate is entitled to be present at the delivery of the candidate's nomination, and may afterwards, so long as the candidate stands nominated, attend the proceedings referred to in paragraph (1) above, but without any such right as is conferred by paragraph (3) above.

(5) The returning officer shall not permit a home address form to be inspected otherwise than in accordance with this rule, or for some other purpose authorised by law.

NOTES

Defined terms

election agent: see s 67

returning officer: see ss 24-27

Decisions as to validity of nomination papers

12(1) Where a nomination paper and the candidate's consent to it and the home address form are delivered and a deposit is made in accordance with these rules, the candidate shall be deemed to stand nominated unless and until—

(a) the returning officer decides that the nomination paper is invalid; or

(aa) the returning officer decides that the home address form does not comply with rule 6(4); or

(b) proof is given to the returning officer's satisfaction of the candidate's death; or

(c) the candidate withdraws.

(2) The returning officer is entitled to hold a nomination paper invalid only on one of the following grounds—
   (a) that the particulars of the candidate or the persons subscribing the paper are not as required by law;
   (b) that the paper is not subscribed as so required; and
   (c) that the candidate is disqualified by the Representation of the People Act 1981.

(3) Subject to paragraph (3A), the returning officer shall give his decision on any objection to a nomination paper—
   (a) as soon as practicable after it is made, and
   (b) in any event, before the end of the period of 24 hours starting with the close of the period for delivery of nomination papers set out in the Table in rule 1.

(3A) If in the returning officer's opinion a nomination paper breaks rule 6A(1) or (1B), he shall give a decision to that effect—
   (a) as soon as practicable after delivery of the nomination paper, and
   (b) in any event, before the end of the period of 24 hours starting with the close of the period for delivery of nomination papers set out in the Table in rule 1.

(4) Where the returning officer decides that a nomination paper is invalid, he shall endorse and sign on the paper the fact and the reasons for his decision.

(5) The returning officer's decision that a nomination paper is valid shall be final and shall not be questioned in any proceeding whatsoever.

(6) Subject to paragraph (5) above nothing in this rule prevents the validity of a nomination being questioned on an election petition.

NOTES
Defined terms
   election petition: s 202(1)
   returning officer: see ss 24-27

Withdrawal of candidates

13(1) A candidate may withdraw his candidature by notice of withdrawal—
   (a) signed by him and attested by one witness, and
   (b) delivered to the returning officer at the place for delivery of nomination papers.

(2) Where a candidate is outside the United Kingdom, a notice of withdrawal signed by his proposer and accompanied by a written declaration also so signed of the candidate's absence from the United Kingdom shall be of the same effect as a notice of withdrawal signed by the candidate; but where the candidate stands nominated by more than one nomination paper a notice of withdrawal under this paragraph shall be effective if, and only if—
   (a) it and the accompanying declaration are signed by all the proposers except any who is, and is stated in that declaration to be, outside the United Kingdom; or
   (b) it is accompanied, in addition to that declaration, by a written statement signed by the candidate that the proposer giving the notice is authorised to do so on the candidate's behalf during his absence from the United Kingdom

NOTES
Defined terms
   returning officer: see ss 24-27
   written: Interpretation Act 1978 Sch 1

Publication of statement of persons nominated

14(1) The returning officer shall prepare and publish a statement showing the persons who have been and stand nominated and any other persons who have been nominated, with the reason why they no longer stand nominated.

(2)   The statement shall show the names, addresses and descriptions of the persons nominated as given in their nomination papers and home address forms, together with the names of the persons subscribing those papers.

(2A)   If a person's nomination paper gives a commonly used surname or forename in addition to another name, the statement shall show the person's commonly used surname or forename (as the case may be) instead of any other name.

(2B)   Paragraph (2A) above does not apply if the returning officer thinks—
   (a)   that the use of the person's commonly used name may be likely to mislead or confuse electors, or
   (b)   that the commonly used name is obscene or offensive.

(2C)   If paragraph (2B) above applies, the returning officer must give notice in writing to the candidate of his reasons for refusing to allow the use of a commonly used name.

(3)   The statement shall show the persons standing nominated arranged alphabetically in order of their surnames, and, if there are two or more of them with the same surname, of their other names.

(3A)   In relation to a nominated person in whose case the home address form (or, if the person is nominated by more than one nomination paper, any of the home address forms) contains—
   (a)   the statement mentioned in rule 6(5)(a), and
   (b)   the information mentioned in rule 6(5)(b),
   the reference in paragraph (2) to the person's address shall be read as a reference to the information mentioned in rule 6(5)(b).

(4)   In the case of a person nominated by more than one nomination paper, the returning officer shall take the particulars required by the foregoing provisions of this rule from such one of the papers as the candidate (or the returning officer in default of the candidate) may select, but if the election is contested a candidate standing nominated may require the returning officer to include in the statement the names of the persons subscribing a second and third nomination.

(4A)   Where—
   (a)   two or more of the names shown on the statement are the same or so similar as to be likely to cause confusion,
   (b)   paragraph (3A) applies in relation to each of the persons in question, and
   (c)   the information mentioned in rule 6(5)(b) is the same for each of them,
   the returning officer may cause any of their particulars to be shown on the statement with such amendments or additions as the officer thinks appropriate in order to reduce the likelihood of confusion.

(4B)   Where it is practicable to do so before the publication of the statement, the returning officer shall consult any person whose particulars are to be amended or added to under paragraph (4A).

(4C)   The returning officer must give notice in writing to any person whose particulars are amended or added to under paragraph (4A).

(4D)   Anything done by a returning officer in pursuance of paragraph (4A) must not be questioned in any proceedings other than proceedings on an election petition.

(4E)   A returning officer must have regard to any guidance issued by the Electoral Commission for the purposes of paragraph (4A).

(5)   The returning officer shall send to the Electoral Commission—
   (a)   a copy of the statement; and

(b) in the case of each candidate standing nominated in respect of whom a certificate has been received by the returning officer in accordance with rule 6A(1) or (1B) above, a copy of that certificate as well.

NOTES

Defined terms
  election petition: s 202(1)
  elector: s 202(1)
  Electoral Commission: see Political Parties, Elections
  and Referendums Act 2000 s 1

returning officer: see ss 24-27
writing: Interpretation Act 1978 Sch 1

Correction of minor errors

14A(1)   A returning officer may, if he thinks fit, at any time before the publication under rule 14 above of the statement of persons nominated, correct minor errors in a nomination paper or home address form.

(2)   Errors which may be corrected include—

    (a)   errors as to a person's electoral number;

    (b)   obvious errors of spelling in relation to the details of a candidate

    (c)   in the home address form, errors as to the information mentioned in rule 6(5)(b).

(3)   Anything done by a returning officer in pursuance of this rule must not be questioned in any proceedings other than proceedings on an election petition.

(4)   A returning officer must have regard to any guidance issued by the Electoral Commission for the purposes of this rule.

NOTES

Defined terms
  election petition: s 202(1)
  Electoral Commission: see Political Parties, Elections
  and Referendums Act 2000 s 1

returning officer: see ss 24-27

Disqualification by Representation of the People Act 1981

15(1)   If it appears to the returning officer that any of the persons nominated might be disqualified by the Representation of the People Act 1981 he shall, as soon as practicable after the expiry of the time allowed for the delivery of nomination papers, prepare and publish a draft of the statement required under rule 14 above.

(2)   The draft shall be headed "Draft statement of persons nominated" and shall omit the names of the persons subscribing the papers but shall contain a notice stating that any person who wishes to object to the nomination of any candidate on the ground that he is disqualified for nomination under the Representation of the People Act 1981 may do so between the hours of 10 in the morning and 4 in the afternoon on the day and at the place specified in the notice; and the day so specified shall be the day next after the last day for the delivery of nomination papers.

NOTES

Defined terms
  returning officer: see ss 24-27

Adjournment of nomination proceedings in case of riot

16(1)   Where the proceedings for or in connection with nomination are on any day interrupted or obstructed by riot or open violence—

    (a)   the proceedings shall be abandoned for that day, and

    (b)   if that day is the last day for the delivery of nomination papers, the proceedings shall be continued on the next day as if that were the last day of such delivery, and that day shall be treated for the purposes of these rules as being the last day for such delivery (subject to any further application of this rule in the event of interruption or obstruction on that day).

(2) Where proceedings are abandoned by virtue of this rule nothing—

    (a) may be done after they are continued if the time for doing it had passed at the time of the abandonment;

    (b) done before the abandonment shall be invalidated by reason of the abandonment.

Method of election

17(1) If the statement of persons nominated shows more than one person standing nominated, a poll shall be taken in accordance with Part III of these rules.

(2) If the statement of persons nominated shows only one person standing nominated, that person shall be declared to be elected in accordance with Part IV of these rules.

PART III
CONTESTED ELECTIONS

General provisions

Poll to be taken by ballot

18 The votes at the poll shall be given by ballot, the result shall be ascertained by counting the votes given to each candidate and the candidate to whom the majority of votes have been given shall be declared to have been elected.

NOTES
Defined terms
  vote: s 202(1)

The ballot papers

19(1) The ballot of every voter shall consist of a ballot paper, and the persons shown in the statement of persons nominated as standing nominated, and no others, shall be entitled to have their names inserted in the ballot paper.

(2) Every ballot paper shall be in the form in the Appendix, and shall be printed in accordance with the directions in that Appendix, and—

    (a) shall contain the names and other particulars of the candidates as shown in the statement of persons nominated;

    (b) shall be capable of being folded up;

    (c) shall have a number and other unique identifying mark printed on the back;

    (d) *Repealed*

(2A) If a candidate who is the subject of a party's authorisation under rule 6A(1) so requests, the ballot paper shall contain, against the candidate's particulars, the party's registered emblem (or, as the case may be, one of the party's registered emblems).

(2AA) If a candidate who is the subject of an authorisation by two or more parties under rule 6A(1B) so requests, the ballot paper shall contain, against the candidate's particulars, the registered emblem (or, as the case may be, one of the registered emblems) of one of those parties.

(2B) A request under paragraph (2A) or (2AA) must—

    (a) be made in writing to the returning officer, and

(b) be received by him during the period for delivery of nomination papers set out in the Table in rule 1.

(3) The order of the names in the ballot paper shall be the same as in the statement of persons nominated.

(4) The Secretary of State may in regulations—

    (a) prescribe a different form of ballot paper from that in the Appendix;

    (b) amend or replace the directions as to printing the ballot paper in the Appendix;

    (c) in consequence of anything done for the purposes of paragraph (a) or (b), amend or replace the Form of directions for the guidance of the voters in voting in the Appendix.

NOTES

Defined terms   writing: Interpretation Act 1978 Sch 1
    returning officer: see ss 24-27
    voter: s 202(1)
    voting: see "vote" s 202(1)

Corresponding number list

19A(1) The returning officer must prepare a list containing the numbers and other unique identifying marks of all of the ballot papers to be issued by him in pursuance of rule 24(1) or provided by him in pursuance of rule 29(1).

(2) The list shall be in such form as the Secretary of State in regulations prescribes

NOTES

Defined terms
    returning officer: see ss 24-27

The official mark

20(1) Every ballot paper must contain an appropriate security marking (the official mark).

(2) The official mark shall be kept secret, and an interval of not less than seven years shall intervene between the use of the same official mark at elections for the same constituency.

(3) The returning officer may use a different official mark for different purposes at the same election

NOTES

Defined terms
    returning officer: see ss 24-27

Prohibition of disclosure of vote

21 No person who has voted at the election shall, in any legal proceeding to question the election or return, be required to state for whom he voted.

NOTES

Defined terms
    vote: s 202(1)

Use of schools and public rooms

22(1) The returning officer may use, free of charge, for the purpose of taking the poll—

    (a) a room in a school to which this rule applies;

    (b) a room the expense of maintaining which is payable out of any rate.

This rule applies—

    (i) in England and Wales, to a school maintained or assisted by a local authority or a school in respect of which grants are made out of moneys provided by Parliament to the person or body of persons responsible for the management of the school;

    (ii) in Scotland, to a school other than an independent school within the meaning of the Education (Scotland) Act 1980;

    (iii) in Northern Ireland, to a school in receipt of a grant out of moneys appropriated by Measure of the Northern Ireland Assembly.

(2)   The returning officer shall make good any damage done to, and defray any expense incurred by the persons having control over, any such room as mentioned above by reason of its being used for the purpose of taking the poll.

(3)   *Repealed*

(4)   In Northern Ireland this rule does not apply to any school adjoining or adjacent to any church or other place of worship nor to any school connected with a nunnery or other religious establishment.

NOTES

Defined terms

  England: Interpretation Act 1978 Sch 1
  local authority (E&W): s 203(1)
  local authority (S): s 204(1)
  person: s 202(1)
  returning officer: see ss 24-27

  vote: s 202(1)
  voter: s 202(1)
  Wales: Interpretation Act 1978 Sch 1

Action to be taken before the poll

Notice of poll

23(1)   The returning officer shall in the statement of persons nominated include a notice of the poll, stating the day on which and hours during which the poll will be taken.

(2)   The returning officer shall also give public notice (which may be combined with the statement of persons nominated) of—

    (a) the situation of each polling station;

    (b) the description of voters entitled to vote there;

    (c) *Repealed*

and he shall as soon as practicable after giving such notice give a copy of it to each of the election agents.

(3)   *Repealed*

NOTES

Defined terms

  election agent: see s 67
  returning officer: see ss 24-27
  vote: s 202(1)

  voter: s 202(1)

Postal ballot papers

24(1)   The returning officer shall, in accordance with regulations, issue to those entitled to vote by post—

    (a) a ballot paper;

    (b) at an election held in England and Wales or Scotland, a postal voting statement in the prescribed form;

    (c) at an election held in Northern Ireland, a declaration of identity in the prescribed form;

together with such envelopes for their return as may be prescribed.

(2)   The returning officer must also issue to those entitled to vote by post such information as he thinks appropriate about how to obtain—

(a) translations into languages other than English of any directions to or guidance for voters sent with the ballot paper;

(b) a translation into Braille of such directions or guidance;

(c) graphical representations of such directions or guidance;

(d) the directions or guidance in any other form (including any audible form).

(3) The prescribed form shall include provision for the form to be signed and for stating the date of birth of the elector or proxy (as the case may be).

(4) In the case of a ballot paper issued to a person resident in the United Kingdom, the returning officer must ensure that the return of the ballot paper and postal voting statement or declaration of identity is free of charge to the voter.

(5) In any other case, regulations may provide that the returning officer must so ensure.

NOTES

Defined terms

elector: s 202(1)
England: Interpretation Act 1978 Sch 1
prescribed: s 202(1)
returning officer: see ss 24-27

vote: s 202(1)
voter: s 202(1)
Wales: Interpretation Act 1978 Sch 1

Provision of polling stations

25(1) The returning officer shall provide a sufficient number of polling stations and, subject to the following provisions of this rule, shall allot the electors to the polling stations in such manner as he thinks most convenient.

(2) One or more polling stations may be provided in the same room.

(3) The polling station allotted to electors from any polling district shall be in the polling place for that district.

(4) In a constituency in Scotland comprising the whole or any part of more local government areas than one, there shall be at least one polling station in each of those local government areas.

(5) The returning officer shall provide each polling station with such number of compartments as may be necessary in which the voters can mark their votes screened from observation.

NOTES

Defined terms

elector: s 202(1)
local government area (E&W): ss 191(1), 203(1)
local government area (S): s 204(1)
returning officer: see ss 24-27

vote: s 202(1)
voter: s 202(1)

Appointment of presiding officers and clerks

26(1) The returning officer shall appoint and pay a presiding officer to attend at each polling station and such clerks as may be necessary for the purposes of the election, but he shall not appoint any person who has been employed by or on behalf of a candidate in or about the election.

(2) The returning officer may, if he thinks fit, preside at a polling station and the provisions of these rules relating to a presiding officer shall apply to a returning officer so presiding with the necessary modifications as to things to be done by the returning officer to the presiding officer or by the presiding officer to the returning officer.

(3) A presiding officer may do, by the clerks appointed to assist him, any act (including the asking of questions) which he is required or authorised by these rules to do at a polling station except order the arrest, exclusion or removal of any person from the polling

station or refuse to deliver a ballot paper under paragraph (1C) of rule 37 (including that paragraph as applied by rule 38, 39 or 40)

NOTES
Defined terms
  returning officer: see ss 24-27

27   *Repealed*

Issue of official poll cards

28(1)   The returning officer shall as soon as practicable after the publication of notice of the election send to electors and their proxies an official poll card.

(1A)   An official poll card shall not be sent to a person registered, or to be registered, in pursuance of an overseas elector's declaration.

(2)   An elector's official poll card shall be sent or delivered to his qualifying address.

(2A)   A proxy's official poll card shall be sent or delivered to the address which—
  (a)   is shown as the proxy's address in the list of proxies; or
  (b)   in the case of a proxy for an elector with an anonymous entry in a register maintained by the Chief Electoral Officer for Northern Ireland, would be so shown but for section 7(4A) of the Representation of the People Act 1985.

(3)   The official poll card shall be in the prescribed form and shall set out—
  (a)   the name of the constituency;
  (b)   the elector's name, qualifying address and number on the register;
  (c)   the date and hours of the poll and the situation of the elector's polling station;
  (d)   such other information as is prescribed;
  (e)   such other information as the returning officer thinks appropriate,
  and different information may be provided in pursuance of sub-paragraph (d) and (e) to different electors or descriptions of elector.

(3A)   In the case of an elector with an anonymous entry, instead of containing the matter mentioned in paragraph (3)(b) above the polling card shall contain such matter as is prescribed.

(4)   Paragraph (6) of rule 7 above applies for the interpretation of this rule.

NOTES
Defined terms
  anonymous entry: ss 9B, 202(1)   prescribed: s 202(1)
  elector: s 202(1)   qualifying address: ss 9(8), 202(1)
  list of proxies: s 202(1)   returning officer: see ss 24-27
  overseas elector's declaration: s 202(1) and RPA 1985
  s 2

Equipment of polling stations

29(1)   The returning officer shall provide each presiding officer with such number of ballot boxes and ballot papers as in the returning officer's opinion may be necessary.

(2)   Every ballot box shall be so constructed that the ballot papers can be put in it, but cannot be withdrawn from it, without the box being unlocked.

(3)   The returning officer shall provide each polling station with—
  (a)   materials to enable voters to mark the ballot papers;
  (b)   *Repealed*
  (c)   copies of the register of electors or such part of it as contains the entries relating to the electors allotted to the station;

(d) the parts of any special lists prepared for the election corresponding to the register of electors or the part of it provided under sub-paragraph (c) above;

(e) a list consisting of that part of the list prepared under rule 19A which contains the numbers (but not the other unique identifying marks) corresponding to those on the ballot papers provided to the presiding officer of the polling station.

(3A) The returning officer shall also provide each polling station with—

(a) at least one large version of the ballot paper which shall be displayed inside the polling station for the assistance of voters who are partially-sighted; and

(b) a device of such description as may be prescribed for enabling voters who are blind or partially-sighted to vote without any need for assistance from the presiding officer or any companion (within the meaning of rule 39(1)).

(4) A notice in the form in the Appendix, giving directions for the guidance of the voters in voting, shall be printed in conspicuous characters and exhibited inside and outside every polling station.

(5) In every compartment of every polling station there shall be exhibited the notice "Vote for one candidate only. Put no other mark on the ballot paper, or your vote may not be counted".

(6) The reference in paragraph (3)(c) to the copies of the registers of electors includes a reference to copies of any notices issued under section 13B(3B) or (3D) of this Act in respect of alterations to the register.

(7) The reference in paragraph (3)(c) to the copies of the register of electors includes a reference to copies of any notices issued under section 13BA(9) in respect of alterations to the register.

NOTES

Defined terms
elector: s 202(1)
prescribed: s 202(1)
register of electors: see s 9
returning officer: see ss 24-27

vote: s 202(1)
voter: s 202(1)
voting: see "vote" s 202(1)

Appointment of polling and counting agents

30(1) Each candidate may, before the commencement of the poll, appoint—

(a) polling agents to attend at polling stations for the purpose of detecting personation; and

(b) counting agents to attend at the counting of the votes.

(2) The returning officer may limit the number of counting agents, so however that—

(a) the number shall be the same in the case of each candidate; and

(b) the number allowed to a candidate shall not (except in special circumstances) be less than the number obtained by dividing the number of clerks employed on the counting by the number of candidates.

(3) Notice in writing of the appointment, stating the names and addresses of the persons appointed, shall be given by the candidate to the returning officer and shall be so given not later than the 5th day (computed like any period of time in the Timetable) before the day of the poll.

(4) If an agent dies, or becomes incapable of acting, the candidate may appoint another agent in his place, and shall forthwith give to the returning officer notice in writing of the name and address of the agent appointed.

(5) *The foregoing provisions of this rule shall be without prejudice to the requirements of section 72(1) of this Act as to the appointment of paid polling agents, and any*

appointment authorised by this rule may be made and the notice of appointment given to the returning officer by the candidate's election agent, instead of by the candidate.

(6) In the following provisions of these rules references to polling and counting agents shall be taken as references to agents—
   (a) whose appointments have been duly made and notified; and
   (b) where the number of agents is restricted, who are within the permitted number.

(7) Any notice required to be given to a counting agent by the returning officer may be delivered at or sent by post to the address stated in the notice of appointment.

(8) A candidate may himself do any act or thing which any polling or counting agent of his, if appointed, would have been authorised to do, or may assist his agent in doing any such act or thing.

(9) A candidate's election agent may do or assist in doing anything which a polling or counting agent of his is authorised to do; and anything required or authorised by these rules to be done in the presence of the polling or counting agents may be done in the presence of a candidate's election agent instead of his polling agent or counting agents.

(10) Where by these rules any act or thing is required or authorised to be done in the presence of the polling or counting agents, the non-attendance of any agents or agent at the time and place appointed for the purpose shall not, if the act or thing is otherwise duly done, invalidate the act or thing done.

NOTES

Defined terms
  election agent: see s 67
  personation: s 60(2)
  returning officer: see ss 24-27

         vote: s 202(1)
         writing: Interpretation Act 1978 Sch 1

Notification of requirement of secrecy

31(1) The returning officer shall make such arrangements as he thinks fit to ensure that—
   (a) every person attending at a polling station (otherwise than for the purpose of voting or assisting a blind voter to vote or as a constable on duty there) has been given a copy in writing of the provisions of subsections (1), (3) and (6) of section 66 of this Act; and
   (b) every person attending at the counting of the votes (other than any constable on duty at the counting) has been given a copy in writing of the provisions of subsections (2) and (6) of that section.

(2) In the application of this rule to an election in England or Wales, a reference to a constable includes a person designated as a community support officer under section 38 of the Police Reform Act 2002 (police powers for employees).

NOTES

Defined terms
  England: Interpretation Act 1978 Sch 1
  returning officer: see ss 24-27
  vote: s 202(1)
  voter: s 202(1)

         voting: see "vote" s 202(1)
         Wales: Interpretation Act 1978 Sch 1
         writing: Interpretation Act 1978 Sch 1

Return of postal ballot papers

31A(1) Where—
   (a) a postal vote has been returned in respect of a person who is entered on the postal voters list, or

(b) a proxy postal vote has been returned in respect of a proxy who is entered on the proxy postal voters list,

the returning officer must mark the list in the prescribed manner.

(1A) Paragraph (1) shall not apply in relation to a vote on a tendered postal ballot paper (see rule 40ZA).

(2) For the purposes of paragraph (1) above, regulations may prescribe the circumstances in which a postal vote or a proxy postal vote (as the case may be) is or is not to be treated as having been returned.

(3) Rule 45(1B) and (2) below does not apply for the purpose of determining whether, for the purposes of this rule, a postal vote or a proxy postal vote is returned

NOTES

Defined terms
  postal voters list: s 202(1)
  prescribed: s 202(1)
  proxy postal voters list: s 202(1)

returning officer: see ss 24-27
vote: s 202(1)

The poll

Admission to polling station

32(1) The presiding officer shall exclude all persons from the polling station except—
    (a) voters;
    (b) persons under the age of 18 who accompany voters to the polling station;
    (c) the candidates and their election agents;
    (d) the polling agents appointed to attend at the polling station;
    (e) the clerks appointed to attend at the polling station;
    (f) persons who are entitled to attend by virtue of any of sections 6A to 6D of the Political Parties, Elections and Referendums Act 2000;
    (g) the constables on duty; and
    (h) the companions of voters with disabilities.

(1A) The presiding officer shall regulate the total number of voters and persons under the age of 18 who accompany them to be admitted to the polling station at the same time.

(2) Not more than one polling agent shall be admitted at the same time to a polling station on behalf of the same candidate.

(3) A constable or person employed by a returning officer shall not be admitted to vote in person elsewhere than at his own polling station under the relevant provision of this Act, except on production and surrender of a certificate as to his employment, which shall be in the prescribed form and signed by the prescribed officer of police or by the returning officer, as the case may be.

(4) Any certificate surrendered under this rule shall forthwith be cancelled.

(5) In the application of this rule to an election in England or Wales, a reference to a constable includes a person designated as a community support officer under section 38 of the Police Reform Act 2002 (police powers for employees).

NOTES

Defined terms
  England: Interpretation Act 1978 Sch 1
  election agent: see s 67
  prescribed: s 202(1)
  returning officer: see ss 24-27

vote: s 202(1)
voter: s 202(1)
Wales: Interpretation Act 1978 Sch 1

Keeping of order in station

33(1)   It is the presiding officer's duty to keep order at his polling station.

(2)   If a person misconducts himself in a polling station, or fails to obey the presiding officer's lawful orders, he may immediately, by the presiding officer's order, be removed from the polling station—

(a)   by a constable in or near that station, or

(b)   by any other person authorised in writing by the returning officer to remove him,

and the person so removed shall not, without the presiding officer's permission, again enter the polling station during the day.

(3)   Any person so removed may, if charged with the commission in the polling station of an offence, be dealt with as a person taken into custody by a constable for an offence without a warrant.

(4)   The powers conferred by this rule shall not be exercised so as to prevent a voter who is otherwise entitled to vote at a polling station from having an opportunity of voting at that station.

NOTES

Defined terms
returning officer: see ss 24-27
vote: s 202(1)
voter: s 202(1)

voting: see "vote" s 202(1)
writing: Interpretation Act 1978 Sch 1

Sealing of ballot boxes

34   Immediately before the commencement of the poll, the presiding officer shall show the ballot box empty to such persons, if any, as are present in the polling station, so that they may see that it is empty, and shall then lock it up and place his seal on it in such a manner as to prevent its being opened without breaking the seal, and shall place it in his view for the receipt of ballot papers, and keep it so locked and sealed.

Questions to be put to voters
England, Wales & Scotland version

35(1)   At the time of the application (but not afterwards), the questions specified in the second column of the following table—

(a)   may be put by the presiding officer to a person who is mentioned in the first column, and

(b)   shall be put if the letter "R" appears after the question and the candidate or his election or polling agent requires the question to be put:

Person applying for ballot paper		*Questions*
1 A person applying as an elector.	(a)	"Are you the person registered in he register of parliamentary eectors for this election as follows (*read out the whole entry from the register*)?" [R]
	(b)	"Have you already voted, here or elsewhere, at this election, otherwise than as proxy for some other person?" [R]
	(c)	At an election held in Northern Ireland, "What is your date of birth?"

Person applying for ballot paper	Questions
2 A person applying as proxy.	(a) "Are you the person whose name appears as A B in the list of proxies for this election as entitled to vote as proxy on behalf of C D?" R
	(b) "Have you already voted here or elsewhere at this election, as proxy on behalf of C D?" R
	(c) "Are you the spouse, civil partner, parent, grandparent, brother/sister, child or grandchild of CD?" R
3 A person applying as proxy for an elector with an anonymous entry (instead of the questions at entry 2 above). *Not in Northern Ireland*	(a) "Are you the person entitled to vote as proxy on behalf of the elector whose number on the register of electors is *(read out the number from the register)*?
	(b) "Have you already voted here or elsewhere as proxy on behalf of the elector whose number on the register of electors is *(read out the number from the register)*?" R
	(c) "Are you the spouse, civil partner, parent, grandparent, brother/sister, child or grandchild of the person whose number on the register of electors is *(read out the number from the register)*?" R
4 Person applying as proxy if the question at entry 2(c) or 3(c) is not answered in the affirmative.	"Have you at this election already voted in this constituency on behalf of two persons of whom you are not the spouse, civil partner, parent, grand-parent, brother/sister, child or grandchild?" R
5 A person applying as an elector in relation to whom there is an entry in the postal voters list.	(a) "Did you apply to vote by post?" (b) "Why have you not voted by post?"
6 A person applying as proxy who is named in the proxy postal voters list.	(a) "Did you apply to vote by post as proxy?" (b) "Why have you not voted by post as proxy?"

(2) In the case of an elector in respect of whom a notice has been issued under section 13B(3B) or (3D) of this Act, the references in the questions at entries 1(a) and 3(a), (b) and (c) to reading from the register must be taken as references to reading from the notice issued under section 13B(3B) or (3D).

(3) A ballot paper shall not be delivered to any person required to answer any of the above questions unless he has answered each question satisfactorily.

(4) Except as authorised by this rule, no inquiry shall be permitted as to the right of any person to vote.

NOTES

Defined terms

anonymous entry: ss 9B, 202(1)
child: cf Family Law Reform Act 1987 s 1
civil partner: Interpretation Act 1978 Sch 1
elector: s 202(1)
list of proxies: s 202(1)
postal voters list: s 202(1)
proxy postal voters list: s 202(1)

register of electors: see s 9
spouse: Marriage (Same Sex Couples) Act 2013 Sch 3 para 1
vote: s 202(1)
voter: s 202(1)

Challenge of voter

36 A person shall not be prevented from voting by reason only that—
   (a) a candidate or his election or polling agent declares that he has reasonable cause to believe that the person has committed an offence of personation, or
   (b) the person is arrested on the grounds that he is suspected of committing or of being about to commit such an offence.

NOTES

Defined terms

personation: s 60(2)
voting: see "vote" s 202(1)

Voting procedure
Version for England, Wales and Scotland

37(1) A ballot paper shall be delivered to a voter who applies for one, and immediately before delivery—
   (a) the number and (unless paragraph (2) applies) name of the elector as stated in the copy of the register of electors shall be called out;
   (b) the number of the elector shall be marked on the list mentioned in rule 29(3)(e) beside the number of the ballot paper to be issued to him;
   (c) a mark shall be placed in the register of electors against the number of the elector to note that a ballot paper has been received but without showing the particular ballot paper which has been received;
   (d) the voter shall sign the list mentioned in rule 29(3)(e) beside the number of the elector marked on the list in accordance with sub-paragraph (b) above; and
   (e) in the case of a person applying for a ballot paper as proxy, a mark shall also be placed against his name in the list of proxies.

(1ZA) In the case of an elector who is added to the register in pursuance of a notice issued under section 13BA(9), paragraph (1) is modified as follows—
   (a) in sub-paragraph (b), for "copy of the register of electors" substitute copy of the notice issued under section 13BA(9);
   (b) in sub-paragraph (d), for "in the register of electors" substitute on the copy of the notice issued under section 13BA(9).

(2) In the case of an elector who has an anonymous entry, he must show the presiding officer his official poll card and only his number shall be called out in pursuance of paragraph (1)(a).

(3) In the case of an elector who is added to the register in pursuance of a notice issued under section 13B(3B) or (3D), paragraph (1) above is modified as follows—
   (a) in sub-paragraph (a), for "copy of the register of electors" substitute "copy of the notice issued under section 13B(3B) or (3D) of this Act";
   (b) in sub-paragraph (c), for "in the register of electors" substitute "on the copy of the notice issued under section 13B(3B) or (3D) of this Act".

(4) Paragraph (1)(d) above does not apply to a voter to whom rule 38 or 39 applies.

(5) The voter, on receiving the ballot paper, shall forthwith proceed into one of the compartments in the polling station and there secretly mark his paper and fold it up so as to conceal his vote, and shall then show to the presiding officer the back of the paper, so as to disclose the number and other unique identifying mark, and put the ballot paper so folded up into the ballot box in the presiding officer's presence.

(6) The voter shall vote without undue delay, and shall leave the polling station as soon as he has put his ballot paper into the ballot box.

Version for Northern Ireland

(1) Subject to paragraphs (1A) to (1G) below, a ballot paper shall be delivered to a voter who applies for one, and immediately before delivery-

    (a) *Repealed*

    (b) the number and name of the elector as stated in the copy of the register of electors shall be called out;

    (c) the number of the elector shall be marked on the list mentioned in rule 29(3)(e) beside the number of the ballot paper to be issued to him;

    (d) a mark shall be placed in the register of electors against the number of the elector to denote that a ballot paper has been received but without showing the particular ballot paper which has been received; and

    (e) in the case of a person applying for a ballot paper as proxy, a mark shall also be placed against his name in the list of proxies.

(1ZA) In the case of an elector who is added to the register in pursuance of a notice issued under section 13BA(9), paragraph (1) is modified as follows-

    (a) in sub-paragraph (b), for "copy of the register of electors" substitute copy of the notice issued under section 13BA(9);

    (b) in sub-paragraph (d), for "in the register of electors" substitute on the copy of the notice issued under section 13BA(9).

(1A) A ballot paper shall not be delivered to a voter unless he has produced a specified document to the presiding officer or a clerk.

(1B) Where a voter produces a specified document, the presiding officer or clerk to whom it is produced shall deliver a ballot paper to the voter unless the officer or clerk decides that

    (a) the document; or

    (b) the apparent age of the voter as compared with his age according to the date supplied as the date of his birth pursuant to section 10(4A)(b), 10A(1A)(b) or 13A(2A)(b) of this Act,

raises a reasonable doubt as to whether the voter is the elector or proxy he represents himself to be.

(1C) Where in such a case it is a presiding officer who so decides, he shall refuse to deliver a ballot paper to the voter.

(1D) Where in such a case it is a clerk who so decides, he shall refer the matter and produce the document to the presiding officer, who shall proceed as if it had been to him that the voter had presented himself and produced the document in the first place.

(1E) For the purposes of this rule a specified document is one which for the time being falls within the following list:-

    (a) a current licence to drive a motor vehicle if the licence bears the photograph of the person to whom it is issued;

    (b) a current passport issued by the Government of the United Kingdom or by the Government of the Republic of Ireland;

    (c)-(g) *Repealed*

(h)   a current electoral identity card issued under section 13C of this Act;

(i)   a Senior SmartPass issued under the Northern Ireland Concessionary Fares Scheme for use from 1st May 2002

In sub-paragraph (a) a licence to drive a motor vehicle is a licence granted under Part 3 of the Road Traffic Act 1972 or Part 3 of the Road Traffic Act 1988 (excluding a provisional licence), or under Article 12 of the Road Traffic (Northern Ireland) Order 1981 or any corresponding enactment for the time being in force.

(1F)   Regulations may make provision varying the list in paragraph (1E) above (whether by adding or deleting documents or varying any description of document).

(1G)   References in this rule to producing a document are to producing it for inspection.

(2)   The voter, on receiving the ballot paper, shall forthwith proceed into one of the compartments in the polling station and there secretly mark his paper and fold it up so as to conceal his vote, and shall then show to the presiding officer the back of the paper, so as to disclose the number and other unique identifying mark, and put the ballot paper so folded up into the ballot box in the presiding officer's presence.

(3)   The voter shall vote without undue delay, and shall leave the polling station as soon as he has put his ballot paper into the ballot box.

NOTES

Defined terms
anonymous entry: ss 9B, 202(1)
elector: s 202(1)
enactment: Interpretation Act 1978 Sch 1
enactment (NI): s 205
list of proxies: s 202(1)

register of electors: see s 9
vote: s 202(1)
voter: s 202(1)

Votes marked by presiding officer

38(1)   *The* Subject to paragraph (1A) below, the presiding officer, on the application of a voter—

(a)   who is incapacitated by blindness or other disability from voting in manner directed by these rules, or

(b)   who declares orally that he is unable to read,

shall, in the presence of the polling agents, cause the voter's vote to be marked on a ballot paper in manner directed by the voter, and the ballot paper to be placed in the ballot box.

(1A)   Paragraphs (1A) to (1G) of rule 37 shall apply in the case of a voter who applies under paragraph (1) above as they apply in the case of a voter who applies under rule 37(1), but reading references to delivering a ballot paper to a voter as references to causing a voter's vote to be marked on a ballot paper.

(2)   The name and number on the register of electors of every voter whose vote is marked in pursuance of this rule, and the reason why it is so marked, shall be entered on a list (in these rules called "the list of votes marked by the presiding officer").

In the case of a person voting as proxy for an elector, the number to be entered together with the voter's name shall be the elector's number.

(3)   In the case of a person in respect of whom a notice has been issued under section 13B(3B) or (3D) of this Act, paragraph (2) above applies as if for "on the register of electors of every voter" there were substituted "relating to every voter in respect of whom a notice has been issued under section 13B(3B) or (3D)".

(4)   In the case of a person in respect of whom a notice has been issued under section 13BA(9), paragraph (2) applies as if for "on the register of electors of every voter" there were substituted "relating to every voter in respect of whom a notice has been issued under section 13BA(9)".

NOTES
Defined terms
  disability: s 202(1)
  elector: s 202(1)
  register of electors: see s 9
  vote: s 202(1)

voter: s 202(1)
voting: see "vote" s 202(1)

Voting by persons with disabilities

39(1) If a voter makes an application to the presiding officer to be allowed, on the ground of—

    (a) blindness or other disability, or

    (b) inability to read,

to vote with the assistance of another person by whom he is accompanied (in these rules referred to as "the companion"), the presiding officer shall require the voter to declare, orally or in writing, whether he is so incapacitated by his blindness or other disability, or by his inability to read, as to be unable to vote without assistance.

  (2) If Subject to paragraph (2A) below, if the presiding officer—

    (a) is satisfied that the voter is so incapacitated, and

    (b) is also satisfied by a written declaration made by the companion (in these rules referred to as "the declaration made by the companion of a voter with disabilities") that the companion—

      (i) is a qualified person within the meaning of this rule, and

      (ii) has not previously assisted more than one voter with disabilities to vote at the election,

the presiding officer shall grant the application, and then anything which is by these rules required to be done to or by that voter in connection with the giving of his vote may be done to, or with the assistance of, the companion.

  (2A) Paragraphs (1A) to (1G) of rule 37 shall apply in the case of a voter who applies under paragraph (1) above as they apply in the case of a voter who applies under rule 37(1), but reading references to delivering a ballot paper to a voter as references to granting a voter's application.

  (3) For the purposes of these rules, a person is a voter with disabilities if he has made such a declaration as is mentioned in paragraph (1) above, and a person shall be qualified to assist a voter with disabilities to vote if that person—

    (a) is a person who is entitled to vote as an elector at the election; or

    (b) is the father, mother, brother, sister, spouse, civil partner, son or daughter of the voter and has attained the age of 18 years.

  (4) The name and number in the register of electors of every voter whose vote is given in accordance with this rule and the name and address of the companion shall be entered on a list (in these rules referred to as "the list of voters with disabilities assisted by companions").

In the case of a person voting as proxy for an elector, the number to be entered together with the voter's name shall be the elector's number.

  (4A) In the case of a person in respect of whom a notice has been issued under section 13B(3B) or (3D) of this Act, paragraph (4) above applies as if for "in the register of electors of every voter" there were substituted "relating to every voter in respect of whom a notice has been issued under section 13B(3B) or (3D)".

  (4B) In the case of a person in respect of whom a notice has been issued under section 13BA(9), paragraph (4) applies as if for "in the register of electors of every voter" there were substituted "relating to every voter in respect of whom a notice has been issued under section 13BA(9)".

(5) The declaration made by the companion—
   (a) shall be in the form in the Appendix; and
   (b) shall be made before the presiding officer at the time when the voter applies to vote with the assistance of a companion and shall forthwith be given to the presiding officer who shall attest and retain it.

(6) No fee or other payment shall be charged in respect of the declaration.

NOTES

Defined terms
age: s 202(2)
brother: cf Family Law Reform Act 1987 s 1
civil partner: Interpretation Act 1978 Sch 1
daughter: cf Family Law Reform Act 1987 s 1
disability: s 202(1)
elector: s 202(1)
father: cf Family Law Reform Act 1987 s 1
mother: cf Family Law Reform Act 1987 s 1
register of electors: see s 9

sister: Family Law Reform Act 1987 s 1
son: cf Family Law Reform Act 1987 s 1
spouse: Marriage (Same Sex Couples) Act 2013 Sch 3 para 1
vote: s 202(1)
voter: s 202(1)
voting: see "vote" s 202(1)
writing: Interpretation Act 1978 Sch 1

Tendered ballot papers

40(1) If a person, representing himself to be—
   (a) a particular elector named on the register and not named in the absent voters list, or
   (b) a particular person named in the list of proxies as proxy for an elector and entitled to vote by post as proxy,

applies for a ballot paper after another person has voted in person either as the elector or his proxy, the applicant shall, on satisfactorily answering the questions permitted by law to be asked at the poll, be entitled, subject to the following provisions of this rule, to mark a ballot paper (in these rules referred to as "a tendered ballot paper") in the same manner as any other voter.

(1ZA) Paragraph (1ZC) applies if—
   (a) a person applies for a ballot paper representing himself to be a particular elector named on the register,
   (b) he is also named in the postal voters list, and
   (c) he claims that he did not make an application to vote by post at the election.

(1ZB) Paragraph (1ZC) also applies if—
   (a) a person applies for a ballot paper representing himself to be a particular person named as a proxy in the list of proxies,
   (b) he is also named in the proxy postal voters list, and
   (c) he claims that he did not make an application to vote by post as proxy.

(1ZC) The person shall, on satisfactorily answering the questions permitted by law to be asked at the poll, be entitled, subject to the following provisions of this rule, to mark a ballot paper (in these rules referred to as a "tendered ballot paper") in the same manner as any other voter.

(1ZD) Paragraph (1ZE) applies if before the close of the poll but after the last time at which a person may apply for a replacement postal ballot paper, a person represents himself to be—
   (a) a particular elector named on the register and who is also named in the postal voters list, or
   (b) a particular person named as a proxy in the list of proxies and who is also named in the proxy postal voters list,
   and claims that he has lost or has not received his postal ballot paper.

(1ZE) The person shall, on satisfactorily answering the questions permitted by law to be asked at the poll, be entitled, subject to the following provisions of this rule, to mark a ballot paper (in these rules referred to as a "tendered ballot paper") in the same manner as any other voter.

(1ZF) A person to whom a ballot paper is not delivered under paragraph (3) of rule 35 following his unsatisfactory answer to the question at entry 1(c) in the table in paragraph (1) of that rule shall, if he satisfactorily answers any other questions permitted by law to be asked at the poll, nevertheless be entitled, subject to the following provisions of this rule, to mark a ballot paper (in these rules referred to as "a tendered ballot paper") in the same manner as any other voter.

(1A) Paragraphs (1A) to (1G) of rule 37 shall apply in the case of a person who seeks to mark a tendered ballot paper under paragraph (1) above as they apply in the case of a voter who applies for a ballot paper under rule 37(1).

(1B) Paragraph (1C) below applies where—
   (a) under paragraph (3) of rule 35 a ballot paper is not delivered to a person following his unsatisfactory answer to the question in paragraph (1A) of that rule; or
   (b) a presiding officer refuses to deliver a ballot paper to a person under paragraph (1C) of rule 37 (including that paragraph as applied by rule 38 or 39 or this rule).

(1C) The person shall, on satisfactorily answering the questions permitted by law to be asked at the poll, nevertheless be entitled, subject to the following provisions of this rule, to mark a ballot paper (in these rules referred to as "a tendered ballot paper") in the same manner as any other voter.

(2) A tendered ballot paper shall—
   (a) be of a colour differing from the other ballot papers;
   (b) instead of being put into the ballot box, be given to the presiding officer and endorsed by him with the name of the voter and his number in the register of electors, and set aside in a separate packet.

(3) The name of the voter and his number on the register of electors shall be entered on a list (in these rules referred to as the "tendered votes list") and the voter must sign the list opposite the entry relating to him.

(4) In the case of a person voting as proxy for an elector, the number to be endorsed or entered together with the voter's name shall be the number of that elector.

(4A) This rule applies to an elector who has an anonymous entry subject to the following modifications—
   (a) in paragraphs (2)(b) and (3) the references to the name of the voter must be ignored;
   (b) otherwise, a reference to a person named on a register or list must be construed as a reference to a person whose number appears on the register or list (as the case may be).

(4B) This rule applies in the case of a person in respect of whom a notice has been issued under section 13B(3B) or (3D) as if—
   (a) in paragraphs (1)(a), (1ZA)(a) and (1ZD)(a) for "named on the register" there were substituted "in respect of whom a notice under section 13B(3B) or (3D) of this Act has been issued";
   (b) in paragraph (2)(b) for "his number in the register of electors" there were substituted "the number relating to him on a notice issued under section 13B(3B) or (3D) of this Act";

(c) in paragraph (3) for "his number on the register of electors" there were substituted "the number relating to him on a notice issued under section 13B(3B) or (3D) of this Act".

(4C) This rule applies in the case of a person in respect of whom a notice has been issued under section 13BA(9) as if—

    (a) in paragraphs (1)(a), (1ZA)(a) and (1ZD)(a) for "named on the register" there were substituted "in respect of whom a notice under section 13BA(9) has been issued";

    (b) in paragraph (2)(b) for "his number in the register of electors" there were substituted "the number relating to him on a notice issued under section 13BA(9)";

    (c) in paragraph (3) for "his number on the register of electors" there were substituted "the number relating to him on a notice issued under section 13BA(9)".

(5) A person who marks a tendered ballot paper under paragraph (1C) above shall sign the paper, unless it was marked after an application was refused under rule 38 or 39.

(6) A paper which is required to be signed under paragraph (5) above and is not so signed shall be void.

(7) This rule does not apply in relation to an elector who has an anonymous entry in a register maintained by the Chief Electoral Officer for Northern Ireland.

NOTES

Defined terms
  anonymous entry: ss 9B, 202(1)
  elector: s 202(1)
  list of proxies: s 202(1)
  postal voters list: s 202(1)
  proxy postal voters list: s 202(1)

  register of electors: see s 9
  vote: s 202(1)
  voter: s 202(1)
  voting: see "vote" s 202(1)

Tendered postal ballot papers: anonymous entries in Northern Ireland

40ZA(1) This rule applies to a person ("P") who—

    (a) is an elector with an anonymous entry in a register maintained by the Chief Electoral Officer for Northern Ireland; or

    (b) is entitled to vote by post as proxy for such an elector,

and who claims to have lost, or not received, a postal ballot paper.

(2) P may apply to the Chief Electoral Officer for a replacement postal ballot paper (in these rules referred to as a "tendered postal ballot paper").

(3) The application—

    (a) may be made by post or in person,

    (b) must be accompanied by a specified document within the meaning of rule 37 (as it extends to Northern Ireland), and

    (c) must be delivered to the Chief Electoral Officer—

        (i) where the application is made by post, before 4 pm on the fourth day before the day of the poll, and

        (ii) where the application is made in person, before 4 pm on the day before the day of the poll.

(4) If the Chief Electoral Officer—

    (a) is satisfied as to P's identity, and

    (b) has no reason to doubt that P has lost, or not received, a postal ballot paper,

the Chief Electoral Officer must issue a tendered postal ballot paper to P in the prescribed manner.

(5) A tendered postal ballot paper must be of a different colour from the other ballot papers.

(6) P, if issued with a tendered postal ballot paper, may mark it, sign it, and send it to the Chief Electoral Officer, in the same manner as a postal ballot paper.

(7) A tendered postal ballot paper which has not been signed, or which does not meet the conditions in rule 45(2) and (2A), is void.

(8) On receipt of a tendered postal ballot paper, the Chief Electoral Officer must deal with it in the prescribed manner.

(9) The Chief Electoral Officer must—

    (a) endorse each tendered postal ballot paper with the entry in the register of the elector in question, and

    (b) set it aside in a separate packet of tendered postal ballot papers.

(10) The Chief Electoral Officer must add the entry in the register of the elector in question to a list (in these rules referred to as the "tendered postal votes list").

(11) The Chief Electoral Officer must seal the packet of tendered postal ballot papers.

(12) This rule applies in the case of a person in respect of whom a notice has been issued under section 13BA(9) (alteration of registers in Northern Ireland: pending elections) as if—

    (a) in paragraph (1) for "in a register maintained" there were substituted "in respect of whom a notice under section 13BA(9) has been issued"; and

    (b) in paragraphs (9)(a) and (10), for "entry in the register of the elector in question" there were substituted "entry relating to the elector in question on a notice issued under section 13BA(9)".

NOTES

Defined terms
  anonymous entry: ss 9B, 202(1)
  elector: s 202(1)
  prescribed: s 202(1)

vote: s 202(1)

Refusal to deliver ballot paper

40A(1) This rule applies where a presiding officer refuses to deliver a ballot paper under paragraph (1C) of rule 37 (including that paragraph as applied by rule 38, 39 or 40).

(2) The refusal shall be subject to review on an election petition but, subject to that, shall be final and shall not be questioned in any proceeding whatsoever.

NOTES

Defined terms
  election petition: s 202(1)

Spoilt ballot papers

41 A voter who has inadvertently dealt with his ballot paper in such manner that it cannot be conveniently used as a ballot paper may, on delivering it to the presiding officer and proving to his satisfaction the fact of the inadvertence, obtain another ballot paper in the place of the ballot paper so delivered (in these rules referred to as "a spoilt ballot paper"), and the spoilt ballot paper shall be immediately cancelled.

NOTES

Defined terms
  voter: s 202(1)

Correction of errors on day of poll

41A The presiding officer shall keep a list of persons to whom ballot papers are delivered in consequence of an alteration to the register made by virtue of section 13B(3B) or (3D) of this Act which takes effect on the day of the poll.

Correction of errors on day of poll: Northern Ireland

41B The presiding officer shall keep a list of persons to whom ballot papers are delivered in consequence of an alteration to the register made by virtue of section 13BA(9) which takes effect on the day of the poll.

Adjournment of poll in case of riot

42(1) Where the proceedings at any polling station are interrupted or obstructed by riot or open violence, the presiding officer shall adjourn the proceedings till the following day and shall forthwith give notice to the returning officer.

(2) Where the poll is adjourned at any polling station—
   (a) the hours of polling on the day to which it is adjourned shall be the same as for the original day; and
   (b) references in this Act to the close of the poll shall be construed accordingly.

NOTES
Defined terms
   returning officer: see ss 24–27

Procedure on close of poll

43(1) As soon as practicable after the close of the poll, the presiding officer shall, in the presence of the polling agents, make up into separate packets, sealed with his own seal and the seals of such polling agents as desire to affix their seals—
   (a) each ballot box in use at the station, sealed so as to prevent the introduction of additional ballot papers and unopened, but with the key attached,
   (b) the unused and spoilt ballot papers placed together,
   (c) the tendered ballot papers,
   (d) the marked copies of the register of electors (including any marked copy notices issued under section 13B(3B) or (3D) of this Act) and of the list of proxies,
   (da) the lists prepared under rule 19A, including the parts which were completed in accordance with rule 37(1)(b) and (d) (together referred to in these rules as "the completed corresponding number lists"),
   (e) the certificates as to employment on duty on the day of the poll,
   (f) the tendered votes list, the list of voters with disabilities assisted by companions, the list of votes marked by the presiding officer, a statement of the number of voters whose votes are so marked by the presiding officer under the heads "disability" and "unable to read", the list maintained under rule 41A, and the declarations made by the companions of voters with disabilities,
   and shall deliver the packets or cause them to be delivered to the returning officer to be taken charge of by him; but if the packets are not delivered by the presiding officer personally to the returning officer, the arrangements for their delivery shall require the returning officer's approval.

(2) The marked copies of the register of electors and of the list of proxies shall be in one packet but shall not be in the same packet as the completed corresponding number lists or the certificates as to employment on duty on the day of the poll.

(3) The packets shall be accompanied by a statement (in these rules referred to as "the ballot paper account") made by the presiding officer showing the number of ballot papers entrusted to him, and accounting for them under the heads of ballot papers issued and not otherwise accounted for, unused, spoilt and tendered ballot papers.

(4) This rule applies in relation to Northern Ireland as if—

   (a) the reference in paragraph (1)(d) to the marked copies of the register of electors included any marked copy notices issued under section 13BA(9), and

   (b) paragraph (1)(f) referred to the list maintained under rule 41B

NOTES

Defined terms
   disability: s 202(1)
   list of proxies: s 202(1)
   returning officer: see ss 24–27
   register of electors: see s 9

vote: s 202(1)
voter: s 202(1)

Counting of votes

Attendance at counting of votes

44(1) The returning officer shall make arrangements for counting the votes in the presence of the counting agents as soon as practicable after the close of the poll, and shall give to the counting agents notice in writing of the time and place at which he will begin to count the votes.

(2) No person other than—

   (a) the returning officer and his clerks,
   (b) the candidates and one other person chosen by each of them,
   (c) the election agents,
   (d) the counting agents,
   (e) persons who are entitled to attend by virtue of any of sections 6A to 6D of the Political Parties, Elections and Referendums Act 2000,

   may be present at the counting of the votes, unless permitted by the returning officer to attend.

(3) A person not entitled to attend at the counting of the votes shall not be permitted to do so by the returning officer unless he—

   (a) is satisfied that the efficient counting of the votes will not be impeded; and
   (b) has either consulted the election agents or thought it impracticable to do so.

(4) The returning officer shall give the counting agents all such reasonable facilities for overseeing the proceedings, and all such information with respect to them, as he can give them consistently with the orderly conduct of the proceedings and the discharge of his duties in connection with them.

(5) In particular, where the votes are counted by sorting the ballot papers according to the candidate for whom the vote is given and then counting the number of ballot papers for each candidate, the counting agents shall be entitled to satisfy themselves that the ballot papers are correctly sorted.

(6) In making arrangements under this rule, the returning officer shall have regard to the duty imposed on him by rule 45(3A) below.

NOTES

Defined terms
   election agent: see s 67
   returning officer: see ss 24–27
   vote: s 202(1)

writing: Interpretation Act 1978 Sch 1

The count

45(1) The returning officer shall—

(a) in the presence of the counting agents open each ballot box and count and record the number of ballot papers in it;

(b) in the presence of the election agents verify each ballot paper account; and

(c) count such of the postal ballot papers as have been duly returned and record the number counted.

(1A) The returning officer shall not count the votes given on any ballot papers until—

(a) in the case of postal ballot papers, they have been mixed with the ballot papers from at least one ballot box, and

(b) in the case of ballot papers from a ballot box, they have been mixed with the ballot papers from at least one other ballot box.

(1B) A postal ballot paper shall not, in England, Wales or Scotland, be taken to be duly returned unless—

(a) it is returned in the prescribed manner and reaches the returning officer or a polling station in the constituency before the close of the poll,

(b) the postal voting statement, duly signed, is also returned in the prescribed manner and reaches him or such a polling station before that time,

(c) the postal voting statement also states the date of birth of the elector or proxy (as the case may be), and

(d) in a case where steps for verifying the date of birth and signature of an elector or proxy have been prescribed, the returning officer (having taken such steps) verifies the date of birth and signature of the elector or proxy (as the case may be).

(1C) A postal ballot paper or postal voting statement that reaches the returning officer or a polling station on or after the close of the poll is treated for the purposes of paragraph (1B) as reaching that officer or polling station before the close of the poll if it is delivered by a person who, at the close of the poll, is in the polling station, or in a queue outside the polling station, for the purpose of returning it.

(2) A postal ballot paper shall not, in Northern Ireland, be deemed to be duly returned unless—

(a) it is returned in the proper envelope so as to reach the returning officer before the close of the poll and is accompanied by the declaration of identity duly signed and authenticated, and

(b) in the case of an elector, that declaration of identity states the date of birth of the elector and the returning officer is satisfied that the date stated corresponds with the date supplied as the date of the elector's birth pursuant to section 10(4A)(b), 10A(1A)(b) or 13A(2A)(b) of this Act.

(2A) In the case of an elector, unless section 10(4B), 10A(1B) or 13A(2B) of this Act applies, the declaration of identity referred to in paragraph (2) shall be taken not to be duly signed unless the returning officer is satisfied that the signature on the declaration corresponds with the signature supplied as the elector's signature pursuant to section 10(4A)(a), 10A(1A)(a) or 13A(2A)(a) of this Act.

(3) The returning officer shall not count any tendered ballot paper or any tendered postal ballot paper.

(3A) The returning officer shall take reasonable steps to begin counting the votes given on the ballot papers as soon as practicable within the period of four hours starting with the close of the poll.

(4) The returning officer, while counting and recording the number of ballot papers and counting the votes, shall keep the ballot papers with their faces upwards and take all proper precautions for preventing any person from seeing the numbers or other unique identifying marks printed on the back of the papers.

(5) The returning officer shall verify each ballot paper account by comparing it with the number of ballot papers recorded by him, and the unused and spoilt ballot papers in his possession and the tendered votes list and tendered postal votes list (opening and re-sealing the packets containing the unused and spoilt ballot papers and the tendered votes list and tendered postal votes list) and shall draw up a statement as to the result of the verification, which any election agent may copy.

(6) The returning officer shall so far as practicable proceed continuously with the votes, allowing only time for refreshment, except that he may, in so far as he and the agents agree, exclude the hours between 7 in the evening and 9 on the following morning.

For the purposes of this exception the agreement of a candidate or his election agent shall be as effective as the agreement of his counting agents.

(7) During the time so excluded the returning officer shall—

(a) place the ballot papers and other documents relating to the election under his own seal and the seals of such of the counting agents as desire to affix their seals; and

(b) otherwise take proper precautions for the security of the papers and documents.

(8) The Electoral Commission shall issue guidance to returning officers on the duty imposed by paragraph (3A) above.

NOTES

Defined terms

England: Interpretation Act 1978 Sch 1
election agent: see s 67
elector: s 202(1)
Electoral Commission: see Political Parties, Elections and Referendums Act 2000 s 1

prescribed: s 202(1)
returning officer: see ss 24-27
vote: s 202(1)
Wales: Interpretation Act 1978 Sch 1

Re-count

46(1) A candidate or his election agent may, if present when the counting or any re-count of the votes is completed, require the returning officer to have the votes re-counted or again re-counted but the returning officer may refuse to do so if in his opinion the request is unreasonable.

(2) No step shall be taken on the completion of the counting or any re-count of votes until the candidates and election agents present at its completion have been given a reasonable opportunity to exercise the right conferred by this rule.

NOTES

Defined terms

election agent: see s 67
returning officer: see ss 24-27

vote: s 202(1)

Rejected ballot papers

47(1) Any ballot paper—

(a) which does not bear the official mark, or

(b) on which votes are given for more than one candidate, or

(c) on which anything is written or marked by which the voter can be identified except the printed number and other unique identifying mark on the back, or

(d) which is unmarked or void for uncertainty,

shall, subject to the provisions of the next following paragraph, be void and not counted.

(2) A ballot paper on which the vote is marked—

(a) elsewhere than in the proper place, or

(b) otherwise than by means of a cross, or
(c) by more than one mark,

shall not for such reason be deemed to be void if an intention that the vote shall be for one or other of the candidates clearly appears, and the way the paper is marked does not itself identify the voter and it is not shown that he can be identified by it.

(3) The returning officer shall endorse the word "rejected" on any ballot paper which under this rule is not to be counted, and shall add to the endorsement the words "rejection objected to" if an objection is made by a counting agent to his decision.

(4) The returning officer shall draw up a statement showing the number of ballot papers rejected under the several heads of—
(a) want of official mark;
(b) voting for more than one candidate;
(c) writing or mark by which voter could be identified;
(d) unmarked or void for uncertainty.

NOTES

Defined terms
  returning officer: see ss 24-27
  vote: s 202(1)
  voter: s 202(1)

voting: see "vote" s 202(1)
writing: Interpretation Act 1978 Sch 1

Decisions on ballot papers

48 The decision of the returning officer on any question arising in respect of a ballot paper shall be final, but shall be subject to review on an election petition.

NOTES

Defined terms
  election petition: s 202(1)
  returning officer: see ss 24-27

Equality of votes

49 Where, after the counting of the votes (including any re-count) is completed, an equality of votes is found to exist between any candidates and the addition of a vote would entitle any of those candidates to be declared elected, the returning officer shall forthwith decide between those candidates by lot, and proceed as if the candidate on whom the lot falls had received an additional vote.

NOTES

Defined terms
  returning officer: see ss 24-27
  vote: s 202(1)

PART IV
FINAL PROCEEDINGS IN CONTESTED AND UNCONTESTED ELECTIONS

Declaration of result

50(1) In a contested election, when the result of the poll has been ascertained, the returning officer shall forthwith—
(a) declare to be elected the candidate to whom the majority of votes has been given;
(b) return his name to the Clerk of the Crown; and
(c) give public notice of his name and of the total number of votes given for each candidate together with the number of rejected ballot papers under each head shown in the statement of rejected ballot papers.

(2) In an uncontested election, the statement of persons nominated, in addition to showing the person standing nominated, shall also declare that person elected, and the returning officer shall forthwith return his name to the Clerk of the Crown.

NOTES
Defined terms
Clerk of the Crown: s 202(1)   vote: s 202(1)
returning officer: see ss 24-27

Return to the writ

51(1) The returning officer shall return the name of the member elected by endorsing on the writ a certificate in the form in the Appendix.

(2) Any rule of law or enactment as to the effect of, or manner of dealing with, the return of a member to serve in Parliament applies to the certificate.

(3) The returning officer may, on receiving a receipt, deliver the writ with the certificate endorsed on it to an official designated for that purpose by a universal postal service provider who is providing a universal postal service (within the meaning of Part 3 of the Postal Services Act 2011) for the area in which the election is being held or to his deputy, provided that the official or deputy is at that time within the area concerned.

(4) The designated official or his deputy shall send the writ so endorsed by the first post, free of charge, under cover to the Clerk of the Crown with the words "Election Writ and Return" endorsed on it.

(5) Any reference in the foregoing provisions of this Part of these rules to the Clerk of the Crown shall be taken, in relation to an election for a constituency in Northern Ireland, as a reference to the Clerk of the Crown for Northern Ireland, but any writ returned to the Clerk of the Crown for Northern Ireland shall be transmitted by him to the Clerk of the Crown in England and the return shall be certified to the House of Commons in the same manner as returns for elections for constituencies in Great Britain.

(6) A copy of each writ returned to the Clerk of the Crown for Northern Ireland and of the certificate endorsed on it shall be attested by the Secretary of State, shall be kept in the office of the Clerk of the Crown for Northern Ireland and may be given in evidence if the originals are lost

NOTES
Defined terms
Clerk of the Crown: s 202(1)   returning officer: see ss 24-27
England: Interpretation Act 1978 Sch 1   universal postal service provider: s 202(1)
enactment: Interpretation Act 1978 Sch 1
enactment (NI): s 205

Record of returns at Crown Office

52(1) The Clerk of the Crown shall from the certificate on each writ returned to him enter the name of the member returned in a book to be kept by him at the Crown Office.

(2) The Clerk of the Crown shall also enter in the book any alteration or amendment made by him in the certificate endorsed on any writ.

(3) The book shall be open to public inspection at reasonable times and any person may, on payment of a reasonable fee, take copies from the book.

NOTES
Defined terms
Clerk of the Crown: s 202(1)

Return or forfeiture of candidate's deposit

53(1) The deposit made under rule 9 of these rules shall either be returned to the person making it or his personal representatives or be forfeited to Her Majesty.

(2) Except in the cases mentioned below in this rule, the deposit shall be returned not later than the next day after that on which the result of the election is declared.

(2A) For the purposes of paragraph (2) above—
    (a) a day shall be disregarded if it would be disregarded under rule 2 above in computing any period of time for the purposes of the timetable for an election of the kind in question; and
    (b) the deposit shall be treated as being returned on a day if a cheque for the amount of the deposit is posted on that day.

(3) If the candidate is not shown as standing nominated in the statement of persons nominated, or if the poll is countermanded or abandoned by reason of his death, the deposit shall be returned as soon as practicable after the publication of the statement or after his death, as the case may be.

(4) Subject to paragraph (3) above the deposit shall be forfeited if a poll is taken and, after the counting of the votes by the returning officer (including any re-count) is completed, the candidate is found not to have polled more than one-twentieth of the total number of votes polled by all the candidates.

(5) Notwithstanding anything in paragraphs (2) to (4) above, if at a general election a candidate is shown as standing nominated in more than one constituency in the statements of persons nominated, not more than one of the deposits shall be returned and, if necessary, the Treasury shall direct which it is to be.

NOTES
Defined terms
  returning officer: see ss 24-27
  vote: s 202(1)

Counting of votes: statement by returning officer

53ZA(1) In a contested election, if the counting of the votes given on the ballot papers did not begin within the period specified in rule 45(3A) above, the returning officer shall before the expiry of the period of 30 days starting with the day on which the poll closed—
    (a) prepare and publish a statement giving the information specified in paragraph (2) below, and
    (b) deliver it to the Electoral Commission.

(2) The statement must—
    (a) specify the time at which the counting of the votes given on the ballot papers began,
    (b) describe the steps taken under rule 45(3A) above, and
    (c) explain why the counting of the votes given on the ballot papers did not start within the period specified in rule 45(3A) above.

(3) Where a statement is delivered to the Electoral Commission under paragraph (1)(b) above, the Commission shall specify in any election report they produce that a statement has been delivered to them under that paragraph in respect of the constituency to which the statement relates.

(4) In paragraph (3) above "election report" means a report under section 5(1) or (2A) of the Political Parties, Elections and Referendums Act 2000 in relation to the parliamentary election in question.

NOTES
Defined terms
  Electoral Commission: see Political Parties, Elections   and Referendums Act 2000 s 1
    parliamentary election: Interpretation Act 1978 Sch 1

report (S): s 204(7)
returning officer: see ss 24-27
vote: s 202(1)

Destruction of home address forms

53A   The returning officer shall destroy each candidate's home address form—

    (a)   on the next working day following the 21st day after the officer has returned the name of the member elected; or

    (b)   if an election petition questioning the election or return is presented before that day, on the next working day following the conclusion of proceedings on the petition or on appeal from such proceedings.

NOTES
Defined terms
   election petition: s 202(1)
   returning officer: see ss 24-27

PART V
DISPOSAL OF DOCUMENTS

Sealing up of ballot papers

54(1)   On the completion of the counting at a contested election the returning officer shall seal up in separate packets the counted and rejected ballot papers.

  (2)   The returning officer shall not open the sealed packets of—

    (a)   tendered ballot papers,

    (aa)   tendered postal ballot papers,

    (b)   the completed corresponding number lists,

    (c)   certificates as to employment on duty on the day of the poll, or

    (d)   marked copies of the register of electors (including any marked copy notices issued under section 13B(3B) or (3D) of this Act) and lists of proxies.

  (3)   This rule applies in relation to Northern Ireland as if the reference in paragraph (2)(d) to section 13B(3B) or (3D) were a reference to section 13BA(9).

NOTES
Defined terms   returning officer: see ss 24-27
   list of proxies: s 202(1)
   register of electors: see s 9

Delivery of documents to registration officer

55(1)   The returning officer shall then forward to the relevant registration officer the following documents—

    (a)   the packets of ballot papers in his possession,

    (b)   the ballot paper accounts and the statements of rejected ballot papers and of the result of the verification of the ballot paper accounts,

    (c)   the tendered votes lists, the tendered postal votes lists, the lists of voters with disabilities assisted by companions, the lists of votes marked by the presiding officer and the related statements, the lists maintained under rule 41A, and the declarations made by the companions of voters with disabilities,

    (ca)   the packets of the completed corresponding number lists,

    (d)   the packets of certificates as to employment on duty on the day of the poll,

    (e)   the packets containing marked copies of registers (including any marked copy notices issued under section 13B(3B) or (3D) of this Act) and of the postal voters list, of lists of proxies and of the proxy postal voters list,

    (f)   such other documents relating to elections as are prescribed, endorsing on each packet a description of its contents, the date of the election to which they relate and the name of the constituency for which the election was held.

(1A) In this rule and in rules 56 and 57 references to the relevant registration officer are to—
  (a) the registration officer of the local authority in whose area the constituency is situated, or
  (b) if the constituency comprises any part of the area of more than one local authority, the registration officer of the local authority in whose area the greater or greatest (as the case may be) number of electors is registered.

(1B) Paragraph (1)(e) does not apply to an election for a constituency in Northern Ireland, but the returning officer shall endorse on each packet containing—
  (a) marked copies of the registers,
  (b) the postal voters list,
  (c) the proxy postal voters list, and
  (d) lists of proxies,
a description of its contents, the date of the election to which it relates and the name of the constituency for which the election was held.

(2) *Repealed*

(3) *Repealed*

(4) *Repealed*

(5) This rule applies in relation to Northern Ireland as if—
  (a) paragraph (1)(c) included a reference to the lists maintained under rule 41B, and
  (b) the reference in paragraph (1B)(a) to marked copies of the registers included any marked copy notices issued under section 13BA(9).

NOTES

Defined terms
elector: s 202(1)
list of proxies: s 202(1)
local authority (E&W): s 203(1)
local authority (S): s 204(1)
postal voters list: s 202(1)
prescribed: s 202(1)
proxy postal voters list: s 202(1)
returning officer: see ss 24-27

Orders for production of documents

56(1) An order—
  (a) for the inspection or production of any rejected ballot papers in the custody of the relevant registration officer, or
  (b) for the opening of a sealed packet of the completed corresponding number lists or of certificates as to employment on duty on the day of the poll or the inspection of any counted ballot papers in his custody,
may be made—
  (i) by the House of Commons; or
  (ii) if satisfied by evidence on oath that the order is required for the purpose of instituting or maintaining a prosecution for an offence in relation to ballot papers, or for the purpose of an election petition, by the High Court or the county court.

(2) An order for the opening of a sealed packet of the completed corresponding number lists or of certificates or for the inspection of any counted ballot papers in the relevant registration officer's custody may be made by an election court.

(3) An order under this rule may be made subject to such conditions as to—
  (a) persons,
  (b) time,

(c) place and mode of inspection,

(d) production or opening,

as the House of Commons or court making the order may think expedient; but in making and carrying into effect an order for the opening of a packet of the completed corresponding number lists or of certificates or for the inspection of counted ballot papers, care shall be taken that the way in which the vote of any particular elector has been given shall not be disclosed until it has been proved—

(i) that his vote was given; and

(ii) that the vote has been declared by a competent court to be invalid.

(4) An appeal lies to the High Court from any order of the county court under this rule.

(5) Any power given under this rule—

(a) to the High Court or, except in Northern Ireland, to the county court, may be exercised by any judge of the court otherwise than in open court; and

(b) in Northern Ireland to a county court, may be exercised in such manner as may be provided by rules of court.

(6) Where an order is made for the production by the relevant registration officer of any document in his possession relating to any specified election—

(a) the production by him or his agent of the document ordered in such manner as may be directed by that order shall be conclusive evidence that the document relates to the specified election; and

(b) any endorsement on any packet of ballot papers so produced shall be prima facie evidence that the ballot papers are what they are stated to be by the endorsement.

(7) The production from proper custody of—

(a) a ballot paper purporting to have been used at any election, and

(b) a completed corresponding number list with a number marked in writing beside the number of the ballot paper,

shall be prima facie evidence that the elector whose vote was given by that ballot paper was the person whose entry in the register of electors (or on a notice issued under section 13B(3B) or (3D) of this Act) at the time of the election contained the same number as the number written as mentioned in sub-paragraph (b).

(8) Save as by this rule provided, no person shall be allowed to inspect any rejected or counted ballot papers in the possession of the relevant registration officer or to open any sealed packets of the completed corresponding number lists or of certificates.

NOTES

Defined terms

county court: Interpretation Act 1978 Sch 1
election court: ss 123, 130, 134, 202(1)
election petition: s 202(1)
elector: s 202(1)
High Court (E, W & NI): Interpretation Act 1978 Sch 1
High Court (S): s 204(3)

oath: Interpretation Act 1978 Sch 1
register of electors: see s 9
rules of court: Interpretation Act 1978 Sch 1
vote: s 202(1)
writing: Interpretation Act 1978 Sch 1

Retention and public inspection of documents

57(1) The relevant registration officer shall retain for a year all documents relating to an election forwarded to him in pursuance of these rules by a returning officer, and then, unless otherwise directed by order of the House of Commons, the High Court, the Crown Court or a magistrates' court, shall cause them to be destroyed.

(1A) The Chief Electoral Officer for Northern Ireland shall retain for a year the documents mentioned in rule 55(1B), and then, unless otherwise directed by order of the House of Commons or the High Court, shall cause them to be destroyed.

(2) The documents mentioned in paragraphs (1) and (1A) except—

    (a)   ballot papers,

    (b)   the completed corresponding number lists,

    (c)   certificates as to employment on duty on the day of the poll,

shall be open to public inspection.

(3)   The relevant registration officer or the Chief Electoral Officer for Northern Ireland (as the case may be) must, on request, supply to any person copies of or extracts from such description of the documents open to public inspection as is prescribed by regulations.

(4)   Each of the following must, on request, be supplied with a copy of the marked copies of the register, the postal voters list, the list of proxies and the proxy postal voters list—

    (a)   a registered party within the meaning of Part 2 of the Political Parties, Elections and Referendums Act 2000;

    (b)   a person who was a candidate at the election in relation to the constituency for which he was a candidate.

(5)   Regulations may impose conditions in relation to—

    (a)   the inspection of any document in pursuance of paragraph (2);

    (b)   the supply of any document or part of a document in pursuance of paragraph (3);

    (c)   the supply of any document or part of a document in pursuance of paragraph (4).

(6)   Regulations may also make provision—

    (a)   as to the form in which any such document or part is supplied;

    (b)   for the payment of a fee in respect of the supply of a document or part.

(7)   Conditions which may be imposed for the purposes of paragraph (5)(a) or (b) include conditions as to—

    (a)   whether a person may take any copy of a document he is permitted to inspect;

    (b)   the manner in which any such copy is to be taken;

    (c)   the purposes for which information contained in any document or part of a document which is inspected or supplied in pursuance of paragraph (2) or (3) may be used.

(8)   Conditions which may be imposed for the purposes of paragraph (5)(b) or (c) include conditions as to the extent to which a person to whom a document or part of a document has been supplied may—

    (a)   supply that document or part to any other person;

    (b)   disclose to any other person any information contained in the document or part;

    (c)   use any such information for a purpose other than that for which the document or part was supplied to him.

(9)   Regulations may also impose conditions corresponding to those mentioned in paragraph (8) in respect of persons who have obtained a document or part of a document mentioned in paragraph (4)—

    (a)   which was supplied to another person in pursuance of paragraph (4), or

    (b)   otherwise than in accordance with regulations under this section.

NOTES

Defined terms

Crown Court: Interpretation Act 1978 Sch 1
High Court (E, W & NI): Interpretation Act 1978 Sch 1
High Court (S): s 204(3)
list of proxies: s 202(1)
Magistrates' court: Interpretation Act 1978 Sch 1

postal voters list: s 202(1)
prescribed: s 202(1)
proxy postal voters list: s 202(1)
returning officer: see ss 24-27

Disposal of documents in Scotland

58(1) This rule modifies rules 55 to 57 in relation to elections in Scotland.

(2) In relation to such elections—

    (a) the documents mentioned in rule 55(1)—

        (i) are not to be forwarded by the returning officer as required by that rule,

        (ii) instead, are to remain in the returning officer's custody (and be endorsed by the officer as required by that rule);

    (b) the references in rules 56 and 57 to the relevant registration officer are to be read as references to the returning officer (and rule 55(1A) is to be disregarded);

    (c) the reference in rule 57(1) to the documents to be retained is to be read as a reference to the documents remaining in the returning officer's custody under sub-paragraph (a)(ii).

NOTES

Defined terms

returning officer: see ss 24–27

PART VI
DEATH OF CANDIDATE

Disposal of documents in Northern Ireland

59 In the application of rules 55 to 57 to elections for a constituency in Northern Ireland, the references to the relevant registration officer shall be taken to be references to the Clerk of the Crown for Northern Ireland.

NOTES

Defined terms

Clerk of the Crown: s 202(1)

Independent candidate

60(1) This rule applies if at a contested election proof is given to the returning officer's satisfaction before the result of the election is declared that one of the persons named or to be named in the ballot papers as an independent candidate has died.

(2) Subject to this rule and rules 61 and 62, these rules apply to the election as if the candidate had not died.

(3) The following provisions of these rules do not apply in relation to the deceased candidate—

    (a) rule 32(1)(c) and (d) (admission to polling station);

    (b) rule 44(2)(b) to (d) (attendance at count);

    (c) rule 53(4) (forfeiture of deposit).

(4) If only two persons are shown as standing nominated in the statement of persons nominated the returning officer must—

    (a) if polling has not begun, countermand the notice of poll;

    (b) if polling has begun, direct that the poll is abandoned;

    (c) subject to rule 65, treat the election as an uncontested election.

(5) For the purposes of this rule a person is named or to be named on the ballot papers as an independent candidate if the description (if any) on his nomination paper is not authorised as mentioned in rule 6A(1) or (1B).

NOTES

Defined terms

returning officer: see ss 24–27

Deceased independent candidate wins

61(1)   This rule applies if at an election mentioned in rule 60(1) the majority of votes is given to the deceased candidate.

(2)   Rule 50(1) (declaration of result) does not apply but the returning officer must—

    (a)   declare that the majority of votes has been given to the deceased candidate,

    (b)   declare that no member is returned, and

    (c)   give public notice of the total number of votes given for each candidate together with the number of rejected ballot papers under each head shown in the statement of rejected ballot papers.

(3)   Rule 53 (return or forfeiture of candidate's deposit) does not apply in relation to the remaining candidates.

(4)   The returning officer must not return the writ and the proceedings with reference to the election must be commenced afresh subject to the following provisions of this rule.

(5)   The writ for the election must be taken to have been received on the first working day after the end of the period of seven days starting on the day of the election mentioned in rule 60(1).

(6)   No fresh nomination is necessary in the case of a person shown in the statement of persons nominated as standing nominated, and no other nomination may be made.

(7)   The last day on which a notice of withdrawal of candidature by a person who stands nominated by virtue of paragraph (6) may be delivered is the seventh working day after the day on which the writ is taken to be received.

(8)   Rule 9 (deposit) does not apply.

(9)   The poll must be held on a day in the period which starts 21 working days after the day on which the writ is taken to have been received and ends 27 working days after that day.

(10)   For the purposes of this rule a working day is a day which is not a day specified in rule 2(1)(a) to (c).

NOTES
Defined terms
  returning officer: see ss 24
  vote: s 202(1)

Deceased independent candidate with equality of votes

62   In an election mentioned in rule 60(1), if—

    (a)   rule 49 applies (equality of votes), and

    (b)   any of the candidates to whom that rule applies is a deceased candidate,

  the deceased candidate must be ignored.

NOTES
Defined terms
  vote: s 202(1)

Party candidate

63(1)   This rule applies if—

    (a)   at a contested election proof is given to the returning officer's satisfaction before the result of the election is declared that one of the persons named or to be named as a candidate in the ballot paper has died, and

    (b)   that person is standing in the name of a registered political party.

(2)   The returning officer must—

    (a)   countermand notice of the poll, or

(b) if polling has begun, direct that the poll be abandoned.

(3) The proceedings with reference to the election must be commenced afresh subject to the following provisions of this rule.

(4) The writ for the election must be taken to have been received on the first working day after the end of the period of seven days starting on the day the proof is given to the returning officer.

(5) No fresh nomination is necessary in the case of a person shown in the statement of persons nominated as standing nominated.

(6) No other nomination may be made except for a person standing in the name of the same registered political party in whose name the deceased candidate was standing.

(7) The last day on which a nomination mentioned in paragraph (6) may be delivered is the seventh working day after the day on which the writ is taken to be received.

(8) The last day on which a notice of withdrawal of candidature by a person who stands nominated by virtue of paragraph (5) or in pursuance of paragraph (6) may be delivered is the seventh working day after the day on which the writ is taken to be received.

(9) The poll must be held on a day in the period which starts 21 working days after the day on which the writ is taken to have been received and ends 27 working days after that day.

(10) For the purposes of this rule—
  (a) a person stands in the name of a registered political party if his nomination paper contains a description which is authorised as mentioned in rule 6A(1) or (1B);
  (b) a registered political party is a party which is registered under Part 2 of the Political Parties, Elections and Referendums Act 2000;
  (c) a working day is a day which is not a day specified in rule 2(1)(a) to (c)

NOTES
Defined terms
  registered political party: s 202(1)
  returning officer: see ss 24-27

Speaker of the House of Commons seeking re-election

64(1) This rule applies if at a contested election—
  (a) one of the candidates is the Speaker of the House of Commons seeking re-election, and
  (b) proof is given to the returning officer's satisfaction before the result of the election is declared that that candidate has died.

(2) The returning officer must—
  (a) countermand notice of the poll, or
  (b) if polling has begun, direct that the poll be abandoned.

(3) The proceedings with reference to the election must be commenced afresh subject to the following provisions of this rule.

(4) The writ for the election must be taken to have been received on the first working day after the end of the period of seven days starting on the day the proof is given to the returning officer.

(5) The last day on which—
  (a) nominations, or
  (b) notice of withdrawal of candidature,

may be delivered is the seventh working day after the day on which the writ is taken to be received.

(6) The poll must be held on a day in the period which starts 21 working days after the day on which the writ is taken to have been received and ends 27 working days after that day.

(7) For the purposes of this rule a working day is a day which is not a day specified in rule 2(1)(a) to (c).

NOTES
Defined terms
returning officer: see ss 24-27

Abandoned poll

65(1) This rule applies to—
    (a) a poll which is abandoned in pursuance of rule 60(4)(b) as if it were a poll at a contested election;
    (b) a poll which is abandoned in pursuance of rule 63(2)(b) or 64(2)(b).

(2) The presiding officer at a polling station must take the like steps (so far as not already taken) for the delivery to the returning officer of ballot boxes and of ballot papers and other documents as he is required to take on the close of the poll.

(3) The returning officer must dispose of ballot papers and other documents in his possession as is he required to do on the completion of the counting of the votes.

(4) It is not necessary for a ballot paper account to be prepared or verified.

(5) No step or further step is to be taken for the counting of the ballot papers or of the votes.

(6) The returning officer must seal up all the ballot papers (whether the votes on them have been counted or not) and it is not necessary to seal up counted and rejected ballot papers in separate packets.

(7) The provisions of these rules as to the inspection, production, retention and destruction of ballot papers and other documents relating to a poll at an election apply subject to paragraphs (8) and (9).

(8) Ballot papers on which the votes were neither counted nor rejected must be treated as counted ballot papers.

(9) No order is to be made for—
    (a) the production or inspection of any ballot papers, or
    (b) the opening of a sealed packet of the completed corresponding number lists or of certificates as to employment on the day of the poll,
unless the order is made by a court with reference to a prosecution.

NOTES
Defined terms
returning officer: see ss 24-27
vote: s 202(1)

APPENDIX OF FORMS

Note— The forms contained in this Appendix may be adapted so far as circumstances require.

Form of writ

[The name of the sovereign may be altered when necessary] Elizabeth the Second by the Grace of God of the United Kingdom of Great Britain and Northern Ireland and of Our other Realms and Territories Queen Head of the Commonwealth Defender of the Faith to the Returning Officer for the .... Constituency Greeting

[This preamble to be omitted except in a case of a general election] Whereas by section 3(1) of the Fixed-term Parliaments Act 2011 Parliament has dissolved We Command you that due notice being first given you do cause election to be made according to law of a Member to serve in Parliament for the said ...... Constituency [Except in a general election insert here *in the place of AB, deceased* or otherwise, stating the cause of vacancy]

And that you do cause the name of such Member when so elected, whether he be present or absent, to be certified to Us in Our Chancery without delay

Witness Ourself at Westminster the .. .. day of .. .. .. in the .. .. year of Our Reign, and in the year of Our Lord 20.....

Label or direction of writ

To the Returning Officer for the .. .. .. Constituency.

A writ of a new election of a Member for the said Constituency.

Endorsement

Received the within Writ on the .. .. .. day of .. .. .., 19 ...

(Signed)

Returning Officer (*or as the case may be.*)

Certificate endorsed on writ

I hereby certify, that the Member elected for the .. .. ..Constituency in pursuance of the within written Writ is .. .. of .. .. in the County of .. .. ..

(Signed)

Returning Officer (*or as the case may be.*)

Note: in relation to any constituency in Wales, "county" in this form refers to a preserved county (as defined by section 64 of the Local Government (Wales) Act 1994).

Form of nomination paper

ELECTION OF A MEMBER to serve in Parliament for the .... Constituency.

We, the undersigned, being electors for the said Constituency, do hereby nominate the under-mentioned person as a candidate at the said election.

Candidate's surname	Other names in full	Commonly used surname (if any)	Commonly used forenames (if any)	Description (if any)
SULLIVAN	Arthur Seymour	GILBERT	WS	Independent

Signatures	Electoral Number (See Note 3)

	Distinctive letter	Number
Proposer	.. ..	.. ..
Seconder	.. ..	.. ..

We, the undersigned, being electors for the said Constituency, do hereby assent to the foregoing nomination.

	Distinctive letter	Number
1.	.. ..	.. ..
2.	.. ..	.. ..
3.	.. ..	.. ..
4.	.. ..	.. ..
5.	.. ..	.. ..
6.	.. ..	.. ..
7.	.. ..	.. ..
8.	.. ..	.. ..

NOTE

1   The attention of candidates and electors is drawn to the rules for filling up nomination papers and other provisions relating to nomination contained in the parliamentary elections rules in Schedule 1 to the Representation of the People Act 1983.

2   Where a candidate is commonly known by some title he may be described by his title as if it were his surname.

2A   Where a candidate commonly uses a name which is different from any other name he has, the commonly used name may also appear on the nomination paper, but if it does so, the commonly used name (instead of any other name) will appear on the ballot paper.

2B   But the ballot paper will show the other name if the returning officer thinks—
   (a)   that the use of the commonly used name may be likely to mislead or confuse electors, or
   (b)   that the commonly used name is obscene or offensive.

3   *Repealed*

4   An elector may not subscribe more than one nomination paper for the same election.

5   A person whose name is entered in the register may not subscribe a nomination paper if the entry gives as the date on which he will become of voting age a date later than the day fixed for the poll.

Form of Ballot Paper
Form of Front of Ballot Paper

1	**BROWN** (JOHN EDWARD Brown, of 52, George Street, Bristol, merchant.)		Counterfoil No. *The counterfoil is to have a number to correspond with that on the back of the Ballot Paper.*

2	**BROWN** (THOMAS WILLIAM Brown, of 136, London Road, Swindon, salesman.)	
3	**JONES** (William David Jones, of High Elms, Wilts., gentleman.)	
4	**MERTON** (Hon. George Travis, commonly called Viscount Merton, of Swansworth, Berks.)	
5	**SMITH** (Mary Smith, of 72 High Street, Bath, married woman)	

Form of back of ballot paper

Election for the .. .. Constituency

on .. .. 19.. ..

Note.— The number on the ballot paper is to correspond with that on the counterfoil.

Directions as to printing the ballot paper

1　Nothing is to be printed on the ballot paper except in accordance with these directions.

2　So far as is practicable, the arrangements set out in paragraphs 3 to 13 must be observed in the printing of the ballot paper.

3　No word may be printed on the face except:
  (a) the heading "Election of the Member of Parliament for the .... constituency";
  (b) within that heading, the name of the constituency;
  (c) the direction "Vote for only one candidate by putting a cross X in the box next to your choice";
  (d) the particulars of the candidates; and
  (e) words forming part of the emblems mentioned at paragraph 10 below.

4　A box must be printed around:
  (a) the heading and name referred to in paragraph 3(a) and (b); and
  (b) the direction referred to in paragraph 3(c);
  and the direction referred to in paragraph 3(c) must be separated from the heading and name referred to in paragraph 3(a) and (b) by a horizontal rule extending across the box.

5　No rule may be printed on the face except:
  (a) as part of the box referred to in paragraph 4;
  (b) the horizontal rule referred to in that paragraph;
  (c) a horizontal rule above the particulars of the first candidate;
  (d) horizontal rules separating the particulars of the candidates from one another;

(e) a horizontal rule below the particulars of the last candidate;

(f) as part of the boxes on the right-hand side of the ballot paper where the vote is to be marked.

6 The horizontal rules referred to in paragraph 5(c), (d) and (e) must be equally spaced and the space between each of them must be a minimum of 2.5 centimetres.

7 The boxes referred to in paragraph 5(f) must not touch any horizontal rule and each one must be equidistant between the horizontal rule above it and the horizontal rule below it.

8 Each of the horizontal rules referred to in paragraph 5(c) and (d) must extend from a point level with the text on the left-hand side of the page to a point directly above the centre of the box below that rule.

9 The horizontal rule referred to in paragraph 5(e) must:

(a) extend from a point level with the text on the left-hand side of the page to a point directly below the right-hand edge of the box above that rule; and

(b) be thicker than the other horizontal rules.

10 here a registered emblem is to be printed against a candidate's particulars:

(a) it must be printed adjacent to and to the right of the candidate's particulars; and

(b) its size as printed must not exceed 2 centimetres square.

11 All the words on the front of the ballot paper must appear in the same large type except that:

(a) the heading and name referred to in paragraph 3(a) and (b) must appear in very large and bold type;

(b) in the direction referred to in paragraph 3(c), the words "only one candidate" must appear in very large and bold type;

(c) the remainder of that direction must appear in very large type;

(d) the names of the candidates and the descriptions, if any, must appear in bold type.

12 The surname of each candidate must appear in capitals and the candidates' other names must be in lower case with initial capitals.

13 The number and other unique identifying mark must be printed close to each other on the back of the ballot paper.

Form of directions for the guidance of the voters in voting
Guidance for Voters

1 When you are given a ballot paper go to one of the compartments. Mark a cross (X) in the box on the right hand side of the ballot paper opposite the name of the candidate you are voting for.

2 Vote for one candidate only. Put no other mark on the ballot paper, or your vote may not be counted. Do not let anyone see your vote.

3 Fold the ballot paper in two. Show the back of the ballot paper to the presiding officer so as to disclose the number and other unique identifying mark. Put the ballot paper in the ballot box and leave the polling station.

4 If by mistake you spoil a ballot paper, show it to the presiding officer and ask for another one.

Form of declaration to be made by the companion of a voter with disabilities
I, *AB*, of .. .. , having been requested to assist *CD*, (*in the case of a voter with disabilities voting as proxy add* voting as proxy for *MN*) whose number on the register is .. .. to record his vote at the election now being held in this constituency, hereby declare that (I am entitled to vote as an elector at the said election) (I am the .. .. (State the relationship of the companion

to the voter) .. .. of the said voter and have attained the age of 18 years), and that I have not previously assisted any voter with disabilities (except *EF*, of .. .. ..) to vote at the said election. (Signed) *AB*,

    day of .. .. .. 19.. .

I, the undersigned, being the presiding officer for the .. .. polling station for the .. ..Constituency, hereby certify that the above declaration, having been first read to the above-named declarant, was signed by the declarant in my presence.

    (Signed) *G. H.*,

day of   19.

minutes past   o'clock [am][pm]

NOTE—

1 If the person making the above declaration knowingly and wilfully makes therein a statement false in a material particular, he will be guilty of an offence.
2 A voter with disabilities is a voter who has made a declaration under the parliamentary elections rules that he is so incapacitated by his blindness or other disability, or by his inability to read, as to be unable to vote without assistance.

SCHEDULE 2

PROVISIONS WHICH MAY BE CONTAINED IN REGULATIONS AS TO REGISTRATION ETC

1(1)   Provisions prescribing the arrangements to be made for the carrying out of his registration duties by a registration officer for part of a constituency, where the constituency is not coterminous with or wholly situated in a district, Welsh county or county borough or London borough.

(2)   Provisions authorising or requiring a registration officer to require persons to give information required for the purpose of his registration duties or to make declarations of any prescribed description as to matters relevant to their entitlement to be registered.

(2A)   Provision made under sub-paragraph (2) authorising or requiring a registration officer in Great Britain to—

    (a)   require a person who has made an application under section 10ZC or 10ZD to provide evidence that he or she is the person named in the application, or

    (b)   require a person who has made an application under section 10ZC or 10ZD, or any person who has an entry in a register, to provide evidence for the purpose of enabling the officer to determine whether a person is entitled to be registered in a register maintained by the officer,

  must specify the kind of evidence that a person may be required to provide (for examples, see paragraph 3ZA(5)).

(2B)   Provision of the kind mentioned in sub-paragraph (2A) may authorise or require the registration officer to require a person to provide the evidence to a registration officer or to some other prescribed person (or person of a prescribed description).

(3)   Provisions authorising a registration officer, where—

    (a)   he has by virtue of regulations under sub-paragraph (2) required any person registered in one of his registers to give him information, or to make any declaration, for the purpose of enabling him to determine whether the person is entitled to be so registered or to determine whether the person is the person who made the application under section 10ZC or 10ZD, and

    (b) the person has not within the prescribed period complied with that requirement in a manner which the officer considers satisfactory (or at all),
to remove the person's entry from the register.

(4) Provisions authorising a registration officer to inspect, for the purpose of his registration duties, records kept (in whatever form) by—

    (a) any local or public authority of any prescribed description, or

    (b) any person providing services to, or authorised to exercise any function of, any such authority,

and to make copies of information contained in such records.

(4A) Provision authorising or requiring any such authority or person, for the purpose mentioned in sub-paragraph (4B), to provide the Chief Electoral Officer for Northern Ireland, at such times or in such circumstances as may be prescribed, with information contained in such records.

(4B) The purpose is assisting the Chief Electoral Officer to meet the relevant registration objectives, and, in particular, assisting him—

    (a) to ascertain to what extent the relevant registration objectives are being met;

    (b) to determine what steps should be taken for meeting those objectives.

(5) Provisions made under sub-paragraph (4) or (4A) above shall have effect despite any statutory or other restriction on the disclosure of information.

(6) But provision made under sub-paragraph (4A) may not permit information obtained under those provisions to be disclosed to a third party except—

    (a) for the purpose mentioned in sub-paragraph (4B);

    (b) for the purposes of any criminal or civil proceedings.

(7) In sub-paragraph (4B) "the relevant registration objectives" has the meaning given by section 10ZB.

(8) In sub-paragraph (6) "third party" means a person other than a person to whom the Chief Electoral Officer for Northern Ireland may delegate his functions.

1A(1) Provision authorising or requiring a person to disclose information to another person for the purpose of assisting a registration officer in Great Britain—

    (a) to verify information relating to a person who is registered in a register maintained by the officer or who is named in an application for registration in, or alteration of, a register,

    (b) to ascertain the names and addresses of people who are not registered but who are entitled to be registered, or

    (c) to identify those people who are registered but who are not entitled to be registered.

(2) Provision made under sub-paragraph (1) may authorise or require the person to whom the information is disclosed—

    (a) to compare it with other information;

    (b) to disclose the results of the comparison to a registration officer for the purpose mentioned in that sub-paragraph.

(3) The provision that may be made under sub-paragraph (1) or (2) includes provision—

    (a) conferring other functions on a person;

    (b) authorising the Secretary of State to make grants to a person on whom functions are conferred;

    (c) authorising a person to disclose or otherwise process information only in accordance with an agreement;

    (d) authorising or requiring a person to disclose or otherwise process information only in accordance with requirements imposed by the Secretary of State;

    (e)   regulating the manner in which information is disclosed;

    (f)   requiring the retention or disposal, or otherwise regulating the processing, of information disclosed.

(4)   Provision made under this paragraph has effect despite any statutory or other restriction on the disclosure of information.

(5)   In this paragraph "processing" has the same meaning as in the Data Protection Act 1998.

1B(1) Provision as to the information that a registration officer may or must require persons to give by virtue of regulations under paragraph 1(2), or must provide to persons, when conducting a canvass in Great Britain (whether as part of a canvass form or otherwise).

(2)   Provision authorising or requiring a registration officer in Great Britain to complete canvass forms in part for people.

(3)   Provision as to the form and contents of declarations to be made by those responding to a canvass in Great Britain.

2   Provisions imposing on registration officers the duty of requiring persons to give information required for the purpose of the officer's duty under section 3(1) of the Juries Act 1974.

2A   Provisions requiring registration officers to remind persons registered in pursuance of declarations or applications of any prescribed description of the need to make fresh declarations or applications in order for them to remain registered.

2B   Provisions requiring registration officers to remind persons with anonymous entries in registers of the need to make a fresh application and declaration in order for them to remain so registered.

3   Provisions laying down a timetable for the preparation of the register and other matters, and providing that notices and other documents received by the registration officer out of time may be or shall be disregarded either altogether or for the purposes of a particular register or election.

3ZA(1) Provision about applications under section 10ZC or 10ZD, including in particular provision about—

    (a)   the form and contents of applications and of any declarations to be made in connection with them;

    (b)   the manner in which applications are to be made.

(2)   Provision made under sub-paragraph (1) may include provision—

    (a)   conferring functions on registration officers, or local or public authorities, to enable applications to be made in a particular manner;

    (b)   conferring other functions on registration officers;

    (c)   conferring functions on the Electoral Commission.

(3)   Provision requiring a person making an application under section 10ZC or 10ZD—

    (a)   to provide evidence that he or she is the person named in the application;

    (b)   to provide evidence of entitlement to be registered.

(4) Provision made under sub-paragraph (3) must specify the kind of evidence that a person is required to provide.

(5) Examples of the evidence that may be specified include a person's date of birth or national insurance number.

(6) Provision made under sub-paragraph (3) may require a person to provide the evidence to a registration officer or to some other prescribed person (or person of a prescribed description).

3A Provisions as to the form and contents of applications for registration in Northern Ireland, including provisions as to any declarations to be made in connection with them.

3B Provisions as to the form and content of applications for an anonymous entry and declarations to be made in connection with such applications.

3C(1) Provision authorising or requiring a registration officer conducting a canvass in Great Britain to take specified steps for the purpose of obtaining information where no response is received in respect of a particular address.

(2) Provision authorising or requiring a registration officer in Great Britain to take specified steps to encourage a person to make an application under section 10ZC or 10ZD in response to an invitation to do so made by the officer.

(3) Examples of the steps that a registration officer may be authorised or required to take under sub-paragraph (1) or (2) include writing to the person or visiting the person's address to speak to the person.

4(1) Provisions as to the manner in which service declarations, and applications and notices from service voters, are to be transmitted to the registration officer.

(2) Provisions as to the manner in which overseas electors' declarations, and applications from persons making such declarations, are to be transmitted to the registration officer.

5(1) Provisions as to the evidence which shall or may be required, or be deemed sufficient or conclusive evidence, of a person's service declaration having ceased to be in force.

(1A) Provisions as to the evidence which shall or may be required, or be deemed sufficient or conclusive evidence, of a person satisfying any of the requirements for qualifying as an overseas elector in respect of any constituency.

(1B) Provisions as to the evidence which shall or may be deemed sufficient or conclusive evidence that a person's safety would be at risk as mentioned in section 9B(10) of this Act.

(2) Provisions as to the evidence of age or nationality which may be required by the Chief Electoral Officer for Northern Ireland in connection with a person's registration otherwise than as a service voter or with his appointment as a proxy.

(3) Provisions requiring any fee payable in connection with the making for the purpose of the regulations of any statutory declaration to be paid by the registration officer.

(4)

5A(1)   Provision requiring applications under paragraph 3 or 4 of Schedule 4 to the Representation of the People Act 2000 or section 6 or 7 of the Representation of the People Act 1985 to be attested and limiting the number of such applications that a person may attest.

(2)   Provision requiring a person applying under paragraph 4 of Schedule 4 to the Representation of the People Act 2000 or section 7 of the Representation of the People Act 1985 to do so in person, producing a document of a prescribed description.

(3)   Provision as to the evidence which shall or may be required, or be deemed sufficient or conclusive evidence, in connection with a person's application to vote by proxy or to vote by post as elector or as proxy.

(4)   Provision authorising or requiring registration officers—
    (a)   to make inquiries of persons included in the record kept under paragraph 3(4) of Schedule 4 to the Representation of the People Act 2000 or section 6(3) of the Representation of the People Act 1985 for the purpose of determining whether there has been a material change of circumstances, and
    (b)   to treat failure to respond to such inquiries as sufficient evidence of such a change.

5B(1)   Provision as to the steps that a registration officer in Great Britain must take, before appointing a person as proxy to vote for another, to ensure that the appointment complies with paragraph 6(3) or (3A) of Schedule 4 to the Representation of the People Act 2000.

(2)   Provision under sub-paragraph (1) may require another registration officer (including the Chief Electoral Officer for Northern Ireland) to provide information about whether the person has or will have an entry in a register maintained by that officer.

6   Provisions as to the cases in which an application or objection may be determined by the registration officer without a hearing, and as to a person's right in any such cases to make written representations to him.

7   Provisions authorising a registration officer to require any person's evidence at a hearing before him to be given on oath and to administer oaths for the purpose.

8   Provisions requiring the registration officer to prepare a special list of those persons entitled to be registered whose addresses are not required to be shown in the register or of any class of such persons, showing the addresses of the person concerned.

8A   Provisions requiring the registration officer to prepare a record of those persons with anonymous entries in the register showing, in relation to each such person, such information as is prescribed.

8B(1)   Provision authorising or requiring a registration officer in determining an application under section 10ZC or 10ZD, in prescribed cases, to treat a prescribed person's statement of a fact as sufficient evidence of that fact.

(2)   In sub-paragraph (1) "prescribed" includes of a prescribed description.

8C(1) Provision requiring the retention or disposal, or otherwise regulating the processing, of—

    (a) information provided in an application under section 10ZC or 10ZD;

    (b) information provided to a person in accordance with a requirement imposed by a registration officer in Great Britain under provision made by virtue of paragraph 1(2);

    (c) information provided to a person by virtue of provision made under paragraph 3ZA.

  (2) In this paragraph "processing" has the same meaning as in the Data Protection Act 1998.

   9 *Repealed*

10(1) Provisions requiring a registration officer to prepare, in addition to the version of the register which he is required to prepare by virtue of the other provisions of this Act ("the full register"), a version of the register which omits the names and addresses of registered electors by or on behalf of whom requests have been made to have their names and addresses excluded from that version of it ("the edited register").

(1A) The edited version shall also omit anonymous entries.

  (2) Provisions specifying a form of words to be used by a registration officer for the purpose of—

    (a) explaining to persons registered or applying to be registered, or persons acting on behalf of such persons, the purposes for which the full register and the edited register may each be used, and

    (b) ascertaining whether the exclusion of their names and addresses from the edited register is requested by or on behalf of such persons.

 10A Provisions requiring copies of the full register and other documents, or prescribed parts of them, to be available for inspection by the public at such places as may be prescribed.

10B(1) Provisions authorising or requiring a registration officer—

    (a) to supply to such persons as may be prescribed copies of the full register and other documents, or prescribed parts of them, whether free of charge or on payment of a prescribed fee;

    (b) to supply to any persons copies of the edited register, or any prescribed part of it, on payment of a prescribed fee.

  (2) Provisions specifying, in relation to any description of persons prescribed by regulations made in pursuance of sub-paragraph (1)(a) above, the purposes for which copies supplied to such persons under such regulations, or information contained in them, may be used whether by such persons or by employees or other persons authorised by them in accordance with regulations to have access to such copies or information contained in them.

  (3) Without prejudice to the generality of sub-paragraph (1) above or paragraph 11A below, regulations made in pursuance of sub-paragraph (1) may contain any such provisions as are authorised by paragraph 11A.

11(1) Provisions imposing prohibitions or restrictions relating to the extent (if any) to which—

    (a) persons inspecting the full register in accordance with regulations made in pursuance of paragraph 10A above may make copies of the register;

    (b) persons to whom copies of the full register are supplied (whether in accordance with regulations made in pursuance of paragraph 10B above or in accordance with any other provision made by or under an Act) may—

        (i) supply those copies, or otherwise disclose any information contained in them, to other persons, or

        (ii) make use of any such information otherwise than for any purposes specified in such regulations or (as the case may be) for which the copies have been supplied in accordance with any such provision.

(2) Provisions imposing, in relation to persons—

    (a) to whom copies of the full register have been supplied, or information contained in such copies has been disclosed, in accordance with regulations made in pursuance of this paragraph, or

    (b) who otherwise have access to such copies or information,

prohibitions or restrictions corresponding to those which may be imposed by virtue of sub-paragraph (1) above.

(3) Provisions imposing, in relation to persons involved in the preparation of the full register, prohibitions with respect to supplying copies of the full register and disclosing information contained in it.

(4) In this paragraph any reference to the full register includes a reference to any part of it.

11A (1) Provisions authorising or requiring registration officers who are data users to supply data, or documents containing information extracted from data and in such form as may be prescribed, to such persons as may be prescribed on payment of a prescribed fee.

(1A) Sub-paragraph (1) is subject to paragraph 1(6).

(2) In this paragraph "data controller" and "data" have the same meanings as in section 1 of the Data Protection Act 1998.

12 Provisions as to the arrangements to be made in relation to the issue and receipt of, and for subsequently dealing with, ballot papers for postal voting, including provisions—

    (a) authorising replacement ballot papers to be issued in any prescribed circumstances;

    (aa) authorising the cancellation or removal of ballot papers in any prescribed circumstances;

    (b) as to the proceedings in connection with the issue and receipt of ballot papers and, in particular—

        (i) the persons who are to be entitled, or may be allowed, to attend, and

        (ii) the rights and obligations of persons attending;

    (c) as to the steps to be taken to ensure the secrecy of the voting and the safe custody (before and after the count) of the ballot papers returned and other documents.

12A Regulations under section 53 making provision as mentioned in paragraph 12 in relation to a local government election in Scotland may also make provision authorising the cancellation or removal of ballot papers at such an election in any prescribed circumstances.

13(1) Provisions making it an offence (punishable on summary conviction by a fine not exceeding level 3 on the standard scale) for a person—

    (a) to have failed to comply with, or given false information in pursuance of, any such requisition of the registration officer as is mentioned in paragraph 1 or paragraph 2 above.

    (b) to have, without lawful authority, destroyed, mutilated, defaced or removed any notice published by the registration officer in connection with his registration duties, or any copies of a document which have been made available for inspection in pursuance of those duties.

(1ZA) Provisions making it an offence (punishable on summary conviction by a fine not exceeding level 5 on the standard scale) for a person to disclose information in contravention of paragraph 1(6).

(1ZB) Provision making it an offence, in prescribed circumstances, for a person to process information in breach of provision made under paragraph 1A(3)(e) or (f) or 8C.

(1ZC) Provision made under sub-paragraph (1ZB) creating an offence may not—

    (a) provide for the offence to be punishable on conviction on indictment by imprisonment for a term exceeding two years;

    (b) provide for the offence to be punishable on summary conviction by imprisonment for a term exceeding the relevant maximum;

    (c) provide for the offence to be punishable on summary conviction by a fine exceeding the statutory maximum or level 5 on the standard scale (as appropriate).

(1ZD) In sub-paragraph (1ZC)(b) "the relevant maximum"—

    (a) in relation to an offence triable either on indictment or summarily, means—

        (i) in England and Wales or Scotland, 12 months, and

        (ii) in Northern Ireland, 6 months;

    (b) in relation to an offence triable only summarily, means—

        (i) in England and Wales, 51 weeks, and

        (ii) in Scotland or Northern Ireland, 6 months.

(1A) Provisions making it an offence (punishable on summary conviction by a fine not exceeding level 5 on the standard scale)—

    (a) for a person to contravene any regulations made in pursuance of paragraph 11 above or to do so in any prescribed circumstances, or

    (b) where such a contravention has occurred on the part of a person in the employment, or otherwise under the direction or control, of a company or other organisation, for—

        (i) a director of the company, or

        (ii) a person concerned with the management of the organisation,

to have failed to take such steps as it was reasonable for him to take to secure the operation of procedures designed to prevent, so far as reasonably practicable, the occurrence of such contraventions on the part of such persons.

(2) Any other provisions incidental or supplemental to those mentioned in the foregoing paragraphs of this Schedule.

NOTES

Defined terms

anonymous entry: ss 9B, 202(1)

election: s 202(1)

elector: s 202(1)

Electoral Commission: see Political Parties, Elections and Referendums Act 2000 s 1

England: Interpretation Act 1978 Sch 1

local government election (S): s 204(1)

prescribed: s 202(1)
service voter: s 202(1)
standard scale: Interpretation Act 1978 Sch 1
statutory declaration: Interpretation Act 1978 Sch 1
statutory maximum: Interpretation Act 1978 Sch 1
summary conviction (NI only): Interpretation Act 1978 Sch 1

vote: s 202(1)
voting: see "vote" s 202(1)
Wales: Interpretation Act 1978 Sch 1
writing: Interpretation Act 1978 Sch 1

SCHEDULE 2A
CONTROL OF DONATIONS TO CANDIDATES

PART I
INTRODUCTORY

Operation and interpretation of Schedule

1(1)   This Schedule has effect for controlling donations to candidates at an election.

(2)   The following provisions have effect for the purposes of this Schedule.

(3)   "Relevant donation", in relation to a candidate at an election, means a donation to the candidate or his election agent for the purpose of meeting election expenses incurred by or on behalf of the candidate.

(4)   In sub-paragraph (3) above the reference to a donation for the purpose of meeting election expenses incurred by or on behalf of a candidate includes a reference to a donation for the purpose of securing that any such expenses are not so incurred; and a donation shall be taken to be a donation for either of those purposes if, having regard to all the circumstances, it must be reasonably assumed to be such a donation.

(5)   "Donation" shall be construed in accordance with paragraphs 2 to 4 below.

(6)   "The 2000 Act" means the Political Parties, Elections and Referendums Act 2000.

(6A)   In relation to a donation received by a candidate at an election in Great Britain, references to a permissible donor falling within section 54(2) of the 2000 Act are to be read as if section 54(2) did not include a party registered in the Northern Ireland register maintained by the Commission under Part 2 of that Act.

(7)   *Repealed*

(8)   "The Commission" means the Electoral Commission established by section 1 of that Act.

(9)   Any reference to a donation received by a candidate when he is (or is deemed to be) his own election agent includes a reference to a donation received by a candidate on a list of candidates to be London members of the London Assembly at an ordinary election who is, or is deemed to be, the election agent of all the candidates on the list.

(10)   Any donation which is received by a candidate as mentioned in sub-paragraph (9) above shall be regarded as received by him in his capacity as election agent.

NOTES
Defined terms
   election: s 202(1)

Donations: general rules

2(1)   "Donation", in relation to a candidate at an election, means (subject to paragraph 4 below)—
   (a)   any gift to the candidate or his election agent of money or other property;

(b) any sponsorship provided in relation to the candidate (as defined by paragraph 3 below);

(c) any money spent (otherwise than by the candidate, his election agent or any sub-agent) in paying any election expenses incurred by or on behalf of the candidate;

(d) any money lent to the candidate or his election agent otherwise than on commercial terms;

(e) the provision otherwise than on commercial terms of any property, services or facilities for the use or benefit of the candidate (including the services of any person).

(2) Where—

(a) any money or other property is transferred to a candidate or his election agent pursuant to any transaction or arrangement involving the provision by or on behalf of the candidate of any property, services or facilities or other consideration of monetary value, and

(b) the total value in monetary terms of the consideration so provided by or on behalf of the candidate is less than the value of the money or (as the case may be) the market value of the property transferred,

the transfer of the money or property shall (subject to sub-paragraph (4) below) constitute a gift to the candidate or (as the case may be) his election agent for the purposes of sub-paragraph (1)(a) above.

(3) In determining—

(a) for the purposes of sub-paragraph (1)(d) above, whether any money lent to a candidate or his election agent is so lent otherwise than on commercial terms, or

(b) for the purposes of sub-paragraph (1)(e) above, whether any property, services or facilities provided for the use or benefit of a candidate is or are so provided otherwise than on such terms,

regard shall be had to the total value in monetary terms of the consideration provided by or on behalf of the candidate in respect of the loan or the provision of the property, services or facilities.

(4) Where (apart from this sub-paragraph) anything would be a donation both by virtue of sub-paragraph (1)(b) above and by virtue of any other provision of this paragraph, sub-paragraph (1)(b) (together with paragraph 3 below) shall apply in relation to it to the exclusion of the other provision of this paragraph.

(5) The reference in sub-paragraph (1)(c) above to money spent as mentioned in that provision is a reference to money so spent by a person, other than the candidate, his election agent or any sub-agent, out of his own resources (with no right to reimbursement out of the resources of any such other person); and where, by virtue of sub-paragraph (1)(c) above, money so spent constitutes a donation to the candidate, the candidate shall be treated as receiving an equivalent amount on the date on which the money is paid to the creditor in respect of the expenses in question.

(6) In this paragraph—

(a) any reference to anything being given or transferred to a candidate or his election agent includes a reference to its being given or transferred either directly or indirectly through any third person;

(b) "gift" includes a bequest or any other form of testamentary disposition.

NOTES

Defined terms
election: s 202(1)
election agent: see s 67

sub-agent: ss 68(1), 202(1)

Sponsorship

3(1)   For the purposes of this Schedule sponsorship is provided in relation to a candidate if—

    (a)   any money or other property is transferred to the candidate or to any person for the benefit of the candidate, and

    (b)   the purpose (or one of the purposes) of the transfer is (or must, having regard to all the circumstances, reasonably be assumed to be)—

        (i)   to help the candidate with meeting, or to meet, to any extent any defined expenses incurred or to be incurred by or on behalf of the candidate, or

        (ii)   to secure that to any extent any such expenses are not so incurred.

(2)   In sub-paragraph (1) above "defined expenses" means expenses in connection with—

    (a)   any conference, meeting or other event organised by or on behalf of the candidate,

    (b)   the preparation, production or dissemination of any publication by or on behalf of the candidate, or

    (c)   any study or research organised by or on behalf of the candidate.

(3)   The following do not, however, constitute sponsorship by virtue of sub-paragraph (1) above—

    (a)   the making of any payment in respect of—

        (i)   any charge for admission to any conference, meeting or other event, or

        (ii)   the purchase price of, or any other charge for access to, any publication;

    (b)   the making of any payment in respect of the inclusion of an advertisement in any publication where the payment is made at the commercial rate payable for the inclusion of such an advertisement in any such publication.

(4)   The Secretary of State may by order made on the recommendation of the Commission amend sub-paragraph (2) or (3) above.

(5)   Any order under sub-paragraph (4) above shall be made by statutory instrument; but no such order shall be made unless a draft of the order has been laid before and approved by a resolution of each House of Parliament.

(6)   In this paragraph "publication" means a publication made available in whatever form and by whatever means (whether or not to the public at large or any section of the public).

Payments etc not to be regarded as donations

4(1)   None of the following shall be regarded as a donation—

    (a)   the provision of any facilities provided in pursuance of any right conferred on a candidate at an election by this Act;

    (b)   the provision by an individual of his own services which he provides voluntarily in his own time and free of charge;

    (c)   any interest accruing to a candidate or his election agent in respect of any donation which is dealt with by the candidate or (as the case may be) his election agent in accordance with section 56(2)(a) or (b) of the 2000 Act (as applied by paragraph 7 below).

(2)   There shall also be disregarded any donation whose value (determined in accordance with paragraph 5 below) is not more than £50.

NOTES

Defined terms
   election: s 202(1)
   election agent: see s 67

Value of donations

5(1) The value of any donation falling within paragraph 2(1)(a) above (other than money) shall be taken to be the market value of the property in question.

(2) Where, however, paragraph 2(1)(a) above applies by virtue of paragraph 2(2) above, the value of the donation shall be taken to be the difference between—
   (a) the value of the money, or the market value of the property, in question, and
   (b) the total value in monetary terms of the consideration provided by or on behalf of the candidate or his election agent.

(3) The value of any donation falling within paragraph 2(1)(b) above shall be taken to be the value of the money, or (as the case may be) the market value of the property, transferred as mentioned in paragraph 3(1) above; and accordingly any value in monetary terms of any benefit conferred on the person providing the sponsorship in question shall be disregarded.

(4) The value of any donation falling within paragraph 2(1)(d) or (e) above shall be taken to be the amount representing the difference between—
   (a) the total value in monetary terms of the consideration that would have had to be provided by or on behalf of the candidate or his election agent in respect of the loan or the provision of the property, services or facilities if—
     (i) the loan had been made, or
     (ii) the property, services or facilities had been provided,
   on commercial terms, and
   (b) the total value in monetary terms of the consideration (if any) actually so provided by or on behalf of the candidate or his election agent.

(5) Where a donation such as is mentioned in sub-paragraph (4) above confers an enduring benefit on the donee over a particular period, the value of the donation—
   (a) shall be determined at the time when it is made, but
   (b) shall be so determined by reference to the total benefit accruing to the donee over that period.

(6) In this paragraph "market value" in relation to any property, means the price which might reasonably be expected to be paid for the property on a sale in the open market.

NOTES
Defined terms
  election agent: see s 67
  person: s 202(1)

PART II
CONTROLS ON DONATIONS

Prohibition on accepting donations from impermissible donors

6(1) A relevant donation received by a candidate or his election agent must not be accepted if—
   (a) the person by whom the donation would be made is not, at the time of its receipt by the candidate or (as the case may be) his election agent, a permissible donor falling within section 54(2) of the 2000 Act; or
   (b) the candidate or (as the case may be) his election agent is (whether because the donation is given anonymously or by reason of any deception or concealment or otherwise) unable to ascertain the identity of the person offering the donation.

(2) For the purposes of this Schedule any relevant donation received by a candidate or his election agent which is an exempt trust donation shall be regarded as a relevant donation received by the candidate or his election agent from a permissible donor; and

section 162 of the 2000 Act (interpretation: exempt trust donations) shall apply for the purposes of this Schedule as it applies for the purposes of that Act.

(3) But, for the purposes of this Schedule, any relevant donation received by a candidate or his election agent from a trustee of any property (in his capacity as such) which is not—

  (a) an exempt trust donation, or

  (b) a relevant donation transmitted by the trustee to the candidate or his election agent on behalf of beneficiaries under the trust who are—

    (i) persons who at the time of its receipt by the candidate or his election agent are permissible donors falling within section 54(2) of the 2000 Act, or

    (ii) the members of an unincorporated association which at that time is such a permissible donor,

shall be regarded as a relevant donation received by the candidate or his election agent from a person who is not such a permissible donor.

(4) Where any person ("the principal donor") causes an amount ("the principal donation") to be received by a candidate or his election agent by way of a relevant donation—

  (a) on behalf of himself and one or more other persons, or

  (b) on behalf of two or more other persons,

then for the purposes of this Part each individual contribution by a person falling within paragraph (a) or (b) of more than £50 shall be treated as if it were a separate donation received from that person.

(5) In relation to each such separate donation, the principal donor must ensure that, at the time when the principal donation is received by the candidate or his election agent, the candidate or (as the case may be) his election agent is given—

  (a) (except in the case of a donation which the principal donor is treated as making) all such details in respect of the person treated as making the donation as are required by virtue of paragraph 11(c) below; and

  (b) (in any case) all such details in respect of the donation as are required by virtue of paragraph 11(a) below.

(6) Where—

  (a) any person ("the agent") causes an amount to be received by a candidate or his election agent by way of a donation on behalf of another person ("the donor"), and

  (b) the amount of the donation is more than £50,

the agent must ensure that, at the time when the donation is received by the candidate or his election agent, the candidate or (as the case may be) his election agent is given all such details in respect of the donor as are required by virtue of paragraph 11(c) below.

(7) A person commits an offence if, without reasonable excuse, he fails to comply with sub-paragraph (5) or (6) above.

(8) A person guilty of an offence under sub-paragraph (7) shall be liable—

  (a) on summary conviction, to a fine not exceeding the statutory maximum or to a term of imprisonment not exceeding months (or both);

  (b) on conviction on indictment, to a fine or to a term of imprisonment not exceeding one year (or both).

NOTES

Defined terms
election agent: see s 67
person: s 202(1)
statutory maximum: Interpretation Act 1978 Sch

summary conviction (NI only): Interpretation Act 1978 Sch 1

Acceptance or return of donations

7(1)   Sections 56 to 60 of the 2000 Act shall apply for the purposes of this Schedule in relation to—

    (a)   a relevant donation received by a candidate or his election agent, and

    (b)   the candidate or (as the case may be) the election agent,

as they apply in relation to a donation received by a registered party and the registered party.

(2)   In the application of sections 56 to 60 of that Act in accordance with sub-paragraph (1)—

    (a)   section 56(1) shall have effect as if the reference to the particulars relating to a donor which would be required to be included in a donation report by virtue of paragraph 2 of Schedule 6 (if the donation were a recordable donation within the meaning of that Schedule) were construed as a reference to the particulars which are required to be included in a return by virtue of paragraph 11(c) below;

    (b)   section 56(3) shall have effect as if the reference to the party were omitted and the reference to the treasurer of the party were construed as a reference to the candidate or (as the case may be) his election agent; and

    (c)   section 56(4) shall have effect as if the reference to the treasurer of the party were construed as a reference to the candidate or (as the case may be) his election agent.

NOTES

Defined terms

    election agent: see s 67

Transfer of donations received by candidate to election agent

8(1)   Sub-paragraph (2) below applies in relation to any relevant donation received by a candidate after the deadline for appointing an election agent (unless the candidate is, or is deemed to be, his own election agent at the time of receipt of the donation).

(2)   The candidate shall, on receipt of any such donation as is mentioned in sub-paragraph (1) above, forthwith deliver to his election agent—

    (a)   the donation,

    (b)   where paragraph 6(5) or (6) above applies in relation to the donation, the information provided to the candidate in pursuance of that provision, and

    (c)   any other information which the candidate has about the donation and its donor which might reasonably be expected to assist the election agent in the discharge of any duties imposed on him, in relation to the donation, under this Part or Part III of this Schedule.

(3)   Where a donation is delivered to an election agent in accordance with sub-paragraph (2) above, the donation shall be treated for the purposes of paragraph 6(1) to (4) above and the provisions applied by paragraph 7 above as if it had been—

    (a)   originally received by the election agent, and

    (b)   so received by him on the date on which it was received by the candidate.

(4)   Where a candidate receives a relevant donation before the deadline for appointing an election agent but at a time when an appointment of a person (other than the candidate himself) as election agent is in force he shall either—

    (a)   forthwith deliver the donation and the information mentioned in sub-paragraph (2)(b) and (c) above to the agent, or

    (b)   (if he fails to do so) deal with the donation in accordance with section 56 of the 2000 Act.

(5)   Sub-paragraph (3) above shall have effect in relation to any relevant donation delivered to an election agent in accordance with sub-paragraph (4)(a) above as it has

effect in relation to a donation delivered to him in accordance with sub-paragraph (2) above.

(6) Sub-paragraph (7) below applies where—

    (a) a relevant donation received by a candidate before the deadline for appointing an election agent has been dealt with by the candidate in accordance with section 56 of the 2000 Act either because—

        (i) it was received by him at a time when no appointment of another person as his election agent was in force, or

        (ii) although such an appointment was in force, he was by virtue of sub-paragraph (4)(b) required to deal with the donation; and

    (b) an appointment of a person (other than the candidate himself) as election agent is in force at, or at any time after—

        (i) the deadline for appointing an election agent, or

        (ii) if later, the time when the candidate has dealt with the donation in accordance with section 56 of the 2000 Act.

(7) Subject to sub-paragraph (9) below, the candidate shall, as soon as reasonably practicable after the relevant time, deliver to the election agent—

    (a) the donation (if it has been accepted by him), and

    (b) any information which he has about the donation and the donor which might reasonably be expected to assist the election agent in the discharge of any duties imposed on him, in relation to the donation, under Part III of this Schedule.

(8) The relevant time for the purposes of sub-paragraph (7) above is—

    (a) the time mentioned in sub-paragraph (6)(b)(i) or (ii) (as the case may be) if the appointment of another person as election agent is in force at that time, or

    (b) otherwise, the time when any such appointment subsequently comes into force.

(9) The duty imposed on a candidate by sub-paragraph (7)(a) above does not apply to any relevant donation to the extent to which it has been lawfully used by the candidate for the purpose of paying election expenses.

(10) In this paragraph—

    (a) any reference to the deadline for appointing an election agent is a reference to the latest time by which an election agent may in accordance with section 67(1) or (1A) of this Act be named as election agent—

        (i) by the candidate, or

        (ii) in the case of a candidate on a list of candidates submitted by a registered political party to be London members of the London Assembly at an ordinary election, by the party; and

    (b) any reference to any provision of section 56 of the 2000 Act is a reference to that provision as applied by paragraph 7 above.

NOTES

Defined terms   registered political party: s 202(1)
   election: s 202(1)
   election agent: see s 67
   person: s 202(1)

Evasion of restrictions on donations

  9 Section 61 of the 2000 Act shall apply for the purposes of this Schedule as if—

    (a) any reference to donations were to relevant donations;

    (b) any reference to a registered party were, in relation to a relevant donation, a reference to a candidate or (as the case may be) his election agent; and

(c) any reference in subsection (2) to the treasurer of a registered party were, in relation to a relevant donation, a reference to either the candidate or his election agent (or both).

NOTES
Defined terms
election agent: see s 67

PART III
REPORTING OF DONATIONS

Statement of relevant donations

10(1) The candidate's election agent must include in any return required to be delivered under section 81 of this Act a statement of relevant donations which complies with paragraphs 11 and 12 below.

(2) If the statement states that the candidate's election agent has seen evidence of such description as is prescribed by the Secretary of State in regulations that an individual donor has an anonymous entry in an electoral register, the statement must be accompanied by a copy of the evidence.

(3) Sub-paragraph (2) does not apply to local government elections in Scotland.

NOTES
Defined terms   prescribed: s 202(1)
anonymous entry: ss 9B, 202(1)
election agent: see s 67
local government election (S): s 204(1)

Donations from permissible donors

11 The statement must record, in relation to each relevant donation accepted by the candidate or his election agent—
(a) the amount of the donation (if a donation of money, in cash or otherwise) or (in any other case) the nature of the donation and its value as determined in accordance with paragraph 5 above;
(b) the date when the donation was accepted by the candidate or his election agent;
(c) the information about the donor which is, in connection with recordable donations to registered parties, required to be recorded in donation reports by virtue of paragraph 2 of Schedule 6 to the 2000 Act; and
(d) such other information as may be required by regulations made by the Commission.

NOTES
Defined terms
election agent: see s 67

Donations from impermissible donors

12(1) This paragraph applies to relevant donations falling within paragraph 6(1)(a) or (b) above.

(2) Where paragraph 6(1)(a) above applies, the statement must record—
(a) the name and address of the donor;
(b) the amount of the donation (if a donation of money, in cash or otherwise) or (in any other case) the nature of the donation and its value as determined in accordance with paragraph 5 above;

   (c) the date when the donation was received, and the date when, and the manner in which, it was dealt with in accordance with section 56(2)(a) of the 2000 Act; and

   (d) such other information as is required by regulations made by the Commission.

(3) Where paragraph 6(1)(b) above applies, the statement must record—

   (a) details of the manner in which the donation was made;

   (b) the amount of the donation (if a donation of money, in cash or otherwise) or (in any other case) the nature of the donation and its value as determined in accordance with paragraph 5 above;

   (c) the date when the donation was received, and the date when, and the manner in which, it was dealt with in accordance with section 56(2)(b) of the 2000 Act; and

   (d) such other information as is required by regulations made by the Commission.

(4) In this paragraph any reference to any provision of section 56 of the 2000 Act is a reference to that provision as applied by paragraph 7 above.

SCHEDULE 3
RETURN AND DECLARATIONS AS TO ELECTION EXPENSES

FORM OF RETURN

Repealed

FORM OF DECLARATIONS

Election in the .. .. constituency (*for a local government election substitute* county of county borough of .. .. , district of .. .. local government area of .. .. , *or as the case may be*).

Date of publication of notice of election .. ..

Name of candidate .. ..

I solemnly and sincerely declare as follows:—

1   I am the person named above as a candidate at this election (and was my own election agent) *or* was at this election the election agent of the person named above as a candidate.

2   I have examined the return of election expenses (about to be) delivered by my election agent (by me) to the returning officer, (*at a local government election, substitute* appropriate officer) of which a copy is now shown to me and marked .. .. .. , and to the best of my knowledge and belief it is a complete and correct return as required by law.

3   To the best of my knowledge and belief, all expenses shown in the return as paid were paid by my election agent (by me), except as otherwise stated.

4   *Repealed*

SCHEDULE 4
ELECTION EXPENSES AT CERTAIN LOCAL ELECTIONS IN ENGLAND AND WALES

1(1) Any claim against any person in respect of any election expenses incurred by or on behalf of a candidate which is not sent in within 14 days after the day of election shall be barred and not paid, and all election expenses incurred as mentioned above shall be paid within 21 days after the day of election and not otherwise.

(2) If any person makes a payment in contravention of this paragraph he shall be guilty of an illegal practice, but a candidate shall not be liable, nor shall his election be avoided, for any illegal practice committed under this sub-paragraph without his consent or connivance.

2 Every agent of a candidate at the election shall, within 23 days after the day of election, make a true return to the candidate in writing of all election expenses incurred by the agent and if he fails so to do he shall be liable on summary conviction to a fine not exceeding level 3 on the standard scale.

3 Within 28 days after the day of election every candidate shall deliver to the proper officer of the authority for which the election is held a return of all election expenses incurred by the candidate or his agents vouched (except in the case of sums under £10) by bills stating the particulars or by receipts and accompanied by a declaration by the candidate as to election expenses.

4(1) After the expiry of the time for making the return and declaration, the candidate, if elected, shall not, until he has made the return and declaration or until the date of the allowance of any authorised excuse under paragraph 7 below, sit or vote in the council and if he does so—
    (a) he shall forfeit £50 for every day on which he so sits or votes; or
    (b) instead of civil proceedings for a penalty, proceedings may be instituted in a magistrates' court, and he shall be liable on conviction to a fine of an amount not exceeding the amount of the penalty which would be recoverable in civil proceedings.

(2) Civil proceedings for a penalty under this paragraph shall be commenced within the period of one year beginning with the day in respect of which the penalty is alleged to have been incurred.

(3) For the purposes of sub-paragraph (2) above the issue of legal process shall be deemed to be a commencement of a proceeding, where the service or execution of the same on or against the alleged offender is prevented by the absconding or concealment or act of the alleged offender, but save as mentioned above the service or execution of the same on or against the alleged offender, and not its issue, shall be deemed to be the commencement of the proceeding.

5 If the candidate fails to make that return and declaration he shall be guilty of an illegal practice, and, if he knowingly makes that declaration falsely, he shall be guilty of a corrupt practice.

6 The High Court, an election court or the county court may, on application either of the candidate or a creditor, allow any claim to be sent in and any expense to be paid after the time limited by this Schedule, and a return of any sum so paid shall forthwith after payment be sent to the proper officer of the authority.

7(1) If the candidate applies to the High Court, an election court or the county court and shows that the failure to make that return and declaration or either of them or any error or false statement in them has arisen by reason of—
    (a) his illness or absence, or
    (b) the absence, death, illness or misconduct of any agent, clerk or officer, or
    (c) inadvertence or any reasonable cause of a like nature,
and not by reason of any want of good faith on the applicant's part, the court may—
        (i) after such notice of the application as it considers fit, and
        (ii) on production of such evidence of the grounds stated in the application, and of the applicant's good faith, and otherwise, as it considers fit,

make such order allowing the authorised excuse for the failure, error or false statement as it considers just.

(2) The order may make the allowance conditional upon compliance with such terms as to the court seem best calculated for carrying into effect the objects of this Schedule, and the order shall relieve the applicant from any liability or consequence under this Act in respect of the matters excused by the order.

(3) The date of the order, or, if conditions and terms are to be complied with, the date on which the applicant fully complies with them, is referred to in this Act as the date of the allowance of the excuse.

8(1) The return and declaration shall be kept at the office of the proper officer of the authority and shall at all reasonable times during the twelve months next after they are received by him be open to inspection by any person on payment of the prescribed fee and the proper officer shall, on demand, provide copies of them, or of any part of them, at the prescribed price.

(2) After the expiry of twelve months the proper officer of the authority may cause the return and declaration to be destroyed or, if the candidate so requires, shall return them to him.

9 For the purposes of this Schedule—

(a) the jurisdiction vested by paragraph 7 in the county court may be exercised otherwise than in open court; and

(b) an appeal lies to the High Court from any order of the county court made by virtue of that paragraph.

NOTES

Defined terms

county court: Interpretation Act 1978 Sch 1
date of the allowance of the excuse: ss 86(8), 118
election court: ss 123, 130, 134, 202(1)
High Court (E, W & NI): Interpretation Act 1978 Sch 1
High Court (S): s 204(3)
legal process: s 202(1)
Magistrates' court: Interpretation Act 1978 Sch 1

person: s 202(1)
prescribed: s 202(1)
summary conviction (NI only): Interpretation Act 1978 Sch 1
standard scale: Interpretation Act 1978 Sch 1
writing: Interpretation Act 1978 Sch 1

SCHEDULE 4A
ELECTION EXPENSES

PART 1
LIST OF MATTERS

1 Advertising of any nature (whatever the medium used).
Expenses in respect of such advertising include agency fees, design costs and other costs in connection with preparing, producing, distributing or otherwise disseminating such advertising or anything incorporating such advertising and intended to be distributed for the purpose of disseminating it.

2 Unsolicited material addressed to electors (whether addressed to them by name or intended for delivery to households within any particular area).

Expenses in respect of such material include design costs and other costs in connection with preparing, producing or distributing such material (including the cost of postage).

3 Transport (by any means) of persons to any place.

Expenses in respect of the transport of such persons include the costs of hiring a means of transport for a particular period.

4   Public meetings (of any kind).

Expenses in respect of such meetings include costs incurred in connection with the attendance of persons at such meetings, the hire of premises for the purposes of such meetings or the provision of goods, services or facilities at them.

5   The services of an election agent or any other person whose services are engaged in connection with the candidate's election.

6   Accommodation and administrative costs.

NOTES
Defined terms   person: s 202(1)
   election: s 202(1)
   election agent: see s 67
   elector: s 202(1)

PART 2
GENERAL EXCLUSIONS

7   The payment of any deposit required by rule 9 of Schedule 1 to this Act.

7A(1) The provision of property, goods, services or facilities where the expenses are incurred for the purpose of removing, or mitigating the effect of, barriers to seeking elected office associated with the candidate's disability.

(2)   But an expense is within sub-paragraph (1) only to the extent that it is defrayed or reimbursed by, and was incurred in accordance with the terms of, a grant awarded by the relevant body out of the Access to Elected Office for Disabled People Fund.

(3)   In this paragraph—

   (a) "the Access to Elected Office for Disabled People Fund" means the fund known by that name comprising money provided by the Secretary of State for the purpose of defraying and reimbursing expenses within sub-paragraph (1);

   (b) "the relevant body" means such body as is making funding decisions and administering payments out of that money pursuant to an agreement with the Secretary of State;

   (c) "disability" has the same meaning as in the Equality Act 2010 (see section 6 of that Act).

(4)   This paragraph ceases to have effect at the end of 30th June 2014; but that does not affect the continued operation of this paragraph in relation to expenses incurred and either defrayed or reimbursed, before that time.

8   The publication of any matter, other than an advertisement, relating to the election in—

   (a) a newspaper or periodical;

   (b) a broadcast made by the British Broadcasting Corporation or by Sianel Pedwar Cymru;

   (c) a programme included in any service licensed under Part 1 or 3 of the Broadcasting Act 1990 or Part 1 or 2 of the Broadcasting Act 1996.

9   The provision of any facilities provided in pursuance of any right conferred on candidates at an election by this Act other than facilities in respect of which expenses fall to be defrayed by virtue of sections 95(4) and 96(4) above.

10   The provision by an individual of his own services which he provides voluntarily in his own time and free of charge.

11(1)   Accommodation which is the candidate's sole or main residence.

(2)   The provision by any other individual of accommodation which is his sole or main residence if the provision is made free of charge.

12(1)   Transport by a means of transport which was acquired by the candidate principally for his own personal use.

(2)   Transport provided free of charge by any other individual if the means of transport was acquired by him principally for his own personal use.

13(1)   Computing or printing equipment which was acquired by the candidate principally for his own personal use.

(2)   The provision by any other individual of computing or printing equipment which was acquired by the individual principally for his own personal use if the provision is made free of charge.

NOTES
Defined terms
   election: s 202(1)

PART 3
SUPPLEMENTAL

Guidance by Commission

14(1)   The Electoral Commission ("the Commission") may prepare, and from time to time revise, a code of practice giving—
   (a)   guidance as to the matters which do, or do not, fall within Part 1 or Part 2 of this Schedule;
   (b)   guidance (supplementing the definition in section 90ZA(3) above) as to the cases or circumstances in which expenses are, or are not, to be regarded as incurred for the purposes of a candidate's election.

(2)   Once the Commission have prepared a draft code under this paragraph, they must submit it to the Secretary of State for his approval.

(3)   The Secretary of State may approve a draft code either without modification or with such modifications as he may determine.

(4)   Once the Secretary of State has approved a draft code he shall lay a copy of the draft, whether—
   (a)   in its original form, or
   (b)   in a form which incorporates any modifications determined under sub-paragraph (3),
   before each House of Parliament.

(5)   If the draft incorporates any such modifications, the Secretary of State must at the same time lay before each House a statement of his reasons for making them.

(6)   If, within the 40-day period, either House resolves not to approve the draft, the Secretary of State must take no further steps in relation to the draft code.

(7)   If no such resolution is made within the 40-day period—
   (a)   the Secretary of State must issue the code in the form of the draft laid before Parliament, and
   (b)   the code is to come into force on such date as the Secretary of State may by order appoint,
   and the Commission must arrange for it to be published in such manner as they think appropriate.

(8) Sub-paragraph (6) does not prevent a new draft code from being laid before Parliament.

(9) In this paragraph, "the 40-day period", in relation to a draft code, means—

(a) if the draft is laid before one House on a day later than the day on which it is laid before the other House, the period of 40 days beginning with the later of the two days, and

(b) in any other case, the period of 40 days beginning with the day on which the draft is laid before each House,

no account being taken of any period during which Parliament is dissolved or prorogued or during which both Houses are adjourned for more than four days.

(10) In this paragraph references to a draft code include a revised draft code.

Power to amend Parts 1 and 2

15(1) The Secretary of State may by order made by statutory instrument make such amendments of Part 1 or 2 of this Schedule as he considers appropriate.

(2) An order under sub-paragraph (1) shall not be made unless a draft of the statutory instrument containing the order has been laid before, and approved by a resolution of, each House of Parliament.

(3) The Secretary of State may make such an order either—

(a) where the order gives effect to a recommendation of the Electoral Commission; or

(b) after consultation with the Electoral Commission.

NOTES

Defined terms
  election: s 202(1)
  disability: s 202(1)
  Electoral Commission: see Political Parties, Elections and Referendums Act 2000 s 1

SCHEDULE 4B
SCOTTISH LOCAL GOVERNMENT ELECTIONS: ELECTION EXPENSES

PART 1
LIST OF MATTERS

1 Advertising of any nature (whatever the medium used).

Expenses in respect of such advertising include agency fees, design costs and other costs in connection with preparing, producing, distributing or otherwise disseminating such advertising or anything incorporating such advertising and intended to be distributed for the purpose of disseminating it.

2 Unsolicited material addressed to electors (whether addressed to them by name or intended for delivery to households within any particular area).

Expenses in respect of such material include design costs and other costs in connection with preparing, producing or distributing such material (including the cost of postage).

3 Transport (by any means) of persons to any place.

Expenses in respect of the transport of such persons include the costs of hiring a means of transport for a particular period.

4 Public meetings (of any kind).

Expenses in respect of such meetings include costs incurred in connection with the attendance of persons at such meetings, the hire of premises for the purposes of such meetings or the provision of goods, services or facilities at them.

5 The services of an election agent or any other person whose services are engaged in connection with the candidate's election.

6 Accommodation and administrative costs.

NOTES
Defined terms
  election: s 202(1)
  election agent: see s 67
  elector: s 202(1)
                           person: s 202(1)

PART 2
GENERAL EXCLUSIONS

7 The publication of any matter, other than an advertisement, relating to the election in—

    (a) a newspaper or periodical;
    (b) a broadcast made by the British Broadcasting Corporation;
    (c) a programme included in any service licensed under Part 1 or 3 of the Broadcasting Act 1990 (c 42) or Part 1 or 2 of the Broadcasting Act 1996 (c 55).

8 The provision of any facilities provided in pursuance of any right conferred on candidates at an election by this Act other than facilities in respect of which expenses fall to be defrayed by virtue of section 96(4) above.

9 The provision by an individual of his own services which he provides voluntarily in his own time and free of charge.

10(1) Accommodation which is the candidate's sole or main residence.

  (2) The provision by any other individual of accommodation which is his sole or main residence if the provision is made free of charge.

11(1) Transport by a means of transport which was acquired by the candidate principally for his own personal use.

  (2) Transport provided free of charge by any other individual if the means of transport was acquired by him principally for his own personal use.

12(1) Computing or printing equipment which was acquired by the candidate principally for his own personal use.

  (2) The provision by any other individual of computing or printing equipment which was acquired by the individual principally for his own personal use if the provision is made free of charge.

NOTES
Defined terms
  election: s 202(1)

PART 3
POWER TO AMEND PARTS 1 AND 2

13(1) The Scottish Ministers may by order made by statutory instrument make such amendment of Part 1 or 2 of this Schedule as they consider appropriate.

  (2) An order under sub-paragraph (1) may contain such incidental, supplemental, saving or transitional provisions as the Scottish Ministers think fit.

(3) No order is to be made under sub-paragraph (1) unless a draft of the instrument containing the order has been laid before and approved by resolution of the Scottish Parliament.

SCHEDULE 5
Use for Parliamentary Election Meetings of Rooms in School Premises and of Meeting Rooms

1(1) Any arrangements for the use of a room in school premises shall be made with the local authority maintaining the school or, in the case of a room in the premises of a foundation or voluntary aided school, with the governing body of the school.

(2) Any question as to the rooms in school premises which a candidate in any constituency is entitled to use, or as to the times at which he is entitled to use them, or as to the notice which is reasonable, shall be determined by the Secretary of State.

2(1) Every local authority shall prepare and revise for their area lists of the rooms in school premises which candidates in any constituency are entitled to use.

(2) The list shall include the rooms in premises outside, as well as those in premises in, the constituency.

3(1) Every district and London borough council and every Welsh county and county borough council shall prepare and revise for their area lists of the meeting rooms which candidates in any constituency are entitled to use.

(2) The list shall indicate the person to whom applications for the use of the room are to be made in each case.

(3) The list shall not include any room if the person maintaining it disputes the right of candidates in the constituency to use it.

4 The lists of rooms in school premises and of meeting rooms prepared for each constituency shall be kept by the re gistration officer, and those lists and particulars of any change made on their revision shall (where necessary) be forwarded to him accordingly.

5 In the event of a dissolution, or of a vacancy occurring in the seat for the constituency, any person stating himself to be, or to be authorised by, a candidate or his election agent shall be entitled at all reasonable hours to inspect those lists or a copy of them.

5A In paragraphs 1 and 2 "local authority" has the meaning given by section 579(1) of the Education Act 1996.

6 In the application of this Schedule to Scotland—
   (a) for the reference in paragraph 1(1) to a local authority substitute a reference to an education authority;
   (aa) *Repealed*
   (b) sub-paragraph (1) of paragraph 2, sub-paragraph (1) of paragraph 3 and paragraph 4 do not apply, and it is the duty of the proper officer of every local authority to prepare and keep for each constituency wholly situated in the area of the council and for each part so situated of any other constituency—
      (i) a list of rooms in school premises, and
      (ii) a list of meeting rooms,
   which candidates in the constituency are entitled to use.

NOTES
Defined terms
   election agent: see s 67

local authority (E&W): s 203(1)
local authority (S): s 204(1)

London borough: s 203(2) and Interpretation Act 1978
Sch 1

SCHEDULE 6
WARD ELECTIONS IN THE CITY

1 Without prejudice to the application of any provision of this Act to elections in the City by virtue of sections 191 to 196 of this Act, this Schedule has effect as regards the operation of Part II of the City of London (Various Powers) Act 1957 (referred to in this Schedule as "the City Act") and the City of London (Ward Elections) Act 2002.

2 Notwithstanding anything in section 6(1) of the City Act—

   (a)   a person qualified (age apart) to vote as an elector at a ward election shall be entitled to do so if he is of the age of 18 years or over on the date of the poll, except that,

   (b)   a person registered in the ward list to be used at a ward election shall not be entitled to vote as an elector at the election if his entry in the ward list gives a date later than the date of the poll as the date on which he will attain the age of 18 years.

3 Ward lists and provisional ward lists shall give for any elector the date which it appears to the town clerk of the City that the elector will attain the age of 18 years, if that date is after the 16th November in the year in which the ward lists are to be published.

4 Claims and objections asking for the omission, insertion or alteration of a date in a ward list as that on which an elector will attain that age may be made as in the case of claims and objections relating to the inclusion of a person's name in the list, and sections 7(4) and 9 of the City Act shall with any necessary modifications apply accordingly.

5 Any power under this Act to prescribe the form of service declaration may be exercised so as to take account of the difference between the qualifying date under this Act and the qualifying date under the City of London (Ward Elections) Act 2002.

6 Nothing in this Act affects the operation of paragraph (a) of subsection (5) of section 5 of the Representation of the People Act 1949 in relation to their application by section 4(2) of the City Act.

NOTES

Defined terms
   age: s 202(2)
   election: s 202(1)
   elector: s 202(1)

the City: s 202(1
vote: s 202(1)

SCHEDULE 7
TRANSITIONAL AND SAVING PROVISIONS, AND INTERPRETATION OF OTHER ACTS

PART I
TRANSITIONAL AND SAVING PROVISIONS

Not reproduced

PART II
INTERPRETATION OF OTHER ACTS
Register, electors, etc

10(1)   A reference in any Act (whenever passed) to—

   (a)   the register of parliamentary and local government electors, or

   (b)   the register of parliamentary electors, or

   (c)   the register of local government electors, or

    (d)   the electors lists for such a register,
shall be taken as a reference to—
            (i)   the register kept under this Act, or
            (ii)   that register so far as it relates to parliamentary electors, or
            (iii) that register so far as it relates to local government electors, or
            (iv)   the electors lists for such a register,
as the case may be, and references in any Act to a parliamentary or local government
elector shall be construed accordingly.

(2)   In relation to a person shown in a register or electors list as attaining voting age on a
specified date the references in sub-paragraph (1) above do not apply except for the
purposes of an fs at which the day fixed for the poll falls on or after that date.

Registration and returning officers

11   A reference in any Act (whenever passed) to—
        (a)   the registration officer for the registration of parliamentary or local government
              electors, or
        (b)   the returning officer for a parliamentary election or constituency,
shall be taken respectively as a reference to the registration officer or returning officer
appointed under this Act.

Registration expenses

12   A reference in any Act (whenever passed) to registration expenses in connection with
the registration of parliamentary or local government electors shall be taken as a
reference to registration expenses under this Act.

Supplemental

13(1)   Subject to this paragraph, the provisions of paragraphs 10 to 12 of this Schedule apply
to a reference—
        (a)   to any of the matters mentioned in those provisions, whatever the terms used in
              that reference; and
        (b)   to any other matter which was to be construed as a reference to any of those
              matters by virtue of an enactment repealed by the Representation of the People
              Act 1948.

(2)   Those provisions so far as they relate to this Act or any other Act passed after that Act
of 1948 do not apply where the context otherwise requires.

(3)   Those provisions so far as they relate to Acts passed before that Act of 1948 may be
excluded in whole or in part by an order of the Secretary of State in any particular case
where they appear to him to be inappropriate.

(4)   That order may make such change in the law which this Act reproduces from the
Representation of the People Act 1949 as might have been made before its
commencement under paragraph 8(1)(c) of Part I of Schedule 10 to that Act of 1948.

(5)   The provisions of paragraphs 10 to 12 may be supplemented by an order made by the
Secretary of State in relation to an Act passed previous to the Representation of the
People Act 1948—
        (a)   where, in any particular case, such an order appears to him necessary for
              harmonising the previous Act with the provisions of this Act; and
        (b)   to the extent that the provisions of this Act re-enact such provisions of the
              Representation of the People Act 1949 as re-enacted provisions of that Act of
              1948.

(6) A power conferred by this paragraph to make an order shall be exercisable by statutory instrument, and any such instrument shall be subject to annulment by resolution of either House of Parliament.

(7) Nothing in paragraphs 10 to 12 shall be taken to prejudice the operation in relation to this Act of any provision of the Interpretation Act 1978 as to repeals.

SCHEDULE 8
CONSEQUENTIAL AMENDMENTS

Not reproduced

SCHEDULE 9
REPEALS AND REVOCATIONS

PART I
REPEAL OF OBSOLETE PROVISIONS

Not reproduced

PART II
CONSEQUENTIAL REPEALS

Not reproduced

PART III
CONSEQUENTIAL REVOCATIONS

Not reproduced

Representation of the People Act 1985

An Act to amend the law relating to parliamentary elections in the United Kingdom and local government elections in Great Britain, to provide for combining polls taken on the same date at such elections and elections to the European Parliament, to extend the franchise at elections to that European Parliament, to amend the law relating to the effect of the demise of the Crown on the summoning and duration of a new Parliament and to repeal section 21(3) of the Representation of the People Act 1918

16th July 1985

SCHEDULES

Extension of franchise to British citizens overseas

Extension of parliamentary franchise

1 (1)   A person is entitled to vote as an elector at a parliamentary election in any constituency if
    (a)   he qualifies as an overseas elector in respect of that constituency on the date on which he makes a declaration under and in accordance with section 2 of this Act ("the relevant date");
    (b)   on that date and on the date of the poll
       (i) he is not subject to any legal incapacity to vote, and
       (ii)   he is a British citizen; and
    (c)   on the date of the poll he is registered in a register of parliamentary electors for that constituency.

(2)   For the purposes of this Act and the principal Act a person qualifies as an overseas elector in respect of a constituency on the relevant date if
    (a)   on that date he is not resident in the United Kingdom, and
    (b)   he satisfies one of the following sets of conditions.

(3)   The first set of conditions is that
    (a)   he was included in a register of parliamentary electors in respect of an address at a place that is situated within the constituency concerned,
    (b)   that entry in the register was made on the basis that he was resident, or to be treated for the purposes of registration as resident, at that address,
    (c)   that entry in the register was in force at any time falling within the period of 15 years ending immediately before the relevant date, and
    (d)   subsequent to that entry ceasing to have effect no entry was made in any register of parliamentary electors on the basis that he was resident, or to be treated for the purposes of registration as resident, at any other address.

(4)   The second set of conditions is that
    (a)   he was last resident in the United Kingdom within the period of 15 years ending immediately before the relevant date,
    (b)   he was by reason only of his age incapable of being included in any register of parliamentary electors in force on the last day on which he was resident in the United Kingdom, and
    (c)   the address at which he was resident on that day was at a place that is situated within the constituency concerned and a parent or guardian of his was included, in respect of that address, in a register of parliamentary electors or a register of local government electors in force on that day.

(5)   The reference in subsection (1) above to a person being subject to a legal incapacity to vote on the relevant date does not include a reference to his being under the age of 18 on that date; and the reference in subsection (4) above to a register of local government electors includes a reference to a register of electors prepared for the

purposes of local elections (within the meaning of the Electoral Law Act (Northern Ireland) 1962).

NOTES
Defined terms
   principal Act: s 27(1)

Registration of British citizens overseas

2 (1)   A person is entitled to be registered in a register of parliamentary electors in pursuance of a declaration made by him under and in accordance with this section (an "overseas elector's declaration") if

(a)   the register is for the constituency or part of the constituency within which is situated the place in the United Kingdom specified in the declaration in accordance with subsection (4) below as having been the address
(i) in respect of which he was registered, or
(ii)   at which he was resident,
as the case may be, and

(b)   the registration officer concerned is satisfied that, on the relevant date, he qualifies as an overseas elector in respect of that constituency for which that register is prepared.

(2)   A person registered in a register of parliamentary electors in pursuance of an overseas elector's declaration is entitled to remain so registered until

(a)   the end of the period of 12 months beginning with the date when the entry in the register first takes effect,

(aa) the registration officer determines in accordance with regulations that the person was not entitled to be registered,

(ab) the registration officer determines in accordance with regulations that the person was registered as the result of an application under section 10ZC of the principal Act made by some other person or that the person's entry has been altered as the result of an application under section 10ZD of that Act made by some other person,

(b)   the declaration is cancelled under subsection (5) below, or

(c)   any entry made in respect of him in any register of parliamentary electors takes effect otherwise than in pursuance of an overseas elector's declaration,

whichever first occurs; and, where the entitlement of such a person to remain so registered terminates by virtue of this subsection, the registration officer concerned shall remove that person's entry from the register, unless he is entitled to remain registered in pursuance of a further overseas elector's declaration.

(3)   An overseas elector's declaration must state

(a)   the date of the declaration,

(b)   that the declarant is a British citizen,

(c)   that the declarant is not resident in the United Kingdom on the relevant date, and

(d)   when he ceased to be so resident or, in the case of a person relying on registration in pursuance of a service declaration, when he ceased to have a service qualification or, if later, ceased to be so resident,

and must contain such other information and satisfy such other requirements (which may include requirements for declarations to be attested and for the charging of fees in respect of their attestation) as may be prescribed.

(3A)   An overseas elector's declaration that specifies an address in Northern Ireland under subsection (4) may, instead of or in addition to including a statement under subsection (3)(b), state that the declarant is an eligible Irish citizen.

(4) An overseas elector's declaration must
   (a) show which set of conditions in section 1 of this Act the declarant claims to satisfy,
   (b) in the case of the first set of conditions, specify the address in respect of which he was registered, and
   (c) in the case of the second set of conditions, specify
       (i) the date of the declarant's birth,
       (ii) the address in the United Kingdom at which he was resident, and
       (iii) the name of the parent or guardian on whose registration in respect of that address he relies, and whether the person named was a parent or guardian,
   and may not, in the case of either set of conditions, specify more than one such address; and if the declarant makes more than one such declaration bearing the same date and specifying different addresses in the United Kingdom as the address in respect of which he was registered or, as the case may be, at which he was resident the declarations shall be void.

(5) An overseas elector's declaration may be cancelled at any time by the declarant.

(6) An overseas elector's declaration shall be of no effect unless it is received by the registration officer concerned within the period of three months beginning with the relevant date.

(7) For the purposes of section 1 of this Act, where a person is registered in a register of parliamentary electors for any constituency or part of a constituency in pursuance of an overseas elector's declaration, it shall be conclusively presumed that he was not resident in the United Kingdom on the relevant date.

(8) In this section "the relevant date" has the meaning given by section 1(1)(a) of this Act.

(9) In this section "eligible Irish citizen" means an Irish citizen who
   (a) was born in Northern Ireland, and
   (b) qualifies as a British citizen (whether or not he identifies himself as such).

(10) A person found abandoned in Northern Ireland as a newborn infant is, unless the contrary is shown, deemed for the purposes of subsection (9) to have been born in Northern Ireland.

NOTES

Defined terms
principal Act: s 27(1)

Subordinate Legislation
Representation of the People (Amendment) Regulations 1990, SI 1990/520.
Representation of the People (England and Wales)

(Amendment) (No 2) Regulations 2006, SI 2006/2910.
Representation of the People (Scotland) (Amendment) Regulations 2007, SI 2007/925.
Representation of the People (Northern Ireland) Regulations 2008, SI 2008/1741.

Extension of franchise for European Parliamentary elections

3 (1) A peer is entitled by virtue of this section to vote as an elector at a European Parliamentary election in any electoral region if
   (a) he qualifies under this section in respect of that region on the date on which he makes a declaration under and in accordance with regulations under this section ("the relevant date"),
   (b) on that date and on the day appointed for the election
       (i) he is not subject to any legal incapacity to vote, and
       (ii) he is a British citizen, and
   (c) on the day so appointed he is registered in the electoral region in a register under this section.

(2) For the purposes of subsection (1) above, a peer qualifies under this section in respect of an electoral region on the relevant date if
    (a) on that date he is not resident in the United Kingdom, and
    (b) he satisfies one of the following sets of conditions.

(3) The first set of conditions is that
    (a) he was included in a register of local government electors in respect of an address at a place that is situated within the electoral region concerned,
    (b) that entry in the register was made on the basis that he was resident, or to be treated for the purposes of registration as resident, at that address,
    (c) that entry in the register was in force at any time falling within the period of 15 years ending immediately before the relevant date, and
    (d) subsequent to that entry ceasing to have effect no entry was made in any register of local government electors on the basis that he was resident, or to be treated for the purposes of registration as resident, at any other address.

(4) The second set of conditions is that
    (a) he was last resident in the United Kingdom within the period of 15 years ending immediately before the relevant date,
    (b) he was by reason only of his age incapable of being included in any register of local government electors in force on the last day on which he was resident in the United Kingdom, and
    (c) the address at which he was resident on that day was at a place that is situated within the electoral region concerned and a parent or guardian of his was included, in respect of that address, in a register of parliamentary electors or a register of local government electors in force on that day.

(4A) For the purposes of subsections (3)(a) and (4)(c) above, a person who has an anonymous entry in a register of parliamentary electors or local government electors is not to be regarded as being included in that register.

(5) Regulations may
    (a) provide for a person seeking registration under this section to make a declaration for the purpose, being a declaration of the prescribed facts and containing the prescribed information;
    (b) require such declarations to be attested and provide for the charging of fees in respect of their attestation;
    (c) make provision for and in connection with the cancellation of such declarations.

(6) Regulations may also
    (a) provide for the registration, subject to prescribed exceptions and on satisfying prescribed conditions, of those peers who (apart from the requirements of registration) may be entitled by virtue of this section to vote as electors at European Parliamentary elections;
    (b) apply with such modifications or exceptions as may be prescribed any provision in respect of the registration of parliamentary or local government electors made by or under the principal Act or this Act.

(7) Regulations under this section shall require each registration officer to prepare and publish, in respect of any year for which any peers are to be registered under this section, a register of the peers so registered; and any such register shall so far as practicable be combined with the registers of parliamentary electors and of local government electors, the entries of peers registered under this section being marked to indicate that fact.

(8) In this section

(a) "legal incapacity" has the same meaning
   (i) in relation to Great Britain as it has in the principal Act for the purposes of local government elections, and
   (ii) in relation to Northern Ireland as it has in the Electoral Law Act (Northern Ireland) 1962 for the purposes of local elections,

but the reference in subsection (1)(b) above to a person being subject to a legal incapacity to vote on the relevant date does not include a reference to his being below the age of 18 on that date,

(b) "local election" has the same meaning as in the Electoral Law Act (Northern Ireland) 1962, and

(c) references to the register of local government elections include a reference to a register of electors prepared
   (i) for the purposes of local elections, or
   (ii) for the purposes of municipal elections in the City of London (that is, elections to the office of mayor, alderman, common councilman or sheriff and also elections of officers elected by the mayor, aldermen and liverymen in common hall).

NOTES

Defined terms
European Parliamentary election: s 27(1)
European Parliamentary general election: s 27(1)
principal Act: s 27(1)

Subordinate Legislation
Representation of the People (Amendment) Regulations 1990, SI 1990/520.
Representation of the People (England and Wales) Regulations 2001, SI 2001/341.

Representation of the People (Scotland) Regulations 2001, SI 2001/497.
Representation of the People (Northern Ireland) Regulations 2008, SI 2008/1741.
Representation of the People (England and Wales) (Description of Electoral Registers and Amendment) Regulations 2013, SI 2013/3198.

Extension of franchise: consequential amendments

4   Repealed

Voting at parliamentary elections in the United Kingdom and local government elections in Great Britain

Manner of voting at parliamentary and local government elections

5 (1)   This section applies to determine the manner of voting of a person entitled to vote as an elector at a parliamentary election.

(2)   He may vote in person at the polling station allotted to him under the appropriate rules, unless he is entitled as an elector to an absent vote at the election.

(3)   He may vote by post if he is entitled as an elector to vote by post at the election.

(4)   If he is entitled to vote by proxy at the election, he may so vote unless, before a ballot paper has been issued for him to vote by proxy, he applies at the polling station allotted to him under the appropriate rules for a ballot paper for the purposes of voting in person, in which case he may vote in person there.

(5)   If he is not entitled as an elector to an absent vote at the election but cannot reasonably be expected to go in person to the polling station allotted to him under the appropriate rules by reason of the particular circumstances of his employment, either as a constable or by the returning officer, on the date of the poll for a purpose connected with the election, he may vote in person at any polling station in the constituency.

(5A)   Nothing in the preceding provisions of this section applies to

(a) a person to whom section 7 of the principal Act (mental patients who are not detained offenders) applies and who is liable, by virtue of any enactment, to be detained in the mental hospital in question, or

(b) a person to whom section 7A of that Act (persons remanded in custody) applies, whether he is registered by virtue of that provision or not; and such a person may only vote by post or by proxy (where he is entitled as an elector to vote by post or, as the case may be, by proxy at the election).

(5AA) Nothing in subsections (1) to (5) applies to a person who has an anonymous entry in the register of parliamentary electors for the constituency; and such a person may only vote by post or by proxy (where entitled as an elector to vote by post or, as the case may be, by proxy at the election).

(5B) Subsection (2) above does not prevent a person, at the polling station allotted to him, marking a tendered ballot paper in pursuance of rule 40(1ZC) or (1ZE) of the parliamentary elections rules.

(6) For the purposes of the provisions of this and the principal Act, a person entitled to vote as an elector at a parliamentary election is entitled as an elector to vote by post or entitled to vote by proxy at the election if he is shown in the absent voters list for the election as so entitled; and references in those provisions to entitlement as an elector to an absent vote at a parliamentary election are references to entitlement as an elector to vote by post or entitlement to vote by proxy at the election.

(7) In this section and sections 6 to 9 of this Act "appropriate rules" means the parliamentary elections rules.

NOTES

Application   principal Act: s 27(1)
  This section now only applies in Northern Ireland.

Defined terms

Absent vote at elections for an indefinite period

6 (1) Where a person applies to the registration officer to vote by post, or to vote by proxy, at parliamentary elections for an indefinite period, the registration officer shall grant the application (subject to subsection (6) below) if

(a) he is satisfied that the applicant is eligible for an absent vote at parliamentary elections for an indefinite period,

(b) he is satisfied that the applicant is or will be registered in the register for such elections.

(ba) the application states the applicant's date of birth and the registration officer is satisfied that the date stated corresponds with the date supplied as the date of the applicant's birth pursuant to section 10(4A)(b), 10A(1A)(b) or 13A(2A)(b) of the principal Act,

(bb) the application is signed and (unless section 10(4B), 10A(1B) or 13A(2B) of the principal Act applies) the registration officer is satisfied that the signature on the application corresponds with the signature supplied as the applicant's signature pursuant to section 10(4A)(a), 10A(1A)(a) or 13A(2A)(a) of the principal Act,

(bc) the application either states the applicant's national insurance number or states that he does not have one, and the registration officer is satisfied as mentioned in subsection (1A) below, and

(c) the application meets the prescribed requirements.

(1A) For the purposes of subsection (1)(bc) above, the registration officer must be satisfied

(a) if the application states a national insurance number, that the requirements of subsection (1B) below are met, or

(b) if the application states that the applicant does not have a national insurance number, that no such number was supplied as his national insurance number pursuant to section 10(4A)(c)(i), 10A(1A)(c)(i) or 13A(2A)(c)(i) of the principal Act.

(1B) The requirements of this subsection are met if
    (a) the number stated as mentioned in subsection (1A)(a) above is the same as the one supplied as the applicant's national insurance number pursuant to section 10(4A)(c)(i), 10A(1A)(c)(i) or 13A(2A)(c)(i) of the principal Act, or
    (b) no national insurance number was supplied under any of those provisions, but the registration officer is not aware of any reason to doubt the authenticity of the application.

(2) For the purposes of this section, a person is eligible for an absent vote at parliamentary elections for an indefinite period
    (za) if he has an anonymous entry,
    (a) if he is or will be registered as a service voter,
    (aa) *repealed*
    (b) if he cannot reasonably be expected
        (i) to go in person to the polling station allotted or likely to be allotted to him under the appropriate rules, or
        (ii) to vote unaided there,
    by reason of blindness or other disability,
    (c) if he cannot reasonably be expected to go in person to that polling station by reason of the general nature of his occupation, service or employment or that of his spouse or civil partner, or by reason of his attendance on a course provided by an educational institution or that of his spouse or civil partner, or
    (d) if he cannot go in person from his qualifying address to that polling station without making a journey by air or sea,
and is also eligible for an absent vote at parliamentary elections for an indefinite period if he is or will be registered in pursuance of an overseas elector's declaration.

(2A) *repealed*

(3) The registration officer shall keep a record of those whose applications under this section have been granted showing
    (a) *repealed*
    (b) in the case of those who may vote by post, the addresses provided by them in their application as the addresses to which their ballot papers are to be sent, and
    (c) in the case of those who may vote by proxy, the names and addresses of those appointed as their proxies.

(4) The registration officer shall remove a person from the record kept under subsection (3) above
    (a) if he applies to the registration officer to be removed,
    (b) in the case of any registered person, if he ceases to be registered or registered at the same qualifying address or ceases to be, or becomes, registered as a service voter or in pursuance of a declaration of local connection or an overseas elector's declaration,
    (ba) if he ceases to have an anonymous entry, or
    (c) if the registration officer gives notice that he has reason to believe there has been a material change of circumstances.

(5) A person shown in the record kept under subsection (3) above as voting by post or, as the case may be, voting by proxy may subsequently alter his choice (subject to subsection (6) below) on an application to the registration officer that meets the

prescribed requirements and the registration officer shall amend the record accordingly.

(6) A person applying to vote by post must provide an address in the United Kingdom as the address to which his ballot paper is to be sent.

NOTES

Application
This section now only applies in Northern Ireland.

Defined terms
principal Act: s 27(1)

Subordinate Legislation
Representation of the People (Northern Ireland) (Amendment) Regulations 2014, SI 2014/1808.

Absent vote at a particular election and absent voters list

7 (1) Where a person applies to the registration officer to vote by post, or to vote by proxy, at a particular parliamentary . . . election, the registration officer shall grant the application (subject to subsection (5) below) if

  (a) he is satisfied that the applicant's circumstances on the date of the poll will be or are likely to be such that he cannot reasonably be expected to vote in person at the polling station allotted or likely to be allotted to him under the appropriate rules,

  (b) he is satisfied that the applicant is or will be registered in the register of parliamentary electors,

  (ba) the application states the applicant's date of birth and the registration officer is satisfied that the date stated corresponds with the date supplied as the date of the applicant's birth pursuant to section 10(4A)(b), 10A(1A)(b) or 13A(2A)(b) of the principal Act,

  (bb) the application is signed and (unless section 10(4B), 10A(1B) or 13A(2B) of the principal Act applies) the registration officer is satisfied that the signature on the application corresponds with the signature supplied as the applicant's signature pursuant to section 10(4A)(a), 10A(1A)(a) or 13A(2A)(a) of the principal Act,

  (bc) the application either states the applicant's national insurance number or states that he does not have one, and the registration officer is satisfied as mentioned in subsection (1A) below, and

  (c) the application meets the prescribed requirements.

(1A) For the purposes of subsection (1)(bc) above, the registration officer must be satisfied

  (a) if the application states a national insurance number, that the requirements of subsection (1B) below are met, or

  (b) if the application states that the applicant does not have a national insurance number, that no such number was supplied as his national insurance number pursuant to section 10(4A)(c)(i), 10A(1A)(c)(i) or 13A(2A)(c)(i) of the principal Act.

(1B) The requirements of this subsection are met if

  (a) the number stated as mentioned in subsection (1A)(a) above is the same as the one supplied as the applicant's national insurance number pursuant to section 10(4A)(c)(i), 10A(1A)(c)(i) or 13A(2A)(c)(i) of the principal Act, or

  (b) no national insurance number was supplied under any of those provisions, but the registration officer is not aware of any reason to doubt the authenticity of the application.

(2) Subsection (1) above does not apply to a person who is included in the record kept under section 6 of this Act, but such a person may, in respect of a particular parliamentary election, apply to the registration officer

  (a) for his ballot paper to be sent to a different address in the United Kingdom, or

(b) to vote by proxy,

if he is shown in the record so kept as voting by post at parliamentary elections.

(3) The registration officer shall grant an application under subsection (2) above if it meets the prescribed requirements.

(4) The registration officer shall, in respect of each parliamentary election, keep a special list ("the absent voters list") consisting of

    (a) a list of

      (i) those whose applications under subsection (1) above to vote by post at the election have been granted, together with the addresses provided by them in their applications as the addresses to which their ballot papers are to be sent, and

      (ii) those who are for the time being shown in the record kept under section 6 of this Act as voting by post at parliamentary elections (excluding those so shown whose applications under subsection (2) above to vote by proxy at the election have been granted), together with the addresses provided by them in their applications under that section or, as the case may be, subsection (2) above as the addresses to which their ballot papers are to be sent, and

    (b) a list ("the list of proxies") of those whose applications under this section to vote by proxy at the election have been granted or who are for the time being shown in the record kept under section 6 of this Act as voting by proxy at parliamentary elections, together with the names and addresses of those appointed as their proxies.

(4A) But in the case of a person who has an anonymous entry, the list mentioned in subsection (4)(a) or (b) must contain only

    (a) the person's electoral number, and

    (b) the date on which the person's entitlement to remain registered anonymously will terminate under section 9C(1A) of the principal Act (in the absence of a further application under section 9B of that Act).

(5) A person applying to vote by post must provide an address in the United Kingdom as the address to which his ballot paper is to be sent.

NOTES

Application
  This section now only applies in Northern Ireland.

Defined terms
  principal Act: s 27(1)

Subordinate Legislation
  Representation of the People (Northern Ireland) (Amendment) Regulations 2014, SI 2014/1808.

Proxies at elections

8 (1) Subject to the provisions of this section, any person is capable of being appointed proxy to vote for another (in this section and section 9 of this Act referred to as "the elector") at any parliamentary election and may vote in pursuance of the appointment.

(2) The elector cannot have more than one person at a time appointed as proxy to vote for him at parliamentary elections (whether in the same constituency or elsewhere).

(3) A person is not capable of being appointed to vote, or voting, as proxy at a parliamentary election

    (a) if he is subject to any legal incapacity (age apart) to vote at that election as an elector, or

    (b) if he is neither a Commonwealth citizen nor a citizen of the Republic of Ireland.

(3A) *Repealed*

(4) A person is not capable of voting as proxy at a parliamentary election unless on the date of the poll he has attained the age of eighteen.

(5) A person is not entitled to vote as proxy at the same parliamentary election in any constituency on behalf of more than two electors of whom that person is not the spouse or civil partner, parent, grandparent, brother, sister, child or grandchild.

(6) Where the elector applies to the registration officer for the appointment of a proxy to vote for him at parliamentary elections for an indefinite period, the registration officer shall make the appointment if the application meets the prescribed requirements and he is satisfied that the elector is or will be

    (a) registered in the register of parliamentary electors, and

    (b) shown in the record kept under section 6 of this Act as voting by proxy at such elections,

and that the proxy is capable of being and willing to be appointed to vote as proxy at such elections.

(7) Where the elector applies to the registration officer for the appointment of a proxy to vote for him at a particular parliamentary election, the registration officer shall make the appointment if the application meets the prescribed requirements and he is satisfied that the elector is or will be

    (a) registered in the register of parliamentary electors for that election, and

    (b) entitled to vote by proxy at that election by virtue of an application under section 7 of this Act,

and that the proxy is capable of being and willing to be appointed.

(8) The appointment of a proxy under this section is to be made by means of a proxy paper issued by the registration officer.

(9) The appointment may be cancelled by the elector by giving notice to the registration officer, and shall also cease to be in force on the issue of a proxy paper appointing a different person to vote for him at any parliamentary election or elections (whether in the same constituency or elsewhere).

(10) Subject to subsection (9) above, the appointment shall remain in force

    (a) in the case of an appointment for a particular election, for that election, and

    (b) in any other case, while the elector is shown as voting by proxy in the record kept under section 6 of this Act in pursuance of the same application under that section.

(11) *Repealed*

NOTES

Application
This section now only applies in Northern Ireland.

Subordinate Legislation
Representation of the People (Northern Ireland) (Amendment) Regulations 2014, SI 2014/1808.

Defined terms
principal Act: s 27(1)

Voting as proxy

9 (1) A person entitled to vote as proxy at a parliamentary election may do so in person at the polling station allotted to the elector under the appropriate rules unless he is entitled to vote by post as proxy for the elector at the election, in which case he may vote by post.

(1A) But in the case of a person entitled to vote as proxy for an elector who has an anonymous entry

    (a) subsection (1) does not apply, and

    (b) the person may only so vote by post (where entitled as a proxy to vote by post).

(2)   Where a person is entitled to vote by post as proxy for the elector at any election, the elector may not apply for a ballot paper for the purpose of voting in person at the election.

(3)   For the purposes of this and the principal Act, a person entitled to vote as proxy for another at a parliamentary election is entitled so to vote by post if he is included in the list kept under subsection (9) below in respect of the election.

(4)   Where a person applies to the registration officer to vote by post as proxy at parliamentary elections for an indefinite period, the registration officer shall (subject to subsections (10) and (12) below) grant the application if
    (a)   the applicant is included in any record kept under section 6 of this Act in respect of a constituency for the whole or any part of which the registration officer acts, or
    (b)   the address provided by the applicant in his application as the address to which his ballot paper is to be sent is not in the same ward as the elector's qualifying address or, where the elector is registered in pursuance of an overseas declaration, the address specified in the declaration in accordance with section 2(4) of this Act, or
    (c)   the elector has an anonymous entry,
and the application meets the prescribed requirements.

(5)   *Repealed*

(6)   The registration officer shall keep a record of those whose applications under subsection (4) above have been granted showing
    (a)   *Repealed*
    (b)   the addresses provided by them in their applications as the addresses to which their ballot papers are to be sent.

(7)   Where a person applies to the registration officer to vote by post as proxy at a particular election and the application meets the prescribed requirements, the registration officer shall (subject to subsections (10) and (12) below) grant the application if
    (a)   he is satisfied that the applicant's circumstances on the date of the poll will be or are likely to be such that he cannot reasonably be expected to vote in person at the polling station allotted or likely to be allotted to the elector under the appropriate rules, or
    (b)   the applicant is, or the registration officer is satisfied that he will be, included in respect of the constituency for the whole or any part of which the registration officer acts in any of the absent voters lists for that election, or
    (c)   the elector has an anonymous entry.

(8)   Where, in the case of a particular election, a person included in the record kept under subsection (6) above applies to the registration officer for his ballot paper to be sent to a different address in the United Kingdom, the registration officer shall grant the application if it meets the prescribed requirements.

(9)   The registration officer shall, in respect of each parliamentary election, keep a special list of
    (a)   those who are for the time being included in the record kept under subsection (6) above, together with the addresses provided by them in their applications under that subsection or, as the case may be, subsection (8) above as the addresses to which their ballot papers are to be sent, and
    (b)   those whose applications under subsection (7) above have been granted in respect of the election concerned, together with the addresses to which their ballot papers are to be sent.

(9A) In the case of a person who has an anonymous entry, the list mentioned in subsection (9)(a) or (b) must contain only
   (a) the person's electoral number, and
   (b) the date on which the entitlement of the person to remain registered anonymously will terminate under section 9C(1A) of the principal Act (in the absence of a further application under section 9B of that Act).

(9B) In the case of a person who is the proxy for an elector who has an anonymous entry, the list mentioned in subsection (9)(a) or (b) must contain only
   (a) the person's electoral number, and
   (b) the date on which the elector's entitlement to remain registered anonymously will terminate under section 9C(1A) of the principal Act (in the absence of a further application under section 9B of that Act).

(10) The registration officer shall not grant any application under this section unless
   (a) he is satisfied that the elector is or will be registered in the register of parliamentary electors. . ., and
   (b) there is in force an appointment of the applicant as the elector's proxy to vote for him at parliamentary elections or, as the case may be, the election concerned.

(11) The registration officer shall remove a person from the record kept under subsection (6) above
   (a) if he applies to the registration officer to be removed,
   (b) where he was included in the record on the ground mentioned in subsection (4)(a) above, if he ceases to be included in any record kept under section 6 of this Act in respect of a constituency for the whole or any part of which the registration officer acts or becomes so included in pursuance of a further application under that section,
   (ba) where he was included in the record on the ground mentioned in subsection (4)(c), if the elector ceases to have an anonymous entry,
   (c) if the elector ceases to be registered as mentioned in subsection (10)(a) above, or
   (d) if the appointment of the person concerned as the elector's proxy ceases to be in force (whether or not he is reappointed).

(11A) Subsection (2) above does not prevent a person, at the polling station allotted to him, marking a tendered ballot paper in pursuance of rule 40(1ZC) or (1ZE) of the parliamentary elections rules.

   12 A person applying to vote by post as proxy must provide an address in the United Kingdom as the address to which his ballot paper is to be sent.

NOTES

Application
   This section now only applies in Northern Ireland.

Defined terms
   European Parliamentary election: s 27(1)

Subordinate Legislation
   Representation of the People (Northern Ireland) (Amendment) Regulations 2014, SI 2014/1808.

Voting at special polling stations in Northern Ireland

10 (1) Schedule 1 to this Act makes provision for those
   (a) whose circumstances on the date of the poll at a particular parliamentary election in Northern Ireland will be or are likely to be such that they cannot reasonably be expected to vote in person as electors at the polling stations allotted or likely to be allotted to them under the parliamentary elections rules, but

(b)   who on that date will be in Northern Ireland.

(2)   The Secretary of State may by order made by statutory instrument bring that Schedule into force if he is satisfied that it is necessary to do so in order to prevent serious abuse of the system of voting by post in the case of ballot papers for elections in Northern Ireland sent to addresses there in pursuance of applications granted under section 7(1) of this Act.

(3)   That Schedule shall cease to be in force if the Secretary of State so provides by order made be statutory instrument (without prejudice to his power to make a further order under subsection (2) above), and an order under this subsection may include such transitional provisions as the Secretary of State considers necessary or expedient.

(4)   No order under this section shall be made unless a draft of the order has been laid before and approved by each House of Parliament.

(5)   While that Schedule is in force, section 7(5) of this Act shall have effect as if it required a person applying under section 7(1) of this Act to vote by post at a particular parliamentary election in Northern Ireland to provide an address in Great Britain as the address to which his ballot paper is to be sent.

NOTES
Application   principal Act: s 27(1)
   This section only applies in Northern Ireland: see s 29(4).

Defined terms

Manner of voting: supplementary provision

11   Schedule 2 to this Act (which
         (a)   in Part I, makes amendments of the principal Act consequential on the provisions of sections 5 to 9 of this Act,
         (b)   and
         (c)   in Part III, makes provision as to absent voting at municipal elections in the City)
shall have effect.

NOTES
Defined terms
   principal Act: s 27(1)

Offences as to declarations, etc

Offences as to declarations, etc

12 (1)   A person who makes an overseas elector's declaration or a declaration purporting to be an overseas elector's declaration
         (a)   when he knows that he is subject to a legal incapacity to vote at parliamentary elections (age apart), or
         (b)   when he knows that it contains a statement which is false,
      is guilty of an offence.

(2)   A person who attests an overseas elector's declaration or a declaration purporting to be an overseas elector's declaration when he knows
         (a)   that he is not authorised to attest such a declaration, or
         (b)   that it contains a statement which is false,
      is guilty of an offence.

(3)   A person who makes a statement which he knows to be false in any declaration or form used for any of the purposes of sections 5 to 9 of this Act or attests an application

under section 6 or 7 of this Act when he knows that he is not authorised to do so or that it contains a statement which is false is guilty of an offence.

(4) A person guilty of an offence under this section shall be liable on summary conviction to a fine not exceeding level 5 on the standard scale.

NOTES
Defined terms
    principal Act: s 27(1)

Deposits and expenses at elections

Deposit by candidates at parliamentary elections
13   *Repealed*

Election expenses
14   *Repealed*

Combination and timing of polls

Combination of polls at parliamentary, Scottish Parliamentary, European Parliamentary and local elections

15 (1)   Where the polls at

   (a)   a parliamentary general election and a European Parliamentary general election;

   (b)   an ordinary local government election and a parliamentary general election; *or*

   (c)   an ordinary local government election and a European Parliamentary general election,

   (d)   a Scottish Parliamentary general election and a parliamentary general election; *or*

   (e)   a Scottish Parliamentary general election and a European Parliamentary general election,

   are to be taken on the same date, they shall be taken together.

   (2)   Where the polls at elections for related areas are to be taken on the same date but are not required by subsection (1) above or section 36 of the principal Act to be taken together, they may nevertheless be so taken if the returning officer for each election thinks fit.

   (3)   In subsection (2) above the reference to elections includes Scottish Parliamentary elections and European Parliamentary elections but does not include elections under the local government Act which are not local government elections; and for the purposes of that subsection two areas are related if one is coterminous with or situated wholly or partly within the other.

(3ZA)   But subsection (2) does not confer power on a returning officer to determine that a Scottish Parliamentary election and a local government election in Scotland are to be taken together.

   (3A)   Where the polls at an election of the Northern Ireland Assembly are to be taken on the same date as the polls at one or more elections of the kind mentioned in subsection (1), the Chief Electoral Officer for Northern Ireland may direct that the polls at the election of the Assembly are to be taken together with the polls at the other election or elections.

(4) Where the polls at any elections are combined under this section the cost of taking the combined polls (excluding any cost solely attributable to one election) and any cost attributable to their combination shall be apportioned equally among the elections.

(5) The Secretary of State may by regulations make such provision as he thinks fit in connection with the combining of polls at any elections under this section including provision modifying the Representation of the People Acts in relation to such elections.

(5A) The power under subsection (5) above to make provision in connection with the combining under this section of polls at
    (a) a local government election in England and Wales, and
    (b) the European Parliamentary general election in 2004,
includes power to make provision modifying, in relation to such elections, any enactment relating to election of members of the European Parliament or any instrument made under any such enactment or under the Representation of the People Acts.

(5B) The power under subsection (5) above to make provision in connection with the combining of polls under subsection (3A) includes power to modify
    (a) Part 2 or 3 of the Schedule to the Elections Act 2001 (in addition to the power conferred by paragraph 32 of that Schedule);
    (b) any provision made under section 34(4) or 84(1) of the Northern Ireland Act 1998 or section 38(1)(a) of the Northern Ireland Constitution Act 1973 (see section 95(1) of the 1998 Act);
    (c) any provision made by or under Northern Ireland legislation relating to local elections.

(5C) Before making provision under subsection (5) in connection with the combination of polls where one of the elections is a Scottish Parliamentary election or a local government election in Scotland, the Secretary of State must consult the Scottish Ministers.

(6) In its application to Northern Ireland, subsection (1) above shall have effect as if the references to an ordinary local government election were to a local election.

NOTES

Provisions not yet in force
Sub-ss (1)(d) and (e), (3ZA) and (5C) are not yet in force. Nor are the words "Scottish Parliamentary elections and" in sub-s (2).

Defined terms
European Parliamentary election: s 27(1)
European Parliamentary general election: s 27(1)
principal Act: s 27(1)

Subordinate Legislation
Representation of the People (Amendment) Regulations 1990, SI 1990/520.
Representation of the People (England and Wales) Regulations 2001, SI 2001/341.

16   *Repealed*

Combination of polls at local elections

17   *Repealed*

Ordinary day of local elections

18   *Repealed*

Timing of elections

9 (1)-(5)   *Repealed*

(6) In the Local Government Act 1972

(a) *Repealed*

(b) for the purposes of subsection (4) of that section, subsection (1) of that section shall have effect as if for the words from "Sunday" to "bank holiday break" there were substituted the words "Saturday, Sunday, Christmas Eve, Christmas Day, Good Friday or bank holiday"; and

(c) *Repealed*

Miscellaneous and supplemental

Demise of the Crown and parliamentary elections etc

20 (1) Subject to what follows, the demise of the Crown does not affect any proclamation summoning a new Parliament issued before the demise (see section 3(4) of the Fixed-term Parliaments Act 2011) (or any other matter relating to a parliamentary election or the summoning of a new Parliament).

(2) Subsections (3) to (6) apply if the demise occurs

(a) on the day of the dissolution of a Parliament by section 3(1) of the 2011 Act, or

(b) after that day but before the polling day for the next parliamentary general election after the dissolution as determined under section 1 of the 2011 Act or appointed under section 2(7) of the 2011 Act ("the current election");

and any relevant writ, notice or other document is to be issued or, if already issued, read accordingly.

(3) In relation to the current election, for the purposes of the timetable in rule 1 in Schedule 1 to the principal Act

(a) the polling day shall be

(i) the 14th day after the day which would otherwise have been the polling day, or

(ii) if the 14th day is not a working day, the next working day after the 14th day;

(b) any working day within the period of 13 days beginning with the day after the demise

(i) shall be disregarded in computing any period of time, and

(ii) shall not be treated as a day for the purpose of any proceedings before the polling day.

(4) If the polling day for the current election was appointed under section 2(7) of the 2011 Act, the reference to the polling day in section 1(4) of the 2011 Act is to be read, in relation to the current election, as a reference to the new polling day under subsection (3)(a).

(5) Section 76 of the principal Act shall have effect in relation to any candidate at the current election as if the maximum amount specified in subsection (2)(a) of that section were increased by one half.

(6) If the proclamation summoning the new Parliament after the current election was issued before the demise, the meeting of the new Parliament shall (subject to any prorogation subsequent to the demise) take place

(a) on the 14th day after the day appointed in the proclamation for the meeting, or

(b) if the 14th day is not a working day, the next working day after the 14th day.

(7) If the demise occurs within the period of seven days before the day of the dissolution of a Parliament by section 3(1) of the 2011 Act, subsections (2) to (6) have effect as if the demise occurred on that day.

(8) In this section "working day" means any day other than one to which rule 2 in Schedule 1 to the principal Act applies in relation to the current election (or would have applied had it fallen before the polling day).

NOTES

Defined terms
   principal Act: s 27(1)

Ordinary elections of parish and community councillors: insufficient nominations

21 (1) This section applies where, at an ordinary election of parish or community councillors in England and Wales, an insufficient number of persons are or remain validly nominated to fill the vacancies in respect of which the election is held.

(2) Unless the number of newly elected members of the council in question is less than the number that constitutes a quorum for meetings of the council

   (a) those members may coopt any person or persons to fill the vacancy or vacancies remaining unfilled,

   (b) the district council or, in the case of a community council, the county council or county borough council may exercise the powers conferred by section 39(4) of the principal Act (power by order to do anything necessary for the proper holding of an election etc) in relation to any such vacancy or vacancies as are not so filled, and

   (c) section 39(1) of that Act (duty of returning officer to order an election) shall not apply;

   but the powers mentioned in paragraph (b) above shall not be exercised before the expiry of the period of 35 days (computed according to section 40 of that Act) beginning with the day on which the election was held.

(3) Subsection (7) of section 39 of that Act (parishes in different districts grouped) shall apply for the purposes of subsection (2) above as it applies for the purposes of subsections (4) and (6) of that section and section 40(3) of that Act (computation of time) shall apply for the purposes of subsection (2) above as it applies for the purposes of section 39.

NOTES

Defined terms
   principal Act: s 27(1)

Welsh forms

22 Section 26 of the Welsh Language Act 1993 (power to prescribe Welsh forms of documents or words specified in Acts), except subsection (3), shall apply in relation to regulations made under the principal Act or this Act and rules made (or having effect as if made) under section 36 of the principal Act as it applies in relation to Acts of Parliament.

Increase in penalties for offences under principal Act, etc

23 Schedule 3 to this Act shall have effect for the purpose of increasing the penalties applying in respect of certain offences under the principal Act and otherwise amending the provisions in that Act concerning such penalties.

Miscellaneous amendments of principal Act

24 The principal Act shall have effect subject to the amendments specified in Schedule 4 to this Act (being miscellaneous amendments including amendments consequential on the provisions of this Act).

Amendments of other enactments

25 (1)   Section 26 of the Police and Criminal Evidence Act 1984 (repeal of statutory powers of arrest) shall not apply to rule 36 in Schedule 1 to the principal Act (power of presiding officer to order constable to arrest person suspected of personation).

(2)   *Repealed*

Expenses

26 (1)   There shall be charged on and paid out of the Consolidated Fund any increase attributable to this Act in the sums to be charged on and paid out of the Fund under any other Act.

(2)   There shall be paid out of money provided by Parliament
   (a)   any increase attributable to this Act in the sums to be paid out of money so provided under any other Act, and
   (b)   any administrative expenses incurred by the Secretary of State by virtue of this Act.

Interpretation

27 (1)   In this Act
   "European Parliamentary election" means an election of a representative to the European Parliament and "European Parliamentary general election" means a general election of such representatives, and
   "principal Act" means the Representation of the People Act 1983.

(2)   The principal Act and sections 1 to 12, 15 to 18 and 21 of and Schedule 1 to this Act shall have effect as if those sections and that Schedule were contained in Part I of that Act, and sections 5 to 7A of the principal Act (residence) apply for the purposes of sections 1 to 3 of this Act as they apply for the purposes of section 4 of that Act.

(2ZA)   See the Chancellor of the Duchy of Lancaster Order 2015, by virtue of which functions of the Secretary of State under this Act are exercisable concurrently with the Chancellor of the Duchy of Lancaster.

(2A)   *Repealed*

(3)   References in any enactment other than an enactment contained in this or the principal Act to Part I of that Act include a reference to sections 1 to 12, 15 to 18 and 21 of and Schedule 1 to this Act.

Repeals

28 (1)   The enactments mentioned in Schedule 5 to this Act are hereby repealed to the extent specified in column 3 of that Schedule.

(2)-(3)   *Repealed*

Citation, commencement and extent

29 (1)   This Act may be cited as the Representation of the People Act 1985 and shall be included among the Acts that may be cited as the Representation of the People Acts.

(2)   This Act (except the provisions mentioned in subsection (3) below) shall come into force on such day as the Secretary of State may by order made by statutory instrument appoint, and different days may be appointed for different provisions and for different purposes.

(3)   Those provisions are

(a) sections 25(1) and 27(1) of this Act, this section, the amendment made by paragraph 18 of Schedule 4 to this Act and the repeal made by the entry in Schedule 5 to this Act relating to the Police and Criminal Evidence Act 1984 (which come into force on the day on which this Act is passed), and

(b) Schedule 1 to this Act (which may be brought into force under section 10 of this Act).

(4) This Act, except the provisions mentioned in subsection (5) below, extends to Northern Ireland; and section 10 of and Schedule 1 to this Act extend to Northern Ireland only.

(5) Those provisions are sections 17 and 18, 21 and 22 of this Act and any amendment or repeal by this Act of an enactment not extending to Northern Ireland.

NOTES

Subordinate Legislation

Representation of the People Act 1985 (Commencement No 1) Order 1985, SI 1985/1185.
Representation of the People Act 1985 (Commencement No 2) Order 1986, SI 1986/639.
Representation of the People Act 1985

(Commencement No 3) Order 1986, SI 1986/1080.
Representation of the People Act 1985 (Commencement No 4) Order 1987, SI 1987/207.

SCHEDULE 1
SPECIAL POLLING STATIONS IN NORTHERN IRELAND

Section 10

Part I
Right to Vote at Special Polling Stations

1 (1) Where, in the case of a person entitled to vote as an elector at a parliamentary election in Northern Ireland, the absent voters list shows that a special polling station is allotted to him he may, notwithstanding anything in section 5 of this Act, vote only in person at that polling station.

(2) Where a person applies to the Chief Electoral Officer for Northern Ireland (in this Schedule referred to as "the electoral officer") to vote at a particular parliamentary election in Northern Ireland at a special polling station, the electoral officer shall grant the application if

(a) he is satisfied that the applicant's circumstances on the date of the poll will be or are likely to be such that he cannot reasonably be expected to vote in person at the polling station allotted or likely to be allotted to him under the parliamentary elections rules,

(b) he is satisfied that the applicant is or will be registered in the register of parliamentary electors, and

(c) the application meets the prescribed requirements.

(3) The electoral officer shall allot a special polling station to any person whose application under this paragraph is granted and shall send him a notice setting out the situation of the special polling station allotted to him and giving such other information as may be prescribed.

(4) There shall be included in the absent voters list in respect of each parliamentary election in Northern Ireland a list of persons whose applications under this paragraph have been granted, setting out, in the case of each person, the situation of the special polling station allotted to him and giving such other information as may be prescribed.

(5) For the purposes of this paragraph, the electoral officer

(a) shall designate special polling places and may by further designations from time to time alter any designation under this paragraph,

(b) shall publish such notice as he thinks is required of the situation of any place or places currently designated under this paragraph, and

(c) shall in respect of each parliamentary election, provide a special polling station in each special polling place, unless he is satisfied that the number of persons likely to vote there at that election does not justify it.

(6) Sub-paragraph (5) above has effect notwithstanding anything in section 18A of the principal Act.

Part II
Rules Relating to Special Polling Stations

2   The following paragraphs in this Part of this Schedule shall have effect for all purposes as additional rules in Schedule 1 to the principal Act.

3   The official mark on the ballot paper of those voting in respect of a constituency at a special polling station

(a) shall be different from the official mark on the ballot papers of those voting at the same election in respect of the constituency at polling stations allotted to them under the parliamentary elections rules, and

(b) shall be kept secret;

and an interval of seven years shall intervene between the use of the same official mark on ballot papers of those voting at special polling stations.

4 (1) The electoral officer shall provide each presiding officer at a special polling station with a list (in this Schedule referred to as "the special polling list") of those electors to whom the special polling station has been allotted, showing for each elector

(a) the constituency in respect of which he is or appears from the electors lists concerned to be entitled to be registered, and

(b) his electoral number.

(2) Rule 7(6) of the parliamentary elections rules applies for the purposes of this paragraph.

5 (1) The electoral officer may, after such consultation as appears to him to be desirable, appoint persons (including a candidates and their election agents) to attend special polling stations as observers, and each appointment of an observer

(a) shall be made in writing, and

(b) shall indicate the polling station or polling stations to which he is assigned,

(2) References in this Schedule to observers are references to observers appointed under this paragraph.

6 (1) When the electoral officer has received the ballot boxes and packets from all the special polling stations, he shall in the presence of each candidate wishing to attend or (if a candidate so chooses) his agent

(a) open each ballot box and count and record the number of ballot papers in it,

(b) verify each ballot paper account, and

(c) in the case of a general election or two or more by-elections, sort the ballot papers into separate packets for each constituency.

(2) The electoral officer shall give notice in writing to the candidates of the time and place at which he will begin to count the ballot papers under this paragraph, and no person

other than the candidates or (where they so choose) their agents may be present unless permitted by the electoral officer.

(3) A person not entitled to attend at the counting of ballot papers under this paragraph shall not be permitted to do so unless the electoral officer
    (a) is satisfied that the efficient counting of the ballot papers will not be impeded, and
    (b) has either consulted the candidates or, as the case may be, their agents or thought it impracticable to do so.

(4) The electoral officer shall give to the candidates or, as the case may be, their agents all such reasonable facilities for overseeing the proceedings, and all such information with respect to them, as he can give them consistently with the orderly conduct of the proceedings and the discharge of his duties in connection with them.

(5) The electoral officer shall verify each ballot paper account by comparing it with the number of ballot papers recorded by him, and the unused and spoilt ballot papers in his possession and the tendered votes list (opening and re-sealing the packets containing unused and spoilt ballot papers) and shall draw up a statement as to the result of the verification, which any candidate or, as the case may be, his agent may copy.

(6) In the case of a general election or two or more by-elections, each packet of ballot papers for a constituency, accompanied by a statement of the number of ballot papers, shall be sent to the place where the votes for that constituency are to be counted and the votes given on the ballot papers may, when
    (a) in the presence of the counting agents appointed under rule 30 of the parliamentary elections rules, the number of ballot papers in the packet has been counted and compared with the statement, and
    (b) those ballot papers have been mixed with the ballot papers from at least one ballot box not used at a special polling station,
be counted in accordance with the parliamentary elections rules (other than rule 45(1), (1A) and (5)).

(7) In any other case, the votes given on any ballot papers counted under this paragraph may, when they have been mixed with the ballot papers from at least one ballot box not used at a special polling station, be counted in accordance with the parliamentary elections rules (other than rule 45(1), (1A) and (5)).

(8) References in this paragraph to a candidate's agent are references to his election agent or to his counting agent appointed under rule 30 of the parliamentary elections rules to attend at the counting of the votes.

7 (1) On the completion of the counting at a contested election, the electoral officer shall, in relation to votes cast at special polling stations, forward to the Clerk of the Crown for Northern Ireland
    (a) the ballot paper accounts and the statements of rejected ballot papers and of the result of the verification of the ballot paper accounts,
    (b) the tendered votes list, the list of votes marked by the presiding officer and the related statements,
    (c) the packets of counterfoils, and
    (d) the special polling lists,
endorsing on each packet a description of its contents and the date of the election to which they relate.

(2) *Repealed*

Part III
Modifications of Parliamentary Elections Rules

8   Subject to the rules in Part II of this Schedule, the parliamentary elections rules shall have effect in relation to special polling stations so far as applicable to them, but subject to the modifications made by this Part of this Schedule.

9   References to the election shall in the case of a general election or two or more by elections be read as references to the elections in all the constituencies concerned in Northern Ireland and references to candidates at the election shall be construed accordingly.

10   References to a candidate's polling agent appointed to attend at a polling station shall be read as references to an observer assigned to that station.

11   References to the register of parliamentary electors for an election shall be read as references to the special polling list for that election.

12   Rule 5(2) shall apply to applications to vote at a special polling station and to other applications and notices about voting at such stations.

13   Rule 20(2) and (3) shall not apply.

14   Rules 23, 24 and 25(1) to (4) shall not apply.

15   Rules 28 and 29(3)(*c*) and (*d*) shall not apply.

16   Rule 30(1) to (9) shall not apply.

17   Rule 31 shall have effect as if
   (a) the reference to counting the votes were a reference to counting the ballot papers under this Schedule, and
   (b) references to provisions of section 66 of the principal Act were references to those provisions as they have effect by virtue of paragraph 27 below.

18   In rule 32
   (a) paragraph (1)(*a*) and (*e*), and
   (b) paragraphs (2), (3) and (4),
   shall not apply and the presiding officer shall not admit a person to a special polling station as observer except on production of his appointment.

19   Rule 35(1) shall have effect as if the question that may be put under sub-paragraph (*a*)(i) were "Are you the person shown in the special polling list for this election as follows?" (*read the whole entry from the list.*)

20   Rule 36(1) shall have effect as if the reference to a candidate or his election agent were omitted.

21   Rule 39 shall not apply.

22   Rule 40(1) shall apply as if, for sub-paragraphs (*a*) and (*b*), there were substituted a reference to a particular elector named in the special polling list.

23   Rules 44 and 45 shall not apply.

Part IV
Modifications of Representations of the People Acts

24   The Representation of the People Acts shall have effect as if the functions of the electoral officer under this Schedule were
    (a)   in the case of functions under paragraph 1(2) and (4) above, functions as registration officer, and
    (b)   in any other case, functions as returning officer.

25   The reference in section 53(1)(*c*) of the principal Act to voting by post or proxy includes a reference to voting at a special polling station.

26   Section 65(3) of the principal Act shall have effect as if the reference to counting the votes included a reference to counting the ballot papers under this Schedule.

27   Section 66 of the principal Act shall have effect as if
    (a)   the duty imposed by subsection (1) were imposed also on observers,
    (b)   the reference to the register of electors included a reference to the special polling list, and
    (c)   references to the counting of the votes included a reference to counting the ballot papers under this Schedule.

28   Paragraph 5A of Schedule 2 to the principal Act shall apply to applications under paragraph 1 above.

29   The second reference in section 5(5) of this Act to a polling station does not include a reference to a special polling station.

30   The references in section 12(3) of this Act to section 7 of this Act include a reference to paragraph 1 above.

SCHEDULE 2
MANNER OF VOTING

Repealed

SCHEDULE 3
PENALTIES

Repealed

SCHEDULE 4
MISCELLANEOUS AMENDMENTS OF THE PRINCIPAL ACT

Repealed

SCHEDULE 5
REPEALS

Not reproduced here

Representation of the People Act 2000

An Act to make new provision with respect to the registration of voters for the purposes of parliamentary and local government elections; to make other provision in relation to voting at such elections; and for connected purposes.

9th March 2000

PART I
ELECTORAL REGISTRATION AND FRANCHISE

PART II
CONDUCT OF ELECTIONS

PART III
MISCELLANEOUS AND GENERAL

PART II
CONDUCT OF ELECTIONS

New electoral procedures

Pilot schemes for local elections in England and Wales

10(1)   Where
   (a) a relevant local authority submit to the Secretary of State proposals for a scheme under this section to apply to particular local government elections held in the authority's area, and
   (b) those proposals are approved by the Secretary of State, either
      (i) without modification, or
      (ii) with such modifications as, after consulting the authority, he considers appropriate,
the Secretary of State shall by order make such provision for and in connection with the implementation of the scheme in relation to those elections as he considers appropriate (which may include provision modifying or disapplying any enactment).

(1A) Subsection (1) applies to proposals falling within that subsection which are submitted by a relevant local authority jointly with the Electoral Commission as if in that subsection
   (a) the first reference to any such authority in paragraph (a), and
   (b) the reference to the authority in paragraph (b)(ii),
were each a reference to the authority and the Commission; and, in a case where any such proposals are not jointly so submitted, the Secretary of State must consult the Commission before making an order under that subsection.

(2) A scheme under this section is a scheme which makes, in relation to local government elections in the area of a relevant local authority, provision differing in any respect from that made under or by virtue of the Representation of the People Acts as regards one or more of the following, namely
   (a) when, where and how voting at the elections is to take place;
   (b) how the votes cast at the elections are to be counted;
   (c) the sending by candidates of election communications free of charge for postage.

(3) Without prejudice to the generality of the preceding provisions of this section, a scheme under this section may make provision
   (a) for voting to take place on more than one day (whether each of those days is designated as a day of the poll or otherwise) and at places other than polling stations,
   (b) for postal charges incurred in respect of the sending of candidates' election communications as mentioned in subsection (2)(c) to be paid by the authority concerned,
and where a scheme makes such provision as is mentioned in paragraph (b), the Secretary of State's order under subsection (1) may make provision for disapplying section 75(1) of the 1983 Act (restriction on third party election expenditure) in relation to the payment of such charges by the authority.

(4) In subsection (2) the reference to local government elections in the area of a relevant local authority is a reference to such elections
   (a) throughout that area, or
   (b) in any particular part or parts of it,
as the scheme may provide.

(5) Where the Secretary of State makes an order under subsection (1)
   (a) he shall send a copy of the order to the authority concerned and to the Electoral Commission; and
   (b) that authority shall publish the order in their area in such manner as they think fit.

(6) Once any elections in relation to which a scheme under this section applied have taken place, the Electoral Commission shall prepare a report on the scheme.

(6A) The report shall be prepared by the Electoral Commission in consultation with the authority concerned; and that authority shall provide the Commission with such assistance as they may reasonably require in connection with the preparation of the report (which may, in particular, include the making by the authority of arrangements for ascertaining the views of voters about the operation of the scheme).

(7) The report shall, in particular, contain
   (a) a description of the scheme and of the respects in which the provision made by it differed from that made by or under the Representation of the People Acts;
   (b) a copy of the order of the Secretary of State under subsection (1); and
   (c) an assessment of the scheme's success or otherwise in facilitating

(i)   voting at the elections in question, and
(ii) (if it made provision as respects the counting of votes cast at those elections) the counting of votes,

or in encouraging voting at the elections in question or enabling voters to make informed decisions at those elections.

(8)   An assessment under subsection (7)(c)(i) shall include a statement by the authority concerned as to whether, in their opinion

(a)   the turnout of voters was higher than it would have been if the scheme had not applied;
(b)   voters found the procedures provided for their assistance by the scheme easy to use;
(c)   the procedures provided for by the scheme led to any increase in personation or other electoral offences or in any other malpractice in connection with elections;
(d)   those procedures led to any increase in expenditure, or to any savings, by the authority.

(9)   If the Secretary of State so requests in writing, the report shall also contain an assessment of such other matters relating to the scheme as are specified in his request.

(10) Once the Electoral Commission have prepared the report, they shall send a copy of the report

(a)   to the Secretary of State, and
(b)   to the authority concerned,

and that authority shall publish the report in their area, in such manner as they think fit, by the end of the period of three months beginning with the date of the declaration of the result of the elections in question.

(11) In this section "relevant local authority" means

(a)   as respects England
(i)   a county council, a district council or a London borough council, or
(ii)   once established, the Greater London Authority;
(b)   as respects Wales, a county council or a county borough council.

(12) For the purposes of this section proposals falling within subsection (1) and submitted to the Secretary of State before the date on which this Act is passed shall be as effective as those so submitted on or after that date.

NOTES

Defined terms   modifications: s 17(2)
  the 1983 Act: s 17(2)
  enactment: s 17(2)
  local government election: s 17(2)

Revision of procedures in the light of pilot schemes

11(1) If it appears to the Secretary of State, in the light of any report made under section 10 on a scheme under that section, that it would be desirable for provision similar to that made by the scheme to apply generally, and on a permanent basis, in relation to

(a)   local government elections in England and Wales, or
(b)   any particular description of such elections,

he may by order make such provision for and in connection with achieving that result as he considers appropriate (which may include provision modifying or disapplying any provision of an Act, including this Act).

The power of the Secretary of State to make such an order shall, however, be exercisable only on a recommendation of the Electoral Commission.

(2) An order under subsection (1)
    (a) may except from the operation of any of its provisions any local government area specified in the order; but
    (b) subject to that, must make the same provision
        (i) in relation to local government elections, or
        (ii) if it applies only to a particular description of such elections, in relation to elections of that description,
throughout England and Wales.

(3) An order under subsection (1) shall be made by statutory instrument; and no such order shall be made unless a draft of the statutory instrument containing the order has been laid before, and approved by a resolution of, each House of Parliament.

(4) When laying such a draft before either House of Parliament the Secretary of State shall also lay before that House a copy of every report under section 10 which relates to a scheme making provision similar to that made by the order.

(5) An order which excepts any local government area as mentioned in subsection (2) shall, if apart from this subsection it would be treated for the purposes of the standing orders of either House of Parliament as a hybrid instrument, proceed in that House as if it were not such an instrument.

(6) Rules made under section 36 of the 1983 Act (local elections in England and Wales) may make such provision as the Secretary of State considers appropriate in connection with any provision made by an order under subsection (1).

(7) Nothing in this section shall be taken as prejudicing the generality of any power contained in any other Act to make subordinate legislation (within the meaning of the Interpretation Act 1978) with respect to elections of any description.

NOTES

Defined terms   modify: s 17(2)
  the 1983 Act: s 17(2)
  local government area: s 17(2)
  local government election: s 17(2)

Manner of voting

Changes relating to absent voting at elections in Great Britain

12(1) Schedule 4 (which makes provision with respect to the manner of voting at elections, and in particular absent voting) shall have effect, as regards both
    (a) parliamentary elections, and
    (b) local government elections,
in relation to England, Wales and Scotland.

(2) Sections 5 to 9 of the Representation of the People Act 1985 (which, so far as applying in relation to England, Wales and Scotland, are superseded by the provisions of Schedule 4)
    (a) shall cease to have effect in relation to those parts of the United Kingdom; and
    (b) shall accordingly continue to have effect only in relation to Northern Ireland as regards parliamentary elections.

(3) Where immediately before the commencement of this section any list or record is kept by a registration officer under any provision of the Representation of the People Act 1985 which ceases to have effect in relation to England, Wales or Scotland in accordance with subsection (2)

(a) the list or record shall be taken, as from that commencement, to be the list or record required to be kept by him under the corresponding provision of Schedule 4 to this Act; and

(b) anything which, immediately before that commencement, is in the process of being done by him in relation to the list or record may be continued in relation to it as the list or record kept under that corresponding provision.

NOTES

Defined terms
    local government election: s 17(2)

Persons with disabilities

Assistance with voting for persons with disabilities

13   *Amends Schedule 1 to the Representation of the People Act 1983: not reproduced here*

PART III
MISCELLANEOUS AND GENERAL

14-16A   *Not reproduced here*

Citation, construction, commencement and extent

17(1)   This Act may be cited as the Representation of the People Act 2000, and shall be included among the Acts that may be cited as the Representation of the People Acts.

(2)   In this Act
    "the 1983 Act" means the Representation of the People Act 1983;
    "enactment" includes
        (a)   any provision of an Act (including this Act),
        (b)   any provision of, or of any instrument made under, an Act of the Scottish Parliament,
        (c)   any provision of, or of any instrument made under, Northern Ireland legislation, and
        (d)   any provision of subordinate legislation (within the meaning of the Interpretation Act 1978);
    "local election" has the same meaning as in the Electoral Law Act (Northern Ireland) 1962;
    "local government area" has the meaning given by section 203(1) of the 1983 Act;
    "local government election" has the meaning given (for England and Wales) by section 203(1) of the 1983 Act or (for Scotland) by section 204(1) of that Act;
    "modifications" includes additions, omissions and amendments (and "modify" has a corresponding meaning).

(3)   Apart from
        (a)   sections 10, 11, 14 and 16 and this section,
        (b)   Schedule 5, and
        (c)   paragraph 6 of Schedule 6,
    this Act does not come into force until such date as the Secretary of State may appoint by order made by statutory instrument; and different dates may be so appointed for different purposes.

(4)   An order under subsection (3) may contain such transitional provisions and savings (including provisions modifying enactments) as the Secretary of State considers appropriate.

(5) Subject to subsections (6) to (9), this Act extends to the whole of the United Kingdom.

(6) The following provisions extend to England, Wales and Scotland
   (a) section 12 and Schedule 4,
   (b) paragraph 7 of Schedule 6, and
   (c) Part II of Schedule 7.

(7) Sections 10 and 11 and paragraph 1 of Schedule 6 extend only to England and Wales.

(8) The amendments made by section 14 have the same extent as the Greater London Authority Act 1999.

(9) The following provisions extend only to Northern Ireland
   (a) Schedule 3,
   (b) paragraphs 13 to 17 of Schedule 6, and
   (c) Part III of Schedule 7.

Scotland Act 1998

An Act to provide for the establishment of a Scottish Parliament and Administration and other changes in the government of Scotland; to provide for changes in the constitution and functions of certain public authorities; to provide for the variation of the basic rate of income tax in relation to income of Scottish taxpayers in accordance with a resolution of the Scottish Parliament; to amend the law about parliamentary constituencies in Scotland; and for connected purposes.

19th November 1998

PART I
THE SCOTTISH PARLIAMENT

PART II
THE SCOTTISH ADMINISTRATION

PART III
FINANCIAL PROVISIONS

PART IVA

PART I

THE SCOTTISH PARLIAMENT

The Scottish Parliament

The Scottish Parliament

1(1)   There shall be a Scottish Parliament.

(2)   One member of the Parliament shall be returned for each constituency (under the simple majority system) at an election held in the constituency.

(3)   Members of the Parliament for each region shall be returned at a general election under the additional member system of proportional representation provided for in this Part and vacancies among such members shall be filled in accordance with this Part.

(4)   The validity of any proceedings of the Parliament is not affected by any vacancy in its membership.

(5)   Schedule 1 (which makes provision for the constituencies and regions for the purposes of this Act and the number of regional members) shall have effect.

NOTES

Defined terms
   constituencies: s 126(1)
   proceedings (in relation to the Parliament): s 126(1)

regions: s 126(1)

General elections

Ordinary general elections

2(1)   The day on which the poll at the first ordinary general election for membership of the Parliament shall be held, and the day, time and place for the meeting of the Parliament following that poll, shall be appointed by order made by the Secretary of State.

(2) The poll at subsequent ordinary general elections shall be held on the first Thursday in May in the fourth calendar year following that in which the previous ordinary general election was held, unless the day of the poll is determined by a proclamation under subsection (5).

(3) If the poll is to be held on the first Thursday in May, the Parliament
    (a) is dissolved by virtue of this section at the beginning of the minimum period which ends with that day, and
    (b) shall meet within the period of seven days beginning immediately after the day of the poll.

(4) In subsection (3), "the minimum period" means the period determined in accordance with an order under section 12(1).

(5) If the Presiding Officer proposes a day for the holding of the poll which is not more than one month earlier, nor more than one month later, than the first Thursday in May, Her Majesty may by proclamation under the Scottish Seal
    (a) dissolve the Parliament,
    (b) require the poll at the election to be held on the day proposed, and
    (c) require the Parliament to meet within the period of seven days beginning immediately after the day of the poll.

(5A) If, under this section as modified by virtue of an Act of the Scottish Parliament, the poll at an ordinary general election would, apart from subsection (5), be held on a day other than that provided by subsection (2) as originally enacted
    (a) references in subsections (3) and (5) to the first Thursday in May are to be read as references to that other day (if it is not the first Thursday in May), and
    (b) subsection (5B) applies to any day proposed under subsection (5).

(5B) The day proposed must not be the same as the day of the poll at
    (a) a parliamentary general election, other than an early parliamentary general election,
    (b) a European parliamentary general election, or
    (c) an ordinary local election.

(5C) In subsection (5B) "ordinary local election" has the meaning given by section 43(1C) of the Representation of the People Act 1983.

(6) In this Act "the Scottish Seal" means Her Majesty's Seal appointed by the Treaty of Union to be kept and used in Scotland in place of the Great Seal of Scotland.

NOTES

Defined terms   Scotland: s 126(1), (2)
    the Parliament: s 126(1)
    Presiding Officer: s 19

Extraordinary general elections

3(1) The Presiding Officer shall propose a day for the holding of a poll if
    (a) the Parliament resolves that it should be dissolved and, if the resolution is passed on a division, the number of members voting in favour of it is not less than two-thirds of the total number of seats for members of the Parliament, or
    (b) any period during which the Parliament is required under section 46 to nominate one of its members for appointment as First Minister ends without such a nomination being made.

(2) If the Presiding Officer makes such a proposal, Her Majesty may by proclamation under the Scottish Seal
    (a) dissolve the Parliament and require an extraordinary general election to be held,

(b) require the poll at the election to be held on the day proposed, and

(c) require the Parliament to meet within the period of seven days beginning immediately after the day of the poll.

(3) If a poll is held under this section within the period of six months ending with the day on which the poll at the next ordinary general election would be held (disregarding section 2(5)), that ordinary general election shall not be held.

(4) Subsection (3) does not affect the year in which the subsequent ordinary general election is to be held.

NOTES

Defined terms   the Scottish Seal: s 2(6)
  the Parliament: s 126(1)
  Presiding Officer: s 19

Calculating time for meeting of the Parliament

4   In calculating any period of days for the purposes of section 2(3)(b) or (5)(c) or section 3(2)(c), Saturday, Sunday, Christmas Eve, Christmas Day, Good Friday, a bank holiday in Scotland or a day appointed for public thanksgiving or mourning shall be disregarded.

Candidates

5(1) At a general election, the candidates may stand for return as constituency members or regional members.

(2) A person may not be a candidate to be a constituency member for more than one constituency.

(3) The candidates to be regional members shall be those included in a list submitted under subsection (4) or individual candidates.

(4) Any registered political party may submit to the regional returning officer a list of candidates to be regional members for a particular region (referred to in this Act, in relation to the region, as the party's "regional list").

(5) A registered political party's regional list has effect in relation to the general election and any vacancy occurring among the regional members after that election and before the next general election.

(6) Not more than twelve persons may be included in the list (but the list may include only one person).

(7) A registered political party's regional list must not include a person

(a) who is included in any other list submitted under subsection (4) for the region or any list submitted under that subsection for another region,

(b) who is an individual candidate to be a regional member for the region or another region,

(c) who is a candidate to be a constituency member for a constituency not included in the region, or

(d) who is a candidate to be a constituency member for a constituency included in the region but is not a candidate of that party.

(8) A person may not be an individual candidate to be a regional member for a particular region if he is

(a) included in a list submitted under subsection (4) for the region or another region,

(b) an individual candidate to be a regional member for another region,

(c) a candidate to be a constituency member for a constituency not included in the region, or

(d) a candidate of any registered political party to be a constituency member for a constituency included in the region.

(9) In this Act, "registered political party" means a party registered under Part II of the Political Parties, Elections and Referendums Act 2000.

NOTES

Defined terms
  constituencies: s 126(1)
  constituency member: s 126(1)
  regional member: s 126(1)

  regional returning officer: s 12(6)
  regions: s 126(1)

Poll for regional members

6(1) This section and sections 7 and 8 are about the return of regional members at a general election.

(2) In each of the constituencies for the Parliament, a poll shall be held at which each person entitled to vote as elector may give a vote (referred to in this Act as a "regional vote") for

(a) a registered political party which has submitted a regional list, or

(b) an individual candidate to be a regional member for the region.

(3) The right conferred on a person by subsection (2) is in addition to any right the person may have to vote in any poll for the return of a constituency member.

NOTES

Defined terms
  constituencies: s 126(1)
  constituency member: s 126(1)
  the Parliament: s 126(1)
  regional list: s 5(4)

  regional member: s 126(1)
  regions: s 126(1)
  registered political party: s 5(9)

Calculation of regional figures

7(1) The persons who are to be returned as constituency members for constituencies included in the region must be determined before the persons who are to be returned as the regional members for the region.

(2) For each registered political party which has submitted a regional list, the regional figure for the purposes of section 8 is

(a) the total number of regional votes given for the party in all the constituencies included in the region,

divided by

(b) the aggregate of one plus the number of candidates of the party returned as constituency members for any of those constituencies.

(3) Each time a seat is allocated to the party under section 8, that figure shall be recalculated by increasing (or further increasing) the aggregate in subsection (2)(b) by one.

(4) For each individual candidate to be a regional member for the region, the regional figure for the purposes of section 8 is the total number of regional votes given for him in all the constituencies included in the region.

NOTES

Defined terms
  constituencies: s 126(1)
  constituency member: s 126(1)
  regional list: s 5(4)
  regional member: s 126(1)

  regions: s 126(1)
  registered political party: s 5(9)

Allocation of seats to regional members

8(1) The first regional member seat shall be allocated to the registered political party or individual candidate with the highest regional figure.

(2) The second and subsequent regional member seats shall be allocated to the registered political party or individual candidate with the highest regional figure, after any recalculation required by section 7(3) has been carried out.

(3) An individual candidate already returned as a constituency or regional member shall be disregarded.

(4) Seats for the region which are allocated to a registered political party shall be filled by the persons in the party's regional list in the order in which they appear in the list.

(5) For the purposes of this section and section 10, a person in a registered political party's regional list who is returned as a member of the Parliament shall be treated as ceasing to be in the list (even if his return is void).

(6) Once a party's regional list has been exhausted (by the return of persons included in it as constituency members or by the previous application of subsection (1) or (2)) the party shall be disregarded.

(7) If (on the application of subsection (1) or any application of subsection (2)) the highest regional figure is the regional figure of two or more parties or individual candidates,
     (a) the subsection in question shall apply to each of them; or
     (b) if paragraph (a) would result in more than the correct number of seats for the region being allocated, the subsection in question shall apply as if the regional figure for each of those parties or candidates had been adjusted in accordance with subsection (8).

(8) The regional figure for a party or candidate is adjusted in accordance with this subsection by
     (a) adding one vote to the total number of regional votes given for the party or candidate in all the constituencies included in the region; and
     (b) (in the case of a party) recalculating the regional figure accordingly.

(9) If, on the application of the subsection in question in accordance with subsection (7)(b), seats would be allocated to two or more parties or individual candidates and that would result in more than the correct number of seats for the region being allocated, the regional returning officer shall decide between them by lot.

NOTES

Defined terms
constituencies: s 126(1)
constituency member: s 126(1)
the Parliament: s 126(1)
regional figure: s 7(2)
regional list: s 5(4)

regional member: s 126(1)
regions: s 126(1)
registered political party: s 5(9)

Vacancies

Constituency vacancies

9(1) Where the seat of a constituency member is vacant, an election shall be held to fill the vacancy (subject to subsection (4)).

(2) The date of the poll shall be fixed by the Presiding Officer.

(3) The date shall fall within the period of three months
     (a) beginning with the occurrence of the vacancy, or

(b) if the vacancy does not come to the notice of the Presiding Officer within the period of one month beginning with its occurrence, beginning when it does come to his notice.

(4) The election shall not be held if the latest date for holding the poll would fall within the period of three months ending with the day on which the poll at the next ordinary general election would be held (disregarding section 2(5)).

(5) For the purposes of this section, the date on which a vacancy is to be treated as occurring shall be determined under standing orders.

(6) A person may not be a candidate at such an election if he is a member of the Parliament or a candidate in another election to fill a vacancy.

NOTES

Defined terms
  constituencies: s 126(1)
  constituency member: s 126(1)
  the Parliament: s 126(1)

Presiding Officer: s 19
standing orders: s 126(1)

Regional vacancies

10(1) This section applies where the seat of a regional member is vacant.

(2) If the regional member was returned as an individual candidate, or the vacancy is not filled in accordance with the following provisions, the seat shall remain vacant until the next general election.

(3) If the regional member was returned (under section 8 or this section) from a registered political party's regional list, the regional returning officer shall notify the Presiding Officer of the name of the person who is to fill the vacancy.

(4) The regional returning officer shall ascertain from that party's regional list the name and address of the person whose name appears highest on that list ("the first choice") and shall take such steps as appear to him to be reasonable to contact the first choice to ask whether he will

(a) state in writing that he is willing and able to serve as a regional member for that region; and

(b) deliver a certificate signed by or on behalf of the nominating officer of the registered party which submitted that regional list stating that the first choice may be returned as a regional member from that list.

(4A) Where

(a) within such period as the regional returning officer considers reasonable

(i) he decides that the steps he has taken to contact the first choice have been unsuccessful; or

(ii) he has not received from that person the statement and certificate referred to in subsection (4); or

(b) the first choice has

(i) stated in writing that he is not willing to serve as a regional member for that region; or

(ii) failed to deliver the certificate referred to in subsection (4)(b),

the regional returning officer shall repeat the procedure required by subsection (4) in respect of the person (if any) whose name appears next in that list ("the second choice") or, where paragraph (a) or (b) of this subsection applies in respect of that person, in respect of the person (if any) whose name appears next highest after the second choice in that list; and the regional returning officer shall continue to repeat the procedure until the regional returning officer has notified the Presiding Officer of the name of the person who is to fill the vacancy or the names in the list are exhausted.

(5) Where a person whose name appears on that list provides the statement and certificate referred to in subsection (4), the regional returning officer shall notify to the Presiding Officer the name of that person.

(5A) Where

    (a) under subsection (4A), the regional returning officer has asked the second choice or a subsequent choice the questions referred to in subsection (4); and

    (b) the person who was asked those questions on an earlier occasion then provides the statement and certificate referred to in that subsection,

that statement and certificate shall have no effect unless and until the circumstances described in paragraph (a) or (b) of subsection (4A) apply in respect of the second choice or, as the case may be, of the subsequent choice.

(6) Where a person's name has been notified under subsection (3), this Act shall apply as if he had been declared to be returned as a regional member for the region on the day on which notification of his name was received by the Presiding Officer.

(7) For the purposes of this section, the date on which a vacancy is to be treated as occurring shall be determined under standing orders.

NOTES

Defined terms

Presiding Officer: s 19
regional list: s 5(4)
regional member: s 126(1)
regional returning officer: s 12(6)

regions: s 126(1)
registered political party: s 5(9)
standing orders: s 126(1)

Franchise and conduct of elections

Electors

11(1) The persons entitled to vote as electors at an election for membership of the Parliament held in any constituency are those who on the day of the poll

    (a) would be entitled to vote as electors at a local government election in an electoral area falling wholly or partly within the constituency, and

    (b) are registered in the register of local government electors at an address within the constituency.

(2) A person is not entitled to vote as elector in any constituency

    (a) more than once at a poll for the return of a constituency member, or

    (b) more than once at a poll for the return of regional members,

or to vote as elector in more than one constituency at a general election.

NOTES

Defined terms

constituencies: s 126(1)
constituency member: s 126(1)
the Parliament: s 126(1)

regional member: s 126(1)

Power of the Scottish Ministers to make provision about elections

12(1) The Scottish Ministers may by order make provision as to

    (a) the conduct of elections for membership of the Parliament, and

    (b) the questioning of such an election and the consequences of irregularities, *Repealed*

    (c) *Repealed*.

(2) The provision that may be made under subsection (1)(a) does not include provision that may be made by the Secretary of State under section 12A but, subject to that, includes, in particular, provision

    (a) about supplying or otherwise dealing with a register of electors,

    (b) *Repealed*

    (c) about the limitation of the election expenses of candidates, and

    (d) for the combination of polls at elections for membership of the Parliament with polls at other elections, if the conduct of the other election falls within the legislative competence of the Parliament,

    (e) *Repealed*

    (f) *Repealed.*

(3) *Repealed*

(4) An order under subsection (1) may

    (a) apply, with or without modifications or exceptions, any provision made by or under the Representation of the People Acts or the European Parliamentary Elections Act 2002 or by any other enactment relating to parliamentary elections, European Parliamentary elections or local government elections,

    (b) *Repealed*

    (c) *Repealed.*

(5) The return of a member of the Parliament at an election may be questioned only under Part III of the Representation of the People Act 1983 as applied by an order under subsection (1).

(6) For the purposes of this Act, the regional returning officer for any region is the person designated as such in accordance with an order made by the Scottish Ministers under this subsection.

(7) Before making an order under this section the Scottish Ministers must consult the Secretary of State.

NOTES

Subordinate Legislation
Scottish Parliament (Regional Returning Officers) (Scotland) Order 1999, SI 1999/270
Scottish Parliament (Elections etc) Order 1999, SI 1999/787
Scottish Parliament (Elections etc) Order 2010, SI 2010/2999
Scottish Parliament (Regional Returning Officers) (Revocation) Order 2015, SI 2015/743
Scottish Parliament (Elections etc) Order 2015, SSI 2015/425
Scottish Parliament Elections (Regional Returning Officers and Constituency Returning Officers) Order

2016, SSI 2016/9

Defined terms
constituency member: s 126(1)
modify: s 126(1)
parliamentary: s 126(1)
the Parliament: s 126(1)
regions: s 126(1)

Power of the Secretary of State to make provision about elections

12A(1) The Secretary of State may by regulations make provision

    (a) about the registration of electors,

    (b) for modifying the application of section 7(1) where the poll at an election for the return of a constituency member is abandoned (or notice of it is countermanded),

    (c) for modifying section 8(7) to ensure the allocation of the correct number of seats for the region, and

    (d) as to the return of members of the Parliament otherwise than at an election.

(2) The provision that may be made under subsection (1)(a) includes

    (a) provision for disregarding alterations in a register of electors, and

    (b) other provision about, or for purposes connected with, the content of a register or the effect of registration,

but subject to that it does not include provision about supplying or otherwise dealing with a register.

(3) The provision that may be made under subsection (1)(d) includes, in particular, provision modifying section 10(4) and (5).

(4) Regulations under subsection (1) may

    (a) apply, with or without modifications or exceptions, any provision made by or under the Representation of the People Acts or the European Parliamentary Elections Act 2002 or by any other enactment relating to parliamentary elections, European Parliamentary elections or local government elections, and

    (b) so far as may be necessary in consequence of any provision made by this Act or regulations under subsection (1), modify any provision made by any enactment relating to the registration of parliamentary electors or local government electors.

(5) Before making regulations under this section the Secretary of State must consult the Scottish Ministers.

NOTES
Defined terms
  constituency member: s 126(1)
  Scottish Ministers: s 44(2)

Duration of membership

Term of office of members

13 The term of office of a member of the Parliament begins on the day on which the member is declared to be returned and ends with the dissolution of the Parliament.

NOTES
Defined terms
  the Parliament: s 126(1)

Resignation of members

14 A member of the Parliament may at any time resign his seat by giving notice in writing to the Presiding Officer.

NOTES
Defined terms
  the Parliament: s 126(1)
  Presiding Officer: s 19

Disqualification

Disqualification from membership of the Parliament

15(1) A person is disqualified from being a member of the Parliament (subject to section 16) if

    (a) he is disqualified from being a member of the House of Commons under paragraphs (a) to (e) of section 1(1) of the House of Commons Disqualification Act 1975 (judges, civil servants, members of the armed forces, members of police forces and members of foreign legislatures),

    (b) he is disqualified otherwise than under that Act (either generally or in relation to a particular parliamentary constituency) from being a member of the House of Commons or from sitting and voting in it,

    (c) *Repealed* or

    (d) he is an officeholder of a description specified in an Order in Council made by Her Majesty under this subsection.

(2) An officeholder of a description specified in an Order in Council made by Her Majesty under this subsection is disqualified from being a member of the Parliament for any constituency or region of a description specified in the Order in relation to the officeholder.

(3) In this section "officeholder" includes employee or other post-holder.

NOTES

Subordinate Legislation
Scottish Parliament (Disqualification) Order 1999, SI 1999/680
Scottish Parliament (Disqualification) Order 2015, SSI 2015/350

Defined terms
constituencies: s 126(1)
the Parliament: s 126(1)
parliamentary: s 126(1)
regions: s 126(1)

Exceptions and relief from disqualification

16(1) A person is not disqualified from being a member of the Parliament merely because
    (a) he is a peer (whether of the United Kingdom, Great Britain, England or Scotland), or
    (b) he is a Lord Spiritual.

(2) A citizen of the European Union who is resident in the United Kingdom is not disqualified from being a member of the Parliament merely because of section 3 of the Act of Settlement (disqualification of persons born outside the United Kingdom other than certain Commonwealth citizens and citizens of the Republic of Ireland).

(3) Subsection (4) applies where a person was, or is alleged to have been, disqualified from being a member of the Parliament (either generally or in relation to a particular constituency or region) on any ground other than one falling within section 15(1)(b).

(4) The Parliament may resolve to disregard any disqualification incurred by that person on the ground in question if it considers that
    (a) the ground has been removed, and
    (b) it is proper to disregard any disqualification so incurred.

(5) A resolution under this section shall not
    (a) affect any proceedings under Part III of the Representation of the People Act 1983 as applied by an order under section 12, or
    (b) enable the Parliament to disregard any disqualification which has been established in such proceedings or in proceedings under section 18.

NOTES

Defined terms
constituencies: s 126(1)
the Parliament: s 126(1)

regions: s 126(1)

Effect of disqualification

17(1) If a person who is disqualified from being a member of the Parliament or from being a member for a particular constituency or region is returned as a member of the Parliament or (as the case may be) as a member for the constituency or region, his return shall be void and his seat vacant.

(2) If a member of the Parliament becomes disqualified from being a member of the Parliament or from being a member for the particular constituency or region for which he is sitting, he shall cease to be a member of the Parliament (so that his seat is vacant).

(3) Subsections (1) and (2) have effect subject to any resolution of the Parliament under section 16.

(4) Subsection (2) also has effect subject to section 427 of the Insolvency Act 1986 (sequestration etc); and where, in consequence of that section, the seat of a disqualified member of the Parliament is not vacant he shall not cease to be a member of the Parliament until his seat becomes vacant but

    (a) he shall not participate in any proceedings of the Parliament, and

    (b) any of his other rights and privileges as a member of the Parliament may be withdrawn by a resolution of the Parliament.

(5) The validity of any proceedings of the Parliament is not affected by the disqualification of any person from being a member of the Parliament or from being a member for the constituency or region for which he purports to sit.

NOTES

Defined terms   regions: s 126(1)

    constituencies: s 126(1)

    the Parliament: s 126(1)

    proceedings (in relation to the Parliament): s 126(1)

Judicial proceedings as to disqualification

18(1) Any person who claims that a person purporting to be a member of the Parliament is disqualified or has been disqualified at any time since being returned may apply to the Court of Session for a declarator to that effect.

(2) An application in respect of any person may be made whether the grounds on which it is made are alleged to have subsisted when the person was returned or to have arisen subsequently.

(3) No declarator shall be made

    (a) on grounds which subsisted when the person was returned, if an election petition is pending or has been tried in which the disqualification on those grounds of the person concerned is or was in issue, or

    (b) on any ground, if a resolution under section 16 requires that any disqualification incurred on that ground by the person concerned is to be disregarded.

(4) The person in respect of whom an application is made shall be the defender.

(5) The applicant shall give such caution for the expenses of the proceedings as the Court of Session may direct; but any such caution shall not exceed £5,000 or such other sum as the Scottish Ministers may by order specify.

(6) The decision of the court on an application under this section shall be final.

(7) In this section "disqualified" means disqualified from being a member of the Parliament or from being a member for the constituency or region for which the person concerned purports to sit.

NOTES

Defined terms   Scottish Ministers: s 44(2)

    constituencies: s 126(1)

    the Parliament: s 126(1)

    regions: s 126(1)

Interpretation of Acts of the Scottish Parliament etc

101(1) This section applies to

    (a) any provision of an Act of the Scottish Parliament, or of a Bill for such an Act, and

    (b) any provision of subordinate legislation made, confirmed or approved, or purporting to be made, confirmed or approved, by a member of the Scottish Government, which could be read in such a way as to be outside competence.

(2) Such a provision is to be read as narrowly as is required for it to be within competence, if such a reading is possible, and is to have effect accordingly.

(3) In this section "competence"
  (a) in relation to an Act of the Scottish Parliament, or a Bill for such an Act, means the legislative competence of the Parliament, and
  (b) in relation to subordinate legislation, means the powers conferred by virtue of this Act.

NOTES

Defined terms

Act of the Scottish Parliament: s 28(1)
Bill: s 28(2)
by virtue of: s 126(11)
legislative competence: s 29

member of the Scottish Government: s 44(1)
the Parliament: s 126(1)
subordinate legislation: s 126(1)

Final provisions

Interpretation

126(1) In this Act
  "body" includes unincorporated association,
  "constituencies" and "regions", in relation to the Parliament, mean the constituencies and regions provided for by Schedule 1,
  "constituency member" means a member of the Parliament for a constituency,
  "the Convention rights" has the same meaning as in the Human Rights Act 1998,
  "document" means anything in which information is recorded in any form (and references to producing a document are to be read accordingly),
  "enactment" includes an Act of the Scottish Parliament, Northern Ireland legislation (within the meaning of the Northern Ireland Act 1998) and an enactment comprised in subordinate legislation, and includes an enactment comprised in, or in subordinate legislation under, an Act of Parliament, whenever passed or made,
  "financial year" means a year ending with 31st March,
  "functions" includes powers and duties, and "confer", in relation to functions, includes impose,
  "government department" means any department of the Government of the United Kingdom,
  "the Human Rights Convention" means
    (a) the Convention for the Protection of Human Rights and Fundamental Freedoms, agreed by the Council of Europe at Rome on 4th November 1950, and
    (b) the Protocols to the Convention,
  as they have effect for the time being in relation to the United Kingdom,
  "Minister of the Crown" includes the Treasury,
  "modify" includes amend or repeal,
  "occupational pension scheme", "personal pension scheme" and "public service pension scheme" have the meanings given by section 1 of the Pension Schemes Act 1993,
  "the Parliament" means the Scottish Parliament,
  "parliamentary", in relation to constituencies, elections and electors, is to be taken to refer to the Parliament of the United Kingdom,
  "prerogative instrument" means an Order in Council, warrant, charter or other instrument made under the prerogative,
  "the principal appointed day" means the day appointed by an order under section 130 which is designated by the order as the principal appointed day,

"proceedings", in relation to the Parliament, includes proceedings of any committee or subcommittee,

"property" includes rights and interests of any description,

"regional member" means a member of the Parliament for a region,

"Scotland" includes so much of the internal waters and territorial sea of the United Kingdom as are adjacent to Scotland,

"Scottish public authority" means any public body (except the Parliamentary corporation), public office or holder of such an office whose functions (in each case) are exercisable only in or as regards Scotland,

"the Scottish zone" means the sea within British fishery limits (that is, the limits set by or under section 1 of the Fishery Limits Act 1976) which is adjacent to Scotland,

"standing orders" means standing orders of the Parliament,

"subordinate legislation" has the same meaning as in the Interpretation Act 1978 and also includes an instrument made under an Act of the Scottish Parliament,

"tribunal" means any tribunal in which legal proceedings may be brought.

(2) Her Majesty may by Order in Council determine, or make provision for determining, for the purposes of this Act any boundary between waters which are to be treated as internal waters or territorial sea of the United Kingdom, or sea within British fishery limits, adjacent to Scotland and those which are not.

(3) For the purposes of this Act

    (a) the question whether any function of a body, government department, office or officeholder relates to reserved matters is to be determined by reference to the purpose for which the function is exercisable, having regard (among other things) to the likely effects in all the circumstances of any exercise of the function, but

    (b) bodies to which paragraph 3 of Part III of Schedule 5 applies are to be treated as if all their functions were functions which relate to reserved matters.

(4) References in this Act to Scots private law are to the following areas of the civil law of Scotland

    (a) the general principles of private law (including private international law),

    (b) the law of persons (including natural persons, legal persons and unincorporated bodies),

    (c) the law of obligations (including obligations arising from contract, unilateral promise, delict, unjustified enrichment and negotiorum gestio),

    (d) the law of property (including heritable and moveable property, trusts and succession), and

    (e) the law of actions (including jurisdiction, remedies, evidence, procedure, diligence, recognition and enforcement of court orders, limitation of actions and arbitration),

and include references to judicial review of administrative action.

(5) References in this Act to Scots criminal law include criminal offences, jurisdiction, evidence, procedure and penalties and the treatment of offenders.

(6) References in this Act and in any other enactment to the Scottish Administration are to the officeholders in the Scottish Administration and the members of the staff of the Scottish Administration.

(7) For the purposes of this Act

    (a) references to officeholders in the Scottish Administration are to

        (i) members of the Scottish Government and junior Scottish Ministers, and

        (ii) the holders of offices in the Scottish Administration which are not ministerial offices, and

(b) references to members of the staff of the Scottish Administration are to the staff of the persons referred to in paragraph (a).

(8) For the purposes of this Act, the offices in the Scottish Administration which are not ministerial offices are
(a) the Registrar General of Births, Deaths and Marriages for Scotland, the Keeper of the Registers of Scotland and the Keeper of the Records of Scotland, and
(b) any other office of a description specified in an Order in Council made by Her Majesty under this subsection.

(9) In this Act
(a) all those rights, powers, liabilities, obligations and restrictions from time to time created or arising by or under the EU Treaties, and
(b) all those remedies and procedures from time to time provided for by or under the EU Treaties,
are referred to as "EU law".

(10) In this Act, "international obligations" means any international obligations of the United Kingdom other than obligations to observe and implement EU law or the Convention rights.

(11) In this Act, "by virtue of" includes "by" and "under".

Index of defined expressions

127 In this Act, the expressions listed in the left-hand column have the meaning given by, or are to be interpreted in accordance with, the provisions listed in the right-hand column.

scheme	
Officeholders in the Scottish Administration	Section 126(7)
Offices in the Scottish Administration which are not ministerial offices	Section 126(8)
Open power	Section 112(3)
The Parliament	Section 126(1)
"parliamentary" (in relation to constituencies, elections and electors)	Section 126(1)
The Parliamentary corporation	Section 21(1)
Pre-commencement enactment	Section 53(3)
Prerogative instrument	Section 126(1)
Presiding Officer	Section 19
Principal appointed day	Section 126(1)
Proceedings	Section 126(1)
Property	Section 126(1)
Regional list (in relation to a party)	Section 5(4)
Regional returning officer	Section 12(6)
Regional vote	Section 6(2)
Regions and regional member	Section 126(1)
Registered political party	Section 5(9)
Reserved matters	Schedule 5
Retained functions (in relation to the Lord Advocate)	Section 52(6)
Scotland	Section 126(1) and (2)
Scots criminal law	Section 126(5)
Scots private law	Section 126(4)
Scottish Administration	Section 126(6)
Scottish Ministers	Section 44(2)
Scottish public authority	Section 126(1)
Scottish public authority with mixed functions or no reserved functions	Paragraphs 1 and 2 of Part III of Schedule 5
Scottish Seal	Section 2(6)
The Scottish zone	Section 126(1)
Staff of the Parliament	Paragraph 3 of Schedule 2
Standing orders	Section 126(1)
Subordinate legislation	Section 126(1)
Tribunal	Section 126(1)

Schedule 1

Constituencies, Regions and Regional Members

General

1(1) There are to be 73 constituencies for the purposes of this Act.

(2) The constituencies are

    (a) the Orkney Islands,

    (b) the Shetland Islands, and

    (c) the constituencies provided for by an Order in Council under paragraph 6.

(3) *Repealed*

2(1) There are to be eight regions for the purposes of this Act.

(2)   The regions are the regions provided for by an Order in Council under paragraph 6.

(3)   Seven regional members are to be returned for each region.

Reports of the Boundary Commission for Scotland

3(1)   The Boundary Commission for Scotland must keep under review the boundaries of the constituencies (other than those mentioned in paragraph 1(2)(a) and (b)).

(2)   The review must be conducted in accordance with the constituency rules.

(3)   The Boundary Commission for Scotland must submit to the Secretary of State a report
      (a) showing the alterations they propose to the boundaries, or
      (b) stating that in their opinion no alteration should be made.

(4)   The first report of the Boundary Commission for Scotland under this paragraph must be submitted to the Secretary of State not later than 30 June 2010.

(5)   Subsequent reports must be submitted not less than eight nor more than twelve years after the date of the submission of the last report.

(6)   The Boundary Commission for Scotland may also from time to time (but not before the submission of their first report) submit to the Secretary of State reports with respect to the area comprised in any two or more constituencies showing the constituencies into which they recommend the area should be divided in order to give effect to the constituency rules.

(7)   A report under sub-paragraph (6) must recommend the same number of constituencies as that in which the area is comprised.

(8)   A report of the Boundary Commission for Scotland which recommends an alteration to the boundaries of constituencies must state as respects each constituency
      (a) the name by which they recommend it is to be known;
      (b) whether they recommend that it is to be a county or a burgh constituency.

(9)   As soon as practicable after the Boundary Commission for Scotland have submitted a report to the Secretary of State under this paragraph he must lay before Parliament
      (a) the report, and
      (b) the draft of an Order in Council for giving effect to the recommendations contained in the report.

(10)   Sub-paragraph (9)(b) does not apply if the report states that no alteration is required to be made to the boundaries of the constituencies.

(11)   The Boundary Commission for Scotland must at the same time as they submit a report in accordance with sub-paragraph (3) or (6) lay any report recommending an alteration in the constituencies before the Parliament.

4(1)   This paragraph applies if the Boundary Commission for Scotland submit a report to the Secretary of State recommending an alteration in a constituency.

(2)   In the report the Boundary Commission for Scotland must recommend any alteration in any of the regions which they think is necessary to give effect to the regional rules.

(3)   A report making a recommendation for an alteration in a region must recommend the name by which the Boundary Commission for Scotland think the region should be known.

5   *Repealed*

Orders in Council

6(1)   The draft of an Order in Council laid before Parliament by the Secretary of State for giving effect to the recommendations contained in a report by the Boundary Commission for Scotland under paragraph 3 may make provision for any matters which he thinks are incidental to or consequential on the recommendations.

(2)   If the draft is approved by resolution of each House of Parliament the Secretary of State must submit it to Her Majesty in Council.

(3)   If a motion for the approval of the draft is rejected by either House of Parliament or withdrawn by leave of the House the Secretary of State may amend the draft and lay the amended draft before Parliament.

(4)   If the draft as so amended is approved by resolution of each House of Parliament the Secretary of State must submit it to Her Majesty in Council.

(5)   If a draft of an Order in Council is submitted to Her Majesty in Council under this Schedule, Her Majesty in Council may make an order in terms of the draft.

(6)   An Order in Council made as mentioned in sub-paragraph (5) comes into force on the date specified in the Order.

(7)   The coming into force of the Order does not affect the return of any member to the Parliament or its constitution until the Parliament is dissolved.

(8)   The validity of an Order in Council purporting to be made under this Schedule and reciting that a draft of the Order has been approved by a resolution of each House of Parliament must not be called in question in any legal proceedings whatsoever.

Notice of proposed report or recommendations

7(1)   If the Boundary Commission for Scotland intend to consider making a report under this Schedule
  (a)   they must inform the Secretary of State by notice in writing;
  (b)   they must publish a copy of the notice in the Edinburgh Gazette.

(2)   If the Boundary Commission for Scotland have provisionally determined to make recommendations affecting a constituency they must publish in at least one newspaper circulating in the constituency a notice stating
  (a)   the effect of the proposed recommendations and (except if the effect is that no alteration should be made in respect of the constituency) that a copy of the recommendations is open to inspection at a specified place in the constituency, and
  (b)   that representations with respect to the proposed recommendations may be made to the Commission before the end of the period of one month starting the day after the notice is published.

(3)   The Boundary Commission for Scotland must take into account any representations made in accordance with the notice.

(4)   If the Boundary Commission for Scotland revise any proposed recommendations after publishing notice of them under sub-paragraph (2) they must comply again with sub-paragraphs (2) and (3) in relation to the revised recommendations as if no earlier notice had been published.

(5)   *Repealed*

8(1)   This paragraph applies if the Boundary Commission for Scotland provisionally determine to make recommendations which would involve any alteration in a constituency.

(2) The Boundary Commission for Scotland must consider whether any alteration within paragraph 4(2) would be required in order to give effect to the regional rules.

(3) *Repealed*

(4) Paragraph 7 applies for the purposes of the proposed recommendations as if for any reference to a constituency there is substituted a reference to a region.

Local inquiries

9(1) The Boundary Commission for Scotland may if they think fit cause a local inquiry to be held in respect of any constituency or constituencies.

(2) If the Boundary Commission for Scotland receive any relevant representations objecting to a proposed recommendation for the alteration of a constituency they must not make the recommendation unless since the publication of the notice under paragraph 7(2) a local inquiry has been held in respect of the constituency.

(3) If a local inquiry was held in respect of the constituency before the publication of the notice under paragraph 7(2), sub-paragraph (2) above does not apply if the Boundary Commission for Scotland after considering
    (a) the matters discussed at the inquiry,
    (b) the nature of the relevant representations received, and
    (c) any other relevant circumstances,
think that a further local inquiry is not justified.

(4) A relevant representation is a representation made in accordance with paragraph 7(2)(b)
    (a) by the council for an area which is wholly or partly comprised in the constituency;
    (b) by a body of not less than 100 persons entitled to vote as electors at an election for membership of the Parliament held in the constituency.

10(1) The Boundary Commission for Scotland may if they think fit cause a local inquiry to be held in respect of any region or regions.

(2) If the Boundary Commission for Scotland receive any relevant representations objecting to a proposed recommendation for the alteration of a region they must not make the recommendation unless since the publication of the notice under paragraph 7(2) a local inquiry has been held in respect of the region.

(3) If a local inquiry was held in respect of the region before the publication of the notice under paragraph 7(2), sub-paragraph (2) above does not apply if the Boundary Commission for Scotland after considering
    (a) the matters discussed at the inquiry,
    (b) the nature of the relevant representations received, and
    (c) any other relevant circumstances,
think that a further local inquiry is not justified.

(4) A relevant representation is a representation made in accordance with paragraph 7(2)(b)
    (a) by the council for an area which is wholly or partly included in the region;
    (b) by a body of not less than 500 persons entitled to vote as electors at an election for membership of the Parliament held in any one or more of the constituencies included in the region.

11 Section 210(4) and (5) of the Local Government (Scotland) Act 1973 (c 69) (attendance of witnesses at inquiries) applies in relation to a local inquiry held under paragraph 9 or 10.

The constituency rules

12 These are the constituency rules.

Rule 1

(1) So far as is practicable, regard must be had to the boundaries of the local government areas having effect from time to time under section 1 of the Local Government etc (Scotland) Act 1994.

(2) *Repealed*

Rule 2

(1) The electorate of a constituency must be as near the electoral quota as is practicable, having regard to Rule 1.

(2) The Boundary Commission for Scotland may depart from the strict application of Rule 1 if they think that it is desirable to do so to avoid an excessive disparity between the electorate of a constituency and the electoral quota or between the electorate of a constituency and that of neighbouring constituencies.

(3) The electoral quota is the number obtained by dividing the total electorate by 71.

(4) The electorate of a constituency is the aggregate of the persons falling within paragraphs (5) and (6) below.

(5) A person falls within this paragraph if his name appears on the register of local government electors in force on the enumeration date under the Representation of the People Acts for a local government area which is situated wholly in the constituency.

(6) A person falls within this paragraph if his name appears on the register of local government electors in force on the enumeration date under the Representation of the People Acts for a local government area which is situated partly in the constituency and his qualifying address is situated in the constituency.

(7) The total electorate is the total number of persons whose names appear on the registers of local government electors in force on the enumeration date under the Representation of the People Acts for all of the local government areas in Scotland (except the local government areas of Orkney and Shetland).

(8) The enumeration date is, in relation to a report of the Boundary Commission for Scotland, the date on which notice with respect to the report is published in the Edinburgh Gazette in accordance with paragraph 7(1) above.

(9) "Qualifying address" and "local government area" have the same meanings as in the Representation

Rule 3

The Boundary Commission for Scotland may depart from the strict application of Rules 1 and 2 if they think that special geographical considerations (including in particular the size, shape and accessibility of a constituency).

Rule 4

The Boundary Commission for Scotland need not aim at giving full effect in all circumstances to Rules 1 to 3 but they must take account (so far as they reasonably can)—

(a) of the inconveniences attendant on alterations of constituencies other than alterations made for the purposes of Rule 1, and

(b) of any local ties which would be broken by such alterations.

The regional rules

13   These are the regional rules.

Rule 1

A constituency must fall wholly within a region.

Rule 2

The regional electorate of a region must be as near the regional electorate of each of the other regions as is practicable, having regard (where appropriate) to special geographical considerations.

14(1) This paragraph applies for the purposes of the regional rules.

(2) For the purposes of a report of the Boundary Commission for Scotland in relation to a region, the regional electorate is the number of persons

(a) whose names appear on the enumeration date on the registers of local government electors in the region, and

(b) who are registered at addresses within a constituency included in the region.

(3) The enumeration date is the date on which notice with respect to the report is published in the Edinburgh Gazette in accordance with paragraph 7(1) above.

(4) *Repealed*

NOTES

Subordinate Legislation
Scottish Parliament (Constituencies and Regions) Order 2010, SI 2010/2691
Scottish Parliament (Constituencies and Regions) Order 2014, SI 2014/501

Defined terms
constituencies: s 126(1)
the Parliament: s 126(1)
regional member: s 126(1)
regions: s 126(1)
Scotland: s 126(1), (2)

Senior Courts Act 1981

142 Selection of judges for trial of election petitions

(1) The judges to be placed on the rota for the trial of parliamentary election petitions in England and Wales under Part III of the Representation of the People Act 1983 in each year shall be selected, in such manner as may be provided by rules of court, from the judges of the Queen's Bench Division of the High Court exclusive of any who are members of the House of Lords.

(2) Notwithstanding the expiry of the year for which a judge has been placed on the rota he may act as if that year had not expired for the purpose of continuing to deal with, giving judgment in, or dealing with any ancillary matter relating to, any case with which he may have been concerned during that year.

(3) Any judge placed on the rota shall be eligible to be placed on the rota again in the succeeding or any subsequent year.

NOTES

Subordinate Legislation
  Election Judges Rota Rules 2015, SI 2015/329

Defined terms
  judgment: s 151(1)

Trade Union and Labour Relations (Consolidation) Act 1992

An Act to consolidate the enactments relating to collective labour relations, that is to say, to trade unions, employers' associations, industrial relations and industrial action

16th July 1992

PART I
TRADE UNIONS

Chapter I
Introductory

Chapters II-V

Chapter VI
Application of Funds for Political Objects

_____

PART I
TRADE UNIONS

Chapter I
Introductory

Meaning of "trade union"

Meaning of "trade union"

1 In this Act a "trade union" means an organisation (whether temporary or permanent)

   (a) which consists wholly or mainly of workers of one or more descriptions and whose principal purposes include the regulation of relations between workers of that description or those descriptions and employers or employers' associations; or

   (b) which consists wholly or mainly of

      (i) constituent or affiliated organisations which fulfil the conditions in paragraph (a) (or themselves consist wholly or mainly of constituent or affiliated organisations which fulfil those conditions), or

      (ii) representatives of such constituent or affiliated organisations, and whose principal purposes include the regulation of relations between workers and employers or between workers and employers' associations, or the regulation of relations between its constituent or affiliated organisations.

2-69   *Not reproduced*

Chapter VI
Application of Funds for Political Objects

Restriction on use of funds for certain political objects

Restriction on use of funds for political objects

71(1)   The funds of a trade union shall not be applied in the furtherance of the political objects to which this Chapter applies unless

(a)   there is in force in accordance with this Chapter a resolution (a "political resolution") approving the furtherance of those objects as an object of the union (see sections 73 to 81), and

(b)   there are in force rules of the union as to

(i)   the making of payments in furtherance of those objects out of a separate fund, and

(ii)   the exemption of any member of the union objecting to contribute to that fund,

which comply with this Chapter (see sections 82, 84 and 85) and have been approved by the Certification Officer.

(2)   This applies whether the funds are so applied directly, or in conjunction with another trade union, association or body, or otherwise indirectly.

NOTES

Defined terms
    rules (of a trade union): ss 119, 299
    trade union: ss 1, 299

Political objects to which restriction applies

72(1)   The political objects to which this Chapter applies are the expenditure of money

(a)   on any contribution to the funds of, or on the payment of expenses incurred directly or indirectly by, a political party;

(b)   on the provision of any service or property for use by or on behalf of any political party;

(c)   in connection with the registration of electors, the candidature of any person, the selection of any candidate or the holding of any ballot by the union in connection with any election to a political office;

(d)   on the maintenance of any holder of a political office;

(e)   on the holding of any conference or meeting by or on behalf of a political party or of any other meeting the main purpose of which is the transaction of business in connection with a political party;

(f)   on the production, publication or distribution of any literature, document, film, sound recording or advertisement the main purpose of which is to persuade people to vote for a political party or candidate or to persuade them not to vote for a political party or candidate.

(2)   Where a person attends a conference or meeting as a delegate or otherwise as a participator in the proceedings, any expenditure incurred in connection with his attendance as such shall, for the purposes of subsection (1)(e), be taken to be expenditure incurred on the holding of the conference or meeting.

(3) In determining for the purposes of subsection (1) whether a trade union has incurred expenditure of a kind mentioned in that subsection, no account shall be taken of the ordinary administrative expenses of the union.

(4) In this section

"candidate" means a candidate for election to a political office and includes a prospective candidate;

"contribution", in relation to the funds of a political party, includes any fee payable for affiliation to, or membership of, the party and any loan made to the party;

"electors" means electors at an election to a political office;

"film" includes any record, however made, of a sequence of visual images, which is capable of being used as a means of showing that sequence as a moving picture;

"local authority" means a local authority within the meaning of section 270 of the Local Government Act 1972 or section 235 of the Local Government (Scotland) Act 1973; and

"political office" means the office of member of Parliament, member of the European Parliament or member of a local authority or any position within a political party.

NOTES
Defined terms
   trade union: ss 1, 299

Application of funds in breach of section 71

72A(1) A person who is a member of a trade union and who claims that it has applied its funds in breach of section 71 may apply to the Certification Officer for a declaration that it has done so.

(2) On an application under this section the Certification Officer
   (a) shall make such enquiries as he thinks fit,
   (b) shall give the applicant and the union an opportunity to be heard,
   (c) shall ensure that, so far as is reasonably practicable, the application is determined within six months of being made,
   (d) may make or refuse the declaration asked for,
   (e) shall, whether he makes or refuses the declaration, give reasons for his decision in writing, and
   (f) may make written observations on any matter arising from, or connected with, the proceedings.

(3) If he makes a declaration he shall specify in it
   (a) the provisions of section 71 breached, and
   (b) the amount of the funds applied in breach.

(4) If he makes a declaration and is satisfied that the union has taken or agreed to take steps with a view to
   (a) remedying the declared breach, or
   (b) securing that a breach of the same or any similar kind does not occur in future,
   he shall specify those steps in making the declaration.

(5) If he makes a declaration he may make such order for remedying the breach as he thinks just under the circumstances.

(6) Where the Certification Officer requests a person to furnish information to him in connection with enquiries made by him under this section, he shall specify the date by which that information is to be furnished and, unless he considers that it would be inappropriate to do so, shall proceed with his determination of the application

notwithstanding that the information has not been furnished to him by the specified date.

(7) A declaration made by the Certification Officer under this section may be relied on as if it were a declaration made by the court.

(8) Where an order has been made under this section, any person who is a member of the union and was a member at the time it was made is entitled to enforce obedience to the order as if he had made the application on which the order was made.

(9) An order made by the Certification Officer under this section may be enforced in the same way as an order of the court.

(10) If a person applies to the Certification Officer under this section in relation to an alleged breach he may not apply to the court in relation to the breach; but nothing in this subsection shall prevent such a person from exercising any right to appeal against or challenge the Certification Officer's decision on the application to him.

(11) If
(a) a person applies to the court in relation to an alleged breach, and
(b) the breach is one in relation to which he could have made an application to the Certification Officer under this section,

he may not apply to the Certification Officer under this section in relation to the breach.

NOTES

Defined terms
the court: ss 121, 299
trade union: ss 1, 299

Political resolution

Passing and effect of political resolution

73(1) A political resolution must be passed by a majority of those voting on a ballot of the members of the trade union held in accordance with this Chapter.

(2) A political resolution so passed shall take effect as if it were a rule of the union and may be rescinded in the same manner and subject to the same provisions as such a rule.

(3) If not previously rescinded, a political resolution shall cease to have effect at the end of the period of ten years beginning with the date of the ballot on which it was passed.

(4) Where before the end of that period a ballot is held on a new political resolution, then
(a) if the new resolution is passed, the old resolution shall be treated as rescinded, and
(b) if it is not passed, the old resolution shall cease to have effect at the end of the period of two weeks beginning with the date of the ballot.

NOTES

Defined terms
date of the ballot: s 96
political resolution: s 71(1)
rules (of a trade union): ss 119, 299

trade union: ss 1, 299

Approval of political ballot rules

74(1) A ballot on a political resolution must be held in accordance with rules of the trade union (its "political ballot rules") approved by the Certification Officer.

(2)   Fresh approval is required for the purposes of each ballot which it is proposed to hold, notwithstanding that the rules have been approved for the purposes of an earlier ballot.

(3)   The Certification Officer shall not approve a union's political ballot rules unless he is satisfied that the requirements set out in
>   section 75 (appointment of independent scrutineer),
>   section 76 (entitlement to vote),
>   section 77 (voting),
>   section 77A (counting of votes etc by independent person), and
>   section 78 (scrutineer's report),

would be satisfied in relation to a ballot held by the union in accordance with the rules.

NOTES

Defined terms   trade union: ss 1, 299
  political resolution: s 71(1)
  rules (of a trade union): ss 119, 299

Appointment of independent scrutineer

75(1)   The trade union shall, before the ballot is held, appoint a qualified independent person ("the scrutineer") to carry out
>   (a)   the functions in relation to the ballot which are required under this section to be contained in his appointment; and
>   (b)   such additional functions in relation to the ballot as may be specified in his appointment.

(2)   A person is a qualified independent person in relation to a ballot if
>   (a)   he satisfies such conditions as may be specified for the purposes of this section by order of the Secretary of State or is himself so specified; and
>   (b)   the trade union has no grounds for believing either that he will carry out any functions conferred on him in relation to the ballot otherwise than competently or that his independence in relation to the union, or in relation to the ballot, might reasonably be called into question.

An order under paragraph (a) shall be made by statutory instrument which shall be subject to annulment in pursuance of a resolution of either House of Parliament.

(3)   The scrutineer's appointment shall require him
>   (a)   to be the person who supervises the production of the voting papers and (unless he is appointed under section 77A to undertake the distribution of the voting papers) their distribution and to whom the voting papers are returned by those voting;
>   (aa)   to
>>   (i)   inspect the register of names and addresses of the members of the trade union, or
>>   (ii)   examine the copy of the register as at the relevant date which is supplied to him in accordance with subsection (5A)(a),

whenever it appears to him appropriate to do so and, in particular, when the conditions specified in subsection (3A) are satisfied;
>   (b)   to take such steps as appear to him to be appropriate for the purpose of enabling him to make his report (see section 78);
>   (c)   to make his report to the trade union as soon as reasonably practicable after the last date for the return of voting papers; and
>   (d)   to retain custody of all voting papers returned for the purposes of the ballot and the copy of the register supplied to him in accordance with subsection (5A)(a)
>>   (i)   until the end of the period of one year beginning with the announcement by the union of the result of the ballot; and

      (ii)   if within that period an application is made under section 79 (complaint of failure to comply with ballot rules), until the Certification Officer or the court authorises him to dispose of the papers or copy.

(3A)   The conditions referred to in subsection (3)(aa) are

     (a)   that a request that the scrutineer inspect the register or examine the copy is made to him during the appropriate period by a member of the trade union who suspects that the register is not, or at the relevant date was not, accurate and uptodate, and

     (b)   that the scrutineer does not consider that the member's suspicion is illfounded.

(3B)   In subsection (3A) "the appropriate period" means the period

     (a)   beginning with the day on which the scrutineer is appointed, and

     (b)   ending with the day before the day on which the scrutineer makes his report to the trade union.

(3C)   The duty of confidentiality as respects the register is incorporated in the scrutineer's appointment.

(4)   The trade union shall ensure that nothing in the terms of the scrutineer's appointment (including any additional functions specified in the appointment) is such as to make it reasonable for any person to call the scrutineer's independence in relation to the union into question.

(5)   The trade union shall, before the scrutineer begins to carry out his functions, either

     (a)   send a notice stating the name of the scrutineer to every member of the union to whom it is reasonably practicable to send such a notice, or

     (b)   take all such other steps for notifying members of the name of the scrutineer as it is the practice of the union to take when matters of general interest to all its members need to be brought to their attention.

(5A)   The trade union shall

     (a)   supply to the scrutineer as soon as is reasonably practicable after the relevant date a copy of the register of names and addresses of its members as at that date, and

     (b)   comply with any request made by the scrutineer to inspect the register.

(5B)   Where the register is kept by means of a computer the duty imposed on the trade union by subsection (5A)(a) is either to supply a legible printed copy or (if the scrutineer prefers) to supply a copy of the computer data and allow the scrutineer use of the computer to read it at any time during the period when he is required to retain custody of the copy.

(6)   The trade union shall ensure that the scrutineer duly carries out his functions and that there is no interference with his carrying out of those functions which would make it reasonable for any person to call the scrutineer's independence in relation to the union into question.

(7)   The trade union shall comply with all reasonable requests made by the scrutineer for the purposes of, or in connection with, the carrying out of his functions.

(8)   In this section "the relevant date" means

     (a)   where the trade union has rules determining who is entitled to vote in the ballot by reference to membership on a particular date, that date, and

     (b)   otherwise, the date, or the last date, on which voting papers are distributed for the purposes of the ballot.

NOTES

Subordinate Legislation

Trade Union Ballots and Elections (Independent Scrutinee Qualifications) Order 1993, SI 1993/1909

Defined terms

the court: ss 121, 299

the duty of confidentiality: ss 24A(3), 299
rules (of a trade union): ss 119, 299
trade union: ss 1, 299

Entitlement to vote

76   Entitlement to vote in the ballot shall be accorded equally to all members of the trade union.

NOTES
Defined terms
   trade union: ss 1, 299

Voting

77(1)   The method of voting must be by the marking of a voting paper by the person voting.

(2)   Each voting paper must
   (a)   state the name of the independent scrutineer and clearly specify the address to which, and the date by which, it is to be returned, and
   (b)   be given one of a series of consecutive whole numbers every one of which is used in giving a different number in that series to each voting paper printed or otherwise produced for the purposes of the ballot, and
   (c)   be marked with its number.

(3)   Every person who is entitled to vote in the ballot must
   (a)   be allowed to vote without interference from, or constraint imposed by, the union or any of its members, officials or employees, and
   (b)   so far as is reasonably practicable, be enabled to do so without incurring any direct cost to himself.

(4)   So far as is reasonably practicable, every person who is entitled to vote in the ballot must
   (a)   have a voting paper sent to him by post at his home address or another address which he has requested the trade union in writing to treat as his postal address, and
   (b)   be given a convenient opportunity to vote by post.

(5)   The ballot shall be conducted so as to secure that
   (a)   so far as is reasonably practicable, those voting do so in secret, and
   (b)   the votes given in the ballot are fairly and accurately counted.
   For the purposes of paragraph (b) an inaccuracy in counting shall be disregarded if it is accidental and on a scale which could not affect the result of the ballot.

NOTES
Defined terms   trade union: ss 1, 299
   employee (generally): ss 295(1), 299
   official (of a trade union): ss 119, 299

Counting of votes etc by independent person

77A(1)   The trade union shall ensure that
   (a)   the storage and distribution of the voting papers for the purposes of the ballot, and
   (b)   the counting of the votes cast in the ballot,
   are undertaken by one or more independent persons appointed by the union.

(2)   A person is an independent person in relation to a ballot if
   (a)   he is the scrutineer, or
   (b)   he is a person other than the scrutineer and the trade union has no grounds for believing either that he will carry out any functions conferred on him in relation

to the ballot otherwise than competently or that his independence in relation to the union, or in relation to the ballot, might reasonably be called into question.

(3)   An appointment under this section shall require the person appointed to carry out his functions so as to minimise the risk of any contravention of requirements imposed by or under any enactment or the occurrence of any unfairness or malpractice.

(4)   The duty of confidentiality as respects the register is incorporated in an appointment under this section.

(5)   Where the person appointed to undertake the counting of votes is not the scrutineer, his appointment shall require him to send the voting papers back to the scrutineer as soon as reasonably practicable after the counting has been completed.

(6)   The trade union
 (a)   shall ensure that nothing in the terms of an appointment under this section is such as to make it reasonable for any person to call into question the independence of the person appointed in relation to the union,
 (b)   shall ensure that a person appointed under this section duly carries out his functions and that there is no interference with his carrying out of those functions which would make it reasonable for any person to call into question the independence of the person appointed in relation to the union, and
 (c)   shall comply with all reasonable requests made by a person appointed under this section for the purposes of, or in connection with, the carrying out of his functions.

NOTES

Defined terms
 contravention: ss 298, 299
 the duty of confidentiality: ss 24A(3), 299
  trade union: ss 1, 299

Scrutineer's report

78(1) The scrutineer's report on the ballot shall state
 (a)   the number of voting papers distributed for the purposes of the ballot,
 (b)   the number of voting papers returned to the scrutineer,
 (c)   the number of valid votes cast in the ballot for and against the resolution,
 (d)   the number of spoiled or otherwise invalid voting papers returned and
 (e)   the name of the person (or of each of the persons) appointed under section 77A or, if no person was so appointed, that fact.

(2) The report shall also state whether the scrutineer is satisfied
 (a)   that there are no reasonable grounds for believing that there was any contravention of a requirement imposed by or under any enactment in relation to the ballot,
 (b)   that the arrangements made (whether by him or any other person) with respect to the production, storage, distribution, return or other handling of the voting papers used in the ballot, and the arrangements for the counting of the votes, included all such security arrangements as were reasonably practicable for the purpose of minimising the risk that any unfairness or malpractice might occur, and
 (c)   that he has been able to carry out his functions without such interference as would make it reasonable for any person to call his independence in relation to the union into question;

and if he is not satisfied as to any of those matters, the report shall give particulars of his reasons for not being satisfied as to that matter.

(2A) The report shall also state
 (a)   whether the scrutineer

       (i)   has inspected the register of names and addresses of the members of the trade union, or

       (ii) has examined the copy of the register as at the relevant date which is supplied to him in accordance with section 75(5A)(a),

  (b) if he has, whether in the case of each inspection or examination he was acting on a request by a member of the trade union or at his own instance,

  (c) whether he declined to act on any such request, and

  (d) whether any inspection of the register, or any examination of the copy of the register, has revealed any matter which he considers should be drawn to the attention of the trade union in order to assist it in securing that the register is accurate and up-to-date,

but shall not state the name of any member who has requested such an inspection or examination.

(2B) Where one or more persons other than the scrutineer are appointed under section 77A, the statement included in the scrutineer's report in accordance with subsection (2)(b) shall also indicate

  (a) whether he is satisfied with the performance of the person, or each of the persons, so appointed, and

  (b) if he is not satisfied with the performance of the person, or any of them, particulars of his reasons for not being so satisfied.

(3) The trade union shall not publish the result of the ballot until it has received the scrutineer's report.

(4) The trade union shall within the period of three months after it receives the report

  (a) send a copy of the report to every member of the union to whom it is reasonably practicable to send such a copy; or

  (b) take all such other steps for notifying the contents of the report to the members of the union (whether by publishing the report or otherwise) as it is the practice of the union to take when matters of general interest to all its members need to be brought to their attention.

(5) Any such copy or notification shall be accompanied by a statement that the union will, on request, supply any member of the union with a copy of the report, either free of charge or on payment of such reasonable fee as may be specified in the notification.

(6) The trade union shall so supply any member of the union who makes such a request and pays the fee (if any) notified to him.

NOTES

Defined terms   trade union: ss 1, 299
  contravention: ss 298, 299
  the scrutineer: s 75(1)

Remedy for failure to comply with ballot rules: general

79(1) The remedy for

  (a) the taking by a trade union of a ballot on a political resolution otherwise than in accordance with political ballot rules approved by the Certification Officer, or

  (b) the failure of a trade union, in relation to a proposed ballot on a political resolution, to comply with the political ballot rules so approved,

is by way of application under section 80 (to the Certification Officer) or 81 (to the court).

(2) An application under those sections may be made only by a person who is a member of the trade union and, where the ballot has been held, was a member at the time when it was held.

References in those sections to a person having a sufficient interest are to such a person.

(3) No such application may be made after the end of the period of one year beginning with the day on which the union announced the result of the ballot.

NOTES

Defined terms
the court: ss 121, 299
political resolution: s 71(1)

trade union: ss 1, 299

Application to Certification Officer

80(1) A person having a sufficient interest (see section 79(2)) who claims that a trade union
    (a) has held a ballot on a political resolution otherwise than in accordance with political ballot rules approved by the Certification Officer, or
    (b) has failed in relation to a proposed ballot on a political resolution to comply with political ballot rules so approved,
may apply to the Certification Officer for a declaration to that effect.

(2) On an application being made to him, the Certification Officer shall
    (a) make such enquiries as he thinks fit, and
    (b) give the applicant and the trade union an opportunity to be heard,
and may make or refuse the declaration asked for.

(3) If he makes a declaration he shall specify in it the provisions with which the trade union has failed to comply.

(4) Where he makes a declaration and is satisfied that steps have been taken by the union with a view to remedying the declared failure, or securing that a failure of the same or any similar kind does not occur in future, or that the union has agreed to take such steps, he shall in making the declaration specify those steps.

(5) Whether he makes or refuses a declaration, he shall give reasons for his decision in writing; and the reasons may be accompanied by written observations on any matter arising from, or connected with, the proceedings.

(5A) Where the Certification Officer makes a declaration he shall also, unless he considers that to do so would be inappropriate, make an enforcement order, that is, an order imposing on the union one or more of the following requirements
    (a) to secure the holding of a ballot in accordance with the order;
    (b) to take such other steps to remedy the declared failure as may be specified in the order;
    (c) to abstain from such acts as may be so specified with a view to securing that a failure of the same or a similar kind does not occur in future.
The Certification Officer shall in an order imposing any such requirement as is mentioned in paragraph (a) or (b) specify the period within which the union must comply with the requirements of the order.

(5B) Where the Certification Officer makes an order requiring the union to hold a fresh ballot, he shall (unless he considers that it would be inappropriate to do so in the particular circumstances of the case) require the ballot to be conducted in accordance with the union's political ballot rules and such other provisions as may be made by the order.

(5C) Where an enforcement order has been made, any person who is a member of the union and was a member at the time the order was made is entitled to enforce obedience to the order as if he had made the application on which the order was made.

(6)   In exercising his functions under this section the Certification Officer shall ensure that, so far as is reasonably practicable, an application made to him is determined within six months of being made.

(7)   Where he requests a person to furnish information to him in connection with enquiries made by him under this section, he shall specify the date by which that information is to be furnished and shall, unless he considers that it would be inappropriate to do so, proceed with his determination of the application notwithstanding that the information has not been furnished to him by the specified date.

(8)   A declaration made by the Certification Officer under this section may be relied on as if it were a declaration made by the court.

(9)   An enforcement order made by the Certification Officer under this section may be enforced in the same way as an order of the court.

(10) The following paragraphs have effect if a person applies under section 81 in relation to a matter
   (a)   that person may not apply under this section in relation to that matter;
   (b)   on an application by a different person under this section in relation to that matter, the Certification Officer shall have due regard to any declaration, order, observations, or reasons made or given by the court regarding that matter and brought to the Certification Officer's notice.

NOTES

Defined terms
   act: ss 298, 299
   the court: ss 121, 299
   political resolution: s 71(1)

trade union: ss 1, 299

Application to court

81(1) A person having a sufficient interest (see section 79(2)) who claims that a trade union
   (a)   has held a ballot on a political resolution otherwise than in accordance with political ballot rules approved by the Certification Officer, or
   (b)   has failed in relation to a proposed ballot on a political resolution to comply with political ballot rules so approved,
   may apply to the court for a declaration to that effect.

(2)   *Repealed*

(3)   If the court makes the declaration asked for, it shall specify in the declaration the provisions with which the trade union has failed to comply.

(4)   Where the court makes a declaration it shall also, unless it considers that to do so would be inappropriate, make an enforcement order, that is, an order imposing on the union one or more of the following requirements
   (a)   to secure the holding of a ballot in accordance with the order;
   (b)   to take such other steps to remedy the declared failure as may be specified in the order;
   (c)   to abstain from such acts as may be so specified with a view to securing that a failure of the same or a similar kind does not occur in future.
   The court shall in an order imposing any such requirement as is mentioned in paragraph (a) or (b) specify the period within which the union must comply with the requirements of the order.

(5)   Where the court makes an order requiring the union to hold a fresh ballot, the court shall (unless it considers that it would be inappropriate to do so in the particular circumstances of the case) require the ballot to be conducted in accordance with the union's political ballot rules and such other provisions as may be made by the order.

(6) Where an enforcement order has been made, any person who is a member of the union and was a member at the time the order was made is entitled to enforce obedience to the order as if he had made the application on which the order was made.

(7) Without prejudice to any other power of the court, the court may on an application under this section grant such interlocutory relief (in Scotland, such interim order) as it considers appropriate.

(8) The following paragraphs have effect if a person applies under section 80 in relation to a matter

(a) that person may not apply under this section in relation to that matter;

(b) on an application by a different person under this section in relation to that matter, the court shall have due regard to any declaration, order, observations or reasons made or given by the Certification Officer regarding that matter and brought to the court's notice.

NOTES

Defined terms

act: ss 298, 299

the court: ss 121, 299

political resolution: s 71(1)

trade union: ss 1, 299

The political fund

Rules as to political fund

82(1) The trade union's rules must provide

(a) that payments in the furtherance of the political objects to which this Chapter applies shall be made out of a separate fund (the "political fund" of the union);

(b) that a member of the union who gives notice in accordance with section 84 that he objects to contributing to the political fund shall be exempt from any obligation to contribute to it;

(c) that a member shall not by reason of being so exempt

(i) be excluded from any benefits of the union, or

(ii) be placed in any respect either directly or indirectly under a disability or at a disadvantage as compared with other members of the union (except in relation to the control or management of the political fund); and

(d) that contribution to the political fund shall not be made a condition for admission to the union.

(2) A member of a trade union who claims that he is aggrieved by a breach of any rule made in pursuance of this section may complain to the Certification Officer.

(2A) On a complaint being made to him the Certification Officer shall make such enquiries as he thinks fit.

(3) Where, after giving the member and a representative of the union an opportunity of being heard, the Certification Officer considers that a breach has been committed, he may make such order for remedying the breach as he thinks just under the circumstances.

(3A) Where the Certification Officer requests a person to furnish information to him in connection with enquiries made by him under this section, he shall specify the date by which that information is to be furnished and, unless he considers that it would be inappropriate to do so, shall proceed with his determination of the application notwithstanding that the information has not been furnished to him by the specified date.

(4A)   Where an order has been made under this section, any person who is a member of the union and was a member at the time it was made is entitled to enforce obedience to the order as if he had made the complaint on which it was made.

(4B)   An order made by the Certification Officer under this section may be enforced
      (a)   in England and Wales, in the same way as an order of the county court;
      (b)   in Scotland, in the same way as an order of the sheriff.

NOTES
Defined terms
   rules (of a trade union): ss 119, 299
   trade union: ss 1, 299

Assets and liabilities of political fund

83(1)   There may be added to a union's political fund only
      (a)   sums representing contributions made to the fund by members of the union or by any person other than the union itself, and
      (b)   property which accrues to the fund in the course of administering the assets of the fund.

(2)   The rules of the union shall not be taken to require any member to contribute to the political fund at a time when there is no political resolution in force in relation to the union.

(3)   No liability of a union's political fund shall be discharged out of any other fund of the union.

This subsection applies notwithstanding any term or condition on which the liability was incurred or that an asset of the other fund has been charged in connection with the liability.

NOTES
Defined terms   rules (of a trade union): ss 119, 299
   political fund: ss 82(1)(a), 299
   political resolution: s 71(1)

Notice of objection to contributing to political fund

84(1)   A member of a trade union may give notice in the following form, or in a form to the like effect, that he objects to contribute to the political fund:
   Name of Trade Union
   POLITICAL FUND (EXEMPTION NOTICE)
   I give notice that I object to contributing to the Political Fund of the Union, and am in consequence exempt, in manner provided by Chapter VI of Part I of the Trade Union and Labour Relations (Consolidation) Act 1992, from contributing to that fund.
   AB
   Address
   day of . . . . 19 . . .

(2)   On the adoption of a political resolution, notice shall be given to members of the union acquainting them
      (a)   that each member has a right to be exempted from contributing to the union's political fund, and
      (b)   that a form of exemption notice can be obtained by or on behalf of a member either by application at or by post from
          (i)   the head office or any branch office of the union, or
          (ii)   the office of the Certification Officer.

(3) The notice to members shall be given in accordance with rules of the union approved for the purpose by the Certification Officer, who shall have regard in each case to the existing practice and character of the union.

(4) On giving an exemption notice in accordance with this section, a member shall be exempt from contributing to the union's political fund

    (a) where the notice is given within one month of the giving of notice to members under subsection (2) following the passing of a political resolution on a ballot held at a time when no such resolution is in force, as from the date on which the exemption notice is given;

    (b) in any other case, as from the 1st January next after the exemption notice is given.

(5) An exemption notice continues to have effect until it is withdrawn.

NOTES

Defined terms

  political fund: ss 82(1)(a), 299

  political resolution: s 71(1)

  rules (of a trade union): ss 119, 299

trade union: ss 1, 299

Manner of giving effect to exemptions

85(1) Effect may be given to the exemption of members from contributing to the political fund of a union either

    (a) by a separate levy of contributions to that fund from the members who are not exempt, or

    (b) by relieving members who are exempt from the payment of the whole or part of any periodical contribution required from members towards the expenses of the union.

(2) In the latter case, the rules shall provide

    (a) that relief shall be given as far as possible to all members who are exempt on the occasion of the same periodical payment, and

    (b) for enabling each member of the union to know what portion (if any) of any periodical contribution payable by him is a contribution to the political fund.

NOTES

Defined terms

  political fund: ss 82(1)(a), 299

  rules (of a trade union): ss 119, 299

Duties of employer who deducts union contributions

Certificate of exemption or objection to contributing to political fund

86(1) If a member of a trade union which has a political fund certifies in writing to his employer that, or to the effect that

    (a) he is exempt from the obligation to contribute to the fund, or

    (b) he has, in accordance with section 84, notified the union in writing of his objection to contributing to the fund,

the employer shall ensure that no amount representing a contribution to the political fund is deducted by him from emoluments payable to the member.

(2) The employer's duty under subsection (1) applies from the first day, following the giving of the certificate, on which it is reasonably practicable for him to comply with that subsection, until the certificate is withdrawn.

(3)   An employer may not refuse to deduct any union dues from emoluments payable to a person who has given a certificate under this section if he continues to deduct union dues from emoluments payable to other members of the union, unless his refusal is not attributable to the giving of the certificate or otherwise connected with the duty imposed by subsection (1).

NOTES

Defined terms

employer: ss 279, 295(1), 296(2), 299
political fund: ss 82(1)(a), 299

trade union: ss 1, 299

Complaint in respect of employer's failure

87(1)   A person who claims his employer has failed to comply with section 86 in deducting or refusing to deduct any amount from emoluments payable to him may present a complaint to an employment tribunal.

(2)   A tribunal shall not consider a complaint under subsection (1) unless it is presented
(a)   within the period of three months beginning with the date of the payment of the emoluments or (if the complaint relates to more than one payment) the last of the payments, or
(b)   where the tribunal is satisfied that it was not reasonably practicable for the complaint to be presented within that period, within such further period as the tribunal considers reasonable.

(2A)   Section 292A (extension of time limits to facilitate conciliation before institution of proceedings) applies for the purposes of subsection (2)(a).

(3)   Where on a complaint under subsection (1) arising out of subsection (3) (refusal to deduct union dues) of section 86 the question arises whether the employer's refusal to deduct an amount was attributable to the giving of the certificate or was otherwise connected with the duty imposed by subsection (1) of that section, it is for the employer to satisfy the tribunal that it was not.

(4)   Where a tribunal finds that a complaint under subsection (1) is wellfounded
(a)   it shall make a declaration to that effect and, where the complaint arises out of subsection (1) of section 86, order the employer to pay to the complainant the amount deducted in contravention of that subsection less any part of that amount already paid to him by the employer, and
(b)   it may, if it considers it appropriate to do so in order to prevent a repetition of the failure, make an order requiring the employer to take, within a specified time, the steps specified in the order in relation to emoluments payable by him to the complainant.

(5)   A person who claims his employer has failed to comply with an order made under subsection (4)(b) on a complaint presented by him may present a further complaint to an employment tribunal; but only one complaint may be presented under this subsection in relation to any order.

(6)   A tribunal shall not consider a complaint under subsection (5) unless it is presented
(a)   after the end of the period of four weeks beginning with the date of the order, but
(b)   before the end of the period of six months beginning with that date.

(7)   Where on a complaint under subsection (5) a tribunal finds that an employer has, without reasonable excuse, failed to comply with an order made under subsection (4)(b), it shall order the employer to pay to the complainant an amount equal to two weeks' pay.

(8) Chapter II of Part XIV of the Employment Rights Act 1996 (calculation of a week's pay) applies for the purposes of subsection (7) with the substitution for section 225 of the following

For the purposes of this Chapter in its application to subsection (7) of section 87 of the Trade Union and Labour Relations (Consolidation) Act 1992, the calculation date is the date of the payment, or (if more than one) the last of the payments, to which the complaint related.

NOTES
Defined terms
  employer: ss 279, 295(1), 296(2), 299

88 *Repealed*

Position where political resolution ceases to have effect

Administration of political fund where no resolution in force

89(1) The following provisions have effect with respect to the political fund of a trade union where there ceases to be any political resolution in force in relation to the union.

(2) If the resolution ceases to have effect by reason of a ballot being held on which a new political resolution is not passed, the union may continue to make payments out of the fund as if the resolution had continued in force for six months beginning with the date of the ballot.

But no payment shall be made which causes the fund to be in deficit or increases a deficit in it.

(3) There may be added to the fund only
  (a) contributions to the fund paid to the union (or to a person on its behalf) before the resolution ceased to have effect, and
  (b) property which accrues to the fund in the course of administering the assets of the fund.

(4) The union may, notwithstanding any of its rules or any trusts on which the fund is held, transfer the whole or part of the fund to such other fund of the union as it thinks fit.

(5) If a new political resolution is subsequently passed, no property held immediately before the date of the ballot by or on behalf of the union otherwise than in its political fund, and no sums representing such property, may be added to the fund.

NOTES
Defined terms
  date of the ballot: s 96
  political fund: ss 82(1)(a), 299
  political resolution: s 71(1)

  rules (of a trade union): ss 119, 299
  trade union: ss 1, 299

Discontinuance of contributions to political fund

90(1) Where there ceases to be any political resolution in force in relation to a trade union, the union shall take such steps as are necessary to ensure that the collection of contributions to its political fund is discontinued as soon as is reasonably practicable.

(2) The union may, notwithstanding any of its rules, pay into any of its other funds any such contribution which is received by it after the resolution ceases to have effect.

(3) If the union continues to collect contributions, it shall refund to a member who applies for a refund the contributions made by him collected after the resolution ceased to have effect.

(4) A member of a trade union who claims that the union has failed to comply with subsection (1) may apply to the court for a declaration to that effect.

(5) Where the court is satisfied that the complaint is well-founded, it may, if it considers it appropriate to do so in order to secure that the collection of contributions to the political fund is discontinued, make an order requiring the union to take, within such time as may be specified in the order, such steps as may be so specified.

Such an order may be enforced by a person who is a member of the union and was a member at the time the order was made as if he had made the application.

(6) The remedy for failure to comply with subsection (1) is in accordance with subsections (4) and (5), and not otherwise; but this does not affect any right to recover sums payable to a person under subsection (3).

NOTES

Rules to cease to have effect

91(1) If there ceases to be any political resolution in force in relation to a trade union, the rules of the union made for the purpose of complying with this Chapter also cease to have effect, except so far as they are required to enable the political fund to be administered at a time when there is no such resolution in force.

(2) If the resolution ceases to have effect by reason of a ballot being held on which a new political resolution is not passed, the rules cease to have effect at the end of the period of six months beginning with the date of the ballot.

In any other case the rules cease to have effect when the resolution ceases to have effect.

(3) Nothing in this section affects the operation of section 82(2) (complaint to Certification Officer in respect of breach of rules) in relation to a breach of a rule occurring before the rule in question ceased to have effect.

(4) No member of a trade union who has at any time been exempt from the obligation to contribute to its political fund shall by reason of his having been exempt

(a) be excluded from any benefits of the union, or

(b) be placed in any respect either directly or indirectly under a disability or at a disadvantage as compared with other members (except in relation to the control or management of the political fund).

NOTES

Supplementary

Manner of making union rules

92 If the Certification Officer is satisfied, and certifies, that rules of a trade union made for any of the purposes of this Chapter and requiring approval by him have been approved

(a) by a majority of the members of the union voting for the purpose, or

(b) by a majority of delegates of the union at a meeting called for the purpose, the rules shall have effect as rules of the union notwithstanding that the rules of the union as to the alteration of rules or the making of new rules have not been complied with.

NOTES
Defined terms
    rules (of a trade union): ss 119, 299
    trade union: ss 1, 299

Effect of amalgamation

93(1) Where on an amalgamation of two or more trade unions
    (a) there is in force in relation to each of the amalgamating unions a political resolution and such rules as are required by this Chapter, and
    (b) the rules of the amalgamated union in force immediately after the amalgamation include such rules as are required by this Chapter,
    the amalgamated union shall be treated for the purposes of this Chapter as having passed a political resolution.

(2) That resolution shall be treated as having been passed on the date of the earliest of the ballots on which the resolutions in force immediately before the amalgamation with respect to the amalgamating unions were passed.

(3) Where one of the amalgamating unions is a Northern Ireland union, the references above to the requirements of this Chapter shall be construed as references to the requirements of the corresponding provisions of the law of Northern Ireland.

NOTES
Defined terms   trade union: ss 1, 299
    Northern Ireland union: s 120
    political resolution: s 71(1)
    rules (of a trade union): ss 119, 299

Overseas members of trade union

94(1) Where a political resolution is in force in relation to the union
    (a) rules made by the union for the purpose of complying with section 74 (political ballot rules) in relation to a proposed ballot may provide for overseas members of the union not to be accorded entitlement to vote in the ballot, and
    (b) rules made by the union for the purpose of complying with section 84 (notice of right to object to contribute to political fund to be given where resolution passed) may provide for notice not to be given by the union to its overseas members.

(2) Accordingly, where provision is made in accordance with subsection (1)(a), the Certification Officer shall not on that ground withhold his approval of the rules; and where provision is made in accordance with subsection (1)(b), section 84(2) (duty to give notice) shall not be taken to require notice to be given to overseas members.

(3) An "overseas member" means a member of the trade union (other than a merchant seaman or offshore worker) who is outside Great Britain throughout the period during which votes may be cast.
    For this purpose
        "merchant seaman" means a person whose employment, or the greater part of it, is carried out on board seagoing ships; and
        "offshore worker" means a person in offshore employment, other than one who is in such employment in an area where the law of Northern Ireland applies.

NOTES
Defined terms   political resolution: s 71(1)
    offshore employment: ss 287, 299   trade union: ss 1, 299

Appeals from Certification Officer

95   An appeal lies to the Employment Appeal Tribunal on any question of law arising in proceedings before or arising from any decision of the Certification Officer under this Chapter.

Meaning of "date of the ballot"

96   In this Chapter the "date of the ballot" means, in the case of a ballot in which votes may be cast on more than one day, the last of those days.

97-118   *Not reproduced*

Interpretation

Expressions relating to trade unions

119   In this Act, in relation to a trade union

"agent" means a banker or solicitor of, or any person employed as an auditor by, the union or any branch or section of the union;

"branch or section", except where the context otherwise requires, includes a branch or section which is itself a trade union;

"executive" means the principal committee of the union exercising executive functions, by whatever name it is called;

"financial affairs" means affairs of the union relating to any fund which is applicable for the purposes of the union (including any fund of a branch or section of the union which is so applicable);

"general secretary" means the official of the union who holds the office of general secretary or, where there is no such office, holds an office which is equivalent, or (except in section 14(4)) the nearest equivalent, to that of general secretary;

"officer" includes

(a)   any member of the governing body of the union, and

(b)   any trustee of any fund applicable for the purposes of the union;

"official" means

(a)   an officer of the union or of a branch or section of the union, or

(b)   a person elected or appointed in accordance with the rules of the union to be a representative of its members or of some of them,

and includes a person so elected or appointed who is an employee of the same employer as the members or one or more of the members whom he is to represent;

"president" means the official of the union who holds the office of president or, where there is no such office, who holds an office which is equivalent, or (except in section 14(4) or Chapter IV) the nearest equivalent, to that of president; and

"rules", except where the context otherwise requires, includes the rules of any branch or section of the union.

Northern Ireland unions

120   In this Part a "Northern Ireland union" means a trade union whose principal office is situated in Northern Ireland.

Meaning of "the court"

121   In this Part "the court" (except where the reference is expressed to be to the county court or sheriff court) means the High Court or the Court of Session.

122-294   *Not reproduced*

Interpretation

Meaning of "employee" and related expressions

295(1) In this Act

"contract of employment" means a contract of service or of apprenticeship,

"employee" means an individual who has entered into or works under (or, where the employment has ceased, worked under) a contract of employment, and

"employer", in relation to an employee, means the person by whom the employee is (or, where the employment has ceased, was) employed.

(2) Subsection (1) has effect subject to section 235 and other provisions conferring a wider meaning on "contract of employment" or related expressions.

Meaning of "worker" and related expressions

296(1) In this Act "worker" means an individual who works, or normally works or seeks to work

(a) under a contract of employment, or

(b) under any other contract whereby he undertakes to do or perform personally any work or services for another party to the contract who is not a professional client of his, or

(c) in employment under or for the purposes of a government department (otherwise than as a member of the naval, military or air forces of the Crown) in so far as such employment does not fall within paragraph (a) or (b) above.

(2) In this Act "employer", in relation to a worker, means a person for whom one or more workers work, or have worked or normally work or seek to work.

(3) This section has effect subject to sections 68(4), 145F(3) and 151(1B).

Associate employers

297 For the purposes of this Act any two employers shall be treated as associated if

(a) one is a company of which the other (directly or indirectly) has control, or

(b) both are companies of which a third person (directly or indirectly) has control;

and "associated employer" shall be construed accordingly.

Minor definitions: general

298 In this Act, unless the context otherwise requires

"act" and "action" each includes omission, and references to doing an act or taking action shall be construed accordingly;

"agency worker" has the meaning given in regulation 3 of the Agency Workers Regulations 2010;

"certificate of independence" means a certificate issued under

(a) section 6(6), or

(b) section 101A(4);

"contravention" includes a failure to comply, and cognate expressions shall be construed accordingly;

"dismiss", "dismissal" and "effective date of termination", in relation to an employee, shall be construed in accordance with Part X of the Employment Rights Act 1996;

"tort", as respects Scotland, means delict, and cognate expressions shall be construed accordingly.

Wales Act 2014

An Act to make provision about elections to and membership of the National Assembly for Wales; to make provision about the Welsh Assembly Government; to make provision about the setting by the Assembly of rates of income tax to be paid by Welsh taxpayers and about the devolution of taxation powers to the Assembly; to make related amendments to Part 4A of the Scotland Act 1998; to make provision about borrowing by the Welsh Ministers; to make miscellaneous amendments in the law relating to Wales; and for connected purposes.

17th December 2014

PART 1

THE ASSEMBLY AND WELSH GOVERNMENT

National Assembly for Wales

Frequency of Assembly ordinary general elections

1   *Amends the Government of Wales Act 2006 and the Fixed-term Parliaments Act 2011: not reproduced here*

Removal of restriction on standing for election for both constituency and electoral region

2   *Amends the Government of Wales Act 2006: not reproduced here*

MPs to be disqualified from membership of Assembly

3   *Amends the Government of Wales Act 2006: not reproduced here*

Welsh Government

The Welsh Government

4(1)   The Welsh Assembly Government is renamed the Welsh Government, or Llywodraeth Cymru.

(2)   Accordingly, in GOWA 2006
   (a)   omit "Assembly" wherever it occurs in the expression "Welsh Assembly Government";
   (b)   omit "Cynulliad" where it occurs in section 45(1) (in both places).

(3)   In the following sections of GOWA 2006, as amended by subsection (2), the references to the Welsh Government include, in relation to any time before the coming into force of this section, references to the Welsh Assembly Government
   (a)   section 37(5) (power to impose requirements on current or former members of staff of the Government);
   (b)   section 52(7)(a) and (8) (power to pay pensions in respect of current or former members of staff of the Government).

(4)   Unless the context requires otherwise, in any enactment, instrument or other document passed or made before the date on which this section comes into force (except GOWA 2006 as to which see subsections (2) and (3))
   (a)   any reference to the Welsh Assembly Government is to be read as, or as including, a reference to the Welsh Government, and
   (b)   any reference to Llywodraeth Cynulliad Cymru is to be read as, or as including, a reference to Llywodraeth Cymru.

NOTES
Defined terms
   enactment: s 27
   GOWA 2006: s 27

First Minister: removal of power to designate after dissolution of Assembly

5   *Amends the Government of Wales Act 2006: not reproduced here*

PART 2
FINANCE

6–11   *Not reproduced*

Referendum on income tax provisions

Referendum about commencement of income tax provisions

12(1)   Her Majesty may by Order in Council cause a referendum to be held throughout Wales about whether the income tax provisions should come into force.

(2) If the majority of the voters in a referendum held by virtue of subsection (1) vote in favour of the income tax provisions coming into force, those provisions are to come into force in accordance with section 14.

(3) But if they do not, that does not prevent the making of a subsequent Order under subsection (1).

(4) No recommendation is to be made to Her Majesty to make an Order under subsection (1) unless a draft of the statutory instrument containing the Order has been laid before, and approved by a resolution of, each House of Parliament and the Assembly.

(5) But subsection (4) is not satisfied unless the resolution of the Assembly is passed on a vote in which the number of Assembly members voting in favour of it is not less than two-thirds of the total number of Assembly seats.

(6) A draft of a statutory instrument containing an Order under subsection (1) may not be laid before either House of Parliament, or the Assembly, until the Secretary of State has undertaken such consultation as the Secretary of State considers appropriate.

(7) For further provision about a referendum held by virtue of subsection (1), see Schedule 1.

(8) In this section "the income tax provisions" means sections 8 and 9.

NOTES
Defined terms
   the Assembly: s 27

Proposal for referendum by Assembly

13(1) This section applies if
   (a) the First Minister or a Welsh Minister appointed under section 48 of GOWA 2006 moves a resolution in the Assembly that, in the Assembly's opinion, a recommendation should be made to Her Majesty to make an Order under section 12(1), and
   (b) the Assembly passes the resolution on a vote in which the number of Assembly members voting in favour of it is not less than two-thirds of the total number of Assembly seats.

(2) A resolution moved under subsection (1)(a) must state whether the voting age at the proposed referendum is to be 16 or 18.

(3) The First Minister must, as soon as practicable after the resolution is passed, ensure that notice in writing of the resolution is given to the Secretary of State.

(4) Within the period of 180 days beginning immediately after the day on which notice under subsection (3) is received by the Secretary of State
   (a) the Secretary of State or the Chancellor of the Duchy of Lancaster must lay a draft of a statutory instrument containing an Order under section 12(1) before each House of Parliament, or
   (b) the Secretary of State must give notice in writing to the First Minister of the refusal to lay a draft under paragraph (a) and the reasons for that refusal.

(5) As soon as practicable after the First Minister receives notice under subsection (4)(b)
   (a) the First Minister must lay a copy of the notice before the Assembly, and
   (b) the Assembly must ensure that the notice is published.

NOTES
Defined terms
   the Assembly: s 27
   GOWA 2006: s 27

Commencement of income tax provisions etc if majority in favour

14(1) This section applies where the majority of the voters in a referendum held by virtue of section 12(1) vote in favour of the income tax provisions coming into force.

(2) The Treasury may bring sections 8 and 9 into force by order.

(3) An order under subsection (2)
- (a) must appoint, in relation to each provision inserted by section 8 or 9, the day on which it comes into force;
- (b) may provide that a provision inserted by section 8 or 9 has effect in relation to
  - (i) a tax year appointed by the order and subsequent tax years, or
  - (ii) a financial year so appointed and subsequent financial years.

(4) A tax year may be appointed under subsection (3)(b) in relation to a provision inserted by section 8 or 9 only if the tax year begins on or after the day appointed under subsection (3)(a) in relation to that provision.

(5) An order under subsection (2) that brings into force section 116D of GOWA 2006 (power to set Welsh rates for Welsh taxpayers) must appoint the first tax year in relation to which a Welsh rate resolution may be made.

(6) The Secretary of State may bring section 10 into force by order.

(7) The Treasury may bring section 11(5), (6), (7)(a) and (8)(a) into force by order.

(8) An order under subsection (7)
- (a) must appoint a day on which the amendments made by the provisions mentioned in that subsection come into force, and
- (b) must provide that those amendments have effect in relation to a tax year appointed by the order and subsequent tax years.

(9) The tax year appointed under subsection (8)(b)
- (a) must begin on or after the day appointed under subsection (8)(a), and
- (b) must not precede the tax year appointed under subsection (5) or under section 25(5) of the Scotland Act 2012 (the first tax year for which Chapter 2 of Part 4A of the Scotland Act 1998 has effect).

(10) An order under this section may make different provision for different purposes.

NOTES

Defined terms   tax year: s 27
    financial year: s 27
    GOWA 2006: s 27
    the income tax provisions: s 12(8)

PART 3
MISCELLANEOUS

24-25   *Not reproduced*

PART 4
GENERAL

26   *Not reproduced*

Interpretation

27   In this Act
    "the Assembly" means the National Assembly for Wales;

"enactment" includes a Measure or Act of the Assembly and subordinate legislation (within the meaning of the Interpretation Act 1978);

"financial year" means the 12 months ending with 31 March;

"GOWA 2006" means the Government of Wales Act 2006;

"modifications" includes amendments, repeals and revocations;

"tax year" means a year beginning on 6 April and ending on the following 5 April.

28-30   *Not reproduced*

SCHEDULE 1
REFERENDUM ABOUT COMMENCEMENT OF INCOME TAX PROVISIONS

Section 12

Entitlement to vote

1(1)   Where a referendum held by virtue of section 12(1) follows on from a youth franchise resolution, a person is entitled to vote in the referendum if, on the date of the poll at the referendum, the person

   (a)   is aged 16 or over,

   (b)   either

      (i)   is registered in the register of local government electors at an address within an Assembly constituency, or

      (ii)   is registered in the register of young voters at such an address in accordance with provision made under paragraph 2,

   (c)   is not subject to any legal incapacity to vote (age apart) within the meaning of section 2(1)(b) of the Representation of the People Act 1983, and

   (d)   is a Commonwealth citizen, a citizen of the Republic of Ireland or a relevant citizen of the Union (within the meaning given by section 202(1) of that Act).

(2)   Where a referendum held by virtue of section 12(1) does not follow on from a youth franchise resolution, a person is entitled to vote in the referendum if the person would be entitled to vote in a general election of Assembly members if one were held on the date of the poll at the referendum.

(3)   For the purposes of this paragraph and paragraph 2, a referendum held by virtue of section 12(1) "follows on from a youth franchise resolution" if

   (a)   a resolution is passed by the Assembly under section 13(1) which states that the voting age at the proposed referendum is to be 16,

   (b)   the First Minister complies with section 13(3) in relation to the resolution, and

   (c)   as a result, a draft of the statutory instrument containing the Order under section 12(1) which causes the referendum to be held is laid in accordance with section 13(4)(a).

(4)   An Order under section 12(1) may include provision for disregarding alterations made in a register of electors or voters after a date specified in the Order and sub-paragraphs (1) and (2) are to be read subject to any such provision.

2(1)   Where an Order under section 12(1) causes a referendum to be held which follows on from a youth franchise resolution, the Order must make provision about the registration of young voters.

(2)   That provision must include

   (a)   provision for the preparation and maintenance of a register of young voters;

   (b)   provision prohibiting the publication or other disclosure of that register, or any entry in it, except as provided by such an Order.

(3) Provision made by virtue of sub-paragraph (1) may, in particular
    (a) apply or incorporate, with or without modifications, any enactment relating to referendums or elections;
    (b) make other modifications of any enactment relating to referendums or elections.

(4) An Order under section 12(1) must make such supplementary, incidental or consequential provision (if any) as appears to Her Majesty to be appropriate for the purposes of, in consequence of, or for giving full effect to
    (a) any provision made by virtue of sub-paragraph (1), or
    (b) the entitlement of 16 and 17 year olds under paragraph 1(1) to vote in the referendum.

(5) Provision made by virtue of sub-paragraph (4) may, in particular
    (a) make modifications of any enactment;
    (b) make transitory, transitional or saving provision.

(6) For the purposes of sub-paragraph (3)(a), "enactment" includes the Scottish Independence Referendum (Franchise) Act 2013 (asp 13).

(7) For the purposes of this paragraph, "young voter" means a person who
    (a) will be aged 16 or 17 on the date of the poll at the referendum, and
    (b) is not registered in the register of local government electors at an address within an Assembly constituency.

Conduct etc of referendum

3(1) An Order under section 12(1) may make provision for and in connection with the referendum which it causes to be held.

(2) Such an Order may, in particular, apply or incorporate, with or without modifications, any enactment relating to referendums, elections or donations.

(3) In sub-paragraph (2) "donations" means anything which is or corresponds to a donation within the meaning of Part 4 of PPERA 2000.

Referendum question and statement

4(1) An Order under section 12(1)
    (a) must specify the question to be included on the ballot paper at the referendum which it causes to be held, and
    (b) may specify a statement to precede the question on that ballot paper.

(2) A question or statement specified under sub-paragraph (1) must be specified in both English and Welsh.

(3) The Secretary of State must, no later than the time at which paragraph (b) of section 104(4) of PPERA 2000 (report stating views as to intelligibility of referendum question expressed by Electoral Commission) is complied with, send to the First Minister a copy of the report laid before Parliament under that paragraph.

(4) As soon as practicable after the First Minister receives a copy of a report under sub-paragraph (3), the First Minister must lay a copy of the report before the Assembly.

Date of referendum

5(1) An Order under section 12(1) must specify the date of the poll at the referendum which it causes to be held.

(2) The Minister may by order vary the date of the poll specified in such an Order (including a date previously set by virtue of this sub-paragraph) if it appears inappropriate for it to be held on that date.

(3) The date of the poll, as specified under sub-paragraph (1) or varied under sub-paragraph (2), must not be within the period

    (a) beginning with the 25th working day before, and

    (b) ending with the 25th working day after,

the date of the poll at an election, or at another referendum, which is held throughout Wales.

(4) But sub-paragraph (3) does not apply if the date of the poll at the election or other referendum is not known to the Minister at the time when

    (a) the recommendation is made to Her Majesty to make the Order (in the case of an Order under section 12(1)), or

    (b) the Minister makes the order (in the case of an order under sub-paragraph (2)).

(5) No order may be made under sub-paragraph (2) without the consent of the Welsh Ministers.

(6) A statutory instrument containing an order under sub-paragraph (2) is subject to annulment in pursuance of a resolution of either House of Parliament.

(7) In this paragraph, "working day" means any day other than

    (a) a Saturday or Sunday;

    (b) a Christmas Eve, Christmas Day or Good Friday;

    (c) a day which is a bank holiday under the Banking and Financial Dealings Act 1971 in any part of the United Kingdom;

    (d) a day appointed for public thanksgiving or mourning.

Referendum period

6 An Order under section 12(1) must determine the referendum period for the purposes of Part 7 of PPERA 2000 in the case of the referendum which it causes to be held.

Combination of polls

7(1) An Order under section 12(1) may make provision for and in connection with the combination of the poll at the referendum which it causes to be held with that at an election or at another referendum (or both).

(2) Sub-paragraph (1) is subject to paragraph 5(3) (which limits the circumstances in which the poll at a referendum held by virtue of section 12(1) can be combined with a poll at an election or another referendum).

Assistance for designated organisations

8(1) An Order under section 12(1) may make provision for the provisions of PPERA 2000 listed in sub-paragraph (2) to apply with specified modifications in relation to a referendum held by virtue of section 12(1).

(2) The provisions are

    (a) sections 108 and 109 of PPERA 2000 (designation of organisations to whom assistance is available);

    (b) section 110 of, and Schedule 12 to, that Act (assistance available to designated organisations).

(3) The modifications specified may include allowing a permitted participant to be designated by the Electoral Commission under section 108(1) of PPERA 2000 in relation

to one of the possible outcomes at the referendum whether or not a permitted participant is designated in relation to the other possible outcome.

Information and encouraging participation

9(1) An Order under section 12(1) may authorise or require the Electoral Commission to do things for the purpose of promoting public awareness and understanding in Wales about one or more of the following

    (a) the referendum which the Order causes to be held;

    (b) the question to be included on the ballot paper at that referendum;

    (c) voting in that referendum.

  (2) An Order under section 12(1) may authorise or require the Chief Counting Officer to do things for the purpose of encouraging participation in the referendum which the Order causes to be held.

  (3) The things which the Commission or the Chief Counting Officer may be authorised or required to do under sub-paragraph (1) or (2) include imposing obligations, or conferring powers, on counting officers or other persons.

Referendum material

10 Section 126 of PPERA 2000 (details to appear on referendum material) does not apply to any material published for the purposes of a referendum held by virtue of section 12(1) if the publication is required under or by virtue of the Order that causes the referendum to be held.

Funding and accounts

11 An Order under section 12(1) must include provision for the funding of costs of the referendum which it causes to be held (and may, in particular, include provision for the costs to be charged on, or payable out of, the Welsh Consolidated Fund).

12 An Order under section 12(1) must include provision as to the preparation and audit of accounts relating to payments made by virtue of provision included in the Order under paragraph 11.

No legal challenge to referendum result

13(1) No court may entertain any proceedings for questioning the number of ballot papers counted or votes cast in a referendum held by virtue of section 12(1) as certified by the Chief Counting Officer or a counting officer unless

    (a) the proceedings are brought by a claim for judicial review, and

    (b) the claim form is filed before the end of the permitted period.

  (2) "The permitted period" means the period of 6 weeks beginning with

    (a) the date on which the Chief Counting Officer or counting officer gives a certificate as to the number of ballot papers counted and votes cast in the referendum, or

    (b) if the Chief Counting Officer or counting officer gives more than one such certificate, the date on which the last is given.

Supplementary

14 An Order under section 12(1) may include provision creating criminal offences.

Interpretation

15(1) In this Schedule

"Assembly constituency" has the same meaning as in GOWA 2006;

"the Minister" means the Secretary of State or the [Chancellor of the Duchy of Lancaster];

"PPERA 2000" means the Political Parties, Elections and Referendums Act 2000.

(2) Expressions used in this Schedule and in Part 7 of PPERA 2000 have the same meaning in this Schedule as in that Part.

NOTES

Defined terms

the Assembly: s 27

enactment: s 27

GOWA 2006: s 27

modifications: s 27

question: Political Parties, Elections and Referendums Act 2000, s 101(2)(b) (by virtue of para 15(2))

referendum: Political Parties, Elections and Referendums Act 2000, s 101(2)(b) (by virtue of para 15(2))

Westminster Secondary Legislation

Civil Procedure Rules 1998

PART 2

APPLICATION AND INTERPRETATION OF THE RULES

Rule 2.1 Application of the Rules

(1) Subject to paragraph (2), these Rules apply to all proceedings in
    (a) the County Court;
    (b) the High Court; and
    (c) the Civil Division of the Court of Appeal.

(2) These Rules do not apply to proceedings of the kinds specified in the first column of the following Table (proceedings for which rules may be made under the enactments specified in the second column) except to the extent that they are applied to those proceedings by another enactment

Proceedings	Enactments
1-6 *Not reproduced*	*Not reproduced*
7 Election petitions in the High Court	Representation of the People Act 1983, s 182

PRACTICE DIRECTION 8A

Terminology

1.1   In this Practice Direction, 'Schedule rules' means provisions contained in the Schedules to the CPR, which were previously contained in the Rules of the Supreme Court (1965) or the County Court Rules (1981).

Application of this Practice Direction

2.1   Section A contains general provisions about claims and applications to which Part 8 applies. Section B comprises a table listing claims, petitions and applications under various enactments which must be made under Part 8. Section C contains certain additions and modifications to the Part 8 procedure that apply to the particular claims and applications identified.

2.2   Some of the claims and applications listed in the table in Section B are dealt with in the Schedule Rules in the CPR. The table in Section B contains cross-reference to the relevant Schedule Rules.

Section A
General Provisions Applicable to Part 8 Claims

Types of claim in which the Part 8 procedure may be used

3.1   The types of claim for which the Part 8 procedure may be used include –
   (1)   a claim by or against a child or protected party, as defined in rule 21.1(2), which has been settled before the commencement of proceedings and the sole purpose of the claim is to obtain the approval of the court to the settlement; or
   (2)   a claim for provisional damages which has been settled before the commencement of proceedings and the sole purpose of the claim is to obtain a consent judgment.

3.2(1)   The Part 8 procedure must be used for those claims, petitions and applications listed in the table in Section B.

   (2)   Where a claim is listed in the table in Section B and is identified as a claim to which particular provisions of Section C apply, the Part 8 procedure shall apply subject to the additions and modifications set out in the relevant paragraphs in Section C.

3.3   The Part 8 procedure must also be used for any claim or application in relation to which an Act, rule or practice direction provides that the claim or application is brought by originating summons, originating motion or originating application.

3.4   Where it appears to a court officer that a claimant is using the Part 8 procedure inappropriately, he may refer the claim to a judge for the judge to consider the point.

3.5   The court may at any stage order the claim to continue as if the claimant had not used the Part 8 procedure and, if it does so, the court will allocate the claim to a track and give such directions as it considers appropriate.

4.1(1)   Part 7 and Practice Direction 7A contain a number of rules and directions applicable to all claims, including those to which Part 8 applies. Those rules and directions should be applied where appropriate.

   (2)   Subject to the provisions in rule 8.1(2A), in the County Court a claim under the Part 8 procedure may be made in any County Court hearing centre. However, when a claim is given a hearing date the court may direct that proceedings should be transferred to another hearing centre if appropriate to do so. A claimant should consider the

potential delay which may result if a claim is not made at the appropriate hearing centre in the first instance.

4.2   Where a claimant uses the Part 8 procedure, the claim form (practice form N208) should be used and must state the matters set out in rule 8.2 and, if rule 8.1(6) applies, must comply with the requirements of the rule or practice direction in question. In particular, the claim form must state that Part 8 applies; a Part 8 claim form means a claim form which so states.

5.1   The provisions of Part 15 (defence and reply) do not apply where the claim form is a Part 8 claim form.

5.2   Where a defendant who wishes to respond to a Part 8 claim form is required to file an acknowledgment of service, that acknowledgment of service should be in practice form N210.

5.3   Where a defendant objects to the use of the Part 8 procedure, and his statement of reasons includes matters of evidence, the acknowledgment of service must be verified by a statement of truth.

6.1   The court may give directions immediately a Part 8 claim form is issued either on the application of a party or on its own initiative. The directions may include fixing a hearing date where –

(1)   there is no dispute, such as in child and protected party settlements; or

(2)   where there may be a dispute, but a hearing date could conveniently be given.

6.2   Where the court does not fix a hearing date when the claim form is issued, it will give directions for the disposal of the claim as soon as practicable after the defendant has acknowledged service of the claim form or, as the case may be, after the period for acknowledging service has expired.

6.3   Certain applications may not require a hearing.

6.4   The court may convene a directions hearing before giving directions.

7.1   A claimant must file the written evidence on which he relies when his Part 8 claim form is issued (unless the evidence is contained in the claim form itself).

7.2   Evidence will normally be in the form of a witness statement or an affidavit but a claimant may rely on the matters set out in his claim form provided that it has been verified by a statement of truth.

(For information about (1) statements of truth see Part 22 and Practice Direction 22, and (2) written evidence see Part 32 and Practice Direction 32.)

7.3   A defendant wishing to rely on written evidence, must file it with his acknowledgment of service.

7.4   A party may apply to the court for an extension of time to serve and file evidence under rule 8.5 or for permission to serve and file additional evidence under rule 8.6(1).

(For information about applications see Part 23 and Practice Direction 23A.)

7.5(1)   The parties may, subject to the following provisions, agree in writing on an extension of time for serving and filing evidence under rule 8.5(3) or rule 8.5(5).

(2)   An agreement extending time for a defendant to file evidence under rule 8.5(3)-
       (a)   must be filed by the defendant at the same time as he files his acknowledgement of service; and

(b) must not extend time by more than 14 days after the defendant files his acknowledgement of service.

(3) An agreement extending time for a claimant to file evidence in reply under rule 8.5(5) must not extend time to more than 28 days after service of the defendant's evidence on the claimant.

8.1 The court may on the hearing date –
    (1) proceed to hear the case and dispose of the claim;
    (2) give case management directions.

8.2 Case management directions may include the specific allocation of a case to a track.

8.3 CPR rules 26.5(3) and (4) and rules 26.6 to 26.10 apply to the allocation of a claim under paragraph 8.2.

Section B
Claims and Applications That Must Be Made Under Part 8

9.1 The claimant must use the Part 8 procedure if the claim is listed in the table below.

9.2 Section C of this Practice Direction contains special provisions modifying the Part 8 procedure, and where it does so, those provisions should be followed. The table below refers to the relevant paragraph of Section C where it applies.

9.3 Some of the claims and applications listed in the table below are dealt with in the Schedule Rules, and those rules modify the Part 8 procedure. A cross-reference to the relevant Schedule Rule is contained in the table below.

9.4 For applications that may or must be brought in the High Court, where no other rule or practice direction assigns the application to a Division of the court, the table specifies the Division to which the application is assigned.

Table not reproduced

Section C
Special Provisions

10.1 The following special provisions apply to the applications indicated.

10A-17 *Not reproduced*

Other proceedings under the Representation of the People Acts

17A.1(1) This paragraph applies to proceedings under the Representation of the People Acts (other than proceedings under section 30 of the Representation of the People Act 1983).

(2) The jurisdiction of the High Court under those Acts in matters relating to Parliamentary and local government elections will be exercised by a Divisional Court except that –
    (a) any jurisdiction, under a provision of any of those Acts, exercisable by a single judge will be exercised by a single judge;
    (b) any jurisdiction, under any such provision, exercisable by a Master will be exercised by a Master; and
    (c) where the court's jurisdiction in matters relating to Parliamentary elections is exercisable by a single judge, that jurisdiction in matters relating to local government elections is also exercisable by a single judge.

18-23 *Not reproduced*

PRACTICE DIRECTION 39A
HEARINGS

1.1 In Part 39, reference to a hearing includes reference to the trial.

1.2 The general rule is that a hearing is to be in public.

.....

1.7A Attention is drawn to paragraph 31.2(8) of Practice Direction 52D, which provides that an appeal to a county court against certain decisions under the Representation of the People Act 1983 is to be heard in private unless the court orders otherwise. Attention is also drawn to paragraph 31.2(9) of that practice direction, which provides that an appeal to the Court of Appeal against such a decision of a county court may be heard in private if the Court of Appeal so orders.

PRACTICE DIRECTION 52D
STATUTORY APPEALS AND APPEALS SUBJECT TO SPECIAL PROVISION

This Practice Direction supplements CPR Part 52

Section I
Introduction

1.1 This Practice Direction applies to all statutory appeals, and to other appeals which are subject to special provision, but not to appeals by way of case stated (to which Practice Direction 52E applies).

Section II
Routes of Appeal

2.1 In this Practice Direction, the court to which an appeal lies is prescribed by statute.

Section III
General Provisions About Statutory Appeals

3.1 This Section contains general provisions about statutory appeals (paragraphs 3.2 – 3.8). For where this Practice Direction or a statute makes additional special provision see also Section 4.

3.2 Where any of the provisions in this Section provide for documents to be filed at the appeal court, those documents are in addition to any documents required under Part 52 or Practice Direction 52B or 52C.

3.3 ....

Service of appellant's notice: rule 52.4(3)

3.4(1) The appellant must serve the appellant's notice on the respondent and on the chairman of the tribunal, Minister of State, government department or other person from whose decision the appeal is brought.

(2) In the case of an appeal from the decision of a tribunal that has no chairman or member who acts as a chairman, the appellant's notice must be served on the member (or members if more than one) of the tribunal.

Variation of time: rule 52.6

3.5 Where any statute prescribes a period within which an appeal must be filed then, unless the statute otherwise provides, the appeal court may not extend that period.

Applications by third parties (rule 52.12A)

3.6 Where all the parties consent, the court may deal with an application under rule 52.12A without a hearing.

3.7 An application for permission must be made by letter to the relevant court office, identifying the appeal, explaining who the applicant is and indicating why and in what form the applicant wants to participate in the hearing.

3.8 If the applicant is seeking a prospective order as to costs, the letter must say what kind of order and on what grounds.

Section IV
Specific Appeals

Provisions about specific appeals

4.1 This Section sets out special provisions about the appeals listed in the Table below. This Section is not exhaustive and does not create, amend or remove any right of appeal.

4.2 Part 52 applies to all appeals to which this Section applies subject to any special provisions set out in this Section.

4.3 Where any of the provisions in this Section provide for documents to be filed at the appeal court, these documents are in addition to any documents required under Part 52 or Practice Direction 52B or 52C.

.....

5.1 ....

Table

Statute (or description of appeal)	Appropriate Court	Relevant paragraph in this Practice Direction
Representation of the People Act 1983, s. 56	County Court	31.1–31.3

....

Representation of the People Act 1983
Appeals against decisions of registration officers

31.1(1) This paragraph applies in relation to an appeal against a decision of a registration officer, being a decision referred to in section 56(1) of the Representation of the People Act 1983 ('the Act').

(2) Where a person ('the appellant') has given notice of such an appeal in accordance with the relevant requirements of section 56, and of the regulations made under section 53 ('the Regulations'), of the Act, the registration officer must, within 7 days after the appellant receives the notice, forward –

    (a) the notice; and

    (b) the statement required by the Regulations,

by post to the County Court.

(3) The respondents to the appeal will be –

    (a) the registration officer; and

(b) if the decision of the registration officer was given in favour of any other person than the appellant, that other person.

(4) On the hearing of the appeal–
    (a) the statement forwarded to the court by the registration officer, and any document containing information submitted to the court by the registration officer pursuant to the Regulations, are admissible as evidence of the facts stated in them; and
    (b) the court –
        (i) may draw any inference of fact that the registration officer might have drawn; and
        (ii) may give any decision and make any order that the registration officer ought to have given or made.

(5) A respondent to an appeal (other than the registration officer) is not liable for nor entitled to costs, unless he appears before the court in support of the registration officer's decision.

(6) Rule 52.4 (appellant's notice) does not apply to an appeal to which this paragraph applies.

Representation of the People Act 1983
Special provision in relation to anonymous entries in the register

31.2(1) In this paragraph –
    (a) 'anonymous entry' has the meaning given by section 9B(4) of the Representation of the People Act 1983;
    (b) 'appeal notice' means the notice required by regulation 32 of the Representation of the People (England and Wales) Regulations 2001.

(2) This paragraph applies to an appeal to the County Court to which paragraph 31.1 (Representation of the People Act 1983 – appeals against decisions of registration officers) applies if a party to the appeal is a person –
    (a) whose entry in the register is an anonymous entry; or
    (b) who has applied for such an entry.

(3) This paragraph also applies to an appeal to the Court of Appeal from a decision of the County Court in an appeal to which paragraph 31.1 applies.

(4) The appellant may indicate in the appeal notice that an application for an anonymous entry has been applied for, or that the entry in the register is an anonymous entry.

(5) The respondent or any other person who applies to become a party to the proceedings may indicate in a respondent's notice or an application to join the proceedings that the entry in the register is an anonymous entry, or that an application has been made for an anonymous entry.

(6) Where the appellant gives such an indication in the appeal notice, the court will refer the matter to a District Judge for directions about the further conduct of the proceedings, and, in particular, directions about how the matter should be listed in the court list.

(7) Where the court otherwise becomes aware that a party to the appeal is a person referred to in sub-paragraph (2), the court will give notice to the parties that no further step is to be taken until the court has given any necessary directions for the further conduct of the matter.

Representation of the People Act 1983
Appeals selected as test cases

31.3(1)   Where two or more appeals to which paragraph 31.1 (Representation of the People Act 1983 – appeals against decisions of registration officers) applies involve the same point of law, the court may direct that one appeal ('the test-case appeal') is to be heard first as a test case.

(2)   The court will send a notice of the direction to each party to all of those appeals.

(3)   Where a notice under sub-paragraph (2) is served on any party to an appeal (other than the test-case appeal), that party may (within 7 days after the notice is served on that party) give notice to the court requesting the appeal to be heard and–

    (a)   the court will hear that appeal after the test-case appeal is disposed of;

    (b)   the court will give the parties to that appeal notice of the day on which it will be heard; and

    (c)   the party who gave the notice is not entitled to receive any costs of the separate hearing of that appeal unless the judge otherwise orders.

(4)   Where no notice is given under sub-paragraph (3) within the period limited by that paragraph –

    (a)   the decision on the test-case appeal binds the parties to each of the other appeals;

    (b)   without further hearing, the court will make, in each other appeal, an order similar to the order in the test-case appeal; and

    (c)   the party to each other appeal who is in the same interest as the unsuccessful party to the selected appeal is liable for the costs of the test-case appeal in the same manner and to the same extent as the unsuccessful party to that appeal and an order directing the party to pay such costs may be made and enforced accordingly.

(5)   Sub-paragraph (4)(a) does not affect the right to appeal to the Court of Appeal of any party to an appeal other than the test-case appeal.

Election Judges Rota Rules 2015
(SI 2015/329)

Made: 18th February 2015
Laid before Parliament: 23rd February 2015
Coming into force: 20th March 2015

The Civil Procedure Rule Committee, being the authority for the time being having power to make rules of court in relation to the Senior Courts, makes the following Rules in exercise of the power conferred by section 142(1) of the Senior Courts Act 1981.

Citation and commencement

1   These Rules may be cited as the Election Judges Rota Rules 2015 and come into force on 20th March 2015.

Placing of judges on rota for trial of election petitions

2(1)   Every year on 1st January, or as soon thereafter as practicable, at least four judges from among the judges of the Queen's Bench Division of the High Court who meet the requirements of section 142 of the Senior Courts Act 1981 (referred to in these Rules as "election judges") shall be placed on the rota for the trial of parliamentary election petitions in England and Wales under Part III of the Representation of the People Act 1983.

(2)   An election judge

    (a)   shall remain on the rota until 31st December of the year in which that judge was placed on the rota, subject to paragraph (4); and

    (b)   is eligible to be placed on the rota again in the succeeding or any subsequent year (unless that judge otherwise ceases to be eligible for any reason).

(3)   The judges to be placed on the rota shall be nominated by the President of the Queen's Bench Division.

(4)   If any election judge ceases to be eligible to be placed on the rota during the year after being placed on the rota, the President of the Queen's Bench Division shall nominate a judge of the Queen's Bench Division to be placed on the rota for the remainder of that year in place of the ineligible judge.

(5)   The President of the Queen's Bench Division may, after consulting the Lord Chief Justice, nominate such number of judges greater than four as the President of the Queen's Bench Division considers appropriate to facilitate the more convenient administration and trial of election petitions, and in that event the greater number of judges shall be placed on the rota.

(6)   Any judge placed on the rota before these Rules come into force shall remain on the rota until 31st December 2015.

Election Petition Rules 1960
(SI 1960/543)

21st March 1960

1   These Rules may be cited as the Election Petition Rules 1960.

2 (1)   The Interpretation Act 1978 shall apply to the interpretation of these Rules as it applies to the interpretation of an Act of Parliament.

(2)   In these Rules, unless the context otherwise requires--

"the Act" means the Representation of the People Act 1983;

"local election petition" means a petition questioning an election under the local government Act as defined in section 203(1) of the Act;

"petition" mean a parliamentary or local election petition;

"election petitions office" means the office of the Queen's Bench Masters' Secretary's Department at the Central Office of the Royal Courts of Justice;

"rota judge" means a judge on the rota for the trial of parliamentary election petitions;

"Divisional Court" means a Divisional Court of the Queen's Bench Division of the High Court;

"constituency" in relation to a local election petition means the local government area to which the petition relates;

"returning officer" means the returning officer of the constituency to which the petition relates.

(3)   The master of the Queen's Bench division who is for the time being nominated under section 157(4) of the Act as the prescribed officer in relation to parliamentary elections shall also be the prescribed officer in relation to elections under the local government Act, and references in these Rules to the prescribed officer shall be construed accordingly.

(4)   Subject to the provisions of the Act and these Rules, the practice and procedure of the High Court shall apply to a petition under these Rules as if it were an ordinary claim within its jurisdiction, notwithstanding any different practice, principle or rule on which the committees of the House of Commons used to act in dealing with election petitions.

(5)   Any document required to be filed in proceedings under these Rules shall be filed in the election petitions office.

NOTES

Defined terms

3 (1)   Any jurisdiction conferred by these Rules on a judge shall, if practicable, be exercised by a rota judge and, if not, by some other judge of the Queen's Bench Division.

(2)   Any jurisdiction conferred by these Rules on a master shall be exercised by the prescribed officer or in his absence by some other master of the Queen's Bench Division.

NOTES

Defined terms

   rota judge: r 2(2)

4 (1)   A petition shall be in the form set out in the Schedule to these Rules or a form to the like effect with such variations as the circumstances may require, and shall state--

  (a) in which of the capacities mentioned in section 121(1) or section 128(1) of the Act the petitioner or each of the petitioners presents the petition;

  (b) the date and result of the election to which the petition relates, showing in the case of a parliamentary election the date on which the return was made to the Clerk of the Crown of the member declared to have been elected;

  (c) in the case of a petition mentioned in subsection (2) or (3) of section 122 or subsection (2), (3) or (4) of section 129 of the Act, the date from which the time for the presentation of the petition is to be calculated; and

  (d) the grounds on which relief is sought, setting out with sufficient particularity the facts relied on but not the evidence by which they are to be proved;

  and shall conclude with a prayer setting out particulars of the relief claimed.

  (2)   The petition shall be presented by filing it and at the same time leaving three copies at the election petitions office.

NOTES

Defined terms
  the Act: r 2(2)
  election petitions office: r 2(2)

petition: r 2(2)

5 (1)   Within three days after the presentation of the petition the petitioner shall apply without notice being served on any Respondent within the meaning of Rule 6 to a master to fix the amount of security for costs which he is to give pursuant to section 136 of the Act.

  (2)   A recognisance as security for costs shall be acknowledged before a person authorised to take affidavits under the Commissioners for Oaths Acts 1889 and 1891 or the Solicitors Act 1974, and shall be filed forthwith after being acknowledged.

  (3)   The recognisance shall be accompanied by an affidavit sworn by each surety and stating that after payment of all his debts he is worth a sum not less than that for which he is bound by his recognisance.

NOTES

Defined terms
  the Act: r 2(2)
  petition: r 2(2)

6 (1)   Within five days after giving the security the petitioner shall serve on the respondent within the meaning of section 121(2) or section 128(2) of the Act and on the Director of Public Prosecutions a notice of the presentation of the petition and of the nature and amount of the security which he has given, together with a copy of the petition and of the affidavit accompanying any recognisance.

  (2)   Service shall be effected in the manner in which a claim form is served and a certificate of service shall be filed as soon as practicable after service has been effected.

NOTES

Defined terms
  the Act: r 2(2)
  petition: r 2(2)

7 (1)   Where the respondent intends to object to a recognisance on any ground mentioned in section 136(4) of the Act, he shall, within fourteen days after service on him of the notice referred to in Rule 6, serve on the petitioner notice of his objection, stating the

grounds thereof, and issue and serve on the petitioner an application notice to determine the validity or otherwise of the objection.

(2) The application shall be heard by a master, subject to an appeal to a judge within five days after the master's decision.

(3) If the objection is allowed, the master or judge having cognisance of the matter shall at the same time determine what sum of money will make the security sufficient, and the petitioner may within five days thereafter remove the objection by deposit of that sum.

NOTES
Defined terms
  the Act: r 2(2)

8   The list of petitions at issue kept by the prescribed officer pursuant to section 138(1) of the Act shall be conspicuously displayed in the election petitions office and shall be available for inspection by the public during office hours.

NOTES
Defined terms   petition: r 2(2)
  the Act: r 2(2)
  election petitions office: r 2(2)

9 (1) Within twenty-eight days after the first day on which a petition is at issue the petitioner shall apply by application notice to a rota judge for a time and place to be fixed for the trial of the petition and, if the petitioner fails to do so, any respondent may, within a further period of twenty-eight days, apply in the same manner as the petitioner could have done.

(2) If no application to fix a time and place for the trial of a petition is made in accordance with the last foregoing paragraph, the prescribed officer shall refer the matter to a rota judge, who shall thereupon fix such a time and place.

(3) In the case of a parliamentary election petition not less than fourteen days, and in any other case not less than seven days, before the day so fixed, the prescribed officer shall cause notice of the time and place of the trial to be displayed in a conspicuous place in the election petitions office and sent by post to–
    (a) the petitioner,
    (b) the respondent,
    (c) the Director of Public Prosecutions, and
    (d) the returning officer.

(4) The returning officers shall upon receipt of the notice forthwith publish it in his constituency.

(5) The rota judge fixing the time and place of trial shall also appoint an officer of the Supreme Court to act as registrar of the election court for the purposes of the trial.

NOTES
Defined terms   returning officer: r 2(2)
  constituency: r 2(2)   rota judge: r 2(2)
  election petitions office: r 2(2)
  petition: r 2(2)

10 (1) Where the petition claims the seat or office for an unsuccessful candidate on the ground that he had a majority of lawful votes, every party shall, not less than seven days before the day fixed for the trial, file a list of the votes which he contends were wrongly admitted or rejected, stating in respect of each such vote the grounds for his contention, and serve a copy of the list on every other party and the Director of Public Prosecutions.

(2) Where the respondent to a petition complaining of an undue election and claiming the seat or office for some other person intends to give evidence, pursuant to section 139(5) of the Act, to prove that that person was not duly elected, the respondent shall, not less than seven days before the day fixed for the trial of the petition, file a list of his objections to the election of that person on which he intends to rely and serve a copy of the list on the petitioner and the Director of Public Prosecutions.

(3) Any party to the petition may inspect and obtain an office copy of any list filed pursuant to either of the two last foregoing paragraphs.

(4) Except by leave of the election court–
   (a) no evidence shall be given by a party against the admission or rejection of any vote, or as to any ground of contention, which is not specified in a list filed by him pursuant to paragraph (1) of this Rule; and
   (b) no evidence shall be given by a respondent of any objection to a person's election which is not specified in a list filed by him pursuant to paragraph (2) of this Rule.

NOTES
Defined terms
   the Act: r 2(2)
   petition: r 2(2)

11 An application for a special case to be stated pursuant to section 146(1) of the Act shall be made by application notice to a Divisional Court.

NOTES
Defined terms
   the Act: r 2(2)
   Divisional Court: r 2(2)

12 (1) An application for leave to withdraw a petition shall be made by application notice to the election court or a Divisional Court at such time and place as the court may appoint.

(2) Not less than seven days before the day so appointed the petitioner shall–
   (a) serve the application notice on the respondent, the returning officer and the Director of Public Prosecutions and lodge a copy in the election petitions office;
   (b) publish notice of the intended application in at least one newspaper circulating in the constituency to which the petition relates.

(3) The application notice shall state the grounds on which the application to withdraw is made and contain a statement to the effect that on the hearing of the application any person who might have been a petitioner in respect of the election may apply to the court to be substituted as a petitioner.

(4) The returning officer shall upon receipt of the application notice forthwith publish it in his constituency.

(5) Where on the hearing of the application a person is substituted as a petitioner, any security required to be given by him shall be given within three days after the order of substitution.

NOTES
Defined terms
   constituency: r 2(2)
   Divisional Court: r 2(2)
   election petitions office: r 2(2)
   petition: r 2(2)
   returning officer: r 2(2)

13 (1) An application by a respondent to stay or dismiss a petition before the day fixed for the trial shall be made by application notice to the election court or a Divisional Court at such time and place as the court may appoint.

(2) Not less than seven days before the date so appointed the respondent shall serve the application notice, stating the grounds thereof, on the petitioner, any other respondent, the returning officer and the Director of Public Prosecutions, and shall lodge a copy at the election petitions office.

NOTES

Defined terms
Divisional Court: r 2(2)
election petitions office: r 2(2)
petition: r 2(2)

returning officer: r 2(2)

14 (1) Where a petition is abated by the death of a sole petitioner or the survivor of several petitioners, the solicitor acting for him in the proceedings at the date of his death or, if he had no such solicitor, any respondent learning of his death shall–

    (a) lodge notice thereof in the election petitions office;

    (b) serve notice thereof on the returning officer, who shall forthwith publish it in his constituency; and

    (c) publish notice thereof in at least one newspaper circulating in the constituency to which the petition relates.

Each such notice shall contain a statement to the effect of the next following paragraph.

(2) Within twenty-eight days after the publication of any notice referred to in sub-paragraph (c) of the last foregoing paragraph any person who might have been a petitioner in respect of the election may apply by application notice to the election court or a Divisional Court, at such time and place as the court may appoint, to be substituted as a petitioner.

NOTES

Defined terms
constituency: r 2(2)
Divisional Court: r 2(2)
election petitions office: r 2(2)

petition: r 2(2)
returning officer: r 2(2)

15 A respondent who does not intend to oppose the petition shall, not less than seven days before the day fixed for the trial, serve notice to that effect on the petitioner and the Director of Public Prosecutions.

NOTES

Defined terms
petition: r 2(2)

16 (1) On the happening of any event mentioned in section 153(1) of the Act, the respondent concerned shall–

    (a) lodge notice thereof in the election petitions office;

    (b) serve notice thereof on the returning officer who shall forthwith publish it in his constituency; and

    (c) publish notice thereof in at least one newspaper circulating in the constituency to which the petition relates.

Each such notice shall contain a statement to the effect of paragraph (3) of this Rule.

(2) The duties imposed by the last foregoing paragraph on the respondent concerned shall, in the case of the death of a respondent, be performed by the solicitor acting for him in the proceedings at the date of his death or, if he had no such solicitor, by any petitioner learning of his death.

(3) Within fourteen days after the publication of any notice referred to in sub-paragraph (c) of paragraph (1) of this Rule any person who might have been a petitioner in respect of the election may apply by application notice to a member of the election court or to a Divisional Court to be admitted as a respondent to oppose the petition.

NOTES

Defined terms
  constituency: r 2(2)
  Divisional Court: r 2(2)
  the Act: r 2(2)
  election petitions office: r 2(2)

petition: r 2(2)
returning officer: r 2(2)

17 A party giving particulars in pursuance of an order or otherwise shall file a copy within twenty-four hours after delivering the particulars to the party requiring them.

NOTES

Defined terms

18 (1) The shorthand writer who is to attend the trial of a local election petition shall be appointed by the commissioner to whom the trial is assigned and shall be entitled to be paid expenses on the same scale as a shorthand writer attending the trial of an action in the Queen's Bench Division .

(2) The commissioner may also appoint a proper person to act as his clerk for the purposes of the trial.

NOTES

Defined terms
  local election petition: r 2(2)

19 (1) Any period of time prescribed by Rules 5, 6 or 7 shall be computed in accordance with section 119 of the Act and shall not be varied by order or otherwise, but save as aforesaid rules 2.8 to 2.11 and 3.1(2)(a) of the Civil Procedure Rules 1998 shall apply to any period of time prescribed by these Rules as if it were prescribed by the Civil Procedure Rules.

(2) Where any period of time limited by the Act for presenting a petition or filing any document expires on a day (not being a day mentioned in section 119(2) of the Act) on which the election petitions office is closed, the petition or document shall be deemed to be duly presented or filed if it is placed in the letter box provided for the purpose at that office and an affidavit stating the time at which this was done is filed on the next day on which the office is open.

NOTES

Defined terms
  the Act: r 2(2)
  election petitions office: r 2(2)

petition: r 2(2)

20 Where by any provision of these Rules a petition or notice is required to be published by the returning officer, the cost of publication shall be paid in the first instance by the petitioner or, as the case may be, by the person by whom the notice was given, without prejudice to the manner in which such cost shall ultimately be borne by one or more of the parties to the petition.

NOTES

Defined terms
  petition: r 2(2)

returning officer: r 2(2)

21 (1) A solicitor appointed to act for a respondent in proceedings on a petition shall forthwith give notice of his appointment to the petitioner and lodge a copy of the notice in the election petitions office.

(2) Any notice required to be served on a respondent to a petition may be served–
> (a) by delivering it or sending it by post to any solicitor who has given notice under the last foregoing paragraph that he is acting for the respondent; or
> (b) if no such notice has been given, in the manner provided by section 184 of the Act.

(3) Any notice required to be served on the returning officer or the Director of Public Prosecutions in proceedings under these Rules may be served by delivering it or sending it by post to him.

NOTES
Defined terms   returning officer: r 2(2)
  the Act: r 2(2)
  election petitions office: r 2(2)
  petition: r 2(2)

23 These Rules shall come into operation on the first day of April 1960 but shall not affect any petition presented before that date.

NOTES
Defined terms
  petition: r 2(2)

SCHEDULE

ELECTION PETITION

Rule 4(1)

In the High Court of Justice,
Queen's Bench Division

In the Matter of the Representation of the People Act 1983

And in the Matter of a Parliamentary (*or* Local Government) Election for (*state place*) .. .. held on the .. ..day of .. ..19 .. ..

The Petition of A.B. of .. ..(and C.D. of .. ..) shows:–
1 That the Petitioner A.B. is a person who voted (*or* had a right to vote) at the above election (*or* was a candidate at the above election) (*or in the case of a parliamentary election* claims to have had a right to be elected or returned at the above election) and the Petitioner C.D. (*state similarly the capacity in which he presents the petition*).

2 That the election was held on the .. ..day of .. .., 19 .. .., when E.F., G.H. and J.K. were candidates, and on the .. ..day of .. ..19 .. .., the Returning Officer returned E.F. and G.H. to the Clerk of the Crown as being duly elected (*or in the case of a local Government election* and E.F. and G.H. were declared to be duly elected).

3 That (*state the facts on which the Petitioner(s) rely*).

4 That (*in the case of a petition mentioned in section 122(2) or (3) or section 129(2), (3) or (4) of*

the above Act state the event on which the time for the presentation of the petition depends and its date).

The Petitioner(s) therefore pray(s):–

(1) That it may be determined that the said E.F. was not duly elected (*or returned*) and that the election was void (*or that the said J.K. was duly elected and ought to have been returned*) (*or as the case may be*).

(2) That the Petitioner'(s) may have such further or other relief as may be just.

Dated this .. ..day of .. ..19 .. ..
　　(Signed)
　　PETITIONER(S)

This petition was presented by .. ..whose address for service is .. .. (and who is agent for .. ..of .. ..) (, solicitor for the said Petitioner).

It is proposed to serve a copy of this petition on .. ..of .. ..(and .. ..of .. ..) and on the Director of Public Prosecutions.

NOTES
Defined terms

European Parliamentary Election Petition Rules 1979
(SI 1979/521)

30th April 1979

1 (1)   These Rules may be cited as the European Parliamentary Election Petition Rules 1979, and shall come into operation on 7th June 1979.

(2)   They extend to England, Wales and Gibraltar.

2 (1)   In these Rules, unless the context otherwise requires:--

"the 2004 Regulations" means the European Parliamentary Elections Regulations 2004;

"combined region" means the electoral region which includes Gibraltar, namely the South West electoral region;

"Director of Public Prosecutions" means the Director of Public Prosecutions for England and Wales;

"Divisional Court" means a Divisional Court of the Queen's Bench Division of the High Court;

"election petitions office" means the office of the Queen's Bench Masters' Secretary's Department at the Central Office of the Royal Court of Justice;

"petition" means a petition questioning an election under the European Parliamentary Elections Act 2002;

"rota judge" means a judge on the rota for the trial of parliamentary election petitions;

"returning officer" means the returning officer for the electoral region to which the petition relates.

(2)   The master of the Queen's Bench Division who is for the time being nominated under section 157(4) of the Representation of the People Act 1983 as the prescribed officer in relation to parliamentary elections shall also be the prescribed officer in relation to European Parliamentary elections, and references in these Rules to the prescribed officer shall be construed accordingly.

(3)   Subject to the provisions of the 2004 Regulations and these Rules, the practice and procedure of the High Court. . . shall apply to a petition under these Rules as if it were an ordinary claim within its jurisdiction, notwithstanding any different practice, principle or rule on which the committees of the House of Commons used to act in dealing with election petitions.

(4)   Any document required to be filed in proceedings under these Rules shall be filed–
   (a)   if the petition relates to an electoral region other than the combined region, in the election petitions office; or
   (b)   if the petition relates to the combined region, in–
      (i)   the election petitions office, or
      (ii)   the Supreme Court Registry of the Gibraltar Supreme Court for transmission to the election petitions office, together with any fee payable.

(5)   *Repealed*

3 (1)   Any jurisdiction conferred by these Rules on a judge shall, if practicable, be exercised by a rota judge and, if not, by some other judge of the Queen's Bench Division.

(2) Any jurisdiction conferred by these Rules on a master shall be exercised by the prescribed officer or in his absence by some other master of the Queen's Bench Division.

4 (1) A petition shall be in the form set out in the Schedule to these Rules or a form to the like effect with such variations as the circumstances may require, and shall state–
    (a) in which of the capacities mentioned in regulation 89(1) of the 2004 Regulations the petitioner or each of the petitioners presents the petition;
    (b) the date and result of the election to which the petition relates;
    (c) . . . and
    (d) the grounds on which relief is sought, setting out with sufficient particularity the facts relied on but not the evidence by which they are to be proved;
and shall conclude with a prayer setting out particulars of the relief claimed.

(2) The petition shall be presented by filing it and at the same time leaving three copies at the election petitions office or the Supreme Court Registry of the Gibraltar Supreme Court (as the case may be).

5 (1) Within three days after the presentation of the petition the petitioner shall apply without notice being served on any Respondent within the meaning of Rule 6 to a master to fix the amount of security for costs which he is to give pursuant to regulation 94 of the 2004 Regulations.

(2) A recognisance as security for costs shall be acknowledged–
    (a) if the petition relates to an electoral region other than the combined region, before a person authorised to take affidavits under the Commissioners for Oaths Acts 1889 and 1891 or the Solicitors Act 1974; or
    (b) if the petition relates to the combined region–
        (i) before a person authorised to take affidavits under the Commissioners for Oaths Acts 1889 and 1891 or the Solicitors Act 1974; or
        (ii) before a person authorised to take affidavits under the Commissioners for Oaths and Public Notaries Act 1953,
and shall be filed forthwith after being acknowledged.

(3) The recognisance shall be accompanied by an affidavit sworn by each surety and stating that after payment of all his debts he is worth a sum not less than that for which he is bound by his recognisance.

(4) A petitioner, when making a payment into court on account of security for costs, may do so–
    (a) if the petition relates to an electoral region other than the combined region, in accordance with rules 7 and 8(1) and (5)(b) of the Court Funds Rules 2011, or
    (b) if the petition relates to the combined region–
        (i) in accordance with rules 7 and 8(1) and (5)(b) of the Court Funds Rules 2011, or
        (ii) at the Supreme Court Registry of the Gibraltar Supreme Court for transmission to the Court Funds Office.

6 (1) Within five days after giving the security the petitioner shall serve on the respondent within the meaning of regulation 89(2) of the 2004 Regulations and on the Director of Public Prosecutions a notice of the presentation of the petition and of the nature and amount of the security which he has given, together with a copy of the petition and of the affidavit accompanying any recognisance.

(2) Service shall be effected in the manner in which a claim form is served and a certificate

of service shall be filed as soon as practicable after service has been effected.

7 (1) Where the respondent intends to object to a recognisance on any ground mentioned in regulation 94(4) of the 2004 Regulations, he shall, within fourteen days after service on him on the notice referred to in Rule 6, serve on the petitioner notice of his objection, stating the grounds thereof, and issue and serve on the petitioner an application notice to determine the validity or otherwise of the objection.

(2) The application shall be heard . . . by a master, subject to an appeal to a judge within five days after the master's decision.

(3) If the objection is allowed, the master or judge having cognisance of the matter shall at the same time determine what sum of money will make the security sufficient, and the petitioner may within five days thereafter remove the objection by deposit of that sum.

8 *Repealed*

9 (1) Within twenty-eight days after the first day on which a petition is at issue, the petitioner shall apply by application notice to a rota judge for a time and place to be fixed for the trial of the petition and, if the petitioner fails to do so, any respondent may, within a further period of twenty-eight days, apply in the same manner as the petitioner could have done.

(2) If no application to fix a time and place for the trial of a petition is made in accordance with the last foregoing paragraph, the prescribed officer shall refer the matter to a rota judge, who shall thereupon fix such a time and place.

(3) Not less than fourteen days before the day so fixed, the prescribed officer shall cause notice of the time and place of the trial to be displayed in a conspicuous place in the election petitions office and sent by post to–
    (a) the petitioner,
    (b) the respondent, and
    (c) the Director of Public Prosecutions.

(4) The rota judge fixing the time and place of trial shall also appoint an officer of the Supreme Court to act as registrar of the election court for the trial.

10 (1) Where the petition claims the office for an unsuccessful candidate on the ground that he had a majority of lawful votes, every party shall, not less than seven days before the day fixed the trial, file a list of the votes which he contends were wrongly admitted or rejected, stating in respect of each such vote the grounds for his contention, and serve a copy of the list on every other party and the Director of Public Prosecutions.

(2) Where the respondent to a petition complaining of an undue election and claiming the office for some other person intends to give evidence, pursuant to regulation 96(4) of the 2004 Regulations, to prove that that person was not duly elected, the respondent shall, not less than seven days before the day fixed for the trial of the petition, file a list of his objections to the election of that person on which he intends to rely and serve a copy of the list on the petitioner and the Director of Public Prosecutions.

(3) Any party to the petition may inspect and obtain an office copy of any list filed pursuant to either of the two last foregoing paragraphs.

(4) Except by leave of the election court–
    (a) no evidence shall be given by a party against the admission or rejection of any vote, or as to any ground of contention, which is not specified in a list filed by him pursuant to paragraph (1) of this Rule; and

(b) no evidence shall be given by a respondent of any objection to a person's election which is not specified in a list filed by him pursuant to paragraph (2) of this Rule.

11 An application for a special case to be stated pursuant to regulation 101(1) of the 2004 Regulations shall be made by application notice to a Divisional Court.

12 (1) An application for leave to withdraw a petition shall be made by application notice to the election court or a Divisional Court at such time and place as the court may appoint.

(2) Not less than seven days before the day so appointed the petitioner shall–
   (a) serve the application notice on–
      (i) the respondent,
      (ii) the returning officer, and
      (iii) the Director of Public Prosecutions;
   (b) file a copy of the application notice in–
      (i) if the petition relates to an electoral region other than the combined region, the election petitions office, or
      (ii) if the petition relates to the combined region in–
      (aa) the election petitions office, or
      (bb) the Supreme Court Registry of the Gibraltar Supreme Court for transmission to the election petitions office; and
   (c) publish notice of the application–
      (i) if the petition relates to an electoral region other than the combined region, in at least one newspaper circulating in the region, or
      (ii) if the petition relates to the combined region, in at least one newspaper circulating in the part of the region which is in the United Kingdom and in at least one newspaper circulating in Gibraltar.

(3) The application notice shall state the grounds on which the application to withdraw is made and contain a statement to the effect that, on the hearing of the application, any person who might have been a petitioner in respect of the election may apply to the court to be substituted as a petitioner.

(4) The returning officer shall upon receipt of the application notice forthwith publish it–
   (a) if the petition relates to an electoral region other than the combined region, in the region, or
   (b) if the petition relates to the combined region, in–
      (i) the part of the region which is in the United Kingdom, and
      (ii) Gibraltar.

(5) Where on the hearing of the application a person is substituted as a petitioner, any security required to be given by him shall be given within three days after the order of substitution.

13 (1) An application by a respondent to stay or dismiss a petition before the day fixed for the trial shall be made by application notice to the election court or a Divisional Court at such time and place as the court may appoint.

(2) Not less than seven days before the date so appointed the respondent–
   (a) shall serve the application notice, stating the grounds thereof, on–
      (i) the petitioner,
      (ii) any other respondent,
      (iii) the returning officer, and
      (iv) the Director of Public Prosecutions; and

(b) file a copy in–
   (i) if the petition relates to an electoral region other than the combined region, the election petitions office, or,
   (ii) if the petition relates to the combined region–
(aa) the election petitions office, or
(bb) the Supreme Court Registry of the Gibraltar Supreme Court for transmission to the election petitions office.

14 (1) Where a petition is abated by the death of a sole petitioner or the survivor of several petitioners, the solicitor acting for him in the proceedings at the date of his death or, if he had no such solicitor, any respondent learning of his death shall–
   (a) file notice thereof–
      (i) if the petition relates to an electoral region other than the combined region, in the election petitions office, or,
      (ii) if the petition relates to the combined region–
   (aa) the election petitions office, or
   (bb) the Supreme Court Registry of the Gibraltar Supreme Court for transmission to the election petitions office;
   (b) serve notice thereof on the returning officer, who shall forthwith publish it–
      (i) if the petition relates to an electoral region other than the combined region, in the region, or
      (ii) if the petition relates to the combined region in–
   (aa) the part of the region which is in the United Kingdom, and
   (bb) Gibraltar; and
   (c) publish notice thereof–
      (i) if the petition relates to an electoral region other than the combined region, in at least one newspaper circulating in the region, or
      (ii) if the petition relates to the combined region, in at least one newspaper circulating in the part of the region which is in the United Kingdom and in at least one newspaper circulating in Gibraltar.
   Each such notice shall contain a statement to the effect of the next following paragraph.

   (2) Within twenty-eight days after the publication of any notice referred to in sub-paragraph (c) of the last foregoing paragraph any person who might have been a petitioner in respect of the election may apply by application notice to the election court or a Divisional Court, at such time and place as the court may appoint, to be substituted as a petitioner.

15 A respondent who does not intend to oppose the petition shall, not less than seven days before the day fixed for the trial, serve notice to that effect on the petitioner and the Director of Public Prosecutions.

16 *Repealed*

17 A party giving particulars in pursuance of an order or otherwise shall file a copy within twenty-four hours after delivering the particulars to the party requiring them.

18 (1) Any period of time prescribed by Rules 5, 6 or 7 shall be computed in accordance with regulation 87 of the 2004 Regulations and shall not be varied by order or otherwise, but save as aforesaid rules 2.8 to 2.11 and 3.1(2)(a) of the Civil Procedure Rules 1998 shall apply to any period of time prescribed by these Rules as if it were prescribed by

the Civil Procedure Rules.

(2) Where any period of time limited by the 2004 Regulations for presenting a petition or filing any document expires on a day (not being a day mentioned in regulation 32(2) of the 2004 Regulations) on which the election petitions office or the Supreme Court Registry of the Gibraltar Supreme Court (as the case may be) is closed, the petition or document shall be deemed to be duly presented or filed if it is placed in the letter box provided for the purpose at that office and an affidavit stating the time at which this was done is filed on the next day on which the office is open.

19 Where, by any provision of these Rules, a petition or notice is required to be published by the returning officer, the cost of publication shall be paid in the first instance by the petitioner or, as the case may be, by the person by whom the notice was given, without prejudice to the manner in which such costs shall ultimately be borne by one or more of the parties to the petition.

20 (1) A solicitor appointed to act for a respondent in proceedings on a petition shall forthwith give notice of his appointment to the petitioner and lodge a copy of the notice in the election petitions office.

(2) Any notice required to be served on a respondent to a petition may be served–
    (a) by delivering it or sending it by post to any solicitor who has given notice under the last foregoing paragraph that he is acting for the respondent; or
    (b) if no such notice has been given, in the manner provided by regulation 122 of the 2004 Regulations.

(3) Any notice required to be served on the returning officer or the Director of Public Prosecutions in proceedings under these Rules may be served by delivering it or sending it by post to him.

SCHEDULE
ELECTION PETITION

Rule 4(1)

In the Matter of the European Parliamentary Elections Regulations 2004,
And in the Matter of a European Parliamentary Election for state electoral region
Held on the.. .. .. ..day of.. .. .. .., 20 .
The Petition of A.B. of .. ..(and C.D. of .. ..) shows:–

1 That the Petitioner A.B. is a person who voted (*or* had a right to vote) at the above election (*or* was a candidate at the above election) (*or* claims to have had a right to be elected or declared to be elected at the above election) and the Petitioner C.D. (*state similarly the capacity in which he represents the petition*).

2 That the election was held on the .. ..day of .. ..20 .. .., when E.F., G.H. and J.K. were candidates, and on the .. ..day of .. .. 20 .. .., the Returning Officer declared E.F. to be duly elected.

3 That (*state the facts on which the Petitioner(s) rely).*

4 The Petitioner(s) therefore pray(s):–
    (1) That it may be determined that the said E.F. was not duly elected (or declared to be elected) and that the election was void (or that the said J.K. was duly elected and ought to have been declared to be elected) (*or as the case may be*).
    (2) That the Petitioner(s) may have such further or other relief as may be just.

Dated this .. ..day of .. ..20 .. ...

(*Signed*)
PETITIONER(S)

This petition was presented by .. ..whose address for service is (and who is agent for .. ..of .. ..) (, solicitor for the said Petitioner).

It is proposed to serve a copy of this petition on .. ..of .. .. (and .. ..of .. ..) and on the Director of Public Prosecutions.

European Parliamentary Elections (Changes to the Franchise and Qualification of Representatives) Regulations 1994
(SI 1994/342)

Made   16th February 1994

PART I
CITATION, COMMENCEMENT AND INTERPRETATION

PART II
CHANGES TO THE QUALIFICATION OF REPRESENTATIVES AND
ASSOCIATED AMENDMENTS ABOUT CITIZENS OF THE UNION

PART III
CHANGES TO THE FRANCHISE AND PROVISIONS ABOUT REGISTRATION

PART IV

PART I
CITATION, COMMENCEMENT AND INTERPRETATION

Citation and commencement

1(1)   These Regulations may be cited as the European Parliamentary Elections (Changes to the Franchise and Qualification of Representatives) Regulations 1994.

(2)   Subject to paragraph (3) below, these Regulations shall come into force on the day after the day on which they are made.

(3)   Part III of these Regulations shall have effect subject to the provisions of Part IV of them (provisions in respect of first registers of relevant citizens of the Union as European Parliamentary electors).

2 Interpretation

(1)   In these Regulations and any provision as applied by Part III of these Regulations
"Act of 1978" means the European Parliamentary Elections Act 1978;
"Act of 1983" means the Representation of the People Act 1983;
.....

PART II
CHANGES TO THE QUALIFICATION OF REPRESENTATIVES AND ASSOCIATED AMENDMENTS ABOUT CITIZENS OF THE UNION

3   *Repealed*

Offence of standing as a candidate in more than one Member State

4(1)   If a person, on any occasion when under article [10] of the Act concerning the election of representatives of the European Parliament by direct universal suffrage annexed to the Council decision 76/787/ECSC, EEC, Euratom of 20th September 1976 elections to the European Parliament are held in all Member States, stands as a candidate at such an election in the United Kingdom and in any other Member State, he shall be guilty of an offence.

(2)   An offence under this regulation shall be an illegal practice within the meaning of the Act of 1983, and the provisions of that Act which relate to illegal practices, as applied by regulations under the Act of 1978, shall accordingly have effect in relation to any such offence.

(3)   . . .

European Parliamentary Elections
(Franchise of Relevant
Citizens of the Union) Regulations 2001
(SI 2001/1184)

Made 26th March 2001

1   Citation, interpretation and extent
2   Revocation
3   Relevant citizens of the Union as European Parliamentary electors
4   Entitlement of relevant citizen of the Union to be registered as European Parliamentary
    elector
5   Registration officers
6   Form of application and declaration required by regulation 4(1)
7   Punishment of false statement in application or declaration made under regulation 6(1)
    and (2)
8   Copies of certain applications and declarations to be sent to the Secretary of State
9   Application, with modifications, of provisions of the 1983 Act and Representation of the
    People Regulations
10 Removal of [entries from the register
11 Consequential amendments

Citation, interpretation and extent

1(1)   These Regulations may be cited as the European Parliamentary Elections (Franchise of
       Relevant Citizens of the Union) Regulations 2001 and shall come into force on the
       expiry of the period of fourteen days beginning with the day on which they are made.

(2)   In these Regulations
       "the 1983 Act" means the Representation of the People Act 1983;
       "citizen of the Union" is to be determined in accordance with Article 17.1 of the
       Treaty establishing the European Community and "relevant citizen of the Union"
       means such a citizen who is not a Commonwealth citizen or citizen of the Republic
       of Ireland.

(3)   These Regulations extend throughout the United Kingdom.

Revocation

2   Regulations 7 to 14 and 17 and 18 of the European Parliamentary Elections (Changes to
    the Franchise and Qualification of Representatives) Regulations 1994 are hereby
    revoked.

Relevant citizens of the Union as European Parliamentary electors

3(1)   A person is entitled to vote as an elector at a European Parliamentary election in an
       electoral region if on the date of the poll he
       (a)   is registered in the region in the register of relevant citizens of the Union
             entitled to vote at European Parliamentary elections (maintained under
             regulation 5(2) below);
       (b)   is not subject to any legal incapacity to vote (age apart);
       (c)   is a relevant citizen of the Union; and
       (d)   is of voting age (that is, 18 years or over).

(2)   A person is not entitled to vote as an elector

1197

     (a) more than once in the same electoral region at any European Parliamentary election, or

     (b) in more than one electoral region at a European Parliamentary general election.

(3)   In this regulation "legal incapacity" has the same meaning in relation to European Parliamentary elections as it has in the 1983 Act in relation to parliamentary elections.

Entitlement of relevant citizen of the Union to be registered as European Parliamentary elector

4(1)   A person is entitled to be registered in the register of relevant citizens of the Union entitled to vote at European Parliamentary elections (maintained under regulation 5(2) below) for part of an electoral region if on the relevant date he

     (a) is resident in that part of the region;

     (b) is not subject to any legal incapacity to vote (age apart);

     (c) is a relevant citizen of the Union; and

     (d) is of voting age;

and the registration officer has received in respect of him an application and declaration made in accordance with regulation 6(1) and (2) below.

(2)   *Repealed*

(3)   The preceding provisions have effect subject to

     (a) any enactment imposing a disqualification for registration as a European Parliamentary elector, and

     (b) compliance with the requirements of these Regulations and any provision applied by these Regulations.

(4)   A person otherwise qualified is (despite paragraph (1)(d) above) entitled to be registered in a register maintained under regulation 5(2) below if he will attain voting age before the end of the period of 12 months beginning with the 1st December next following the relevant date, but

     (a) his entry in the register shall give the date on which he will attain that age; and

     (b) until the date given in the entry, he shall not by virtue of the entry be treated as an elector for any purposes other than those of an election the date of the poll for which is the date so given or any later date.

(4A) If a person entitled to be registered by virtue of paragraph (4) above has an anonymous entry in the register, the references in paragraphs (a) and (b) of that paragraph to his entry in the register are to be read as references to his entry in the record of anonymous entries prepared under regulation 45A of the Representation of the People (England and Wales) Regulations 2001, regulation 45A of the Representation of the People (Scotland) Regulations 2001, or regulation 53A of the Representation of the People Regulations 2008, as applied by these Regulations.

(5)   In this regulation

     "enactment" includes

        (a) any provision of an Act, and

        (b) any provision of subordinate legislation (within the meaning of the Interpretation Act 1978); and

     "the relevant date" means the date on which the application and declaration required by regulation 6(1) and (2) below were made.

Registration officers

5(1)   The officer who

     (a) under subsections (2) to (4) of section 8 of the 1983 Act is the registration officer for any of the areas referred to in those subsections for the purposes of that Act;

and

(b) under the provision substituted by the Schedule to the Isles of Scilly Order 1978 is the registration officer for the Isles of Scilly for those purposes,

shall be the registration officer for the area in question for the purposes of the registration of relevant citizens of the Union as European Parliamentary electors.

(2) Each registration officer shall maintain a register of any person or persons entitled to be registered under regulation 4 above.

(3) Such a register shall, so far as practicable, be combined with

(a) the registers of parliamentary and local government electors, and

(b) any register of peers kept under section 3 of the Representation of the People Act 1985;

and the entries for persons registered under this regulation shall be marked to indicate that fact.

Form of application and declaration required by regulation 4(1)

6(1) An application under this regulation may be made by a relevant citizen of the Union ("the applicant"), shall be signed and dated by him and shall state

(a) the full name of the applicant;

(b) the address in respect of which the applicant claims to be registered and whether he is resident there on the relevant date;

(c) *Repealed*

(d) if the applicant is not resident on the relevant date at the address in respect of which he claims to be registered, whether he has made a declaration of local connection;

(e) if the applicant is a merchant seaman on the relevant date, that fact; . . .

(f) either that the applicant is aged 18 or over or, if not, the date of his birth; and

(g) in the case of an applicant whose application is accompanied by an application for an anonymous entry, that fact.

(2) An application under this regulation shall include a declaration stating

(a) the nationality of the applicant;

(b) the applicant's address in the United Kingdom, if different from the address given under paragraph (1)(b) above;

(c) where the applicant's name has been entered in a register of electors in a locality or constituency in the Member State of which he is a national, the name of the locality or constituency where, so far as he knows, his name was last so entered; and

(d) that the applicant will exercise any right which he has to vote at European Parliamentary elections at any such election only in the United Kingdom during the period for which any entry in the register of electors made in pursuance of this application remains in force.

(3) The registration officer shall supply free of charge as many copies of forms for use in connection with applications and declarations under paragraphs (1) and (2) above as appear to that officer reasonable in the circumstances to any person who satisfies that officer of his intention to use the forms in connection with the registration of relevant citizens of the Union as European Parliamentary electors.

(4) An application under paragraph (1) above and a declaration under paragraph (2) above shall be of no effect unless they are received by the registration officer concerned within the period of three months beginning with the date on which they are made.

(5) In any case where the registration officer is not required to notify the applicant of the result of the application under the regulations applied by regulation 9 below, he shall

so notify the applicant under this paragraph.

(6) In this regulation

"locality or constituency" has the same meaning as it has in the directive of the Council of the European Commissioners No 93/109/EC; and

"relevant date" has the same meaning as in regulation 4 above.

Punishment of false statement in application or declaration made under regulation 6(1) and (2)

7(1) A person who makes a statement which he knows to be false in an application or declaration required by regulation 6(1) and (2) above is guilty of an offence and liable on summary conviction to a fine not exceeding level 3 on the standard scale.

(2) The provisions of Part III of the 1983 Act relating to the prosecution of offences, as applied by regulations made under the European Parliamentary Elections Act 1978, shall have effect in relation to an offence under this regulation as they have effect in relation to an offence under the 1983 Act as so applied.

Copies of certain applications and declarations to be sent to the Secretary of State

8(1) As soon as practicable after the registration officer has registered the entry for a relevant citizen of the Union in the register maintained under regulation 5(2) above in the circumstances set out in paragraph (2) below, he shall send information contained in the application and declaration made in pursuance of regulation 6(1) and (2) above by virtue of which he registered the entry in the register to the person shown as the representative of the State in respect of which the applicant is a national in a direction containing a list of such representatives issued by the Secretary of State or the Chancellor of the Duchy of Lancaster in accordance with paragraph (3) below.

(2) Those circumstances are where the relevant citizen of the Union would be entitled to vote at a European Parliamentary general election in pursuance of the registration.

(3) The Secretary of State or the Chancellor of the Duchy of Lancaster shall issue directions identifying the representative for each Member State of the European Union to whom the information referred to in paragraph (1) above is to be sent.

Application, with modifications, of provisions of the 1983 Act and Representation of the People Regulations

9(1) The provisions of

(a) the 1983 Act which are set out in column 1 of Part I of the Schedule to these Regulations, and

(b) the Representation of the People (England and Wales) Regulations 2001 the Representation of the People (Scotland) Regulations 2001 and the Representation of the People (Northern Ireland) Regulations 2008 which are set out in column 1 of Part II of that Schedule,

shall apply for the purposes of the registration of relevant citizens of the Union as European Parliamentary electors as they apply for the purposes of the registration of parliamentary and local government electors subject to

(i) any modification and exceptions specified in relation to those provisions in column 2 of the Schedule to these Regulations, and

(ii) paragraph (2) below.

(2) Unless the context otherwise requires, in the provisions applied by the Schedule to these Regulations

(a) any reference to a parliamentary elector is a reference to a European Parliamentary elector;

(b) any reference to a register is to the register maintained under regulation 5(2) above;

(c) any reference to a constituency is a reference to an electoral region; and

(d) any reference in such a provision to another provision which is so applied, is to that provision as so applied.

Removal of entries from the register

10(1) A declaration under regulation 6(2) above may be cancelled at any time by the declarant.

(2) A relevant citizen of the Union registered in a register of electors maintained under regulation 5(2) above is entitled to remain so registered until

(a) the end of the period of 12 months beginning with the date when the entry in the register first takes effect,

(b) the declaration under regulation 6(2) above is cancelled under paragraph (1) above;

(c) the citizen applies for his entry to be removed;

(d) any entry made in respect of him in any other register of electors maintained under regulation 5(2) above takes effect,

whichever occurs first.

(3) Where the entitlement of such a person to remain registered terminates by virtue of paragraph (2) above, the registration officer concerned shall remove the person's entry from the register, unless he is entitled to remain in pursuance of a further application and declaration under regulation 6(1) and (2) above.

(4) The registration officer shall remove the entry for a relevant citizen of the Union from the register maintained under regulation 5(2) above where the Secretary of State sends to that officer a copy of any information provided by the Member State of which that citizen is a national to show that he has lost the right to vote there.

Consequential amendments

11 In

(a) *Repealed*

(b) section 54(8)(b) of the Political Parties, Elections and Referendums Act 2000,

for "Part III of the European Parliamentary Elections (Changes to the Franchise and the Qualifications of Representatives) Regulations 1994" substitute "the European Parliamentary Elections (Franchise of Relevant Citizens of the Union) Regulations 2001".

SCHEDULE

APPLICATION WITH MODIFICATIONS OF THE 1983 ACT AND

VARIOUS REPRESENTATION OF THE PEOPLE REGULATIONS FOR REGISTRATION UNDER THESE REGULATIONS

1 Provision applied	2 Modification
	PART I THE 1983 ACT
Section 5 (residence: general)	In subsection (1) from the words "section 4" to the end substitute "regulation 4 of the 2001 Regulations falls to be determined for the purposes of that regulation.". In subsections (3) and (6) for "section 4 above" substitute "regulation 4 of the 2001 Regulations".

1 Provision applied	2 Modification
Section 6 (residence: merchant seamen)	For "section 4 above" substitute "regulation 4 of the 2001 Regulations".
Section 7 (residence: patients in mental hospitals who are not detained offenders or on remand)	In subsection (1)(b) omit "section 3A above or".
	In subsection (2) for "section 4 above" substitute "regulation 4 of the 2001 Regulations".
	In subsection (3)(aa) for "regulations" substitute "the Representation of the People Regulations as applied by the 2001 Regulations".
Section 7A (residence: persons remanded in custody etc)	In subsection (2) for "section 4 above" substitute "regulation 4 of the 2001 Regulations".
	In subsection (3)(aa) for "regulations" substitute "the Representation of the People Regulations as applied by the 2001 Regulations".
Section 7B (notional residence: declarations of local connection)	In subsection (2)(c) for "section 4 above" substitute "regulation 4 of the 2001 Regulations".
	In subsection (3)(e) omit the words from "a Commonwealth citizen" to "elections)".
	Omit subsections (6) and (7).
Section 7C (effect of declaration of local connection)	In subsection (1) for "section 4 above" substitute "regulation 4 of the 2001 Regulations".
	In subsection (2)(aa) for "regulations" substitute "the Representation of the People Regulations as applied by the 2001 Regulations".
Section 9 (registers of electors), subsections (2), (3), (4), (7) and (8)	
Section 9B (anonymous registration)	In subsection (1)(a), for "section 10ZC or 10A(1)(a)" substitute "regulation 6 of the 2001 Regulations".
	In subsection (4) after "this Act" insert "and the 2001 Regulations".
	In subsection (6), for "section 10ZC or 10A(1)(a)" substitute "regulation 6 of the 2001 Regulations".
	In subsection (7)(b) omit the words from "(including" to the end.
	For subsection (11) substitute
	"(11) In this section, "determines" means determines in accordance with the Representation of the People Regulations as applied by the 2001 Regulations."
	After subsection (11) insert
	"(12) A relevant citizen of the Union who (a) applies to be registered in a register of European Parliamentary electors, and (b) has an existing anonymous entry in a register of local government electors, shall be anonymously registered in a register of European Parliamentary electors maintained under regulation 5(2) of the 2001 Regulations.".
Section 9C (removal of anonymous entry)	After subsection (1E) insert

1 Provision applied	2 Modification
	"(1F) A person's entitlement to an anonymous entry in a register of European Parliamentary electors maintained under regulation 5(2) of the 2001 Regulations by virtue of section 9B(12) terminates at the same time as his entitlement to have an anonymous entry in a register of local government electors terminates by virtue of this section.".
	In subsection (2) omit "other" and for "the Representation of the People Act 1985" substitute "the 2001 Regulations".
Section 10A (maintenance of registers: registration of electors), subsections (1)(a), (1A), (1B), (3), (3A), (3B), (4) and (9)	In subsection (1)(a) for "the prescribed requirements, or" substitute "regulations 4 and 6 of the 2001 Regulations.".
	In subsection (1A) omit the words from "and the power in subsection (1)" to the end.
	For subsection (9) substitute "(9) In this section "determines" means determines in accordance with the Representation of the People Regulations as applied by the 2001 Regulations.".
Section 13 (publication of registers)	For subsections (1) to (3) substitute
	"(1) Where a register maintained under regulation 5(2) of the 2001 Regulations is in force, a revised version of it shall be published when a revised version of the registers of parliamentary and local government electors is published under subsection (1) or (3) of this section, as it has effect for the purposes of such registers.".
Section 13A (alteration of registers)	In subsection (1)
	(a) in paragraph (a), for "prescribed requirements" substitute " requirements in regulations 4 and 6 of the 2001 Regulations"; and
	(b) in paragraph (b), after "this Act" insert "or of the 2001 Regulations".
	In subsection (2A) omit the words from "and the power in subsection (1)(a)" to the end.
	In subsection (3)
	(a) for paragraph (a) substitute
	"(a) at the beginning of the month containing the date on which revised versions of the registers of parliamentary and local government electors are next due to be published in accordance with section 13(1) or (3) as they have effect for the purposes of such registers, or"
	(b) for paragraph (b) substitute

1 Provision applied	2 Modification
	"(b) at the beginning of either of the two months preceding that containing the date on which revised versions of the registers of parliamentary or local government electors are next due to be published in accordance with section 13(1)(a) as it has effect for the purposes of such registers,".
	In subsection (6)
	(a) for "regulations" substitute "the Representation of the People Regulations as applied by the 2001 Regulations"; and
	(b) omit "as if it were contained in Part II of this Act".
Section 13AB (alteration of registers: interim publication dates)	For subsection (8) substitute
	"(8) This section applies to elections to the European Parliament in England, Wales and Scotland."
Section 13B (alteration of registers: pending elections)	For subsection (4) substitute
	"(4) This section applies to elections to the European Parliament in England, Wales or Scotland.".
	In subsection (6) omit from "as if" to the end.
Section 13BA (alteration of registers in Northern Ireland: pending elections)	For subsection (12) substitute
	"(12) This section applies to elections in Northern Ireland to the European Parliament.".
Section 13C (electoral identity card: Northern Ireland)	For subsection (7) substitute
	"(7) In this section "determine" means determine in accordance with the Representation of the People Regulations as applied by the 2001 Regulations.".
Section 50 (effect of misdescription)	
Section 52 (discharge of registration duties)	In subsections (1) and (4) after "this Act" insert "and the 2001 Regulations".
Section 54 (payment of expenses of registration)	In subsection (1) for "under this Act" substitute "under the 2001 Regulations". Omit subsection (3).
Section 56 (registration appeals: England and Wales)	In subsection (1)
	(a) in paragraph (a), after "this Act" insert "or the 2001 Regulations";
	(b) for paragraph (aa) substitute
	"(aa) from any decision under the 2001 Regulations of the registration officer that a person registered in the register of European Parliamentary electors maintained under regulation (5)(2) of the 2001 Regulations was not entitled to be

1	2
Provision applied	Modification
	registered,"; and
	(c) omit paragraph (b).
Section 57 (registration appeals: Scotland)	
Section 58 (registration appeals: Northern Ireland)	In subsection (1)
	(a) in paragraph (a) after "this Act" insert "or the 2001 Regulations";
	(b) for paragraph (b) substitute
	"(b) from any decision under the 2001 Regulations of the Chief Electoral Officer that a person registered in the register of European Parliamentary electors maintained under regulation (5)(2) of the 2001 Regulations was not entitled to be registered,"; and
	(c) omit paragraph (c).
Section 62 (offences as to declarations)	In subsection (1)(a)
	(a) omit "or a service declaration";
	(b) in sub-paragraph (i) omit "or section 15(1)"; and
	(c) in sub-paragraph (iii) at the end omit "or".
	Omit subsections (1)(b) and (2).
Section 63 (breach of official duty), subsections (1) to (3)	In subsection (3)
	(a) for paragraphs (a) to (d) substitute
	"(a) any registration officer.";
	(b) in paragraph (e) for "any of paragraphs (a) to (d)" substitute "paragraph (a)"; and
	(c) for the words from "relating to" to the end, substitute "relating to the registration of relevant citizens of the Union as European Parliamentary electors".
Section 119 (computation of time for purposes of Part II)	In the heading for "Part II" substitute "section 13A and 13B".
	In subsection (1)
	(a) for "this Part of this Act" substitute "section 13A or 13B"; and
	(b) in paragraph (b) for "this Part" substitute "section 13A or 13B".
Section 202 (general provisions as to interpretation)	In subsection (1)
	(a) omit all of the definitions except "anonymous entry", "citizen of the Union", "dwelling" and "qualifying address"; and
	(b) insert, at the appropriate places
	""2001 Regulations" means the European Parliamentary Elections (Franchise of Relevant Citizens of the Union) Regulations 2001,".
	""prescribed" in the following sections means prescribed by the Representation of the People

1	2
Provision applied	Modification
	Regulations as applied by the 2001 Regulations 9(2)(a) and (b); 9B(1)(a) and (c) and (3)(b); 10A(3); 13A(2); 13B(3), (3A)(a), (3B), (3C)(a), (3D) and (3E); 13BA(3), (7)(a), (8)(a), (10) and (11)(a); 13C(1); 56(1) and (5); and 58(2) and (6)(a),".
	""Representation of the People Regulations" means (a) in relation to England and Wales, the Representation of the People (England and Wales) Regulations 2001; (b) in relation to Scotland, the Representation of the People (Scotland) Regulations 2001; and (c) in relation to Northern Ireland, the Representation of the People (Northern Ireland) Regulations 2008;"."

PART II

THE REPRESENTATION OF THE PEOPLE (ENGLAND AND WALES) REGULATIONS 2001

Regulation 3 (interpretation)	
Regulation 5 (communication of applications, notices etc)	
Regulation 6 (electronic signatures and related certificates)	
Regulation 7 (copies of documents)	Omit paragraph (6).
Regulation 8 (time)	
Regulation 11 (interference with notices etc)	
Regulation 24 (evidence as to age and nationality)	In paragraph (2) for sub-paragraphs (b) to (d) substitute "(b) evidence of his status as a national of a Member State or a statutory declaration as to that nationality.".
Regulation 27 (objections to registration)	
Regulation 28 (inspection of applications and objections)	
Regulation 29 (procedure for determining applications for registration and objections without a hearing)	Omit paragraph (8).
Regulation 30 (notice of hearing)	
Regulation 31 (hearing of applications and objections)	
Regulation 31A (objections relating to applications that have been allowed, but before alterations to register have	

1	2
Provision applied	Modification

taken effect)

Regulation 31B (other determinations by registration officer of entitlement to registration)	In paragraph (1) for "regulations 31C to 31F" substitute "regulations 31D to 31F".
	In paragraph (2) (a) in sub-paragraph (a) (i) in paragraph (i) for ", 7C(2)(aa), and 15(2)(aa) of the 1983 Act, and" substitute "and 7C(2)(aa) of the 1983 Act."; and (ii) omit paragraph (ii); and (b) omit sub-paragraph (b).
Regulation 31D (procedure for reviewing entitlement to registration)	In paragraphs (5) and (8) omit "or, as the case may be, has ceased to satisfy the conditions for registration set out in section 4 of the 1983 Act".
Regulation 31E (list of reviews)	
Regulation 31F (hearing of reviews)	In paragraph (6) omit "or, as the case may be, has ceased to satisfy the conditions for registration set out in section 4 of the 1983 Act".
Regulation 31G (anonymous registration: applications and declarations)	In paragraph (1)(b) for "regulation 26(1)(b)" substitute "regulation 6(1)(b) of the 2001 Regulations".
Regulation 31H (anonymous registration: determination of applications by registration officer)	
Regulation 31I (anonymous registration: evidence consisting of relevant court orders or injunctions)	
Regulation 31J (anonymous registration: evidence by attestation)	
Regulation 32 (registration appeals)	In paragraph (1), for sub-paragraph (b) substitute "(b) under section 56(1)(aa) of the 1983 Act, from the decision of a registration officer made in accordance with regulations 31D to 31F that a person was not entitled to be registered;"
Regulation 32A (representations regarding clerical errors)	
Regulation 36(2) and (3) (notices in connection with registration)	In paragraph (2) (a) for "that Act" substitute "the 1983 Act"; and (b) in sub-paragraph (b) omit "except in a case falling within regulation 31C(2)(b) above,".
Regulation 36A (communication of notices made on polling day)	
Regulation 38 (separate part of a register for each parliamentary polling district)	
Regulation 39 (different letter for each parliamentary polling district)	
Regulation 40 (qualifying addresses which are not included in the register)	In paragraph (1) (a) in sub-paragraph (a), at the end omit "or";

1	2
Provision applied	Modification
	and
	(b) omit sub-paragraph (b).
	Omit paragraph (2)(a) and the "or" following it.
Regulation 41 (order of names)	
Regulation 41A (anonymous entries)	
Regulation 45A (record of anonymous entries)	
Regulation 45B (duties of registration officer and his staff in relation to record of anonymous entries)	
Regulation 45C (supply of record of anonymous entries to returning and counting officers)	
Regulation 45E (supply of record of anonymous entries to the security services)	
Regulation 45F (supply of the record of anonymous entries to police forces and other organisations)	
Regulation 45G (certificate of anonymous registration)	
THE REPRESENTATION OF THE PEOPLE (SCOTLAND) REGULATIONS 2001	
Regulation 3 (interpretation)	
Regulation 5 (communication of applications, notices etc)	
Regulation 6 (electronic signatures and related certificates)	
Regulation 7 (copies of documents)	Omit paragraph (6).
Regulation 8 (time)	
Regulation 11 (interference with notices etc)	
Regulation 24 (evidence as to age and nationality)	In paragraph (2) for sub-paragraphs (b) to (d) substitute "(b) evidence of his status as a national of a Member State or a statutory declaration as to that nationality.".
Regulation 27 (objections to registration)	
Regulation 28 (inspection of applications and objections)	
Regulation 29 (procedure for determining applications for registration and objections without a hearing)	Omit paragraph (8).
Regulation 30 (notice of hearing)	
Regulation 31 (hearing of applications and objections)	
Regulation 31A (objections relating to applications that have been allowed, but before alterations to register have taken effect)	

1	2
Provision applied	*Modification*
Regulation 31B (other determinations by registration officer of entitlement to registration)	In paragraph (1) for "regulations 31C to 31F" substitute "regulations 31D to 31F". In paragraph (2) (a) in sub-paragraph (a) (i) in paragraph (i) for ", 7C(2)(aa), and 15(2)(aa) of the 1983 Act, and" substitute "and 7C(2)(aa) of the 1983 Act."; and (ii) omit paragraph (ii); and (b) omit sub-paragraph (b).
Regulation 31D (procedure for reviewing entitlement to registration)	In paragraphs (5) and (8) omit "or, as the case may be, has ceased to satisfy the conditions for registration set out in section 4 of the 1983 Act".
Regulation 31E (list of reviews)	
Regulation 31F (hearing of reviews)	In paragraph (6) omit "or, as the case may be, has ceased to satisfy the conditions for registration set out in section 4 of the 1983 Act".
Regulation 31G (anonymous registration: applications and declarations)	In paragraph (1)(b) for "regulation 26(1)(b)" substitute "regulation 6(1)(b) of the 2001 Regulations".
Regulation 31H (anonymous registration: determination of applications by registration officer)	
Regulation 31I (anonymous registration: evidence consisting of relevant court orders or injunctions)	
Regulation 31J (anonymous registration: evidence by attestation)	
Regulation 32 (registration appeals)	In paragraph (1), for sub-paragraph (b) substitute "(b) under section 56(1)(aa) of the 1983 Act, from the decision of a registration officer made in accordance with regulations 31D to 31F that a person was not entitled to be registered;".
Regulation 32A (representations regarding clerical errors)	
Regulation 36(2) and (3) (notices in connection with registration)	In paragraph (2) (a) for "that Act" substitute "the 1983 Act"; and (b) in sub-paragraph (b) omit "except in a case falling within regulation 31C(2)(b) above,".
Regulation 36A (communication of notices made on polling day)	
Regulation 38 (separate part of a register for each parliamentary polling district)	
Regulation 39 (different letter, number or combination of letter and number for each parliamentary polling district)	
Regulation 40 (qualifying addresses	In paragraph (1)

1 *Provision applied*	2 *Modification*
which are not included in the register)	(a) in sub-paragraph (a), at the end omit "or"; and (b) omit sub-paragraph (b). Omit paragraph (2)(a) and the "or" following it.
Regulation 41 (order of names)	
Regulation 41A (anonymous entries)	
Regulation 45A (record of anonymous entries)	
Regulation 45B (duties of registration officer and his staff in relation to record of anonymous entries)	
Regulation 45C (supply of record of anonymous entries to returning and counting officers)	
Regulation 45D (supply of record of anonymous entries to the security services)	
Regulation 45E (supply of the record of anonymous entries to police forces and other organisations)	
Regulation 45F (certificate of anonymous registration)	

THE REPRESENTATION OF THE PEOPLE (NORTHERN IRELAND) REGULATIONS 2008

Regulation 3 (interpretation)	
Regulation 5 (communication of applications, notices, etc)	
Regulation 6 (electronic signatures and related certificates)	
Regulation 7 (copies of documents)	
Regulation 8 (time)	
Regulation 11 (interference with notices, etc)	
Regulation 13 (applications for an electoral identity card)	For paragraph (2)(a) substitute "(a) a person who is registered in a register of European Parliamentary electors maintained under regulation 5(2) of the 2001 Regulations; or".
Regulation 25 (alteration of registers under section 13BA(3) of the 1983 Act)	In paragraph (3) (a) omit sub-paragraph (d); and (b) in sub-paragraph (e) omit "a qualifying Commonwealth citizen or citizen of Ireland or". In paragraph (4) (a) omit sub-paragraph (c); (b) in sub-paragraph (d) omit "a qualifying Commonwealth citizen or citizen of Ireland

1 Provision applied	2 Modification
	or"; and (c) for sub-paragraph (e) substitute "(e) a passport issued by a Member State of the European Union.". In paragraph (6) for "section 4 of the 1983 Act" substitute "regulation 4 of the 2001 Regulations".
Regulation 28 (objections to registration)	
Regulation 29 (inspection of applications and objections)	
Regulation 30 (procedure for determining applications for registration and objections without a hearing)	Omit paragraph (15).
Regulation 31 (notice of hearing)	
Regulation 32 (hearing of applications and objections)	
Regulation 33 (objections relating to applications which have been allowed, but before alterations to the register have taken effect)	
Regulation 34 (other determinations by registration officer of entitlement to registration)	In paragraph (1) for "regulations 35 to 38" substitute "regulations 36 to 38". In paragraph (2) (a) in sub-paragraph (a) (i) in paragraph (i) for ", 7C(2)(aa), and 15(2)(aa) of the 1983 Act, and" substitute "and 7C(2)(aa) of the 1983 Act."; and (ii) omit paragraph (ii); and (b) omit sub-paragraph (b).
Regulation 36 (procedure for reviewing entitlement to registration)	In paragraphs (4) and (7) omit "or, as the case may be, has ceased to satisfy the conditions for registration set out in section 4 of the 1983 Act".
Regulation 37 (list of reviews)	
Regulation 38 (hearing of reviews)	In paragraph (6) omit "or, as the case may be, has ceased to satisfy the conditions for registration set out in section 4 of the 1983 Act".
Regulation 38A (anonymous registration: applications and declarations)	In paragraph (1)(b), for "regulation 27(1)(b)" substitute "regulation 6(1)(b) of the 2001 Regulations". For paragraph (7) substitute "(7) In this regulation, "an application for an absent vote" means an application under regulation 8 of the European Parliamentary Elections (Northern Ireland) Regulations 2004.";
Regulation 38B (anonymous registration: determination of applications by the registration officer)	

1	2
Provision applied	Modification
Regulation 38C (anonymous registration: evidence consisting of relevant court orders or injunctions)	
Regulation 38D (anonymous registration: evidence by attestation)	
Regulation 38E (anonymous registration: review of entitlement to an anonymous entry)	
Regulation 39 (registration appeals)	In paragraph (1) for sub-paragraph (b) substitute "(b) the decision of the registration officer made under section 58(1)(b) of the 1983 Act in accordance with regulations 36 to 38 that a person was not entitled to be registered.".
Regulation 40 (representations regarding clerical errors)	
Regulation 44(2) and (3) (notices in connection with registration)	In paragraph (2) (a) for "that Act" substitute "the 1983 Act"; and (b) in sub-paragraph (c) omit "except in a case falling within regulation 35(2)(d),".
Regulation 45 (communication of notices made on polling day)	
Regulation 47 (separate part of register for each parliamentary polling district)	
Regulation 48 (different letter for each parliamentary polling district)	
Regulation 49 (qualifying addresses which are not included in the register)	In paragraph (1) (a) in sub-paragraph (a), at the end omit "or"; and (b) omit sub-paragraph (b). Omit paragraph (2)(a) and the "or" following it."
Regulation 50 (order of names)	
Regulation 50A (anonymous entries);	
Regulation 53A (record of anonymous entries)	In paragraph (4), for the words from "section 6(6) or 9(12) of the 1985 Act" to the end substitute "regulation 8(8) or 11(11) of the European Parliamentary Elections (Northern Ireland) Regulations 2004".
Regulation 53B (duties of registration officer and his staff in relation to record of anonymous entries)	
Regulation 53C (supply of the record of anonymous entries to police forces and other organisations)	
Regulation 53D (certificate of anonymous registration)	

European Parliamentary Elections (Returning Officers' and Local Returning Officers' Charges) (Great Britain and Gibraltar) Order 2014 (SI 2014/325)

Made 13th February 2014

Citation, commencement and extent

1(1)   This Order may be cited as the European Parliamentary Elections (Returning Officers' and Local Returning Officers' Charges) (Great Britain and Gibraltar) Order 2014 and comes into force on the day after the day on which it is made.

(2)   This Order extends to Great Britain and Gibraltar.

Interpretation

2   In this Order
"the 2004 Regulations" means the European Parliamentary Elections Regulations 2004;
"relevant election or referendum" means an election or referendum referred to in regulation 11 of the 2004 Regulations (other than a European Parliamentary election).

Revocations

3   The following Orders are revoked
(a)   the European Parliamentary Elections (Returning Officers' Charges) (Great Britain and Gibraltar) Order 2009;
(b)   the European Parliamentary Elections (Local Returning Officers' Charges) (England, Wales and Gibraltar) Order 2009; and
(c)   the European Parliamentary Elections (Local Returning Officers' Charges) (Scotland) Order 2009.

Returning officers: overall maximum recoverable amount

4   The overall maximum amount recoverable by the returning officer for an electoral region listed in column 1 of the table in Schedule 1 is the amount listed in the corresponding entry in column 4 of that table.

Returning officers: maximum recoverable amount for specified services

5(1)   The total of the charges recoverable by the returning officer for an electoral region listed in column 1 of the table in Schedule 1 in respect of the services specified in paragraph (2) must not exceed the amount listed in the corresponding entry in column 2 of that table.

(2)   The specified services are
   (a)   discharging the returning officer's duties at the election; and
   (b)   making arrangements for the election.

Returning officers: maximum recoverable amount for specified expenses

6(1)   The total of the charges recoverable by the returning officer for an electoral region listed in column 1 of the table in Schedule 1 in respect of the expenses specified in paragraph (2) must not exceed the amount listed in the corresponding entry in column 3 of that table.

(2)   The specified expenses are those incurred in
   (a)   the appointment and payment of persons to assist the returning officer;
   (b)   travel and overnight subsistence for the returning officer and any person appointed to assist the returning officer;
   (c)   the nomination process;
   (d)   printing or otherwise producing the ballot papers;
   (e)   printing or otherwise producing and, where appropriate, publishing notices and any other documents required by any enactment or instrument for or in connection with a European Parliamentary election;
   (f)   renting, heating, lighting, cleaning, adapting or restoring any building or room;
   (g)   providing and transporting equipment;
   (h)   providing information communications technology equipment and software and associated costs;
   (i)   providing security, including secure storage of ballot boxes, ballot papers and verification documents;
   (j)   conducting the count;
   (k)   providing and receiving training; and
   (l)   providing stationery and meeting postage, telephone, printing, translation and banking costs and the costs of other miscellaneous items.

Local returning officers: overall maximum recoverable amount

7   The overall maximum amount recoverable by the local returning officer for a local counting area
   (a)   listed in column 1 of the table in Schedule 2 is the amount listed in the corresponding entry in column 4 of that table;
   (b)   listed in column 1 of the table in Schedule 3 (being an area in which the poll at a European Parliamentary election in 2014 is to be taken together with the poll at a relevant election or referendum) is the amount listed in the corresponding entry in column 4 of that table.

Local returning officers: maximum recoverable amount for specified services

8(1)   The total of the charges recoverable in respect of the services specified in paragraph (2) by the local returning officer for a local counting area
   (a)   listed in column 1 of the table in Schedule 2 must not exceed the amount listed in the corresponding entry in column 2 of that table;
   (b)   listed in column 1 of the table in Schedule 3 (being an area in which the poll at a European Parliamentary election in 2014 is to be taken together with the poll at

a relevant election or referendum) must not exceed the amount listed in the corresponding entry in column 2 of that table.

(2) The specified services are
  (a) conducting the election;
  (b) discharging the local returning officer's duties at the election; and
  (c) making arrangements for the election.

Local returning officers: maximum recoverable amount for specified expenses

9(1) The total of the charges recoverable in respect of the expenses specified in paragraph (2) by the local returning officer for a local counting area
  (a) listed in column 1 of the table in Schedule 2 must not exceed the amount listed in the corresponding entry in column 3 of that table;
  (b) listed in column 1 of the table in Schedule 3 (being an area in which the poll at a European Parliamentary election is to be taken together with the poll at a relevant election or referendum) must not exceed the amount listed in the corresponding entry in column 3 of that table.

(2) The specified expenses are those incurred in
  (a) the appointment and payment of persons to assist the local returning officer;
  (b) travel and overnight subsistence for the local returning officer and any person appointed to assist the local returning officer;
  (c) printing or otherwise producing the ballot papers;
  (d) printing, producing or purchasing postal voting documents and arranging for the delivery and payment of the costs of return by voters of such documents;
  (e) printing or otherwise producing and arranging for the delivery of poll cards;
  (f) printing or otherwise producing and, where appropriate, publishing notices and any other documents required by any enactment or instrument for or in connection with a European Parliamentary election;
  (g) renting, heating, lighting, cleaning, adapting or restoring any building or room;
  (h) providing and transporting equipment;
  (i) providing information and communications technology equipment and software and associated costs;
  (j) providing security, including secure storage of ballot boxes, ballot papers and verification documents;
  (k) conducting the verification and the count;
  (l) providing and receiving training; and
  (m) providing stationery and meeting postage, telephone, printing, translation and banking costs and the costs of other miscellaneous items.

Overall maximum recoverable amount at an uncontested election

10 At an uncontested election
  (a) articles 4 to 9 do not apply;
  (b) the overall maximum recoverable amount for each electoral region is £350; and
  (c) the overall maximum recoverable amount for each local counting area is £1,750.

SCHEDULE 1
RETURNING OFFICERS: MAXIMUM RECOVERABLE AMOUNTS FOR ELECTORAL REGIONS

Not reproduced

SCHEDULE 2
LOCAL RETURNING OFFICERS: MAXIMUM RECOVERABLE AMOUNTS FOR LOCAL COUNTING AREAS

Not reproduced

SCHEDULE 3
LOCAL RETURNING OFFICERS: MAXIMUM RECOVERABLE AMOUNTS
FOR LOCAL COUNTING AREAS WHERE A RELEVANT ELECTION OR REFERENDUM IS TO BE HELD

Not reproduced

European Parliamentary Elections Regulations 2004
(SI 2004/293)

22nd March 2004

PART 1
GENERAL

PART 2
THE ELECTION CAMPAIGN

Election Agents of Registered Parties

126   Revocation
      Signature(s)

<h2 style="text-align:center">SCHEDULES</h2>

<h1 style="text-align:center">PART 1</h1>
<h2 style="text-align:center">GENERAL</h2>

Citation, commencement and extent

1 (1)   These Regulations may be cited as the European Parliamentary Elections Regulations 2004.

   (2)   They shall come into force on the day after the day on which they are made.

   (3)   They shall extend to England, Wales, Scotland and Gibraltar.

Interpretation

2 (1)   Unless the context otherwise requires, in these Regulations–
"1983 Act" means the Representation of the People Act 1983;
"1985 Act" means the Representation of the People Act 1985;
"1986 (Scotland) Regulations" means the Representation of the People (Scotland) Regulations 1986;
"2000 Act" means the Political Parties, Elections and Referendums Act 2000;
"2001 Franchise Regulations" means the European Parliamentary Elections (Franchise of Relevant Citizens of the Union) Regulations 2001;
"2001 Regulations" means the Representation of the People (England and Wales) Regulations 2001;
"2001 (Scotland) Regulations" means the Representation of the People (Scotland) Regulations 2001;
"2002 Act" means the European Parliamentary Elections Act 2002;
"2003 Act" means the European Parliament (Representation) Act 2003;
"2004 Act" means the European Parliamentary Elections Act 2004 passed by the Gibraltar Parliament;
"2006 Act" means the Electoral Administration Act 2006;
"anonymous entry" in relation to a register of electors, other than the Gibraltar register, is to be construed in accordance with section 9B of the 1983 Act and
"the record of anonymous entries" means the record prepared in pursuance of regulations made under paragraph 8A of Schedule 2 to the 1983 Act; and in relation to the Gibraltar register "anonymous entry" and "the record of anonymous entries" are to be construed in accordance with the equivalent provisions forming part of the law of

Gibraltar;

"bank or public holiday" in relation to Gibraltar means a day which is a bank or public holiday under the Banking and Financial Dealings Act and the Interpretation and General Clauses Act;

"citizen of the Union" is to be construed in accordance with Article 8 of the Treaty establishing the European Community, and "relevant citizen of the Union" means such a citizen who is not a Commonwealth citizen or a citizen of the Republic of Ireland;

"the City" means the City of London;

"Combination of Polls Regulations" means the Representation of the People (Combination of Polls) (England and Wales) Regulations 2004;

"Common Council" means the Common Council of the City;

"completed corresponding number list" means a list prepared under rule 23 of the European Parliamentary elections rules including the parts which are completed in accordance with rules 32(3)(d) and 41(1)(b) of those rules or paragraph 48(1) of Schedule 2;

"disability", in relation to doing a thing, includes a short term inability to do it;

"dwelling" includes any part of a building where that part is occupied separately as a dwelling;

"election" means a European Parliamentary election;

"elector", in relation to an election, means any person who has for the time being an entry in a register of electors, but does not include those shown in such a register (or, in the case of a person with an anonymous entry in the register, in the record of anonymous entries) as below voting age on the day fixed for the poll;

"European Parliamentary elections rules" means the rules in Schedule 1 to these Regulations;

"European Parliamentary election petition" means a petition presented in pursuance of Part 4 of these Regulations;

"European Parliamentary overseas elector" means a person falling within section 8(4) of the 2002 Act;

"European Parliamentary overseas elector's declaration" means a declaration made in pursuance of regulations made under section 3 of the 1985 Act;

"Gibraltar elector", in relation to an election, means any person who has for the time being an entry in the Gibraltar register, but does not include those shown in such a register as below voting age on the day fixed for the poll;

"legal incapacity" includes (in addition to any incapacity by virtue of any subsisting provision of the common law) any disqualification imposed by these Regulations or by any Act;

"legal process" means a claim form, application, notice, writ, summons or other process;

"list" means a list of candidates submitted by a registered party to accompany its nomination for election;

"local counting area" means any of the following as it exists on the day of an election—

    (a) a district in England for which there is a district council,

    (b) a county in England in which there are no districts with councils,

    (c) a London borough,

    (d) the City of London (including the Inner and Middle Temples),

    (e) the Isles of Scilly,

    (f) a county or county borough in Wales,

    (g) a local government area in Scotland, or

    (h) Gibraltar;

"the list of proxies" has, in relation to any election, the meaning given by paragraph 5(3) of Schedule 2 to these Regulations;

"mayoral election" means an election conducted under the Local Authorities (Mayoral Elections) (England and Wales) Regulations 2007;

"marked register" is the copy of a register of electors marked in accordance with rule 41(1)(c) of the European Parliamentary elections rules;

"marked copy of the postal voters list or the proxy postal voters list" is the copy of that list marked as mentioned in paragraph 60 of Schedule 2 to these Regulations for the purposes of rule 35 of the European Parliamentary elections rules;

"national election agent" means the person appointed under regulation 33;

"nominating officer" means the person registered under the 2000 Act as the officer with responsibility for the matters referred to in section 24(3) of that Act in respect of a registered party;

"overseas elector" means a person falling within section 8(2)(b) of the 2002 Act or in relation to Gibraltar, a person falling within section 16(2) of the 2003 Act;

"overseas elector's declaration" has the meaning given by section 2 of the 1985 Act or, in relation to Gibraltar, paragraph 15 of Schedule 4 to these Regulations;

"postal voters list" means the list of persons kept in pursuance of paragraph 5(2) of Schedule 2 to these Regulations (persons whose applications to vote by post have been granted);

"the proxy postal voters list" means the list of persons kept in pursuance of paragraph 7(8) of Schedule 2 to these Regulations (persons whose applications to vote by post as proxy have been granted);

"proper officer" in England and Wales means a proper officer within the meaning of section 270(3) and (4) of the Local Government Act 1972, or in Scotland, section 235(3) of the Local Government etc (Scotland) Act 1973;

"referendum" means a referendum conducted under the Local Authorities (Conduct of Referendums) (England) Regulations 2007;

"register of electors" means any part of–

(a) a register of parliamentary or, in the case of peers, local government electors,

(b) a register under section 3 of the 1985 Act,

(c) a register under regulation 5 of the 2001 Franchise Regulations, and

(d) the Gibraltar register,

in force within an electoral region at the time of a European Parliamentary election in that region;

"registered party" means a party registered under Part 2 of the 2000 Act;

"registration officer" means an officer appointed under section 8 of the 1983 Act or, in relation to Gibraltar, the European electoral registration officer for Gibraltar;

"relevant disqualifying decision" has the meaning given by section 10(5A) of the 2002 Act;

"relevant registration officer" (except where otherwise provided) means–

(a) the registration officer of the local authority in whose area the election is held; or

(b) *Repealed* or

(c) in relation to the City of London, the registration officer for the London borough of Westminster; or

(d) in relation to the Scottish electoral region, the returning officer designated under section 6(3) of the 2002 Act; or

(e) the European electoral registration officer for Gibraltar as regards documents issued for use in Gibraltar;

"service voter" means a person who has made a service declaration and is registered or entitled to be registered in pursuance of it;

"sub-agent" has the meaning given by regulation 35(1) in relation to registered parties under Part 2 of the 2000 Act or regulation 39(1) in relation to individual candidates;

"universal postal service provider" means a universal service provider within the meaning of Part 3 of the Postal Services Act 2011 and, in relation to Gibraltar, such person or persons with the right to exercise the functions of a universal service provider within the meaning of Council Directive No 97/67/EC; and "voter" means a person voting at an election and includes a person voting as proxy and, except in the European Parliamentary elections rules, a person voting by proxy; and

"vote" (whether noun or verb) is to be construed accordingly, except that in those rules any reference to an elector voting or an elector's vote is to include a reference to an elector voting by proxy or an elector's vote given by proxy.

(2) Part 1 of these Regulations shall (subject to any express provision contained in it) apply to the City as if the City were a London Borough and the Common Council were a London borough council.

For the purposes of this paragraph the Inner Temple and the Middle Temple shall be treated as forming part of the City.

(3) The modifications made by paragraph (2) do not affect regulation 19(3).

General application in relation to local government elections in England and Wales

3   In the application of these Regulations in relation to England and Wales, as respects local government elections–

"the 1999 Act" means the Greater London Authority Act 1999;

"Assembly constituency" has the same meaning as in the 1999 Act (see section 2(4) and (5) of that Act);

"Authority election" means–

    (a)   any election of the Mayor of London;

    (b)   any election of a constituency member of the London Assembly; or

    (c)   the election of the London members of the London Assembly at an ordinary election;

"constituency member", in relation to the London Assembly, has the same meaning as in the 1999 Act;

"election of a constituency member of the London Assembly" means–

    (a)   any such election at an ordinary election; or

    (b)   an election under section 10 of the 1999 Act (election to fill a vacancy in an Assembly constituency);

"election of the Mayor of London" means–

    (a)   any such election at an ordinary election; or

    (b)   an election under section 10 of the 1999 Act (election to fill a vacancy in the office of Mayor of London);

"electoral area" means–

    (a)   any electoral division or ward or, in the case of a parish or community in which there are no wards, the parish or community, for which the election of councillors is held under the local government Act;

    (b)   Greater London, in the case of–

        (i)   any election of the Mayor of London; or

        (ii)   the election of the London members of the London Assembly at an ordinary election;

    (c)   any Assembly constituency for which the election of a constituency member of the London Assembly is held;

"local authority" means the Greater London Authority, a county council, a county borough council, a district council, a London borough council or a parish or community council;

"local government Act" means the Local Government Act 1972;

"local government area" means Greater London, a county, county borough, London borough, district, parish or community;

"local government election" means–

    (a)   the election of councillors for any electoral area; or

(b)   any Authority election; and

"London member", in relation to the London Assembly, has the same meaning as in the 1999 Act.

General application to Scotland

4 (1)   This regulation has (in addition to any express application elsewhere in these Regulations) effect for the general application of these Regulations to Scotland, and accordingly–

"electoral area", in relation to a local government election, means the electoral ward for which the election is held;

"local authority" means a council constituted under section 2 of the Local Government etc (Scotland) Act 1994;

"local government area" means the area of a local authority; and

"local government election" means an election of councillors by local government electors for an electoral area.

(2)   For a reference to the High Court substitute a reference to the Court of Session and for a reference to the county court or a judge of that court substitute a reference to the sheriff.

(3)   The power conferred by regulation 22 on the Court of Session to make acts of sederunt for the appointment of judges to hear appeals under that regulation or to fill any vacancy among the judges so appointed is not required to be exercised by statutory instrument.

(4)   For a reference to the Director of Public Prosecutions or the Attorney General substitute a reference to the Lord Advocate.

(5)   For a reference to a plaintiff or defendant substitute respectively a reference to a pursuer or defender, for a reference to a recognisance substitute a reference to a bond of caution and for a reference to an injunction substitute a reference to an interdict.

(6)   *Repealed*

General application to Gibraltar

5 (1)   This regulation has (in addition to any express application elsewhere in these Regulations) effect for the general application of these Regulations to Gibraltar.

(2)   "Gibraltar court", as respects any purpose, means the court determined by or under the law of Gibraltar to be the court for that purpose.

(3)   Except where the contrary intention appears, any reference to–

(a)   a level of a fine on the standard scale shall be construed as a reference to that level on the standard scale pursuant to section 550 of, and Part A of Schedule 9 to, the Criminal Procedure and Evidence Act 2011; and

(b)   a fine not exceeding the statutory maximum shall be construed as a reference to a fine not exceeding level 5 on the standard scale pursuant to section 550 of, and Part A of Schedule 9 to, that Act.

(4)   Where reference is made to a time of day, in Gibraltar that reference shall be taken to be the time of day in Gibraltar (and in the United Kingdom that time shall be taken to be the time of day in the United Kingdom) unless otherwise stated.

(5)   References in these Regulations to a named Act are to the Gibraltar Act of that name.

(6)   Any reference to a "civil partner" (wherever it appears) is omitted.

(7)   Any reference to section 13B(3B), 13B(3C) or 13B(3D) of the 1983 Act is to be construed as a reference to the equivalent provision forming part of the law of Gibraltar.

Conduct of poll and count in each local counting area

6 (1) The local returning officer for each local counting area wholly or partly comprised in an electoral region shall be responsible for–

    (a) the conduct of the poll in that area;

    (b) unless the returning officer otherwise directs, the printing of the ballot papers;

    (c) the issue and receipt of postal ballot papers for electors in that area and their proxies;

    (d) the verification of the ballot paper accounts; and

    (e) the counting of the votes given in that area.

  (2) The local returning officer for a local counting area that is–

    (a) a district in England,

    (b) a county in England,

    (c) a London borough, or

    (d) a county or county borough in Wales,

shall be the person who, by virtue of section 35 of the 1983 Act, is the returning officer for elections of councillors for the district, county, borough or county borough.

(2A) The local returning officer for the City of London shall be the person who, by virtue of that section, is the returning officer for elections of councillors for the London borough of Westminster.

(2B) The local returning officer for the Isles of Scilly shall be the person who, by virtue of that section, is the returning officer for elections to the Council of the Isles of Scilly.

(2C) The local returning officer for a local government area in Scotland shall be the person who, by virtue of section 41 of the 1983 Act, is the returning officer for elections of councillors for the local authority for that local government area.

  (3) The local returning officer pursuant to section 6(5A)(b) of the 2002 Act shall be the local returning officer for the Gibraltar local counting area.

Deputies and assistance

7 (1) A returning officer and a local returning officer may, in writing, appoint deputies to discharge all or any of the functions imposed on them under these Regulations or the provisions applied by these Regulations.

  (2) A returning officer may appoint such clerks as may be necessary to assist him in his functions in relation to an election.

Polling districts and places

8 (1) Every electoral region shall be divided into polling districts and subject to the provisions of this regulation there shall be a polling place designated for each polling district.

  (2) Subject to paragraph (4), the polling districts and polling places designated under this regulation shall be the same as those used or designated for parliamentary elections, except where it appears to those responsible for designating parliamentary polling districts and places that special circumstances make it desirable for some other polling district or place to be designated.

  (3) An election shall not be questioned by reason of–

    (a) any non-compliance with the provisions of this regulation; or

    (b) any informality relative to polling districts or polling places.

  (4) In Gibraltar the polling districts and polling places designated for each district shall be the same as those used or designated for elections to the Gibraltar Parliament.

Rules for European Parliamentary elections and general duty of returning officers and local returning officers

9 (1)   The proceedings at a European Parliamentary election shall be conducted in accordance with the European Parliamentary elections rules in Schedule 1 to these Regulations.

(2)   It is the returning officer's and the local returning officer's general duty at a European Parliamentary election to do all such acts and things as may be necessary for effectually conducting the election in the manner provided by those rules.

(3)   The returning officer may give to any local returning officer for a local counting area in the electoral region for which he acts directions relating to the discharge of his functions, including directions requiring the provision to him of any information which that person has or is entitled to have.

(4)   It shall be the duty of any local returning officer to whom directions are given under paragraph (3) to discharge his functions in accordance with the directions.

(4A)   A returning officer or a local returning officer for a European Parliamentary election may take such steps as he thinks appropriate to remedy any act or omission on his part, or on the part of a relevant person, which–
   (a)   arises in connection with any function the returning officer or local returning officer or relevant person has in relation to the election, and
   (b)   is not in accordance with the European Parliamentary elections rules or other requirements applicable to the election.

(4B)   A returning officer or local returning officer may not under paragraph (4A) re-count the votes given at an election after the result has been declared.

(4C)   These are the relevant persons–
   (a)   a registration officer;
   (b)   a presiding officer;
   (c)   a person providing goods or services to the returning officer or local returning officer;
   (d)   a deputy of any person mentioned in sub-paragraphs (a) to (c) or a person appointed to assist, or in the course of his employment assisting, such a person in connection with any function he has in relation to the European Parliamentary election.

(4D)   A returning officer or local returning officer for a European Parliamentary election must take such steps as he thinks appropriate to encourage the participation by electors in the electoral process in the area or region for which he acts.

(4E)   A returning officer or local returning officer must have regard to any guidance issued by the Electoral Commission for the purposes of paragraph (4D) of this Regulation.

(5)   No European Parliamentary election shall be declared invalid by reason of any act or omission by the returning officer, local returning officer or any other person in breach of his official duty in connection with the election or otherwise of the European Parliamentary elections rules if it appears to the tribunal having cognisance of the question that–
   (a)   the election was so conducted as to be substantially in accordance with the law as to elections; and
   (b)   the act or omission did not affect its result.

Absent voting

10   Schedule 2, which makes provision with respect to the manner of voting at elections, and in particular absent voting, shall have effect.

Combination of polls

11   Where the poll at a European Parliamentary election is to be taken together with–

    (a)   the poll at a parliamentary or local government election under section 15(1) or (2) of the 1985 Act; or

    (b)   the poll at a mayoral election or a referendum in accordance with regulations made under sections 9HE and 105, 9MG and 105 or 44 and 105 of the Local Government Act 2000,

or two or more such polls, the European Parliamentary elections rules shall have effect subject to–

    (i)   in England and Wales, the modifications in Part 1 of Schedule 3 to these Regulations, and

    (ii) in Scotland, the modifications in Part 2 of that Schedule.

Entitlement to registration and legal incapacity to vote in Gibraltar

12   Schedule 4, which makes provision as to–

    (a)   legal incapacity to vote in Gibraltar as an elector at a European Parliamentary election; and

    (b)   entitlement to registration in the Gibraltar register,

shall have effect.

Title of returning officers and local returning officers

14   A European Parliamentary election is not liable to be questioned by reason of a defect in the title, or want of title, of the person presiding at or conducting the election, if that person was then in actual possession of, or acting in, the office giving the right to preside at or conduct the election.

13   *Repealed*

Payments by and to returning officers and local returning officers

15 (1)   Subject to regulation 15A, a returning officer or a local returning officer may recover his charges in respect of services rendered, or expenses incurred, for or in connection with a European Parliamentary election if–

    (a)   the services were necessarily rendered, or the expenses were necessarily incurred, for the efficient and effective conduct of the election; and

    (b)   the total of his charges does not exceed the amount ("the overall maximum recoverable amount") specified in, or determined in accordance with, an order made by the Secretary of State.

(2)   An order under paragraph (1) may specify, or make provision for determining in accordance with the order, a maximum recoverable amount for services or expenses of any specified description and, subject to paragraph (3), the returning officer or local returning officer may not recover more than that amount in respect of any such services or expenses.

(3)   The Secretary of State may, in a particular case, authorise the payment of–

    (a)   more than the overall recoverable amount, or

    (b)   more than the specified maximum recoverable amount for any specified services or expenses,

if he is satisfied that the conditions in paragraph (4) are met.

(4)   The conditions referred to in paragraph (3) are–

    (a)   that it was reasonable for the returning officer concerned to render the services or incur the expenses; and

(b)   that the charges in question are reasonable.

(5)   The power to make orders under paragraph (1) shall be exercised by statutory instrument and section 1 of the Statutory Instruments Act 1946 shall apply accordingly; and any such order may make different provision for different cases, circumstances or areas and may contain such incidental, supplemental, saving or transitional provisions as the Secretary of State thinks fit.

(6)   The amount of any charges recoverable in accordance with this regulation shall be charged on and paid out of the Consolidated Fund on an account being submitted to the Secretary of State, but the Secretary of State may if he thinks fit before payment, apply for the account to be taxed under the provisions of regulation 16.

(7)   Where the superannuation contributions required to be paid by a local authority in respect of any person are increased by any fee paid under this regulation as part of a returning officer's or local returning officer's charges at a European Parliamentary election, then on an account being submitted to the Secretary of State a sum equal to the increase shall be charged on and paid out of the Consolidated Fund to the authority.

(8)   On the returning officer's or local returning officer's request for an advance on account of his charges, the Secretary of State may, on such terms as he thinks fit, make such an advance.

(9)   Regulations by the Secretary of State may make provision as to the time when and the manner and form in which accounts are to be rendered to the Secretary of State for the purposes of the payment of a returning officer's or local returning officer's charges, and may include different provision for different cases, circumstances or areas.

(10) Any exercise by the Secretary of State of his functions under paragraph (1) shall require the consent of the Treasury.

Inadequate performance of returning officer or local returning officer: reduction of charges

15A (1)   This regulation applies to a service rendered by a returning officer or a local returning officer (referred to in this regulation as the "relevant officer") for or in connection with a European Parliamentary election which, in the opinion of the Electoral Commission, was inadequately performed.

(2)   The Commission may recommend to the Secretary of State that the relevant officer is entitled under regulation 15(1) to no more than a specified amount (which may be nil) in respect of that service.

(3)   In making a recommendation under paragraph (2), the Commission must have regard to–
(a)   if the election concerned is a general election of MEPs, any report prepared under section 5 of the 2000 Act on the administration of that election;
(b)   any assessment of the level of performance of the relevant officer in relation to that election under section 9B(4) of the 2000 Act;
(c)   any representations made to the Commission by the relevant officer in respect of the performance of the service; and
(d)   any other information relating to the performance of the service by the relevant officer that has been provided to the Commission.

(4)   Where the Commission makes a recommendation under paragraph (2), the relevant officer is entitled under regulation 15(1) to no more than the amount (which may be nil) determined by the Secretary of State, having regard to the recommendation by the Commission.

Taxation of returning officer's and local returning officer's account

16 (1)   An application for a returning officer's or local returning officer's account to be taxed shall be made–
    (a)   where the account relates to an election in an electoral region in England or Wales, to the county court,
    (b)   where the account relates to an election in Scotland, to the Auditor of the Court of Session,
    (c)   where the account is the account of the local returning officer for the Gibraltar local counting area, to the Gibraltar court,
and in this regulation the expression "the court" means that court or Auditor.

(2)   On any such application the court has jurisdiction to tax the account in such manner and at such time and place as the court thinks fit, and finally to determine the amount payable to the returning officer.

(3)   On any such application the returning officer or local returning officer may apply to the court to examine any claim made by any person against him in respect of matters charged in the account; and the court, after notice given to the claimant and after giving him an opportunity to be heard and to tender any evidence, may allow or disallow or reduce the claim objected to with or without costs; and the determination of the court shall be final for all purposes and as against all persons.

(4)   In paragraph (1)(a), the reference to an account which relates to an electoral region in England shall be construed as including a reference to an account which relates to the whole of the combined region.

Effect of registers

17 (1)   Any entry in the register of electors, if it gives a date as that on which the person named will attain voting age, shall for any purpose of this Part relating to him as elector be conclusive that until the date given in the entry he is not of voting age nor entitled to be treated as an elector except for the purposes of an election at which the day fixed for the poll is that or a later date.

(1A)   Paragraph (1) applies to an entry in the record of anonymous entries as it applies to an entry in the register of electors.

(2)   A person whose registration as an elector or entry in the list of proxies entitles him to vote shall not be excluded from voting on any of the following grounds: but this shall not prevent the rejection of the vote on a scrutiny, or affect his liability to any penalty for voting.
The grounds are–
    (a)   that he is not of voting age;
    (b)   that he does not or did not at any particular time satisfy any requirement for voting which relates to citizenship;
    (c)   that he is or was at any particular time otherwise subject to any other legal incapacity to vote.

(3)   In the case of the persons referred to in paragraph (4), for "at any particular time" in each of paragraph (2)(b) and (c), substitute "on the relevant date or the date of his appointment (as the case may be).

(4)   "The relevant date" in paragraph (3)–
    (a)   in the case of a Gibraltar elector, is the date on which an application for registration is made or treated as having been made by virtue of paragraph 6 of Schedule 4;
    (b)   in the case of a person registered as an elector by virtue of being a relevant

citizen of the Union, is the date which is the relevant date for the purposes of regulation 4 of the 2001 Franchise Regulations;

    (c)   in the case of a peer entitled to vote by virtue of section 3 of the 1985 Act, is the date which is the relevant date for the purposes of that section.

Effect of misdescription

18   No misnomer or inaccurate description of any person or place named–

    (a)   in the register of electors, or

    (b)   in any list, record, proxy paper, nomination paper, ballot paper, notice or other document required for the purposes of this Part of these Regulations,

affects the full operation of the document with respect to that person or place in any case where the description of the person or place is such as to be commonly understood.

Discharge of registration duties

19 (1)   Any of the duties and powers of a registration officer may be performed and exercised by any deputy for the time being approved by the council which appointed the registration officer, and the provisions of these Regulations apply to any such deputy so far as respects any duties or powers to be performed or exercised by him as they apply to the registration officer.

  (2)   In England and Wales, any acts authorised or required to be done by or with respect to the registration officer may, in the event of his incapacity to act or of a vacancy, be done by or with respect to the proper officer of the council by whom the registration officer was appointed.

  (3)   It shall be the duty–

    (a)   in England, of a district council or London borough council,

    (b)   in Wales, of a county or county borough council, and

    (c)   in Scotland, of every local authority,

to assign such officers to assist the registration officer as may be required for carrying out his functions under these Regulations.

  (4)   This regulation shall apply as respects the European Parliamentary electoral registration officer for Gibraltar with the following modifications–

    (a)   in paragraph (1), for "approved by the council which appointed the registration officer", substitute "appointed for that purpose by the Clerk of the Gibraltar Parliament";

    (b)   in paragraph (2)–

       (i) for "In England and Wales", substitute "In Gibraltar"; and

       (ii)   for the words from "the proper officer" to the end, substitute "any deputy appointed under paragraph (1)"; and

    (c)   in paragraph (3), insert after sub-paragraph (c)–

    "(d) in Gibraltar, the Government of Gibraltar,".

Payment of expenses of registration

20 (1)   Any expenses properly incurred by a registration officer in the performance of his functions under these Regulations (in these Regulations referred to as "registration expenses") shall be paid by the local authority by whom the registration officer was appointed.

  (2)   Any fees paid to the registration officer under these Regulations shall be accounted for by him and paid to the local authority by whom he was appointed.

(3) On the request of a registration officer for an advance on account of registration expenses the local authority by whom the registration officer was appointed may, if they think fit, make such an advance to him of such an amount and subject to such conditions as they may approve.

(4) Any registration expenses or contributions to them paid by the Common Council shall be paid out of the general rate and any sums paid to the Common Council under this regulation shall be placed to the credit of that rate.

(5) This regulation does not apply to the European Parliamentary electoral registration officer for Gibraltar.

Registration appeals: England and Wales

21 (1) Subject to paragraph (2), an appeal lies to the county court from any decision under these Regulations of the registration officer–
    (a) disallowing a person's application to vote by post or proxy as elector or to vote by post as proxy, or
    (b) to remove a person's entry from the lists of postal voters or of proxy postal voters,
in any case where the application or entry is not related to a particular election only.

(2) No appeal lies where the person desiring to appeal has not availed himself of a prescribed right to be heard by or make representations to the registration officer on the matter which is the subject of the appeal, or has not given the prescribed notice of appeal within the prescribed time.

(3) No appeal lies from the decision of the Court of Appeal on appeal from a decision of the county court under this regulation.

(4) An appeal to the county court or Court of Appeal by virtue of this regulation which is pending when notice of an election is given shall not prejudice the operation as respects the election of the decision appealed against, and anything done in pursuance of the decision shall be as good as if no such appeal had been brought and shall not be affected by the decision of the appeal.

(5) Notice shall be sent to the registration officer in manner provided by rules of court of the decision of the county court or of the Court of Appeal on any appeal by virtue of this regulation.

(6) The registration officer shall undertake such duties in connection with appeals brought by virtue of this regulation as are set out in paragraph 21 of Schedule 2 and shall on any such appeal be deemed to be a party to the proceedings, and the registration expenses payable to a registration officer shall include any expenses properly incurred by him by virtue of this paragraph.

(7) In paragraph (2) "prescribed" means prescribed by paragraph 21 of Schedule 2.

(8) This regulation applies to Gibraltar subject to the following modifications–
    (a) any reference to the county court shall be construed as a reference to the Gibraltar court; and
    (b) any reference to the Court of Appeal shall be construed as a reference to the Gibraltar Court of Appeal.

Registration appeals: Scotland

22 (1) Regulation 21 applies to Scotland subject to the following modifications–
    (a) paragraph (3) shall be omitted;
    (b) an appeal lies on any point of law from any decision of the sheriff under this regulation to the court of three judges constituted under paragraph (2); and

(c)   for any reference to the Court of Appeal there shall be substituted a reference to that court of three judges.

(2)   The court for hearing appeals under sub-paragraph (b) of paragraph (1) shall consist of three judges of the Court of Session who shall be appointed by the Court of Session by act of sederunt and of whom one judge shall be appointed from each division of the Inner House and one from the Lords Ordinary in the Outer House; and the Principal Clerk of Session shall be clerk of the court.

(3)   The Court of Session may by act of sederunt fill any vacancy in the court of three judges, and regulate its sittings and forms of process so as to carry out the provisions of these Regulations; and acts of sederunt under this regulation may be made, and the court of three judges may sit, either during the sitting of the Court of Session or in vacation or recess.

Personation

23 (1)   A person shall be guilty of a corrupt practice if he commits, or aids, abets, counsels or procures the commission of, the offence of personation.

(2)   A person shall be deemed to be guilty of personation at a European Parliamentary election if he–

(a)   votes in person or by post as some other person, whether as an elector or as proxy, and whether that other person is living or dead or is a fictitious person; or

(b)   votes in person or by post as proxy–

(i)   for a person whom he knows or has reasonable grounds for supposing to be dead or to be a fictitious person; or

(ii)   when he knows or has reasonable grounds for supposing that his appointment as proxy is no longer in force.

(3)   For the purposes of this regulation, a person who has applied for a ballot paper for the purpose of voting in person or who has marked, whether validly or not, and returned a ballot paper issued for the purpose of voting by post, shall be deemed to have voted.

Other voting offences

24 (1)   A person shall be guilty of an offence if–

(a)   he votes in person or by post, whether as an elector or as proxy, or applies to vote by proxy or by post as elector at a European Parliamentary election knowing that he is subject to a legal incapacity to vote at the election; or

(b)   he applies for the appointment of a proxy to vote for him at any European Parliamentary election knowing that he is or the person to be appointed is subject to a legal incapacity to vote at the election; or

(c)   he votes, whether in person or by post, as proxy for some other person at a European Parliamentary election, knowing that that person is subject to a legal incapacity to vote.

For the purposes of this paragraph references to a person being subject to a legal incapacity to vote do not, in relation to things done before polling day at the election or first election at or for which they are done, include his being below voting age if he will be of voting age on that day.

(2)   References in paragraph (1) to legal incapacity to vote at a European Parliamentary election include incapacity to vote at the kind of election from which the entitlement to vote at a European Parliamentary election derives.

(3)   A person shall be guilty of an offence if–

(a)   he votes as elector otherwise than by proxy either–

(i)   more than once in the same electoral region at any European Parliamentary election; or

(ii)   in more than one electoral region at a European Parliamentary election, or

(iii) in any electoral region at a European Parliamentary election when there is in force an appointment of a person to vote as his proxy at the election in respect of an address other than the address by virtue of which he votes as elector; or

(b)   he votes as elector in person at a European Parliamentary election at which he is entitled to vote by post; or

(c)   he votes as elector in person at a European Parliamentary election, knowing that a person appointed to vote as his proxy at the election either has already voted in person at the election or is entitled to vote by post at the election; or

(d)   he applies for a person to be appointed as his proxy to vote for him at European Parliamentary elections in any electoral region without applying for the cancellation of a previous appointment of a third person then in force in respect of that or another electoral region or without withdrawing a pending application for such an appointment in respect of that or another electoral region.

(4)   A person shall be guilty of an offence if–

(a)   he votes as proxy for the same elector either–

(i)   more than once in the same electoral region at any European Parliamentary election; or

(ii) in more than one electoral region at a European Parliamentary election; or

(b)   he votes in person as proxy for an elector at a European Parliamentary election at which he is entitled to vote by post as proxy for that elector; or

(c)   he votes in person as proxy for an elector at a European Parliamentary election knowing that the elector has already voted in person at the election.

(5)   A person shall also be guilty of an offence if he votes at a European Parliamentary election in any electoral region as proxy for more than two persons of whom he is not the spouse, civil partner, parent, grandparent, brother, sister, child or grandchild.

(6)   A person shall also be guilty of an offence if he knowingly induces or procures some other person to do an act which is, or but for that other person's want of knowledge would be, an offence by that other person under the foregoing paragraphs of this regulation.

(7)   For the purposes of this regulation a person who has applied for a ballot paper for the purpose of voting in person, or who has marked, whether validly or not, and returned a ballot paper issued for the purpose of voting by post, shall be deemed to have voted, but for the purpose of determining whether an application for a ballot paper constitutes an offence under paragraph (5), a previous application made in circumstances which entitle the applicant only to mark a tendered ballot paper shall, if he does not exercise that right, be disregarded.

(7A) A person is not guilty of an offence under paragraph (3)(b) or (4)(b) only by reason of his having marked a tendered ballot paper in pursuance of rule 44(4) or 44(6) of the European Parliamentary elections rules.

(8)   An offence under this regulation shall be an illegal practice, but the court before whom a person is convicted of any such offence may, if they think it just in the special circumstances of the case, mitigate or entirely remit any incapacity imposed by virtue of regulation 107.

Breach of official duty

25 (1) If a person to whom this regulation applies is, without reasonable cause, guilty of any act or omission in breach of his official duty, he shall be liable on summary conviction to a fine not exceeding level 5 on the standard scale.

(2) No person to whom this regulation applies shall be liable for breach of his official duty to any penalty at common law and no action for damages shall lie in respect of the breach by such a person of his official duty.

(3) The persons to whom this regulation applies are–

    (a) any sheriff clerk, registration officer, returning officer, local returning officer or presiding officer,

    (b) any official designated by a universal postal service provider,

    (ba) *Repealed*

    (bb) any other person whose duty it is to be responsible after a European Parliamentary election for the used ballot papers and other documents (including returns and declarations as to expenses), and

    (c) any deputy of a person mentioned in any of sub-paragraphs (a), (b) and (bb) or any person appointed to assist or in the course of his employment assisting a person so mentioned in connection with his official duties;

and "official duty" shall for the purposes of this regulation be construed accordingly, but shall not include duties imposed otherwise than by the law relating to European Parliamentary elections or the registration of parliamentary or local government electors.

(4) Where–

    (a) a local returning officer to whom regulation 9 applies is guilty of an act or omission in breach of his official duty, but

    (b) remedies that act or omission in full by taking steps under paragraph (4A) of that regulation,

he shall not be guilty of an offence under paragraph (1) of this regulation.

(5) Paragraph (4) does not affect any conviction which takes place, or any penalty which is imposed, before the date on which the act or omission is remedied in full.

Tampering with nomination papers, ballot papers, etc

26 (1) A person shall be guilty of an offence, if, at a European Parliamentary election, he–

    (a) fraudulently defaces or fraudulently destroys any nomination paper, or the list of candidates submitted by a registered party; or

    (b) fraudulently defaces or fraudulently destroys any ballot paper, or the official mark on any ballot paper, or any postal voting statement or official envelope used in connection with voting by post; or

    (c) without due authority supplies any ballot paper to any person; or

    (d) fraudulently puts into any ballot box any paper other than the ballot paper which he is authorised by law to put in; or

    (e) fraudulently takes out of the polling station any ballot paper; or

    (f) without due authority destroys, takes, opens or otherwise interferes with any ballot box or packet of ballot papers then in use for the purposes of the election; or

    (g) fraudulently or without due authority, as the case may be, attempts to do any of the foregoing acts.

(2) In Scotland, a person shall be guilty of an offence if–

    (a) at a European Parliamentary election, he forges any nomination paper, delivers to the returning officer any nomination paper knowing it to be forged, or forges or counterfeits any ballot paper or the official mark on any ballot paper; or

    (b) he fraudulently or without due authority, as the case may be, attempts to do any of the foregoing acts.

(3) If a returning officer, a local returning officer, a presiding officer or a clerk appointed to assist in taking the poll, counting the votes or assisting at the proceedings in

connection with the issue or receipt of postal ballot papers is guilty of an offence under this section, he shall be liable–

    (a) on conviction on indictment to a fine, or to imprisonment for a term not exceeding 2 years, or to both;

    (b) on summary conviction, to a fine not exceeding the statutory maximum, or to imprisonment for a term not exceeding 6 months, or to both.

(4) If any other person is guilty of an offence under this regulation, he shall be liable on summary conviction to a fine not exceeding level 5 on the standard scale, or to imprisonment for a term not exceeding 6 months, or to both.

False statement in nomination papers

27 A person is guilty of a corrupt practice if, in the case of a European Parliamentary election, he causes or permits to be included in a document delivered or otherwise furnished to a returning officer for use in connection with the election a statement of the name or home address of a candidate at the election which he knows to be false in any particular.

Offences in connection with candidature

28 (1) A person who makes a statement which he knows to be false in the declaration required by rule 9(4) of the European Parliamentary elections rules is guilty of an offence and is liable on summary conviction to a fine not exceeding level 3 on the standard scale .

(2) A person who, at a general election of MEPs–

    (a) consents to nomination as an individual candidate in more than one electoral region,

    (b) consents to nomination as an individual candidate in an electoral region and consents to being nominated in a list submitted by a registered party, whether in that region or some other,

    (c) consents to being nominated in the list submitted by more than one registered party in the same region, or

    (d) consents to being nominated in the lists submitted by a registered party or parties for more than one region,

  is guilty of an illegal practice.

(3) An individual candidate or a candidate being nominated in a list submitted by a registered party at a European Parliamentary election is guilty of a corrupt practice if, in any document in which he gives his consent to his nomination in accordance with rule 8 of the European Parliamentary elections rules, he makes–

    (a) a statement of his date of birth, or

    (b) a statement as to his qualification for being elected at that election,

  which he knows to be false in any particular.

(4) For the purposes of paragraph (3), a statement as to a candidate's qualification is a statement–

    (a) that he is qualified for being elected,

    (b) that he will be qualified for being elected, or

    (c) that to the best of his knowledge and belief he is not disqualified for being elected.

Requirement of secrecy

29 (1) The following persons–

    (a) every local returning officer and every presiding officer or clerk attending at a polling station,

     (b) every candidate or election agent or polling agent so attending,

     (c) every person so attending by virtue of any of sections 6A to 6D of the 2000 Act,

shall maintain and aid in maintaining the secrecy of voting and shall not, except for some purpose authorised by law, communicate to any person before the poll is closed any information as to–

         (i)   the name of any elector or proxy for an elector who has or has not applied for a ballot paper or voted at a polling station;

        (ii) the number on the register of electors of any elector who, or whose proxy, has or has not applied for a ballot paper or voted at a polling station; or

       (iii) the official mark.

(2) Every person attending at the verification of the ballot paper accounts or the counting of the votes shall maintain and aid in maintaining the secrecy of voting and shall not–

     (a) ascertain or attempt to ascertain at the counting of the votes the number or other unique identifying mark on the back of any ballot paper;

     (b) communicate any information obtained at the verification of the ballot paper accounts or the counting of the votes as to the way in which any vote is given on any particular ballot paper.

(3) No person attending at the verification of the ballot paper accounts shall express to any person an opinion based on information obtained at that verification as to the likely result of the election.

(4) No person shall–

     (a) interfere with or attempt to interfere with a voter when recording his vote;

     (b) otherwise obtain or attempt to obtain in a polling station information as to the way in which a voter in that station is about to vote or has voted;

     (c) communicate at any time to any person any information obtained in a polling station as to the way in which a voter in that station is about to vote or has voted, or as to the number or other unique identifying mark on the back of the ballot paper given to a voter at that station;

     (d) directly or indirectly induce a voter to display his ballot paper after he has marked it so as to make known to any person the way in which he has voted.

(5) Every person attending the proceedings in connection with the issue or the receipt of ballot papers for persons voting by post shall maintain and aid in maintaining the secrecy of the voting and shall not–

     (a) except for some purpose authorised by law, communicate, before the poll is closed, to any person any information obtained at those proceedings as to the official mark; or

     (b) except for some purpose authorised by law, communicate to any person at any time any information obtained at those proceedings as to the number or other unique identifying mark on the back of the ballot paper sent to any person; or

     (c) except for some purpose authorised by law, attempt to ascertain at the proceedings in connection with the receipt of ballot papers the number or other unique identifying mark on the back of any ballot paper; or

     (d) attempt to ascertain at the proceedings in connection with the receipt of the ballot papers the way in which any vote is given in any particular ballot paper or communicate any information with respect thereto obtained at those proceedings.

(6) No person having undertaken to assist a voter with disabilities to vote shall communicate at any time to any person any information as to the way in which that voter intends to vote or has voted, or as to the number or other unique identifying mark on the back of the ballot paper given for the use of that voter.

(7) If a person acts in contravention of this regulation he shall be liable on summary

conviction to a fine not exceeding level 5 on the standard scale or to imprisonment for a term not exceeding 6 months.

Prohibition on publication of exit polls

30 (1) No person shall in the case of a European Parliamentary election publish before the close of the poll–

    (a) any statement relating to the way in which voters have voted at the election where that statement is (or might reasonably be taken to be) based on information given by voters after they have voted, or

    (b) any forecast as to the result of the election which is (or might reasonably be taken to be) based on information so given.

  (2) If a person acts in contravention of paragraph (1), he shall be liable on summary conviction to a fine not exceeding level 5 on the standard scale or to imprisonment for a term not exceeding 6 months.

  (3) In this regulation–

"close of the poll" means, in the case of a general election of MEPs, the close of the polling in the Member State whose electors are the last to vote in the election;

"forecast" includes estimate;

"publish" means make available to the public at large, or any section of the public, in whatever form and by whatever means;

and any reference to the result of an election is a reference to the result of the election either as a whole or so far as any particular registered party or individual candidate at the election is or are concerned.

PART 2
THE ELECTION CAMPAIGN

Interpretation of Part 2

31 (1) In this Part of these Regulations, unless the context otherwise requires–

"appropriate officer" means the returning officer;

"candidate" shall be construed in accordance with paragraph (2) below;

"committee room" does not include any house or room occupied by a candidate as a dwelling, by reason only of the candidate transacting business there with his agents in relation to the election, and no room or building shall be deemed to be a committee room by reason only of the candidate or any agent of the candidate addressing in it electors, committee members or others;

"declaration as to election expenses" means a declaration made under regulation 52;

"disputed claim" has the meaning given by regulation 49(1) as extended by regulation 50;

"election expenses", in relation to a European Parliamentary election, shall be construed in accordance with regulations 60 and 62;

"individual candidate" means a person to whom paragraph (2)(b) applies;

"money" and "pecuniary reward" shall (except in regulations 42, 77 and 78 and Schedule 6 to these Regulations) be deemed to include–

    (a) any office, place or employment, and

    (b) any valuable security or other equivalent of money, and

    (c) any valuable consideration,

and expressions referring to money shall be construed accordingly;

"payment" includes any pecuniary or other reward;

"personal expenses" as used with respect to the expenditure of a candidate in relation to any European Parliamentary election includes the reasonable travelling expenses of the candidate, and the reasonable expenses of his living at hotels or elsewhere for the purposes of and in relation to the election; and

"return as to election expenses" means a return (including the bills and receipts to be delivered with it) to be made under regulation 51(1).

(2) A person becomes a candidate at an election–

    (a) in the case of a person included in the list of candidates of a registered party to accompany its nomination for election, on the day on which the list is submitted by the party; or

    (b) in the case of a person not included in the list of candidates of a registered party to accompany its nomination for election–

        (i) on the last day for publication of the notice of the election if on or before that day he is declared by himself or by others to be a candidate at the election, and

        (ii) otherwise, on the day on which he is so declared by himself or by others or on which he is nominated as a candidate at the election (whichever is the earlier).

Computation of time for purposes of Part 2

32 (1) Where the day or last day on which anything is required or permitted to be done by or in pursuance of this Part of these Regulations is any of the days mentioned in paragraph (2)–

    (a) the requirement or permission shall be deemed to relate to the first day thereafter which is not one of those days; and

    (b) in computing any period of not more than 7 days for the purposes of this Part any of the days so mentioned shall be disregarded.

(2) The days referred to in paragraph (1) are Saturday, Sunday, Christmas Eve, Christmas Day, Good Friday, a bank holiday or a day appointed for public thanksgiving or mourning.

(3) In this regulation "bank holiday", in relation to any European Parliamentary election, means–

    (a) in relation to the combined region, a day which is a bank holiday under the Banking and Financial Dealings Act 1971 in England and Wales or a Bank or Public Holiday in Gibraltar not otherwise falling within paragraph (2);

    (b) in relation to an electoral region other than the combined region, a day which is a bank holiday under the Banking and Financial Dealings Act 1971 in the part of the United Kingdom in which the electoral region is situated.

Election Agents of Registered Parties

Appointment of national election agent of registered party

33 (1) This regulation applies where, at a general election of MEPs, the nominating officer of a registered party (in accordance with the European Parliamentary elections rules) nominates, or authorises the nomination of, that party to stand for election in more than one electoral region.

(2) Not later than the latest date for the delivery of notices of withdrawal for an election, that officer shall name himself, or some other person, as the party's national election agent.

(3) The name and address of the person so named shall be declared in writing by or on behalf of the party's nominating officer to the Secretary of State not later than that time.

(4) One national election agent only shall be appointed for each registered party but the appointment (whether or not the national election agent appointed is the party's nominating officer) may be revoked.

(5) If (whether before, during or after the general election of MEPs) the appointment or deemed appointment of a national election agent is revoked or a national election agent dies, another national election agent shall be appointed forthwith and his name and address declared to the Secretary of State.

(6) The declaration as a party's national election agent of a person other than the nominating officer of that party shall be of no effect under this regulation unless it is made and signed by that person or is accompanied by a written declaration of acceptance signed by him.

(7) Upon the name and address of a national election agent being declared to the Secretary of State, the Secretary of State shall forthwith give public notice of that name and address.

(8) Where for any reason the nominating officer of a registered party is unable to act, functions conferred on him by this regulation shall be discharged by–
   (a) the person registered as leader of that party under the 2000 Act, or
   (b) where that person is also the nominating officer, the person who holds some other office in the party and is registered in pursuance of it under section 24 of that Act.

(9) In the following provisions of these Regulations, except regulations 38 to 41–
   (a) any reference to an election agent shall, in the case of a registered party to which this regulation applies, be construed as a reference to a national election agent, and
   (b) any reference to the election agent of a candidate shall, in the case of a registered party to which this regulation applies, be construed as a reference to that party's national election agent.

Appointment of election agent by a registered party standing in one electoral region only

34 (1) This regulation applies where a registered party is nominated for election in one electoral region only.

(2) Not later than the latest date for the delivery of notices of withdrawal for an election, the nominating officer of a registered party shall name himself, or some other person, as the party's election agent.

(3) The name and address of the person so named shall be declared in writing by or on behalf of the party's nominating officer to the appropriate officer not later than that time.

(4) One election agent only shall be appointed for each registered party, but the appointment (whether or not the election agent appointed is the party's nominating officer) may be revoked.

(5) If (whether before, during or after the election) the appointment or deemed appointment of an election agent is revoked or an election agent dies, another election agent shall be appointed forthwith and his name and address declared to the appropriate officer.

(6) The declaration as a party's election agent of a person other than the nominating officer of that party shall be of no effect under this regulation unless it is made and signed by that person or is accompanied by a written declaration of acceptance signed by him.

(7) Upon the name and address of an election agent being declared to the appropriate officer, the appropriate officer shall forthwith give public notice of that name and address.

(8) Regulation 33(8) above applies for the purposes of this regulation as it applies for the purposes of that regulation.

(9) In the following provisions of these Regulations, except regulations 38 to 41, any reference to the election agent of a candidate shall, in the case of a registered party to which this regulation applies, be construed as a reference to that party's election agent.

Appointment of sub-agent for registered parties

35 (1) A national election agent or a person authorised by him may appoint to act in any electoral region one, but not more than one, deputy election agent and in any part of an electoral region one, but not more than one, deputy election agent (referred to in these Regulations as a sub-agent).

(2) An election agent of a registered party may appoint to act in any part of the electoral region one, but not more than one, deputy election agent (referred to in these Regulations as a sub-agent).

(3) As regards matters in the area for which there is a sub-agent, the election agent (including the national election agent), may act by the sub-agent and–
    (a) anything done for the purposes of these Regulations, by or to the sub-agent in his area shall be deemed to be done by or to the election agent (including the national election agent); and
    (b) any act or default of a sub-agent which, if he were the election agent (including the national election agent), would be an illegal practice or other offence against these Regulations, shall be an illegal practice and offence against these Regulations committed by the sub-agent and the sub-agent shall be liable to punishment accordingly.

(4) Not later than the fifth day before the day of the poll (calculated in accordance with regulation 32) the national election agent or a person acting on his behalf or, as the case may be, the election agent shall declare in writing to the returning officer–
    (a) the name and address of every sub-agent, and
    (b) the area for which he is appointed to act.

(5) The appointment of a sub-agent shall not be vacated by the national election agent or, as the case may be, the election agent who appointed him ceasing to be such an agent.

(6) The appointment of a sub-agent may be revoked by whoever is for the time being the national election agent or, as the case may be, election agent.

(7) Where the appointment of a sub-agent is revoked or the sub-agent dies, another sub-agent may be appointed, and the national election agent or a person acting on his behalf or, as the case may be, the election agent shall forthwith declare in writing to the returning officer–
    (a) the name and address of the sub-agent, and
    (b) the area for which he is appointed to act.

(8) On receipt of a declaration under paragraph (4) or (7) above, the returning officer shall forthwith give public notice of the name, address and area so declared.

(9) References in this regulation to an election agent are to the election agent of a registered party.

Office of agents of registered parties

36 (1) Every national election agent, every election agent and every sub-agent of a registered party shall have an office to which all claims, notices, legal process and other documents may be sent.

(2) The office of a national election agent shall be in the United Kingdom and shall be–
   (a) declared to the Secretary of State at the same time as the appointment of the agent is declared to him; and
   (b) stated in the public notice of the name of the agent.

(3) The office of the election agent or sub-agent of a registered party shall be within the United Kingdom or, in the case of a party standing for election in the combined region, Gibraltar and shall be–
   (a) declared to the appropriate officer at the same time as the appointment of the agent is declared to him; and
   (b) stated in the public notice of the name of the agent.

(4) Any claim, notice, legal process or other document delivered at the address of the national election agent, election agent or sub-agent and addressed to him, shall be deemed to have been served on him and every national election agent, election agent or sub-agent may in respect of any matter connected with the election in which he is acting be sued in any court having jurisdiction at the place where his office is situated.

Effect of default in appointment of agents of registered parties

37 (1) If no person's name and address are given as required by–
   (a) regulation 33 as the national election agent of a registered party, or
   (b) regulation 34 (where regulation 33 does not apply) as the election agent of a registered party for an electoral region,
   by the latest time for delivery of notices of withdrawals, the nominating officer shall be deemed to have named himself as the national election agent or, as the case may be, the election agent and to have revoked any appointment of another person as that agent.

(2) If–
   (a) the person whose name and address have been so given as those of the party's national election agent or, as the case may be, election agent (not being the party's nominating officer) dies, and
   (b) a new appointment is not made on the day of the death or the following day,
   the party's nominating officer shall be deemed to have appointed himself as from the time of the death to the office in question.

(3) If the appointment of a party's national election agent or, as the case may be, election agent is revoked without a new appointment being made, the party's nominating officer shall be deemed to have been appointed (or re-appointed) to the office in question.

(4) The deemed appointment of a nominating officer as his party's national election agent or, as the case may be, election agent may be revoked as if it were an actual appointment.

(5) Regulation 33(8) applies for the purposes of this regulation as it applies for the purposes of that regulation.

(6) Where a party's nominating officer or officer determined under regulation 33(8), as applied by paragraph (5) above, is by virtue of this regulation to be treated as the party's national election agent or, as the case may be, election agent, he shall be deemed to have his office at the address registered under the 2000 Act as the party's headquarters (or, if it has no headquarters, the address to which communications to

the party may be sent).

(7) On being satisfied that a party's nominating officer or officer determined under paragraph (5) above is by virtue of this regulation to be treated as–

    (a) the party's national election agent, or

    (b) the party's election agent,

the Secretary of State or the appropriate officer (as the case may be) shall forthwith proceed to publish the like notice as if that officer's name and address and the address of his office had been duly given to him under regulations 33 and 36 or, as the case may be, regulations 34 and 36.

Election Agents of Individual Candidates

Appointment of election agent for individual candidate

38 (1) Not later than the latest time for the delivery of notices of withdrawals for an election, a person shall be named by or on behalf of each individual candidate as the individual candidate's election agent, and the name and address of the individual candidate's election agent shall be declared in writing by the individual candidate or some other person on his behalf to the appropriate officer not later than that time.

(2) An individual candidate may name himself as election agent, and upon doing so shall, so far as circumstances admit, be subject to the provisions of these Regulations both as an individual candidate and as an election agent, and, except where the context otherwise requires, any reference in these Regulations to an election agent shall be construed to refer to the individual candidate acting in his capacity of election agent.

(3) One election agent only shall be appointed for each individual candidate, but the appointment, whether the election agent appointed be the individual candidate himself or not, may be revoked.

(4) If (whether before, during or after the election) the appointment (or deemed appointment) of an election agent is revoked or an election agent dies, another election agent shall be appointed forthwith and his name and address declared in writing to the appropriate officer.

(5) The declaration as an individual candidate's election agent of a person other than the individual candidate shall be of no effect under this regulation unless it is made and signed by that person or is accompanied by a written declaration of acceptance signed by him.

(6) Upon the name and address of an election agent being declared to the appropriate officer, the appropriate officer shall forthwith give public notice of that name and address.

Appointment of sub-agent for individual candidate

39 (1) An election agent for an individual candidate may appoint to act in any part of the electoral region one, but not more than one, deputy election agent (in these Regulations referred to as a sub-agent).

(2) As regards matters in a part of the electoral region for which there is a sub-agent the election agent may act by the sub-agent and–

    (a) anything done for the purposes of these Regulations by or to the sub-agent in his part of the electoral region shall be deemed to be done by or to the election agent; and

    (b) any act or default of a sub-agent which, if he were the election agent, would be an illegal practice or other offence against these Regulations shall be an illegal practice and offence against these Regulations committed by the sub-agent, and the sub-agent shall be liable to punishment accordingly.

(3) Not later than the fifth day before the day of the poll the election agent shall declare in writing the name and address of every sub-agent to the appropriate officer, and the appropriate officer shall forthwith give public notice of the name and address of every sub-agent so declared.

(4) The appointment of a sub-agent–
   (a) shall not be vacated by the election agent who appointed him ceasing to be election agent, but
   (b) may be revoked by whoever is for the time being the individual candidate's election agent,

and in the event of the revocation of the appointment or of the death of a sub-agent another sub-agent may be appointed, and his name and address shall be forthwith declared in writing to the appropriate officer, who shall forthwith give public notice of the name and address so declared.

(5) The declaration to be made to the appropriate officer, and the notice to be given by him, under paragraph (3) or paragraph (4) shall specify the part of the electoral region within which any sub-agent is appointed to act.

(6) In paragraphs (2) to (4) references to an election agent are to an election agent of an individual candidate.

Office of election agent and sub-agent for individual candidate

40 (1) Every election agent and every sub-agent shall have an office to which all claims, notices, writs, summonses and legal process and other documents may be sent, and the address of the office shall be–
   (a) declared to the appropriate officer at the same time as the appointment of the agent is declared to him; and
   (b) stated in the public notice of the name of the agent.

(2) The office of the elections agent or sub-agent shall be within the United Kingdom or, in the case of a candidate standing for election in the combined region, Gibraltar.

(3) Any claim, notice, writ, summons or legal process or other document delivered at the office of the election agent or sub-agent and addressed to him, shall be deemed to have been served on him and every election agent or sub-agent may in respect of any matter connected with the election in which he is acting be sued in any court having jurisdiction at the place where his office is situated.

(4) In this regulation, references to an election agent and sub-agent are to an election agent or sub-agent of an individual candidate.

Effect of default in election agent's appointment

41 (1) If no person's name and address is given as required by regulation 38 as the election agent of an individual candidate who remains validly nominated at the latest time for delivery of notices of withdrawals, the individual candidate shall be deemed at that time to have named himself as election agent and to have revoked any appointment of another person as his election agent.

(2) If–
   (a) the person whose name and address have been so given as those of the individual candidate's election agent (not being the individual candidate himself) dies, and
   (b) a new appointment is not made on the day of the death or on the following day, the individual candidate shall be deemed to have appointed himself as from the time of death.

(3)   If the appointment of an individual candidate's election agent is revoked without a new appointment being made, the individual candidate himself shall be deemed to have been appointed (or re-appointed) election agent.

(4)   The deemed appointment of an individual candidate as his own election agent may be revoked as if it were an actual appointment.

(5)   Where an individual candidate is by virtue of this regulation to be treated as his own election agent, he shall be deemed to have his office at his address as given in the statement as to persons nominated.

(6)   The appropriate officer on being satisfied that an individual candidate is by virtue of this regulation to be treated as his own election agent, shall forthwith proceed to publish the like notice as if the name and address of the individual candidate and the address of his office had been duly given to him under regulations 38 and 40.

Election Expenses

Control of donations to individual candidates

42 (1)   In the case of any individual candidate at a European Parliamentary election, any money or other property provided (whether as a gift or loan)–
    (a)   by any person other than the candidate or his election agent, and
    (b)   for the purpose of meeting election expenses incurred by or on behalf of the candidate,
must be provided to the candidate or his election agent.

(2)   Paragraph (1) does not apply to any money or other property so provided for the purpose of meeting any such expenses which may be lawfully paid by a person other than the candidate, his election agent or any sub-agent.

(3)   A person who provides any money or other property in contravention of paragraph (1) shall be guilty of an illegal practice.

(4)   Schedule 6 to these Regulations shall have effect for the purpose of controlling donations to individual candidates.

(5)   In this regulation and that Schedule "property" includes any description of property, and references to the provision of property accordingly include the supply of goods.

Payment of expenses of individual candidates through election agent

43 (1)   Subject to paragraph (5), no payment (of whatever nature) shall be made by–
    (a)   an individual candidate at an election, or
    (b)   any other person,
in respect of election expenses incurred by or on behalf of an individual candidate unless it is made by or through the candidate's election agent.

(2)   Every payment made by an election agent in respect of any election expenses shall, except where less than £20, be vouched for by a bill stating the particulars or by a receipt.

(3)   The references in the foregoing provisions of this regulation to an election agent shall be taken as references to the election agent acting by himself or a sub-agent or a person authorised in writing by the election agent or sub-agent.

(4)   All money provided by any person other than the individual candidate for any election expenses, whether as gift, loan, advance or deposit, shall be paid to the candidate or his election agent or sub-agent and not otherwise.

(5)   This regulation does not apply to–

(a) any expenses which are, in accordance with regulations 44(1) or (2), 48(6) or 49(2), paid by the individual candidate;

(b) any expenses which are paid in accordance with regulation 44(4) by a person authorised as mentioned in that provision;

(c) any expenses included in a declaration made by the election agent under regulation 45; or

(d) any expenses which are to be regarded as incurred by or on behalf of the individual candidate by virtue of regulation 60(5).

(6) A person who makes any payment (of whatever nature) in contravention of paragraph (1), or pays in contravention of paragraph (4) any money so provided as mentioned above, shall be guilty of an illegal practice.

Individual candidate's personal expenses, and petty expenses

44 (1) An individual candidate at a European Parliamentary election may pay any personal expenses incurred by him on account of or in connection with or incidental to the election, but the amount which the candidate may pay shall not exceed £900, and where this applies any further personal expenses so incurred by him shall be paid by his election agent.

(2) An individual candidate at a European Parliamentary election may also pay any election expenses (other than expenses falling within paragraph (1)) which were incurred by him or on his behalf and in respect of which payment falls to be made before the date on which he appoints (or is deemed to have appointed) an election agent.

(3) The candidate shall send to his election agent within the time limited by these Regulations for sending in claims a written statement of the amount of expenses paid as mentioned in paragraph (1) or (2) by the candidate.

(4) Any person may, if so authorised in writing by an election agent or sub-agent, pay any election expenses to a total amount not exceeding that named in the authority, but any excess above that amount so named shall be paid by the agent who authorised that person.

(5) A statement of the particulars of payments made by any person so authorised shall be sent to the agent who authorised them within the time limited by these Regulations for sending in claims, and shall be vouched for by a bill containing that person's receipt and, where that agent is the sub-agent, he shall forward the statement, together with his authority, to the election agent.

(6) Regulations 48 and 49 do not apply to expenses which, in accordance with any provision of this regulation, are paid otherwise than by the candidate's election agent.

Expenses of individual candidate incurred otherwise than for elections purposes

45 (1) Neither regulation 43 nor regulations 48 and 49 shall apply to election expenses–

(a) which are incurred by or on behalf of an individual candidate otherwise than for the purposes of the candidate's election, but

(b) which by virtue of regulation 60(1) fall to be regarded as election expenses by reason of the property, services or facilities in respect of which they were incurred being used for the purposes of the candidate's election.

(2) The individual candidate's election agent shall make a declaration of the amount of any election expenses falling within paragraph (1).

(3) In this regulation "for the purposes of the candidate's election" has the same meaning as in regulations 60 and 62.

Prohibition of expenses of individual candidate not authorised by election agent

46 (1)   No expenses shall, with a view to promoting or procuring the election of an individual candidate at an election, be incurred after he becomes a candidate by any person other than the candidate, his election agent and persons authorised in writing by the election agent on account–

(a)   of holding public meetings or organising any public display; or

(b)   of issuing advertisements, circulars or publications; or

(c)   of otherwise representing to the electors that candidate or his views or the extent or nature of his backing or disparaging a registered party or its candidates or an independent candidate.

(1A)   Sub-paragraph (c) of paragraph (1) does not restrict the publication of any matter relating to the election in–

(a)   a newspaper or other periodical,

(b)   a broadcast made by the British Broadcasting Corporation, the Gibraltar Broadcasting Corporation, or by Sianel Pedwar Cymru, or

(c)   a programme included in any service licensed under Part 1 or 3 of the Broadcasting Act 1990or Part 1 or 2 of the Broadcasting Act 1996.

(1B)   Paragraph (1) does not apply to any expenses incurred by any person–

(a)   which do not exceed in the aggregate the permitted sum (and are not incurred by that person as part of a concerted plan of action), or

(b)   in travelling or living away from home or similar personal expenses.

(2)   For the purposes of paragraph (1B), the "permitted sum" means £5,000; and expenses must be regarded as incurred by a person "as part of a concerted plan of action" if they are incurred by that person in pursuance of any plan or other arrangement whereby that person and one or more other persons are to incur, with a view to promoting or procuring the election of the same candidate, expenses which (disregarding paragraph (1B)(a)) fall within paragraph (1).

(2A)   For the purposes of paragraph (1), expenditure incurred before or on the date when a person becomes an individual candidate or a candidate included in the list of candidates submitted by a registered party at the election, is to be treated as having been incurred after that date if it is incurred in connection with any thing which is used or takes place after that date.

(3)   Where a person incurs any expenses required by this regulation to be authorised by the election agent–

(a)   that person shall, within 21 days after the day on which the result of the election is declared, deliver to the agent who authorised the expenses a return of the amount of them, and

(b)   the return shall be accompanied by a declaration made by that person (or in the case of an association or body of persons, by a director, general manager, secretary or other similar officer of the association or body) verifying the return and giving particulars of the matters for which the expenses were incurred,

but this paragraph does not apply to any person engaged or employed for payment or promise of payment by the individual candidate or his election agent.

(4)   The authority of the agent who authorised the incurring of the expenses shall be annexed to and deemed to form part of the return.

(5)   If a person–

(a)   incurs, or aids, abets, counsels or procures any other person to incur, any expenses in contravention of this regulation, or

(b)   knowingly makes the declaration required by paragraph (3) falsely,

he shall be guilty of a corrupt practice; and if a person fails to deliver any declaration or return as required by this regulation he shall be guilty of an illegal practice, but the court before whom a person is convicted under this paragraph may, if they think it just in the special circumstances of the case, mitigate or entirely remit any incapacity imposed by virtue of regulation 107.

(6) Where any act or omission of an association or body of persons, corporate or unincorporate, is an offence declared to be a corrupt or illegal practice by this regulation, any person who at the time of the act or omission was a director, general manager, secretary or other similar officer of the association or body, or was purporting to act in any such capacity, shall be deemed to be guilty of that offence, unless he proves–

   (a) that the act or omission took place without his consent or connivance; and

   (b) that he exercised all such diligence to prevent the commission of the offence as he ought to have exercised having regard to the nature of his functions in that capacity and to all the circumstances.

(7) References in this regulation to an election agent include a sub-agent.

Limitation of election expenses for individual candidates

47 (1) Sums paid out and election expenses incurred by or on behalf of an individual candidate at an election must not in the aggregate exceed the maximum amount specified in paragraph (4).

(2) The references in paragraph (1) to sums paid out and expenses incurred on behalf of an individual candidate include sums being paid and expenses being incurred by the election agent or by a person acting on the written authority of an election agent or sub-agent.

(3) Where any election expenses are incurred in excess of a maximum amount specified in paragraph (4), any candidate or election agent who–

   (a) incurred, or authorised the incurring of, the election expenses, and

   (b) knew or ought reasonably to have known that the expenses would be incurred in excess of that maximum amount,

   shall be guilty of an illegal practice.

(4) That maximum amount is £45,000 multiplied by the number of MEPs to be returned for the electoral region at that election.

(5) The maximum amount mentioned above for an individual candidate at a European Parliamentary election is not required to cover the individual candidate's personal expenses.

Time for sending in and paying claims: individual candidates

48 (1) Every claim against an individual candidate or his election agent in respect of election expenses which is not sent in to the agent who incurred the expense not later than 21 days after the day on which the result of the election is declared shall be barred and not paid.

(2) All election expenses of an individual candidate shall be paid not later than 28 days after that day.

(3) Where the agent who incurred the expense is not the election agent, he shall send to that agent, forthwith on payment of the expense, the bill and a record of the fact that he has paid it and, on receiving a receipt for that payment, shall send that receipt to that agent.

(4) An election agent or the agent who incurred the expense who pays a claim in contravention of paragraph (1) or makes a payment in contravention of paragraph (2) shall be guilty of an illegal practice.

(5)   The claimant or the agent or individual candidate who incurred the expense may apply to the High Court or to a county court for leave to pay a claim for any election expenses, although sent in after that period of 21 days or although sent in to the individual candidate and not to the agent who incurred the expense, and the court on cause shown to their satisfaction may by order grant the leave.

(6)   Any sum specified in the order of leave may be paid by the agent or candidate who incurred the expense and when paid in pursuance of the leave shall not be deemed to be in contravention of paragraph (2); and paragraph (3) shall apply to any such payment.

(7)   References in this regulation to the agent who incurred the expense are references to the election agent or sub-agent or an agent who did so on the written authority of such an agent.

(8)   In the application of this regulation to Gibraltar, for the reference in paragraph (5) to the High Court or a county court, substitute a reference to the Gibraltar court.

Disputed claims: individual candidates

49 (1)   If the agent who incurred the expense disputes any claim sent in to him within the period of 21 days mentioned in regulation 48 or refuses or fails to pay the claim within the period of 28 days so mentioned, the claim shall be deemed to be a disputed claim.

(2)   The claimant may, if he thinks fit, bring an action for a disputed claim in any competent court, including, in Gibraltar, the Gibraltar court, and any sum paid by the agent or individual candidate who incurred the expense in pursuance of the judgment or order of the court shall not be deemed to be in contravention of regulation 43(1) or of regulation 48(2).

(3)   If the defendant in the action admits his liability but disputes the amount of the claim, that amount shall, unless the court on the claimant's application otherwise directs, be forthwith referred for taxation–
   (a)   to a Circuit judge nominated under subsection (1)(a) of section 68 of the Senior Courts Act 1981, or
   (b)   to the master, registrar or other proper officer of the court, or
   (c)   in an action in a Gibraltar court, the registrar,
and the amount found due on the taxation shall be the amount to be recovered in the action in respect of the claim.

(4)   Paragraphs (5) to (7) of regulation 48 apply in relation to a disputed claim as they apply in relation to a claim for election expenses sent in after that period of 21 days.

Election agent's claim

50   So far as circumstances admit, these Regulations apply to an election agent's claim for his remuneration and to its payment in like manner as if he were any other creditor, and if any difference arises about the amount of the claim, the claim shall be a disputed claim within the meaning of these Regulations and be dealt with accordingly.

Return as to election expenses: individual candidates

51 (1)   Within 50 days after the day on which the result of the election is declared, the election agent of every individual candidate at the election shall deliver or cause to be delivered to the appropriate officer a true return containing as respects that candidate–
   (a)   a statement of all election expenses incurred by or on behalf of the candidate; and
   (b)   a statement of all payments made by the election agent together with all bills or

receipts relating to the payments.

(2) A return under this regulation must–

    (a) specify the poll by virtue of which the return is required;

    (b) specify the name of the candidate to whom the return relates and of the candidate's election agent; and

    (c) under a separate heading with any expenses in respect of which a return is required by virtue of regulation 46(2).

(3) The return shall also contain as respects that candidate–

    (a) a statement of all payments made–

        (i) by the candidate in accordance with regulation 44(1) or (2), or

        (ii) by any other person in accordance with regulation 44(4),

together with all bills or receipts relating to any such payments made in accordance with regulation 44(2) or 44(4);

    (b) a statement of all disputed claims of which the election agent is aware;

    (c) a statement of all the unpaid claims, if any, of which the election agent is aware, in respect of which application has been or is about to be made to the High Court, county court or Gibraltar court;

    (d) any declarations of value falling to be made by the candidate's election agent by virtue of regulation 45(2) or 62(2);

    (e) a declaration of the amount of expenses which are to be regarded as election expenses incurred by or on behalf of the candidate by virtue of regulation 60(5);

    (f) a statement of donations made to the candidate or his election agent which complies with the requirements of paragraphs 11 and 12 of Schedule 6 to these Regulations; and

    (g) a statement of the amount, if any, of money provided by the candidate from his own resources for the purpose of meeting election expenses incurred by him or on his behalf.

(4) Where after the date at which the return as to election expenses is delivered, leave is given by the court under regulation 48(5) for any claim to be paid, the agent of the candidate who incurred the expenses shall, within seven days after its payment, deliver or cause to be delivered to the appropriate officer a return of the sums paid in pursuance of the leave, accompanied by a copy of the order of the court giving the leave, and in default he shall be deemed to have failed to comply with the requirements of this regulation without such authorised excuse as is mentioned in regulation 55.

(5) Regulation 48(7) applies for the interpretation of paragraph (4) as it applies for the interpretation of regulation 48.

Declarations as to election expenses: individual candidates

52 (1) A return delivered under regulation 51(1) shall be accompanied by a declaration made by the election agent in the appropriate form.

(2) At the same time that the election agent delivers or causes to be delivered that return, or within seven days afterwards, the candidate shall deliver or cause to be delivered to the appropriate officer a declaration made by him in the appropriate form.

(3) For the purposes of paragraphs (1) and (2), "the appropriate form" is the form in Schedule 7 to this Act.

(4) Where the candidate is out of the United Kingdom or, in the case of an individual candidate resident in Gibraltar standing for election in the combined region, Gibraltar when the return is so delivered–

    (a) the declaration required by paragraph (2) may be made by him within 14 days after his return to the United Kingdom or Gibraltar (as the case may be), and

(b) in that case, the declaration shall be forthwith delivered to the appropriate officer,

but the delay authorised by this provision in making the declaration shall not exonerate the election agent from complying with the provisions of these Regulations relating to the return and declaration as to election expenses.

(5) Where the candidate is his own election agent, the declaration by an election agent as to election expenses need not be made and the declaration by the candidate as to election expenses shall be modified as specified in the form in Schedule 7.

(6) If a candidate or election agent knowingly makes the declaration required by this regulation falsely, he shall be guilty of a corrupt practice.

Return as to personal expenses: candidates on party lists

53 (1) Within 50 days after the day on which the result of the election is declared, every candidate on the list of a registered party shall deliver or cause to be delivered to the appropriate officer a true return containing as respects that candidate a statement of all personal expenses incurred by him on account of or incidental to the election.

(2) If a candidate knowingly makes the return required by this regulation falsely, he shall be guilty of a corrupt practice.

Penalty for failure as respects return or declarations: individual candidates

54 Subject to the provisions of regulation 55 if an individual candidate or election agent fails to comply with the requirements of regulation 51 or regulation 52 he shall be guilty of an illegal practice.

Authorised excuses for failures as to return and declarations: individual candidates

55 (1) An individual candidate or his election agent may apply for relief under this regulation to–

    (a) the High Court;

    (b) an election court; or

    (c) a county court.

(2) Where a person makes an application under this regulation he shall notify the Director of Public Prosecutions of the application and the Director or his assistant or any barrister, advocate or solicitor duly appointed as the Director's representative may attend the hearing of the application and make representations at the hearing in respect of it.

(3) Relief under this regulation may be granted–

    (a) to a candidate, in respect of any failure to deliver the return and declarations as to election expenses, or any part of them, or in respect of any error or false statement in them; or

    (b) to an election agent, in respect of the failure to deliver the return and declarations which he was required to deliver, or any part of them, or in respect of any error or false statement in them.

(4) The application for relief may be made on the ground that the failure, error or false statement arose–

    (a) by reason of the applicant's illness; or

    (b) where the applicant is the candidate, by reason of the absence, death, illness or misconduct of his election agent or sub-agent or of any clerk or officer of such agent; or

    (c) where the applicant is the election agent, by reason of the death or illness of any prior election agent of the candidate, or of the absence, death, illness or misconduct of any sub-agent, clerk or officer of any election agent of the candidate; or

(d) by reason of inadvertence or any reasonable cause of a like nature,

and not by reason of any want of good faith on the applicant's part.

(5) The court may–

(a) after such notice of the application in the electoral region as it considers fit, and

(b) on production of such evidence of the grounds stated in the application and of the good faith of the application, and otherwise, as it considers fit,

make such order for allowing an authorised excuse for the failure, error or false statement as it considers just.

(6) An order under paragraph (5) may make the allowance conditional on the making of the return and declaration in a modified form or within an extended time, and upon the compliance with such other terms as to the court seem best calculated for carrying into effect the objects of this Part of these Regulations.

(7) An order under paragraph (5) shall relieve the applicant for the order from any liability or consequences under these Regulations in respect of the matter excused by the order.

(8) In the application of this regulation to Gibraltar, for the reference in paragraph (1) to a county court, substitute a reference to the Gibraltar court.

(9) Where a person makes an application under this regulation to the Gibraltar court, references in paragraph (2) to the Director of Public Prosecutions shall be construed as references to the Attorney General for Gibraltar.

Court's power to require information from election agent or sub-agent of individual candidate

56 (1) Where on an application under regulation 55 it appears to the court that any person who is or has been an election agent or sub-agent of an individual candidate has refused or failed to make such return, or to supply such particulars, as will enable the candidate and his election agent to comply with the provisions of these Regulations as to the return or declarations as to election expenses, the court, before making an order under that regulation, shall order that person to attend before the court.

(2) The court shall on the attendance of that person, unless he shows cause to the contrary, order him–

(a) to make the return and declaration, or

(b) to deliver a statement of the particulars required to be contained in the return,

as the court considers just, within such time, to such person and in such manner as it may direct, or may order him to be examined with respect to the particulars.

(3) If a person fails to comply with any order of the court under this section, the court may order him to pay a fine *not exceeding the amount of the maximum fine to which he would be liable if at the time the order is made he were convicted of a summary offence on conviction of which he was liable to a fine of level 5 on the standard scale.*

(4) References in this regulation to the election agent or sub-agent include a person authorised in writing by the election agent or any sub-agent to incur election expenses.

Duty of appropriate officer to forward returns and declarations to Electoral Commission

57 Where the appropriate officer receives any return or declaration under regulations 46, 51, 52 or 53 in respect of a European Parliamentary election he shall as soon as reasonably practicable after receiving the return or declaration deliver a copy of it to the Electoral Commission and, if so requested by the Commission, he shall also deliver to them a copy of any accompanying documents.

Publication of time and place for inspection of returns and declarations

58 (1) At a European Parliamentary election–

    (a) the returning officer shall, within 10 days after the end of the time allowed for delivering to him returns as to election expenses, publish in at least one newspaper circulating in the electoral region for which the election was held a notice of the time and place at which the returns and declarations (including the accompanying documents) can be inspected; but

    (b) if any return or declaration has not been received by the returning officer before the notice is despatched for publication, the notice shall so state, and a like notice about that return or declaration, if afterwards received, shall within 10 days after the receipt be published in like manner.

  (2) In the application of this regulation to the combined region, for the words "the electoral region" substitute "that part of the region which is in England and in at least one newspaper circulating in that part which is in Gibraltar".

Inspection of returns and declaration

59 (1) Where the appropriate officer receives any return or declaration under regulations 51(1) or 52 he shall–

    (a) as soon as reasonably practicable after receiving the return or declaration make a copy of it, and any accompanying documents, available for public inspection at his office, or some other convenient place chosen by him, for a period of 12 months beginning with the date when the return is received by him;

    (b) if requested to do so by any person, and on payment of the prescribed fee, supply that person with a copy of the return or declaration and any accompanying documents.

  (2) If any such return contains a statement of donations in accordance with regulation 51(3)(f), the appropriate officer shall secure that the copy of the statement made available for public inspection under paragraph (a) or (as the case may be) supplied under paragraph (b) does not include, in the case of any donation by an individual, the donor's address.

  (3) After the expiry of those 12 months the appropriate officer may cause the returns or declarations (including the accompanying documents) to be destroyed.

Meaning of "election expenses"

60 (1) In this Part of these Regulations "election expenses" in relation to a candidate at an election means (subject to paragraph (2) and regulation 62) any expenses incurred at any time in respect of any matter specified in Part 1 of Schedule 7A which is used for the purposes of the candidate's election after the date when he becomes a candidate at the election.

  (2) No election expenses are to be regarded as incurred by virtue of paragraph (1) or regulation 62 in respect of any matter specified in Part 2 of Schedule 7A.

  (3) In this regulation and regulation 62 "for the purposes of the candidate's election" means with a view to, or otherwise in connection with, promoting or procuring the candidate's election at the election.

  (4) For the purposes of this Part of these Regulations and in Schedule 7A, election expenses are incurred by or on behalf of a candidate at an election if they are incurred–

    (a) by the candidate or his election agent, or

    (b) by any person authorised in writing by the candidate or his election agent to incur expenses.

(5) In this Part of these Regulations and in Schedule 7A, any reference to election expenses incurred by or on behalf of a candidate at an election includes expenses–
  (a) which are incurred as mentioned in paragraph (1) before the date when he becomes a candidate at the election, but
  (b) which by virtue of that paragraph fall to be regarded as election expenses.

(6) In this Part of these Regulations and in Part 4 and in Schedule 7A, any reference (in whatever terms) to promoting or procuring a candidate's election at an election includes doing so by prejudicing the electoral prospects of another candidate at the election.

Incurring of election expenses for purposes of regulation 60

61 Schedule 7A, which makes provision for election expenses, has effect.

Property, goods, services etc provided free of charge or at a discount

62 (1) This regulation applies where, in the case of a candidate at an election–
  (a) either–
    (i) property or goods is or are transferred to the candidate or his election agent free of charge or at a discount of more than 10 per cent of the market value of the property or goods, or
    (ii) property, goods, services or facilities is or are provided for the use or benefit of the candidate free of charge or at a discount of more than 10 per cent of the commercial rate for the use of the property or for the provision of the goods, services or facilities, and
  (b) the property, goods, services or facilities is or are made use of by or on behalf of the candidate in circumstances such that, if any expenses were to be (or are) actually incurred by or on behalf of the candidate in respect of that use, they would be (or are) election expenses incurred by or on behalf of the candidate.

(2) Where this regulation applies–
  (a) an amount of election expenses determined in accordance with this regulation ("the appropriate amount") shall be treated, for the purposes of this Part of these Regulations, as incurred by the candidate, and
  (b) in the case of an individual candidate, the candidate's election agent shall make a declaration of that amount, unless that amount is not more than £50.
  This paragraph has effect subject to Part 2 of Schedule 7A to these Regulations.

(3) Where paragraph (1)(a)(i) applies, the appropriate amount is such proportion of either–
  (a) the market value of the property or goods (where the property or goods is or are transferred free of charge), or
  (b) the difference between the market value of the property or goods and the amount of expenses actually incurred by or on behalf of the candidate in respect of the property or goods (where the property or goods is or are transferred at a discount),
  as is reasonably attributable to the use made of the property or goods as mentioned in paragraph (1)(b).

(4) Where paragraph (1)(a)(ii) applies, the appropriate amount is such proportion of either–
  (a) the commercial rate for the use of the property or the provision of the goods, services or facilities (where the property, goods, services or facilities is or are provided free of charge), or
  (b) the difference between that commercial rate and the amount of expenses

actually incurred by or on behalf of the candidate in respect of the use of the property or the provision of the services or facilities (where the property, goods, services or facilities is or are provided at a discount),

as is reasonably attributable to the use made of the property, goods, services or facilities as mentioned in paragraph (1)(b).

(5)   Where the services of an employee are made available by his employer for the use or benefit of a candidate, then for the purposes of this regulation the commercial rate for the provision of those services shall be the amount of the remuneration and allowances payable to the employee by his employer in respect of the period for which his services are so made available (but shall not include any amount in respect of any contributions or other payments for which the employer is liable in respect of the employee).

(6)   In this regulation "market value", in relation to any property or goods, means the price which might reasonably be expected to be paid for the property or goods on a sale in the open market; and paragraph 2(6)(a) of Schedule 6 to these Regulations shall apply with any necessary modifications for the purpose of determining, for the purposes of paragraph (1), whether property or goods is or are transferred to a candidate or his election agent.

General

Candidate's right to send election address post free

63 (1)   An individual candidate and the nominating officer of a registered party which is included in the statement of parties and individual candidates nominated for the election or a person authorised in writing by that officer at a European Parliamentary election is, subject to such reasonable terms and conditions as the universal service provider concerned may specify, entitled to send free of any charge for postage which would otherwise be made by a universal service provider either–

    (a)   one unaddressed postal communication, containing matter relating to the election only and not exceeding 60 grammes in weight, to each place in the electoral region which, in accordance with those terms and conditions, constitutes a delivery point for the purposes of this paragraph; or

    (b)   one such postal communication addressed to each elector.

(2)   An individual candidate and the nominating officer of a registered party which is included in the statement of parties and individual candidates nominated for the election or a person authorised in writing by that officer is also, subject as mentioned above, entitled to send free of any such charge for postage as mentioned above to each person entered in the list of proxies for the election one such communication as mentioned above for each appointment in respect of which that person is so entered.

(2A)   The individual candidate and the nominating officer of a registered party which are included in the statement of parties and individual candidates nominated for the election or a person authorised in writing by that officer may also require the local returning officer to make arrangements with the universal postal service provider for communications under paragraph (1)(b) to be sent to persons who have anonymous entries in the register.

(2B)   Arrangements under paragraph (2A) must be such as to ensure that it is not disclosed to any other person that the addressee of such a communication has an anonymous entry.

(3)   A person shall not be deemed to be an individual candidate for the purposes of this regulation unless he is shown as standing nominated in the statement of persons

nominated, but until the publication of that statement any person who declares himself to be an individual candidate shall be entitled to exercise the right of free postage conferred by this regulation if he gives such security as may be required by the universal service provider concerned for the payment of postage should he not be shown as standing nominated as mentioned above.

(4) Until the publication of the statement of parties and individual candidates nominated for the election in an electoral region, the nominating officer of a registered party or a person authorised in writing by him shall be entitled to exercise in that region the right of free postage conferred by this regulation if he gives such security as may be required by the universal service provider concerned for the payment of postage should that party not be included in that statement as standing nominated.

(5) For the purposes of this regulation "elector" means a person–
   (a) who is registered in the register of electors to be used at the election in the electoral region on the last day for publication of notice of the election; and
   (b) includes a person who is registered in such a register (or, in the case of a person who has an anonymous entry in the register, in the record of anonymous entries) as below voting age if (but only if) it appears from the register (or from the record) that he will be of voting age on the day fixed for the poll.

(6) In this regulation "universal service provider" has the same meaning as in Part 3 of the Postal Services Act 2011.

Broadcasting from outside United Kingdom

64 (1) No person shall, with intent to influence persons to give or refrain from giving their votes at a European Parliamentary election, include, or aid, abet, counsel or procure the inclusion of, any matter relating to the election in any programme service (within the meaning of the Broadcasting Act 1990) or in any service which would, if Gibraltar were part of the United Kingdom, be a programme service provided from a place outside the United Kingdom and Gibraltar otherwise than in pursuance of arrangements made with–
   (a) in the United Kingdom,
      (i) the British Broadcasting Corporation;
      (ii) Sianel Pedwar Cymru;
      (iii) the holder of any licence granted by the Office of Communications;
   (b) in Gibraltar, the Gibraltar Broadcasting Corporation,
   for the reception and re-transmission of that matter by that body or the holder of that licence.

(2) An offence under this regulation shall be an illegal practice, but the court before whom a person is convicted of an offence under this regulation may, if they think it just in the special circumstances of the case, mitigate or entirely remit any incapacity imposed by virtue of regulation 107.

(3) Where any act or omission of an association or body of persons, corporate or unincorporate, is an illegal practice under this regulation, any person who at the time of the act or omission was a director, general manager, secretary or other similar officer of the association or body, or was purporting to act in any such capacity, shall be deemed to be guilty of the illegal practice, unless he proves–
   (a) that the act or omission took place without his consent or connivance; and
   (b) that he exercised all such diligence to prevent the commission of the illegal practice as he ought to have exercised having regard to the nature of his functions in that capacity and to all the circumstances.

Broadcasting of local items during election period

65 (1) Each broadcasting authority shall adopt a code of practice with respect to the participation of candidates at a European Parliamentary election in items about the electoral region in question which are included in relevant services during the election period.

(2) The code for the time being adopted by a broadcasting authority under this section shall be either–

(a) a code drawn up by that authority, whether on their own or jointly with one or more other broadcasting authorities, or

(b) a code drawn up by one or more other such authorities;

and a broadcasting authority shall from time to time consider whether the code for the time being so adopted by them should be replaced by a further code falling within paragraph (a) or (b).

(3) Before drawing up a code under this section a broadcasting authority shall have regard to any views expressed by the Electoral Commission for the purposes of this regulation; and any such code may make different provision for different cases.

(4) The Office of Communications and the Gibraltar Regulatory Authority shall each do all that they can to secure that the code for the time being adopted by them under this regulation is observed in the provision of relevant services; and the British Broadcasting Corporation, the Gibraltar Broadcasting Corporation and Sianel Pedwar Cymru shall each observe in the provision of relevant services the code so adopted by them.

(5) For the purposes of paragraph (1) "the election period", in relation to an election, means the period beginning with the last date for publication of notice of the election, and ending with the close of the poll.

(6) In this regulation–

"broadcasting authority" means the British Broadcasting Corporation, the Office of Communications, Sianel Pedwar Cymru or the Gibraltar Regulatory Authority;

"candidate", in relation to an election, means a candidate standing nominated at the election or included in a list of candidates submitted in connection with it;

"relevant services"–

(a) in relation to the British Broadcasting Corporation or Sianel Pedwar Cymru, means services broadcast by that body;

(b) in relation to the Office of Communications, means services licensed under Part 1 or 3 of the Broadcasting Act 1990 or Part 1 or 2 of the Broadcasting Act 1996; and

(c) in relation to the Gibraltar Regulatory Authority, means services broadcast by the Gibraltar Broadcasting Corporation.

Imitation poll cards

66 No person shall for the purpose of promoting or procuring the election of a registered party or any individual candidate at a European Parliamentary election issue any poll card or document so closely resembling an official poll card as to be calculated to deceive, and paragraphs (2) and (3) of regulation 64 apply as if an offence under this regulation were an offence under that regulation.

Schools and rooms for European Parliamentary election meetings

67 (1) Subject to the provisions of this regulation, a candidate at a European Parliamentary election is entitled for the purpose of holding public meetings in furtherance of his candidature or that of his party to the use free of charge at reasonable times between the last date on which notice of election may be published in accordance with the

European Parliamentary elections rules and the day preceding the date of the poll of–
- (a) a suitable room in the premises of a school to which this regulation applies;
- (b) any meeting room to which this regulation applies.

(2) This regulation applies–
- (a) in England and Wales, to community, foundation and voluntary schools of which the premises are situated in the electoral region,
- (b) in Scotland, to any school of which the premises are so situated, not being an independent school within the meaning of the Education (Scotland) Act 1980; and
- (c) in Gibraltar, to a school the expense of maintaining which is payable wholly or partly out of public funds or out of any rate, or by a body whose expenses are so payable.

(3) This regulation applies to meeting rooms situated in the electoral region, the expense of maintaining which is payable wholly or mainly out of public funds or out of any rate, or by a body whose expenses are so payable.

(4) Where a room is used for a meeting in pursuance of the rights conferred by this regulation, the person by whom or on whose behalf the meeting is convened–
- (a) shall defray any expenses incurred in preparing, warming, lighting and cleaning the room and providing attendance for the meeting and restoring the room to its usual condition after the meeting; and
- (b) shall defray any damage done to the room or the premises in which it is situated, or to the furniture, fittings or apparatus in the room or premises.

(5) A candidate is not entitled to exercise the rights conferred by this regulation except on reasonable notice; and this regulation does not authorise any interference with the hours during which a room in school premises is used for educational purposes, or any interference with the use of a meeting room either for the purposes of the person maintaining it or under a prior agreement for its letting for any purpose.

(6) The provisions of Schedule 8 to these Regulations have effect with respect to the rights conferred by this regulation and the arrangements to be made for their exercise.

(7) For the purposes of this regulation (except those of paragraph (b) of paragraph (4)), the premises of a school shall not be taken to include any private dwelling, and in this regulation–
- (a) the expression "meeting room" means any room which it is the practice to let for public meetings; and
- (b) the expression "room" includes a hall, gallery or gymnasium.

Disturbances at election meetings

68 (1) A person who at a lawful public meeting to which this regulation applies acts, or incites others to act, in a disorderly manner for the purpose of preventing the transaction of the business for which the meeting was called together shall be guilty of an illegal practice.

(2) This regulation applies to a political meeting held in an electoral region in connection with a European Parliamentary election between the last date on which notice of election may be published in accordance with the European Parliamentary elections rules and the date of the poll.

(3) If a constable reasonably suspects any person of committing an offence under paragraph (1), he may if requested so to do by the chairman of the meeting require that person to declare to him immediately his name and address and, if that person refuses or fails so to declare his name and address or gives a false name and address, he shall be liable on summary conviction to a fine not exceeding level 1 on the

standard scale .

Officials not to act for candidates

69 (1) If–

    (a) any returning officer or local returning officer at a European Parliamentary election, or

    (b) any officer or clerk appointed under the European Parliamentary elections rules, or

    (c) any partner or clerk of any such person,

acts as an agent of a registered party which has submitted a list, a candidate on that list or an individual candidate in the conduct or management of the election, he shall be guilty of an offence, but nothing in this paragraph prevents an individual candidate from acting as his own election agent.

  (2) A person guilty of an offence under this regulation shall be liable on summary conviction to a fine not exceeding level 4 on the standard scale .

Illegal canvassing by police officers

70 (1) No member of a police force shall by word, message, writing or in any other manner, endeavour to persuade any person to give, or dissuade any person from giving, his vote, whether as an elector or as proxy at any European Parliamentary election for an electoral region wholly or partly within the police area.

  (2) A person acting in contravention of paragraph (1) shall be liable on summary conviction to a fine not exceeding level 3 on the standard scale , but nothing in that paragraph shall subject a member of a police force to any penalty for anything done in the discharge of his duty as a member of the force.

  (3) In the application of this regulation to Gibraltar, the reference in paragraph (1) to the police area shall be construed as a reference to Gibraltar.

False statements as to candidates

71 (1) A person who, or any director of any body or association corporate which–

    (a) before or during an election,

    (b) for the purpose of affecting the return of any registered party or individual candidate at the election,

makes or publishes any false statement of fact in relation to the personal character or conduct of a candidate on the list of that party or of that individual candidate shall be guilty of an illegal practice, unless he can show that he had reasonable grounds for believing, and did believe, the statement to be true.

  (2) A person making or publishing any false statement of fact as mentioned above may be restrained by interim or perpetual injunction by the High Court or the county court from any repetition of that false statement or of a false statement of a similar character in relation to the candidate and, for the purpose of granting an interim injunction, prima facie proof of the falsity of the statement shall be sufficient.

  (3) In the application of this regulation to Gibraltar, in paragraph (2) for the reference to the county court substitute a reference to the Gibraltar court.

Corrupt withdrawal from candidature

72 Any person who corruptly induces or procures any other person to withdraw from being an individual candidate at an election, in consideration of any payment or promise of payment, and any person withdrawing in pursuance of the inducement or

procurement, shall be guilty of an illegal payment.

Payments for exhibition of election notices

73 (1)   No payment or contract for payment shall for the purpose of promoting or procuring the election of a registered party or an individual candidate at an election be made to an elector or his proxy on account of the exhibition of, or the use of any house, land, building or premises for the exhibition of, any address, bill or notice, unless–

    (a)   it is the ordinary business of the elector or proxy as an advertising agent to exhibit for payment bills and advertisements; and

    (b)   the payment or contract is made in the ordinary course of that business.

(2)   If any payment or contract for payment is knowingly made in contravention of this regulation either before, during or after an election–

    (a)   the person making the payment or contract, and

    (b)   if he knew it to be in contravention of these Regulations, any person receiving the payment or being a party to the contract,

shall be guilty of an illegal practice.

Details to appear on election publications

74 (1)   This regulation applies to any material which can reasonably be regarded as intended to promote or procure the election of a candidate at an election (whether or not it can be so regarded as intended to achieve any other purpose as well).

(2)   No material to which this regulation applies is to be published unless in the case of material which is, or is contained in, such a printed document as is mentioned in paragraph (4), (5) or (6), the requirements of that paragraph are complied with.

(3)   For the purposes of paragraphs (4) to (6), the following details are "the relevant details" in the case of any material falling within paragraph (2), namely–

    (a)   the name and address of the printer of the document;

    (b)   the name and address of the promoter of the material; and

    (c)   the name and address of any person on behalf of whom the material is being published (and who is not the promoter).

(4)   Where the material is a document consisting (or consisting principally) of a single side of printed matter, the relevant details must appear on the face of the document.

(5)   Where the material is a printed document other than one to which paragraph (4) applies, the relevant details must appear either on the first or the last page of the document.

(6)   Where the material is an advertisement contained in a newspaper or periodical–

    (a)   the name and address of the printer of the newspaper or periodical must appear either on its first or last page; and

    (b)   the relevant details specified in paragraph (3)(b) and (c) must be included in the advertisement.

(7)   Where any material falling within paragraph (1) is published in contravention of paragraph (2), then (subject to paragraphs (8) and (9))–

    (a)   the promoter of the material,

    (b)   any other person by whom the material is so published, and

    (c)   the printer of the document,

shall be guilty of an offence and liable on summary conviction to a fine not exceeding level 5 on the standard scale.

(8)   It shall be a defence for a person charged with an offence under this regulation to prove–

    (a)   that the contravention of paragraph (2) arose from circumstances beyond his control; and

(b) that he took all reasonable steps, and exercised all due diligence, to ensure that the contravention would not arise.

(9) Where a candidate or his election agent would (apart from this paragraph) be guilty of an offence under paragraph (7), he shall instead be guilty of an illegal practice.

(10) In this regulation–
"print" means print by whatever means, and "printer" is to be construed accordingly;
"the promoter", in relation to any election material, means the person causing the material to be published; and
"publish" means make available to the public at large, or any section of the public, in whatever form and by whatever means.

(11) For the purpose of determining whether any material is material such as is mentioned in paragraph (1), it is immaterial that it does not expressly mention the name of any candidate.

Prohibition of paid canvassers

75 If a person is, either before, during or after a European Parliamentary election, engaged or employed for payment or promise of payment as a canvasser for the purpose of promoting or procuring the election of a registered party or an individual candidate–
(a) the person so engaging or employing him, and
(b) the person so engaged or employed,
shall be guilty of illegal employment.

Providing money for illegal purposes

76 Where a person knowingly provides money–
(a) for any payment which is contrary to the provisions of these Regulations, or
(b) for any expenses incurred in excess of the maximum amount allowed by these Regulations, or
(c) for replacing any money expended in any such payment or expenses,
except where the payment or the incurring of the expenses may have been previously allowed in pursuance of regulation 108 to be an exception, that person shall be guilty of an illegal payment.

Bribery

77 (1) A person shall be guilty of a corrupt practice if he is guilty of bribery.

(2) A person shall be guilty of bribery if he, directly or indirectly, by himself or by any other person on his behalf–
(a) gives any money or procures any office to or for any voter or to or for any other person on behalf of any voter or to or for any other person in order to induce any voter to vote or refrain from voting, or
(b) corruptly does any such act as mentioned above on account of any voter having voted or refrained from voting, or
(c) makes any such gift or procurement as mentioned above to or for any person in order to induce that person to procure, or endeavour to procure, the return of any individual candidate or registered party at a European Parliamentary election or the vote of any voter,
or if upon or in consequence of any such gift or procurement as mentioned above he procures or engages, promises or endeavours to procure the return of any person or registered party at a European Parliamentary election or the vote of any voter.
For the purposes of this paragraph–

(i) references to giving money include references to giving, lending, agreeing to give or lend, offering, promising, or promising to procure or endeavour to procure any money or valuable consideration; and

(ii) references to procuring any office include references to giving, procuring, agreeing to give or procure, offering, promising, or promising to procure or to endeavour to procure any office, place or employment.

(3) A person shall be guilty of bribery if he advances or pays or causes to be paid any money to or for the use of any other person with the intent that that money or any part of it shall be expended in bribery at any European Parliamentary election or knowingly pays or causes to be paid any money to any person in discharge or repayment of any money wholly or in part expended in bribery at any election.

(4) The foregoing provisions of this regulation shall not extend or be construed to extend to any money paid or agreed to be paid for or on account of any legal expenses incurred in good faith at or concerning a European Parliamentary election.

(5) A voter shall be guilty of bribery if before or during a European Parliamentary election he directly or indirectly by himself or by any other person on his behalf receives, agrees, or contracts for any money, gift, loan or valuable consideration, office, place or employment for himself or for any other person for voting or agreeing to vote or for refraining or agreeing to refrain from voting.

(6) A person shall be guilty of bribery if after a European Parliamentary election he directly or indirectly by himself or by any other person on his behalf receives any money or valuable consideration on account of any person having voted or refrained from voting or having induced any other person to vote or refrain from voting.

(7) In this regulation the expression "voter" includes any person who has or claims to have a right to vote.

Treating

78 (1) A person shall be guilty of a corrupt practice if he is guilty of treating.

(2) A person shall be guilty of treating if he corruptly, by himself or by any other person, either before, during or after a European Parliamentary election, directly or indirectly gives or provides, or pays wholly or in part the expense of giving or providing, any meat, drink, entertainment or provision to or for any person–
(a) for the purpose of corruptly influencing that person or any other person to vote or refrain from voting; or
(b) on account of that person or any other person having voted or refrained from voting, or being about to vote or refrain from voting.

(3) Every elector or his proxy who corruptly accepts or takes any such meat, drink, entertainment or provision shall also be guilty of treating.

Undue influence

79 (1) A person shall be guilty of a corrupt practice if he is guilty of undue influence.

(2) A person shall be guilty of undue influence–
(a) if he, directly or indirectly, by himself or by any other person on his behalf, makes use of or threatens to make use of any force, violence or restraint, or inflicts or threatens to inflict, by himself or by any other person, any temporal or spiritual injury, damage, harm or loss upon or against any person in order to induce or compel that person to vote or refrain from voting, or on account of that person having voted or refrained from voting; or
(b) if, by abduction, duress or any fraudulent device or contrivance, he impedes or prevents or intends to impede or prevent the free exercise of the franchise of an

elector or proxy for an elector, or so compels, induces or prevails upon or intends so to compel, induce or prevail upon an elector or proxy for an elector either to vote or to refrain from voting.

Rights of creditors

80 The provisions of this Part of these Regulations prohibiting–

    (a) payments and contracts for payments,

    (b) the payment or incurring of election expenses in excess of the maximum amount allowed by these Regulations; or

    (c) the incurring of expenses not authorised by the election agent,

do not affect the right of any creditor, who, when the contract was made or the expense was incurred, was ignorant of that contract or expense being in contravention of these Regulations.

Savings as to European Parliamentary elections

81 (1) Nothing in this Part makes it illegal for an employer to permit European Parliamentary electors or their proxies to absent themselves from his employment for a reasonable time for the purpose of voting at the poll at a European Parliamentary election without having any deduction from their salaries or wages on account of their absence, if the permission–

    (a) is (so far as practicable without injury to the employer's business) given equally to all persons alike who are at the time in his employment, and

    (b) is not given with a view to inducing any person to record his vote for any particular registered party or individual candidate at the election, and

    (c) is not refused to any person for the purpose of preventing him from recording his vote for any particular registered party or individual candidate at the election,

but this paragraph shall not be construed as making illegal any act which would not be illegal apart from this paragraph.

PART 3
VACANCIES

Initial response to vacancies

82 (1) Subject to paragraphs (2) and (5), as soon as practicable after the Secretary of State has–

    (a) received information of a vacancy in the seat of an MEP from the President of the European Parliament under the Act annexed to Council Decision 76/787, or

    (b) informed the European Parliament under that Act that a vacancy exists,

he shall send a notice in accordance with paragraph (4) to the returning officer for the electoral region in which the vacancy exists.

(2) Paragraph (1) does not apply where it appears from the declaration of the result of the election that the person whose seat is now vacant was an individual candidate.

(3) Subject to regulation 85(2), a by-election shall be held in the circumstances described in paragraph (2) to fill the vacancy and the period within which the poll at that election must take place is six months from the occurrence of the event specified in paragraph (1)(a) or (b), as the case may be.

(4) The notice referred to in paragraph (1) shall–

    (a) state that a vacancy exists, and

    (b) set out the name of the person who had been returned in the seat which is vacant, together with the name of the registered party on whose list his name was included.

(5) Paragraph (1) shall not apply where the event referred to in sub-paragraph (a) or (b) of that paragraph occurred less than six months before the Thursday of the period of the next general election of MEPs.

(6) For the purpose of paragraph (5) and regulation 83(1), the period of the next general election of MEPs is that during which the next general election would take place in accordance with the Act annexed to Council Decision 76/787.

Filling of vacancies from a registered party's list

83 (1) On receipt of a notice under regulation 82(4), the returning officer shall ascertain from the list submitted by the registered party named in the notice ("the relevant list") the name and address of the person whose name appears highest on that list ("the first choice"), disregarding the name of any person who has been returned as an MEP or who has died.

(2) The returning officer shall take such steps as appear to him to be reasonable to contact the first choice to ask whether he will–
   (a) state in writing that he is willing and able to be returned as an MEP, and
   (b) deliver a certificate signed by or on behalf of the nominating officer of the registered party which submitted the relevant list stating that he may be returned as that party's MEP.

(3) Paragraph (4) applies where–
   (a) within such period as the returning officer considers reasonable–
      (i)   he decides that the steps he has taken to contact the first choice have been unsuccessful, or
      (ii) he has not received from the first choice the statement and certificate referred to in paragraph (2), or
   (b) the first choice has–
      (i)   stated in writing that he is not willing or able to be returned as an MEP, or
      (ii) failed to deliver the certificate referred to in paragraph (2)(b).

(4) In the circumstances set out in paragraph (3), the returning officer shall repeat the procedure required by paragraph (2) in respect of the person (if any) whose name and address appears next in the relevant list ("the second choice") or, where paragraph (3)(a) or (b) applies in respect of that person, in respect of the person (if any) whose name and address appear next highest after the second choice in that list and the returning officer shall continue to repeat the procedure until the seat is filled or the names in the list exhausted.

(5) Where a person whose name appears on the relevant list provides the statement and certificate referred to in paragraph (2), the returning officer shall (subject to paragraph (6)) declare in writing that person to be returned as an MEP.

(6) Where–
   (a) the returning officer has, in accordance with paragraph (4), asked a second or other subsequent choice the questions in paragraph (2), and
   (b) the person who was previously asked those questions then provides the statement and certificate referred to in paragraph (2),
   that statement and certificate shall have no effect unless and until the circumstances described in sub-paragraph (a) or (b) of paragraph (3) apply in respect of the second or other subsequent choice.

(7) The returning officer shall give public notice of a declaration given under paragraph (5) and send a copy of it to the Secretary of State.

(8) Where the returning officer is unable to fill the seat under this regulation, he shall notify the Secretary of State that he is unable to do so.

By-election to fill certain vacancies

84 (1) Subject to regulation 85(2), where the Secretary of State has received a notice from a returning officer under regulation 83(8), a by-election shall be held to fill that vacancy.

(2) The period within which the poll at any by-election which is required to be held under paragraph (1) must take place is six months from the date on which the Secretary of State receives the notice referred to in that paragraph.

When a by-election is not needed

85 (1) The circumstances in which this regulation applies are where the latest date for the poll for a by-election would fall on or after the Thursday of the period of the next general election of MEPs (within the meaning of regulation 82(6)).

(2) In the circumstances in which this regulation applies, regulations 82(3) and 84(1) shall not apply and the Secretary of State shall not appoint a day for the poll for a by-election.

PART 4
LEGAL PROCEEDINGS

Interpretation of Part 4

86 In this Part of these Regulations, unless the context otherwise requires–
"appropriate officer" means the returning officer;
"candidate" has the same meaning as in Part 2 of these Regulations;
"costs" includes charges and expenses;
"declaration as to election expenses" means a declaration made under regulation 52;
"elective office" means any office to which a local government election is held in England or Wales;
"judicial office" includes the office of justice of the peace;
"Licensing Acts" means the Licensing Act 2003 or, in relation to Scotland, the Licensing (Scotland) Act 2005, or in relation to Gibraltar, the Licensing and Fees Act, the Clubs Act, the Entertainment Act and the Leisure Areas (Licensing) Act 2001;
"money" and "pecuniary reward" shall be deemed to include–
(a) any office, place or employment, and
(b) any valuable security or other equivalent of money, and
(c) any valuable consideration,
and expressions referring to money shall be construed accordingly;
"payment" includes any pecuniary or other reward;
"prescribed" means prescribed by rules of court; and
"public office" in relation to Scotland means any office held in Scotland–
(a) under the Crown, or
(b) under the charter of a city or burgh, or
(c) under the Acts relating to local government or public health or public education,
whether the office is that–
(i) of mayor, provost, chief magistrate, chairman, alderman, councillor, member of a board, commission or other local authority in any local government or other area; or
(ii) of proper officer or other officer under a council, board, commission or

other authority; or

    (iii) of any other office to which a person is elected or appointed under any such charter or enactment as is mentioned above, including any other municipal or parochial office; and

"return as to election expenses" means a return made under regulation 51.

Computation of time for purposes of Part 4

87   Regulation 32 applies in computing any period of time for the purposes of this Part of these Regulations as for the purposes of Part 2 of these Regulations.

Method of questioning European Parliamentary elections

88 (1) No European Parliamentary election and no declaration of the result by the returning officer under rule 56 of the European Parliamentary elections rules shall be questioned except by a petition complaining of an undue election or undue declaration ("a European Parliamentary election petition") presented in accordance with this Part of these Regulations.

(2) A petition complaining that no declaration of the result has been given by the returning officer shall be deemed to be a European Parliamentary election petition and the High Court–

    (a) may make such order on the petition as they think expedient for compelling a declaration to be made; or

    (b) may allow the petition to be heard by an election court as provided with respect to ordinary European Parliamentary election petitions.

(3) No European Parliamentary election petition may be brought on the grounds of the commission of corrupt or illegal practices, except those in regulations 23 and 24.

(4) No European Parliamentary election petition may be brought where an application may be made under section 11 of the 2002 Act.

Presentation and service of European Parliamentary election petitions

89 (1) A European Parliamentary election petition may be presented by one or more of the following persons–

    (a) a person who voted as an elector at the election or who had a right so to vote; or

    (b) a person claiming to have had a right to be elected or returned at the election; or

    (c) a person alleging himself to have been a candidate at the election.

(1A) The reference in paragraph (1)(a) to a person who voted as an elector at an election or who had the right so to vote does not include a person who had an anonymous entry in a register of electors.

(2) If the petition complains of the conduct of–

    (a) the returning officer,

    (b) any local returning officer,

the officer (or officers) in question shall be deemed to be the respondent (or respondents), together with any MEP returned at the election.

(3) The petition shall be in the prescribed form, state the prescribed matters and be signed by the petitioner, or all the petitioners if more than one, and shall be presented to–

    (a) the High Court, where it relates to the combined region or any electoral region wholly in England and Wales,

    (b) the Court of Session, where it relates to Scotland.

(4) The petition shall be presented by delivering it to the prescribed officer or otherwise

dealing with it in the prescribed manner; and the prescribed officer shall send a copy of it to the returning officer of the electoral region to which the petition relates, who shall forthwith publish it in that electoral region.

(5) The petition shall be served in such manner as may be prescribed.

Time for presentation or amendment of European Parliamentary election petition

90 A European Parliamentary election petition shall be presented within 21 days after the day on which the result of the election was declared under rule 56 of the European Parliamentary elections rules.

Constitution of election court and place of trial

91 (1) A European Parliamentary election petition shall be tried by two judges on the rota for the trial of parliamentary election petitions, and the judges for the time being on that rota shall, unless they otherwise agree, try the European Parliamentary election petitions standing for trial according to their seniority, and the judges presiding at the trial of a European Parliamentary election petition are hereinafter referred to as the election court.

(2) The election court has, subject to the provisions of these Regulations, the same powers, jurisdiction and authority as a judge of the High Court (or, in Scotland, a judge of the Court of Session presiding at the trial of a civil cause without a jury) and shall be a court of record.

(3) In the application of this regulation to a European Parliamentary election relating to the combined region, in paragraph (1), after the word "petitions", in the first place where it occurs, insert "and a judge of the Gibraltar Supreme court".

Judges' expenses and reception: England and Wales

92 In relation to the trial of a European Parliamentary election petition in England (including the combined region) and Wales, the travelling and other expenses of the judges and all expenses properly incurred in providing them with necessary accommodation and with a proper court shall be defrayed by the Treasury out of moneys provided by Parliament.

Judges' expenses and reception: Scotland

93 In relation to the trial of a European Parliamentary election petition in Scotland the travelling and other expenses of the judges, and of the officer or officers in attendance on them, and all expenses properly incurred in providing the judges with a proper court shall be defrayed by the Treasury out of moneys provided by Parliament.

Security for costs

94 (1) At the time of presenting a European Parliamentary election petition or within three days afterwards the petitioner shall give security for all costs which may become payable by him to any witness summoned on his behalf or to any respondent.

(2) The security shall be such amount not exceeding £5,000 as the High Court or a judge of the High Court directs on an application made by the petitioner; and shall be given in the prescribed manner by recognisance entered into by any number of sureties not exceeding four or by a deposit of money, or partly in one way and partly in the other; but in Scotland–

(a) the amount mentioned above shall be such amount not exceeding £5,000 as the Court of Session or a judge of the Court of Session directs and the amount mentioned in sub-paragraph (b) shall be such amount not exceeding £2,500 as the election court or the sheriff directs; and

(b) the persons finding caution for that amount may exceed four.

(3) Within the prescribed time after giving the security the petitioner shall serve on the respondent in the prescribed manner–

    (a) a notice of the presentation of the petition and of the amount and nature of the security, and

    (b) a copy of the petition.

(4) Within a further prescribed time, the respondent may object in writing to any recognisance on the ground that any surety is insufficient or is dead or cannot be found or ascertained for want of a sufficient description in the recognisance, or that a person named in the recognisance has not duly acknowledged the recognisance.

(5) An objection to a recognisance shall be decided in the prescribed manner.

(6) If the objection is allowed, the petitioner may within a further prescribed time, remove it by a deposit in the prescribed manner of such sum of money as will, in the opinion of the court or officer having cognisance of the matter, make the security sufficient.

(7) If no security is given as required by this regulation or any objection is allowed and not removed as mentioned above, no further proceedings shall be had on the petition.

Petition at issue

95 (1) The petition shall be at issue as from the relevant time, as defined by paragraph (2).

(2) In this paragraph "the relevant time" means–

    (a) where the petitioner gives the security for costs required by regulation 94 by a deposit of money equal to the amount of the security so required, the time when the security is so given; and

    (b) in any other case, the time when–

        (i) the time prescribed for the making of objections under regulation 94(4) expires, or

        (ii) if such an objection is made, that objection is disallowed or removed,

    whichever happens later.

Trial of election issue

96 (1) A European Parliamentary election petition shall be tried in open court, without a jury, and notice of the time and place of trial shall be given in the prescribed manner, not less than 14 days before the day of trial.

(2) The election court may in its discretion adjourn the trial from time to time, but the trial shall, so far as is practicable consistently with the interests of justice in respect of the trial, be continued from day to day on every lawful day until its conclusion.

(3) The trial of a European Parliamentary election petition shall be proceeded with notwithstanding that one (or more) of the respondents is no longer an MEP.

(4) On the trial of a petition complaining of an undue election and claiming the seat or office for some person, the respondent may give evidence to prove that that person was not duly elected, in the same manner as if he had presented a petition against the election of that person.

(5) If the petition relates to an election conducted under the European Parliamentary elections rules and it appears that there is an equality of votes between any registered parties or individual candidates at the election, and that the addition of a vote would entitle any of those registered parties or individual candidates to be declared elected then–

    (a) any decision under the provisions as to equality of votes in the European Parliamentary elections rules, as the case may be, shall in so far as it determines the question between those registered parties or individual candidates, be effective also for the purposes of the petition; and

(b) in so far as that question is not determined by such a decision, the court shall decide between them by lot and proceed as if the one on whom the lot then falls had received an additional vote.

Witnesses

97 (1) Witnesses shall be summoned and sworn in the same manner as nearly as circumstances admit as in an action tried in the High Court.

(2) On the trial a member of the election court may, by order signed by him, require any person who appears to him to have been concerned in the election to attend as a witness, and any person refusing to obey the order shall be guilty of contempt of court.

(3) The election court may examine any person so required to attend or who is in court although he is not called and examined by any party to the petition.

(4) A witness may, after his examination by the court, be cross-examined by or on behalf of the petitioner and respondent, or either of them.

(5) In Scotland one of the deputies of the Lord Advocate or the procurator-fiscal of the district may, if the Lord Advocate so decides, and shall, if the election court so requests attend the trial of the petition as part of his official duty.

Duty to answer relevant questions

98 (1) A person called as a witness respecting an election before any election court shall not be excused from answering any question relating to any offence at or connected with the election–
   (a) on the ground that the answer to it may incriminate or tend to incriminate–
      (i) that person or that person's spouse or civil partner, or
      (ii) in Scotland, that person; or
   (b) on the ground of privilege.

(2) An answer by a person to a question put by or before any election court shall not, except in the case of any criminal proceeding for perjury in respect of the evidence, be in any proceeding, civil or criminal, admissible in evidence against–
   (a) that person or that person's spouse or civil partner; or
   (b) in Scotland, that person.

Expenses of witnesses

99 (1) The reasonable expenses incurred by any person in appearing to give evidence at the trial of a European Parliamentary election petition, according to the scale allowed to witnesses on the trial of civil actions, may be allowed to him by a certificate of the election court or of the prescribed officer.

(2) If the witness was called and examined by virtue of regulation 97(2), the expenses referred to in paragraph (1) shall be deemed part of the expenses of providing a court, but otherwise they shall be deemed costs of the petition.

Conclusion of trial of European Parliamentary election petition

00 (1) At the conclusion of the trial of a European Parliamentary election petition, the election court shall determine whether–
   (a) the member or members whose election is complained of were duly elected,
   (b) some other person or persons should have been declared to be elected, or
   (c) the election of all members for that electoral region was void,
   and the determination so certified shall be final to all intents as to the matters at issue

on the petition.

(2) The election court shall forthwith certify in writing the determination to the Secretary of State.

(3) If the judges constituting the election court differ as to any matter which they are required to determine, they shall certify that difference and, to the extent that there is such a difference, the result of the election shall stand.

Special case for determination of the High Court

101 (1) If, on the application of any party to a petition made in the prescribed manner to the High Court, it appears to the High Court that the case raised by the petition can be conveniently stated as a special case, the High Court may direct it to be stated accordingly and the special case shall be heard before the High Court.

(2) In the case of a European Parliamentary election petition, the High Court shall certify to the Secretary of State its decision on the special case.

(3) If it appears to the election court on the trial of a European Parliamentary election petition that any question of law as to the admissibility of evidence or otherwise requires further consideration by the High Court, the election court may postpone the granting of a certificate until the question has been determined by the High Court, and for this purpose may reserve the question by stating a case for the decision of the High Court.

(4) In Scotland the decision of the Court of Session on a special case under paragraph (1) shall be final.

Withdrawal of petition

102 (1) A petitioner shall not withdraw a European Parliamentary election petition without the leave of the election court or High Court on special application, made in the prescribed manner and at the prescribed time and place.

(2) The application shall not be made until the prescribed notice of the intention to make it has been given in the electoral region to which the petition relates.

(3) Where there are more petitioners than one, the application shall not be made except with the consent of all the petitioners.

(4) If a petition is withdrawn the petitioner shall be liable to pay the costs of the respondent.

103   *Repealed*

Costs of petition

104 (1) All costs of and incidental to the presentation of a European Parliamentary election petition and the proceedings consequent on it, except such as are by these Regulations otherwise provided for, shall be defrayed by the parties to the petition in such manner and in such proportions as the election court or High Court may determine.

(2) In particular–

(a) any costs which in the opinion of the election court or High Court have been caused by vexatious conduct, unfounded allegations or unfounded objections on the part either of the petitioner or of the respondent, and

(b) any needless expense incurred or caused on the part of the petitioner or respondent,

may be ordered to be defrayed by the parties by whom it has been incurred or caused whether or not they are on the whole successful.

Neglect or refusal to pay costs

105 (1)   Paragraph (2) applies if, in the case of a European Parliamentary election petition a petitioner neglects or refuses for six months after demand to pay to any person summoned as a witness on his behalf or to the respondent any sum certified to be due to that person or the respondent for his costs, and the neglect or refusal is, within one year after the demand, proved to the satisfaction of the High Court, or, in Scotland, the election court.

(2)   Where paragraph (1) applies, every person who under these Regulations entered into a recognisance relating to that petition shall be held to be in default of the recognisance, and–

(a)   the prescribed officer shall thereupon certify the recognisance to be forfeited, and

(b)   it shall be dealt with as if forfeited by the Crown Court,

but in Scotland the prescribed officer shall, where otherwise competent under the provisions of this paragraph–

(i)   certify that the conditions contained in the bond of caution have not been fulfilled; and

(ii)   it shall then be competent for the party or parties interested to register that bond, and do diligence upon it as accords of law.

Appeals and jurisdiction

106 (1)   No appeal lies without the special leave of the High Court from the decision of the High Court on any question of law, whether on appeal or otherwise, under the foregoing provisions of this Part of these Regulations, and if leave to appeal is granted the decision of the Court of Appeal in the case shall be final and conclusive.

(2)   The High Court has, subject to the provisions of these Regulations, the same powers, jurisdiction and authority with respect to a European Parliamentary election petition and the proceedings on it as if the petition were an ordinary action within its jurisdiction.

(3)   The duties to be performed in relation to European Parliamentary elections by the prescribed officer under this Part shall be performed by such one or more of the masters of the Supreme Court (Queen's Bench Division) as the Lord Chief Justice may determine.

(4)   In the application of this regulation to Scotland, paragraphs (1) and (3) shall be omitted, but the duties to be performed in relation to European Parliamentary elections by the prescribed officer under this Part shall be performed by the Principal Clerk of Session.

Persons convicted of corrupt or illegal practices

107 (1)   Subject to the provisions of paragraph (2) and regulation 112, a candidate or other person convicted of a corrupt or illegal practice–

(a)   shall during the relevant period specified in paragraph (3) be incapable of–

(i)   being registered as an elector or voting at any parliamentary or European Parliamentary election in the United Kingdom or at any local government election in Great Britain,

(ii)   being registered as a European Parliamentary elector or voting at any European Parliamentary election in Gibraltar,

(iii)   being elected to the House of Commons or the European Parliament, or

(iv)   holding any elective office; and

(b) if already elected to a seat in the House of Commons or the European Parliament, or holding any such office, shall vacate the seat or office as from the date of the conviction.

(2) The incapacity imposed by paragraph (1)(a)(i) applies only to a candidate or other person convicted of a corrupt practice under regulation 23 or of an illegal practice under regulation 24.

(3) For the purposes of paragraph (1) the relevant period is the period beginning with the date of the conviction and ending–
    (a) in the case of a person convicted of a corrupt practice, five years after that date, or
    (b) in the case of a person convicted of an illegal practice, three years after that date,
except that if (at any time within that period of five or three years) a court determines on an appeal by that person against the conviction that it should not be upheld, the relevant period shall end at that time instead.

(4) Where paragraph (1)(b) applies to any person, he shall (subject to paragraph (5)) vacate the seat or office in question at the appropriate time for the purposes of this regulation, namely–
    (a) the end of the period which is the period prescribed by law within which notice of appeal may be given, or an application for leave to appeal may be made, by him in respect of the conviction, or
    (b) if (at any time within that period) that period is extended–
        (i) the end of the period as so extended, or
        (ii) the end of the period of three months beginning with the date of the conviction,
    whichever is the earlier.

(5) If (before the appropriate time mentioned in paragraph (4)) notice of appeal is given, or an application for leave to appeal is made, by such a person in respect of the conviction, he shall vacate the seat or office in question at the end of the period of three months beginning with the date of the conviction unless–
    (a) such an appeal is dismissed or abandoned at any earlier time (in which case he shall vacate the seat or office at that time), or
    (b) at any time within that period of three months the court determines on such an appeal that the conviction should not be upheld (in which case the seat or office shall not be vacated by him).

(6) Where such a person vacates a seat or office in accordance with paragraph (4) or (5), no subsequent determination of a court that his conviction should not be upheld shall entitle him to resume the seat or office.

(7) If a person convicted of a corrupt or illegal practice has already been elected to a seat in the House of Commons or the European Parliament or to any elective office, he shall (in addition to being subject to the incapacities mentioned in paragraph (1)(a)) be suspended from performing any of his functions as a Member of Parliament or a Member of the European Parliament, or (as the case may be) any of the functions of that office, during the period of suspension specified in paragraph (8).

(8) For the purposes of paragraph (7) the period of suspension is the period beginning with the date of the conviction and ending with–
    (a) the date on which the seat or office is vacated in accordance with paragraph (4) or (5), or
    (b) where paragraph (5)(b) applies, the date on which the court determines that the conviction should not be upheld.

(9) Any incapacities or other requirement applying to a person by virtue of paragraph (1)

or (7) applies in addition to any punishment imposed under regulation 109 or 110; but each of those regulations has effect subject to regulation 112.

(10) Subject to the provisions of regulation 112 but in addition to any incapacity arising by virtue of paragraph (1) or (7), a candidate or other person convicted of a corrupt practice–
    (a) shall for the period of five years beginning with the date of the conviction, be incapable of holding any public or judicial office in Scotland, and
    (b) if already holding such an office, shall vacate it as from that date.

Application for relief

.08 (1) An application for relief under this regulation may be made to the High Court or an election court or else, if in respect of a payment made in contravention of regulation 48(1) or (2), to a county court.

(2) Where a person makes an application under this regulation he shall notify the Director of Public Prosecutions of the application and the Director or his assistant or representative may attend the hearing of the application and make representations at the hearing in respect of it.

(3) If it is shown to the court by such evidence as to the court seems sufficient–
    (a) that any act or omission of any person would apart from this regulation by reason of being in contravention of these Regulations be an illegal practice, payment, employment or hiring,
    (b) that the act or omission arose from inadvertence or from accidental miscalculation or from some other reasonable cause of a like nature, and in any case did not arise from any want of good faith, and
    (c) that such notice of the application has been given in the electoral region as to the court seems fit,
and under the circumstances it seems to the court to be just that either that or any other person should not be subject to any of the consequences under these Regulations of the act or omission, the court may make an order allowing the act or omission to be an exception from the provisions of these Regulations making it an illegal practice, payment, employment or hiring and upon the making of the order no person shall be subject to any of the consequences under these Regulations of that act or omission.

(4) This regulation shall apply to Gibraltar subject to the following modifications–
    (a) in paragraph (1), for "a county court", substitute "the Gibraltar court";
    (b) in paragraph (2), in the case of an application to the Gibraltar court, references in paragraph (2) to the Director of Public Prosecutions shall be construed as references to the Attorney General for Gibraltar.

Prosecution for corrupt practices

109 (1) A person who is guilty of a corrupt practice shall be liable–
    (a) on conviction on indictment–
        (i) in the case of a corrupt practice under regulation 23 or paragraph 11 of Schedule 2, to imprisonment for a term not exceeding two years, or to a fine, or to both,
        (ii) in any other case, to imprisonment for a term not exceeding one year, or to a fine, or to both;
    (b) on summary conviction, to imprisonment for a term not exceeding 6 months, or to a fine not exceeding the statutory maximum, or to both.

(2) If it appears to the court by which any person holding a licence or certificate under the Licensing Acts is convicted of the offence of bribery or treating that the offence was

committed on his licensed premises–

> (a) the court shall direct the conviction to be entered in the proper register of licences, and
> (b) the entry shall be taken into consideration by the licensing authority in determining whether they will or will not grant a renewal of the licence or certificate, and may be a ground, if the authority think fit, for refusing its renewal.

Prosecutions for illegal practices

110   A person who is guilty of an illegal practice shall be liable to a fine not exceeding level 5 on the standard scale; and on a prosecution for an illegal practice it shall be sufficient to allege that the person charged was guilty of an illegal practice.

Conviction of illegal practice on charge of corrupt practice

111   A person charged with a corrupt practice may, if the circumstances warrant such finding, be found guilty of an illegal practice (which offence shall for that purpose be an indictable offence), and a person charged with an illegal practice may be found guilty of that offence notwithstanding that the act constituting the offence amounted to a corrupt practice.

Mitigation and remission etc

112 (1)   Where any person is subject to any incapacity by virtue of a conviction and any witness who gave evidence against that person upon the proceeding for the conviction is convicted of perjury in respect of that evidence, the incapacitated person may apply to the High Court, and the court, if satisfied that the conviction so far as respects that person was based upon perjury, may order that the incapacity shall thenceforth cease.

(2)   In the application of this regulation to Gibraltar, for "High Court" substitute "Gibraltar court".

Illegal payments

113 (1)   A person guilty of an offence of illegal payment or employment shall, on summary conviction, be liable to a fine not exceeding level 5 on the standard scale; and on a prosecution for such an offence it shall be sufficient to allege that the person charged was guilty of an illegal payment or employment as the case may be.

(2)   A candidate or election agent who is personally guilty of an offence of illegal payment or employment shall be guilty of an illegal practice.

(3)   Any person charged with an offence of illegal payment or employment may be found guilty of that offence, notwithstanding that the act constituting the offence amounted to a corrupt or illegal practice.

Time limit for prosecution

114 (1)   A proceeding against a person in respect of any offence under any provision contained in these Regulations shall be commenced within one year after the offence was committed, and the time so limited by this regulation shall, in the case of any proceedings under the Magistrates' Court Act 1980 or, in the case of Gibraltar, the Criminal Procedure and Evidence Act 2011, for any such offence be substituted for any limitation of time contained in those Acts.

(2)   A magistrates' court in England, Wales or Gibraltar may act under paragraph (3) if it is satisfied on an application by a constable or Crown Prosecutor, or in Gibraltar, the Attorney General–

(a) that there are exceptional circumstances which justify the granting of the application, and

(b) that there has been no undue delay in the investigation of the offence to which the application relates.

(3) A magistrates' court may extend the time within which proceedings must be commenced in pursuance of paragraph (1) to not more than 24 months after the offence was committed.

(4) If a magistrates' court acts under paragraph (3), it may also make an order under paragraph (5) if it is satisfied, on an application by a constable or Crown Prosecutor, or in Gibraltar, the Attorney General, that documents retained by the relevant registration officer in pursuance of rule 66 of the European Parliamentary elections rules may provide evidence relating to the offence.

(5) An order under this paragraph is an order–
(a) directing the relevant registration officer not to cause the documents to be destroyed at the expiry of the period of one year mentioned in rule 66 of the European Parliamentary elections rules, and
(b) extending the period for which he is required to retain them under that rule by such further period not exceeding 12 months as is specified in the order.

(6) The making of an order under paragraph (5) does not affect any other power to require the retention of the documents.

(7) An application under this regulation must be made not more than one year after the offence was committed.

(8) Any party to–
(a) an application under paragraph (2), or
(b) an application under paragraph (4),
who is aggrieved by the refusal of the magistrates' court to act under paragraph (3) or to make an order under paragraph (5) (as the case may be) may appeal to the Crown Court or, in Gibraltar, the Supreme Court.

(9) For the purposes of this regulation–
(a) in England and Wales, the laying of information;
(b) in Gibraltar, the laying of information; and
(c) in Scotland, the granting of a warrant to apprehend or cite the accused (if, in relation to an offence alleged to have been committed within the United Kingdom, such warrant is executed without delay),
shall be deemed to be the commencement of the proceeding.

Prosecution of offences committed outside the United Kingdom

115 Proceedings in respect of an offence under these Regulations alleged to have been committed outside the United Kingdom or Gibraltar by a Commonwealth citizen or citizen of the Union may be taken, and the offence may for all incidental purposes be treated as having been committed, in any place in the United Kingdom or Gibraltar.

Offences by associations

116 Where–
(a) any corrupt or illegal practice or any illegal payment, employment or hiring, or
(b) any offence under regulation 74,
is committed by any association or body of persons, corporate or unincorporate, the members of the association or body who have taken part in the commission of the offence shall be liable to any fine or punishment imposed for that offence by these Regulations.

Evidence by certificate of holding of elections

117 On any prosecution for a corrupt or illegal practice or for any illegal payment, employment or hiring, the certificate of the returning officer at a European Parliamentary election–

    (a) that the election mentioned in the certificate was duly held, and

    (b) that the person named in the certificate was a candidate at the election, and

    (c) that a registered party named in the certificate submitted a list at the election,

shall be sufficient evidence of the facts stated in it.

Evidence by certificate of electoral registration

118 The certificate of a registration officer that any person is or is not, or was or was not at any particular time, duly registered in one of the officer's registers in respect of any address shall be sufficient evidence of the facts stated in it; and a document purporting to be such a certificate shall be received in evidence and presumed to be such a certificate unless the contrary is proved.

Director of Public Prosecutions

119 (1) Where information is given to the Director of Public Prosecutions that any offence under these Regulations has been committed, it is his duty to make such inquiries and institute such prosecutions as the circumstances of the case appear to him to require.

  (2) The Director by himself or by his assistant or by his representative appointed under paragraph (3) may and, if the election court so requests him, shall attend the trial of every European Parliamentary election petition.

  (3) The Director may nominate a barrister or solicitor to be his representative for the purposes of this Part of these Regulations.

  (4) There shall be allowed to the Director and his assistant or representative for the purposes of this Part (other than his general duties under paragraph (1)) such allowances for expenses as the Treasury may approve.

  (5) The costs incurred in defraying the expenses of the Director incurred for those purposes (including the remuneration of his representative) shall, in the first instance, be paid by the Treasury, and shall be deemed to be expenses of the election court; but if for any reasonable cause it seems just to the court so to do, the court shall order all or part of those costs to be repaid to the Treasury by the parties to the petition, or such of them as the court may direct.

  (6) In the application of this regulation to Scotland, paragraphs (2) to (5) shall be omitted.

  (7) In the application of this regulation to Gibraltar, in paragraph (1) the reference to the Director of Public Prosecutions shall be construed as a reference to the Attorney General for Gibraltar.

Rules of procedure

120 (1) The authority having for the time being power to make rules of court for the Supreme Court may make rules for the purposes of Part 2 and this Part of these Regulations.

  (2) In relation to the power conferred by paragraph (1) to make rules–

    (a) that power shall be exercisable by statutory instrument, and be treated for the purposes of the Statutory Instruments Act 1946 as if conferred by an Act on a Minister of the Crown; and

    (b) a statutory instrument containing rules under paragraph (1) shall be subject to annulment in pursuance of a resolution of either House of Parliament; and section 5 of the Statutory Instruments Act 1946 shall apply accordingly.

(3) The above provisions of this regulation do not apply to Scotland, but the Court of Session has power to make acts of sederunt for the purposes of Part 2 and this Part.

(4) The above provisions of this regulation do not apply to Gibraltar courts, but in those courts Gibraltar rules of court apply.

Costs

121 (1) The rules of the Supreme Court with respect to costs to be allowed in actions, causes and matters in the High Court shall in principle and so far as practicable apply to the costs of petition and other proceedings under Part 2 or this Part of these Regulations, and the taxing officer shall not allow any costs higher than would be allowed in any action, cause or matter in the High Court on a common fund basis.

(2) Where any costs or other sums are, under the order of an election court or otherwise under this Part, to be paid by any person, those costs or sums shall be due from that person to the person or persons to whom they are to be paid and, if payable to the Treasury, shall be a debt due to Her Majesty and in either case may be recovered accordingly.

(3) The above provisions of this regulation do not apply to Scotland, but those costs shall, subject to any provision which the Court of Session may make by act of sederunt, be taxed as nearly as possible according to the same principles as expenses between solicitor and client are taxed in a cause in the Court of Session.

(4) The above provisions of this regulation do not apply to Gibraltar courts, but those costs shall be taxed as nearly as possible according to the same principles as expenses between solicitor and client are taxed in a cause in the Gibraltar court.

Services of notices

122 (1) Any notice, legal process or other document required to be served on any person with reference to any proceeding respecting an election for the purpose of causing him to appear before the High Court, the county court, or any election court, or otherwise or of giving him an opportunity of making a statement, or showing cause, or being heard by himself before any court for any purpose of this Part of these Regulations may be served–
   (a) by delivering it to that person, or by leaving it at, or sending it by post by a registered letter or by the recorded delivery service, to his last known place of abode in the electoral region or, as the case may be, the area of the authority for which the election was held; or
   (b) if the proceeding is before any court in such other manner as the court may direct.

(2) In proving service by post under this regulation it shall be sufficient to prove that the letter was prepaid, properly addressed, and registered or recorded with the postal operator (within the meaning of Part 3 of the Postal Services Act 2011) concerned.

(3) In the application of the above provisions to post sent in Gibraltar, references to the postal operator shall be construed as references to the Gibraltar Post Office.

(4) This regulation does not apply in respect of any proceedings before the Gibraltar court.

PART 5
MISCELLANEOUS

Translations etc of certain documents

122A (1) Paragraphs (2) and (3) apply to any document which by virtue of these Regulations is required or authorised to be given to voters or displayed in any place for the purposes of a European Parliamentary election.

(2) The person who is required or authorised to give or display the document must, as he thinks appropriate, give or display or otherwise make available in such form as he thinks appropriate–

   (a) the document in Braille;

   (b) the document in languages other than English;

   (c) graphical representations of the information contained in the document;

   (d) other means of making the information contained in the document accessible to persons who might not otherwise have reasonable access to the information.

(3) The person required or authorised to give or display the document must also, as he thinks appropriate, make available the information contained in the document in such audible form as he thinks appropriate.

(4) Paragraphs (2) and (3) do not apply to–

   (a) the nomination paper; and

   (b) the ballot paper.

(5) The local returning officer at a European Parliamentary election must cause to be displayed at every polling station in the election an enlarged sample copy of the ballot paper in accordance with rule 32(5)(a) of the European Parliamentary elections rules.

(6) The sample copy mentioned in paragraph (5)–

   (a) must have printed the words "Vote only once by putting a cross X in the box next to your choice" at the top; and

   (b) may include a translation of those words into such other languages as the local returning officer thinks appropriate.

(7) The local returning officer at a European Parliamentary election must provide at every polling station in the election an enlarged hand-held sample copy of the ballot paper for the assistance of voters who are partially sighted.

(8) The sample copy mentioned in paragraph (7) must be clearly marked as a specimen provided only for the guidance of voters.

Public notices and declarations

123 (1) A public notice required by or under these Regulations to be given by a returning officer for a European Parliamentary election shall be given by posting the notice in some conspicuous place or places in the electoral region and may also be given in such other manner as he thinks desirable for publicising it.

(2) A public notice required by or under these Regulations to be given by a local returning officer shall be given by posting the notice in some conspicuous place or places in the local counting area and may also be given in such other manner as he thinks fit.

(3) Any person before whom a declaration is authorised to be made under these Regulations may take the declaration.

(4) In the application of paragraph (1) to the combined region, the notice shall be given by posting it in some conspicuous place or places in that part of the combined region which is in the United Kingdom and in some conspicuous place or places in that part which is in Gibraltar.

Remuneration for free postal services provided under the Regulations

124 (1) This regulation applies where any postal services are provided without charge by a

universal service provider in pursuance of these Regulations.

(2)   The universal service provider shall be entitled to be remunerated for having provided the services–

   (a)   at the rate fixed in relation to them by virtue of a scheme under section 89 of the Postal Services Act 2000; or

   (b)   in the case of any postal communication sent to a place or an elector in the combined region in pursuance of regulation 63 for which there is no such scheme for those services, at a rate fixed in relation to those services in accordance with paragraph (3).

(3)   The rate referred to in paragraph (2)(b) must correspond substantially to the rate fixed in relation to the provision of services in pursuance of regulation 63 which would apply by virtue of a scheme under section 89 of the Postal Services Act 2000 if the whole of the combined region were in England, except that it may include an element for additional expenses associated with providing such services in the combined region.

(4)   A sum which a universal service provider is entitled to receive by virtue of this regulation shall be charged on, and issued out of, the Consolidated Fund.

(5)   In this regulation "postal services" and "universal service provider" have the same meanings as in Part 3 of the Postal Services Act 2011.

Application of Local Government Finance Act 1988 for European Parliamentary Elections

125   Section 65(6) of the Local Government Finance Act 1988 (hereditaments to be treated as unoccupied notwithstanding use for election purposes) shall apply in relation to a European Parliamentary election as it applies in relation to a parliamentary election and as though the reference in section 65(6) to a person's candidature included a reference to a registered party's; and as though the reference to a returning officer was a reference to a local returning officer.

Requirement to provide information about candidate standing in other Member State

25A (1)   This regulation applies when the Secretary of State receives a notice from another Member State in accordance with Article 6 of Council Directive 93/109/EC that a person who falls to be treated as a national of the United Kingdom for the purposes of the EU treaties has made a declaration in that Member State under Article 10 of that Directive.

(2)   The Secretary of State must, within the period specified in paragraph (3), provide the Member State with any information that is available to the Secretary of State as to whether the person has been deprived of the right to stand as a candidate at European Parliamentary elections through a relevant disqualifying decision in the United Kingdom.

(3)   The period referred to in paragraph (2) is five days calculated in accordance with rule 2 of Schedule 1 and beginning with the day the notice is received by the Secretary of State, or such shorter period as is requested by the Member State if it is possible for the Secretary of State to provide the information within that period.

Revocation

126   The European Parliamentary Elections Regulations 1999 are hereby revoked.
Initial Commencement

SCHEDULE 1
EUROPEAN PARLIAMENTARY ELECTIONS RULES

Timetable

1   The proceedings at the election must be conducted in accordance with the following

Timetable.
Timetable

Proceeding	Time
Publication of notice of election	Not later than the twenty-fifth day before the date of poll.
Delivery of nomination papers and list of candidates of registered parties	Between the hours of 10 am and 4 pm on any day after the date of the publication of the notice of election but not later than the nineteenth day before the date of the poll
Delivery of notices of withdrawals of candidature	Within the time for the delivery of nomination papers and lists of candidates at the election
The making of objections to nomination papers or list of candidates of registered parties	During the hours allowed for delivery of nomination papers and lists of candidates on the last day for their delivery and the hour following; but (a) no objection may be made in the afternoon of that last day except to a nomination paper delivered within 24 hours of the last time for its delivery and, in the case of a nomination paper so delivered, no objection may be so made to the sufficiency or nature of the particulars of a registered party or candidate on the party's list or individual candidate unless made at or immediately after the time of the delivery of the nomination paper; and (b) the foregoing provisions do not apply to objections made in pursuance of rule18(2).
Publication of statement of parties and individual candidates nominated	If no objections to nomination papers or lists of candidates of registered parties are made, at the close of the time for doing so, or if any such objections are made to nomination papers or lists of candidates of registered parties, not before they are disposed of, but not later than 24 hours after the last time for delivery of nomination papers or lists (as the case may be).
Polling	Between the hours of 7 am and 10 pm on the day of the poll.

Computation of time

2 (1) In computing any period of time for the purposes of the Timetable in rule 1–
    (a) a Saturday or Sunday,
    (b) Christmas Eve, Christmas Day, Good Friday or a bank holiday, or
    (c) a day appointed for public thanksgiving or mourning,
must be disregarded, and any such day must not be treated as a day for the purpose of any proceedings up to the completion of the poll nor must the returning officer or local returning officer be obliged to proceed with the counting of the votes on such a day.

  (2) In this rule "bank holiday" means–
    (a) in relation to a general election in the combined region, a day which is a bank holiday under the Banking and Financial Dealings Act 1971 in any part of the United Kingdom or a bank or public holiday in Gibraltar not otherwise falling

within sub-paragraph (b) of paragraph (1);

(b)　in relation to a by-election in the combined region, a day which is a bank holiday under the Banking and Financial Dealings Act 1971 in England and Wales or a bank or public holiday in Gibraltar not otherwise falling within sub-paragraph (b) of paragraph (1);

(c)　in relation to a general election in a region other than the combined region, a day which is a bank holiday under the Banking and Financial Dealings Act 1971 in any part of the United Kingdom; and

(d)　in relation to a by-election in a region other than the combined region, a day which is a bank holiday under the Banking and Financial Dealings Act 1971 in that part of the United Kingdom in which the region is situated,

but at a general election sub-paragraph (b) or (d) and not sub-paragraph (a) or (c) (as the case may be) of this paragraph applies in relation to any proceedings extending, by reason of riot or open violence, beyond the time laid down by the Timetable in rule 1.

Part 2
Stages Common to Contested and Uncontested Elections

Notice of election

3 (1)　The returning officer must publish notice of the election stating–
    (a)　the place and times at which nomination papers are to be delivered; and
    (b)　the date of the poll in the event of a contest,
     and the notice must state that forms of nomination papers may be obtained at that place and those times.

(2)　The notice of election must also state the arrangements which apply for the payment of the deposit required by rule 10 to be made by means of the electronic transfer of funds.

(3)　The notice of election must state the date by which–
    (a)　applications to vote by post or by proxy; and
    (b)　other applications and notices about postal or proxy voting,
must reach the registration officer in order that they may be effective for the election.

(4)　The returning officer must send a copy of the notice to the local returning officer for each local counting area in the electoral region; and each local returning officer must publish the copy of the notice at a place within the area in which he acts.

Nomination of individual candidates

4 (1)　Each individual candidate must be nominated by a separate nomination paper, which is signed and delivered by the individual candidate himself or a person authorised in writing by him.

(2)　The nomination paper must state the individual candidate's–
    (a)　full names;
    (b)　home address in full; and
    (c)　if desired, description,
and the surname must be placed first in the list of his names.

(3)　If an individual candidate commonly uses–
    (a)　a surname which is different from any other surname he has; or
    (b)　a forename which is different from any other forename he has,
the nomination paper may state the commonly used surname or forename in addition to the other name.

(4)　The description (if any) can only be–

    (a) in the case of an individual candidate standing on behalf of a registered party at a by-election, the name of the party registered under section 28 of the 2000 Act and, if desired, a description which is authorised as mentioned in rule 5(2) or (4); or

    (b) the word "Independent".

(5) Where a nomination paper is delivered in respect of the same person after an earlier paper in respect of that person has been delivered, that later paper must be deemed to supersede the earlier one.

Nomination papers: name of registered party at a by-election

5 (1) The nomination paper of an individual candidate standing on behalf of a registered party at a by-election must state the name of the party registered under section 28 of the 2000 Act.

(2) A nomination paper may not include a description of an individual candidate which is likely to lead electors to associate the candidate with a registered party unless–

    (a) the individual candidate is standing on behalf of a registered party at a by-election;

    (b) the party is a qualifying party in relation to the electoral region; and

    (c) the description is authorised by a certificate–

        (i) issued by or on behalf of the registered nominating officer of the party; and

        (ii) received by the returning officer before the last time for the delivery of nomination papers set out in the Timetable in rule 1.

(3) In paragraph (2) an authorised description must be a description of the party registered under section 28A of the 2000 Act.

(4) A nomination paper may not include a description of an individual candidate which is likely to lead electors to associate the candidate with two or more registered political parties unless–

    (a) the individual candidate is standing on behalf of two or more registered parties at a by-election;

    (b) each of the parties are qualifying parties in relation to the electoral region; and

    (c) the description is a registered description authorised by a certificate–

        (i) issued by or on behalf of the registered nominating officer of each of the parties; and

        (ii) received by the returning officer before the last time for the delivery of nomination papers set out in the Timetable in rule 1.

(5) For the purposes of paragraph (4), an authorised description is a registered description if it is a description registered for use by the parties under section 28B of the 2000 Act.

(6) A person shall be guilty of a corrupt practice if he fraudulently purports to be authorised to issue a certificate under paragraph (2) or (4) on behalf of a registered party's nominating officer.

(7) For the purposes of the application of this rule in relation to an election–

    (a) "registered party" means a party which was registered under Part 2 of the 2000 Act on the day ("the relevant day") which is two days before the last day for the delivery of nomination papers at that election; and

    (b) a registered party is a qualifying party in relation to an electoral region if the region is in England, Wales, Scotland or the combined region and the party was on the relevant day registered in respect of that part of Great Britain or the combined region in the Great Britain register mentioned under that Part of that Act.

(8) For the purposes of paragraph (7)(a) any day falling within rule 2(1) must be

disregarded.

Nomination papers: name of registered party at a general election

6 (1) A registered party which is to stand for election in the electoral region must be nominated by a nomination paper delivered to the returning officer at the place which he has fixed for the purpose, by the party's nominating officer or a person authorised in writing by him.

  (2) The nomination paper must state the name of the party registered under section 28 of the 2000 Act.

  (3) The nomination paper may state the description by which the registered party is to stand for election.

  (4) In paragraph (3) a description must be a description of the party registered under section 28A of the 2000 Act.

  (5) The nomination paper must be accompanied by a list of candidates which complies with rule 7.

  (6) The nomination paper must include a statement that the party is nominated by or on behalf of the nominating officer of the registered party in question and must be signed by the person making it.

  (7) Where a nomination paper and list of candidates are delivered in respect of the same registered party after an earlier paper and list have been delivered in respect of that party, that later paper and list must be deemed to supersede the earlier ones.

  (8) A person shall be guilty of a corrupt practice if he fraudulently purports to be authorised to make the statement required by paragraph (6) on behalf of a registered party's nominating officer.

List of candidates

7 (1) The number of candidates in the list of a registered party's candidates which must accompany its nomination paper must not exceed the number of MEPs to be elected in the electoral region at the election.

  (2) The list must set out the full names and home addresses in full of each candidate.

  (3) If a person on the list of a registered party's candidates commonly uses–
     (a) a surname which is different from any other surname he has; or
     (b) a forename which is different from any other forename he has,
the list may state the person's commonly used surname or forename in addition to the other name.

Consent to nomination

8 (1) A person shall not be validly nominated as an individual candidate or a candidate on a registered party's list unless his consent to nomination–
     (a) is given in writing on or within one month before the day fixed as the last day for the delivery of nomination papers;
     (b) is attested by one witness;
     (c) in the case of a candidate on a registered party's list, identifies the party in question; and
     (d) is delivered at the place and within the time for the delivery of nomination papers, subject to paragraph (2).

  (2) If the returning officer is satisfied that, owing to the absence of a person from the United Kingdom or Gibraltar (as the case may be) it has not been reasonably

practicable for his consent in writing to be given, a telegram (or any similar means of communication) consenting to his nomination and purporting to have been sent by him shall be deemed for the purposes of this rule to be consent in writing given by him on the day on which it purports to have been sent, and attestation of his consent is not required.

(3) A candidate's consent given under this rule must state the day, month and year of his birth; and–
  (a) that he is aware of the provisions of section 10 of the European Parliamentary Elections Act 2002; and
  (b) that to the best of his knowledge and belief he is not disqualified for the office of MEP.

(4) For the purpose of paragraph (3)(b), a candidate is not disqualified for the office of MEP by virtue of his being a life peer at the time of his nomination.

Candidature by relevant citizen of the Union

9 (1) A candidate who is a relevant citizen of the Union is not validly nominated as an individual candidate or as a candidate on a registered party's list unless one of Conditions A and B is met.

(2) Condition A is that a declaration under paragraph (4) is delivered to the returning officer, whether before or after the notice of election is published, but not later than 4 pm on the twenty-fourth day before the date of the poll.

(3) Condition B is that a declaration under paragraph (4) and information under paragraph (5) are delivered at the place and within the time for the delivery of nomination papers.

(4) The declaration referred to in paragraphs (2) and (3) must be made by the candidate and must state, in addition to the candidate's name–
  (a) the candidate's nationality, date and place of birth, last address in the Member State of which the candidate is a national and home address in the United Kingdom or Gibraltar;
  (b) that the candidate is not standing for election to the European Parliament in any other Member State;
  (c) where the candidate's name has been entered on an electoral roll in a locality or constituency in the Member State of which the candidate is a national, the name of the locality or constituency where, so far as the candidate knows, the candidate's name was last entered; and
  (d) that the candidate has not been deprived of the right to stand as a candidate through a relevant disqualifying decision in the Member State of which the candidate is a national.

(5) The information referred to in paragraph (3) is information which–
  (a) has been provided to the candidate by the designated contact point in the Member State of which the candidate is a national; and
  (b) states either that the candidate has not been deprived of the right to stand as a candidate in that State through a relevant disqualifying decision or that no such disqualification is known to the designated contact point.

(6) Where the returning officer receives a declaration under paragraph (4) delivered in accordance with Condition A or B, the returning officer must send a copy to the Secretary of State as soon as practicable after the declaration is received.

(7) In this rule and in rule 9A, "electoral roll" and "locality or constituency" have the same meaning as they have in Council Directive 93/109/EC, and "designated contact point" means a contact point designated by a Member State in accordance with Article 6(3) of

that Directive.

Request for information where candidate is relevant citizen of the Union

9A (1) This rule applies where the candidate is a relevant citizen of the Union and the Secretary of State has received a copy of a declaration in accordance with rule 9(6).

(2) The Secretary of State must send a notice to the designated contact point in the Member State of which the candidate is a national.

(3) The notice referred to in paragraph (2)–
  (a) must notify the Member State of the declaration made by the candidate under rule 9(4);
  (b) must ask whether the candidate has been deprived of the right to stand as a candidate through a relevant disqualifying decision in that Member State; and
  (c) may request a response by a specified date.

(4) The Secretary of State must send to the returning officer a copy of any response to the notice as soon as practicable after the response is received.

Deposit

10 (1) A person shall not be validly nominated as an individual candidate unless the sum of £5,000 is deposited by him or on his behalf with the returning officer at the place and during the time for delivery of nomination papers.

(2) A registered party shall not be validly nominated unless the sum of £5,000 is deposited on its behalf with the returning officer at the place and during the time for the delivery of nomination papers.

(3) The deposit may be made either–
  (a) by the deposit of any legal tender, or
  (b) by means of a banker's draft, or
  (c) with the returning officer's consent, in any other manner (including by means of a debit or credit card or the electronic transfer of funds),
  but the returning officer may refuse to accept a deposit sought to be made by means of a banker's draft if he does not know that the drawer carries on a business as a banker in the United Kingdom or Gibraltar.

(4) Where the deposit is made on behalf of the registered party or individual candidate, the person making the deposit must at the time he makes it give his name and address to the returning officer (unless they have previously been given to him under regulation 33, 34 or 38 of these Regulations).

Place for delivery of nomination papers

11 The returning officer must fix the place in the electoral region at which nomination papers are to be delivered to him, and must attend there during the time for their delivery and for the making of objections to them.

Right to attend nomination

12 (1) Except for the purpose of delivering a nomination paper or of assisting the returning officer, no person is entitled to attend the proceedings during the time for delivery of nomination papers or for making objections to them unless he is–
  (a) a person standing nominated as an individual candidate or included in a list under rule 7; or
  (b) the election agent of a registered party which has submitted a nomination

paper or of an individual candidate; or

   (c)   a person authorised in writing to deliver a nomination paper; or

   (d)   a person who is entitled to attend by virtue of section 6A or 6B of the 2000 Act.

(2)   The right to attend conferred by this rule includes the right–

   (a)   to inspect; and

   (b)   to object to the validity of,

any nomination paper or list of candidates.

(3)   Paragraph (2) does not apply to a person mentioned in paragraph (1)(d).

(4)   One other person chosen by each candidate is entitled to be present at the delivery of the candidate's nomination, and may afterwards, so long as the candidate stands nominated, attend the proceedings referred to in paragraph (1) but without any such right as is conferred by paragraph (2).

Decisions as to validity of nomination papers

13 (1)   Where, in the case of an individual candidate, a nomination paper and the candidate's consent to it (and, where required, a declaration under rule 9(4) or, as the case may be, a declaration under rule 9(4) and information under rule 9(5)) are delivered and a deposit is made in accordance with these rules, the candidate must be deemed to stand nominated unless and until–

   (a)   the returning officer decides that the nomination paper is invalid; or

   (b)   proof is given to the returning officer's satisfaction of the candidate's death; or

   (c)   the candidate withdraws.

(2)   Where, in the case of a registered party, a nomination paper and list under rule 7 are delivered and a deposit is made in accordance with these rules, the party and (subject to paragraph (5)) the candidates on its list must be deemed to stand nominated unless and until the returning officer determines that the nomination paper or list is invalid.

(3)   The returning officer is entitled to hold a nomination paper of an individual candidate invalid only on one of the following grounds–

   (a)   that the particulars of the candidate are not as required by law;

   (b)   that the candidate is disqualified by the Representation of the People Act 1981 (which applies in respect of the office of MEP by virtue of section 10(1)(a) of the 2002 Act) or any corresponding provision in respect of detained offenders in Gibraltar made under section 10(4A) of the 2002 Act;

   (c)   the candidate is a relevant citizen of the Union and the returning officer has received, under rule 9A(4), information that the candidate has been deprived of the right to stand as a candidate through a relevant disqualifying decision in the Member State of which the candidate is a national.

(4)   The returning officer is entitled to hold a nomination paper of a registered party, together with the list of candidates accompanying it, invalid only on one of the following grounds–

   (a)   that the contents of the nomination paper are not as required by law; and

   (b)   that the number of candidates in the list breaches rule 7(1).

(5)   Where–

   (a)   the particulars of any candidate in the list of candidates accompanying the nomination paper of a registered party are not as required by law;

   (b)   the consent to nomination of any such candidate is not delivered in accordance with these rules;

   (c)   any such candidate is a relevant citizen of the Union and neither Condition A nor Condition B in rule 9 has been met in relation to that candidate; or

   (d)   any such candidate is a relevant citizen of the Union and the returning officer has received, under rule 9A(4), information that the candidate has been deprived of the right to stand as a candidate through a relevant disqualifying decision in the Member State of which the candidate is a national,

the returning officer must delete the name and address of that candidate from the list.

(6) The returning officer must give his decision on any objection to a nomination paper–
    (a) as soon as practicable after it is made; and
    (b) in any event, before the end of the period of 24 hours starting with the close of the

period for delivery of nomination papers set out in the Timetable in rule 1.

(7) If, in the returning officer's opinion a nomination paper breaches rule 5(2) or (4), he must give a decision to that effect–
    (a) as soon as practicable after the delivery of the nomination paper; and
    (b) in any event, before the end of the period of 24 hours starting with the close of the period for delivery of nomination papers set out in the Timetable in rule 1.

(8) Where the returning officer decides that a nomination paper is invalid, he must endorse on the paper the fact and the reasons for his decision and sign the paper.

(9) Where the returning officer deletes any name from the list of candidates of a registered party, he must endorse on the nomination paper the fact and the reasons for his decision to do so and sign the paper.

(10) The returning officer's decision that a nomination paper and, where applicable, its accompanying list, is valid is final and may not be questioned in any proceedings whatsoever.

(11) Subject to paragraph (10), nothing in this rule prevents the validity of a nomination being questioned on an election petition.

Withdrawal of candidates

14 (1) An individual candidate may withdraw his candidature by notice of withdrawal–
    (a) signed by him and attested by one witness, and
    (b) delivered to the returning officer at the place for delivery of nomination papers.

(2) The nominating officer of a registered party or a person authorised in writing by him may withdraw that party's nomination by notice of withdrawal signed by him and delivered to the returning officer at the place for delivery of nomination papers.

Publication of statement of persons nominated

15 (1) The returning officer must prepare and publish a statement ("the statement of parties and individual candidates nominated") showing–
    (a) the registered parties which have been and stand nominated, together with the list of persons who stand as candidates of those parties;
    (b) persons who have been and stand nominated as individual candidates; and
    (c) any other persons or parties who have been nominated (whether on a list of a registered party or as individual candidates) together with the reason why they no longer stand nominated.

(2) The statement must show the names followed by the descriptions, if any, of registered parties which have been and stand nominated in alphabetical order, with the names, home addresses of the candidates who appear on the list of each party as given in that list and arranged in the order in which their names appear on that list.

(3) The statement must show the names followed by descriptions, if any, and addresses of the persons nominated as individual candidates as given in their nomination papers.

(4) If a nomination paper or list gives a commonly used surname or forename of a candidate in addition to another name, the statement must show the person's commonly used surname or forename (as the case may be) instead of any other name.

(5) Paragraph (4) does not apply if the returning officer thinks–
    (a) that the use of the person's commonly used name may be likely to mislead or confuse electors, or
    (b) that the commonly used name is obscene or offensive.

(6) If paragraph (5) applies, the returning officer must give notice in writing to the candidate and party whose list contains the candidate's name of his reasons for refusing to allow the use of a commonly used name.

(7) The statement must show the persons standing nominated as individual candidates after the names of the registered parties standing nominated and the names of those candidates must be arranged alphabetically in order of their surnames, and, if there are two or more of them with the same surname, of their other names.

(8) The returning officer must send to the Electoral Commission a copy of the statement.

Correction of minor errors

16 (1) A returning officer may, if he thinks fit, at any time before the publication under rule 15 of the statement of parties and individual candidates nominated, correct minor errors in a nomination paper or list.

(2) Errors which may be corrected include obvious errors of spelling in relation to the details of a candidate or the authorised description of a registered party.

(3) Anything done by a returning officer in pursuance of this rule may not be questioned in any proceedings other than proceedings on an election petition.

(4) A returning officer must have regard to any guidance issued by the Electoral Commission for the purposes of this rule.

Local publication of statement under rule 15

17 (1) Immediately following publication of the statement of parties and individual candidates nominated, the returning officer must forward a copy of it to the local returning officer for each local counting area in the electoral region.

(2) As soon as practicable after receipt of the copy of the statement, each local returning officer must publish it at a place within the area for which he acts.

Disqualification by Representation of the People Act 1981

18 (1) If it appears to the returning officer that any of the persons nominated as an individual candidate might be disqualified by the Representation of the People Act 1981 (which applies in respect of the office of MEP by virtue of section 10(1)(a) of the 2002 Act) or any corresponding provision in respect of detained offenders in Gibraltar made under section 10(4A) of the 2002 Act he must, as soon as practicable after the expiry of the time allowed for the delivery of nomination papers, prepare and publish a draft of that part of the statement of parties and individual candidates nominated as is required by rule 15(1)(b).

(2) The draft must be headed "draft statement of individual candidates nominated" and must contain a notice stating that any person who wishes to object to the nomination of any individual candidate on the ground that he is disqualified for nomination under the Representation of the People Act 1981 or any corresponding provision in respect of detained offenders in Gibraltar made under section 10(4A) of the 2002 Act may do so

between the hours of 10 am and 4 pm and at the place specified in the notice; and the day so specified must be the day after the last day for the delivery of nomination papers.

Adjournment of nomination proceedings in case of riot

19 (1) Where the proceedings for or in connection with nomination are on any day interrupted or obstructed by riot or open violence–

    (a) the proceedings must be abandoned for that day; and

    (b) if that day is the last day for the delivery of nomination papers, the proceedings must be continued on the next day as if that were the last day of such delivery,

and that day must be treated for the purposes of these rules as being the last day for such delivery (subject to any further application of this rule in the event of interruption or obstruction on that day).

(2) Where proceedings are abandoned by virtue of this rule, nothing–

    (a) may be done after they are continued if the time for doing it had passed at the time of the abandonment;

    (b) done before the abandonment is invalidated by reason of the abandonment.

Method of election

20 (1) If the statement of parties and individual candidates nominated shows more candidates than there are seats to be filled, a poll must be taken in accordance with Part 3 of these rules.

(2) If the statement of parties and individual candidates nominated shows a number of candidates (whether on a registered party's list or individual candidates) which is the same as or less than the number of seats to be filled, those candidates must be declared to be elected in accordance with Part 4 of these rules.

Part 3
Contested Elections

Chapter 1
General Provisions

Poll to be taken by ballot

21 The votes at the poll must be given by ballot in accordance with subsection (4) of section 2 of the 2002 Act and the seats must be allocated in accordance with subsections (5) to (9) of that section.

The ballot papers

22 (1) The ballot of every voter must consist of a ballot paper, and the registered parties, together with their candidates shown in the statement of parties and individual candidates nominated and the individual candidates shown as standing nominated, and no others, are entitled to have their names inserted in the ballot paper.

(2) Every ballot paper must be in Form A in the Appendix, and must be printed in accordance with the directions in that Appendix, and–

    (a) must contain the names followed by the descriptions, if any, of the registered parties shown in the statement of parties and individual candidates nominated, together with the names of the candidates of those parties and the names, followed by the descriptions if any, of any individual candidate so shown;

    (b)   must be capable of being folded up; and

    (c)   must have a number and other unique identifying mark printed on the back.

(3)   If a request is made by or on behalf of a nominating officer of a registered party, the ballot paper must contain adjacent to the party's name the party's registered emblem (or, as the case may be, one of the party's registered emblems).

(4)   The request must–

    (a)   be made in writing to the returning officer; and

    (b)   be received by him before the last time for the delivery of nomination papers set out in the Timetable in rule 1.

(5)   The order of the names of the registered parties, together with their candidates, and of the individual candidates in the ballot paper must be the same as in the statement of parties and individual candidates nominated.

The corresponding number list

23 (1)   The local returning officer must prepare a list ("the corresponding number list") containing the numbers and other unique identifying marks of all the ballot papers to be issued by him in pursuance of rule 28(1) or provided by him in pursuance of rule 32(1).

(2)   The form of corresponding number list to be prepared by a local returning officer for the purpose of rule 28(1) and paragraph 48(1) of Schedule 2 must be in Form B in the Appendix.

(3)   The form of corresponding number list to be prepared by the local returning officer for the purposes of rule 32(3)(d) and 41(1)(b) must be in Form C in the Appendix.

(4)   The form of corresponding number list to be prepared by the local returning officer for the purpose of rule 28(1) and paragraph 48(1) of Schedule 2 when the poll at a European Parliamentary election is to be taken with–

    (a)   the poll at an election under subsection (1) or (2) of section 15 of the 1985 Act (combination of polls at parliamentary, European Parliamentary and local government elections), or

    (b)   the poll at a mayoral election or a referendum in accordance with regulations made under sections 9HE and 105, 9MG and 105 or 44 and 105 of the Local Government Act 2000,

   must be in Form D in the Appendix.

(5)   The form of corresponding number list to be prepared by the local returning officer for the purposes of rules 32(3)(d) and 41(1)(b) when the poll at a European Parliamentary election is to be taken with–

    (a)   the poll at an election under subsection (1) or (2) of section 15 of the 1985 Act (combination of polls at parliamentary, European Parliamentary and local government elections), or

    (b)   the poll at a mayoral election or referendum in accordance with regulations made under sections 9HE and 105, 9MG and 105 or 44 and 105 of the Local Government Act 2000,

   must be in Form E in the Appendix.

The official mark

24 (1)   Every ballot paper must contain an appropriate security marking (the official mark).

(2)   The official mark must be kept secret, and an interval of not less than five years must intervene between the use of the same official mark at elections for the same local counting area.

(3) The local returning officer may use a different official mark for different purposes at the same election.

Prohibition of disclosure of vote

25   No person who has voted at the election must, in any legal proceeding to question the election, be required to state for whom he has voted.

Use of schools and public rooms

26 (1) The local returning officer may use, free of charge, for the purpose of taking the poll–
    (a) a room in a school to which this rule applies;
    (b) a room the expense of maintaining which is payable out of any rate.

(2) This rule applies–
    (a) in England and Wales, to a school maintained or assisted by a local authority (as defined in the Education Act 1996) or a school in respect of which grants are made out of moneys provided by Parliament to the person or body of persons responsible for the management of the school;
    (b) in Scotland, to a school other than an independent school within the meaning of the Education (Scotland) Act 1980;
    (c) in Gibraltar, to a school, club or sports house or other premises, the expense of maintaining which is payable wholly or partly out of public funds or out of any rate, or by a body whose expenses are so payable.

(3) The local returning officer must make good any damage done to, and defray any expense incurred by the persons having control over, any room which has been used in accordance with this rule by reason of its being used for the purpose of taking the poll.

Chapter 2
Action to be Taken Before the Poll

Notice of poll

27 (1) The returning officer must in the statement of parties and individual candidates nominated include a notice of the poll stating the day on which and hours during which the poll will be taken.

(2) In respect of each local counting area or part of an area contained in the electoral region, the local returning officer must also give public notice of–
    (a) the situation of each polling station;
    (b) the description of voters entitled to vote there;
and he must as soon as practicable after giving such notice give a copy of it to each of the election agents.

Postal ballot papers and postal voting statements

28 (1) The local returning officer must, in accordance with Schedule 2, issue to those entitled to vote by post a ballot paper and postal voting statement in the appropriate form prescribed by paragraph 42 of that Schedule, together with such envelopes for their return as are required for the purposes of paragraph 50 of that Schedule.

(2) The local returning officer must also issue to those entitled to vote by post such information as he thinks appropriate about how to obtain–
    (a) translations into languages other than English of any directions to or guidance for voters sent with the ballot paper;

    (b)   a translation into Braille of such directions or guidance;

    (c)   graphical representations of such directions or guidance;

    (d)   the directions or guidance in any other form (including any audible form).

(3) In the case of a ballot paper issued to a person at an address in the United Kingdom or Gibraltar, the local returning officer must ensure that the return of the ballot paper and postal voting statement is free of charge to the voter.

Provision of polling stations

29 (1) The local returning officer must provide a sufficient number of polling stations and, subject to the following provisions of this rule, must allot the electors to the polling stations in such manner as he thinks most convenient.

(2) One or more polling stations may be provided in the same room.

(3) The polling station allotted to electors from any polling district must be in the polling place for that district.

(4) The local returning officer must provide each polling station with such number of compartments as may be necessary in which the voters can mark their votes screened from observation.

Appointment of presiding officers and clerks

30 (1) The local returning officer must appoint and pay a presiding officer to attend at each polling station and such clerks as may be necessary for the purposes of the election, but he must not appoint any person who has been employed by or on behalf of a registered party or individual candidate in or about the election.

(2) The local returning officer may, if he thinks fit, preside at a polling station and the provisions of these rules relating to a presiding officer apply to a local returning officer so presiding with the necessary modifications as to things to be done by the local returning officer to the presiding officer or by the presiding officer to the local returning officer.

(3) A presiding officer may do, by the clerks appointed to assist him, any act (including the asking of questions) which he is required or authorised by these rules to do at a polling station except order the arrest, exclusion or removal of any person from the polling station.

Issue of official poll cards

31 (1) The local returning officer must as soon as practicable after the publication of the notice of election send to electors and their proxies the appropriate official poll card, but a card must not be sent to any person registered, or to be registered, in pursuance of an overseas elector's declaration.

(2) An elector's official poll card must be sent or delivered to his qualifying address, and a proxy's to his address as shown in the list of proxies.

(3) The official poll card issued to an elector must be in Form F in the Appendix.

(4) The official postal poll card issued to an elector must be in Form G in the Appendix.

(5) The official poll card issued to the proxy of an elector must be in Form H in the Appendix.

(6) The official postal poll card issued to the proxy of an elector must be in Form J in the Appendix.

(7) The official poll card must set out–

(a) the name of the electoral region and electoral area;

(b) the elector's name, qualifying address and number on the register;

(c) the date and hours of the poll and the situation of the elector's polling station;

(d) such other information as the local returning officer thinks appropriate,

and different information may be provided in pursuance of sub-paragraph (d) to different electors or descriptions of elector.

(8) In the case of an elector with an anonymous entry, instead of containing the matter mentioned in paragraph (7)(b), the polling card must contain such matter as is specified in Forms F to J in the Appendix.

Equipment of polling stations

32 (1) The local returning officer must provide each presiding officer with such number of ballot boxes and ballot papers as in the local returning officer's opinion may be necessary.

(2) Every ballot box must be so constructed that the ballot papers can be put in it, but cannot be withdrawn from it, without the box being unlocked or, where the box has no lock, the seal being broken.

(3) The local returning officer must provide each polling station with–

(a) materials to enable voters to mark the ballot papers;

(b) copies of the register of electors or such part of it as contains the entries relating to the electors allotted to the polling station;

(c) the parts of any special lists prepared for the election corresponding to the register of electors or such part of it as provided under sub-paragraph (b);

(d) Form C prepared under rule 23(3) (or where applicable, Form E prepared under rule 23(5)) which contains the numbers (but not the other unique identifying marks) corresponding to those on the ballot papers provided to the presiding officer of the polling station.

(4) The reference in paragraph (3)(b) to the copies of the registers of electors includes a reference to copies of any notices issued under section 13B(3B) or (3D) of the 1983 Act in respect of alterations to the register.

(5) The local returning officer must also provide each polling station with–

(a) at least one large version of the ballot paper which must be displayed inside the polling station for the assistance of voters who are partially sighted; and

(b) a device of such description as is set out in paragraph (8) for enabling voters who are blind or partially sighted to vote without any need for assistance from the presiding officer or any companion (within the meaning of rule 43).

(6) A notice in Form K in the Appendix, giving directions for the guidance of voters in voting, must be printed in conspicuous characters and exhibited inside and outside every polling station.

(7) In every compartment of every polling station there must be exhibited the notice "Vote only once by putting a cross X in the box next to your choice. Put no other mark on the ballot paper, or your vote may not count.

(8) The device referred to in paragraph (5)(b) must–

(a) allow a ballot paper to be inserted into and removed from or attached to and detached from the device, easily and without damage to the paper;

(b) keep the ballot paper firmly in place during use;

(c) provide suitable means for the voter to–

(i) identify the spaces on the ballot paper on which he may mark his vote;

(ii) identify the registered party or individual candidate to which each such space refers; and

        (iii) mark his vote on the space he has chosen.

(9)   Where proof has been given to the returning officer's satisfaction of the death of a candidate on a registered party's list or an individual candidate, he must request each local returning officer to provide each presiding officer with a sufficient number of notices to this effect for display in every compartment of every polling station.

Appointment of polling and counting agents

33 (1)   The election agent or sub-agent of a registered party standing nominated or the election agent or sub-agent of an individual candidate or any person authorised in writing by such an agent or candidate may, before commencement of the poll, appoint–

     (a) polling agents to attend at polling stations for the purpose of detecting personation; and

     (b) counting agents to attend at the verification of the ballot paper accounts and the counting of the votes.

(2)   For each count one (but no more than one) counting agent of each registered party or individual candidate may be authorised by the terms of his appointment to require a re-count at that count.

(3)   The local returning officer may limit the number of counting agents, so that–

     (a) the number must be the same in the case of each registered party standing nominated or individual candidate; and

     (b) the number allowed to a registered party standing nominated or individual candidate must not (except in special circumstances) be less than the number obtained by dividing the number of clerks employed on the verification of the ballot paper accounts or the counting of the votes by the number obtained by adding together the number of registered parties standing nominated and the number of individual candidates.

(4)   Notice in writing of the appointment, stating the names and addresses of the persons appointed, must be given by the person by whom the appointment was made to the local returning officer and must be so given not later than the fifth day (computed like any period of time in the Timetable in rule 1) before the day of the poll.

(5)   If an agent dies, or becomes incapable of acting, the person by whom the appointment was made may appoint another agent in his place, and must forthwith give to the local returning officer notice in writing of the name and address of the agent appointed.

(6)   In the following provisions of these rules references to polling agents and counting agents must be taken as references to agents–

     (a) whose appointments have been duly made and notified; and

     (b) where the number of agents is restricted, who are within the permitted numbers.

(7)   Any notice required to be given to a counting agent by the local returning officer may be delivered at, or sent by post to, the address stated in the notice of appointment.

(8)   A candidate may himself do any act or thing which any polling or counting agent of his, if appointed, would have been authorised to do, or may assist his agent in doing any such act or thing.

(9)   A candidate's election agent may do or assist in doing anything which a polling or counting agent of his or of his registered party, if appointed, would have been authorised to do; and anything required or authorised by these rules to be done in the presence of the polling or counting agents may be done in the presence of the candidate's election agent instead of the polling agent or counting agent.

(10) An election agent or sub-agent of a registered party standing nominated or the election agent or sub-agent of an individual candidate may do or assist in doing anything which a polling or counting agent of that party or candidate is authorised to do; and anything required or authorised by these rules to be done in the presence of the polling or counting agents may be done in the presence of an election agent or sub-agent of a registered party standing nominated or the election agent or sub-agent of an individual candidate instead of that party's or candidate's polling agent or counting agents.

(11) Where by these rules any act or thing is required or authorised to be done in the presence of the polling or counting agents, the non-attendance of any agent or agents at the time and place appointed for the purpose shall not, if the act or thing is otherwise duly done, invalidate the act or thing done.

Notification of requirement of secrecy

34 (1) The local returning officer must make such arrangements as he thinks fit to ensure that–

    (a) every person attending at a polling station (otherwise than for the purpose of voting or assisting a voter with disabilities to vote or as a constable on duty there or as a person under the age of 18 accompanying a voter) has been given a copy in writing of the provisions of paragraphs (1), (4) and (7) of regulation 29 of these Regulations; and

    (b) every person attending at the verification of the ballot paper accounts or the counting of the votes (other than any constable on duty at the counting) has been given a copy in writing of the provisions of paragraphs (2), (3) and (7) of regulation 29 of these Regulations.

(2) In the application of this rule to an election in England or Wales, a reference to a constable includes a person designated as a community support officer under section 38 of the Police Reform Act 2002 (police powers for civilian staff).

Return of postal ballot papers

35 (1) Where–

    (a) a postal vote has been returned in respect of a person who is entered on the postal voters list, or

    (b) a proxy postal vote has been returned in respect of a proxy who is entered on the proxy postal voters list,

the local returning officer must mark the list as provided for in paragraph 60 of Schedule 2.

(2) Rule 51(2) does not apply for the purpose of determining whether, for the purpose of this rule, a postal vote or a proxy postal vote is returned.

Chapter 3
The Poll

Admission to polling station

36 (1) The presiding officer must exclude all persons from the polling station except–

    (a) voters;

    (b) persons under the age of 18 who accompany voters to the polling station;

    (c) the candidates and the election agents of any registered party standing nominated and any individual candidate and their election agents;

(d)   the polling agents appointed to attend at the polling station;

(e)   the clerks appointed to attend at the polling station;

(f)   persons who are entitled to attend by virtue of any of sections 6A to 6D of the 2000 Act ;

(g)   the constables on duty; and

(h)   the companions of voters with disabilities.

(2)   The presiding officer must regulate the total number of voters and persons under the age of 18 who accompany them to be admitted to the polling station at the same time.

(3)   Not more than one polling agent may be admitted at the same time to a polling station on behalf of the same registered party standing nominated and any individual candidate.

(4)   A constable or person employed by a local returning officer must not be admitted to vote in person elsewhere than at his own polling station under rule 29(1), except on production and surrender of a certificate as to his employment which must be in Form L in the Appendix and signed by an officer of police of or above the rank of inspector or by the local returning officer, as the case may be.

(5)   Any certificate surrendered under this rule must forthwith be cancelled.

(6)   In the application of this rule to an election in England or Wales, a reference to a constable includes a person designated as a community support officer under section 38 of the Police Reform Act 2002 (police powers for civilian staff).

Keeping of order in station

37 (1)   It is the presiding officer's duty to keep order at his polling station.

(2)   If a person misconducts himself in a polling station, or fails to obey the presiding officer's lawful orders, he may immediately, by the presiding officer's order, be removed from the polling station–

(a)   by a constable in or near that station; or

(b)   by any other person authorised in writing by the local returning officer to remove him,

and the person so removed must not, without the presiding officer's permission, again enter the polling station during the day.

(3)   Any person so removed may, if charged with the commission in the polling station of an offence, be dealt with as a person taken into custody by a constable for an offence without a warrant.

(4)   The powers conferred by this rule must not be exercised so as to prevent a voter who is otherwise entitled to vote at a polling station from having an opportunity of voting at that station.

Sealing of ballot boxes

38   Immediately before the commencement of the poll, the presiding officer must–

(a)   show the ballot box empty to such persons, if any, as are present in the polling station, so that they may see that it is empty;

(b)   then lock it up, if it has a lock;

(c)   place his seal on it in such a manner so as to prevent it being opened without breaking the seal;

(d)   place it in his view for the receipt of ballot papers; and

(e)   keep it so sealed or, if it has a lock, both sealed and locked.

Questions to be put to voters

39 (1)   At the time of the application (but not afterwards), the questions specified in the second column of the following table–

  (a)   may be put by the presiding officer to a person applying for a ballot paper who is mentioned in the first column; and

  (b)   must be put if the letter "R" appears after the question and if the candidate or the election or polling agent of a registered party standing nominated, an individual candidate or the election agent or polling agent of an individual candidate requires the question to be put:

Q No	Person applying for ballot paper	Question
1	A person applying as an elector	(a)–Are you the person registered in the register of electors for this election as follows *read the whole entry from the register* R?
		(b)–Have you already voted, (here in the UK or in another Member State at this general election of MEPs) (here or elsewhere at this by-election) otherwise than as proxy for some other person? R
2	A person applying as proxy	(a)–Are you the person whose name appears as AB in the list of proxies for this election as entitled to vote as proxy on behalf of CD? R
		(b)–Have you already voted here or elsewhere at this (general election of MEPs) (by-election), as proxy on behalf of CD? R
		(c)–Are you the spouse, civil partner, parent, grandparent, brother, sister, child or grandchild of CD? R
3	A person applying as proxy for an elector with an anonymous entry (instead of the questions at entry 2)	(a)–Are you the person entitled to vote as proxy on behalf of the elector whose number on the register of electors is (*read out the number*)? R
		(b)–Have you already voted here or elsewhere at this (general election of MEPs) (by-election), as proxy on behalf of the elector whose number on the register of electors is (*read out the number*)? R
		(c)–Are you the spouse, civil partner, parent, grandparent, brother, sister, child or grandchild of the person whose number on the register of electors is (*read out the number*)? R
4	Person applying as proxy if the question at entry 2(c) or 3(c) is not answered in the affirmative	Have you at this (general election of MEPs) (by-election) already voted in this electoral region on behalf of two persons of whom you are not the spouse, civil partner, parent, grandparent, brother, sister, child or grandchild? R
5	Person applying as an elector in relation to whom there is an entry in the postal voters list	(a)–Did you apply to vote by post?
		(b)–Why have you not voted by post?
6	A person applying as proxy who is named in the proxy	(a)–Did you apply to vote by post as proxy?
		(b)–Why have you not voted by post as

postal voters list	proxy?

(2) In the case of an elector in respect of whom a notice has been issued under section 13B(3B) or (3D) of the 1983 Act, the references in the questions at entries 1(a) and 3(a), (b) and (c) to reading from the register must be taken as references to reading from the notice issued under section 13B(3B) or (3D) of the 1983 Act.

(3) A ballot paper must not be delivered to any person required to answer any of the above questions unless he has answered each question satisfactorily.

(4) Except as authorised by this rule, no inquiry may be permitted as to the right of any person to vote.

Challenge of voter

40   A person must not be prevented from voting by reason only that–
   (a) a candidate or the election or polling agent of a registered party standing nominated or of an individual candidate or his election or polling agent declares that he has reasonable cause to believe that the person has committed an offence of personation, or
   (b) the person is arrested on the grounds that he is suspected of committing or of being about to commit such an offence.

Voting procedure

41 (1)   A ballot paper must be delivered to a voter who applies for one, and immediately before delivery–
   (a) the number and (unless paragraph (2) applies) name of the elector as stated in the copy of the register of electors must be called out;
   (b) the number of the elector must be marked on the list mentioned in rule 32(3)(d) beside the number of the ballot paper to be issued to him;
   (c) a mark must be placed in the copy of the register of electors against the number of the elector to note that a ballot paper has been received but without showing the particular ballot paper which has been received; and
   (d) in the case of a person applying for a ballot paper as proxy, a mark must also be placed against his name in the list of proxies.

(2) In the case of an elector who has an anonymous entry, he must show the presiding officer his official poll card and only his number must be called out in pursuance of paragraph (1)(a).

(3) In the case of an elector who is added to the register in pursuance of a notice issued under section 13B(3B) or (3D) of the 1983 Act, paragraph (1) is modified as follows–
   (a) in sub-paragraph (a), for "copy of the register of electors" substitute "copy of the notice issued under section 13B(3B) or (3D) of the 1983 Act";
   (b) in sub-paragraph (c), for "in the copy of the register of electors" substitute "on the copy of the notice issued under section 13B(3B) or (3D) of the 1983 Act".

(4) The voter, on receiving the ballot paper, must forthwith proceed into one of the compartments in the polling station and there secretly mark his paper and fold it up so as to conceal his vote, and must then show to the presiding officer the back of the paper, so as to disclose the number and other unique identifying mark, and put the ballot paper so folded up into the ballot box in the presiding officer's presence.

(5) The voter must vote without undue delay, and must leave the polling station as soon as he has put his ballot paper into the ballot box.

(6) A voter who at the close of the poll is in the polling station, or in a queue outside the

polling station, for the purpose of voting is (despite the close of the poll) entitled to apply for a ballot paper under paragraph (1); and these rules apply in relation to such a voter accordingly.

Votes marked by presiding officer

42 (1) The presiding officer, on the application of a voter–
    (a) who is incapacitated by blindness or other disability from voting in the manner directed by these rules; or
    (b) who declares orally that he is unable to read,
must, in the presence of the polling agents, cause the voter's vote to be marked on a ballot paper in the manner directed by the voter, and the ballot paper to be placed in the ballot box.

(2) The name and number on the copy of the register of electors of every voter whose vote is marked in pursuance of this rule, and the reason why it is so marked, must be entered on a list (in these rules called "the list of votes marked by the presiding officer").

(3) In the case of a person voting as proxy for an elector, the number to be entered together with the voter's name must be the elector's number.

(4) In the case of a person in respect of whom a notice has been issued under section 13B(3B) or (3D) of the 1983 Act, paragraph (2) applies as if for "on the copy of the register of electors of every voter" there were substituted "relating to every voter in respect of whom a notice has been issued under section 13B(3B) or (3D) of the 1983 Act".

Voting by persons with disabilities

43 (1) If a voter makes an application to the presiding officer to be allowed, on the ground of–
    (a) blindness or other disability; or
    (b) inability to read,
to vote with the assistance of another person by whom he is accompanied (in these rules referred to as "the companion"), the presiding officer must require the voter to declare, orally or in writing, whether he is so incapacitated by his blindness or other disability, or by his inability to read, as to be unable to vote without assistance.

(2) If the presiding officer–
    (a) is satisfied that the voter is so incapacitated, and
    (b) is also satisfied by a written declaration made by the companion (in these rules referred to as "the declaration made by the companion of a voter with disabilities") that the companion–
        (i) is a qualified person within the meaning of these rules; and
        (ii) has not previously assisted more than one voter with disabilities to vote at the election,
the presiding officer must grant the application, and then anything which is by these rules required to be done to or by that voter in connection with the giving of his vote may be done to, or with the assistance of, the companion.

(3) For the purposes of these rules, a person is a voter with disabilities if he has made such a declaration as is mentioned in paragraph (1), and a person is qualified to assist a voter with disabilities to vote if that person–
    (a) is a person who is entitled to vote as an elector at the election; or
    (b) is the father, mother, brother, sister, spouse, civil partner, son or daughter of the voter and has attained the age of 18 years.

(4) The name and number in the copy of the register of electors of every voter whose vote

is given in accordance with this rule and the name and address of the companion must be entered on a list (in these rules referred to as "the list of voters with disabilities assisted by companions").

(5)   In the case of a person voting as proxy for an elector, the number to be entered together with the voter's name must be the elector's number.

(6)   In the case of a person in respect of whom a notice has been issued under section 13B(3B) or (3D) of the 1983 Act, paragraph (4) applies as if for "in copy of the register of electors of every voter" there were substituted "relating to every voter in respect of whom a notice has been issued under section 13B(3B) or (3D) of the 1983 Act".

(7)   The declaration made by the companion–
   (a)   must be in Form M in the Appendix; and
   (b)   must be made before the presiding officer at the time when the voter applies to vote with the assistance of a companion,
and must forthwith be given to the presiding officer who must attest and retain it.

(8)   No fee or other payment may be charged in respect of the declaration.

Tendered ballot papers: circumstances where available

44 (1)   If a person, representing himself to be–
   (a)   a particular elector named on the register and not named in the postal voters list; or
   (b)   a particular person named in the list of proxies as proxy for an elector and not entitled to vote by post as proxy,
applies for a ballot paper after another person has voted in person either as the elector or his proxy, the applicant must, on satisfactorily answering the questions permitted by rule 39(1) to be asked at the poll, be entitled, subject to the following provisions of this rule and rule 45, to mark a ballot paper (in these rules referred to as "a tendered ballot paper") in the same manner as any other voter.

(2)   Paragraph (4) applies if–
   (a)   a person applies for a ballot paper representing himself to be a particular elector named on the register;
   (b)   he is also named in the postal voters list; and
   (c)   he claims that he did not make an application to vote by post at the election.

(3)   Paragraph (4) also applies if–
   (a)   a person applies for a ballot paper representing himself to be a particular person named as a proxy in the list of proxies;
   (b)   he is also named in proxy postal voters list; and
   (c)   he claims that he did not make an application to vote by post as proxy.

(4)   The person must, on satisfactorily answering the questions permitted by rule 39(1) to be asked at the poll, be entitled, subject to the following provisions of this rule and rule 45, to mark a ballot paper (in these rules referred to as a "tendered ballot paper") in the same manner as any other voter.

(5)   Paragraph (6) applies if before the close of the poll but after the last time at which a person may apply for a replacement postal ballot paper, a person represents himself to be–
   (a)   a particular elector named on the register who is also named in the postal voters list; or
   (b)   a particular person named as a proxy in the list of proxies and who is also named in the proxy postal voters list,
and claims that he has lost or has not received his postal ballot paper.

(6) The person must, on satisfactorily answering the questions permitted by rule 39(1) to be asked at the poll, be entitled, subject to the provisions of rule 45, to mark a ballot paper (in these rules referred to as a "tendered ballot paper") in the same manner as any other voter.

Tendered ballot papers: general provisions

45 (1) A tendered ballot paper must–
    (a) be of a colour differing from the other ballot papers;
    (b) instead of being put into the ballot box, be given to the presiding officer and endorsed by him with the name of the voter and his number in the copy of the register of electors, and set aside in a separate packet.

(2) The name of the voter and his number on the register of electors must be entered on a list (in these rules referred to as the "tendered votes list").

(3) In the case of a person voting as proxy for an elector, the number to be endorsed or entered together with the voter's name must be the number of that elector.

(4) In the case of an elector who has an anonymous entry, this rule and rule 44 apply subject to the following modifications–
    (a) in paragraphs (1)(b), (2) and (3) of this rule, the references to the name of the voter must be ignored;
    (b) otherwise, a reference to a person named on a register or list must be construed as a reference to a person whose number appears on the register or list (as the case may be).

(5) In the case of a person in respect of whom a notice has been issued under section 13B(3B) or (3D) of the 1983 Act, this rule and rule 44 apply as if–
    (a) in rule 44(1)(a), (2)(a) and (5)(a), for "named on the register" there were substituted "in respect of whom a notice under section 13B(3B) or (3D) of the 1983 Act has been issued";
    (b) in paragraph (1)(b) of this rule for "his number in the copy of the register of electors" there were substituted "the number relating to him on a notice issued under section 13B(3B) or (3D) of the 1983 Act"; and
    (c) in paragraph (2) of this rule, for "his number on the register of electors" there were substituted "the number relating to him on a notice issued under section 13(3B) or (3D) of the 1983 Act".

Spoilt ballot papers

46 A voter who has inadvertently dealt with his ballot paper in such manner that it cannot conveniently be used as a ballot paper may, on delivering it to the presiding officer and proving to his satisfaction the fact of the inadvertence, obtain another ballot paper in the place of the ballot paper so delivered (in these rules referred to as "a spoilt ballot paper"), and the spoilt ballot paper must be immediately cancelled.

Alteration of registers

47 (1) The presiding officer must keep a list of persons to whom ballot papers are delivered in consequence of an alteration to the register made by virtue of section 13B(3B) or (3D) of the 1983 Act which takes effect on the day of the poll.

(2) For the purposes of section 13B(3C) of the 1983 Act, a representation may be made orally or in writing.

(3) Where a representation under section 13B(3C) is made in a polling station to a presiding officer, the presiding officer must as soon as practicable communicate that

representation to the appropriate registration officer.

(4) Where a notice is issued under section 13B(3B) or (3D) of the 1983 Act on the day of the poll, the registration officer must take reasonable steps to ensure that the notice comes to the attention of the appropriate presiding officer.

(5) Such steps may include communication to the presiding officer by telephone.

(6) Where a notice issued under section 13(3B) or (3D) of the 1983 Act is communicated to a presiding officer by telephone, the presiding officer must make a written record of that notice.

(7) For the purposes of section 13B(3A) and (3C) of the 1983 Act the prescribed time on the day of the poll is 9pm.

Adjournment of poll in case of riot

48 (1) Where the proceedings at any polling station are interrupted or obstructed by riot or open violence, the presiding officer must adjourn the proceedings till the following day and must forthwith give notice to the local returning officer.

(2) Where the poll is adjourned at any polling station–
    (a) the hours of polling on the day to which it is adjourned must be the same as for the original day; and
    (b) references in these rules to the close of the poll must be construed accordingly.

Procedure on close of poll

49 (1) As soon as practicable after the close of the poll, the presiding officer must, in the presence of the polling agents, make up into separate packets, sealed with his own seal and the seals of such polling agents as desire to affix their seals–
    (a) each ballot box in use at the station, sealed so as to prevent the introduction of additional ballot papers and unopened, but with the key, if any, attached;
    (b) the unused and spoilt ballot papers placed together;
    (c) the tendered ballot papers;
    (d) the marked copies of the register of electors (including any marked copy notices issued under section 13B(3B) or (3D) of the 1983 Act) and of the list of proxies;
    (e) the lists prepared under rule 23 including the parts which were marked with the numbers of electors in accordance with rule 41(1)(b) (together referred to in these rules as "the completed corresponding number lists");
    (f) the certificates as to employment on duty on the day of the poll;
    (g) the tendered votes list, the list of voters with disabilities assisted by companions, the list of votes marked by the presiding officer, a statement of the number of voters whose votes are so marked by the presiding officer under the heads "disability" and "unable to read", the list maintained under rule 47, and the declarations made by the companions of voters with disabilities;
and must deliver the packets or cause them to be delivered to the local returning officer to be taken charge of by him; but if the packets are not delivered by the presiding officer personally to the local returning officer, the arrangements for their delivery must be approved by the local returning officer.

(2) The marked copies of the register of electors and of the list of proxies mentioned in paragraph (1)(d) must be in one packet but must not be in the same packet as the completed corresponding number lists mentioned in paragraph (1)(e) or the certificates as to employment on duty on the day of the poll mentioned in paragraph (1)(f).

(3) The packets must be accompanied by a statement (in these rules referred to as "the ballot paper account") made by the presiding officer showing the number of ballot

papers entrusted to him, and accounting for them under the heads of ballot papers issued and not otherwise accounted for, unused, spoilt and tendered ballot papers.

Chapter 4
Counting of Votes

Attendance at verification of ballot paper accounts

50 (1) The local returning officer must make arrangements for the verification of the ballot paper accounts in the presence of the counting agents as soon as practicable after the close of the poll, and must give to the returning officer and the counting agents notice in writing of the time and place at which he will begin such verification.

(2) No person other than–
   (a) the returning officer, the local returning officer and his clerks;
   (b) the candidates and one other person chosen by each of them;
   (c) the election agents;
   (d) the counting agents; and
   (e) persons who are entitled to attend by virtue of any of sections 6A to 6D of the 2000 Act;
   may attend the verification of the ballot paper accounts, unless permitted by the local returning officer to attend.

(3) A person not entitled to attend the verification of ballot paper accounts must not be permitted to do so by the local returning officer unless he is satisfied that the efficient verification of the ballot paper accounts will not be impeded.

(4) The local returning officer must give the counting agents all such reasonable facilities for observing the proceedings, and all such information with respect to them, as he can give them consistently with the orderly conduct of the proceedings and the discharge of his duties in connection with them.

Procedure at verification of ballot paper accounts

51 (1) The local returning officer must in the presence of the counting agents–
   (a) open each ballot box and count and record the number of ballot papers in it and verify each ballot paper account; and
   (b) count such of the postal ballot papers as have been duly returned and record the number counted.

(2) A postal ballot paper must not be deemed to be duly returned unless–
   (a) subject to paragraph (2A), it is returned in the manner prescribed in paragraph 55 of Schedule 2 so as to reach the local returning officer or any polling station in the local counting area in question before the close of the poll;
   (b) the postal voting statement duly signed is also returned in that manner before that time;
   (c) the postal voting statement also states the date of birth of the elector or proxy (as the case may be); and
   (d) the local returning officer verifies the date of birth and the signature of the elector or proxy (as the case may be) under paragraph 63 of Schedule 2.

(2A) A postal ballot paper or postal voting statement that reaches the local returning officer or a polling station on or after the close of poll is treated for the purposes of this rule as reaching that officer or polling station before the close of the poll if it is delivered by a person who, at the close of the poll, is in the polling station, or in a queue outside the polling station, for the purpose of returning it.

(3) The local returning officer must not count any tendered ballot paper.

(4) The local returning officer, while counting and recording the number of ballot papers, must keep the ballot papers with their faces downwards.

(5) The local returning officer must verify each ballot paper account by comparing it with the number of ballot papers recorded by him, the unused and spoilt ballot papers in his possession and the tendered votes list (opening and re-sealing the packets containing the unused and spoilt ballot papers and the tendered votes list) and must draw up a statement as to the result of the verification, which any counting agent may copy.

(6) The local returning officer must determine the hours during which the procedure under this rule is proceeded with.

(7) The local returning officer must take proper precautions for the security of the ballot papers and documents.

(8) On completion of the procedure under this rule, the local returning officer must–
    (a) place the ballot papers and other documents relating to the election in packets under his own seal and the seals of such counting agents as desire to affix their seals, unless he proceeds immediately to the counting of the votes under rule 53;
    (b) otherwise take proper precautions for the security of the papers and documents; and
    (c) inform the returning officer of the total number of ballot papers counted.

Attendance at counting of votes

52 (1) The local returning officer must make arrangements for counting the votes in the presence of the counting agents–
    (a) in the case of a general election of MEPs, before or after the material time and in either case so that the requirements of rule 57(1) are satisfied as soon as practicable after the material time; and
    (b) in the case of a by-election, as soon as practicable after the close of the poll,
and must give to the counting agents and the returning officer notice in writing of the time and place at which he will begin to count the votes.

(2) For the purposes of paragraph (1), the "material time" means, in relation to a general election of MEPs, the close of the polling in the Member State whose electors are the last to vote in the election.

(3) No person other than–
    (a) the returning officer, the local returning officer and his clerks;
    (b) the candidates and one other person chosen by each of them;
    (c) the election agents;
    (d) the counting agents; and
    (e) persons who are entitled to attend by virtue of any of sections 6A to 6D of the 2000 Act,
may be present at the counting of the votes, unless permitted by the local returning officer to attend.

(4) A person not entitled to attend at the counting of the votes must not be permitted to do so by the local returning officer unless he–
    (a) is satisfied that the efficient counting of the votes will not be impeded; and
    (b) has either consulted the election agents or thought it impracticable to do so.

(5) The local returning officer must give the counting agents all such reasonable facilities for overseeing the proceedings, and all such information with respect to them, as he

can give them consistently with the orderly conduct of the proceedings and the discharge of his duties in connection with them.

(6) In particular, where the votes are counted by sorting the ballot papers according to the registered party or individual candidate for whom the vote is given and then counting the number of ballot papers for each registered party or individual candidate, the counting agents must be allowed to satisfy themselves that the ballot papers are correctly sorted.

The count

53 (1) The local returning officer must–

    (a) where the ballot papers and other documents have been placed in packets under rule 51(8), open the packets of ballot papers other than unused, spoilt and tendered ballot papers;

    (b) mix together the ballot papers with the exception of the unused, spoilt and tendered ballot papers.

(2) The local returning officer must not count any tendered ballot paper.

(3) The local returning officer, while counting the votes, must keep the ballot papers with their faces upwards and take all proper precautions for preventing any person from seeing the numbers or other unique identifying marks printed on the back of the papers.

(4) The local returning officer must so far as practicable proceed continuously with counting the votes, allowing only time for refreshment, except that he may, in so far as he and the agents agree, exclude the hours between 7 pm and 9 am

(5) For the purposes of paragraph (4), the agreement of an individual candidate or the election agent of a registered party shall be as effective as the agreement of the counting agents of that individual candidate or party.

(6) During the time so excluded the local returning officer must–

    (a) place the ballot papers and other documents relating to the election under his own seal and the seals of such of the counting agents as desire to affix their seals; and

    (b) otherwise take proper precautions for the security of the papers and documents.

(7) In the case of a general election of MEPs, if the counting of the votes has commenced before the material time (within the meaning of rule 52(1)), the local returning officer or his clerks must not disclose the number of votes given for each registered party and individual candidate to anyone other than the returning officer or his clerks until after that time and the counting of the votes must be deemed not to have been completed until after that time.

Re-count

54 (1) If any of the persons in paragraph (2) are present when the counting of the votes is completed (or, if later, deemed to be completed under rule 53(7)) or any re-count of the votes is completed, they may require the local returning officer to have the votes re-counted or again re-counted but the local returning officer may refuse to do so if in his opinion the request is unreasonable.

(2) The persons mentioned in paragraph (1) are–

    (a) a candidate;

    (b) the election agent of a registered party;

    (c) the election agent of an individual candidate; and

(d) a counting agent authorised under rule 33(2).

(3) No step may be taken on the completion of the counting (or, if later, its deemed completion) or any re-count of the votes until any persons referred to in paragraph (2) who are present at its completion (or, if later, its deemed completion) have been given a reasonable opportunity to exercise the right conferred by this rule.

Rejected ballot papers

55 (1) Any ballot paper–
    (a) which does not bear the official mark; or
    (b) on which votes are given for more than one registered party or individual candidate or for both a registered party and an individual candidate; or
    (c) on which anything is written or marked by which the voter can be identified except the printed number and other unique identifying mark on the back; or
    (d) which is unmarked or void for uncertainty,
shall, subject to the provisions of paragraphs (2) and (3), be void and not counted.

(2) A ballot paper on which the vote is marked–
    (a) elsewhere than in the proper place; or
    (b) otherwise than by means of a cross; or
    (c) by more than one mark,
must not for such reason be deemed to be void if an intention that the vote shall be for one or other of the registered parties or individual candidates clearly appears, and the way the paper is marked does not itself identify the voter and it is not shown that he can be identified by it.

(3) A ballot paper on which a vote is marked for a particular candidate on a party's list of candidates must, if otherwise valid, be treated as a vote for that party, whether or not there is also a vote for that party.

(4) The local returning officer must endorse the word "rejected" on any ballot paper which under this rule is not to be counted, and must add to the endorsement the words "rejection objected to" if any objection is made by a counting agent to his decision.

(5) The local returning officer must draw up a statement showing the number of ballot papers rejected under the several heads of–
    (a) want of official mark;
    (b) voting for more than one registered party or individual candidate;
    (c) writing or mark by which voter could be identified; and
    (d) unmarked or void for uncertainty.

Decisions on ballot papers

56 The decision of the local returning officer on any question arising in respect of a ballot paper is final, but may be subject to review on an election petition.

Notification of local result

57 (1) As soon as practicable after the completion of the count (or, if later, its deemed completion under rule 53(7)) the local returning officer must draw up a statement showing the number of votes given for each registered party and individual candidate, excluding any votes given on ballot papers rejected under rule 55.

(2) The local returning officer must forthwith inform the returning officer of the contents of that statement.

(3) The local returning officer must give public notice of the statements prepared under this rule and under rule 55 as soon as practicable after the returning officer has agreed

that he should do so.

Attendance at allocation of seats

58 (1) The returning officer must make arrangements for making the calculation and allocation required by rule 59.

(2) No person other than–
   (a) the returning officer and his clerks;
   (b) the election agent of each registered party standing at the election or a person acting on his behalf;
   (c) each candidate on the list of such a party and one other person chosen by each of them;
   (d) each individual candidate and one person chosen by each of them;
   (e) the election agent of each individual candidate or a person acting on his behalf;
   (f) the nominating officer of each registered party which is contesting the election to the European Parliament in the electoral region;
   (g) persons who are entitled to attend by virtue of any of sections 6A to 6D of the 2000 Act ,

may be present at that calculation and allocation unless permitted by the returning officer to attend.

(3) The returning officer must give to–
   (a) the election agent of each registered party standing at the election; and
   (b) each individual candidate,

notice in writing of the place at which he will conduct the proceedings under rule 59 and of the time at which he will begin those proceedings.

Allocation of seats

59 (1) The returning officer, as soon as practicable after he has been informed of the contents of the statements prepared under rule 57(1) by local returning officers in his region must calculate the total number of votes given to each registered party and individual candidate in all of the local counting areas within the electoral region, as shown in those statements.

(2) Subject to paragraph (4), rule 60 and rule 60A, the returning officer must then allocate the seats in accordance with subsections (5) to (9) of section 2 of the 2002 Act.

(3) The returning officer must give the persons entitled to be present reasonable facilities for satisfying themselves that the results of the calculation and allocation which he is required to make are accurate; and in particular, a person entitled to be present may require the returning officer to make a calculation or allocation again but the returning officer may refuse to do so if in his opinion the request is unreasonable.

(4) At a by-election at which there is only one vacancy, subsections (5) to (9) of section 2 of the 2002 Act are to have effect as though they provided that the party or individual candidate to whom the majority of the votes have been given must be declared to be elected.

Equality of seats

60 (1) Where in the case of the last seat to be allocated, two or more registered parties or individual candidates have an equal number of votes and that number is greater than the number of votes of any other party or candidate, one vote must be added to the votes of each party or individual candidate having such an equal number and the rules in subsections (5) to (9) of section 2 of the 2002 Act must be applied again.

(2) Where, after the application of the procedure set out in paragraph (1), two or more parties or individual candidates still have an equal number of votes and that number is greater than the number of votes of any other party or candidate, the returning officer must forthwith decide between the parties and individual candidates having such an equal number by lot, and allocate the seat to the party or candidate on whom the lot falls.

(3) Where the lot falls on a party, the returning officer must comply with section 2(8) of the 2002 Act.

Disqualification in home Member State

60A (1) This rule applies where a candidate is a relevant citizen of the Union and, after the publication of the statement of parties and individual candidates standing nominated, the returning officer receives, under rule 9A(4), information that the candidate has been deprived of the right to stand as a candidate through a relevant disqualifying decision in the Member State of which the candidate is a national.

(2) Any votes given to the candidate are to be disregarded for the purpose of applying–
    (a) rules 59 and 60, and
    (b) subsections (5) to (9) of section 2 to the 2002 Act (voting system in Great Britain and Gibraltar).

(3) For the purpose of subsections (7) and (8) of section 2 of the 2002 Act, the candidate is to be treated as being omitted from a party's list of candidates.

Part 4
Final Proceedings in Contested and Uncontested Elections

Declaration of result

61 (1) In a contested election, when the result of the allocation and filling of seats has been ascertained, the returning officer must–
    (a) forthwith declare to be elected those candidates on a registered party's list by whom seats are filled and those individual candidates to whom seats are allocated under rules 59, 60 and 60A;
    (b) prepare a statement setting out–
        (i) the total number of valid votes (as notified to him) given to each registered party and individual candidate;
        (ii) the number of votes which such a party or candidate had, after the application of subsections (5) to (9) of section 2 of the 2002 Act, at any stage when a seat was allocated to that party or candidate;
        (iii) the names in full and home address in full of each candidate who fills a seat or to whom a seat has been allocated; and
        (iv) whether, in the case of a party, there are remaining candidates on that party's list who have not been declared to be elected; and
        (v) give public notice of that statement and send a copy to the Secretary of State.

(2) In the case of an uncontested election, the statement of parties and individual candidates nominated, in addition to showing the registered parties, the candidates on the list of those parties and individual candidates standing nominated, must also declare to be elected any candidate so shown; and the returning officer must send a copy of that statement and declaration to the Secretary of State.

(3) The returning officer for the combined region must also send a copy of the statement

in paragraphs (1)(b) and (2) to the Chief Secretary of the Government of Gibraltar.

Return or forfeiture of candidate's deposit

62 (1) The deposit made under rule 10 of these rules must either be returned to the person making it or his personal representatives or be forfeited to Her Majesty.

(2) Except in the cases mentioned in paragraphs (4) and (5), the deposit must be returned not later than the next day after that on which the result of the election is declared.

(3) For the purposes of paragraph (2)–
    (a) a day must be disregarded if it would be disregarded under rule 2(1) in computing any period of time for the purposes of the Timetable in rule 1 for an election of the kind in question; and
    (b) the deposit must be treated as being returned on a day if a cheque for the amount of the deposit is posted on that day.

(4) Where–
    (a) a registered party or an individual candidate is not shown as standing nominated in the statement of parties and individual candidates nominated, or
    (b) in the case of an individual candidate, the candidate has died,
the deposit must be returned as soon as practicable after the publication of that statement or the time when the returning officer is satisfied of the candidate's death, as the case may be.

(5) Subject to paragraph (4), the deposit must be forfeited if a poll is taken and, after the total number of valid votes for each registered party and individual candidate has been ascertained under rule 59(1), the party or candidate is found not to have polled more than one-fortieth of the total number of votes polled by all the parties and candidates.

Part 5
Disposal of Documents

Sealing up of ballot papers

63 (1) On the completion of the counting at a contested election (or, if later, its deemed completion under rule 53(7)) the local returning officer must seal up in separate packets the counted and rejected ballot papers.

(2) The local returning officer must not open the sealed packets of–
    (a) tendered ballot papers;
    (b) the completed corresponding number lists;
    (c) certificates as to employment on duty on the day of the poll; or
    (d) marked copies of the register of electors (including any marked copy notices issued under section 13B(3B) or (3D) of the 1983 Act) and lists of proxies.

Delivery and retention of documents

64 (1) The local returning officer must then forward to the relevant registration officer the following documents–
    (a) the packets of ballot papers in his possession;
    (b) the ballot paper accounts and the statements of rejected ballot papers and of the result of the verification of the ballot paper accounts;
    (c) the tendered votes lists, the lists of voters with disabilities assisted by companions, the lists of votes marked by the presiding officer and the related statements, the lists maintained under rule 47, and the declarations made by the companions of voters with disabilities;

    (d) the packets of the completed corresponding number lists;

    (e) the packets of certificates as to employment on duty on the day of the poll;

    (f) the packets containing marked copies of registers (including any marked copy notices issued under section 13B(3B) or (3D) of the 1983 Act) and of the postal voters list, of the lists of proxies and of the proxy postal voters list,

endorsing on each packet a description of its contents.

(2) In the case of the electoral region of Scotland, paragraph (1) is to apply as if for the words "forward to the relevant registration officer" there were substituted "retain on behalf of the returning officer", and references to documents in the custody or possession of the relevant registration officer shall include documents held by the local returning officer on his behalf.

(3) In the case of an election held in Gibraltar, paragraph (1) is to apply as if for the words "forward to the relevant registration officer" there were substituted "retain on behalf of the local returning officer in his capacity as registration officer for the purposes of European Parliamentary elections", and references to documents in the custody or possession of the relevant registration officer shall include documents held by the local returning officer on his behalf.

Orders for production of documents

65 (1) An order–

    (a) for the inspection or production of any rejected ballot papers in the custody of the relevant registration officer; or

    (b) for the opening of a sealed packet of completed corresponding number lists and certificates as to employment on duty on the day of the poll or for the inspection of any counted ballot papers in his custody,

may be made, if the court is satisfied by evidence on oath that the order is required for the purpose of instituting or maintaining a prosecution for an offence in relation to ballot papers, or for the purpose of a European Parliamentary election petition, by the High Court or a county court, or, in Gibraltar, the Supreme Court.

(2) An order for the opening of a sealed packet of completed corresponding number lists and certificates or for the inspection of any counted ballot papers in the custody of the relevant registration officer may be made by an election court.

(3) Subject to paragraph (4), an order under this rule may be made subject to such conditions as to–

    (a) persons;

    (b) time;

    (c) place and mode of inspection;

    (d) production or opening,

as the court making the order thinks expedient.

(4) In making and carrying into effect an order under paragraph (3) for the opening of a packet of completed corresponding number lists or of certificates or for the inspection of counted ballot papers, care must be taken that the way in which the vote of any particular elector has been given must not be disclosed until it has been proved–

    (a) that his vote was given; and

    (b) that the vote has been declared by a competent court to be invalid.

(5) An appeal lies to the High Court from any order of a county court under this rule, or in Gibraltar, an appeal lies to the Court of Appeal from any order of the Supreme Court under this rule.

(6) Any power given under this rule to the High Court or a county court or, in Gibraltar, the Supreme Court, may be exercised by any judge of the court otherwise than in open

court.

(7) Where an order is made for the production by the relevant registration officer of any document in his possession relating to any specified election–

    (a) the production by him or his agent of the document ordered in such manner as may be directed by that order shall be conclusive evidence that the document relates to the specified election; and

    (b) any endorsement on any packet of ballot papers so produced shall be prima facie evidence that the ballot papers are what they are stated to be by the endorsement.

(8) The production from proper custody of–

    (a) a ballot paper purporting to have been used at any election; and

    (b) a completed corresponding number list with a number marked in writing,

shall be prima facie evidence that the elector whose vote was given by that ballot paper was the person whose entry in the register of electors or on a notice issued under section 13B(3B) or (3D) of the 1983 Act at the time of the election contained the same number as the number written as mentioned in sub-paragraph (b) of this paragraph.

(9) Save as provided by this rule, no person shall be allowed to inspect any rejected or counted ballot papers in the possession of the relevant registration officer or open any sealed packets of completed corresponding number lists and certificates.

Retention of documents by relevant registration officer

66 (1) The relevant registration officer must retain or cause to be retained for one year all documents relating to an election forwarded to him in pursuance of these rules by a local returning officer, and then, unless otherwise directed by an order of the High Court, the Crown Court, a magistrates' court, an election court or, in Gibraltar, the Supreme Court or Court of Appeal, must cause them to be destroyed.

(2) The documents mentioned in paragraph (1) except–

    (a) ballot papers;

    (b) the completed corresponding number lists;

    (c) certificates as to the employment on duty on the day of the poll,

shall be open to public inspection.

(3) In the application of this rule to Scotland, paragraph (1) shall have effect as if for "the High Court, the Crown Court, a magistrates' court, an election court" there were substituted "the Court of Session, an election court".

Part 6
Access to Marked Registers and Other Documents
Open to Public Inspection After an Election

Interpretation and general

67 (1) In this Part–

    "enactment" includes–

    (a) any provision of an Act, including any provision of an Act of the Gibraltar Parliament;

    (b) any provision of, or of any instrument made under, an Act of the Scottish Parliament,

    (c) any provision of, or of any instrument made under, Northern Ireland legislation, and

    (d) any provision of subordinate legislation (within the meaning of the

Interpretation Act 1978);

"the full register" means the version of the register published under section 13(1) or (3) of the 1983 Act or, as the case may be, paragraph 11(1) or (3) of Schedule 1 to the 2004 Act;

"marked register or lists" means any part of the marked copies of the full register, list of proxies, postal voters list and proxy postal voters list forwarded to the relevant registration officer under rule 64;

"processor" means any person who provides a service which consists of putting information into data form or processing information in data form and any reference to a processor includes a reference to his employees; and

"research purposes" includes statistical or historical purposes.

(2) The processor of the register may not disclose the full register or the information contained in it except to the person who supplied the information to the processor or an employee of that person or a person who is entitled to obtain a copy of the full register under the 2001 Regulations, under the 2001 (Scotland) Regulations, or, in Gibraltar, under the 2004 Act, or any employee of such a person.

(3) In paragraph (2), any reference to an employee of any person who has access to a copy of the full register shall be deemed to include a person working or providing services for the purposes of that person or employed by or on behalf of, or working for, any person who is so working or who is supplying such a service.

(4) For the purposes of this Part any period of days shall be calculated in accordance with rule 2(1).

(5) Subject to any direction by the Secretary of State under section 52(1) of the 1983 Act or paragraph 21 of Schedule 4, any duty on a relevant registration officer to supply records or lists or make them available for inspection under this Part imposes only a duty to provide that information in the form in which he holds it.

Supply of marked registers and lists after a European Parliamentary election

68 (1) Any person entitled to be supplied in accordance with–
   (a) regulation 100, 103, 105, 106, 108, 109 or 113 of the 2001 Regulations; or
   (b) regulation 99, 102, 104, 105, 107, 108 or 112 of the 2001 (Scotland) Regulations; or
   (c) paragraph 50, 52, 53, 54, 55, 56 or 57 of Schedule 1 to the 2004 Act,

   with copies of the full register at a particular European Parliamentary election is also a person entitled, subject to this rule and rule 70, to request that a relevant registration officer supply copies of the relevant part (within the meaning of those regulations) of the marked register or lists he is required to keep.

(2) A person whose entitlement to request copies of the marked register or lists under paragraph (1) arises from being in a category of persons to whom–
   (a) regulation 103, 105, 106, or 108 of the 2001 Regulations; or
   (b) regulation 102, 104, 105 or 107 of the 2001 (Scotland) Regulations; or
   (c) paragraph 52, 53, 54 or 56 of Schedule 1 to the 2004 Act,

   applies before a particular European Parliamentary election, shall be entitled to request those documents regardless of whether, after that election, he remains in a category of persons which is entitled under those provisions.

(3) A request under paragraph (1) must be made in writing and must–
   (a) specify which of the marked register or lists (or the relevant part of the register or lists) are requested;
   (b) state whether a printed copy of the records or lists or a copy in data form is requested; and
   (c) state the purposes for which the marked register or lists shall be used and why

the supply or purchase of a copy of the full register or unmarked lists would not be sufficient to achieve those purposes.

(4) The relevant registration officer must supply a copy of the relevant part of the marked register or lists where a request is duly made, and–

    (a) he is satisfied that the requestor needs to see the marks on the marked register or lists in order to achieve the purpose for which it is requested; and

    (b) he has received payment of a fee calculated in accordance with rule 71.

(5) If the relevant registration officer is not satisfied in accordance with paragraph (4)(a) he may treat the request for a marked register or list as a request for–

    (a) information in unmarked lists under paragraph 32 of Schedule 2; or

    (b) the published copy of the full register in accordance with regulation 102 of the 2001 Regulations, or

    (c) the published copy of the full register in accordance with regulation 101 of the 2001 (Scotland) Regulations,

or both (a) and (b) or, as the case may be, (a) and (c), and must provide the requestor with information concerning the availability of the unmarked lists, full register or both as the case may be.

(6) A person who obtains a copy of any part of a marked register or list under this rule and whose entitlement arose under paragraph (1)(a) may use it only for the permitted purposes specified in rule 70(2), and any conditions–

    (a) specified in that rule, or

    (b) which would apply to the use of the full register under whichever of regulations 100, 103, 105, 106, 108, 109 and 113 of the 2001 Regulations entitled that person to obtain that document,

shall apply to such use.

(7) A person who obtains a copy of any part of a marked register or list under this rule and whose entitlement arose under paragraph (1)(b) may only use it for the permitted purposes specified in rule 70(2), and any conditions–

    (a) specified in that rule; or

    (b) which would apply to the use of the full register under whichever of regulations 99, 102, 104, 105,107, 108 and 112 of the 2001 (Scotland) Regulations entitled that person to obtain that document,

shall apply to such use.

(8) A person who obtains a copy of any part of a marked register or list under this rule and whose entitlement arose under paragraph (1)(c) may use it only for the permitted purposes specified in rule 70(2), and any conditions–

    (a) specified in that rule; or

    (b) which would apply to the use of the full register under whichever of paragraphs 50, 52, 53, 54, 55, 56 or 57 of Schedule 1 to the 2004 Act entitled that person to obtain that document,

shall apply to such use.

(9) The conditions referred to in paragraph (6), or as the case may be paragraphs (7) or (8), apply to a person to whom a copy of marked register or list, or any information contained in them (that is not contained in the edited register) has been supplied or disclosed under these rules as they apply to a person to whom those regulations apply.

(10) Any person who has obtained or is entitled to obtain a copy of the marked register or lists under this rule may–

    (a) supply a copy of the marked register or lists to a processor for the purpose of processing the information contained therein,

    (b) procure that a processor processes and supplies to them any copy of the information in the marked register or lists which the processor has obtained under this rule,

for use in respect of the purposes for which that person is entitled to obtain such copy or information (as the case may be).

Inspection of documents open to public inspection

69 (1) Any person is entitled to request that the relevant registration officer make available for inspection a copy of any of the following documents (referred to in this rule and rule 70 as the "documents open to public inspection")–

    (a) the marked register or lists;

    (b) such other documents relating to an election as the relevant registration officer is required by or under any enactment to retain for any period except–

        (i) ballot papers;

        (ii) completed corresponding number lists;

        (iii) certificates as to employment on duty on the day of the election; and

        (v) any list produced under paragraph 67(4) of Schedule 2 (reasons for rejection of postal voting statements).

  (2) A request under paragraph (1) must be made in writing and must specify–

    (a) which documents are requested;

    (b) the purposes for which the information in any document will be used;

    (c) where the request is to inspect the marked register or lists, any reason why inspecting the full register or unmarked lists would not be sufficient to achieve that purpose;

    (d) who will inspect the documents;

    (e) the date on which they wish to inspect the documents; and

    (f) whether they would prefer to inspect the documents in printed or data form.

  (3) Subject to paragraph (4), the relevant registration officer must make the documents open to public inspection available for inspection under supervision not later than 10 days after the date of receipt of a request that has been duly made.

  (4) Where a request has been made to inspect copies of the marked register or lists under paragraph (1) and the relevant registration officer is not satisfied that the purposes of the requestor cannot be met by inspection of the full register, he must inform the requestor–

    (a) of his decision under this paragraph; and

    (b) provide the requestor with information concerning the availability of the published full register for inspection in accordance with regulation 43 of the 2001 Regulations, or in Scotland, regulation 43 of the 2001 (Scotland) Regulations or, in Gibraltar, paragraph 41 of Schedule 1 to the 2004 Act.

  (5) A person who obtains a copy of or information in any document open to public inspection under this rule may use it only for the permitted purposes specified in rule 70, and any conditions–

    (a) specified in that rule;

    (b) specified in paragraph (7); or

    (c) which would apply to the use of the full register under regulation 109 of the 2001 Regulations, or as the case may be, regulation 108 of the 2001 (Scotland) Regulations, or paragraph 57 of Schedule 1 to the 2004 Act, where such a person has obtained a copy of that document under paragraph (8),

shall apply to such use.

  (6) Where inspection takes place by providing the records or lists on a computer screen or otherwise in data form, the relevant registration officer must ensure the manner in, and the equipment on which, that copy is provided do not permit any person consulting that copy to–

      (a)   search it by electronic means by reference to the name of any person; or

      (b)   copy or transmit any part of that copy by electronic or any other means.

(7)   Subject to paragraph (8), a person who inspects a copy of a document open to public inspection, whether in printed copy or in data form, may not–

      (a)   make copies of any part of it; or

      (b)   record any particulars in it,

    except that a person who inspects a copy of the marked register or lists may make hand written notes.

(8)   The relevant registration officer must, on request, supply free of charge copies of any documents open to public inspection to a person who has inspected those documents and who is entitled to be supplied with a copy of the marked register or lists by virtue of being a person to whom regulation 109 of the 2001 Regulations, or, in Scotland, regulation 108 of the 2001 (Scotland) Regulations, or, in Gibraltar, paragraph 57 of Schedule 1 to the 2004 Act, applies.

Conditions on the use, supply and disclosure of documents open to public inspection

70 (1)   Subject to paragraphs (2) and (3) the restrictions on the supply, disclosure and use of information in regulations 94 and 96 of the 2001 Regulations, or, in Scotland, regulations 94 and 95 of the 2001 (Scotland) Regulations, or, in Gibraltar, paragraphs 46 and 47 of Schedule 1 to the 2004 Act, shall apply to the documents open to public inspection as they apply to the full register.

(2)   Where a person–

      (a)   obtains copies of information in the marked register or lists in accordance with rule 68(1); or

      (b)   a person inspects information in accordance with rule 69(1),

    the permitted purposes means either research purposes or electoral purposes.

(3)   Where a copy of any information was supplied in the circumstances to which rule 69(8) applies, the permitted purposes means the purposes set out in regulation 109(4) of the 2001 Regulations, or, in Scotland, regulation 108(4) of the 2001 (Scotland) Regulations, or, in Gibraltar, paragraph 57(2) of Schedule 1 to the 2004 Act.

Fees relating to the marked registers and lists

71 (1)   The fee to be paid in accordance with rule 68(4)(b) by a person making a request for a copy of the whole or of any part of the marked register or lists is set out in paragraph (2).

(2)   The fee shall be the sum of £10, plus for a copy–

      (a)   in printed form, £2 for each 1,000 entries (or remaining part of 1,000 entries) covered by the request; and

      (b)   in data form, £1 for each 1,000 entries (or remaining part of 1,000 entries) covered by the request.

(3)   For the purposes of this rule, a request for a copy of the whole or the same part of the marked register or lists in both a printed and data form may be treated as two separate requests.

Access to marked registers and other election documents: contravention of conditions

72 (1)   A person is guilty of an offence–

      (a)   if he fails to comply with any of the conditions imposed under rule 70; or

      (b)   he is an appropriate supervisor of a person (P) who fails to comply with any such condition and he failed to take appropriate steps.

(2) P is not guilty of an offence under paragraph (1) if–
- (a) he has an appropriate supervisor, and
- (b) he has complied with the requirements imposed on him by his appropriate supervisor.

(3) A person who is not P or an appropriate supervisor is not guilty of an offence under paragraph (1) if he takes all reasonable steps to ensure that he complies with the conditions.

(4) In paragraphs (1)(b) and (2)–
- (a) an appropriate supervisor is a person who is a director of a company concerned in the management of an organisation in which P is employed or under whose direction or control P is;
- (b) appropriate steps are such steps as it was reasonable for the appropriate supervisor to take to secure the operation of procedures designed to prevent, so far as reasonably practicable, the occurrence of failure to comply with the conditions.

(5) A person guilty of an offence as mentioned in paragraph (1) is liable on summary conviction to a fine not exceeding level 5 on the standard scale.

Part 7
Appendix of Forms

Not reproduced

SCHEDULE 2
ABSENT VOTING

Part 1
Entitlement

Interpretation

1 (1) In this Schedule–
"absent voter" means an elector who is entitled to vote by proxy or an elector or proxy who is entitled to vote by post, ;
"allotted polling station" has the meaning set out in paragraph 23(8);
"valid postal voting statement" means a postal voting statement which, in accordance with paragraph 62 or 63, the local returning officer is satisfied has been duly completed.

(2) A reference in this Schedule to a form identified by means of a letter is to be construed as a reference to the form so identified in the Appendix to this Schedule.

(3) Unless otherwise stated, a reference in this Schedule to a numbered paragraph or Part is to a paragraph or Part bearing that number in this Schedule.

Manner of voting at European Parliamentary elections

2 (1) This paragraph applies to determine the manner of voting of a person entitled to vote as an elector at a European Parliamentary election.

(2) He may vote in person at his allotted polling station, unless he is entitled as an elector to an absent vote at the election.

(3) He may vote by post if he is entitled as an elector to vote by post at the election.

(4) If he is entitled to vote by proxy at the election, he may so vote unless, before a ballot paper has been issued for him to vote by proxy, he applies at the polling station allotted to him under European Parliamentary elections rules for a ballot paper for the purpose of voting in person, in which case he may vote in person there.

(5) If–
    (a) he is not entitled as an elector to an absent vote at the election, but
    (b) he cannot reasonably be expected to go in person to the allotted polling station by reason of the particular circumstances of his employment, either as a constable or by the local returning officer, on the date of the poll for a purpose connected with the election,
  he may vote in person at any polling station in the local counting area.

(5A) In the application of sub-paragraph (5) to an election in England or Wales, a reference to a constable includes a person designated as a community support officer under section 38 of the Police Reform Act 2002 (police powers for civilian staff).

(6) Nothing in the preceding provisions of this paragraph applies to a person to whom section 7 of the 1983 Act (residence: patients in mental hospitals who are not detained offenders or on remand) or, in Gibraltar, paragraph 10 of Schedule 4 to these Regulations applies and who is liable, by virtue of any enactment, to be detained in the mental hospital in question, whether he is registered by virtue of that provision or not; and such a person may vote–
    (a) in person (where he is granted permission to be absent from the hospital and voting in person does not breach any condition attached to that permission), or
    (b) by post or by proxy (where he is entitled as an elector to vote by post or, as the case may be, by proxy at the election).

(7) Nothing in the preceding provisions of this paragraph applies to a person to whom section 7A of the 1983 Act (residence: persons remanded in custody etc) or in Gibraltar, paragraph 11 of Schedule 4 to these Regulations applies, whether he is registered by virtue of that provision or not; and such a person may only vote by post or by proxy (where he is entitled as an elector to vote by post or, as the case may be, by proxy at the election).

(8) Sub-paragraph (2) does not prevent a person, at his allotted polling station, marking a tendered ballot paper in pursuance of rule 44(4) or (6) of the European Parliamentary elections rules.

(9) For the purposes of the provisions of–
    (a) these Regulations, and
    (b) the 1983 Act, the 2002 Act and the 2003 Act,
  a person entitled to vote as an elector at a European Parliamentary election is entitled as an elector to vote by post or entitled to vote by proxy at the election if sub-paragraph (10) or (11) (as the case may be) applies to him in relation to that election; and references in those provisions to entitlement as an elector to an absent vote at a European Parliamentary election are references to entitlement as an elector to vote by post or entitlement to vote by proxy at the election.

(10) This sub-paragraph applies to a person who is shown in the postal voters list mentioned in paragraph 5(2) as entitled to vote by post at an election.

(11) This sub-paragraph applies to a person who is shown in the list of proxies mentioned in paragraph 5(3) as entitled to vote by proxy at an election.

Absent vote at elections for definite or indefinite period

3 (1) Where a person applies to the registration officer to vote by post at European Parliamentary elections (whether for an indefinite period or for a particular period specified in his application), the registration officer must grant the application if–

    (a) he is satisfied that the applicant is or will be registered in the register of electors; and

    (b) the application contains the applicant's signature and date of birth and meets the requirements of Part 2.

(2) Where a person applies to the registration officer to vote by proxy at European Parliamentary elections (whether for an indefinite period or for a particular period specified in his application), the registration officer must grant the application if–

    (a) he is satisfied that the applicant is eligible to vote by proxy at elections to which the application relates;

    (b) he is satisfied that the applicant is or will be registered in the register of electors; and

    (c) the application contains the applicant's signature and date of birth and meets the requirements of Part 2.

(3) For the purposes of this paragraph a person is eligible to vote by proxy at European Parliamentary elections if–

    (a) he is or will be registered as a service voter;

    (b) he has an anonymous entry in the register of electors for the election;

    (c) he cannot reasonably be expected–

        (i) to go in person to the polling station allotted or likely to be allotted to him under the European Parliamentary elections rules, or

        (ii) to vote unaided there,

  by reason of blindness or other disability;

    (d) he cannot reasonably be expected to go in person to that polling station by reason of the general nature of his occupation, service or employment or that of his spouse or civil partner, or by reason of his attendance on a course provided by an educational institution or that of his spouse or civil partner; or

    (e) he cannot go in person from his qualifying address to that polling station without making a journey by air or sea,

and a person is also eligible to vote by proxy at European Parliamentary elections if he is or will be registered in pursuance of an overseas elector's declaration or a European Parliamentary overseas elector's declaration.

(4) The registration officer must keep a record of those whose applications under this paragraph have been granted showing–

    (a) whether their applications were to vote by post or proxy for an indefinite or a particular period (specifying that period);

    (b) in the case of those who may vote by post, the addresses provided by them in their applications as the addresses to which their ballot papers are to be sent; and

    (c) in the case of those who may vote by proxy, the names and addresses of those appointed as their proxies.

(5) The registration officer must remove a person from the record–

    (a) if he applies to the registration officer to be removed;

    (b) in the case of a person who is eligible to vote by proxy by virtue of having an anonymous entry, if he ceases to have an anonymous entry;

    (c) in the case of any registered person, if he ceases to be registered or registered at the same qualifying address or ceases to be, or becomes, registered in pursuance of–

        (i) a service declaration,

(ii)   a declaration of local connection, or

(iii) an overseas elector's declaration,

(d) in the case of any person shown in the record as voting by proxy, if the registration officer gives notice that he has reason to believe there has been a material change of circumstances; or

(e) in the case of a person who applied to vote by post or proxy for a particular period, once that period has expired.

(6) A person shown in the record as voting by post may subsequently alter his choice by applying to the registration officer to vote by proxy instead (whether for an indefinite period or for a particular period specified in his application); and, if the registration officer would be required to grant that application if it were one made under sub-paragraph (2), the registration officer must amend the record accordingly.

(7) A person shown in the record as voting by proxy may subsequently alter his choice by applying to the registration officer to vote by post instead (whether for an indefinite period or for a particular period specified in his application); and, if the application meets the requirements of Part 2, the registration officer must amend the record accordingly.

(8) The registration officer may dispense with the requirement under sub-paragraph (1)(b) or sub-paragraph (2)(c) for the applicant to provide a signature if he is satisfied that the applicant is unable–

(a)   to provide a signature because of any disability the applicant has;

(b)   to provide a signature because the applicant is unable to read or write; or

(c)   to sign in a consistent and distinctive way because of any such disability or inability.

(9) The registration officer must also keep a record in relation to those whose applications under this paragraph have been granted showing–

(a)   their dates of birth;

(b)   except in cases where the registration officer in pursuance of sub-paragraph (8) has dispensed with the requirement to provide a signature, their signatures.

(10) The record kept under sub-paragraph (9) must be retained by the registration officer for the period calculated by reference to paragraph 18(1).

Absent vote at a particular election

4 (1) Where a person applies to the registration officer to vote by post at a particular European Parliamentary election, the registration officer must grant the application if–

(a)   he is satisfied that the applicant is or will be registered in the register of electors; and

(b)   the application contains the applicant's signature and date of birth and meets the requirements of Part 2.

(2) Where a person applies to the registration officer to vote by proxy at a particular European Parliamentary election, the registration officer must grant the application if–

(a)   he is satisfied that the applicant's circumstances on the date of the poll will be or are likely to be such that he cannot reasonably be expected to vote in person at the polling station allotted or likely to be allotted to him under the European Parliamentary elections rules;

(b)   he is satisfied that the applicant is or will be registered in the register of electors; and

(c)   the application contains the applicant's signature and date of birth and meets the requirements of Part 2.

(3) Where a person who has an anonymous entry in the register of electors applies to the

registration officer to vote by proxy at a particular election the registration officer must grant the application if it meets the requirements of Part 2.

(4)   Nothing in sub-paragraph (1) or (2) applies to a person who is included in the record by virtue of paragraph 3, but such a person may, in respect of a particular European Parliamentary election, apply to the registration officer–

    (a)   for his ballot paper to be sent to a different address from that shown in the record; or

    (b)   to vote by proxy;

if he is shown in the record as voting by post at elections of the kind in question.

(5)   The registration officer must grant an application under sub-paragraph (4) if–

    (a)   (in the case of any application) it meets the requirements of Part 2; and

    (b)   (in the case of an application to vote by proxy) the registration officer is satisfied that the applicant's circumstances on the date of the poll will be or are likely to be such that he cannot reasonably be expected to vote in person at the polling station allotted or likely to be allotted to him under the European Parliamentary elections rules.

(6)   The registration officer may dispense with the requirement under sub-paragraph (1)(b) or (2)(c) for the applicant to provide a signature if he is satisfied that the applicant is unable–

    (a)   to provide a signature because of any disability the applicant has;

    (b)   to provide a signature because the applicant is unable to read or write; or

    (c)   to sign in a consistent and distinctive way because of any such disability or inability.

(7)   The registration officer must also keep a record in relation to those whose applications under this paragraph have been granted showing–

    (a)   their dates of birth;

    (b)   except in cases where the registration officer in pursuance of sub-paragraph (6) has dispensed with the requirement to provide a signature, their signatures.

(8)   The record kept under sub-paragraph (7) must be retained by the registration officer for the period required by paragraph 18(1).

Absent voters list

5   (1)   The registration officer must, in respect of each European Parliamentary election, keep two special lists mentioned in sub-paragraphs (2) and (3) respectively.

(2)   The first of those lists is a list ("the postal voters list") of–

    (a)   those whose applications under paragraph 4(1) to vote by post at the election have been granted, together with the addresses provided by them in their applications as the addresses to which their ballot papers are to be sent; and

    (b)   those who are for the time being shown in the record kept under paragraph 3 as voting by post at European Parliamentary elections (excluding those so shown whose applications under paragraph 4(4)(b) to vote by proxy at the election have been granted), together with the addresses provided by them in their applications under paragraph 3 or, as the case may be, paragraph 4(4)(a) as the addresses to which their ballot papers are to be sent.

(3)   The second of the lists mentioned in sub-paragraph (1) is a list ("the list of proxies") of–

    (a)   those whose applications under paragraph 4(2) or 4(4) to vote by proxy at the election have been granted; and

    (b)   those who are for the time being shown in the record kept under paragraph 3 as voting by proxy at elections of the kind in question,

together with (in each case) the names and addresses of those appointed as their proxies.

(4) In the case of a person who has an anonymous entry in a register the postal voters list or list of proxies (as the case may be) must show in relation to the person only–

    (a) his electoral number, and

    (b) the period for which the anonymous entry has effect.

(5) The registration officer must, forthwith on completion of the compilation of those special lists, or at any time at the request of the local returning officer, supply to the local returning officer for any local counting area within the area for which he acts so much of those lists as relate to that counting area.

Proxies at elections

6 (1) Subject to the provisions of this paragraph, any person is capable of being appointed proxy to vote for an elector at any European Parliamentary election and may vote in pursuance of the appointment.

(2) The elector cannot have more than one person at a time appointed as proxy to vote for him at European Parliamentary elections (whether in the same electoral region or elsewhere).

(2A) A person is not capable of being appointed to vote, or voting, as proxy in Great Britain at a European Parliamentary election unless the person is entitled to vote at that election in accordance with section 8 of the 2002 Act.

(3) A person is not capable of being appointed to vote, or voting, as proxy in Gibraltar at a European Parliamentary election–

    (a) if he is subject to any legal incapacity (age apart) to vote at that election as an elector; or

    (b) he is neither a Commonwealth citizen nor a citizen of the Union.

(4) A person is not capable of voting as proxy in Gibraltar at a European Parliamentary election unless on the date of the poll he has attained the age of 18.

(5) A person is not entitled to vote as proxy at the same European Parliamentary election in any electoral region, on behalf of more than two electors of whom that person is not the spouse, civil partner, parent, grandparent, brother, sister, child or grandchild.

(6) Where the elector applies to the registration officer for the appointment of a proxy to vote for him at European Parliamentary elections, the registration officer must make the appointment if the application meets the requirements of Part 2 and he is satisfied that the elector is or will be–

    (a) registered in the register of electors; and

    (b) shown in the record kept under paragraph 3 as voting by proxy at such elections,

and that the proxy is capable of being, and willing to be, appointed at such elections.

(7) Where the elector applies to the registration officer for the appointment of a proxy to vote for him at a particular European Parliamentary election, the registration officer must make the appointment if the application meets the requirements of Part 2 and he is satisfied that the elector is or will be registered in the register of electors and entitled to vote by proxy at that election by virtue of an application under paragraph 4(2) or 4(4) and that the proxy is capable of being, and willing to be, appointed.

(8) The appointment of a proxy under this paragraph is to be made by means of a proxy paper in Form N in the Appendix issued by the registration officer.

(9) The appointment may be cancelled by the elector by giving notice to the registration officer and shall also cease to be in force–

    (a) where the appointment related to a particular European Parliamentary election or elections, on the issue of a proxy paper appointing a different person to vote for him at a European Parliamentary election or elections (whether in the same electoral region or elsewhere); or

(b) where the appointment was for a particular period, once that period expires.

(10) Subject to sub-paragraph (9), the appointment remains in force–

(a) in the case of an appointment for a particular election, for that election; and

(b) in any other case, while the elector is shown as voting by proxy in the record kept under paragraph 3 in pursuance of the same application under that paragraph.

Voting as proxy

7 (1) A person entitled to vote as proxy at a European Parliamentary election may do so in person at his allotted polling station unless he is entitled to vote by post as proxy for the elector at the election, in which case he may vote by post.

(2) Where a person is entitled to vote by post as proxy for the elector at any election, the elector may not apply for a ballot paper for the purpose of voting in person at the election.

(3) For the purposes of these Regulations, the 1983 Act, the 2002 Act and the 2003 Act, a person entitled to vote as proxy for another at a European Parliamentary election is entitled so to vote by post if he is included in the list kept under sub-paragraph (8) in respect of the election.

(4) Where a person applies to the registration officer to vote by post–

(a) as proxy at European Parliamentary elections (whether for an indefinite period or for a particular period specified in his application); or

(b) as proxy at a particular European Parliamentary election,

the registration officer must grant the application if the conditions set out in sub-paragraph (5) are satisfied.

(5) Those conditions are–

(a) that the registration officer is satisfied that the elector is or will be registered in the register of electors;

(b) that there is in force an appointment of the applicant as the elector's proxy to vote for him at European Parliamentary elections, or, as the case may be, the election concerned; and

(c) that the application contains the applicant's signature and date of birth and meets the requirements of Part 2.

(6) The registration officer must keep a record of those whose applications under sub-paragraph (4)(a) have been granted showing–

(a) whether their applications were to vote by post or by proxy for an indefinite or particular period (specifying that period); and

(b) the addresses provided by them in their applications as the addresses to which their ballot papers are to be sent.

(7) Where, in the case of a particular European Parliamentary election, a person included in the record kept under sub-paragraph (6) applies to the registration officer for his ballot paper to be sent to a different address from that shown in the record, the registration officer must grant the application if it meets the requirements of Part 2.

(8) The registration officer must, in respect of each European Parliamentary election, keep a special list ("the proxy postal voters list") of–

(a) those who are for the time being included in the record kept under sub-paragraph (6), together with the addresses provided by them in their applications under sub-paragraph (4)(a) or, as the case may be, sub-paragraph (7) as the addresses to which their ballot papers are to be sent; and

(b) those whose applications under sub-paragraph (4)(b) have been granted in respect of the election concerned, together with the addresses provided by them in their applications as the addresses to which their ballot papers are to be sent,

and, forthwith on completion of the compilation of that list, supply to the local returning officer for any local counting area wholly or partly within the area for which he acts so much of that list as relates to any such area.

(9) In the case of a person who has an anonymous entry in a register, the list mentioned in sub-paragraph (8) must contain only–
   (a) the person's electoral number, and
   (b) the period for which the anonymous entry has effect.

(10) The registration officer must remove a person from the record kept under sub-paragraph (6)–
   (a) if he applies to the registration officer to be removed;
   (b) if the elector ceases to be registered in the register of electors;
   (c) if the appointment of the person concerned as the elector's proxy ceases to be in force (whether or not he is re-appointed); or
   (d) in the case of a person who applied to vote by post as proxy for a particular period, once that period expires.

(11) Sub-paragraph (2) does not prevent a person, at the polling station allotted to him, marking a tendered ballot paper in pursuance of rule 44(4) or (6) of the European Parliamentary elections rules.

(12) The registration officer may dispense with the requirement under sub-paragraph (5)(c) for the applicant to provide a signature if he is satisfied that the applicant is unable–
   (a) to provide a signature because of any disability the applicant has;
   (b) to provide a signature because the applicant is unable to read or write; or
   (c) to sign in a consistent and distinctive way because of any such disability or inability.

(13) The registration officer must also keep a record in relation to those whose applications under sub-paragraph (4)(a) or (b) have been granted showing–
   (a) their dates of birth;
   (b) except in cases where the registration officer in pursuance of sub-paragraph (12) has dispensed with the requirement to provide a signature, their signatures.

(14) The record kept under sub-paragraph (13) must be retained by the registration officer for the period calculated by reference to paragraph 18(1).

Provision of fresh signatures

8 (1) A person who remains on the record kept under paragraph 3(4) or 7(6) may, at any time, provide the registration officer with a fresh signature.

(2) Anything required or authorised to be done for the purposes of any enactment in relation to a signature required to be provided in pursuance of this Schedule must be done in relation to a signature provided as mentioned in sub-paragraph (1) instead of in relation to a signature provided on any earlier occasion.

Use of personal identifier information

9 (1) The registration officer must either–
   (a) provide the local returning officer for an election with a copy of the information contained in records kept by the registration officer in pursuance of paragraph 3(9), 4(7) and 7(13) in relation to electors at the election; or
   (b) give the local returning officer access to such information.

(2) Information contained in records kept by a registration officer in pursuance of paragraphs 3(9), 4(7) and 7(13) may be disclosed by him to–

    (a) any other registration officer if he thinks that to do so will assist the other registration officer in the performance of his duties; and

    (b) any person exercising functions in relation to the preparation or conduct of legal proceedings under these Regulations.

Offences

10 A person who–

    (a) in any declaration or form used for any of the purposes of this Schedule, makes a statement which he knows to be false; or

    (b) attests an application under paragraph 3 or 4 when he knows that he is not authorised to do so or that it contains a statement which is false,

is guilty of an offence and liable on summary conviction to a fine not exceeding level 5 on the standard scale.

Offences relating to applications for postal or proxy votes

11 (1) A person commits an offence if he–

    (a) engages in an act specified in sub-paragraph (2) at a European Parliamentary election; and

    (b) intends, by doing so, to deprive another of an opportunity to vote or to make for himself or another a gain of a vote to which he or the other is not otherwise entitled or a gain of money or property.

(2) These are the acts–

    (a) applying for a postal or proxy vote as some other person (whether that other person is living or dead or is a fictitious person);

    (b) otherwise making a false statement in, or in connection with, an application for a postal or proxy vote;

    (c) inducing the registration officer or local returning officer to send a postal ballot paper or any communication relating to a postal or proxy vote to an address which has not been agreed to by the person entitled to the vote;

    (d) causing a communication relating to a postal or proxy vote or containing a postal ballot paper not to be delivered to the intended recipient.

(3) In sub-paragraph (1)(b) property includes any description of property.

(4) In sub-paragraph (2) a reference to a postal vote or a postal ballot paper includes a reference to a proxy postal vote or a proxy postal ballot paper (as the case may be).

(5) A person who commits an offence under sub-paragraph (1) or who aids, abets, counsels or procures the commission of such an offence is guilty of a corrupt practice.

Part 2
Applications

Forms

12 (1) The registration officer must supply free of charge as many forms for use in connection with applications made under this Part, Part 3 and Part 4 as appear to that officer reasonable in the circumstances to any person who satisfies that officer of his intention to use the forms in connection with an election.

(2) The forms set out in the Appendix to this Schedule or forms substantially to the like

effect may be used with such variations as the circumstances may require.

Communication of applications, notices etc

13 The requirement in this Part, Part 3 and Part 4 that any application, notice, representation or objection should be in writing is satisfied where (apart from the usual meaning of that expression) the text of it–

   (a) is transmitted by electronic means;
   (b) is received in legible form; and
   (c) is capable of being used for subsequent reference.

Electronic signatures and related certificates

14 (1) A requirement in this Part, Part 3 and Part 4 for an application, notice, representation or objection to be signed is satisfied (as an alternative to the signature given by hand) where there is–

   (a) an electronic signature incorporated into or otherwise logically associated with a particular electronic communication; and
   (b) the certification by any person of such a signature.

(2) For the purposes of this paragraph an electronic signature is so much of anything in electronic form as–

   (a) is incorporated into or otherwise logically associated with any electronic communication or both; and
   (b) purports to be so incorporated or associated for the purpose of being used in establishing the authenticity of the communication, the integrity of the communication or both.

(3) For the purposes of this paragraph an electronic signature incorporated into or associated with a particular electronic communication is certified by any person if that person (whether before or after the making of the communication) has made a statement confirming that–

   (a) the signature;
   (b) a means of producing, communicating or verifying the signature; or
   (c) a procedure applied to the signature,

   is (either alone or in combination with other factors) a valid means of establishing the authenticity of the communication, the integrity of the communication or both.

(4) This paragraph does not apply to the provision of signatures under paragraphs 17(4), 31(1)(a) and 36(2) which must be given by hand.

Time

15 (1) Where the day or last day of the time allowed by this Part, Part 3 and Part 4 for the doing of any thing falls on any of the days mentioned in sub-paragraph (3), that time must be extended until the next following day which is not one of those days.

(2) Subject to paragraph 26(7), in computing any period of not more than 7 days for the purposes of this Part, Part 3 and Part 4 any of the days mentioned in sub-paragraph (3) must be disregarded.

(3) The days referred to in sub-paragraphs (1) and (2) are a Saturday, Sunday, Christmas Eve, Christmas Day, Good Friday or a bank holiday.

(4) In sub-paragraph (3) "bank holiday" means–

   (a) as respects the combined region, a day which is a bank holiday under the Banking and Financial Dealings Act 1971 in England and Wales and a bank or public holiday in Gibraltar not otherwise falling within sub-paragraph (3);

(b) as respects an electoral region other than Scotland or the combined region, a day which is a bank holiday under the Banking and Financial Dealings Act 1971 in England and Wales; and

(c) as respects Scotland, a day which is a bank holiday under the Banking and Financial Dealings Act 1971 in Scotland.

Interference with notices etc

16 Any person who without lawful authority destroys, mutilates, defaces or removes any notice published by the registration officer in connection with his registration duties or any copies of a document which have been made available for inspection in pursuance of those duties, is liable on summary conviction to a fine not exceeding level 3 on the standard scale.

General requirements for applications for an absent vote

17 (1) An application under this Part must comply with the requirements of this paragraph and such further requirements in this Part as are relevant to the application.

(2) The application must state–

(a) the full name of the applicant;

(b) the address in respect of which the applicant is registered or has applied to be (or is treated as having applied to be) registered in the register except in the case of an application under paragraph 7(4) or (7);

(c) in the case of such an application, the proxy's address, together with the name of the elector for whom he will act as proxy and the elector's address for the purposes of sub-paragraph (2)(b);

(d) in the case of a person applying to vote by post, the address to which the ballot paper should be sent;

(e) in the case of an application to vote by proxy, the grounds on which the elector claims to be entitled to an absent vote;

(f) in the case of a person who is unable to provide a signature, the reasons for his request for waiver of any requirement under paragraph 3, 4 or 7 to provide a signature and the name and address of any person who has assisted him to complete his application; and

(g) where the applicant has, or has applied for, an anonymous entry, that fact.

(3) The application must be made in writing and must be dated.

(4) Where an application is required to contain a signature and date of birth, the information must be set out in a manner that is sufficiently clear and unambiguous as to be capable of electronic scanning into his record by configuring the information as follows–

(a) the signature must appear against a background of white unlined paper of at least five centimetres long and two centimetres high; and

(b) the applicant's date of birth must be set out numerically configured in the sequence of date, month and year, namely ddmmyyyy.

(5) Where the application contains a request that the registration officer waive the requirement for a signature, sub-paragraph (4)(a) does not apply.

(6) An application under this Schedule which is made for an indefinite period or the period specified in the application must state–

(a) that it is so made; and

(b) that it is made for European Parliamentary elections.

(7) An application under this Schedule which is made for a particular European Parliamentary election must–

      (a) state that it is so made; and

      (b) identify the election in question.

(8) Where an application is made to vote by proxy, it must include an application for the appointment of a proxy which meets the requirements of paragraph 22.

(9) An application under this Part may be combined with an application for an absent vote made under the 2001 Regulations, including those Regulations as applied by regulations under sections 9HE and 105, 9MG and 105 or 44 and 105 of the Local Government Act 2000, or the 2001 (Scotland) Regulations.

The personal identifiers record

18 (1) The registration officer must maintain a record ("the personal identifiers record"), apart from the other records and lists which he is required to keep under this Schedule, of the signatures and dates of birth provided by persons whose applications under paragraph 3(1) or (2), paragraph 4(1) or (2) or paragraph 7(4)(a) or (b) were granted, until the expiry of 12 months from–

      (a) the date on which a person is removed from the record kept pursuant to paragraph 3(4) or 7(6); or

      (b) the date of the poll for the purposes of which the person's application for an absent vote was granted under paragraph 4(1) or (2) or 7(4)(b).

(2) The personal identifiers record must contain the following information in respect of each absent voter on the postal voters list, list of proxies or proxy postal voters list–

      (a) his name;

      (b) his date of birth; and

      (c) his signature, or a record of the waiver by the registration officer of the requirement for a signature.

(3) The registration officer may allow the disclosure of information held in the personal identifiers record to–

      (a) any candidate or agent attending proceedings on receipt of postal ballot papers, in accordance with and for the purposes of paragraphs 62 and 63;

      (b) any person attending proceedings on receipt of postal ballot papers, who is entitled to do so by virtue of any of sections 6A to 6D of the 2000 Act, but only to the extent required to permit them to observe the proceedings.

Additional provision concerning the requirement that an application for an absent vote must be signed by the applicant

19 The registration officer may satisfy himself–

      (a) that an application under this Schedule meets any requirements that it has been signed by the applicant and states his date of birth by referring to any signature and date of birth–

          (i) previously provided by the applicant to the registration officer or the returning officer; or

          (ii) previously provided by the applicant to the council that appointed the registration officer or to a registrar of births and deaths, which the registration officer is authorised to inspect by virtue of regulation 35 of the 2001 Regulations or regulation 35 of the 2001 (Scotland) Regulations or paragraph 8(4) of Schedule 1 to the 2004 Act for the purposes of his registration duties; and

      (b) as to whether the applicant is unable to provide a signature or a consistent signature due to any disability or inability to read or write.

Additional requirement for applications for ballot papers to be sent to different address from that stated in application

20 (1) Sub-paragraph (2) applies where–

    (a) in the case of an application to vote by post under paragraph 3(1) or (7) or 4(1), the addresses stated in accordance with paragraph 17(2)(b) and (d) are different;

    (b) in the case of an application by a proxy to vote by post under paragraph 7(4), the proxy's address stated in accordance with paragraph 17(2)(c) and the address stated in accordance with paragraph 17(2)(d) are different.

  (2) The application must set out why the applicant's circumstances will be or are likely to be such that he requires the ballot paper to be sent to the address stated in accordance with paragraph 17(2)(d).

  (3) This paragraph does not apply where an applicant has, or has applied for, an anonymous entry.

Additional requirements for applications for ballot papers to be sent to different address from that shown in the record kept under paragraph 3(4) or 7(6)

21 (1) An application under–

    (a) paragraph 4(4)(a) by a person shown as voting by post in the record kept under paragraph 3(4); or

    (b) paragraph 7(7) by a person shown as voting by post in the record kept under paragraph 7(6),

for his ballot paper to be sent to a different address from that shown in the records must set out why the applicant's circumstances will be or are likely to be such that he requires his ballot paper to be sent to that address.

  (2) This paragraph does not apply where an applicant has, or has applied for, an anonymous entry.

Additional requirements for applications for the appointment of a proxy

  22 An application for the appointment of a proxy under paragraph 3 or 4 must state the full name and address of the person whom the applicant wishes to appoint as his proxy, together with his family relationship, if any, with the applicant, and–

    (a) if it is signed only by the applicant, must contain a statement by him that he has consulted the person so named and that that person is capable of being and willing to be appointed to vote as his proxy; or

    (b) if it is also signed by the person to be appointed, must contain a statement by that person that he is capable of being and willing to be appointed to vote as the applicant's proxy.

Additional requirements for applications for a proxy vote for a definite or indefinite period on grounds of blindness or other disability

23 (1) An application to vote by proxy for a particular or indefinite period under paragraph 3(3)(c) must specify the disability by reason of which it is made.

  (2) Subject to sub-paragraphs (3) and (6), such an application must be attested and signed by–

    (a) a registered medical practitioner;

    (b) a registered nurse;

    (c) a registered dentist as defined by section 53(1) of the Dentists Act 1984;

    (d) a registered dispensing optician or a registered optometrist within the meaning of section 36(1) of the Opticians Act 1989;

    (e) a registered pharmacist within the meaning of article 3(1) of the Pharmacists and Pharmacy Technicians Order 2007;

    (f) a registered osteopath as defined by section 41 of the Osteopaths Act 1993;

    (g) a registered chiropractor as defined by section 43 of the Chiropractors Act 1994;

    (h) a Christian Science practitioner;

    (i) a person for the time being listed in the British Psychological Society's Register of Chartered Psychologists;

    (j) a person who is registered as a member of a relevant profession for the purposes of the Health and Social Work Professions Order 2001;

    (k) the person registered–

        (i) in England and Wales, as carrying on a care home registered under Part 2 of the Care Standards Act 2000, or

        (ii) in Scotland, as managing a care home service registered under Part 5 of the Public Services Reform (Scotland) Act 2010;

where the applicant states that he is resident in such a home;

    (l) the warden of premises forming one of a group of premises provided for persons of pensionable age or disabled persons for which there is a resident warden, where the applicant states that he resides in such premises;

    (m) a manager–

        (i) in England and Wales, within the meaning of section 145(1) of the Mental Health Act 1983, or

        (ii) in Scotland, within the meaning of section 329 of the Mental Health (Care and Treatment) (Scotland) Act 2003 responsible for the administration of a hospital within the meaning of that section,

or a person authorised to act on behalf of such a manager for these purposes;

    (n) a person registered in the register of social workers maintained–

        (i) in Wales, in accordance with section 56 of the Care Standards Act 2000, or

        (ii) in Scotland, in accordance with section 44 of the Regulation of Care (Scotland) Act 2001,

    (o) in Gibraltar, in the case of an applicant who is resident in a residential home for persons of pensionable age or for physically disabled persons, a senior nursing officer of the home; and

    (p) in Gibraltar, any person registered under the provisions of the Medical and Health Act 1997.

(3) A person who qualifies–

    (a) by virtue of any of sub-paragraphs (2)(a) to (j) may not attest an application for these purposes unless–

        (i) he is treating the applicant for the disability specified in the application; or

        (ii) the applicant is receiving care from him in respect of that disability; or

        (iii) the person is a social worker who qualifies by virtue of sub-paragraph (2)(j), and has arranged care or assistance for the applicant in respect of that disability; or

    (b) by virtue of sub-paragraph (2)(n) may not attest an application for these purposes unless–

        (i) he is treating the applicant for the disability specified in the application;

        (ii) the applicant is receiving care from him in respect of that disability; or

        (iii) he has arranged care or assistance for the applicant in respect of that disability.

(4) The person attesting the application must state–

    (a) his name and address and the qualification by virtue of which he attests the application;

    (b) where the person who attests the application is a person referred to in sub-paragraph (3)(a), that–

         (i)   he is treating the applicant for the disability specified in the application; or

         (ii) the applicant is receiving care from him in respect of that disability;

    (c) where the person who attests the application is a person referred to in sub-paragraph (3)(b), that–

         (i)   he is treating the applicant for the disability specified in the application;

         (ii) the applicant is receiving care from him in respect of that disability; or

         (iii) he has arranged care or assistance for the applicant in respect of that disability;

    (d) that, to the best of his knowledge and belief, the applicant has the disability specified in the application and that he cannot reasonably be expected to go in person to his allotted polling station or to vote unaided there by reason of that disability; and

    (e) that, to the best of his knowledge and belief, the disability specified in the application is likely to continue either indefinitely or for a period specified by the person attesting the application.

(5) A manager (or person authorised to act on behalf of such a manager) attesting an application by virtue of sub-paragraph (2)(m) must, instead of the matters specified in sub-paragraph (4)(a), state in the attestation–

    (a) the name of the person attesting the application;

    (b) that the person is authorised to attest the application;

    (c) the position of the person in the hospital at which the applicant is liable to be detained or at which he is receiving treatment;

    (d) the statutory provision under which the applicant is detained, or liable to be detained, at the hospital, where applicable.

(6) Sub-paragraphs (2), (4) and (5) do not apply where–

    (a) in Wales, the application is based on the applicant's blindness and the applicant is registered as a blind person by the local authority which is specified in the application and which has made arrangements for the applicant under section 29(1) of the National Assistance Act 1948;

    (aa) in England, the application is based on the applicant's severe sight-impairment and the applicant is registered, under section 77(1) of the Care Act 2014 (registers of sight-impaired adults), as a severely sight-impaired person by the local authority which is specified in the application;

    (b) in Gibraltar, the application is based on the applicant's blindness and the applicant is registered as a blind person by the Gibraltar Health Authority;

    (c) in Scotland, the application is based on the applicant's blindness and the applicant is registered as a blind person by a local authority which is specified in the application;

    (d) the application states that the applicant is in receipt of the higher rate of the mobility component of a disability living allowance (payable under section 73 of the Social Security Contributions and Benefits Act 1992) because of the disability specified in the application;

    (e) the application states that the applicant is in receipt of the enhanced rate of the mobility component of personal independence payment (payable under section 79(2) of the Welfare Reform Act 2012) because of the disability specified in the application; or

    (f) the application states that the applicant is in receipt of armed forces independence payment under the Armed Forces and Reserve Forces (Compensation Scheme) Order 2011 because of the disability specified in the application.

(7) The fact that an applicant is registered with a local authority, or the Gibraltar Health Authority, as mentioned in sub-paragraph (6) shall be deemed sufficient evidence that

he is eligible to vote by proxy on the grounds set out in paragraph 3(3)(c).

(8) In this paragraph and in paragraphs 24 and 25 "allotted polling station", in relation to an elector, means the polling station to which the elector is allotted or likely to be allotted under rule 29(1) of the European Parliamentary elections rules.

Additional requirements for applications for a proxy vote for a definite or indefinite period based on occupation, service, employment or attendance on a course

24 (1) An application to vote by proxy for a particular or indefinite period under paragraph 3(3)(d) must state–
    (a) whether the occupation, service or employment in respect of which it is made is that of the applicant or his spouse or civil partner or, as the case may be, it is the applicant or his spouse or civil partner who is attending the course provided by an educational institution in respect of which the application is made;
    (b) the nature of the occupation, service or employment or course provided by an educational institution giving rise to the application;
    (c) where the person in respect of whose occupation, service or employment it is made (in this regulation referred to as "the employed person") is self employed, that fact; and in any other case the name of that person's employer;
    (d) the reason, relevant to the general nature of the employment, service or occupation in question or the course provided by an educational institution, why the applicant cannot reasonably be expected to go in person to his allotted polling station.

(2) Such an application must be attested and signed–
    (a) where the person is self-employed, by a person who–
        (i) is aged 18 years or over;
        (ii) knows the self-employed person; and
        (iii) is not related to him;
    (b) by the employer of the employed person or by another employee to whom this function is delegated by the employer; and
    (c) in the case of a course provided by an educational institution, by the director or tutor of that course or by the principal or head of that institution or an employee to whom this function is delegated by the principal or head.

(3) The person attesting an application under sub-paragraph (2) must–
    (a) where the applicant is the employed person, self-employed person or the person attending the course, certify that the statements required by sub-paragraph (1)(a) to (d) to be included in the application are true; or
    (b) where the applicant is the spouse or civil partner of the employed person, self-employed person or the person attending the course, certify that the statements included in the application in accordance with the requirements of sub-paragraph (1)(a) to (c) are true.

(4) The person attesting an application under sub-paragraph (2) must also state–
    (a) his name and address, that he is aged 18 years or over, that he knows the employed person, self-employed person or person attending a course provided by an educational institution but is not related to him; and
    (b) if he is attesting as or on behalf of the employer of the employed person, that he is the employer or the position he holds in the employment of that employer; or
    (c) if he is attesting an application made on the grounds of attendance at a course provided by an educational institution, the post he holds at that institution.

(5) For the purposes of this paragraph, one person is related to another if he is the spouse, civil partner, parent, grandparent, brother, sister, child or grandchild of the other.

Additional requirements for applications for a proxy vote in respect of a particular election

25 (1) An application under paragraph 4(2) to vote by proxy at a particular election must set out why the applicant's circumstances on the date of the poll for that election in respect of which it is made will be or are likely to be such that he cannot reasonably be expected to vote in person at his allotted polling station.

(2) Where an application under paragraph 4(2)–
  (a) is made on the grounds of the applicant's disability; and
  (b) is made after 5 pm on the sixth day before the date of the poll at the election for which it is made,
the requirements of paragraph 23 as to the matters to be specified and the attestation shall apply.

(3) Where an application mentioned in sub-paragraph (2) is made, the person who attests the application must state, in addition to those matters specified in paragraph 23, to the best of his knowledge and belief, the date upon which the applicant became disabled.

(3A) Where an application under paragraph 4(2) is made–
  (a) on grounds relating to the applicant's occupation, service or employment; and
  (b) after 5 pm on the sixth day before the date of the poll at the election for which it is made,
the requirements of paragraph 25A as to the matters to be specified and the attestation shall apply.

(4) Where an application under paragraph 4(2) is made by a person to whom paragraph 2(6) applies after 5 pm on the sixth day before the date of the poll at the election for which it is made, the requirements of sub-paragraph (5) as to the matters to be specified and as to attestation shall apply.

(5) Where an application mentioned in sub-paragraph (4) is made–
  (a) the application must additionally state the name and address of the hospital at which the applicant is liable to be detained; and
  (b) the application must be attested by the manager, within the meaning of section 145(1) of the Mental Health Act 1983, or section 329 of the Mental Health (Care and Treatment)(Scotland) Act 2003, responsible for the administration of the hospital at which the applicant is liable to be detained, or a person authorised to act on behalf of such a manager for these purposes, or, in Gibraltar, by the Chief Executive of the Gibraltar Health Authority or a person authorised to act on his behalf, and the attestation must state–
    (i) the name of the person, attesting the application;
    (ii) that the person, is authorised to attest the application;
    (iii) the position of the person in the hospital at which the applicant is liable to be detained; and
    (iv) the statutory provision under which the applicant is detained, or liable to be detained, at the hospital, where applicable.

(6) This paragraph does not apply where the applicant has an anonymous entry.

Additional requirements for application for an emergency proxy vote in respect of a particular election based on occupation, service or employment

25A (1) This paragraph sets out the requirements referred to in paragraph 25(3A).

(2) The application must (in addition to providing the information required by paragraph 25(1)) state–
  (a) where the applicant is self-employed, that fact; and in any other case the name

of the applicant's employer;

    (b) that the reason provided in accordance with paragraph 25(1) relates to the applicant's occupation, service or employment; and

    (c) the date on which the applicant became aware of that reason.

(3) Sub-paragraphs (4), (5) and (6) apply unless the applicant is or will be registered as a service voter.

(4) The application must be attested and signed–

    (a) where the applicant is self-employed, by a person who–

        (i) is aged 18 years or over;

        (ii) knows the applicant; and

        (iii) is not related to the applicant,

    (b) where the applicant is not self-employed, by the applicant's employer or by another employee to whom this function is delegated by the employer.

(5) The person attesting an application under sub-paragraph (4) (the "attestor") must certify that the statements required by sub-paragraph (2) and the information required by paragraph 25(1) are true to the best of their knowledge and belief.

(6) The attestor must also state–

    (a) the attestor's name and address; and

    (b) if the attestor is attesting where the applicant is self-employed, that the attestor is aged 18 years or over, and that the attestor knows, but is not related to, the applicant; or

    (c) if the attestor is attesting as or on behalf of the employer of the applicant, that the attestor is the employer or the position the attestor holds in the employment of that employer.

(7) For the purposes of this paragraph, one person ('A') is related to another ('B') if A is the spouse, civil partner, parent, grandparent, brother, sister, child or grandchild of B.

Closing date for applications

26 (1) An application under paragraph 3(1), (6) and (7) or 7(4) must be disregarded for the purposes of a particular European Parliamentary election and an application under paragraph 4(4) must be refused if it is received by the registration officer after 5 pm on the eleventh day before the date of the poll at that election.

(2) An application under paragraph 3(2) or 6(6) must be disregarded for the purposes of a particular European Parliamentary election if it is received by the registration officer after 5 pm on the sixth day before the date of the poll at that election.

(3) Subject to sub-paragraph (4), an application under paragraph 4(2) or 6(7) must be refused if it is received by the registration officer after 5 pm on the sixth day before the date of the poll at the election for which it is made.

(4) Where an application made under paragraph 4(2) is made–

    (a) on the grounds of the applicant's disability and the applicant became disabled after 5 pm on the sixth day before the date of the poll at the election for which it is made; or

    (aa) on grounds relating to the applicant's occupation, service or employment and the applicant became aware of those grounds after 5 pm on the sixth day before the date of the poll at the election for which it is made; or

    (b) by a person to whom paragraph 2(6) applies,

the application, or an application under paragraph 6(7) made by virtue of that application, must be refused if it is received after 5 pm on the day of the poll at the election for which it is made.

(5) An application under paragraph 4(1) or 7(7) must be refused if it is received by the registration officer after 5 pm on the eleventh day before the date of the poll at the election for which it is made.

(6) An application under–
 (a) paragraph 3(5)(a) by an elector to be removed from the record kept under paragraph 3(4); or
 (b) paragraph 7(10)(a) by a proxy to be removed from the record kept under paragraph 7(6),

and a notice under paragraph 6(9) by an elector cancelling a proxy's appointment must be disregarded for the purposes of a particular European Parliamentary election if it is received by the registration officer after 5 pm on the eleventh day before the date of the poll at that election.

(6A) Any application or notice mentioned in this paragraph must be disregarded for the purposes of a particular European Parliamentary election if, before the application or notice is considered by the registration officer, the elector or proxy has returned a postal ballot paper to the local returning officer (except where it has been returned in accordance with paragraph 53 or 54 (spoilt and lost postal ballot papers)).

(7) In computing a period of days for the purposes of this paragraph, Saturday, Sunday, Christmas Eve, Christmas Day, Good Friday or a bank holiday must be disregarded.

(8) In sub-paragraph (7) "bank holiday" means–
 (a) in relation to a general election in the combined region, a day which is a bank holiday under the Banking and Financial Dealings Act 1971 in any part of the United Kingdom or a bank or public holiday in Gibraltar not otherwise falling within sub-paragraph (7);
 (b) in relation to a by-election in the combined region a day, which is a bank holiday under the Banking and Financial Dealings Act 1971 in England and Wales or a bank or public holiday in Gibraltar not otherwise falling within sub-paragraph (7);
 (c) in relation to a general election in a region other than the combined region, a day which is a bank holiday under the Banking and Financial Dealings Act 1971 in any part of the United Kingdom; and
 (d) in relation to a by-election in a region other than the combined region, a day which is a bank holiday under that Act in that part of the United Kingdom in which the electoral region is situated.

Grant or refusal of applications

27 (1) Where the registration officer grants an application to vote by post, he must notify the applicant of his decision.

(2) Where the registration officer grants an application for the appointment of a proxy, he must confirm in writing to the elector that the proxy has been appointed, his name and address, and the duration of the appointment.

(3) Where the registration officer refuses an application under this Part, he must notify the applicant of his decision and of the reason for it.

(4) Where the returning officer grants an application made under–
 (a) paragraph 4(4)(a) by a person shown as voting by post in the record kept under paragraph 3(4); or
 (b) paragraph 7(7) by a person shown as voting by post in the record kept under paragraph 7(6),
he must notify the applicant of this.

(5) Where a person is removed from the record kept pursuant to paragraph 3(4) or 7(6),

the registration officer must where practicable notify him of this and the reason for it.

(6) Where the appointment of a proxy is cancelled by the elector or otherwise ceases to be in force, the registration officer must notify the elector that the appointment has been cancelled or, as the case may be, notify him that the appointment has ceased to be in force and the reason for it.

(7) Where, under paragraph 26, a registration officer disregards an application for the purposes of any particular European Parliamentary election, he must notify the applicant of this.

(8) At a European Parliamentary election where the registration officer is not the local returning officer for any local counting area in the area for which he is the registration officer, he must send to that officer details of any application to vote by post which he has granted as soon as practicable after doing so.

Notice of appeal

28 (1) A person desiring to appeal under regulation 21(1) against the decision of a registration officer must give notice of the appeal to the registration officer within 14 days of the receipt of the notice given under paragraph 27(3) specifying the grounds of appeal.

(2) The registration officer must forward any such notice to the appropriate county court or, in Gibraltar, the Gibraltar Court in the manner directed by rules of court together in each case with a statement of the material facts which in his opinion have been established in the case, of his decision upon the whole case and on any point which may be specified as a ground of appeal.

(3) In Scotland, the registration officer must forward any such notice to the sheriff with a statement of the material facts which in his opinion have been established in the case, of his decision upon the whole case and on any point which may be specified as a ground of appeal; and he must give to the sheriff any other information which the sheriff may require and which the registration officer is able to give.

(4) Where it appears to the registration officer that any notices of appeal given to him are based on similar grounds, he must inform the county court, sheriff or, in Gibraltar, the Gibraltar Court of this to enable the court or sheriff (if it or he thinks fit) to consolidate the appeals or select a case as a test case.

Cancellation of proxy appointment

29 Where the appointment of a proxy is cancelled by notice given to the registration officer under paragraph 6(9) or ceases to be in force under that provision or is no longer in force under paragraph 6(10)(b), the registration officer must–

(a) notify the person whose appointment as proxy has been cancelled, expired or is no longer in force, unless the registration officer has previously been notified by that person that he no longer wishes to act as proxy; and

(b) remove his name from the record kept under paragraph 3(4)(c).

Inquiries by registration officer

30 (1) The registration officer may, at such times as he thinks fit, make inquiries of a person who is shown as voting by proxy in the record kept under paragraph 3(4) in pursuance of an application granted on the grounds set out in paragraph 3(3)(c) or (d) for the purpose of determining whether there has been a material change of circumstances.

(2) Where the grant of an application for a proxy vote for an indefinite or particular period was based on the grounds referred to in paragraph 3(3)(d), the registration officer

must make the inquiries referred to not later than three years after the granting of the application or the last such inquiries, as the case may be.

(3) The registration officer may treat the failure by a person of whom inquiries have been made to respond to such inquiries within one month of the date on which they were made as sufficient evidence of a material change in circumstances.

Requirement to provide fresh signatures at five yearly intervals

31 (1) The registration officer must every year by 31st January send every person who remains an absent voter at European Parliamentary elections and whose signature held on the personal identifiers record is more than five years old a notice in writing–
    (a) requiring him to provide a fresh signature; and
    (b) informing him of the date (6 weeks from the date of sending the notice) on which he would cease to be entitled to vote by post or by proxy in the event of a failure or refusal to provide a fresh signature.

(2) The notice must be sent by the registration officer to the current or last known address of the absent voter.

(3) The registration officer must, if the absent voter has not responded to the notice within 3 weeks from the date on which the notice was sent, as soon as practicable send a copy of the notice to him.

(4) Where a notice or copy of a notice is sent by post, the registration officer may use–
    (a) a universal postal service provider; or
    (b) a commercial delivery firm,
and postage must be prepaid.

(5) A notice or copy of a notice sent to an absent voter in accordance with sub-paragraph (1) or (3) must be accompanied by a pre-addressed reply envelope and, in the case of any notice or copy of a notice sent to an address in the United Kingdom or Gibraltar, return postage must be prepaid.

(6) The registration officer must determine, not later than the date specified in the notice sent to the absent voter, whether the absent voter has failed or refused to provide a fresh signature.

(7) Where the registration officer determines that the absent voter has refused or failed to provide a fresh signature, he must from the date specified in the notice sent to the absent voter in accordance with sub-paragraph (1)(b) remove that person's entry from the records kept pursuant to paragraph 3(4) or 7(6) and from the postal voters list, list of proxies or proxy postal voters list (as the case may be) kept under paragraph 5(2), 5(3) or 7(8).

(8) Where a registration officer removes an absent voter's entry in the circumstances to which sub-paragraph (7) refers–
    (a) the registration officer must inform the absent voter, where appropriate, of the location of his allotted polling station or the polling station to which he is likely to be allotted (as determined in accordance with the European Parliamentary elections rules);
    (b) paragraph 27(3) and paragraph 28 shall apply as if the registration officer were refusing an application under this Schedule; and
    (c) in the case of an entry removed from the proxy postal voters list, the registration officer must also notify the elector who appointed the proxy whose entry has been removed.

(9) The registration officer must include in the notice to be sent to an absent voter regarding his removal from the records kept pursuant to paragraph 3(4) or 7(6) and

from the postal voters list, list of proxies or proxy postal voters list (as the case may be) kept under paragraph 5(2), 5(3) or 7(8), information–

    (a) explaining the effect of such removal; and

    (b) reminding the absent voter that he may make a fresh application under Part 2 to vote by post or by proxy (as the case may be).

(10) Where a person to whom sub-paragraph (1) applies has provided a registration officer with the required personal identifiers under paragraph 3, 4 or 7 of Schedule 4 to the Representation of the People Act 2000, the 2001 Regulations, the 2001 (Scotland) Regulations, the Scottish Parliament (Elections etc) Order 2007 or the National Assembly for Wales (Representation of the People) Order 2007 before the date specified in the notice sent to the absent voter in accordance with sub-paragraph (1)(b), the registration officer may use them and enter them in his records in accordance with paragraphs 3(9), 4(7), 7(13) and 18.

Notification of a rejected postal voting statement

31A (1) Where an absent voter (whether an elector or proxy) appears on the list created under paragraph 67(4) then–

    (a) the registration officer responsible for the personal identifiers record that contains information in respect of the absent voter must notify the absent voter (and the elector if the absent voter is a proxy) that the ballot paper concerned was rejected because the local returning officer was not satisfied that the postal voting statement was duly completed;

    (b) the registration officer must send the notification within the period of three months beginning with the date of the poll at which the ballot paper was rejected; and

    (c) the notification must include information as to which of the specified reasons referred to in paragraph 67(5) applied to the postal voting statement.

(2) The registration officer is not obliged to send a notification–

    (a) to any person who is no longer shown as voting by post in the relevant record at the time the registration officer proposes to send the notification; or

    (b) where the registration officer suspects that an offence may have been committed in relation to the postal ballot paper, the postal voting statement or the absent voter's registration as an elector.

(3) A notification issued under paragraph (1) may also include any other information that the registration officer considers appropriate, but a notification must not include information held on the personal identifiers record.

Requirement to provide fresh signatures following rejection of a postal voting statement

31B (1) Where an absent voter is notified under paragraph 31A that the signature does not match the example held on the personal identifiers record, and the absent voter continues to be shown on the relevant record as voting by post, the registration officer may require the absent voter to provide a fresh signature for the personal identifiers record.

(2) In doing so, the registration officer must–

    (a) issue a notice in writing to the absent voter, requiring the provision of a fresh signature; and

    (b) inform the absent voter of the date (six weeks from the sending of the notice) on which the absent voter would cease to be entitled to vote by post in the event of a failure or refusal to provide a fresh signature.

(3)   The registration officer must, if the absent voter has not responded to the notice within three weeks from the date on which the notice was sent, as soon as practicable send a copy of the notice to the absent voter.

(4)   The notice and any copy must be sent by the registration officer to the current or last known address of the absent voter.

(5)   Where a notice or copy of a notice is sent by post, the registration officer may use–
    (a)   a universal postal service provider; or
    (b)   a commercial delivery firm,
and postage must be prepaid.

(6)   A notice or copy of a notice sent to an absent voter in accordance with sub-paragraph (2) or (3) must be accompanied by a pre-addressed reply envelope and, in the case of any notice or copy of a notice sent to an address in the United Kingdom or Gibraltar, return postage must be prepaid.

(7)   Following the date specified in the notice sent to the absent voter, the registration officer must determine whether the absent voter has failed or refused to provide a fresh signature.

(8)   Where the registration officer determines that the absent voter has refused or failed to provide a fresh signature, the registration officer must remove that person's entry from the records kept pursuant to paragraph 3(4) or 7(6) and from the postal voters list or proxy postal voters list (as the case may be) kept under paragraph 5(2) or 7(8).

(9)   Where a registration officer removes an absent voter's entry in the circumstances to which sub-paragraph (8) refers–
    (a)   the registration officer must inform the absent voter, where appropriate, of the location of the absent voter's allotted polling station or the polling station to which the absent voter is likely to be allotted (as determined in accordance with the European Parliamentary elections rules);
    (b)   paragraph 27(3) and paragraph 28 shall apply as if the registration officer were refusing an application under this Schedule; and
    (c)   in the case of an entry removed from the proxy postal voters list, the registration officer must also notify the elector who appointed the proxy whose entry has been removed.

(10) The registration officer must include in the notice to be sent to an absent voter regarding the removal from the records kept pursuant to paragraph 3(4) or 7(6) and from the postal voters list or proxy postal voters list (as the case may be) kept under paragraph 5(2) or 7(8), information–
    (a)   explaining the effect of such removal; and
    (b)   reminding the absent voter that they may make a fresh application under Part 2 to vote by post or by proxy (as the case may be).

(11) Where an absent voter has provided a registration officer with a fresh signature in response to a notice issued by the registration officer under this paragraph, or in response to a notice issued by the registration officer under any other enactment following the rejection of the absent voter's postal voting statement at an election or referendum, the registration officer may use that signature and enter it in the records kept in accordance with paragraphs 3(9), 4(7), 7(13) and 18.

Further notification of a rejected postal voting statement

31C (1)   Where a registration officer notifies an absent voter of a rejected postal statement under paragraph 31A, in relation to the European Parliamentary election on 22nd May 2014, that officer must–

(a) send that voter a further notification that the ballot paper concerned was rejected because the returning officer was not satisfied that the postal voting statement was duly completed; and

(b) do so within a period of 10 days beginning on 19thMarch 2015.

(2) The further notification must include–

    (a) details of the poll where the rejection occurred,

    (b) an indication that a notification was previously sent under paragraph 31A, and

    (c) general information on the requirements for a duly completed postal voting statement.

(3) A registration officer need not send a further notification–

    (a) to any person who is no longer shown as voting by post in the relevant record; or

    (b) if the officer suspects that an offence has been committed in relation to the registration as an elector of the person who would otherwise receive it, or that person's postal ballot paper or postal voting statement.

(4) Sub-paragraph (1) applies in relation to a notification of a rejected postal statement made under paragraph 31A before the coming into force of this paragraph as it applies to one made after the coming into force of this paragraph.

Records and lists kept under this Schedule

32 (1) Any person entitled to be supplied in accordance with regulation 103, 105, 106 or 108 of the 2001 Regulations, or in accordance with regulation 102, 104, 105 or 107 of the 2001 (Scotland) Regulations, or in accordance with paragraphs 52, 53, 54 or 56 of Schedule 1 to the 2004 Act, with copies of the full register is also a person entitled, subject to this paragraph and to paragraph 33, to request that the registration officer supply free of charge the relevant part (within the meaning of those regulations) of a copy of any of the following information which he keeps–

    (a) the current version of the information which would, in the event of a particular European Parliamentary election, be included in the postal voters lists, the list of proxies or the proxy postal voters lists, which he is required to keep under paragraph 5 or 7(8);

    (b) the current or final version of the postal voters list, the list of proxies or the proxy postal voters lists kept under paragraph 5 or 7(8).

(2) A request under paragraph (1) must be made in writing and must specify–

    (a) the information (or the relevant parts of the information) requested;

    (b) whether the request is made only in respect of the current lists or whether it includes a request for the supply of any final list; and

    (c) whether a printed copy of the records or lists is requested or a copy in data form.

(3) A person who obtains any information under this paragraph may use it only for the permitted purposes specified in paragraph 33, and any restrictions–

    (a) specified in that paragraph; or

    (b) which would apply to the use of the full register under whichever of regulation 103, 105, 106 or 108 of the 2001 Regulations, or regulation 102, 104, 105 or 107 of the 2001 (Scotland) Regulations or paragraphs 53 or 56 of Schedule 1 to the 2004 Act, entitled that person to obtain that information,

shall apply to such use.

(4) The registration officer must supply a current copy of the information requested under sub-paragraph (1), as soon as practicable after receipt of a request that is duly made.

(5) The registration officer must supply a final copy of the postal voters list kept under

paragraph 5(2), as soon as practicable after 5pm on the eleventh day before the day of the poll, in response to a request under sub-paragraph (1) that has been duly made.

(6) As soon as practicable after 5pm on the sixth day before the day of the poll the registration officer must–

    (a) make a copy of the lists kept under paragraphs 5 and 7(8) available for inspection at his office in accordance with sub-paragraphs (10) to (15);

    (b) if he is not the local returning officer for the local counting area for which he is registration officer, send that officer a copy of those lists; and

    (c) supply a final copy of the postal voters lists or the list of proxies in response to every request under sub-paragraph (1) that has been duly made.

(7) The registration officer must supply a final copy of the list of proxies kept under paragraph 5(3), updated to include any additions to that list made in consequence of any applications granted in accordance with paragraph 26(4), as soon as practicable after 5pm on the day of the poll, to every person who received that list in accordance with sub-paragraph (6)(b).

(8) Any person who has obtained or is entitled to obtain a copy of information specified in sub-paragraph (1) may–

    (a) supply a copy of the information to a processor, within the meaning of rule 67 of the European Parliamentary elections rules, for the purpose of processing the information; or

    (b) procure that a processor processes and supplies to them any copy of the information which the processor has obtained under this paragraph,

for use in respect of the purposes for which that person is entitled to obtain such information.

(9) Paragraphs (2) and (3) of regulation 92 of the 2001 regulations and the condition in paragraph (9) of that regulation, or paragraph (4) of regulation 114 of the 2001 (Scotland) Regulations, or, as appropriate, paragraph 44(9) of Schedule 1 to the 2004 Act, shall be taken to apply to the supply and processing of information supplied under this paragraph as they apply to the supply and processing of the full register under Part 6 of the 2001 Regulations, under Part 6 of the 2001 (Scotland) Regulations or under Part 3 of Schedule 1 to the 2004 Act.

(10) Any person is entitled to request that the registration officer make available for inspection a copy of any of the information specified in sub-paragraph (1).

(11) A request under sub-paragraph (10) must be made in writing and must specify–

    (a) the information (or relevant parts of the information) requested;

    (b) whether the request is made only in respect of the current lists or whether it includes a request for the inspection of any final list;

    (c) who will inspect the information;

    (d) the date on which they wish to inspect the information; and

(e) whether they would prefer to inspect the information in printed or data form.

(12) The registration officer must make a copy of the information available for inspection under supervision as soon as practicable after the date of receipt of a request that has been duly made.

(13) Where inspection takes place by providing a copy of the information on a computer screen or otherwise in data form, the registration officer must ensure that the manner in, and equipment on, which that copy is provided do not permit any person consulting that copy to–

    (a) search it by electronic means by reference to the name of any person; or

    (b) copy or transmit any part of that copy by electronic, or any other means.

(14) A person who inspects a copy of the information, whether a printed copy or in data form,

may not–
  (a) make copies of any part of it; or
  (b) record any particulars in it;
  otherwise than by means of hand-written notes.

(15) Subject to any direction by the Secretary of State under section 52(1) of the 1983 Act or paragraph 21 of Schedule 4 to these Regulations, any duty on a registration officer to supply a copy or make information available for inspection under this paragraph imposes only a duty to provide that information in the form in which he holds it.

(16) For the purposes of this paragraph–
  (a) a "current copy" of records or lists is a copy of the records or lists as kept by the registration officer at 9 am on the date it is supplied; and
  (b) any period of days is to be calculated in accordance with paragraph 26(7).

(17) The registration officer must ensure that where he supplies or discloses information specified in sub-paragraph (1)(a) in accordance with this paragraph, he does not supply or disclose any record relating to a person specified in sub-paragraph (18).

(18) The persons specified in this paragraph are–
  (a) a person who has an anonymous entry;
  (b) the proxy of a person who has an anonymous entry.

Conditions on the use, supply and inspection of absent voter records or lists

33 The restrictions on the supply, disclosure and use of the full register in regulations 94 and 96 of the 2001 Regulations or, as appropriate, regulations 94 and 95 of the 2001 (Scotland) Regulations or paragraphs 46 and 47 of Schedule 1 to the 2004 Act, apply to information specified in paragraph 32(1)(a) and (b) as they apply to the full register, except that the permitted purpose is to mean either–
  (a) research purposes, including statistical or historical purposes; or
  (b) electoral purposes.

Marked register for polling stations

34 To indicate that an elector or his proxy is entitled to vote by post and is for that reason not entitled to vote in person, the letter "A" must be placed against the entry of that elector in any copy of the register, or part of it, provided for a polling station.

Part 3

Repealed

Part 4
Issue and Receipt of Postal Ballot Papers

Interpretation of Part 4

40 (1) For the purposes of this Part, unless the context otherwise requires–
  "agent" includes the election agent and a person appointed to attend in the election agent's place;
  "ballot paper envelope" and "covering envelope" mean the envelopes referred to in paragraph 50;
  "postal ballot paper" means a ballot paper issued to a postal voter;
  "postal voter" means an elector or proxy who is entitled to vote by post;
  "postal voters' ballot box" means the ballot box referred to in paragraph 57(1)(a);
  "receptacle for ballot paper envelopes", and other references to specified receptacles,

means the receptacles referred to in paragraph 57(5);

"relevant election or referendum" means one or more of the following–

    (a) a parliamentary election,

    (b) a local government election,

    (c) a mayoral election,

    (ca) an election of a police and crime commissioner in accordance with Chapter 6 of Part 1 of the Police Reform and Social Responsibility Act 2011;

    (d) referendum conducted under the Local Authorities (Conduct of Referendums)(England) Regulations 2007,

the poll at which is taken together with the poll at the European Parliamentary election; and

"spoilt postal ballot paper" means a ballot paper referred to in paragraph 53(1).

(2) In the case of a referendum, a reference to–

    (a) a candidate must be construed as a reference to a petition organiser, within the meaning of regulation 2(1) of the Local Authorities (Conduct of Referendums) (England) Regulations 2007;

    (b) an election agent or counting agent must be construed as a reference to a counting observer, within the meaning of that regulation;

    (c) a polling agent must be construed as a reference to a polling observer, within the meaning of that regulation; and

    (d) a returning officer or local returning officer must be construed as a reference to a counting officer, within the meaning of that regulation.

Issue of Postal Ballot Papers

Combination of poll

41   Where the poll at the European Parliamentary election is to be taken together with–

    (a) the poll at an election under subsection (1) or (2) of section 15 of the 1985 Act (combination of polls at parliamentary, European Parliamentary and local government elections); or

    (b) the poll at a mayoral election or a referendum in accordance with regulations made under sections 9HE and 105, 9MG and 105 or 44 and 105 of the Local Government Act 2000,

or two or more such polls, the proceedings on the issue and receipt of postal ballot papers in respect of each election or referendum may, if all the returning officers concerned agree, be taken together.

Form of postal voting statement

42   The form of the postal voting statement for the purposes of rule 28 of the European Parliamentary elections rules in Schedule 1 to these Regulations must be–

    (a) in Form O in the Appendix at a European Parliamentary election taken alone;

    (b) in Form P in the Appendix at a European Parliamentary election where the proceedings on the issue and receipt of postal ballot papers are taken together with those proceedings at a relevant election or referendum; and

    (c) in Form Q in the Appendix at a European Parliamentary election where the poll is taken together with the poll at a relevant election or referendum, but where the proceedings on the issue and receipt of postal ballot papers are not.

Persons entitled to be present at proceedings on issue of postal ballot papers

43   Without prejudice to the provisions of sections 6A to 6E of the 2000 Act, no person may be present at the proceedings on the issue of postal ballot papers other than the local returning officer and his clerks.

Persons entitled to be present at proceedings on receipt of postal ballot papers

44   Without prejudice to the provisions of sections 6A to 6E of the 2000 Act, no person may be present at the proceedings on the receipt of postal ballot papers other than–

    (a)   the local returning officer and his clerks;

    (b)   a candidate;

    (c)   an election agent or a person appointed by him to attend in his place;

    (d)   a sub-agent;

    (e)   any agents appointed under paragraph 45; and

    (f)   where the proceedings on the receipt of postal ballot papers are taken together with the proceedings for a relevant election or referendum, persons entitled to be present at the proceedings for the relevant election or referendum.

Agents of candidates who may attend proceedings on receipt of postal ballot papers

45 (1)   The election agent or sub-agent of each registered party standing nominated or the election agent or sub-agent of each individual candidate may appoint one or more agents to attend the proceedings on the receipt of the postal ballot papers up to the number he may be authorised by the local returning officer to appoint so that the number authorised must be the same in the case of each registered party standing nominated or each individual candidate.

  (2)   Notice in writing of the appointment stating the names and addresses of the persons appointed must be given by the election agent or sub-agent to the local returning officer before the time fixed for the opening of the postal voters' ballot box.

  (3)   Where postal ballot papers for more than one election or referendum are issued together under paragraph 41, the returning officer to whom notice must be given under sub-paragraph (2) and sub-paragraph (4) is the returning officer who issues the postal ballot papers.

  (4)   If an agent dies or becomes incapable of acting, the candidate or election agent of a registered party may appoint another agent in his place and must forthwith give to the local returning officer notice in writing of the name and address of the agent appointed.

  (5)   In this Part references to agents must be taken as references to agents whose appointments have been duly made and notified and, in the case of agents appointed under sub-paragraph (1), who are within the number authorised by the local returning officer.

  (6)   A candidate may himself do any act or thing which any agent of his or his party, if appointed, would have been authorised to do, or may assist his agent or the agent of his party in doing any such act or thing.

  (7)   Where in this Part any act or thing is required or authorised to be done in the presence of the candidates or their agents, the non-attendance of any such person at the time and place appointed for the purpose shall not, if the act or thing is otherwise duly done, invalidate the act or thing done.

Notification of requirement of secrecy

46   The local returning officer must make such arrangements as he thinks fit to ensure that every person attending the proceedings in connection with the issue or receipt of postal ballot papers has been given a copy in writing of the provisions of regulation 29(5) and (7).

Time when postal ballot papers are to be issued

47 Postal ballot papers (and postal voting statements) must be issued by the local returning officer as soon as it is practicable to do so.

Procedure on issue of postal ballot paper

48 (1) The number of the elector as stated in the copy of the register of electors must be marked on the corresponding number list, next to the number and unique identifying mark of the ballot paper issued to that elector.

(2) A mark must be placed in the postal voters list or the proxy postal voters list against the number of the elector to denote that a ballot paper has been issued to the elector or his proxy, but without showing the particular ballot paper issued.

(3) The number of a postal ballot paper must be marked on the postal voting statement sent with that paper.

(4) Where postal ballot papers for the European Parliamentary election and a relevant election or referendum are issued together under paragraph 41–

(a) one mark must be placed in the postal voters list or the proxy postal voters list under sub-paragraph (2) to denote that ballot papers have been issued in respect of each election or referendum; except that, where ballot papers are not so issued, a different mark must be placed in the postal voters list or proxy postal voters list to identify the election or referendum in respect of which the ballot paper was issued; and

(b) the number of each ballot paper must be marked on the postal voting statement under sub-paragraph (3).

(5) Where the poll at a European Parliamentary election is taken with the poll at a relevant election or referendum (under the provisions referred to in paragraph 41) but not the proceedings on the issue and receipt of postal ballot papers, the colour of the postal ballot paper must also be marked on the postal voting statement sent with that paper.

(6) Subject to sub-paragraph (7), the address to which the postal ballot paper, postal voting statement and the envelopes referred to in paragraph 50 are to be sent is–

(a) in the case of an elector, the address shown in the postal voters list;

(b) in the case of a proxy, the address shown in the proxy postal voters list.

(7) Where a person has an anonymous entry in the register, the items specified in sub-paragraph (6) must be sent (as the case may be) to the address to which postal ballot papers should be sent–

(a) as shown in the record kept under paragraph 3(4) or 7(6); or

(b) as given in pursuance of an application made under paragraph 4(1) or 7(4)(b).

Refusal to issue postal ballot paper

49 Where a local returning officer is satisfied that two or more entries in the postal voters list, or in the proxy postal voters list or in each of those lists relate to the same elector, he must not issue more than one ballot paper in respect of that elector at any one election.

Envelopes

50 (1) Sub-paragraphs (2) and (3) prescribe the envelopes which are to be issued to a postal voter in addition to the ballot paper and postal voting statement (which are issued under rule 28 of the European Parliamentary elections rules).

(2) There must be issued an envelope for the return of the postal ballot paper or, as the case may be, ballot papers and the postal voting statement (referred to as a "covering

envelope") which must be marked with the letter "B".

(3) There must also be issued a smaller envelope (referred to as a "ballot paper envelope") which must be marked with–
   (a) the letter "A";
   (b) the words "ballot paper envelope"; and
   (c) unless the envelope has a window through which the number on the ballot paper (or ballot papers) can be displayed, the number of the ballot paper or, as the case may be, ballot papers.

(4) Where polls are taken together (under the provisions referred to in paragraph 41) but not the proceedings on the issue and receipt of postal ballot papers–
   (a) the envelope referred to in sub-paragraph (2) must also be marked "Covering envelope for the *insert colour of ballot paper* coloured ballot paper"; and
   (b) on the envelope referred to in sub-paragraph (3), after the words "Ballot paper envelope" there must be added the words "for the *insert colour of ballot paper* coloured ballot paper".

Sealing up of completed corresponding number lists and security of special lists

51 (1) As soon as practicable after the issue of each batch of postal ballot papers, the local returning officer must make up into a packet the completed corresponding number lists of those ballot papers which have been issued and must seal such a packet.

(2) Until the time referred to in paragraph 60(11), the local returning officer must take proper precautions for the security of the marked copy of the postal voters list and the proxy postal voters list.

Delivery of postal ballot papers

52 (1) For the purposes of delivering postal ballot papers, the local returning officer may use–
   (a) a universal postal service provider;
   (b) a commercial delivery firm; or
   (c) clerks appointed under rule 30(1) of the European Parliamentary elections rules.

(2) Where the services of a universal postal service provider or a commercial delivery firm are to be used, envelopes addressed to postal voters must be counted and delivered by the local returning officer with such form of receipt to be endorsed by that provider or firm as may be arranged.

(3) Postage must be prepaid on envelopes addressed to the postal voters (except where sub-paragraph (1)(c) applies).

(4) Return postage must be prepaid on all covering envelopes where the address provided by the postal voter for the receipt of the postal ballot paper is within the United Kingdom or Gibraltar.

Spoilt postal ballot papers

53 (1) Where a postal voter has inadvertently dealt with his postal ballot paper or postal voting statement in such manner that it cannot be conveniently used as a ballot paper (referred to as "a spoilt postal ballot paper") or, as the case may be, a postal voting statement (referred to as "a spoilt postal voting statement") he may return (either by hand or by post) to the local returning officer the spoilt postal ballot paper or, as the case may be, the spoilt postal voting statement.

(2) Where a postal voter exercises the entitlement conferred by sub-paragraph (1), he must also return–

(a) the postal ballot paper or, as the case may be, the postal voting statement, whether spoilt or not;

(b) where postal ballot papers for more than one election have been issued together under paragraph 41, all other ballot papers so issued, whether spoilt or not; and

(c) the envelopes supplied for the return of the documents mentioned in paragraph 50.

(3) Subject to sub-paragraph (4), on receipt of the documents referred to in sub-paragraph (1) and, where applicable, sub-paragraph (2), the local returning officer must issue another postal ballot paper or, as the case may be, ballot papers except where those documents are received after 5 pm on the day of the poll.

(4) Where the local returning officer receives the documents referred to in sub-paragraph (1) and, where applicable, sub-paragraph (2), after 5 pm on the day before the day of the poll, he must only issue another postal ballot paper or, as the case may be, ballot papers if the postal voter returned the documents in person.

(5) Paragraphs 48 (except sub-paragraph (2)), 50, 51 and, subject to sub-paragraph (8), 52 apply to the issue of a replacement postal ballot paper under sub-paragraph (3).

(6) Any postal ballot paper or postal voting statement, whether spoilt or not, returned in accordance with sub-paragraph (1) or (2) must be immediately cancelled.

(7) The local returning officer, as soon as practicable after cancelling those documents, must make up those documents in a separate packet and must seal the packet; and if on any subsequent occasion documents are cancelled under sub-paragraph (6), the sealed packet must be opened and the additional cancelled documents included in it and the packet must be sealed again.

(8) Where a postal voter applies in person for a replacement ballot paper–

(a) by 5 pm on the day before the day of the poll, the local returning officer may hand a replacement postal ballot paper to him; or

(b) after 5 pm on the day before the day of the poll, the local returning officer may only hand a replacement postal ballot paper to him,

instead of delivering it in accordance with paragraph 52.

(9) The local returning officer must enter in a list kept for the purpose ("the list of spoilt postal ballot papers")–

(a) the name and number of the elector as stated in the register (or, in the case of an elector who has an anonymous entry, his electoral number alone);

(b) the number of the postal ballot paper (or papers) issued under this paragraph; and

(c) where the postal voter whose ballot paper is spoilt is a proxy, his name and address.

Lost postal ballot papers

54 (1) Where a postal voter claims either to have lost or not to have received–

(a) his postal ballot paper; or

(b) the postal voting statement; or

(c) one or more of the envelopes supplied for their return,

by the fourth day before the day of the poll, he may apply (whether or not in person) to the local returning officer for a replacement ballot paper.

(2) Such an application must include evidence of the voter's identity.

(3) Where a postal voter exercises the entitlement conferred by sub-paragraph (1), he must return–

(a) the documents referred to in sub-paragraph (1)(a) to (c); and

(b) where the postal ballot papers for more than one election have been issued together under paragraph 41, all other ballot papers so issued,

which he has received and which have not been lost.

(4) Any postal ballot paper or postal voting statement returned in accordance with sub-paragraph (3) must be immediately cancelled.

(5) The local returning officer as soon as practicable after cancelling those documents, must make up those documents in a separate packet and must seal the packet; and if on any subsequent occasion documents are cancelled as mentioned above, the sealed packet must be opened and additional cancelled documents included in it and the packet must be sealed again.

(6) Subject to sub-paragraph (7), where the application is received by the local returning officer before 5 pm on the day of the poll and the local returning officer–

    (a) is satisfied as to the voter's identity; and

    (b) has no reason to doubt that the postal voter has either lost or has not received the original ballot paper or postal voting statement or one or more of the envelopes provided for their return,

he must issue another postal ballot paper or, as the case may be, postal ballot papers.

(7) Where the application is received by the local returning officer after 5pm on the day before the day of the poll, he must only issue another postal ballot paper or, as the case may be, other ballot papers if the postal voter applies in person.

(8) The local returning officer must enter in a list kept for the purpose ("the list of lost postal ballot papers")–

    (a) the name and number of the elector as stated in the register (or, in the case of an elector who has an anonymous entry, his electoral number alone);

    (b) the number of the replacement postal ballot paper issued under this paragraph; and

    (c) where the postal voter is a proxy, his name and address.

(9) Paragraphs 48 (except sub-paragraph (2)), 50, 51 and, subject to sub-paragraph (10), 52 shall apply to the issue of a replacement postal ballot paper under sub-paragraph (6).

(10) Where a postal ballot voter applies in person–

    (a) by 5 pm on the day before the day of the poll, the returning officer may hand a replacement postal ballot paper to him; or

    (b) after 5 pm on the day before the day of the poll, the returning officer may only hand a replacement postal ballot paper to him,

instead of delivering it in accordance with paragraph 52.

Receipt of Postal Ballot Papers

Cancellation of postal ballot papers

54A (1) Where, after the nineteenth day before the date of the poll at an election, an application under–

    (a) paragraph 3(5)(a) (application to be removed from record of absent voters),

    (b) paragraph 3(6) or 4(4)(b) (application to vote by proxy by person recorded as voting by post),

    (c) paragraph 3(7) (application to vote by post by person recorded as voting by proxy),

    (d) paragraph 4(4)(a) (application for postal ballot paper to be sent to different address),

    (e) paragraph 6(7) (appointment of proxy),

    (f) paragraph 7(7) (application from postal proxy voter for postal ballot paper to be sent to different address), or

(g) paragraph 7(10)(a) (application by proxy to be removed from record of postal proxies),

is granted or a notice under paragraph 6(9) (cancellation of proxy appointment) is received, and the application or notice is not to be disregarded for the purposes of that election under paragraph 26, the registration officer must notify the local returning officer who must immediately cancel any postal ballot paper issued to the elector or proxy and, in the case of an application under paragraph 4(4)(a) or 7(7), must issue a replacement postal ballot paper.

(2) Where a person returns a postal ballot paper that has been or is to be cancelled in accordance with sub-paragraph (1) (whether to the registration officer or the local returning officer), it must be dealt with as follows–

(a) the ballot paper, together with any other ballot papers, postal voting statements or covering envelopes which are returned to the registration officer, must be given by the registration officer to the local returning officer;

(b) any document returned in accordance with this sub-paragraph but not cancelled in accordance with sub-paragraph (1) must be immediately cancelled;

(c) the local returning officer, as soon as practicable after receiving and cancelling those documents, must make up those documents in a separate packet and must seal the packet, and if on any subsequent occasion documents are returned in accordance with this sub-paragraph, the sealed packet must be opened, the additional cancelled documents included in it and the packet must be again made up and sealed;

(3) The local returning officer must enter in a list kept for the purpose of recording postal ballot papers cancelled under this paragraph ("the list of cancelled postal ballot papers")–

(a) the name and number of the elector as stated in the register of electors (or, in the case of an elector who has an anonymous entry, their electoral number alone);

(b) the number of the cancelled postal ballot paper;

(c) the number of any replacement postal ballot paper issued under sub-paragraph (1); and

(d) where the postal voter is a proxy, their name and address.

(4) Paragraphs 48 (except sub-paragraph (2)), 50, 51 and 52 apply to a replacement postal ballot paper issued under sub-paragraph (1).

(5) Rule 2 of Schedule 1 applies to the computation of the period of nineteen days for the purposes of sub-paragraph (1) as it applies to the computation of a period for the purposes of rule 1 of that Schedule.

Means of returning postal ballot paper or postal voting statement

55 (1) The manner in which a postal ballot paper or postal voting statement may be returned to the local returning officer is by post or by hand, unless it is returned to the polling station in which case it must be returned by hand.

(2) Subject to sub-paragraph (3), the presiding officer of a polling station must deliver, or cause to be delivered, any postal ballot paper or postal voting statement returned to that station to the local returning officer in the same manner and at the same time as he delivers, or causes to be delivered, the packets referred to in rule 49(1) of the European Parliamentary elections rules.

(3) The local returning officer may collect, or cause to be collected, any postal ballot paper or postal voting statement which by virtue of sub-paragraph (2) the presiding officer of a polling station would otherwise be required to deliver or cause to be delivered to him.

(4)   Where the local returning officer collects, or causes to be collected, any postal ballot paper or postal voting statement in accordance with sub-paragraph (3) the presiding officer must first make it (or them) into a packet sealed with his own seal and the seals of such polling agents as are present and desire to affix their seals.

Notice of opening of postal ballot paper envelopes

56 (1)   The local returning officer must give to each election agent or sub-agent, where appointments of sub-agents have been made, not less than 48 hours' notice in writing of each occasion on which a postal voters' ballot box and the envelopes contained in it is to be opened.

(2)   Such a notice must specify–
    (a)   the time and place at which such an opening is to take place; and
    (b)   the number of agents the election agent or sub-agent may appoint under paragraph 45(1) to attend each opening.

Postal ballot boxes and receptacles

57 (1)   The local returning officer must provide a separate ballot box for the reception of–
    (a)   the covering envelopes when returned by the postal voters ("postal voters' ballot box"); and
    (b)   postal ballot papers ("postal ballot box").

(2)   Each such ballot box must be marked "postal voters' ballot box" or "postal ballot box", as the case may be, and with the name of the local counting area or parliamentary constituency or electoral area (or areas) or voting area for which the election (or elections) or referendum is (or are) held.

(3)   The postal ballot box must be shown to the agents present on the occasion of opening the first postal voters' ballot box as being empty.

(4)   The local returning officer must then lock the ballot box, if it has a lock, and apply his seal in such manner as to prevent its being opened without breaking the seal; any of the agents present who wish to add their seals may then do likewise.

(5)   The local returning officer must provide the following receptacles–
    (a)   the receptacle for rejected votes;
    (b)   *Repealed*
    (c)   the receptacle for ballot paper envelopes;
    (d)   the receptacle for rejected ballot paper envelopes;
    (e)   the receptacle for rejected votes (verification procedure); and
    (f)   the receptacle for postal voting statements (verification procedure).

(6)   The local returning officer must take proper precautions for the safe custody of every ballot box and receptacle referred to in this paragraph.

Receipt of covering envelope

58 (1)   The local returning officer must, immediately on receipt (whether by hand or by post) of a covering envelope (or an envelope which is stated to include a postal vote) before the close of the poll, place it unopened in a postal voters' ballot box.

(2)   Where an envelope, other than a covering envelope issued by the local returning officer–
    (a)   has been opened; and
    (b)   contains a ballot paper envelope, postal voting statement or ballot paper,
the first-mentioned envelope, together with its contents, must be placed in a postal voters' ballot box.

Opening of postal voters' ballot box

59 (1) Each postal voters' ballot box must be opened by the local returning officer in the presence of the agents, if in attendance.

   (2) So long as the local returning officer ensures that there is at least one sealed postal voters' ballot box for the reception of covering envelopes up to the time of the close of the poll, the other postal voters' ballot boxes may previously be opened by him.

   (3) The last postal voters' ballot box and the postal ballot box must be opened at the verification of the ballot paper accounts under rule 51 of the European Parliamentary elections rules.

Opening of covering envelopes

60 (1) When a postal voters' ballot box is opened, the local returning officer must count and record the number of covering envelopes (including any envelope which is stated to include a postal vote and any envelope described in paragraph 58(2)).

   (2) *Repealed*

   (3) The local returning officer must open separately each covering envelope (including an envelope described in paragraph 58(2)).

   (4) The procedure in paragraph 63 applies where a covering envelope (including an envelope to which paragraph 58(2) applies) contains a postal voting statement.

   (5) Where the covering envelope does not contain the postal voting statement separately, the local returning officer must open the ballot paper envelope to ascertain whether the postal voting statement is inside.

   (6) Where a covering envelope does not contain a postal voting statement (whether separately or not) the local returning officer must mark the covering envelope "provisionally rejected", attach its contents (if any) and place it in the receptacle for rejected votes.

   (7) *Repealed*

   (8) In carrying out the procedures in this paragraph and paragraphs 61 to 68, the local returning officer–
       (a) must keep the ballot papers face downwards and must take proper precautions for preventing any person from seeing the votes made on the ballot papers; and
       (b) must not be permitted to view the corresponding number list used at the issue of postal ballot papers.

   (9) Where an envelope opened in accordance with sub-paragraph (3) contains a postal voting statement, the local returning officer must place a mark in the marked copy of the postal voters list or proxy postal voters list in a place corresponding to the number of the elector to denote that a postal vote has been returned as provided for in rule 35 of the European Parliamentary election rules.

   (10) A mark made under sub-paragraph (9) must be distinguishable from and must not obscure the mark made under paragraph 48(2).

   (11) As soon as practicable after the last covering envelope has been opened, the local returning officer must make up into a packet the copy of the marked postal voters list and proxy postal voters list that have been marked in accordance with sub-paragraph (9) and must seal such a packet.

Confirming receipt of postal voting statements

61 (1) An elector or a proxy voter who is shown in the postal voters list or proxy postal voters

list may make a request, at any time between the first issue of postal ballots under paragraph 47 and the close of the poll, that the local returning officer confirm–

(a) whether a mark is shown in the marked copy of the postal voters list or proxy postal voters list in a place corresponding to the number of the elector to denote that a postal vote has been returned; and

(b) whether the number of the ballot paper issued to the elector or his proxy has been recorded on either of the lists of provisionally rejected votes kept by the returning officer under sub-paragraphs (2) and (3) of paragraph 67.

(2) A request under sub-paragraph (1) must–

(a) be made by any method specified; and

(b) include any evidence of the voter's identity requested,

by the local returning officer.

(3) Where a request is received in accordance with sub-paragraph (2) the local returning officer must satisfy himself that the request has been made by the elector or their proxy and where he is so satisfied provide confirmation of the matters under sub-paragraph (1).

62 *Repealed*

Procedure in relation to postal voting statements: personal identifier verification

63 (1) This paragraph applies in the circumstances described in paragraph 60(4).

(2) The local returning officer must satisfy himself that the postal voting statement is duly completed and as part of that process must compare the date of birth and the signature on the postal voting statement against the date of birth and signature contained in the personal identifier record relating to the person to whom the postal ballot paper was addressed.

(3) Where the local returning officer is not so satisfied, he must mark the statement "rejected", attach to it the ballot paper envelope, or if there is no such envelope but there is a ballot paper, the ballot paper, and, subject to sub-paragraph (4), place it in the receptacle for rejected votes (verification procedure).

(4) Before placing a postal voting statement in the receptacle for rejected votes (verification procedure), the local returning officer must show it to the agents and must permit them to view the entries in the personal identifiers record which relate to the person to whom the postal ballot paper was addressed and, if any of them object to his decision, he must add the words "rejection objected to".

(5) The local returning officer must then examine the number on the postal voting statement against the number on the ballot paper envelope and, where they are the same, he must place the statement and the ballot paper envelope respectively in the receptacle for postal voting statements (verification procedure) and the receptacle for ballot paper envelopes.

(6) Where–

(a) the number on a valid postal voting statement is not the same as the number on the ballot paper envelope; or

(b) that envelope has no number on it (or only one number when the postal voting statement has more than one),

the local returning officer must open the envelope.

(7) Sub-paragraph (8) applies where–

(a) there is a valid postal voting statement but no ballot paper envelope; or

(b) the ballot paper envelope has been opened under paragraph 60(5) or sub-paragraph (6).

(8)   In the circumstances described in sub-paragraph (7), the local returning officer must place–

    (a)   in the postal ballot box, any ballot paper the number on which is the same as the number on the valid postal voting statement;

    (b)   in the receptacle for rejected votes (verification procedure), any other ballot paper, with the valid postal voting statement attached and marked "provisionally rejected";

    (c)   in the receptacle for rejected votes (verification procedure), any valid postal voting statement marked "provisionally rejected" where–

        (i)   there is no ballot paper; or

        (ii)   in the case of a statement on which the number of more than one ballot paper appears, there is not a sufficient number of ballot papers and, in such a case, must mark the statement to indicate which ballot paper is missing;

    (d)   in the receptacle for postal voting statements (verification procedure), any valid statement not disposed of under paragraph (b) or (c).

64   *Repealed*

Opening of ballot paper envelopes

65 (1)   The local returning officer must open separately each ballot paper envelope placed in the receptacle for ballot paper envelopes.

  (2)   He must place–

    (a)   in the postal ballot box, any ballot paper the number on which is the same as the number (or one of the numbers) on the ballot paper envelope;

    (b)   in the receptacle for rejected votes, any other ballot paper which must be marked "provisionally rejected" and to which must be attached the ballot paper envelope; and

    (c)   in the receptacle for rejected ballot paper envelopes, any ballot paper envelope which must be marked "provisionally rejected" because it does not contain either a ballot paper or, where more than one number appears on the ballot paper envelope, a sufficient number of ballot papers (and indicating, in such a case, the missing ballot paper).

Retrieval of cancelled postal ballot papers

66 (1)   Where it appears to the local returning officer that a postal ballot paper which has been cancelled in accordance with paragraph 53(6), 54(4), 54A(1) or (2) has been placed–

    (a)   in a postal voters' ballot box;

    (b)   in the receptacle for ballot paper envelopes; or

    (c)   in a postal ballot box,

he must proceed as follows.

  (2)   He must, on at least one occasion on which a postal voters' ballot box is opened in accordance with paragraph 59, also open any postal ballot box and the receptacle for ballot paper envelopes and–

    (a)   retrieve the cancelled ballot paper;

    (b)   show the ballot paper number on the cancelled ballot paper to the agents;

    (c)   retrieve the postal voting statement that relates to a cancelled ballot paper from the receptacle for postal voting statements (verification procedure);

    (d)   attach any cancelled postal ballot paper to the postal voting statement to which it relates;

   (e)   place the cancelled documents in a separate packet and deal with that packet in the manner provided for by paragraph 53(7) or 54A(2); and

   (f)   unless the postal ballot box has been opened for the purposes of the counting of votes under rule 53 of the European Parliamentary elections rules, re-lock or re-seal (or both re-lock and re-seal), the postal ballot box in the presence of the agents.

   (3)   Whilst retrieving a cancelled ballot paper in accordance with sub-paragraph (2), the local returning officer and his staff–

   (a)   must keep the ballot papers face downwards and must take proper precautions for preventing any person seeing the votes made on the ballot papers; and

   (b)   must not be permitted to view the corresponding number list used at the issue of postal ballot papers.

Lists of rejected postal ballot papers

67 (1)   In respect of any election, the local returning officer must keep lists relating to rejected postal ballot papers as required by this paragraph.

   (2)   In the first list, he must record the ballot paper number of any postal ballot paper for which no valid postal voting statement was received with it.

   (3)   In the second list, he must record the ballot paper number of any postal ballot paper which is entered on a valid postal voting statement where that ballot paper is not received with the postal voting statement.

   (4)   In the third list, the local returning officer must record, for every postal voting statement in the receptacle for rejected votes (verification procedure) immediately prior to sealing–

   (a)   the elector's name and address (and the name and address of the proxy if the elector has a proxy);

   (b)   the elector's number on the register of electors (and that of the proxy if the elector has a proxy);

   (c)   the specified reason or reasons for the rejection of the postal voting statement; and

   (d)   any other information relating to the rejection that the local returning officer considers appropriate, but not the ballot paper number.

   (5)   The specified reasons that may be given under sub-paragraph (4)(c) for the rejection of a postal voting statement are as follows–

   (a)   the signature does not match the example held on the personal identifiers record;

   (b)   the date of birth does not match the one held on the personal identifiers record;

   (c)   the signature field is blank; or

   (d)   the date of birth field is blank.

   (6)   Sub-paragraphs (4) and (5) do not apply to the local returning officer for Gibraltar.

Checking of lists kept under paragraph 67

68 (1)   Where the local returning officer receives a valid postal voting statement without the postal ballot paper (or papers or, as the case may be, all of the papers) to which it relates, he may, at any time prior to the close of the poll, check the list kept under paragraph 67(2) to see whether the number (or numbers) of a postal ballot paper to which the statement relates is entered in that list.

   (2)   Where the local returning officer receives a postal ballot paper without the postal voting statement to which it relates, he may, at any time prior to the close of the poll,

check the list kept under paragraph 67(3) to see whether the number of that ballot paper is entered in that list.

(3) The local returning officer must conduct the checks required by sub-paragraphs (1) and (2) as soon as practicable after the receipt of packets from every polling station in the local counting area, parliamentary constituency, electoral area or, as the case may be, voting area under rule 49(1) of the European Parliamentary elections rules.

(4) Where the ballot paper number in the list matches that number on a valid postal voting statement or, as the case may be, the postal ballot paper, the local returning officer must retrieve that statement or paper.

(5) The local returning officer must then take the appropriate steps under this Part as though any document earlier marked "provisionally rejected" had not been so marked and must amend the document accordingly.

Sealing of receptacles

69 (1) As soon as practicable after the completion of the procedure under paragraph 68(3) and (4), the local returning officer must make up into separate packets the contents of–
   (a) the receptacle of rejected votes;
   (b) *Repealed*
   (c) the receptacle of rejected ballot paper envelopes;
   (d) the lists of spoilt, lost or cancelled postal ballot papers;
   (e) the receptacle of rejected votes (verification procedure); and
   (f) the receptacle of postal voting statements (verification procedure),
   and must seal up such packets.

(2) Any document in those packets marked "provisionally rejected" must be deemed to be marked "rejected".

Forwarding of documents

70 (1) Subject to sub-paragraphs (2) and (7), the local returning officer must forward to the relevant registration officer, at the same time as he forwards the documents mentioned in rule 64 of the European Parliamentary elections rules–
   (a) the packets referred to in paragraphs 51(1), 53(7), 54(5), 54A(2), 60(11) and 69, endorsing on each a description of the contents;
   (b) any list compiled under paragraph 67(4); and
   (c) a completed statement in Form R in the Appendix.

(2) Where the proceedings on the issue and receipt of postal ballot papers are taken together under paragraph 41, the returning officer or local returning officer discharging those functions must forward the packets containing–
   (a) the marked copies of the postal voters list and proxy postal voters list; and
   (b) the postal voting statements,
   to the same person, and at the same time and in the same manner, as he is required to forward those documents as respects the election or referendum for which he is the returning officer.

(3) Where–
   (a) any covering envelopes are received by the local returning officer after the close of the poll (apart from those delivered in accordance with the provisions of paragraph 55(2));
   (b) any envelopes addressed to postal voters are returned as undelivered and are too late to be readdressed; or
   (c) any spoilt postal ballot papers are returned too late to enable other postal

ballot papers to be issued,

the local returning officer must put them unopened in a separate packet, seal up such packet and endorse and retain it and subsequently deal with it in the manner described in sub-paragraph (1).

(4) Rules 65 and 66 of the European Parliamentary elections rules apply to any packet or document retained under this paragraph except that in applying those rules the list compiled under paragraph 67(4) must be treated in the same manner as a counted ballot paper.

(5) A completed statement in Form R in the Appendix must be provided by the local returning officer to the Secretary of State and the Electoral Commission in the period which starts 10 days after the day of the poll and ends 15 days after that day.

(6) The statement referred to in sub-paragraph (5) must identify the local counting areas within the electoral region for which it is prepared.

(7) In the case of the Scottish electoral region, sub-paragraph (1) does not apply and the local returning officer must retain on behalf of the returning officer the packets and documents to which it refers.

Forwarding copy of list of rejected postal voting statements in Scotland

71 (1) As soon as practicable after the declaration of the result under rule 61 of the European Parliamentary elections rules, the local returning officer for each local government area in Scotland must send a copy of the list compiled under paragraph 67(4) (rejected postal voting statements) to the registration officer for that local government area.

(2) A registration officer may only use the copy of the list sent under sub-paragraph (1) for the purposes of notifying voters of rejected postal voting statements in accordance with paragraph 31A and requiring fresh signatures to be provided in accordance with paragraph 31B.

(3) Rule 65 (orders for the production of documents) of the European Parliamentary elections rules shall apply to the copy of the list sent in accordance with sub-paragraph (1) as if–

(a) references to counted ballot papers in the custody of the relevant registration officer were references to the copy of the list sent to a registration officer in accordance with sub-paragraph (1); and

(b) references to the relevant registration officer were references to the registration officer who was sent a copy of a list in accordance with sub-paragraph (1).

(4) Except as provided for by virtue of sub-paragraph (3), no other person may be allowed to inspect the copy of the list sent to a registration officer in accordance with sub-paragraph (1).

(5) The registration officer must cause the copy of the list sent in accordance with sub-paragraph (1) to be destroyed–

(a) as soon as practicable after the registration officer has complied with the requirements of paragraph 31A and issued any notices under paragraph 31B in relation to the information provided in the copy of the list; and

(b) in any event, within four months of receipt.

Part 5

Appendix of Forms

Not reproduced

SCHEDULE 3
MODIFICATION OF EUROPEAN PARLIAMENTARY ELECTIONS RULES FOR COMBINED POLLS

Part 1
England and Wales

1   This Part of this Schedule applies in the circumstances set out in regulation 11(i) of these Regulations.

2 (1)   In this Part of this Schedule, and in any provision of the European Parliamentary elections rules modified by this Schedule–
"police and crime commissioner election" means an election of a police and crime commissioner in accordance with Chapter 6 of Part 1 of the Police Reform and Social Responsibility Act 2011;
"relevant election or referendum" means one or more of the following–
    (a)   parliamentary election,
    (b)   local government election,
    (c)   mayoral election,
    (d)   referendum,
    (e)   a police and crime commissioner election,
the poll at which is taken together with a poll at the European Parliamentary election; and
"GLRO" means the Greater London Returning Officer, being the person who is for the time being a proper officer of the Greater London Authority for the purposes of section 35(2C) of the 1983 Act.

   (2)   In the case of a referendum, a reference to–
    (a)   an election agent or counting agent shall be construed as a reference to a counting officer within the meaning of regulation 2(1) of the Local Authorities (Conduct of Referendums) (England) Regulations 2007;
    (b)   a polling agent shall be construed as a reference to a polling observer, within the meaning of that regulation; and
    (c)   the returning officer or local returning officer shall be construed as a reference to a counting officer, within the meaning of that regulation.

3 (1)   In rule 22 (the ballot papers) at the end of paragraph (2)(b) omit "and".
   (2)   At the end of paragraph (2) insert–
"; and
    (d)   must be of a different colour from that of any ballot papers used at any relevant election or referendum.".

4   At the end of rule 27 (notice of poll) insert–
"(3) A notice published under paragraph (2) must, in addition–
    (a)   state that the poll at the European Parliamentary election is to be taken together with the poll at a relevant election or referendum;
    (b)   specify the relevant parliamentary constituency, local authority or, as the case may be, voting area and, in the case of a local government election to fill a casual vacancy, the electoral area for which the election is held; and
    (c)   where the polls are to be taken together in part of the local counting area only, specify that part."

5   At the end of rule 31 (issue of official poll cards) insert–
"(9) If the returning officer for each relevant election or referendum agrees, an official

poll card issued under this rule may be combined with an official poll card issued at each relevant election or referendum, with necessary adaptations."

6 After paragraph (1) of rule 32 (equipment of polling stations) insert–
"(1A) The same ballot box may be used for the poll at the European Parliamentary election and the poll at each relevant election or referendum, if the returning officer who discharges the functions specified in regulation 5 of the Combination of Polls Regulations thinks fit.

(1B) Where the same ballot box is not used under paragraph (1A), each ballot box must be clearly marked with–
  (a) the election or referendum to which it relates, as shown on the ballot papers for that election or referendum; and
  (b) the words "Please insert the *specify colour of ballot papers in question* coloured ballot papers in here."".

7 After paragraph (5) of rule 32 (equipment of polling stations) insert–
"(5A) The large version of the ballot paper referred to in paragraph (5)(a) must be printed on paper of the same colour as that of the ballot papers for use at the European Parliamentary election.".

8 For paragraph (7) of rule 32 (equipment of polling stations) substitute the following–
"(7) In every compartment of every polling station there must be exhibited the notice:
*PARLIAMENTARY ELECTION
(*Specify colour* ballot paper)
Vote for ONLY ONE CANDIDATE by putting a cross X in the box next to your choice.
*EUROPEAN PARLIAMENTARY ELECTION
(*Specify colour* ballot paper)
Vote ONLY ONCE by putting a cross X in the box next to your choice.
*Specify name of council COUNCIL ELECTION
(*Specify colour* ballot paper)
*Vote for NO MORE THAN ... CANDIDATES by putting a cross X in the box next to EACH of your choices
*Vote ONLY ONCE by putting a cross X in the box next to your choice
*ELECTION OF THE MAYOR OF LONDON
(*Specify colour* ballot paper)
#On the ballot paper for the election of the Mayor, vote ONCE for your first choice and ONCE for your second choice.
*ELECTION OF THE LONDON ASSEMBLY
#On the constituency members ballot paper (specify colour) vote for ONE candidate only.
#On the London members ballot paper (specify colour) vote for ONE party or individual candidate only.
*Specify other ELECTION/REFERENDUM
(*Specify colour* ballot paper)
Specify voting instructions in accordance with the legislation governing the election or referendum
PUT NO OTHER MARK ON THE BALLOT PAPER(S)*
OR YOUR VOTE(S)* MAY NOT COUNT
*PLEASE DO NOT FOLD THE BALLOT PAPERS FOR *specify the elections at which the votes are to be counted electronically*. *Post them, face downwards, in the *appropriate ballot box.
Complete or omit as necessary

#Alternatively, insert such information as the GLRO may decide".

9　In paragraph (1)(b) of rule 33 (appointment of polling and counting agents) omit the words "the verification of the ballot paper accounts and" and in paragraph (3)(b) of that rule omit the words "the verification of the ballot paper accounts or".

10　At the end of paragraph (4) of rule 33 (appointment of polling and counting agents) insert–
"Notices of the appointment of polling agents and counting agents which are required by this paragraph and paragraph (5) to be given to the local returning officer must be given to the returning officer who discharges the functions specified in regulation 5 of the Combination of Polls Regulations".

11　In rule 34(1)(b) (notification of requirement of secrecy) omit the words "the verification of the ballot paper accounts or" and ", (3)".

12 (1)　In rule 36(1) (admission to polling station), after sub-paragraph (g) omit "and".

　(2)　After sub-paragraph (h), insert–
"; and
　　　(i)　persons entitled to be admitted to the polling station at a relevant election or referendum.".

13　In rule 39 (questions to be put to voters) in questions 1(b), 2(b), 3(b) and 4 specified in the second column of the table set out in paragraph (1) after the words "at this" (wherever they occur) insert "European Parliamentary".

14　At the end of rule 41 (voting procedure) insert–
"(7)　The same copy of a register of electors or, where paragraph (3) applies, the same copy of the notice issued under section 13B(3B) or (3D) of the 1983 Act, may be used under paragraph (1) for each relevant election or referendum, and
　(a)　one mark may be placed in that register or on that notice under paragraph (1)(c) or in the list of proxies under paragraph (1)(d), to denote that a ballot paper has been issued in respect of each election or referendum; and
　(b)　where a ballot paper has not been issued in respect of a relevant election or referendum, a different mark must be placed in the register, or on the notice or list so as to identify each election or referendum in respect of which the ballot paper was issued.".

15　At the end of paragraph (2) of rule 42 (votes marked by presiding officer) insert–
"The same list may be used for each relevant election or referendum and, where it is so used, an entry in that list shall be taken to mean that the ballot papers were so marked in respect of each election or referendum, unless the list identifies the election or referendum at which the vote was so marked.".

16　At the end of paragraph (4) of rule 43 (voting by persons with disabilities) insert–
"The same list may be used for each relevant election or referendum and, where it is so used, an entry in that list shall be taken to mean that votes were so given in respect of each election or referendum, unless the list identifies the election or referendum at which the vote was given.".

17 At the end of paragraph (2) of rule 45 (tendered ballot papers: general provisions) insert–
"The same list may be used for each relevant election or referendum and, where it is so used, an entry in that list shall be taken to mean that tendered ballot papers were marked in respect of each election or referendum, unless the list identifies the election or referendum at which a tendered ballot paper was marked".

18 At the end of paragraph (1) of rule 47 (alteration of registers) insert–
"The same list may be used for each relevant election or referendums and, where it is so used, an entry in that list shall be taken to mean that ballot papers were issued in respect of each election or referendum, unless the list identifies the election or referendum for which a ballot paper was issued.".

19 In paragraph (1) of rule 48 (adjournment of poll in case of riot) omit "local" and after "returning officer" insert "who discharges the functions specified in regulation 5 of the Combination of Polls Regulations".

20 In paragraph (1) of rule 49 (procedure on close of poll) after the words "polling agents", in the first place where they occur, insert "appointed for the purpose of the European Parliamentary election and those appointed for the purposes of each relevant election or referendum".

21 After paragraph (1) of rule 49 (procedure on close of poll) insert–
"(1A) The contents of the packets referred to in sub-paragraphs (b), (c) and (f) of paragraph (1) must not be combined with the contents of packets made up under the corresponding rule that applies at each relevant election or referendum; nor shall the statement prepared under paragraph (3) be so combined.

(1B) References to the local returning officer in paragraph (1) above are references to the returning officer who discharges the functions specified in regulation 5 of the Combination of Polls Regulations".

22 Omit rules 50 (attendance at verification of ballot paper accounts) and 51 (procedure at verification of ballot paper accounts).

23 For paragraph (1) of rule 52 (attendance at counting of votes) substitute–
"(1) The local returning officer must make arrangements for counting the votes in the presence of the counting agents after the delivery of the ballot papers to him by the returning officer who discharges the functions specified in regulation 5 of the Combination of Polls Regulations–
(a) in the case of a general election of MEPs, before or after the material time and in either case so that the requirements of rule 57(1) are satisfied as soon as practicable after the material time;
(b) in the case of a by-election, as soon as practicable after that delivery,
and must give to the counting agents and the returning officer notice in writing of the time after which he will begin to count the votes if by then he has received the ballot papers and of the place at which the count will take place."

24 For paragraph (1) of rule 53 (the count) substitute–

"(1) The local returning officer must–
    (a) on receipt of the containers of ballot papers from the returning officer who discharges the functions specified in regulation 5 of the Combination of Polls Regulations and after the time specified in the notice given under rule 52(1) in the presence of the counting agents open each container;
    (b) where the proceedings on the issue and receipt of postal ballot papers are not taken together with those proceedings at another relevant election or referendum under paragraph 41 of Schedule 2, count such of the postal ballot papers as have been duly returned and record the number counted; and
    (c) mix together the postal ballot papers and the ballot papers from the containers and count the votes given on them.

(1A) Where separate ballot boxes have been used, no vote for any individual candidate or registered party shall be rendered invalid by the ballot paper being placed in the ballot box used at any relevant election or referendum.

(1B) A postal ballot paper must not be deemed to be duly returned unless–
    (a) it is returned in the manner prescribed in paragraph 55 of Schedule 2 so as to reach the local returning officer or any polling station in the appropriate area before the close of the poll;
    (b) the postal voting statement duly signed (unless the requirement for a signature has been waived) is also returned in that manner before that time;
    (c) the postal voting statement states the date of birth of the elector or proxy (as the case may be), and
    (d) the local returning officer verifies the date of birth and the signature of the elector or proxy (as the case may be) under paragraph 63 of Schedule 2.

(1C) In paragraph (1B) the "appropriate area" means–
    (a) the area in the local counting area common to the parliamentary constituency, electoral area or voting area (as the case may be) in which the polls at the European Parliamentary election and a relevant election or referendum are being taken together; and
    (b) in respect of which polls the voter has been issued with a postal ballot paper.

(1D) A postal ballot paper or postal voting statement that reaches the local returning officer or a polling station on or after the close of the poll is treated for the purposes of this rule as reaching that officer or polling station before the close of the poll if it is delivered by a person who, at the close of the poll, is in the polling station, or in a queue outside the polling station, for the purpose of returning it."

25 In paragraph (3) of rule 53 (the count) after the word "while" insert "counting and recording the number of postal ballot papers and".

26 For paragraph (2) of rule 63 (sealing up of ballot papers) substitute–

"(2) The local returning officer must not open the sealed packets of–
    (a) tendered ballot papers, or
    (b) certificates as to employment on duty on the day of the poll.

(3) Where he is the returning officer who discharges the functions referred to in regulation 5 of the Combination of Polls Regulations, the local returning officer must not open the sealed packets of–
    (a) the completed corresponding number lists, or
    (b) marked copies of a register of electors (including any marked copy notices

issued under section 13B(3B) or (3D) of the 1983 Act) and lists of proxies".

27 In paragraph (1) of rule 64 (delivery and retention of documents), omit sub-paragraphs (c) and (f).

28 In the Appendix of Forms, for Form K (form of directions for guidance of voters in voting) substitute Form K1 in the Appendix of Forms to this Schedule.

29 In the Appendix of Forms, for Form M (form of declaration by companion of voter with disabilities) substitute Form M1 in the Appendix of Forms to this Schedule.

Part 2
Scotland

1 This Part of this Schedule applies in the circumstances set out in regulation 11(ii) of these Regulations.

2 (1) In rule 22 (the ballot papers) at the end of paragraph (2)(b) omit "and".

(2) At the end of paragraph (2) insert–
"; and
(d) must be of a different colour from that of any ballot papers used at an election the poll for which is taken together with the poll for the European Parliamentary election."

3 At the end of rule 27 (notice of poll) insert–
"(3) The notice published under paragraph (2) must, in addition:
(a) state that the poll at the European Parliamentary election is to be taken together with the poll at a parliamentary or, as the case may be, local government election;
(b) specify the relevant parliamentary constituency or, as the case may be, local authority and, in the case of a local government election to fill a casual vacancy, the electoral area for which the election is held; and
(c) where the polls are to be taken together in part of the European Parliamentary electoral region only, specify that part.".

4 At the end of rule 31 (issue of official poll cards) insert–
"(9) An official poll card issued under this rule may be combined with an official poll card issued at a parliamentary election or, as the case may be, local government election."

5 After paragraph (1) of rule 32 (equipment of polling stations) insert–
"(1A) The same ballot box may be used for the poll at the European Parliamentary election and the poll at the parliamentary election or, as the case may be, local government election, if the returning officer who discharges the functions specified in regulation 96 of the 1986 (Scotland) Regulations thinks fit.

(1B) Where the same ballot box is not used under paragraph (1A), each ballot box must be clearly marked with–

(a)   the election to which it relates, as shown on the ballot papers for that election; and

(b)   the words "Please insert the *specify colour of ballot papers in question* coloured ballot papers in here.""

6   After paragraph (5) of rule 32 (equipment of polling stations) insert–
"(5A)   The large version of the ballot paper referred to in paragraph (5)(a) must be printed on paper of the same colour as that of the ballot papers for use at the European Parliamentary election."

7   For paragraph (7) of rule 32 (equipment of polling stations) substitute–
"(7)   In every compartment of every polling station there must be exhibited the notice:
*PARLIAMENTARY ELECTION
(Specify colour) ballot paper)
Vote for ONLY ONE CANDIDATE by putting a cross X in the box next to your choice.
EUROPEAN PARLIAMENTARY ELECTION
(Specify colour ballot paper)
Vote ONLY ONCE by putting a cross X in the box next to your choice.
*LOCAL GOVERNMENT ELECTION
On the Local Government ballot paper (coloured Specify colour) you vote using numbers. Put the number 1 in the box next to the name of the candidate who is your first choice, then put the number 2 in the box next to the name of the candidate who is your second choice, the number 3 in the box next to your third choice, the number 4 in the box next to your fourth choice, and so on. You can mark as many choices as you wish.
PUT NO OTHER MARK ON THE BALLOT PAPER(S)*
OR YOUR VOTE(S)* MAY NOT COUNT
Delete as necessary".

8   In paragraph (1)(b) of rule 33 (appointment of polling and counting agents) omit the words "the verification of the ballot paper accounts and" and in paragraph (3)(b) of that rule omit the words "verification of the ballot papers accounts or".

9   At the end of paragraph (4) of rule 33 (appointment of polling and counting agents) insert–
"Notices of the appointment of polling agents and counting agents which are required by this paragraph and paragraph (5) to be given to the local returning officer must be given to the returning officer who discharges the functions specified in regulation 96 of the 1986 (Scotland) Regulations.".

10   In rule 34(1)(b) (notification of requirement of secrecy) omit the words "the verification of the ballot paper accounts or" and "(3)".

11 (1)   In rule 36(1)(admission to polling station), after sub-paragraph (g) omit "and".

(2)   (2)After sub-paragraph (h) insert the following–
"; and
(i)   persons entitled to be admitted to the polling station at an election the poll for which is taken together with the poll for the European Parliamentary election."

12 In rule 39 (questions to be put to voters) in questions 1(b), 2(b), 3(b) and 4 specified in the second column of the table set out in paragraph (1) after the words "at this" (wherever they occur) insert "European Parliamentary".

13 At the end of rule 41 (voting procedure) insert–
"(7) The same copy of a register of electors or, where paragraph (3) applies, the same copy of the notice issued under section 13B(3B) or (3D) of the 1983 Act, may be used under paragraph (1) for each election, and
(a) one mark may be placed in that register or on that notice under paragraph (1)(c) or in the list of proxies under paragraph (1)(d) to denote that a ballot paper has been issued in respect of each election; and
(b) where a ballot paper has not been issued in respect of one election only, a different mark must be placed in the register, on the notice or list so as to identify the election in respect of which the ballot paper was issued."

14 At the end of paragraph (2) of rule 42 (votes marked by presiding officer) insert–
"The same list may be used for each election and, where it is so used, an entry in that list shall be taken to mean that the ballot papers were so marked in respect of each election, unless the list identifies the election at which the ballot paper was so marked."

15 At the end of paragraph (4) of rule 43 (voting by person with disabilities) insert–
"The same list may be used for each election and, where it is so used, an entry in that list shall be taken to mean that votes were so given in respect of each election, unless the list identifies the election at which the vote was given."

16 At the end of paragraph (2) of rule 45 (tendered ballot papers: general provisions) insert–
"The same list may be used for each election and, where it is so used, an entry in that list shall be taken to mean that tendered ballot papers were marked in respect of each election, unless the list identifies the election at which the ballot papers were so marked."

17 At the end of paragraph (1) of rule 47 (alteration of registers) insert–
"The same list may be used for each election and, where it is so used, an entry in that list shall be taken to mean that ballot papers were issued in respect of each election, unless the list identifies the election for which a ballot paper was issued."

18 At the end of paragraph (1) of rule 48 (adjournment of poll in case of riot) insert "who discharges the functions specified in regulation 96 of the 1986 (Scotland) Regulations".

19 In rule 49 (1) (procedure on close of poll), after the words "polling agents", in the first place where they occur, insert "for the European Parliamentary election and for the parliamentary, or as the case may be, local government election".

20 After paragraph (1) of rule 49 (procedure on close of poll) insert–
"(1A) The contents of the packets referred to in sub-paragraphs (b), (c) and (f) of paragraph (1) must not be combined with the contents of packets made up under the corresponding rule that applies at a parliamentary election or, as the case may

be, local government election; nor shall the statement prepared under paragraph (3) be so combined.

(1B) References to the local returning officer in paragraph (1) above are references to the returning officer who discharges the functions specified in regulation 96 of the 1986 (Scotland) Regulations."

21 Omit rules 50 (attendance at verification of ballot paper accounts) and 51 (procedure at verification of ballot paper accounts).

22 For paragraph (1) of rule 52 (attendance at counting of votes) substitute–

"(1) The local returning officer must make arrangements for counting the votes in the presence of the counting agents after the delivery of the ballot papers to him by the returning officer who discharges the functions specified in regulation 96 of the 1986 (Scotland) Regulations–

(a) in the case of a general election of MEPs, before or after the material time and in either case so that the requirements of rule 57(1) are satisfied as soon as practicable after the material time;

(b) in the case of a by-election, as soon as practicable after that delivery,

and must give to the counting agents and the returning officer notice in writing of the time after which he will begin to count the votes if by then he has received the ballot papers and of the place at which the count will take place."

23 For paragraph (1) of rule 53 (the count) substitute–

"(1) The local returning officer must–

(a) on receipt of the containers of ballot papers from the returning officer who discharges the functions specified in regulation 96 of the 1986 (Scotland) Regulations and after the time specified in the notice given under rule 52(1), in the presence of the counting agents open each container;

(b) where the proceedings on the issue and receipt of postal ballot papers are not taken together with those proceedings at another election under paragraph 41 of Schedule 2, count such of the postal ballot papers as have been duly returned and record the number counted; and

(c) mix together the postal ballot papers and the ballot papers from the containers and count the votes given on them.

(1A) Where separate ballot boxes have been used, no vote for any individual candidate or registered party shall be rendered invalid by the ballot paper being placed in the ballot box used for another election.

(1B) A postal ballot paper must not be deemed to be duly returned unless–

(a) it is returned in the manner prescribed in paragraph 55 of Schedule 2 so as to reach the local returning officer or any polling station in the local counting area before the close of the poll;

(b) the duly completed postal voting statement is also returned in that manner before that time;

(c) the local returning officer verifies the date of birth and the signature of the elector or proxy (as the case may be) under paragraph 63 of Schedule 2.

(1C) A postal ballot paper or postal voting statement that reaches the local returning officer or a polling station on or after the close of the poll is treated for the purposes of this rule as reaching that officer or polling station before the close of the poll if it is delivered by a person who, at the close of the poll, is in the polling station, or in a queue outside the polling station, for the purpose of returning it."

24 In paragraph (3) of rule 53 (the count) after the word "while" insert "counting and recording the number of postal ballot papers and".

25 For paragraph (2) of rule 63 (sealing up of ballot papers) substitute–
    "(2) The local returning officer must not open the sealed packets of–
        (a) tendered ballot papers, or
        (b) certificates as to employment on duty on the day of the poll.
    (3) Where he is the returning officer who discharges the functions referred to in regulation 96 of the 1986 (Scotland) Regulations, the local returning officer must not open the sealed packets of–
        (a) the completed corresponding number lists, or
        (b) marked copies of a register of electors (including any marked copy notices issued under section 13B(3B) or (3D) of the 1983 Act) and lists of proxies."

26 In paragraph (1) of rule 64 (delivery and retention of documents) omit sub-paragraphs (c) and (f).

27 In the Appendix of Forms, for Form K (form of directions for the guidance of voters in voting) substitute Form K1 in the Appendix of Forms to this Schedule.

28 In the Appendix of Forms, for Form M (form of declaration by companion of voter with disabilities) substitute Form M1 in the Appendix of Forms to this Schedule.

Appendix of Forms
Not reproduced

SCHEDULE 4
ENTITLEMENT TO REGISTRATION AND LEGAL INCAPACITY TO VOTE IN GIBRALTAR
Regulation 12

Part 1
General Application and Interpretation

1 (1) This Schedule makes provision as to–
    (a) legal incapacity to vote in Gibraltar as an elector at a European Parliamentary election; and
    (b) entitlement to registration in the Gibraltar register.

  (2) For the purposes of this Schedule, "the register" means the Gibraltar register.

Time

2 (1) Where the day or last day of the time allowed by this Schedule for the doing of any thing falls on any of the days mentioned in sub-paragraph (3), that time shall be extended until the next following day which is not one of those days.

  (2) In computing any period of not more than 7 days for the purposes of this Schedule any of the days mentioned in sub-paragraph (3) shall be disregarded.

  (3) The days referred to in sub-paragraphs (1) and (2) are a Saturday, Sunday, Christmas Eve, Christmas Day, Good Friday or a bank holiday.

  (5) In this regulation "bank holiday" means a day which is a Bank or Public Holiday in

Gibraltar not otherwise falling within sub-paragraph (3).

Part 2
Entitlement to Registration and Legal Incapacity

Legal Incapacity
Legal incapacity to vote of offenders in prison etc

3 (1)   A convicted person during the time that he is detained in a penal institution in Gibraltar in pursuance of his sentence or unlawfully at large when he would otherwise be so detained is legally incapable of voting at any European Parliamentary election.

(2)   For this purpose–

(a)   "convicted person" means any person found guilty of an offence (whether under the law of Gibraltar or not), including a person found guilty by a court-martial, but not including a person dealt with by committal or other summary process for contempt of court; and

(b)   a person detained for default in complying with his sentence shall not be treated as detained in pursuance of the sentence, whether or not the sentence provided for detention in the event of default, but a person detained by virtue of a conditional pardon in respect of an offence shall be treated as detained in pursuance of his sentence for the offence.

(3)   It is immaterial for the purposes of this paragraph whether a conviction or sentence was before or after the coming into force of these Regulations.

Legal incapacity to vote of offenders detained in mental hospitals

4 (1)   A person to whom this paragraph applies is, during the time that he is–

(a)   detained at any place in pursuance of the order by virtue of which this paragraph applies to him, or

(b)   unlawfully at large when he would otherwise be so detained,

legally incapable of voting at any European Parliamentary election.

(2)   This paragraph applies to the following persons–

(a)   any person in respect of whom an order has been made under sections 662(2)(a) or (b) of the Criminal Procedure and Evidence Act 2011;

(b)   a convicted person, within the meaning of paragraph 3, in respect of whom an order has been made under section 668 or 669 of the Criminal Procedure and Evidence Act 2011; and

(c)   any person in respect of whom a hospital order has been made under section 169(2)(a) of the Armed Forces Act 2006.

(3)   Any reference in any of sub-paragraphs (2)(a) to (c) to a provision of any Act includes a reference to any earlier provision (whether of that Act as originally enacted or made or as previously amended, or otherwise) to the like effect.

Persons under the Age of 18
Entitlement to registration of person under the age of 18

5 (1)   A person otherwise qualified for registration is (despite sections 15(1)(d) and 16(1)(d) and (2)(d) of the 2003 Act) entitled to be registered in the register if he will attain voting age before the end of the period of 12 months beginning with the 1st December next following the relevant date, but–

(a)   his entry in the register shall give the date on which he will attain that age; and

(b)   until the date given in the entry he shall not by virtue of the entry be treated as an elector for any purposes other than those of an election the date of the poll for which is the date so given or any later date.

(2) In this paragraph "the relevant date", in relation to a person, means–

    (a) the date on which an application for registration is made (or, by virtue of paragraph 6, is treated as having been made) by him;

    (b) in the case of a person applying for registration in pursuance of a declaration of local connection or a service declaration, the date on which the declaration was made.

Circumstances in which an application for registration in the Gibraltar register may be treated as having been made

6 Where–

    (a) in connection with a canvass under paragraph 9 of Schedule 1 to the 2004 Act, the form completed in respect of any address specifies any person as a person who is entitled to be registered in the register, and

    (b) that person is not for the time being registered in the register in respect of that address,

he shall be treated as having made, on the canvass date (within the meaning of that Act) in question, an application for registration in the register in respect of that address.

7 *Repealed*

Residence

Residence: general

8 (1) This paragraph applies where the question whether a person is resident at a particular address on the relevant date for the purposes of section 16(1)(a) of the 2003 Act falls to be determined for the purposes of that section.

(2) Regard shall be had, in particular, to the purpose and other circumstances, as well as to the fact, of his presence at, or absence from, the address on that date.

For example, where at a particular time a person is staying at any place otherwise than on a permanent basis, he may in all the circumstances be taken to be at that time–

    (a) resident there if he has no home elsewhere, or

    (b) not resident there if he does have a home elsewhere.

(3) For the purpose of determining whether a person is resident in a dwelling on the relevant date for the purposes of section 16(1)(a) of the 2003 Act, his residence in the dwelling shall not be taken to have been interrupted by reason of his absence in the performance of any duty arising from or incidental to any office, service or employment held or undertaken by him if–

    (a) he intends to resume actual residence within six months of giving up such residence, and will not be prevented from doing so by the performance of that duty; or

    (b) the dwelling serves as a permanent place of residence (whether for himself or for himself and other persons) and he would be in actual residence there but for his absence in the performance of that duty.

(4) For the purposes of sub-paragraph (3) any temporary period of unemployment shall be disregarded.

(5) Sub-paragraph (3) shall apply in relation to a person's absence by reason of his attendance on a course provided by an educational institution as it applies in relation to a person's absence in the performance of any duty such as is mentioned in that subsection.

(6)   Subject to paragraphs 10 and 11, a person who is detained at any place in legal custody shall not, by reason of his presence there, be treated for the purposes of section 16(1)(a) of the 2003 Act as resident there.

Residence: merchant seamen

9   At any time when a merchant seaman is not resident in Gibraltar and would have been resident there but for the nature of his occupation, he shall be entitled to be treated for the purposes of section 16(1)(a) of the 2003 Act as resident–
   (a)   at any place at which he would have been resident but for the nature of his occupation; or
   (b)   at any hostel or club providing accommodation for merchant seamen at which he commonly stays in the course of his occupation.

For this purpose "merchant seaman" means any person not having a service qualification whose employment or the greater part of it is carried out on board seagoing ships, and includes any such person while temporarily without employment.

Residence: patients in mental hospitals who are not detained offenders or on remand

10 (1)   This paragraph applies to a person who–
   (a)   is a patient in a mental hospital in Gibraltar (whether or not he is liable to be detained there), but
   (b)   is not a person to whom paragraph 4 or paragraph 11 applies.

(2)   A person to whom this paragraph applies shall (subject to sub-paragraph (5)) be regarded for the purposes of section 16(1)(a) of the 2003 Act as resident at the mental hospital in question if the length of the period which he is likely to spend at the hospital is sufficient for him to be regarded as being resident there for the purposes of electoral registration.

(3)   A person registered in the register in pursuance of an application for registration made by virtue of sub-paragraph (2) is entitled to remain so registered until–
   (a)   the end of the period of 12 months beginning with the date when the entry in the register first takes effect, or
   (b)   another entry made in respect of him in the register takes effect (whether or not in pursuance of an application made by virtue of sub-paragraph (2)),
   whichever first occurs.

(4)   Where the entitlement of such a person to remain so registered terminates by virtue of sub-paragraph (3), the registration officer concerned shall remove that person's entry from the register, unless he is entitled to remain registered in pursuance of a further application made by virtue of sub-paragraph (2).

(5)   Sub-paragraph (2) shall not be taken as precluding the registration of a person to whom this paragraph applies–
   (a)   by virtue of his residence at some place other than the mental hospital in which he is a patient, or
   (b)   in pursuance of a declaration of local connection.

(6)   In this paragraph "mental hospital" means any establishment (or part of an establishment) maintained wholly or mainly for the reception and treatment of persons suffering from any form of mental disorder; and for this purpose "mental disorder", has the same meaning as in section 3(1) of the Mental Health Act.

Residence: persons remanded in custody etc

11 (1)   This paragraph applies to a person who is detained at any place in Gibraltar pursuant

to a relevant order or direction and is so detained otherwise than after–
- (a) being convicted of any offence, or
- (b) a finding in criminal proceedings that he did the act or made the omission charged.

(2) A person to whom this paragraph applies shall (subject to sub-paragraph (5)) be regarded for the purposes of section 16(1)(a) of the 2003 Act as resident at the place at which he is detained if the length of the period which he is likely to spend at that place is sufficient for him to be regarded as being resident there for the purposes of electoral registration.

(3) A person registered in the register in pursuance of an application for registration made by virtue of sub-paragraph (2) is entitled to remain so registered until–
- (a) the end of the period of 12 months beginning with the date when the entry in the register first takes effect, or
- (b) another entry made in respect of him in the register takes effect (whether or not in pursuance of an application made by virtue of sub-paragraph (2)),

whichever first occurs.

(4) Where the entitlement of such a person to remain so registered terminates by virtue of sub-paragraph (3), the registration officer concerned shall remove that person's entry from the register, unless he is entitled to remain registered in pursuance of a further application made by virtue of sub-paragraph (2).

(5) Sub-paragraph (2) shall not be taken as precluding the registration of a person to whom this section applies–
- (a) by virtue of his residence at some place other than the place at which he is detained, or
- (b) in pursuance of a declaration of local connection.

(6) In this section "a relevant order or direction" means–
- (a) a remand or committal in custody;
- (b) a remand to a hospital under section 249(6)(c), 250(4) or (5) of the Criminal Procedure Act;
- (c) a direction for removal to a hospital under section 257 of that Act.

Notional residence: declarations of local connection

12 (1) A declaration under this paragraph ("a declaration of local connection")–
- (a) may be made only by a person to whom this paragraph applies, but
- (b) may be made by such a person despite the fact that by reason of his age he is not entitled to vote.

(2) This paragraph applies to any person who on the date when he makes such a declaration is–
- (a) a person to whom paragraph 10 applies and who would not be entitled to be registered by virtue of residence at any place other than the mental hospital (within the meaning of that paragraph) at which he is a patient, or
- (b) a person to whom paragraph 11 applies and who would not be entitled to be registered by virtue of residence at any place other than the place at which he is detained as mentioned in sub-paragraph (1) of that paragraph, or
- (c) a person who does not fall within paragraph (a) or (b) (and is not otherwise in legal custody) and who is not, for the purposes of section 16(1)(a) of the 2003 Act, resident at any address in Gibraltar (a "homeless person").

(3) A declaration of local connection shall state–
- (a) the name of the declarant and either–
    - (i) an address to which correspondence for him from the registration officer or the returning officer can be delivered, or

    (ii) that he is willing to collect such correspondence periodically from the registration officer's office;

  (b) the date of the declaration;

  (c) that on the date of the declaration the declarant falls into one of the categories of persons to whom this paragraph applies, specifying–

    (i) the category in question, and

    (ii) (in the case of a person falling within sub-paragraph (2)(a) or (b)) the name and address of the mental hospital at which he is a patient or (as the case may be) of the place at which he is detained;

  (d) the required address (as defined by sub-paragraph (4));

  (e) the nationality of the declarant on the date of the declaration confirming that he is a Commonwealth citizen or a relevant citizen of the Union;

  (f) whether the declarant has on the date of the declaration attained the age of 18 years, and, if he has not, the date of his birth.

(4) For the purposes of this paragraph "the required address" is–

  (a) in the case of a person falling within sub-paragraph (2)(a) or (b)–

    (i) the address in Gibraltar where he would be residing if he were not such a patient, or detained, as mentioned in that provision, or

    (ii) if he cannot give such an address, an address in Gibraltar at which he has resided;

  (b) in the case of a homeless person, the address of, or which is nearest to, a place in Gibraltar where he commonly spends a substantial part of his time (whether during the day or at night).

(5) If a person–

  (a) makes a declaration of local connection stating more than one address under sub-paragraph (3)(d), or

  (b) makes more than one declaration of local connection bearing the same date and stating different addresses under that provision,

the declaration or declarations shall be void.

(6) A declaration of local connection may be cancelled at any time by the declarant.

(7) A declaration of local connection shall be of no effect unless it is received by the registration officer within the period of three months beginning with the date of the declaration.

Effect of declaration of local connection

13 (1) Where a person's declaration of local connection is in force when he applies for registration, he shall be regarded for the purposes of section 16(1)(a) of the 2003 Act as resident on the date of the declaration at the address stated in it in accordance with paragraph 12.

(2) A person registered in the register in pursuance of a declaration of local connection is entitled to remain so registered until–

  (a) the end of the period of 12 months beginning with the date when the entry in the register first takes effect,

  (b) the declaration is cancelled under paragraph 12(6), or

  (c) another entry made in respect of him in the register takes effect (whether or not in pursuance of a declaration of local connection),

whichever first occurs.

(3) Where the entitlement of such a person to remain so registered terminates by virtue of sub-paragraph (2), the registration officer shall remove that person's entry from the register, unless he is entitled to remain registered in pursuance of a further declaration

of local connection.

(4)　This paragraph shall not be taken as precluding the registration of a person falling within paragraph 12(2)(a) or (b) in pursuance of an application made by virtue of paragraph 10(2) or 11(2).

Overseas Electors

Registration of overseas electors

14 (1)　A person qualifies for registration in Gibraltar as an overseas elector, for the purposes of section 16(2)(a) of the 2003 Act and these Regulations, if–

(a)　he makes a declaration under and in accordance with paragraph 15; and

(b)　on that date ("the relevant date")–

(i)　he is not resident in Gibraltar; and

(ii)　he satisfies one of the following sets of conditions.

(2)　The first set of conditions is that–

(a)　he was included in the register in respect of an address at a place that is situated within Gibraltar,

(b)　that entry in the register was made on the basis that he was resident, or to be treated for the purposes of registration as resident, at that address,

(c)　that entry in the register was in force at any time falling within the period of 15 years ending immediately before the relevant date, and

(d)　subsequent to that entry ceasing to have effect no entry was made in the register on the basis that he was resident, or to be treated for the purposes of registration as resident, at any other address.

(3)　The second set of conditions is that–

(a)　the was last resident in Gibraltar within the period of 15 years ending immediately before the relevant date,

(b)　he was by reason only of his age incapable of being included in the register in force on the last day on which he was resident in Gibraltar, and

(c)　the address at which he was resident on that day was at a place that is situated within Gibraltar and a parent or guardian of his was included, in respect of that address, in the register in force on that day.

Overseas elector's declaration

15 (1)　A declaration made by an elector under and in accordance with this paragraph is referred to in these Regulations as an "overseas elector's declaration".

(2)　A person registered in the register in pursuance of an overseas elector's declaration is entitled to remain so registered until–

(a)　the end of the period of 12 months beginning with the date when the entry in the register first takes effect,

(b)　the declaration is cancelled under sub-paragraph (5), or

(c)　any entry made in respect of him in the register takes effect otherwise than in pursuance of an overseas elector's declaration,

whichever first occurs; and, where the entitlement of such a person to remain so registered terminates by virtue of this sub-paragraph, the registration officer shall remove that person's entry from the register, unless he is entitled to remain registered in pursuance of a further overseas elector's declaration.

(3)　An overseas elector's declaration must state–

(a)　the date of the declaration,

(b)　the declarant's nationality confirming that he is a Commonwealth citizen,

(c)　that the declarant is not resident in Gibraltar on the relevant date, and

(d)　when he ceased to be so resident or, in the case of a person relying on registration in pursuance of a service declaration, when he ceased to have a service qualification or, if later, ceased to be so resident,

and must also satisfy the requirements of sub-paragraph (4) and paragraph 14 of Schedule 1 to the 2004 Act.

(4)   An overseas elector's declaration must–

    (a)   show which set of conditions in paragraph 14 the declarant claims to satisfy,

    (b)   in the case of the first set of conditions, specify the address in respect of which he was registered, and

    (c)   in the case of the second set of conditions, specify–

        (i)   the date of the declarant's birth,

        (ii)   the address in Gibraltar at which he was resident, and

        (iii)   the name of the parent or guardian on whose registration in respect of that address he relies, and whether the person named was a parent or guardian,

and may not, in the case of either set of conditions, specify more than one such address; and if the declarant makes more than one such declaration bearing the same date and specifying different addresses in Gibraltar as the address in respect of which he was registered or, as the case may be, at which he was resident the declarations shall be void.

(5)   An overseas elector's declaration may be cancelled at any time by the declarant.

(6)   An overseas elector's declaration shall be of no effect unless it is received by the registration officer concerned within the period of three months beginning with the relevant date.

(7)   For the purposes of paragraph 12, where a person is registered in the register in pursuance of an overseas elector's declaration, it shall be conclusively presumed that he was not resident in Gibraltar on the relevant date.

(8)   In this paragraph "the relevant date" has the meaning given by paragraph 14(1).

Service Voters

Service qualification

16   A person has a service qualification for the purposes of these Regulations who–

    (a)   is a member of the Royal Gibraltar regiment,

    (b)   is the wife or husband of a member of the Royal Gibraltar regiment.

Service declaration

17 (1)   A service declaration shall be made only by a person who has a service qualification, and a service declaration may be made by such a person notwithstanding the fact that by reason of his age he is not yet entitled to vote.

(2)   Where a person is registered in the Gibraltar register in pursuance of a service declaration, the person is entitled to remain so registered until–

    (a)   the end of the period of 3 years beginning with the date when the entry in the register first takes effect,

    (b)   the declaration is cancelled under sub-paragraph (5), or

    (c)   another entry made in respect of him in the register takes effect (whether or not in pursuance of a service declaration),

whichever first occurs.

(3)   Where the entitlement of such a person to remain so registered terminates by virtue of sub-paragraph (2), the registration officer shall remove that person's entry from the register, unless he is entitled to remain registered in pursuance of a further service declaration.

(4) If a person–
   (a) makes a service declaration declaring to more than one address, or
   (b) makes more than one service declaration bearing the same date and declaring to different addresses,
   the declaration or declarations shall be void.

(5) A service declaration may at any time be cancelled by the declarant.

(6) A service declaration shall be of no effect unless it is received by the registration officer within the period of three months beginning with the date of the declaration.

(7) Arrangements shall be made by the Gibraltar Ministry of Defence for securing that (so far as circumstances permit) every person having a service qualification by virtue of sub-paragraph (a) or (b)of paragraph 16 shall–
   (a) have an effective opportunity of exercising from time to time as occasion may require the rights conferred on him by these Regulations in relation to the making and cancellation of service declarations and of appointments of a proxy, and in relation to voting by post; and
   (b) receive such instructions as to the effect of these Regulations, and such other assistance, as may be reasonably sufficient in connection with the exercise by him and any wife of his or, as the case may be, by her and any husband of hers, of any rights conferred on them as mentioned above.

Contents of service declaration

18 A service declaration shall state–
   (a) the date of the declaration,
   (b) that on that date the declarant is, or but for the circumstances entitling him to make the declaration would have been, residing in Gibraltar,
   (c) the address where the declarant is or, as the case may be, would have been residing in Gibraltar or, if he cannot give any such address, an address at which he has resided in Gibraltar,
   (d) the nationality of the declarant on the date of the declaration confirming that he is a Commonwealth citizen or a relevant citizen of the Union,
   (e) whether the declarant had on the date of the declaration attained the age of 18 years, and, if he had not, the date of his birth, and
   (f) such particulars (if any) of the declarant's identity and service qualifications as are required by paragraph 19 of Schedule 1 to the 2004 Act.

Effect of service declaration

19 (1) Where a person's service declaration is in force when he applies for registration, he shall be regarded for the purposes of section 16(1)(a) of the 2003 Act as–
   (a) resident on the date of the declaration at the address specified in it in accordance with paragraph 18(c);
   (b) until the contrary is proved, as being a Commonwealth citizen or a relevant citizen of the Union of the age appearing from the declaration and as not being subject to any legal incapacity except as so appearing.

(2) Where a service declaration appearing to be properly made out and (where required) attested is transmitted to the registration officer in the proper manner, the declarant shall, until the contrary is proved, be treated for the purposes of registration as having had from the date of the declaration or such later date, if any, as appears from it, and as continuing to have, a service qualification.

Relevant Citizens of the Union

Notification of and removal of names of relevant citizens of the Union from the register

20 (1)   As soon as practicable after the registration officer has entered the name of a relevant citizen of the Union in the register where he would be entitled to vote at a European Parliamentary election in pursuance of the registration, he shall send a copy of the application and declaration by virtue of which he entered the name in the register to the person shown as the representative of the State in respect of which the applicant is a national in a direction containing a list of such representatives issued by the Lord Chancellor under regulation 8(3) of the 2001 Franchise Regulations.

   (2)   A declaration under paragraph 25(3)(b) of Schedule 1 to the European Parliamentary Elections Ordinance 2004 may be cancelled at any time by the declarant.

   (3)   A relevant citizen of the Union registered in the register is entitled to remain so registered until–
   (a)   the end of the period of 12 months beginning with the date when the entry in the register first takes effect;
   (b)   the declaration under paragraph 25(3)(b) of Schedule 1 to the 2004 Act is cancelled under sub-paragraph (2);
   (c)   the citizen applies for his name to be removed,
   whichever first occurs.

   (4)   Where the entitlement of such a person to remain registered terminates by virtue of sub-paragraph (3), the registration officer shall remove the person's entry from the register, unless he is entitled to remain in pursuance of a further application and declaration under paragraph 25 of Schedule 1 to the 2004 Act.

   (6)   The registration officer shall remove the name of a relevant citizen of the Union from the register where the Secretary of State sends to that officer a copy of information provided by the Member State of which that citizen is a national to show that he has lost the right to vote there.

Part 3
Discharge of Registration Duties

21 (1) The registration officer shall comply with any general or special directions which may be given by the Secretary of State with respect to the arrangements to be made by the registration officer for carrying out his functions under this Schedule.

   (2)   Without prejudice to the generality of sub-paragraph (1), the directions which may be given under sub-paragraph (1) include directions requiring the registration officer to maintain the register in a specified electronic form; and any such directions may in particular specify–
   (a)   the software which is to be used in connection with the maintenance of the register in that form;
   (b)   the standards in accordance with which that software is to be maintained and updated;
   (c)   how information required by this Schedule to be included in the register is to be recorded and stored in that form.

SCHEDULE 5

Revoked

SCHEDULE 6
CONTROL OF DONATIONS TO INDIVIDUAL CANDIDATES

Part 1
Introductory

Operation and interpretation of Schedule

1 (1)   This Schedule has effect for controlling donations to individual candidates at an election.

   (2)   The following provisions have effect for the purposes of this Schedule.

   (3)   In accordance with sub-paragraph (1), references to a candidate are to an individual candidate.

   (4)   "Relevant donation", in relation to a candidate at an election, means a donation to the candidate or his election agent for the purpose of meeting election expenses incurred by or on behalf of the candidate.

   (5)   In sub-paragraph (4) above the reference to a donation for the purpose of meeting election expenses incurred by or on behalf of a candidate includes a reference to a donation for the purpose of securing that any such expenses are not so incurred; and a donation shall be taken to be a donation for either of those purposes if, having regard to all the circumstances, it must be reasonably assumed to be such a donation.

   (6)   "Donation" shall be construed in accordance with paragraphs 2 to 4 below.

   (7)   In relation to a donation received by a candidate at an election in Great Britain or Gibraltar, references to a permissible donor falling within section 54(2) of the 2000 Act are to be read as if section 54(2) did not include a party registered in the Northern Ireland register maintained by the Commission under Part 2 of that Act.

   (8)   "The Commission" means the Electoral Commission established by section 1 of that Acct.

Donations: general rules

2 (1)   "Donation", in relation to an individual candidate at an election, means (subject to paragraph 4 below)–

   (a)   any gift to the candidate or his election agent of money or other property;

   (b)   any sponsorship provided in relation to the candidate (as defined by paragraph 3 below);

   (c)   any money spent (otherwise than by the candidate, his election agent or any sub-agent) in paying any election expenses incurred by or on behalf of the candidate;

   (d)   any money lent to the candidate or his election agent otherwise than on commercial terms;

   (e)   the provision otherwise than on commercial terms of any property, services or facilities for the use or benefit of the candidate (including the services of any person).

   (2)   Where–

   (a)   any money or other property is transferred to a candidate or his election agent pursuant to any transaction or arrangement involving the provision by or on behalf of the candidate of any property, services or facilities or other consideration of monetary value, and

   (b)   the total value in monetary terms of the consideration so provided by or on behalf of the candidate is less than the value of the money or (as the case may be) the market value of the property transferred, the transfer of the money or property shall (subject to sub-paragraph (4) below) constitute a gift to the candidate or (as the case may be) his election agent for the purposes of sub-paragraph (1)(a) above.

(3) In determining–

    (a) for the purposes of sub-paragraph (1)(d) above, whether any money lent to a candidate or his election agent is so lent otherwise than on commercial terms, or

    (b) for the purposes of sub-paragraph (1)(e) above, whether any property, services or facilities provided for the use or benefit of a candidate is or are so provided otherwise than on such terms,

regard shall be had to the total value in monetary terms of the consideration provided by or on behalf of the candidate in respect of the loan or the provision of the property, services or facilities.

(4) Where (apart from this sub-paragraph) anything would be a donation both by virtue of sub-paragraph (1)(b) above and by virtue of any other provision of this paragraph, sub-paragraph (1)(b) (together with paragraph 3 below) shall apply in relation to it to the exclusion of the other provision of this paragraph.

(5) The reference in sub-paragraph (1)(c) above to money spent as mentioned in that provision is a reference to money so spent by a person, other than the candidate, his election agent or any sub-agent, out of his own resources (with no right to reimbursement out of the resources of any such other person); and where, by virtue of sub-paragraph (1)(c) above, money so spent constitutes a donation to the candidate, the candidate shall be treated as receiving an equivalent amount on the date on which the money is paid to the creditor in respect of the expenses in question.

(6) In this paragraph–

    (a) any reference to anything being given or transferred to a candidate or his election agent includes a reference to its being given or transferred either directly or indirectly through any third person;

    (b) "gift" includes a bequest or any other form of testamentary disposition.

Sponsorship

3 (1) For the purposes of this Schedule sponsorship is provided in relation to a candidate if–

    (a) any money or other property is transferred to the candidate or to any person for the benefit of the candidate, and

    (b) the purpose (or one of the purposes) of the transfer is (or must, having regard to all the circumstances, reasonably be assumed to be)–

        (i) to help the candidate with meeting, or to meet, to any extent any defined expenses incurred or to be incurred by or on behalf of the candidate, or

        (ii) to secure that to any extent any such expenses are not so incurred.

(2) In sub-paragraph (1) above "defined expenses" means expenses in connection with–

    (a) any conference, meeting or other event organised by or on behalf of the candidate,

    (b) the preparation, production or dissemination of any publication by or on behalf of the candidate, or

    (c) any study or research organised by or on behalf of the candidate.

(3) The following do not, however, constitute sponsorship by virtue of sub-paragraph (1) above–

    (a) the making of any payment in respect of–

        (i) any charge for admission to any conference, meeting or other event, or

        (ii) the purchase price of, or any other charge for access to, any publication;

    (b) the making of any payment in respect of the inclusion of an advertisement in any publication where the payment is made at the commercial rate payable for the inclusion of such an advertisement in any such publication.

(4)   In this paragraph "publication" means a publication made available in whatever form and by whatever means (whether or not to the public at large or any section of the public).

Payments etc not to be regarded as donations

4 (1)   None of the following shall be regarded as a donation–

    (a)   the provision of any facilities provided in pursuance of any right conferred on a candidate at an election by these Regulations;

    (b)   the provision by an individual of his own services which he provides voluntarily in his own time and free of charge;

    (c)   any interest accruing to a candidate or his election agent in respect of any donation which is dealt with by the candidate or (as the case may be) his election agent in accordance with section 56(2)(a) or (b) of the 2000 Act (as applied by paragraph 7 below).

(2)   There shall also be disregarded any donation whose value (determined in accordance with paragraph 5 below) is not more than £50.

Value of donations

5 (1)   The value of any donation falling within paragraph 2(1)(a) above (other than money) shall be taken to be the market value of the property in question.

(2)   Where, however, paragraph 2(1)(a) above applies by virtue of paragraph 2(2) above, the value of the donation shall be taken to be the difference between–

    (a)   the value of the money, or the market value of the property, in question, and

    (b)   the total value in monetary terms of the consideration provided by or on behalf of the candidate or his election agent.

(3)   The value of any donation falling within paragraph 2(1)(b) above shall be taken to be the value of the money, or (as the case may be) the market value of the property, transferred as mentioned in paragraph 3(1) above; and accordingly any value in monetary terms of any benefit conferred on the person providing the sponsorship in question shall be disregarded.

(4)   The value of any donation falling within paragraph 2(1)(d) or (e) above shall be taken to be the amount representing the difference between–

    (a)   the total value in monetary terms of the consideration that would have had to be provided by or on behalf of the candidate or his election agent in respect of the loan or the provision of the property, services or facilities if–

      (i)   the loan had been made, or

      (ii)   the property, services or facilities had been provided,

on commercial terms, and

    (b)   the total value in monetary terms of the consideration (if any) actually so provided by or on behalf of the candidate or his election agent.

(5)   Where a donation such as is mentioned in sub-paragraph (4) above confers an enduring benefit on the donee over a particular period, the value of the donation–

    (a)   shall be determined at the time when it is made, but

    (b)   shall be so determined by reference to the total benefit accruing to the donee over that period.

(7)   In this paragraph "market value" in relation to any property, means the price which might reasonably be expected to be paid for the property on a sale in the open market.

Part 2
Controls on Donations

Prohibition on accepting donations from impermissible donors

6 (1) A relevant donation received by an individual candidate or his election agent must not be accepted if–
   (a) the person by whom the donation would be made is not, at the time of its receipt by the candidate or (as the case may be) his election agent, a permissible donor falling within section 54(2) of the 2000 Act; or
   (b) the candidate or (as the case may be) his election agent is (whether because the donation is given anonymously or by reason of any deception or concealment or otherwise) unable to ascertain the identity of the person offering the donation.

(2) For the purposes of this Schedule any relevant donation received by a candidate or his election agent which is an exempt trust donation shall be regarded as a relevant donation received by the candidate or his election agent from a permissible donor; and section 162 of the 2000 Act (interpretation: exempt trust donations) shall apply for the purposes of this Schedule as it applies for the purposes of that Act.

(3) But, for the purposes of this Schedule, any relevant donation received by a candidate or his election agent from a trustee of any property (in his capacity as such) which is not–
   (a) an exempt trust donation, or
   (b) a relevant donation transmitted by the trustee to the candidate or his election agent on behalf of beneficiaries under the trust who are–
      (i) persons who at the time of its receipt by the candidate or his election agent are permissible donors falling within section 54(2) of the 2000 Act, or
      (ii) the members of an unincorporated association which at that time is such a permissible donor,
   shall be regarded as a relevant donation received by the candidate or his election agent from a person who is not such a permissible donor.

(4) Where any person ("the principal donor") causes an amount ("the principal donation") to be received by a candidate or his election agent by way of a relevant donation–
   (a) on behalf of himself and one or more other persons, or
   (b) on behalf of two or more other persons,
   then for the purposes of this Part each individual contribution by a person falling within paragraph (a) or (b) of more than £50 shall be treated as if it were a separate donation received from that person.

(5) In relation to each such separate donation, the principal donor must ensure that, at the time when the principal donation is received by the candidate or his election agent, the candidate or (as the case may be) his election agent is given–
   (a) (except in the case of a donation which the principal donor is treated as making) all such details in respect of the person treated as making the donation as are required by virtue of paragraph 11(c) below; and
   (b) (in any case) all such details in respect of the donation as are required by virtue of paragraph 11(a) below.

(6) Where–
   (a) any person ("the agent") causes an amount to be received by a candidate or his election agent by way of a donation on behalf of another person ("the donor"), and

(b) the amount of the donation is more than £50,

the agent must ensure that, at the time when the donation is received by the candidate or his election agent, the candidate or (as the case may be) his election agent is given all such details in respect of the donor as are required by virtue of paragraph 11(c) below.

(7) A person commits an offence if, without reasonable excuse, he fails to comply with sub-paragraph (5) or (6) above.

(8) A person guilty of an offence under sub-paragraph (7) shall be liable–
    (a) on summary conviction, to a fine not exceeding the statutory maximum or to a term of imprisonment not exceeding 6 months (or both);
    (b) on conviction on indictment, to a fine or to a term of imprisonment not exceeding one year (or both).

(9) In the application of this paragraph to an individual candidate (or his election agent) at an election in the combined region–
    (a) the references in sub-paragraphs (1)(a) and (3)(b)(i) to a permissible donor falling within section 54(2) include references to persons listed in section 54(2A)(a) to (g) of the 2000 Act;
    (b) in sub-paragraph (3)(b)(ii) the reference to an unincorporated association which is a permissible donor includes a reference to an unincorporated association falling within section 54(2A)(g) of the 2000 Act; and
    (c) in sub-paragraph (2) and (3)(a) the references to an exempt trust donation include a reference to an exempt Gibraltar trust donation (within the meaning of section 162 of the 2000 Act).

Acceptance or return of donations

7 (1) Sections 56 to 60 of the 2000 Act shall apply for the purposes of this Schedule in relation to–
    (a) a relevant donation received by a candidate or his election agent, and
    (b) the candidate or (as the case may be) the election agent,
as they apply in relation to a donation received by a registered party and the registered party.

(2) In the application of sections 56 to 60 of that Act in accordance with sub-paragraph (1)–
    (a) section 56(1) shall have effect as if the reference to the particulars relating to a donor which would be required to be included in a donation report by virtue of paragraph 2 of Schedule 6 (if the donation were a recordable donation within the meaning of that Schedule) were construed as a reference to the particulars which are required to be included in a return by virtue of paragraph 11(c) below;
    (b) section 56(3) shall have effect as if the reference to the party were omitted and the reference to the treasurer of the party were construed as a reference to the candidate or (as the case may be) his election agent; and
    (c) section 56(4) shall have effect as if the reference to the treasurer of the party were construed as a reference to the candidate or (as the case may be) his election agent.

Transfer of donations received by candidate to election agent

8 (1) Sub-paragraph (2) below applies in relation to any relevant donation received by a candidate after the deadline for appointing an election agent (unless the candidate is, or is deemed to be, his own election agent at the time of receipt of the donation).

(2) The candidate shall, on receipt of any such donation as is mentioned in sub-paragraph (1) above, forthwith deliver to his election agent–

  (a)   the donation,
  (b)   where paragraph 6(5) or (6) above applies in relation to the donation, the information provided to the candidate in pursuance of that provision, and
  (c)   any other information which the candidate has about the donation and its donor which might reasonably be expected to assist the election agent in the discharge of any duties imposed on him, in relation to the donation, under this Part or Part 3 of this Schedule.

(3)   Where a donation is delivered to an election agent in accordance with sub-paragraph (2) above, the donation shall be treated for the purposes of paragraph 6(1) to (4) above and the provisions applied by paragraph 7 above as if it had been–
  (a)   originally received by the election agent, and
  (b)   so received by him on the date on which it was received by the candidate.

(4)   Where a candidate receives a relevant donation before the deadline for appointing an election agent but at a time when an appointment of a person (other than the candidate himself) as election agent is in force he shall either–
  (a)   forthwith deliver the donation and the information mentioned in sub-paragraph (2)(b) and (c) above to the agent, or
  (b)   (if he fails to do so) deal with the donation in accordance with section 56 of the 2000 Act.

(5)   Sub-paragraph (3) above shall have effect in relation to any relevant donation delivered to an election agent in accordance with sub-paragraph (4)(a) above as it has effect in relation to a donation delivered to him in accordance with sub-paragraph (2) above.

(6)   Sub-paragraph (7) below applies where–
  (a)   a relevant donation received by a candidate before the deadline for appointing an election agent has been dealt with by the candidate in accordance with section 56 of the 2000 Act either because–
    (i)   it was received by him at a time when no appointment of another person as his election agent was in force, or
    (ii)   although such an appointment was in force, he was by virtue of sub-paragraph (4)(b) required to deal with the donation; and
  (b)   an appointment of a person (other than the candidate himself) as election agent is in force at, or at any time after–
    (i)   the deadline for appointing an election agent, or
    (ii)   if later, the time when the candidate has dealt with the donation in accordance with section 56 of the 2000 Act.

(7)   Subject to sub-paragraph (9) below, the candidate shall, as soon as reasonably practicable after the relevant time, deliver to the election agent–
  (a)   the donation (if it has been accepted by him), and
  (b)   any information which he has about the donation and the donor which might reasonably be expected to assist the election agent in the discharge of any duties imposed on him, in relation to the donation, under Part 3 of this Schedule.

(8)   The relevant time for the purposes of sub-paragraph (7) above is–
  (a)   the time mentioned in sub-paragraph (6)(b)(i) or (ii) (as the case may be) if the appointment of another person as election agent is in force at that time, or
  (b)   otherwise, the time when any such appointment subsequently comes into force.

(9)   The duty imposed on a candidate by sub-paragraph (7)(a) above does not apply to any relevant donation to the extent to which it has been lawfully used by the candidate for the purpose of paying election expenses.

(10) In this paragraph–
  (a) any reference to the deadline for appointing an election agent is a reference to the latest time by which an election agent may in accordance with regulation 38(1) be named as election agent by the candidate; and
  (b) any reference to any provision of section 56 of the 2000 Act is a reference to that provision as applied by paragraph 7 above.

Evasion of restrictions on donations

9 Section 61 of the 2000 Act shall apply for the purposes of this Schedule as if–
  (a) any reference to donations were to relevant donations;
  (b) any reference to a registered party were, in relation to a relevant donation, a reference to an individual candidate or (as the case may be) his election agent; and
  (d) any reference in subsection (2) to the treasurer of a registered party were, in relation to a relevant donation, a reference to either the candidate or his election agent (or both).

Part 3
Reporting of Donations

Statement of relevant donations

10 (1) The candidate's election agent must include in any return required to be delivered under regulation 51 a statement of relevant donations which complies with paragraphs 11 and 12 below.

(2) If the statement states that the candidate's election agent has seen a certificate of anonymous registration issued pursuant to regulation 45G of the 2001 Regulations, regulation 45F of the 2001 (Scotland) Regulations, regulation 53D of the Representation of the People (Northern Ireland) Regulations 2008 or the equivalent provision forming part of the law of Gibraltar, which is evidence that an individual donor has an anonymous entry in an electoral register, the statement must be accompanied by a copy of that certificate of anonymous registration.

Donations from permissible donors

11 The statement must record, in relation to each relevant donation accepted by the candidate or his election agent–
  (a) the amount of the donation (if a donation of money, in cash or otherwise) or (in any other case) the nature of the donation and its value as determined in accordance with paragraph 5 above;
  (b) the date when the donation was accepted by the candidate or his election agent;
  (c) the information about the donor which is, in connection with recordable donations to registered parties, required to be recorded in donation reports by virtue of paragraph 2 of Schedule 6 to the 2000 Act; and
  (d) such other information as may be required by regulations made by the Commission.

Donations from impermissible donors

12 (1) This paragraph applies to relevant donations falling within paragraph 6(1)(a) or (b) above.

(2) Where paragraph 6(1)(a) above applies, the statement must record–

(a) the name and address of the donor;

(b) the amount of the donation (if a donation of money, in cash or otherwise) or (in any other case) the nature of the donation and its value as determined in accordance with paragraph 5 above;

(c) the date when the donation was received, and the date when, and the manner in which, it was dealt with in accordance with section 56(2)(a) of the 2000 Act; and

(d) such other information as is required by regulations made by the Commission.

(3) Where paragraph 6(1)(b) above applies, the statement must record–

(a) details of the manner in which the donation was made;

(b) the amount of the donation (if a donation of money, in cash or otherwise) or (in any other case) the nature of the donation and its value as determined in accordance with paragraph 5 above;

(c) the date when the donation was received, and the date when, and the manner in which, it was dealt with in accordance with section 56(2)(b) of the 2000 Act; and

(d) such other information as is required by regulations made by the Commission.

(4) In this paragraph any reference to any provision of section 56 of the 2000 Act is a reference to that provision as applied by paragraph 7 above.

SCHEDULE 7
DECLARATION AS TO ELECTION EXPENSES
Regulation 51

FORM OF DECLARATION
*General election of MEPs on (*insert date of poll*)
*European Parliamentary election in . . . . .electoral region on (*insert date of poll*)
Name of candidate
I solemnly and sincerely declare as follows:–

1 I am the person named above as a candidate at this election (and was my own election agent) or was at this election the election agent of the person named above as a candidate.

2 I have examined the return of election expenses (about to be) delivered by my election agent (by me) to the returning officer, of which a copy is now shown to me and marked. . . . ., and to the best of my knowledge and belief it is a complete and correct return as required by law.

3 To the best of my knowledge and belief, all expenses shown in the return as paid were paid by my election agent (by me), except as otherwise stated.

Signature of declarant. . . . .
Signed and declared by the above named declarant on the . . . . . . .day of . . . .,
before me,
(Signed) . . . .
(NOTE–Where there has been a change of election agent, suitable variations may be introduced into the declaration as to expenses.)

SCHEDULE 7A

ELECTION EXPENSES

Part 1

List of Matters

1   Advertising of any nature (whatever the medium used).

Expenses in respect of such advertising include agency fees, design costs and other costs in connection with preparing, producing, distributing or otherwise disseminating such advertising or anything incorporating such advertising and intended to be distributed for the purpose of disseminating it.

2   Unsolicited material addressed to electors (whether addressed to them by name or intended for delivery to households within any particular area).

Expenses in respect of such material include design costs and other costs in connection with preparing, producing or distributing such material (including the cost of postage).

3   Transport (by any means) of persons to any place.

Expenses in respect of the transport of such persons include the costs of hiring a means of transport for a particular period.

4   Public meetings (of any kind).

Expenses in respect of such meetings include costs incurred in connection with the attendance of persons at such meetings, the hire of premises for the purposes of such meetings or the provision of goods, services or facilities at them.

5   The services of an election agent or any other person whose services are engaged in connection with the candidate's election.

6   Accommodation and administrative costs.

Part 2

General Exclusions

7   The payment of any deposit required by rule 10 of the European Parliamentary elections rules.

8   The publication of any matter, other than an advertisement, relating to the election in–
    (a)   a newspaper or periodical;
    (b)   a broadcast made by the British Broadcasting Corporation, the Gibraltar Broadcasting Corporation, or by Sianel Pedwar Cymru;
    (c)   a programme included in any service licensed under Part 1 or 3 of the Broadcasting Act 1990 or Part 1 or 2 of the Broadcasting Act 1996.

9   The provision of any facilities provided in pursuance of any right conferred on candidates at an election by these Regulations other than facilities in respect of which expenses fall to be defrayed by virtue of regulation 67(4).

10 The provision by an individual of his own services which he provides voluntarily in his own time and free of charge.

11 (1)   Accommodation which is the candidate's sole or main residence.

   (2)   The provision by any other individual of accommodation which is his sole or main residence if the provision is made free of charge.

12 (1)   Transport by a means of transport which was acquired by the candidate principally for his own personal use.

   (2)   Transport provided free of charge by any other individual if the means of transport was acquired by him principally for his own personal use.

13 (1)   Computing or printing equipment which was acquired by the candidate principally for his own personal use.

   (2)   The provision by any other individual of computing or printing equipment which was acquired by the individual principally for his own personal use if the provision is made free of charge.

SCHEDULE 8
USE FOR EUROPEAN PARLIAMENTARY ELECTION MEETINGS OF ROOMS IN SCHOOL PREMISES AND OF MEETING ROOMS

Regulation 66

1 Any arrangements for the use of a room in school premises shall be made with the local authority (within the meaning of the Education Act 1996) maintaining the school or, in the case of a room in the premises of a foundation or voluntary aided school, with the governing body of the school.

2 Any question as to the rooms in school premises which a candidate in any local counting area is entitled to use, or as to the times at which he is entitled to use them, or as to the notice which is reasonable, shall be determined by the Secretary of State.

3 Any person stating himself to be, or to be authorised by, a candidate or the election agent of a registered party or an individual candidate shall be entitled at all reasonable hours to inspect the lists of rooms in school premises and of meeting rooms prepared under Schedule 5 to the 1983 Act, or a copy of those lists.

4 In the application of this Schedule to Scotland, for any reference to a local authority (within the meaning of the Education Act 1996) substitute a reference to an education authority.

5 In the application of this Schedule to Gibraltar–
   (a)   in paragraph 1, for the reference to the local authority (within the meaning of the Education Act 1996) substitute a reference to the Department of Education and Training;

(b)   in paragraph 2, for the reference to the Secretary of State substitute a reference to the Government of Gibraltar;

(c)   for paragraph 3, substitute the following paragraph–

"3(1)   The Department of Education and Training shall prepare and revise lists of the rooms in school premises in Gibraltar which candidates are entitled to use.

(2)   The Government of Gibraltar shall prepare and revise lists of the meeting rooms in Gibraltar which candidates are entitled to use, and the list shall-

    (a)   indicate the person to whom applications for the use of the room are to be made in each case; and

    (b)   not include any room if the person maintaining it disputes the right of candidates to use it.

(3)   The list of rooms in school premises and of meeting rooms prepared under sub-paragraphs (1) and (2) shall be kept by the European Parliamentary electoral registration officer for Gibraltar, and those lists and particulars of any change made on their revision shall be forwarded to him accordingly.

(4)   Any person stating himself to be, or to be authorised by, a candidate or the election agent of a registered party or an individual candidate shall be entitled at all reasonable hours to inspect the lists of rooms in school premises and of meeting rooms prepared under this paragraph."

European Union Referendum (Conduct) Regulations 2016
2016 no 209

Made 25th February 2016

73   Application to vote by post or by proxy in the referendum
74   Absent voters lists
75   Proxies
76
77   Voting as proxy
78   Offences

PART 4
APPLICATION AND AMENDMENT OF EXISTING LEGISLATION
79   Application of provisions of the Representation of the People Act 1983
80   Application of provisions of other acts
81   Application of existing provisions of regulations
82   Amendment of the European Parliamentary Elections Regulations 2004

PART 5
SUPPLEMENTARY
83   Forms

SCHEDULE 1 Application of Provisions of the Representation of the People Act 1983
SCHEDULE 2 Application of Provisions of other Acts
SCHEDULE 3 Application of Existing Provisions of Regulations
SCHEDULE 4 Forms

PART 1
INTRODUCTORY

Citation and commencement
1   These Regulations may be cited as the European Union Referendum (Conduct) Regulations 2016 and come into force on the day after the day on which they are made.

Extent
2(1)   These Regulations extend to the whole of the United Kingdom.

(2)   The following provisions extend also to Gibraltar
   (a)   this Part,
   (b)   regulation 82,
   (c)   paragraphs 3 and 9 of Schedule 1 (extent and application and modification of section 52 of the 1983 Act) and regulation 79 (introduction of Schedule 1) to the extent that it introduces those paragraphs,
   (d)   Part 1 of Schedule 2 (application of provisions of the Political Parties, Elections and Referendums Act 2000) and regulation 80 (introduction of Schedule 2) to the extent that it introduces that Part, and
   (e)   paragraph 112 of Schedule 3 (right of audience and right to conduct litigation of Gibraltar persons in referendum proceedings), paragraphs 114 and 115 of that Schedule (persons convicted of corrupt or illegal practices: Gibraltar) and regulation 81 (introduction of Schedule 3) to the extent that it introduces those paragraphs.

Interpretation
3   In these Regulations "the 2015 Act" means the European Union Referendum Act 2015.

PART 2

REGULATIONS FOR THE CONDUCT OF THE REFERENDUM IN THE UNITED KINGDOM

Application and Interpretation

Part to apply in United Kingdom and not Gibraltar

4   This Part applies in England and Wales, Scotland and Northern Ireland (and not in Gibraltar).

Interpretation

5   In this Part —

"anonymous entry", in relation to a register of electors, is to be read in accordance with section 9B of the 1983 Act;

"ballot paper account" has the meaning given by regulation 44(6);

"certificate as to employment on duty on the day of the poll" has the meaning given by regulation 26(4);

"companion" has the meaning given by regulation 36(1);

"the completed corresponding number lists" has the meaning given by regulation 44(1)(e);

"counting agent" is to be read in accordance with regulation 23(10);

"declaration made by the companion of a voter with disabilities" has the meaning given by regulation 36(2)(c);

"declaration of identity" is to be read in accordance with regulation 17(1)(c);

"elector" means a person who is entitled to vote on his or her own behalf in the referendum;

"list of proxies" —

(a)   in relation to England and Wales and Scotland, means the list kept under regulation 63(3);

(b)   in relation to Northern Ireland, means the list kept under regulation 74(3);

"the list of voters with disabilities assisted by companions" has the meaning given by regulation 36(8);

"the list of votes marked by the presiding officer" has the meaning given by regulation 35(4);

"official mark" has the meaning given by regulation 12(1);

"parliamentary polling district" means a polling district for parliamentary elections (see sections 18A and 18AA of the 1983 Act);

"parliamentary polling place", in relation to a parliamentary polling district, means the polling place designated for that district in accordance with section 18B of the 1983 Act;

"peer" means a peer who is a member of the House of Lords;

"polling agent" is to be read in accordance with regulation 23(10);

"postal voters list" —

(a)   in relation to England and Wales and Scotland, means the list kept under regulation 63(2);

(b)   in relation to Northern Ireland, means the list kept under regulation 74(2);

"postal voting statement" is to be read in accordance with regulation 17(1)(b);

"presiding officer" is to be read in accordance with regulation 19(1) and (2);

"proxy postal voters list" —

(a)   in relation to England and Wales and Scotland, means the list kept under regulation 66(6);

(b)   in relation to Northern Ireland, means the list kept under regulation 77(8);

"referendum agent" means a person appointed under paragraph 15 of Schedule 1 to the 2015 Act;

"the relevant postal voting provisions"
  (a) in relation to England and Wales, means Part 5 of the Representation of the People (England and Wales) Regulations 2001 as applied by Part 1 of Schedule 3;
  (b) in relation to Scotland, means Part 5 of the Representation of the People (Scotland) Regulations 2001 as so applied;
  (c) in relation to Northern Ireland, means Part 5 of the Representation of the People (Northern Ireland) Regulations 2008 as applied by Part 2 of Schedule 3;
"the relevant regulations"
  (a) in relation to England and Wales, means the Representation of the People (England and Wales) Regulations 2001 as applied by Part 1 of Schedule 3;
  (b) in relation to Scotland, means the Representation of the People (Scotland) Regulations 2001 as so applied;
  (c) in relation to Northern Ireland, means the Representation of the People (Northern Ireland) Regulations 2008 as applied by Part 2 of Schedule 3;
"a spoilt ballot paper" has the meaning given by regulation 41(1)(a);
"tendered ballot paper" has the meaning given by regulation 37(1);
"tendered postal ballot paper" has the meaning given by regulation 39(2);
"the tendered postal votes list" has the meaning given by regulation 39(10);
"tendered votes list" has the meaning given by regulation 38(7);
"voter" means a person voting in the referendum and includes a person voting as proxy and "vote" (whether noun or verb) is to be construed accordingly; and a reference to an elector voting or an elector's vote includes a reference to an elector voting by proxy or an elector's vote given by proxy.

Time

Timetable

6 The proceedings at the referendum are to be conducted in accordance with the following table.

Proceeding	Time
Publication of notice of referendum	Not later than the 25th day before the day of the referendum
Notice of poll	Not later than the 15th day before the day of the referendum
Hours of polling	Between 7am and 10pm on the day of the referendum

Computation of time

7(1) In calculating any period of time (other than a year) for the purposes of this Part, the following are to be disregarded
  (a) Saturdays and Sundays,
  (b) Christmas Eve, Christmas Day, Good Friday and any other day that is a bank holiday under the Banking and Financial Dealings Act 1971 in any part of the United Kingdom,
  (c) any day that is a bank holiday or public holiday in Gibraltar under the Gibraltar Acts titled the Banking and Financial Dealings Act and the Interpretation and General Clauses Act, and
  (d) any day appointed in any part of the United Kingdom or Gibraltar as a day of public thanksgiving or mourning.

(2) In relation to proceedings adjourned by a presiding officer under regulation 43 (riot or

open violence)

    (a)   the reference in paragraph (1)(b) to a day that is a bank holiday in any part of the United Kingdom is to be read as a reference to a day that is a bank holiday in the part of the United Kingdom where the proceedings are adjourned ("the relevant part of the United Kingdom"),

    (b)   paragraph (1)(c) is to be treated as omitted, and

    (c)   the reference in paragraph (1)(d) to a day that is appointed as a day of public thanksgiving or mourning in any part of the United Kingdom or Gibraltar is to be read as a reference to a day that is appointed as a day of public thanksgiving or mourning in the relevant part of the United Kingdom.

General Provisions

Notice of referendum

8   Each counting officer must give public notice of the referendum stating

    (a)   the date of the poll;

    (b)   the date by which

        (i)   applications to vote by post or by proxy, and

        (ii) other applications and notices about postal or proxy voting,

must reach the registration officer in order that they may be effective for the referendum.

Poll to be taken by ballot

9   The votes at the poll are to be given by ballot.

The ballot paper

10(1)   The ballot of every voter is to consist of a ballot paper, which is to be printed in the form set out in Form 1 in Schedule 4 according to the directions specified in that Schedule.

(2)   Each ballot paper

    (a)   must set out the question and the alternative answers to that question as specified in section 1 of the 2015 Act;

    (b)   must be capable of being folded up; and

    (c)   must have a number and other unique identifying mark printed on the back.

Corresponding number list

11(1)   The counting officer must prepare a list containing the numbers and other unique identifying marks of all of the ballot papers to be

    (a)   issued by the officer in pursuance of regulation 17(1), or

    (b)   provided by the officer in pursuance of regulation 22(1).

(2)   The list must be in the form set out in Form 2 in Schedule 4.

The official mark

12(1)   Every ballot paper must contain an appropriate security marking (referred to in these Regulations as the "official mark").

(2)   The official mark must be kept secret.

(3)   The counting officer may use a different official mark for different purposes.

Prohibition of disclosure of vote

13   A person who has voted in the referendum may not be required, in any legal proceeding to question the referendum, to state for which answer he or she voted.

Use of schools and public rooms

14(1) The counting officer may use, free of charge, for the purpose of taking the poll
    (a) a room in a school within paragraph (3);
    (b) a room the expense of maintaining which is met by any local authority (in England and Wales or Scotland) or is payable out of any rate (in Northern Ireland).

(2) The counting officer must
    (a) make good any damage done to any such room, and
    (b) defray any expense incurred by the persons having control over any such room, by reason of its being used for that purpose.

(3) The schools within this paragraph are
    (a) in England and Wales
      (i) a school maintained or assisted by a local authority;
      (ii) a school in respect of which grants are made out of moneys provided by Parliament to the person or body of persons responsible for the management of the school;
    (b) in Scotland, a school that is not an independent school within the meaning of the Education (Scotland) Act 1980;
    (c) in Northern Ireland, a school in receipt of a grant out of moneys appropriated by Act of the Northern Ireland Assembly, other than a school that
      (i) adjoins or is adjacent to a church or other place of worship, or
      (ii) is connected with a nunnery or other religious establishment.

Modification of forms

15(1) The Chief Counting Officer may, for the purpose of making a relevant form easier for voters to understand or use, specify modifications that are to be made to the wording or appearance of the form.

(2) In paragraph (1) "relevant form" means any of the following
    (a) the forms in Schedule 4, except Forms 1 (ballot paper), 2 (corresponding number list), 13 (corresponding number list for use in polling stations), 16 (certificate of employment Great Britain) or 17 (certificate of employment Northern Ireland);
    (b) the forms of the notices set out in regulation 22(8).

(3) In these Regulations a reference to such a form is to be read as a reference to that form with any modifications specified under paragraph (1).

(4) Where a form is modified by virtue of paragraph (1), section 26(2) of the Welsh Language Act 1993 applies as if the modified form were specified by these Regulations.

Action to be Taken before the Poll

Notice of poll

16(1) The counting officer must give public notice of the poll stating
    (a) the day and hours fixed for the poll;
    (b) the question that is to appear on the ballot paper.

(2) The notice of the poll must be published not later than the 15th day before the day of the referendum.

(3) No later than the time of the publication of the notice of the poll, the counting officer must also give public notice of
    (a) the situation of each polling station;

(b)   the description of voters entitled to vote there.

(4)   As soon as practicable after giving the notice under paragraph (3), the counting officer must give a copy of it to each of the referendum agents appointed for the officer's area.

Postal Ballot papers

17(1)   The counting officer must, in accordance with the relevant postal voting provisions, issue to those entitled to vote by post
>   (a)   a ballot paper,
>   (b)   in the case of those entitled to vote in England and Wales or Scotland, a postal voting statement in the form set out in Form 3 in Schedule 4, and
>   (c)   in the case of those entitled to vote in Northern Ireland, a declaration of identity in the form set out in Form 4 in Schedule 4,

together with envelopes for their return complying with the requirements prescribed by the relevant postal voting provisions.

(2)   The counting officer must also issue to those entitled to vote by post whatever information the officer thinks appropriate about how to obtain
>   (a)   translations into languages other than English of any directions to, or guidance for, voters sent with the ballot paper;
>   (b)   a translation into Braille of those directions or guidance;
>   (c)   graphical representations of those directions or guidance;
>   (d)   those directions or guidance in any other form (including any audible form).

(3)   In the case of a ballot paper issued to a person resident in the United Kingdom, the counting officer must ensure that the return of the ballot paper and postal voting statement or declaration of identity is free of charge to the voter.

Provision of polling stations

18(1)   The counting officer must provide a sufficient number of polling stations and, subject to the following provisions of this regulation, must allot the electors to the polling stations in whatever manner the officer thinks most convenient.

(2)   One or more polling stations may be provided in the same room.

(3)   The polling station allotted to electors from any parliamentary polling district wholly or partly within a particular voting area must, in the absence of special circumstances, be in the parliamentary polling place for that district unless the parliamentary polling place is outside the voting area.

(4)   The number of ballot papers counted or votes cast as certified by the Chief Counting Officer or a Regional Counting Officer or counting officer may not be questioned by reason of
>   (a)   any non-compliance with paragraph (3), or
>   (b)   any informality relative to polling districts or polling places.

(5)   The counting officer must provide each polling station with however many compartments are necessary in which the voters can mark their votes screened from observation.

Appointment of presiding officers and clerks

19(1)   The counting officer must appoint and pay
>   (a)   a presiding officer to attend at each polling station;
>   (b)   however many clerks are necessary for the purposes of the referendum.

But the officer may not employ a person who has been employed by or on behalf of a permitted participant in or about the referendum.

(2)   The counting officer may, if the officer thinks fit, preside at a polling station.

The provisions of this Part relating to a presiding officer apply to a counting officer so presiding, with the necessary modifications as to things to be done by the counting officer to the presiding officer or by the presiding officer to the counting officer.

(3)   A presiding officer may do, by the clerks appointed to assist the officer, any act (including the asking of questions) which the officer is required or authorised by this Part to do at a polling station except order the arrest, exclusion or removal of a person from the polling station.

Issue of official poll cards

20(1)   The counting officer must, as soon as practicable after the publication of notice of the referendum, send to electors and their proxies an official poll card.

This paragraph is subject to paragraph (2).

(2)   An official poll card must not be sent to a person registered, or to be registered, in pursuance of

    (a)   an overseas elector's declaration, within the meaning of section 2 of the Representation of the People Act 1985 (registration of British citizens overseas), or

    (b)   a declaration made by virtue of subsection (5) of section 3 of that Act (extension of franchise for European Parliamentary Elections).

(3)   An elector's official poll card must be sent or delivered to his or her qualifying address.

(4)   A proxy's official poll card must be sent or delivered to the address which

    (a)   is shown as the proxy's address in the list of proxies, or

    (b)   in the case of a proxy for an elector with an anonymous entry in a register maintained by the Chief Electoral Officer for Northern Ireland, would be so shown but for regulation 74(4).

(5)   In the case of an elector who is entitled to vote in the referendum in England and Wales or Scotland

    (a)   an official poll card sent to the elector must be in the form set out in Form 5 in Schedule 4;

    (b)   an official postal poll card sent to the elector must be in the form set out in Form 6 in Schedule 4;

    (c)   an official poll card sent to the proxy of the elector must be in the form set out in Form 7 in Schedule 4;

    (d)   an official postal poll card sent to the proxy of the elector must be in the form set out in Form 8 in Schedule 4.

(6)   In the case of an elector who is entitled to vote in the referendum in Northern Ireland

    (a)   an official poll card sent to the elector must be in the form set out in Form 9 in Schedule 4;

    (b)   an official postal poll card sent to the elector must be in the form set out in Form 10 in Schedule 4;

    (c)   an official poll card sent to the proxy of the elector must be in the form set out in Form 11 in Schedule 4;

    (d)   an official postal poll card sent to the proxy of the elector must be in the form set out in Form 12 in Schedule 4.

(7)   An official poll card or official postal poll card may set out whatever information, in addition to that required by virtue of paragraph (5) or (6), the counting officer thinks appropriate.

(8)   Different information may be provided in pursuance of paragraph (7) to different electors or descriptions of elector.

(9)   In this regulation
"qualifying address" means the address in respect of which a person is entitled to be registered on the register of electors;
"elector" includes only those electors who, on the last day for publication of notice of the referendum, appear on a register to be used for the referendum.

Notification that certain electors entitled to absent vote

21(1)   As soon as practicable after the publication of notice of the referendum, a registration officer must
  (a)   notify those peers who are within entry 2, 4 or 5 of the table in regulation 63(2) or 74(2) that they are entitled to vote by post in the referendum;
  (b)   notify those electors who are within entry 2, 3, 4 or 5 of the table in regulation 63(3) or 74(3) that they are entitled to vote by proxy in the referendum.

 (2)   A notice given to a person under paragraph (1)(b) must
  (a)   in the case of a person within entry 2 of the table, state that the person's entitlement to vote by proxy in the referendum arises by virtue of the person's inclusion in the list of proxies for a specified poll mentioned in that entry;
  (b)   in the case of a person within entry 3 of the table, state that the person's entitlement to vote by proxy in the referendum arises by virtue of the person's inclusion in the record kept under paragraph 3 of Schedule 4 to the Representation of the People Act 2000 or (as the case may be) section 6 of the Representation of the People Act 1985 as voting by proxy at parliamentary elections;
  (c)   in the case of a peer within entry 4 of the table, state that the peer's entitlement to vote by proxy in the referendum arises by virtue of the peer's inclusion in the record kept under paragraph 3 of Schedule 4 to the Representation of the People Act 2000 or (as the case may be) paragraph 1 of Schedule 2 to the Local Elections (Northern Ireland) Order 1985 as voting by proxy;
  (d)   in the case of a peer within entry 5 of the table, state that the peer's entitlement to vote by proxy in the referendum arises by virtue of the peer's inclusion in the record kept under paragraph 3 of Schedule 2 to the European Parliamentary Elections Regulations 2004 or (as the case may be) regulation 8 of the European Parliamentary Elections (Northern Ireland) Regulations 2004 as voting by proxy.

Equipment of polling stations

22(1)   The counting officer must provide each presiding officer with however many ballot boxes and ballot papers the counting officer thinks are necessary.

 (2)   Every ballot box must be constructed so that the ballot papers can be put in it, but cannot be withdrawn from it, without the box being unlocked or (in the case of a box without a lock) the seal being broken.

 (3)   The counting officer must provide each polling station with
  (a)   materials to enable voters to mark the ballot papers;
  (b)   copies of each register of electors used for the referendum that contains the entries relating to the electors allotted to the station (or, in the case of a register only part of which contains those entries, that part);
  (c)   the parts of any special lists prepared for the referendum corresponding to each register or part of a register provided under sub-paragraph (b);
  (d)   a list consisting of that part of the list prepared under regulation 11 that contains the numbers (but not the other unique identifying marks) corresponding to those on the ballot papers provided to the presiding officer of the polling station.

The list provided under sub-paragraph (d) must be in the form set out in Form 13 in Schedule 4.

(4) The counting officer must also provide each polling station with

    (a) at least one large version of the ballot paper, which must be displayed inside the polling station for the assistance of voters who are partially sighted;

    (b) a device for enabling voters who are blind or partially sighted to vote without any need for assistance from the presiding officer or any companion (see regulation 36(1)).

(5) The device mentioned in paragraph (4)(b) must

    (a) allow a ballot paper to be inserted into and removed from the device, or attached to and detached from it, easily and without damage to the paper;

    (b) keep the ballot paper firmly in place during use;

    (c) provide suitable means for the voter

        (i) to identify the spaces on the ballot paper on which the voter may mark his or her vote,

        (ii) to identify the answer to which each such space refers, and

        (iii) to mark his or her vote on the space the voter has chosen.

(6) A notice giving directions for the guidance of the voters in voting must be printed in conspicuous characters and exhibited inside and outside every polling station.

(7) That notice must be in the form set out in Form 14 in Schedule 4 (for a polling station in England, Wales or Scotland) or Form 15 in that Schedule (for a polling station in Northern Ireland).

(8) In every compartment of every polling station there must be exhibited the notice

    "Put a cross [X] in one box only. Put no other mark on the ballot paper, or your vote may not be counted".

(9) The reference in paragraph (3)(b) to the copies of a register of electors includes a reference to copies of any notices issued under section 13B(3B) or (3D) or 13BA(9) of the 1983 Act in respect of alterations to the register.

Appointment of polling and counting agents

23(1) A referendum agent may, before the commencement of the poll, appoint

    (a) polling agents to attend at polling stations for the purpose of detecting personation;

    (b) counting agents to attend at the counting of the votes.

(2) A referendum agent may, for each count, designate one counting agent as a person authorised to require a recount under regulation 47.

A designation under this paragraph must be made at the same time as the person's appointment as a counting agent.

(3) In paragraph (2) "count" includes a recount and "recount" includes a further recount.

(4) The counting officer may limit the number of counting agents that may be appointed, so long as

    (a) the number that may be appointed by each referendum agent is the same, and

    (b) the number that may be appointed by each referendum agent is not (except in special circumstances) less than the number obtained by dividing the number of clerks employed on the counting by the number of referendum agents.

(5) For the purposes of paragraph (4)(b), a counting agent appointed by more than one referendum agent is to be treated as a separate agent for each of them.

(6) A referendum agent who appoints a polling or counting agent must give the counting officer notice of the appointment by no later than the 5th day before the day of the

poll.

(7) If a polling or counting agent dies, or becomes incapable of acting, the referendum agent may appoint another agent and must give the counting officer notice of the new appointment as soon as practicable.

(8) If a referendum agent designates a counting agent under paragraph (2) the notice under paragraph (6) or (7) must include notice of that fact.

(9) A notice under paragraph (6) or (7)
    (a) must be in writing, and
    (b) must give the name and address of the appointee.

(10) In the following provisions of this Part, references to polling agents and counting agents are to be read as references to polling or counting agents appointed under paragraph (1) or (7)
    (a) whose appointments have been duly made and notified, and
    (b) where the number of agents is restricted, who are within the permitted numbers.

(11) Any notice required to be given to a counting agent by the counting officer may be delivered at, or sent by post to, the address stated in the notice of appointment.

(12) A referendum agent may do or assist in doing anything that a polling or counting agent appointed by him or her is authorised to do; and anything required or authorised by this Part to be done in the presence of the polling or counting agents may be done in the presence of a referendum agent instead of his or her polling or counting agents.

(13) Where by this Part anything is required or authorised to be done in the presence of the polling or counting agents, the nonattendance of any agent or agents at the time and place appointed for the purpose does not invalidate the thing (if the thing is otherwise duly done).

Notification of requirement of secrecy

24(1) The counting officer must make whatever arrangements the officer thinks are appropriate to ensure that
    (a) every person attending at a polling station (otherwise than for the purpose of voting, or assisting a voter with disabilities to vote, or as a constable on duty there) has been given a copy in writing of the provisions of subsections (1), (3) and (6) of section 66 of the 1983 Act as modified by Schedule 1;
    (b) every person attending at the counting of the votes (other than any constable on duty at the counting) has been given a copy in writing of the provisions of subsections (2) and (6) of that section as so modified.

(2) In the application of this regulation in England and Wales, a reference to a constable includes a person designated as a community support officer under section 38 of the Police Reform Act 2002 (police powers for employees).

Return of postal ballot papers

25(1) Where
    (a) a postal vote has been returned in respect of a person who is entered in the postal voters list, or
    (b) a proxy postal vote has been returned in respect of a proxy who is entered in the proxy postal voters list,
the counting officer must mark the list in the manner prescribed by the relevant postal voting provisions.

(2) Paragraph (1) does not apply in relation to a vote on a tendered postal ballot paper

(see regulation 39).

(3) Regulation 46(3) and (5) does not apply for the purpose of determining whether, for the purposes of this regulation, a postal vote or a proxy postal vote is returned.

The Poll

Admission to Polling station

26(1) The presiding officer must exclude from the polling station everyone except
    (a) voters,
    (b) persons under the age of 18 who accompany voters to the polling station,
    (c) the Chief Counting Officer, the Regional Counting Officer (in the case of a polling station in a region for which a Regional Counting Officer is appointed) and the counting officer,
    (d) the referendum agents,
    (e) the polling agents appointed to attend at the polling station,
    (f) the clerks appointed to attend at the polling station,
    (g) persons who are entitled to attend by virtue of any of sections 6A to 6D of the 2000 Act,
    (h) the constables on duty, and
    (i) the companions of voters with disabilities attending at the polling station.

(2) The presiding officer must regulate the total number of voters and persons under the age of 18 who accompany them to be admitted to the polling station at the same time.

(3) No more than one polling agent may be admitted at the same time to a polling station on behalf of the same referendum agent.

(4) A constable or person employed by a counting officer may be admitted to vote in person elsewhere than at the polling station allotted under this Part only on production and surrender of a certificate (referred to in this Part as a "certificate as to employment on duty on the day of the poll") that
    (a) confirms that the person is a constable or, as the case may be, is employed by a counting officer,
    (b) is in the form set out in Form 16 in Schedule 4 (for a person in Great Britain) or Form 17 in that Schedule (for a person in Northern Ireland), and
    (c) is signed
        (i) in the case of a certificate for a person in Great Britain, by an officer of police of or above the rank of inspector or, as the case may be, by the counting officer, or
        (ii) in the case of a certificate for a person in Northern Ireland, by an officer of the Police Service of Northern Ireland of or above the rank of chief inspector or, as the case may be, by the counting officer.

(5) A certificate surrendered under this regulation must be cancelled immediately.

(6) In the application of this regulation in England and Wales, a reference to a constable includes a person designated as a community support officer under section 38 of the Police Reform Act 2002 (police powers for employees).

Keeping of order in polling station

27(1) It is the presiding officer's duty to keep order at the officer's polling station.

(2) If a person engages in misconduct in a polling station or fails to obey the presiding officer's lawful orders, the person may immediately, by the presiding officer's order, be removed from the polling station
    (a) by a constable, or
    (b) by any other person authorised in writing by the counting officer to discharge

this function.

(3) A person so removed may not, without the presiding officer's permission, reenter the polling station that day.

(4) The powers conferred by this regulation may not be exercised so as to prevent a voter who is otherwise entitled to vote at a polling station from having an opportunity to vote at that station.

Sealing of ballot boxes

28(1) Immediately before the commencement of the poll, the presiding officer must show anyone present in the polling station that the ballot box is empty.

(2) The presiding officer must then
    (a) lock the box (if it has a lock) and place his or her seal on it in a manner that prevents it from being opened without breaking the seal, and
    (b) place the box in his or her view for the receipt of ballot papers, and keep it so locked (if it has a lock) and sealed.

Questions to be put to voters

29(1) When an application is made for a ballot paper (but not afterwards), the questions specified in the second column of the table following paragraph (4)
    (a) may be put by the presiding officer to a person who is mentioned in the first column, and
    (b) must be put if the letter "R" appears after the question and a referendum or polling agent requires the question to be put.

(2) In the case of a voter in respect of whom a notice has been issued under section 13B(3B) or (3D) or 13BA(9) of the 1983 Act, references in the table to reading from the register are to be read as references to reading from that notice.

(3) A ballot paper must not be delivered to any person required to answer any of the questions in the table unless the person has answered each question satisfactorily.

(4) Except as authorised by this regulation, no inquiry is permitted as to the right of any person to vote.

Person applying for ballot paper	Questions
(1) A person applying as an elector	(a) "Are you the person registered in the register of electors as follows (read out the whole entry from the register)?" [R]
	(b) "Have you already voted in the referendum on the United Kingdom's membership of the European Union, here or elsewhere, otherwise than as proxy for some other person?" [R]
	(c) In Northern Ireland, "What is your date of birth?"
(2) A person applying as proxy	(a) "Are you the person whose name appears as A B in the list of proxies for the referendum on the United Kingdom's membership of the European Union as entitled to vote as proxy on behalf of C D?" [R]
	(b) "Have you already voted in the referendum on the United Kingdom's membership of the European Union, here

Person applying for ballot paper	Questions
	or elsewhere, as proxy on behalf of C D?" [R]
	(c) "Are you the spouse, civil partner, parent, grandparent, brother/sister, child or grandchild of C D?" [R]
(3) A person applying in England and Wales or Scotland as proxy for an elector with an anonymous entry (instead of the questions at entry (2))	(a) "Are you the person entitled to vote as proxy on behalf of the elector whose number on the register of electors is (read out the number from the register)?" [R]
	(b) "Have you already voted in the referendum on the United Kingdom's membership of the European Union, here or elsewhere, as proxy on behalf of the elector whose number on the register of electors is (read out the number from the register)?" [R]
	(c) "Are you the spouse, civil partner, parent, grandparent, brother/sister, child or grandchild of the person whose number on the register of electors is (read out the number from the register)?" [R]
(4) Person applying as proxy if the question at entry (2)(c), or (3)(c) (if applicable), is not answered in the affirmative	"Have you already voted in the referendum on the United Kingdom's membership of the European Union on behalf of two persons of whom you are not the spouse, civil partner, parent, grandparent, brother/sister, child or grandchild?" [R]
(5) A person applying as an elector in relation to whom there is an entry in the postal voters list	(a) "Did you apply to vote by post?" (b) "Why have you not voted by post?"
(6) A person applying as proxy who is named in the proxy postal voters list	(a) "Did you apply to vote by post as proxy?" (b) "Why have you not voted by post as proxy?"

Challenge of voter

30 A person is not to be prevented from voting by reason only that
    (a) a referendum or polling agent declares that there is reasonable cause to believe that the person has committed an offence of personation, or
    (b) the person is arrested on suspicion of committing or of being about to commit an offence of personation.

Voting procedure

31 A ballot paper must be delivered to a voter who applies for one, subject to any provision of this Part to the contrary.

32(1) In Northern Ireland a ballot paper must not be delivered to a voter unless the voter has produced a specified document to the presiding officer or a clerk.

(2) A clerk or presiding officer in Northern Ireland to whom a specified document is produced must not deliver a ballot paper to the voter if the clerk or officer decides that
    (a) the document raises a reasonable doubt as to whether the voter is the elector or proxy he or she claims to be, or

(b) the apparent age of the voter as compared with the date of birth supplied in pursuance of section 10(4A)(b), 10A(1A)(b) or 13A(2A)(b) of the 1983 Act raises a reasonable doubt as to whether the voter is the elector or proxy he or she claims to be.

(3) Where such a decision is made by a clerk, the clerk must refer the case to the presiding officer, who must deal with it under this regulation as if the specified document had been produced to the officer in the first place.
The presiding officer must deal with the case in person (and accordingly regulation 19(3) does not apply).

(4) For the purposes of this regulation a specified document is one that for the time being falls within the following list
(a) a licence to drive a motor vehicle if the licence bears the photograph of the person to whom it is issued;
(b) a passport issued by the Government of the United Kingdom or by the Government of the Republic of Ireland;
(c) an electoral identity card, issued under section 13C of the 1983 Act;
(d) a Senior SmartPass issued under the Northern Ireland Concessionary Fares Scheme for use from 1st May 2002;
(e) a Blind Person's SmartPass, issued under the Northern Ireland Concessionary Fares Scheme for use from 1st May 2002;
(f) a War Disabled SmartPass, issued under the Northern Ireland Concessionary Fares Scheme for use from 1st May 2002;
(g) a 60+ SmartPass issued under the Northern Ireland Concessionary Fares Scheme for use from 1st October 2008.

(5) In paragraph (4)(a) "licence to drive a motor vehicle" means a licence granted under
(a) Part 3 of the Road Traffic Act 1972 or Part 3 of the Road Traffic Act 1988, or
(b) the Road Traffic (Northern Ireland) Order 1981,
and includes a Community licence within the meaning of those enactments.

(6) References in this regulation to producing a document are to producing it for inspection.

33(1) This regulation applies where there is a duty to deliver a ballot paper to a voter under regulation 31.

(2) Immediately before delivery of the ballot paper
(a) the number and (unless paragraph (3) applies) name of the elector as stated in the copy of the register of electors must be called out;
(b) the number of the elector must be marked on the list mentioned in regulation 22(3)(d) beside the number of the ballot paper to be issued to the elector;
(c) a mark must be placed in the register of electors against the number of the elector to note that a ballot paper has been received but without showing the particular ballot paper which has been received;
(d) in the case of a person applying for a ballot paper as proxy, a mark must also be placed against the person's name in the list of proxies.

(3) An elector who has an anonymous entry in a register maintained by a registration officer in Great Britain must show the presiding officer his or her official poll card and only the number is to be called out in pursuance of paragraph (2)(a).

(4) In the case of an elector who is added to the register in pursuance of a notice issued under section 13B(3B) or (3D) or 13BA(9) of the 1983 Act
(a) the reference in paragraph (2)(a) to the copy of the register of electors is to be read as a reference to the copy of the notice;

(b) the reference in paragraph (2)(c) to a mark being placed in the register of electors is to be read as a reference to a mark being made on the copy of the notice.

34(1) Immediately after receiving a ballot paper the voter must

    (a) proceed into one of the compartments in the polling station and there secretly mark the paper and fold it up so as to conceal the vote, and then

    (b) show to the presiding officer the back of the paper, so as to disclose the number and other unique identifying mark, and put the ballot paper so folded up into the ballot box in the presiding officer's presence.

(2) The voter must vote without undue delay, and must leave the polling station as soon as he or she has put the ballot paper into the ballot box.

(3) A voter who at the close of the poll is in the polling station, or in a queue outside the polling station, for the purpose of voting is (despite the close of the poll) entitled to apply for a ballot paper under regulation 31; and this Part applies in relation to the voter accordingly.

Votes marked by presiding officer

35(1) This regulation applies where a voter applies to the presiding officer to mark the voter's ballot paper and the voter

    (a) is incapacitated by blindness or other disability from voting in the manner directed by this Part, or

    (b) declares orally that he or she is unable to read.

(2) The presiding officer must, in the presence of the polling agents

    (a) cause the voter's vote to be marked on a ballot paper in the manner directed by the voter, and

    (b) cause the ballot paper to be placed in the ballot box,

but in Northern Ireland this is subject to paragraph (3).

(3) In the case of a voter who makes an application in Northern Ireland under this regulation, regulation 32 applies as if the references to delivering a ballot paper were references to causing the voter's vote to be marked on the ballot paper.

(4) The name of every voter whose vote is marked in pursuance of this regulation must be entered on a list (called in this Part "the list of votes marked by the presiding officer"), together with

    (a) the voter's number on the register of electors, and

    (b) the reason for the vote being marked in pursuance of this regulation.

(5) In the case of a person voting as proxy for an elector, the number to be entered together with the voter's name is the elector's number.

(6) In the case of a person in respect of whom a notice has been issued under section 13B(3B) or (3D) or 13BA(9) of the 1983 Act, the reference in paragraph (4)(a) to the voter's number on the register of electors is to be read as a reference to the number relating to the voter on the notice.

Voting by people with disabilities

36(1) Paragraph (2) applies where a voter applies to the presiding officer, on the ground of blindness or other disability or inability to read, to be allowed to vote with the assistance of an accompanying person (referred to in this Part as the "companion").

(2) The presiding officer must grant the application if

    (a) the voter makes an oral or written declaration that he or she is so incapacitated by blindness or other disability, or by an inability to read, as to be unable to vote without assistance,

    (b)   the presiding officer is satisfied that the voter is so incapacitated, and

    (c)   the presiding officer is satisfied by a written declaration made by the companion (referred to in this Part as a "declaration made by the companion of a voter with disabilities") that the companion

        (i)   is a person qualified to assist the voter, and

        (ii) has not previously assisted more than one voter with disabilities to vote in the referendum,

but in Northern Ireland this paragraph is subject to paragraph (3).

(3)   In the case of a voter who makes an application in Northern Ireland under this regulation, regulation 32 applies as if the references to delivering a ballot paper were references to granting the voter's application.

(4)   For the purposes of paragraph (2)(c) a person is qualified to assist a voter with disabilities to vote if the person

    (a)   is entitled to vote as an elector in the referendum, or

    (b)   is the father, mother, brother, sister, spouse, civil partner, son or daughter of the voter and has attained the age of 18 years.

(5)   The declaration made by the companion

    (a)   must be in the form set out in Form 18 in Schedule 4 (for a companion in Great Britain) or Form 19 in that Schedule (for a companion in Northern Ireland),

    (b)   must be made before the presiding officer at the time when the voter applies to vote with the assistance of the companion, and

    (c)   must be given immediately to the presiding officer,

and the presiding officer must attest and retain the declaration.

(6)   No fee or other payment may be charged in respect of the declaration.

(7)   If the presiding officer grants an application under this regulation, anything which is by this Part required to be done to or by the voter in connection with the giving of his or her vote may be done to, or with the assistance of, the companion.

(8)   The name of every voter whose vote is given in accordance with this regulation must be entered on a list (referred to in this Part as "the list of voters with disabilities assisted by companions") together with

    (a)   the voter's number on the register of electors, and

    (b)   the name and address of the companion.

(9)   In the case of a person voting as proxy for an elector, the number to be entered together with the voter's name is the elector's number.

(10)   In the case of a person in respect of whom a notice has been issued under section 13B(3B) or (3D) or 13BA(9) of the 1983 Act, the reference in paragraph (8)(a) to the voter's number on the register of electors is to be read as a reference to the number relating to the voter on the notice.

(11)   For the purposes of this Part a person is a voter with disabilities if the person has made a declaration under this regulation.

Tendered ballot papers

37(1) In the following cases a person is entitled to mark a ballot paper (referred to in this Part as a "tendered ballot paper") in the same manner as any other voter if

    (a)   in cases 1 to 7, the person satisfactorily answers the questions permitted by law to be asked at the poll;

    (b)   in case 8, the person satisfactorily answers the questions permitted by law to be asked at the poll other than the question at entry (1)(c) in the table in regulation

29.

Regulation 38 makes further provision about tendered ballot papers.

(2) Case 1 is that
- (a) a person applies for a ballot paper,
- (b) the person claims
  - (i) to be a particular elector named on the register, and
  - (ii) not to be named in the postal voters list or the list of proxies, and
- (c) another person has already voted in person either as that elector or as proxy for that elector.

(3) Case 2 is that
- (a) a person applies for a ballot paper,
- (b) the person claims to be
  - (i) a particular person named in the list of proxies as proxy for an elector, and
  - (ii) not entitled to vote by post as proxy, and
- (c) another person has already voted in person either as that elector or as proxy for that elector.

(4) Regulation 32 applies in relation to a voter in Northern Ireland who seeks to mark a tendered ballot paper in reliance on Case 1 or 2 as it applies in relation to a voter who applies for a ballot paper under regulation 31.

(5) Case 3 is that
- (a) a person applies for a ballot paper,
- (b) the person claims to be a particular elector named on the register,
- (c) the person is also named in the postal voters list, and
- (d) the person claims not to have made an application to vote by post.

(6) Case 4 is that
- (a) a person applies for a ballot paper,
- (b) the person claims to be a particular person named as a proxy in the list of proxies,
- (c) the person is also named in the proxy postal voters list, and
- (d) the person claims not to have made an application to vote by post as proxy.

(7) Case 5 is that, before the close of the poll but after the last time at which a person may apply for a replacement postal ballot paper
- (a) a person claims to be a particular elector named on the register and also named in the postal voters list, and
- (b) the person claims to have lost or not received the postal ballot paper.

(8) Case 6 is that, before the close of the poll but after the last time at which a person may apply for a replacement postal ballot paper
- (a) a person claims to be a particular person named as a proxy in the list of proxies and also named in the proxy postal voters list, and
- (b) the person claims to have lost or not received the postal ballot paper.

(9) Case 7 is that
- (a) a person applies for a ballot paper in Northern Ireland, and
- (b) there has been a refusal under paragraph (2) of regulation 32 (including that paragraph as applied by regulation 35 or 36 or this regulation) by a presiding officer.

(10) Case 8 is that
- (a) a person applies for a ballot paper in Northern Ireland, and
- (b) the person fails to answer the question at entry 1(c) in the table in regulation 29 satisfactorily.

(11) In the case of an elector who has an anonymous entry, the references in this regulation

to a person named on a register or list are to be read as references to a person whose number appears on the register or list (as the case may be).

(12) In the case of a person in respect of whom a notice has been issued under section 13B(3B) or (3D) or 13BA(9) of the 1983 Act, the references in this regulation to a person named on the register are to be read as references to a person in respect of whom such a notice has been issued.

(13) This regulation does not apply in relation to an elector who has an anonymous entry in a register maintained by the Chief Electoral Officer for Northern Ireland.

38(1) Tendered ballot papers must be a different colour from the other ballot papers.

(2) A person in Northern Ireland who marks a tendered ballot paper in reliance on Case 7 or 8 in regulation 37 must sign the paper, unless it is marked after an application was refused under regulation 35 or 36.

(3) If a tendered ballot paper is required to be signed under paragraph (2) and the paper is not signed, the paper is void.

(4) Tendered ballot papers must be given to the presiding officer instead of being put into the ballot box.

(5) On receiving a tendered ballot paper from a voter the presiding officer must endorse it with the voter's name and number on the register of electors.

(6) The presiding officer must set tendered ballot papers aside in a separate packet.

(7) The name and number on the register of electors of every voter whose vote is marked in pursuance of regulation 37 must be entered on a list (referred to in this Part as the "tendered votes list") and the voter must sign the list opposite the entry relating to him or her.

(8) In the case of a person voting as proxy for an elector, the number to be endorsed or entered together with the voter's name is the elector's number.

(9) In the case of an elector who has an anonymous entry, the references in paragraphs (5) and (7) to the name of the voter are to be ignored.

(10) In the case of a person in respect of whom a notice has been issued under section 13B(3B) or (3D) or 13BA(9) of the 1983 Act, the references in paragraphs (5) and (7) to the voter's number on the register of electors are to be read as references to the number relating to the voter on the notice.

(11) This regulation does not apply in relation to an elector who has an anonymous entry in a register maintained by the Chief Electoral Officer for Northern Ireland.

Tendered postal ballot papers: anonymous entries in Northern Ireland

39(1) This regulation applies to a person ("P") who
    (a) is an elector with an anonymous entry in a register maintained by the Chief Electoral Officer for Northern Ireland, or
    (b) is entitled to vote by post as a proxy for such an elector,
and who claims to have lost, or not received, a postal ballot paper.

(2) P may apply to the counting officer for a replacement postal ballot paper (referred to in this Part as a "tendered postal ballot paper").

(3) The application
    (a) may be made by post or in person,
    (b) must be accompanied by a specified document within the meaning of regulation 32,

      (c) must be delivered to the counting officer
           (i)   where the application is made by post, before 4pm on the fourth day before the day of the poll, or
           (ii) where the application is made in person, before 4pm on the day before the day of the poll.

(4)   If the counting officer
      (a) is satisfied as to P's identity, and
      (b) has no reason to doubt that P has lost, or not received, a postal ballot paper,
the counting officer must issue a tendered postal ballot paper to P in accordance with the relevant postal voting provisions.

(5)   A tendered postal ballot paper must be of a different colour from the other ballot papers.

(6)   P, if issued with a tendered postal ballot paper, may mark it, sign it, and send it to the counting officer, in the same manner as a postal ballot paper.

(7)   A tendered postal ballot paper which has not been signed, or which does not meet the conditions in regulation 46(5) and (6), is void.

(8)   On receipt of a tendered postal ballot paper, the counting officer must deal with it in accordance with the relevant postal voting provisions.

(9)   The counting officer must
      (a) endorse each tendered postal ballot paper with the entry in the register of the elector in question, and
      (b) set it aside in a separate packet of tendered postal ballot papers.

(10) The counting officer must add the entry in the register of the elector in question to a list (referred to in this Part as "the tendered postal votes list").

(11) The counting officer must seal the packet of tendered postal ballot papers.

(12) This regulation applies in the case of a person in respect of whom a notice has been issued under section 13BA(9) of the 1983 Act (alteration of registers in Northern Ireland: pending elections) as if
      (a) in paragraph (1), for "in a register maintained" there were substituted "in respect of whom a notice under section 13BA(9) of the 1983 Act has been issued", and
      (b) in paragraphs (9)(a) and (10), for "entry in the register of the elector in question" there were substituted "entry relating to the elector in question on a notice issued under section 13BA(9) of the 1983 Act".

Refusal to deliver ballot paper

40   A decision by a presiding officer taken under paragraph (2) of regulation 32, including that paragraph as applied by regulation 35, 36 or 37, is final (except that it is subject to review in proceedings brought by an application for judicial review).

Spoilt ballot papers

41(1) This regulation applies if a voter has inadvertently dealt with his or her ballot paper in a manner which means that it cannot conveniently be used as a ballot paper and
      (a) the voter delivers the ballot paper (referred to in this Part as "a spoilt ballot paper") to the presiding officer, and
      (b) proves the fact of the inadvertence to the satisfaction of the officer.

(2)   The voter may obtain a replacement ballot paper and the spoilt ballot paper must be cancelled immediately.

Correction of errors on day of poll

42   The presiding officer must keep a list of persons to whom ballot papers are delivered in consequence of an alteration to the register made by virtue of section 13B(3B) or (3D) or 13BA(9) of the 1983 Act that takes effect on the day of the poll.

Adjournment of poll in case of riot

43(1)   Where the proceedings at a polling station are interrupted or obstructed by riot or open violence, the presiding officer must adjourn the proceedings till the following day and must give notice to the counting officer as soon as practicable.

(2)   Where the poll is adjourned at a polling station
   (a)   the hours of polling on the day to which it is adjourned must be the same as for the original day, and
   (b)   references in this Part to the close of the poll are to be read accordingly.

Procedure on close of poll

44(1)   As soon as practicable after the close of the poll, the presiding officer must, in the presence of any polling agents, make up into separate packets
   (a)   each ballot box in use at the station, sealed so as to prevent the introduction of additional ballot papers and unopened, but with the key (if any) attached;
   (b)   the unused and spoilt ballot papers placed together;
   (c)   the tendered ballot papers;
   (d)   the marked copies of the registers of electors (including any marked copy notices issued under section 13B(3B) or (3D) or 13BA(9) of the 1983 Act) and of the list of proxies;
   (e)   the lists prepared under regulation 11, including the parts that were completed in accordance with regulation 33(2)(b) (together referred to in this Part as "the completed corresponding number lists");
   (f)   the certificates as to employment on duty on the day of the poll;
   (g)   the tendered votes list, the list of voters with disabilities assisted by companions, the list of votes marked by the presiding officer, a statement of the number of voters whose votes are so marked by the presiding officer under the heads "disability" and "unable to read", the list maintained under regulation 42, and the declarations made by the companions of voters with disabilities.

(2)   The marked copies of the registers of electors (including any marked copy notices issued under section 13B(3B) or (3D) or 13BA(9) of the 1983 Act) and of the list of proxies must be in one packet and must not be in the same packet as the completed corresponding number lists or the certificates as to employment on duty on the day of the poll.

(3)   The packets must be sealed with
   (a)   the presiding officer's seal, and
   (b)   the seals of any polling agents who want to affix their seals.

(4)   The presiding officer must deliver the packets, or cause them to be delivered, to the counting officer to be taken charge of by that officer.

(5)   If the packets are not delivered by the presiding officer personally to the counting officer, their delivery must be in accordance with arrangements approved by the counting officer.

(6)   The packets must be accompanied by a statement (referred to in this Part as "the ballot paper account") made by the presiding officer showing the number of ballot papers entrusted to him or her, and accounting for them under the following heads
   (a)   ballot papers issued and not otherwise accounted for,

(b)   unused ballot papers,

(c)   spoilt ballot papers, and

(d)   tendered ballot papers.

Counting of Votes

Attendance at the count

45(1)   The counting officer must make arrangements for counting the votes in the presence of the counting agents as soon as practicable after the close of the poll.

(2)   The counting officer must give the counting agents notice in writing of the time and place at which the counting of votes will begin.

(3)   A person may be present at the counting of the votes only if
(a)   the person falls within paragraph (4), or
(b)   the person is permitted by the counting officer to attend.

(4)   The persons within this paragraph are
(a)   the Chief Counting Officer, the Regional Counting Officer (where the voting area is in a region for which a Regional Counting Officer is appointed) and the counting officer;
(b)   the counting officer's clerks;
(c)   the referendum agents;
(d)   the counting agents;
(e)   persons who are entitled to attend by virtue of any of sections 6A to 6D of the 2000 Act.

(5)   The counting officer may give a person permission under paragraph (3)(b) only if
(a)   the officer is satisfied that the person's attendance will not impede the efficient counting of the votes, and
(b)   the officer has consulted the referendum agents or thinks it impracticable to do so.

(6)   The counting officer must give the counting agents
(a)   whatever reasonable facilities for overseeing the proceedings, and
(b)   whatever information with respect to the proceedings,
the officer can give them consistently with the orderly conduct of the proceedings and the discharge of the officer's duties.

(7)   In particular, where the votes are counted by sorting the ballot papers according to the answer for which the vote is given and then counting the number of ballot papers for each answer, the counting agents are entitled to satisfy themselves that the ballot papers are correctly sorted.

The count

46(1)   The counting officer must
(a)   in the presence of the counting agents open each ballot box and count and record the number of ballot papers in it;
(b)   in the presence of the referendum agents verify each ballot paper account;
(c)   count the postal ballot papers that have been duly returned and record the number counted.

(2)   The counting officer must not count the votes given on any ballot papers until
(a)   in the case of postal ballot papers, they have been mixed with the ballot papers from at least one ballot box;
(b)   in the case of ballot papers from a ballot box, they have been mixed with the ballot papers from at least one other ballot box.

(3)   In England and Wales and Scotland, a postal ballot paper is not to be taken to be duly

returned unless

    (a)   it is returned in the manner prescribed by the relevant postal voting provisions and reaches the counting officer or a polling station in the appropriate area before the close of the poll,

    (b)   the postal voting statement, duly signed, is also returned in the manner prescribed by the relevant postal voting provisions and reaches the counting officer or such a polling station before that time,

    (c)   the postal voting statement also states the date of birth of the elector or proxy (as the case may be), and

    (d)   in a case where an elector's or proxy's date of birth and signature are to be verified in accordance with the relevant postal voting provisions, the counting officer verifies the date of birth and signature of the elector or proxy (as the case may be).

In paragraph (a) "the appropriate area" means the voting area containing the address in respect of which the elector is registered.

(4)   A postal ballot paper or postal voting statement that reaches the counting officer or a polling station on or after the close of the poll is treated for the purposes of paragraph (3) as reaching that officer or polling station before the close of the poll if it is delivered by a person who, at the close of the poll, is in the polling station, or in a queue outside the polling station, for the purpose of returning it.

(5)   In Northern Ireland a postal ballot paper is not to be taken to be duly returned unless

    (a)   it is returned in the proper envelope so as to reach the counting officer before the close of the poll and is accompanied by the declaration of identity duly signed and authenticated, and

    (b)   in the case of an elector, the declaration of identity states the elector's date of birth and the counting officer is satisfied that the date stated corresponds with the date supplied as the elector's date of birth in pursuance of section 10(4A)(b), 10A(1A)(b) or 13A(2A)(b) of the 1983 Act.

(6)   In the case of an elector in Northern Ireland, unless section 10(4B), 10A(1B) or 13A(2B) of the 1983 Act applies, the declaration of identity referred to in paragraph (5) is not to be taken to be duly signed unless the counting officer is satisfied that the signature on the declaration corresponds with the signature supplied as the elector's signature in pursuance of section 10(4A)(a), 10A(1A)(a) or 13A(2A)(a) of that Act.

(7)   The counting officer must not count any tendered ballot papers or (in Northern Ireland) tendered postal ballot papers.

(8)   The counting officer, while counting and recording the number of ballot papers and counting the votes, must

    (a)   keep the ballot papers with their faces upwards, and

    (b)   take all proper precautions for preventing anyone from seeing the numbers or other unique identifying marks printed on the back of the papers.

(9)   The counting officer must

    (a)   verify each ballot paper account by comparing it with the number of ballot papers recorded by the officer, and the unused and spoilt ballot papers in the officer's possession and the tendered votes list and, in Northern Ireland, the tendered postal votes list (opening and re-sealing the packets containing the unused and spoilt ballot papers and the lists);

    (b)   draw up a statement as to the result of the verification.

(10)   Any counting agent present at the verification may copy the statement drawn up under paragraph (9)(b).

(11)   Once the statement is drawn up the counting officer must

   (a) in the case of a voting area in a region for which a Regional Counting Officer is appointed, inform the Regional Counting Officer of the contents of the statement;

   (b) in the case of any other voting area, inform the Chief Counting Officer of the contents of the statement.

(12) The counting officer must so far as practicable proceed continuously with the counting of votes, allowing only time for refreshment, except that

   (a) the officer may, with the agreement of the counting agents, exclude the whole or any part of the period between 7pm and 9am on the next day;

   (b) the officer may exclude a day mentioned in regulation 7(1).

(13) During the time so excluded the counting officer must

   (a) place the ballot papers and other documents relating to the referendum under the officer's own seal and the seals of any of the counting agents who want to affix their seals, and

   (b) otherwise take proper precautions for the security of the papers and documents.

(14) For the purposes of paragraph (12)(a) the agreement of a referendum agent is effective as the agreement of his or her counting agents.

Recount

47(1) A person within paragraph (2) who is present at the completion of the counting (or any recount) of the votes in a voting area may require the counting officer to have the votes for that area recounted (or again recounted), but the counting officer may refuse to do so if in the officer's opinion the requirement is unreasonable.

(2) The persons within this paragraph are

   (a) referendum agents;

   (b) counting agents who, in relation to the count (or recount), are designated under regulation 23(2).

(3) No step is to be taken on the completion of the counting (or any recount) of the votes until the persons within paragraph (2) present at its completion have been given a reasonable opportunity to exercise the right conferred by this regulation.

(4) A counting officer may not conduct a recount once a direction has been given under regulation 49(3)(b).

Rejected ballot papers

48(1) Any ballot paper

   (a) that does not bear the official mark, or

   (b) on which a vote is given for both answers to the referendum question, or

   (c) on which anything is written or marked by which the voter can be identified (except the printed number and other unique identifying mark on the back), or

   (d) which is unmarked or does not indicate the voter's intention with certainty,

   is void and not to be counted.

(2) But a ballot paper on which the vote is marked

   (a) elsewhere than in the proper place, or

   (b) otherwise than by means of a cross, or

   (c) by more than one mark,

   is not to be treated as void for that reason if the voter's intended answer to the referendum question is apparent, and the way the paper is marked does not itself identify the voter and it is not shown that the voter can be identified by it.

(3) The counting officer must endorse the word "rejected" on any ballot paper which

under this regulation is not to be counted, and must add to the endorsement the words "rejection objected to" if an objection is made by a counting agent to the officer's decision.

(4) The counting officer must draw up a statement showing the number of ballot papers rejected under each of the following heads

    (a) no official mark;

    (b) both answers voted for;

    (c) writing or mark by which voter could be identified;

    (d) unmarked or void for uncertainty.

(5) Once the statement is drawn up the counting officer must

    (a) in the case of a voting area in a region for which a Regional Counting Officer is appointed, inform the Regional Counting Officer of the contents of the statement;

    (b) in the case of any other voting area, inform the Chief Counting Officer of the contents of the statement.

Direction to conduct recount

49(1) On the completion of the counting of the votes (including any recount under regulation 47), and on the completion of any recount under this regulation, the counting officer must draw up a statement showing

    (a) the total number of ballot papers counted, and

    (b) the number of votes cast in favour of each answer to the question asked in the referendum.

(2) Once the statement is drawn up the counting officer must

    (a) in the case of a voting area in a region for which a Regional Counting Officer is appointed, inform the Regional Counting Officer of the contents of the statement;

    (b) in the case of any other voting area, inform the Chief Counting Officer of the contents of the statement.

(3) The Regional Counting Officer or Chief Counting Officer must then either

    (a) direct the counting officer to have the votes recounted, or

    (b) direct the counting officer to make the certification under section 128(5) of the 2000 Act.

(4) The Regional Counting Officer or Chief Counting Officer may give a direction under paragraph (3)(a) only if the officer thinks that there is reason to doubt the accuracy of the counting of the votes in the counting officer's voting area.

(5) A counting officer who is given a direction under paragraph (3)(a) must

    (a) begin the recount as soon as practicable, and

    (b) if the officer does not begin the recount immediately, notify the counting agents of the time and place at which it will take place.

(6) A counting officer may not make the certification under section 128(5) of the 2000 Act until directed to do so under paragraph (3)(b).

Decisions on ballot papers

50 The decision of the counting officer on any question arising in respect of a ballot paper is final (subject to review in accordance with paragraph 19 of Schedule 3 to the 2015 Act).

Final Proceedings

Declaration by counting officers

51(1) This regulation applies to the counting officer for a voting area in a region for which a Regional Counting Officer is appointed.

(2) After making the certification under section 128(5) of the 2000 Act, the counting officer must

    (a) immediately give to the Regional Counting Officer notice of the matters certified;

    (b) as soon as practicable give to the Regional Counting Officer notice of the number of rejected ballot papers under each head shown in the statement of rejected ballot papers.

(3) When authorised to do so by the Regional Counting Officer, the counting officer must

    (a) make a declaration of the matters certified under section 128(5) of the 2000 Act;

    (b) give public notice of the matters certified together with the number of rejected ballot papers under each head shown in the statement of rejected ballot papers.

52(1) This regulation applies to

    (a) the counting officer for Northern Ireland;

    (b) the counting officer for a voting area in a region for which no Regional Counting Officer is appointed.

(2) After making the certification under section 128(5) of the 2000 Act, the counting officer must

    (a) immediately give to the Chief Counting Officer notice of the matters certified;

    (b) as soon as practicable give to the Chief Counting Officer notice of the number of rejected ballot papers under each head shown in the statement of rejected ballot papers.

(3) When authorised to do so by the Chief Counting Officer, the counting officer must

    (a) make a declaration of the matters certified under section 128(5) of the 2000 Act;

    (b) give public notice of the matters certified together with the number of rejected ballot papers under each head shown in the statement of rejected ballot papers.

Declaration by regional counting officers

53(1) After making the certification under paragraph 7(4) of Schedule 3 to the 2015 Act, a Regional Counting Officer must

    (a) immediately give to the Chief Counting Officer notice of the matters certified;

    (b) as soon as practicable give to the Chief Counting Officer notice of the number of rejected ballot papers for the region under each head shown in the statements of rejected ballot papers.

(2) When authorised to do so by the Chief Counting Officer, a Regional Counting Officer must

(a) make a declaration of the matters certified under paragraph 7(4) of Schedule 3 to the 2015 Act;

(b) give public notice of the matters certified together with the number of rejected ballot papers for the region under each head shown in the statements of rejected ballot papers.

Declaration of referendum result by chief counting officer

54 After making the certification under section 128(6) of the 2000 Act, the Chief Counting Officer must

(a) immediately make a declaration of the matters certified under that provision;
(b) as soon as practicable give public notice of the matters certified together with the number of rejected ballot papers under each head shown in the statements of rejected ballot papers.

Disposal of Documents

Sealing up of ballot papers

55(1) On the completion of the counting the counting officer must seal up in separate packets
  (a) the counted ballot papers, and
  (b) the rejected ballot papers.

(2) The counting officer may not open the sealed packets of
  (a) tendered ballot papers,
  (b) tendered postal ballot papers (in Northern Ireland),
  (c) the completed corresponding number lists,
  (d) certificates as to employment on duty on the day of the poll, or
  (e) marked copies of the registers of electors (including any marked copy notices issued under section 13B(3B) or (3D) or 13BA(9) of the 1983 Act) and lists of proxies.

Delivery or retention of documents

56(1) The counting officer must endorse on each of the sealed packets a description of its contents and the name of the voting area and must
  (a) in the case of a counting officer for a voting area in England and Wales, forward the documents specified in paragraph (2) to the registration officer of the local authority in whose area that voting area is situated;
  (b) in the case of a counting officer for a voting area in Scotland or the counting officer for Northern Ireland, retain the documents.

(2) The documents referred to above are
  (a) the packets of ballot papers;
  (b) the ballot paper accounts and the statements of
    (i) rejected ballot papers, and
    (ii) the result of the verification of the ballot paper accounts;
  (c) the tendered votes lists, the lists of voters with disabilities assisted by companions, the lists of votes marked by the presiding officer and the related statements, the lists maintained under regulation 42 and the declarations made by the companions of voters with disabilities;
  (d) in the case of the counting officer for Northern Ireland, the tendered postal votes list;
  (e) the packets of the completed corresponding number lists;
  (f) the packets of certificates as to employment on duty on the day of the poll;
  (g) the packets containing marked copies of the registers (including any marked copy notices issued under section 13B(3B) or (3D) or 13BA(9) of the 1983 Act) and marked copies of the postal voters list, of lists of proxies and of the proxy postal voters list;
  (h) any other documents prescribed for the purposes of this paragraph by the relevant postal voting provisions.

(3) In paragraph (1) "local authority" has the same meaning as in paragraph 6 of Schedule 3 to the 2015 Act.

Orders for production of documents

57(1) The High Court or county court or, in the case of a voting area in Scotland, the Court of Session or sheriff, may make an order

(a) for the inspection or production of any rejected ballot papers in the custody of a registration officer or (as the case may be) a counting officer,

(b) for the opening of a sealed packet of the completed corresponding number lists or of certificates as to employment on duty on the day of the poll, or

(c) for the inspection of any counted ballot papers in the officer's custody,

if satisfied by evidence on oath that the order is required for the purpose of instituting or maintaining a prosecution for an offence in relation to ballot papers or for the purpose of proceedings brought as mentioned in paragraph 19 of Schedule 3 to the 2015 Act.

(2) An order under this regulation may be made subject to whatever conditions the court or sheriff thinks expedient as to

(a) persons,

(b) time,

(c) place and mode of inspection, or

(d) production or opening.

(3) In making and carrying into effect an order for the opening of a packet of the completed corresponding number lists or of certificates or for the inspection of counted ballot papers, care must be taken to avoid disclosing the way in which the vote of any particular voter has been given until it has been proved

(a) that the vote was given, and

(b) that the vote has been declared by a competent court to be invalid.

(4) An appeal lies to the High Court from any order of the county court under this regulation, and to the Court of Session from any order of the sheriff under this regulation.

(5) A power given under this regulation to a court (other than a county court in Northern Ireland) or the sheriff may be exercised by any judge of the court, or by the sheriff, otherwise than in open court.

(6) A power given under this regulation to a county court in Northern Ireland may be exercised in whatever manner rules of court provide.

(7) Where an order is made for the production by a registration officer or a counting officer of a document in the officer's possession relating to the referendum

(a) the production by the officer or the officer's agent of the document ordered in the manner directed by the order is conclusive evidence that the document relates to the referendum;

(b) any endorsement on any packet of ballot papers so produced is prima facie evidence that the ballot papers are what they are stated to be by the endorsement.

(8) The production from proper custody of

(a) a ballot paper purporting to have been used at the referendum, and

(b) a completed corresponding number list with a number marked in writing beside the number of the ballot paper,

is prima facie evidence that the elector whose vote was given by that ballot paper was the person whose entry on the register of electors (or on a notice issued under section 13B(3B) or (3D) or 13BA(9) of the 1983 Act) at the time of the referendum contained the same number as the number written as mentioned in sub-paragraph (b).

(9) Except as provided by this regulation (or a court order) nobody may

    (a) inspect any rejected or counted ballot papers in the possession of a registration officer or counting officer, or

    (b) open any sealed packets of the completed corresponding number lists or of certificates.

Retention and public inspection of documents

58(1) A registration officer or (as the case may be) counting officer must retain for a year all documents relating to the referendum and then, unless otherwise directed by an order of a competent court, must have them destroyed.

  (2) For the purposes of paragraph (1) a competent court is

    (a) in relation to a registration officer in England and Wales, the High Court, the Crown Court or a magistrates' court;

    (b) in relation to a counting officer in Scotland, the Court of Session;

    (c) in relation to the counting officer for Northern Ireland, the High Court.

  (3) While documents are retained under paragraph (1) they must be open to public inspection.

    This does not apply to

    (a) ballot papers;

    (b) the completed corresponding number lists;

    (c) certificates as to employment on duty on the day of the poll.

  (4) The registration officer or (as the case may be) counting officer must, on request, supply to any person copies of or extracts from any description of the documents open to public inspection that is prescribed by the relevant regulations.

  (5) A right to inspect or be supplied with a document or part of a document under this regulation is subject to

    (a) any conditions imposed by the relevant regulations, and

    (b) the payment of any fee required by the relevant regulations.

PART 3

ABSENT VOTING IN THE REFERENDUM IN THE UNITED KINGDOM

CHAPTER 1

GREAT BRITAIN

Overview and interpretation

59(1) This Chapter of this Part contains provision about voting in the referendum in England and Wales and Scotland.

  (2) In this Chapter of this Part

    "anonymous entry", in relation to a register of electors, is to be read in accordance with section 9B of the 1983 Act;

    "peer" means a peer who is a member of the House of Lords;

    "relevant register" means

    (a) a register of parliamentary electors, or

    (b) in relation to a peer

      (i) a register of local government electors, or

      (ii) a register of peers maintained under section 3 of the Representation of the People Act 1985 (peers resident outside the United Kingdom);

    "the relevant regulations"

    (a) in relation to England and Wales, means the Representation of the People (England and Wales) Regulations 2001 as applied by Part 1 of Schedule 3;

(b) in relation to Scotland, means the Representation of the People (Scotland) Regulations 2001 as so applied;

"the RPA 2000" means the Representation of the People Act 2000.

Manner of voting in the referendum

60(1) This regulation applies to determine the manner of voting in England and Wales or Scotland of a person entitled to vote in the referendum.

(2) The person may vote in person at the polling station allotted to him or her under Part 2, unless the person is entitled to vote by post or by proxy in the referendum.

(3) The person may vote by post if the person is entitled to vote by post in the referendum.

(4) If the person is entitled to vote by proxy in the referendum, the person may so vote unless, before a ballot paper has been issued for the person to vote by proxy, the person applies at the polling station allotted to him or her under Part 2 for a ballot paper for the purpose of voting in person, in which case he or she may vote in person there.

(5) If the person is not entitled to vote by post or by proxy in the referendum, the person may vote in person at any polling station in the same voting area as the polling station allotted to him or her under Part 2 if paragraph (6) applies.

(6) This paragraph applies if the person cannot reasonably be expected to go in person to the polling station allotted to him or her under Part 2 by reason of his or her employment on the date of the poll for a purpose connected with the referendum, if that employment is

(a) as a constable or as a person designated as a community support officer under section 38 of the Police Reform Act 2002 (police powers for employees), or

(b) by the counting officer.

(7) Nothing in this regulation applies to a person to whom section 7 of the 1983 Act (mental patients who are not detained offenders) applies and who is liable, by virtue of any enactment, to be detained in the mental hospital in question, whether the person is registered by virtue of that provision or not; and such a person may vote

(a) in person (where the person is granted permission to be absent from the hospital and voting in person does not breach any condition attached to that permission), or

(b) by post or by proxy (where the person is entitled to vote by post or, as the case may be, by proxy in the referendum).

(8) Nothing in this paragraph applies to a person to whom section 7A of the 1983 Act (persons remanded in custody) applies, whether the person is registered by virtue of that provision or not; and such a person may vote only by post or by proxy (where the person is entitled to vote by post or, as the case may be, by proxy in the referendum).

(9) Paragraph (2) does not prevent a person, at the polling station allotted to him or her, marking a tendered ballot paper in pursuance of regulation 37.

Entitlement to vote by post or by proxy

61(1) A person entitled to vote in the referendum is entitled to vote by post or by proxy if paragraph (2) or (3) (as the case may be) applies to the person.

(2) This paragraph applies to a person who is shown in the postal voters list mentioned in regulation 63(2) as entitled to vote by post in the referendum.

(3) This paragraph applies to a person who is shown in the list of proxies mentioned in regulation 63(3) as entitled to vote by proxy in the referendum.

Application to vote by post or by proxy in the referendum

62(1)   Where a person applies to the registration officer to vote by post in the referendum, the registration officer must grant the application if
    (a)   the officer is satisfied that the applicant is or will be registered in a relevant register, and
    (b)   the application contains the applicant's signature and date of birth and meets the requirements prescribed by the relevant regulations.

(2)   Where a person applies to the registration officer to vote by proxy in the referendum, the registration officer must grant the application if
    (a)   the officer is satisfied that the applicant's circumstances on the date of the poll will be or are likely to be such that the applicant cannot reasonably be expected to vote in person at the polling station allotted or likely to be allotted to the applicant under Part 2,
    (b)   the officer is satisfied that the applicant is or will be registered in a relevant register, and
    (c)   the application contains the applicant's signature and date of birth and meets the requirements prescribed by the relevant regulations.

(3)   Where a person
    (a)   has an anonymous entry in a relevant register, and
    (b)   applies to the registration officer to vote by proxy in the referendum,
    the registration officer must grant the application if it meets the requirements prescribed by the relevant regulations.

(4)   Nothing in paragraph (1), (2) or (3) applies to
    (a)   a person who is included in the record kept under paragraph 3 of Schedule 4 to the RPA 2000 (absent vote at elections for definite or indefinite period) in respect of parliamentary elections,
    (b)   a peer who is included in the record kept under paragraph 3 of Schedule 4 to the RPA 2000 (absent vote at elections for definite or indefinite period) in respect of local government elections, or
    (c)   a peer who is included in the record kept under paragraph 3 of Schedule 2 to the European Parliamentary Elections Regulations 2004 (absent vote at elections for definite or indefinite period).

(5)   But if a person is included in a record mentioned in paragraph (4) and is shown in the record as voting by post, the person may, in respect of the referendum, apply to the registration officer
    (a)   for his or her ballot paper to be sent to a different address from that shown in the record, or
    (b)   to vote by proxy.

(6)   The registration officer must grant an application under paragraph (5) if
    (a)   (in the case of any application) it meets the requirements prescribed by the relevant regulations, and
    (b)   (in the case of an application to vote by proxy) the registration officer is satisfied that the applicant's circumstances on the date of the poll will be or are likely to be such that the applicant cannot reasonably be expected to vote in person at the polling station allotted or likely to be allotted to the applicant under Part 2.

(7)   The registration officer may dispense with the requirement under paragraph (1)(b) or (2)(c) for the applicant to provide a signature if the officer is satisfied that the applicant
    (a)   is unable to provide a signature because of any disability the applicant has,
    (b)   is unable to provide a signature because the applicant is unable to read or write, or
    (c)   is unable to sign in a consistent and distinctive way because of any such

disability or inability.

(8) The registration officer must keep a record of those whose applications under this paragraph have been granted, showing
    (a) their dates of birth, and
    (b) except in cases where the registration officer in pursuance of paragraph (7) has dispensed with the requirement to provide a signature, their signatures.

(9) The record kept under paragraph (8) must be retained by the registration officer for the period of twelve months beginning with the date of the poll for the referendum.

Absent voters lists

63(1) The registration officer must, for the purposes of the referendum, keep the two special lists mentioned in paragraphs (2) and (3) respectively.

(2) The first of those lists is a list ("the postal voters list") of those within column 2 of the following table, together with the addresses provided as mentioned in column 3 as the addresses to which their ballot papers are to be sent.

	Description of person voting by post	Address
1	A person whose application under regulation 62(1) to vote by post in the referendum has been granted.	Address provided in the person's application under regulation 62(1).
2	A person who (a) is entitled to vote in the referendum and in a poll that is taken together with the referendum, (b) is included in the postal voters list for that poll, and (c) is not within entry 1 in this table or entry 1 in the table in paragraph (3).	Address provided in the application that gave rise to the person being included in the postal voters list or, if the person is included in more than one, the address provided in the latest of those applications.
3	A person who (a) is for the time being shown in the record kept under paragraph 3 of Schedule 4 to the RPA 2000 as voting by post at parliamentary elections, and (b) is not within entry 1 or 2 of this table or entry 1 or 2 in the table in paragraph (3).	Address provided in the person's application under paragraph 3 of Schedule 4 to the RPA 2000 or (as the case may be) regulation 62(5)(a).
4	A peer who (a) is for the time being shown in the record kept under paragraph 3 of Schedule 4 to the RPA 2000 as voting by post at local government elections, (b) is not for the time being shown in the record kept under paragraph 3 of Schedule 2 to the European Parliamentary Elections Regulations 2004 as voting by post, or was included in that record before being included in the record mentioned in paragraph (a) above, and (c) is not within entry 1 or 2 of this table or entry 1 or 2 in the table in paragraph (3).	Address provided in the peer's application under paragraph 3 of Schedule 4 to the RPA 2000 or (as the case may be) regulation 62(5)(a).
5	A peer who (a) is for the time being shown in the record kept under paragraph 3 of Schedule 2 to	Address provided in the peer's application under paragraph 3 of Schedule 2 to the European

Description of person voting by post	Address
the European Parliamentary Elections Regulations 2004 as voting by post, (b) is not for the time being shown in the record kept under paragraph 3 of Schedule 4 to the RPA 2000 as voting by post at local government elections, or was included in that record before being included in the record mentioned in paragraph (a) above, and (c) is not within entry 1 or 2 in this table or entry 1 or 2 in the table in paragraph (3).	Parliamentary Elections Regulations 2004 or (as the case may be) regulation 62(5)(a).

(3) The second of the lists mentioned in paragraph (1) is a list ("the list of proxies") of those within column 2 of the following table, together with the names and addresses of their proxies appointed as mentioned in column 3.

Description of person voting by proxy	Proxy
1 A person (not within entry 1 in the table in paragraph (2)) whose application under regulation 62(2), (3) or (5)(b) to vote by proxy in the referendum has been granted.	Proxy appointed under regulation 64.
2 A person who (a) is entitled to vote in the referendum and in a poll that is taken together with the referendum, (b) is included in the list of proxies for that poll, and (c) is not within entry 1 in this table or entry 1 or 2 in the table in paragraph (2).	Proxy appointed for the purposes of that poll or, if there is more than one, the proxy appointed for the poll in respect of which the latest of the person's applications to vote by proxy was made.
3 A person who (a) is for the time being shown in the record kept under paragraph 3 of Schedule 4 to the RPA 2000 as voting by proxy at parliamentary elections, and (b) is not within entry 1 or 2 of this table or entry 1 or 2 in the table in paragraph (2).	Proxy appointed under paragraph 6 of Schedule 4 to the RPA 2000 for parliamentary elections.
4 A peer who (a) is for the time being shown in the record kept under paragraph 3 of Schedule 4 to the RPA 2000 as voting by proxy at local government elections, (b) is not for the time being shown in the record kept under paragraph 3 of Schedule 2 to the European Parliamentary Elections Regulations 2004 as voting by proxy, or was included in that record before being included in the record mentioned in paragraph (a) above, and (c) is not within entry 1 or 2 of this table or entry 1, 2 or 5 in the table in paragraph (2).	Proxy appointed under paragraph 6 of Schedule 4 to the RPA 2000 for local government elections.
5 A peer who (a) is for the time being shown in the record kept under paragraph 3 of Schedule 2 to the European Parliamentary Elections Regulations 2004 as voting by proxy,	Proxy appointed under paragraph 6 of Schedule 2 to the European

Description of person voting by proxy	Proxy
(b) is not for the time being shown in the record kept under paragraph 3 of Schedule 4 to the RPA 2000 as voting by proxy at local government elections, or was included in that record before being included in the record mentioned in paragraph (a) above, and (c) is not within entry 1 or 2 in this table or entry 1, 2 or 4 in the table in paragraph (2).	Parliamentary Elections Regulations 2004.

(4) In the case of a person who has an anonymous entry in a register, the postal voters list or list of proxies (as the case may be) must show in relation to the person only
  (a) his or her electoral number, and
  (b) the period for which the anonymous entry has effect.

Proxies

64(1) Subject to what follows, any person is capable of being appointed under this paragraph to vote as proxy for another (the "principal") in the referendum.

(2) The principal cannot have more than one person at a time appointed as proxy to vote for him or her in the referendum.

(3) A person is capable of being appointed to vote as proxy only if
  (a) the person is not subject to any legal incapacity (age apart) to vote in the referendum in his or her own right, and
  (b) the person is or will on the date of the poll for the referendum be registered in a relevant register.

(4) Where the principal applies to the registration officer for the appointment of a proxy under this regulation, the registration officer must make the appointment if the application meets the requirements prescribed by the relevant regulations and the officer is satisfied that the principal is or will be
  (a) registered in a relevant register, and
  (b) entitled to vote by proxy in the referendum by virtue of an application under regulation 62(2), (3) or (5)(b),
  and that the proxy is capable of being, and willing to be, appointed.

(5) The appointment of a proxy under this paragraph is to be made by means of a proxy paper issued by the registration officer in the form set out in Form 20 in Schedule 4.

(6) The appointment may be cancelled by the principal by giving notice to the registration officer and also ceases to be in force on the issue of a proxy paper appointing a different person under this paragraph to vote for the principal in the referendum.

65(1) Subject to what follows, where a relevant proxy appointment is in force, the person appointed is entitled to vote as proxy for the person for whom the appointment was made (the "principal").

(2) In paragraph (1) "relevant proxy appointment" means
  (a) in relation to a principal who is included in the list of proxies by virtue of entry 1 in the table in regulation 63(3), an appointment under regulation 64;
  (b) in relation to a principal who is included in the list of proxies by virtue of entry 2 in that table, the appointment of the person mentioned in column 3 of that entry;
  (c) in relation to a principal who is included in the list of proxies by virtue of entry 3 in that table, an appointment under paragraph 6 of Schedule 4 to the RPA 2000 for parliamentary elections;
  (d) in relation to a principal who is a peer included in the list of proxies by virtue of

entry 4 in that table, an appointment under paragraph 6 of Schedule 4 to the RPA 2000 for local government elections;

(e) in relation to a principal who is a peer included in the list of proxies by virtue of entry 5 in that table, an appointment under paragraph 6 of Schedule 2 to the European Parliamentary Elections Regulations 2004.

(3) A person is capable of voting as proxy in the referendum only if

(a) the person is not subject to any legal incapacity (age apart) to vote in the referendum in his or her own right, and

(b) the person is registered in a relevant register.

(4) A person is not capable of voting as proxy in the referendum unless on the date of the poll the person has attained the age of 18.

(5) A person is not entitled to vote as proxy in the referendum on behalf of more than two others of whom that person is not the spouse, civil partner, parent, grandparent, brother, sister, child or grandchild.

Voting as proxy

66(1) A person entitled to vote as proxy for another (the "principal") in the referendum may do so in person at the polling station allotted to the principal under Part 2 unless the proxy is entitled to vote by post as proxy for the principal in the referendum, in which case the proxy may vote by post.

(2) Where a person is entitled to vote by post as proxy for the principal in the referendum, the principal may not apply for a ballot paper for the purpose of voting in person in the referendum.

(3) For the purposes of this Chapter of this Part and the 1983 Act a person entitled to vote as proxy for another in the referendum is entitled so to vote by post if the person is included in the list kept under paragraph (6).

(4) Where a person applies to the registration officer to vote by post as proxy in the referendum the officer must grant the application if
(a) the officer is satisfied that the principal is or will be registered in a relevant register,
(b) the applicant is the subject of a relevant proxy appointment within the meaning of regulation 65(2), and
(c) the application contains the applicant's signature and date of birth and meets the requirements prescribed by the relevant regulations.

(5) A person who is the subject of a relevant proxy appointment within the meaning of regulation 65(2)(b), (c) or (d) and who
(a) is included in the record kept under paragraph 7(6) of Schedule 4 to the RPA 2000 (record of proxies who have applied to vote by post) in respect of parliamentary elections,
(b) is included in the record kept under paragraph 7(6) of Schedule 4 to the RPA 2000 (record of proxies who have applied to vote by post) in respect of local government elections, or
(c) is included in the record kept under paragraph 7(6) of Schedule 2 to the European Parliamentary Elections Regulations 2004 (record of proxies who have applied to vote by post),
may apply to the registration officer for his or her referendum ballot paper to be sent to a different address from that shown in the record, and the officer must grant the application if it meets the requirements prescribed by the relevant regulations.

(6) The registration officer must, in respect of the referendum, keep a special list ("the

proxy postal voters list") of those within column 2 of the following table, together with the addresses provided as mentioned in column 3 as the addresses to which their ballot papers are to be sent.

	Description of proxy postal voters	Address
1	A proxy whose application under paragraph (4) has been granted.	Address provided in the proxy's application under paragraph (4).
2	A proxy who (a) was appointed as mentioned in column 3 of entry 2 in the table in regulation 63(3) for a person mentioned in column 2 of that entry, and (b) is included in the proxy postal voters list for the poll in respect of which that appointment was made.	Address provided in the proxy's application to vote by post as proxy in that poll.
3	A proxy who (a) was appointed as mentioned in column 3 of entry 3 in the table in regulation 63(3) for a person mentioned in column 2 of that entry, and (b) is for the time being included in the record kept under paragraph 7(6) of Schedule 4 to the RPA 2000 (record of proxies who have applied to vote by post).	Address provided in the proxy's application under paragraph 7(4)(a) of Schedule 4 to the RPA 2000 or (as the case may be) paragraph (5) above.
4	A proxy who (a) was appointed as mentioned in column 3 of entry 4 in the table in regulation 63(3) for a peer mentioned in column 2 of that entry, and (b) is for the time being included in the record kept under paragraph 7(6) of Schedule 4 to the RPA 2000 (record of proxies who have applied to vote by post).	Address provided in the proxy's application under paragraph 7(4)(a) of Schedule 4 to the RPA 2000 or (as the case may be) paragraph (5) above.
5	A proxy who (a) was appointed as mentioned in column 3 of entry 5 in the table in regulation 63(3) for a peer mentioned in column 2 of that entry, and (b) is for the time being included in the record kept under paragraph 7(6) of Schedule 2 to the European Parliamentary Elections Regulations 2004.	Address provided in the proxy's application under paragraph 7(4)(a) of Schedule 2 to the European Parliamentary Elections Regulations 2004 or (as the case may be) paragraph (5) above.

(7) In the case of a person who has an anonymous entry in a register, the special list mentioned in paragraph (6) must contain only
   (a) the person's electoral number, and
   (b) the period for which the anonymous entry has effect.

(8) Paragraph (2) does not prevent a person, at the polling station allotted to him or her, marking a tendered ballot paper in pursuance of regulation 37.

(9) The registration officer may dispense with the requirement under paragraph (4)(c) for the applicant to provide a signature if the officer is satisfied that the applicant
   (a) is unable to provide a signature because of any disability the applicant has,
   (b) is unable to provide a signature because the applicant is unable to read or write, or
   (c) is unable to sign in a consistent and distinctive way because of any such

disability or inability.

(10) The registration officer must also keep a record in relation to those whose applications under paragraph (4) have been granted showing
    (a) their dates of birth, and
    (b) except in cases where the registration officer in pursuance of paragraph (9) has dispensed with the requirement to provide a signature, their signatures.

(11) The record kept under paragraph (10) must be retained by the registration officer for the period of twelve months beginning with the date of the poll for the referendum.

Use of personal identifier information

67 The registration officer must either
    (a) provide the counting officer with a copy of the information contained in records kept by the registration officer in pursuance of
        (i) paragraphs 3(9) and 7(12) of Schedule 4 to the RPA 2000 (dates of birth and signatures of certain electors and proxies) in relation to persons entitled to vote in the referendum,
        (ii) paragraphs 3(9) and 7(13) of Schedule 2 to the European Parliamentary Elections Regulations 2004 (dates of birth and signatures of certain electors and proxies) in relation to peers entitled to vote in the referendum, and
        (iii) regulations 62(8) and 66(10), or
    (b) give the counting officer access to such information.

68 Information contained in records kept by a registration officer in pursuance of regulation 62(8) or 66(10) may be disclosed by the officer to
    (a) any other registration officer if the officer thinks that to do so will assist the other registration officer in the performance of his or her duties;
    (b) any person exercising functions in relation to the preparation or conduct of legal proceedings under the 2015 Act or the Representation of the People Acts.

Offences

69(1) If a person
    (a) in any declaration or form used for any of the purposes of this Chapter of this Part, makes a statement knowing it to be false, or
    (b) attests an application under regulation 62 knowing
        (i) that he or she is not authorised to do so, or
        (ii) that it contains a statement which is false,
that person commits an offence.

(2) A person guilty of an offence under paragraph (1) is liable
    (a) on summary conviction in England and Wales, to a fine;
    (b) on summary conviction in Scotland, to a fine not exceeding level 5 on the standard scale.

(3) If a person provides false information in connection with an application under regulation 62(1) or (2) or 66(4), that person commits an offence.

(4) In relation to a signature, "false information" for the purposes of paragraph (3), means a signature which
    (a) is not the usual signature of, or
    (b) was written by a person other than,
the person whose signature it purports to be.

(5) A person does not commit an offence under paragraph (3) if the person did not know, and had no reason to suspect, that the information was false.

(6) Where sufficient evidence is adduced to raise an issue with respect to the defence under paragraph (5), the court is to assume that the defence is satisfied unless the prosecution proves beyond reasonable doubt that it is not.

(7) A person guilty of an offence under paragraph (3) is liable

    (a) on summary conviction in England and Wales, to imprisonment for a term not exceeding 51 weeks or to a fine, or to both;

    (b) on summary conviction in Scotland, to imprisonment for a term not exceeding 6 months or to a fine not exceeding level 5 on the standard scale, or to both.

(8) The reference in paragraph (7)(a) to 51 weeks is to be read as a reference to 6 months in relation to an offence committed before the commencement of section 281(5) of the Criminal Justice Act 2003.

CHAPTER 2
NORTHERN IRELAND

Overview and interpretation

70(1) This Chapter of this Part contains provision about voting in the referendum in Northern Ireland.

(2) In this Chapter of this Part

"anonymous entry", in relation to a register of electors, is to be read in accordance with section 9B of the 1983 Act;

"peer" means a peer who is a member of the House of Lords;

"relevant register" means

    (a) a register of parliamentary electors, or

    (b) in relation to a peer

        (i) a register of local electors, or

        (ii) a register of peers maintained under section 3 of the Representation of the People Act 1985 (peers resident outside the United Kingdom);

"the 2008 Regulations" means the Representation of the People (Northern Ireland) Regulations 2008 as applied by Part 2 of Schedule 3;

"the 1985 Act" means the Representation of the People Act 1985.

Manner of voting in the referendum

71(1) This regulation applies to determine the manner of voting in Northern Ireland of a person entitled to vote in the referendum.

(2) The person may vote in person at the polling station allotted to him or her under Part 2, unless the person is entitled to vote by post or by proxy in the referendum.

(3) The person may vote by post if the person is entitled to vote by post in the referendum.

(4) If the person is entitled to vote by proxy in the referendum, the person may so vote unless, before a ballot paper has been issued for the person to vote by proxy, the person applies at the polling station allotted to him or her under Part 2 for a ballot paper for the purpose of voting in person, in which case he or she may vote in person there.

(5) If the person is not entitled to vote by post or by proxy in the referendum, the person may vote in person at any polling station in Northern Ireland if paragraph (6) applies.

(6) This paragraph applies if the person cannot reasonably be expected to go in person to the polling station allotted to him or her under Part 2 by reason of his or her employment on the date of the poll for a purpose connected with the referendum, if that employment is

    (a) as a constable, or

    (b) by the counting officer.

(7) Nothing in this regulation applies to

    (a) a person to whom section 7 of the 1983 Act (mental patients who are not detained offenders) applies and who is liable, by virtue of any enactment, to be detained in the mental hospital in question, whether the person is registered by virtue of that provision or not;

    (b) a person to whom section 7A of the 1983 Act (persons remanded in custody) applies, whether the person is registered by virtue of that provision or not;

    (c) a person who has an anonymous entry in a register maintained by the Chief Electoral Officer for Northern Ireland;

and such a person may vote only by post or by proxy (where the person is entitled to vote by post or, as the case may be, by proxy in the referendum).

(8) Paragraph (2) does not prevent a person, at the polling station allotted to him or her, marking a tendered ballot paper in pursuance of regulation 37.

Entitlement to vote by post or by proxy

72(1) A person entitled to vote in the referendum is entitled to vote by post or by proxy if paragraph (2) or (3) (as the case may be) applies to the person.

(2) This paragraph applies to a person who is shown in the postal voters list mentioned in regulation 74(2) as entitled to vote by post in the referendum.

(3) This paragraph applies to a person who is shown in the list of proxies mentioned in regulation 74(3) as entitled to vote by proxy in the referendum.

Application to vote by post or by proxy in the referendum

73(1) Where a person applies to the registration officer to vote by post, or to vote by proxy, in the referendum, the registration officer must grant the application if

    (a) the officer is satisfied that the applicant is or will be registered in a relevant register,

    (b) the officer is satisfied that the applicant's circumstances on the date of the poll will be or are likely to be such that the applicant cannot reasonably be expected to vote in person at the polling station allotted or likely to be allotted to the applicant under Part 2,

    (c) the application states the applicant's date of birth and the registration officer is satisfied that the date stated corresponds with the date supplied as the date of the applicant's birth in pursuance of section 10(4A)(b), 10A(1A)(b) or 13A(2A)(b) of the 1983 Act,

    (d) the application is signed and (unless section 10(4B), 10A(1B) or 13A(2B) of the 1983 Act applies) the registration officer is satisfied that the signature on the application corresponds with the signature supplied as the applicant's signature in pursuance of section 10(4A)(a), 10A(1A)(a) or 13A(2A)(a) of the 1983 Act,

    (e) the application either states the applicant's national insurance number or states that the applicant does not have one, and the registration officer is satisfied as mentioned in paragraph (2) below, and

    (f) the application meets the requirements prescribed by the 2008 Regulations.

(2) For the purposes of paragraph (1)(e), the registration officer must be satisfied

    (a) if the application states a national insurance number, that the requirements of paragraph (3) are met, or

    (b) if the application states that the applicant does not have a national insurance number, that no such number was supplied as the applicant's national insurance number in pursuance of section 10(4A)(c)(i), 10A(1A)(c)(i) or

13A(2A)(c)(i) of the 1983 Act.

(3) The requirements of this paragraph are met if
   (a) the number stated as mentioned in paragraph (2)(a) is the same as the one supplied as the applicant's national insurance number in pursuance of section 10(4A)(c)(i), 10A(1A)(c)(i) or 13A(2A)(c)(i) of the 1983 Act, or
   (b) no national insurance number was supplied under any of those provisions, but the registration officer is not aware of any reason to doubt the authenticity of the application.

(4) Nothing in paragraph (1) applies to
   (a) a person who is included in the record kept under section 6 of the 1985 Act (absent vote at parliamentary elections for indefinite period),
   (b) a peer who is included in the record kept under paragraph 1 of Schedule 2 to the Local Elections (Northern Ireland) Order 1985 (absent vote at local elections for indefinite period), or
   (c) a peer who is included in the record kept under regulation 8 of the European Parliamentary Elections (Northern Ireland) Regulations 2004 (absent vote at elections for indefinite period).

(5) But if a person is included in a record mentioned in paragraph (4)(a), (b) or (c) and is shown in the record as voting by post, the person may, in respect of the referendum, apply to the registration officer
   (a) for his or her ballot paper to be sent to a different address in the United Kingdom from that shown in the record, or
   (b) to vote by proxy.

(6) The registration officer must grant an application under paragraph (5) if it meets the requirements prescribed by the 2008 Regulations.

(7) A person applying to vote by post must provide an address in the United Kingdom as the address to which the person's ballot paper is to be sent.

Absent voters lists

74(1) The registration officer must, for the purposes of the referendum, keep the two special lists mentioned in paragraphs (2) and (3) respectively.

(2) The first of those lists is a list ("the postal voters list") of those within column 2 of the following table, together with the addresses provided as mentioned in column 3 as the addresses to which their ballot papers are to be sent.

	Description of person voting by post	Address
1	A person whose application under regulation 73(1) to vote by post in the referendum has been granted.	Address provided in the person's application under regulation 73(1).
2	A person who (a) is entitled to vote in the referendum and in a poll that is taken together with the referendum, (b) is shown in the absent voters list for that poll as voting by post, and (c) is not within entry 1 in this table or entry 1 in the table in paragraph (3).	Address provided in the application that gave rise to the person being included in the absent voters list or, if the person is included in more than one, the address provided in the latest of those applications.
3	A person who (a) is for the time being shown in the record kept under section 6 of the 1985 Act as voting by post at	Address provided in the person's application under section 6 of the

Description of person voting by post	Address
	parliamentary elections, and (b) is not within entry 1 or 2 of this table or entry 1 or 2 in the table in paragraph (3).	1985 Act or (as the case may be) regulation 73(5)(a).
4	A peer who (a) is for the time being shown in the record kept under paragraph 1 of Schedule 2 to the Local Elections (Northern Ireland) Order 1985, (b) is not for the time being shown in the record kept under regulation 8 of the European Parliamentary Elections (Northern Ireland) Regulations 2004 as voting by post, or was included in that record before being included in the record mentioned in paragraph (a) above, and (c) is not within entry 1 or 2 of this table or entry 1 or 2 in the table in paragraph (3).	Address provided in the peer's application under paragraph 1 of Schedule 2 to the Local Elections (Northern Ireland) Order 1985 or (as the case may be) regulation 73(5)(a).
5	A peer who (a) is for the time being shown in the record kept under regulation 8 of the European Parliamentary Elections (Northern Ireland) Regulations 2004 as voting by post, (b) is not for the time being shown in the record kept under paragraph 1 of Schedule 2 to the Local Elections (Northern Ireland) Order 1985, or was included in that record before being included in the record mentioned in paragraph (a) above, and (c) is not within entry 1 or 2 in this table or entry 1 or 2 in the table in paragraph (3).	Address provided in the peer's application under regulation 8 of the European Parliamentary Elections (Northern Ireland) Regulations 2004 or (as the case may be) regulation 73(5)(a).

(3) The second of the lists mentioned in paragraph (1) is a list ("the list of proxies") of those within column 2 of the following table, together with the names and addresses of their proxies appointed as mentioned in column 3.

	Description of person voting by proxy	Proxy
1	A person (not within entry 1 in the table in paragraph (2)) whose application under regulation 73(1) or (5)(b) to vote by proxy in the referendum has been granted.	Proxy appointed under regulation 75.
2	A person who (a) is entitled to vote in the referendum and in a poll that is taken together with the referendum, (b) is shown in the absent voters list for that poll as voting by proxy, and (c) is not within entry 1 in this table or entry 1 or 2 in the table in paragraph (2).	Proxy appointed for the purposes of that poll or, if there is more than one, the proxy appointed for the poll in respect of which the latest of the person's applications to vote by proxy was made.
3	A person who (a) is for the time being shown in the record kept under section 6 of the 1985 Act as voting by proxy at parliamentary elections, and (b) is not within entry 1 or 2 of this table or entry 1 or 2 in the table in paragraph (2).	Proxy appointed under section 8 of the 1985 Act for parliamentary elections.
4	A peer who (a) is for the time being shown in the record kept under	Proxy appointed under paragraph 3 of Schedule

	Description of person voting by proxy	Proxy
	paragraph 1 of Schedule 2 to the Local Elections (Northern Ireland) Order 1985 as voting by proxy, (b) is not for the time being shown in the record kept under regulation 8 of the European Parliamentary Elections (Northern Ireland) Regulations 2004 as voting by proxy, or was included in that record before being included in the record mentioned in paragraph (a) above, and (c) is not within entry 1 or 2 of this table or entry 1, 2 or 5 in the table in paragraph (2).	2 to the Local Elections (Northern Ireland) Order 1985.
5	A peer who (a) is for the time being shown in the record kept under regulation 8 of the European Parliamentary Elections (Northern Ireland) Regulations 2004 as voting by proxy, (b) is not for the time being shown in the record kept under paragraph 1 of Schedule 2 to the Local Elections (Northern Ireland) Order 1985 as voting by proxy, or was included in that record before being included in the record mentioned in paragraph (a) above, and (c) is not within entry 1 or 2 in this table or entry 1, 2 or 4 in the table in paragraph (2).	Proxy appointed under regulation 10 of the European Parliamentary Elections (Northern Ireland) Regulations 2004.

(4)   In the case of a person who has an anonymous entry in a register, the postal voters list or list of proxies (as the case may be) must show in relation to the person only

   (a)   his or her electoral number, and

   (b)   the date on which the person's entitlement to remain registered anonymously will terminate under section 9C(1A) of the 1983 Act (in the absence of a further application under section 9B of that Act).

Proxies

75(1)   Subject to what follows, any person is capable of being appointed under this paragraph to vote as proxy for another (the "principal") in the referendum.

   (2)   The principal cannot have more than one person at a time appointed as proxy to vote for him or her in the referendum.

   (3)   A person is capable of being appointed to vote as proxy only if

   (a)   the person is not subject to any legal incapacity (age apart) to vote in the referendum in his or her own right, and

   (b)   the person is either a Commonwealth citizen or a citizen of the Republic of Ireland.

   (4)   Where the principal applies to the registration officer for the appointment of a proxy under this regulation, the registration officer must make the appointment if the application meets the requirements prescribed by the 2008 Regulations and the officer is satisfied that the principal is or will be

   (a)   registered in a relevant register, and

   (b)   entitled to vote by proxy in the referendum by virtue of an application under regulation 73(1) or (5)(b),

   and that the proxy is capable of being, and willing to be, appointed.

   (5)   The appointment of a proxy under this paragraph is to be made by means of a proxy paper, in the form set out in Form 21 in Schedule 4, issued by the registration officer.

(6) The appointment may be cancelled by the principal by giving notice to the registration officer and also ceases to be in force on the issue of a proxy paper appointing a different person under this paragraph to vote for the principal in the referendum.

76(1) Subject to what follows, where a relevant proxy appointment is in force, the person appointed is entitled to vote as proxy for the person for whom the appointment was made (the "principal").

(2) In paragraph (1) "relevant proxy appointment" means

    (a) in relation to a principal who is included in the list of proxies by virtue of entry 1 in the table in regulation 74(3), an appointment under regulation 75;

    (b) in relation to a principal who is included in the list of proxies by virtue of entry 2 in that table, the appointment of the person mentioned in column 3 of that entry;

    (c) in relation to a principal who is included in the list of proxies by virtue of entry 3 in that table, an appointment under section 8 of the 1985 Act for parliamentary elections;

    (d) in relation to a principal who is a peer included in the list of proxies by virtue of entry 4 in that table, an appointment under paragraph 3 of Schedule 2 to the Local Elections (Northern Ireland) Order 1985;

    (e) in relation to a principal who is a peer included in the list of proxies by virtue of entry 5 in that table, an appointment under regulation 10 of the European Parliamentary Elections (Northern Ireland) Regulations 2004.

(3) A person is capable of voting as proxy in the referendum only if

    (a) the person is not subject to any legal incapacity (age apart) to vote in the referendum in his or her own right, and

    (b) the person is either a Commonwealth citizen or a citizen of the Republic of Ireland.

(4) A person is not capable of voting as proxy in the referendum unless on the date of the poll the person has attained the age of 18.

(5) A person is not entitled to vote as proxy in the referendum on behalf of more than two others of whom that person is not the spouse, civil partner, parent, grandparent, brother, sister, child or grandchild.

Voting as proxy

77(1) A person entitled to vote as proxy for another (the "principal") in the referendum may do so in person at the polling station allotted to the principal under Part 2 unless the proxy is entitled to vote by post as proxy for the principal in the referendum, in which case the proxy may vote by post.

(2) But in the case of a person entitled to vote as proxy for an elector who has an anonymous entry in a register

    (a) paragraph (1) does not apply, and

    (b) the person may only so vote by post (where the person is entitled as a proxy to vote by post in the referendum).

(3) Where a person is entitled to vote by post as proxy for the principal in the referendum, the principal may not apply for a ballot paper for the purpose of voting in person in the referendum.

(4) For the purposes of this Chapter of this Part and the 1983 Act a person entitled to vote as proxy for another in the referendum is entitled so to vote by post if the person is included in the list kept under paragraph (8).

(5) Where a person applies to the registration officer to vote by post as proxy in the referendum the officer must grant the application if
    (a) the officer is satisfied that the principal is or will be registered in a relevant register,
    (b) the applicant is the subject of a relevant proxy appointment within the meaning of regulation 76(2),
    (c) any of the conditions in paragraph (6) are met,
    (d) the application specifies an address in the United Kingdom as the address to which the ballot paper is to be sent, and
    (e) the application meets the requirements prescribed by the 2008 Regulations.

(6) The conditions in this paragraph are that
    (a) the officer is satisfied that the applicant's circumstances on the date of the poll will be or are likely to be such that the applicant cannot reasonably be expected to vote in person at the polling station allotted or likely to be allotted to the principal under Part 2,
    (b) the applicant is, or the officer is satisfied that the applicant will be, included in the postal voters list or the list of proxies, or
    (c) the principal is an elector who has an anonymous entry in a register.

(7) A person who is the subject of a relevant proxy appointment within the meaning of regulation 76(2)(b), (c) or (d) and who
    (a) is included in the record kept under section 9(6) of the 1985 Act (record of proxies who have applied to vote by post) in respect of parliamentary elections,
    (b) is included in the record kept under paragraph 4(5) of Schedule 2 to the Local Elections (Northern Ireland) Order 1985 (record of proxies who have applied to vote by post), or
    (c) is included in the record kept under regulation 11(5) of the European Parliamentary Elections (Northern Ireland) Regulations 2004 (record of proxies who have applied to vote by post),
may apply to the registration officer for his or her referendum ballot paper to be sent to a different address in the United Kingdom from that shown in the record, and the officer must grant the application if it meets the requirements prescribed by the 2008 Regulations.

(8) The registration officer must, in respect of the referendum, keep a special list ("the proxy postal voters list") of those within column 2 of the following table, together with the addresses provided as mentioned in column 3 as the addresses to which their ballot papers are to be sent.

	Description of proxy postal voters	Address
1	A proxy whose application under paragraph (5) has been granted.	Address provided in the proxy's application under paragraph (5).
2	A proxy who (a) was appointed as mentioned in column 3 of entry 2 in the table in regulation 74(3) for a person mentioned in column 2 of that entry, and (b) is included in the proxy postal voters list for the poll in respect of which that appointment was made.	Address provided in the proxy's application to vote by post as proxy in that poll.
3	A proxy who (a) was appointed as mentioned in column 3 of entry 3 in the table in regulation 74(3) for a person mentioned in column 2 of that entry,	Address provided in the proxy's application under section 9(4) of the 1985 Act or (as the case may be)

Description of proxy postal voters	Address
and (b) is for the time being included in the record kept under section 9(6) of the 1985 Act.	paragraph (7) above.
4	A proxy who (a) was appointed as mentioned in column 3 of entry 4 in the table in regulation 74(3) for a peer mentioned in column 2 of that entry, and (b) is for the time being included in the record kept under paragraph 4(5) of Schedule 2 to the Local Elections (Northern Ireland) Order 1985.	Address provided in the proxy's application under paragraph 4(4) of Schedule 2 to the Local Elections (Northern Ireland) Order 1985 or (as the case may be) paragraph (7) above.
5	A proxy who (a) was appointed as mentioned in column 3 of entry 5 in the table in regulation 74(3) for a peer mentioned in column 2 of that entry, and (b) is for the time being included in the record kept under regulation 11(5) of the European Parliamentary Elections (Northern Ireland) Regulations 2004.	Address provided in the proxy's application under regulation 11(4) of the European Parliamentary Elections (Northern Ireland) Regulations 2004 or (as the case may be) paragraph (7) above.

(9)   In the case of a person who has an anonymous entry in a register, the proxy postal voters list must contain only

    (a)   the person's electoral number, and

    (b)   the date on which the person's entitlement to remain registered anonymously will terminate under section 9C(1A) of the 1983 Act (in the absence of a further application under section 9B of that Act).

(10) Paragraph (3) does not prevent a person, at the polling station allotted to him or her, marking a tendered ballot paper in pursuance of regulation 37.

Offences

78(1) If a person

    (a)   in any declaration or form used for any of the purposes of this Chapter of this Part, makes a statement knowing it to be false, or

    (b)   attests an application under regulation 73 knowing

        (i)   that he or she is not authorised to do so, or

        (ii)   that it contains a statement which is false,

that person commits an offence.

(2)   A person guilty of an offence under paragraph (1) is liable on summary conviction to a fine not exceeding level 5 on the standard scale.

(3)   If a person provides false information in connection with an application under regulation 73(1) or 77(5), that person is guilty of an offence.

(4)   In relation to a signature, "false information" for the purposes of paragraph (3), means a signature which

    (a)   is not the usual signature of, or

    (b)   was written by a person other than,

the person whose signature it purports to be.

(5)   A person does not commit an offence under paragraph (3) if the person did not know, and had no reason to suspect, that the information was false.

(6)   Where sufficient evidence is adduced to raise an issue with respect to Act) the defence under paragraph (5), the court is to assume that the defence is satisfied unless the

prosecution proves beyond reasonable doubt that it is not.

(7)   A person guilty of an offence under paragraph (3) is liable on summary conviction to imprisonment for a term not exceeding 6 months or to a fine not exceeding level 5 on the standard scale, or to both.

PART 4
APPLICATION AND AMENDMENT OF EXISTING LEGISLATION

Application of provisions of the Representation of the People Act 1983

79   Schedule 1 makes provision about the application of provisions of the 1983 Act for the purposes of the referendum.

Application of provisions of other acts

80   Schedule 2 makes provision about the application of Acts (other than the 1983 Act) for the purposes of the referendum.

Application of existing provisions of regulations

81   Schedule 3 makes provision about the application of existing provisions of regulations for the purposes of the referendum.

Amendment of the European Parliamentary Elections Regulations 2004

82   Schedule 4 to the European Parliamentary Elections Regulations 2004 (Entitlement to Registration and Legal Incapacity to Vote in Gibraltar) is amended as follows:
   (a)   The existing words of paragraph 6 become sub-paragraph (1).
   (b)   After that sub-paragraph insert
   "(2)   Where
      (a)   on the date this sub-paragraph comes into force, a person is registered under the law of Gibraltar as an elector for elections to the Gibraltar Parliament in respect of an address, and
      (b)   that person is not for the time being registered in the register in respect of that address,
      that person is to be treated as having made, on the date this sub-paragraph comes into force, an application for registration in the register in respect of that address."

PART 5
SUPPLEMENTARY

Forms

83   Schedule 4 specifies forms referred to in Parts 2 and 3.

Regulation 79

Part 1
Interpretation and Extent

Interpretation of applied provisions: general

1(1) In any provision of the 1983 Act as applied by this Schedule

"Chief Counting Officer" has the meaning given by section 11(1) of the 2015 Act;

"counting agent" is to be read in accordance with regulation 23(10);

"counting officer" has the meaning given by paragraph 3 of Schedule 3 to the 2015 Act;

"declaration of identity" is to be read in accordance with regulation 17(1)(c);

"document" means a document in whatever form;

"Gibraltar conduct law" has the meaning given by section 11(1) of the 2015 Act;

"the Gibraltar registration officer" means the European electoral registration officer for Gibraltar (see section 14 of the European Parliament (Representation) Act 2003);

"list of proxies" has the meaning given by regulation 5;

"official mark" has the meaning given by regulation 12(1);

"permitted participant" has the meaning given by section 11(1) of the 2015 Act;

"polling agent" is to be read in accordance with regulation 23(10);

"postal voting statement" is to be read in accordance with regulation 17(1)(b);

"presiding officer" is to be read in accordance with regulation 19(1) and (2);

"the referendum" has the meaning given by section 11(1) of the 2015 Act;

"referendum agent" means a person appointed under paragraph 15 of Schedule 1 to the 2015 Act;

"Regional Counting Officer" has the meaning given by section 11(1) of the 2015 Act;

"tendered ballot paper" has the meaning given by regulation 37(1);

"vote" and "voter" have the meaning given by paragraph 2;

"voting area" has the meaning given by section 11(2) of the 2015 Act.

(2) Except where the context otherwise requires, in any provision of the 1983 Act as applied by this Schedule expressions defined for the purposes of that provision by any other provision of the 1983 Act have the meaning given by that other provision (see, in particular, the following provisions of the 1983 Act

section 118 (interpretation of Part 2),

section 185 (interpretation of Part 3), and

section 202 (general interpretation), as modified by paragraph 46 of this Schedule).

(3) Nothing in this Schedule which provides for a particular reference to a provision to be read as, or as including, a reference to that provision as applied by another provision is to be taken to limit the effect of section 20(2) of the Interpretation Act 1978.

Meaning of "vote" in applied provisions

2(1) In any provision of the 1983 Act as applied by this Schedule "vote" as a verb means vote in the referendum and includes (where the context allows)

(a) voting as proxy, and

(b) voting by proxy,

but does not include voting in Gibraltar; and "vote" as a noun and "voter" are to be construed accordingly.

(2) For the purposes of sub-paragraph (1) a person votes "in Gibraltar" if

(a) that person votes (on his or her own behalf or as proxy) in person in Gibraltar or by post under the law of Gibraltar relating to postal voting, or

(b)   that person votes by proxy and the proxy votes in person in Gibraltar or by post under the law of Gibraltar relating to postal voting.

Extent of section 52 of the 1983 Act

3   For the purposes of the referendum, section 52(1), (1ZA), (1ZB) and (1A) of the 1983 Act (which extends to the whole of the United Kingdom) extends also to Gibraltar.

Part 2
Application of Provisions

Alteration of registers pending the referendum: England, Wales and Scotland

4(1)   In relation to England, Wales and Scotland, section 13AB of the 1983 Act applies for the purposes of the referendum but as if

(a)   in subsection (1)(b) for "the relevant election area" there were substituted "the area for which the registration officer acts",

(b)   in subsection (4) for "an election to which this section applies" there were substituted "the referendum",

(c)   in subsection (5) for "the last day on which nomination papers may be delivered to the returning officer for the purposes of the election" there were substituted "the nineteenth working day before the date of the poll for the referendum",

(d)   subsection (8) were omitted,

(e)   the reference in subsection (9) to subsection (5) of section 13B were to that subsection as applied by sub-paragraph (2) below, and

(f)   after subsection (9) there were inserted

"(10)   In this section "working day" means a day that is not

(a)   a Saturday or Sunday,

(b)   Christmas Eve, Christmas Day, Good Friday or any other day that is a bank holiday under the Banking and Financial Dealings Act 1971 in any part of the United Kingdom,

(c)   a bank holiday or public holiday in Gibraltar under the Gibraltar Acts titled the Banking and Financial Dealings Act and the Interpretation and General Clauses Act, or

(d)   a day appointed in any part of the United Kingdom or Gibraltar as a day of public thanksgiving or mourning."

(2)   In relation to England, Wales and Scotland, section 13B of the 1983 Act applies for the purposes of the referendum but as if

(a)   in subsection (1), for each of "an election to which this section applies" and "the election" there were substituted "the referendum",

(b)   in each of subsections (2), (3A) and (3C)

(i)   for "an election to which this section applies" there were substituted "the referendum", and

(ii)   for "the relevant election area" there were substituted "the area for which the registration officer acts",

(c)   subsection (4) were omitted, and

(d)   in subsection (5)

(i)   in the definition of "the appropriate publication date", for "an election to which this section applies" there were substituted "the referendum", and

(ii)   the definitions of "the final nomination day" and "the relevant election area" were omitted.

(3)   A reference in any enactment to section 13AB or 13B of the 1983 Act includes (where

the context allows) a reference to that section as applied by this paragraph.

(4) Sub-paragraph (3) has effect, in relation to any register, until the first publication after the referendum of a revised version of the register under section 13 of the 1983 Act.

Alteration of registers pending the referendum: Northern Ireland

5(1) In relation to Northern Ireland, section 13BA of the 1983 Act applies for the purposes of the referendum but as if
   (a) in subsection (1)
      (i) for the words from "the final nomination day" to "this section applies" there were substituted "the eleventh day before the date of the poll for the referendum", and
      (ii) for "that election" there were substituted "the referendum",
   (b) in subsection (2)
      (i) for "an election to which this section applies" there were substituted "the referendum", and
      (ii) for "the final nomination day" there were substituted "the eleventh day before the date of the poll for the referendum",
   (c) in subsection (3A) for "the final nomination day" there were substituted "the eleventh day before the date of the poll for the referendum",
   (d) in subsection (5), for "an election to which this section applies" there were substituted "the referendum",
   (e) in each of subsections (7) and (8)
      (i) for "an election to which this section applies" there were substituted "the referendum", and
      (ii) for "the relevant election area" there were substituted "the area for which the registration officer acts",
   (f) subsection (12) were omitted, and
   (g) the reference in subsection (13) to subsection (5) of section 13B were to that subsection as applied by paragraph 4(2) of this Schedule.

(2) A reference in any enactment to section 13BA of the 1983 Act includes (where the context allows) a reference to that section as applied by this paragraph.

(3) Sub-paragraph (2) has effect, in relation to any register, until the first publication after the referendum of a revised version of the register under section 13 of the 1983 Act.

Loan of equipment

6 Section 47 of the 1983 Act applies for the purposes of the referendum but as if
   (a) in subsection (1) the reference to the returning officer at a local government election included a counting officer for the referendum for a voting area anywhere in the United Kingdom, and
   (b) in subsection (2) the reference to the returning officer at an election mentioned there included a counting officer for the referendum for a voting area in England, Wales or Scotland.

Effect of registers

7(1) Section 49 of the 1983 Act applies for the purposes of the referendum but with the following modifications.

(2) Subsection (4) has effect for those purposes as if
   (a) for "any purpose of this Part relating to him as elector" there were substituted "any purpose of this Part, the European Union Referendum Act 2015 or the European Union Referendum (Conduct) Regulations 2016", and
   (b) for "as an elector except" to the end there were substituted "as a person

entitled to vote by virtue of that entry unless the day fixed for the poll for the referendum is that or a later date".

(3) Subsection (5) has effect for the purposes of the referendum as if the following were omitted
    (a) the words "prevent the rejection of the vote on a scrutiny, or", and
    (b) paragraph (b)(iv).

(4) For the avoidance of doubt, in section 49 of the 1983 Act as applied by this paragraph
    (a) "voting age" has the same meaning as in section 49 as it has effect apart from this Schedule, but
    (b) "vote" as a verb is to be read in accordance with paragraph 2 of this Schedule.

Effect of misdescription

8   Section 50 of the 1983 Act applies for the purposes of the referendum but as if
    (a) the words "nomination paper," were omitted, and
    (b) for the words "and the parliamentary election rules" there were substituted "or by the European Union Referendum Act 2015 or the European Union Referendum (Conduct) Regulations 2016".

Discharge of registration duties

9(1)   Section 52 of the 1983 Act applies for the purposes of the referendum but with the following modifications.

(2) For those purposes, the following subsections are to be treated as substituted for subsection (1)
    "(1) A registration officer shall comply with any general or special directions which may be given by the Secretary of State for the purposes of the referendum with respect to the arrangements to be made by that officer for carrying out
    (a) any of that officer's functions under Schedule 3 to the European Union Referendum Act 2015,
    (b) any of that officer's functions under the European Union Referendum (Conduct) Regulations 2016, or
    (c) any of that officer's functions under this Act.
    (1ZA) In subsection (1) the reference to a registration officer includes the Gibraltar registration officer, and in relation to that officer
    (a) the reference in subsection (1)(b) to "the European Union Referendum (Conduct) Regulations 2016" is to be read as a reference to any regulations under section 4 of the European Union Referendum Act 2015 that extend to Gibraltar and Gibraltar conduct law, and
    (b) the reference in subsection (1)(c) to "this Act" is to be read as a reference to the Gibraltar Act titled the European Parliamentary Elections Act 2004.
    (1ZB) The Secretary of State may give a direction under subsection (1) only if it is in accordance with a recommendation made by the Electoral Commission."

(3) Subsection (1A) has effect for the purposes of the referendum as if after "registration officer" there were inserted "or the Gibraltar registration officer".

(4) Subsections (2) and (4) each have effect for the purposes of the referendum as if after "this Act" there were inserted ", the European Union Referendum Act 2015 and the European Union Referendum (Conduct) Regulations 2016".

Payment of expenses of registration

10   Section 54 of the 1983 Act applies for the purposes of the referendum but as if in subsection (1) after "2013" there were inserted "or the European Union Referendum

Act 2015 or the European Union Referendum (Conduct) Regulations 2016".

Registration appeals: England and Wales and Scotland

11(1) In subsection (3) of section 56 of the 1983 Act, the references to "an election" and "the election" include the referendum.

(2) For the purposes of the referendum the following subsection is to be treated as substituted for subsection (4A) of section 56 of the 1983 Act

"(4A) Where, as a result of the decision on an appeal, an alteration in the register made in pursuance of subsection (4) takes effect under section 13(5), 13A(2), 13AB(3), 13B(3) or (3B) or 13BC(3) or (6) on or before the date of the poll for the referendum, subsection (3) does not apply to that appeal as respects the referendum."

(3) References in this paragraph to section 56 of the 1983 Act include that section as applied by section 57 of that Act (registration appeals: Scotland).

Registration appeals: Northern Ireland

12(1) In subsection (3) of section 58 of the 1983 Act, the references to "an election" and "the election" include the referendum.

(2) For the purposes of the referendum, the following subsection is to be treated as substituted for subsection (5) of section 58 of the 1983 Act

"(5) Where, as a result of the decision on an appeal, an alteration in the register made in pursuance of subsection (4) takes effect under section 13(5), 13A(2), 13BA(6) or (9) or 13BC(3) or (6) on or before the date of the poll for the referendum, subsection (3) does not apply to that appeal as respects the referendum."

Offence of personation

13 Section 60 of the 1983 Act applies for the purposes of the referendum but as if in subsection (2)

(a) for "at a parliamentary or local government election" there were substituted "in the referendum", and

(b) for "whether as an elector or as proxy" there were substituted "whether or not as proxy".

Other voting offences

14(1) Section 61 of the 1983 Act applies for the purposes of the referendum but with the modifications in sub-paragraphs (2) to (4) below.

(2) For the purposes of the referendum, the following subsections are to be treated as substituted for subsections (1) to (4)

"(1) A person shall be guilty of an offence if

(a) he votes in person or by post, whether on his own behalf or as proxy, or applies to vote by proxy or by post on his own behalf, knowing that he is subject to a legal incapacity to vote; or

(b) he applies for the appointment of a proxy to vote for him knowing that he is or the person to be appointed is subject to a legal incapacity to vote; or

(c) he votes, whether in person or by post, as proxy for some other person knowing that that person is subject to a legal incapacity to vote.

For the purposes of this subsection references to a person being subject to a legal incapacity to vote do not, in relation to things done before polling day, include his being below voting age if he will be of voting age on that day.

(2) A person shall be guilty of an offence if
   (a) he votes on his own behalf otherwise than by proxy more than once; or
   (b) he votes on his own behalf in person when he is entitled to vote by post; or
   (c) he votes on his own behalf in person knowing that a person appointed to vote as his proxy either has already voted in person or is entitled to vote by post; or
   (d) he applies under Part 3 of the European Union Referendum (Conduct) Regulations 2016 for a person to be appointed as his proxy to vote for him without applying for the cancellation of a previous appointment of a third person then in force under that Part or without withdrawing a pending application for such an appointment.

(3) A person shall be guilty of an offence if
   (a) he votes as proxy for the same person more than once; or
   (b) he votes in person as proxy for another person and he is entitled to vote by post as proxy for that person; or
   (c) he votes in person as proxy for another person and he knows that other person has already voted in person.

(4) A person shall also be guilty of an offence if he votes as proxy for more than two persons of whom he is not the spouse, civil partner, parent, grandparent, brother, sister, child or grandchild."

(3) Subsection (6A) has effect for the purposes of the referendum as if for the words from "in pursuance of" to the end there were substituted "in reliance on Case 3, 4, 5 or 6 in regulation 37 of the European Union Referendum (Conduct) Regulations 2016".

(4) For the purposes of the referendum the following are to be treated as omitted
   (a) subsection (6B);
   (b) subsection (7)(b).

(5) Paragraph 2(1) of this Schedule (meaning of "vote") does not apply for the purposes of
   (a) subsection (2)(a) and (c), or
   (b) subsection (3)(a) and (c),
of section 61 of the 1983 Act as applied by this paragraph, and in those provisions "vote" is to be read in accordance with sub-paragraphs (6) and (7).

(6) In subsections (2)(a) and (3)(a) "vote" means vote in the referendum (and does not exclude voting in Gibraltar).

(7) In subsections (2)(c) and (3)(c)
   (a) references to voting in person are to voting in the referendum in person either in the United Kingdom or Gibraltar, and
   (b) references to voting by post are to voting in the referendum by post, either under the law of the United Kingdom relating to postal voting or under the law of Gibraltar relating to postal voting.

(8) But
   (a) a person does not commit an offence under subsection (2)(a) or (3)(a) of section 61 of the 1983 Act as applied by this paragraph unless at least one of the votes mentioned in subsection (2)(a) or (3)(a) (as the case may be) is a vote in the United Kingdom;
   (b) a person does not commit an offence under subsection (2)(c) of section 61 of the 1983 Act as so applied unless either or both of the following apply
     (i) the person's vote on his own behalf is a vote in person in the United Kingdom;
     (ii) the proxy's vote (or entitlement to a postal vote) is a vote in (or an entitlement to a postal vote in) the United Kingdom;
   (c) a person does not commit an offence under subsection (3)(c) of section 61 of the

1983 Act as so applied unless at least one of the votes mentioned in subsection (3)(c) is a vote in person in the United Kingdom.

(9)   In sub-paragraph (6) the reference to voting "in Gibraltar" is to voting
    (a)   in person in Gibraltar, or
    (b)   by post under the law of Gibraltar relating to postal voting,
and in sub-paragraph (8) references to a vote "in the United Kingdom" are to be read accordingly.

Offences relating to applications for absent voting

15   Section 62A(1) to (5) of the 1983 Act applies for the purposes of the referendum but as if
    (a)   in subsection (1)(a) the words "at a parliamentary or local government election" were omitted, and
    (b)   in subsection (2)(c) for "returning officer" there were substituted "counting officer".

Breach of official duty

16   Section 63 of the 1983 Act applies for the purposes of the referendum but as if for subsections (3) and (4) there were substituted
    "(3) The persons to whom this section applies are
        (a)   the Chief Counting Officer,
        (b)   any Regional Counting Officer,
        (c)   any counting officer,
        (d)   any registration officer,
        (e)   the Gibraltar registration officer,
        (f)   any presiding officer, or any equivalent officer in Gibraltar,
        (g)   any official designated by a universal postal service provider (within the meaning given by section 202), and
        (h)   any deputy of a person mentioned in any of paragraphs (a) to (g) above or any person appointed to assist, or in the course of his employment assisting, a person so mentioned in connection with his official duties;
and "official duty" shall for the purposes of this section be construed accordingly, but shall not include duties imposed otherwise than by this Act, the European Union Referendum Act 2015 or regulations under section 4 of that Act, Gibraltar conduct law, the Gibraltar Act titled the European Parliamentary Elections Act 2004 or the law of the United Kingdom or of Gibraltar relating to referendums.

(4)   Where
    (a)   a Regional Counting Officer or counting officer is guilty of an act or omission in breach of his official duty, but
    (b)   he remedies that act or omission in full by taking steps under paragraph 9 of Schedule 3 to the European Union Referendum Act 2015,
he shall not be guilty of an offence under subsection (1) above."

Tampering with papers

17(1)   Section 65 of the 1983 Act applies for the purposes of the referendum but with the following modifications.

(2)   Subsection (1) has effect for those purposes as if
    (a)   for "at a parliamentary or local government election" there were substituted "in the referendum",
    (b)   paragraph (a) were omitted, and
    (c)   in paragraph (f), for "election" there were substituted "referendum".

(3) But nothing in that subsection is to be taken to apply to anything done in connection with the referendum so far as held in Gibraltar.

(4) For the purposes of the referendum the following subsection is to be treated as substituted for subsection (2)

"(2) In Scotland, a person shall be guilty of an offence if

(a) in the referendum, he forges or counterfeits any ballot paper or the official mark on any ballot paper; or

(b) he fraudulently or without due authority, as the case may be, attempts to do any of those things."

(5) Subsection (3) has effect for the purposes of the referendum as if for "a returning officer" there were substituted "the Chief Counting Officer, a Regional Counting Officer, a counting officer".

Requirement of secrecy

18(1) Section 66(1) to (6) of the 1983 Act applies for the purposes of the referendum but with the following modifications.

(2) Subsection (1) has effect for those purposes as if

(a) for paragraphs (a) to (c) there were substituted

"(a) the Chief Counting Officer, and every Regional Counting Officer and counting officer, attending at a polling station in the United Kingdom,

(b) every deputy of such an officer so attending,

(c) every presiding officer and clerk so attending,

(d) every referendum agent, polling agent and counting agent so attending, and

(e) every person so attending by virtue of any of sections 6A to 6D of the Political Parties, Elections and Referendums Act 2000,",

(b) in paragraph (i) for "elector or proxy for an elector" there were substituted "person", and

(c) in paragraph (ii) for "elector" there were substituted "person".

(3) The references in subsections (1) and (4) to the closure of the poll are to be read, in relation to the referendum, as references to the closure of the poll in the United Kingdom or Gibraltar, whichever is the later.

(4) Subsections (2)(b), (3)(b) and (c), (4)(d) and (5) have effect for the purposes of the referendum as if for "the candidate for whom" there were substituted "the referendum answer for which".

(5) Subsection (3)(d) has effect for those purposes as if for "the name of the candidate for whom" there were substituted "the referendum answer for which".

(6) Subsection (5) has effect for those purposes as if

(a) for "blind voter" there were substituted "voter with disabilities", and

(b) at the end there were inserted

"Voter with disabilities" has the meaning given by regulation 36(11) of the European Union Referendum (Conduct) Regulations 2016."

Prohibition on publication of exit polls

19(1) Section 66A of the 1983 Act applies for the purposes of the referendum but with the following modifications.

(2) Subsection (1) has effect for those purposes as if "the referendum" were substituted for each of the following

(a) "an election to which this section applies", and

(b)   "the election" (in both places).

(3)   For the purposes of the referendum subsection (2) is to be treated as omitted.

(4)   Subsection (4) has effect for the purposes of the referendum as if for the words after "whatever means" there were substituted

"and the reference to a forecast as to the result of the referendum includes a forecast as to the number or proportion of votes expected to be cast for each answer to the referendum question in any region, voting area or other area."

(5)   In section 66A of the 1983 Act as applied by this paragraph

(a)   the reference in subsection (1) to the closure of the poll is to be read as a reference to the closure of the poll in the United Kingdom or Gibraltar, whichever is the later, and

(b)   the references in subsection (1)(a) to "voters" include any voters in the referendum, whether voting in the United Kingdom or Gibraltar, and "vote" is to be read accordingly,

and, accordingly, paragraph 2(1) of this Schedule (meaning of "vote") does not apply in relation to that section.

(6)   In subsection (4) of that section as so applied, the references to the public are to the public in the United Kingdom.

Failure to comply with conditions relating to supply etc of documents

20   Section 66B of the 1983 Act applies for the purposes of the referendum, but as if in subsection (1)(a) for "imposed in pursuance of regulations under rule 57 of the parliamentary election rules" there were substituted "to which the right to inspect or be supplied with a document or part of document under regulation 58 of the European Union Referendum (Conduct) Regulations 2016 is subject under paragraph (5)(a) of that regulation".

Broadcasting from outside UK

21   Section 92 of the 1983 Act applies for the purposes of the referendum but as if in subsection (1)

(a)   for "at a parliamentary or local government election" there were substituted "in the referendum", and

(b)   for "the election" there were substituted "the referendum".

Imitation poll cards

22(1)   Section 94(1) of the 1983 Act applies for the purposes of the referendum but as if for "the election of any candidate at a parliamentary election or a local government election to which this section applies" there were substituted "a particular result in the referendum".

(2)   The references in section 94(1) to poll cards do not include poll cards for the purposes of the referendum so far as held in Gibraltar.

Disturbances at meetings

23   Section 97 of the 1983 Act applies for the purposes of the referendum but as if for subsection (2) there were substituted

"(2) This section applies to a meeting in connection with the referendum which

(a)   is held by a permitted participant during the referendum period (within the meaning given by paragraph 1 of Schedule 1 to the European Union Referendum Act 2015), and

(b)   is held in the United Kingdom."

Premises used for referendum meetings in Scotland or Northern Ireland

24   Section 98 of the 1983 Act applies for the purposes of the referendum but as if the reference to public meetings in furtherance of any person's candidature at a parliamentary or local government election included public meetings to promote or procure a particular result in the referendum.

Officials not to act for candidates

25   Section 99 of the 1983 Act applies for the purposes of the referendum but as if for subsection (1) there were substituted

"(1) If
   (a)   the Chief Counting Officer,
   (b)   any Regional Counting Officer,
   (c)   any counting officer for a voting area in the United Kingdom,
   (d)   any officer, deputy or clerk appointed by a person mentioned in paragraph (a), (b) or (c), or
   (e)   any officer whose services have been placed at the disposal of a counting officer or Regional Counting Officer under paragraph 6(1) of Schedule 3 to the European Union Referendum Act 2015,

   acts as a referendum agent for a permitted participant, he shall be guilty of an offence."

Illegal canvassing by police officers

26   Section 100 of the 1983 Act applies for the purposes of the referendum but as if in subsection (1)
   (a)   for "as an elector" there were substituted "on that person's own behalf", and
   (b)   the words after "proxy" were omitted.

Payments for exhibition of election notices

27   Section 109 of the 1983 Act applies for the purposes of the referendum but as if
   (a)   in subsection (1) for "the election of a candidate at an election" there were substituted "a particular result in the referendum",
   (b)   in subsection (2) for "an election" there were substituted "the referendum", and
   (c)   after subsection (2) there were inserted
      "(3) In this section "elector" means a person entitled to vote on his own behalf."

Prohibition of paid canvassers

28(1)   Section 111 of the 1983 Act applies for the purposes of the referendum but as if
   (a)   for "an election" there were substituted "the referendum", and
   (b)   for "a candidate's election" there were substituted "a particular result in the referendum".

   (2)   But nothing in that section applies in relation to canvassing in Gibraltar in connection with the referendum.

Providing money etc for illegal purposes

29   Section 112 of the 1983 Act applies for the purposes of the referendum but as if
   (a)   the reference in paragraph (a) to the provisions of the 1983 Act were to any provision of the 1983 Act as applied by this Schedule, and
   (b)   the following were omitted
      (i)   paragraph (b),
      (ii)   in paragraph (c) the words "or expenses", and

(iii) the words "or the incurring of the expenses".

Bribery

30(1) Section 113 of the 1983 Act applies for the purposes of the referendum but with the following modifications.

(2) Subsection (2) has effect for those purposes as if
  (a) for "the return of any person at an election" (in the first two places) there were substituted "a particular result in the referendum", and
  (b) paragraph (iii) were omitted.

(3) Subsection (3) has effect for those purposes as if for "at any election" (in both places) there were substituted "in the referendum".

(4) Each of subsections (4), (5) and (6) has effect for those purposes as if for "an election" there were substituted "the referendum".

Treating

31 Section 114 of the 1983 Act applies for the purposes of the referendum but as if
  (a) in subsection (2) for "an election" there were substituted "the referendum", and
  (b) in subsection (3) for "Every elector or his proxy" there were substituted "Every person entitled to vote on his own behalf, and every proxy of such a person,".

Undue influence

32 Section 115 of the 1983 Act applies for the purposes of the referendum but as if after subsection (2) there were inserted
  "(3) In this section "elector" means a person entitled to vote on his own behalf."

Rights of creditors where applied provision prohibits payments

33 In section 116 of the 1983 Act the reference to the provisions of Part 2 of that Act prohibiting payments and contracts for payments includes any such provision as applied by this Schedule.

Saving for employees to be absent for voting

34 Section 117(2) of the 1983 Act applies for the purposes of the referendum but as if
  (a) for "parliamentary electors or their proxies" there were substituted "persons entitled to vote (on their own behalf or as proxies)",
  (b) the words "at a parliamentary election" were omitted, and
  (c) in paragraphs (b) and (c), for "any particular candidate at the election" there were substituted "a particular answer in the referendum".

Computation of time

35(1) Section 119 of the 1983 Act, in its application for the purposes of any provision of the 1983 Act as applied by this Schedule, has effect as if for subsection (3) there were substituted
  "(3) In this section, in relation to a voting area
    (a) "bank holiday" means any day that is a bank holiday under the Banking and Financial Dealings Act 1971 in the part of the United Kingdom in which the voting area is situated, and
    (b) "a day appointed for public thanksgiving or mourning" means a day appointed in the part of the United Kingdom in which the voting area is situated as a day of public thanksgiving or mourning."

(2) The reference in sub-paragraph (1) to section 119 of the 1983 Act includes that section

as applied by any other provision of that Act.

Application for relief

36(1) Section 167(1) to (2) applies for the purposes of the referendum but with the following modifications.

(2) For the purposes of the referendum the following subsection is to be treated as substituted for subsection (1)
"(1) An application for relief under this section may be made to the High Court."

(3) Subsection (2)(c) has effect for those purposes as if the words from "in the constituency" to "was held," were omitted.

Powers of court on conviction of corrupt practice

37 In section 168 of the 1983 Act
(a) the reference in subsection (1) to a person who is guilty of a corrupt practice includes a person who is guilty of a corrupt practice under a provision of the 1983 Act as applied by this Schedule,
(b) the reference in subsection (1)(a) to section 60 or 62A includes either of those sections as so applied, and
(c) the reference in subsection (7) to the offence of bribery or treating includes an offence under section 113 or 114 of the 1983 Act as applied by this Schedule.

Prosecution and conviction of illegal practice and illegal payments

38 In sections 169, 170, 173, 173A and 175(1) and (3) of the 1983 Act
(a) references to an illegal practice include an illegal practice under a provision of the 1983 Act as applied by this Schedule,
(b) references to a corrupt practice include a corrupt practice under such a provision, and
(c) references to an offence of illegal payment or employment include an offence of illegal payment or employment under such a provision;
and in section 173(2) any reference to a corrupt practice or illegal practice under a section mentioned there includes a reference to a corrupt practice or illegal practice under that section as applied by this Schedule.

Time limit for prosecutions

39(1) In section 176 of the 1983 Act, the reference in subsection (1) to any offence under any provision contained in the 1983 Act includes any offence under any such provision as applied by this Schedule.

(2) Subsections (2) to (2G) of section 176 of the 1983 Act have effect in relation to such an offence ("a referendum offence") with the following modifications.

(3) Subsection (2C) has effect in relation to a referendum offence as if for "rule 57 of the parliamentary elections rules" there were substituted "regulation 58 of the European Union Referendum (Conduct) Regulations 2016".

(4) Subsection (2D) has effect in relation to a referendum offence as if for paragraph (a) there were substituted
"(a) directing the registration officer not to cause the documents to be destroyed at the expiry of the period of one year mentioned in regulation 58 of the European Union Referendum (Conduct) Regulations 2016,".

Prosecution of offences committed outside the United Kingdom

40 In section 178 of the 1983 Act the reference to an offence under that Act includes an

offence under any provision of that Act as applied by this Schedule.

Offences by associations

41   In section 179 of the 1983 Act
    (a)   the reference to any corrupt or illegal practice includes any corrupt or illegal practice under any provision of the 1983 Act as applied by this Schedule, and
    (b)   the reference to any illegal payment, employment or hiring includes any illegal payment or employment under any such provision.

Director of Public Prosecutions

42   In section 181(1) of the 1983 Act the reference to any offence under that Act includes any offence under any provision of that Act as applied by this Schedule.

Service of notices

43   Section 184 of the 1983 Act applies for the purposes of the referendum but as if in subsection (1)
    (a)   for "an election" there were substituted "the referendum",
    (b)   for the words from "the High Court" to "any election court" there were substituted "the High Court or the county court", and
    (c)   in paragraph (a), the words from "in the constituency" to "held" were omitted.

Computation of time for purposes of Part 3

44   In section 186 of the 1983 Act the reference to Part 3 of that Act includes any provision of that Part as applied by this Schedule.

Translations etc of certain documents

45(1)   Section 199B(1) to (9) of the 1983 Act applies for the purposes of the referendum but with the following modifications.

(2)   For those purposes, the following subsection is to be treated as substituted for subsection (1)
    "(1) Subsections (2) and (3) below apply to any document which under or by virtue of this Act, the European Union Referendum Act 2015 or the European Union Referendum (Conduct) Regulations 2016 is required or authorised
    (a)   to be given to voters, or
    (b)   to be displayed in any place in the United Kingdom, for the purposes of the referendum."

(3)   Subsection (4) has effect for the purposes of the referendum as if paragraph (a) were omitted.

(4)   For the purposes of the referendum the following subsections are to be treated as substituted for subsections (5) to (7)
    "(5) The counting officer for a voting area in the United Kingdom may cause to be displayed at every polling station in that area an enlarged sample copy of the ballot paper.
    (6)   The sample copy mentioned in subsection (5) above
    (a)   must have printed on it the words "Put a cross (X) in one box only" both at the top and immediately below the referendum question, and
    (b)   below the second occurrence of those words, may include a translation of those words into such other languages as the counting officer thinks appropriate.
    (7)   The counting officer for a voting area in the United Kingdom must provide at

every polling station in that area an enlarged handheld sample copy of the ballot paper for the assistance of voters who are partially sighted."

(5)   Subsection (9) has effect for the purposes of the referendum as if for "returning officer" there were substituted "counting officer".

General interpretation

46   In its application for the purposes of any provision of the 1983 Act as applied by this Schedule, section 202 of the 1983 Act has effect as if in subsection (1)
    (a)   for the definition of "list of proxies" there were substituted
        "'list of proxies' is to be read in accordance with paragraph 1(1) of Schedule 1 to the European Union Referendum (Conduct) Regulations 2016;", and
    (b)   for the definition of "voter" and "vote" there were substituted
        "'vote' and 'voter' are to be read in accordance with paragraph 2(1) of Schedule 1 to the European Union Referendum (Conduct) Regulations 2016 (subject to any provision to the contrary in that Schedule)."

General application to Scotland

47   Section 204(3), (5) and (8) of the 1983 Act applies for the purposes of any provision of the 1983 Act as applied by this Schedule, so far as that provision applies to Scotland.

General application to Northern Ireland

48   Section 205 of the 1983 Act applies for the purposes of any provision of the 1983 Act as applied by this Schedule, so far as that provision applies to Northern Ireland.

Premises used for poll: Scotland and Northern Ireland

49   Rule 22(3) in Schedule 1 to the 1983 Act applies for the purposes of the referendum but as if the reference to use for the purpose of taking the poll in an election included use by a counting officer for the purpose of taking the poll in the referendum.

SCHEDULE 2
APPLICATION OF PROVISIONS OF OTHER ACTS

Regulation 80

Part 1
Political Parties, Elections and Referendums Act 2000

Attendance of representatives of Electoral Commission at referendum proceedings

1   Section 6A of the 2000 Act has effect for the purposes of the referendum as if for subsection (4) there were substituted
    "(4) In this section, "the relevant counting officer" means, in relation to proceedings at the referendum under section 1 of the European Union Referendum Act 2015, the counting officer for the voting area to which the proceedings relate (determined in accordance with paragraph 3 of Schedule 3 to that Act)."

Observation of working practices by representatives of the Electoral Commission

2   Section 6B of the 2000 Act has effect for the purposes of the referendum as if
    (a)   for subsection (1)(c) there were substituted
        "(c) a counting officer for the referendum under section 1 of the European Union Referendum Act 2015", and
    (b)   subsection (2)(a) were omitted.

Accredited observers of referendum proceedings

3 Section 6C of the 2000 Act has effect for the purposes of the referendum as if the following subsection were inserted after subsection (1)

   "(1A) In subsection (1)(c) the reference to "proceedings at the counting of votes" includes proceedings of

   (a) a Regional Counting Officer in connection with the officer's duty to certify the matters specified in paragraph 7(4) of Schedule 3 to the European Union Referendum Act 2015, and

   (b) the Chief Counting Officer in connection with the officer's duty to certify the matters specified in section 128(6)."

4 Section 6D of the 2000 Act has effect for the purposes of the referendum as if the following subsection were inserted after subsection (1)

   "(1A) In subsection (1)(c) the reference to "proceedings at the counting of votes" includes proceedings of

   (a) a Regional Counting Officer in connection with the officer's duty to certify the matters specified in paragraph 7(4) of Schedule 3 to the European Union Referendum Act 2015, and

   (b) the Chief Counting Officer in connection with the officer's duty to certify the matters specified in section 128(6)."

Provision to the Electoral Commission of information about expenditure

5 Section 9C of the 2000 Act has effect for the purposes of the referendum as if for subsection (2)(c) there were substituted

   "(c) in the case of a counting officer for the referendum under section 1 of the European Union Referendum Act 2015, expenditure in connection with that referendum."

Right to use rooms for holding public meetings

6 Paragraph 2(3) of Schedule 12 to the 2000 Act has effect for the purposes of the referendum as if after "public funds" there were inserted ", Gibraltar public funds".

Part 2
Application of other Enactments

Premises used for referendum purposes in England and Wales

7 Section 65(6) of the Local Government Finance Act 1988 (which makes provision for England and Wales corresponding to section 98 of and rule 22(3) in Schedule 1 to the 1983 Act) applies for the purposes of the referendum but as if

   (a) the reference in paragraph (a) to public meetings in furtherance of a person's candidature at a parliamentary or local government election included public meetings to promote or procure a particular result in the referendum, and

   (b) the reference in paragraph (b) to use by a returning officer for the purpose of taking the poll in a parliamentary or local government election included use by a counting officer for the purpose of taking the poll in the referendum.

Restriction on powers of arrest at polling station by persons other than constables

8 Section 71 of the Electoral Administration Act 2006 applies for the purposes of the referendum but as if the reference to an offence under section 60 of the 1983 Act were a reference to an offence under that section as applied by Schedule 1.

SCHEDULE 3
APPLICATION OF EXISTING PROVISIONS OF REGULATIONS

Regulation 81

Part 1
The 2001 Regulations (England and Wales) and the 2001 Regulations (Scotland)

Preliminary

1(1)   In this Part of this Schedule the "relevant regulations" means

(a)   the Representation of the People (England and Wales) Regulations 2001 (referred to in this Part of this Schedule as "the England and Wales Regulations"), and

(b)   the Representation of the People (Scotland) Regulations 2001 (referred to in this Part of this Schedule as "the Scotland Regulations").

(2)   In any provision of the relevant regulations as applied by this Part of this Schedule

(a)   expressions defined by section 11 of the 2015 Act have the meaning given by that section, and

(b)   expressions defined by regulation 5 have the meaning given by that regulation.

(3)   Sub-paragraph (2) does not apply to the extent that the context otherwise requires.

2   The following provisions of the relevant regulations apply for the purposes of the referendum

(a)   regulation 3(1) and (3) (interpretation);

(b)   regulation 5 (applications, notices etc);

(c)   regulation 6 (electronic signatures);

(d)   regulation 11 (interference with notices etc);

(e)   regulation 32A (representations regarding clerical errors);

(f)   regulation 36A (communication of notices issued on polling day);

(g)   regulation 55A (additional requirements for applications for an emergency proxy vote);

(h)   regulation 62 (marked register for polling stations);

(i)   regulation 120 (calculating the fee for supply of marked registers or lists).

Forms

3(1)   Regulation 4 of the relevant regulations (forms) applies for the purposes of the referendum but with the following modifications.

(2)   Paragraph (1) has effect for the purposes of the referendum as if

(a)   after paragraph (b) there were inserted

", and

(c)   applications made under Chapter 1 of Part 3 of the European Union Referendum (Conduct) Regulations 2016."

(b)   after "an election" there were inserted "or the referendum".

(3)   Paragraph (2) has effect for the purposes of the referendum only in so far as it relates to Form K in Schedule 3 to the relevant regulations.

Computation of time

4   Regulation 8 of the relevant regulations (time) has effect for the purposes of the referendum as if in paragraph (2) for "regulation 56(6)" there were substituted

"regulations 56(6) and 78A(5)".

Restriction on supply etc of record of anonymous entries

5   Regulation 45B(2) of the Scotland Regulations (duties of registration officers etc in relation to record of anonymous entries) has effect for the purposes of the referendum as if
    (a)   after sub-paragraph (a) there were treated as inserted
        "(aa)   a deputy of the registration officer acting in that other capacity;", and
    (b)   the references in sub-paragraph (b) to "that officer" were treated as references to "a person mentioned in sub-paragraph (a) or (aa)".

General requirements for applications for an absent vote

6(1)   Regulation 51 of the relevant regulations (general requirements for applications for an absent vote) has effect for the purposes of the referendum with the following modifications.

(2)   Paragraph (1) has effect for those purposes as if after "Schedule 4" there were inserted "or Chapter 1 of Part 3 of the European Union Referendum (Conduct) Regulations 2016".

(3)   Paragraph (2) has effect for the purposes of the referendum as if
    (a)   in sub-paragraph (b), after "Schedule 4" there were inserted "or regulation 66(4) or (5) of the European Union Referendum (Conduct) Regulations 2016", and
    (b)   in sub-paragraph (f), after "Schedule 4" there were inserted "or regulation 62 or 66 of the European Union Referendum (Conduct) Regulations 2016,".

(4)   For the purposes of the referendum the following paragraph is to be treated as inserted after paragraph (5)
        "(5A)   An application that is made under Chapter 1 of Part 3 of the European Union Referendum (Conduct) Regulations 2016 for the purposes of the referendum must state that it is so made."

Signature of application for absent vote

7   Regulation 51A(a) of the relevant regulations (requirements that applications for an absent vote must be signed) has effect for the purposes of the referendum as if
    (a)   after "Schedule 4" there were inserted "or Chapter 1 of Part 3 of the European Union Referendum (Conduct) Regulations 2016", and
    (b)   for "or the returning officer" there were substituted ", the returning officer or the counting officer".

Address to which to send ballot paper: requirements if different to address in application

8   Regulation 51AA(1) of the relevant regulations (additional requirement for applications for ballot paper to be sent to different address from that in application) has effect for the purposes of the referendum as if
    (a)   in sub-paragraph (a), after "Schedule 4" there were inserted "or regulation 62(1) of the European Union Referendum (Conduct) Regulations 2016", and
    (b)   in sub-paragraph (b), after "Schedule 4" there were inserted "or regulation 66(4) of the European Union Referendum (Conduct) Regulations 2016".

Address to which to send ballot paper: requirements if different to address in records

9   Regulation 51B of the relevant regulations (additional requirement for applications for ballot paper to be sent to different address from that in records) applies for the

purposes of the referendum but as if for sub-paragraphs (a) and (b) of paragraph (1) there were substituted "regulation 62(5)(a) or 66(5) of the European Union Referendum (Conduct) Regulations 2016 by a person shown as voting by post in the record referred to in that provision."

Applications for appointment of a proxy

10 Regulation 52 of the relevant regulations (additional requirements for applications for appointment of proxy) has effect for the purposes of the referendum as if after "Schedule 4" there were inserted "or regulation 64(4) of the European Union Referendum (Conduct) Regulations 2016".

Additional requirements for applications for proxy to vote

11(1) Regulation 55 of the relevant regulations (additional requirement for applications for proxy to vote) applies for the purposes of the referendum but with the following modifications.

(2) For those purposes the following paragraph is to be treated as substituted for paragraph (1)

"(1) An application under regulation 62(2) of the European Union Referendum (Conduct) Regulations 2016 to vote by proxy in the referendum is to set out why the applicant's circumstances on the date of the poll will be or are likely to be such that the applicant cannot reasonably be expected to vote in person at the polling station allotted to the applicant under Part 2 of those Regulations."

(3) Paragraph (2) has effect for the purposes of the referendum as if
  (a) for "paragraph 4(2) of Schedule 4" there were substituted "regulation 62(2) of the European Union Referendum (Conduct) Regulations 2016", and
  (b) for "at the election for which it is made" there were substituted "for the referendum".

(4) Paragraph (3A) of the England and Wales Regulations and paragraph (4) of the Scotland Regulations has effect for the purposes of the referendum as if
  (a) for "paragraph 4(2) of Schedule 4" there were substituted "regulation 62(2) of the European Union Referendum (Conduct) Regulations 2016", and
  (b) for "at the election for which it is made" there were substituted "for the referendum".

(5) Paragraph (4) of the England and Wales Regulations and paragraph (3A) of the Scotland Regulations has effect for the purposes of the referendum as if
  (a) for "paragraph 4(2) of Schedule 4" there were substituted "regulation 62(2) of the European Union Referendum (Conduct) Regulations 2016",
  (b) for "paragraph 2(5A) of that Schedule" there were substituted "regulation 60(7) of those Regulations", and
  (c) for "at the election for which it is made" there were substituted "for the referendum".

Closing date for applications

12(1) Regulation 56 of the relevant regulations (closing date for applications) has effect for the purposes of the referendum with the following modifications.

(2) For those purposes the following paragraph is to be treated as substituted for paragraph (1)

"(1) An application under paragraph 3(1), (6) or (7) or 7(4) of Schedule 4 to the 2000 Act or an application under regulation 66(4) of the European Union Referendum (Conduct) Regulations 2016 shall be disregarded for the purposes of the referendum, and an application under regulation 62(5) of the European Union Referendum (Conduct) Regulations 2016 shall be refused, if it is received by the registration officer after 5 pm on the eleventh day before the date of the poll for the referendum."

(3) Paragraph (2) has effect for the purposes of the referendum as if
   (a) for "a particular parliamentary or local government election" there were substituted "the referendum", and
   (b) for "at that election" there were substituted "for the referendum".

(4) For the purposes of the referendum the following paragraphs are to be treated as substituted for paragraphs (3) and (3A)
   "(3) Subject to paragraph (3A), an application under regulation 62(2) or 64(4) of the European Union Referendum (Conduct) Regulations 2016 shall be refused if it is received by the registration officer after 5 pm on the sixth day before the date of the poll for the referendum.
   (3A) Where an application made under regulation 62(2) of the European Union Referendum (Conduct) Regulations 2016 is made
      (a) on the grounds of the applicant's disability and the applicant became disabled after 5 pm on the sixth day before the date of the poll for the referendum; or
      (b) on grounds relating to the applicant's occupation, service or employment and the applicant became aware of those grounds after 5 pm on the sixth day before the date of the poll for the referendum; or
      (c) by a person to whom regulation 60(7) of those Regulations applies,
      the application, or an application under regulation 64(4) of those Regulations made by virtue of that application, is to be refused if it is received after 5pm on the day of the poll for the referendum."

(5) For the purposes of the referendum the following paragraph is to be treated as substituted for paragraph (4)
   "(4) An application under regulation 62(1) or 66(5) of the European Union Referendum (Conduct) Regulations 2016 is to be refused if it is received by the registration officer after 5 pm on the eleventh day before the date of the poll for the referendum."

(6) Paragraph (5) has effect for the purposes of the referendum as if
   (a) after "paragraph 6(10) of that Schedule by an elector" there were treated as inserted ", or a notice under regulation 64(6) of the European Union Referendum (Conduct) Regulations 2016 by a person,",
   (b) for "a particular parliamentary or local government election" there were substituted "the referendum", and
   (c) for "at that election" there were substituted "for the referendum".

(7) Paragraph (5A) has effect for the purposes of the referendum as if for "a particular parliamentary or local government election" there were substituted "the referendum".

(8) For the purposes of the referendum the following paragraph is to be treated as substituted for paragraphs (6) and (7)
   "(6) In computing a period of days for the purposes of this regulation the following days are to be disregarded
      (a) a Saturday or Sunday, and
      (b) Christmas Eve, Christmas Day, Good Friday and any other day that is a bank holiday under the Banking and Financial Dealings Act 1971 in any part of the United Kingdom."

Grant or refusal of applications

13(1) Regulation 57 of the relevant regulations (grant or refusal of applications) has effect for the purposes of the referendum with the following modifications.

(2) For those purposes, paragraph (3) is treated as omitted.

(3) Paragraph (4) has effect for the purposes of the referendum as if after "Schedule 4" there were inserted "or Chapter 1 of Part 3 of the European Union Referendum (Conduct) Regulations 2016".

(4) Paragraph (4A) has effect for the purposes of the referendum as if after sub-paragraph (b) there were inserted
", or
　(c)　regulation 62(5)(a) of the European Union Referendum (Conduct) Regulations 2016 by a person shown as voting by post in a record mentioned in that provision, or
　(d)　regulation 66(5) of those Regulations by a person shown as voting by post in a record mentioned in that provision,".

(5) Paragraph (4B) has effect for the purposes of the referendum as if after "Schedule 4" there were inserted "or regulation 62(5)(a) or 66(5) of the European Union Referendum (Conduct) Regulations 2016".

(6) Paragraph (5) has effect for the purposes of the referendum as if for "any particular parliamentary or local government election," there were substituted "the referendum".

(7) For the purposes of the referendum the following paragraph is to be treated as inserted after paragraph (6)
"(7) Where the registration officer is not the counting officer for any voting area or part of a voting area in the area for which he is the registration officer, he shall send to that officer details of any application to vote by post which he has granted as soon as practicable after doing so."

Cancellation of proxy appointment

14 Regulation 59 of the relevant regulations (cancellation of proxy appointment) has effect for the purposes of the referendum as if
　(a)　after "paragraph 6(10) of Schedule 4" there were inserted "or regulation 64(6) of the European Union Referendum (Conduct) Regulations 2016",
　(b)　for "that provision" there were substituted "either of those provisions",
　(c)　for "of that Schedule" there were substituted "of Schedule 4", and
　(d)　after "paragraph 3(4)(c) of Schedule 4" there were inserted "or the list of proxies kept under regulation 63(3) of the European Union Referendum (Conduct) Regulations 2016".

Requirement to provide fresh signatures every 5 years

15(1) Regulation 60A of the relevant regulations (requirement to provide fresh signatures) has effect for the purposes of the referendum with the following modifications.

(2) Paragraph (7) has effect for those purposes as if for the words from "kept under" to the end there were substituted "kept under regulation 63(2), 63(3) or 66(6) of the European Union Referendum (Conduct) Regulations 2016."

(3) Paragraph (8) has effect for the purposes of the referendum as if
　(a)　in sub-paragraph (a), at the end there were inserted "or under Part 2 of the European Union Referendum (Conduct) Regulations 2016 (as the case may be)", and
　(b)　in sub-paragraph (b), after "Schedule 4" there were inserted "or Chapter 1 of

Part 3 of the European Union Referendum (Conduct) Regulations 2016".

(4)   Paragraph (9) has effect for the purposes of the referendum as if for the words from "kept under" to the end there were substituted

"kept under regulation 63(2), 63(3) or 66(6) of the European Union Referendum (Conduct) Regulations 2016, information

(a)   explaining the effect of such removal, and

(b)   reminding the absent voter that he may make a fresh application to vote by post or by proxy (as the case may be)."

Records and lists

16(1)   Regulation 61 of the relevant regulations (records and lists) applies for the purposes of the referendum but with the following modifications.

(2)   Paragraph (1) has effect for those purposes as if for the words from "any of the following" to the end there were substituted "the current or final version of the postal voters list, the list of proxies or the proxy postal voters lists which he is required to keep under regulation 63(2), 63(3) or 66(6) of the European Union Referendum (Conduct) Regulations 2016."

(3)   Paragraph (3) of the Scotland Regulations has effect for the purposes of the referendum as if after sub-paragraph (b) there were inserted

"or

(c)   purposes connected with the referendum,".

(4)   Paragraph (5) has effect for the purposes of the referendum as if for "paragraph 5(2) of Schedule 4" there were substituted "regulation 63(2) of the European Union Referendum (Conduct) Regulations 2016."

(5)   Paragraph (6) has effect for the purposes of the referendum as if

(a)   in sub-paragraph (a), for "paragraphs 5 and 7(8) of Schedule 4" there were substituted "regulations 63 and 66(6) of the European Union Referendum (Conduct) Regulations 2016", and

(b)   for sub-paragraph (b) there were substituted

"(b) if he is not the counting officer for any voting area or part of a voting area in the area for which he is the registration officer, send to that officer a copy of those lists and provide any subsequent revised lists or revisions to the lists;".

(6)   Paragraph (6A) has effect for the purposes of the referendum as if

(a)   for "parliamentary election" there were substituted "the referendum",

(b)   for "acting returning officer" there were substituted "counting officer",

(c)   for "any constituency or part of a constituency" there were substituted "any voting area or part of a voting area", and

(d)   for "paragraphs 5 and 7(8) of Schedule 4" there were substituted "regulations 63 and 66(6)of the European Union Referendum (Conduct) Regulations 2016".

(7)   Paragraph (7) has effect for the purposes of the referendum as if for "the proxy voters list kept under paragraph 5(3) of Schedule 4" there were substituted "the list of proxies kept under regulation 63(3) of the European Union Referendum (Conduct) Regulations 2016".

Conditions on use, supply and inspection of absent voter records or lists

17   Regulation 61A of the relevant regulations (conditions on the use, supply and inspection of absent voter records or lists) applies for the purposes of the referendum but as if

(a)   for "regulations 61(1)(a) and (b)" there were substituted "regulation 61(1)",

(b) the word "either" were omitted, and

(c) after sub-paragraph (b) there were inserted

", or

(c) purposes connected with the referendum."

Personal identifiers record

18(1) Regulation 61B of the relevant regulations (personal identifiers record) has effect for the purposes of the referendum with the following modifications.

(2) For those purposes the following paragraph is to be treated as substituted for paragraph (1)

"(1) In these Regulations "personal identifiers record" means a record kept by a registration officer in pursuance of

(a) paragraph 3(9) or 7(12) of Schedule 4 to the Representation of the People Act 2000 in relation to persons entitled to vote in the referendum,

(b) paragraph 3(9) or 7(13) of Schedule 2 to the European Parliamentary Elections Regulations 2004 in relation to peers entitled to vote in the referendum, or

(c) regulation 62(8) or 66(10) of the European Union Referendum (Conduct) Regulations 2016."

(3) Paragraph (3) has effect for the purposes of the referendum as if the following were substituted for sub-paragraph (a)

"(a) any agent attending proceedings on receipt of postal ballot papers, in accordance with regulation 85A(4)."

Notification of rejected postal voting statement

19 Regulation 61C of the relevant regulations (notification of rejected postal voting statement) applies for the purposes of the referendum but as if, in paragraphs (1)(a) and (2)(b), for "returning officer" there were substituted "counting officer".

Interpretation of Part 5

20 Regulation 64 of the relevant regulations (interpretation of Part 5) has effect for the purposes of the referendum as if

(a) the following were substituted for the definition of "agent"

"'agent', except in regulation 69, means a referendum agent or an agent appointed under regulation 69;", and

(b) in the definition of "valid postal voting statement", for "returning officer" there were substituted "counting officer".

Persons entitled to be present at proceedings on issue of postal ballot papers

21 Regulation 67 of the relevant regulations (persons entitled to be present at proceedings on issue of postal ballot papers) applies for the purposes of the referendum but as if for "returning officer" there were substituted "counting officer".

Persons entitled to be present at proceedings on receipt of postal ballot papers

22 Regulation 68 of the relevant regulations (persons entitled to be present at proceedings on receipt of postal ballot papers) applies for the purposes of the referendum but as if for sub-paragraphs (a) to (c) there were substituted

"(a) the counting officer and his clerks,

(b) a referendum agent,".

Agents of candidate who may attend proceedings on receipt of postal ballot papers

23 Regulation 69 of the relevant regulations (agents of candidates who may attend proceedings on receipt of postal ballot papers) applies for the purposes of the referendum but as if

  (a) for "candidate" (in each place) there were substituted "referendum agent",

  (b) for "returning officer" (in each place) there were substituted "counting officer", and

  (c) paragraphs (3) and (5) were omitted.

Notification of requirement of secrecy

24 Regulation 70 of the relevant regulations (notification of requirement of secrecy) applies for the purposes of the referendum but as if for "returning officer" there were substituted "counting officer".

Time when postal ballot papers are to be issued

25 Regulation 71 of the relevant regulations (time when postal ballot papers are to be issued) applies for the purposes of the referendum but as if for the words from "be issued" to the end there were substituted

  "not be issued by a counting officer so as to be received by persons entitled to vote in the referendum before the beginning of the relevant period within the meaning of section 125 of the Political Parties, Elections and Referendums Act 2000 (restriction on campaigning by certain persons or bodies)."

Procedure on issue of postal ballot papers

26 Regulation 72 of the relevant regulations (procedure on issue of postal ballot papers) applies for the purposes of the referendum but as if in paragraph (8) for sub-paragraphs (a) and (b) there were substituted "as mentioned in column 3 of the table in regulation 63(2) or 66(6) of the European Union Referendum (Conduct) Regulations 2016."

Refusal to issue ballot paper

27 Regulation 73 of the relevant regulations (refusal to issue ballot paper) has effect for the purposes of the referendum as if

  (a) for "returning officer" there were substituted "counting officer", and

  (b) for "at any one election" there were substituted "for the referendum".

Envelopes

28 Regulation 74 of the relevant regulations (envelopes) applies for the purposes of the referendum but as if in paragraph (1) for "rule 24 of the elections rules" there were substituted "regulation 17 of the European Union Referendum (Conduct) Regulations 2016".

Sealing up of completed corresponding number lists

29 Regulation 75 of the relevant regulations (sealing up of completed corresponding number lists) applies for the purposes of the referendum but as if for "returning officer" (in both places) there were substituted "counting officer".

Delivery of postal ballot papers

30(1) Regulation 76 of the relevant regulations (delivery of postal ballot papers) applies for the purposes of the referendum but with the following modifications.

(2) For those purposes paragraph (1) has effect as if

    (a) for "returning officer" there were substituted "counting officer", and

    (b) in sub-paragraph (c), for "rule 26(1) of the elections rules" there were substituted "regulation 19 of the European Union Referendum (Conduct) Regulations 2016."

(3) For the purposes of the referendum paragraph (2) has effect as if for "returning officer" there were substituted "counting officer".

Spoilt postal ballot papers

31 Regulation 77 of the relevant regulations (spoilt postal ballot papers) applies for the purposes of the referendum but as if for "returning officer" (in each place) there were substituted "counting officer".

Lost postal ballot papers

32 Regulation 78 of the relevant regulations (lost postal ballot papers) applies for the purposes of the referendum but as if for "returning officer" (in each place) there were substituted "counting officer".

Cancellation of postal ballot papers

33(1) Regulation 78A of the relevant regulations (cancellation of postal ballot papers) applies for the purposes of the referendum but with the following modifications.

(2) Paragraph (1) has effect for those purposes as if

    (a) for the words from "final" to "application under" there were substituted "nineteenth day before the day of the poll for the referendum, an application under",

    (b) in sub-paragraph (b), for the reference to "or 4(3)(b) of that Schedule" there were substituted "of Schedule 4 or regulation 62(5)(b) of the European Union Referendum (Conduct) Regulations 2016",

    (c) in sub-paragraph (c), for the reference to "that Schedule" there were substituted "Schedule 4",

    (d) in sub-paragraph (d), for the reference to "paragraph 4(3)(a) of that Schedule" there were substituted "regulation 62(5)(a) of the European Union Referendum (Conduct) Regulations 2016",

    (e) in sub-paragraph (e), for the reference to "or (8) of that Schedule" there were substituted "of Schedule 4 or regulation 64(4) of the European Union Referendum (Conduct) Regulations 2016",

    (f) in sub-paragraph (f), for the reference to "paragraph 7(7) of that Schedule" there were substituted "regulation 66(5) of the European Union Referendum (Conduct) Regulations 2016",

    (g) in sub-paragraph (g), for the reference to "that Schedule" there were substituted "Schedule 4",

    (h) for the reference to "paragraph 6(10) of that Schedule" there were substituted "paragraph 6(10) of Schedule 4 or regulation 64(4) of the European Union Referendum (Conduct) Regulations 2016", and

    (i) for the reference to "that election" there were substituted "the referendum".

(3) For the purposes of the referendum, paragraphs (1), (2) and (3) have effect as if for "returning officer" (in each place) there were substituted "counting officer".

(4) For the purposes of the referendum the following paragraph is treated as substituted for paragraph (5)

"(5) In computing a period of days for the purposes of this regulation the following

days are to be disregarded
(a) a Saturday or Sunday,
(b) Christmas Eve, Christmas Day, Good Friday and any other day that is a bank holiday under the Banking and Financial Dealings Act 1971 in any part of the United Kingdom,
(c) any day that is a bank or public holiday in Gibraltar under the Gibraltar Acts titled the Banking and Financial Dealings Act and the Interpretation and General Clauses Act, and
(d) any day appointed in any part of the United Kingdom or Gibraltar as a day of public thanksgiving or mourning."

Alternative means of returning postal ballot paper or postal voting statement: England and Wales

34 Regulation 79 of the England and Wales Regulations (alternative means of returning postal ballot paper or postal voting statement) applies for the purposes of the referendum but as if
(a) for "returning officer" (in each place) there were substituted "counting officer",
(b) in paragraph (1) for "rule 45(1B) of the rules in Schedule 1 to the 1983 Act" there were substituted "regulation 46(3) of the European Union Referendum (Conduct) Regulations 2016", and
(c) in paragraph (3) for "rule 43(1) of the elections rules" there were substituted "regulation 44(1) of the European Union Referendum (Conduct) Regulations 2016".

Alternative means of returning postal ballot paper or postal voting statement: Scotland

35 Regulation 79 of the Scotland Regulations (alternative means of returning postal ballot paper or postal voting statement) applies for the purposes of the referendum but as if
(a) for "returning officer" (in each place) there were substituted "counting officer",
(b) in paragraph (1) for "rule 45(1B) of the elections rules" there were substituted "regulation 46(3) of the European Union Referendum (Conduct) Regulations 2016", and
(c) in paragraph (2) for "rule 43(1) of the elections rules" there were substituted "regulation 44(1) of the European Union Referendum (Conduct) Regulations 2016".

Notice of opening of postal ballot paper envelopes

36(1) Regulation 80 of the relevant regulations (notice of opening of postal ballot paper envelopes) applies for the purposes of the referendum but with the following modifications.

(2) Paragraph (1) has effect for those purposes as if
(a) for "returning officer" there were substituted "counting officer", and
(b) for "candidate" there were substituted "referendum agent".

(3) Paragraph (2) has effect for the purposes of the referendum as if for "candidate" there were substituted "referendum agent".

Postal ballot boxes and receptacles

37 Regulation 81 of the relevant regulations (postal ballot boxes and receptacles) applies for the purposes of the referendum but as if
(a) for "returning officer" (in each place) there were substituted "counting officer",
(b) in paragraph (2) for the words from "constituency" to the end there were substituted "voting area", and

(c) in paragraph (4) after "box" there were inserted "(if it has a lock)".

Receipt of covering envelope

38 Regulation 82 of the relevant regulations (receipt of covering envelope) applies for the purposes of the referendum but as if for "returning officer" (in both places) there were substituted "counting officer".

Opening of postal voters' ballot box

39 Regulation 83 of the relevant regulations (opening of postal voters' ballot box) applies for the purposes of the referendum but as if
(a) for "returning officer" (in both places) there were substituted "counting officer", and
(b) in paragraph (3) for "rule 45 of the elections rules" there were substituted "regulation 46 of the European Union Referendum (Conduct) Regulations 2016".

Opening of covering envelopes

40 Regulation 84 of the relevant regulations (opening of covering envelopes) applies for the purposes of the referendum but as if for "returning officer" (in each place) there were substituted "counting officer".

Confirming receipt of postal voting statements

41 Regulation 84A of the relevant regulations (confirming receipt of postal voting statements) applies for the purposes of the referendum but as if for "returning officer" (in each place) there were substituted "counting officer".

Procedure in relation to postal voting statements: personal identifier verification

42 Regulation 85A of the relevant regulations (procedure in relation to postal voting statements: personal identifier verification) applies for the purposes of the referendum but as if for "returning officer" (in each place) there were substituted "counting officer".

Opening of ballot paper envelopes

43 Regulation 86 of the relevant regulations (opening of ballot paper envelopes) applies for the purposes of the referendum but as if, in paragraph (1), for "returning officer" there were substituted "counting officer".

Retrieval of cancelled postal ballot papers

44(1) Regulation 86A of the relevant regulations (retrieval of cancelled postal ballot papers) applies for the purposes of the referendum but with the following modifications.

(2) Paragraphs (1) and (3) have effect for those purposes as if for "returning officer" (in each place) there were substituted "counting officer".

(3) Paragraph (2)(f) has effect for the purposes of the referendum as if for "rule 45 of the elections rules" there were substituted "regulation 46 of the European Union Referendum (Conduct) Regulations 2016".

Lists of rejected postal ballot papers

45 Regulation 87 of the relevant regulations (lists of rejected postal ballot papers) applies for the purposes of the referendum but as if in paragraph (1) for "In respect of any election, the returning officer" there were substituted "The counting officer".

Checking of lists of rejected postal ballot papers

46 Regulation 88 of the relevant regulations (checking of lists of rejected postal ballot papers) applies for the purposes of the referendum but as if

    (a) for "returning officer" (in each place) there were substituted "counting officer", and

    (b) in paragraph (3), for the words from "constituency" to the end there were substituted "voting area under regulation 44(4) of the European Union Referendum (Conduct) Regulations 2016".

Sealing of receptacles

47 Regulation 89 of the relevant regulations (sealing of receptacles) applies for the purposes of the referendum but as if, in paragraph (1), for "returning officer" there were substituted "counting officer".

Forwarding or retention of documents: England and Wales

48(1) Regulation 91 of the England and Wales Regulations (forwarding of documents) applies for the purposes of the referendum but with the following modifications.

    (2) For those purposes the following paragraph is to be treated as substituted for paragraph (1)

      "(1) When the counting officer forwards the documents mentioned in regulation 56 of the European Union Referendum (Conduct) Regulations 2016, he shall forward to the same registration officer

        (a) any packets referred to in regulations 75, 77(6), 78(2C), 78A(2), 84(9) and 89, endorsing on each packet a description of its contents, the date of the referendum and the name of the voting area, and

        (b) a completed statement in Form K of the number of postal ballot papers issued."

    (3) Paragraph (3) has effect for the purposes of the referendum as if for "returning officer" (in both places) there were substituted "counting officer".

    (4) Paragraph (3A) has effect for the purposes of the referendum as if

      (a) for "returning officer" (in both places) there were substituted "counting officer",

      (b) the following were substituted for sub-paragraph (a)

      "(a) forward to the registration officer mentioned in that paragraph the list required to be compiled under regulation 87(4),", and

      (c) in sub-paragraph (b) for "constituency" there were substituted "voting area".

    (5) Paragraph (4) has effect for the purposes of the referendum as if for "Rules 56 and 57 of the elections rules" there were substituted "Regulations 57 and 58 of the European Union Referendum (Conduct) Regulations 2016".

    (6) Paragraph (5) has effect for the purposes of the referendum as if for "returning officer" there were substituted "counting officer".

Retention of documents: Scotland

49(1) Regulation 91 of the Scotland Regulations (retention of documents) applies for the purposes of the referendum but with the following modifications.

    (2) For those purposes the following paragraph is to be treated as substituted for paragraph (1)

      "(1) The counting officer shall retain together with the documents mentioned in regulation 56 of the European Union Referendum (Conduct) Regulations 2016

        (a) any packets referred to in regulations 75, 77(6), 78(2C), 78A(2), 84(8) and 89, endorsing on each packet a description of its contents, the date of the referendum and the name of the voting area,

    (b)   a completed statement in Form K of the number of postal ballot papers issued, and

    (c)   any list compiled under regulation 87(4)."

(3)   Paragraph (2) has effect for the purposes of the referendum as if for "returning officer" (in both places) there were substituted "counting officer".

(4)   Paragraph (4) has effect for the purposes of the referendum as if
    (a)   for "Rules 56, 57 and 58 of the elections rules" there were substituted "Regulations 57 and 58 of the European Union Referendum (Conduct) Regulations 2016", and
    (b)   for "rules 56 and 57" there were substituted "those regulations".

(5)   Paragraph (5) has effect for the purposes of the referendum as if for "returning officer" there were substituted "counting officer".

Forwarding of documents: Scotland

50(1)   Regulation 91A of the Scotland Regulations (forwarding of documents) applies for the purposes of the referendum but with the following modifications.

(2)   For those purposes the following paragraph is to be treated as substituted for paragraph (1)
    "(1) Before the counting officer seals up the counted and rejected ballot papers as provided by regulation 55 of the European Union Referendum (Conduct) Regulations 2016, the counting officer must send a copy of any list compiled under regulation 87(4) to the registration officer for the local government area for which the counting officer is appointed."

(3)   Paragraph (2) has effect for the purposes of the referendum as if the words from "and requiring" to the end were omitted.

(4)   Paragraph (3) has effect for the purposes of the referendum as if
    (a)   for "Rule 56 of the elections rules, as modified by rule 58 of those rules," there were substituted "Regulation 57 of the European Union Referendum (Conduct) Regulations 2016",
    (b)   the words ", or extracts of the list," were omitted,
    (c)   for "returning officer" (in both places) there were substituted "counting officer",
    (d)   in sub-paragraph (a)
        (i)   for "rule 56" there were substituted "regulation 57", and
        (ii) the words ", or extracts of the list," were omitted, and
    (e)   in sub-paragraph (b)
        (i)   the words "(as modified by rule 58 of the elections rules)" were omitted, and
        (ii) the words ", or extracts of a list," were omitted.

(5)   Paragraph (4) has effect for the purposes of the referendum as if the words ", or extracts of the list," were omitted.

(6)   Paragraph (5) has effect for the purposes of the referendum as if
    (a)   the words ", or extracts of the list," (in both places) were omitted, and
    (b)   the words ", and issued any notices under regulation 60B," were omitted.

Interpretation and application of Part 6: England and Wales

51   Regulation 92 of the England and Wales Regulations (interpretation and application of Part 6) applies for the purposes of the referendum but as if
    (a)   in paragraph (7), for the words from "under regulations" to the first "may" there were substituted "under regulation 98 may", and

(b) in paragraph (10), for the words from "in regulations" to "below" there were substituted "in regulations 94(3) and 98(9) below".

Restriction on supply etc of full register: England and Wales

52   Regulation 94 of the England and Wales Regulations (restrictions on supply etc of full register) has effect for the purposes of the referendum as if, in paragraph (1), after sub-paragraph (b) there were inserted
"(ba)   the Chief Counting Officer and any Regional Counting Officer; and
(bb) any deputy of the Chief Counting Officer or of any Regional Counting Officer; and".

Restriction on supply etc of full register: Scotland

53(1)   Regulation 94 of the Scotland Regulations (restrictions on supply etc of full register) has effect for the purposes of the referendum with the following modifications.

(2)   Paragraph (1) has effect for those purposes as if after sub-paragraph (a) there were inserted
"(aa)   the Chief Counting Officer and any Regional Counting Officer, and
(ab) any deputy of the Chief Counting Officer or of any Regional Counting Officer, and".

(3)   Paragraph (2) has effect for the purposes of the referendum as if
(a)   after sub-paragraph (a) there were inserted
"(aa)   any deputy of the registration officer acting in that other capacity, and", and
(b)   the references in sub-paragraph (b) to "that officer" were treated as references to "a person mentioned in sub-paragraph (a) or (aa)".

Supply of free copy of full register for electoral purposes and restrictions on use: Scotland

54   For the purposes of the referendum the following is treated as substituted for regulation 97 of the Scotland Regulations
"97 Supply of free copy of full register for electoral purposes and restrictions on use
(1)   By no later than the publication of the notice of the referendum, the registration officer shall supply each relevant counting officer with as many printed copies of the following as he may reasonably require for the purposes of the referendum
(a)   the latest version of the relevant registers,
(b)   any notice, published under section 13A(2), 13AB(2) or 13B(3), (3B) or (3D) of the 1983 Act, setting out an alteration to the latest version of a relevant register, and
(c)   the latest version of the list of overseas electors.
(2)   In this regulation
"relevant counting officer" in relation to a registration officer
(a)   means a counting officer for a voting area that is the same as, or falls wholly or partly within, the registration officer's registration area, but
(b)   does not include a counting officer who is the same individual as the registration officer;
"relevant register" means
(a)   the register of parliamentary electors, published under section 13(1) or (3) of the 1983 Act,
(b)   the register of local government electors, published under section 13(1) or (3) of that Act, or

(c) the register of peers, maintained under section 3 of the 1985 Act, and published under section 13(1) or (3) of the 1983 Act (as applied by regulation 13(4) of, and Schedule 4 to, these regulations).

(3) If at any time after a registration officer has complied with paragraph (1)

(a) a revised version of a relevant register is published,

(b) a notice is published, under section 13A(2), 13AB(2) or 13B(3), (3B) or (3D) of the 1983 Act, setting out an alteration to the latest version of a relevant register, or

(c) a revised version of the list of overseas electors is published,

the registration officer shall supply the counting officer with as many printed copies of the register, notice or list as he may reasonably require for the purposes of the referendum.

(4) Where a registration officer is under a duty to supply a counting officer with printed copies of a register, notice or list under this regulation, he must also supply a copy of the register, notice or list in data form.

(5) A register notice or list supplied under this regulation shall be supplied free of charge.

(6) No person to whom a copy of any register has been supplied under this regulation may

(a) supply a copy of the full register,

(b) disclose any information contained in it (that is not contained in the edited register), or

(c) make use of any such information,

except for the purposes of the referendum."

Supply of free copy of full register for electoral purposes and restrictions on use: England and Wales

55 For the purposes of the referendum the following is treated as substituted for regulation 98 of the England and Wales Regulations

"98 Supply of free copy of full register for electoral purposes and restrictions on use

(1) By no later than the publication of the notice of the referendum, the registration officer shall supply each relevant counting officer with as many printed copies of the following as he may reasonably require for the purposes of the referendum

(a) the latest version of the relevant registers,

(b) any notice, published under section 13A(2), 13AB(2) or 13B(3), (3B) or (3D) of the 1983 Act, setting out an alteration to the latest version of a relevant register, and

(c) the latest version of the list of overseas electors.

(2) In this regulation

"relevant counting officer" in relation to a registration officer

(a) means a counting officer for a voting area that is the same as, or falls wholly or partly within, the registration officer's registration area, but

(b) does not include a counting officer who is the same individual as the registration officer;

"relevant register" means

(a) the register of parliamentary electors, published under section 13(1) or (3) of the 1983 Act,

(b) the register of local government electors, published under section 13(1) or (3) of that Act, or

(c) the register of peers, maintained under section 3 of the 1985 Act, and published under section 13(1) or (3) of the 1983 Act (as applied by regulation 13(4) of, and Schedule 4 to, these regulations).

(3) If at any time after a registration officer has complied with paragraph (1)

    (a) a revised version of a relevant register is published,

    (b) a notice is published, under section 13A(2), 13AB(2) or 13B(3), (3B) or (3D) of the 1983 Act, setting out an alteration to the latest version of a relevant register, or

    (c) a revised version of the list of overseas electors is published,

the registration officer shall supply the counting officer with as many printed copies of the register, notice or list as he may reasonably require for the purposes of the referendum.

(4) Where a registration officer is under a duty to supply a counting officer with printed copies of a register, notice or list under this regulation, he must also supply a copy of the register, notice or list in data form.

(5) A register notice or list supplied under this regulation shall be supplied free of charge.

(6) No person to whom a copy of any register has been supplied under this regulation may

    (a) supply a copy of the full register,

    (b) disclose any information contained in it (that is not contained in the edited register), or

    (c) make use of any such information,

except for the purposes of the referendum."

Offences: England and Wales

56 Regulation 115 of the England and Wales Regulations (offences) has effect for the purposes of the referendum as if in paragraph (2) for "98(9)" there were substituted "98(6)".

Offences: Scotland

57 Regulation 115 of the Scotland Regulations (offences) has effect for the purposes of the referendum as if in paragraph (2) for "97(7)" there were substituted "97(6)".

Interpretation of Part 7: England and Wales

58 Regulation 116 of the England and Wales Regulations (interpretation of Part 7) has effect for the purposes of the referendum as if

    (a) in paragraph (1) for "rule 55(1)(e) of the elections rules" there were substituted "by virtue of regulation 56(2)(g) of the European Union Referendum (Conduct) Regulations 2016", and

    (b) after paragraph (1) there were inserted

        "(1A) In this Part references to "the relevant registration officer" means the registration officer to whom packets are forwarded under regulation 56(1) of the European Union Referendum (Conduct) Regulations 2016."

Interpretation of Part 7: Scotland

59(1) Regulation 116 of the Scotland Regulations (interpretation of Part 7) has effect for the purposes of the referendum with the following modifications.

  (2) Paragraph (1) has effect for those purposes as if

    (a) for "returning officer" there were substituted "counting officer", and

    (b) for "rule 58 of the elections rules" there were substituted "by virtue of regulation 56(2)(g) of the European Union Referendum (Conduct) Regulations 2016".

(3) Paragraph (4) has effect for the purposes of the referendum as if for "returning officer" there were substituted "counting officer".

Supply of marked registers and lists after an election: England and Wales

60(1) Regulation 117 of the England and Wales Regulations (supply of marked registers and lists) applies for the purposes of the referendum but with the following modifications.

(2) Paragraph (1) has effect for those purposes as if
   (a) for the words from "regulation 100" to "local government election" there were substituted "regulation 100, 106, 109 or 113 with copies of the full register", and
   (b) at the end there were treated as inserted
      "The reference to a person entitled to be supplied in accordance with regulation 106 with copies of the full register does not include a person mentioned in regulation 106(1)(b)."

(3) Paragraph (2) has effect for the purposes of the referendum as if
   (a) for "regulation 103, 105, 106 or 108 before a particular election" there were substituted "regulation 106(1)(a) or (c) before the referendum", and
   (b) for "that election for which the marked register or list was prepared" there were substituted "the referendum".

(4) Paragraph (6)(b) has effect for the purposes of the referendum as if for "regulations 100, 103, 105, 106, 108, 109 or 113" there were substituted "regulations 100, 106, 109 and 113".

(5) Paragraph (7) has effect for the purposes of the referendum as if for "regulations 100(3), 105(4), 106(3), 108(5) and 109(3)" there were substituted "regulations 100(3), 106(3) and 109(3)".

Supply of marked registers and lists after an election: Scotland

61(1) Regulation 117 of the Scotland Regulations (supply of marked registers and lists) applies for the purposes of the referendum but with the following modifications.

(2) The regulation has effect for those purposes as if for "returning officer" (in each place) there were substituted "counting officer".

(3) Paragraph (1) has effect for the purposes of the referendum as if
   (a) for the words from "regulation 99" to "parliamentary election" there were substituted "regulation 99, 105, 108 or 112 with copies of the full register", and
   (b) at the end there were treated as inserted
      "The reference to a person entitled to be supplied in accordance with regulation 105 with copies of the full register does not include a person mentioned in regulation 105(1)(b)."

(4) Paragraph (2) has effect for the purposes of the referendum as if
   (a) for "regulation 102, 104, 105 or 107 before a particular election" there were substituted "regulation 105(1)(a) or (c) before the referendum", and
   (b) for "that election for which the marked register or list was prepared" there were substituted "the referendum".

(5) Paragraph (6)(b) has effect for the purposes of the referendum as if for "regulations 99, 102, 104, 105, 107, 108 or 112" there were substituted "regulations 99, 105, 108 and 112".

(6) Paragraph (7) has effect for the purposes of the referendum as if for "regulations 99(3), 102(3), 104(4), 105(3), 107(5) or 108(3)" there were substituted "regulations 99(3), 105(3) or 108(3)".

Inspection of documents open to public inspection

62   Regulation 118 of the relevant regulations (inspection of documents) applies for the purposes of the referendum but as if in paragraph (1)

    (a)   for "an election" there were substituted "the referendum", and

    (b)   for "the election" there were substituted "the referendum".

63   For the purposes of the referendum, in regulation 118 of the Scotland Regulations, for "returning officer" (in each place) there is to be treated as substituted "counting officer".

Conditions on use, supply and disclosure of documents open to public inspection

64   Regulation 119 of the relevant regulations (conditions on the use, supply and disclosure of documents) applies for the purposes of the referendum but as if, in paragraph (2)(b)

    (a)   the word "either" were omitted, and

    (b)   the following were treated as inserted after paragraph (ii)

        "; or

    (iii)   any purpose in connection with the referendum."

Form K: statement as to postal ballot papers

65   Form K in Schedule 3 to the relevant regulations (statement as to postal ballot papers) applies for the purposes of the referendum but as if

    (a)   for the heading "REPRESENTATION OF THE PEOPLE ACTS PARLIAMENTARY ELECTION" there were substituted "REFERENDUM ON THE UNITED KINGDOM'S MEMBERSHIP OF THE EUROPEAN UNION",

    (b)   for "constituency" there were substituted "voting area", and

    (c)   for "Returning Officer" (in each place) there were substituted "Counting Officer".

Part 2
The 2008 Regulations (Northern Ireland)

Preliminary

66(1)   In this Part of this Schedule the "2008 Regulations" means the Representation of the People (Northern Ireland) Regulations 2008.

  (2)   In any provision of the 2008 Regulations as applied by this Part of this Schedule

    (a)   expressions defined by section 11 of the 2015 Act have the meaning given by that section, and

    (b)   expressions defined by regulation 5 have the meaning given by that regulation.

  (3)   Sub-paragraph (2) does not apply to the extent that the context otherwise requires.

67   The following provisions of the 2008 Regulations apply for the purposes of the referendum

    (a)   regulation 3 (interpretation);

    (b)   regulation 5 (applications, notices etc);

    (c)   regulation 6 (electronic signatures);

    (d)   regulation 8 (time);

    (e)   regulation 11 (interference with notices etc);

    (f)   regulation 25 (alteration of registers under section 13BA(3) of the 1983 Act);

    (g)   regulation 40 (representations regarding clerical errors);

(h) regulation 119 (fees relating to the supply of marked registers and lists).

Forms

68(1) Regulation 4 of the 2008 Regulations (forms) applies for the purposes of the referendum but with the following modifications.

(2) Paragraph (1) has effect for those purposes as if for "an election" there were substituted "the referendum".

(3) Paragraph (2) has effect for the purposes of the referendum only in so far as it relates to Form N in Schedule 3 to the 2008 Regulations.

Communication of notices made on polling day

69 Regulation 45 of the 2008 Regulations (communication of notices made on polling day) applies for the purposes of the referendum but as if in paragraph (3) for "returning officer" there were substituted "counting officer".

Interpretation of Part 4

70 Regulation 54 of the 2008 Regulations (interpretation of Part 4) has effect for the purposes of the referendum as if after "his allotted polling station" there were inserted "(apart from in regulation 59)".

General requirements for applications for an absent vote

71(1) Regulation 55 of the 2008 Regulations (general requirements for applications for an absent vote) has effect for the purposes of the referendum with the following modifications.

(2) Paragraph (1) has effect for those purposes as if after "the 1985 Act" there were inserted "or Chapter 2 of Part 3 of the European Union Referendum (Conduct) Regulations 2016".

(3) Paragraph (2) has effect for the purposes of the referendum as if
  (a) after "section 6(1) or 7(1)" there were inserted "of the 1985 Act or regulation 73(1) or 77(5) of the European Union Referendum (Conduct) Regulations 2016",
  (b) after "section 7(1)(ba) to (bc) of the 1985 Act" there were inserted "regulation 73(1)(c) to (e) or 77(5)(d) of those Regulations",
  (c) in sub-paragraph (b), after "the 1985 Act" there were inserted "or regulation 77(5) of the European Union Referendum (Conduct) Regulations 2016",
  (d) in sub-paragraph (c) for "such an application" there were substituted "an application under section 9 of the 1985 Act", and
  (e) in sub-paragraph (d), after "the 1985 Act" there were inserted "or regulation 73(1) or 77(5) of the European Union Referendum (Conduct) Regulations 2016".

Address to which to send ballot paper: requirements if different to address in application

72 Regulation 55A of the 2008 Regulations (additional requirement for applications for ballot paper to be sent to different address to that in register) has effect for the purposes of the referendum as if
  (a) after paragraph (1)(c) there were inserted
    "(d) in the case of an application to vote by post under regulation 73(1) of the European Union Referendum (Conduct) Regulations 2016, the address provided in accordance with regulation 73(7) of those Regulations and regulation 55(2)(b) above are different.", and
  (b) in paragraph (2) "of the 1985 Act" were omitted.

Address to which to send ballot paper: requirements if different to address in records

73   Regulation 55B of the 2008 Regulations (additional requirement for applications for ballot paper to be sent to different address from that in records) applies for the purposes of the referendum but as if for sub-paragraphs (a) and (b) of paragraph (1) there were inserted "regulation 73(5)(a) or 77(7) of the European Union Referendum (Conduct) Regulations 2016 by a person ("A") shown as voting by post in the record referred to in that provision".

Additional requirements for applications for appointment of a proxy

74   Regulation 56 of the 2008 Regulations (additional requirement for applications for the appointment of a proxy) applies for the purposes of the referendum but as if
     (a)   in paragraph (1), after "the 1985 Act" there were inserted "or regulation 75(4) of the European Union Referendum (Conduct) Regulations 2016", and
     (b)   after paragraph (2)(b) there were inserted
           "; or
     (c)   regulation 77(5) of the European Union Referendum (Conduct) Regulations 2016."

Additional requirements for applications in respect of a particular election

75(1) Regulation 59 of the 2008 Regulations (additional requirements for applications in respect of a particular election) applies for the purposes of the referendum but with the following modifications.
   (2) For those purposes the following paragraph is to be treated as substituted for paragraph (1)
        "(1) An application under regulation 73(1) of the European Union Referendum (Conduct) Regulations 2016 shall set out why the applicant's circumstances on the date of the poll will be or are likely to be such that he cannot reasonably be expected to vote in person at the polling station allotted to him under Part 2 of the European Union Referendum (Conduct) Regulations 2016."
   (3) Paragraphs (2)(d) and (3)(e) have effect for the purposes of the referendum as if the words from "in respect" to the end of the paragraph were omitted.
   (4) Paragraphs (4), (6) and (8) have effect for the purposes of the referendum as if for "section 7(1) of the 1985 Act" there were substituted "regulation 73(1) of the European Union Referendum (Conduct) Regulations 2016".
   (5) Paragraph (6)(a) has effect for the purposes of the referendum as if for "at the election in question" there were substituted "for the referendum".
   (6) For the purposes of the referendum the following paragraph is to be treated as substituted for paragraph (8)(b)
        "(b) in which the circumstances set out in accordance with paragraph (1) relate to the applicant's employment either as a constable or by a counting officer on the date of the poll for the referendum for a purpose connected with the referendum;".

Additional requirements for applications by proxies to vote by post at a particular election

76   Regulation 60 of the 2008 Regulations (additional requirements for applications by proxies to vote by post at a particular election) applies for the purposes of the referendum but as if for "section 9(7)(a) of the 1985 Act" there were substituted "regulation 77(5) of the European Union Referendum (Conduct) Regulations 2016".

Closing date for applications

77(1) Regulation 61 of the 2008 Regulations (closing date for applications) has effect for the purposes of the referendum with the following modifications.

(2) For those purposes the following paragraphs are to be treated as substituted for paragraphs (1) to (3)

"(1) An application under section 6(1) or (5), 8(6) or 9(4) of the 1985 Act shall be disregarded for the purposes of the referendum if it is received by the registration officer after 5 pm on the fourteenth day before the date of the poll for the referendum.

(2) Subject to paragraph (3), an application under regulation 73(1) or (5), 75(4) or 77(5) of the European Union Referendum (Conduct) Regulations 2016 shall be refused if it is received by the registration officer after 5 pm on the fourteenth day before the date of the poll for the referendum.

(3) Paragraph (2) shall not apply to an application which satisfies the requirements of either paragraphs (6) and (7) or paragraph (8) of regulation 59; and such an application shall be refused if it is received by the registration officer after 5 pm on the sixth day before the date of the poll for the referendum."

(3) Paragraph (4) has effect for the purposes of the referendum as if

(a) after "section 8(9) of that Act by an elector" there were inserted ", or a notice under regulation 75(6) of the European Union Referendum (Conduct) Regulations 2016 by a person,",

(b) for "a particular election" there were substituted "the referendum", and

(c) for "at that election" there were substituted "for the referendum".

(4) For the purposes of the referendum the following paragraph is to be treated as substituted for paragraphs (5) and (6)

"(5) In computing a period of days for the purposes of this regulation the following days are to be disregarded

(a) a Saturday or Sunday, and

(b) Christmas Eve, Christmas Day, Good Friday and any other day that is a bank holiday under the Banking and Financial Dealings Act 1971 in any part of the United Kingdom."

Grant or refusal of applications

78(1) Regulation 62 of the 2008 Regulations (grant or refusal of applications) has effect for the purposes of the referendum with the following modifications.

(2) Paragraph (1) has effect for those purposes as if after "section 6, 7, 8 or 9 of the 1985 Act" there were inserted "or Chapter 2 of Part 3 of the European Union Referendum (Conduct) Regulations 2016".

(3) For the purposes of the referendum, paragraph (3) is to be treated as omitted.

(4) For the purposes of the referendum paragraph (4) has effect as if after "the 1985 Act" there were inserted "or Chapter 2 of Part 3 of the European Union Referendum (Conduct) Regulations 2016"

(5) Paragraph (5) has effect for the purposes of the referendum as if after "a particular election" there were inserted "or the referendum".

Cancellation of proxy appointment

79 Regulation 64 of the 2008 Regulations (cancellation of proxy appointment) has effect for the purposes of the referendum as if

(a) after "the 1985 Act" there were inserted "or regulation 75(6) of the European

Union Referendum (Conduct) Regulations 2016,

(b) for "that provision" there were substituted "either of those provisions",

(c) for "that Act" there were substituted "the 1985 Act", and

(d) before "remove his name" there were inserted "in the case where an application was made under section 8 of the 1985 Act,".

Records and lists

80(1) Regulation 66 of the 2008 Regulations (records and lists) applies for the purposes of the referendum but with the following modifications.

(2) Paragraph (1) has effect for those purposes as if
(a) for "sections 7(4) and 9(9) of the 1985 Act" there were substituted "regulations 74(2) or (3) or 77(8) of the European Union Referendum (Conduct) Regulations 2016", and
(b) for "candidate at a parliamentary election or his election agent" there were substituted "referendum agent".

(3) For the purposes of the referendum paragraphs (2) and (2A) are to be treated as omitted.

(4) Paragraph (3) has effect for the purposes of the referendum as if for "sections 7(4) and 9(9) of the 1985 Act" there were substituted "regulations 74(2) or (3) or 77(8) of the European Union Referendum (Conduct) Regulations 2016".

Interpretation of Part 5

81(1) Regulation 70 of the 2008 Regulations (interpretation of Part 5) has effect for the purposes of the referendum with the following modifications.

(2) For those purposes the definition of "absent voters list" has effect as if for "section 7(4) of the 1985 Act" there were substituted "regulations 74(2) or (3) of the European Union Referendum (Conduct) Regulations 2016".

(3) For the purposes of the referendum the definition of "agent" has effect as if the following were substituted for it
"'agent', except in regulation 73, means a referendum agent or an agent appointed under regulation 73;".

(4) For the purposes of the referendum the definition of "list of postal proxies" has effect as if for "section 9(9) of the 1985 Act" there were substituted "regulation 77(8) of the European Union Referendum (Conduct) Regulations 2016".

Time when postal ballot papers are to be issued

82 For the purposes of the referendum, the following regulation is to be treated as inserted after regulation 70 of the 2008 Regulations

"70A Time when postal ballot papers are to be issued

Postal ballot papers (and declarations of identity) must not be issued by the counting officer so as to be received by persons entitled to vote in the referendum before the beginning of the relevant period within the meaning of section 125 of the Political Parties, Elections and Referendums Act 2000 (restriction on campaigning by certain persons and bodies)."

Persons entitled to be present at proceedings on issue and receipt of postal ballot papers

83(1) Regulation 72 of the 2008 Regulations (persons entitled to be present at proceedings on issue of postal ballot papers) applies for the purposes of the referendum but with the following modifications.

(2) Paragraph (1) has effect for those purposes as if
    (a) For "a parliamentary election" there were substituted "the referendum", and
    (b) for sub-paragraphs (a) to (c) there were substituted
        "(a) the counting officer and his clerks;
        (b) a referendum agent;".

(3) Paragraph (2) has effect for the purposes of the referendum as if
    (a) for "sub-paragraphs (b), (c) and (d)" there were substituted "sub-paragraphs (b) and (d)", and
    (b) for "rule 40ZA of the elections rules" there were substituted "regulation 39 of the European Union Referendum (Conduct) Regulations 2016".

Agents of candidate who may attend proceedings on issue or receipt of postal ballot papers

84 Regulation 73 of the 2008 Regulations (agents of candidates who may attend proceedings on issue or receipt of postal ballot papers) applies for the purposes of the referendum but as if
    (a) for "candidate" (in each place) there were substituted "referendum agent",
    (b) for "returning officer" (in each place) there were substituted "counting officer",
    (c) paragraph (6) were treated as omitted, and
    (d) in paragraph (10), for "rule 40ZA of the elections rules" there were substituted "regulation 39 of the European Union Referendum (Conduct) Regulations 2016".

Notification of requirement of secrecy

85 Regulation 74 of the 2008 Regulations (notification of requirement of secrecy) applies for the purposes of the referendum but as if for "returning officer" there were substituted "counting officer".

Notice of issue of postal ballot papers

86 Regulation 75 of the 2008 Regulations (notice of issue of postal ballot papers) applies for the purposes of the referendum but as if
    (a) for "returning officer" (in both places) there were substituted "counting officer",
    (b) for "candidate" (in each place) there were substituted "referendum agent", and
    (c) in paragraph (3), for "rule 40ZA of the elections rules" there were substituted "regulation 39 of the European Union Referendum (Conduct) Regulations 2016".

Procedure on issue of postal ballot paper

87(1) Regulation 76 of the 2008 Regulations (procedure on issue of postal ballot paper) applies for the purposes of the referendum but with the following modifications.

(2) For those purposes paragraph (5) has effect as if
    (a) in sub-paragraph (a) for "section 7(4A) of the 1985 Act" there were substituted "regulation 74(4) of the European Union Referendum (Conduct) Regulations 2016", and
    (b) in sub-paragraph (b)
        (i) for "section 9(9) of the 1985 Act" there were substituted "regulation 77(8) of those Regulations", and
        (ii) for "section 9(9A) or (9B) of that Act" there were substituted "regulation 77(9) of those Regulations".

Refusal to issue ballot paper

88 Regulation 77 of the 2008 Regulations (refusal to issue ballot paper) applies for the

purposes of the referendum but as if for "returning officer" there were substituted "counting officer".

Envelopes

89 Regulation 78 of the 2008 Regulations (envelopes) applies for the purposes of the referendum but as if in paragraph (1) for "rule 24 of the elections rules" there were substituted "regulation 17 of the European Union Referendum (Conduct) Regulations 2016".

Sealing up of completed corresponding number lists

90 Regulation 79 of the 2008 Regulations (sealing up of completed corresponding number lists) applies for the purposes of the referendum but as if for "returning officer" (in each place) there were substituted "counting officer".

Delivery of postal ballot papers

91(1) Regulation 80 of the 2008 Regulations (delivery of postal ballot papers) applies for the purposes of the referendum but with the following modifications.

(2) For those purposes paragraph (1) has effect as if
    (a) for "returning officer" there were substituted "counting officer", and
    (b) in sub-paragraph (c), for "rule 26(1) of the elections rules" there were substituted "regulation 19 of the European Union Referendum (Conduct) Regulations 2016."

(3) For the purposes of the referendum paragraph (2) has effect as if for "returning officer" there were substituted "counting officer".

Spoilt postal ballot papers

92 Regulation 81 of the 2008 Regulations (spoilt postal ballot papers) applies for the purposes of the referendum but as if for "returning officer" (in each place) there were substituted "counting officer".

Tendered postal ballot papers

93(1) Regulation 81A of the 2008 Regulations (tendered postal ballot papers) applies for the purposes of the referendum but with the following modifications.

(2) Paragraph (1) has effect for those purposes as if for "rule 40ZA of the elections rules" there were substituted "regulation 39 of the European Union Referendum (Conduct) Regulations 2016".

(3) Paragraph (2) has effect for the purposes of the referendum as if
    (a) for "a parliamentary election" there were substituted "the referendum", and
    (b) for "section 15 of the 1985 Act" there were substituted "regulations under section 4(2) of the European Union Referendum Act 2015".

(4) Paragraph (4) has effect for the purposes of the referendum as if
    (a) in sub-paragraph (a), for "section 7(4A) of the 1985 Act" there were substituted "regulation 74(4) of the European Union Referendum (Conduct) Regulations 2016", and
    (b) in sub-paragraph (b), for the words from "section 9(9)" to the end there were substituted "regulation 77(8) of the European Union Referendum (Conduct) Regulations 2016 but for regulations 74(4) or 77(9) of those Regulations."

(5) Paragraphs (5) to (11) have effect for the purposes of the referendum as if for "Chief Electoral Officer" (in each place) there were substituted "counting officer".

(6)   Paragraph (9) has effect for the purposes of the referendum as if
    (a)   for "rule 40ZA(9) of the elections rules" there were substituted "regulation 39(9) of the European Union Referendum (Conduct) Regulations 2016", and
    (b)   for "rule 40ZA(7) of the elections rules" there were substituted "regulation 39(7) of the European Union Referendum (Conduct) Regulations 2016".

Notice of opening of postal ballot paper envelopes

94(1)   Regulation 82 of the 2008 Regulations (notice of opening of postal ballot paper envelopes) applies for the purposes of the referendum but with the following modifications.

(2)   Paragraph (1) has effect for those purposes as if
    (a)   for "returning officer" there were substituted "counting officer", and
    (b)   for "candidate" there were substituted "referendum agent".

(3)   Paragraph (2) has effect for the purposes of the referendum as if for "candidate" there were substituted "referendum agent".

Postal ballot boxes and receptacles

95   Regulation 83 of the 2008 Regulations (postal ballot boxes and receptacles) applies for the purposes of the referendum but as if
    (a)   for "returning officer" (in each place) there were substituted "counting officer",
    (b)   in paragraph (2), for the words from "constituency" to the end there were substituted "voting area", and
    (c)   in paragraph (4), after "box" there were inserted "(if it has a lock)".

Receipt of covering envelope

96   Regulation 84 of the 2008 Regulations (receipt of covering envelope) applies for the purposes of the referendum but as if for "returning officer" there were substituted "counting officer".

Opening of postal voters' ballot box

97   Regulation 85 of the 2008 Regulations (opening of postal voters' ballot box) applies for the purposes of the referendum but as if
    (a)   for "returning officer" (in both places) there were substituted "counting officer", and
    (b)   in paragraph (3), for "rule 45 of the elections rules" there were substituted "regulation 46 of the European Union Referendum (Conduct) Regulations 2016".

Opening of covering envelopes

98   Regulation 86 of the 2008 Regulations (opening of covering envelopes) applies for the purposes of the referendum but as if
    (a)   for "returning officer" (in each place) there were substituted "counting officer", and
    (b)   after paragraph (4) there were inserted
        "(5) Where an envelope opened in accordance with paragraph (1) contains a declaration of identity (whether separate or not), the counting officer must place a mark in the marked copy of the postal voters list or the proxy postal voters list in a place corresponding to the number of the elector to denote that a postal vote has been returned.
        (6) A mark made under paragraph (5) must be distinguishable from and must not obscure the mark made under regulation 76.

(7) As soon as practicable after the last covering envelope has been opened, the counting officer must make up into a packet the copy of the postal voters list and the proxy postal voters list that has been marked in accordance with paragraph (5) and must seal the packet."

Procedure in relation to declarations of identity

99   Regulation 87 of the 2008 Regulations (procedure in relation to declarations of identity) applies for the purposes of the referendum but as if

    (a)   for "returning officer" (in each place) there were substituted "counting officer", and

    (b)   in paragraph (1)(b) for "rule 45(2)(b) and (2A) of the elections rules" there were substituted "regulation 46(5)(b) and (6) of the European Union Referendum (Conduct) Regulations 2016".

Opening of ballot paper envelopes

100   Regulation 88 of the 2008 Regulations (opening of ballot paper envelopes) applies for the purposes of the referendum but as if, in paragraph (1), for "returning officer" there were substituted "counting officer".

Sealing of receptacles

101   Regulation 89 of the 2008 Regulations (sealing of receptacles) applies for the purposes of the referendum but as if for "returning officer" there were substituted "counting officer".

Forwarding of documents

102   Regulation 91 of the 2008 Regulations (forwarding of documents) applies for the purposes of the referendum but as if

    (a)   for "returning officer" (in each place) there were substituted "counting officer",

    (b)   the following were treated as substituted for paragraph (1)

"(1) The Chief Electoral Officer for Northern Ireland shall retain together with the documents mentioned in regulation 56 of the European Union Referendum (Conduct) Regulations 2016

    (a)   any packets referred to in regulation 79, 81(5), 81A(11) and 89, endorsing on each packet a description of its contents, the date of the referendum and the name of the voting area,

    (b)   the list of spoilt ballot papers and the list of tendered ballot papers, and

    (c)   a completed statement in Form N.",

    (c)   in paragraph (2), for the words from "and endorse" to the end there were substituted ", endorse the packet as mentioned in paragraph (1)(a) and retain the packet",

    (d)   the following were treated as substituted for paragraph (3)

"(3) Regulations 57 and 58 of the European Union Referendum (Conduct) Regulations 2016 shall apply to any packet or document retained under this regulation.", and

    (e)   in paragraph (4) for "(1)(b)" there were substituted "(1)(c)".

Restriction on supply etc of full register

103   Regulation 94(1) of the 2008 Regulations (restrictions on supply etc of full register) has effect for the purposes of the referendum as if

    (a)   after sub-paragraph (b) there were inserted

"(ba)   the Chief Counting Officer;

(bb) any deputy of the Chief Counting Officer;", and

(b) the references in sub-paragraph (c) to "any such officer" were treated as references to "a person mentioned in sub-paragraph (a), (b), (ba) or (bb)".

Interpretation of Part 7

104 Regulation 115 of the 2008 Regulations (interpretation of Part 7) has effect for the purposes of the referendum as if, in paragraph (1), for "rule 57(1A) of the elections rules" there were substituted "regulation 56(1)(b) of the European Union Referendum (Conduct) Regulations 2016".

Supply of marked registers and lists after an election

105(1) Regulation 116 of the 2008 Regulations (supply of marked registers and lists) applies for the purposes of the referendum but with the following modifications.

(2) Paragraph (1) has effect for those purposes as if
  (a) for the words from "regulation 99" to "local government election" there were substituted "regulations 99, 105, 107 or 111, with copies of the full register", and
  (b) at the end there were treated as inserted
  "The reference to a person entitled to be supplied in accordance with regulation 105 with copies of the full register does not include a person mentioned in regulation 105(1)(b)."

(3) Paragraph (2) has effect for the purposes of the referendum as if
  (a) for the words from "regulation 102" to "particular election" there were substituted "regulation 105(1)(a) or (c) applies before the referendum", and
  (b) for "that election" there were substituted "the referendum".

(4) Paragraph (6)(b) has effect for the purposes of the referendum as if for "regulations 99, 102, 104, 105, 106, 107 or 111" there were substituted "regulations 99, 105, 107 or 111".

Inspection of documents open to public inspection

106 Regulation 117 of the 2008 Regulations (inspection of documents) applies for the purposes of the referendum but as if in paragraph (1)(b) for "an election" there were substituted "the referendum".

Conditions on use, supply and disclosure of documents open to public inspection

107 Regulation 118 of the 2008 Regulations (conditions on the use, supply and disclosure of documents) applies for the purposes of the referendum but as if, in paragraph (2)
  (a) the word "either" were omitted, and
  (b) at the end, there was inserted "or any purpose in connection with the referendum".

Form N: statement as to postal ballot papers

108 Form N in Schedule 3 of the 2008 Regulations (statement as to postal ballot papers) applies for the purposes of the referendum but as if
  (a) for the heading "REPRESENTATION OF THE PEOPLE ACTS PARLIAMENTARY ELECTION" there were substituted "REFERENDUM ON THE UNITED KINGDOM'S MEMBERSHIP OF THE EUROPEAN UNION",
  (b) for "constituency" there were substituted "voting area", and
  (c) for "Returning Officer" (in each place) there were substituted "Counting Officer".

Part 3
Other Regulations
Control of advertisements

109 The Town and Country Planning (Control of Advertisements) Regulations 1992 apply in relation to the display on any site in Wales of an advertisement relating specifically to the referendum as they apply in relation to the display of an advertisement relating specifically to a pending parliamentary election.

110 The Town and Country Planning (Control of Advertisements) (Scotland) Regulations 1984 apply in relation to the display on any site in Scotland of an advertisement relating specifically to the referendum as they apply in relation to the display of an advertisement relating specifically to a pending parliamentary election.

111 The Planning (Control of Advertisements) Regulations (Northern Ireland) 2015 apply in relation to the display on any site in Northern Ireland of an advertisement relating specifically to the referendum as they apply in relation to the display of an advertisement relating specifically to a pending parliamentary election.

Right of audience and right to conduct litigation

112 Article 6 of the European Parliamentary Elections (Combined Region and Campaign Expenditure) (United Kingdom and Gibraltar) Order 2004 applies for the purposes of the referendum but as if for "European Parliamentary elections in the combined region" (in each place) there were substituted "the referendum under section 1 of the European Union Referendum Act 2015 in the South West and Gibraltar Region within the meaning of that Act (see paragraph 5 of Schedule 3 to that Act)".

Provision of information regarding proxies

113 Regulation 2 of the Representation of the People (Provision of Information Regarding Proxies) Regulations 2013 has effect for the purposes of the referendum as if
   (a) the following paragraph were treated as substituted for paragraph (1)
      "(1) A registration officer in Great Britain may require a registration officer in Great Britain or Northern Ireland to provide information as soon as reasonably practicable about
         (a) whether the person, whom an elector wishes to be appointed as their proxy under paragraph 6(7) or (8) of Schedule 4 to the Representation of the People Act 2000, has or will have an entry in a relevant register maintained by that officer under section 9(1) of the Representation of the People Act 1983; or
         (b) whether the person, whom the principal wishes to be appointed as their proxy under regulation 64 of the European Union Referendum (Conduct) Regulations 2016, has or will have an entry in a relevant register maintained by that officer.", and
   (b) the following paragraphs were treated as substituted for paragraph (2)
      "(2) In paragraph (1)(a) "relevant register" means a register which relates to elections of the same kind as those to which the proxy appointment relates.
      (3) In paragraph (1)(b) "relevant register" means
         (a) a register of parliamentary electors, or
         (b) in relation to a peer
            (i) a register of local government electors in Great Britain, or
            (ii) a register of local electors in Northern Ireland, or
            (iii) a register of peers maintained under section 3 of the

Representation of the People Act 1985 (peers resident outside the United Kingdom)."

Persons convicted of corrupt or illegal practices: Gibraltar

114   Regulation 107 of the European Parliamentary Elections Regulations 2004 applies for the purposes of the referendum but as if

(a)   references to an illegal practice included an illegal practice under any provision of Gibraltar conduct law,

(b)   references to a corrupt practice included a corrupt practice under any such provision,

(c)   in paragraph (1) for "paragraph (2)" there were substituted "paragraphs (1A) and (2)",

(d)   after that paragraph there were inserted

"(1A)   Paragraph (1) does not apply in relation to an act or omission that is an illegal practice by reason of being a contravention of Gibraltar conduct law (within the meaning of section 11(1) of the European Union Referendum Act 2015) in respect of which the Gibraltar court has made an order under any provision of Gibraltar conduct law making provision corresponding to regulation 108.",

(e)   the reference in paragraph (2) to regulation 23 included any provision of Gibraltar conduct law making provision corresponding to that regulation, and

(f)   the reference in that paragraph to regulation 24 included any provision of Gibraltar conduct law making provision corresponding to that regulation.

115   Regulation 112 of the European Parliamentary Elections Regulations 2004 applies for the purposes of the referendum.

SCHEDULE 4
Forms

Regulation 83

Form 1 – Form of ballot paper
Front of ballot paper

Referendum on the United Kingdom's membership of the European Union
Vote only once by putting a cross **X** in the box next to your choice
Should the United Kingdom remain a member of the European Union or leave the European Union?
Remain a member of the European Union
Leave the European Union

Back of ballot paper

Number

[Other unique identifying mark]

Referendum on the United Kingdom's membership of the European Union

[insert voting area]

Other forms not reproduced

European Union Referendum (Counting Officers' and Regional Counting Officers' Charges) Regulations 2016
2016 No 419

Made 22nd March 2016

1 Citation, commencement and extent

(1)   These Regulations may be cited as the European Union Referendum (Counting Officers' and Regional Counting Officers' Charges) Regulations 2016 and come into force on the day after the day on which they are made.

(2)   These Regulations extend to the whole of the United Kingdom and to Gibraltar.

2 Counting officers: overall maximum recoverable amount

The overall maximum recoverable amount in respect of a counting officer for a voting area is the amount given in the entry in column 4 of the table in Schedule 1 that corresponds to that voting area.

3 Counting officers: maximum recoverable amount for specified services

(1)   In respect of the services specified in paragraph (2), the maximum amount recoverable by a counting officer for a voting area is the amount given in the entry in column 2 of the table in Schedule 1 that corresponds to that voting area.

(2)   The specified services are
    (a)   making arrangements for the referendum;
    (b)   discharging the counting officer's duties at the referendum;
    (c)   conducting the referendum.

(3)   This regulation does not apply to the counting officer for the Northern Ireland voting area.

4 Counting officers: maximum recoverable amount for specified expenses

(1)   In respect of the expenses specified in paragraph (2), the maximum amount recoverable by a counting officer for a voting area is the amount given in the entry in column 3 of the table in Schedule 1 that corresponds to that voting area.

(2)   The specified expenses are those incurred in
    (a)   the appointment and payment of persons to assist the counting officer;
    (b)   travel and overnight subsistence for the counting officer and any person appointed to assist the counting officer;
    (c)   printing or otherwise producing the ballot papers;

    (d)   printing, or otherwise producing, or buying the postal vote stationery;

    (e)   printing, or otherwise producing, and arranging for the delivery of poll cards;

    (f) printing, or otherwise producing, and where appropriate publishing, notices and any other documents required by any enactment for or in connection with the referendum;

    (g)   renting, heating, lighting, cleaning, adapting or restoring any building or room;

    (h)   providing and transporting equipment;

    (i) providing information and communications technology equipment and software, and associated costs;

    (j) providing for the safekeeping and security of ballot papers (including, where necessary, the secure storage of ballot boxes) and any verification documents kept by the counting officer;

    (k)   conducting the verification and the count;

    (l) providing and receiving training;

    (m)   providing stationery and meeting postage, telephone, printing, translation and banking costs and the costs of other miscellaneous items.

5 Regional Counting Officers: overall maximum recoverable amount

The overall maximum recoverable amount in respect of a Regional Counting Officer appointed for a region is the amount given in the entry in column 4 of the table in Schedule 2 that corresponds to that region.

6 Regional Counting Officers: maximum recoverable amount for specified services

(1)   In respect of the services specified in paragraph (2), the maximum amount recoverable by a Regional Counting Officer appointed for a region is the amount given in the entry in column 2 of the table in Schedule 2 that corresponds to that region.

(2)   The specified services are

    (a)   making arrangements for the referendum;

    (b)   discharging the Regional Counting Officer's duties at the referendum.

7 Regional Counting Officers: maximum recoverable amount for specified expenses

(1)   In respect of the expenses specified in paragraph (2), the maximum amount recoverable by a Regional Counting Officer appointed for a region is the amount given in the entry in column 3 of the table in Schedule 2 that corresponds to that region.

(2)   The specified expenses are those incurred in

    (a)   the appointment and payment of persons to assist the Regional Counting Officer;

    (b)   travel and overnight subsistence for the Regional Counting Officer and any person appointed to assist the Regional Counting Officer;

    (c)   printing or otherwise producing the ballot papers;

    (d)   printing, or otherwise producing, and where appropriate publishing, notices and any other documents required by any enactment for or in connection with the referendum;

    (e)   renting, heating, lighting, cleaning, adapting or restoring any building or room;

    (f) providing and transporting equipment;

    (g)   providing security;

    (h)   providing and receiving training;

    (i) collating the results of the referendum in voting areas within the region and submitting the regional result to the Chief Counting Officer;

    (j) providing stationery and meeting postage, telephone, printing, translation and banking costs and the costs of other miscellaneous items.

European Union Referendum (Counting Officers' and
Regional Counting Officers' Charges) Regulations 2016

SCHEDULE 1

MAXIMUM RECOVERABLE AMOUNTS FOR COUNTING OFFICERS

Regulations 2, 3 and 4

1	2	3	4
Voting area	Maximum recoverable amount for specified services	Maximum recoverable amount for specified expenses	Overall maximum recoverable amount
Aberdeen, City of	£7,266	£588,081	£595,347
Aberdeenshire	£8,966	£626,848	£635,814
Adur	£2,500	£93,707	£96,207
Allerdale	£3,404	£172,843	£176,247
Amber Valley	£4,293	£207,454	£211,747
Angus	£4,040	£280,744	£284,784
Argyll and Bule	£3,111	£245,689	£248,800
Arun	£5,349	£190,752	£196,101
Ashfield	£4,264	£191,736	£196,000
Ashford	£4,083	£206,292	£210,375
Aylesbury Vale	£6,077	£260,318	£266,395
8abergh	£3,219	£129,279	£132,498
Barking and Dagenham	£5,255	£245,844	£251,099
Barnet	£9,893	£530,871	£540,764
Bamsley	£7,923	£397,391	£405,314
Barrow-in-Furness	£2,500	£98,171	£100,671
Basildon	£5,944	£206,507	£212,451
Basingstoke and Deane	£5,866	£228,279	£234,145
Bassetlaw	£3,945	£203,676	£207,621
Bath and North East Somerset	£6,105	£286,148	£292,253
Bedford	£5,579	£420,399	£425,978
Bexley	£7,797	£398,829	£406,626
Binningham	£32,382	£1,334,604	£1,366,986
Blaby	£3,397	£132,383	£135,780
Blackburn with Darwen	£4,568	£199,234	£203,802
Blackpool	£4,601	£220,069	£224,670
Blaenau Gwent	£2,500	£115,686	£118,186
Bolsover	£2,668	£123,737	£126,405
Bolton	£8,93\	£373,404	£382,335
Boston	£2,500	£86,252	£88,752

1	2	3	4
Voting area	*Maximum recoverable amount for specified services*	*Maximum recoverable amount for specified expenses*	*Overall maximum recoverable amount*
Bournemouth	£6,164	£263,291	£269,455
Bracknell Forest	£3,863	£137,965	£141,828
Bradford	£15,411	£709,909	£725,320
Braintree	£5,129	£212,796	£217,925
Breckland	£4,613	£251,160	£255,773
Brent	£8,603	£412,151	£420,754
Brentwood	£2,659	£138,850	£141,509
Bridgend	£4,805	£211,426	£216,231
Brighton and Hove	£8,642	£403,241	£411,883
Bristol, City of	£14,199	£606,626	£620,825
Broadland	£4,476	£185,108	£189,584
Bromley	£10,652	£570,650	£581,302
Bromsgrove	£3,396	£145,604	£149,000
Broxboume	£3,122	£110,613	£113,735
Broxtowe	£3,803	£169,760	£173,563
Burnley	£2,983	£152,349	£155,332
Bury	£6,354	£271,065	£277,419
Caerphilly	£5,941	£248,464	£254,405
Calderda1e	£6,739	£282,972	£289,711
Cambridge	£3,442	£126,558	£130,000
Camden	£6,149	£316,008	£322,157
Cannock Chase	£3,467	£145,127	£148,594
Canterbury	£4,743	£186,986	£191,729
Cardiff	£\0,751	£556,579	£567,330
Carlisle	£3,632	£202,000	£205,632
Cannarthenshire	£6,321	£346,094	£352,415
Castle Point	£3,197	£102,339	£105,536
Central Bedfordshire	£9,306	£390,079	£399,385
Cerooigion	£2,500	£114,988	£117,488
Chamwood	£6,018	£226,568	£232,586
Chelmsford	£6,021	£205,750	£211,771
Cheltenham	£4,047	£177,300	£181,347
Cherwell	£4,910	£213,978	£218,888
Cheshire East	£12,775	£686,022	£698,797
Cheshire West and Chester	£12,114	£547,562	£559,676

*European Union Referendum (Counting Officers' and
Regional Counting Officers' Charges) Regulations 2016*

1	2	3	4
Voting area	Maximum recoverable amount for specified services	Maximum recoverable amount for specified expenses	Overall maximum recoverable amount
Chesterfield	£3,725	£166,587	£170,312
Chichester	£4,061	£179,630	£183,691
Chiltern	£3,234	£99,247	£\02,481
Chorley	£3,852	£187,877	£191,729
Christchurch	£2,500	£86,949	£89,449
City of London	£2,500	£21,754	£24,254
C1ackmannanshire	£2,500	£121,612	£124,112
Colchester	£5,661	£250,260	£255,921
Conwy	£4,196	£211,560	£215,756
Copeland	£2,502	£133,354	£135,856
Corby	£2,500	£96,174	£98,674
Cornwall	£18,553	£823,925	£842,478
Cotswo1d	£3,107	£172,743	£175,850
County Durham	£17,813	£718,414	£736,227
Coventry	£9,907	£476,375	£486,282
Craven	£2,500	£112,365	£114,865
Crawley	£3,333	£120,712	£124,045
Croydon	£11,057	£464,099	£475,156
Dacorum	£4,910	£198,472	£203,382
Darlington	£3,535	£165,122	£168,657
Dartford	£3,404	£152,737	£156,141
Daventry	£2,752	£155,088	£157,840
Denbyshire	£3,494	£171,894	£175,388
Derby	£8,030	£293,282	£301,312
Derbyshire Dales	£2,590	£167,292	£169,882
Doncaster	£9,972	£377,358	£387,330
Dover	£3,959	£176,892	£180,851
Dudley	£11,296	£420,800	£432,096
Dumfries and Galloway	£5,346	£371,942	£377,288
Dundee City	£4,853	£307,071	£311,924
Ealing	£9,872	£572,542	£582,414
East Ayrshire	£4,243	£204,665	£208,908
East Cambridgeshire	£2,860	£137,085	£139,945
East Devon	£5,069	£197,924	£202,993
East Dorset	£3,297	£126,294	£129,591

1	2	3	4
Voting area	Maximum recoverable amount for specified services	Maximum recoverable amount for specified expenses	Overall maximum recoverable amount
East Dunbartonshire	£3,865	£218,010	£221,875
East Hampshire	£4,076	£185,474	£189,550
East Hertfordshire	£4,764	£156,213	£160,977
East Lindsey	£4,857	£246,540	£251,397
East Lothian	£3,582	£219,010	£222,592
East Northamptonshire	£3,050	£159,694	£162,744
East Renfrewshire	£3,192	£236,890	£240,082
East Riding of Yorkshire	£12,007	£489,601	£501,608
East Staffordshire	£3,840	£180,576	£184,416
Eastbourne	£3,236	£143,668	£146,904
Eastleigh	£4,439	£202,014	£206,453
Eden	£2,500	£124,535	£127,035
Edinburgh, City of	£15,492	£1,372,546	£1,388,038
Elmbridge	£4,423	£222,863	£227,286
Enfield	£9,085	£431,776	£440,861
Epping Forest	£4,607	£216,515	£221,122
Epsom and Ewell	£2,581	£156,815	£159,396
Erewash	£3,996	£185,883	£189,879
Exeter	£3,833	£159,419	£163,252
Falkirk	£5,437	£282,985	£288,422
Fareham	£4,113	£131,117	£135,230
Fenland	£3,266	£178,026	£181,292
Fife	£12,663	£646,500	£659,163
Flintshire	£5,319	£241,779	£247,098
Forest Heath	£2,500	£88,419	£90,919
Forest of Dean	£3,074	£135,784	£138,858
Fylde	£2,806	£131,923	£134,729
Gateshead	£6,657	£336,322	£342,979
Gedling	£4,049	£181,600	£185,649
Gibraltar	£2,500	£56,005	£58,505
Glasgow City	£21,111	£1,558,097	£1,579,208
Gloucester	£4,078	£140,792	£144,870
Gosport	£2,873	£112,713	£115,586
Gravesham	£3,322	£163,089	£166,411
Great Yarmouth	£3,299	£123,201	£126,500

1	2	3	4
Voting area	Maximum recoverable amount for specified services	Maximum recoverable amount for specified expenses	Overall maximum recoverable amount
Greenwich	£7,565	£418,127	£425,692
Guildford	£4,646	£189,086	£193,732
Gwynedd	£3,788	£177,141	£180,929
Hackncy	£7,025	£355,788	£362,813
Halton	£4,390	£144,578	£148,968
Hambleton	£3,174	£131,530	£134,704
Hammersmith and Fulham	£4,980	£298,850	£303,830
Harborough	£2,994	£143,234	£146,228
Haringey	£6,682	£307,318	£314,000
Harlow	£2,713	£85,015	£87,728
Harrogate	£5,472	£252,792	£258,264
Harrow	£7,602	£419,400	£427,002
Hart	£3,193	£135,265	£138,458
Hartlepool	£3,221	£124,418	£127,639
Hastings	£2,712	£105,899	£108,611
Havant	£4,350	£141,327	£145,677
Havering	£8,348	£319,383	£327,731
Herefordshire, County of	£6,275	£319,280	£325,555
Hertsmere	£3,289	£172,743	£176,032
High Peak	£3,362	£199,037	£202,399
Highland	£8,131	£461,187	£469,318
Hillingdon	£8,684	£335,735	£344,419
Hinckley and Bosworth	£3,944	£142,747	£146,691
Horsham	£4,725	£231,452	£236,177
Hounslow	£7,519	£390,522	£398,041
Huntingdonshire	£5,853	£234,457	£240,310
Hyndburn	£2,825	£103,507	£106,332
Inverclyde	£2,703	£171,274	£173,977
Ipswich	£4,137	£206,139	£210,276
Isle of Anglesey	£2,500	£134,222	£136,722
Isle of Wight	£4,985	£155,720	£160,705
Isles of Scilly	£2,500	£8,535	£11,035
Islington	£6,351	£289,455	£295,806
Kensington and Chelsea	£3,622	£220,638	£224,260
Kettering	£3,221	£184,435	£187,656

1	*2*	*3*	*4*
Voting area	Maximum recoverable amount for specified services	Maximum recoverable amount for specified expenses	Overall maximum recoverable amount
King's Lynn and West Norfolk	£5,231	£162,850	£168,081
Kingston upon Hull, City of	£8,291	£288,870	£297,161
Kingston upon Thames	£4,925	£347,880	£352,805
Kirklees	£13,925	£561,324	£575,249
Knowsley	£5,186	£218,664	£223,850
Lambeth	£8,910	£384,130	£393,040
Lancaster	£4,547	£180,189	£184,736
Leeds	£24,303	£1,006,440	£1,030,743
Leicester	£9,907	£418,087	£427,994
Lewes	£3,345	£144,084	£147,429
Lewisham	£7,909	£371,360	£379,269
Lichfield	£3,666	£193,153	£196,819
Lincoln	£2,727	£127,693	£130,420
Liverpool	£14,351	£606,126	£620,477
Luton	£5,843	£262,422	£268,265
Maidstone	£5,126	£249,839	£254,965
Maldon	£2,500	£82,633	£85,133
Malvern Hills	£2,762	£108,402	£111,164
Manchester	£16,308	£984,481	£1,000,789
Mansfield	£3,496	£208,307	£211,803
Medway	£8,599	£477,482	£486,081
Melton	£2,500	£96,838	£99,338
Mendip	£3,769	£189,471	£193,240
Merthyr Tydfil	£2,500	£94,460	£96,960
Merton	£6,111	£310,501	£316,612
Mid Devon	£2,732	£190,248	£192,980
Mid Suffolk	£3,587	£142,569	£146,156
Mid Sussex	£4,925	£167,809	£172,734
Middlesbrough	£4,264	£175,830	£180,094
Midlothian	£3,073	£202,119	£205,192
Milton Keynes	£8,031	£283,876	£291,907
Mole Valley	£3,054	£173,207	£176,261
Monmouthshire	£3,228	£168,487	£171,715
Moray	£3,276	£165,282	£168,558

European Union Referendum (Counting Officers' and Regional Counting Officers' Charges) Regulations 2016

1	2	3	4
Voting area	Maximum recoverable amount for specified services	Maximum recoverable amount for specified expenses	Overall maximum recoverable amount
Na h-Eileanan Siar	£2,500	£79,839	£82,339
Neath Port Talbot	£4,865	£263,946	£268,811
New Forest	£6,509	£236,019	£242,528
Newark and Sherwood	£3,909	£189,806	£193,715
Newcastle upon Tyne	£8,528	£482,189	£490,717
Neweastle-under-Lyme	£4,219	£167,368	£171,587
Newham	£8,021	£369,799	£377,820
Newport	£4,767	£219,142	£223,909
North Ayrshire	£4,847	£280,668	£285,515
North Devon	£3,454	£153,874	£157,328
North Dorset	£2,500	£132,149	£134,649
North East Derbyshire	£3,641	£188,574	£192,215
North East Lincolnshire	£5,314	£228,449	£233,763
North Hertfordshire	£4,504	£170,405	£174,909
North Kesteven	£3,918	£173,015	£176,933
North Lanarkshire	£11,807	£768,440	£780,247
North Lincolnshire	£5,665	£200,396	£206,061
North Norfolk	£3,820	£216,412	£220,232
North Somerset	£7,152	£301,447	£308,599
North Tyneside	£7,132	£303,796	£310,928
North Warwickshire	£2,500	£97,635	£100,135
North West Leicestershire	£3,365	£160,367	£163,732
Northampton	£6,501	£288,858	£295,359
Northern Ireland	£3,292,686	£3,292,686	£3,292,686
Northumberland	£10,985	£476,009	£486,994
Norwich	£4,404	£160,266	£164,670
Nottingham	£8,848	£440,333	£449,181
Nuneaton and Bedworth	£4,274	£153,349	£157,623
Oadby and Wigston	£2,500	£79,654	£82,154
Oldham	£7,260	£243,984	£251,244
Orkney Islands	£2,500	£57,013	£59,513
Oxford	£4,199	£161,211	£165,410
Pembrokeshire	£4,119	£225,816	£229,935
Pendle	£2,969	£131,513	£134,482
Perth and Kinross	£5,064	£347,952	£353,016

1	2	3	4
Voting area	*Maximum recoverable amount for specified services*	*Maximum recoverable amount for specified expenses*	*Overall maximum recoverable amount*
Peterborough	£5,574	£316,496	£322,070
Plymouth	£8,352	£414,745	£423,097
Poole	£5,112	£235,604	£240,716
Portsmouth	£6,374	£188,684	£195,058
Powys	£4,683	£220,384	£225,067
Preston	£4,281	£187,283	£191,564
Purbeck	£2,500	£90,346	£92,846
Reading	£4,536	£266,893	£271,429
Redbridge	£8,403	£355,491	£363,894
Redcar and Cleveland	£4,740	£212,262	£217,002
Redditch	£2,808	£117,153	£119,961
Reigate and Banstead	£4,715	£205,949	£210,664
Renfrewshire	£5,803	£374,197	£380,000
Rhondda Cynon Taff	£7,893	£321,500	£329,393
Ribble Valley	£2,500	£119,738	£122,238
Richmond upon Thames	£5,964	£317,658	£323,622
Richmondshire	£2,500	£96,066	£98,566
Rochdale	£7,013	£264,165	£271,178
Rochford	£3,041	£109,043	£112,084
Rossendale	£2,500	£98,247	£100,747
Rother	£3,301	£145,872	£149,173
Rotherham	£9,035	£479,355	£488,390
Rugby	£3,359	£157,081	£160,440
Runnymede	£2,618	£126,541	£129,159
RushclifTe	£3,967	£221,876	£225,843
Rushmoor	£2,948	£161,811	£164,759
Rutland	£2,500	£68,997	£71,497
Ryedale	£2,500	£113,854	£116,354
Salford	£7,677	£396,095	£403,772
Sandwell	£10,163	£455,639	£465,802
Scarborough	£3,772	£167,109	£170,881
Scottish Borders	£4,028	£267,710	£271,738
Sedgemoor	£4,102	£169,840	£173,942
Sefton	£9,409	£390,300	£399,709
Selby	£2,978	£115,766	£118,744

European Union Referendum (Counting Officers' and
Regional Counting Officers' Charges) Regulations 2016

1	2	3	4
Voting area	Maximum recoverable amount for specified services	Maximum recoverable amount for specified expenses	Overall maximum recoverable amount
Sevenoaks	£4,047	£164,136	£168,183
Sheffield	£18,036	£621,464	£639,500
Shepway	£3,657	£161,577	£165,234
Shetland Islands	£2,500	£52,208	£54,708
Shropshire	£10,853	£500,982	£511,835
Slough	£3,792	£184,818	£188,610
Solihull	£7,258	£290,518	£297,776
South Ayrshire	£4,052	£246,760	£250,812
South Bucks	£2,500	£99,731	£102,231
South Cambridgeshire	£5,194	£260,354	£265,548
South Derbyshire	£3,378	£126,585	£129,963
South Gloucestershire	£9,576	£393,621	£403,197
South Hams	£3,104	£134,211	£137,315
South Holland	£3,002	£121,643	£124,645
South Kesteven	£4,793	£196,136	£200,929
South Lakeland	£3,738	£159,283	£163,021
South Lanarkshire	£11,515	£654,832	£666,347
South Norfolk	£4,650	£225,143	£229,793
South Northamptonshire	£3,239	£130,036	£133,275
South Oxfordshire	£4,711	£175,897	£180,608
South Ribble	£3,854	£144,204	£148,058
South Somerset	£5,572	£268,648	£274,220
South Staffordshire	£3,932	£159,498	£163,430
South Tyneside	£5,406	£316,390	£321,796
Southampton	£6,994	£254,724	£261,718
Southend-on-Sea	£5,806	£241,376	£247,182
Southwark	£8,833	£397,501	£406,334
Spelthorne	£3,320	£145,022	£148,342
St. Albans	£4,782	£187,494	£192,276
St. Edmundsbury	£3,626	£175,613	£179,239
St. Helens	£6,168	£263,487	£269,655
Stafford	£4,507	£246,257	£250,764
Staffordshire Moorlands	£3,696	£204,110	£207,806
Stevenage	£2,816	£90,000	£92,816
Stirling	£3,002	£203,701	£206,703

1	2	3	4
Voting area	Maximum recoverable amount for specified services	Maximum recoverable amount for specified expenses	Overall maximum recoverable amount
Stockport	£9,999	£511,703	£521,702
Stockton-on-Tees	£6,507	£305,088	£311,595
Stoke-on-Trent	£8,502	£292,664	£301,166
Stratford-on-Avon	£4,447	£229,006	£233,453
Stroud	£4,302	£159,848	£164,150
Suffolk Coastal	£4,437	£182,516	£186,953
Sunderland	£9,716	£514,363	£524,079
Surrey Heath	£2,951	£152,078	£155,029
Sutton	£6,401	£284,959	£291,360
Swale	£4,530	£162,700	£167,230
Swansea	£7,885	£307,798	£315,683
Swindon	£7,011	£312,979	£319,990
Tameside	£7,758	£385,341	£393,099
Tamworth	£2,678	£138,003	£140,681
Tandridge	£2,852	£105,208	£108,060
Taunton Deane	£3,696	£162,381	£166,077
Teignbridge	£4,700	£182,929	£187,629
Telford and Wrekin	£5,610	£227,839	£233,449
Tendring	£5,138	£206,269	£211,407
Test Valley	£4,286	£186,343	£190,629
Tewkesbury	£3,107	£109,998	£113,105
Thanet	£4,581	£189,294	£193,875
Three Rivers	£3,123	£110,948	£114,071
Thurrock	£5,038	£212,202	£217,240
Tonbridge and Malling	£4,228	£161,518	£165,746
Torbay	£4,630	£204,164	£208,794
Torfaen	£3,132	£125,937	£129,069
Torridge	£2,500	£125,306	£127,806
Tower Hamlets	£7,142	£398,719	£405,861
Trafford	£7,525	£487,127	£494,652
Tunbridge Wells	£3,602	£145,442	£149,044
Uttlesford	£2,902	£160,383	£163,285
Vale of Glamorgan	£4,296	£241,168	£245,464
Vale of White Horse	£4,267	£154,022	£158,289
Wakefield	£11,203	£522,310	£533,513

European Union Referendum (Counting Officers' and
Regional Counting Officers' Charges) Regulations 2016

1	2	3	4
Voting area	Maximum recoverable amount for specified services	Maximum recoverable amount for specified expenses	Overall maximum recoverable amount
Walsall	£8,826	£456,037	£464,863
Waltham Forest	£7,358	£419,318	£426,676
Wandsworth	£9,520	£473,591	£483,111
Warrington	£7,205	£318,520	£325,725
Warwick	£4,623	£211,516	£216,139
Watford	£2,997	£134,892	£137,889
Waveney	£4,139	£155,384	£159,523
Waverley	£4,158	£145,126	£149,284
Wealden	£5,499	£274,532	£280,031
Wellingborough	£2,500	£98,543	£101,043
Welwyn Hatfield	£3,461	£121,778	£125,239
West Berkshire	£5,398	£234,236	£239,634
West Devon	£2,500	£108,652	£111,152
West Dorset	£3,674	£149,635	£153,309
West Dunbartonshire	£3,147	£170,206	£173,353
West Lancashire	£3,905	£177,166	£181,071
West Lindsey	£3,414	£172,291	£175,705
West Lothian	£6,012	£382,142	£388,154
West Oxfordshire	£3,700	£155,759	£159,459
West Somerset	£2,500	£79,128	£81,628
Westminster	£5,270	£272,595	£277,865
Weymouth and Portland	£2,500	£109,756	£112,256
Wigan	£10,770	£375,033	£385,803
Wiltshire	£16,371	£750,370	£766,741
Winchester	£4,044	£184,753	£188,797
Windsor and Maidenhead	£4,572	£162,847	£167,419
Wirral	£11,088	£368,637	£379,725
Woking	£3,190	£149,315	£152,505
Wokingham	£5,558	£216,946	£222,504
Wolverhampton	£8,028	£408,331	£416,359
Worcester	£3,325	£139,265	£142,590
Worthing	£3,662	£138,756	£142,418
Wrexham	£4,523	£193,450	£197,973
Wychavon	£4,332	£192,697	£197,029
Wycombe	£5,624	£198,967	£204,591

1	2	3	4
Voting area	Maximum recoverable amount for specified services	Maximum recoverable amount for specified expenses	Overall maximum recoverable amount
Wyre	£3,875	£178,079	£181,954
Wyre Forest	£3,553	£146,478	£150,031
York	£6,985	£341,230	£348,215

SCHEDULE 2
MAXIMUM RECOVERABLE AMOUNTS FOR REGIONAL COUNTING OFFICERS

Regulations 5, 6 and 7

1	2	3	4
Region	Maximum recoverable amount for specified services	Maximum recoverable amount for specified expenses	Overall maximum recoverable amount
East Midlands	£12,000	£22,383	£34,383
Eastern	£12,000	£22,670	£34,670
London	£12,000	£22,861	£34,861
North East	£12,000	£10,019	£22,019
North West	£12,000	£55,910	£67,910
Scotland	£12,000	£43,794	£55,794
South East	£12,000	£36,520	£48,520
South West and Gibraltar	£12,000	£35,000	£47,000
Wales	£12,000	£38,118	£50,118
West Midlands	£12,000	£22,273	£34,273
Yorkshire and the Humber	£12,000	£10,938	£22,938

Greater London Authority (Declaration of Acceptance of Office) Order 2002 (SI 2002/1044)

Made 10th April 2002

Citation, commencement and application

1(1)   This Order may be cited as the Greater London Authority (Declaration of Acceptance of Office) Order 2002 and shall come into force on 6th May 2002.

(2)   This Order applies to the Greater London Authority only.

Form of declaration of acceptance of office

2   The declaration of acceptance of the office of
- (a)   Mayor;
- (b)   Assembly member; and
- (c)   acting Mayor by virtue of being Deputy mayor,

shall be in the form in the Schedule to this Order or a form to the like effect.

Revocation of the Greater London Authority (Elections and Acceptance of Office) Order 2000

3   The Greater London Authority (Elections and Acceptance of Office) Order 2000 shall be revoked.

Amendment to the Local Authorities (Model Code of Conduct) (England) Order 2001

Not reproduced

SCHEDULE
DECLARATION OF ACCEPTANCE OF OFFICE

I [(**1**)] having assumed the office of [(**2**)] declare that I take that office upon myself, and will duly and faithfully fulfil the duties of it according to the best of my judgement and ability.

* or

I [(**1**)] being for the time being Deputy Mayor of London, declare that I take upon myself the office of acting Mayor of London, and will duly and faithfully fulfil the duties of it according to the best of my judgement and ability.

Signed   Date

This declaration was made and signed before me,

Signed

Proper officer of the Greater London Authority (**3**)

(**1**)   *Insert the name of the person making the declaration.*

(**2**)   *Insert "Mayor of London" or "member of the London Assembly" as appropriate.*

(**3**)   *Where the declaration is made before another person authorised by section 28(3) of the Greater London Authority Act 1999, state the capacity in which that person takes the declaration.*

*delete the appropriate paragraph

Greater London Authority
(Disqualification) Order 2000
(SI 2000/432)

Made 23rd February 2000

Citation, commencement and interpretation

1(1)   This Order may be cited as the Greater London Authority (Disqualification) Order 2000 and shall come into force on the day after the day on which it is made.

(2)   In this Order "the 1999 Act" means the Greater London Authority Act 1999.

Designation of disqualifying offices and appointments

2   There are hereby designated as offices and appointments disqualifying persons from being the Mayor or an Assembly member
    (a)   the office of member of any of the bodies specified in Part I of the Schedule;
    (b)   the offices and appointments specified in Part II of the Schedule.

SCHEDULE
OFFICES AND APPOINTMENTS DISQUALIFYING PERSONS
FROM BEING THE MAYOR OF LONDON OR A MEMBER OF THE LONDON ASSEMBLY

Part I
Bodies whose Members are Disqualified

1 The Audit Commission for Local Authorities and the National Health Service in England and Wales.
2 The Central Arbitration Committee.
3 The Commission for Local Administration in England.
4 The Council of the Advisory, Conciliation and Arbitration Service.
5 The Health and Safety Executive.
6 The Local Government Commission.
7 The London Pension Fund Authority.
7A   The Office for Nuclear Regulation.
8 The Police Complaints Authority.

Part II
Other Disqualifying Offices and Appointments

9 Any office or appointment which would disqualify the holder from membership of the House of Commons by virtue of section 1(1)(a), (b), (c), (d) or (e) of the House of Commons Disqualification Act 1975 (judges, civil servants, members of the armed forces, members of police forces and members of foreign legislatures).
10   Chair of the Health and Safety Executive.
11   Commissioner or Assistant Commissioner of Police of the Metropolis.
12   Commissioner of the City of London Police.
13   *Repealed*
14   Information Commissioner.
15   Director of Passenger Rail Franchising.
16   Greater London returning officer and returning officer at an election of a constituency member of the London Assembly.
17   Her Majesty's Chief Inspector of Constabulary.
18   Her Majesty's Chief Inspector of Fire Services.

19 Member of the Metropolitan Police Authority appointed under paragraph 5 of Schedule 2A to the Police Act 1996 (magistrate members).
20 Member or employee of the National Audit Office.
20A Member of staff of the Office for Nuclear Regulation (within the meaning of Part 3 of the Energy Act 2013).
21 Parking adjudicator appointed under section 73 of the Road Traffic Act 1991.
22 Person appointed under paragraph 2 of Schedule 10 to the 1999 Act (penalty fares appeals adjudicators).
23 Person appointed under paragraph 20 of Schedule 24 to the 1999 Act (persons to hear work place parking levy appeals).
24 Person appointed under regulations under paragraph 12(1) of Schedule 23 to the 1999 Act (road user charging appeals adjudicators).
25 Public -Private Partnership Agreement Arbiter.
26 Office of Rail Regulation.

Greater London Authority Elections Rules 2007
(SI 2007/3541)

17th December 2007

Citation, commencement and revocation

1 (1) These Rules may be cited as the Greater London Authority Elections Rules 2007 and will come into force on 14th January 2008

   (2) The following Rules are revoked—

      (a) the Greater London Authority Elections (No 2) Rules 2000;

      (b) the Greater London Authority Elections (No 2) (Amendment) Rules 2000;

      (c) the Greater London Authority Elections (Amendment) Rules 2001; and

      (d) the Greater London Authority Elections (Amendment) Rules 2004.

Interpretation

2 (1) In these Rules–

     "1983 Act" means the Representation of the People Act 1983;

     "1999 Act" means the Greater London Authority Act 1999;

     "2000 Act" means the Political Parties, Elections and Referendums Act 2000;

     "2002 Act" means the Police Reform Act 2002;

     "2006 Act" means the Electoral Administration Act 2006;

     "appropriate form" means, in relation to a particular rule, the form relevant to that rule set out in the Forms Schedule or where more than one form is so set out, the form indicated by the relevant rule as being appropriate to the particular circumstances;

"Assembly constituency" means a constituency area specified in an order made under section 2(4) of the 1999 Act;

"Authority election" means an election, whether at an ordinary election or in the circumstances mentioned in sections 10, 11 or 16 of the 1999 Act (filling a vacancy in an Assembly constituency or the office of Mayor), held under–

(a)   the Constituency Members Election Rules,

(b)   the London Members Election Rules, or

(c)   the Mayoral Election Rules;

"Combination of Polls Regulations" means the Representation of the People (Combination of Polls) (England and Wales) Regulations 2004;

"Combined Manual Count Rules" means the Rules in Schedule 8;

"constituency member" has the same meaning as in section 2 of the 1999 Act;

"Constituency Members Election Rules" means the Rules in Schedule 1 or 5;

"CRO" (constituency returning officer) means, in relation to an Assembly constituency and an election, the person (or person fitting the description) for the time being designated by an order under section 35(2B) of the 1983 Act;

"elector", except where the context provides otherwise, has the same meaning as in section 202 of the 1983 Act;

"election booklet" has the same meaning as in article 7 of the Greater London Authority Elections (Election Addresses) Order 2003;

"electronic counting system" means such computer hardware, software and other equipment or services as may be provided by the GLRO to the CRO in accordance with the rules applying at the election, for the purpose of counting the number of ballot papers to verify the ballot paper accounts and to count the votes cast on them;

"European Parliamentary election" has the same meaning as in section 27(1) of the Representation of the People Act 1985;

"Forms Schedule" means Schedule 10;

"GLRO" (Greater London returning officer) means the person who is for the time being the proper officer of the Greater London Authority for the purposes of section 35(2C) of the 1983 Act (returning officer at the election of the Mayor and London Members);

"local authority mayoral election" means an election conducted under the Local Authorities (Mayoral Elections) (England and Wales) Regulations 2007;

"London Assembly" has the same meaning as in section 2 of the 1999 Act;

"London members" has the same meaning as in section 2 of the 1999 Act;

"London Members Election Rules" means the Rules in Schedule 2 or 6;

"Manual Count Rules" means the Rules in Schedule 4;

"Mayor" means the Mayor of London.

"mayoral by-election" means an election for the Mayor or London held in the circumstances mentioned in section 16 (filling a vacancy in the office of Mayor) of the 1999 Act;

"mayoral election" means an election for the return of the Mayor, whether at an ordinary election or an election held in the circumstances mentioned in section 16 (filling a vacancy in the office of Mayor) of the 1999 Act;

"Mayoral Election Rules" means the Rules in Schedule 3 or 7;

"Notices Schedule" means the rules in Schedule 9;

"referendum" means a referendum conducted under the Referendum Regulations;

"Referendum Regulations" means the Local Authorities (Conduct of Referendums) (England) Regulations 2007;

"relevant registration officer" means the registration officer within the meaning of subsection (3)(a) of section 44 of the 2006 Act, or appointed by an order made under subsection (3)(b) of that section;

"ward" has the same meaning as in paragraph 7(1) of Schedule 2 to the Local Government Act 1972.

(2) References in these rules–

    (a) to the CRO include references to any person appointed by him under subsection (4) of section 35 (returning officers: local elections in England and Wales) of the 1983 Act, and

    (b) to the GLRO include references to any person appointed by him under that subsection.

(3) Other expressions used both in these Rules and in Part 1 (the Greater London Authority) of the 1999 Act have the same meaning in these Rules as they have in that Part.

Rules for Authority elections

3 (1) Subject to rules 4, 5 and 7, Authority elections shall be conducted in accordance with the rules specified in paragraphs (2) to (4) of this rule.

(2) The Constituency Members Election Rules in Schedule 1 have effect for the purposes of any election of constituency members at an ordinary election, and any election under section 10 (filing a vacancy in an Assembly constituency) of the 1999 Act.

(3) The London Members Election Rules in Schedule 2, with the exception of Part 7, have effect for the purposes of any election of London members; and Part 7 of those rules has effect for the purposes of section 11 (filing a vacancy among the London members) of the 1999 Act.

(4) The Mayoral Election Rules in Schedule 3 have effect for the purposes of any election of the Mayor of London at an ordinary election, and any election under section 16 (filing a vacancy in the office of Mayor) of the 1999 Act.

Modification to the Rules where votes are counted manually

4 Where some or all of the votes cast at a Authority election to which rule 3 applies, are to be counted without the use of an electronic counting system, the Constituency Members Election Rules, the London Members Election Rules and the Mayoral Election Rules have effect, with respect to those votes counted manually, subject to the modifications set out in the Manual Count Rules in Schedule 4.

Rules for Authority elections combined with a relevant election or referendum

5 (1) This rule applies to an Authority election that is taken together with the poll at–

    (a) a parliamentary election, European Parliamentary election or local government election (other than an Authority election), under section 15(1) or (2) of the Representation of the People Act 1985; or

    (b) a local authority mayoral election or referendum in accordance with regulations made under sections 44 and 105, or 45 and 105, of the Local Government Act 2000.

(2) For the purposes of an election to which this rule applies–

    (a) rules 3 and 4 will not apply; and

    (b) subject to rules 6 and 7, the election must be conducted in accordance with the rules specified in paragraphs (3) to (5) of this rule.

(3) The Constituency Members Election Rules in Schedule 5 have effect for the purposes of any election of constituency members of the London Assembly at an ordinary election, and any election under section 10 (filing a vacancy in an Assembly constituency) of the 1999 Act.

(4) The London Members Election Rules in Schedule 6, with the exception of Part 7, have effect for the purposes of any election of London members; and Part 7 of those rules

has effect for the purposes of section 11 (filling a vacancy among the London members) of the 1999 Act.

(5)   The Mayoral Election Rules in Schedule 7 have effect for the purposes of any election of the Mayor of London at an ordinary election, and any election under section 16 (filing a vacancy in the Office of Mayor) of the 1999 Act.

Modifications to the combined Rules where votes are counted manually

6   Where some or all of the votes cast at an Authority election to which rule 5 applies, are to be counted without the use of an electronic counting system, then Constituency Members Election Rules, the London Members Election Rules and the Mayoral Election Rules have effect, with respect to those votes counted manually, subject to the modifications in the Combined Manual Count Rules in Schedule 8.

Modifications to the election timetable at by-elections

7 (1)   For the purposes of a constituency member or mayoral by-election, for the timetable in rule 3 of–
   (a)   the Constituency Members Election Rules in Schedule 1 or 5;
   (b)   the Mayoral Election Rules in Schedule 3 or 7, substitute–

"By-election timetable

Proceedings	Time
Publication of notice of election	Not later than the twenty-fifth day before the day of election.
Delivery of nomination papers	Not later than 4 in the afternoon on the nineteenth day before the day of election.
Delivery of notices of withdrawals of candidature	Not later than 4 in the afternoon on the nineteenth day before the day of election
Publication of statement as to persons nominated	Not later than 4 in the afternoon on the eighteenth day before the day of election.
Notice of poll	Not later than the sixth day before the day of election.
Polling	Between the hours of 7 in the morning and 10 at night on the day of election."

Notices

8   Schedule 9 (requirements for notices for guidance of voters) has effect.

Forms

9   Schedule 10 (forms) has effect.

Returning officers' duties

10 (1)   At an ordinary election, it is the duty of the CROs and the GLRO to co-operate with each other in the discharge of their functions.

(2)   Where a poll is to be taken–
   (a)   for the return of the London members; or
   (b)   for the return of the Mayor,
   it is the duty of CROs to perform any of the functions they are required to perform by the rules applying to those elections, including verifying the ballot papers at the poll (or each poll if both are to be taken) and counting the votes cast in that poll (or each poll, if both are to be taken).

GLRO's power of direction

11 (1)   The GLRO may give to any CRO a direction–

    (a)   as to the manner in which he must discharge any of his functions set out in these Rules; or

    (b)   requiring him to provide the GLRO with any information which the CRO has or is entitled to have in accordance with these rules.

  (2)   It is the duty of each CRO to whom a direction is given under paragraph (1) to discharge his functions in accordance with that direction.

  (3)   Without prejudice to the generality of the preceding provisions of this rule, a GLRO may exercise the power conferred by paragraph (1) to give the directions set out in paragraph (4) subject to the requirements in paragraphs (5) and (6).

  (4)   The GLRO may direct the CRO to–

    (a)   include alternative information in the appropriate form of postal voting statement, in place of the paragraphs beneath the heading "Instructions for voting by post";

    (b)   issue additional information to those entitled to vote by post; or

    (c)   exercise his discretion to include additional information in poll cards.

  (5)   Where the GLRO has decided to direct the CRO in accordance with paragraph (4), he must–

    (a)   supply the alternative or additional information which the CRO is to issue to voters either electronically or in a printed form; and

    (b)   direct the CRO in writing as to how the information is to be used,

by no later than the date of the notice of election.

  (6)   Where the CRO does not discharge the functions specified in regulation 5 (functions at combined polls) of the Combination of Polls Regulations, the GLRO may give a direction under paragraph (4) to the returning officer who does discharge those functions.

  (7)   The alternative or additional information supplied under (5)(a) must–

    (a)   comply with paragraph 4 of the Notices Schedule (as though that information were to be included in a notice);

    (b)   and must relate to–

      (i)   the system of voting at the Authority election;

      (ii)   how many votes a voter has at each Authority election;

      (iii)   the marks to be used, and the manner in which they should be used, in order to ensure that a vote is counted for any candidate.

  (8)   For the purposes of this rule–

    (a)   "postal voting statement"; and

    (b)   "poll card",

mean the documents issued under the relevant rules in the Schedule pertaining to the election, and set out in the Forms Schedule.

Supply of postal voters lists, etc

12 (1)   Paragraphs (2) and (3) apply where a registration officer ("R") for any part of an Assembly constituency is not the CRO for that constituency.

  (2)   As soon as practicable after 5pm on the sixth day before the day of the poll at an Authority election, R must send the CRO a copy of the lists R is required to keep in respect of that election under paragraphs 5 and 7(8) of Schedule 4 to the Representation of the People Act 2000 (absent voters lists and proxy postal voters list).

(3) R must, on a request made at any time, supply the CRO with a copy of the lists mentioned in paragraph (2).

(4) In relation to an Authority election, for the purposes of paragraph (2), "the sixth day before the day of the poll" is to be computed in the same way as a period of time mentioned in the timetable for that election.

SCHEDULE 1
THE CONSTITUENCY MEMBERS ELECTION RULES

Rule 3(2)

Part 1
General Provisions

Part 2
Provisions as to Time

Part 3
Stages Common to Contested and Uncontested Elections

Part 4
Contested Elections

Part 5
Final Proceedings in Contested and Uncontested Elections

Part 6
Disposal of Documents

Part 7
Death of Candidate

Part 1
General Provisions

Citation

1   This Schedule may be cited as the Constituency Members Election Rules.

Interpretation

2   In the rules in this Schedule–
   (a)   unless the context indicates otherwise, "election" means an election of a constituency member;
   (b)   reference to a rule by number alone is a reference to the rule so numbered in this Schedule.

Part 2
Provisions as to Time

Timetable

3   The proceedings at the election must be conducted in accordance with the following timetable:

Timetable

Proceedings	Time
Publication of notice of election	Not later than the thirtieth day before the day of election.
Delivery of nomination papers	Not later than 4 in the afternoon on the twenty-fourth day before the day of election.
Delivery of notices of withdrawals of candidature	Not later than 4 in the afternoon on the twenty-fourth day before the day of election
Publication of statement as to persons nominated	Not later than 4 in the afternoon on the twenty-second day before the day of election.
Notice of poll	Not later than the sixth day before the day of election.
Polling	Between the hours of 7 in the morning and 10 at night on the day of election.

Computation of time

4 (1)   In computing any period of time for the purposes of the timetable–
   (a)   a Saturday or Sunday,
   (b)   Christmas Eve, Christmas Day, Good Friday or a bank holiday, or
   (c)   a day appointed for public thanksgiving or mourning,
   must be disregarded, and any such day must not be treated as a day for the purpose of any proceedings up to the completion of the poll nor may the CRO be obliged to proceed with the counting of the votes on such a day.

   (2)   In this rule, "bank holiday" means a day which is a bank holiday under the Banking and Financial Dealings Act 1971 in England and Wales.

Part 3
Stages Common to Contested and Uncontested Elections

Notice of election

5 (1)   The CRO must publish notice of the election stating–
   (a)   the place and times at which nomination papers are to be delivered, and
   (b)   the date of the poll in the event of a contest,
   and the notice must state that forms of nomination papers may be obtained at that place and those times.

   (2)   The notice of election must state the arrangements (if any) which apply for the payment of the deposit required by rule 8 by means of the electronic transfer of funds.

   (3)   The notice of election must state the date by which–
   (a)   applications to vote by post or by proxy, and
   (b)   other applications and notices about postal or proxy voting,
   must reach the registration officer for local government electors in order that they may be effective for the election.

Nomination of candidates

6 (1) Each candidate must be nominated by a separate nomination paper, which must be–
   (a) in the appropriate form, and
   (b) delivered to the place fixed for the purpose by the CRO, which must be at the offices of a local authority within the Assembly constituency, before the last time for the delivery of nomination papers.

  (2) The nomination paper must state the candidate's–
   (a) full names,
   (b) home address, in full, and
   (c) if desired, description,
and the surname must be placed first in the list of names.

  (3) If a candidate commonly uses–
   (a) a surname which is different from any other surname he has, or
   (b) a forename which is different from any other forename he has,
the nomination paper may state the commonly used surname or forename, or both surname and forename, in addition to the other name.

  (4) The description (if any) can only be–
   (a) one authorised as mentioned in paragraph (5) or (7), or
   (b) the word "Independent".

  (5) A nomination paper may not include a description of a candidate that is likely to lead electors to associate the candidate with a registered party unless–
   (a) the party is a qualifying party in relation to the electoral area, and
   (b) the description is authorised by a certificate–
    (i) issued by or on behalf of the registered nominating officer of the party, and
    (ii) received by the CRO before the last time for the delivery of nomination papers set out in the timetable in rule 3.

  (6) In paragraph (5) an authorised description may be either–
   (a) the name of the party registered under section 28 of the 2000 Act, or
   (b) a description of the party registered under section 28A of that Act.

  (7) A nomination paper may not include a description of a candidate which is likely to lead electors to associate the candidate with two or more registered political parties unless the parties are each qualifying parties in relation to the electoral area and the description is a registered description authorised by a certificate–
   (a) issued by or on behalf of the registered nominating officer of each of the parties, and
   (b) received by the CRO before the last time for the delivery of nomination papers set out in the timetable in rule 3.

  (8) For the purposes of paragraph (7), a description is a registered description if it is a description registered for use by the parties under section 28B of the 2000 Act.

  (9) A person will be guilty of a corrupt practice if he fraudulently purports to be authorised to issue a certificate under paragraph (5) or (7) on behalf of a registered party's nominating officer.

  (10) For the purposes of the application of these rules in relation to an election–
   (a) "registered party" means a party which was registered under Part 2 of the 2000 Act on the day ("the relevant day") which is two days before the last day for the delivery of nomination papers at that election,
   (b) a registered party is a qualifying party in relation to an electoral area if on the relevant day the party was registered in respect of England in the Great Britain register maintained under that Part of that Act.

  (11) For the purposes of paragraph (10)(a), any day falling within rule 4(1) must be

disregarded.

Consent to nomination

7 (1)   A person will not be validly nominated unless his consent to nomination–
    (a)   is given in writing in the appropriate form, or a form to like effect, on or within one month before the last day for the delivery of nomination papers;
    (b)   is attested by one witness whose name and address must be given; and
    (c)   is delivered at the place and within the time for delivery of nomination papers.

(2)   A candidate's consent given under this rule must–
    (a)   state the day, month and year of his birth; and
    (b)   contain a statement that to the best of the candidate's knowledge and belief he is not disqualified from being elected by reason of–
        (i)   any disqualification set out in section 21 (disqualification from being the Mayor or an Assembly member) of the 1999 Act,
        (ii)   a decision made under section 78A of the Local Government Act 2000 (decisions of First-tier tribunal), or
        (iii)   an order made under section 34(4) of the Localism Act 2011(offences).

Deposits

8 (1)   A person will not be validly nominated unless the sum of £1,000 is deposited by him, or on his behalf, with the CRO at the place and within the time for delivery of nomination papers.

(2)   The deposit may be made either–
    (a)   by the deposit of any legal tender, or
    (b)   by means of a banker's draft, or
    (c)   with the CRO's consent, in any other manner including by means of a debit or credit card or the electronic transfer of funds,
but the CRO may refuse to accept a deposit sought to be made by means of a banker's draft if he does not know that the drawer carries on business as a banker in the United Kingdom.

(3)   Where the deposit is made on behalf of the candidate, the person making the deposit must at the time he makes it give his name and address to the CRO, unless they have previously been given to him under section 67 (appointment of election agent) of the 1983 Act.

Decisions as to validity of nomination papers

9 (1)   Where a nomination paper and the candidate's consent to it are delivered, and the deposit is made, in accordance with this Part of these Rules, the candidate must be deemed to stand nominated unless and until–
    (a)   the CRO decides that the nomination paper is invalid, or
    (b)   proof is given to the CRO's satisfaction of the candidate's death, or
    (c)   the candidate withdraws.

(2)   The CRO is entitled to hold a nomination paper invalid only on the grounds–
    (a)   that the particulars of the candidate on the nomination paper are not as required by law; or
    (b)   that the paper breaks rule 6(5) or (7).

(3)   Subject to paragraph (4), the CRO must, as soon as practicable after each nomination paper has been delivered, examine it and decide whether the candidate has been validly nominated.

(4)   If in the CRO's opinion a nomination paper breaks rule 6(5) or (7), he must give a

decision to that effect–
   (a)   as soon as practicable after the delivery of the nomination paper, and
   (b)   in any event, before the end of the period of 24 hours starting with the end of the period for the delivery of nomination papers set out in the timetable in rule 3.

(5)   Where the CRO decides that a nomination paper is invalid, he must endorse and sign on the paper the fact and the reasons for his decision.

(6)   The CRO must, as soon as practicable after making a decision under paragraph (3) or (4) that a nomination paper is valid or invalid, send notice of that decision to the candidate at his home address as given in his nomination paper.

(7)   The CRO's decision that a nomination paper is valid is final and must not be questioned in any proceeding whatsoever.

(8)   Subject to paragraph (7), nothing in this rule prevents the validity of a nomination being questioned on an election petition.

Publication of statement of persons nominated

10 (1)   The CRO must prepare and (subject to paragraph (11)) publish a statement showing the persons who have been and stand nominated and any other persons who have been nominated together with the reason why they no longer stand nominated.

(2)   The statement must show the names, addresses and descriptions of the persons nominated as given in their nomination papers.

(3)   If a person's nomination paper gives a commonly used surname or forename, or both surname and forename, in addition to another name, the statement must show the person's commonly used surname or forename, or both surname and forename (as the case may be) instead of any other name.

(4)   Paragraph (3) does not apply if the CRO thinks–
   (a)   that the use of the person's commonly used name may be likely to mislead or confuse electors, or
   (b)   that the commonly used name is obscene or offensive.

(5)   If paragraph (4) applies, the CRO must give notice in writing to the candidate of his reasons for refusing to allow the use of a commonly used name.

(6)   The statement must show the persons standing nominated arranged alphabetically in the order of their surnames, and if there are two or more of them with the same surname, of their other names.

(7)   In the case of a person nominated by more than one nomination paper, the CRO must take the particulars required by the foregoing provisions of this rule from such one of the papers as the candidate (or the CRO in default of the candidate) may select.

(8)   Paragraphs (9) to (11) apply at an ordinary election.

(9)   As soon as possible after all decisions under rule 9 which are required to be made have been made, the CRO must arrange for a copy of the statement that the CRO has prepared and proposes to publish to be delivered to the GLRO.

(10)   If, after having delivered the statement mentioned in paragraph (9) to the GLRO, the CRO receives notification from the GLRO under rule 13(4) that a candidate is deemed to have withdrawn his or her candidature, the CRO must amend that statement accordingly.

(11)   The CRO may not publish the statement under paragraph (1) until–
   (a)   the CRO has made any amendments required under paragraph (10), or
   (b)   where no notification under rule 13(4) is received from the GLRO, the time by

which the GLRO must give such a notification has passed.

Correction of minor errors

11 (1)   A CRO may, if he thinks fit, at any time before the publication under rule 10 of the statement of persons nominated, correct minor errors in a nomination paper.

(2)   Errors which may be corrected include–
    (a)   errors as to a person's electoral number,
    (b)   obvious errors of spelling in relation to the details of a candidate.

(3)   Anything done by a CRO in pursuance of this rule may not be questioned in any proceedings other than proceedings on an election petition.

(4)   A CRO must have regard to any guidance issued by the Electoral Commission for the purposes of this rule.

Inspection of nomination papers and consent to nomination

12 (1)   During ordinary office hours, in the period starting 24 hours after the latest time for the delivery of nomination papers and before the date of the poll, any person may inspect and take copies of, or extracts from, nomination papers and consents to nomination.

(2)   Inspection under paragraph (1) may not take place on a day that is specified in rule 4(1).

Nomination in more than one Assembly constituency

13 (1)   This rule applies at an ordinary election.

(2)   A candidate who is validly nominated in more than one Assembly constituency must withdraw his or her candidature, in accordance with rule 14, in all but one of those constituencies.

(3)   Where a candidate does not withdraw his or her candidature as mentioned in paragraph (2), he or she is deemed, after the last time for delivery of notices of withdrawals, to have withdrawn his or her candidature from all the Assembly constituencies in which he or she is, but for this rule, validly nominated.

(4)   Where, having reviewed the proposed statements of persons nominated delivered under rule 10(9), it appears to the GLRO that a candidate ("C") appears (but for this rule) to have been validly nominated in more than one Assembly constituency ("a relevant constituency"), the GLRO must at least one hour before the last time for publication of the statement as to persons nominated as set out in the timetable in rule 3, notify the CRO for each relevant constituency that C's candidature is deemed to have been withdrawn in that constituency.

(5)   A CRO must, as soon as practicable after receiving the notification mentioned in paragraph (4), notify C that C's candidature is deemed to have been withdrawn in that constituency.

Withdrawal of candidates

14 (1)   A candidate may withdraw his candidature by notice of withdrawal–
    (a)   signed by him and attested by one witness, whose name and address must be given, and
    (b)   delivered to the CRO at the place for delivery of nomination papers,
by the end of the period for the delivery of notices of withdrawals of candidature in the timetable in rule 3.

(2)   Where a candidate is outside the United Kingdom, a notice of withdrawal signed by his

election agent and accompanied by a written declaration also so signed of the candidate's absence from the United Kingdom will be of the same effect as a notice of withdrawal signed by the candidate; but where the candidate stands nominated by more than one nomination paper a notice of withdrawal under this paragraph will be effective if, and only if, it is accompanied, in addition to that declaration, by a written statement signed by the candidate that the person giving the notice is authorised to do so on the candidate's behalf during his absence from the United Kingdom.

Method of election

15 (1) If, after any withdrawals in accordance with these Rules, the number of persons remaining validly nominated for the Assembly constituency exceeds one, a poll must be taken in accordance with Part 4 of these Rules.

(2) If, after any withdrawals in accordance with these Rules, only one person remains validly nominated for the Assembly constituency, that person must be declared to be elected in accordance with Part 5.

Part 4
Contested Elections

Poll to be taken by ballot

16 The votes at the poll must be given by ballot, the result must be ascertained by counting the votes given to each candidate, and the candidate to whom more votes have been given than to the other candidates must be declared to have been elected.

The ballot papers

17 (1) The ballot of every voter must consist of a ballot paper that must be in the appropriate form.

(2) Each person remaining validly nominated for the election, after any withdrawals, and no other, is entitled to have their name inserted in the ballot paper.

(3) Every ballot paper–
(a) must, so far as practicable for the purposes of electronic counting, be printed in accordance with the directions set out in the Forms Schedule,
(b) must contain the names and other particulars of the candidates as shown in the statement of persons nominated,
(c) must have a number and other unique identifying mark printed on the back, and
(d) may, in the case of ballot papers for use at polling stations, be marked with the words "do not fold".

(4) If a candidate who is the subject of a party's authorisation under rule 6(5) so requests, the ballot paper must contain, against the candidate's particulars, the party's registered emblem (or, as the case may be, one of the party's registered emblems).

(4A) If a candidate who is the subject of an authorisation by two or more parties under rule 6(7) so requests, the ballot paper must contain, against the candidate's particulars, the registered emblem (or, as the case may be, one of the registered emblems) of one of those parties.

(5) The candidate's request under paragraph (4) or paragraph (4A) must–
(a) be made in writing to the CRO, and
(b) be received by him within the period for delivery of nomination papers set out

in the timetable in rule 3.

(6) The order of the names in the ballot paper must be the same as in the statement of persons nominated.

(7) At an ordinary election, the GLRO must supply the ballot papers for use at the election to the CRO by such date as may be agreed between them.

(8) The ballot papers supplied under paragraph (7) must be of a different colour from those used at any other Authority election with which the election is taken.

The corresponding number list

18 (1) The CRO must prepare a list containing the numbers and other unique identifying marks of all of the ballot papers to be issued by him in pursuance of rule 23(1) or provided by him in pursuance of rule 28(1).

(2) The list must be in the appropriate form or a form to like effect.

(3) At an ordinary election, the same list may be used for each Authority election.

The official mark

19 (1) Every ballot paper must contain an appropriate security marking (the official mark).

(2) The official mark must be kept secret, and an interval of not less than five years must intervene between the use of the same official mark at any Authority election.

(3) The CRO, or at an ordinary election the GLRO, may use a different official mark for different purposes at the same election.

Prohibition of disclosure of vote

20 No person who has voted at the election may, in any legal proceeding to question the election, be required to state for whom he has voted.

Use of schools and public rooms

21 (1) The CRO may use, free of charge, for the purpose of taking the poll or counting the votes–
   (a) a room in a school maintained or assisted by a local authority (as defined in the Education Act 1996) or a school in respect of which grants are made out of moneys provided by Parliament to the person or body of persons responsible for the management of the school,
   (b) a room the expense of maintaining which is met by any local authority.

(2) The CRO must make good any damage done to, and defray any expense incurred by the persons having control over, any such room as mentioned in paragraph (1) by reason of its being used for the purpose of taking the poll or counting the votes.

Notice of poll

22 (1) The CRO must, in accordance with the timetable in rule 3, publish notice of the poll stating–
   (a) the day and hours fixed for the poll, and
   (b) the particulars of each candidate remaining validly nominated (the names and other particulars of the candidates, and the order of the candidates' names being the same as in the statement of persons nominated).

(2) The CRO must, not later than the time of the publication of the notice of the poll, also

give public notice of–
- (a) the situation of each polling station, and
- (b) the description of voters entitled to vote there,

and he must as soon as practicable after giving such a notice give a copy of it to each of the election agents.

(3) At an ordinary election, the notice of poll must include the heading "GREATER LONDON AUTHORITY ELECTION".

Postal ballot papers

23 (1) The CRO must, in accordance with regulations made under the 1983 Act, issue to those entitled to vote by post a ballot paper and a postal voting statement, together with such envelopes for their return as may be prescribed in such regulations.

(2) The postal voting statement must be in the appropriate form or a form to like effect.

(3) The postal voting statement must include provision for the form to be signed and for stating the date of birth of the elector or proxy (as the case may be).

(4) The CRO must also issue to those entitled to vote by post such information as he thinks appropriate about how to obtain–
- (a) translations into languages other than English of any directions to or guidance for voters sent with the ballot paper,
- (b) a translation into Braille of such directions or guidance,
- (c) graphical representations of such directions or guidance,
- (d) the directions or guidance in any other form (including any audible form).

(5) In the case of a ballot paper issued to a person at an address in the United Kingdom, the CRO must ensure that the return of the ballot paper and postal voting statement is free of charge to the voter.

(6) Where the proceedings on the issue and receipt of postal ballot papers at the election are taken together with any other Authority election the appropriate form of postal voting statement under paragraph (2) may be the joint postal voting statement which must be in the appropriate form or form to like effect.

Provision of polling stations

24 (1) The CRO must provide a sufficient number of polling stations and, subject to the following provisions of this rule, must allot the electors to the polling stations in such manner as he thinks most convenient.

(2) One or more polling stations may be provided in the same room.

(3) The polling station allotted to electors from any parliamentary polling district wholly or partly within the Assembly constituency must, in the absence of special circumstances, be in the parliamentary polling place for that district, unless that place is outside the Assembly constituency.

(4) The CRO must provide each polling station with such number of compartments as may be necessary in which the voters can mark their votes screened from observation.

Appointment of presiding officers and clerks

25 (1) The CRO must appoint and pay a presiding officer to attend at each polling station and such clerks and technical assistants as may be necessary for the purposes of the election, but he must not appoint any person who has been employed by or on behalf of a candidate in or about the election.

(2) The CRO may, if he thinks fit, preside at a polling station and the provisions of this Part

relating to a presiding officer apply to a CRO so presiding with the necessary modifications as to things to be done by the CRO to the presiding officer or by the presiding officer to the CRO.

(3) A presiding officer may do, by the clerks appointed to assist him, any act (including the asking of questions) which he is required or authorised by this Part to do at a polling station except order the arrest, exclusion or removal of any person from the polling station.

Issue of official poll cards

26 (1) The CRO must as soon as practicable after the publication of the notice of election, send to electors and their proxies an official poll card.

(2) An elector's official poll card must be sent or delivered to his qualifying address, and a proxy's to his address as shown in the list of proxies.

(3) The official poll card must be in the appropriate form or a form to like effect, and must set out–
    (a) the name of the Assembly constituency for which a constituency member is to be elected,
    (b) the elector's name, qualifying address and number on the register,
    (c) the date and hours of the poll and the situation of the elector's polling station, and
    (d) such other information as the CRO thinks appropriate,
and different information may be provided in pursuance of sub-paragraph (d) to different electors or descriptions of elector.

(4) In the case of an elector with an anonymous entry, instead of containing the matter mentioned in paragraph (3)(b), the polling card must contain such matter as is specified in the appropriate form.

(5) At an ordinary election, the CRO must issue a combined poll card in the appropriate form.

(6) In this rule "elector" means–
    (a) an elector with an entry on the register to be used at the election on the last day for the publication of the notice of the election, and
    (b) includes a person then shown in the register as below voting age if (but only if) it appears from the register that he will be of voting age on the day fixed for the poll.

Information for voters

27 (1) At an ordinary election, the GLRO may, in addition to a statement by him in an election booklet, include in the booklet information for voters that has been agreed by him with the Electoral Commission.

(2) The information for voters given in the election booklet may include information about–
    (a) the office of the Mayor and the London Assembly,
    (b) the system of voting at each Authority election,
    (c) how to vote in a manner that will ensure a vote is regarded as validly cast, and
subject to paragraph (3), may include any other information given in exercise of the GLRO's duty under section 69 (encouraging electoral participation) of the 2006 Act.

(3) The information for voters must not contain–
    (a) any advertising material,
    (b) any material referring to a candidate or a registered party, other than by

reproduction of a ballot paper which refers equally to all candidates and parties at the ordinary election,

    (c)   any material referring to the holder, at any time, of the office of Mayor or Assembly member, other than under paragraph (b) as a candidate at the ordinary election.

(4)   Information published in an election booklet under this rule must be printed on not more than two sides of A5 paper.

Equipment of polling stations

28 (1)   The CRO must provide each presiding officer with–
    (a)   such ballot papers as may be necessary, and
    (b)   such ballot boxes as may be necessary having taken account of any direction made by the GLRO in accordance with paragraph (9).

(2)   Every ballot box must be so constructed that the ballot papers can be put in it, but cannot be withdrawn from it, without the box being unlocked or, where the box has no lock, the seal being broken.

(3)   The CRO must provide each polling station with–
    (a)   materials to enable voters to mark the ballot papers,
    (b)   copies of the register of electors for the Assembly constituency or such part of it as contains the entries relating to the electors allotted to the station,
    (c)   the parts of any special lists prepared for the election corresponding to the register of electors for the Assembly constituency or the part of it provided under sub-paragraph (b),
    (d)   a list consisting of that part of the list prepared under rule 18 which contains the numbers (but not the other unique identifying marks) corresponding to those on the ballot papers provided to the presiding officer of the polling station.

(4)   The reference in paragraph (3)(b) to the copies of the register of electors includes a reference to copies of any notices issued under section 13B(3B) or (3D) of the 1983 Act in respect of alterations to the register.

(5)   The CRO must also provide each polling station with a device for enabling voters who are blind or partially sighted to vote without any need for assistance from the presiding officer or any companion within the meaning of rule 40.

(6)   The device referred to in paragraph (5) above must–
    (a)   allow a ballot paper to be inserted into and removed from or attached to and detached from the device, easily and without damage to the paper,
    (b)   keep the ballot paper firmly in place during use,
    (c)   provide suitable means for the voter to–
        (i)   identify the spaces on the ballot paper on which he may mark his vote,
        (ii)   identify the candidate to whom each such space refers, and
        (iii)   mark his vote on the space he has chosen.

(7)   The enlarged sample copies of the ballot paper that the CRO provides to, or causes to be displayed at, every polling station (in accordance with section 199B(5) and (7) of the 1983 Act) must be printed on paper of the same colour as the ballot paper at the election.

(8)   The CRO must also provide each polling station with notices for the guidance of voters, which must be exhibited–
    (a)   outside the polling station,
    (b)   inside the polling station–
        (i)   in the communal areas, and
        (ii)   in every voting compartment.

(9) If the GLRO thinks fit he may, not later than the date of the notice of election, direct the CRO that joint ballot boxes must be used for the ballot papers at the election and any or all Authority elections with which the election is taken.

Notices for the guidance of voters

29 (1) The CRO must prepare the notices to be exhibited under rule 28(8).

(2) The CRO may prepare versions of the notices in such other form as he thinks appropriate, in accordance with section 199B (translations etc of certain documents) of the 1983 Act.

(3) Notices for the guidance of voters exhibited under rule 28(8) or paragraph (2) must be in the appropriate form, but may include such alternative information relating to Authority elections as–
    (a) meets with the requirements of the Notices Schedule, and
    (b) the CRO may decide.

(4) Notices provided under paragraph (2) may, if the CRO agrees, be exhibited at any polling station–
    (a) outside the polling station,
    (b) inside the polling station–
        (i) in the communal areas,
        (ii) in every voting compartment.

(5) At an ordinary election, the GLRO must prepare the notices and versions of notices to be exhibited under rule 28(8) and supply them to the CRO, and for paragraph (3)(b) there must substituted–
    "(b) the GLRO may decide."

Appointment of polling and counting agents

30 (1) Before the commencement of the poll, each candidate may appoint–
    (a) polling agents to attend at polling stations for the purpose of detecting personation, and
    (b) counting agents to attend at the counting of votes.

(2) The same person may be appointed as a polling agent or counting agent by more than one candidate.

(3) For the count, one (but no more than one) counting agent of each candidate may be authorised by the terms of his appointment to require a re-count at that count.

(4) Not more than four polling agents, or such greater number as the CRO may by notice allow, may be permitted to attend at any particular polling station.

(5) If the number of such agents appointed to attend at a particular polling station exceeds that number, the CRO must determine by lot which agents are permitted to attend, and only the agents on whom the lot falls will be deemed to have been duly appointed.

(6) The CRO may limit the number of counting agents, but in doing so must ensure that–
    (a) the number is the same in the case of each candidate, and
    (b) the number allowed to a candidate must not (except in special circumstances) be less than the number obtained by dividing the number of clerks employed on the counting by the number of candidates.

(7) For the purposes of the calculations required by paragraph (6), a counting agent who has been appointed by more than one candidate is a separate agent for each of the candidates by whom he has been appointed.

(8) Notice in writing of the appointment of polling and counting agents, stating the names and addresses of the persons appointed, must be given by the candidate to the CRO and must be so given not later than the fifth day (computed in accordance with rule 4) before the day of the poll.

(9) If an agent dies, or becomes incapable of acting, the candidate may appoint another agent in his place, and must forthwith give to the CRO notice in writing of the name and address of the agent appointed.

(10) Any appointment authorised by this rule may be made and the notice of appointment given to the CRO by the candidate's election agent, instead of by the candidate.

(11) In the following provisions of this Part references to polling agents and counting agents must be taken as references to agents–
    (a) whose appointments have been duly made and notified, and
    (b) where the number of agents is restricted, who are within the permitted numbers.

(12) Any notice required to be given to a counting agent by the CRO may be delivered at, or sent by post to, the address stated in the notice of appointment.

(13) A candidate may himself do any act or thing which any polling or counting agent of his, if appointed, would have been authorised to do, or may assist his agent in doing any such act or thing.

(14) A candidate's election agent may do or assist in doing anything which a polling or counting agent of his is authorised to do; and anything required or authorised by these Rules to be done in the presence of the polling or counting agent may be done in the presence of a candidate's election agent instead of his polling agent or counting agent.

(15) Where by these Rules any act or thing is required or authorised to be done in the presence of the polling or counting agents, the non-attendance of any agent or agents at the time and place appointed for the purpose will not, if the act or thing is otherwise duly done, invalidate the act or thing done.

Notification of requirement of secrecy

31 (1) The CRO must make such arrangements as he thinks fit to ensure that–
    (a) every person attending a polling station (otherwise than for the purpose of voting or assisting a voter with disabilities to vote or as a constable on duty there) has been given a copy of the provisions of subsections (1), (3) and (6) of section 66 (requirement of secrecy) of the 1983 Act, and
    (b) every person attending at the counting of the votes (other than any constable on duty at the counting) has been given a copy of the provisions of subsections (2) and (6) of that section.

(2) In paragraph (1) a reference to a constable includes a person designated as a community support officer under section 38 of the 2002 Act (police powers for employees).

Return of postal ballot papers

32 (1) Where–
    (a) a postal vote has been returned in respect of a person who is entered on the postal voters list, or
    (b) a proxy postal vote has been returned in respect of a proxy who is entered on the proxy postal voters list,
the CRO must mark the list in the manner prescribed by regulations made under the 1983 Act.

(2) Rule 49(2) does not apply for the purpose of determining whether, for the purposes of this rule, a postal vote or a proxy postal vote is returned.

Admission to polling station

33 (1) The presiding officer must exclude all persons from the polling station except–
    (a) voters,
    (b) persons under the age of 18 who accompany voters to the polling station,
    (c) the candidates and their election agents,
    (d) the polling agents appointed to attend at the polling station,
    (e) the clerks appointed to attend at the polling station,
    (f) persons who are entitled to attend by virtue of any of sections 6A to 6D of the 2000 Act,
    (g) the constables on duty, and
    (h) the companions of voters with disabilities.

(2) The presiding officer must regulate the total number of voters and persons under the age of 18 who accompany them to be admitted to the polling station at the same time.

(3) Not more than one polling agent may be admitted at the same time to a polling station on behalf of the same candidate.

(4) A constable or person employed by the CRO must not be admitted to vote in person elsewhere than at his own polling station allotted to him under these Rules, except on production and surrender of a certificate as to his employment which must be in the appropriate form and signed by an officer of the police of or above the rank of inspector or by the CRO, as the case may be.

(5) Any certificate surrendered under this rule must forthwith be cancelled.

(6) In this rule a reference to a constable includes a person designated as a community support officer under section 38 of the 2002 Act.

Keeping of order in station

34 (1) It is the presiding officer's duty to keep order at his polling station.

(2) If a person misconducts himself in a polling station, or fails to obey the presiding officer's lawful orders, he may immediately, by the presiding officer's order, be removed from the polling station–
    (a) by a constable in or near that station, or
    (b) by any other person authorised in writing by the CRO to remove him,
and the person so removed must not, without the presiding officer's permission, again enter the polling station during the day.

(3) Any person so removed may, if charged with the commission in the polling station of an offence, be dealt with as a person taken into custody by a constable for an offence without a warrant.

(4) The powers conferred by this rule must not be exercised so as to prevent a voter who is otherwise entitled to vote at a polling station from having an opportunity of voting at that station.

Sealing of ballot boxes

35 Immediately before the commencement of the poll, the presiding officer must–
    (a) show each ballot box, empty, to such persons, if any, as are present in the polling station, so that they may see that the boxes are empty,
    (b) lock up such of the boxes as have locks,

    (c) place his seal–
        (i)   on each lock, and
        (ii)   on each ballot box which has no lock,
in such a manner as to prevent its being opened without breaking the seal,
    (d) place each box in his view for the receipt of ballot papers, and
    (e) keep each box locked and sealed or, as the case may be, sealed.

Questions to be put to voters

36 (1) At the time of the application (but not afterwards), the questions specified in the second column of the following table–
    (a) may be put by the presiding officer to a person who is mentioned in the first column, and
    (b) must be put if the letter "R" appears after the question and the candidate or his election or polling agent requires the question to be put.

Q No	Person applying for ballot paper	Question
1	A person applying as an elector	(a)–Are you the person registered in the register of local government electors for this election as follows (*read the whole entry from the register*)? R (b)–Have you already voted, here or elsewhere at this election for a constituency member, otherwise than as proxy for some other person? R
2	A person applying as proxy	(a)–Are you the person whose name appears as AB in the list of proxies for this election as entitled to vote as proxy on behalf of CD? R (b)–Have you already voted here or elsewhere at this election for a constituency member, as proxy on behalf of CD? R (c)–Are you the spouse, civil partner, parent, grandparent, brother, sister, child or grandchild of CD? R
3	A person applying as proxy for an elector with an anonymous entry (instead of the questions at entry 2)	(a)–Are you the person entitled to vote as proxy on behalf of the elector whose number on the register of electors is (*read out the number*)? R (b)–Have you already voted here or elsewhere as proxy on behalf of the elector whose number on the register of electors is (*read out the number*)?" R (c)–Are you the spouse, civil partner, parent, grandparent, brother, sister, child or grandchild of the person whose number on the register of electors is (*read out the number*)? R
4	A person applying as proxy if the question at entry 2(c) or 3(c) is not answered in the affirmative	Have you already voted here or elsewhere at this election for a constituency member, on behalf of two persons of whom you are not the spouse, civil partner, parent,

		grandparent, brother, sister, child or grandchild? R
5	A person applying as an elector in relation to whom there is an entry in the postal voters list	(a)–Did you apply to vote by post?
		(b)–Why have you not voted by post?
6	A person applying as proxy who is named in the proxy postal voters list	(a)–Did you apply to vote by post as proxy?
		(b)–Why have you not voted by post as proxy?

(2) In the case of an elector in respect of whom a notice has been issued under section 13B(3B) or (3D) of the 1983 Act, the references in the questions at entries 1(a) and 3(a), (b) and (c) to reading from the register must be taken as references to reading from the notice issued under those subsections.

(3) A ballot paper must not be delivered to any person required to answer any of the above questions unless he has answered each question satisfactorily.

(4) Except as authorised by this rule, no inquiry may be permitted as to the right of any person to vote.

Challenge of voter

37 A person must not be prevented from voting because–
    (a) a candidate or his election or polling agent declares that he has reasonable cause to believe that the person has committed an offence of personation, or
    (b) the person is arrested on the grounds that he is suspected of committing or of being about to commit such an offence.

Voting procedure

38 (1) A ballot paper must be delivered to a voter who applies for one, and immediately before delivery–
    (a) the number and (unless paragraph (2) applies) name of the elector as stated in the copy of the register of electors must be called out,
    (b) the number of the elector must be marked on the list mentioned in rule 28(3)(d) beside the number of the ballot paper to be issued to him,
    (c) a mark must be placed in the register of electors against the number of the elector to note that a ballot paper has been applied for but without showing the particular ballot paper which may be delivered,
    (d) in the case of a person applying for a ballot paper as proxy, a mark must also be placed against his name in the list of proxies.

(2) In the case of an elector who has an anonymous entry, he must show the presiding officer his official poll card and only his number may be called out in pursuance of paragraph (1)(a).

(3) In the case of an elector who is added to the register in pursuance of a notice issued under section 13B(3B) or (3D) of the 1983 Act, paragraph (1) is modified as follows–
    (a) in sub-paragraph (a), for "copy of the register of electors" substitute "copy of the notice issued under section 13B(3B) or (3D) of the 1983 Act",
    (b) in sub-paragraph (c), for "in the register of electors" substitute "on the copy of the notice issued under section 13B(3B) or (3D) of the 1983 Act".

(4) The voter, on receiving the ballot paper, must forthwith proceed into one of the compartments in the polling station and there secretly mark his paper, and must then show to the presiding officer the back of the paper, so as to disclose the number and other unique identifying mark, and put the ballot paper into the ballot box in the presiding officer's presence, but so as to conceal his vote.

(5) The voter must vote without undue delay, and must leave the polling station as soon as he has put his ballot paper into the ballot box.

(6) A voter who has had a ballot paper delivered to him under paragraph (1), but has decided not to mark it, may return it to the presiding officer and where the voter does so, the presiding officer must–
   (a) immediately cancel the ballot paper, and for the purposes of these rules treat it as a spoilt ballot paper,
   (b) place a mark beside the number of that ballot paper on the corresponding number list to show that the ballot paper has been cancelled.

(7) At an ordinary election, the same copy of–
   (a) the list of proxies,
   (b) the list mentioned in rule 28(3)(d),
   (c) the register of electors,
   (d) any notice issued under section 13B(3B) or (3D) of the 1983 Act (marked in the case of an elector who is added to the register in pursuance of such a notice),
   may be used for each Authority election and one mark may be placed in the list, register or notice (as the case may be) to denote that a ballot paper has been delivered in respect of each Authority election; except that, where a ballot paper has not been issued in respect of any Authority election, a different mark must be placed in the list, register or notice so as to identify the elections in respect of which a ballot paper was issued.

(8) A voter who at the close of the poll is in the polling station, or in a queue outside the polling station, for the purpose of voting must (despite the close of the poll) be entitled to apply for a ballot paper under paragraph (1); and these rules apply in relation to such a voter accordingly.

Votes marked by presiding officer

39 (1) The presiding officer, on the application of a voter–
   (a) who is incapacitated by blindness or other disability from voting in the manner directed by these Rules, or
   (b) who declares orally that he is unable to read,
   must, in the presence of the polling agents, cause the voter's vote to be marked on a ballot paper in the manner directed by the voter, and the ballot paper to be placed in the ballot box.

(2) The name and number on the register of electors of every voter whose vote is marked in pursuance of this rule, and the reason why it is so marked, must be entered on a list (in these Rules called "the list of votes marked by the presiding officer").
   In the case of a person voting as proxy for an elector, the number to be entered together with the voter's name must be the elector's number.

(3) In the case of a person in respect of whom a notice has been issued under section 13B(3B) or (3D) of the 1983 Act, paragraph (2) applies as if for "on the register of electors of every voter" there were substituted "relating to every voter in respect of whom a notice has been issued under section 13B(3B) or (3D) of the 1983 Act".

(4) At an ordinary election, the same list may be used for each Authority election, and where it is so used, an entry in that list must be taken to mean that the ballot papers

were so marked in respect of each Authority election, unless the list identifies the election for which the ballot paper was so marked.

Voting by persons with disabilities

40 (1)   If a voter makes an application to the presiding officer to be allowed, on the ground of–
(a)   blindness or other disability, or
(b)   inability to read,
to vote with the assistance of another person by whom he is accompanied (in these Rules referred to as "the companion"), the presiding officer must require the voter to declare, orally or in writing, whether he is so incapacitated by his blindness or other disability, or by his inability to read, as to be unable to vote without assistance.

(2)   If the presiding officer–
(a)   is satisfied that the voter is so incapacitated, and
(b)   is also satisfied by a written declaration made by the companion (in these Rules referred to as "the declaration made by the companion of a voter with disabilities") that the companion–
(i)   is a qualified person within the meaning of these Rules, and
(ii)   has not previously assisted more than one voter with disabilities to vote at the election,
the presiding officer must grant the application, and then anything which is by these Rules required to be done to, or by that voter in connection with the giving of his vote may be done to, or with the assistance of, the companion.

(3)   For the purpose of these Rules, a person is a voter with disabilities if he has made such a declaration as is mentioned in paragraph (1) above, and a person may be qualified to assist a voter with disabilities to vote if that person–
(a)   is a person who is entitled to vote as an elector at the election, or
(b)   is the father, mother, brother, sister, spouse, civil partner, son or daughter of the voter and has attained the age of 18 years.

(4)   The name and number in the register of electors of every voter whose vote is given in accordance with this rule and the name and address of the companion must be entered on a list (in these Rules referred to as the "list of voters with disabilities assisted by companions").
In the case of a person voting as proxy for an elector, the number to be entered together with the voter's name must be the elector's number.

(5)   In the case of a person in respect of whom a notice has been issued under section 13B(3B) or (3D) of the 1983 Act, paragraph (4) applies as if for "in the register of electors of every voter" there were substituted "relating to every voter in respect of whom a notice has been issued under section 13B(3B) or (3D) of the 1983 Act".

(6)   The declaration made by the companion–
(a)   must be in the appropriate form,
(b)   must be made before the presiding officer at the time when the voter applies to vote with the assistance of a companion, and
(c)   must forthwith be given to the presiding officer who must attest and retain it.

(7)   No fee or other payment may be charged in respect of the declaration.

(8)   At an ordinary election, the same list of voters with disabilities assisted by companions may be used for each Authority election, and where it is so used, an entry in that list must be taken to mean that the votes were so given in respect of each Authority election, unless the list identifies the election for which the vote was so given.

Tendered ballot papers: circumstances where available

41 (1) If a person, representing himself to be–
- (a) a particular elector named in the register and not named in the absent voters list, or
- (b) a particular person named in the list of proxies as proxy for an elector and not entitled to vote by post as proxy,

applies for a ballot paper after another person has voted in person either as the elector or his proxy, the applicant must, on satisfactorily answering the questions permitted by law to be asked at the poll, be entitled, subject to the following provisions of this rule and rule 42, to mark a ballot paper (in these Rules referred to as "a tendered ballot paper") in the same manner as any other voter.

(2) Paragraph (4) applies if–
- (a) a person applies for a ballot paper representing himself to be a particular elector named in the register,
- (b) he is also named in the postal voters list, and
- (c) he claims that he did not make an application to vote by post at the election.

(3) Paragraph (4) also applies if–
- (a) a person applies for a ballot paper representing himself to be a particular person named as a proxy in the list of proxies,
- (b) he is also named in the proxy postal voters list, and
- (c) he claims that he did not make an application to vote by post as proxy.

(4) The person must, on satisfactorily answering the questions permitted by law to be asked at the poll, be entitled, subject to the following provisions of this rule and rule 42, to mark a ballot paper (in these Rules referred to as a "tendered ballot paper") in the same manner as any other voter.

(5) Paragraph (6) applies if before the close of the poll but after the last time at which a person may apply for a replacement postal ballot paper, a person represents himself to be–
- (a) a particular elector named in the register who is also named in the postal voters list, or
- (b) a particular person named as a proxy in the list of proxies and who is also named in the proxy postal voters list,

and claims that he has lost or has not received his postal ballot paper.

(6) The person must, on satisfactorily answering the questions permitted by law to be asked at the poll, be entitled, subject to the provisions of this rule and rule 42, to mark a ballot paper (in these Rules referred to as a "tendered ballot paper") in the same manner as any other voter.

Tendered ballot papers: general provisions

42 (1) A tendered ballot paper must–
- (a) be of a colour differing from the other ballot papers,
- (b) instead of being put into the ballot box, be given to the presiding officer and endorsed by him with the name of the voter and his number on the register of electors, and set aside in a separate packet.

(2) The name of the voter and his number on the register of electors must be entered on a list (in these Rules referred to as the "tendered votes list").

(3) In the case of a person voting as proxy for an elector, the number to be endorsed or entered together with the voter's name must be the number of that elector.

(4) In the case of an elector who has an anonymous entry, this rule and rule 41 apply

subject to the following modifications–
    (a) in paragraphs (1)(b) and (2) above, the references to the name of the voter must be ignored,
    (b) otherwise, a reference to a person named on a register or list must be construed as a reference to a person whose number appears in the register or list (as the case may be).

(5) In the case of a person in respect of whom a notice has been issued under section 13B(3B) or (3D) of the 1983 Act, this rule and rule 41 apply as if–
    (a) in rule 41(1)(a), (2)(a) and (5)(a), for "named in the register" there were substituted "in respect of whom a notice under section 13B(3B) or (3D) of the 1983 Act has been issued",
    (b) in paragraph (1)(b) of this rule for "his number in the register of electors" there were substituted "the number relating to him on a notice issued under section 13B(3B) or (3D) of the 1983 Act",
    (c) in paragraph (2) of this rule, for "his number in the register of electors" there were substituted "the number relating to him on a notice issued under section 13B(3B) or (3D) of the 1983 Act".

(6) At an ordinary election, the same list may be used for each Authority election, and where it is so used, an entry in that list must be taken to mean that tendered ballot papers were marked in respect of each Authority election, unless the list identifies the election for which a tendered ballot paper was delivered.

Spoilt and replacement ballot papers

43 (1) A voter who has inadvertently dealt with his ballot paper in such manner that it cannot be conveniently used as a ballot paper may, on delivering it to the presiding officer and proving to his satisfaction the fact of the inadvertence, obtain a replacement for the ballot paper so delivered (in these Rules referred to as "a spoilt ballot paper"), and the spoilt ballot paper must be immediately cancelled.

(2) If a voter decides, after he has returned his ballot paper and it has been cancelled in accordance with rule 38(6), but before the close of the poll, that he wishes to vote in the election, he may obtain a replacement for the returned ballot paper.

(3) Before a replacement ballot paper is obtained, the presiding officer must mark the corresponding number list that was marked under rule 39(1) (the corresponding number list)–
    (a) in the case of a ballot paper being replaced under paragraph (1) or (2), beside the number of the replacement ballot paper obtained to show–
        (i)   the number of the elector, and
        (ii) the number of the ballot paper which is being replaced; and
    (b) in the case of a ballot paper being replaced under paragraph (1), beside the number of the spoilt ballot paper to show that the ballot paper was replaced.

(4) At an ordinary election, the voter must only receive a replacement for a spoilt or returned ballot paper.

(5) If the same corresponding number list is used for more than one Authority election in accordance with rule 38(7)–
    (a) the marks made under paragraph (3) must identify the election for which a ballot paper has been replaced, and
    (b) any ballot paper which the voter has not applied for or obtained as a replacement, but which bears the same ballot paper number as a ballot paper delivered under rule 38(1), or obtained under paragraph (1) or (2) of this rule–
        (i)   must not be delivered to the voter,
        (ii) must be cancelled, and

(iii) for the purposes of these rules, must be treated as a spoilt ballot paper.

Correction of errors on day of poll

44 (1) The presiding officer must keep a list of persons to whom ballot papers are delivered in consequence of an alteration to the register made by virtue of section 13B(3B) or (3D) of the 1983 Act which takes effect on the day of the poll.

(2) At an ordinary election, the same list may be used for each Authority election, and where it is so used, an entry in that list must be taken to mean that ballot papers were delivered in respect of each Authority election, unless the list identifies the election for which a tendered ballot paper was delivered.

Adjournment of poll in case of riot

45 (1) Where the proceedings at any polling station are interrupted or obstructed by riot or open violence, the presiding officer must adjourn the proceedings till the following day and must forthwith inform the CRO.

(2) Where the poll is adjourned at any polling station–
   (a) the hours of polling on the day to which it is adjourned must be the same as for the original day, and
   (b) references in these Rules to the close of the poll must be construed accordingly.

(3) As soon as practicable after being informed of the adjournment of a poll, the CRO must inform the GLRO of that fact and of the cause of its adjournment.

Procedure on close of poll

46 (1) As soon as practicable after the close of the poll, the presiding officer must, in the presence of the polling agents, make up into separate packets, sealed with his own seal and the seals of such polling agents as desire to affix their seals–
   (a) each ballot box in use at the station, sealed so as to prevent the introduction of additional ballot papers and unopened, but with any key attached,
   (b) the unused and spoilt ballot papers placed together,
   (c) the tendered ballot papers,
   (d) the marked copies of the register of electors (including any marked copy notices issued under section 13B(3B) or (3D) of the 1983 Act) and of the list of proxies,
   (e) the list prepared under rule 18, including the part completed in accordance with rule 38(1)(b) (together referred to in these Rules as "the completed corresponding number list"),
   (f) the certificates as to employment on duty on the day of the poll,
   (g) the tendered votes list, the list of voters with disabilities assisted by companions, the list of votes marked by the presiding officer, a statement of the number of voters whose votes are so marked by the presiding officer under the heads "disability" and "unable to read", the list maintained under rule 44, and the declarations made by the companions of voters with disabilities,
   and must deliver the packets or cause them to be delivered to the CRO to be taken charge of by him; but if the packets are not delivered by the presiding officer personally to the CRO, the arrangements for their delivery must be approved by the CRO.

(2) The contents of the packets referred to in paragraph (1)(b), (c) and (f) must not be combined with the contents of the packets made under the corresponding rule that applies at any other Authority election.

(3) The marked copies of the register of electors and of the list of proxies must be in one packet but must not be in the same packet as the completed corresponding number

list or the certificates as to employment on duty on the day of the poll.

(4) The packets must be accompanied by a statement ("the ballot paper account") showing the number of ballot papers entrusted to the presiding officer, and accounting for them under the heads–

    (a) ballot papers issued and not otherwise accounted for,

    (b) unused ballot papers,

    (c) spoilt ballot papers, and

    (d) tendered ballot papers.

(5) At an ordinary election, the statement referred to in paragraph (4) may be combined with the statements produced in relation to other Authority elections and the combined statement must be arranged in such manner as the GLRO may direct.

Attendance at verification and the counting of votes

47 (1) As soon as practicable after the close of the poll, the CRO must make arrangements for carrying out, in the presence of the counting agents, the verification and counting of votes at the election and must give to the counting agents notice in writing of the time and place at which he will begin to verify and count the votes.

(2) No person other than–

    (a) the CRO and his clerks and technical assistants,

    (b) the GLRO,

    (c) the candidates and one other person chosen by each of them,

    (d) the election agents,

    (e) the counting agents,

    (f) persons who are entitled to attend by virtue of any of sections 6A to 6D of the 2000 Act,

may be present at the verification and counting of the votes, unless permitted by the CRO to attend.

(3) A person not entitled to attend at the verification and counting of the votes must not be permitted to do so by the CRO unless the CRO–

    (a) is satisfied that the efficient conduct of those proceedings will not be impeded, and

    (b) has either consulted the candidates or thought it impracticable to do so.

(4) The CRO must give the counting agents all such reasonable facilities for overseeing the proceedings, and all such information with respect to them, as he can give them consistently with the orderly conduct of the proceedings and the discharge of his duties in connection with them.

Use of the electronic counting system

48 (1) The GLRO may provide the CRO with an electronic counting system consisting of computer hardware, software and other equipment or services, for the purpose of counting the number of ballot papers, to verify the ballot paper accounts and to count the votes cast on them.

(2) Any verification of ballot paper accounts, count or re-count at the election conducted using the electronic counting system must be conducted in accordance with rule 49.

(3) If the GLRO has provided the CRO with an electronic counting system for use at the election, the CRO must obtain the prior written consent of the GLRO before he may conduct the verification of ballot paper accounts or count the votes manually.

(4) If the verification of ballot paper accounts, count or re-count has commenced using the electronic counting system but has not been completed, the CRO may, if he

considers it appropriate, discontinue the count and instead count the votes manually.

(5) Where the count or a re-count has been conducted using the electronic counting system, the CRO may, if he considers it appropriate, conduct any re-count without using that system.

(6) Where verification or any count or re-count is conducted using the electronic counting system, any of the steps referred to rule 49, in so far as practicable, may be undertaken–
    (a) concurrently with any other of those steps, or
    (b) in a different order.

Verification and the count

49 (1) The CRO must–
    (a) open the ballot boxes from each polling station together, in the presence of the counting agents appointed for the purposes of the election and any other Authority election with which is its combined,
    (b) cause the electronic counting system to count such of the postal ballot papers as have been duly returned in accordance with paragraphs (2) and (3) and record separately the number counted,
    (c) not mix the contents of any ballot box with the contents of any other ballot box during the conduct of any count or re-count.

(2) A postal ballot paper must not be taken to be duly returned unless–
    (a) it is returned in the manner set out in paragraph (3) and reaches the CRO or any polling station in the Assembly constituency that includes the electoral area for which the elector is registered as a local government elector, before the close of the poll,
    (b) the postal voting statement, duly signed, is also returned in the manner set out in paragraph (3) and reaches him or such polling station before that time,
    (c) the postal voting statement also states the date of birth of the elector or proxy (as the case may be), and
    (d) in a case where the steps for verifying the date of birth and signature of an elector or proxy have been prescribed by regulations made under the 1983 Act, the CRO (having taken such steps) verifies the date of birth and signature of the elector or proxy (as the case may be).

(3) The manner in which any postal paper or postal voting statement may be returned–
    (a) to the CRO, is by hand or by post,
    (b) to a polling station in the Assembly constituency, is by hand.

(3A) A postal ballot paper or postal voting statement that reaches the CRO or a polling station mentioned in sub-paragraph (a) of paragraph (2) at or after the close of the poll is treated for the purposes of paragraph (2) as reaching that officer or polling station before the close of the poll if it is delivered by a person who, at the close of the poll, is in the polling station, or in a queue outside the polling station, for the purpose of returning it.

(4) After completing the proceedings under paragraph (1), the CRO must cause the electronic counting system to process the ballot papers so as to count–
    (a) the number of ballot papers, and
    (b) votes given on the ballot papers.

(5) The CRO must not cause the electronic counting system to count any tendered ballot paper.

(6) The CRO must verify each ballot paper account by comparing it with the number of ballot papers processed by the electronic counting system, and the unused and spoilt

ballot papers in his possession and the tendered votes list (opening and re-sealing the packets containing the unused and spoilt ballot papers and the tendered votes list) and must draw up a statement as to the result of the verification, which any election agent may copy.

(7) The CRO, while verifying the ballot paper accounts and counting the votes, must take all proper precautions for preventing any person from seeing the numbers printed on the back of the papers.

(8) The CRO must so far as practicable proceed continuously with counting the votes, allowing only time for refreshment, except that the hours between 5 in the afternoon and 10 on the following morning may be excluded.

(9) At an ordinary election, the hours between 5 in the afternoon and 10 on the following morning may only be excluded with the prior consent of the GLRO.

(10) During the time so excluded the CRO must–
    (a) place the ballot papers and other documents relating to the election under his own seal and the seals of such of the counting agents as desire to affix their seals, and
    (b) otherwise take proper precautions for the security of the papers and documents.

Rejected ballot papers

50 (1) Any ballot paper–
    (a) which does not bear the official mark,
    (b) on which votes are given for more than one candidate,
    (c) on which anything is written or marked by which the voter can be identified except the printed number and other unique identifying mark on the back,
    (d) which is unmarked, or
    (e) which is void for uncertainty,
is, subject to paragraph (2), void and must not be counted.

(2) A ballot paper on which the vote is marked–
    (a) elsewhere than in the proper place, or
    (b) otherwise than by means of a cross, or
    (c) by more than one mark,
must not for such reason be void if an intention that the vote be given for one only of the candidates clearly appears, and the way the paper is marked does not itself identify the voter and it is not shown that he can be identified by it.

(3) Where the electronic counting system identifies a ballot paper that has been marked, but which appears for whatever reason to be void, it must be examined by a clerk appointed by the CRO in the manner referred to in paragraph (6).

(4) If the clerk, having examined the ballot, considers that the vote is void then the CRO must examine it in the manner referred to in paragraph (6).

(5) After the CRO examines the ballot paper, he must give his decision as to the validity of the vote.

(6) An examination under paragraph (3) or (4) is to be made by the clerk or CRO examining an image of the ballot paper which is shown on a screen so as to be visible to those attending the count.

(7) The CRO may examine any ballot paper that he is not required to examine in accordance with paragraph (4)–
    (a) either in the manner referred to in paragraph (6), or
    (b) by examining a paper copy,

and where the CRO does so, he must give a decision on that paper in accordance with paragraph (5).

(8) No person attending the count is to be entitled to require the clerk or CRO to examine a ballot paper or to provide a paper copy for inspection.

(9) A record of the CRO's decision must be retained in the electronic counting system together with, in the case of a decision that the ballot paper is void, his reasons by reference to paragraph (1).

(10) If a counting agent objects to the CRO's decision the CRO must record on the electronic counting system that the decision was objected to.

(11) The CRO must draw up a statement showing the number of ballot papers rejected under the several heads of–
    (a) want of an official mark,
    (b) voting for more than one candidate,
    (c) writing or mark by which the voter could be identified,
    (d) unmarked ballot paper, or
    (e) void for uncertainty.

(12) As soon as practicable after the completion of the statement under paragraph (11) the CRO must inform–
    (a) such candidates, election agents and counting agents as are present at the count, and
    (b) the GLRO,
of its contents.

Decisions on ballot papers

51 The decision of the CRO on any question arising in respect of a ballot paper will be final, but may be subject to review on an election petition.

Re-count

52 (1) A candidate or his election agent or a counting agent authorised under rule 30(3) may, if present when the counting or any re-count of the votes, is completed, require the CRO to have the votes re-counted or again re-counted but the CRO may refuse to do so if in his opinion the request is unreasonable.

(2) No step may be taken on the completion of the counting or any re-count of votes until the candidates and election agents present at its completion have been given a reasonable opportunity to exercise the right conferred by this rule.

(3) The CRO may determine the extent to which any re-count involves the electronic counting of votes.

(4) When the returning officer uses the electronic counting system for the re-counting of votes, he must not re-consider any decision made on any ballot paper under rule 50(5).

Equality of votes

53 Where, after the counting of the votes (including any re-count) is completed, an equality of votes is found to exist between any candidates and the addition of a vote would entitle any of those candidates to be declared elected, the CRO must forthwith decide between those candidates by lot, and proceed as if the candidate on whom the lot falls had received an additional vote.

Part 5
Final Proceedings in Contested and Uncontested Elections

Declaration of result

54 (1) In a contested election, when the result of the poll has been ascertained, the CRO must forthwith–
  (a) declare to be elected the candidate to whom the majority of votes has been given,
  (b) give public notice of–
      (i) the name of the person declared to be elected,
      (ii) the person's authorised description, if any, within the meaning of rule 6(5) or (7),
      (iii) the total number of votes given for each candidate together with the number of rejected ballot papers under each head shown in the statement of rejected ballot papers.

  (2) Subject to paragraph (3), after the CRO complies with paragraph (1), he may give public notice of the information referred to paragraph (1)(b)(iii) so as to set out the number of votes falling under each of the heads in that sub-paragraph, in respect of each ward.

  (3) Where the sum of votes given for all candidates in any ward does not exceed 500, the GLRO must not give notice under paragraph (2) in respect of that ward alone, but must amalgamate the figures for that ward with those for any other ward in which more than 500 votes have been given, in the same Assembly constituency.

  (4) In an uncontested election, the CRO must as soon as practicable after the latest time for the delivery of notices of withdrawals of candidature–
  (a) declare to be elected the candidate remaining validly nominated,
  (b) give public notice of–
      (i) the name of the person declared to be elected, and
      (ii) the person's authorised description, if any, within the meaning of rule 6(5) or (7).

  (5) The CRO must as soon as practicable notify the GLRO and the proper officer of the Authority of the information in the notice given under (1)(b).

Return or forfeiture of candidate's deposit

55 (1) Unless forfeited in accordance with paragraph (5), the deposit made under rule 8 must be returned to the person making it or his personal representative.

  (2) Subject to paragraphs (3) and (4), the deposit must be returned not later than the next day after that on which the result of the election is declared.

  (3) For the purposes of paragraph (2)–
  (a) a day must be disregarded if, in accordance with rule 4, it would be disregarded in computing any period of time for the purposes of the timetable for the election, and
  (b) the deposit must be treated as being returned on a day if a cheque for the amount of the deposit is posted on that day.

  (4) If the candidate is not shown as standing nominated in the statement of persons nominated, or if the poll is countermanded or abandoned by reason of his death, the deposit must be returned as soon as practicable after the publication of the statement or after his death, as the case may be.

  (5) Where a poll is taken, if, after the counting of the votes by the CRO (including any re-

count) is completed, the candidate is found not to have polled more than one-twentieth of the total number of votes polled by all the candidates, the deposit must be forfeited to the Greater London Authority.

Part 6
Disposal of Documents

Sealing up of ballot papers

56 (1) On the completion of the counting at a contested election the CRO must seal up in separate packets the counted and rejected ballot papers.

(2) Where some or all of the votes have been counted using the electronic counting system, the CRO must also seal up in a separate packet a complete electronic record ("the electronic record") of the information stored in the electronic counting system, held in such device as may be suitable for the purpose of its storage.

(3) After making the electronic record under paragraph (2), the CRO must arrange for the original records in the electronic counting system to be removed from it and destroyed in a manner that ensures that the secrecy of those records is preserved.

(4) The CRO must not open the sealed packets of–
   (a) tendered ballot papers,
   (b) certificates as to employment on duty on the day of the poll,
   (c) the completed corresponding number lists, or
   (d) marked copies of the register of electors (including any marked copy notices issued under section 13B(3B) or (3D) of the 1983 Act) and list of proxies.

Delivery and retention of documents

57 (1) The CRO must then forward the following documents to the relevant registration officer–
   (a) the packets of ballot papers in his possession,
   (b) the packet containing the electronic record (if any),
   (c) the ballot paper accounts and the statements of rejected ballot papers and of the result of the verification of the ballot paper accounts,
   (d) the tendered votes lists, the lists of voters with disabilities assisted by companions, the lists of votes marked by the presiding officer and the related statements, the lists maintained under rule 44 and the declarations made by the companions of voters with disabilities,
   (e) the packets of the completed corresponding number lists,
   (f) the packets of certificates as to employment on duty on the day of the poll, and
   (g) the packets containing marked copies of registers (including any marked copy notices issued under section 13B(3B) or (3D) of the 1983 Act) and of the postal voters list, of the lists of proxies and of the proxy postal voters list,
   endorsing on each packet a description of its contents, the date of the election to which they relate and the name of the Assembly constituency for which the election was held.

Orders for production of documents

58 (1) An order–
   (a) for the inspection or production of any rejected ballot papers in the custody of the relevant registration officer, or
   (b) for the opening of a packet containing the electronic record or a sealed packet of completed corresponding number lists or certificates as to employment on

duty on the day of the poll or the inspection of any counted ballot papers, in the custody of the relevant registration officer,

may be made by a county court, if the court is satisfied by evidence on oath that the order is required for the purpose of instituting or maintaining a prosecution for an offence in relation to ballot papers, or for the purpose of an election petition.

(2) An election court may make an order for the opening of a packet containing the electronic record or a sealed packet of completed corresponding number lists or certificates or for the inspection of any counted ballot papers in the custody of the relevant registration officer.

(3) An order under this rule may be made subject to such conditions as to–
    (a) persons,
    (b) time,
    (c) place and mode of inspection,
    (d) production or opening,
as the court making the order thinks expedient; but in making and carrying into effect an order for the opening of a packet containing the electronic record or a packet of completed corresponding number lists or certificates or for the inspection of counted ballot papers, care must be taken that the way in which the vote of any particular elector has been given must not be disclosed until it has been proved–
    (i) that his vote was given, and
    (ii) that the vote has been declared by a competent court to be invalid.

(4) An appeal lies to the High Court from any order of a county court under this rule.

(5) Any power given under this rule to a county court may be exercised by any judge of the court otherwise than in open court.

(6) Where an order is made for the production by the relevant registration officer of any document or electronic record in his custody relating to any specified election–
    (a) the production by him or his agent of the document or electronic record ordered in such manner as may be directed by that order will be conclusive evidence that the document or electronic record relates to the specified election, and
    (b) any endorsement on any packet of ballot papers or so produced will be *prima facie* evidence that the ballot papers are what they are stated to be by the endorsement.

(7) The production from proper custody of–
    (a) a ballot paper purporting to have been used at any election, or
    (b) a copy of the electronic record which purports to record that a particular ballot paper was used at any election, and
a completed corresponding number list with a number written beside the number of the ballot paper, will be *prima facie* evidence that the elector whose vote was given by that ballot paper was the person who, at the time of the election, had affixed to his entry in the register of electors or on the notice issued under section 13B(3B) or (3D) of the 1983 Act, the same number as was written on the completed corresponding number list.

(8) Unless authorised by this rule, no person may be allowed to inspect any rejected or counted ballot papers in the custody of the relevant registration officer or open any sealed packets of completed corresponding number lists, certificates of employment on the day of the poll or containing the electronic record.

Retention and destruction of documents and records

59   The relevant registration officer must retain or cause to be retained for one year all

documents and, where applicable, the electronic record relating to an election forwarded to him in pursuance of these Rules by a CRO, and then, unless otherwise directed by an order of a county court, a Crown Court, a magistrate's court or an election court, must cause them to be destroyed.

Part 7
Death of Candidate

Countermand or abandonment of poll on death of candidate

60 (1) If at a contested election proof is given to the CRO's satisfaction before the result of the election is declared that one of the persons named or to be named as candidate in the ballot papers has died, the CRO–

    (a) must countermand notice of the poll or, if polling has begun, direct that the poll be abandoned,

    (b) must inform the GLRO of the countermand or abandonment of the poll and of the name of the candidate who has died.

(2) Subsection (1) of section 39 (local elections void etc in England and Wales) of the 1983 Act applies in respect of any vacancy which remains unfilled as if for the reference to the returning officer there were substituted a reference to the CRO.

(3) Where the poll is abandoned by reason of a candidate's death, no further ballot papers may be issued, and the presiding officer at any polling station must take the like steps (so far as not already taken) for the delivery to the CRO of ballot boxes and of ballot papers and other documents in his possession as he is required to take on the close of the poll in due course.

(4) The CRO must dispose of the ballot papers and other documents in his possession as he is required to do on the completion in due course of the counting of the votes, subject to paragraphs (5) and (6).

(5) It is not be necessary for any ballot paper account to be prepared or verified.

(6) The CRO must seal up all the ballot papers, whether the votes on them have been counted or not, and it will not be necessary to seal up counted and rejected ballot papers in separate packets.

(7) The provisions of these Rules as to the inspection, production, retention and destruction of ballot papers and other documents relating to a poll at an election apply to any such documents relating to a poll abandoned by reason of a candidate's death, subject to paragraphs (8) and (9).

(8) Ballot papers on which the votes were neither counted nor rejected must be treated as counted ballot papers.

(9) No order may be made for–

    (a) the production or inspection of any ballot papers, or

    (b) for the opening of a sealed packet of completed corresponding number lists or certificates as to employment on duty on the day of the poll,

unless the order is made by a court with reference to a prosecution.

SCHEDULE 2

THE LONDON MEMBERS ELECTION RULES

Rule 3(3)

Part 1

General Provisions

Part 1
General Provisions

Citation

1   This Schedule may be cited as the London Members Election Rules.

Interpretation

2 (1)   In the rules in this Schedule, unless the context indicates otherwise–
"election" means an election for the return of the London members;
"individual candidate" means a candidate other than a list candidate at an election for

the return of London members;

"list candidate" means a person included on a party list;

"local count" means the count of the London votes given for a registered party or, as the case may be, an individual candidate, at an election in an Assembly constituency;

"London vote" has the same meaning as in Part 1 of the 1999 Act;

"party list" means a list delivered to the GLRO in accordance with paragraph 5 (party lists and individual candidates) of Part 2 of Schedule 2 to the 1999 Act on behalf of a party registered under Part 2 (registration of political parties) of the 2000 Act.

(2)   Reference to a rule by number alone is a reference to the rule so numbered in this Schedule.

Part 2
Provisions as to Time

Timetable

3   The proceedings at the election must be conducted in accordance with the following timetable:

Timetable

Proceedings	Time
Publication of notice of election	Not later than the thirtieth day before the day of election.
Delivery of nomination papers and party lists	Not later than 4 in the afternoon on the twenty-fourth day before the day of election.
Delivery of notices of withdrawals of candidature	Not later than 4 in the afternoon on the twenty-fourth day before the day of election
Publication of statement as to persons nominated	Not later than 4 in the afternoon on the twenty-second day before the day of election.
Notice of poll	Not later than the sixth day before the day of election.
Polling	Between the hours of 7 in the morning and 10 at night on the day of election.

Computation of time

4 (1)   In computing any period of time for the purposes of the Timetable–

(a)   a Saturday or Sunday,

(b)   Christmas Eve, Christmas Day, Good Friday or a bank holiday, or

(c)   a day appointed for public thanksgiving or mourning,

must be disregarded, and any such day must not be treated as a day for the purpose of any proceedings up to the completion of the poll nor must the CRO be obliged to proceed with the counting of the votes on such a day.

(2)   In this rule, "bank holiday" means a day which is a bank holiday under the Banking and Financial Dealings Act 1971 in England and Wales.

Part 3
Stages Common to Contested and Uncontested Elections

Notice of election

5 (1)   The GLRO must publish in each Assembly constituency notice of the election stating–

    (a)   the place and times at which nomination papers and party lists are to be delivered, and

    (b)   the date of the poll in the event of a contest,

and the notice must state that forms of nomination papers and party lists may be obtained at that place and those times.

(2)   The notice of election must state the arrangements (if any) which apply for the payment of the deposit required by rule 10 by means of the electronic transfer of funds.

(3)   The notice of election must state the date by which–

    (a)   applications to vote by post or proxy, and

    (b)   other applications and notices about postal or proxy voting,

must reach the registration officer for local government electors in order that they may be effective for the election.

Nomination of candidates: individual candidates

6 (1)   Each individual candidate must be nominated by a separate nomination paper that must be–

    (a)   in the appropriate form, and

    (b)   delivered to the GLRO in accordance with the following provisions of this rule and rule 8.

(2)   The nomination paper of an individual candidate must state the candidate's–

    (a)   full names,

    (b)   home address, in full, and

    (c)   if desired, a description consisting of the word "independent",

and the surname must be placed first in the list of names.

Nomination of candidates: list candidates

7 (1)   A registered party which is a qualifying party and is to stand at the election of London members must be nominated by the delivery of a nomination paper which must be–

    (a)   in the appropriate form, and

    (b)   delivered to the GLRO by the party's registered nominating officer, or a person authorised in writing by him, in accordance with the following provisions of this rule and rule 8.

(2)   The registered party's nomination paper must–

    (a)   state the authorised description by which the registered party is to stand for election,

    (b)   include a statement, signed by the person issuing the paper, that it is issued either–

        (i)   by the party's registered nominating officer, or

        (ii)   on behalf of the party's registered nominating officer by a person authorised in writing by him, and

    (c)   be accompanied by a party list which sets out the full names and home addresses of each candidate included in that list.

(3)   An authorised description for the purposes of paragraph (2)(a) must be either–

    (a)   the name of the party registered under section 28 of the 2000 Act, or

    (b)   a description of the party, registered under section 28A of that Act.

(4)   A person will be guilty of a corrupt practice if he fraudulently purports to be authorised to make the statement required by paragraph (2)(b) by or on behalf of a registered

party's nominating officer.

(5) For the purposes of the application of these rules in relation to an election–
    (a) "registered party" means a party which was registered under Part 2 of the 2000 Act on the day ("the relevant day") which is two days before the last day for the delivery of nomination papers and party lists at that election,
    (b) a registered party is a qualifying party if on the relevant day the party was registered in respect of England in the Great Britain register maintained under that Part of that Act.

Nomination papers: general provisions

8 (1) The following provisions of this rule have effect in relation to nomination papers delivered under rules 6 and 7.

(2) If an individual candidate or a candidate included on a party list commonly uses–
    (a) a surname which is different from any other surname he has, or
    (b) a forename which is different from any other forename he has,
the nomination paper and party list may state the commonly used surname or forename, or both surname and forename in addition to the other name.

(3) Each nomination paper must be delivered to the GLRO at the place specified by him in the notice of election, which must be at one of the offices of the Greater London Authority, and must be received by the GLRO before the last time for the delivery of nomination papers.

(4) Where a nomination paper is delivered in respect of–
    (a) the same registered party, or
    (b) the same individual candidate,
after an earlier nomination paper has been delivered, that later paper must be deemed to supersede the earlier one.

(5) In this rule and in the following provisions of these rules, unless the context requires otherwise–
    (a) "nomination paper" includes a reference to–
        (i) the nomination paper of a registered party, and
        (ii) the nomination paper of an individual candidate;
    (b) "nomination paper of a registered party" includes a reference to a party list.

Consent to nomination

9 (1) A person will not be validly nominated (whether as an individual candidate or a list candidate) unless his consent to nomination–
    (a) is given in writing in the appropriate form, or a form to like effect, on or within one month before the last day for the delivery of nomination papers;
    (b) is attested by one witness whose name and address must be given; and
    (c) is delivered at the place and within the time for delivery of nomination papers.

(2) A candidate's consent given under this rule must–
    (a) state the day, month and year of his birth;
    (b) contain a statement that he has read whichever of sub-paragraphs (5) and (6) of paragraph 5 of Schedule 2 to the 1999 Act (persons who many not be candidates) applies in his case; and
    (c) contain a statement that to the best of the candidate's knowledge and belief he is not disqualified from being elected by reason of–
        (i) any disqualification set out in section 21 (disqualification from being the Mayor or an Assembly member) of the 1999 Act,
        (ii) a decision made under section 78A of the Local Government Act 2000 (decisions of First-tier tribunal), or

(iii) an order made under section 34(4) of the Localism Act 2011(offences).

Deposits

10 (1) A person will not be validly nominated as an individual candidate at the election unless the sum of £5,000 is deposited by him, or on his behalf, with the GLRO at the place and during the time for delivery of nomination papers and party lists.

(2) A registered party (and anyone on its party list) will not be validly nominated unless the sum of £5,000 is deposited on its behalf with the GLRO at the place and during the time for delivery of nomination papers and party lists.

(3) The deposit may be made either–
  (a) by the deposit of any legal tender, or
  (b) by means of a banker's draft, or
  (c) with the GLRO's consent, in any other manner including by means of a debit or credit card or the electronic transfer of funds,

but the GLRO may refuse to accept a deposit sought to be made by means of a banker's draft if he does not know that the drawer carries on business as a banker in the United Kingdom.

(4) Where the deposit is made on behalf of an individual candidate, the person making the deposit must at the time he makes it give his name and address to the GLRO, unless they have previously been given to him under section 67 (appointment of election agent) of the 1983 Act.

Decisions as to validity of nomination papers

11 (1) Where, in the case of an individual candidate, a nomination paper ("individual nomination paper") and the candidate's consent to it are delivered, and a deposit is made, in accordance with these Rules, the candidate will be deemed to stand nominated unless and until–
  (a) the GLRO decides that the nomination paper is invalid, or
  (b) proof is given to the GLRO's satisfaction of the candidate's death, or
  (c) the candidate withdraws.

(2) Where the nomination paper of a registered party and the consent of each candidate included in that party's list are delivered, and a deposit is made, in accordance with these Rules, that party and (subject to paragraph (6)) each candidate on its list must be deemed to stand nominated unless and until the GLRO decides that the nomination paper is invalid.

(3) As soon as practicable after each nomination paper has been delivered, the GLRO must examine it and decide whether the individual candidate, or as the case may be each registered party and each candidate included in that party's list, has been validly nominated.

(4) The GLRO is entitled to hold an individual nomination paper invalid only on the grounds that the particulars of the candidate on the nomination paper are not as required by law.

(5) The GLRO is entitled to hold the nomination paper of a registered party invalid only on one of the following grounds–
  (a) that the authorised description stated under rule 7(2)(a) breaches rule 7(3);
  (b) that the nomination paper does not contain the statement referred to in rule 7(2)(b);
  (c) that the number of candidates on the list is greater than 25.

(6) Where, in respect of a candidate included in a party list–

    (a) proof is given to the GLRO's satisfaction of his death;

    (b) he withdraws or his candidature is withdrawn in accordance with rule 15;

    (c) his particulars in that list are not as required by law;

    (d) the consent to nomination of that candidate is not delivered in accordance with rule 9,

the GLRO must delete the name and address of that candidate from the list.

(7)   Where the GLRO has decided under paragraph (3)–

    (a) that an individual nomination paper is invalid,

    (b) that the nomination paper of a registered party is invalid or that the name and address of a list candidate must be deleted from the list,

he must endorse and sign on the nomination paper to record that decision and the reasons for his decision.

(8)   The GLRO must, as soon as practicable after making such a decision under paragraph (3) that a nomination paper is valid or invalid, send notice of that decision–

    (a) to the candidate at his home address as given in his nomination paper, and

    (b) in the case of a list candidate, also to the nominating officer.

(9)   Where in the GLRO's opinion the nomination paper of a registered party is invalid on the grounds in paragraphs (5)(a) or (b), then he must give a decision to that effect–

    (a) as soon as practicable after the delivery of the nomination paper, and

    (b) in any event, before the end of the period of 24 hours starting with the end of the period for the delivery of nomination papers set out in the timetable in rule 3.

(10)   The GLRO's decision that a nomination paper is valid is final and may not be questioned in any proceeding whatsoever.

(11)   Subject to paragraph (10), nothing in this rule prevents the validity of a nomination being questioned on an election petition.

Publication of statement of persons nominated

12 (1)   The GLRO must prepare and publish a statement showing–

    (a) each registered party which has been and stands nominated, together with that party's list,

    (b) the persons who have been and stand nominated as individual candidates, and

    (c) any other parties or persons who have been nominated, together with the reason why they no longer stand nominated.

(2)   If an individual's nomination paper or person's entry on a party list gives a commonly used surname or forename, or both surname and forename, in addition to another name, the statement must show the person's commonly used surname or forename, or both surname and forename (as the case may be) instead of any other name.

(3)   Paragraph (2) does not apply if the GLRO thinks–

    (a) that the use of the person's commonly used name may be likely to mislead or confuse electors, or

    (b) that the commonly used name is obscene or offensive.

(4)   If paragraph (3) applies, the GLRO must give notice in writing to the candidate of his reasons for refusing to allow the use of a commonly used name.

(5)   The statement must show, in the following order–

    (a) the registered parties which have been and stand nominated, set out in alphabetical order according to the authorised descriptions given in the nomination papers,

    (b) the names and home addresses of the list candidates as given in party lists, arranged in the order in which their names appear in those lists,

    (c)   the names, addresses and descriptions (if any) of the persons standing nominated as individual candidates, arranged alphabetically in the order of their surnames and, if there are two or more of them with the same surname, of their other names.

(6)   In the case of an individual candidate nominated by more than one nomination paper, the GLRO must take the particulars required by the foregoing provisions of this rule from such one of the papers as the candidate (or the GLRO in default of the candidate) may select.

Correction of minor errors

13 (1)   The GLRO may, if he thinks fit, at any time before the publication under rule 12 of the statement of parties and persons nominated, correct minor errors in a nomination paper.

(2)   Errors which may be corrected include–

    (a)   errors as to a person's electoral number,

    (b)   obvious errors of spelling in relation to the details of a party or candidate.

(3)   Anything done by the GLRO in pursuance of this rule may not be questioned in any proceedings other than proceedings on an election petition.

(4)   The GLRO must have regard to any guidance issued by the Electoral Commission for the purposes of this rule.

Inspection of nomination papers and consent to nomination

14 (1)   During ordinary office hours, in the period starting 24 hours after the latest time for the delivery of nomination papers and before the date of the poll, any person may inspect and take copies of, or extracts from–

    (a)   a nomination paper, or

    (b)   the consents to nomination.

(2)   Inspection under paragraph (1) may not take place on a day that is specified in rule 4(1).

Withdrawal or death of candidate

15 (1)   An individual candidate or a candidate on a party's list may withdraw his candidature by notice of withdrawal–

    (a)   signed by him and attested by one witness, whose name and address must be given, and

    (b)   delivered to the GLRO at the place for delivery of nomination papers and party lists,

by the end of the period for the delivery of notices of withdrawals of candidature in the timetable in rule 3.

(2)   The nominating officer of a registered party, or a person authorised in writing by him may withdraw that party's nomination by a notice of withdrawal signed by him and delivered to the returning officer at the place for delivery of nomination papers and party lists.

(3)   Where a candidate is outside the United Kingdom, a notice of withdrawal signed by his election agent and accompanied by a written declaration also so signed of the candidate's absence from the United Kingdom will be of the same effect as a notice of withdrawal signed by the candidate; but where the candidate stands nominated by more than one nomination paper a notice of withdrawal under this paragraph will be

effective if, and only if, it is accompanied, in addition to that declaration, by a written statement signed by the candidate that the person giving the notice is authorised to do so on the candidate's behalf during his absence from the United Kingdom.

(4) If before the result of the election is declared, proof is given to the GLRO's satisfaction that an individual candidate who is named (or is to be named) in the ballot papers or a candidate whose name appears on a party list has died, then (in addition to complying with any other requirement of these rules relevant to that event) the GLRO must–
   (a) inform each CRO of the death of the candidate;
   (b) in the case of a person whose name is included in a party list, remove that person's name from that list.

Method of election

16 If, after any withdrawals under rule 15, the number of persons remaining validly nominated exceeds the number of seats available for allocation to London members, then, unless all of those persons are named on the same party list, a poll must be taken in accordance with Part 4 of these Rules.

Part 4
Contested Elections

Poll to be taken by ballot

17 The votes at the poll must be given by ballot to enable the seats for London members to be allocated to registered parties and individual candidates in accordance with paragraphs 7 and 8 of Part 2 of Schedule 2 to the 1999 Act.

The ballot papers

18 (1) The ballot of every voter must consist of a ballot paper which must be in the appropriate form.

(2) Each registered party that remains validly nominated at the election and whose party list includes a person who remains validly nominated as a list candidate, after any withdrawals, and no other, is entitled to have its authorised description inserted in the ballot paper.

(3) Each person remaining validly nominated as an individual candidate at the election, after any withdrawals, and no other, is entitled to have their name inserted in the ballot paper.

(4) Every ballot paper–
   (a) must, so far as practicable for the purposes of electronic counting, be printed in accordance with the directions set out in the Forms Schedule,
   (b) must contain the authorised descriptions of the registered parties; and the names and other particulars of the individual candidates as shown in the statement of persons nominated,
   (c) must have a number and other unique identifying mark printed on the back, and
   (d) may, in the case of ballot papers for use at polling stations, be marked with the words "do not fold".

(5) If a request is made by or on behalf of a registered party's nominating officer, the ballot paper must contain, against the party's authorised description, the party's registered emblem (or, as the case may be, one of the party's registered emblems).

(6) The request under paragraph (5) must–

      (a) be made in writing to the GLRO, and

      (b) be received by him during the period for delivery of nomination papers and party lists set out in the timetable in rule 3.

(7)   The order of the authorised descriptions of the registered parties and the names of the individual candidates must be in the same order as in the statement of parties and persons nominated.

(8)   The GLRO must supply the ballot papers for use at the election to the CRO by such date as may be agreed between them.

(9)   The ballot papers supplied under paragraph (8) must be of a different colour from those used at any other Authority election.

The corresponding number list

19 (1) The CRO must prepare a list containing the numbers and other unique identifying marks of all of the ballot papers to be issued by him in pursuance of rule 24(1) or provided by him in pursuance of rule 29(1).

(2)   The list must be in the appropriate form or a form to like effect.

(3)   At an ordinary election, the same list may be used for each Authority election with which the election is combined.

The official mark

20 (1) Every ballot paper must contain an appropriate security marking (the official mark).

(2)   The official mark must be kept secret, and an interval of not less than five years must intervene between the use of the same official mark at any Authority election.

(3)   The GLRO may use a different official mark for different purposes at the same election.

Prohibition of disclosure of vote

21   No person who has voted at the election may, in any legal proceeding to question the election, be required to state for which candidate or party he has voted.

Use of schools and public rooms

22 (1) The CRO may use, free of charge, for the purpose of taking the poll or counting the votes–

      (a) a room in a school maintained or assisted by a local authority (as defined in the Education Act 1996) or a school in respect of which grants are made out of moneys provided by Parliament to the person or body of persons responsible for the management of the school,

      (b) a room the expense of maintaining which is met by any local authority.

(2)   The CRO must make good any damage done to, and defray an expense incurred by the persons having control over, any such room as mentioned in paragraph (1) by reason of its being used for the purpose of taking the poll or counting the votes.

Notice of poll

23 (1) The GLRO must, in accordance with the timetable in rule 3, publish notice of the poll stating–

      (a) the day and hours fixed for the poll,

      (b) the number of seats for London members available for allocation at that election,

(c) the authorised description of each registered party whose party list includes persons who remain validly nominated as list candidates, and

(d) the name and description (if any) of each individual candidate remaining validly nominated,

and rule 12(5) applies in relation to the order in which that information appears on the notice of the poll as it applies in relation to the statement of persons nominated.

(2) The CRO must, not later than the time of the publication of the notice of the poll, also give public notice of–

(a) the situation of each polling station, and

(b) the description of voters entitled to vote there,

and he must as soon as practicable after giving such a notice give a copy of it to each of the election agents.

(3) The notice of poll must include the heading "GREATER LONDON AUTHORITY ELECTION".

Postal ballot papers

24 (1) The CRO must, in accordance with regulations made under the 1983 Act, issue to those entitled to vote by post a ballot paper and a postal voting statement, together with such envelopes for their return as may be prescribed in such regulations.

(2) The postal voting statement must be in the appropriate form, or a form to the like effect.

(3) The postal voting statement must include provision for the form to be signed and for stating the date of birth of the elector or proxy (as the case may be).

(4) The CRO must also issue to those entitled to vote by post such information as he thinks appropriate about how to obtain–

(a) translations into languages other than English of any directions to or guidance for voters sent with the ballot paper,

(b) a translation into Braille of such directions or guidance,

(c) graphical representations of such directions or guidance,

(d) the directions or guidance in any other form (including any audible form).

(5) In the case of a ballot paper issued to a person at an address in the United Kingdom, the CRO must ensure that the return of the ballot paper and postal voting statement is free of charge to the voter.

(6) Where the proceedings on the issue and receipt of postal ballot papers at the election are taken together with any other Authority election the appropriate form of postal voting statement under paragraph (2) may be the joint postal voting statement which must be in the appropriate form or form to like effect.

Provision of polling stations

25 (1) The CRO must provide a sufficient number of polling stations and, subject to the following provisions of this rule, must allot the electors to the polling stations in such manner as he thinks most convenient.

(2) One or more polling stations may be provided in the same room.

(3) The polling station allotted to electors from any parliamentary polling district wholly or partly within the Assembly constituency must, in the absence of special circumstances, be in the parliamentary polling place for that district, unless that place is outside the Assembly constituency.

(4) The CRO must provide each polling station with such number of compartments as may

be necessary in which the voters can mark their votes screened from observation.

Appointment of presiding officers and clerks

26 (1) The CRO must appoint and pay a presiding officer to attend at each polling station and such clerks and technical assistants as may be necessary for the purposes of the election, but he must not appoint any person who has been employed in or about the election by or on behalf of a candidate or a registered party which has been nominated.

(2) The CRO may, if he thinks fit, preside at a polling station and the provisions of this Part relating to a presiding officer apply to the CRO so presiding with the necessary modifications as to things to be done by the CRO to the presiding officer or by the presiding officer to the CRO.

(3) A presiding officer may do, by the clerks appointed to assist him, any act (including the asking of questions) which he is required or authorised by this Part to do at a polling station except order the arrest, exclusion or removal of any person from the polling station.

Issue of official poll cards

27 (1) The CRO must as soon as practicable after the publication of the notice of election, send to electors and their proxies an official poll card.

(2) An elector's official poll card must be sent or delivered to his qualifying address, and a proxy's to his address as shown in the list of proxies.

(3) The official poll card must be in the appropriate form or a form to like effect, and must set out–

(a) that the election is of the London members of the London Assembly at an ordinary election,

(b) the elector's name, qualifying address and number on the register,

(c) the date and hours of the poll and the situation of the elector's polling station, and

(d) such other information as the CRO thinks appropriate,

and different information may be provided in pursuance of sub-paragraph (d) to different electors or descriptions of elector.

(4) In the case of an elector with an anonymous entry, instead of containing the matter mentioned in paragraph (3)(b), the polling card must contain such matter as is specified in the appropriate form.

(5) Where the ordinary elections for constituency members and the Mayor are contested, the CRO must issue a combined poll card in the appropriate form.

(6) In this rule "elector" means–

(a) an elector with an entry on the register to be used at the election on the last day for the publication of the notice of the election, and

(b) includes a person then shown in the register as below voting age if (but only if) it appears from the register that he will be of voting age on the day fixed for the poll.

Information for voters

28 (1) At an ordinary election, the GLRO may, in addition to a statement by him in an election booklet, include in the booklet information for voters that has been agreed by him with the Electoral Commission.

(2) The information for voters given in the election booklet may include information

about–
(a) the office of the Mayor and the London Assembly,
(b) the system of voting at each Authority election,
(c) how to vote in a manner that will ensure a vote is regarded as validly cast, and

subject to paragraph (3), may include any other information given in exercise of the GLRO's duty under section 69 (encouraging electoral participation) of the 2006 Act.

(3) The information for voters must not contain–
(a) any advertising material,
(b) any material referring to a candidate or a registered party, other than by reproduction of a ballot paper which refers equally to all candidates and parties at the ordinary election,
(c) any material referring to the holder, at any time, of the office of Mayor or Assembly member, other than under paragraph (b) as a candidate at the ordinary election.

(4) Information published in an election booklet under this rule must be printed on not more than two sides of A5 paper.

Equipment of polling stations

29 (1) The CRO must provide each presiding officer with–
(a) such ballot papers as may be necessary, and
(b) such ballot boxes as may be necessary having taken account of any direction made by the GLRO in accordance with paragraph (9).

(2) Every ballot box must be so constructed that the ballot papers can be put in it, but cannot be withdrawn from it, without the box being unlocked or, where the box has no lock, the seal being broken.

(3) The CRO must provide each polling station with–
(a) materials to enable voters to mark the ballot papers,
(b) copies of the register of electors or such part of it as contains the entries relating to the electors allotted to the station,
(c) the parts of any special lists prepared for the election corresponding to the register of electors or the part of it provided under sub-paragraph (b),
(d) a notice of the death of any person of whose death he has been informed as mentioned in rule 15(4),
(e) a list consisting of that part of the list prepared under rule 19 which contains the numbers (but not the other unique identifying marks) corresponding to those on the ballot papers provided to the presiding officer of the polling station.

(4) The reference in paragraph (3)(b) to the copies of the register of electors includes a reference to copies of any notices issued under section 13B(3B) or (3D) of the 1983 Act in respect of alterations to the register.

(5) The CRO must also provide each polling station with a device for enabling voters who are blind or partially sighted to vote without any need for assistance from the presiding officer or any companion within the meaning of rule 41.

(6) The device referred to in paragraph (5) above must–
(a) allow a ballot paper to be inserted into and removed from or attached to and detached from the device, easily and without damage to the paper,
(b) keep the ballot paper firmly in place during use,
(c) provide suitable means for the voter to–
(i) identify the spaces on the ballot paper on which he may mark his vote,
(ii) identify the candidate to whom each such space refers, and
(iii) mark his vote on the space he has chosen.

(7) The enlarged sample copies of the ballot paper that the GLRO is required to provide, or cause to be displayed at every polling station (in accordance with section 199B(5) and (7) of the 1983 Act) must–

    (a) be provided to the CRO who will deliver them to the polling stations, and

    (b) be of the same colour as the ballot paper at the election.

(8) The CRO must also provide each polling station with notices for the guidance of voters, which must be exhibited–

    (a) outside the polling station,

    (b) inside the polling station–

        (i) in the communal areas, and

        (ii) in every voting compartment.

(9) If the GLRO thinks fit he may, not later than the date of the notice of election, direct the CRO that joint ballot boxes must be used for the ballot papers at the election and any or all Authority elections with which the election is taken.

Notices for the guidance of voters

30 (1) The GLRO must prepare and provide each CRO with the notices to be exhibited under rule 29(8).

(2) The GLRO may also provide each CRO with versions of the notices in such other form as he thinks appropriate, in accordance with section 199B (translations etc of certain documents) of the 1983 Act.

(3) Notices for the guidance of voters exhibited under rule 28(8) or paragraph (2) must be in the appropriate form, but may include such alternative information relating to Authority elections as–

    (a) meets with the requirements of the Notices Schedule, and

    (b) the GLRO may decide.

(4) Notices provided under paragraph (2) may, if the CRO agrees, be exhibited at any polling station–

    (a) outside the polling station,

    (b) inside the polling station, or

    (c) in every compartment of the polling station.

Appointment of polling and counting agents

31 (1) Before the commencement of the poll–

    (a) each individual candidate, and

    (b) the election agent of each list candidate,

may appoint–

        (i) polling agents to attend at polling stations for the purpose of detecting personation, and

        (ii) counting agents to attend at the local count.

(2) The same person may be appointed as a polling agent or counting agent by, or in the case of list candidates on behalf of, more than one candidate.

(3) For each local count, one (but no more than one) counting agent of each registered party standing nominated or individual candidate, as the case may be, may be authorised by the terms of his appointment to require a re-count at that count.

(4) Not more than four polling agents, or such greater number as the CRO may by notice allow, may be permitted to attend at any particular polling station.

(5) If the number of such agents appointed to attend at a particular polling station exceeds that number, the CRO must determine by lot which agents are permitted to

attend, and only the agents on whom the lot falls will be deemed to have been duly appointed.

(6) The CRO may limit the number of counting agents, but in doing so must ensure that–

   (a) the number is the same in the case of each candidate, and

   (b) the number allowed to a candidate must not (except in special circumstances) be less than the number obtained by dividing the number of clerks employed on the counting by the number of candidates.

(7) For the purposes of the calculations required by paragraph (6)–

   (a) a counting agent appointed for more than one list candidate must be deemed to be appointed for all the candidates on that list,

   (b) a counting agent appointed for more than one candidate (other than a list candidate) is a separate agent for each of the candidates for whom he has been appointed.

(8) Notice in writing of the appointment of polling and counting agents, stating the names and addresses of the persons appointed, must be given by the candidate to the CRO and must be so given not later than the fifth day (computed in accordance with rule 4) before the day of the poll.

(9) If an agent dies, or becomes incapable of acting, the candidate or, as the case may be, the election agent, may appoint another person in his place, and must forthwith give to the CRO notice in writing of the name and address of that other person.

(10) Any appointment authorised by this rule may be made and the notice of appointment given to the CRO by the candidate's election agent, instead of by the candidate.

(11) In the following provisions of these Rules references to polling agents and counting agents must be taken as references to agents–

   (a) whose appointments have been duly made and notified, and

   (b) where the number of agents is restricted, who are within the permitted numbers.

(12) Any notice required to be given to a counting agent by the CRO may be delivered at, or sent by post to, the address stated in the notice of appointment.

(13) A candidate may himself do any act or thing which any polling or counting agent of his, if appointed, would have been authorised to do, or may assist his agent in doing any such act or thing.

(14) A candidate's election agent may do or assist in doing anything which a polling or counting agent of his is authorised to do; and anything required or authorised by these Rules to be done in the presence of the polling or counting agent may be done in the presence of a candidate's election agent instead of his polling agent or counting agent.

(15) Where by these Rules any act or thing is required or authorised to be done in the presence of the polling or counting agents, the non-attendance of any agent or agents at the time and place appointed for the purpose will not, if the act or thing is otherwise duly done, invalidate the act or thing done.

Notification of requirement of secrecy

32 (1) The CRO must make such arrangements as he thinks fit to ensure that–

   (a) every person attending at a polling station (otherwise than for the purpose of voting or assisting a voter with disabilities to vote or as a constable on duty there) has been given a copy of the provisions of subsections (1), (3) and (6) of section 66 (requirement of secrecy) of the Representation of the People Act 1983, and

   (b) every person attending at the counting of the votes (other than any constable on duty at the counting) has been given a copy of the provisions of subsections (2) and (6) of that section.

(2) In paragraph (1) a reference to a constable includes a person designated as a community support officer under section 38 of the 2002 Act (police powers for employees).

Return of postal ballot papers

33 (1) Where–

    (a) a postal vote has been returned in respect of a person who is entered on the postal voters list, or

    (b) a proxy postal vote has been returned in respect of a proxy who is entered on the proxy postal voters list,

the CRO must mark the list in the manner prescribed by regulations made under the 1983 Act.

(2) Rule 50(2) does not apply for the purpose of determining whether, for the purposes of this rule, a postal vote or a proxy postal vote is returned.

Admission to polling station

34 (1) The presiding officer must exclude all persons from the polling station except–

    (a) voters,

    (b) persons under the age of 18 who accompany voters to the polling station,

    (c) the candidates and their election agents,

    (d) the polling agents appointed to attend at the polling station,

    (e) the clerks appointed to attend at the polling station,

    (f) persons who are entitled to attend by virtue of any of sections 6A to 6D of the 2000 Act,

    (g) the constables on duty, and

    (h) the companions of voters with disabilities.

(2) The presiding officer must regulate the total number of voters and persons under the age of 18 who accompany them to be admitted to the polling station at the same time.

(3) Not more than one polling agent may be admitted at the same time to a polling station on behalf of the same party or individual candidate.

(4) A constable or person employed by the CRO must not be admitted to vote in person elsewhere than at his own polling station allotted to him under these Rules, except on production and surrender of a certificate as to his employment which must be in the appropriate form and signed by an officer of the police of or above the rank of inspector or by the CRO, as the case may be.

(5) Any certificate surrendered under this rule must forthwith be cancelled.

(6) In this rule a reference to a constable includes a person designated as a community support officer under section 38 of the 2002 Act.

Keeping of order in station

35 (1) It is the presiding officer's duty to keep order at his polling station.

(2) If a person misconducts himself in a polling station, or fails to obey the presiding officer's lawful orders, he may immediately, by the presiding officer's order, be removed from the polling station–

    (a) by a constable in or near that station, or

    (b) by any other person authorised in writing by the CRO to remove him, and the person so removed must not, without the presiding officer's permission, again enter the polling station during the day.

(3) Any person so removed may, if charged with the commission in the polling station of an offence, be dealt with as a person taken into custody by a constable for an offence without a warrant.

(4) The powers conferred by this rule must not be exercised so as to prevent a voter who is otherwise entitled to vote at a polling station from having an opportunity of voting at that station.

Sealing of ballot boxes

36 Immediately before the commencement of the poll, the presiding officer must–
    (a) show each ballot box, empty, to such persons, if any, as are present in the polling station, so that they may see that the boxes are empty,
    (b) lock up such of the boxes as have locks,
    (c) place his seal–
        (i) on each lock, and
        (ii) on each ballot box which has no lock,
in such a manner as to prevent its being opened without breaking the seal,
    (d) place each box in his view for the receipt of ballot papers, and
    (e) keep each box locked and sealed or, as the case may be, sealed.

Questions to be put to voters

37 (1) At the time of the application (but not afterwards), the questions specified in the second column of the following table–
    (a) may be put by the presiding officer to a person who is mentioned in the first column, and
    (b) must be put if the letter "R" appears after the question and the candidate or his election or polling agent requires the question to be put.

Q No	Person applying for ballot paper	Question
1	A person applying as an elector	(a)–Are you the person registered in the register of local government electors for this election as follows (*read the whole entry from the register*)? R (b)–Have you already voted, here or elsewhere in Greater London at this election for London members, otherwise than as proxy for some other person? R
2	A person applying as proxy	(a)–Are you the person whose name appears as AB in the list of proxies for this election as entitled to vote as proxy on behalf of CD?R (b)–Have you already voted here or elsewhere in Greater London at this election for London members, as proxy on behalf of CD?R (c)–Are you the spouse, civil partner, parent, grandparent, brother, sister, child or grandchild of CD?R
3	A person applying as proxy for an elector with an anonymous entry (instead of the questions at entry 2)	(a)–Are you the person entitled to vote as proxy on behalf of the elector whose number on the register of electors is

		(*read out the number*)? R
		(b)–Have you already voted here or elsewhere as proxy on behalf of the elector whose number on the register of electors is (*read out the number*)? R
		(c)–Are you the spouse, civil partner, parent, grandparent, brother, sister, child or grandchild of the person whose number on the register of electors is (*read out the number*)? R
4	A person applying as proxy if the question at entry 2(c) or 3(c) is not answered in the affirmative	Have you already voted here or elsewhere in Greater London at this election for London members, on behalf of two persons of whom you are not the spouse, civil partner, parent, grandparent, brother, sister, child or grandchild? R
5	A person applying as an elector in relation to whom there is an entry in the postal voters list	(a)–Did you apply to vote by post?
		(b)–Why have you not voted by post?
6	A person applying as proxy who is named in the proxy postal voters list	(a)–Did you apply to vote by post as proxy?
		(b)–Why have you not voted by post as proxy?

(2)   In the case of an elector in respect of whom a notice has been issued under section 13B(3B) or (3D) of the 1983 Act, the references in the questions at entries 1(a) and 3(a), (b) and (c) to reading from the register must be taken as references to reading from the notice issued under those subsections.

(3)   A ballot paper must not be delivered to any person required to answer any of the above questions unless he has answered each question satisfactorily.

(4)   Except as authorised by this rule, no inquiry may be permitted as to the right of any person to vote.

Challenge of voter

38   A person must not be prevented from voting because–
   (a)   a candidate or his election or polling agent declares that he has reasonable cause to believe that the person has committed an offence of personation, or
   (b)   the person is arrested on the grounds that he is suspected of committing or of being about to commit such an offence.

Voting procedure

39 (1)   A ballot paper must be delivered to a voter who applies for one, and immediately before delivery–
   (a)   the number and (unless paragraph (2) applies) name of the elector as stated in the copy of the register of electors must be called out,
   (b)   the number of the elector must be marked on the list mentioned in rule 29(3)(e) beside the number of the ballot paper to be delivered to him,
   (c)   a mark must be placed in the register of electors against the number of the elector to note that a ballot paper has been applied for but without showing the particular ballot paper which may be delivered,

(d) in the case of a person applying for a ballot paper as proxy, a mark must also be placed against his name in the list of proxies.

(2) In the case of an elector who has an anonymous entry, he must show the presiding officer his official poll card and only his number may be called out in pursuance of paragraph (1)(a).

(3) In the case of an elector who is added to the register in pursuance of a notice issued under section 13B(3B) or (3D) of the 1983 Act, paragraph (1) is modified as follows–
   (a) in sub-paragraph (a), for "copy of the register of electors" substitute "copy of the notice issued under section 13B(3B) or (3D) of the 1983 Act",
   (b) in sub-paragraph (c), for "in the register of electors" substitute "on the copy of the notice issued under section 13B(3B) or (3D) of the 1983 Act".

(4) The voter, on receiving the ballot paper, must forthwith proceed into one of the compartments in the polling station and there secretly mark his paper, and must then show to the presiding officer the back of the paper, so as to disclose the number and other unique identifying mark, and put the ballot paper into the ballot box in the presiding officer's presence, but so as to conceal his vote.

(5) The voter must vote without undue delay, and must leave the polling station as soon as he has put his ballot paper into the ballot box.

(6) A voter who has had a ballot paper delivered to him under paragraph (1), but has decided not to mark it, may return it to the presiding officer and where the voter does so, the presiding officer must–
   (a) immediately cancel the ballot paper, and for the purposes of these rules treat it as a spoilt ballot paper,
   (b) place a mark beside the number of that ballot paper on the corresponding number list to show that the ballot paper has been cancelled.

(7) Where any other ordinary Authority election in the Assembly constituency is contested, the same copy of–
   (a) the list of proxies,
   (b) the list mentioned in rule 29(3)(e),
   (c) the register of electors,
   (d) any notice issued under section 13B(3B) or (3D) of the 1983 Act (marked in the case of an elector who is added to the register in pursuance of such a notice),
   may be used for each Authority election and one mark may be placed in the list, register or notice (as the case may be) to denote that a ballot paper has been delivered in respect of each Authority election; except that, where a ballot paper has not been issued in respect of any Authority election, a different mark must be placed in the list, register or notice so as to identify the elections in respect of which a ballot paper was issued.

(8) A voter who at the close of the poll is in the polling station, or in a queue outside the polling station, for the purpose of voting must (despite the close of the poll) be entitled to apply for a ballot paper under paragraph (1); and these rules apply in relation to such a voter accordingly.

Votes marked by presiding officer

40 (1) The presiding officer, on the application of a voter–
   (a) who is incapacitated by blindness or other disability from voting in the manner directed by these Rules, or
   (b) who declares orally that he is unable to read,
   must, in the presence of the polling agents, cause the voter's vote to be marked on a ballot paper in the manner directed by the voter, and the ballot paper to be placed in

the ballot box.

(2) The name and number on the register of electors of every voter whose vote is marked in pursuance of this rule, and the reason why it is so marked, must be entered on a list (in these Rules called "the list of votes marked by the presiding officer").

In the case of a person voting as proxy for an elector, the number to be entered together with the voter's name must be the elector's number.

(3) In the case of a person in respect of whom a notice has been issued under section 13B(3B) or (3D) of the 1983 Act, paragraph (2) applies as if for "on the register of electors of every voter" there were substituted "relating to every voter in respect of whom a notice has been issued under section 13B(3B) or (3D) of the 1983 Act".

(4) The same list of votes marked by the presiding officer may be used for the election and each Authority election, and where it is so used, an entry in that list must be taken to mean that the ballot papers were so marked in respect of each Authority election, unless the list identifies the election for which the ballot paper was so marked.

Voting by persons with disabilities

41 (1) If a voter makes an application to the presiding officer to be allowed, on the ground of–
   (a) blindness or other disability, or
   (b) inability to read,

to vote with the assistance of another person by whom he is accompanied (in these Rules referred to as "the companion"), the presiding officer must require the voter to declare, orally or in writing, whether he is so incapacitated by his blindness or other disability, or by his inability to read, as to be unable to vote without assistance.

(2) If the presiding officer–
   (a) is satisfied that the voter is so incapacitated, and
   (b) is also satisfied by a written declaration made by the companion (in these Rules referred to as "the declaration made by the companion of a voter with disabilities") that the companion–
      (i) is a qualified person within the meaning of these Rules, and
      (ii) has not previously assisted more than one voter with disabilities to vote at the election,

the presiding officer must grant the application, and then anything which is by these Rules required to be done to, or by that voter in connection with the giving of his vote may be done to, or with the assistance of, the companion.

(3) For the purpose of these Rules, a person is a voter with disabilities if he has made such a declaration as is mentioned in paragraph (1) above, and a person may be qualified to assist a voter with disabilities to vote if that person–
   (a) is a person who is entitled to vote as an elector at the election, or
   (b) is the father, mother, brother, sister, spouse, civil partner, son or daughter of the voter and has attained the age of 18 years.

(4) The name and number in the register of electors of every voter whose vote is given in accordance with this rule and the name and address of the companion must be entered on a list (in these Rules referred to as the "list of voters with disabilities assisted by companions").

In the case of a person voting as proxy for an elector, the number to be entered together with the voter's name must be the elector's number.

(5) In the case of a person in respect of whom a notice has been issued under section 13B(3B) or (3D) of the 1983 Act, paragraph (4) applies as if for "in the register of electors of every voter" there were substituted "relating to every voter in respect of whom a notice has been issued under section 13B(3B) or (3D) of the 1983 Act".

(6) The declaration made by the companion–
  (a) must be in the appropriate form,
  (b) must be made before the presiding officer at the time when the voter applies to vote with the assistance of a companion, and
  (c) must forthwith be given to the presiding officer who must attest and retain it.

(7) No fee or other payment may be charged in respect of the declaration.

(8) Where any other ordinary Authority election in the Assembly constituency is contested, the same list of voters with disabilities assisted by companions may be used for the election and each Authority election, and where it is so used, an entry in that list must be taken to mean that the votes were so given in respect of each Authority election, unless the list identifies the election for which the vote was so given.

Tendered ballot papers: circumstances where available

42 (1) If a person, representing himself to be–
  (a) a particular elector named in the register and not named in the absent voters list, or
  (b) a particular person named in the list of proxies as proxy for an elector and not entitled to vote by post as proxy,
  applies for a ballot paper after another person has voted in person either as the elector or his proxy, the applicant must, on satisfactorily answering the questions permitted by law to be asked at the poll, be entitled, subject to the following provisions of this rule and rule 43, to mark a ballot paper (in these Rules referred to as "a tendered ballot paper") in the same manner as any other voter.

(2) Paragraph (4) applies if–
  (a) a person applies for a ballot paper representing himself to be a particular elector named in the register,
  (b) he is also named in the postal voters list, and
  (c) he claims that he did not make an application to vote by post at the election.

(3) Paragraph (4) also applies if–
  (a) a person applies for a ballot paper representing himself to be a particular person named as a proxy in the list of proxies,
  (b) he is also named in the proxy postal voters list, and
  (c) he claims that he did not make an application to vote by post as proxy.

(4) The person must, on satisfactorily answering the questions permitted by law to be asked at the poll, be entitled, subject to the following provisions of this rule and rule 43, to mark a ballot paper (in these Rules referred to as a "tendered ballot paper") in the same manner as any other voter.

(5) Paragraph (6) applies if before the close of the poll but after the last time at which a person may apply for a replacement postal ballot paper, a person represents himself to be–
  (a) a particular elector named in the register who is also named in the postal voters list, or
  (b) a particular person named as a proxy in the list of proxies and who is also named in the proxy postal voters list,
  and claims that he has lost or has not received his postal ballot paper.

(6) The person must, on satisfactorily answering the questions permitted by law to be asked at the poll, be entitled, subject to the provisions of this rule and rule 43, to mark a ballot paper (in these Rules referred to as a "tendered ballot paper") in the same manner as any other voter.

Tendered ballot papers: general provisions

43 (1) A tendered ballot paper must–
    (a) be of a colour differing from the other ballot papers,
    (b) instead of being put into the ballot box, be given to the presiding officer and endorsed by him with the name of the voter and his number on the register of electors, and set aside in a separate packet.

(2) The name of the voter and his number on the register of electors must be entered on a list (in these Rules referred to as the "tendered votes list").

(3) In the case of a person voting as proxy for an elector, the number to be endorsed or entered together with the voter's name must be the number of that elector.

(4) In the case of an elector who has an anonymous entry, this rule and rule 42 apply subject to the following modifications–
    (a) in paragraphs (1)(b) and (2) above, the references to the name of the voter must be ignored,
    (b) otherwise, a reference to a person named on a register or list must be construed as a reference to a person whose number appears in the register or list (as the case may be).

(5) In the case of a person in respect of whom a notice has been issued under section 13B(3B) or (3D) of the 1983 Act, this rule and rule 42 apply as if–
    (a) in rule 42(1)(a), (2)(a) and (5)(a), for "named in the register" there were substituted "in respect of whom a notice under section 13B(3B) or (3D) of the 1983 Act has been issued",
    (b) in paragraph (1)(b) of this rule for "his number in the register of electors" there were substituted "the number relating to him on a notice issued under section 13B(3B) or (3D) of the 1983 Act",
    (c) in paragraph (2) of this rule, for "his number in the register of electors" there were substituted "the number relating to him on a notice issued under section 13B(3B) or (3D) of the 1983 Act".

(6) Where any other ordinary Authority election in the Assembly constituency is contested, the same tendered votes list may be used for the election and each Authority election, and where it is so used, an entry in that list must be taken to mean that tendered ballot papers were marked in respect of each Authority election, unless the list identifies the election for which a tendered ballot paper was delivered.

Spoilt and replacement ballot papers

44 (1) A voter who has inadvertently dealt with his ballot paper in such manner that it cannot be conveniently used as a ballot paper may, on delivering it to the presiding officer and proving to his satisfaction the fact of the inadvertence, obtain a replacement for the ballot paper so delivered (in these Rules referred to as "a spoilt ballot paper"), and the spoilt ballot paper must be immediately cancelled.

(2) If a voter decides, after he has returned his ballot paper and it has been cancelled in accordance with rule 39(6), but before the close of the poll, that he wishes to vote in the election, he may obtain a replacement for the returned ballot paper.

(3) Before a replacement ballot paper is obtained, the presiding officer must mark the corresponding number list that was marked under rule 39(1) (the corresponding number list)–
    (a) in the case of a ballot paper being replaced under paragraph (1) or (2), beside the number of the replacement ballot paper obtained to show–

      (i)   the number of the elector, and

      (ii) the number of the ballot paper which is being replaced; and

  (b) in the case of a ballot paper being replaced under paragraph (1), beside the number of the spoilt ballot paper to show that the ballot paper was replaced.

(4) Where any other ordinary Authority election in the Assembly constituency is contested, the voter must only receive a replacement for a spoilt or returned ballot paper.

(5) If the same corresponding number list is used for more than one Authority election in accordance with rule 39(7)–

  (a) the marks made under paragraph (3) must identify the election for which a ballot paper has been replaced, and

  (b) any ballot paper which the voter has not applied for or obtained as a replacement, but which bears the same ballot paper number as a ballot paper delivered under rule 39(1), or obtained under paragraph (1) or (2) of this rule–

      (i)   must not be delivered to the voter,

      (ii) must be cancelled, and

      (iii) for the purposes of these rules, must be treated as a spoilt ballot paper.

Correction of errors on day of poll

45 (1) The presiding officer must keep a list of persons to whom ballot papers are delivered in consequence of an alteration to the register made by virtue of section 13B(3B) or (3D) of the 1983 Act which takes effect on the day of the poll.

(2) Where any other ordinary Authority election in the Assembly constituency is contested, the same list referred to in paragraph (1) may be used for the election and each Authority election, and where it is so used, an entry in that list must be taken to mean that ballot papers were delivered in respect of each Authority election, unless the list identifies the election for which a tendered ballot paper was delivered.

Adjournment of poll in case of riot

46 (1) Where the proceedings at any polling station are interrupted or obstructed by riot or open violence, the presiding officer must adjourn the proceedings till the following day and must forthwith give notice to the CRO.

(2) Where the poll is adjourned at any polling station–

  (a) the hours of polling on the day to which it is adjourned must be the same as for the original day, and

  (b) references in these Rules to the close of the poll must be construed accordingly.

(3) As soon as practicable after being informed of the adjournment of a poll, the CRO must inform the GLRO of that fact and of the cause of its adjournment.

Procedure on close of poll

47 (1) As soon as practicable after the close of the poll, the presiding officer must, in the presence of the polling agents, make up into separate packets, sealed with his own seal and the seals of such polling agents as desire to affix their seals–

  (a) each ballot box in use at the station, sealed so as to prevent the introduction of additional ballot papers and unopened, but with the key attached,

  (b) the unused and spoilt ballot papers placed together,

  (c) the tendered ballot papers,

  (d) the marked copies of the register of electors (including any marked copy notices issued under section 13B(3B) or (3D) of the 1983 Act) and of the list of proxies,

  (e) the list prepared under rule 19, including the part completed in accordance with rule 39(1)(b) (together referred to in these Rules as "the completed corresponding number list"),

    (f)   the certificates as to employment on duty on the day of the poll,

    (g)   the tendered votes list, the list of voters with disabilities assisted by companions, the list of votes marked by the presiding officer, a statement of the number of voters whose votes are so marked by the presiding officer under the heads "disability" and "unable to read", the list maintained under rule 45, and the declarations made by the companions of voters with disabilities,

and must deliver the packets or cause them to be delivered to the CRO to be taken charge of by him; but if the packets are not delivered by the presiding officer personally to the CRO, the arrangements for their delivery must be approved by the CRO.

(2)   The contents of the packets referred to in paragraph (1)(b), (c) and (f) must not be combined with the contents of the packets made under the corresponding rule that applies at any other Authority election.

(3)   The marked copies of the register of electors and of the list of proxies must be in one packet but must not be in the same packet as the completed corresponding number list or the certificates as to employment on duty on the day of the poll.

(4)   The packets must be accompanied by a statement ("ballot paper account") showing the number of ballot papers entrusted to the presiding officer, and accounting for them under the heads–

    (a)   ballot papers issued and not otherwise accounted for,

    (b)   unused ballot papers,

    (c)   spoilt ballot papers, and

    (d)   tendered ballot papers.

(5)   The statement referred to in paragraph (4) may be combined with the statements produced in relation to other Authority elections and the combined statement must be arranged in such manner as the GLRO may direct.

Attendance at verification and the local count

48 (1)   As soon as practicable after the close of the poll, the CRO must make arrangements for carrying out, in the presence of the counting agents, the verification and the counting of the votes at the election and must give to the counting agents notice in writing of the time and place at which he will begin to verify and count the votes.

(2)   No person other than–

    (a)   the CRO and his clerks and technical assistants,

    (b)   the GLRO,

    (c)   the candidates and one other person chosen by each of them,

    (d)   the election agents,

    (e)   the counting agents,

    (f)   persons who are entitled to attend by virtue of any of sections 6A to 6D of the 2000 Act,

may be present at the verification and counting of the votes, unless permitted by the CRO to attend.

(3)   A person not entitled to attend the local verification and count must not be permitted to do so by the CRO unless he–

    (a)   is satisfied that the efficient conduct of those proceedings will not be impeded, and

    (b)   has either consulted the election agents or thought it impracticable to do so.

(4)   The CRO must give the counting agents all such reasonable facilities for overseeing the proceedings, and all such information with respect to them, as he can give them

consistently with the orderly conduct of the proceedings and the discharge of his duties in connection with them.

Use of the electronic counting system

49 (1) The GLRO may provide the CRO with an electronic counting system consisting of computer hardware, software and other equipment or services, for the purpose of counting the number of ballot papers, to verify the ballot paper accounts and to count the votes cast on them.

(2) Any verification of ballot paper accounts, count or re-count at the election conducted using the electronic counting system must be conducted in accordance with rule 50.

(3) If the GLRO has provided the CRO with an electronic counting system for use at the election, the CRO must obtain the prior written consent of the GLRO before he may conduct the verification of ballot paper accounts or count the votes manually.

(4) If the verification of ballot paper accounts, count or re-count has commenced using the electronic counting system but has not been completed, the CRO may, if he considers it appropriate, discontinue the count and instead count the votes manually.

(5) Where the count or a re-count has been conducted using the electronic counting system, the CRO may, if he considers it appropriate, conduct any re-count without using that system.

(6) Where verification or any count or re-count is conducted using the electronic counting system, any of the steps referred to rule 50, in so far as practicable, may be undertaken–
      (a) concurrently with any other of those steps, or
      (b) in a different order.

Verification and the local count

50 (1) The CRO must–
      (a) open the ballot boxes from each polling station together, in the presence of the counting agents appointed for the purposes of the election and any other Authority election,
      (b) cause the electronic counting system to count such of the postal ballot papers as have been duly returned in accordance with paragraphs (2) and (3) and record separately the number counted,
      (c) not mix the contents of any ballot box with the contents of any other ballot box during the conduct of any count or re-count.

(2) A postal ballot paper must not be taken to be duly returned unless–
      (a) it is returned in the manner set out in paragraph (3) and reaches the CRO or any polling station in the Assembly constituency that includes the electoral area for which the elector is registered as a local government elector, before the close of the poll,
      (b) the postal voting statement, duly signed, is also returned in the manner set out in paragraph (3) and reaches him or such polling station before that time,
      (c) the postal voting statement also states the date of birth of the elector or proxy (as the case may be), and
      (d) in a case where the steps for verifying the date of birth and signature of an elector or proxy have been prescribed by regulations made under the 1983 Act, the CRO (having taken such steps) verifies the date of birth and signature of the elector or proxy (as the case may be).

(3) The manner in which any postal paper or postal voting statement may be returned–
      (a) to the CRO, is by hand or by post,

(b) to a polling station in the Assembly constituency, is by hand.

(3A) A postal ballot paper or postal voting statement that reaches the CRO or a polling station mentioned in sub-paragraph (a) of paragraph (2) at or after the close of the poll is treated for the purposes of paragraph (2) as reaching that officer or polling station before the close of the poll if it is delivered by a person who, at the close of the poll, is in the polling station, or in a queue outside the polling station, for the purpose of returning it.

(4) After completing the proceedings under paragraph (1), the CRO must cause the electronic counting system to process the ballot papers so as to count–
    (a) the number of ballot papers, and
    (b) votes given on the ballot papers.

(5) The CRO must not cause the electronic counting system to count any tendered ballot paper.

(6) The CRO must verify each ballot paper account by comparing it with the number of ballot papers processed by the electronic counting system, and the unused and spoilt ballot papers in his possession and the tendered votes list (opening and re-sealing the packets containing the unused and spoilt ballot papers and the tendered votes list) and must draw up a statement as to the result of the verification, which any election agent may copy.

(7) The CRO, while verifying the ballot paper accounts and counting the votes, must take all proper precautions for preventing any person from seeing the numbers printed on the back of the papers.

(8) The CRO must so far as practicable proceed continuously with counting the votes, allowing only time for refreshment, except that the hours between 5 in the afternoon and 10 on the following morning may be excluded with the prior consent of the GLRO.

(9) During the time so excluded the CRO must–
    (a) place the ballot papers and other documents relating to the election under his own seal and the seals of such of the counting agents as desire to affix their seals, and
    (b) otherwise take proper precautions for the security of the papers and documents.

Rejected ballot papers

51 (1) Any ballot paper–
    (a) which does not bear the official mark,
    (b) on which votes are given for more than one party or individual candidate,
    (c) on which anything is written or marked by which the voter can be identified except the printed number and other unique identifying mark on the back,
    (d) which is unmarked, or
    (e) which is void for uncertainty,
is, subject to paragraph (2), void and must not be counted.

(2) A ballot paper on which the vote is marked–
    (a) elsewhere than in the proper place, or
    (b) otherwise than by means of a cross, or
    (c) by more than one mark,
must not for such reason be void if an intention that the vote be given for one only of the party or individual candidates clearly appears, and the way the paper is marked does not itself identify the voter and it is not shown that he can be identified by it.

(3) Where the electronic counting system identifies a ballot paper that has been marked, but which appears for whatever reason to be void, it must be examined by a clerk

appointed by the CRO in the manner referred to in paragraph (6).

(4)   If the clerk, having examined the ballot, considers that the vote is void then the CRO must examine it in the manner referred to in paragraph (6).

(5)   After the CRO examines the ballot paper, he must give his decision as to the validity of the vote.

(6)   An examination under paragraph (3) or (4) is to be made by the clerk or CRO examining an image of the ballot paper which is shown on a screen so as to be visible to those attending the count.

(7)   The CRO may examine any ballot paper that he is not required to examine in accordance with paragraph (4)–

      (a)   either in the manner referred to in paragraph (6), or

      (b)   by examining a paper copy,

and where the CRO does so, he must give a decision on that paper in accordance with paragraph (5).

(8)   No person attending the count is to be entitled to require the clerk or CRO to examine a ballot paper or to provide a paper copy for inspection.

(9)   A record of the CRO's decision must be retained in the electronic counting system together with, in the case of a decision that the ballot paper is void, his reasons by reference to paragraph (1).

(10)   Where a counting agent objects to the CRO's decision the CRO must record on the electronic counting system that the decision was objected to.

(11)   The CRO must draw up a statement showing the number of ballot papers rejected under the several heads of–

      (a)   want of an official mark,

      (b)   voting for more than one party or individual candidate,

      (c)   writing or mark by which the voter could be identified,

      (d)   unmarked ballot paper, or

      (e)   void for uncertainty.

(12)   As soon as practicable after the completion of the statement under paragraph (11) the CRO must inform–

      (a)   such candidates, election agents and counting agents as are present at the count, and

      (b)   the GLRO,

of its contents.

Decision on ballot papers

52   The decision of the CRO on any question arising in respect of a ballot paper is final, but may be subject to review on an election petition.

Re-count

53 (1)   A candidate or his election agent (including, in the case of a list candidate, the election agent for that list) or a counting agent authorised under rule 31(3) may, if present when the counting or any re-count of the votes is completed, require the CRO to have the votes re-counted or again re-counted but the CRO may refuse to do so if in his opinion the request is unreasonable.

(2)   No step may be taken on the completion of the counting or any re-count of votes until the candidates and election agents and counting agents authorised under rule 31(1) present at its completion have been given a reasonable opportunity to exercise the right conferred by this rule.

(3) The CRO may determine the extent to which any re-count involves the electronic counting of votes.

(4) When the returning officer uses the electronic counting system for the re-counting of votes, he must not re-consider any decision made on any ballot paper under rule 51(5).

Procedure at conclusion of local count

54 (1) As soon as practicable after the conclusion of the local count (including any re-count), the CRO must draw up a statement showing–
    (a) the total number of votes cast,
    (b) the total number of votes rejected under rule 51,
    (c) the number of votes given for each registered party, and
    (d) the number of votes cast for each individual candidate.

(2) As soon as practicable after the statement is drawn up under paragraph (1), the CRO must inform the GLRO of its contents, and if it is practicable to do so, must also provide that information so as to show the total number of votes under each of those heads in each ward.

(3) As soon as practicable after the GLRO has authorised him to do so, the CRO must–
    (a) inform such of the candidates and their election agents as are then present of the content of the statements prepared in accordance with rule 51 and paragraph (1) of this rule, and
    (b) give public notice of the contents of those statements.

Attendance at allocation of seats

55 (1) The GLRO must make arrangements for making the allocation of seats in the presence of the election agents of the individual candidates (including, in the case of a list candidate, the election agent for that list), and he must give to those agents notice in writing of the time and place at which he will begin the allocation.

(2) No person other than–
    (a) the GLRO and his clerks,
    (b) the CROs and a clerk or technical assistant chosen by each of them,
    (c) the individual candidates and one person chosen by each of them,
    (d) candidates included on a party list and one person chosen by each of them,
    (e) the election agents,
    (f) the nominating officers of those registered parties standing nominated at the election,
    (g) persons who are entitled to attend by virtue of any of sections 6A to 6D of the 2000 Act,
    (h) persons permitted to be present at the central calculation at the election of the Mayor of London,
may be present at an allocation, unless permitted by the GLRO to attend.

(3) A person not entitled to attend an allocation must not be permitted to do so by the GLRO unless the GLRO–
    (a) is satisfied that the efficiency of the allocation will not be impeded, and
    (b) has either consulted the election agents or thought it impracticable to do so.

The calculation

56 (1) As soon as the GLRO has received from every CRO the information required by rule 54 he must calculate the London figure for each registered party and individual candidate.

(2) As soon as the GLRO has ascertained the result of the calculation, he must inform such of the election agents for the candidates as are then present of the relevant figures and must give them a reasonable opportunity to satisfy themselves as to the accuracy of the calculation.

(3) Where information of the description mentioned in paragraph (4)(e) is given in accordance with paragraph (2), the GLRO must provide the persons to whom it was given with a statement containing–
    (a) the names of the persons concerned, and
    (b) with respect to each such person, the name of the party from whose list his name has been omitted or treated as omitted, and the reason therefor.

(4) In this rule, "the relevant figures" means–
    (a) the number of London votes given in the Assembly constituencies for each registered party and for each individual candidate at that election,
    (b) in respect of each party, the number of successful candidates to be constituency members, who were the subject of that party's authorisation under rule 6(5) or 6(7) of the Constituency Members Election Rules,
    (c) the calculation of the London figure,
    (d) any recalculation required by paragraph 8(3), or carried out in the circumstances mentioned in paragraph 8(8), of Schedule 2 to the 1999 Act, and
    (e) the number of persons whose names have been omitted from, or (pursuant to paragraph 8(10) of Schedule 2 to the 1999 Act) who are to be treated as ceasing to be on, a party list.

(5) Paragraph (6) applies where the GLRO is notified under rule 54(5) of the Constituency Members Election Rules that a candidate who is returned as a constituency member is the candidate with a description authorised under rule 6(7)(a) of those rules (a using a description registered by more than one party).

(6) Where this paragraph applies, the GLRO must, in calculating the London figure of each registered party whose nominating officer issued a certificate to which rule 6(7)(a) of the Constituency Members Election Rules refers, include that candidate as a candidate of that party; and in doing so must disregard the fact that for the purposes of calculating the London figure of another registered party, the candidate is also included as the candidate of that other registered party.

Part 5
Final Proceedings in Contested and Uncontested Elections

Declaration of result

57 (1) The GLRO must declare the allocation of the seats for London members and, where seats are allocated to a registered party, the names of the persons on the party list who, in accordance with paragraph 8(5) of Schedule 2 to the 1999 Act, are to fill those seats.

(2) The GLRO must give public notice of–
    (a) the registered parties to which seats for London members have been allocated and the names of the list candidates by whom those seats are to be filled,
    (b) the names of the successful individual candidates,
    (c) the total number of London votes given for each registered party and each individual candidate,
    (d) the total number of candidates of registered parties returned as constituency members,
    (e) the number of rejected ballot papers under each head shown in the statement

of rejected ballot papers,

(f) the name of every person included on a party list who has been omitted from, or (pursuant to paragraph 8(10) of Schedule 2 to the 1999 Act) is to be treated as ceasing to be on, that list, together with the reason for the omission or cessation, as the case may be.

(3) Subject to paragraph (4), after the GLRO complies with paragraphs (1) and (2), he may give public notice of the information referred to paragraph (2)(c) and (e) so as to set out the number of votes falling under each of those heads, in respect of each ward.

(4) Where the sum of votes given for all registered parties and individual candidates in any ward does not exceed 500, the GLRO must not give notice under paragraph (3) in respect of that ward alone, but must amalgamate the figures for that ward with those for any other ward in which more than 500 votes have been given, in the same Assembly constituency.

Return or forfeiture of candidate's deposit

58 (1) Unless forfeited in accordance with paragraph (5), the deposit made under rule 10 must be returned to the person making it or his personal representative.

(2) Subject to paragraph (4), the deposit must be returned not later than the next day after that on which the result of the election is declared.

(3) For the purposes of paragraph (2)–
   (a) a day must be disregarded if, in accordance with rule 4, it would be disregarded in computing any period of time for the purposes of the timetable for the election, and
   (b) the deposit will be treated as being returned on a day if a cheque for the amount of the deposit is posted on that day.

(4) If the individual candidate or registered party is not shown as standing nominated in the statement of persons nominated, or if proof has been given to the GLRO before the allocation of seats of the death of an individual candidate, then the deposit must be returned as soon as practicable after the publication of the statement or after the individual candidate's death, as the case may be.

(5) Where a poll is taken, if, after the declaration under rule 57, a candidate or registered party is found not to have polled more than one-fortieth of the total number of votes polled by all the candidates and registered parties, the deposit must be forfeited to the Greater London Authority.

Part 6
Disposal of Documents

Sealing up of ballot papers

59 (1) On the completion of the counting at a contested election the CRO must seal up in separate packets the counted and rejected ballot papers.

(2) Where some or all of the votes have been counted using the electronic counting system, the CRO must also seal up in a separate packet a complete electronic record ("the electronic record") of the information stored in the electronic counting system, held in such device as may be suitable for the purpose of its storage.

(3) After making the electronic record under paragraph (2), the CRO must arrange for the original records in the electronic counting system to be removed from it and destroyed in a manner that ensures that the secrecy of those records is preserved.

(4)   The CRO must not open the sealed packets of–
    (a)   tendered ballot papers,
    (b)   certificates as to employment on duty on the day of the poll,
    (c)   the completed corresponding number lists, or
    (d)   marked copies of the register of electors (including any marked copy notices issued under section 13B(3B) or (3D) of the 1983 Act) and lists of proxies.

Delivery and retention of documents

60 (1)   The CRO must then forward the following documents to the relevant registration officer–
    (a)   the packets of ballot papers in his possession,
    (b)   the packet containing the electronic record (if any),
    (c)   the ballot paper accounts and the statements of rejected ballot papers and of the result of the verification of the ballot paper accounts,
    (d)   the tendered votes lists, the lists of voters with disabilities assisted by companions, the lists of votes marked by the presiding officer and the related statements, the lists maintained under rule 45 and the declarations made by the companions of voters with disabilities,
    (e)   the packets of the completed corresponding number lists,
    (f)   the packets of certificates as to employment on duty on the day of the poll, and
    (g)   the packets containing marked copies of registers (including any marked copy notices issued under section 13B(3B) or (3D) of the 1983 Act) and of the postal voters list, of the lists of proxies and of the proxy postal voters list,

endorsing on each packet a description of its contents, the date of the election to which they relate and the name of the Assembly constituency for which the election was held.

Orders for production of documents

61 (1)   An order–
    (a)   for the inspection or production of any rejected ballot papers in the custody of the relevant registration officer, or
    (b)   for the opening of a packet containing the electronic record or a sealed packet of completed corresponding number lists or certificates as to employment on duty on the day of the poll or the inspection of any counted ballot papers in the custody of the relevant registration officer,

may be made by a county court, if the court is satisfied by evidence on oath that the order is required for the purpose of instituting or maintaining a prosecution for an offence in relation to ballot papers, or for the purpose of an election petition.

(2)   An election court may make an order for the opening of a packet containing the electronic record or a sealed packet of completed corresponding number lists or certificates or for the inspection of any counted ballot papers in the custody of the relevant registration officer.

(3)   An order under this rule may be made subject to such conditions as to–
    (a)   persons,
    (b)   time,
    (c)   place and mode of inspection,
    (d)   production or opening,

as the court making the order thinks expedient; but in making and carrying into effect an order for the opening of a packet containing the electronic record or a packet of completed corresponding number lists or certificates or for the inspection of counted ballot papers, care must be taken that the way in which the vote of any particular elector has been given must not be disclosed until it has been proved–

(i)   that his vote was given, and

(ii)   that the vote has been declared by a competent court to be invalid.

(4)   An appeal lies to the High Court from any order of a county court under this rule.

(5)   Any power given under this rule to a county court may be exercised by any judge of the court otherwise than in open court.

(6)   Where an order is made for the production by the relevant registration officer of any document or electronic record in his custody relating to any specified election—

(a)   the production by him or his agent of the document or electronic record ordered in such manner as may be directed by that order will be conclusive evidence that the document or electronic record relates to the specified election, and

(b)   any endorsement on any packet of ballot papers so produced will be *prima facie* evidence that the ballot papers are what they are stated to be by the endorsement.

(7)   The production from proper custody of—

(a)   a ballot paper purporting to have been used at any election, or

(b)   a copy of the electronic record which purports to record that a particular ballot paper was used at any election, and

a completed corresponding number list with a number written beside the number of the ballot paper, will be *prima facie* evidence that the elector whose vote was given by that ballot paper was the person who, at the time of the election, had affixed to his entry in the register of electors or on the notice issued under section 13B(3B) or (3D) of the 1983 Act, the same number as was written on the completed corresponding number list.

(8)   Unless authorised by this rule, no person may be allowed to inspect any rejected or counted ballot papers in the custody of the relevant registration officer or open any sealed packets of completed corresponding number lists, certificates as to employment on the day of the poll or containing the electronic record.

Retention and destruction of documents and records

62   The relevant registration officer must retain or cause to be retained for one year all documents and, where applicable, the electronic record relating to an election forwarded to him in pursuance of these Rules by a CRO, and then, unless otherwise directed by an order of a county court, a Crown Court, a magistrate's court or an election court, must cause them to be destroyed.

Part 7
List Candidates and the Filling of Vacancies

Interpretation of Part 7

63   In this Part—

"dual candidate" means a person—

(a)   whose name, subject to rule 65, falls to be notified as mentioned in subsection (6) of section 11 (filling a vacancy among the London members) of the 1999 Act, and

(b)   who is a candidate (otherwise than at an ordinary election) for election—

(i)   as the Mayor of London, or

(ii)   as a constituency member,

"nominating officer", in relation to a registered party and a vacancy in the office of a London member, means the person who holds that office in the party at the time at which the vacancy arises, and

"paragraph (1) notice" has the meaning given by rule 65(1).

Removal from a party list on election as Mayor or as a constituency member

64 (1)   Where a person whose name is for the time being included in a party list is elected (otherwise than at an ordinary election)–

    (a)   as the Mayor of London, or

    (b)   as a constituency member,

his name must be removed from that list.

(2)   For the purposes of this Part, the name of a person to whom paragraph (1) applies must be treated as ceasing to be included in the list from the date on which he is returned as the Mayor or a constituency member, as the case may be (even if his return is void).

(3)   Where proof is given to the GLRO's satisfaction that a person whose name is for the time being included in a party list has died, then the GLRO must remove that person's name from that list.

Notification of vacancy

65 (1)   As soon as the office of a London member who was returned from a registered party's list becomes vacant, the GLRO must simultaneously give or send to–

    (a)   the party's nominating officer, and

    (b)   the person whose name would, in accordance with subsection (6) of section 11 (filling a vacancy among the London members) of the 1999 Act (and on the assumption that he satisfies the conditions in subsection (4) of that section), be so notified,

written notice ("paragraph (1) notice") of the matters specified in paragraph (2).

(2)   The matters specified in this paragraph are–

    (a)   the vacancy,

    (b)   that the nominating officer may, by notice in writing delivered to the GLRO not later than one month after the date of the paragraph (1) notice, give the notice referred to in subsection (5)(b) of section 11 of the 1999 Act, and

    (c)   that the person must, by notice in writing delivered to the GLRO not later than one month after the date of the paragraph (1) notice, indicate whichever of the following apply to him–

        (i)   that he is willing to serve as a London member ("notice of willingness"),

        (ii)   that he is not willing to serve as a London member, and

        (iii)   that he is a dual candidate.

(3)   The GLRO must not notify the Chair of the London Assembly as mentioned in section 11(3) of the 1999 Act until–

    (a)   the period mentioned in paragraph (2)(b) has elapsed, and

    (b)   he has received a notice of willingness, and

    (c)   if the person by whom notice of willingness has been given is a dual candidate, the result of the election for which he is a Mayoral or constituency member candidate has been declared.

Unwilling candidate or objection by registered party

66   Where the GLRO receives a notice under rule 65(2)(c)(ii) or section 11(5)(b) of the 1999 Act he must again send a paragraph (1) notice, but with the substitution, for the name of the person to whom the first such notice was sent, of the name of the person who, on the same assumption, would be the next person whose name would be notified in accordance with section 11(6) of that Act; and so on until, in respect of such a person–

(a) no notice is given under section 11(5)(b) of that Act, and

(b) a notice of willingness has been received.

Acceptance of office and further notification

67 (1) As soon as practicable after the GLRO has identified the person who is to fill the vacancy, he must invite him to attend at his office to sign the declaration of acceptance of office.

(2) In a case to which section 11(3) of the 1999 Act applies, as soon as practicable after the declaration of acceptance of office has been signed, the GLRO must notify the Chair of the London Assembly as mentioned in that subsection.

Part 8
Returns and Declarations as to Election Expenses

Declarations as to election expenses

68 (1) Subject to paragraph (2), the form of the declaration required by section 82(1) of the 1983 Act (agent's declaration as to election expenses), in the circumstances mentioned in subsection (2A)(a) of that section, is that set out in part 1 of Form 20 of the Forms Schedule.

(2) In a case to which section 82(5A) of the 1983 Act applies, the declaration referred to in paragraph (1) must be modified as specified in part 2 of Form 20.

(3) Subject to paragraph (4), the form of the declaration required by section 82(2) of the 1983 Act (candidate's declaration as to election expenses), in the circumstances mentioned in subsection (2A)(b) of that section must be that set out in part 1 of the Form 21 of the Forms Schedule.

(4) In a case to which section 82(5A) of the 1983 Act applies, the declaration referred to in paragraph (3) must be modified as specified in part 2 of Form 21.

SCHEDULE 3
THE MAYORAL ELECTION RULES

Rule 3(4)

Part 1
General Provisions
1 Citation
2 Interpretation

Part 2
Provisions as to Time
3 Timetable
4 Computation of time

Part 3
Stages Common to Contested and Uncontested Elections
5 Notice of election
6 Nomination of candidates
7 Subscription of nomination papers
8 Consent to nomination
9 Deposits
10 Decisions as to validity of nomination papers
11 Publication of statement of persons nominated
12 Correction of minor errors
13 Inspection of nomination papers and consent to nomination
14 Withdrawal of candidature
15 Method of election

Part 4
Contested Elections
16 Poll to be taken by ballot
17 The ballot papers
18 The corresponding number list
19 The official mark
20 Prohibition of disclosure of vote
21 Use of schools and public rooms
22 Notice of poll
23 Postal ballot papers
24 Provision of polling stations
25 Appointment of presiding officers and clerks
26 Issue of official poll cards
27 Information for voters
28 Equipment of polling stations
29 Notices for the guidance of voters
30 Appointment of polling and counting agents
31 Notification of requirement of secrecy
32 Return of postal ballot papers
33 Admission to polling station
34 Keeping of order in station
35 Sealing of ballot boxes
36 Questions to be put to voters
37 Challenge of voter
38 Voting procedure
39 Votes marked by presiding officer

Part 5
Further Provision: More Than Two Candidates

Part 6
Final Proceedings in Contested and Uncontested Elections

Part 7
Disposal of Documents

Part 8
Death of Candidate

Part 1
General Provisions

Citation

1   This Schedule may be cited as the Mayoral Election Rules.

Interpretation

2 (1)   In the rules in this Schedule, unless the context indicates otherwise–
      "candidate" means a candidate to be the Mayor;
      "election" means an election for the return of the Mayor;

(2)   Reference to a rule by number alone is a reference to the rule so numbered in this Schedule.

Part 2
Provisions as to Time

Timetable

3   The proceedings at the election must be conducted in accordance with the following timetable:

Timetable

Proceedings	Time
Publication of notice of election	Not later than the thirtieth day before the day of election.
Delivery of nomination papers	Not later than 4pm on the twenty-fourth day before the day of election.
Delivery of notices of withdrawals of candidature	Not later than 4 in the afternoon on the twenty-fourth day before the day of election
Publication of statement as to persons nominated	Not later than 4 in the afternoon on the twenty-second day before the day of election.
Notice of poll	Not later than the sixth day before the day of election.
Polling	Between the hours of 7 in the morning and 10 at night on the day of election.

Computation of time

4 (1)   In computing any period of time for the purposes of the Timetable–
    (a)   a Saturday or Sunday,
    (b)   Christmas Eve, Christmas Day, Good Friday or a bank holiday, or
    (c)   a day appointed for public thanksgiving or mourning,
must be disregarded, and any such day must not be treated as a day for the purpose of any proceedings up to the completion of the poll nor must the CRO be obliged to proceed with the counting of the votes on such a day.

(2)   In this rule, "bank holiday" means a day which is a bank holiday under the Banking and Financial Dealings Act 1971 in England and Wales.

Part 3
Stages Common to Contested and Uncontested Elections

Notice of election

5 (1)   The GLRO must publish in each Assembly constituency notice of the election stating–
    (a)   the place and times at which nomination papers are to be delivered, and
    (b)   the date of the poll in the event of a contest,
and the notice must state that forms of nomination papers may be obtained at that place and those times.

(2)   The notice of election must state the arrangements (if any) which apply for the payment of the deposit required by rule 9 by means of the electronic transfer of funds.

(3)   The notice of election must state the date by which–

(a) applications to vote by post or proxy, and

(b) other applications and notices about postal or proxy voting,

must reach the registration officer for local government electors in order that they may be effective for the election.

Nomination of candidates

6 (1) Each candidate must be nominated by a separate nomination paper which must be–

    (a) in the appropriate form, and

    (b) delivered to the place fixed for the purpose by the GLRO, which must be at one of the offices of the Greater London Authority, before the last time for the delivery of nomination papers.

(2) A nomination paper must state the candidate's–

    (a) full names,

    (b) home address, in full, and

    (c) if desired, description,

and the surname must be placed first in the list of names.

(3) If a candidate commonly uses–

    (a) a surname which is different from any other surname he has, or

    (b) a forename which is different from any other forename he has,

the nomination paper may state the commonly used surname or forename, or both surname and forename, in addition to the other name.

(4) The description (if any) can only be–

    (a) one authorised as mentioned in paragraph (5) or (7), or

    (b) the word "Independent".

(5) A nomination paper may not include a description of a candidate that is likely to lead electors to associate the candidate with a registered party unless–

    (a) the party is a qualifying party in relation to Greater London, and

    (b) the description is authorised by a certificate–

        (i) issued by or on behalf of the registered nominating officer of the party, and

        (ii) received by the GLRO before the last time for the delivery of nomination papers set out in the timetable in rule 3.

(6) In paragraph (5) an authorised description may be either–

    (a) the name of the party registered under section 28 of the 2000 Act, or

    (b) a description of the party registered under section 28A of that Act.

(7) A nomination paper may not include a description of a candidate which is likely to lead electors to associate the candidate with two or more registered political parties unless the parties are each qualifying parties in relation to Greater London and the description is a registered description authorised by a certificate–

    (a) issued by or on behalf of the registered nominating officer of each of the parties, and

    (b) received by the GLRO before the last time for the delivery of nomination papers set out in the timetable in rule 3.

(8) For the purposes of paragraph (7), a description is a registered description if it is a description registered for use by the parties under section 28B of the 2000 Act.

(9) A person will be guilty of a corrupt practice if he fraudulently purports to be authorised to issue a certificate under paragraph (5) or (7) on behalf of a registered party's nominating officer.

(10) For the purposes of the application of these rules in relation to an election–

    (a) "registered party" means a party which was registered under Part 2 of the 2000 Act on the day ("the relevant day") which is two days before the last day for the delivery of nomination papers at that election,

    (b) a registered party is a qualifying party in relation to Greater London if on the relevant day the party was registered in respect of England in the Great Britain register maintained under that Part of that Act.

(11) For the purposes of paragraph (10)(a), any day falling within rule 4(1) must be disregarded.

Subscription of nomination papers

7 (1) The nomination paper of a candidate must be subscribed by at least 330 persons each of whom is entitled to vote at the election; and in relation to each London borough and the City, at least ten of the subscribers must be electors who are ordinarily resident in the borough or, as the case may be, the City.

  (2) Where a nomination paper has the signatures of more than the required number of persons as assenting to the nomination of a candidate, the signatures (up to the required number) appearing first on the paper must be taken into account to the exclusion of any others.

  (3) The nomination paper must give the electoral number of each person subscribing it.

(3A) A person must not subscribe more than one nomination paper at the same election.

(3B) Paragraph (3A) does not prevent a person subscribing a further nomination paper where the previously nominated candidate has either died or withdrawn.

  (4) The GLRO–

    (a) must supply any elector with as many forms of nomination paper and forms of consent to nomination as may be required at the place and during the time for delivery of nomination papers, and

    (b) must, at any elector's request, prepare a nomination paper for signature,

but it is not necessary for a nomination or consent to nomination to be on a form supplied by the GLRO.

  (5) In this rule–

"elector" means a person named as a local government elector in the register being used at the election in that Assembly constituency, and includes a person shown in the register as below voting age if it appears from the register that he will be of voting age on the day fixed for the poll, but does not include a person who has an anonymous entry in the register.

"electoral number" means–

    (a) a person's number in that register, or

    (b) pending publication of the register, his number (if any) in the electors list for that register.

Consent to nomination

8 (1) A person will not be validly nominated unless his consent to nomination–

    (a) is given in writing in the appropriate form, or a form to like effect, on or within one month before the last day for the delivery of nomination papers;

    (b) is attested by one witness whose name and address must be given; and

    (c) is delivered at the place and within the time for delivery of nomination papers.

  (2) A candidate's consent given under this rule must–

    (a) state the day, month and year of his birth; and

    (b) contain a statement that to the best of the candidate's knowledge and belief he is not disqualified from being elected by reason of–

      (i) any disqualification set out in section 21 (disqualification from being the

Mayor or an Assembly member) of the 1999 Act,

(ii) a decision made under section 78A of the Local Government Act 2000 (decisions of First-tier tribunal), or

(iii) an order made under section 34(4) of the Localism Act 2011(offences).

Deposits

9 (1) A person will not be validly nominated as a candidate unless the sum of £10,000 is deposited by him, or on his behalf, with the GLRO at the place and during the time for delivery of nomination papers.

(2) The deposit may be made either–
    (a) by the deposit of any legal tender, or
    (b) by means of a banker's draft, or
    (c) with the GLRO's consent, in any other manner including by means of a debit or credit card or the electronic transfer of funds,

but the GLRO may refuse to accept a deposit sought to be made by means of a banker's draft if he does not know that the drawer carries on business as a banker in the United Kingdom.

(3) Where the deposit is made on behalf of the candidate, the person making the deposit must at the time he makes it give his name and address to the GLRO, unless they have previously been given to him under section 67 (appointment of election agent) of the 1983 Act.

Decisions as to validity of nomination papers

10 (1) Where a nomination paper and the candidate's consent to it are delivered, and the deposit is made, in accordance with these Rules, the candidate must be deemed to stand nominated unless and until–
    (a) the GLRO decides that the nomination paper is invalid, or
    (b) proof is given to the GLRO's satisfaction of the candidate's death, or
    (c) the candidate withdraws.

(2) The GLRO is entitled to hold the nomination paper of a person invalid only on one of the following grounds–
    (a) that the particulars of the candidate or of the persons subscribing the paper are not as required by law,
    (b) that the paper is not subscribed as so required;,
    (c) that the paper breaks rule 6(5) or (7).

(2A) If, contrary to rule 7(3A), a person subscribes more than one nomination paper the GLRO, in determining whether a paper is subscribed as so required under paragraph (2)(b)–
    (a) must only take the person's signature into account in respect of the first nomination paper delivered under rule 6(1)(b) on which the person's signature appears,
    (b) must, where the person's signature appears on a nomination paper delivered subsequently, find that the paper is not subscribed as so required if the signature appears within the first 330 signatures on the paper, regardless of whether the paper contains more than 330 signatures.

(3) Subject to paragraph (4), the GLRO must, as soon as practicable after each nomination paper has been delivered, examine it and decide whether the candidate has been validly nominated.

(4) If in the GLRO's opinion a nomination paper breaks rule 6(5) or (7), he must give a decision to that effect–

(a) as soon as practicable after the delivery of the nomination paper, and

(b) in any event, before the end of the period of 24 hours starting with the end of the period for the delivery of nomination papers set out in the timetable in rule 3.

(5) Where the GLRO decides that a nomination paper is invalid, he must endorse and sign on the paper the fact and the reasons for his decision.

(6) The GLRO must, as soon as practicable after making such a decision in accordance with paragraph (3) or (4) that a nomination paper is valid or invalid, send notice of it to the candidate at his home address as given in his nomination paper.

(7) The GLRO's decision that a nomination paper is valid is final and may not be questioned in any proceeding whatsoever.

(8) Subject to paragraph (7), nothing in this rule prevents the validity of a nomination being questioned on an election petition.

Publication of statement of persons nominated

11 (1) The GLRO must prepare and publish a statement showing the persons who have been and stand nominated and any other persons who have been nominated together with the reason why they no longer stand nominated.

(2) The statement must show the names, addresses and descriptions of the persons nominated as given in their nomination papers.

(3) If a person's nomination paper gives a commonly used surname or forename, or both surname and forename in addition to another name, the statement must show the person's commonly used surname or forename, or both surname and forename (as the case may be) instead of any other name.

(4) Paragraph (3) does not apply if the GLRO thinks–
(a) that the use of the person's commonly used name may be likely to mislead or confuse electors, or
(b) that the commonly used name is obscene or offensive.

(5) If paragraph (4) applies, the GLRO must give notice in writing to the candidate of his reasons for refusing to allow the use of a commonly used name.

(6) The statement must show the persons standing nominated arranged alphabetically in the order of their surnames, and if there are two or more of them with the same surname, of their other names.

(7) In the case of a person nominated by more than one nomination paper, the GLRO must take the particulars required by the foregoing provisions of this rule from such one of the papers as the candidate (or the GLRO in default of the candidate) may select.

Correction of minor errors

12 (1) The GLRO may, if he thinks fit, at any time before the publication under rule 11 of the statement of persons nominated, correct minor errors in a nomination paper.

(2) Errors which may be corrected include–
(a) errors as to a person's electoral number,

(b) obvious errors of spelling in relation to the details of a candidate.

(3) Anything done by the GLRO in pursuance of this rule may not be questioned in any proceedings other than proceedings on an election petition.

(4) The GLRO must have regard to any guidance issued by the Electoral Commission for the purposes of this rule.

Inspection of nomination papers and consent to nomination

13 (1)   During ordinary office hours, in the period starting 24 hours after the latest time for the delivery of nomination papers and before the date of the poll, any person may inspect and take copies of, or extracts from, nomination papers and consents to nomination.

(2)   Inspection under paragraph (1) may not take place on a day that is specified in rule 4(1).

Withdrawal of candidature

14 (1)   A candidate may withdraw his candidature by notice of withdrawal–
   (a)   signed by him and attested by one witness, whose name and address must be given, and
   (b)   delivered to the GLRO at the place for delivery of nomination papers,
   by the end of the period for the delivery of notices of withdrawals of candidature in the timetable in rule 3.

(2)   Where a candidate is outside the United Kingdom, a notice of withdrawal signed by his election agent and accompanied by a written declaration also so signed of the candidate's absence from the United Kingdom will be of the same effect as a notice of withdrawal signed by the candidate; but where the candidate stands nominated by more than one nomination paper a notice of withdrawal under this paragraph will be effective if, and only if, it is accompanied, in addition to that declaration, by a written statement signed by the candidate that the person giving the notice is authorised to do so on the candidate's behalf during his absence from the United Kingdom.

Method of election

15   If, after any withdrawals under rule 14–
   (a)   more than two candidates remain validly nominated, a poll must be taken in accordance with Parts 4 and 5 of these Rules;
   (b)   only two candidates remain validly nominated, a poll must be taken in accordance with Part 4;
   (c)   only one candidate remains validly nominated, that person must be declared to be elected in accordance with Part 6.

Part 4
Contested Elections

Poll to be taken by ballot

16   The votes at the poll must be given by ballot.

The ballot papers

17 (1)   The ballot of every person entitled to a mayoral vote at the election must consist of a ballot paper which must be in the appropriate form.

(2)   Each person remaining validly nominated at the election, after any withdrawals, and no other, is entitled to have their name inserted in the ballot paper at that election.

(3)   Every ballot paper–
   (a)   must, so far as practicable for the purposes of electronic counting, be printed in accordance with the directions set out in the Forms Schedule,
   (b)   must contain the names and other particulars of the candidates as shown in the

statement of persons nominated,

    (c)   must have a number and other unique identifying mark printed on the back, and

    (d)   may, in the case of ballot papers for use at polling stations, be marked with the words "do not fold".

(4)   If a candidate who is the subject of a party's authorisation under rule 6(5) so requests, the ballot paper must contain, against the candidate's particulars, the party's registered emblem (or, as the case may be, one of the party's registered emblems).

(4A) If a candidate who is the subject of an authorisation by two or more parties under rule 6(7) so requests, the ballot paper must contain, against the candidate's particulars, the registered emblem (or, as the case may be, one of the registered emblems) of one of those parties.

(5)   The candidate's request under paragraph (4) or paragraph (4A) must–

    (a)   be made in writing to the GLRO, and

    (b)   be received by him during the period for delivery of nomination papers set out in the timetable in rule 3.

(6)   The names of the candidates must be arranged alphabetically in order of their surnames and, if there are two or more of them with the same surname, of their other names.

(7)   The GLRO must supply the ballot papers for use at the election to the CRO by such date as may be agreed between them.

(8)   The ballot papers supplied under paragraph (7) must be of a different colour from those used at any other Authority election with which the election is taken.

The corresponding number list

18 (1) The CRO must prepare a list containing the numbers and other unique identifying marks of all of the ballot papers to be issued by him in pursuance of rule 23(1) or provided by him in pursuance of rule 28(1).

(2)   The list must be in the appropriate form or a form to like effect.

(3)   At an ordinary election, the same list may be used for each Authority election with which the election is combined.

The official mark

19 (1) Every ballot paper must contain an appropriate security marking (the official mark).

(2)   The official mark must be kept secret, and an interval of not less than five years must intervene between the use of the same official mark at any Authority election.

(3)   The GLRO may use a different official mark for different purposes at the same election.

Prohibition of disclosure of vote

20   No person who has voted at the election may, in any legal proceeding to question the election, be required to state for whom he has voted.

Use of schools and public rooms

21 (1) The CRO may use, free of charge, for the purpose of taking the poll or counting the votes–

    (a)   a room in a school maintained or assisted by a local authority (as defined in the Education Act 1996) or a school in respect of which grants are made out of moneys provided by Parliament to the person or body of persons responsible for the management of the school,

(b)   a room the expense of maintaining which is met by any local authority.

(2)   In relation to an election to fill a vacancy in the office of the Mayor, the CRO must make good any damage done to, and defray any expense incurred by the persons having control over, any such room as is mentioned in paragraph (1) by reason of its being used for the purpose of taking the poll or counting the votes.

Notice of poll

22 (1)   The GLRO must, in accordance with the timetable in rule 3, publish notice of the poll stating–
(a)   the day and hours fixed for the poll,
(b)   particulars of each candidate remaining validly nominated,
and rule 11(6) applies in relation to the order in which names and particulars appear on the notice of the poll as it applies in relation to the statement of persons nominated.

(2)   The CRO must, not later than the time of the publication of the notice of the poll, also give public notice of–
(a)   the situation of each polling station, and
(b)   the description of voters entitled to vote there,
and he must as soon as practicable after giving such a notice give a copy of it to each of the election agents.

(3)   At an ordinary election, the notice of poll must include the heading "GREATER LONDON AUTHORITY ELECTION".

Postal ballot papers

23 (1)   The CRO must, in accordance with regulations made under the 1983 Act, issue to those entitled to vote by post a ballot paper and a postal voting statement, together with such envelopes for their return as may be prescribed in such regulations.

(2)   The postal voting statement must be in the appropriate form or a form to like effect.

(3)   The postal voting statement must include provision for the form to be signed and for stating the date of birth of the elector or proxy (as the case may be).

(4)   The CRO must also issue to those entitled to vote by post such information as he thinks appropriate about how to obtain–
(a)   translations into languages other than English of any directions to or guidance for voters sent with the ballot paper,
(b)   a translation into Braille of such directions or guidance,
(c)   graphical representations of such directions or guidance,
(d)   the directions or guidance in any other form (including any audible form).

(5)   In the case of a ballot paper issued to a person at an address in the United Kingdom, the CRO must ensure that the return of the ballot paper and postal voting statement is free of charge to the voter.

(6)   Where the proceedings on the issue and receipt of postal ballot papers at the election are taken together with any other Authority election the appropriate form of postal voting statement under paragraph (2) may be the joint postal voting statement which must be in the appropriate form or form to like effect.

Provision of polling stations

24 (1)   The CRO must provide a sufficient number of polling stations and, subject to the following provisions of this rule, must allot the electors to the polling stations in such manner as he thinks most convenient.

(2)   One or more polling stations may be provided in the same room.

(3)   The polling station allotted to electors from any parliamentary polling district wholly or partly within the Assembly constituency must, in the absence of special circumstances, be in the parliamentary polling place for that district, unless that place is outside the Assembly constituency.

(4)   The CRO must provide each polling station with such number of compartments as may be necessary in which the voters can mark their votes screened from observation.

Appointment of presiding officers and clerks

25 (1)   The CRO must appoint and pay a presiding officer to attend at each polling station and such clerks and technical assistants as may be necessary for the purposes of the election, but he must not appoint any person who has been employed by or on behalf of a candidate in or about the election.

(2)   The CRO may, if he thinks fit, preside at a polling station and the provisions of this Part relating to a presiding officer apply to the CRO so presiding with the necessary modifications as to things to be done by the CRO to the presiding officer or by the presiding officer to the CRO.

(3)   A presiding officer may do, by the clerks appointed to assist him, any act (including the asking of questions) which he is required or authorised by this Part to do at a polling station except order the arrest, exclusion or removal of any person from the polling station.

Issue of official poll cards

26 (1)   The CRO must as soon as practicable after the publication of the notice of election, send to electors and their proxies an official poll card.

(2)   An elector's official poll card must be sent or delivered to his qualifying address, and a proxy's to his address as shown in the list of proxies.

(3)   The official poll card must be in the appropriate form or a form to like effect, and must set out–
    (a)   that the election is a mayoral election,
    (b)   the elector's name, qualifying address and number on the register,
    (c)   the date and hours of the poll and the situation of the elector's polling station, and
    (d)   such other information as the CRO thinks appropriate,
and different information may be provided in pursuance of sub-paragraph (d) to different electors or descriptions of elector.

(4)   In the case of an elector with an anonymous entry, instead of containing the matter mentioned in paragraph (3)(b), the polling card must contain such matter as is specified in the appropriate form.

(5)   At an ordinary election, the CRO must issue a combined poll card in the appropriate form.

(6)   In this rule "elector" means–
    (a)   an elector with an entry on the register to be used at the election on the last day for the publication of the notice of the election, and
    (b)   includes a person then shown in the register as below voting age if (but only if)

it appears from the register that he will be of voting age on the day fixed for the poll.

Information for voters

27 (1) At an ordinary election, the GLRO may, in addition to a statement by him in an election booklet, include in the booklet information for voters that has been agreed by him with the Electoral Commission.

(2) The information for voters given in the election booklet may include information about–
    (a) the office of the Mayor and the London Assembly,
    (b) the system of voting at each Authority election,
    (c) how to vote in a manner that will ensure a vote is regarded as validly cast, and subject to paragraph (3), may include any other information given in exercise of the GLRO's duty under section 69 (encouraging electoral participation) of the 2006 Act.

(3) The information for voters must not contain–
    (a) any advertising material,
    (b) any material referring to a candidate or a registered party other than by reproduction of a ballot paper which refers equally to all candidates and parties at the ordinary election,
    (c) any material referring to the holder, at any time, of the office of Mayor or Assembly member, other than under paragraph (b) as a candidate at the ordinary election.

(4) Information published in an election booklet under this rule must be printed on not more than two sides of A5 paper.

Equipment of polling stations

28 (1) The CRO must provide each presiding officer with–
    (a) such ballot papers as may be necessary, and
    (b) such ballot boxes as may be necessary having taken account of any direction made by the GLRO in accordance with paragraph (9).

(2) Every ballot box must be so constructed that the ballot papers can be put in it, but cannot be withdrawn from it, without the box being unlocked or, where the box has no lock, the seal being broken.

(3) The CRO must provide each polling station with–
    (a) materials to enable voters to mark the ballot papers,
    (b) copies of the register of electors for such part of it as contains the entries relating to the electors allotted to the station,
    (c) the parts of any special lists prepared for the election corresponding to the register of electors or the part of it provided under sub-paragraph (b),
    (d) a list consisting of that part of the list prepared under rule 18 which contains the numbers (but not the other unique identifying marks) corresponding to those on the ballot papers provided to the presiding officer of the polling station.

(4) The reference in paragraph (3)(b) to the copies of the register of electors includes a reference to copies of any notices issued under section 13B(3B) or (3D) of the 1983 Act in respect of alterations to the register.

(5) The CRO must also provide each polling station with a device for enabling voters who are blind or partially sighted to vote without any need for assistance from the presiding officer or any companion within the meaning of rule 40.

(6) The device referred to in paragraph (5) above must–

(a) allow a ballot paper to be inserted into and removed from or attached to and detached from the device, easily and without damage to the paper,

(b) keep the ballot paper firmly in place during use, and

(c) provide suitable means for the voter to–

    (i) identify the spaces on the ballot paper on which he may mark his vote,

    (ii) identify the candidate to whom each such space refers, and

    (iii) mark his vote on the space he has chosen.

(7) The enlarged sample copies of the ballot paper that the GLRO is required to provide, or cause to be displayed at every polling station (in accordance with section 199B(5) and (7) of the 1983 Act) must–

    (a) be provided to the CRO who will deliver them to the polling stations, and

    (b) be printed on paper of the same colour as the ballot paper at the election.

(8) The CRO must also provide each polling station with notices for the guidance of voters, which must be exhibited–

    (a) outside the polling station,

    (b) inside the polling station–

        (i) in the communal areas, and

        (ii) in every voting compartment.

(9) If the GLRO thinks fit he may, not later than the date of the notice of election, direct the CRO that joint ballot boxes must be used for the ballot papers at the election and any or all Authority elections with which the election is taken.

Notices for the guidance of voters

29 **(1)** The GLRO must prepare and provide each CRO with the notices to be exhibited under rule 28(8).

(2) The GLRO may provide each CRO with versions of the notices in such other form as he thinks appropriate, in accordance with section 199B (translations etc of certain documents) of the 1983 Act.

(3) Notices for the guidance of voters exhibited under rule 28(8) or paragraph (2) must be in the appropriate form, but may include such alternative information relating to Authority elections as–

    (a) meets with the requirements of the Notices Schedule, and

    (b) the GLRO may decide.

(4) Notices provided under paragraph (2) may, if the CRO agrees, be exhibited at any polling station–

    (a) outside the polling station,

    (b) inside the polling station–

        (i) in the communal areas,

        (ii) in every voting compartment.

Appointment of polling and counting agents

30 (1) Before the commencement of the poll, each candidate may appoint–

    (a) polling agents to attend at polling stations for the purpose of detecting personation, and

    (b) counting agents to attend at the mayoral count.

(2) The same person may be appointed as a polling agent or counting agent by more than one candidate.

(3) For each local count, one (but no more than one) counting agent of each candidate may be authorised by the terms of his appointment to require a re-count at that count.

(4) Not more than four polling agents, or such greater number as the CRO may by notice allow, may be permitted to attend at any particular polling station.

(5) If the number of such agents appointed to attend at a particular polling station exceeds that number, the CRO must determine by lot which agents are permitted to attend, and only the agents on whom the lot falls will be deemed to have been duly appointed.

(6) The CRO may limit the number of counting agents, but in doing so must ensure that–
    (a) the number is the same in the case of each candidate, and
    (b) the number allowed to a candidate must not (except in special circumstances) be less than the number obtained by dividing the number of clerks employed on the counting by the number of candidates.

(7) For the purposes of the calculations required by paragraph (6) a counting agent appointed for more than one candidate is a separate agent for each of the candidates for whom he has been appointed.

(8) Notice in writing of the appointment of polling and counting agents, stating the names and addresses of the persons appointed, must be given by the candidate to the CRO and must be so given not later than the fifth day (computed in accordance with rule 4) before the day of the poll.

(9) If an agent dies, or becomes incapable of acting, the candidate or, as the case may be, the election agent, may appoint another person in his place, and must forthwith give to the CRO notice in writing of the name and address of that other person.

(10) Any appointment authorised by this rule may be made and the notice of appointment given to the CRO by the candidate's election agent, instead of by the candidate.

(11) In the following provisions of this Part references to polling agents and counting agents must be taken as reference to agents–
    (a) whose appointments have been duly made and notified, and
    (b) where the number of agents is restricted, who are within the permitted numbers.

(12) Any notice required to be given to a counting agent by the CRO may be delivered at, or sent by post to, the address stated in the notice of appointment.

(13) A candidate may himself do any act or thing which any polling or counting agent of his, if appointed, would have been authorised to do, or may assist his agent in doing any such act or thing.

(14) A candidate's election agent may do or assist in doing anything which a polling or counting agent of his is authorised to do, and anything required or authorised by these Rules to be done in the presence of the polling or counting agent may be done in the presence of a candidate's election agent instead of his polling agent or counting agent.

(15) Where by these Rules any act or thing is required or authorised to be done in the presence of the polling or counting agents, the non-attendance of any agent or agents at the time and place appointed for the purpose will not, if the act or thing is otherwise duly done, invalidate the act or thing done.

Notification of requirement of secrecy

31 (1) The CRO must make such arrangements as he thinks fit to ensure that–
    (a) every person attending at a polling station (otherwise than for the purpose of voting or assisting a voter with disabilities to vote or as a constable on duty there) has been given a copy of the provisions of subsections (1), (3) and (6) of section 66 (requirement of secrecy) of the Representation of the People Act

1983, and

    (b)   every person attending at the counting of the votes (other than any constable on duty at the counting) has been given a copy of the provisions of subsections (2) and (6) of that section.

  (2) In paragraph (1) a reference to a constable includes a person designated as a community support officer under section 38 of the 2002 Act (police powers for employees).

Return of postal ballot papers

32 (1) Where–

    (a)   a postal vote has been returned in respect of a person who is entered on the postal voters list, or

    (b)   a proxy postal vote has been returned in respect of a proxy who is entered on the proxy postal voters list,

the CRO must mark the list in the manner prescribed by regulations made under the 1983 Act.

  (2) Rule 49(2) does not apply for the purpose of determining whether, for the purposes of this rule, a postal vote or a proxy postal vote is returned.

Admission to polling station

33 (1) The presiding officer must exclude all persons from the polling station except–

    (a)   voters,

    (b)   persons under the age of 18 who accompany voters to the polling station,

    (c)   the candidates and their election agents,

    (d)   the polling agents appointed to attend at the polling station,

    (e)   the clerks appointed to attend at the polling station,

    (f)   persons who are entitled to attend by virtue of any of sections 6A to 6D of the 2000 Act,

    (g)   the constables on duty, and

    (h)   the companions of voters with disabilities.

  (2) The presiding officer must regulate the total number of voters and persons under the age of 18 who accompany them to be admitted to the polling station at the same time.

  (3) Not more than one polling agent may be admitted at the same time to a polling station on behalf of the same candidate.

  (4) A constable or person employed by the CRO must not be admitted to vote in person elsewhere than at his own polling station allotted to him under these Rules, except on production and surrender of a certificate as to his employment which must be in the appropriate form and signed by an officer of the police of or above the rank of inspector or by the CRO, as the case may be.

  (5) Any certificate surrendered under this rule must forthwith be cancelled.

  (6) In this rule a reference to a constable includes a person designated as a community support officer under section 38 of the 2002 Act.

Keeping of order in station

34 (1) It is the presiding officer's duty to keep order at his polling station.

  (2) If a person misconducts himself in a polling station, or fails to obey the presiding officer's lawful orders, he may immediately, by the presiding officer's order, be removed from the polling station–

    (a) by a constable in or near that station, or

    (b) by any other person authorised in writing by the CRO to remove him,

and the person so removed must not, without the presiding officer's permission, again enter the polling station during the day.

(3) Any person so removed may, if charged with the commission in the polling station of an offence, be dealt with as a person taken into custody by a constable for an offence without a warrant.

(4) The powers conferred by this rule must not be exercised so as to prevent a voter who is otherwise entitled to vote at a polling station from having an opportunity of voting at that station.

Sealing of ballot boxes

35 Immediately before the commencement of the poll, the presiding officer must–

    (a) show each ballot box, empty, to such persons, if any, as are present in the polling station, so that they may see that the boxes are empty,

    (b) lock up such of the boxes as have locks,

    (c) place his seal–

        (i)   on each lock, and

        (ii) on each ballot box which has no lock,

in such a manner as to prevent its being opened without breaking the seal,

    (d) place each box in his view for the receipt of ballot papers, and

    (e) keep each box locked and sealed or, as the case may be, sealed.

Questions to be put to voters

36 (1) At the time of the application (but not afterwards), the questions specified in the second column of the following table–

    (a) may be put by the presiding officer to a person who is mentioned in the first column, and

    (b) must be put if the letter "R" appears after the question and the candidate or his election or polling agent requires the question to be put.

Q No	Person applying for ballot paper	Question
1	A person applying as an elector	(a)–Are you the person registered in the register of local government electors for this election as follows (*read the whole entry from the register*)? R (b)–Have you already voted, here or elsewhere in Greater London at this election for the Mayor of London, otherwise than as proxy for some other person?R
2	A person applying as proxy	(a)–Are you the person whose name appears as AB in the list of proxies for this election as entitled to vote as proxy on behalf of CD? R (b)–Have you already voted here or elsewhere in Greater London at this election for the Mayor of London, as proxy on behalf of CD? R (c)–Are you the spouse, civil partner, parent, grandparent, brother, sister, child or grandchild of CD? R

3	A person applying as proxy for an elector with an anonymous entry (instead of the questions at entry 2)	(a)–Are you the person entitled to vote as proxy on behalf of the elector whose number on the register of electors is (*read out the number*)? R (b)–Have you already voted here or elsewhere in Greater London as proxy on behalf of the elector whose number on the register of electors is (*read out the number*)? R (c)–Are you the spouse, civil partner, parent, grandparent, brother, sister, child or grandchild of the person whose number on the register of electors is (*read out the number*)? R
4	A person applying as proxy if the question at entry 2(c) or 3(c) is not answered in the affirmative	Have you already voted here or elsewhere in Greater London at this election for the Mayor of London, on behalf of two persons of whom you are not the spouse, civil partner, parent, grandparent, brother, sister, child or grandchild? R
5	A person applying as an elector in relation to whom there is an entry in the postal voters list	(a)–Did you apply to vote by post? (b)–Why have you not voted by post?
6	A person applying as proxy who is named in the proxy postal voters list	(a)–Did you apply to vote by post as proxy? (b)–Why have you not voted by post as proxy?

(2) In the case of an elector in respect of whom a notice has been issued under section 13B(3B) or (3D) of the 1983 Act, the references in the questions at entries 1(a) and 3(a), (b) and (c) to reading from the register must be taken as references to reading from the notice issued under those subsections.

(3) A ballot paper must not be delivered to any person required to answer any of the above questions unless he has answered each question satisfactorily.

(4) Except as authorised by this rule, no inquiry may be permitted as to the right of any person to vote.

Challenge of voter

37 A person must not be prevented from voting because–

    (a) a candidate or his election or polling agent declares that he has reasonable cause to believe that the person has committed an offence of personation, or

    (b) the person is arrested on the grounds that he is suspected of committing or of being about to commit such an offence.

Voting procedure

38 (1) A ballot paper must be delivered to a voter who applies for one, and immediately before delivery–

    (a) the number and (unless paragraph (2) applies) name of the elector as stated in the copy of the register of electors must be called out,

(b) the number of the elector must be marked on the list mentioned in rule 28(3)(d) beside the number of the ballot paper to be issued to him,

(c) a mark must be placed in the register of electors against the number of the elector to note that a ballot paper has been applied for but without showing the particular ballot paper which may be delivered,

(d) in the case of a person applying for a ballot paper as proxy, a mark must also be placed against his name in the list of proxies.

(2) In the case of an elector who has an anonymous entry, he must show the presiding officer his official poll card and only his number may be called out in pursuance of paragraph (1)(a).

(3) In the case of an elector who is added to the register in pursuance of a notice issued under section 13B(3B) or (3D) of the 1983 Act, paragraph (1) is modified as follows–

(a) in sub-paragraph (a), for "copy of the register of electors" substitute "copy of the notice issued under section 13B(3B) or (3D) of the 1983 Act",

(b) in sub-paragraph (c), for "in the register of electors" substitute "on the copy of the notice issued under section 13B(3B) or (3D) of the 1983 Act".

(4) The voter, on receiving the ballot paper, must forthwith proceed into one of the compartments in the polling station and there secretly mark his paper, and must then show to the presiding officer the back of the paper, so as to disclose the number and other unique identifying mark, and put the ballot paper into the ballot box in the presiding officer's presence, but so as to conceal his vote.

(5) The voter must vote without undue delay, and must leave the polling station as soon as he has put his ballot paper into the ballot box.

(6) A voter who has had a ballot paper delivered to him under paragraph (1), but has decided not to mark it, may return it to the presiding officer and where the voter does so, the presiding officer must–

(a) immediately cancel the ballot paper, and for the purposes of these rules treat it as a spoilt ballot paper,

(b) place a mark beside the number of that ballot paper on the corresponding number list to show that the ballot paper has been cancelled.

(7) At an ordinary election, the same copy of–

(a) the list of proxies,

(b) the list mentioned in rule 28(3)(d),

(c) the register of electors,

(d) any notice issued under section 13B(3B) or (3D) of the 1983 Act (marked in the case of an elector who is added to the register in pursuance of such a notice),

may be used for each Authority election and one mark may be placed in the list, register or notice (as the case may be) to denote that a ballot paper has been delivered in respect of each Authority election; except that, where a ballot paper has not been issued in respect of any Authority election, a different mark must be placed in the list, register or notice so as to identify the elections in respect of which a ballot paper was issued.

(8) A voter who at the close of the poll is in the polling station, or in a queue outside the polling station, for the purpose of voting must (despite the close of the poll) be entitled to apply for a ballot paper under paragraph (1); and these rules apply in relation to such a voter accordingly.

Votes marked by presiding officer

39 (1) The presiding officer, on the application of a voter–

(a)   who is incapacitated by blindness or other disability from voting in the manner directed by these Rules, or

(b)   who declares orally that he is unable to read,

must, in the presence of the polling agents, cause the voter's vote to be marked on a ballot paper in the manner directed by the voter, and the ballot paper to be placed in the ballot box.

(2)   The name and number on the register of electors of every voter whose vote is marked in pursuance of this rule, and the reason why it is so marked, must be entered on a list (in these Rules called "the list of votes marked by the presiding officer").

In the case of a person voting as proxy for an elector, the number to be entered together with the voter's name must be the elector's number.

(3)   In the case of a person in respect of whom a notice has been issued under section 13B(3B) or (3D) of the 1983 Act, paragraph (2) applies as if for "on the register of electors of every voter" there were substituted "relating to every voter in respect of whom a notice has been issued under section 13B(3B) or (3D) of the 1983 Act".

(4)   At an ordinary election, the same list may be used for each Authority election, and where it is so used, an entry in that list must be taken to mean that the ballot papers were so marked in respect of each Authority election, unless the list identifies the election for which the ballot paper was so marked.

Voting by persons with disabilities

40 (1)   If a voter makes an application to the presiding officer to be allowed, on the ground of–
(a)   blindness or other disability, or
(b)   inability to read,

to vote with the assistance of another person by whom he is accompanied (in these Rules referred to as "the companion"), the presiding officer must require the voter to declare, orally or in writing, whether he is so incapacitated by his blindness or other disability, or by his inability to read, as to be unable to vote without assistance.

(2)   If the presiding officer–
(a)   is satisfied that the voter is so incapacitated, and
(b)   is also satisfied by a written declaration made by the companion (in these Rules referred to as "the declaration made by the companion of a voter with disabilities") that the companion–
(i)   is a qualified person within the meaning of these Rules, and
(ii)   has not previously assisted more than one voter with disabilities to vote at the election,

the presiding officer must grant the application, and then anything which is by these Rules required to be done to, or by that voter in connection with the giving of his vote may be done to, or with the assistance of, the companion.

(3)   For the purpose of these Rules, a person is a voter with disabilities if he has made such a declaration as is mentioned in paragraph (1) above, and a person may be qualified to assist a voter with disabilities to vote if that person–
(a)   is a person who is entitled to vote as an elector at the election, or
(b)   is the father, mother, brother, sister, spouse, civil partner, son or daughter of the voter and has attained the age of 18 years.

(4)   The name and number in the register of electors of every voter whose vote is given in accordance with this rule and the name and address of the companion must be entered on a list (in these Rules referred to as the "list of voters with disabilities assisted by companions").

In the case of a person voting as proxy for an elector, the number to be entered together with the voter's name must be the elector's number.

(5) In the case of a person in respect of whom a notice has been issued under section 13B(3B) or (3D) of the 1983 Act, paragraph (4) applies as if for "in the register of electors of every voter" there were substituted "relating to every voter in respect of whom a notice has been issued under section 13B(3B) or (3D) of the 1983 Act".

(6) The declaration made by the companion–
   (a) must be in the appropriate form, and
   (b) must be made before the presiding officer at the time when the voter applies to vote with the assistance of a companion, and
   (c) must forthwith be given to the presiding officer who must attest and retain it.

(7) No fee or other payment may be charged in respect of the declaration.

(8) At an ordinary election, the same list of voters with disabilities assisted by companions may be used for each Authority election, and where it is so used, an entry in that list must be taken to mean that the votes were so given in respect of each Authority election, unless the list identifies the election for which the vote was so given.

Tendered ballot papers: circumstances where available

41 (1) If a person, representing himself to be–
   (a) a particular elector named in the register and not named in the absent voters list, or
   (b) a particular person named in the list of proxies as proxy for an elector and not entitled to vote by post as proxy,
   applies for a ballot paper after another person has voted in person either as the elector or his proxy, the applicant must, on satisfactorily answering the questions permitted by law to be asked at the poll, be entitled, subject to the following provisions of this rule and rule 42, to mark a ballot paper (in these Rules referred to as "a tendered ballot paper") in the same manner as any other voter.

(2) Paragraph (4) applies if–
   (a) a person applies for a ballot paper representing himself to be a particular elector named in the register,
   (b) he is also named in the postal voters list, and
   (c) he claims that he did not make an application to vote by post at the election.

(3) Paragraph (4) also applies if–
   (a) a person applies for a ballot paper representing himself to be a particular person named as a proxy in the list of proxies,
   (b) he is also named in the proxy postal voters list, and
   (c) he claims that he did not make an application to vote by post as proxy.

(4) The person must, on satisfactorily answering the questions permitted by law to be asked at the poll, be entitled, subject to the following provisions of this rule and rule 42, to mark a ballot paper (in these Rules referred to as a "tendered ballot paper") in the same manner as any other voter.

(5) Paragraph (6) applies if before the close of the poll but after the last time at which a person may apply for a replacement postal ballot paper, a person represents himself to be–
   (a) a particular elector named in the register who is also named in the postal voters list, or
   (b) a particular person named as a proxy in the list of proxies and who is also named in the proxy postal voters list,
   and claims that he has lost or has not received his postal ballot paper.

(6) The person must, on satisfactorily answering the questions permitted by law to be

asked at the poll, be entitled, subject to the provisions of this rule and rule 42, to mark a ballot paper (in these Rules referred to as a "tendered ballot paper") in the same manner as any other voter.

Tendered ballot papers: general provisions

42 (1)   A tendered ballot paper must–

    (a)   be of a colour differing from the other ballot papers,

    (b)   instead of being put into the ballot box, be given to the presiding officer and endorsed by him with the name of the voter and his number on the register of electors, and set aside in a separate packet.

(2)   The name of the voter and his number on the register of electors must be entered on a list (in these Rules referred to as the "tendered votes list").

(3)   In the case of a person voting as proxy for an elector, the number to be endorsed or entered together with the voter's name must be the number of that elector.

(4)   In the case of an elector who has an anonymous entry, this rule and rule 41 apply subject to the following modifications–

    (a)   in paragraphs (1)(b) and (2) above, the references to the name of the voter must be ignored,

    (b)   otherwise, a reference to a person named on a register or list must be construed as a reference to a person whose number appears in the register or list (as the case may be).

(5)   In the case of a person in respect of whom a notice has been issued under section 13B(3B) or (3D) of the 1983 Act, this rule and rule 41 apply as if–

    (a)   in rule 41(1)(a), (2)(a) and (5)(a), for "named in the register" there were substituted "in respect of whom a notice under section 13B(3B) or (3D) of the 1983 Act has been issued",

    (b)   in paragraph (1)(b) of this rule for "his number in the register of electors" there were substituted "the number relating to him on a notice issued under section 13B(3B) or (3D) of the 1983 Act",

    (c)   in paragraph (2) of this rule, for "his number in the register of electors" there were substituted "the number relating to him on a notice issued under section 13B(3B) or (3D) of the 1983 Act".

(6)   At an ordinary election, the same list may be used for each Authority election, and where it is so used, an entry in that list must be taken to mean that tendered ballot papers were marked in respect of each Authority election, unless the list identifies the election for which a tendered ballot paper was delivered.

Spoilt and replacement ballot papers

43 (1)   A voter who has inadvertently dealt with his ballot paper in such manner that it cannot be conveniently used as a ballot paper may, on delivering it to the presiding officer and proving to his satisfaction the fact of the inadvertence, obtain a replacement for the ballot paper so delivered (in these Rules referred to as "a spoilt ballot paper"), and the spoilt ballot paper must be immediately cancelled.

(2)   If a voter decides, after he has returned his ballot paper and it has been cancelled in accordance with rule 38(6), but before the close of the poll, that he wishes to vote in the election, he may obtain a replacement for the returned ballot paper.

(3)   Before a replacement ballot paper is obtained, the presiding officer must mark the corresponding number list that was marked under rule 38(1) (the corresponding number list)–

(a)   in the case of a ballot paper being replaced under paragraph (1) or (2), beside the number of the replacement ballot paper obtained to show–
   (i)   the number of the elector, and
   (ii)   the number of the ballot paper which is being replaced; and

(b)   in the case of a ballot paper being replaced under paragraph (1), beside the number of the spoilt ballot paper to show that the ballot paper was replaced.

(4)   At an ordinary election, the voter must only receive a replacement for a spoilt or returned ballot paper.

(5)   If the same corresponding number list is used for more than one Authority election in accordance with rule 38(7)–
   (a)   the marks made under paragraph (3) must identify the election for which a ballot paper has been replaced, and
   (b)   any ballot paper which the voter has not applied for or obtained as a replacement, but which bears the same ballot paper number as a ballot paper delivered under rule 38(1), or obtained under paragraph (1) or (2) of this rule–
      (i)   must not be delivered to the voter,
      (ii)   must be cancelled, and
      (iii)   for the purposes of these rules, must be treated as a spoilt ballot paper.

Correction of errors on day of poll

44 (1)   The presiding officer must keep a list of persons to whom ballot papers are delivered in consequence of an alteration to the register made by virtue of section 13B(3B) or (3D) of the 1983 Act which takes effect on the day of the poll.

(2)   At an ordinary election, the same list may be used for each Authority election, and where it is so used, an entry in that list must be taken to mean that ballot papers were delivered in respect of each Authority election, unless the list identifies the election for which a tendered ballot paper was delivered.

Adjournment of poll in case of riot

45 (1)   Where the proceedings at any polling station are interrupted or obstructed by riot or open violence, the presiding officer must adjourn the proceedings till the following day and must forthwith give notice to the CRO.

(2)   Where the poll is adjourned at any polling station–
   (a)   the hours of polling on the day to which it is adjourned must be the same as for the original day, and
   (b)   references in these Rules to the close of the poll must be construed accordingly.

(3)   As soon as practicable after the CRO has received notice of the adjournment of a poll he must inform the GLRO of that fact and of the cause of its adjournment.

Procedure on close of poll

46 (1)   As soon as practicable after the close of the poll, the presiding officer must, in the presence of the polling agents, make up into separate packets, sealed with his own seal and the seals of such polling agents as desire to affix their seals–
   (a)   each ballot box in use at the station, sealed so as to prevent the introduction of additional ballot papers and unopened, but with the key attached,
   (b)   the unused and spoilt ballot papers placed together,
   (c)   the tendered ballot papers,
   (d)   the marked copies of the register of electors (including any marked copy notices issued under section 13B(3B) or (3D) of the 1983 Act) and of the list of proxies,
   (e)   the list prepared under rule 18, including the part completed in accordance with

rule 38(1)(b) (together referred to in these Rules as "the completed corresponding number list"),

(f)   the certificates as to employment on duty on the day of the poll,

(g)   the tendered votes list, the list of voters with disabilities assisted by companions, the list of votes marked by the presiding officer, a statement of the number of voters whose votes are so marked by the presiding officer under the heads "disability" and "unable to read", the list maintained under rule 44, and the declarations made by the companions of voters with disabilities,

and must deliver the packets or cause them to be delivered to the CRO to be taken charge of by him; but if the packets are not delivered by the presiding officer personally to the CRO, the arrangements for their delivery must be approved by the CRO.

(2)   The contents of the packets referred to in paragraph (1)(b), (c) and (f) must not be combined with the contents of the packets made under the corresponding rule that applies at any other Authority election.

(3)   The marked copies of the register of electors and of the list of proxies must be in one packet but must not be in the same packet as the completed corresponding number list or the certificates as to employment on duty on the day of the poll.

(4)   The packets must be accompanied by a statement ("the ballot paper account") showing the number of ballot papers entrusted to the presiding officer, and accounting for them under the heads–

(a)   ballot papers issued and not otherwise accounted for,

(b)   unused ballot papers,

(c)   spoilt ballot papers, and

(d)   tendered ballot papers.

(5)   At an ordinary election, the statement referred to in paragraph (4) may be combined with the statements produced in relation to other Authority elections and the combined statement must be arranged in such manner as the GLRO may direct.

Attendance at verification and the local count

47 (1)   As soon as practicable after the close of the poll, the CRO must make arrangements for carrying out, in the presence of the counting agents appointed for the purposes of the election, the verification and the counting of votes and must give to the counting agents notice in writing of the time and place at which he will begin to verify and count the votes.

(2)   No person other than–

(a)   the CRO and his clerks and technical assistants,

(b)   the GLRO,

(c)   the candidates and one other person chosen by each of them,

(d)   the election agents,

(e)   the counting agents,

(f)   persons who are entitled to attend by virtue of any of sections 6A to 6D of the 2000 Act,

may be present at the verification and counting of the votes, unless permitted by the CRO to attend.

(3)   A person not entitled to attend the verification and local count must not be permitted to do so by the CRO unless he–

(a)   is satisfied that the efficient conduct of those proceedings will not be impeded, and

(b)   has either consulted the election agents or thought it impracticable to do so.

(4) The CRO must give the counting agents all such reasonable facilities for overseeing the proceedings, and all such information with respect to them, as he can give them consistently with the orderly conduct of the proceedings and the discharge of his duties in connection with them.

Use of the electronic counting system

48 (1) The GLRO may provide the CRO with an electronic counting system consisting of computer hardware, software and other equipment or services, for the purpose of counting the number of ballot papers, to verify the ballot paper accounts and to count the votes cast on them.

(2) Any verification of ballot paper accounts, count or re-count at the election conducted using the electronic counting system must be conducted in accordance with rule 49.

(3) If the GLRO has provided the CRO with an electronic counting system for use at the election, the CRO must obtain the prior written consent of the GLRO before he may conduct the verification of ballot paper accounts or count the votes manually.

(4) If the verification of ballot paper accounts, count or re-count has commenced using the electronic counting system but has not been completed, the CRO may, if he considers it appropriate, discontinue the count and instead count the votes manually.

(5) Where the count or a re-count has been conducted using the electronic counting system, the CRO may, if he considers it appropriate, conduct any re-count without using that system.

(6) Where verification or any count or re-count is conducted using the electronic counting system, any of the steps referred to in rule 49, in so far as practicable, may be undertaken–
   (a) concurrently with any other of those steps, or
   (b) in a different order.

Verification and the local count

49 (1) The CRO must–
   (a) open the ballot boxes from each polling station together, in the presence of the counting agents appointed for the purposes of the election and any other Authority election with which is its combined,
   (b) cause the electronic counting system to count such of the postal ballot papers as have been duly returned in accordance with paragraphs (2) and (3) and record separately the number counted,
   (c) not mix the contents of any ballot box with the contents of any other ballot box during the conduct of any count or re-count.

(2) A postal ballot paper must not be taken to be duly returned unless–
   (a) it is returned in the manner set out in paragraph (3) and reaches the CRO or any polling station in the Assembly constituency that includes the electoral area for which the elector is registered as a local government elector, before the close of the poll,
   (b) the postal voting statement, duly signed, is also returned in the manner set out in paragraph (3) and reaches him or such polling station before that time,
   (c) the postal voting statement also states the date of birth of the elector or proxy (as the case may be), and
   (d) in a case where the steps for verifying the date of birth and signature of an elector or proxy have been prescribed by regulations made under the 1983 Act, the CRO (having taken such steps) verifies the date of birth and signature of the elector or proxy (as the case may be).

(3) The manner in which any postal paper or postal voting statement may be returned–
    (a) to the CRO, is by hand or by post,
    (b) to a polling station in the Assembly constituency, is by hand.

(3A) A postal ballot paper or postal voting statement that reaches the CRO or a polling station mentioned in sub-paragraph (a) of paragraph (2) at or after the close of the poll is treated for the purposes of paragraph (2) as reaching that officer or polling station before the close of the poll if it is delivered by a person who, at the close of the poll, is in the polling station, or in a queue outside the polling station, for the purpose of returning it.

(4) After completing the proceedings under paragraph (1), the CRO must cause the electronic counting system to process the ballot papers so as to–
    (a) count the number of ballot papers,
    (b) count the number of first preference votes given for each candidate, and
    (c) record the way that second preference votes have been given on the ballot papers.

(5) The CRO must not cause the electronic counting system to count any tendered ballot paper.

(6) The CRO must verify each ballot paper account by comparing it with the number of ballot papers processed by the electronic counting system, and the unused and spoilt ballot papers in his possession and the tendered votes list (opening and re-sealing the packets containing the unused and spoilt ballot papers and the tendered votes list) and must draw up a statement as to the result of the verification, which any election agent may copy.

(7) The CRO, while verifying the ballot paper accounts and counting the votes, must take all proper precautions for preventing any person from seeing the numbers printed on the back of the papers.

(8) The CRO must so far as practicable proceed continuously with counting the votes, allowing only time for refreshment, except that the hours between 5 in the afternoon and 10 on the following morning may be excluded with the prior consent of the GLRO.

(9) During the time so excluded the CRO must–
    (a) place the ballot papers and other documents relating to the election under his own seal and the seals of such of the counting agents as desire to affix their seals, and
    (b) otherwise take proper precautions for the security of the papers and documents.

Rejected ballot papers

50 (1) Any ballot paper–
    (a) which does not bear the official mark,
    (b) on which anything is written or marked by which the voter can be identified except the printed number and other unique identifying mark on the back,
    (c) which is unmarked,
    (d) which is void for uncertainty,
is, subject to paragraph (2), void and must not be counted.

(2) A ballot paper on which a vote is marked–
    (a) elsewhere than in the proper place, or
    (b) otherwise than by means of a cross, or
    (c) by more than one mark,
must not for such reason be void if–
        (i) at an election at which more than two candidates remain validly

nominated, an intention that a first preference vote be given for not more than one of the candidates clearly appears,

    (ii) at any other election, an intention that a vote is for one only of the candidates clearly appears.

(3) A ballot paper–
    (a) which is not void, and
    (b) on which an intention that a second preference vote be given for not more than one of the candidates clearly appears,
will be valid as respects that second preference vote and must be counted accordingly.

(4) Where the electronic counting system identifies a ballot paper that has been marked, but which appears–
    (a) to be void, or
    (b) to contain a first preference vote that can be counted, and another mark that cannot be counted as a second preference vote,
then that ballot paper must be examined by a clerk appointed by the CRO in the manner referred to in paragraph (7).

(5) If the clerk, having examined the ballot paper, considers that–
    (a) it is void, or
    (b) that it is marked with a first preference vote that can be counted, but that it is not marked with a second preference vote that can be counted,
then the CRO must examine it in the manner referred to in paragraph (7).

(6) After the CRO examines the ballot paper, he must give his decision as to whether or not–
    (a) it is void, or
    (b) it is marked with a second preference vote that can be counted.

(7) An examination under paragraph (4) or (5) is to be made by the clerk or CRO examining an image of the ballot paper which is shown on a screen so as to be visible to those attending the count.

(8) The CRO may examine any ballot paper that he is not required to examine in accordance with paragraphs (5)–
    (a) either in the manner referred to in paragraph (7), or
    (b) by examining a paper copy,
and where the CRO does so, he must give a decision on that paper in accordance with paragraph (6),

(9) No person attending the count is to be entitled to require the clerk or CRO to examine a ballot paper or to provide a paper copy for inspection.

(10) A record of the CRO's decision under paragraph (6) must be retained in the electronic counting system together, in the case of a decision that the ballot is void, with his reasons by reference to paragraph (1).

(11) If a counting agent objects to the CRO's decision that the ballot paper–
    (a) is void, or
    (b) is marked with a second preference vote that cannot be counted,
the CRO must record on the electronic counting system that the decision was objected to.

(12) A record must be retained in the electronic counting system of the number of ballot papers which are not void, but on which a second preference vote has not been counted because–
    (a) a vote has not been marked,
    (b) a vote has been given for more than one candidate, or
    (c) there is uncertainty as to for whom a vote was given.

(13) The CRO must draw up a statement showing the number of rejected ballot papers under the several heads of–
    (a) want of an official mark,
    (b) voting for more than one candidate as to first preference vote,
    (c) writing or mark by which the voter could be identified,
    (d) unmarked as to the first preference vote, and
    (e) void for uncertainty.

(14) As soon as practicable after the completion of the statement under paragraph (13) the CRO must inform–
    (a) such candidates, election agents and counting agents as are present at the count, and
    (b) the GLRO,
of its contents.

(15) The CRO must also include in the statement drawn up under paragraph (13), the numbers of second preference votes for which a record has been retained, set out under the several heads in sub-paragraphs (12)(a) to (c).

Decisions on ballot papers

51 The decision of the CRO on any question arising in respect of a ballot paper is final, but may be subject to review on an election petition.

Re-count

52 (1) A candidate or his election agent or a counting agent authorised under rule 30(3) may, if present when the counting or any re-count of the votes, is completed, require the CRO to have the votes re-counted or again re-counted but the CRO may refuse to do so if in his opinion the request is unreasonable.

(2) No step may be taken on the completion of the counting or any re-count of votes, until the candidates and election agents and counting agents authorised under rule 30(1) present at its completion have been given a reasonable opportunity to exercise the right conferred by this rule.

(3) The CRO may determine the extent to which any re-count involves the electronic counting of votes.

(4) When the returning officer uses the electronic counting system for the re-counting of votes, he must not re-consider any decision made on any ballot paper under rule 50(6).

Procedure at conclusion of local count

53 (1) As soon as practicable after the conclusion of the local count (including any re-count), the CRO must draw up a statement showing–
    (a) the total number of ballot papers used,
    (b) the total number of rejected ballot papers,
    (c) at an election contested by more than two candidates–
        (i) the total number of first preference votes given,
        (ii) the number of first preference votes given for each candidate, and
        (iii) the total number second preference votes given for each candidate correlated with the way the first preference votes have been cast.
    (d) at an election contested by only two candidates, the number of votes given for each candidate.

(2) As soon as practicable after the statement is drawn up under paragraph (1), the CRO must inform the GLRO of its contents, and if it is practicable to do so, must also provide

that information so as to show the total number of votes under each of those heads in each ward .

(3)   As soon as practicable after the GLRO has authorised him to do so, the CRO must–

(a)   inform such of the candidates and their election agents as are then present of the contents of the statements prepared in accordance with rule 50 and paragraph (1) of this rule, and

(b)   give public notice of the contents of those statements.

Attendance at the central calculation

54 (1)   The GLRO must make arrangements for making the calculations made under rules 55 and 56 in the presence of the election agents and he must give to those agents notice in writing of the time and place at which he will begin the calculation.

(2)   No person other than–

(a)   the GLRO and his clerks,

(b)   the CROs and a clerk or technical assistant chosen by each of them,

(c)   the candidates and one person chosen by each of them,

(d)   the election agents,

(e)   persons who are entitled to attend by virtue of any of sections 6A to 6D of the Political Parties, Elections and Referendums Act 2000,

(f)   at an ordinary election, the persons permitted to be present at the allocation of seats for London Members of the London Assembly,

may be present at a calculation, unless permitted by the GLRO to attend.

(3)   A person not entitled to attend a calculation must not be permitted to do so by the GLRO unless he–

(a)   is satisfied that the efficiency of the calculation will not be impeded, and

(b)   has either consulted the election agents or thought it impracticable to do so.

The first calculation and resolution of equality

55 (1)   As soon as the GLRO has received the information required by rule 53 from every CRO he must–

(a)   in relation to an election contested by more than two candidates, ascertain the total of the first preference votes given in the Assembly constituencies to each candidate, and

(b)   in relation to an election contested by only two candidates, ascertain the total number of votes given in the Assembly constituencies to each candidate.

(2)   As soon as the GLRO has ascertained the result of the calculation, he must inform such of the election agents as are then present of the relevant figures and must give them a reasonable opportunity to satisfy themselves as to the accuracy of the calculation.

(3)   In paragraph (2), "the relevant figures" means–

(a)   in the case of an election contested by more than two candidates, the number of first preference votes given in each of the Assembly constituencies for each candidate and the calculation undertaken by the GLRO for the purposes of ascertaining whether a candidate is to be returned in accordance with paragraph 3 of Schedule 2 to the 1999 Act (candidate with overall majority of first preference votes),

(b)   in the case of an election contested by only two candidates, the number of votes given in each Assembly constituency for each candidate and the total number of votes given for each candidate.

(4)   Where an election is contested by more than two candidates–

(a)   if paragraph 3 of Schedule 2 to the 1999 Act applies (candidate with overall majority of first preference votes) the declaration of the person to be returned as the Mayor must be made in accordance with rule 57, or

    (b) if paragraph 4(1) of that Schedule applies (no candidate with overall majority of first preference votes), the GLRO must proceed with the second calculation in accordance with Part 5.

(5) Where an election is contested by only two candidates and the total number of votes given for each of them is unequal the person to be returned as the Mayor is the candidate to whom the majority of the votes is given.

(6) Where an election is contested by only two candidates and the total number of votes given for each of them is equal, the person to be returned as the Mayor is the person whom the GLRO decides, in accordance with paragraph 4(8) of Schedule 2 to the 1999 Act, is to be returned as the Mayor.

(7) In a case to which paragraph (5) or (6) applies, the declaration of the person to be returned as the Mayor must be made in accordance with rule 57.

Part 5
Further Provision: More Than Two Candidates

The second calculation and resolution of equality

56 (1) As soon as the GLRO has determined that paragraph 4(1) of Schedule 2 to the 1999 Act applies he must comply with paragraphs 4(5) and (6) of Schedule 2 to the 1999 Act.

(2) As soon as the GLRO has ascertained the result of the second calculation, he must provide such of the election agents for those candidates who remain in the contest as are then present with a copy of the relevant figures and must give them a reasonable opportunity to satisfy themselves as to the accuracy of the calculation.

(3) In paragraph (2), "the relevant figures" means–

    (a) the number of second preference votes given in each of the Assembly constituencies for each of the candidates remaining in the contest, and

    (b) the calculation undertaken by the GLRO for the purpose of ascertaining the total number of first and second preference votes given to each of those candidates.

(4) If, after the second calculation, the total number of votes given for two or more candidates is equal, the person to be returned as the Mayor is the person whom the GLRO decides, in accordance with paragraph 4(8) of Schedule 2 to the 1999 Act, is to be returned as the Mayor.

Part 6
Final Proceedings in Contested and Uncontested Elections

Declaration of result

57 (1) The GLRO must declare to be elected as the Mayor of London the candidate who, in accordance with section 4(2) of the 1999 Act or Part I of Schedule 2 to that Act (including those provisions as applied by section 16(4) at an election to fill a vacancy), as the case may be, is to be returned as the Mayor at that election.

(2) The GLRO must give public notice of–

    (a) the name of the of the person declared to be elected and his authorised description, if any, within the meaning of rule 6(5) or (7),

    (b) the total number of first preference votes given for each candidate,

    (c) the total number of second preference votes given for each of the candidates remaining in the contest after the count of the first preference votes,

(d) the number of rejected ballot papers at the election under each head shown in the statement of rejected ballot papers, and

(e) the number of ballot papers on which no second preference vote was counted under each head shown in the statement of rejected ballot papers,

(3) In an uncontested election, the GLRO must as soon as practicable after the latest time for the delivery of notices of withdrawals of candidature–

(a) declare to be elected the candidate remaining validly nominated, and

(b) give public notice of the name of the person declared to be elected and his authorised description, if any, within the meaning of rule 6(5) or (7).

(4) Subject to paragraph (5), after the GLRO complies with paragraphs (1) and (2), he may, in so far as is practicable, give public notice of the information referred to paragraph (2)(b) to (e) so as to set out the number of votes falling under each of those heads, in respect of each ward.

(5) Where the sum of first preference votes given for all candidates in any ward does not exceed 500, the GLRO must not give notice under paragraph (4) in respect of that ward alone, but must amalgamate the figures for that ward with those for any other ward in which more than 500 votes have been given, in the same Assembly constituency.

Return or forfeiture of candidate's deposit

58 (1) Unless forfeited in accordance with paragraph (5), the deposit made under rule 9 must be returned to the person making it or his personal representative.

(2) Subject to paragraph (4), the deposit must be returned not later than the next day after that on which the result of the election is declared.

(3) For the purposes of paragraph (2)–

(a) a day must be disregarded if, in accordance with rule 4, it would be disregarded in computing any period of time for the purposes of the timetable for the election, and

(b) the deposit must be treated as being returned on a day if a cheque for the amount of the deposit is posted on that day.

(4) If the candidate is not shown as standing nominated in the statement of persons nominated, or if proof of his death has been given to the GLRO before the first calculation under rule 55, the deposit must be returned as soon as practicable after the publication of the statement or after his death, as the case may be.

(5) Where a poll is taken, if, after the first calculation under rule 55, the candidate is found not to have polled more than one-twentieth of the total number of first preference votes polled by all the candidates, the deposit must be forfeited to the Greater London Authority.

Part 7
Disposal of Documents

Sealing up of ballot papers

59 (1) On the completion of the counting at a contested election the CRO must seal up in separate packets the counted and rejected ballot papers.

(2) Where some or all of the votes have been counted using the electronic counting system, the CRO must also seal up in a separate packet a complete electronic record ("the electronic record") of the information stored in the electronic counting system,

held in such device as may be suitable for the purpose of its storage.

(3) After making the electronic record under paragraph (2), the CRO must arrange for the original records in the electronic counting system to be removed from it and destroyed in a manner that ensures that the secrecy of those records is preserved.

(4) The CRO must not open the sealed packets of–
   (a) tendered ballot papers,
   (b) certificates as to employment on duty on the day of the poll,
   (c) the completed corresponding number lists, or
   (d) marked copies of the register of electors (including any marked copy notices issued under section 13B(3B) or (3D) of the 1983 Act) and lists of proxies.

Delivery and retention of documents

60 (1) The CRO must then forward the following documents to the relevant registration officer–
   (a) the packets of ballot papers in his possession,
   (b) the packet containing the electronic record (if any),
   (c) the ballot paper accounts and the statements of rejected ballot papers and of the result of the verification of the ballot paper accounts,
   (d) the tendered votes lists, the lists of voters with disabilities assisted by companions, the lists of votes marked by the presiding officer and the related statements, the lists maintained under rule 44 and the declarations made by the companions of voters with disabilities,
   (e) the packets of the completed corresponding number lists,
   (f) the packets of certificates as to employment on duty on the day of the poll, and
   (g) the packets containing marked copies of registers (including any marked copy notices issued under section 13B(3B) or (3D) of the 1983 Act) and of the postal voters list, of the lists of proxies and of the proxy postal voters list,

endorsing on each packet a description of its contents, the date of the election to which they relate and the name of the Assembly constituency for which the election was held.

Orders for production of documents

61 (1) An order–
   (a) for the inspection or production of any rejected ballot papers in the custody of the relevant registration officer, or
   (b) for the opening of a packet containing the electronic record or a sealed packet of completed corresponding number lists or certificates as to employment on duty on the day of the poll or the inspection of any counted ballot papers in the custody of the relevant registration officer,

may be made by a county court, if the court is satisfied by evidence on oath that the order is required for the purpose of instituting or maintaining a prosecution for an offence in relation to ballot papers, or for the purpose of an election petition.

(2) An election court may make an order for the opening of a packet containing the electronic record or a sealed packet of completed corresponding number lists or certificates or for the inspection of any counted ballot papers in the custody of the relevant registration officer.

(3) An order under this rule may be made subject to such conditions as to–
   (a) persons,
   (b) time,
   (c) place and mode of inspection,
   (d) production or opening,

as the court making the order thinks expedient; but in making and carrying into effect an order for the opening of a packet containing the electronic record or a packet of completed corresponding number lists or certificates or for the inspection of counted ballot papers, care must be taken that the way in which the vote of any particular elector has been given must not be disclosed until it has been proved–

    (i)   that his vote was given, and

    (ii) that the vote has been declared by a competent court to be invalid.

(4)   An appeal lies to the High Court from any order of a county court under this rule.

(5)   Any power given under this rule to a county court may be exercised by any judge of the court otherwise than in open court.

(6)   Where an order is made for the production by the relevant registration officer of any document in his custody relating to any specified election–

    (a) the production by him or his agent of the document or electronic record ordered in such manner as may be directed by that order will be conclusive evidence that the document or electronic record relates to the specified election, and

    (b) any endorsement on any packet of ballot papers so produced will be *prima facie* evidence that the ballot papers are what they are stated to be by the endorsement.

(7)   The production from proper custody of–

    (a) a ballot paper purporting to have been used at any election, or

    (b) a copy of the electronic record which purports to record that a particular ballot paper was used at any election, and

a completed corresponding number list with a number written beside the number of the ballot paper, will be *prima facie* evidence that the elector whose vote was given by that ballot paper was the person who, at the time of the election, had affixed to his entry in the register of electors or on the notice issued under section 13B(3B) or (3D) of the 1983 Act, the same number as was written on the completed corresponding number list.

(8)   Unless authorised by this rule, no person may be allowed to inspect any rejected or counted ballot papers in the custody of the relevant registration officer or open any sealed packets of completed corresponding number lists, certificates of employment on the day of the poll or containing the electronic record.

Retention and destruction of documents and records

62   The relevant registration officer must retain or cause to be retained for one year all documents and, where applicable, electronic records relating to an election forwarded to him in pursuance of these Rules by a CRO, and then, unless otherwise directed by an order of a county court, a Crown Court, a magistrate's court or an election court, must cause them to be destroyed.

Part 8
Death of Candidate

Deceased independent candidate

63 (1) This rule applies if at a contested election proof is given to the GLRO's satisfaction before the result of the election is declared that one of the persons named or to be named in the ballot papers as an independent candidate has died.

(2)   Subject to this rule and rules 65 and 66, these rules apply to the election as if the

candidate had not died.

(3) The following provisions of these rules do not apply in relation to the deceased candidate–
    (a) rule 33(1)(c) and (d) (admission to polling station),
    (b) rule 47(2)(c) to (e) (attendance at count),
    (c) rule 58(5) (forfeiture of deposit).

(4) If only two persons are shown as standing nominated in the statement of persons nominated the GLRO must–
    (a) if polling has not begun, countermand the notice of poll,
    (b) if polling has begun, direct that the poll is abandoned, and
    (c) subject to rule 66, treat the election as an uncontested election.

(5) For the purposes of this rule a person is named or to be named on the ballot papers as an independent candidate if the description (if any) on his nomination paper is not authorised as mentioned in rule 6(5) or (7).

Deceased independent candidate wins

64 (1) This rule applies if at an election mentioned in rule 63 either–
    (a) the deceased candidate is given a majority of votes in accordance with rules 55(5) or (6),
    (b) the deceased candidate is given more than half of all the first preference votes in accordance with rule 55(4)(a), or
    (c) the deceased candidate is given the greatest total number of votes following the second calculation in accordance with rule 56.

(2) Rule 57 (declaration of result) does not apply but the GLRO must–
    (a) declare that the majority or greatest total number of votes has been given to the deceased candidate,
    (b) declare that no person is returned, and
    (c) give public notice of the relevant figures supplied to election agents in accordance with rules 56(2) and 57(2) together with the number of rejected ballot papers under each head shown in the statement of rejected ballot papers.

(3) The provisions of these Rules as to the inspection, production, retention and destruction of ballot papers and other documents apply to any documents relating to a poll to which paragraph (1) applies as they would if the election had resulted in a declaration under rule 57.

(4) Rule 58 (return or forfeiture of candidate's deposit) does not apply in relation to the remaining candidates.

(5) The election must be commenced afresh within the period of 35 days (computed in accordance with rule 4) beginning with the day of the election to which paragraph (1) applies.

(6) The proceedings with reference to the recommenced election must be conducted in accordance with these Rules as modified by the following provisions of this rule and the provisions in the By-election timetable.

(7) No fresh nomination is necessary in the case of a person shown in the statement of persons nominated for the election to which paragraph (1) applies, and no other nomination may be made for the recommenced election.

(8) Instead of the information required by rule 5(1)(a) (date by which nomination papers must be received), the notice of election issued at the recommenced election must state that no fresh nomination may be made.

(9)   Rule 9 (deposit) does not apply.

Deceased party candidate

65 (1)   This rule applies if–
- (a)   at a contested election, proof is given to the GLRO's satisfaction before the result of the election is declared that one of the persons named or to be named as a candidate in the ballot paper has died, and
- (b)   that person is standing in the name of a registered party.

(2)   The GLRO must–
- (a)   countermand notice of the poll, or
- (b)   if polling has begun, direct that the poll be abandoned,

and the provisions of section 39(1) and (5) (local elections void etc in England and Wales) of the 1983 Act apply in respect of the unfilled vacancy.

(3)   For the purposes of this rule–
- (a)   a person stands in the name of a registered party if his nomination paper contains a description which is authorised as mentioned in rule 6(5) or (7),
- (b)   a registered party is a party which is registered under Part 2 of the 2000 Act.

Abandoned poll

66 (1)   This rule applies to–
- (a)   a poll which is abandoned in pursuance of rule 63(4)(b) as if it were a poll at a contested election, or
- (b)   a poll which is abandoned in pursuance of rule 65(2)(b)

(2)   The presiding officer at any polling station must take the like steps (so far as not already taken) for the delivery to the CRO of the ballot box and of ballot papers and other documents in his possession as he is required to do on the close of the poll.

(3)   The CRO must dispose of the ballot papers and other documents in his possession as he is required to do on the completion of the counting of the votes.

(4)   It is not necessary for a ballot paper account to be prepared or verified.

(5)   The CRO must take no step or further step for the counting of the ballot papers or of the votes.

(6)   The CRO must seal up all the ballot papers (whether the votes on them have been counted or not) and it will not be necessary to seal up counted and rejected ballot papers in separate packets.

(7)   The provisions of these Rules as to the inspection, production, retention and destruction of ballot papers and other documents relating to a poll at an election apply subject to the modifications in paragraphs (8) and (9).

(8)   Ballot papers on which the votes were neither counted nor rejected must be treated as counted ballot papers.

(9)   No order is to be made for–
- (a)   the production or inspection of any ballot papers, or
- (b)   for the opening of a sealed packet of completed corresponding number lists or certificates as to employment on duty on the day of the poll,

unless the order is made by a court with reference to a prosecution.

SCHEDULE 4
MANUAL COUNT RULES

Rule 4

Citation

1 This Schedule may be cited as the Manual Count Rules.

Interpretation

2 (1) In this Schedule–
"CMER" means the Constituency Members Election Rules in Schedule 1;
"LMER" means the London Members Election Rules in Schedule 2;
"MER" means the Mayoral Election Rules in Schedule 3.

3 If the votes at an Authority election are counted without the use of an electronic counting system, the CMER, the LMER and the MER will have effect as if the provisions listed in column (1) of Table 1 were modified as shown in column (2).

Table 1

(1) Rule(s)	(2) Modification
CMER rule 17 (ballot papers)	In paragraph (3)(a) omit ", so far as practicable for the purposes of electronic counting,".
LMER rule 18 (ballot papers)	In paragraph (4)(a) omit ", so far as practicable for the purposes of electronic counting,".
MER rule 17 (ballot papers)	In paragraph (3)(a) omit ", so far as practicable for the purposes of electronic counting,".
CMER rule 47 (attendance at verification and the counting of votes)	In paragraph (1), before "verification" insert "separation," and after "begin to" insert "separate,".
LMER rule 48 (attendance at verification and the local count)	In paragraph (2)(a) omit "and technical assistants".
MER rule 47 (attendance at verification and the local count)	After paragraph (4) insert–
	"(5) In particular, where the votes are counted by sorting the ballot papers according to the candidate for whom the vote is given and then counting the number of ballot papers for each candidate, the counting agents are entitled to satisfy themselves that the ballot papers are correctly sorted.".
CMER rule 49 (verification and the count)	For paragraph (1) substitute the following paragraphs–
	"(1) Where the election is at an ordinary election, the CRO must–
	(a) in the presence of the counting agents appointed for the purposes of the constituency members election, the London members election and the mayoral election, open each ballot box and record separately the number of ballot papers used in each

Authority election,

(b) in the presence of the election agents appointed for the purposes of those elections, verify each ballot paper account,

(c) count such of the postal ballot papers as have been duly returned and record separately the number counted at each Authority election,

(d) separate the ballot papers relating to the election from those relating to the other Authority elections.

(1A) Where the election is a not at an ordinary election, the CRO must–

(a) in the presence of the counting agents open each ballot box and count and record the number of ballot papers in it,

(b) in the presence of the election agents verify each ballot paper account, and

(c) count such of the postal ballot papers as have been duly returned and record the number counted.".

For paragraph (4) substitute–

"(4) After completing the proceedings under paragraph (1) or (1A), the CRO must mix together all of the ballot papers used in the election in the Assembly constituency and must count the votes given on them.".

In paragraph (5) omit the words "cause the electronic counting system to".

For paragraph (6) substitute–

"(6) The CRO must verify each ballot paper account by comparing it with the number of ballot papers recorded by him, the unused and spoilt ballot papers in his possession and the tendered votes list (opening and re-sealing the packets containing the unused and spoilt ballot papers and the tendered votes list) and must draw up a statement as to the result of the verification, which any election agent may copy.".

| LMER rule 50 (verification and the local count) | For paragraph (1) substitute–

"(1) The CRO must–
(a) in the presence of the counting agents appointed for the purposes of the constituency members election, the London members election and the mayoral election, open each ballot box and record separately the number |

of ballot papers used in each Authority election,

(b) in the presence of the election agents appointed for the purposes of those elections, verify each ballot paper account,

(c) count such of the postal ballot papers as have been duly returned and record separately the number counted at each Authority election,

(d) separate the ballot papers relating to the election from those relating to the other Authority elections.".

For paragraph (4) substitute–

"(4) After completing the proceedings under paragraph (1), the CRO must mix together all of the ballot papers used in the election in the Assembly constituency and must count the votes given on them.".

In paragraph (5) omit the words "cause the electronic counting system to".

For paragraph (6) substitute–

"(6) The CRO must verify each ballot paper account by comparing it with the number of ballot papers recorded by him, the unused and spoilt ballot papers in his possession and the tendered votes list (opening and re-sealing the packets containing the unused and spoilt ballot papers and the tendered votes list) and must draw up a statement as to the result of the verification, which any election agent may copy.".

MER rule 49 (verification and the local count)

For paragraph (1) substitute the following paragraphs–

"(1) Where the election is held at an ordinary election, the CRO must–

(a) in the presence of the counting agents appointed for the purposes of the constituency members election, the London members election and the mayoral election, open each ballot box and record separately the number of ballot papers used in each Authority election,

(b) in the presence of the election agents appointed for the purposes of those elections, verify each ballot paper account,

(c) count such of the postal ballot papers as have been duly returned and record separately the number counted at each Authority election,

(d) separate the ballot papers relating to the election from those relating to the other Authority elections.

(1A) Where the election is a not held at an ordinary election, the CRO must–

(a) in the presence of the counting agents open each ballot box and count and record the number of ballot papers in it,

(b) in the presence of the election agents verify each ballot paper account, and

(c) count such of the postal ballot papers as have been duly returned and record the number counted.".

For paragraph (4) substitute–

"(4) After completing the proceedings under paragraph (1) or (1A), the CRO must mix together all of the ballot papers used at that election in the Assembly constituency and–

(a) where the election is contested by more than two candidates, count the first preference votes given on them,

(b) where the election is contested by only two candidates, count the votes given on them.".

In paragraph (5) omit the words "cause the electronic counting system to".

For paragraph (6) substitute–

"(6) The CRO must verify each ballot paper account by comparing it with the number of ballot papers recorded by him, and the unused and spoilt ballot papers in his possession and the tendered votes list (opening and re-sealing the packets containing the unused and spoilt ballot papers and the tendered votes list) and must draw up a statement as to the result of the verification, which any election agent may copy.".

CMER rule 50 LMER rule 51 (rejected ballot papers)	For paragraph (3) substitute– "(3) The CRO must endorse the word "rejected" on any ballot paper which under this rule is not to be counted, and must add to the endorsement the words "rejection objected to" if any objection to his decision is made by a counting agent.". Omit paragraphs (4)-(10).
MER rule 50 (rejected ballot papers)	For paragraph (4) substitute–

	"(4) The CRO must endorse the word "rejected" on any ballot paper which under this rule is not to be counted, and must add to the endorsement the words "rejection objected to" if any objection to his decision is made by a counting agent.".
	Omit paragraphs (5) to (12).
	Omit paragraph (13)(e) and for paragraph (13)(d) substitute–
	"(d) unmarked or void for uncertainty as to the first preference vote.".
LMER rule 54 (procedure at conclusion of local count)	For paragraph (2) substitute–
	"(2) As soon as practicable after the statement is drawn up under paragraph (1), the CRO must inform the GLRO of its contents.".
MER rule 53 (procedure at conclusion of local count)	Omit paragraph (1)(c)(iii).
	For paragraph (2) substitute–
	"(2) As soon as practicable after the statement is drawn up under paragraph (1), the CRO must inform the GLRO of its contents.".
LMER rule 55 (attendance at allocation of seats)	In paragraph (2)(b) omit "or technical assistant".
MER rule 54 (attendance at the central calculation)	In paragraph (2)(b) omit "or technical assistant".
MER rule 55 (the first calculation and resolution of equality)	For paragraph (4)(b) substitute–
	"(b) if paragraph 4(1) of that Schedule applies (no candidate with overall majority of first preference votes), the GLRO must direct every CRO at the election who has counted manually to count the second preference votes given as mentioned in paragraph 4(5) of that Schedule.".

In Part 5, before rule 56 insert–

"56ZA The count of second preference votes

(1) As soon as the CRO has received such a direction as is mentioned in rule 55(4)(b) he must count the number of second preference votes for each of the candidates remaining in the contest given by voters who did not give their first preference vote to any of those candidates.

(2) A ballot paper which is not otherwise void and on which not more than one second preference vote is marked will be valid as respects that vote and

must be counted accordingly if, but only if, a valid first preference vote has also been marked.

(3) Rules 47, 49, 50, 53 and 55 will apply in relation to the count of second preference votes as they apply in relation to the count of first preference votes, and as if references to first preference votes were references to second preference votes.

(4) The CRO may not be required to re-examine any decision taken under rule 50.

(5) As soon as practicable after the second preference votes have been counted, the CRO must inform the GLRO of the number of second preference votes cast for each of the candidates remaining in the contest.".

MER rule 56 (the second calculation and resolution of equality)	For paragraph (1) substitute–
	(1) As soon as the GLRO has received the information required by rule 56ZA(5) from every CRO, he must comply with paragraph 4(5) and (6) of Schedule 2 to the 1999 Act.".
CMER rule 54 (declaration of result)	Omit paragraphs (2) and (3).
LMER rule 57 (declaration of result)	Omit paragraphs (3) and (4).
MER rule 57 (declaration of result)	Omit paragraphs (2)(e), (4) and (5).

SCHEDULE 5
THE CONSTITUENCY MEMBERS ELECTION RULES

Rule 5(3)

Part 5
Final Proceedings in Contested and Uncontested Elections

Part 6
Disposal of Documents

Part 7
Death of Candidate

Part 1
General Provisions

Citation

1   This Schedule may be cited as the Constituency Members Election Rules.

Interpretation

2 (1)   In the rules in this Schedule, unless the context indicates otherwise–
"Combination of Polls Regulations" means the Representation of the People (Combination of Polls) (England and Wales) Regulations 2004;
"counting observer" has the same meaning as in regulation 2 of the Referendum Regulations;
"counting officer" has the same meaning as in regulation 9 of the Referendum Regulations;
"election" means an election of a constituency member of the London Assembly;
"electoral area" where the Authority election is held together with a referendum, includes a voting area where the referendum is held;
"European Parliamentary election" has the same meaning as in section 27(1) of the Representation of the People Act 1985;
"local authority mayoral election" means an election conducted under the Local

Authorities (Mayoral Elections) (England and Wales) Regulations 2007;

"local counting area" has the same meaning as in regulation 2(1) of the European Parliamentary Elections Regulations 2004;

"petition organiser" has the same meaning as in regulation 3 of the Local Authorities (Referendums) (Petitions and Directions) (England) Regulations 2000;

"polling observer" has the same meaning as in regulation 2 of the Referendum Regulations;

"referendum" means a referendum conducted under the Referendum Regulations;

"Referendum Regulations" means the Local Authorities (Conduct of Referendums) (England) Regulations 2007;

"relevant election or referendum" means one or more of the following–
(a) a Parliamentary election,
(b) a European Parliamentary election,
(c) a local government election (including another Authority election where more than one is taken together),
(d) a local authority mayoral election or referendum in accordance with regulations made under sections 44 and 105, or 45 and 105, of the Local Government Act 2000;

"voting area" has the same meaning as in regulation 2 of the Referendum Regulations.

(2) In the case of a referendum, a reference to–
(a) a "candidate" shall be construed as a reference to a counting observer,
(b) a "election agent" shall be construed as a reference to a counting observer,
(c) a "polling agent" shall be construed as a reference to polling observer,
(d) a "returning officer" shall be construed as a reference to a counting officer.

(3) Reference to a rule by number alone is a reference to the rule so numbered in this Schedule.

Part 2
Provisions as to Time

Timetable

3   The proceedings at the election must be conducted in accordance with the following timetable:

Timetable

Proceedings	Time
Publication of notice of election	Not later than the thirtieth day before the day of election.
Delivery of nomination papers	Not later than 4 in the afternoon on the twenty-fourth day before the day of election.
Delivery of notices of withdrawals of candidature	Not later than 4 in the afternoon on the twenty-fourth day before the day of election
Publication of statement as to persons nominated	Not later than 4 in the afternoon on the twenty-second day before the day of election.
Notice of poll	Not later than the sixth day before the day of election.
Polling	Between the hours of 7 in the morning and 10 at night on the day of election.

Computation of time

4 (1)   In computing any period of time for the purposes of the Timetable–
  (a)   a Saturday or Sunday,
  (b)   Christmas Eve, Christmas Day, Good Friday or a bank holiday, or
  (c)   a day appointed for public thanksgiving or mourning,
  must be disregarded, and any such day must not be treated as a day for the purpose of any proceedings up to the completion of the poll nor may the CRO be obliged to proceed with the counting of the votes on such a day.

  (2)   In this rule, "bank holiday" means a day which is a bank holiday under the Banking and Financial Dealings Act 1971 in England and Wales.

Part 3
Stages Common to Contested and Uncontested Elections

Notice of election

5 (1)   The CRO must publish notice of the election stating–
  (a)   the place and times at which nomination papers are to be delivered, and
  (b)   the date of the poll in the event of a contest,
  and the notice must state that forms of nomination papers may be obtained at that place and those times.

  (2)   The notice of election must state the arrangements (if any) which apply for the payment of the deposit required by rule 8 by means of the electronic transfer of funds.

  (3)   The notice of election must state the date by which–
  (a)   applications to vote by post or by proxy, and
  (b)   other applications and notices about postal or proxy voting,
  must reach the registration officer for local government electors in order that they may be effective for the election.

Nomination of candidates

6 (1)   Each candidate must be nominated by a separate nomination paper, which must be–
  (a)   in the appropriate form, and
  (b)   delivered to the place fixed for the purpose by the CRO, which must be at the offices of a local authority within the Assembly constituency, before the last time for the delivery of nomination papers.

  (2)   The nomination paper must state the candidate's–
  (a)   full names,
  (b)   home address, in full, and
  (c)   if desired, description,
  and the surname must be placed first in the list of names.

  (3)   If a candidate commonly uses–
  (a)   a surname which is different from any other surname he has, or
  (b)   a forename which is different from any other forename he has,
  the nomination paper may state the commonly used surname or forename, or both surname and forename, in addition to the other name.

  (4)   The description (if any) can only be–
  (a)   one authorised as mentioned in paragraph (5) or (7), or
  (b)   the word "Independent".

  (5)   A nomination paper may not include a description of a candidate that is likely to lead electors to associate the candidate with a registered party unless–

(a) the party is a qualifying party in relation to the electoral area, and

(b) the description is authorised by a certificate–

    (i) issued by or on behalf of the registered nominating officer of the party, and

    (ii) received by the CRO before the last time for the delivery of nomination papers set out in the timetable in rule 3.

(6) In paragraph (5) an authorised description may be either–

    (a) the name of the party registered under section 28 of the Political Parties, Elections and Referendums Act 2000, or

    (b) a description of the party registered under section 28A of that Act.

(7) A nomination paper may not include a description of a candidate which is likely to lead electors to associate the candidate with two or more registered political parties unless the parties are each qualifying parties in relation to the electoral area and the description is a registered description authorised by a certificate–

    (a) issued by or on behalf of the registered nominating officer of each of the parties, and

    (b) received by the CRO before the last time for the delivery of nomination papers set out in the timetable in rule 3.

(8) For the purposes of paragraph (7), a description is a registered description if it is a description registered for use by the parties under section 28B of the 2000 Act.

(9) A person will be guilty of a corrupt practice if he fraudulently purports to be authorised to issue a certificate under paragraph (5) or (7) on behalf of a registered party's nominating officer.

(10) For the purposes of the application of these rules in relation to an election–

    (a) "registered party" means a party which was registered under Part 2 of the 2000 Act on the day ("the relevant day") which is two days before the last day for the delivery of nomination papers at that election,

    (b) a registered party is a qualifying party in relation to an electoral area if on the relevant day the party was registered in respect of England in the Great Britain register maintained under that Part of that Act.

(11) For the purposes of paragraph (10)(a), any day falling within rule 4(1) must be disregarded.

Consent to nomination

7 A person will not be validly nominated unless his consent to nomination–

    (a) is given in writing in the appropriate form, or a form to like effect, on or within one month before the last day for the delivery of nomination papers,

    (b) is attested by one witness whose name and address must be given, and

    (c) is delivered at the place and within the time for delivery of nomination papers.

(2) A candidate's consent given under this rule must–

    (a) state the day, month and year of his birth, and

    (b) contain a statement that to the best of the candidate's knowledge and belief he is not disqualified from being elected by reason of–

        (i) any disqualification set out in section 21 (disqualification from being the Mayor or an Assembly member) of the 1999 Act,

        (ii) a decision made under section 78A of the Local Government Act 2000 (decisions of First-tier tribunal), or

        (iii) an order made under section 34(4) of the Localism Act 2011(offences).

Deposits

8 (1) A person will not be validly nominated unless the sum of £1,000 is deposited by him or

on his behalf with the CRO at the place and within the time for delivery of nomination papers.

(2) The deposit may be made either–

   (a) by the deposit of any legal tender, or

   (b) by means of a banker's draft, or

   (c) with the CRO's consent, in any other manner including by means of a debit or credit card or the electronic transfer of funds,

   but the CRO may refuse to accept a deposit sought to be made by means of a banker's draft if he does not know that the drawer carries on business as a banker in the United Kingdom.

(3) Where the deposit is made on behalf of the candidate, the person making the deposit must at the time he makes it give his name and address to the CRO, unless they have previously been given to him under section 67 (appointment of election agent) of the 1983 Act.

Decisions as to validity of nomination papers

9 (1) Where a nomination paper and the candidate's consent to it are delivered, and the deposit is made, in accordance with this Part of these Rules, the candidate must be deemed to stand nominated unless and until–

   (a) the CRO decides that the nomination paper is invalid, or

   (b) proof is given to the CRO's satisfaction of the candidate's death, or

   (c) the candidate withdraws.

(2) The CRO is entitled to hold a nomination paper invalid only on the grounds–

   (a) that the particulars of the candidate on the nomination paper are not as required by law; or

   (b) that the paper breaks rule 6(5) or (7).

(3) Subject to paragraph (4), the CRO must, as soon as practicable after each nomination paper has been delivered, examine it and decide whether the candidate has been validly nominated.

(4) If in the CRO's opinion a nomination paper breaks rule 6(5) or (7), he must give a decision to that effect–

   (a) as soon as practicable after the delivery of the nomination paper, and

   (b) in any event, before the end of the period of 24 hours starting with the end of the period for the delivery of nomination papers set out in the timetable in rule 3.

(5) Where the CRO decides that a nomination paper is invalid, he must endorse and sign on the paper the fact and the reasons for his decision.

(6) The CRO must, as soon as practicable after making a decision under paragraph (3) or (4) that a nomination paper is valid or invalid, send notice of that decision to the candidate at his home address as given in his nomination paper.

(7) The CRO's decision that a nomination paper is valid is final and must not be questioned in any proceeding whatsoever.

(8) Subject to paragraph (7), nothing in this rule prevents the validity of a nomination being questioned on an election petition.

Publication of statement of persons nominated

10(1) The CRO must prepare and (subject to paragraph (11)) publish a statement showing the persons who have been and stand nominated and any other persons who have been nominated together with the reason why they no longer stand nominated.

(2) The statement must show the names, addresses and descriptions of the persons nominated as given in their nomination papers.

(3) If a person's nomination paper gives a commonly used surname or forename, or both surname and forename, in addition to another name, the statement must show the person's commonly used surname or forename, or both surname and forename (as the case may be) instead of any other name.

(4) Paragraph (3) does not apply if the CRO thinks–
    (a) that the use of the person's commonly used name may be likely to mislead or confuse electors, or
    (b) that the commonly used name is obscene or offensive.

(5) If paragraph (4) applies, the CRO must give notice in writing to the candidate of his reasons for refusing to allow the use of a commonly used name.

(6) The statement must show the persons standing nominated arranged alphabetically in the order of their surnames, and if there are two or more of them with the same surname, of their other names.

(7) In the case of a person nominated by more than one nomination paper, the CRO must take the particulars required by the foregoing provisions of this rule from such one of the papers as the candidate (or the CRO in default of the candidate) may select.

(8) Paragraphs (9) to (11) apply at an ordinary election.

(9) As soon as possible after all decisions under rule 9 which are required to be made have been made, the CRO must arrange for a copy of the statement that the CRO has prepared and proposes to publish to be delivered to the GLRO.

(10) If, after having delivered the statement mentioned in paragraph (9) to the GLRO, the CRO receives notification from the GLRO under rule 13(4) that a candidate is deemed to have withdrawn his or her candidature, the CRO must amend that statement accordingly.

(11) The CRO may not publish the statement under paragraph (1) until–
    (a) the CRO has made any amendments required under paragraph (10), or
    (b) where no notification under rule 13(4) is received from the GLRO, the time by which the GLRO must give such notification has passed.

Correction of minor errors

11(1) A CRO may, if he thinks fit, at any time before the publication under rule 10 of the statement of persons nominated, correct minor errors in a nomination paper.

(2) Errors which may be corrected include–
    (a) errors as to a person's electoral number,
    (b) obvious errors of spelling in relation to the details of a candidate.

(3) Anything done by a CRO in pursuance of this rule may not be questioned in any proceedings other than proceedings on an election petition.

(4) A CRO must have regard to any guidance issued by the Electoral Commission for the purposes of this rule.

Inspection of nomination papers and consent to nomination

12(1) During ordinary office hours, in the period starting 24 hours after the latest time for the delivery of nomination papers and before the date of the poll, any person may inspect and take copies of, or extracts from, nomination papers and consents to nomination.

(2) Inspection under paragraph (1) may not take place on a day that is specified in rule

4(1).

Nomination in more than one Assembly constituency

13(1)   This rule applies at an ordinary election.

(2)   A candidate who is validly nominated in more than one Assembly constituency must withdraw his or her candidature, in accordance with rule 14, in all but one of those constituencies.

(3)   Where a candidate does not withdraw his or her candidature as mentioned in paragraph (2), he or she is deemed, after the last time for delivery of notices of withdrawals, to have withdrawn his or her candidature from all the Assembly constituencies in which he or she is, but for this rule, validly nominated.

(4)   Where, having reviewed the proposed statements of persons nominated delivered under rule 10(9), it appears to the GLRO that a candidate ("C") appears (but for this rule) to have been validly nominated in more than one Assembly constituency ("a relevant constituency"), the GLRO must at least one hour before the last time for publication of the statement as to persons nominated as set out in the timetable in rule 3, inform the CRO for each relevant constituency that C's candidature is deemed to have been withdrawn in that constituency.

(5)   A CRO must, as soon as practicable, after receiving the notification mentioned in paragraph (4), notify C that C's candidature is deemed to have been withdrawn in that constituency.

Withdrawal of candidates

14(1)   A candidate may withdraw his candidature by notice of withdrawal–
(a)   signed by him and attested by one witness, whose name and address must be given, and
(b)   delivered to the CRO at the place for delivery of nomination papers,
by the end of the period for the delivery of notices of withdrawals of candidature in the timetable in rule 3.

(2)   Where a candidate is outside the United Kingdom, a notice of withdrawal signed by his election agent and accompanied by a written declaration also so signed of the candidate's absence from the United Kingdom will be of the same effect as a notice of withdrawal signed by the candidate; but where the candidate stands nominated by more than one nomination paper a notice of withdrawal under this paragraph will be effective if, and only if, it is accompanied, in addition to that declaration, by a written statement signed by the candidate that the person giving the notice is authorised to do so on the candidate's behalf during his absence from the United Kingdom.

Method of election

15(1)   If, after any withdrawals in accordance with these Rules, the number of persons remaining validly nominated for the Assembly constituency exceeds one, a poll must be taken in accordance with Part 4 of these Rules.

(2)   If, after any withdrawals in accordance with these Rules, only one person remains validly nominated for the Assembly constituency, that person must be declared to be elected in accordance with Part 5.

Part 4
Contested Elections

Poll to be taken by ballot

16   The votes at the poll must be given by ballot, the result must be ascertained by counting the votes given to each candidate, and the candidate to whom more votes have been given than to the other candidates must be declared to have been elected.

The ballot papers

17(1)   The ballot of every voter must consist of a ballot paper which must be in the appropriate form.

(2)   Each person remaining validly nominated for the election, after any withdrawals, and no other, is entitled to have their name inserted in the ballot paper.

(3)   Every ballot paper—

    (a)   must, so far as practicable for the purposes of electronic counting, be printed in accordance with the directions set out in the Forms Schedule,

    (b)   must contain the names and other particulars of the candidates as shown in the statement of persons nominated,

    (c)   must have a number and other unique identifying mark printed on the back, and

    (d)   may, in the case of ballot papers for use at polling stations, be marked with the words "do not fold".

(4)   If a candidate who is the subject of a party's authorisation under rule 6(5) so requests, the ballot paper must contain, against the candidate's particulars, the party's registered emblem (or, as the case may be, one of the party's registered emblems).

(4A)   If a candidate who is the subject of an authorisation by two or more parties under rule 6(7) so requests, the ballot paper must contain, against the candidate's particulars, the registered emblem (or, as the case may be, one of the registered emblems) of one of those parties.

(5)   The candidate's request under paragraph (4) or paragraph (4A) must—

    (a)   be made in writing to the CRO, and

    (b)   be received by him within the period for delivery of nomination papers set out in the timetable in rule 3.

(6)   The order of the names in the ballot paper must be the same as in the statement of persons nominated.

(7)   At an ordinary election, the GLRO must supply the ballot papers for use at the election to the CRO by such date as may be agreed between them.

(8)   The ballot papers supplied under paragraph (7) must be of a different colour from the ballot papers used at any other relevant election or referendum.

The corresponding number list

18(1)   The CRO must prepare a list containing the numbers and other unique identifying marks of all of the ballot papers to be issued by him in pursuance of rule 23(1) or provided by him in pursuance of rule 28(1).

(2)   The list must be in the appropriate form or a form to like effect.

(3)   At an ordinary election, the same list may be used for each Authority election with which the election is combined.

The official mark

19(1)   Every ballot paper must contain an appropriate security marking (the official mark).

(2)   The official mark must be kept secret, and an interval of not less than five years must intervene between the use of the same official mark at any Authority election.

(3)   The CRO, or at an ordinary election the GLRO, may use a different official mark for different purposes at the same election.

Prohibition of disclosure of vote

20   No person who has voted at the election may, in any legal proceeding to question the election, be required to state for whom he has voted.

Use of schools and public rooms

21(1)   The CRO may use, free of charge, for the purpose of taking the poll or counting the votes–
   (a)   a room in a school maintained or assisted by a local authority (as defined in the Education Act 1996) or a school in respect of which grants are made out of moneys provided by Parliament to the person or body of persons responsible for the management of the school,
   (b)   a room the expense of maintaining which is met by any local authority.

(2)   The CRO must make good any damage done to, and defray any expense incurred by the persons having control over, any such room as mentioned in paragraph (1) by reason of its being used for the purpose of taking the poll or counting the votes.

Notice of poll

22(1)   The CRO must, in accordance with the timetable in rule 3, publish notice of the poll stating–
   (a)   the day and hours fixed for the poll, and
   (b)   the particulars of each candidate remaining validly nominated (the names and other particulars of the candidates, and the order of the candidates' names being the same as in the statement of persons nominated).

(2)   The CRO must, not later than the time of the publication of the notice of the poll, also give public notice of–
   (a)   the situation of each polling station, and
   (b)   the description of voters entitled to vote there,
   and he must as soon as practicable after giving such a notice give a copy of it to each of the election agents.

(3)   The notice published under paragraph (2) shall–
   (a)   state that the poll at the election is to be taken together with the poll at a relevant election or referendum as the case may be,
   (b)   specify the parliamentary constituency, European Parliamentary local counting area, relevant London borough, or voting area; and in the case of an election to fill a casual vacancy, the electoral area for which the relevant election or referendum is held, and
   (c)   where the polls are to be taken together in part of the Borough only, specify that part.

(4)   At an ordinary election, the notice of poll must include the heading "GREATER LONDON AUTHORITY ELECTION".

Postal ballot papers

23(1) The CRO must, in accordance with regulations made under the 1983 Act, issue to those entitled to vote by post a ballot paper and a postal voting statement, together with such envelopes for their return as may be prescribed in such regulations.

(2) The postal voting statement must be in the appropriate form or a form to like effect.

(3) The postal voting statement must include provision for the form to be signed and for stating the date of birth of the elector or proxy (as the case may be).

(4) The CRO must also issue to those entitled to vote by post such information as he thinks appropriate about how to obtain–
    (a) translations into languages other than English of any directions to or guidance for voters sent with the ballot paper,
    (b) a translation into Braille of such directions or guidance,
    (c) graphical representations of such directions or guidance,
    (d) the directions or guidance in any other form (including any audible form).

(5) In the case of a ballot paper issued to a person at an address in the United Kingdom, the CRO must ensure that the return of the ballot paper and postal voting statement is free of charge to the voter.

(6) Where the proceedings on the issue and receipt of postal ballot papers at the election are taken together with a relevant election or referendum the appropriate form of postal voting statement under paragraph (2) may be the joint postal voting statement which must be in the appropriate form or form to like effect.

Provision of polling stations

24(1) The CRO must provide a sufficient number of polling stations and, subject to the following provisions of this rule, must allot the electors to the polling stations in such manner as he thinks most convenient.

(2) One or more polling stations may be provided in the same room.

(3) The polling station allotted to electors from any parliamentary polling district wholly or partly within the Assembly constituency must, in the absence of special circumstances, be in the parliamentary polling place for that district, unless that place is outside the Assembly constituency.

(4) The CRO must provide each polling station with such number of compartments as may be necessary in which the voters can mark their votes screened from observation.

Appointment of presiding officers and clerks

25(1) The CRO must appoint and pay a presiding officer to attend at each polling station and such clerks and technical assistants as may be necessary for the purposes of the election, but he must not appoint any person who has been employed by or on behalf of a candidate in or about the election.

(2) The CRO may, if he thinks fit, preside at a polling station and the provisions of this Part relating to a presiding officer apply to a CRO so presiding with the necessary modifications as to things to be done by the CRO to the presiding officer or by the presiding officer to the CRO.

(3) A presiding officer may do, by the clerks appointed to assist him, any act (including the asking of questions) which he is required or authorised by this Part to do at a polling station except order the arrest, exclusion or removal of any person from the polling station.

Issue of official poll cards

26(1) The CRO must as soon as practicable after the publication of the notice of election, send to electors and their proxies an official poll card.

(2) An elector's official poll card must be sent or delivered to his qualifying address, and a proxy's to his address as shown in the list of proxies.

(3) The official poll card must be in the appropriate form, or a form to like effect, and must set out–
  (a) the name of the Assembly constituency for which a constituency member is to be elected,
  (b) the elector's name, qualifying address and number on the register,
  (c) the date and hours of the poll and the situation of the elector's polling station, and
  (d) such other information as the CRO thinks appropriate,
  and different information may be provided in pursuance of sub-paragraph (d) to different electors or descriptions of elector.

(4) In the case of an elector with an anonymous entry, instead of containing the matter mentioned in paragraph (3)(b), the polling card must contain such matter as is specified in the appropriate form.

(5) At an ordinary election, the CRO must issue a combined poll card in the appropriate form.

(6) If the CRO and the returning officer for each relevant election or referendum agree, the poll card issued under this rule may be combined with the official poll card for the relevant election or referendum, with necessary adaptations.

(7) In this rule "elector" means–
  (a) an elector with an entry on the register to be used at the election on the last day for the publication of the notice of the election, and
  (b) includes a person then shown in the register as below voting age if (but only if) it appears from the register that he will be of voting age on the day fixed for the poll.

Information for voters

27(1) At an ordinary election, the GLRO may, in addition to a statement by him in an election booklet, include in the booklet information for voters that has been agreed by him with the Electoral Commission.

(2) The information for voters given in the election booklet may include information about–
  (a) the office of the Mayor and the London Assembly,
  (b) the system of voting at each Authority election,
  (c) how to vote in a manner that will ensure a vote is regarded as validly cast, and subject to paragraph (3), may include any other information given in exercise of the GLRO's duty under section 69 (encouraging electoral participation) of the 2006 Act.

(3) The information for voters must not contain–
  (a) any advertising material,
  (b) any material referring to a candidate or a registered party, other than by reproduction of a ballot paper which refers equally to all candidates and parties at the ordinary election,
  (c) any material referring to the holder, at any time, of the office of Mayor or Assembly member, other than under paragraph (b) as a candidate at the ordinary election.

(4) Information published in an election booklet under this rule must be printed on not more than two sides of A5 paper.

Equipment of polling stations

28(1) The CRO must provide each presiding officer with–
  (a) such ballot papers as may be necessary, and
  (b) such ballot boxes as may be necessary having taken account of any direction made by the GLRO in accordance with paragraph (9).

(2) Every ballot box must be so constructed that the ballot papers can be put in it, but cannot be withdrawn from it, without the box being unlocked or, where the box has no lock, the seal being broken.

(3) The CRO must provide each polling station with–
  (a) materials to enable voters to mark the ballot papers,
  (b) copies of the register of electors for the Assembly constituency or such part of it as contains the entries relating to the electors allotted to the station,
  (c) the parts of any special lists prepared for the election corresponding to the register of electors for the Assembly constituency or the part of it provided under sub-paragraph (b),
  (d) a list consisting of that part of the list prepared under rule 18 which contains the numbers (but not the other unique identifying marks) corresponding to those on the ballot papers provided to the presiding officer of the polling station.

(4) The reference in paragraph (3)(b) to the copies of the register of electors includes a reference to copies of any notices issued under section 13B(3B) or (3D) of the 1983 Act in respect of alterations to the register.

(5) The CRO must also provide each polling station with a device for enabling voters who are blind or partially sighted to vote without any need for assistance from the presiding officer or any companion within the meaning of rule 40.

(6) The device referred to in paragraph (5) above must–
  (a) allow a ballot paper to be inserted into and removed from or attached to and detached from the device, easily and without damage to the paper,
  (b) keep the ballot paper firmly in place during use,
  (c) provide suitable means for the voter to–
    (i) identify the spaces on the ballot paper on which he may mark his vote,
    (ii) identify the candidate to whom each such space refers, and
    (iii) mark his vote on the space he has chosen.

(7) The enlarged sample copies of the ballot paper that the CRO is required to provide, or cause to be displayed at every polling station (in accordance with section 199B(5) and (7) of the 1983 Act) must be printed on paper of the same colour as the ballot paper at the election.

(8) The CRO must also provide each polling station with notices for the guidance of voters, which must be exhibited–
  (a) outside the polling station,
  (b) inside the polling station–
    (i) in the communal areas, and
    (ii) in every voting compartment.

(9) If the GLRO thinks fit he may, not later than the date of the notice of election, direct the CRO that joint ballot boxes must be used for the ballot papers at the election and any or all relevant elections or referendums with which the election is taken.

(10) Where separate ballot boxes are to be used for the election and every relevant election

or referendum, each ballot box shall be clearly marked with–

    (a)   the election or referendum to which it relates, as shown on the ballot papers for that election or referendum, and

    (b)   the words "Place the *specify colour of ballot papers in question* ballot paper here".

(11)   Where the CRO does not discharge the functions specified in regulation 5 of the Combination of Polls Regulations, references in this rule to the CRO should be read as references to the returning officer who does discharge those functions.

Notices for the guidance of voters

29(1)   The CRO must prepare the notices to be exhibited under rule 28(8).

(2)   The CRO may prepare versions of the notices in such other form as he thinks appropriate, in accordance with section 199B (translations etc of certain documents) of the 1983 Act.

(3)   Notices for the guidance of voters exhibited under rule 28(8) or paragraph (2) must be in the appropriate form, but may include such alternative information relating to Authority elections as–

    (a)   meets with the requirements of the Notices Schedule, and

    (b)   the CRO may decide.

(4)   Notices provided under paragraph (2) may, if the CRO agrees, be exhibited at any polling station–

    (a)   outside the polling station,

    (b)   inside the polling station–

        (i)   in the communal areas,

        (ii)   in every voting compartment.

(5)   At an ordinary election, the GLRO must prepare the notices and versions of notices to be exhibited under rule 28(8) and supply them to the CRO, and for paragraph (3)(b) of this rule there is substituted–

    "(b) the GLRO may decide."

(6)   Where the CRO does not discharge the functions specified in regulation 5 of the Combination of Polls Regulations, then references to the CRO in this rule must be read as references to the returning officer who does discharge those functions.

Appointment of polling and counting agents

30(1)   Before the commencement of the poll, each candidate may appoint–

    (a)   polling agents to attend at polling stations for the purpose of detecting personation, and

    (b)   counting agents to attend at the counting of votes.

(2)   The same person may be appointed as a polling agent or counting agent by more than one candidate.

(3)   For the count, one (but no more than one) counting agent of each candidate may be authorised by the terms of his appointment to require a re-count at that count.

(4)   Not more than four polling agents, or such greater number as the CRO may by notice allow, may be permitted to attend at any particular polling station.

(5)   If the number of such agents appointed to attend at a particular polling station exceeds that number, the CRO must determine by lot which agents are permitted to attend, and only the agents on whom the lot falls will be deemed to have been duly appointed.

(6) The CRO may limit the number of counting agents, but in doing so must ensure that–
   (a) the number is the same in the case of each candidate, and
   (b) the number allowed to a candidate must not (except in special circumstances) be less than the number obtained by dividing the number of clerks employed on the counting by the number of candidates.

(7) For the purposes of the calculations required by paragraph (6), a counting agent who has been appointed by more than one candidate is a separate agent for each of the candidates by whom he has been appointed.

(8) Notice in writing of the appointment of polling and counting agents, stating the names and addresses of the persons appointed, must be given by the candidate to the CRO and must be so given not later than the fifth day (computed in accordance with rule 4) before the day of the poll.

(9) If an agent dies, or becomes incapable of acting, the candidate may appoint another agent in his place, and must forthwith give to the CRO notice in writing of the name and address of the agent appointed.

(10) Any appointment authorised by this rule may be made and the notice of appointment given to the CRO by the candidate's election agent, instead of by the candidate.

(11) In the following provisions of this Part references to polling agents and counting agents must be taken as references to agents–
   (a) whose appointments have been duly made and notified, and
   (b) where the number of agents is restricted, who are within the permitted numbers.

(12) Any notice required to be given to a counting agent by the CRO may be delivered at, or sent by post to, the address stated in the notice of appointment.

(13) A candidate may himself do any act or thing which any polling or counting agent of his, if appointed, would have been authorised to do, or may assist his agent in doing any such act or thing.

(14) A candidate's election agent may do or assist in doing anything which a polling or counting agent of his is authorised to do; and anything required or authorised by these Rules to be done in the presence of the polling or counting agent may be done in the presence of a candidate's election agent instead of his polling agent or counting agent.

(15) Where by these Rules any act or thing is required or authorised to be done in the presence of the polling or counting agents, the non-attendance of any agent or agents at the time and place appointed for the purpose will not, if the act or thing is otherwise duly done, invalidate the act or thing done.

(16) Where the CRO does not discharge the functions specified in regulation 5 of the Combination of Polls Regulations, then notices of the appointment of polling agents and counting agents which are required by this rule to be given to the CRO shall be given to the returning officer who discharges those functions.

Notification of requirement of secrecy

31(1) The CRO must make such arrangements as he thinks fit to ensure that–
   (a) every person attending a polling station (otherwise than for the purpose of voting or assisting a voter with disabilities to vote or as a constable on duty there) has been given a copy of the provisions of subsections (1), (3) and (6) of section 66 (requirement of secrecy) of the 1983 Act, and
   (b) every person attending at the counting of the votes (other than any constable on duty at the counting) has been given a copy of the provisions of subsections (2) and (6) of that section.

(2) In paragraph (1) a reference to a constable includes a person designated as a community support officer under section 38 of the 2002 Act (police powers for employees).

Return of postal ballot papers

32(1) Where–
  (a) a postal vote has been returned in respect of a person who is entered on the postal voters list, or
  (b) a proxy postal vote has been returned in respect of a proxy who is entered on the proxy postal voters list,
  the CRO must mark the list in the manner prescribed by regulations made under the 1983 Act.

(2) Rule 49(5) does not apply for the purpose of determining whether, for the purposes of this rule, a postal vote or a proxy postal vote is returned.

Admission to polling station

33(1) The presiding officer must exclude all persons from the polling station except–
  (a) voters,
  (b) persons under the age of 18 who accompany voters to the polling station,
  (c) the candidates and their election agents,
  (d) the polling agents appointed to attend at the polling station,
  (e) the clerks appointed to attend at the polling station,
  (f) persons who are entitled to attend by virtue of any of sections 6A to 6D of the 2000 Act,
  (g) the constables on duty,
  (h) the companions of voters with disabilities, and
  (i) persons entitled to be admitted to the polling station at a relevant election or referendum.

(2) The presiding officer must regulate the total number of voters and persons under the age of 18 who accompany them to be admitted to the polling station at the same time.

(3) Not more than one polling agent may be admitted at the same time to a polling station on behalf of the same candidate.

(4) A constable or person employed by the CRO must not be admitted to vote in person elsewhere than at his own polling station allotted to him under these Rules, except on production and surrender of a certificate as to his employment which must be in the appropriate form and signed by an officer of the police of or above the rank of inspector or by the CRO, as the case may be.

(5) Any certificate surrendered under this rule must forthwith be cancelled.

(6) In this rule a reference to a constable includes a person designated as a community support officer under section 38 of the 2002 Act.

Keeping of order in station

34(1) It is the presiding officer's duty to keep order at his polling station.

(2) If a person misconducts himself in a polling station, or fails to obey the presiding officer's lawful orders, he may immediately, by the presiding officer's order, be removed from the polling station–
  (a) by a constable in or near that station, or
  (b) by any other person authorised in writing by the CRO to remove him,

and the person so removed must not, without the presiding officer's permission, again enter the polling station during the day.

(3) Any person so removed may, if charged with the commission in the polling station of an offence, be dealt with as a person taken into custody by a constable for an offence without a warrant.

(4) The powers conferred by this rule must not be exercised so as to prevent a voter who is otherwise entitled to vote at a polling station from having an opportunity of voting at that station.

Sealing of ballot boxes

35 Immediately before the commencement of the poll, the presiding officer must–

    (a) show each ballot box, empty, to such persons, if any, as are present in the polling station, so that they may see that the boxes are empty,

    (b) lock up such of the boxes as have locks,

    (c) place his seal–

        (i) on each lock, and

        (ii) on each ballot box which has no lock,

in such a manner as to prevent its being opened without breaking the seal,

    (d) place each box in his view for the receipt of ballot papers, and

    (e) keep each box locked and sealed or, as the case may be, sealed.

Questions to be put to voters

36(1) At the time of the application (but not afterwards), the questions specified in the second column of the following table–

    (a) may be put by the presiding officer to a person who is mentioned in the first column, and

    (b) must be put if the letter "R" appears after the question and the candidate or his election or polling agent requires the question to be put.

Q No	Person applying for ballot paper	Question
1	A person applying as an elector	(a)–Are you the person registered in the register of local government electors for this election as follows (*read the whole entry from the register*)? R (b)–Have you already voted, here or elsewhere at this election for a constituency member otherwise than as proxy for some other person? R
2	A person applying as proxy	(a)–Are you the person whose name appears as AB in the list of proxies for this election as entitled to vote as proxy on behalf of CD? R (b)–Have you already voted here or elsewhere at this election for a constituency member as proxy on behalf of CD? R (c)–Are you the spouse, civil partner, parent, grandparent, brother, sister, child or grandchild of CD? R
3	A person applying as proxy for an elector with an anonymous entry (instead of the questions at entry 2)	(a)–Are you the person entitled to vote as proxy on behalf of the elector whose number on the register of electors is

		(*read out the number*)? R
		(b)–Have you already voted here or elsewhere as proxy on behalf of the elector whose number on the register of electors is (*read out the number*)? R
		(c)–Are you the spouse, civil partner, parent, grandparent, brother, sister, child or grandchild of the person whose number on the register of electors is (*read out the number*)? R
4	A person applying as proxy if the question at entry 2(c) or 3(c) is not answered in the affirmative	Have you already voted here or elsewhere at this election for a constituency member, on behalf of two persons of whom you are not the spouse, civil partner, parent, grandparent, brother, sister, child or grandchild? R
5	A person applying as an elector in relation to whom there is an entry in the postal voters list	(a)–Did you apply to vote by post? (b)–Why have you not voted by post?
6	A person applying as proxy who is named in the proxy postal voters list	(a)–Did you apply to vote by post as proxy? (b)–Why have you not voted by post as proxy?

(2) In the case of an elector in respect of whom a notice has been issued under section 13B(3B) or (3D) of the 1983 Act, the references in the questions at entries 1(a) and 3(a), (b) and (c) to reading from the register must be taken as references to reading from the notice issued under those subsections.

(3) A ballot paper must not be delivered to any person required to answer any of the above questions unless he has answered each question satisfactorily.

(4) Except as authorised by this rule, no inquiry may be permitted as to the right of any person to vote.

Challenge of voter

37 A person must not be prevented from voting because–
  (a) a candidate or his election or polling agent declares that he has reasonable cause to believe that the person has committed an offence of personation, or
  (b) the person is arrested on the grounds that he is suspected of committing or of being about to commit such an offence.

Voting procedure

38 (1) A ballot paper must be delivered to a voter who applies for one, and immediately before delivery–
  (a) the number and (unless paragraph (2) applies) name of the elector as stated in the copy of the register of electors must be called out,
  (b) the number of the elector must be marked on the list mentioned in rule 28(3)(d) beside the number of the ballot paper to be issued to him,
  (c) a mark must be placed in the register of electors against the number of the

elector to note that a ballot paper has been applied for but without showing the particular ballot paper which may be delivered,

    (d) in the case of a person applying for a ballot paper as proxy, a mark must also be placed against his name in the list of proxies.

(2) In the case of an elector who has an anonymous entry, he must show the presiding officer his official poll card and only his number may be called out in pursuance of paragraph (1)(a).

(3) In the case of an elector who is added to the register in pursuance of a notice issued under section 13B(3B) or (3D) of the 1983 Act, paragraph (1) is modified as follows–

    (a) in sub-paragraph (a), for "copy of the register of electors" substitute "copy of the notice issued under section 13B(3B) or (3D) of the 1983 Act",

    (b) in sub-paragraph (c), for "in the register of electors" substitute "on the copy of the notice issued under section 13B(3B) or (3D) of the 1983 Act".

(4) The voter, on receiving the ballot paper, must forthwith proceed into one of the compartments in the polling station and there secretly mark his paper, and must then show to the presiding officer the back of the paper, so as to disclose the number and other unique identifying mark, and put the ballot paper into the ballot box in the presiding officer's presence, but so as to conceal his vote.

(5) The voter must vote without undue delay, and must leave the polling station as soon as he has put his ballot paper into the ballot box.

(6) A voter who has had a ballot paper delivered to him under paragraph (1), but has decided not to mark it, may return it to the presiding officer and where the voter does so, the presiding officer must–

    (a) immediately cancel the ballot paper, and for the purposes of these rules treat it as a spoilt ballot paper,

    (b) place a mark beside the number of that ballot paper on the corresponding number list to show that the ballot paper has been cancelled.

(7) The same copy of–

    (a) the list of proxies,

    (b) the register of electors,

    (c) any notice issued under section 13B(3B) or (3D) of the 1983 Act (marked in the case of an elector who is added to the register in pursuance of such a notice),

may be used for the election and each relevant election and referendum and one mark may be placed in the list, register or notice (as the case may be) to denote that a ballot paper has been delivered in respect of each election and referendum; except that, where a ballot paper has not been issued in respect of any election or referendum, a different mark must be placed in the list, register or notice so as to identify the election or referendum in respect of which a ballot paper was issued.

(8) At an ordinary election, the same copy of the list mentioned in rule 28(3)(d), may be used for each Authority election and one mark may be placed in the list, to denote that a ballot paper has been delivered in respect of each Authority election; except that, where a ballot paper has not been issued in respect of any Authority election, a different mark must be placed in the list, so as to identify the elections in respect of which a ballot paper was issued.

(9) A voter who at the close of the poll is in the polling station, or in a queue outside the polling station, for the purpose of voting must (despite the close of the poll) be entitled to apply for a ballot paper under paragraph (1); and these rules apply in relation to such a voter accordingly.

Votes marked by presiding officer

39(1) The presiding officer, on the application of a voter–
   (a) who is incapacitated by blindness or other disability from voting in the manner directed by these Rules, or
   (b) who declares orally that he is unable to read,
   must, in the presence of the polling agents, cause the voter's vote to be marked on a ballot paper in the manner directed by the voter, and the ballot paper to be placed in the ballot box.

   (2) The name and number on the register of electors of every voter whose vote is marked in pursuance of this rule, and the reason why it is so marked, must be entered on a list (in these Rules called "the list of votes marked by the presiding officer").
   In the case of a person voting as proxy for an elector, the number to be entered together with the voter's name must be the elector's number.

   (3) In the case of a person in respect of whom a notice has been issued under section 13B(3B) or (3D) of the 1983 Act, paragraph (2) applies as if for "on the register of electors of every voter" there were substituted "relating to every voter in respect of whom a notice has been issued under section 13B(3B) or (3D) of the 1983 Act".

   (4) The same list may be used for each relevant election or referendum, and where it is so used, an entry in that list must be taken to mean that the ballot papers were so marked in respect of each election or referendum, unless the list identifies the election or referendum at which the ballot paper was so marked.

Voting by persons with disabilities

40 (1) If a voter makes an application to the presiding officer to be allowed, on the ground of–
   (a) blindness or other disability, or
   (b) inability to read,
   to vote with the assistance of another person by whom he is accompanied (in these Rules referred to as "the companion"), the presiding officer must require the voter to declare, orally or in writing, whether he is so incapacitated by his blindness or other disability, or by his inability to read, as to be unable to vote without assistance.

   (2) If the presiding officer–
   (a) is satisfied that the voter is so incapacitated, and
   (b) is also satisfied by a written declaration made by the companion (in these Rules referred to as "the declaration made by the companion of a voter with disabilities") that the companion–
       (i) is a qualified person within the meaning of these Rules, and
       (ii) has not previously assisted more than one voter with disabilities to vote at the election,
   the presiding officer must grant the application, and then anything which is by these Rules required to be done to, or by that voter in connection with the giving of his vote may be done to, or with the assistance of, the companion.

   (3) For the purpose of these Rules, a person is a voter with disabilities if he has made such a declaration as is mentioned in paragraph (1) above, and a person may be qualified to assist a voter with disabilities to vote if that person–
   (a) is a person who is entitled to vote as an elector at the election, or
   (b) is the father, mother, brother, sister, spouse, civil partner, son or daughter of the voter and has attained the age of 18 years.

   (4) The name and number in the register of electors of every voter whose vote is given in accordance with this rule and the name and address of the companion must be entered on a list (in these Rules referred to as the "list of voters with disabilities

assisted by companions").

In the case of a person voting as proxy for an elector, the number to be entered together with the voter's name must be the elector's number.

(5) In the case of a person in respect of whom a notice has been issued under section 13B(3B) or (3D) of the 1983 Act, paragraph (4) applies as if for "in the register of electors of every voter" there were substituted "relating to every voter in respect of whom a notice has been issued under section 13B(3B) or (3D) of the 1983 Act".

(6) The declaration made by the companion–

    (a) must be in the appropriate form, and

    (b) must be made before the presiding officer at the time when the voter applies to vote with the assistance of a companion, and

    (c) must forthwith be given to the presiding officer who must attest and retain it.

(7) No fee or other payment may be charged in respect of the declaration.

(8) The same list of voters with disabilities assisted by companions may be used for each relevant election or referendum, and where it is so used, an entry in that list must be taken to mean that the votes were so given in respect of each election and referendum, unless the list identifies the election or referendum for which the vote was so given.

Tendered ballot papers: circumstances where available

41 (1) If a person, representing himself to be–

    (a) a particular elector named in the register and not named in the absent voters list, or

    (b) a particular person named in the list of proxies as proxy for an elector and not entitled to vote by post as proxy,

applies for a ballot paper after another person has voted in person either as the elector or his proxy, the applicant must, on satisfactorily answering the questions permitted by law to be asked at the poll, be entitled, subject to the following provisions of this rule and rule 42, to mark a ballot paper (in these Rules referred to as "a tendered ballot paper") in the same manner as any other voter.

(2) Paragraph (4) applies if–

    (a) a person applies for a ballot paper representing himself to be a particular elector named in the register,

    (b) he is also named in the postal voters list, and

    (c) he claims that he did not make an application to vote by post at the election.

(3) Paragraph (4) also applies if–

    (a) a person applies for a ballot paper representing himself to be a particular person named as a proxy in the list of proxies,

    (b) he is also named in the proxy postal voters list, and

    (c) he claims that he did not make an application to vote by post as proxy.

(4) The person must, on satisfactorily answering the questions permitted by law to be asked at the poll, be entitled, subject to the following provisions of this rule and rule 42, to mark a ballot paper (in these Rules referred to as a "tendered ballot paper") in the same manner as any other voter.

(5) Paragraph (6) applies if before the close of the poll but after the last time at which a person may apply for a replacement postal ballot paper, a person represents himself to be–

    (a) a particular elector named in the register who is also named in the postal voters list, or

    (b) a particular person named as a proxy in the list of proxies and who is also named in the proxy postal voters list,

and claims that he has lost or has not received his postal ballot paper.

(6) The person must, on satisfactorily answering the questions permitted by law to be asked at the poll, be entitled, subject to the provisions of this rule and rule 42, to mark a ballot paper (in these Rules referred to as a "tendered ballot paper") in the same manner as any other voter.

Tendered ballot papers: general provisions

42 (1) A tendered ballot paper must–
  (a) be of a colour differing from the other ballot papers,
  (b) instead of being put into the ballot box, be given to the presiding officer and endorsed by him with the name of the voter and his number on the register of electors, and set aside in a separate packet.

(2) The name of the voter and his number on the register of electors must be entered on a list (in these Rules referred to as the "tendered votes list").

(3) In the case of a person voting as proxy for an elector, the number to be endorsed or entered together with the voter's name must be the number of that elector.

(4) In the case of an elector who has an anonymous entry, this rule and rule 41 apply subject to the following modifications–
  (a) in paragraphs (1)(b) and (2) above, the references to the name of the voter must be ignored,
  (b) otherwise, a reference to a person named on a register or list must be construed as a reference to a person whose number appears in the register or list (as the case may be).

(5) In the case of a person in respect of whom a notice has been issued under section 13B(3B) or (3D) of the 1983 Act, this rule and rule 41 apply as if–
  (a) in rule 41(1)(a), (2)(a) and (5)(a), for "named in the register" there were substituted "in respect of whom a notice under section 13B(3B) or (3D) of the 1983 Act has been issued",
  (b) in paragraph (1)(b) of this rule for "his number in the register of electors" there were substituted "the number relating to him on a notice issued under section 13B(3B) or (3D) of the 1983 Act",
  (c) in paragraph (2) of this rule, for "his number in the register of electors" there were substituted "the number relating to him on a notice issued under section 13B(3B) or (3D) of the 1983 Act".

(6) The same list may be used for each relevant election or referendum, and where it is so used, an entry in that list must be taken to mean that tendered ballot papers were marked in respect of each election or referendum, unless the list identifies the election or referendum at which a tendered ballot paper was marked.

Spoilt and replacement ballot papers

43 (1) A voter who has inadvertently dealt with his ballot paper in such manner that it cannot be conveniently used as a ballot paper may, on delivering it to the presiding officer and proving to his satisfaction the fact of the inadvertence, obtain a replacement for the ballot paper so delivered (in these Rules referred to as "a spoilt ballot paper"), and the spoilt ballot paper must be immediately cancelled.

(2) If a voter decides, after he has returned his ballot paper and it has been cancelled in accordance with rule 38(6), but before the close of the poll, that he wishes to vote in the election, he may obtain a replacement for the returned ballot paper.

(3) Before a replacement ballot paper is obtained, the presiding officer must mark the

corresponding number list that was marked under rule 38(1) (the corresponding number list)–

    (a) in the case of a ballot paper being replaced under paragraph (1) or (2), beside the number of the replacement ballot paper obtained to show–

        (i)   the number of the elector, and

        (ii) the number of the ballot paper which is being replaced; and

    (b) in the case of a ballot paper being replaced under paragraph (1), beside the number of the spoilt ballot paper to show that the ballot paper was replaced.

(4) Where the election is taken with a relevant election or referendum the voter must only receive a replacement for a spoilt or returned ballot paper.

(5) If the same corresponding number list is used for more than one Authority election in accordance with rule 38(8)–

    (a) the marks made under paragraph (3) must identify the election for which a ballot paper has been replaced, and

    (b) any ballot paper which the voter has not applied for or obtained as a replacement, but which bears the same ballot paper number as a ballot paper delivered under rule 38(1), or obtained under paragraph (1) or (2) of this rule–

        (i)   must not be delivered to the voter,

        (ii) must be cancelled, and

        (iii) for the purposes of these rules, must be treated as a spoilt ballot paper.

Correction of errors on day of poll

44 (1) The presiding officer must keep a list of persons to whom ballot papers are delivered in consequence of an alteration to the register made by virtue of section 13B(3B) or (3D) of the 1983 Act which takes effect on the day of the poll.

(2) The same list may be used for each relevant election or referendum, and where it is so used, an entry in that list must be taken to mean that ballot papers were delivered in respect of each election or referendum, unless the list identifies the election or referendum at which a tendered ballot paper was marked.

Adjournment of poll in case of riot

45 (1) Where the proceedings at any polling station are interrupted or obstructed by riot or open violence, the presiding officer must adjourn the proceedings till the following day and must forthwith inform the CRO.

(2) Where the poll is adjourned at any polling station–

    (a) the hours of polling on the day to which it is adjourned must be the same as for the original day, and

    (b) references in these Rules to the close of the poll must be construed accordingly.

(3) As soon as practicable after being informed of the adjournment of a poll, the CRO must inform the GLRO of that fact and of the cause of its adjournment.

(4) If the CRO does not discharge the functions specified in regulation 5 of the Combination of Polls Regulations, then references in this rule to the CRO must be taken as references to the returning officer who discharges those functions.

Procedure on close of poll

46 (1) As soon as practicable after the close of the poll, the presiding officer must, in the presence of the polling agents appointed for the purposes of the election and each relevant election or referendum, make up into separate packets, sealed with his own seal and the seals of such polling agents as desire to affix their seals–

(a) each ballot box in use at the station, sealed so as to prevent the introduction of additional ballot papers and unopened, but with any key attached,

(b) the unused and spoilt ballot papers placed together,

(c) the tendered ballot papers,

(d) the marked copies of the register of electors (including any marked copy notices issued under section 13B(3B) or (3D) of the 1983 Act) and of the list of proxies,

(e) the list prepared under rule 18, including the part completed in accordance with rule 38(1)(b) (together referred to in these Rules as "the completed corresponding number list"),

(f) the certificates as to employment on duty on the day of the poll,

(g) the tendered votes list, the list of voters with disabilities assisted by companions, the list of votes marked by the presiding officer, a statement of the number of voters whose votes are so marked by the presiding officer under the heads "disability" and "unable to read", the list maintained under rule 44, and the declarations made by the companions of voters with disabilities,

and must deliver the packets or cause them to be delivered to the CRO to be taken charge of by him; but if the packets are not delivered by the presiding officer personally to the CRO, the arrangements for their delivery must be approved by the CRO.

(2) The contents of the packets referred to in paragraph (1)(b), (c) and (f) must not be combined with the contents of the packets made under the corresponding rule that applies at any other relevant election or referendum except for an Authority election.

(3) The marked copies of the register of electors and of the list of proxies must be in one packet but must not be in the same packet as the completed corresponding number list or the certificates as to employment on duty on the day of the poll.

(4) The packets must be accompanied by a statement ("the ballot paper account") showing the number of ballot papers entrusted to the presiding officer, and accounting for them under the heads–

(a) ballot papers issued and not otherwise accounted for,

(b) unused ballot papers,

(c) spoilt ballot papers, and

(d) tendered ballot papers.

(5) At an ordinary election, the statement referred to in paragraph (4) may be combined with the statements produced in relation to any other Authority election, but not with those for a relevant election or referendum, and the combined statement must be arranged in such manner as the GLRO may direct.

(6) Where the CRO does not discharge the functions specified in regulation 5 of the Combination of Polls Regulations, references in paragraph (1) to the CRO must be taken as references to the returning officer who discharges those functions.

Attendance at verification and the counting of votes

47 (1) Where the CRO discharges the functions specified in regulation 5 of the Combination of Polls Regulations, he must–

(a) make arrangements for–

(i) carrying out the functions in rule 49(1) (separating ballot papers and verifying ballot paper accounts) at the election in the presence of the counting agents appointed for the purposes of the election and each relevant election and referendum as soon as practicable after the close of the poll, and

(ii) for counting the votes in the presence of the counting agents appointed for the purposes of the election,

(b) give to the counting agents appointed for the purposes of the election and each relevant election and referendum, notice in writing of the time and place at which he will begin carrying out the functions in rule 49(1).

(2) Where the CRO does not discharge the functions specified in regulation 5 of the Combination of Polls Regulations he must make arrangements for counting the votes in the presence of the counting agents appointed for the purposes of the election as soon as practicable after the delivery of the ballot papers to him by the returning officer who does discharge those functions; and the CRO must give to the counting agents for the election notice in writing of the time and place at which he will begin to count the votes.

(3) No person other than a person entitled to be present at the counting of the votes at the election and at each relevant election or referendum may be present at the proceedings under rule 49(1) (separating ballot papers and verifying ballot paper accounts) unless permitted by the CRO to attend.

(4) No person other than–
    (a) the CRO and his clerks and technical assistants,
    (b) the GLRO,
    (c) the candidates and one other person chosen by each of them,
    (d) the election agents,
    (e) the counting agents,
    (f) persons who are entitled to attend by virtue of any of sections 6A to 6D of the 2000 Act,

may be present at the counting of the votes in accordance with rule 49(2) to (15), unless permitted by the CRO to attend

(5) A person not entitled to attend at the separation and verification or the counting of the votes must not be permitted to do so by the CRO unless the CRO–
    (a) is satisfied that the efficient separation and verification of the ballot paper accounts or, as the case may be, the efficient counting of the votes will not be impeded, and
    (b) has either consulted the candidates or thought it impracticable to do so.

(6) The CRO must give the counting agents all such reasonable facilities for overseeing the proceedings, and all such information with respect to them, as he can give them consistently with the orderly conduct of the proceedings and the discharge of his duties in connection with them.

Use of the electronic counting system

48 (1) The GLRO may provide the CRO with an electronic counting system consisting of computer hardware, software and other equipment or services, for the purpose of counting the number of ballot papers, to verify the ballot paper accounts and to count the votes cast on them.

(2) Any verification of ballot paper accounts, count or re-count at the election conducted using the electronic counting system must be conducted in accordance with rule 49.

(3) If the GLRO has provided the CRO with an electronic counting system for use at the election, the CRO must obtain the prior written consent of the GLRO before he may conduct the verification of ballot paper accounts or count the votes manually.

(4) If the verification of ballot paper accounts, count or re-count has commenced using the electronic counting system but has not been completed, the CRO may, if he considers it appropriate, discontinue the count and instead count the votes manually.

(5) Where the count or a re-count has been conducted using the electronic counting

system, the CRO may, if he considers it appropriate, conduct any re-count without using that system.

(6) Where verification or any count or re-count is conducted using the electronic counting system, any of the steps referred to rule 49, in so far as practicable, may be undertaken–

    (a) concurrently with any other of those steps, or

    (b) in a different order.

Verification and the count

49 (1) Where the CRO discharges the functions specified in regulation 5 of the Combination of Polls Regulations, he must–

    (a) in the presence of the counting agents appointed for the purposes of the election and each relevant election or referendum, open each ballot box from each polling station together, and record separately the number of ballot papers used in the election and each relevant election or referendum with which is it is taken,

    (b) in the presence of the counting agents appointed for the purposes of the election and each relevant election or referendum, verify each ballot paper account at the election and for each relevant election or referendum,

    (c) count such of the postal ballot papers as have been duly returned and record separately the number counted at the election and each relevant election or referendum,

    (d) where the same ballot boxes have been used for the election and each relevant election or referendum, separate the ballot papers for all of the Authority elections from those for any other relevant election or referendum.

    (e) make up into packets the ballot papers for each relevant election or referendum (not including those for any Authority election) and seal them up in separate containers endorsing on each a description of the area to which the ballot papers relate,

    (f) deliver or cause to be delivered to the returning officer for the relevant election or referendum to which the ballot papers relate–

      (i) those containers, together with a list of them and of the contents of each, and

      (ii) the ballot paper accounts together with a copy of the statement as to the result of their verification in respect of that relevant election or referendum, and

    (g) at the same time deliver to that officer the packets that so relate containing–

      (i) the unused and spoilt ballot papers,

      (ii) the tendered ballot papers, and

      (iii) the completed corresponding number lists of the used ballot papers and the certificates as to employment on duty on the day of the poll.

(2) Where the CRO does not discharge the functions specified in regulation 5 of the Combination of Polls Regulations, and the votes on the ballot papers are not to be counted concurrently with the votes on the ballot papers at a relevant election or referendum, he must–

    (a) on receipt of the containers of ballot papers from the returning officer who does discharge those functions, and after the time specified in the notice given by him in writing to the counting agents under rule 47(2), open each container in the presence of the counting agents;

    (b) where the proceedings on the issue and receipt of postal ballot papers at the election are not taken together with those proceedings at a relevant election or referendum under regulation 65 of the Representation of the People (England

and Wales) Regulations 2001, or under that regulation as applied by regulations made under sections 44 and 105, or 45 and 105, of the Local Government Act 2000, count such of the postal ballot papers as have been duly returned and record the number counted,

and paragraph (10) below does not apply to these proceedings.

(3) Where separate ballot boxes are used for the ballots at the election and each relevant election and referendum, no vote for any candidate shall be rendered invalid by the ballot paper being placed in the ballot box used at any relevant election or referendum.

(4) Where the same ballot boxes are used for the election and other Authority elections, but not for other relevant elections or referendums–

    (a) the CRO must not mix the ballot papers for Authority elections from any ballot box or container with the contents of any other ballot box or container (including a postal ballot box) during the conduct of verification (where this occurs under paragraph (1)), the count or any re-count;

    (b) the ballot boxes from each polling station for the Authority elections shall be opened together and the ballot papers counted (but not necessarily the votes on them) and verified together.

(5) A postal ballot paper must not be taken to be duly returned unless–

    (a) it is returned in the manner set out in paragraph (6) and reaches the CRO or any polling station in the appropriate area (as defined in paragraph (7)) before the close of the poll,

    (b) the postal voting statement, duly signed, is also returned in the manner set out in paragraph (6) and reaches him or such polling station before that time,

    (c) the postal voting statement also states the date of birth of the elector or proxy (as the case may be), and

    (d) in a case where the steps for verifying the date of birth and signature of an elector or proxy have been prescribed by regulations made under the 1983 Act, the CRO (having taken such steps) verifies the date of birth and signature of the elector or proxy (as the case may be).

(6) The manner in which any postal paper or postal voting statement may be returned–

    (a) to the CRO, is by hand or by post,

    (b) to a polling station in the appropriate area, is by hand.

(6A) A postal ballot paper or postal voting statement that reaches the CRO or a polling station in the appropriate area at or after the close of the poll is treated for the purposes of paragraph (5) as reaching that officer or polling station before the close of the poll if it is delivered by a person who, at the close of the poll, is in the polling station, or in a queue outside the polling station, for the purpose of returning it.

(7) For the purposes of paragraphs (5), (6) and (6A), "polling station in the appropriate area" means a polling station–

    (a) in the area which is common to the Assembly constituency, and parliamentary constituency, local counting area, electoral area or voting area, as the case may be, in which the polls at the Authority election and a relevant election or referendum are being taken together, and

    (b) in respect of which polls the voter has been issued with a postal ballot paper.

(8) After the completing the proceedings in paragraph (1) or (2), the CRO must cause the electronic counting system to process the ballot papers for the election so as to count–

    (a) the number of ballot papers, and

    (b) votes given on the ballot papers.

(9) The CRO must not cause the electronic counting system to count any tendered ballot paper.

(10) Subject to paragraph (11), the CRO must verify each ballot paper account by comparing it with the number of ballot papers recorded by him, and the unused and spoilt ballot papers in his possession and the tendered votes list (opening and re-sealing the packets containing the unused and spoilt ballot papers and the tendered votes list) and must draw up a statement as to the result of the verification, which any election agent may copy.

(11) The CRO may verify each ballot paper account for the election by comparing it with the number of ballot papers processed by the electronic counting system, and the unused and spoilt ballot papers in his possession and the tendered votes list (opening and re-sealing the packets containing the unused and spoilt ballot papers and the tendered votes list).

(12) The CRO, while verifying the ballot paper accounts and counting the votes, must take all proper precautions for preventing any person from seeing the numbers printed on the back of the papers.

(13) The CRO must so far as practicable proceed continuously with counting the votes, allowing only time for refreshment, except that the hours between 5 in the afternoon and 10 on the following morning may be excluded.

(14) At an ordinary election, the hours between 5 in the afternoon and 10 on the following morning may only be excluded with the prior consent of the GLRO.

(15) During the time so excluded the CRO must–
    (a) place the ballot papers and other documents relating to the election under his own seal and the seals of such of the counting agents as desire to affix their seals, and
    (b) otherwise take proper precautions for the security of the papers and documents.

Rejected ballot papers

50 (1) Any ballot paper–
    (a) which does not bear the official mark,
    (b) on which votes are given for more than one candidate,
    (c) on which anything is written or marked by which the voter can be identified except the printed number and other unique identifying mark on the back,
    (d) which is unmarked, or
    (e) which is void for uncertainty,
is, subject to paragraph (2), void and must not be counted.

(2) A ballot paper on which the vote is marked–
    (a) elsewhere than in the proper place, or
    (b) otherwise than by means of a cross, or
    (c) by more than one mark,
must not for such reason be void if an intention that the vote be given for one only of the candidates clearly appears, and the way the paper is marked does not itself identify the voter and it is not shown that he can be identified by it.

(3) Where the electronic counting system identifies a ballot paper that has been marked, but which appears for whatever reason to be void, it must be examined by a clerk appointed by the CRO in the manner referred to in paragraph (6).

(4) If the clerk, having examined the ballot, considers that the vote is void then the CRO must examine it in the manner referred to in paragraph (6).

(5) After the CRO examines the ballot paper, he must give his decision as to the validity of the vote.

(6) An examination under paragraph (3) or (4) is to be made by the clerk or CRO examining an image of the ballot paper which is shown on a screen so as to be visible to those attending the count.

(7) The CRO may examine any ballot paper that he is not required to examine in accordance with paragraph (4)–
    (a) either in the manner referred to in paragraph (6), or
    (b) by examining a paper copy,
and where the CRO does so, he must give a decision on that paper in accordance with paragraph (5).

(8) No person attending the count is to be entitled to require the clerk or CRO to examine a ballot paper or to provide a paper copy for inspection.

(9) A record of the CRO's decision must be retained in the electronic counting system together with, in the case of a decision that the ballot paper is void, his reasons by reference to paragraph (1).

(10) If a counting agent objects to the CRO's decision the CRO must record on the electronic counting system that the decision was objected to.

(11) The CRO must draw up a statement showing the number of ballot papers rejected under the several heads of–
    (a) want of an official mark,
    (b) voting for more than one candidate,
    (c) writing or mark by which the voter could be identified,
    (d) unmarked ballot paper, or
    (e) void for uncertainty.

(12) As soon as practicable after the completion of the statement under paragraph (11) the CRO must inform–
    (a) such candidates, election agents and counting agents as are present at the count, and
    (b) the GLRO,
of its contents.

Decisions on ballot papers

51 The decision of the CRO on any question arising in respect of a ballot paper will be final, but may be subject to review on an election petition.

Re-count

52 (1) A candidate or his election agent or a counting agent authorised under rule 30(3) may, if present when the counting or any re-count of the votes, is completed, require the CRO to have the votes re-counted or again re-counted but the CRO may refuse to do so if in his opinion the request is unreasonable.

(2) No step may be taken on the completion of the counting or any re-count of votes until the candidates and election agents present at its completion have been given a reasonable opportunity to exercise the right conferred by this rule.

(3) The CRO may, in his discretion, decide the extent to which any re-count involves the electronic counting of votes.

(4) When the returning officer uses the electronic counting system for the re-counting of votes, he must not re-consider any decision made on any ballot paper under rule 50(5).

Equality of votes

53   Where, after the counting of the votes (including any re-count) is completed, an equality of votes is found to exist between any candidates and the addition of a vote would entitle any of those candidates to be declared elected, the CRO must forthwith decide between those candidates by lot, and proceed as if the candidate on whom the lot falls had received an additional vote.

Part 5
Final Proceedings in Contested and Uncontested Elections

Declaration of result

54 (1)   In a contested election, when the result of the poll has been ascertained, the CRO must forthwith–
   (a)   declare to be elected the candidate to whom the majority of votes has been given,
   (b)   give public notice of–
      (i)   the name of the person declared to be elected,
      (ii)   the person's authorised description, if any, within the meaning of rule 6(5) or (7),
      (iii) the total number of votes given for each candidate together with the number of rejected ballot papers under each head shown in the statement of rejected ballot papers.

   (2)   Subject to paragraph (3), after the CRO complies with paragraph (1), he may give public notice of the information referred to paragraph (1)(b)(iii) so as to set out the number of votes falling under each of the heads in that sub-paragraph, in respect of each ward.

   (3)   Where the sum of votes given for all candidates in any ward does not exceed 500, the GLRO must not give notice under paragraph (2) in respect of that ward alone, but must amalgamate the figures for that ward with those for any other ward in which more than 500 votes have been given, in the same Assembly constituency.

   (4)   In an uncontested election, the CRO must as soon as practicable after the latest time for the delivery of notices of withdrawals of candidature–
   (a)   declare to be elected the candidate remaining validly nominated,
   (b)   give public notice of–
      (i)   the name of the person declared to be elected, and
      (ii)   the person's authorised description, if any, within the meaning of rule 6(5) or (7).

   (5)   The CRO must as soon as practicable notify the GLRO and the proper officer of the Authority of the information in the notice given under (1)(b).

Return or forfeiture of candidate's deposit

55 (1)   Unless forfeited in accordance with paragraph (5), the deposit made under rule 8 must be returned to the person making it or his personal representative.

   (2)   Subject to paragraphs (3) and (4), the deposit must be returned not later than the next day after that on which the result of the election is declared.

   (3)   For the purposes of paragraph (2)–
   (a)   a day must be disregarded if, in accordance with rule 4, it would be disregarded in computing any period of time for the purposes of the timetable for the election, and

(b) the deposit must be treated as being returned on a day if a cheque for the amount of the deposit is posted on that day.

(4) If the candidate is not shown as standing nominated in the statement of persons nominated, or if the poll is countermanded or abandoned by reason of his death, the deposit must be returned as soon as practicable after the publication of the statement or after his death, as the case may be.

(5) Where a poll is taken, if, after the counting of the votes by the CRO (including any re-count) is completed, the candidate is found not to have polled more than one-twentieth of the total number of votes polled by all the candidates, the deposit must be forfeited to the Greater London Authority.

Part 6
Disposal of Documents

Sealing up of ballot papers

56 (1) On the completion of the counting at a contested election the CRO must seal up in separate packets the counted and rejected ballot papers.

(2) Where some or all of the votes have been counted using the electronic counting system, the CRO must also seal up in a separate packet a complete electronic record ("the electronic record") of the information stored in the electronic counting system, held in such device as may be suitable for the purpose of its storage.

(3) After making the electronic record under paragraph (2), the CRO must arrange for the original records in the electronic counting system to be removed from it and destroyed in a manner that ensures that the secrecy of those records is preserved.

(4) The CRO must not open the sealed packets of–
(a) tendered ballot papers, or
(b) certificates as to employment on duty on the day of the poll.

(5) Where the CRO discharges the functions referred to in regulation 5 of the Combination of Polls Regulations, he must also not open the sealed packets of–
(a) the completed corresponding number lists,
(b) marked copies of the register of electors (including any marked copy notices issued under section 13B(3B) or (3D) of the 1983 Act) and lists of proxies.

Delivery and retention of documents

57 (1) The CRO must then forward the following documents to the relevant registration officer–
(a) the packets of ballot papers in his possession,
(b) the packet containing the electronic record (if any),
(c) the ballot paper accounts and the statements of rejected ballot papers and of the result of the verification of the ballot paper accounts,
(d) the tendered votes lists, the lists of voters with disabilities assisted by companions, the lists of votes marked by the presiding officer and the related statements, the lists maintained under rule 44 and the declarations made by the companions of voters with disabilities,
(e) the packets of the completed corresponding number lists,
(f) the packets of certificates as to employment on duty on the day of the poll, and
(g) the packets containing marked copies of registers (including any marked copy notices issued under section 13B(3B) or (3D) of the 1983 Act) and of the postal voters list, of the lists of proxies and of the proxy postal voters list,
endorsing on each packet a description of its contents, the date of the election to

which they relate and the name of the Assembly constituency for which the election was held.

(2)   At an election where the returning officer does not discharge the functions referred to in regulation 5 of the Combination of Polls Regulations, paragraph (1) must have effect as if sub paragraphs (d), (e) and (f) were omitted.

Orders for production of documents

58 (1)   An order–
  (a)   for the inspection or production of any rejected ballot papers in the custody of the relevant registration officer, or
  (b)   for the opening of a packet containing the electronic record or a sealed packet of completed corresponding number lists or certificates as to employment on duty on the day of the poll or the inspection of any counted ballot papers, in the custody of the relevant registration officer,

may be made by a county court, if the court is satisfied by evidence on oath that the order is required for the purpose of instituting or maintaining a prosecution for an offence in relation to ballot papers, or for the purpose of an election petition.

(2)   An election court may make an order for the opening of a packet containing the electronic record or a sealed packet of completed corresponding number lists or certificates or for the inspection of any counted ballot papers in the custody of the relevant registration officer.

(3)   An order under this rule may be made subject to such conditions as to–
  (a)   persons,
  (b)   time,
  (c)   place and mode of inspection,
  (d)   production or opening,

as the court making the order thinks expedient; but in making and carrying into effect an order for the opening of a packet containing the electronic record or a packet of completed corresponding number lists or certificates or for the inspection of counted ballot papers, care must be taken that the way in which the vote of any particular elector has been given must not be disclosed until it has been proved–
  (i)   that his vote was given, and
  (ii)   that the vote has been declared by a competent court to be invalid.

(4)   An appeal lies to the High Court from any order of a county court under this rule.

(5)   Any power given under this rule to a county court may be exercised by any judge of the court otherwise than in open court.

(6)   Where an order is made for the production by the relevant registration officer of any document or electronic record in his custody relating to any specified election–
  (a)   the production by him or his agent of the document or electronic record ordered in such manner as may be directed by that order will be conclusive evidence that the document or electronic record relates to the specified election, and
  (b)   any endorsement on any packet of ballot papers or so produced will be *prima facie* evidence that the ballot papers are what they are stated to be by the endorsement.

(7)   The production from proper custody of–
  (a)   a ballot paper purporting to have been used at any election, or
  (b)   a copy of the electronic record which purports to record that a particular ballot paper was used at any election, and

a completed corresponding number list with a number written beside the number of the ballot paper, will be *prima facie* evidence that the elector whose vote was given by that ballot paper was the person who, at the time of the election, had affixed to his entry in the register of electors or on the notice issued under section 13B(3B) or (3D) of the 1983 Act, the same number as was written on the completed corresponding number list.

(8) Unless authorised by this rule, no person may be allowed to inspect any rejected or counted ballot papers in the custody of the relevant registration officer or open any sealed packets of completed corresponding number lists, certificates of employment on the day of the poll or containing the electronic record.

Retention and destruction of documents and records

59 The relevant registration officer must retain or cause to be retained for one year all documents and, where applicable, the electronic record relating to an election forwarded to him in pursuance of these Rules by a CRO, and then, unless otherwise directed by an order of a county court, a Crown Court, a magistrate's court or an election court, must cause them to be destroyed.

Part 7
Death of Candidate

Countermand or abandonment of poll on death of candidate

60 (1) If at a contested election proof is given to the CRO's satisfaction before the result of the election is declared that one of the persons named or to be named as candidate in the ballot papers has died, the CRO–
   (a) must countermand notice of the poll or, if polling has begun, direct that the poll be abandoned,
   (b) must inform the GLRO of the countermand or abandonment of the poll and of the name of the candidate who has died.

(2) Subsection (1) of section 39 (local elections void etc in England and Wales) of the 1983 Act applies in respect of any vacancy which remains unfilled as if for the reference to the returning officer there were substituted a reference to the CRO.

(3) Where the poll is abandoned by reason of a candidate's death, no further ballot papers may be issued, and the presiding officer at any polling station must take the like steps (so far as not already taken) for the delivery to the CRO of ballot boxes and of ballot papers and other documents in his possession as he is required to take on the close of the poll in due course.

(4) The CRO must dispose of the ballot papers and other documents in his possession as he is required to do on the completion in due course of the counting of the votes, subject to paragraphs (5) and (6).

(5) It is not be necessary for any ballot paper account to be prepared or verified.

(6) The CRO must seal up all the ballot papers, whether the votes on them have been counted or not, and it will not be necessary to seal up counted and rejected ballot papers in separate packets.

(7) The provisions of these Rules as to the inspection, production, retention and destruction of ballot papers and other documents relating to a poll at an election apply to any such documents relating to a poll abandoned by reason of a candidate's death, subject to paragraphs (8) and (9).

(8) Ballot papers on which the votes were neither counted nor rejected must be treated as

counted ballot papers.

(9) No order may be made for–

    (a) the production or inspection of any ballot papers, or

    (b) for the opening of a sealed packet of completed corresponding number lists or certificates as to employment on duty on the day of the poll,

unless the order is made by a court with reference to a prosecution or election petition.

(10) The countermand of the notice of poll or abandonment of the poll at the election, will not effect the poll at each relevant election or referendum.

SCHEDULE 6

THE LONDON MEMBERS ELECTION RULES

Rule 5(4)

Part 1

General Provisions

Part 2

Provisions as to Time

Part 3

Stages Common to Contested and Uncontested Elections

Part 4

Contested Elections

Part 1
General Provisions

Citation

1   This Schedule may be cited as the London Members Election Rules.

Interpretation

2 (1)   In the rules in this Schedule, unless the context indicates otherwise–
"Combination of Polls Regulations" means the Representation of the People (Combination of Polls) (England and Wales) Regulations 2004;

"counting observer" has the same meaning as in regulation 2 of the Referendum Regulations;

"counting officer" has the same meaning as in regulation 9 of the Referendum Regulations;

"election" means an election for the return of the London members;

"electoral area" where the Authority election is held together with a referendum, includes a voting area where the referendum is held;

"European Parliamentary election" has the same meaning as in section 27(1) of the Representation of the People Act 1985;

"individual candidate" means a candidate other than a list candidate at an election for the return of London members of the London Assembly;

"list candidate" means a person included on a party list;

"local authority mayoral election" means an election conducted under the Local Authorities (Mayoral Elections) (England and Wales) Regulations 2007;

"local count" means the count of the London votes given for a registered party or, as the case may be, an individual candidate, at an election in an Assembly constituency;

"local counting area" has the same meaning as in regulation 2(1) of the European Parliamentary Elections Regulations 2004;

"London vote" has the same meaning as in Part 1 of the 1999 Act;

"party list" means a list delivered to the GLRO in accordance with paragraph 5 (party lists and individual candidates) of Part 2 of Schedule 2 to the 1999 Act on behalf of a party registered under Part 2 (registration of political parties) of the 2000 Act;

"petition organiser" has the same meaning as in regulation 3 of the Local Authorities (Referendums) (Petitions and Directions) (England) Regulations 2000;

"polling observer" has the same meaning as in regulation 2 of the Referendum Regulations;

"referendum" means a referendum conducted under the Referendum Regulations;

"Referendum Regulations" means the Local Authorities (Conduct of Referendums) (England) Regulations 2007;

"relevant election or referendum" means one or more of the following–

    (a) a Parliamentary election,

    (b) a European Parliamentary election,

    (c) a local government election (including another Authority election where more than one is taken together),

    (d) a local authority mayoral election or referendum in accordance with regulations made under sections 44 and 105, or 45 and 105, of the Local Government Act 2000;

"voting area" has the same meaning as in regulation 2 of the Referendum Regulations.

(2)   In the case of a referendum, a reference to a–

    (a) "candidate" shall be construed as a reference to a counting observer,

    (b) "election agent" shall be construed as a reference to a counting observer,

    (c) "polling agent" shall be construed as a reference to polling observer,

    (d) "returning officer" shall be construed as a reference to a counting officer.

(3)   Reference to a rule by number alone is a reference to the rule so numbered in this Schedule.

Part 2
Provisions as to Time

Timetable

3   The proceedings at the election must be conducted in accordance with the following

timetable:

Timetable

Proceedings	Time
Publication of notice of election	Not later than the thirtieth day before the day of election.
Delivery of nomination papers and party lists	Not later than 4 in the afternoon on the twenty-fourth day before the day of election.
Delivery of notices of withdrawals of candidature	Not later than 4 in the afternoon on the twenty-fourth day before the day of election
Publication of statement as to persons nominated	Not later than 4 in the afternoon on the twenty-second day before the day of election.
Notice of poll	Not later than the sixth day before the day of election.
Polling	Between the hours of 7 in the morning and 10 at night on the day of election.

Computation of time

4 (1)   In computing any period of time for the purposes of the timetable–

      (a)   a Saturday or Sunday,

      (b)   Christmas Eve, Christmas Day, Good Friday or a bank holiday, or

      (c)   a day appointed for public thanksgiving or mourning,

must be disregarded, and any such day must not be treated as a day for the purpose of any proceedings up to the completion of the poll nor must the CRO be obliged to proceed with the counting of the votes on such a day.

(2)   In this rule, "bank holiday" means a day which is a bank holiday under the Banking and Financial Dealings Act 1971 in England and Wales.

Part 3
Stages Common to Contested and Uncontested Elections

Notice of election

5 (1)   The GLRO must publish in each Assembly constituency notice of the election stating–

      (a)   the place and times at which nomination papers and party lists are to be delivered, and

      (b)   the date of the poll in the event of a contest,

and the notice must state that forms of nomination papers and party lists may be obtained at that place and those times.

(2)   The notice of election must state the arrangements (if any) which apply for the payment of the deposit required by rule 10 by means of the electronic transfer of funds.

(3)   The notice of election must state the date by which–

      (a)   applications to vote by post or proxy, and

      (b)   other applications and notices about postal or proxy voting,

must reach the registration officer for local government electors in order that they may be effective for the election.

Nomination of candidates: individual candidates

6 (1) Each individual candidate must be nominated by a separate nomination paper that must be–
    (a) in the appropriate form, and
    (b) delivered to the GLRO in accordance with the following provisions of this rule and rule 8.

  (2) The nomination paper of an individual candidate must state the candidate's–
    (a) full names,
    (b) home address, in full, and
    (c) if desired, a description consisting of the word "Independent",
and the surname must be placed first in the list of names.

Nomination of candidates: list candidates

7 (1) A registered party which is a qualifying party and is to stand at the election of London members must be nominated by the delivery of a nomination paper that must be–
    (a) in the appropriate form, and
    (b) delivered to the GLRO, by the party's registered nominating officer or a person authorised in writing by him, in accordance with the following provisions of this rule and rule 8.

  (2) The registered party's nomination paper must–
    (a) state the authorised description by which the registered party is to stand for election,
    (b) include a statement, signed by the person issuing the paper, that it is issued either–
      (i) by the party's registered nominating officer, or
      (ii) on behalf of the party's registered nominating officer, by a person authorised in writing by him, and
    (c) be accompanied by a party list which sets out the full names and home addresses of each candidate included in that list.

  (3) An authorised description for the purposes of paragraph (2)(a) must be either–
    (a) the name of the party registered under section 28 of the 2000 Act, or
    (b) a description of the party, registered under section 28A of that Act.

  (4) A person will be guilty of a corrupt practice if he fraudulently purports to be authorised to make the statement required by paragraph (2)(b) by or on behalf of a registered party's nominating officer.

  (5) For the purposes of the application of these rules in relation to an election–
    (a) "registered party" means a party which was registered under Part 2 of the 2000 Act on the day ("the relevant day") which is two days before the last day for the delivery of nomination papers and party lists at that election,
    (b) a registered party is a qualifying party if on the relevant day the party was registered in respect of England in the Great Britain register maintained under that Part of that Act.

Nomination papers: general provisions

8 (1) The following provisions of this rule have effect in relation to nomination papers delivered under rules 6 and 7.

  (2) If an individual candidate or a candidate included on a party list commonly uses–
    (a) a surname which is different from any other surname he has, or
    (b) a forename which is different from any other forename he has,
the nomination paper and party list may state the commonly used surname or

forename, or both surname and forename in addition to the other name.

(3) Each nomination paper must be delivered to the GLRO at the place specified by him in the notice of election, which must be at one of the offices of the Greater London Authority, and must be received by the GLRO before the last time for the delivery of nomination papers and party lists.

(4) Where a nomination paper is delivered in respect of–
   (a) the same registered party, or
   (b) the same individual candidate,
   after an earlier nomination paper has been delivered, that later paper must be deemed to supersede the earlier one.

(5) In this rule and in the following provisions of these rules, unless the context requires otherwise–
   (a) "nomination paper" includes a reference to–
      (i) the nomination paper of a registered party, and
      (ii) the nomination paper of an individual candidate;
   (b) "nomination paper of a registered party" includes a reference to a party list.

Consent to nomination

9 (1) A person will not be validly nominated (whether as an individual candidate or a list candidate) unless his consent to nomination–
   (a) is given in writing in the appropriate form, or a form to like effect, on or within one month before the last day for the delivery of nomination papers;
   (b) is attested by one witness whose name and address must be given; and
   (c) is delivered at the place and within the time for delivery of nomination papers.

(2) A candidate's consent given under this rule must–
   (a) state the day, month and year of his birth;
   (b) contain a statement that he has read whichever of sub-paragraphs (5) and (6) of paragraph 5 of Schedule 2 to the 1999 Act (persons who many not be candidates) applies in his case; and
   (c) contain a statement that to the best of the candidate's knowledge and belief he is not disqualified from being elected by reason of–
      (i) any disqualification set out in section 21 (disqualification from being the Mayor or an Assembly member) of the 1999 Act,
      (ii) a decision made under section 78A of the Local Government Act 2000 (decisions of First-tier tribunal), or
      (iii) an order made under section 34(4) of the Localism Act 2011(offences).

Deposits

10 (1) A person will not be validly nominated as an individual candidate at the election unless the sum of £5,000 is deposited by him or on his behalf with the GLRO at the place and during the time for delivery of nomination papers and party lists.

(2) A registered party (and anyone on its party list) will not be validly nominated unless the sum of £5,000 is deposited on its behalf with the GLRO at the place and during the time for delivery of nomination papers and party lists.

(3) The deposit may be made either–
   (a) by the deposit of any legal tender, or
   (b) by means of a banker's draft, or
   (c) with the GLRO's consent, in any other manner including by means of a debit or credit card or the electronic transfer of funds,
   but the GLRO may refuse to accept a deposit sought to be made by means of a banker's draft if he does not know that the drawer carries on business as a banker in

the United Kingdom.

(4) Where the deposit is made on behalf of an individual candidate, the person making the deposit must at the time he makes it give his name and address to the GLRO, unless they have previously been given to him under section 67 (appointment of election agent) of the 1983 Act.

Decisions as to validity of nomination papers

11 (1) Where, in the case of an individual candidate, a nomination paper ("individual nomination paper") and the candidate's consent to it are delivered and a deposit is made, in accordance with these Rules, the candidate will be deemed to stand nominated unless and until–
    (a) the GLRO decides that the nomination paper is invalid, or
    (b) proof is given to the GLRO's satisfaction of the candidate's death, or
    (c) the candidate withdraws.

(2) Where, the nomination paper of a registered party and the consent of each candidate included in that party's list are delivered, and a deposit is made, in accordance with these Rules, that party and (subject to paragraph (6)) each candidate on its list must be deemed to stand nominated unless and until the GLRO decides that the nomination paper is invalid.

(3) As soon as practicable after each nomination paper has been delivered, the GLRO must examine it and decide whether the individual candidate, or as the case may be, each registered party and each candidate included in that party's list has been validly nominated.

(4) The GLRO is entitled to hold an individual nomination paper invalid only on the grounds that the particulars of the candidate on the nomination paper are not as required by law.

(5) The GLRO is entitled to hold the nomination paper of a registered party invalid only on one of the following grounds–
    (a) that the authorised description stated under rule 7(2)(a) breaches rule 8(3),
    (b) that the nomination paper does not contain the statement referred to in rule 7(2)(b),
    (c) that the number of candidates on the list is greater than 25.

(6) Where, in respect of a candidate included in a party list–
    (a) proof is given to the GLRO's satisfaction of his death,
    (b) he withdraws or his candidature is withdrawn in accordance with rule 15,
    (c) his particulars in that list are not as required by law, or
    (d) the consent to nomination of that candidate is not delivered in accordance with rule 9,
the GLRO must delete the name and address of that candidate from the list.

(7) Where the GLRO has decided under paragraph (3)–
    (a) that an individual nomination paper is invalid,
    (b) that the nomination paper of a registered party is invalid or that the name and address of a list candidate must be deleted from the list,
he must endorse and sign on the nomination paper to record that decision and the reasons for his decision.

(8) The GLRO must, as soon as practicable after making such a decision under paragraph (3) that a nomination paper is valid or invalid, send notice of that decision–
    (a) to the candidate at his home address as given in his nomination paper, and
    (b) in the case of a list candidate, also to the nominating officer.

(9) Where in the GLRO's opinion the nomination paper of a registered party is invalid on the grounds in paragraphs (5)(a) or (b), then he must give a decision to that effect–
   (a) as soon as practicable after the delivery of the nomination paper, and
   (b) in any event, before the end of the period of 24 hours starting with the end of the period for the delivery of nomination papers set out in the timetable in rule 3.

(10) The GLRO's decision that a nomination paper is valid is final and may not be questioned in any proceeding whatsoever.

(11) Subject to paragraph (10), nothing in this rule prevents the validity of a nomination being questioned on an election petition.

Publication of statement of persons nominated

12 (1) The GLRO must prepare and publish a statement showing–
   (a) each registered party which has been and stands nominated, together with that party's list,
   (b) the persons who have been and stand nominated as individual candidates, and
   (c) any other parties or persons who have been nominated, together with the reason why they no longer stand nominated.

(2) If an individual's nomination paper or person's entry on a party list gives a commonly used surname or forename, or both surname and forename, in addition to another name, the statement must show the person's commonly used surname or forename, or both surname and forename (as the case may be) instead of any other name.

(3) Paragraph (2) does not apply if the GLRO thinks–
   (a) that the use of the person's commonly used name may be likely to mislead or confuse electors, or
   (b) that the commonly used name is obscene or offensive.

(4) If paragraph (3) applies, the GLRO must give notice in writing to the candidate of his reasons for refusing to allow the use of a commonly used name.

(5) The statement must show, in the following order–
   (a) the registered parties which have been and stand nominated, arranged in alphabetical order according to the authorised descriptions given in the nomination papers,
   (b) the names and home addresses of the list candidates as given in party lists, arranged in the order in which their names appear in those lists,
   (c) the names, addresses and descriptions (if any) of the persons standing nominated as individual candidates, arranged alphabetically in the order of their surnames and, if there are two or more of them with the same surname, of their other names.

(6) In the case of an individual candidate nominated by more than one nomination paper, the GLRO must take the particulars required by the foregoing provisions of this rule from such one of the papers as the candidate (or the GLRO in default of the candidate) may select.

Correction of minor errors

13(1) The GLRO may, if he thinks fit, at any time before the publication under rule 12 of the statement of parties and persons nominated, correct minor errors in a nomination paper.

(2) Errors which may be corrected include–
   (a) errors as to a person's electoral number,

(b)   obvious errors of spelling in relation to the details of a party or candidate.

(3)   Anything done by the GLRO in pursuance of this rule may not be questioned in any proceedings other than proceedings on an election petition.

(4)   The GLRO must have regard to any guidance issued by the Electoral Commission for the purposes of this rule.

Inspection of nomination papers and consent to nomination

14 (1)   During ordinary office hours, in the period starting 24 hours after the latest time for the delivery of nomination papers and before the date of the poll, any person may inspect and take copies of, or extracts from–

(a)   a nomination paper, or

(b)   the consents to nomination.

(2)   Inspection under paragraph (1) may not take place on a day that is specified in rule 4(1).

Withdrawal or death of candidate

15 (1)   An individual candidate may withdraw his candidature by notice of withdrawal–

(a)   signed by him and attested by one witness, whose name and address must be given, and

(b)   delivered to the GLRO at the place for delivery of nomination papers and party lists,

by the end of the period for the delivery of notices of withdrawals of candidature in the timetable in rule 3.

(2)   The nominating officer of a registered party, or a person authorised in writing by him may withdraw that party's nomination by a notice of withdrawal signed by him and delivered to the returning officer at the place for delivery of nomination papers and party lists.

(3)   Where a candidate is outside the United Kingdom, a notice of withdrawal signed by his election agent and accompanied by a written declaration also so signed of the candidate's absence from the United Kingdom will be of the same effect as a notice of withdrawal signed by the candidate; but where the candidate stands nominated by more than one nomination paper a notice of withdrawal under this paragraph will be effective if, and only if, it is accompanied, in addition to that declaration, by a written statement signed by the candidate that the person giving the notice is authorised to do so on the candidate's behalf during his absence from the United Kingdom.

(4)   If before the result of the election is declared, proof is given to the GLRO's satisfaction that an individual candidate who is named (or is to be named) in the ballot papers or a candidate whose name appears on a party list has died, then (in addition to complying with any other requirement of these rules relevant to that event) the GLRO must–

(a)   inform each CRO of the death of the candidate;

(b)   in the case of a person whose name is included in a party list, remove that person's name from that list.

Method of election

16   If, after any withdrawals under rule 15, the number of persons remaining validly nominated exceeds the number of seats available for allocation to London members, then, unless all of those persons are named on the same party list, a poll must be taken in accordance with Part 4 of these Rules.

Part 4
Contested Elections

Poll to be taken by ballot

17   The votes at the poll must be given by ballot to enable the seats for London members to be allocated to registered parties and individual candidates in accordance with paragraphs 7 and 8 of Part 2 of Schedule 2 to the 1999 Act.

The ballot papers

18 (1)   The ballot of every voter must consist of a ballot paper, which must be in the appropriate form.

(2)   Each registered party which remains validly nominated at the election and whose party list includes a person who remains validly nominated as a list candidate, after any withdrawals, and no other, is entitled to have their authorised description inserted in the ballot paper.

(3)   Each person remaining validly nominated as an individual candidate at the election, after any withdrawals, and no other, is entitled to have their name inserted in the ballot paper.

(4)   Every ballot paper–
   (a)   must, so far as practicable for the purposes of electronic counting, be printed in accordance with the directions set out in the Forms Schedule,
   (b)   must contain the authorised descriptions of the registered parties; and the names and other particulars of the individual candidates as shown in the statement of persons nominated,
   (c)   must have a number and other unique identifying mark printed on the back, and
   (d)   may, in the case of ballot papers for use at polling stations, be marked with the words "do not fold".

(5)   If a request is made by or on behalf of a registered party's nominating officer, the ballot paper must contain, against the party's authorised description, the party's registered emblem (or, as the case may be, one of the party's registered emblems).

(6)   The request under paragraph (5) must–
   (a)   be made in writing to the GLRO, and
   (b)   be received by him during the period for delivery of nomination papers and party lists set out in the timetable in rule 3.

(7)   The order of the authorised descriptions of the registered parties and the names of the individual candidates must be in the same order as in the statement of parties and persons nominated.

(8)   The GLRO must supply the ballot papers for use at the election to the CRO by such date as may be agreed between them.

(9)   The ballot papers supplied under paragraph (8) must be of a different colour from those used at any relevant election or referendum with which the election is taken.

The corresponding number list

19 (1)   The CRO must prepare a list containing the numbers and other unique identifying marks of all of the ballot papers to be issued by him in pursuance of rule 24(1) or provided by him in pursuance of rule 29(1).

(2) The list must be in the appropriate form or a form to like effect.

(3) At an ordinary election, the same list may be used for each Authority election with which the election is combined.

The official mark

20 (1) Every ballot paper must contain an appropriate security marking (the official mark).

(2) The official mark must be kept secret, and an interval of not less than five years must intervene between the use of the same official mark at any Authority election.

(3) The GLRO may use a different official mark for different purposes at the same election.

Prohibition of disclosure of vote

21 No person who has voted at the election may, in any legal proceeding to question the election, be required to state for which candidate or party he has voted.

Use of schools and public rooms

22 (1) The CRO may use, free of charge, for the purpose of taking the poll or counting the votes–

    (a) a room in a school maintained or assisted by a local authority (as defined in the Education Act 1996) or a school in respect of which grants are made out of moneys provided by Parliament to the person or body of persons responsible for the management of the school,

    (b) a room the expense of maintaining which is met by any local authority.

(2) The CRO must make good any damage done to, and defray an expense incurred by the persons having control over, any such room as mentioned in paragraph (1) by reason of its being used for the purpose of taking the poll or counting the votes.

Notice of poll

23 (1) The GLRO must, in accordance with the timetable in rule 3, publish notice of the poll stating–

    (a) the day and hours fixed for the poll,

    (b) the number of seats for London members available for allocation at that election,

    (c) the authorised description of each registered party whose party list includes persons who remain validly nominated as list candidates, and

    (d) the name and description (if any) of each individual candidate remaining validly nominated,

and rule 12(5) applies in relation to the order in which that information appears on the notice of the poll as it applies in relation to the statement of persons nominated.

(2) The CRO must, not later than the time of the publication of the notice of the poll, also give public notice of–

    (a) the situation of each polling station, and

    (b) the description of voters entitled to vote there,

and he must as soon as practicable after giving such a notice give a copy of it to each of the election agents.

(3) The notice published under paragraph (2) shall–

    (a) state that the poll at the election is to be taken together with the poll at a relevant election or referendum as the case may be,

    (b) specify the parliamentary constituency, European Parliamentary local counting area, relevant London borough, or voting area; and in the case of an election to fill a casual vacancy, the electoral area for which the relevant election or referendum is held, and

(c) where the polls are to be taken together in part of the Borough only, specify that part.

(4) The notice of poll must include the heading "GREATER LONDON AUTHORITY ELECTION".

Postal ballot papers

24 (1) The CRO must, in accordance with regulations made under the 1983 Act, issue to those entitled to vote by post a ballot paper and a postal voting statement, together with such envelopes for their return as may be prescribed in such regulations.

(2) The postal voting statement must be in the appropriate form or a form to like effect.

(3) The postal voting statement must include provision for the form to be signed and for stating the date of birth of the elector or proxy (as the case may be).

(4) The CRO must also issue to those entitled to vote by post such information as he thinks appropriate about how to obtain–
    (a) translations into languages other than English of any directions to or guidance for voters sent with the ballot paper,
    (b) a translation into Braille of such directions or guidance,
    (c) graphical representations of such directions or guidance,
    (d) the directions or guidance in any other form (including any audible form).

(5) In the case of a ballot paper issued to a person at an address in the United Kingdom, the CRO must ensure that the return of the ballot paper and postal voting statement is free of charge to the voter.

(6) Where the proceedings on the issue and receipt of postal ballot papers at the election are taken together with a relevant election or referendum the appropriate form of postal voting statement under paragraph (2) may be the joint postal voting statement which must be in the appropriate form or form to like effect.

Provision of polling stations

25 (1) The CRO must provide a sufficient number of polling stations and, subject to the following provisions of this rule, must allot the electors to the polling stations in such manner as he thinks most convenient.

(2) One or more polling stations may be provided in the same room.

(3) The polling station allotted to electors from any parliamentary polling district wholly or partly within the Assembly constituency must, in the absence of special circumstances, be in the parliamentary polling place for that district, unless that place is outside the Assembly constituency.

(4) The CRO must provide each polling station with such number of compartments as may be necessary in which the voters can mark their votes screened from observation.

Appointment of presiding officers and clerks

26 (1) The CRO must appoint and pay a presiding officer to attend at each polling station and such clerks and technical assistants as may be necessary for the purposes of the election, but he must not appoint any person who has been employed by or on behalf of a candidate in or about the election.

(2) The CRO may, if he thinks fit, preside at a polling station and the provisions of this Part

relating to a presiding officer apply to the CRO so presiding with the necessary modifications as to things to be done by the CRO to the presiding officer or by the presiding officer to the CRO.

(3) A presiding officer may do, by the clerks appointed to assist him, any act (including the asking of questions) which he is required or authorised by this Part to do at a polling station except order the arrest, exclusion or removal of any person from the polling station.

Issue of official poll cards

27 (1) The CRO must as soon as practicable after the publication of the notice of election, send to electors and their proxies an official poll card.

(2) An elector's official poll card must be sent or delivered to his qualifying address, and a proxy's to his address as shown in the list of proxies.

(3) The official poll card must be in the appropriate form or a form to like effect, and must set out–
  (a) that the election is of London members of the London Assembly at an ordinary election,
  (b) the elector's name, qualifying address and number on the register,
  (c) the date and hours of the poll and the situation of the elector's polling station, and
  (d) such other information as the CRO thinks appropriate,
and different information may be provided in pursuance of sub-paragraph (d) to different electors or descriptions of elector.

(4) In the case of an elector with an anonymous entry, instead of containing the matter mentioned in paragraph (3)(b), the polling card must contain such matter as is specified in the appropriate form.

(5) At an ordinary election, the CRO must issue a combined poll card in the appropriate form.

(6) If the CRO and the returning officer for each relevant election or referendum agree, the poll card issued under this rule may be combined with the official poll card for the relevant election or referendum, with necessary adaptations.

(7) In this rule "elector" means–
  (a) an elector with an entry on the register to be used at the election on the last day for the publication of the notice of the election, and
  (b) includes a person then shown in the register as below voting age if (but only if) it appears from the register that he will be of voting age on the day fixed for the poll.

Information for voters

28 (1) At an ordinary election, the GLRO may, in addition to a statement by him in an election booklet, include in the booklet information for voters that has been agreed by him with the Electoral Commission.

(2) The information for voters given in the election booklet may include information about–
  (a) the office of the Mayor and the London Assembly,
  (b) the system of voting at each Authority election,
  (c) how to vote in a manner that will ensure a vote is regarded as validly cast, and
subject to paragraph (3), may include any other information given in exercise of the GLRO's duty under section 69 (encouraging electoral participation) of the 2006 Act.

(3)   The information for voters must not contain–
   (a)   any advertising material,
   (b)   any material referring to a candidate or a registered party, other than by reproduction of a ballot paper which refers equally to all candidates and parties at the ordinary election,
   (c)   any material referring to the holder, at any time, of the office of Mayor or Assembly member, other than under paragraph (b) as a candidate at the ordinary election.

(4)   Information published in an election booklet under this rule must be printed on not more than two sides of A5 paper.

Equipment of polling stations

29 (1)   The CRO must provide each presiding officer with–
   (a)   such ballot papers as may be necessary, and
   (b)   such ballot boxes as may be necessary having taken account of any direction made by the GLRO in accordance with paragraph (9).

(2)   Every ballot box must be so constructed that the ballot papers can be put in it, but cannot be withdrawn from it, without the box being unlocked or, where the box has no lock, the seal being broken.

(3)   The CRO must provide each polling station with–
   (a)   materials to enable voters to mark the ballot papers,
   (b)   copies of the register of electors or such part of it as contains the entries relating to the electors allotted to the station,
   (c)   the parts of any special lists prepared for the election corresponding to the register of electors or the part of it provided under sub-paragraph (b),
   (d)   a notice of the death of any person of whose death he has been informed as mentioned in rule 15(4),
   (e)   a list consisting of that part of the list prepared under rule 19 which contains the numbers (but not the other unique identifying marks) corresponding to those on the ballot papers provided to the presiding officer of the polling station.

(4)   The reference in paragraph (3)(b) to the copies of the register of electors includes a reference to copies of any notices issued under section 13B(3B) or (3D) of the 1983 Act in respect of alterations to the register.

(5)   The CRO must also provide each polling station with a device for enabling voters who are blind or partially sighted to vote without any need for assistance from the presiding officer or any companion within the meaning of rule 41.

(6)   The device referred to in paragraph (5) above must–
   (a)   allow a ballot paper to be inserted into and removed from or attached to and detached from the device, easily and without damage to the paper,
   (b)   keep the ballot paper firmly in place during use,
   (c)   provide suitable means for the voter to–
      (i)   identify the spaces on the ballot paper on which he may mark his vote,
      (ii)   identify the candidate to whom each such space refers, and
      (iii) mark his vote on the space he has chosen.

(7)   The enlarged sample copies of the ballot paper that the GLRO is required to provide, or cause to be displayed at every polling station (in accordance with section 199B(5) and (7) of the 1983 Act) must–
   (a)   be provided to the CRO who will deliver them to the polling stations, and
   (b)   be printed on paper of the same colour as the ballot paper at the election.

(8) The CRO must also provide each polling station with notices for the guidance of voters, which must be exhibited–
    (a) outside the polling station,
    (b) inside the polling station–
        (i) in the communal areas, and
        (ii) in every voting compartment.

(9) If the GLRO thinks fit he may, not later than the date of the notice of election, direct the CRO that joint ballot boxes must be used for the ballot papers at the election and any or all relevant elections or referendums with which the election is taken.

(10) Where separate ballot boxes are to be used for the election and every relevant election or referendum, each ballot box shall be clearly marked with–
    (a) the election or referendum to which it relates, as shown on the ballot papers for that election or referendum, and
    (b) the words "Place the *specify colour of ballot papers in question* ballot paper here".

(11) Where the CRO does not discharge the functions specified in regulation 5 of the Combination of Polls Regulations, references in this rule to the CRO should be read as references to the returning officer who does discharge those functions.

Notices for the guidance of voters

30 (1) The GLRO must prepare and provide each CRO with the notices to be exhibited under rule 29(8).

(2) The GLRO may also provide each CRO with versions of the notices in such other form as he thinks appropriate, in accordance with section 199B (translations etc of certain documents) of the 1983 Act.

(3) Notices for the guidance of voters exhibited under rule 29(8) or paragraph (2) must be in the appropriate form, but may include such alternative information relating to Authority elections as–
    (a) meets with the requirements of the Notices Schedule, and
    (b) the GLRO may decide.

(4) Notices provided under paragraph (2) may, if the CRO agrees, be exhibited at any polling station–
    (a) outside the polling station,
    (b) inside the polling station–
        (i) in the communal areas,
        (ii) in every voting compartment.

(5) Where the CRO does not discharge the functions specified in regulation 5 of the Combination of Polls Regulations, references in this rule to the CRO should be read as references to the returning officer who does discharge those functions.

Appointment of polling and counting agents

31 (1) Before the commencement of the poll–
    (a) each individual candidate, and
    (b) the election agent of each list candidate,
    may appoint–
        (i) polling agents to attend at polling stations for the purpose of detecting personation, and
        (ii) counting agents to attend at the local count.

(2) The same person may be appointed as a polling agent or counting agent by, or in the

case of list candidates on behalf of, more than one candidate.

(3) For each local count, one (but no more than one) counting agent of each registered party standing nominated or individual candidate, as the case may be, may be authorised by the terms of his appointment to require a re-count at that count.

(4) Not more than four polling agents, or such greater number as the CRO may by notice allow, may be permitted to attend at any particular polling station.

(5) If the number of such agents appointed to attend at a particular polling station exceeds that number, the CRO must determine by lot which agents are permitted to attend, and only the agents on whom the lot falls will be deemed to have been duly appointed.

(6) The CRO may limit the number of counting agents, but in doing so must ensure that–
    (a) the number is the same in the case of each candidate, and
    (b) the number allowed to a candidate must not (except in special circumstances) be less than the number obtained by dividing the number of clerks employed on the counting by the number of candidates.

(7) For the purposes of the calculations required by paragraph (6)–
    (a) a counting agent appointed for more than one list candidate must be deemed to be appointed for all the candidates on that list,
    (b) a counting agent appointed for more than one candidate (other than a list candidate) is a separate agent for each of the candidates for whom he has been appointed.

(8) Notice in writing of the appointment of polling and counting agents, stating the names and addresses of the persons appointed, must be given by the candidate to the CRO and must be so given not later than the fifth day (computed in accordance with rule 4) before the day of the poll.

(9) If an agent dies, or becomes incapable of acting, the candidate or, as the case may be, the election agent, may appoint another person in his place, and must forthwith give to the CRO notice in writing of the name and address of that other person.

(10) Any appointment authorised by this rule may be made and the notice of appointment given to the CRO by the candidate's election agent, instead of by the candidate.

(11) In the following provisions of these Rules references to polling agents and counting agents must be taken as references to agents–
    (a) whose appointments have been duly made and notified, and
    (b) where the number of agents is restricted, who are within the permitted numbers.

(12) Any notice required to be given to a counting agent by the CRO may be delivered at, or sent by post to, the address stated in the notice of appointment.

(13) A candidate may himself do any act or thing which any polling or counting agent of his, if appointed, would have been authorised to do, or may assist his agent in doing any such act or thing.

(14) A candidate's election agent may do or assist in doing anything which a polling or counting agent of his is authorised to do; and anything required or authorised by these Rules to be done in the presence of the polling or counting agent may be done in the presence of a candidate's election agent instead of his polling agent or counting agent.

(15) Where by these Rules any act or thing is required or authorised to be done in the presence of the polling or counting agents, the non-attendance of any agent or agents at the time and place appointed for the purpose will not, if the act or thing is otherwise duly done, invalidate the act or thing done.

(16) Where the CRO does not discharge the functions specified in regulation 5 of the Combination of Polls Regulations, then notices of the appointment of polling agents and counting agents which are required by this rule to be given to the CRO shall be given to the returning officer who discharges those functions.

Notification of requirement of secrecy

32 (1) The CRO must make such arrangements as he thinks fit to ensure that–

    (a) every person attending at a polling station (otherwise than for the purpose of voting or assisting a voter with disabilities to vote or as a constable on duty there) has been given a copy of the provisions of subsections (1), (3) and (6) of section 66 (requirement of secrecy) of the Representation of the People Act 1983, and

    (b) every person attending at the counting of the votes (other than any constable on duty at the counting) has been given a copy of the provisions of subsections (2) and (6) of that section.

(2) In paragraph (1) a reference to a constable includes a person designated as a community support officer under section 38 of the 2002 Act (police powers for employees).

Return of postal ballot papers

33 (1) Where–

    (a) a postal vote has been returned in respect of a person who is entered on the postal voters list, or

    (b) a proxy postal vote has been returned in respect of a proxy who is entered on the proxy postal voters list,

    the CRO must mark the list in the manner prescribed by regulations made under the 1983 Act.

(2) Rule 50(5) does not apply for the purpose of determining whether, for the purposes of this rule, a postal vote or a proxy postal vote is returned.

Admission to polling station

34 (1) The presiding officer must exclude all persons from the polling station except–

    (a) voters,

    (b) persons under the age of 18 who accompany voters to the polling station,

    (c) the candidates and their election agents,

    (d) the polling agents appointed to attend at the polling station,

    (e) the clerks appointed to attend at the polling station,

    (f) persons who are entitled to attend by virtue of any of sections 6A to 6D of the 2000 Act,

    (g) the constables on duty,

    (h) the companions of voters with disabilities, and

    (i) persons entitled to be admitted to the polling station at a relevant election or referendum.

(2) The presiding officer must regulate the total number of voters and persons under the age of 18 who accompany them to be admitted to the polling station at the same time.

(3) Not more than one polling agent may be admitted at the same time to a polling station on behalf of the same party or individual candidate.

(4) A constable or person employed by the CRO must not be admitted to vote in person elsewhere than at his own polling station allotted to him under these Rules, except on

production and surrender of a certificate as to his employment which must be in the appropriate form and signed by an officer of the police of or above the rank of inspector or by the CRO, as the case may be.

(5) Any certificate surrendered under this rule must forthwith be cancelled.

(6) In this rule a reference to a constable includes a person designated as a community support officer under section 38 of the 2002 Act.

Keeping of order in station

35 (1) It is the presiding officer's duty to keep order at his polling station.

(2) If a person misconducts himself in a polling station, or fails to obey the presiding officer's lawful orders, he may immediately, by the presiding officer's order, be removed from the polling station–
    (a) by a constable in or near that station, or
    (b) by any other person authorised in writing by the CRO to remove him,
and the person so removed must not, without the presiding officer's permission, again enter the polling station during the day.

(3) Any person so removed may, if charged with the commission in the polling station of an offence, be dealt with as a person taken into custody by a constable for an offence without a warrant.

(4) The powers conferred by this rule must not be exercised so as to prevent a voter who is otherwise entitled to vote at a polling station from having an opportunity of voting at that station.

Sealing of ballot boxes

36 Immediately before the commencement of the poll, the presiding officer must–
    (a) show each ballot box, empty, to such persons, if any, as are present in the polling station, so that they may see that the boxes are empty,
    (b) lock up such of the boxes as have locks,
    (c) place his seal–
        (i) on each lock, and
        (ii) on each ballot box which has no lock,
in such a manner as to prevent its being opened without breaking the seal,
    (d) place each box in his view for the receipt of ballot papers, and
    (e) keep each box locked and sealed or, as the case may be, sealed.

Questions to be put to voters

37 (1) At the time of the application (but not afterwards), the questions specified in the second column of the following table–
    (a) may be put by the presiding officer to a person who is mentioned in the first column, and
    (b) must be put if the letter "R" appears after the question and the candidate or his election or polling agent requires the question to be put.

Q No	Person applying for ballot paper	Question
1	A person applying as an elector	(a)–Are you the person registered in the register of local government electors for this election as follows (*read the whole entry from the register*)? R (b)–Have you already voted, here or elsewhere in Greater London at this

		election for London members, otherwise than as proxy for some other person? R
2	A person applying as proxy	(a)–Are you the person whose name appears as AB in the list of proxies for this election as entitled to vote as proxy on behalf of CD? R (b)–Have you already voted here or elsewhere in Greater London at this election for London members, as proxy on behalf of CD? R (c)–Are you the spouse, civil partner, parent, grandparent, brother, sister, child or grandchild of CD?R
3	A person applying as proxy for an elector with an anonymous entry (instead of the questions at entry 2)	(a)–Are you the person entitled to vote as proxy on behalf of the elector whose number on the register of electors is (*read out the number*)? R (b)–Have you already voted here or elsewhere in Greater London as proxy on behalf of the elector whose number on the register of electors is (*read out the number*)? R (c)–Are you the spouse, civil partner, parent, grandparent, brother, sister, child or grandchild of the person whose number on the register of electors is (*read out the number*)?R
4	A person applying as proxy if the question at entry 2(c) or 3(c) is not answered in the affirmative	Have you already voted here or elsewhere in Greater London at this election for London members, on behalf of two persons of whom you are not the spouse, civil partner, parent, grandparent, brother, sister, child or grandchild? R
5	A person applying as an elector in relation to whom there is an entry in the postal voters list	(a)–Did you apply to vote by post? (b)–Why have you not voted by post?
6	A person applying as proxy who is named in the proxy postal voters list	(a)–Did you apply to vote by post as proxy? (b)–Why have you not voted by post as proxy?

(2) In the case of an elector in respect of whom a notice has been issued under section 13B(3B) or (3D) of the 1983 Act, the references in the questions at entries 1(a) and 3(a), (b) and (c) to reading from the register must be taken as references to reading from the notice issued under those subsections.

(3) A ballot paper must not be delivered to any person required to answer any of the above questions unless he has answered each question satisfactorily.

(4) Except as authorised by this rule, no inquiry may be permitted as to the right of any person to vote.

Challenge of voter

38   A person must not be prevented from voting because–

    (a)   a candidate or his election or polling agent declares that he has reasonable cause to believe that the person has committed an offence of personation, or

    (b)   the person is arrested on the grounds that he is suspected of committing or of being about to commit such an offence.

Voting procedure

39 (1)   A ballot paper must be delivered to a voter who applies for one, and immediately before delivery–

    (a)   the number and (unless paragraph (2) applies) name of the elector as stated in the copy of the register of electors must be called out,

    (b)   the number of the elector must be marked on the list mentioned in rule 29(3)(e) beside the number of the ballot paper to be issued to him,

    (c)   a mark must be placed in the register of electors against the number of the elector to note that a ballot paper has been applied for but without showing the particular ballot paper which may be delivered,

    (d)   in the case of a person applying for a ballot paper as proxy, a mark must also be placed against his name in the list of proxies.

  (2)   In the case of an elector who has an anonymous entry, he must show the presiding officer his official poll card and only his number may be called out in pursuance of paragraph (1)(a).

  (3)   In the case of an elector who is added to the register in pursuance of a notice issued under section 13B(3B) or (3D) of the 1983 Act, paragraph (1) is modified as follows–

    (a)   in sub-paragraph (a), for "copy of the register of electors" substitute "copy of the notice issued under section 13B(3B) or (3D) of the 1983 Act",

    (b)   in sub-paragraph (c), for "in the register of electors" substitute "on the copy of the notice issued under section 13B(3B) or (3D) of the 1983 Act".

  (4)   The voter, on receiving the ballot paper, must forthwith proceed into one of the compartments in the polling station and there secretly mark his paper, and must then show to the presiding officer the back of the paper, so as to disclose the number and other unique identifying mark, and put the ballot paper into the ballot box in the presiding officer's presence, but so as to conceal his vote.

  (5)   The voter must vote without undue delay, and must leave the polling station as soon as he has put his ballot paper into the ballot box.

  (6)   A voter who has had a ballot paper delivered to him under paragraph (1), but has decided not to mark it, may return it to the presiding officer and where the voter does so, the presiding officer must–

    (a)   immediately cancel the ballot paper, and for the purposes of these rules treat it as a spoilt ballot paper,

    (b)   place a mark beside the number of that ballot paper on the corresponding number list to show that the ballot paper has been cancelled.

  (7)   The same copy of–

    (a)   the list of proxies,

    (b)   the register of electors,

    (c)   any notice issued under section 13B(3B) or (3D) of the 1983 Act (marked in the case of an elector who is added to the register in pursuance of such a notice),

    may be used for the election and each relevant election and referendum and one mark may be placed in the list, register or notice (as the case may be) to denote that a ballot paper has been delivered in respect of each election and referendum; except that, where a ballot paper has not been issued in respect of any election or referendum, a different mark must be placed in the list, register or notice so as to identify the election or referendum in respect of which a ballot paper was issued.

(8) At an ordinary election, the same copy of the list mentioned in rule 29(3)(e), may be used for each Authority election and one mark may be placed in the list, to denote that a ballot paper has been delivered in respect of each Authority election; except that, where a ballot paper has not been issued in respect of any Authority election, a different mark must be placed in the list, so as to identify the elections in respect of which a ballot paper was issued.

(9) A voter who at the close of the poll is in the polling station, or in a queue outside the polling station, for the purpose of voting must (despite the close of the poll) be entitled to apply for a ballot paper under paragraph (1); and these rules apply in relation to such a voter accordingly.

Votes marked by presiding officer

40 (1) The presiding officer, on the application of a voter–
   (a) who is incapacitated by blindness or other disability from voting in the manner directed by these Rules, or
   (b) who declares orally that he is unable to read,
must, in the presence of the polling agents, cause the voter's vote to be marked on a ballot paper in the manner directed by the voter, and the ballot paper to be placed in the ballot box.

(2) The name and number on the register of electors of every voter whose vote is marked in pursuance of this rule, and the reason why it is so marked, must be entered on a list (in these Rules called "the list of votes marked by the presiding officer").
In the case of a person voting as proxy for an elector, the number to be entered together with the voter's name must be the elector's number.

(3) In the case of a person in respect of whom a notice has been issued under section 13B(3B) or (3D) of the 1983 Act, paragraph (2) applies as if for "on the register of electors of every voter" there were substituted "relating to every voter in respect of whom a notice has been issued under section 13B(3B) or (3D) of the 1983 Act".

(4) The same list may be used for each relevant election or referendum, and where it is so used, an entry in that list must be taken to mean that the ballot papers were so marked in respect of each election or referendum, unless the list identifies the election or referendum at which the ballot paper was so marked.

Voting by persons with disabilities

41 (1) If a voter makes an application to the presiding officer to be allowed, on the ground of–
   (a) blindness or other disability, or
   (b) inability to read,
to vote with the assistance of another person by whom he is accompanied (in these Rules referred to as "the companion"), the presiding officer must require the voter to declare, orally or in writing, whether he is so incapacitated by his blindness or other disability, or by his inability to read, as to be unable to vote without assistance.

(2) If the presiding officer–
   (a) is satisfied that the voter is so incapacitated, and
   (b) is also satisfied by a written declaration made by the companion (in these Rules referred to as "the declaration made by the companion of a voter with disabilities") that the companion–
     (i) is a qualified person within the meaning of these Rules, and
     (ii) has not previously assisted more than one voter with disabilities to vote at

the election,

the presiding officer must grant the application, and then anything which is by these Rules required to be done to, or by that voter in connection with the giving of his vote may be done to, or with the assistance of, the companion.

(3) For the purpose of these Rules, a person is a voter with disabilities if he has made such a declaration as is mentioned in paragraph (1) above, and a person may be qualified to assist a voter with disabilities to vote if that person–
  (a) is a person who is entitled to vote as an elector at the election, or
  (b) is the father, mother, brother, sister, spouse, civil partner, son or daughter of the voter and has attained the age of 18 years.

(4) The name and number in the register of electors of every voter whose vote is given in accordance with this rule and the name and address of the companion must be entered on a list (in these Rules referred to as the "list of voters with disabilities assisted by companions").

In the case of a person voting as proxy for an elector, the number to be entered together with the voter's name must be the elector's number.

(5) In the case of a person in respect of whom a notice has been issued under section 13B(3B) or (3D) of the 1983 Act, paragraph (4) applies as if for "in the register of electors of every voter" there were substituted "relating to every voter in respect of whom a notice has been issued under section 13B(3B) or (3D) of the 1983 Act".

(6) The declaration made by the companion–
  (a) must be in the appropriate form,
  (b) must be made before the presiding officer at the time when the voter applies to vote with the assistance of a companion, and
  (c) must forthwith be given to the presiding officer who must attest and retain it.

(7) No fee or other payment may be charged in respect of the declaration.

(8) The same list of voters with disabilities assisted by companions may be used for each relevant election or referendum, and where it is so used, an entry in that list must be taken to mean that the votes were so given in respect of each election or referendum, unless the list identifies the election or referendum for which the vote was so given.

Tendered ballot papers: circumstances where available

42 (1) If a person, representing himself to be–
  (a) a particular elector named in the register and not named in the absent voters list, or
  (b) a particular person named in the list of proxies as proxy for an elector and not entitled to vote by post as proxy,

applies for a ballot paper after another person has voted in person either as the elector or his proxy, the applicant must, on satisfactorily answering the questions permitted by law to be asked at the poll, be entitled, subject to the following provisions of this rule and rule 43, to mark a ballot paper (in these Rules referred to as "a tendered ballot paper") in the same manner as any other voter.

(2) Paragraph (4) applies if–
  (a) a person applies for a ballot paper representing himself to be a particular elector named in the register,
  (b) he is also named in the postal voters list, and
  (c) he claims that he did not make an application to vote by post at the election.

(3) Paragraph (4) also applies if–
  (a) a person applies for a ballot paper representing himself to be a particular person named as a proxy in the list of proxies,

> (b) he is also named in the proxy postal voters list, and
>
> (c) he claims that he did not make an application to vote by post as proxy.

(4) The person must, on satisfactorily answering the questions permitted by law to be asked at the poll, be entitled, subject to the following provisions of this rule and rule 43, to mark a ballot paper (in these Rules referred to as a "tendered ballot paper") in the same manner as any other voter.

(5) Paragraph (6) applies if before the close of the poll but after the last time at which a person may apply for a replacement postal ballot paper, a person represents himself to be–

> (a) a particular elector named in the register who is also named in the postal voters list, or
>
> (b) a particular person named as a proxy in the list of proxies and who is also named in the proxy postal voters list,

and claims that he has lost or has not received his postal ballot paper.

(6) The person must, on satisfactorily answering the questions permitted by law to be asked at the poll, be entitled, subject to the provisions of this rule and rule 43, to mark a ballot paper (in these Rules referred to as a "tendered ballot paper") in the same manner as any other voter.

Tendered ballot papers: general provisions

43 (1) A tendered ballot paper must–

> (a) be of a colour differing from the other ballot papers,
>
> (b) instead of being put into the ballot box, be given to the presiding officer and endorsed by him with the name of the voter and his number on the register of electors, and set aside in a separate packet.

(2) The name of the voter and his number on the register of electors must be entered on a list (in these Rules referred to as the "tendered votes list").

(3) In the case of a person voting as proxy for an elector, the number to be endorsed or entered together with the voter's name must be the number of that elector.

(4) In the case of an elector who has an anonymous entry, this rule and rule 42 apply subject to the following modifications–

> (a) in paragraphs (1)(b) and (2) above, the references to the name of the voter must be ignored,
>
> (b) otherwise, a reference to a person named on a register or list must be construed as a reference to a person whose number appears in the register or list (as the case may be).

(5) In the case of a person in respect of whom a notice has been issued under section 13B(3B) or (3D) of the 1983 Act, this rule and rule 42 apply as if–

> (a) in rule 42(1)(a), (2)(a) and (5)(a), for "named in the register" there were substituted "in respect of whom a notice under section 13B(3B) or (3D) of the 1983 Act has been issued",
>
> (b) in paragraph (1)(b) of this rule for "his number in the register of electors" there were substituted "the number relating to him on a notice issued under section 13B(3B) or (3D) of the 1983 Act",
>
> (c) in paragraph (2) of this rule, for "his number in the register of electors" there were substituted "the number relating to him on a notice issued under section 13B(3B) or (3D) of the 1983 Act".

(6) The same list may be used for each relevant election or referendum, and where it is so used, an entry in that list must be taken to mean that tendered ballot papers were marked in respect of each election or referendum, unless the list identifies the election

or referendum at which a tendered ballot paper was marked.

Spoilt and replacement ballot papers

44 (1) A voter who has inadvertently dealt with his ballot paper in such manner that it cannot be conveniently used as a ballot paper may, on delivering it to the presiding officer and proving to his satisfaction the fact of the inadvertence, obtain a replacement for the ballot paper so delivered (in these Rules referred to as "a spoilt ballot paper"), and the spoilt ballot paper must be immediately cancelled.

(2) If a voter decides, after he has returned his ballot paper and it has been cancelled in accordance with rule 39(6), but before the close of the poll, that he wishes to vote in the election, he may obtain a replacement for the returned ballot paper.

(3) Before a replacement ballot paper is obtained, the presiding officer must mark the corresponding number list that was marked under rule 39(1) (the corresponding number list)–
    (a) in the case of a ballot paper being replaced under paragraph (1) or (2), beside the number of the replacement ballot paper obtained to show–
        (i) the number of the elector, and
        (ii) the number of the ballot paper which is being replaced; and
    (b) in the case of a ballot paper being replaced under paragraph (1), beside the number of the spoilt ballot paper to show that the ballot paper was replaced.

(4) Where the election is taken with a relevant election or referendum the voter must only receive a replacement for a spoilt or returned ballot paper.

(5) If the same corresponding number list is used for more than one Authority election in accordance with rule 39(8)–
    (a) the marks made under paragraph (3) must identify the election for which a ballot paper has been replaced, and
    (b) any ballot paper which the voter has not applied for or obtained as a replacement, but which bears the same ballot paper number as a ballot paper delivered under rule 39(1), or obtained under paragraph (1) or (2) of this rule–
        (i) must not be delivered to the voter,
        (ii) must be cancelled, and
        (iii) for the purposes of these rules, must be treated as a spoilt ballot paper.

Correction of errors on day of poll

45 (1) The presiding officer must keep a list of persons to whom ballot papers are delivered in consequence of an alteration to the register made by virtue of section 13B(3B) or (3D) of the 1983 Act which takes effect on the day of the poll.

(2) The same list may be used for each relevant election or referendum, and where it is so used, an entry in that list must be taken to mean that ballot papers were delivered in respect of each election or referendum, unless the list identifies the election or referendum at which a tendered ballot paper was marked.

Adjournment of poll in case of riot

46 (1) Where the proceedings at any polling station are interrupted or obstructed by riot or open violence, the presiding officer must adjourn the proceedings till the following day and must forthwith give notice to the CRO.

(2) Where the poll is adjourned at any polling station–
    (a) the hours of polling on the day to which it is adjourned must be the same as for the original day, and

(b) references in these Rules to the close of the poll must be construed accordingly.

(3) As soon as practicable after being informed of the adjournment of a poll, the CRO must inform the GLRO of that fact and of the cause of its adjournment.

(4) If the CRO does not discharge the functions specified in regulation 5 of the Combination of Polls Regulations, then references in this rule to the CRO must be read as references to the returning officer who discharges those functions.

Procedure on close of poll

47 (1) As soon as practicable after the close of the poll, the presiding officer must, in the presence of the polling agents appointed for the purposes of the election and each relevant election or referendum, make up into separate packets, sealed with his own seal and the seals of such polling agents as desire to affix their seals–

    (a) each ballot box in use at the station, sealed so as to prevent the introduction of additional ballot papers and unopened, but with the key attached,

    (b) the unused and spoilt ballot papers placed together,

    (c) the tendered ballot papers,

    (d) the marked copies of the register of electors (including any marked copy notices issued under section 13B(3B) or (3D) of the 1983 Act) and of the list of proxies,

    (e) the list prepared under rule 19, including the part completed in accordance with rule 39(1)(b) (together referred to in these Rules as "the completed corresponding number list"),

    (f) the certificates as to employment on duty on the day of the poll,

    (g) the tendered votes list, the list of voters with disabilities assisted by companions, the list of votes marked by the presiding officer, a statement of the number of voters whose votes are so marked by the presiding officer under the heads "disability" and "unable to read", the list maintained under rule 45, and the declarations made by the companions of voters with disabilities,

and must deliver the packets or cause them to be delivered to the CRO to be taken charge of by him; but if the packets are not delivered by the presiding officer personally to the CRO, the arrangements for their delivery must be approved by the CRO.

(2) The contents of the packets referred to in paragraph (1)(b), (c) and (f) must not be combined with the contents of the packets made under the corresponding rule that applies at any other relevant election or referendum except for an Authority election.

(3) The marked copies of the register of electors and of the list of proxies must be in one packet but must not be in the same packet as the completed corresponding number list or the certificates as to employment on duty on the day of the poll.

(4) The packets must be accompanied by a statement ("ballot paper account") showing the number of ballot papers entrusted to the presiding officer, and accounting for them under the heads–

    (a) ballot papers issued and not otherwise accounted for,

    (b) unused ballot papers,

    (c) spoilt ballot papers, and

    (d) tendered ballot papers.

(5) The statement referred to in paragraph (4) may be combined with the statements produced in relation to any other Authority election, but not with those for a relevant election or referendum, and the combined statement must be arranged in such manner as the GLRO may direct.

(6) Where the CRO does not discharge the functions specified in regulation 5 of the Combination of Polls Regulations, references in paragraph (1) to the CRO must be

taken as references to the returning officer who discharges those functions.

Attendance at verification and the counting of votes

48 (1) Where the CRO discharges the functions specified in regulation 5 of the Combination of Polls Regulations, he must–
(a) make arrangements for–
(i) carrying out the functions in rule 50(1) (separating ballot papers and verifying ballot paper accounts) at the election in the presence of the counting agents appointed for the purposes of the election and each relevant election and referendum as soon as practicable after the close of the poll, and
(ii) for counting the votes in the presence of the counting agents appointed for the purposes of the election,
(b) give to the counting agents appointed for the purposes of the election and each relevant election and referendum, notice in writing of the time and place at which he will begin carrying out the functions in rule 50(1).

(2) Where the CRO does not discharge the functions specified in regulation 5 of the Combination of Polls Regulations he must make arrangements for counting the votes in the presence of the counting agents appointed for the purposes of the election as soon as practicable after the delivery of the ballot papers to him by the returning officer who does discharge those functions; and the CRO must give to the counting agents for the election notice in writing of the time and place at which he will begin to count the votes.

(3) No person other than a person entitled to be present at the counting of the votes at the election and at each relevant election or referendum may be present at the proceedings under rule 50(1) (separating ballot papers and verifying ballot paper accounts) unless permitted by the CRO to attend.

(4) No person other than–
(a) the CRO and his clerks and technical assistants,
(b) the GLRO,
(c) the candidates and one other person chosen by each of them,
(d) the election agents,
(e) the counting agents,
(f) persons who are entitled to attend by virtue of any of sections 6A to 6D of the 2000 Act,
may be present at the counting of the votes in accordance with rule 50(2) to (14), unless permitted by the CRO to attend

(5) A person not entitled to attend at the separation and verification or the counting of the votes must not be permitted to do so by the CRO unless the CRO–
(a) is satisfied that the efficient separation and verification of the ballot paper accounts or, as the case may be, the efficient counting of the votes will not be impeded, and
(b) has either consulted the candidates or thought it impracticable to do so.

(6) The CRO must give the counting agents all such reasonable facilities for overseeing the proceedings, and all such information with respect to them, as he can give them consistently with the orderly conduct of the proceedings and the discharge of his duties in connection with them.

Use of the electronic counting system

49 (1) The GLRO may provide the CRO with an electronic counting system consisting of

computer hardware, software and other equipment or services, for the purpose of counting the number of ballot papers, to verify the ballot paper accounts and to count the votes cast on them.

(2) Any verification of ballot paper accounts, count or re-count at the election conducted using the electronic counting system must be conducted in accordance with rule 50.

(3) If the GLRO has provided the CRO with an electronic counting system for use at the election, the CRO must obtain the prior written consent of the GLRO before he may conduct the verification of ballot paper accounts or count the votes manually.

(4) If the verification of ballot paper accounts, count or re-count has commenced using the electronic counting system but has not been completed, the CRO may, if he considers it appropriate, discontinue the count and instead count the votes manually.

(5) Where the count or a re-count has been conducted using the electronic counting system, the CRO may, if he considers it appropriate, conduct any re-count without using that system.

(6) Where verification or any count or re-count is conducted using the electronic counting system, any of the steps referred to rule 50, in so far as practicable, may be undertaken–
   (a) concurrently with any other of those steps, or
   (b) in a different order.

Verification and the local count

50 (1) Where the CRO discharges the functions specified in regulation 5 of the Combination of Polls Regulations, he must–
   (a) in the presence of the counting agents appointed for the purposes of the election and each relevant election or referendum, open each ballot box from each polling station together, and record separately the number of ballot papers used in the election and each relevant election or referendum with which is it is taken,
   (b) in the presence of the counting agents appointed for the purposes of the election and each relevant election or referendum, verify each ballot paper account at the election and for each relevant election or referendum,
   (c) count such of the postal ballot papers as have been duly returned and record separately the number counted at the election and each relevant election or referendum,
   (d) where the same ballot boxes have been used for the election and each relevant election or referendum, separate the ballot papers for all of the Authority elections from those for any other relevant election or referendum.
   (e) make up into packets the ballot papers for each relevant election or referendum (not including those for any Authority election) and seal them up in separate containers endorsing on each a description of the area to which the ballot papers relate,
   (f) deliver or cause to be delivered to the returning officer for the relevant election or referendum to which the ballot papers relate–
      (i) those containers, together with a list of them and of the contents of each, and
      (ii) the ballot paper accounts together with a copy of the statement as to the result of their verification in respect of that relevant election or referendum, and
   (g) at the same time deliver to that officer the packets that so relate containing–
      (i) the unused and spoilt ballot papers,
      (ii) the tendered ballot papers, and

      (iii) the completed corresponding number lists of the used ballot papers and the certificates as to employment on duty on the day of the poll.

(2) Where the CRO does not discharge the functions specified in regulation 5 of the Combination of Polls Regulations, and the votes on the ballot papers are not to be counted concurrently with the votes on the ballot papers at a relevant election or referendum, he must–

     (a) on receipt of the containers of ballot papers from the returning officer who does discharge those functions, and after the time specified in the notice given by him in writing to the counting agents under rule 48(2), open each container in the presence of the counting agents;

     (b) where the proceedings on the issue and receipt of postal ballot papers at the election are not taken together with those proceedings at a relevant election or referendum under regulation 65 of the Representation of the People (England and Wales) Regulations 2001, or under that regulation as applied by regulations made under sections 44 and 105, or 45 and 105, of the Local Government Act 2000, count such of the postal ballot papers as have been duly returned and record the number counted,

and paragraph (10) below does not apply to these proceedings.

(3) Where separate ballot boxes are used for the ballots at the election and each relevant election and referendum, no vote for any candidate shall be rendered invalid by the ballot paper being placed in the ballot box used at any relevant election or referendum.

(4) Where the same ballot boxes are used for the election and other Authority elections, but not for other relevant elections or referendums–

     (a) the CRO must not mix the ballot papers for Authority elections from any ballot box or container with the contents of any other ballot box or container (including a postal ballot box) during the conduct of verification (where this occurs under paragraph (1)), the count or any re-count;

     (b) the ballot boxes from each polling station for the Authority elections shall be opened together and the ballot papers counted (but not necessarily the votes on them) and verified together.

(5) A postal ballot paper must not be taken to be duly returned unless–

     (a) it is returned in the manner set out in paragraph (6) and reaches the CRO or any polling station in the appropriate area (as defined in paragraph (7)) before the close of the poll,

     (b) the postal voting statement, duly signed, is also returned in the manner set out in paragraph (6) and reaches him or such polling station before that time,

     (c) the postal voting statement also states the date of birth of the elector or proxy (as the case may be), and

     (d) in a case where the steps for verifying the date of birth and signature of an elector or proxy have been prescribed by regulations made under the 1983 Act, the CRO (having taken such steps) verifies the date of birth and signature of the elector or proxy (as the case may be).

(6) The manner in which any postal paper or postal voting statement may be returned–

     (a) to the CRO, is by hand or by post,

     (b) to a polling station in the appropriate area, is by hand.

(6A) A postal ballot paper or postal voting statement that reaches the CRO or a polling station in the appropriate area at or after the close of the poll is treated for the purposes of paragraph (5) as reaching that officer or polling station before the close of the poll if it is delivered by a person who, at the close of the poll, is in the polling station, or in a queue outside the polling station, for the purpose of returning it.

(7) For the purposes of paragraphs (5), (6) and (6A), "polling station in the appropriate area" means a polling station–

    (a) in the area which is common to the Assembly constituency, and parliamentary constituency, local counting area, electoral area or voting area, as the case may be, in which the polls at the Authority election and a relevant election or referendum are being taken together, and

    (b) in respect of which polls the voter has been issued with a postal ballot paper.

(8) After completing the proceedings under paragraph (1) or (2), the CRO must cause the electronic counting system to process the ballot papers for the election so as to count–

    (a) the number of ballot papers, and

    (b) votes given on the ballot papers.

(9) The CRO must not cause the electronic counting system to count any tendered ballot paper.

(10) Subject to paragraph (11), the CRO must verify each ballot paper account by comparing it with the number of ballot papers recorded by him, and the unused and spoilt ballot papers in his possession and the tendered votes list (opening and re-sealing the packets containing the unused and spoilt ballot papers and the tendered votes list) and must draw up a statement as to the result of the verification, which any election agent may copy.

(11) The CRO may verify each ballot paper account for the election by comparing it with the number of ballot papers processed by the electronic counting system, and the unused and spoilt ballot papers in his possession and the tendered votes list (opening and re-sealing the packets containing the unused and spoilt ballot papers and the tendered votes list).

(12) The CRO, while verifying the ballot paper accounts and counting the votes, must take all proper precautions for preventing any person from seeing the numbers and unique identifying marks printed on the back of the papers.

(13) The CRO must so far as practicable proceed continuously with counting the votes, allowing only time for refreshment, except that the hours between 5 in the afternoon and 10 on the following morning may be excluded with the prior consent of the GLRO.

(14) During the time so excluded the CRO must–

    (a) place the ballot papers and other documents relating to the election under his own seal and the seals of such of the counting agents as desire to affix their seals, and

    (b) otherwise take proper precautions for the security of the papers and documents.

Rejected ballot papers

51 (1) Any ballot paper–

    (a) which does not bear the official mark,

    (b) on which votes are given for more than one party or individual candidate,

    (c) on which anything is written or marked by which the voter can be identified except the printed number and other unique identifying mark on the back,

    (d) which is unmarked, or

    (e) which is void for uncertainty,

is, subject to paragraph (2), void and must not be counted.

(2) A ballot paper on which the vote is marked–

    (a) elsewhere than in the proper place, or

    (b) otherwise than by means of a cross, or

    (c) by more than one mark,

must not for such reason be void if an intention that the vote be given for one only of the party or individual candidates clearly appears, and the way the paper is marked does not itself identify the voter and it is not shown that he can be identified by it.

(3) Where the electronic counting system identifies a ballot paper that has been marked, but which appears for whatever reason to be void, it must be examined by a clerk appointed by the CRO in the manner referred to in paragraph (6).

(4) If the clerk, having examined the ballot, considers that the vote is void then the CRO must examine it in the manner referred to in paragraph (6).

(5) After the CRO examines the ballot paper, he must give his decision as to the validity of the vote.

(6) An examination under paragraph (3) or (4) is to be made by the clerk or CRO examining an image of the ballot paper which is shown on a screen so as to be visible to those attending the count.

(7) The CRO may examine any ballot paper that he is not required to examine in accordance with paragraph (4)–
    (a) either in the manner referred to in paragraph (6), or
    (b) by examining a paper copy,
and where the CRO does so, he must give a decision on that paper in accordance with paragraph (5).

(8) No person attending the count is to be entitled to require the clerk or CRO to examine a ballot paper or to provide a paper copy for inspection.

(9) A record of the CRO's decision must be retained in the electronic counting system together with, in the case of a decision that the ballot paper is void, his reasons by reference to paragraph (1).

(10) Where a counting agent objects to the CRO's decision the CRO must record on the electronic counting system that the decision was objected to.

(11) The CRO must draw up a statement showing the number of ballot papers rejected under the several heads of–
    (a) want of an official mark,
    (b) voting for more than one party or individual candidate,
    (c) writing or mark by which the voter could be identified,
    (d) unmarked ballot paper, or
    (e) void for uncertainty.

(12) As soon as practicable after the completion of the statement under paragraph (11) the CRO must inform–
    (a) such candidates, election agents and counting agents as are present at the count, and
    (b) the GLRO,
of its contents.

Decision on ballot papers

52 The decision of the CRO on any question arising in respect of a ballot paper is final, but may be subject to review on an election petition.

Re-count

53 (1) A candidate or his election agent (including, in the case of a list candidate, the election agent for that list) or a counting agent authorised under rule 31(3) may, if present when the counting or any re-count of the votes is completed, require the CRO to have the votes re-counted or again re-counted but the CRO may refuse to do so if in his

opinion the request is unreasonable.

(2) No step may be taken on the completion of the counting or any re-count of votes until the candidates and election agents and counting agents authorised under rule 31(1) present at its completion have been given a reasonable opportunity to exercise the right conferred by this rule.

(3) The CRO may determine the extent to which any re-count involves the electronic counting of votes.

(4) When the returning officer uses the electronic counting system for the re-counting of votes, he must not re-consider any decision made on any ballot paper under rule 51(5).

Procedure at conclusion of local count

54 (1) As soon as practicable after the conclusion of the local count (including any re-count), the CRO must draw up a statement showing–
    (a) the total number of votes cast,
    (b) the total number of votes rejected under rule 51,
    (c) the number of votes given for each registered party, and
    (d) the number of votes cast for each individual candidate.

(2) As soon as practicable after the statement is drawn up under paragraph (1), the CRO must inform the GLRO of its contents, and if it is practicable to do so, must also provide that information so as to show the total number of votes under each of those heads in each ward.

(3) Where practicable, the CRO must provide the information in the statement under paragraph (1) to the GLRO so as to show and the number of rejected ballot papers in each ward.

(4) As soon as practicable after the GLRO has authorised him to do so, the CRO must–
    (a) inform such of the candidates and their election agents as are then present of the content of the statements prepared in accordance with rule 51 and paragraph (1) of this rule, and
    (b) give public notice of the contents of those statements.

Attendance at allocation of seats

55 (1) The GLRO must make arrangements for making the allocation of seats in the presence of the election agents of the individual candidates (including, in the case of a list candidate, the election agent for that list); and he must give to those agents notice in writing of the time and place at which he will begin the allocation.

(2) No person other than–
    (a) the GLRO and his clerks,
    (b) the CROs and a clerk or technical assistant chosen by each of them,
    (c) the individual candidates and one person chosen by each of them,
    (d) candidates included on a party list and one person chosen by each of them,
    (e) the election agents,
    (f) the nominating officers of those registered parties standing nominated at the election,
    (g) persons who are entitled to attend by virtue of any of sections 6A to 6D of the 2000 Act,
    (h) persons permitted to be present at the central calculation at the election of the Mayor of London,
may be present at an allocation, unless permitted by the GLRO to attend.

(3) A person not entitled to attend an allocation must not be permitted to do so by the

GLRO unless the GLRO–

(a) is satisfied that the efficiency of the allocation will not be impeded, and

(b) has either consulted the election agents or thought it impracticable to do so.

The calculation

56 (1) As soon as the GLRO has received from every CRO the information required by rule 54 he must calculate the London figure for each registered party and individual candidate.

(2) As soon as the GLRO has ascertained the result of the calculation, he must inform such of the election agents for the candidates as are then present of the relevant figures and must give them a reasonable opportunity to satisfy themselves as to the accuracy of the calculation.

(3) Where information of the description mentioned in paragraph (4)(e) is given in accordance with paragraph (2), the GLRO must provide the persons to whom it was given with a statement containing–

(a) the names of the persons concerned, and

(b) with respect to each such person, the name of the party from whose list his name has been omitted or treated as omitted, and the reason therefor.

(4) In this rule, "the relevant figures" means–

(a) the number of London votes given in the Assembly constituencies for each registered party and individual candidate at that election,

(b) in respect of each party, the number of successful candidates to be constituency members, who were the subject of that party's authorisation under rule 6(5) or 6(7) of the Constituency Members Election Rules,

(c) the calculation of the London figure,

(d) any recalculation required by paragraph 8(3), or carried out in the circumstances mentioned in paragraph 8(8), of Schedule 2 to the 1999 Act, and

(e) the number of persons whose names have been omitted from, or (pursuant to paragraph 8(10) of Schedule 2 to the 1999 Act) who are to be treated as ceasing to be on, a party list.

(5) Paragraph (6) applies where the GLRO is notified under rule 54(5) of the Constituency Members Election Rules that a candidate who is returned as a constituency member is the candidate with a description authorised under rule 6(7)(a) of those Rules (a using a description registered by more than one party).

(6) Where this paragraph applies, the GLRO must, in calculating the London figure of each registered party whose nominating officer issued a certificate to which rule 6(7)(a) of the Constituency Members Election Rules refers, include that candidate as a candidate of that party; and in doing so must disregard the fact that for the purposes of calculating the London figure of another registered party, the candidate is also included as the candidate of that other registered party.

Part 5
Final Proceedings in Contested and Uncontested Elections

Declaration of result

57 (1) The GLRO must declare the allocation of the seats for London members and, where seats are allocated to a registered party, the names of the persons on the party list who, in accordance with paragraph 8(5) of Schedule 2 to the 1999 Act, are to fill those seats.

(2) The GLRO must give public notice of–

(a)   the registered parties to which seats for London members have been allocated and the names of the list candidates by whom those seats are to be filled,

(b)   the names of the successful individual candidates,

(c)   the total number of London votes given for each registered party and individual candidate,

(d)   the total number of candidates of registered parties returned as constituency members,

(e)   the number of rejected ballot papers under each head shown in the statement of rejected ballot papers,

(f)   the name of every person included on a party list who has been omitted from, or (pursuant to paragraph 8(10) of Schedule 2 to the 1999 Act) is to be treated as ceasing to be on, that list, together with the reason for the omission or cessation, as the case may be.

(3)   Subject to paragraph (4), after the GLRO complies with paragraphs (1) and (2), he may give public notice of the information referred to paragraph (2)(c) and (e) so as to set out the number of votes falling under each of those heads, in respect of each ward.

(4)   Where the sum of votes given for all registered parties and individual candidates in any ward does not exceed 500, the GLRO must not give notice under paragraph (3) in respect of that ward alone, but must amalgamate the figures for that ward with those for any other ward in which more than 500 votes have been given, in the same Assembly constituency.

Return or forfeiture of candidate's deposit

58 (1)   Unless forfeited in accordance with paragraph (5), the deposit made under rule 10 must be returned to the person making it or his personal representative.

(2)   Subject to paragraph (4), the deposit must be returned not later than the next day after that on which the result of the election is declared.

(3)   For the purposes of paragraph (2)–

(a)   a day must be disregarded if, in accordance with rule 4, it would be disregarded in computing any period of time for the purposes of the timetable for the election, and

(b)   the deposit will be treated as being returned on a day if a cheque for the amount of the deposit is posted on that day.

(4)   If the individual candidate or registered party is not shown as standing nominated in the statement of persons nominated, or if proof has been given to the GLRO before the allocation of seats of the death of an individual candidate, then the deposit must be returned as soon as practicable after the publication of the statement or after the individual candidate's death, as the case may be.

(5)   Where a poll is taken, if, after the declaration under rule 57, a candidate or registered party is found not to have polled more than one-fortieth of the total number of votes polled by all the candidates and registered parties, the deposit must be forfeited to the Greater London Authority.

Part 6
Disposal of Documents

Sealing up of ballot papers

59 (1)   On the completion of the counting at a contested election the CRO must seal up in separate packets the counted and rejected ballot papers.

(2) Where some or all of the votes have been counted using the electronic counting system, the CRO must also seal up in a separate packet a complete electronic record ("the electronic record") of the information stored in the electronic counting system, held in such device as may be suitable for the purpose of its storage.

(3) After making the electronic record under paragraph (2), the CRO must arrange for the original records in the electronic counting system to be removed from it and destroyed in a manner that ensures that the secrecy of those records is preserved.

(4) The CRO must not open the sealed packets of–
    (a) tendered ballot papers, or
    (b) certificates as to employment on duty on the day of the poll.

(5) Where the CRO discharges the functions referred to in regulation 5 of the Combination of Polls Regulations, he must also not open the sealed packets of–
    (a) the completed corresponding number lists,
    (b) marked copies of the register of electors (including any marked copy notices issued under section 13B(3B) or (3D) of the 1983 Act) and lists of proxies.

Delivery and retention of documents

60 (1) The CRO must then forward the following documents to the relevant registration officer–
    (a) the packets of ballot papers in his possession,
    (b) the packet containing the electronic record (if any),
    (c) the ballot paper accounts and the statements of rejected ballot papers and of the result of the verification of the ballot paper accounts,
    (d) the tendered votes lists, the lists of voters with disabilities assisted by companions, the lists of votes marked by the presiding officer and the related statements, the lists maintained under rule 45 and the declarations made by the companions of voters with disabilities,
    (e) the packets of the completed corresponding number lists,
    (f) the packets of certificates as to employment on duty on the day of the poll, and
    (g) the packets containing marked copies of registers (including any marked copy notices issued under section 13B(3B) or (3D) of the 1983 Act) and of the postal voters list, of the lists of proxies and of the proxy postal voters list,
endorsing on each packet a description of its contents, the date of the election to which they relate and the name of the Assembly constituency for which the election was held.

(2) At an election where the returning officer does not discharge the functions referred to in regulation 5 of the Combination of Polls Regulations, paragraph (1) must have effect as if sub paragraphs (d), (e) and (f) were omitted.

Orders for production of documents

61 (1) An order–
    (a) for the inspection or production of any rejected ballot papers in the custody of the relevant registration officer, or
    (b) for the opening of a packet containing the electronic record or a sealed packet of completed corresponding number lists or certificates as to employment on duty on the day of the poll or the inspection of any counted ballot papers in the custody of the relevant registration officer,
may be made by a county court, if the court is satisfied by evidence on oath that the order is required for the purpose of instituting or maintaining a prosecution for an offence in relation to ballot papers, or for the purpose of an election petition.

(2)   An election court may make an order for the opening of a packet containing the electronic record or a sealed packet of completed corresponding number lists or certificates or for the inspection of any counted ballot papers in the custody of the relevant registration officer.

(3)   An order under this rule may be made subject to such conditions as to–
    (a)   persons,
    (b)   time,
    (c)   place and mode of inspection,
    (d)   production or opening,
as the court making the order thinks expedient; but in making and carrying into effect an order for the opening of a packet containing the electronic record or a packet of completed corresponding number lists or certificates or for the inspection of counted ballot papers, care must be taken that the way in which the vote of any particular elector has been given must not be disclosed until it has been proved–
    (i)   that his vote was given, and
    (ii)   that the vote has been declared by a competent court to be invalid.

(4)   An appeal lies to the High Court from any order of a county court under this rule.

(5)   Any power given under this rule to a county court may be exercised by any judge of the court otherwise than in open court.

(6)   Where an order is made for the production by the relevant registration officer of any document or electronic record in his custody relating to any specified election–
    (a)   the production by him or his agent of the document or electronic record ordered in such manner as may be directed by that order will be conclusive evidence that the document or electronic record relates to the specified election, and
    (b)   any endorsement on any packet of ballot papers so produced will be *prima facie* evidence that the ballot papers are what they are stated to be by the endorsement.

(7)   The production from proper custody of–
    (a)   a ballot paper purporting to have been used at any election, or
    (b)   a copy of the electronic record which purports to record that a particular ballot paper was used at any election, and
a completed corresponding number list with a number written beside the number of the ballot paper, will be *prima facie* evidence that the elector whose vote was given by that ballot paper was the person who, at the time of the election, had affixed to his entry in the register of electors or on the notice issued under section 13B(3B) or (3D) of the 1983 Act, the same number as was written on the completed corresponding number list.

(8)   The Electoral Commission may require the production and opening of any sealed packet of ballot papers and of any sealed packet containing an electronic copy of information made pursuant to rule 59(2), but only–
    (a)   in connection with any review which they are conducting under section 6(2) of the 2000 Act, and
    (b)   if the request that they undertake that review includes a request that they examine ballot papers.

(9)   In their review of any documents or records to which they have access by virtue of paragraph (8), the Electoral Commission must take care to ensure that the way in which a particular elector has given their vote is not ascertained.

(10) At the termination of their review, the Electoral Commission must re-seal in their packets the documents and records produced under paragraph (8), return them to the

relevant registration officer, and destroy any copies of those documents and records that have been made.

(11) Unless authorised by this rule, no person may be allowed to inspect any rejected or counted ballot papers in the custody of the relevant registration officer or open any sealed packets of completed corresponding number lists, certificates of employment on the day of the poll or containing the electronic record.

Retention and destruction of documents and records

62 The relevant registration officer must retain or cause to be retained for one year all documents and, where applicable, the electronic record relating to an election forwarded to him in pursuance of these Rules by a CRO, and then, unless otherwise directed by an order of a county court, a Crown Court, a magistrate's court or an election court, must cause them to be destroyed.

Part 7
List Candidates and the Filling of Vacancies

Interpretation of Part 7

63 In this Part–
"dual candidate" means a person–
    (a) whose name, subject to rule 65, falls to be notified as mentioned in subsection (6) of section 11 of the 1999 Act, and
    (b) who is a candidate (otherwise than at an ordinary election) for election–
        (i) as the Mayor of London, or
        (ii) as a constituency member,
"nominating officer", in relation to a registered party and a vacancy in the office of a London member, means the person who holds that office in the party at the time at which the vacancy arises; and
"paragraph (1) notice" has the meaning given by rule 65(1).

Removal from a party list on election as Mayor or as a constituency member

64 (1) Where a person whose name is for the time being included in a party list is elected (otherwise than at an ordinary election)–
    (a) as the Mayor of London, or
    (b) as a constituency member,
his name must be removed from that list.

(2) For the purposes of this Part, the name of a person to whom paragraph (1) applies must be treated as ceasing to be included in the list from the date on which he is returned as the Mayor or a constituency member, as the case may be (even if his return is void).

(3) Where proof is given to the GLRO's satisfaction that a person whose name is for the time being included in a party list has died, then the GLRO must remove that person's name from that list.

Notification of vacancy

65 (1) As soon as the office of a London member who was returned from a registered party's list becomes vacant, the GLRO must simultaneously give or send to–
    (a) the party's nominating officer, and
    (b) the person whose name would, in accordance with subsection (6) of section 11

of the 1999 Act (filling a vacancy among the London members) (and on the assumption that he satisfies the conditions in subsection (4)), be so notified, written notice ("paragraph (1) notice") of the matters specified in paragraph (2).

(2) The matters specified in this paragraph are–
    (a) the vacancy,
    (b) that the nominating officer may, by notice in writing delivered to the GLRO not later than one month after the date of the paragraph (1) notice, give the notice referred to in subsection (5)(b) of section 11 of the 1999 Act, and
    (c) that the person must, by notice in writing delivered to the GLRO not later than one month after the date of the paragraph (1) notice, indicate whichever of the following apply to him–
        (i)   that he is willing to serve as a London member ("notice of willingness"),
        (ii) that he is not willing to serve as a London member, and
        (iii) that he is a dual candidate.

(3) The GLRO must not notify the Chair of the London Assembly as mentioned in section 11(3) of the 1999 Act until–
    (a) the period mentioned in paragraph (2)(b) has elapsed, and
    (b) he has received a notice of willingness, and
    (c) if the person by whom notice of willingness has been given is a dual candidate, the result of the election for which he is a Mayoral or constituency member candidate has been declared.

Unwilling candidate or objection by registered party

66   Where the GLRO receives a notice under rule 65(2)(c)(ii) or section 11(5)(b) of the 1999 Act he must again send a paragraph (1) notice, but with the substitution, for the name of the person to whom the first such notice was sent, of the name of the person who, on the same assumption, would be the next person whose name would be notified in accordance with section 11(6) of that Act; and so on until, in respect of such a person–
    (a) no notice is given under section 11(5)(b) of that Act, and
    (b) a notice of willingness has been received.

Acceptance of office and further notification

67 (1) As soon as practicable after the GLRO has identified the person who is to fill the vacancy, he must invite him to attend at his office to sign the declaration of acceptance of office.

(2) In a case to which section 11(3) of the 1999 Act applies, as soon as practicable after the declaration of acceptance of office has been signed, the GLRO must notify the Chair of the London Assembly as mentioned in that subsection.

Part 8
Returns and Declarations as to Election Expenses

Declarations as to election expenses

68 (1) Subject to paragraph (2), the form of the declaration required by section 82(1) of the 1983 Act (agent's declaration as to election expenses), in the circumstances mentioned in subsection (2A)(a) of that section, is that set out in part 1 of Form 20 of the Forms Schedule.

(2) In a case to which section 82(5A) of the 1983 Act applies, the declaration referred to in paragraph (1) must be modified as specified in part 2 of Form 20.

(3) Subject to paragraph (4), the form of the declaration required by section 82(2) of the

1983 Act (candidate's declaration as to election expenses), in the circumstances mentioned in subsection (2A)(b) of that section must be that set out in part 1 of the Form 21 of the Forms Schedule.

(4) In a case to which section 82(5A) of the 1983 Act applies, the declaration referred to in paragraph (3) must be modified as specified in part 2 of Form 21.

SCHEDULE 7
THE MAYORAL ELECTION RULES

Rule 5(5)

Part 1
General Provisions

Part 1
General Provisions

Citation

1   This Schedule may be cited as the Mayoral Election Rules.

Interpretation

2 (1)   In the rules in this Schedule, unless the context indicates otherwise–
        "candidate" means a candidate to be the Mayor;
        "Combination of Polls Regulations" means the Representation of the People
        (Combination of Polls) (England and Wales) Regulations 2004;
        "counting observer" has the same meaning as in regulation 2 of the Referendum

Regulations;

"counting officer" has the same meaning as in regulation 9 of the Referendum Regulations;

"election" mean an election for the return of the Mayor;

"electoral area" where the Authority election is held together with a referendum, includes a voting area where the referendum is held;

"European Parliamentary election" has the same meaning as in section 27(1) of the Representation of the People Act 1985;

"local authority mayoral election" means an election conducted under the Local Authorities (Mayoral Elections) (England and Wales) Regulations 2007;

"local counting area" has the same meaning as in regulation 2(1) of the European Parliamentary Elections Regulations 2004;

"petition organiser" has the same meaning as in regulation 3 of the Local Authorities (Referendums) (Petitions and Directions) (England) Regulations 2000;

"polling observer" has the same meaning as in regulation 2 of the Referendum Regulations;

"referendum" means a referendum conducted under the Referendum Regulations;

"Referendum Regulations" means the Local Authorities (Conduct of Referendums) (England) Regulations 2007;

"relevant election or referendum" means one or more of the following–

- (a) a Parliamentary election,
- (b) a European Parliamentary election,
- (c) a local government election (including another Authority election where more than one is taken together),
- (d) a local authority mayoral election or referendum in accordance with regulations made under sections 44 and 105, or 45 and 105, of the Local Government Act 2000;

"voting area" has the same meaning as in regulation 2 of the Referendum Regulations.

(2) In the case of a referendum, a reference to a–
- (a) "candidate" shall be construed as a reference to a counting observer,
- (b) "election agent" shall be construed as a reference to a counting observer,
- (c) "polling agent" shall be construed as a reference to polling observer,
- (d) "returning officer" shall be construed as a reference to a counting officer.

(3) Reference to a rule by number alone is a reference to the rule so numbered in this Schedule.

Part 2
Provisions as to Time

Timetable

3   The proceedings at the election must be conducted in accordance with the following timetable:

Timetable

Proceedings	Time
Publication of notice of election	Not later than the thirtieth day before the day of election.
Delivery of nomination papers	Not later than 4 in the afternoon on the twenty-fourth day before the day of election.
Delivery of notices of withdrawals of candidature	Not later than 4 in the afternoon on the twenty-fourth day before the day

	of election
Publication of statement as to persons nominated	Not later than 4 in the afternoo on the twenty-second day before the day of election.
Notice of poll	Not later than the sixth day before the day of election.
Polling	Between the hours of 7 in the morning and 10 at night on the day of election.

Computation of time

4 (1)   In computing any period of time for the purposes of the timetable–
      (a)   a Saturday or Sunday,
      (b)   Christmas Eve, Christmas Day, Good Friday or a bank holiday, or
      (c)   a day appointed for public thanksgiving or mourning,
must be disregarded, and any such day must not be treated as a day for the purpose of any proceedings up to the completion of the poll nor must the CRO be obliged to proceed with the counting of the votes on such a day.

(2)   In this rule, "bank holiday" means a day which is a bank holiday under the Banking and Financial Dealings Act 1971 in England and Wales.

Part 3
Stages Common to Contested and Uncontested Elections

Notice of election

5 (1)   The GLRO must publish in each Assembly constituency notice of the election stating–
      (a)   the place and times at which nomination papers are to be delivered, and
      (b)   the date of the poll in the event of a contest,
and the notice must state that forms of nomination papers may be obtained at that place and those times.

(2)   The notice of election must state the arrangements (if any) which apply for the payment of the deposit required by rule 9 by means of the electronic transfer of funds.

(3)   The notice of election must state the date by which–
      (a)   applications to vote by post or proxy, and
      (b)   other applications and notices about postal or proxy voting,
must reach the registration officer for local government electors in order that they may be effective for the election.

Nomination of candidates

6 (1)   Each candidate must be nominated by a separate nomination paper, which must be–
      (a)   in the appropriate form, and
      (b)   delivered to the place fixed for the purpose by the GLRO, which must be at one of the offices of the Greater London Authority before the last time for the delivery of nomination papers.

(2)   A nomination paper must state the candidate's–
      (a)   full names,
      (b)   home address, in full, and
      (c)   if desired, description,
and the surname must be placed first in the list of names.

(3)   If a candidate commonly uses–

(a) a surname which is different from any other surname he has, or

(b) a forename which is different from any other forename he has,

the nomination paper may state the commonly used surname or forename, or both surname and forename, in addition to the other name.

(4) The description (if any) can only be–

    (a) one authorised as mentioned in paragraph (5) or (7), or

    (b) the word "Independent".

(5) A nomination paper may not include a description of a candidate that is likely to lead electors to associate the candidate with a registered party unless–

    (a) the party is a qualifying party in relation to Greater London, and

    (b) the description is authorised by a certificate–

        (i) issued by or on behalf of the registered nominating officer of the party, and

        (ii) received by the GLRO before the last time for the delivery of nomination papers set out in the timetable in rule 3.

(6) In paragraph (5) an authorised description may be either–

    (a) the name of the party registered under section 28 of the 2000 Act, or

    (b) a description of the party registered under section 28A of that Act.

(7) A nomination paper may not include a description of a candidate which is likely to lead electors to associate the candidate with two or more registered political parties unless the parties are each qualifying parties in relation to Greater London and the description is a registered description authorised by a certificate–

    (a) issued by or on behalf of the registered nominating officer of each of the parties, and

    (b) received by the GLRO before the last time for the delivery of nomination papers set out in the timetable in rule 3.

(8) For the purposes of paragraph (7), a description is a registered description if it is a description registered for use by the parties under section 28B of the 2000 Act.

(9) A person will be guilty of a corrupt practice if he fraudulently purports to be authorised to issue a certificate under paragraph (5) or (7) on behalf of a registered party's nominating officer.

(10) For the purposes of the application of these rules in relation to an election–

    (a) "registered party" means a party which was registered under Part 2 of the 2000 Act on the day ("the relevant day") which is two days before the last day for the delivery of nomination papers at that election,

    (b) a registered party is a qualifying party in relation to Greater London if on the relevant day the party was registered in respect of England in the Great Britain register maintained under that Part of that Act.

(11) For the purposes of paragraph (10)(a), any day falling within rule 4(1) must be disregarded.

Subscription of nomination papers

7 (1) The nomination paper of a candidate must be subscribed by at least 330 persons each of whom is entitled to vote at the election; and in relation to each London borough and the City, at least ten of the subscribers must be electors who are ordinarily resident in the borough or, as the case may be, the City.

(2) Where a nomination paper has the signatures of more than the required number of persons as assenting to the nomination of a candidate, the signatures (up to the required number) appearing first on the paper must be taken into account to the exclusion of any others.

(3)   The nomination paper must give the electoral number of each person subscribing it.

(3A) A person must not subscribe more than one nomination paper at the same election.

(3B) Paragraph (3A) does not prevent a person subscribing a further nomination paper where the previously nominated candidate has either died or withdrawn.

(4)   The GLRO–
  (a)   must supply any elector with as many forms of nomination paper and forms of consent to nomination as may be required at the place and during the time for delivery of nomination papers, and
  (b)   must, at any elector's request, prepare a nomination paper for signature,
  but it is not necessary for a nomination or consent to nomination to be on a form supplied by the GLRO.

(5)   In this rule–
  "elector" means a person named as a local government elector in the register being used at the election in that Assembly constituency, and includes a person shown in the register as below voting age if it appears from the register that he will be of voting age on the day fixed for the poll, but does not include a person who has an anonymous entry in the register, and
  "electoral number" means–
  (a)   a person's number in that register, or
  (b)   pending publication of the register, his number (if any) in the electors list for that register.

Consent to nomination

8 (1)   A person will not be validly nominated unless his consent to nomination–
  (a)   is given in writing in the appropriate form, or a form to like effect, on or within one month before the last day for the delivery of nomination papers;
  (b)   is attested by one witness whose name and address must be given; and
  (c)   is delivered at the place and within the time for delivery of nomination papers.

(2)   A candidate's consent given under this rule must–
  (a)   state the day, month and year of his birth; and
  (b)   contain a statement that to the best of the candidate's knowledge and belief he is not disqualified from being elected by reason of–
    (i)   any disqualification set out in section 21 (disqualification from being the Mayor or an Assembly member) of the 1999 Act,
    (ii)   a decision made under section 78A of the Local Government Act 2000 (decisions of First-tier tribunal), or
    (iii) an order made under section 34(4) of the Localism Act 2011(offences).

Deposits

9 (1)   A person will not be validly nominated as a candidate unless the sum of £10,000 is deposited by him or on his behalf with the GLRO at the place and during the time for delivery of nomination papers.

(2)   The deposit may be made either–
  (a)   by the deposit of any legal tender, or
  (b)   by means of a banker's draft, or
  (c)   with the GLRO's consent, in any other manner including by means of a debit or credit card or the electronic transfer of funds,
  but the GLRO may refuse to accept a deposit sought to be made by means of a banker's draft if he does not know that the drawer carries on business as a banker in the United Kingdom.

(3)   Where the deposit is made on behalf of the candidate, the person making the deposit must at the time he makes it give his name and address to the GLRO, unless they have previously been given to him under section 67 (appointment of election agent) of the 1983 Act.

Decisions as to validity of nomination papers

10 (1)   Where a nomination paper and the candidate's consent to it are delivered, and the deposit is made, in accordance with these Rules, the candidate must be deemed to stand nominated unless and until–
    (a)   the GLRO decides that the nomination paper is invalid, or
    (b)   proof is given to the GLRO's satisfaction of the candidate's death, or
    (c)   the candidate withdraws.

(2)   The GLRO is entitled to hold the nomination paper of a person invalid only on one of the following grounds–
    (a)   that the particulars of the candidate or of the persons subscribing the paper are not as required by law,
    (b)   that the paper is not subscribed as so required, and
    (c)   that the paper breaks rule 6(5) or (7).

(2A)   If, contrary to rule 7(3A), a person subscribes more than one nomination paper the GLRO, in determining whether a paper is subscribed as so required under paragraph (2)(b)–
    (a)   must only take the person's signature into account in respect of the first nomination paper delivered under rule 6(1)(b) on which the person's signature appears,
    (b)   must, where the person's signature appears on a nomination paper delivered subsequently, find that the paper is not subscribed as so required if the signature appears within the first 330 signatures on the paper, regardless of whether the paper contains more than 330 signatures.

(3)   Subject to paragraph (4), the GLRO must, as soon as practicable after each nomination paper has been delivered, examine it and decide whether the candidate has been validly nominated.

(4)   If in the GLRO's opinion a nomination paper breaks rule 6(5) or (7), he must give a decision to that effect–
    (a)   as soon as practicable after the delivery of the nomination paper, and
    (b)   in any event, before the end of the period of 24 hours starting with the end of the period for the delivery of nomination papers set out in the timetable in rule 3.

(5)   Where the GLRO decides that a nomination paper is invalid, he must endorse and sign on the paper the fact and the reasons for his decision.

(6)   The GLRO must, as soon as practicable after making such a decision in accordance with paragraph (3) or (4) that a nomination paper is valid or invalid, send notice of it to the candidate at his home address as given in his nomination paper.

(7)   The GLRO's decision that a nomination paper is valid is final and may not be questioned in any proceeding whatsoever.

(8)   Subject to paragraph (7), nothing in this rule prevents the validity of a nomination being questioned on an election petition.

Publication of statement of persons nominated

11 (1)   The GLRO must prepare and publish a statement showing the persons who have been

and stand nominated and any other persons who have been nominated together with the reason why they no longer stand nominated.

(2) The statement must show the names, addresses and descriptions of the persons nominated as given in their nomination papers.

(3) If a person's nomination paper gives a commonly used surname or forename, or both surname and forename in addition to another name, the statement must show the person's commonly used surname or forename, or both surname and forename (as the case may be) instead of any other name.

(4) Paragraph (3) does not apply if the GLRO thinks–
    (a) that the use of the person's commonly used name may be likely to mislead or confuse electors, or
    (b) that the commonly used name is obscene or offensive.

(5) If paragraph (4) applies, the GLRO must give notice in writing to the candidate of his reasons for refusing to allow the use of a commonly used name.

(6) The statement must show the persons standing nominated arranged alphabetically in the order of their surnames, and if there are two or more of them with the same surname, of their other names.

(7) In the case of a person nominated by more than one nomination paper, the GLRO must take the particulars required by the foregoing provisions of this rule from such one of the papers as the candidate (or the GLRO in default of the candidate) may select.

Correction of minor errors

12 (1) The GLRO may, if he thinks fit, at any time before the publication under rule 11 of the statement of persons nominated, correct minor errors in a nomination paper.

(2) Errors which may be corrected include–
    (a) errors as to a person's electoral number,
    (b) obvious errors of spelling in relation to the details of a candidate.

(3) Anything done by the GLRO in pursuance of this rule may not be questioned in any proceedings other than proceedings on an election petition.

(4) The GLRO must have regard to any guidance issued by the Electoral Commission for the purposes of this rule.

Inspection of nomination papers and consent to nomination

13 (1) During ordinary office hours, in the period starting 24 hours after the latest time for the delivery of nomination papers and before the date of the poll, any person may inspect and take copies of, or extracts from, nomination papers and consents to nomination.

(2) Inspection under paragraph (1) may not take place on a day that is specified in rule 4(1).

Withdrawal of candidature

14 (1) A candidate may withdraw his candidature by notice of withdrawal–
    (a) signed by him and attested by one witness, whose name and address must be given, and
    (b) delivered to the GLRO at the place for delivery of nomination papers,
by the end of the period for the delivery of notices of withdrawals of candidature in the timetable in rule 3.

(2) Where a candidate is outside the United Kingdom, a notice of withdrawal signed by his

election agent and accompanied by a written declaration also so signed, of the candidate's absence from the United Kingdom will be of the same effect as a notice of withdrawal signed by the candidate; but where the candidate stands nominated by more than one nomination paper a notice of withdrawal under this paragraph will be effective if, and only if, it is accompanied, in addition to that declaration, by a written statement signed by the candidate that the person giving the notice is authorised to do so on the candidate's behalf during his absence from the United Kingdom.

Method of election

15 If, after any withdrawals under rule 14–

    (a) more than two candidates remain validly nominated, a poll must be taken in accordance with Parts 4 and 5 of these Rules;

    (b) only two candidates remain validly nominated, a poll must be taken in accordance with Part 4;

    (c) only one candidate remains validly nominated, that person must be declared to be elected in accordance with Part 6.

Part 4
Contested Elections

Poll to be taken by ballot

16 The votes at the poll must be given by ballot.

The ballot papers

17 (1) The ballot of every person entitled to a mayoral vote at the election must consist of a ballot paper which must be in the appropriate form.

  (2) Each person remaining validly nominated at the election, after any withdrawals, and no other, is entitled to have their name inserted in the ballot paper.

  (3) Every ballot paper–

    (a) must, so far as practicable for the purposes of electronic counting, be printed in accordance with the directions set out in the Forms Schedule,

    (b) must contain the names and other particulars of the candidates as shown in the statement of persons nominated,

    (c) must have a number and other unique identifying mark printed on the back, and

    (d) may, in the case of ballot papers for use at polling stations, be marked with the words "do not fold".

  (4) If a candidate who is the subject of a party's authorisation under rule 6(5) so requests, the ballot paper must contain, against the candidate's particulars, the party's registered emblem (or, as the case may be, one of the party's registered emblems).

  (4A) If a candidate who is the subject of an authorisation by two or more parties under rule 6(7) so requests, the ballot paper must contain, against the candidate's particulars, the registered emblem (or, as the case may be, one of the registered emblems) of one of those parties.

  (5) The candidate's request under paragraph (4) or paragraph (4A) must–

    (a) be made in writing to the GLRO, and

    (b) be received by him during the period for delivery of nomination papers set out in the timetable in rule 3.

(6) The names of the candidates must be arranged alphabetically in order of their surnames and, if there are two or more of them with the same surname, of their other names.

(7) The GLRO must supply the ballot papers for use at the election to the CRO by such date as may be agreed between them.

(8) The papers supplied under paragraph (7) must be of a different colour from those used at any other relevant election or referendum.

The corresponding number list

18 (1) The CRO must prepare a list containing the numbers and other unique identifying marks of all of the ballot papers to be issued by him in pursuance of rule 23(1) or provided by him in pursuance of rule 28(1).

(2) The list must be in the appropriate form or a form to like effect.

(3) At an ordinary election, the same list may be used for each Authority election with which the election is combined.

The official mark

19 (1) Every ballot paper must contain an appropriate security marking (the official mark).

(2) The official mark must be kept secret, and an interval of not less than five years must intervene between the use of the same official mark at any Authority election.

(3) The GLRO may use a different official mark for different purposes at the same election.

Prohibition of disclosure of vote

20 No person who has voted at the election may, in any legal proceeding to question the election, be required to state for whom he has voted.

Use of schools and public rooms

21 (1) The CRO may use, free of charge, for the purpose of taking the poll or counting the votes–
  (a) a room in a school maintained or assisted by a local authority (as defined in the Education Act 1996) or a school in respect of which grants are made out of moneys provided by Parliament to the person or body of persons responsible for the management of the school,
  (b) a room the expense of maintaining which is met by any local authority.

(2) In relation to an election to fill a vacancy in the office of the Mayor, the CRO must make good any damage done to, and defray any expense incurred by the persons having control over, any such room as is mentioned in paragraph (1) by reason of its being used for the purpose of taking the poll or counting the votes.

Notice of poll

22 (1) The GLRO must, in accordance with the timetable in rule 3, publish notice of the poll stating–
  (a) the day and hours fixed for the poll,
  (b) particulars of each candidate remaining validly nominated,
and rule 11(2) applies in relation to the order in which names and particulars appear on the notice of the poll as it applies in relation to the statement of persons nominated.

(2)   The CRO must, not later than the time of the publication of the notice of the poll, also give public notice of–
   (a)   the situation of each polling station, and
   (b)   the description of voters entitled to vote there,
and he must as soon as practicable after giving such a notice give a copy of it to each of the election agents.

(3)   The notice published under paragraph (2) shall–
   (a)   state that the poll at the election is to be taken together with the poll at a relevant election or referendum as the case may be,
   (b)   specify the parliamentary constituency, European Parliamentary local counting area, relevant London borough, or voting area; and in the case of an election to fill a casual vacancy, the electoral area for which the relevant election or referendum is held, and
   (c)   where the polls are to be taken together in part of the Borough only, specify that part.

(4)   At an ordinary election, the notice of poll must include the heading "GREATER LONDON AUTHORITY ELECTION".

Postal ballot papers

23 (1)   The CRO must, in accordance with regulations made under the 1983 Act, issue to those entitled to vote by post a ballot paper and a postal voting statement, together with such envelopes for their return as may be prescribed in such regulations.

(2)   The postal voting statement must be in the appropriate form or a form to like effect.

(3)   The postal voting statement must include provision for the form to be signed and for stating the date of birth of the elector or proxy (as the case may be).

(4)   The CRO must also issue to those entitled to vote by post such information as he thinks appropriate about how to obtain–
   (a)   translations into languages other than English of any directions to or guidance for voters sent with the ballot paper,
   (b)   a translation into Braille of such directions or guidance,
   (c)   graphical representations of such directions or guidance,
   (d)   the directions or guidance in any other form (including any audible form).

(5)   In the case of a ballot paper issued to a person at an address in the United Kingdom, the CRO must ensure that the return of the ballot paper and postal voting statement is free of charge to the voter.

(6)   Where the proceedings on the issue and receipt of postal ballot papers at the election are taken together with a relevant election or referendum the appropriate form of postal voting statement under paragraph (2) may be the joint postal voting statement which must be in the appropriate form or form to like effect.

Provision of polling stations

24 (1)   The CRO must provide a sufficient number of polling stations and, subject to the following provisions of this rule, must allot the electors to the polling stations in such manner as he thinks most convenient.

(2)   One or more polling stations may be provided in the same room.

(3)   The polling station allotted to electors from any parliamentary polling district wholly or partly within the Assembly constituency must, in the absence of special circumstances, be in the parliamentary polling place for that district, unless that place

is outside the Assembly constituency.

    (4)   The CRO must provide each polling station with such number of compartments as may be necessary in which the voters can mark their votes screened from observation.

Appointment of presiding officers and clerks

25 (1)   The CRO must appoint and pay a presiding officer to attend at each polling station and such clerks and technical assistants as may be necessary for the purposes of the election, but he must not appoint any person who has been employed by or on behalf of a candidate in or about the election.

   (2)   The CRO may, if he thinks fit, preside at a polling station and the provisions of this Part relating to a presiding officer apply to the CRO so presiding with the necessary modifications as to things to be done by the CRO to the presiding officer or by the presiding officer to the CRO.

   (3)   A presiding officer may do, by the clerks appointed to assist him, any act (including the asking of questions) which he is required or authorised by this Part to do at a polling station except order the arrest, exclusion or removal of any person from the polling station.

Issue of official poll cards

26 (1)   The CRO must as soon as practicable after the publication of the notice of election, send to electors and their proxies an official poll card.

   (2)   An elector's official poll card must be sent or delivered to his qualifying address, and a proxy's to his address as shown in the list of proxies.

   (3)   The official poll card must be in the appropriate form or a form to like effect, and must set out–
       (a)   that the election is a mayoral election,
       (b)   the elector's name, qualifying address and number on the register,
       (c)   the date and hours of the poll and the situation of the elector's polling station, and
       (d)   such other information as the CRO thinks appropriate,
and different information may be provided in pursuance of sub-paragraph (d) to different electors or descriptions of elector.

   (4)   In the case of an elector with an anonymous entry, instead of containing the matter mentioned in paragraph (3)(b), the polling card must contain such matter as is specified in the appropriate form.

   (5)   At an ordinary election, the CRO must issue a combined poll card in the appropriate form.

   (6)   If the CRO and the returning officer for each relevant election or referendum agree, the poll card issued under this rule may be combined with the official poll card for the relevant election or referendum, with necessary adaptations.

   (7)   In this rule "elector" means–
       (a)   an elector with an entry on the register to be used at the election on the last day for the publication of the notice of the election, and
       (b)   includes a person then shown in the register as below voting age if (but only if) it appears from the register that he will be of voting age on the day fixed for the poll.

Information for voters

27 (1)   At an ordinary election, the GLRO may, in addition to a statement by him in an election booklet, include in the booklet information for voters that has been agreed by him with the Electoral Commission.

(2)   The information for voters given in the election booklet may include information about–
    (a)   the office of the Mayor and the London Assembly,
    (b)   the system of voting at each Authority election,
    (c)   how to vote in a manner that will ensure a vote is regarded as validly cast, and subject to paragraph (3), may include any other information given in exercise of the GLRO's duty under section 69 (encouraging electoral participation) of the 2006 Act.

(3)   The information for voters must not contain–
    (a)   any advertising material,
    (b)   any material referring to a candidate or a registered party other than by reproduction of a ballot paper which refers equally to all candidates and parties at the ordinary election,
    (c)   any material referring to the holder, at any time, of the office of Mayor or Assembly member, other than under paragraph (b) as a candidate at the ordinary election.

(4)   Information published in an election booklet under this rule must be printed on not more than two sides of A5 paper.

Equipment of polling stations

28 (1)   The CRO must provide each presiding officer with–
    (a)   such ballot papers as may be necessary, and
    (b)   such ballot boxes as may be necessary having taken account of any direction made by the GLRO in accordance with paragraph (9).

(2)   Every ballot box must be so constructed that the ballot papers can be put in it, but cannot be withdrawn from it, without the box being unlocked or, where the box has no lock, the seal being broken.

(3)   The CRO must provide each polling station with–
    (a)   materials to enable voters to mark the ballot papers,
    (b)   copies of the register of electors for such part of it as contains the entries relating to the electors allotted to the station,
    (c)   the parts of any special lists prepared for the election corresponding to the register of electors or the part of it provided under sub-paragraph (b),
    (d)   a list consisting of that part of the list prepared under rule 18 which contains the numbers (but not the other unique identifying marks) corresponding to those on the ballot papers provided to the presiding officer of the polling station.

(4)   The reference in paragraph (3)(b) to the copies of the register of electors includes a reference to copies of any notices issued under section 13B(3B) or (3D) of the 1983 Act in respect of alterations to the register.

(5)   The CRO must also provide each polling station with a device for enabling voters who are blind or partially sighted to vote without any need for assistance from the presiding officer or any companion within the meaning of rule 40.

(6)   The device referred to in paragraph (5) above must–
    (a)   allow a ballot paper to be inserted into and removed from or attached to and detached from the device, easily and without damage to the paper,
    (b)   keep the ballot paper firmly in place during use, and
    (c)   provide suitable means for the voter to–

      (i)   identify the spaces on the ballot paper on which he may mark his vote,

      (ii) identify the candidate to whom each such space refers, and

      (iii) mark his vote on the space he has chosen.

(7)   The enlarged sample copies of the ballot paper that the GLRO is required to provide, or cause to be displayed at every polling station (in accordance with section 199B(5) and (7) of the 1983 Act) must–

      (a) be provided to the CRO who will deliver them to the polling stations, and

      (b) be printed on paper of the same colour as the ballot paper at the election.

(8)   The CRO must also provide each polling station with notices for the guidance of voters, which must be exhibited–

      (a) outside the polling station,

      (b) inside the polling station–

         (i)   in the communal areas, and

         (ii) in every voting compartment.

(9)   If the GLRO thinks fit he may, not later than the date of the notice of election, direct the CRO that joint ballot boxes must be used for the ballot papers at the election and any or all relevant elections or referendums with which the election is taken.

(10) Where separate ballot boxes are to be used for the election and every relevant election or referendum, each ballot box shall be clearly marked with–

      (a) the election or referendum to which it relates, as shown on the ballot papers for that election or referendum, and

      (b) the words "Place the *specify colour of ballot papers in question* ballot paper here".

(11) Where the CRO does not discharge the functions specified in regulation 5 of the Combination of Polls Regulations, references in this rule to the CRO should be read as references to the returning officer who does discharge those functions.

Notices for the guidance of voters

29 (1) The GLRO must prepare and provide each CRO with the notices to be exhibited under rule 28(8).

(2)   The GLRO may provide each CRO with versions of the notices in such other form as he thinks appropriate, in accordance with section 199B (translations etc of certain documents) of the 1983 Act.

(3)   Notices for the guidance of voters exhibited under rule 28(8) or paragraph (2) must be in the appropriate form, but may include such alternative information relating to Authority elections as–

      (a) meets with the requirements of the Notices Schedule, and

      (b) the GLRO may decide.

(4)   Notices provided under paragraph (2) may, if the CRO agrees, be exhibited at any polling station–

      (a) outside the polling station,

      (b) inside the polling station–

         (i)   in the communal areas,

         (ii) in every voting compartment.

(5)   Where the CRO does not discharge the functions specified in regulation 5 of the Combination of Polls Regulations, references in this rule to the CRO should be read as references to the returning officer who does discharge those functions.

Appointment of polling and counting agents

30 (1)   Before the commencement of the poll, each candidate may appoint–
    (a)   polling agents to attend at polling stations for the purpose of detecting personation, and
    (b)   counting agents to attend at the mayoral count.

(2)   The same person may be appointed as a polling agent or counting agent by more than one candidate.

(3)   For each local count, one (but no more than one) counting agent of each candidate may be authorised by the terms of his appointment to require a re-count at that count.

(4)   Not more than four polling agents, or such greater number as the CRO may by notice allow, may be permitted to attend at any particular polling station.

(5)   If the number of such agents appointed to attend at a particular polling station exceeds that number, the CRO must determine by lot which agents are permitted to attend, and only the agents on whom the lot falls will be deemed to have been duly appointed.

(6)   The CRO may limit the number of counting agents, but in doing so must ensure that–
    (a)   the number is the same in the case of each candidate, and
    (b)   the number allowed to a candidate must not (except in special circumstances) be less than the number obtained by dividing the number of clerks employed on the counting by the number of candidates.

(7)   For the purposes of the calculations required by paragraph (6) a counting agent appointed for more than one candidate is a separate agent for each of the candidates for whom he has been appointed.

(8)   Notice in writing of the appointment of polling and counting agents, stating the names and addresses of the persons appointed, must be given by the candidate to the CRO and must be so given not later than the fifth day (computed in accordance with rule 4) before the day of the poll.

(9)   If an agent dies, or becomes incapable of acting, the candidate or, as the case may be, the election agent, may appoint another person in his place, and must forthwith give to the CRO notice in writing of the name and address of that other person.

(10)   Any appointment authorised by this rule may be made and the notice of appointment given to the CRO by the candidate's election agent, instead of by the candidate.

(11)   In the following provisions of this Part references to polling agents and counting agents must be taken as reference to agents–
    (a)   whose appointments have been duly made and notified, and
    (b)   where the number of agents is restricted, who are within the permitted numbers.

(12)   Any notice required to be given to a counting agent by the CRO may be delivered at, or sent by post to, the address stated in the notice of appointment.

(13)   A candidate may himself do any act or thing which any polling or counting agent of his, if appointed, would have been authorised to do, or may assist his agent in doing any such act or thing.

(14)   A candidate's election agent may do or assist in doing anything which a polling or counting agent of his is authorised to do; and anything required or authorised by these Rules to be done in the presence of the polling or counting agent may be done in the presence of a candidate's election agent instead of his polling agent or counting agent.

(15)   Where by these Rules any act or thing is required or authorised to be done in the presence of the polling or counting agents, the non-attendance of any agent or agents

at the time and place appointed for the purpose will not, if the act or thing is otherwise duly done, invalidate the act or thing done.

(16) Where the CRO does not discharge the functions specified in regulation 5 of the Combination of Polls Regulations, then notices of the appointment of polling agents and counting agents which are required by this rule to be given to the CRO shall be given to the returning officer who discharges those functions.

Notification of requirement of secrecy

31 (1) The CRO must make such arrangements as he thinks fit to ensure that–
  (a) every person attending at a polling station (otherwise than for the purpose of voting or assisting a voter with disabilities to vote or as a constable on duty there) has been given a copy of the provisions of subsections (1), (3) and (6) of section 66 (requirement of secrecy) of the Representation of the People Act 1983, and
  (b) every person attending at the counting of the votes (other than any constable on duty at the counting) has been given a copy of the provisions of subsections (2) and (6) of that section.

(2) In paragraph (1) a reference to a constable includes a person designated as a community support officer under section 38 of the 2002 Act (police powers for employees).

Return of postal ballot papers

32 (1) Where–
  (a) a postal vote has been returned in respect of a person who is entered on the postal voters list, or
  (b) a proxy postal vote has been returned in respect of a proxy who is entered on the proxy postal voters list,
  the CRO must mark the list in the manner prescribed by regulations made under the 1983 Act.

(2) Rule 49(5) does not apply for the purpose of determining whether, for the purposes of this rule, a postal vote or a proxy postal vote is returned.

Admission to polling station

33 (1) The presiding officer must exclude all persons from the polling station except–
  (a) voters,
  (b) persons under the age of 18 who accompany voters to the polling station,
  (c) the candidates and their election agents,
  (d) the polling agents appointed to attend at the polling station,
  (e) the clerks appointed to attend at the polling station,
  (f) persons who are entitled to attend by virtue of any of sections 6A to 6D of the 2000 Act,
  (g) the constables on duty,
  (h) the companions of voters with disabilities, and
  (i) persons entitled to be admitted to the polling station at a relevant election or referendum.

(2) The presiding officer must regulate the total number of voters and persons under the age of 18 who accompany them to be admitted to the polling station at the same time.

(3) Not more than one polling agent may be admitted at the same time to a polling station on behalf of the same candidate.

(4) A constable or person employed by the CRO must not be admitted to vote in person elsewhere than at his own polling station allotted to him under these Rules, except on production and surrender of a certificate as to his employment which must be in the appropriate form and signed by an officer of the police of or above the rank of inspector or by the CRO, as the case may be.

(5) Any certificate surrendered under this rule must forthwith be cancelled.

(6) In this rule a reference to a constable includes a person designated as a community support officer under section 38 of the 2002 Act.

Keeping of order in station

34 (1) It is the presiding officer's duty to keep order at his polling station.

(2) If a person misconducts himself in a polling station, or fails to obey the presiding officer's lawful orders, he may immediately, by the presiding officer's order, be removed from the polling station–
   (a) by a constable in or near that station, or
   (b) by any other person authorised in writing by the CRO to remove him,
and the person so removed must not, without the presiding officer's permission, again enter the polling station during the day.

(3) Any person so removed may, if charged with the commission in the polling station of an offence, be dealt with as a person taken into custody by a constable for an offence without a warrant.

(4) The powers conferred by this rule must not be exercised so as to prevent a voter who is otherwise entitled to vote at a polling station from having an opportunity of voting at that station.

Sealing of ballot boxes

35 Immediately before the commencement of the poll, the presiding officer must–
   (a) show each ballot box, empty, to such persons, if any, as are present in the polling station, so that they may see that the boxes are empty,
   (b) lock up such of the boxes as have locks,
   (c) place his seal–
      (i) on each lock, and
      (ii) on each ballot box which has no lock,
in such a manner as to prevent its being opened without breaking the seal,
   (d) place each box in his view for the receipt of ballot papers, and
   (e) keep each box locked and sealed or, as the case may be, sealed.

Questions to be put to voters

36 (1) At the time of the application (but not afterwards), the questions specified in the second column of the following Table–
   (a) may be put by the presiding officer to a person who is mentioned in the first column, and
   (b) must be put if the letter "R" appears after the question and the candidate or his election or polling agent requires the question to be put.

Q No	Person applying for ballot paper	Question
1	A person applying as an elector	(a)–Are you the person registered in the register of local government electors for this election as follows

		(read the whole entry from the register)? R
		(b)–Have you already voted, here or elsewhere in Greater London at this election for the Mayor of London, otherwise than as proxy for some other person? R
2	A person applying as proxy	(a)–Are you the person whose name appears as AB in the list of proxies for this election as entitled to vote as proxy on behalf of CD? R
		(b)–Have you already voted here or elsewhere in Greater London at this election for the Mayor of London, as proxy on behalf of CD.? R
		(c)–Are you the spouse, civil partner, parent, grandparent, brother, sister, child or grandchild of CD? R
3	A person applying as proxy for an elector with an anonymous entry (instead of the questions at entry 2)	(a)–Are you the person entitled to vote as proxy on behalf of the elector whose number on the register of electors is *(read out the number)*? R
		(b)–Have you already voted here or elsewhere in Greater London as proxy on behalf of the elector whose number on the register of electors is *(read out the number)*? R
		(c)–Are you the spouse, civil partner, parent, grandparent, brother, sister, child or grandchild of the person whose number on the register of electors is *(read out the number)*? R
4	A person applying as proxy if the question at entry 2(c) or 3(c) is not answered in the affirmative	Have you already voted here or elsewhere in Greater London at this election for the Mayor of London, on behalf of two persons of whom you are not the spouse, civil partner, parent, grandparent, brother, sister, child or grandchild? R
5	A person applying as an elector in relation to whom there is an entry in the postal voters list	(a)–Did you apply to vote by post?
		(b)–Why have you not voted by post?
6	A person applying as proxy who is named in the proxy postal voters list	(a)–Did you apply to vote by post as proxy?
		(b)–Why have you not voted by post as proxy?

(2) In the case of an elector in respect of whom a notice has been issued under section 13B(3B) or (3D) of the 1983 Act, the references in the questions at entries 1(a) and 3(a), (b) and (c) to reading from the register must be taken as references to reading from the

notice issued under those subsections.

(3) A ballot paper must not be delivered to any person required to answer any of the above questions unless he has answered each question satisfactorily.

(4) Except as authorised by this rule, no inquiry may be permitted as to the right of any person to vote.

Challenge of voter

37 A person must not be prevented from voting because–

(a) a candidate or his election or polling agent declares that he has reasonable cause to believe that the person has committed an offence of personation, or

(b) the person is arrested on the grounds that he is suspected of committing or of being about to commit such an offence.

Voting procedure

38 (1) A ballot paper must be delivered to a voter who applies for one, and immediately before delivery–

(a) the number and (unless paragraph (2) applies) name of the elector as stated in the copy of the register of electors must be called out,

(b) the number of the elector must be marked on the list mentioned in rule 28(3)(d) beside the number of the ballot paper to be issued to him,

(c) a mark must be placed in the register of electors against the number of the elector to note that a ballot paper has been applied for but without showing the particular ballot paper which may be delivered,

(d) in the case of a person applying for a ballot paper as proxy, a mark must also be placed against his name in the list of proxies.

(2) In the case of an elector who has an anonymous entry, he must show the presiding officer his official poll card and only his number may be called out in pursuance of paragraph (1)(a).

(3) In the case of an elector who is added to the register in pursuance of a notice issued under section 13B(3B) or (3D) of the 1983 Act, paragraph (1) is modified as follows–

(a) in sub-paragraph (a), for "copy of the register of electors" substitute "copy of the notice issued under section 13B(3B) or (3D) of the 1983 Act",

(b) in sub-paragraph (c), for "in the register of electors" substitute "on the copy of the notice issued under section 13B(3B) or (3D) of the 1983 Act".

(4) The voter, on receiving the ballot paper, must forthwith proceed into one of the compartments in the polling station and there secretly mark his paper, and must then show to the presiding officer the back of the paper, so as to disclose the number and other unique identifying mark, and put the ballot paper into the ballot box in the presiding officer's presence, but so as to conceal his vote.

(5) The voter must vote without undue delay, and must leave the polling station as soon as he has put his ballot paper into the ballot box.

(6) A voter who has had a ballot paper delivered to him under paragraph (1), but has decided not to mark it, may return it to the presiding officer and where the voter does so, the presiding officer must–

(a) immediately cancel the ballot paper, and for the purposes of these rules treat it as a spoilt ballot paper,

(b) place a mark beside the number of that ballot paper on the corresponding number list to show that the ballot paper has been cancelled.

(7) The same copy of–

(a) the list of proxies,

(b) the register of electors,

(c) any notice issued under section 13B(3B) or (3D) of the 1983 Act (marked in the case of an elector who is added to the register in pursuance of such a notice),

may be used for the election and each relevant election and referendum and one mark may be placed in the list, register or notice (as the case may be) to denote that a ballot paper has been delivered in respect of each election and referendum; except that, where a ballot paper has not been issued in respect of any election or referendum, a different mark must be placed in the list, register or notice so as to identify the election or referendum in respect of which a ballot paper was issued.

(8) At an ordinary election, the same copy of the list mentioned in rule 28(3)(d), may be used for each Authority election and one mark may be placed in the list, to denote that a ballot paper has been delivered in respect of each Authority election; except that, where a ballot paper has not been issued in respect of any Authority election, a different mark must be placed in the list, so as to identify the elections in respect of which a ballot paper was issued.

(9) A voter who at the close of the poll is in the polling station, or in a queue outside the polling station, for the purpose of voting must (despite the close of the poll) be entitled to apply for a ballot paper under paragraph (1); and these rules apply in relation to such a voter accordingly.

Votes marked by presiding officer

39 (1) The presiding officer, on the application of a voter–

(a) who is incapacitated by blindness or other disability from voting in the manner directed by these Rules, or

(b) who declares orally that he is unable to read,

must, in the presence of the polling agents, cause the voter's vote to be marked on a ballot paper in the manner directed by the voter, and the ballot paper to be placed in the ballot box.

(2) The name and number on the register of electors of every voter whose vote is marked in pursuance of this rule, and the reason why it is so marked, must be entered on a list (in these Rules called "the list of votes marked by the presiding officer").

In the case of a person voting as proxy for an elector, the number to be entered together with the voter's name must be the elector's number.

(3) In the case of a person in respect of whom a notice has been issued under section 13B(3B) or (3D) of the 1983 Act, paragraph (2) applies as if for "on the register of electors of every voter" there were substituted "relating to every voter in respect of whom a notice has been issued under section 13B(3B) or (3D) of the 1983 Act".

(4) The same list may be used for each relevant election or referendum, and where it is so used, an entry in that list must be taken to mean that the ballot papers were so marked in respect of each election or referendum, unless the list identifies the election or referendum at which the ballot paper was so marked.

Voting by persons with disabilities

40 (1) If a voter makes an application to the presiding officer to be allowed, on the ground of–

(a) blindness or other disability, or

(b) inability to read,

to vote with the assistance of another person by whom he is accompanied (in these Rules referred to as "the companion"), the presiding officer must require the voter to declare, orally or in writing, whether he is so incapacitated by his blindness or other disability, or by his inability to read, as to be unable to vote without assistance.

(2) If the presiding officer–

    (a) is satisfied that the voter is so incapacitated, and

    (b) is also satisfied by a written declaration made by the companion (in these Rules referred to as "the declaration made by the companion of a voter with disabilities") that the companion–

        (i) is a qualified person within the meaning of these Rules, and

        (ii) has not previously assisted more than one voter with disabilities to vote at the election,

the presiding officer must grant the application, and then anything which is by these Rules required to be done to, or by that voter in connection with the giving of his vote may be done to, or with the assistance of, the companion.

(3) For the purpose of these Rules, a person is a voter with disabilities if he has made such a declaration as is mentioned in paragraph (1) above, and a person may be qualified to assist a voter with disabilities to vote if that person–

    (a) is a person who is entitled to vote as an elector at the election, or

    (b) is the father, mother, brother, sister, spouse, civil partner, son or daughter of the voter and has attained the age of 18 years.

(4) The name and number in the register of electors of every voter whose vote is given in accordance with this rule and the name and address of the companion must be entered on a list (in these Rules referred to as the "list of voters with disabilities assisted by companions").

In the case of a person voting as proxy for an elector, the number to be entered together with the voter's name must be the elector's number.

(5) In the case of a person in respect of whom a notice has been issued under section 13B(3B) or (3D) of the 1983 Act, paragraph (4) applies as if for "in the register of electors of every voter" there were substituted "relating to every voter in respect of whom a notice has been issued under section 13B(3B) or (3D) of the 1983 Act".

(6) The declaration made by the companion–

    (a) must be in the appropriate form, and

    (b) must be made before the presiding officer at the time when the voter applies to vote with the assistance of a companion, and

    (c) must forthwith be given to the presiding officer who must attest and retain it.

(7) No fee or other payment may be charged in respect of the declaration.

(8) The same list of voters with disabilities assisted by companions may be used for each relevant election and referendum, and where it is so used, an entry in that list must be taken to mean that the votes were so given in respect of each election and referendum, unless the list identifies the election or referendum for which the vote was so given.

Tendered ballot papers: circumstances where available

41 (1) If a person, representing himself to be–

    (a) a particular elector named in the register and not named in the absent voters list, or

    (b) a particular person named in the list of proxies as proxy for an elector and not entitled to vote by post as proxy,

applies for a ballot paper after another person has voted in person either as the elector or his proxy, the applicant must, on satisfactorily answering the questions permitted by law to be asked at the poll, be entitled, subject to the following provisions of this rule and rule 42, to mark a ballot paper (in these Rules referred to as "a tendered ballot paper") in the same manner as any other voter.

(2) Paragraph (4) applies if–
- (a) a person applies for a ballot paper representing himself to be a particular elector named in the register,
- (b) he is also named in the postal voters list, and
- (c) he claims that he did not make an application to vote by post at the election.

(3) Paragraph (4) also applies if–
- (a) a person applies for a ballot paper representing himself to be a particular person named as a proxy in the list of proxies,
- (b) he is also named in the proxy postal voters list, and
- (c) he claims that he did not make an application to vote by post as proxy.

(4) The person must, on satisfactorily answering the questions permitted by law to be asked at the poll, be entitled, subject to the provisions of this rule and rule 42, to mark a ballot paper (in these Rules referred to as a "tendered ballot paper") in the same manner as any other voter.

(5) Paragraph (6) applies if before the close of the poll but after the last time at which a person may apply for a replacement postal ballot paper, a person represents himself to be–
- (a) a particular elector named in the register who is also named in the postal voters list, or
- (b) a particular person named as a proxy in the list of proxies and who is also named in the proxy postal voters list,

and claims that he has lost or has not received his postal ballot paper.

(6) The person must, on satisfactorily answering the questions permitted by law to be asked at the poll, be entitled, subject to the provisions of this rule and rule 42, to mark a ballot paper (in these Rules referred to as a "tendered ballot paper") in the same manner as any other voter.

Tendered ballot papers: general provisions

42 (1) A tendered ballot paper must–
- (a) be of a colour differing from the other ballot papers,
- (b) instead of being put into the ballot box, be given to the presiding officer and endorsed by him with the name of the voter and his number on the register of electors, and set aside in a separate packet.

(2) The name of the voter and his number on the register of electors must be entered on a list (in these Rules referred to as the "tendered votes list").

(3) In the case of a person voting as proxy for an elector, the number to be endorsed or entered together with the voter's name must be the number of that elector.

(4) In the case of an elector who has an anonymous entry, this rule and rule 41 apply subject to the following modifications–
- (a) in paragraphs (1)(b) and (2) above, the references to the name of the voter must be ignored,
- (b) otherwise, a reference to a person named on a register or list must be construed as a reference to a person whose number appears in the register or list (as the case may be).

(5) In the case of a person in respect of whom a notice has been issued under section 13B(3B) or (3D) of the 1983 Act, this rule and rule 41 apply as if–
- (a) in rule 41(1)(a), (2)(a) and (5)(a), for "named in the register" there were substituted "in respect of whom a notice under section 13B(3B) or (3D) of the 1983 Act has been issued",

(b) in paragraph (1)(b) of this rule, for "his number in the register of electors" there were substituted "the number relating to him on a notice issued under section 13B(3B) or (3D) of the 1983 Act",

(c) in paragraph (2) of this rule, for "his number in the register of electors" there were substituted "the number relating to him on a notice issued under section 13B(3B) or (3D) of the 1983 Act".

(6) The same list may be used for each relevant election or referendum, and where it is so used, an entry in that list must be taken to mean that tendered ballot papers were marked in respect of each election or referendum, unless the list identifies the election for which a tendered ballot paper was delivered.

Spoilt and replacement ballot papers

43 (1) A voter who has inadvertently dealt with his ballot paper in such manner that it cannot be conveniently used as a ballot paper may, on delivering it to the presiding officer and proving to his satisfaction the fact of the inadvertence, obtain a replacement for the ballot paper so delivered (in these Rules referred to as "a spoilt ballot paper"), and the spoilt ballot paper must be immediately cancelled.

(2) If a voter decides, after he has returned his ballot paper and it has been cancelled in accordance with rule 38(6), but before the close of the poll, that he wishes to vote in the election, he may obtain a replacement for the returned ballot paper.

(3) Before a replacement ballot paper is obtained, the presiding officer must mark the corresponding number list that was marked under rule 38(1) (the corresponding number list)–

(a) in the case of a ballot paper being replaced under paragraph (1) or (2), beside the number of the replacement ballot paper obtained to show–

(i) the number of the elector, and

(ii) the number of the ballot paper which is being replaced; and

(b) in the case of a ballot paper being replaced under paragraph (1), beside the number of the spoilt ballot paper to show that the ballot paper was replaced.

(4) Where the election is taken with a relevant election or referendum the voter must only receive a replacement for a spoilt or returned ballot paper.

(5) If the same corresponding number list is used for more than one Authority election in accordance with rule 38(8)–

(a) the marks made under paragraph (3) must identify the election for which a ballot paper has been replaced, and

(b) any ballot paper which the voter has not applied for or obtained as a replacement, but which bears the same ballot paper number as a ballot paper delivered under rule 38(1), or obtained under paragraph (1) or (2) of this rule–

(i) must not be delivered to the voter,

(ii) must be cancelled, and

(iii) for the purposes of these rules, must be treated as a spoilt ballot paper.

Correction of errors on day of poll

44 (1) The presiding officer must keep a list of persons to whom ballot papers are delivered in consequence of an alteration to the register made by virtue of section 13B(3B) or (3D) of the 1983 Act which takes effect on the day of the poll.

(2) The same list may be used for each relevant election or referendum, and where it is so used, an entry in that list must be taken to mean that ballot papers were delivered in respect of each election or referendum, unless the list identifies the election or referendum at which a tendered ballot paper was marked.

Adjournment of poll in case of riot

45 (1)   Where the proceedings at any polling station are interrupted or obstructed by riot or open violence, the presiding officer must adjourn the proceedings till the following day and must forthwith give notice to the CRO.

(2)   Where the poll is adjourned at any polling station–
    (a)   the hours of polling on the day to which it is adjourned must be the same as for the original day, and
    (b)   references in these Rules to the close of the poll must be construed accordingly.

(3)   As soon as practicable after the CRO has received notice of the adjournment of a poll he must inform the GLRO of that fact and of the cause of its adjournment.

(4)   If the CRO does not discharge the functions specified in regulation 5 of the Combination of Polls Regulations, then references in this rule to the CRO must be read as references to the returning officer who discharges those functions.

Procedure on close of poll

46 (1)   As soon as practicable after the close of the poll, the presiding officer must, in the presence of the polling agents appointed for the purposes of the election and each relevant election or referendum, make up into separate packets, sealed with his own seal and the seals of such polling agents as desire to affix their seals–
    (a)   each ballot box in use at the station, sealed so as to prevent the introduction of additional ballot papers and unopened, but with the key attached,
    (b)   the unused and spoilt ballot papers placed together,
    (c)   the tendered ballot papers,
    (d)   the marked copies of the register of electors (including any marked copy notices issued under section 13B(3B) or (3D) of the 1983 Act) and of the list of proxies,
    (e)   the list prepared under rule 18, including the part completed in accordance with rule 38(1)(b) (together referred to in these Rules as "the completed corresponding number list"),
    (f)   the certificates as to employment on duty on the day of the poll,
    (g)   the tendered votes list, the list of voters with disabilities assisted by companions, the list of votes marked by the presiding officer, a statement of the number of voters whose votes are so marked by the presiding officer under the heads "disability" and "unable to read", the list maintained under rule 44, and the declarations made by the companions of voters with disabilities,

and must deliver the packets or cause them to be delivered to the CRO to be taken charge of by him; but if the packets are not delivered by the presiding officer personally to the CRO, the arrangements for their delivery must be approved by the CRO.

(2)   The contents of the packets referred to in paragraph (1)(b), (c) and (f) must not be combined with the contents of the packets made under the corresponding rule that applies at any other relevant election or referendum except for an Authority election.

(3)   The marked copies of the register of electors and of the list of proxies must be in one packet but must not be in the same packet as the completed corresponding number list or the certificates as to employment on duty on the day of the poll.

(4)   The packets must be accompanied by a statement ("the ballot paper account") showing the number of ballot papers entrusted to the presiding officer, and accounting for them under the heads–
    (a)   ballot papers issued and not otherwise accounted for,
    (b)   unused ballot papers,

(c)   spoilt ballot papers, and

(d)   tendered ballot papers.

(5)   At an ordinary election, the statement referred to in paragraph (4) may be combined with the statements produced in relation to any other Authority elections, but not with those for a relevant election or referendum, and the combined statement must be arranged in such manner as the GLRO may direct.

(6)   Where the CRO does not discharge the functions specified in regulation 5 of the Combination of Polls Regulations, references in paragraph (1) to the CRO must be taken as references to the returning officer who discharges those functions.

Attendance at verification and the counting of votes

47 (1)   Where the CRO discharges the functions specified in regulation 5 of the Combination of Polls Regulations, he must–

(a)   make arrangements for–

(i)   carrying out the functions in rule 49(1) (separating ballot papers and verifying ballot paper accounts) at the election in the presence of the counting agents appointed for the purposes of the election and each relevant election and referendum as soon as practicable after the close of the poll, and

(ii)   for counting the votes in the presence of the counting agents appointed for the purposes of the election,

(b)   give to the counting agents appointed for the purposes of the election and each relevant election and referendum, notice in writing of the time and place at which he will begin carrying out the functions in rule 49(1).

(2)   Where the CRO does not discharge the functions specified in regulation 5 of the Combination of Polls Regulations he must make arrangements for counting the votes in the presence of the counting agents appointed for the purposes of the election as soon as practicable after the delivery of the ballot papers to him by the returning officer who does discharge those functions; and the CRO must give to the counting agents for the election notice in writing of the time and place at which he will begin to count the votes.

(3)   No person other than a person entitled to be present at the counting of the votes at the election and at each relevant election or referendum may be present at the proceedings under rule 49(1) (separating ballot papers and verifying ballot paper accounts) unless permitted by the CRO to attend.

(4)   No person other than–

(a)   the CRO and his clerks and technical assistants,

(b)   the GLRO,

(c)   the candidates and one other person chosen by each of them,

(d)   the election agents,

(e)   the counting agents,

(f)   persons who are entitled to attend by virtue of any of sections 6A to 6D of the 2000 Act,

may be present at the counting of the votes in accordance with rule 49(2) to (14), unless permitted by the CRO to attend

(5)   A person not entitled to attend at the separation and verification or the counting of the votes must not be permitted to do so by the CRO unless the CRO–

(a)   is satisfied that the efficient separation and verification of the ballot paper accounts or, as the case may be, the efficient counting of the votes will not be impeded, and

(b)   has either consulted the candidates or thought it impracticable to do so.

(6)   The CRO must give the counting agents all such reasonable facilities for overseeing the proceedings, and all such information with respect to them, as he can give them consistently with the orderly conduct of the proceedings and the discharge of his duties in connection with them.

Use of the electronic counting system

48 (1)   The GLRO may provide the CRO with an electronic counting system consisting of computer hardware, software and other equipment or services, for the purpose of counting the number of ballot papers, to verify the ballot paper accounts and to count the votes cast on them.

(2)   Any verification of ballot paper accounts, count or re-count at the election conducted using the electronic counting system must be conducted in accordance with rule 49.

(3)   If the GLRO has provided the CRO with an electronic counting system for use at the election, the CRO must obtain the prior written consent of the GLRO before he may conduct the verification of ballot paper accounts or count the votes manually.

(4)   If the verification of ballot paper accounts, count or re-count has commenced using the electronic counting system but has not been completed, the CRO may, if he considers it appropriate, discontinue the count and instead count the votes manually.

(5)   Where the count or a re-count has been conducted using the electronic counting system, the CRO may, if he considers it appropriate, conduct any re-count without using that system.

(6)   Where verification or any count or re-count is conducted using the electronic counting system, any of the steps referred to rule 49, in so far as practicable, may be undertaken–

    (a)   concurrently with any other of those steps, or

    (b)   in a different order.

Verification and the local count

49 (1)   Where the CRO discharges the functions specified in regulation 5 of the Combination of Polls Regulations, he must–

    (a)   in the presence of the counting agents appointed for the purposes of the election and each relevant election or referendum, open each ballot box from each polling station together, and record separately the number of ballot papers used in the election and each relevant election or referendum with which is it is taken,

    (b)   in the presence of the counting agents appointed for the purposes of the election and each relevant election or referendum, verify each ballot paper account at the election and for each relevant election or referendum,

    (c)   count such of the postal ballot papers as have been duly returned and record separately the number counted at the election and each relevant election or referendum,

    (d)   where the same ballot boxes have been used for the election and each relevant election or referendum, separate the ballot papers for all of the Authority elections from those for any other relevant election or referendum.

    (e)   make up into packets the ballot papers for each relevant election or referendum (not including those for any Authority election) and seal them up in separate containers endorsing on each a description of the area to which the ballot papers relate,

    (f)   deliver or cause to be delivered to the returning officer for the relevant election or referendum to which the ballot papers relate–

   (i) those containers, together with a list of them and of the contents of each, and

   (ii) the ballot paper accounts together with a copy of the statement as to the result of their verification in respect of that relevant election or referendum, and

  (g) at the same time deliver to that officer the packets that so relate containing–

   (i) the unused and spoilt ballot papers,

   (ii) the tendered ballot papers, and

   (iii) the completed corresponding number lists of the used ballot papers and the certificates as to employment on duty on the day of the poll.

(2) Where the CRO does not discharge the functions specified in regulation 5 of the Combination of Polls Regulations, and the votes on the ballot papers are not to be counted concurrently with the votes on the ballot papers at a relevant election or referendum, he must–

  (a) on receipt of the containers of ballot papers from the returning officer who does discharge those functions, and after the time specified in the notice given by him in writing to the counting agents under rule 47(2), open each container in the presence of the counting agents;

  (b) where the proceedings on the issue and receipt of postal ballot papers at the election are not taken together with those proceedings at a relevant election or referendum under regulation 65 of the Representation of the People (England and Wales) Regulations 2001, or under that regulation as applied by regulations made under sections 44 and 105, or 45 and 105, of the Local Government Act 2000, count such of the postal ballot papers as have been duly returned and record the number counted,

 and paragraph (10) below does not apply to these proceedings.

(3) Where separate ballot boxes are used for the ballots at the election and each relevant election and referendum, no vote for any candidate shall be rendered invalid by the ballot paper being placed in the ballot box used at any relevant election or referendum.

(4) Where the same ballot boxes are used for the election and other Authority elections, but not for other relevant elections or referendums–

  (a) the CRO must not mix the ballot papers for Authority elections from any ballot box or container with the contents of any other ballot box or container (including a postal ballot box) during the conduct of verification (where this occurs under paragraph (1)), the count or any re-count;

  (b) the ballot boxes from each polling station for the Authority elections shall be opened together and the ballot papers counted (but not necessarily the votes on them) and verified together.

(5) A postal ballot paper must not be taken to be duly returned unless–

  (a) it is returned in the manner set out in paragraph (6) and reaches the CRO or any polling station in the appropriate area (as defined in paragraph (7)) before the close of the poll,

  (b) the postal voting statement, duly signed, is also returned in the manner set out in paragraph (6) and reaches him or such polling station before that time,

  (c) the postal voting statement also states the date of birth of the elector or proxy (as the case may be), and

  (d) in a case where the steps for verifying the date of birth and signature of an elector or proxy have been prescribed by regulations made under the 1983 Act, the CRO (having taken such steps) verifies the date of birth and signature of the elector or proxy (as the case may be).

(6) The manner in which any postal paper or postal voting statement may be returned–

(a)   to the CRO, is by hand or by post,

(b)   to a polling station in the appropriate area, is by hand.

(6A)   A postal ballot paper or postal voting statement that reaches the CRO or a polling station in the appropriate area at or after the close of the poll is treated for the purposes of paragraph (5) as reaching that officer or polling station before the close of the poll if it is delivered by a person who, at the close of the poll, is in the polling station, or in a queue outside the polling station, for the purpose of returning it.

(7)   For the purposes of paragraphs (5), (6) and (6A), "polling station in the appropriate area" means a polling station–

(a)   in the area which is common to the Assembly constituency, and parliamentary constituency, local counting area, electoral area or voting area, as the case may be, in which the polls at the Authority election and a relevant election or referendum are being taken together, and

(b)   in respect of which polls the voter has been issued with a postal ballot paper.

(8)   After completing the proceedings in paragraph (1) or (2), the CRO must cause the electronic counting system to process the ballot papers for the election so as to count–

(a)   the number of ballot papers, and

(b)   votes given on the ballot papers.

(9)   The CRO must not cause the electronic counting system to count any tendered ballot paper.

(10)   Subject to paragraph (11), the CRO must verify each ballot paper account by comparing it with the number of ballot papers recorded by him, and the unused and spoilt ballot papers in his possession and the tendered votes list (opening and re-sealing the packets containing the unused and spoilt ballot papers and the tendered votes list) and must draw up a statement as to the result of the verification, which any election agent may copy.

(11)   The CRO may verify each ballot paper account for the election by comparing it with the number of ballot papers processed by the electronic counting system, and the unused and spoilt ballot papers in his possession and the tendered votes list (opening and re-sealing the packets containing the unused and spoilt ballot papers and the tendered votes list).

(12)   The CRO, while verifying the ballot paper accounts and counting the votes, must take all proper precautions for preventing any person from seeing the numbers printed on the back of the papers.

(13)   The CRO must so far as practicable proceed continuously with counting the votes, allowing only time for refreshment, except that the hours between 5 in the afternoon and 10 on the following morning may be excluded with the prior consent of the GLRO.

(14)   During the time so excluded the CRO must–

(a)   place the ballot papers and other documents relating to the election under his own seal and the seals of such of the counting agents as desire to affix their seals, and

(b)   otherwise take proper precautions for the security of the papers and documents.

Rejected ballot papers

50 (1)   Any ballot paper–

(a)   which does not bear the official mark,

(b)   on which anything is written or marked by which the voter can be identified except the printed number and other unique identifying mark on the back,

(c)   which is unmarked,

(d) which is void for uncertainty,

is, subject to paragraph (2), void and must not be counted.

(2) A ballot paper on which a vote is marked–

(a) elsewhere than in the proper place, or

(b) otherwise than by means of a cross, or

(c) by more than one mark,

must not for such reason be void if–

(i) at an election at which more than two candidates remain validly nominated, an intention that a first preference vote be given for not more than one of the candidates clearly appears,

(ii) at any other election, an intention that a vote is for one only of the candidates clearly appears.

(3) A ballot paper which–

(a) is not void, and

(b) on which an intention that a second preference vote be given for not more than one of the candidates clearly appears,

will be valid as respects that second preference vote and must be counted accordingly.

(4) Where the electronic counting system identifies a ballot paper that has been marked, but which appears–

(a) to be void, or

(b) to contain a first preference vote that can be counted, and another mark that cannot be counted as a second preference vote,

then that ballot paper must be examined by a clerk appointed by the CRO in the manner referred to in paragraph (7).

(5) If the clerk, having examined the ballot paper, considers that–

(a) it is void, or

(b) that it is marked with a first preference vote that can be counted, but that it is not marked with a second preference vote that can be counted,

then the CRO must examine it in the manner referred to in paragraph (7).

(6) After the CRO examines the ballot paper, he must give his decision as to whether or not–

(a) it is void, or

(b) it is marked with a second preference vote that can be counted.

(7) An examination under paragraph (4) or (5) is to be made by the clerk or CRO examining an image of the ballot paper which is shown on a screen so as to be visible to those attending the count.

(8) The CRO may examine any ballot paper that he is not required to examine in accordance with paragraphs (5)–

(a) either in the manner referred to in paragraph (7), or

(b) by examining a paper copy,

and where the CRO does so, he must give a decision on that paper in accordance with paragraph (6),

(9) No person attending the count is to be entitled to require the clerk or CRO to examine a ballot paper or to provide a paper copy for inspection.

(10) A record of the CRO's decision under paragraph (6) must be retained in the electronic counting system together, in the case of a decision that the ballot is void, with his reasons by reference to paragraph (1).

(11) If a counting agent objects to the CRO's decision that the ballot paper–

(a) is void, or

(b) is marked with a second preference vote that cannot be counted, the CRO must record on the electronic counting system that the decision was objected to.

(12) A record must be retained in the electronic counting system of the number of ballot papers which are not void, but on which a second preference vote has not been counted because–

    (a) a vote has not been marked,

    (b) a vote has been given for more than one candidate, or

    (c) there is uncertainty as to for whom a vote was given.

(13) The CRO must draw up a statement showing the number of rejected ballot papers under the several heads of–

    (a) want of an official mark,

    (b) voting for more than one candidate as to first preference vote,

    (c) writing or mark by which the voter could be identified,

    (d) unmarked as to the first preference vote, and

    (e) void for uncertainty.

(14) As soon as practicable after the completion of the statement under paragraph (13) the CRO must inform–

    (a) such candidates, election agents and counting agents as are present at the count, and

    (b) the GLRO,

of its contents.

(15) The CRO must also include in the statement drawn up under paragraph (13), the numbers of second preference votes for which a record has been retained, set out under the several heads in sub-paragraphs (12)(a) to (c).

Decisions on ballot papers

51 The decision of the CRO on any question arising in respect of a ballot paper is final, but may be subject to review on an election petition.

Re-count

52 (1) A candidate or his election agent or a counting agent authorised under rule 30(3) may, if present when the counting or any re-count of the votes, is completed, require the CRO to have the votes re-counted or again re-counted but the CRO may refuse to do so if in his opinion the request is unreasonable.

(2) No step may be taken on the completion of the counting or any re-count of votes, until the candidates and election agents and counting agents authorised under rule 30(1) present at its completion have been given a reasonable opportunity to exercise the right conferred by this rule.

(3) The CRO may determine the extent to which any re-count involves the electronic counting of votes.

(4) When the returning officer uses the electronic counting system for the re-counting of votes, he must not re-consider any decision made on any ballot paper under rule 50(6).

Procedure at conclusion of local count

53 (1) As soon as practicable after the conclusion of the local count (including any re-count), the CRO must draw up a statement showing–

    (a) the total number of ballot papers used,

    (b) the total number of rejected ballot papers,

    (c) at an election contested by more than two candidates–

> (i) the total number of first preference votes given,
>
> (ii) the number of first preference votes given for each candidate, and
>
> (iii) the total number of second preference votes given for each candidate correlated with the way the first preference votes have been cast.

(d) at an election contested by only two candidates, the number of votes given for each candidate.

(2) As soon as practicable after the statement is drawn up under paragraph (1), the CRO must inform the GLRO of its contents, and if it is practicable to do so, must also provide that information so as to show the total number of votes under each of those heads in each ward.

(3) As soon as practicable after the GLRO has authorised him to do so, the CRO must–

(a) inform such of the candidates and their election agents as are then present of the contents of the statements prepared in accordance with rule 50 and paragraph (1) of this rule, and

(b) give public notice of the contents of those statements.

Attendance at the central calculation

54 (1) The GLRO must make arrangements for making the calculations made under rules 55 and 56 in the presence of the election agents and he must give to those agents notice in writing of the time and place at which he will begin the calculation.

(2) No person other than–

(a) the GLRO and his clerks,

(b) the CROs and a clerk or technical assistant chosen by each of them,

(c) the candidates and one person chosen by each of them,

(d) the election agents,

(e) persons who are entitled to attend by virtue of any of sections 6A to 6D of the 2000 Act,

(f) at an ordinary election, the persons permitted to be present at the central calculation at the election of the Mayor of London,

may be present at a calculation, unless permitted by the GLRO to attend.

(3) A person not entitled to attend a calculation must not be permitted to do so by the GLRO unless he–

(a) is satisfied that the efficiency of the calculation will not be impeded, and

(b) has either consulted the election agents or thought it impracticable to do so.

The first calculation and resolution of equality

55 (1) As soon as the GLRO has received the information required by rule 53 from every CRO he must–

(a) in relation to an election contested by more than two candidates, ascertain the total of the first preference votes given in the Assembly constituencies to each candidate, and

(b) in relation to an election contested by only two candidates, ascertain the total number of votes given in the Assembly constituencies to each candidate.

(2) As soon as the GLRO has ascertained the result of the calculation, he must inform such of the election agents as are then present of the relevant figures and must give them a reasonable opportunity to satisfy themselves as to the accuracy of the calculation.

(3) In paragraph (2), "the relevant figures" means–

(a) in the case of an election contested by more than two candidates, the number of first preference votes given in each of the Assembly constituencies for each candidate and the calculation undertaken by the GLRO for the purposes of ascertaining whether a candidate is to be returned in accordance with paragraph 3 of Schedule 2 to the 1999 Act (candidate with overall majority of first preference votes),

(b) in the case of an election contested by only two candidates, the number of votes given in each Assembly constituency for each candidate and the total number of votes given for each candidate.

(4) Where an election is contested by more than two candidates–

(a) if paragraph 3 of Schedule 2 to the 1999 Act applies (candidate with overall majority of first preference votes) the declaration of the person to be returned as the Mayor must be made in accordance with rule 58, or

(b) if paragraph 4(1) of that Schedule applies (no candidate with overall majority of first preference votes), the GLRO must proceed with the second calculation in accordance with Part 5.

(5) Where an election is contested by only two candidates and the total number of votes given for each of them is unequal the person to be returned as the Mayor is the candidate to whom the majority of the votes is given.

(6) Where an election is contested by only two candidates and the total number of votes given for each of them is equal, the person to be returned as the Mayor is the person whom the GLRO decides, in accordance with paragraph 4(8) of Schedule 2 to the 1999 Act, is to be returned as the Mayor.

(7) In a case to which paragraph (5) or (6) applies, the declaration of the person to be returned as the Mayor must be made in accordance with rule 58.

Part 5
Further Provision: More Than Two Candidates

The second calculation and resolution of equality

56 (1) As soon as the GLRO has determined that paragraph 4(1) of Schedule 2 to the 1999 Act applies he must comply with paragraphs 4(5) and (6) of Schedule 2 to the 1999 Act.

(2) As soon as the GLRO has ascertained the result of the second calculation, he must provide such of the election agents for those candidates who remain in the contest as are then present with a copy of the relevant figures and must give them a reasonable opportunity to satisfy themselves as to the accuracy of the calculation.

(3) In paragraph (2), "the relevant figures" means–

(a) the number of second preference votes given in each of the Assembly constituencies for each of the candidates remaining in the contest, and

(b) the calculation undertaken by the GLRO for the purpose of ascertaining the total number of first and second preference votes given to each of those candidates.

(4) If, after the second calculation, the total number of votes given for two or more candidates is equal, the person to be returned as the Mayor is the person whom the GLRO decides, in accordance with paragraph 4(8) of Schedule 2 to the 1999 Act, is to be returned as the Mayor.

Part 6
Final Proceedings in Contested and Uncontested Elections

Declaration of result

57 (1) The GLRO must declare to be elected as the Mayor of London the candidate who, in

accordance with section 4(2) of the 1999 Act or Part I of Schedule 2 to that Act (including those provisions as applied by section 16(4) at an election to fill a vacancy), as the case may be, is to be returned as the Mayor at that election.

(2) The GLRO must give public notice of–
- (a) the name of the of the person declared to be elected and his authorised description, if any, within the meaning of rule 6(5) or (7),
- (b) the total number of first preference votes given for each candidate,
- (c) the total number of second preference votes given for each of the candidates remaining in the contest after the count of the first preference votes,
- (d) the number of rejected ballot papers at the election under each head shown in the statement of rejected ballot papers, and
- (e) the number of ballot papers on which no second preference vote was counted under each head shown in the statement of rejected ballot papers,

(3) In an uncontested election, the GLRO must as soon as practicable after the latest time for the delivery of notices of withdrawals of candidature–
- (a) declare to be elected the candidate remaining validly nominated, and
- (b) give public notice of the name of the person declared to be elected and his authorised description, if any, within the meaning of rule 6(5) or (7).

(4) Subject to paragraph (5), after the GLRO complies with paragraphs (1) and (2), he may in so far as is practicable, give public notice of the information referred to paragraph (2)(b) to (e) so as to set out the number of votes falling under each of those heads, in respect of each ward.

(5) Where the sum of first preference votes given for all candidates in any ward does not exceed 500, the GLRO must not give notice under paragraph (4) in respect of that ward alone, but must amalgamate the figures for that ward with those for any other ward in which more than 500 votes have been given, in the same Assembly constituency.

Return or forfeiture of candidate's deposit

58 (1) Unless forfeited in accordance with paragraph (5), the deposit made under rule 9 must be returned to the person making it or his personal representative.

(2) Subject to paragraph (4), the deposit must be returned not later than the next day after that on which the result of the election is declared.

(3) For the purposes of paragraph (2)–
- (a) a day must be disregarded if, in accordance with rule 4, it would be disregarded in computing any period of time for the purposes of the timetable for the election, and
- (b) the deposit must be treated as being returned on a day if a cheque for the amount of the deposit is posted on that day.

(4) If the candidate is not shown as standing nominated in the statement of persons nominated, or if proof of his death has been given to the GLRO before the first calculation under rule 55, the deposit must be returned as soon as practicable after the publication of the statement or after his death, as the case may be.

(5) Where a poll is taken, if, after the first calculation under rule 55, the candidate is found not to have polled more than one-twentieth of the total number of first preference votes polled by all the candidates, the deposit must be forfeited to the Greater London Authority.

Part 7
Disposal of Documents

Sealing up of ballot papers

59 (1) On the completion of the counting at a contested election the CRO must seal up in separate packets the counted and rejected ballot papers.

(2) Where some or all of the votes have been counted using the electronic counting system, the CRO must also seal up in a separate packet a complete electronic record ("the electronic record") of the information stored in the electronic counting system, held in such device as may be suitable for the purpose of its storage.

(3) After making the electronic record under paragraph (2), the CRO must arrange for the original records in the electronic counting system to be removed from it and destroyed in a manner that ensures that the secrecy of those records is preserved.

(4) The CRO must not open the sealed packets of–
    (a) tendered ballot papers, or
    (b) certificates as to employment on duty on the day of the poll.

(5) Where the CRO discharges the functions referred to in regulation 5 of the Combination of Polls Regulations, he must also not open the sealed packets of–
    (a) the completed corresponding number lists,
    (b) marked copies of the register of electors (including any marked copy notices issued under section 13B(3B) or (3D) of the 1983 Act) and lists of proxies.

Delivery and retention of documents

60 (1) The CRO must then forward the following documents to the relevant registration officer–
    (a) the packets of ballot papers in his possession,
    (b) the packet containing the electronic record (if any),
    (c) the ballot paper accounts and the statements of rejected ballot papers and of the result of the verification of the ballot paper accounts,
    (d) the tendered votes lists, the lists of voters with disabilities assisted by companions, the lists of votes marked by the presiding officer and the related statements, the lists maintained under rule 44 and the declarations made by the companions of voters with disabilities,
    (e) the packets of the completed corresponding number lists,
    (f) the packets of certificates as to employment on duty on the day of the poll, and
    (g) the packets containing marked copies of registers (including any marked copy notices issued under section 13B(3B) or (3D) of the 1983 Act) and of the postal voters list, of the lists of proxies and of the proxy postal voters list,

endorsing on each packet a description of its contents, the date of the election to which they relate and the name of the Assembly constituency for which the election was held.

(2) At an election where the returning officer does not discharge the functions referred to in regulation 5 of the Combination of Polls Regulations, paragraph (1) must have effect as if sub paragraphs (d), (e) and (f) were omitted.

Orders for production of documents

61 (1) An order–
    (a) for the inspection or production of any rejected ballot papers in the custody of the relevant registration officer, or
    (b) for the opening of a packet containing the electronic record or a sealed packet of completed corresponding number lists or certificates as to employment on duty on the day of the poll or the inspection of any counted ballot papers in the

custody of the relevant registration officer,

may be made by a county court, if the court is satisfied by evidence on oath that the order is required for the purpose of instituting or maintaining a prosecution for an offence in relation to ballot papers, or for the purpose of an election petition.

(2)   An election court may make an order for the opening of a packet containing the electronic record or a sealed packet of completed corresponding number lists or certificates or for the inspection of any counted ballot papers in the custody of the relevant registration officer.

(3)   An order under this rule may be made subject to such conditions as to–
    (a)   persons,
    (b)   time,
    (c)   place and mode of inspection,
    (d)   production or opening,

as the court making the order thinks expedient; but in making and carrying into effect an order for the opening of a packet containing the electronic record or a packet of completed corresponding number lists or certificates or for the inspection of counted ballot papers, care must be taken that the way in which the vote of any particular elector has been given must not be disclosed until it has been proved–
    (i)   that his vote was given, and
    (ii)   that the vote has been declared by a competent court to be invalid.

(4)   An appeal lies to the High Court from any order of a county court under this rule.

(5)   Any power given under this rule to a county court may be exercised by any judge of the court otherwise than in open court.

(6)   Where an order is made for the production by the relevant registration officer of any document in his custody relating to any specified election–
    (a)   the production by him or his agent of the document or electronic record ordered in such manner as may be directed by that order will be conclusive evidence that the document or electronic record relates to the specified election, and
    (b)   any endorsement on any packet of ballot papers so produced will be *prima facie* evidence that the ballot papers are what they are stated to be by the endorsement.

(7)   The production from proper custody of–
    (a)   a ballot paper purporting to have been used at any election, or
    (b)   a copy of the electronic record which purports to record that a particular ballot paper was used at any election, and

a completed corresponding number list with a number written beside the number of the ballot paper, will be *prima facie* evidence that the elector whose vote was given by that ballot paper was the person who, at the time of the election, had affixed to his entry in the register of electors or on the notice issued under section 13B(3B) or (3D) of the 1983 Act, the same number as was written on the completed corresponding number list.

(8)   Unless authorised by this rule, no person may be allowed to inspect any rejected or counted ballot papers in the custody of the relevant registration officer or open any sealed packets of completed corresponding number lists, certificates of employment on the day of the poll or containing the electronic record.

Retention and destruction of documents and records

62   The relevant registration officer must retain or cause to be retained for one year all documents and, where applicable, electronic records relating to an election forwarded

to him in pursuance of these Rules by a CRO, and then, unless otherwise directed by an order of a county court, a Crown Court, a magistrate's court or an election court, must cause them to be destroyed.

Part 8
Death of Candidate

Deceased independent candidate

63 (1) This rule applies if at a contested election proof is given to the GLRO's satisfaction before the result of the election is declared that one of the persons named or to be named in the ballot papers as an independent candidate has died.

(2) Subject to this rule and rules 65 and 66, these rules apply to the election as if the candidate had not died.

(3) The following provisions of these rules do not apply in relation to the deceased candidate–
    (a) rule 33(1)(c) and (d) (admission to polling station),
    (b) rule 47(3)(c) to (e) (attendance at count),
    (c) rule 58(5) (forfeiture of deposit).

(4) If only two persons are shown as standing nominated in the statement of persons nominated the GLRO must–
    (a) if polling has not begun, countermand the notice of poll,
    (b) if polling has begun, direct that the poll is abandoned, and
    (c) subject to rule 66, treat the election as an uncontested election.

(5) For the purposes of this rule a person is named or to be named on the ballot papers as an independent candidate if the description (if any) on his nomination paper is not authorised as mentioned in rule 6(5) or (7).

Deceased independent candidate wins

64 (1) This rule applies if at an election mentioned in rule 63 either–
    (a) the deceased candidate is given a majority of votes in accordance with rules 55(5) or (6),
    (b) the deceased candidate is given more than half of all the first preference votes in accordance with rule 55(4)(a), or
    (c) the deceased candidate is given the greatest total number of votes following the second calculation in accordance with rule 56.

(2) Rule 57 (declaration of result) does not apply but the GLRO must–
    (a) declare that the majority or greatest total number of votes has been given to the deceased candidate,
    (b) declare that no person is returned, and
    (c) give public notice of the relevant figures supplied to election agents in accordance with rules 56(2) and 57(2) together with the number of rejected ballot papers under each head shown in the statement of rejected ballot papers.

(3) The provisions of these Rules as to the inspection, production, retention and destruction of ballot papers and other documents apply to any documents relating to a poll to which paragraph (1) applies as they would if the election had resulted in a declaration under rule 57.

(4) Rule 58 (return or forfeiture of candidate's deposit) does not apply in relation to the remaining candidates.

(5)   The election must be commenced afresh within the period of 35 days (computed in accordance with rule 4) beginning with the day of the election to which paragraph (1) applies.

(6)   The proceedings with reference to the recommenced election must be conducted in accordance with these Rules as modified by the following provisions of this rule and the provisions in the By-election timetable.

(7)   No fresh nomination is necessary in the case of a person shown in the statement of persons nominated for the election to which paragraph (1) applies, and no other nomination may be made for the recommenced election.

(8)   Instead of the information required by rule 5(1)(a) (date by which nomination papers must be received), the notice of election issued at the recommenced election must state that no fresh nomination may be made.

(9)   Rule 9 (deposit) does not apply.

Party candidate

65 (1)   This rule applies if–
   (a)   at a contested election, proof is given to the GLRO's satisfaction before the result of the election is declared that one of the persons named or to be named as a candidate in the ballot paper has died, and
   (b)   that person is standing in the name of a registered party.

(2)   The GLRO must–
   (a)   countermand notice of the poll, or
   (b)   if polling has begun, direct that the poll be abandoned,
   and the provisions of section 39(1) and (5) (local elections void etc in England and Wales) of the 1983 Act apply in respect of the unfilled vacancy.

(3)   For the purposes of this rule–
   (a)   a person stands in the name of a registered party if his nomination paper contains a description which is authorised as mentioned in rule 6(5) or (7).
   (b)   a registered party is a party which is registered under Part 2 of the 2000 Act.

Abandoned poll

66 (1)   This rule applies to–
   (a)   a poll which is abandoned in pursuance of rule 63(4)(b) as if it were a poll at a contested election, or
   (b)   a poll which is abandoned in pursuance of rule 65(2)

(2)   The presiding officer at any polling station must take the like steps (so far as not already taken) for the delivery to the CRO of the ballot box and of ballot papers and other documents in his possession as he is required to do on the close of the poll.

(3)   The CRO must dispose of the ballot papers and other documents in his possession as he is required to do on the completion of the counting of the votes.

(4)   It is not necessary for a ballot paper account to be prepared or verified.

(5)   The CRO must take no step or further step for the counting of the ballot papers or of the votes.

(6)   The CRO must seal up all the ballot papers (whether the votes on them have been counted or not) and it will not be necessary to seal up counted and rejected ballot papers in separate packets.

(7)   The provisions of these Rules as to the inspection, production, retention and destruction of ballot papers and other documents relating to a poll at an election

apply subject to the modifications in paragraphs (8) and (9).

(8) Ballot papers on which the votes were neither counted nor rejected must be treated as counted ballot papers.

(9) No order is to be made for–

    (a) the production or inspection of any ballot papers, or

    (b) for the opening of a sealed packet of completed corresponding number lists or certificates as to employment on duty on the day of the poll,

unless the order is made by a court with reference to a prosecution.

(10) The countermand of the notice of poll or abandonment of the poll at the election, will not effect the poll at each relevant election or referendum.

SCHEDULE 8
COMBINED MANUAL COUNT RULES

Rule 6

Citation

1   This Schedule may be cited as the Combined Manual Count Rules.

Interpretation

2 (1)   In this Schedule–

"CMER" means the Constituency Members Election Rules in Schedule 5;

"LMER" means the London Members Election Rules in Schedule 6;

"MER" means the Mayoral Election Rules in Schedule 7;

"relevant election or referendum" means one or more of the following–

(a)   a Parliamentary election,

(b)   a European Parliamentary election,

(c)   a local government election (including another Authority election where more than one is taken together),

(d)   a local authority mayoral election or referendum in accordance with regulations made under sections 44 and 105, or 45 and 105, of the Local Government Act 2000.

(2)   If the votes at an Authority election, which is combined with a relevant election or referendum, are counted without the use of an electronic counting system, the CMER, the LMER and the MER, will have effect as if the provisions listed in column (1) of Table 1 were modified as shown in column (2).

Table 1

(1) Rule(s)	(2) Modification
CMER rule 17 (ballot papers)	In paragraph (3)(a) omit ", so far as practicable for the purposes of electronic counting,".
LMER rule 18 (ballot papers)	In paragraph (4)(a) omit ", so far as practicable for the purposes of electronic counting,".
MER rule 17 (ballot papers)	In paragraph (3)(a) omit ", so far as practicable for the purposes of electronic counting,".
CMER rule 47 (attendance at verification and the Counting of votes)	In paragraph (4)(a) omit the words "and technical assistants".
LMER rule 48 (attendance at verification and the local count)	After paragraph (6) insert–
MER rule 47 (attendance at verification and the local count)	"(7) In particular, where the votes are counted by sorting the ballot papers according to the candidate for whom the vote is given and then counting the number of ballot papers for each candidate, the counting agents must be entitled to satisfy themselves that the ballot papers are correctly sorted.".
CMER rule 49 (verification and the count)	After paragraph (1)(d) insert–
LMER rule 50 (verification and the	"(da) separate the ballot papers relating to

local count)	the election from those relating to the other Authority elections.". After paragraph (2)(b) insert– "(c) mix together the postal ballot papers and the ballot papers from all of the containers and count the votes given on them,". Omit paragraph (4). For paragraph (8) substitute– "(8) After completing the proceedings under paragraph (1) or (2), the CRO must mix together the ballot papers used at the election and count the votes given on them." In paragraph (9) omit "cause the electronic counting system to". Omit paragraph (11).
MER rule 49 (verification and the local count)	After paragraph (1)(d) insert– "(da) separate the ballot papers relating to the election from those relating to the other Authority elections.". After paragraph (2)(b) insert– "(c) mix together the postal ballot papers and the ballot papers from all of the containers and count the votes given on them,". Omit paragraph (4). For paragraph (8) substitute– "(8) After completing the proceedings under paragraph (1) and (2), the CRO must mix together all of the ballot papers used at the election in the Assembly constituency and– (a) where the election is contested by more than two candidates, count the first preference votes given on them, (b) where the election is contested by only two candidates, count the votes given on them.". In paragraph (9) omit "cause the electronic counting system to". Omit paragraph (11).
CMER rule 50 LMER rule 51(rejected ballot papers)	For paragraph (3) substitute– "(3) The CRO must endorse the word "rejected" on any ballot paper which under this rule is not to be counted, and must add to the endorsement the words "rejection objected to" if any objection to his decision is made by a counting agent.". Omit paragraphs (4)-(10).
MER rule 50 (rejected ballot Papers)	For paragraph (4) substitute– "(4) The CRO must endorse the word

"rejected" on any ballot paper which under this rule is not to be counted, and must add to the endorsement the words "rejection objected to" if any objection to his decision is made by a counting agent."

Omit paragraphs (5) to (12).

Omit sub-paragraph (13)(e) and for sub-paragraph (13)(d) substitute–

"(d) unmarked or void for uncertainty as to the first preference vote.".

LMER rule 54 (procedure at conclusion of local count)	For paragraph (2) substitute– "(2) As soon as practicable after the statement is drawn up under paragraph (1), the CRO must inform the GLRO of its contents.".
MER rule 53 (procedure at Conclusion of local count)	Omit paragraph (1)(c)(iii). For paragraph (2) substitute– "(2) As soon as practicable after the statement is drawn up under paragraph (1), the CRO must inform the GLRO of its contents.".
LMER rule 55 (attendance at allocation of seats) MER rule 54 (attendance at the central calculation)	In paragraph (2)(b) omit "or technical assistant".
MER rule 55 (the first calculation and resolution of equality)	For paragraph (4)(b) substitute– "(b) if paragraph 4(1) of that Schedule applies (no candidate with overall majority of first preference votes), the GLRO must direct every CRO at the election who has counted manually to count the second preference votes given as mentioned in paragraph 4(5) of that Schedule.".

In Part 5, before rule 56 insert–

"56ZA The count of second preference votes

(1) As soon as the CRO has received such a direction as is mentioned in rule 55(4)(b) he must count the number of second preference votes for each of the candidates remaining in the contest given by voters who did not give their first preference vote to any of those candidates.

(2) A ballot paper which is not otherwise void and on which not more than one second preference vote is marked will be valid as respects that vote and must be counted accordingly if, but only if, a valid

first preference vote has also been
marked.

(3) Rules 47, 49, 50, 53 and 55 will apply in
relation to the count of second
preference votes as they apply in relation
to the count of first preference votes,
and as if references to first preference
votes were references to second
preference votes.

(4) The CRO may not be required to re-
examine any decision taken under rule
50.

(5) As soon as practicable after the second
preference votes have been counted, the
CRO must inform the GLRO of the
number of second preference votes cast
for each of the candidates remaining in
the contest.".

MER rule 56 (the second calculation and resolution of equality)	For paragraph (1) substitute–
	"(1) As soon as the GLRO has received the information required by rule 56ZA(5) from every CRO he must comply with paragraph 4(5) and (6) of Schedule 2 to the 1999 Act.".
CMER rule 54 (declaration of result)	Omit paragraphs (2) and (3).
LMER rule 57 (declaration of result)	Omit paragraphs (3) and (4).
MER rule 57 (declaration of result)	Omit paragraphs (2)(e), (4) and (5).

SCHEDULE 9

REQUIREMENTS FOR NOTICES FOR GUIDANCE OF VOTERS

Rule 9

Interpretation

1   In this Schedule–
"CMER" means the Constituency Members Election Rules in Schedule 1 or 5;
"LMER" means the London Members Election Rules in Schedule 2 or 6;
"MER" means the Mayoral Election Rules in Schedule 3 or 7.

Requirement relating to all notices

2   Notices must be provided by the GLRO for the guidance of voters in accordance with the CMER, LMER, MER.

3   Notices for the guidance of voters to be exhibited–
  (a)   outside the polling station,
  (b)   inside the polling station–
    (i)   in the communal areas, and
    (ii)   in a voting compartment,
may differ depending on where they are to be displayed.

4   Notices provided must be of the same description and appearance or in a form to the like effect for use at all polling stations in all Assembly constituencies.

5   Notices may contain any information providing guidance to voters as to how to exercise their vote in a manner that will ensure that it is regarded as validly cast and can be efficiently processed by the electronic counting system if one is in use, but must not contain–
  (a)   any material referring to or promoting any candidate or party at the election, other than such name and particulars of such candidate or registered party as may appear on a ballot paper at the election, or
  (b)   any example or illustration referring to a candidate or a registered party that does not equally refer to all candidates and registered parties (as the case may be) at the election.

Requirements relating to specific notices

6   Notices for display inside a polling station must contain information explaining–
  (a)   which election each ballot paper is for,
  (b)   how many votes a voter has in each election,
  (c)   the marks to be used, and the manner in which they should be used, in order to ensure that a vote is counted for any candidate or party (as the case may be),
  (d)   whether or not the voter should fold the ballot paper in two before showing the presiding officer the number and the other unique identifying mark on the back and putting it in the ballot box,
  (e)   which ballot box the voter is to put their ballot paper into after recording their vote, and
  (f)   what to do if the voter spoils a ballot paper.

7   Notices for display inside a polling station may also contain information giving examples or illustrating of any of the kinds of information in paragraph 5 of this Schedule.

8   Notices for display inside a voting compartment shall contain information explaining–
  (a)   which election each ballot paper is for,
  (b)   how many votes a voter has in each election.

9   Notices for display inside a polling booth may also contain–

    (a) the information mentioned in paragraph 6(c) to (f) of this Schedule, and

    (b) information giving examples or illustration of any of the information mentioned in paragraph 6(a) to (f) of this Schedule.

10   All notices shall be easily legible.

SCHEDULE 10

SCHEDULE OF FORMS

Interpretation

1   In this Schedule–

"CMER" means the Constituency Members Election Rules in Schedule 1 or 5;

"LMER" means the London Members Election Rules in Schedule 2 or 6;

"MER" means the Mayoral Election Rules in Schedule 3 or 7.

2   The forms in this Schedule may be adapted so far as circumstances require (and in particular, for the purposes of electronic counting), but any adaptation made by the CRO must, where appropriate, be in compliance with any direction issued by the GLRO under rule 11.

Forms

Form 1:   Nomination paper (constituency and individual London member candidates)

Form 2:   Nomination paper (London member party list candidates)

Form 3:   Nomination paper (Mayor of London candidates)

Form 4:   Candidates consent to nomination

Form 5:   Ballot paper for constituency member elections
Directions as to printing the ballot paper

Form 6:   Ballot paper for London members elections
Directions as to printing the ballot paper

Form 7:   Ballot paper for mayoral elections
Directions as to printing the ballot paper

Form 8:   Corresponding number list L1

Form 9:   Corresponding number list L2

Form 10:   *Repealed*

Form 11:   postal voting statement (ordinary elections or constituency member or mayoral by-election)

Form 11A: Postal voting statement: for use at a combined election where issue and receipt of postal ballot papers are taken together

Form 11B: Postal voting statement: for use at a combined election where issue and receipt of postal ballot papers are not taken together

Form 12:   Official poll card

Form 13:   Official postal poll card

Form 14:   Official proxy poll card

Form 15:   Official proxy postal poll card

Form 16:   Notices for the guidance of voters at by -elections and Ordinary elections

Form 17:   Notices for guidance of voters at Authority elections combined with another election

Form 18:   Certificate of employment

Form 19:   Declaration to be made by the companion of a voter with disabilities

Form 19A: Declaration to be made by the companion of a voter with disabilities: combined election

Form 20:   Election agent's declaration as to election expenses (list candidates)

Form 21:   List candidate's declaration as to election expenses

Greater London Authority Elections (Election Addresses) Order 2003 (SI 2003/1907)

Made 16th July 2003

Citation and commencement

1 This Order may be cited as the Greater London Authority Elections (Election Addresses) Order 2003 and shall come into force on the day after it is made.

Interpretation

2(1) In this Order—

"the 1983 Act" means the Representation of the People Act 1983;

"the 1999 Act" means the Greater London Authority Act 1999;

"the PPER Act" means the Political Parties, Elections and Referendums Act 2000;

"the Authority" means the Greater London Authority;

"candidate" means, unless the context otherwise requires, a person who stands nominated as a candidate for the office of Mayor at the election;

"election" means, unless the context otherwise requires, an election for the return of the Mayor at an ordinary election;

"election address" shall be construed in accordance with article 4;

"election booklet" shall be construed in accordance with article 7;

"elector" in relation to an "election"—

(i) means a person who is registered in the register of local government electors for an electoral area in Greater London on the last day permitted for publication of notice of the election; and

(ii) includes a person then shown in any such register (or, in the case of a person who has an anonymous entry in any such register, in the record of anonymous entries for that electoral area) as below voting age if (but only if) it appears from the register (or from the record) that he will be of voting age on the day fixed for the poll;

"the GLRO" means the Greater London returning officer;

"individual candidate" means a candidate other than a list candidate;

"list candidate" means a person included on a party list;

"party list" means a list submitted to the GLRO in accordance with paragraph 5 (party lists and individual candidates) of Part II of Schedule 2 to the 1999 Act on behalf of a party registered under Part II (registration of political parties) of the Political Parties, Elections and Referendums Act 2000;

"print" means print by whatever means (and "printer" shall be construed accordingly);

"registered political party" means a party which is registered under Part II (registration of political parties) of the PPER Act at the latest time by which the notice of election is required to be published;

(2)   In paragraph (ii) of the definition of "elector" in article 2, "anonymous entry" and "record of anonymous entries" have the meaning given in section 202(1) of the 1983 Act.

Mayoral candidate's right to delivery of an election address

3   Each candidate at an election shall be entitled (subject to and in accordance with the provisions of this Order) to have an election address prepared on behalf of the candidate included in an election booklet prepared by the GLRO delivered at the Authority's expense.

Election address

4   An election address, in relation to a candidate, is a statement prepared by the candidate's election agent which complies with the provisions of articles 5 and 6.

Contents of election addresses

5(1)   An election address must contain matter relating to the election only.

(2)   In particular, an election address must not contain

    (a)   any advertising material (other than material promoting the candidate as a candidate at the election); or

    (b)   any material referring to any other candidate or to a candidate for election to the Assembly; or

    (c)   any material appearing to the GLRO

        (i)   to be included with a view to commercial gain; or

        (ii)   to be indecent, obscene or offensive; or

        (iii)   to be such that its publication or distribution would be likely to amount to the commission of an offence.

(3)   An election address may include a representation of the registered emblem, or (as the case may be) one of the registered emblems, of a registered political party, if the address is prepared on behalf of an authorised party candidate.

(3A)   Where an election address is prepared on behalf of an authorised party candidate, the address may contain a description registered under section 28A or, if the description is registered for use by candidates of two or more parties, under section 28B of the PPER Act.

(4)   In paragraphs (3) and (3A) "authorised party candidate", in relation to a registered political party, means a candidate who has been authorised to use the emblem or description in question by a certificate

    (a)   issued by or on behalf of the registered nominating officer of the party where the description is registered under section 28A of the PPER Act, or of each of the parties where the description is registered under section 28B of that Act, and

    (b)   received by the GLRO before the last time for the delivery of nomination papers for the election.

(5)   An election address must

    (a)   contain a statement to the effect that it has been prepared by the candidate's election agent; and

    (b)   give the name and address of the election agent.

Form of election addresses

6(1) Subject to any requirements imposed by or under this article, the format of a candidate's election address may be determined by the candidate (and, in particular, may consist of a combination of words, pictures and artwork).

(2) An election address must be printed on not more than two sides of A5 paper, but if such an address is printed on two sides of such paper

    (a) it must, when submitted to the GLRO for inclusion in the election booklet, be accompanied by a second version printed on a single side of such paper; and

    (b) if the total number of candidates from whom election addresses have been accepted by the GLRO by the last time for the delivery of nomination papers for the election exceeds 15, the version to be included in the election booklet shall be the second version.

(3) An election address must

    (a) comply with such requirements as to typographical layout, margins and the use of colour as the GLRO may specify; and

    (b) comply with such other requirements as he may specify with a view to facilitating its reproduction as a page or pages of the election booklet.

(4) An election address must, when submitted to the GLRO for inclusion in the election booklet, be accompanied

    (a) where the address is to contain a photograph of the candidate, by two identical copies of the photograph, of which one is signed on the back by the candidate; and

    (b) in any case, by such copies of anything contained in the address as the GLRO may reasonably require in connection with the reproduction of the address.

The election booklet

7(1) The election booklet is a document prepared by the GLRO which contains the election addresses of all candidates who

    (a) desire their election addresses to be included in the booklet, and

    (b) have submitted

        (i) those addresses, and

        (ii) any additional material required under article 6(4) above,

to the GLRO by the last time for the delivery of nomination papers for the election.

(2) If

    (a) it appears to the GLRO that any of the requirements of articles 5 and 6 above have not been complied with in relation to an election address, or

    (b) a candidate fails to make the payment required by article 10 below in respect of an election address,

the GLRO shall decline to include the address in the election booklet.

Form of election booklet

8(1) The order in which the candidates' election addresses appear in the election booklet shall be determined by lot drawn by the GLRO, as soon as reasonably practicable after the last time for the delivery of nomination papers for the election.

(2) The election booklet shall include, in addition to candidates' election addresses, a statement by the GLRO

    (a) giving the date of the election and explaining the nature and purpose of the election booklet;

    (b) listing all the candidates for the office of Mayor (whether or not their election addresses are included in the booklet), in the order they are to appear on the ballot paper;

   (c) listing all the candidates at the ordinary election for the return of London members by

      (i) the names of the registered political parties that have been nominated (including thereunder the names of list candidates appearing in the order in which they appear on the party list); and

      (ii) the names of individual candidates;

     in the order they are to appear on the ballot paper;

   (d) listing all the candidates at the ordinary election for the return of constituency members, in alphabetical order by constituency and with the names of candidates for each constituency in the order they are to appear on the ballot paper.

(3) The GLRO shall include in a listing of candidates under paragraphs (2)(b) to (d) any description of the candidate as stated on his nomination paper.

(4) The election booklet may also include such other information as the GLRO is required or permitted by or under any enactment to publish in the booklet.

(5) The election booklet must

   (a) contain a statement that it has been published by the GLRO; and

   (b) give the name and address of the GLRO and those of the printer of the booklet.

(6) Subject to paragraphs (1) to (5) above, the form of the election booklet shall be determined by the GLRO.

(7) The election agent of each candidate whose election address has been accepted by the GLRO for inclusion in the booklet shall be given an opportunity to attend at a time and place notified to him by the GLRO in order to check, and submit to the GLRO typographical corrections to, the proof of the candidate's address, by such time as the GLRO may require.

(8) If the election agent of any such candidate fails to avail himself of that opportunity, the GLRO may

   (a) make such typographical corrections to the proof as appear to him to be appropriate; and

   (b) proceed with the printing and distribution of the election booklet without further reference to the candidate or his election agent (and without incurring any liability for any errors in the candidate's address).

(9) No person other than

   (a) the candidate in respect of whom an election address is included in the election booklet, or

   (b) the candidate's election agent,

shall incur any civil or criminal liability in respect of the publication of that address in the election booklet or its dissemination in accordance with article 9 below.

Distribution of election booklets

9(1) The GLRO shall cause copies of the election booklet to be addressed and delivered to each elector at the Authority's expense.

(2) The election booklets shall be delivered by a postal operator within the meaning of Part 3 of the Postal Services Act 2011.

(3) The GLRO may in addition disseminate the contents of the election booklet by

   (a) the publication by the GLRO of the contents on a website;

   (b) making printed copies, or copies of the booklet in any electronic format, available to anyone who makes a request to the GLRO for such copies;

   (c) making the contents available, so far as practicable, in large print, in Braille, and on audio tape, to anyone who makes a request to the GLRO for a copy of the contents in such a format;

(d) making copies of the booklet available at

   (i) the offices of the Authority. . ., the Metropolitan Police Authority, the London Fire and Emergency Planning Authority, and Transport for London;

   (ii) the offices of London borough councils and the Common Council of the City of London;

   (iii) public libraries.

Contributions by candidates towards cost of printing

10(1) Each candidate by whom an election address is submitted to the GLRO for inclusion in the election booklet shall pay the sum of £10,000 to the GLRO as a contribution towards the expenses incurred by him in respect of the printing of the election booklet.

(2) The payment required by paragraph (1) above shall be made at such time, and in such manner, as the GLRO may determine.

(3) A candidate shall be entitled to a full refund of any such payment if, but only if, the candidate has given notice of withdrawal of his candidature before the last time for the withdrawal of candidates.

(4) If the total amount of the payments made by candidates under this article exceeds the total amount of the expenses incurred by the GLRO in respect of the printing of the election booklet, the GLRO shall

   (a) divide the amount of the excess between those candidates in equal shares, and

   (b) send to each of those candidates a payment in respect of his share.

Contributions to printing cost as candidates' election expenses

11(1) The amount of any payment made by a candidate under article 10 above (or if paragraph (4) of that article applies, the net amount of any such payment after deducting the payment under that paragraph) shall be taken, for the purposes of Part II of the 1983 Act (the election campaign), to be an amount of election expenses incurred by the candidate in relation to the election.

(2) Nothing in section 75(1) of the 1983 Act (restriction on third party expenditure) shall be taken to apply, in relation to any candidate, to any expenses incurred by the GLRO in consequence of the provisions of this Order.

Greater London Authority Elections
(Expenses) Order 2000
(SI 2000/789)

Made 16th March 2000

Citation and commencement

1   This Order may be cited as the Greater London Authority Elections (Expenses) Order 2000 and shall come into force on the day after the day on which it is made.

Third parties' expenses

2   In relation to an Authority election, for the monetary sum specified in section 75(1)(ii) of the Representation of the People Act 1983 (limit on expenses incurred by a person other than a candidate, agent, or person authorised by an agent), there shall be substituted the following sums

    (a)   in relation to an election of the Mayor of London £25,000;

    (b)   in relation to an election of a constituency member of the London Assembly £1,800; and

    (c)   in relation to an election of the London members of the London Assembly at an ordinary election £25,000.

Candidates' and agents' expenses

3   As respects Authority elections the maximum amounts of the sums which may be paid and the expenses which may be incurred by a candidate or his election agent shall be as follows

    (a)   £420,000 for a candidate in an election of the Mayor of London;

    (b)   £35,000 for a candidate in an election of a constituency member of the London Assembly;

    (c)   £330,000 for an individual candidate in an election of the London members of the London Assembly at an ordinary election;

    (d)   £330,000 for the purposes of section 76(1A) of the Representation of the People Act 1983 (expenses of candidates to be London Members of the London Assembly on a list submitted by a registered political party).

Holders of Hereditary Peerages (Overseas Electors) (Transitional Provisions) Order 2001 (SI 2001/84)

1(1)   This Order may be cited as the Holders of Hereditary Peerages (Overseas Electors) (Transitional Provisions) Order 2001 and shall come into force on 16th February 2001.

(2)   The Holders of Hereditary Peerages (Extension of the Franchise) (Transitional Provisions) Order 1999 is hereby revoked.

2   In the case of the holder of a hereditary peerage to whom section 3(1) of the House of Lords Act 1999 applies, any reference in section 1(3) or (4)(b) of the Representation of the People Act 1985 (conditions as to qualification as an overseas elector) to a register of parliamentary electors shall include
   (a)   any register of local government electors in Great Britain; and
   (b)   any register of local electors in Northern Ireland,
which was required to be published on any date not later than 15th February 2000.

Local and European Parliamentary Elections (Registration of Citizens of Accession States) Regulations 2003
(SI 2003/1557)

Made 12th June 2003

Citation and interpretation

1(1) These Regulations may be cited as the Local and European Parliamentary Elections (Registration of Citizens of Accession States) Regulations 2003 and shall come into force on 9th July 2003.

(2) In these Regulations
   "the 1983 Act" means the Representation of the People Act 1983, and expressions defined in the 1983 Act shall have the same meaning in these Regulations;
   "the 1989 Act" means the Elected Authorities (Northern Ireland) Act 1989, and expressions defined in the 1989 Act shall have the same meaning in these Regulations;
   "the 2001 Franchise Regulations" means the European Parliamentary Elections (Franchise of Relevant Citizens of the Union) Regulations 2001;
   "Accession State" means any of the following states
   (a) the Czech Republic,
   (b) the Republic of Estonia,
   (c) the Republic of Cyprus,
   (d) the Republic of Latvia,
   (e) the Republic of Lithuania,
   (f) the Republic of Hungary,
   (g) the Republic of Malta,
   (h) the Republic of Poland,
   (i) the Republic of Slovenia, or
   (j) the Slovak Republic;
   "citizen of an Accession State" means a national of one of the Accession States and "relevant citizen of an Accession State" means such a citizen who is not a Commonwealth citizen or a citizen of the Republic of Ireland; and
   "Treaty of Athens" means the Treaty signed at Athens on 16th April 2003 concerning the accession of the Czech Republic, the Republic of Estonia, the Republic of Cyprus, the Republic of Latvia, the Republic of Lithuania, the Republic of Hungary, the Republic of Malta, the Republic of Poland, the Republic of Slovenia and the Slovak Republic to the European Union.

Modification of the 1983 Act

2(1) The provisions of the 1983 Act shall apply for the purposes of

    (a) the registration of relevant citizens of the Accession States as local government electors before 1st May 2004,

    (b) making arrangements for persons so registered to exercise the right to vote if they become relevant citizens of the Union on 1st May 2004, and

    (c) the alteration or removal of entries on the register in relation to relevant citizens of the Accession States after that date,

subject to the following modifications.

(2) In section 4 (entitlement to registration), insert after subsection (3)

"(3A) The entry in the register of local government electors for a relevant citizen of an Accession State shall, subject to subsection (3B) below, include a mark against his name in the register consisting of the letter "Y" to indicate that he is registered as a relevant citizen of an Accession State and, before the date on which that Accession State accedes to the European Union, he shall not be treated as an elector for any purposes other than those of an election the poll for which is held on or after that date.

(3B) Where a relevant citizen of an Accession State is registered in the register of local government electors, and that State accedes to the European Union on 1st May 2004, the mark referred to in subsection (3A) above shall be removed from his entry in the register.

(3C) From 1st May 2004, no relevant citizen of an Accession State shall be entitled to be registered in the register of local government electors under subsection (3)(c) unless he has become a relevant citizen of the Union following the accession to the European Union of the Accession State of which he is a national.".

(3) In

    (a) section 4(3)(c);

    (b) section 7B(3)(e);

    (c) section 7B(7)(a);

    (d) section 15(5)(a);

    (e) section 16(e); and

    (f) section 17(1)(c),

for "relevant citizen of the Union" substitute in each case "relevant citizen of the Union or of an Accession State".

(4) In section 49 (effect of registers), insert after subsection (5)

"(5A) Nothing in subsection (5) shall prevent a relevant citizen of an Accession State from being excluded from voting on the ground that the Accession State of which he is a national has not acceded to the European Union.".

(5) In section 61(1) (other voting offences), for the words "For the purposes of this subsection" to the end of the subsection, substitute

"For the purposes of this subsection, references to a person being subject to a legal incapacity to vote do not, in relation to things done before polling day at the election or first election at which or for which they are done

    (i) include his being below voting age if he will be of voting age on that day;

    (ii) include his being a citizen of an Accession State, and therefore not entitled to vote until the Accession State in question accedes to the European Union on 1st May 2004.".

(6) In section 62 (offences as to declarations), insert after subsection (2)

"(3) For the purposes of subsection (1), a person shall not be treated as being subject to a legal incapacity to vote because he is a citizen of an Accession

State, and therefore not entitled to vote until the Accession State in question accedes to the European Union on 1st May 2004.".

(7) In section 202(1) of the 1983 Act
  (a) there shall be inserted at the appropriate place
  """Accession State" means any of the following States
    (a) the Czech Republic,
    (b) the Republic of Estonia,
    (c) the Republic of Cyprus,
    (d) the Republic of Latvia,
    (e) the Republic of Lithuania,
    (f) the Republic of Hungary,
    (g) the Republic of Malta,
    (h) the Republic of Poland,
    (i) the Republic of Slovenia, or
    (j) the Slovak Republic;";
  """citizen of an Accession State" means a national of one of the Accession States and "relevant citizen of an Accession State" means such a citizen who is not a Commonwealth citizen or a citizen of the Republic of Ireland"; and
  (b) in the definition of "elector", after the word "age", insert ", or, subject to section 4(3A), those shown in the register as a relevant citizen of an Accession State,".

Modification of the Electoral Law (Northern Ireland) Act 1962

3(1) Paragraph 12A (supplementary provisions about voting offences) of Schedule 9 to the Electoral Law (Northern Ireland) Act 1962, shall for the purposes of
  (a) the registration of relevant citizens of the Accession States as local electors before 1st May 2004, and
  (b) making arrangements for persons so registered to exercise the right to vote if they become relevant citizens of the Union on 1st May 2004,
  apply subject to the modification in paragraph (2).

(2) In sub-paragraph (1), for the words "For the purposes of this sub-paragraph" to the end of the sub-paragraph, substitute
  "For the purposes of this sub-paragraph, references to a person being subject to a legal incapacity to vote do not, in relation to things done before polling day at the election or first election at which or for which they are done
    (i) include his being below voting age if he will be of voting age on that day;
    (ii) include his being a citizen of an Accession State, and therefore not entitled to vote until the Accession State in question accedes to the European Union on 1st May 2004.".

Modification of the 1989 Act as regards the application of the 1983 Act to local elections in Northern Ireland

4 Section 2 of, and Schedule 1 to, the 1989 Act (application of provisions of Representation of the People Act 1983 to local elections in Northern Ireland) shall for the purposes of
  (a) the registration of relevant citizens of the Accession States as local electors before 1st May 2004,
  (b) making arrangements for persons so registered to exercise the right to vote if they become relevant citizens of the Union on 1st May 2004, and
  (c) the alteration or removal of entries on the register in relation to relevant citizens of the Accession States after that date,
  apply subject to the further modifications to the 1983 Act made in regulation 2 above.

Amendment of the 2001 Franchise Regulations: applications and declarations to be sent to the appointed person

5   Regulation 8 (copies of certain applications and declarations to be sent to the Secretary of State) of the 2001 Franchise Regulations shall be amended as follows

    (a)   in paragraph (1), for "Secretary of State" substitute "the person shown as the representative of the State in respect of which the applicant is a national in a direction containing a list of such representatives issued by the Lord Chancellor in accordance with paragraph (3) below".

    (b)   insert after paragraph (2)

        "(3)   The Lord Chancellor shall issue directions identifying the representative for each Member State of the European Union to whom the documents referred to in paragraph (1) above are to be sent.".

Modification of the 2001 Franchise Regulations

6   The provisions of the 2001 Franchise Regulations shall apply for the purposes of

    (a)   the registration of relevant citizens of the Accession States as European Parliamentary electors before 1st May 2004,

    (b)   making arrangements for persons so registered to exercise the right to vote if they become relevant citizens of the Union on 1st May 2004, and

    (c)   the alteration or removal of entries on the register in relation to relevant citizens of the Accession States after that date,

subject to the modifications made in Schedule 1 to these Regulations.

Consequential modifications

7   The provisions of the Representation of the People (England and Wales) Regulations 2001, the Representation of the People (Scotland) Regulations 2001, the Representation of the People (Northern Ireland) Regulations 2001, the Local Elections (Northern Ireland) Order 1985, the Scottish Parliament (Elections etc) Order 2002 and the National Assembly for Wales (Representation of the People) Order 2003 shall apply for the purposes of

    (a)   the registration of relevant citizens of the Accession States as local electors before 1st May 2004,

    (b)   making arrangements for persons so registered to exercise the right to vote if they become relevant citizens of the Union on 1st May 2004, and

    (c)   the alteration or removal of entries on the register in relation to relevant citizens of the Accession States after that date,

subject to the modifications made in Schedule 2 to these Regulations.

SCHEDULE 1

APPLICATION OF THE 2001 FRANCHISE REGULATIONS WITH MODIFICATIONS

Regulation 6

Modification of the 2001 Franchise Regulations: interpretation

1(1)   Regulation 1(2) of the 2001 Franchise Regulations (citation, interpretation and extent) is modified as follows.

(2)   After the definition of "the 1983 Act" insert

    ""Accession State" means any of the following states

      (a)   the Czech Republic,

      (b)   the Republic of Estonia,

      (c)   the Republic of Cyprus,

      (d)   the Republic of Latvia,

      (e)   the Republic of Lithuania,

    (f) the Republic of Hungary,

    (g) the Republic of Malta,

    (h) the Republic of Poland,

    (i) the Republic of Slovenia, or

    (j) the Slovak Republic;"; and

""citizen of an Accession State" means a national of one of the Accession States and "relevant citizen of an Accession State" means such a citizen who is not a Commonwealth citizen or a citizen of the Republic of Ireland;".

Modification of the 2001 Franchise Regulations: entitlement to be registered

2   In regulation 4 of the 2001 Franchise Regulations (entitlement of relevant citizen of the Union to be registered as European parliamentary elector)

    (a) in paragraph (1)(c), after "is a relevant citizen of the Union" insert "or, subject to paragraph (1C) below, a relevant citizen of an Accession State".

    (b) after paragraph (1), insert

       "(1A) The entry in the register maintained under regulation 5(2) below for a relevant citizen of an Accession State shall, subject to paragraph (1B) below, include a mark against his name in the register consisting of the letter "Y" to indicate that he is registered as a relevant citizen of an Accession State and, before the date on which that State accedes to the European Union, he shall not be treated as an elector for any purposes other than those of an election the poll for which is held on or after that date.

       (1B) Where a relevant citizen of an Accession State is registered in the register maintained under regulation 5(2) below, and that State accedes to the European Union on 1st May 2004, the mark referred to in paragraph (1A) above shall be removed from his entry in the register.

       (1C) From 1st May 2004, no relevant citizen of an Accession State shall be entitled to be registered in the register maintained under regulation 5(2) below under paragraph (3)(c) unless he has become a relevant citizen of the Union following the accession to the European Union of the Accession State of which he is a national.".

Modification of the 2001 Franchise Regulations: registration officers

3   In regulation 5(1) (registration officers), after "registration of relevant citizens of the Union" insert "and relevant citizens of the Accession States".

Modification of the 2001 Franchise Regulations: application for registration

4   In regulation 6 (form of application and declaration required by regulation 4(1))

    (a) in paragraph (1), after "relevant citizen of the Union" insert "or of an Accession State";

    (b) in paragraph (2)(c), after "in the Member State" insert "or Accession State";

    (c) in paragraph (3), after "relevant citizens of the Union" insert "or of an Accession State".

Modification of the 2001 Franchise Regulations: applications and declarations to be sent to the appointed person

5   In regulation 8 (copies of certain applications and declarations to be sent to the Secretary of State) as amended by regulation 5 of these Regulations

    (a) in paragraph (1), after "relevant citizen of the Union" insert "or of an Accession State";

    (b) in paragraph (2), after "relevant citizen of the union" insert "or of an Accession

State";

   (c) in paragraph (3), after "Member State" insert "and Accession State".

Modification of the 2001 Franchise Regulations: application of the 1983 Act

6 In regulation 9(1) (application, with modifications, of provisions of the 1983 Act and Representation of the People Regulations), after "relevant citizens of the Union" insert "and of the Accession States".

Modification of the 2001 Franchise Regulations: removal of names from the register

7 In regulation 10 (removal of names from the register)

   (a) in paragraph (2), after "relevant citizen of the Union" insert "and, subject to paragraph (5) below, a relevant citizen of an Accession State";

   (b) in paragraph (4), substitute "Lord Chancellor" for "Secretary of State";

   (c) after paragraph (4), insert

    "(5) The registration officer shall remove the name of a relevant citizen of an Accession State registered in a register of electors maintained under regulation 5(2) if the Accession State of which he is a citizen does not accede to the European Union on 1st May 2004.".

Modification of the 2001 Franchise Regulations: Schedule

8(1) The Schedule (application, with modifications, of provisions of the 1983 Act and Representation of the People Regulations) shall be modified as follows.

(2) In Part I, in column 2, for the entry (b) relating to subsection (3) of section 63 of the 1983 Act, substitute

   "(b) for the words from "relating to" to the end, substitute "relating to the registration of relevant citizens of the Union or relevant citizens of the Accession States as European Parliamentary electors".".

(3) In column 2, in the entry relating to section 202 of the 1983 Act, add the following additional definitions

   ""Accession State" means any of the following states

   (a) the Czech Republic,

   (b) the Republic of Estonia,

   (c) the Republic of Cyprus,

   (d) the Republic of Latvia,

   (e) the Republic of Lithuania,

   (f) the Republic of Hungary,

   (g) the Republic of Malta,

   (h) the Republic of Poland,

   (i) the Republic of Slovenia, or

   (j) the Slovak Republic;"; and

   ""citizen of an Accession State" means a national of one of the Accession States and "relevant citizen of an Accession State" means such a citizen who is not a Commonwealth citizen or a citizen of the Republic of Ireland;".

(4) In column 2, for the entry relating to regulation 24 of the Representation of the People (England and Wales) Regulations 2001, substitute

   "In paragraph (2), for sub-paragraphs (b) to (d) substitute "(b) evidence of his status as a national of a Member State or of an Accession State or a statutory declaration as to that nationality.".".

(5) In column 2, for the entry relating to regulation 24 of the Representation of the People (Scotland) Regulations 2001, substitute

"In paragraph (2), for sub-paragraphs (b) to (d) substitute "(b) evidence of his status as a national of a Member State or of an Accession State or a statutory declaration as to that nationality.".".

(6)   In column 2, for the entry relating to regulation 24 of the Representation of the People (Northern Ireland) Regulations 2002, substitute
"In paragraph (2), for sub-paragraphs (b) to (d) substitute "(b) evidence of his status as a national of a Member State or of an Accession State or a statutory declaration as to that nationality.".".

SCHEDULE 2

**MODIFICATIONS CONSEQUENTIAL UPON THE REGISTRATION
OF CITIZENS OF ACCESSION STATES AS LOCAL ELECTORS**

Regulation 7

Modification of the Representation of the People (England and Wales) Regulations 2001

1(1)   The Representation of the People (England and Wales) Regulations 2001 shall be modified as follows.

(2)   In regulation 3 (interpretation), there shall be inserted in the appropriate place
""Accession State" means any of the following states
(a)   the Czech Republic,
(b)   the Republic of Estonia,
(c)   the Republic of Cyprus,
(d)   the Republic of Latvia,
(e)   the Republic of Lithuania,
(f)   the Republic of Hungary,
(g)   the Republic of Malta,
(h)   the Republic of Poland,
(i)   the Republic of Slovenia, or
(j)   the Slovak Republic;";
""citizen of an Accession State" means a national of one of the Accession States and "relevant citizen of an Accession State" means such a citizen who is not a Commonwealth citizen or a citizen of the Republic of Ireland;"; and
""Treaty of Athens" means the Treaty signed at Athens on 16th April 2003 concerning the accession of the Czech Republic, the Republic of Estonia, the Republic of Cyprus, the Republic of Latvia, the Republic of Lithuania, the Republic of Hungary, the Republic of Malta, the Republic of Poland, the Republic of Slovenia and the Slovak Republic to the European Union;".

(3)   In
(a)   regulation 24(2)(d)(ii);
(b)   regulation 26(3)(b); and
(c)   regulation 42(3),
for "relevant citizen of the Union" substitute in each case "relevant citizen of the Union or of an Accession State".

(4)   In regulation 33(2)
(i)   at the end of sub-paragraph (d), omit "or";
(ii)   insert after sub-paragraph (3)(e)
"; or
(f)   has been informed by the Lord Chancellor that the Accession State of which the relevant citizen is a national has not acceded to the European Union".

(5) In regulation 71
   (a) insert at the beginning of paragraph (2), "Subject to paragraph (3) below,";
   (b) after paragraph (2), insert "(3) In the case of a relevant citizen of an Accession State, no postal ballot paper or declaration of identity may be issued by the returning officer before he has been informed by the Lord Chancellor that the Accession State in question has ratified the Treaty of Athens.".

Modification of the Representation of the People (Scotland) Regulations 2001

2(1) The Representation of the People (Scotland) Regulations 2001 shall be modified as follows.

(2) In regulation 3 (interpretation), there shall be inserted in the appropriate place
   ""Accession State" means any of the following states
   (a) the Czech Republic,
   (b) the Republic of Estonia,
   (c) the Republic of Cyprus,
   (d) the Republic of Latvia,
   (e) the Republic of Lithuania,
   (f) the Republic of Hungary,
   (g) the Republic of Malta,
   (h) the Republic of Poland,
   (i) the Republic of Slovenia, or
   (j) the Slovak Republic;";
   ""citizen of an Accession State" means a national of one of the Accession States and "relevant citizen of an Accession State" means such a citizen who is not a Commonwealth citizen or a citizen of the Republic of Ireland;"; and
   ""Treaty of Athens" means the Treaty signed at Athens on 16th April 2003 concerning the accession of the Czech Republic, the Republic of Estonia, the Republic of Cyprus, the Republic of Latvia, the Republic of Lithuania, the Republic of Hungary, the Republic of Malta, the Republic of Poland, the Republic of Slovenia and the Slovak Republic to the European Union;".

(3) In
   (a) regulation 24(2)(d)(ii);
   (b) regulation 26(3)(b); and
   (c) regulation 42(2),
   for "relevant citizen of the Union" substitute in each case "relevant citizen of the Union or of an Accession State".

(4) In regulation 33(2)(a)
   (a) at the end of sub-paragraph (iv), omit "or";
   (b) at the end of sub-paragraph (v), substitute "or" for "and";
   (c) insert after sub-paragraph (v)
   "; or
      (vi) has been informed by the Secretary of State that the Accession State of which the relevant citizen is a national has not acceded to the European Union; and".

(5) In regulation 71
   (a) insert at the beginning of paragraph (2) "Subject to paragraph (3) below,";
   (b) after paragraph (2), insert
   "(3) In the case of a relevant citizen of an Accession State, no postal ballot paper or declaration of identity may be issued by the returning officer before he has been informed by the Secretary of State that the Accession State in question has ratified the Treaty of Athens.".

Modification of the Local Elections (Northern Ireland) Order 1985

3(1) Part III of Schedule 2 to the Local Elections (Northern Ireland) Order 1985 is modified as follows.

  (2) In paragraph 3 (interpretation), there shall be inserted in the appropriate place
""Accession State" means any of the following states
- (a) the Czech Republic,
- (b) the Republic of Estonia,
- (c) the Republic of Cyprus,
- (d) the Republic of Latvia,
- (e) the Republic of Lithuania,
- (f) the Republic of Hungary,
- (g) the Republic of Malta,
- (h) the Republic of Poland,
- (i) the Republic of Slovenia, or
- (j) the Slovak Republic;";

""citizen of an Accession State" means a national of one of the Accession States and "relevant citizen of an Accession State" means such a citizen who is not a Commonwealth citizen or a citizen of the Republic of Ireland;"; and

""Treaty of Athens" means the Treaty signed at Athens on 16th April 2003 concerning the accession of the Czech Republic, the Republic of Estonia, the Republic of Cyprus, the Republic of Latvia, the Republic of Lithuania, the Republic of Hungary, the Republic of Malta, the Republic of Poland, the Republic of Slovenia and the Slovak Republic to the European Union;".

  (3) After paragraph 7 (refusal to issue ballot paper) insert
"7A In the case of a relevant citizen of an Accession State, no postal ballot paper may be issued by the returning officer before he has been informed by the Secretary of State that the Accession State in question has ratified the Treaty of Athens."

4 *Repealed*

Modification of the Scottish Parliament (Elections etc) Order 2002

5(1) The Scottish Parliament (Elections etc) Order 2002 shall be modified as follows.

  (2) In article 3 (interpretation), there shall be inserted in the appropriate place
""Accession State" means any of the following states
- (a) the Czech Republic,
- (b) the Republic of Estonia,
- (c) the Republic of Cyprus,
- (d) the Republic of Latvia,
- (e) the Republic of Lithuania,
- (f) the Republic of Hungary,
- (g) the Republic of Malta,
- (h) the Republic of Poland,
- (i) the Republic of Slovenia, or
- (j) the Slovak Republic;"; and

""citizen of an Accession State" means a national of one of the Accession States and "relevant citizen of an Accession State" means such a citizen who is not a Commonwealth citizen or a citizen of the Republic of Ireland;"; and

""Treaty of Athens" means the Treaty signed at Athens on 16th April 2003 concerning the accession of the Czech Republic, the Republic of Estonia, the Republic of Cyprus, the Republic of Latvia, the Republic of Lithuania, the Republic of

Hungary, the Republic of Malta, the Republic of Poland, the Republic of Slovenia and the Slovak Republic to the European Union;".

(3) In article 22 (effect of register), insert after paragraph (3)

"(3A) Nothing in paragraphs (2) and (3) shall prevent a relevant citizen of an Accession State from being excluded from voting on the ground that the Accession State of which he is a national has not acceded to the European Union.".

(4) In paragraph 7 of Schedule 4

(a) insert at the beginning of sub-paragraph (2) "Subject to sub-paragraph (3) below,";

(b) after sub-paragraph (2) insert

"(3) In the case of a relevant citizen of an Accession State, no postal ballot paper or declaration of identity may be issued by the constituency returning officer before he has been informed by the Secretary of State that the Accession State in question has ratified the Treaty of Athens.".

Modification of the National Assembly for Wales (Representation of the People) Order 2003

6(1) The National Assembly for Wales (Representation of the People) Order 2003 shall be modified as follows.

(2) In article 2 (interpretation), there shall be inserted in the appropriate place

"'Accession State' means any of the following states

(a) the Czech Republic,

(b) the Republic of Estonia,

(c) the Republic of Cyprus,

(d) the Republic of Latvia,

(e) the Republic of Lithuania,

(f) the Republic of Hungary,

(g) the Republic of Malta,

(h) the Republic of Poland,

(i) the Republic of Slovenia, or

(j) the Slovak Republic;";

""citizen of an Accession State" means a national of one of the Accession States and "relevant citizen of an Accession State" means such a citizen who is not a Commonwealth citizen or a citizen of the Republic of Ireland;"; and

""Treaty of Athens" means the Treaty signed at Athens on 16th April 2003 concerning the accession of the Czech Republic, the Republic of Estonia, the Republic of Cyprus, the Republic of Latvia, the Republic of Lithuania, the Republic of Hungary, the Republic of Malta, the Republic of Poland, the Republic of Slovenia and the Slovak Republic to the European Union;".

(3) In article 24 (effect of registers), insert after paragraph (3)

"(3A) Nothing in paragraphs (2) and (3) shall prevent a relevant citizen of an Accession State from being excluded from voting on the ground that the Accession State of which he is a national has not acceded to the European Union".

(4) In paragraph 8 of Schedule 3

(a) insert at the beginning of sub-paragraph (2) "Subject to sub-paragraph (3) below,"; and

(b) after sub-paragraph (2) insert

"(3) In the case of a relevant citizen of an Accession State, no postal ballot paper or declaration of identity may be issued by the constituency returning officer before he has been informed by the Lord Chancellor that the Accession State in question has ratified the Treaty of Athens.".

Local Authorities (Elected Mayors)
(Elections, Terms of Office nd Casual Vacancies)
(England) Regulations 2012
(SI 2012/336)

Made 8th February 2012

Citation and commencement

1   These Regulations may be cited as the Local Authorities (Elected Mayors) (Elections, Terms of Office and Casual Vacancies) (England) Regulations 2012 and shall come into force on 9th March 2012.

Interpretation

2(1)   In these Regulations
"the 2000 Act" means the Local Government Act 2000;
"election", except in regulation 9, does not include an election to fill a casual vacancy;
"first election" means the first election for the return of an elected mayor following (as the case may be)
    (a)   a referendum in which proposals for a mayor and cabinet executive are approved; or
    (b)   a mayoral resolution;
"further referendum" means a referendum held in pursuance of the order of an election court under paragraph (5) of regulation 17 (determination of referendum petitions) of the Referendums Regulations;
"mayoral resolution" means a resolution of a local authority under section 9KC(1) to change to a mayor and cabinet executive without holding a referendum;
"the ordinary day of election", in relation to any year, means the day in that year on which, in accordance with section 37 of the Representation of the People Act 1983, councillors are elected for local government areas;
"petition organiser" has the same meaning as in regulation 3 of the Petitions Regulations;
"the Petitions Regulations" means the Local Authorities (Referendums) (Petitions) (England) Regulations 2011;
"referendum" means a referendum held under section 9M (cases in which change is subject to approval in a referendum etc), or by virtue of regulations or an order made under any provision of Part 1A of the 2000 Act, other than a further

referendum;

"referendum petition" has the same meaning as in regulation 15 of the Referendums Regulations;

"the Referendums Regulations" means the Local Authorities (Conduct of Referendums) (England) Regulations 2012;

"relevant day" means

(a) the first Thursday in May; or

(b) the third Thursday in October;

"returning officer" has the same meaning as in the Local Authorities (Mayoral Elections)(England and Wales) Regulations 2007;

"second election" means an election for the return of an elected mayor as successor to an elected mayor who was elected at the first election.

(2) Any reference in the following provisions of these Regulations to a section followed by a number is, unless the context otherwise requires, a reference to the section of the 2000 Act that bears that number.

First election of mayor

3(1) Subject to paragraph (1A) and regulation 5, if a local authority so resolves the first election shall take place on the first relevant day after (as the case may be) the date of the referendum or the date the mayoral resolution was passed.

(1A) Where the following conditions are satisfied, the first election shall take place on the first ordinary day of election after the end of the period of 3 months beginning with the date of the referendum under Part 2 of the Petitions Regulations

(a) the petition organiser made a request in writing, at the time a valid petition was presented to the local authority in accordance with regulation 9 of the Petitions Regulations, for the first election to take place on the first ordinary day of election after the end of the period of 3 months beginning with the date of the referendum under Part 2 of the Petitions Regulations, and

(b) the local authority resolves, prior to the publication of the notice under regulation 4(1) of the Referendum Regulations, that if the proposals are approved the first election shall take place on the first ordinary day of election after the period of 3 months beginning with the date of the referendum under Part 2 of the Petitions Regulations.

(2) Subject to regulation 5, where the date of the referendum or the date the mayoral resolution was passed is before 15th November 2012, the local authority may resolve that the first election shall take place on 15th November 2012.

(3) If no resolution is passed by the local authority under either paragraph (1), (1A) or (2) the first election shall take place on the first relevant day after (as the case may be) the end of the period of three months beginning with the date of the referendum or the date the mayoral resolution was passed.

(4) Paragraphs (1), (1A), (2) and (3) apply with the modifications specified in paragraph (5) if

(a) an election court

(i) dismisses a referendum petition; or

(ii) in accordance with section 145(1A)(b) of the Representation of the People Act 1983, reverses the result of a referendum; or

(b) the High Court declines to grant leave for the presentation of a referendum petition on the ground mentioned in paragraph (1)(d) of regulation 15 (procedures for questioning referendum) of the Referendums Regulations.

(5) In

(a) each of paragraphs (1) and (3) for the words from "the date" to the end substitute the words "the date of the decision of the election court or the High Court"; . . .

(aa) paragraph (1A) for the words "the date of the referendum under Part 2 of the Petitions Regulations" the first time they occur substitute the words "the date of the decision of the election court or the High Court"; and

(b) paragraph (2) for the words from "the date" to "was passed" substitute the words "the date of the decision of the election court or the High Court".

Second election of mayor

4(1) Subject to regulation 6, the second election shall take place on the ordinary day of election in a year in which ordinary elections of councillors of the local authority are held, as may be specified in or determined under the local authority's executive arrangements.

(2) The second election may not take place before the end of the period of 23 months beginning with the date on which the first election took place.

(3) The second election must take place no later than 67 months beginning with the date on which the first election took place.

First election of mayor in section 9N order authorities

5(1) Subject to the other paragraphs of this regulation, where a referendum held by virtue of an order under section 9N (requiring referendum on change to mayor and cabinet executive) made before 1st April 2012 approves the change to a mayor and cabinet executive, the first election for the return of an elected mayor in such an authority shall take place on 15th November 2012.

(2) Paragraphs (3) and (4) apply where

(a) an election court

(i) dismisses a referendum petition; or

(ii) in accordance with section 145(1A)(b) of the Representation of the People Act 1983, reverses the result of a referendum; or

(b) the High Court declines to grant leave for the presentation of a referendum petition on the ground mentioned in paragraph (1)(d) of regulation 15 (procedures for questioning referendum) of the Referendums Regulations.

(3) If a local authority so resolves, the first election shall take place on the first relevant day after (as the case may be) the date of the decision of the election court or the High Court.

(4) If no resolution is passed by the local authority, the first election shall take place on the first relevant day after (as the case may be) the end of the period of three months beginning with the date of the decision of the election court or the High Court.

Second election of mayor in section 9N order authorities

6 Where the change to a mayor and cabinet executive was approved by a referendum held by virtue of an order under section 9N made before 1st April 2012, the second election for the return of an elected mayor in such an authority shall take place on the ordinary day of election in May 2016.

Elections after the second election

7 Elections for the return of elected mayors, other than elections under regulations 3, 4, 5 or 6 shall take place on the ordinary day of elections in every fourth year commencing with the fourth year after that in which the second election takes place.

Term of office of elected mayor

8(1) An individual elected as elected mayor shall come into office on the fourth day after the election at which he or she was elected and, unless he or she resigns or otherwise ceases to hold office, shall hold office (subject to paragraphs (2) and (3)) until his or her successor comes into office.

(2) Where a local authority which operates a mayor and cabinet executive passes a resolution to make a change in governance arrangements of the kind set out in section 9K or 9KA, the elected mayor under the existing arrangements shall continue to hold office until the fourth day after the date on which, but for the resolution, a second or subsequent election would have been held in accordance with (as the case may be) regulation 4, 6 or 7 or section 9H(6).

(3) Where the result of a further referendum is to reject the continuation of the existing mayor and cabinet executive, the incumbent elected mayor shall continue to hold office until the local authority concerned implements the operation of the governance arrangements it operated at the time of the tainted referendum.

(4) In paragraph (3) "tainted referendum" means a referendum which an election court has declared tainted under regulation 17(5) of the Referendums Regulations.

Filling of casual vacancies

9(1) Subject to paragraph (2), on a casual vacancy occurring in the office of an elected mayor, an election to fill the vacancy shall be held
  (a) in a case in which the High Court or the local authority has declared the office to be vacant, within 35 days (computed in accordance with paragraph (3)) from the date of the declaration;
  (b) in any other case, within 35 days (computed in accordance with paragraph (3)) after notice in writing of the vacancy has been given to the proper officer of the authority by two local government electors for the area.

(2) A casual vacancy in the office of elected mayor
  (a) shall not be filled if the authority has passed a resolution to make a change in governance arrangements of the kind set out in section 9K or 9KA;
  (b) if it occurs within six months before the day on which the elected mayor would have retired, shall be filled at the election on the day determined (as the case may be) by reference to regulation 4, 6 or 7 or by section 9H(6).

(3) The day of election under paragraph (1) shall be fixed by the returning officer; and in computing a period for the purposes of that paragraph, the following shall be disregarded
  (a) a Saturday or Sunday;
  (b) Christmas Eve, Christmas Day, Good Friday or a day which is a bank holiday under the Banking and Financial Dealings Act 1971 in England; and
  (c) any day appointed as a day of public thanksgiving or mourning.

(4) Where, between the giving of notice of the poll and the completion of the poll, a day is declared to be a bank holiday or a day of public thanksgiving or mourning, paragraph (3) shall not operate to invalidate any act which would have been valid apart from that paragraph.

Filling of casual vacancies: supplementary

10(1) For the purposes of filling a casual vacancy in the office of elected mayor, the date on which the vacancy is to be taken to have occurred shall be
  (a) in the case of nonacceptance of office, the date of the expiration of the period appointed under section 83 (declaration of acceptance of office) of the Local

Government Act 1972 for the delivery of the declaration;

    (b) in the case of resignation, the date of the receipt of the notice of resignation by the person to whom the notice is required to be delivered;

    (c) in the case of death, the date of death;

    (d) in the case of his or her election being declared void on the determination of an election petition, the date of the report or certificate of the election court;

    (e) in the case of the elected mayor's ceasing to be qualified to be a member of a local authority, or becoming disqualified for any reason other than one mentioned in sub-paragraphs (a) to (d), or ceasing to be a member of a local authority by reason of failure to attend meetings, the date on which the elected mayor's office is declared to have been vacated by (as the case may be) the High Court or the local authority.

(2) Public notice of a casual vacancy in the office of elected mayor shall be given by the local authority in which the office exists; and the steps to be taken to give public notice in accordance with section 232 (public notices) of the Local Government Act 1972 shall be taken

    (a) in a case where the local authority declares the office to be vacant, immediately after the declaration;

    (b) in any other case, as soon as practicable after the date on which, by virtue of paragraph (1) of this regulation, the vacancy is treated as occurring.

Term of office of persons filling casual vacancies

11A person elected to fill a casual vacancy in the office of elected mayor shall hold office until the date on which the person in whose place he or she is elected would have ceased to hold office (in accordance with regulation 8).

Transitional provision

12 Where a local authority has, before the date on which these Regulations come into force, passed a mayoral resolution, that resolution is to have effect for the purpose of determining the date of the first election under regulation 3.

Revocation

13 The Local Authorities (Elected Mayors)(Elections, Terms of Office and Casual Vacancies) (England) Regulations 2001 are revoked.

Local Authorities (Mayoral Elections) (England and Wales) Regulations 2007 (SI 2007/1024)

26th March 2007

Citation, Commencement and Revocation

1 (1)   These Regulations may be cited as the Local Authorities (Mayoral Elections) (England and Wales) Regulations 2007.

(2)   These Regulations come into force on the day after that on which they are made except for the purposes of an election if the last date for the publication of the notice of election for that election is on or before 26 March 2007.

(3)   The following instruments are revoked–

(a)   The Local Authorities (Mayoral Elections) (England and Wales) Regulations 2002;

(b)   The Local Authorities (Mayoral Elections) (England and Wales) (Amendment) Regulations 2004;

(c)   The Civil Partnership Act 2004 (Amendments to Subordinate Legislation) Order 2005 to the extent of Part 4 of Schedule 12.

Interpretation

2   In these Regulations,–

"the 2000 Act" means the Local Government Act 2000;

"the 1983 Act" means the Representation of the People Act 1983;

"the Elections Regulations" means the Representation of the People (England and Wales) Regulations 2001;

"the Mayoral Elections Rules" means the rules set out in Schedule 1 to these Regulations;

"the Referendums Regulations" means the Local Authorities (Conduct of Referendums) (England) Regulations 2012;

"candidate" means a candidate to be an elected mayor;

"election" or "mayoral election" means an election for the return of an elected mayor;

"electoral area"–

(a)   in relation to a mayoral election in England, means the county, district or London borough in which the election is held;

(b)   in relation to a mayoral election in Wales, means the county or county borough in which the election is held;

"European Parliamentary election" shall have the same meaning as in section 27(1) of the Representation of the People Act 1985;

"local government election" shall have the same meaning as in section 203(1) of the 1983 Act;

"police and crime commissioner election" means an election of a police and crime commissioner in accordance with Chapter 6 of Part 1 of the 2011 Act;

"proper officer" has the meaning given by section 270(3) of the Local Government Act 1972;

"referendum" means a referendum conducted under the Referendums Regulations;

"relevant election or referendum" means one or more of the following–
(a)   a Parliamentary election;
(b)   a European Parliamentary election;
(c)   a local government election;
(d)   another mayoral election; and
(e)   a referendum,
(f)   a police and crime commissioner election,
the poll at which is taken together with the poll at the mayoral election;

"returning officer", in relation to a mayoral election, means––
(a)   the proper officer of the London borough concerned or, as the case may be, the person appointed as the returning officer for the election in accordance with subsection (1) or (1A) of section 35 (returning officers: local elections in England and Wales) of the 1983 Act as applied by these Regulations; and
(b)   any person appointed under subsection (4) of that section by a person of a description mentioned in paragraph (a).

Conduct of mayoral elections

3 (1)   An election for the return of an elected mayor shall be conducted in accordance with the Rules set out in Schedule 1 ("the Mayoral Elections Rules").

(2)   The relevant provisions in the enactments referred to in paragraph (3), shall have effect–
(a)   in relation to the conduct of a mayoral election in England, as they have effect in relation to the conduct of an election of councillors for any county electoral division or district or London borough ward,
(b)   in relation to the conduct of a mayoral election in Wales, as they have effect in relation to the conduct of an election of councillors for any county electoral division or county borough ward,
subject to the modifications set out in paragraph (4).

(3)   The enactments referred to in paragraph (2) are–
(a)   the 1983 Act;
(b)   the Representation of the People Act 1985;
(c)   the Representation of the People Act 2000;
(d)   the Elections Regulations, and
(e)   the Electoral Administration Act 2006.

(4)   The modifications referred to in paragraph (2) are–
(a)   references in the relevant provisions to "local government elections" shall be taken to include mayoral elections;
(b)   references in the relevant provisions to a "candidate" shall be taken to include a

candidate at a mayoral election;

    (c)   subject to paragraph (4A), the other modifications set out in Schedule 2.

(4A)   Where the poll at a mayoral election is taken alone, or is taken together with a poll at a police and crime commissioner election but not with a poll at any other relevant election or referendum, section 199B of the 1983 Act (translation of certain documents) has effect in relation to the conduct of the mayoral election subject to the modification in the Table in Schedule 2A instead of the modification to that section in Table 1 of Schedule 2.

(5)   In this regulation "relevant provisions" means the provisions which have effect in relation to the conduct of the election of councillors for any county electoral division or district or London borough ward (in England) or any county electoral division or county borough ward (in Wales).

Combination of polls

4 (1)   Where the poll at a mayoral election is taken together with the poll at a relevant election or referendum, the Mayoral Elections Rules shall be modified so as to have effect as set out in Schedule 3.

(2)   Where the poll at a mayoral election is taken together with a poll at a police and crime commissioner election and is not also taken together with a poll at any other relevant election or referendum, Schedule 3 has effect subject to the modifications set out in Schedule 3A.

Questioning of mayoral election

5   For the purposes of sections 9HE(6) and 44(4) of the 2000 Act, Part 3 (legal proceedings) of the 1983 Act shall have effect in relation to the questioning of an election for the return of an elected mayor as it has effect in relation to the questioning of an election under the local government Act.

Free delivery of election addresses

6 (1)   Each candidate at a mayoral election shall be entitled (subject to and in accordance with the provisions of Schedule 4) to have an election address prepared on behalf of the candidate included in a booklet of election addresses–

    (a)   prepared by the returning officer; and

    (b)   delivered by that officer to each person entitled to vote at that election.

(2)   Candidates' election addresses shall be delivered at the expense of the local authority for whose electoral area the election is held.

(3)   Schedule 4 (which makes provisions supplementing paragraph (1) above) shall have effect.

SCHEDULE 1
THE MAYORAL ELECTIONS RULES
Regulation 3(1)

Part 1
General Provisions

Part 2
Provisions as to Time

Part 3
Stages Common to Contested and Uncontested Elections

Part 4
Contested Elections

Part 1
General Provisions

Citation
1   These Rules may be cited as the Mayoral Elections Rules.

Interpretation
2 (1)   In these Rules, "the Appendix" means the Appendix to these Rules.

   (2)   Other expressions used both in these Rules and in the 1983 Act (as it applies to local government elections), except for those defined in regulation 2 or modified by regulation 3, shall have the same meaning in these Rules as they have in that Act.

Part 2
Provisions as to Time

Timetable

3 The proceedings at the election shall be conducted in accordance with the following Timetable:

Proceeding	Time
Publication of notice of election	Not later than the twenty-fifth day before the day of election
Delivery of nomination papers	Not later than 4 in the afternoon on the nineteenth day before the day of election
Publication of statement as to persons nominated	Not later than 4 in the afternoon on the eighteenth day before the day of election
Delivery of notices of withdrawal of candidature	Not later than 4 in the afternoon on the nineteenth day before the day of election
Notice of poll	Not later than the sixth day before the day of election
Polling	Between the hours of 7 in the morning and 10 at night on the day of election

Computation of time

4 (1) In computing any period of time for the purposes of the Timetable–

    (a) a Saturday or Sunday,

    (b) Christmas Eve, Christmas Day, Good Friday or a bank holiday, or

    (c) a day appointed for public thanksgiving or mourning,

shall be disregarded, and any such day shall not be treated as a day for the purpose of any proceedings up to the completion of the poll nor shall the returning officer be obliged to proceed with the counting of the votes on such a day.

(2) In this rule, "bank holiday" means a day which is a bank holiday under the Banking and Financial Dealings Act 1971 in England and Wales.

Part 3
Stages Common to Contested and Uncontested Elections

Notice of Election

5 (1) The returning officer must publish notice of the election stating–

    (a) the place and times at which nomination papers are to be delivered, and

    (b) the date of the poll in the event of a contest,

and the notice must state that forms of nomination papers may be obtained at that place and those times.

(2) The notice of election must also state the arrangements which apply for the payment of the deposit required by rule 10 to be made by means of the electronic transfer of funds.

(3) The notice of election must state the date by which–

    (a)   applications to vote by post or by proxy, and

    (b)   other applications and notices about postal or proxy voting,

must reach the registration officer in order that they may be effective for the election.

Nomination of candidates

6 (1)   Each candidate must be nominated by a separate nomination paper.

  (2)   A nomination paper must be in the appropriate form in the Appendix or a form to the like effect and shall be delivered at the place fixed for the purpose by the returning officer, which shall be at the offices of the council of the county, county borough, district or London borough in which the electoral area wholly or mainly lies.

  (3)   A nomination paper must state the candidate's–

      (a)   full names,

      (b)   home address, in full, and

      (c)   if desired, description,

and the surname must be placed first in the list of names.

  (4)   If a candidate commonly uses–

      (a)   a surname which is different from any other surname he has, or

      (b)   a forename which is different from any other forename he has,

the nomination paper may state the commonly used surname or forename in addition to the other name.

  (5)   The description (if any) can only be–

      (a)   one authorised as mentioned in rule 7(1) or (3); or

      (b)   the word "Independent".

Nomination papers: name of registered political party

7 (1)   A nomination paper may not include a description of a candidate which is likely to lead electors to associate the candidate with a registered political party unless the party is a qualifying party in relation to the electoral area and the description is authorised by a certificate–

      (a)   issued by or on behalf of the registered nominating officer of the party, and

      (b)   received by the returning officer before the last time for the delivery of nomination papers set out in the Timetable in rule 3.

  (2)   In paragraph (1) an authorised description may be either–

      (a)   the name of the party registered under section 28 of the Political Parties, Elections and Referendums Act 2000, or

      (b)   a description of the party registered under section 28A of that Act.

  (3)   A nomination paper may not include a description of a candidate which is likely to lead electors to associate the candidate with two or more registered political parties unless the parties are each qualifying parties in relation to the electoral area and the description is a registered description authorised by a certificate–

      (a)   issued by or on behalf of the registered nominating officer of each of the parties, and

      (b)   received by the returning officer before the last time for the delivery of nomination papers set out in the Timetable in rule 3.

  (4)   For the purposes of paragraph (3), a description is a registered description if it is a description registered for use by the parties under section 28B of the Political Parties, Elections and Referendums Act 2000.

  (5)   A person shall be guilty of a corrupt practice if he fraudulently purports to be authorised to issue a certificate under paragraph (1) or (3) on behalf of a registered political party's nominating officer.

(6) For the purposes of the application of this rule in relation to an election–

    (a) "registered political party" means a party which was registered under Part 2 of the Political Parties, Elections and Referendums Act 2000 on the day ("the relevant day") which is two days before the last day for the delivery of nomination papers at that election;

    (b) a registered political party is a qualifying party in relation to an electoral area if the electoral area is in England or Wales and the party was on the relevant day registered in respect of that part of Great Britain in the Great Britain register maintained under that Part of that Act.

(7) For the purposes of paragraph (6)(a), any day falling within rule 4(1) must be disregarded.

Subscription of nomination paper

8 (1) The nomination paper must be subscribed by two electors as proposer and seconder, and by twenty-eight other electors as assenting to the nomination.

(2) Where a nomination paper has the signatures of more than the required number of persons as proposing, seconding or assenting to the nomination of a candidate, the signature or signatures (up to the required number) appearing first on the paper in each category must be taken into account to the exclusion of any others in that category.

(3) The nomination paper must give the electoral number of each person subscribing it.

(4) The returning officer–

    (a) must supply any elector with as many forms of nomination paper and forms of consent to nomination as may be required at the place and during the time for delivery of nomination papers, and

    (b) must at any elector's request prepare a nomination paper for signature,

but it is not necessary for a nomination or consent to nomination to be on a form supplied by the returning officer.

(5) In this rule "elector"–

    (a) means a person who is registered in the register of local government electors for the electoral area in question on the last day for the publication of notice of the election; and

    (b) includes a person then shown in the register as below voting age if (but only if) it appears from the register that he will be of voting age on the day fixed for the poll.

(6) But, in this rule, "elector" does not include a person who has an anonymous entry in the register.

Consent to nomination

9 A person shall not be validly nominated unless his consent to nomination–

    (a) is given in writing, on or within one month before the last day for the delivery of nomination papers,

    (b) is in the appropriate form in the Appendix or a form to the like effect and includes–

        (i) for a nomination in England, a copy of sections 80 and 81 of the Local Government Act 1972, section 78A of the Local Government Act 2000 and section 34 of the Localism Act 2011; or

        (ii) for a nomination in Wales, a copy of sections 80 and 81 of the Local Government Act 1972 and sections 78A and 79 of the Local Government Act

2000,

    (c) is attested by one witness, and

    (d) is delivered at the place and within the time for the delivery of nomination papers.

Deposits

10 (1) A person shall not be validly nominated unless the sum of £500 is deposited by him or on his behalf, with the returning officer at the place and within the time for delivery of nomination papers.

  (2) The deposit may be made either–

    (a) by the deposit of any legal tender, or

    (b) by means of a banker's draft, or

    (c) with the returning officer's consent, in any other manner (including by means of a debit or credit card or the electronic transfer of funds),

but the returning officer may refuse to accept a deposit sought to be made by means of a banker's draft if he does not know that the drawer carries on business as a banker in the United Kingdom.

  (3) Where the deposit is made on behalf of the candidate, the person making the deposit must at the time he makes it give his name and address to the returning officer (unless they have previously been given to him under section 67 (appointment of election agent) of the 1983 Act).

Decisions as to validity of nomination papers

11 (1) Where a nomination paper and the candidate's consent to nomination are delivered in accordance with these Rules, the candidate shall be deemed to stand nominated unless and until–

    (a) the returning officer decides that the nomination paper is invalid, or

    (b) proof is given to the returning officer's satisfaction of the candidate's death, or

    (c) the candidate withdraws.

  (2) The returning officer is entitled to hold the nomination paper of a person invalid only on one of the following grounds–

    (a) that the particulars of the candidate or of the persons subscribing the paper are not as required by law; and

    (b) that the paper is not subscribed as so required.

  (3) Subject to paragraph (4), the returning officer must, as soon as practicable after each nomination paper has been delivered, examine it and decide whether the candidate has been validly nominated.

  (4) If in the returning officer's opinion a nomination paper breaks rule 7(1) or (3), he must give a decision to that effect–

    (a) as soon as practicable after the delivery of the nomination paper, and

    (b) in any event, before the end of the period of 24 hours starting with the last time for delivery of nomination papers set out in the Timetable in rule 3.

  (5) Where the returning officer decides that a nomination paper is invalid, he must endorse and sign on the paper the fact and the reasons for his decision.

  (6) The returning officer must send notice of his decision that a nomination paper is valid or invalid to each candidate at his home address as given in his nomination paper.

  (7) The returning officer's decision that a nomination paper is valid shall be final and shall not be questioned in any proceeding whatsoever.

  (8) Subject to paragraph (7), nothing in this rule prevents the validity of a nomination

being questioned on an election petition.

Publication of statement of persons nominated

12 (1) The returning officer must prepare and publish a statement showing the persons who have been and stand nominated and any other persons who have been nominated, with the reason why they no longer stand nominated.

(2) The statement must show the names, addresses and descriptions of the persons nominated as given in their nomination papers.

(3) If a person's nomination paper gives a commonly used surname or forename in addition to another name, the statement must show the person's commonly used surname or forename (as the case may be) instead of any other name.

(4) Paragraph (3) does not apply if the returning officer thinks–
    (a) that the use of the person's commonly used name may be likely to mislead or confuse electors, or
    (b) that the commonly used name is obscene or offensive.

(5) If paragraph (4) applies, the returning officer must give notice in writing to the candidate of his reasons for refusing to allow the use of a commonly used name.

(6) The statement must show the persons standing nominated arranged alphabetically in the order of their surnames, and if there are two or more of them with the same surname, of their other names.

(7) In the case of a person nominated by more than one nomination paper, the returning officer must take the particulars required by the foregoing provisions of this rule from such one of the papers as the candidate (or the returning officer in default of the candidate) may select.

Inspection of nomination papers and consent to nomination

13 During ordinary office hours on any day, other than a day specified in rule 4(1), after the latest time for delivery of nomination papers and before the date of the poll, any person may inspect and take copies of, or extracts from, nomination papers and consents to nomination.

Correction of minor errors

14 (1) A returning officer may, if he thinks fit, at any time before the publication under rule 12 of the statement of persons nominated, correct minor errors in a nomination paper.

(2) Errors which may be corrected include–
    (a) errors as to a person's electoral number;
    (b) obvious errors of spelling in relation to the details of a candidate.

(3) Anything done by a returning officer in pursuance of this rule shall not be questioned in any proceedings other than proceedings on an election petition.

(4) A returning officer must have regard to any guidance issued by the Electoral Commission for the purposes of this rule.

Withdrawal of candidature

15 (1) A candidate may withdraw his candidature by notice of withdrawal–
    (a) signed by him and attested by one witness, and
    (b) delivered to the returning officer at the place for delivery of nomination papers.

(2) Where a candidate is outside the United Kingdom, a notice of withdrawal signed by his

proposer and accompanied by a written declaration also so signed of the candidate's absence from the United Kingdom shall be of the same effect as a notice of withdrawal signed by the candidate; but where the candidate stands nominated by more than one nomination paper a notice of withdrawal under this paragraph shall be effective if, and only if–

    (a) it and the accompanying declaration are signed by all the proposers except any who is, and is stated in that declaration to be, outside the United Kingdom; or

    (b) it is accompanied, in addition to that declaration, by a written statement signed by the candidate that the proposer giving the notice is authorised to do so on the candidate's behalf during his absence from the United Kingdom.

Method of election

16   If, after any withdrawals under rule 15–

    (a) more than two candidates remain validly nominated, a poll shall be taken in accordance with Parts 4 and 5 of these Rules;

    (b) only two candidates remain validly nominated, a poll shall be taken in accordance with Part 4;

    (c) only one candidate remains validly nominated, that person shall be declared to be elected in accordance with Part 6.

Part 4

Contested Elections

Poll to be taken by ballot

17   The votes at the poll shall be given by ballot.

The ballot papers

18 (1)   The ballot of every person entitled to a vote at the election shall consist of a ballot paper.

  (2)   The persons remaining validly nominated for election to the office of mayor, after any withdrawals, and no others, shall be entitled to have their names inserted in the ballot paper at that election.

  (3)   Every ballot paper must be in the appropriate form, and must be printed in accordance with the appropriate directions set out in the Appendix, and–

    (a) must contain the names and other particulars of the candidates as shown in the statement of persons nominated;

    (b) must be capable of being folded up; and

    (c) must have a number and other unique identifying mark printed on the back.

  (4)   If a candidate who is the subject of a party's authorisation under rule 7(1) so requests, the ballot paper must contain, against the candidate's particulars, the party's registered emblem (or, as the case may be, one of the party's registered emblems).

  (4A)   If a candidate who is the subject of an authorisation by two or more parties under rule 7(3) so requests, the ballot paper must contain, against the candidate's particulars, the registered emblem (or, as the case may be, one of the registered emblems) of one of those parties.

  (5)   The candidate's request under paragraph (4) or (4A) must–

    (a) be made in writing to the returning officer, and

    (b) be received by him before the last time for the delivery of nomination papers set out in the Timetable in rule 3.

(6)   The order of the names in the ballot paper must be the same as in the statement of persons nominated.

The corresponding number list

19 (1)   The returning officer must prepare a list containing the numbers and other unique identifying marks of all of the ballot papers to be issued by him in pursuance of rule 24 or provided by him in pursuance of rule 28.

(2)   The list must be in the appropriate form in the Appendix or a form to like effect.

The official mark

20 (1)   Every ballot paper must contain an appropriate security marking (the official mark).

(2)   The official mark must be kept secret, and an interval of not less than five years shall intervene between the use of the same official mark at an election (of whatever description) for the same county, county borough, district or London borough, as the case may be.

(3)   The returning officer may use a different official mark for different purposes at the same election.

Prohibition of disclosure of vote

21   No person who has voted at the election shall, in any legal proceeding to question the election, be required to state for whom he has voted.

Use of schools and public rooms

22 (1)   The returning officer may use, free of charge, for the purpose of taking the poll or counting the votes–
  (a)   a room in a school maintained or assisted by a local authority (as defined in the Education Act 1996) or a school in respect of which grants are made out of moneys provided by Parliament to the person or body of persons responsible for the management of the school;
  (b)   a room the expense of maintaining which is met by any local authority.

(2)   The use of a room in an unoccupied hereditament for that purpose or those purposes does not render a person liable to any payment by way of council tax or non-domestic rate in respect of that hereditament and any day on which it is so used.

(3)   The returning officer must make good any damage done to, and defray any expense incurred by the persons having control over, any such room as is mentioned in paragraph (1) by reason of its being used for the purpose of taking the poll or counting the votes.

Notice of poll

23 (1)   The returning officer must publish notice of the poll stating–
  (a)   the day and hours fixed for the poll;
  (b)   the particulars of each candidate remaining validly nominated (the names and other particulars of the candidates, and the order of the candidates' names being the same as in the statement of persons nominated); and
  (c)   the names of all persons signing a candidate's nomination paper.

(2)   Where a candidate is nominated by more than one nomination paper, the nomination paper referred to in paragraph (1)(c) must be that from which the names and other

particulars of the candidate shown in the statement of persons nominated are taken.

(3) The returning officer must, not later than the time of the publication of the notice of the poll, also give public notice of–

    (a) the situation of each polling station; and

    (b) the description of voters entitled to vote there,

and he must as soon as practicable after giving such a notice give a copy of it to each of the election agents.

Postal ballot papers

24 (1) The returning officer must, in accordance with regulations made under the 1983 Act, issue to those entitled to vote by post a ballot paper and a postal voting statement in the appropriate form in the Appendix, or a form to the like effect, together with such envelopes for their return as may be prescribed by such regulations.

(2) The returning officer must also issue to those entitled to vote by post such information as he thinks appropriate about how to obtain–

    (a) translations into languages other than English of any directions to or guidance for voters sent with the ballot paper;

    (b) a translation into Braille of such directions or guidance;

    (c) graphical representations of such directions or guidance;

    (d) the directions or guidance in any other form (including any audible form).

(3) The postal voting statement must include provision for the form to be signed and for stating the date of birth of the elector or proxy (as the case may be).

(4) In the case of a ballot paper issued to a person at an address in the United Kingdom, the returning officer must ensure that the return of the ballot paper and postal voting statement is free of charge to the voter.

Provision of polling stations

25 (1) The returning officer must provide a sufficient number of polling stations and, subject to the following provisions of this rule, must allot the electors to the polling stations in such manner as he thinks most convenient.

(2) One or more polling stations may be provided in the same room.

(3) The polling station allotted to electors from any parliamentary polling district wholly or partly within the electoral area must, in the absence of special circumstances, be in the parliamentary polling place for that district, unless that place is outside the electoral area.

(4) The returning officer must provide each polling station with such number of compartments as may be necessary in which the voters can mark their votes screened from observation.

Appointment of presiding officers and polling clerks

26 (1) The returning officer must appoint and pay a presiding officer to attend at each polling station and such clerks as may be necessary for the purposes of the election, but he must not appoint any person who has been employed by or on behalf of a candidate in or about the election.

(2) The returning officer may, if he thinks fit, preside at a polling station and the provisions of these Rules relating to a presiding officer shall apply to a returning officer so presiding with the necessary modifications as to things to be done by the returning officer to the presiding officer or by the presiding officer to the returning officer.

(3) A presiding officer may do, by the clerks appointed to assist him, any act (including the asking of questions) which he is required or authorised by these Rules to do at a polling station except order the arrest, exclusion or removal of any person from the polling station.

Issue of official poll cards

27 (1) The returning officer must as soon as practicable after the publication of the notice of the election send to electors and their proxies an official poll card.

(2) An elector's official poll card must be sent or delivered to his qualifying address, and a proxy's to his address as shown in the list of proxies.

(3) The official poll card must be in the appropriate form in the Appendix, or a form to the like effect, and must set out–
   (a) the name of the local authority to which the election relates;
   (b) that the election is a mayoral election;
   (c) the elector's name, qualifying address and number on the register;
   (d) the date and hours of the poll and the situation of the elector's polling station;
   (e) such other information as the returning officer thinks appropriate,
and different information may be provided in pursuance of sub-paragraph (e) to different electors or descriptions of elector.

(4) In the case of an elector with an anonymous entry, instead of containing the matter mentioned in paragraph (3)(c), the poll card must contain such matter as is specified in the appropriate form in the Appendix.

(5) Paragraph (5) of rule 8 shall apply for the interpretation of this rule.

Equipment of polling stations

28 (1) The returning officer must provide each presiding officer with such number of ballot boxes and ballot papers as in the returning officer's opinion may be necessary.

(2) Every ballot box must be so constructed that the ballot papers can be put in it, but cannot be withdrawn from it, without the box being unlocked or, where the box has no lock, the seal being broken.

(3) The returning officer must provide each polling station with–
   (a) materials to enable voters to mark the ballot papers;
   (b) copies of the register of electors for the electoral area or such part of it as contains the names of the electors allotted to the station;
   (c) the parts of any special lists prepared for the election corresponding to the register of electors for the electoral area or the part of it provided under sub-paragraph (b);
   (d) a list consisting of that part of the list prepared under rule 19 which contains the numbers (but not the other unique identifying marks) corresponding to those on the ballot papers provided to the presiding officer of the polling station.

(4) The reference in paragraph (3)(b) to the copies of the register of electors includes a reference to copies of any notices issued under section 13B(3B) or (3D) of the 1983 Act in respect of alterations to the register.

(5) The returning officer must also provide each polling station with–
   (a) at least one large version of the ballot paper which must be displayed inside the polling station for the assistance of voters who are partially sighted; and
   (b) a device of such description as is set out in paragraph (8) for enabling voters who are blind or partially sighted to vote without any need for assistance from the presiding officer or any companion (within the meaning of rule 39(1)).

(6) A notice in the appropriate form in the Appendix giving directions for the guidance of voters in voting, must be printed in conspicuous characters and exhibited inside and outside every polling station.

(7) The returning officer may also provide copies of the notice mentioned in paragraph (6) in Braille or translated into languages other than English as he considers appropriate, provided that these notices are accurate reproductions in Braille or that other language of that notice.

(8) The device referred to in paragraph (5)(b) must–
  (a) allow a ballot paper to be inserted into and removed from, or attached to and detached from, the device easily and without damage to the paper;
  (b) hold the ballot paper firmly in place during use; and
  (c) provide suitable means for the voter to–
    (i) identify the spaces on the ballot paper on which he may mark his vote; and
    (ii) identify the candidate to which each such space refers; and
    (iii) mark his vote on the space he has chosen.

Appointment of polling and counting agents

29 (1) Subject to paragraphs (3), (4) and (5), before the commencement of the poll each candidate may appoint–
  (a) polling agents to attend at polling stations for the purpose of detecting personation; and
  (b) counting agents to attend at the counting of the votes.

(2) The same person may be appointed as a polling agent or counting agent by more than one candidate.

(3) Not more than four polling agents, or such greater number as the returning officer may by notice allow, shall be permitted to attend at any particular polling station.

(4) If the number of such agents appointed to attend at a particular polling station exceeds the allowed number, the returning officer must determine which agents are permitted to attend by lot, and only the agents on whom the lot falls shall be deemed to have been duly appointed.

(5) The returning officer may limit the number of counting agents, but in doing so must ensure that–
  (a) the number is the same in the case of each candidate; and
  (b) the number allowed to a candidate must not (except in special circumstances) be less than the number obtained by dividing the number of clerks employed on the counting by the number of candidates.

(6) For the purposes of the calculations required by paragraph (5), a counting agent appointed for more than one candidate is a separate agent for each of the candidates for whom he has been appointed.

(7) Notice in writing of the appointment, stating the names and addresses of the persons appointed, must be given by the candidate to the returning officer and must be so given not later than the fifth day (disregarding any referred to in rule 4 (1)) before the day of the poll.

(8) If an agent dies, or becomes incapable of acting, the candidate may appoint another person in his place, and must forthwith give to the returning officer notice in writing of the name and address of that other person.

(9) Any appointment for a candidate authorised by this rule may be made and the notice of appointment given to the returning officer by the candidate's election agent, instead of by the candidate.

(10) In the following provisions of these Rules references to polling agents and counting agents shall be taken as references to agents–
  (a) whose appointments have been duly made and notified; and
  (b) where the number of agents is restricted, who are within the permitted numbers.

(11) Any notice required to be given to a counting agent by the returning officer may be delivered at, or sent by post to, the address stated in the notice of appointment.

(12) A candidate may himself do any act or thing which any polling or counting agent of his, if appointed, would have been authorised to do, or may assist his agent in doing any such act or thing.

(13) A candidate's election agent may do or assist in doing anything which the candidate's polling or counting agent is authorised to do; and anything required or authorised by these Rules to be done in the presence of the polling or counting agent may be done in the presence of a candidate's election agent instead of his polling agent or counting agent.

(14) Where by these Rules any act or thing is required or authorised to be done in the presence of the polling or counting agent, the non-attendance of any agent or agents at the time and place appointed for the purpose shall not, if the act or thing is otherwise duly done, invalidate the act or thing done.

Notification of requirement of secrecy

30 (1) The returning officer must make such arrangements as he thinks fit to ensure that–
  (a) every person attending at a polling station (otherwise than for the purpose of voting or assisting a voter with disabilities to vote or as a constable on duty there) has been given a copy in writing of the provisions of subsections (1), (3) and (6) of section 66 of the 1983 Act; and
  (b) every person attending at the counting of the votes (other than any constable on duty at the counting) has been given a copy in writing of the provisions of subsections (2) and (6) of that section.

(2) In this rule, a reference to a constable includes a person designated as a community support officer under section 38 of the Police Reform Act 2002 (police powers for employees).

Return of postal ballot papers

31 (1) Where–
  (a) a postal vote has been returned in respect of a person who is entered on the postal voters list, or
  (b) a proxy postal vote has been returned in respect of a proxy who is entered on the proxy postal voters list,
the returning officer must mark the list in the manner prescribed by regulations made under the 1983 Act.

(2) Rule 47(4) does not apply for the purpose of determining whether, for the purposes of this rule, a postal vote or a proxy postal vote is returned.

Admission to polling station

32 (1) The presiding officer must exclude all persons from the polling station except–
  (a) voters;
  (b) persons under the age of 18 who accompany voters to the polling station;
  (c) the candidates and their election agents;

(d) the polling agents appointed to attend at the polling station;

(e) the clerks appointed to attend at the polling station;

(f) persons who are entitled to attend by virtue of any of sections 6A to 6D of the Political Parties, Elections and Referendums Act 2000;

(g) the constables on duty; and

(h) the companions of voters with disabilities.

(2) The presiding officer must regulate the total number of voters and persons under the age of 18 who accompany them to be admitted to the polling station at the same time.

(3) Not more than one polling agent shall be admitted at the same time to a polling station on behalf of the same candidate.

(4) A constable or person employed by a returning officer must not be admitted to vote in person elsewhere than at his own polling station allotted to him under these Rules, except on production and surrender of a certificate as to his employment which must be in the appropriate form in the Appendix, or a form to the like effect, and signed by an officer of police of or above the rank of inspector or by the returning officer, as the case may be.

(5) Any certificate surrendered under this rule must forthwith be cancelled.

(6) In this rule, a reference to a constable includes a person designated as a community support officer under section 38 of the Police Reform Act 2002 (police powers for employees).

Keeping of order in station

33 (1) It is the presiding officer's duty to keep order at his polling station.

(2) If a person misconducts himself in a polling station, or fails to obey the presiding officer's lawful orders, he may immediately, by the presiding officer's order, be removed from the polling station–

(a) by a constable in or near that station, or

(b) by any other person authorised in writing by the returning officer to remove him,

and the person so removed shall not, without the presiding officer's permission, again enter the polling station during the day.

(3) Any person so removed may, if charged with the commission in the polling station of an offence, be dealt with as a person taken into custody by a constable for an offence without a warrant.

(4) The powers conferred by this rule must not be exercised so as to prevent a voter who is otherwise entitled to vote at a polling station from having an opportunity of voting at that station.

Sealing of ballot boxes

34 Immediately before the commencement of the poll, the presiding officer must–

(a) show the ballot box, empty, to such persons, if any, as are present in the polling station, so that they may see that the box is empty;

(b) lock up the box (if it has a lock);

(c) place his seal–

(i) on the lock; or

(ii) where the ballot box has no lock, on the box,

in such a manner as to prevent its being opened without breaking the seal;

(d) place the box in his view for the receipt of ballot papers; and

(e) keep the box locked and sealed or, as the case may be, sealed.

Questions to be put to voters

35 (1) At the time of the application for a ballot paper (but not afterwards), the questions specified in the second column of the following Table–

(a) may be put by the presiding officer to a person applying for a ballot paper who is mentioned in the first column, and

(b) must be put if the letter "R" appears after the question and the candidate or his election or polling agent requires the question to be put:

Q No	Person applying for ballot paper	Question
1	A person applying as an elector	(a)–Are you the person registered in the register of local government electors for this election as follows? *read the whole entry from the register* R (b)–Have you already voted here or elsewhere at this election otherwise than as proxy for some other person? R
2	A person applying as proxy	(a)–Are you the person whose name appears as A.B. in the list of proxies for this election as entitled to vote as proxy on behalf of CD? R (b)–Have you already voted here or elsewhere at this election as proxy on behalf of CD? R (c)–Are you the spouse, civil partner, parent, grandparent, brother, sister, child or grandchild of CD? R
3	A person applying as proxy for an elector with an anonymous entry (instead of the questions at entry 2)	(a)–Are you the person entitled to vote as proxy on behalf of the elector whose number on the register of electors is *(read out the number)*? R (b)–Have you already voted here or elsewhere as proxy on behalf of the elector whose number on the register of electors is *(read out the number)*? R (c)–Are you the spouse, civil partner, parent, grandparent, brother, sister, child or grandchild of the person whose number on the register of electors is *(read out the number)*? R
4	A person applying as proxy if the question at entry 2(c) or 3(c) is not answered in the affirmative	Have you already voted at this election on behalf of two persons of whom you are not the spouse, civil partner, parent, grandparent, brother, sister, child or grandchild? R
5	A person applying as an elector in relation to whom there is an entry in the postal voters list	(a)–Did you apply to vote by post? (b)–Why have you not voted by post?
6	A person applying as proxy who is named in the proxy postal voters list	(a)–Did you apply to vote by post as proxy? (b)–Why have you not voted by post as proxy?

(2) In the case of an elector in respect of whom a notice has been issued under section 13B(3B) or (3D) of the 1983 Act, the references in the questions at entries 1(a) and 3(a), (b) and (c) to reading from the register shall be taken as references to reading from the notice issued under section 13B(3B) or (3D) of the 1983 Act.

(3) A ballot paper must not be delivered to any person required to answer any of the

above questions unless he has answered each question satisfactorily.

(4) Except as authorised by this rule, no inquiry shall be permitted as to the right of any person to vote.

Challenge of voter

36   A person must not be prevented from voting by reason only that–

    (a)   a candidate or his election or polling agent declares that he has reasonable cause to believe that the person has committed an offence of personation, or

    (b)   the person is arrested on the grounds that he is suspected of committing or of being about to commit such an offence.

Voting procedure

37 (1)   A ballot paper must be delivered to a voter who applies for one, and immediately before delivery–

    (a)   the number and (unless paragraph (2) applies) name of the elector as stated in the copy of the register of electors must be called out;

    (b)   the number of the elector must be marked on the list mentioned in rule 28(3)(d) beside the number of the ballot paper to be issued to him;

    (c)   a mark must be placed in the copy of the register of electors against the number of the elector to note that a ballot paper has been received but without showing the particular ballot paper which has been received; and

    (d)   in the case of a person applying for a ballot paper as proxy, a mark must also be placed against his name in the list of proxies.

(2)   In the case of an elector who has an anonymous entry, he must show the presiding officer his official poll card and only his number shall be called out in pursuance of paragraph (1)(a).

(3)   In the case of an elector who is added to the register in pursuance of a notice issued under section 13B(3B) or (3D) of the 1983 Act, paragraph (1) is modified as follows–

    (a)   in sub-paragraph (a), for "copy of the register of electors" substitute "copy of the notice issued under section 13B(3B) or (3D) of the 1983 Act";

    (b)   in sub-paragraph (c), for "in the register of electors" substitute "on the copy of the notice issued under section 13B(3B) or (3D) of the 1983 Act".

(4)   The voter, on receiving the ballot paper, must forthwith proceed into one of the compartments in the polling station and there secretly mark his paper and fold it up so as to conceal his vote, and must then show to the presiding officer the back of the paper, so as to disclose the number and other unique identifying mark, and put the ballot paper so folded up into the ballot box in the presiding officer's presence.

(5)   The voter must vote without undue delay, and must leave the polling station as soon as he has put his ballot paper into the ballot box.

(6)   A voter who at the close of the poll is in the polling station, or in a queue outside the polling station, for the purposes of voting shall (despite the close of the poll) be entitled to apply for a ballot paper under paragraph (1); and these rules apply in relation to such a voter accordingly.

Votes marked by presiding officer

38 (1)   The presiding officer, on the application of a voter–

    (a)   who is incapacitated by blindness or other disability from voting in the manner directed by these Rules, or

    (b)   who declares orally that he is unable to read,

must, in the presence of the polling agents, cause the voter's vote to be marked on a ballot paper in the manner directed by the voter, and the ballot paper to be placed in the ballot box.

(2) The name and number on the register of electors of every voter whose vote is marked in pursuance of this rule, and the reason why it is so marked, must be entered on a list (in these Rules called "the list of votes marked by the presiding officer").

(3) In the case of a person voting as proxy for an elector, the number to be entered together with the voter's name shall be the elector's number.

(4) In the case of a person in respect of whom a notice has been issued under section 13B(3B) or (3D) of the 1983 Act, paragraph (2) applies as if for "on the register of electors of every voter" there were substituted "relating to every voter in respect of whom a notice has been issued under section 13B(3B) or (3D) of the 1983 Act".

Voting by persons with disabilities

39 (1) If a voter makes an application to the presiding officer to be allowed, on the ground of–
  (a) blindness or other disability, or
  (b) inability to read,
  to vote with the assistance of another person by whom he is accompanied (in these Rules referred to as "the companion"), the presiding officer must require the voter to declare, orally or in writing, whether he is so incapacitated by his blindness or other disability, or by his inability to read, as to be unable to vote without assistance.

(2) If the presiding officer–
  (a) is satisfied that the voter is so incapacitated, and
  (b) is also satisfied by a written declaration made by the companion (in these Rules referred to as "the declaration made by the companion of a voter with disabilities") that the companion–
    (i) is a qualified person within the meaning of this rule; and
    (ii) has not previously assisted more than one voter with disabilities to vote at the election,
  the presiding officer must grant the application, and then anything which is by these Rules required to be done to or by that voter in connection with the giving of his vote may be done to, or with the assistance of, the companion.

(3) For the purposes of these Rules–
  (a) a person is a voter with disabilities if he has made such a declaration as is mentioned in paragraph (1); and
  (b) a person shall be qualified to assist a voter with disabilities to vote if that person is either–
    (i) a person who is entitled to vote as an elector at the election; or
    (ii) the father, mother, brother, sister, spouse, civil partner, son or daughter of the voter and has attained the age of 18 years.

(4) Subject to paragraph (5), the name and number in the register of electors of every voter whose vote is given in accordance with this rule and the name and address of the companion must be entered on a list (in these Rules referred to as "the list of voters with disabilities assisted by companions").

(5) In the case of a person voting as proxy for an elector, the number to be entered together with the voter's name shall be the elector's number.

(6) In the case of a person in respect of whom a notice has been issued under section 13B(3B) or (3D) of the 1983 Act, paragraph (4) applies as if for "in the register of electors of every voter" there were substituted "relating to every voter in respect of whom a notice has been issued under section 13B(3B) or (3D) of the 1983 Act".

(7) The declaration made by the companion of a voter with disabilities–
    (a) must be in the appropriate form in the Appendix or a form to the like effect,
    (b) must be made before the presiding officer at the time when the voter applies to vote with the assistance of the companion, and
    (c) must forthwith be given to the presiding officer who must attest and retain it.

(8) No fee or other payment shall be charged in respect of the declaration.

Tendered ballot papers–circumstances where available

40 (1) If a person, representing himself to be–
    (a) a particular elector named on the register and not named in the absent voters list, or
    (b) a particular person named in the list of proxies as proxy for an elector and not entitled to vote by post as proxy,

applies for a ballot paper after another person has voted in person either as the elector or his proxy, the applicant shall, on satisfactorily answering the questions permitted by law to be asked at the poll, be entitled, subject to the provisions of rule 41, to mark a ballot paper (in these Rules referred to as "a tendered ballot paper") in the same manner as any other voter.

(2) Paragraph (4) applies if–
    (a) a person applies for a ballot paper representing himself to be a particular elector named on the register,
    (b) he is also named in the postal voters list, and
    (c) he claims that he did not make an application to vote by post at the election.

(3) Paragraph (4) also applies if–
    (a) a person applies for a ballot paper representing himself to be a particular person named as a proxy in the list of proxies,
    (b) he is also named in the proxy postal voters list, and
    (c) he claims that he did not make an application to vote by post as proxy.

(4) The person shall, on satisfactorily answering the questions permitted by law to be asked at the poll, be entitled, subject to the provisions of rule 41, to mark a ballot paper (in these Rules referred to as a "tendered ballot paper") in the same manner as any other voter.

(5) Paragraph (6) applies if, before the close of the poll but after the last time at which a person may apply for a replacement postal ballot paper, a person represents himself to be–
    (a) a particular elector named on the register who is also named in the postal voters list, or
    (b) a particular person named as a proxy in the list of proxies and who is also named in the proxy postal voters list,

and claims that he has lost or has not received his postal ballot paper.

(6) The person shall, on satisfactorily answering the questions permitted by law to be asked at the poll, be entitled, subject to the provisions of rule 41, to mark a ballot paper (in these Rules referred to as a "tendered ballot paper") in the same manner as any other voter.

Tendered ballot papers–general provisions

41 (1) A tendered ballot paper must–
    (a) be of a colour differing from that of the other ballot papers;
    (b) instead of being put into the ballot box, be given to the presiding officer and

endorsed by him with the name of the voter and his number in the register of electors, and set aside in a separate packet.

(2) The name of the voter and his number in the register of electors must be entered on a list (in these Rules referred to as the "tendered votes list").

(3) In the case of a person voting as proxy for an elector, the number to be endorsed or entered together with the voter's name shall be the number of that elector.

(4) In the case of an elector who has an anonymous entry, this rule and rule 40 apply subject to the following modifications–

    (a) in paragraphs (1)(b) and (2) above, the references to the name of the voter shall be ignored;

    (b) otherwise, a reference to a person named on a register or list shall be construed as a reference to a person whose number appears in the register or list (as the case may be).

(5) In the case of a person in respect of whom a notice has been issued under section 13B(3B) or (3D) of the 1983 Act, this rule and rule 40 shall apply as if–

    (a) in rule 40(1)(a), (2)(a) and (5)(a), for "named on the register" there were substituted "in respect of whom a notice under section 13B(3B) or (3D) of the 1983 Act has been issued";

    (b) in paragraph (1)(b) of this rule for "his number in the register of electors" there were substituted "the number relating to him on a notice issued under section 13B(3B) or (3D) of the 1983 Act";

    (c) in paragraph (2) of this rule, for "his number in the register of electors" there were substituted "the number relating to him on a notice issued under section 13B(3B) or (3D) of the 1983 Act".

Spoilt ballot papers

42 A voter who has inadvertently dealt with his ballot paper in such manner that it cannot be conveniently used as a ballot paper may, on delivering it to the presiding officer and proving to his satisfaction the fact of the inadvertence, obtain another ballot paper in the place of the ballot paper so delivered (in these Rules referred to as "a spoilt ballot paper"), and the spoilt ballot paper must be immediately cancelled.

Correction of errors on day of poll

43 The presiding officer must keep a list of persons to whom ballot papers are delivered in consequence of an alteration to the register made by virtue of section 13B(3B) or (3D) of the 1983 Act which takes effect on the day of the poll.

Adjournment of poll in case of riot

44 (1) Where the proceedings at any polling station are interrupted or obstructed by riot or open violence, the presiding officer must adjourn the proceedings till the following day and must forthwith give notice to the returning officer.

    (2) Where the poll is adjourned at any polling station–

        (a) the hours of polling on the day to which it is adjourned must be the same as for the original day; and

        (b) references in these Rules to the close of the poll shall be construed accordingly.

Procedure on close of poll

45 (1) As soon as practicable after the close of the poll, the presiding officer must, in the presence of the polling agents, make up into separate packets, sealed with his own

seal and the seals of such polling agents as desire to affix their seals–
- (a) each ballot box in use at the station, sealed so as to prevent the introduction of additional ballot papers and unopened, but with the key, if any, attached,
- (b) the unused and spoilt ballot papers placed together,
- (c) the tendered ballot papers,
- (d) the marked copies of the register of electors (including any marked copy notices issued under section 13B(3B) or (3D) of the 1983 Act) and of the list of proxies,
- (e) the lists prepared under rule 19 including the parts which were completed in accordance with rule 37(1)(b) (together referred to in these Rules as "the completed corresponding number lists"),
- (f) the certificates as to employment on duty on the day of the poll,
- (g) the tendered votes list, the list of voters with disabilities assisted by companions, the list of votes marked by the presiding officer, a statement of the number of voters whose votes are so marked by the presiding officer under the heads "disability" and "unable to read", the list maintained under rule 43 (correction of errors on day of poll), and the declarations made by the companions of voters with disabilities,

and must deliver the packets or cause them to be delivered to the returning officer to be taken charge of by him; but if the packets are not delivered by the presiding officer personally to the returning officer, the arrangements for their delivery shall require the returning officer's approval.

(2) The marked copies of the register of electors and of the list of proxies must be in one packet but must not be in the same packet as the completed corresponding number lists or the certificates as to employment on duty on the day of the poll.

(3) The packets must be accompanied by a statement (in these Rules referred to as "the ballot paper account") made by the presiding officer showing the number of ballot papers entrusted to him, and accounting for them under the heads–
- (a) ballot papers issued and not otherwise accounted for,
- (b) unused ballot papers,
- (c) spoilt ballot papers and
- (d) tendered ballot papers.

Attendance at the count

46 (1) The returning officer must make arrangements for counting the votes in the presence of the counting agents as soon as practicable after the close of the poll, and must give to the counting agents notice in writing of the time and place–
- (a) at which he will begin to count the votes; and
- (b) at which he will begin any count of the second preference votes.

(2) No person other than–
- (a) the returning officer and his clerks,
- (b) the candidates and one other person chosen by each of them,
- (c) the election agents,
- (d) the counting agents,
- (e) persons who are entitled to attend by virtue of any of sections 6A to 6D of the Political Parties, Elections and Referendums Act 2000,

may be present at the counting of the votes, unless permitted by the returning officer to attend.

(3) A person not entitled to attend at the counting of the votes shall not be permitted to do so by the returning officer unless he–
- (a) is satisfied that the efficient counting of the votes will not be impeded; and
- (b) has either consulted the election agents or thought it impracticable to do so.

(4) The returning officer must give the counting agents all such reasonable facilities for overseeing the proceedings, and all such information with respect to them, as he can give them consistently with the orderly conduct of the proceedings and the discharge of his duties in connection with them.

(5) In particular, where the votes are counted by sorting the ballot papers according to the candidate for whom the vote is given and then counting the number of ballot papers for each candidate, the counting agents shall be entitled to satisfy themselves that the ballot papers are correctly sorted.

The first count

47 (1) The returning officer must–
    (a) in the presence of the counting agents open each ballot box and count and record the number of ballot papers in it;
    (b) in the presence of the election agents verify each ballot paper account; and
    (c) count such of the postal ballot papers as have been duly returned and record the number counted.

(2) The returning officer must not count the votes given on any ballot papers until–
    (a) in the case of postal ballot papers, they have been mixed with the ballot papers from at least one ballot box, and
    (b) in the case of ballot papers from a ballot box, they have been mixed with the ballot papers from at least one other ballot box.

(3) The returning officer shall then–
    (a) where the election is contested by more than two candidates, count the first preference votes given on them;
    (b) where the election is contested by only two candidates, count the votes given on them.

(4) A postal ballot paper must not be taken to be duly returned unless–
    (a) it is returned in the manner set out in paragraph (5) and reaches the returning officer or any polling station in the electoral area in question before the close of the poll; and
    (b) the postal voting statement, duly signed, is also returned in the manner set out in paragraph (5) and reaches him or such a polling station before that time;
    (c) the postal voting statement also states the date of birth of the elector or proxy (as the case may be), and
    (d) in a case where steps for verifying the date of birth and signature of an elector or proxy have been prescribed by regulations made under the 1983 Act, the returning officer (having taken such steps) verifies the date of birth and signature of the elector or proxy (as the case may be).

(5) The manner in which any postal ballot paper or postal voting statement may be returned–
    (a) to the returning officer, is by hand or by post;
    (b) to a polling station, is by hand.

(5A) A postal ballot paper or postal voting statement that reaches the returning officer or a polling station on or after the close of the poll is treated for the purposes of this rule as reaching that officer or polling station before the close of the poll if it is delivered by a person who, at the close of the poll, is in the polling station, or in a queue outside the polling station, for the purpose of returning it.

(6) The returning officer must not count any tendered ballot paper.

(7) The returning officer, while counting and recording the number of ballot papers and

counting the votes, must keep the ballot papers with their faces upwards and take all proper precautions for preventing any person from seeing the numbers or other unique identifying marks printed on the back of the papers.

(8)   The returning officer must verify each ballot paper account by comparing it with the number of ballot papers recorded by him, and the unused and spoilt ballot papers in his possession and the tendered votes list (opening and re-sealing the packets containing the unused and spoilt ballot papers and the tendered votes list) and must draw up a statement as to the result of the verification, which any election agent may copy.

(9)   The returning officer must so far as practicable proceed continuously with counting the votes, allowing only time for refreshment, except that he may exclude the hours between 7 in the evening and 9 on the following morning.

(10) During the time so excluded the returning officer must–

    (a)   place the ballot papers and other documents relating to the election under his own seal and the seals of such of the counting agents as desire to affix their seals; and

    (b)   otherwise take proper precautions for the security of the papers and documents.

Rejected ballot papers

48 (1) Any ballot paper–

    (a)   which does not bear the official mark, or

    (b)   on which more than one first preference vote is given, or

    (c)   on which anything is written or marked by which the voter can be identified except the printed number and other unique identifying mark on the back, or

    (d)   which is unmarked or void for uncertainty as to the first preference vote,

shall, subject to paragraph (2), be void and not counted.

(2)   A ballot paper on which the vote is marked–

    (a)   elsewhere than in the proper place, or

    (b)   otherwise than by means of a cross, or

    (c)   by more than one mark,

shall not for such reason be deemed to be void if–

    (i)   at an election at which more than two candidates remain validly nominated, an intention that a vote shall be given, by way of a first preference vote, for not more than one of the candidates clearly appears; or

    (ii) at any other election, an intention that a vote shall be for one only of the candidates clearly appears,

and (in either case) the way the paper is marked does not itself identify the voter and it is not shown that he can be identified by it.

(3)   A ballot paper which is not otherwise void and on which not more than one first preference vote is marked (whether or not a second preference vote is marked) shall be valid as respects that vote, and counted accordingly.

(4)   The returning officer must endorse the word "rejected" on any ballot paper which under this rule is not to be counted, and shall add to the endorsement the words "rejection objected to" if any objection is made to his decision by a counting agent.

(5)   The returning officer must draw up a statement showing the number of ballot papers rejected, under the several heads of–

    (a)   want of official mark;

    (b)   voting for more than one candidate as to the first preference vote;

    (c)   writing or mark by which the voter could be identified; and

(d)   unmarked or void for uncertainty as to the first preference vote.

(6)   In the case of an election where only two candidates remain validly nominated, this rule is to apply as if–

(a)   in paragraph (1)(b), for "first preference vote" there were substituted "vote";

(b)   in paragraphs (1)(d), (5)(b) and (d), the words "as to the first preference vote" were omitted;

(c)   paragraph (3) were omitted.

Decisions on ballot papers

49   The decision of the returning officer on any question arising in respect of a ballot paper shall be final, but shall be subject to review on an election petition.

Re-count

50 (1)   A candidate or his election agent may, if present when the counting or any re-count of the votes or, as the case may be, the first preference votes, is completed, require the returning officer to have the votes re-counted or again re-counted but the returning officer may refuse to do so if in his opinion the request is unreasonable.

(2)   No step shall be taken on the completion of the counting or any re-count of votes, or as the case may be, the first preference votes, until the candidates and election agents present at its completion have been given a reasonable opportunity to exercise the right conferred by this rule.

Procedure at conclusion of first count

51 (1)   As soon as practicable after the conclusion of the first count (including any re-count), the returning officer must draw up a statement showing–

(a)   the total number of ballot papers used;

(b)   the total number of rejected ballot papers;

(c)   at an election contested by more than two candidates–

(i)   the number of first preference votes given for each candidate; and

(ii)   the total number of first preference votes given; and

(d)   at an election contested by only two candidates, the number of votes given for each candidate.

(2)   As soon as practicable after completion of the statement, the returning officer must–

(a)   inform such of the candidates and their election agents as are then present of the contents of the statements prepared in accordance with rule 48(5) and paragraph (1) of this rule; and

(b)   give public notice of the contents of those statements.

(3)   Where an election is contested by more than two candidates, the returning officer must–

(a)   if paragraph 2 of Schedule 2 to the 2000 Act applies (candidate with overall majority of first preference votes), make the declaration required by rule 54(1); or

(b)   if paragraph 3 of that Schedule applies, count the second preference votes at the time and place notified in writing to the counting agents.

(4)   Where–

(a)   an election is contested by only two candidates; and

(b)   the total number of votes for each of them is unequal,

the person to be returned as the elected mayor is the candidate to whom the majority of the votes is given.

(5)   Where–
    (a)   an election is contested by only two candidates; and
    (b)   the total number of votes given for each of them is equal,
the returning officer shall decide by lot which of them is to be returned as the elected mayor.

(6)   In a case to which paragraph (4) or (5) applies, the declaration of the person to be returned as the elected mayor shall be made in accordance with rule 54.

Part 5
Further Provision: More than Two Candidates

The count of second preference votes

52 (1)   The returning officer must count the number of second preference votes for each of the candidates remaining in the contest given by voters who did not give their first preference vote to any of those candidates.

(2)   A ballot paper which is not otherwise void and on which not more than one second preference vote is marked shall be valid as respects that vote and shall be counted accordingly if, but only if, a valid first preference vote has also been marked.

(3)   Rules 46(2) to (5), 47(6), (7), (9) and (10), 48 (except paragraph (3)) and 50 (except the words "the votes, or as the case may be," in both paragraphs where they appear) shall apply in relation to the count of second preference votes as they apply in relation to the count of first preference votes as if references to first preference votes were references to second preference votes.

(4)   The returning officer shall not be required to re-examine any decision taken under rule 49.

The calculation of total votes and resolution of equality

53 (1)   The returning officer must comply with paragraph 3(6) of Schedule 2 to the 2000 Act.

(2)   The returning officer must then draw up a statement showing–
    (a)   the total number of first preference votes given for each candidate,
    (b)   the total number of second preference votes given for each of the candidates remaining in the contest after the count of the first preference votes,
    (c)   the total number of votes given for each of those candidates, and
    (d)   the number of ballot papers that were–
        (i)   valid as respects a first preference vote given for a candidate who did not remain in the contest after the count of the first preference votes; and
        (ii)   rejected for the purposes of the count of second preference votes on the ground that they were unmarked or void for uncertainty as to the second preference vote.

(3)   As soon as practicable after completion of the statement, the returning officer must provide such of the election agents for those candidates who remain in the contest as are then present with a copy of the statement, and shall give them a reasonable opportunity to satisfy themselves as to the accuracy of the calculation.

(4)   If, after the second preference votes have been counted, the total number of votes given for two or more candidates remaining in the contest is equal, the person to be returned as the elected mayor is the person whom the returning officer decides, in accordance with paragraph 3(8) of Schedule 2 to the 2000 Act, is to be returned as the elected mayor.

Part 6
Final Proceedings in Contested and Uncontested Elections

Declaration of result

54 (1) The returning officer must declare the elected mayor to be the candidate who, in accordance with section 9HC(2) or (3) or section 42(2) or (3) of the 2000 Act or, as the case may be, Schedule 2 to that Act, is to be returned as the elected mayor at that election.

   (2) The returning officer must give public notice of–
   - (a) the name of the successful candidate,
   - (b) the total number of first preference votes given for each candidate,
   - (c) the number of rejected ballot papers at the election under each head shown in the statement of rejected ballot papers (rule 48(5)), and
   - (d) if second preference votes were counted–
       - (i)   the total number of second preference votes given for each of the candidates remaining in the contest after the count of the first preference votes, and
       - (ii) the number of ballot papers rejected for the purposes of the count of second preference votes on the ground that they were unmarked or void for uncertainty as to the second preference vote.

   (3) In an uncontested election, the returning officer must as soon as practicable after the latest time for the delivery of notices of withdrawals of candidature–
   - (a)   declare to be elected the person remaining validly nominated;
   - (b)   give public notice of the name of the person declared to be elected.

   (4) The returning officer must inform the proper officer of the local authority concerned of the result of the election.

Return or forfeiture of candidate's deposit

55 (1) Unless forfeited in accordance with paragraph (5), the deposit made under rule 10 of these Rules shall be returned to the person making it or his personal representative.

   (2) Subject to paragraph (4), the deposit shall be returned not later than the next day after that on which the result of the election is declared.

   (3) For the purposes of paragraph (2)–
   - (a) a day shall be disregarded if it would be disregarded under rule 4 in computing any period of time for the purpose of the timetable for a mayoral election; and
   - (b) the deposit shall be treated as being returned on a day if a cheque for the amount of the deposit is posted on that day.

   (4) If the candidate is not shown as standing nominated in the statement of persons nominated, or if proof of his death has been given to the returning officer before the conclusion of the first count, the deposit shall be returned as soon as practicable after the publication of the statement or after his death, as the case may be.

   (5) Where a poll is taken, if, after the conclusion of the first count, the candidate is found not to have polled more than one-twentieth of the total number of first preference votes polled by all the candidates, the deposit shall be forfeited to the local authority of the electoral areas concerned.

Part 7

Disposal of Documents

Sealing up of ballot papers

56 (1)   On the completion of the counting at a contested election the returning officer must seal up in separate packets the counted and rejected ballot papers, including ballot papers rejected in part.

(2)   The returning officer must not open the sealed packets of–

(a)   tendered ballot papers,

(b)   the completed corresponding number lists,

(c)   certificates as to employment on duty on the day of the poll, or

(d)   marked copies of the register of electors (including any marked copy notices issued under section 13B(3B) or (3D) of the 1983 Act) and lists of proxies.

Delivery and retention of documents

57   The returning officer must then forward to the relevant registration officer of the local authority concerned the following documents–

(a)   the packets of ballot papers in his possession,

(b)   the ballot paper accounts and the statements of rejected ballot papers and of the result of the verification of the ballot paper accounts,

(c)   the tendered votes lists, the lists of voters with disabilities assisted by companions, the lists of votes marked by the presiding officer and the related statements, the lists maintained under rule 43 and the declarations made by the companions of voters with disabilities,

(d)   the packets of the completed corresponding number lists,

(e)   the packets of certificates as to employment on duty on the day of the poll,

(f)   the packets containing marked copies of registers (including any marked copy notices issued under section 13B(3B) or (3D) of the 1983 Act) and of the postal voters list, of the lists of proxies and of the proxy postal voters list,

endorsing on each packet a description of its contents, the date of the election to which they relate and the name of the electoral area for which the election was held.

Orders for production of documents

58 (1)   An order–

(a)   for the inspection or production of any rejected ballot papers, including ballot papers rejected in part, in the custody of the relevant registration officer; or

(b)   for the opening of a sealed packet of the completed corresponding number lists or certificates as to employment on duty on the day of the poll or for the inspection of any counted ballot papers in his custody,

may be made by a county court, if the court is satisfied by evidence on oath that the order is required for the purpose of instituting or maintaining a prosecution for an offence in relation to ballot papers, or for the purpose of an election petition.

(2)   An order for the opening of a sealed packet of completed corresponding number lists or of certificates as to employment on duty on the day of the poll or for the inspection of any counted ballot papers in the custody of the relevant registration officer may be made by an election court.

(3)   An order under this rule may be made subject to such conditions as to–

(a)   persons,

(b)   time,

(c)   place and mode of inspection,

(d)   production or opening,

as the court making the order may think expedient.

(4) In making and carrying into effect an order for the opening of a packet of completed corresponding number lists or of certificates as to employment on duty on the day of the poll or for the inspection of counted ballot papers, care must be taken that the way in which the vote of any particular elector has been given shall not be disclosed until it has been proved–

    (i)   that his vote was given; and

    (ii) that the vote has been declared by a competent court to be invalid.

(5) An appeal lies to the High Court from any order of a county court under this rule.

(6) Any power given under this rule to a county court may be exercised by any judge of the court otherwise than in open court.

(7) Where an order is made for the production by the relevant registration officer of any document in his possession relating to any specified election–

    (a) the production by him or his agent of the document ordered in such manner as may be directed by that order shall be conclusive evidence that the document relates to the specified election; and

    (b) any endorsement on any packet of ballot papers so produced shall be prima facie evidence that the ballot papers are what they are stated to be by the endorsement.

(8) The production from proper custody of–

    (a) a ballot paper purporting to have been used at any election, and

    (b) a completed corresponding number list with a number marked in writing beside the number of the ballot paper,

shall be prima facie evidence that the elector whose vote was given by that ballot paper was the person whose entry in the register of electors or on a notice issued under section 13B(3B) or (3D) of the 1983 Act at the time of the election contained the same number as the number written as mentioned in sub-paragraph (b) of this paragraph.

(9) Save as by this rule provided, no person shall be allowed to inspect any rejected or counted ballot papers in the possession of the relevant registration officer or open any sealed packets of completed corresponding number lists or of certificates as to employment on duty on the day of the poll.

Retention of documents

59 The relevant registration officer must retain for one year all documents relating to an election forwarded to him in pursuance of these Rules by a returning officer, and then, unless otherwise directed by an order of a county court, the Crown Court, a magistrates' court or an election court, must cause them to be destroyed.

Part 8
Death of Candidate

Countermand or abandonment of poll on death of a candidate

60 (1) If at a contested election proof is given to the returning officer's satisfaction before the result of the election is declared that one of the persons named or to be named as candidate in the ballot papers has died, then the returning officer must countermand notice of the poll or, if polling has begun, direct that the poll be abandoned, and the provisions of subsections (1) and (5) of section 39 of the 1983 Act apply in respect of any vacancy which remains unfilled.

(2) Subject to paragraph (4), where the poll is abandoned by reason of a candidate's death no further ballot papers shall be issued, and the presiding officer at any polling station must take the like steps (so far as not already taken) for the delivery to the returning officer of ballot boxes and ballot papers and other documents as he is required to take on the close of the poll in due course.

(3) The returning officer must dispose of ballot papers and other documents in his possession as he is required to do on the completion in due course of the counting of the votes, subject to paragraphs (4) and (5).

(4) It is not necessary for any ballot paper account to be prepared or verified.

(5) The returning officer must seal up all the ballot papers, whether the votes on them have been counted or not, and it is not necessary to seal up counted and rejected ballot papers in separate packets.

(6) The provisions of these Rules as to the inspection, production, retention and destruction of ballot papers and other documents relating to a poll at an election apply to any such documents relating to a poll abandoned by reason of a candidate's death subject to paragraphs (7) and (8).

(7) Ballot papers on which the votes were neither counted nor rejected must be treated as counted ballot papers.

(8) No order is to be made for–
    (a) the inspection or production of any ballot papers, or
    (b) for the opening of a sealed packet of the completed corresponding number lists or certificates as to employment on duty on the day of the poll,
unless the order is made by a court with reference to a prosecution.

Appendix of Forms

Notes: In this Appendix any reference to a numbered rule is a reference to the rule of that number in the Mayoral Elections Rules.

The forms contained in this Appendix may be adapted so far as circumstances require.

Forms

Form 1:   Nomination paper
Form 2:   Candidate's consent to nomination
Form 3:   Ballot paper (two candidates)
Form 4:   Ballot paper (three or more candidates)
Form 5:   Corresponding Number List L1
Form 6:   Corresponding Number List L2
Form 7:   Postal Voting Statement
Form 8:   Elector's official poll card
Form 9:   Official postal poll card
Form 10:   Official proxy poll card
Form 11:   Official proxy postal poll card
Form 12:   Directions for guidance of voters
Form 13:   Certificate of employment
Form 14:   Declaration to be made by the companion of a voter with disabilities.

The forms have not been reproduced

SCHEDULE 2
MODIFICATIONS OF ACTS AND STATUTORY INSTRUMENT

Regulation 3(2)&(4)

Table 1
The Representation of the People Act 1983

(1) Provision	*(2)* Modification
Section 31 (polling districts and stations at local government elections)	In subsection (1)– (a) after "county councillors" insert "or elected mayors of county councils," and (b) after "district councillors", insert "or elected mayors of London borough or district councils". In subsection (1A), after "county borough councillors", insert "or elected mayors of county or county borough councils,".
Section 35 (returning officers: local elections in England and Wales)	In subsection (1)– (a) after "councillors of the county", insert "and elected mayors of the county council"; and (b) after "councillors of the district", insert "and elected mayors of the district council". In subsection (1A), in paragraph (a), after "councillors of the county or county borough", insert "and elected mayors of the county or county borough council". In subsection (3), after "London borough councillors", insert "or the election of an elected mayor of a London borough council".
Section 36 (local elections in England and Wales)	In subsection (3) in paragraph (a), after "such a councillor," insert "or the election of an elected mayor of a district council". In subsection (3AB), in paragraph (a), after "such a councillor", insert "or the election of an elected mayor of a Welsh county or county borough council". In subsection (3AC), in paragraph (a), after "such a councillor", insert "or the election of an elected mayor of the council of a county in England in which there are no district councils". In subsection (4), after "a London borough)" insert "or the election of an elected mayor of the council of such an area," In subsection (6), after "Wales", insert "or at an election of an elected mayor of the council of any such area,".
Section 39 (local elections void etc in England and Wales	In subsection (2), after "other reason", insert "a mayoral election or". In subsection (5), in paragraph (a), after "section 36 above", insert "or, in the case of a mayoral election, regulations under section 9HE or 44 of that Act,". In subsection (6), in paragraph (a)– (a) in sub-paragraph (i), after "section 36)", insert "or under Part 1A or Part 2 of the 2000 Act (and the regulations under section 9HE or 44)"; and (b) omit ", or, as the case may be, the district council, or Welsh county or county borough council,".

Section 40 (timing as to local elections in England and Wales)	In subsection (1), after "the 1999 Act", insert "or regulations under section 9HE or 44 of the 2000 Act". In subsection (2), after "the 1999 Act" insert "and (in the case of a mayoral election) regulations under section 9HE or 44 of the 2000 Act". In subsection (3)– (a) after "section 36 above", insert "or regulations under section 9HE or 44 of the 2000 Act"; and (b) after "such rules" (in both places) and "those rules", insert "or regulations (as the case may be)".
Section 46 (further provision as to local election voting)	Omit subsection (1).
Section 47 (loan of equipment for local elections)	In subsection (2)– (a) omit paragraph (b); and (b) for "those Acts", substitute "that Act or Part 1A or Part II of the 2000 Act".
Section 48 (validity of local elections and legal costs)	In subsection (1), after "section 42 above", insert "or regulations under section 9HE or 44 of the 2000 Act".
Section 50 (effect of misdescription)	In paragraph (c)– (a) after "this Part of this Act", insert "(as applied for the purposes of mayoral elections), and regulations under section 9HE or 44 of the 2000 Act"; and (b) omit "and the parliamentary elections rules,".
Section 52 (discharge of registration duties)	In subsections (1) and (4), after "this Act", insert "(including any such functions in relation to mayoral elections)".
Section 54 (payment of expenses of registration)	In subsection (1) after "this Act", at the first place where these words appear, insert "(including any such functions in relation to mayoral elections)".
Section 61 (other voting offences)	In subsection (2), in paragraph (a)– (a) in sub-paragraph (ii), after "councillors" insert "or a mayoral election"; and (b) in sub-paragraph (iii), after "ordinary election", insert "or mayoral election". In subsection (3) in paragraph (a) (ii) after "councillors", insert "or at a mayoral election". In subsection (6A), for "rule 40 (1ZC) or (1ZE) of the parliamentary elections rules", substitute "rule 40 (4) or (6) of the Mayoral Elections Rules".
Section 67 (appointment of election agent)	In subsection (2)– (a) after "this Act", where it first appears, insert "or, in the case of a mayoral election, such of the provisions of this Act as are applied by regulations under section 9HE or 44 of the 2000 Act,"; and (b) after "this Act", in the second place, insert "or, in the case of a mayoral election, any applicable provision of this Act,".
Section 76 (limitation of election expenses)	For subsection (2), substitute– "(2) That maximum amount is £2,362 together with an additional 5.9p for every entry in the register of electors to be used at the election."
Section 85 (penalty for "sitting or voting" where no return and declarations	Omit subsection (2).

transmitted)	
Section 85A (disqualification where no return and declarations transmitted after election of Mayor of London)	In subsection (1)– (a) for "an election of the Mayor of London" substitute "a mayoral election"; and (b) for "Mayor of London", in the second place, substitute "elected mayor".
Section 87A (duty of appropriate officer to forward returns and declarations to Electoral Commission).	In subsection (1) after paragraph (b) insert "or, (c) a mayoral election".
Section 94 (imitation of poll cards)	In subsection (2)– (a) after "section 36" insert "above, or regulations made under section 44 of the 2000 Act"; and (b) after "the rules", insert "or, as the case may be, the regulations".
Section 96 (schools and rooms for local election meetings)	In subsection (1), after "section 36", insert "above, or regulations made under section 44 of the 2000 Act".
Section 97 (disturbances at election meetings)	In subsection (2), in paragraph (b), after "section 36", insert "above, or regulations made under section 44 of the 2000 Act".
Section 99 (officials not to act for candidates)	In subsection (1), in paragraph (b), after "section 36", insert "above, or regulations made under section 44 of the 2000 Act".
Section 118A (meaning of candidate)	In subsection (3), after "local government Act", insert "or at an election for a mayor under the 2000 Act".
Section 199B (translation of certain documents)	In subsection (6), insert after paragraph (b)– "(ba) in the case of an election for a mayor under the 2000 Act, must have printed at the top of the list of candidates the words "Vote (x) for one candidate only" if there are only two candidates, or the words "Vote once (x) in column 1 for your first choice, and Vote once (x) in column 2 for your second choice" if there are more than two candidates;".
Section 203 (local government provisions as to England and Wales)	In subsection (1)– (a) after the definition of "the 1999 Act", insert, ""the 2000 Act" means the Local Government Act 2000;" (b) in the definition of "local government election", at the end of paragraph (b), insert "or (c) any mayoral election;" and (c) after the definition of "London member", insert– ""mayoral election" means the election of an elected mayor under Part 1A or Part II of the 2000 Act.". In subsection (1A), at the end, insert "or a mayoral election". In subsection (2), in paragraph (b), after "Authority elections", insert "or mayoral elections".

Table 2
The Representation of the People Act 1985

(1) Provision	(2) Modification
Section 15 (combination of	In subsection (1), at the end of paragraph (c), insert–

polls at parliamentary, European Parliamentary and local elections)	"or, (d) a mayoral election and an election of one or more of the descriptions specified in paragraphs (a) to (c),". Omit subsections (5) and (5A).

Table 3
The Representation of the People Act 2000

(1) Provision	(2) Modification
Schedule 4 (absent voting in Great Britain)	In paragraph 1, in sub-paragraph (1)– (a) in the definition of "the appropriate rules", at the end of paragraph (b), insert "and (c) in the case of a mayoral election, the Mayoral Elections Rules, within the meaning of the Local Authorities (Mayoral Elections) (England and Wales) Regulations 2007"; (b) in the definition of "local government election", at the end insert "and includes a mayoral election"; and (c) after that definition, insert the following definition– ""mayoral election" means an election under regulations under section 9HE or 44 of the Local Government Act 2000;". In paragraph 2, in sub-paragraph (6A) for "rule 40(1ZC) or (1ZE) of the parliamentary elections rules", substitute "rule 40(4) or (6) of the Mayoral Elections Rules". In paragraph 7, in sub-paragraph (10) for "rule 40(1ZC) or (1ZE) of the parliamentary elections rules", substitute "rule 40(4) or (6) of the Mayoral Elections Rules".

Table 4
The Representation of the People (England and Wales) Regulations 2001

(1) Provision	(2) Modification
Regulation 3 (interpretation)	At the end of paragraph (2)(b) insert– ", or (c) the corresponding rule in the regulations made under section 44 of the 2000 Act in the case of a mayoral election.". At the end of paragraph (4), insert– "(5) A reference in these Regulations to a local government election shall, except in paragraph (2)(b) above, include a mayoral election under Part 1A or Part 2 of the 2000 Act."
Regulation 50 (interpretation of Part 4)	At the end of the definition of "Schedule 4" insert "as modified by Schedule 2 to the Local Authorities (Mayoral Elections) (England and Wales) Regulations 2007."
Regulation 64 (interpretation of Part 5)	At the appropriate place, insert–"candidates" includes a candidate at a mayoral election under Part 1A or Part 2 of the 2000 Act;".
Regulation 65 (combination of polls)	After paragraph (b) insert– ", or (c) subsection (3), (3AB) or (3AC), as modified by Schedule 2 to the Local Authorities (Mayoral Elections) (England and Wales) Regulations 2007,".

Table 5

The Electoral Administration Act 2006

(1) Provision	(2) Modification
Section 32 (photographs on ballot papers: piloting)	In subsection (10)– (a) in paragraph (a) in the definition of "local government election" at the end insert "and includes a mayoral election under regulations made under section 44 of the Local Government Act 2000"; (b) for paragraph (b) substitute– "(b) a reference to the area of a local authority means a county, county borough, London borough or district.".
Section 44 (access to other election documents: supplementary)	In paragraph (12), at the end insert "subject to modifications made by regulations made under section 44 of the 2000 Act.".
Section 69 (encouraging electoral participation)	In paragraph (9) at the end, insert– "(g) mayoral elections under regulations made under section 44 of the 2000 Act.".

SCHEDULE 3
MAYORAL ELECTION (COMBINATION OF POLLS) RULES

Regulation 4

Part 1
General Provisions

Part 2
Provisions as to Time

Part 3
Stages Common to Contested and Uncontested Elections

Part 4
Contested Elections

Part 1
General Provisions

Citation

1   These Rules may be cited as the Mayoral Elections (Combination of Polls) Rules.

Interpretation

2 (1)   In these Rules, unless the context indicates otherwise–
"the Appendix" means the Appendix to these Rules;
"Assembly constituency" shall have the meaning as in section 2(4) and (5) of the Greater London Authority Act 1999;
"candidate" means a candidate to be an elected mayor;
"the Combination of Polls Regulations" means the Representation of the People (Combination of Polls) (England and Wales) Regulations 2004;
"counting observer" shall have the same meaning as in regulation 2(1) of the Referendums

Regulations;

"counting officer" shall have the same meaning as in regulation 2(1) of the Referendums Regulations;

"local counting area" shall have the same meaning as in regulation 2(1) of the European Parliamentary Elections Regulations 2004;

"petition organiser" shall have the same meaning as in regulation 3 of the Local Authorities (Referendums) (Petitions and Directions) (England) Regulations 2000;

"polling observer" shall have the same meaning as in regulation 2(1) of the Referendums Regulations;

"returning officer", in relation to an election means–

    (a) the proper officer of the London borough concerned or, as the case may be, the person appointed as the returning officer for the election in accordance with subsection (1) or (1A) of section 35 (returning officers: local elections in England and Wales) of the 1983 Act; and

    (b) any person appointed under subsection (4) of that section by a person of a description mentioned in paragraph (a);

"voting area" shall have the same meaning as in regulation 2 of the Referendums Regulations.

(2) In the case of a referendum, a reference to–

    (a) a "candidate" shall be construed as a reference to a petition organiser;

    (b) an "election agent" or a "counting agent" shall be construed as a reference to a counting observer;

    (c) a "polling agent" shall be construed as a reference to a polling observer; and

    (d) a "returning officer" shall be construed as a reference to a counting officer.

(3) Subject to paragraph (4), other expressions used both in these Rules and in the 1983 Act (as it applies to local government elections) have the same meaning in these Rules as they have in that Act.

(4) Where such expressions are used in relation to a mayoral election, they have the meaning as defined in regulation 2 or modified by regulation 3.

Part 2
Provisions as to Time

Timetable

3 The proceedings at the election shall be conducted in accordance with the following Timetable:

Proceedings	Time
Publication of notice of election	Not later than the twenty-fifth day before the day of election.
Delivery of nomination papers	Not later than 4 in the afternoon on the nineteenth day before the day of election.
Publication of statement as to persons nominated	Not later than 4 in the afternoon on the eighteenth day before the day of election.
Delivery of notices of withdrawal of candidature	Not later than 4 in the afternoon on the nineteenth day before the day of election.
Notice of poll	Not later than the sixth day before the day of election.
Polling	Between the hours of 7 in the morning and 10 at night on the day of election.

Computation of time

4 (1) In computing any period of time for the purposes of the Timetable–
      (a) a Saturday or Sunday,
      (b) Christmas Eve, Christmas Day, Good Friday or a bank holiday, or
      (c) a day appointed for public thanksgiving or mourning,
shall be disregarded, and any such day shall not be treated as a day for the purpose of any proceedings up to the completion of the poll nor shall the returning officer be obliged to proceed with the counting of votes on such a day.

  (2)   In this rule, "bank holiday" means a day which is a bank holiday under the Banking and Financial Dealings Act 1971 in England and Wales.

Part 3
Stages Common to Contested and Uncontested Elections

Notice of election

5 (1)   The returning officer shall publish notice of the election stating–
      (a) the place and times at which nomination papers are to be delivered, and
      (b) the date of the poll in the event of a contest,
and the notice must state that forms of nomination papers may be obtained at that place and those times.

  (2)   The notice of election must also state the arrangements which apply for the payment of the deposit required by rule 10 to be made by means of the electronic transfer of funds.

  (3)   The notice of election must state the date by which–
      (a) applications to vote by post or by proxy, and
      (b) other applications and notices about postal or proxy voting,
must reach the registration officer in order that they may be effective for the election.

Nomination of candidates

6 (1)   Each candidate must be nominated by a separate nomination paper.

  (2)   A nomination paper must be in the appropriate form in the Appendix or a form to the like effect and shall be delivered at the place fixed for the purpose by the returning officer, which shall be at the offices of the council of the county, county borough, district or London borough in which the electoral area wholly or mainly lies.

  (3)   A nomination paper must state the candidate's–
      (a) full names,
      (b) home address, in full, and
      (c) if desired, description,
and the surname must be placed first in the list of names.

  (4)   If a candidate commonly uses–
      (a) a surname which is different from any other surname he has, or
      (b) a forename which is different from any other forename he has,
the nomination paper may state the commonly used surname or forename in addition to the other name.

  (5)   The description, if any, which may not comprise more than six words, must consist of either–
      (a) that authorised as mentioned in paragraph rule 7(1) or (3); or
      (b) the word "Independent".

Nomination papers: name of registered political party

7 (1) A nomination paper may not include a description of a candidate which is likely to lead electors to associate the candidate with a registered political party unless the party is a qualifying party in relation to the electoral area and the description is authorised by a certificate–

    (a) issued by or on behalf of the registered nominating officer of the party, and

    (b) received by the returning officer before the last time for the delivery of nomination papers set out in the Timetable in rule 3.

(2) In paragraph (1) an authorised description may be either–

    (a) the name of the party registered under section 28 of the Political Parties, Elections and Referendums Act 2000, or

    (b) a description of the party registered under section 28A of that Act.

(3) A nomination paper may not include a description of a candidate which is likely to lead electors to associate the candidate with two or more registered political parties unless the parties are each qualifying parties in relation to the electoral area and the description is a registered description authorised by a certificate–

    (a) issued by or on behalf of the registered nominating officer of each of the parties, and

    (b) received by the returning officer before the last time for the delivery of nomination papers set out in the Timetable in rule 3.

(4) For the purposes of paragraph (3), a description is a registered description if it is a description registered for use by the parties under section 28B of the Political Parties, Elections and Referendums Act 2000.

(5) A person shall be guilty of a corrupt practice if he fraudulently purports to be authorised to issue a certificate under paragraph (1) or (3) on behalf of a registered political party's nominating officer.

(6) For the purposes of the application of this rule in relation to an election–

    (a) "registered political party" means a party which was registered under Part 2 of the Political Parties, Elections and Referendums Act 2000 on the day ("the relevant day") which is two days before the last day for the delivery of nomination papers at that election;

    (b) a registered political party is a qualifying party in relation to an electoral area if the electoral area is in England or Wales and the party was on the relevant day registered in respect of that part of Great Britain in the Great Britain register maintained under that Part of that Act.

(7) For the purposes of paragraph (6)(a), any day falling within rule 4(1) must be disregarded.

Subscription of nomination paper

8 (1) The nomination paper must be subscribed by two electors as proposer and seconder, and by twenty-eight other electors as assenting to the nomination.

(2) Where a nomination paper has the signatures of more than the required number of persons as proposing, seconding or assenting to the nomination of a candidate, the signature or signatures (up to the required number) appearing first on the paper in each category must be taken into account to the exclusion of any others in that category.

(3) The nomination paper must give the electoral number of each person subscribing it.

(4) The returning officer–

(a) must supply any elector with as many forms of nomination paper and forms of consent to nomination as may be required at the place and during the time for delivery of nomination papers, and

(b) must at any elector's request prepare a nomination paper for signature,

but it is not necessary for a nomination or consent to nomination to be on a form supplied by the returning officer.

(5) In this rule "elector"–

(a) means a person who is registered in the register of local government electors for the electoral area in question on the last day for the publication of notice of the election; and

(b) includes a person then shown in the register as below voting age if (but only if) it appears from the register that he will be of voting age on the day fixed for the poll.

(6) But, in this rule, "elector" does not include a person who has an anonymous entry in the register.

Consent to nomination

9 A person shall not be validly nominated unless his consent to nomination–

(a) is given in writing, on or within one month before the last day for the delivery of nomination papers,

(b) is in the appropriate form in the Appendix or a form to the like effect and includes–

(i) for a nomination in England, a copy of sections 80 and 81 of the Local Government Act 1972, section 78A of the Local Government Act 2000 and section 34 of the Localism Act 2011; or

(ii) for a nomination in Wales, a copy of sections 80 and 81 of the Local Government Act 1972 and sections 78A and 79 of the Local Government Act 2000,

(c) is attested by one witness, and

(d) is delivered at the place and within the time for the delivery of nomination papers.

Deposits

10 (1) A person shall not be validly nominated unless the sum of £500 is deposited by him or on his behalf, with the returning officer at the place and within the time for delivery of nomination papers.

(2) The deposit may be made either–

(a) by the deposit of any legal tender, or

(b) by means of a banker's draft, or

(c) with the returning officer's consent, in any other manner (including by means of a debit or credit card or the electronic transfer of funds),

but the returning officer may refuse to accept a deposit sought to be made by means of a banker's draft if he does not know that the drawer carries on business as a banker in the United Kingdom.

(3) Where the deposit is made on behalf of the candidate, the person making the deposit must at the time he makes it give his name and address to the returning officer (unless they have previously been given to him under section 67 (appointment of election agent) of the 1983 Act).

Decisions as to validity of nomination papers

11 (1) Where a nomination paper and the candidate's consent to nomination are delivered in accordance with these Rules, the candidate shall be deemed to stand nominated unless and until–
    (a) the returning officer decides that the nomination paper is invalid, or
    (b) proof is given to the returning officer's satisfaction of the candidate's death, or
    (c) the candidate withdraws.

(2) The returning officer is entitled to hold the nomination paper of a person invalid only on one of the following grounds–
    (a) that the particulars of the candidate or of the persons subscribing the paper are not as required by law; and
    (b) that the paper is not subscribed as so required.

(3) Subject to paragraph (4), the returning officer must, as soon as practicable after each nomination paper has been delivered, examine it and decide whether the candidate has been validly nominated.

(4) If in the returning officer's opinion a nomination paper breaks rule 7(1) or (3), he must give a decision to that effect–
    (a) as soon as practicable after the delivery of the nomination paper, and
    (b) in any event, before the end of the period of 24 hours starting with the close of the period for delivery of nomination papers set out in the Timetable in rule 3.

(5) Where the returning officer decides that a nomination paper is invalid, he must endorse and sign on the paper the fact and the reasons for his decision.

(6) The returning officer must send notice of his decision that a nomination paper is valid or invalid to each candidate at his home address as given in his nomination paper.

(7) The returning officer's decision that a nomination paper is valid shall be final and shall not be questioned in any proceeding whatsoever.

(8) Subject to paragraph (7), nothing in this rule prevents the validity of a nomination being questioned on an election petition.

Publication of statement of persons nominated

12 (1) The returning officer must prepare and publish a statement showing the persons who have been and stand nominated and any other persons who have been nominated, with the reason why they no longer stand nominated.

(2) The statement must show the names, addresses and descriptions of the persons nominated as given in their nomination papers.

(3) If a person's nomination paper gives a commonly used surname or forename in addition to another name, the statement must show the person's commonly used surname or forename (as the case may be) instead of any other name.

(4) Paragraph (3) does not apply if the returning officer thinks–
    (a) that the use of the person's commonly used name may be likely to mislead or confuse electors, or
    (b) that the commonly used name is obscene or offensive.

(5) If paragraph (4) applies, the returning officer must give notice in writing to the candidate of his reasons for refusing to allow the use of a commonly used name.

(6) The statement must show the persons standing nominated arranged alphabetically in the order of their surnames, and if there are two or more of them with the same surname, of their other names.

(7)   In the case of a person nominated by more than one nomination paper, the returning officer must take the particulars required by the foregoing provisions of this rule from such one of the papers as the candidate (or the returning officer in default of the candidate) may select.

Inspection of nomination papers and consent to nomination

13   During ordinary office hours on any day, other than a day specified in rule 4(1), after the latest time for delivery of nomination papers and before the date of the poll, any person may inspect and take copies of, or extracts from, nomination papers and consents to nomination.

Correction of minor errors

14 (1)   A returning officer may, if he thinks fit, at any time before the publication under rule 12 of the statement of persons nominated, correct minor errors in a nomination paper.

(2)   Errors which may be corrected include–
  (a)   errors as to a person's electoral number;
  (b)   obvious errors of spelling in relation to the details of a candidate.

(3)   Anything done by a returning officer in pursuance of this rule shall not be questioned in any proceedings other than proceedings on an election petition.

(4)   A returning officer must have regard to any guidance issued by the Electoral Commission for the purposes of this rule.

Withdrawal of candidature

15 (1)   A candidate may withdraw his candidature by notice of withdrawal–
  (a)   signed by him and attested by one witness; and
  (b)   delivered to the returning officer at the place for delivery of nomination papers.

(2)   Where a candidate is outside the United Kingdom, a notice of withdrawal signed by his election proposer and accompanied by a written declaration also so signed of the candidate's absence from the United Kingdom shall be of the same effect as a notice of withdrawal signed by the candidate; but where the candidate stands nominated by more than one nomination paper a notice of withdrawal under this paragraph shall be effective if, and only if–
  (a)   it and the accompanying declaration are signed by all the proposers except any who is, and is stated in that declaration to be, outside the United Kingdom; or
  (b)   it is accompanied, in addition to that declaration, by a written statement signed by the candidate that the proposer giving the notice is authorised to do so on the candidate's behalf during his absence from the United Kingdom.

Method of election

16   If, after any withdrawals under rule 15–
  (a)   more than two candidates remain validly nominated, a poll shall be taken in accordance with Parts 4 and 5 of these Rules,
  (b)   only two candidates remain validly nominated, a poll shall be taken in accordance with Part 4;
  (c)   only one candidate remains validly nominated, that person shall be declared to be elected in accordance with Part 6.

Part 4
Contested Elections

Poll to be taken by ballot

17　The votes at the poll shall be given by ballot.

The ballot papers

18 (1)　The ballot of every person entitled to a vote at the election shall consist of a ballot paper.

(2)　The persons remaining validly nominated for election to the office of mayor, after any withdrawals, and no others, shall be entitled to have their names inserted in the ballot paper at that election.

(3)　Every ballot must be in the appropriate form, and must be printed in accordance with the appropriate directions, set out in the Appendix, and–

　　(a)　must contain the names and other particulars of the candidates as shown in the statement of persons nominated;

　　(b)　must be capable of being folded up;

　　(c)　must have a number and other unique identifying mark printed on the back;

　　(d)　must be of a different colour from that of any ballot papers used at any relevant election or referendum.

(4)　If a candidate who is the subject of a party's authorisation under rule 7(1) so requests, the ballot paper must contain, against the candidate's particulars, the party's registered emblem (or, as the case may be, one of the party's registered emblems).

(4A)　If a candidate who is the subject of an authorisation by two or more parties under rule 7(3) so requests, the ballot paper must contain, against the candidate's particulars, the registered emblem (or, as the case may be, one of the registered emblems) of one of those parties.

(5)　The candidate's request under paragraph (4) or (4A) must–

　　(a)　be made in writing to the returning officer, and

　　(b)　be received by him during the period for delivery of nomination papers set out in the Timetable in rule 3.

(6)　The order of the names in the ballot paper must be the same as in the statement of persons nominated.

The corresponding number list

19 (1)　The returning officer must prepare a list containing the numbers and other unique identifying marks of all of the ballot papers to be issued by him in pursuance of rule 24 or provided by him in pursuance of rule 28.

(2)　The list must be in the appropriate form in the Appendix or a form to like effect.

The official mark

20 (1)　Every ballot paper must contain an appropriate security marking (the official mark).

(2)　The official mark must be kept secret, and an interval of not less than five years shall intervene between the use of the same official mark at an election (of whatever description) for the same county, county borough, district or London borough, as the case may be.

(3) The returning officer may use a different official mark for different purposes at the same election.

Prohibition of disclosure of vote

21   No person who has voted at the election shall, in any legal proceeding to question the election, be required to state for whom he has voted.

Use of schools and public rooms

22 (1) The returning officer may use, free of charge, for the purpose of taking the poll or counting the votes–
    (a)   a room in a school maintained or assisted by a local authority (as defined in the Education Act 1996) or a school in respect of which grants are made out of moneys provided by Parliament to the person or body of persons responsible for the management of the school;
    (b)   a room the expense of maintaining which is met by any local authority.

(2) The use of a room in an unoccupied hereditament for that purpose or those purposes does not render a person liable to any payment by way of council tax or non-domestic rate in respect of that hereditament and any day on which it is so used.

(3) The returning officer must make good any damage done to, and defray any expense incurred by the persons having control over, any such room as is mentioned in paragraph (1) by reason of its being used for the purpose of taking the poll or counting the votes.

Notice of poll

23 (1) The returning officer must publish notice of the poll stating–
    (a)   the day and hours fixed for the poll;
    (b)   particulars of each candidate remaining validly nominated (the names and other particulars of the candidates, and the order of their names being the same as in the statement of persons nominated); and
    (c)   the names of all persons signing a candidate's nomination paper.

(2) Where a candidate is nominated by more than one nomination paper, the nomination paper referred to in paragraph (1)(c) must be that from which the names and other particulars of the candidate shown in the statement of persons nominated are taken.

(3) The returning officer must, not later than the time of the publication of the notice of the poll, also give public notice of–
    (a)   the situation of each polling station; and
    (b)   the description of voters entitled to vote there,
and he must as soon as practicable after giving such a notice give a copy of it to each of the election agents.

(4) The notice published under paragraph (3) above shall–
    (a)   state that the poll at the mayoral election is to be taken together with the poll at a relevant election or referendum;
    (b)   specify the parliamentary constituency, local counting area, Assembly constituency, voting area or, as the case may be, the relevant local authority and, in the case of an election to fill a casual vacancy, the electoral area for which the relevant election is held, and
    (c)   where the polls are to be taken together in part of the electoral area only, specify that part.

Postal ballot papers

24 (1) The returning officer must, in accordance with regulations made under the 1983 Act, issue to those entitled to vote by post a ballot paper and a postal voting statement in the appropriate form in the Appendix, or a form to like effect, together with such envelopes for their return as may be prescribed by such regulations.

(2) The returning officer must also issue to those entitled to vote by post such information as he thinks appropriate about how to obtain–
- (a) translations into languages other than English of any directions to or guidance for voters sent with the ballot paper;
- (b) a translation into Braille of such directions or guidance;
- (c) graphical representations of such directions or guidance;
- (d) the directions or guidance in any other form (including any audible form).

(3) The postal voting statement must include provision for the form to be signed and for stating the date of birth of the elector or proxy (as the case may be).

(4) In the case of a ballot paper issued to a person at an address in the United Kingdom, the returning officer must ensure that the return of the ballot paper and postal voting statement is free of charge to the voter.

Provision of polling stations

25 (1) The returning officer must provide a sufficient number of polling stations and, subject to the following provisions of this rule, must allot the electors to the polling stations in such manner as he thinks most convenient.

(2) One or more polling stations may be provided in the same room.

(3) The polling station allotted to electors from any parliamentary polling district wholly or partly within the electoral area must, in the absence of special circumstances, be in the parliamentary polling place for that district, unless that place is outside the electoral area.

(4) The returning officer must provide each polling station with such number of compartments as may be necessary in which the voters can mark their votes screened from observation.

Appointment of presiding officers and polling clerks

26 (1) The returning officer must appoint and pay a presiding officer to attend at each polling station and such clerks as may be necessary for the purposes of the election, but he must not appoint any person who has been employed by or on behalf of a candidate in or about the election.

(2) The returning officer may, if he thinks fit, preside at a polling station and the provisions of these Rules relating to a presiding officer shall apply to a returning officer so presiding with the necessary modifications as to things to be done by the returning officer to the presiding officer or by the presiding officer to the returning officer.

(3) A presiding officer may do, by the clerks appointed to assist him, any act (including the asking of questions) which he is required or authorised by these Rules to do at a polling station except order the arrest, exclusion or removal of any person from the polling station.

Issue of official poll cards

27 (1) The returning officer must as soon as practicable after the publication of the notice of the election send to electors and their proxies an official poll card.

(2) An elector's official poll card must be sent or delivered to his qualifying address, and a proxy's to his address as shown in the list of proxies.

(3) The official poll card must be in the appropriate form in the Appendix, or a form to the like effect, and must set out–
   (a) the name of the local authority to which the election relates;
   (b) that the election is a mayoral election;
   (c) the elector's name, qualifying address and number on the register;
   (d) the date and hours of the poll and the situation of the elector's polling station; and
   (e) such other information as the returning officer thinks appropriate,
   and different information may be provided in pursuance of sub-paragraph (e) to different electors or descriptions of elector.

(4) In the case of an elector with an anonymous entry, instead of containing the matter mentioned in paragraph (3)(c), the poll card must contain such matter as is specified in the appropriate form in the Appendix.

(5) Paragraph (5) of rule 8 shall apply for the interpretation of this rule.

(6) If the returning officer and the returning officer for each relevant election or referendum think fit, an official poll card issued under this rule may be combined with the official poll card issued at every relevant election or referendum.

Equipment of polling stations

28 (1) The returning officer must provide each presiding officer with such number of ballot boxes and ballot papers as in the returning officer's opinion may be necessary.

(2) The same ballot box may be used for the poll at the mayoral election and the poll at every relevant election or referendum, if the returning officer thinks fit.

(3) Every ballot box must be so constructed that the ballot papers can be put in it, but cannot be withdrawn from it, without the box being unlocked or, where the box has no lock, the seal being broken.

(4) The returning officer must provide each polling station with–
   (a) materials to enable voters to mark the ballot papers;
   (b) copies of the register of electors for the electoral area or such part of it as contains the names of the electors allotted to the station;
   (c) the parts of any special lists prepared for the election corresponding to the register of electors or the part of it provided under sub-paragraph (b);
   (d) a list consisting of that part of the list prepared under rule 19 which contains the numbers (but not the other unique identifying marks) corresponding to those on the ballot papers provided to the presiding officer of the polling station.

(5) The reference in paragraph (4)(b) to the copies of the register of electors includes a reference to copies of any notices issued by section 13B(3B) or (3D) of the 1983 Act in respect of alterations to the register.

(6) The returning officer must also provide each polling station with–
   (a) at least one large version of each ballot paper which must be printed on the same colour paper as the corresponding ballot paper and must be displayed inside the polling station for the assistance of voters who are partially sighted; and
   (b) a device of such description as is set out in paragraph (11) below for enabling voters who are blind or partially sighted to vote without any need for assistance from the presiding officer or any companion (within the meaning of rule 39(1)).

(7) Where notwithstanding paragraph (2) above separate ballot boxes are to be used, each

ballot box must be clearly marked with–

(a) the election or referendum to which it relates, as shown on the ballot papers for that election or referendum;

(b) the words "Place the *specify colour of ballot papers in question* ballot papers in here".

(8) A notice in the appropriate form in the Appendix giving directions for the guidance of voters in voting, must be printed in conspicuous characters and exhibited inside and outside every polling station.

(9) The returning officer may also provide copies of the notice mentioned in paragraph (8) in Braille or translated into languages other than English as he considers appropriate, provided that these notices are accurate reproductions in Braille or that other language of that notice.

(10) In every compartment of every polling station there must be exhibited the notice:

"PARLIAMENTARY ELECTION

(*Specify colour* ballot paper)

Vote for ONLY ONE CANDIDATE by putting a cross X in the box next to your choice.

*EUROPEAN PARLIAMENTARY ELECTION

(*Specify colour* ballot paper)

Vote ONLY ONCE by putting a cross X in the box next to your choice.

*Specify name of council COUNCIL ELECTION

(*Specify colour* ballot paper)

*Vote for NO MORE THAN … CANDIDATES by putting a cross X in the box next to EACH of your choices.

*Vote ONLY ONCE by putting a cross X in the box next to your choice.

*ELECTION OF THE MAYOR OF LONDON

(*Specify colour* ballot paper)

On the ballot paper for the election of the Mayor, vote ONCE for your first choice and ONCE for your second choice.

*ELECTION OF THE LONDON ASSEMBLY

On the constituency members ballot paper (*specify colour*) vote for ONE candidate only.

On the London members ballot paper (*specify colour*) vote for ONE party or individual candidate only.

*LOCAL MAYORAL ELECTION

(*Specify colour* ballot paper)

*Vote for ONLY ONE CANDIDATE by putting a cross X in the box next to your choice.

*Vote by putting a cross X in the box

In column 1 next to your FIRST CHOICE candidate

In column 2 next to your SECOND CHOICE candidate

Your first and second choices should be different.

Specify other ELECTION/REFERENDUM

(*Specify colour* ballot paper)

Specify voting instructions in accordance with the legislation governing the election or referendum

PUT NO OTHER MARK ON THE BALLOT PAPER OR YOUR VOTE MAY NOT COUNT.

*PLEASE DO NOT FOLD THE BALLOT PAPERS FOR *specify the elections and/or referendum(s) at which the votes are to be counted electronically*. Post them, face downwards, in the *appropriate ballot box.

*Complete or omit as necessary.

Alternatively, insert such information as the GLRO may decide."

(11) The device referred to in paragraph (6)(b) must–
    (a) allow a ballot paper to be inserted into and removed from, or attached to and detached from, the device easily and without damage to the paper;
    (b) hold the ballot paper firmly in place during use; and
    (c) provide suitable means for the voter to–
        (i) identify the spaces on the ballot paper on which he may mark his vote; and
        (ii) identify the registered party or individual candidate to which each such space refers; and
        (iii) mark his vote on the space he has chosen.

Appointment of polling and counting agents

29 (1) Subject to paragraphs (3), (4) and (5), before the commencement of the poll each candidate may appoint–
    (a) polling agents to attend at polling stations for the purpose of detecting personation; and
    (b) counting agents to attend at the counting of the votes.

(2) The same person may be appointed as a polling agent or counting agent by more than one candidate.

(3) Not more than four polling agents, or such greater number as the returning officer may by notice allow, shall be permitted to attend at any particular polling station.

(4) If the number of such agents appointed to attend at a particular polling station exceeds that number, the returning officer must determine by lot which agents are permitted to attend, and only the agents on whom the lot falls shall be deemed to have been duly appointed.

(5) The returning officer may limit the number of counting agents, but in doing so must ensure that–
    (a) the number is the same in the case of each candidate; and
    (b) the number allowed to a candidate must not (except in special circumstances) be less than the number obtained by dividing the number of clerks employed on the counting by the number of candidates.

(6) For the purposes of the calculations required by paragraph (5), a counting agent appointed for more than one candidate is a separate agent for each of the candidates for whom he has been appointed.

(7) Notice in writing of the appointment, stating the names and addresses of the persons appointed, must be given by the candidate to the returning officer and must be so given not later than the fifth day (disregarding any day referred to in rule 4(1)) before the day of the poll.

(8) Notices of the appointment of polling agents and counting agents which are required by paragraphs (7) and (9) to be given to the returning officer must be given to that returning officer who discharges the functions specified in regulation 5 of the Combination of Polls Regulations.

(9) If an agent dies, or becomes incapable of acting, the candidate may appoint another person in his place, and must forthwith give to the returning officer notice in writing of the name and address of that other person.

(10) Any appointment for a candidate authorised by this rule may be made and the notice of appointment given to the returning officer by the candidate's election agent, instead of by the candidate.

(11) In the following provisions of these Rules references to polling agents and counting agents shall be taken as references to agents–
   (a) whose appointments have been duly made and notified; and
   (b) where the number of agents is restricted, who are within the permitted numbers.

(12) Any notice required to be given to a counting agent by the returning officer may be delivered at, or sent by post to, the address stated in the notice of appointment.

(13) A candidate may himself do any act or thing which any polling or counting agent of his, if appointed, would have been authorised to do, or may assist his agent in doing any such act or thing.

(14) A candidate's election agent may do or assist in doing anything which the candidate's polling or counting agent is authorised to do; and anything required or authorised by these Rules to be done in the presence of the polling or counting agent may be done in the presence of a candidate's election agent instead of his polling agent or counting agent.

(15) Where by these Rules any act or thing is required or authorised to be done in the presence of the polling or counting agent, the non-attendance of any agent or agents at the time and place appointed for the purpose shall not, if the act or thing is otherwise duly done, invalidate the act or thing done.

Notification of requirement of secrecy

30 (1) The returning officer must make such arrangements as he thinks fit to ensure that–
   (a) every person attending at a polling station (otherwise than for the purpose of voting or assisting a voter with disabilities to vote or as a constable on duty there) has been given a copy in writing of the provisions of subsections (1), (3) and (6) of section 66 of the 1983 Act; and
   (b) every person attending at the counting of the votes (other than any constable on duty at the counting) has been given a copy in writing of the provisions of subsections (2) and (6) of that section.

(2) In this rule, a reference to a constable includes a person designated as a community support officer under section 38 of the Police Reform Act 2002 (police powers for employees).

Return of postal ballot papers

31 (1) Where–
   (a) a postal vote has been returned in respect of a person who is entered on the postal voters list, or
   (b) a proxy postal vote has been returned in respect of a proxy who is entered on the proxy postal voters list,
   the returning officer must mark the list in the manner prescribed by regulations made under the 1983 Act.

(2) Rule 47(7) does not apply for the purpose of determining whether, for the purposes of this rule, a postal vote or a proxy postal vote is returned.

Admission to polling station

32 (1) The presiding officer must exclude all persons from the polling station except–
   (a) voters;
   (b) persons under the age of 18 who accompany voters to the polling station;
   (c) the candidates and their election agents;
   (d) the polling agents appointed to attend at the polling station;
   (e) the clerks appointed to attend at the polling station;
   (f) persons who are entitled to attend by virtue of any of sections 6A to 6D of the Political Parties, Elections and Referendums Act 2000;
   (g) the constables on duty;
   (h) the companions of voters with disabilities; and
   (i) persons entitled to be admitted to the polling station at a relevant election or referendum with which the poll at the mayoral election is combined.

   (2) The presiding officer must regulate the total number of voters and persons under the age of 18 who accompany them to be admitted to the polling station at the same time.

   (3) Not more than one polling agent shall be admitted at the same time to a polling station on behalf of the same candidate.

   (4) A constable or person employed by a returning officer must not be admitted to vote in person elsewhere than at his own polling station allotted to him under these Rules, except on production and surrender of a certificate as to his employment which must be in the appropriate form in the Appendix, or a form to the like effect, and signed by an officer of police of or above the rank of inspector or by the returning officer, as the case may be.

   (5) Any certificate surrendered under this rule must forthwith be cancelled.

   (6) In this rule, a reference to a constable includes a person designated as a community support officer under section 38 of the Police Reform Act 2002 (police powers for employees).

Keeping of order in station

33 (1) It is the presiding officer's duty to keep order at his polling station.

   (2) If a person misconducts himself in a polling station, or fails to obey the presiding officer's lawful orders, he may immediately, by the presiding officer's order, be removed from the polling station–
   (a) by a constable in or near that station, or
   (b) by any other person authorised in writing by the returning officer to remove him,
   and the person so removed shall not, without the presiding officer's permission, again enter the polling station during the day.

   (3) Any person so removed may, if charged with the commission in the polling station of an offence, be dealt with as a person taken into custody by a constable for an offence without a warrant.

   (4) The powers conferred by this rule must not be exercised so as to prevent a voter who is otherwise entitled to vote at a polling station from having an opportunity of voting at that station.

Sealing of ballot boxes

34 Immediately before the commencement of the poll, the presiding officer must–

(a) show the ballot box, empty, to such persons, if any, as are present in the polling station, so that they may see that the box is empty;

(b) lock up the box (if it has a lock);

(c) place his seal–

    (i) on the lock; or

    (ii) where the ballot box has no lock, on the box,

in such a manner as to prevent its being opened without breaking the seal;

(d) place the box in his view for the receipt of ballot papers; and

(e) keep the box locked and sealed or, as the case may be, sealed.

Questions to be put to voters

35 (1) At the time of the application for a ballot paper (but not afterwards), the questions specified in the second column of the following Table–

(a) may be put by the presiding officer to a person applying for a ballot paper who is mentioned in the first column, and

(b) must be put if the letter "R" appears after the question and the candidate or his election or polling agent requires the question to be put:

Q No	Person applying for ballot paper	Question
1	A person applying as an elector	(a)–Are you the person registered in the register of local government electors for this election as follows? *read the whole entry from the register* R (b)–Have you already voted here or elsewhere at this election otherwise than as proxy for some other person? R
2	A person applying as proxy	(a)–Are you the person whose name appears as AB in the list of proxies for this election as entitled to vote as proxy on behalf of CD? R (b)–Have you already voted here or elsewhere at this election as proxy on behalf of CD? R (c)–Are you the spouse, civil partner, parent, grandparent, brother, sister, child or grandchild of CD? R
3	A person applying as proxy for an elector with an anonymous entry (instead of the questions at entry 2)	(a)–Are you the person entitled to vote as proxy on behalf of the elector whose number on the register of electors is *(read out the number)*? R (b)–Have you already voted here or elsewhere as proxy on behalf of the elector whose number on the register of electors is *(read out the number)*? R (c)–Are you the spouse, civil partner, parent, grandparent, brother, sister, child or grandchild of the person whose number on the register of electors is *(read out the number)*? R
4	A person applying as proxy if the question at entry 2(c) or 3(c) is not	Have you already voted at this election on behalf of two persons of whom you are not the spouse, civil partner, parent,

	answered in the affirmative	grandparent, brother, sister, child or grandchild?. R
5	A person applying as an elector in relation to whom there is an entry in the postal voters list	(a)–Did you apply to vote by post? (b)–Why have you not voted by post?
6	A person applying as proxy who is named in the proxy postal voters list	(a)–Did you apply to vote by post as proxy? (b)–Why have you not voted by post as proxy?

(2) In the case of an elector in respect of whom a notice has been issued under section 13B(3B) or (3D) of the 1983 Act, the references in the questions at entries 1(a) and 3(a), (b) and (c) to reading from the register shall be taken as references to reading from the notice issued under section 13B(3B) or (3D) of the 1983 Act.

(3) A ballot paper must not be delivered to any person required to answer any of the above questions unless he has answered each question satisfactorily.

(4) Except as authorised by this rule, no inquiry shall be permitted as to the right of any person to vote.

Challenge of voter

36 A person must not be prevented from voting by reason only that–
    (a) a candidate or his election or polling agent declares that he has reasonable cause to believe that the person has committed an offence of personation, or
    (b) the person is arrested on the grounds that he is suspected of committing or of being about to commit such an offence.

Voting procedure

37 (1) A ballot paper must be delivered to a voter who applies for one, and immediately before delivery–
    (a) the number and (unless paragraph (2) applies) name of the elector as stated in the copy of the register of electors must be called out;
    (b) the number of the elector must be marked on the list mentioned in rule 28(4)(d) beside the number of the ballot paper to be issued to him;
    (c) a mark must be placed in the copy of the register of electors against the number of the elector to note that a ballot paper has been received but without showing the particular ballot paper which has been received;
    (d) in the case of a person applying for a ballot paper as proxy, a mark must also be placed against his name in the list of proxies.

(2) In the case of an elector who has an anonymous entry, he must show the presiding officer his official poll card and only his number shall be called out in pursuance of paragraph (1)(a).

(3) In the case of an elector who is added to the register in pursuance of a notice issued under section 13B(3B) or (3D) of the 1983 Act, paragraph (1) is modified as follows–
    (a) in sub-paragraph (a), for "copy of the register of electors" substitute "copy of the notice issued under section 13B(3B) or (3D) of the 1983 Act";
    (b) in sub-paragraph (c), for "in the register of electors" substitute "on the copy of the notice issued under section 13B(3B) or (3D) of the 1983 Act".

(4) The voter, on receiving the ballot paper, must forthwith proceed into one of the compartments in the polling station and there secretly mark his paper and fold it up so as to conceal his vote, and must then show to the presiding officer the back of the

paper, so as to disclose the number and other unique identifying mark, and put the ballot paper so folded up into the ballot box in the presiding officer's presence.

(5) The voter must vote without undue delay, and must leave the polling station as soon as he has put his ballot paper into the ballot box.

(6) The same copy of the register of electors which is used under paragraph (1) for the mayoral election or, where paragraph (3) applies, the same copy of the notice issued under section 13B(3B) or (3B) in the 1983 Act, may be used for each relevant election or referendum, and–

    (a) one mark may be placed in that copy of the register or on that notice under paragraph (1)(c) or in the list of proxies under paragraph (1)(d) to denote that a ballot paper has been issued in respect of each election or referendum; but

(7) A voter who at the close of the poll is in the polling station, or in a queue outside the polling station, for the purposes of voting shall (despite the close of the poll) be entitled to apply for a ballot paper under paragraph (1); and these rules apply in relation to such a voter accordingly.

Votes marked by presiding officer

38 (1) The presiding officer, on the application of a voter–

    (a) who is incapacitated by blindness or other disability from voting in the manner directed by these Rules, or

    (b) who declares orally that he is unable to read,

must, in the presence of the polling agents, cause the voter's vote to be marked on a ballot paper in the manner directed by the voter, and the ballot paper to be placed in the ballot box.

(2) The name and number on the register of electors of every voter whose vote is marked in pursuance of this rule, and the reason why it is so marked, must be entered on a list (in these Rules called "the list of votes marked by the presiding officer").

(3) In the case of a person voting as proxy for an elector, the number to be entered together with the voter's name shall be the elector's number.

(4) In the case of a person in respect of whom a notice has been issued under section 13B(3B) or (3D) of the 1983 Act, paragraph (2) applies as if for "on the register of electors of every voter" there were substituted "relating to every voter in respect of whom a notice has been issued under section 13B(3B) or (3D) of the 1983 Act".

(5) The same list may be used for the mayoral election and each relevant election or referendum and, where it is so used, an entry in that list shall be taken to mean that the ballot papers were so marked in respect of each election or referendum, unless the list identifies the election or referendum at which the ballot paper was so marked.

Voting by persons with disabilities

39 (1) If a voter makes an application to the presiding officer to be allowed, on the ground of–

    (a) blindness or other disability, or

    (b) inability to read,

to vote with the assistance of another person by whom he is accompanied (in these Rules referred to as "the companion"), the presiding officer must require the voter to declare, orally or in writing, whether he is so incapacitated by his blindness or other disability, or by his inability to read, as to be unable to vote without assistance.

(2) If the presiding officer–

    (a) is satisfied that the voter is so incapacitated, and

    (b) is also satisfied by a written declaration made by the companion (in these Rules referred to as "the declaration made by the companion of a voter with disabilities") that the companion–

    (i)   is a qualified person within the meaning of this rule; and

    (ii)   has not previously assisted more than one voter with disabilities to vote at the election,

the presiding officer must grant the application, and then anything which is by these Rules required to be done to or by that voter in connection with the giving of his vote may be done to, or with the assistance of, the companion.

(3)   For the purposes of these Rules–

    (a)   a person is a voter with disabilities if he has made such a declaration as is mentioned in paragraph (1); and

    (b)   a person shall be qualified to assist a voter with disabilities to vote if that person is either–

        (i)   a person who is entitled to vote as an elector at the election; or

        (ii)   the father, mother, brother, sister, spouse, civil partner, son or daughter of the voter and has attained the age of 18 years.

(4)   Subject to paragraph (5), the name and number in the register of electors of every voter whose vote is given in accordance with this rule and the name and address of the companion must be entered on a list (in these Rules referred to as "the list of voters with disabilities assisted by companions").

(5)   In the case of a person voting as proxy for an elector, the number to be entered together with the voter's name shall be the elector's number.

(6)   In the case of a person in respect of whom a notice has been issued under section 13B(3B) or (3D) of the 1983 Act, paragraph (4) applies as if for "in the register of electors of every voter" there were substituted "relating to every voter in respect of whom a notice has been issued under section 13B(3B) or (3D) of the 1983 Act".

(7)   The same list may be used for the mayoral election and each relevant election or referendum and, where it is so used, an entry in that list shall be taken to mean that the votes were so given in respect of each election or referendum, unless the list identifies the election or referendum at which the vote was so given.

(8)   The declaration made by the companion of a voter with disabilities–

    (a)   must be in the appropriate form in the Appendix or a form to the like effect,

    (b)   must be made before the presiding officer at the time when the voter applies to vote with the assistance of the companion, and

    (c)   must forthwith be given to the presiding officer who must attest and retain it.

(9)   No fee or other payment shall be charged in respect of the declaration.

Tendered ballot papers–circumstances where available

40 (1)   If a person, representing himself to be–

    (a)   a particular elector named on the register and not named in the absent voters list, or

    (b)   a particular person named in the list of proxies as proxy for an elector and not entitled to vote by post as proxy,

applies for a ballot paper after another person has voted in person either as the elector or his proxy, the applicant shall, on satisfactorily answering the questions permitted by law to be asked at the poll, be entitled, subject to the provisions of rule 41, to mark a ballot paper (in these Rules referred to as "a tendered ballot paper") in the same manner as any other voter.

(2)   Paragraph (4) applies if–

    (a)   a person applies for a ballot paper representing himself to be a particular elector named on the register,

    (b) he is also named in the postal voters list, and

    (c) he claims that he did not make an application to vote by post at the election.

(3) Paragraph (4) also applies if–

    (a) a person applies for a ballot paper representing himself to be a particular person named as a proxy in the list of proxies,

    (b) he is also named in the proxy postal voters list, and

    (c) he claims that he did not make an application to vote by post as proxy.

(4) The person shall, on satisfactorily answering the questions permitted by law to be asked at the poll, be entitled, subject to the provisions of rule 41, to mark a ballot paper (in these Rules referred to as a "tendered ballot paper") in the same manner as any other voter.

(5) Paragraph (6) applies if, before the close of the poll but after the last time at which a person may apply for a replacement postal ballot paper, a person represents himself to be–

    (a) a particular elector named on the register who is also named in the postal voters list, or

    (b) a particular person named as a proxy in the list of proxies and who is also named in the proxy postal voters list,

and claims that he has lost or has not received his postal ballot paper.

(6) The person shall, on satisfactorily answering the questions permitted by law to be asked at the poll, be entitled, subject to the provisions of rule 41, to mark a ballot paper (in these Rules referred to as a "tendered ballot paper") in the same manner as any other voter.

Tendered ballot papers–general provisions

41 (1) A tendered ballot paper must–

    (a) be of a colour differing from that of the other ballot papers;

    (b) instead of being put into the ballot box, be given to the presiding officer and endorsed by him with the name of the voter and his number in the register of electors, and set aside in a separate packet.

(2) The name of the voter and his number in the register of electors must be entered on a list (in these Rules referred to as the "tendered votes list").

(3) The same list may be used for the mayoral election and each relevant election or referendum and, where it so used, an entry in that list shall be taken to mean that tendered ballot papers were marked in respect of each election or referendum, unless the list identifies the election or referendum at which a tendered ballot paper was marked.

(4) In the case of a person voting as proxy for an elector, the number to be endorsed or entered together with the voter's name shall be the number of that elector.

(5) In the case of an elector who has an anonymous entry, this rule and rule 40 apply subject to the following modifications–

    (a) in paragraphs (1)(b) and (2) above, the references to the name of the voter shall be ignored;

    (b) otherwise, a reference to a person named on a register or list shall be construed as a reference to a person whose number appears in the register or list (as the case may be).

(6) In the case of a person in respect of whom a notice has been issued under section 13B(3B) or (3D) of the 1983 Act, this rule and rule 40 shall apply as if–

(a) in rule 40(1)(a), (2)(a) and (5)(a), for "named on the register" there were substituted "in respect of whom a notice under section 13B(3B) or (3D) of the 1983 Act has been issued";

(b) in paragraph (1)(b) of this rule for "his number in the register of electors" there were substituted "the number relating to him on a notice issued under section 13B(3B) or (3D) of the 1983 Act";

(c) in paragraph (2) of this rule, for "his number in the register of electors" there were substituted "the number relating to him on a notice issued under section 13B(3B) or (3D) of the 1983 Act".

Spoilt ballot papers

42 A voter who has inadvertently dealt with his ballot paper in such manner that it cannot be conveniently used as a ballot paper may, on delivering it to the presiding officer and proving to his satisfaction the fact of the inadvertence, obtain another ballot paper in the place of the ballot paper so delivered (in these Rules referred to as "a spoilt ballot paper"), and the spoilt ballot paper must be immediately cancelled.

Correction of errors on day of poll

43 (1) The presiding officer must keep a list of persons to whom ballot papers are delivered in consequence of an alteration to the register made by virtue of section 13B(3B) or (3D) of the 1983 Act which takes effect on the day of the poll.

(2) The same list may be used for each relevant election or referendum and, where it so used, an entry in that list shall be taken to mean that ballot papers were issued in respect of each election or referendum, unless the list identifies the election or referendum for which a ballot paper was issued.

Adjournment of poll in case of riot

44 (1) Where the proceedings at any polling station are interrupted or obstructed by riot or open violence, the presiding officer must adjourn the proceedings till the following day and must forthwith give notice to the returning officer who discharges the functions specified in regulation 5 of the Combinations of Polls Regulations.

(2) Where the poll is adjourned at any polling station–

(a) the hours of polling on the day to which it is adjourned must be the same as for the original day; and

(b) references in these Rules to the close of the poll shall be construed accordingly.

Procedure on close of poll

45 (1) As soon as practicable after the close of the poll, the presiding officer must, in the presence of the polling agents appointed for the purposes of the mayoral election and those appointed for the purposes of each relevant election or referendum, make up into separate packets, sealed with his own seal and the seals of such polling agents as desire to affix their seals–

(a) each ballot box in use at the station, sealed so as to prevent the introduction of additional ballot papers and unopened, but with the key, if any, attached,

(b) the unused and spoilt ballot papers placed together,

(c) the tendered ballot papers,

(d) the marked copies of the register of electors (including any marked copy notices issued under section 13B(3B) or (3D) of the 1983 Act) and of the list of proxies,

(e) the lists prepared under rule 19 including the parts which were completed in accordance with rule 37(1)(b) (together referred to in these Rules as "the completed corresponding number lists"),

(f) the certificates as to employment on duty on the day of the poll,

(g) the tendered votes list, the list of voters with disabilities assisted by companions, the list of votes marked by the presiding officer, a statement of the number of voters whose votes are so marked by the presiding officer under the heads "disability" and "unable to read", the list maintained under rule 43 (correction of errors on day of poll), and the declarations made by the companions of voters with disabilities,

and must deliver the packets or cause them to be delivered to the returning officer to be taken charge of by him; but if the packets are not delivered by the presiding officer personally to the returning officer, the arrangements for their delivery shall require the returning officer's approval.

(2) The contents of the packets referred to in sub-paragraphs (b), (c) and (f) of paragraph (1) above must not be combined with the contents of the packets made under the corresponding rule that applies at any relevant election or referendum; nor shall the statement prepared under paragraph (5) below be so combined.

(3) References to the returning officer in paragraph (1) above are references to the returning officer who discharges the functions specified in regulation 5 of the Combination of Polls Regulations.

(4) The marked copies of the register of electors and of the list of proxies must be in one packet but must not be in the same packet as the completed corresponding number lists or the certificates as to employment on duty on the day of the poll.

(5) The packets must be accompanied by a statement (in these Rules referred to as "the ballot paper account") made by the presiding officer showing the number of ballot papers entrusted to him, and accounting for them under the heads–

(a) ballot papers issued and not otherwise accounted for,

(b) unused ballot papers,

(c) spoilt ballot papers and

(d) tendered ballot papers.

Attendance at the count

46 (1) Where the returning officer at the mayoral election discharges the functions specified in regulation 5 of the Combination of Polls Regulations, he must–

(a) make arrangements for–

(i) discharging the functions referred to in rule 47(1) in the presence of the counting agents appointed for the purposes of the mayoral election and those appointed for the purpose of each relevant election or referendum as soon as practicable after the close of the poll, and

(ii) thereafter counting the votes at the mayoral election in the presence of the agents appointed for the purpose of that election, and

(b) give to the counting agents appointed for the purposes of the mayoral election and those appointed for the purpose of each relevant election or referendum notice in writing of the time and place at which he will begin to discharge the functions under rule 47(1).

(2) Where the returning officer at the mayoral election does not discharge the functions specified in regulation 5 of the Combination of Polls Regulations, he shall–

(a) make arrangements for counting the votes in the presence of the counting agents as soon as practicable after the delivery of the ballot papers to him by the person who does discharge those functions; and

(b) give to the counting agents notice in writing of the time, if by then he has received the ballot papers, and of the place at which he will begin to count the votes; and

(3)   No person other than–
  (a)   the returning officer and his clerks,
  (b)   the candidates and one other person chosen by each of them,
  (c)   the election agents,
  (d)   the counting agents, and
  (e)   persons who are entitled to attend by virtue of any of sections 6A to 6D of the Political Parties, Elections and Referendums Act 2000,
may be present at the counting of the votes under rule 47(2) to (13), unless permitted by the returning officer to attend.

(4)   No person other than a person entitled to be present at the counting of the votes at the mayoral election under rule 47(2) to (13) or at a relevant election or referendum may be present at the proceedings under rule 47(1) unless permitted by the returning officer to attend.

(5)   A person not entitled to attend at the proceedings under rule 47(1) or the counting of the votes under rule 47(2) to (13) shall not be permitted to do so by the returning officer unless he–
  (a)   is satisfied that the efficient separation of the ballot papers or, as the case may be, the efficient counting of the votes will not be impeded; and
  (b)   has either consulted the election agents or thought it impracticable to do so.

(6)   The returning officer must give the counting agents all such reasonable facilities for overseeing the proceedings, and all such information with respect to them, as he can give them consistently with the orderly conduct of the proceedings and the discharge of his duties in connection with them.

(7)   In particular, where the votes are counted by sorting the ballot papers according to the candidate for whom the vote is given and then counting the number of ballot papers for each candidate, the counting agents shall be entitled to satisfy themselves that the ballot papers are correctly sorted.

The first count

47 (1)   Where the returning officer at the mayoral election discharges the functions specified in regulation 5 of the Combination of Polls Regulations, he must–
  (a)   in the presence of the counting agents appointed for the purposes of the mayoral election and each relevant election or referendum open each ballot box and count and record separately the number of ballot papers used in each election;
  (b)   in the presence of the election agents appointed for the purposes of the mayoral election and each relevant election or referendum verify each ballot paper account;
  (c)   count such of the postal ballot papers as have been duly returned and record separately the number counted at the mayoral election and each relevant election or referendum;
  (d)   separate the ballot papers relating to the mayoral election from the ballot papers relating to each relevant election or referendum;
  (e)   make up into packets the ballot papers for each relevant election or referendum and seal them up into separate containers endorsing on each a description of the area to which the ballot papers relate;
  (f)   deliver or cause to be delivered to the returning officer for the relevant election or referendum to which the ballot papers relate–
    (i)   those containers, together with a list of them and of the contents of each; and
    (ii)   the ballot paper accounts together with a copy of the statement as to the

result of their verification in respect of that election; and

    (g) at the same time deliver or cause to be delivered to that officer packets that so relate containing–

        (i)   the unused and spoilt ballot papers,

        (ii) the tendered ballot papers.

        (iii) the certificates as to employment on duty on the day of the poll.

(2)   After completion of the proceedings under paragraph (1), the returning officer shall mix together all of the ballot papers used at the mayoral election and count the votes given on them.

(3)   Where separate ballot boxes are used, no vote for any candidate shall be rendered invalid by the ballot paper being placed in the ballot box intended for use at any relevant election or referendum.

(4)   Where the returning officer at the mayoral election does not discharge the functions specified in regulation 5 of the Combination of Polls Regulations, he must–

    (a) on receipt of containers containing the ballot papers from the returning officer who does discharge those functions, and after the time specified in the notice given under rule 46(2), in the presence of the counting agents, open each container;

    (b) where the proceedings on the issue and receipt of postal ballot papers are not taken together with those proceedings at a relevant election or referendum under regulation 65 of the Elections Regulations, or under that regulation as applied by these Regulations or regulations made under sections 9MG and 105 or sections 45 and 105 of the Local Government Act 2000(, count such of the postal ballot papers as have been duly returned and record the number counted; and

    (c) mix together the postal ballot papers and the ballot papers from all of the containers and count the votes given on them.

(5)   Paragraph (12) does not apply to proceedings under paragraph (4).

(6)   The returning officer must then–

    (a) where the election is contested by more than two candidates, count the first preference votes given on them;

    (b) where the election is contested by only two candidates, count the votes given on them

(7)   A postal ballot paper must not be taken to be duly returned unless–

    (a) it is returned in the manner set out in paragraph (8) and reaches the returning officer or any polling station in the appropriate electoral area before the close of the poll;

    (b) the postal voting statement, duly signed, is also returned in the manner set out in paragraph (8) and reaches him or such a polling station before that time;

    (c) the postal voting statement also states the date of birth of the elector or proxy (as the case may be), and

    (d) in a case where steps for verifying the date of birth and signature of an elector or proxy have been prescribed by regulations made under the 1983 Act, the returning officer (having taken such steps) verifies the date of birth and signature of the elector or proxy.

(8)   The manner in which any postal ballot paper or postal voting statement may be returned–

    (a) to the returning officer, is by hand or by post;

    (b) to a polling station, is by hand.

(8A) A postal ballot paper or postal voting statement that reaches the returning officer or a polling station on or after the close of the poll is treated for the purposes of this rule as reaching that officer or polling station before the close of the poll if it is delivered by a person who, at the close of the poll, is in the polling station, or in a queue outside the polling station, for the purpose of returning it.

(9)   The appropriate electoral area in respect of any voter shall be–
   (a)   the area which is common to the parliamentary constituency, electoral area, local counting area, local authority area or voting area (as the case may be) in which the polls at the mayoral election and any relevant election or referendum are being taken together; and
   (b)   in respect of which polls the voter has been issued with a postal ballot paper.

(10)   The returning officer must not count any tendered ballot papers.

(11)   While counting and recording the number of ballot papers and counting the votes, the returning officer must keep the ballot papers with their faces upwards and take all proper precautions for preventing any person from seeing the numbers or other unique identifying marks printed on the back of the papers.

(12)   The returning officer must verify each ballot paper account by comparing it with the number of ballot papers recorded by him, and the unused and spoilt ballot papers in his possession and the tendered votes list (opening and re-sealing the packets containing the unused and spoilt ballot papers and the tendered votes list) and must draw up a statement as to the result of the verification, which any election agent may copy.

(13)   The returning officer must so far as practicable proceed continuously with counting the votes, allowing only time for refreshment, except that he may exclude the hours between 7 in the evening and 9 on the following morning.

(14)   During the time so excluded the returning officer must–
   (a)   place the ballot papers and other documents relating to the election under his own seal and the seals of such of the counting agents as desire to affix their seals; and
   (b)   otherwise take proper precautions for the security of the papers and documents.

Rejected ballot papers

48 (1)   Any ballot paper–
   (a)   which does not bear the official mark, or
   (b)   on which more than one first preference vote is given, or
   (c)   on which anything is written or marked by which the voter can be identified except the printed number and other unique identifying mark on the back, or
   (d)   which is unmarked or void for uncertainty as to the first preference vote,
   shall, subject to paragraphs (2) and (3), be void and not counted.

(2)   A ballot paper on which the vote is marked–
   (a)   elsewhere than in the proper place, or
   (b)   otherwise than by means of a cross, or
   (c)   by more than one mark,
   shall not for such reason be deemed to be void if–
      (i)   at an election at which more than two candidates remain validly nominated, an intention that votes shall be given, by way of a first preference vote, for not more than one of the candidates clearly appears;
      (ii)   at any other election, an intention that a vote shall be for one only of the candidates clearly appears,
   and (in each case) the way the paper is marked does not itself identify the voter and it is not shown that he can be identified by it.

(3)   A ballot paper which is not otherwise void and on which not more than one first preference vote is marked (whether or not a second preference vote is marked) shall be valid as respects that vote, and counted accordingly.

(4)   The returning officer must endorse the word "rejected" on any ballot paper which under this rule is not to be counted, and shall add to the endorsement the words "rejection objected to" if any objection is made to his decision by a counting agent.

(5)   The returning officer must draw up a statement showing the number of ballot papers rejected under the several heads of–
    (a)   want of official mark;
    (b)   voting for more than one candidate as to the first preference vote;
    (c)   writing or mark by which the voter could be identified; and
    (d)   unmarked or void for uncertainty as to the first preference vote.

(6)   In the case of an election where only two candidates remain validly nominated, this rule is to apply as if–
    (a)   in paragraph (1)(b), for "first preference vote" there were substituted "vote";
    (b)   in paragraphs (1)(d), (5)(b) and (d), the words "as to the first preference vote" were omitted;
    (c)   paragraph (3) were omitted.

Decisions on ballot papers

49   The decision of the returning officer on any question arising in respect of a ballot paper shall be final, but shall be subject to review on an election petition.

Re-count

50 (1)   A candidate or his election agent may, if present when the counting or any re-count of the votes, or as the case may be, the first preference votes, is completed, require the returning officer to have the votes re-counted or again re-counted but the returning officer may refuse to do so if in his opinion the request is unreasonable.

(2)   No step shall be taken on the completion of the counting or any re-count of votes, or as the case may be, the first preference votes, until the candidates and election agents present at its completion have been given a reasonable opportunity to exercise the right conferred by this rule.

Procedure at conclusion of first count

51 (1)   As soon as practicable after the conclusion of the first count (including any re-count), the returning officer must draw up a statement showing–
    (a)   the total number of ballot papers used;
    (b)   the total number of rejected ballot papers;
    (c)   at an election contested by more than two candidates–
        (i)   the number of first preference votes given for each candidate; and
        (ii)   the total number of first preference votes given; and
    (d)   at an election contested by only two candidates, the number of votes given for each candidate.

(2)   As soon as practicable after completion of the statement, the returning officer shall–
    (a)   inform such of the candidates and their election agents as are then present of the contents of the statements prepared in accordance with rule 48(5) and paragraph (1) of this rule; and
    (b)   give public notice of the contents of those statements.

(3)   Where an election is contested by more than two candidates, the returning officer

shall–
- (a) if paragraph 2 of Schedule 2 to the 2000 Act applies (candidate with overall majority of first preference votes), make the declaration required by rule 54(1); or
- (b) if paragraph 3 of that Schedule applies, count the second preference votes at the time and place notified in writing to the counting agents.

(4) Where–
- (a) an election is contested by only two candidates; and
- (b) the total number of votes for each of them is unequal,

the person to be returned as the elected mayor is the candidate to whom the majority of the votes is given.

(5) Where–
- (a) an election is contested by only two candidates; and
- (b) the total number of votes given for each of them is equal,

the returning officer shall decide by lot which of them is to be returned as the elected mayor.

(6) In a case to which paragraph (4) or (5) applies, the declaration of the person to be returned as the elected mayor shall be made in accordance with rule 54.

Part 5
Further Provision: More than Two Candidates

The count of second preference votes

52 (1) The returning officer must count the number of second preference votes for each of the candidates remaining in the contest given by voters who did not give their first preference vote to any of those candidates.

(2) A ballot paper which is not otherwise void and on which not more than one second preference vote is marked shall be valid as respects that vote and shall be counted accordingly if, but only if, a valid first preference vote has also been marked.

(3) Rules 46(3) to (7), 47(10), (11), (13) and (14), 48 (except paragraph (3)) and 50 (except the words "the votes, or as the case may be," in both paragraphs where they appear) shall apply in relation to the count of second preference votes as they apply in relation to the count of first preference votes as if references to first preference votes were references to second preference votes.

(4) The returning officer shall not be required to re-examine any decision taken under rule 49.

The calculation of total votes and resolution of equality

53 (1) The returning officer must comply with paragraph 3(6) of Schedule 2 to the 2000 Act.

(2) The returning officer must then draw up a statement showing–
- (a) the total number of first preference votes given for each candidate,
- (b) the total number of second preference votes given for each of the candidates remaining in the contest after the count of the first preference votes,
- (c) the total number of votes given for each of those candidates, and
- (d) the number of ballot papers that were–
  - (i) valid as respects a first preference vote given for a candidate who did not remain in the contest after the count of the first preference votes; and
  - (ii) rejected for the purposes of the count of second preference votes on the ground that they were unmarked or void for uncertainty as to the second

preference vote.

(3) As soon as practicable after completion of the statement, the returning officer shall provide such of the election agents for those candidates who remain in the contest as are then present with a copy of the statement, and must give them a reasonable opportunity to satisfy themselves as to the accuracy of the calculation.

(4) If, after the second preference votes have been counted, the total number of votes given for two or more candidates remaining in the contest is equal, the person to be returned as the elected mayor is the person whom the returning officer decides, in accordance with paragraph 3(8) of Schedule 2 to the 2000 Act, is to be returned as the elected mayor.

Part 6
Final Proceedings in Contested and Uncontested Elections

Declaration of result

54 (1) The returning officer must declare the elected mayor to be the candidate who, in accordance with section 9HC(2) or (3), section 42(2) or (3) of the 2000 Act or, as the case may be, Schedule 2 to that Act, is to be returned as the elected mayor at that election.

(2) The returning officer must give public notice of–
    (a) the name of the successful candidate,
    (b) the total number of first preference votes given for each candidate,
    (c) the number of rejected ballot papers at the election under each head shown in the statement of rejected ballot papers (rule 48(5)), and
    (d) if second preference votes were counted–
        (i) the total number of second preference votes given for each of the candidates remaining in the contest after the count of the first preference votes, and
        (ii) the number of ballot papers rejected for the purposes of the count of second preference votes on the ground that they were unmarked or void for uncertainty as to the second preference vote.

(3) In an uncontested election, the returning officer must as soon as practicable after the latest time for the delivery of notices of withdrawals of candidature–
    (a) declare to be elected the person remaining validly nominated;
    (b) give public notice of the name of the person declared to be elected.

(4) The returning officer must inform the proper officer of the local authority concerned of the result of the election.

Return or forfeiture of candidate's deposit

55 (1) Unless forfeited in accordance with paragraph (5), the deposit made under rule 10 of these Rules shall be returned to the person making it or his personal representative.

(2) Subject to paragraph (4), the deposit shall be returned not later than the next day after that on which the result of the election is declared.

(3) For the purposes of paragraph (2)–
    (a) a day shall be disregarded if it would be disregarded under rule 4 in computing any period of time for the purpose of the timetable for an election of the kind in question; and
    (b) the deposit shall be treated as being returned on a day if a cheque for the amount of the deposit is posted on that day.

(4) If the candidate is not shown as standing nominated in the statement of persons nominated, or if proof of his death has been given to the returning officer before the first calculation under rule 51, the deposit shall be returned as soon as practicable after the publication of the statement or after his death, as the case may be.

(5) Where a poll is taken, if, after the conclusion of the first count, the candidate is found not to have polled more than one-twentieth of the total number of first preference votes polled by all the candidates, the deposit shall be forfeited to the local authority of the electoral areas concerned.

Part 7
Disposal of Documents

Sealing up of ballot papers

56 (1) On the completion of the counting at a contested election the returning officer must seal up in separate packets the counted and rejected ballot papers.

(2) The returning officer must not open the sealed packets of–
   (a) tendered ballot papers, or
   (b) certificates as to employment on duty on the day of the poll.

(3) Where the returning officer discharges the functions referred to in regulation 5 of the Combinations of Polls Regulations, he must also not open the sealed packets of–
   (a) the completed corresponding number lists, or
   (b) the marked copies of the register of electors (including any marked copy notices issued under section 13B(3B) or (3D) of the 1983 Act) and lists of proxies.

Delivery and retention of documents

57 (1) The returning officer must then forward to the relevant registration officer the following documents–
   (a) the packets of ballot papers in his possession,
   (b) the ballot paper accounts and the statements of rejected ballot papers and of the result of the verification of the ballot paper accounts,
   (c) the tendered votes lists, the lists of voters with disabilities assisted by companions, the lists of votes marked by the presiding officer and the related statements, the lists maintained under rule 43 and the declarations made by the companions of voters with disabilities,
   (d) the packets of the completed corresponding number lists,
   (e) the packets of certificates as to employment on duty on the day of the poll,
   (f) the packets containing marked copies of registers (including any marked copy notices issued under section 13B(3B) or (3D) of the 1983 Act) and of the postal voters list, of the lists of proxies and of the proxy postal voters list, and
   endorsing on each packet a description of its contents, the date of the election to which they relate and the name of the electoral area for which the election was held.

(2) At an election where the returning officer does not discharge the functions referred to in regulation 5 of the Combination of Polls Regulations, paragraph (1) shall have effect as if sub-paragraphs (c), (d) and (f) were omitted.

(3) In this rule and in rules 58, 59 and 60 references to the relevant registration officer are to–
   (a) the registration officer for the local authority in whose area the mayoral election is held;
   (b) if the electoral area of the relevant election or referendum comprises any part of the area of more than one local authority, the registration officer of the local

authority in whose area the greater or greatest (as the case may be) number of electors is registered;

(c) if the returning officer discharges the functions referred to in regulation 5 of the Combination of Polls Regulations, the registration officer of the local authority in whose area the mayoral election is held,

and for these purposes "local authority" does not include the Greater London Authority.

Orders for production of documents

58 (1) An order–

(a) for the inspection or production of any rejected ballot papers, in the custody of the relevant registration officer; or

(b) for the opening of a sealed packet of the completed corresponding number lists or certificates as to employment on duty on the day of the poll or for the inspection of any counted ballot papers in his custody,

may be made by a county court, if the court is satisfied by evidence on oath that the order is required for the purpose of instituting or maintaining a prosecution for an offence in relation to ballot papers, or for the purpose of an election petition.

(2) An order for the opening of a sealed packet of completed corresponding number lists or of certificates as to employment on duty on the day of the poll or for the inspection of any counted ballot papers in the custody of the relevant registration officer may be made by an election court.

(3) An order under this rule may be made subject to such conditions as to–

(a) persons,

(b) time,

(c) place and mode of inspection,

(d) production or opening,

as the court making the order may think expedient.

(4) In making and carrying into effect an order for the opening of a packet of completed corresponding number lists or of certificates as to employment on duty on the day of the poll or for the inspection of counted ballot papers, care must be taken that the way in which the vote of any particular elector has been given shall not be disclosed until it has been proved–

(i) that his vote was given; and

(ii) that the vote has been declared by a competent court to be invalid.

(5) An appeal lies to the High Court from any order of a county court under this rule.

(6) Any power given under this rule to a county court may be exercised by any judge of the court otherwise than in open court.

(7) Where an order is made for the production by the relevant registration officer of any document in his possession relating to any specified election–

(a) the production by him or his agent of the document ordered in such manner as may be directed by that order shall be conclusive evidence that the document relates to the specified election; and

(b) any endorsement on any packet of ballot papers so produced shall be prima facie evidence that the ballot papers are what they are stated to be by the endorsement.

(8) The production from proper custody of–

(a) a ballot paper purporting to have been used at any election, and

(b) a completed corresponding number list with a number marked in writing beside the number of the ballot paper,

shall be prima facie evidence that the elector whose vote was given by that ballot paper was the person whose entry in the register of electors or on a notice issued under section 13B(3B) or (3D) of the 1983 Act at the time of the election contained the same number as the number written as mentioned in sub-paragraph (b) of this paragraph.

(9) Save as by this rule provided, no person shall be allowed to inspect any rejected or counted ballot papers in the possession of the relevant registration officer or open any sealed packets of completed corresponding number lists or of certificates as to employment on duty on the day of the poll.

Retention of documents

59 The relevant registration officer must retain for one year all documents relating to an election forwarded to him in pursuance of these Rules by a returning officer, and then, unless otherwise directed by an order of a county court, the Crown Court, a magistrates' court or an election court, must cause them to be destroyed.

Part 8
Death of Candidate

Countermand or abandonment of poll on death of a candidate

60 (1) If at a contested election proof is given to the returning officer's satisfaction before the result of the election is declared that one of the persons named or to be named as candidate in the ballot papers has died, then the returning officer must countermand notice of the poll or, if polling has begun, direct that the poll be abandoned, and the provisions of subsections (1) and (5) of section 39 (local elections void etc in England and Wales) of the 1983 Act apply in respect of any vacancy which remains unfilled.

(2) Neither the countermand of the poll at the mayoral election nor the direction that the poll be abandoned shall affect the poll at each relevant election or referendum.

(3) Where the poll at the mayoral election is abandoned by reason of a candidate's death no further ballot papers shall be issued.

(4) Subject to paragraph (6), at the close of the poll at any relevant election or referendum the presiding officer must take the like steps (so far as not already taken) for the delivery to the returning officer of ballot boxes and ballot papers and other documents as he would be required to do if the poll at the mayoral election had not been abandoned.

(5) The returning officer must dispose of ballot papers used at the mayoral election (at which the candidate has died) as he is required to do on the completion in due course of the counting of the votes subject to paragraphs (6) and (7).

(6) It is not necessary for any ballot paper account at that election to be prepared or verified.

(7) The returning officer, having separated the ballot papers relating to each relevant election or referendum must take no step or further step for the counting of the ballot papers used at the mayoral election (at which a candidate has died) or of the votes cast at that mayoral election.

(8) The returning officer must seal up all those ballot papers used at the mayoral election, whether the votes on them have been counted or not, and it is not necessary to seal up counted and rejected ballot papers in separate packets.

(9) The provisions of these Rules as to the inspection, production, retention and destruction of ballot papers and other documents by the relevant registration officer

relating to a poll at the mayoral election apply to any such documents relating to a poll abandoned by reason of a candidate's death, subject to paragraphs (10) and (11).

(10)   Ballot papers on which the votes were neither counted nor rejected must be treated as counted ballot papers.

(11)   No order is to be made for–
>   (a)   the inspection or production of any ballot papers, or
>   (b)   for the opening of a sealed packet of the completed corresponding number lists or of certificates as to employment on duty on the day of the poll,

unless the order is made by a court with reference to a prosecution.

Appendix of Forms

Notes: In this Appendix any reference to a numbered rule is a reference to the rule of that number in the Mayoral Elections (Combination of Polls) Rules.

The forms contained in this Appendix may be adapted so far as circumstances require.

Forms

Form 1:   Nomination paper
Form 2:   Candidate's consent to nomination
Form 3:   Ballot paper (two candidates)
Form 4:   Ballot paper (three or more candidates)
Form 5:   Corresponding number list M1
Form 6:   Corresponding number list M2
Form 7(1);   Postal voting statement
Form 7(2):   Postal voting statement
Form 8:   Elector's official poll card
Form 9:   Official postal poll card
Form 10:   Official proxy poll card
Form 11:   Official proxy postal poll card
Form 12:   Directions for guidance of voters
Form 13:   Certificate of employment
Form 14:   Declaration to be made by the companion of a voter with disabilities.

The forms are not reproduced here

SCHEDULE 4

FREE DELIVERY OF ELECTION ADDRESSES

Regulation 6

1   In this Schedule–
>   "candidate" means a person who stands nominated as a candidate at the election;
>   "election" means an election for the return of an elected mayor;
>   "election address" shall be construed in accordance with paragraph 2;
>   "elector" in relation to an election, means a person entitled, in accordance with section 9HD(1) or 43(1) of the 2000 Act, to vote at that election;
>   "election booklet" shall be construed in accordance with paragraph 5;
>   "print" means print by whatever means (and "printer" shall be construed accordingly); and
>   "registered political party" means a party which was registered under Part 2 (registration of political parties) of the Political Parties, Elections and Referendums Act 2000 at the time by which the notice of election is required to be

published.

2 For the purposes of regulation 6 and this Schedule, an election address, in relation to a candidate, is a statement prepared by the candidate's election agent which complies with the provisions of paragraphs 3 and 4.

3 (1) An election address must contain matter relating to the election only.

(2) In particular, an election address must not contain–

    (a) any advertising material (other than material promoting the candidate as a candidate at the election);

    (b) any other material appearing to be included with a view to commercial gain; or

    (c) any material referring to any other candidate.

(3) An election address may include representations of the registered emblem, or (as the case may be) one of the registered emblems, of a registered political party if the address is prepared on behalf of an authorised party candidate.

(4) Where an election address is prepared on behalf of an authorised party candidate, the address may contain a description registered under section 28A or, if the description is registered for use by candidates of two or more parties, under section 28B of the Political Parties, Elections and Referendums Act 2000.

(5) In sub-paragraph (3) "authorised party candidate", in relation to a registered political party, means a candidate who has been authorised to use the emblem or description in question by a certificate–

    (a) issued by or on behalf of the registered nominating officer of the party; and

    (b) received by the returning officer before the last time for the delivery of nomination papers for the election.

(6) An election address must–

    (a) contain a statement to the effect that it has been prepared by the candidate's election agent;

    (b) give the name and address of the election agent; and

    (c) give the name and address of the candidate on whose behalf it has been prepared.

4 (1) Subject to any requirements imposed by or under this paragraph, the format of a candidate's election address may be determined by the candidate (and, in particular, may consist of a combination of words, pictures and artwork).

(2) An election address must be printed on not more than two sides of A5 paper, but if such an address is printed on two sides of such paper–

    (a) it must, when submitted to the returning officer for inclusion in the election booklet, be accompanied by a second version printed on a single side of such paper; and

    (b) if the total number of candidates from whom election addresses have been accepted by the returning officer by the last time for delivery of nomination papers for the election exceeds 15, the version to be included in the election booklet shall be the second version.

(3) An election address must–

    (a) comply with such requirements as to typographical layout, margins and use of colour as the returning officer may determine; and

    (b) comply with such other requirements as he may determine with a view to facilitating its reproduction as a page or pages of the election booklet.

(4) An election address must, when submitted to the returning officer for inclusion in the election booklet, be accompanied–

    (a) where the address is to contain a photograph of the candidate, by two identical copies of the photograph, of which one is signed on the back by the candidate; and

    (b) in any case, by such copies of anything contained in the address as the returning officer may reasonably require in connection with the reproduction of the address.

5 (1) For the purposes of this Schedule, the election booklet is a document prepared by the returning officer which contains the election addresses of all candidates who–

    (a) desire their election addresses to be included in the booklet; and

    (b) have submitted–

      (i) those addresses, and

      (ii) any additional material required under paragraph 4(4),

to the returning officer before the last time for the delivery of nomination papers for the election.

(2) If–

    (a) it appears to the returning officer that any of the requirements of paragraphs 3 and 4 has not been complied with in relation to an election address, or

    (b) a candidate fails to make the payment required by paragraph 8 in respect of an election address,

the returning officer shall decline to include the address in the election booklet.

6 (1) The order in which the candidates' election addresses appear in the election booklet shall be determined by lot drawn by the returning officer as soon as reasonably practicable after the last time for the delivery of nomination papers for the election.

(2) The election booklet may include, in addition to candidates' election addresses, a statement by the returning officer–

    (a) explaining the nature and purpose of the election booklet;

    (b) listing in alphabetical order, the names of all the candidates at the election (whether or not their election addresses are included in the booklet); and

    (c) giving the date of the election and such other information about it as the returning officer may determine.

(3) The election booklet must–

    (a) contain a statement that it has been published by the returning officer; and

    (b) give the name and address of the returning officer and those of the printer of the booklet.

(4) Subject to sub-paragraphs (1) to (3), the form of the election booklet shall be determined by the returning officer.

(5) The election agent of each candidate whose election address has been accepted by the returning officer for inclusion in the booklet shall be given an opportunity to attend at a time and place notified to him by the returning officer in order to check, and submit to the returning officer typographical corrections to, the proof of the candidate's address.

(6) If the election agent of any such candidate fails to avail himself of that opportunity, the returning officer may–

    (a) make such typographical corrections to the proof as appear to him to be appropriate; and

    (b) proceed with the printing and distribution of the election booklet without further reference to the candidate or his election agent (and without incurring any liability for any errors in the candidate's address).

(7) No person other than–

    (a) the candidate on whose behalf an election address included in the election booklet was prepared, or

    (b) the candidate's election agent,

shall incur any civil or criminal liability in respect of the publication of that address in the election booklet or its dissemination in accordance with paragraph 7.

7 (1) Copies of the election booklet shall be delivered by the returning officer, in envelopes addressed to individual electors, at such time and by such means as the returning officer may determine.

(2) The returning officer may disseminate the contents of the election booklet by such other means as he may determine.

8 (1) Each candidate by whom an election address is submitted to the returning officer for inclusion in the election booklet shall pay to the returning officer such reasonable sum (which shall be the same for each such candidate) as the returning officer may determine by way of contribution towards the expenses incurred by him in respect of the printing of the election booklet.

(2) The payment required by sub-paragraph (1) shall be made at such time, and in such manner, as the returning officer may determine.

(3) A candidate shall be entitled to a full refund of any such payment if, but only if, the candidate has given notice of withdrawal of his candidature before the last time for the withdrawal of candidates.

(4) If the total amount of the payments made by candidates under this paragraph exceeds the total amount of the expenses incurred by the returning officer in respect of the printing of the election booklet, the returning officer shall

    (a) divide the amount of the excess between those candidates in equal shares, and

    (b) send to each of those candidates a payment in respect of his share.

9 (1) The amount of any payment made by a candidate under paragraph 8 (or, if sub-paragraph (4) of that paragraph applies, the net amount of any such payment after deducting the payment under that sub-paragraph) shall be taken, for the purposes of Part 2 (the Election campaign) of the 1983 Act (as modified for the purposes of mayoral elections by regulation 3(2) and (4) of, and Table 1 of Schedule 2 to, these Regulations), to be an amount of election expenses incurred by the candidate in relation to the election.

(2) Nothing in section 75(1) (restriction on third party election expenditure) of the 1983 Act (as modified as mentioned in sub-paragraph (1)) shall be taken to apply, in relation to any candidate, to any expenses incurred by the returning officer in consequence of the relevant provisions.

Local Authorities (Referendums) (Petitions) (England) Regulations 2011
(SI 2011/2914)

Made 5th December 2011

Part 1
General

Citation, commencement and interpretation

1 These Regulations may be cited as the Local Authorities (Referendums) (Petitions) (England) Regulations 2011 and shall come into force on 23rd January 2012.

2(1) In these Regulations
"the 1972 Act" means the Local Government Act 1972;
"the 1983 Act" means the Representation of the People Act 1983
"the 2000 Act" means the Local Government Act 2000.

(2) Except where expressly stated to the contrary, any reference in these Regulations to a section followed by a number is a reference to the section bearing that number in the 2000 Act.

Part 2
Petitions and Referendums

Interpretation of Part 2

3 In this Part
"amalgamated petition" means the single petition resulting from an amalgamation of petitions in accordance with paragraph (1) or (2) of regulation 8;
"constituent petitions" means petitions that have been amalgamated;
"constitutional change"
  (a) in relation to an authority which are operating a leader and cabinet executive (England), means a proposal that the authority should start to operate a mayor and cabinet executive or the committee system instead;
  (b) in relation to an authority which are operating a mayor and cabinet executive, means a proposal that the authority should start to operate a leader and cabinet executive (England) or the committee system instead;
  (c) in relation to an authority which are operating the committee system, means a proposal that the authority should start to operate a mayor and cabinet executive or a leader and cabinet executive (England) instead;
"electoral register" must be construed in accordance with section 9 of the 1983 Act;
"electoral registration officer" has the meaning given by section 8 of the 1983 Act;
"moratorium period", in relation to a local authority's area and a petition, means the period of nine years commencing with the day on which a referendum ("referendum A") was last held under Part 1A of the 2000 Act in relation to that area, except where
  (a) referendum A was held by virtue of an order under section 9N; and
  (b) the proposal for the authority to operate a mayor and cabinet executive was rejected;
"notice period", in relation to a petition means the period of one month beginning with the petition date;
"ordinary day of election" has the meaning given by section 37 of the 1983 Act;
"petition", unless the context otherwise requires, includes an amalgamated petition;
"petition date"
  (a) in relation to a petition submitted prior to the publication of the verification number in accordance with regulation 4(1) means the date on which that verification number is published;
  (b) subject to paragraph (d), in relation to constituent petitions amalgamated in accordance with regulation 8(2), means the latest date on which any of the petitions amalgamated was received by the authority;

(c)   subject to paragraph (d), in relation to any other petition, means the date on which it was received by the authority;

(d)   in relation to a petition received within the period of six months beginning with the date that is twelve months before the earliest date on which a second (or subsequent) referendum may lawfully be held in the area of the authority to whom the petition is addressed, means the date on which that period of six months ends;

"petition organiser"

(a)   in relation to constituent petitions amalgamated in accordance with paragraph (1) of regulation 8, means the person determined in accordance with paragraph (5) of regulation 10;

(b)   in any other case, has the meaning given by paragraph (4) of regulation 10;

"post-announcement petition" means a petition received in the circumstances mentioned in regulation 7(1);

"proper officer" has the meaning given by section 270(3) of the 1972 Act;

"publish" in relation to a local authority or a proper officer's duty to publish, means to make the specified information available to those persons who live in the area in whatever manner the local authority considers likely to bring it to the attention of those persons;

"revised version of the register" must be construed in accordance with section 13 of the 1983 Act;

"valid petition" has the meaning given by regulation 9(1);

"verification number", in relation to a petition, means the number to be used for verification purposes by virtue of paragraphs (3) or (4) of regulation 4, as the case may be; and

"verification purposes" means the purposes of establishing the matters mentioned in regulations 8(3) and 9(1)(a).

Verification number

4(1)   Subject to paragraph (2), in each year the proper officer of each local authority shall, within the period of 14 days beginning with 15th February, publish the number that is equal to 5 per cent of the number of local government electors for the authority's area shown in the revised version of the register or, as the case may be, the registers having effect for that area on that 15th February.

(2)   Where the whole period of 12 months beginning with 1st April in any year to which paragraph (1) applies falls within a moratorium period, that paragraph shall not apply as respects the years in which part of that period of 12 months falls.

(3)   The number published in each year in accordance with paragraph (1) shall be used for verification purposes in relation to any petition presented to the authority in the period of 12 months beginning with1st April in that year.

(4)   Where the verification number published in any year in accordance with paragraph (1) is less than the number published in the preceding year, the number to be used for verification purposes, in relation to any petition presented to the authority in the period beginning on the date of publication of the lesser number and ending immediately before 1st April in that year, shall be that lesser number.

(5)   The proper officer may, in connection with the discharge of the duty imposed by paragraph (1), require an electoral registration officer to provide him or her with information relevant to the number that is to be published in accordance with that paragraph; and an electoral registration officer who receives such a request shall comply with it within the period of seven days beginning with the day on which the request is received.

Publicity for verification numbers

5   As soon as reasonably practicable after the publication of a verification number in accordance with regulation 4(1), the authority shall publish a notice which contains a statement
  (a) that the authority's proper officer has published the number that is equal to 5 per cent of the number of local government electors shown in the electoral register or registers having effect on 15th February in that year;
  (b) of the number so published;
  (c) that the number so published will have effect for the purposes of determining the validity of petitions presented after 31st March in the year of publication and before 1st April in the following year, unless a different number has effect by virtue of paragraph (4) of regulation 4;
  (d) the effect of paragraph (4) of regulation 4; and
  (e) of the address of the authority's principal office.

Petitions for a referendum

6(1) Subject to regulation 7, a local authority shall hold a referendum by virtue of this Part where they receive a valid petition (but shall not be required to hold such a referendum where they receive a petition which is not a valid petition).

  (2) A petition may be presented to a local authority
  (a) by properly addressing, prepaying and posting it to any office of the authority; or
  (b) by delivering it to any such office.

Post-announcement petitions

7(1) In relation to a petition received after an authority have given notice of their intention to hold a referendum and of the date on which that referendum will be held (whether pursuant to this Part, or section 9M (cases in which change subject to approval in a referendum)), nothing in this Part shall require an authority to hold a referendum or to take any steps other than those specified in paragraph (2) and regulation 12.

  (2) The steps specified in this paragraph are to secure that the proper officer, as soon as reasonably practicable after the receipt of the petition notifies the petition organiser (if any)
  (a) of the receipt of the petition;
  (b) that the petition is a post-announcement petition; and
  (c) that the authority propose to take no further action in relation to it.

Amalgamation of petitions

  (1) Where more than one petition relating to the same area and proposing the same constitutional change has been prepared, those petitions may, at any time before their presentation to the authority, be amalgamated; and those petitions shall then be treated for all other purposes of this Part as a single petition.

  (2) Subject to paragraph (3), where an authority receive more than one petition relating to the same area, the proper officer shall, if satisfied as to their validity in every respect other than that mentioned in regulation 9(1)(a), amalgamate those petitions in accordance with paragraph (4); and those petitions shall then be treated for all other purposes of this Part as a single petition.

  (3) The proper officer shall not amalgamate petitions
  (a) if he or she is satisfied that the first petition received by the authority (including constituent petitions amalgamated in accordance with paragraph (1)) contains

a number of signatures of local government electors for the authority's area that equals or exceeds the verification number and is, in other respects, a valid petition;

    (b) if he or she is satisfied that the first and other constituent petitions amalgamated in accordance with paragraph (2) contain numbers of signatures of local government electors for the authority's area that in aggregate equal or exceed the verification number and are, in other respects, valid petitions; or

    (c) that do not propose the same constitutional change.

(4) Petitions shall be amalgamated in the order in which they are received except that, where more than one petition is received on the same day

    (a) the petition that contains the greatest number of signatures shall be treated as the first to be received;

    (b) any other petitions shall be treated in the following order

        (i) the petition that contains the greatest number of signatures;

        (ii) the petition that contains the next greatest number of signatures; and so on.

Validity of petitions

9(1) Subject to paragraph (2) a petition shall be a valid petition if

    (a) it is signed (whether before or after the coming into force of these Regulations) by not less than the number of local government electors for the authority's area that is the verification number; and

    (b) it satisfies the requirements of regulation 10; and

    (c) it is presented to the local authority to whom it is addressed on a day other than one which falls within a moratorium period.

(2) A petition shall not be invalid by reason only of a failure to satisfy the requirements of regulation 10(1) or 10(2) if the constitutional change in relation to which the referendum is sought can be ascertained.

(3) Where a person signs a petition but the information referred to in regulation 10(3)(a) is not included, or is not included in a legible form, that person's signature shall be disregarded in determining whether the petition satisfies the requirements of paragraph (1)(a).

(4) If a person signs a petition more than once, that person's second or subsequent signature shall be disregarded in determining whether the petition satisfies the requirements of paragraph (1)(a).

(5) Any signature on a petition which bears a date earlier than 12 months before the petition date shall be disregarded in determining whether the petition satisfies the requirements of paragraph (1)(a).

Formalities of petition

10(1) A petition shall on each sheet state

    (a) the name of the local authority to whom it is addressed; and

    (b) the constitutional change in relation to which the referendum is sought.

(2) A petition shall, on each sheet, contain a statement in the terms set out in the Schedule to these Regulations or in terms to similar effect.

(3) In relation to each person who signs a petition the following information shall be given

    (a) that person's first name and surname and address; and

    (b) the date on which he or she signs the petition.

(4) A petition shall contain, or shall be accompanied by a statement that contains, the name and full address of the person ("the petition organiser") to whom

correspondence relating to the petition is to be sent.

(5) Where petitions are amalgamated before they are presented to the authority
    (a) the petition organisers of each of the constituent petitions shall determine the identity of the person (whether or not that person is the petition organiser of any of the constituent petitions) who is to be the petition organiser for the purposes of the amalgamated petition; and
    (b) the petition organiser of the amalgamated petition shall notify the authority of his or her name and full address.

Procedure on receipt of petition

11(1) As soon as reasonably practicable after receipt of a petition, the proper officer shall
    (a) if paragraph (2) of regulation 8 applies in relation to the petition
      (i) amalgamate it in accordance with that paragraph; and
      (ii) notify the petition organiser (if any) of each of the constituent petitions, of the petition date of the amalgamated petition; or
    (b) in any other case, notify the petition organiser (if any) of the petition date.

(2) As soon as reasonably practicable after receipt of a petition, and not later than the end of the notice period, the proper officer shall, subject to paragraph (3), satisfy himself or herself as to the validity of the petition.

(3) Where the petition is a second (or subsequent) petition ("later petition") which cannot lawfully be amalgamated with an earlier petition for a reason mentioned in paragraph (3) of regulation 8, the proper officer shall take the steps specified in paragraph (4).

(4) The steps specified in this paragraph are that, within the notice period, the proper officer shall notify the petition organiser (if any)
    (a) of the receipt of the petition and of its petition date;
    (b) of the receipt of every earlier petition and of its petition date;
    (c) of the reason why the later petition cannot be amalgamated with any earlier petition; and
    (d) that, by reason of the receipt of an earlier valid petition, the proper officer proposes to take no further action in relation to the later petition.

Public inspection of petitions

12 The authority shall secure that for the period of six years beginning with the petition date, a petition is available at their principal office for inspection by members of the public at all reasonable times and free of charge.

Publicity for valid petitions

13(1) Where the proper officer is satisfied that a petition is valid, he or she shall, within the notice period, notify the petition organiser
    (a) of his or her conclusion; and
    (b) that a referendum will be held.

(2) In a case to which paragraph (1) applies, the authority shall, as soon as reasonably practicable after the paragraph (1) requirement has been met, publish a notice which contains a statement
    (a) that a valid petition has been received;
    (b) of the constitutional change sought by the petition;
    (c) of the petition date;
    (d) that the petition is available at the authority's principal office for inspection by members of the public at all reasonable times and free of charge;
    (e) of the address of the authority's principal office; and

(f)   that a referendum will be held.

Publicity for invalid petitions

14(1)   Where the proper officer is satisfied that a petition is not a valid petition, he or she shall, within the notice period, notify the petition organiser (if any) of his or her conclusion and of the reasons for that conclusion.

(2)   In a case to which paragraph (1) applies, the authority shall, as soon as reasonably practicable after the paragraph (1) requirement has been met, publish a notice which contains a statement
    (a)   that a petition has been received which has been determined to be an invalid petition;
    (b)   of the reasons for that determination;
    (c)   of the constitutional change sought by the petition;
    (d)   of the petition date;
    (e)   that the petition is available at the authority's principal office for inspection by members of the public at all reasonable times and free of charge; and
    (f)   of the address of the authority's principal office.

(3)   Where a petition is invalid only because it does not comply with regulation 9(1)(a), the notification under paragraph (1) and the statement to be published by the authority under paragraph (2) shall also include a statement that the invalid petition may be amalgamated with any subsequent petitions which are submitted to the authority.

Restrictions relating to publicity

15(1)   An authority shall not incur any expenditure for the purpose of
    (a)   publishing any material which, in whole or in part, appears designed to influence local government electors in deciding whether or not to sign a petition under this Part;
    (b)   assisting any person to publish any such material; or
    (c)   influencing or assisting any person to influence, by any other means, local government electors in deciding whether or not to sign a petition under this Part.

(2)   Nothing in paragraph (1) shall be taken to prevent an authority from incurring expenditure on publishing or otherwise providing to any person (whether or not in pursuance of any duty to do so) any factual information so far as it is presented fairly.

(3)   In determining for the purposes of paragraph (2) whether any information is presented fairly, regard shall be had to any guidance for the time being issued by the Secretary of State under section 9Q.

Timing of referendum in consequence of valid petition

16(1)   Subject to paragraphs (2) and (3), a referendum in consequence of a valid petition shall be held no later than the end of the next ordinary day of election after the petition date.

(2)   Paragraph (1) shall not apply where
    (a)   the petition date falls 4 months or less before the next ordinary day of election; or
    (b)   the next ordinary day of election falls within the period of six months beginning with the date that is six months before the earliest date on which a second (or subsequent) referendum may lawfully be held in the area of the authority to whom the petition is addressed,
and, in such a case, a referendum in consequence of a valid petition shall be held no

later than the end of the period of six months beginning with the petition date.

(3)   Paragraph (1) shall not apply where the Secretary of State holds a referendum in exercise of the power conferred by regulation 20.

(4)   A referendum under this Part may not be held on
   (a)   a Saturday or Sunday;
   (b)   Christmas Eve, Christmas Day, Maundy Thursday, Good Friday or a day which is a bank holiday under the Banking and Financial Dealings Act 1971 in England; or
   (c)   any day appointed as a day of public thanksgiving or mourning.

Action before referendum

17(1)   Before the holding of a referendum under this Part, the authority shall decide the extent to which the functions specified in regulations under section 9D(3)(b) are to be the responsibility of the executive (if applicable) should the form of governance that is the constitutional change proposed in the petition be approved.

(2)   Before the holding of a referendum under this Part, the authority shall draw up proposals for the operation of the form of governance that is the constitutional change proposed in the petition.

(3)   In drawing up proposals under paragraph (2) the authority shall have regard to any guidance for the time being issued by the Secretary of State under section 9Q.

Part 3
Action to be Taken After Referendums

Action where referendum proposals approved

18   If the result of a referendum held under Part 2 of these Regulations is to approve the proposals that were the subject of the referendum the authority shall implement the proposals that were the subject of the referendum.

Action where referendum proposals rejected

19   If the result of a referendum held under Part 2 of these Regulations is to reject the proposals that were the subject of the referendum
   (a)   the authority may not implement those proposals; and
   (b)   shall continue to operate their existing form of governance arrangements.

Part 4
Default Powers of the Secretary of State

Default powers of the Secretary of State

20   The Secretary of State may, in the event of any failure by an authority to take any action which may or must be taken by the authority under any of Parts 2 and 3 of these Regulations, take that action.

Part 5
Revocations

21   The following Regulations are revoked
   (a)   the Local Authorities (Referendums) (Petitions and Directions) (England) Regulations 2000;
   (b)   the Local Authorities (Referendums) (Petitions and Directions) (England) (Amendment) Regulations 2001;
   (c)   the Local Authorities (Referendums) (Petitions and Directions) (England)

(Amendment) (No 2) Regulations 2001; and

(d) the Local Authorities (Referendums) (Petitions and Directions) (England) (Amendment) (No 3) Regulations 2001.

SCHEDULE
PETITION STATEMENT

Regulation 10(2)

The terms of the statement referred to in regulation 10(2) are

"We, the undersigned, being local government electors for the area of [*insert name of local authority*], to whom this petition is addressed, seek a referendum on whether the council should be run in a different way by *(a mayor who is elected by voters for the area which the council serves) **(a leader who is an elected councillor chosen by a vote of the other elected councillors) ***(one or more committees made up of elected councillors)."

*Note: The phrase marked * or ** or *** to be omitted or retained as the petitioners require.*

Local Authorities (Referendums) (Petitions and Directions) (Wales) Regulations 2001 (SI 2001/2292)

Made 21st June 2001

SCHEDULES

Part I
General

Citation, commencement and application

1(1) These Regulations are called the Local Authorities (Referendums) (Petitions and Directions) (Wales) Regulations 2001 and shall come into force on 28 July 2001.

(2) These Regulations apply to Wales only.

General interpretation

2(1) In these Regulations

"the Act" ("*y Ddeddf*") means the Local Government Act 2000;

"authority" ("*awdurdod*") means a county or county borough council in Wales; and

"outline fallback proposals" ("*cynigion wrthgefn amlinellol*") means an outline of the proposals that an authority intend to implement if proposals that are to be the subject of a referendum under Part II or Part III of these Regulations are rejected in that referendum.

(2) Except in the definition of "proper officer" in regulation 3, any reference in these Regulations to a section followed by a number is a reference to the section bearing that number in the Act.

Part II
Petitions and Referendums

Interpretation of Part II

3 In this Part

"amalgamated petition"("*deiseb gyfun*") means the single petition resulting from an amalgamation of petitions in accordance with paragraph (1) or (3) of regulation 8;

"constituent petitions" ("*deisebau cyfansoddol*") means petitions that have been amalgamated;

"constitutional change" ("*newid cyfansoddiadol*") means

(a) unless a local authority is operating executive arrangements which involve an elected mayor, a proposal that the authority should operate executive arrangements

(i) under which the executive takes the form specified in subsection (2) or (4) of section 11 (local authority executives), or otherwise involves an elected mayor; or,

(ii) in a form that is not specified in the proposal;

(b) where a local authority are operating executive arrangements which involve an elected mayor ("existing executive arrangements"), a proposal that the authority should operate executive arrangements under which the executive takes a form which

(i) is specified in the proposal;

(ii) involves an elected mayor; and

(iii) differs from the form of executive under the existing executive arrangements;

"first petition period" ("*cyfnod deisebu cyntaf*") has the meaning given by regulation 3A;

"moratorium period" ("*cyfnod moratoriwm*") means the period of five years commencing on the date on which an authority holds a referendum under Part II of the Act;

"notice period" ("*cyfnod hysbysu*"), in relation to a petition, means the period of one month beginning with the petition date;

"petition" ("*deiseb*"), unless the context otherwise requires, includes an amalgamated petition;

"petition date" ("*dyddiad y ddeiseb*")

    (a) *Repealed*

    (b) in relation to constituent petitions amalgamated in accordance with regulation 8(3), means the latest date on which a constituent petition was received by the authority;

    (c) in relation to any other petition, means the date on which it was received by the authority;

    (d) *Repealed*;

"petition organiser" ("*trefnydd deiseb*")

    (a) in relation to constituent petitions amalgamated in accordance with paragraph (1) of regulation 8, means the person determined in accordance with paragraph (5) of regulation 10;

    (b) in any other case, has the meaning given by paragraph (4) of regulation 10;

"petition period" ("*cyfnod deisebu*") has the meaning given by regulation 3A;

"post-announcement petition" ("*deiseb ôlgyhoeddiad*") means a petition received in the circumstances mentioned in regulation 7(1);

"proper officer" ("*swyddog priodol*") has the meaning given by section 270(3) of the Local Government Act 1972;

"valid petition" ("*deiseb ddilys*") has the meaning given by regulation 9(1);

"verification date" ("*dyddiad dilysu*") means, other than in relation to the first petition period, the date that is seven months before the commencement of a petition period;

"verification number" ("*Rhif dilysu*"), in relation to a petition, means the number to be used for verification purposes by virtue of paragraphs (2) or (4) of regulation 4; and

"verification purposes" ("*dibenion dilysu*") means the purposes of establishing whether a petition is a valid petition.

Petition periods

3A(1) The local government electorate for an authority's area may present petitions to that authority during a petition period.

(2) The duration of a petition period is six months.

(3) The first petition period will commence on the date that is twelve months before the date on which the ordinary local government elections in 2004 are to be held.

(4) Subject to the following paragraphs of this regulation, subsequent petition periods for an authority will commence on the date that is twelve months before the date on which each subsequent ordinary local government elections are to be held.

(5) If part or the whole of one or more of an authority's petition periods as determined in accordance with paragraph (4) or the following paragraphs are to fall within a moratorium period, that petition period, or those petition periods (which, for the purposes of this regulation, are to be treated as a single petition period), will commence on the date during that moratorium period that is twelve months before the earliest date on which a second (or subsequent) referendum may lawfully be held in the area of that authority.

(6) Where an authority does not receive a valid petition during a petition period determined in accordance with paragraph (5), the date on which the next petition period for that authority will commence is the date that is twelve months before the date on which the next ordinary local government elections are to be held.

(7) Paragraph (6) will not apply where part or the whole of a petition period determined in accordance with that paragraph will fall within a year in which part or the whole of a petition period determined in accordance with paragraph (5) falls.

(8)   Where an authority does not receive a valid petition during a petition period determined in accordance with paragraph (5) and, by virtue of paragraph (7), paragraph (6) does not apply, the next petition period for that authority will commence on the date that is twelve months before the date on which the ordinary local government elections which are subsequent to the next ordinary local government elections are to be held.

Verification number

4(1) Not later than four weeks after 4th April 2003, the proper officer of each authority shall publish the number that is equal to 10% of the number of local government electors for the authority's area shown in the electoral register or registers published and having effect for the authority's area on 4th April 2003.

(2)   The number published in accordance with paragraph (1) will be used for verification purposes in relation to any petition presented to the authority during the first petition period.

(3)   For the purposes of each subsequent petition period, the proper officer of each authority must, within the period of 14 days beginning with the verification date, publish the number that is equal to 10% of the number of local government electors for the authority's area shown in the revised version of the registers having effect for the area on the verification date.

(4)   The number published in accordance with paragraph (3) will be used for verification purposes in relation to any petition presented to the authority during the petition period that is to commence seven months after the verification date to which that number relates.

(5)   The proper officer may, in connection with the discharge of the duty imposed by paragraphs (1) or (3), make a request in writing to an electoral registration officer to provide the proper officer with information relevant to the number that is to be published in accordance with those paragraphs; and an electoral registration officer who receives such a request must comply with it within the period of seven days beginning with the day on which the request is received.

Publicity for verification number and petition period

5   As soon as reasonably practicable after the publication of a verification number, the authority must publish in at least one newspaper circulating in its area a notice containing a statement

   (a) that the authority's proper officer has published the number that is equal to 10% of the number of local government electors shown in the electoral register or registers having effect for the authority's area on the date that
       (i)   for the purposes of the first petition period, is the date of the coming into force of these Regulations; or
       (ii) for the purposes of a subsequent petition period, is the verification date;
   (b) of the number so published;
   (c) that the number so published will have effect for the purposes of determining the validity of petitions presented to the authority during the first petition period or (as is appropriate) the petition period for that authority that will commence seven months after the verification date referred to in paragraph (a)(ii);
   (d) of the date on which that petition period (be it the first petition period or a subsequent petition period) for the authority will
       (i)   commence; and
       (ii) end; and

(e) of the address of the authority's principal office.

Petitions for a referendum

6(1) Subject to regulations 7, 8(8) and 19, an authority shall hold a referendum by virtue of this Part where it receives a valid petition (but shall not be required to hold such a referendum where it receives a petition which is not a valid petition).

(2) A petition may be presented to a local authority
  (a) by properly addressing, prepaying and posting it to the authority's principal office; or
  (b) by delivering it to the authority's principal office.

Post-announcement and post-direction petitions

7(1) In relation to a petition received after an authority has given notice of its intention to hold a referendum and of the date on which that referendum will be held (whether pursuant to this Part, a direction under regulation 18, or section 27 (referendum in case of proposals involving elected mayor)) on proposals which involve a directly elected mayor, nothing in this Part shall require an authority to hold a referendum or to take any steps other than those specified in paragraph (2) and regulation 12.

(2) The steps specified in this paragraph are to secure that the proper officer, as soon as reasonably practicable after the receipt of the petition
  (a) notifies the National Assembly for Wales and the petition organiser
    (i) of the receipt of the petition;
    (ii) that the petition is a post-announcement petition; and
    (iii) that the authority propose to take no further action in relation to it;
  and
  (b) notifies the petition organiser that the petition organiser may, within the period of two months beginning with the date of the notice, request the National Assembly for Wales to consider the exercise of any power conferred on it by Part III of these Regulations.

(3) Where
  (a) a petition is received by an authority
    (i) after it has received a direction under regulation 18(1); and
    (ii) before it has given notice of the date on which the referendum is to be held pursuant to the direction; and
  (b) the constitutional change proposed in the petition is the same as that in relation to which the direction requires the referendum to be held,
  the authority shall take no further action in relation to the petition and shall, as soon as reasonably practicable, comply with the requirements of paragraph (4).

(4) The authority shall notify the National Assembly for Wales and the petition organiser
  (a) of the receipt of the petition; and
  (b) that it proposes to take no further action in relation to the petition because it proposes the same constitutional change as that in relation to which the referendum is to be held pursuant to the direction.

(5) Where
  (a) a petition is received by an authority
    (i) after it has received a direction under regulation 18(1); and
    (ii) before it has given notice of the date on which the referendum is to be held pursuant to the direction; and
  (b) the constitutional change proposed in the petition is not the same as that in relation to which the direction requires the referendum to be held,
  the authority shall secure that the proper officer determines, in accordance with this

Part, whether the petition is a valid petition.

(6) Where the proper officer determines that a petition of the description in paragraph (5) is not a valid petition, the proper officer shall comply with regulation 14(1) but, subject to that

    (a) the authority shall take no further action in relation to the petition; and

    (b) for the purposes of regulation 21, the date of the direction shall be the date of the proper officer's determination.

(7) For the purposes of paragraphs (3) to (5)

    (a) in relation to a direction under regulation 18(1) that requires an authority to hold a referendum on a form of executive that includes an elected mayor, a petition received subsequently by that authority in which the form of executive is not specified, shall be treated as proposing the same constitutional change; and

    (b) other constitutional changes shall be treated as the same if they propose executive arrangements under which the executive takes the same form.

Amalgamation of petitions

8(1) Where more than one petition relating to the same area has been prepared, those petitions may, at any time before their presentation to the authority, be amalgamated; and those petitions shall then be treated for all other purposes of this Part as a single petition.

(2) Where constituent petitions amalgamated under paragraph (1) do not propose the same constitutional change, the amalgamated petition shall not be entertained by the authority unless it is accompanied by a statement, signed by the petition organiser in relation to the amalgamated petition, that the amalgamated petition is presented with the agreement of the petition organiser of each of the constituent petitions.

(3) Subject to paragraphs (4), (5) and (6), where an authority receives more than one petition relating to the same area, the proper officer shall, if satisfied as to their validity in every respect other than that mentioned in regulation 9(1)(a), amalgamate those petitions in accordance with paragraph (7); and those petitions shall then be treated for all other purposes of this Part as a single petition.

(4) The proper officer shall not amalgamate petitions if satisfied that the first petition received by the authority (including constituent petitions amalgamated in accordance with paragraph (1)) contains a number of signatures of local government electors for the authority's area that equals or exceeds the verification number and is, in other respects, a valid petition.

(5) Once an amalgamated petition (amalgamated in accordance with paragraph (3)) contains a number of signatures of local government electors for the authority's area that equals or exceeds the verification number and is, in other respects, a valid petition, the proper officer shall not amalgamate any other petition with that amalgamated petition.

(6) The proper officer

    (a) shall not amalgamate petitions that do not propose the same constitutional change unless the proper officer has obtained in writing the agreement of the petition organiser of each petition that would, after amalgamation, be a constituent petition.

    (b) shall inform each petition organiser whose agreement is required for the purposes of sub-paragraph (a) of the consequence of amalgamation specified in paragraph (10) below.

(7) Petitions shall be amalgamated in the order in which they are received except that,

where more than one petition is received on the same day
- (a) the petition that contains the greatest number of signatures shall be treated as the first to be received;
- (b) the petition that proposes the same constitutional change as that proposed in the petition identified in accordance with sub-paragraph (a) shall be treated as the second to be received; and if there is more than one such petition, those petitions shall be treated as received in sequence, beginning with the petition that contains the greater number of signatures;
- (c) any other petitions shall be treated as received in the following order
  - (i) the petition that contains the greatest number of signatures;
  - (ii) the petition, if any, that proposes the same constitutional change as the petition identified in accordance with paragraph (i);
  - (iii) the petition that contains the next greatest number of signatures;
  - (iv) the petition, if any, that proposes the same constitutional change as the petition identified in accordance with paragraph (iii);
  - (v) the petition that contains the next greatest number of signatures; and so on.

(8) Where
- (a) an authority receives more than one petition on the same day; and
- (b) those petitions each contain a number of signatures of local government electors for the authority's area that equals or exceeds the verification number and are, in other respects, valid petitions; and
- (c) those petitions do not propose the same constitutional change,

that authority shall make a determination as to the petition in relation to which it will hold a referendum.

(9) Before making a determination under paragraph (8)
- (a) the authority shall take into account the outcome of any prior consultation undertaken by that authority in pursuance of sections 25 or 31 or regulations 17 or 19; and
- (b) if the authority considers it necessary, undertake further consultation with the local government electors for, and other interested persons in, the authority's area.

(10) Where an amalgamated petition results from the combination of constituent petitions which do not propose the same constitutional change, the amalgamated petition shall be treated for the purposes of this Part as proposing that the authority should operate executive arrangements under which the proposed form of executive is not specified.

(11) For the purposes of this regulation, constitutional changes shall be treated as the same
- (a) if they propose executive arrangements under which the executive takes the same form; or
- (b) if the proposed form of executive is not specified.

Validity of petitions

9(1) Subject to paragraph (2), a petition shall be a valid petition if
- (a) it is signed (whether before or after the passing of the Act or the coming into force of these Regulations) by not less than the verification number;
- (b) it satisfies the requirements of regulation 10; and
- (c) it is presented to the authority to which it is addressed on a day that falls within a petition period for that authority.

(2) A petition shall not be invalid by reason only of a failure to satisfy any requirement of regulation 10 if the constitutional change in relation to which the referendum is sought can be ascertained.

(3)   Where a person signs a petition but the information referred to in regulation 10(3)(a) is not included, or is not included in a legible form, that person's signature shall be disregarded in determining whether the petition satisfies the requirements of paragraph (1)(a).

(4)   If a person signs a petition more than once, that person's second or subsequent signature shall be disregarded in determining whether the petition satisfies the requirements of paragraph (1)(a).

(5)   Any signature on a petition which bears a date earlier than 6 months before the petition date shall be disregarded in determining whether the petition satisfies the requirements of paragraph (1)(a).

Formalities of petition

10(1)   A petition shall on each sheet state
    (a)   the name of the authority to whom it is addressed; and
    (b)   the constitutional change in relation to which the referendum is sought.

(2)   A petition shall, on each sheet, contain a statement in the terms set out in Schedule 1 to these Regulations or in terms to similar effect.

(3)   In relation to each person who signs a petition the following information shall be given
    (a)   that person's first name and surname and address; and
    (b)   the date on which that person signs the petition.

(4)   A petition shall contain, or shall be accompanied by a statement that contains, the name and full address of the person (in this Part referred to as the "petition organiser") to whom correspondence relating to the petition is to be sent.

(5)   Where petitions are amalgamated before they are presented to the authority
    (a)   the petition organiser of each of the constituent petitions shall determine the identity of the person (whether or not that person is the petition organiser of any of the constituent petitions) who is to be the petition organiser for the purposes of the amalgamated petition; and
    (b)   the petition organiser of the amalgamated petition shall notify the authority of the petition organiser's name and full address.

Procedure on receipt of petition

11(1)   As soon as reasonably practicable after receipt of a petition, the proper officer shall
    (a)   if paragraph (3) of regulation 8 applies in relation to the petition, notify the petition organiser of each of the constituent petitions, of the petition date of the amalgamated petition; or
    (b)   in any other case, notify the petition organiser of the petition date.

(2)   As soon as reasonably practicable after receipt of a petition, and not later than the end of the notice period, the proper officer shall determine the validity of the petition.

(3)   Where the petition is a second (or subsequent) petition ("later petition") which cannot lawfully be amalgamated with an earlier petition for a reason mentioned in paragraph (4), (5) or (6) of regulation 8, the proper officer shall take steps specified in paragraph (4) below, and such other steps as the National Assembly for Wales may direct.

(4)   The steps specified in this paragraph are that, within the notice period, the proper officer
    (a)   shall notify the National Assembly for Wales and the petition organiser
        (i)   of the receipt of the petition and of its petition date;
        (ii)   of the receipt of every earlier petition and of its petition date;
        (iii)   of the reason why the later petition cannot be amalgamated with any

          earlier petition; and

          (iv) that, by reason of the receipt of an earlier valid petition, the proper officer proposes to take no further action in relation to the later petition; and

     (b) shall notify the petition organiser that the petition organiser may, within the period of two months beginning with the date of the notice, request the National Assembly for Wales to consider the exercise of any power conferred on it by regulation 18.

Public inspection of petitions

12   The authority shall secure that, for the period of six years beginning with the petition date, a petition is available at its principal office for inspection by members of the public at all reasonable times and free of charge.

Publicity for valid petitions

13(1)   Where the proper officer is satisfied that a petition is valid, the proper officer shall, within the notice period, notify the National Assembly for Wales and either the petition organiser or where the petition has been amalgamated in accordance with regulation 8(3) the petition organiser of each of the constituent petitions

        (a) of the proper officer's conclusion; and

        (b) that a referendum will be held.

   (2)   In a case to which paragraph (1) applies, the authority shall publish in at least one newspaper circulating in its area a notice which contains a statement

        (a) that a valid petition has been received;

        (b) of the constitutional change sought or, as the case may be, treated as sought, by the petition;

        (c) of the petition date;

        (d) that the petition is available at the authority's principal office for inspection by members of the public at all reasonable times and free of charge;

        (e) of the address of the authority's principal office; and

        (f) that a referendum will be held.

Publicity for invalid petitions and those petitions in relation to which the authority will not act

14(1)   Where the proper officer is satisfied that a petition is not a valid petition, the proper officer shall, within the notice period, and, if possible, where that petition satisfies the requirements of regulation 9(1)(c), within that petition period, notify the National Assembly for Wales and the petition organiser (if any) of his determination and of the reasons for that determination.

   (2)   Where the authority has made a determination under regulation 8(8) the proper officer shall, within the notice period, notify the National Assembly for Wales and the petition organiser of the authority's determination and the reasons for that determination.

   (3)   In a case to which paragraph (1) applies and subject to paragraph (3A), the authority shall publish in at least one newspaper circulating in its area a notice which contains a statement

        (a) that a petition has been received which has been determined to be an invalid petition;

        (b) of the reasons for that determination;

        (c) of the constitutional change sought or, as the case may be, treated as sought, by the petition;

        (d) of the petition date;

        (e) that the petition is available at the authority's principal office for inspection by

members of the public at all reasonable times and free of charge; and
    (f)   of the address of the authority's principal office.

(3A) Where a petition in relation to which a notice is to be published in accordance with paragraph (3) satisfies the requirements of regulation 9(1)(c) the authority must, if possible, publish that notice within that petition period and within the notice period.

(4) Where a petition is invalid only because it does not comply with regulation 9(1)(a), the notification under paragraph (1) and the statement to be published by the authority under paragraph (3) shall also include a statement that the invalid petition may be amalgamated with any subsequent petitions which are submitted to the authority.

(5) In a case to which paragraph (2) applies, the authority shall publish in at least one newspaper circulating in its area a notice which contains a statement
    (a)   that a valid petition has been received;
    (b)   that the authority will not take any action in relation to that petition on account of it having made a determination under regulation 8(8) of these Regulations;
    (c)   of the reasons for that determination;
    (d)   of the constitutional change sought by the petition;
    (e)   of the petition date;
    (f)   that the petition is available at the authority's principal office for inspection by members of the public at all reasonable times and free of charge; and
    (g)   of the address of the authority's principal office.

Restrictions relating to publicity

15(1) An authority shall not incur any expenditure for the purpose of
    (a)   publishing any material which, in whole or in part, appears designed to influence local government electors in deciding whether or not to sign a petition under this Part;
    (b)   assisting any person to publish any such material; or
    (c)   influencing or assisting any person to influence, by any other means, local government electors in deciding whether or not to sign a petition under this Part.

(2) Nothing in paragraph (1) shall be taken to prevent an authority from incurring expenditure on publishing or otherwise providing to any person (whether or not in pursuance of any duty to do so) any factual information so far as it is presented fairly.

(3) In determining for the purposes of paragraph (2) whether any information is presented fairly, regard shall be had to any guidance for the time being issued by the National Assembly for Wales under section 38.

Timing of referendum

16(1) Subject to paragraphs (1A), (2) and (3) and regulation 21, a referendum in consequence of a valid petition shall be held not later than
    (a)   the end of the period of six months beginning with the petition date; or
    (b)   the end of the period of two months beginning with the date on which regulations under section 45 (with respect to the referendum) come into force, whichever is the later.

(1A) Where
    (a)   an authority's petition period commences (by virtue of regulation 3A(5)) on the date that is twelve months before the earliest date on which that authority may hold a second (or subsequent) referendum; and
    (b)   a valid petition is presented to that authority within that petition period,
that authority must hold a referendum on the earliest date on which it may lawfully

hold a second (or subsequent) referendum.

(2) A referendum shall not be held before the end of the period of two months beginning with the date on which proposals and a statement are sent to the National Assembly for Wales in accordance with regulation 17(9).

(3) Paragraph (1) shall not apply where the National Assembly for Wales holds a referendum in exercise of the power conferred by regulation 25.

(4) A referendum under this Part may not be held on
   (a) a Saturday or Sunday,
   (b) Christmas Eve, Christmas Day, Maundy Thursday, Good Friday or a day which is a bank holiday under the Banking and Financial Dealings Act 1971 in Wales, or
   (c) any day appointed as a day of public thanksgiving or mourning.

Action before referendum

17(1) Before the holding of a referendum under this Part, the authority shall
   (a) where the petition does not specify, or is treated as not specifying, the form proposed for the authority's executive
      (i) subject to paragraph (2), decide which form the executive is to take; and
      (ii) decide the extent to which the functions specified in regulations under section 13(3)(b) are to be the responsibility of the executive; or
   (b) where the petition specifies the form proposed for the authority's executive, decide the extent to which the functions specified in regulations under section 13(3)(b) are to be the responsibility of the executive.

(2) The form of executive determined under paragraph (1)(a)(i) must include an elected mayor.

(3) Before the holding of a referendum under this Part, the authority shall also
   (a) draw up proposals for the operation of executive arrangements; and
   (b) draw up outline fallback proposals.

(4) Before drawing up proposals under paragraph (3)(a) and (b) the authority shall take reasonable steps to consult the local government electors for, and other interested persons in, the authority's area.

(5) The authority's proposals under paragraph (3)(a) shall include
   (a) such details of the executive arrangements as the National Assembly for Wales may direct,
   (b) a timetable with respect to the implementation of the proposals, and
   (c) details of any transitional arrangements which are necessary for the implementation of the proposals.

(6) In drawing up proposals under paragraph (3)(a) the authority shall consider the extent to which the proposals, if implemented, are likely to assist in securing continuous improvement in the way in which the authority's functions are exercised, having regard to a combination of economy, efficiency and effectiveness.

(7) The authority's proposals under paragraph (3)(b)
   (a) where the authority is not then operating executive arrangements
      (i) shall include such details of the executive arrangements to which they relate as the National Assembly for Wales may direct;
      (ii) shall include a timetable with respect to the implementation of detailed fallback proposals which are based on the outline fallback proposals in the event that the proposals that are to be the subject of the referendum are rejected; and
      (iii) may include, as the authority's outline fallback proposals, any proposals under subsection (1) of section 28 (approval of outline fallback proposals)

approved by the National Assembly for Wales;

(b) where the authority is then operating executive arrangements shall consist of a summary of those arrangements.

(8) In drawing up proposals under paragraph (3)(a) and (b) the authority shall have regard to any guidance for the time being issued by the National Assembly for Wales under section 38.

(9) Not later than two months before the date on which the referendum is to be held, the authority shall send to the National Assembly for Wales

(a) a copy of the proposals drawn up under paragraph (3)(a) and (b); and

(b) a statement which describes

(i)   the steps which the authority took to consult the local government electors for, and other interested persons in, the authority's area, and

(ii) the outcome of that consultation and the extent to which that outcome is reflected in the proposals.

(10) The authority shall comply with any directions given by the National Assembly for Wales for the purposes of this regulation.

Part III
Directions and Referendums

Circumstances in which the National Assembly for Wales may require referendum

18(1) The National Assembly for Wales may by a direction in writing to the authority, require the authority, subject to paragraphs (3) and (4), to hold a referendum on whether it should operate executive arrangements involving an executive which takes such form permitted by or under section 11 as may be specified in the direction

(a) where it appears to it that the circumstances are as mentioned in any paragraph of Schedule 2 to these Regulations;

(b) where it has rejected an authority's application under section 28 (approval of outline fallback proposals);

(c) where it appears to it that a direction is necessary to further compliance with the requirements of Part I of the Local Government Act 1999 (best value);

(d) if an authority request it to do so; or

(e) if a petition organiser requests it to do so.

(2) Where the National Assembly for Wales gives a direction pursuant to paragraph (1)(a), it may specify in the direction

(a) the form of executive to be included in proposals drawn up under regulation 19(1)(c);

(b) details (whether or not in the form of proposals that are to be the subject of the referendum) of

(i)   the executive arrangements and their operation; and

(ii) any transitional arrangements necessary for the implementation of the proposals on which the referendum is to be held;

(c) a timetable with respect to the implementation of the proposals;

(d) the principles or matters to which the authority is to have regard in drawing up the proposals;

(e) except in a case where details in the form of proposals are specified pursuant to sub-paragraph (b), in relation to the consultation to be undertaken in drawing up those proposals

(i)   the persons with whom consultation is required;

(ii) the manner of the consultation; and

(iii) the matters about which those persons are to be consulted;

(f) the outline fallback proposals;

    (g) details (whether or not in the form of proposals) of the detailed fallback proposals that are to be implemented if the proposals that are to be the subject of the referendum are rejected.

(3) Where a form of executive involving an elected mayor is specified in a petition, a direction given in response to the request of the person who is the petition organiser in relation to that petition shall not require the authority to hold a referendum on proposals involving any other form of executive.

(4) Where a form of executive involving an elected mayor is specified in a petition in consequence of which proposals are drawn up under regulation 17(3), a direction given pursuant to paragraph (1)(a) in respect of those proposals shall not require the authority to hold a referendum on proposals involving any other form of executive.

Action following direction

19(1) Subject to paragraphs (2) and (5), on receipt of a direction under regulation 18 in which a matter referred to in any of sub-paragraphs (a) to (e) of paragraph (2) of that regulation is specified, the authority to which the direction is given shall immediately

    (a) abandon any arrangements made for the holding of a referendum (whether in consequence of a petition or an earlier direction of the National Assembly for Wales) to the extent that those arrangements are inconsistent with the arrangements necessary to conduct the referendum required by the direction;

    (b) abandon all action in respect of any petition received on or before the day on which they receive the direction;

    (c) in accordance with paragraphs (1), (2) and (4) of regulation 20, draw up proposals for the operation of executive arrangements;

    (d) in accordance with paragraphs (3) and (4) of regulation 20, draw up outline fallback proposals; and

    (e) make arrangements for the holding of a referendum on the proposals drawn up in accordance with sub-paragraph (c) (to the extent required to supplement any arrangements that may continue by virtue of sub-paragraph (a)).

(2) Where, on the day on which the direction is received, the authority

    (a) is in possession of the first petition submitted to it under Part II of these Regulations (including the single petition resulting from an amalgamation of petitions in accordance with regulation 8(1)), and

    (b) has not complied with regulation 11(2) in relation to it,

the authority shall satisfy itself as to the validity of the petition in accordance with Part II of these Regulations; and, subject to paragraph (3)(b), the direction shall be of no further effect.

(3) Where, in a case to which paragraph (2) applies

    (a) the authority is satisfied that the petition is valid, it shall comply with regulation 13; and the direction under regulation 18 shall be treated as revoked with effect from the date on which notice is given under regulation 13(1);

    (b) the authority is satisfied that the petition is invalid, it shall comply with regulation 14; and the direction under regulation 18 shall be treated as effective from the date on which notice is given under regulation 14(1).

(4) On receipt of a direction under regulation 18 in which a matter referred to in sub-paragraph (f) or (g) of paragraph (2) of that regulation is specified, the authority to which the direction is given shall immediately take the steps necessary to give effect to the direction.

(5) Where

    (a) the authority to which a direction under regulation 18 has been given receives a petition submitted to it under Part II of these Regulations (including the single petition resulting from an amalgamation of petitions in accordance with regulation 8(1));

(b) the petition is received before it has given notice of the date on which the referendum is to be held pursuant to the direction;

(c) the petition proposes a constitutional change different from that in relation to which the direction requires a referendum to be held; and

(d) the proper officer determines, in accordance with Part II, that the petition is a valid petition,

the direction shall be treated as revoked with effect from the date of the proper officer's determination.

(6) In a case to which paragraph (5) applies, the authority shall notify the National Assembly for Wales and the petition organiser of the date of the proper officer's determination; and shall include that notification in the notification required by regulation 13(1).

Requirements as to proposals

20(1) In drawing up proposals under regulation 19(1)(c) the authority shall

(a) where the direction specifies details, a form of executive or a timetable, include those details, that form of executive or that timetable;

(b) where the direction requires regard to be had to principles or matters, have regard to those principles or matters;

(c) where the direction requires consultation with specified persons, or in a specified manner or about specified matters, consult those persons, in that manner or about those matters, as the case may be;

(d) consider the extent to which its proposals, if implemented, are likely to assist in securing continuous improvement in the way in which its functions are exercised, having regard to a combination of economy, efficiency and effectiveness;

(e) subject to sub-paragraphs (a) to (d)

(i) decide which form the executive is to take;

(ii) decide the extent to which the functions specified in regulations under section 13(3)(b) are to be the responsibility of the executive; and

(iii) take reasonable steps to consult the local government electors for, and other interested persons in, the authority's area.

(2) Without prejudice to paragraph (1)(a), proposals under regulation 19(1) (c) shall include

(a) such details of the executive arrangements as the National Assembly for Wales may direct,

(b) a timetable with respect to the implementation of the proposals, and

(c) details of any transitional arrangements which are necessary for the implementation of the proposals.

(3) The authority's proposals under regulation 19(1)(d)

(a) where the authority is not then operating executive arrangements

(i) may not be drawn up before the authority has taken reasonable steps to consult the local government electors for, and other interested persons in, its area;

(ii) shall include such details of the executive arrangements to which they relate as the National Assembly for Wales may direct;

(iii) shall include a timetable with respect to the implementation of the detailed fallback proposals in the event that the proposals that are to be the subject of the referendum are rejected; and

(iv) may include, as the authority's outline fallback proposals, any proposals under subsection (1) of section 28 (approval of outline fallback proposals) approved by the National Assembly for Wales;

    (b) where the authority is then operating executive arrangements, shall consist of a summary of those arrangements.

(4) In drawing-up proposals under regulation 19(1)(c) and (d) an authority

    (a) shall comply with any directions given by the National Assembly for Wales; and

    (b) shall have regard to any guidance for the time being issued by the National Assembly for Wales under section 38.

(5) Not later than two months before the date on which the referendum is to be held, the authority shall send to the National Assembly for Wales

    (a) a copy of the proposals drawn up under regulation 19(1)(c) and (d); and

    (b) a statement which describes

      (i) the steps which the authority took to consult the local government electors for, and other interested persons in, the authority's area, and

      (ii) the outcome of that consultation and the extent to which that outcome is reflected in the proposals.

Time for holding referendum required by direction

21(1) Subject to paragraphs (2) to (4), a referendum required by a direction under regulation 18 shall be held not later than the end of the period of six months beginning with the date of the direction or, in a case to which paragraph (6) of regulation 7 applies, the date that is treated, in accordance with that paragraph, as the date of the direction.

(2) A referendum shall not be held before the end of the period of two months beginning with the date on which proposals and a statement are sent to the National Assembly for Wales in accordance with regulation 20(5).

(3) A referendum under this Part may not be held on

    (a) a Saturday or Sunday,

    (b) Christmas Eve, Christmas Day, Maundy Thursday, Good Friday or a day which is a bank holiday under the Banking and Financial Dealings Act 1971 in Wales, or

    (c) any day appointed as a day of public thanksgiving or mourning.

(4) Paragraph (1) shall not apply where the National Assembly for Wales holds a referendum in exercise of the power conferred by regulation 25.

(5) Where the National Assembly for Wales

    (a) in exercise of the power conferred by regulation 25, draws up outline fallback proposals or proposals for the operation of executive arrangements; and

    (b) directs an authority to hold a referendum on those proposals,

the authority shall hold the referendum not later than the end of the period of two months beginning with the date of the National Assembly for Wales' direction.

Publicity for referendum required by direction

22(1) The authority to which a direction under regulation 18 is given shall, not later than one month after the date of the direction, publish in at least one newspaper circulating in its area a notice which

    (a) sets out the terms of the direction; and

    (b) contains a statement

      (i) that a direction in the terms set out in the notice has been given by the National Assembly for Wales requiring a referendum to be held;

      (ii) of the form of executive to be included in the proposals that are to be the subject of the referendum; and

      (iii) that a referendum will be held.

(2) An authority may include in the notice to be published in accordance with paragraph (1), or may otherwise provide to any person (whether or not in pursuance of any duty to do so), any other factual information relating to the direction so far as it is presented fairly.

(3) In determining for the purposes of paragraph (2) whether any information is presented fairly, regard shall be had to any guidance for the time being issued by the National Assembly for Wales under section 38.

Part IV
Action to be Taken After Referendums

Action where referendum proposals approved

23 If the result of a referendum held under Part II or in pursuance of a direction under Part III is to approve the proposals that were the subject of the referendum

    (a) the authority shall implement the proposals that were the subject of the referendum in accordance with the timetable included in the proposals under regulation 17(3)(a) or, as the case may be, regulation 19(1)(c); and

    (b) where the authority is then operating executive arrangements that take a form that differs from those that were the subject of the referendum, section 29 (operation of, and publicity for, executive arrangements) shall apply for the purpose of enabling the authority to operate the executive arrangements that were the subject of the referendum as it applies for the purpose of enabling an authority to operate executive arrangements in other circumstances as if, for references to the arrangements, there were substituted references to the different executive arrangements that were the subject of the referendum.

Action where referendum proposals rejected

24(1) If the result of a referendum held under Part II or in pursuance of a direction under Part III is to reject the proposals that were the subject of the referendum

    (a) the authority may not implement those proposals; and

    (b) if the authority is not then operating executive arrangements, it shall draw up detailed fallback proposals which are based on its outline fallback proposals; or

    (c) if the authority is then operating executive arrangements, it shall continue to operate those arrangements until it is authorised or required to operate different executive arrangements; or

    (d) *Repealed.*

(2) Detailed fallback proposals shall comprise

    (a) the details (if any) specified in a direction under regulation 18(1);

    (b) such other details of the executive arrangements to which they relate as the National Assembly for Wales may direct; and

    (c) details of any transitional arrangements which are necessary for the implementation of the fallback proposals.

(3) In drawing up detailed fallback proposals the authority

    (a) shall comply with any directions given by the National Assembly for Wales; and

    (b) where those proposals involve executive arrangements shall, unless a direction has been given in relation to that matter, decide the extent to which the functions specified in regulations under section 13(3)(b) are to be the responsibility of the executive.

(4) Except to the extent that detailed fallback proposals involving executive arrangements are specified in a direction under regulation 18(1)

    (a) before drawing up proposals in accordance with paragraph (1)(b) above, the authority shall take reasonable steps to consult the local government electors for, and other interested persons in, the authority's area; and

(b) in drawing up those proposals, the authority shall consider the extent to which the proposals, if implemented, are likely to assist in securing continuous improvement in the way in which the authority's functions are exercised, having regard to a combination of economy, efficiency and effectiveness.

(5) Where detailed fallback proposals are drawn up in accordance with paragraph (1)(b), the authority shall send a copy of them to the National Assembly for Wales.

(6) Subject to paragraph (7), the authority shall implement detailed fallback proposals in accordance with the timetable included pursuant to regulation 17(7)(a)(ii) or, as the case may be, regulation 20(3)(a)(iii).

(7) Where detailed fallback proposals are based on proposals approved under subsection (1) of section 28 (approval of outline fallback proposals), the timetable referred to in paragraph (6) shall be extended to the extent that there is any delay in making the necessary regulations under section 11(5) or 32 (as the case may be).

Part V
Default Powers of The National Assembly for Wales

Default powers of the National Assembly for Wales

25 The National Assembly for Wales may, in the event of any failure by an authority to take any action which may or must be taken by the authority under any of Parts II to IV, itself take that action.

SCHEDULE 1
PETITION STATEMENT

Regulation 10(2)

The terms of the statement referred to in regulation 10(2) are
"We, the undersigned, being local government electors for the area of insert name of local authority, to whom this petition is addressed, seek a referendum on whether the electors for that area should elect a mayor who * (, with a ** cabinet ** council manager) will be in charge of our local services and lead insert name of local authority.".

*Note: The phrase marked * to be omitted or retained as the petitioners require.*
*If the phrase marked * is retained, the petitioners should select one of the alternatives marked **.*

SCHEDULE 2
PARTICULAR CIRCUMSTANCES IN WHICH THE NATIONAL ASSEMBLY
FOR WALES MAY REQUIRE REFERENDUM TO BE HELD

Regulation 18(1)(a)

Part I
Circumstances Relating to Proposals

1 The authority has not drawn up proposals under section 25, section 31, regulation 17(3)(a) or, as the case may be, regulation 19(1)(c), and is unlikely to do so unless the National Assembly for Wales so directs.

2 The authority has drawn up proposals under section 25 or, as the case may be, section 31, regulation 17(3)(a) or regulation 19(1)(c),or regulations under section 30 and 33
   (a) without having taken reasonable steps to undertake the consultation required by section 25(2) or, as the case may be, section 31(5), regulation 17(4), regulation 20(1)(c) or (e)(iii) or regulations under section 30, 33 or 31(7); or
   (b) without having had due regard to the response to that consultation; or
   (c) without having undertaken that consultation in a manner which is fair and consistent with guidance as to the matter of such consultation.

3 The authority's proposals
   (a) do not comply with the requirements of subsections (3) and (6) of section 25 or, as the case may be, regulation 17(1)(a) or (b) and (5) or regulation 20(1)(a) and (b), (e)(i) and (ii) and (2) or any comparable provision of regulations under sections 30 and 33;
   (b) do not comply with the requirements specified in regulations under section 31(7) of the Act; or
   (c) are unsatisfactory in any other respect.

4 The interval between any consecutive actions proposed in the timetable with respect to the implementation of the authority's proposals included in proposals drawn up under section 25, or, as the case may be, regulation 17(3)(a), regulation 19(1)(c) or regulations under section 30, 33 or 31(7)
   (a) is unreasonably long; or
   (b) contravenes any requirement imposed by or under Part II of the Act.

5 The authority has failed to implement its proposals in accordance with the timetable included in those proposals.

6 The authority has failed to comply with any directions given by the National Assembly for Wales for the purposes of Part II of the Act.

Part II

Circumstances Relating to Fall-Back Proposals

7 The authority has not drawn up outline fallback proposals under section 27(1)(b) or, as the case may be, regulation 17(3)(b) or regulation 19(1)(d), and is unlikely to do so unless the National Assembly for Wales so directs.

8 The authority has drawn up outline fallback proposals
   (a) without having taken reasonable steps to undertake the consultation required by section 27(3) or, as the case may be, regulation 17(4) or regulation 20(3)(a);
   (b) without having undertaken that consultation in a manner which is fair and consistent with guidance as to the manner of such consultation; or
   (c) without having had due regard to the response to that consultation;

9 The interval between any consecutive actions proposed in the timetable with respect to the implementation of the authority's outline fallback proposals in the event that the referendum rejects the proposals drawn up under section 25 or, as the case may be, regulation 17(3)(a) or regulation 19(1)(c), is unreasonably long.

10 The authority's outline fallback proposals
    (a) do not comply with the requirements of subsections (4) and (10) of section 27 or, as the case may be, regulation 17(7)(a) or regulation 20(3)(a)(ii); or
    (b) are unsatisfactory in any other respect.

11 The authority has failed to comply with any directions given by the National Assembly for Wales for the purposes of Part II of the Act.

Local Elections (Declaration of Acceptance of Office) Order 2012 (SI 2012/1465)

Made 6th June 2012

1 Citation, commencement and application
2 Form of declaration of acceptance of office
3 Revocation of order

Citation, commencement and application

1(1) This Order may be cited as the Local Elections (Declaration of Acceptance of Office) Order 2012 and comes into force on 9th July 2012.

(2) This Order applies in relation to England only.

Form of declaration of acceptance of office

2 For the purposes of section 83(1) and (4) of the Local Government Act 1972, the prescribed form of the declaration of acceptance of office is as set out in the Schedule to this Order.

Revocation of order

3 The Local Elections (Declaration of Acceptance of Office) Order 2001 is revoked.

SCHEDULE
DECLARATION OF ACCEPTANCE OF OFFICE

I [**(1)**] having been elected to the office of [**(2)**] of [**(3)**] declare that I take that office upon myself, and will duly and faithfully fulfil the duties of it according to the best of my judgment and ability.
Signed
Date
This declaration was made and signed before me,
Signed
Date
Proper officer of the council **(4)**.

(1) *Insert the name of the person making the declaration.*
(2) *Insert "member" or "Mayor" as appropriate.*
(3) *Insert the name of the authority of which the person making the declaration is a member or mayor.*
(4) *Where the declaration is made before another person authorised by section 83(3) of the Local Government Act 1972, state instead the capacity in which that person takes the declaration(a).*

(a) Under section 83(3) of the Local Government Act 1972, a declaration for members or elected mayors of a county, district or London borough council shall be made before two members of the council, its elected mayor, its proper officer, a justice of the peace or magistrate in the United Kingdom, the Channel Isles or the Isle of Man, or a commissioner appointed to administer oaths in the Supreme Court. A declaration for members of parish councils shall be made before a member or the proper officer of the council.

Local Elections (Declaration of Acceptance of Office) (Wales) Order 2004 (SI 2004/1508)

Made 15 June 2004

1   Name, commencement and application
2   Interpretation
3   Form of declaration of acceptance of office
4   Revocation of orders
Schedules

Name, commencement and application

1(1)   This Order may be called the Local Elections (Declaration of Acceptance of Office) (Wales) Order 2004, and shall come into force on 1 September 2004.

(2)   This Order applies to each authority in Wales.

Interpretation

2   In this Order
"authority" ("*awdurdod*") means
(a)   a county council,
(b)   a county borough council, and
(c)   a community council.

Form of declaration of acceptance of office

3   Where an authority has adopted the mandatory provisions of a model code of conduct made under section 50(2) of the Local Government Act 2000 that is applicable to that council, or the mandatory provisions of such a code apply to the members of that council pursuant to section 51(5)(b) of that Act, the declaration of acceptance of office of
(a)   a member; and
(b)   an elected mayor,
shall be either in the English form set out in Schedule 1 to this Order or the Welsh form set out in Schedule 2, or a form to the like effect.

Revocation of orders

4   The following orders shall be revoked on 1 September 2004
(a)   the Local Elections (Principal Areas) (Declaration of Acceptance of Office) Order 1990;
(b)   the Local Elections (Parishes and Communities) (Declaration of Acceptance of Office) Order 1990;
(c)   the Local Elections (Declaration of Acceptance of Office) (Welsh Forms) Order 1991; and
(d)   the Local Elections (Declaration of Acceptance of Office) (Amendment) (Wales) Order 2001.

SCHEDULE 1
DECLARATION OF ACCEPTANCE OF OFFICE

I [**(1)**] having been elected to the office of [**(2)**] of [**(3)**] declare that I take that office upon myself, and will duly and faithfully fulfil the duties of it according to the best of my judgement and ability.

I undertake to observe the code for the time being as to the conduct which is expected of members of [**(4)**] and which may be revised from time to time.
Signed ; Date ;
This declaration was made and signed before me,
Signed
Proper officer of the council **(5)**.

(1)   *Insert the name of the person making the declaration.*
(2)   *Insert "member" or "Mayor" as appropriate.*
(3) and (4)   *Insert the name of the authority of which the person making the declaration is a member or mayor.*
(5)   *Where the declaration is made before another person authorised by section 83(3) or (4) of the Local Government Act 1972, state instead the capacity in which that person takes the declaration.*

SCHEDULE 2
DATGANIAD DERBYN SWYDD

Yr wyf i [**(1)**], a minnau wedi fy ethol i swydd [**(2)**] [**(3)**], yn datgan fy mod yn cymryd arnaf fy hun y swydd honno, ac y byddaf yn cyflawni dyletswyddau'r swydd yn briodol ac yn ffyddlon hyd eithaf fy marn a'm gallu.
Yr wyf yn ymrwymo i barchu'r cod ymddygiad a ddisgwylir oddi wrth aelodau ac sy'n bodoli am y tro ac a allai gael ei adolygu o dro i dro [**(4)**].
Llofnodwyd ; Dyddiad ;
Cafodd y datganiad hwn ei wneud a'i lofnodi ger fy mron,
Llofnodwyd:
Swyddog priodol y cyngor **(5)**.

(1)   *Mewnosoder enw'r person sy'n gwneud y datganiad.*
(2)   *Mewnosoder "aelod" neu "Maer" fel y bo'n briodol.*
(3) a (4)   *Mewnosoder enw'r awdurdod y mae'r person sy'n gwneud y datganiad yn aelod ohono neu'n faer yr awdurdod.*
(5)   *Pan wneir y datganiad gerbron person arall a awdurdodwyd gan adran 83(3) neu (4) o Ddeddf Llywodraeth Leol 1972, dylid datgan, yn lle hynny, yn rhinwedd pa swydd y mae'r person hwnnw'n derbyn y datganiad.*

Local Elections (Parishes and Communities) (England and Wales) Rules 2006 (SI 2006/3305)

12th December 2006

1 Citation, commencement, extent and revocations
2 Interpretation
3 Elections Rules
4 Combination of polls
5 Filling of casual vacancies
6 Modification of the 1983 Act
7 Form of declaration
Schedules

Citation, commencement, extent and revocations

1 (1) These Rules may be cited as The Local Elections (Parishes and Communities) (England and Wales) Rules 2006.

(2) These Rules come into force on 2 January 2007 except for the purposes of an election if the last date for the publication of the notice of election for that election was, or will be, prior to 27 March 2007.

(3) These Rules do not extend to Scotland or Northern Ireland.

(4) Subject to paragraph (2), the Rules specified in Schedule 1 to these Rules are revoked.

Interpretation

2 (1) In these Rules,

"1983 Act" means the Representation of the People Act 1983;

"the Combination of Polls Regulations" means the Representation of the People (Combination of Polls) (England and Wales) Regulations 2004;

"counting observer" shall have the same meaning as in regulation 2(1) of the Local Authorities (Conduct of Referendums) (England) Regulations 2012];

"counting officer" shall have the same meaning as in regulation 2(1) of the Local Authorities (Conduct of Referendums) (England) Regulations 2012];

"European Parliamentary election" shall have the same meaning as in section 27(1) of the Representation of the People Act 1985;

"local counting area" shall have the same meaning as in regulation 2(1) of the European Parliamentary Elections Regulations 2004;

"mayoral election" means an election conducted under the Local Authorities (Mayoral Elections) (England and Wales) Regulations 2007];

"petition organiser" shall have the same meaning as in regulation 3 of the Local Authorities (Referendums) (Petitions and Directions) (England) Regulations 2000;

"police and crime commissioner election" means an election of a police and crime commissioner in accordance with Chapter 6 of Part 1 of the 2011 Act;]

"polling observer" shall have the same meaning as in regulation 2(1) of the Local Authorities (Conduct of Referendums) (England) Regulations 2012];

"principal area" means, in England, a county or district and, in Wales, a county or county borough;

"referendum" means a referendum conducted under the Local Authorities (Conduct of Referendums) (England) Regulations 2012];

"voting area" shall have the same meaning as in regulation 2 of the Local Authorities (Conduct of Referendums) (England) Regulations 2012.

(2) In these Rules, "relevant election or referendum" means one or more of the following--
    (a) a Parliamentary election;
    (b) a European Parliamentary election;
    (c) another local government election;
    (d) a mayoral election; and
    (e) a referendum,
    (f) a police and crime commissioner election,
the poll at which is taken together with the poll at the parish or community election.

(3) In the case of a referendum, a reference to--
    (a) a "candidate" shall be construed as a reference to a petition organiser;
    (b) an "election agent" or a "counting agent" shall be construed as a reference to a counting observer;
    (c) a "polling agent" shall be construed as a reference to a polling observer; and
    (d) a "returning officer" shall be construed as a reference to a counting officer.

(4) Any reference in these Rules to a district shall be construed as a reference to a county in the case of a county in which there are no district councils.

Elections Rules

3   In the application of the parliamentary elections rules to the election of councillors of the council of a parish or community where the poll at that election is not taken together with the poll at another election under section 36(3), (3AB) or (3AC) of the 1983 Act or section 15(1) or (2) of the Representation of the People Act 1985, adaptations, alterations and exceptions shall be made to those rules so that the election shall be conducted in accordance with the Rules set out in Schedule 2 to these Rules.

Combination of polls

4   Where the poll at an election of councillors to the council of a parish or community is to be taken together with the poll at a relevant election or referendum, the Rules set out in Schedule 2 shall apply to the parish or community election as shown modified in Schedule 3.

Filling of casual vacancies

5 (1) A request may be made in accordance with paragraph (2) for an election to fill a casual vacancy in the office of a parish or community councillor.

(2) Any request must be made--
    (a) to the proper officer of the council of the district in which the parish is situate or the county or county borough in which the community is situate,
    (b) by 10 persons who are named on the register in use at the time of the request as local government electors for the electoral area in which the vacancy has occurred, and
    (c) within 14 days (computed in accordance with rule 2 of the elections rules in Schedule 2 to these Rules) after public notice of the vacancy has been given in accordance with section 87(2) of the Local Government Act 1972.

(3) An election must be held, if requested in accordance with paragraph (2), if the casual

vacancy in the office of the parish or community councillor occurs other than within six months before the day on which that councillor would regularly have retired.

(4) Where a casual vacancy in any such office is required to be filled by election, the election must be held on a day appointed by the returning officer, being a day falling within the period of 60 days (so computed) beginning with the day on which public notice of the vacancy was given.

(5) Subject to paragraph (6) below, where a casual vacancy in any such office is not required to be filled by election, the parish or community council must, as soon as practicable after the expiry of the period of 14 days referred to in paragraph (2)(c), co-opt a person to fill the vacancy.

(6) In the case of a casual vacancy occurring in the office of a parish or community councillor within six months before the day on which that councillor would regularly have retired, paragraph (5) shall have effect with the substitution of the word "may" for "must"; and any vacancy not so filled must be filled at the next ordinary election.

Modification of the 1983 Act

6 In the application of those provisions of the 1983 Act referred to in section 187(1) of that Act to an election of parish or community councillors or an election of the chairman of a parish or community council the following modifications shall have effect--

    (a) for any reference to the proper officer of the authority there shall be substituted a reference to the returning officer, and

    (b) in section 136(2)(b) of that Act for the words "£2,500" there shall be substituted "£1,500".

Form of declaration

7 A declaration as to election expenses at an election of parish or community councillors must be in the form in Schedule 4 to these Rules, or a form to the like effect.

SCHEDULE 1
Revocations

Not reproduced

SCHEDULE 2

**RULES FOR CONDUCT OF AN ELECTION OF COUNCILLORS OF
A PARISH OR COMMUNITY WHERE POLL IS NOT TAKEN
TOGETHER WITH POLL AT ANOTHER ELECTION**

Part 1
Provisions as to Time

Timetable

1   The proceedings at the election shall be conducted in accordance with the following Table.

Timetable

Proceedings	Time
Publication of notice of election	Not later than the twenty-fifth day before the day of election.
Delivery of nomination papers	Not later than 4 in the afternoon on the nineteenth day before the day of election
Publication of statement as to persons nominated	Not later than 4 in the afternoon on the eighteenth day before the day of election
Delivery of notices of withdrawals of candidature	Not later than 4 in the afternoon on the nineteenth day before the day of election
Notice of poll	Not later than the sixth day before the day of election.
Polling	Between the hours of 7 in the morning and 10 at night on the day of election.

Computation of time

2(1)   In computing any period of time for the purposes of the Timetable—

     (a)   a Saturday or Sunday,

     (b)   Christmas Eve, Christmas Day, Good Friday or a bank holiday, or

     (c)   a day appointed for public thanksgiving or mourning,

shall be disregarded, and any such day shall not be treated as a day for the purpose of any proceedings up to the completion of the poll nor shall the returning officer be obliged to proceed with the counting of the votes on such a day.

  (2)   In this rule "bank holiday" means a day which is a bank holiday under the Banking and Financial Dealings Act 1971 in England and Wales.

Part 2
Stages Common to Contested and Uncontested Elections

Notice of election

3(1) The returning officer must publish notice of the election stating—
    (a) the place and times at which nomination papers are to be delivered, and
    (b) the date of the poll in the event of a contest,
and the notice must state that forms of nomination papers may be obtained at that place and those times.

  (2) The notice of election must state the date by which—
    (a) applications to vote by post or by proxy, and
    (b) other applications and notices about postal or proxy voting,
must reach the registration officer in order that they may be effective for the election.

Nomination of candidates

4(1) Each candidate must be nominated by a separate nomination paper, in the form in the Appendix, delivered at the place fixed for the purpose by the returning officer.

  (2) The nomination paper must state the candidate's—
    (a) full names,
    (b) home address in full, and
    (c) if desired, description,
and the surname must be placed first in the list of names.

  (3) If a candidate commonly uses—
    (a) a surname which is different from any other surname he has, or
    (b) a forename which is different from any other forename he has,
the nomination paper may state the commonly used surname or forename in addition to the other name.

  (4) The description, if any, must not exceed 6 words in length, and need not refer to his rank, profession or calling so long as, with the candidate's other particulars, it is sufficient to identify him.

Nomination papers: name of registered political party

5(1) A nomination paper may not include a description of a candidate which is likely to lead electors to associate the candidate with a registered political party unless the party is a qualifying party in relation to the electoral area and the description is authorised by a certificate—
    (a) issued by or on behalf of the registered nominating officer of the party, and
    (b) received by the returning officer before the last time for the delivery of nomination papers set out in the Table in rule 1.

  (2) In paragraph (1) an authorised description may be either—
    (a) the name of the party registered under section 28 of the Political Parties, Elections and Referendums Act 2000 , or
    (b) a description of the party registered under section 28A of that Act.

  (3) A nomination paper may not include a description of a candidate which is likely to lead electors to associate the candidate with two or more registered political parties unless the parties are each qualifying parties in relation to the electoral area and the description is a registered description authorised by a certificate—
    (a) issued by or on behalf of the registered nominating officer of each of the parties, and
    (b) received by the returning officer before the last time for the delivery of nomination papers set out in the Table in rule 1.

  (4) For the purposes of paragraph (3), a description is a registered description if it is a description registered for use by the parties under section 28B of the Political Parties,

Elections and Referendums Act 2000 .

(5) A person shall be guilty of a corrupt practice if he fraudulently purports to be authorised to issue a certificate under paragraph (1) or (3) on behalf of a registered political party's nominating officer.

(6) For the purposes of the application of this rule in relation to an election—

    (a) "registered political party" means a party which was registered under Part 2 of the Political Parties, Elections and Referendums Act 2000 on the day ("the relevant day") which is two days before the last day for the delivery of nomination papers at that election;

    (b) a registered political party is a qualifying party in relation to an electoral area if the electoral area is in England or Wales and the party was on the relevant day registered in respect of that part of Great Britain in the Great Britain register maintained under that Part of that Act.

(7) For the purposes of paragraph (6)(a) of this rule, any day falling within rule 2(1) must be disregarded.

Subscription of nomination paper

6(1) The nomination paper must be subscribed by two electors as proposer and seconder.

(2) Where a nomination paper has the signatures of more than the required number of persons as proposing or seconding the nomination of a candidate, the signature appearing first on the paper in each category must be taken into account to the exclusion of any others in that category.

(3) The nomination paper must give the electoral number of each person subscribing it.

(4) The returning officer—

    (a) must supply any elector with as many forms of nomination paper and forms of consent to nomination as may be required at the place and during the time for delivery of nomination papers, and

    (b) must at any elector's request prepare a nomination paper for signature,

but it is not necessary for a nomination or consent to nomination to be on a form supplied by the returning officer.

(5) A person must not subscribe more nomination papers than there are vacancies to be filled in the electoral area; nor subscribe any nomination paper in respect of an election in any other ward of the same parish or community whilst the election in the first-mentioned ward is taking place:

Provided that a person shall not be prevented from subscribing a nomination paper by reason only of his having subscribed that of a candidate who has died or withdrawn before delivery of the first-mentioned paper.

(6) If a person subscribes any nomination paper in contravention of paragraph (5), his signature shall be inoperative on all but those papers (up to the permitted number) which are first delivered.

(7) In this rule "elector"—

    (a) means a person who is registered in the register of local government electors for the electoral area in question on the last day for the publication of notice of the election, and

    (b) includes a person then shown in the register as below voting age if (but only if) it appears from the register that he will be of voting age on the day fixed for the poll.

(8) But, in this rule, "elector" does not include a person who has an anonymous entry in the register.

Consent to nomination

7   A person shall not be validly nominated unless his consent to nomination—
- (a)   is given in writing on or within one month before the last day for the delivery of nomination papers,
- (b)   is in the appropriate form in the Appendix or a form to the like effect and includes—
  - (i)   for a nomination in England, a copy of sections 80 and 81 of the Local Government Act 1972, section 78A of the Local Government Act 2000 and section 34 of the Localism Act 2011; or
  - (ii)   for a nomination in Wales, a copy of sections 80 and 81 of the Local Government Act 1972 and sections 78A and 79 of the Local Government Act 2000.
- (c)   is attested by one witness, and
- (d)   is delivered at the place and within the time for the delivery of nomination papers.

Decisions as to validity of nomination papers

8(1)   Where a nomination paper and the candidate's consent to it are delivered in accordance with these Rules, the candidate shall be deemed to stand nominated unless and until—
- (a)   the returning officer decides that the nomination paper is invalid; or
- (b)   proof is given to the returning officer's satisfaction of the candidate's death; or
- (c)   the candidate withdraws.

(2)   The returning officer is entitled to hold a nomination paper invalid only on one of the following grounds—
- (a)   that the particulars of the candidate or the persons subscribing the paper are not as required by law; and
- (b)   that the paper is not subscribed as so required.

(3)   Subject to paragraph (4), the returning officer must, as soon as practicable after each nomination paper has been delivered, examine it and decide whether the candidate has been validly nominated.

(4)   If in the returning officer's opinion a nomination paper breaks rule 5(1) or (3), he must give a decision to that effect—
- (a)   as soon as practicable after the delivery of the nomination paper, and
- (b)   in any event before the end of the period of 24 hours starting with the close of the period for delivery of nomination papers set out in the Table in rule 1.

(5)   Where the returning officer decides that a nomination paper is invalid, he must endorse and sign on the paper the fact and the reasons for his decision.

(6)   The returning officer must send notice of his decision that a nomination paper is valid or invalid to each candidate at his home address as given in his nomination paper.

(7)   The returning officer's decision that a nomination paper is valid shall be final and shall not be questioned in any proceeding whatsoever.

(8)   Subject to paragraph (7), nothing in this rule prevents the validity of a nomination being questioned on an election petition.

Publication of statement of persons nominated

9(1)   The returning officer must prepare and publish a statement showing the persons who have been and stand nominated and any other persons who have been nominated, with the reason why they no longer stand nominated.

(2)   The statement must show the names, addresses and descriptions of the persons nominated as given in their nomination papers.

(3)   If a person's nomination paper gives a commonly used surname or forename in addition to another name, the statement must show the person's commonly used surname or forename (as the case may be) instead of any other name.

(4)   Paragraph (3) does not apply if the returning officer thinks—
   (a)   that the use of the person's commonly used name may be likely to mislead or confuse electors, or
   (b)   that the commonly used name is obscene or offensive.

(5)   If paragraph (4) applies, the returning officer must give notice in writing to the candidate of his reasons for refusing to allow the use of a commonly used name.

(6)   The statement must show the persons standing nominated arranged alphabetically in the order of their surnames, and if there are two or more of them with the same surname, of their other names.

(7)   In the case of a person nominated by more than one nomination paper, the returning officer must take the particulars required by the foregoing provisions of this rule from such one of the papers as the candidate (or the returning officer in default of the candidate) may select.

Correction of minor errors

10(1)   A returning officer may, if he thinks fit, at any time before the publication under rule 9 of the statement of persons nominated, correct minor errors in a nomination paper.

(2)   Errors which may be corrected include—
   (a)   errors as to a person's electoral number;
   (b)   obvious errors of spelling in relation to the details of a candidate.

(3)   Anything done by a returning officer in pursuance of this rule shall not be questioned in any proceedings other than proceedings on an election petition.

(4)   A returning officer must have regard to any guidance issued by the Electoral Commission for the purposes of this rule.

Inspection of nomination papers and consents to nomination

11   During ordinary office hours on any day, other than a day specified in rule 2(1), after the latest time for delivery of nomination papers and before the date of the poll, any person may inspect and take copies of, or extracts from, nomination papers and consents to nomination.

Nomination in more than one ward

12   A candidate who is validly nominated for more than one ward of the same parish or community must withdraw from his candidature in all those wards except one, and if he does not so withdraw, he shall be deemed to have withdrawn from his candidature in all those wards.

Withdrawal of candidates

13(1)   A candidate may withdraw his candidature by notice of withdrawal—
   (a)   signed by him and attested by one witness, and
   (b)   delivered to the returning officer at the place for delivery of nomination papers.

(2)   Where a candidate is outside the United Kingdom, a notice of withdrawal signed by his proposer and accompanied by a written declaration also so signed of the candidate's

absence from the United Kingdom shall be of the same effect as a notice of withdrawal signed by the candidate; but where the candidate stands nominated by more than one nomination paper a notice of withdrawal under this paragraph shall be effective if, and only if—

    (a) it and the accompanying declaration are signed by all the proposers except any who is, and is stated in that declaration to be, outside the United Kingdom; or

    (b) it is accompanied, in addition to that declaration, by a written statement signed by the candidate that the proposer giving the notice is authorised to do so on the candidate's behalf during his absence from the United Kingdom.

Method of election

14(1) If the number of persons remaining validly nominated for the electoral area after any withdrawals under these Rules exceeds the number of councillors to be elected, a poll must be taken in accordance with Part 3 of these Rules.

  (2) If the number of persons remaining validly nominated for the electoral area after any withdrawals under these Rules does not exceed the number of councillors to be elected, such person or persons must be declared to be elected in accordance with Part 4 of these Rules.

Part 3
Contested Elections

Chapter 1
General Provisions

Poll to be taken by ballot

15 The votes at the poll must be given by ballot, the result must be ascertained by counting the votes given to each candidate and the candidate or candidates to whom more votes have been given than to the other candidates, up to the number of councillors to be elected, must be declared to have been elected.

The ballot papers

16(1) The ballot of every voter must consist of a ballot paper, and the persons remaining validly nominated for the electoral area after any withdrawals under these Rules, and no others, shall be entitled to have their names inserted in the ballot paper.

  (2) Every ballot paper must be in the form in the Appendix, and must be printed in accordance with the directions in that Appendix, and—

    (a) must contain the names and other particulars of the candidates as shown in the statement of persons nominated;

    (b) must be capable of being folded up; and

    (c) must have a number and other unique identifying mark printed on the back.

  (3) If a candidate who is the subject of a party's authorisation under rule 5(1) so requests, the ballot paper must contain, against the candidate's particulars, the party's registered emblem (or, as the case may be, one of the party's registered emblems).

  (3A) If a candidate who is the subject of an authorisation by two or more parties under rule 5(3) so requests, the ballot paper must contain, against the candidate's particulars, the registered emblem (or, as the case may be, one of the registered emblems) of one of those parties.

  (4) The candidate's request under paragraph (3) or (3A) must—

    (a) be made in writing to the returning officer, and

(b)   be received by him before the last time for the delivery of nomination papers set out in the Table in rule 1.

(5)   The order of the names in the ballot paper must be the same as in the statement of persons nominated.

The corresponding number list

17(1)   The returning officer must prepare a list containing the numbers and other unique identifying marks of all of the ballot papers to be issued by him in pursuance of rule 22(1) or provided by him in pursuance of rule 26(1).

(2)   The list must be in the appropriate form in the Appendix or a form to like effect.

The official mark

18(1)   Every ballot paper must contain an appropriate security marking (the official mark).

(2)   The official mark must be kept secret, and an interval of not less than five years shall intervene between the use of the same official mark at elections for the same parish or community.

(3)   The returning officer may use a different official mark for different purposes at the same election.

Prohibition of disclosure of vote

19   No person who has voted at the election shall, in any legal proceeding to question the election, be required to state for whom he has voted.

Use of schools and public rooms

20(1)   The returning officer may use, free of charge, for the purpose of taking the poll or counting the votes—

(a)   a room in a school maintained or assisted by a local authority (within the meaning of the Education Act 1996) or a school in respect of which grants are made out of moneys provided by Parliament to the person or body of persons responsible for the management of the school;

(b)   a room the expense of maintaining which is payable out of any rate.

(2)   The returning officer must make good any damage done to, and defray any expense incurred by the persons having control over, any such room as mentioned above by reason of its being used for the purpose of taking the poll or counting the votes.

Chapter 2
Action to be Taken Before the Poll

Notice of poll

21(1)   The returning officer must publish notice of the poll stating—

(a)   the day and hours fixed for the poll;

(b)   the number of councillors to be elected;

(c)   the particulars of each candidate remaining validly nominated (the names and other particulars of the candidates, and the order of the candidates' names being the same as in the statement of persons nominated); and

(d)   the names of the proposer and seconder signing a candidate's nomination paper.

(2)   Where a candidate is nominated by more than one nomination paper, the nomination paper referred to in paragraph (1)(d) must be that from which the names and other particulars of the candidate shown in the statement of persons nominated are taken.

(3) The returning officer must, not later than the time of the publication of the notice of the poll, also give public notice of—
   (a) the situation of each polling station; and
   (b) the description of voters entitled to vote there,
   and he must as soon as practicable after giving such a notice give a copy of it to each of the election agents (if appointed).

Postal ballot papers

22(1) The returning officer must, in accordance with regulations made under the 1983 Act, issue to those entitled to vote by post a ballot paper and a postal voting statement in the appropriate form in the Appendix, or a form to like effect together with such envelopes for their return as may be prescribed by such regulations.

(2) The returning officer must also issue to those entitled to vote by post such information as he thinks appropriate about how to obtain—
   (a) translations into languages other than English of any directions to or guidance for voters sent with the ballot paper;
   (b) a translation into Braille of such directions or guidance;
   (c) graphical representations of such directions or guidance;
   (d) the directions or guidance in any other form (including any audible form).

(3) The postal voting statement must include provision for the form to be signed and for stating the date of birth of the elector or proxy (as the case may be).

(4) In the case of a ballot paper issued to a person at an address in the United Kingdom, the returning officer must ensure that the return of the ballot paper and postal voting statement is free of charge to the voter.

Provision of polling stations

23(1) The returning officer must provide a sufficient number of polling stations and, subject to the following provisions of this rule, must allot the electors to the polling stations in such manner as he thinks most convenient.

(2) One or more polling stations may be provided in the same room.

(3) The polling station allotted to electors from any parliamentary polling district wholly or partly within the electoral area must, in the absence of special circumstances, be in the parliamentary polling place for that district, unless that place is outside the electoral area.

(4) The returning officer must provide each polling station with such number of compartments as may be necessary in which the voters can mark their votes screened from observation.

Appointment of presiding officers and polling clerks

24(1) The returning officer must appoint and pay a presiding officer to attend at each polling station and such clerks as may be necessary for the purposes of the election, but he must not appoint any person who has been employed by or on behalf of a candidate in or about the election.

(2) The returning officer may, if he thinks fit, preside at a polling station and the provisions of these Rules relating to a presiding officer shall apply to a returning officer so presiding with the necessary modifications as to things to be done by the returning officer to the presiding officer or by the presiding officer to the returning officer.

(3) A presiding officer may do, by the clerks appointed to assist him, any act (including the asking of questions) which he is required or authorised by these Rules to do at a

polling station except order the arrest, exclusion or removal of any person from the polling station.

Issue of official poll cards

25(1)   Where the poll at a parish or community election is not to be taken together with the poll at some other election, the council of the parish or community may, not later than 4 in the afternoon on the nineteenth day before the day of election, request the returning officer to issue official poll cards for that election.

(2)   Where the returning officer receives a request under paragraph (1) he must as soon as practicable send to electors and their proxies an official poll card.

(3)   An elector's official poll card must be sent or delivered to his qualifying address, and a proxy's to his address as shown in the list of proxies.

(4)   The official poll card must be in the appropriate form in the Appendix, or a form to the like effect, and must set out—
    (a)   the name of the council and, where appropriate, of the ward to which councillors are to be elected;
    (b)   the elector's name, qualifying address and number on the register;
    (c)   the date and hours of the poll and the situation of the elector's polling station;
    (d)   such other information as the returning officer thinks appropriate,
and different information may be provided in pursuance of sub-paragraph (d) to different electors or descriptions of elector.

(5)   In the case of an elector with an anonymous entry—
    (a)   the returning officer must issue an official poll card in the appropriate form in the Appendix to every such elector or to his proxy (if appointed) whether or not the local council of the parish or community make the request mentioned in paragraph (1);
    (b)   instead of containing the elector's name and qualifying address, the polling card must contain the elector's number on the register and such other matter as is specified in the appropriate form in the Appendix; and
    (c)   the official poll card must be sent in an envelope or other form of covering so as not to disclose that the elector has an anonymous entry in the register.

(6)   Paragraph (7) of rule 6 shall apply for the interpretation of this rule.

Equipment of polling stations

26(1)   The returning officer must provide each presiding officer with such number of ballot boxes and ballot papers as in the returning officer's opinion may be necessary.

(2)   Every ballot box must be so constructed that the ballot papers can be put in it, but cannot be withdrawn from it, without the box being unlocked or, where the box has no lock, the seal being broken.

(3)   The returning officer must provide each polling station with—
    (a)   materials to enable voters to mark the ballot papers;
    (b)   copies of the register of electors for the electoral area or such part of it as contains the names of the electors allotted to the station;
    (c)   the parts of any special lists prepared for the election corresponding to the register of electors for the electoral area or the part of it provided under sub-paragraph (b);
    (d)   a list consisting of that part of the list prepared under rule 17 which contains the numbers (but not the other unique identifying marks) corresponding to those on the ballot papers provided to the presiding officer of the polling station.

(4)   The reference in paragraph (3)(b) to the copies of the register of electors includes a

reference to copies of any notices issued under section 13B(3B) or (3D) of the 1983 Act in respect of alterations to the register.

(5) The returning officer must also provide each polling station with—

    (a) at least one large version of the ballot paper which must be displayed inside the polling station for the assistance of voters who are partially sighted; and

    (b) and a device of such description as is set out in paragraph (9) for enabling voters who are blind or partially sighted to vote without any need for assistance from the presiding officer or any companion (within the meaning of rule 37(1)).

(6) A notice in the form in the Appendix, giving directions for the guidance of voters in voting, must be printed in conspicuous characters and exhibited inside and outside every polling station.

(7) The returning officer may also provide copies of the notice mentioned in paragraph (6) in Braille or translated into languages other than English as he considers appropriate, provided that these notices are accurate reproductions in Braille or that other language of that notice.

(8) In every compartment of every polling station there must be exhibited the notice:

    "Vote for NO MORE THAN … CANDIDATES by putting a cross X in the box next to EACH of your choices.
    Vote ONLY ONCE by putting a cross X in the box next to your choice.
    PUT NO OTHER MARK ON THE BALLOT PAPER OR YOUR VOTE MAY NOT COUNT."

(9) The device referred to in paragraph (5)(b) must—

    (a) allow a ballot paper to be inserted into and removed from, or attached to and detached from, the device easily and without damage to the paper;

    (b) hold the ballot paper firmly in place during use; and

    (c) provide suitable means for the voter to—

        (i) identify the spaces on the ballot paper on which he may mark his vote;

        (ii) identify the candidate to which each such space refers; and

        (iii) mark his vote on the space he has chosen.

Appointment of polling agents and counting agents

27(1) Subject to paragraphs (3) and (4), each candidate may, before the commencement of the poll, appoint—

    (a) polling agents to attend at polling stations for the purpose of detecting personation; and

    (b) counting agents to attend at the counting of the votes.

(2) The same person may be appointed as a polling agent or counting agent by more than one candidate.

(3) Not more than four polling agents, or such greater number as the returning officer may by notice allow, shall be permitted to attend at any particular polling station and if the number of such agents appointed to attend at a particular polling station exceeds that number, the returning officer must determine which agents are permitted to attend by lot and only the agents on whom the lot falls shall be deemed to have been duly appointed.

(4) The returning officer may limit the number of counting agents, so however that—

    (a) the number must be the same in the case of each candidate; and

    (b) the number allowed to a candidate must not (except in special circumstances) be less than the number obtained by dividing the number of clerks employed on the counting by the number of candidates.

For the purposes of the calculations required by this paragraph, a counting agent who has been appointed for more than one candidate is a separate agent for each of the candidates by whom he has been appointed.

(5) Notice in writing of the appointment, stating the names and addresses of the persons appointed, must be given by the candidate to the returning officer and must be so given not later than the fifth day (disregarding any day referred to in rule 2(1)) before the day of the poll.

(6) If an agent dies, or becomes incapable of acting, the candidate may appoint another agent in his place, and must forthwith give to the returning officer notice in writing of the name and address of the agent appointed.

(7) In the following provisions of these Rules references to polling agents and counting agents shall be taken as references to agents—

    (a) whose appointments have been duly made and notified; and

    (b) where the number of agents is restricted, who are within the permitted numbers.

(8) Any notice required to be given to a counting agent by the returning officer may be delivered at, or sent by post to, the address stated in the notice of appointment.

(9) A candidate may himself do any act or thing which his polling or counting or election agent, if appointed, would have been authorised to do, or may assist his agent in doing any such act or thing.

(10) Where by these Rules any act or thing is required or authorised to be done in the presence of the polling or counting agents, the nonattendance of any agent or agents at the time and place appointed for the purpose shall not, if the act or thing is otherwise duly done, invalidate the act or thing done.

Notification of requirement of secrecy

(1) The returning officer must make such arrangements as he thinks fit to ensure that—

    (a) every person attending at a polling station (otherwise than for the purpose of voting or assisting a voter with disabilities to vote or as a constable on duty there) has been given a copy in writing of the provisions of subsections (1), (3) and (6) of section 66 of the 1983 Act; and

    (b) every person attending at the counting of the votes (other than any constable on duty at the counting) has been given a copy in writing of the provisions of subsections (2) and (6) of that section.

(2) In this rule, a reference to a constable includes a person designated as a community support officer under section 38 of the Police Reform Act 2002 (police powers for employees).

Return of postal ballot papers

29(1) Where—

    (a) a postal vote has been returned in respect of a person who is entered on the postal voters list, or

    (b) a proxy postal vote has been returned in respect of a proxy who is entered on the proxy postal voters list,

the returning officer must mark the list in the manner prescribed by regulations made under the 1983 Act.

(2) Rule 45(3) does not apply for the purpose of determining whether, for the purposes of this rule, a postal vote or a proxy postal vote is returned.

Chapter 3
The Poll

Admission to the polling station

30(1)   The presiding officer must exclude all persons from the polling station except—

    (a)   voters;

    (b)   persons under the age of 18 who accompany voters to the polling station;

    (c)   the candidates and their election agents (if appointed);

    (d)   the polling agents appointed to attend at the polling station;

    (e)   the clerks appointed to attend at the polling station;

    (f) persons who are entitled to attend by virtue of any of sections 6A to 6D of the Political Parties, Elections and Referendums Act 2000 ;

    (g) the constables on duty; and

    (h) the companions of voters with disabilities.

(2)   The presiding officer must regulate the total number of voters and persons under the age of 18 who accompany them to be admitted to the polling station at the same time.

(3)   Not more than one polling agent shall be admitted at the same time to a polling station on behalf of the same candidate.

(4)   A constable or person employed by a returning officer must not be admitted to vote in person elsewhere than at his own polling station allotted to him under these Rules, except on production and surrender of a certificate as to his employment which must be in the form in the Appendix or a form to the like effect, and signed by an officer of police of or above the rank of inspector or by the returning officer, as the case may be.

(5)   Any certificate surrendered under this rule must forthwith be cancelled.

(6)   In this rule, a reference to a constable includes a person designated as a community support officer under section 38 of the Police Reform Act 2002 (police powers for employees).

Keeping of order in station

31(1)   It is the presiding officer's duty to keep order at his polling station.

(2)   If a person misconducts himself in a polling station, or fails to obey the presiding officer's lawful orders, he may immediately, by the presiding officer's order, be removed from the polling station—

    (a)   by a constable in or near that station, or

    (b)   by any other person authorised in writing by the returning officer to remove him,

and the person so removed shall not, without the presiding officer's permission, again enter the polling station during the day.

(3)   Any person so removed may, if charged with the commission in the polling station of an offence, be dealt with as a person taken into custody by a constable for an offence without a warrant.

(4)   The powers conferred by this rule must not be exercised so as to prevent a voter who is otherwise entitled to vote at a polling station from having an opportunity of voting at that station.

Sealing of ballot boxes

32   Immediately before the commencement of the poll, the presiding officer must show the ballot box empty to such persons, if any, as are present in the polling station, so that they may see that it is empty, and must then lock it up if it has a lock and (in any case) place his seal on it in such a manner as to prevent its being opened without breaking the seal and must place it in his view for the receipt of ballot papers, and keep it so locked and sealed or sealed (as the case may be).

Questions to be put to voters

33(1) At the time of the application (but not afterwards), the questions specified in the second column of the following Table—

    (a) may be put by the presiding officer to a person applying for a ballot paper who is mentioned in the first column, and

    (b) must be put if the letter "R" appears after the question and the candidate or his election or polling agent requires the question to be put:

Q. No.	Person applying for ballot paper	Question
1	A person applying as an elector	(a)—Are you the person registered in the register of local government electors for this election as follows? read the whole entry from the register R (b)—Have you already voted at this election for *(this parish) *(this community), * delete whichever is inapplicable (adding, in the case of an election for several wards , in this or any other ward) otherwise than as proxy for some other person? R
2	A person applying as proxy	(a)—Are you the person whose name appears as A.B. in the list of proxies for this election as entitled to vote as proxy on behalf of C.D.? R (b)—Have you already voted at this election for *(this parish) *(this community), * delete whichever is inapplicable (adding in the case of an election for several wards , in this or any other ward) as proxy on behalf of C.D.? R (c)—Are you the spouse, civil partner, parent, grandparent, brother, sister, child or grandchild of C.D.? R
3	A person applying as proxy for an elector with an anonymous entry (instead of the questions at entry 2)	(a)—Are you the person entitled to vote as proxy on behalf of the elector whose number on the register of electors is (read out the number)? R (b)—Have you already voted as proxy on behalf of the elector whose number on the register of electors is (read out the number)? R

		(c)—Are you the spouse, civil partner, parent, grandparent, brother, sister, child or grandchild of the person whose number on the register of electors is (read out the number)? R
4	A person applying as proxy if the question at entry 2(c) or 3(c) is not answered in the affirmative	Have you already voted at this election in *(this parish) *(this community) * delete whichever is inapplicable (adding in the case of an election for several wards , in this or any other ward) on behalf of two persons of whom you are not the spouse, civil partner, parent, grandparent, brother, sister, child or grandchild? R
5	A person applying as an elector in relation to whom there is an entry in the postal voters list	(a)—Did you apply to vote by post? (b)—Why have you not voted by post?
6	A person applying as proxy who is named in the proxy postal voters list	(a)—Did you apply to vote by post as proxy? (b)—Why have you not voted by post as proxy?

(2) In the case of an elector in respect of whom a notice has been issued under section 13B(3B) or (3D) of the 1983 Act, the references in the questions at entries 1(a) and 3(a), (b) and (c) to reading from the register shall be taken as references to reading from the notice issued under section 13B(3B) or (3D) of the 1983 Act.

(3) A ballot paper must not be delivered to any person required to answer any of the above questions unless he has answered each question satisfactorily.

(4) Except as authorised by this rule, no inquiry shall be permitted as to the right of any person to vote.

Challenge of voter

34 A person must not be prevented from voting by reason only that—
   (a) a candidate or his polling agent declares that he has reasonable cause to believe that the person has committed an offence of personation, or
   (b) the person is arrested on the grounds that he is suspected of committing or of being about to commit such an offence.

Voting procedure

35(1) A ballot paper must be delivered to a voter who applies for one, and immediately before delivery—
   (a) the number and (unless paragraph (2) applies) name of the elector as stated in the copy of the register of electors must be called out;
   (b) the number of the elector must be marked on the list mentioned in rule 26(3)(d) beside the number of the ballot paper to be issued to him;

(c) a mark must be placed in the register of electors against the number of the elector to note that a ballot paper has been received but without showing the particular ballot paper which has been received;

(d) in the case of a person applying for a ballot paper as proxy, a mark must also be placed against his name in the list of proxies.

(2) In the case of an elector who has an anonymous entry, he must show the presiding officer his official poll card and only his number shall be called out in pursuance of paragraph (1)(a).

(3) In the case of an elector who is added to the register in pursuance of a notice issued under section 13B(3B) or (3D) of the 1983 Act, paragraph (1) is modified as follows—

(a) in sub-paragraph (a), for "copy of the register of electors" substitute "copy of the notice issued under section 13B(3B) or (3D) of the 1983 Act";

(b) in sub-paragraph (c), for "in the register of electors" substitute "on the copy of the notice issued under section 13B(3B) or (3D) of the 1983 Act".

(4) The voter, on receiving the ballot paper, must forthwith proceed into one of the compartments in the polling station and there secretly mark his paper and fold it up so as to conceal his vote, and must then show to the presiding officer the back of the paper, so as to disclose the number and other unique identifying mark, and put the ballot paper so folded up into the ballot box in the presiding officer's presence.

(5) The voter must vote without undue delay, and must leave the polling station as soon as he has put his ballot paper into the ballot box.

(6) A voter who at the close of the poll is in the polling station, or in a queue outside the polling station, for the purposes of voting shall (despite the close of the poll) be entitled to apply for a ballot paper under paragraph (1); and these rules apply in relation to such a voter accordingly.

Votes marked by presiding officer

36(1) The presiding officer, on the application of a voter—

(a) who is incapacitated by blindness or other disability from voting in the manner directed by these Rules, or

(b) who declares orally that he is unable to read,

must, in the presence of the polling agents, cause the voter's vote to be marked on a ballot paper in the manner directed by the voter, and the ballot paper to be placed in the ballot box.

(2) The name and number on the register of electors of every voter whose vote is marked in pursuance of this rule, and the reason why it is so marked, must be entered on a list (in these Rules called "the list of votes marked by the presiding officer").

In the case of a person voting as proxy for an elector, the number to be entered together with the voter's name shall be the elector's number.

(3) In the case of a person in respect of whom a notice has been issued under section 13B(3B) or (3D) of the 1983 Act, paragraph (2) applies as if for "on the register of electors of every voter" there were substituted "relating to every voter in respect of whom a notice has been issued under section 13B(3B) or (3D) of the 1983 Act".

Voting by persons with disabilities

37(1) If a voter makes an application to the presiding officer to be allowed on the ground of—

(a) blindness or other disability, or

(b) inability to read,

to vote with the assistance of another person by whom he is accompanied (in these

Rules referred to as "the companion"), the presiding officer must require the voter to declare, orally or in writing, whether he is so incapacitated by his blindness or other disability, or by his inability to read, as to be unable to vote without assistance.

(2) If the presiding officer—
    (a) is satisfied that the voter is so incapacitated, and
    (b) is also satisfied by a written declaration made by the companion (in these Rules referred to as "the declaration made by the companion of a voter with disabilities") that the companion—
        (i) is a qualified person within the meaning of this rule, and
        (ii) has not previously assisted more than one voter with disabilities to vote at the election,

the presiding officer must grant the application, and then anything which is by these Rules required to be done to or by that voter in connection with the giving of his vote may be done to, or with the assistance of, the companion.

(3) For the purposes of these Rules, a person is a voter with disabilities if he has made such a declaration as is mentioned in paragraph (1), and a person shall be qualified to assist a voter with disabilities to vote, if that person—
    (a) is a person who is entitled to vote as an elector at the election; or
    (b) is the father, mother, brother, sister, spouse, civil partner, son or daughter of the voter and has attained the age of 18 years.

(4) The name and number in the register of electors of every voter whose vote is given in accordance with this rule and the name and address of the companion must be entered on a list (in these Rules referred to as "the list of voters with disabilities assisted by companions").

In the case of a person voting as proxy for an elector, the number to be entered together with the voter's name shall be the elector's number.

(5) In the case of a person in respect of whom a notice has been issued under section 13B(3B) or (3D) of the 1983 Act, paragraph (4) applies as if for "in the register of electors of every voter" there were substituted "relating to every voter in respect of whom a notice has been issued under section 13B(3B) or (3D) of the 1983 Act".

(6) The declaration made by the companion—
    (a) must be in the form in the Appendix;
    (b) must be made before the presiding officer at the time when the voter applies to vote with the assistance of a companion; and
    (c) must forthwith be given to the presiding officer who must attest and retain it.

(7) No fee or other payment shall be charged in respect of the declaration.

Tendered ballot papers: circumstances where available

38(1) If a person, representing himself to be—
    (a) a particular elector named on the register and not named in the absent voters list, or
    (b) a particular person named in the list of proxies as proxy for an elector and not entitled to vote by post as proxy,

applies for a ballot paper after another person has voted in person either as the elector or his proxy, the applicant shall, on satisfactorily answering the questions permitted by law to be asked at the poll, be entitled, subject to the following provisions of this rule and rule 39, to mark a ballot paper (in these Rules referred to as "a tendered ballot paper") in the same manner as any other voter.

(2) Paragraph (4) applies if—
    (a) a person applies for a ballot paper representing himself to be a particular elector named on the register,

(b)   he is also named in the postal voters list, and

(c)   he claims that he did not make an application to vote by post at the election.

(3)   Paragraph (4) also applies if—

(a)   a person applies for a ballot paper representing himself to be a particular person named as a proxy in the list of proxies,

(b)   he is also named in the proxy postal voters list, and

(c)   he claims that he did not make an application to vote by post as proxy.

(4)   The person shall, on satisfactorily answering the questions permitted by law to be asked at the poll, be entitled, subject to the following provisions of this rule and rule 39, to mark a ballot paper (in these Rules referred to as a "tendered ballot paper") in the same manner as any other voter.

(5)   Paragraph (6) applies if before the close of the poll but after the last time at which a person may apply for a replacement postal ballot paper, a person represents himself to be—

(a)   a particular elector named on the register who is also named in the postal voters list, or

(b)   a particular person named as a proxy in the list of proxies and who is also named in the proxy postal voters list,

and claims that he has lost or has not received his postal ballot paper.

(6)   The person shall, on satisfactorily answering the questions permitted by law to be asked at the poll, be entitled, subject to the provisions of this rule and rule 39, to mark a ballot paper (in these Rules referred to as a "tendered ballot paper") in the same manner as any other voter.

Tendered ballot papers: general provisions

39(1)   A tendered ballot paper must—

(a)   be of a colour differing from the other ballot papers;

(b)   instead of being put into the ballot box, be given to the presiding officer and endorsed by him with the name of the voter and his number in the register of electors, and set aside in a separate packet.

(2)   The name of the voter and his number in the register of electors must be entered on a list (in these Rules referred to as the "tendered votes list".

(3)   In the case of a person voting as proxy for an elector, the number to be endorsed or entered together with the voter's name shall be the number of that elector.

(4)   In the case of an elector who has an anonymous entry, this rule and rule 38 apply subject to the following modifications—

(a)   in paragraphs (1)(b) and (2) of this rule, the references to the name of the voter shall be ignored;

(b)   otherwise, a reference to a person named on a register or list shall be construed as a reference to a person whose number appears on the register or list (as the case may be).

(5)   In the case of a person in respect of whom a notice has been issued under section 13B(3B) or (3D) of the 1983 Act, this rule and rule 38 shall apply as if—

(a)   in rule 38(1)(a), (2)(a) and (5)(a), for "named on the register" there were substituted "in respect of whom a notice under section 13B(3B) or (3D) of the 1983 Act has been issued";

(b)   in paragraph (1)(b) of this rule, for "his number in the register of electors" there were substituted "the number relating to him on a notice issued under section 13B(3B) or (3D) of the 1983 Act";

(c)   in paragraph (2) of this rule, for "his number in the register of electors" there were substituted "the number relating to him on a notice issued under section 13B(3B) or (3D) of the 1983 Act".

Spoilt ballot papers

40 A voter who has inadvertently dealt with his ballot paper in such manner that it cannot be conveniently used as a ballot paper may, on delivering it to the presiding officer and proving to his satisfaction the fact of the inadvertence, obtain another ballot paper in the place of the ballot paper so delivered (in these Rules referred to as "a spoilt ballot paper"), and the spoilt ballot paper must be immediately cancelled.

Correction of errors on day of poll

41 The presiding officer must keep a list of persons to whom ballot papers are delivered in consequence of an alteration to the register made by virtue of section 13B(3B) or (3D) of the 1983 Act which takes effect on the day of the poll.

Adjournment of poll in case of riot

42(1) Where the proceedings at any polling station are interrupted or obstructed by riot or open violence, the presiding officer must adjourn the proceedings till the following day and must forthwith give notice to the returning officer.

(2) Where the poll is adjourned at any polling station—
    (a) the hours of polling on the day to which it is adjourned must be the same as for the original day; and
    (b) references in these Rules to the close of the poll shall be construed accordingly.

Procedure on close of poll

43(1) As soon as practicable after the close of the poll, the presiding officer must, in the presence of the polling agents, make up into separate packets, sealed with his own seal and the seals of such polling agents as desire to affix their seals—
    (a) each ballot box in use at the station, sealed so as to prevent the introduction of additional ballot papers and unopened, but with the key, if any, attached,
    (b) the unused and spoilt ballot papers placed together,
    (c) the tendered ballot papers,
    (d) the marked copies of the register of electors (including any marked copy notices issued under section 13B(3B) or (3D) of the 1983 Act) and of the list of proxies,
    (e) the lists prepared under rule 17 including the parts which were completed in accordance with rule 35(1)(b) (together referred to in these Rules as "the completed corresponding number lists"),
    (f) the certificates as to employment on duty on the day of the poll,
    (g) the tendered votes list, the list of voters with disabilities assisted by companions, the list of votes marked by the presiding officer, a statement of the number of voters whose votes are so marked by the presiding officer under the heads "disability" and "unable to read", the list maintained under rule 41 (correction of errors on day of poll), and the declarations made by the companions of voters with disabilities,

and must deliver the packets or cause them to be delivered to the returning officer to be taken charge of by him; but if the packets are not delivered by the presiding officer personally to the returning officer, the arrangements for their delivery shall require the returning officer's approval.

(2) The marked copies of the register of electors and of the list of proxies must be in one packet but must not be in the same packet as the completed corresponding number lists or the certificates as to employment on duty on the day of the poll.

(3) The packets must be accompanied by a statement (in these Rules referred to as "the ballot paper account") made by the presiding officer showing the number of ballot papers entrusted to him, and accounting for them under the heads of ballot papers issued and not otherwise accounted for, unused, spoilt and tendered ballot papers.

Chapter 4
Counting of Votes

Attendance at counting of votes

44(1) The returning officer must make arrangements for counting the votes in the presence of the counting agents as soon as practicable after the close of the poll, and must give to the counting agents notice in writing of the time and place at which he will begin to count the votes.

(2) No person other than—
    (a) the returning officer and his clerks,
    (b) the candidates and one other person chosen by each of them,
    (c) the election agents (if appointed),
    (d) the counting agents,
    (e) persons who are entitled to attend by virtue of any of sections 6A to 6D of the Political Parties, Elections and Referendums Act 2000,
may be present at the counting of the votes, unless permitted by the returning officer to attend.

(3) A person not entitled to attend at the counting of the votes shall not be permitted to do so by the returning officer unless he—
    (a) is satisfied that the efficient counting of the votes will not be impeded; and
    (b) has either consulted the candidates or thought it impracticable to do so.

(4) The returning officer must give the counting agents all such reasonable facilities for overseeing the proceedings, and all such information with respect to them, as he can give them consistently with the orderly conduct of the proceedings and the discharge of his duties in connection with them.

(5) In particular, where the votes are counted by sorting the ballot papers according to the candidate for whom the vote is given and then counting the number of ballot papers for each candidate, the counting agents shall be entitled to satisfy themselves that the ballot papers are correctly sorted.

The count

45(1) The returning officer must—
    (a) in the presence of the counting agents open each ballot box and count and record the number of ballot papers in it;
    (b) in the presence of the counting agents verify each ballot paper account; and
    (c) count such of the postal ballot papers as have been duly returned and record the number counted.

(2) The returning officer must not count the votes given on any ballot papers until—
    (a) in the case of postal ballot papers, they have been mixed with the ballot papers from at least one ballot box, and
    (b) in the case of ballot papers from a ballot box, they have been mixed with the ballot papers from at least one other ballot box.

(3) A postal ballot paper must not be taken to be duly returned unless—
    (a) it is returned in the manner set out in paragraph (4) and reaches the returning officer or any polling station in the electoral area in question before the close of the poll;

    (b)   the postal voting statement, duly signed, is also returned in the manner set out in paragraph (4) and reaches him or such a polling station before that time;

    (c)   the postal voting statement also states the date of birth of the elector or proxy (as the case may be), and

    (d)   in a case where steps for verifying the date of birth and signature of the elector or proxy have been prescribed by regulations made under the 1983 Act ,

the returning officer (having taken such steps) verifies the date of birth and signature of the elector or proxy (as the case may be).

(4)   The manner in which any postal ballot paper or postal voting statement may be returned—

    (a)   to the returning officer, is by hand or by post;

    (b)   to a polling station, is by hand.

(4A)   A postal ballot paper or postal voting statement that reaches the returning officer or a polling station on or after the close of the poll is treated for the purposes of this rule as reaching that officer or polling station before the close of the poll if it is delivered by a person who, at the close of the poll, is in the polling station, or in a queue outside the polling station, for the purpose of returning it.

(5)   The returning officer must not count any tendered ballot paper.

(6)   The returning officer, while counting and recording the number of ballot papers and counting the votes, must keep the ballot papers with their faces upwards and take all proper precautions for preventing any person from seeing the numbers or other unique identifying marks printed on the back of the papers.

(7)   The returning officer must verify each ballot paper account by comparing it with the number of ballot papers recorded by him, and the unused and spoilt ballot papers in his possession and the tendered votes list (opening and re-sealing the packets containing the unused and spoilt ballot papers and the tendered votes list) and must draw up a statement as to the result of the verification, which any counting agent may copy.

(8)   The returning officer must so far as practicable proceed continuously with counting the votes, allowing only time for refreshment, except that he may exclude the hours between 7 in the evening and 9 on the following morning.

(9)   During the time so excluded the returning officer must—

    (a)   place the ballot papers and other documents relating to the election under his own seal and the seals of such of the counting agents as desire to affix their seals; and

    (b)   otherwise take proper precautions for the security of the papers and documents.

Recount

46(1)   A candidate may, if present when the counting or any recount of the votes is completed, require the returning officer to have the votes recounted or again recounted but the returning officer may refuse to do so if in his opinion the request is unreasonable.

(2)   No step shall be taken on the completion of the counting or any recount of votes until the candidates present at its completion have been given a reasonable opportunity to exercise the right conferred by this rule.

Rejected ballot papers

47(1)   Any ballot paper—

    (a)   which does not bear the official mark, or

      (b) on which votes are given for more candidates than the voter is entitled to vote for, or

      (c) on which anything is written or marked by which the voter can be identified except the printed number and other unique identifying mark on the back, or

      (d) which is unmarked or void for uncertainty,

shall, subject to paragraphs (2) and (3), be void and not counted.

(2) Where the voter is entitled to vote for more than one candidate, a ballot paper shall not be deemed to be void for uncertainty as respects any vote as to which no uncertainty arises and that vote must be counted.

(3) A ballot paper on which the vote is marked—

      (a) elsewhere than in the proper place, or

      (b) otherwise than by means of a cross, or

      (c) by more than one mark,

shall not for such reason be deemed to be void (either wholly or as respects that vote) if an intention that the vote shall be for one or other of the candidates clearly appears, and the way the paper is marked does not itself identify the voter and it is not shown that he can be identified by it.

(4) The returning officer must—

      (a) endorse the word "rejected" on any ballot paper which under this rule is not to be counted; and

      (b) in the case of a ballot paper on which any vote is counted under paragraph (2), endorse the words "rejected in part" on the ballot paper and indicate which vote or votes have been counted;

and must add to the endorsement the words "rejection objected to" if any objection is made by a counting agent to his decision.

(5) The returning officer must draw up a statement showing the number of ballot papers rejected, including those rejected in part, under the several heads of—

      (a) want of official mark;

      (b) voting for more candidates than the voter is entitled to;

      (c) writing or mark by which the voter could be identified;

      (d) unmarked or void for uncertainty;

and the statement must record the number of ballot papers rejected in part.

Decisions on ballot papers

48   The decision of the returning officer on any question arising in respect of a ballot paper shall be final, but shall be subject to review on an election petition.

Equality of votes

49   Where after the counting of the votes (including any recount) is completed, an equality of votes is found to exist between any candidates and the addition of a vote would entitle any of those candidates to be declared elected, the returning officer must forthwith decide between those candidates by lot, and proceed as if the candidate on whom the lot falls had received an additional vote.

Part 4
Final Proceedings in Contested and Uncontested Elections
Declaration of result

50(1) In a contested election, when the result of the poll has been ascertained, the returning officer must forthwith—

      (a) declare to be elected the candidate or candidates to whom more votes have been given than to the other candidates, up to the number of councillors to be elected;

(b) give notice of the name of each candidate to whom sub-paragraph (a) applies to—

(i)   the proper officer of the parish or community council, and

(ii) the proper officer of the council of the district in which the parish is situate or the county or county borough in which the community is situate; and

(c) give public notice of the name of each candidate elected and of the total number of votes given for each candidate (whether elected or not) together with the number of rejected ballot papers under each head shown in the statement of rejected ballot papers.

(2) In an uncontested election, the returning officer must as soon as practicable after the latest time for the delivery of notices of withdrawals of candidature—

(a) declare to be elected the person or persons remaining validly nominated;

(b) give notice of the name of each person to whom sub-paragraph (a) applies to—

(i)   the proper officer of the parish or community council, and

(ii) the proper officer of the council of the district in which the parish is situate or the county or county borough in which the community is situate; and

(c) give public notice of the name of each such person.

Part 5
Disposal of Documents
Sealing up of ballot papers

51(1) On the completion of the counting at a contested election the returning officer must seal up in separate packets the counted and rejected ballot papers, including ballot papers rejected in part.

(2) The returning officer must not open the sealed packets of—

(a) tendered ballot papers,

(b) the completed corresponding number lists,

(c) certificates as to employment on duty on the day of the poll, or

(d) marked copies of the register of electors (including any marked copy notices issued under section 13B(3B) or (3D) of the 1983 Act) and lists of proxies.

Delivery of documents to relevant registration officer

52(1) The returning officer must then forward to the relevant registration officer the following documents—

(a) the packets of ballot papers in his possession,

(b) the ballot paper accounts and the statements of rejected ballot papers and of the result of the verification of the ballot paper accounts,

(c) the tendered votes lists, the lists of voters with disabilities assisted by companions, the lists of votes marked by the presiding officer and the related statements, the lists maintained under rule 41 and the declarations made by the companions of voters with disabilities,

(d) the packets of the completed corresponding number lists,

(e) the packets of certificates as to employment on duty on the day of the poll, and

(f)   the packets containing marked copies of registers (including any marked copy notices issued under section 13B(3B) or (3D) of the 1983 Act) and of the postal voters list, of the lists of proxies and of the proxy postal voters list.

(2) In this rule and in rules 53, 54 and 55, references to the relevant registration officer are to the registration officer of the local authority in whose area the election is held and in which the parish or community is situate.

Orders for production of documents

53(1) An order—

    (a) for the inspection or production of any rejected ballot papers, including ballot papers rejected in part, in the custody of the relevant registration officer; or

    (b) for the opening of a sealed packet of the completed corresponding number lists or certificates as to employment on duty on the day of the poll or for the inspection of any counted ballot papers in his custody,

    may be made by a county court, if the court is satisfied by evidence on oath that the order is required for the purpose of instituting or maintaining a prosecution for an offence in relation to ballot papers, or for the purpose of an election petition.

(2) An order for the opening of a sealed packet of completed corresponding number lists or certificates as to employment on duty on the day of the poll or for the inspection of any counted ballot papers in the custody of the relevant registration officer may be made by an election court.

(3) An order under this rule may be made subject to such conditions as to—

    (a) persons,

    (b) time,

    (c) place and mode of inspection,

    (d) production or opening,

    as the court making the order may think expedient; but in making and carrying into effect an order for the opening of a packet of completed corresponding number lists or of certificates as to employment on duty on the day of the poll or for the inspection of counted ballot papers, care must be taken that the way in which the vote of any particular elector has been given shall not be disclosed until it has been proved—

    (i) that his vote was given; and

    (ii) that the vote has been declared by a competent court to be invalid.

(4) An appeal lies to the High Court from any order of a county court under this rule.

(5) Any power given under this rule to a county court may be exercised by any judge of the court otherwise than in open court.

(6) Where an order is made for the production by the relevant registration officer of any document in his possession relating to any specified election—

    (a) the production by him or his agent of the document ordered in such manner as may be directed by that order shall be conclusive evidence that the document relates to the specified election; and

    (b) any endorsement on any packet of ballot papers so produced shall be prima facie evidence that the ballot papers are what they are stated to be by the endorsement.

(7) The production from proper custody of—

    (a) a ballot paper purporting to have been used at any election, and

    (b) a completed corresponding number list with a number marked in writing beside the number of the ballot paper,

    shall be prima facie evidence that the elector whose vote was given by that ballot paper was the person whose entry in the register of electors or on a notice issued under section 13B(3B) or (3D) of the 1983 Act at the time of the election contained the same number as the number written as mentioned in sub-paragraph (b) of this paragraph.

(8) Save as by this rule provided, no person shall be allowed to inspect any rejected or counted ballot papers in the possession of the relevant registration officer or open any sealed packets of the completed corresponding number lists or of certificates as to employment on duty on the day of the poll.

Retention of documents

54   The relevant registration officer must retain for one year all documents relating to an election forwarded to him in pursuance of these Rules by a returning officer, and then, unless otherwise directed by an order of a county court, a Crown Court, a magistrates' court or an election court, must cause them to be destroyed.

Part 6
Death of Candidate

Countermand or abandonment of poll on death of a candidate

55(1)   If at a contested election proof is given to the returning officer's satisfaction before the result of the election is declared that one of the persons named or to be named as candidate in the ballot papers has died, then the returning officer must countermand notice of the poll or, if polling has begun, direct that the poll be abandoned, and the provisions of subsections (1) and (5) of section 39 of the 1983 Act apply in respect of any vacancy which remains unfilled.

(2)   Where the poll is abandoned by reason of a candidate's death no further ballot papers shall be issued, and the presiding officer at any polling station must take the like steps (so far as not already taken) for the delivery to the returning officer of ballot boxes and ballot papers and other documents as he is required to take on the close of the poll in due course.

(3)   The returning officer must dispose of ballot papers and other documents in his possession as he is required to do on the completion in due course of the counting of the votes, subject to paragraphs (4) and (5).

(4)   It is not necessary for any ballot paper account to be prepared or verified.

(5)   The returning officer must seal up all the ballot papers, whether the votes on them have been counted or not, and it shall not be necessary to seal up counted and rejected ballot papers in separate packets.

(6)   The provisions of these Rules as to the inspection, production, retention and destruction of ballot papers and other documents by the relevant registration officer relating to a poll at an election shall apply to any such documents relating to a poll abandoned by reason of a candidate's death, subject to paragraphs (7) and (8).

(7)   Ballot papers on which the votes were neither counted nor rejected must be treated as counted ballot papers.

(8)   No order is to be made for—
  (a)   the inspection or production of any ballot papers, or
  (b)   for the opening of a sealed packet of the completed corresponding number lists or of certificates as to employment on duty on the day of the poll,
unless the order is made by a court with reference to a prosecution.

Part 7
Appendix of Forms

The forms are not reproduced

SCHEDULE 3

RULES FOR CONDUCT OF AN ELECTION OF COUNCILLORS OF A PARISH OR
COMMUNITY WHERE THE POLL IS TAKEN TOGETHER
WITH THE POLL AT A RELEVANT ELECTION OF REFERENDUM

Rule 4

Part 1
Provisions as to Time

Timetable

1   The proceedings at the election shall be conducted in accordance with the following Table.

Proceedings	Time
Publication of notice of election	Not later than the twenty-fifth day before the day of election.
Delivery of nomination papers	Not later than 4 in the afternoon on the nineteenth day before the day of election
Publication of statement as to persons nominated	Not later than 4 in the afternoon on the eighteenth day before the day of election
Delivery of notices of withdrawals of candidature	Not later than 4 in the afternoon on the nineteenth day before the day of election
Notice of poll	Not later than the sixth day before the day of election.
Polling	Between the hours of 7 in the morning and 10 at night on the day of election.

Computation of time

2(1)   In computing any period of time for the purposes of the Timetable—
    (a)   a Saturday or Sunday,
    (b)   Christmas Eve, Christmas Day, Good Friday or a bank holiday, or
    (c)   a day appointed for public thanksgiving or mourning,
shall be disregarded, and any such day shall not be treated as a day for the purpose of any proceedings up to the completion of the poll nor shall the returning officer be obliged to proceed with the counting of the votes on such a day.

(2)   In this rule "bank holiday" means a day which is a bank holiday under the Banking and Financial Dealings Act 1971 in England and Wales.

Part 2
Stages Common to Contested and Uncontested Elections

Notice of election

3(1) The returning officer must publish notice of the election stating—

(a) the place and times at which nomination papers are to be delivered, and

(b) the date of the poll in the event of a contest,

and the notice must state that forms of nomination papers may be obtained at that place and those times.

(2) The notice of election must state the date by which—

(a) applications to vote by post or by proxy, and

(b) other applications and notices about postal or proxy voting,

must reach the registration officer in order that they may be effective for the election.

Nomination of candidates

4(1) Each candidate must be nominated by a separate nomination paper, in the form in the Appendix, delivered at the place fixed for the purpose by the returning officer.

(2) The nomination paper must state the candidate's—

(a) full names,

(b) home address in full, and

(c) if desired, description,

and the surname must be placed first in the list of names.

(3) If a candidate commonly uses—

(a) a surname which is different from any other surname he has, or

(b) a forename which is different from any other forename he has,

the nomination paper may state the commonly used surname or forename in addition to the other name.

(4) The description, if any, must not exceed 6 words in length, and need not refer to his rank, profession or calling so long as, with the candidate's other particulars, it is sufficient to identify him.

Nomination papers: name of registered political party

5(1) A nomination paper may not include a description of a candidate which is likely to lead electors to associate the candidate with a registered political party unless the party is a qualifying party in relation to the electoral area and the description is authorised by a certificate—

(a) issued by or on behalf of the registered nominating officer of the party, and

(b) received by the returning officer before the last time for the delivery of nomination papers set out in the Table in rule 1.

(2) In paragraph (1) an authorised description may be either—

(a) the name of the party registered under section 28 of the Political Parties, Elections and Referendums Act 2000, or

(b) a description of the party registered under section 28A of that Act.

(3) A nomination paper may not include a description of a candidate which is likely to lead electors to associate the candidate with two or more registered political parties unless the parties are each qualifying parties in relation to the electoral area and the description is a registered description authorised by a certificate—

(a) issued by or on behalf of the registered nominating officer of each of the parties, and

(b) received by the returning officer before the last time for the delivery of nomination papers set out in the Table in rule 1.

(4) For the purposes of paragraph (3), a description is a registered description if it is a description registered for use by the parties under section 28B of the Political Parties,

Elections and Referendums Act 2000.

(5) A person shall be guilty of a corrupt practice if he fraudulently purports to be authorised to issue a certificate under paragraph (1) or (3) on behalf of a registered political party's nominating officer.

(6) For the purposes of the application of this rule in relation to an election—

    (a) "registered political party" means a party which was registered under Part 2 of the Political Parties, Elections and Referendums Act 2000 on the day ("the relevant day") which is two days before the last day for the delivery of nomination papers at that election;

    (b) a registered political party is a qualifying party in relation to an electoral area if the electoral area is in England or Wales and the party was on the relevant day registered in respect of that part of Great Britain in the Great Britain register maintained under that Part of that Act.

(7) For the purposes of paragraph (6)(a) of this rule, any day falling within rule 2(1) must be disregarded.

Subscription of nomination paper

6(1) The nomination paper must be subscribed by two electors as proposer and seconder.

(2) Where a nomination paper has the signatures of more than the required number of persons as proposing or seconding the nomination of a candidate, the signature appearing first on the paper in each category must be taken into account to the exclusion of any others in that category.

(3) The nomination paper must give the electoral number of each person subscribing it.

(4) The returning officer—

    (a) must supply any elector with as many forms of nomination paper and forms of consent to nomination as may be required at the place and during the time for delivery of nomination papers, and

    (b) must at any elector's request prepare a nomination paper for signature,

but it is not necessary for a nomination or consent to nomination to be on a form supplied by the returning officer.

(5) A person must not subscribe more nomination papers than there are vacancies to be filled in the electoral area; nor subscribe any nomination paper in respect of an election in any other ward of the same parish or community whilst the election in the first-mentioned ward is taking place:

Provided that a person shall not be prevented from subscribing a nomination paper by reason only of his having subscribed that of a candidate who has died or withdrawn before delivery of the first-mentioned paper.

(6) If a person subscribes any nomination paper in contravention of paragraph (5), his signature shall be inoperative on all but those papers (up to the permitted number) which are first delivered.

(7) In this rule "elector"—

    (a) means a person who is registered in the register of local government electors for the electoral area in question on the last day for the publication of notice of the election, and

    (b) includes a person then shown in the register as below voting age if (but only if) it appears from the register that he will be of voting age on the day fixed for the poll.

(8) But, in this rule, "elector" does not include a person who has an anonymous entry in the register.

Consent to nomination

7.   A person shall not be validly nominated unless his consent to nomination—
     (a)   is given in writing on or within one month before the last day for the delivery of nomination papers,
     (b)   is in the appropriate form in the Appendix or a form to the like effect and includes—
           (i)   for a nomination in England, a copy of sections 80 and 81 of the Local Government Act 1972, section 78A of the Local Government Act 2000 and section 34 of the Localism Act 2011; or
           (ii)   for a nomination in Wales, a copy of sections 80 and 81 of the Local Government Act 1972 and sections 78A and 79 of the Local Government Act 2000,
     (c)   is attested by one witness, and
     (d)   is delivered at the place and within the time for the delivery of nomination papers.

Decisions as to validity of nomination papers

8(1)   Where a nomination paper and the candidate's consent to it are delivered in accordance with these Rules, the candidate shall be deemed to stand nominated unless and until—
       (a)   the returning officer decides that the nomination paper is invalid; or
       (b)   proof is given to the returning officer's satisfaction of the candidate's death; or
       (c)   the candidate withdraws.

(2)   The returning officer is entitled to hold a nomination paper invalid only on one of the following grounds—
       (a)   that the particulars of the candidate or the persons subscribing the paper are not as required by law; and
       (b)   that the paper is not subscribed as so required.

(3)   Subject to paragraph (4), the returning officer must, as soon as practicable after each nomination paper has been delivered, examine it and decide whether the candidate has been validly nominated.

(4)   If in the returning officer's opinion a nomination paper breaks rule 5(1) or (3), he must give a decision to that effect—
       (a)   as soon as practicable after the delivery of the nomination paper, and
       (b)   in any event before the end of the period of 24 hours starting with the close of the period for delivery of nomination papers set out in the Table in rule 1.

(5)   Where the returning officer decides that a nomination paper is invalid, he must endorse and sign on the paper the fact and the reasons for his decision.

(6)   The returning officer must send notice of his decision that a nomination paper is valid or invalid to each candidate at his home address as given in his nomination paper.

(7)   The returning officer's decision that a nomination paper is valid shall be final and shall not be questioned in any proceeding whatsoever.

(8)   Subject to paragraph (7), nothing in this rule prevents the validity of a nomination being questioned on an election petition.

Publication of statement of persons nominated

9(1)   The returning officer must prepare and publish a statement showing the persons who have been and stand nominated and any other persons who have been nominated, with the reason why they no longer stand nominated.

(2) The statement must show the names, addresses and descriptions of the persons nominated as given in their nomination papers.

(3) If a person's nomination paper gives a commonly used surname or forename in addition to another name, the statement must show the person's commonly used surname or forename (as the case may be) instead of any other name.

(4) Paragraph (3) does not apply if the returning officer thinks—
    (a) that the use of the person's commonly used name may be likely to mislead or confuse electors, or
    (b) that the commonly used name is obscene or offensive.

(5) If paragraph (4) applies, the returning officer must give notice in writing to the candidate of his reasons for refusing to allow the use of a commonly used name.

(6) The statement must show the persons standing nominated arranged alphabetically in the order of their surnames, and if there are two or more of them with the same surname, of their other names.

(7) In the case of a person nominated by more than one nomination paper, the returning officer must take the particulars required by the foregoing provisions of this rule from such one of the papers as the candidate (or the returning officer in default of the candidate) may select.

Correction of minor errors

10(1) A returning officer may, if he thinks fit, at any time before the publication under rule 9 of the statement of persons nominated, correct minor errors in a nomination paper.

(2) Errors which may be corrected include—
    (a) errors as to a person's electoral number;
    (b) obvious errors of spelling in relation to the details of a candidate.

(3) Anything done by a returning officer in pursuance of this rule shall not be questioned in any proceedings other than proceedings on an election petition.

(4) A returning officer must have regard to any guidance issued by the Electoral Commission for the purposes of this rule.

Inspection of nomination papers and consents to nomination

11 During ordinary office hours on any day, other than a day specified in rule 2(1), after the latest time for delivery of nomination papers and before the date of the poll, any person may inspect and take copies of, or extracts from, nomination papers and consents to nomination.

Nomination in more than one ward

12 A candidate who is validly nominated for more than one ward of the same parish or community must withdraw from his candidature in all those wards except one, and if he does not so withdraw, he shall be deemed to have withdrawn from his candidature in all those wards.

Withdrawal of candidates

13(1) A candidate may withdraw his candidature by notice of withdrawal—
    (a) signed by him and attested by one witness, and
    (b) delivered to the returning officer at the place for delivery of nomination papers.

(2) Where a candidate is outside the United Kingdom, a notice of withdrawal signed by his proposer and accompanied by a written declaration also so signed of the candidate's

absence from the United Kingdom shall be of the same effect as a notice of withdrawal signed by the candidate; but where the candidate stands nominated by more than one nomination paper a notice of withdrawal under this paragraph shall be effective if, and only if—

    (a) it and the accompanying declaration are signed by all the proposers except any who is, and is stated in that declaration to be, outside the United Kingdom; or

    (b) it is accompanied, in addition to that declaration, by a written statement signed by the candidate that the proposer giving the notice is authorised to do so on the candidate's behalf during his absence from the United Kingdom.

Method of election

14(1) If the number of persons remaining validly nominated for the electoral area after any withdrawals under these Rules exceeds the number of councillors to be elected, a poll must be taken in accordance with Part 3 of these Rules.

  (2) If the number of persons remaining validly nominated for the electoral area after any withdrawals under these Rules does not exceed the number of councillors to be elected, such person or persons must be declared to be elected in accordance with Part 4 of these Rules.

Part 3
Contested Elections

Chapter 1
General Provisions

Poll to be taken by ballot

15 The votes at the poll must be given by ballot, the result must be ascertained by counting the votes given to each candidate and the candidate or candidates to whom more votes have been given than to the other candidates, up to the number of councillors to be elected, must be declared to have been elected.

The ballot papers

16(1) The ballot of every voter must consist of a ballot paper, and the persons remaining validly nominated for the electoral area after any withdrawals under these Rules, and no others, shall be entitled to have their names inserted in the ballot paper.

  (2) Every ballot paper must be in the form in the Appendix, and must be printed in accordance with the directions in that Appendix, and—

    (a) must contain the names and other particulars of the candidates as shown in the statement of persons nominated;

    (b) must be capable of being folded up; and

    (c) must have a number and other unique identifying mark printed on the back.

  (3) If a candidate who is the subject of a party's authorisation under rule 5(1) so requests, the ballot paper must contain, against the candidate's particulars, the party's registered emblem (or, as the case may be, one of the party's registered emblems).

  (3A) If a candidate who is the subject of an authorisation by two or more parties under rule 5(3) so requests, the ballot paper must contain, against the candidate's particulars, the registered emblem (or, as the case may be, one of the registered emblems) of one of those parties.

  (4) The candidate's request under paragraph (3) or (3A) must—

    (a) be made in writing to the returning officer, and

    (b) be received by him before the last time for the delivery of nomination papers set out in the Table in rule 1.

(5) The order of the names in the ballot paper must be the same as in the statement of persons nominated.

The corresponding number list

17(1) The returning officer must prepare a list containing the numbers and other unique identifying marks of all of the ballot papers to be issued by him in pursuance of rule 22(1) or provided by him in pursuance of rule 26(1).

(2) The list must be in the appropriate form in the Appendix or a form to like effect.

The official mark

18(1) Every ballot paper must contain an appropriate security marking (the official mark).

(2) The official mark must be kept secret, and an interval of not less than five years shall intervene between the use of the same official mark at elections for the same parish or community.

(3) The returning officer may use a different official mark for different purposes at the same election.

Prohibition of disclosure of vote

19 No person who has voted at the election shall, in any legal proceeding to question the election, be required to state for whom he has voted.

Use of schools and public rooms

20(1) The returning officer may use, free of charge, for the purpose of taking the poll or counting the votes—

    (a) a room in a school maintained or assisted by a local authority (within the meaning of the Education Act 1996) or a school in respect of which grants are made out of moneys provided by Parliament to the person or body of persons responsible for the management of the school;

    (b) a room the expense of maintaining which is payable out of any rate.

(2) The returning officer must make good any damage done to, and defray any expense incurred by the persons having control over, any such room as mentioned above by reason of its being used for the purpose of taking the poll or counting the votes.

Chapter 2
Action to be Taken Before the Poll

Notice of poll

21(1) The returning officer must publish notice of the poll stating—

    (a) the day and hours fixed for the poll;

    (b) the number of councillors to be elected;

    (c) the particulars of each candidate remaining validly nominated (the names and other particulars of the candidates, and the order of the candidates' names being the same as in the statement of persons nominated); and

    (d) the names of the proposer and seconder signing a candidate's nomination paper.

(2) Where a candidate is nominated by more than one nomination paper, the nomination paper referred to in paragraph (1)(d) must be that from which the names and other

particulars of the candidate shown in the statement of persons nominated are taken.

(3) The returning officer must, not later than the time of the publication of the notice of the poll, also give public notice of—

    (a) the situation of each polling station; and

    (b) the description of voters entitled to vote there,

and he must as soon as practicable after giving such a notice give a copy of it to each of the candidates or their election agents (if appointed).

(4) The notice published under paragraph (3) must—

    (a) state that the poll at the parish or community election is to be taken together with the poll at a relevant election or referendum;

    (b) specify the parliamentary constituency, local counting area, voting area or, as the case may be, the relevant local authority and, in the case of an election to fill a casual vacancy, the electoral area for which the relevant election is held; and

    (c) where any of the polls are to be taken together in part of the local government area only, specify that part.

Postal ballot papers

22(1) The returning officer must, in accordance with regulations made under the 1983 Act, issue to those entitled to vote by post a ballot paper and a postal voting statement in the appropriate form in the Appendix, or a form to like effect together with such envelopes for their return as may be prescribed by such regulations.

(2) The returning officer must also issue to those entitled to vote by post such information as he thinks appropriate about how to obtain—

    (a) translations into languages other than English of any directions to or guidance for voters sent with the ballot paper;

    (b) a translation into Braille of such directions or guidance;

    (c) graphical representations of such directions or guidance;

    (d) the directions or guidance in any other form (including any audible form).

(3) The postal voting statement must include provision for the form to be signed and for stating the date of birth of the elector or proxy (as the case may be).

(4) In the case of a ballot paper issued to a person at an address in the United Kingdom, the returning officer must ensure that the return of the ballot paper and postal voting statement is free of charge to the voter.

Provision of polling stations

23(1) The returning officer must provide a sufficient number of polling stations and, subject to the following provisions of this rule, must allot the electors to the polling stations in such manner as he thinks most convenient.

(2) One or more polling stations may be provided in the same room.

(3) The polling station allotted to electors from any parliamentary polling district wholly or partly within the electoral area must, in the absence of special circumstances, be in the parliamentary polling place for that district, unless that place is outside the electoral area.

(4) The returning officer must provide each polling station with such number of compartments as may be necessary in which the voters can mark their votes screened from observation.

Appointment of presiding officers and clerks

24(1)   The returning officer must appoint and pay a presiding officer to attend at each polling station and such clerks as may be necessary for the purposes of the election, but he must not appoint any person who has been employed by or on behalf of a candidate in or about the election.

(2)   The returning officer may, if he thinks fit, preside at a polling station and the provisions of these Rules relating to a presiding officer shall apply to a returning officer so presiding with the necessary modifications as to things to be done by the returning officer to the presiding officer or by the presiding officer to the returning officer.

(3)   A presiding officer may do, by the clerks appointed to assist him, any act (including the asking of questions) which he is required or authorised by these Rules to do at a polling station except order the arrest, exclusion or removal of any person from the polling station.

Issue of official poll cards

25(1)   The council of the parish or community may, not later than 4 in the afternoon on the nineteenth day before the day of the election, request the returning officer to issue official poll cards for that election.

(2)   Where the returning officer receives a request under paragraph (1), he must, as soon as practicable, send to electors and their proxies an official poll card.

(3)   An elector's official poll card must be sent or delivered to his qualifying address, and a proxy's to his address as shown in the list of proxies.

(4)   The official poll card must be in the appropriate form in the Appendix, or a form to the like effect, and must set out—
   (a)   the name of the council and, where appropriate, of the ward to which councillors are to be elected;
   (b)   the elector's name, qualifying address and number on the register;
   (c)   the date and hours of the poll and the situation of the elector's polling station;
   (d)   such other information as the returning officer thinks appropriate,
and different information may be provided in pursuance of sub-paragraph (d) to different electors or descriptions of elector.

(5)   In the case of an elector with an anonymous entry—
   (a)   the returning officer must issue an official poll card in the appropriate form in the Appendix to every such elector or to his proxy (if appointed) whether or not the local council of the parish or community make the request mentioned in paragraph (1);
   (b)   instead of containing the elector's name and qualifying address, the polling card must contain the elector's number on the register and such other matter as is specified in the appropriate form in the Appendix; and
   (c)   the official poll card must be sent in an envelope or other form of covering so as not to disclose that the elector has an anonymous entry in the register.

(6)   Paragraph (7) of rule 6 shall apply for the interpretation of this rule.

(7)   If the returning officer and the returning officer for each relevant election or referendum think fit, an official poll card issued under this rule may be combined with the official poll card issued at every relevant election or referendum.

Equipment of polling stations

26(1)   The returning officer must provide each presiding officer with such number of ballot boxes and ballot papers as in the returning officer's opinion may be necessary.

(2)   The same ballot box may be used for the poll at the parish or community election and

the poll at every relevant election or referendum, if the returning officer thinks fit.

(3) Every ballot box must be so constructed that the ballot papers can be put in it, but cannot be withdrawn from it, without the box being unlocked or, where the box has no lock, the seal being broken.

(4) The returning officer must provide each polling station with—
(a) materials to enable voters to mark the ballot papers;
(b) copies of the register of electors for the electoral area or such part of it as contains the names of the electors allotted to the station;
(c) the parts of any special lists prepared for the election corresponding to the register of electors for the electoral area or the part of it provided under sub-paragraph (b);
(d) a list consisting of that part of the list prepared under rule 17 which contains the numbers (but not the other unique identifying marks) corresponding to those on the ballot papers provided to the presiding officer of the polling station.

(5) The reference in paragraph (4)(b) to the copies of the register of electors includes a reference to copies of any notices issued under section 13B(3B) or (3D) of the 1983 Act in respect of alterations to the register.

(6) The returning officer must also provide each polling station with—
(a) at least one large version of the ballot paper which must be printed on the same colour paper as the ballot papers and displayed inside the polling station for the assistance of voters who are partially sighted; and
(b) a device of such description as is set out in paragraph (11) for enabling voters who are blind or partially sighted to vote without any need for assistance from the presiding officer or any companion (within the meaning of rule 37(1)).

(7) Where notwithstanding paragraph (2) separate ballot boxes are to be used, each ballot box must be clearly marked with—
(a) the election or referendum to which it relates, as shown on the ballot papers for that election or referendum; and
(b) the words "Place the specify colour of ballot papers in question ballot papers in here".

(8) A notice in the form in the Appendix, giving directions for the guidance of voters in voting, must be printed in conspicuous characters and exhibited inside and outside every polling station.

(9) The returning officer may also provide copies of the notice mentioned in paragraph (8) in Braille or translated into languages other than English as he considers appropriate, provided that these notices are accurate reproductions in Braille or that other language of that notice.

(10) In every compartment of every polling station there must be exhibited the notice—
*PARLIAMENTARY ELECTION
(Specify colour ballot paper)
Vote for ONLY ONE CANDIDATE by putting a cross X in the box next to your choice.
*EUROPEAN PARLIAMENTARY ELECTION
(Specify colour ballot paper)
Vote ONLY ONCE by putting a cross X in the box next to your choice.
*Specify name of council COUNCIL ELECTION
(Specify colour ballot paper)
*Vote for NO MORE THAN … CANDIDATES by putting a cross X in the box next to EACH of your choices.
*Vote ONLY ONCE by putting a cross X in the box next to your choice.
*ELECTION OF THE MAYOR OF LONDON
(Specify colour ballot paper)

#On the ballot paper for the election of the Mayor, vote ONCE for your first choice and ONCE for your second choice.

*ELECTION OF THE LONDON ASSEMBLY

#On the constituency members ballot paper (specify colour) vote for ONE candidate only.

#On the London members ballot paper (specify colour) vote for ONE party or individual candidate only.

* Specify other ELECTION/REFERENDUM

(Specify colour ballot paper)

Specify voting instructions in accordance with the legislation governing the election or referendum

PUT NO OTHER MARK ON THE BALLOT PAPER OR YOUR VOTE MAY NOT COUNT.

*PLEASE DO NOT FOLD THE BALLOT PAPERS FOR specify the election(s) and/or referendum(s) at which the votes are to be counted electronically . Post them, face downwards, in the *appropriate ballot box.

*Complete or omit as necessary.

Alternatively, insert such information as the GLRO may decide."

(11)   The device referred to in paragraph (6)(b) must—

    (a)   allow a ballot paper to be inserted into and removed from, or attached to and detached from, the device easily and without damage to the paper;

    (b)   hold the ballot paper firmly in place during use; and

    (c)   provide suitable means for the voter to—

        (i)   identify the spaces on the ballot paper on which he may mark his vote;

        (ii)   identify the registered party or individual candidate to which each such space refers; and

        (iii)   mark his vote on the space he has chosen.

Appointment of polling and counting agents

27(1)   Subject to paragraphs (3) and (4), each candidate may, before the commencement of the poll, appoint—

    (a)   polling agents to attend at polling stations for the purpose of detecting personation; and

    (b)   counting agents to attend at the counting of the votes.

(2)   The same person may be appointed as a polling agent or counting agent by more than one candidate.

(3)   Not more than four polling agents, or such greater number as the returning officer may by notice allow, shall be permitted to attend at any particular polling station and if the number of such agents appointed to attend at a particular polling station exceeds that number, the returning officer must determine which agents are permitted to attend by lot and only the agents on whom the lot falls shall be deemed to have been duly appointed.

(4)   The returning officer may limit the number of counting agents, so however that—

    (a)   the number must be the same in the case of each candidate; and

    (b)   the number allowed to a candidate must not (except in special circumstances) be less than the number obtained by dividing the number of clerks employed on the counting by the number of candidates.

    For the purposes of the calculations required by this paragraph, a counting agent who has been appointed for more than one candidate is a separate agent for each of the candidates by whom he has been appointed.

(5)   Notice in writing of the appointment, stating the names and addresses of the persons appointed, must be given by the candidate to the returning officer and must be so

given not later than the fifth day (computed like any period of time in the Timetable) before the day of the poll.

(6) Notices of the appointment of polling agents and counting agents which are required by paragraph (5) above and paragraph (7) below to be given to the returning officer shall be given to that returning officer who discharges the functions specified in regulation 5 of the Combination of Polls Regulations.

(7) If an agent dies, or becomes incapable of acting, the candidate may appoint another agent in his place, and must forthwith give to the returning officer notice in writing of the name and address of the agent appointed.

(8) In the following provisions of these Rules references to polling agents and counting agents must be taken as references to agents—
    (a) whose appointments have been duly made and notified; and
    (b) where the number of agents is restricted, who are within the permitted numbers.

(9) Any notice required to be given to a counting agent by the returning officer may be delivered at, or sent by post to, the address stated in the notice of appointment.

(10) A candidate may himself do any act or thing which any polling or counting or election agent of his, if appointed, would have been authorised to do, or may assist his agent in doing any such act or thing.

(11) Where by these Rules any act or thing is required or authorised to be done in the presence of the polling or counting agents, the nonattendance of any agent or agents at the time and place appointed for the purpose shall not, if the act or thing is otherwise duly done, invalidate the act or thing done.

Notification of requirement of secrecy

28(1) The returning officer must make such arrangements as he thinks fit to ensure that—
    (a) every person attending at a polling station (otherwise than for the purpose of voting or assisting a voter with disabilities to vote or as a constable on duty there) has been given a copy in writing of the provisions of subsections (1), (3) and (6) of section 66 of the 1983 Act; and
    (b) every person attending at the counting of the votes (other than any constable on duty at the counting) has been given a copy in writing of the provisions of subsections (2) and (6) of that section.

(2) In this rule, a reference to a constable includes a person designated as a community support officer under section 38 of the Police Reform Act 2002 (police powers for employees).

Return of postal ballot papers

29(1) Where—
    (a) a postal vote has been returned in respect of a person who is entered on the postal voters list, or
    (b) a proxy postal vote has been returned in respect of a proxy who is entered on the proxy postal voters list,
the returning officer must mark the list in the manner prescribed by regulations made under the 1983 Act.

(2) Rule 45(5) does not apply for the purpose of determining whether, for the purposes of this rule, a postal vote or a proxy postal vote is returned.

Chapter 3
The Poll

Admission to polling station

30(1) The presiding officer must exclude all persons from the polling station except—
    (a) voters;
    (b) persons under the age of 18 who accompany voters to the polling station;
    (c) the candidates and their election agents (if appointed);
    (d) the polling agents appointed to attend at the polling station;
    (e) the clerks appointed to attend at the polling station;
    (f) persons who are entitled to attend by virtue of any of sections 6A to 6D of the Political Parties, Elections and Referendums Act 2000;
    (g) the constables on duty;
    (h) the companions of voters with disabilities; and
    (i) persons entitled to be admitted to the polling station at a relevant election or referendum with which the poll at the parish or community election is combined.

(2) The presiding officer must regulate the total number of voters and persons under the age of 18 who accompany them to be admitted to the polling station at the same time.

(3) Not more than one polling agent shall be admitted at the same time to a polling station on behalf of the same candidate.

(4) A constable or person employed by a returning officer must not be admitted to vote in person elsewhere than at his own polling station allotted to him under these Rules, except on production and surrender of a certificate as to his employment which must be in the form in the Appendix, or a form to the like effect, and signed by an officer of police of or above the rank of inspector or by the returning officer, as the case may be.

(5) Any certificate surrendered under this rule must forthwith be cancelled.

(6) In this rule, a reference to a constable includes a person designated as a community support officer under section 38 of the Police Reform Act 2002 (police powers for employees).

Keeping of order in station

31(1) It is the presiding officer's duty to keep order at his polling station.

(2) If a person misconducts himself in a polling station, or fails to obey the presiding officer's lawful orders, he may immediately, by the presiding officer's order, be removed from the polling station—
    (a) by a constable in or near that station, or
    (b) by any other person authorised in writing by the returning officer to remove him,
and the person so removed shall not, without the presiding officer's permission, again enter the polling station during the day.

(3) Any person so removed may, if charged with the commission in the polling station of an offence, be dealt with as a person taken into custody by a constable for an offence without a warrant.

(4) The powers conferred by this rule must not be exercised so as to prevent a voter who is otherwise entitled to vote at a polling station from having an opportunity of voting at that station.

Sealing of ballot boxes

32 Immediately before the commencement of the poll, the presiding officer must show the ballot box empty to such persons, if any, as are present in the polling station, so that they may see that it is empty, and must then lock it up, if it has a lock and (in any case) place his seal on it in such a manner as to prevent its being opened without breaking the seal

and must place it in his view for the receipt of ballot papers, and keep it so locked and sealed or sealed (as the case may be).

Questions to be put to voters

33(1) At the time of the application (but not afterwards), the questions specified in the second column of the following Table—

(a) may be put by the presiding officer to a person applying for a ballot paper who is mentioned in the first column, and

(b) must be put if the letter "R" appears after the question and the candidate or his polling agent requires the question to be put:

Q. No.	Persons applying for ballot paper	Question
1	A person applying as an elector	(a)—Are you the person registered in the register of local government electors for this election as follows ? read the whole entry from the register R
		(b)—Have you already voted at this election for *(this parish) *(this community), * delete whichever is inapplicable (adding, in the case of an election for several wards , in this or any other ward) otherwise than as proxy for some other person? R
2	A person applying as proxy	(a)—Are you the person whose name appears as A.B. in the list of proxies for this election as entitled to vote as proxy on behalf of C.D.? R
		(b)—Have you already voted at this election for *(this parish) *(this community), * delete whichever is inapplicable (adding in the case of an election for several wards , in this or any other ward) as proxy on behalf of C.D.? R
		(c)—Are you the spouse, civil partner, parent, grandparent, brother, sister, child or grandchild of C.D.? R
3	A person applying as proxy for an elector with an anonymous entry (instead of the questions at entry 2)	(a)—Are you the person entitled to vote as proxy on behalf of the elector whose number on the register of electors is (read out the number)? [R]
		(b)—Have you already voted as proxy on behalf of the elector whose number on the register of electors is (read out the number)? R

Q. No.	Persons applying for ballot paper	Question
		(c)—Are you the spouse, civil partner, parent, grandparent, brother, sister, child or grandchild of the person whose number on the register of electors is (read out the number)? R
4	A person applying as proxy if the question at entry 2(c) or 3(c) is not answered in the affirmative	Have you already voted at this election for *(this parish) *(this community) * delete whichever is inapplicable (adding in the case of an election for several wards , in this or any other ward) on behalf of two persons of whom you are not the spouse, civil partner, parent, grandparent, brother, sister, child or grandchild? R
5	A person applying as an elector in relation to whom there is an entry in the postal voters list	(a)—Did you apply to vote by post? (b)—Why have you not voted by post?
6	A person applying as proxy who is named in the proxy postal voters list	(a)—Did you apply to vote by post as proxy? (b)—Why have you not voted by post as proxy?

(2) In the case of an elector in respect of whom a notice has been issued under section 13B(3B) or (3D) of the 1983 Act, the references in the questions at entries 1(a) and 3(a), (b) and (c) to reading from the register shall be taken as references to reading from the notice issued under section 13B(3B) or (3D) of the 1983 Act.

(3) A ballot paper must not be delivered to any person required to answer any of the above questions unless he has answered each question satisfactorily.

(4) Except as authorised by this rule, no inquiry shall be permitted as to the right of any person to vote.

Challenge of voter

34 A person must not be prevented from voting by reason only that—

    (a) a candidate or his polling agent declares that he has reasonable cause to believe that the person has committed an offence of personation, or

    (b) the person is arrested on the grounds that he is suspected of committing or of being about to commit such an offence.

Voting procedure

35(1) A ballot paper must be delivered to a voter who applies for one, and immediately before delivery—

    (a) the number and (unless paragraph (2) applies) name of the elector as stated in the copy of the register of electors must be called out;

    (b) the number of the elector must be marked on the list mentioned in rule 26(4)(d) beside the number of the ballot paper to be issued to him;

(c) a mark must be placed in the register of electors against the number of the elector to note that a ballot paper has been received but without showing the particular ballot paper which has been received;

(d) in the case of a person applying for a ballot paper as proxy, a mark must also be placed against his name in the list of proxies.

(2) In the case of an elector who has an anonymous entry, he must show the presiding officer his official poll card and only his number shall be called out in pursuance of paragraph (1)(a).

(3) In the case of an elector who is added to the register in pursuance of a notice issued under section 13B(3B) or (3D) of the 1983 Act, paragraph (1) is modified as follows—

(a) in sub-paragraph (a), for "copy of the register of electors" substitute "copy of the notice issued under section 13B(3B) or (3D) of the 1983 Act";

(b) in sub-paragraph (c), for "in the register of electors" substitute "on the copy of the notice issued under section 13B(3B) or (3D) of the 1983 Act".

(4) The voter, on receiving the ballot paper, must forthwith proceed into one of the compartments in the polling station and there secretly mark his paper and fold it up so as to conceal his vote, and must then show to the presiding officer the back of the paper, so as to disclose the number and other unique identifying mark, and put the ballot paper so folded up into the ballot box in the presiding officer's presence.

(5) The voter must vote without undue delay, and must leave the polling station as soon as he has put his ballot paper into the ballot box.

(6) The same copy of the register of electors or, where paragraph (3) applies, the same copy of the notice issued under section 13(3B) or (3D) of the 1983 Act, which is used under paragraph (1) for the parish or community election may be used for each relevant election or referendum—

(a) and one mark may be placed in that register or on that notice under paragraph (1)(c) or in the list of proxies under paragraph (1)(d) to denote that a ballot paper has been issued in respect of each election or referendum;

(b) but where a ballot paper has not been issued in respect of a relevant election or referendum, a different mark must be placed in the register or, as the case may be, on that notice or in that list so as to identify each election or referendum in respect of which a ballot paper was issued.

(7) A voter who at the close of the poll is in the polling station, or in a queue outside the polling station, for the purposes of voting shall (despite the close of the poll) be entitled to apply for a ballot paper under paragraph (1); and these rules apply in relation to such a voter accordingly.

Votes marked by presiding officer

36(1) The presiding officer, on the application of a voter—

(a) who is incapacitated by blindness or other disability from voting in the manner directed by these Rules, or

(b) who declares orally that he is unable to read,

must, in the presence of the polling agents, cause the voter's vote to be marked on a ballot paper in the manner directed by the voter, and the ballot paper to be placed in the ballot box.

(2) The name and number on the register of electors of every voter whose vote is marked in pursuance of this rule, and the reason why it is so marked, must be entered on a list (in these Rules called "the list of votes marked by the presiding officer").

In the case of a person voting as proxy for an elector, the number to be entered together with the voter's name shall be the elector's number.

(3) In the case of a person in respect of whom a notice has been issued under section 13B(3B) or (3D) of the 1983 Act, paragraph (2) applies as if for "on the register of electors of every voter" there were substituted "relating to every voter in respect of whom a notice has been issued under section 13B(3B) or (3D) of the 1983 Act".

(4) The same list may be used for the parish or community election and each relevant election or referendum and, where it is so used, an entry in that list shall be taken to mean that the ballot papers were so marked in respect of each election or referendum, unless the list identifies the election or referendum at which the ballot paper was so marked.

Voting by persons with disabilities

37(1) If a voter makes an application to the presiding officer to be allowed, on the ground of—

    (a) blindness or other disability, or

    (b) inability to read,

to vote with the assistance of another person by whom he is accompanied (in these Rules referred to as "the companion"), the presiding officer must require the voter to declare, orally or in writing, whether he is so incapacitated by his blindness or other disability, or by his inability to read, as to be unable to vote without assistance.

(2) If the presiding officer—

    (a) is satisfied that the voter is so incapacitated, and

    (b) is also satisfied by a written declaration made by the companion (in these Rules referred to as "the declaration made by the companion of a voter with disabilities") that the companion—

        (i) is a qualified person within the meaning of these Rules; and

        (ii) has not previously assisted more than one voter with disabilities to vote at the election,

the presiding officer must grant the application, and then anything which is by these Rules required to be done to, or by that voter in connection with the giving of his vote may be done to, or with the assistance of, the companion.

(3) For the purposes of these Rules, a person is a voter with disabilities if he has made such a declaration as is mentioned in paragraph (1), and a person shall be qualified to assist a voter with disabilities to vote if that person—

    (a) is a person who is entitled to vote as an elector at the election; or

    (b) is the father, mother, brother, sister, spouse, civil partner, son or daughter of the voter and has attained the age of 18 years.

(4) The name and number in the register of electors of every voter whose vote is given in accordance with this rule and the name and address of the companion must be entered on a list (in these Rules referred to as "the list of voters with disabilities assisted by companions").

In the case of a person voting as proxy for an elector, the number to be entered together with the voter's name shall be the elector's number.

(5) In the case of a person in respect of whom a notice has been issued under section 13B(3B) or (3D) of the 1983 Act, paragraph (4) applies as if for "in the register of electors of every voter" there were substituted "relating to every voter in respect of whom a notice has been issued under section 13B(3B) or (3D) of the 1983 Act".

(6) The same list may be used for the parish or community election and each relevant election and referendum and, where it is so used, an entry in that list shall be taken to mean that the votes were so given in respect of each election or referendum, unless the list identifies the election or referendum at which the vote was so given.

(7) The declaration made by the companion—

    (a) must be in the form in the Appendix;

    (b) must be made before the presiding officer at the time when the voter applies to vote with the assistance of a companion; and

    (c) must forthwith be given to the presiding officer who must attest and retain it.

(8) No fee or other payment shall be charged in respect of the declaration.

Tendered ballot papers: circumstances where available

38(1) If a person, representing himself to be—

    (a) a particular elector named on the register and not named in the absent voters list, or

    (b) a particular person named in the list of proxies as proxy for an elector and not entitled to vote by post as proxy,

applies for a ballot paper after another person has voted in person either as the elector or his proxy, the applicant shall, on satisfactorily answering the questions permitted by law to be asked at the poll, be entitled, subject to the following provisions of this rule and rule 39, to mark a ballot paper (in these Rules referred to as "a tendered ballot paper") in the same manner as any other voter.

(2) Paragraph (4) applies if—

    (a) a person applies for a ballot paper representing himself to be a particular elector named on the register,

    (b) he is also named in the postal voters list, and

    (c) he claims that he did not make an application to vote by post at the election.

(3) Paragraph (4) also applies if—

    (a) a person applies for a ballot paper representing himself to be a particular person named as a proxy in the list of proxies,

    (b) he is also named in the proxy postal voters list, and

    (c) he claims that he did not make an application to vote by post as proxy.

(4) The person shall, on satisfactorily answering the questions permitted by law to be asked at the poll, be entitled, subject to the following provisions of this rule and rule 39, to mark a ballot paper (in these Rules referred to as a "tendered ballot paper") in the same manner as any other voter.

(5) Paragraph (6) applies if before the close of the poll but after the last time at which a person may apply for a replacement postal ballot paper, a person represents himself to be—

    (a) a particular elector named on the register who is also named in the postal voters list, or

    (b) a particular person named as a proxy in the list of proxies and who is also named in the proxy postal voters list,

and he claims that he has lost or has not received his postal ballot paper.

(6) The person shall, on satisfactorily answering the questions permitted by law to be asked at the poll, be entitled, subject to the provisions of this rule and rule 39, to mark a ballot paper (in these Rules referred to as a "tendered ballot paper") in the same manner as any other voter.

Tendered ballot papers: general provisions

39(1) A tendered ballot paper must—

    (a) be of a colour differing from the other ballot papers;

    (b) instead of being put into the ballot box, be given to the presiding officer and endorsed by him with the name of the voter and his number in the register of electors, and set aside in a separate packet.

(2)   The name of the voter and his number in the register of electors must be entered on a list (in these Rules referred to as the "tendered votes list").

(3)   The same list may be used for the parish or community election and each relevant election or referendum and, where it is so used, an entry in that list shall be taken to mean that tendered ballot papers were marked in respect of each election or referendum, unless the list identifies the election or referendum at which a tendered ballot paper was marked.

(4)   In the case of a person voting as proxy for an elector, the number to be endorsed or entered together with the voter's name shall be the number of that elector.

(5)   In the case of an elector who has an anonymous entry, this rule and rule 38 apply subject to the following modifications—

  (a)   in paragraphs (1)(b) and (2) of this rule, the references to the name of the voter shall be ignored;

  (b)   otherwise, a reference to a person named on a register or list shall be construed as a reference to a person whose number appears on the register or list (as the case may be).

(6)   In the case of a person in respect of whom a notice has been issued under section 13B(3B) or (3D) of the 1983 Act, this rule and rule 38 shall apply as if—

  (a)   in rule 38(1)(a), (2)(a) and (5)(a), for "named on the register" there were substituted "in respect of whom a notice under section 13B(3B) or (3D) of the 1983 Act has been issued";

  (b)   in paragraph (1)(b) of this rule, for "his number in the register of electors" there were substituted "the number relating to him on a notice issued under section 13B(3B) or (3D) of the 1983 Act";

  (c)   in paragraph (2) of this rule, for "his number in the register of electors" there were substituted "the number relating to him on a notice issued under section 13B(3B) or (3D) of the 1983 Act".

Spoilt ballot papers

40   A voter who has inadvertently dealt with his ballot paper in such manner that it cannot be conveniently used as a ballot paper may, on delivering it to the presiding officer and proving to his satisfaction the fact of the inadvertence, obtain another ballot paper in the place of the ballot paper so delivered (in these Rules referred to as "a spoilt ballot paper"), and the spoilt ballot paper must be immediately cancelled.

Correction of errors on day of poll

41(1)   The presiding officer must keep a list of persons to whom ballot papers are delivered in consequence of an alteration to the register made by virtue of section 13B(3B) or (3D) of the 1983 Act which takes effect on the day of the poll.

(2)   The same list may be used for each relevant election or referendum and, where it is so used, an entry in that list shall be taken to mean that ballot papers were issued in respect of each election or referendum, unless the list identifies the election or referendum for which a ballot paper was issued.

Adjournment of poll in case of riot

42(1)   Where the proceedings at any polling station are interrupted or obstructed by riot or open violence, the presiding officer must adjourn the proceedings till the following day and must forthwith give notice to the returning officer who discharges the functions specified in regulation 5 of the Combination of Polls Regulations.

(2)   Where the poll is adjourned at any polling station—

    (a)   the hours of polling on the day to which it is adjourned must be the same as for the original day; and

    (b)   references in these Rules to the close of the poll shall be construed accordingly.

Procedure on close of poll

43(1)   As soon as practicable after the close of the poll, the presiding officer must, in the presence of the polling agents appointed for the purposes of the parish or community election and those appointed for the purposes of each relevant election or referendum, make up into separate packets, sealed with his own seal and the seals of such polling agents as desire to affix their seals—

    (a)   each ballot box in use at the station, sealed so as to prevent the introduction of additional ballot papers and unopened, but with the key, if any, attached,

    (b)   the unused and spoilt ballot papers placed together,

    (c)   the tendered ballot papers,

    (d)   the marked copies of the register of electors (including any marked copy notices issued under section 13B(3B) or (3D) of the 1983 Act) and of the list of proxies,

    (e)   the lists prepared under rule 17 including the parts which were completed in accordance with rule 35(1)(b) and (d) (together referred to in these Rules as "the completed corresponding number lists"),

    (f)   the certificates as to employment on duty on the day of the poll,

    (g)   the tendered votes list, the list of voters with disabilities assisted by companions, the list of votes marked by the presiding officer, a statement of the number of voters whose votes are so marked by the presiding officer under the heads "disability" and "unable to read", the list maintained under rule 41 (correction of errors on day of poll), and the declarations made by the companions of voters with disabilities,

and must deliver the packets or cause them to be delivered to the returning officer to be taken charge of by him; but if the packets are not delivered by the presiding officer personally to the returning officer, the arrangements for their delivery shall require the returning officer's approval.

(2)   The contents of the packets referred to in sub-paragraphs (b), (c) and (f) of paragraph (1) must not be combined with the contents of the packets made under the corresponding rule that applies at any relevant election or referendum; nor shall the statement prepared under paragraph (5) be so combined.

(3)   References to the returning officer in paragraph (1) are references to the returning officer who discharges the functions specified in regulation 5 of the Combination of Polls Regulations.

(4)   The marked copies of the register of electors and of the list of proxies must be in one packet but must not be in the same packet as the completed corresponding number lists or the certificates as to employment on duty on the day of the poll.

(5)   The packets must be accompanied by a statement (in these Rules referred to as "the ballot paper account") made by the presiding officer showing the number of ballot papers entrusted to him, and accounting for them under the heads of ballot papers issued and not otherwise accounted for, unused, spoilt and tendered ballot papers.

Chapter 4

Counting of Votes

Attendance at counting of votes

44(1)   Where the returning officer at the parish or community election discharges the functions specified in regulation 5 of the Combination of Polls Regulations, he must—

    (a)   make arrangements for—

        (i)   discharging the functions under rule 45(1) in the presence of the counting agents appointed for the purposes of the parish or community election and those appointed for the purpose of each relevant election or referendum as soon as practicable after the close of the poll, and

        (ii) thereafter counting the votes at that election in the presence of the agents appointed for the purpose of that election; and

    (b)   give to the counting agents appointed for the purposes of the parish or community election and those appointed for the purpose of each relevant election or referendum notice in writing of the time and place at which he will begin to discharge the functions under rule 45(1).

(2)   Where the returning officer at the parish or community election does not discharge the functions specified in regulation 5 of the Combination of Polls Regulations, he must—

    (a)   make arrangements for counting the votes in the presence of the counting agents as soon as practicable after the delivery of the ballot papers to him by the returning officer who does discharge those functions; and

    (b)   give to the counting agents notice in writing of the time after which he will begin to count the votes if by then he has received the ballot papers and of the place at which that count will take place.

(3)   No person other than—

    (a)   the returning officer and his clerks,

    (b)   the candidates and one other person chosen by each of them,

    (c)   the election agents (if appointed),

    (d)   the counting agents,

    (e)   persons who are entitled to attend by virtue of any of sections 6A to 6D of the Political Parties, Elections and Referendums Act 2000,

may be present at the counting of the votes under paragraphs (4) to (12) of rule 45, unless permitted by the returning officer to attend.

(4)   No person other than a person entitled to be present at the counting of the votes at the parish or community election under paragraphs (4) to (12) of rule 45 or at a relevant election or referendum may be present at the proceedings under rule 45(1), unless permitted by the returning officer to attend.

(5)   A person not entitled to attend at the proceedings under rule 45(1) or the counting of the votes shall not be permitted to do so by the returning officer unless he—

    (a)   is satisfied that the efficient separation of the ballot papers or, as the case may be, the efficient counting of the votes will not be impeded; and

    (b)   has either consulted the election agents (if appointed) or thought it impracticable to do so.

(6)   The returning officer must give the counting agents all such reasonable facilities for overseeing the proceedings, and all such information with respect to them, as he can give them consistently with the orderly conduct of the proceedings and the discharge of his duties in connection with them.

(7)   In particular, where the votes are counted by sorting the ballot papers according to the candidate for whom the vote is given and then counting the number of ballot papers for each candidate, the counting agents shall be entitled to satisfy themselves that the ballot papers are correctly sorted.

The count

45(1) Where the returning officer at the parish or community election discharges the functions specified in regulation 5 of the Combination of Polls Regulations, he must—

    (a)   in the presence of the counting agents appointed for the purposes of the poll at the parish or community election and each relevant election or referendum open each ballot box and record separately the number of ballot papers used in each election;

(b) in the presence of the counting agents appointed for the purposes of the poll at the parish or community election and the election agents appointed for the purposes of the poll at each relevant election or referendum, verify each ballot paper account;

(c) count such of the postal ballot papers as have been duly returned and record separately the number counted at the poll at the parish or community election and each relevant election or referendum;

(d) separate the ballot papers relating to the parish or community election from the ballot papers relating to each relevant election or referendum;

(e) make up into packets the ballot papers for each relevant election or referendum and seal them up in separate containers endorsing on each a description of the area to which the ballot papers relate;

(f) deliver or cause to be delivered to the returning officer for the relevant election or referendum to which the ballot papers relate—

  (i) those containers, together with a list of them and of the contents of each; and

  (ii) the ballot paper accounts together with a copy of the statement as to the result of their verification in respect of that election; and

(g) at the same time deliver or cause to be delivered to that officer packets that so relate containing—

  (i) the unused and spoilt ballot papers,

  (ii) the tendered ballot papers, and

  (iii) the certificates as to employment on duty on the day of the poll.

(2) Where separate ballot boxes are used, no vote for any candidate shall be rendered invalid by the ballot paper being placed in the ballot box intended for use at any relevant election or referendum.

(3) After completion of the proceedings under paragraph (1), the returning officer must mix together all of the ballot papers used at the parish or community election and count the votes given on them.

(4) Where the returning officer at the parish or community election does not discharge the functions specified in regulation 5 of the Combination of Polls Regulations, he must—

(a) on receipt of containers from the returning officer who does discharge those functions, and after the time specified in the notice given under rule 44(2)(b), in the presence of the counting agents open each container;

(b) where the proceedings on the issue and receipt of postal ballot papers are not taken together with those proceedings at a relevant election or referendum under regulation 65 of the Representation of the People (England and Wales) Regulations 2001 or under that regulation as applied by regulations made under section 9HE, 9MG, 44 or 45, whether or not in addition to 105 of the Local Government Act 2000, count such of the postal ballot papers as have been duly returned and record the number counted; and

(c) mix together the postal ballot papers and the ballot papers from all of the containers and count the votes given on them,

and paragraph (10) shall not apply to these proceedings.

(5) A postal ballot paper must not be taken to be duly returned unless—

(a) it is returned in the manner set out in paragraph (6) and reaches the returning officer or any polling station in the appropriate electoral area (as defined in paragraph (7)) before the close of the poll;

(b) the postal voting statement, duly signed, is also returned in the manner set out in paragraph (6) and reaches him or such a polling station before that time;

    (c)   the postal voting statement also states the date of birth of the elector or proxy (as the case may be); and

    (d)   in a case where steps for verifying the date of birth and signature of the voter have been prescribed by regulations made under the 1983 Act, the returning officer (having taken such steps) verifies the date of birth and signature of the voter.

(6)   The manner in which any postal ballot paper or postal voting statement may be returned—

    (a)   to the returning officer, is by hand or by post; and

    (b)   to a polling station, is by hand.

(6A) A postal ballot paper or postal voting statement that reaches the returning officer or a polling station on or after the close of the poll is treated for the purposes of this rule as reaching that officer or polling station before the close of the poll if it is delivered by a person who, at the close of the poll, is in the polling station, or in a queue outside the polling station, for the purpose of returning it.

(7)   The appropriate electoral area in respect of any voter shall be—

    (a)   the area which is common to the parliamentary constituency, electoral area, local counting area, local authority area or voting area (as the case may be) in which the polls at the parish or community election and any relevant election or referendum are being taken together; and

    (b)   in respect of which polls the postal voter has been issued with a ballot paper.

(8)   The returning officer must not count any tendered ballot papers.

(9)   The returning officer, while counting and recording the number of ballot papers and counting the votes, must keep the ballot papers with their faces upwards and take all proper precautions for preventing any person from seeing the numbers or other unique identifying marks printed on the back of the papers.

(10) The returning officer must verify each ballot paper account by comparing it with the number of ballot papers recorded by him, and the unused and spoilt ballot papers in his possession and the tendered votes list (opening and re-sealing the packets containing the unused and spoilt ballot papers and the tendered votes list) and must draw up a statement as to the result of the verification, which any election agent (if appointed) may copy.

(11) The returning officer must so far as practicable proceed continuously with counting the votes, allowing only time for refreshment, except that he may exclude the hours between 7 in the evening and 9 on the following morning.

(12) During the time so excluded the returning officer must—

    (a)   place the ballot papers and other documents relating to the election under his own seal and the seals of such of the counting agents as desire to affix their seals; and

    (b)   otherwise take proper precautions for the security of the papers and documents.

Recount

46(1) A candidate or his election agent (if appointed) may, if present when the counting or any recount of the votes is completed, require the returning officer to have the votes recounted or again recounted but the returning officer may refuse to do so if in his opinion the request is unreasonable.

(2)   No step shall be taken on the completion of the counting or any recount of votes until the candidates and election agents (if appointed) present at its completion have been

given a reasonable opportunity to exercise the right conferred by this rule.

Rejected ballot papers

47(1) Any ballot paper—

(a) which does not bear the official mark, or

(b) on which votes are given for more candidates than the voter is entitled to vote for, or

(c) on which anything is written or marked by which the voter can be identified except the printed number and other unique identifying mark on the back, or

(d) which is unmarked or void for uncertainty, shall, subject to paragraphs (2) and (3), be void and not counted.

(2) Where the voter is entitled to vote for more than one candidate, a ballot paper shall not be deemed to be void for uncertainty as respects any vote as to which no uncertainty arises and that vote must be counted.

(3) A ballot paper on which the vote is marked—

(a) elsewhere than in the proper place, or

(b) otherwise than by means of a cross, or

(c) by more than one mark,

shall not for such reason be deemed to be void (either wholly or as respects that vote) if an intention that the vote shall be for one or other of the candidates clearly appears, and the way the paper is marked does not itself identify the voter and it is not shown that he can be identified by it.

(4) The returning officer must—

(a) endorse the word "rejected" on any ballot paper which under this rule is not to be counted; and

(b) in the case of a ballot paper on which any vote is counted under paragraph (2), endorse the words "rejected in part" on the ballot paper and indicate which vote or votes have been counted,

and must add to the endorsement the words "rejection objected to" if any objection is made by a counting agent to his decision.

(5) The returning officer must draw up a statement showing the number of ballot papers rejected, including those rejected in part, under the several heads of—

(a) want of official mark;

(b) voting for more candidates than the voter is entitled to;

(c) writing or mark by which the voter could be identified;

(d) unmarked or void for uncertainty,

and the statement must record the number of ballot papers rejected in part.

Decisions on ballot papers

48 The decision of the returning officer on any question arising in respect of a ballot paper shall be final, but shall be subject to review on an election petition.

Equality of votes

49 Where, after the counting of the votes (including any recount) is completed, an equality of votes is found to exist between any candidates and the addition of a vote would entitle any of those candidates to be declared elected, the returning officer must forthwith decide between those candidates by lot, and proceed as if the candidate on whom the lot falls had received an additional vote.

Part 4
Final Proceedings in Contested and Uncontested Elections

Declaration of result

50(1) In a contested election, when the result of the poll has been ascertained, the returning officer must forthwith—

   (a) declare to be elected the candidate or candidates to whom more votes have been given than to the other candidates, up to the number of councillors to be elected;

   (b) give notice of the name of each candidate to whom sub-paragraph (a) applies to—

      (i) the proper officer of the parish or community council, and

      (ii) the proper officer of the council of the district in which the parish is situate or the county or county borough in which the community is situate; and

   (c) give public notice of the name of each candidate elected and of the total number of votes given for each candidate (whether elected or not) together with the number of rejected ballot papers under each head shown in the statement of rejected ballot papers.

   (2) In an uncontested election, the returning officer must as soon as practicable after the latest time for the delivery of notices of withdrawals of candidature—

   (a) declare to be elected the person or persons remaining validly nominated;

   (b) give notice of the name of each person to whom sub-paragraph (a) applies to—

      (i) the proper officer of the parish or community council, and

      (ii) the proper officer of the council of the district in which the parish is situate or the county or county borough in which the community is situate; and

   (c) give public notice of the name of each such person.

Part 5
Disposal of Documents

Sealing up of ballot papers

51(1) On the completion of the counting at a contested election the returning officer must seal up in separate packets the counted and rejected ballot papers, including ballot papers rejected in part.

   (2) The returning officer must not open the sealed packets of—

   (a) tendered ballot papers, or

   (b) certificates as to employment on duty on the day of the poll.

   (3) Where the returning officer discharges the functions referred to in regulation 5 of the Combination of Polls Regulations, he must also not open the sealed packets of—

   (a) the completed corresponding number lists, or

   (b) the marked copies of the register of electors (including any marked copy notices issued under section 13B(3B) or (3D) of the 1983 Act) and lists of proxies.

Delivery of documents to relevant registration officer

52(1) The returning officer must then forward to the relevant registration officer the following documents—

   (a) the packets of ballot papers in his possession,

   (b) the ballot paper accounts and the statements of rejected ballot papers and of the result of the verification of the ballot paper accounts,

   (c) the tendered votes lists, the lists of voters with disabilities assisted by companions, the lists of votes marked by the presiding officer and the related statements, the lists maintained under rule 41 and the declarations made by the companions of voters with disabilities,

(d)   the packets of the completed corresponding number lists,

(e)   the packets of certificates as to employment on duty on the day of the poll, and

(f)   the packets containing marked copies of registers (including any marked copy notices issued under section 13B(3B) or (3D) of the 1983 Act) and of the postal voters list, of the lists of proxies and of the proxy postal voters list.

(2)   At an election where the returning officer does not discharge the functions referred to in regulation 5 of the Combination of Polls Regulations, paragraph (1) shall have effect as if sub-paragraphs (c), (d) and (e) were omitted.

(3)   In this rule and in rules 53, 54 and 55 references to the relevant registration officer are to—

(a)   the registration officer of the local authority in whose area the election is held and in which the parish or community is situate;

(b)   if the electoral area for the relevant election or referendum comprises any part of the area of more than one local authority, the registration officer of the local authority in whose area the greater or greatest (as the case may be) number of electors is registered;

(c)   if the returning officer discharges the functions referred to in regulation 5 of the Combination of Polls Regulations, the registration officer of the local authority in whose area the parish or community election is held and in which the parish or community is situate.

Orders for production of documents

53(1)   An order—

(a)   for the inspection or production of any rejected ballot papers, including ballot papers rejected in part, in the custody of the relevant registration officer, or

(b)   for the opening of a sealed packet of the completed corresponding number lists or certificates as to employment on duty on the day of the poll or the inspection of any counted ballot papers in his custody,

may be made by a county court, if the court is satisfied by evidence on oath that the order is required for the purpose of instituting or maintaining a prosecution for an offence in relation to ballot papers, or for the purpose of an election petition.

(2)   An order for the opening of a sealed packet of the completed corresponding number lists or of certificates as to employment on duty on the day of the poll or for the inspection of any counted ballot papers in the custody of the relevant registration officer may be made by an election court.

(3)   An order under this rule may be made subject to such conditions as to—

(a)   persons,

(b)   time,

(c)   place and mode of inspection,

(d)   production or opening,

as the court making the order may think expedient; but in making and carrying into effect an order for the opening of a packet of the completed corresponding number lists or certificates as to employment on duty on the day of the poll or for the inspection of counted ballot papers, care must be taken that the way in which the vote of any particular elector has been given shall not be disclosed until it has been proved—

(i)   that his vote was given; and

(ii)   that the vote has been declared by a competent court to be invalid.

(4) An appeal lies to the High Court from any order of a county court under this rule.

(5) Any power given under this rule to a county court may be exercised by any judge of the court otherwise than in open court.

(6) Where an order is made for the production by the relevant registration officer of any document in his possession relating to any specified election—

    (a) the production by him or his agent of the document ordered in such manner as may be directed by that order shall be conclusive evidence that the document relates to the specified election; and

    (b) any endorsement on any packet of ballot papers so produced shall be prima facie evidence that the ballot papers are what they are stated to be by the endorsement.

(7) The production from proper custody of—

    (a) a ballot paper purporting to have been used at any election, and

    (b) a completed corresponding number list with a number marked in writing beside the number of the ballot paper,

shall be prima facie evidence that the elector whose vote was given by that ballot paper was the person whose entry in the register of electors or on a notice issued under section 13B(3B) or (3D) of the 1983 Act at the time of the election contained the same number as the number written as mentioned in sub-paragraph (b) of this paragraph.

(8) Save as by this rule provided, no person shall be allowed to inspect any rejected or counted ballot papers in the possession of the relevant registration officer or open any sealed packets of the completed corresponding number lists or of certificates as to employment on duty on the day of the poll.

Retention of documents

54 The relevant registration officer must retain for one year all documents relating to an election forwarded to him in pursuance of these Rules by a returning officer, and then, unless otherwise directed by an order of a county court, the Crown Court, a magistrates' court or an election court, must cause them to be destroyed.

Part 6
Death of Candidate

Countermand or abandonment of poll on death of a candidate

55(1) If at a contested election proof is given to the returning officer's satisfaction before the result of the election is declared that one of the persons named or to be named as candidate in the ballot papers has died, then the returning officer must countermand notice of the poll or, if polling has begun, direct that the poll be abandoned, and the provisions of subsections (1) and (5) of section 39 of the 1983 Act apply in respect of any vacancy which remains unfilled.

(2) Neither the countermand of the poll at the parish or community election nor the direction that that poll be abandoned shall affect the poll at each relevant election or referendum.

(3) Where the poll at the parish or community election is abandoned by reason of a candidate's death, no further ballot papers shall be issued.

(4) At the close of the poll at each relevant election or referendum the presiding officer must take the like steps (so far as not already taken) for the delivery to the returning

officer of ballot boxes and ballot papers and other documents as he would be required to do if the poll at the parish or community election had not been abandoned.

(5)   The returning officer must dispose of ballot papers used at the parish or community election (at which a candidate has died) as he is required to do on the completion in due course of the counting of the votes, subject to paragraphs (6) and (7).

(6)   It is not necessary for any ballot paper account at that election to be prepared or verified.

(7)   Having separated the ballot papers relating to each relevant election or referendum, the returning officer must take no step or further step for the counting of the ballot papers used at the parish or community election (at which a candidate has died) or of the votes cast at that parish or community election.

(8)   The returning officer must seal up all the ballot papers used at the parish or community election (whether the votes on them have been counted or not) and it shall not be necessary to seal up counted and rejected ballot papers in separate packets.

(9)   The provisions of these Rules as to the inspection, production, retention and destruction of ballot papers and other documents by the relevant registration officer relating to a poll at a parish or community election apply to any such documents relating to a poll abandoned by reason of a candidate's death subject to paragraphs (10) and (11).

(10) Ballot papers on which the votes were neither counted nor rejected must be treated as counted ballot papers.

(11) No order is to be made for—
  (a) the production or inspection of any ballot papers, or
  (b) for the opening of a sealed packet of the completed corresponding number lists or of certificates as to employment on duty on the day of the poll,
unless the order is made by a court with reference to a prosecution.

Part 7
Appendix of Forms
Forms not reproduced

SCHEDULE 4
Rule 7

Parishes and Communities Elections
Declaration as to Expenses
Election for the .... ward of the
Parish/Community of ....
Day of Election ....
Full name of candidate ....
I declare as follows–
1 The amount paid by me or on my behalf for my election expenses at the above election was £ ....
2 To the best of my knowledge and belief no other election expenses have been paid or incurred by me or by any other person or organisation in connection with my candidature.
3 To the best of my knowledge and belief the accompanying return of election expenses is complete and correct as required by law.

4 I understand that the law does not allow any election expenses not mentioned in the return to be defrayed except in pursuance of a court order.

Signature of candidate . . . .

Date . . . .

Local Elections (Principal Areas) (England and Wales) Rules 2006 (SI 2006/3304)

12th December 2006

Citation, commencement, extent and revocations

1 (1)   These Rules may be cited as The Local Elections (Principal Areas) (England and Wales) Rules 2006.

(2)   These Rules come into force on 2 January 2007 except for the purposes of an election if the last date for the publication of the notice of election for that election was, or will be, prior to 27 March 2007.

(3)   These Rules shall not extend to Scotland or Northern Ireland.

(4)   Subject to paragraph (2), the statutory instruments listed in column 1 of Schedule 1 to these Rules (which have the reference listed in column 2) are revoked to the extent indicated in column 3 of that Schedule.

Interpretation

2 (1)   In these Rules,

"1983 Act" means the Representation of the People Act 1983;

"Assembly constituency" shall have the same meaning as in section 2(4) and (5) of the Greater London Authority Act 1999;

"the Combination of Polls Regulations" means the Representation of the People (Combination of Polls) (England and Wales) Regulations 2004;

"counting observer" shall have the same meaning as in regulation 2(1) of the Local Authorities (Conduct of Referendums) (England) Regulations 2012;

"counting officer" shall have the same meaning as in regulation 2(1) of the Local Authorities (Conduct of Referendums) (England) Regulations 2012;

"European Parliamentary election" shall have the same meaning as in section 27(1) of the Representation of the People Act 1985;

"GLRO" means the Greater London returning officer, being the person who is for the time being the proper officer of the Greater London Authority for the purposes of section 35(2C) of the 1983 Act or any person acting on his behalf;

"local counting area" shall have the same meaning as in regulation 2(1) of the

European Parliamentary Elections Regulations 2004;

"mayoral election" means an election conducted under the Local Authorities (Mayoral Elections) (England and Wales) Regulations 2007;

"petition organiser" shall have the same meaning as in regulation 3 of the Local Authorities (Referendums) (Petitions and Directions) (England) Regulations 2000;

"police and crime commissioner election" means an election of a police and crime commissioner in accordance with Chapter 6 of Part 1 of the 2011 Act;

"polling observer" shall have the same meaning as in regulation 2(1) of the Local Authorities (Conduct of Referendums) (England) Regulations 2012;

"principal area" means, in England, a county, district or London borough and, in Wales, a county or county borough;

"referendum" means a referendum conducted under the Local Authorities (Conduct of Referendums) (England) Regulations 2012;

"voting area" shall have the same meaning as in regulation 2 of the Local Authorities (Conduct of Referendums) (England) Regulations 2012.

(2) In these Rules, "relevant election or referendum" means one or more of the following–
    (a) a Parliamentary election;
    (b) a European Parliamentary election;
    (c) another local government election;
    (d) a mayoral election; and
    (e) a referendum,
    (f) a police and crime commissioner election,
the poll at which is taken together with the poll at the principal area election.

(3) In the case of a referendum, a reference to--
    (a) a "candidate" shall be construed as a reference to a petition organiser;
    (b) an "election agent" or a "counting agent" shall be construed as a reference to a counting observer;
    (c) a "polling agent" shall be construed as a reference to a polling observer; and
    (d) a "returning officer" shall be construed as a reference to a counting officer.

Elections Rules

3 In the application of the parliamentary elections rules to the election of councillors of the council of a principal area where the poll at that election is not taken together with the poll at another election under section 36(3), (3AB) or (3AC) of the 1983 Act or section 15(1) or (2) of the Representation of the People Act 1985, adaptations, alterations and exceptions shall be made to those rules so that the election shall be conducted in accordance with the Rules set out in Schedule 2 to these Rules.

Combination of polls

4 Where the poll at an election of councillors to the council of a principal area is to be taken together with the poll at a relevant election or referendum, the Rules set out in Schedule 2 shall apply to the principal area election as shown modified in Schedule 3.

SCHEDULE 1
Revocations

Not reproduced

SCHEDULE 2

Rules for Conduct of an Election of Councillors of a Principal Area where Poll is Not Taken Together with Poll at Another Election

Rule 3

Part 1
Provisions as to Time

Part 2
Stages Common to Contested and Uncontested Elections

Part 3
Contested Elections

Chapter 1
General Provisions

Chapter 2
Action to be Taken Before the Poll

Chapter 3
The Poll

Part 1
Provisions as to Time

Timetable

1   The proceedings at the election shall be conducted in accordance with the following
Table.

Proceedings	Time
Publication of notice of election	Not later than the twenty-fifth day before the day of election.

Proceedings	Time
Delivery of nomination papers	Not later than 4 in the afternoon on the nineteenth day before the day of election
Publication of statement as to persons nominated	Not later than 4 in the afternoon on the eighteenth day before the day of election
Delivery of notices of withdrawals of candidature	Not later than 4 in the afternoon on the nineteenth day before the day of election
Notice of poll	Not later than the sixth day before the day of election.
Polling	Between the hours of 7 in the morning and 10 at night on the day of election.

Computation of time

2(1) In computing any period of time for the purposes of the Timetable-
   (a) a Saturday or Sunday,
   (b) Christmas Eve, Christmas Day, Good Friday or a bank holiday, or
   (c) a day appointed for public thanksgiving or mourning,
shall be disregarded, and any such day shall not be treated as a day for the purpose of any proceedings up to the completion of the poll nor shall the returning officer be obliged to proceed with the counting of the votes on such a day.

(2) In this rule "bank holiday" means a day which is a bank holiday under the Banking and Financial Dealings Act 1971 in England and Wales.

Part 2
Stages Common to Contested and Uncontested Elections

Notice of election

3(1) The returning officer must publish notice of the election stating-
   (a) the place and times at which nomination papers are to be delivered, and
   (b) the date of the poll in the event of a contest,
and the notice must state that forms of nomination papers may be obtained at that place and those times.

(2) The notice of election must state the date by which-
   (a) applications to vote by post or by proxy, and
   (b) other applications and notices about postal or proxy voting,
must reach the registration officer in order that they may be effective for the election.

Nomination of candidates

4(1)   Each candidate must be nominated by a separate nomination paper, in the form in the Appendix, delivered at the place fixed for the purpose by the returning officer, which shall be at the offices of the council of the district or London borough in which the electoral area wholly or mainly lies.

(2)   The nomination paper must state the candidate's-
   (a)   full names,
   (b)   home address in full, and
   (c)   if desired, description,
   and the surname must be placed first in the list of names.

(3)   If a candidate commonly uses-
   (a)   a surname which is different from any other surname he has, or
   (b)   a forename which is different from any other forename he has,
   the nomination paper may state the commonly used surname or forename in addition to the other name.

(4)   The description (if any) can only be-
   (a)   one authorised as mentioned in rule 5(1) or (3); or
   (b)   the word "Independent".

Nomination papers: name of registered political party

5(1)   A nomination paper may not include a description of a candidate which is likely to lead electors to associate the candidate with a registered political party unless the party is a qualifying party in relation to the electoral area and the description is authorised by a certificate-
   (a)   issued by or on behalf of the registered nominating officer of the party, and
   (b)   received by the returning officer before the last time for the delivery of nomination papers set out in the Table in rule 1.

(2)   In paragraph (1) an authorised description may be either-
   (a)   the name of the party registered under section 28 of the Political Parties, Elections and Referendums Act 2000, or
   (b)   a description of the party registered under section 28A of that Act.

(3)   A nomination paper may not include a description of a candidate which is likely to lead electors to associate the candidate with two or more registered political parties unless the parties are each qualifying parties in relation to the electoral area and the description is a registered description authorised by a certificate-
   (a)   issued by or on behalf of the registered nominating officer of each of the parties, and
   (b)   received by the returning officer before the last time for the delivery of nomination papers set out in the Table in rule 1.

(4)   For the purposes of paragraph (3), a description is a registered description if it is a description registered for use by the parties under section 28B of the Political Parties, Elections and Referendums Act 2000.

(5)   A person shall be guilty of a corrupt practice if he fraudulently purports to be authorised to issue a certificate under paragraph (1) or (3) on behalf of a registered political party's nominating officer.

(6)   For the purposes of the application of this rule in relation to an election-
   (a)   "registered political party" means a party which was registered under Part 2 of the Political Parties, Elections and Referendums Act 2000 on the day ("the relevant day") which is two days before the last day for the delivery of nomination papers at that election;

(b) a registered political party is a qualifying party in relation to an electoral area if the electoral area is in England or Wales and the party was on the relevant day registered in respect of that part of Great Britain in the Great Britain register maintained under that Part of that Act.

(7) For the purposes of paragraph (6)(a), any day falling within rule 2(1) must be disregarded.

Subscription of nomination paper

6(1) The nomination paper must be subscribed by two electors as proposer and seconder, and by eight other electors as assenting to the nomination.

(2) Where a nomination paper has the signatures of more than the required number of persons as proposing, seconding or assenting to the nomination of a candidate, the signature or signatures (up to the required number) appearing first on the paper in each category must be taken into account to the exclusion of any others in that category.

(3) The nomination paper must give the electoral number of each person subscribing it.

(4) The returning officer-

    (a) must supply any elector with as many forms of nomination paper and forms of consent to nomination as may be required at the place and during the time for delivery of nomination papers, and

    (b) must at any elector's request prepare a nomination paper for signature,

but it is not necessary for a nomination or consent to nomination to be on a form supplied by the returning officer.

(5) A person must not subscribe more nomination papers than there are vacancies to be filled in the electoral area; nor subscribe any nomination paper in respect of an election in any other electoral area of the same local government area whilst the election in the first-mentioned electoral area is taking place:

Provided that a person shall not be prevented from subscribing a nomination paper by reason only of his having subscribed that of a candidate who has died or withdrawn before delivery of the first mentioned paper.

(6) If a person subscribes any nomination paper in contravention of paragraph (5), his signature shall be inoperative on all but those papers (up to the permitted number) which are first delivered.

(7) In this rule "elector"-

    (a) means a person who is registered in the register of local government electors for the electoral area in question on the last day for the publication of notice of the election; and

    (b) includes a person then shown in the register as below voting age if (but only if) it appears from the register that he will be of voting age on the day fixed for the poll.

(8) But, in this rule, "elector" does not include a person who has an anonymous entry in the register.

Consent to nomination

7 A person shall not be validly nominated unless his consent to nomination-

    (a) is given in writing on or within one month before the last day for the delivery of nomination papers,

    (b) is in the appropriate form in the Appendix or a form to the like effect and includes-

        (i) for a nomination in England, a copy of sections 80 and 81 of the Local

Government Act 1972, section 78A of the Local Government Act 2000 and section 34 of the Localism Act 2011; or

    (ii) for a nomination in Wales, a copy of sections 80 and 81 of the Local Government Act 1972 and sections 78A and 79 of the Local Government Act 2000,

(c) is attested by one witness, and

(d) is delivered at the place and within the time for the delivery of nomination papers.

Decisions as to validity of nomination papers

8(1) Where a nomination paper and the candidate's consent to it are delivered in accordance with these Rules, the candidate shall be deemed to stand nominated unless and until-

    (a) the returning officer decides that the nomination paper is invalid; or

    (b) proof is given to the returning officer's satisfaction of the candidate's death; or

    (c) the candidate withdraws.

(2) The returning officer is entitled to hold a nomination paper invalid only on one of the following grounds-

    (a) that the particulars of the candidate or the persons subscribing the paper are not as required by law; and

    (b) that the paper is not subscribed as so required.

(3) Subject to paragraph (4), the returning officer must, as soon as practicable after each nomination paper has been delivered, examine it and decide whether the candidate has been validly nominated.

(4) If in the returning officer's opinion a nomination paper breaks rule 5(1) or (3), he must give a decision to that effect-

    (a) as soon as practicable after the delivery of the nomination paper, and

    (b) in any event, before the end of the period of 24 hours starting with the close of the period for delivery of nomination papers set out in the Table in rule 1.

(5) Where the returning officer decides that a nomination paper is invalid, he must endorse and sign on the paper the fact and the reasons for his decision.

(6) The returning officer must send notice of his decision that a nomination paper is valid or invalid to each candidate at his home address as given in his nomination paper.

(7) The returning officer's decision that a nomination paper is valid shall be final and shall not be questioned in any proceeding whatsoever.

(8) Subject to paragraph (7), nothing in this rule prevents the validity of a nomination being questioned on an election petition.

Publication of statement of persons nominated

9(1) The returning officer must prepare and publish a statement showing the persons who have been and stand nominated and any other persons who have been nominated, with the reason why they no longer stand nominated.

(2) The statement must show the names, addresses and descriptions of the persons nominated as given in their nomination papers.

(3) If a person's nomination paper gives a commonly used surname or forename in addition to another name, the statement must show the person's commonly used surname or forename (as the case may be) instead of any other name.

(4) Paragraph (3) does not apply if the returning officer thinks-

    (a) that the use of the person's commonly used name may be likely to mislead or confuse electors, or

   (b) that the commonly used name is obscene or offensive.

(5) If paragraph (4) applies, the returning officer must give notice in writing to the candidate of his reasons for refusing to allow the use of a commonly used name.

(6) The statement must show the persons standing nominated arranged alphabetically in the order of their surnames, and if there are two or more of them with the same surname, of their other names.

(7) In the case of a person nominated by more than one nomination paper, the returning officer must take the particulars required by the foregoing provisions of this rule from such one of the papers as the candidate (or the returning officer in default of the candidate) may select.

Correction of minor errors

10(1) A returning officer may, if he thinks fit, at any time before the publication under rule 9 of the statement of persons nominated, correct minor errors in a nomination paper.

(2) Errors which may be corrected include-
   (a) errors as to a person's electoral number;
   (b) obvious errors of spelling in relation to the details of a candidate.

(3) Anything done by a returning officer in pursuance of this rule shall not be questioned in any proceedings other than proceedings on an election petition.

(4) A returning officer must have regard to any guidance issued by the Electoral Commission for the purposes of this rule.

Inspection of nomination papers and consents to nomination

11 During ordinary office hours on any day, other than a day specified in rule 2(1), after the latest time for delivery of nomination papers and before the date of the poll, any person may inspect and take copies of, or extracts from, nomination papers and consents to nomination.

Nomination in more than one electoral area

12 A candidate who is validly nominated for more than one electoral area of the same local government area, must withdraw from his candidature in all those electoral areas except one, and if he does not so withdraw, he shall be deemed to have withdrawn from his candidature in all those electoral areas.

Withdrawal of candidates

13(1) A candidate may withdraw his candidature by notice of withdrawal-
   (a) signed by him and attested by one witness, and
   (b) delivered to the returning officer at the place for delivery of nomination papers.

(2) Where a candidate is outside the United Kingdom, a notice of withdrawal signed by his proposer and accompanied by a written declaration also so signed of the candidate's absence from the United Kingdom shall be of the same effect as a notice of withdrawal signed by the candidate; but where the candidate stands nominated by more than one nomination paper a notice of withdrawal under this paragraph shall be effective if, and only if-
   (a) it and the accompanying declaration are signed by all the proposers except any who is, and is stated in that declaration to be, outside the United Kingdom; or
   (b) it is accompanied, in addition to that declaration, by a written statement signed by the candidate that the proposer giving the notice is authorised to do so on

the candidate's behalf during his absence from the United Kingdom.

Method of election

14(1) If the number of persons remaining validly nominated for the electoral area after any withdrawals under these Rules exceeds the number of councillors to be elected, a poll must be taken in accordance with Part 3 of these Rules.

(2) If the number of persons remaining validly nominated for the electoral area after any withdrawals under these Rules does not exceed the number of councillors to be elected, such person or persons must be declared to be elected in accordance with Part 4 of these Rules.

Part 3
Contested Elections

Chapter 1
General Provisions

Poll to be taken by ballot

15 The votes at the poll must be given by ballot, the result must be ascertained by counting the votes given to each candidate and the candidate or candidates to whom more votes have been given than to the other candidates, up to the number of councillors to be elected, must be declared to have been elected.

The ballot papers

16(1) The ballot of every voter must consist of a ballot paper, and the persons remaining validly nominated for the electoral area after any withdrawals under these Rules, and no others, shall be entitled to have their names inserted in the ballot paper.

(2) Every ballot paper must be in the form in the Appendix, and must be printed in accordance with the directions in that Appendix, and-
    (a) must contain the names and other particulars of the candidates as shown in the statement of persons nominated;
    (b) must be capable of being folded up; and
    (c) must have a number and other unique identifying mark printed on the back.

(3) If a candidate who is the subject of a party's authorisation under rule 5(1) so requests, the ballot paper must contain, against the candidate's particulars, the party's registered emblem (or, as the case may be, one of the party's registered emblems).

(3A) If a candidate who is the subject of an authorisation by two or more parties under rule 5(3) so requests, the ballot paper must contain, against the candidate's particulars, the registered emblem (or, as the case may be, one of the registered emblems) of one of those parties.

(4) The candidate's request under paragraph (3) or (3A) must-
    (a) be made in writing to the returning officer, and
    (b) be received by him before the last time for the delivery of nomination papers set out in the Table in rule 1.

(5) The order of the names in the ballot paper must be the same as in the statement of persons nominated.

The corresponding number list

17(1) The returning officer must prepare a list containing the numbers and other unique identifying marks of all of the ballot papers to be issued by him in pursuance of rule

22(1) or provided by him in pursuance of rule 26(1).

(2) The list must be in the appropriate form in the Appendix or a form to like effect.

The official mark

18(1) Every ballot paper must contain an appropriate security marking (the official mark).

(2) The official mark must be kept secret, and an interval of not less than five years shall intervene between the use of the same official mark at elections for the same county, county borough, district or London borough, as the case may be.

(3) The returning officer may use a different official mark for different purposes at the same election.

Prohibition of disclosure of vote

19 No person who has voted at the election shall, in any legal proceeding to question the election, be required to state for whom he has voted.

Use of schools and public rooms

20(1) The returning officer may use, free of charge, for the purpose of taking the poll or counting the votes-
   (a) a room in a school maintained or assisted by a local authority (as defined in the Education Act 1996) or a school in respect of which grants are made out of moneys provided by Parliament to the person or body of persons responsible for the management of the school;
   (b) a room the expense of maintaining which is payable out of any rate.

(2) The returning officer must make good any damage done to, and defray any expense incurred by the persons having control over, any such room as mentioned above by reason of its being used for the purpose of taking the poll or counting the votes.

Chapter 2
Action to be Taken Before the Poll

Notice of poll

21(1) The returning officer must publish notice of the poll stating-
   (a) the day and hours fixed for the poll;
   (b) the number of councillors to be elected;
   (c) the particulars of each candidate remaining validly nominated (the names and other particulars of the candidates, and the order of the candidates' names being the same as in the statement of persons nominated); and
   (d) the names of all persons signing a candidate's nomination paper.

(2) Where a candidate is nominated by more than one nomination paper, the nomination paper referred to in paragraph (1)(d) must be that from which the names and other particulars of the candidate shown in the statement of persons nominated are taken.

(3) The returning officer must, not later than the time of the publication of the notice of the poll, also give public notice of-
   (a) the situation of each polling station; and
   (b) the description of voters entitled to vote there,
   and he must as soon as practicable after giving such a notice give a copy of it to each of the election agents.

Postal ballot papers

22(1) The returning officer must, in accordance with regulations made under the 1983 Act, issue to those entitled to vote by post a ballot paper and a postal voting statement in the appropriate form in the Appendix, or a form to like effect, together with such envelopes for their return as may be prescribed by such regulations.

(2) The returning officer must also issue to those entitled to vote by post such information as he thinks appropriate about how to obtain-

    (a) translations into languages other than English of any directions to or guidance for voters sent with the ballot paper;

    (b) a translation into Braille of such directions or guidance;

    (c) graphical representations of such directions or guidance;

    (d) the directions or guidance in any other form (including any audible form).

(3) The postal voting statement must include provision for the form to be signed and for stating the date of birth of the elector or proxy (as the case may be).

(4) In the case of a ballot paper issued to a person at an address in the United Kingdom, the returning officer must ensure that the return of the ballot paper and postal voting statement is free of charge to the voter.

Provision of polling stations

23(1) The returning officer must provide a sufficient number of polling stations and, subject to the following provisions of this rule, must allot the electors to the polling stations in such manner as he thinks most convenient.

(2) One or more polling stations may be provided in the same room.

(3) The polling station allotted to electors from any parliamentary polling district wholly or partly within the electoral area must, in the absence of special circumstances, be in the parliamentary polling place for that district, unless that place is outside the electoral area.

(4) The returning officer must provide each polling station with such number of compartments as may be necessary in which the voters can mark their votes screened from observation.

Appointment of presiding officers and polling clerks

24(1) The returning officer must appoint and pay a presiding officer to attend at each polling station and such clerks as may be necessary for the purposes of the election, but he must not appoint any person who has been employed by or on behalf of a candidate in or about the election.

(2) The returning officer may, if he thinks fit, preside at a polling station and the provisions of these Rules relating to a presiding officer shall apply to a returning officer so presiding with the necessary modifications as to things to be done by the returning officer to the presiding officer or by the presiding officer to the returning officer.

(3) A presiding officer may do, by the clerks appointed to assist him, any act (including the asking of questions) which he is required or authorised by these Rules to do at a polling station except order the arrest, exclusion or removal of any person from the polling station.

Issue of official poll cards

25(1) The returning officer must as soon as practicable after the publication of the notice of the election send to electors and their proxies an official poll card.

(2) An elector's official poll card must be sent or delivered to his qualifying address, and a proxy's to his address as shown in the list of proxies.

(3) The official poll card must be in the appropriate form in the Appendix, or a form to the

like effect, and must set out-

    (a) the name of the council and of the electoral division or ward to which councillors are to be elected;

    (b) the elector's name, qualifying address and number on the register;

    (c) the date and hours of the poll and the situation of the elector's polling station;

    (d) such other information as the returning officer thinks appropriate,

and different information may be provided in pursuance of sub-paragraph (d) to different electors or descriptions of elector.

(4) In the case of an elector with an anonymous entry, instead of containing the matter mentioned in paragraph (3)(b), the polling card must contain such matter as is specified in the appropriate form in the Appendix.

(5) Paragraph (7) of rule 6 shall apply for the interpretation of this rule.

Equipment of polling stations

26(1) The returning officer must provide each presiding officer with such number of ballot boxes and ballot papers as in the returning officer's opinion may be necessary.

(2) Every ballot box must be so constructed that the ballot papers can be put in it, but cannot be withdrawn from it, without the box being unlocked or, where the box has no lock, the seal being broken.

(3) The returning officer must provide each polling station with-

    (a) materials to enable voters to mark the ballot papers;

    (b) copies of the register of electors for the electoral area or such part of it as contains the names of the electors allotted to the station;

    (c) the parts of any special lists prepared for the election corresponding to the register of electors for the electoral area or the part of it provided under sub-paragraph (b);

    (d) a list consisting of that part of the list prepared under rule 17 which contains the numbers (but not the other unique identifying marks) corresponding to those on the ballot papers provided to the presiding officer of the polling station.

(4) The reference in paragraph (3)(b) to the copies of the register of electors includes a reference to copies of any notices issued under section 13B(3B) or (3D) of the 1983 Act in respect of alterations to the register.

(5) The returning officer must also provide each polling station with-

    (a) at least one large version of the ballot paper which must be displayed inside the polling station for the assistance of voters who are partially sighted; and

    (b) a device of such description as is set out in paragraph (9) for enabling voters who are blind or partially sighted to vote without any need for assistance from the presiding officer or any companion (within the meaning of rule 37(1)).

(6) A notice in the form in the Appendix, giving directions for the guidance of voters in voting, must be printed in conspicuous characters and exhibited inside and outside every polling station.

(7) The returning officer may also provide copies of the notice mentioned in paragraph (6) in Braille or translated into languages other than English as he considers appropriate, provided that these notices are accurate reproductions in Braille or that other language of that notice.

(8) In every compartment of every polling station there must be exhibited the notice:
"Vote for NO MORE THAN . CANDIDATES by putting a cross X in the box next to EACH of your choices.
Vote ONLY ONCE by putting a cross X in the box next to your choice.
PUT NO OTHER MARK ON THE BALLOT PAPER OR YOUR VOTE MAY NOT COUNT."

(9)   The device referred to in paragraph (5)(b) must-
- (a)   allow a ballot paper to be inserted into and removed from, or attached to and detached from, the device easily and without damage to the paper;
- (b)   hold the ballot paper firmly in place during use; and
- (c)   provide suitable means for the voter to-
  - (i)   identify the spaces on the ballot paper on which he may mark his vote;
  - (ii)   identify the candidate to which each such space refers; and
  - (iii)   mark his vote on the space he has chosen.

Appointment of polling and counting agents

27(1)   Subject to paragraphs (3) and (4), each candidate may, before the commencement of the poll, appoint-
- (a)   polling agents to attend at polling stations for the purpose of detecting personation; and
- (b)   counting agents to attend at the counting of the votes.

(2)   The same person may be appointed as a polling agent or counting agent by more than one candidate.

(3)   Not more than four polling agents, or such greater number as the returning officer may by notice allow, shall be permitted to attend at any particular polling station and if the number of such agents appointed to attend at a particular polling station exceeds that number, the returning officer must determine which agents are permitted to attend by lot and only the agents on whom the lot falls shall be deemed to have been duly appointed.

(4)   The returning officer may limit the number of counting agents, so however that-
- (a)   the number must be the same in the case of each candidate; and
- (b)   the number allowed to a candidate must not (except in special circumstances) be less than the number obtained by dividing the number of clerks employed on the counting by the number of candidates.

For the purposes of the calculations required by this paragraph, a counting agent who has been appointed for more than one candidate is a separate agent for each of the candidates by whom he has been appointed.

(5)   Notice in writing of the appointment, stating the names and addresses of the persons appointed, must be given by the candidate to the returning officer and must be so given not later than the fifth day (disregarding any day specified in rule 2(1)) before the day of the poll.

(6)   If an agent dies, or becomes incapable of acting, the candidate may appoint another agent in his place, and must forthwith give to the returning officer notice in writing of the name and address of the agent appointed.

(7)   In the following provisions of these Rules references to polling agents and counting agents shall be taken as references to agents-
- (a)   whose appointments have been duly made and notified; and
- (b)   where the number of agents is restricted, who are within the permitted numbers.

(8)   Any notice required to be given to a counting agent by the returning officer may be delivered at, or sent by post to, the address stated in the notice of appointment.

(9)   A candidate may himself do any act or thing which any polling or counting agent of his, if appointed, would have been authorised to do, or may assist his agent in doing any such act or thing.

(10)   A candidate's election agent may do or assist in doing anything which the candidate's

polling or counting agent is authorised to do; and anything required or authorised by these Rules to be done in the presence of the polling or counting agents may be done in the presence of a candidate's election agent instead of his polling agent or counting agents.

(11) Where by these Rules any act or thing is required or authorised to be done in the presence of the polling or counting agents, the non-attendance of any agent or agents at the time and place appointed for the purpose shall not, if the act or thing is otherwise duly done, invalidate the act or thing done.

Notification of requirement of secrecy

28(1) The returning officer must make such arrangements as he thinks fit to ensure that-
- (a) every person attending at a polling station (otherwise than for the purpose of voting or assisting a voter with disabilities to vote or as a constable on duty there) has been given a copy in writing of the provisions of subsections (1), (3) and (6) of section 66 of the 1983 Act; and
- (b) every person attending at the counting of the votes (other than any constable on duty at the counting) has been given a copy in writing of the provisions of subsections (2) and (6) of that section.

(2) In this rule, a reference to a constable includes a person designated as a community support officer under section 38 of the Police Reform Act 2002 (police powers for employees).

Return of postal ballot papers

29(1) Where-
- (a) a postal vote has been returned in respect of a person who is entered on the postal voters list, or
- (b) a proxy postal vote has been returned in respect of a proxy who is entered on the proxy postal voters list,

the returning officer must mark the list in the manner prescribed by regulations made under the 1983 Act.

(2) Rule 45(3) does not apply for the purpose of determining whether, for the purposes of this rule, a postal vote or a proxy postal vote is returned.

Chapter 3
The Poll

Admission to polling station

30(1) The presiding officer must exclude all persons from the polling station except-
- (a) voters;
- (b) persons under the age of 18 who accompany voters to the polling station;
- (c) the candidates and their election agents;
- (d) the polling agents appointed to attend at the polling station;
- (e) the clerks appointed to attend at the polling station;
- (f) persons who are entitled to attend by virtue of any of sections 6A to 6D of the Political Parties, Elections and Referendums Act 2000;
- (g) the constables on duty; and
- (h) the companions of voters with disabilities.

(2) The presiding officer must regulate the total number of voters and persons under the age of 18 who accompany them to be admitted to the polling station at the same time.

(3) Not more than one polling agent shall be admitted at the same time to a polling station on behalf of the same candidate.

(4) A constable or person employed by a returning officer must not be admitted to vote in person elsewhere than at his own polling station allotted to him under these Rules, except on production and surrender of a certificate as to his employment which must be in the form in the Appendix, or a form, to the like effect, and signed by an officer of police of or above the rank of inspector or by the returning officer, as the case may be.

(5) Any certificate surrendered under this rule must forthwith be cancelled.

(6) In this rule, a reference to a constable includes a person designated as a community support officer under section 38 of the Police Reform Act 2002 (police powers for employees).

Keeping of order in station

31(1) It is the presiding officer's duty to keep order at his polling station.

(2) If a person misconducts himself in a polling station, or fails to obey the presiding officer's lawful orders, he may immediately, by the presiding officer's order, be removed from the polling station-
   (a) by a constable in or near that station, or
   (b) by any other person authorised in writing by the returning officer to remove him,
   and the person so removed shall not, without the presiding officer's permission, again enter the polling station during the day.

(3) Any person so removed may, if charged with the commission in the polling station of an offence, be dealt with as a person taken into custody by a constable for an offence without a warrant.

(4) The powers conferred by this rule must not be exercised so as to prevent a voter who is otherwise entitled to vote at a polling station from having an opportunity of voting at that station.

Sealing of ballot boxes

32 Immediately before the commencement of the poll, the presiding officer must show the ballot box empty to such persons, if any, as are present in the polling station, so that they may see that it is empty, and must then lock it up, if it has a lock and (in any case) place his seal on it in such a manner as to prevent its being opened without breaking the seal and must place it in his view for the receipt of ballot papers, and keep it so locked and sealed or sealed (as the case may be).

Questions to be put to voters

33(1) At the time of the application (but not afterwards), the questions specified in the second column of the following Table-
   (a) may be put by the presiding officer to a person applying for a ballot paper who is mentioned in the first column, and
   (b) must be put if the letter "R" appears after the question and the candidate or his election or polling agent requires the question to be put:

Q. No.	Person applying for ballot paper	Question
1	A person applying as an elector	(a)—Are you the person registered in the register of local government electors for this election as follows? read the whole entry from the register [R]
		(b)—Have you already voted here or elsewhere at this election for *(this county) *(this district) *(this London borough) *(this county borough), *delete whichever is inapplicable (adding, in the case of an election for several electoral areas , in this or any other electoral area) otherwise than as proxy for some other person? [R]
2	A person applying as proxy	(a)—Are you the person whose name appears as A.B. in the list of proxies for this election as entitled to vote as proxy on behalf of C.D.? [R]
		(b)—Have you already voted here or elsewhere at this election for *(this county) *(this district) *(this London borough) *(this county borough), *delete whichever is inapplicable (adding in the case of an election for several electoral areas , in this or any other electoral area) as proxy on behalf of C.D.? [R]
		(c)—Are you the spouse, civil partner, parent, grandparent, brother, sister, child or grandchild of C.D.? [R]
3	A person applying as proxy for an elector with an anonymous entry (instead of the questions at entry 2)	(a)—Are you the person entitled to vote as proxy on behalf of the elector whose number on the register of electors is (read out the number)? [R]

Q. No.	Person applying for ballot paper	Question
		(b)—Have you already voted here or elsewhere as proxy on behalf of the elector whose number on the register of electors is (read out the number)? [R]
		(c)—Are you the spouse, civil partner, parent, grandparent, brother, sister, child or grandchild of the person whose number on the register of electors is (read out the number)? [R]
4	A person applying as proxy if the question at entry 2(c) or 3(c) is not answered in the affirmative	Have you already voted at this election for *(this county) *(this district) *(this London borough) *(this county borough), *delete whichever is inapplicable (adding, in the case of an election for several electoral areas , in this or any other electoral area) on behalf of two persons of whom you are not the spouse, civil partner, parent, grandparent, brother, sister, child or grandchild? [R]
5	A person applying as an elector in relation to whom there is an entry in the postal voters list	(a)—Did you apply to vote by post?
		(b)—Why have you not voted by post?
6	A person applying as proxy who is named in the proxy postal voters list	(a)—Did you apply to vote by post as proxy?
		(b)—Why have you not voted by post as proxy?

(2) In the case of an elector in respect of whom a notice has been issued under section 13B(3B) or (3D) of the 1983 Act, the references in the questions at entries 1(a) and 3(a), (b) and (c) to reading from the register shall be taken as references to reading from the notice issued under section 13B(3B) or (3D) of the 1983 Act.

(3) A ballot paper must not be delivered to any person required to answer any of the above questions unless he has answered each question satisfactorily.

(4) Except as authorised by this rule, no inquiry shall be permitted as to the right of any

person to vote.

Challenge of voter

34   A person must not be prevented from voting by reason only that-

    (a) a candidate or his election or polling agent declares that he has reasonable cause to believe that the person has committed an offence of personation, or

    (b) the person is arrested on the grounds that he is suspected of committing or of being about to commit such an offence.

Voting procedure

35(1) A ballot paper must be delivered to a voter who applies for one, and immediately before delivery-

    (a) the number and (unless paragraph (2) applies) name of the elector as stated in the copy of the register of electors must be called out;

    (b) the number of the elector must be marked on the list mentioned in rule 26(3)(d) beside the number of the ballot paper to be issued to him;

    (c) a mark must be placed in the register of electors against the number of the elector to note that a ballot paper has been received but without showing the particular ballot paper which has been received; and

    (d) in the case of a person applying for a ballot paper as proxy, a mark must also be placed against his name in the list of proxies.

  (2) In the case of an elector who has an anonymous entry, he must show the presiding officer his official poll card and only his number shall be called out in pursuance of paragraph (1)(a).

  (3) In the case of an elector who is added to the register in pursuance of a notice issued under section 13B(3B) or (3D) of the 1983 Act, paragraph (1) is modified as follows-

    (a) in sub-paragraph (a), for "copy of the register of electors" substitute "copy of the notice issued under section 13B(3B) or (3D) of the 1983 Act";

    (b) in sub-paragraph (c), for "in the register of electors" substitute "on the copy of the notice issued under section 13B(3B) or (3D) of the 1983 Act".

  (4) The voter, on receiving the ballot paper, must forthwith proceed into one of the compartments in the polling station and there secretly mark his paper and fold it up so as to conceal his vote, and must then show to the presiding officer the back of the paper, so as to disclose the number and other unique identifying mark, and put the ballot paper so folded up into the ballot box in the presiding officer's presence.

  (5) The voter must vote without undue delay, and must leave the polling station as soon as he has put his ballot paper into the ballot box.

  (6) A voter who at the close of the poll is in the polling station, or in a queue outside the polling station, for the purposes of voting shall (despite the close of the poll) be entitled to apply for a ballot paper under paragraph (1); and these rules apply in relation to such a voter accordingly.

Votes marked by presiding officer

36(1) The presiding officer, on the application of a voter-

    (a) who is incapacitated by blindness or other disability from voting in the manner directed by these Rules, or

    (b) who declares orally that he is unable to read,

must, in the presence of the polling agents, cause the voter's vote to be marked on a ballot paper in the manner directed by the voter, and the ballot paper to be placed in the ballot box.

(2) The name and number on the register of electors of every voter whose vote is marked in pursuance of this rule, and the reason why it is so marked, must be entered on a list (in these Rules called "the list of votes marked by the presiding officer").

In the case of a person voting as proxy for an elector, the number to be entered together with the voter's name shall be the elector's number.

(3) In the case of a person in respect of whom a notice has been issued under section 13B(3B) or (3D) of the 1983 Act, paragraph (2) applies as if for "on the register of electors of every voter" there were substituted "relating to every voter in respect of whom a notice has been issued under section 13B(3B) or (3D) of the 1983 Act".

Voting by persons with disabilities

37(1) If a voter makes an application to the presiding officer to be allowed, on the ground of-
    (a) blindness or other disability, or
    (b) inability to read,
to vote with the assistance of another person by whom he is accompanied (in these Rules referred to as "the companion"), the presiding officer must require the voter to declare, orally or in writing, whether he is so incapacitated by his blindness or other disability, or by his inability to read, as to be unable to vote without assistance.

(2) If the presiding officer-
    (a) is satisfied that the voter is so incapacitated, and
    (b) is also satisfied by a written declaration made by the companion (in these Rules referred to as "the declaration made by the companion of a voter with disabilities") that the companion-
        (i) is a qualified person within the meaning of this rule; and
        (ii) has not previously assisted more than one voter with disabilities to vote at the election,
the presiding officer must grant the application, and then anything which is by these Rules required to be done to or by that voter in connection with the giving of his vote may be done to, or with the assistance of, the companion.

(3) For the purposes of these Rules, a person is a voter with disabilities if he has made such a declaration as is mentioned in paragraph (1), and a person shall be qualified to assist a voter with disabilities to vote if that person-
    (a) is a person who is entitled to vote as an elector at the election; or
    (b) is the father, mother, brother, sister, spouse, civil partner, son or daughter of the voter and has attained the age of 18 years.

(4) The name and number in the register of electors of every voter whose vote is given in accordance with this rule and the name and address of the companion must be entered on a list (in these Rules referred to as "the list of voters with disabilities assisted by companions").

In the case of a person voting as proxy for an elector, the number to be entered together with the voter's name shall be the elector's number.

(5) In the case of a person in respect of whom a notice has been issued under section 13B(3B) or (3D) of the 1983 Act, paragraph (4) applies as if for "in the register of electors of every voter" there were substituted "relating to every voter in respect of whom a notice has been issued under section 13B(3B) or (3D) of the 1983 Act".

(6) The declaration made by the companion-
    (a) must be in the form in the Appendix,
    (b) must be made before the presiding officer at the time when the voter applies to vote with the assistance of a companion, and
    (c) must forthwith be given to the presiding officer who must attest and retain it.

(7)   No fee or other payment shall be charged in respect of the declaration.

Tendered ballot papers: circumstances where available

38(1)   If a person, representing himself to be-
- (a)   a particular elector named on the register and not named in the absent voters list, or
- (b)   a particular person named in the list of proxies as proxy for an elector and not entitled to vote by post as proxy,

applies for a ballot paper after another person has voted in person either as the elector or his proxy, the applicant shall, on satisfactorily answering the questions permitted by law to be asked at the poll, be entitled, subject to the following provisions of this rule and rule 39, to mark a ballot paper (in these Rules referred to as "a tendered ballot paper") in the same manner as any other voter.

(2)   Paragraph (4) applies if-
- (a)   a person applies for a ballot paper representing himself to be a particular elector named on the register,
- (b)   he is also named in the postal voters list, and
- (c)   he claims that he did not make an application to vote by post at the election.

(3)   Paragraph (4) also applies if-
- (a)   a person applies for a ballot paper representing himself to be a particular person named as a proxy in the list of proxies,
- (b)   he is also named in the proxy postal voters list, and
- (c)   he claims that he did not make an application to vote by post as proxy.

(4)   The person shall, on satisfactorily answering the questions permitted by law to be asked at the poll, be entitled, subject to the following provisions of this rule and rule 39, to mark a ballot paper (in these Rules referred to as a "tendered ballot paper") in the same manner as any other voter.

(5)   Paragraph (6) applies if before the close of the poll but after the last time at which a person may apply for a replacement postal ballot paper, a person represents himself to be-
- (a)   a particular elector named on the register who is also named in the postal voters list, or
- (b)   a particular person named as a proxy in the list of proxies and who is also named in the proxy postal voters list,

and claims that he has lost or has not received his postal ballot paper.

(6)   The person shall, on satisfactorily answering the questions permitted by law to be asked at the poll, be entitled, subject to the provisions of this rule and rule 39, to mark a ballot paper (in these Rules referred to as a "tendered ballot paper") in the same manner as any other voter.

Tendered ballot papers: general provisions

39(1)   A tendered ballot paper must-
- (a)   be of a colour differing from the other ballot papers;
- (b)   instead of being put into the ballot box, be given to the presiding officer and endorsed by him with the name of the voter and his number in the register of electors, and set aside in a separate packet.

(2)   The name of the voter and his number in the register of electors must be entered on a list (in these Rules referred to as the "tendered votes list").

(3)   In the case of a person voting as proxy for an elector, the number to be endorsed or entered together with the voter's name shall be the number of that elector.

(4) In the case of an elector who has an anonymous entry, this rule and rule 38 apply subject to the following modifications-

    (a) in paragraphs (1)(b) and (2) above, the references to the name of the voter shall be ignored;

    (b) otherwise, a reference to a person named on a register or list shall be construed as a reference to a person whose number appears in the register or list (as the case may be).

(5) In the case of a person in respect of whom a notice has been issued under section 13B(3B) or (3D) of the 1983 Act, this rule and rule 38 shall apply as if-

    (a) in rule 38(1)(a), (2)(a) and (5)(a), for "named on the register" there were substituted "in respect of whom a notice under section 13B(3B) or (3D) of the 1983 Act has been issued";

    (b) in paragraph (1)(b) of this rule for "his number in the register of electors" there were substituted "the number relating to him on a notice issued under section 13B(3B) or (3D) of the 1983 Act";

    (c) in paragraph (2) of this rule, for "his number in the register of electors" there were substituted "the number relating to him on a notice issued under section 13B(3B) or (3D) of the 1983 Act".

Spoilt ballot papers

40 A voter who has inadvertently dealt with his ballot paper in such manner that it cannot be conveniently used as a ballot paper may, on delivering it to the presiding officer and proving to his satisfaction the fact of the inadvertence, obtain another ballot paper in the place of the ballot paper so delivered (in these Rules referred to as "a spoilt ballot paper"), and the spoilt ballot paper must be immediately cancelled.

Correction of errors on day of poll

41 The presiding officer must keep a list of persons to whom ballot papers are delivered in consequence of an alteration to the register made by virtue of section 13B(3B) or (3D) of the 1983 Act which takes effect on the day of the poll.

Adjournment of poll in case of riot

42(1) Where the proceedings at any polling station are interrupted or obstructed by riot or open violence, the presiding officer must adjourn the proceedings till the following day and must forthwith give notice to the returning officer.

(2) Where the poll is adjourned at any polling station-

    (a) the hours of polling on the day to which it is adjourned must be the same as for the original day; and

    (b) references in these Rules to the close of the poll shall be construed accordingly.

Procedure on close of poll

43(1) As soon as practicable after the close of the poll, the presiding officer must, in the presence of the polling agents, make up into separate packets, sealed with his own seal and the seals of such polling agents as desire to affix their seals-

    (a) each ballot box in use at the station, sealed so as to prevent the introduction of additional ballot papers and unopened, but with the key, if any, attached,

    (b) the unused and spoilt ballot papers placed together,

    (c) the tendered ballot papers,

    (d) the marked copies of the register of electors (including any marked copy notices issued under section 13B(3B) or (3D) of the 1983 Act) and of the list of proxies,

    (e) the lists prepared under rule 17 including the parts which were completed in accordance with rule 35(1)(b) (together referred to in these Rules as "the completed corresponding number lists"),

(f) the certificates as to employment on duty on the day of the poll,

(g) the tendered votes list, the list of voters with disabilities assisted by companions, the list of votes marked by the presiding officer, a statement of the number of voters whose votes are so marked by the presiding officer under the heads "disability" and "unable to read", the list maintained under rule 41 (correction of errors on day of poll), and the declarations made by the companions of voters with disabilities,

and must deliver the packets or cause them to be delivered to the returning officer to be taken charge of by him; but if the packets are not delivered by the presiding officer personally to the returning officer, the arrangements for their delivery shall require the returning officer's approval.

(2) The marked copies of the register of electors and of the list of proxies must be in one packet but must not be in the same packet as the completed corresponding number lists or the certificates as to employment on duty on the day of the poll.

(3) The packets must be accompanied by a statement (in these Rules referred to as "the ballot paper account") made by the presiding officer showing the number of ballot papers entrusted to him, and accounting for them under the heads of ballot papers issued and not otherwise accounted for, unused, spoilt and tendered ballot papers.

Chapter 4
Counting of Votes

Attendance at counting of votes

44

(1) The returning officer must make arrangements for counting the votes in the presence of the counting agents as soon as practicable after the close of the poll, and must give to the counting agents notice in writing of the time and place at which he will begin to count the votes.

(2) No person other than-

(a) the returning officer and his clerks,

(b) the candidates and one other person chosen by each of them,

(c) the election agents,

(d) the counting agents,

(e) persons who are entitled to attend by virtue of any of sections 6A to 6D of the Political Parties, Elections and Referendums Act 2000,

may be present at the counting of the votes, unless permitted by the returning officer to attend.

(3) A person not entitled to attend at the counting of the votes shall not be permitted to do so by the returning officer unless he-

(a) is satisfied that the efficient counting of the votes will not be impeded; and

(b) has either consulted the election agents or thought it impracticable to do so.

(4) The returning officer must give the counting agents all such reasonable facilities for overseeing the proceedings, and all such information with respect to them, as he can give them consistently with the orderly conduct of the proceedings and the discharge of his duties in connection with them.

(5) In particular, where the votes are counted by sorting the ballot papers according to the candidate for whom the vote is given and then counting the number of ballot papers for each candidate, the counting agents shall be entitled to satisfy themselves that the ballot papers are correctly sorted.

The count

45(1)   The returning officer must-
- (a)   in the presence of the counting agents open each ballot box and count and record the number of ballot papers in it;
- (b)   in the presence of the election agents verify each ballot paper account; and
- (c)   count such of the postal ballot papers as have been duly returned and record the number counted.

(2)   The returning officer must not count the votes given on any ballot papers until-
- (a)   in the case of postal ballot papers, they have been mixed with the ballot papers from at least one ballot box, and
- (b)   in the case of ballot papers from a ballot box, they have been mixed with the ballot papers from at least one other ballot box.

(3)   A postal ballot paper must not be taken to be duly returned unless-
- (a)   it is returned in the manner set out in paragraph (4) and reaches the returning officer or any polling station in the electoral area in question before the close of the poll;
- (b)   the postal voting statement, duly signed, is also returned in the manner set out in paragraph (4) and reaches him or such a polling station before that time;
- (c)   the postal voting statement also states the date of birth of the elector or proxy (as the case may be), and
- (d)   in a case where steps for verifying the date of birth and signature of an elector or proxy have been prescribed by regulations made under the 1983 Act, the returning officer (having taken such steps) verifies the date of birth and signature of the elector or proxy (as the case may be).

(4)   The manner in which any postal ballot paper or postal voting statement may be returned-
- (a)   to the returning officer, is by hand or by post;
- (b)   to a polling station, is by hand.

(4A)   A postal ballot paper or postal voting statement that reaches the returning officer or a polling station on or after the close of the poll is treated for the purposes of this rule as reaching that officer or polling station before the close of the poll if it is delivered by a person who, at the close of the poll, is in the polling station, or in a queue outside the polling station, for the purpose of returning it.

(5)   The returning officer must not count any tendered ballot paper.

(6)   The returning officer, while counting and recording the number of ballot papers and counting the votes, must keep the ballot papers with their faces upwards and take all proper precautions for preventing any person from seeing the numbers or other unique identifying marks printed on the back of the papers.

(7)   The returning officer must verify each ballot paper account by comparing it with the number of ballot papers recorded by him, and the unused and spoilt ballot papers in his possession and the tendered votes list (opening and re-sealing the packets containing the unused and spoilt ballot papers and the tendered votes list) and must draw up a statement as to the result of the verification, which any election agent may copy.

(8)   The returning officer must so far as practicable proceed continuously with counting the votes, allowing only time for refreshment, except that he may exclude the hours between 7 in the evening and 9 on the following morning.

(9)   During the time so excluded the returning officer must-
- (a)   place the ballot papers and other documents relating to the election under his own seal and the seals of such of the counting agents as desire to affix their

seals; and
   (b) otherwise take proper precautions for the security of the papers and documents.

Re-count

46(1) A candidate or his election agent may, if present when the counting or any re-count of the votes is completed, require the returning officer to have the votes re-counted or again re-counted but the returning officer may refuse to do so if in his opinion the request is unreasonable.

   (2) No step shall be taken on the completion of the counting or any re-count of votes until the candidates and election agents present at its completion have been given a reasonable opportunity to exercise the right conferred by this rule.

Rejected ballot papers

47(1) Any ballot paper-
   (a) which does not bear the official mark, or
   (b) on which votes are given for more candidates than the voter is entitled to vote for, or
   (c) on which anything is written or marked by which the voter can be identified except the printed number and other unique identifying mark on the back, or
   (d) which is unmarked or void for uncertainty,
   shall, subject to paragraphs (2) and (3), be void and not counted.

   (2) Where the voter is entitled to vote for more than one candidate, a ballot paper shall not be deemed to be void for uncertainty as respects any vote as to which no uncertainty arises and that vote must be counted.

   (3) A ballot paper on which the vote is marked-
   (a) elsewhere than in the proper place, or
   (b) otherwise than by means of a cross, or
   (c) by more than one mark,
   shall not for such reason be deemed to be void (either wholly or as respects that vote) if an intention that the vote shall be for one or other of the candidates clearly appears, and the way the paper is marked does not itself identify the voter and it is not shown that he can be identified by it.

   (4) The returning officer must-
   (a) endorse the word "rejected" on any ballot paper which under this rule is not to be counted; and
   (b) in the case of a ballot paper on which any vote is counted under paragraph (2), endorse the words "rejected in part" on the ballot paper and indicate which vote or votes have been counted;
   and must add to the endorsement the words "rejection objected to" if any objection is made by a counting agent to his decision.

   (5) The returning officer must draw up a statement showing the number of ballot papers rejected, including those rejected in part, under the several heads of-
   (a) want of official mark;
   (b) voting for more candidates than the voter is entitled to;
   (c) writing or mark by which the voter could be identified;
   (d) unmarked or void for uncertainty;
   and the statement must record the number of ballot papers rejected in part.

Decisions on ballot papers

48 The decision of the returning officer on any question arising in respect of a ballot paper

shall be final, but shall be subject to review on an election petition.

Equality of votes

49   Where, after the counting of the votes (including any re-count) is completed, an equality of votes is found to exist between any candidates and the addition of a vote would entitle any of those candidates to be declared elected, the returning officer must forthwith decide between those candidates by lot, and proceed as if the candidate on whom the lot falls had received an additional vote.

Part 4
Final Proceedings in Contested and Uncontested Elections

Declaration of result

50(1)   In a contested election, when the result of the poll has been ascertained, the returning officer must forthwith-

    (a)   declare to be elected the candidate or candidates to whom more votes have been given than to the other candidates, up to the number of councillors to be elected;

    (b)   give notice of the name of each candidate to whom sub-paragraph (a) applies to the proper officer of the council for which the election is held; and

    (c)   give public notice of the name of each candidate elected and of the total number of votes given for each candidate (whether elected or not) together with the number of rejected ballot papers under each head shown in the statement of rejected ballot papers.

  (2)   In an uncontested election, the returning officer must as soon as practicable after the latest time for the delivery of notices of withdrawals of candidature-

    (a)   declare to be elected the person or persons remaining validly nominated;

    (b)   give notice of the name of each person to whom sub-paragraph (a) applies to the proper officer of the council for which the election is held; and

    (c)   give public notice of the name of each such person.

Part 5
Disposal of Documents

Sealing up of ballot papers

51(1)   On the completion of the counting at a contested election the returning officer must seal up in separate packets the counted and rejected ballot papers, including ballot papers rejected in part.

  (2)   The returning officer must not open the sealed packets of-

    (a)   tendered ballot papers,

    (b)   the completed corresponding number lists,

    (c)   certificates as to employment on duty on the day of the poll, or

    (d)   marked copies of the register of electors (including any marked copy notices issued under section 13B(3B) or (3D) of the 1983 Act) and lists of proxies.

Delivery of documents to relevant registration officer

52(1)   The returning officer must then forward to the relevant registration officer the following documents-

    (a)   the packets of ballot papers in his possession,

    (b)   the ballot paper accounts and the statements of rejected ballot papers and of the result of the verification of the ballot paper accounts,

    (c)   the tendered votes lists, the lists of voters with disabilities assisted by companions, the lists of votes marked by the presiding officer and the related statements, the lists maintained under rule 41, and the declarations made by the companions of voters with disabilities,

    (d)   the packets of the completed corresponding number lists,

    (e)   the packets of certificates as to employment on duty on the day of the poll, and

    (f)   the packets containing marked copies of registers (including any marked copy notices issued under section 13B(3B) or (3D) of the 1983 Act) and of the postal voters list, of the lists of proxies and of the proxy postal voters list.

(2)   In this rule and in rules 53, 54 and 55 references to the relevant registration officer are to the registration officer of the local authority in whose area the election is held.

Orders for production of documents

53(1)   An order-

    (a)   for the inspection or production of any rejected ballot papers, including ballot papers rejected in part, in the custody of the relevant registration officer; or

    (b)   for the opening of a sealed packet of the completed corresponding number lists or certificates as to employment on duty on the day of the poll or for the inspection of any counted ballot papers in his custody,

may be made by a county court, if the court is satisfied by evidence on oath that the order is required for the purpose of instituting or maintaining a prosecution for an offence in relation to ballot papers, or for the purpose of an election petition.

(2)   An order for the opening of a sealed packet of the completed corresponding number lists or of certificates as to employment on duty on the day of the poll or for the inspection of any counted ballot papers in the custody of the relevant registration officer may be made by an election court.

(3)   An order under this rule may be made subject to such conditions as to-

    (a)   persons,

    (b)   time,

    (c)   place and mode of inspection,

    (d)   production or opening,

as the court making the order may think expedient; but in making and carrying into effect an order for the opening of a packet of the completed corresponding number lists or of certificates as to employment on duty on the day of the poll or for the inspection of counted ballot papers, care must be taken that the way in which the vote of any particular elector has been given shall not be disclosed until it has been proved-

    (i)   that his vote was given; and

    (ii)   that the vote has been declared by a competent court to be invalid.

(4)   An appeal lies to the High Court from any order of a county court under this rule.

(5)   Any power given under this rule to a county court may be exercised by any judge of the court otherwise than in open court.

(6)   Where an order is made for the production by the relevant registration officer of any document in his possession relating to any specified election-

    (a)   the production by him or his agent of the document ordered in such manner as may be directed by that order shall be conclusive evidence that the document relates to the specified election; and

    (b)   any endorsement on any packet of ballot papers so produced shall be prima facie evidence that the ballot papers are what they are stated to be by the endorsement.

(7) The production from proper custody of-
    (a) a ballot paper purporting to have been used at any election, and
    (b) a completed corresponding number list with a number marked in writing beside the number of the ballot paper,
shall be prima facie evidence that the elector whose vote was given by that ballot paper was the person whose entry in the register of electors or on a notice issued under section 13B(3B) or (3D) of the 1983 Act at the time of the election contained the same number as the number written as mentioned in sub-paragraph (b) of this paragraph.

(8) Save as by this rule provided, no person shall be allowed to inspect any rejected or counted ballot papers in the possession of the relevant registration officer or open any sealed packets of the completed corresponding number lists or of certificates as to employment on duty on the day of the poll.

Retention of documents

54 The relevant registration officer must retain for one year all documents relating to an election forwarded to him in pursuance of these Rules by a returning officer, and then, unless otherwise directed by an order of a county court, a Crown Court, a magistrates' court or an election court, must cause them to be destroyed.

Part 6
Death of Candidate

Countermand or abandonment of poll on death of a candidate

55(1) If at a contested election proof is given to the returning officer's satisfaction before the result of the election is declared that one of the persons named or to be named as candidate in the ballot papers has died, then the returning officer must countermand notice of the poll or, if polling has begun, direct that the poll be abandoned, and the provisions of subsections (1) and (5) of section 39 of the 1983 Act apply in respect of any vacancy which remains unfilled.

(2) Where the poll is abandoned by reason of a candidate's death no further ballot papers shall be issued, and the presiding officer at any polling station must take the like steps (so far as not already taken) for the delivery to the returning officer of ballot boxes and ballot papers and other documents as he is required to take on the close of the poll in due course.

(3) The returning officer must dispose of ballot papers and other documents in his possession as he is required to do on the completion in due course of the counting of the votes, subject to paragraphs (4) and (5).

(4) It is not necessary for any ballot paper account to be prepared or verified.

(5) The returning officer must seal up all the ballot papers, whether the votes on them have been counted or not, and it shall not be necessary to seal up counted and rejected ballot papers in separate packets.

(6) The provisions of these Rules as to the inspection, production, retention and destruction of ballot papers and other documents by the relevant registration officer relating to a poll at an election shall apply to any such documents relating to a poll abandoned by reason of a candidate's death, subject to paragraphs (7) and (8).

(7) Ballot papers on which the votes were neither counted nor rejected must be treated as counted ballot papers.

(8) No order is to be made for-

(a) the inspection or production of any ballot papers, or

(b) for the opening of a sealed packet of the completed corresponding number lists or certificates as to employment on duty on the day of the poll,

unless the order is made by a court with reference to a prosecution.

Part 7

Appendix of Forms

Forms not reproduced

SCHEDULE 3

RULES FOR CONDUCT OF AN ELECTION OF COUNCILLORS OF A
PRINCIPAL AREA WHERE THE POLL IS TAKEN TOGETHER
WITH THE POLL AT A RELEVANT ELECTION OR REFERENDUM

Rule 4

Part 1

Provisions as to Time

Timetable

1. The proceedings at the election shall be conducted in accordance with the following Table.

Timetable

Proceedings	Time
Publication of notice of election	Not later than the twenty-fifth day before the day of election.
Delivery of nomination papers	Not later than 4 in the afternoon on the nineteenth day before the day of election
Publication of statement as to persons nominated	Not later than 4 in the afternoon on the eighteenth day before the day of election
Delivery of notices of withdrawals of candidature	Not later than 4 in the afternoon on the nineteenth day before the day of election
Notice of poll	Not later than the sixth day before the day of election.
Polling	Between the hours of 7 in the morning and 10 at night on the day of election.

Computation of time

2(1) In computing any period of time for the purposes of the Timetable—

    (a) a Saturday or Sunday,

    (b) Christmas Eve, Christmas Day, Good Friday or a bank holiday, or

    (c) a day appointed for public thanksgiving or mourning,

shall be disregarded, and any such day shall not be treated as a day for the purpose of any proceedings up to the completion of the poll nor shall the returning officer be obliged to proceed with the counting of the votes on such a day.

(2)   In this rule "bank holiday" means a day which is a bank holiday under the Banking and Financial Dealings Act 1971 in England and Wales.

Part 2
Stages Common to Contested and Uncontested Elections

Notice of election

3(1)   The returning officer must publish notice of the election stating—
    (a)   the place and times at which nomination papers are to be delivered, and
    (b)   the date of the poll in the event of a contest,
and the notice must state that forms of nomination papers may be obtained at that place and those times.

(2)   The notice of election must state the date by which—
    (a)   applications to vote by post or by proxy, and
    (b)   other applications and notices about postal or proxy voting,
must reach the registration officer in order that they may be effective for the election.

Nomination of candidates

4(1)   Each candidate must be nominated by a separate nomination paper, in the form in the Appendix, delivered at the place fixed for the purpose by the returning officer, which shall be at the offices of the council of the district or London borough in which the electoral area wholly or mainly lies.

(2)   The nomination paper must state the candidate's—
    (a)   full names,
    (b)   home address in full, and
    (c)   if desired, description,
and the surname must be placed first in the list of names.

(3)   If a candidate commonly uses—
    (a)   a surname which is different from any other surname he has, or
    (b)   a forename which is different from any other forename he has,
the nomination paper may state the commonly used surname or forename in addition to the other name.

(4)   The description (if any) can only be—
    (a)   one authorised as mentioned in rule 5(1) or (3); or
    (b)   the word "Independent".

Nomination papers: name of registered political party

5(1)   A nomination paper may not include a description of a candidate which is likely to lead electors to associate the candidate with a registered political party unless the party is a qualifying party in relation to the electoral area and the description is authorised by a certificate—
    (a)   issued by or on behalf of the registered nominating officer of the party, and
    (b)   received by the returning officer before the last time for the delivery of nomination papers set out in the Table in rule 1.

(2)   In paragraph (1) an authorised description may be either—
    (a)   the name of the party registered under section 28 of the Political Parties,

Elections and Referendums Act 2000, or

(b)   a description of the party registered under section 28A of that Act.

(3)   A nomination paper may not include a description of a candidate which is likely to lead electors to associate the candidate with two or more registered political parties unless the parties are each qualifying parties in relation to the electoral area and the description is a registered description authorised by a certificate—

(a)   issued by or on behalf of the registered nominating officer of each of the parties, and

(b)   received by the returning officer before the last time for the delivery of nomination papers set out in the Table in rule 1.

(4)   For the purposes of paragraph (3), a description is a registered description if it is a description registered for use by the parties under section 28B of the Political Parties, Elections and Referendums Act 2000.

(5)   A person shall be guilty of a corrupt practice if he fraudulently purports to be authorised to issue a certificate under paragraph (1) or (3) on behalf of a registered political party's nominating officer.

(6)   For the purposes of the application of this rule in relation to an election—

(a)   "registered political party" means a party which was registered under Part 2 of the Political Parties, Elections and Referendums Act 2000 on the day ("the relevant day") which is two days before the last day for the delivery of nomination papers at that election;

(b)   a registered political party is a qualifying party in relation to an electoral area if the electoral area is in England or Wales and the party was on the relevant day registered in respect of that part of Great Britain in the Great Britain register maintained under that Part of that Act.

(7)   For the purposes of paragraph (6)(a), any day falling within rule 2(1) shall be disregarded.

Subscription of nomination paper

6(1)   The nomination paper must be subscribed by two electors as proposer and seconder, and by eight other electors as assenting to the nomination.

(2)   Where a nomination paper has the signatures of more than the required number of persons as proposing, seconding or assenting to the nomination of a candidate, the signature or signatures (up to the required number) appearing first on the paper in each category must be taken into account to the exclusion of any others in that category.

(3)   The nomination paper must give the electoral number of each person subscribing it.

(4)   The returning office

(a)   must supply any elector with as many forms of nomination paper and forms of consent to nomination as may be required at the place and during the time for delivery of nomination papers, and

(b)   must at any elector's request prepare a nomination paper for signature,

but it is not necessary for a nomination or consent to nomination to be on a form supplied by the returning officer.

(5)   A person must not subscribe more nomination papers than there are vacancies to be filled in the electoral area; nor subscribe any nomination paper in respect of an election in any other electoral area of the same local government area whilst the election in the first-mentioned electoral area is taking place:

Provided that a person shall not be prevented from subscribing a nomination paper by reason only of his having subscribed that of a candidate who has died or withdrawn before delivery of the first mentioned paper.

(6) If a person subscribes any nomination paper in contravention of paragraph (5), his signature shall be inoperative on all but those papers (up to the permitted number) which are first delivered.

(7) In this rule "elector"—

    (a) means a person who is registered in the register of local government electors for the electoral area in question on the last day for the publication of notice of the election; and

    (b) includes a person then shown in the register as below voting age if (but only if) it appears from the register that he will be of voting age on the day fixed for the poll.

(8) But, in this rule, "elector"does not include a person who has an anonymous entry in the register.

Consent to nomination

7 A person shall not be validly nominated unless his consent to nomination—

    (a) is given in writing on or within one month before the last day for the delivery of nomination papers,

    (b) is in the appropriate form in the Appendix or a form to the like effect and includes—

       (i) for a nomination in England, a copy of sections 80 and 81 of the Local Government Act 1972, section 78A of the Local Government Act 2000 and section 34 of the Localism Act 2011; or

       (ii) for a nomination in Wales, a copy of sections 80 and 81 of the Local Government Act 1972 and sections 78A and 79 of the Local Government Act 2000,

    (c) is attested by one witness, and

    (d) is delivered at the place and within the time for the delivery of nomination papers.

Decisions as to validity of nomination papers

8(1) Where a nomination paper and the candidate's consent to it are delivered in accordance with these Rules, the candidate shall be deemed to stand nominated unless and until—

    (a) the returning officer decides that the nomination paper is invalid; or

    (b) proof is given to the returning officer's satisfaction of the candidate's death; or

    (c) the candidate withdraws.

(2) The returning officer is entitled to hold a nomination paper invalid only on one of the following grounds—

    (a) that the particulars of the candidate or the persons subscribing the paper are not as required by law; and

    (b) that the paper is not subscribed as so required.

(3) Subject to paragraph (4), the returning officer must, as soon as practicable after each nomination paper has been delivered, examine it and decide whether the candidate has been validly nominated.

(4) If in the returning officer's opinion a nomination paper breaks rule 5(1) or (3), he must give a decision to that effect—

    (a) as soon as practicable after the delivery of the nomination paper, and

    (b) in any event, before the end of the period of 24 hours starting with the close of the period for delivery of nomination papers set out in the Table in rule 1.

(5) Where the returning officer decides that a nomination paper is invalid, he must endorse and sign on the paper the fact and the reasons for his decision.

(6) The returning officer must send notice of his decision that a nomination paper is valid or invalid to each candidate at his home address as given in his nomination paper.

(7) The returning officer's decision that a nomination paper is valid shall be final and shall not be questioned in any proceeding whatsoever.

(8) Subject to paragraph (7), nothing in this rule prevents the validity of a nomination being questioned on an election petition.

Publication of statement of persons nominated

9(1) The returning officer must prepare and publish a statement showing the persons who have been and stand nominated and any other persons who have been nominated, with the reason why they no longer stand nominated.

(2) The statement must show the names, addresses and descriptions of the persons nominated as given in their nomination papers.

(3) If a person's nomination paper gives a commonly used surname or forename in addition to another name, the statement must show the person's commonly used surname or forename (as the case may be) instead of any other name.

(4) Paragraph (3) does not apply if the returning officer thinks—
    (a) that the use of the person's commonly used name may be likely to mislead or confuse electors, or
    (b) that the commonly used name is obscene or offensive.

(5) If paragraph (4) applies, the returning officer must give notice in writing to the candidate of his reasons for refusing to allow the use of a commonly used name.

(6) The statement must show the persons standing nominated arranged alphabetically in the order of their surnames, and if there are two or more of them with the same surname, of their other names.

(7) In the case of a person nominated by more than one nomination paper, the returning officer must take the particulars required by the foregoing provisions of this rule from such one of the papers as the candidate (or the returning officer in default of the candidate) may select.

Correction of minor errors

10(1) A returning officer may, if he thinks fit, at any time before the publication under rule 9 of the statement of persons nominated, correct minor errors in a nomination paper.

(2) Errors which may be corrected include—
    (a) errors as to a person's electoral number;
    (b) obvious errors of spelling in relation to the details of a candidate.

(3) Anything done by a returning officer in pursuance of this rule shall not be questioned in any proceedings other than proceedings on an election petition.

(4) A returning officer must have regard to any guidance issued by the Electoral Commission for the purposes of this rule.

Inspection of nomination papers and consents to nomination

11 During ordinary office hours on any day, other than a day specified in rule 2(1), after the latest time for delivery of nomination papers and before the date of the poll, any person may inspect and take copies of, or extracts from, nomination papers and

consents to nomination.

Nomination in more than one electoral area

12   A candidate who is validly nominated for more than one electoral area of the same local government area, must withdraw from his candidature in all those electoral areas except one, and if he does not so withdraw, he shall be deemed to have withdrawn from his candidature in all those electoral areas.

Withdrawal of candidates

13(1)   A candidate may withdraw his candidature by notice of withdrawal—

    (a)   signed by him and attested by one witness, and

    (b)   delivered to the returning officer at the place for delivery of nomination papers.

(2)   Where a candidate is outside the United Kingdom, a notice of withdrawal signed by his proposer and accompanied by a written declaration also so signed of the candidate's absence from the United Kingdom shall be of the same effect as a notice of withdrawal signed by the candidate; but where the candidate stands nominated by more than one nomination paper a notice of withdrawal under this paragraph shall be effective if, and only if—

    (a)   it and the accompanying declaration are signed by all the proposers except any who is, and is stated in that declaration to be, outside the United Kingdom; or

    (b)   it is accompanied, in addition to that declaration, by a written statement signed by the candidate that the proposer giving the notice is authorised to do so on the candidate's behalf during his absence from the United Kingdom.

Method of election

14(1)   If the number of persons remaining validly nominated for the electoral area after any withdrawals under these Rules exceeds the number of councillors to be elected, a poll must be taken in accordance with Part 3 of these Rules.

(2)   If the number of persons remaining validly nominated for the electoral area after any withdrawals under these Rules does not exceed the number of councillors to be elected, such person or persons must be declared to be elected in accordance with Part 4 of these Rules.

Part 3
Contested Elections

Chapter 1
General Provisions

Poll to be taken by ballot

15   The votes at the poll must be given by ballot, the result must be ascertained by counting the votes given to each candidate and the candidate or candidates to whom more votes have been given than to the other candidates, up to the number of councillors to be elected, must be declared to have been elected.

The ballot papers

16(1)   The ballot of every voter must consist of a ballot paper, and the persons remaining validly nominated for the electoral area after any withdrawals under these Rules, and no others, shall be entitled to have their names inserted in the ballot paper.

(2)   Every ballot paper must be in the form in the Appendix, and must be printed in accordance with the directions in that Appendix, and—

(a) must contain the names and other particulars of the candidates as shown in the statement of persons nominated;

(b) must be capable of being folded up;

(c) must have a number and other unique identifying mark printed on the back; and

(d) must be of a different colour from that of any ballot papers used at any relevant election or referendum.

(3)   If a candidate who is the subject of a party's authorisation under rule 5(1) so requests, the ballot paper must contain, against the candidate's particulars, the party's registered emblem (or, as the case may be, one of the party's registered emblems).

(3A)   If a candidate who is the subject of an authorisation by two or more parties under rule 5(3) so requests, the ballot paper must contain, against the candidate's particulars, the registered emblem (or, as the case may be, one of the registered emblems) of one of those parties.

(4)   The candidate's request under paragraph (3) or (3A) must—

(a) be made in writing to the returning officer, and

(b) be received by him before the last time for the delivery of nomination papers set out in the Table in rule 1.

(5)   The order of the names in the ballot paper must be the same as in the statement of persons nominated.

The corresponding number list

17(1)   The returning officer must prepare a list containing the numbers and other unique identifying marks of all of the ballot papers to be issued by him in pursuance of rule 22(1) or provided by him in pursuance of rule 26(1).

(2)   The list must be in the appropriate form in the Appendix or a form to like effect.

The official mark

18(1)   Every ballot paper must contain an appropriate security marking (the official mark).

(2)   The official mark must be kept secret, and an interval of not less than five years shall intervene between the use of the same official mark at elections for the same county, county borough, district or London borough as the case may be.

(3)   The returning officer may use a different official mark for different purposes at the same election.

Prohibition of disclosure of vote

19   No person who has voted at the election shall, in any legal proceeding to question the election, be required to state for whom he has voted.

Use of schools and public rooms

20(1)   The returning officer may use, free of charge, for the purpose of taking the poll or counting the votes—

(a) a room in a school maintained or assisted by a local authority (as defined in the Education Act 1996) or a school in respect of which grants are made out of moneys provided by Parliament to the person or body of persons responsible for the management of the school;

(b) a room the expense of maintaining which is payable out of any rate.

(2)   The returning officer must make good any damage done to, and defray any expense incurred by the persons having control over, any such room as mentioned above by

reason of its being used for the purpose of taking the poll or counting the votes.

Chapter 2
Action to be Taken Before the Poll

Notice of Poll

21(1) The returning officer must publish notice of the poll stating—
    (a) the day and hours fixed for the poll;
    (b) the number of councillors to be elected;
    (c) the particulars of each candidate remaining validly nominated (the names and other particulars of the candidates, and the order of the candidates' names being the same as in the statement of persons nominated); and
    (d) the names of all persons signing a candidate's nomination paper.

(2) Where a candidate is nominated by more than one nomination paper, the nomination paper referred to in paragraph (1)(d) must be that from which the names and other particulars of the candidate shown in the statement of persons nominated are taken.

(3) The returning officer must, not later than the time of the publication of the notice of the poll, also give public notice of—
    (a) the situation of each polling station; and
    (b) the description of voters entitled to vote there,
and he must as soon as practicable after giving such a notice give a copy of it to each of the election agents.

(4) The notice published under paragraph (3) must—
    (a) state that the poll at the principal area election is to be taken together with the poll at a relevant election or referendum;
    (b) specify the parliamentary constituency, local counting area, Assembly constituency, voting area or, as the case may be, the relevant local authority and, in the case of an election to fill a casual vacancy, the electoral area for which the relevant election is held; and
    (c) where any of the polls are to be taken together in part of the local government area only, specify that part.

Postal ballot papers

22(1) The returning officer must, in accordance with regulations made under the 1983 Act, issue to those entitled to vote by post a ballot paper and a postal voting statement in the appropriate form in the Appendix, or a form to like effect, together with such envelopes for their return as may be prescribed by such regulations.

(2) The returning officer must also issue to those entitled to vote by post such information as he thinks appropriate about how to obtain—
    (a) translations into languages other than English of any directions to or guidance for voters sent with the ballot paper;
    (b) a translation into Braille of such directions or guidance;
    (c) graphical representations of such directions or guidance;
    (d) the directions or guidance in any other form (including any audible form).

(3) The postal voting statement must include provision for the form to be signed and for stating the date of birth of the elector or proxy (as the case may be).

(4) In the case of a ballot paper issued to a person at an address in the United Kingdom, the returning officer must ensure that the return of the ballot paper and postal voting statement is free of charge to the voter.

Provision of polling stations

23(1) The returning officer must provide a sufficient number of polling stations and, subject to the following provisions of this rule, must allot the electors to the polling stations in such manner as he thinks most convenient.

(2) One or more polling stations may be provided in the same room.

(3) The polling station allotted to electors from any parliamentary polling district wholly or partly within the electoral area must, in the absence of special circumstances, be in the parliamentary polling place for that district, unless that place is outside the electoral area.

(4) The returning officer must provide each polling station with such number of compartments as may be necessary in which the voters can mark their votes screened from observation.

Appointment of presiding officers and clerks

24(1) The returning officer must appoint and pay a presiding officer to attend at each polling station and such clerks as may be necessary for the purposes of the election, but he must not appoint any person who has been employed by or on behalf of a candidate in or about the election.

(2) The returning officer may, if he thinks fit, preside at a polling station and the provisions of these Rules relating to a presiding officer shall apply to a returning officer so presiding with the necessary modifications as to things to be done by the returning officer to the presiding officer or by the presiding officer to the returning officer.

(3) A presiding officer may do, by the clerks appointed to assist him, any act (including the asking of questions) which he is required or authorised by these Rules to do at a polling station except order the arrest, exclusion or removal of any person from the polling station.

Issue of official poll cards

25(1) The returning officer must as soon as practicable after the publication of the notice of election send to electors and their proxies an official poll card.

(2) An elector's official poll card must be sent or delivered to his qualifying address, and a proxy's to his address as shown in the list of proxies.

(3) The official poll card must be in the appropriate form in the Appendix, or a form to the like effect, and must set out—

    (a) the name of the council and of the electoral division or ward to which councillors are to be elected;

    (b) the elector's name, qualifying address and number on the register;

    (c) the date and hours of the poll and the situation of the elector's polling station;

    (d) such other information as the returning officer thinks appropriate,

and different information may be provided in pursuance of sub-paragraph (d) to different electors or descriptions of elector.

(4) In the case of an elector with an anonymous entry, instead of containing the matter mentioned in paragraph (3)(b), the polling card must contain such matter as is specified in the appropriate form in the Appendix.

(5) Paragraph (7) of rule 6 shall apply for the interpretation of this rule.

(6) If the returning officer and the returning officer for each relevant election or referendum think fit, an official poll card issued under this rule may be combined with the official poll card issued at every relevant election or referendum.

Equipment of polling stations

26(1)   The returning officer must provide each presiding officer with such number of ballot boxes and ballot papers as in the returning officer's opinion may be necessary.

(2)   The same ballot box may be used for the poll at the principal area election and the poll at every relevant election or referendum, if the returning officer thinks fit.

(3)   Every ballot box must be so constructed that the ballot papers can be put in it, but cannot be withdrawn from it, without the box being unlocked or, where the box has no lock, the seal being broken.

(4)   The returning officer must provide each polling station with—

   (a)   materials to enable voters to mark the ballot papers;

   (b)   copies of the register of electors for the electoral area or such part of it as contains the names of the electors allotted to the station;

   (c)   the parts of any special lists prepared for the election corresponding to the register of electors for the electoral area or the part of it provided under sub-paragraph (b);

   (d)   a list consisting of that part of the list prepared under rule 17 which contains the numbers (but not the other unique identifying marks) corresponding to those on the ballot papers provided to the presiding officer of the polling station.

(5)   The reference in paragraph (4)(b) to the copies of the register of electors includes a reference to copies of any notices issued under section 13B(3B) or (3D) of the 1983 Act in respect of alterations to the register.

(6)   The returning officer must also provide each polling station with—

   (a)   at least one large version of the ballot paper which must be printed on the same colour paper as the ballot papers and displayed inside the polling station for the assistance of voters who are partially sighted; and

   (b)   a device of such description as is set out in paragraph (11) for enabling voters who are blind or partially sighted to vote without any need for assistance from the presiding officer or any companion (within the meaning of rule 37(1)).

(7)   Where notwithstanding paragraph (2) separate ballot boxes are to be used, each ballot box must be clearly marked with—

   (a)   the election or referendum to which it relates, as shown on the ballot papers for that election or referendum; and

   (b)   the words "Place the specify colour of ballot papers in question ballot papers in here".

(8)   A notice in the form in the Appendix, giving directions for the guidance of voters in voting, must be printed in conspicuous characters and exhibited inside and outside every polling station.

(9)   The returning officer may also provide copies of the notice mentioned in paragraph (8) in Braille or translated into languages other than English as he considers appropriate, provided that these notices are accurate reproductions in Braille or that other language of that notice.

(10)   In every compartment of every polling station there must be exhibited the notice—

   *PARLIAMENTARY ELECTION

   (Specify colour ballot paper)

   Vote for ONLY ONE CANDIDATE by putting a cross X in the box next to your choice.

   *EUROPEAN PARLIAMENTARY ELECTION

   (Specify colour ballot paper)

   Vote ONLY ONCE by putting a cross X in the box next to your choice.

   *Specify name of council COUNCIL ELECTION

   (Specify colour ballot paper)

*Vote for NO MORE THAN … CANDIDATES by putting a cross X in the box next to EACH of your choices.

*Vote ONLY ONCE by putting a cross X in the box next to your choice.

*ELECTION OF THE MAYOR OF LONDON

(Specify colour ballot paper)

#On the ballot paper for the election of the Mayor, vote ONCE for your first choice and ONCE for your second choice.

*ELECTION OF THE LONDON ASSEMBLY

#On the constituency members ballot paper (specify colour) vote for ONE candidate only.

#On the London members ballot paper (specify colour) vote for ONE party or individual candidate only.

* Specify other ELECTION/REFERENDUM

(Specify colour ballot paper)

Specify voting instructions in accordance with the legislation governing the election or referendum

PUT NO OTHER MARK ON THE BALLOT PAPER OR YOUR VOTE MAY NOT COUNT.

*PLEASE DO NOT FOLD THE BALLOT PAPERS FOR specify the election(s) and/or referendum(s) at which the votes are to be counted electronically . Post them, face downwards, in the *appropriate ballot box.

*Complete or omit as necessary.

Alternatively, insert such information as the GLRO may decide.

(11) The device referred to in paragraph (6)(b) must—

    (a) allow a ballot paper to be inserted into and removed from, or attached to and detached from, the device easily and without damage to the paper;

    (b) hold the ballot paper firmly in place during use; and

    (c) provide suitable means for the voter to—

        (i) identify the spaces on the ballot paper on which he may mark his vote;

        (ii) identify the registered party or individual candidate to which each such space refers; and

        (iii) mark his vote on the space he has chosen.

Appointment of polling and counting agents

27(1) Subject to paragraphs (3) and (4), each candidate may, before the commencement of the poll, appoint—

    (a) polling agents to attend at polling stations for the purpose of detecting personation; and

    (b) counting agents to attend at the counting of the votes.

(2) The same person may be appointed as a polling agent or counting agent by more than one candidate.

(3) Not more than four polling agents, or such greater number as the returning officer may by notice allow, shall be permitted to attend at any particular polling station and if the number of such agents appointed to attend at a particular polling station exceeds that number, the returning officer must determine which agents are permitted to attend by lot and only the agents on whom the lot falls shall be deemed to have been duly appointed.

(4) The returning officer may limit the number of counting agents, so however that—

    (a) the number must be the same in the case of each candidate; and

    (b) the number allowed to a candidate must not (except in special circumstances) be less than the number obtained by dividing the number of clerks employed on the counting by the number of candidates.

For the purposes of the calculations required by this paragraph, a counting agent who has been appointed for more than one candidate is a separate agent for each of the candidates by whom he has been appointed.

(5) Notice in writing of the appointment, stating the names and addresses of the persons appointed, must be given by the candidate to the returning officer and must be so given not later than the fifth day (disregarding any day referred to in rule 2(1)) before the day of the poll.

(6) Notices of the appointment of polling agents and counting agents which are required by paragraph (5) above and paragraphs (7) and (8) below to be given to the returning officer must be given to that returning officer who discharges the functions specified in regulation 5 of the Combination of Polls Regulations.

(7) If an agent dies, or becomes incapable of acting, the candidate may appoint another agent in his place, and must forthwith give to the returning officer notice in writing of the name and address of the agent appointed.

(8) Any appointment authorised by this rule may be made and the notice of appointment given to the returning officer by the candidate's election agent, instead of by the candidate.

(9) In the following provisions of these Rules references to polling agents and counting agents shall be taken as references to agents—
   (a) whose appointments have been duly made and notified; and
   (b) where the number of agents is restricted, who are within the permitted numbers.

(10) Any notice required to be given to a counting agent by the returning officer may be delivered at, or sent by post to, the address stated in the notice of appointment.

(11) A candidate may himself do any act or thing which any polling or counting agent of his, if appointed, would have been authorised to do, or may assist his agent in doing any such act or thing.

(12) A candidate's election agent may do or assist in doing anything which the candidate's polling or counting agent is authorised to do; and anything required or authorised by these Rules to be done in the presence of the polling or counting agents may be done in the presence of a candidate's election agent instead of his polling agent or counting agents.

(13) Where by these Rules any act or thing is required or authorised to be done in the presence of the polling or counting agents, the non-attendance of any agent or agents at the time and place appointed for the purpose shall not, if the act or thing is otherwise duly done, invalidate the act or thing done.

Notification of requirement of secrecy

28(1) The returning officer must make such arrangements as he thinks fit to ensure that—
   (a) every person attending at a polling station (otherwise than for the purpose of voting or assisting a voter with disabilities to vote or as a constable on duty there) has been given a copy in writing of the provisions of subsections (1), (3) and (6) of section 66 of the 1983 Act and
   (b) every person attending at the counting of the votes (other than any constable on duty at the counting) has been given a copy in writing of the provisions of subsections (2) and (6) of that section.

(2) In this rule, a reference to a constable includes a person designated as a community support officer under section 38 of the Police Reform Act 2002 (police powers for employees).

Return of postal ballot papers

29(1)   Where—

    (a)   a postal vote has been returned in respect of a person who is entered on the postal voters list, or

    (b)   a proxy postal vote has been returned in respect of a proxy who is entered on the proxy postal voters list,

the returning officer must mark the list in the manner prescribed by regulations made under the 1983 Act.

(2)   Rule 45(6) does not apply for the purpose of determining whether, for the purposes of this rule, a postal vote or a proxy postal vote is returned.

Chapter 3
The Poll

Admission to the polling station

30(1)   The presiding officer must exclude all persons from the polling station except—

    (a)   voters;

    (b)   persons under the age of 18 who accompany voters to the polling station;

    (c)   the candidates and their election agents;

    (d)   the polling agents appointed to attend at the polling station;

    (e)   the clerks appointed to attend at the polling station;

    (f)   persons who are entitled to attend by virtue of any of sections 6A to 6D of the Political Parties, Elections and Referendums Act 2000;

    (g)   the constables on duty;

    (h)   the companions of voters with disabilities; and

    (i)   persons entitled to be admitted to the polling station at a relevant election or referendum with which the poll at the principal area election is combined.

(2)   The presiding officer must regulate the total number of voters and persons under the age of 18 who accompany them to be admitted to the polling station at the same time.

(3)   Not more than one polling agent shall be admitted at the same time to a polling station on behalf of the same candidate.

(4)   A constable or person employed by a returning officer must not be admitted to vote in person elsewhere than at his own polling station allotted to him under these Rules, except on production and surrender of a certificate as to his employment which must be in the form in the Appendix, or a form to the like effect, and signed by an officer of police of or above the rank of inspector or by the returning officer, as the case may be.

(5)   Any certificate surrendered under this rule must forthwith be cancelled.

(6)   In this rule, a reference to a constable includes a person designated as a community support officer under section 38 of the Police Reform Act 2002 (police powers for employees).

Keeping of order in station

31(1)   It is the presiding officer's duty to keep order at his polling station.

(2)   If a person misconducts himself in a polling station, or fails to obey the presiding officer's lawful orders, he may immediately, by the presiding officer's order, be removed from the polling station—

    (a)   by a constable in or near that station, or

    (b)   by any other person authorised in writing by the returning officer to remove him,

and the person so removed shall not, without the presiding officer's permission, again enter the polling station during the day.

(3) Any person so removed may, if charged with the commission in the polling station of an offence, be dealt with as a person taken into custody by a constable for an offence without a warrant.

(4) The powers conferred by this rule must not be exercised so as to prevent a voter who is otherwise entitled to vote at a polling station from having an opportunity of voting at that station.

Sealing of ballot boxes

32 Immediately before the commencement of the poll, the presiding officer must show the ballot box empty to such persons, if any, as are present in the polling station, so that they may see that it is empty, and must then lock it up, if it has a lock and (in any case) place his seal on it in such a manner as to prevent its being opened without breaking the seal and must place it in his view for the receipt of ballot papers, and keep it so locked and sealed or sealed (as the case may be).

Questions to be put to voters

33(1) At the time of the application (but not afterwards), the questions specified in the second column of the following Table—

(a) may be put by the presiding officer to a person applying for a ballot paper who is mentioned in the first column, and

(b) must be put if the letter "R" appears after the question and the candidate or his election or polling agent requires the question to be put:

Q. No	Person applying for ballot paper	Question
1	A person applying as an elector	(a)—Are you the person registered in the register of local government electors for this election as follows? read the whole entry from the register R
		(b)—Have you already voted here or elsewhere at this election for *(this county) *(this district) *(this London borough) *(this county borough), * delete whichever is inapplicable (adding, in the case of an election for several electoral areas, in this or any other electoral area) otherwise than as proxy for some other person? R
2	A person applying as proxy	(a)—Are you the person whose name appears as A.B. in the list of proxies for this election as entitled to vote as proxy on behalf of C.D.? R
		(b)—Have you already voted here or elsewhere at this election for

Q. No	Person applying for ballot paper	Question
		*(this county) *(this district) *(this London borough) *(this county borough), * delete whichever is inapplicable (adding in the case of an election for several electoral areas , in this or any other electoral area) as proxy on behalf of C.D.? R
		(c)—Are you the spouse, civil partner, parent, grandparent, brother, sister, child or grandchild of C.D.? R
3	A person applying as proxy for an elector with an anonymous entry (instead of the questions at entry 2)	(a)—Are you the person entitled to vote as proxy on behalf of the elector whose number on the register of electors is (read out the number)? R
		(b)—Have you already voted here or elsewhere as proxy on behalf of the elector whose number on the register of electors is (read out the number)? R
		(c)—Are you the spouse, civil partner, parent, grandparent, brother, sister, child or grandchild of the person whose number on the register of electors is (read out the number)? R
4	A person applying as proxy if the question at entry 2(c) or 3(c) is not answered in the affirmative	Have you already voted at this election for *(this county) *(this district) *(this London borough) *(this county borough), * delete whichever is inapplicable (adding, in the case of an election for several electoral areas , in this or any other electoral area) on behalf of two persons of whom you are not the spouse, civil partner, parent, grandparent, brother, sister, child or grandchild? R
5	A person applying as an elector in relation to whom there is an entry in the postal voters list	(a)—Did you apply to vote by post?
		(b)—Why have you not voted by post?

Q. No	Person applying for ballot paper	Question
6	A person applying as proxy who is named in the proxy postal voters list	(a)—Did you apply to vote by post as proxy? (b)—Why have you not voted by post as proxy?

(2) In the case of an elector in respect of whom a notice has been issued under section 13B(3B) or (3D) of the 1983 Act, the references in the questions at entries 1(a) and 3(a), (b) and (c) to reading from the register shall be taken as references to reading from the notice issued under section 13B(3B) or (3D) of the 1983 Act.

(3) A ballot paper must not be delivered to any person required to answer any of the above questions unless he has answered each question satisfactorily.

(4) Except as authorised by this rule, no inquiry shall be permitted as to the right of any person to vote.

Challenge of voter

34 A person must not be prevented from voting by reason only that—
    (a) a candidate or his election or polling agent declares that he has reasonable cause to believe that the person has committed an offence of personation, or
    (b) the person is arrested on the grounds that he is suspected of committing or of being about to commit such an offence.

Voting procedure

35(1) A ballot paper must be delivered to a voter who applies for one, and immediately before delivery—
    (a) the number and (unless paragraph (2) applies) name of the elector as stated in the copy of the register of electors must be called out;
    (b) the number of the elector must be marked on the list mentioned in rule 26(4)(d) beside the number of the ballot paper to be issued to him;
    (c) a mark must be placed in the register of electors against the number of the elector to note that a ballot paper has been received but without showing the particular ballot paper which has been received; and
    (d) in the case of a person applying for a ballot paper as proxy, a mark must also be placed against his name in the list of proxies.

(2) In the case of an elector who has an anonymous entry, he must show the presiding officer his official poll card and only his number shall be called out in pursuance of paragraph (1)(a).

(3) In the case of an elector who is added to the register in pursuance of a notice issued under section 13B(3B) or (3D) of the 1983 Act, paragraph (1) is modified as follows—
    (a) in sub-paragraph (a), for "copy of the register of electors" substitute "copy of the notice issued under section 13B(3B) or (3D) of the 1983 Act";
    (b) in sub-paragraph (c), for "in the register of electors" substitute "on the copy of the notice issued under section 13B(3B) or (3D) of the 1983 Act".

(4) The voter, on receiving the ballot paper, must forthwith proceed into one of the compartments in the polling station and there secretly mark his paper and fold it up so as to conceal his vote, and must then show to the presiding officer the back of the paper, so as to disclose the number and other unique identifying mark, and put the

ballot paper so folded up into the ballot box in the presiding officer's presence.

(5) The voter must vote without undue delay, and must leave the polling station as soon as he has put his ballot paper into the ballot box.

(6) The same copy of the register of electors which is used under paragraph (1) for the principal area election or, where paragraph (3) applies, the same copy of the notice issued under section 13B(3B) or (3D) of the 1983 Act, may be used for each relevant election or referendum—

    (a) and one mark may be placed in that register or on that notice under paragraph (1)(c) or in the list of proxies under paragraph (1)(d) to denote that a ballot paper has been issued in respect of each election or referendum;

    (b) but where a ballot paper has not been issued in respect of a relevant election or referendum, a different mark must be placed in the register or, as the case may be, on that notice or in that list so as to identify each election or referendum in respect of which a ballot paper was issued.

(7) A voter who at the close of the poll is in the polling station, or in a queue outside the polling station, for the purposes of voting shall (despite the close of the poll) be entitled to apply for a ballot paper under paragraph (1); and these rules apply in relation to such a voter accordingly.

Votes marked by presiding officer

36(1) The presiding officer, on the application of a voter—

    (a) who is incapacitated by blindness or other disability from voting in the manner directed by these Rules, or

    (b) who declares orally that he is unable to read,

must, in the presence of the polling agents, cause the voter's vote to be marked on a ballot paper in the manner directed by the voter, and the ballot paper to be placed in the ballot box.

(2) The name and number on the register of electors of every voter whose vote is marked in pursuance of this rule, and the reason why it is so marked, must be entered on a list (in these Rules called "the list of votes marked by the presiding officer").

In the case of a person voting as proxy for an elector, the number to be entered together with the voter's name shall be the elector's number.

(3) In the case of a person in respect of whom a notice has been issued under section 13B(3B) or (3D) of the 1983 Act, paragraph (2) applies as if for "on the register of electors of every voter" there were substituted "relating to every voter in respect of whom a notice has been issued under section 13B(3B) or (3D) of the 1983 Act".

(4) The same list may be used for the principal area election and each relevant election or referendum and, where it is so used, an entry in that list shall be taken to mean that the ballot papers were so marked in respect of each election or referendum, unless the list identifies the election or referendum at which the ballot paper was so marked.

Voting by persons with disabilities

37(1) If a voter makes an application to the presiding officer to be allowed, on the ground of—

    (a) blindness or other disability, or

    (b) inability to read,

to vote with the assistance of another person by whom he is accompanied (in these Rules referred to as "the companion"), the presiding officer must require the voter to declare, orally or in writing, whether he is so incapacitated by his blindness or other disability, or by his inability to read, as to be unable to vote without assistance.

(2) If the presiding officer—

    (a) is satisfied that the voter is so incapacitated, and

    (b) is also satisfied by a written declaration made by the companion (in these Rules referred to as "the declaration made by the companion of a voter with disabilities") that the companion—

        (i) is a qualified person within the meaning of this rule; and

        (ii) has not previously assisted more than one voter with disabilities to vote at the election,

the presiding officer must grant the application, and then anything which is by these Rules required to be done to, or by that voter in connection with the giving of his vote may be done to, or with the assistance of, the companion.

(3) For the purposes of these Rules, a person is a voter with disabilities if he has made such a declaration as is mentioned in paragraph (1), and a person shall be qualified to assist a voter with disabilities to vote if that person—

    (a) is a person who is entitled to vote as an elector at the election; or

    (b) is the father, mother, brother, sister, spouse, civil partner, son or daughter of the voter and has attained the age of 18 years.

(4) The name and number in the register of electors of every voter whose vote is given in accordance with this rule and the name and address of the companion must be entered on a list (in these Rules referred to as "the list of voters with disabilities assisted by companions").

In the case of a person voting as proxy for an elector, the number to be entered together with the voter's name shall be the elector's number.

(5) In the case of a person in respect of whom a notice has been issued under section 13B(3B) or (3D) of the 1983 Act, paragraph (4) applies as if for "in the register of electors of every voter" there were substituted "relating to every voter in respect of whom a notice has been issued under section 13B(3B) or (3D) of the 1983 Act".

(6) The same list may be used for the principal area election and each relevant election and referendum and, where it is so used, an entry in that list shall be taken to mean that the votes were so given in respect of each election or referendum, unless the list identifies the election or referendum at which the vote was so given.

(7) The declaration made by the companion—

    (a) must be in the form in the Appendix,

    (b) must be made before the presiding officer at the time when the voter applies to vote with the assistance of a companion, and

    (c) must forthwith be given to the presiding officer who must attest and retain it.

(8) No fee or other payment shall be charged in respect of the declaration.

Tendered ballot papers: circumstances where available

38(1) If a person, representing himself to be—

    (a) a particular elector named on the register and not named in the absent voters list, or

    (b) a particular person named in the list of proxies as proxy for an elector and not entitled to vote by post as proxy,

applies for a ballot paper after another person has voted in person either as the elector or his proxy, the applicant shall, on satisfactorily answering the questions permitted by law to be asked at the poll, be entitled, subject to the following provisions of this rule and rule 39, to mark a ballot paper (in these Rules referred to as "a tendered ballot paper") in the same manner as any other voter.

(2) Paragraph (4) applies if—

     (a) a person applies for a ballot paper representing himself to be a particular elector named on the register,

     (b) he is also named in the postal voters list, and

     (c) he claims that he did not make an application to vote by post at the election.

(3) Paragraph (4) also applies if—

     (a) a person applies for a ballot paper representing himself to be a particular person named as a proxy in the list of proxies,

     (b) he is also named in the proxy postal voters list, and

     (c) he claims that he did not make an application to vote by post as proxy.

(4) The person shall, on satisfactorily answering the questions permitted by law to be asked at the poll, be entitled, subject to the following provisions of this rule and rule 39, to mark a ballot paper (in these Rules referred to as a "tendered ballot paper") in the same manner as any other voter.

(5) Paragraph (6) applies if before the close of the poll but after the last time at which a person may apply for a replacement postal ballot paper, a person represents himself to be—

     (a) a particular elector named on the register who is also named in the postal voters list, or

     (b) a particular person named as a proxy in the list of proxies and who is also named in the proxy postal voters list,

  and claims that he has lost or has not received his postal ballot paper.

(6) The person shall, on satisfactorily answering the questions permitted by law to be asked at the poll, be entitled, subject to the provisions of this rule and rule 39, to mark a ballot paper (in these Rules referred to as a "tendered ballot paper") in the same manner as any other voter.

Tendered ballot papers: general provisions

39(1) A tendered ballot paper must—

     (a) be of a colour differing from the other ballot papers;

     (b) instead of being put into the ballot box, be given to the presiding officer and endorsed by him with the name of the voter and his number in the register of electors, and set aside in a separate packet.

(2) The name of the voter and his number in the register of electors must be entered on a list (in these Rules referred to as the "tendered votes list").

(3) The same list may be used for the principal area election and each relevant election or referendum and, where it is so used, an entry in that list shall be taken to mean that tendered ballot papers were marked in respect of each election or referendum, unless the list identifies the election or referendum at which a tendered ballot paper was marked.

(4) In the case of a person voting as proxy for an elector, the number to be endorsed or entered together with the voter's name shall be the number of that elector.

(5) In the case of an elector who has an anonymous entry, this rule and rule 38 apply subject to the following modifications—

     (a) in paragraphs (1)(b) and (2) above, the references to the name of the voter shall be ignored;

     (b) otherwise, a reference to a person named on a register or list shall be construed as a reference to a person whose number appears on the register or list (as the case may be).

(6) In the case of a person in respect of whom a notice has been issued under section 13B(3B) or (3D) of the 1983 Act, this rule and rule 38 shall apply as if—

(a) in rule 38(1)(a), (2)(a) and (5)(a), for "named on the register" there were substituted "in respect of whom a notice under section 13B(3B) or (3D) of the 1983 Act has been issued";

(b) in paragraph (1)(b) of this rule, for "his number in the register of electors" there were substituted "the number relating to him on a notice issued under section 13B(3B) or (3D) of the 1983 Act";

(c) in paragraph (2) of this rule, for "his number in the register of electors" there were substituted "the number relating to him on a notice issued under section 13B(3B) or (3D) of the 1983 Act".

Spoilt ballot papers

40 A voter who has inadvertently dealt with his ballot paper in such manner that it cannot be conveniently used as a ballot paper may, on delivering it to the presiding officer and proving to his satisfaction the fact of the inadvertence, obtain another ballot paper in the place of the ballot paper so delivered (in these Rules referred to as "a spoilt ballot paper"), and the spoilt ballot paper must be immediately cancelled.

Correction of errors on day of poll

41(1) The presiding officer must keep a list of persons to whom ballot papers are delivered in consequence of an alteration to the register made by virtue of section 13B(3B) or (3D) of the 1983 Act which takes effect on the day of the poll.

(2) The same list may be used for each relevant election or referendum and, where it is so used, an entry in that list shall be taken to mean that ballot papers were issued in respect of each election or referendum, unless the list identifies the election or referendum for which a ballot paper was issued.

Adjournment of poll in case of riot

42(1) Where the proceedings at any polling station are interrupted or obstructed by riot or open violence, the presiding officer must adjourn the proceedings till the following day and must forthwith give notice to the returning officer who discharges the functions specified in regulation 5 of the Combination of Polls Regulations.

(2) Where the poll is adjourned at any polling station—
  (a) the hours of polling on the day to which it is adjourned must be the same as for the original day; and
  (b) references in these Rules to the close of the poll shall be construed accordingly.

Procedure on close of poll

43(1) As soon as practicable after the close of the poll, the presiding officer must, in the presence of the polling agents appointed for the purposes of the principal area election and those appointed for the purposes of each relevant election or referendum, make up into separate packets, sealed with his own seal and the seals of such polling agents as desire to affix their seals—
  (a) each ballot box in use at the station, sealed so as to prevent the introduction of additional ballot papers and unopened, but with the key, if any, attached,
  (b) the unused and spoilt ballot papers placed together,
  (c) the tendered ballot papers,
  (d) the marked copies of the register of electors (including any marked copy notices issued under section 13B(3B) or (3D) of the 1983 Act) and of the list of proxies,
  (e) the lists prepared under rule 17 including the parts which were completed in accordance with rule 35(1)(b) (together referred to in these Rules as "the completed corresponding number lists"),

(f)   the certificates as to employment on duty on the day of the poll,

(g)   the tendered votes list, the list of voters with disabilities assisted by companions, the list of votes marked by the presiding officer, a statement of the number of voters whose votes are so marked by the presiding officer under the heads "disability" and "unable to read", the list maintained under rule 41 (correction of errors on day of poll) and the declarations made by the companions of voters with disabilities,

and must deliver the packets or cause them to be delivered to the returning officer to be taken charge of by him; but if the packets are not delivered by the presiding officer personally to the returning officer, the arrangements for their delivery shall require the returning officer's approval.

(2)   The contents of the packets referred to in sub-paragraphs (b), (c) and (f) of paragraph (1) must not be combined with the contents of the packets made under the corresponding rule that applies at any relevant election or referendum; nor shall the statement prepared under paragraph (5) be so combined.

(3)   References to the returning officer in paragraph (1) are references to the returning officer who discharges the functions specified in regulation 5 of the Combination of Polls Regulations.

(4)   The marked copies of the register of electors and of the list of proxies must be in one packet but must not be in the same packet as the completed corresponding number lists or the certificates as to employment on duty on the day of the poll.

(5)   The packets must be accompanied by a statement (in these Rules referred to as "the ballot paper account") made by the presiding officer showing the number of ballot papers entrusted to him, and accounting for them under the heads of ballot papers issued and not otherwise accounted for, unused, spoilt and tendered ballot papers.

Chapter 4
Counting of Votes

Attendance at counting of votes

44(1)   Where the returning officer at the principal area election discharges the functions specified in regulation 5 of the Combination of Polls Regulations, he must

   (a)   make arrangements for—

      (i)   discharging the functions under rule 45(1) in the presence of the counting agents appointed for the purposes of the principal area election and those appointed for the purpose of each relevant election or referendum as soon as practicable after the close of the poll, and

      (ii)   thereafter counting the votes at the principal area election in the presence of the agents appointed for the purpose of that election; and

   (b)   give to the counting agents appointed for the purposes of the principal area election and those appointed for the purpose of each relevant election or referendum notice in writing of the time and place at which he will begin to discharge the functions under rule 45(1).

(2)   Where the returning officer at the principal area election does not discharge the functions specified in regulation 5 of the Combination of Polls Regulations, he must—

   (a)   make arrangements for counting the votes in the presence of the counting agents as soon as practicable after the delivery of the ballot papers to him by the returning officer who does discharge those functions; and

   (b)   give to the counting agents notice in writing of the time after which he will begin to count the votes if by then he has received the ballot papers and of the place at which that count will take place.

(3)   No person other than—

    (a) the returning officer and his clerks,

    (b) the candidates and one other person chosen by each of them,

    (c) the election agents,

    (d) the counting agents,

    (e) persons who are entitled to attend by virtue of any of sections 6A to 6D of the Political Parties, Elections and Referendums Act 2000,

may be present at the counting of the votes, unless permitted by the returning officer to attend.

(4) No person other than a person entitled to be present at the counting of the votes at the principal area election under paragraphs (4) to (13) of rule 45 or at a relevant election or referendum may be present at the proceedings under rule 45(1) unless permitted by the returning officer to attend.

(5) A person not entitled to attend at the proceedings under rule 45(1) or the counting of the votes under paragraphs (4) to (13) of rule 45 must not be permitted to do so by the returning officer unless he—

    (a) is satisfied that the efficient separation of the ballot papers or, as the case may be, the efficient counting of the votes will not be impeded; and

    (b) has either consulted the election agents or thought it impracticable to do so.

(6) The returning officer must give the counting agents all such reasonable facilities for overseeing the proceedings, and all such information with respect to them, as he can give them consistently with the orderly conduct of the proceedings and the discharge of his duties in connection with them.

(7) In particular, where the votes are counted by sorting the ballot papers according to the candidate for whom the vote is given and then counting the number of ballot papers for each candidate, the counting agents shall be entitled to satisfy themselves that the ballot papers are correctly sorted.

The count

45(1) Where the returning officer at the principal area election discharges the functions specified in regulation 5 of the Combination of Polls Regulations, he must—

    (a) in the presence of the counting agents appointed for the purposes of the poll at the principal area election and each relevant election or referendum open each ballot box and record separately the number of ballot papers used in each election;

    (b) in the presence of the election agents appointed for the purposes of the poll at the principal area election and each relevant election or referendum verify each ballot paper account;

    (c) count such of the postal ballot papers as have been duly returned and record separately the number counted at the principal area election and each relevant election or referendum;

    (d) separate the ballot papers relating to the principal area election from the ballot papers relating to each relevant election or referendum;

    (e) make up into packets the ballot papers for each relevant election or referendum and seal them up in separate containers endorsing on each a description of the area to which the ballot papers relate;

    (f) deliver or cause to be delivered to the returning officer for the relevant election or referendum to which the ballot papers relate—

        (i) those containers, together with a list of them and of the contents of each; and

        (ii) the ballot paper accounts together with a copy of the statement as to the result of their verification in respect of that election; and

    (g) at the same time deliver or cause to be delivered to that officer packets that so

relate containing—
  (i)   the unused and spoilt ballot papers,
  (ii) the tendered ballot papers, and
  (iii) the certificates as to employment on duty on the day of the poll.

(2) In the application of paragraph (1) to combined polls at county and district council elections, it shall have effect as if after the words "principal area election" in the first place where they occur and in sub-paragraphs (a) to (d), there are inserted the words "for which he is the returning officer".

(3) Where separate ballot boxes are used, no vote for any candidate shall be rendered invalid by the ballot paper being placed in the ballot box intended for use at any relevant election or referendum.

(4) After completion of the proceedings under paragraph (1), the returning officer must mix together all of the ballot papers used at the principal area election and count the votes given on them.

(5) Where the returning officer at the principal area election does not discharge the functions specified in regulation 5 of the Combination of Polls Regulations, he must—
  (a) on receipt of containers from the returning officer who does discharge those functions, and after the time specified in the notice given under rule 44(2)(b), in the presence of the counting agents open each container;
  (b) where the proceedings on the issue and receipt of postal ballot papers are not taken together with those proceedings at a relevant election or referendum under regulation 65 of the Representation of the People (England and Wales) Regulations 2001, or under that regulation as applied by regulations made under section 9HE, 9MG, 44 or 45, whether or not in addition to 105 of the Local Government Act 2000, count such of the postal ballot papers as have been duly returned and record the number counted; and
  (c) mix together the postal ballot papers and the ballot papers from all of the containers and count the votes given on them,
and paragraph (11) shall not apply to these proceedings.

(6) A postal ballot paper must not be taken to be duly returned unless—
  (a) it is returned in the manner set out in paragraph (7) and reaches the returning officer or any polling station in the appropriate electoral area (as defined in paragraph (8)) before the close of the poll;
  (b) the postal voting statement, duly signed, is also returned in the manner set out in paragraph (7) and reaches him or such a polling station before that time;
  (c) the postal voting statement also states the date of birth of the elector or proxy (as the case may be); and
  (d) in a case where steps for verifying the date of birth and signature of an elector or proxy have been prescribed by regulations made under the 1983 Act, the returning officer (having taken such steps) verifies the date of birth and signature of the elector or proxy.

(7) The manner in which any postal ballot paper or postal voting statement may be returned—
  (a) to the returning officer, is by hand or by post;
  (b) to a polling station, is by hand.

(7A) A postal ballot paper or postal voting statement that reaches the returning officer or a polling station on or after the close of the poll is treated for the purposes of this rule as reaching that officer or polling station before the close of the poll if it is delivered by a person who, at the close of the poll, is in the polling station, or in a queue outside the polling station, for the purpose of returning it.

(8) The appropriate electoral area in respect of any voter shall be—

(a) the area which is common to the parliamentary constituency, electoral area, local counting area, local authority area or voting area (as the case may be) in which the polls at the principal area election and any relevant election or referendum are being taken together; and

(b) in respect of which polls the voter has been issued with a postal ballot paper.

(9) The returning officer must not count any tendered ballot papers.

(10) The returning officer, while counting and recording the number of ballot papers and counting the votes, must keep the ballot papers with their faces upwards and take all proper precautions for preventing any person from seeing the numbers or other unique identifying marks printed on the back of the papers.

(11) The returning officer must verify each ballot paper account by comparing it with the number of ballot papers recorded by him, and the unused and spoilt ballot papers in his possession and the tendered votes list (opening and re-sealing the packets containing the unused and spoilt ballot papers and the tendered votes list) and must draw up a statement as to the result of the verification, which any election agent may copy.

(12) The returning officer must so far as practicable proceed continuously with counting the votes, allowing only time for refreshment, except that he may exclude the hours between 7 in the evening and 9 on the following morning.

(13) During the time so excluded the returning officer must—

(a) place the ballot papers and other documents relating to the election under his own seal and the seals of such of the counting agents as desire to affix their seals; and

(b) otherwise take proper precautions for the security of the papers and documents.

Re-count

46(1) A candidate or his election agent may, if present when the counting or any re-count of the votes is completed, require the returning officer to have the votes re-counted or again recounted but the returning officer may refuse to do so if in his opinion the request is unreasonable.

(2) No step shall be taken on the completion of the counting or any re-count of votes until the candidates and election agents present at its completion have been given a reasonable opportunity to exercise the right conferred by this rule.

Rejected ballot papers

47(1) Any ballot paper—

(a) which does not bear the official mark, or

(b) on which votes are given for more candidates than the voter is entitled to vote for, or

(c) on which anything is written or marked by which the voter can be identified except the printed number on the back and other unique identifying mark, or

(d) which is unmarked or void for uncertainty,

shall, subject to paragraphs (2) and (3), be void and not counted.

(2) Where the voter is entitled to vote for more than one candidate, a ballot paper shall not be deemed to be void for uncertainty as respects any vote as to which no uncertainty arises and that vote must be counted.

(3) A ballot paper on which the vote is marked—

(a) elsewhere than in the proper place, or

(b) otherwise than by means of a cross, or

(c) by more than one mark,

shall not for such reason be deemed to be void (either wholly or as respects that vote) if an intention that the vote shall be for one or other of the candidates clearly appears, and the way the paper is marked does not itself identify the voter and it is not shown that he can be identified by it.

(4) The returning officer must—
   (a) endorse the word "rejected" on any ballot paper which under this rule is not to be counted; and
   (b) in the case of a ballot paper on which any vote is counted under paragraph (2), endorse the words "rejected in part" on the ballot paper and indicate which vote or votes have been counted,

and must add to the endorsement the words "rejection objected to" if any objection is made by a counting agent to his decision.

(5) The returning officer must draw up a statement showing the number of ballot papers rejected, including those rejected in part, under the several heads of—
   (a) want of official mark;
   (b) voting for more candidates than voter is entitled to;
   (c) writing or mark by which the voter could be identified;
   (d) unmarked or void for uncertainty,

and the statement must record the number of ballot papers rejected in part.

Decisions on ballot papers

48 The decision of the returning officer on any question arising in respect of a ballot paper shall be final, but shall be subject to review on an election petition.

Equality of votes

49 Where, after the counting of the votes (including any re-count) is completed, an equality of votes is found to exist between any candidates and the addition of a vote would entitle any of those candidates to be declared elected, the returning officer must forthwith decide between those candidates by lot, and proceed as if the candidate on whom the lot falls had received an additional vote.

Part 4
Final Proceedings in Contested and Uncontested Elections

Declaration of result

50(1) In a contested election, when the result of the poll has been ascertained, the returning officer must forthwith—
   (a) declare to be elected the candidate or candidates to whom more votes have been given than to the other candidates, up to the number of councillors to be elected;
   (b) give notice of the name of each candidate to whom sub-paragraph (a) applies to the proper officer of the council for which the election is held; and
   (c) give public notice of the name of each candidate elected and of the total number of votes given for each candidate (whether elected or not) together with the number of rejected ballot papers under each head shown in the statement of rejected ballot papers.

(2) In an uncontested election, the returning officer must as soon as practicable after the latest time for the delivery of notices of withdrawals of candidature—
   (a) declare to be elected the person or persons remaining validly nominated;

(b)   give notice of the name of each person to whom sub-paragraph (a) applies to the proper officer of the council for which the election is held; and

(c)   give public notice of the name of each such person.

Part 5
Disposal of Documents

Sealing up of ballot papers

51(1)   On the completion of the counting at a contested election the returning officer must seal up in separate packets the counted and rejected ballot papers, including ballot papers rejected in part.

(2)   The returning officer must not open the sealed packets of—
(a)   tendered ballot papers, or
(b)   certificates as to employment on duty on the day of the poll.

(3)   Where the returning officer discharges the functions referred to in regulation 5 of the Combination of Polls Regulations, he must also not open the sealed packets of—
(a)   the completed corresponding number lists, or
(b)   the marked copies of the register of electors (including any marked copy notices issued under section 13B(3B) or (3D) of the 1983 Act) and lists of proxies.

Delivery of documents to relevant registration officer

52(1)   The returning officer must then forward to the relevant registration officer the following documents—
(a)   the packets of ballot papers in his possession,
(b)   the ballot paper accounts and the statements of rejected ballot papers and of the result of the verification of the ballot paper accounts,
(c)   the tendered votes lists, the lists of voters with disabilities assisted by companions, the lists of votes marked by the presiding officer and the related statements, the lists maintained under rule 41, and the declarations made by the companions of voters with disabilities,
(d)   the packets of the completed corresponding number lists,
(e)   the packets of certificates as to employment on duty on the day of the poll, and
(f)   the packets containing marked copies of registers (including any marked copy notices issued under section 13B(3B) or (3D) of the 1983 Act) and of the postal voters list, of the lists of proxies and of the proxy postal voters list.

(2)   At an election where the returning officer does not discharge the functions referred to in regulation 5 of the Combination of Polls Regulations, paragraph (1) shall have effect as if sub-paragraphs (c), (d) and (e) were omitted.

(3)   In this rule and in rules 53, 54 and 55 references to the relevant registration officer are to—
(a)   the registration officer of the local authority in whose area the principal area election is held;
(b)   if the electoral area of the relevant election or referendum comprises any part of the area of more than one local authority, the registration officer of the local authority in whose area the greater or greatest (as the case may be) number of electors is registered;
(c)   if the returning officer discharges the functions referred to in regulation 5 of the Combination of Polls Regulations, the registration officer of the local authority in whose area the principal area election is held,
and for these purposes "local authority"does not include the Greater London

Authority.

Orders for production of documents

53(1) An order—

(a) for the inspection or production of any rejected ballot papers, including ballot papers rejected in part, in the custody of the relevant registration officer, or

(b) for the opening of a sealed packet of the completed corresponding number lists or certificates as to employment on duty on the day of the poll or for the inspection of any counted ballot papers in his custody,

may be made by a county court, if the court is satisfied by evidence on oath that the order is required for the purpose of instituting or maintaining a prosecution for an offence in relation to ballot papers, or for the purpose of an election petition.

(2) An order for the opening of a sealed packet of the completed corresponding number lists or certificates as to employment on duty on the day of the poll or for the inspection of any counted ballot papers in the custody of the relevant registration officer may be made by an election court.

(3) An order under this rule may be made subject to such conditions as to—

(a) persons,

(b) time,

(c) place and mode of inspection,

(d) production or opening,

as the court making the order may think expedient; but in making and carrying into effect an order for the opening of a packet of the completed corresponding number lists or certificates as to employment on duty on the day of the poll or for the inspection of counted ballot papers, care must be taken that the way in which the vote of any particular elector has been given shall not be disclosed until it has been proved—

(i) that his vote was given; and

(ii) that the vote has been declared by a competent court to be invalid.

(4) An appeal lies to the High Court from any order of a county court under this rule.

(5) Any power given under this rule to a county court may be exercised by any judge of the court otherwise than in open court.

(6) Where an order is made for the production by the relevant registration officer of any document in his possession relating to any specified election—

(a) the production by him or his agent of the document ordered in such manner as may be directed by that order shall be conclusive evidence that the document relates to the specified election; and

(b) any endorsement on any packet of ballot papers so produced shall be prima facie evidence that the ballot papers are what they are stated to be by the endorsement.

(7) The production from proper custody of—

(a) a ballot paper purporting to have been used at any election, and

(b) a completed corresponding number list with a number marked in writing beside the number of the ballot paper,

shall be prima facie evidence that the elector whose vote was given by that ballot paper was the person whose entry in the register of electors or on a notice issued under section 13B(3B) or (3D) of the 1983 Act at the time of the election contained the same number as the number written as mentioned in sub-paragraph (b) of this paragraph.

(8) Save as by this rule provided, no person shall be allowed to inspect any rejected or counted ballot papers in the possession of the relevant registration officer or open any

sealed packets of the completed corresponding number lists or of certificates as to employment on duty on the day of the poll.

Retention of documents

54   The relevant registration officer must retain for one year all documents relating to an election forwarded to him in pursuance of these Rules by a returning officer, and then, unless otherwise directed by an order of a county court, the Crown Court, a magistrates' court or an election court, must cause them to be destroyed.

Part 6
Death of Candidate

Countermand or abandonment of poll on death of a candidate

55(1)   If at a contested election proof is given to the returning officer's satisfaction before the result of the election is declared that one of the persons named or to be named as candidate in the ballot papers has died, then the returning officer must countermand notice of the poll or, if polling has begun, direct that the poll be abandoned, and the provisions of subsections (1) and (5) of section 39 of the 1983 Act apply in respect of any vacancy which remains unfilled.

(2)   Neither the countermand of the poll at the principal area election nor the direction that that poll be abandoned shall affect the poll at each relevant election or referendum.

(3)   Where the poll at the principal area election is abandoned by reason of a candidate's death, no further ballot papers shall be issued.

(4)   At the close of the poll at each relevant election or referendum the presiding officer must take the like steps (so far as not already taken) for the delivery to the returning officer of ballot boxes and ballot papers and other documents as he would be required to do if the poll at the principal area election had not been abandoned.

(5)   The returning officer must dispose of ballot papers used at the principal area election (at which a candidate has died) as he is required to do on the completion in due course of the counting of the votes, subject to paragraphs (6) and (7).

(6)   It is not necessary for any ballot paper account at that election to be prepared or verified.

(7)   Having separated the ballot papers relating to each relevant election or referendum, the returning officer must take no step or further step for the counting of the ballot papers used at the principal area election (at which a candidate has died) or of the votes cast at that principal area election.

(8)   The returning officer must seal up all the ballot papers used at the principal area election (whether the votes on them have been counted or not) and it shall not be necessary to seal up counted and rejected ballot papers in separate packets.

(9)   The provisions of these Rules as to the inspection, production, retention and destruction of ballot papers and other documents by the relevant registration officer relating to a poll at a principal area election apply to any such documents relating to a poll abandoned by reason of a candidate's death subject to paragraphs (10) and (11).

(10)   Ballot papers on which the votes were neither counted nor rejected must be treated as counted ballot papers.

(11)   No order is to be made for—
   (a)   the production or inspection of any ballot papers, or

(b) for the opening of a sealed packet of the completed corresponding number lists or of certificates as to employment on duty on the day of the poll,

unless the order is made by a court with reference to a prosecution.

Part 7
Appendix of Forms

Forms not reproduced

Local Government Officers (Political Restrictions) Regulations 1990 (SI 1990/851)

Made 4th April 1990

Citation and commencement

1   These Regulations may be cited as the Local Government Officers (Political Restrictions) Regulations 1990 and shall come into force on 1st May 1990.

Interpretation

2   In these Regulations

"the Act" means the Local Government and Housing Act 1989;

"Deputy Mayor for Policing and Crime" means a person appointed under section 19(1) of the Police Reform and Social Responsibility Act 2011;

references to the appointee are references to a person holding such a post as is mentioned in regulation 3(1) and references to the holding of an appointment shall be construed accordingly;

references to a political party do not include references to an organisation whose objects relate solely to matters arising in, or connected with, a state which is not a member State; and

references to speaking to the public include references to the giving of an interview which, to the knowledge of the person giving it, is likely to result in the publication of statements made, or opinions expressed, during the course of the interview.

Terms of appointment and conditions of employment

3(1) Subject to paragraph (3), the terms of appointment and conditions of employment of every person holding a politically restricted post under a local authority (including persons appointed to such posts before the coming into force of these Regulations) shall be deemed to incorporate

(a)   in all cases, the terms and conditions set out in Part I of the Schedule hereto;

(b)   in the case of persons appointed otherwise than pursuant to section 9 of the Act (political assistants), the further terms and conditions set out in Part II of that Schedule; and

(c)   in the case of persons appointed pursuant to that section, the further terms and conditions set out in Part III of that Schedule.

(2)   The terms and conditions referred to in paragraph (1)(a) to (c) apply to the appointee at all times while he holds his appointment.

(3)   Paragraphs 4, 5, 6, 7 and 8 of the Schedule do not apply where the appointee is the Deputy Mayor for Policing and Crime.

Incidental and supplementary provisions

4   In determining whether a person is in breach of a term or condition set out in Part II of the Schedule hereto, regard shall be had, in particular, to the following matters

(a)   whether the appointee referred to a political party or to persons identified with a political party, or whether anything said by him or the relevant work promotes or opposes a point of view identifiable as the view of one political party and not of another; and

(b)   where the appointee spoke or the work was published as part of a campaign, the effect which the campaign appears to be designed to achieve.

SCHEDULE
TERMS OF APPOINTMENT AND CONDITIONS OF EMPLOYMENT

Part I
General

1   The appointee shall not announce or cause, authorise or permit anyone else to announce that he is, or intends to be, a candidate for election as a member of

    (a)   the House of Commons;

    (aa) the Scottish Parliament;

    (ab) the National Assembly for Wales;

    (ab) the Welsh Assembly;

    (b)   the European Parliament; or

    (c)   a local authority within the meaning of section 21(1) or (2) of the Act.

1B   Where prior to 1st April 1999 an announcement has been made that the appointee is, or intends to be, a candidate for election as a member of the Scottish Parliament at the first ordinary general election for membership of that Parliament, the appointee shall not act, or continue to act, as such a candidate.

1C   Where prior to 1st April 1999 an announcement has been made that the appointee is, or intends to be, a candidate for election as a member of the Welsh Assembly at the first ordinary general election for membership of that Assembly, the appointee shall not act, or continue to act, as such a candidate.

2(1)   Notwithstanding any contrary provision in his terms of appointment or his contract of employment, upon the appointee giving notice in writing to the local authority under which he holds his appointment that he wishes to resign his appointment because he intends to announce or cause, authorise or permit anyone else to announce that he is, or intends to be, a candidate for election to the House of Commons at a pending election, his appointment shall terminate forthwith.

  (2)   For the purposes of this paragraph an election shall be taken to be pending

    (a)   in the case of a general election, if the date proposed for the dissolution of Parliament preceding that election has been officially announced;

    (b)   in the case of a by-election, if the vacancy giving rise to that election has occurred.

2B   Notwithstanding any contrary provision in his terms of appointment or his contract of employment, upon the appointee giving notice in writing to the local authority under which he holds his appointment that he wishes to resign his appointment because he intends to become, or to continue as, a candidate for election as a member of the Scottish Parliament at the first ordinary general election for membership of that Parliament, his appointment shall terminate forthwith.

2C   Notwithstanding any contrary provision in his terms of appointment or his contract of employment, upon the appointee giving notice in writing to the local authority under which he holds his appointment that he wishes to resign his appointment because he intends to become, or to continue as, a candidate for election as a member of the Welsh Assembly at the first ordinary general election for membership of that Assembly, his appointment shall terminate forthwith.

2D   Notwithstanding any contrary provision in his terms of appointment or his contract of employment, upon the appointee giving notice in writing to the local authority under which he holds his appointment that he wishes to resign his appointment because he intends to announce or cause, authorise or permit anyone else to announce that he is, or intends to be a candidate for election as a member of the National Assembly for Wales, his appointment shall terminate forthwith.

3   The appointee shall not act as an election agent or sub-agent within the meaning of section 67 or section 68 of the Representation of the People Act 1983 for a candidate for election as a member of a body mentioned in paragraph 1.

4   The appointee shall not be an officer of a political party or of any branch of such a party or a member of any committee or subcommittee of such a party or branch if his duties as such an officer or member would be likely to require him
    (a) to participate in the general management of the party or the branch; or
    (b) to act on behalf of the party or branch in dealings with persons other than members of the party or members of another political party associated with the party.

5   The appointee shall not canvass on behalf of a political party or on behalf of a person who is, or proposes to be, a candidate for election to any of the bodies mentioned in paragraph 1.

Part II
Additional terms and conditions in the case of Officers not appointed under section 9 of the Act

6   The appointee shall not speak to the public at large or to a section of the public with the apparent intention of affecting public support for a political party.

7(1)   The appointee shall not
    (a) publish any written or artistic work of which he is the author (or one of the authors) or any written work or collection of artistic works in relation to which he has acted in an editorial capacity; or
    (b) cause, authorise or permit any other person to publish such a work or collection,
  if the work appears to be intended to affect public support for a political party.

(2)   Sub-paragraph (1) only applies to publication to the public at large or to a section of the public; and nothing in that sub-paragraph shall preclude the display of a poster or other document on property occupied by the appointee as his dwelling or on a vehicle or article used by him.

8   Nothing in paragraph 6 or 7 shall be construed as precluding the appointee from engaging in the activities there mentioned to such extent as is necessary for the proper performance of his official duties.

Part III
Further terms and conditions in the case of officers appointed under section 9 of the Act

9   The appointee shall not speak to the public at large or to a section of the public in

circumstances or terms which are likely to create the impression that he is speaking as an authorised representative of a political party, whether he is so authorised or not.

10   The appointee shall not publish any written or artistic work of which he is the author (or one of the authors) or any written work or collection of artistic works in relation to which he has acted in an editorial capacity or cause, authorise or permit any other person to publish such a work or collection in circumstances which are likely to create the impression that the publication is authorised by a political party, whether or not it is so authorised.

Magistrates' Courts (Forfeiture of Political Donations) Rules 2003 (SI 2003/1645)

Made 22nd June 2003

Citation, commencement and interpretation

1(1)   These Rules may be cited as the Magistrates' Courts (Forfeiture of Political Donations) Rules 2003 and shall come into force on 24th July 2003.

(2)   In these Rules
   (a)   a reference to a section by number alone or reference to a schedule by number alone is a reference to the section so numbered or schedule so numbered respectively in the Political Parties, Elections and Referendums Act 2000;
   (b)   any reference to a form is a reference to a form set out in the Schedule to these Rules or a form to like effect.
   (c)   "applicant" means the Commission.
   (d)   "forfeiture order" means an order pursuant to section 58(2) and includes orders made under section 58(2) as applied by
      (i)   paragraph 8 of Schedule 7;
      (ii)   paragraph 7 of Schedule 11;
      (iii)   paragraph 7 of Schedule 15; and
      (iv)   paragraph 7 of Schedule 2A to the Representation of the People Act 1983; or
      (v)   an order made under section 65(6); or
      (vi)   an order made under paragraph 12(4) of Schedule 7.
   (e)   "respondent" means the registered party, regulated donee, recognised third party, permitted participant or candidate or election agent (as appropriate) respectively, against whom a forfeiture order is sought.

Application for forfeiture

2(1)   An application for a forfeiture order shall be in Form A, A1, A2, A3, A4, B, or B1 as appropriate, and shall be addressed to the designated officer for a magistrates' court.

(2)   The justices' clerk shall, as soon as reasonably practicable, fix a date for the hearing, give notice in writing to the applicant of it and give notice in writing to the respondent of the application and of the date, time and place fixed for the hearing.

Transfer

3(1)   The court may, of its own initiative or on the application of any party to the proceedings, order that the hearing be transferred to the court of another local justice area having regard to
   (a)   whether it would be more convenient or fair for the hearing to be held in some other court;
   (b)   the importance of the outcome of the hearing to the public in general;
   (c)   the facilities available at the court where the application for a forfeiture order was lodged and whether they may be inadequate because of
      (i)   any disability of any party to the proceedings or representative of any such party (as appropriate) or any potential witness;
      (ii)   press and public interest;
   (d)   any other matters that may affect the just disposal of the hearing.

(2)   If the court makes an order under paragraph (1) the designated officer for the court shall give notice to the parties to the proceedings.

(3)   Any order of the court made before the transfer of proceedings shall not be affected by the order for transfer.

Joinder

4(1)   The court may order that any person who is not already a party to the proceedings ("the joined party") be made one, if it thinks it is desirable to do so.

(2)   The court may make an order under paragraph (1), on the application of an existing party to the proceedings, or otherwise, including of its own initiative.

(3)   If the court makes an order under paragraph (1) the designated officer for the court shall give notice to the parties to the proceedings.

(4)   The court may give such further directions as to the joinder of the joined party as it thinks fit.

(5)   If the court makes an order under paragraph (4) the designated officer for the court shall give notice to the other parties to the proceedings.

Procedure at hearing

5(1)   Any person
    (a)   to whom notice of the application has been given; or
    (b)   who has been joined as a party to the proceedings under rule 4;
may attend and be heard on the question of whether a forfeiture order should be made.

(2)   If any person referred to in paragraph (1) fails to attend or to be represented at the hearing of which he has been duly notified the court may unless it is satisfied that there is good and sufficient reason for such absence
    (a)   hear and determine the proceedings in the absence of the party to the proceedings or his representative, or
    (b)   postpone or adjourn the hearing.

(3)   Before deciding to hear and determine any proceedings in the absence of a party to the proceedings or his representative, the court shall
    (a)   consider any representations in writing; or
    (b)   otherwise submitted by or on behalf of that party in response to the notice of the hearing; and
    (c)   shall give any party to the proceedings present at the hearing an opportunity to be heard in regard to those representations.

(4)   The designated officer for the court shall, as soon as reasonably practicable after the hearing, send a copy of any order made at the hearing to any person referred to in paragraph (1) who has failed to attend or to be represented at the hearing.

(5)   Subject to the foregoing provisions of these Rules
    (a)   proceedings on an application for a forfeiture order shall be regulated in the same manner as proceedings on complaint; and
    (b)   accordingly, for the purpose of this rule
        (i)   the application shall be deemed to be a complaint;
        (ii)   the applicant to be the complainant;
        (iii)   the respondent to be the defendant; and
        (iv)   any notice given under rule 2(2) of these Rules to be a summons;
but nothing in this rule shall be construed as enabling a warrant of arrest to be issued for failure to appear in answer to any such notice.

SCHEDULE

Form A

Application for Forfeiture Pursuant to section 58(2)Registered Party

. . . . .Magistrates' Court
. . . . .Code
Date. . . . .
. . . .(name of applicant) of. . . . .(address of applicant)
applies for an order for forfeiture pursuant to section 58(2) of the Political Parties, Elections
and Referendums Act 2000, against. . . . .(name of registered party) of. . . .
. . . .(address of registered party) of an amount equal to the value of the
donation made on. . . . . .and accepted by the registered party on. . . . .
. . . ., on the following grounds:
To: The Designated Officer
. . . . .Magistrates' Court

Form A1

Application for Forfeiture Pursuant to Section 58(2)Regulated Donee

. . . . .Magistrates' Court
. . . . .Code
Date. . . . .
. . . .(name of applicant) of. . . . .(address of applicant)
applies for an order for forfeiture pursuant to section 58(2) of the Political Parties, Elections
and Referendums Act 2000, as applied by paragraph 8 of Schedule 7 to that Act against. . . . .
. . . .(name of regulated donee) of. . . . .(address of regulated
donee) of an amount equal to the value of the controlled donation made on. . . . .
. . . .and accepted by the regulated donee on. . . . ., on the following
grounds:
To: The Designated Officer
. . . . .Magistrates' Court

Form A2

Application for Forfeiture Pursuant to Section 58(2)Recognised Third Party

. . . . .Magistrates' Court
. . . . .Code
Date. . . . .
. . . .(name of applicant) of. . . . .(address of applicant)
applies for an order for forfeiture pursuant to section 58(2) of the Political Parties, Elections
and Referendums Act 2000, as applied by paragraph 7 of Schedule 11 to that Act, against. . . .
. . . .(name of recognised third party) of. . . . .(address of
recognised third party) of an amount equal to the value of the relevant donation made on. . .
. . . . .and accepted by the recognised third party on. . . . . ,
on the following grounds:
To: The Designated Officer
. . . . .Magistrates' Court

Form A3

Application for Forfeiture Pursuant to Section 58(2)Permitted Participants

. . . . .Magistrates' Court
. . . . .Code
Date. . . . .
. . . .(name of applicant) of. . . . .(address of applicant) applies for an order for forfeiture pursuant to section 58(2) of the Political Parties, Elections and Referendums Act 2000, as applied by paragraph 7 of Schedule 15 to that Act, against. . . . .(name of permitted participant) of. . . . .(address of permitted participant) of an amount equal to the value of the relevant donation made on. . . . . .and accepted by the permitted participant on. . . . ., on the following grounds:
To: The Designated Officer
. . . . .Magistrates' Court

Form A4

Application for Forfeiture Pursuant to Section 58(2)Candidates or Election Agents

. . . . .Magistrates' Court
. . . . .Code
Date. . . . .
. . . .(name of applicant) of. . . . .(address of applicant) applies for an order for forfeiture pursuant to section 58(2) of the Political Parties, Elections and Referendums Act 2000, as applied by paragraph 7 of Schedule 2A to the Representation of the People Act 1983, against. . . . .(name of candidate/election agent as appropriate) of. . . . .(address of candidate/election agent as appropriate) of an amount equal to the value of the relevant donation made on. . . . . .and accepted by the candidate/election agent (delete as appropriate) on. . . . ., on the following grounds:
To: The Designated Officer
. . . . .Magistrates' Court

Form B

Application for Forfeiture Pursuant to Section 65(6)Registered Party

. . . . .Magistrates' Court
. . . . .Code
Date. . . . .
. . . .(name of applicant) of. . . . .(address of applicant) applies for an order for forfeiture pursuant to section 65(6) of the Political Parties, Elections and Referendums Act 2000, against. . . . .(name of registered party) of. . . . .(address of registered party) of an amount equal to the value of the donation made on. . . . . .and accepted by the registered party on. . . . . , on the following grounds:
To: The Designated Officer

. . . . .Magistrates' Court

Form B1

Application for Forfeiture Pursuant to Paragraph 12(4) of Schedule 7regulated Donee

. . . . .Magistrates' Court

. . . . .Code

Date. . . . .

. . . .(name of applicant) of. . . . .(address of applicant) applies for an order for forfeiture pursuant to paragraph 12(4) of Schedule 7 to the Political Parties, Elections and Referendums Act 2000, against. . . . .(name of regulated donee) of. . . . .(address of regulated donee) of an amount equal to the value of the controlled donation made on. . . . . .and accepted by the regulated donee on. . . . . , on the following grounds:

To: The Designated Officer

. . . . .Magistrates' Court

National Assembly for Wales (Elections: Nomination Papers) (Welsh Form) Order 2001
(SI 2001/2914)

Made 15th August 2001

Citation and Commencement

1   This Order may be cited as the National Assembly for Wales (Elections : Nomination Papers) (Welsh Form) Order 2001 and shall come into force on 16th August 2001.

Welsh Form

2(1)   "Annibynnol" is hereby prescribed as the form of words in Welsh for the word "Independent" which is specified by section 22(3)(a)(i) of the Political Parties, Elections and Referendums Act 2000.

(2)   The form of words in Welsh which is prescribed by paragraph (1) may be used as well as or in place of the equivalent word in English at an election to the National Assembly for Wales.

National Assembly for Wales (Representation of the People) Order 2007 (SI 2007/236)

Made 31st January 2007

PART 1
GENERAL

PART 2
ASSEMBLY FRANCHISE AND ITS EXERCISE

PART 3
THE ELECTION CAMPAIGN

PART 5
MISCELLANEOUS AND SUPPLEMENTAL

Schedules

_____

Part 1
General

Citation, commencement and revocation

1(1)   This Order may be cited as the National Assembly for Wales (Representation of the People) Order 2007 and shall come into force on the day after the day on which it is made.

(2)   Subject to article 149 and rule 69(2) of Schedule 5, this Order revokes the National Assembly for Wales (Representation of the People) Order 2003 and the National Assembly for Wales (Representation of the People) (Amendment) Order 2006.

Interpretation

2(1)   In this Order, except where the context requires otherwise
         "the 1983 Act" means the Representation of the People Act 1983;
         "the 1985 Act" means the Representation of the People Act 1985;
         "the 1998 Act" means the Government of Wales Act 1998;
         "the 2000 Act" means the Representation of the People Act 2000;
         "the 2000 Political Parties Act" means the Political Parties, Elections and Referendums Act 2000;
         "the 2001 Regulations" means the Representation of the People (England and Wales) Regulations 2001;
         "the 2006 Act" means the Government of Wales Act 2006;
         "the 2007 Assembly general election" means the Assembly general election held in 2007 under section 3 of the 1998 Act;
         "absent voter" means an elector who is entitled to vote by proxy or an elector or proxy who is entitled to vote by post;
         "anonymous entry" in relation to a register shall be construed in accordance with

section 9B of the 1983 Act and "record of anonymous entries" means the record prepared in pursuance of regulations made by virtue of paragraph 8A of Schedule 2 to the 1983 Act;

"appropriate returning officer" means a constituency returning officer in relation to a constituency election and a regional returning officer in relation to a regional election;

"the Assembly" means

(a) in relation to elections and returns under Part 1 of the 1998 Act (except the 2007 Assembly general election) the National Assembly for Wales constituted by the 1998 Act; and

(b) in relation to the 2007 Assembly general election and elections and returns under Part 1 of the 2006 Act, the National Assembly for Wales constituted by the 2006 Act,

and all related expressions shall be construed accordingly; but

(i) in articles 16(4), 18(2)(b) and (3)(b), 23(1), (3) and (6) to (10), 24(4)(a), 62(7) and 65(9) and paragraph 3(3) of Schedule 4, it means the National Assembly for Wales constituted by the 1998 Act; and

(ii) in article 91 and rule 69(2) of Schedule 5, it means, until the day of election for the 2007 Assembly general election, the National Assembly for Wales constituted by the 1998 Act, but thereafter the National Assembly for Wales Commission;

"Assembly Constituency" is to be construed in accordance with section 2(1) of the 2006 Act;

"Assembly election" means a constituency election or a regional election;

"Assembly election petition" means a petition presented in pursuance of Part 4 of this Order;

"Assembly election rules" means the rules for the conduct of Assembly elections set out in Schedule 5;

"Assembly electoral region" is to be construed in accordance with section 2(3) of, and Schedule 1 to, the 2006 Act;

"Assembly general election" means the holding of constituency and regional elections for the return of all Assembly members;

"available for inspection" means available for inspection during ordinary office hours;

"candidate" means a constituency candidate, an individual candidate or a party list candidate;

"the Clerk" shall be construed in accordance with section 26 of the 2006 Act;

"the Commission" means the Electoral Commission established by section 1 of the 2000 Political Parties Act;

"constituency candidate" means a candidate at an Assembly constituency election;

"constituency election" means an election to return an Assembly member for an Assembly constituency;

"constituency returning officer" means the person who is the returning officer for a constituency election;

"constituency vote" means a vote given to a candidate to be an Assembly member for an Assembly constituency;

"declaration as to election expenses" means a declaration made under article 53 or 54;

"disability" in relation to doing a thing, includes the short term inability to do it;

"dwelling" includes any part of a building where that part is occupied separately as a dwelling;

"election to fill a casual vacancy" means a constituency election held otherwise than at an Assembly general election;

"election court" means the judges presiding at the trial of an Assembly election petition;

"elector" means any person whose name is for the time being on the register to be used at an Assembly election (or in the case of a person who has an anonymous entry in the register, in the record of anonymous entries) but does not include those shown on the register as below voting age on the day fixed for the poll;

"electoral number" means a person's number in the register to be used at the election or, pending publication of the register, his number (if any) in the electors lists for that register;

"electoral region vote" means a vote given for

(a) a registered political party which has submitted a list of candidates to be Assembly members for an Assembly electoral region; or

(b) an individual who is a candidate to be an Assembly member for that Assembly electoral region;

"European Parliamentary election" has the same meaning as in section 27(1) of the 1985 Act;

"individual candidate" means a candidate at an Assembly regional election other than a party list candidate;

"legal incapacity" includes (in addition, where applicable, to any incapacity arising by virtue of any subsisting provision of the common law) any disqualification imposed by this Order or by any other enactment;

"legal process" means a claim form, application notice, writ, summons or other process;

"the list of proxies" in relation to an Assembly election, has the meaning given by article 10(3),

"local government election" includes a mayoral election;

"mayoral election" means an election for the return of an elected mayor of a local authority in Wales;

"nomination paper" means a constituency nomination paper, an individual nomination paper or a party nomination paper;

"ordinary local government election" means an election at which all the councillors of a county or county borough or community council in Wales are returned

"party list" means a list of not more than twelve candidates (but it may be a list of only one candidate) to be Assembly members for an Assembly electoral region which is to be or has been submitted to a regional returning officer by a registered political party;

"party list candidate" means a candidate included on a party list;

"person" includes (without prejudice to the provisions of the Interpretation Act 1978) an association corporate or unincorporate;

"postal ballot paper" means a ballot paper issued to a postal voter;

"postal proxy" means a person entitled to vote by post as proxy at an election;

"postal voter" means an elector or proxy who is entitled to vote by post;

"postal voters list" means the list kept under article 10(2);

"presiding officer", in relation to a polling station, means a person holding the office set out in rule 35 of Schedule 5;

"Presiding Officer of the Assembly" shall

(a) in relation to the Assembly constituted by the 1998 Act, be construed in accordance with section 52 of the 1998 Act; and

(b) in relation to the Assembly constituted by the 2006 Act, be construed in accordance with, section 25 of the 2006 Act;

"proxy postal voters list" means the list kept under article 12(8);

"qualifying address" has the same meaning as in section 9(8)(b) of the 1983 Act "qualifying Commonwealth citizen" means a Commonwealth citizen who is either

(a) not a person who requires leave under the Immigration Act 1971 to enter or remain in the United Kingdom; or

(b) is such a person but for the time being has (or is, by virtue of any enactment, to be treated as having) indefinite leave to remain within the meaning of that Act,

but a person is not a qualifying Commonwealth citizen if he does not require leave to enter or remain in the United Kingdom by virtue only of Section 8 of the Immigration Act 1971 (exemptions to requirement for leave in special cases);

"regional election" means an election to return Assembly members for an Assembly electoral region;

"regional returning officer" means the person who is the returning officer for a regional election;

"register" means the register of local government electors;

"registered emblem" means an emblem registered by a registered political party under Part 2 of the 2000 Political Parties Act;

"registered nominating officer" means the person registered under Part 2 of the 2000 Political Parties Act as the officer with responsibility for the matters referred to in section 24(3) of that Act in respect of a registered political party;

"registered political party" means (subject to rule 80 of Schedule 5) a party registered under Part 2 of the 2000 Political Parties Act;

"registration officer" means an electoral registration officer;

"relevant citizen of the Union" means a citizen of the Union who is not a qualifying Commonwealth citizen or a citizen of the Republic of Ireland and "citizen of the Union" shall be construed in accordance with Article 20(1) of the Treaty on the Functioning of the European Union;

"relevant registration officer" is to be construed in accordance with sections 42(1) and 44(1) to (3) and (5) of the Electoral Administration Act 2006;

"service voter" means a person who has made a service declaration in accordance with section 15 of the 1983 Act and is registered or entitled to be registered in pursuance of it;

"sub-agent" has the meaning given by article 38(1);

"universal service provider" shall have the same meaning as in Part 3 of the Postal Services Act 2011;

"valid postal voting statement" means a postal voting statement, which, in accordance with paragraph 22 or 23 of Schedule 3, the returning officer is satisfied has been duly completed; and

"voter" means a person voting at an Assembly election and includes a person voting as proxy and, except in Schedule 5, a person voting by proxy, and "vote" (whether noun or verb) shall be construed accordingly, except that in that Schedule any reference to an elector voting or an elector's vote shall include a reference to an elector voting by proxy or elector's vote given by proxy, and absent vote shall be construed accordingly.

(2) References in this Order to the giving of two votes refer to the giving of a constituency vote and an electoral region vote where the polls at a constituency election and at a regional election are to be taken together on the same date.

(3) For the purposes of this Order a person shall be deemed not to have attained a given age until the commencement of the relevant anniversary of the day of his birth.

Part 2
Assembly Franchise and its Exercise

Voting at Assembly elections

3   At an Assembly general election, both constituency and electoral region votes shall be given in an Assembly constituency.

Registers of electors etc

4   An alteration in a published version of a register of electors under section 13A or 56 of the 1983 Act (alteration of registers and registration appeals) shall not have effect for the purposes of an Assembly election if it is to take effect after the fifth day before the date of the poll.

Registration appeals

5(1) Subject to giving notice of the appeal in accordance with paragraph 9(1) of Schedule 1, an appeal from any decision under this Order of the registration officer disallowing a person's application to vote

(a)   by proxy or by post as elector; or

(b)   by post as proxy,

lies to the county court in any case where the application is not made for a particular Assembly election only.

(2)   No appeal lies from the decision of the Court of Appeal on appeal from a decision of the county court under this article.

(3)   An appeal to the county court or Court of Appeal by virtue of this article or section 56 of the 1983 Act which is pending when notice of an Assembly election is given shall not prejudice the operation as respects the Assembly election of the decision appealed against, and anything done in pursuance of the decision shall be as good as if no such appeal had been brought and shall not be affected by the decision of the appeal.

(4)   Notice shall be sent to the registration officer in the manner provided by rules of court of the decision of the county court or of the Court of Appeal on any appeal by virtue of this article, and the registration officer shall make such alterations in the

(a)   record kept under article 8(3); or

(b)   record kept under article 12(6),

as may be required to give effect to the decision.

(5)   Where, as a result of the decision on an appeal by virtue of this article or section 56 of the 1983 Act, an alteration in the register or record takes effect under this article or under section 13(5) or 13A(2),13B(3) or (3B) of the 1983 Act on or before the date of the poll, paragraph (3) shall not apply to that appeal as respects that Assembly election.

(6)   The registration officer shall on an appeal brought under this article be deemed to be a party to the proceedings, and the registration expenses payable to a registration officer shall include any expenses properly incurred by him by virtue of this paragraph.

(7)   CCR Order 45, rule 2 of the Civil Procedure Rules 1998 (appeal from decision of registration officer) shall have effect in relation to appeals under this article subject to the following modifications

(a)   in rule 2(1), "regulations made under section 53 of the said Act of 1983"; and

(b)   in rule 2(4)(a), "to the regulations mentioned in paragraph (1)",

shall be construed as including a reference to paragraph 9 of Schedule 1.

Polling districts and places at Assembly elections

6(1) For the purpose of Assembly elections every Assembly constituency shall be divided into polling districts and there shall be a polling place for each polling district unless the size or other circumstances of a polling district are such that the situation of the polling stations does not materially affect the convenience of the electors or any body of them.

(2)   The polling districts and polling places for the purpose of Assembly elections shall be the districts and places designated for parliamentary elections.

(3)   An election shall not be questioned by reason of
    (a)   any non-compliance with the provisions of this article; or
    (b)   any irregularity relating to polling districts or polling places.

Manner of voting at Assembly elections

7(1)   This article applies to determine the manner of voting of a person entitled to vote as an elector at an Assembly election.

(2)   He may vote in person at the polling station allotted to him under this Order, unless he is entitled as an elector to an absent vote at the Assembly election.

(3)   He may vote by post if he is entitled as an elector to vote by post at the Assembly election.

(4)   If he is entitled to vote by proxy at the Assembly election, he may so vote unless, before a ballot paper has been issued for him to vote by proxy, he applies at the polling station allotted to him under this Order for a ballot paper for the purpose of voting in person, in which case he may vote in person there.

(5)   If he is not entitled as an elector to an absent vote at an Assembly election but cannot reasonably be expected to go in person to the polling station allotted to him under this Order by reason of the particular circumstances of his employment
    (a)   as a constable;
    (b)   by a constituency returning officer, in the case of a constituency election;
    (c)   by a regional returning officer, in the case of a regional election; or
    (d)   by a constituency returning officer, in the case of a regional election where that officer is exercising functions in relation to the election,
on the date of the poll for a purpose connected with the election (subject to paragraph (7)), he may vote in person at any polling station in an Assembly constituency as set out in paragraph (6).

(6)   A person to whom paragraph (5) applies may vote in person at a polling station in the Assembly constituency
    (a)   for which the election is being held, in the case of a constituency election; or
    (b)   in which he is entitled to give his vote, in the case of a regional election.

(7)   Where the polls at a constituency election and a regional election are to be taken together and a person is employed at those elections for a purpose connected with only one of those two elections at which he is entitled to give a vote, he shall be treated for the purposes of paragraph (5) as employed for a purpose connected with both elections; provided that, if a person is so treated, in exercising the right conferred by paragraph (5) those votes shall be given at the same polling station.

(8)   Nothing in the preceding provisions of this article applies to a person to whom section 7 of the 1983 Act (mental patients who are not detained offenders) applies and who is liable, by virtue of any enactment, to be detained in the mental hospital in question, whether he is registered by virtue of that provision or not; and such a person may vote
    (a)   in person (where he is granted permission to be absent from the hospital and voting in person does not breach any condition attached to that permission); or
    (b)   by post or by proxy (where he is entitled as an elector to vote by post or, as the case may be, by proxy at the election).

(9)   Nothing in the preceding provisions of this article applies to a person to whom section 7A of the 1983 Act (persons remanded in custody) applies whether he is registered by virtue of that provision or not; and such a person may only vote by post or by proxy

(where he is entitled as an elector to vote by post or, as the case may be, by proxy at the election).

(10) For the purposes of this Order a person entitled to vote as an elector at an Assembly election is entitled to vote by post or entitled to vote by proxy at the election if paragraph (11) or (12) (as the case may be) applies to him in relation to the election.

(11) This paragraph applies to a person who is shown in the postal voters list mentioned in article 10(2) as entitled to vote by post at an election.

(12) This paragraph applies to a person who is shown in the list of proxies mentioned in article 10(3) as entitled to vote by proxy at an election.

(13) Paragraph (2) does not prevent a person, at the polling station allotted to him, marking a tendered ballot paper in pursuance of rule 49(4) or (6) of Schedule 5.

Absent vote at Assembly elections for a particular or an indefinite period

8(1) Where a person applies to the registration officer to vote by post, or to vote by proxy, at Assembly elections (whether for an indefinite period or for a particular period specified in his application), the registration officer shall grant the application if
   (a) in the case of an application to vote by proxy, he is satisfied that the applicant is eligible to vote by proxy at Assembly elections;
   (b) he is satisfied that the applicant is or will be registered in the register; and
   (c) the application contains the applicant's signature and date of birth and meets the requirements set out in Schedule 1.

(2) For the purposes of this article, a person is eligible to vote by proxy at Assembly elections if
   (a) he is or will be registered as a service voter;
   (b) he has an anonymous entry in the register of electors for the election;
   (c) he cannot reasonably be expected
      (i) to go in person to the polling station allotted or likely to be allotted to him under this Order; or
      (ii) to vote unaided there,
   by reason of blindness or other disability;
   (d) he cannot reasonably be expected to go in person to that polling station by reason of the general nature of his occupation, service or employment or that of his spouse or civil partner, or by reason of his attendance on a course provided by an educational institution or that of his spouse or civil partner; or
   (e) he cannot go in person from his qualifying address to that polling station without making a journey by air or sea.

(3) The registration officer shall keep a record of those whose applications under this article have been granted showing whether their applications were to vote by post or proxy for an indefinite or a particular period and specifying that period.

(4) The record kept under paragraph (3) shall also show
   (a) in the case of those who may vote by post, the addresses provided by them in their applications as the addresses to which their ballot papers are to be sent; and
   (b) in the case of those who may vote by proxy, the names and addresses of those appointed as their proxies.

(5) The registration officer shall remove a person from the record kept under paragraph (3)
   (a) if he applies to the registration officer to be removed;
   (b) in the case of a person who is eligible to vote by proxy by virtue of having an anonymous entry, if he ceases to have an anonymous entry;

    (c)   in the case of any registered person, if he ceases to be registered or registered at the same qualifying address or ceases to be, or becomes, registered in pursuance of

        (i)   a service declaration; or

        (ii) a declaration of local connection;

    (d)   in the case of any person shown in the record as voting by proxy, if the registration officer gives notice that he has reason to believe there has been a material change of circumstances; or

    (e)   in the case of a person who applied to vote by post or proxy for a particular period, once that period has expired.

(6)   A person shown in the record kept under paragraph (3) as voting by post may subsequently alter his choice by applying to the registration officer to vote by proxy instead (whether for an indefinite period or for a particular period specified in his application); and if the registration officer would be required to grant that application if it were an application to vote by proxy under paragraph (1), the registration officer shall amend the record accordingly.

(7)   A person shown in the record kept under paragraph (3) as voting by proxy may subsequently alter his choice by applying to the registration officer to vote by post instead (whether for an indefinite period or for a particular period specified in his application); and if the application meets the requirements of Schedule 1, the registration officer shall amend the record accordingly.

(8)   The registration officer may dispense with the requirement under paragraph (1)(c) for the applicant to provide a signature if he is satisfied that the applicant is unable

    (a)   to provide a signature because of any disability the applicant has; or

    (b)   to provide a signature because the applicant is unable to read or write; or

    (c)   to sign in a consistent and distinctive way because of any such disability or inability.

(9)   The registration officer shall also keep a record in relation to those whose applications under this article have been granted showing

    (a)   their dates of birth; and

    (b)   except in cases where the registration officer in pursuance of paragraph (8) has dispensed with the requirement to provide a signature, their signatures.

(10)   The record kept under paragraph (9) must be retained by the registration officer for the period prescribed in paragraph 2 of Schedule 1.

9 Absent vote at a particular Assembly election

(1)   Where a person applies to the registration officer to vote by post, or to vote by proxy, at a particular Assembly election, the registration officer shall grant the application if

    (a)   he is satisfied in the case of an application to vote by proxy, that the applicant's circumstances on the date of the poll will be or are likely to be such that he cannot reasonably be expected to vote in person at the polling station allotted or likely to be allotted to him under this Order;

    (b)   he is satisfied that the applicant is or will be registered in the register; and

    (c)   the application contains the applicant's signature and date of birth and meets the requirements set out in Schedule 1.

(2)   Where a person who has an anonymous entry in the register applies to the registration officer to vote by proxy at a particular Assembly election, the registration officer shall grant the application if it meets the requirements set out in Schedule 1.

(3)   Paragraph (1) does not apply to a person who is included in the record kept under article 8 but such a person may, in respect of a particular Assembly election, apply to

the registration officer

    (a) for his ballot paper to be sent to a different address from that shown in the record; or

    (b) to vote by proxy,

if he is shown in the record as voting by post at Assembly elections.

(4) The registration officer shall grant an application under paragraph (3) if

    (a) in the case of any application, it meets the requirements set out in Schedule 1; and

    (b) in the case of an application to vote by proxy, he is satisfied that the applicant's circumstances on the date of the poll will be or are likely to be such that he cannot reasonably be expected to vote in person at the polling station allotted or likely to be allotted to him under this Order.

(5) The registration officer may dispense with the requirement under paragraph (1)(c) for the applicant to provide a signature if he is satisfied that the applicant is unable

    (a) to provide a signature because of any disability the applicant has; or

    (b) to provide a signature because the applicant is unable to read or write; or

    (c) to sign in a consistent and distinctive way because of any such disability or inability.

(6) The registration officer shall also keep a record in relation to those whose applications under this article have been granted showing

    (a) their dates of birth; and

    (b) except in cases where the registration officer in pursuance of paragraph (5) has dispensed with the requirement to provide a signature, their signatures.

(7) The record kept under paragraph (6) must be retained by the registration officer for the period prescribed in paragraph 2 of Schedule 1.

(8) For the purposes of this article, articles 11 and 12 and Schedule 1, "particular election", shall, where a person (whether as elector or as proxy) is entitled to give two votes, refer to both elections at which he is entitled to so vote; and references to an absent vote at a particular Assembly election shall be construed accordingly.

10 Absent voters lists at Assembly elections

(1) The registration officer shall, in respect of each Assembly election, keep the two special lists mentioned in paragraphs (2) and (3).

(2) The first of those lists ("the postal voters list") is a list of

    (a) those who are for the time being shown in the record kept under article 8 as voting by post at Assembly elections (excluding those so shown whose applications under article 9(3)(b) to vote by proxy at the election, have been granted) together with the addresses provided by them in their application under article 8 or 9(3)(a) as the addresses to which their ballot papers are to be sent; and

    (b) those whose applications under article 9(1) to vote by post at the election have been granted, together with the addresses provided by them in their applications as the addresses to which their ballot papers are to be sent.

(3) The second list is a list ("the list of proxies") of those who are for the time being shown in the record kept under article 8 as voting by proxy at Assembly elections or whose applications under article 9 to vote by proxy at the election have been granted, together with the names and addresses of those appointed as their proxies.

(4) In the case of a person who has an anonymous entry in the register the postal voters list or list of proxies (as the case may be) must show in relation to that person only

    (a) his electoral number; and

(b) the period for which the anonymous entry has effect.

(5) Where electors are entitled to give two votes, only one list shall be kept under each of paragraphs (2) and (3) and those lists shall have effect in relation to both elections.

11 Proxies at Assembly elections

(1) Subject to the provisions of this article, any person is capable of being appointed proxy to vote for another (in this article and article 12 referred to as "the elector") at any Assembly election and may vote in pursuance of the appointment.

(2) The elector cannot have more than one person at a time appointed as proxy to vote for him at an Assembly election (whether in the same Assembly constituency or elsewhere).

(3) A person is not capable of being appointed to vote, or voting, as proxy at an Assembly election
  (a) if he is subject to any legal incapacity (age apart) to vote at that election as an elector; or
  (b) if he is neither a qualifying Commonwealth citizen nor a citizen of the Republic of Ireland nor a relevant citizen of the Union.

(4) A person is not capable of voting as proxy at an Assembly election unless on the date of the poll he has attained the age of eighteen.

(5) A person is not entitled to vote as proxy
  (a) in the case of an Assembly general election in the same Assembly constituency, or constituencies in the same electoral region;
  (b) in the case of a constituency election other than at an Assembly general election, in the same constituency election;
  (c) in a regional election,
on behalf of more than two persons of whom he is not the spouse, civil partner, parent, grandparent, brother, sister, child or grandchild.

(6) Where the elector applies to the registration officer for the appointment of a proxy to vote for him at Assembly elections (whether for an indefinite period or for a particular period specified in his application), the registration officer shall make the appointment if the application meets the requirements set out in Schedule 1 and he is satisfied that the elector is or will be
  (a) registered in the register; and
  (b) shown in the record kept under article 8 as voting by proxy at such elections,
and that the proxy is capable of being and willing to be appointed to vote as proxy at such elections.

(7) Where the elector applies to the registration officer for the appointment of a proxy to vote for him at a particular Assembly election, the registration officer shall make the appointment if the application contains the signature and date of birth of the applicant and meets the requirements set out in Schedule 1 and he is satisfied that the elector is or will be
  (a) registered in the register for that election; and
  (b) entitled to vote by proxy at that election by virtue of an application under article 9,
and that the proxy is capable of being, and willing to be, appointed.

(8) The appointment of a proxy under this article is to be made by means of a proxy paper issued by the registration officer.

(9) The appointment may be cancelled by the elector by giving notice to the registration officer and shall also cease to be in force on the issue of a proxy paper appointing a different person to vote for him at an Assembly election or Assembly elections

(whether in the same Assembly constituency or elsewhere), and where the appointment was for a particular period, the appointment shall cease to be in force once that period expires.

(10) Subject to paragraph (9), the appointment shall remain in force
    (a) in the case of an appointment for a particular election, for that election; and
    (b) in any other case, while the elector is shown as voting by proxy in the record kept under article 8 in pursuance of the same application under that article.

Voting as proxy at Assembly elections

12(1) A person entitled to vote as proxy at an Assembly election may do so in person at the polling station allotted to the elector under this Order unless he is entitled to vote by post as proxy for the elector at the election, in which case he may vote by post.

(2) Where a person is entitled to vote by post as proxy for the elector at any Assembly election, the elector may not apply for a ballot paper for the purpose of voting in person at the election.

(3) For the purposes of this Order, a person entitled to vote as proxy for another at an Assembly election is entitled so to vote by post if he is included in the list kept under paragraph (8) in respect of the election.

(4) Where a person applies to the registration officer to vote by post
    (a) as proxy at Assembly elections (whether for an indefinite period or for a particular period specified in his application); or
    (b) as proxy at a particular Assembly election,
the registration officer shall grant the application if the conditions set out in paragraph (5) are satisfied.

(5) Those conditions are
    (a) that the registration officer is satisfied that the elector is or will be registered in the register; and
    (b) that there is in force an appointment of the applicant as the elector's proxy to vote for him at Assembly elections or, as the case may be, the Assembly election concerned; and
    (c) that the application contains the applicant's signature and date of birth and meets the requirements set out in Schedule 1.

(6) The registration officer shall keep a record of those whose applications under paragraph (4)(a) have been granted showing
    (a) whether their applications were to vote by post as proxy for an indefinite or a particular period (specifying that period); and
    (b) the addresses provided by them in their applications as the addresses to which their ballot papers are to be sent.

(7) Where, in the case of a particular election, a person included in the record kept under paragraph (6) applies to the registration officer for his ballot paper to be sent to a different address from that shown in the record, the registration officer shall grant the application if it meets the requirements set out in Schedule 1.

(8) The registration officer shall, in respect of each Assembly election, keep a special list ("the proxy postal voters list") of
    (a) those who are for the time being included in the record kept under paragraph (6), together with the addresses provided by them in their applications under paragraph (4)(a) or paragraph (7) as the addresses to which their ballot papers are to be sent; and
    (b) those whose applications under paragraph (4)(b) have been granted in respect of the election concerned, together with the addresses to which their ballot

papers are to be sent,

provided that where the polls at a constituency election and at a regional election are to be taken together, only one list shall be kept under this paragraph and that list shall have effect in relation to both elections.

(9) In the case of a person who has an anonymous entry in the register the special list mentioned in paragraph (8) must contain only the person's electoral number and the period for which the anonymous entry has effect.

(10) The registration officer shall remove a person from the record kept under paragraph (6)

    (a) if he applies to the registration officer to be removed;

    (b) in the case of a person who applied to vote by post as proxy for a particular period, once that period expires;

    (c) if the elector ceases to be registered as mentioned in paragraph (5)(a); or

    (d) if the appointment of the person concerned as the elector's proxy ceases to be in force (whether or not he is reappointed).

(11) Paragraph (2) does not prevent a person, at the polling station allotted to him, marking a tendered ballot paper in pursuance of rule 49 (4) or (6) of Schedule 5.

(12) The registration officer may dispense with the requirement under paragraph (5)(c) for the applicant to provide a signature if he is satisfied that the applicant is unable

    (a) to provide a signature because of any disability the applicant has; or

    (b) to provide a signature because the applicant is unable to read or write; or

    (c) to sign in a consistent and distinctive way because of any such disability or inability.

(13) The registration officer shall also keep a record in relation to those whose applications under paragraph (4)(a) or (b) have been granted showing

    (a) their dates of birth; and

    (b) except in cases where the registration officer in pursuance of paragraph (12) has dispensed with the requirement to provide a signature, their signatures.

(14) The record kept under paragraph (13) must be retained by the registration officer for the period prescribed in paragraph 2 of Schedule 1.

Electors' signatures and use of personal identifier information

13(1) An application for an absent vote or postal proxy made in accordance with article 8, 9, 11 or 12 must comply with paragraph 1 of Schedule 1 (relating to personal identifiers).

(2) A registration officer shall comply with the transitional provisions of Schedule 2 in relation to a person who, on 1st February 2007 has an entry as an absent voter or postal proxy in his absent voting record.

(3) A person who remains on the record kept under article 8(3) or 12(6) may, at any time, provide the registration officer with a fresh signature.

(4) Anything required or authorised to be done for the purposes of any enactment in relation to a signature required to be provided in pursuance of the absent vote provisions of this Order must be done in relation to a signature provided as mentioned in paragraph (3) instead of in relation to a signature provided on any earlier occasion.

(5) The registration officer shall either

    (a) provide the constituency returning officer for an Assembly election with a copy of the information contained in records kept by the registration officer in pursuance of articles 8(9), 9(6) and 12(13) in relation to electors at the election; or

    (b) give that returning officer access to such information.

(6)   Information contained in records kept by a registration officer in pursuance of article 8(9), 9(6) or 12(13) may be disclosed by him (subject to the conditions prescribed in paragraphs 13 and 14 of Schedule 1) to

    (a)   any other registration officer if he thinks that to do so will assist the other registration officer in the performance of his duties;

    (b)   any person exercising functions in relation to the preparation or conduct of legal proceedings under the Representation of the People Acts or this Order;

    (c)   such other persons for such other purposes relating to elections as are prescribed in paragraphs 13 and 14 of Schedule 1.

Offences

14(1)   A person who provides false information in connection with an application to which article 8, 9, 11 or 12 applies is guilty of an offence.

(2)   For the purposes of paragraph (1), "false information" means a signature which

    (a)   is not the usual signature of; or

    (b)   was written by a person other than,

the person whose signature it purports to be.

(3)   A person does not commit an offence under paragraph (1) if he did not know and had no reason to suspect that the information was false.

(4)   Where sufficient evidence is adduced to raise an issue with respect to the defence under paragraph (3), the court shall assume that the defence is satisfied unless the prosecution proves beyond reasonable doubt that it is not.

(5)   A person guilty of an offence under paragraph (1) shall be liable on summary conviction to

    (a)   imprisonment for a term not exceeding 51 weeks; or

    (b)   a fine not exceeding level 5 on the standard scale,

or both.

(6)   In relation to an offence committed before the commencement of section 281(5) of the Criminal Justice Act 2003, the reference in paragraph (5)(a) to 51 weeks must be taken to be a reference to 6 months.

(7)   A person also commits an offence if he

    (a)   engages in an act specified in paragraph (8) at an Assembly election; and

    (b)   intends, by doing so, to deprive another of an opportunity to vote or to make for himself or another a gain of a vote to which he or the other is not otherwise entitled or a gain of money or property.

(8)   These are the acts

    (a)   applying for a postal or proxy vote as some other person (whether that other person is living or dead or is a fictitious person);

    (b)   otherwise making a false statement in, or in connection with, an application for a postal or proxy vote;

    (c)   inducing the registration officer or constituency returning officer to send a postal ballot paper or any communication relating to a postal or proxy vote to an address which has not been agreed to by the person entitled to the vote; and

    (d)   causing a communication relating to a postal or proxy vote or containing a postal ballot paper not to be delivered to the intended recipient.

(9)   In paragraph (7)(b), property includes any description of property.

(10)   In paragraph (8) a reference to a postal vote or a postal ballot paper includes a reference to a proxy postal vote or a proxy postal ballot paper (as the case may be).

(11)   A person who commits an offence under paragraph (7) or who aids, abets, counsels or

procures the commission of such an offence is guilty of a corrupt practice and shall be liable on conviction in accordance with article 120.

Absent voting at Assembly elections: miscellaneous

15(1) For the purposes of section 59 of the 1983 Act (supplemental provisions as to members of forces and service voters)

    (a) subsections (3)(b) and (c) shall be construed as including a reference to this Order in connection with the rights conferred by this Order on a person having a service qualification by virtue of section 14(1)(a) or (b) of that Act in relation to the making and cancellation of appointments of a proxy and in relation to voting in person, by post or by proxy; and

    (b) subsection (3A) shall be similarly construed.

(2) Schedule 1 (which makes further provision in connection with absent voting at Assembly elections) has effect.

(3) Schedule 2 (which makes transitional provision in connection with absent voting at Assembly elections) has effect.

(4) Schedule 3 (which makes further provision in connection with the issue and receipt of postal ballot papers) has effect.

Combination of polls at Assembly and local government elections

16(1) Where the polls at an Assembly general election and an ordinary local government election are to be taken on the same date, they shall be taken together.

(2) Where the polls at an Assembly election and local government election for related areas are to be taken on the same date but are not required by paragraph (1) to be taken together, they may nevertheless be so taken if the returning officer for each election thinks fit.

(3) For the purposes of paragraph (2), two areas are related if one is coterminous with or situated wholly or partly within the other.

(4) Where the polls at an Assembly general election and an ordinary local government election are combined under paragraph (1) the cost of taking the combined polls (excluding any cost solely attributable to one election) and any cost attributable to their combination shall be apportioned among the elections in such proportions as the Assembly may by order specify; and an order under this paragraph may specify different proportions in relation to different functions.

(5) Where the polls at an Assembly election and another election are combined under paragraph (2) the cost of taking the combined polls (excluding any cost solely attributable to one election) and any cost attributable to their combination shall be apportioned equally among the elections.

(6) The power to make orders under paragraph (4) shall be exercised by statutory instrument and for the purposes of section 1 of the Statutory Instruments Act 1946 this provision shall have effect as if contained in an Act of Parliament..

(7) Schedule 4 (which makes provision in connection with the combination of polls at Assembly and local government elections) has effect but, where the poll at an Assembly election is combined with a mayoral election, only Parts 1 and 2 of Schedule 4 shall apply.

Rules for Assembly elections

17(1) The proceedings at Assembly elections including the return of Assembly members shall be conducted in accordance with the Assembly election rules set out in Schedule

5.

(2) In addition to the functions otherwise conferred or imposed on a constituency or regional returning officer at an Assembly election it is the general duty of such an officer to do all such acts as may be necessary for effectively conducting the election in the manner provided by those rules.

(3) No Assembly election shall be declared invalid by reason of any act or omission by such a returning officer or any other person in breach of his official duty in connection with the election or otherwise of those rules if it appears to the tribunal having cognizance of the question that
    (a) the election was so conducted as to be substantially in accordance with the law as to Assembly elections; and
    (b) the act or omission did not affect the result.

Returning officers

18(1) For the purpose of Assembly elections there shall be
    (a) a constituency returning officer for each Assembly constituency; and
    (b) a regional returning officer for each Assembly electoral region, and
such persons shall hold office in accordance with the following provisions of this article.

(2) A constituency returning officer shall be the person
    (a) who is appointed under section 35(1A)(a) of the 1983 Act to be the returning officer for elections of councillors of a county or county borough situated wholly or partly in the Assembly constituency; and
    (b) in the case where there is more than one such person, who is for the time being designated by the Assembly as returning officer for the constituency.

(3) A regional returning officer shall be the person
    (a) who is appointed under section 35(1A)(a) of the 1983 Act to be the returning officer for elections of councillors of a county or county borough situated wholly or partly in the Assembly electoral region; and
    (b) in the case where there is more than one such person, who is for the time being designated by the Assembly as returning officer for the electoral region.

(4) A designation made under this article shall be in writing.

(5) The office of returning officer is a distinct office from that by virtue of which the person becomes returning officer.

(6) Where a person takes any office by virtue of which he becomes a returning officer, he (and not the outgoing holder of the office) shall complete the conduct of any outstanding election in accordance with the Assembly election rules.

Officers of councils to be placed at disposal of returning officers

19(1) The council of each county or county borough shall place the services of its officers at the disposal of any constituency returning officer for an Assembly constituency wholly or partly situated in its area.

(2) The services placed at the disposal of a constituency returning officer under paragraph (1) may relate to the exercise of that officer's functions in connection with a constituency election, a regional election or both such elections.

(3) The council of each county or county borough shall also place the services of its officers at the disposal of any regional returning officer for an Assembly electoral region partly situated in its area.

Returning officers: discharge of functions

20(1) A constituency or a regional returning officer at an Assembly election may, in writing, appoint one or more persons to discharge all or any of his functions.

(2) Paragraph (1) applies to a constituency returning officer at a constituency or a regional election.

(3) Except in the case of an election to fill a casual vacancy, it shall be the duty of each regional returning officer and each constituency returning officer for an Assembly constituency in the Assembly electoral region to co-operate with each other in the discharge of their functions.

(4) The duty imposed by paragraph (3) applies as between constituency returning officers in an Assembly electoral region as well as between such officers and the regional returning officer for the electoral region.

(5) In this Order, a reference to a constituency returning officer in relation to the discharge of functions at a regional election is a reference to the discharge of such functions in relation to the Assembly constituency for which he is the returning officer.

Returning officers: correction of procedural errors

21(1) A constituency or a regional returning officer at an Assembly election may take such steps as he thinks appropriate to remedy any act or omission on his part, or on the part of a relevant person, which

(a) arises in connection with any function the returning officer or relevant person has in relation to the election; and

(b) is not in accordance with the rules or any other requirements applicable to the election.

(2) But a returning officer may not under paragraph (1) recount the votes given at an election after the result has been declared.

(3) These are the relevant persons

(a) an electoral registration officer;

(b) in relation to a regional election, a relevant returning officer at that election;

(c) a presiding officer;

(d) a person providing goods or services to the returning officer; and

(e) a deputy of any person mentioned in sub paragraphs (a) to (c) or a person appointed to assist, or in the course of his employment assisting, such a person in connection with any function he has in relation to the election.

(4) In paragraph (3)(b), "a relevant returning officer" means

(a) in the case of a regional returning officer taking steps under paragraph (1), a constituency returning officer at that regional election; and

(b) in the case of a constituency returning officer taking steps under paragraph (1), the regional returning officer at that regional election.

(5) Where the act or omission to be remedied is that of a relevant returning officer, then, before taking steps under paragraph (1)

(a) the regional returning officer must consult the constituency returning officer whose act or omission is to be remedied; and

(b) a constituency returning officer must consult the regional returning officer.

Returning officers: general

22(1) An Assembly election is not liable to be questioned by reason of a defect in the title, or want of title, of the person presiding at or conducting the election, if that person was then in actual possession of, or acting in, the office giving the right to preside at or conduct the election.

(2) A person is not subject to any incapacity to vote at an Assembly election by reason of being or acting as returning officer at that election.

Payments by and to returning officer

23(1) A constituency or a regional returning officer shall be entitled to recover his charges in respect of services rendered, or expenses incurred, for, or in connection with, an Assembly election if

    (a) the services were necessarily rendered, or the expenses were necessarily incurred, for the efficient and effective conduct of the election; and

    (b) the total of his charges does not exceed the amount ("the overall maximum recoverable amount") specified in, or determined in accordance with, an order made by the Assembly for the purposes of this paragraph,

and in the case of a constituency returning officer, this paragraph applies to services rendered or expenses incurred for, or in connection with, a constituency or a regional election.

(2) An order under paragraph (1) may specify, or make provision for determining in accordance with the order, a maximum recoverable amount for services or expenses of any specified description and, subject to paragraph (3), the returning officer may not recover more than that amount in respect of any such services or expenses.

(3) The Assembly may, in a particular case, authorise the payment of

    (a) more than the overall maximum recoverable amount; or

    (b) more than the specified maximum recoverable amount for any specified services or expenses,

if the Assembly is satisfied that the conditions in paragraph (4) are met.

(4) The conditions referred to in paragraph (3) are

    (a) that it was reasonable for the returning officer concerned to render the services or incur the expenses; and

    (b) that the charges in question are reasonable.

(5) The power to make orders under paragraph (1) shall be exercised by statutory instrument and for the purpose of section 1 of the Statutory Instruments Act 1946 this provision shall have effect as if contained in an Act of Parliament.

(6) Any order under paragraph (1) may make different provision for different purposes and may contain such incidental supplemental saving or transitional provision as the Assembly thinks fit.

(7) The Assembly shall pay the amount of any charges recoverable in accordance with this article on an account being submitted to it but the Assembly may if it thinks fit, before payment, apply for the account to be assessed under the provisions of article 24.

(8) Where the superannuation contributions required to be paid by a local authority in respect of any person are increased by any fee paid under this article as part of a returning officer's charges at an Assembly election; then on an account being submitted to the Assembly, a sum equal to the increase shall be paid by the Assembly to the authority.

(9) On a returning officer's request for an advance on account of his charges, the Assembly may, on such terms as it thinks fit, make such an advance.

(10) The Assembly may by regulations make provision as to the time when and the manner and form in which accounts are to be rendered to the Assembly for the purpose of the payment of a returning officer's charges; and such regulations may make different provision for different purposes.

(11) Any sums payable by the Assembly or the Welsh Ministers under paragraph (7) or (8) in the financial year beginning on 1st April 2007 and in subsequent years shall be charged on the Welsh Consolidated Fund

Detailed assessment of returning officer's account

24(1) An application for a returning officer's account to be assessed shall be made to the county court and in this article the expression "the court" means the county court.

(2) On any such application the court has jurisdiction to assess the account in such manner and at such time and place as the court thinks fit, and finally to determine the amount payable to the returning officer.

(3) On any such application the returning officer may apply to the court to examine any claim made by any person against him in respect of matters charged in the account; and the court, after notice given to the claimant and after giving him an opportunity to be heard and to tender any evidence, may allow or disallow or reduce the claim objected to with or without costs; and the determination of the court shall be final for all purposes and against all persons.

(4) CCR Order 45, rule 1 of the Civil Procedure Rules 1998 (application for detailed assessment of returning officer's account under section 30 of the 1983 Act) shall have effect in relation to applications made under this article and, in relation to such applications, that rule shall apply with the following modifications
   (a) references to the Secretary of State shall be construed as references to the Assembly; and
   (b) references to returning officers shall be construed as references to
       (i)   constituency returning officers in relation to a constituency election; and
       (ii) constituency and regional returning officers in relation to a regional election.

Loan of equipment for Assembly elections

25(1) Any ballot boxes, fittings and compartments provided for parliamentary elections out of money provided by Parliament may, on request, be lent to a constituency returning officer at an Assembly election on such terms and conditions as the Commission may determine.

(2) Any ballot boxes, fittings and compartments provided by or belonging to a local authority within the meaning of the Local Government Act 1972 shall, on request (if not required for immediate use by that authority), be lent to a constituency returning officer at an Assembly election on such terms and conditions as may be agreed.

Effect of registers

26(1) Any entry in the register of electors, if it gives a date as that on which the person named will attain voting age, shall for any purpose of this Part relating to him as elector be conclusive that until the date given in the entry he is not of voting age nor entitled to be treated as an elector except for the purposes of an Assembly election at which the date fixed for the poll is that or a later date.

(2) A person registered as a local government elector, or entered in the list of proxies, shall not be excluded from voting at an Assembly election on any of the grounds set out in paragraph (3); but this shall not prevent the rejection of the vote on a scrutiny, or affect his liability to any penalty for voting.

(3) The grounds referred to in paragraph (2) are
   (a) that he is not of voting age;
   (b) that he is not, or on the relevant date or the date of his appointment (as the

            case may be), was not

              (i)   a qualifying Commonwealth citizen;

              (ii)   a citizen of the Republic of Ireland; or

              (iii) a relevant citizen of the Union; or

       (c)   that he is or, on the relevant date or the date of his appointment (as the case may be) was, otherwise subject to any other legal incapacity to vote.

  (4)   In paragraph (3), the "relevant date" means

       (a)   in relation to a person registered in the register as published in accordance with section 13(1) of the 1983 Act, the 15th October immediately preceding the date of publication of the register;

       (b)   in relation to any other person registered in the register, the relevant date for the purposes of section 4 of the 1983 Act.

  (5)   Paragraph (1) applies to an entry in the record of anonymous entries as it applies to an entry in the register of electors.

Effect of misdescription

27   In relation to an Assembly election no misnomer or inaccurate description of any person or place named

       (a)   in the register of electors; or

       (b)   in any list, record, proxy paper, nomination paper, ballot paper, notice or other document required for the purposes of this Order,

shall affect the full operation of the document with respect to that person or place in any case where the description of the person or place is such as to be commonly understood.

Discharge of registration duties

28(1)   A registration officer shall comply with any general or specific directions which may be given by the Secretary of State, in accordance with and on the recommendation of the Commission, with respect to the arrangements to be made by the registration officer in carrying out his functions under this Order.

  (2)   Any of the duties and powers of a registration officer under this Order may be performed and exercised by any deputy for the time being approved by the county or county borough council which appointed the registration officer; and the provisions of this Order apply to any such deputy so far as respects any duties or powers to be performed or exercised by him as they apply to the registration officer.

  (3)   Any acts authorised or required to be done by or with respect to the registration officer under this Order may, in the event of his incapacity to act or of a vacancy, be done by or with respect to the proper officer of the county or county borough council by whom the registration officer was appointed.

  (4)   A county or county borough council by whom a registration officer is appointed shall assign such officers to assist him as may be required in carrying out his functions under this Order.

Payment of expenses of registration

29(1)   Any expenses properly incurred by a registration officer in the performance of his functions under this Order (in this Order referred to as "registration expenses") shall be paid by the county or county borough council by whom the registration officer was appointed.

  (2)   Any fees paid to the registration officer under this Order shall be accounted for by him and paid to the county or county borough council by whom he was appointed.

  (3)   On the request of a registration officer for an advance on account of registration

expenses, the county or county borough council by whom the registration officer was appointed may, if it thinks fit, make such an advance to him of such an amount and subject to such conditions as it may approve.

Personation

30(1)   In relation to an Assembly election a person shall be guilty of a corrupt practice if he commits, or aids, abets, counsels or procures the commission of, the offence of personation.

(2)   A person shall be deemed to be guilty of personation at an Assembly election if he

    (a)   votes in person or by post as some other person, whether as an elector or as proxy, and whether that other person is living or dead or is a fictitious person; or

    (b)   votes in person or by post as proxy

        (i)   for a person whom he knows or has reasonable grounds for supposing to be dead or to be a fictitious person; or

        (ii)   when he knows or has reasonable grounds for supposing that his appointment as proxy is no longer in force.

(3)   For the purposes of this article, a person who has applied for a ballot paper for the purpose of voting in person or who has marked, whether validly or not, and returned a ballot paper issued for the purpose of voting by post, shall be deemed to have voted.

(4)   Section 24A of the Police and Criminal Evidence Act 1984 (arrest without warrant: other persons) does not permit a person other than a constable to arrest, inside a polling station, a person who commits or is suspected of committing an offence under the preceding provisions of this article.

Other voting offences

31(1)   For the purposes of this article a person who has applied for a ballot paper for the purpose of voting in person, or who has marked, whether validly or not, and returned a ballot paper issued for the purpose of voting by post, shall be deemed to have voted, but for the purpose of determining whether an application for a ballot paper constitutes an offence under paragraph (6), a previous application made in circumstances which entitle the applicant only to mark a tendered ballot paper shall, if he does not exercise that right, be disregarded.

(2)   A person shall be guilty of an offence if

    (a)   he votes in person or by post, whether as an elector or as proxy, or applies to vote by proxy or by post as elector at an Assembly election, or at Assembly elections, knowing that he is subject to a legal incapacity to vote at the election or, as the case may be, at elections of that kind;

    (b)   he applies for the appointment of a proxy to vote for him at an Assembly election or at Assembly elections, knowing that he or the person to be appointed is subject to a legal incapacity to vote at the election or, as the case may be, at elections of that kind; or

    (c)   he votes, whether in person or by post, as proxy for some other person at an Assembly election, knowing that that person is subject to a legal incapacity to vote.

(3)   For the purposes of paragraph (2), references to a person being subject to a legal incapacity to vote do not, in relation to things done before polling day at the election or first election at or for which they are done, include his being below voting age if he will be of voting age on that day.

(4)   A person shall be guilty of an offence if

    (a)   he votes as elector otherwise than by proxy either

    (i)   more than once in the same Assembly constituency at any Assembly election;

    (ii) in more than one Assembly constituency at an Assembly general election; or

    (iii) in any Assembly constituency at an Assembly election when there is in force an appointment of a person to vote as his proxy at the election in some other constituency;

 (b) he votes as elector in person at an Assembly election at which he is entitled to vote by post;

 (c) he votes as elector in person at an Assembly election, knowing that a person appointed to vote as his proxy at the election either has already voted in person at the election or is entitled to vote by post at the election; or

 (d) he applies for a person to be appointed as his proxy to vote for him at Assembly elections in any Assembly constituency without applying for the cancellation of a previous appointment of a third person then in force in respect of that or another constituency or without withdrawing a pending application for such an appointment in respect of that or another constituency.

(5) A person shall be guilty of an offence if

 (a) he votes as proxy for the same elector either

    (i)   more than once in the same Assembly constituency at any Assembly election; or

    (ii) in more than one Assembly constituency at an Assembly general election;

 (b) he votes in person as proxy for an elector at an Assembly election at which he is entitled to vote by post as proxy for that elector; or

 (c) he votes in person as proxy for an elector at an Assembly election knowing that the elector has already voted in person at the election.

(6) A person shall also be guilty of an offence if he votes as proxy

 (a) in the case of an Assembly general election, at constituency elections in Assembly constituencies in an Assembly electoral region (or in one such election);

 (b) in the case of a constituency election other than at an Assembly general election, at a constituency election; or

 (c) at a regional election (whether or not at an Assembly general election);

for more than two persons of whom he is not the spouse, civil partner, parent, grandparent, brother, sister, child or grandchild.

(7) A person shall also be guilty of an offence if he knowingly induces or procures some other person to do an act which is, or but for that other person's want of knowledge would be, an offence by that other person under the foregoing paragraphs of this article.

(8) A person is not guilty of an offence under paragraph (4)(b) or (5)(b) only by reason of his having marked a tendered ballot paper in pursuance of rule 49(4) or (6) of Schedule 5.

(9) An offence under this article shall be an illegal practice, but

 (a) the court before whom a person is convicted of any such offence may, if they think it just in the special circumstances of the case, mitigate or entirely remit any incapacity imposed by virtue of article 123; and

 (b) a candidate shall not be liable, nor shall his election be avoided, for an illegal practice under this article of any agent of his other than an offence under paragraph (7).

(10) Where a person is entitled to give two votes (whether in person as elector or by proxy, or by post as elector or by proxy) he votes once in relation to each Assembly election

for which his votes are given.

Breach of official duty

32(1)   If a person to whom this article applies is, without reasonable cause, guilty of any act or omission in breach of his official duty, he shall be liable on summary conviction to a fine not exceeding level 5 on the standard scale.

(2)   No person to whom this article applies shall be liable for breach of his official duty to any penalty at common law and no action for damages shall lie in respect of the breach by such a person of his official duty.

(3)   The persons to whom this article applies are
- (a)   any registration officer, returning officer or presiding officer;
- (b)   any other person whose duty it is to be responsible after an Assembly election for the used ballot papers and other documents (including returns and declarations as to expenses);
- (c)   any official designated by a universal service provider; and
- (d)   any deputy of a person mentioned in any of sub-paragraphs (a) to (c) or any person appointed to assist or in the course of his employment assisting a person so mentioned in connection with his official duties,

and "official duty" shall for the purpose of this article be construed accordingly, but shall not include duties imposed otherwise than by the law relating to Assembly elections or the registration of local government electors.

(4)   Where
- (a)   a returning officer for an Assembly election is guilty of an act or omission in breach of his official duty; but
- (b)   he remedies that act or omission in full by taking steps under paragraph (1) of article 21,

he shall not be guilty of an offence under paragraph (1).

(5)   Paragraph (4) does not affect any conviction which takes place, or any penalty which is imposed, before the date on which the act or omission is remedied in full.

Tampering with nomination papers, ballot papers etc

33(1)   A person shall be guilty of an offence if, at an Assembly election, he
- (a)   fraudulently defaces or fraudulently destroys any constituency, individual or party nomination paper;
- (b)   fraudulently defaces or fraudulently destroys any ballot paper, or the official mark on any ballot paper, or postal voting statement or official envelope used in connection with voting by post;
- (c)   without due authority supplies any ballot paper to any person;
- (d)   fraudulently puts into any ballot box any paper other than the ballot paper which he is authorised by law to put in;
- (e)   fraudulently takes out of the polling station any ballot paper;
- (f)   without due authority destroys, takes, opens or otherwise interferes with any ballot box or packet of ballot papers then in use for the purposes of the election; or
- (g)   fraudulently or without due authority, as the case may be, attempts to do any of the foregoing acts.

(2)   If a returning officer, a presiding officer or a clerk appointed to assist in taking the poll and counting the votes, or at the proceedings in connection with the issue or receipt of postal ballot papers, is guilty of an offence under this article, he shall be liable
- (a)   on conviction on indictment to a fine, or to imprisonment for a term not exceeding two years, or to both; or

    (b) on summary conviction, to a fine not exceeding the statutory maximum, or to imprisonment for a term not exceeding 6 months, or to both.

(3) If any other person is guilty of an offence under this article he shall be liable on summary conviction to a fine not exceeding level 5 on the standard scale, or to imprisonment for a term not exceeding 6 months, or to both.

(4) In relation to an offence committed after commencement of section 281(5) of the Criminal Justice Act 2003, the reference in paragraphs (2)(b) and (3) to 6 months must be taken to be a reference to 51 weeks.

False statements in nomination papers etc

34(1) A person shall be guilty of a corrupt practice if, in the case of an Assembly election, he causes or permits to be included in a document delivered or otherwise furnished to a returning officer for use in connection with the election

    (a) a statement of the name or home address of a candidate at the election which he knows to be false in any particular; or

    (b) anything which purports to be the signature of a person who subscribes a nomination paper but which he knows

        (i) was not written by the person by whom it purports to have been written; or

        (ii) if written by that person, was not written by him for the purpose of subscribing that nomination paper; or

    (c) a certificate under rule 5 of the Assembly election rules authorising the use by a constituency candidate of a description if he knows that the candidate is a candidate in another Assembly constituency election in which the poll is to be held on the same day as the poll at the election to which the certificate relates; or

    (d) a certificate under rule 8 of the Assembly election rules authorising the use by a registered political party of a description if he knows that a candidate on that party's list of candidates is also an individual candidate or a party list candidate for another registered political party at that Assembly election or is a candidate in another Assembly election in which the poll is to be held on the same day as the poll at the election to which the certificate relates.

(2) A person is guilty of a corrupt practice if, in the case of a constituency election, he makes in any document in which he gives his consent to nomination as a candidate

    (a) a statement of his date of birth;

    (b) a statement as to his qualification for membership of the Assembly; or

    (c) a statement that he is not a candidate at an election for any other constituency the poll for which is to be held on the same day as the poll at the election to which the consent relates,

which he knows to be false in any particular.

(3) A person is guilty of a corrupt practice if, in the case of an individual candidate at a regional election, he makes in any document in which he gives his consent to nomination as a candidate

    (a) a statement of his date of birth;

    (b) a statement as to his qualification for membership of the Assembly; or

    (c) a statement that he is not a party list candidate at that regional election nor a candidate in another Assembly election the poll for which is to be held on the same day as the poll at the election to which the consent relates,

which he knows to be false in any particular.

(4) A person is guilty of a corrupt practice if, in the case of a party list candidate at a regional election, he makes in any document in which he gives his consent to nomination as a candidate

    (a)   a statement of his date of birth;

    (b)   a statement as to his qualification for membership of the Assembly; or

    (c)   a statement that he is not an individual candidate or a candidate on the list submitted by another registered political party at that regional election or a candidate at another Assembly election in which the poll is to be held on the same day as the poll at the election to which the consent relates,

which he knows to be false in any particular.

(5)   For the purposes of paragraphs (2), (3), and (4) a statement as to the candidate's qualification is a statement that

    (a)   he is qualified for being elected;

    (b)   he will be qualified for being elected; or

    (c)   to the best of his knowledge and belief he is not disqualified for being elected or to the best of his knowledge and belief he is disqualified only under section 16(1)(za) of the 2006 Act (disqualification of MPs).

Requirement of secrecy

35(1)   The following persons attending at a polling station, namely

    (a)   a returning officer;

    (b)   a presiding officer or clerk;

    (c)   a candidate or election agent or polling agent; or

    (d)   a person attending by virtue of any of sections 6A to 6D of the 2000 Political Parties Act,

shall maintain and aid in maintaining the secrecy of voting and shall not, except for some purpose authorised by law, communicate to any person before the poll is closed any information as to

    (i)   the name of any elector or proxy for an elector who has or has not applied for a ballot paper or voted at a polling station;

    (ii)   the number on the register of electors of any elector who, or whose proxy, has or has not applied for a ballot paper or voted at a polling station; or

    (iii)   the official mark on any ballot paper.

(2)   Every person attending at the counting of the votes shall maintain and aid in maintaining the secrecy of voting and shall not

    (a)   ascertain or attempt to ascertain at the counting of votes the number or other unique identifying mark on the back of any ballot paper; or

    (b)   communicate any information obtained at the counting of votes as to how any vote is given on any particular ballot paper.

(3)   No person shall

    (a)   interfere with or attempt to interfere with a voter when giving his vote;

    (b)   otherwise obtain or attempt to obtain in a polling station information as to how a voter in that station is about to vote or has voted;

    (c)   communicate at any time to any person any information obtained in a polling station as to how a voter in that station is about to vote or has voted, or as to the number or other unique identifying mark on the back of a ballot paper given to a voter at that station; or

    (d)   directly or indirectly induce a voter to display a ballot paper after he has marked it so as to make known to any person how he has or has not voted.

(4)   Every person attending the proceedings in connection with the issue or the receipt of ballot papers for persons voting by post shall maintain and aid in maintaining the secrecy of the voting and shall not

    (a)   except for some purpose authorised by law, communicate, before the poll is closed, to any person any information obtained at those proceedings as to the official mark;

    (b) except for some purpose authorised by law, communicate to any person at any time any information obtained at those proceedings as to the number or other unique identifying mark on the back of the ballot paper sent to any person;

    (c) except for some purpose authorised by law, attempt to ascertain at the proceedings in connection with the receipt of ballot papers the number or other unique identifying mark on the back of any ballot paper; or

    (d) attempt to ascertain at the proceedings in connection with the receipt of the ballot papers how any vote is given on any particular ballot paper or communicate any information with respect thereto obtained at those proceedings.

(5) No person having undertaken to assist a voter with disabilities shall communicate at any time to any person any information as to how that voter intends to vote or has voted, or as to the number or other unique identifying mark on the back of the ballot paper given for the use of that voter.

(6) If a person acts in contravention of this article he shall be liable on summary conviction to a fine not exceeding level 5 on the standard scale or to imprisonment for a term not exceeding 6 months.

(7) In relation to an offence committed after commencement of section 281(5) of the Criminal Justice Act 2003, the reference in paragraph (6) to 6 months must be taken to be a reference to 51 weeks.

Prohibition on publication of exit polls

36(1) No person shall, in the case of an Assembly election, publish before the poll is closed

    (a) any statement relating to the way in which voters have voted at the election where that statement is (or might reasonably be taken to be) based on information given by voters after they have voted; or

    (b) any forecast as to the result of the election which is (or might reasonably be taken to be) based on information so given.

(2) If a person acts in contravention of paragraph (1), he shall be liable on summary conviction to a fine not exceeding level 5 on the standard scale or to imprisonment for a term not exceeding 6 months.

(3) In relation to an offence committed after commencement of section 281(5) of the Criminal Justice Act 2003, the reference in paragraph (2) to 6 months must be taken to be a reference to 51 weeks.

(4) In this article

    "forecast" includes estimate;

    "publish" means make available to the public at large, or any section of the public, in whatever form and by whatever means,

and any reference to the result of an election is a reference to the result of the election either as a whole or so far as any particular candidate or candidates at the election is or are concerned.

Part 3
The Election Campaign

Appointment of election agent

37(1) At an Assembly election, not later than the latest time for delivery of notices of withdrawal of candidature, a person shall be named by, or on behalf of

    (a) each constituency candidate; and

      (b) each individual candidate, in the case of a regional election,

as the candidate's election agent, and the name and address of the candidate's election agent shall be declared in writing by the candidate, or some other person on his behalf, to the appropriate returning officer not later than that time.

(2) A constituency or an individual candidate at a regional election may name himself as election agent.

(3) At a regional election, not later than the latest time for delivery of notices of withdrawal of candidature, a person shall be named by, or on behalf of, each registered political party submitting a party list as the election agent for that party in relation to that list, and that person's name and address shall be declared in writing by or on behalf of that party's registered nominating officer to the regional returning officer not later than that time.

(4) A candidate included on a registered political party's party list may be named as election agent for that party in relation to that party list.

(5) Where a candidate has been named or has named himself as an election agent, so far as circumstances permit, he shall be subject to the provisions of this Order both as a candidate and as an election agent and, except where the context otherwise requires, any reference in this Order to an election agent shall be construed to refer to the candidate acting in his capacity as election agent.

(6) One election agent only shall be appointed for
    (a) each constituency candidate;
    (b) each individual candidate at a regional election; and
    (c) each registered political party that has submitted a party list at a regional election,

but the appointment, whether the election agent appointed be a candidate himself or not, may be revoked.

(7) If (whether before, during or after the election) the appointment (or deemed appointment) of an election agent is revoked or an election agent dies, another election agent shall be appointed forthwith and his name and address declared in writing to the appropriate returning officer.

(8) The declaration as an election agent of a person other than
    (a) a constituency or an individual candidate; or
    (b) in relation to a registered political party that has submitted a party list, the candidate whose name appears first on the list,

shall be of no effect under this article unless it is made and signed by that person or is accompanied by a written declaration of acceptance signed by him.

(9) Upon the name and address of an election agent being declared to the appropriate returning officer
    (a) the appropriate returning officer shall forthwith give public notice of that name and address; and
    (b) in the case of a regional election, the regional returning officer shall forthwith give notice of that name and address to the constituency returning officer for each Assembly constituency in the Assembly electoral region.

Nomination of sub-agent

38(1) At an Assembly election an election agent, subject to the provisions of this article, may appoint to act in any part of
    (a) the Assembly constituency, in the case of a constituency election; or
    (b) the Assembly electoral region, in the case of a regional election,
one, but not more than one, deputy election agent (in this Order referred to as a sub-

agent).

(2) As regards matters in the part of an Assembly constituency or electoral region for which there is a sub-agent the election agent may act by the sub-agent and

   (a) anything done for the purposes of this Order by or to the sub-agent in his part of the Assembly constituency or electoral region shall be deemed to be done by or to the election agent;

   (b) any act or default of a sub-agent which, if he were the election agent, would be an illegal practice or other offence against this Order shall be an illegal practice or offence against this Order committed by the sub-agent, and the sub-agent shall be liable to punishment accordingly; and

   (c) a candidate shall suffer the like incapacity as if that act or default had been the election agent's act or default.

(3) Not later than the second day before the day of the poll the election agent shall declare in writing the name and address of every sub-agent to the appropriate returning officer, and

   (a) the returning officer shall forthwith give public notice of the name and address of every sub-agent so declared; and

   (b) in the case of a regional election, the regional returning officer shall forthwith give notice of that name and address to the constituency returning officer for each Assembly constituency in any part of which the sub-agent is appointed to act.

(4) The appointment of a sub-agent

   (a) shall not be vacated by the election agent who appointed him ceasing to be election agent; but

   (b) may be revoked by whoever is for the time being the election agent,

   and in the event of the revocation of the appointment or of the death of a sub-agent another sub-agent may be appointed, and his name and address shall be forthwith declared in writing to the appropriate returning officer, who shall forthwith give the like notice required by paragraph (3)(a) and, if applicable, (b).

(5) The declaration to be made to the appropriate returning officer, and such notice to be given by him, under paragraph (3) or (4) shall specify the part of the Assembly constituency or electoral region within which any sub-agent is appointed to act.

Office of election agent and sub-agent

39(1) Every election agent and every sub-agent shall have an office to which all claims, notices, legal processes and other documents may be sent, and the address of the office shall be

   (a) declared to the appropriate returning officer at the same time as the appointment of the agent is declared to him;

   (b) stated in the public notice under article 37(9)(a) or 38(3)(a); and

   (c) in the case of a regional election, stated in the notice to the constituency returning officers under article 37(9)(b) or 38(3)(b).

(2) The office

   (a) of an election agent for a constituency election shall be

      (i) in the Assembly constituency for which the election is held or an adjoining Assembly constituency; or

      (ii) in a county or county borough which is partly comprised in or adjoins the first mentioned Assembly constituency;

   (b) of an election agent for a regional election shall be in Wales; and

   (c) of a sub-agent shall be in the area within which he is appointed to act.

(3) Any claim, notice, legal process or other document delivered at the office of the

election agent or sub-agent and addressed to him, shall be deemed to have been served on him and every election agent or sub-agent may, in respect of any matter connected with the election in which he is acting, be sued in any court having jurisdiction at the place where his office is situated.

Effect of default in election agent's appointment

40(1) If no person's name and address is given as required by article 37 as the election agent of a constituency or individual candidate who remains validly nominated at the latest time for delivery of notices of withdrawal of candidature, the candidate shall be deemed at that time to have named himself as election agent and to have revoked any appointment of another person as his election agent.

(2) If no person's name and address is given as required by article 37 as the election agent of a registered political party which has submitted a party list at the latest time for delivery of notices of withdrawal of candidature, the candidate whose name appears first on the list shall be deemed at that time to have been named as election agent and any appointment of another person as that party's election agent shall be deemed to have been revoked.

(3) This paragraph applies if
   (a) the person whose name and address have been so given as those of an election agent for a constituency or an individual candidate (not being the candidate himself) or a registered political party dies; and
   (b) a new appointment is not made on the day of the death or on the following day.

(4) Where paragraph (3) applies
   (a) in the case of a constituency candidate or an individual candidate at a regional election, he shall be deemed to have appointed himself as from the time of death; and
   (b) in the case of the death of an election agent for a registered political party at a regional election
      (i) the candidate whose name appears first on the list shall be deemed to have been appointed from the time of death; or
      (ii) where paragraph (3) applies through the death of such a candidate, the candidate whose name appears next highest on the list shall be deemed to have been appointed from the time of death.

(5) If the appointment of an election agent is revoked without a new appointment being made
   (a) in the case of a constituency candidate or an individual candidate at a regional election, the candidate himself shall be deemed to have been appointed (or reappointed) election agent; and
   (b) in the case of a registered political party the candidate whose name appears first on that party's list shall be deemed to have been appointed (or reappointed) election agent.

(6) The deemed appointment of an election agent may be revoked as if it were an actual appointment.

(7) Where a candidate is by virtue of this article to be treated as an election agent he shall be deemed to have his office at his address as given for that purpose in his consent to nomination under rule 9 of Schedule 5.

(8) The appropriate returning officer on being satisfied that a person is by virtue of this article to be treated as an election agent, shall forthwith proceed to give such like notice as if the name and address of the person and the address of his office had been duly given to him under articles 37 and 39.

Control of donations to constituency and individual candidates

41(1) In the case of any constituency or individual candidate at an Assembly election, any money or other property provided (whether as a gift or loan)

    (a) by any person other than the candidate or his election agent; and

    (b) for the purpose of meeting election expenses incurred by or on behalf of the candidate,

must be provided to the candidate or his election agent.

  (2) Paragraph (1) does not apply to any money or other property so provided for the purpose of meeting any such expenses which may be lawfully paid by a person other than the candidate, his election agent or any sub-agent.

  (3) A person who provides any money or other property in contravention of paragraph (1) shall be guilty of an illegal practice.

  (4) Schedule 6 has effect for the purpose of controlling donations to constituency and individual candidates at an Assembly election.

  (5) In this article and that Schedule "property" includes any description of property and references to the provision of property accordingly include the supply of goods.

Expenses of constituency candidate

42 For the purpose of this Part of this Order, sums paid or expenses incurred by, or in respect of, a candidate at a constituency election in respect of whom the constituency returning officer has received a certificate issued by the registered nominating officer of a registered political party under rule 5(1) or, as the case may be, (3) of Schedule 5, are not to be regarded as having been paid or incurred by that party.

Constituency and individual candidates: payment of expenses by or through election agent

43(1) Subject to paragraph (4), no payment (of whatever nature) shall be made by

    (a) a constituency or individual candidate at an Assembly election; or

    (b) any other person,

in respect of election expenses incurred by or on behalf of the candidate unless it is made by or through the candidate's election agent.

  (2) Every payment made by an election agent in respect of any election expenses shall, except where less than £20, be vouched for by a bill stating the particulars or by a receipt.

  (3) The references in paragraphs (1) and (2) to an election agent shall be taken as references to the election agent acting by himself or by a sub-agent.

  (4) This article does not apply to

    (a) any expenses which are, in accordance with article 44(1) or (2), 49(6) or 50(2), paid by the candidate;

    (b) any expenses which are paid in accordance with article 44(4) by a person authorised as mentioned in that provision;

    (c) any expenses included in a declaration made by the election agent under article 45; or

    (d) any expenses which are regarded as incurred by or on behalf of the candidate by virtue of article 63(5).

  (5) A person who makes any payment (of whatever nature) in contravention of paragraph (1) shall be guilty of an illegal practice.

Expenses which may be paid otherwise than by election agent

44(1)   A candidate at an Assembly election may pay any personal expenses incurred by him on account of or in connection with or incidental to the election, but the amount which a candidate may pay shall not exceed

(a)   £600, in the case of a constituency candidate; or

(b)   £900, in the case of a candidate at a regional election,

and any further personal expenses incurred by him shall be paid by the election agent.

(2)   A candidate at an Assembly election may also pay any election expenses (other than expenses falling within paragraph (1)) which were incurred by him or on his behalf and in respect of which payment falls to be made before the date on which he appoints (or is deemed to have appointed) an election agent.

(3)   A candidate shall send to the election agent within the time permitted by this Order for sending in claims a written statement of the amount of expenses paid as mentioned in paragraph (1) or (2) by the candidate.

(4)   Any person may, if so authorised in writing by an election agent, at an Assembly election pay any necessary expenses of stationery, postage, telephonic communication (or any other similar means of communication) and other petty expenses, to a total amount not exceeding that named in the authority, but any excess above the total amount so named shall be paid by the election agent.

(5)   A statement of the particulars of payments made by any person so authorised shall be sent to the election agent within the time limited by this Order for sending in claims, and shall be vouched for by a bill containing that person's receipt.

(6)   Articles 49 and 50 do not apply to expenses which, in accordance with any provision of this article, are paid otherwise than by the candidate's election agent.

Expenses incurred otherwise than for election purposes

45(1)   Articles 43, 49 and 50 shall not apply to election expenses

(a)   which are incurred by or on behalf of the candidate otherwise than for the purposes of the candidate's election; but

(b)   which by virtue of article 63(1) fall to be regarded as election expenses by reason of the property, services or facilities in respect of which they are incurred being used for the purposes of the candidate's election.

(2)   The candidate's election agent shall make a declaration of the amount of any election expenses falling within paragraph (1).

(3)   In this article "for the purposes of the candidate's election" has the same meaning as in articles 63 and 64.

Constituency and individual candidates: prohibition of expenses not authorised by election agent etc

46(1)   No expenses shall, with a view to promoting or procuring the election of a constituency or individual candidate at an Assembly election, be incurred after he becomes a candidate at that election by any person other than the candidate, his election agent and persons authorised in writing by the election agent on account

(a)   of holding public meetings or organising any public display; or

(b)   of issuing advertisements, circulars or publications; or

(c)   in the case of a constituency election, of otherwise presenting to the electors the candidate or his views or the extent or nature of his backing or disparaging another candidate; or

(d)   in the case of a regional election, of otherwise presenting to the electors the candidate or his views or the extent or nature of his backing or disparaging another individual candidate or a registered political party or any or all of its party list candidates.

(2) Sub-paragraph (c) or (d) of paragraph (1) does not restrict the publication of any matter relating to the election in

    (a) a newspaper or other periodical;

    (b) a broadcast made by the British Broadcasting Corporation or by Sianel Pedwar Cymru; or

    (c) a programme included in any service licensed under Part 1 or 3 of the Broadcasting Act 1990 or Part 1 or 2 of the Broadcasting Act 1996.

(3) Paragraph (1) does not apply to any expenses incurred by any person

    (a) which do not exceed in the aggregate the permitted sum (and are not incurred by that person as part of a concerted plan of action); or

    (b) in travelling or living away from home or similar personal expenses.

(4) For the purposes of paragraph (3)(a)

    (a) expenses shall be regarded as incurred by a person "as part of a concerted plan of action" if they are incurred by that person in pursuance of any plan or other arrangement whereby that person and one or more other persons are to incur, with a view to promoting or procuring the election of the same candidate, expenses which (disregarding paragraph (3)(a)) fall within paragraph (1); and

    (b) "the permitted sum" is £500 in the case of a constituency election and £1,000 in the case of a regional election.

(5) Where a person incurs any expenses in respect of a candidate required by this article to be authorised by the election agent

    (a) that person shall within 21 days after the day on which the result of the election is declared deliver to the appropriate returning officer a return of the amount of those expenses stating the constituency or regional election at which, and the candidate in whose support, they were incurred; and

    (b) the return shall be accompanied by a declaration made by that person (or, in the case of an association or body of persons, by a director, general manager, secretary or other similar officer of the association or body) verifying the return and giving particulars of the matters for which the expenses were incurred,

but this paragraph does not apply to any person engaged or employed for payment or promise of payment by a candidate or his election agent.

(6) The return and declaration under the foregoing provisions of this article shall be in forms CU and CV set out in English and Welsh in Schedule 10, and the authority received from the election agent shall be annexed to and deemed to be part of the return.

(7) The appropriate returning officer shall forward to the relevant registration officer every document sent to him in pursuance of paragraph (5), and rule 69(1) of Schedule 5 shall apply to any document sent to the relevant registration officer under this paragraph.

(8) If a person

    (a) incurs, or aids, abets, counsels or procures any other person to incur any expenses in contravention of this article; or

    (b) knowingly makes the declaration required by paragraph (5) falsely,

he shall be guilty of a corrupt practice.

(9) If a person fails to deliver or send any declaration or return or a copy of it as required by this article he shall be guilty of an illegal practice.

(10) The court before whom a person is convicted under paragraph (8) or (9) may, if they think it just in the special circumstances of the case, mitigate or entirely remit any incapacity imposed by virtue of article 123.

(11) A candidate shall not be liable, nor shall his election be avoided, for a corrupt or illegal practice under paragraph (8) or (9) committed by an agent without his consent or connivance.

(12) Where any act or omission of an association or body of persons, corporate or unincorporate, is an offence declared to be a corrupt or illegal practice by this article, any person who at the time of the act or omission was a director, general manager, secretary or other similar officer of the association or body, or was purporting to act in any such capacity, shall be deemed to be guilty of that offence, unless he proves
    (a) that the act or omission took place without his consent or connivance; and
    (b) that he exercised all such diligence to prevent the commission of the offence as he ought to have exercised having regard to the nature of his functions in that capacity and to all the other circumstances.

(13) For the purposes of paragraph (1) expenditure incurred before the date when a person becomes a candidate at the election is to be treated as having been incurred after that date if it is incurred in connection with anything which is used or takes place after that date.

Constituency and individual candidates: limitation of election expenses

47(1) The election expenses incurred by or on behalf of a constituency or individual candidate at an Assembly election must not in the aggregate exceed the appropriate maximum amount specified in paragraph (3).

(2) Where any election expenses are incurred in excess of the appropriate maximum amount specified in paragraph (3), any candidate or election agent who
    (a) incurred, or authorised the incurring of, the election expenses; and
    (b) knew or ought reasonably to have known that the expenses would be incurred in excess of that maximum amount,
shall be guilty of an illegal practice.

(3) The maximum amount is
    (a) at an Assembly general election, for a constituency candidate
        (i) for an Assembly constituency which is coterminous with a parliamentary constituency which is a county constituency, £7,150 together with an additional 7p for every entry in the register of electors; and
        (ii) for an Assembly constituency which is coterminous with a parliamentary constituency which is a borough constituency, £7,150 together with an additional 5p for every entry in the register of electors;
    (b) for a constituency candidate at an election to fill a casual vacancy, £100,000; and
    (c) for an individual candidate at a regional election, the aggregate of the maximum amounts under sub-paragraph (a)(i) or (ii) as apply, or would apply, at that time at a constituency election in respect of each Assembly constituency in the Assembly electoral region for which the election is held.

(4) In paragraph (3) "the register of electors" means the register for the Assembly constituency or Assembly electoral region in question as it has effect on the last day for publication of notice of the election.

(5) The maximum amount mentioned in paragraph (3) for a candidate at an Assembly election is not required to cover his personal expenses.

(6) Where at a constituency election
    (a) notice of poll is countermanded or the poll is abandoned by reason of a candidate's death pursuant to rule 73 of Schedule 5; or
    (b) the majority of votes at a poll is given to a deceased candidate and a new notice

of election is published pursuant to rule 71 of Schedule 5,

the maximum amount of election expenses shall, for any of the other candidates who then remain validly nominated, be twice, or if there has been a previous increase under this paragraph, three times what it would have been but for any increase under this paragraph.

(7) The maximum amount mentioned in paragraph (3) for a candidate shall not be affected by the change in the timing of an Assembly election or of any step in the proceedings at an Assembly election.

Power to vary provisions concerning election expenses

48(1) The Secretary of State may by order vary any of the sums to which this article applies

    (a) where he considers that the variation is expedient in consequence of changes in the value of money; or

    (b) in order to give effect to a recommendation of the Commission.

(2) This article applies to any of the sums for the time being specified in articles 43(2), 44(1), or 47(3).

(3) A statutory instrument containing an order under paragraph (1) shall be subject to annulment in pursuance of a resolution of either House of Parliament and for the purpose of section 1 of the Statutory Instruments Act 1946 this provision shall have effect as if contained in an Act of Parliament.

Time for sending in and paying claims

49(1) Every claim against

    (a) a constituency candidate or his election agent; or

    (b) an individual candidate or his election agent at a regional election,

in respect of election expenses which is not sent in to the election agent within 21 days after the day on which the result or results of the election are declared shall be barred and not paid.

(2) All election expenses shall be paid not later than 28 days after the day set out in paragraph (1).

(3) Any person who pays a claim in contravention of paragraph (1) or makes a payment in contravention of paragraph (2) shall be guilty of an illegal practice.

(4) Where the election court reports that it has been proved to the court that any payment so made was by an election agent without the sanction or connivance of the candidate

    (a) the candidate's election shall not be void;

    (b) nor shall he be subject to any incapacity under this Order by reason only of that payment having been made in contravention of this article.

(5) In respect of a claim, the payment of which is otherwise barred by paragraph (1)

    (a) a claimant; or

    (b) a constituency or individual candidate or his election agent,

may apply to the High Court or to a county court for leave to pay the claim although sent in after the period of 21 days or although sent in to a candidate and not as required to the election agent, and the court on cause shown to their satisfaction may by order grant the leave.

(6) Any sum specified in the order of leave under paragraph (5) may be paid by a candidate or his election agent, and when paid in pursuance of the leave shall not be deemed to be in contravention of paragraph (2).

Disputed claims

50(1) If an election agent disputes any claim sent in within the period of 21 days mentioned in article 49(1) or refuses or fails to pay the claim within the period of 28 days mentioned in article 49(2) the claim shall be deemed to be a disputed claim.

(2) The claimant may, if he thinks fit, bring an action for a disputed claim in any competent court and any sum paid by a constituency or an individual candidate in pursuance of the judgement or order of the court shall not be deemed to be in contravention of article 43(1) or 49(2).

(3) Article 49(5) and (6), applies in relation to a disputed claim as it applies in relation to a claim for election expenses sent in after the period of 21 days.

Election agent's claim

51 So far as circumstances admit, this Order applies to an election agent's claim for his remuneration and to its payment in like manner as if he were any other creditor, and if any difference arises about the amount of the claim, the claim shall be a disputed claim within the meaning of this Order and shall be dealt with accordingly.

Constituency and individual candidates: return as to election expenses

52(1) Within 35 days after the day on which the result or results of an Assembly election are declared the election agent of every
    (a) candidate, in the case of a constituency election; and
    (b) individual candidate, in the case of a regional election,
at the election shall deliver to the appropriate returning officer a true return in manner as provided for in paragraph (8), containing as respects that candidate
      (i) a statement of all election expenses incurred by or on behalf of the candidate; and
      (ii) a statement of all payments made by the election agent together with all bills or receipts relating to the payments.

(2) A return under this section must
    (a) specify the poll by virtue of which the return is required;
    (b) specify the name of the candidate to whom the return relates and of the candidate's election agent; and
    (c) deal under a separate heading with any expenses in respect of which a return is required by virtue of article 46(5).

(3) The return shall also contain as respects that candidate
    (a) a statement relating to such other expenses in connection with which provision is made by this Part as the Commission provide in regulations;
    (b) a statement relating to such claims (whether paid, unpaid or disputed) in connection with such election expenses or such other expenses mentioned in sub-paragraph (a) as the Commission so provide; and
    (c) a statement relating to such other matters as the Commission may provide in regulations.

(4) Until the coming into force of the first regulations made by the Commission under paragraph (3), the return shall also contain as respects that candidate
    (a) a statement of all payments made
      (i) by the candidate in accordance with article 44(1) or (2); or
      (ii) by any other person in accordance with article 44(4),
together with all bills or receipts relating to any such payments made;
    (b) a statement of all disputed claims of which the election agent is aware;
    (c) a statement of all the unpaid claims, if any, of which the election agent is aware, in respect of which application has been or is about to be made to the High

Court or county court;

- (d) any declarations of value falling to be made by the candidate's election agent by virtue of article 45(2) or 64(2);
- (e) a declaration of the amount of expenses which are to be regarded as election expenses incurred by or on behalf of the candidate by virtue of article 63(5)(b);
- (f) a statement of donations made to the candidate or his election agent which complies with the requirements of paragraphs 11 and 12 of Schedule 6; and
- (g) a statement of the amount, if any, of money provided by the candidate from his own resources for the purpose of meeting election expenses incurred by him or on his behalf.

(5) Paragraph (6) shall apply where, after the date at which the return as to election expenses is delivered, leave is given by the court under article 49(5) for any claims to be paid.

(6) The candidate or, as the case may be, his election agent shall, within seven days after its payment, deliver to the appropriate returning officer a return of the sums paid in pursuance of the leave accompanied by a copy of the order of the court giving the leave and in default he shall be deemed to have failed to comply with the requirements of this article without such authorised excuse as is mentioned in article 58.

(7) Any regulations under paragraph (3) may make different provision for different purposes and may contain such incidental, supplemental, saving or transitional provisions as the Commission thinks fit.

(8) The return shall be in form CW set out in English and Welsh in Schedule 10.

Constituency and individual candidates: declaration as to election expenses

53(1) Each return delivered under article 52(1) shall be accompanied by a declaration made by the election agent in form CX set out in English and Welsh in Schedule 10.

(2) At the same time as the election agent delivers that return, or within seven days thereafter each constituency or individual candidate shall deliver to the appropriate returning officer a declaration made by him in the form CX set out in English and Welsh in that Schedule.

(3) Where a candidate is out of the United Kingdom when the return is so delivered
- (a) the declaration required by paragraph (2) may be made by him within 14 days after his return to the United Kingdom; and
- (b) in that case, the declaration shall be forthwith delivered to the appropriate returning officer,

but the delay authorised by this provision in making the declaration shall not exonerate the election agent from complying with the provisions of this Order relating to the return and declaration as to election expenses.

(4) Where a constituency candidate or an individual candidate is his own election agent, the declaration by the election agent as to the election expenses need not be made and the declaration by the candidate as to election expenses shall be modified as specified in the form CX set out in English and Welsh in Schedule 10.

(5) If a candidate or election agent knowingly makes the declaration required by this article falsely, he shall be guilty of a corrupt practice.

Party list candidates: declarations as to election expenses

54(1) At the same time as the treasurer of a registered political party delivers a return under section 80 of the 2000 Political Parties Act, or within 7 days thereafter, each candidate on a party list submitted by that party shall deliver to the regional returning officer a declaration made by that candidate in form CY set out in English and Welsh in

Schedule 10.

(2) Where any such candidate is out of the United Kingdom when the return is so delivered

   (a) the declaration required by paragraph (1) may be made by him within 14 days after his return to the United Kingdom; and

   (b) in that case, the declaration shall forthwith be delivered to the regional returning officer,

but the delay authorised by this article in making the declaration shall not exonerate the treasurer of the registered political party from complying with the provisions of the 2000 Political Parties Act relating to the return of party expenditure.

(3) If a person knowingly makes the declaration required by this article falsely, he shall be guilty of a corrupt practice.

Circumstances in which no return or declaration is required

55 Notwithstanding anything in article 52, 53 or 54, no return or declaration as to election expenses shall be required in the case of a person

   (a) who is a candidate at an Assembly election, but is so only because he has been declared by others to be a candidate; and

   (b) who has not consented to the declaration or taken any part as a candidate at the election.

Penalty for failure as respects return or declarations

56 Subject to the provisions of article 58, if any candidate or election agent fails to comply with the requirements of article 52, 53 or 54 he shall be guilty of an illegal practice.

57 Penalty for sitting or voting where no return and declarations are delivered etc

(1) If

   (a) in the case of a constituency or individual candidate, the return and declarations as to election expenses; or

   (b) in the case of a party list candidate, his declaration as to election expenses,

are not delivered before the expiry of the time limited for the purpose, the candidate shall not, after the expiry of that time, sit or vote in the Assembly as member for the Assembly constituency or electoral region for which the election was held until either

   (i) where sub-paragraph (a) applies, that return and those declarations have been delivered; or

   (ii) where sub-paragraph (b) applies, that declaration has been delivered; or

   (iii) the date of the allowance of an authorised excuse for the failure to deliver that return and those declarations or, as the case may be, that declaration.

(2) If he sits or votes in contravention of paragraph (1) he shall forfeit £100 for every day on which he so sits or votes.

(3) Civil proceedings for a penalty under this article shall be commenced within the period of one year beginning with the day in respect of which the penalty is alleged to have been incurred.

(4) For the purpose of paragraph (3)

   (a) where the service or execution of legal process on or against the alleged offender is prevented by the absconding or concealment or act of the alleged offender, the issue of legal process shall be deemed to be a commencement of a proceeding; but,

   (b) where sub-paragraph (a) does not apply, the service or execution of legal process on or against the alleged offender, and not its issue, shall be deemed to be the commencement of the proceeding.

Authorised excuses for failures as to return and declarations

58(1) A candidate or an election agent may apply for relief under this article to the High Court, an election court or a county court.

(2) Where an application is made under this article the person or persons making the application shall notify the Director of Public Prosecutions of the application and the Director or his assistant or any barrister, advocate or solicitor duly appointed as the Director's representative may attend the hearing of the application and make representations at the hearing in respect of it.

(3) Relief under this article may be granted
   (a) to a candidate, in respect of any failure to deliver the return and declarations as to election expenses, or any part of them, or in respect of any error or false statement in them; or
   (b) to an election agent, in respect of any failure to deliver the return and declaration as to election expenses which he was required to deliver, or any part of them or in respect of any error or false statement in them.

(4) The application for relief may be made on the ground that the failure, error or false statement arose
   (a) by reason of the applicant's illness;
   (b) where the applicant is a candidate, by reason of the absence, death, illness or misconduct
      (i) of his election agent or sub-agent; or
      (ii) of any clerk or officer of such agent;
   (c) where the applicant is an election agent
      (i) by reason of the death or illness of any prior election agent of the candidate; or
      (ii) by reason of the absence, death, illness or misconduct of any sub-agent, clerk or officer of any election agent of the candidate; or
   (d) by reason of inadvertence or any reasonable cause of a like nature,
   and not by reason of any want of good faith on the applicant's part.

(5) The court may
   (a) after such notice of the application in the Assembly constituency or electoral region for which the election was held, as it considers fit; and
   (b) on production of such evidence of the grounds stated in the application and of the good faith of the application, and otherwise, as it considers fit,
   make such order for allowing an authorised excuse for the failure, error or false statement as it considers just.

(6) Where it is proved to the court by a candidate
   (a) that any act or omission of the election agent in relation to the return or declarations was without the sanction or connivance of the candidate; and
   (b) that the candidate took all reasonable means for preventing the act or omission,
   the court shall relieve the candidate from the consequences of the act or omission of his election agent.

(7) An order under paragraph (5) may make the allowance conditional on the making of the return and declaration in a modified form or within an extended time, and upon the compliance with such other terms as to the court seem best calculated for carrying into effect the objects of this Part.

(8) An order under paragraph (5) shall relieve the applicant for the order from any liability or consequences under this Order in respect of the matter excused by the order.

(9) The date of the order, or if conditions and terms are to be complied with, the date at which the applicant fully complies with them, is referred to in this Order as the date of the allowance of the excuse.

Court's power to require information from election agent or sub-agent

59(1) Where on an application under article 58 it appears to the court that any person who is or has been an election agent or sub-agent has refused or failed to make such return, or to supply such particulars, as will enable
    (a) a candidate and his election agent at a constituency election; or
    (b) an individual candidate and his election agent at a regional election,
to comply with the provisions of this Order as to the return or declarations as to election expenses the court, before making an order under that article, shall order that person to attend before the court.

(2) The court shall on the attendance of that person, unless he shows cause to the contrary, order him
    (a) to make the return and declaration; or
    (b) to deliver a statement of the particulars required to be contained in the return,
as the court considers just, within such time, to such person and in such manner as it may direct, or may order him to be examined with respect to the particulars.

(3) If a person fails to comply with any order of the court under this article, the court may order him to pay a fine.

Duty of appropriate returning officer to forward returns and declarations to the Commission

60 Where the appropriate returning officer receives any return or declaration under article 46, 52, 53 or 54, he shall as soon as reasonably practicable after receiving the return or declaration deliver a copy of it to the Commission and, if so requested by the Commission, he shall also deliver to them a copy of any accompanying documents.

Publication of time and place of inspection of returns and declarations

61(1) At an Assembly election the appropriate returning officer, within ten days after the end of the time allowed for delivering to him returns as to election expenses, shall
    (a) publish in not less than
        (i) two newspapers circulating in the Assembly constituency; or
        (ii) three newspapers circulating in the Assembly electoral region,
    for which the election was held, and
    (b) send
        (i) in the case of a constituency election, to each of the election agents; and
        (ii) in the case of a regional election, to the registered nominating officer of each registered political party that stood nominated and to each of the election agents for individual candidates,
a notice of the time and place at which the returns and declarations (including the accompanying documents) can be inspected.

(2) But if any return or declaration has not been received by the appropriate returning officer before the notice is despatched for publication, the notice shall so state and a like notice about that return and declaration, if afterwards received, shall within ten days after the receipt be published in like manner and sent to such persons to whom the first notice is sent other than an election agent who is in default or an election agent for a candidate who is in default.

Constituency and individual candidates: inspection of returns and declarations

62(1) Where the appropriate returning officer receives any return or declaration under article 46, 52, 53 or 54 he shall

(a) as soon as reasonably practicable after receiving the return or declaration make a copy of it, and any accompanying documents, available for public inspection at his office, or some other convenient place chosen by him, for a period of two years beginning with the date when the return is received by him; and

(b) if requested to do so by any person, and on payment of the fee specified in paragraph (4), supply that person with a copy of the return or declaration and any accompanying documents.

(2) If any such return contains a statement of donations in accordance with paragraph 10 of Schedule 6, the appropriate officer shall secure that the copy of the statement made available for public inspection under sub-paragraph (1)(a) or (as the case may be) supplied under sub-paragraph (1)(b) does not include, in the case of any donation by an individual, the donor's address.

(3) The fee for inspecting a copy of a return or declaration (including any accompanying documents) referred to in sub-paragraph (1)(a) shall be £1.50.

(4) The fee payable for a copy of any such return, declaration or document referred to in sub-paragraph (1)(b) shall be at the rate of 15p for each side of each page.

(5) After the expiry of those two years the appropriate returning officer

(a) may cause those returns and declarations (including the accompanying documents) to be destroyed; or

(b) if the candidate or where appropriate, his election agent so requires, shall return them to the candidate.

(6) Any returns or declarations delivered under article 46 shall be returned not to a candidate (if he or his election agent so requires) but to the person delivering them if he so requires.

(7) The Assembly may by order vary the amount of any fee payable under paragraph (3) or (4).

(8) The power to make orders under paragraph (7) shall be exercisable by statutory instrument and for the purpose of section 1 of the Statutory Instruments Act 1946 this provision shall have effect as if contained in an Act of Parliament.

Meaning of "election expenses"

63(1) In this Part "election expenses", in relation to a constituency or individual candidate, means (subject to paragraph (3) and article 64) any expenses incurred at any time in respect of any matter specified in Part 1 of Schedule 7 which is used for the purposes of the candidate's election after the date when he becomes a candidate at the election.

(2) No election expenses are to be regarded as incurred by virtue of paragraph (1) or article 64 in respect of any matter specified in Part 2 of Schedule 7.

(3) In this article and in article 64, "for the purposes of the candidate's election" means with a view to, or otherwise in connection with, promoting or procuring the candidate's election at the election.

(4) For the purposes of this Part, election expenses are incurred by or on behalf of a candidate at an Assembly election if they are incurred

(a) by the candidate or his election agent; or

(b) by any person authorised by the candidate or his election agent to incur the expenses.

(5) In this Part, any reference to election expenses incurred by or on behalf of a candidate at an Assembly election includes expenses

    (a) which are incurred as mentioned in paragraph (1) before the date when he becomes a candidate at the election but

    (b) which by virtue of that paragraph fall to be regarded as election expenses.

(6) In this Part and in Part 4, any reference (in whatever terms) to promoting or procuring a candidate's election at an election includes doing so by prejudicing the electoral prospects of another candidate or registered political party at the election.

(7) Schedule 7 has effect.

(8) A Code of Practice issued by the Secretary of State under the provisions of paragraph 14 of Schedule 4A to the 1983 Act shall apply to Schedule 7 as it does to Schedule 4A to the 1983 Act.

Property, goods, services etc provided free of charge or at a discount

64(1) This article applies where, in the case of a constituency or individual candidate at an Assembly election

    (a) either

        (i) property or goods is or are transferred to the candidate or his election agent free of charge or at a discount of more than 10 per cent of the market value of the property or goods; or

        (ii) property, goods, services or facilities is or are provided for the use or benefit of the candidate free of charge or at a discount of more than 10 per cent of the commercial rate for the use of the property or for the provision of the goods, services or facilities,

  and

    (b) the property, goods, services or facilities is or are made use of by or on behalf of the candidate in circumstances such that, if any expenses were to be (or are) actually incurred by or on behalf of the candidate in respect of that use, they would be (or are) election expenses incurred by or on behalf of the candidate.

(2) Where this article applies

    (a) an amount of election expenses determined in accordance with this article ("the appropriate amount") shall be treated, for the purposes of this Part, as incurred by the candidate; and (in that case),

    (b) the candidate's election agent shall make a declaration of that amount,

  unless that amount is not more than £50.

  This paragraph has effect subject to Part 2 of Schedule 7.

(3) Where paragraph (1)(a)(i) applies, the appropriate amount is such proportion of either

    (a) the market value of the property or goods (where the property or goods is or are transferred free of charge); or

    (b) the difference between the market value of the property or goods and the amount of expenses actually incurred by or on behalf of the candidate in respect of the property or goods (where the property or goods is or are transferred at a discount),

  as is reasonably attributable to the use made of the property or goods as mentioned in paragraph (1)(b).

(4) Where paragraph (1)(a)(ii) applies, the appropriate amount is such proportion of either

    (a) the commercial rate for the use of the property or the provision of the goods, services or facilities (where the property, goods, services or facilities is or are provided free of charge); or

    (b) the difference between that commercial rate and the amount of expenses actually incurred by or on behalf of the candidate in respect of the use of the property or the provision of the services or facilities (where the property, goods, services or facilities is or are provided at a discount), as is reasonably attributable to the use made of the property, goods, services or facilities as mentioned in paragraph (1)(b).

(5) Where the services of an employee are made available by his employer for the use or benefit of a candidate, then for the purposes of this article the commercial rate for the provision of those services shall be the amount of the remuneration and allowances payable to the employee by his employer in respect of the period for which his services are so made available (but shall not include any amount in respect of any contributions or other payments for which the employer is liable in respect of the employee).

(6) In this article "market value", in relation to any property or goods, means the price which might reasonably be expected to be paid for the property or goods on a sale in the open market; and paragraph 2(6)(a) of Schedule 6 shall apply with any necessary modifications for the purpose of determining, for the purposes of paragraph (1), whether property or goods is or are transferred to a candidate or his election agent.

Right to send election address post free

65(1) At an Assembly election, each constituency or individual candidate or registered nominating officer of a registered political party which has submitted a list of candidates at such an election (subject to such reasonable terms and conditions as the universal service provider concerned may specify) is entitled to send free of any charge for postage which would otherwise be made by a universal service provider either

(a) one unaddressed postal communication, containing matter relating to such election wholly and not exceeding 60 grammes in weight, to each place in the Assembly constituency or electoral region for which the election is being held at which he or they are a candidate or candidates which, in accordance with those terms and conditions, constitutes a delivery point for the purposes of this article; or

(b) one such postal communication addressed to each elector.

(2) Any such candidate or, as the case may be, registered nominating officer shall also, subject as mentioned in paragraph (1), be entitled to send free of any such charge for postage as is mentioned in that paragraph to each person entered in the list of proxies for the election one such communication as mentioned in paragraph (1) for each appointment in respect of which that person is so entered.

(3) Any such candidate or, as the case may be, registered nominating officer may require the returning officer to make arrangements with the universal service provider for communications under paragraph (1)(b) to be sent to persons who have anonymous entries in the register.

(4) Arrangements under paragraph (3) shall be such as to ensure that it is not disclosed to any other person that the addressee of such a communication has an anonymous entry.

(5) In relation to a candidate at a constituency election or to an individual candidate at a regional election, a person shall not be deemed to be a candidate for the purposes of this article unless he is shown as standing nominated in the statement of persons nominated; but, until the publication of that statement, any person who declares himself to be a candidate shall be entitled to exercise the right of free postage conferred by this article if he gives such security as may be required by the universal service provider concerned for the payment of postage should he not be shown as standing nominated as mentioned above.

(6) In relation to a registered political party at a regional election, such a party shall not be deemed to have submitted a list of candidates for the purposes of this article unless

the party is shown as standing nominated in the statement of parties and other persons nominated; but, until the publication of that statement, the registered nominating officer of a party which has submitted a list of candidates shall be entitled to exercise the right of free postage conferred by this article if he gives such security as may be required by the universal service provider should the party not be shown as standing nominated as mentioned above.

(7) The regional returning officer shall be entitled to treat any purported exercise by the registered nominating officer of a registered political party of the right of free postage conferred by this article through the party election agent as a valid exercise of that right.

(8) If at a regional election the area of the regional returning officer is situated in the area of more than one official designated by a universal service provider, the controlling designated official shall be determined by that regional returning officer.

(9) A universal service provider who provides a postal service free of charge pursuant to this article shall be entitled to be remunerated for that service at the rate determined by or in accordance with a scheme made under section 89 of the Postal Services Act 2000 and the amount of such remuneration shall be paid by the Assembly.

(10) In respect of any Assembly election after the 2007 Assembly general election, the sums payable by the Welsh Ministers under paragraph (9) shall be charged on the Welsh Consolidated Fund.

(11) For the purposes of this article "elector"
    (a) means a person who is registered in the register of electors for the Assembly constituency or electoral region on the last day for publication of notice of the election; and
    (b) includes a person then shown in that register (or, in the case of a person who has an anonymous entry in the register, in the record of anonymous entries) as below voting age if (but only if) it appears from the register (or from the record) that he will be of voting age on the day fixed for the poll.

Broadcasting from outside United Kingdom

66(1) No person shall, with intent to influence persons to give or refrain from giving their votes at an Assembly election, include, or aid, abet, counsel or procure the inclusion of, any matter relating to the election in any programme service (within the meaning of the Broadcasting Act 1990) provided from a place outside the United Kingdom otherwise than in pursuance of arrangements made with
    (a) the British Broadcasting Corporation;
    (b) Sianel Pedwar Cymru; or
    (c) the holder of any licence granted by the Office of Communications,
for the reception and retransmission of that matter by that body or the holder of that licence.

(2) An offence under this article shall be an illegal practice, but the court before whom a person is convicted of an offence under this article may, if they think it just in the special circumstances of the case, mitigate or entirely remit any incapacity imposed by virtue of article 123.

(3) Where any act or omission of an association or body of persons, corporate or unincorporate, is an illegal practice under this article, any person who at the time of the act or omission was a director, general manager, secretary or other similar officer of the association or body, or was purporting to act in any such capacity, shall be deemed to be guilty of the illegal practice, unless he proves
    (a) that the act or omission took place without his consent or connivance; and

(b) that he exercised all such diligence to prevent the commission of the illegal practice as he ought to have exercised having regard to the nature of his functions in that capacity and to all the circumstances.

Broadcasting of local items during election period.

67(1) Each broadcasting authority shall adopt a code of practice with respect to the participation of candidates at an Assembly election in items about the constituency or electoral region in question which are included in relevant services during the election period.

(2) The code for the time being adopted by a broadcasting authority under this article shall be either
  (a) a code drawn up by that authority, whether on their own or jointly with one or more other broadcasting authorities; or
  (b) a code drawn up by one or more other such authorities,
and a broadcasting authority shall from time to time consider whether the code for the time being so adopted by them should be replaced by a further code falling within sub-paragraph (a) or (b).

(3) Before drawing up a code under this article a broadcasting authority shall have regard to any views expressed by the Commission and any such code may make different provision for different cases.

(4) The Office of Communications shall do all that they can to secure that the code for the time being adopted by them under this article is observed in the provision of relevant services; and the British Broadcasting Corporation and Sianel Pedwar Cymru shall each observe in the provision of relevant services the code so adopted by them.

(5) For the purpose of paragraph (1) "the election period", means the period beginning with
  (a) in relation to the 2007 Assembly general election, the last date for publication of notice of the election;
  (b) in relation to any other Assembly general election, the date of dissolution of the Assembly; and
  (c) in relation to any election to fill a casual vacancy, the date of the occurrence of the vacancy, and
in each case ending with the close of the poll.

(6) In this article
  "broadcasting authority" means the British Broadcasting Corporation, the Office of Communications or Sianel Pedwar Cymru;
  "candidate", means a candidate (including a party list candidate) standing nominated; and
  "relevant services"
  (a) in relation to the British Broadcasting Corporation or Sianel Pedwar Cymru, means services broadcast by that body; and
  (b) in relation to the Office of Communications, means services licensed under Part 1 or 3 of the Broadcasting Act 1990 or Part 1 or 2 of the Broadcasting Act 1996.

Imitation poll cards

68 No person shall for the purpose of promoting or procuring a particular result at an Assembly election issue any poll card or document so closely resembling an official poll card as to be calculated to deceive, and article 66(2) and (3) shall apply as if an offence under this article were an offence under that article.

Schools and rooms for Assembly election meetings

69(1) Subject to the provisions of this article, a candidate at an Assembly election is entitled for the purpose of holding public meetings to promote or procure the giving of votes at that election

    (a) for himself, in the case of a constituency or an individual candidate; or

    (b) for the registered political party on whose list he is included, in the case of a party list candidate,

to the use free of charge at reasonable times between the last day on which notice of the election may be published in accordance with the Table in rule 1(1) of Schedule 5 and the day preceding the date of the poll of

    (i) a suitable room in the premises of a school to which this article applies; or

    (ii) any meeting room to which this article applies.

(2) This article applies to a community, foundation or voluntary school of which

    (a) in the case of a constituency election, the premises are situated in the Assembly constituency for which the election is held or an adjoining Assembly constituency; and

    (b) in the case of a regional election, the premises are situated in the Assembly electoral region for which the election is held,

but, in relation to sub-paragraph (a), a constituency candidate is not entitled under this article to the use of a room in school premises outside the Assembly constituency if there is a suitable room in premises in the constituency which are reasonably accessible from the same parts of the constituency as those outside and are premises of a school to which this article applies.

(3) This article applies to a meeting room situated

    (a) in the case of a constituency election, in the Assembly constituency for which the election is held; or

    (b) in the case of a regional election, in the Assembly electoral region for which the election is held,

the expense of maintaining which is payable wholly or mainly out of public funds or by a body whose expenses are so payable.

(4) Where a room is used for a meeting in pursuance of the rights conferred by this article, the person by whom or on whose behalf the meeting is convened

    (a) shall defray any expenses incurred in preparing, warming, lighting and cleaning the room and providing attendance for the meeting and restoring the room to its usual condition after the meeting; and

    (b) shall defray any damage done to the room or the premises in which it is situated, or the furniture, fittings or apparatus in the room or premises.

(5) A candidate is not entitled to exercise the rights conferred by this article except on reasonable notice; and this article does not authorise any interference with the hours during which a room in school premises is used for education purposes, or any interference with the use of a meeting room either for the purposes of the person maintaining it or under a prior agreement for its letting for any purpose.

(6) Schedule 8 (which makes provision with respect to the rights conferred by this article and the arrangements to be made for their exercise) has effect.

(7) For the purposes of this article (except those of paragraph (4)(b)), the premises of a school shall not be taken to include any private dwelling, and in this article

    (a) the expression "meeting room" means any room which it is the practice to let for public meetings; and

    (b) the expression "room" includes a hall, gallery or gymnasium.

Disturbances at Assembly election meetings

70(1) A person who at a lawful public meeting to which this article applies acts, or incites others to act, in a disorderly manner for the purpose of preventing the transaction of the business for which the meeting was called together shall be guilty of an illegal practice.

(2) This article applies to a political meeting held

(a) in relation to a constituency election, in the Assembly constituency for which the election is held; and

(b) in relation to a regional election, in the Assembly electoral region for which the election is held,

during the period beginning with the last day on which notice of election may be published in accordance with the Table set out in rule 1(1) of Schedule 5 and ending with the day of election.

(3) If a constable reasonably suspects any person of committing an offence under paragraph (1), he may if requested so to do by the chairman of the meeting require that person to declare to him immediately his name and address and, if that person refuses or fails so to declare his name and address, or gives a false name and address, he shall be liable on summary conviction to a fine not exceeding level 1 on the standard scale.

Officials not to act for candidates

71(1) If

(a) any constituency or regional returning officer at a constituency election;

(b) any constituency or regional returning officer at a regional election;

(c) any person appointed under article 20(1);

(d) any officer or clerk appointed under Schedule 5; or

(e) any partner or clerk of any such person,

acts as an agent for any candidate or registered political party which has submitted a list of candidates in the conduct or management of the election, he shall be guilty of an offence, but nothing in this article prevents a constituency or an individual candidate from acting as his own election agent or a party list candidate from acting as election agent for the registered political party on whose list he is a candidate.

(2) A person guilty of an offence under this article shall be liable on summary conviction to a fine not exceeding level 4 on the standard scale.

Illegal canvassing by police officers

72(1) No member of a police force shall by word, message, writing or in any other manner, endeavour to persuade any person to give, or dissuade any person from giving, his vote, whether as an elector or as proxy

(a) at any constituency election for an Assembly constituency; or

(b) at any regional election for an Assembly electoral region,

wholly or partly within the police area.

(2) A person acting in contravention of paragraph (1) shall be liable on summary conviction to a fine not exceeding level 3 on the standard scale; but nothing in that paragraph shall subject a member of a police force to any penalty for anything done in the discharge of his duty as a member of the force.

False statements as to candidates

73(1) A person who, or any director of any body or association corporate which

(a) before or during an Assembly election; and

(b) for the purpose of affecting how a vote is given at the election, makes or publishes any false statement of fact in relation to the personal character or conduct of any candidate shall be guilty of an illegal practice, unless he can show that he had reasonable grounds for believing, and did believe, the statement to be true.

(2) Except in a case to which paragraph (3) applies, a candidate shall not be liable, nor shall his election be avoided, for any illegal practice under paragraph (1) committed
    (a) in the case of a constituency or an individual candidate, by his agent other than his election agent;
    (b) in the case of a party list candidate, by the agent of the registered political party on whose list he is a candidate other than its election agent in relation to that list.

(3) This paragraph applies where
    (i) it can be shown that the candidate (including, in the case of a party list candidate another candidate on the list) or the election agent has authorised or consented to the committing of the illegal practice by the other agent or has paid for the circulation of the false statement constituting the illegal practice; or
    (ii) an election court find and report that the election of the candidate was procured or materially assisted in consequence of the making or publishing of such false statements.

(4) A person making or publishing any false statement of fact as mentioned above may be restrained by interim or perpetual injunction by the High Court or county court from any repetition of that false statement or of a false statement of a similar character in relation to the candidate or candidates and, for the purpose of granting an interim injunction, prima facie proof of the falsity of the statement shall be sufficient.

(5) Any person who, before or during an Assembly election, knowingly publishes a false statement of the withdrawal of any candidate at the election for the purpose of promoting or procuring a particular result at the election shall be guilty of an illegal practice.

(6) A candidate shall not be liable, nor shall his election be avoided, for any illegal practice under paragraph (5) committed
    (a) in the case of a constituency or an individual candidate, by his agent other than his election agent; or
    (b) in the case of a party list candidate, by the agent of the registered political party on whose list he is a candidate other than that party's election agent in relation to that list.

Corrupt withdrawal from candidature

74 Any person who corruptly induces or procures any other person to withdraw from being a candidate at an Assembly election, in consideration of any payment or promise of payment, and any person withdrawing in pursuance of the inducement or procurement, shall be guilty of an illegal payment.

Payments for exhibition of election notices

75(1) No payment or contract for payment for the purpose of promoting or procuring a particular result at an Assembly election shall be made to an elector or his proxy on account of the exhibition of, or the use of any house, land, building or premises for the exhibition of, any address, bill or notice, unless
    (a) it is the ordinary business of the elector or proxy as an advertising agent to exhibit for payment bills and advertisements; and
    (b) the payment or contract is made in the ordinary course of that business.

(2) If any payment or contract for payment is knowingly made in contravention of this article either before, during or after such an election
- (a) the person making the payment or contract; and
- (b) if he knew it to be in contravention of this Order, any person receiving the payment or being a party to the contract,

shall be guilty of an illegal practice.

Printer's name and address on election publications

76(1) This article applies to any material which can reasonably be regarded as intended to promote or procure a particular result at an Assembly election (whether or not it can be so regarded as intended to achieve any other purpose as well).

(2) No material to which this article applies shall be published unless
- (a) in the case of material which is, or is contained in, such a document as is mentioned in paragraph (4), (5) or (6), the requirements of the relevant paragraph are complied with; or
- (b) in the case of any other material, any requirements falling to be complied with in relation to the material by virtue of regulations under paragraph (7) are complied with.

(3) For the purposes of paragraphs (4) to (6), the following details are "the relevant details" in the case of any material falling within paragraph (2)(a), namely
- (a) the name and address of the printer of the document;
- (b) the name and address of the promoter of the material; and
- (c) the name and address of any person on behalf of whom the material is being published (and who is not the promoter).

(4) Where the material is a document consisting (or consisting principally) of a single side of printed matter, the relevant details must appear on the face of the document.

(5) Where the material is a printed document other than one to which paragraph (4) applies, the relevant details must appear either on the first or the last page of the document.

(6) Where the material is an advertisement contained in a newspaper or periodical
- (a) the name and address of the printer of the newspaper or periodical must appear either on its first or last page; and
- (b) the relevant details specified in paragraph(3)(b) and (c) must be included in the advertisement.

(7) The Secretary of State may, after consulting the Commission, by regulations make provision for and in connection with the imposition of requirements as to the inclusion in material falling within paragraph (2)(b) of the following details, namely
- (a) the name and address of the promoter of the material; and
- (b) the name and address of any person on behalf of whom the material is being published (and who is not the promoter).

(8) Regulations under paragraph (7) may in particular specify
- (a) the manner and form in which such details must be included in any such material for the purpose of complying with any such requirement;
- (b) circumstances in which
  - (i) any such requirement does not have to be complied with by any person of any description specified in the regulations; or
  - (ii) a breach of any such requirement by a person of any description so specified is not to result in the commission of an offence under this article by that person or by a person of any other description;
- (c) circumstances in which material is, or is not, to be taken for the purposes of the

        regulations to be published or, as the case may be, published by a person of any description so specified.

(9)   Where any material within paragraph (2)(a) is published in contravention of paragraph (2), then, subject to paragraphs (11) and (12)

      (a) the promoter of the material;

      (b) any other person by whom the material is so published; and

      (c) the printer of the document,

shall be guilty of an offence and liable on summary conviction to a fine not exceeding level 5 on the standard scale.

(10) Where any material falling within paragraph (2)(b) is published in contravention of paragraph (2), then, subject to regulations made by virtue of paragraph (8)(b) and to paragraphs (11) and (12)

      (a) the promoter of the material; and

      (b) any other person by whom the material is so published,

shall be guilty of an offence and liable on summary conviction to a fine not exceeding level 5 on the standard scale.

(11) It shall be a defence for a person charged with an offence under this article to prove that

      (a) the contravention of paragraph (2) arose from circumstances beyond his reasonable control; and

      (b) he took all reasonable steps, and exercised due diligence, to ensure that the contravention would not arise.

(12) Where

      (a) a constituency or individual candidate or his election agent; or

      (b) a party list candidate or the election agent of the registered political party in relation to that party's list,

would (apart from this paragraph) be guilty of an offence under paragraph (9) or (10), he shall instead be guilty of an illegal practice.

(13) The power to make regulations under paragraph (7) shall be

      (a) exercisable by statutory instrument; and

      (b) subject to annulment in pursuance of a resolution of either House of Parliament,

and for the purpose of section 1 of the Statutory Instruments Act 1946 this provision shall have effect as if contained in an Act of Parliament.

(14) For the purpose of determining whether any material is such material as is mentioned in paragraph (1), it is immaterial that it does not expressly mention the name of any candidate.

(15) In this article

      "print" means print by whatever means, and "printer" shall be construed accordingly;

      "the promoter" in relation to any material to which this article applies, means the person causing the material to be published; and

      "publish" means to make available to the public at large, or any section of the public, in whatever form or by whatever means.

Prohibition of paid canvassers

77   If a person is, either before, during or after an Assembly election, engaged or employed for payment or promise of payment as a canvasser for the purpose of promoting or procuring a particular result at the Assembly election

      (a) the person so engaging or employing him; and

(b)   the person so engaged or employed,

shall be guilty of illegal employment.

Providing money for illegal purposes

78   Where a person knowingly provides money

(a)   for any payment which is contrary to the provisions of this Order;

(b)   for any expenses incurred in excess of the maximum amount allowed by this Order; or

(c)   for replacing any money expended in any such payment or expenses,

except where the payment or the incurring of the expenses may have been previously allowed in pursuance of article 119 to be an exception, that person shall be guilty of an illegal payment.

Bribery

79(1)   A person shall be guilty of a corrupt practice if he is guilty of bribery.

(2)   A person shall be guilty of bribery if he, directly or indirectly, by himself or by any other person on his behalf

(a)   gives any money or procures any office

(i)   to or for any voter;

(ii)   to or for any other person on behalf of any voter; or

(iii)   to or for any other person,

in order to induce any voter to vote or refrain from voting;

(b)   corruptly does any such act as mentioned above on account of any voter having voted or refrained from voting; or

(c)   makes any such gift or procurement as mentioned above to or for any person in order to induce that person to procure, or endeavour to procure, a particular result at an Assembly election or the vote of any voter,

or if upon or in consequence of any such gift or procurement as mentioned above he procures or engages, promises or endeavours to procure a particular result at an Assembly election or the vote of any voter.

(3)   For the purposes of paragraph (2)

(a)   references to giving money include references to giving, lending, agreeing to give or lend, offering, promising, or promising to procure or endeavour to procure any money or valuable consideration; and

(b)   references to procuring any office include references to giving, procuring, agreeing to give or procure, offering, promising, or promising to procure or to endeavour to procure any office, place or employment.

(4)   A person shall be guilty of bribery if he advances or pays or causes to be paid any money to or for the use of any other person with the intent that that money or any part of it shall be expended in bribery at an Assembly election or knowingly pays or causes to be paid any money to any person in discharge or repayment of any money wholly or in part expended in bribery at any such election.

(5)   The foregoing provisions of this article shall not extend or be construed to extend to any money paid or agreed to be paid for or on account of any legal expenses incurred in good faith at or concerning an Assembly election.

(6)   A voter shall be guilty of bribery if before or during an Assembly election he, directly or indirectly, by himself or by any other person on his behalf receives, agrees, or contracts for any money, gift, loan or valuable consideration, office, place or employment for himself or for any other person for voting or agreeing to vote or for refraining or agreeing to refrain from voting.

(7)   A person shall be guilty of bribery if after an Assembly election he, directly or indirectly, by himself or by any other person on his behalf receives any money or valuable consideration on account of any person having voted or refrained from voting or having induced any other person to vote or refrain from voting.

(8)   In this article the expression "voter" includes any person who has or claims to have a right to vote.

Treating

80(1)   A person shall be guilty of a corrupt practice if he is guilty of treating.

(2)   A person shall be guilty of treating if he corruptly, by himself or by any other person, either before, during or after an Assembly election, directly or indirectly gives or provides, or pays wholly or in part the expense of giving or providing, any meat, drink, entertainment or provision to or for any person

(a)   for the purpose of corruptly influencing that person or any other person to vote or refrain from voting; or

(b)   on account of that person or any other person having voted or refrained from voting, or being about to vote or refrain from voting.

(3)   Every elector or his proxy who corruptly accepts or takes any such meat, drink, entertainment or provision shall also be guilty of treating.

Undue influence

81(1)   A person shall be guilty of a corrupt practice if he is guilty of undue influence.

(2)   A person shall be guilty of undue influence

(a)   if he, directly or indirectly, by himself or by any other person on his behalf, makes use of or threatens to make use of any force, violence or restraint, or inflicts or threatens to inflict, by himself or by any other person, any temporal or spiritual injury, damage, harm or loss upon or against any person in order to induce or compel that person to vote or refrain from voting, or on account of that person having voted or refrained from voting; or

(b)   if, by abduction, duress or any fraudulent device or contrivance, he impedes or prevents, or intends to impede or prevent, the free exercise of the franchise of an elector or proxy for an elector, or so compels, induces or prevails upon, or intends so to compel, induce or prevail upon, an elector or proxy for an elector either to vote or to refrain from voting.

Rights of creditors

82   The provisions of this Part prohibiting

(a)   payments and contracts for payments;

(b)   the payment or incurring of election expenses in excess of the maximum amount allowed by this Order; or

(c)   the incurring of expenses not authorised by an election agent,

do not affect the right of any creditor who, when the contract was made or the expense was incurred, was ignorant of that contract or expense being in contravention of this Order.

Savings as to Assembly elections

83(1)   Where a person has been declared by others to be a candidate at an Assembly election without his consent, nothing in this Part shall be construed to impose any liability on that person, unless he has afterwards given his assent to the declaration or has been nominated.

(2)   Nothing in this Part makes it illegal for an employer to permit electors at Assembly

elections or their proxies to absent themselves from his employment for a reasonable time for the purpose of voting at the poll at an Assembly election without having any deduction from their salaries or wage on account of their absence, if the permission

(a) is (so far as practicable without injury to the employer's business) given equally to all persons alike who are at the time in his employment;

(b) is not given with a view to inducing any person to give his vote in a particular way at the election; and

(c) is not refused to any person for the purpose of preventing him from giving his vote in a particular way at the election,

but this paragraph shall not be construed as making illegal any act which would not be illegal apart from this paragraph.

Interpretation of Part 3

84(1) In this Part, except where the context otherwise requires

"candidate" shall be construed in accordance with paragraph (2);

"date of the allowance of an authorised excuse" has the meaning given by article 58(9);

"disputed claim" has the meaning given by article 50(1) as extended by article 51;

"money" and "pecuniary reward" shall (except in articles 41, 79 and 80 and Schedule 6) be deemed to include

(a) any office, place or employment;

(b) any valuable security or other equivalent of money; and

(c) any valuable consideration;

and expressions referring to money shall be construed accordingly;

"payment" includes any pecuniary or other reward;

"personal expenses" as used with respect to the expenditure of any candidate in relation to any Assembly election includes the reasonable travelling expenses of the candidate, and the reasonable expenses of his living at hotels or elsewhere for the purposes of and in relation to the election; and

"return as to election expenses" means a return (including the bills and receipts to be delivered with it) to be made under article 52(1).

(2) A person becomes a "candidate" in relation to

(a) the 2007 Assembly general election

(i) on the last day for publication of notice of the election if on or before that day he is declared by himself or by others to be a candidate at the election; and

(ii) otherwise, on the day on which he is so declared by himself or by others or on which he is nominated as a candidate at the election (whichever is the earlier); and

(b) in relation to any subsequent Assembly election

(i) on the date

(aa) of the dissolution of the Assembly; or

(bb) in the case of an election to fill a casual vacancy, of the occurrence of the vacancy if on or before that date he is declared by himself or others to be a candidate at the election; and

(ii) otherwise, on the day on which he is so declared by himself or others or on which he is nominated as a candidate at the election (whichever is the earlier).

Computation of time for purposes of Part 3

85(1) Where the day or last day on which anything is required or permitted to be done by or in pursuance of this Part is any of the days mentioned in paragraph (2)

(a) the requirement or permission shall be deemed to relate to the first day thereafter which is not one of those days; and

(b) in computing any period of not more than seven days for the purposes of this Part any of the days so mentioned shall be disregarded.

(2) The days referred to in paragraph (1) are

    (a) a Saturday or a Sunday;

    (b) Christmas Eve, Christmas Day, or Good Friday;

    (c) a day which is a bank holiday in Wales under the Banking and Financial Dealings Act 1971; or

    (d) a day appointed for public thanksgiving or mourning.

Part 4
Legal Proceedings

Method of questioning Assembly election

86(1) No Assembly election and no return to the Assembly shall be questioned except by a petition complaining of an undue election or undue return ("an Assembly election petition") presented in accordance with this Part; and "Assembly election petition" includes a petition complaining of an undue return in respect of a vacancy in an electoral region.

(2) A petition complaining of no return shall be deemed to be an Assembly election petition and the High Court

    (a) may make such order on the petition as they think expedient for compelling a return to be made; or

    (b) may allow the petition to be heard by an election court as provided with respect to ordinary Assembly election petitions.

(3) In this Part, the expression "return" as the context requires refers to a return following an Assembly election and "vacancy return" refers to a return in respect of a vacancy in an electoral region.

Presentation and service of Assembly election petition

87(1) An Assembly election petition may be presented by one or more of the following persons

    (a) a person who voted as an elector at the election or who had a right so to vote;

    (b) a person claiming to have had a right to be elected or returned at the election;

    (c) a person alleging himself to have been a candidate at the election; or

    (d) a person claiming to have had a right to be returned in an electoral region vacancy.

(2) The reference in paragraph (1)(a) to a person who voted as an elector at the election or who had the right so to vote does not include a person who had an anonymous entry in the register of electors.

(3) Any Assembly member whose election or return is complained of is hereinafter referred to as a respondent but if the petition complains of the conduct of a constituency or a regional returning officer, the returning officer shall for the purposes of this Part be deemed to be a respondent.

(4) Paragraph (3) also applies if the petition complains of the conduct of a constituency returning officer in the exercise of his functions in relation to a regional election.

(5) The petition shall be in the prescribed form, state the prescribed matters and be signed by the petitioner, or all the petitioners if more than one, and shall be presented

to the High Court.

(6) The petition shall be presented by delivering it to the prescribed officer or otherwise dealing with it in the prescribed manner; and the prescribed officer shall send a copy of it to the returning officer of the Assembly constituency or electoral region to which the petition relates, who shall forthwith publish it in that Assembly constituency or electoral region.

(7) The petition shall be served in such manner as may be prescribed.

Time for presentation or amendment of Assembly election petition

88(1) Subject to the provisions of this article, an Assembly election petition shall be presented within 21 days after the day on which the name of any member to whose election or return the petition relates has been returned to the Clerk or, as the case may be, notified to the Presiding Officer of the Assembly in accordance with Schedule 5 (the Assembly election rules).

(2) If the petition questions the election or return upon an allegation of corrupt practices and specifically alleges a payment of money or other reward to have been made by such member or on his account or with his privity since the time of that return in pursuance or in furtherance of the alleged corrupt practice, it may be presented within 28 days after the date of the payment.

(3) A petition questioning the election or return upon an allegation of an illegal practice may, so far as respects that illegal practice, be presented

 (a) within 21 days after the day specified in paragraph (4), or

 (b) if specifically alleging a payment of money or some other act to have been made or done since the day so specified by such member to whose election or return the petition relates or an agent of his, or with the privity of that member or the election agent, in pursuance or in furtherance of the alleged illegal practice, within 28 days after the date of the payment or other act.

(4) The day referred to in paragraph (3) is the tenth day after the end of the time allowed for delivering returns as to election expenses at the election or, if later

 (a) where that member was a constituency or an individual candidate, that day on which the appropriate returning officer receives the return and declarations as to election expenses by that member and his election agent;

 (b) where that member was a party list candidate, that day on which

  (i) the Commission receives the return and declaration as to election expenses by the treasurer of the registered political party, and

  (ii) the regional returning officer receives the declaration as to election expenses by that member;

 (c) where the return and declarations are received on different days, the last of those days; or

 (d) where there is an authorised excuse for failing to make the return and declarations, the date of the allowance of the excuse, or if there was a failure as regards two or more of them, and the excuse was allowed at different times, the date of the allowance of the last excuse.

(5) An Assembly election petition presented within the time limited by paragraph (1) or (2) may, for the purpose of questioning the election or return upon an allegation of an illegal practice, be amended with the leave of the High Court within the time within which a petition questioning the election upon the allegation of that illegal practice could be presented under paragraph (3).

(6) Paragraphs (3), (4) and (5) apply

 (a) notwithstanding that the act constituting the alleged illegal practice amounted to a corrupt practice; and

(b) to a corrupt practice under article 46, as if it were an illegal practice.

(7) For the purposes of this article, an allegation that an election is avoided under article 116 shall be deemed to be an allegation of corrupt practices, notwithstanding that the offences alleged are or include offences other than corrupt practices.

Constitution of election court and place of trial

89(1) An Assembly election petition shall be tried by two judges on the rota for the trial of parliamentary election petitions, and the judges for the time being on that rota shall, unless they otherwise agree, try the election petitions standing for trial according to their seniority, and the judges presiding at the trial of an Assembly election petition are hereinafter referred to as the election court.

(2) The election court has, subject to the provisions of this Order, the same powers, jurisdiction and authority as a judge of the High Court and shall be a court of record.

(3) The place of trial shall be within the Assembly constituency or electoral region for which the election was held (or, where article 87(1)(d) applies, within the Assembly electoral region for which a person claims to have had a right to be returned to fill an electoral region vacancy), but the High Court, may on being satisfied that special circumstances exist rendering it desirable that the petition should be tried elsewhere, appoint some other convenient place for the trial.

(4) The election court may adjourn the trial from one place to another within the Assembly constituency or electoral region.

Judges' expenses and reception

90 In relation to the trial of an Assembly election petition, the travelling and other expenses of the judges and all expenses properly incurred in providing them with necessary accommodation and with a proper court shall be defrayed by the Secretary of State out of money provided by Parliament.

Attendance of shorthand writer

91(1) The Assembly shall require a shorthand writer to attend the trial of an Assembly election petition and that person shall be sworn by one of the judges of the election court faithfully and truly to take down the evidence given at the trial and from time to time as occasion requires to transcribe that evidence or cause it to be transcribed.

(2) The shorthand writer shall take down the evidence and from time to time transcribe it or cause it to be transcribed and a copy of the evidence shall accompany the certificate given by the election court to the Presiding Officer of the Assembly.

Security for costs

92(1) At the time of presenting an Assembly election petition or within three days afterwards the petitioner shall give security for all costs which may become payable by him to any witness summoned on his behalf or to any respondent.

(2) The security shall be such amount not exceeding £5,000 as the High Court, or a judge of the High Court, directs on an application made by the petitioner, and shall be given in the prescribed manner by recognisance entered into by any number of sureties not exceeding four or by a deposit of money, or partly in one way and partly in the other.

(3) Within the prescribed time after giving the security the petitioner shall serve on the respondent in the prescribed manner

(a) a notice of the presentation of the petition and of the amount and nature of the security; and

(b) a copy of the petition.

(4) Within a further prescribed time, the respondent may object in writing to any recognisance on the ground that any surety is insufficient or is dead or cannot be found or ascertained for want of a sufficient description in the recognisance, or that a person named in the recognisance has not duly acknowledged the recognisance.

(5) An objection to a recognisance shall be decided in the prescribed manner.

(6) If the objection is allowed, the petitioner may within a further prescribed time remove it by deposit in the prescribed manner of such sum of money as will, in the opinion of the court or officer having cognisance of the matter, make the security sufficient.

(7) If no security is given as required by this article or any objection is allowed and not removed as mentioned above, no further proceedings shall be had on the petition.

Petition at issue

93(1) The Assembly election petition shall be at issue as from the relevant time, as defined by paragraph (2).

(2) In this article "the relevant time" means
    (a) where the petitioner gives the security for costs required by article 92 by a deposit of money equal to the amount of the security required, the time when the security is given; and
    (b) in any other case, the time when
        (i) the time prescribed for the making of objections under article 92(4) expires; or
        (ii) if such an objection is made, that objection is disallowed or removed, whichever happens later.

List of petitions

94(1) The prescribed officer shall
    (a) as soon as may be, make out a list of all Assembly election petitions at issue presented to the court of which he is officer, placing them in the order in which they were presented; and
    (b) keep at his office a copy of the list, open to inspection in the prescribed manner.

(2) The petitions shall, so far as convenient, be tried in the order in which they stand in the list.

(3) Where more petitions than one are presented relating to the same Assembly election (or the return in respect of the same electoral region), all those petitions shall be bracketed together in the election list and shall be dealt with as one petition, standing, unless the High Court otherwise direct, in the election list in the place where the last of them would have stood if it had been the only petition presented.

Trial of petition

95(1) An Assembly election petition shall be tried in open court, without a jury, and notice of the time and place of trial shall be given in the prescribed manner not less than fourteen days before the day of trial.

(2) The election court may in its discretion adjourn the trial from time to time, but the trial shall, so far as is practicable consistent with the interests of justice in respect of the trial, be continued from day to day on every lawful day until its conclusion.

(3) The trial of an Assembly election petition shall be proceeded with notwithstanding a respondent resigning his seat or becoming disqualified from being an Assembly

member so that the seat is vacant.

(4) On the trial of an Assembly election petition, unless the court otherwise directs, any charge of a corrupt practice may be gone into, and evidence in relation to it received, before any proof has been given of agency on behalf of any candidate in respect of the corrupt practice.

(5) On the trial of an Assembly election petition complaining of an undue election or return and claiming a seat for some person, a respondent may give evidence to prove that that person was not duly elected or was incapable of being duly returned in the same manner as if he had presented a petition against the election or return of that person.

(6) This paragraph applies if, in relation to an Assembly election petition, it appears that
    (a) there is an equality of votes between any candidates at a constituency election; or
    (b) two or more individual candidates or registered political parties at a regional election have the same electoral region figure,
and that the addition of a vote would entitle any of those individual candidates or any party list candidate of those parties to be declared elected, as provided for in the Assembly Election Rules (Schedule 5).

(7) Where paragraph (6) applies
    (a) any decision under the provisions in
        (i) rule 60 of Schedule 5, in the case of a constituency election; or
        (ii) rule 63 of Schedule 5, in the case of a regional election,
as to equality of votes shall, in so far as it determines the question as to who is elected, be effective also for the purposes of the petition; and
    (b) in so far as that question is not determined by such a decision, the court shall decide between them by lot and proceed as if the one on whom the lot then falls had received an additional vote.

Witnesses

96(1) At the trial of an Assembly election petition witnesses shall be summoned and sworn in the same manner as nearly as circumstances admit as in an action tried in the High Court.

(2) On the trial a member of the election court may, by order signed by him, require any person who appears to him to have been concerned in the Assembly election or return to a vacancy in an electoral region to attend as a witness, and any person refusing to obey the order shall be guilty of contempt of court.

(3) The election court may examine any person so required to attend or who is in court although he is not called and examined by any party to the Assembly election petition.

(4) A witness may, after his examination by the court, be crossexamined by or on behalf of the petitioner and a respondent, or either of them.

(5) The Director of Public Prosecutions shall without any direction from the court cause any person appearing to him to be able to give material evidence as to the subject of the trial to attend the trial and shall, with the leave of the court, examine him as a witness.

Duty to answer relevant questions

97(1) A person called as a witness respecting an Assembly election or return to a vacancy in an electoral region before any election court shall not be excused from answering any question relating to any offence at or connected with the election or return
    (a) on the ground that the answer to it may incriminate or tend to incriminate that

    person or that person's spouse or civil partner; or

    (b)   on the ground of privilege.

(2)   An answer by a person to a question put by or before any election court shall not, except in the case of any criminal proceeding for perjury in respect of the evidence, be in any proceeding, civil or criminal, admissible in evidence against that person or that person's spouse or civil partner.

Expenses of witnesses

98(1)   The reasonable expenses incurred by any person in appearing to give evidence at the trial of an Assembly election petition, according to the scale allowed to witnesses on the trial of civil actions, may be allowed to him by a certificate of the election court or of the prescribed officer.

(2)   If the witness was called and examined by virtue of article 96(2), the expenses referred to in paragraph (1) shall be deemed part of the expenses of providing a court, but otherwise they shall be deemed costs of the petition.

Conclusion of trial of Assembly election petition

99(1)   Subject to paragraph (2), at the conclusion of the trial of an Assembly election petition, the election court shall determine whether the Assembly member whose election or return is complained of, or any and what other person, was duly elected or returned, or if applicable, the election was void, and the determination so certified shall be final to all intents as to the matters at issue on the petition.

(2)   Where the election court determine that at a regional election an Assembly member for an Assembly electoral region was not duly elected or returned, the court in addition shall determine that the regional election was void.

(3)   The election court shall forthwith certify in writing the determination to the Presiding Officer of the Assembly.

(4)   If the judges constituting the election court
    (a)   subject to paragraph (2), differ as to whether any Assembly member whose election or return is complained of was duly elected or returned, they shall certify that difference and
        (i)   the member shall be deemed to be duly elected or returned; or
        (ii)   some other person or persons shall be declared to be elected or returned; or
        (iii)   the election of all members for that electoral region was void.
    (b)   where the petition relates to a constituency election, determine that such member was not duly elected or returned but differ as to the rest of the determination, they shall certify that difference and the election shall be deemed to be void.

(5)   Where any charge is made in the petition of any corrupt or illegal practice having been committed at an Assembly election the court shall, in addition to giving a certificate, and at the same time, make a report to the Presiding Officer of the Assembly as required by articles 108 and 110 and also stating whether corrupt or illegal practices have, or whether there is reason to believe that corrupt or illegal practices have, extensively prevailed at the election.

(6)   The election court may at the same time make a special report to the Presiding Officer of the Assembly as to matters arising in the course of the trial an account of which in the judgement of the court ought to be submitted to the Assembly.

(7)   Every report sent to the Presiding Officer of the Assembly under this article shall be signed by both judges of the election court and if the judges differ as to the subject of

the report, they shall certify that difference and make no report on the subject on which they so differ.

(8) The Presiding Officer of the Assembly shall publish any certificate or report of an election court received by him under this article.

Election court determination in respect of a constituency election etc

100(1) Where by virtue of article 99 the election court determine at a constituency election that

    (a) an Assembly member was not duly elected or returned; or

    (b) the election was void,

and the return of the member at that election was taken into account for the purposes of deciding which members were to be returned for the Assembly electoral region in which the Assembly constituency is situated

    (i) the determination by the election court; or

    (ii) the subsequent return of an Assembly member for that constituency,

shall not affect the validity of the return of those members for that electoral region.

(2) Where by virtue of article 99(4)(b) a constituency election is deemed to be void, the election court shall be treated as having determined that election to be void for the purposes of paragraph (1)(b).

Regional election determined to be void by election court

101(1) Where by virtue of article 99 the election court determine that a regional election was void, the Presiding Officer of the Assembly shall (subject to paragraph (3)) forthwith after receipt of the certificate from the election court under article 99(3)

    (a) fix a date in accordance with paragraph (2) for a poll to be held at another election in the Assembly electoral region for which the regional election is determined to be void, and

    (b) send a notice in accordance with paragraph (4) to the returning officer for the Assembly electoral region in which the election was held.

(2) The date fixed shall not be later than three months after receipt of the certificate from the election court.

(3) But an election shall not be held if it appears to the Presiding Officer of the Assembly that the latest date which may be fixed for the poll would fall within the period of three months preceding an Assembly general election.

(4) A notice under paragraph (1)(b) shall

    (a) state that the election has been determined to be void;

    (b) require that the election is held again for the purpose of returning the members for that Assembly electoral region; and

    (c) state the date fixed for the poll at the election.

(5) The regional returning officer shall on receipt of a notice under paragraph (1)(b) inform each constituency returning officer for an Assembly constituency in the Assembly electoral region as to the contents of that notice.

(6) The results of the constituency elections in the Assembly electoral region for which the election is held at the last Assembly general election shall have effect for the purposes of ascertaining the results of the regional election.

Special case for determination of High Court

102(1) If, on the application of any party to an Assembly election petition made in the prescribed manner to the High Court, it appears to the High Court that the case raised by the petition can be conveniently stated as a special case, the High Court may direct it to be stated accordingly and the special case shall be heard before the High Court.

(2)   The High Court shall certify to the Presiding Officer of the Assembly its decision on the special case.

(3)   If it appears to the election court on the trial of an Assembly election petition that any question of law as to the admissibility of evidence or otherwise requires further consideration by the High Court, the election court may postpone the granting of a certificate until the question has been determined by the High Court, and for this purpose may reserve the question by stating a case for the decision of the High Court.

(4)   The Presiding Officer of the Assembly shall publish any certificate received by him under paragraph (2).

Withdrawal of petition

103(1)   A petitioner shall not withdraw an Assembly election petition without the leave of the election court or High Court on special application, made in the prescribed manner and at the prescribed time and place.

(2)   The application shall not be made until the prescribed notice of the intention to make it has been given in the Assembly constituency or electoral region to which the petition relates.

(3)   Where there is more than one petitioner, the application shall not be made except with the consent of all the petitioners.

(4)   If a petition is withdrawn the petitioner shall be liable to pay the costs of a respondent.

Costs of petition

104(1)   All costs of and incidental to the presentation of an Assembly election petition and the proceedings consequent on it, except such as are by this Order otherwise provided for, shall be defrayed by the parties to the petition in such manner and in such proportions as the election court or High Court may determine.

(2)   In particular

    (a)   any costs which in the opinion of the election court or High Court have been caused by vexatious conduct, unfounded allegations or unfounded objections on the part either of a petitioner or of a respondent; and

    (b)   any needless expense incurred or caused on the part of a petitioner or respondent,

    may be ordered to be defrayed by the parties by whom it has been incurred or caused whether or not they are on the whole successful.

Neglect or refusal to pay costs

105(1)   Paragraph (2) applies if, in relation to an Assembly election petition, a petitioner neglects or refuses, for six months after demand, to pay to any person summoned as a witness on his behalf, or to the respondent, any sum certified to be due to that person or the respondent for his costs, and the neglect or refusal is, within one year after the demand, proved to the satisfaction of the High Court.

(2)   Where paragraph (1) applies, every person who under this Order entered into a recognisance relating to that petition shall be held to be in default of the recognisance; and

    (a)   the prescribed officer shall thereupon certify the recognisance to be forfeited; and

    (b)   it shall be dealt with as if forfeited by the Crown Court.

Further provision as to costs

106(1) Where upon the trial of an Assembly election petition it appears to the election court

   (a) that a corrupt practice has not been proved to have been committed in relation to an Assembly election by or with the knowledge and consent of the respondent to the petition; and

   (b) that the respondent took all reasonable means to prevent corrupt practices being committed on his behalf,

   the court may, subject to the provisions of paragraph (2), make such order with respect to the whole or part of the costs of the petition as is mentioned in that paragraph.

   (2) If it appears to the court that any person or persons is or are proved, whether by providing money or otherwise, to have been extensively engaged in corrupt practices, or to have encouraged or promoted extensive corrupt practices in relation to the Assembly election, the court may, after giving that person or those persons an opportunity of being heard by counsel or solicitor and examining and cross examining witnesses to show cause why the order should not be made

   (a) order the whole or part of the costs to be paid by that person, or those persons or any of them; and

   (b) order that if the costs cannot be recovered from one or more of those persons they shall be paid by some other of those persons or by either of the parties to the petition.

   (3) Where any person appears to the court to have been guilty of a corrupt or illegal practice, the court may, after giving that person an opportunity of making a statement to show why the order should not be made, order the whole or any part of the costs of or incidental to any proceedings before the court in relation to that offence or to that person to be paid by that person to such person or persons as the court may direct.

Appeals and jurisdiction

107(1) No appeal lies without the special leave of the High Court from the decision of the High Court on any question of law, whether on appeal or otherwise, under the foregoing provisions of this Part, and if leave to appeal is granted the decision of the Court of Appeal in the case shall be final and conclusive.

   (2) Subject to the provisions of this Order, the principles, practice and rules on which committees of the House of Commons used to act in dealing with parliamentary election petitions shall be observed, so far as may be, by the High Court and election court in the case of Assembly election petitions.

   (3) The High Court has, subject to the provisions of this Order, the same powers, jurisdiction and authority with respect to an Assembly election petition and the proceedings on it as if the petition were an ordinary action within its jurisdiction.

   (4) The duties to be performed in relation to Assembly elections by the prescribed officer under this Part shall be performed by such one or more of the masters of the Supreme Court (Queen's Bench Division) as the Lord Chief Justice may determine.

Report as to candidate guilty of a corrupt or illegal practice

108(1) Other than where the petition relates to a vacancy return, the report of an election court under article 99 shall state whether any corrupt or illegal practice has or has not been proved to have been committed by or with the knowledge and consent of any candidate at the Assembly election, and the nature of the corrupt or illegal practice.

   (2) For the purposes of articles 109 and 110

   (a) if it is reported that a corrupt practice other than treating or undue influence was committed with the knowledge and consent of a candidate, he shall be treated as having been reported personally guilty of that corrupt practice; and

    (b) if it is reported that an illegal practice was committed with the knowledge and consent of a candidate, he shall be treated as having been reported personally guilty of that illegal practice.

(3) The report shall also state whether any of the candidates has at that Assembly election been guilty by his agents of any corrupt or illegal practice in relation to the election; but if a candidate is reported guilty by his agents of treating, undue influence or any illegal practice, and the court further reports that the candidate has proved to the court

    (a) that no corrupt or illegal practice was committed at the election by the candidate or his election agent and the offences mentioned in the report were committed contrary to the orders and without the sanction or connivance of the candidate or his election agent;

    (b) that the candidate and his election agent took all reasonable means for preventing the commission of corrupt and illegal practices at the election;

    (c) that the offences mentioned in the report were of a trivial, unimportant and limited character; and

    (d) that in all other respects the election was free from any corrupt or illegal practice on the part of the candidate and of his agents,

then the candidate shall not be treated for the purposes of article 109 as having been reported guilty by his agents of the offences mentioned in the report.

(4) References in this article to a candidate and his agent, or as the case may be, his election agent shall as appropriate apply to a party list candidate and the agent or, as the case may be, the election agent of the registered political party in relation to the list submitted by that party and on which that party list candidate is included.

Candidate reported guilty of corrupt or illegal practice

109 If a candidate who has been elected is reported by an election court personally guilty or guilty by his agents of any corrupt or illegal practice his election shall be void.

Persons reported personally guilty of corrupt or illegal practices

110(1) Other than where the petition relates to a vacancy return, the report of the election court under article 99 shall state the names of all persons (if any) who have been proved at the trial to have been guilty of any corrupt or illegal practice, but in the case of someone

    (a) who is not a party to the petition; or

    (b) who is not a candidate on behalf of whom the seat is claimed by the petition,

the election court shall first cause notice to be given to him, and if he appears in pursuance of the notice shall give him an opportunity of being heard by himself and of calling evidence in his defence to show why he should not be so reported.

(2) The report shall be laid before the Director of Public Prosecutions.

(3) Subject to the provisions of paragraph (4) and article 126, a candidate or other person reported by an election court personally guilty of a corrupt or illegal practice shall during the relevant period specified in paragraph (5) be incapable

    (a) of being registered as an elector or voting at any

        (i)   Assembly election;

        (ii) election to the House of Commons;

        (iii) election to the European Parliament;

        (iv) election to the Scottish Parliament;

        (v) election to the Northern Ireland Assembly; or

        (vi) local government election; or

       (b) of being elected to the Assembly, the House of Commons, the European Parliament, the Scottish Parliament, the Northern Ireland Assembly or as a member of a local authority, and if already elected to a seat in the Assembly or holding another elective office, shall vacate the seat or office as from the date of the report.

(4) The incapacities imposed by paragraph (3)(a) apply only to a candidate or other person reported personally guilty of a corrupt practice under article 14(11) or 30 or of an illegal practice under article 31.

(5) For the purposes of paragraph (3) the relevant period is the period beginning with the date of the report and ending

       (a) in the case of a person reported personally guilty of a corrupt practice, five years after that date; and

       (b) in the case of a person reported personally guilty of an illegal practice, three years after that date.

(6) The provisions of this article as to the consequences of the report that a candidate was guilty by his agents of a corrupt or illegal practice have effect subject to the express provisions of this Order relating to particular acts which are declared to be corrupt or illegal practices.

Persons reported personally guilty of corrupt or illegal practices at parliamentary elections or local government elections

111 Subject to the provisions of section 174 of the 1983 Act, if a person is reported by an election court personally guilty of a corrupt or illegal practice under that Act, in addition to being subject to the incapacities set out in section 160 of that Act, he shall for the relevant period specified in article 110(5) from the date of that report be incapable of being elected to and sitting in the Assembly, and if already elected to the Assembly, he shall from that date vacate the seat.

Persons reported personally guilty of corrupt or illegal practices at European parliamentary elections

112 A person reported by an election court personally guilty of a corrupt or illegal practice under the European Parliamentary Elections Regulations 2004 in addition to being subject to the incapacities set out in regulation 107 of those regulations shall, for the relevant period specified in article 110(5), from the date of that report be incapable of being elected to and sitting in the Assembly and, if already elected to the Assembly, he shall from that date vacate the seat.

Justice of the peace

113 Where a justice of the peace is reported by an election court to have been guilty of any corrupt practice in relation to an Assembly election the court shall report the case to the Lord Chancellor and the Lord Chief Justice, or in the case of a justice of the peace for any area in Scotland to the Secretary of State with such evidence as may have been given of the corrupt practice.

Members of legal and certain other professions

114 Where a barrister, advocate, solicitor or any person who belongs to any profession the admission to which is regulated by law is reported by an election court to have been guilty of any corrupt practice in relation to an Assembly election

       (a) the court shall bring the matter before the Inn of Court, Faculty of Advocates, High Court, tribunal or other body having power to take cognizance of any misconduct of the person in his profession; and

(b) the Inn of Court, Faculty of Advocates, High Court, tribunal or other body may deal with him as if the corrupt practice were misconduct by him in his profession.

Holder of licence or certificate under Licensing Acts

115(1) If it appears to an election court that a person holding a licence or certificate under the Licensing Acts has knowingly permitted any bribery or treating in relation to any Assembly election to take place upon his licensed premises

    (a) the court shall, after affording him such rights as are conferred on those about to be reported under article 110(1), report the fact; and

    (b) the court shall bring the report before the licensing authority from whom, or on whose certificate, that person obtained his licence, and the licensing authority shall cause the report to be entered in the proper register of licences.

(2) The entry of the report in that register shall be taken into consideration by the licensing authority in determining whether they will or will not grant a renewal of the licence or certificate of the person reported and may be a ground, if the authority think fit, for refusing renewal.

Avoidance of election for general corruption etc

116(1) Where on an Assembly election petition it is shown that corrupt or illegal practices or illegal payments or employments committed in relation to an Assembly election for the purpose of promoting or procuring the election of any person at the election have so extensively prevailed that they may be reasonably supposed to have affected the result

    (a) his election, if he has been elected, shall be void; and

    (b) he shall be incapable of being elected to fill the vacancy or any of the vacancies for which the election was held.

(2) Where on an Assembly election petition it is shown that corrupt or illegal practices or illegal payments or employments have prevailed in relation to a regional election for the purpose of promoting or procuring the giving of votes for a registered political party at the election, such acts, for the purposes of paragraph (1), shall be treated as having prevailed for the purpose of promoting or procuring the election of each candidate on that party's list.

(3) An election shall not be liable to be avoided otherwise than under this article by reason of general corruption, bribery, treating or intimidation.

Avoidance of election for employing corrupt agent

117(1) Subject to paragraph (3),

    (a) if a constituency or an individual candidate for an Assembly constituency or a regional election or his election agent personally engages; or

    (b) if a party list candidate or the election agent of the registered political party on whose list he is a candidate personally engages,

as a canvasser or agent for the conduct or management of the election any person whom he knows or has reasonable grounds for supposing to be subject to an incapacity to vote at the election, the candidate shall be incapable of being elected to fill the vacancy or any of the vacancies for which the election is held.

(2) For the purposes of paragraph (1) a person shall be subject to an incapacity to vote if

    (a) he has been convicted of or reported for any corrupt or illegal practice within the meaning of this Order, the 1983 Act, or of any enactment relating to elections to the European Parliament, the Northern Ireland Assembly or the Scottish Parliament;

(b) *Repealed,*

(3) In relation to party list candidates at a regional election, the incapacity imposed by paragraph (1) shall apply

    (a) where the election agent engages such a person, to each candidate on the list; or

    (b) where the election agent does not engage such a person, only to that candidate who engages, or those candidates who engage, that person.

(4) A vote given

    (a) at a constituency or regional election for a constituency or, (as the case may be) individual candidate who, at the time of the election, was by virtue of this article incapable of being elected; or

    (b) at a regional election for a registered political party where, at the time of the election, each candidate included on the party's list was by virtue of this article incapable of being elected,

shall not, by reason of that incapacity, be deemed to be thrown away so as to entitle another candidate to be declared elected, unless given at a poll consequent on the decision of an election court that he was so incapable.

Votes to be struck off for corrupt or illegal practices

118(1) Where, on an Assembly election petition claiming the seat for any person, a candidate is proved to have been guilty by himself, or by any person on his behalf, of bribery, treating or undue influence in respect of any person who voted at the Assembly election there shall, on a scrutiny, be struck off from the number of votes appearing to have been given

    (a) to that individual candidate in either a constituency or an electoral region; or

    (b) to the registered political party in an electoral region where the candidate is a candidate on that party's list of candidates,

one vote for every person who voted at the election and is proved to have been so bribed, treated or unduly influenced.

(2) If any person who is guilty of a corrupt or illegal practice or of illegal payment or employment at an Assembly election votes at the election, his vote shall be void.

(3) If any person who is subject under any enactment relating to corrupt or illegal practices to an incapacity to vote at

    (a) an Assembly election;

    (b) an election to the House of Commons;

    (c) an election to the European Parliament;

    (d) an election to the Scottish Parliament;

    (e) an election to the Northern Ireland Assembly; or

    (f) a local government election,

votes at that Assembly election, his vote shall be void.

Application for relief

119(1) An application for relief under this article may be made to the High Court or an election court or else, if in respect of a payment made in contravention of article 49(1), (2) or (3), to a county court.

(2) Where a person makes an application under this article he shall notify the Director of Public Prosecutions of the application and the Director or his assistant or representative may attend the hearing of the application and make representations at the hearing in respect of it.

(3) If it is shown to the court by such evidence as to the court seems sufficient

(a) that any act or omission of any person would apart from this article by reason of being in contravention of this Order be an illegal practice, payment or employment;

(b) that the act or omission arose from inadvertence or from accidental miscalculation or from some other reasonable cause of a like nature, and in any case did not arise from any want of good faith; and

(c) that such notice of the application has been given in the Assembly constituency or electoral region for which the election was held, as to the court seems fit,

and under the circumstances it seems to the court to be just that either that or any other person should not be subject to any of the consequences under this Order of the act or omission, the court may make an order allowing the act or omission to be an exception from the provisions of this Order making it an illegal practice, payment or employment and upon the making of the order no person shall be subject to any of the consequences under this Order of that act or omission.

Prosecutions for corrupt practices

120(1) A person who is guilty of a corrupt practice shall be liable
    (a) on conviction on indictment
      (i) in the case of a corrupt practice under article 14(11) or 30, to imprisonment for a term not exceeding two years, or to a fine, or to both;
      (ii) in any other case, to imprisonment for a term not exceeding one year, or to a fine, or to both; or
    (b) on summary conviction, to imprisonment for a term not exceeding 6 months, or to a fine not exceeding the statutory maximum, or to both.

(2) In relation to an offence committed after commencement of section 281(5) of the Criminal Justice Act 2003, the reference in paragraph (1)(b) to 6 months must be taken to be a reference to 51 weeks.

(3) If it appears to the court by which any person holding a licence or certificate under the Licensing Acts is convicted of the offence of bribery or treating that the offence was committed on his licensed premises
    (a) the court shall direct the conviction to be entered in the proper register of licences; and
    (b) the entry shall be taken into consideration by the licensing authority in determining whether they will or will not grant a renewal of the licence or certificate, and may be a ground, if the authority think fit, for refusing its renewal.

Prosecutions for illegal practices

121 A person guilty of an illegal practice shall on summary conviction be liable to a fine not exceeding level 5 on the standard scale; and on a prosecution for an illegal practice it shall be sufficient to allege that the person charged was guilty of an illegal practice.

Conviction of illegal practice on charge of corrupt practice etc

122 A person charged with a corrupt practice may, if the circumstances warrant such finding, be found guilty of an illegal practice (which offence shall for that purpose be an indictable offence), and a person charged with an illegal practice may be found guilty of that offence notwithstanding that the act constituting the offence amounted to a corrupt practice.

Incapacities on conviction of corrupt or illegal practice

123(1) Subject to paragraph (3), a person convicted of a corrupt or illegal practice shall during the relevant period specified in sub-paragraph (4) be incapable of

    (a) being registered as an elector or voting at any

        (i)   Assembly election;

        (ii) election to the House of Commons;

        (iii) election to the European Parliament;

        (iv) election to the Scottish Parliament;

        (v)   election to the Northern Ireland Assembly; or

        (vi) local government election; or

    (b) being elected to the Assembly, the House of Commons, the European Parliament, the Scottish Parliament, the Northern Ireland Assembly or as a member of a local authority.

(2)   If already elected to a seat in the Assembly or holding an elective office (as listed in paragraph (1)(b)), a person convicted of a corrupt or illegal practice shall vacate the seat or office in accordance with paragraphs (5) and (6).

(3)   The incapacity imposed by paragraph (1)(a) applies only to a person convicted of a corrupt practice under article 14(11) or 30, or of an illegal practice under article 31.

(4)   For the purposes of paragraph (1) the relevant period is the period beginning with the date of conviction and ending

    (a) in the case of a person convicted of a corrupt practice, five years after that date; or

    (b) in the case of a person convicted of an illegal practice, three years after that date,

except that if (at any time within that period of five or three years) a court determines on an appeal by that person against the conviction that it should not be upheld, the relevant period shall end at that time instead.

(5)   Where paragraph (2) applies to any person, he shall (subject to paragraph (6)) vacate the seat or office in question at the appropriate time for the purposes of this section, namely

    (a) the end of the period which is the period prescribed by law within which notice of appeal may be given, or an application for leave to appeal may be made, by him in respect of the conviction; or

    (b) if (at any time within that period) that period is extended

        (i)   the end of the period as so extended; or

        (ii) the end of the period of three months beginning with the date of the conviction,

whichever is the earlier.

(6)   If (before the appropriate time mentioned in paragraph (5)) notice of appeal is given, or an application for leave to appeal is made, by such a person in respect of the conviction, he shall vacate the seat or office in question at the end of the period of three months beginning with the date of conviction unless

    (a) such an appeal is dismissed or abandoned at any earlier time (in which case he shall vacate the seat or office at that time); or

    (b) at any time within that period of three months the court determines on such an appeal that the conviction should not be upheld (in which case the seat or office shall not be vacated by him).

(7)   Where such a person vacates a seat or office in accordance with paragraph (5) or (6), no subsequent determination of a court that his conviction should not be upheld shall entitle him to resume his seat or office.

(8)   If a person convicted of a corrupt or illegal practice has already been elected to a seat in the Assembly or to an elective office as listed in paragraph (1)(b), he shall (in addition to being subject to the incapacities mentioned in paragraph(1)(a) and (b)) be

suspended from performing any of his functions as an Assembly member, or (as the case may be) any of the functions of that office, during the period of suspension specified in paragraph (9).

(9) For the purposes of paragraph (8) the period of suspension is the period beginning with the date of the conviction and ending with

    (a) the date on which the seat or office is vacated in accordance with paragraph (5) or (6); or

    (b) where paragraph (6)(b) applies, the date on which the court determines that the conviction should not be upheld.

(10) Any incapacity or other requirement applying to a person by virtue of paragraphs (1), (2) and (8) apply in addition to any punishment imposed under articles 120 or 121 but each of those paragraphs has effect subject to article 126.

Incapacities on conviction of corrupt or illegal practice at parliamentary or local government elections

124(1) A person convicted of a corrupt or illegal practice under the 1983 Act shall be subject to the incapacities imposed by article 111 as if at the date of the conviction he had been reported personally guilty of that corrupt or illegal practice.

(2) Section 174 of the 1983 Act shall apply to any incapacity imposed under this article as if the incapacity was imposed under section 160 of that Act.

Incapacities on conviction of corrupt or illegal practice at European parliamentary elections

125 A person convicted of a corrupt or illegal practice under the European Parliamentary Regulations 2004, in addition to the incapacities set out in those regulations, shall for the relevant period set out in article 123(4) be incapable of being elected to or sitting in the Assembly, and if already elected to the Assembly, he shall vacate the seat as from the date of conviction.

Mitigation and remission etc

126(1) Where

    (a) any person is subject to any incapacity by virtue of the report of an election court; and

    (b) he or some other person in respect of whose acts the incapacity was imposed is on a prosecution acquitted of any of the matters in respect of which the incapacity was imposed,

the court may order that the incapacity shall thenceforth cease so far as it is imposed in respect of those matters.

(2) Where any person who is subject to any incapacity as mentioned above is on a prosecution convicted of any such matters as are mentioned above, no further incapacity shall be taken to be imposed by reason of the conviction, and the court shall have the like power (if any) to mitigate or remit for the future the incapacity so far as it is imposed by article 110 in respect of the matters of which he is convicted, as if the incapacity had been imposed by reason of the conviction.

(3) A court exercising any of the powers conferred by paragraphs (1) and (2) shall make an order declaring how far, if at all, the incapacities imposed by virtue of the relevant report remain unaffected by the exercise of that power, and that order shall be conclusive for all purposes.

(4) Where a person convicted of a corrupt or illegal practice is subsequently reported to have been guilty of that practice by an election court, no further incapacity shall be

imposed on him under article 110 by reason of the report.

(5) Where any person is subject to any incapacity by virtue of a conviction or of the report of an election court, and any witness who gave evidence against that person upon the proceeding for the conviction or report is convicted of perjury in respect of that evidence, the incapacitated person may apply to the High Court, and the court, if satisfied that the conviction or report so far as respects that person was based upon perjury, may order that the incapacity shall thenceforth cease.

Illegal payments etc

127(1) A person guilty of an offence of illegal payment or employment shall, on summary conviction, be liable to a fine not exceeding level 5 on the standard scale; and on a prosecution for such an offence it shall be sufficient to allege that the person charged was guilty of an illegal payment or employment as the case may be.

(2) A candidate or election agent who is personally guilty of an offence of illegal payment or employment shall be guilty of an illegal practice.

(3) Any person charged with an offence of illegal payment or employment may be found guilty of that offence, notwithstanding that the act constituting the offence amounted to a corrupt or illegal practice.

Time limit for prosecutions

128(1) A proceeding against a person in respect of any offence under any provision contained in this Order shall be commenced within one year after the offence was committed, and the time so limited by this article shall, in the case of any proceedings under the Magistrates' Courts Act 1980 for any such offence, be substituted for any limitation of time contained in that Act.

(2) For the purposes of this article the laying of an information shall be deemed to be the commencement of a proceeding.

(3) A magistrates' court may act under paragraph (4) if it is satisfied on an application by a constable or Crown Prosecutor

(a) that there are exceptional circumstances which justify the granting of the application; and

(b) that there has been no undue delay in the investigation of the offence to which the application relates.

(4) The magistrates' court may extend the time within which the proceedings must be commenced in pursuance of paragraph (1) to not more than 24 months after the offence was committed.

(5) If the magistrates' court acts under paragraph (4), it may also make an order under paragraph (6) if it is satisfied, on an application by a constable or Crown Prosecutor, that documents retained by the relevant registration officer in pursuance of rule 69 of Schedule 5 may provide evidence relating to the offence.

(6) An order under this paragraph is an order

(a) directing the relevant registration officer not to cause the documents to be destroyed at the expiry of the period of one year mentioned in rule 69 of Schedule 5; and

(b) extending the period for which he is required to retain them under that rule by such further period not exceeding 12 months as is specified in the order.

(7) The making of an order under paragraph (6) does not affect any other power to require the retention of the documents.

(8) An application under this article must be made not more than one year after the

offence was committed.

(9) Any party to
   (a) an application under paragraph (3); or
   (b) an application under paragraph (5),

who is aggrieved by the refusal of the magistrates' court to act under paragraph (4) or to make an order under paragraph(6) (as the case may be) may appeal to the Crown Court.

Prosecution of offences committed outside the United Kingdom

129 Proceedings in respect of an offence under this Order alleged to have been committed outside the United Kingdom by a Commonwealth citizen or citizen of the Republic of Ireland or a relevant citizen of the Union may be taken, and the offence may for all incidental purposes be treated as having been committed, in any place in the United Kingdom.

Offences by associations

130 Where
   (a) any corrupt or illegal practice or any illegal payment or employment; or
   (b) any offence under article 76,

is committed by any association or body of persons, corporate or unincorporate, the members of the association or body who have taken part in the commission of the offence shall be liable to any fine or punishment imposed for that offence by this Order.

Evidence by certificate of holding of Assembly elections

131 On
   (a) any prosecution for a corrupt or illegal practice or for any illegal payment or employment; and
   (b) any proceedings for a penalty under article 57,

the certificate of the appropriate returning officer at an Assembly election
   (i) that the election mentioned in the certificate was duly held; and
   (ii) that the person named in the certificate was a candidate at the election,

shall be sufficient evidence of the facts stated in it.

Evidence by certificate of electoral registration

132 The certificate of a registration officer that any person is or is not, or was or was not at any particular time, duly registered in his register in respect of any address shall be sufficient evidence of the facts stated in it; and a document purporting to be such a certificate shall be received in evidence and presumed to be such a certificate unless the contrary is proved.

Director of Public Prosecutions

133(1) Where information is given to the Director of Public Prosecutions that any offence under this Order has been committed it is his duty to make such inquiries and institute such prosecutions as the circumstances of the case appear to him to require.

(2) The Director by himself or by his assistant or by his representative appointed under paragraph (3) may and, if the election court so requests him, shall attend the trial of every Assembly election petition.

(3) The Director may nominate a barrister, a solicitor or an authorised person to be his representative for the purposes of this Part.

(3A) In paragraph (3) "authorised person" means a person (other than a barrister or solicitor) who, for the purposes of the Legal Services Act 2007, is an authorised person in relation to an activity which constitutes the exercise of a right of audience (within the meaning of that Act).

(4) There shall be allowed to the Director and his assistant or representative for the purposes of this Part (other than his general duties under paragraph (1)) such allowances for expenses as the Treasury may approve.

(5) The costs incurred in defraying the expenses of the Director incurred for those purposes (including the remuneration of his representative) shall, in the first instance, be paid by the Treasury, and shall be deemed to be expenses of the election court; but if for any reasonable cause it seems just to the court so to do, the court shall order all or part of those costs to be repaid to the Treasury by the parties to the petition, or such of them as the court may direct.

Rules of procedure

134(1) The authority having for the time being power to make rules of court for the Supreme Court may make rules for the purposes of Part 3 of this Order and this Part.

(2) In relation to the power conferred under paragraph (1) to make rules
  (a) that power shall be exercisable by statutory instrument, and be treated for the purposes of the Statutory Instruments Act 1946 as if conferred by an Act of Parliament on a Minister of the Crown, and
  (b) a statutory instrument containing rules under paragraph (1) shall be subject to annulment in pursuance of a resolution of either House of Parliament.

(3) Subject to any rules made under paragraph 1, the Election Petition Rules 1960 shall have effect (subject to the modifications set out in Schedule 9) in relation to an Assembly election petition as if made in the exercise of the power conferred by paragraph (1).

Costs

135(1) The rules of the Supreme Court with respect to costs to be allowed in actions, causes and matters in the High Court shall in principle and so far as practicable apply to the costs of petition and other proceedings under Part 3 of this Order or this Part and the taxing officer shall not allow any costs higher than would be allowed in any action, cause or matter in the High Court on a standard basis.

(2) Where any costs or other sums are, under the order of an election court or otherwise under this Part, to be paid by any person, those costs or sums shall be due from that person to the person or persons to whom they are to be paid and, if payable to the Treasury, shall be a debt due to Her Majesty and in either case may be recovered accordingly.

Service of notices

136(1) Any notice, legal process or other document required to be served on any person with reference to any proceeding for the purpose of causing him to appear before the High Court, a county court, or any election court, or otherwise or of giving him an opportunity of making a statement, or showing cause, or being heard by himself before any court for any purpose of this Part may be served
  (a) by delivering it to that person, or by leaving it at, or sending it by post by a registered letter or by the recorded delivery service to his last known place of abode in the Assembly constituency or, as the case may be, electoral region for which the election was held; or

(b) if the proceeding is before any court in such other manner as the court may direct.

(2) In proving service by post under this article it shall be sufficient to prove that the letter was prepaid, properly addressed, and registered or recorded with the postal operator (within the meaning of Part 3 of the Postal Services Act 2011) concerned.

Interpretation of Part 4

137(1) In this Part, unless the context otherwise requires

"candidate" has the same meaning as in Part 3 of this Order and the saving in article 83(1) applies in relation to this Part as in relation to Part 3;

"costs" include charges and expenses;

"date of the allowance of an authorised excuse" has the meaning assigned to it by article 58(9);

"Licensing Acts" means the Licensing Act 2003 and the Acts amending that Act, or the corresponding enactments forming part of the law of Scotland or Northern Ireland;

"money" and "pecuniary reward" shall be deemed to include

(a) any office, place or employment;

(b) any valuable security or other equivalent of money; and

(c) any valuable consideration,

and expressions referring to money shall be construed accordingly;

"payment" includes any pecuniary or other reward;

"prescribed" means prescribed by rules of court; and

"return as to election expenses" means a return made under article 52.

(2) For the purposes of section 119 of the 1998 Act anything required by this Part to be published by the Presiding Officer of the Assembly shall be treated as being required to be published by the Assembly.

Computation of time for purposes of Part 4

138 Article 85 applies in computing any period of time for the purposes of this Part as it applies for the purposes of Part 3 of this Order.

Part 5
Miscellaneous and Supplemental

Advertisements

139 The Town and Country Planning (Control of Advertisement) Regulations 1992 shall have effect in relation to the display, on any site in Wales, of an advertisement relating specifically to an Assembly election or Assembly elections as they have effect in relation to the display of an advertisement relating specifically to a parliamentary election.

Assembly constituencies not wholly within a county or county borough

140 Where an Assembly constituency is not coterminous with, or wholly situated in, a county or county borough

(a) the registration officer for any part of the Assembly constituency shall, if he is not the returning officer for the constituency, consult him concerning the form of so much of

(i) the register;

(ii) the electors lists; or

(iii) the postal voters list, the list of proxies and the proxy postal voters list,

as relate to the constituency in order to ensure that, so far as practicable, they are in a form similar to those in use elsewhere in the constituency, and

(b) if the registration officer for any part of the Assembly constituency at an Assembly election is not the returning officer for the constituency, he shall forthwith supply to the constituency returning officer a copy of the lists compiled under article 10 and 12(8) on completion of the compilation of them.

Translations etc of certain documents

141(1) Paragraphs (2) and (3) apply to any document which under or by virtue of this Order is required or authorised to be given to voters or displayed in any place for the purposes of an Assembly election.

(2) The person who is required or authorised to give or display the document must give or display or otherwise make available in such form as he thinks appropriate
   (a) the document in Braille;
   (b) the document in languages other than English and Welsh;
   (c) graphical representations of the information contained in the document; and
   (d) other means of making the information contained in the document accessible to persons who might not otherwise have reasonable access to the information.

(3) The person required or authorised to give or display the document must also make available the information contained in the document in such audible form as he thinks appropriate.

(4) Paragraphs (2) and (3) do not apply to
   (a) the nomination paper;
   (b) the ballot paper.

(5) The constituency returning officer at an Assembly election must cause to be displayed at every polling station in the election an enlarged sample copy of the ballot paper.

(6) The sample copy mentioned in paragraph (5)
   (a) in the case of a constituency election, must have printed the words "VOTE FOR ONE CANDIDATE ONLY" and "PLEIDLEISIWCH DROS UN YMGEISYDD YN UNIG" both at the top and immediately below the list of candidates;
   (b) in the case of a regional election, must have printed the words "VOTE ONCE ONLY" and "PLEIDLEISIWCH UNWAITH YN UNIG" both at the top and bottom of the front of the ballot paper; and
   (c) in each case, below the second occurrence of those words may include a translation of those words into such other languages as the constituency returning officer thinks appropriate.

(7) The constituency returning officer at an Assembly election must provide at every polling station in the election an enlarged handheld sample copy of the ballot paper for the assistance of voters who are partially sighted.

(8) The sample copy mentioned in paragraph (7) must be clearly marked as a specimen provided only for the guidance of voters.

Forms: general

142(1) Subject to paragraph (2), the forms set out in this Order may be used with such variations as the circumstances may require.

(2) Paragraph (1) does not apply to the forms of ballot paper to be used at constituency and regional elections set out in Schedule 10.

(3) Without prejudice to the power conferred by paragraph (1), where any form to which

that paragraph applies is set out in English and Welsh in this Order so that it is set out in English first and then in Welsh, that form may be varied so that

(a)   the English and Welsh parts are combined; or

(b)   it is set out in Welsh first and then in English.

(4)   Where any form is required to be completed by any person, and it is a form set out in this Order referred to in paragraph (3), such form may be validly completed by completion of either the English or Welsh parts.

Public notices, and declarations

143(1)   A public notice required by or under this Order to be given by a constituency or regional returning officer at an Assembly election shall be given by posting the notice in some conspicuous place or places

(a)   in the case of a constituency election, in the Assembly constituency; and

(b)   in the case of a regional election, in each Assembly constituency in the Assembly electoral region for which the election is held,

and may also be given in such other manner as he thinks desirable for publicising it.

(2)   Any person before whom a declaration is authorised to be made under this Order may take the declaration.

Sending of applications and notices; electronic signatures and related certificates

144(1)   The requirement in this Order that any application, notice, representation or objection should be in writing is satisfied where (apart from the usual meaning of that expression) the text of it

(a)   is transmitted by electronic means;

(b)   is received in legible form; and

(c)   is capable of being used for future reference.

(2)   The requirement in this Order for an application, notice, representation or objection to be signed is satisfied (as an alternative to a signature given by hand) where there is

(a)   an electronic signature incorporated into or logically associated with a particular electronic communication; and

(b)   the certification by any person of such a signature.

(3)   For the purposes of this Order an electronic signature is so much of anything in electronic form as

(a)   is incorporated into or otherwise logically associated with any electronic communication or both; and

(b)   purports to be so incorporated or associated for the purpose of being used in establishing the authenticity of the communication, the integrity of the communication or both.

(4)   For the purposes of this Order an electronic signature incorporated into or associated with a particular electronic communication is certified by any person if that person (whether before or after the making of the communication) has made a statement confirming that

(a)   the signature;

(b)   a means of producing, communicating or verifying the signature; or

(c)   a procedure applied to the signature,

is (either alone or in combination with other factors) a valid means of establishing the authenticity of the communication, the integrity of the communication or both.

Publication of documents

145(1)   Any failure to publish a document in accordance with this Order shall not invalidate the document, but this provision shall not relieve any person from any penalty for such a failure.

(2) Where a document is made available for inspection, any person may make a copy (whether in handwriting or by other means) of the whole or any part of such a document.

Interference with notices etc

146 If any person without lawful authority destroys, mutilates, defaces or removes any notice published by a registration officer in connection with his registration duties under this Order or any copies of a document which have been made available for inspection in pursuance of those duties, he shall be liable on summary conviction to a fine not exceeding level 3 on the standard scale.

Premises used for election purposes

147 In relation to premises in Wales, section 65(6) of the Local Government Finance Act 1988 (occupation for election meetings and polls) shall have effect as if
  (a) the reference to public meetings in furtherance of a person's candidature at an election included a reference to public meetings promoting a particular result at an Assembly election; and
  (b) the reference to use by a returning officer for the purpose of taking the poll in an election included a reference to use by a constituency returning officer in taking a poll at an Assembly election in accordance with Schedule 5.

Dissolution of the Assembly

148 The "minimum period" for the purpose of section 3(2)(a) of the 2006 Act is a period of 21 days, computed in accordance with rule 2 of Schedule 5.

Saving and transitional provision as to incapacities in respect of Assembly elections

149(1) Any incapacity imposed by or under Part 4 of the National Assembly for Wales (Representation of the People) Order 2003 or by or under Part 4 of this Order (legal proceedings) on any person from
  (a) voting in any election under Part 1 of the 1998 Act; or
  (b) being, acting as or remaining a member of the Assembly constituted by that Act,
shall also apply to the like extent in relation to that person
    (i) voting in any election under Part 1 of the 2006 Act; or
    (ii) being, acting as or remaining a member of the Assembly constituted by the 2006 Act.

(2) Nothing in paragraph (1) prejudices the operation of sections 16 and 17 of the Interpretation Act 1978 in respect of the revocation of the National Assembly for Wales (Representation of the People) Order 2003 by this Order.

SCHEDULE 1
ABSENT VOTING AT ASSEMBLY ELECTIONS

Article 15(2)

Contents

General requirements for applications

1(1)   Applications under article 8, 9, 11 or 12 must state

   (a)   the applicant's full name;

   (b)   the address in respect of which the applicant is registered or has applied to be (or is treated as having applied to be) registered in the register except in the case of an application under article 12(4) and (7);

   (c)   in the case of such an application, the proxy's address together with the name of the elector for whom he will act as proxy and the elector's address for the purposes of sub-paragraph (b);

   (d)   in the case of a person applying to vote by post, the address to which the ballot paper should be sent;

   (e)   in the case of an application to vote by proxy, the grounds on which the elector claims to be entitled to an absent vote;

   (f) in the case of a person who is unable to provide a signature, the reasons for his request for a waiver of any requirement under article 8, 9 or 12 to provide a signature and the name and address of any person who has assisted him to complete his application; and

   (g)   where the applicant has, or has applied for, an anonymous entry, that fact.

(2)   The application shall be made in writing and be dated.

(3)   Where an application is required to contain a signature and date of birth, the information must be set out in a manner that is sufficiently clear and unambiguous as to be capable of electronic scanning into the record by configuring the information as follows

   (a)   the signature shall appear against a background of white unlined paper of at least five centimetres long and two centimetres high; and

   (b)   the applicant's date of birth shall be set out numerically configured in the sequence of date, month, year namely dd mm yyyy.

(4)   Where the application contains a request that the registration officer dispense with a requirement for a signature, sub-paragraph (3)(a) shall not apply.

(5)

   (a)   An application under article 8(1), 11(6) or 12(4)(a) which is made for an indefinite period or the period specified in the application must state that it is so made;

(b) an application under article 9(1), (2), (3), 11(7) or 12(7) which is made for a particular Assembly election must state that it is so made,

but, where the poll for an Assembly election falls on the same day as the poll at another election, the same application may be used for both elections.

(6) The registration officer may satisfy himself

(a) that an application under articles 8, 9, 11 or 12 meets any requirements that it has been signed by the applicant and states his date of birth by referring to any signature and date of birth

(i) previously provided by the applicant to the registration officer or the returning officer; or

(ii) previously provided by the applicant to the county or county borough council, or registrar of births and deaths which the registration officer is authorised to inspect for the purposes of his registration duties; and

(b) as to whether the applicant is unable to provide a signature or a consistent signature due to disability or inability to read or write.

(7)

(a) Where

(i) in the case of an application to vote by post under articles 8(1), (7) or 9(1) the addresses stated in accordance with sub-paragraph (1)(b) and (d) are different; or

(ii) in the case of an application by a proxy to vote by post under article 12(4), the proxy's address stated in accordance with sub-paragraph (1)(c) and the address stated in accordance with sub-paragraph (1)(d) are different,

the application must set out why the applicant's circumstances will be or are likely to be such that he requires the ballot paper to be sent to the address stated in accordance with sub-paragraph (1)(d).

(b) This sub-paragraph does not apply where an applicant has, or has applied for, an anonymous entry.

(8)

(a) An application under

(i) article 9(3)(a) by a person shown as voting by post in the record kept under Article 8; or

(ii) article 12(7) by a person shown as voting by post in the record kept under Article 12 (6),

for his ballot paper to be sent to a different address from that shown in the record shall set out why the applicant's circumstances will be or are likely to be such that he requires his ballot paper to be sent to that address.

(b) this paragraph does not apply where the applicant has, or has applied for, an anonymous entry.

(9) For the purposes of sub-paragraph (1)(b), the address in respect of which the applicant is or has applied to be (or is treated as having applied to be) registered includes

(a) in the case of a service voter, the address given in the service declaration in accordance with section 16(d) of the 1983 Act;

(b) in the case of a person to whom section 7 of the 1983 Act applies (mental patients who are not detained offenders), the address of the mental hospital or the address shown on the declaration of local connection in accordance with section 7B(3)(d) of the 1983 Act;

(c) in the case of a person to whom section 7A of the 1983 Act applies (person remanded in custody), the address of the place at which he is detained or the address shown on the declaration of local connection in accordance with section 7B(3)(d) of the 1983 Act; and

    (d) in the case of a homeless person, the address shown on the declaration of local connection in accordance with section 7B(3)(d) of the 1983 Act.

The personal identifiers record

2(1) The registration officer shall maintain a record ("the personal identifiers record") apart from the other records and lists which he is required to keep under this Order, of the signatures and dates of birth provided by persons whose applications under article 8(1), 9(1) or 12(4)(a) or (b) were granted, until the expiry of twelve months from

    (a) the date on which a person is removed from the record kept pursuant to article 8(3) or 12(6); or

    (b) the date of the poll for the purposes of which the person's application for an absent vote was granted under article 9(1) or 12(4)(b).

(2) The personal identifiers record shall contain the following information in respect of each absent voter on the postal voters list, list of proxies or proxy postal voters list

    (a) his name;

    (b) his date of birth; and

    (c) his signature, or a record of waiver by the registration officer of the requirement for his signature.

(3) The registration officer may disclose information held in the personal identifiers record to

    (a) any candidate or agent attending proceedings on receipt of postal ballot papers, in accordance with and for the purposes referred to in paragraph 23 and 24 of Schedule 3;

    (b) any person attending proceedings on receipt of postal ballot papers, who is entitled to do so by virtue of any of sections 6A to 6D of the 2000 Political Parties Act but only to the extent required to permit them to observe the proceedings.

Additional requirements for applications for appointment of a proxy

3 An application for the appointment of a proxy under article 8 or 9 shall state the full name and address of the person whom the applicant wishes to appoint as his proxy, together with his family relationship, if any, with the applicant, and

    (a) if it is signed only by the applicant, shall contain a statement by him that he has consulted the person so named and that that person is capable of being and willing to be appointed to vote as his proxy; or

    (b) if it is also signed by the person to be appointed, shall contain a statement by that person that he is capable of being and willing to be appointed to vote as the applicant's proxy.

Additional requirements for applications on grounds of blindness or other disability

4(1) An application to vote by proxy for a particular or indefinite period under article 8(2)(c) shall specify the disability by reason of which the application is made.

(2) Subject to sub-paragraph (3) such an application shall be attested and signed by:

    (a) a registered medical practitioner;

    (b) a nurse registered on the register maintained by the Nursing and Midwifery Council under article 5 of the Nursing and Midwifery Order 2001 by virtue of qualifications in nursing;

    (c) a registered dentist as defined by section 53(1) of the Dentists Act 1984;

    (d) a registered dispensing optician or a registered optometrist within the meaning of the Opticians Act 1989;

    (e) a registered pharmacist as defined by article 3(1) of the Pharmacy Order 2010;

   (f)   a registered osteopath as defined by section 41 of the Osteopaths Act 1993;

   (g)   a registered chiropractor as defined by section 43 of the Chiropractors Act 1994;

   (h)   a Christian Science practitioner;

   (j)   a person registered as a member of a profession to which the Health and Social Work Professions Order 2001 for the time being extends;

   (k)   the person carrying on a care home registered under Part 2 of the Care Standards Act 2000;

   (l)   the warden of premises forming one of a group of premises provided for persons of pensionable age or disabled persons for which there is a resident warden, where the applicant states that he resides in such premises;

   (m)   a manager within the meaning of section 145(1) of the Mental Health Act 1983 or on behalf of such a manager; or

   (n)   a person registered in a register for social workers maintained in accordance with section 56 of the Care Standards Act 2000.

(3)   A person who qualifies

   (a)   by virtue of any of sub-paragraph (a) to (j) of paragraph (2), may not attest an application for these purposes unless

      (i)   he is treating the applicant for the disability specified in the application; or

      (ii)   the applicant is receiving care from him in respect of that disability; or

      (iii)   the person is a social worker who qualifies by virtue of sub-paragraph (2)(j), and has arranged care or assistance for the applicant in respect of that disability; or

   (b)   by virtue of sub-paragraph (2)(n), may not attest an application for these purposes unless

      (i)   he is treating the applicant for the disability specified in the application;

      (ii)   the applicant is receiving care from him in respect of that disability; or

      (iii)   he has arranged care or assistance for the person in respect of his disability.

(4)   The person attesting the application shall state

   (a)   his name and address and the qualification by virtue of which he attests the application,

   (b)   where the person who attests the application is a person referred to in paragraph (3)(a), that

      (i)   he is treating the applicant for the disability specified in the application; or

      (ii)   the applicant is receiving care from him in respect of that disability;

   (c)   where the person who attests the application is a person referred to in paragraph (3)(b), that

      (i)   he is treating the applicant for the disability specified in the application;

      (ii)   the applicant is receiving care from him in respect of that disability; or

      (iii)   he has arranged care or assistance for the applicant in respect of that disability;

   (d)   that, to the best of his knowledge and belief, the applicant has the disability specified in the application and that he cannot reasonably be expected to go in person to his allotted polling station or to vote unaided there by reason of that disability; and

   (e)   that, to the best of his knowledge and belief, the disability specified in the application is likely to continue either indefinitely or for a period specified by the person attesting the application.

(5)   Sub-paragraphs (2) to (4) shall not apply where

   (a)   the application is based on the applicant's blindness and the applicant is registered as a blind person by a local authority, which is specified in the application, under section 29(4)(g) of the National Assistance Act 1948; or

(b) the application states that the applicant is in receipt of the higher rate of the mobility component of a disability living allowance (payable under section 73 of the Social Security Contributions and Benefits Act 1992) because of the disability specified in the application; ...

(c) the application states that the applicant is in receipt of the enhanced rate of the mobility component of personal independence payment (payable under section 79(2) of the Welfare Reform Act 2012) because of the disability specified in the application; or

(d) the application states that the applicant is in receipt of armed forces independence payment under the Armed Forces and Reserve Forces (Compensation Scheme) Order 2011 because of the disability specified in the application.

(6) A person who qualifies by virtue of sub-paragraph (3)(m) shall, instead of the matters specified in sub-paragraph (4)(a), state in the attestation

(a) his name;

(b) his position in the hospital at which the applicant is liable to be detained or at which he is receiving treatment;

(c) that he is a person authorised to make the attestation; and

(d) in the case of an applicant who is liable to be detained in hospital, the statutory provision under which the applicant is liable to be so detained.

(7) The fact that an applicant is registered with a local authority under section 29(4)(g) of the National Assistance Act 1948 shall be deemed sufficient evidence that he is eligible for an absent vote on the grounds set out in article 8(2)(c).

(8) In this paragraph and paragraphs 5 and 6, "his allotted polling station", in relation to an elector, means the polling station allotted or likely to be allotted to him under this Order.

Additional requirements for applications for a proxy vote based on occupation, service, employment or attendance on a course

5(1) An application to vote by proxy for a particular or indefinite period under article 8(2)(d) shall state

(a) whether the occupation, service or employment, in respect of which it is made, is that of the applicant or his spouse or civil partner or, as the case may be, whether it is the applicant or his spouse or civil partner who is attending the course provided by an educational institution in respect of which the application is made;

(b) the nature of the occupation, service, employment or course provided by an educational institution giving rise to the application;

(c) where the person in respect of whose occupation, service or employment it is made (in this paragraph referred to as "the employed person") is self-employed, that fact; and, in any other case, the name of that person's employer; and

(d) the reason relevant to the general nature of the occupation, service or employment in question or the course provided by an educational institution, why the applicant cannot reasonably be expected to go in person to his allotted polling station.

(2) Such an application shall be attested and signed

(a) where the employed person is self-employed, by a person who

(i) is aged 18 years or over;

(ii) knows the employed person; and

(iii) is not related to him;

(b) by the employer of the employed person or by another employee to whom this function is delegated by the employer; or

 (c) in the case of a course provided by an educational institution, by the director or tutor of that course or by the principal or head of that institution or an employee to whom this function is delegated by the principal or head.

(3) The person attesting an application under sub-paragraph (2) shall

 (a) where the applicant is the employed person or the person attending the course, certify that the statements included in the application in accordance with the requirements of sub-paragraph (1)(a) to (d) are true; or

 (b) where the applicant is the spouse or civil partner of the employed person or the person attending the course, certify that the statements included in the application in accordance with the requirements of sub-paragraph (1)(a) to (c) are true.

(4) The person attesting an application under sub-paragraph (2) shall also state

 (a) in the case of a person who attests an application under sub-paragraph (2)(a), his name and address, and that he is aged 18 years or over, knows the employed person, but is not related to him; or

 (b) in the case of a person who attests an application under sub-paragraph (2)(b), either that he is the employer of the employed person or the position he holds in the employment of that employer; or

 (c) in the case of a person who attests under sub-paragraph (2)(c), the post he holds at the institution.

(5) For the purpose of sub-paragraphs (2)(a) and (4)(a), one person is related to another if he is the spouse, civil partner, parent, grandparent, brother, sister, child or grandchild of the other.

Additional requirements for applications to vote by proxy in respect of a particular Assembly election

6(1) An application under article 9(1) to vote by proxy at a particular election shall set out why the applicant's circumstances on the date of the poll for that election in respect of which it is made will be or are likely to be such that he cannot reasonably be expected to vote in person at his allotted polling station.

(2) Where an application under article 9(1)

 (a) is made on the grounds of the applicant's disability; and

 (b) is made after 5 pm on the sixth day before the date of the poll at the election for which it is made,

the requirements of paragraphs 1 and 4 of this Schedule as to the matters to be specified and the attestation shall apply.

(3) Where an application mentioned in sub-paragraph (2) is made, the person who attests the application shall state, in addition to those matters specified in paragraph 3, to the best of his knowledge and belief, the date upon which the applicant became disabled.

(4) Where an application under article 9(1) is made by a person to whom article 7(7) applies after 5 pm on the sixth day before the date of the poll at the election for which it is made, the requirements of sub-paragraph (5) as to the matters to be specified and as to attestation shall apply.

(5) Where an application mentioned in paragraph (4) is made

 (a) the application shall additionally state the name and address of the hospital at which the applicant is liable to be detained;

 (b) the application shall be attested by or on behalf of the managers responsible for the administration of the hospital within the meaning of section 145(1) of the Mental Health Act 1983 at which the applicant is liable to be detained, and the

attestation shall state
- (i) the name of the person attesting the application;
- (ii) his position in the hospital at which the applicant is liable to be detained;
- (iii) that he is a person authorised to make the attestation; and
- (iv) the statutory provision under which the applicant is liable to be detained in the hospital.

(6) This paragraph does not apply where the applicant has an anonymous entry.

Closing dates for applications

7(1) An application
- (a) to vote by post under article 8(1) or 9(1); or
- (b) from a proxy to vote by post under article 12(4),

shall be disregarded for the purposes of any particular Assembly election if it is received by the registration officer after 5pm on the eleventh day before the date of the poll at that election.

(2) Subject to sub-paragraph (3) an application
- (a) to vote by proxy under article 8(1) or 9(1); or
- (b) for the appointment of a proxy under article 11(6) or (7),

shall be disregarded for the purposes of any particular Assembly election if it is received by the registration officer after 5pm on the sixth day before the date of the poll at that election.

(3) Where an application under article 9(1) is made
- (a) on the grounds of the applicant's disability and the applicant became disabled after 5pm on the sixth day before the poll at the election for which it is made; or
- (b) by a person to whom article 7(8) applies,

the application, or an application under article 11(7) made by virtue of that application, shall be refused if it is received after 5pm on the day of the poll at the election for which it is made.

(4) An application
- (a) by an absent voter to alter his choice as to the manner of absent voting under article 8(6) or (7);
- (b) by a postal voter for his ballot paper to be sent to a different address or to vote instead by proxy at a particular election under article 9(3); or
- (c) from a postal proxy for his ballot paper to be sent to a different address at a particular election under article 12(7),

shall be refused for the purposes of any particular Assembly election if it is received by the registration officer after 5 pm on the eleventh day before the date of the poll at that election.

(5) The following, namely
- (a) an application under article 8(5)(a) by an elector to be removed from the record kept under article 8(3);
- (b) an application under article 12(10)(a) by a proxy to be removed from the record kept under article 12(6); and
- (c) a notice under article 11(9) of the cancellation of a proxy's appointment,

shall be disregarded for the purposes of any particular Assembly election if it is received by the registration officer after 5 pm on the eleventh day before the date of the poll at that election for which it is made.

(6) In computing a period of days for the purposes of this paragraph, Saturday, Sunday, Christmas Eve, Christmas Day, Good Friday, or a bank holiday shall be disregarded.

(7) In paragraph (6) "bank holiday" means a day which is a bank holiday under the

Banking and Financial Dealings Act 1971 in Wales.

Grant or refusal of applications

8(1) Where the registration officer grants an application to vote by post he shall notify the applicant of his decision.

(2) Where the registration officer grants an application for the appointment of a proxy, he shall confirm in writing to the elector that the proxy has been appointed, his name and address and the duration of the appointment.

(3) The proxy paper to be issued by the registration officer on the appointment of a proxy shall be in form CA set out in English and Welsh in Schedule 10 (but this may be combined with another form of proxy paper if the registration officer is issuing a proxy paper appointing that person as proxy for the same elector in respect of another election or other elections).

(4) Where the registration officer refuses an application for an absent vote he shall notify the applicant of his decision and the reason for it.

(5) Where the registration officer grants an application made under
   (a) article 9(3)(a) by a person shown as voting by post in the record kept under article 8(3); or
   (b) article 12(7) by a person shown as voting by post in the record kept under article 12(6),
   he shall notify the applicant of this.

(6) Where a person is removed from the record kept pursuant to article 8(3), the registration officer shall, where practicable notify him of this and the reason for it.

(7) Where the appointment of a proxy is cancelled by the elector or otherwise ceases to be in force, the registration officer shall, where practicable notify the elector that the appointment has been cancelled or, as the case may be, notify him that the appointment has ceased and the reason for it.

(8) Where under paragraph 7 of this Schedule the registration officer refuses or disregards an application for the purposes of any Assembly election, he shall notify the applicant of this.

(9) At an Assembly election where the registration officer is not the returning officer for any constituency or part of a constituency in the area for which he is the registration officer, he shall send to that returning officer details of any application to vote by post which he has granted as soon as practicable after doing so.

Notice of appeal

9(1) A person desiring to appeal under article 5(1) against the decision of a registration officer must give notice of the appeal to the registration officer within 14 days of the receipt of the notice given under paragraph 8(4) of this Schedule specifying the grounds of the appeal.

(2) The registration officer shall forward any such notice to the county court in the manner directed by rules of court together in each case with a statement of the material facts which in his opinion have been established in the case, of his decision upon the whole case and on any point which may be specified as a ground of appeal.

(3) Where it appears to the registration officer that any notices of appeal given to him are based on similar grounds, he shall inform the county court of this to enable the court (if it thinks fit) to consolidate the appeals or select a case as a test case.

Cancellation of proxy appointment

10   Where the appointment of a proxy is cancelled by notice given to the registration officer under article 11(9) or ceases to be in force under that provision or is no longer in force under article 11(10)(b), the registration officer shall

    (a)   notify the person whose appointment as proxy has been cancelled, expired or ceases to be or is no longer in force, unless the registration officer has previously been notified by that person that he no longer wishes to act as proxy; and

    (b)   remove his name from the record kept under article 8(3).

Inquiries by registration officer

11(1)   The registration officer may, at such times as he thinks fit, make inquiries of a person

    (a)   who is shown as voting by proxy in the record kept under article 8(3) in pursuance of an application granted on the grounds set out in article 8(2)(c) or (d); or

    (b)   who immediately before 11th March 1999 was entitled to vote by proxy at parliamentary elections or local government elections or both in pursuance of an application granted on grounds corresponding to those set out in article 8(2)(c) or (d) (disability, blindness, occupation, service or employment),

for the purpose of determining whether there has been a material change of circumstances.

(2)   Where the grant of an application for a proxy vote for an indefinite or particular period was based on grounds referred to in article 8(2)(d) (or grounds corresponding to those grounds), the registration officer shall make the inquiries referred to not later than three years after the granting of the application or the last such inquiries as the case may be.

(3)   The registration officer may treat the failure by a person of whom inquiries have been made under sub-paragraph (1) or (2) to respond to such inquiries within one month of the date on which they were made as sufficient evidence of a material change in circumstances.

Requirement to provide fresh signatures at five yearly intervals

12(1)   The registration officer shall, every year by 31st January send to every person who remains an absent voter and whose signature held on the personal identifiers record is more than five years old a notice in writing

    (a)   requiring him to provide a fresh signature; and

    (b)   informing him of the date (six weeks from the date of sending the notice) on which he would cease to be entitled to vote by post or proxy in the event of a failure or refusal to provide a fresh signature.

(2)   The notice must be sent by the registration officer to the current or last known address of the absent voter.

(3)   The registration officer must, if the absent voter has not responded to the notice within three weeks from the date on which the notice was sent, as soon as practicable send a copy of the notice to him.

(4)   Where a notice or copy of a notice is sent by post, the registration officer may use

    (a)   a universal service provider; or

    (b)   a commercial delivery firm,

and postage shall be prepaid.

(5)   A notice or copy of a notice sent to an absent voter in accordance with sub-paragraph (1) or (3) must be accompanied by a pre-addressed reply paid envelope and, in the case of a notice or copy of a notice sent to an address in the United Kingdom, return

postage must be prepaid.

(6) Upon the expiration of the period specified in the notice sent to the absent voter the registration officer shall determine whether the absent voter has failed or refused to provide a fresh signature.

(7) Where the registration officer determines that the absent voter has refused or failed to provide a fresh signature within the specified period, he must remove that person's entry from the records kept pursuant to article 8(3) or 12(6) and from the postal voters list, list of proxies or proxy postal voters list (as the case may be) kept under article 10(2), 10(3) or 12(8).

(8) Where the registration officer removes an absent voter's entry in the circumstances to which sub-paragraph (7) refers

   (a) the registration officer shall inform the absent voter, where appropriate, of the location of the polling station allotted or likely to be allotted to him under this Order;

   (b) paragraphs 8(4), 8(6), 8(7) and 9 of this Schedule shall apply as if the registration officer were refusing an application in accordance with this Schedule;

   (c) in the case of an entry removed from the proxy postal voters list, the registration officer must also notify the elector who appointed the proxy whose entry has been removed.

(9) The registration officer shall include in the notice to be sent to an absent voter regarding his removal from the records kept pursuant to article 8(3) or 12(6) and from the postal voters list, list of proxies or proxy postal voters list (as the case may be) kept pursuant to articles 10(2), 10(3) or 12(8), information

   (a) explaining the effect of such removal; and

   (b) reminding the absent voter that he may make a fresh application under article 8(1), 9(1) or 12(4) to vote by post or proxy (as the case may be).

Records and lists kept under articles 8, 10 and 12

13(1) Any of the persons listed in sub-paragraph (2) entitled to copies of the full register in accordance with the provisions of regulations 103, 105, 106 and 108 of the 2001 Regulations are also entitled, subject to this paragraph and paragraph 14 of this Schedule, to request that the registration officer supply free of charge the relevant parts (within the meaning of the 2001 Regulations) of a copy of any of the following information which he keeps

   (a) the current version of the information which would, in the event of a particular Assembly election, be included in the postal voters lists, the list of proxies or the proxy postal voters lists which he is required to keep under article 10 or 12(8);

   (b) the current or final version of the postal voters list, the list of proxies or the proxy postal voters list kept under article 10 or 12(8).

(2) The persons are

   (a) each member of the National Assembly for Wales for any constituency or Assembly electoral region wholly or partly within the registration area;

   (b) a candidate or his agent for an Assembly constituency election;

   (c) an individual candidate or the candidates or election agent for a registered political party standing nominated in an Assembly electoral region; or

   (d) any person nominated to act for the purposes of this paragraph by the registered nominating officer of a registered political party provided that not more than one person may be nominated in respect of the same registered political party and registration area.

(3) A request under sub-paragraph (1) shall be made in writing and shall

   (a) specify which records or lists (or the relevant parts of such records or lists) are requested;

    (b) state whether the request is made only in respect of current lists or whether it includes a request for the supply of any final list; and

    (c) state whether a printed copy of the records or lists is requested or a copy in data form.

(4)   A person who obtains a copy of a list under this paragraph may use it only for the permitted purposes specified in paragraph 14 of this Schedule, and any restrictions

    (a) specified in that paragraph; or

    (b) which would apply to the use of the full register under whichever of regulations 103, 105, 106 and 108 of the 2001 Regulations entitled that person to obtain that document,

shall apply to such use.

(5)   The registration officer shall supply a current copy of relevant information requested under sub-paragraph (1)(a) or (b) as soon as practicable after receipt of a request duly made.

(6)   The registration officer shall supply a final copy of the postal voters list kept under article 10(2)(a) as soon as practicable after 5pm on the eleventh day before the day of the poll, in response to a request that has been duly made under sub-paragraph (1).

(7)   As soon as practicable after 5pm on the sixth day before the day of the poll the registration officer shall

    (a) make a copy of the lists kept under articles 10 and 12(8) available for inspection at his office in accordance with sub-paragraphs (11) to (16); and

    (b) supply a final copy of the postal voters list or the list of proxies in response to every request that has been duly made under sub-paragraph (1).

(8)   The registration officer shall supply a final copy of the list of proxies kept under article 10(3), updated to include any additions to those lists made in consequence of any applications granted in accordance with paragraph 6 of this Schedule, as soon as practicable after 5pm on the day of the poll, to every person who received that list in accordance with sub-paragraph 7(b).

(9)   Any person who has obtained or is entitled to obtain a copy of information covered by sub-paragraph (1) may

    (a) supply a copy of the information to a processor for the purpose of processing the information contained in the information; or

    (b) procure that a processor processes and supplies to them any copy of the information which the processor has obtained under this paragraph,

for use in respect of the purposes for which that person is entitled to obtain such information.

(10) The provisions contained in paragraphs (2), (3) and (9) of regulation 92 of the 2001 Regulations shall be taken to apply to the supply and processing of information or lists supplied under this paragraph as they apply to the supply and processing of the full register.

(11) Any person is entitled to request that the registration officer make available for inspection a copy of any of the information specified in (a) and (b) of sub-paragraph (1).

(12) A request under sub-paragraph (11) shall be made in writing and shall specify

    (a) the information (or relevant parts of the information) requested;

    (b) whether the request is made only in respect of the current lists or whether it includes a request for the inspection of any final list;

    (c) who will be inspecting the information;

    (d) the date on which he wishes to inspect the information; and

(e) whether he would prefer to inspect the information in a printed or data form.

(13) The registration officer shall make a copy of the information available for inspection under supervision as soon as practicable after the date of receipt of a request that has been duly made.

(14) Where inspection takes place by providing a copy of the information on a computer screen or otherwise in data form, the registration officer shall ensure that the manner in, and equipment on, which that copy is provided do not permit any person consulting that copy to

(a) search it by electronic means by reference to the name of any person; or

(b) copy or transmit any part of that copy by electronic, or any other means.

(15) A person who inspects a copy of the information, whether a printed copy or in data form, may not

(a) make copies of any part of it; nor

(b) record any particulars in it,

otherwise than by means of hand-written notes.

(16) Subject to any direction by the Secretary of State under section 52(1) of the 1983 Act, any duty on a registration officer to supply a copy or make information available for inspection under this paragraph, imposes only a duty to provide that information in the form in which he holds it.

(17) For the purposes of this paragraph

(a) a "current copy" of records or lists is a copy of the records or lists as kept by the registration officer at 9am on the date it is supplied; and

(b) any period of days shall be calculated in accordance with paragraph 7.

(18)(a) The registration officer shall ensure that where he supplies or discloses information covered by sub-paragraph (1)(a) in accordance with this paragraph, he does not supply or disclose any record relating to a person specified in (b).

(b) The persons specified in this sub-paragraph are

(i) a person who has an anonymous entry; and

(ii) the proxy of a person who has an anonymous entry.

Conditions on the use, supply and inspection of absent voter records or lists

14 The provisions of regulations 94 and 96 of the 2001 Regulations shall apply to information covered by paragraph 13(1)(a) and (b) of this Schedule as they apply to restrictions on the supply, disclosure and use of the full register, except that permitted purposes for the purpose of paragraph 13(1)(a) and (b) means either

(a) research purposes within the meaning of that term in section 33 of the Data Protection Act 1998; or

(b) electoral purposes.

Marked register for polling stations

15 To indicate that an elector or his proxy is entitled to vote by post and is for that reason not entitled to vote in person, the letter "A" shall be placed against the entry for that elector in any copy of the register, or part of it, provided for a polling station.

Certificate of employment at an Assembly election

16 The certificate as to the employment of constables and persons employed by a returning officer on the date of the poll at an Assembly election (to enable such a constable or person to vote elsewhere than at his own polling station) shall be in form CB set out in English and Welsh in Schedule 10 and shall be signed, in the case of a constable, by an officer of a police force of or above the rank of inspector.

Notification by registration officer

17   Where a registration officer is required by this Schedule to notify any person, such notification shall be in writing and may be sent by post

    (a)   in the case of a person other than a service voter, to the address provided by that person for the purpose of such notification or of any record or, if there is no such address, to the last known place of abode of that person;

    (b)   in the case of a service voter, to any address provided by him for the purpose of such notification or of any record or to the address provided for the purpose by the appropriate government department (as defined by section 59(3B) of the 1983 Act) or, as the case may be, the British Council.

SCHEDULE 2

ABSENT VOTING (TRANSITIONAL PROVISIONS)

Article 15(3)

Contents

Requiring personal identifiers from existing absent voters

1(1) A registration officer must, by 7th February 2007, send a notice in writing to every person who has on 1st February 2007 an entry as an absent elector or postal proxy in his absent voting records kept in accordance with the National Assembly for Wales (Representation of the People) Order 2003.

(2) The notice must require the absent elector or postal proxy (as the case may be) to provide the registration officer within 42 days with a specimen of his signature and his date of birth ("the required personal identifiers") in accordance with this Schedule.

(3) The notice must be sent by the registration officer to the current or last known address of the absent elector or postal proxy (as the case may be).

(4) Where a notice is sent by post, the registration officer may use
   (a) a universal service provider; or
   (b) a commercial delivery firm,
and postage shall be prepaid on any such notice sent by post.

(5) Any notice must be accompanied by a reply envelope addressed to the registration officer and, in the case of any notice sent to an address within the United Kingdom, return postage shall be prepaid.

(6) Where a registration officer has been provided with the required personal identifiers by an applicant for an absent vote under the Representation of the People (England and Wales)(Amendment)(No 2) Regulations 2006 or the Absent Voting (Transitional Provisions)(England and Wales) Regulations 2006 before the date specified in the notice in accordance with paragraph 2(2)(d), he may use them for the purposes of Assembly elections and enter them in his records kept in accordance with article 12(13).

Required information to be provided to existing absent voters

2(1) Where a registration officer sends a notice pursuant to paragraph 1, he must also provide information
   (a) explaining how the required personal identifiers will be used and how the personal identifiers will assist in deterring misuse of the entitlement to vote;
   (b) explaining that, in the event of a failure or refusal to provide the required personal identifiers, the absent elector will lose his entitlement to vote by post or by proxy, and a postal proxy will cease to be entitled to vote by post as proxy;
   (c) explaining the circumstances in which a registration officer may dispense with the requirement to provide a signature; and
   (d) explaining that loss of the entitlement to vote by post or by proxy or as a postal proxy under this Order does not prevent him from making a fresh application under articles 8, 9 or 12 to be entitled to vote by post or by proxy or to act as a postal proxy.

(2) The notice must specify the following matters

(a) that the absent elector or postal proxy would cease to be entitled to vote by post or by proxy, or to act as a postal proxy in Assembly elections if he does not provide the required personal identifiers;

(b) whether the person has an entry in the absent voting records as voting by post, by proxy or as a postal proxy or in more than one capacity;

(c) as regards a postal proxy, the names and addresses of each absent elector for whom he is entitled to vote;

(d) in the case of an absent elector, the date (not less than 49 days from the sending of the initial notice) from which he will cease to be entitled to vote by post or by proxy in the event of his failure or refusal to provide the required personal identifiers; and

(e) in the case of a postal proxy, the date (not less than 49 days from the sending of the initial notice) from which he will cease to be entitled to act as a postal proxy in the event of his failure or refusal to provide the required personal identifiers.

Additional steps and determination by registration officer

3(1) The registration officer must, if the absent elector or postal proxy has not responded to the notice within 21 days from the date on which the notice was sent, send a second copy of the notice.

(2) The registration officer must, no later than the date specified in the notice sent to the absent elector or postal proxy in accordance with paragraph 2(2)(d) or (e), determine whether the absent elector or postal proxy has refused or failed to provide the required personal identifiers.

Removal from absent voting records

4(1) Where the registration officer determines that there has been a refusal or failure to provide the required personal identifiers, he shall forthwith remove the entry relating to the absent voter or the postal proxy (as the case may be) from his records and special lists kept under articles 10(2), (3) and 12(8).

(2) Paragraph 8(4), (6) and (7) of Schedule 1 shall apply upon the removal of an absent elector from the absent voting records as if the registration officer had refused an application by an elector to vote by post.

(3) The registration officer shall include in the written notice to be sent to the elector, to any person appointed as his proxy and to any postal proxy regarding his removal from the absent voting records, information

(a) explaining the effect of removal from the absent voting records;

(b) reminding the elector that he may make a fresh application under article 8, 9 or 11 to vote by post or proxy;

(c) reminding a person who was a postal proxy that he may make a fresh application under article 12 to act as postal proxy; and

(d) informing the elector or the proxy, where appropriate, of the location of the polling station allotted or likely to be allotted to him under rule 34 of Schedule 5.

Pending applications

5 Where a person has made an application under article 8(1), 9(1), or 12(4) of the National Assembly for Wales (Representation of the People) Order 2003 prior to 31st January 2007 that has not been determined on or before 31st January 2007, the registration officer must not grant the application unless the applicant has provided to the registration officer a specimen of their signature and their date of birth.

SCHEDULE 3

ISSUE AND RECEIPT OF POSTAL BALLOT PAPERS

Article 15(4)

Contents

Interpretation

1   For the purposes of this Schedule, unless the context requires otherwise
"agent" includes an election agent and a person appointed to attend in the election agent's place;
"ballot paper envelope" and "covering envelope" mean the envelopes referred to in paragraph 11;
"issue" includes the original and any subsequent issue;
"postal ballot box" means the ballot box referred to in paragraph 17(1)(b);

"postal voters' ballot box" means the ballot box referred to in paragraph 17(1)(a); "receptacle for ballot paper envelopes", and other references to specified receptacles, means the receptacles referred to in paragraph 17(5); and "spoilt postal ballot paper" means a ballot paper referred to in paragraph 14(1);

Issue of Postal Ballot Papers

Combination of polls

2   Where the polls at elections are taken together under article 16(1) or (2) the proceedings on the issue and receipt of postal ballot papers in respect of each election may, if the returning officers agree, be taken together.

Form of postal voting statement

3   The form of the postal voting statement sent with the postal ballot paper (prescribed in Rule 33 of Schedule 5) to a postal voter shall be
  (a) in form CC1 set out in English and Welsh in Schedule 10 at an Assembly election the poll at which is not taken together with another election under article 16(1) or (2);
  (b) in form CC2 set out in English and Welsh in Schedule 10 at an Assembly election where the proceedings on the issue and receipt of postal ballot papers are taken together under paragraph 2 with those proceedings at another election;
  (c) in form CC3 set out in English and Welsh in Schedule 10 at an Assembly election, the polls at which are taken together with the poll at another election under article 16(1) or (2) in any part of an Assembly constituency, but where the proceedings on the issue and receipt of postal ballot papers are not taken together under paragraph 2, for use in that part of the constituency in which polls at more than one election are taken together under article 16(1) or (2).

Regional elections

4   At a regional election the functions connected with the issue and receipt of postal ballot papers are to be exercised in relation to each Assembly constituency in an Assembly electoral region by the returning officer for such a constituency.

Persons entitled to be present at proceedings on issue of postal ballot papers.

5   Without prejudice to the provisions of section 6A, 6B, 6C, 6D or 6E of the 2000 Political Parties Act, no person may be present at the proceedings on the issue of postal ballot papers other than the constituency returning officer and his clerks.

Persons entitled to be present at proceedings on receipt of postal ballot papers

6(1) Without prejudice to the provisions of section 6A, 6B, 6C, 6D or 6E of the 2000 Political Parties Act, no person may be present at the proceedings on the receipt of postal ballot papers other than
  (a) the constituency returning officer and his clerks;
  (b) the regional returning officer in the case of a regional election;
  (c) a candidate;
  (d) an election agent or any person appointed by
    (i)   a candidate to attend in his election agent's place in the case of a constituency election;
    (ii) an individual candidate to attend in his election agent's place in the case of a regional election; or
    (iii) the election agent of a registered political party standing nominated or by the registered nominating officer of that party to attend in the place of that party's election agent in the case of a regional election; or

      (e) any agents appointed under sub-paragraph (2).

(2) Each
      (a) candidate in the case of a constituency election; and
      (b) individual candidate and election agent for a registered political party standing nominated, in the case of a regional election,

may appoint one or more agents up to the number as may be authorised by the constituency returning officer to appoint; provided, however, that the number authorised shall be the same in the case of each candidate or, as the case may be, election agent for a registered political party standing nominated.

(3) Notice in writing of the appointment stating the names and addresses of the persons appointed shall be given by the candidate or election agent to the constituency returning officer before the time fixed for the opening of the postal voters' ballot boxes.

(4) Where the postal ballot papers for more than one election are issued together under paragraph 2, the constituency returning officer to whom notice shall be given under sub-paragraphs (3), (5) and (6) is the returning officer who issues the postal ballot papers.

(5) If an agent dies or becomes incapable of acting, the candidate or election agent for a registered political party, as the case may be, may appoint another agent in his place and shall forthwith give to the constituency returning officer notice in writing of the name and address of the agent appointed.

(6) Agents may be appointed and notice of appointment given to the constituency returning officer by the election agent for a candidate who is otherwise authorised to make an appointment under sub-paragraph (2).

(7) In this Schedule references to agents shall be taken as references to agents whose appointments have been duly made and notified and, in the case of agents appointed under sub-paragraph (2), who are within the number authorised by the constituency returning officer.

(8) Any of the following persons, namely
      (a) a candidate in a constituency election;
      (b) an individual candidate in a regional election; or
      (c) the election agent of a registered political party standing nominated,

may himself do any act or thing which any agent of his or of the registered political party on whose list he is a candidate, if appointed, would have been authorised to do, or may assist his agent in doing any such act or thing.

(9) Where in this Schedule any act or thing is required or authorised to be done in the presence of the candidates or their agents, the nonattendance of any such person at the time and place appointed for the purpose shall not, if the act or thing is otherwise duly done, invalidate the act or thing done.

Notification of requirement of secrecy

7   The constituency returning officer shall make such arrangements as he thinks fit to ensure that every person attending the proceedings in connection with the issue or receipt of postal ballot papers has been given a copy in writing of the provisions of article 35(4) and (6).

Time when postal ballot papers are to be issued

8(1)   In the case of a person shown in the record kept under
      (a) article 8(3); or
      (b) article 12(6),

no postal ballot paper and postal voting statement shall be issued until after 5 pm on the eleventh day before the date of the poll (computed in accordance with paragraph 7(6) of Schedule 1).

(2)   In the case of any other person, the postal ballot paper and postal voting statement shall be issued by the constituency returning officer as soon as practicable after the registration officer has granted the application to vote by post.

Procedure on issue of postal ballot paper

9(1)   The number of the elector as stated in the register shall be marked on the corresponding number list, next to the number and unique identifying mark of the ballot paper issued to that elector.

(2)   Where an elector is entitled to give two votes, the constituency ballot paper and the regional ballot paper shall have the same number.

(3)   A mark shall be placed in the postal voters list or the proxy postal voters list against the number of the elector to denote that a ballot paper has been issued to the elector or his proxy but without showing the particular ballot paper issued.

(4)   The number of a postal ballot paper shall be marked on the postal voting statement sent with that paper.

(5)   Where postal ballot papers for more than one election are issued together
        (a)   one mark shall be placed in the postal voters list or the proxy postal voters list under sub-paragraph (3) to denote that ballot papers have been issued in respect of all of those elections; except that, where ballot papers are not so issued a different mark shall be placed in the postal voters list or proxy postal voters list to identify the election in respect of which the ballot paper was issued; and
        (b)   the number of each ballot paper shall be marked on the postal voting statement under sub-paragraph (4).

(6)   Where the poll at an Assembly election is taken with the poll at another election under article 16(1) or (2) but the proceedings on the issue and receipt of postal ballot papers are not taken together under paragraph 2, the colour of the postal ballot paper (or colours of the postal ballot papers) shall also be marked on the postal voting statement sent with that paper.

(7)   Subject to sub-paragraph (8), the address to which the postal ballot paper, postal voting statement and the envelopes referred to in paragraph 11 are to be sent is
        (a)   in the case of an elector, the address shown in the postal voters list;
        (b)   in the case of a proxy, the address shown in the proxy postal voters list.

(8)   Where a person has an anonymous entry in the register, the items specified in sub-paragraph (7) must be sent (as the case may be) to the address to which postal ballot papers should be sent
        (a)   as shown in the record kept under article 8(3) or 12(6); or
        (b)   as given in pursuance of an application made under article 9(1) or 12(4)(b).

Refusal to issue postal ballot papers

10   Where a constituency returning officer is satisfied that two or more entries in either the postal voters list, or the proxy postal voters list or in each of those lists relate to the same elector he shall not issue more than one ballot paper in respect of the same elector for the same Assembly election.

Envelopes

11(1) The envelope which the constituency returning officer is required by rule 33 of Schedule 5 to send to a postal voter for the return of the postal ballot paper or, as the case may be, ballot papers and the postal voting statement (referred to as a "covering envelope") shall be marked with the letter "B".

(2) In addition to the documents referred to in sub-paragraph (1), the constituency returning officer shall send to a postal voter a smaller envelope (referred to as a "ballot paper envelope") which shall be marked with
    (a) the letter "A";
    (b) the words
        (i) "Ballot paper envelope";
        (ii) "Amlen papur pleidleisio"; and
    (c) the number of the ballot paper or, as the case may be, ballot papers.

(3) Where the poll at an Assembly election is taken together with the poll at another election under article 16(1) or (2) but the proceedings on the issue and receipt of postal ballot papers are not to be taken together under paragraph 2
    (a) the envelope referred to in sub-paragraph (1) shall also be marked
        (i) "Covering envelope for the *insert colour of ballot paper(s)* coloured ballot paper(s)";
        (ii) "Prif amlen ar gyfer y papur(au) pleidleisio lliw *nodwch liw'r papur(au) pleidleisio*"; and
    (b) on the envelope referred to in sub-paragraph (2), after the words
        (i) "Ballot paper envelope" there shall be added the words "for the *insert colour of ballot paper(s)* coloured ballot paper(s)"; and
        (ii) "Amlen papur pleidleisio" there shall be added "ar gyfer y papur(au) pleidleisio lliw *nodwch liw'r papur(au) pleidleisio*".

Sealing up of completed corresponding number lists and security of special lists

12(1) As soon as practicable after the issue of each batch of postal ballot papers, the constituency returning officer shall make up into a packet the completed corresponding number lists of those ballot papers which have been issued and shall seal such a packet.

(2) Until the time referred to in paragraph 20(11), the returning officer shall take all proper precautions for the security of the marked copy of the postal voters list and the proxy postal voters list.

Delivery of postal ballot papers

13(1) For the purposes of delivering postal ballot papers, the constituency returning officer may use
    (a) a universal service provider;
    (b) a commercial delivery firm; or
    (c) persons appointed under rule 35(1) of Schedule 5.

(2) Where the services of a universal service provider or commercial delivery firm are to be used, envelopes addressed to postal voters shall be counted and delivered by the constituency returning officer with such form of receipt to be endorsed by that provider or firm as may be arranged.

(3) Postage shall be prepaid on envelopes addressed to the postal voters (except where sub-paragraph (1)(c) applies).

(4) Return postage shall be prepaid on all covering envelopes where the address provided by the postal voter for the receipt of the postal ballot paper is within the United Kingdom.

Spoilt postal ballot paper

14(1) If a postal voter has inadvertently dealt with his ballot paper or postal voting statement in such a manner that it cannot be conveniently used as a ballot paper (referred to as "a spoilt ballot paper") or, as the case may be, a postal voting statement (referred to as "a spoilt postal voting statement") he may return (either by hand or by post) to the constituency returning officer the spoilt ballot paper or, as the case may be, the spoilt postal voting statement.

(2) Where the postal voter exercises the entitlement conferred by sub-paragraph (1), he shall also return

    (a) the postal ballot paper or, as the case may be, the postal voting statement, whether spoilt or not;

    (b) where postal ballot papers for more than one election have been issued together (including under paragraph 2 of this Schedule), all other ballot papers so issued, whether spoilt or not; and

    (c) the envelopes supplied for the return of the documents mentioned in sub-paragraph (1) and paragraphs (a) and (b) of this sub-paragraph.

(3) Subject to sub-paragraph (4) on receipt of the documents referred to in sub-paragraphs (1) and, where applicable, (2) the constituency returning officer shall issue another postal ballot paper or, as the case may be, ballot papers except where those documents are received after 5 pm on the day of the poll.

(4) Where the constituency returning officer receives the documents referred to in sub-paragraph (1) and, where applicable sub-paragraph (2), after 5pm on the day before the day of the poll, he shall only issue another postal ballot paper or, as the case may be, ballot papers if the postal voter returned the documents by hand.

(5) Paragraphs 9 (except sub-paragraph(3))to 12 and, subject to sub-paragraph (8), 13 shall apply to the issue of a replacement postal ballot paper under sub-paragraph (3).

(6) Any postal ballot paper or postal voting statement, whether spoilt or not, returned in accordance with paragraph (1) or (2) shall be immediately cancelled.

(7) The constituency returning officer, as soon as practicable after cancelling those documents, shall make up those documents in a separate packet and shall seal the packet; and if on any subsequent occasion documents are cancelled as mentioned above, the sealed packet shall be opened and the additional cancelled documents included in it and the packet shall then be again made up and sealed.

(8) Where a postal voter applies in person

    (a) by 5pm on the day before the day of the poll, the constituency returning officer may hand a replacement postal ballot paper to him; or

    (b) after 5pm on the day before the day of the poll, the constituency returning officer may only hand a replacement postal ballot paper to him,

  instead of delivering it in accordance with paragraph 13.

(9) The constituency returning officer shall enter in a list kept for the purpose ("the list of spoilt postal ballot papers")

    (a) the name and number of the elector as stated in the register (or, in the case of an elector who has an anonymous entry, his electoral number alone);

    (b) the number of the postal ballot paper (or papers) issued under this paragraph; and

    (c) where the postal voter whose ballot paper is spoilt is a proxy, his name and address.

Lost postal ballot papers

15(1) Where a postal voter claims either to have lost or not to have received

    (a) his postal ballot paper; or

    (b) the postal voting statement; or

    (c) one or more of the envelopes supplied for their return,

by the fourth day before the day of the poll, he may apply (whether or not in person) to the constituency returning officer for a replacement ballot paper.

(2) Such an application shall include evidence of the voter's identity.

(3) Where a postal voter exercises the entitlement conferred by sub-paragraph (1), he shall return

    (a) the documents referred to in sub-paragraph (1)(a), (b) and (c); and

    (b) where postal ballot papers for more than one election have been issued together (including under paragraph 2 of this Schedule), all other ballot papers so issued,

which he has received and which have not been lost.

(4) Any postal ballot paper or postal voting statement returned in accordance with sub-paragraph (3) shall be immediately cancelled.

(5) The constituency returning officer, as soon as practicable after cancelling those documents, shall make up those documents in a separate packet and shall seal the packet; and if on any subsequent occasion documents are cancelled as mentioned above, the sealed packet shall be opened and the additional cancelled documents included in it and the packet shall be again made up and sealed.

(6) Subject to sub-paragraph (7) where the application is received by the constituency returning officer before 5 pm on the day of the poll and the constituency returning officer

    (a) is satisfied as to the voter's identity; and

    (b) has no reason to doubt that the postal voter has lost or did not receive the original postal ballot paper or the postal voting statement or one or more of the envelopes provided for their return,

he shall issue another postal ballot paper or, as the case may be, postal ballot papers.

(7) Where the application is received by the constituency returning officer after 5pm on the day before the day of the poll, he shall only issue another postal ballot paper or, as the case may be, other ballot papers if the postal voter applied in person.

(8) The constituency returning officer shall enter in a list kept for the purpose ("the list of lost postal ballot papers")

    (a) the name and number of the elector as stated in the register (or, in the case of an elector who has an anonymous entry, his electoral number alone);

    (b) the number of the postal ballot paper which has been lost or not received and of its replacement issued under this paragraph; and

    (c) where the postal voter is a proxy, his name and address.

(9) Paragraphs 9 (except sub-paragraph (3)) to 12, and subject to sub-paragraph (10), 13 of this Schedule shall apply to the issue of a replacement postal ballot papers under sub-paragraph (6).

(10) Where the postal voter applies in person

    (a) by 5pm on the day before the day of the poll, the constituency returning officer may hand a replacement paper to him; or

    (b) after 5pm on the day before the day of the poll, the constituency returning officer may only hand a replacement postal ballot paper to him,

instead of delivering it in accordance with paragraph 13 of this Schedule.

(11) Where the constituency returning officer issues another postal ballot paper, or as the

case may be, postal ballot papers under sub-paragraph (6), the ballot paper which has been lost or not received shall be cancelled and of no effect.

Receipt of Postal Ballot Papers

Notice of opening of postal ballot paper envelopes

16(1) The constituency returning officer shall give not less than 48 hours' notice in writing of each occasion on which a postal voters' ballot box and the envelopes contained in it are to be opened to

    (a) each candidate in a constituency election; and

    (b) in the case of an election for an Assembly electoral region, each individual candidate and the election agent for each registered party standing nominated.

  (2) Such a notice shall specify

    (a) the time and place at which such an opening is to take place; and

    (b) the number of agents a candidate or registered political party may appoint under paragraph 6(2) to attend each opening.

Postal ballot boxes and receptacles

17(1) The constituency returning officer shall provide a separate ballot box for the reception of

    (a) the covering envelopes when returned by the postal voters ("postal voters' ballot box"); and

    (b) postal ballot papers ("postal ballot box").

  (2) Each such ballot box shall be marked "postal voters' ballot box" or "postal ballot box", as the case may be, and with the name of the constituency or electoral region for which the election is, or elections are, held.

  (3) The postal ballot box shall be shown to the agents present on the occasion of opening the first postal voters' ballot box as being empty.

  (4) The constituency returning officer shall then apply his seal in such manner as to prevent its being opened without breaking the seal; any of the agents present who wish to add their seals may then do likewise.

  (5) The constituency returning officer shall provide the following receptacles

    (a) the receptacle for rejected votes;

    (b) the receptacle for postal voting statements;

    (c) the receptacle for ballot paper envelopes;

    (d) the receptacle for rejected ballot paper envelopes;

    (e) the receptacle for rejected votes (verification procedure); and

    (f) the receptacle for postal voting statements (verification procedure).

  (6) The constituency returning officer shall take proper precautions for the safe custody of every ballot box and receptacle referred to in this paragraph.

Receipt of covering envelope

18(1) The constituency returning officer shall, immediately on receipt (whether by hand or by post) of a covering envelope (or an envelope which is stated to include a postal vote) before the close of the poll, place it unopened in a postal voters' ballot box.

  (2) Where an envelope, other than a covering envelope issued by the constituency returning officer

    (a) has been opened; and

    (b) contains a ballot paper envelope, postal voting statement or ballot paper,

the first-mentioned envelope together with its contents, shall be placed in a postal voters' ballot box.

Opening of postal voters' ballot box

19(1) Each postal voters' ballot box shall be opened by the constituency returning officer in the presence of any agents, if in attendance.

(2) So long as the constituency returning officer ensures that there is at least one sealed postal voters' ballot box for the reception of covering envelopes up to the time of the close of the poll, the other postal voters' ballot boxes may previously be opened by him.

(3) The last postal voters' ballot box and the postal ballot box shall be opened at the counting of the votes under rule 55 of Schedule 5.

Opening of covering envelopes

20(1) When a postal voters' ballot box is opened, the constituency returning officer shall count and record the number of covering envelopes (including any envelope which is stated to include a postal vote and any envelope described in paragraph 18).

(2) He shall set aside for personal identifier verification a percentage, not less than 20%, of the envelopes recorded on that occasion.

(3) He shall open separately each covering envelope (including an envelope described in paragraph 18(2)).

(4) The procedure in paragraph 22 or 23 applies where a covering envelope (including an envelope to which paragraph 18 applies) contains both

    (a) a postal voting statement; and

    (b) a ballot paper envelope, or if there is no ballot paper envelope, a ballot paper (or ballot papers).

(5) Where the covering envelope does not contain the postal voting statement separately, the constituency returning officer shall open the ballot paper envelope to ascertain whether the postal voting statement is inside.

(6) Where a covering envelope does not contain both

    (a) a postal voting statement (whether separately or not); and

    (b) a ballot paper envelope or, if there is no ballot paper envelope, a ballot paper, (or ballot papers),

the constituency returning officer shall mark the covering envelope "provisionally rejected", attach its contents (if any) and place it in the receptacle for rejected votes.

(7) Where

    (a) an envelope contains the postal voting statement of an elector with an anonymous entry; and

    (b) sub-paragraph (6) does not apply,

the constituency returning officer shall set aside that envelope and its contents for personal identifier verification in accordance with paragraph 23.

(8) In carrying out the procedures in this paragraph and paragraphs 22 to 28 the returning officer

    (a) shall keep the ballot papers face downwards and shall take all proper precautions for preventing any person from seeing the votes made on the ballot papers; and

    (b) shall not be permitted to view the corresponding number list used at the issue of postal ballot papers.

(9) Where an envelope opened in accordance with sub-paragraph (3) contains a postal voting statement, the constituency returning officer shall place a mark in the marked copy of the postal voters list or proxy postal voters list in a place corresponding to the

number of the elector to denote that a postal vote has been returned.

(10) A mark made under sub-paragraph (9) shall be distinguishable from and shall not obscure the mark made under paragraph 9 of this schedule.

(11) As soon as practicable after the last covering envelope has been opened, the constituency returning officer shall make up into a packet the copies of the marked postal voters list and proxy postal voters list that have been marked in accordance with sub-paragraph (9) and shall seal such a packet.

Confirming receipt of postal voting statements

21(1) An elector or a proxy voter who is shown in the postal voters list or proxy postal voters list may make a request, at any time between the first issue of postal ballots under paragraph 9 of this Schedule and the close of poll, that the constituency returning officer confirm

    (a) whether a mark is shown in the marked copy of the postal voters list or proxy postal voters list in a place corresponding to the number of the elector to denote that a postal vote has been returned; and

    (b) whether the number of the ballot paper issued to the elector or his proxy has been recorded on either of the lists of provisionally rejected votes kept by the constituency returning officer under paragraph 27.

(2) A request under sub-paragraph (1) shall

    (a) be made by any method specified by the returning officer; and

    (b) include any evidence of the voter's identity requested by the constituency returning officer.

(3) Where a request is received in accordance with sub-paragraph (2) the constituency returning officer shall satisfy himself that the request has been made by the elector or his proxy and where he is so satisfied provide confirmation of the matters under sub-paragraph (1).

Procedure in relation to postal voting statements

22(1) This paragraph applies to any postal voting statement contained in an envelope that has not been set aside for personal identifier verification in accordance with paragraph 20(2) or (7).

(2) The constituency returning officer must satisfy himself that the postal voting statement is duly completed.

(3) Where the constituency returning officer is not so satisfied, he shall mark the statement "rejected", attach to it the ballot paper envelope, or if there is no such envelope, the ballot paper (or ballot papers), and, subject to sub-paragraph (4), place it in the receptacle for rejected votes.

(4) The constituency returning officer shall then examine the number (or numbers) on the postal voting statement against the number (or numbers) on the ballot paper envelope and, where they are the same, he shall place the statement and the ballot paper envelope respectively in the receptacle for postal voting statements and the receptacle for ballot paper envelopes.

(5) Where

    (a) the number (or numbers) on a valid postal voting statement is not the same as the number (or numbers) on the ballot paper envelope; or

    (b) the envelope has no number on it (or only one number when the postal voting statement has more than one),

the constituency returning officer shall open the envelope.

(6) Sub-paragraph (7) applies where
- (a) there is a valid postal voting statement but no ballot paper envelope; or
- (b) the ballot paper envelope has been opened under paragraph 20(5) or sub-paragraph (7).

(7) In the circumstances described in sub-paragraph (6), the constituency returning officer shall place
- (a) in the postal ballot box any ballot paper the number on which is the same as the number (or one of the numbers) on the valid postal voting statement;
- (b) in the receptacle for rejected votes any other ballot paper, with the postal voting statement attached and marked "provisionally rejected";
- (c) in the receptacle for rejected votes any valid postal voting statement marked "provisionally rejected" where
  - (i) there is no ballot paper; or
  - (ii) in the case of a statement on which the number of more than one ballot paper appears, there is not a sufficient number of ballot papers and, in such a case, shall mark the statement to indicate which ballot paper is missing;
- (d) in the receptacle for postal voting statements, any valid statement not disposed of under sub-paragraph (b) or (c).

Procedure in relation to postal voting statements: personal identifier verification

23(1) This paragraph applies to any postal voting statement contained in an envelope that is set aside for personal identifier verification in accordance with paragraph 20(2)or (7).

(2) The constituency returning officer must satisfy himself that the postal voting statement is duly completed and as part of that process must compare the date of birth and the signature on the postal voting statement against the date of birth and signature contained in the personal identifier record relating to the person to whom the postal ballot paper was addressed.

(3) Where the constituency returning officer is not so satisfied, he shall mark the statement "rejected", attach to it the ballot paper envelope, or if there is no such envelope, the ballot paper, and subject to sub-paragraph (4), place it in the receptacle for rejected votes (verification procedure).

(4) Before placing any postal voting statement in the receptacle for rejected votes (verification procedure), the constituency returning officer must show it to the agents and, must permit them to view the entries in the personal identifiers record which relate to the person to whom the postal voting statement was addressed, and if any of them object to his decision, he shall add the words "rejection objected to".

(5) The constituency returning officer shall then examine the number (or numbers) on the postal voting statement against the number (or numbers) on the ballot paper envelope and, where they are the same, he shall place the statement and the ballot paper envelope respectively in the receptacle for postal voting statements (verification procedure) and the receptacle for ballot paper envelopes.

(6) Where
- (a) the number on a valid postal voting statement is not the same as the number on the ballot paper envelope; or
- (b) the envelope has no number on it (or only one number when the postal voting statement has more than one),
the constituency returning officer shall open the envelope.

(7) Sub-paragraph (8) applies where
- (a) there is a valid postal voting statement but no ballot paper envelope; or

(b) the ballot paper envelope has been opened under paragraph 20(5) or sub-paragraph (6).

(8)   In the circumstances described in sub-paragraph (7), the constituency returning officer shall place

(a)   in the postal ballot box any ballot paper the number on which is the same as the number on the valid postal voting statement;

(b)   in the receptacle for rejected votes (verification procedure), any other ballot paper, with the postal voting statement attached and marked "provisionally rejected";

(c)   in the receptacle for rejected votes (verification procedure) any valid postal voting statement marked "provisionally rejected" where

(i)   there is no ballot paper; or

(ii)   in the case of a statement on which the number of more than one ballot paper appears, there is not a sufficient number of ballot papers and, in such a case, shall mark the statement to indicate which ballot paper is missing; and

(d)   in the receptacle for postal voting statements (verification procedure), any valid statement not disposed of under sub-paragraph (b) or (c).

Postal voting statements: additional personal identifier verification

24(1)   The constituency returning officer may on any occasion at which a postal voters' ballot box is opened in accordance with paragraph 19 undertake verification of the personal identifiers on any postal voting statement that has on a prior occasion been placed in the receptacle for postal voting statements.

(2)   Where the returning officer undertakes additional verification of personal identifiers, he must

(a)   remove as many postal voting statements from the receptacle for postal voting statements as he wishes to subject to additional verification; and

(b)   compare the date of birth and the signature on each such postal voting statement against the date of birth and signature contained in the personal identifiers record relating to the person to whom the postal ballot paper was addressed.

(3)   Where the constituency returning officer is no longer satisfied that the postal voting statement has been duly completed he must mark the statement "rejected", and before placing the postal voting statement in the receptacle for rejected votes (verification procedure) he must

(a)   show it to the agents and must permit them to view the entries in the personal identifiers record which relate to the person to whom the postal ballot paper was addressed, and if any of them object to his decision, he must add the words "rejection objected to";

(b)   open any postal ballot box and retrieve the ballot paper corresponding to the ballot paper on the postal voting statement;

(c)   show the ballot paper number on the retrieved ballot paper to the agents; and

(d)   attach the ballot paper to the postal voting statement.

(4)   Following the removal of a postal ballot paper from a postal ballot box the constituency returning officer must re-seal the postal ballot box in the presence of the agents.

Opening of ballot paper envelopes

25(1)   The constituency returning officer shall open separately each ballot paper envelope placed in the receptacle for ballot paper envelopes.

(2) He shall place

    (a) in the postal ballot box, any ballot paper the number on which is the same as the number (or one of the numbers) on the ballot paper envelope;

    (b) in the receptacle for rejected votes, any other ballot paper which shall be marked "provisionally rejected" and to which shall be attached the ballot paper envelope; and

    (c) in the receptacle for rejected ballot paper envelopes, any ballot paper envelope which shall be marked "provisionally rejected" because it does not contain either a ballot paper or, where more than one number appears on the ballot paper envelope, a sufficient number of ballot papers (and indicating, in such a case, the missing ballot paper).

Retrieval of cancelled postal ballot papers

26(1) Where it appears to the constituency returning officer that a cancelled postal ballot paper has been placed

    (a) in a postal voters' ballot box; or

    (b) in the receptacle for ballot paper envelopes; or

    (c) a postal ballot box,

he shall proceed as follows.

(2) He shall, on at least one occasion on which a postal voters ballot box is opened in accordance with paragraph 19 of this Schedule, also open any postal ballot box and the receptacle for ballot paper envelopes and

    (a) retrieve the cancelled ballot paper;

    (b) show the ballot paper number on the cancelled ballot paper to the agents;

    (c) retrieve the postal voting statement that relates to a cancelled ballot paper from the receptacle for postal voting statements;

    (d) attach any cancelled postal ballot paper to the postal voting statement to which it relates;

    (e) place the cancelled documents in a separate packet and deal with that packet in the manner provided for by paragraph 14(7) of this Schedule; and

    (f) unless the postal ballot box has been opened for the purposes of counting the votes under rule 55 of Schedule 5 re-seal the postal ballot box in the presence of the agents.

Lists of rejected postal ballot papers

27(1) In respect of any Assembly election, the constituency returning officer shall keep two separate lists of rejected postal ballot papers.

(2) In the first list, he shall record the ballot paper number of any postal ballot paper for which no valid postal voting statement was received with it.

(3) In the second list, he shall record the ballot paper number of any postal ballot paper which is entered on a valid postal voting statement where that ballot paper is not received with the postal voting statement.

Checking of lists kept under paragraph 27

28(1) Where the constituency returning officer receives a valid postal voting statement without the postal ballot paper (or papers or, as the case may be, all of the papers) to which it relates, he may, at any time prior to the close of the poll, check the list referred to in paragraph 27(2) to see whether the number (or numbers) of a postal ballot paper to which the statement relates is entered in that list.

(2) Where the constituency returning officer receives a postal ballot paper without the

postal voting statement to which it relates, he may, at any time prior to the close of the poll, check the list referred to in paragraph 27(3) to see whether the number of that ballot paper is entered in that list.

(3) The constituency returning officer shall conduct the checks required by sub-paragraphs (1) and (2) as soon as practicable after the receipt of packets from every polling station in the constituency or, as the case may be, electoral area under rule 53 of Schedule 5.

(4) Where the ballot paper number in the list matches that number on a valid postal voting statement or, as the case may be, the postal ballot paper, the constituency returning officer shall retrieve that statement or paper.

(5) The constituency returning officer shall then take the appropriate steps under this Schedule as though any document earlier marked "provisionally rejected" had not been so marked and shall amend the document accordingly.

Sealing of receptacles

29(1) As soon as practicable after the completion of the procedure under paragraph 28(3) and (4), the constituency returning officer shall make up into separate packets the contents of
  (a) the receptacle of rejected votes;
  (b) the receptacle of postal voting statements;
  (c) the receptacle of rejected ballot paper envelopes;
  (d) the lists of spoilt and lost postal ballot papers; and
  (e) the receptacle of rejected votes (verification procedure); and
  (f) the receptacle of postal voting statements (verification procedure),
  and shall seal up such packets.

(2) Any document in those packets marked "provisionally rejected" shall be deemed to be marked "rejected".

Abandoned poll

30(1) Where a poll is abandoned or countermanded after postal ballot papers have been issued, by reason of the death of a candidate, the constituency returning officer
  (a) shall not take any step or further step to open covering envelopes or deal with the contents in accordance with the provisions of this Schedule; and
  (b) shall, notwithstanding paragraphs 20 to 26, treat all unopened covering envelopes and the contents of those that have been opened as if they were counted ballot papers.

(2) Sub-paragraph (1) shall not apply where postal ballot papers for more than one election have been issued together under paragraph 2.

Forwarding of documents

31(1) The constituency returning officer shall forward to the relevant registration officer at the same time as he forwards the documents mentioned in rule 67 of Schedule 5
  (a) any packets referred to in paragraphs 12, 14(7), 15(5), 20(11) and 29, subject to paragraph 30, endorsing on each packet a description of its contents, the date of the election to which it relates and the name of the constituency or electoral area for which the election (or elections) was (or were) held; and
  (b) a completed statement in the form CD "Statement as to postal ballot papers" set out in English and Welsh in Schedule 10, of the number of postal ballot papers issued.

(2) Where

(a) any covering envelopes are received by the constituency returning officer after the close of the poll (apart from those delivered in accordance with rule 55(7) of Schedule 5);

(b) any envelopes addressed to postal voters are returned as undelivered too late to be readdressed; or

(c) any spoilt postal ballot papers are returned too late to enable other postal ballot papers to be issued,

the constituency returning officer shall put them unopened in a separate packet, seal up such packet and endorse and forward it at a subsequent date in the manner described in sub-paragraph (1).

(3) Rules 68 and 69 of Schedule 5 shall apply to any packet or document forwarded under this paragraph.

(4) A copy of the statement referred to in sub-paragraph (1)(b) shall be provided by the constituency returning officer to the Commission in the period which starts 10 days after the day of the poll and ends 15 days after that day.

SCHEDULE 4
COMBINATION OF POLLS

Article 16(7)

Contents
PART 1
GENERAL

PART 2
MODIFICATIONS TO SCHEDULE 5 TO APPLY WHERE THE POLL AT AN ASSEMBLY ELECTION IS TAKEN TOGETHER WITH A POLL AT A LOCAL GOVERNMENT ELECTION UNDER ARTICLE 16(1) OR (2)

PART 3
MODIFICATIONS TO ELECTION RULES TO APPLY WHERE THE POLL AT AN ELECTION OF COUNTY OR COUNTY BOROUGH COUNCILLORS IS TAKEN TOGETHER WITH A POLL AT AN ASSEMBLY ELECTION UNDER ARTICLE 16(1) OR (2)

PART 4

MODIFICATIONS TO ELECTION RULES TO APPLY WHERE THE POLL AT AN ELECTION OF COMMUNITY COUNCILLORS IS TAKEN TOGETHER WITH THE POLL AT AN ASSEMBLY ELECTION UNDER ARTICLE 16(1) OR (2)

made by the companion of a voter with disabilities)

Part 1
General

Returning officers and polling stations

1(1) Where the polls at an Assembly general election and an ordinary local government election are taken together under article 16(1)

(a) those functions of the returning officer at the local government election which are specified in paragraph 2 shall be discharged by the constituency returning officer for an Assembly constituency for such part of the local government area as is situated in the constituency; and

(b) only polling stations used for the Assembly general election shall be used for the local government election.

(2) Subject to sub-paragraph (4) where the polls at an Assembly and a local government election for related areas (within the meaning of article 16(3)) are taken together under article 16(2)

(a) the returning officers for those elections shall decide which returning officer shall discharge in the area in which the polls are combined ("the combined area") those functions of the other which are specified in paragraph 2; and

(b) the only polling stations which shall be used in the combined area at such elections are the polling stations used at the election for which the returning officer who discharges the functions referred to in paragraph (a) acts as returning officer.

(3) Where by virtue of sub-paragraph (2)(a) functions in respect of another election fall to be discharged by a regional returning officer, he in turn shall delegate the discharge of those functions to the constituency returning officer for an Assembly constituency that is wholly or partly situated in the combined area in relation to such part of the combined area as is situated in the Assembly constituency; and where functions are so delegated subsequent references in this Part to the returning officer who discharges the functions specified in paragraph 2 are to be treated as references to such a constituency returning officer.

(4) Where the polls at an Assembly general election and a local government election for related areas are taken together under article 16(2), sub-paragraphs (1)(a) and (b) shall apply.

Functions at combined polls

2(1) The functions referred to in paragraph 1 are the functions conferred

(a) in the case of an Assembly election, by Schedule 5 and which are specified in sub-paragraph (2);

(b) in the case of a local government election which is not a mayoral election, by those of the rules made under section 36 of the 1983 Act which correspond to the provisions specified in sub-paragraph (2); and

(c) in the case of a local government election which is a mayoral election, by those rules made under section 44 of the Local Government Act 2000 which correspond to the provisions specified in sub-paragraph (2),

and where the proceedings on the issue and receipt of postal ballot papers at two or more elections are taken together under paragraph 2 of Schedule 3, the functions conferred by that Schedule and by Part 5 of the 2001 Regulations.

(2) The functions referred to in sub-paragraph (1) are those functions in Schedule 5

conferred or by

    (a) rule 27 (corresponding number list);

    (b) rule 32(2) and (3) (notice of situation of polling stations etc);

    (c) rule 33 (postal ballot papers) where the proceedings on the issue and receipt of postal ballot papers at two or more elections are taken together under paragraph 2 of Schedule 3 and rule 55 (the count) of Schedule 5;

    (d) rule 34 (provision of polling stations);

    (e) rule 35(1) and (3) (appointment of presiding officers and clerks) to the extent that the paragraph concerns the appointment of presiding officers and clerks to assist them;

    (f) rule 37 (equipment of polling stations);

    (g) rule 39(a) (notification of requirement of secrecy at polling station);

    (h) rule 40 (return of postal ballot papers) where the proceedings on the issue and receipt of postal ballot papers at two or more elections are taken together under paragraph 2 of Schedule 3;

    (i) rule 41(5) (signature of certificate as to employment);

    (j) rule 42(2)(b) (authorisation to order removal from polling station); and

    (k) paragraphs (1)(as substituted by paragraph 20 of this Schedule) and paragraph (8) of rule 55 (the count).

Modification of provisions about expenses in this Order and the 1983 Act

3(1)   Where those functions of a returning officer at an election which are specified in paragraph 2 are discharged by the returning officer at another election under paragraph 1, references to the returning officer or his charges or expenditure

    (a) in article 23(1) to (4), (7), (9) and (10) (payments by and to returning officer);

    (b) in article 24 (detailed assessment of returning officer's account); and

    (c) in section 36(4) and (5A) of the 1983 Act (expenses at local elections),

shall, to the extent that such functions are so discharged, be construed as references to the returning officer who discharges those functions and his charges or expenditure in respect of those functions.

  (2)   The reference in section 36(6) of the 1983 Act to the returning officer or person acting as returning officer requesting an advance in respect of his expenses shall, to the extent that those expenses relate to the functions specified in paragraph 2, include a reference to the returning officer who under paragraph 1 discharges those functions at the local government election.

  (3)   In relation to elections the polls at which are taken together under article 16(1) or (2), the Assembly may under article 23(1) include special provision for services properly rendered, or expenses properly incurred, in respect of the discharge of functions specified in paragraph 2, and in respect of the remuneration of presiding officers and clerks, by the returning officer who discharges those functions by virtue of paragraph 1.

  (4)   In relation to elections the polls at which are taken together under article 16(1) or (2), a county or county borough council may, in fixing a scale under

    (a) section 36(4) of the 1983 Act (fixing a scale at an election to the council etc); or

    (b) section 36(5A) of that Act (fixing a scale at an election for a community within the area of the council etc),

include special provision for expenses incurred in respect of the discharge of functions specified in paragraph 2, and in respect of the remuneration of presiding officers and clerks, by the returning officer who discharges those functions by virtue of paragraph 1.

Part 2
Modifications to Schedule 5 to Apply Where the Poll
at an Assembly Election is Taken Together with a Poll at
a Local Government Election Under Article 16(1) or (2)

Modifications to Schedule 5: general provision

4   Where the poll at an Assembly election is taken with the poll at a local government election under article 16(1) or (2), Schedule 5 shall have effect subject to the modifications set out in the remaining paragraphs of this Part.

Rule 28 of Schedule 5 (colour of ballot papers)

5   At the end of rule 28 of Schedule 5 add
  "And the ballot paper to be used at an Assembly election shall be of a different colour from that of any ballot paper to be used at a local government election the poll for which is taken together with the poll for the Assembly election.".

Rule 32 of Schedule 5 (notice of poll)

6   At the end of rule 32 of Schedule 5 add
  "(5) Where the poll at an Assembly election is taken together with a poll at a local government election the notice published under paragraph (2) or (3) shall
    (a)   state that the poll at the Assembly election is to be taken together with the poll at a local government election;
    (b)   specify the relevant local authority and, in the case of a local government election to fill a casual vacancy, the electoral area for which the election is held; and
    (c)   where the polls are to be taken together in part of an Assembly constituency only, specify that part.".

Rule 36 of Schedule 5 (issue of official poll cards)

7   At the end of rule 36 of Schedule 5 add
  "(10)   Where a poll at an Assembly election is taken together with a poll at a local government election an official poll card issued under this paragraph may be combined with an official poll card issued at the local government election.".

Rule 37 of Schedule 5 (equipment of polling stations)

8(1)   After rule 37(4) of Schedule 5 insert
  "(4A)   The same ballot box may be used for the poll at the Assembly election and for the poll at the local government election.
  (4B) Where the same ballot box is not used under paragraph (4A) each ballot box shall be clearly marked with
    (a)   the election to which it relates, as shown on the ballot papers for that election; and
    (b)   the words "Place the *specify the colour of the ballot papers in question* ballot paper here, Rhowch y papur pleidleisio *nodwch liw'r papurau pleidleisio dan sylw* yma."".

  (2)   For rules 37(14) to (15) of Schedule 5 substitute
  "(14)   Where a poll at an Assembly election is taken together with a poll at a local government election, the notice in form CP set out in English and Welsh in Schedule 10, giving directions for the guidance of the voters in voting, shall be printed in conspicuous characters and exhibited inside and outside every polling station.

(15) Where the poll at an Assembly election is taken together with a poll at a local government election in every compartment of every polling station there shall be exhibited the notice

(a) in respect of a constituency election

"Vote for one candidate only on the constituency ballot paper coloured *colour of ballot paper*. Put no other mark on the ballot paper or your vote may not be counted.

Pleidleisiwch dros un ymgeisydd yn unig ar y papur pleidleisio etholaeth lliw *lliw'r papur pleidleisio*. Peidiwch â rhoi unrhyw farc arall ar y papur pleidleisio, neu fe all na chaiff eich pleidlais ei chyfrif.";

(b) in respect of a regional election

"Vote once only on the regional ballot paper coloured *colour of ballot paper* . Put no other mark on the ballot paper or your vote may not be counted.

Pleidleisiwch unwaith yn unig ar y papur pleidleisio rhanbarthol lliw *lliw'r papur pleidleisio*. Peidiwch â rhoi unrhyw farc arall ar y papur pleidleisio, neu fe all na chaiff eich pleidlais ei chyfrif.";

(c) in respect of a local government election

(i) where there is more than one candidate to be returned for an electoral area

"Vote for no more than . . . . candidates on the local government ballot paper coloured *colour of ballot paper*. Put no other marks on the ballot paper or your votes may not be counted.

Peidiwch â phleidleisio dros fwy na(g) . . . . o ymgeiswyr ar y papur pleidleisio llywodraeth leol lliw *lliw'r papur pleidleisio*. Peidiwch â rhoi unrhyw farciau eraill ar y papur pleidleisio, neu fe all na chaiff eich pleidleisiau eu cyfrif."; or

(ii) where there is one candidate to be returned for an electoral area

"Vote for no more than one candidate on the local government ballot paper coloured *colour of ballot paper*. Put no other mark on the ballot paper or your vote may not be counted.

Peidiwch â phleidleisio dros fwy nag un ymgeisydd ar y papur pleidleisio llywodraeth leol lliw *lliw' papur pleidleisio*. Peidiwch â rhoi unrhyw farc arall ar y papur pleidleisio, neu fe all na chaiff eich pleidlais ei chyfrif."; and

(d) in respect of a local government election which is a mayoral election

"*Vote for one candidate only Vote once for your first choice and once for your second choice* on the mayoral ballot paper coloured *colour of ballot paper*. Put no other mark on the ballot paper or your vote may not be counted.

Pleidleisiwch dros un ymgeisydd yn unig Pleidleisiwch unwaith dros eich dewisiad cyntaf ac unwaith dros eich ail ddewisiad ar y papur pleidleisio maerol lliw *lliw'r papur pleidleisio*. Peidiwch â rhoi unrhyw farc arall ar y papur pleidleisio, neu fe all na chaiff eich pleidlais ei chyfrif.",

and paragraph (16) does not apply.".

Rule 38 of Schedule 5 (appointment of polling and counting agents)

9   After rule 38(7) of Schedule 5 insert

"(7A) Where the poll at an Assembly election is taken together with a poll at a local government election notices of the appointment of polling agents which are required by paragraphs (5), (6) and (7) to be given to the returning officer shall be given to the returning officer who discharges the functions specified in paragraph 2 of Schedule 4.".

Rule 41 of Schedule 5 (admission to polling station)

10   After paragraph (1)(h) of rule 41 insert

"(i) persons entitled to be admitted to the polling station at the local government election.".

Rule 44 of Schedule 5 (questions to be put to voters)

11(1)   In questions 1(b), 2, 3(a) and (b), 4, 5(b), 6 and 7 in column (2) of the Table to rule 44 of Schedule 5, before "election" insert "Assembly".

(2)   In questions 1(b), 2, 3(a) and (b), 4, 5(b), 6 and 7 in column (2) of the Table to rule 44 of Schedule 5, after "yr etholiad hwn" insert "i'r Cynulliad".

Rule 46 of Schedule 5 (voting procedure)

12   At the end of rule 46 of Schedule 5 add

"(8) Where the poll at an Assembly election is taken together with a poll at a local government election the same copy of the register of electors or where paragraph (3) applies, the same copy of the notice may be used under paragraph (1) for each election and

(a) one mark may be placed in that register or on that notice under paragraph (1)(c) or in the list of proxies under paragraph (1)(d) to denote that a ballot paper has been received in respect of each election; and

(b) where a ballot paper has not been issued in respect of each election, a different mark shall be placed in the register, on the notice or list so as to identify the election in respect of which the ballot paper was issued.".

Rule 47 of Schedule 5 (votes marked by presiding officer)

13   At the end of rule 47 of Schedule 5 add

"(6) Where the poll at an Assembly election is taken together with a poll at a local government election the same list of votes marked by the presiding officer may be used for each election and, where it is so used, an entry in that list shall be taken to mean that the ballot papers were so marked in respect of each election, unless the list identifies the election at which a ballot paper was so marked.".

Rule 48 of Schedule 5 (voting by persons with disabilities)

14   At the end of rule 48 of Schedule 5 add

"(10) Where the poll at an Assembly election is taken together with a poll at a local government election the same list of voters with disabilities assisted by companions may be used for each election and, where it is so used, an entry in that list shall be taken to mean the votes were so given in respect of each election, unless the list identifies the election at which a vote was so given.".

Rule 49 of Schedule 5 (tendered ballot papers)

15   At the end of rule 49 of Schedule 5 add

"(13) Where the poll at an Assembly election is taken together with a poll at a local government election the same tendered votes list may be used for each election and, where it is so used, an entry in that list shall be taken to mean that tendered ballot papers were so marked in respect of each election, unless the list identifies the election at which a tendered ballot paper was so marked.".

Rule 51 of Schedule 5 (correction of errors on the day of poll)

16   At the end of rule 51 of Schedule 5 add

"Where the poll at an Assembly election is taken together with a poll at a local government election the same list may be used for each election and, where it is so used, an entry in that list shall be taken to mean that ballot papers were issued in respect of each election, unless the list identifies the election for which a ballot paper was issued".

Rule 52 of Schedule 5 (adjournment of poll in case of riot)

17   After rule 52(1) of Schedule 5 insert

"(1A)   Where the poll at an Assembly election is taken together with a poll at a local government election, and the returning officer who discharges the functions specified in paragraph 2 of Schedule 4 is not a constituency returning officer, the notice required to be given under paragraph (1)(b) or (c) shall also be given to the first mentioned returning officer.".

Rule 53 of Schedule 5 (procedure on close of poll)

18(1)   After rule 53(1) of Schedule 5 insert

"(1A)   Where paragraph (1) applies and the poll is taken together with a poll at a local government election the contents of the packets referred to in paragraph (1)(b) to (e), (g) and (h) shall not be combined with the contents of packets made under the corresponding rule that applies at a local government election; nor shall the statement prepared under paragraph (4) be so combined.".

(2)   After rule 53(2) of Schedule 5 insert

"(2A)   Where paragraph (2) applies and the poll is taken together with a poll at a local government election

(a)   the contents of the packets referred to in paragraph (2)(b), (c), (e) and (f) shall not be combined with the contents of packets made under the corresponding rule that applies at a local government election; nor shall the statement prepared under paragraph (4) be so combined; and

(b)   references to the constituency returning officer in paragraph (3) are references to the returning officer who discharges the functions specified in paragraph 2 of Schedule 4.".

Rule 54 of Schedule 5 (time of, and attendance at, counting of votes)

19(1)   After rule 54(2) of Schedule 5 insert

"(2A)   Where the poll at an Assembly election is taken together with a poll at a local government election and a constituency returning officer at the Assembly election does not discharge the functions specified in paragraph 2 of Schedule 4 (so that sub-paragraph (1) does not apply), the constituency returning officer shall make arrangements for counting the votes in the presence of the counting agents after the delivery of the ballot papers to him by the returning officer who does discharge those functions, and he shall also give to the counting agents notice in writing of the time and place he will begin to count the votes if he has by then received the ballot papers.

(2B)   At a regional election notice under paragraph (2A) shall also be given to the regional returning officer.".

(2)   In rule 54(6), before "the efficient" insert "the efficient separating of the ballot papers or, as the case may be,".

Rule 55 of Schedule 5 (the count)

20(1)   For rules 55(1) to (3) of Schedule 5 substitute

"(1)   Where the poll at an Assembly election is taken together with the poll at a local government election and if the constituency returning officer for the Assembly constituency discharges the functions specified in paragraph 2 of Schedule 4, he must

(a)   in the presence of the counting agents appointed for the purposes of the Assembly and local government elections open each ballot box and record separately the number of ballot papers in each box for each election;

(b)   in the presence of the election agents appointed for the purposes of the Assembly and local government elections verify each ballot paper account;

(c)   count such of the postal ballot papers as have been duly returned and record separately the number counted at each election;

(d)   separate the ballot papers relating to each election;

(e)   make up into packets the ballot papers for each election other than the Assembly elections and seal them up in separate containers endorsing on each a description of the area to which the ballot papers relate;

(f)   deliver, or cause to be delivered, to the returning officer at the election to which the ballot papers relate

(i)   those containers, together with a list of them and of the contents of each; and

(ii)   the ballot paper accounts together with a copy of the statement as to the result of their verification in respect of that election; and

(g)   at the same time deliver, or cause to be delivered, to that officer packets that so relate containing,

(i)   the unused and spoilt ballot papers;

(ii)   the tendered ballot papers; and

(iii)   the completed corresponding number lists and the certificates as to employment on duty on the day of the poll.

(2)   Where separate ballot boxes have been used, no vote shall be rendered invalid solely by the ballot paper being placed in the wrong ballot box.

(2A)   After the completion of the proceedings under paragraph (1) the returning officer shall separately mix together all the ballot papers used at the Assembly constituency election and those used at the Assembly regional election (or if only one poll is held in respect of an Assembly election, the ballot papers used at that election) and count the votes given on them.

(2B)   Where the poll at an Assembly election is taken together with a poll at a local government election and a constituency returning officer does not discharge the functions specified in paragraph 2 of Schedule 4 he must

(a)   on receipt of containers from the returning officer who does discharge those functions, and after the time specified in the notice given under rule 54(2A), in the presence of the counting agents open each container;

(b)   where the proceedings on the issue and receipt of postal ballot papers are not taken together with those proceedings at another election under paragraph 2 of Schedule 3, count such of the postal ballot papers as have been duly returned and record the number counted; and

(c)   in respect of each Assembly election, mix together the postal ballot papers and the ballot papers from all of the containers and count the votes given on them;

and paragraph (12) shall not apply to these proceedings

(3)   The proceedings described in paragraph (1) may be undertaken at a different place (or at different places) than a place at which the votes at an Assembly election are counted; but if the power is so exercised paragraph (4) does not

apply with respect to the ballot papers and other documents relating to the local government election.".

(2) Paragraphs (16) to (18) of rule 55 shall not apply to these proceedings.

Rule 67 of Schedule 5 (delivery of documents to relevant registration officer)

21 After rule 67(2) of Schedule 5 insert

"(3) Where the poll at an Assembly election is taken together with a poll at a local government election and a constituency returning officer does not discharge the functions specified in paragraph 2 of Schedule 4, paragraph (2) shall have effect as if paragraphs (c) and (f) were omitted.".

Rule 70 of Schedule 5 (constituency election: death of independent candidate)

22 After rule 70(5) of Schedule 5 insert

"(6) neither the countermand of the notice of poll at the Assembly election nor the direction that the poll be abandoned shall affect the poll at the local government election.".

Rule 73 of Schedule 5 (constituency election: death of party candidate)

23(1) After rule 73(2) of Schedule 5 insert

"(2A) Neither the countermand of the notice of poll at the Assembly election nor the direction that the poll be abandoned shall affect the poll at the local government election.".

(2) In paragraph (4) after "with reference to the" insert "Assembly".

Rule 76 of Schedule 5 (abandoned poll)

24 After rule 76(10) of Schedule 5 insert

"(11) Where the poll at an Assembly election is taken together with a poll at a local government election and the poll at the Assembly election is abandoned by reason of a candidate's death (and paragraph (10) does not apply) the steps required by the presiding officer at such a polling station by paragraph (2) shall take place at the close of poll; and in paragraph (3)

(a) references to the constituency returning officer shall be construed as references to the returning officer who discharges the functions specified in paragraph 2 of Schedule 5; and

(b) "having separated the ballot papers relating to the local government election,", shall be construed as having been inserted after "constituency returning officer".".

Schedule 10 (appendix of forms) (form CP)

25 In Schedule 10, after form CP insert
    form not reproduced

Schedule 10 (appendix of forms) (form CQ)

26(1) In Schedule 10, the form CQ shall be amended in accordance with sub-paragraphs (2) and (3).

(2) In that part of the form in English for "the Assembly election now being held in this constituency and electoral region" substitute "the elections now being held in this Assembly constituency , Assembly electoral region and, in the case of a local government election which is not a mayoral election, *name of electoral area for which election is held and name of local government area* or, in the case of a local government

election which is a mayoral election, *name of local government area*".

(3) In that part of the form in Welsh for "yn etholiad y Cynulliad a gynhelir yn awr yn yr etholaeth hon a'r rhanbarth etholiadol hwn" substitute "yr etholiadau a gynhelir yn awr yn yr etholaeth y cynulliad hon , y rhanbarth etholiadol Cynulliad hwn ac, yn achos etholiad llywodraeth leol nad yw yn etholiad maerol, *enw'r ardal etholiadol y cynhelir yr etholiad hwn ar ei chyfer ac enw'r ardal llywodraeth leol* neu, yn achos etholiad llywadraeth leol sydd yn etholiad maerol, *enw'r ardal llywodraeth leol*".

Part 3
Modifications to Election Rules to Apply Where the Poll at an Election of County or County Borough Councillors is Taken Together with a Poll at an Assembly Election Under Article 16(1) or (2)

Modifications to principal area election rules: general provision

27(1) Where the poll at an election of county or county borough councillors is taken together with the poll at an Assembly election under article 16(1) or (2), Schedule 3 to the Local Elections (Principal Areas) (England and Wales) Rules 2006 (rules for conduct of an election of councillors of a principal area) shall have effect subject to the modifications set out in the remaining paragraphs of this Part.

(2) In this Part the rules in that Schedule referred to in sub-paragraph (1) are referred to as the principal area election rules.

Rule 16 of principal area election rules (the ballot papers)

28(1) After rule 16(2)(d) of the principal area election rules insert
    "(e) must be of a different colour from that of any ballot papers used at an Assembly election and at any local government election the polls of which are taken together with the poll at the principal area election.".

(2) At the end of rule 16 of the principal area election rules add
    "(6) References to an Assembly election in paragraph (2)(e) and elsewhere in these rules refer to an election to the National Assembly for Wales; and references to an Assembly election (and to a poll at such an election) include a reference to Assembly elections (and to polls at such elections) where the context so requires.".

Rule 21 of principal area election rules (notice of poll)

29 In rule 21 of the principal area election rules for paragraph (4) substitute
    "(4) The notice published under paragraph (3) must:
        (a) state that the poll at the principal area election is to be taken together with the poll at an Assembly election and any other local government election;
        (b) specify the Assembly constituency or electoral region and any relevant local authority and, in the case of an election to fill a casual vacancy, the electoral area for which the other election is held; and
        (c) where the polls are to be taken together in part of the local government area only, specify that part.".

Rule 25 of principal area election rules (issue of official poll cards)

30 At the end of rule 25 add
    "(7) An official poll card issued under this rule may be combined with the official poll card issued at an Assembly election and any other local government election.".

Rule 26 of principal area election rules (equipment of polling stations)

31(1) For rule 26(2) of the principal area election rules substitute

"(2) The same ballot box may be used for the poll at the principal area election and for the polls at the Assembly election and any other local government election if the returning officer who discharges the functions specified in paragraph 2 of Schedule 4 to the National Assembly for Wales (Representation of the People) Order 2007 so decides and a decision may make different provision for different polling stations.".

(2) For rule 26(7) of the principal area election rules substitute

"(7) Where the same ballot box is not used under paragraph (2) each ballot box shall be clearly marked with

(a) the election to which it relates, as shown on the ballot papers for that election; and

(b) the words "Place the *specify the colour of the ballot papers in question* ballot paper here, Rhowch y papur pleidleisio *nodwch liw'r papurau pleidleisio dan sylw* yma.".".

(3) For rule 26(10) of the principal area election rules substitute

"(10) In every compartment of every polling station there shall be exhibited the notice

(a) in respect of a local government election

(i) where there is more than one candidate to be returned for an electoral area

"Vote for no more than . . . . candidates on the local government ballot paper coloured *colour of ballot paper*. Put no other marks on the ballot paper or your votes may not be counted.

Peidiwch â phleidleisio dros fwy nag . . . . . o ymgeiswyr ar y papur pleidleisio llywodraeth leol lliw *lliw'r papur pleidleisio*. Peidiwch â rhoi unrhyw farciau eraill ar y papur pleidleisio, neu fe all na chaiff eich pleidleisiau eu cyfrif."; or

(ii) where there is one candidate to be returned for an electoral area

"Vote for no more than one candidate on the local government ballot paper coloured *colour of ballot paper*. Put no other mark on the ballot paper or your vote may not be counted.

Peidiwch â phleidleisio dros fwy nag un ymgeisydd ar y papur pleidleisio llywodraeth leol lliw *lliw'r papur pleidleisio*. Peidiwch â rhoi unrhyw farc arall ar y papur pleidleisio, neu fe all na chaiff eich pleidlais ei chyfrif.";

(b) in respect of an Assembly election for an Assembly constituency

"Vote for one candidate only on the constituency ballot paper coloured *colour of ballot paper*. Put no other mark on the ballot paper or your vote may not be counted.

Pleidleisiwch dros un ymgeisydd yn unig ar y papur pleidleisio etholaeth lliw *lliw'r papur pleidleisio*. Peidiwch â rhoi unrhyw farc arall ar y papur pleidleisio, neu fe all na chaiff eich pleidlais ei chyfrif."; and

(c) in respect of an Assembly election for an Assembly electoral region

"Vote once only on the regional ballot paper coloured *colour of ballot paper*. Put no other mark on the ballot paper or your vote may not be counted.

Pleidleisiwch unwaith yn unig ar y papur pleidleisio rhanbarthol lliw *lliw'r papur pleidleisio*. Peidiwch â rhoi unrhyw farc arall ar y papur pleidleisio, neu fe all na chaiff eich pleidlais ei chyfrif.".".

Rule 27 of principal area election rules (appointment of polling and counting agents)

32 For rule 27(6) of the principal area election rules substitute

"(6) Notices of the appointment of polling agents which are required by this paragraph and paragraphs (7) and (8) to be given to the returning officer shall be given to that returning officer who discharges the functions specified in paragraph 2 of Schedule 4 to the National Assembly for Wales (Representation of the People) Order 2007.".

Rule 35 of principal area election rules (voting procedure)

33   For rule 35(6) of the principal area election rules substitute

"(6) The same copy of the register of electors which is used under paragraph (1) for the principal area election or, where paragraph (3) applies, the same copy of the notice issued under section 13(3B) or (3D) of the 1983 Act may be used for the Assembly election

(a)   and one mark may be placed in that register under paragraph (1)(c) or in the list of proxies under paragraph (1)(d) to denote that a ballot paper has been received in respect of each election;

(b)   but where a ballot paper has been issued in respect of one election only, a different mark must be placed in the register or, as the case may be, on that notice or in that list so as to identify the election in respect of which the ballot paper was issued.".

Rule 36 of principal area election rules (votes marked by presiding officer)

34   For rule 36(4) of the principal area election rules substitute

"The same list may be used for each election and, where it is so used, an entry in that list shall be taken to mean that the ballot papers were so marked in respect of each election, unless the list identifies the election at which the ballot paper was so marked.".

Rule 37 of principal area election rules (voting by persons with disabilities)

35   For rule 37(6) of the principal area election rules substitute

"The same list may be used for each election and, where it is so used, an entry in that list shall be taken to mean that the votes were so given in respect of each election, unless the list identifies the election at which the vote was so given.".

Rule 39 of principal area election rules (tendered ballot papers, general provisions)

36   For rule 39(3) of the principal area election rules substitute

"(3) The same list may be used for each election and, where it is so used, an entry in that list shall be taken to mean that tendered ballot papers were so marked in respect of each election, unless the list identifies the election at which a tendered ballot paper was so marked.".

Rule 42 of principal area election rules (adjournment of poll in case of riot)

37   In rule 42(1) of the principal area election rules substitute

"(1) Where the proceedings at any polling station are interrupted or obstructed by riot or open violence, the presiding officer must adjourn the proceedings until the following day and must forthwith give notice

(a)   to the returning officer who discharges the functions specified in paragraph 2 of Schedule 4 to the National Assembly for Wales (Representation of the People) Order 2007; and

(b)   in the case of a regional election, whether or not the poll is taken with the poll at a constituency election, to the regional returning officer.".

Rule 43 of principal area election rules (procedure on close of poll)

38(1) For rule 43(2) of the principal area election rules substitute

"(2) The contents of the packets referred to in paragraph (1)(b), (c) (e) and (f) shall not be combined with the contents of the packets made under the corresponding provisions that apply to an Assembly election and any other local government election; nor shall the statement prepared under paragraph (3) be so combined.".

(2) For rule 43(3) of the principal area election rules substitute

"(3) References to the returning officer in paragraph (1) are references to the returning officer who discharges the functions specified in paragraph 2 of Schedule 4 to the National Assembly for Wales (Representation of the People) Order 2007.".

Rule 44 of principal area election rules (attendance at counting of votes)

39 For rule 44(1) and (2) of the principal area election rules substitute

"(1) Where the returning officer at the principal area election discharges the functions specified in paragraph 2 of Schedule 4 to the National Assembly for Wales (Representation of the People) Order 2007, he must

(a) make arrangements for

(i)   discharging the functions under rule 45(1) (as substituted by Schedule 4 to the National Assembly for Wales (Representation of the People) Order 2007) in the presence of the counting agents appointed for the purposes of the principal area election and Assembly election as soon as practicable after the close of the poll; and

(ii) thereafter counting the votes at the principal area election in the presence of the agents appointed for the purpose of that election; and

(b) give to the counting agents appointed for the purpose of those elections notice in writing of the time and place at which he will begin to discharge the functions under rule 45(1) (as so substituted).

(2) Where the returning officer at the principal area election does not discharge the functions specified in paragraph 2 of Schedule 4 to the National Assembly for Wales (Representation of the People) Order 2007, he shall make arrangements for counting the votes in the presence of the counting agents appointed for the purposes of the principal area election as soon as practicable after the delivery of the ballot papers to him by the returning officer who does discharge those functions, and shall give to the counting agents notice in writing of the time at which he will begin to count the votes if by then he has received the ballot papers and of the place at which that count will take place.".

Rule 45 of principal area election rules (the count)

40 For rule 45(1) of the principal area election rules substitute

"(1) Where the returning officer at the principal area election discharges the functions specified in paragraph 2 of Schedule 4 to the National Assembly for Wales (Representation of the People) Order 2007, he shall

(a) in the presence of the counting agents appointed for the purposes of the principal area election and Assembly election open each ballot box and record separately the number of ballot papers used in each election;

(b) in the presence of the election agents appointed for the purposes of the principal area election and Assembly election verify each ballot paper account;

(c) count such of the postal ballot papers as have been duly returned and record separately the number counted at each election;

(d) separate the ballot papers relating to each election;

> (e) make up into packets the ballot papers for each election other than the principal area election and seal them up in separate containers endorsing on each a description of the election to which the ballot papers relate;
>
> (f) deliver, or cause to be delivered, to the returning officer for the election to which the ballot papers relate (or, in the case of a regional election, to the constituency returning officer for the Assembly constituency in which the votes were given on those ballot papers)
>
> > (i) those containers, together with a list of them and of the contents of each; and
> >
> > (ii) the ballot paper accounts together with a copy of the statement as to the result of their verification in respect of that election; and
>
> (g) at the same time deliver, or cause to be delivered, to that officer packets that so relate containing (as appropriate)
>
> > (i) the unused and spoilt ballot papers;
> >
> > (ii) the tendered ballot papers;
> >
> > (iii) the completed corresponding number lists; and
> >
> > (iv) the certificates as to employment on duty on the day of the poll.
>
> (1A) Where the returning officer at the principal area election does not discharge the functions specified in paragraph 2 of Schedule 4 to the National Assembly for Wales (Representation of the People) Order 2007, he shall
>
> > (a) on receipt of containers from the returning officer who does discharge those functions, and after the time specified in the notice given under rule 44(2) (as substituted by Schedule 4 to the National Assembly for Wales (Representation of the People) Order 2007), in the presence of the counting agents open each container;
> >
> > (b) where the proceedings on the issue and receipt of postal ballot papers are not taken together with those proceedings at another election under paragraph 2 of Schedule 4 to the National Assembly for Wales (Representation of the People) Order 2007, count such of the postal ballot papers as have been duly returned and record the number counted; and
> >
> > (c) mix together the postal ballot papers and the ballot papers from all of the containers and count the votes given on them.
>
> Paragraph (11) does not apply to these proceedings.".

Rule 52 of principal area election rules (delivery of documents to relevant registration officer)

41 At the end of rule 52(1) of the principal area election rules add

> "At an election where the returning officer does not discharge the functions specified in paragraph 2 of Schedule 4 to the National Assembly for Wales (Representation of the People) Order 2007, this paragraph shall have effect as if sub-paragraphs (c) and (f) were omitted.".

Rule 55 of principal area election rules (countermand or abandonment of poll on death of candidate)

42(1) For rule 55(2) of the principal area election rules substitute

> "(2) Neither the countermand of the notice of the poll at the principal area election nor the direction that that poll be abandoned shall affect the poll at the Assembly election and any other local government election.".

(2) For rule 55(3) of the principal area election rules substitute

> "(3) Where the poll at the principal area election is abandoned by reason of a candidate's death, no further ballot papers shall be delivered in any polling station and, at the close of the poll for the Assembly election and any other local

government election, the presiding officer shall take the like steps for the delivery to the returning officer of ballot boxes and of ballot papers and other documents as he would be required to do if the poll at the principal area election had not been abandoned, and the returning officer shall dispose of ballot papers used at the principal area election as he is required to do on the completion in due course of the counting of the votes, but

(a) it shall not be necessary for any ballot paper account at that election to be prepared or verified; and

(b) the returning officer, having separated the ballot papers relating to the Assembly election and any other local government election, shall take no step or further step for the counting of the ballot papers used at the principal area election or of the votes and shall seal up all of those ballot papers, whether the votes on them have been counted or not, and it shall not be necessary to seal up counted and rejected ballot papers in separate packets.".

(3) Paragraphs (4) to (8) of rule 53 shall not apply.

Appendix of forms to principal area election rules (postal voting statement)

43(1) In the Appendix of forms to the principal area election rules, for the form of postal voting statement substitute

(a) the form set out in sub-paragraph (2) where the proceedings on the issue and receipt of postal ballot papers at the principal area election are taken together with those proceedings at an Assembly election under paragraph 2 of Schedule 3 to the National Assembly for Wales (Representation of the People) Order 2007; and

(b) the form set out in sub-paragraph (3) where those proceedings are not taken together.

(2) Where sub-paragraph (1)(a) applies, substitute form CC2 in English and Welsh referred to in paragraph 3(b) in Schedule 3 and shown in Schedule 10.

(3) The following form shall be substituted where sub-paragraph (1)(b) applies
Form not reproduced

Appendix of forms to principal area election rules (directions for the guidance of the voters in voting)

44 In the Appendix of forms to the principal area election rules, for the form of directions for the guidance of the voters in voting there shall be substituted the same form of directions as is set out in paragraph 25.

Appendix of forms to principal area election rules (declaration to be made by the companion of a voter with disabilities)

45 In the Appendix of forms in the principal area election rules, for the form of declaration to be made by the companion of a voter with disabilities there shall be substituted the following form
Form not reproduced

Part 4
Modifications to Election Rules to Apply Where the
Poll at an Election of Community Councillors is Taken Together
with the Poll at an Assembly Election Under Article 16(1) or (2)

Modifications to community election rules: general provision

46(1) Where the poll at an election of community councillors is taken together with the poll at an Assembly election under article 16(1) or (2), Schedule 3 to the Local Elections (Parishes and Communities)(England and Wales) Rules 2006 shall have effect subject to the modifications set out in to the remaining paragraphs of this Part.

(2) In this Part the rules in that Schedule referred to in sub-paragraph (1) are referred to as the community election rules.

Rule 16 of community election rules (the ballot papers)

47(1) At the end of rule 16(2) of the community election rules add
"(e) must be of a different colour from that of any ballot papers used at an Assembly election and any local government election the polls at which are taken together with the poll at the community election.".

(2) At the end of rule 16 of the community election rules add
"(6) References to an Assembly election in paragraph (2)(e) and elsewhere in these rules refer to an election to the National Assembly for Wales; and references to an Assembly election (and to a poll at such an election) include a reference to Assembly elections (and to polls at such elections) where the context so requires.".

Rule 21 of community election rules (notice of poll)

48 For rule 21(4) of the community election rules substitute
"(4) The notice published under paragraph (3) shall:
(a) state that the poll at the community election is to be taken together with the poll at an Assembly election and any other local government election;
(b) specify the Assembly constituency or electoral region and any relevant local authority and, in the case of an election to fill a casual vacancy, the electoral area for which the other election is held; and
(c) where the polls are to be taken together in part of the local government area only, specify that part.".

Rule 25 of community election rules (issue of official poll cards)

49 At the end of rule 25 to the community election rules add
"(8) An official poll card issued under this rule may be combined with the official poll card issued at an Assembly election and any other local government election.".

Rule 26 of community election rules (equipment of polling stations)

50(1) For rule 26(2) of the community election rules substitute
"(2) The same ballot box may be used for the poll at the community election and for the polls at the Assembly election and any other local government election if the returning officer who discharges the functions specified in paragraph 2 of Schedule 4 to the National Assembly for Wales (Representation of the People) Order 2007 so decides and a decision may make different provision for different polling stations.".

(2) For rule 26(7) of the community election rules substitute
"(7) Where the same ballot box is not used under paragraph (2) each ballot box shall be clearly marked with
(a) the election to which it relates, as shown on the ballot papers for that election; and
(b) the words "Place the *specify the colour of the ballot papers in question* ballot paper here, Rhowch y papur pleidleisio *nodwch liw'r papurau pleidleisio*

        dan sylw yma.”.”

(3)   For rule 26(10) of the community election rules substitute

      “(10) In every compartment of every polling station there shall be exhibited the notice

        (a) in respect of a local government election

          (i) where there is more than one candidate to be returned for an electoral area

            “Vote for no more than . . . . candidates on the local government ballot paper coloured **colour of ballot paper*. Put no other marks on the ballot paper or your votes may not be counted.

            Peidiwch â phleidleisio dros fwy nag . . . . o ymgeiswyr ar y papur pleidleisio llywodraeth leol lliw *lliw'r papur pleidleisio*. Peidiwch â rhoi unrhyw farciau eraill ar y papur pleidleisio, neu fe all na chaiff eich pleidlais ei chyfrif.”; or

          (ii) where there is one candidate to be returned for an electoral area

            “Vote for no more than one candidate on the local government ballot paper coloured *colour of ballot paper*. Put no other mark on the ballot paper or your vote may not be counted.

            Peidiwch â phleidleisio dros fwy nag un ymgeisydd ar y papur pleidleisio llywodraeth leol lliw *lliw'r papur pleidleisio*. Peidiwch â rhoi unrhyw farc arall ar y papur pleidleisio, neu fe all na chaiff eich pleidlais ei chyfrif.”;

        (b) in respect of an Assembly election for an Assembly constituency

          “Vote for one candidate only on the constituency ballot paper coloured *colour of ballot paper*. Put no other mark on the ballot paper or your vote may not be counted.

          Pleidleisiwch dros un ymgeisydd yn unig ar y papur pleidleisio etholaeth lliw *lliw'r papur pleidleisio*. Peidiwch â rhoi unrhyw farc arall ar y papur pleidleisio, neu fe all na chaiff eich pleidlais ei chyfrif.”; and

        (c) in respect of an Assembly election for an Assembly electoral region

          “Vote once only on the regional ballot paper coloured *colour of ballot paper*. Put no other mark on the ballot paper or your vote may not be counted.

          Pleidleisiwch unwaith yn unig ar y papur pleidleisio rhanbarthol lliw *lliw'r papur pleidleisio*. Peidiwch â rhoi unrhyw farc arall ar y papur pleidleisio, neu fe all na chaiff eich pleidlais ei chyfrif.”.”.

Rule 27 of community election rules (appointment of polling and counting agents)

51   For rule 27(6) of the community election rules substitute

     “(6) Notices of appointment of polling and election agents which are required by paragraphs (5) and (7) to be given to the returning officer shall be given to that returning officer who discharges the functions specified in paragraph 2 of Schedule 4 to the National Assembly for Wales (Representation of the People) Order 2007”.

Rule 35 of community election rules (voting procedure)

52   For rule 35(6) of the community election rules substitute

     “(6) The same copy of the register of electors which is used for the community election under paragraph (1), or where paragraph (3) applies, the same copy of the notice issued under section 13(3B) or (3D) of the 1983 Act, may be used for the Assembly election

      (a) and one mark may be placed in that register or on that notice under paragraph (1)(c) or in the list of proxies under paragraph (1)(d) to denote that a ballot paper has been issued in respect of each election;

(b) but where a ballot paper has been issued in respect of one election only, a different mark must be placed in the register or, as the case may be, on that notice or in that list so as to identify the election in respect of which a ballot paper was issued.".

Rule 36 of community election rules (votes marked by presiding officer)

53 For rule 36(4) of the community election rules substitute

"(4) The same list may be used for the community election and for an Assembly election and, where it is so used, an entry in that list shall be taken to mean that the ballot papers were so marked in respect of each election, unless the list identifies an election at which a ballot paper was so marked.".

Rule 37 of community election rules (voting by persons with disabilities)

54 For rule 37(6) of the community election rules substitute

"(6) The same list may be used for the community election and for an Assembly election, and where it is so used, an entry in that list shall be taken to mean that the votes were so given in respect of each election, unless the list identifies an election at which a vote was so given.".

Rule 39 of community election rules (tendered ballot papers; general provisions)

55 For rule 39(3) of the community election rules substitute

"(3) The same list may be used for each election and, where it is so used, an entry in that list shall be taken to mean that tendered ballot papers were so marked in respect of the community election and an Assembly election, unless the list identifies an election at which a tendered ballot paper was so marked.".

Rule 42 of community election rules (adjournment of poll in case of riot)

56 For rule 42(1) of the community election rules substitute

"(1) Where the proceedings at any polling station are interrupted or obstructed by riot or open violence, the presiding officer must adjourn the proceedings until the following day and must forthwith give notice

(a) to the returning officer who discharges the functions specified in paragraph 2 of Schedule 4 to the National Assembly for Wales (Representation of the People) Order 2007; and

(b) in the case of a regional election, whether or not the poll is taken with the poll at a constituency election, to the regional returning officer.".

Rule 43 of community election rules (procedure on close of poll)

57(1) For rule 43(2) of the community election rules substitute

"(2) The contents of the packets referred to in paragraph (1)(b), (c), (e) and (f) shall not be combined with the contents of the packets made under the corresponding provisions that apply at an Assembly election and any other local government election; nor shall the statement prepared under paragraph (5) be so combined".

(2) For rule 43(3) substitute

"(3) References to the returning officer in paragraph (1) are references to the returning officer who discharges the functions specified in paragraph 2 of Schedule 4 to the National Assembly for Wales (Representation of the People) Order 2007.".

Rule 44 of community election rules (attendance at counting of votes)

58(1) For rule 44(1) and (2) of the community election rules substitute

"(1) Where the returning officer at the community election discharges the functions specified in paragraph 2 of Schedule 4 to the National Assembly for Wales (Representation of the People) Order 2007, he must

    (a) make arrangements for

        (i) discharging the functions under rule 45(1) (as substituted by Schedule 4 to the National Assembly for Wales (Representation of the People) Order 2007) in the presence of the counting agents appointed for the purposes of the community election and Assembly election as soon as practicable after the close of the poll; and

        (ii) thereafter counting the votes at the community election in the presence of the agents appointed for that election; and

    (b) give to those counting agents appointed for the purposes of the community election and Assembly election notice in writing of the time and place at which he will begin to discharge the functions under rule 45(1).

  (2) Where the returning officer at the community election does not discharge the functions specified in paragraph 2 of Schedule 4 to the National Assembly for Wales (Representation of the People) Order 2007, he must

    (a) make arrangements for counting the votes in the presence of the counting agents appointed for the purposes of the community election as soon as practicable after the delivery of the ballot papers to him by the returning officer who does discharge those functions; and

    (b) must give to the counting agents notice in writing of the time at which he will begin to count the votes, if by then he has received the ballot papers and the place at which the count will take place.".

  (2) In rule 44(3) of the community election rules after "at the counting of the votes" insert "in accordance with rule 45(1) (as substituted) or".

Rule 45 of community election rules (the count)

59(1) For rule 45(1) of the community election rules substitute

"(1) Where the returning officer at the community election discharges the functions specified in paragraph 2 of Schedule 4 to the National Assembly for Wales (Representation of the People) Order 2007, he must

    (a) in the presence of the counting agents appointed for the purposes of the poll at the community election and Assembly election open each ballot box and count and record separately the number of ballot papers used in each election;

    (b) in the presence of the counting agents appointed for the purposes of the poll at the community election and the election agents appointed for the purposes of the Assembly elections, verify each ballot paper account;

    (c) count such of the postal ballot papers as have been duly returned and record separately the number counted at each election;

    (d) separate the ballot papers relating to each election;

    (e) make up into packets the ballot papers for each election other than the community election and seal them up in separate containers endorsing on each a description of the election to which the ballot papers relate;

    (f) deliver, or cause to be delivered, to the returning officer for the election to which the ballot papers relate (or, in the case of a regional election, to the constituency returning officer for the Assembly constituency in which the votes were given on those ballot papers)

      (i)   those containers, together with a list of them and of the contents of each; and

      (ii) the ballot paper accounts together with a copy of the statement as to the result of their verification in respect of that election; and

    (g) at the same time deliver, or cause to be delivered, to that officer packets that so relate containing (as appropriate)

      (i)   the unused and spoilt ballot papers;

      (ii) the tendered ballot papers;

      (iii) the completed corresponding number lists; and

      (iv) the certificates as to employment on duty on the day of the poll.".

(2)   For rule 45(2) substitute

    "(2) Where separate ballot boxes are used for the community election and Assembly election no vote for any candidate shall be rendered invalid by the ballot papers being placed in the wrong ballot box.".

(3)   For rule 45(3) and (4) substitute

    "(3) After completion of the proceedings under paragraph (1), the returning officer shall mix together all of the ballot papers used at the community election and count the votes given on them.

    (4) Where the returning officer at the community election does not discharge the functions specified in paragraph 2 of Schedule 4 to the National Assembly for Wales (Representation of the People) Order 2007, he shall

      (a) on receipt of containers from the returning officer who does discharge those functions, and after the time specified in the notice given under rule 44(2) (as substituted by Schedule 4 to the National Assembly for Wales (Representation of the People) Order 2007), in the presence of the counting agents open each container;

      (b) where the proceedings on the issue and receipt of postal ballot papers are not taken together with those proceedings at another election under paragraph 2 of Schedule 3 to the National Assembly for Wales (Representation of the People) Order 2007, count such of the postal ballot papers as have been duly returned and record the number counted; and

      (c) mix together the postal ballot papers and the ballot papers from all of the containers and count the votes given on them.".

(4)   Rule 45(10) does not apply to these proceedings.

Rule 55 of community election rules (countermand or abandonment of poll on death of candidate)

60(1) For rule 55(2) of the community election rules substitute

    "(2) Neither the countermand of the notice of the poll at the community election nor the direction that that poll be abandoned shall affect the poll at the Assembly election and any other local government election.".

(2)   For rule 55(4) of the community election rules substitute

    "(4) At the close of the poll for the Assembly election and any other local government election, the presiding officer shall take the like steps (so far as not already taken) for the delivery to the returning officer of ballot boxes and of ballot papers and other documents as he would be required to do if the poll at the community election had not been abandoned.".

(3)   For rule 55(7) substitute

    "(7) Having separated the ballot papers relating to the Assembly election and local government election (as the case may be) the returning officer must take no step or further step for the counting of the ballot papers used at the community election (at which the candidate has died) or of the votes.".

Appendix of forms to community election rules (postal voting statement)

61   In the Appendix of forms to the community election rules, for the form of postal voting statement substitute

    (a)   the form set out in paragraph 43(2) where the proceedings on the issue and receipt of postal ballot papers at the community election are taken together with those proceedings at an Assembly election under paragraph 2 of Schedule 3 to the National Assembly for Wales (Representation of the People) Order 2007; and

    (b)   the form set out in paragraph 43(3) where those proceedings are not taken together.

Appendix of forms to community election rules (directions for the guidance of the voters in voting)

62   In the Appendix of forms to the community election rules, for the form of directions for the guidance of the voters in voting substitute the same form of directions as is set out in paragraph 25.

Appendix of forms to community election rules (declaration to be made by the companion of a voter with disabilities)

63   In the Appendix of forms to the community election rules, for the form of declaration to be made by the companion of a voter with disabilities, substitute the form set out in paragraph 45.

SCHEDULE 5
ASSEMBLY ELECTION RULES

Article 17(1)

Contents

PART 1
PROVISION AS TO TIME

PART 2
STAGES COMMON TO CONTESTED AND UNCONTESTED ELECTIONS

Notice of Election

Nomination

PART 3
CONTESTED ELECTIONS

General Provisions

PART 7
MISCELLANEOUS

Part 1
Provision as to Time

Timetable

1(1)   The proceedings at an Assembly election shall be conducted in accordance with the
       following Table

Proceeding	Time
Publication of notice of election.	Not later than the twentyfifth day before the day of election
Delivery of nomination papers.	Between (a) the hours of 10 in the morning and 4 in the afternoon on any day after the date of publication of notice of election but before the nineteenth day before the day of election, and (b) the hours of 10 in the morning and noon on the nineteenth day before the day of election.
The making of objections to nomination papers.	During the hours allowed for delivery of nomination papers on the last day for their delivery and the hour following, but (a) no objection may be made in the afternoon of that last day except to a nomination paper delivered within 24 hours of the last time for its delivery and, in the case of a nomination paper so delivered, no objection may be so made to the sufficiency or nature of the particulars of a candidate unless made at or immediately after the time of the delivery of the nomination paper, and (b) the foregoing provisions do not apply to objections made under rule 19(2).
Delivery of notices of withdrawal of candidature.	Not later than noon on the seventeenth day before the day of election.
Publication of	Not later than noon on the sixteenth day before the day

statement of persons nominated.	of the election.
Polling.	Between the hours of 7 in the morning and 10 at night on the day of election.

(2)   In the Table, "making of objections to nomination papers", in the case of making of an objection to a party nomination paper includes the making of an objection to the nomination of any party list candidate on the list of candidates accompanying a party nomination paper.

Computation of time

2   In computing any period of time for the purposes of the Timetable
     (a)   a Saturday or a Sunday;
     (b)   Christmas Eve, Christmas Day or Good Friday;
     (c)   a day which is a bank holiday in Wales under the Banking and Financial Dealings Act 1971; or
     (d)   a day appointed for public thanksgiving or mourning,
shall be disregarded, and any such day shall not be treated as a day for the purpose of any proceedings up to the completion of the poll nor shall a constituency returning officer be obliged to proceed with the counting of votes on such a day.

Part 2
Stages Common to Contested and Uncontested Elections

Notice of Election
Notice of election: constituency election and regional election

3(1)   At a constituency election, the constituency returning officer shall publish notice of the election stating
     (a)   the place and times at which nomination papers are to be delivered;
     (b)   that forms of nomination paper may be obtained at that place and at those times; and
     (c)   the date of the poll in the event of a contest.

(2)   At a regional election, the regional returning officer shall prepare a notice of election stating
     (a)   the place or places and times at which nomination papers are to be delivered;
     (b)   that forms of nomination papers may be obtained at that place or those places and at those times; and
     (c)   the date of the poll in the event of a contest,
and he shall deliver, or cause to be delivered, the notice to each constituency returning officer for an Assembly constituency in the Assembly electoral region.

(3)   A notice of election under paragraph (1) or (2) must also state
     (a)   the arrangements which apply for the payment of the deposit required by rule 10 to be made by means of electronic transfer of funds; and
     (b)   the date by which
        (i)   applications to vote by post or proxy; and
        (ii)   other applications and notices about postal or proxy voting,
must reach the registration officer in order that they may be effective for the election.

(4)   On receipt of a notice under paragraph (2) a constituency returning officer shall publish it.

Nomination

Nomination of candidates at a constituency election

4(1) Each candidate at a constituency election shall be nominated by a separate nomination paper ("constituency nomination paper"), in form CE set out in English and Welsh in Schedule 10, delivered

    (a) by the candidate himself; or

    (b) in a case where in respect of the candidate a certificate issued under rule 5(1) or (3) is also delivered, by the registered nominating officer of a registered political party,

to the constituency returning officer at the place fixed for the purpose, but the paper may be so delivered on the candidate's behalf by his election agent if the agent's name and address have been previously given to the returning officer as required by article 37 or are so given at the time the paper is delivered.

(2) The constituency nomination paper shall state the candidate's

    (a) full names;

    (b) home address in full; and

    (c) if desired (but subject to paragraph (4)), description,

and the surname shall be placed first in the list of his names.

(3) If a candidate commonly uses

    (a) a surname which is different from any other surname he has; or

    (b) a forename which is different from any other forename he has,

the constituency nomination paper may state the commonly used surname or forename in addition to the other name.

(4) The description, if any, must consist of either

    (a) a description which is authorised as mentioned in rule 5(1) or (3); or

    (b) the word "Independent" or the word "Annibynnol" or both.

(5) Each constituency nomination paper delivered under this rule shall be subscribed by one person who shall also (if he is not the candidate) set out his full name and address.

(6) The constituency returning officer shall supply any person upon request with a form of constituency nomination paper at the place, and during the time, for delivery of nomination papers but it is not necessary for a nomination to be on a form supplied by the constituency returning officer.

Constituency nomination paper: name or description of registered political party

5(1) A constituency nomination paper may not include a description of a candidate which is likely to lead electors to associate the candidate with a registered political party unless the party is a qualifying party in relation to the constituency and the description is authorised by a certificate in form CF set out in English and Welsh in Schedule 10

    (a) issued by the party's registered nominating officer; and

    (b) received by the constituency returning officer at some time during the period for the delivery of nomination papers set out in the Table in rule 1(1).

(2) In paragraph (1) an authorised description may be either

    (a) the name or names of the party registered under section 28 of the 2000 Political Parties Act; or

    (b) a description of the party registered under section 28A of that Act.

(3) A nomination paper may not include a description of a candidate which is likely to lead electors to associate the candidate with two or more registered political parties unless the parties are each qualifying parties in relation to the constituency and the description is a registered description authorised by a certificate in form CG set out in English and Welsh in Schedule 10

(a) issued by the registered nominating officer of each of the parties; and

(b) received by the constituency returning officer at some time during the period for the delivery of nomination papers set out in the Table in rule 1(1).

(4) For the purposes of paragraph (3), a description is a registered description if it is a description registered for use by the parties under section 28B of the 2000 Political Parties Act.

(5) If it is proposed that a party's registered emblem is to be shown on the ballot paper against the candidate's particulars, a certificate issued under paragraph (1) or (3) shall request that it be so shown; but so that

(a) in a case in which a party has more than one registered emblem, only one of its emblems may be requested to be shown on the ballot paper; and

(b) in a case to which paragraph (3) applies, the registered emblem of only one of the parties may be requested to be shown on the ballot paper.

(6) A certificate issued under paragraph (1) or (3) may be combined with a constituency nomination paper delivered under rule 4(1).

(7) A person shall be guilty of a corrupt practice if he fraudulently purports to be authorised, by virtue of rule 81, to issue a certificate under paragraph (1) or (3) on behalf of a party's registered nominating officer.

Nomination of individual candidates at a regional election

6(1) Each individual candidate at a regional election shall be nominated by a separate nomination paper ("individual nomination paper"), in form CH set out in English and Welsh in Schedule 10, delivered by the candidate himself to the regional returning officer at the place or a place fixed for the purpose, but the paper may be so delivered on the candidate's behalf by his election agent if the agent's name and address have been previously given to the returning officer as required by article 37 or are so given at the time the paper is delivered.

(2) The individual nomination paper shall state the candidate's

(a) full names;

(b) home address in full; and

(c) if desired, a description consisting of the word "Independent" or the word "Annibynnol" or both,

and the surname shall be placed first in the list of his names.

(3) If a candidate commonly uses

(a) a surname which is different from any other surname he has; or

(b) a forename which is different from any other forename he has,

the nomination paper may state the commonly used surname or forename in addition to the other name.

(4) Each individual nomination paper delivered under this rule shall be subscribed by one person who shall also (if he is not the candidate) set out his full name and address.

(5) The regional returning officer shall supply any person upon request with a form of individual nomination paper at the place or a place, and during the time, for delivery of individual or party nomination papers but it is not necessary for a nomination to be on a form supplied by the regional returning officer.

Nomination of parties and party list candidates at a regional election

7(1) A registered political party may stand for election at a regional election if it is a qualifying party in relation to that region and is nominated by a separate nomination paper ("party nomination paper") in form CI set out in English and Welsh in Schedule 10 and delivered by that party's registered nominating officer to the regional returning officer at the place or a place fixed for the purpose.

(2)   A party nomination paper shall, in accordance with rule 8, include either
    (a)   the name or names of the party registered under section 28 of the 2000 Political Parties Act; or
    (b)   a description of the party registered under section 28A of that Act.

(3)   A party nomination paper shall include the list ("party list") of candidates ("party list candidates") submitted by the party for that regional election and the party nomination paper shall be the nomination paper for each candidate on that list.

(4)   In respect of each party list candidate, the party list shall state the candidate's
    (a)   full names; and
    (b)   home address in full,
and the surname shall be placed first in the list of his names.

(5)   If a party list candidate commonly uses
    (a)   a surname which is different from any other surname he has; or
    (b)   a forename which is different from any other forename he has,
the party list may state as regards that candidate the commonly used surname or forename in addition to the other name.

(6)   A party nomination paper shall be subscribed by one person who shall also (if he is not a party list candidate) set out his full name and address.

(7)   The regional returning officer shall supply any person on request with a form of party nomination paper at the place or a place, and during the time, for delivery of individual or party nomination papers but it is not necessary for a party nomination paper to be on a form supplied by the regional returning officer.

Party nomination paper: name or description of registered political party

8(1)   The name (or, as the case may be, names) or description required by rule 7(2) to be contained in a party nomination paper shall be authorised by a certificate in form CJ set out in English and Welsh in Schedule 10 issued by the registered nominating officer of the registered political party.

(2)   If it is proposed that the party's registered emblem is to be shown on the ballot paper against the party's name or description the certificate issued under paragraph (1) shall request that it be so shown; but so that in a case in which a party has more than one registered emblem, only one of its emblems may be requested to be shown on the ballot paper.

(3)   A certificate issued under paragraph (1) shall be combined with the party nomination paper delivered under rule 7(1).

(4)   A person shall be guilty of a corrupt practice if he fraudulently purports to be authorised by virtue of rule 81 to issue a certificate under paragraph (1) on behalf of a party's registered nominating officer.

Consent to nomination

9(1)   Subject to paragraph (3), at a constituency election a person shall not be validly nominated unless his consent to nomination
    (a)   is given and dated in writing on, or within one month before, the day fixed as the last day for the delivery of constituency nomination papers;
    (b)   is attested by one witness; and
    (c)   is delivered at the place, and within the time, for the delivery of nomination papers.

(2)   Subject to paragraph (3), at a regional election a person shall not be validly nominated

(whether as an individual or party list candidate) unless his consent to nomination

    (a) is given and dated in writing on, or within one month before, the day fixed as the last day for the delivery of individual nomination papers or party nomination papers;

    (b) is attested by one witness; and

    (c) is delivered at the place or a place, and within the time, for the delivery of individual nomination papers or party nomination papers.

(3) If the appropriate returning officer is satisfied that owing to the absence of a person from the United Kingdom it has not been reasonably practicable for his consent in writing to be given as mentioned, a facsimile communication (or any similar means of communication) consenting to his nomination and purporting to have been sent by him shall be deemed for the purposes of this rule to be consent in writing by him on the day on which it purports to have been sent, and attestation of his consent shall not be required.

(4) Subject to paragraph (7), a candidate's consent given under this rule

    (a) shall state the day, month and year of his birth;

    (b) shall state an address within the relevant area that shall be deemed to be his office as an election agent for the purposes of article 40(7);

    (c) shall state

        (i) that he is aware of the provisions of sections 12 to 15 of the 1998 Act (disqualification) and of any Order in Council under section 12(1)(b) of that Act; and

        (ii) that to the best of his knowledge and belief he is not disqualified for membership of the Assembly or that to the best of his knowledge and belief he is disqualified for membership of the Assembly only under section 16(1)(za) of the 2006 Act (disqualification of MPs);

    (d) shall, in the case of a candidate at a constituency election, state that he is not a candidate at an election for any other constituency, the poll for which is to be held on the same day as that for the election to which the consent relates or, in the case of an election to fill a casual vacancy, that he is not an Assembly member;

    (e) shall, in the case of an individual candidate at a regional election, state that he is not

        (i) a party list candidate in the election for that region; nor

        (ii) a candidate at a constituency election; nor

        (iii) an individual or party list candidate at an election for any other region,

        the poll for which is to be held on the same day as that for the election to which the consent relates; and

    (f) shall, in the case of a party list candidate at a regional election, state that he is not

        (i) an individual candidate or a candidate on any other party list in the election for that region; nor

        (ii) a candidate at a constituency election; nor

        (iii) an individual or party list candidate at an election for any other region,

        the poll for which is to be held on the same day as that for the election to which the consent relates.

(5) A candidate is required to give his consent under this rule notwithstanding that he has subscribed the nomination paper by virtue of which he is nominated.

(6) For the purposes of paragraph (4)(b), "the relevant area" shall be construed in accordance with

    (a) in relation to a constituency election, article 39(2)(a); and

    (b) in relation to a regional election, article 39(2)(b).

(7)   In respect of an Assembly election after the 2007 Assembly general election, rule 4(c)(i) shall have effect as if

    (a)   the references to sections 12 to 15 of the 1998 Act were a reference to sections 16 to 19 of the 2006 Act; and

    (b)   the reference to any Order in Council under section 12(1)(b) of the 1998 Act included a reference to any Order in Council under section 16(1)(b) of the 2006 Act.

Deposit

10(1)   A person shall not be validly nominated as a candidate at a constituency election unless the sum of £500 is deposited by him, or on his behalf, with the constituency returning officer at the place and during the time for delivery of constituency nomination papers.

(2)   A person shall not be validly nominated as an individual candidate at a regional election unless the sum of £500 is deposited by him, or on his behalf, with the regional returning officer at the place or a place, and during the time, for delivery of individual nomination papers.

(3)   A registered political party and each of the party list candidates on the list it has submitted shall not be validly nominated at a regional election unless the sum of £500 is deposited by the party's registered nominating officer (or by or on behalf of one of the party list candidates) with the regional returning officer at the place or a place, and during the time, for delivery of a party list.

(4)   The deposit may be made either

    (a)   by the deposit of any legal tender;

    (b)   by means of a banker's draft; or

    (c)   with the appropriate returning officer's consent, in any other manner (including by means of a debit or credit card or the electronic transfer of funds),

but the appropriate returning officer may refuse to accept a deposit sought to be made by means of a banker's draft if he does not know that the drawer carries on business as a banker in the United Kingdom.

(5)   Where the deposit is made on behalf of a candidate at a constituency election or an individual candidate at a regional election, the person making the deposit shall at the time he makes it give his name and address to the appropriate returning officer unless that information has previously been given to him under article 37.

(6)   Where the deposit is made on behalf of a registered political party and its party list candidates at a regional election the person making the deposit shall at the time he makes it

    (a)   if he is the registered political party's registered nominating officer, state that fact to the regional returning officer; or

    (b)   if he is not the party's registered nominating officer, give his name and address to the regional returning officer unless that information has previously been given to him under article 37.

Place for delivery of nomination papers

11(1)   In relation to a constituency election, the constituency returning officer shall fix the place at which constituency nomination papers are to be delivered to him, and shall attend there during the time for their delivery and for the making of objections to them.

(2)   The place in relation to a constituency election shall be in

    (a)   the Assembly constituency; or

(b) the registration area which includes the whole or any part of the Assembly constituency.

(3) In relation to a regional election, the regional returning officer shall fix the place or places at which individual nomination papers or party nomination papers are to be delivered to him, and he shall attend there during the time for their delivery and for the making of objections to them.

(4) A place in relation to a regional election shall be in the Assembly electoral region.

(5) For the purposes of paragraph (2)(b) "registration area" means the area of two or more Assembly constituencies which have the same registration officer.

Right to attend nomination

12(1) In relation to a constituency election, except for the purpose of delivering a constituency nomination paper or of assisting the constituency returning officer, and subject to paragraph (6), no person is entitled to attend the proceedings during the time for delivery of nomination papers or for making objections to them unless he is

    (a) a person standing nominated as a candidate;

    (b) the election agent of such a person;

    (c) the registered nominating officer of a registered political party that has delivered a certificate under paragraph 5(1) or (3) in respect of a candidate; or

    (d) a person who is entitled to attend by virtue of section 6A or 6B of the 2000 Political Parties Act,

but where a candidate acts as his own election agent he may name one other person who shall be entitled to attend in place of his election agent.

(2) In relation to a regional election, except for the purpose of delivering an individual nomination paper or a party nomination paper or of assisting the regional returning officer, and subject to paragraph (6), no person is entitled to attend the proceedings during the time for delivery of individual nomination papers or party nomination papers or for making objections to them unless he is

    (a) a person standing nominated as an individual candidate;

    (b) the election agent of such a person;

    (c) a party list candidate;

    (d) the registered nominating officer of a registered political party that has submitted a party list, or the election agent of that party in respect of that list;

    (e) a person who is entitled to attend by virtue of section 6A or 6B of the 2000 Political Parties Act,

but where an individual candidate acts as his own election agent, or a party list candidate acts as election agent of that party in relation to that list, he may name one other person who shall be entitled to attend in place of the election agent for that individual candidate or, as the case may be party.

(3) In relation to a constituency election, the right to attend conferred by this rule includes the right

    (a) to inspect; and

    (b) to object to the validity of,

any constituency nomination paper.

(4) In relation to a regional election, the right to attend conferred by this rule includes the right

    (a) to inspect; and

    (b) to object to the validity of,

any individual nomination paper or any party nomination paper (including the nomination of any party list candidate on the party list submitted with that party nomination paper).

(5) Paragraphs (3) and (4) do not apply to a person mentioned in paragraph (1)(d) or (2)(e).

(6) One other person chosen by the candidate is entitled to be present at the delivery of the nomination paper by which that candidate is nominated, and may afterwards, so long as the candidate stands nominated, attend the proceedings referred to in paragraph (1) or, as the case may be, (2), but without any such right as is conferred by paragraph (3) or, as the case may be, (4).

Decisions as to validity of individual and constituency nomination papers

13(1) A candidate to whom this rule applies shall be deemed to stand nominated where the nomination paper by which he is nominated and his consent to nomination are delivered and a deposit is made in accordance with these rules; and such candidate shall be deemed to stand nominated unless and until

    (a) the appropriate returning officer decides that the nomination paper is invalid;

    (b) proof is given to the appropriate returning officer's satisfaction of the candidate's death; or

    (c) the candidate withdraws.

(2) The appropriate returning officer is entitled to hold a nomination paper invalid only on one of the following grounds

    (a) that the particulars of the candidate are not as required by law (including, at a constituency election, that a nomination paper breaches rule 5(1) or (3));

    (b) that the paper is not subscribed as so required;

    (c) that the candidate is disqualified by the Representation of the People Act 1981;

    (d) in the case of an individual candidate at a regional election, that his candidature is in breach of section 5(6) of the 1998 Act; or

    (e) in the case of a candidate at a constituency election, that his candidature is in breach of section 4(7) of the 1998 Act.

(3) Subject to paragraph (4), the appropriate returning officer shall give his decision on any objection to a nomination paper

    (a) as soon as practicable after it is made; and

    (b) in any event, before the end of the period of 24 hours starting with the close of the period for delivery of constituency nomination papers set out in the Table in rule 1(1).

(4) If in the constituency returning officer's opinion a constituency nomination paper breaches rule 5(1) or (3), he shall give a decision to that effect

    (a) as soon as practicable after the delivery of the nomination paper; and

    (b) in any event, before the end of the period of 24 hours starting with the close of the period for delivery of nomination papers set out in the Table in rule 1(1).

(5) Where the appropriate returning officer decides that a nomination paper is invalid, he shall endorse and sign on the paper the fact and the reasons for his decision.

(6) The appropriate returning officer's decision that a nomination paper is valid shall be final and shall not be questioned in any proceedings whatsoever.

(7) Subject to paragraph (6), nothing in this rule prevents the validity of a nomination being questioned on an Assembly election petition.

(8) In respect of an Assembly election held after the 2007 Assembly general election, paragraph (2) shall have effect as if

    (a) in sub-paragraph (d) the reference to section 5(6) of the 1998 Act were a reference to section 7(6) of the 2006 Act; and

    (b) in sub-paragraph (e) the reference to section 4(7) of the 1998 Act were a reference to section 7(1), or as the case may be, section 10(9) of the 2006 Act.

(9)   This rule applies to a constituency candidate and an individual candidate.

Decisions as to validity of party nomination papers

14(1)   Where a party nomination paper, together with its party list and the consent of each candidate in that list, is delivered and a deposit is made in accordance with these rules the party and (subject to paragraphs (3) and (4)) each candidate on its list shall be deemed to stand nominated unless and until the regional returning officer decides that the party nomination paper is invalid.

(2)   The regional returning officer is entitled to hold a party nomination paper invalid only on one of the following grounds
    (a)   that it breaches rule 7(2) or (3);
    (b)   that it breaches rule 8(1) or (3);
    (c)   that it is not subscribed as so required;
    (d)   that the party list includes more than twelve persons; or
    (e)   that each candidate included on the party list has, in accordance with paragraphs (3) and (4), ceased to stand nominated.

(3)   Where, in respect of a party list candidate
    (a)   proof is given to the regional returning officer's satisfaction of his death; or
    (b)   he withdraws or his candidature is withdrawn in accordance with rule 15(4),
    he shall cease to stand nominated.

(4)   The regional returning officer is entitled to hold that a party list candidate shall cease to stand nominated where
    (a)   his particulars are not as required by law; or
    (b)   he is disqualified by the Representation of the People Act 1981; or
    (c)   his candidature is in breach of section 5(5) of the 1998 Act .

(5)   Where a candidate ceases to stand nominated by virtue of paragraph (4) it shall not of itself prevent any other candidate included on the party list from continuing to stand nominated.

(6)   Subject to paragraph (7), the regional returning officer shall give his decision on any objection to a party nomination paper or to a party list candidate
    (a)   as soon as practicable after it is made; and
    (b)   in any event, before the end of the period of 24 hours starting with the close of the period for delivery of nomination papers set out in the Table in rule 1(1).

(7)   If in the regional returning officer's opinion a party nomination paper breaches rule 7(2), 8(1) or 8(3), he shall give a decision to that effect
    (a)   as soon as practicable after the delivery of the nomination paper; and
    (b)   in any event before the end of the period of 24 hours starting with the close of the period for delivery of nomination papers set out in the Table in rule 1(1).

(8)   Where the regional returning officer decides that
    (a)   a party nomination paper is invalid; or
    (b)   the name and address of a candidate shall be deleted from a party list,
    he shall endorse and sign on the paper the fact and reasons for his decision.

(9)   The regional returning officer's decision that
    (a)   a party nomination paper is valid; or
    (b)   the name and address of a candidate should not be removed from a party list,
    shall be final and shall not be questioned in any proceedings whatsoever.

(10)   Subject to paragraph (9), nothing in this rule prevents the validity of a nomination being questioned on an Assembly election petition.

(11)   In respect of an Assembly election held after the 2007 Assembly general election,

paragraph (4)(c) shall have effect as if the reference to section 5(5) of the 1998 Act were a reference to section 7(5) of the 2006 Act.

Withdrawal of candidates

15(1) Subject to paragraph (3), a candidate at a constituency election may withdraw his candidature by notice of withdrawal
    (a) signed by him and attested by one witness; and
    (b) delivered to the constituency returning officer at the place for delivery of constituency nomination papers.

(2) Subject to paragraph (3), an individual or party list candidate at a regional election may withdraw his candidature by notice of withdrawal
    (a) signed by him and attested by one witness; and
    (b) delivered to the regional returning officer at the place or a place for delivery of individual nomination papers or party nomination papers.

(3) Where a candidate is outside the United Kingdom, a notice of withdrawal signed by a person and accompanied
    (a) by a written declaration also so signed of the candidate's absence from the United Kingdom; and
    (b) by a written statement signed by the candidate that the person giving the notice is authorised to do so on the candidate's behalf during his absence from the United Kingdom,
shall be of the same effect as a notice of withdrawal signed by the candidate.

(4) At a regional election a registered political party may withdraw the candidature of any or all of the candidates included in a party list of that party by notice of withdrawal
    (a) signed by the party's registered nominating officer; and
    (b) delivered to the regional returning officer at the place or a place for the delivery of individual nomination papers or party nomination papers.

Constituency election: publication of statement of persons nominated

16(1) At a constituency election the constituency returning officer shall prepare and publish a statement showing the persons who have been and stand nominated and any other persons who have been nominated, with the reason why they no longer stand nominated.

(2) The statement shall show the names, addresses and descriptions of the persons nominated as given in their constituency nomination papers.

(3) If a person's constituency nomination paper gives a commonly used surname or forename in addition to another name, the statement shall show the person's commonly used surname or forename (as the case may be) instead of any other name.

(4) Paragraph (3) does not apply if the returning officer thinks
    (a) that the use of the person's commonly used name may be likely to mislead or confuse electors; or
    (b) that the commonly used name is obscene or offensive.

(5) If paragraph (4) applies, the returning officer must give notice in writing to the candidate of his reasons for refusing to allow the use of a commonly used name.

(6) The statement shall show the persons standing nominated arranged alphabetically in the order of their surnames and, if there are two or more of them with the same surname, of their other names.

(7) In the case of a person nominated by more than one constituency nomination paper, the constituency returning officer shall take the particulars required by the foregoing

provisions of this rule from such one of the papers as the candidate (or the returning officer in default of the candidate) may select.

(8) The constituency returning officer shall send to the Commission
    (a) a copy of the statement; and
    (b) in the case of each candidate standing nominated in respect of whom a certificate has been received by the returning officer in accordance with rule 5(1) or (3), a copy of that certificate as well.

Regional election: publication of statement of parties and other persons nominated

17(1) At a regional election the regional returning officer shall prepare a statement showing
    (a) the names of the persons who have been and stand nominated as individual candidates;
    (b) the registered political parties which have been and stand nominated (together with in respect of each such party the list of candidates it has submitted and who have been and stand nominated as the candidates of that party); and
    (c) any other persons or parties who have been nominated together with the reason why they are no longer nominated,
and he shall deliver, or cause to be delivered, the statement to each constituency returning officer for an Assembly constituency in the Assembly electoral region.

(2) On receipt of a statement under paragraph (1) a constituency returning officer shall publish it.

(3) The statement shall show
    (a) in respect of individual candidates, the names, addresses and descriptions of the persons nominated as given in their individual nomination papers; and
    (b) in respect of the registered political parties who have submitted a party list, the names of those parties together with, in respect of each such party
        (i) the name, names or description referred to in rule 7(2); and
        (ii) the names and addresses of the persons nominated as appear in that party's list.

(4) If an individual candidate's nomination paper gives a commonly used surname or forename in addition to another name, the statement shall show the person's commonly used surname or forename (as the case may be) instead of any other name.

(5) If as regards a candidate included in a party list, the party list gives a commonly used surname or forename in addition to another name, the statement shall show the person's commonly used surname or forename (as the case may be) instead of any other name.

(6) Paragraph (4) and (5) do not apply if the regional returning officer thinks
    (a) that the use of the person's commonly used name may be likely to mislead or confuse electors, or
    (b) that the commonly used name is obscene or offensive.

(7) If paragraph (6) applies, the regional returning officer must give notice in writing to the candidate of his reasons for refusing to allow the use of a commonly used name.

(8) The statement shall show
    (a) the individual candidates standing nominated arranged together alphabetically; and
    (b) the registered political parties which have submitted a party list arranged together alphabetically and (in respect of each such party) the candidates standing nominated arranged (immediately after the entry for the relevant party) in the order that they appear on the party list.

(9) The arrangement of registered political parties referred to in paragraph (8)(b) is to be

shown in the statement before the arrangement of individual candidates referred to in paragraph (8)(a) is so shown.

(10) For the purposes of paragraph (8)(a) alphabetical order is to be determined by reference to the surnames of the individual candidates and, if there are two or more of them with the same surname, of their other names.

(11) For the purposes of paragraph (8)(b)

    (a) a registered political party is to be shown in the statement by reference to the name (or names) or, as the case may be, the description referred to in rule 7(2) in respect of the party; and

    (b) alphabetical order is to be determined by disregarding the definite or indefinite article and, where there are two or more words in the name or names or, as the case may be, description (having disregarded the definite or indefinite article), by reference to the first of those words and, if there are two or more parties with the same first word, of the other words.

(12) In the case of a person nominated by more than one individual nomination paper, the regional returning officer shall take the particulars required by the foregoing provisions of this paragraph from such one of the papers as the candidate (or the returning officer in default of the candidate) may select.

(13) In the case of a registered political party which has delivered more than one party nomination paper (and where party list candidates of that party stand nominated by more than one party list submitted with those papers), the regional returning officer shall take the particulars required by the foregoing provisions of this paragraph from such one of the papers and the party list with that paper as the registered nominating officer of the party (or the returning officer in default of that registered nominating officer) may select; and if any candidate is shown standing nominated by a list not so selected but is not so shown in the selected list he shall no longer stand nominated.

(14) The regional returning officer shall send to the Commission a copy of the statement.

(15) Other than in rule 19 the statement required by this paragraph is referred to in this Order as a statement of persons nominated.

Correction of minor errors

18(1) A returning officer may, if he thinks fit, at any time before the publication under paragraph 16 or 17 of the statement of persons nominated, correct minor errors in a nomination paper (including in a party list submitted with a party nomination paper).

(2) Errors which may be corrected include obvious errors of spelling in relation to the details of a candidate or of those of a registered political party.

(3) Anything done by a returning officer in pursuance of this rule must not be questioned in any proceedings other than proceedings on an Assembly election petition.

(4) A returning officer must have regard to any guidance issued by the Commission for the purposes of this rule.

Disqualification by Representation of the People Act 1981

19(1) If it appears to the appropriate returning officer that any person nominated as a constituency candidate or as an individual candidate or as a party list candidate might be disqualified by the Representation of the People Act 1981 he shall, as soon as practicable after the expiry of the time allowed for the delivery of

    (a) constituency nomination papers, in the case of a constituency election; or

    (b) individual nomination papers or party nomination papers, in the case of a regional election, prepare and publish a draft of the statement required by rule 16 or, as the case may be, 17.

(2) The draft shall be headed

    (a) in the case of a constituency election

        "Draft statement of persons nominated

        Datganiad drafft o'r personau a enwebwyd"; or

    (b) in the case of a regional election

        "Draft statement of registered political parties and other persons nominated

        Datganiad drafft y pleidiau gwleidyddol cofrestredig a phobl eraill a enwebwyd",

and shall contain a notice stating that any person who wishes to object to the nomination of any candidate on the ground that he is disqualified for nomination under the Representation of the People Act 1981 may do so between the hours of 10 in the morning and 4 in the afternoon on the day and at the place specified in the notice; and the day so specified shall be the day next after the last day for the delivery of nomination papers.

Adjournment of nomination proceedings in the case of riot

20(1) Where, the proceedings for, or in connection with, nomination are on any day interrupted or obstructed by riot or open violence

    (a) the proceedings shall be abandoned for that day; and

    (b) if that day is the last day for the delivery of

        (i) constituency nomination papers, in the case of a constituency election; or

        (ii) individual nomination papers and party nomination papers, in the case of a regional election,

the proceedings shall be continued on the next day as if that were the last day of such delivery, and that day shall be treated for the purposes of these rules as being the last day for such delivery (subject to any further application of this paragraph in the event of interruption or obstruction on that day).

(2) Where proceedings are abandoned by virtue of this rule nothing

    (a) may be done after they are continued if the time for doing it had passed at the time of the abandonment; or

    (b) done before the abandonment shall be invalidated by reason of the abandonment.

Method of election at a constituency election

21 At a constituency election

    (a) if the statement of persons nominated shows more than one person standing nominated, a poll shall be taken in accordance with Part 3 of these rules; or

    (b) if the statement of persons nominated shows only one person standing nominated, that person shall be declared to be elected in accordance with Part 4 of these rules.

Method of election at a regional election

22(1) Subject to paragraph (2), if the statement of persons standing nominated at a regional election shows more persons standing nominated (whether as individual candidates or party list candidates) than the number of seats for that Assembly electoral region a poll shall be taken in accordance with Part 3 of these rules.

(2) Where each person is included on the same party list, those persons shall be declared to be elected in accordance with Part 4 of these rules in the order that they are included on that list (starting with the highest) up to the number of seats for the

Assembly electoral region.

(3) But if the statement of persons standing nominated shows the number of persons standing nominated (whether as individual candidates or party list candidates) is the same as, or fewer than, the number of seats for the Assembly electoral region, those persons standing nominated shall be declared to be elected in accordance with Part 4 of these rules.

(4) Paragraph (2) or, as the case may be, (3) shall also apply where notice of poll at a regional election is countermanded or the poll is abandoned under rule 75(1) (election becomes uncontested through death of candidate).

Part 3
Contested Elections

General Provisions

Poll to be taken by ballot

23(1)   At a constituency election the votes at the poll shall be given by ballot and the result shall be ascertained, after counting the votes given to each candidate, in accordance with section 4(4) of the 1998 Act; and the candidate to whom the majority of votes has been given shall be declared to have been elected.

(2)   At a regional election the votes at the poll shall be given by ballot and the results shall be ascertained, after counting the electoral region votes given to each individual candidate or registered political party, in accordance with sections 4(5) and (6) and 5 to 7 of the 1998 Act; and the candidates who, in accordance with those provisions, are returned as Assembly members shall be declared to have been elected.

(3)   In respect of an Assembly election held after the 2007 Assembly general election
  (a)   paragraph (1) shall have effect as if the reference to section 4(4) of the 1998 Act were a reference to section 6(4) of the 2006 Act; and
  (b)   paragraph (2) shall have effect as if the references to sections 4(5) and (6) and 5 to 7 of the 1998 Act were a reference to sections 6(5) and 7 to 9 of the 2006 Act.

The ballot paper at a constituency election

24(1)   At a constituency election, the ballot of every voter shall consist of a ballot paper.

(2)   The persons shown in the statement of persons nominated as standing nominated, and no others, shall be entitled to have their names inserted in the ballot paper.

(3)   Every ballot paper shall be in form CK in Schedule 10, and shall be printed in accordance with the directions in form CK1 in that Schedule and
  (a)   shall contain the names and other particulars of the candidates shown in the statement of persons nominated;
  (b)   shall be capable of being folded up; and
  (c)   shall have a number and other unique identifying mark printed on the back.

(4)   The order of the names in the ballot paper shall be the same as in the statement of persons nominated.

(5)   If a certificate received by the constituency returning officer under rule 5(1) or (3) has requested that a registered political party's registered emblem (or, as the case may be, one of the party's registered emblems) is to be shown on the ballot paper against the candidate's particulars, the ballot paper shall contain that emblem in that way.

The ballot paper at a regional election

25(1) At a regional election, the ballot of every voter shall consist of a ballot paper.

(2) The following, namely

    (a) the persons shown in the statement of persons nominated standing nominated as individual candidates; and

    (b) the registered political parties which have submitted a party list and are shown in the statement of persons nominated as standing nominated, together with the party list candidates appearing on the party list of each such party and as standing nominated,

and no others, shall be entitled to have their names and descriptions inserted in the ballot paper.

(3) Every ballot paper shall be in form CL in Schedule 10, and shall be printed in accordance with the directions in form CL1 in that Schedule, and

    (a) shall contain the names and descriptions of the individual candidates shown in the statement of persons nominated;

    (b) shall contain the names or, as the case may be, descriptions of the registered political parties shown in the statement of persons nominated together with the names of the candidates included on those parties' lists;

    (c) shall be capable of being folded up; and

    (d) shall have a number and other unique identifying mark printed on the back (together with a mark or other distinguishing feature by which the Assembly constituency can be identified in which the vote is to be given in relation to the ballot paper).

(4) The order of

    (a) the names of the individual candidates; and

    (b) the names or, as the case may be, descriptions of the registered political parties (together with, in respect of each such name (or names) or, as the case may be, description of a registered political party, the names of its party list candidates),

in the ballot paper shall be the same order as in the statement of persons nominated.

(5) If a certificate received by the regional returning officer under rule 8(1) has requested that the registered political party's registered emblem (or, as the case may be, one of the party's registered emblems) is to be shown on the ballot paper against the party's description, the ballot paper shall contain that emblem in that way.

Polls with two ballot papers

26(1) Where the poll at a regional election is to be taken together with the poll at a constituency election for a relevant constituency, the constituency returning officer shall ensure that the number on the back of a constituency ballot paper is the same as the number on the back of one (but not more than one) regional ballot paper.

(2) A constituency is a relevant constituency for the purposes of paragraph (1) if it is situated in the region in respect of which the regional election is being held.

Corresponding number list

27(1) The constituency returning officer must prepare a list containing the numbers and other unique identifying marks of all ballot papers to be issued by him in pursuance of rule 33(1) or provided by him in pursuance of rule 37(1).

(2) The list shall be in form CM as set out in English and Welsh in Schedule 10.

Colour of ballot papers

28 Where at Assembly elections, an elector is entitled to give two votes, the ballot paper for each vote shall be of a different colour.

The official mark

29(1) Every ballot paper must contain an appropriate security marking (in this rule and in rule 58 referred to as "the official mark").

(2) The official mark shall be kept secret, and an interval of not less than seven years shall intervene between the use of the same official mark

    (a) at elections for the same Assembly constituency; or

    (b) in relation to the same Assembly constituency, at elections in the same Assembly electoral region.

(3) The appropriate returning officer may use a different official mark for different purposes at the same election.

Prohibition of disclosure of vote

30 No person who has voted at an Assembly election shall, in any legal proceedings to question the election or return, be required to state how he voted.

Use of schools and public rooms

31(1) At an Assembly election the constituency returning officer may use, free of charge, for the purpose of taking the poll

    (a) a room in a school to which this paragraph applies; or

    (b) a room, the expense of maintaining which is payable wholly or mainly out of public funds.

(2) This rule applies to a school maintained or assisted by a local authority (within the meaning of section 579(1) of the Education Act 1996), or a school in respect of which grants are made out of money provided by the Assembly or by Parliament to the person or body of persons responsible for the management of the school.

(3) The constituency returning officer shall make good any damage done to, and defray any expense incurred by the persons having control over, any such room as mentioned by reason of its being used for the purpose of taking the poll.

Action to be Taken Before the Poll

Notice of poll

32(1) The appropriate returning officer shall in the statement of persons nominated include a notice of the poll, stating the day on which and the hours during which the poll will be taken.

(2) In the case of a constituency election, the constituency returning officer shall also prepare and publish a notice (which may be combined with the statement of persons nominated under paragraph 16) setting out

    (a) the situation of each polling station; and

    (b) the description of voters entitled to vote there,

and he shall as soon as practicable after publishing such notice give a copy of it to each of the election agents.

(3) In the case of a regional election, the constituency returning officer for each Assembly constituency in the Assembly electoral region shall prepare and publish a notice (which may be combined with the statement of persons nominated under rule 17) setting out

    (a) the situation of each polling station in the Assembly constituency for which he is returning officer; and

    (b) the description of voters entitled to vote there,

and he shall as soon as practicable after publishing such notice

(i)   give a copy of it to each of the election agents; and

(ii)   deliver, or cause to be delivered, a copy of it to the regional returning officer.

(4)   Where the polls at a constituency election and a regional election are to be taken together the notices prepared by a constituency returning officer under paragraphs (2) and (3) may be combined.

Postal ballot papers

33(1)   Subject to paragraph (2), at an Assembly election the constituency returning officer shall in accordance with Schedule 3 issue to those entitled to vote by post

(a)   a ballot paper; and

(b)   a postal voting statement,

in the appropriate forms set out in Schedule 10 together with such envelopes for their return in accordance with paragraph 11 of Schedule 3.

(2)   In the case of a person who is entitled to give a constituency vote and an electoral region vote by post the provisions of paragraph (1) shall apply save the reference in paragraph (1) to "a ballot paper" shall be construed as a reference to a constituency ballot paper and a regional ballot paper and following references in this rule to "ballot paper" shall be construed accordingly.

(3)   In the case of a ballot paper issued to a person resident in the United Kingdom, the constituency returning officer must ensure that the return of the ballot paper and postal voting statement is free of charge to the voter.

(4)   The constituency returning officer must also issue to those entitled to vote by post such information as he thinks appropriate about how to obtain

(a)   translations into languages other than English and Welsh of any directions to and guidance for voters sent with the ballot paper;

(b)   a translation into Braille of such directions or guidance;

(c)   graphical representations of such directions or guidance; or

(d)   the directions or guidance in any other form (including any audible form).

Provision of polling stations

34(1)   At an Assembly election the constituency returning officer shall provide a sufficient number of polling stations and, subject to the following provisions of this rule, shall allot the electors to the polling stations in such manner as he thinks most convenient.

(2)   One or more polling stations may be provided in the same room.

(3)   The polling station allotted to electors from any polling district shall be in the polling place for that district.

(4)   The constituency returning officer shall provide each polling station with such number of compartments as may be necessary in which the voters can mark their votes screened from observation.

Appointment of presiding officers and clerks

35(1)   At an Assembly election the constituency returning officer shall appoint and pay a presiding officer to attend at each polling station and such clerks as may be necessary for the purposes of the election, but he shall not appoint any person who has been employed by or on behalf of

(a)   a candidate; or

(b)   a registered political party,

in or about the election.

(2) At a regional election the regional returning officer shall appoint and pay such clerks as may be necessary for the purposes of the election, but he shall not appoint any person who has been employed in the circumstances described in paragraph (1)(a) or (b).

(3) The constituency returning officer may, if he thinks fit, preside at a polling station and the provisions of these rules relating to a presiding officer shall apply to a constituency returning officer so presiding with the necessary modifications as to things to be done by the constituency returning officer to the presiding officer or by the presiding officer to the constituency returning officer.

(4) A presiding officer may do, by the clerks appointed to assist him, any act (including the asking of questions) which he is required or authorised by these rules to do at a polling station except order the arrest, exclusion or removal of any person from the polling station.

Issue of official poll cards

36(1) At an Assembly election the constituency returning officer shall as soon as practicable after the publication of notice of the election send to electors and their proxies an official poll card.

(2) An elector's official poll card shall be sent or delivered to his qualifying address, and a proxy's to his address as shown in the list of proxies.

(3) In accordance with the following provisions of this rule, the official poll card shall set out

    (a) the name of the Assembly constituency or electoral region for which the election is to be held, or, where the polls at a constituency election and a regional election are to be taken together, both such areas;

    (b) the elector's name, qualifying address and number on the register;

    (c) the date and hours of the poll and the situation of the elector's polling station; and

    (d) such other information, not relating to any candidate or registered political party, as the constituency returning officer considers appropriate,

and different information may be provided in pursuance of sub-paragraph (d) to different electors or descriptions of electors.

(4) In the case of an elector with an anonymous entry, instead of containing the matter mentioned in paragraph (3)(b), the official poll card shall contain such matter as is specified in the appropriate form referred to in paragraph (5), (6), (7) or (8).

(5) The official poll card issued to an elector shall be in form CN1 set out in English and Welsh in Schedule 10.

(6) The official poll card issued to the proxy of an elector shall be in form CN2 set out in English and Welsh in Schedule 10.

(7) The official postal poll card issued to an elector shall be in form CN3 set out in English and Welsh in Schedule 10.

(8) The official postal poll card issued to the proxy of an elector shall be in form CN4 set out in English and Welsh in Schedule 10.

(9) In this rule

    "elector" means a person

        (a) who is registered in the register for the Assembly constituency or as the case may be, Assembly electoral region on the last day for publication of notice of the election in question; and

        (b) includes a person then shown in that register as below voting age if (but only if) it appears from the register that he will be of voting age on the day fixed for the poll.

Equipment of polling stations

37(1) At an Assembly election the constituency returning officer shall provide each presiding officer with such number of ballot boxes and ballot papers as in the constituency returning officer's opinion may be necessary.

(2) Where the polls at a constituency election and a regional election are to be taken together, the same ballot box may be used for the receipt of ballot papers at the regional election and at the constituency election if the constituency returning officer so determines and a determination may make different provision for different polling stations.

(3) Where separate ballot boxes are to be used for the receipt of ballot papers at a constituency election and at a regional election, each ballot box shall be clearly marked with

    (a) the Assembly election to which it relates; and

    (b) the words "Place the *specify the colour of the ballot papers in question* ballot paper here, Rhowch y papur pleidleisio *nodwch liw'r papurau pleidleisio dan sylw* yma".

(4) Every ballot box shall be so constructed that the ballot papers can be put in it, but cannot be withdrawn from it without the seal being broken.

(5) The constituency returning officer shall provide each polling station with

    (a) materials to enable voters to mark the ballot papers;

    (b) copies of the register or such part of it as contains the entries relating to the electors allotted to the station;

    (c) the parts of any special lists prepared for the election corresponding to the register of electors or the part of it provided under sub-paragraph (b); and

    (d) a list consisting of that part of the list prepared under rule 27 which contains the numbers (but not the other unique identifying marks) corresponding to those on the ballot papers provided to the presiding officer of the polling station in the form CO set out in Schedule 10.

(6) The reference in paragraph (5)(b) to the copies of the register of electors includes a reference to copies of any notices issued under section 13B(3B) or (3D) of the 1983 Act in respect of alterations to the register.

(7) The constituency returning officer shall for the assistance of voters who are partially-sighted provide each polling station with

    (a) at least one large version of the ballot paper which complies with the relevant provision of article 141(6) and which shall be displayed inside the polling station;

    (b) an enlarged handheld copy of the ballot paper which complies with the relevant provisions of article 141(7) and (8); and

    (c) a device of the description set out in paragraphs (8) and (9), for enabling voters who are blind or partially-sighted to vote without any need for assistance from the presiding officer or any companion (within the meaning of rule 48(1)).

(8) The device referred to in paragraph (7)(c) must be capable of being attached firmly to a ballot paper and of being removed from it after use without damage to the paper.

(9) On one side of the device there shall be tabs of equal size which satisfy the conditions in paragraphs (10) to (13).

(10) The tabs must be capable of being positioned on the ballot paper so that each one is above one of the spaces to the right of

    (a) in the case of a constituency election, the particulars of a constituency candidate; or,

(b) in the case of a regional election

    (i) the name or names or, as the case may be, description of a registered political party; or

    (ii) the particulars of an individual candidate,

and on which the vote is to be marked ("the relevant space").

(11) Each tab shall be numbered so that when the device is positioned over a ballot paper, the number of each tab corresponds to that of the candidate, or as the case may be, registered political party, whose details (as referred to in paragraph (10)) are to the left of the relevant space covered by the tab in question.

(12) Each number on a tab shall be in raised form so that it can be clearly identified by touch.

(13) Each tab shall be capable of being lifted so as to reveal the relevant space and so that there is sufficient room to allow a voter to mark a cross on that space.

(14) A notice in the form of form CP set out in English and Welsh in Schedule 10, giving directions for the guidance of the voters in voting, shall be printed in conspicuous characters and exhibited inside and outside every polling station.

(15) Where there is a contested constituency election, in every compartment of every polling station there shall be exhibited the notice

(a) in the case where votes are also given at the polling station in respect of a contested regional election

"Vote for one candidate only on the constituency ballot paper coloured *colour of ballot paper*. Put no other mark on the ballot paper or your vote may not be counted.

Pleidleisiwch dros un ymgeisydd yn unig ar y papur pleidleisio etholaeth lliw *lliw'r papur pleidleisio*. Peidiwch â rhoi unrhyw farc arall ar y papur pleidleisio, neu fe all na chaiff eich pleidlais ei chyfrif."; or

(b) in any other case

"Vote for one candidate only on the ballot paper. Put no other mark on the ballot paper or your vote may not be counted.

Pleidleisiwch dros un ymgeisydd yn unig ar y papur pleidleisio. Peidiwch â rhoi unrhyw farc arall ar y papur pleidleisio, neu fe all na chaiff eich pleidlais ei chyfrif.".

(16) Where there is a contested regional election, in every compartment of every polling station there shall be exhibited the notice

(a) in the case where votes are also given at the polling station in respect of a contested constituency election

"Vote once only on the regional ballot paper coloured *colour of ballot paper*. Put no other mark on the ballot paper or your vote may not be counted.

Pleidleisiwch unwaith yn unig ar y papur pleidleisio rhanbarthol lliw *lliw'r papur pleidleisio*. Peidiwch â rhoi unrhyw farc arall ar y papur pleidleisio, neu fe all na chaiff eich pleidlais ei chyfrif."; or

(b) in any other case

"Vote once only on the ballot paper. Put no other mark on the ballot paper or your vote may not be counted.

Pleidleisiwch unwaith yn unig ar y papur pleidleisio. Peidiwch â rhoi unrhyw farc arall ar y papur pleidleisio, neu fe all na chaiff eich pleidlais ei chyfrif.".

(17) The appropriate statement of persons nominated referred to in rule 16 and rule 17 shall be printed in conspicuous characters and exhibited inside and outside every polling station.

Appointment of polling and counting agents

38(1)   Subject to paragraph (2), at a constituency election each candidate may, before the commencement of the poll, appoint
     (a)   polling agents to attend at polling stations for the purpose of detecting personation; and
     (b)   counting agents to attend at the counting of the votes.

(2)   The constituency returning officer may limit the number of counting agents that may be appointed under paragraph (1), so that
     (a)   the number shall be the same in the case of each candidate; and
     (b)   the number allowed to a candidate shall not (except in special circumstances) be less than the number obtained by dividing the number of clerks employed on the counting by the number of candidates.

(3)   Subject to paragraph (4), at a regional election each
     (a)   individual candidate; and
     (b)   election agent for a registered political party standing nominated,
may, before the commencement of the poll, appoint in relation to each Assembly constituency in the Assembly electoral region
     (i)   polling agents to attend at polling stations for the purpose of detecting personation; and
     (ii)   counting agents to attend at the counting of the votes.

(4)   The constituency returning officer may, in relation to the Assembly constituency for which he is the returning officer, limit the number of counting agents that may be appointed under paragraph (3), so that
     (a)   the number shall be the same in the case of each individual candidate or registered political party; and
     (b)   the number allowed to an individual candidate or registered political party shall not (except in special circumstances) be less than the number obtained by dividing the number of clerks employed on the counting by the total of the number of individual candidates and registered political parties standing nominated.

(5)   Notice in writing of an appointment under paragraph (1) or (3), stating the name and address of the person appointed, shall be given by the person making the appointment to the constituency returning officer and shall be so given not later than the second day (computed like any period of time set out in the Table in rule 1(1)) before the day of the poll.

(6)   If an agent dies, or becomes incapable of acting, the person who appointed him may appoint another agent in his place, and shall forthwith give to the constituency returning officer notice in writing of the name and address of the agent appointed.

(7)   Any appointment authorised by this rule to be made by a constituency or an individual candidate may be made, and the notice of appointment given to the constituency returning officer, by the candidate's election agent instead of by the candidate.

(8)   In the following provisions of these rules references to polling and counting agents shall be taken as references to agents
     (a)   whose appointments have been duly made and notified; and
     (b)   where the number of agents is restricted, who are within the permitted number.

(9)   Any notice required to be given to a counting agent by the constituency returning officer may be delivered at or sent by post to the address stated in the notice of appointment.

(10)   Any candidate may do himself any act or thing which any polling or counting agent, if appointed by him or on his behalf, would have been authorised to do, or may assist

such agent in doing any such act or thing.

(11) An election agent for a constituency or an individual candidate or a registered political party standing nominated may do or assist in doing anything which a polling or counting agent of that candidate or party is authorised to do; and anything required or authorised by these rules to be done in the presence of the polling or counting agents may be done in the presence of such an election agent instead of such polling or counting agents.

(12) Where by these rules any act or thing is required or authorised to be done in the presence of the polling or counting agents, the nonattendance of any agents or agent at the time and place appointed for the purpose shall not, if the act or thing is otherwise duly done, invalidate the act or thing done.

Notification of requirement of secrecy

39 At an Assembly election the constituency returning officer shall make such arrangements as he thinks fit to ensure that
    (a) every person attending at a polling station (otherwise than for the purpose of voting or assisting a voter with disabilities to vote or as a constable on duty there) has been given a copy in writing of the provisions of article 35(1), (3) and (6); and
    (b) every person attending at the counting of the votes (other than any constable on duty at the counting) has been given a copy in writing of the provisions of article 35(2) and (6).

Return of postal ballot papers

40(1) Where
    (a) a postal vote has been returned in respect of a person who is entered on the postal voters list; or
    (b) a proxy postal vote has been returned in respect of a proxy who is entered on the proxy postal voters list,
the constituency returning officer must mark the appropriate list accordingly.

(2) Rule 55(6) does not apply for the purposes of determining whether, for the purposes of this paragraph, a postal vote or a proxy postal vote is returned.

The Poll

Admission to polling station

41(1) The presiding officer shall exclude all persons from the polling station except
    (a) voters;
    (b) persons under the age of 18 who accompany voters to the polling station;
    (c) the candidates and the election agents of any constituency or individual candidates or in relation to any registered political party standing nominated, the election agent of such party in respect of the list it has submitted;
    (d) the polling agents appointed to attend at the polling station;
    (e) the clerks appointed to attend the polling station;
    (f) persons who are entitled to attend by virtue of any of sections 6A to 6D of the 2000 Political Parties Act;
    (g) the constables on duty; and
    (h) the companions of voters with disabilities.

(2) The presiding officer shall regulate the total number of voters and persons under the age of 18 who accompany them to be admitted to the polling station at the same time.

(3)   Not more than one party list candidate from the same party list submitted by a registered political party shall be admitted at the same time to a polling station.

(4)   Not more than one polling agent shall be admitted at the same time to a polling station on behalf of the same constituency or individual candidate or on behalf of the same registered political party.

(5)   A constable or person employed by a constituency or regional returning officer shall not be admitted to vote in person elsewhere than at his own polling station under the relevant provision of this Order, except on production and surrender of a certificate as to his employment, which shall be in form CB set out in Schedule 10 and signed by an officer of police of the rank of inspector or above or by the returning officer, as the case may be.

(6)   Any certificate surrendered under this rule shall forthwith be cancelled.

Keeping of order in the polling station

42(1)   It is the presiding officer's duty to keep order at his polling station.

(2)   If a person misconducts himself in a polling station, or fails to obey the presiding officer's lawful orders, he may immediately, by the presiding officer's order, be removed from the polling station

(a)   by a constable in or near that station; or

(b)   by any other person authorised in writing by the constituency returning officer to remove him,

and the person so removed shall not, without the presiding officer's permission, enter the polling station again during the day.

(3)   Any person so removed may, if charged with the commission in the polling station of an offence, be dealt with as a person taken into custody by a constable for an offence without a warrant.

(4)   The powers conferred by this rule shall not be exercised so as to prevent a voter who is otherwise entitled to vote at a polling station from having an opportunity of voting at that station.

Sealing of ballot boxes

43 Immediately before the commencement of the poll, the presiding officer shall

(a)   show each ballot box proposed to be used for the purposes of the poll empty to such persons, if any, as are present in the polling station, so that they may see that each box is empty;

(b)   place his seal on it in such a manner as to prevent it being opened without breaking the seal;

(c)   place each box in his view for the receipt of ballot papers; and

(d)   keep it so sealed.

Questions to be put to voters

44(1)   At the time that a person described in an entry in column 1 of the Table to this rule ("the Table") applies for a ballot paper (but not afterwards) the presiding officer may put to that person the appropriate question (or if more than one any of them) set out opposite that entry.

(2)   A question may be asked in English (as set out in column (2) of the Table) or Welsh (as set out in column (3) of the Table).

(3)   In respect of a person described in entries 2, 4 or 6 of the Table, the questions set out opposite those entries may be asked only where the polls at a constituency election

and a regional election are taken together.

(4)   Where the letter "R" appears after a question the presiding officer shall put that question to the person described opposite if the candidate or his election or polling agent (including such an agent of a registered political party standing nominated) so requires.

(5)   In the case of an elector in respect of whom a notice has been issued under section 13B (3B) or 13B(3D) of the 1983 Act, the references in the questions at 1(a), 5(a), (b) (c) and 6 to reading from the register must be taken as references to reading from the notice issued under section 13B (3B) or 13B (3D).

(6)   A ballot paper shall not be delivered to any person required to answer any of the questions unless that person has answered each question satisfactorily.

(7)   Except as authorised by this rule, no inquiry shall be permitted as to the right of any person to vote.

Table

Column (1)	Column (2)	Column (3)
Person applying for a ballot paper	Question to be asked in English	Question to be asked in Welsh
1 A person applying as an elector	(a) "Are you the person registered in the register of local government electors as follows (*read out the whole entry from the register*) ?"R (b) "Have you already voted, here or elsewhere, at this election, otherwise than as proxy for some other person?"R	(a) "Ai chi yw'r person sydd wedi ei gofrestru ar y gofrestr o etholwyr llywodraeth leol fel a ganlyn (*darllen allan y cofnod cyfan o'r gofrestr)*?"R (b) "A ydych eisoes wedi pleidleisio, yma neu yn rhywle arall, yn yr etholiad hwn, ar wahân i fel dirprwy dros berson arall?"R
2 A person applying as an elector where that person is entitled to give two votes at the polling station and the presiding officer has asked that person one or more of the questions at entry 1(a) and 1(b)	"Have you already cast a constituency vote and an electoral region vote at this election, here or elsewhere, otherwise than as a proxy for some person?"R	"A ydych eisoes wedi bwrw pleidlais etholaedol a phleidlais rhanbarth etholiadol yn yr etholiad hwn, yma neu yn rhywle arall, ar wahân i fel dirprwy dros berson arall?"R
3 A person applying as proxy	(a) "Are you the person whose name appears as AB in the list of proxies for this election as entitled to vote as proxy on behalf of CD?"R (b) "Have you already voted, here or elsewhere, at this election, as proxy on behalf of CD?"R (c) "Are you the spouse,	(a) "Ai chi yw'r person y mae eich enw yn ymddangos fel AB ar y rhestr o ddirprwyon ar gyfer yr etholiad hwn fel rhywun sydd â hawl i fwrw pleidlais ddirprwy ar ran CD?"R (b) "A ydych eisoes wedi pleidleisio, yma neu yn rhywle arall, yn yr etholiad hwn, fel dirprwy ar ran CD?"R (c) "Ai chi yw priod,

	civil partner, parent, grandparent, brother/ sister, child or grandchild of CD?"R	partner sifil, rhiant, nain neu daid, brawd / chwaer, plentyn neu ŵyr / wyres CD?"R
4 A person applying as proxy on behalf of an elector who is entitled to give two votes at the polling station if the presiding officer has asked that person one or more of the questions at entry 3(a) and 3(b).	"Have you already cast a constituency vote and an electoral region vote, at this election here or elsewhere, on behalf of CD?"R	"A ydych eisoes wedi bwrw pleidlais etholiadol a phleidlais rhanbarth etholiadol, yn yr etholiad hwn neu yn rhywle arall, ar ran CD?"R
5 A person applying as proxy for an elector with an anonymous entry, instead of the questions at entry 3.	(a) "Are you the person entitled to vote as proxy on behalf of the elector whose number on the register of electors is *(read out the number from the register)* ?"R (b) "Have you already voted, here or elsewhere, at this election, as proxy on behalf of the elector whose number on the register of electors is *(read out the number from the register)* ?"R (c) "Are you the spouse, civil partner, parent, grandparent, brother/ sister, child or grandchild of the elector whose number on the register of electors is *(read out the number from the register)* ?"R	(a) "Ai chi yw'r person sydd â hawl i bleidleisio fel dirprwy ar ran yr etholwr sydd â'r rhif canlynol ar y gofrestr etholwyr ar ei gyfer *(darllen allan y rhif o'r gofrestr)*?"R (b) "A ydych eisoes wedi pleidleisio, yma neu yn rhywle arall, yn yr etholiad hwn, fel dirprwy ar ran yr etholwr sydd â'r rhif canlynol ar y gofrestr etholwyr ar ei gyfer *(darllen allan y rhif o'r gofrestr)*?"R (c) " Ai chi yw priod, partner sifil, rhiant, nain neu daid, brawd / chwaer, plentyn neu ŵyr / wyres yr etholwr sydd â'r rhif canlynol ar y gofrestr etholwyr *(darllen allan y rhif o'r gofrestr)*?"R
6 A person applying as proxy on behalf of an elector with an anonymous entry and that elector is entitled to give two votes at the polling station, if the presiding officer has asked the person applying to vote as proxy one or more of the questions at entry 5(a) and 5(b).	"Have you already cast a constituency vote and an electoral region vote, here or elsewhere, at this election, on behalf of the elector whose number on the register of electors is *(read out the number from the register)*?"R	"A ydych eisoes wedi bwrw pleidlais etholiadol a phleidlais rhanbarth etholiadol, yma neu yn rhywle arall, yn yr etholiad hwn, ar ran yr etholwr sydd â'r rhif canlynol ar y gofrestr etholwyr ar ei gyfer *(darllen allan y rhif o'r gofrestr)*?"R
7 A person applying as proxy, if the question at entry 3(c) or 5(c) is not	"Have you at this election already voted in this constituency on behalf of	"A ydych yn yr etholiad hwn eisoes wedi pleidleisio yn yr

answered in the affirmative.	two persons of whom you are not the spouse, civil partner, parent, grandparent, brother/ sister, child or grandchild?"R	etholaeth hon ar ran dau berson a chithau heb fod yn briod, partner sifil, rhiant, nain neu daid, brawd / chwaer, plentyn neu ŵyr / wyres iddynt?"R
8 A person applying as an elector in relation to whom there is an entry in the postal voters list.	(a) "Did you apply to vote by post?" (b) "Why have you not voted by post?"	(a) "A wnaethoch wneud cais i bleidleisio drwy'r post?" (b) "Pam na wnaethoch bleidleisio drwy'r post?"
9 A person applying as proxy who is named in the proxy postal voters list.	(a) "Did you apply to vote by post as proxy?" (b) "Why have you not voted by post as proxy?"	(a) "A wnaethoch wneud cais i bleidleisio drwy'r post fel dirprwy?" (b) "Pam na wnaethoch bleidleisio drwy'r post fel dirprwy?"

Challenge of voter

45 A person shall not be prevented from voting by reason only that

    (a) a candidate or his election or polling agent declares that he has reasonable cause to believe that the person has committed an offence of personation; or

    (b) the person is arrested on the grounds that he is suspected of committing or of being about to commit such an offence.

Voting procedure

46(1) A ballot paper shall be delivered to a voter who applies for one, and immediately before delivery

    (a) the number and (unless paragraph (2) applies) name of the elector as stated in the copy of the register shall be called out;

    (b) the number of the elector shall be marked on the list mentioned in rule 37(5)(d) beside the number of the ballot paper to be issued to him;

    (c) a mark shall be placed in that copy of the register against the number of the elector to note that a ballot paper has been received but without showing the particular ballot paper which has been received; and

    (d) in the case of a person applying for a ballot paper as proxy, a mark shall also be placed against his name in the list of proxies.

(2) In the case of an elector who has an anonymous entry, he must show the presiding officer his official poll card and only his number shall be called out in pursuance of paragraph (1)(a).

(3) In the case of an elector who is added to the register in pursuance of a notice issued under section 13B(3B) or (3D) of the 1983 Act paragraph (1) is modified as follows

    (a) in paragraph 1(a), for "copy of the register of electors" substitute "copy of the notice issued under section 13B(3B) or (3D) of the 1983 Act";

    (b) in paragraph 1(c), for "in the register of electors" substitute "on the copy of the notice issued under section 13B(3B) or (3D) of the 1983 Act".

(4) The voter, on receiving the ballot paper, shall forthwith proceed into one of the compartments in the polling station and there secretly mark his paper and fold it up so as to conceal his vote, and shall then show to the presiding officer the back of the paper, so as to disclose the number and other unique identifying mark, and put the

ballot paper so folded up into the ballot box in the presiding officer's presence.

(5) The voter shall vote without undue delay, and shall leave the polling station as soon as he has put his ballot paper into the ballot box.

(6) Where the polls at a constituency election and a regional election are to be taken together the same copy of the register of electors or copy of the notice may be used under paragraph (1) for a constituency election and a regional election and one mark may be placed in that register or on that copy under paragraph (1)(c) or in the list of proxies under paragraph (1)(d) to denote that a ballot paper has been received in respect of each election except that, where a ballot paper has been issued in respect of one election only, a different mark shall be placed in the register or, as the case may be, on the copy or in the list so as to identify the election in respect of which the ballot paper was issued.

(7) Subject to rule 50(4) where a voter is entitled to two votes, the constituency ballot paper and the regional ballot paper delivered to a voter shall bear the same number.

Votes marked by presiding officer

47(1) The presiding officer on the application of a voter
   (a) who is incapacitated by blindness or other disability from voting in a manner directed by these rules; or
   (b) who declares orally that he is unable to read,
shall, in the presence of the polling agents, cause the voter's vote to be marked on a ballot paper in a manner directed by the voter, and the ballot paper to be placed in the ballot box.

(2) The name and number on the register of every voter whose vote is marked in pursuance of this rule, and the reason why it is so marked, shall be entered on a list (in this Schedule called "the list of votes marked by the presiding officer").

(3) For the purposes of paragraph (2) in the case of a person voting as proxy for an elector, the number to be entered together with the voter's name shall be the elector's number.

(4) In the case of a person in respect of whom a notice has been issued under section 13B(3B) or (3D) of the 1983 Act, paragraph (2) applies as if for "on the register of electors of every voter" there were substituted "relating to every voter in respect of whom a notice has been issued under section 13B(3B) or (3D) of the 1983 Act".

(5) Where the polls at a constituency election and a regional election are to be taken together, the same list of votes marked by the presiding officer may be used for the constituency and regional elections at which the voters are entitled to vote and, where it is so used, an entry in that list shall be taken to mean that the ballot papers were so marked in respect of each election, unless the list identifies the election at which the ballot paper was so marked.

Voting by persons with disabilities

48(1) If a voter makes an application to the presiding officer to be allowed, on the ground of
   (a) blindness or other disability; or
   (b) inability to read,
to vote with the assistance of another person by whom he is accompanied (in these rules referred to as "the companion"), the presiding officer shall require the voter to declare, orally or in writing, whether he is so incapacitated by his blindness or other disability, or by his inability to read, as to be unable to vote without assistance.

(2) If the presiding officer
   (a) is satisfied that the voter is so incapacitated; and

(b) is also satisfied by a written declaration made by the companion (in these rules referred to as "the declaration made by the companion of a voter with disabilities") that the companion

    (i) is a qualified person within the meaning of these rules; and

    (ii) has not previously assisted more than one voter with disabilities to vote at the Assembly election,

the presiding officer shall grant the application, and then anything which is by this Schedule required to be done to or by that voter in connection with the giving of his vote may be done to, or with the assistance of, the companion.

(3) For the purposes of this rule, a person is a voter with disabilities if he has made such a declaration as is mentioned in paragraph (1), and a person shall be qualified to assist a voter with disabilities to vote, if that person is either

    (a) a person who is entitled to vote as an elector at the Assembly election; or

    (b) the father, mother, brother, sister, spouse, civil partner, son or daughter of the voter with disabilities and has attained the age of 18 years.

(4) The name and number in the register of every voter whose vote is given in accordance with this paragraph and the name and address of the companion shall be entered on a list (in these rules referred to as "the list of voters with disabilities assisted by companions").

(5) For the purposes of paragraph (4), in the case of a person voting as proxy for an elector, the number to be entered together with the voter's name shall be the elector's number.

(6) In the case of a person in respect of whom a notice has been issued under section 13B(3B) or (3D) of the 1983 Act, paragraph (4) applies as if for "in the register of every voter" there were substituted "relating to every voter in respect of whom a notice has been issued under section 13B(3B) or (3D) of the 1983 Act".

(7) The declaration made by the companion

    (a) shall be in form CQ set out in English and Welsh in Schedule 10;

    (b) shall be made before the presiding officer at the time when the voter applies to vote with the assistance of a companion and shall forthwith be given to the presiding officer who shall attest and retain it.

(8) No fee or other payment shall be charged in respect of the declaration.

(9) Where the polls at a constituency election and a regional election are to be taken together, the same list of voters with disabilities assisted by companions may be used for the constituency and regional elections at which the voters are entitled to vote and, where it is so used, an entry in that list shall be taken to mean that the votes were so given in respect of each election, unless the list identifies the election at which a vote was so given.

Tendered ballot papers

49(1) If a person, representing himself to be

    (a) a particular elector named on the register and not named in the postal voters list; or

    (b) a particular person named in the list of proxies as proxy for an elector and not entitled to vote by post as proxy,

applies for a ballot paper after another person has voted in person either as the elector or his proxy, the applicant shall, on satisfactorily answering the questions permitted by law to be asked at the poll, be entitled, subject to the following provisions of this rule, to mark a ballot paper (in these rules referred to as "a tendered ballot paper") in the same manner as any other voter.

(2) Paragraph (4) applies if
    (a) a person applies for a ballot paper representing himself to be a particular elector named on the register;
    (b) he is also named in the postal voters list; and
    (c) he claims that he did not make an application to vote by post at the election.

(3) Paragraph (4) also applies if
    (a) a person applies for a ballot paper representing himself to be a particular person named as a proxy in the list of proxies;
    (b) he is also named in the proxy postal voters list; and
    (c) he claims that he did not make an application to vote by post as proxy.

(4) The person shall, on satisfactorily answering the questions permitted by law to be asked at the poll, be entitled, subject to the following provisions of this rule, to mark a ballot paper (in these rules referred to as a "tendered ballot paper") in the same manner as any other voter.

(5) Paragraph (6) applies if before the close of the poll but after the last time at which a person may apply for a replacement postal ballot paper, a person represents himself to be
    (a) a particular elector named on the register and who is also named in the postal voters list; or
    (b) a particular person named as a proxy in the list of proxies and who is also named in the proxy postal voters list,
and claims that he has lost or has not received his postal ballot paper.

(6) The person shall, on satisfactorily answering the questions permitted by law to be asked at the poll, be entitled, subject to the following provisions of this rule, to mark a ballot paper (in these rules referred to as a "tendered ballot paper") in the same manner as any other voter.

(7) A tendered ballot paper shall
    (a) be of a colour different from the other ballot papers; and
    (b) instead of being put into the ballot box, be given to the presiding officer and endorsed by him with the name of the voter and his number on the register, and set aside in a separate packet.

(8) The name of the voter and his number on the register shall be entered on a list (in these rules referred to as the "tendered votes list").

(9) In the case of a person voting as proxy for an elector, the number to be endorsed or entered together with the voter's name shall be the number of that elector.

(10) This rule applies to an elector who has an anonymous entry subject to the following modifications
    (a) in paragraphs (7)(b) and (8) the references to the name of the voter must be ignored;
    (b) otherwise, a reference to a person named on a register or in a list must be construed as a reference to a person whose number appears on the register or in the list (as the case may be).

(11) This rule applies in the case of a person in respect of whom a notice has been issued under section 13B(3B) or (3D) of the 1983 Act as if
    (a) in paragraphs (1)(a), (2)(a) and (5)(a) for "named on the register" there were substituted "in respect of whom a notice under section 13B(3B) or (3D) of the 1983 Act has been issued"; and
    (b) in paragraphs (7)(b) and (8) for "his number on the register of electors" there were substituted "the number relating to him on a notice issued under section 13B(3B) or (3D) of the 1983 Act".

(12) Where the polls at a constituency election and a regional election are to be taken together, the same tendered votes list for the constituency and regional elections at which the voters are entitled to vote may be used and, where it is so used, an entry in that list shall be taken to mean that tendered ballot papers were so marked in respect of each election, unless the list identifies the election at which a tendered ballot paper was so marked.

Spoilt ballot papers

50(1) A voter who has inadvertently dealt with his ballot paper in such manner that it cannot be conveniently used as a ballot paper may, on delivering it to the presiding officer and proving to his satisfaction the fact of the inadvertence, obtain another ballot paper ("the replacement ballot paper") in the place of the ballot paper so delivered (in these rules referred to as a "spoilt ballot paper"), and the spoilt ballot paper shall be immediately cancelled.

(2) Paragraph (1) shall also apply in a case where a voter is entitled to give two votes at a polling station, but subject to paragraphs (3) and (4).

(3) Subject to paragraph (4), if the voter proves to the satisfaction of the presiding officer that only one ballot paper is spoilt inadvertently
(a) he shall nevertheless deliver both ballot papers ("the surrendered ballot papers") to the presiding officer;
(b) the presiding officer shall deliver to the voter two replacement ballot papers; and
(c) the presiding officer shall treat both of the surrendered ballot papers as spoilt ballot papers and shall immediately cancel them.

(4) If a voter proves to the satisfaction of the presiding officer that one ballot paper is spoilt inadvertently and that the other ballot paper ("the used ballot paper") has been placed in the ballot box
(a) the voter shall deliver the spoilt ballot paper ("the returned ballot paper") to the presiding officer;
(b) the presiding officer shall deliver to the voter a replacement ballot paper in place of the returned ballot paper notwithstanding that the number on the replacement ballot paper is not the same as the number on the used ballot paper previously delivered to the voter; and
(c) the presiding officer in addition to cancelling the returned ballot paper shall treat the constituency or, as the case may be, regional ballot paper that has the same number as the replacement ballot paper delivered to the voter as a spoilt ballot paper and shall also immediately cancel it.

Correction of errors on the day of poll

51 The presiding officer shall keep a list of persons to whom ballot papers are delivered in consequence of an alteration to the register made by virtue of section 13B(3B) or (3D) of the 1983 Act which takes effect on the day of the poll.

Adjournment of poll in case of riot

52(1) Where the proceedings at any polling station are interrupted or obstructed by riot or open violence, the presiding officer shall adjourn the proceedings till the following day and shall forthwith give notice
(a) in the case where the polls at a constituency election and at a regional election are taken together, to the constituency and to the regional returning officer; but otherwise
(b) in the case of a constituency election, to the constituency returning officer; or

(c) in the case of a regional election, to the constituency returning officer for the Assembly constituency in which the polling station is situated and to the regional returning officer.

(2) Where the poll is adjourned at any polling station

    (a) the hours of polling on the day to which it is adjourned shall be the same as for the original day; and

    (b) references in this Order to the close of the poll shall be construed accordingly.

Procedure on close of poll

53(1) As soon as practicable after the close of the polls where the polls at a constituency election and at a regional election have been taken together, the presiding officer shall, in the presence of the polling agents, make up into separate packets, sealed with his own seal and the seals of such polling agents as desire to affix their seals

    (a) each ballot box in use at the station, sealed so as to prevent the introduction of additional ballot papers and unopened;

    (b) the unused and spoilt ballot papers placed together relating to the constituency election;

    (c) the unused and spoilt ballot papers placed together relating to the regional election;

    (d) the tendered ballot papers relating to the constituency election;

    (e) the tendered ballot papers relating to the regional election;

    (f) the marked copies of the register of electors (including any marked copy notices issued under section 13B(3B) or (3D) of the 1983 Act) and of the list of proxies;

    (g) the lists prepared under rule 27, including the parts which were completed in accordance with rule 46(1)(b) (together referred to in these rules as "the completed corresponding number lists");

    (h) the certificates as to employment on duty on the day of the poll; and

    (i) the tendered votes list, the list of voters with disabilities assisted by companions, the list of votes marked by the presiding officer, a statement of the number of voters whose votes are so marked by the presiding officer under the heads "disability" and "unable to read", the list maintained under rule 51 and the declarations made by the companions of voters with disabilities.

(2) Where paragraph (1) does not apply at an Assembly election, as soon as practicable after the close of the poll, the presiding officer shall, in the presence of the polling agents, make up into separate packets, sealed with his own seal and the seals of such polling agents as desire to affix their seals

    (a) each ballot box in use at the station, sealed so as to prevent the introduction of additional ballot papers and unopened;

    (b) the unused and spoilt ballot papers placed together;

    (c) the tendered ballot papers;

    (d) the marked copies of the register of electors (including any marked copy notices issued under section 13B(3B) or (3D) of the 1983 Act) and of the list of proxies;

    (e) the completed corresponding number lists;

    (f) the certificates as to employment on duty on the day of the poll; and

    (g) the tendered votes list, the list of voters with disabilities assisted by companions, the list of votes marked by the presiding officer, a statement of the number of voters whose votes are so marked by the presiding officer under the heads "disability" and "unable to read", the list maintained under rule 51 and the declarations made by the companions of voters with disabilities.

(3) The presiding officer shall deliver the packets made up under paragraph (1) or (2), or cause them to be delivered, to the constituency returning officer to be taken charge of

by him; but if the packets are not delivered by the presiding officer personally to the constituency returning officer, the arrangements for their delivery shall require the constituency returning officer's approval.

(4) The packets shall be accompanied by

    (a) a separate statement relating to each Assembly election where paragraph (1) applies; or

    (b) a statement relating to the Assembly election where paragraph (2) applies,

(in these rules referred to as "the ballot paper account") made by the presiding officer showing the number of ballot papers entrusted to him, and accounting for them under the heads of ballot papers issued and not otherwise accounted for, unused, spoilt and tendered ballot papers.

Counting of Votes

Time of, and attendance at, counting of votes

54(1) At an Assembly election the constituency returning officer shall

    (a) (subject to paragraph (2)) make arrangements for counting the votes in the presence of the counting agents as soon as practicable after the close of the poll; and

    (b) give to the counting agents and, in the case of a regional election, to the regional returning officer, notice in writing

        (i) of the time and place at which the proceedings described in rule 55(1) will begin;

        (ii) in the case where the power conferred by rule 55(3) is exercised, of the time and the place at which he will count the votes following completion of the proceedings described in rule 55(1); and

        (iii) in the case of a direction under paragraph (2), of the time and the place at which he will count the votes following completion of the proceedings described in rule 55(1),

and a notice under this paragraph may be combined with another such notice.

(2) At an Assembly general election where there are polls at

    (a) a regional election; and

    (b) constituency elections in the Assembly electoral region for which the regional election is held,

the Secretary of State may direct each constituency returning officer for any constituency within that Assembly electoral region that the counting of votes (as provided for in rule 55(5)) in respect of the regional and each constituency election shall not begin before such time between the hours of 9 in the morning and noon on the day following the close of polls for those elections (disregarding any day mentioned in rule 2) as is specified in the direction.

(3) A direction given under paragraph (2) shall be given not later than 28 days before the date of the poll at the Assembly general election in question.

(4) Where a direction is given under paragraph (2), then during the period beginning with the conclusion of the proceedings described in rule 55(1) and ending with the time specified in the direction, the constituency returning officer shall

    (a) place the ballot papers and other documents relating to each election under his own seal and the seals of such of the counting agents as desire to affix their seals; and

    (b) otherwise take proper precautions for the security of the papers and documents.

(5) No person other than

    (a)   the constituency returning officer and his clerks;

    (b)   the candidates and one other person chosen by each of them;

    (c)   the election agents;

    (d)   the counting agents;

    (e)   persons who are entitled to attend by virtue of any of sections 6A to 6D of the 2000 Political Parties Act; and

    (f)   in the case of a regional election, the regional returning officer,

may be present at the proceedings described in rule 55(1) or at the counting of the votes, unless permitted by the constituency returning officer.

(6)   A person not entitled to attend at the proceedings described in rule 55(1) or at the counting of the votes shall not be permitted to do so by the constituency returning officer unless he

    (a)   is satisfied that the efficient counting of the votes will not be impeded; and

    (b)   has either consulted the election agents or thought it impracticable to do so.

(7)   The constituency returning officer shall give the counting agents all such reasonable facilities for overseeing the proceedings, and all such information with respect to them, as he can give them consistently with the orderly conduct of the proceedings and the discharge of his duties in connection with them.

(8)   In particular, where the votes are counted by sorting the ballot papers according to

    (a)   a candidate for whom a vote is given in the case of a constituency election; or

    (b)   an individual candidate for whom, or a registered political party for which, a vote is given in the case of a regional election,

and then counting the number of ballot papers for each such candidate or party, the counting agents shall be entitled to satisfy themselves that the ballot papers are correctly sorted.

The count

55(1)   Subject to paragraph (8) where the polls at a regional election and at a constituency election for a constituency situated in that region are held on the same day, the constituency returning officer shall

    (a)   in the presence of the counting agents appointed for the purposes of each election open each ballot box and count and record separately the number of ballot papers in each box for each election;

    (b)   in the presence of the election agents appointed for the purposes of each election verify each ballot paper account;

    (c)   count such of the postal ballot papers as have been duly returned and record separately the number counted for each election; and

    (d)   separate the ballot papers relating to each election.

(2)   Where separate ballot boxes are used at polls in respect of a regional election and a constituency election for a constituency situated within that region, no vote shall be rendered invalid solely by the ballot paper being placed in the wrong ballot box.

(3)   The proceedings described in paragraph (1) may be undertaken at a different place (or at different places) than a place at which the votes given on ballot papers are counted.

(4)   But if the power in paragraph (3) is exercised, during the period beginning with the conclusion of the proceedings described in paragraph (1) and ending with the commencement of proceedings described in paragraph (5), the constituency returning officer shall

    (a)   place the ballot papers and other documents relating to each election under his own seal and the seals of such of the counting agents as desire to affix their seals; and

    (b)   otherwise take proper precautions for the security of the papers and documents.

(5) Subject to paragraphs (3) and (4) and any direction under rule 54(2), following completion of the proceedings described in sub-paragraph (1) the constituency returning officer shall in respect of the ballot papers relating to each election mix together all the ballot papers used at that election and count the votes given on them.

(6) A postal ballot paper shall not be taken to be duly returned unless
    (a) before the close of the poll
        (i) it is returned by hand or post and reaches the constituency returning officer; or
        (ii) it is returned by hand to a polling station in the same constituency as that for which that returning officer is appointed;
    (b) the postal voting statement duly signed is, before that time also returned either
        (i) by hand or post and reaches the constituency returning officer; or
        (ii) by hand and reaches such a polling station;
    (c) the postal voting statement also states the date of birth of the elector or, as the case may be, proxy; and
    (d) in a case where the constituency returning officer takes steps to verify the date of birth and signature of the elector or, as the case may be, proxy in accordance with paragraph 23 or, as the case may be, 24 of Schedule 3, he so verifies the date of birth and signature of that elector or, as the case may be, proxy.

(7) The presiding officer of the polling station shall deliver or cause to be delivered any postal ballot paper or postal voting statement returned to that polling station to the constituency returning officer in the same manner and at the same time as he delivers, or causes to be delivered, the packets referred to in rule 53.

(8) The constituency returning officer may collect, or cause to be collected, any postal ballot paper or postal voting statement which by virtue of paragraph (7) the presiding officer of a polling station would otherwise be required to deliver or cause to be delivered to him.

(9) Where the constituency returning officer collects, or causes to be collected, any postal ballot paper or postal voting statement in accordance with paragraph (8) the presiding officer shall first make it (or them) up into a packet (or packets) sealed with his own seal and the seals of such polling agents as are present and desire to affix their seals.

(10) The constituency returning officer shall not count any tendered ballot paper.

(11) The constituency returning officer, while counting and recording the number of ballot papers and counting the votes, shall keep the ballot papers with their faces upwards and take all proper precautions for preventing any person from seeing the numbers or other unique identifying marks printed on the back of the papers.

(12) The constituency returning officer shall verify each ballot paper account by comparing it with the number of ballot papers recorded by him, and the unused and spoilt ballot papers in his possession and the tendered votes list (opening and re-sealing the packets containing the unused and spoilt ballot papers and the tendered votes list) and shall draw up a statement as to the result of the verification, which any election agent appointed for the purposes of that election may copy; but where the power conferred by paragraph (3) is exercised in respect of more than one place a statement shall be drawn up in respect of each such place.

(13) The constituency returning officer shall so far as practicable proceed continuously with counting the votes, allowing only time for refreshment, except that he may, in so far as he and the agents appointed for the purpose of that election agree, exclude the hours between 7 in the evening and 9 on the following morning.

(14) For the purposes of the exception in paragraph (13), the agreement of

    (a)   in the case of a constituency election, a candidate or his election agent; or

    (b)   in the case of a regional election, an individual candidate or his election agent or the election agent for a registered political party,

shall be as effective as the agreement of his or its counting agents.

(15)   During the time so excluded the constituency returning officer shall

    (a)   place the ballot papers and other documents relating to the election under his own seal and the seals of such of the counting agents as desire to affix their seals; and

    (b)   otherwise take proper precautions for the security of the papers and documents.

(16)   In relation to an Assembly election to which paragraph (1) does not apply

    (a)   paragraph (17) shall apply in its place;

    (b)   the references in paragraphs (3) and (4) and in rule 54(1), (5) and (6) to paragraph (1) shall be construed as references to paragraph (17);

    (c)   "each election" in paragraph (4)(a) shall be construed as a reference to "the election"; and

    (d)   paragraph (18) shall apply in place of paragraph (5) and the reference to paragraph (5) in paragraph (4) shall be construed as a reference to paragraph (18).

(17)   The constituency returning officer shall

    (a)   in the presence of the counting agents open each ballot box and count and record the number of ballot papers in those boxes;

    (b)   in the presence of the election agents verify each ballot paper account; and

    (c)   count such of the postal ballot papers as have been duly returned and record the number counted.

(18)   Subject to paragraphs (3) and (4), following completion of the proceedings described in paragraph (17) the constituency returning officer shall count the votes given on the ballot papers after

    (a)   in the case of postal ballot papers, they have been mixed with the ballot papers from at least one ballot box; and

    (b)   in the case of ballot papers from a ballot box, they have been mixed with the ballot papers from at least one other ballot box.

Recount at a constituency election

56(1)   At a constituency election a candidate or his election agent may, if present when the counting or any recount of the votes is completed, require the constituency returning officer to have the votes recounted or again recounted but the constituency returning officer may refuse to do so if in his opinion the request is unreasonable.

(2)   No step shall be taken on the completion of the counting or any recount of votes until the candidates and election agents present at its completion have been given a reasonable opportunity to exercise the right conferred by this rule.

Recount of electoral region votes in an Assembly constituency

57(1)   At a regional election and prior to the certification required by rule 61(1)

    (a)   an individual candidate or his election agent;

    (b)   a party list candidate or an election agent for a registered political party standing nominated; or

    (c)   subject to paragraph (3), a counting agent for an individual candidate or a registered political party standing nominated,

may, if present when the counting or any recount of the votes is completed in a constituency, require the constituency returning officer to have the votes recounted or again recounted but the constituency returning officer may refuse to do so if in his opinion the request is unreasonable.

(2) No step shall be taken on the completion of the counting or any recount of votes until the candidates, election agents and counting agents present at its completion have been given a reasonable opportunity to exercise the right conferred by this rule.

(3) Where no candidate or election agent is present on the completion of the counting or any recount of votes, the right conferred on that person by this rule (if he had been present) may be exercised by a counting agent referred to in paragraph (1)(c) so present provided that in his terms of appointment as a counting agent he is authorised to exercise the right conferred by this rule; but not more than one such counting agent for the same individual candidate or registered political party standing nominated may be appointed for the purposes of this rule in relation to the same Assembly constituency.

Rejected ballot papers

58(1) Any ballot paper
  (a) which does not bear the official mark;
  (b) on which more than one vote is given;
  (c) on which anything is written or marked by which the voter can be identified except the printed number or other unique identifying mark on the back; or
  (d) which is unmarked or void for uncertainty,
shall, subject to the provisions of paragraph (2), be void and not counted.

(2) A ballot paper on which the vote is marked
  (a) elsewhere than in the proper place;
  (b) otherwise than by means of a cross; or
  (c) by more than one mark,
shall not for such reason be deemed to be void if an intention how the vote is to be given clearly appears, and the way the paper is marked does not of itself identify the voter and it is not shown that he can be identified by it.

(3) At a regional election, a ballot paper on which a vote is marked for a particular party list candidate on the party list of a registered political party shall, if otherwise valid, be treated as a vote for that party, whether or not there is also a vote marked for that party.

(4) The constituency returning officer shall endorse the word "rejected" on any ballot paper which under this rule is not to be counted, and shall add to the endorsement the words "rejection objected to" if an objection is made by a counting agent to his decision.

(5) The constituency returning officer shall draw up a statement showing the number of ballot papers rejected under the several heads of
  (a) want of official mark;
  (b) giving more than one vote;
  (c) writing or mark by which voter could be identified; and
  (d) unmarked or void for uncertainty.

Decisions on ballot papers

59 The decision of the constituency returning officer at an Assembly election on any question arising in respect of a ballot paper shall be final, but shall be subject to review on an Assembly election petition.

Equality of votes at a constituency election

60   At a constituency election, where, after the counting of the votes (including any recount) is completed, an equality of votes is found to exist between any candidates and the addition of a vote would entitle any of those candidates to be declared elected, the constituency returning officer shall forthwith decide between those candidates by lot, and proceed as if the candidate on whom the lot falls had received an additional vote.

Regional election: conveying results of count etc to regional returning officer

61(1) At the conclusion of the count of ballot papers in an Assembly constituency at a regional election the constituency returning officer shall, in accordance with any directions given by the regional returning officer, certify
    (a) the number of ballot papers counted by him and the total number of votes given for each individual candidate or registered political party; and
    (b) the number of rejected ballot papers under each head shown in the statement under rule 58(5), and
forthwith convey that information to the regional returning officer.

(2) Where the regional returning officer has received the information required to be conveyed to him under paragraph (1) from each constituency returning officer for an Assembly constituency in the Assembly electoral region, he shall certify the totals of the numbers referred to in paragraph (1) for the electoral region.

(3) After a constituency returning officer has conveyed to the regional returning officer the information required to be conveyed under paragraph (1) he may, subject to paragraph (4) give public notice in such manner as he considers appropriate of the information so conveyed.

(4) The regional returning officer may direct that the constituency returning officer may only give the notice referred to in paragraph (3) after the regional returning officer has given the notice that he is required to give under rule 64(1)(d).

Part 4
Final Proceedings in Contested and Uncontested Elections

Declaration of result at a constituency election

62(1) At a contested constituency election, when the result of the poll has been ascertained, the constituency returning officer shall forthwith
    (a) declare to be elected the candidate to whom the majority of votes has been given;
    (b) return his name and, if a certificate has been received by the constituency returning officer issued by the registered nominating officer of one or more registered political parties under rule 5(1) or (3) in respect of the candidate, the name of the party or, as the case may be, parties to the Clerk in accordance with paragraph (4);
    (c) give public notice of
        (i)   his name and, if applicable, the name of any registered political party referred to in paragraph (1)(b); and
        (ii) the total number of votes given for each candidate together with the number of rejected ballot papers under each head shown in the statement of rejected ballot papers under rule 58(5).

(2) At an uncontested constituency election, the statement of persons nominated, in addition to showing the person standing nominated, shall also declare that person elected, and the constituency returning officer shall forthwith return his name and, if a

certificate has been received by the constituency returning officer issued by the registered nominating officer of one or more registered political parties under rule 5(1) or (3) in respect of the candidate, the name of the party or, as the case may be, parties to the Clerk in accordance with paragraph (4).

(3) Where paragraph (1) or (2) applies at an Assembly general election, the constituency returning officer shall forthwith also notify the regional returning officer for the Assembly electoral region in which the Assembly constituency is situated as to
    (a) the name of the candidate who has been returned; and
    (b) if applicable, the name of the registered political party or parties referred to in paragraph (1)(b), or as the case may be, paragraph (2) and for which party or parties the candidate is, for the purposes of ascertaining the result at that regional election, returned as the Assembly member for that constituency.

(4) For the purposes of paragraph (1)(b) and (2), the constituency returning officer shall return those names required to be returned by
    (a) completing a certificate in form CR set out in English and Welsh in Schedule 10 declaring the candidate to be returned; and
    (b) delivering it, or causing it to be delivered, to the Clerk.

(5) References to "the Clerk" in paragraphs (1), (2) and (4) and in rule 64 shall, in relation to the 2007 Assembly general election, include the Clerk to the Assembly constituted by the 1998 Act.

(6) In this rule and in rule 63, references to "ascertaining the result" shall in relation to a contested regional election, mean
    (a) calculating the electoral region figure of each individual candidate and of each registered political party standing nominated at that election; and
    (b) allocating the seats to the electoral region members for that region,
and like terms shall be construed accordingly.

Ascertainment of results at a contested regional election

63(1) At a contested regional election, the regional returning officer shall make arrangements for ascertaining the results of the poll as soon as practicable after he has
    (a) given the certification required by rule 61(2); and
    (b) subject to rule 74(1), received the notification required by rule 62(3) from each constituency returning officer for an Assembly constituency in the Assembly electoral region.

(2) At a contested regional election the regional returning officer shall give notice in writing to the election agents and to each constituency returning officer for an Assembly constituency in the Assembly electoral region for which the election is held of the place and time at which he will begin to ascertain the results of the poll (together with such other information as he considers appropriate).

(3) No person other than
    (a) the regional returning officer and his clerks;
    (b) the individual and party list candidates and one other person chosen by each of them;
    (c) the election agents;
    (d) persons who are entitled to attend by virtue of any of sections 6A to 6D of the 2000 Political Parties Act; and
    (e) the constituency returning officer for any Assembly constituency in the Assembly electoral region for which the election is held,
may be present at the proceedings on the ascertainment of the results, unless permitted by the regional returning officer to attend.

(4) A person not entitled to attend at the proceedings shall not be permitted to do so by the regional returning officer unless he
    (a) is satisfied that the efficient ascertainment of the results will not be impeded; and
    (b) has either consulted the election agents or thought it impracticable to do so.

(5) The regional returning officer shall give the election agents and candidates all such reasonable facilities for overseeing the proceedings and all such information with respect to them (including for satisfying themselves that the ascertainment of the result that he is required to make is accurate), as he can give them consistent with the orderly conduct of the proceedings and the discharge of his duties in connection with them.

(6) The regional returning officer shall provisionally ascertain the results of the poll and notify that provisional ascertainment to such of the following persons who are present, namely
    (a) an individual candidate or his election agent; and
    (b) the election agent for a registered political party standing nominated or (in his absence) one of the candidates on the list submitted by that party.

(7) A person to whom notification under paragraph (6) has been given may require the regional returning officer to ascertain provisionally those results again but the regional returning officer may refuse to do so if in his opinion the request is unreasonable.

(8) No step shall be taken to complete the ascertainment of the result until the persons notified under paragraph (6) have been given a reasonable opportunity to exercise the right conferred under paragraph (7).

(9) Where the regional returning officer has provisionally ascertained the results again under paragraph (7), paragraphs (6), (7) and (8) and this paragraph shall apply to the further provisional ascertainment.

(10) If in ascertaining the results of the poll the regional returning officer is required to draw lots, he shall allocate the seat to the individual candidate or party on whom the lot falls.

(11) The regional returning officer shall have completed ascertaining the results of the poll when following a provisional ascertainment
    (a) there is no request under paragraph (7) for him to make a further provisional ascertainment; or
    (b) if there is such a request, the regional returning officer refuses to make a further provisional ascertainment.

(12) This paragraph applies where the regional returning officer is notified under rule 62(3) that a candidate who is returned as the Assembly member for a constituency is the candidate of more than one registered political party.

(13) In a case to which paragraph (12) applies, the regional returning officer shall, in calculating the electoral region figure of a registered political party named in the notification, include that candidate as a candidate of that party; and in doing so shall disregard the fact that, for the purposes of calculating the electoral region figure of another registered political party named in that notification, the candidate is also included as the candidate of that other registered political party.

Declaration of results at a regional election

64(1) After the regional returning officer has ascertained the results of the poll, he shall forthwith
    (a) announce the individual candidates or the registered political parties to whom

    seats have been allocated (together with the names of the party list candidates who are to fill such seats);

  (b) declare those individual or party list candidates to have been elected;

  (c) return the names of those persons to the Clerk (and, in respect of any party list candidate, the name of the registered political party for which he was such a candidate) in accordance with paragraph (3); and

  (d) give public notice

     (i) of the name of any individual candidate elected;

    (ii) of the name of any party list candidate elected (and the name of the registered political party for which he was such a candidate);

    (iii) of the total number of votes given for each individual candidate or registered political party together with the number of rejected ballot papers under each head shown in the statement of rejected ballot papers; and

    (iv) in respect of the number of votes referred to in sub-paragraph (iii), a breakdown of the number of votes given for each such candidate or party in each Assembly constituency in the Assembly electoral region.

(2) At an uncontested regional election the statement of persons nominated, in addition to showing the registered political parties and other persons standing nominated, shall also

  (a) set out the individual candidates or the registered political parties to whom seats have been allocated (together with the names of the party list candidates who are to fill such seats); and

  (b) declare those individual or party list candidates to have been elected and returned,

and the regional returning officer shall forthwith return the names of those persons to the Clerk (and, in respect of any party list candidate, the name of the registered political party for which he was such a candidate) in accordance with paragraph (3).

(3) For the purposes of paragraphs (1)(c) and (2) the regional returning officer shall return those names required to be returned, by

  (a) completing a certificate in form CS set out in English and Welsh in Schedule 10, (declaring the candidate to be returned); and

  (b) delivering it, or causing it to be delivered, to the Clerk.

Return or forfeiture of deposit

65(1) The deposit made at an Assembly election under rule 10 shall either be

  (a) returned to the person making it or his personal representatives, in the case of a candidate at a constituency election or an individual candidate at a regional election;

  (b) returned to the registered nominating officer of a registered political party which has submitted a party list, in the case of a regional election; or

  (c) forfeited to the Secretary of State.

(2) Except in the cases mentioned in this rule, the deposit shall be returned not later than the next day after that on which the result or results of the election are declared.

(3) For the purposes of paragraph (2)

  (a) a day shall be disregarded if it would be disregarded under rule 2 in computing any period of time for the purposes of the timetable for the election; and

  (b) the deposit shall be treated as being returned on a day if a cheque for the amount of the deposit is posted on that day.

(4) If, in the case of a constituency election, a candidate is not shown as standing nominated in the statement of persons nominated, or if the poll is countermanded or

abandoned by reason of his death, his deposit shall be returned as soon as practicable after the publication of the statement or after his death, as the case may be.

(5) If, in the case of a regional election, an individual candidate or a registered political party is not shown as standing nominated in the statement of persons nominated, his or their deposit shall be returned as soon as practicable after publication of the statement.

(6) Subject to paragraph (4) the deposit shall be forfeited if in the case of a candidate for return as a constituency member, a poll is taken and after the counting of the votes by the constituency returning officer (including any recount) is completed, the candidate is found to have polled not more than one twentieth of the total number of votes polled by all candidates in the constituency.

(7) Subject to paragraph (5), the deposit shall be forfeited if, in the case of a registered political party standing nominated or an individual candidate for return as a regional member, a poll is taken and after the total number of votes given for each registered party and each individual candidate has been counted, the registered political party or individual candidate is found to have polled not more than one twentieth of the total number of votes polled by all registered political parties and individual candidates in the region.

(8) Notwithstanding anything in paragraphs (2) to (7), if at an Assembly election a person is standing nominated as
    (a) a candidate at a constituency election; or
    (b) an individual or party list candidate at a regional election,
and by virtue of such nomination he is in breach of
        (i) in relation to a constituency candidate, section 4(7) or section 8(7) of the 1998 Act; or
        (ii) in relation to an individual or party list candidate, section 5(5) or, as the case may be section 5(6) of the 1998 Act,
then not more than one of the deposits shall be returned and, if necessary, the Secretary of State shall determine which it is to be.

(9) In respect of an Assembly election held after the 2007 Assembly general election, paragraph (8) shall have effect as if
    (a) in sub-paragraph (i), the references to sections 4(7) and 8(7)of the 1998 Act were respectively a reference to sections 7(1) and 10(9) of the 2006 Act; and
    (b) in sub-paragraph (ii), the references to section 5(5) and section 5(6) of the 1998 Act, were respectively a reference to section 7(5) and section 7(6) of the 2006 Act.

Part 5
Disposal of Documents

Sealing up of ballot papers

66(1) On the completion of the counting at a contested Assembly election the constituency returning officer shall seal up in separate packets the counted and rejected ballot papers.

(2) Where the polls at a constituency election and a regional election are taken together packets sealed up under paragraph (1) shall not contain ballot papers relating to different elections.

(3) The constituency returning officer shall not open the sealed packets of
    (a) tendered ballot papers;

(b)   the completed corresponding number lists;

(c)   certificates as to employment on duty on the day of the poll; or

(d)   marked copies of the register of electors (including any marked copy notices issued under section 13B(3B) or (3D) of the 1983 Act) and lists of proxies.

Delivery of documents to relevant registration officer

67(1)   Where a constituency returning officer has conducted a count where the poll at a constituency election and a regional election have been taken together , he shall then forward to the relevant registration officer the following documents

(a)   the packets of ballot papers in his possession relating to a constituency election;

(b)   the packets of ballot papers in his possession relating to a regional election;

(c)   the ballot paper accounts and the statements of rejected ballot papers and of the result of the verification of the ballot paper accounts relating to a constituency election;

(d)   the ballot paper accounts and the statements of rejected ballot papers and of the result of the verification of the ballot paper accounts relating to a regional election;

(e)   the tendered votes lists, the lists of voters with disabilities assisted by companions, the lists of votes marked by the presiding officer and the related statements, the lists maintained under rule 51 and the declarations made by the companions of voters with disabilities relating to the election, or as the case may be, elections;

(f)   the packets of the completed corresponding number lists;

(g)   the packets of the certificates as to employment on duty on the day of the poll relating to the election, or as the case may be, elections; and

(h)   the packets containing marked copies of registers (including any marked copy notices issued under section 13B(3B) or (3D) of the 1983 Act) and of the postal voters list, of lists of proxies and of the proxy postal voters list relating to the election, or as the case may be elections,

endorsing on each packet

(i)   a description of its contents;

(ii)   the date of the election or elections to which they relate;

(iii)   where the packet relates to a constituency election, the name of the Assembly constituency for which the election was held;

(iv)   where the packet relates to a regional election, the name of the Assembly electoral region for which the election was held and the name of the Assembly constituency in which the electoral region votes were given; and

(v)   where the packet relates to both a constituency and a regional election, the name of the Assembly constituency and electoral region for which the elections were held.

(2)   Where a constituency returning officer has conducted a count at an Assembly election and paragraph (1) does not apply, he shall then forward to the relevant registration officer the following documents

(a)   the packets of ballot papers in his possession;

(b)   the ballot paper accounts and the statements of rejected ballot papers and of the result of the verification of the ballot paper accounts;

(c)   the tendered votes lists, the lists of voters with disabilities assisted by companions, the lists of votes marked by the presiding officer and the related statements, the lists maintained under rule 51 and the declarations made by the companions of voters with disabilities;

(d)   the packets of the completed corresponding number lists;

(e)   the packets of the certificates as to employment on duty on the day of the poll;

and

(f) the packets containing marked copies of registers (including any marked copy notices issued under section 13B(3B) or (3D) of the 1983 Act) and of the postal voters list, of lists of proxies and of the proxy postal voters list,

endorsing on each packet

    (i) a description of its contents;

    (ii) the date of the election to which they relate;

    (iii) the name of the Assembly constituency or electoral region for which the election was held; and

    (iv) in the case of a regional election, the name of the Assembly constituency in which the electoral region votes were given.

Order for production of documents

68(1) An order

    (a) for the inspection or production of any rejected ballot papers in the custody of the relevant registration officer; or

    (b) for the opening of a sealed packet of the completed corresponding number lists or of certificates as to employment on duty on the day of the poll or the inspection of any counted ballot papers in his custody,

may be made if satisfied by evidence on oath that the order is required for the purpose of instituting or maintaining a prosecution for an offence in relation to ballot papers, or for the purpose of an Assembly election petition, by the High Court or a county court.

(2) An order for the opening of a sealed packet referred to in paragraph (1)(b) or for the inspection of any counted ballot papers in the relevant registration officer's custody may be made by an election court.

(3) An order under this paragraph may be made subject to such conditions as to

    (a) persons;

    (b) time;

    (c) place and mode of inspection; or

    (d) production or opening,

as the court making the order may think expedient; but in making and carrying into effect an order for the opening of a sealed packet referred to in paragraph (1)(b) or for the inspection of counted ballot papers, care shall be taken that the way in which the vote of any particular elector has been given shall not be disclosed until it has been proved

    (i) that his vote was given; and

    (ii) that the vote has been declared by a competent court to be invalid.

(4) An appeal lies to the High Court from any order of a county court under this paragraph.

(5) Any power given under this rule to the High Court, or to a county court, may be exercised by any judge of the court otherwise than in open court.

(6) Where an order is made for the production by the relevant registration officer of any document in his possession relating to any specified election

    (a) the production by him or his agent of the document ordered in such manner as may be directed by that order shall be conclusive evidence that the document relates to the specified election; and

    (b) any endorsement on any packet of ballot papers so produced shall be prima facie evidence that the ballot papers are what they are stated to be by the endorsement.

(7) The production from proper custody of

    (a) a ballot paper purporting to have been used at any election; and

(b) a completed corresponding number list with a number marked in writing beside the number of the ballot paper,

shall be prima facie evidence that the elector whose vote was given by that ballot paper was the person whose entry in the register of electors or on a notice issued under section 13B(3B) or(3D) of the 1983 Act at the time of the election contained the same number as the number written as mentioned in sub-paragraph (b).

(8) Save as provided by this rule, no person shall be allowed to inspect any rejected or counted ballot papers in the possession of the relevant registration officer or to open any sealed packets referred to in paragraph (1)(b).

Retention and public inspection of documents

69(1) The relevant registration officer shall retain for a year all documents relating to an election forwarded to him in pursuance of these rules by a constituency returning officer and then, unless otherwise directed by order of the High Court, the Crown Court or a magistrates' court, shall cause them to be destroyed.

(2) Notwithstanding the revocation of the National Assembly for Wales (Representation of the People) Order 2003, rule 64 of Schedule 5 to that Order shall, in relation to documents forwarded to the Assembly under that Schedule and to which that paragraph applied, continue to have effect as if incorporated in this Order.

Part 6
Death of Candidate

Constituency election: death of independent candidate

70(1) This rule applies if at a contested constituency election proof is given to the constituency returning officer's satisfaction before the result of the election is declared that one of the persons named or to be named in the ballot paper as an independent candidate has died.

(2) Subject to this rule and rules 71 and 72, these rules apply to the election as if the candidate had not died.

(3) The following provisions of these rules do not apply in relation to the deceased candidate
  (a) rule 41(1)(c) and (d) (admission to polling station);
  (b) rule 54(5)(b) to (d) (attendance at count); and
  (c) rule 65(6) (forfeiture of deposit).

(4) If only two persons are shown as standing nominated in the statement of persons nominated the returning officer must
  (a) if polling has not begun, countermand the notice of poll;
  (b) if polling has begun, direct that the poll is abandoned; and
  (c) subject to rule 76, treat the election as an uncontested election.

(5) For the purposes of this rule a person is named or to be named in the ballot paper as an independent candidate if the description (if any) on his nomination paper is not authorised as mentioned in rule 5(1) or (3).

Constituency election: deceased independent candidate wins

71(1) This rule applies if at an election mentioned in rule 70(1) the majority of votes is given to the deceased candidate.

(2) Rule 62(1) (declaration of result) does not apply and the constituency returning officer must not complete a certificate under rule 62(4) but must

(a) declare that the majority of votes has been given to the deceased candidate;

(b) declare that no member is returned;

(c) give public notice of the total number of votes given for each candidate together with the number of rejected ballot papers under each head shown in the statement under rule 58(5); and

(d) at an Assembly general election, forthwith notify the regional returning officer for the region containing that constituency that the majority of votes has been given to the deceased candidate and that no member is returned for that constituency.

(3) Rule 65 (return or forfeiture of deposit) does not apply in relation to the remaining candidates.

(4) The proceedings with reference to the election must be commenced afresh subject to the following provisions of this rule.

(5) A new notice of the election ("the new notice") must be published on the first working day after the end of the period of seven days starting on the day of the poll of the election mentioned in rule 70(1).

(6) No fresh nomination is necessary in the case of a person shown in the previous statement of persons nominated, and no other nomination may be made.

(7) The last day on which a notice of withdrawal of candidature by a person who stands nominated by virtue of paragraph (6) may be delivered is the seventh working day after the day on which the new notice is published.

(8) Rule 10 (deposit) does not apply.

(9) Subject to paragraphs (10) and (11), the poll must be held on a day in the period ("the first period") which starts 15 working days after the day on which the new notice is published and ends 19 working days after that day.

(10) If any of the days within the first period is Maundy Thursday, then

(a) the poll must not be held on Maundy Thursday; but

(b) the constituency returning officer may fix the day of the poll to be held in the period which starts 20 working days after the day on which the new notice is published and ends 24 working days after that day.

(11) If any of the days within the first period is a day in the period which starts with 22nd December and ends with 2nd January following, the constituency returning officer may fix the day of the poll to be held in the period which starts 20 working days after the day on which the new notice is published and ends 24 working days after that day.

(12) For the purposes of this rule

(a) a working day is a day which is not a day mentioned in rule 2; and

(b) "previous statement of persons nominated" means the statement of persons nominated in operation at the time of the death of the deceased candidate.

Constituency election: deceased independent candidate with equality of votes

72   In an election mentioned in rule 70(1), if

(a) rule 60 (equality of votes) applies; and

(b) any of the candidates to whom that paragraph applies is a deceased candidate,

the deceased candidate must be ignored.

Constituency election: death of party candidate

73(1)   This rule applies if

(a) at a contested constituency election proof is given to the constituency returning officer's satisfaction before the result of the election is declared that one of the persons named or to be named in the ballot paper has died; and

(b)   that person is standing in the name of a registered political party.

(2)   The returning officer must

    (a)   countermand notice of the poll; or

    (b)   if polling has begun, direct that the poll be abandoned.

(3)   At an Assembly general election, the constituency returning officer must forthwith notify the regional returning officer for the region containing that constituency that notice of the poll at that constituency election has been countermanded or, as the case may be, that the poll has been abandoned and that no member is returned for that constituency.

(4)   The proceedings with reference to the election must be commenced afresh subject to the following provisions of this rule.

(5)   A new notice of the election ("the new notice") must be published on the first working day after the end of the period of seven days starting on the day the proof of death is given to the constituency returning officer.

(6)   No fresh nomination is necessary in the case of a person shown in the previous statement of persons nominated as standing nominated.

(7)   No other nomination may be made except for a person standing in the name of the same registered political party in whose name the deceased candidate was standing.

(8)   The last day on which a nomination mentioned in paragraph (7) may be delivered is the seventh working day after the day on which the new notice of the election is published.

(9)   The last day on which a notice of withdrawal of candidature by a person who stands nominated by virtue of paragraph (6) or in pursuance of paragraph (7) may be delivered is the seventh working day after the day on which the new notice of the election is published.

(10)   Subject to paragraphs (11) and (12) the poll must be held on a day in the period ("the first period") which starts 15 working days after the day on which the new notice is published and ends 19 working days after that day.

(11)   If any of the days within the first period is Maundy Thursday, then

    (a)   the poll must not be held on Maundy Thursday; but

    (b)   the constituency returning officer may fix the day of the poll to be held in the period which starts 20 working days after the day on which the new notice is published and ends 24 working days after that day.

(12)   If any of the days within the first period is a day in the period which starts with 22nd December and ends with 2nd January following, the constituency returning officer may fix the day of the poll to be held in the period which starts 20 working days after the day on which the new notice is published and ends 24 working days after that day.

(13)   For the purposes of this rule

    (a)   a person stands in the name of a registered political party if his nomination paper contains a description which is authorised as mentioned in rule 5(1) or (3) and where the description is authorised under rule 5(3), references to "party" shall be construed as referring to each party by whom use of that description is authorised;

    (b)   a working day is a day which is not specified in rule 2(a) to (d); and

    (c)   "previous statement of person nominated" means the statement of persons nominated in operation at the time of the death of the person standing in the name of the registered political party.

Regional election: effect of countermand or abandonment of constituency poll

74(1)   Where at an Assembly general election, there is a contested regional election and the poll or declaration of result at a constituency election for an Assembly constituency in the Assembly electoral region is postponed in accordance with rule 71 or 73, rule 63(1)(b) shall be satisfied when the regional returning officer has received the notification required by rule 62(3) in respect of each of the other Assembly constituencies in the Assembly electoral region (other than in respect of an Assembly constituency to which this sub-paragraph also applies).

   (2)   Where paragraph (1) applies, the subsequent election of a candidate for the Assembly constituency shall have no effect upon the validity of the election and return of any member at the regional election.

Regional election: death of candidate

75(1)   If at a contested regional election proof is given to the regional returning officer's satisfaction before the results of the election are declared that one of the persons named or to be named as a candidate on the ballot paper (whether as an individual or party list candidate) has died and as a result of that death the election becomes uncontested, then the regional returning officer shall
   (a)   countermand notice of the poll; or
   (b)   if polling has begun, direct that the poll be abandoned; and
   (c)   in either case, forthwith notify each constituency returning officer in the Assembly electoral region of the action that he has taken.

   (2)   If at a contested regional election proof is given to the regional returning officer's satisfaction before the results of the election are declared that one of the persons named or to be named as a candidate on the ballot paper (whether as an individual or party list candidate) has died, but notwithstanding that death the election continues to be contested, the notice of poll shall not be countermanded nor shall the poll be abandoned; and in the event of such a death it shall have no effect upon the validity of the election and return of any other candidate at the regional election.

   (3)   But where paragraph (2) applies, the regional returning officer shall take such steps as he considers reasonable to publicise in the Assembly electoral region for which the election is held
   (a)   the name of that candidate and the fact of his death;
   (b)   whether that candidate was an individual or party list candidate; and
   (c)   if he was a party list candidate, the name of the registered political party for which he was such a candidate,
   and the regional returning officer shall, in particular, consider whether he should publicise as required by this paragraph by causing notices to be placed outside polling stations.

   (4)   In respect of an election to which paragraph (1) or (2) applies, rules 41(1)(c) and (d) (admission to polling station) and 54(5)(b) to (d) (attendance at count) do not apply in relation to the deceased candidate; and where the deceased candidate is an individual candidate, rule 65(6) (forfeiture of deposit) also does not apply in relation to that deceased candidate.

Abandoned poll

76(1)   This rule applies to
   (a)   a poll which is abandoned in pursuance of rule 70(4)(b) or 75(1)(b) as if it were a poll at a contested election; and
   (b)   a poll which is abandoned in pursuance of rule 73(2)(b).

(2) Subject to paragraph (10) the presiding officer at a polling station must take the like steps (so far as not already taken) for the delivery to the constituency returning officer of ballot boxes and of ballot papers and other documents as he is required to take on the close of the poll.

(3) The constituency returning officer must dispose of ballot papers and other documents in his possession as he is required to do on the completion of the counting of the votes.

(4) It is not necessary for a ballot paper account to be prepared or verified.

(5) No step or further step is to be taken for the counting of the ballot papers or of the votes.

(6) The constituency returning officer must seal up all the ballot papers (whether the votes on them have been counted or not) and it is not necessary to seal up counted and rejected ballot papers in separate packets.

(7) The provisions of these rules as to the inspection, production, retention and destruction of ballot papers and other documents relating to a poll at an election apply subject to paragraphs (8) and (9).

(8) Ballot papers on which the votes were neither counted nor rejected must be treated as counted ballot papers.

(9) No order is to be made for
    (a) the production or inspection of any ballot papers; or
    (b) the opening of a sealed packet of the completed corresponding number lists or of certificates as to employment on the day of the poll,
unless the order is made by a court with reference to a prosecution.

(10) Where the polls at a regional election and at a constituency election for a constituency within that region are held on the same day but the poll at one election is abandoned in any of the circumstances mentioned in paragraph (1)
    (a) the steps which the presiding officer is required to take at such a polling station by sub-paragraph (2) shall take place at the close of the poll at the other election; and
    (b) sub-paragraph (3) shall have effect as if after "the constituency returning officer", there was inserted "having separated the ballot papers relating to the other Assembly election,", and
paragraphs (4) to (9) shall apply only to the election at which the poll has been abandoned.

Part 7
Miscellaneous

Vacancies: Assembly constituency seats

77 Where the date of the poll to fill a vacant seat for an Assembly constituency is fixed by the Presiding Officer of the Assembly he shall forthwith send a notice to the returning officer for the Assembly constituency stating
    (a) that the vacancy exists; and
    (b) the date fixed for the poll to fill that vacancy.

Vacancies: return of electoral region members

78(1) Other than where article 101 applies, where it comes to the notice of the Presiding Officer of the Assembly that the seat of an Assembly member returned from a party list for an Assembly electoral region is vacant, he shall forthwith send a notice in accordance with paragraph (2) to the returning officer for the Assembly electoral region.

(2) A notice under paragraph (1) shall
    (a) state that a vacancy exists; and
    (b) set out the name of the person who had been returned to fill that seat, together with the name of the registered political party on whose list he was included.

(3) Where a regional returning officer receives a notice under paragraph (1), he shall ascertain from the list submitted at the previous Assembly general election by the registered political party named in the notice the name and address of the person whose name now appears highest on that list ("the prospective member").

(4) The regional returning officer shall take such steps as appear to him to be reasonable
    (a) to contact the prospective member to ask whether he will state that he is willing to serve as an Assembly member for the Assembly electoral region; and
    (b) to contact the registered nominating officer of the registered political party on whose list that person is included and notify that officer of the action he is taking under sub-paragraph (a).

(5) Where within such period as the regional returning officer considers reasonable
    (a) he decides that the steps he has taken to contact the prospective member have been unsuccessful; or
    (b) he has not received from the prospective member a statement in writing that he is willing to serve as an Assembly member for the Assembly electoral region; or
    (c) the prospective member has stated in writing he is not willing to so serve as an Assembly member; or
    (d) the regional returning officer
        (i) is satisfied that the prospective member is not a member of the registered political party on whose list he is included; and
        (ii) receives notice signed by the registered nominating officer of that party that the prospective member's name is not to be notified to the Presiding Officer of the Assembly as the name of the person who is to fill the vacancy,
the prospective member shall be treated as ceasing to be included on that list for the purposes of filling that vacancy.

(6) Where a person is so treated, the regional returning officer shall repeat the procedure required by paragraph (4) in respect of the person (if any) whose name and address appears next highest on that list; and paragraph (5) and this paragraph shall also apply with respect to that person.

(7) The regional returning officer shall continue to repeat the procedure until he has notified to the Presiding Officer of the Assembly the name of the person who is to fill the vacancy or the names on that list are exhausted.

(8) Subject to paragraph (5)(d), where a prospective member states in writing in response to the question from the regional returning officer under paragraph (4)(a) (including that sub-paragraph as applied by paragraph (6)) that he is willing to serve as an Assembly member for the Assembly electoral region, the regional returning officer shall forthwith notify to the Presiding Officer of the Assembly the name of that person as the person to fill the vacancy.

(9) The regional returning officer shall forthwith give public notice of the name
    (a) of the member to be returned; and
    (b) of the registered political party for which such a member was a party list candidate.

(10) Where following the application of this rule the seat continues to be vacant the regional returning officer shall forthwith

(a) give public notice that the vacancy cannot be filled and that the seat will remain vacant until the next Assembly general election by virtue of the relevant enactment;

(b) complete a certificate in form CT set out in English and Welsh in Schedule 10; and

(c) deliver it, or cause it to be delivered, to the Clerk.

(11) In paragraph (10) "the relevant enactment" means, in respect of a vacancy occurring before the 2007 Assembly general election, section 9(7)(b) of the 1998 Act and in respect of vacancies occurring after that election, section 11(7)(b) of the 2006 Act.

(12) References to "the Clerk" in paragraph (10)(c) and in rule 79(1) shall, in relation to any vacancy in an Assembly electoral region occurring before the 2007 Assembly general election, be construed as references to the Clerk to the Assembly constituted by the 1998 Act.

Return of Assembly members and record of returns etc

79(1) The Clerk shall on receipt of a certificate delivered under rule 62(4), 64(3) or 78(10) enter the information contained in the certificate in a book kept for that purpose at the Assembly (in this paragraph referred to as "the returns book").

(2) Where the Presiding Officer of the Assembly sends a notice under rule 77 or 78(1), he shall record in the returns book the fact of the vacancy in the Assembly constituency or electoral region concerned.

(3) Where the Presiding Officer of the Assembly is notified under rule 78(8) of the name of the person who is to fill an Assembly electoral region vacancy, he shall record in the returns book the name of that person, the name of the relevant Assembly electoral region and also the date on which he received that notification.

(4) Where a vacancy in an Assembly constituency can not be filled because, under the relevant enactment, an election to fill that vacancy must not be held, the Presiding Officer of the Assembly shall record in the returns book that

(a) there is a vacancy in the Assembly constituency concerned; and

(b) under the relevant enactment, the seat is to remain vacant until the next Assembly general election.

(5) Where it comes to the notice of the Presiding Officer of the Assembly that

(a) the seat of an Assembly member returned for an Assembly electoral region is vacant; and

(b) the person was returned as an individual candidate,

he shall record in the returns book that

(i) there is a vacancy in the Assembly electoral region concerned; and

(ii) under the relevant enactment, the seat is to remain vacant until the next Assembly general election.

(6) The returns book shall be open to public inspection at reasonable times and any person may, on payment of a reasonable fee, obtain copies from the book.

(7) "The relevant enactment" means in relation to

(a) a vacancy in an Assembly constituency, section 8(6) of the 1998 Act, in respect of a vacancy occurring before the 2007 Assembly general election and section 10(7) of the 2006 Act in relation to a vacancy occurring after that election; and

(b) a vacancy in an Assembly electoral region for which an individual candidate was the member, section 9(7)(a) of the 1998 Act, in respect of a vacancy occurring before the 2007 Assembly general election and section 11(7)(a) of the 2006 Act in relation to a vacancy occurring after that election.

Registered political parties

80(1) For the purposes of the application of these rules in relation to an Assembly election "registered political party" means a party which was registered under Part 2 of the 2000 Political Parties Act on the day ("the relevant day") which is two days before the last day for the delivery of nomination papers at the election in accordance with the Table in rule 1(1).

(2) A registered political party is a qualifying party in relation to an Assembly constituency or electoral region if the party was on the relevant day registered in respect of Wales in the Great Britain register maintained under that Part of that Act.

(3) For the purposes of paragraph (1) any day as mentioned in rule 2 should be disregarded.

Party's registered nominating officer: discharge of functions

81(1) A registered nominating officer for a registered political party may, in writing, appoint one or more persons to discharge all or any of his functions conferred or imposed by these rules.

(2) Where an appointment is made under paragraph (1), a copy of the document which records the writing required by that paragraph shall be delivered

(a) to the constituency returning officer, in the case of a constituency election;

(b) to the regional returning officer, in the case of a regional election; and

(c) to each constituency returning officer for an Assembly constituency in the Assembly electoral region, in the case of a regional election.

(3) Where a returning officer does not receive a copy of the document required to be delivered to him under paragraph (2), he shall be entitled to treat any function of the registered nominating officer purportedly exercised (or to be exercised) on his behalf by another person as not so exercised (or exercisable).

SCHEDULE 6
CONTROL OF DONATIONS TO CANDIDATES

Contents

PART 1
GENERAL

PART 2
CONTROLS ON DONATIONS

PART 3
REPORTING OF DONATIONS

Part 1
General

Interpretation

1(1) This Schedule has effect for controlling donations to constituency and individual candidates at an Assembly election and in the following provisions of this Schedule references to "candidate" shall be construed accordingly.

(2) For the purposes of this Schedule, except where the context otherwise requires
"relevant donation", in relation to a candidate at an Assembly election, means a donation to the candidate or his election agent for the purpose of meeting election expenses incurred by or on behalf of the candidate; and
"donation" shall be construed in accordance with paragraphs 2 to 4.

(3) In the definition of "relevant donation", the reference to a donation for the purpose of meeting election expenses incurred by or on behalf of a candidate includes a reference to a donation for the purpose of securing that any such expenses are not so incurred; and a donation shall be taken to be a donation for either of those purposes if, having regard to all the circumstances, it must reasonably be assumed to be such a donation.

(4) In relation to a donation received by a candidate at an Assembly election, references to a permissible donor falling within section 54(2) of the 2000 Political Parties Act are to be read as if section 54(2) did not include a party registered in the Northern Ireland register maintained by the Commission under Part 2 of that Act of 2000.

Donations: general rules

2(1) "Donation", in relation to a candidate at an Assembly election, means (subject to paragraph 4)

(a) any gift to the candidate or his election agent of money or other property;

    (b)   any sponsorship provided in relation to a candidate (as defined by paragraph 3);

    (c)   any money spent (otherwise than by the candidate, his election agent or any sub-agent) in paying any election expenses incurred by or on behalf of the candidate;

    (d)   any money lent to the candidate or his election agent otherwise than on commercial terms; or

    (e)   the provision otherwise than on commercial terms of any property, services or facilities for the use or benefit of the candidate (including the services of any person).

(2)   Where

    (a)   any money or other property is transferred to a candidate or his election agent pursuant to any transaction or arrangement involving the provision by or on behalf of the candidate of any property, services or facilities or other consideration of monetary value; and

    (b)   the total value in monetary terms of the consideration so provided by or on behalf of the candidate is less than the value of the money or (as the case may be) the market value of the property transferred,

the transfer of the money or property shall (subject to sub-paragraph (4)) constitute a gift to the candidate or (as the case may be) his election agent for the purposes of sub-paragraph (1)(a).

(3)   In determining

    (a)   for the purposes of sub-paragraph (1)(d), whether any money lent to a candidate or his election agent is so lent otherwise than on commercial terms; or

    (b)   for the purposes of sub-paragraph (1)(e), whether any property, services or facilities provided for the use or benefit of a candidate is or are so provided otherwise than on such terms,

regard shall be had to the total value in monetary terms of the consideration provided by or on behalf of the candidate in respect of the loan or the provision of the property, services or facilities.

(4)   Where (apart from this sub-paragraph) anything would be a donation both by virtue of sub-paragraph (1)(b) and by virtue of any other provision of this paragraph, sub-paragraph (1)(b) (together with paragraph 3) shall apply in relation to it to the exclusion of the other provision of this paragraph.

(5)   The reference in sub-paragraph (1)(c) to money spent as mentioned in that provision is a reference to money so spent by a person, other than the candidate, his election agent or any sub-agent, out of his own resources (with no right to reimbursement out of the resources of any such other person); and where, by virtue of sub-paragraph (1)(c), money so spent constitutes a donation to the candidate, the candidate shall be treated as receiving an equivalent amount on the date on which the money is paid to the creditor in respect of the expenses in question.

(6)   In this paragraph

    (a)   any reference to anything being given or transferred to a candidate or his election agent includes a reference to its being given or transferred either directly or indirectly through any third person; and

    (b)   "gift" includes a bequest or any other form of testamentary disposition.

Sponsorship

3(1) For the purposes of this Schedule sponsorship is provided in relation to a candidate if

    (a)   any money or other property is transferred to the candidate or to any person for the benefit of the candidate; and

    (b)   the purpose (or one of the purposes) of the transfer is (or must, having regard to all the circumstances, reasonably be assumed to be)

    (i)   to help the candidate with meeting, or to meet, to any extent any defined expenses incurred or to be incurred by or on behalf of the candidate; or

    (ii)   to secure that to any extent any such expenses are not so incurred.

(2)   In sub-paragraph (1) "defined expenses" means expenses in connection with

    (a)   any conference, meeting or other event organised by or on behalf of the candidate;

    (b)   the preparation, production or dissemination of any publication by or on behalf of the candidate; or

    (c)   any study or research organised by or on behalf of the candidate.

(3)   The following do not, however, constitute sponsorship by virtue of sub-paragraph (1)

    (a)   the making of any payment in respect of

    (i)   any charge for admission to any conference, meeting or other event; or

    (ii)   the purchase price of, or any charge for access to, any publication; or

    (b)   the making of any payment in respect of the inclusion of an advertisement in any publication where the payment is made at the commercial rate payable for the inclusion of such an advertisement in any such publication.

(4)   In this paragraph "publication" means a publication made available in whatever form and by whatever means (whether or not to the public at large or any section of the public).

Payments etc not to be regarded as donations

4(1)   None of the following shall be regarded as a donation

    (a)   the provision of any facilities provided in pursuance of any right conferred on a candidate at an election by this Order;

    (b)   the provision by an individual of his own services which he provides voluntarily in his own time and free of charge; or

    (c)   any interest accruing to a candidate or his election agent in respect of any donation which is dealt with by the candidate or (as the case may be) his election agent in accordance with section 56(2)(a) or (b) of the 2000 Political Parties Act (as applied by paragraph 7).

(2)   There shall also be disregarded any donation whose value (determined in accordance with paragraph 5) is not more than £50.

Value of donations

5(1)   The value of any donation falling within paragraph 2(1)(a) (other than money) shall be taken to be the market value of the property in question.

(2)   Where, however, paragraph 2(1)(a) applies by virtue of paragraph 2(2), the value of the donation shall be taken to be the difference between

    (a)   the value of the money, or the market value of the property, in question; and

    (b)   the total value in monetary terms of the consideration provided by or on behalf of the candidate or his election agent.

(3)   The value of any donation falling within paragraph 2(1)(b) shall be taken to be the value of the money, or (as the case may be) the market value of the property, transferred as mentioned in paragraph 3(1); and accordingly any value in monetary terms of any benefit conferred on the person providing the sponsorship in question shall be disregarded.

(4)   The value of any donation falling within paragraph 2(1)(d) or (e) shall be taken to be the amount representing the difference between

    (a)   the total value in monetary terms of the consideration that would have had to be provided by or on behalf of the candidate or his election agent in respect of the loan or the provision of the property, services or facilities if

    (i)   the loan had been made; or

    (ii) the property, services or facilities had been provided,

on commercial terms; and

  (b) the total value in monetary terms of the consideration (if any) actually so provided by or on behalf of the candidate or his election agent.

(5) Where a donation such as is mentioned in sub-paragraph (4) confers an enduring benefit on the donee over a particular period, the value of the donation

  (a) shall be determined at the time when it is made; but

  (b) shall be so determined by reference to the total benefit accruing to the donee over that period.

(6) In this paragraph "market value" in relation to any property, means the price which might reasonably be expected to be paid for the property on a sale in the open market.

Part 2
Controls on Donations

Prohibition on accepting donations from impermissible donors

6(1) A relevant donation received by a candidate or his election agent must not be accepted if

  (a) the person by whom the donation would be made is not, at the time of its receipt by the candidate or (as the case may be) his election agent, a permissible donor falling within section 54(2) of the 2000 Political Parties Act; or

  (b) the candidate or (as the case may be) his election agent is (whether because the donation is given anonymously or by reason of any deception or concealment or otherwise) unable to ascertain the identity of the person offering the donation.

(2) For the purposes of this Schedule any relevant donation received by a candidate or his election agent which is an exempt trust donation shall be regarded as a relevant donation received by the candidate or his election agent from a permissible donor; and section 162 of the 2000 Political Parties Act (interpretation: exempt trust donations) shall apply for the purposes of this Schedule as is applies for the purposes of that Act.

(3) But, for the purposes of this Schedule, any relevant donation received by a candidate or his election agent from a trustee of any property (in his capacity as such) which is not

  (a) an exempt trust donation; or

  (b) a relevant donation transmitted by the trustee to the candidate or his election agent on behalf of beneficiaries under the trust who are

    (i)   persons who at the time of its receipt by the candidate or his election agent are permissible donors falling within section 54(2) of the 2000 Political Parties Act; or

    (ii) the members of an unincorporated association which at that time is such a permissible donor,

shall be regarded as a relevant donation received by the candidate or his election agent from a person who is not such a permissible donor.

(4) Where any person ("the principal donor") causes an amount ("the principal donation") to be received by a candidate or his election agent by way of a relevant donation

  (a) on behalf of himself and one or more other persons; or

  (b) on behalf of two or more other persons,

then for the purposes of this Part each individual contribution by a person falling within paragraph (a) or (b) of more than £50 shall be treated as if it were a separate donation received from that person.

(5) In relation to each such separate donation, the principal donor must ensure that, at the time when the principal donation is received by the candidate or his election agent, the candidate or (as the case may be) his election agent is given

    (a) (except in the case of a donation which the principal donor is treated as making) all such details in respect of the person treated as making the donation as are required by virtue of paragraph 11(c); and

    (b) (in any case) all such details in respect of the donation as are required by virtue of paragraph 11(a).

(6) Where

    (a) any person ("the agent") causes an amount to be received by a candidate or his election agent by way of a donation on behalf of another person ("the donor"); and

    (b) the amount of the donation is more than £50,

the agent must ensure that, at the time when the donation is received by the candidate or his election agent, the candidate or (as the case may be) his election agent is given all such details in respect of the donor as are required by virtue of paragraph 11(c).

(7) A person commits an offence if, without reasonable excuse, he fails to comply with sub-paragraph (5) or (6).

(8) A person guilty of an offence under sub-paragraph (7) shall be liable

    (a) on summary conviction, to a fine not exceeding the statutory maximum or to a term of imprisonment not exceeding 6 months (or both);

    (b) on conviction on indictment, to a fine or to a term of imprisonment not exceeding one year (or both).

(9) In relation to an offence committed after commencement of section 281(5) of the Criminal Justice Act 2003, the reference in sub-paragraph (8)(a) to 6 months must be taken to be a reference to 51 weeks.

Acceptance or return of donations

7(1) Sections 56 to 60 of the 2000 Political Parties Act shall apply for the purposes of this Schedule in relation to

    (a) a relevant donation received by a candidate or by his election agent; and

    (b) the candidate or (as the case may be) the election agent,

as they apply in relation to a donation received by a registered party and the registered party.

(2) In the application of sections 56 to 60 of that Act in accordance with sub-paragraph (1)

    (a) section 56(1) shall have effect as if the reference to the particulars relating to a donor which would be required to be included in a donation report by virtue of paragraph 2 of Schedule 6 to the 2000 Political Parties Act (if the donation were a recordable donation within the meaning of that Schedule) were construed as a reference to the particulars which are required to be included in a return by virtue of paragraph 11(c);

    (b) section 56(3) shall have effect as if the reference to the party were omitted and the reference to the treasurer of the party were construed as a reference to the candidate or (as the case may be) his election agent; and

    (c) section 56(4) shall have effect as if the reference to the treasurer of the party were construed as a reference to the candidate or (as the case may be) his election agent.

Transfer of donations received by candidate to election agent

8(1)   Sub-paragraph (2) applies in relation to any relevant donation received by a candidate after the deadline for appointing an election agent (unless the candidate is, or is deemed to be, his own election agent at the time of receipt of the donation).

(2)   The candidate shall, on receipt of any such donation as is mentioned in sub-paragraph (1), forthwith deliver to his election agent

  (a)   the donation;

  (b)   where paragraph 6(5) or (6) applies in relation to the donation, the information provided to the candidate in pursuance of that provision; and

  (c)   any other information which the candidate has about the donation and its donor which might reasonably be expected to assist the election agent in the discharge of any duties imposed on him, in relation to the donation, under this Part or Part 3 of this Schedule.

(3)   Where a donation is delivered to an election agent in accordance with sub-paragraph (2), the donation shall be treated for the purposes of paragraph 6(1) to (4) and the provisions applied by paragraph 7 as if it had been

  (a)   originally received by the election agent; and

  (b)   so received by him on the date on which it was received by the candidate.

(4)   Where a candidate receives a relevant donation before the deadline for appointing an election agent but at a time when an appointment of a person (other than the candidate himself) as election agent is in force he shall either

  (a)   forthwith deliver the donation and the information mentioned in sub-paragraph (2)(b) and (c) to the agent; or

  (b)   (if he fails to do so) deal with the donation in accordance with section 56 of the 2000 Political Parties Act.

(5)   Sub-paragraph (3) shall have effect in relation to any relevant donation delivered to an election agent in accordance with sub-paragraph (4)(a) as it has effect in relation to a donation delivered to him in accordance with sub-paragraph (2).

(6)   Sub-paragraph (7) applies where

  (a)   a relevant donation received by a candidate before the deadline for appointing an election agent has been dealt with by the candidate in accordance with section 56 of the 2000 Political Parties Act either because

    (i)   it was received by him at a time when no appointment of another person as his election agent was in force; or

    (ii)   although such an appointment was in force, he was by virtue of sub-paragraph (4)(b) required to deal with the donation; and

  (b)   an appointment of a person (other than the candidate himself) as election agent is in force at, or at any time after

    (i)   the deadline for appointing an election agent; or

    (ii)   if later, the time when the candidate has dealt with the donation in accordance with section 56 of the 2000 Political Parties Act.

(7)   Subject to sub-paragraph (9), the candidate shall, as soon as reasonably practicable after the relevant time, deliver to the election agent

  (a)   the donation (if it has been accepted by him); and

  (b)   any information which he has about the donation and the donor which might reasonably be expected to assist the election agent in the discharge of any duties imposed on him, in relation to the donation, under Part 3 of this Schedule.

(8)   The relevant time for the purposes of sub-paragraph (7) is

  (a)   the time mentioned in sub-paragraph (6)(b)(i) or (ii) (as the case may be) if the

> appointment of another person as election agent is in force at that time; or

(b) otherwise, the time when any such appointment subsequently comes into force.

(9) The duty imposed on a candidate by sub-paragraph (7)(a) does not apply to any relevant donation to the extent to which it has been lawfully used by the candidate for the purpose of paying election expenses.

(10) In this paragraph

(a) any reference to the deadline for appointing an election agent is a reference to the latest time by which an election agent may in accordance with article 37 of this Order be named as election agent by the candidate; and

(b) any reference to any provision of section 56 of the 2000 Political Parties Act is a reference to that provision as applied by paragraph 7.

Evasion of restrictions on donations

9 Section 61 of the 2000 Political Parties Act shall apply for the purposes of this Schedule as if

(a) any reference to donations were to relevant donations;

(b) any reference to a registered political party were, in relation to a relevant donation, a reference to a candidate or (as the case may be) his election agent; and

(c) any reference in subsection (2) to the treasurer of a registered political party were, in relation to a relevant donation, a reference to either the candidate or his election agent (or both).

Part 3
Reporting of Donations

Statement of relevant donations

10(1) The candidate's election agent must include in any return to be delivered under article 52 of this Order a statement of relevant donations which complies with paragraphs 11 and 12.

(2) If the statement states that the election agent has seen, in relation to an individual donor, a certificate of anonymous registration, the statement must be accompanied by a copy of that certificate.

(3) For the purpose of sub-paragraph (2), "certificate of anonymous registration" means a certificate issued in pursuance of regulation 45G of the 2001 Regulations.

Donations from permissible donors

11 The statement must record, in relation to each relevant donation accepted by the candidate or his election agent

(a) the amount of the donation (if a donation of money, in cash or otherwise) or (in any other case) the nature of the donation and its value as determined in accordance with paragraph 5;

(b) the date when the donation was accepted by the candidate or his election agent;

(c) the information about the donor which is, in connection with recordable donations to registered political parties, required to be recorded in donation reports by virtue of paragraph 2 of Schedule 6 to the 2000 Political Parties Act; and

(d) such other information as may be required by regulations made by the

Commission.

Donations from impermissible donors

12(1)   This paragraph applies to relevant donations falling within paragraph 6(1)(a) or (b).

(2)   Where paragraph 6(1)(a) applies, the statement must record
- (a)   the name and address of the donor;
- (b)   the amount of the donation (if a donation of money, in cash or otherwise) or (in any other case) the nature of the donation and its value as determined in accordance with paragraph 5;
- (c)   the date when the donation was received, and the date when, and the manner in which, it was dealt with in accordance with section 56(2)(a) of the 2000 Political Parties Act; and
- (d)   such other information as is required by regulations made by the Commission.

(3)   Where paragraph 6(1)(b) applies, the statement must record
- (a)   details of the manner in which the donation was made;
- (b)   the amount of the donation (if a donation of money, in cash or otherwise) or (in any other case) the nature of the donation and its value as determined in accordance with paragraph 5;
- (c)   the date when the donation was received, and the date when, and the manner in which, it was dealt with in accordance with section 56(2)(b) of the 2000 Political Parties Act; and
- (d)   such other information as is required by regulations made by the Commission.

(4)   In this paragraph any reference to any provision of section 56 of the 2000 Political Parties Act is a reference to that provision as applied by paragraph 7.

SCHEDULE 7
ELECTION EXPENSES

Article 63(7)

Part 1
List of Matters

1 Advertising of any nature (whatever the medium used).
   Expenses in respect of such advertising include agency fees, design costs and other costs in connection with preparing, producing, distributing or otherwise disseminating such advertising or anything incorporating such advertising and intended to be distributed for the purpose of disseminating it.

2 Unsolicited material addressed to electors (whether addressed to them by name or intended for delivery to households within any particular area).
   Expenses in respect of such material include design costs and other costs in connection with preparing, producing or distributing such material (including the cost of postage).

3 Transport (by any means) of persons to any place.
   Expenses in respect of the transport of such persons include the costs of hiring a means of transport for a particular period.

4 Public meetings (of any kind).
   Expenses in respect of such meetings include costs incurred in connection with the attendance of persons at such meetings, the hire of premises for the purposes of such meetings or the provision of goods, services or facilities at them.

5 The services of an election agent or any other person whose services are engaged in connection with the candidate's election.

6 Accommodation and administrative costs.

Part 2
General Exclusions

7 The payment of any deposit required by rule 10 of Schedule 5.

8 The publication of any matter, other than an advertisement, relating to the election in
   (a) a newspaper or periodical;
   (b) a broadcast made by the British Broadcasting Corporation or by Sianel Pedwar Cymru; or
   (c) a programme included in any service licensed under Part 1 or 3 of the Broadcasting Act 1990 or Part 1 or 2 of the Broadcasting Act 1996.

9 The provision of any facilities provided in pursuance of any right conferred on candidates at an election by this Order other than facilities in respect of which expenses fall to be defrayed by virtue of article 69(4).

10 The provision by an individual of his own services which he provides voluntarily in his own time and free of charge.

11(1) Accommodation which is the candidate's sole or main residence.
   (2) The provision by any other individual of accommodation which is his sole or main

residence if the provision is made free of charge.

12(1) Transport by a means of transport which was acquired by the candidate principally for his own personal use.

(2) Transport provided free of charge by any other individual if the means of transport was acquired by him principally for his own personal use.

13(1) Computing or printing equipment which was acquired by the candidate principally for his own personal use.

(2) The provision by any other individual of computing or printing equipment which was acquired by the individual principally for his own personal use if the provision is made free of charge.

SCHEDULE 8
USE FOR ASSEMBLY ELECTION MEETINGS OF ROOMS IN SCHOOL PREMISES AND OF MEETING ROOMS

Article 69(6)

Contents

Use of rooms in school premises

1(1) Any arrangements for the use of a room in school premises shall be made with the local authority (within the meaning of section 579(1) of the Education Act 1996) maintaining the school or, in the case of a room in the premises of a foundation or voluntary aided school, with the governing body of the school.

(2) Any question
(a) as to the rooms in school premises which a candidate in any Assembly constituency or electoral region is entitled to use;
(b) as to the times at which he is entitled to use them; or
(c) as to the notice which is reasonable,
shall be determined by the Secretary of State.

Lists of rooms in school premises

2(1) Every local authority (within the meaning of section 579(1) of the Education Act 1996) shall prepare, keep under review and from time to time, as it considers appropriate, revise for its area, lists of the rooms in school premises which candidates for return as Assembly members are entitled to use.

(2) In relation to an Assembly constituency, the list shall include the rooms in premises within any of the authority's area outside, as well as those in premises in, the constituency.

Lists of meeting rooms

3(1) Each county and county borough council shall prepare, keep under review and from time to time, as it considers appropriate, revise for its area a list of the meeting rooms which candidates for return as Assembly members are entitled to use.

(2) The list shall indicate the person to whom applications for the use of such a room are to be made in each case.

(3) The list shall not include any room if the person maintaining it disputes the right of candidates at an Assembly election to use it.

Lists to be kept by registration officer etc

4 The lists of rooms in school premises and of meeting rooms prepared for each Assembly constituency and electoral region shall be kept by the registration officer, and those lists and particulars of any change made on their revision shall (where necessary) be forwarded to him by the relevant local authority (within the meaning of section 579(1) of the Education Act 1996) or, as the case may be county or county borough council.

Inspection etc of lists

5 In the event of notice of election being published in accordance with the Table in paragraph 1(1) of Schedule 5, any person stating himself to be, or to be authorised by,

(a) a constituency or individual candidate at that election or his election agent; or

(b) a party list candidate at that election or the registered nominating officer of the registered political party on whose list he is a candidate or that party's election agent in relation to that list of candidates,

shall be entitled at all reasonable hours to inspect those lists or a copy of them.

SCHEDULE 9
MODIFICATION OF ELECTION PETITION RULES 1960

Article 134(3)

Contents

1 Assembly election petition: modification of the Election Petition Rules 1960
2 Rule 2(2) of the 1960 Rules (definitions)
3 Rule 2(3) of the 1960 Rules (prescribed officer)
4 Rule 4(1) of the 1960 Rules (form of petition)
5 Rule 9(3) of the 1960 Rules (display etc of notice of time and place of trial)
6 Rule 10(1) of the 1960 Rules (identifying votes at issue)
7 References to "election" in the 1960 Rules
8 Form of election petition in the 1960 Rules
9 References to the 1983 Act

Assembly election petition: modification of the Election Petition Rules 1960

1 The Election Petition Rules 1960 ("the 1960 Rules") shall apply to an Assembly election petition subject to the following modifications.

Rule 2(2) of the 1960 Rules (definitions)

2 In rule 2(2) of the 1960 Rules, the following definitions shall be modified as follows

(a) "the Act" shall (except in rule 2(3)) be construed as meaning this Order and a reference to a provision of the 1983 Act in the 1960 Rules shall be construed as a reference to the corresponding provision in this Order as set out in paragraph 9 of this Schedule;

(b) "local election petition" shall be disregarded as shall be rule 18 of the 1960 Rules and any reference in the 1960 Rules which is a reference to a provision of the 1983 Act that applies only to such a local election petition;

(c) "petition" shall be construed as meaning an Assembly election petition;

(d) "constituency" shall be construed as meaning

    (i)   in the case of a petition relating to a constituency election, the Assembly constituency to which the petition relates;

    (ii) in the case of a petition relating to a regional election, to the Assembly electoral region to which the petition relates; and

    (iii) in the case of a petition relating to a return in respect of an electoral region vacancy, to the Assembly electoral region to which the petition relates; and

(e) "returning officer" shall be construed as meaning the constituency returning officer in the case of a petition relating to a constituency election and the regional returning officer in the case of a petition relating to a regional election, or as the case may be, an electoral regional vacancy.

Rule 2(3) of the 1960 Rules (prescribed officer)

3   Rule 2(3) of the 1960 Rules shall apply as if for "the prescribed officer in relation to elections under the Local Government Act" there were substituted "the prescribed officer in relation to elections under Part 1 of the Government of Wales Act 1998 or, as the case may be, under Part 1 of the Government of Wales Act 2006".

Rule 4(1) of the 1960 Rules (form of petition)

4(1)   Rule 4 of the 1960 Rules shall apply with the following modifications.

(2)   In rule 4(1)(b)

    (a)   "in the case of a parliamentary election" shall be disregarded;

    (b)   "the Clerk of the Crown" shall be construed as a reference to the Assembly constituted by the 1998 Act in respect of a return made before the 2007 Assembly general election and as a reference to the Clerk in respect of any subsequent return; and

    (c)   in the case of a regional election, "result", "return was" and "member" shall be construed as "results", "returns were" and "members" respectively.

(3)   Rule 4(1) shall be construed as if after paragraph (1)(b) there were inserted

    "(ba) in the case of a petition relating to a return in respect of an electoral region vacancy the date on which the person was declared to be returned as an Assembly member;".

Rule 9(3) of the 1960 Rules (display etc of notice of time and place of trial)

5   In rule 9(3) of the 1960 Rules

    (a)   "a parliamentary election petition" shall be construed as "an Assembly election petition"

    (b)   "and in any other case not less than seven days" shall be disregarded.

Rule 10(1) of the 1960 Rules (identifying votes at issue)

6   In rule 10(1) of the 1960 Rules, in the case of a regional election, "he had a majority of lawful votes," shall be construed as "he or the registered political party on whose list he was a candidate had a higher electoral figure than that of another individual candidate or of another registered party to whom a seat in that Assembly electoral region was allocated.

References to "election" in the 1960 Rules

7(1) Rule 10(2) and (4)(b) of the 1960 rules shall apply to an Assembly election petition complaining of an undue return in respect of an electoral regional vacancy as it applies to an Assembly election petition complaining of an undue election; and references in those paragraphs to "undue election" "duly elected", and "election" shall be construed accordingly.

(2) In rules 12(3), 14(2) and 16(3) of the 1960 Rules, references to "election" shall, in the case of an Assembly election petition relating to a return in respect of an electoral region vacancy, be construed as references to such a return.

Form of election petition in the 1960 Rules

8 The form of election petition in the Schedule to the 1960 Rules shall apply in relation to an Assembly election petition as if

  (a) for the words after "Queen's Bench Division" to before "The Petition of AB of", there were substituted

    (i) in the case of an electoral region vacancy occurring before the 2007 Assembly general election

    "In the Matter of the Government of Wales Act 1998 and the National Assembly for Wales (Representation of the People) Order 2007

    And in the Matter of a return of an Assembly member under section 9 of the Government of Wales Act 1998 for the. . . . . .electoral region and made on the. . . .day of. . . . .20. . . .";

    (ii) in the case of any subsequent electoral regional vacancy

    "In the Matter of the Government of Wales Act 2006 and the National Assembly for Wales (Representation of the People) Order 2007

    And in the Matter of a return of an Assembly member under section 11 of the Government of Wales Act 2006 for. . . . . .electoral region and made on the. . . .day of. . . .20. . . .";

    (iii) in the case of an Assembly election at the 2007 Assembly general election

    "In the Matter of the Government of Wales Act 1998 and the National Assembly for Wales (Representation of the People) Order 2007

    And in the Matter of an Assembly election for *state place* held on the. . . . .day of. . . . .2007"; and

    (iv) in the case of any subsequent Assembly election

    "In the Matter of the Government of Wales Act 2006 and the National Assembly for Wales (Representation of the People) Order 2007

    And in the Matter of an Assembly election for *state place* held on the. . . . .day of. . . . .20. . . . .";

  (b) but subject to sub-paragraph (c), for paragraphs 1 and 2, there were substituted

    "1 That the Petitioner A.B. is a person who voted *or* had a right to vote at the above election *or* was a candidate at the above election*or* claims to have had a right to be elected or returned at the above election *or, in the case of a return under section 9 of the Government of Wales Act 1998 or, as the case may be, under section 11 of the Government of Wales Act 2006*, claims to have had a right to be returned under section 9 of the Government of Wales Act 1998 (*or, as the case may be,* section 11 of the Government of Wales Act 2006) and the Petitioner CD *state similarly the capacity in which he presents the petition.*

    2 That the election was held on the. . . . .day of. . . . .20. . . . .when *in the case of an election for an Assembly constituency, insert names of candidates* were candidates*or, in the case of a regional election insert names* were individual candidates and there were candidates for *insert names of registered political parties appearing on the ballot paper* the names of those

candidates in respect of each such party are set down below*/annexed hereto* (*delete as appropriate*), and on the. . . . .day of. . . . .20. . . . ., the returning officer returned *insert names of candidates* to the Clerk of the National Assembly for Wales as being duly elected. *at an election for an Assembly electoral region set out the name of each registered political party appearing on the ballot paper and after the name of each party the names of the candidates of that party appearing on the ballot paper.*";

(c) in the case of a petition relating to a return in respect of an electoral region vacancy instead of paragraph 2 set out in sub-paragraph (b) substitute

"2 That in respect of a vacancy in the *insert name of Assembly electoral region* electoral region, on the . . . . .day of. . . . . .20. . . . . .the returning officer notified the Presiding Officer of the National Assembly for Wales that EF was to fill that vacancy and pursuant to *section 9(6) of the Government of Wales Act 1998/ *section 11(6) of the Government of Wales Act 2006 (*delete as appropriate*) was on the . . . . . .day of. . . . .20. . . . . treated as having been declared to be returned.";

(d) in paragraph 4, for "section 122(2) or (3) or section 129(2), (3) or (4) of the above Act" there were substituted "article 88(2) or (3) of the above Order"; and

(e) for paragraph (1) of the prayer, there were substituted

(i) in the case of a petition in relation to an election

"(1) That it may be determined that the said *insert name* was not duly elected *or* returned and that the election was void *or* that the said *insert name* was duly elected and ought to have been returned *or as the case may be*."; and

(ii) in the case of a petition in relation to a vacancy in respect of an electoral region

"(1) That it may be determined that the said *insert name* was not duly returned and that the said *insert* name ought to have been returned under *section 9 of the Government of Wales Act 1998 / *under section 11 of the Government of Wales Act 2006 (*delete as appropriate*) *or as the case may be*.".

References to the 1983 Act

9   In the Table below references in column (2) to a numbered section of the 1983 Act set out opposite to a numbered rule of the 1960 Rules in column (1) shall be construed as a reference to the appropriate numbered article in this Order set out in column (3)

Column (1)	Column (2)	Column (3)
rule 4(1)(a)	section 121(1)	article 87(1)
rule 4(1)(c)	section 122(2) or (3)	article 88(2) or (3)
rule 5(1)	section 136	article 92
rule 6(1)	section 121(2)	article 87(3)
rule 7	section 136(4)	article 92(4)
rule 8	section 138(1)	article 94(1)
rule 10(2)	section 139(5)	article 95(5)
rule 11	section 146(1)	article 102(1)
rule 19(1)	section 119	article 85
rule 19(2)	section 119(2)	article 85(2)
rule 21(2)(b)	section 184	article 136

Parliamentary Constituencies (England) Order 2007 (SI 2007/1681)

Made 13th June 2007

1 Citation and commencement
2 Parliamentary constituencies in England
3 Electoral registers
4 Revocation
Schedules

Citation and commencement

1(1) This Order may be cited as the Parliamentary Constituencies (England) Order 2007.

(2) This Order shall come into force on the fourteenth day after the day on which it is made.

Parliamentary constituencies in England

2(1) England shall be divided into the parliamentary constituencies
   (a) which are named in column 1 of the Table in the Schedule to this Order;
   (b) which are designated as being either county constituencies or borough constituencies by inclusion of those words beneath the name in column 1 of the Table in the Schedule; and
   (c) which comprise the areas which are set out in column 2 of the Table in the Schedule opposite the name of the constituency.

(2) The areas set out in column 2 of the Table in the Schedule to this Order are local government areas as they existed on 12th April 2005.

Electoral registers

3(1) Each electoral registration officer for the constituencies referred to in article 2 shall make such rearrangement or adaptation of the registers of parliamentary electors as may be necessary to give effect to this Order.

Revocation

4 The following Orders are revoked
   (a) The Parliamentary Constituencies (England) Order 1995,
   (b) The Parliamentary Constituencies (England) (Miscellaneous Changes) Order 1996,
   (c) The Parliamentary Constituencies (England) (Miscellaneous Changes) Order 1998.

SCHEDULE

NAME, DESIGNATION AND COMPOSITION OF CONSTITUENCIES IN ENGLAND

Table

Name and Designation	Composition
GREATER LONDON	
In the London boroughs of Barking and Dagenham, and Havering	
Barking (borough	The Borough of Barking and Dagenham wards: Abbey, Alibon, Becontree, Eastbury, Gascoigne, Goresbrook,

constituency)	Longbridge, Mayesbrook, Parsloes, Thames, Valence.
Dagenham and Rainham (borough constituency)	*The Borough of Barking and Dagenham wards:* Chadwell Heath, Eastbrook, Heath, River, Village, Whalebone. *The Borough of Havering wards:* Elm Park, Rainham and Wennington, South Hornchurch.
Hornchurch and Upminster (borough constituency)	*The Borough of Havering wards:* Cranham, Emerson Park, Gooshays, Hacton, Harold Wood, Heaton, St Andrew's, Upminster.
Romford (borough constituency)	*The Borough of Havering wards:* Brooklands, Havering Park, Hylands, Mawneys, Pettits, Romford Town, Squirrel's Heath.

In the London borough of Barnet

Chipping Barnet (borough constituency)	*The Borough of Barnet wards:* Brunswick Park, Coppetts, East Barnet, High Barnet, Oakleigh, Totteridge, Underhill.
Finchley and Golders Green (borough constituency)	*The Borough of Barnet wards:* Childs Hill, East Finchley, Finchley Church End, Garden Suburb, Golders Green, West Finchley, Woodhouse.
Hendon (borough constituency)	*The Borough of Barnet wards:* Burnt Oak, Colindale, Edgware, Hale, Hendon, Mill Hill, West Hendon.

In the London boroughs of Bexley and Greenwich

Bexleyheath and Crayford (borough constituency)	*The Borough of Bexley wards:* Barnehurst, Brampton, Christchurch, Colyers, Crayford, Danson Park, North End, St Michael's.
Eltham (borough constituency)	*The Borough of Greenwich wards:* Coldharbour and New Eltham, Eltham North, Eltham South, Eltham West, Kidbrooke with Hornfair, Middle Park and Sutcliffe, Shooters Hill.
Erith and Thamesmead (borough constituency)	*The Borough of Bexley wards:* Belvedere, Erith, Lesnes Abbey, Northumberland Heath, Thamesmead East. *The Borough of Greenwich wards:* Abbey Wood, Plumstead, Thamesmead Moorings.
Greenwich and Woolwich (borough constituency)	*The Borough of Greenwich wards:* Blackheath Westcombe, Charlton, Glyndon, Greenwich West, Peninsula, Woolwich Common, Woolwich Riverside.
Old Bexley and Sidcup (borough constituency)	*The Borough of Bexley wards:* Blackfen and Lamorbey, Blendon and Penhill, Cray Meadows, East Wickham, Falconwood and Welling, Longlands, St Mary's, Sidcup.

In the London boroughs of Brent and Camden

Brent Central (borough constituency)	*The Borough of Brent wards:* Dollis Hill, Dudden Hill, Harlesden, Kensal Green, Mapesbury, Stonebridge, Tokyngton, Welsh Harp, Willesden Green.
Brent North	*The Borough of Brent wards:*

(borough constituency)	Alperton, Barnhill, Fryent, Kenton, Northwick Park, Preston, Queensbury, Sudbury, Wembley Central.
Hampstead and Kilburn (borough constituency)	*The Borough of Brent wards:* Brondesbury Park, Kilburn, Queens Park. *The Borough of Camden wards:* Belsize, Fortune Green, Frognal and Fitzjohns, Hampstead Town, Kilburn, Swiss Cottage, West Hampstead.
Holborn and St Pancras (borough constituency)	*The Borough of Camden wards:* Bloomsbury, Camden Town with Primrose Hill, Cantelowes, Gospel Oak, Haverstock, Highgate, Holborn and Covent Garden, Kentish Town, King's Cross, Regent's Park, St Pancras and Somers Town.

In the London boroughs of Bromley and Lewisham

Beckenham (borough constituency)	*The Borough of Bromley wards:* Bromley Common and Keston, Copers Cope, Hayes and Coney Hall, Kelsey and Eden Park, Shortlands, West Wickham.
Bromley and Chislehurst (borough constituency)	*The Borough of Bromley wards:* Bickley, Bromley Town, Chislehurst, Cray Valley West, Mottingham and Chislehurst North, Plaistow and Sundridge.
Lewisham, Deptford (borough constituency)	*The Borough of Lewisham wards:* Brockley, Crofton Park, Evelyn, Ladywell, Lewisham Central, New Cross, Telegraph Hill.
Lewisham East (borough constituency)	*The Borough of Lewisham wards:* Blackheath, Catford South, Downham, Grove Park, Lee Green, Rushey Green, Whitefoot.
Lewisham West and Penge (borough constituency)	*The Borough of Bromley wards:* Clock House, Crystal Palace, Penge and Cator. *The Borough of Lewisham wards:* Bellingham, Forest Hill, Perry Vale, Sydenham.
Orpington (borough constituency)	*The Borough of Bromley wards:* Biggin Hill, Chelsfield and Pratts Bottom, Cray Valley East, Darwin, Farnborough and Crofton, Orpington, Petts Wood and Knoll.

In the London borough of Croydon

Croydon Central (borough constituency)	*The Borough of Croydon wards:* Addiscombe, Ashburton, Fairfield, Fieldway, Heathfield, New Addington, Shirley, Woodside.
Croydon North (borough constituency)	*The Borough of Croydon wards:* Bensham Manor, Broad Green, Norbury, Selhurst, South Norwood, Thornton Heath, Upper Norwood, West Thornton.
Croydon South (borough constituency)	*The Borough of Croydon wards:* Coulsdon East, Coulsdon West, Croham, Kenley, Purley, Sanderstead, Selsdon and Ballards, Waddon.

In the London borough of Ealing

Ealing Central and Acton (borough constituency)	*The Borough of Ealing wards:* Acton Central, Ealing Broadway, Ealing Common, East Acton, Hanger Hill, South Acton, Southfield, Walpole.
Ealing North	*The Borough of Ealing wards:*

(borough constituency)	Cleveland, Greenford Broadway, Greenford Green, Hobbayne, North Greenford, Northolt Mandeville, Northolt West End, Perivale.
Ealing, Southall (borough constituency)	*The Borough of Ealing wards:* Dormers Wells, Elthorne, Lady Margaret, Northfield, Norwood Green, Southall Broadway, Southall Green.

The London borough of Enfield

Edmonton (borough constituency)	*The Borough of Enfield wards:* Bush Hill Park, Edmonton Green, Haselbury, Jubilee, Lower Edmonton, Ponders End, Upper Edmonton.
Enfield North (borough constituency)	*The Borough of Enfield wards:* Chase, Enfield Highway, Enfield Lock, Highlands, Southbury, Town, Turkey Street.
Enfield, Southgate (borough constituency)	*The Borough of Enfield wards:* Bowes, Cockfosters, Grange, Palmers Green, Southgate, Southgate Green, Winchmore Hill.

In the London borough of Hackney

Hackney North and Stoke Newington (borough constituency)	*The Borough of Hackney wards:* Brownswood, Cazenove, Clissold, Dalston, Hackney Downs, Leabridge, Lordship, New River, Springfield, Stoke Newington Central.
Hackney South and Shoreditch (borough constituency)	*The Borough of Hackney wards:* Chatham, De Beauvoir, Hackney Central, Haggerston, Hoxton, King's Park, Queensbridge, Victoria, Wick.

In the London borough of Hammersmith and Fulham, and the Royal borough of Kensington and Chelsea

Chelsea and Fulham (borough constituency)	*The Borough of Hammersmith and Fulham wards:* Fulham Broadway, Munster, Palace Riverside, Parsons Green and Walham, Sands End, Town. *The Royal Borough of Kensington and Chelsea wards:* Cremorne, Hans Town, Redcliffe, Royal Hospital, Stanley.
Hammersmith (borough constituency)	*The Borough of Hammersmith and Fulham wards:* Addison, Askew, Avonmore and Brook Green, College Park and Old Oak, Fulham Reach, Hammersmith Broadway, North End, Ravenscourt Park, Shepherd's Bush Green, Wormholt and White City.
Kensington (borough constituency)	*The Royal Borough of Kensington and Chelsea wards:* Abingdon, Brompton, Campden, Colville, Courtfield, Earl's Court, Golborne, Holland, Norland, Notting Barns, Pembridge, Queen's Gate, St Charles.

In the London borough of Haringey

Hornsey and Wood Green (borough constituency)	*The Borough of Haringey wards:* Alexandra, Bounds Green, Crouch End, Fortis Green, Highgate, Hornsey, Muswell Hill, Noel Park, Stroud Green, Woodside.
Tottenham (borough constituency)	*The Borough of Haringey wards:* Bruce Grove, Harringay, Northumberland Park, St Ann's, Seven Sisters, Tottenham Green, Tottenham Hale, West Green, White Hart Lane.

In the London boroughs of Harrow and Hillingdon

Harrow East (borough constituency)	*The Borough of Harrow wards:* Belmont, Canons, Edgware, Harrow Weald, Kenton East, Kenton West, Queensbury, Stanmore Park, Wealdstone.

Harrow West (borough constituency)	The Borough of Harrow wards: Greenhill, Harrow on the Hill, Headstone North, Headstone South, Marlborough, Rayners Lane, Roxbourne, Roxeth, West Harrow.
Hayes and Harlington (borough constituency)	The Borough of Hillingdon wards: Barnhill, Botwell, Charville, Heathrow Villages, Pinkwell, Townfield, West Drayton, Yeading.
Ruislip, Northwood and Pinner (borough constituency)	The Borough of Harrow wards: Hatch End, Pinner, Pinner South. The Borough of Hillingdon wards: Eastcote and East Ruislip, Harefield, Ickenham, Northwood, Northwood Hills, West Ruislip.
Uxbridge and South Ruislip (borough constituency)	The Borough of Hillingdon wards: Brunel, Cavendish, Hillingdon East, Manor, South Ruislip, Uxbridge North, Uxbridge South, Yiewsley.

In the London borough of Hounslow

Brentford and Isleworth (borough constituency)	The Borough of Hounslow wards: Brentford, Chiswick Homefields, Chiswick Riverside, Hounslow Central, Hounslow Heath, Hounslow South, Isleworth, Osterley and Spring Grove, Syon, Turnham Green.
Feltham and Heston (borough constituency)	The Borough of Hounslow wards: Bedfont, Cranford, Feltham North, Feltham West, Hanworth, Hanworth Park, Heston Central, Heston East, Heston West, Hounslow West.

In the London borough of Islington

Islington North (borough constituency)	The Borough of Islington wards: Finsbury Park, Highbury East, Highbury West, Hillrise, Junction, Mildmay, St George's, Tollington.
Islington South and Finsbury (borough constituency)	The Borough of Islington wards: Barnsbury, Bunhill, Caledonian, Canonbury, Clerkenwell, Holloway, St Mary's, St Peter's.

In the Royal borough of Kingston upon Thames and the London borough of Richmond upon Thames

Kingston and Surbiton (borough constituency)	The Royal Borough of Kingston upon Thames wards: Alexandra, Berrylands, Beverley, Chessington North and Hook, Chessington South, Grove, Norbiton, Old Malden, St James, St Mark's, Surbiton Hill, Tolworth and Hook Rise.
Richmond Park (borough constituency)	The Royal Borough of Kingston upon Thames wards: Canbury, Coombe Hill, Coombe Vale, Tudor. The Borough of Richmond upon Thames wards: Barnes, East Sheen, Ham, Petersham and Richmond Riverside, Kew, Mortlake and Barnes Common, North Richmond, South Richmond.
Twickenham (borough constituency)	The Borough of Richmond upon Thames wards: Fulwell and Hampton Hill, Hampton, Hampton North, Hampton Wick, Heathfield, St Margarets and North Twickenham, South Twickenham,

Teddington, Twickenham Riverside, West Twickenham, Whitton.

The London boroughs of Lambeth and Southwark	
Bermondsey and Old Southwark (borough constituency)	*The Borough of Southwark wards:* Cathedrals, Chaucer, East Walworth, Grange, Newington, Riverside, Rotherhithe, South Bermondsey, Surrey Docks.
Camberwell and Peckham (borough constituency)	*The Borough of Southwark wards:* Brunswick Park, Camberwell Green, Faraday, Livesey, Nunhead, Peckham, Peckham Rye, South Camberwell, The Lane.
Dulwich and West Norwood (borough constituency)	*The Borough of Lambeth wards:* Coldharbour, Gipsy Hill, Herne Hill, Knight's Hill, Thurlow Park. *The Borough of Southwark wards:* College, East Dulwich, Village.
Streatham (borough constituency)	*The Borough of Lambeth wards:* Brixton Hill, Clapham Common, St Leonard's, Streatham Hill, Streatham South, Streatham Wells, Thornton, Tulse Hill.
Vauxhall (borough constituency)	*The Borough of Lambeth wards:* Bishop's, Clapham Town, Ferndale, Larkhall, Oval, Prince's, Stockwell, Vassall.
The London borough of Merton	
Mitcham and Morden (borough constituency)	*The Borough of Merton wards:* Colliers Wood, Cricket Green, Figge's Marsh, Graveney, Lavender Fields, Longthornton, Lower Morden, Pollards Hill, Ravensbury, St Helier.
Wimbledon (borough constituency)	*The Borough of Merton wards:* Abbey, Cannon Hill, Dundonald, Hillside, Merton Park, Raynes Park, Trinity, Village, West Barnes, Wimbledon Park.
In the London borough of Newham	
East Ham (borough constituency)	*The Borough of Newham wards:* Beckton, Boleyn, East Ham Central, East Ham North, East Ham South, Green Street East, Little Ilford, Manor Park, Royal Docks, Wall End.
West Ham (borough constituency)	*The Borough of Newham wards:* Canning Town North, Canning Town South, Custom House, Forest Gate North, Forest Gate South, Green Street West, Plaistow North, Plaistow South, Stratford and New Town, West Ham.
The London boroughs of Redbridge and Waltham Forest	
Chingford and Woodford Green (borough constituency)	*The Borough of Redbridge wards:* Church End, Monkhams. *The Borough of Waltham Forest wards:* Chingford Green, Endlebury, Hale End and Highams Park, Hatch Lane, Larkswood, Valley.
Ilford North (borough constituency)	*The Borough of Redbridge wards:* Aldborough, Barkingside, Bridge, Clayhall, Fairlop, Fullwell, Hainault, Roding.
Ilford South (borough	*The Borough of Redbridge wards:* Chadwell, Clementswood, Cranbrook, Goodmayes, Loxford, Mayfield,

constituency)	Newbury, Seven Kings, Valentines.
Leyton and Wanstead (borough constituency)	*The Borough of Redbridge wards:* Snaresbrook, Wanstead. *The Borough of Waltham Forest wards:* Cann Hall, Cathall, Forest, Grove Green, Leyton, Leytonstone.
Walthamstow (borough constituency)	*The Borough of Waltham Forest wards:* Chapel End, Higham Hill, High Street, Hoe Street, Lea Bridge, Markhouse, William Morris, Wood Street.
In the London borough of Sutton	
Carshalton and Wallington (borough constituency)	*The Borough of Sutton wards:* Beddington North, Beddington South, Carshalton Central, Carshalton South and Clockhouse, St Helier, The Wrythe, Wallington North, Wallington South, Wandle Valley.
Sutton and Cheam (borough constituency)	*The Borough of Sutton wards:* Belmont, Cheam, Nonsuch, Stonecot, Sutton Central, Sutton North, Sutton South, Sutton West, Worcester Park.
In the London borough of Tower Hamlets	
Bethnal Green and Bow (borough constituency)	*The Borough of Tower Hamlets wards:* Bethnal Green North, Bethnal Green South, Bow East, Bow West, Mile End and Globe Town, St Dunstan's and Stepney Green, Spitalfields and Banglatown, Weavers, Whitechapel.
Poplar and Limehouse (borough constituency)	*The Borough of Tower Hamlets wards:* Blackwall and Cubitt Town, BromleybyBow, East India and Lansbury, Limehouse, Mile End East, Millwall, St Katharine's and Wapping, Shadwell.
In the London borough of Wandsworth	
Battersea (borough constituency)	*The Borough of Wandsworth wards:* Balham, Fairfield, Latchmere, Northcote, Queenstown, St Mary's Park, Shaftesbury.
Putney (borough constituency)	*The Borough of Wandsworth wards:* East Putney, Roehampton, Southfields, Thamesfield, West Hill, West Putney.
Tooting (borough constituency)	*The Borough of Wandsworth wards:* Bedford, Earlsfield, Furzedown, Graveney, Nightingale, Tooting, Wandsworth Common.
In the City of Westminster and the City of London	
Cities of London and Westminster (borough constituency)	*The City of Westminster wards:* Bryanston and Dorset Square, Churchill, Hyde Park, Knightsbridge and Belgravia, Marylebone High Street, St James's, Tachbrook, Vincent Square, Warwick, West End. *The City of London.*
Westminster North (borough constituency)	*The City of Westminster wards:* Abbey Road, Bayswater, Church Street, Harrow Road, Lancaster Gate, Little Venice, Maida Vale, Queen's Park, Regent's Park, Westbourne.
THE METROPOLITAN COUNTIES	
IN GREATER MANCHESTER	

Altrincham and Sale West (borough constituency)	*The Borough of Trafford wards:* Altrincham, Ashton upon Mersey, Bowdon, Broadheath, Hale Barns, Hale Central, St Mary's, Timperley, Village.
AshtonunderLyne (borough constituency)	*The Borough of Oldham wards:* Failsworth East, Failsworth West. *The Borough of Tameside wards:* Ashton Hurst, Ashton St Michael's, Ashton Waterloo, Droylsden East, Droylsden West, St Peter's.
Blackley and Broughton (borough constituency)	*The City of Manchester wards:* Charlestown, Cheetham, Crumpsall, Harpurhey, Higher Blackley. *The City of Salford wards:* Broughton, Kersal.
Bolton North East (borough constituency)	*The Borough of Bolton wards:* Astley Bridge, Bradshaw, Breightmet, Bromley Cross, Crompton, Halliwell, Tonge with the Haulgh.
Bolton South East (borough constituency)	*The Borough of Bolton wards:* Farnworth, Great Lever, Harper Green, Hulton, Kearsley, Little Lever and Darcy Lever, Rumworth.
Bolton West (county constituency)	*The Borough of Bolton wards:* Heaton and Lostock, Horwich and Blackrod, Horwich North East, Smithills, Westhoughton North and Chew Moor, Westhoughton South. *The Borough of Wigan ward:* Atherton.
Bury North (borough constituency)	*The Borough of Bury wards:* Church, East, Elton, Moorside, North Manor, Ramsbottom, Redvales, Tottington.
Bury South (borough constituency)	*The Borough of Bury wards:* Besses, Holyrood, Pilkington Park, Radcliffe East, Radcliffe North, Radcliffe West, St Mary's, Sedgley, Unsworth.
Cheadle (borough constituency)	*The Borough of Stockport wards:* Bramhall North, Bramhall South, Cheadle and Gatley, Cheadle Hulme North, Cheadle Hulme South, Heald Green, Stepping Hill.
Denton and Reddish (borough constituency)	*The Borough of Stockport wards:* Reddish North, Reddish South. *The Borough of Tameside wards:* Audenshaw, Denton North East, Denton South, Denton West, Dukinfield.
Hazel Grove (county constituency)	*The Borough of Stockport wards:* Bredbury and Woodley, Bredbury Green and Romiley, Hazel Grove, Marple North, Marple South, Offerton.
Heywood and Middleton (county constituency)	*The Borough of Rochdale wards:* Bamford, Castleton, East Middleton, Hopwood Hall, Norden, North Heywood, North Middleton, South Middleton, West Heywood, West Middleton.
Leigh (county constituency)	*The Borough of Wigan wards:* Astley Mosley Common, Atherleigh, Golborne and Lowton West, Leigh East, Leigh South, Leigh West, Lowton East, Tyldesley.

Makerfield (county constituency)	*The Borough of Wigan wards:* Abram, Ashton, Bryn, Hindley, Hindley Green, Orrell, Winstanley, Worsley Mesnes.
Manchester Central (borough constituency)	*The City of Manchester wards:* Ancoats and Clayton, Ardwick, Bradford, City Centre, Hulme, Miles Platting and Newton Heath, Moss Side, Moston.
Manchester, Gorton (borough constituency)	*The City of Manchester wards:* Fallowfield, Gorton North, Gorton South, Levenshulme, Longsight, Rusholme, Whalley Range.
Manchester, Withington (borough constituency)	*The City of Manchester wards:* Burnage, Chorlton, Chorlton Park, Didsbury East, Didsbury West, Old Moat, Withington.
Oldham East and Saddleworth (county constituency)	*The Borough of Oldham wards:* Alexandra, Crompton, Saddleworth North, Saddleworth South, Saddleworth West and Lees, St James', St Mary's, Shaw, Waterhead.
Oldham West and Royton (borough constituency)	*The Borough of Oldham wards:* Chadderton Central, Chadderton North, Chadderton South, Coldhurst, Hollinwood, Medlock Vale, Royton North, Royton South, Werneth.
Rochdale (county constituency)	*The Borough of Rochdale wards:* Balderstone and Kirkholt, Central Rochdale, Healey, Kingsway, Littleborough Lakeside, Milkstone and Deeplish, Milnrow and Newhey, Smallbridge and Firgrove, Spotland and Falinge, Wardle and West Littleborough.
Salford and Eccles (borough constituency)	*The City of Salford wards:* Claremont, Eccles, Irwell Riverside, Langworthy, Ordsall, Pendlebury, Swinton North, Swinton South, Weaste and Seedley.
Stalybridge and Hyde (county constituency)	*The Borough of Tameside wards:* Dukinfield Stalybridge, Hyde Godley, Hyde Newton, Hyde Werneth, Longdendale, Mossley, Stalybridge North, Stalybridge South.
Stockport (borough constituency)	*The Borough of Stockport wards:* Brinnington and Central, Davenport and Cale Green, Edgeley and Cheadle Heath, Heatons North, Heatons South, Manor.
Stretford and Urmston (borough constituency)	*The Borough of Trafford wards:* BucklowSt Martins, Clifford, Davyhulme East, Davyhulme West, Flixton, Gorse Hill, Longford, Stretford, Urmston.
Wigan (county constituency)	*The Borough of Wigan wards:* Aspull New Springs Whelley, Douglas, Ince, Pemberton, Shevington with Lower Ground, Standish with Langtree, Wigan Central, Wigan West.
Worsley and Eccles South (county constituency)	*The City of Salford wards:* Barton, Boothstown and Ellenbrook, Cadishead, Irlam, Little Hulton, Walkden North, Walkden South, Winton, Worsley.
Wythenshawe and Sale East (borough constituency)	*The City of Manchester wards:* Baguley, Brooklands, Northenden, Sharston, Woodhouse Park. *The Borough of Trafford wards:*

Brooklands, Priory, Sale Moor.

IN MERSEYSIDE	
Birkenhead (borough constituency)	*The Borough of Wirral wards:* Bidston and St James, Birkenhead and Tranmere, Claughton, Oxton, Prenton, Rock Ferry.
Bootle (borough constituency)	*The Borough of Sefton wards:* Church, Derby, Ford, Linacre, Litherland, Netherton and Orrell, St Oswald, Victoria.
Garston and Halewood (borough constituency)	*The Borough of Knowsley wards:* Halewood North, Halewood South, Halewood West. *The City of Liverpool wards:* Allerton and Hunts Cross, Belle Vale, Cressington, SpekeGarston, Woolton.
Knowsley (borough constituency)	*The Borough of Knowsley wards:* Cherryfield, Kirkby Central, Longview, Northwood, Page Moss, Park, Prescot West, Roby, St Bartholomews, St Gabriels, St Michaels, Shevington, Stockbridge, Swanside, Whitefield.
Liverpool, Riverside (borough constituency)	*The City of Liverpool wards:* Central, Greenbank, Kirkdale, Mossley Hill, Princes Park, Riverside, St Michael's.
Liverpool, Walton (borough constituency)	*The City of Liverpool wards* Anfield, Clubmoor, County, Everton, Fazakerley, Warbreck.
Liverpool, Wavertree (borough constituency)	*The City of Liverpool wards:* Childwall, Church, Kensington and Fairfield, Old Swan, Picton, Wavertree.
Liverpool, West Derby (borough constituency)	*The City of Liverpool wards:* Croxteth, Knotty Ash, Norris Green, Tuebrook and Stoneycroft, West Derby, Yew Tree.
Sefton Central (county constituency)	*The Borough of Sefton wards:* Blundellsands, Harington, Manor, Molyneux, Park, Ravenmeols, Sudell.
Southport (borough constituency)	*The Borough of Sefton wards:* Ainsdale, Birkdale, Cambridge, Duke's, Kew, Meols, Norwood.
St Helens North (borough constituency)	*The Borough of St Helens wards:* Billinge and Seneley Green, Blackbrook, Earlestown, Haydock, Moss Bank, Newton, Parr, Rainford, Windle.
St Helens South and Whiston (borough constituency)	*The Borough of Knowsley wards:* Prescot East, Whiston North, Whiston South. *The Borough of St Helens wards:* Bold, Eccleston, Rainhill, Sutton, Thatto Heath, Town Centre, West Park.
Wallasey (borough constituency)	*The Borough of Wirral wards:* Leasowe and Moreton East, Liscard, Moreton West and Saughall Massie, New Brighton, Seacombe, Wallasey.
Wirral South	*The Borough of Wirral wards:*

(county constituency)	Bebington, Bromborough, Clatterbridge, Eastham, Heswall.
Wirral West (county constituency)	*The Borough of Wirral wards:* Greasby, Frankby and Irby, Hoylake and Meols, Pensby and Thingwall, Upton, West Kirby and Thurstaston.

IN SOUTH YORKSHIRE

Barnsley Central (borough constituency)	*The Borough of Barnsley wards:* Central, Darton East, Darton West, Kingstone, Monk Bretton, Old Town, Royston, St Helens.
Barnsley East (county constituency)	*The Borough of Barnsley wards:* Cudworth, Darfield, Hoyland Milton, North East, Rockingham, Stairfoot, Wombwell, Worsbrough.
Don Valley (county constituency)	*The Borough of Doncaster wards:* Conisbrough and Denaby, Edlington and Warmsworth, Finningley, Hatfield, Rossington, Thorne, Torne Valley.
Doncaster Central (borough constituency)	*The Borough of Doncaster wards:* Armthorpe, Balby, Bessacarr and Cantley, Central, Edenthorpe, Kirk Sandall and Barnby Dun, Town Moor, Wheatley.
Doncaster North (county constituency)	*The Borough of Doncaster wards:* Adwick, Askern Spa, Bentley, Great North Road, Mexborough, Sprotbrough, Stainforth and Moorends.
Penistone and Stocksbridge (county constituency)	*The Borough of Barnsley wards:* Dodworth, Penistone East, Penistone West. *The City of Sheffield wards:* East Ecclesfield, Stocksbridge and Upper Don, West Ecclesfield.
Rother Valley (county constituency)	*The Borough of Rotherham wards:* Anston and Woodsetts, Dinnington, Hellaby, Holderness, Maltby, Rother Vale, Sitwell, Wales.
Rotherham (borough constituency)	*The Borough of Rotherham wards:* Boston Castle, Brinsworth and Catcliffe, Keppel, Rotherham East, Rotherham West, Valley, Wingfield.
Sheffield, Brightside and Hillsborough (borough constituency)	*The City of Sheffield wards:* Burngreave, Firth Park, Hillsborough, Shiregreen and Brightside, Southey.
Sheffield Central (borough constituency)	*The City of Sheffield wards:* Broomhill, Central, Manor Castle, Nether Edge, Walkley.
Sheffield, Hallam (county constituency)	*The City of Sheffield wards:* Crookes, Dore and Totley, Ecclesall, Fulwood, Stannington.
Sheffield, Heeley (borough constituency)	*The City of Sheffield wards:* Arbourthorne, Beauchief and Greenhill, Gleadless Valley, Graves Park, Richmond.
Sheffield South East (borough constituency)	*The City of Sheffield wards:* Beighton, Birley, Darnall, Mosborough, Woodhouse.
Wentworth and Dearne (county constituency)	*The Borough of Barnsley wards:* Dearne North, Dearne South.

	The Borough of Rotherham wards:
	Hoober, Rawmarsh, Silverwood, Swinton, Wath, Wickersley.

IN TYNE AND WEAR

Blaydon (borough constituency)	*The Borough of Gateshead wards:* Birtley, Blaydon, Chopwell and Rowlands Gill, Crawcrook and Greenside, Dunston Hill and Whickham East, Lamesley, Ryton, Crookhill and Stella, Whickham North, Whickham South and Sunniside, Winlaton and High Spen.
Gateshead (borough constituency)	*The Borough of Gateshead wards:* Bridges, Chowdene, Deckham, Dunston and Teams, Felling, High Fell, Lobley Hill and Bensham, Low Fell, Saltwell, Windy Nook and Whitehills.
Houghton and Sunderland South (borough constituency)	*The City of Sunderland wards:* Copt Hill, Doxford, Hetton, Houghton, St Chad's, Sandhill, Shiney Row, Silksworth.
Jarrow (borough constituency)	*The Borough of Gateshead wards:* Pelaw and Heworth, Wardley and Leam Lane. *The Borough of South Tyneside wards:* Bede, Boldon Colliery, Cleadon and East Boldon, Fellgate and Hedworth, Hebburn North, Hebburn South, Monkton, Primrose.
Newcastle upon Tyne Central (borough constituency)	*The City of Newcastle upon Tyne wards:* Benwell and Scotswood, Blakelaw, Elswick, Fenham, Kenton, Westgate, West Gosforth, Wingrove.
Newcastle upon Tyne East (borough constituency)	*The City of Newcastle upon Tyne wards:* Byker, Dene, North Heaton, North Jesmond, Ouseburn, South Heaton, South Jesmond, Walker, Walkergate.
Newcastle upon Tyne North (borough constituency)	*The City of Newcastle upon Tyne wards:* Castle, Denton, East Gosforth, Fawdon, Lemington, Newburn, Parklands, Westerhope, Woolsington.
North Tyneside (borough constituency)	*The Borough of North Tyneside wards:* Battle Hill, Benton, Camperdown, Howdon, Killingworth, Longbenton, Northumberland, Riverside, Wallsend, Weetslade.
South Shields (borough constituency)	*The Borough of South Tyneside wards:* Beacon and Bents, Biddick and All Saints, Cleadon Park, Harton, Horsley Hill, Simonside and Rekendyke, Westoe, West Park, Whitburn and Marsden, Whiteleas.
Sunderland Central (borough constituency)	*The City of Sunderland wards:* Barnes, Fulwell, Hendon, Millfield, Pallion, Ryhope, St Michael's, St Peter's, Southwick.
Tynemouth (borough constituency)	*The Borough of North Tyneside wards:* Chirton, Collingwood, Cullercoats, Monkseaton North, Monkseaton South, Preston, St Mary's, Tynemouth, Valley, Whitley Bay.
Washington and Sunderland West (borough constituency)	*The City of Sunderland wards:* Castle, Redhill, St Anne's, Washington Central, Washington East, Washington North, Washington South, Washington West.

IN THE WEST MIDLANDS

AldridgeBrownhills	*The Borough of Walsall wards:*

(borough constituency)	Aldridge Central and South, Aldridge North and Walsall Wood, Brownhills, Pelsall, RushallShelfield, Streetly.
Birmingham, Edgbaston (borough constituency)	*The City of Birmingham wards:* Bartley Green, Edgbaston, Harborne, Quinton.
Birmingham, Erdington (borough constituency)	*The City of Birmingham wards:* Erdington, Kingstanding, Stockland Green, Tyburn.
Birmingham, Hall Green (borough constituency)	*The City of Birmingham wards:* Hall Green, Moseley and Kings Heath, Sparkbrook, Springfield.
Birmingham, Hodge Hill (borough constituency)	*The City of Birmingham wards:* Bordesley Green, Hodge Hill, Shard End, Washwood Heath.
Birmingham, Ladywood (borough constituency)	*The City of Birmingham wards:* Aston, Ladywood, Nechells, Soho.
Birmingham, Northfield (borough constituency)	*The City of Birmingham wards:* Kings Norton, Longbridge, Northfield, Weoley.
Birmingham, Perry Barr (borough constituency)	*The City of Birmingham wards:* Handsworth Wood, Lozells and East Handsworth, Oscott, Perry Barr.
Birmingham, Selly Oak (borough constituency)	*The City of Birmingham wards:* Billesley, Bournville, Brandwood, Selly Oak.
Birmingham, Yardley (borough constituency)	*The City of Birmingham wards:* Acocks Green, Sheldon, South Yardley, Stechford and Yardley North.
Coventry North East (borough constituency)	*The City of Coventry wards:* Foleshill, Henley, Longford, Lower Stoke, Upper Stoke, Wyken.
Coventry North West (borough constituency)	*The City of Coventry wards:* Bablake, Holbrook, Radford, Sherbourne, Whoberley, Woodlands.
Coventry South (borough constituency)	*The City of Coventry wards:* Binley and Willenhall, Cheylesmore, Earlsdon, St Michael's, Wainbody, Westwood.
Dudley North (borough constituency)	*The Borough of Dudley wards:* Castle and Priory, Gornal, St James's, St Thomas's, Sedgley, Upper Gornal and Woodsetton.
Dudley South (borough	*The Borough of Dudley wards:* Brierley Hill, Brockmoor and Pensnett, Kingswinford North and Wall

constituency)	Heath, Kingswinford South, Netherton, Woodside and St Andrews, Wordsley.
Halesowen and Rowley Regis (borough constituency)	*The Borough of Dudley wards:* Belle Vale, Halesowen North, Halesowen South, Hayley Green and Cradley South. *The Borough of Sandwell wards:* Blackheath, Cradley Heath and Old Hill, Rowley.
Meriden (county constituency)	*The Borough of Solihull wards:* Bickenhill, Blythe, Castle Bromwich, Chelmsley Wood, Dorridge and Hockley Heath, Kingshurst and Fordbridge, Knowle, Meriden, Smith's Wood.
Solihull (borough constituency)	*The Borough of Solihull wards:* Elmdon, Lyndon, Olton, St Alphege, Shirley East, Shirley South, Shirley West, Silhill.
Stourbridge (borough constituency)	*The Borough of Dudley wards:* Amblecote, Cradley and Foxcote, Lye and Wollescote, Norton, Pedmore and Stourbridge East, Quarry Bank and Dudley Wood, Wollaston and Stourbridge Town.
Sutton Coldfield (borough constituency)	*The City of Birmingham wards:* Sutton Four Oaks, Sutton New Hall, Sutton Trinity, Sutton Vesey.
Walsall North (borough constituency)	*The Borough of Walsall wards:* Birchills Leamore, Blakenall, Bloxwich East, Bloxwich West, Short Heath, Willenhall North, Willenhall South.
Walsall South (borough constituency)	*The Borough of Walsall wards:* Bentley and Darlaston North, Darlaston South, Paddock, Palfrey, Pheasey Park Farm, Pleck, St Matthew's.
Warley (borough constituency)	*The Borough of Sandwell wards:* Abbey, Bristnall, Langley, Old Warley, St Pauls, Smethwick, Soho and Victoria.
West Bromwich East (borough constituency)	*The Borough of Sandwell wards:* Charlemont with Grove Vale, Friar Park, Great Barr with Yew Tree, Greets Green and Lyng, Hateley Heath, Newton, West Bromwich Central.
West Bromwich West (borough constituency)	*The Borough of Sandwell wards:* Great Bridge, Oldbury, Princes End, Tipton Green, Tividale, Wednesbury North, Wednesbury South.
Wolverhampton North East (borough constituency)	*The City of Wolverhampton wards:* Bushbury North, Bushbury South and Low Hill, Fallings Park, Heath Town, Oxley, Wednesfield North, Wednesfield South.
Wolverhampton South East (borough constituency)	*The Borough of Dudley ward:* Coseley East. *The City of Wolverhampton wards:* Bilston East, Bilston North, Blakenhall, East Park, Ettingshall, Spring Vale.
Wolverhampton South West (borough	*The City of Wolverhampton wards:* Graiseley, Merry Hill, Park, Penn, St Peter's, Tettenhall Regis,

constituency)	Tettenhall Wightwick.
IN WEST YORKSHIRE	
Batley and Spen (borough constituency)	*The Borough of Kirklees wards:* Batley East, Batley West, Birstall and Birkenshaw, Cleckheaton, Heckmondwike, Liversedge and Gomersal.
Bradford East (borough constituency)	*The City of Bradford wards:* Bolton and Undercliffe, Bowling and Barkerend, Bradford Moor, Eccleshill, Idle and Thackley, Little Horton.
Bradford South (borough constituency)	*The City of Bradford wards:* Great Horton, Queensbury, Royds, Tong, Wibsey, Wyke.
Bradford West (borough constituency)	*The City of Bradford wards:* City, Clayton and Fairweather Green, Heaton, Manningham, Thornton and Allerton, Toller.
Calder Valley (county constituency)	*The Borough of Calderdale wards:* Brighouse, Calder, Elland, Greetland and Stainland, Hipperholme and Lightcliffe, Luddendenfoot, Rastrick, Ryburn, Todmorden.
Colne Valley (county constituency)	*The Borough of Kirklees wards:* Colne Valley, Crosland Moor and Netherton, Golcar, Holme Valley North, Holme Valley South, Lindley.
Dewsbury (county constituency)	*The Borough of Kirklees wards:* Denby Dale, Dewsbury East, Dewsbury South, Dewsbury West, Kirkburton, Mirfield.
Elmet and Rothwell (county constituency)	*The City of Leeds wards:* Garforth and Swillington, Harewood, Kippax and Methley, Rothwell, Wetherby.
Halifax (borough constituency)	*The Borough of Calderdale wards:* Illingworth and Mixenden, Northowram and Shelf, Ovenden, Park, Skircoat, Sowerby Bridge, Town, Warley.
Hemsworth (county constituency)	*The City of Wakefield wards:* Ackworth, North Elmsall and Upton, Crofton, Ryhill and Walton, Featherstone, Hemsworth, South Elmsall and South Kirkby, Wakefield South.
Huddersfield (borough constituency)	*The Borough of Kirklees wards:* Almondbury, Ashbrow, Dalton, Greenhead, Newsome.
Keighley (county constituency)	*The City of Bradford wards:* Craven, Ilkley, Keighley Central, Keighley East, Keighley West, Worth Valley.
Leeds Central (borough constituency)	*The City of Leeds wards:* Beeston and Holbeck, Burmantofts and Richmond Hill, City and Hunslet, Hyde Park and Woodhouse, Middleton Park.
Leeds East (borough constituency)	*The City of Leeds wards:* Cross Gates and Whinmoor, Gipton and Harehills, Killingbeck and Seacroft, Temple Newsam.
Leeds North East (borough constituency)	*The City of Leeds wards:* Alwoodley, Chapel Allerton, Moortown, Roundhay.
Leeds North West (borough constituency)	*The City of Leeds wards:* Adel and Wharfedale, Headingley, Otley and Yeadon, Weetwood.
Leeds West (borough constituency)	*The City of Leeds wards:* Armley, Bramley and Stanningley, Farnley and Wortley, Kirkstall.

constituency)	
Morley and Outwood (county constituency)	*The City of Leeds wards:* Ardsley and Robin Hood, Morley North, Morley South, *The City of Wakefield wards:* Stanley and Outwood East, Wrenthorpe and Outwood West.
Normanton, Pontefract and Castleford (county constituency)	*The City of Wakefield wards:* Airedale and Ferry Fryston, Altofts and Whitwood, Castleford Central and Glasshoughton, Knottingley, Normanton, Pontefract North, Pontefract South.
Pudsey (borough constituency)	*The City of Leeds wards:* Calverley and Farsley, Guiseley and Rawdon, Horsforth, Pudsey.
Shipley (county constituency)	*The City of Bradford wards:* Baildon, Bingley, Bingley Rural, Shipley, Wharfedale, Windhill and Wrose.
Wakefield (county constituency)	*The City of Wakefield wards:* Horbury and South Ossett, Ossett, Wakefield East, Wakefield North, Wakefield Rural, Wakefield West.

THE Non-metropolITAN COUNTIES

IN BATH AND NORTH EAST SOMERSET

Bath (borough constituency)	*The District of Bath and North East Somerset wards:* Abbey, Bathwick, Combe Down, Kingsmead, Lambridge, Lansdown, Lyncombe, Newbridge, Odd Down, Oldfield, Southdown, Twerton, Walcot, Westmoreland, Weston, Widcombe.
North East Somerset (county constituency)	*The District of Bath and North East Somerset wards:* Bathavon North, Bathavon South, Bathavon West, Chew Valley North, Chew Valley South, Clutton, Farmborough, High Littleton, Keynsham East, Keynsham North, Keynsham South, Mendip, Midsomer Norton North, Midsomer Norton Redfield, Paulton, Peasedown, Publow and Whitchurch, Radstock, Saltford, Timsbury, Westfield.

IN BEDFORDSHIRE AND LUTON

Bedford (borough constituency)	*The Borough of Bedford wards:* Brickhill, Castle, Cauldwell, De Parys, Goldington, Harpur, Kempston East, Kempston North, Kempston South, Kingsbrook, Newnham, Putnoe, Queen's Park.
Luton North (borough constituency)	*The Borough of Luton wards:* Barnfield, Bramingham, Challney, Icknield, Leagrave, Lewsey, Limbury, Northwell, Saints, Sundon Park.
Luton South (borough constituency)	*The Borough of Luton wards:* Biscot, Crawley, Dallow, Farley, High Town, Round Green, South, Stopsley, Wigmore. *The District of South Bedfordshire ward:* Caddington, Hyde and Slip End.
Mid Bedfordshire (county constituency)	*The Borough of Bedford wards:* Turvey, Wilshamstead, Wootton. *The District of Mid Bedfordshire wards:* Ampthill, Aspley Guise, Clifton and Meppershall, Cranfield, Flitton,

Greenfield and Pulloxhill, Flitwick East, Flitwick West, Harlington, Houghton, Haynes, Southill and Old Warden, Marston, Maulden and Clophill, Shefford, Campton and Gravenhurst, Shillington, Stondon and Henlow Camp, Silsoe, Westoning and Tingrith, Woburn.
The District of South Bedfordshire wards:
BartonleClay, Streatley, Toddington.

North East Bedfordshire (county constituency)	*The Borough of Bedford wards:* Bromham, Carlton, Clapham, Eastcotts, Great Barford, Harrold, Oakley, Riseley, Roxton, Sharnbrook. *The District of Mid Bedfordshire wards:* Arlesey, Biggleswade Holme, Biggleswade Ivel, Biggleswade Stratton, Langford and Henlow Village, Northill and Blunham, Potton and Wensley, Sandy Ivel, Sandy Pinnacle, Stotfold.
South West Bedfordshire (county constituency)	*The District of South Bedfordshire wards:* All Saints, Chiltern, Dunstable Central, Eaton Bray, Grovebury, Heath and Reach, Houghton Hall, Icknield, Kensworth and Totternhoe, Linslade, Manshead, Northfields, Parkside, Planets, Plantation, Southcott, Stanbridge, Tithe Farm, Watling.

IN BERKSHIRE

Bracknell (county constituency)	*The Borough of Bracknell Forest wards:* Bullbrook, Central Sandhurst, College Town, Crown Wood, Crowthorne, Great Hollands North, Great Hollands South, Hanworth, Harmans Water, Little Sandhurst and Wellington, Old Bracknell, Owlsmoor, Priestwood and Garth, Wildridings and Central. *The District of Wokingham wards:* Finchampstead North, Finchampstead South, Wokingham Without.
Maidenhead (county constituency)	*The Royal Borough of Windsor and Maidenhead wards:* Belmont, Bisham and Cookham, Boyn Hill, Bray, Cox Green, Furze Platt, Hurley and Walthams, Maidenhead Riverside, Oldfield, Pinkneys Green. *The District of Wokingham wards:* Charvil, Coronation, Hurst, Remenham, Wargrave and Ruscombe, Sonning, Twyford.
Newbury (county constituency)	*The District of West Berkshire wards:* Aldermaston, Basildon, Bucklebury, Chieveley, Clay Hill, Cold Ash, Compton, Downlands, Falkland, Greenham, Hungerford, Kintbury, Lambourn Valley, Northcroft, St Johns, Speen, Thatcham Central, Thatcham North, Thatcham South and Crookham, Thatcham West, Victoria.
Reading East (borough constituency)	*The Borough of Reading wards:* Abbey, Caversham, Church, Katesgrove, Mapledurham, Park, Peppard, Redlands, Thames. *The District of Wokingham wards:* Bulmershe and Whitegates, Loddon, South Lake.
Reading West (county constituency)	*The Borough of Reading wards:* Battle, Kentwood, Minster, Norcot, Southcote, Tilehurst, Whitley. *The District of West Berkshire wards:* Birch Copse, Calcot, Pangbourne, Purley on Thames, Theale, Westwood.
Slough	*The Borough of Slough wards:*

(borough constituency)	Baylis and Stoke, Britwell, Central, Chalvey, Cippenham Green, Cippenham Meadows, Farnham, Foxborough, Haymill, Kedermister, Langley St Mary's, Upton, Wexham Lea.
Windsor (county constituency)	*The Borough of Bracknell Forest wards:* Ascot, Binfield with Warfield, Warfield Harvest Ride, Winkfield and Cranbourne. *The Borough of Slough ward:* Colnbrook with Poyle. *The Royal Borough of Windsor and Maidenhead wards:* Ascot and Cheapside, Castle Without, Clewer East, Clewer North, Clewer South, Datchet, Eton and Castle, Eton Wick, Horton and Wraysbury, Old Windsor, Park, Sunningdale, Sunninghill and South Ascot.
Wokingham (county constituency)	*The District of West Berkshire wards:* Burghfield, Mortimer, Sulhamstead. *The District of Wokingham wards:* Arborfield, Barkham, Emmbrook, Evendons, Hawkedon, Hillside, Maiden Erlegh, Norreys, Shinfield North, Shinfield South, Swallowfield, Wescott, Winnersh.

IN BRISTOL

Bristol East (borough constituency)	*The City of Bristol wards:* Brislington East, Brislington West, Eastville, Frome Vale, Hillfields, St George East, St George West, Stockwood.
Bristol North West (borough constituency)	*The City of Bristol wards:* Avonmouth, Henbury, Henleaze, Horfield, Kingsweston, Lockleaze, Southmead, Stoke Bishop, WestburyonTrym.
Bristol South (borough constituency)	*The City of Bristol wards:* Bedminster, Bishopsworth, Filwood, Hartcliffe, Hengrove, Knowle, Southville, Whitchurch Park, Windmill Hill.
Bristol West (borough constituency)	*The City of Bristol wards:* Ashley, Bishopston, Cabot, Clifton, Clifton East, Cotham, Easton, Lawrence Hill, Redland.

IN BUCKINGHAMSHIRE

Aylesbury (county constituency)	*The District of Aylesbury Vale wards:* Aston Clinton, Aylesbury Central, Bedgrove, Coldharbour, Elmhurst and Watermead, Gatehouse, Mandeville and Elm Farm, Oakfield, Quarrendon, Southcourt, Walton Court and Hawkslade, Wendover. *The District of Wycombe wards:* Bledlow and Bradenham, Greater Hughenden, Lacey Green, Speen and the Hampdens, Stokenchurch and Radnage.
Beaconsfield (county constituency)	*The District of South Bucks wards:* Beaconsfield North, Beaconsfield South, Beaconsfield West, Burnham Beeches, Burnham Church, Burnham Lent Rise, Denham North, Denham South, Dorney and Burnham South, Farnham Royal, Gerrards Cross East and Denham South West, Gerrards Cross North, Gerrards Cross South, Hedgerley and Fulmer, Iver Heath, Iver Village and Richings Park, Stoke Poges, Taplow, Wexham and Iver West. *The District of Wycombe wards:* Bourne EndcumHedsor, Flackwell Heath and Little Marlow, Marlow North and West, Marlow South East, The Wooburns.
Buckingham (county	*The District of Aylesbury Vale wards:* Bierton, Brill, Buckingham North, Buckingham South, Cheddington,

constituency)	Edlesborough, Great Brickhill, Great Horwood, Grendon Underwood, Haddenham, Long Crendon, Luffield Abbey, Marsh Gibbon, Newton Longville, Pitstone, Quainton, Steeple Claydon, Stewkley, Tingewick, Waddesdon, Weedon, Wing, Wingrave, Winslow.
	The District of Wycombe wards: Icknield, The Risboroughs.
Chesham and Amersham (county constituency)	*The District of Chiltern wards:* Amersham Common, AmershamontheHill, Amersham Town, Asheridge Vale and Lowndes, Ashley Green, Latimer and Chenies, Austenwood, Ballinger, South Heath and Chartridge, Central, Chalfont Common, Chalfont St Giles, Chesham Bois and Weedon Hill, Cholesbury, The Lee and Bellingdon, Gold Hill, Great Missenden, Hilltop and Townsend, Holmer Green, Little Chalfont, Little Missenden, Newtown, Penn and Coleshill, Prestwood and Heath End, Ridgeway, St Mary's and Waterside, Seer Green, Vale.
Wycombe (county constituency)	*The District of Wycombe wards:* Abbey, Booker and Cressex, Bowerdean, Chiltern Rise, Disraeli, Downley and Plomer Hill, Greater Marlow, Hambleden Valley, Hazlemere North, Hazlemere South, Micklefield, Oakridge and Castlefield, Ryemead, Sands, Terriers and Amersham Hill, Totteridge, Tylers Green and Loudwater.

IN CAMBRIDGESHIRE AND PETERBOROUGH

Cambridge (borough constituency)	*The City of Cambridge wards:* Abbey, Arbury, Castle, Cherry Hinton, Coleridge, East Chesterton, King's Hedges, Market, Newnham, Petersfield, Romsey, Trumpington, West Chesterton.
Huntingdon (county constituency)	*The District of Huntingdonshire wards:* Alconbury and The Stukeleys, Brampton, Buckden, Fenstanton, Godmanchester, Gransden and The Offords, Huntingdon East, Huntingdon North, Huntingdon West, Kimbolton and Staughton, Little Paxton, St Ives East, St Ives South, St Ives West, St Neots Eaton Ford, St Neots Eaton Socon, St Neots Eynesbury, St Neots Priory Park, The Hemingfords.
North East Cambridgeshire (county constituency)	*The District of East Cambridgeshire wards:* Downham Villages, Littleport East, Littleport West, Sutton. *The District of Fenland wards:* Bassenhally, Benwick, Coates and Eastrea, Birch, Clarkson, Delph, Doddington, Elm and Christchurch, Hill, Kingsmoor, Kirkgate, Lattersey, Manea, March East, March North, March West, Medworth, Parson Drove and Wisbech St Mary, Peckover, Roman Bank, St Andrews, St Marys, Slade Lode, Staithe, The Mills, Waterlees, Wenneye, Wimblington.
North West Cambridgeshire (county constituency)	*The City of Peterborough wards:* Barnack, Fletton, Glinton and Wittering, Northborough, Orton Longueville, Orton Waterville, Orton With Hampton, Stanground Central, Stanground East, *The District of Huntingdonshire wards:* Earith, Ellington, Elton and Folksworth, Ramsey, Sawtry, Somersham,

Stilton, Upwood and The Raveleys, Warboys and Bury, Yaxley and Farcet

Peterborough (borough constituency)	*The City of Peterborough wards:* Bretton North, Bretton South, Central, Dogsthorpe, East, Eye and Thorney, Newborough, North, Park, Paston, Ravensthorpe, Walton, Werrington North, Werrington South, West.
South Cambridgeshire (county constituency)	*The City of Cambridge ward:* Queen Edith's. *The District of South Cambridgeshire wards:* Bar Hill, Barton, Bassingbourn, Bourn, Caldecote, Comberton, Cottenham, Duxford, Fowlmere and Foxton, Gamlingay, Girton, Hardwick, Harston and Hauxton, Haslingfield and The Eversdens, Longstanton, Melbourn, Meldreth, Orwell and Barrington, Papworth and Elsworth, Sawston, Swavesey, The Abingtons, The Mordens, The Shelfords and Stapleford, Whittlesford.
South East Cambridgeshire (county constituency)	*The District of East Cambridgeshire wards:* Bottisham, Burwell, Cheveley, Dullingham Villages, Ely East, Ely North, Ely South, Ely West, Fordham Villages, Haddenham, Isleham, Soham North, Soham South, Stretham, The Swaffhams. *The District of South Cambridgeshire wards:* Balsham, Fulbourn, Histon and Impington, Linton, Milton, Teversham, The Wilbrahams, Waterbeach, Willingham and Over.

IN CHESHIRE AND HALTON

City of Chester (county constituency)	*The City of Chester wards:* Blacon Hall, Blacon Lodge, Boughton, Boughton Heath, Christleton, City & St Anne's, College, Curzon & Westminster, Dodleston, Handbridge & St Mary's, Hoole All Saints, Hoole Groves, Huntington, Lache Park, Mollington, Newton Brook, Newton St Michaels, Saughall, Upton Grange, Upton Westlea, Vicars Cross.
Congleton (county constituency)	*The Borough of Congleton wards:* Alsager Central, Alsager East, Alsager West, Astbury, Brereton, Buglawton, Congleton Central, Congleton North, Congleton North West, Congleton South, Congleton West, Dane Valley, Holmes Chapel, Lawton, Middlewich Cledford, Middlewich Kinderton, Odd Rode, Sandbach East, Sandbach North, Sandbach West.
Crewe and Nantwich (county constituency)	*The Borough of Crewe and Nantwich wards:* Alexandra, Barony Weaver, Birchin, Coppenhall, Delamere, Englesea, Grosvenor, Haslington, Leighton, Maw Green, St Barnabas, St John's, St Mary's, Shavington, Valley, Waldron, Wellington, Wells Green, Willaston, Wistaston Green, Wybunbury.
Eddisbury (county constituency)	*The City of Chester wards:* Barrow, Farndon, Kelsall, Malpas, Tarvin, Tattenhall, Tilston, Waverton. *The Borough of Crewe and Nantwich wards:* Acton, Audlem, Bunbury, Minshull, Peckforton, Wrenbury. *The Borough of Vale Royal wards:* Cuddington & Oakmere, Davenham & Moulton, Mara, Tarporley & Oulton, Winsford Dene, Winsford Gravel, Winsford Over, Winsford Swanlow, Winsford Verdin, Winsford Wharton.

Ellesmere Port and Neston (county constituency)	*The City of Chester wards:*
	Elton, Mickle Trafford.
	The Borough of Ellesmere Port & Neston wards:
	Burton & Ness, Central, Grange, Groves, Ledsham, Little Neston, Neston, Parkgate, Pooltown, Rivacre, Riverside, Rossmore, Stanlow & Wolverham, Strawberry Fields, Sutton, Sutton Green & Manor, Westminster, Whitby, Willaston & Thornton.
Halton (county constituency)	*The Borough of Halton wards:*
	Appleton, Birchfield, Broadheath, Castlefields, Ditton, Farnworth, Grange, Hale, Halton Brook, Halton View, Heath, Hough Green, Kingsway, Mersey, Riverside.
Macclesfield (county constituency)	*The Borough of Macclesfield wards:*
	Bollington Central, Bollington East, Bollington West, Disley & Lyme Handley, Gawsworth, Henbury, Macclesfield Bollinbrook, Macclesfield Broken Cross, Macclesfield Central, Macclesfield East, Macclesfield Hurdsfield, Macclesfield Ivy, Macclesfield Ryles, Macclesfield South, Macclesfield Tytherington, Macclesfield West, Poynton Central, Poynton East, Poynton West, Prestbury, Rainow, Sutton.
Tatton (county constituency)	*The Borough of Macclesfield wards:*
	Alderley Edge, Chelford, Dean Row, Fulshaw, Handforth, High Legh, Hough, Knutsford Bexton, Knutsford Nether, Knutsford Norbury Booths, Knutsford Over, Lacey Green, Mere, Mobberley, Morley & Styal, Plumley.
	The Borough of Vale Royal wards:
	Barnton, Cogshall, Lostock & Wincham, Rudheath & South Witton, Seven Oaks & Marston, Shakerley.
Weaver Vale (county constituency)	*The Borough of Halton wards:*
	Beechwood, Daresbury, Halton Lea, Norton North, Norton South, Windmill Hill.
	The Borough of Vale Royal wards:
	Forest, Frodsham North, Frodsham South, Hartford & Whitegate, Helsby, Kingsley, Leftwich & Kingsmead, Milton Weaver, Northwich Castle, Northwich Winnington, Northwich Witton, Weaverham.

IN CORNWALL AND THE ISLES OF SCILLY

Camborne and Redruth (county constituency)	*The District of Carrick ward:* Mount Hawke.
	The District of Kerrier wards:
	Camborne North, Camborne South, Camborne West, Constantine, Gweek and Mawnan, Illogan North, Illogan South, Mabe and Budock, Redruth North, Redruth South, St Day, Lanner and Carharrack, Stithians, Wendron.
	The District of Penwith wards:
	Gwinear, Gwithian and Hayle East, Hayle North, Hayle South.
North Cornwall (county constituency)	*The District of North Cornwall wards:*
	Allan, Altarnun, Blisland and St Breward, Bodmin St Mary's, Bodmin St Petroc, Bude, Camelford, Camelot, Grenville, Lanivet, Launceston, Marhamchurch, North Petherwin, Padstow and District, Poughill and Stratton, St

	Endellion and St Kew, St Minver, South Petherwin, Stokeclimsland, Tremaine, Valency, Wadebridge, Week St Mary and Whitstone.
South East Cornwall (county constituency)	*The District of Caradon wards:* Callington, Calstock, Deviock and Sheviock, Dobwalls and District, Duloe, Lansallos and Pelynt, Landrake and St Dominick, Lanteglos and St Veep, Liskeard North, Liskeard South, Looe and St Martin, Lynher, Menheniot and St Ive, Millbrook, Rame Peninsula, St Cleer and St Neot, St Germans, Saltash Burraton, Saltash Essa, Saltash Pill, Saltash St Stephens, Torpoint East, Torpoint West. *The Borough of Restormel ward:* Lostwithiel.
St Austell and Newquay (county constituency)	*The Borough of Restormel wards:* Bethel, Crinnis, Edgcumbe North, Edgcumbe South, Fowey and Tywardreath, Gannel, Gover, Mevagissey, Mount Charles, Poltair, Rialton, Rock, St Blaise, St Columb, St Enoder, St Ewe, St Stephen, Treverbyn.
St Ives (county constituency)	*The District of Kerrier wards:* Breage and Crowan, GradeRuan and Landewednack, Helston North, Helston South, Meneage, Mullion, Porthleven and Sithney, St Keverne. *The District of Penwith wards:* Goldsithney, Gulval and Heamoor, Lelant and Carbis Bay, Ludgvan and Towednack, Madron and Zennor, Marazion and Perranuthnoe, Morvah, Pendeen and St Just, Penzance Central, Penzance East, Penzance Promenade, Penzance South, St Buryan, St Erth and St Hilary, St Ives North, St Ives South. *The Isles of Scilly.*
Truro and Falmouth (county constituency)	*The District of Carrick wards:* Arwenack, Boscawen, Boslowick, Carland, Feock and Kea, Kenwyn and Chacewater, Moresk, Mylor, Newlyn and Goonhavern, Penryn, Penwerris, Perranporth, Probus, Roseland, St Agnes, Tregolls, Trehaverne and Gloweth, Trescobeas.
IN CUMBRIA	
Barrow and Furness (county constituency)	*The Borough of BarrowinFurness wards:* Barrow Island, Central, Dalton North, Dalton South, Hawcoat, Hindpool, Newbarns, Ormsgill, Parkside, Risedale, Roosecote, Walney North, Walney South. *The District of South Lakeland wards:* Broughton, Crake Valley, Low Furness & Swarthmoor, Ulverston Central, Ulverston East, Ulverston North, Ulverston South, Ulverston Town, Ulverston West.

Carlisle (borough constituency)	*The City of Carlisle wards:* Belah, Belle Vue, Botcherby, Burgh, Castle, Currock, Dalston, Denton Holme, Harraby, Morton, St Aidans, Stanwix Urban, Upperby, Wetheral, Yewdale.
Copeland (county constituency)	*The Borough of Allerdale wards:* Crummock, Dalton, Derwent Valley, Keswick. *The Borough of Copeland wards:* Arlecdon, Beckermet, Bootle, Bransty, Cleator Moor North, Cleator Moor South, Distington, Egremont North, Egremont South, Ennerdale, Frizington, Gosforth, Harbour, Haverigg, Hensingham, Hillcrest, Holborn Hill, Kells, Millom Without, Mirehouse, Moresby, Newtown, St Bees, Sandwith, Seascale.
Penrith and The Border (county constituency)	*The Borough of Allerdale wards:* Warnell, Wigton. *The City of Carlisle wards:* Brampton, Great Corby and Geltsdale, Hayton, Irthing, Longtown & Rockcliffe, Lyne, Stanwix Rural. *The District of Eden wards:* Alston Moor, Appleby (Appleby), Appleby (Bongate), Askham, Brough, Crosby Ravensworth, Dacre, Eamont, Greystoke, Hartside, Hesket, Kirkby Stephen, Kirkby Thore, Kirkoswald, Langwathby, Lazonby, Long Marton, Morland, Orton With Tebay, Penrith Carleton, Penrith East, Penrith North, Penrith Pategill, Penrith South, Penrith West, Ravenstonedale, Shap, Skelton, Ullswater, Warcop.
Westmorland and Lonsdale (county constituency)	*The District of South Lakeland wards:* Arnside & Beetham, Burneside, Burton & Holme, Cartmel, Coniston, Crooklands, Grange, Hawkshead, Holker, Kendal Castle, Kendal Far Cross, Kendal Fell, Kendal Glebelands, Kendal Heron Hill, Kendal Highgate, Kendal Kirkland, Kendal Mintsfeet, Kendal Nether, Kendal Oxenholme, Kendal Parks, Kendal Stonecross, Kendal Strickland, Kendal Underley, Kirkby Lonsdale, Lakes Ambleside, Lakes Grasmere, Levens, Lyth Valley, Milnthorpe, Natland, Sedbergh, StaveleyinCartmel, StaveleyinWestmorland, Whinfell, Windermere Applethwaite, Windermere Bowness North, Windermere Bowness South, Windermere Town.
Workington (county constituency)	*The Borough of Allerdale wards:* All Saints, Aspatria, Boltons, Broughton St Bridget's, Christchurch, Clifton, Ellen, Ellenborough, Ewanrigg, Flimby, Harrington, Holme, Marsh, Moorclose, Moss Bay, Netherhall, St John's, St Michael's, Seaton, Silloth, Solway,

Stainburn, Wampool, Waver, Wharrels.

IN DERBYSHIRE AND DERBY	
Amber Valley (county constituency)	*The Borough of Amber Valley wards:* Alfreton, Codnor and Waingroves, Heage and Ambergate, Heanor and Loscoe, Heanor East, Heanor West, Ironville and Riddings, Kilburn, Denby and Holbrook, Langley Mill and Aldercar, Ripley, Ripley and Marehay, Shipley Park, Horsley and Horsley Woodhouse, Somercotes, Swanwick, Wingfield.
Bolsover (county constituency)	*The District of Bolsover wards:* Barlborough, Blackwell, Bolsover North West, Bolsover South, Bolsover West, Clowne North, Clowne South, ElmtonwithCreswell, Pinxton, Pleasley, Scarcliffe, Shirebrook East, Shirebrook Langwith, Shirebrook North West, Shirebrook South East, Shirebrook South West, South Normanton East, South Normanton West, Tibshelf, Whitwell. *The District of North East Derbyshire wards:* Holmewood and Heath, Pilsley and Morton, Shirland, Sutton.
Chesterfield (borough constituency)	*The Borough of Chesterfield wards:* Brimington North, Brimington South, Brockwell, Dunston, Hasland, Hollingwood and Inkersall, Holmebrook, Linacre, Loundsley Green, Middlecroft and Poolsbrook, Moor, Old Whittington, Rother, St Helen's, St Leonard's, Walton, West.
Derby North (borough constituency)	*The City of Derby wards:* Abbey, Chaddesden, Darley, Derwent, Littleover, Mackworth, Mickleover.
Derby South (borough constituency)	*The City of Derby wards:* Alvaston, Arboretum, Blagreaves, Boulton, Chellaston, Normanton, Sinfin.
Derbyshire Dales (county constituency)	*The Borough of Amber Valley wards:* Alport, Crich, South West Parishes. *The District of Derbyshire Dales wards:* Ashbourne North, Ashbourne South, Bakewell, Bradwell, Brailsford, Calver, Carsington Water, Chatsworth, Clifton and Bradley, Darley Dale, Dovedale and Parwich, Doveridge and Sudbury, Hartington and Taddington, Hathersage and Eyam, Hulland, Lathkill and Bradford, Litton and Longstone, Masson, Matlock All Saints, Matlock St Giles, Norbury, Stanton, Tideswell, Winster and South Darley, Wirksworth.
Erewash (county constituency)	*The Borough of Erewash wards:* Abbotsford, Breaston, Cotmanhay, Derby Road East, Derby Road West, Draycott, Hallam Fields, Ilkeston Central, Ilkeston North, Kirk Hallam, Little Hallam, Long Eaton Central, Nottingham Road, Old Park, Sandiacre North, Sandiacre

	South, Sawley, Wilsthorpe.
High Peak (county constituency)	*The Borough of High Peak wards:* Barms, Blackbrook, Burbage, Buxton Central, Chapel East, Chapel West, Corbar, Cote Heath, Dinting, Gamesley, Hadfield North, Hadfield South, Hayfield, Hope Valley, Howard Town, Limestone Peak, New Mills East, New Mills West, Old Glossop, Padfield, St John's, Sett, Simmondley, Stone Bench, Temple, Tintwistle, Whaley Bridge, Whitfield.
Mid Derbyshire (county constituency)	*The Borough of Amber Valley wards:* Belper Central, Belper East, Belper North, Belper South, Duffield. *The City of Derby wards:* Allestree, Oakwood, Spondon. *The Borough of Erewash wards:* Little Eaton and Breadsall, Ockbrook and Borrowash, Stanley, West Hallam and Dale Abbey.
North East Derbyshire (county constituency)	*The Borough of Chesterfield wards:* Barrow Hill and New Whittington, Lowgates and Woodthorpe. *The District of North East Derbyshire wards:* Ashover, Barlow and Holmesfield, Brampton and Walton, Clay Cross North, Clay Cross South, Coal Aston, Dronfield North, Dronfield South, Dronfield Woodhouse, Eckington North, Eckington South, Gosforth Valley, Grassmoor, Killamarsh East, Killamarsh West, North Wingfield Central, Renishaw, Ridgeway and Marsh Lane, Tupton, Unstone, Wingerworth.
South Derbyshire (county constituency)	*The District of South Derbyshire wards:* Aston, Church Gresley, Etwall, Hartshorne and Ticknall, Hatton, Hilton, Linton, Melbourne, Midway, Newhall and Stanton, North West, Repton, Seales, Stenson, Swadlincote, Willington and Findern, Woodville.
IN DEVON, PLYMOUTH, AND TORBAY	
Central Devon (county constituency)	*The District of East Devon ward:* Exe Valley. *The District of Mid Devon wards:* Boniface, Bradninch, Cadbury, Lawrence, Newbrooke, Sandford and Creedy, Silverton, Taw, Taw Vale, Upper Yeo, Way, Yeo. *The District of Teignbridge wards:* Ashburton and Buckfastleigh, Bovey, Chudleigh, Haytor, Kenn Valley, Moorland, Teignbridge North, Teign Valley. *The Borough of West Devon wards:* Chagford, Drewsteignton, Exbourne, Hatherleigh, Lew Valley, North Tawton, Okehampton East, Okehampton West, South Tawton.

East Devon (county constituency)	*The District of East Devon wards:* Broadclyst, Budleigh, Clyst Valley, Exmouth Brixington, Exmouth Halsdon, Exmouth Littleham, Exmouth Town, Exmouth Withycombe Raleigh, Newton Poppleford and Harpford, Ottery St Mary Rural, Ottery St Mary Town, Raleigh, Sidmouth Rural, Sidmouth Sidford, Sidmouth Town, Whimple, Woodbury and Lympstone *The City of Exeter wards:* St Loyes, Topsham.
Exeter (borough constituency)	*The City of Exeter wards:* Alphington, Cowick, Duryard, Exwick, Heavitree, Mincinglake, Newtown, Pennsylvania, Pinhoe, Polsloe, Priory, St David's, St James, St Leonard's, St Thomas, Whipton & Barton.
Newton Abbot (county constituency)	*The District of Teignbridge wards:* Ambrook, Bishopsteignton, Bradley, Buckland and Milber, Bushell, College, Dawlish Central and North East, Dawlish South West, Ipplepen, Kenton with Starcross, KerswellwithCombe, Kingsteignton East, Kingsteignton West, Shaldon and Stokeinteignhead, Teignmouth Central, Teignmouth East, Teignmouth West.
North Devon (county constituency)	*The District of North Devon wards:* Bickington and Roundswell, Bishop's Nympton, Bratton Fleming, Braunton East, Braunton West, Central Town, Chittlehampton, Chulmleigh, Combe Martin, Forches and Whiddon Valley, Fremington, Georgeham and Mortehoe, Heanton Punchardon, Ilfracombe Central, Ilfracombe East, Ilfracombe West, Instow, Landkey, Swimbridge and Taw, Longbridge, Lynton and Lynmouth, Marwood, Newport, North Molton, Pilton, South Molton, Witheridge, Yeo Valley.
Plymouth, Moor View (borough constituency)	*The City of Plymouth wards:* Budshead, Eggbuckland, Ham, Honicknowle, Moor View, St Budeaux, Southway.
Plymouth, Sutton and Devonport (borough constituency)	*The City of Plymouth wards:* Compton, Devonport, Drake, Efford and Lipson, Peverell, St Peter and the Waterfront, Stoke, Sutton and Mount Gould.
South West Devon (county constituency)	*The City of Plymouth wards:* Plympton Chaddlewood, Plympton Erle, Plympton St Mary, Plymstock Dunstone, Plymstock Radford. *The District of South Hams wards:* Bickleigh and Shaugh, Charterlands, Cornwood and Sparkwell, Erme Valley, Ivybridge Central, Ivybridge Filham, Ivybridge Woodlands, Newton and Noss, Wembury and Brixton, Yealmpton.
Tiverton and Honiton	*The District of East Devon wards:*

(county constituency)	Axminster Rural, Axminster Town, Beer and Branscombe, Coly Valley, Dunkeswell, Feniton and Buckerell, Honiton St Michael's, Honiton St Paul's, Newbridges, Otterhead, Seaton, Tale Vale, Trinity, Yarty. *The District of Mid Devon wards:* Canonsleigh, Castle, Clare and Shuttern, Cranmore, Cullompton North, Cullompton Outer, Cullompton South, Halberton, Lower Culm, Lowman, Upper Culm, Westexe.
Torbay (borough constituency)	*The Borough of Torbay wards:* CliftonwithMaidenway, CockingtonwithChelston, Ellacombe, GoodringtonwithRoselands, Preston, RoundhamwithHyde, St Marychurch, ShiphaywiththeWillows, Tormohun, Watcombe, Wellswood.
Torridge and West Devon (county constituency)	*The District of Torridge wards:* Appledore, Bideford East, Bideford North, Bideford South, Broadheath, Clinton, Clovelly Bay, Coham Bridge, Forest, Hartland and Bradworthy, Holsworthy, Kenwith, Monkleigh and Littleham, Northam, Orchard Hill, Shebbear and Langtree, Tamarside, Three Moors, Torrington, Two Rivers, Waldon, Westward Ho!, Winkleigh. *The Borough of West Devon wards:* Bere Ferrers, Bridestowe, Buckland Monachorum, Burrator, Lydford, Mary Tavy, Milton Ford, Tamarside, Tavistock North, Tavistock South, Tavistock South West, Thrushel, Walkham.
Totnes (county constituency)	*The District of South Hams wards:* Allington and Loddiswell, Avon and Harbourne, Dartington, Dartmouth and Kingswear, Dartmouth Townstal, East Dart, Eastmoor, Kingsbridge East, Kingsbridge North, Marldon, Salcombe and Malborough, Saltstone, Skerries, South Brent, Stokenham, Thurlestone, Totnes Bridgetown, Totnes Town, West Dart, Westville and Alvington. *The Borough of Torbay wards:* Berry HeadwithFurzeham, Blatchcombe, ChurstonwithGalmpton, St Mary'swithSummercombe.

IN DORSET, BOURNEMOUTH, AND POOLE

Bournemouth East (borough constituency)	*The Borough of Bournemouth wards:* Boscombe East, Boscombe West, East Cliff and Springbourne, East Southbourne and Tuckton, Littledown and Iford, Moordown, Queen's Park, Strouden Park, Throop and Muscliff, West Southbourne.
Bournemouth West	*The Borough of Bournemouth wards:*

(borough constituency)	Central, Kinson North, Kinson South, Redhill and Northbourne, Talbot and Branksome Woods, Wallisdown and Winton West, Westbourne and West Cliff, Winton East. *The Borough of Poole wards:* Alderney, Branksome East.
Christchurch (county constituency)	*The Borough of Christchurch wards:* Burton and Winkton, Grange, Highcliffe, Jumpers, Mudeford and Friars Cliff, North Highcliffe and Walkford, Portfield, Purewell and Stanpit, St Catherine's and Hurn, Town Centre, West Highcliffe. *The District of East Dorset wards:* Ameysford, Ferndown Central, Ferndown Links, Longham, Parley, St Leonards and St Ives East, St Leonards and St Ives West, Stapehill, West Moors.
Mid Dorset and North Poole (county constituency)	*The District of East Dorset wards:* Colehill East, Colehill West, Corfe Mullen Central, Corfe Mullen North, Corfe Mullen South, Wimborne Minster. *The Borough of Poole wards:* Broadstone, Canford Heath East, Canford Heath West, Merley and Bearwood. *The District of Purbeck wards:* Bere Regis, Lytchett Matravers, Lytchett Minster and Upton East, Lytchett Minster and Upton West, St Martin, Wareham.
North Dorset (county constituency)	*The District of East Dorset wards:* Alderholt, Crane, Handley Vale, Holt, Stour, Three Cross and Potterne, Verwood Dewlands, Verwood Newtown, Verwood Stephen's Castle. *The District of North Dorset wards:* Abbey, Blackmore, Blandford Damory Down, Blandford Hilltop, Blandford Langton St Leonards, Blandford Old Town, Blandford Station, Bourton and District, Bulbarrow, Cranborne Chase, Gillingham Town, Hill Forts, Lodbourne, Lydden Vale, Marnhull, Milton, Motcombe and Ham, Portman, Riversdale, Shaftesbury Central, Shaftesbury Christy's, Shaftesbury Grosvenor, Shaftesbury Underhill, Stour Valley, The Beacon, The Lower Tarrants, The Stours, Wyke.
Poole (borough constituency)	*The Borough of Poole wards:* Branksome West, Canford Cliffs, Creekmoor, Hamworthy East, Hamworthy West, Newtown, Oakdale, Parkstone, Penn Hill, Poole Town.
South Dorset (county constituency)	*The District of Purbeck wards:* Castle, Creech Barrow, Langton, Swanage North, Swanage South, West Purbeck, Winfrith, Wool. *The District of West Dorset ward:*

Owermoigne.
The Borough of Weymouth and Portland wards:
Littlemoor, Melcombe Regis, Preston, Radipole, Tophill East, Tophill West, Underhill, Upwey and Broadwey, Westham East, Westham North, Westham West, Wey Valley, Weymouth East, Weymouth West, Wyke Regis.

West Dorset (county constituency)	*The District of West Dorset wards:* Beaminster, Bradford Abbas, Bradpole, Bridport North, Bridport South and Bothenhampton, Broadmayne, Broadwindsor, Burton Bradstock, Cam Vale, Charminster and Cerne Valley, Charmouth, Chesil Bank, Chickerell, Chideock and Symondsbury, Dorchester East, Dorchester North, Dorchester South, Dorchester West, Frome Valley, Halstock, Loders, Lyme Regis, Maiden Newton, Marshwood Vale, Netherbury, Piddle Valley, Puddletown, Queen Thorne, Sherborne East, Sherborne West, Winterborne St Martin, Yetminster.

IN DURHAM AND DARLINGTON

Bishop Auckland (county constituency)	*The Borough of Sedgefield wards:* Byerley, Low Spennymoor and Tudhoe Grange, Middlestone, Spennymoor, Sunnydale, Thickley, Tudhoe. *The District of Teesdale wards:* Barnard Castle East, Barnard Castle North, Barnard Castle West, Barningham and Ovington, Cockfield, Cotherstone with Lartington, Eggleston, Etherley, Evenwood, Ramshaw and Lands, Gainford and Winston, Greta, Hamsterley and South Bedburn, Ingleton, Lynesack, MiddletoninTeesdale, Romaldkirk, Staindrop, Startforth, Streatlam and Whorlton. *The District of Wear Valley wards:* Bishop Auckland Town, Cockton Hill, Coundon, Dene Valley, Escomb, Henknowle, West Auckland, Woodhouse Close.
City of Durham (county constituency)	*The City of Durham wards:* Bearpark and Witton Gilbert, Belmont, Brancepeth, Langley Moor and Meadowfield, Brandon, Carrville and Gilesgate Moor, CassopcumQuarrington, Coxhoe, Crossgate and Framwelgate, Deerness, Elvet, Framwellgate Moor, Neville's Cross, New Brancepeth and Ushaw Moor, Newton Hall North, Newton Hall South, Pelaw and Gilesgate, Pittington and West Rainton, St Nicholas, Shadforth and Sherburn, Shincliffe.
Darlington (borough constituency)	*The Borough of Darlington wards:* Bank Top, Central, Cockerton East, Cockerton West, College, Eastbourne, Faverdale, Harrowgate Hill, Haughton East, Haughton

North, Haughton West, Hummersknott, Lascelles, Lingfield, Mowden, Northgate, North Road, Park East, Park West, Pierremont.

Easington (county constituency)	*The District of Easington wards:* Acre Rigg, Blackhalls, Dawdon, Dene House, Deneside, Easington Colliery, Easington Village and South Hetton, Eden Hill, Haswell and Shotton, Horden North, Horden South, Howletch, Hutton Henry, Murton East, Murton West, Passfield, Seaham Harbour, Seaham North.
North Durham (county constituency)	*The District of ChesterleStreet wards:* Bournmoor, Chester Central, Chester East, Chester North, Chester South, Chester West, Edmondsley and Waldridge, Grange Villa and West Pelton, Kimblesworth and Plawsworth, Lumley, North Lodge, Ouston, Pelton, Pelton Fell, Sacriston, Urpeth. *The District of Derwentside wards:* Annfield Plain, Catchgate, Craghead and South Stanley, Havannah, South Moor, Stanley Hall, Tanfield.
North West Durham (county constituency)	*The District of Derwentside wards:* Benfieldside, Blackhill, Burnhope, Burnopfield, Castleside, Consett East, Consett North, Consett South, Cornsay, Delves Lane, Dipton, Ebchester and Medomsley, Esh, Lanchester, Leadgate. *The District of Wear Valley wards:* Crook North, Crook South, Howden, Hunwick, St John's Chapel, Stanhope, Tow Law and Stanley, Wheatbottom and Helmington Row, Willington Central, Willington West End, Wolsingham and WittonleWear.
Sedgefield (county constituency)	*The Borough of Darlington wards:* Heighington and Coniscliffe, Hurworth, Middleton St George, Sadberge and Whessoe. *The District of Easington wards:* Thornley and Wheatley Hill, Wingate. *The Borough of Sedgefield wards:* Bishop Middleham and Cornforth, Broom, Chilton, Ferryhill, Fishburn and Old Trimdon, Greenfield Middridge, Neville and Simpasture, New Trimdon and Trimdon Grange, Sedgefield, Shafto St Marys, West, Woodham.

IN THE EAST RIDING OF YORKSHIRE, KINGSTON UPON HULL, NORTH EAST LINCOLNSHIRE, AND NORTH LINCOLNSHIRE

Beverley and Holderness (county constituency)	*The District of East Riding of Yorkshire wards:* Beverley Rural, Mid Holderness, Minster and Woodmansey, North Holderness, St Mary's, South East Holderness, South West Holderness.
Brigg and Goole (county constituency)	*The District of East Riding of Yorkshire wards:* Goole North, Goole South, Snaith, Airmyn, Rawcliffe and Marshland.

	The Borough of North Lincolnshire wards: Axholme Central, Axholme North, Axholme South, Brigg and Wolds, Broughton and Appleby, Burringham and Gunness, Burton upon Stather and Winterton.
Cleethorpes (county constituency)	The Borough of North East Lincolnshire wards: Croft Baker, Haverstoe, Humberston and New Waltham, Immingham, Sidney Sussex, Waltham, Wolds.
	The Borough of North Lincolnshire wards: Barton, Ferry.
East Yorkshire (county constituency)	The District of East Riding of Yorkshire wards: Bridlington Central and Old Town, Bridlington North, Bridlington South, Driffield and Rural, East Wolds and Coastal, Pocklington Provincial, Wolds Weighton.
Great Grimsby (borough constituency)	The Borough of North East Lincolnshire wards: East Marsh, Freshney, Heneage, Park, Scartho, South, West Marsh, Yarborough.
Haltemprice and Howden (county constituency)	The District of East Riding of Yorkshire wards: Cottingham North, Cottingham South, Dale, Howden, Howdenshire, South Hunsley, Tranby, Willerby and Kirk Ella.
Kingston upon Hull East (borough constituency)	The City of Kingston upon Hull wards: Drypool, Holderness, Ings, Longhill, Marfleet, Southcoates East, Southcoates West, Sutton.
Kingston upon Hull North (borough constituency)	The City of Kingston upon Hull wards: Avenue, Beverley, Bransholme East, Bransholme West, Bricknell, Kings Park, Newland, Orchard Park and Greenwood, University.
Kingston upon Hull West and Hessle (borough constituency)	The District of East Riding of Yorkshire ward: Hessle.
	The City of Kingston upon Hull wards: Boothferry, Derringham, Myton, Newington, Pickering, St Andrew's.
Scunthorpe (county constituency)	The Borough of North Lincolnshire wards: Ashby, Bottesford, Brumby, Crosby and Park, Frodingham, Kingsway with Lincoln Gardens, Ridge, Town.
IN EAST SUSSEX, AND BRIGHTON AND HOVE	
Bexhill and Battle (county constituency)	The District of Rother wards: Battle Town, Central, Collington, Crowhurst, Darwell, Ewhurst and Sedlescombe, Kewhurst, Old Town, Rother Levels, Sackville, St Marks, St Michaels, St Stephens, Salehurst, Sidley, Ticehurst and Etchingham. The District of Wealden wards: Cross In Hand/Five Ashes, Heathfield East, Heathfield North and Central, Herstmonceux, Ninfield and Hooe with Wartling, Pevensey and Westham.
Brighton, Kemptown (borough constituency)	The City of Brighton and Hove wards: East Brighton, Moulsecoomb and Bevendean,

	Queen's Park, Rottingdean Coastal, Woodingdean.
	The District of Lewes wards:
	East Saltdean and Telscombe Cliffs, Peacehaven East, Peacehaven North, Peacehaven West.
Brighton, Pavilion (borough constituency)	*The City of Brighton and Hove wards:* Hanover and Elm Grove, Hollingbury and Stanmer, Patcham, Preston Park, Regency, St Peter's and North Laine, Withdean.
Eastbourne (borough constituency)	*The Borough of Eastbourne wards:* Devonshire, Hampden Park, Langney, Meads, Old Town, Ratton, St Anthony's, Sovereign, Upperton.
	The District of Wealden ward: Willingdon.
Hastings and Rye (county constituency)	*The Borough of Hastings wards:* Ashdown, Baird, Braybrooke, Castle, Central St Leonards, Conquest, Gensing, Hollington, Maze Hill, Old Hastings, Ore, St Helens, Silverhill, Tressell, West St Leonards, Wishing Tree.
	The District of Rother wards: Brede Valley, Eastern Rother, Marsham, Rye.
Hove (borough constituency)	*The City of Brighton and Hove wards:* Brunswick and Adelaide, Central Hove, Goldsmid, Hangleton and Knoll, North Portslade, South Portslade, Stanford, Westbourne, Wish.
Lewes (county constituency)	*The District of Lewes wards:* Barcombe and Hamsey, Chailey and Wivelsfield, Ditchling and Westmeston, Kingston, Lewes Bridge, Lewes Castle, Lewes Priory, Newhaven Denton and Meeching, Newhaven Valley, Newick, Ouse Valley and Ringmer, Plumpton, Streat, East Chiltington and St John (Without), Seaford Central, Seaford East, Seaford North, Seaford South, Seaford West.
	The District of Wealden wards: Alfriston, East Dean, Polegate North, Polegate South.
Wealden (county constituency)	*The District of Wealden wards:* Buxted and Maresfield, Chiddingly and East Hoathly, Crowborough East, Crowborough Jarvis Brook, Crowborough North, Crowborough St Johns, Crowborough West, Danehill/Fletching/Nutley, Forest Row, Framfield, Frant/Withyham, Hailsham Central and North, Hailsham East, Hailsham South and West, Hartfield, Hellingly, Horam, Mayfield, Rotherfield, Uckfield Central, Uckfield New Town, Uckfield North, Uckfield Ridgewood, Wadhurst.

IN ESSEX, SOUTHENDONSEA, AND THURROCK

Basildon and Billericay	*The District of Basildon wards:*

(borough constituency)	Billericay East, Billericay West, Burstead, Crouch, Fryerns, Laindon Park, Lee Chapel North, St Martin's.
Braintree (county constituency)	*The District of Braintree wards:* Bocking Blackwater, Bocking North, Bocking South, Braintree Central, Braintree East, Braintree South, Bumpstead, Cressing and Stisted, Gosfield and Greenstead Green, Great Notley and Braintree West, Halstead St Andrews, Halstead Trinity, Hedingham and Maplestead, Panfield, Rayne, Stour Valley North, Stour Valley South, The Three Colnes, Three Fields, Upper Colne, Yeldham.
Brentwood and Ongar (county constituency)	*The Borough of Brentwood wards:* Brentwood North, Brentwood South, Brentwood West, Brizes and Doddinghurst, Herongate, Ingrave and West Horndon, Hutton Central, Hutton East, Hutton North, Hutton South, Ingatestone, Fryerning and Mountnessing, Pilgrims Hatch, Shenfield, South Weald, Tipps Cross, Warley. *The District of Epping Forest wards:* Chipping Ongar, Greensted and Marden Ash, High Ongar, Willingale and The Rodings, Lambourne, Moreton and Fyfield, North Weald Bassett, Passingford, Shelley.
Castle Point (borough constituency)	*The Borough of Castle Point wards:* Appleton, Boyce, Canvey Island Central, Canvey Island East, Canvey Island North, Canvey Island South, Canvey Island West, Canvey Island Winter Gardens, Cedar Hall, St George's, St James, St Mary's, St Peter's, Victoria.
Chelmsford (borough constituency)	*The Borough of Chelmsford wards:* Chelmer Village and Beaulieu Park, Galleywood, Goat Hall, Great Baddow East, Great Baddow West, Marconi, Moulsham and Central, Moulsham Lodge, Patching Hall, St Andrews, Springfield North, The Lawns, Trinity, Waterhouse Farm.
Clacton (county constituency)	*The District of Tendring wards:* Alton Park, Beaumont and Thorpe, Bockings Elm, Burrsville, Frinton, Golf Green, Hamford, Haven, Holland and Kirby, Homelands, Little Clacton and Weeley, Peter Bruff, Pier, Rush Green, St Bartholomews, St James, St Johns, St Marys, St Osyth and Point Clear, St Pauls, Walton.
Colchester (borough constituency)	*The Borough of Colchester wards:* Berechurch, Castle, Christ Church, Harbour, Highwoods, Lexden, Mile End, New Town, Prettygate, St Andrew's, St Anne's, St John's, Shrub End.
Epping Forest	*The District of Epping Forest wards:*

(county constituency)	Broadley Common, Epping Upland and Nazeing, Buckhurst Hill East, Buckhurst Hill West, Chigwell Row, Chigwell Village, Epping Hemnall, Epping Lindsey and Thornwood Common, Grange Hill, Loughton Alderton, Loughton Broadway, Loughton Fairmead, Loughton Forest, Loughton Roding, Loughton St John's, Loughton St Mary's, Theydon Bois, Waltham Abbey High Beach, Waltham Abbey Honey Lane, Waltham Abbey North East, Waltham Abbey Paternoster, Waltham Abbey South West.
Harlow (county constituency)	*The District of Epping Forest wards:* Hastingwood, Matching and Sheering Village, Lower Nazeing, Lower Sheering, Roydon. *The District of Harlow wards:* Bush Fair, Church Langley, Great Parndon, Harlow Common, Little Parndon and Hare Street, Mark Hall, Netteswell, Old Harlow, Staple Tye, Sumners and Kingsmoor, Toddbrook.
Harwich and North Essex (county constituency)	*The Borough of Colchester wards:* Dedham and Langham, East Donyland, Fordham and Stour, Great Tey, Pyefleet, West Bergholt and Eight Ash Green, West Mersea, Wivenhoe Cross, Wivenhoe Quay. *The District of Tendring wards:* Alresford, Ardleigh and Little Bromley, Bradfield, Wrabness and Wix, Brightlingsea, Great and Little Oakley, Great Bentley, Harwich East, Harwick East Central, Harwich West, Harwich West Central, Lawford, Manningtree, Mistley, Little Bentley and Tendring, Ramsey and Parkeston, Thorrington, Frating, Elmstead and Great Bromley.
Maldon (county constituency)	*The Borough of Chelmsford wards:* Bicknacre and East and West Hanningfield, Little Baddow, Danbury and Sandon, Rettendon and Runwell, South Hanningfield, Stock and Margaretting, South WoodhamChetwood and Collingwood, South WoodhamElmwood and Woodville. *The District of Maldon wards:* Althorne, BurnhamonCrouch North, BurnhamonCrouch South, Heybridge East, Heybridge West, Maldon East, Maldon North, Maldon South, Maldon West, Mayland, Purleigh, Southminster, Tillingham.
Rayleigh and Wickford (county constituency)	*The District of Basildon wards:* Wickford Castledon, Wickford North, Wickford Park. *The District of Rochford wards:* Ashingdon and Canewdon, Downhall and Rawreth, Grange, Hawkwell North, Hawkwell South, Hawkwell West, Hockley Central, Hockley

	North, Hockley West, Hullbridge, Lodge, Rayleigh Central, Sweyne Park, Trinity, Wheatley, Whitehouse.
Rochford and Southend East (county constituency)	*The District of Rochford wards:* Barling and Sutton, Foulness and Great Wakering, Rochford. *The Borough of SouthendonSea wards:* Kursaal, Milton, St Luke's, Shoeburyness, Southchurch, Thorpe, Victoria, West Shoebury.
Saffron Walden (county constituency)	*The Borough of Chelmsford wards:* Boreham and The Leighs, Broomfield and The Walthams, Chelmsford Rural West, Writtle. *The District of Uttlesford wards:* Ashdon, Barnston and High Easter, Birchanger, Broad Oak and the Hallingburys, Clavering, Elsenham and Henham, Felsted, Great Dunmow North, Great Dunmow South, Hatfield Heath, Littlebury, Newport, Saffron Walden Audley, Saffron Walden Castle, Saffron Walden Shire, Stansted North, Stansted South, Stebbing, Stort Valley, Takeley and the Canfields, Thaxted, The Chesterfords, The Eastons, The Rodings, The Sampfords, Wenden Lofts, Wimbish and Debden.
South Basildon and East Thurrock (county constituency)	*The District of Basildon wards:* Langdon Hills, Nethermayne, Pitsea North West, Pitsea South East, Vange. *The Borough of Thurrock wards:* Corringham and Fobbing, East Tilbury, Orsett, Stanford East and Corringham Town, StanfordleHope West, The Homesteads.
Southend West (borough constituency)	*The Borough of SouthendonSea wards:* Belfairs, Blenheim Park, Chalkwell, Eastwood Park, Leigh, Prittlewell, St Laurence, Westborough, West Leigh.
Thurrock (borough constituency)	*The Borough of Thurrock wards:* Aveley and Uplands, Belhus, Chadwell St Mary, Chafford and North Stifford, Grays Riverside, Grays Thurrock, Little Thurrock Blackshots, Little Thurrock Rectory, Ockendon, South Chafford, Stifford Clays, Tilbury Riverside and Thurrock Park, Tilbury St Chads, West Thurrock and South Stifford.
Witham (county constituency)	*The District of Braintree wards:* Black Notley and Terling, Bradwell, Silver End and Rivenhall, Coggeshall and North Feering, Hatfield Peverel, Kelvedon, Witham Chipping Hill and Central, Witham North, Witham South, Witham West. *The Borough of Colchester wards:* Birch and Winstree, Copford and West Stanway, Marks Tey, Stanway, Tiptree. *The District of Maldon wards:*

	Great Totham, Tollesbury, Tolleshunt D'Arcy, Wickham Bishops and Woodham.
IN GLOUCESTERSHIRE	
Cheltenham (borough constituency)	*The Borough of Cheltenham wards:* All Saints, Battledown, Benhall and The Reddings, Charlton Kings, Charlton Park, College, Hesters Way, Lansdown, Leckhampton, Oakley, Park, Pittville, St Mark's, St Paul's, St Peter's, Springbank, Up Hatherley, Warden Hill.
Forest of Dean (county constituency)	*The District of Forest of Dean wards:* Alvington, Aylburton and West Lydney, Awre, Berry Hill, Blaisdon and Longhope, Bream, Bromesberrow and Dymock, Christchurch and English Bicknor, Churcham and Huntley, Cinderford East, Cinderford West, Coleford Central, Coleford East, Hartpury, Hewelsfield and Woolaston, Littledean and Ruspidge, Lydbrook and Ruardean, Lydney East, Lydney North, Mitcheldean and Drybrook, Newent Central, Newland and St Briavels, Newnham and Westbury, Oxenhall and Newent North East, Pillowell, Redmarley, Tibberton, Tidenham. *The Borough of Tewkesbury ward:* Highnam with Haw Bridge.
Gloucester (borough constituency)	*The City of Gloucester wards:* Abbey, Barnwood, Barton and Tredworth, Elmbridge, Grange, Hucclecote, Kingsholm and Wotton, Matson and Robinswood, Moreland, Podsmead, Quedgeley Fieldcourt, Quedgeley Severn Vale, Tuffley, Westgate.
Stroud (county constituency)	*The District of Stroud wards:* Amberley and Woodchester, Berkeley, Bisley, Cainscross, Cam East, Cam West, Central, Chalford, Coaley and Uley, Dursley, Eastington and Standish, Farmhill and Paganhill, Hardwicke, Nailsworth, Over Stroud, Painswick, Rodborough, Severn, Slade, Stonehouse, The Stanleys, Thrupp, Trinity, Uplands, Upton St Leonards, Vale, Valley.
Tewkesbury (county constituency)	*The Borough of Cheltenham wards:* Prestbury, Swindon Village. *The City of Gloucester ward:* Longlevens. *The Borough of Tewkesbury wards:* Ashchurch with Walton Cardiff, Badgeworth, Brockworth, Churchdown Brookfield, Churchdown St John's, Cleeve Grange, Cleeve Hill, Cleeve St Michael's, Cleeve West, Coombe Hill, Hucclecote, Innsworth with Down Hatherley, Isbourne, Northway, Oxenton Hill, Shurdington, Tewkesbury Newtown, Tewkesbury Prior's Park, Tewkesbury Town With Mitton, Twyning, Winchcombe.

The Cotswolds (county constituency)	*The District of Cotswold wards:* AmpneyColn, Avening, BeaconStow, Blockley, BourtonontheWater, CampdenVale, Chedworth, Churn Valley, Cirencester Beeches, Cirencester Chesterton, Cirencester Park, Cirencester StrattonWhiteway, Cirencester Watermoor, Ermin, Fairford, Fosseridge, Grumbolds Ash, Hampton, KempsfordLechlade, MoretoninMarsh, Northleach, Rissingtons, Riversmeet, Sandywell, Tetbury, Thames Head, Three Rivers, Water Park. *The District of Stroud wards:* Kingswood, Minchinhampton, WottonunderEdge.

IN HAMPSHIRE AND SOUTHAMPTON

Aldershot (borough constituency)	*The District of Hart wards:* Blackwater and Hawley, Frogmore and Darby Green. *The Borough of Rushmoor wards:* Cove and Southwood, Empress, Fernhill, Grange, Heron Wood, Knellwood, Manor Park, Mayfield, North Town, Rowhill, St John's, St Mark's, Wellington, Westheath.
Basingstoke (borough constituency)	*The Borough of Basingstoke and Deane wards:* Basing, Brighton Hill North, Brighton Hill South, Brookvale and Kings Furlong, Buckskin, Chineham, Eastrop, Grove, Hatch Warren and Beggarwood, Kempshott, Norden, Popley East, Popley West, Rooksdown, South Ham, Winklebury.
East Hampshire (county constituency)	*The District of East Hampshire wards:* Alton Amery, Alton Ashdell, Alton Eastbrooke, Alton Westbrooke, Alton Whitedown, Alton Wooteys, Binstead and Bentley, Bramshott and Liphook, Downland, East Meon, Four Marks and Medstead, Froxfield and Steep, Grayshott, Headley, Holybourne and Froyle, Lindford, Liss, Petersfield Bell Hill, Petersfield Causeway, Petersfield Heath, Petersfield Rother, Petersfield St Marys, Petersfield St Peters, Ropley and Tisted, Selborne, The Hangers and Forest, Whitehill Chase, Whitehill Deadwater, Whitehill Hogmoor, Whitehill Pinewood, Whitehill Walldown.
Eastleigh (borough constituency)	*The Borough of Eastleigh wards:* Bishopstoke East, Bishopstoke West, Botley, Bursledon and Old Netley, Eastleigh Central, Eastleigh North, Eastleigh South, Fair Oak and Horton Heath, HambleleRice and Butlocks Heath, Hedge End Grange Park, Hedge End St John's, Hedge End Wildern, Netley Abbey, West End North, West End South.
Fareham	*The Borough of Fareham wards:*

(county constituency)	Fareham East, Fareham North, Fareham NorthWest, Fareham South, Fareham West, Locks Heath, Park Gate, Portchester East, Portchester West, Sarisbury, Titchfield, Titchfield Common, Warsash.
Gosport (borough constituency)	*The Borough of Fareham wards:* Hill Head, Stubbington. *The Borough of Gosport wards:* Alverstoke, Anglesey, Bridgemary North, Bridgemary South, Brockhurst, Christchurch, Elson, Forton, Grange, Hardway, Lee East, Lee West, Leesland, Peel Common, Privett, Rowner and Holbrook, Town.
Havant (borough constituency)	*The Borough of Havant wards:* Barncroft, Battins, Bedhampton, Bondfields, Emsworth, Hayling East, Hayling West, Purbrook, St Faith's, Stakes, Warren Park.
Meon Valley (county constituency)	*The District of East Hampshire wards:* Clanfield and Finchdean, Horndean Catherington and Lovedean, Horndean Downs, Horndean Hazleton and Blendworth, Horndean Kings, Horndean Murray, Rowlands Castle. *The Borough of Havant wards:* Cowplain, Hart Plain, Waterloo. *The City of Winchester wards:* Bishops Waltham, Boarhunt and Southwick, Cheriton and Bishops Sutton, Denmead, Droxford, Soberton and Hambledon, Owslebury and Curdridge, Shedfield, Swanmore and Newtown, Upper Meon Valley, Whiteley, Wickham.
New Forest East (county constituency)	*The District of New Forest wards:* Ashurst, Copythorne South and Netley Marsh, Boldre and Sway, Bramshaw, Copythorne North and Minstead, Brockenhurst and Forest South East, Butts Ash and Dibden Purlieu, Dibden and Hythe East, Fawley, Blackfield and Langley, Furzedown and Hardley, Holbury and North Blackfield, Hythe West and Langdown, Lyndhurst, Marchwood, Totton Central, Totton East, Totton North, Totton South, Totton West.
New Forest West (county constituency)	*The District of New Forest wards:* Barton, Bashley, Becton, Bransgore and Burley, Buckland, Downlands and Forest, Fernhill, Fordingbridge, Forest North West, Hordle, Lymington Town, Milford, Milton, Pennington, Ringwood East and Sopley, Ringwood North, Ringwood South.
North East Hampshire (county constituency)	*The Borough of Basingstoke and Deane wards:* Calleva, Pamber, Sherborne St John, Upton Grey and The Candovers. *The District of Hart wards:* Church Crookham East, Church Crookham West,

	Crondall, Eversley, Fleet Central, Fleet Courtmoor, Fleet North, Fleet Pondtail, Fleet West, Hartley Wintney, Hook, Long Sutton, Odiham, Yateley East, Yateley North, Yateley West.
North West Hampshire (county constituency)	*The Borough of Basingstoke and Deane wards:* Baughurst, Burghclere, East Woodhay, Highclere and Bourne, Kingsclere, Oakley and North Waltham, Overton, Laverstoke and Steventon, Tadley North, Tadley South, Whitchurch.
	The Borough of Test Valley wards: Alamein, Amport, Anna, Bourne Valley, Charlton, Harroway, Millway, Penton Bellinger, St Mary's, Winton.
Romsey and Southampton North (county constituency)	*The City of Southampton wards:* Bassett, Swaythling.
	The Borough of Test Valley wards: Abbey, Ampfield and Braishfield, Blackwater, Broughton and Stockbridge, Chilworth, Nursling and Rownhams, Cupernham, Dun Valley, Harewood, Kings Somborne and Michelmersh, North Baddesley, Over Wallop, Romsey Extra, Tadburn, Valley Park.
Southampton, Itchen (borough constituency)	*The City of Southampton wards:* Bargate, Bitterne, Bitterne Park, Harefield, Peartree, Sholing, Woolston.
Southampton, Test (borough constituency)	*The City of Southampton wards:* Bevois, Coxford, Freemantle, Millbrook, Portswood, Redbridge, Shirley.
Winchester (county constituency)	*The Borough of Eastleigh wards:* Chandler's Ford East, Chandler's Ford West, Hiltingbury East, Hiltingbury West.
	The City of Winchester wards: Colden Common and Twyford, Compton and Otterbourne, Itchen Valley, Kings Worthy, Littleton and Harestock, Olivers Battery and Badger Farm, St Barnabas, St Bartholomew, St John and All Saints, St Luke, St Michael, St Paul, Sparsholt, The Alresfords, Wonston and Micheldever.
IN HARTLEPOOL	
Hartlepool (borough constituency)	*The Borough of Hartlepool wards:* Brus, Burn Valley, Dyke House, Elwick, Fens, Foggy Furze, Grange, Greatham, Hart, Owton, Park, Rift House, Rossmere, St Hilda, Seaton, Stranton, Throston.
IN HEREFORDSHIRE	
Hereford and South Herefordshire (county constituency)	*The County and District of Herefordshire wards:* Aylestone, Belmont, Central, Golden Valley North, Golden Valley South, Hollington, Kerne Bridge, Llangarron, Penyard, Pontrilas, RossonWye East, RossonWye West, St Martins

	and Hinton, St Nicholas, Stoney Street, Three Elms, Tupsley, Valletts.
North Herefordshire (county constituency)	*The County and District of Herefordshire wards:* Backbury, Bircher, Bringsty, Bromyard, Burghill, Holmer and Lyde, Castle, Credenhill, Frome, Golden Cross with Weobley, Hagley, Hampton Court, Hope End, Kington Town, Ledbury, Leominster North, Leominster South, Mortimer, Old Gore, Pembridge and Lyonshall with Titley, Sutton Walls, Upton, Wormsley Ridge.

IN HERTFORDSHIRE

Broxbourne (borough constituency)	*The Borough of Broxbourne wards:* Broxbourne, Bury Green, Cheshunt Central, Cheshunt North, Flamstead End, Goffs Oak, Hoddesdon North, Hoddesdon Town, Rosedale, Rye Park, Theobalds, Waltham Cross, Wormley & Turnford. *The District of Welwyn Hatfield ward:* Northaw.
Hemel Hempstead (county constituency)	*The District of Dacorum wards:* Adeyfield East, Adeyfield West, Apsley, Ashridge, Bennetts End, Boxmoor, Chaulden & Shrubhill, Corner Hall, Gadebridge, Grove Hill, Hemel Hempstead Central, Highfield & St Pauls, Kings Langley, Leverstock Green, Nash Mills, Warners End, Watling, Woodhall.
Hertford and Stortford (county constituency)	*The District of East Hertfordshire wards:* Bishop's Stortford All Saints, Bishop's Stortford Central, Bishop's Stortford Meads, Bishop's Stortford Silverleys, Bishop's Stortford South, Great Amwell, Hertford Bengeo, Hertford Castle, Hertford Heath, Hertford Kingsmead, Hertford Sele, Hunsdon, Much Hadham, Sawbridgeworth, Stanstead Abbots, Ware Chadwell, Ware Christchurch, Ware St Mary's, Ware Trinity.
Hertsmere (county constituency)	*The Borough of Hertsmere wards:* Aldenham East, Aldenham West, Borehamwood Brookmeadow, Borehamwood Cowley Hill, Borehamwood Hillside, Borehamwood Kenilworth, Bushey Heath, Bushey North, Bushey Park, Bushey St James, Elstree, Potters Bar Furzefield, Potters Bar Oakmere, Potters Bar Parkfield, Shenley
Hitchin and Harpenden (county constituency)	*The District of North Hertfordshire wards:* Cadwell, Graveley & Wymondley, Hitchin Bearton, Hitchin Highbury, Hitchin Oughton, Hitchin Priory, Hitchin Walsworth, Hitchwood, Hoo, Kimpton, Offa. *The City of St Albans wards:* Harpenden East, Harpenden North, Harpenden South, Harpenden West, Redbourn, Sandridge, Wheathampstead.

North East Hertfordshire (county constituency)	*The District of East Hertfordshire wards:* Braughing, Buntingford, Hertford Rural North, Hertford Rural South, Little Hadham, Mundens and Cottered, Puckeridge, Thundridge & Standon, Walkern, WattonatStone. *The District of North Hertfordshire wards:* Arbury, Baldock East, Baldock Town, Ermine, Letchworth East, Letchworth Grange, Letchworth South East, Letchworth South West, Letchworth Wilbury, Royston Heath, Royston Meridian, Royston Palace, Weston and Sandon.
South West Hertfordshire (county constituency)	*The District of Dacorum wards:* Aldbury and Wigginton, Berkhamsted Castle, Berkhamsted East, Berkhamsted West, Bovingdon, Flaunden & Chipperfield, Northchurch, Tring Central, Tring East, Tring West. *The District of Three Rivers wards:* Ashridge, Chorleywood East, Chorleywood West, Croxley Green, Croxley Green North, Croxley Green South, Hayling, Maple Cross & Mill End, Moor Park & Eastbury, Northwick, Penn, Rickmansworth, Rickmansworth West, Sarratt.
St Albans (county constituency)	*The City of St Albans wards:* Ashley, Batchwood, Clarence, Colney Heath, Cunningham, London Colney, Marshalswick North, Marshalswick South, Park Street, St Peters, St Stephen, Sopwell, Verulam. *The District of Three Rivers ward:* Bedmond & Primrose Hill.
Stevenage (county constituency)	*The District of East Hertfordshire ward:* Datchworth & Aston. *The District of North Hertfordshire wards:* Codicote, Knebworth. *The Borough of Stevenage wards:* Bandley Hill, Bedwell, Chells, Longmeadow, Manor, Martins Wood, Old Town, Pin Green, Roebuck, St Nicholas, Shephall, Symonds Green, Woodfield.
Watford (borough constituency)	*The District of Three Rivers wards:* Abbots Langley, Carpenders Park, Langleybury, Leavesden, Oxhey Hall. *The Borough of Watford wards:* Callowland, Central, Holywell, Leggatts, Meriden, Nascot, Oxhey, Park, Stanborough, Tudor, Vicarage, Woodside.
Welwyn Hatfield (county constituency)	*The District of Welwyn Hatfield wards:* Brookmans Park and Little Heath, Haldens, Handside, Hatfield Central, Hatfield East, Hatfield North, Hatfield South, Hatfield West, Hollybush, Howlands, Panshanger, Peartree, Sherrards, Welham Green, Welwyn North, Welwyn South.

2205

IN THE ISLE OF WIGHT

Isle of Wight (county constituency)	*Isle of Wight electoral divisions:* Ashey, Bembridge North, Bembridge South, Binstead, Brading and St Helens, Brighstone and Calbourne, Carisbrooke East, Carisbrooke West, Central Rural, Chale, Niton and Whitwell, Cowes Castle East, Cowes Castle West, Cowes Central, Cowes Medina, East Cowes North, East Cowes South, Fairlee, Freshwater Afton, Freshwater Norton, Gurnard, Lake North, Lake South, Mount Joy, Newchurch, Newport North, Newport South, Northwood, Osborne, Pan, Parkhurst, Ryde North East, Ryde North West, Ryde South East, Ryde South West, St Johns East, St Johns West, Sandown North, Sandown South, Seaview and Nettlestone, Shalfleet and Yarmouth, Shanklin Central, Shanklin North, Shanklin South, Totland, Ventnor East, Ventnor West, Wootton, Wroxall and Godshill.

IN KENT AND MEDWAY

Ashford (county constituency)	*The Borough of Ashford wards:* Aylesford Green, Beaver, Biddenden, Bockhanger, Boughton Aluph and Eastwell, Bybrook, Charing, Downs North, Downs West, Godinton, Great Chart with Singleton North, Highfield, Isle of Oxney, Kennington, Little Burton Farm, Norman, North Willesborough, Park Farm North, Park Farm South, Rolvenden and Tenterden West, St Michaels, Singleton South, South Willesborough, Stanhope, Stour, Tenterden North, Tenterden South, Victoria, Washford, Weald Central, Weald East, Weald North, Weald South, Wye.
Canterbury (county constituency)	*The City of Canterbury wards:* Barham Downs, Barton, Blean Forest, Chartham and Stone Street, Chestfield and Swalecliffe, Gorrell, Harbledown, Harbour, Little Stour, North Nailbourne, Northgate, St Stephens, Seasalter, Sturry North, Sturry South, Tankerton, Westgate, Wincheap.
Chatham and Aylesford (county constituency)	*The Borough of Medway wards:* Chatham Central, Lordswood and Capstone, Luton and Wayfield, Princes Park, Walderslade. *The Borough of Tonbridge and Malling wards:* Aylesford, Blue Bell Hill and Walderslade, Burham, Eccles and Wouldham, Ditton, Larkfield North, Larkfield South, Snodland East, Snodland West.
Dartford (county constituency)	*The Borough of Dartford wards:* Bean and Darenth, Brent, Castle, Greenhithe, Heath, Joyce Green, Joydens Wood, Littlebrook, Longfield, New Barn and Southfleet, Newtown, Princes, Stone, SuttonatHone and Hawley,

	Swanscombe, Town, West Hill, Wilmington.
	The District of Sevenoaks ward:
	Hartley and Hodsoll Street.
Dover	*The District of Dover wards:*
(county constituency)	Aylesham, Buckland, CapelleFerne, Castle,
	Eastry, Eythorne and Shepherdswell, Lydden
	and Temple Ewell, Maxton, Elms Vale and
	Priory, Middle Deal and Sholden, Mill Hill, North
	Deal, Ringwould, River, St Margaret'satCliffe, St
	Radigunds, Tower Hamlets, Town and Pier,
	Walmer, Whitfield.
Faversham and Mid Kent	*The Borough of Maidstone wards:*
(county constituency)	Bearsted, Boughton, Monchelsea and Chart
	Sutton, Boxley, Detling and Thurnham,
	Downswood and Otham, Harrietsham and
	Lenham, Headcorn, Leeds, North Downs, Park
	Wood, Shepway North, Shepway South, Sutton
	Valence and Langley.
	The Borough of Swale wards:
	Abbey, Boughton and Courtenay, Davington
	Priory, East Downs, St Ann's, Watling.
Folkestone and Hythe	*The Borough of Ashford ward:*
(county constituency)	Saxon Shore.
	The District of Shepway wards:
	Dymchurch and St Mary's Bay, Elham and
	Stelling Minnis, Folkestone Cheriton, Folkestone
	East, Folkestone Foord, Folkestone Harbour,
	Folkestone Harvey Central, Folkestone Harvey
	West, Folkestone Morehall, Folkestone Park,
	Folkestone Sandgate, Hythe Central, Hythe
	East, Hythe West, Lydd, Lympne and Stanford,
	New Romney Coast, New Romney Town, North
	Downs East, North Downs West, Romney Marsh,
	Tolsford.
Gillingham and Rainham	*The Borough of Medway wards:*
(borough constituency)	Gillingham North, Gillingham South,
	Hempstead and Wigmore, Rainham Central,
	Rainham North, Rainham South, Twydall,
	Watling.
Gravesham	*The Borough of Gravesham wards:*
(county constituency)	Central, Chalk, Coldharbour, Higham, Istead
	Rise, Meopham North, Meopham South and
	Vigo, Northfleet North, Northfleet South,
	Painters Ash, Pelham, Riverside, Riverview,
	Shorne, Cobham and Luddesdown, Singlewell,
	Westcourt, Whitehill, Woodlands.
Maidstone and The Weald	*The Borough of Maidstone wards:*
(county constituency)	Allington, Barming, Bridge, Coxheath and
	Hunton, East, Fant, Heath, High Street, Loose,
	Marden and Yalding, North, South, Staplehurst.
	The Borough of Tunbridge Wells wards:
	Benenden and Cranbrook, Frittenden and
	Sissinghurst.

North Thanet (county constituency)	*The City of Canterbury wards:* Greenhill and Eddington, Herne and Broomfield, Heron, Marshside, Reculver, West Bay. *The District of Thanet wards:* Birchington North, Birchington South, Dane Valley, Garlinge, Margate Central, Salmestone, Thanet Villages, Westbrook, WestgateonSea.
Rochester and Strood (county constituency)	*The Borough of Medway wards:* Cuxton and Halling, Peninsula, River, Rochester East, Rochester South and Horsted, Rochester West, Strood North, Strood Rural, Strood South.
Sevenoaks (county constituency)	*The District of Sevenoaks wards:* Ash, Brasted, Chevening and Sundridge, Crockenhill and Well Hill, Dunton Green and Riverhead, Eynsford, Farningham, Horton Kirby and South Darenth, Fawkham and West Kingsdown, Halstead, Knockholt and Badgers Mount, Hextable, Kemsing, Otford and Shoreham, Seal and Weald, Sevenoaks Eastern, Sevenoaks Kippington, Sevenoaks Northern, Sevenoaks Town and St John's, Swanley Christchurch and Swanley Village, Swanley St Mary's, Swanley White Oak, Westerham and Crockham Hill.
Sittingbourne and Sheppey (county constituency)	*The Borough of Swale wards:* Borden, Chalkwell, Grove, Hartlip, Newington and Upchurch, Iwade and Lower Halstow, Kemsley, Leysdown and Warden, Milton Regis, Minster Cliffs, Murston, Queenborough and Halfway, Roman, St Michaels, Sheerness East, Sheerness West, Sheppey Central, Teynham and Lynsted, West Downs, Woodstock.
South Thanet (county constituency)	*The District of Dover wards:* Little Stour and Ashstone, Sandwich. *The District of Thanet wards:* Beacon Road, Bradstowe, Central Harbour, Cliffsend and Pegwell, Cliftonville East, Cliftonville West, Eastcliff, Kingsgate, Nethercourt, Newington, Northwood, St Peters, Sir Moses Montefiore, Viking.
Tonbridge and Malling (county constituency)	*The District of Sevenoaks wards:* Cowden and Hever, Edenbridge North and East, Edenbridge South and West, Leigh and Chiddingstone Causeway, Penshurst, Fordcombe and Chiddingstone. *The Borough of Tonbridge and Malling wards:* Borough Green and Long Mill, Cage Green, Castle, Downs, East Malling, East Peckham and Golden Green, Hadlow, Mereworth and West Peckham, Higham, Hildenborough, Ightham, Judd, Kings Hill, Medway, Trench, Vauxhall, Wateringbury, West Malling and Leybourne, Wrotham.

Tunbridge Wells (county constituency)	*The Borough of Tunbridge Wells wards:* Brenchley and Horsmonden, Broadwater, Capel, Culverden, Goudhurst and Lamberhurst, Hawkhurst and Sandhurst, Paddock Wood East, Paddock Wood West, Pantiles and St Mark's, Park, Pembury, Rusthall, St James', St John's, Sherwood, Southborough and High Brooms, Southborough North, Speldhurst and Bidborough.

IN LANCASHIRE, BLACKBURN WITH DARWEN, AND BLACKPOOL

Blackburn (borough constituency)	*The Borough of Blackburn with Darwen wards:* Audley, Bastwell, Beardwood with Lammack, Corporation Park, Ewood, Higher Croft, Little Harwood, Livesey with Pleasington, Meadowhead, Mill Hill, Queen's Park, Roe Lee, Shadsworth with Whitebirk, Shear Brow, Wensley Fold.
Blackpool North and Cleveleys (borough constituency)	*The Borough of Blackpool wards:* Anchorsholme, Bispham, Claremont, Greenlands, Ingthorpe, Layton, Norbreck, Park, Warbreck. *The Borough of Wyre wards:* Bourne, Cleveleys Park, Jubilee, Victoria.
Blackpool South (borough constituency)	*The Borough of Blackpool wards:* Bloomfield, Brunswick, Clifton, Hawes Side, Highfield, Marton, Squires Gate, Stanley, Talbot, Tyldesley, Victoria, Waterloo.
Burnley (borough constituency)	*The Borough of Burnley wards:* Bank Hall, Briercliffe, Brunshaw, Cliviger with Worsthorne, Coal Clough with Deerplay, Daneshouse with Stoneyholme, Gannow, Gawthorpe, Hapton with Park, Lanehead, Queensgate, Rosegrove with Lowerhouse, Rosehill with Burnley Wood, Trinity, Whittlefield with Ightenhill.
Chorley (county constituency)	*The Borough of Chorley wards:* Adlington and Anderton, Astley and Buckshaw, Brindle and Hoghton, Chisnall, Chorley East, Chorley North East, Chorley North West, Chorley South East, Chorley South West, ClaytonleWoods and WhittleleWoods, ClaytonleWoods North, ClaytonleWoods West and Cuerden, Coppull, Euxton North, Euxton South, Heath Charnock and Rivington, Pennine, Wheelton and Withnell.
Fylde (county constituency)	*The Borough of Fylde wards:* Ansdell, Ashton, Central, Clifton, Elswick and Little Eccleston, Fairhaven, Freckleton East, Freckleton West, Heyhouses, Kilnhouse, Kirkham North, Kirkham South, MedlarwithWesham, Newton and Treales, Park, RibbywithWrea, St Johns, St Leonards, Singleton and Greenhalgh, Staining and

	Weeton, Warton and Westby.
	The City of Preston ward:
	Lea.
Hyndburn (borough constituency)	*The Borough of Hyndburn wards:* Altham, Barnfield, Baxenden, Central, Church, ClaytonleMoors, Huncoat, Immanuel, Milnshaw, Netherton, Overton, Peel, Rishton, St Andrew's, St Oswald's, Spring Hill. *The Borough of Rossendale wards:* Greenfield, Worsley.
Lancaster and Fleetwood (county constituency)	*The City of Lancaster wards:* Bulk, Castle, Duke's, Ellel, John O'Gaunt, Lower Lune Valley, Scotforth East, Scotforth West, University. *The Borough of Wyre wards:* Mount, Park, Pharos, Pilling, Preesall, Rossall, Warren, Wyresdale.
Morecambe and Lunesdale (county constituency)	*The City of Lancaster wards:* Bare, BoltonleSands, Carnforth, HaltonwithAughton, Harbour, Heysham Central, Heysham North, Heysham South, Kellet, Overton, Poulton, Silverdale, Skerton East, Skerton West, SlynewithHest, Torrisholme, Upper Lune Valley, Warton, Westgate.
Pendle (borough constituency)	*The Borough of Pendle wards:* Barrowford, Blacko and Higherford, Boulsworth, Bradley, Brierfield, Clover Hill, Coates, Craven, Earby, Foulridge, Higham and Pendleside, Horsfield, Marsden, Old Laund Booth, Reedley, Southfield, Vivary Bridge, Walverden, Waterside, Whitefield.
Preston (borough constituency)	*The City of Preston wards:* Ashton, Brookfield, Deepdale, Fishwick, Ingol, Larches, Moor Park, Ribbleton, Riversway, St George's, St Matthew's, Town Centre, Tulketh, University.
Ribble Valley (county constituency)	*The Borough of Ribble Valley wards:* Aighton, Bailey and Chaigley, Alston and Hothersall, Billington and Old Langho, Bowland, Newton and Slaidburn, Chatburn, Chipping, ClaytonleDale with Ramsgreave, Derby and Thornley, Dilworth, Edisford and Low Moor, Gisburn, Rimington, Langho, Littlemoor, Mellor, Primrose, Read and Simonstone, Ribchester, Sabden, St Mary's, Salthill, Waddington and West Bradford, Whalley, Wilpshire, Wiswell and Pendleton. *The Borough of South Ribble wards:* Bamber Bridge East, Bamber Bridge North, Bamber Bridge West, Coupe Green and Gregson Lane, Farington East, Farington West, Lostock Hall, Samlesbury and Walton, Tardy Gate, WaltonleDale.

Rossendale and Darwen (borough constituency)	*The Borough of Blackburn with Darwen wards:* Earcroft, East Rural, Fernhurst, Marsh House, North Turton with Tockholes, Sudell, Sunnyhurst, Whitehall. *The Borough of Rossendale wards:* Cribden, Eden, Facit and Shawforth, Goodshaw, Greensclough, Hareholme, Healey and Whitworth, Helmshore, Irwell, Longholme, Stacksteads, Whitewell.
South Ribble (county constituency)	*The Borough of Chorley wards:* Eccleston and Mawdesley, Lostock. *The Borough of South Ribble wards:* Broad Oak, Charnock, Earnshaw Bridge, Golden Hill, Howick and Priory, Kingsfold, Leyland Central, Leyland St Ambrose, Leyland St Mary's, Little Hoole and Much Hoole, Longton and Hutton West, Lowerhouse, Middleforth, Moss Side, New Longton and Hutton East, Seven Stars, Whitefield. *The District of West Lancashire wards:* HeskethwithBecconsall, North Meols, Rufford, Tarleton.
West Lancashire (county constituency)	*The District of West Lancashire wards:* Ashurst, Aughton and Downholland, Aughton Park, Bickerstaffe, Birch Green, Burscough East, Burscough West, Derby, Digmoor, Halsall, Knowsley, Moorside, Newburgh, Parbold, Scarisbrick, Scott, Skelmersdale North, Skelmersdale South, Tanhouse, Up Holland, Wrightington.
Wyre and Preston North (county constituency)	*The City of Preston wards:* Cadley, College, Garrison, Greyfriars, Preston Rural East, Preston Rural North, Sharoe Green. *The Borough of Wyre wards:* Breck, Brock, Cabus, Calder, Carleton, Catterall, Garstang, Great Eccleston, Hambleton and StalminewithStaynall, Hardhorn, High Cross, Norcross, Staina, Tithebarn.
IN LEICESTER	
Leicester East (borough constituency)	*The City of Leicester wards:* Belgrave, Charnwood, Coleman, Evington, Humberstone and Hamilton, Latimer, Rushey Mead, Thurncourt.
Leicester South (borough constituency)	*The City of Leicester wards:* Aylestone, Castle, Eyres Monsell, Freemen, Knighton, Spinney Hills, Stoneygate.
Leicester West (borough constituency)	*The City of Leicester wards:* Abbey, Beaumont Leys, Braunstone Park and Rowley Fields, Fosse, New Parks, Westcotes, Western Park.
IN LEICESTERSHIRE AND RUTLAND	
Bosworth (county constituency)	*The Borough of Hinckley and Bosworth wards:* Ambien, Barlestone, Nailstone and Osbaston,

	Barwell, Burbage, St Catherines and Lash Hill, Burbage, Sketchley and Stretton, Cadeby, Carlton and Market Bosworth with Shackerstone, Earl Shilton, Hinckley Castle, Hinckley Clarendon, Hinckley De Montfort, Hinckley Trinity, Markfield, Stanton and Fieldhead, Newbold Verdon with Desford and Peckleton, Ratby, Bagworth and Thornton, Twycross and Witherley with Sheepy.
Charnwood (county constituency)	*The District of Blaby wards:* Ellis, Fairestone, Forest, Muxloe. *The Borough of Charnwood wards:* Anstey, Birstall Wanlip, Birstall Watermead, East Goscote, Forest Bradgate, Mountsorrel, Queniborough, Rothley and Thurcaston, Syston East, Syston West, Thurmaston, Wreake Villages. *The Borough of Hinckley and Bosworth ward:* Groby.
Harborough (county constituency)	*The District of Harborough wards:* Bosworth, Fleckney, Glen, Kibworth, Lubenham, Market HarboroughGreat Bowden and Arden, Market HarboroughLittle Bowden, Market HarboroughLogan, Market HarboroughWelland. *The Borough of Oadby and Wigston wards:* Oadby Brocks Hill, Oadby Grange, Oadby St Peter's, Oadby Uplands, Oadby Woodlands, South Wigston, Wigston All Saints, Wigston Fields, Wigston Meadowcourt, Wigston St Wolstan's.
Loughborough (county constituency)	*The Borough of Charnwood wards:* Barrow and Sileby West, Loughborough Ashby, Loughborough Dishley and Hathern, Loughborough Garendon, Loughborough Hastings, Loughborough Lemyngton, Loughborough Nanpantan, Loughborough Outwoods, Loughborough Shelthorpe, Loughborough Southfields, Loughborough Storer, Quorn and Mountsorrel Castle, Shepshed East, Shepshed West, Sileby, The Wolds.
North West Leicestershire (county constituency)	*The District of North West Leicestershire wards:* Appleby, Ashby Castle, Ashby Holywell, Ashby Ivanhoe, Bardon, Breedon, Castle Donington, Coalville, Greenhill, Hugglescote, Ibstock and Heather, Kegworth and Whatton, Measham, Moira, Oakthorpe and Donisthorpe, Ravenstone and Packington, Snibston, Thringstone, Valley, Whitwick.
Rutland and Melton (county constituency)	*The District of Harborough wards:* Billesdon, Nevill, Thurnby and Houghton, Tilton. *The Borough of Melton wards:* Asfordby, Bottesford, Croxton Kerrial, FrisbyontheWreake, Gaddesby, Long Clawson

	and Stathern, Melton Craven, Melton Dorian, Melton Egerton, Melton Newport, Melton Sysonby, Melton Warwick, Old Dalby, Somerby, WalthamontheWolds, Wymondham.
	The District of Rutland wards:
	Braunston and Belton, Cottesmore, Exton, Greetham, Ketton, Langham, Lyddington, Martinsthorpe, Normanton, Oakham North East, Oakham North West, Oakham South East, Oakham South West, Ryhall and Casterton, Uppingham, Whissendine.
South Leicestershire (county constituency)	*The District of Blaby wards:*
	Blaby South, Cosby with South Whetstone, Countesthorpe, Croft Hill, Enderby and St John's, Millfield, Narborough and Littlethorpe, Normanton, North Whetstone, Pastures, Ravenhurst and Fosse, Saxondale, Stanton and Flamville, Winstanley.
	The District of Harborough wards:
	Broughton AstleyAstley, Broughton AstleyBroughton, Broughton AstleyPrimethorpe, Broughton AstleySutton, Dunton, Lutterworth Brookfield, Lutterworth Orchard, Lutterworth Springs, Lutterworth Swift, Misterton, Peatling, Ullesthorpe.

IN LINCOLNSHIRE

Boston and Skegness (county constituency)	*The Borough of Boston wards:*
	Central, Coastal, Fenside, Fishtoft, Five Village, Frampton and Holme, Kirton, North, Old Leake and Wrangle, Pilgrim, Skirbeck, South, Staniland North, Staniland South, Swineshead and Holland Fen, West, Witham, Wyberton.
	The District of East Lindsey wards:
	Burgh le Marsh, Croft, Frithville, Ingoldmells, St Clement's, Scarbrough, Seacroft, Sibsey, Stickney, Wainfleet and Friskney, Winthorpe.
Gainsborough (county constituency)	*The District of East Lindsey ward:*
	Wragby.
	The District of West Lindsey wards:
	Bardney, Caistor, Cherry Willingham, Dunholme, Fiskerton, Gainsborough East, Gainsborough North, Gainsborough SouthWest, Hemswell, Kelsey, Lea, Market Rasen, Middle Rasen, Nettleham, Saxilby, Scampton, Scotter, Stow, Sudbrooke, Thonock, Torksey, Waddingham and Spital, Welton, Wold View, Yarborough.
Grantham and Stamford (county constituency)	*The District of South Kesteven wards:*
	All Saints, Aveland, Belmont, Bourne East, Bourne West, Earlesfield, Forest, Glen Eden, Grantham St John's, Green Hill, Greyfriars, Harrowby, Hillsides, Isaac Newton, Lincrest, Morkery, Ringstone, St Anne's, St George's, St Mary's, St Wulfram's, Stamford St John's,

	Thurlby, Toller, Truesdale.
Lincoln (borough constituency)	*The City of Lincoln wards:* Abbey, Birchwood, Boultham, Bracebridge, Carholme, Castle, Glebe, Hartsholme, Minster, Moorland, Park. *The District of North Kesteven wards:* Bracebridge Heath and Waddington East, Skellingthorpe.
Louth and Horncastle (county constituency)	*The District of East Lindsey wards:* Alford, Binbrook, Chapel St Leonards, Coningsby and Tattershall, Grimoldby, Halton Holegate, Holton le Clay, Horncastle, Hundleby, Legbourne, Ludford, Mablethorpe Central, Mablethorpe East, Mablethorpe North, Mareham le Fen, Marshchapel, North Holme, North Somercotes, North Thoresby, Priory, Roughton, St James', St Margaret's, St Mary's, St Michael's, Skidbrooke with Saltfleet Haven, Spilsby, Sutton on Sea North, Sutton on Sea South, Tetford, Tetney, Trinity, Trusthorpe and Mablethorpe South, Willoughby with Sloothby, Withern with Stain, Woodhall Spa.
Sleaford and North Hykeham (county constituency)	*The District of North Kesteven wards:* Ashby de la Launde, Bassingham, Billinghay, Branston and Mere, Brant Broughton, Cliff Villages, Cranwell and Byard's Leap, Eagle and North Scarle, Heckington Rural, Heighington and Washingborough, Kyme, Leasingham and Roxholm, Martin, Metheringham, North Hykeham Forum, North Hykeham Memorial, North Hykeham Mill, North Hykeham Moor, North Hykeham Witham, Osbournby, Ruskington, Sleaford Castle, Sleaford Holdingham, Sleaford Mareham, Sleaford Navigation, Sleaford Quarrington, Sleaford Westholme, Waddington West. *The District of South Kesteven wards:* Barrowby, Ermine, Heath, Loveden, Peascliffe, Saxonwell, Witham Valley.
South Holland and The Deepings (county constituency)	*The District of South Holland wards:* Crowland, Deeping St Nicholas, Donington, Fleet, Gedney, Gosberton Village, Holbeach Hurn, Holbeach St John's, Holbeach Town, Long Sutton, Pinchbeck, Spalding Castle, Spalding Monks House, Spalding St John's, Spalding St Mary's, Spalding St Paul's, Spalding Wygate, Surfleet, Sutton Bridge, The Saints, Weston and Moulton, Whaplode. *The District of South Kesteven wards:* Deeping St James, Market and West Deeping.

IN MIDDLESBROUGH, REDCAR AND CLEVELAND

Middlesbrough (borough constituency)	*The Borough of Middlesbrough wards:* Acklam, Ayresome, Beckfield, Beechwood,

	Brookfield, Clairville, Gresham, Kader, Linthorpe, Middlehaven, North Ormesby and Brambles Farm, Pallister, Park, Thorntree, University.
Middlesbrough South and East Cleveland (county constituency)	*The Borough of Middlesbrough wards:* Coulby Newham, Hemlington, Ladgate, Marton, Marton West, Nunthorpe, Park End, Stainton and Thornton. *The Borough of Redcar and Cleveland wards:* Brotton, Guisborough, Hutton, Lockwood, Loftus, Saltburn, Skelton, Westworth.
Redcar (borough constituency)	*The Borough of Redcar and Cleveland wards:* Coatham, Dormanstown, Eston, Grangetown, Kirkleatham, Longbeck, Newcomen, Normanby, Ormesby, St Germain's, South Bank, Teesville, West Dyke, Zetland.

IN MILTON KEYNES

Milton Keynes North (county constituency)	*The Borough of Milton Keynes wards:* Bradwell, Campbell Park, Hanslope Park, Linford North, Linford South, Middleton, Newport Pagnell North, Newport Pagnell South, Olney, Sherington, Stantonbury, Wolverton.
Milton Keynes South (borough constituency)	*The Borough of Milton Keynes wards:* Bletchley and Fenny Stratford, Danesborough, Denbigh, Eaton Manor, Emerson Valley, Furzton, Loughton Park, Stony Stratford, Walton Park, Whaddon, Woughton.

IN NORFOLK

Broadland (county constituency)	*The District of Broadland wards:* Acle, Aylsham, Blofield with South Walsham, Brundall, Burlingham, Buxton, Coltishall, Drayton North, Drayton South, Eynesford, Great Witchingham, Hevingham, Horsford and Felthorpe, Marshes, Plumstead, Reepham, Spixworth with St Faiths, Taverham North, Taverham South, Wroxham. *The District of North Norfolk wards:* Astley, Lancaster North, Lancaster South, The Raynhams, Walsingham, Wensum.
Great Yarmouth (county constituency)	*The Borough of Great Yarmouth wards:* Bradwell North, Bradwell South and Hopton, Caister North, Caister South, Central and Northgate, Claydon, East Flegg, Fleggburgh, Gorleston, Lothingland, Magdalen, Nelson, Ormesby, St Andrews, Southtown and Cobholm, West Flegg, Yarmouth North.
Mid Norfolk (county constituency)	*The District of Breckland wards:* All Saints, Buckenham, Burgh and Haverscroft, DerehamCentral, DerehamHumbletoft, DerehamNeatherd, DerehamToftwood, Eynsford, Haggard De Toni, Hermitage, Launditch, Necton, Queen's, Shipdham, Springvale and Scarning, Swanton Morley,

	Taverner, Templar, Two Rivers, Upper Wensum, Upper Yare, Watton, Wissey.
	The District of South Norfolk wards: Abbey, Cromwells, Hingham and Deopham, Northfields, Rustens, Town, Wicklewood.
North Norfolk (county constituency)	*The District of North Norfolk wards:* Briston, Chaucer, Corpusty, Cromer Town, Erpingham, Glaven Valley, Gaunt, Happisburgh, High Heath, Holt, Hoveton, Mundesley, North Walsham East, North Walsham North, North Walsham West, Poppyland, Priory, Roughton, Scottow, St Benet, Sheringham North, Sheringham South, Stalham and Sutton, Suffield Park, The Runtons, Waterside, Waxham, Worstead.
North West Norfolk (county constituency)	*The Borough of King's Lynn and West Norfolk wards:* Brancaster, Burnham, Clenchwarton, Dersingham, Docking, Fairstead, Gayton, Gaywood Chase, Gaywood North Bank, Grimston, Heacham, Hunstanton, North Lynn, North Wootton, Old Gaywood, Priory, Rudham St Margarets with St Nicholas, Snettisham, South and West Lynn, South Wootton, Spellowfields, Springwood, Valley Hill, Walpole, West Winch.
Norwich North (borough constituency)	*The District of Broadland wards:* Hellesdon North West, Hellesdon South East, Old Catton and Sprowston West, Sprowston Central, Sprowston East, Thorpe St Andrew North West, Thorpe St Andrew South East. *The City of Norwich wards:* Catton Grove, Crome, Mile Cross, Sewell.
Norwich South (borough constituency)	*The City of Norwich wards:* Bowthorpe, Eaton, Lakenham, Mancroft, Nelson, Thorpe Hamlet, Town Close, University, Wensum. *The District of South Norfolk ward:* New Costessey.
South Norfolk (county constituency)	*The District of South Norfolk wards:* Beck Vale, Bressingham and Burston, Brooke, Bunwell, Chedgrave and Thurton, Cringleford, Dickleburgh, Diss, Ditchingham and Broome, Earsham, Easton, Forncett, Gillingham, Harleston, Hempnall, Hethersett, Loddon, Mulbarton, Newton Flotman, Old Costessey, Poringland with The Framinghams, Rockland, Roydon, Scole, Stoke Holy Cross, Stratton, Tasburgh, Thurlton.
South West Norfolk (county constituency)	*The District of Breckland wards:* Conifer, East Guiltcross, Harling and Heathlands, Mid Forest, Nar Valley, Swaffham, ThetfordAbbey, ThetfordCastle,

ThetfordGuildhall, ThetfordSaxon, Wayland, Weeting, West Guiltcross.

The Borough of King's Lynn and West Norfolk wards:
Airfield, Denton, Downham Old Town, East Downham, Emneth with Outwell, Hilgay with Denver, Mershe Lande, North Downham, St Lawrence, South Downham, Upwell and Delph, Walton, Watlington, Wiggenhall, Wimbotsham with Fincham Wissey.

IN NORTHAMPTONSHIRE

Corby (county constituency)	*The Borough of Corby wards:* Central, Danesholme, East, Hazelwood, Hillside, Kingswood, Lloyds, Lodge Park, Rural East, Rural North, Rural West, Shire Lodge, West. *The District of East Northamptonshire wards:* Barnwell, Dryden, Fineshade, Irthlingborough, King's Forest, Lower Nene, Lyveden, Oundle, Prebendal, Raunds Saxon, Raunds Windmill, Ringstead, Stanwick, Thrapston, Woodford.
[Daventry (county constituency)	*The District of Daventry wards:* Abbey North, Abbey South, Badby, Barby and Kilsby, Boughton and Pitsford, Brampton, Braunston, Brixworth, Byfield, Clipston, Crick, Drayton, Flore, Hill, Long Buckby, Moulton, Ravensthorpe, Spratton, Walgrave, Weedon, Welford, West Haddon and Guilsborough, Woodford, Yelvertoft. *The District of South Northamptonshire wards:* Harpole and Grange, Heyfords and Bugbrooke. *The Borough of Wellingborough wards:* Earls Barton, West.]
Kettering (county constituency)	*The Borough of Kettering wards:* All Saints, Avondale, Barton, Brambleside, Buccleuch, Latimer, Loatland, Millbrook, Pipers Hill, Plessy, Queen Eleanor, St Andrew's, St Giles, St Mary's, St Michael's, St Peter's, Slade, Spinney, Tresham, Trinity, Warkton, Welland, Wicksteed.
Northampton North (borough constituency)	*The Borough of Northampton wards:* Abington, Boughton Green, Eastfield, Headlands, Kingsley, Kingsthorpe, Lumbertubs, Parklands, St David, Thorplands.
Northampton South (borough constituency)	*The Borough of Northampton wards:* Billing, Castle, Delapre, Ecton Brook, New Duston, Old Duston, St Crispin, St James, Spencer, Weston.
[South Northamptonshire (county constituency)	*The Borough of Northampton wards:* East Hunsbury, Nene Valley, West Hunsbury. *The District of South Northamptonshire wards:* Astwell, Blakesley and Cote, Blisworth and Roade, Brackley East, Brackley South, Brackley West, Brafield and Yardley, Cosgrove and

	Grafton, Danvers and Wardoun, Deanshanger, Grange Park, Hackleton, Kings Sutton, Kingthorn, Little Brook, Middleton Cheney, Old Stratford, Salcey, Silverstone, Steane, Tove, Towcester Brook, Towcester Mill, Washington, Whittlewood.]
Wellingborough (county constituency)	*The District of East Northamptonshire wards:* Higham Ferrers, Rushden East, Rushden North, Rushden South, Rushden West. *The Borough of Wellingborough wards:* Brickhill, Castle, Croyland, Finedon, Great Doddington and Wilby, Hemmingwell, Irchester, North, Queensway, Redwell East, Redwell West, South, Swanspool, Wollaston.

IN NORTH SOMERSET

North Somerset (county constituency)	*The District of North Somerset wards:* Backwell, Clevedon Central, Clevedon East, Clevedon North, Clevedon South, Clevedon Walton, Clevedon West, Clevedon Yeo, EastoninGordano, Gordano, Nailsea East, Nailsea North and West, Pill, Portishead Central, Portishead Coast, Portishead East, Portishead Redcliffe Bay, Portishead South and North Weston, Portishead West, Winford, Wraxall and Long Ashton, Wrington, Yatton.
WestonSuperMare (county constituency)	*The District of North Somerset wards:* Banwell and Winscombe, Blagdon and Churchill, Congresbury, Hutton and Locking, Kewstoke, WestonSuperMare Central, WestonSuperMare Clarence and Uphill, WestonSuperMare East, WestonSuperMare Milton and Old Worle, WestonSuperMare North Worle, WestonSuperMare South, WestonSuperMare South Worle, WestonSuperMare West.

IN NORTHUMBERLAND

BerwickuponTweed (county constituency)	*The District of Alnwick wards:* Alnmouth and Lesbury, Alnwick Castle, Alnwick Clayport, Alnwick Hotspur, Amble Central, Amble East, Amble West, Embleton, Harbottle and Elsdon, Hedgeley, Longframlington, Longhoughton with Craster and Rennington, Rothbury and South Rural, Shilbottle, Warkworth, Whittingham. *The Borough of BerwickuponTweed wards:* Bamburgh, Beadnell, Belford, Cheviot, Edward, Elizabeth, Flodden, Ford, Islandshire, Lowick, Norhamshire, North Sunderland, Prior, Seton, Shielfield, Spittal, Wooler. *The Borough of Castle Morpeth wards:* Chevington, Ellington, Hartburn, Longhorsley, Lynemouth, Ulgham.
Blyth Valley	*The Borough of Blyth Valley wards:*

(borough constituency)	Cowpen, Cramlington East, Cramlington Eastfield with East Hartford, Cramlington North, Cramlington Parkside, Cramlington South East, Cramlington Village, Cramlington West, Croft, Hartley, Holywell, Isabella, Kitty Brewster, Newsham and New Delaval, Plessey, Seaton Delaval, Seghill, South Beach, South Newsham, Wensleydale.
Hexham (county constituency)	*The Borough of Castle Morpeth wards:* HeddonontheWall, Ponteland East, Ponteland North, Ponteland South, Ponteland West, Stamfordham, Stannington. *The District of Tynedale wards:* Acomb, Allendale, Bellingham, Broomhaugh and Riding, Chollerton with Whittington, Corbridge, East Tynedale, Hadrian, Haltwhistle, Haydon, Hexham Gilesgate, Hexham Hencotes, Hexham Leazes, Hexham Priestpopple, Humshaugh and Wall, Ovingham, Prudhoe Castle, Prudhoe North, Prudhoe South, Prudhoe West, Redesdale, Sandhoe with Dilston, Slaley and Hexhamshire, South Tynedale, Stocksfield with Mickley, Upper North Tyne, Wanney, Warden and Newbrough, Wark, West Tynedale, Wylam.
Wansbeck (county constituency)	*The Borough of Castle Morpeth wards:* Hebron, Hepscott and Mitford, Morpeth Central, Morpeth Kirkhill, Morpeth North, Morpeth South, Morpeth Stobhill, Pegswood. *The District of Wansbeck wards:* Bedlington Central, Bedlington East, Bedlington West, Bothal, Central, Choppington, College, Guide Post, Haydon, Hirst, Newbiggin East, Newbiggin West, Park, Seaton, Sleekburn, Stakeford.

IN NORTH YORKSHIRE

Harrogate and Knaresborough (county constituency)	*The Borough of Harrogate wards:* Bilton, Boroughbridge, Claro, Granby, Harlow Moor, High Harrogate, Hookstone, Killinghall, Knaresborough East, Knaresborough King James, Knaresborough Scriven Park, Low Harrogate, New Park, Pannal, Rossett, Saltergate, Starbeck, Stray, Woodfield.
Richmond (Yorks) (county constituency)	*The District of Hambleton wards:* Bedale, Brompton, Broughton and Greenhow, Cowtons, Crakehall, Great Ayton, Leeming, Leeming Bar, MortononSwale, Northallerton Broomfield, Northallerton Central, Northallerton North, Osmotherley, Romanby, Rudby, Stokesley, Swainby, Tanfield. *The District of Richmondshire wards:* Addlebrough, Barton, Bolton Castle, BromptononSwale and Scorton, Catterick,

	Colburn, Croft, Gilling West, Hawes and High Abbotside, Hipswell, Hornby Castle, Leyburn, Lower Wensleydale, Melsonby, Middleham, Middleton Tyas, Newsham with Eppleby, Penhill, Reeth and Arkengarthdale, Richmond Central, Richmond East, Richmond West, Scotton, Swaledale.
Scarborough and Whitby (county constituency)	*The Borough of Scarborough wards:* Castle, Cayton, Central, Danby, Derwent Valley, Eastfield, Esk Valley, Falsgrave Park, Fylingdales, Lindhead, Mayfield, Mulgrave, Newby, North Bay, Northstead, Ramshill, Scalby, Hackness and Staintondale, Seamer, Stepney, Streonshalh, Weaponness, Whitby West Cliff, Woodlands.
Selby and Ainsty (county constituency)	*The Borough of Harrogate wards:* Marston Moor, Ouseburn, Ribston, Spofforth with Lower Wharfedale. *The District of Selby wards:* Appleton Roebuck, Barlby, Brayton, Camblesforth, Cawood with Wistow, Eggborough, Fairburn with Brotherton, Hambleton, Hemingbrough, Monk Fryston and South Milford, North Duffield, Riccall with Escrick, Saxton and Ulleskelf, Selby North, Selby South, Selby West, Sherburn in Elmet, Tadcaster East, Tadcaster West, Whitley.
Skipton and Ripon (county constituency)	*The District of Craven wards:* Aire Valley with Lothersdale, Barden Fell, Bentham, Cowling, EmbsaywithEastby, Gargrave and Malhamdale, Glusburn, Grassington, Hellifield and Long Preston, Ingleton and Clapham, Penyghent, Settle and Ribblebanks, Skipton East, Skipton North, Skipton South, Skipton West, SuttoninCraven, Upper Wharfedale, West Craven. *The Borough of Harrogate wards:* Bishop Monkton, Kirkby Malzeard, Lower Nidderdale, Mashamshire, Newby, Nidd Valley, Pateley Bridge, Ripon Minster, Ripon Moorside, Ripon Spa, Washburn, Wathvale.
Thirsk and Malton (county constituency)	*The District of Hambleton wards:* Easingwold, Helperby, Huby and Sutton, Shipton, Sowerby, Stillington, Thirsk, Thorntons, Tollerton, Topcliffe, White Horse, Whitestonecliffe. *The District of Ryedale wards:* Amotherby, Ampleforth, Cropton, Dales, Derwent, Helmsley, Hovingham, Kirkbymoorside, Malton, Norton East, Norton West, Pickering East, Pickering West, Rillington, Ryedale South West, Sherburn, Sheriff Hutton, Sinnington, Thornton Dale, Wolds.

	The Borough of Scarborough wards: Filey, Hertford.
IN NOTTINGHAM	
Nottingham East (borough constituency)	*The City of Nottingham wards:* Arboretum, Berridge, Dales, Mapperley, St Ann's, Sherwood.
Nottingham North (borough constituency)	*The City of Nottingham wards:* Aspley, Basford, Bestwood, Bilborough, Bulwell, Bulwell Forest.
Nottingham South (borough constituency)	*The City of Nottingham wards:* Bridge, Clifton North, Clifton South, Dunkirk and Lenton, Leen Valley, Radford and Park, Wollaton East and Lenton Abbey, Wollaton West.
IN NOTTINGHAMSHIRE	
Ashfield (county constituency)	*The District of Ashfield wards:* Jacksdale, Kirkby in Ashfield Central, Kirkby in Ashfield East, Kirkby in Ashfield West, Selston, Sutton in Ashfield Central, Sutton in Ashfield East, Sutton in Ashfield North, Sutton in Ashfield West, Underwood, Woodhouse. *The Borough of Broxtowe wards:* Brinsley, Eastwood North and Greasley (Beauvale), Eastwood South.
Bassetlaw (county constituency)	*The District of Bassetlaw wards:* Beckingham, Blyth, Carlton, Clayworth, East Retford East, East Retford North, East Retford South, East Retford West, Everton, Harworth, Langold, Misterton, Ranskill, Sturton, Sutton, Welbeck, Worksop East, Worksop North, Worksop North East, Worksop North West, Worksop South, Worksop South East.
Broxtowe (county constituency)	*The Borough of Broxtowe wards:* Attenborough, Awsworth, Beeston Central, Beeston North, Beeston Rylands, Beeston West, Bramcote, Chilwell East, Chilwell West, Cossall and Kimberley, Greasley (Giltbrook and Newthorpe), Nuthall East and Strelley, Nuthall West and Greasley (Watnall), Stapleford North, Stapleford South East, Stapleford South West, Toton and Chilwell Meadows, Trowell.
Gedling (county constituency)	*The Borough of Gedling wards:* Bonington, Burton Joyce and Stoke Bardolph, Carlton, Carlton Hill, Daybrook, Gedling, Killisick, Kingswell, Mapperley Plains, Netherfield and Colwick, Phoenix, Porchester, St James, St Marys, Valley, Woodthorpe.
Mansfield (county constituency)	*The District of Mansfield wards:* Berry Hill, Birklands, Broomhill, Cumberlands, Eakring, Forest Town East, Forest Town West, Grange Farm, Ladybrook, Leeming, Lindhurst, Meden, Oak Tree, Pleasley Hill, Portland, Priory, Ravensdale, Robin Hood, Sherwood.
Newark	*The District of Bassetlaw wards:*

(county constituency)	East Markham, Rampton, Tuxford and Trent. *The District of Newark and Sherwood wards:* Balderton North, Balderton West, Beacon, Bridge, Castle, Caunton, Collingham and Meering, Devon, Farndon, Lowdham, Magnus, Muskham, Southwell East, Southwell North, Southwell West, SuttononTrent, Trent, Winthorpe. *The Borough of Rushcliffe wards:* Bingham East, Bingham West, Cranmer, Oak, Thoroton.
Rushcliffe (county constituency)	*The Borough of Rushcliffe wards:* Abbey, Compton Acres, Cotgrave, Edwalton Village, Gamston, Gotham, Keyworth North, Keyworth South, Lady Bay, Leake, Lutterell, Manvers, Melton, Musters, Nevile, Ruddington, Soar Valley, Stanford, Tollerton, Trent, Trent Bridge, Wiverton, Wolds.
Sherwood (county constituency)	*The District of Ashfield wards:* Hucknall Central, Hucknall East, Hucknall North, Hucknall West. *The Borough of Gedling wards:* Bestwood Village, Calverton, Lambley, Newstead, Ravenshead, Woodborough. *The District of Newark and Sherwood wards:* Bilsthorpe, Blidworth, Boughton, Clipstone, Edwinstowe, Farnsfield, Ollerton, Rainworth.
IN OXFORDSHIRE	
Banbury (county constituency)	*The District of Cherwell wards:* Adderbury, Ambrosden and Chesterton, Banbury Calthorpe, Banbury Easington, Banbury Grimsbury and Castle, Banbury Hardwick, Banbury Neithrop, Banbury Ruscote, Bicester East, Bicester North, Bicester South, Bicester Town, Bicester West,Bloxham and Bodicote, Caversfield, Cropredy, Deddington, Fringford, Hook Norton, Launton, Sibford, The Astons and Heyfords, Wroxton.
Henley (county constituency)	*The District of Cherwell wards:* Kirtlington, Otmoor. *The District of South Oxfordshire wards:* Aston Rowant, Benson, Berinsfield, Chalgrove, Chiltern Woods, Chinnor, Crowmarsh, Forest Hill and Holton, Garsington, Goring, Great Milton, Henley North, Henley South, Sandford, Shiplake, Sonning Common, Thame North, Thame South, Watlington, Wheatley, Woodcote.
Oxford East (borough constituency)	*The City of Oxford wards:* Barton and Sandhills, Blackbird Leys, Carfax, Churchill, Cowley, Cowley Marsh, Headington, Headington Hill and Northway, Hinksey Park, Holywell, Iffley Fields, Littlemore, Lye Valley, Marston, Northfield Brook, Quarry and

	Risinghurst, Rose Hill and Iffley, St Clement's, St Mary's.
Oxford West and Abingdon (county constituency)	*The District of Cherwell wards:* Kidlington North, Kidlington South, Yarnton, Gosford and Water Eaton. *The City of Oxford wards:* Jericho and Osney, North, St Margaret's, Summertown, Wolvercote. *The District of Vale of White Horse wards:* Abingdon Abbey and Barton, Abingdon Caldecott, Abingdon Dunmore, Abingdon Fitzharris, Abingdon Northcourt, Abingdon Ock Meadow, Abingdon Peachcroft, Appleton and Cumnor, Kennington and South Hinksey, North Hinksey and Wytham, Radley, Sunningwell and Wootton.
Wantage (county constituency)	*The District of South Oxfordshire wards:* Brightwell, Cholsey and Wallingford South, Didcot All Saints, Didcot Ladygrove, Didcot Northbourne, Didcot Park, Hagbourne, Wallingford North. *The District of Vale of White Horse wards:* Blewbury and Upton, Craven, Drayton, Faringdon and The Coxwells, Greendown, Grove, Hanneys, Harwell, Hendreds, Kingston Bagpuize with Southmoor, Longworth, Marcham and Shippon, Shrivenham, Stanford, Sutton Courtenay and Appleford, Wantage Charlton, Wantage Segsbury.
Witney (county constituency)	*The District of West Oxfordshire wards:* Alvescot and Filkins, Ascott and Shipton, Bampton and Clanfield, Brize Norton and Shilton, Burford, Carterton North East, Carterton North West, Carterton South, Chadlington and Churchill, Charlbury and Finstock, Chipping Norton, Ducklington, Eynsham and Cassington, Freeland and Hanborough, Hailey, Minster Lovell and Leafield, Kingham, Rollright and Enstone, MiltonunderWychwood, North Leigh, Standlake, Aston and Stanton Harcourt, Stonesfield and Tackley, The Bartons, Witney Central, Witney East, Witney North, Witney South, Witney West, Woodstock and Bladon.

IN PORTSMOUTH

Portsmouth North (borough constituency)	*The City of Portsmouth wards:* Baffins, Copnor, Cosham, Drayton and Farlington, Hilsea, Nelson, Paulsgrove.
Portsmouth South (borough constituency)	*The City of Portsmouth wards:* Central Southsea, Charles Dickens, Eastney and Craneswater, Fratton, Milton, St Jude, St Thomas.

IN SHROPSHIRE, AND TELFORD AND WREKIN

Ludlow (county constituency)	*The District of Bridgnorth wards:* Alveley, Bridgnorth Castle, Bridgnorth East, Bridgnorth Morfe, Bridgnorth West, Broseley East, Broseley West, Claverley, Ditton Priors, Glazeley, Harrington, Highley, Morville, Much Wenlock, Stottesdon, Worfield. *The District of South Shropshire wards:* Apedale, Bishop's Castle with Onny Valley, Bitterley with Stoke St Milborough, Bucknell, Burford, Caynham with Ashford, Chirbury, Church Stretton North, Church Stretton South, Clee, Cleobury Mortimer, Clun, Clun Forest, Corve Valley, Kemp Valley, Ludlow Henley, Ludlow St Laurence's, Ludlow St Peter's, Ludlow Sheet with Ludford, Stokesay, Upper Corvedale, Wistanstow with Hopesay, Worthen.
North Shropshire (county constituency)	*The District of North Shropshire wards:* Baschurch, Clive and Myddle, Cockshutt, Dudleston Heath, Ellesmere and Welshampton, Hinstock, Hodnet, Hordley, Tetchill and Lyneal, Market Drayton East, Market Drayton North, Market Drayton South, Prees, Shavington, Shawbury, Sutton, Wem East, Wem Rural, Wem West, Whitchurch North, Whitchurch Rural, Whitchurch South, Whitchurch West, Whixhall, Woore. *The Borough of Oswestry wards:* Cabin Lane, Cambrian, Carreg Llwyd, Castle, Gatacre, Gobowen, Kinnerley, Llanyblodwel and Pant, Maserfield, Ruyton and West Felton, St Martin's, Sweeney and Trefonen, Weston Rhyn, Whittington.
Shrewsbury and Atcham (county constituency)	*The Borough of Shrewsbury and Atcham wards:* Bagley, Battlefield and Heathgates, Bayston Hill, Belle Vue, Bowbrook, Castlefields and Quarry, Column, Condover, Copthorne, Hanwood and Longden, Harlescott, Haughmond and Attingham, Lawley, Meole Brace, Monkmoor, Montford, Pimhill, Porthill, Rea Valley, Rowton, Severn Valley, Sundorne, Sutton and Reabrook, Underdale.
Telford (borough constituency)	*The Borough of Telford and Wrekin wards:* Brookside, Cuckoo Oak, Dawley Magna, Horsehay and Lightmoor, Ironbridge Gorge, Ketley and Oakengates, Lawley and Overdale, Madeley, Malinslee, Priorslee, St Georges, The Nedge, Woodside, Wrockwardine Wood and Trench.
The Wrekin (county constituency)	*The District of Bridgnorth wards:* Albrighton South, Donington and Albrighton North, Shifnal Idsall, Shifnal Manor, Shifnal Rural. *The Borough of Telford and Wrekin wards:*

Apley Castle, Arleston, Church Aston and Lilleshall, College, Donnington, Dothill, Edgmond, Ercall, Ercall Magna, Hadley and Leegomery, Haygate, Muxton, Newport East, Newport North, Newport South, Newport West, Park, Shawbirch, Wrockwardine.

IN SOMERSET

Bridgwater and West Somerset (county constituency)	*The District of Sedgemoor wards:* Bridgwater Bower, Bridgwater Eastover, Bridgwater Hamp, Bridgwater Quantock, Bridgwater Sydenham, Bridgwater Victoria, Cannington and Quantocks, East Poldens, Huntspill and Pawlett, King's Isle, North Petherton, Puriton, Sandford, West Poldens, Woolavington. *The District of West Somerset wards:* Alcombe East, Alcombe West, Aville Vale, Brompton Ralph and Haddon, Carhampton and Withycombe, Crowcombe and Stogumber, Dulverton and Brushford, Dunster, Exmoor, Minehead North, Minehead South, Old Cleeve, Porlock and District, Quantock Vale, Quarme, Watchet, West Quantock, Williton.
[Somerton and Frome (county constituency)	*The District of Mendip wards:* Ammerdown, Beckington and Selwood, Butleigh and Baltonsborough, Coleford and Holcombe, Cranmore, Doulting and Nunney, Creech, Frome Berkley Down, Frome College, Frome Keyford, Frome Market, Frome Oakfield, Frome Park, Postlebury, Rode and Norton St Philip, the Pennards and Ditcheat. *The District of South Somerset wards:* Blackmoor Vale, Bruton, Burrow Hill, Camelot, Cary, Curry Rivel, Islemoor, Langport and Huish, Martock, Milborne Port, Northstone, Tower, Turn Hill, Wessex, Wincanton.]
Taunton Deane (county constituency)	*The Borough of Taunton Deane wards:* Bishop's Hull, Bishop's Lydeard, Blackdown, BradfordonTone, Comeytrowe, Milverton and North Deane, Monument, Neroche, North Curry, Norton Fitzwarren, Ruishton and Creech, Staplegrove, Stoke St Gregory, Taunton Blackbrook and Holway, Taunton Eastgate, Taunton Fairwater, Taunton Halcon, Taunton Killams and Mountfield, Taunton Lyngford, Taunton Manor and Wilton, Taunton Pyrland and Rowbarton, Trull, Wellington East, Wellington North, Wellington Rockwell Green and West, West Monkton, Wiveliscombe and West Deane.
[Wells (county constituency)	*The District of Mendip wards:* Ashwick, Chilcompton and Stratton, Chewton Mendip and Ston Easton, Croscombe and Pilton,

	Glastonbury St Benedict's, Glastonbury St Edmund's, Glastonbury St John's, Glastonbury St Mary's, Moor, Rodney and Westbury, St Cuthbert Out North, Shepton East, Shepton West, Street North, Street South, Street West, Wells Central, Wells St Cuthbert's, Wells St Thomas', Wookey and St Cuthbert Out West. *The District of Sedgemoor wards:* Axbridge, Axe Vale, Berrow, Brent North, Burnham North, Burnham South, Cheddar and Shipham, Highbridge, Knoll, Wedmore and Mark.]
Yeovil (county constituency)	*The District of South Somerset wards:* Blackdown, Brympton, Chard Avishayes, Chard Combe, Chard Crimchard, Chard Holyrood, Chard Jocelyn, Coker, Crewkerne, Eggwood, Hamdon, Ilminster, Ivelchester, Neroche, Parrett, St Michael's, South Petherton, Tatworth and Forton, Windwhistle, Yeovil Central, Yeovil East, Yeovil South, Yeovil West, Yeovil Without.

IN SOUTH GLOUCESTERSHIRE

Filton and Bradley Stoke (county constituency)	*The District of South Gloucestershire wards:* Almondsbury, Bradley Stoke Baileys Court, Bradley Stoke Bowsland, Bradley Stoke Sherbourne, Downend, Filton, Patchway, Pilning and Severn Beach, Staple Hill, Stoke Gifford, Winterbourne.
Kingswood (borough constituency)	*The District of South Gloucestershire wards:* Bitton, Hanham, Kings Chase, Longwell Green, Oldland Common, Parkwall, Rodway, Siston, Woodstock.
Thornbury and Yate (county constituency)	*The District of South Gloucestershire wards:* Alveston, Boyd Valley, Charfield, Chipping Sodbury, Cotswold Edge, Dodington, Frampton Cotterell, Ladden Brook, Severn, Thornbury North, Thornbury South, Westerleigh, Yate Central, Yate North, Yate West.

IN STAFFORDSHIRE AND STOKEONTRENT

Burton (county constituency)	*The Borough of East Staffordshire wards:* Abbey, Anglesey, Branston, Brizlincote, Burton, Churnet, Crown, Eton Park, Heath, Horninglow, Rolleston on Dove, Shobnall, Stapenhill, Stretton, Town, Tutbury and Outwoods, Weaver, Winshill.
Cannock Chase (county constituency)	*The District of Cannock Chase wards:* Brereton and Ravenhill, Cannock East, Cannock North, Cannock South, Cannock West, Etching Hill and The Heath, Hagley, Hawks Green, Heath Hayes East and Wimblebury, Hednesford Green Heath, Hednesford North, Hednesford South, Norton Canes, Rawnsley, Western Springs.
Lichfield (county constituency)	*The Borough of East Staffordshire wards:* Bagots, Needwood, Yoxall.

The District of Lichfield wards:
All Saints, Alrewas and Fradley, Armitage with Handsacre, Boley Park, Boney Hay, Burntwood Central, Chadsmead, Chase Terrace, Chasetown, Colton and Mavesyn Ridware, Curborough, Hammerwich, Highfield, King's Bromley, Leomansley, Longdon, St John's, Stowe, Summerfield, Whittington.

NewcastleunderLyme (borough constituency)	*The Borough of NewcastleunderLyme wards:* Audley and Bignall End, Bradwell, Chesterton, Clayton, Cross Heath, Halmerend, Holditch, Keele, Knutton and Silverdale, May Bank, Porthill, Seabridge, Silverdale and Parksite, Thistleberry, Town, Westlands, Wolstanton.
South Staffordshire (county constituency)	*The District of South Staffordshire wards:* Bilbrook, Brewood and Coven, Cheslyn Hay North and Saredon, Cheslyn Hay South, Codsall North, Codsall South, Essington, Featherstone and Shareshill, Great Wyrley Landywood, Great Wyrley Town, Himley and Swindon, Huntington and Hatherton, Kinver, Pattingham and Patshull, Perton Dippons, Perton East, Perton Lakeside, Trysull and Seisdon, Wombourne North and Lower Penn, Wombourne South East, Wombourne South West.
Stafford (county constituency)	*The District of South Staffordshire wards:* Penkridge North East and Acton Trussell, Penkridge South East, Penkridge West, Wheaton Aston, Bishopswood and Lapley. *The Borough of Stafford wards:* Baswich, Common, Coton, Forebridge, Haywood and Hixon, Highfields and Western Downs, Holmcroft, Littleworth, Manor, Milford, Penkside, Rowley, Seighford, Tillington, Weeping Cross.
Staffordshire Moorlands (county constituency)	*The Borough of NewcastleunderLyme ward:* Newchapel. *The District of Staffordshire Moorlands wards:* Alton, Bagnall and Stanley, Biddulph East, Biddulph Moor, Biddulph North, Biddulph South, Biddulph West, Brown Edge and Endon, Caverswall, Cellarhead, Cheddleton, Churnet, Dane, Hamps Valley, Horton, Ipstones, Leek East, Leek North, Leek South, Leek West, Manifold, Werrington.
StokeonTrent Central (borough constituency)	*The City of StokeonTrent wards:* Abbey Green, Bentilee and Townsend, Berryhill and Hanley East, Hanley West and Shelton, Hartshill and Penkhull, Northwood and Birches Head, Stoke and Trent Vale.
StokeonTrent North (borough constituency)	*The Borough of NewcastleunderLyme wards:* Butt Lane, Kidsgrove, Ravenscliffe, Talke. *The City of StokeonTrent wards:*

	Burslem North, Burslem South, Chell and Packmoor, East Valley, Norton and Bradeley, Tunstall.
StokeonTrent South (borough constituency)	*The City of StokeonTrent wards:* Blurton, Fenton, Longton North, Longton South, Meir Park and Sandon, Trentham and Hanford, Weston and Meir North.
Stone (county constituency)	*The Borough of NewcastleunderLyme wards:* Loggerheads and Whitmore, Madeley. *The Borough of Stafford wards:* Barlaston and Oulton, Chartley, Church Eaton, Eccleshall, Fulford, Gnosall and Woodseaves, Milwich, St Michael's, Stonefield and Christchurch, Swynnerton, Walton. *The District of Staffordshire Moorlands wards:* Cheadle North East, Cheadle South East, Cheadle West, Checkley, Forsbrook.
Tamworth (county constituency)	*The District of Lichfield wards:* Bourne Vale, Fazeley, Little Aston, Mease and Tame, Shenstone, Stonnall. *The Borough of Tamworth wards:* Amington, Belgrave, Bolehall, Castle, Glascote, Mercian, Spital, Stonydelph, Trinity, Wilnecote.

IN STOCKTONONTEES

Stockton North (borough constituency)	*The Borough of StocktononTees wards:* Billingham Central, Billingham East, Billingham North, Billingham South, Billingham West, Hardwick, Newtown, Northern Parishes, Norton North, Norton South, Norton West, Roseworth, Stockton Town Centre, Western Parishes,
Stockton South (borough constituency)	*The Borough of StocktononTees wards:* Bishopsgarth and Elm Tree, Eaglescliffe, Fairfield, Grangefield, Hartburn, Ingleby Barwick East, Ingleby Barwick West, Mandale and Victoria, Parkfield and Oxbridge, Stainsby Hill, Village, Yarm.

IN SUFFOLK

Bury St Edmunds (county constituency)	*The District of Mid Suffolk wards:* Bacton and Old Newton, Badwell Ash, Elmswell and Norton, Gislingham, Haughley and Wetherden, Needham Market, Onehouse, Rattlesden, Rickinghall and Walsham, Ringshall, Stowmarket Central, Stowmarket North, Stowmarket South, Stowupland, Thurston and Hessett, Woolpit. *The Borough of St Edmundsbury wards:* Abbeygate, Eastgate, Fornham, Great Barton, Horringer and Whelnetham, Minden, Moreton Hall, Northgate, Pakenham, Risbygate, Rougham, St Olaves, Southgate, Westgate.
Central Suffolk and North Ipswich (county constituency)	*The Borough of Ipswich wards:* Castle Hill, Whitehouse, Whitton. *The District of Mid Suffolk wards:*

	Barking and Somersham, Bramford and Blakenham, Claydon and Barham, Debenham, Eye, Fressingfield, Helmingham and Coddenham, Hoxne, Mendlesham, Palgrave, Stradbroke and Laxfield, The Stonhams, Wetheringsett, Worlingworth. *The District of Suffolk Coastal wards:* Earl Soham, Framlingham, Grundisburgh, Hacheston, Kesgrave East, Kesgrave West, Otley, Rushmere St Andrew, Wickham Market, Witnesham.
Ipswich (borough constituency)	*The Borough of Ipswich wards:* Alexandra, Bixley, Bridge, Gainsborough, Gipping, Holywells, Priory Heath, Rushmere, St John's, St Margaret's, Sprites, Stoke Park, Westgate.
South Suffolk (county constituency)	*The District of Babergh wards:* Alton, Berners, Boxford, Brett Vale, Brook, Bures St Mary, Chadacre, Dodnash, Glemsford and Stanstead, Great Cornard North, Great Cornard South, Hadleigh North, Hadleigh South, Holbrook, Lavenham, Leavenheath, Long Melford, Lower Brett, Mid Samford, Nayland, North Cosford, Pinewood, South Cosford, Sudbury East, Sudbury North, Sudbury South, Waldingfield. *The Borough of St Edmundsbury wards:* Cavendish, Clare.
Suffolk Coastal (county constituency)	*The District of Suffolk Coastal wards:* Aldeburgh, Farlingaye, Felixstowe East, Felixstowe North, Felixstowe South, Felixstowe South East, Felixstowe West, Hollesley with Eyke, Kyson, Leiston, Martlesham, Melton and Ufford, Nacton, Orford and Tunstall, Peasenhall, Rendlesham, Riverside, Saxmundham, Seckford, Snape, Sutton, Trimleys with Kirton, Walberswick and Wenhaston, Yoxford. *The District of Waveney wards:* Blything, Halesworth, Southwold and Reydon, Wrentham.
Waveney (county constituency)	*The District of Waveney wards:* Beccles North, Beccles South, Bungay, Carlton, Carlton Colville, Gunton and Corton, Harbour, Kessingland, Kirkley, Lothingland, Normanston, Oulton, Oulton Broad, Pakefield, St Margaret's, The Saints, Wainford, Whitton, Worlingham.
West Suffolk (county constituency)	*The District of Forest Heath wards:* All Saints, Brandon East, Brandon West, Eriswell and The Rows, Exning, Great Heath, Iceni, Lakenheath, Manor, Market, Red Lodge, St Mary's, Severals, South. *The Borough of St Edmundsbury wards:* Bardwell, Barningham, Barrow, Chedburgh,

Haverhill East, Haverhill North, Haverhill South, Haverhill West, Hundon, Ixworth, Kedington, Risby, Stanton, Wickhambrook, Withersfield.

East Surrey (county constituency)	*The Borough of Reigate and Banstead wards:* Horley Central, Horley East, Horley West. *The District of Tandridge wards:* Bletchingley and Nutfield, Burstow, Horne and Outwood, Chaldon, Dormansland and Felcourt, Felbridge, Godstone, Harestone, Limpsfield, Lingfield and Crowhurst, Oxted North and Tandridge, Oxted South, Portley, Queens Park, Tatsfield and Titsey, Valley, Warlingham East and Chelsham and Farleigh, Warlingham West, Westway, Whyteleafe, Woldingham.
Epsom and Ewell (borough constituency)	*The Borough of Epsom and Ewell wards:* Auriol, College, Court, Cuddington, Ewell, Ewell Court, Nonsuch, Ruxley, Stamford, Stoneleigh, Town, West Ewell, Woodcote. *The District of Mole Valley wards:* Ashtead Common, Ashtead Park, Ashtead Village. *The Borough of Reigate and Banstead wards:* Nork, Tattenhams.
Esher and Walton (borough constituency)	*The Borough of Elmbridge wards:* Claygate, Cobham and Downside, Cobham Fairmile, Esher, Hersham North, Hersham South, Hinchley Wood, Long Ditton, Molesey East, Molesey North, Molesey South, Oxshott and Stoke D'Abernon, Thames Ditton, Walton Ambleside, Walton Central, Walton North, Walton South, Weston Green.
Guildford (county constituency)	*The Borough of Guildford wards:* Burpham, Christchurch, Friary and St Nicolas, Holy Trinity, Merrow, Onslow, Pilgrims, Shalford, Stoke, Stoughton, Westborough, Worplesdon. *The Borough of Waverley wards:* Alfold, Cranleigh Rural and Ellens Green, Blackheath and Wonersh, Cranleigh East, Cranleigh West, Ewhurst, Shamley Green and Cranleigh North.
Mole Valley (county constituency)	*The Borough of Guildford wards:* Clandon and Horsley, Effingham, Lovelace, Send, Tillingbourne. *The District of Mole Valley wards:* Beare Green, Bookham North, Bookham South, Box Hill and Headley, Brockham, Betchworth and Buckland, Capel, Leigh and Newdigate, Charlwood, Dorking North, Dorking South, Fetcham East, Fetcham West, Holmwoods, Leatherhead North, Leatherhead South, Leith Hill, Mickleham, Westhumble and Pixham,

	Okewood, Westcott.
Reigate (borough constituency)	*The Borough of Reigate and Banstead wards:* Banstead Village, Chipstead, Hooley and Woodmansterne, Earlswood and Whitebushes, Kingswood with Burgh Heath, Meadvale and St John's, Merstham, Preston, Redhill East, Redhill West, Reigate Central, Reigate Hill, Salfords and Sidlow, South Park and Woodhatch, Tadworth and Walton.
Runnymede and Weybridge (county constituency)	*The Borough of Elmbridge wards:* Oatlands Park, St George's Hill, Weybridge North, Weybridge South. *The Borough of Runnymede wards:* Addlestone Bourneside, Addlestone North, Chertsey Meads, Chertsey St Ann's, Chertsey South and Row Town, Egham Hythe, Egham Town, Englefield Green East, Englefield Green West, Foxhills, New Haw, Thorpe, Virginia Water, Woodham.
South West Surrey (county constituency)	*The Borough of Waverley wards:* Bramley, Busbridge and Hascombe, Chiddingfold and Dunsfold, Elstead and Thursley, Farnham Bourne, Farnham Castle, Farnham Firgrove, Farnham Hale and Heath End, Farnham Moor Park, Farnham Shortheath and Boundstone, Farnham Upper Hale, Farnham Weybourne and Badshot Lea, Farnham Wrecclesham and Rowledge, Frensham, Dockenfield and Tilford, Godalming Binscombe, Godalming Central and Ockford, Godalming Charterhouse, Godalming Farncombe and Catteshall, Godalming Holloway, Haslemere Critchmere and Shottermill, Haslemere East and Grayswood, Hindhead, Milford, Witley and Hambledon.
Spelthorne (borough constituency)	*The Borough of Spelthorne wards:* Ashford Common, Ashford East, Ashford North and Stanwell South, Ashford Town, Halliford and Sunbury West, Laleham and Shepperton Green, Riverside and Laleham, Shepperton Town, Staines, Staines South, Stanwell North, Sunbury Common, Sunbury East.
Surrey Heath (county constituency)	*The Borough of Guildford wards:* Ash South and Tongham, Ash Vale, Ash Wharf. *The Borough of Surrey Heath wards:* Bagshot, Bisley, Chobham, Frimley, Frimley Green, Heatherside, Lightwater, Mytchett And Deepcut, Old Dean, Parkside, St Michaels, St Pauls, Town, Watchetts, West End, Windlesham.
Woking (county constituency)	*The Borough of Guildford wards:* Normandy, Pirbright. *The Borough of Woking wards:* Brookwood, Byfleet, Goldsworth East,

Goldsworth West, Hermitage and Knaphill South, Horsell East and Woodham, Horsell West, Kingfield and Westfield, Knaphill, Maybury and Sheerwater, Mayford and Sutton Green, Mount Hermon East, Mount Hermon West, Old Woking, Pyrford, St John's and Hook Heath, West Byfleet.

IN SWINDON	
North Swindon (county constituency)	*The Borough of Swindon wards:* Abbey Meads, Blunsdon, Covingham and Nythe, Gorse Hill and Pinehurst, Haydon Wick, Highworth, Moredon, Penhill, St Margaret, St Philip, Western.
South Swindon (county constituency)	*The Borough of Swindon wards:* Central, Dorcan, Eastcott, Freshbrook and Grange Park, Old Town and Lawn, Parks, Ridgeway, Shaw and Nine Elms, Toothill and Westlea, Walcot, Wroughton and Chiseldon.
IN WARRINGTON	
Warrington North (borough constituency)	*The Borough of Warrington wards:* Birchwood, Burtonwood and Winwick, Culcheth, Glazebury and Croft, Fairfield and Howley, Orford, Poplars and Hulme, Poulton North, Poulton South, Rixton and Woolston, Westbrook.
Warrington South (borough constituency)	*The Borough of Warrington wards:* Appleton, Bewsey and Whitecross, Grappenhall and Thelwall, Great Sankey North, Great Sankey South, Hatton, Stretton and Walton, Latchford East, Latchford West, Lymm, Penketh and Cuerdley, Stockton Heath, Whittle Hall.
IN WARWICKSHIRE	
Kenilworth and Southam (county constituency)	*The Borough of Rugby wards:* Dunchurch and Knightlow, Leam Valley, RytononDunsmore. *The District of Stratford on Avon wards:* Burton Dassett, Fenny Compton, Harbury, Kineton, Long Itchington, Southam, Stockton and Napton, Wellesbourne. *The District of Warwick wards:* Abbey, Cubbington, Lapworth, Leek Wootton, Park Hill, Radford Semele, St John's, Stoneleigh.
North Warwickshire (county constituency)	*The Borough of North Warwickshire wards:* Atherstone Central, Atherstone North, Atherstone South and Mancetter, Baddesley and Grendon, Coleshill North, Coleshill South, Curdworth, Dordon, Fillongley, Hurley and Wood End, Kingsbury, Newton Regis and Warton, Polesworth East, Polesworth West, Water Orton. *The Borough of Nuneaton and Bedworth wards:* Bede, Exhall, Heath, Poplar, Slough.
Nuneaton	*The Borough of North Warwickshire wards:*

(county constituency)	Arley and Whitacre, Hartshill. *The Borough of Nuneaton and Bedworth wards:* Abbey, Arbury, Attleborough, Bar Pool, Camp Hill, Galley Common, Kingswood, St Nicolas, Weddington, Wem Brook, Whitestone.
Rugby (county constituency)	*The Borough of Nuneaton and Bedworth ward:* Bulkington. *The Borough of Rugby wards:* Admirals, Avon and Swift, Benn, Bilton, Brownsover North, Brownsover South, Caldecott, Earl Craven and Wolston, Eastlands, Fosse, Hillmorton, Lawford and King's Newnham, New Bilton, Newbold, Overslade, Paddox, Wolvey.
StratfordonAvon (county constituency)	*The District of Stratford on Avon wards:* Alcester, Aston Cantlow, Bardon, Bidford and Salford, Brailes, Claverdon, Ettington, Henley, Kinwarton, Long Compton, Quinton, Sambourne, Shipston, Snitterfield, Stratford Alveston, Stratford Avenue and New Town, Stratford Guild and Hathaway, Stratford Mount Pleasant, Studley, Tanworth, Tredington, Vale of the Red Horse, Welford.
Warwick and Leamington (borough constituency)	*The District of Warwick wards:* Bishop's Tachbrook, Brunswick, Budbrooke, Clarendon, Crown, Manor, Milverton, Warwick North, Warwick South, Warwick West, Whitnash, Willes.
IN WEST SUSSEX	
Arundel and South Downs (county constituency)	*The District of Arun wards:* Angmering, Arundel, Barnham, Findon, Walberton. *The District of Chichester wards:* Bury, Petworth, Wisborough Green. *The District of Horsham wards:* Bramber, Upper Beeding and Woodmancote, Chanctonbury, Chantry, Cowfold, Shermanbury and West Grinstead, Henfield, Pulborough and Coldwatham, Steyning. *The District of Mid Sussex wards:* Hassocks, Hurstpierpoint and Downs.
Bognor Regis and Littlehampton (county constituency)	*The District of Arun wards:* Aldwick East, Aldwick West, Beach, Bersted, Brookfield, Felpham East, Felpham West, Ham, Hotham, Marine, MiddletononSea, Orchard, Pagham and Rose Green, Pevensey, River, Wick with Toddington, Yapton.
Chichester (county constituency)	*The District of Chichester wards:* Bosham, Boxgrove, Chichester East, Chichester North, Chichester South, Chichester West, Donnington, Easebourne, East Wittering, Fernhurst, Fishbourne, Funtington, Harting,

	Lavant, Midhurst, North Mundham, Plaistow, Rogate, Selsey North, Selsey South, Sidlesham, Southbourne, Stedham, Tangmere, West Wittering, Westbourne.
Crawley (borough constituency)	*The Borough of Crawley wards:* Bewbush, Broadfield North, Broadfield South, Furnace Green, Gossops Green, Ifield, Langley Green, Maidenbower, Northgate, Pound Hill North, Pound Hill South and Worth, Southgate, Three Bridges, Tilgate, West Green.
East Worthing and Shoreham (county constituency)	*The District of Adur wards:* Buckingham, Churchill, Cokeham, Eastbrook, Hillside, Manor, Marine, Mash Barn, Peverel, St Mary's, St Nicolas, Southlands, Southwick Green, Widewater. *The Borough of Worthing wards:* Broadwater, Gaisford, Offington, Selden.
Horsham (county constituency)	*The District of Horsham wards:* Billingshurst and Shipley, Broadbridge Heath, Denne, Forest, Holbrook East, Holbrook West, Horsham Park, Itchingfield, Slinfold and Warnham, Nuthurst, Roffey North, Roffey South, Rudgwick, Rusper and Colgate, Southwater, Trafalgar. *The District of Mid Sussex wards:* Ardingly and Balcombe, Copthorne and Worth, Crawley Down and Turners Hill.
Mid Sussex (county constituency)	*The District of Mid Sussex wards:* Ashurst Wood, Bolney, Burgess Hill Dunstall, Burgess Hill Franklands, Burgess Hill Leylands, Burgess Hill Meeds, Burgess Hill St Andrews, Burgess Hill Victoria, Cuckfield, East Grinstead Ashplats, East Grinstead Baldwins, East Grinstead Herontye, East Grinstead Imberhorne, East Grinstead Town, Haywards Heath Ashenground, Haywards Heath Bentswood, Haywards Heath Franklands, Haywards Heath Heath, Haywards Heath Lucastes, High Weald, Lindfield.
Worthing West (borough constituency)	*The District of Arun wards:* East Preston with Kingston, Ferring, Rustington East, Rustington West. *The Borough of Worthing wards:* Castle, Central, Durrington, Goring, Heene, Marine, Northbrook, Salvington, Tarring.
IN WILTSHIRE	
Chippenham (county constituency)	*The District of North Wiltshire wards:* Cepen Park, Chippenham Allington, Chippenham Audley, Chippenham Avon, Chippenham Hill Rise, Chippenham London Road, Chippenham Monkton Park, Chippenham Park, Chippenham Pewsham, Chippenham Redland, Chippenham Westcroft/Queens,

	Corsham, Lacock with Neston and Gastard, Pickwick. *The District of West Wiltshire wards:* Atworth and Whitley, BradfordonAvon North, BradfordonAvon South, Holt, Manor Vale, Melksham North, Melksham Spa, Melksham Without, Melksham Woodrow, Paxcroft.
Devizes (county constituency)	*The District of Kennet wards:* Aldbourne, All Cannings, Bedwyn, Bishops Cannings, Bromham and Rowde, Burbage, Cheverell, Collingbourne, Devizes East, Devizes North, Devizes South, Lavingtons, Ludgershall, Marlborough East, Marlborough West, Milton Lilbourne, Netheravon, Ogbourne, Pewsey, Pewsey Vale, Potterne, Ramsbury, Roundway, Seend, Shalbourne, Tidworth, Perham Down and Ludgershall South, Upavon, Urchfont, West Selkley. *The District of Salisbury wards:* Bulford, Durrington.
North Wiltshire (county constituency)	*The District of North Wiltshire wards:* Ashton Keynes and Minety, Box, Bremhill, Brinkworth and The Somerfords, Calne Abberd, Calne Chilvester, Calne Lickhill, Calne Marden, Calne Priestley, Calne Quemerford, Calne Without, Colerne, Cricklade, Hilmarton, Kington Langley, Kington St Michael, Lyneham, Malmesbury, Nettleton, Purton, St Paul Malmesbury Without and Sherston, The Lydiards and Broad Town, Wootton Bassett North, Wootton Bassett South.
Salisbury (county constituency)	*The District of Salisbury wards:* Alderbury and Whiteparish, Amesbury East, Amesbury West, Bemerton, Bishopdown, Chalke Valley, Downton and Redlynch, Ebble, Fisherton and Bemerton Village, Harnham East, Harnham West, Laverstock, Lower Wylye and Woodford Valley, St Edmund and Milford, St Mark and Stratford, St Martin and Milford, St Paul, Till Valley and Wylye, Upper Bourne, Idmiston and Winterbourne, Wilton, Winterslow.
South West Wiltshire (county constituency)	*The District of Salisbury wards:* Donhead, Fonthill and Nadder, Knoyle, Tisbury and Fovant, Western and Mere. *The District of West Wiltshire wards:* Dilton Marsh, Ethandune, Mid Wylye Valley, Shearwater, Southwick and Wingfield, Summerham, Trowbridge Adcroft, Trowbridge College, Trowbridge Drynham, Trowbridge John of Gaunt, Trowbridge Park, Warminster East, Warminster West, Westbury Ham, Westbury Laverton.

IN WORCESTERSHIRE

Bromsgrove (county constituency)	*The District of Bromsgrove wards:* Alvechurch, Beacon, Catshill, Charford, Drakes Cross and Walkers Heath, Furlongs, Hagley, Hillside, Hollywood and Majors Green, Linthurst, Marlbrook, Norton, St Johns, Sidemoor, Slideslow, Stoke Heath, Stoke Prior, Tardebigge, Uffdown, Waseley, Whitford, Woodvale, Wythall South.
Mid Worcestershire (county constituency)	*The District of Wychavon wards:* Badsey, Bengeworth, Bowbrook, Bretforton and Offenham, Broadway and Wickhamford, Dodderhill, Drakes Broughton, Droitwich Central, Droitwich East, Droitwich South East, Droitwich South West, Droitwich West, Evesham North, Evesham South, Fladbury, Great Hampton, Hartlebury, Harvington and Norton, Honeybourne and Pebworth, Little Hampton, Lovett and North Claines, Norton and Whittington, Ombersley, Pinvin, The Littletons, Upton Snodsbury.
Redditch (county constituency)	*The Borough of Redditch wards:* Abbey, Astwood Bank and Feckenham, Batchley, Central, Church Hill, Crabbs Cross, Greenlands, Headless Cross and Oakenshaw, Lodge Park, Matchborough, West, Winyates. *The District of Wychavon ward:* Inkberrow.
West Worcestershire (county constituency)	*The District of Malvern Hills wards:* Alfrick and Leigh, Baldwin, Broadheath, Chase, Dyson Perrins, Hallow, Kempsey, Lindridge, Link, Longdon, Martley, Morton, Pickersleigh, Powick, Priory, Ripple, Teme Valley, Tenbury, Upton and Hanley, Wells, West, Woodbury. *The District of Wychavon wards:* Bredon, Eckington, Elmley Castle and Somerville, Pershore, South Bredon Hill.
Worcester (borough constituency)	*The City of Worcester wards:* Arboretum, Battenhall, Bedwardine, Cathedral, Claines, Gorse Hill, Nunnery, Rainbow Hill, St Clement, St John, St Peter's Parish, St Stephen, Warndon, Warndon Parish North, Warndon Parish South.
Wyre Forest (county constituency)	*The District of Wyre Forest wards:* Aggborough and Spennells, Areley Kings, Bewdley and Arley, Blakedown and Chaddesley, Broadwaters, Cookley, Franche, Greenhill, Habberley and Blakebrook, Lickhill, Mitton, Offmore and Comberton, Oldington and Foley Park, Rock, Sutton Park, Wolverley, Wribbenhall.

IN YORK

York Central (borough constituency)	*The City of York wards:* Acomb, Clifton, Fishergate, Guildhall, Heworth, Holgate, Hull Road, Micklegate, Westfield.

York Outer (county constituency)	*The City of York wards:* Bishopthorpe, Derwent, Dringhouses and Woodthorpe, Fulford, Haxby and Wigginton, Heslington, Heworth Without, Huntington and New Earswick, Osbaldwick, Rural West York, Skelton, Rawcliffe and Clifton Without, Strensall, Wheldrake.

Parliamentary Constituencies (Scotland) Order 2005
(SI 2005/250)

Made 9th February 2005

1(1) This Order may be cited as the Parliamentary Constituencies (Scotland) Order 2005.

(2) Subject to section 4(6) of the Parliamentary Constituencies Act 1986, this Order shall come into force on the day after the day on which it is made.

(3) In this Order
  (a) any reference to a ward is a reference to the ward of the local government area in which that ward is situated; and
  (b) any reference to a local government area is a reference to that area as it existed on 30th November 2004.

2 Scotland shall be divided into the constituencies
  (a) which are named in column 1 of the Schedule to this Order;
  (b) which comprise the areas which are set out in column 2 of that Schedule opposite the name of the constituency; and
  (c) which are designated as being either county constituencies or burgh constituencies according to the name in column 1 of that Schedule.

3 Each electoral registration officer for the constituencies referred to in Article 2 above shall make such rearrangement or adaptation of the registers of parliamentary electors as may be necessary to give effect to this Order.

4 The Parliamentary Constituencies (Scotland) Order 1995 is revoked.

SCHEDULE

Name and Designation	Composition
Aberdeen North Burgh Constituency	**The Aberdeen City Council Wards**
	7 Donmouth
	8 Newhills
	9 Auchmill
	10 Cummings Park
	11 Springhill
	12 Mastrick
	13 Sheddocksley
	14 Summerhill
	15 Hilton
	16 Woodside
	17 St Machar
	18 Seaton
	19 Kittybrewster
	20 Stockethill
	21 Berryden
	22 Sunnybank
	23 Pittodrie
	24 Midstocket
	28 Castlehill

Aberdeen South Burgh Constituency	**The Aberdeen City Council Wards**
	25 Queens Cross
	26 Gilcomston
	27 Langstane
	29 Hazlehead
	30 Peterculter
	31 Murtle
	32 Cults
	33 Seafield
	34 Ashley
	35 Broomhill
	36 Garthdee
	37 Gairn
	38 Duthie
	39 Torry
	40 Tullos Hill
	41 Kincorth West
	42 Nigg
	43 Loirston
Banff and Buchan County Constituency	**The Aberdeenshire Council Wards**
	1 Durn
	2 Banff West and Boyndie
	3 Banff
	4 Aberchirder
	5 Macduff
	6 Gamrie King Edward
	7 Buchan North
	8 Fraserburgh West
	9 Fraserburgh North
	10 Fraserburgh East
	11 Fraserburgh South
	12 Buchan North East
	13 South Buchan
	14 Central Buchan
	15 Lonmay and St Fergus
	16 Mintlaw Old Deer
	17 Mintlaw Longside
	18 Boddam Inverugie
	19 Blackhouse
	20 Buchanhaven
	21 Peterhead Central Roanheads
	22 Clerkhill
	23 Dales Towerhill
	24 Cruden
	25 Turriff West
	26 Turriff East
	27 Upper Ythan
	28 Fyvie Methlick
Gordon County Constituency	**The Aberdeenshire Council Wards**
	29 Tarves
	30 Ythan
	31 Ellon Town

	32 Logie Buchan
	33 Meldrum
	34 UdnySlains
	35 Belhelvie
	36 Insch
	37 Chapel and Gadie
	38 Inverurie North
	39 Inverurie Central
	40 Inverurie South and Port Elphinstone
	41 Kintore and Keithhall
	42 Newmachar and Fintray
	48 Huntly West
	49 Huntly East
	50 Strathbogie
	The Aberdeen City Council Wards
	1 Pitmedden
	2 Bankhead/Stoneywood
	3 Danestone
	4 Jesmond
	5 Oldmachar
	6 Bridge of Don
West Aberdeenshire and Kincardine County Constituency	**The area of the Aberdeenshire Council other than those parts in the Banff and Buchan County Constituency and the Gordon County Constituency**
Angus County Constituency	**The Angus Council Wards**
	1 Kirriemuir West
	2 Kirriemuir East
	3 Brechin West
	4 Brechin North Esk
	5 Westfield and Dean
	6 Forfar West
	7 Forfar Central
	8 Forfar East
	9 Brechin South Esk
	10 Montrose Ferryden
	11 Montrose Central
	12 Montrose West
	13 Montrose Hillside
	14 Forfar South
	15 Letham and Friockheim
	23 Arbirlot and Hospitalfield
	24 Keptie
	25 Arbroath North
	26 Brothock
	27 Hayshead and Lunan
	28 Harbour
	29 Cliffburn
Dundee East Burgh Constituency	**The Angus Council Wards**
	17 Sidlaw East and Ashludie
	18 Monifieth West
	19 Monifieth Central
	20 Carnoustie West
	21 Carnoustie Central

	22 Carnoustie East
	The Dundee City Council Wards
	9 Claverhouse
	10 Whitfield
	11 Longhaugh
	12 Pitkerro
	13 Douglas
	14 Barnhill
	15 Balgillo
	16 Broughty Ferry
	17 West Ferry
	18 Craigiebank
	24 East Port
	25 Baxter Park
Dundee West Burgh Constituency	**The Angus Council Ward** 16 Sidlaw West **and the area of the Dundee City Council other than that part in the Dundee East Burgh Constituency.**
Argyll and Bute County Constituency	**The area of the Argyll and Bute Council**
Ochil and South Perthshire County Constituency	**The Perth and Kinross Council Wards** 11 Comrie 12 Crieff North 13 Crieff South 14 Strathord and Logiealmond 15 Strathalmond 34 Earn 35 Auchterarder Mid Earn 36 Strathallan and Glendevon 37 Auchterarder Craig Rossie 38 Abernethy and Glenfarg 39 Milnathort and North Kinross 40 Kinross Town 41 Kinrossshire **and the area of the Clackmannanshire Council**
Perth and North Perthshire County Constituency	**The area of the Perth and Kinross Council other than that part in the Ochil and South Perthshire County Constituency**
Na hEileanan an Iar County Constituency	**The area of Comhairle nan Eilean Siar**
Berwickshire, Roxburgh and Selkirk County Constituency	**The area of the Scottish Borders Council other than that part in the Dumfriesshire, Clydesdale and Tweeddale County Constituency**
Dumfries and Galloway County Constituency	**The area of the Dumfries and Galloway Council other than that part in the Dumfriesshire, Clydesdale and Tweeddale County Constituency**
Dumfriesshire, Clydesdale and Tweeddale County Constituency	**The Scottish Borders Council Wards** 30 Innerleithen and Walkerburn 31 Peebles and District South 32 Peebles and District East

	33 Peebles and Upper Tweed
	34 West Linton and District
	The Dumfries and Galloway Council Wards
	20 Sanquhar and District
	21 Kirkconnel
	22 Mid Nithsdale
	32 Nithsdale East
	35 Caerlaverock
	36 Hoddom and Kinmount
	37 Annan West
	38 Annan Central
	39 Annan East
	40 Chapelcross
	41 Solway Border
	42 Canonbie and Kirtle
	43 Langholm and Upper Eskdale
	44 Dryfe and Lockerbie East
	45 Lockerbie and Upper Annandale
	46 Lochmaben
	47 Moffat
	The South Lanarkshire Council Wards
	6 Biggar/Symington and Black Mount
	7 Duneaton/Carmichael
	9 Douglas
East Kilbride, Strathaven and Lesmahagow County Constituency	**The South Lanarkshire Council Wards**
	3 Lesmahagow
	4 Blackwood
	14 Long Calderwood
	15 Calderglen
	16 Blacklaw
	17 Morrishall
	18 Maxwellton
	19 East Mains
	20 West Mains
	21 Duncanrig
	22 Westwoodhill
	23 Headhouse
	24 Heatheryknowe
	25 Greenhills
	26 Whitehills
	27 Hairmyres/Crosshouse
	28 Mossneuk/Kittoch
	29 Stewartfield
	30 Lindsay
	31 Avondale North
	32 Avondale South
	55 Stonehouse
Lanark and Hamilton East County Constituency	**The South Lanarkshire Council Wards**
	1 Lanark North
	2 Lanark South
	5 Clyde Valley

	8 Carstairs/Carnwath
	10 Carluke/Whitehill
	11 Carluke/Crawforddyke
	12 Forth
	13 Law/Carluke
	37 Hamilton Centre North
	38 Whitehill
	39 Bothwell South
	40 Uddingston South/Bothwell
	41 Uddingston
	47 Hamilton Centre/Ferniegair
	48 Low Waters
	49 Silvertonhill
	50 Cadzow
	51 Dalserf
	52 Larkhall East
	53 Larkhall West
	54 Larkhall South
Midlothian County Constituency	**The area of the Midlothian Council**
Rutherglen and Hamilton West Burgh Constituency	**The area of the South Lanarkshire Council other than those parts in the Dumfriesshire, Clydesdale and Tweeddale County Constituency, the East Kilbride, Strathaven and Lesmahagow County Constituency and the Lanark and Hamilton East County Constituency**
Ayr, Carrick and Cumnock County Constituency	**The East Ayrshire Council Wards**
	25 Drongan, Stair and Rankinston
	26 Ochiltree, Skares, Netherthird and Craigens
	28 Cumnock West
	29 Cumnock East
	30 Patna and Dalrymple
	31 Dalmellington
	32 New Cumnock
	The South Ayrshire Council Wards
	10 Ayr Newton
	11 Ayr Lochside
	12 Ayr Whitletts
	13 Ayr Craigie
	14 Ayr Central
	15 Ayr Fort
	16 Ayr Old Belmont
	17 Ayr Forehill
	18 Ayr Masonhill
	19 Ayr Belmont
	20 Ayr Doonfoot and Seafield
	21 Ayr Rozelle
	25 Coylton and Minishant
	26 North Carrick and Maybole West
	27 North Carrick and Maybole East
	28 South Carrick
	29 Girvan Ailsa
	30 Girvan Glendoune

Central Ayrshire County Constituency	**The North Ayrshire Council Wards** 1 Irvine West 2 Irvine Townhead 3 Irvine Vineburgh and Woodlands South 4 Irvine North 5 Eglinton and Lawthorn 6 Dreghorn 7 Irvine Landward 8 Bourtreehill 9 Woodlands North and Girdle Toll **and the area of the South Ayrshire Council other than that part in the Ayr, Carrick and Cumnock County Constituency**
Kilmarnock and Loudon County Constituency	**The area of the East Ayrshire Council, other than that part in the Ayr, Carrick and Cumnock County Constituency**
North Ayrshire and Arran County Constituency	**The area of the North Ayrshire Council, other than that part in the Central Ayrshire County Constituency**
Airdrie and Shotts County Constituency	**The North Lanarkshire Council Wards** 16 Newmains 17 Stane 18 Dykehead 20 Benhar 27 Holytown 29 Newarthill 41 Whinhall 42 Academy 43 Airdrie Central 44 Clarkston 45 New Monkland West 46 Plains and Caldercruix 47 North Cairnhill and Coatdyke 48 South East Cairnhill and Gartlea 49 Craigneuk and Petersburn 50 Calderbank 51 Chapelhall 52 Salsburgh
Coatbridge, Chryston and Bellshill Burgh Constituency	**The North Lanarkshire Council Wards** 21 Tannochside 22 Fallside 23 Viewpark 24 Bellshill North 30 Hattonrig 31 Townhead 32 Blairpark 33 North Central and Glenboig 34 Coatbridge Central 35 Sikeside and Carnbroe 36 Bargeddie and Langloan 37 Kirkwood 38 Kirkshaws

	39 Shawhead
	40 Old Monkland
	67 Moodiesburn East and Blackwood West
	68 Moodiesburn West and Gartcosh
	69 Chryston and Auchinloch
	70 Stepps
Cumbernauld, Kilsyth and Kirkintilloch East County Constituency	**The East Dunbartonshire Council Wards**
	11 Hillhead and Broomhill
	12 Rosebank and Waterside
	13 East Harestanes and Twechar
	17 Campsie
	18 Milton
	The North Lanarkshire Council Wards
	53 Kildrum and Park
	54 Seafar and The Village
	55 Balloch East and Ravenswood
	56 Balloch West, Blackwood East and Craigmarloch
	57 Westerwood, Carrickstone and Dullatur
	58 Abronhill South
	59 Abronhill Central and North
	60 Carbrain East
	61 Carbrain West and Greenfaulds
	62 Condorrat Central
	63 Condorrat North and Westfield
	64 Croy, Kilsyth South and Smithstone
	65 Queenzieburn and Kilsyth West
	66 Banton and Kilsyth East
East Dunbartonshire County Constituency	**The area of the East Dunbartonshire Council other than that part in the Cumbernauld, Kilsyth and Kirkintilloch East County Constituency**
Motherwell and Wishaw Burgh Constituency	**The area of the North Lanarkshire Council other than those parts in the Airdrie and Shotts County Constituency, the Coatbridge, Chryston and Bellshill Burgh Constituency and the Cumbernauld, Kilsyth and Kirkintilloch East County Constituency**
Edinburgh East Burgh Constituency	**The City of Edinburgh Council Wards**
	32 Tollcross
	33 Southside
	34 Holyrood
	35 Meadowbank
	36 Mountcastle
	37 Leith Links
	38 Restalrig
	39 Portobello
	40 Milton
	50 Prestonfield
	57 Craigmillar
	58 Duddingston
Edinburgh North and Leith Burgh Constituency	**The City of Edinburgh Council Wards**
	8 Craigleith

	9 Pilton
	10 Granton
	11 Trinity
	12 Newhaven
	16 Dean
	17 Stockbridge
	18 New Town
	19 Broughton
	20 Calton
	21 Harbour
	22 Lorne
Edinburgh South West Burgh Constituency	**The City of Edinburgh Council Wards** 1 Balerno 2 Baberton 25 Parkhead 26 Craiglockhart 28 Moat 29 Shandon 30 Dalry 31 Fountainbridge 41 Murray Burn 42 Sighthill 43 Colinton 44 Firrhill
Edinburgh South Burgh Constituency	**The City of Edinburgh Council Wards** 45 Merchiston 46 North Morningside/Grange 47 Marchmont 48 Sciennes 49 Newington 51 South Morningside 52 Fairmilehead 53 Alnwickhill 54 Kaimes 55 Moredun 56 Gilmerton
Edinburgh West Burgh Constituency	**The City of Edinburgh Council Wards** 3 Dalmeny/Kirkliston 4 Queensferry 5 Cramond 6 Davidson's Mains 7 Muirhouse/Drylaw 13 East Craigs 14 N.E. Corstorphine 15 Murrayfield 23 Gyle 24 S.E. Corstorphine 27 Stenhouse
East Lothian County Constituency	**The area of the East Lothian Council**
East Renfrewshire County	**The area of the East Renfrewshire Council**

Constituency	
Falkirk County Constituency	**The area of the Falkirk Council other than that part in the Linlithgow and East Falkirk County Constituency**
Linlithgow and East Falkirk County Constituency	**The Falkirk Council Wards**
	9 Zetland
	10 Beancross
	11 Inchyra
	12 Dundas/Kerse
	13 Grange and Blackness
	14 Dean
	15 Borrowstoun
	16 Kinneil and Whitecross
	31 Reddingmuirhead, Brightons and Rumford
	32 Avon
	and the West Lothian Council Wards
	1 St Michael's
	2 Kingsfield
	3 Preston
	4 Boghall
	6 Armadale West
	7 Armadale Central
	8 Easton
	9 Newland
	10 Durhamtoun
	20 Polkemmet
	21 Croftmalloch
	22 Almond
Livingston County Constituency	**The area of the West Lothian Council other than that part in the Linlithgow and East Falkirk County Constituency**
Dunfermline and West Fife County Constituency	**The Fife Council Wards**
	1 Kincardine, Culross and Low Valleyfield
	2 Blairhall, High Valleyfield and Torryburn
	3 Oakley, Saline and Steelend
	4 Cairneyhill, Carnock and Milesmark
	5 Crossford and Dunfermline Central
	6 Baldridgeburn
	7 Wellwood and Headwell
	8 Townhill and Bellyeoman
	9 Garvock and Carnegie
	10 Halbeath, Hill of Beath and Kingseat
	11 Woodmill
	12 Linburn
	13 Brucefield and Nethertown
	14 Pitcorthie
	15 Limekilns and Pitreavie
	16 Rosyth West
	17 Rosyth East
	18 Inverkeithing West and Rosyth South
	19 Inverkeithing East and North Queensferry
	22 Crossgates and Mossside
Glenrothes County	**The Fife Council Wards**

Constituency	
	37 Cardenden, Cluny and Chapel
	38 Kinglassie, Bowhill and Dundonald
	44 Wemyss and Muiredge
	45 Buckhaven and Denbeath
	46 Methilhill
	47 Methil
	49 Leven West and Kirkland
	50 Kennoway
	51 Windygates, Star and Balgonie
	52 Markinch and Woodside East
	53 Auchmuty and Woodside West
	54 Pitteuchar and Finglassie North
	55 Thornton, Stenton and Finglassie South
	56 Caskieberran and Rimbleton
	57 Newcastle and Tanshall
	58 South Parks and Macedonia
	59 Leslie and Whinnyknowe
	60 Balgeddie and Collydean
	61 Cadham, Pitcoudie and Balfarg
Kirkcaldy and Cowdenbeath County Constituency	**The Fife Council Wards**
	20 Dalgety Bay West and Hillend
	21 Dalgety Bay East
	23 Cowdenbeath Central
	24 Oakfield and Cowdenbeath North
	25 Kelty
	26 Ballingry and Lochore
	27 Crosshill and Lochgelly North
	28 Lumphinnans and Lochgelly South
	29 Aberdour and Burntisland West
	30 Auchtertool and Burntisland East
	31 Kinghorn and Invertiel
	32 Linktown and Kirkcaldy Central
	33 Raith and Longbraes
	34 Bennochy and Valley
	35 Templehall East
	36 Templehall West
	39 Dunnikier
	40 Hayfield and Balsusney
	41 Smeaton and Overton
	42 Glebe Park, Pathhead and Sinclairtown
	43 Dysart and Gallatown
North East Fife County Constituency	**The area of the Fife Council other than those parts in the Dunfermline and West Fife County Constituency, the Glenrothes County Constituency and the Kirkcaldy and Cowdenbeath County Constituency**
Glasgow Central Burgh Constituency	**The Glasgow City Council Wards**
	16 Kelvingrove
	17 Anderston
	27 Merchant City
	34 Calton
	35 Bridgeton/Dalmarnock

	54 Kingston 65 Pollokshields East 66 Hutchesontown 67 Govanhill 68 Strathbungo 75 Toryglen
Glasgow East Burgh Constituency	**The Glasgow City Council Wards** 36 Parkhead 40 Queenslie 41 Greenfield 42 Barlanark 43 Shettleston 44 Tollcross Park 45 Braidfauld 46 Mount Vernon 47 Baillieston 48 Garrowhill 49 Garthamlock 50 Easterhouse
Glasgow North East Burgh Constituency	**The Glasgow City Council Wards** 23 Milton 24 Ashfield 26 Keppochhill 28 Royston 29 Cowlairs 30 Springburn 31 Wallacewell 32 Milnbank 33 Dennistoun 37 Carntyne 38 Robroyston 39 Gartcraig
Glasgow North West Burgh Constituency	**The Glasgow City Council Wards** 1 Drumry 2 Summerhill 3 Blairdardie 4 Knightswood Park 5 Knightswood South 6 Yoker 7 Anniesland 8 Jordanhill 10 Scotstoun 11 Victoria Park 12 Hayburn
Glasgow North Burgh Constituency	**The Glasgow City Council Wards** 9 Kelvindale 13 Hyndland 14 Hillhead 15 Partick 18 Woodlands

	19 North Kelvin
	20 Wyndford
	21 Maryhill
	22 Summerston
	25 Firhill
Glasgow South West Burgh Constituency	**The Glasgow City Council Wards**
	51 Drumoyne
	52 Govan
	53 Ibrox
	55 Mosspark
	56 North Cardonald
	57 Penilee
	58 Cardonald
	59 Pollok
	60 Crookston
	61 Nitshill
	62 Darnley
Glasgow South Burgh Constituency	**The Glasgow City Council Wards**
	63 Carnwadric
	64 Maxwell Park
	69 Battlefield
	70 Langside
	71 Pollokshaws
	72 Newlands
	73 Cathcart
	74 Mount Florida
	76 King's Park
	77 Castlemilk
	78 Carmunnock
	79 Glenwood
Caithness, Sutherland and Easter Ross County Constituency	**The Highland Council Wards**
	1 Caithness North West
	2 Thurso West
	3 Thurso Central
	4 Thurso East
	5 Caithness Central
	6 Caithness North East
	7 Wick
	8 Wick West
	9 Pulteneytown
	10 Caithness South East
	11 Sutherland North West
	12 Tongue and Farr
	13 Sutherland Central
	14 Golspie and Rogart
	15 Brora
	16 Dornoch Firth
	18 Alness and Ardross
	19 Tain West
	20 Tain East

	21 Seaboard
	22 Invergordon
	23 Rosskeen and Saltburn
	26 Ferindonald
Inverness, Nairn, Badenoch and Strathspey County Constituency	**The Highland Council Wards**
	42 Kirkhill
	43 Scorguie
	44 Muirtown
	45 Merkinch
	46 Inverness Central
	47 Culloden
	48 Ardersier, Croy and Petty
	49 Loch Ness West
	50 Inverness West
	51 Canal
	52 Ballifeary
	53 Lochardil
	54 Hilton
	55 Milton
	56 Crown
	57 Raigmore
	58 Loch Ness East
	59 Culduthel
	60 Inshes
	61 Drumossie
	62 Westhill and Smithton
	63 Balloch
	64 Nairn Alltan
	65 Nairn Ninian
	66 Nairn Cawdor
	67 Nairn Auldearn
	68 Badenoch West
	69 Badenoch East
	70 Strathspey South
	71 Strathspey North East
	72 Grantown on Spey
Ross, Skye and Lochaber County Constituency	**The area of the Highland Council other than those parts in the Caithness, Sutherland and Easter Ross County Constituency and the Inverness, Nairn, Badenoch and Strathspey County Constituency**
Inverclyde County Constituency	**The area of the Inverclyde Council**
Moray County Constituency	**The area of the Moray Council**
Orkney and Shetland County Constituency	**The areas of the Orkney Islands Council and the Shetland Islands Council**
Paisley and Renfrewshire North County Constituency	**The Renfrewshire Council Wards**
	1 Shortroods
	3 Ferguslie
	4 Linwood East
	5 Linwood West
	18 Gallowhill and Whitehaugh

	19 Sandyford
	20 Ralston
	26 Blythswood
	27 Deanside
	28 Townhead
	29 Arkleston and Newmains
	30 Moorpark
	32 Bridge of Weir South and Brookfield
	34 Bridge of Weir North and Craigends
	35 Houston and Langbank
	36 Erskine S E and Inchinnan
	37 Parkmains
	38 Erskine Central
	39 Erskine West
	40 Bishopton
Paisley and Renfrewshire South County Constituency	**The area of the Renfrewshire Council other than that part in the Paisley and Renfrewshire North County Constituency**
Stirling County Constituency	**The area of the Stirling Council**
West Dunbartonshire County Constituency	**The area of the West Dunbartonshire Council**

Parliamentary Constituencies (Northern Ireland) Order 2008 (SI 2008/1486)

Made 11th June 2008

Citation and commencement

1   This Order may be cited as the Parliamentary Constituencies (Northern Ireland) Order 2008 and shall come into force on the fourteenth day after the day on which it is made.

Parliamentary Constituencies in Northern Ireland

2(1)   For all the constituencies in Northern Ireland there shall be substituted the constituencies which

    (a)   are named in the left-hand column of the Schedule to this Order;

    (b)   are designated in that column as either county constituencies or borough constituencies; and

    (c)   comprise the areas set out in the right-hand column of that Schedule.

(2)   The areas set out in the right-hand column of the Schedule to this Order are local government areas as they existed on 14th September 2007.

(3)   The Chief Electoral Officer for Northern Ireland shall make such rearrangement or adaptation of the register of parliamentary electors as may be necessary to give effect to this Order.

SCHEDULE
NAMES, DESIGNATION AND COMPOSITION OF CONSTITUENCIES IN NORTHERN IRELAND

Name and designation	Composition
Belfast East (borough constituency)	(i) The following wards of Belfast local government district: Ballyhackamore, Ballymacarrett, Belmont, Bloomfield, Cherryvalley, Island, Knock, Orangefield, Stormont, Sydenham and The Mount; and (ii) the following wards of Castlereagh local government district: Ballyhanwood, Carrowreagh, Cregagh, Downshire, Dundonald, Enler, Gilnahirk, Graham's Bridge, Lisnasharragh, Lower Braniel, Tullycarnet and Upper Braniel.
Belfast North (borough constituency)	(i) The following wards of Belfast local government district: Ardoyne, Ballysillan, Bellevue, Castleview, Cavehill, Chichester Park, Cliftonville, Crumlin, Duncairn, Fortwilliam, Legoniel, New Lodge, Water Works and Woodvale; and (ii) the following wards of Newtownabbey local government district: Abbey, Ballyhenry, Cloughfern, Collinbridge, Coole, Dunanney, Glebe, Glengormley, Hightown, Valley and Whitehouse.
Belfast South (borough constituency)	(i) The following wards of Belfast local government district: Ballynafeigh, Blackstaff, Botanic, Finaghy, Malone,

	Musgrave, Ravenhill, Rosetta, Shaftesbury, Stranmillis, Upper Malone, Windsor and Woodstock; and (ii) the following wards of Castlereagh local government district: Beechill, Cairnshill, Carryduff East, Carryduff West, Galwally, Hillfoot, Knockbracken, Minnowburn, Newtownbreda and Wynchurch.
Belfast West (borough constituency)	(i) The following wards of Belfast local government district: Andersonstown, Beechmount, Clonard, Falls, Falls Park, Glencairn, Glencolin, Glen Road, Highfield, Ladybrook, Shankill, Upper Springfield and Whiterock; (ii) the following wards of Lisburn City local government district: Collin Glen, Dunmurry, Kilwee, Poleglass, and Twinbrook; and (iii) in Lisburn City local government district, that part of Derryaghy ward lying to the north of the Derryaghy and Lagmore townland boundary.
East Antrim (county constituency)	(i) The local government district of Carrickfergus; (ii) the local government district of Larne; (iii) the following wards of Moyle local government district: Glenaan, Glenariff and Glendun; and (iv) the following wards of Newtownabbey local government district: Jordanstown, Monkstown and Rostulla.
East Londonderry (county constituency)	(i) The local government district of Coleraine; (ii) the following wards of Derry local government district: Banagher and Claudy; and (iii) the local government district of Limavady.
Fermanagh and South Tyrone (county constituency)	(i) The following wards of Dungannon and South Tyrone Borough local government district: Augher, Aughnacloy, Ballygawley, Ballysaggart, Benburb, Caledon, Castlecaulfield, Clogher, Coolhill, Drumglass, Fivemiletown, Killyman, Killymeal, Moy, Moygashel and Mullaghmore; and (ii) the local government district of Fermanagh.
Foyle (county constituency)	The following wards of Derry local government district: Altnagelvin, Ballynashallog, Beechwood, Brandywell, Carn Hill, Caw, Clondermot, Creggan

	Central, Creggan South, Crevagh, Culmore, Ebrington, Eglinton, Enagh, Foyle Springs, Holly Mount, Kilfennan, Lisnagelvin, New Buildings, Pennyburn, Rosemount, Shantallow East, Shantallow West, Springtown, Strand, The Diamond, Victoria and Westland.
Lagan Valley (county constituency)	(i) The following wards of Banbridge local government district: Dromore North, Dromore South, Gransha and Quilly; (ii) the following wards of Lisburn City local government district: Ballinderry, Ballymacash, Ballymacbrennan, Ballymacoss, Blaris, Dromara, Drumbo, Harmony Hill, Hilden, Hillhall, Hillsborough, Knockmore, Lagan Valley, Lambeg, Lisnagarvey, Maghaberry, Magheralave, Maze, Moira, Old Warren, Seymour Hill, Tonagh and Wallace Park; and (iii) in Lisburn City local government district, that part of Derryaghy ward lying to the south and east of the Derryaghy and Lagmore townland boundary.
Mid Ulster (county constituency)	(i) The local government district of Cookstown; (ii) the following wards of Dungannon and South Tyrone Borough local government district: Altmore, Coalisland North, Coalisland South, Coalisland West and Newmills, Donaghmore and Washing Bay; and (iii) the local government district of Magherafelt.
Newry and Armagh (county constituency)	(i) The local government district of Armagh City and District; and (ii) the following wards of Newry and Mourne local government district: Ballybot, Bessbrook, Camlough, Creggan, Crossmaglen, Daisy Hill, Derrymore, Drumalane, Drumgullion, Fathom, Forkhill, Newtownhamilton, St Mary's, St Patrick's, Silver Bridge, Tullyhappy and Windsor Hill.
North Antrim (county constituency)	(i) The local government district of Ballymena; (ii) the local government district of Ballymoney; and (iii) the following wards of Moyle local government district: Armoy, Ballylough, Bushmills, Bonamargy and Rathlin, Carnmoon, Dalriada, Dunseverick,

	Glenshesk, Glentaisie, Kinbane, Knocklayd, MossSide and Moyarget.
North Down (county constituency)	(i) The following wards of Ards local government district: Donaghadee North, Donaghadee South and Millisle; and (ii) the local government district of North Down.
South Antrim (county constituency)	(i) The local government district of Antrim; (ii) the following ward of Lisburn City local government district: Glenavy; and (iii) the following wards of Newtownabbey local government district: Ballyclare North, Ballyclare South, Ballyduff, Ballynure, Ballyrobert, Burnthill, Carnmoney, Doagh, Hawthorne, Mallusk and Mossley.
South Down (county constituency)	(i) The following wards of Banbridge local government district: Ballyward, Bannside, Katesbridge and Rathfriland; (ii) the following wards of Down local government district: Ardglass, Audley's Acre, Ballymote, Castlewellan, Cathedral, Crossgar, Donard, Drumaness, Dundrum, Dunmore, Killough, Murlough, Quoile, Seaforde, Shimna, Strangford and Tollymore; and (iii) the following wards of Newry and Mourne local government district: Annalong, Binnian, Burren and Kilbroney, Clonallan, Derryleckagh, Donaghmore, Kilkeel Central, Kilkeel South, Lisnacree, Mayobridge, Rostrevor, Seaview and Spelga.
Strangford (county constituency)	(i) The following wards of Ards local government district: Ballygowan, Ballyrainey, Ballywalter, Bradshaw's Brae, Carrowdore, Central, Comber East, Comber North, Comber West, Glen, Gregstown, Killinchy, Kircubbin, Lisbane, Loughries, Movilla, Portaferry, Portavogie, Scrabo and Whitespots; (ii) the following ward of Castlereagh local government district: Moneyreagh; and (iii) the following wards of Down local government district: Ballymaglave, Ballynahinch East, Derryboy, Killyleagh, Kilmore and Saintfield.
Upper Bann (county constituency)	(i) The following wards of Banbridge local government district: Ballydown, Banbridge West, Edenderry, Fort, Gilford, Lawrencetown, Loughbrickland, Seapatrick, The Cut; and

	(ii) the local government district of Craigavon.
West Tyrone (county constituency)	(i) The local government district of Omagh; and
	(ii) the local government district of Strabane.

Parliamentary Constituencies and Assembly Electoral Regions (Wales) Order 2006 (SI 2006/1041)

Made 11th April 2006

Citation, commencement and interpretation

1(1)   This Order may be cited as the Parliamentary Constituencies and Assembly Electoral Regions (Wales) Order 2006.

(2)   Subject to section 4(6) of the Parliamentary Constituencies Act 1986 and paragraph 9(2) of Schedule 1 to the Government of Wales Act 1998, this Order shall come into force on the fourteenth day after the day on which it is made.

(3)   In this Order
   (a)   any reference to an electoral division is a reference to the electoral division of the local government area in which that electoral division is situated;
   (b)   subject to paragraph (4), any reference to a local government area is a reference to that area as it existed on 1st April 2005; and
   (c)   "the Assembly" means the Assembly for Wales which was established by section 1 of the Government of Wales Act 1998 and which is known as the National Assembly for Wales or Cynulliad Cenedlaethol Cymru.

(4)   Any reference in this Order to an electoral division or a local government area, where it relates to an Assembly constituency (as referred to in article 2A), is a reference to that division or area as it existed on 1st December 2010.

Parliamentary constituencies in Wales

2   Wales shall be divided into the parliamentary constituencies
   (a)   which are named in column 1 of Schedule 1 to this Order;
   (b)   which comprise the areas which are set out in column 2 of that Schedule opposite the name of the constituency; and
   (c)   which are designated as being either county constituencies or borough constituencies according to the name in column 1 of that Schedule.

Assembly constituencies

2A   For the purposes of Part 1 of the Government of Wales Act 2006 the Assembly constituencies shall be the constituencies
   (a)   which are named in column 1 of Schedule 1 to this Order; and
   (b)   which comprise the areas which are set out in column 2 of that Schedule opposite the name of the constituency.

Assembly electoral regions

3(1)   The Assembly electoral regions shall be the regions
   (a)   which are named in column 1 of Schedule 2 to this Order; and
   (b)   which comprise the areas which are set out in column 2 of that Schedule opposite the name of the Assembly electoral region.

(2)   The areas set out in column 2 of that Schedule are the Assembly constituencies referred to in article 2A and named in column 1 of Schedule 1 to this Order.

Electoral registers

4   Each electoral registration officer for
   (a)   the constituencies referred to in article 2; and

(b) the Assembly electoral regions referred to in article 3

shall make such rearrangement or adaptation of the registers of parliamentary or, as the case may be, local government electors as may be necessary to give effect to this Order.

Revocation

5   The Parliamentary Constituencies (Wales) Order 1995 is revoked.

SCHEDULE 1

NAME, DESIGNATION AND COMPOSITION OF
PARLIAMENTARY CONSTITUENCIES AND ASSEMBLY CONSTITUENCIES IN WALES

IN THE PRESERVED COUNTY OF CLWYD	
Name and Designation	*Composition*
Aberconwy County Constituency	**The Conwy County Borough electoral divisions**
	BetwsyCoed
	Bryn
	Caerhun
	Capelulo
	Conwy
	CraigyDon
	Crwst
	Deganwy
	Eglwysbach
	Gogarth
	Gower
	Llansanffraid
	Marl
	Mostyn
	Pandy
	Pantyrafon/Penmaenan
	Penrhyn
	Pensarn
	Trefriw
	Tudno
	Uwch Conwy
Alyn and Deeside County Constituency	**Flintshire County electoral divisions**
	Aston
	Broughton North East
	Broughton South
	Buckley Bistre East
	Buckley Bistre West
	Buckley Mountain
	Buckley Pentrobin
	Caergwrle
	Connah's Quay Central
	Connah's Quay Golftyn
	Connah's Quay South
	Connah's Quay Wepre
	Ewloe
	Hawarden

	Higher Kinnerton
	Hope
	Llanfynydd
	Mancot
	Penyffordd
	Queensferry
	Saltney Mold Junction
	Saltney Stonebridge
	Sealand
	Shotton East
	Shotton Higher
	Shotton West
	Treuddyn
Clwyd South County Constituency	**Denbighshire County electoral divisions**
	Corwen
	Llandrillo
	Llangollen
	Wrexham County Borough electoral divisions
	Bronington
	Brymbo
	Bryn Cefn
	Cefn
	Dyffryn Ceiriog/Ceiriog Valley
	Chirk North
	Chirk South
	Coedpoeth
	Esclusham
	Gwenfro
	Johnstown
	Llangollen Rural
	Marchwiel
	Minera
	New Broughton
	Overton
	Pant
	Penycae
	Penycae and Ruabon South
	Plas Madoc
	Ponciau
	Ruabon
Clwyd West County Constituency	**Conwy County Borough electoral divisions**
	Abergele Pensarn
	Betws yn Rhos
	Colwyn
	Eirias
	Gele
	Glyn
	Kinmel Bay
	Llanddulas
	Llandrillo yn Rhos
	Llangernyw
	Llansannan
	Llysfaen
	Mochdre

	Pentre Mawr
	Rhiw
	Towyn
	Uwchaled
	Denbighshire County electoral divisions
	Efenechtyd
	LlanarmonynIal/Llandegla
	Llanbedr Dyffryn Clwyd/Llangynhafal
	Llanfair Dyffryn Clwyd/Gwyddelwern
	LlanrhaeadryngNghinmeirch
	Ruthin
Delyn County Constituency	**Flintshire County electoral divisions**
	Argoed
	Bagillt East
	Bagillt West
	Brynford
	Caerwys
	Cilcain
	Ffynnongroyw
	Flint Castle
	Flint Coleshill
	Flint Oakenholt
	Flint Trelawney
	Greenfield
	Gronant
	Gwernaffield
	Gwernymynydd
	Halkyn
	Holywell Central
	Holywell East
	Holywell West
	Leeswood
	Mold Broncoed
	Mold East
	Mold South
	Mold West
	Mostyn
	New Brighton
	Northop
	Northop Hall
	Trelawnyd and Gwaenysgor
	Whitford
Vale of Clwyd County Constituency	**Denbighshire County electoral divisions**
	Bodelwyddan
	Denbigh Central
	Denbigh Lower
	Denbigh Upper/Henllan
	Dyserth
	Llandyrnog
	Prestatyn Central
	Prestatyn East
	Prestatyn Meliden
	Prestatyn North

	Prestatyn South West
	Rhuddlan
	Rhyl East
	Rhyl South
	Rhyl South East
	Rhyl South West
	Rhyl West
	St Asaph East
	St Asaph West
	Trefnant
	Tremeirchion
Wrexham County Constituency	**Wrexham County electoral divisions**
	Acton
	Borras Park
	Brynyffynnon
	Cartrefle
	Erddig
	Garden Village
	Gresford East and West
	Grosvenor
	Gwersyllt East and South
	Gwersyllt North
	Gwersyllt West
	Hermitage
	Holt
	Little Acton
	Llay
	Maesydre
	Marford and Hoseley
	Offa
	Queensway
	Rhosnesni
	Rossett
	Smithfield
	Stansty
	Whitegate
	Wynnstay

IN THE PRESERVED COUNTY OF DYFED	
Name and Designation	*Composition*
Carmarthen East and Dinefwr County Constituency	**Carmarthenshire County electoral divisions**
	Abergwili
	Ammanford
	Betws
	Cenarth
	Cilycwm
	Cynwyl Gaeo
	Garnant
	Glanamman
	Gorslas
	Llanddarog

	Llandeilo
	Llandovery
	Llandybie
	Llanegwad
	Llanfihangel Aberbythych
	LlanfihangelarArth
	Llangadog
	Llangeler
	Llangunnor
	Llangyndeyrn
	Llanybydder
	Manordeilo and Salem
	Penygroes
	Pontamman
	Quarter Bach
	St Ishmael
	Saron
Carmarthen West and South Pembrokeshire County Constituency	**Carmarthenshire County electoral divisions**
	Carmarthen Town North
	Carmarthen Town South
	Carmarthen Town West
	Cynwyl Elfed
	Laugharne Township
	Llanboidy
	Llansteffan
	St Clears
	Trelech
	Whitland
	Pembrokeshire County electoral divisions
	Amroth
	Carew
	East Williamston
	Hundleton
	Kilgetty/Begelly
	Lampeter Velfrey
	Lamphey
	Manorbier
	Martletwy
	Narberth
	Narberth Rural
	Pembroke Dock: Central
	Pembroke Dock: Llanion
	Pembroke Dock: Market
	Pembroke Dock: Pennar
	Pembroke: Monkton
	Pembroke: St Mary North
	Pembroke: St Mary South
	Pembroke: St Michael
	Penally
	Saundersfoot
	Tenby: North
	Tenby: South
Ceredigion County Constituency	**The County of Ceredigion**

Llanelli County Constituency	Carmarthenshire County electoral divisions
	Bigyn
	Burry Port
	Bynea
	Dafen
	Elli
	Felinfoel
	Glanymor
	Glyn
	Hendy
	Hengoed
	Kidwelly
	Llangennech
	Llannon
	Lliedi
	Llwynhendy
	Pembrey
	Pontyberem
	Swiss Valley
	Trimsaran
	Tycroes
	Tyisha
Preseli Pembrokeshire County Constituency	Pembrokeshire County electoral divisions
	Burton
	Camrose
	Cilgerran
	Clydau
	Crymych
	Dinas Cross
	Fishguard North East
	Fishguard North West
	Goodwick
	Haverfordwest: Castle
	Haverfordwest: Garth
	Haverfordwest: Portfield
	Haverfordwest: Prendergast
	Haverfordwest: Priory
	Johnston
	Letterston
	Llangwm
	Llanrhian
	Maenclochog
	Merlin's Bridge
	Milford: Central
	Milford: East
	Milford: Hakin
	Milford: Hubberston
	Milford: North
	Milford: West
	Newport
	Neyland: East
	Neyland: West
	Rudbaxton

	St David's
	St Dogmaels
	St Ishmael's
	Scleddau
	Solva
	The Havens
	Wiston

IN THE PRESERVED COUNTY OF GWENT AND MID GLAMORGAN	
Name and designation	*Composition*
Blaenau Gwent County Constituency	**The County Borough of Blaenau Gwent**
Bridgend County Constituency	**The Bridgend County Borough electoral divisions** Brackla Bryntirion, Laleston and Merthyr Mawr Cefn Glas Coity Cornelly Coychurch Lower Litchard Llangewydd and Brynhyfryd Morfa Newcastle Newton Nottage Oldcastle Pendre Penyfai Porthcawl East Central Porthcawl West Central Pyle Rest Bay
Caerphilly County Constituency	**Caerphilly County Borough electoral divisions** Aber Valley Bargoed Bedwas, Trethomas and Machen Gilfach Hengoed Llanbradach Morgan Jones Nelson Penyrheol St Cattwg St James St Martins Ystrad Mynach
Cynon Valley County Constituency	**Rhondda Cynon Taff County Borough electoral divisions** Aberaman North Aberaman South Abercynon Aberdare East

	Aberdare West/Llwydcoed
	Cilfynydd
	Cwmbach
	Glyncoch
	Hirwaun
	Mountain Ash East
	Mountain Ash West
	Penrhiwceiber
	Penywaun
	Rhigos
	Ynysybwl
Islwyn County Constituency	**Caerphilly County Borough electoral divisions**
	Aberbargoed
	Abercarn
	Argoed
	Blackwood
	Cefn Fforest
	Crosskeys
	Crumlin
	Maesycwmmer
	Newbridge
	Pengam
	Penmaen
	Pontllanfraith
	Risca East
	Risca West
	Ynysddu
Merthyr Tydfil and Rhymney County Constituency	**Merthyr Tydfil County Borough electoral divisions**
	Bedlinog
	Cyfarthfa
	Dowlais
	Gurnos
	Merthyr Vale
	Park
	Penydarren
	Plymouth
	Town
	Treharris
	Vaynor
	Caerphilly County Borough electoral divisions
	Darran Valley
	Moriah
	New Tredegar
	Pontlottyn
	Twyn Carno
Monmouth County Constituency	**Monmouthshire County electoral divisions**
	Caerwent
	Cantref
	Castle
	Croesonen
	Crucorney
	Devauden
	Dixton with Osbaston

	Drybridge
	Goetre Fawr
	Grofield
	Lansdown
	Larkfield
	Llanbadoc
	Llanelly Hill
	Llanfoist Fawr
	Llangybi Fawr
	Llanover
	Llantilio Crossenny
	Llanwenarth Ultra
	Mardy
	Mitchel Troy
	Overmonnow
	Portskewett
	Priory
	Raglan
	St Arvans
	St Christopher's
	St Kingsmark
	St Mary's
	Shirenewton
	Thornwell
	Trellech United
	Usk
	Wyesham
	Torfaen County Borough electoral divisions
	Croesyceiliog North
	Croesyceiliog South
	Llanyrafon North
	Llanyrafon South
Newport East County Constituency	**Newport County Borough electoral divisions**
	Alway
	Beechwood
	Langstone
	Liswerry
	Llanwern
	Ringland
	St Julians
	Victoria
	Monmouthshire County electoral divisions
	Caldicot Castle
	Dewstow
	Green Lane
	Mill
	Rogiet
	Severn
	The Elms
	West End
Newport West County Constituency	**Newport County Borough electoral divisions**
	Alltyryn
	Bettws
	Caerleon

	Gaer
	Graig
	Malpas
	Marshfield
	Pillgwenlly
	Rogerstone
	Shaftesbury
	Stow Hill
	Tredegar Park
Ogmore County Constituency	**Bridgend County Borough electoral divisions**
	Aberkenfig
	Bettws
	Blackmill
	Blaengarw
	Bryncethin
	Bryncoch
	Caerau
	Cefn Cribwr
	Felindre
	Hendre
	Llangeinor
	Llangynwyd
	Maesteg East
	Maesteg West
	Nantymoel
	Ogmore Vale
	Penprysg
	Pontycymmer
	Sarn
	Ynysawdre
	Rhondda Cynon Taff County Borough electoral divisions
	Brynna
	Gilfach Goch
	Llanharan
	Llanharry
Pontypridd County Constituency	**Rhondda Cynon Taff County Borough electoral divisions**
	Beddau
	Church Village
	Graig
	Hawthorn
	Llantrisant Town
	Llantwit Fardre
	Pontyclun
	Pontypridd Town
	Rhondda
	Rhydfelen Central/Ilan
	Taffs Well
	Talbot Green
	Tonteg
	Tonyrefail East
	Tonyrefail West
	Trallwng

	Treforest
	Tynynant
Rhondda County Constituency	**Rhondda Cynon Taff County Borough electoral divisions**
	Cwm Clydach
	Cymmer
	Ferndale
	Llwynypia
	Maerdy
	Pentre
	Penygraig
	Porth
	Tonypandy
	Trealaw
	Treherbert
	Treorchy
	Tylorstown
	Ynyshir
	Ystrad
Torfaen County Constituency	**Torfaen County Borough electoral divisions**
	Abersychan
	Blaenavon
	Brynwern
	Coed Eva
	Cwmyniscoy
	Fairwater
	Greenmeadow
	Llantarnam
	New Inn
	Panteg
	Pontnewydd
	Pontnewynydd
	Pontypool
	St Cadocs and Penygarn
	St Dials
	Snatchwood
	Trevethin
	Two Locks
	Upper Cwmbran
	Wainfelin

IN THE PRESERVED COUNTY OF GWYNEDD	
Name and Designation	*Composition*
Arfon County Constituency	**Gwynedd County electoral divisions**
	Arllechwedd
	Bethel
	Bontnewydd
	Cadnant
	CwmyGlo
	Deiniol
	Deiniolen
	Dewi

	Garth
	Gerlan
	Glyder
	Groeslon
	Hendre
	Hirael
	Llanberis
	Llanllyfni
	Llanrug
	Llanwnda
	Marchog
	Menai (Bangor)
	Menai (Caernarfon)
	Ogwen
	Peblig (Caernarfon)
	Penisarwaun
	Pentir
	Penygroes
	Seiont
	Talysarn
	Tregarth & Mynydd Llandygai
	Waunfawr
	Y Felinheli
Dwyfor Meirionnydd County Constituency	**Gwynedd County electoral divisions**
	Aberdaron
	Aberdovey
	Aberech
	Abermaw
	Abersoch
	Bala
	Botwnnog
	Bowydd & Rhiw
	Brithdir & Llanfachreth/Ganllwyd/Llanelltyd
	Bryncrug/Llanfihangel
	Clynnog
	Corris/Mawddwy
	Criccieth
	Diffwys & Maenofferen
	Dolbenmaen
	Dolgellau North
	Dolgellau South
	Dyffryn Ardudwy
	Efailnewydd/Buan
	Harlech
	Llanaelhaearn
	Llanbedr
	Llanbedrog
	Llandderfel
	Llanengan
	Llangelynin
	Llanuwchllyn
	Llanystumdwy
	Morfa Nefyn

	Nefyn
	Penrhyndeudraeth
	Porthmadog East
	Porthmadog West
	PorthamadogTremadog
	Pwllheli North
	Pwllheli South
	Teigl
	Trawsfynydd
	Tudweiliog
	Tywyn
Ynys Môn County Constituency	**The County of the Isle of Anglesey**

IN THE PRESERVED COUNTY OF POWYS	
Name and Designation	*Composition*
Brecon and Radnorshire County Constituency	**Powys County electoral divisions**
	Abercraf
	Beguildy
	Bronllys
	Builth
	Bwlch
	Crickhowell
	Cwmtwrch
	Disserth and Trecoed
	Felinfâch
	Glasbury
	Gwernyfed
	Hay
	Knighton
	Llanafanfawr
	Llanbadarn Fawr
	Llandrindod East/Llandrindod West
	Llandrindod North
	Llandrindod South
	Llanelwedd
	Llangattock
	Llangors
	Llangunllo
	Llangynidr
	Llanwrtyd Wells
	Llanyre
	Maescar/Llywel
	Nantmel
	Old Radnor
	Presteigne
	Rhayader
	St David Within
	St John
	St Mary
	Talgarth
	TalybontonUsk

	TaweUchaf
	Ynyscedwyn
	Yscir
	Ystradgynlais
Montgomeryshire County Constituency	**Powys County electoral divisions**
	Banwy
	Berriew
	Blaen Hafren
	Caersws
	Churchstoke
	Dolforwyn
	Forden
	Glantwymyn
	Guilsfield
	Kerry
	Llanbrynmair
	Llandinam
	Llandrinio
	Llandysilio
	Llanfair Caereinion
	Llanfihangel
	Llanfyllin
	Llanidloes
	LlanrhaeadrymMochnant
	LlanrhaeadrymMochnant/Llansilin
	Llansantffraid
	Machynlleth
	Meifod
	Montgomery
	Newtown Central
	Newtown East
	Newtown Llanllwchaiarn North
	Newtown Llanllwchaiarn West
	Newtown South
	Rhiwcynon
	Trewern
	Welshpool Castle
	Welshpool Gungrog
	Welshpool Llanerchyddol

IN THE PRESERVED COUNTY OF SOUTH GLAMORGAN	
Name and Designation	*Composition*
Cardiff Central Borough Constituency	**Cardiff County electoral divisions**
	Adamsdown
	Cathays
	Cyncoed
	Pentwyn
	Penylan
	Plasnewydd
Cardiff North Borough Constituency	**Cardiff County electoral divisions**

	Gabalfa
	Heath
	Lisvane
	Llandaff North
	Llanishen
	Pontprennau/Old St Mellons
	Rhiwbina
	Whitchurch and Tongwynlais
Cardiff South and Penarth Borough Constituency	**Cardiff County electoral divisions**
	Butetown
	Grangetown
	Llanrumney
	Rumney
	Splott
	Trowbridge
	The Vale of Glamorgan County Borough electoral divisions
	Cornerswell
	Llandough
	Plymouth
	St Augustine's
	Stanwell
	Sully
Cardiff West Borough Constituency	**Cardiff County electoral divisions**
	Caerau
	Canton
	Creigiau/St Fagans
	Ely
	Fairwater
	Llandaff
	Pentyrch
	Radyr
	Riverside
Vale of Glamorgan County Constituency	**The Vale of Glamorgan County Borough electoral divisions**
	Baruc
	Buttrills
	Cadoc
	Castleland
	Court
	Cowbridge
	Dinas Powys
	Dyfan
	Gibbonsdown
	Illtyd
	Llandow/Ewenny
	Llantwit Major
	PeterstonsuperEly
	Rhoose
	St Athan
	St Bride's Major
	Wenvoe

IN THE PRESERVED COUNTY OF WEST GLAMORGAN	
Name and Designation	*Composition*
Aberavon County Constituency	**Neath Port Talbot County Borough electoral division** Aberavon Baglan Briton Ferry East Briton Ferry West Bryn and Cwmavon Coedffranc Central Coedffranc North Coedffranc West Cymmer Glyncorrwg Gwynfi Margam Port Talbot Sandfields East Sandfields West Taibach
Gower County Constituency	**Swansea County electoral divisions** Bishopston Clydach Fairwood Gorseinon Gower Gowerton Kingsbridge Llangyfelach Lower Loughor Mawr Newton Oystermouth Penclawdd Penllergaer Pennard Penyrheol Pontardulais Upper Loughor West Cross
Neath County Constitutency	**Neath Port Talbot County Borough electoral divisions** Aberdulais Alltwen Blaengwrach Bryncôch North Bryncôch South Cadoxton Cimla Crynant Cwmllynfell Dyffryn

	Glynneath
	Godre'r graig
	GwaunCaeGurwen
	Lower Brynamman
	Neath East
	Neath North
	Neath South
	Onllwyn
	Pelenna
	Pontardawe
	Resolven
	Rhos
	Seven Sisters
	Tonna
	Trebanos
	Ystalyfera
Swansea East Borough Constituency	**Swansea County electoral divisions**
	Bonymaen
	Cwmbwrla
	Landore
	Llansamlet
	Morriston
	Mynyddbach
	Penderry
	St Thomas
Swansea West Borough Constituency	**Swansea County electoral divisions**
	Castle
	Cockett
	Dunvant
	Killay North
	Killay South
	Mayals
	Sketty
	Townhill
	Uplands

SCHEDULE 2

NAME AND COMPOSITION OF ASSEMBLY ELECTORAL REGIONS

Name	Composition
North Wales	Aberconwy County Constituency
	Alyn and Deeside County Constituency
	Arfon County Constituency
	Clwyd South County Constituency
	Clwyd West County Constituency
	Delyn County Constituency
	Vale of Clwyd County Constituency
	Wrexham County Constituency
	Ynys Môn County Constituency
Mid and West Wales	Brecon and Radnorshire County Constituency

	Carmarthen East and Dinefwr County Constituency
	Carmarthen West and South Pembrokeshire County Constituency
	Ceredigion County Constituency
	Dwyfor Meirionnydd County Constituency
	Llanelli County Constituency
	Montgomeryshire County Constituency
	Preseli Pembrokeshire County Constituency
South Wales West	Aberavon County Constituency
	Bridgend County Constituency
	Gower County Constituency
	Neath County Constituency
	Ogmore County Constituency
	Swansea East Borough Constituency
	Swansea West Borough Constituency
South Wales Central	Cardiff Central Borough Constituency
	Cardiff North Borough Constituency
	Cardiff South and Penarth Borough Constituency
	Cardiff West Borough Constituency
	Cynon Valley County Constituency
	Pontypridd County Constituency
	Rhondda County Constituency
	Vale of Glamorgan County Constituency
South Wales East	Blaenau Gwent County Constituency
	Caerphilly County Constituency
	Islwyn County Constituency
	Merthyr Tydfil and Rhymney County Constituency
	Monmouth County Constituency
	Newport East County Constituency
	Newport West County Constituency
	Torfaen County Constituency

Parliamentary Elections (Returning Officers' Charges) Order 2015 (SI 2015/476)

Made 26th February 2015

Citation, commencement, extent and interpretation

1(1) This Order may be cited as the Parliamentary Elections (Returning Officers' Charges) Order 2015 and comes into force on the day after the day on which it is made.

(2) This Order extends to England, Wales and Scotland except articles 3(3), 4(3) and 5(3) which extend to England and Wales only and article 5(o) which extends to Scotland only.

(3) In this Order

"an ordinary election of councillors" means an ordinary election of councillors under section 37(1) of the Representation of the People Act 1983;

"an ordinary election of a mayor" means an ordinary election of a mayor under section 9H of the Local Government Act 2000.

Revocation

2 The Parliamentary Elections (Returning Officers' Charges) Order 2010 is revoked.

Returning officers: overall maximum recoverable amount

3(1) Except in a case described in paragraph (2) or (3), the overall maximum recoverable amount for each constituency is the amount listed in the corresponding entry in column 4 of the table in Schedule 1.

(2) Where, in a constituency listed in the table in Schedule 2, the poll at a parliamentary general election in 2015 is taken together only with the poll at an ordinary election of councillors, the overall maximum recoverable amount for that constituency is the amount listed in the corresponding entry in column 4 of that table.

(3) Where, in a constituency listed in the table in Schedule 3, the poll at a parliamentary general election in 2015 is taken together with the poll at an ordinary election of councillors and also the poll at an ordinary election of a mayor, the overall maximum recoverable amount for that constituency is the amount listed in the corresponding entry in column 4 of that table.

Returning officers: maximum recoverable amount for specified services

4(1) Except in a case described in paragraph (2) or (3), the maximum recoverable amount in respect of specified services for each constituency is the amount listed in the corresponding entry in column 2 of the table in Schedule 1.

(2) Where, in a constituency listed in the table in Schedule 2, the poll at a parliamentary general election in 2015 is taken together only with the poll at an ordinary election of councillors, the maximum recoverable amount in respect of specified services for that constituency is the amount listed in the corresponding entry in column 2 of that table.

(3) Where, in a constituency listed in the table in Schedule 3, the poll at a parliamentary general election in 2015 is taken together with the poll at an ordinary election of councillors and also the poll at an ordinary election of a mayor, the maximum recoverable amount in respect of specified services for that constituency is the amount listed in the corresponding entry in column 2 of that table.

(4) The specified services are

(a) making arrangements for the parliamentary election;

(b) discharging the returning officer's duties at the parliamentary election.

Returning officers: maximum recoverable amount for specified expenses

5(1) Except in a case described in paragraph (2) or (3), the maximum recoverable amount in respect of specified expenses for each constituency is the amount listed in the corresponding entry in column 3 of the table in Schedule 1.

(2) Where, in a constituency listed in the table in Schedule 2, the poll at a parliamentary general election in 2015 is taken together only with the poll at an ordinary election of councillors, the maximum recoverable amount in respect of specified expenses for that constituency is the amount listed in the corresponding entry in column 3 of that table.

(3) Where, in a constituency listed in the table in Schedule 3, the poll at a parliamentary general election in 2015 is taken together with the poll at an ordinary election of councillors and also the poll at an ordinary election of a mayor, the maximum recoverable amount in respect of specified expenses for that constituency is the amount listed in the corresponding entry in column 3 of that table.

(4) The specified expenses are those incurred in
   (a) the appointment and payment of persons to assist the returning officer;
   (b) travel and overnight subsistence for the returning officer and any person appointed to assist the returning officer;
   (c) the costs of the nomination process;
   (d) printing or otherwise producing the ballot papers;
   (e) printing or otherwise producing or purchasing postal vote stationery;
   (f) printing or otherwise producing and arranging for the delivery of poll cards;
   (g) printing or otherwise producing and, where appropriate, publishing notices and any other documents required by any enactment or instrument for or in connection with the parliamentary election;
   (h) renting, heating, lighting, cleaning, adapting or restoring any building or room;
   (i) providing and transporting equipment;
   (j) providing information and communications technology equipment and software and associated costs;
   (k) providing security, including secure storage of ballot boxes, ballot papers and verification documents;
   (l) conducting the verification and the count;
   (m) providing and receiving training;
   (n) providing stationery and meeting postage, telephone, printing, translation and banking costs and the costs of other miscellaneous items;
   (o) in a constituency in Scotland, the supply of copies of the register of electors for use in the conduct of the parliamentary election.

Overall maximum recoverable amount at an uncontested parliamentary election

6 At an uncontested parliamentary election
   (a) articles 3 to 5 do not apply; and
   (b) the overall maximum recoverable amount for each constituency is £1,750.

SCHEDULE 1

**OVERALL MAXIMUM RECOVERABLE AMOUNTS AND MAXIMUM RECOVERABLE AMOUNTS
FOR SPECIFIED SERVICES AND SPECIFIED EXPENSES FOR EACH
CONSTITUENCY WHERE A PARLIAMENTARY ELECTION IS A STANDALONE POLL**

Not reproduced

SCHEDULES 2 AND 3

Schedules 2 and 3 relate only to the 2015 General Election, and are not reproduced

Parliamentary Elections (Returning Officer's Charges) (Northern Ireland) Order 2015 (SI 2015/885)

Made 20th March 2015

Citation, commencement and extent

1(1)   This Order may be cited as the Parliamentary Elections (Returning Officer's Charges) (Northern Ireland) Order 2015 and it comes into force on the day after the day on which it is made.

(2)   This Order extends to Northern Ireland only.

Overall maximum recoverable amount

2   For the purposes of section 29(3) of the Representation of the People Act 1983 the amount specified as the overall maximum recoverable amount at
   (a)   an uncontested parliamentary election in each constituency is £1,750;
   (b)   a contested parliamentary election in a constituency is the amount specified in respect of that constituency in the table in the Schedule to this Order.

Revocation

3   The Parliamentary Elections (Returning Officer's Charges) (Northern Ireland) Order 2010 is revoked.

SCHEDULE
OVERALL MAXIMUM RECOVERABLE AMOUNT FOR EACH CONSTITUENCY

Constituency	Overall maximum recoverable amount
Belfast East	£196,500
Belfast North	£204,000
Belfast South	£180,000
Belfast West	£178,500
East Antrim	£164,000
East Londonderry	£181,000
Fermanagh and South Tyrone	£198,000
Foyle	£182,500
Lagan Valley	£175,500
Mid Ulster	£181,500
Newry and Armagh	£194,000
North Antrim	£202,500
North Down	£156,000
South Antrim	£170,000
South Down	£188,000
Strangford	£155,500
Upper Bann	£193,000
West Tyrone	£177,500

Parliamentary Writs Order 1983
(SI 1983/605)

Made   20th April 1983

Citation, commencement and extent

1(1)   This Order may be cited as the Parliamentary Writs Order 1983 and shall come into operation forthwith.

(2)   This Order shall not extend to Northern Ireland.

Interpretation

2   In this Order
"appropriate official" means the official referred to in Article 10(1) below;
"elections rules" means the parliamentary elections rules set out in Schedule 1 to the Representation of the People Act 1983;
"parliamentary writs list" means the list prepared and kept in accordance with Article 6 below;
"registered post service" has the same meaning as in the Postal Services Act 2000;
"the relevant universal postal service provider" means the universal service provider (within the meaning of Part 3 of the Postal Services Act 2011) responsible for conveying writs;
"writ" means the writ for a parliamentary election.

Form of notices to Clerk of the Crown

3(1)   A notice given under sub-paragraph (a) of rule 4(1) of the elections rules (by which the returning officer for a constituency in England and Wales requests that the writ shall be conveyed to the acting returning officer) shall be in the form set out in paragraph 1 of the Schedule to this Order (or a form to the like effect).

(2)   A notice revoking the notice prescribed by paragraph (1) above shall be in the form set out in paragraph 2 of the Schedule to this Order (or a form to the like effect).

Duty to notify acting returning officer

4   A returning officer shall forthwith copy any notice he has given under sub-paragraph (a) of rule 4(1) of the elections rules to the appropriate acting returning officer in order that the acting returning officer may comply with Article 5(2) below.

Duty to provide address to the relevant universal postal service provider

5(1)   Every returning officer for a constituency shall
(a)   if requested by the relevant universal postal service provider so to do, or
(b)   on the revocation of any notice given under sub-paragraph (a) of rule 4(1) of the elections rules
provide to the relevant universal postal service provider an address at which the writ may be conveyed to him and, on any change of that address, he shall as soon as possible provide to the relevant universal postal service provider a new address for that purpose.

(2)   Every acting returning officer for a constituency in England and Wales to whom the writ is to be delivered by virtue of a notice given under sub-paragraph (a) of rule 4(1) of the elections rules shall
(a)   on being informed that such a notice has been given, or
(b)   if requested by the relevant universal postal service provider so to do,
provide to the relevant universal postal service provider an address at which the writ

may be conveyed to him and, on any change of that address, he shall as soon as possible provide to the relevant universal postal service provider a new address for that purpose.

Parliamentary writs list

6   The relevant universal postal service provider shall prepare and keep up to date a list (in this Order referred to as the "parliamentary writs list") setting out

    (a) by the title of his office, each returning officer in respect of whom a notice under sub-paragraph (a) of rule 4(1) of the elections rules is not in force, together with, as the address of the office of that officer, the address provided under Article 5(1) above, and

    (b) by the title of his office, each acting returning officer in respect of whom a notice under sub-paragraph (a) of rule 4(1) of the elections rules is in force, together with, as the address of the office of that officer, the address provided under Article 5(2) above.

Appointment of postal officials

    (1) The relevant universal postal service provider shall, in respect of each returning officer or acting returning officer set out in the parliamentary writs list, appoint a postal official as the person responsible for securing the delivery of any writ required under rules 3 and 4 of the elections rules to be conveyed to that officer.

  (2) The designation and address of the officer appointed under paragraph (1) above shall be entered in the parliamentary writs list together with a reference to the officer to whom he is required to secure the delivery of any writ.

Copy of the list or alterations to it

8   The relevant universal postal service provider shall, as soon as practicable after

    (a) a new parliamentary writs list has been prepared, or

    (b) alterations have been made to a parliamentary writs list,

send a copy of the list or, as the case may be, the alterations to the Clerk of the Crown.

Writs to be conveyed by post

9   Writs for parliamentary elections shall be conveyed by sending them through the post in accordance with Articles 10 and 11 below.

Conveyance of writ to appropriate official

10(1) As soon as may be after the issue of the writ for a parliamentary election in a constituency, the Clerk of the Crown shall cause a package containing the writ and other items mentioned in paragraph (2) below to be sent by the registered post service of the relevant universal postal service provider to the postal official appearing from the parliamentary writs list to be charged with the duty of securing the delivery of the writ (in this Order referred to as the "appropriate office").

  (2) The package referred to in paragraph (1) above shall contain, in addition to the writ

    (a) instructions from the relevant universal postal service provider to the appropriate official as to the delivery of the writ; and

    (b) a form of receipt for the writ to be signed by the person to whom it is delivered.

Conveyance of writ by appropriate official

11(1) The appropriate official shall forthwith on receipt of the package referred to in Article 10 above convey the writ, or cause it to be conveyed, to the returning officer or, as the case may be, acting returning officer to whom it is addressed: but delivery of the writ to a person found in and for the time being in charge of the place which is recorded in the parliamentary writs list as being the office of the returning officer or, as the case may be, acting returning officer, shall be as good as delivery to that officer.

(2) The person to whom the writ is delivered in accordance with paragraph (1) above shall sign the receipt referred to in Article 10(2)(b) above and shall hand it to the appropriate official or person acting on his behalf.

(3) The appropriate official shall as soon as practicable send the receipt which has been signed in accordance with paragraph (2) above to the Clerk of the Crown by the registered post service of the relevant universal postal service provider.

Revocation and savings

12(1) *Repealed*

(2) Without prejudice to the interpretation Act 1978, the parliamentary writs list which was prepared under the Order revoked by paragraph (1) above shall continue to have effect as if made under this Order, as shall any notice which was given under that Order and remains in force on the coming into operation of this Order.

SCHEDULE
FORMS

1 Form of notice by returning officer requesting that the writ be conveyed to the acting returning officer.

To the Clerk of the Crown in Chancery

In pursuance of rule 4(1) of the parliamentary elections rules in Schedule 1 to the Representation of the People Act 1983, I hereby request that any writ for a parliamentary election in the constituency of .. .. which is issued one month after the receipt by you of this notice shall be conveyed to the acting returning officer.

Dated this .. .. day of .. .. 19.. .. .. ..

(*Signed*) (Delete whichever is inappropriate)

Sheriff of .. ..

Chairman of the Council of .. ..

Mayor of the London Borough of .. ..

Chairman of the London Borough of .. ..

2 Form of notice by returning officer revoking the notice set out in paragraph 1 above.

To the Clerk of the Crown in Chancery

In pursuance of rule 4(1) of the parliamentary elections rules in Schedule 1 to the Representation of the People Act 1983, I hereby revoke, as respects any writ for a parliamentary election issued one month after the receipt by you of this notice, the notice given on the .. .. day of .. .. 19 .. .. requesting that any writ for a parliamentary election in the constituency of .. .. be conveyed to the acting returning officer.

Dated this .. .. day of .. .. 19.. .. .. ..

(*Signed*) (Delete whichever is inappropriate)

Sheriff of .. ..

Chairman of the Council of .. ..

Mayor of the London Borough of .. ..

Chairman of the London Borough of .. ..

Political Parties, Elections and Referendums (Civil Sanctions) Order 2010 (SI 2010/2860)

Made 29th November 2010

Citation and commencement

1   This Order may be cited as the Political Parties, Elections and Referendums (Civil Sanctions) Order 2010 and comes into force on 1st December 2010.

Interpretation

2   In this Order
"the 2000 Act" means the Political Parties, Elections and Referendums Act 2000;
"compliance notice" means a notice imposing a requirement under paragraph 5(5)(b) of Schedule 19C;
"final notice" means a notice under paragraph 2(4) or 6(5) of Schedule 19C;
"restoration notice" means a notice imposing a requirement under paragraph 5(5)(c) of Schedule 19C; and
"Schedule 19C" means Schedule 19C to the 2000 Act.

Provision made by Schedule 1

3(1)   Part 1 of Schedule 1 makes provision for fixed monetary penalties.

(2)   Part 2 of Schedule 1 makes provision for discretionary requirements.

(3)   Part 3 of Schedule 1 makes provision for stop notices.

(4)   Part 4 of Schedule 1 makes provision for enforcement undertakings.

Prescribed offences and prescribed restrictions and requirements

4(1)   Part 1 of Schedule 2 lists the offences prescribed for the purposes of paragraphs 1(1)(a)[, (2)(a), (3)(a) and (4)(a)] (fixed monetary penalties), 5(1)(a)[, (2)(a), (3)(a) and (4)(a)] (discretionary requirements), 10(2)(b)(i) and (3)(b)(i) (stop notices) and 15(1)(a)(i) (enforcement undertakings) of Schedule 19C.

(2)   Part 2 of Schedule 2 lists the restrictions and requirements prescribed for the purposes of paragraphs 1(1)(b), 5(1)(b), 10(2)(b)(ii) and (3)(b)(ii) and 15(1)(a)(ii) of Schedule 19C.

(3)   Part 3 of Schedule 2 lists the restrictions and requirements prescribed for the purposes of paragraphs 1(2)(b), (3)(b) and (4)(b) (fixed monetary penalties) and 5(2)(b), (3)(b) and (4)(b) (discretionary requirements) of Schedule 19C.

Recovery of payments

5(1)   In England and Wales and Northern Ireland, the Commission may recover a fixed monetary penalty, variable monetary penalty, [non-compliance penalty,] or any interest or other financial penalty for late payment on the order of a court, as if payable under a court order.

(2)   In Scotland, the Commission may recover a fixed monetary penalty, variable monetary penalty, [non-compliance penalty,] or any interest or other financial penalty for late payment as a civil debt.

Non-compliance penalties

6(1)   The amount of a non-compliance penalty must be determined by the Commission having regard to all the circumstances of the case and must not be less than £500 nor more than £20,000.

(2) The notice imposing a non-compliance penalty must include information as to
    (a) the grounds for imposing the non-compliance penalty;
    (b) the amount of the penalty;
    (c) the period within which payment must be made, which must not be less than 28 days beginning with the day on which the notice imposing the penalty is received;
    (d) rights of appeal; and
    (e) the consequences of failure to mak
    e payment within the specified period.

(3) A non-compliance penalty must be paid to the Commission.

(4) If the steps specified in the compliance notice or restoration notice are completed, and a certificate is issued by the Commission under paragraph 6 of Schedule 1, within the period set for payment of the non-compliance penalty the Commission may by notice waive, or reduce the amount of, a non-compliance penalty.

(5) An appeal under paragraph 9(3) of Schedule 19C against a notice imposing a non-compliance penalty must be made within 28 days of the day on which the notice was received.

Withdrawal or variation of notices

7(1) The Commission may by notice in writing at any time withdraw, reduce the monetary amount payable under, or reduce the steps to be taken under, any final notice.

(2) The Commission may by notice in writing at any time withdraw a stop notice (without prejudice to their power to serve another in respect of the activity specified in the withdrawn notice).

Appeals

8(1) Where an appeal under paragraph 13(1) or (2) of Schedule 19C is made, the stop notice is not suspended unless suspended or varied on the order of the county court or (in Scotland) the sheriff.

(2) On an appeal under paragraph 2(6), 6(6), 9(3) or 13(1) of Schedule 19C the county court or (in Scotland) the sheriff may
    (a) withdraw, confirm or vary the requirement or notice;
    (b) take such steps as the Commission could take in relation to the act or omission giving rise to the requirement or notice;
    (c) remit the decision whether to confirm the requirement or notice, or any matter relating to that decision, to the Commission.

(3) On an appeal under paragraph 13(2) of Schedule 19C or paragraph 8 or 16 of Schedule 1 to this Order, the county court or (in Scotland) the sheriff may make an order requiring the Commission to issue a certificate under paragraph 12 of Schedule 19C or, as the case may be, paragraph 6 or 15 of Schedule 1 to this Order.

SCHEDULE 1

Part 1
Fixed Monetary Penalties

Prescribed amount

1 For the purposes of paragraph 1(5) of Schedule 19C (fixed monetary penalty) the amount

prescribed is £200.

Discharge of liability

2 For the purposes of paragraph 2(2) of Schedule 19C (sum by which penalty may be discharged) the sum prescribed is £200.

Appeals

3(1) An appeal under paragraph 2(6) of Schedule 19C against the decision to impose a fixed monetary penalty must be made within 28 days of the day on which the final notice was received.

(2) The penalty is suspended from the day on which the appeal is made.

(3) The suspension has effect until the day on which the appeal is determined or withdrawn.

Late payment

4(1) Subject to sub-paragraphs (4) and (5), the fixed monetary penalty must be paid within 28 days of the day on which the final notice was received.

(2) If the penalty is not paid within that period the amount payable is increased by 25%.

(3) If the penalty (as increased by sub-paragraph (2)) is not paid within 56 days of the day on which the final notice was received, the amount payable is the amount of the fixed monetary penalty originally imposed increased by 50%.

(4) In the case of an appeal, any penalty which falls to be paid, whether because the court upheld the penalty or varied it, or because the appeal was withdrawn, is payable within 28 days of the day of determination or withdrawal of the appeal, and if not paid within that period the amount payable is increased by 25%.

(5) If the penalty (as increased by sub-paragraph (4)) is not paid within 56 days of the day of the determination or withdrawal of the appeal, the amount payable is the amount of the fixed monetary penalty originally imposed increased by 50%.

Part 2

Discretionary Requirements

Variable monetary penalties: maximum amount

5 The maximum amount that the Commission may impose as a variable monetary penalty is £20,000.

Completion

6(1) Where, after the service of a compliance notice or a restoration notice on a person, the Commission are satisfied that the person has taken the steps specified in the notice, they must issue a certificate to that effect.

(2) A compliance notice or a restoration notice ceases to have effect on the issue of a certificate relating to that notice.

(3) A person on whom a compliance notice or a restoration notice has been served may at any time apply for a certificate and the Commission must make a decision whether to issue a certificate within 28 days of the day on which they receive such an application.

(4) An application under sub-paragraph (3) must be accompanied by such information as is reasonably necessary to enable the Commission to determine whether the compliance notice or restoration notice has been complied with.

(5) Where, on an application under sub-paragraph (3), the Commission decide not to issue a certificate they must notify the applicant and provide the applicant with information as to

    (a) the grounds for the decision not to issue a certificate; and

    (b) rights of appeal.

(6) The Commission may revoke a certificate if it was granted on the basis of inaccurate, incomplete or misleading information, and if the Commission revoke a certificate, the compliance notice or restoration notice has effect as if the certificate had not been issued.

Appeals

7(1) An appeal under paragraph 6(6) of Schedule 19C against the decision to impose a discretionary requirement must be made within 28 days of the day on which the final notice was received.

(2) The requirement is suspended from the day on which the appeal is made.

(3) The suspension has effect until the day on which the appeal is determined or withdrawn.

8(1) A person served with a compliance notice or a restoration notice may appeal to a county court or (in Scotland) the sheriff against a decision not to issue a certificate under paragraph 6 on the ground that the decision was

    (a) based on an error of fact;

    (b) wrong in law; or

    (c) unfair or unreasonable.

(2) An appeal must be made within 28 days of the day on which notification of the decision was received.

Late payment

9(1) Subject to sub-paragraphs (4) and (5), the variable monetary penalty must be paid within 28 days of the day on which the final notice was received.

(2) If the penalty is not paid within that period the amount payable is increased by 25%.

(3) If the penalty (as increased by sub-paragraph (2)) is not paid within 56 days of the day on which the final notice was received, the amount payable is the amount of the variable monetary penalty originally imposed increased by 50%.

(4) In the case of an appeal, any penalty which falls to be paid, whether because the court upheld the penalty or varied it, or because the appeal was withdrawn, is payable within 28 days of the day of determination or withdrawal of the appeal, and if it is not paid within that period the amount payable is increased by 25%.

(5) If the penalty (as increased by sub-paragraph (4)) is not paid within 56 days of the day of determination or withdrawal of the appeal the amount payable is the amount of the variable monetary penalty originally imposed increased by 50%.

Part 3
Stop Notices

Completion certificates

10(1) An application for a completion certificate must be accompanied by such information as is reasonably necessary to enable the Commission to determine whether the stop notice has been complied with.

(2) Where, on an application under paragraph 12(3) of Schedule 19C, the Commission decide not to issue a completion certificate they must notify the applicant and provide the applicant with information as to
  (a) the grounds for the decision not to issue a completion certificate; and
  (b) rights of appeal.

11 The Commission may revoke a completion certificate if it was granted on the basis of inaccurate, incomplete or misleading information, and if the Commission revoke a completion certificate, the stop notice has effect as if the certificate had not been issued.

Appeals

12(1) An appeal under paragraph 13(1) of Schedule 19C against the decision to serve a stop notice must be made within 28 days of the day on which the notice was received.

(2) An appeal under paragraph 13(2) of Schedule 19C against a decision not to issue a completion certificate must be made within 28 days of the day on which notification of the decision was received.

Part 4
Enforcement Undertakings

Contents of an enforcement undertaking

13(1) An enforcement undertaking must be in writing and include
  (a) a statement that the undertaking is an enforcement undertaking regulated by the 2000 Act and this Order;
  (b) the terms of the undertaking;
  (c) the period within which the action specified in the undertaking must be completed;
  (d) details of how and when a person is to be considered to have complied with the undertaking; and
  (e) information as to the consequences of failure to comply in full or in part with the undertaking, including reference to the effect of paragraph 15(2) of Schedule 19C.

(2) The enforcement undertaking may be varied or extended if both parties agree.

Publication of enforcement undertakings

14 The Commission may publish any enforcement undertaking which they accept in whatever manner they see fit.

Compliance with an enforcement undertaking

15(1) Where, after accepting an enforcement undertaking from a person, the Commission are satisfied that the undertaking has been complied with in full they must issue a certificate to that effect.

(2) An enforcement undertaking ceases to have effect on the issue of a certificate relating to that undertaking.

(3) A person who has given an enforcement undertaking may at any time apply for a certificate, and the Commission must make a decision whether to issue a certificate within 28 days of the day on which they receive such an application.

(4) An application under sub-paragraph (3) must be accompanied by such information as is reasonably necessary to enable the Commission to determine whether the undertaking has been complied with.

(5) Where, on an application under sub-paragraph (3), the Commission decide not to issue a certificate they must notify the applicant and provide the applicant with information as to

    (a) the grounds for the decision not to issue a certificate; and

    (b) rights of appeal.

(6) The Commission may revoke a certificate if it was granted on the basis of inaccurate, incomplete or misleading information, and if the Commission revoke a certificate, the enforcement undertaking has effect as if the certificate had not been issued.

Appeals

16(1) A person who has given an enforcement undertaking may appeal to a county court or (in Scotland) the sheriff against a decision not to issue a certificate under paragraph 15 on the ground that the decision was

    (a) based on an error of fact;

    (b) wrong in law; or

    (c) unfair or unreasonable.

(2) An appeal must be made within 28 days of the day on which notification of the decision was received.

SCHEDULE 2

PRESCRIBED OFFENCES, RESTRICTIONS AND REQUIREMENTS

Part 1

Prescribed Offences

Provision creating offence	Offence
section 24(8)	registration as treasurer where convicted of certain offences
section 43(7)	failure to deliver statement relating to auditor's resignation etc
section 47(1)(a)	failure to deliver proper statement of accounts
section 47(1)(b)	failure to deliver accounts within time limits
section 54(7)	failure to provide information about donors
section 56(3), (3B) or (4)	failure to return donations
section 65(3)	failure to deliver donation reports to Commission within time limits
section 65(4)	failure to comply with requirements for recording donations in donation report
section 71L(1)	registered party entering into regulated transaction with unauthorised participant
section 71L(2)	treasurer of party entering into regulated transaction with unauthorised participant
section 71L(3)	party liable if treasurer fails to repay money obtained under regulated transaction with unauthorised participant
section 71L(4)	treasurer failing to repay money obtained under regulated transaction with unauthorised participant
section 71L(5)	party benefiting from connected transaction to which

Provision creating offence	Offence
	an unauthorised participant is a party
section 71L(6)	treasurer of registered party which benefits from connected transaction to which an unauthorised participant is a party
section 71L(7)	party liable if treasurer fails to repay benefit obtained in consequence of security given by unauthorised participant
section 71L(8)	treasurer failing to repay benefit obtained in consequence of security given by unauthorised participant
section 71S(4)	failure to deliver transaction reports to Commission within time limits
section 71S(5)	failure to comply with requirements for recording transactions in transaction report
section 74(4)	acceptance by ineligible person of office of deputy treasurer
section 75(2)	incurring campaign expenditure without authority
section 76(4)(a)	making payments in respect of campaign expenditure without authority
section 76(4)(b)	failure to notify treasurer of payments in respect of campaign expenditure
section 77(3)(a)	paying claim in respect of campaign expenditure where failure to comply with procedure
section 77(3)(b)	paying claim in respect of campaign expenditure outside specified time period
section 79(2)	exceeding limits on campaign expenditure
section 82(4)(a)	failure of treasurer to deliver return and auditor's report to Commission
section 82(4)(b)	failure to comply with requirements for returns
section 82(4)(c)	failure of treasurer to deliver return and court order to Commission
section 83(3)(b)	failure to deliver signed declaration with return to Commission
section 90(2)	incurring controlled expenditure without authority
section 91(4)(a)	making payments in respect of controlled expenditure without authority
section 91(4)(b)	failure to notify responsible person of payments in respect of controlled expenditure
section 92(3)(a)	paying claim in respect of controlled expenditure where failure to comply with procedure
section 92(3)(b)	paying claim in respect of controlled expenditure outside specified time period
section 94(2) or (4)	exceeding limits on controlled expenditure
[section 94E(2) or (3)	exceeding limits on targeted controlled expenditure when not authorised]
[section 95C(1)(a)	failure of responsible person to deliver quarterly or weekly report to Commission]
[section 95C(1)(b)	failure to deliver signed declaration with quarterly or weekly report to the Commission]
[section 95C(1)(c)	failure to comply with requirements for quarterly or weekly reports]
section 98(4)(a)	failure of responsible person to deliver return and

Provision creating offence	Offence
	auditor's report to Commission
[section 98(4)(aa)	failure of responsible person to deliver statement of accounts and auditor's report to Commission]
section 98(4)(b)	failure to comply with requirements for returns
[section 98(4)(ba)	failure to comply with requirements for statements of accounts]
section 98(4)(c)	failure to deliver return and court order to Commission
section 99(4)(b)	failure to deliver signed declaration with return to Commission
[section 99A(3)(b)	failure to deliver signed declaration with statement of accounts to Commission]
section 113(2)	incurring referendum expenses without authority
section 114(4)(a)	making payments in respect of referendum expenses without authority
section 114(4)(b)	failure to notify responsible person of payments in respect of referendum expenses
section 115(3)(a)	paying claim in respect of referendum expenses where failure to comply with procedure
section 115(3)(b)	paying claim in respect of referendum expenses outside specified time period
section 117(2)	individual (other than permitted participant) exceeding limits on referendum expenses
section 117(3) or (4)	body (other than permitted participant) exceeding limits on referendum expenses
section 118(2)	permitted participant exceeding limits on referendum expenses
section 122(4)(a)	failure to deliver return and auditor's report to Commission
section 122(4)(b)	failure to comply with requirements for returns
section 122(4)(c)	failure to deliver return and court order to Commission
section 123(4)(b)	failure to deliver signed declaration with return to Commission
section 126(8) and (9)	printing or publishing referendum material without details of printer or publisher
section 143(8) or (9)	printing or publishing election material without details of printer or publisher
section 148(2)(a)	failure to supply relevant person with information
paragraph 1B of Schedule 7	failure by members association to comply with requirement to appoint responsible person
paragraph 6(5) of Schedule 7	failure to provide information about donors
paragraph 12(1) of Schedule 7	failure to deliver donation report to Commission within time limit
paragraph 12(2) of Schedule 7	failure to comply with requirements for recording donations in donation reports
paragraph 8(3) of Schedule 7A	individual regulated participant failing to repay money obtained under controlled transaction with unauthorised participant
paragraph 8(4) of Schedule 7A	responsible person failing to repay money obtained by members association under controlled transaction with unauthorised participant
paragraph 8(7) of Schedule	individual regulated participant failing to repay value

Provision creating offence	Offence
7A	of benefit obtained in consequence of connected transaction involving unauthorised participant
paragraph 8(8) of Schedule 7A	responsible person failing to repay value of benefit obtained by members association in consequence of connected transaction involving unauthorised participant
paragraph 12(1) of Schedule 7A	failure to deliver transaction report to Commission within time limit
paragraph 12(2) of Schedule 7A	failure to comply with requirements for recording transactions on transaction reports
paragraph 6(7) of Schedule 11	failure to provide information about donors
paragraph 6(8) of Schedule 15	failure to provide information about donors
paragraph 6(1) of Schedule 19A	failure to give notification or report within specified period
paragraph 6(2) of Schedule 19A	giving notification or report that fails to comply with requirements of that Schedule
paragraph 13(1) of Schedule 19B	failure to comply with investigation requirement

Part 2
Prescribed Restrictions and Requirements

Provision containing restriction or requirement	Restriction or requirement
section 31(1) or (3A)	notification required to be given by the treasurer of a registered party
section 34(3)	requirement to submit annual notification of minor party details on time
section 41(1)	requirement to keep accounts
section 41(4) or (5)	requirement to maintain accounts for six years
section 74(6)	requirement for the treasurer to notify the Commission of change of details
paragraph 4(1) and (3) of Schedule 6	requirement to give details of the nature and value of a noncash donation

Part 3
Prescribed Restrictions or Requirements for which
Party or Organisation May be Liable for Actions of
an Office Holder or Responsible Person

Provision containing restriction or requirement	Restriction or requirement
section 31(1) or (3A)	notification required to be given by the treasurer of a registered party
section 34(3)	requirement to submit annual notification of minor party details on time
section 41(1)	requirement to keep accounts

Provision containing restriction or requirement	Restriction or requirement
section 41(4) or (5)	requirement to maintain accounts for six years
section 45(1) or (2)	requirement to deliver any statement of accounts, notification or auditor's report relating to a registered party or any accounting unit of such a party
section 65(1) or (2)	requirement to deliver any donation report relating to a registered party
section 74(6)	requirement for the treasurer to notify the Commission of change of details
section 82(1), (2) or (3)	requirement in relation to any return or auditor's report relating to a registered party
section 98(1), (2) or (3)	requirement in relation to any return or auditor's report relating to a recognised third party
section 122(1), (2) or (3)	requirement in relation to any return or auditor's report relating to a permitted participant
paragraph 4(1) and (3) of Schedule 6	requirement in relation to any requirement to give details of the nature and value of a noncash donation

Political Parties, Elections and Referendums Act 2000 (Northern Ireland Political Parties) Order 2007 (SI 2007/2501)

Made 20th August 2007

1 Citation, commencement and extent
2 Interpretation

PART 1
EXTENSION OF CATEGORIES OF PERMISSIBLE DONORS IN RELATION TO NORTHERN IRELAND RECIPIENTS

3 Donations by Irish citizens
4 Donations by Irish bodies
5 Northern Ireland reports
6 Minor and consequential amendments

PART 2
DUTY OF THE COMMISSION DURING THE PRESCRIBED PERIOD

7 Steps to be taken by the Commission for the purpose of verifying information given in Northern Ireland reports
8 Selection of Northern Ireland donations
9 Verification of donations to Northern Ireland recipients
10 Disclosure of information relating to a donation which was required to be dealt with in accordance with section 56(2) of the 2000 Act
11 Disclosure of information by the Commission

SCHEDULES

Citation, commencement and extent

1 This Order may be cited as the Political Parties, Elections and Referendums Act 2000 (Northern Ireland Political Parties) Order 2007 and shall come into force on 1st November 2007.

Interpretation

2 In this Order

"the 1983 Act" means the Representation of the People Act 1983;

"the 2000 Act" means the Political Parties, Elections and Referendums Act 2000;

"the 2006 Act" means the Northern Ireland (Miscellaneous Provisions) Act 2006;

"individual donor" means an individual who is a permissible donor by virtue of

(a) section 54(2)(a) of the 2000 Act (individuals registered in the electoral register), or

(b) section 71B(1)(a) of that Act (Irish citizen making a donation to a Northern Ireland recipient);

"Northern Ireland report" means a report to the Commission which is prepared by a Northern Ireland recipient and contains, or purports to contain, information required to be given by Schedule 6 or 7 to the 2000 Act, but does not include a report required to be prepared by virtue of section 63 of that Act;

"prescribed bodies" has the meaning given by article 4(2);

"reporting period" has the meaning given by section 62(2) of the 2000 Act in relation to reports prepared pursuant to that section but, in relation to reports which contain, or purport to contain, information required to be given pursuant to Schedule 7 to the 2000 Act, it means each month; and

"selected Northern Ireland donation" means a donation made to a Northern Ireland recipient which is selected by the Commission for verification under article 8.

Part 1
Extension of Categories of Permissible Donors in relation to Northern Ireland Recipients

Donations by Irish citizens

3 For the purposes of section 71B(1)(a) of the 2000 Act, the prescribed condition in relation to an Irish citizen is that at the time of making a donation to a Northern Ireland recipient he must be eligible to obtain one of the following documents
  (a) an Irish passport;
  (b) a certificate of nationality; or
  (c) a certificate of naturalisation.

Donations by Irish bodies

4(1) The description or category of bodies prescribed for the purposes of section 71B(1)(b) of the 2000 Act, are such of the bodies set out in paragraph (2) which keep an office in Ireland or Northern Ireland being an office from which the carrying on of one or more of its principal activities is directed.

  (2) The prescribed bodies are
    (a) a company
      (i)   appearing on the Register of Companies of Ireland; and
      (ii) incorporated within Ireland or another member State;
    (b) a political party appearing on the Register of Political Parties of Ireland;
    (c) a trade union registered by the Registrar of Friendly Societies of Ireland;
    (d) a building society registered by the Central Bank and Financial Services Authority of Ireland;
    (e) a limited liability partnership registered by the Registrar of Companies of Ireland;
    (f) a friendly society or industrial and provident society registered by the Registrar of Friendly Societies of Ireland;
    (g) a trust created in Ireland before 1st November 2007 to which no property has been transferred on or after that date otherwise than by a person who was a permissible donor at the time of the transfer or under the will of a permissible donor;
    (h) a trust created in Ireland on or after 1st November 2007
      (i)   which was created by a person who was a permissible donor at the time the trust was created or by the will of a permissible donor; and
      (ii) to which no property has been transferred otherwise than by a person who was a permissible donor at the time of the transfer or under the will of a permissible donor; and
    (i) any unincorporated association of two or more persons which does not fall within any of the preceding paragraphs but which carries on business or other activities wholly or mainly in Ireland and whose main office is there.

  (3) In sub-paragraphs (2)(g) and (h) "permissible donor" means a person who falls within section 71B(1)(a) or (b) of the 2000 Act.

Northern Ireland reports

5 Schedule 1 (which amends the 2000 Act in connection with the recording of donations

made to Northern Ireland recipients) has effect.

Minor and consequential amendments

6   Schedule 2 (minor and consequential amendments) has effect.

Part 2
Duty of the Commission During the Prescribed Period

Steps to be taken by the Commission for the purpose of verifying information given in Northern Ireland reports

7   For the purposes of section 71D(1) of the 2000 Act the prescribed steps which the Commission must take for the purpose of verifying the information given in Northern Ireland reports during the prescribed period are set out in articles 8 and 9.

Selection of Northern Ireland donations

8(1)   In each reporting period, in relation to each Northern Ireland recipient who has provided a Northern Ireland report, the Commission must
   (a)   select for verification 50 per cent of all donations made by individual donors reported by that recipient in accordance with paragraphs (2) and (3); and
   (b)   select for verification every donation which has not been made by an individual donor.

  (2)   In the case of a Northern Ireland recipient who has reported an odd number of donations from individual donors during any reporting period, the Commission must determine the number of donations from individual donors to be selected for verification by adding one to the number of donations from individual donors reported by that Northern Ireland recipient and dividing the resulting number by two.

  (3)   In the case of a Northern Ireland recipient who has reported only one donation from an individual donor during any reporting period, the Commission must select that donation for verification.

Verification of donations to Northern Ireland recipients

  (1)   The Commission must take the following steps in relation to each selected Northern Ireland donation.

  (2)   In relation to a Northern Ireland report made in respect of a selected Northern Ireland donation, and any documentation provided with it, the Commission must take reasonable steps to ascertain whether
   (a)   the information provided in the report in relation to that donation is accurate; and
   (b)   any documentation provided with the report in relation to that donation is genuine.

  (3)   The steps taken by the Commission under paragraph (2) may include, but are not limited to, contacting a relevant body set out in article 11.

Disclosure of information relating to a donation which was required to be dealt with in accordance with section 56(2) of the 2000 Act

10   If, after taking the steps prescribed by articles 8 and 9, the Commission believes on reasonable grounds that a donation reported in a Northern Ireland report fell to be dealt with under section 56(2) of the 2000 Act, and that it has not been dealt with in this manner, the Commission must
   (a)   write to the Northern Ireland recipient who provided the report informing him

of the Commission's intention to publish the information in accordance with paragraph (b); and

(b) publish the following information
- (i) the name of the Northern Ireland recipient;
- (ii) the amount of the donation;
- (iii) the date of the donation;
- (iv) whether the donation was received from an individual or from a body; and
- (v) in the case of a donation received from a body, the type of body which made the donation with reference to article 4(2) or section 54(2) of the 2000 Act.

Disclosure of information by the Commission

11 The following bodies are prescribed for the purposes of section 71E(2)(b) of the 2000 Act

- (a) a firm of solicitors in Ireland which has provided a statement in accordance with paragraph 2A(12) of Schedule 6 to the 2000 Act;
- (b) the Central Bank and Financial Services Authority of Ireland;
- (c) the office of the Certification Officer;
- (d) the Corporate Officer of the House of Commons;
- (e) the Corporate Officer of the House of Lords;
- (f) the office of the Northern Ireland Certification Officer;
- (g) Companies House (meaning that part of the Department for Business, Innovation and Skills known as the Companies House Executive Agency);
- (h) the Department of Enterprise, Trade and Investment;
- (i) the Department of Foreign Affairs of Ireland;
- (j) the Electoral Office for Northern Ireland;
- (k) the Financial Conduct Authority;
- (ka) the Prudential Regulation Authority;
- (l) the Northern Ireland Assembly Commission;
- (m) the office of any electoral registration officer;
- (n) the Registrar of Companies of Ireland;
- (o) the Registrar of Friendly Societies of Ireland; and
- (p) the Registrar of Political Parties of Ireland.

SCHEDULE 1
DETAILS TO BE GIVEN IN NORTHERN IRELAND REPORTS
Not reproduced

SCHEDULE 2
MINOR AND CONSEQUENTIAL AMENDMENTS
Not reproduced

Political Parties, Elections and Referendums Act 2000
Northern Ireland Political Parties) Order 2008
(SI 2008/1737)

Made 30th June 2008

PART I
CITATION, COMMENCEMENT AND INTERPRETATION

1   Citation and commencement
2   Interpretation

PART II
EXTENSION OF CATEGORIES OF AUTHORISED PARTICIPANTS
IN RELATION TO NORTHERN IRELAND PARTICIPANTS

3   Irish citizens as authorised participants
4   Irish bodies as authorised participants
5   Northern Ireland reports
6   Minor and consequential amendments

PART IIII
DUTY OF THE COMMISSION DURING THE PRESCRIBED PERIOD

7   Steps to be taken by the Commission for the purpose of verifying information given in Northern Ireland reports
8   Selection of Northern Ireland recordable transactions
9   Verification of recordable transactions involving Northern Ireland participants
10 Disclosure of information relating to transactions which are required to be dealt with in accordance with section 71I or 71J of, or paragraph 5 or 6 of Schedule 7A to, the 2000 Act
11 Disclosure of information by the Commission

SCHEDULES

Part I
Citation, Commencement and Interpretation

Citation and commencement

1   This Order may be cited as the Political Parties, Elections and Referendums Act 2000 (Northern Ireland Political Parties) Order 2008 and shall come into force on 1st July 2008.

Interpretation

2   In this Order
"the 2000 Act" means the Political Parties, Elections and Referendums Act 2000;
"individual participant" means an individual who is an authorised participant by virtue of
  (a) section 71H(3) of the 2000 Act, or
  (b) section 71Z1(1)(a) of that Act (Irish citizen entering into a regulated transaction with a Northern Ireland participant);
"Northern Ireland participant" has the meaning given in section 71Z of the 2000 Act;

"Northern Ireland report" means a report to the Commission which is prepared by a Northern Ireland participant and contains, or purports to contain, information required to be given by Schedule 6A or 7A to the 2000 Act, but does not include a report required to be prepared by virtue of section 71Q of that Act;

"prescribed bodies" has the meaning given by article 4(2);

"recordable transaction", other than in Schedule 1, means a transaction which is required to be recorded in a Northern Ireland report;

"reporting period" has the meaning given by section 71M(3) of the 2000 Act in relation to reports prepared pursuant to that section but, in relation to reports which contain, or purport to contain, information required to be given pursuant to Schedule 7A to the 2000 Act, it means each month; and

"selected Northern Ireland transaction" means a recordable transaction involving a Northern Ireland participant which is selected by the Commission for verification under article 8.

Part II
Extension of Categories of Authorised Participants in Relation to Northern Ireland Participants

Irish citizens as authorised participants

3 For the purposes of section 71Z1(1)(a) of the 2000 Act, the prescribed condition in relation to an Irish citizen is that at the time he enters into a regulated transaction or controlled transaction relating to a Northern Ireland participant he must be eligible to obtain one of the following documents
  (a) an Irish passport;
  (b) a certificate of nationality; or
  (c) a certificate of naturalisation.

Irish bodies as authorised participants

4(1) The description or category of body prescribed, for the purposes of section 71Z1(1)(b) of the 2000 Act, is any of the bodies set out in paragraph (2) which keeps an office in Ireland or Northern Ireland being an office from which the carrying on of one or more of its principal activities is directed.

(2) The prescribed bodies are
  (a) a company
    (i) appearing on the Register of Companies of Ireland; and
    (ii) incorporated within Ireland or another member State;
  (b) a political party appearing on the Register of Political Parties of Ireland;
  (c) a trade union registered by the Registrar of Friendly Societies of Ireland;
  (d) a building society registered by the Central Bank and Financial Services Authority of Ireland;
  (e) a limited liability partnership registered by the Registrar of Companies of Ireland;
  (f) a friendly society or industrial and provident society registered by the Registrar of Friendly Societies of Ireland; and
  (g) any unincorporated association of two or more persons which does not fall within any of the preceding paragraphs but which carries on business or other activities wholly or mainly in Ireland and whose main office is there.

Northern Ireland reports

5 Schedule 1 (which amends the 2000 Act in connection with the recording of

transactions to which Northern Ireland participants are a party) has effect.

Minor and consequential amendments

6   Schedule 2 (minor and consequential amendments) has effect.

Part III
Duty of the Commission During the Prescribed Period

Steps to be taken by the Commission for the purpose of verifying information given in Northern Ireland reports

7   For the purposes of section 71Z3(1) of the 2000 Act the prescribed steps which the Commission must take for the purpose of verifying the information given in Northern Ireland reports during the prescribed period are set out in articles 8 and 9.

Selection of Northern Ireland recordable transactions

8(1)   In each reporting period, in relation to each Northern Ireland participant who has provided a Northern Ireland report, the Commission must
    (a)   select for verification 50 per cent of all recordable transactions to which an individual participant is a party and which have been reported by that Northern Ireland participant in accordance with paragraphs (2) and (3); and
    (b)   select for verification every recordable transaction to which an individual participant is not a party.

  (2)   In the case of a Northern Ireland participant who has reported an odd number of recordable transactions to which individual participants are a party during any reporting period, the Commission must determine the number of recordable transactions involving individual participants to be selected for verification by adding one to the number of recordable transactions involving individual participants reported by that Northern Ireland participant and dividing the resulting number by two.

  (3)   In the case of a Northern Ireland participant who has reported only one recordable transaction to which an individual participant is a party during any reporting period, the Commission must select that transaction for verification.

Verification of recordable transactions involving Northern Ireland participants

9(1)   The Commission must take the following steps in relation to each selected Northern Ireland transaction.

  (2)   In relation to a Northern Ireland report made in respect of a selected Northern Ireland transaction, and any documentation provided with it, the Commission must take reasonable steps to ascertain whether
    (a)   the information provided in the report in relation to that transaction is accurate; and
    (b)   any documentation provided with the report in relation to that transaction is genuine.

  (3)   The steps taken by the Commission under paragraph (2) may include, but are not limited to, contacting a body set out in article 11.

Disclosure of information relating to transactions which are required to be dealt with in accordance with section 71I or 71J of, or paragraph 5 or 6 of Schedule 7A to, the 2000 Act

10   If, after taking the steps prescribed by articles 8 and 9, the Commission believes on

reasonable grounds that a transaction recorded in a Northern Ireland report fell to be dealt with under section 71I or 71J of, or paragraph 5 or 6 of Schedule 7A to, the 2000 Act, and that it has not been dealt with in this manner, the Commission must

    (a) write to the Northern Ireland participant who provided the report informing him of the Commission's intention to publish the information in accordance with paragraph (b); and

    (b) publish the following information

        (i)   the name of the Northern Ireland participant;

        (ii) the value of the transaction;

        (iii) the date the transaction was entered into;

        (iv) whether the parties to the transaction (other than the Northern Ireland participant) are individuals or bodies; and

        (v) in the case of a transaction involving a body, the type of body which is a party to the transaction with reference to article 4(2) or section 54(2) of the 2000 Act.

Disclosure of information by the Commission

11   The following bodies are prescribed for the purposes of section 71Z4(2)(b) of the 2000 Act

    (a) a firm of solicitors in Ireland which has provided a statement in accordance with paragraph 2A(11) of Schedule 6A to the 2000 Act;

    (b) the Central Bank and Financial Services Authority of Ireland;

    (c) the office of the Certification Officer;

    (d) the Corporate Officer of the House of Commons;

    (e) the Corporate Officer of the House of Lords;

    (f) the office of the Northern Ireland Certification Officer;

    (g) Companies House (meaning that part of the Department for Business, Innovation and Skills known as the Companies House Executive Agency);

    (h) the Department of Enterprise, Trade and Investment;

    (i)   the Department of Foreign Affairs of Ireland;

    (j)   the Electoral Office for Northern Ireland;

    (k) the Financial Conduct Authority;

    (ka) the Prudential Regulation Authority;

    (l)   the Northern Ireland Assembly Commission;

    (m) the office of any electoral registration officer;

    (n) the Registrar of Companies of Ireland;

    (o) the Registrar of Friendly Societies of Ireland; and

    (p) the Registrar of Political Parties of Ireland.

SCHEDULE 1

DETAILS TO BE GIVEN IN NORTHERN IRELAND REPORTS

Amends the 2000 Act. Not reproduced here

SCHEDULE 2

MINOR AND CONSEQUENTIAL AMENDMENTS

Not reproduced here

Registered Parties (Non-constituent and Non-affiliated Organisations) Order 2000 (SI 2000/3183)

Made 4th December 2000

1 This Order may be cited as the Registered Parties (Non-constituent and Nonaffiliated Organisations) Order 2000 and shall come into force on 14th December 2000.

2 The organisations specified in Part I of the Schedule to this Order and the organisations of a description specified in Part II of that Schedule are hereby specified as falling within section 26(8) of the Political Parties, Elections and Referendums Act 2000 (organisations which are not constituent or affiliated organisations in relation to a party for the purposes of schemes falling within section 26).

SCHEDULE

ORGANISATIONS WHICH ARE NOT CONSTITUENT OR AFFILIATED IN RELATION TO A PARTY FOR THE PURPOSES OF SECTION 26 OF THE POLITICAL PARTIES, ELECTIONS AND REFERENDUMS ACT 2000

Part I
Specified Organisations

Association of Conservative Peers
[Association of Loyal Orange Women of Ireland]
Black and Asian Society
Christian Socialist Movement
Conservative Animal Welfare Group
Conservative Christian Fellowship
Conservative Disability Group
Conservative Foreign Affairs Forum
Conservative Foreign and Commonwealth Council
Conservative Friends of Israel
Conservative Lawyers
Conservative Medical Society
Conservative National Education Society
Conservative Transport Group
Conservatives at Work
[County Grand Lodges of the Loyal Orange Institution of Ireland]
Fabian Society
Hurst Park Residents Association
Labour Housing Group
Labour Irish Group
National Union of Labour and Socialist Clubs
Poale Zion
Socialist Health Association
Socialist Education Association
Socialist Environment and Resources Association
Society of Labour Lawyers

The Association of Conservative Clubs
The Conservative Councillors Association
The Countryside Forum
The 1922 Committee
The Society of Conservative Accountants
The Tory Green Initiative

Part II
Organisations of Specified Description

Any organisation which is not a permissible donor by virtue of coming within paragraph (b), (e), (f) or (h) of section 54(2) of the Political Parties, Elections and Referendums Act 2000.

Any branch of a students' organisation which is wholly or mainly funded from resources provided by a students' union within the meaning of Part II of the Education Act 1994, and defined by section 20 of that Act.

Registration of Political Parties (Fees) Order 2001
(SI 2001/83)

Made 15th January 2001

1(1)   This Order may be cited as the Registration of Political Parties (Fees) Order 2001.

(2)   This Order shall come into force on 16th February 2001.

(3)   In this Order "the Act" means the Political Parties, Elections and Referendums Act 2000.

(4)   The Registration of Political Parties (Fees) Order 1998 is hereby revoked.

2   The fee for an application by a party under section 28 of, and Part I of Schedule 4 to, the Act for registration under Part II of the Act is £150.

3   The fee for an application under section 30 of, and Part II of Schedule 4 to, the Act by a party to have its entry in the register altered is £25.

4   The fee for a notification under section 32 or 34(3) of, or paragraph 11(2) of Schedule 23 to, the Act is £25.

Registration of Political Parties (Prohibited Words and Expressions) Order 2001 (SI 2001/82)

Made 15th January 2001

1(1)   This Order may be cited as the Registration of Political Parties (Prohibited Words and Expressions) Order 2001.

(2)   This Order shall come into force on 16th February 2001.

(3)   The Registration of Political Parties (Prohibited Words and Expressions) Order 1998 is hereby revoked.

2(1)   Subject to paragraph (2), the registered name or registered description of a party shall not include any word or expression which is listed in any Part of the Schedule to this Order.

(2)   Paragraph (1) shall not apply to a word or expression listed in
- (a)   Part I of the Schedule where it forms part of the name of a place, institution or local government area;
- (b)   Part II of the Schedule where it is qualified by another word or expression other than the registered name or registered description of a party (other than the applicant party) which is already registered in respect of the relevant part of the United Kingdom;
- (c)   Part III of the Schedule where it is qualified by another word or expression other than
  - (i)   the registered name of a registered party;
  - (ii)   a word listed in that Part;
  - (iii)   the word "party" or;
  - (iv)   the registered description of a registered party;
- (d)   Part IV of the Schedule where it is qualified by the name of a local government or geographical area;
- (e)   Part V of the Schedule, if the words are used otherwise than as part of an expression prohibited in that Part.

(2A)   Paragraph (1) shall not apply as respects a party established in Gibraltar, in connection with the registration of that party in the Great Britain register in respect of England (including the combined region), to the word "Gibraltar" or "Gibraltarian" where it is qualified by the registered name or registered description of a party which is already registered in respect of England (including the combined region).

(3)   In paragraph (2)(b)
- (a)   the reference to another word or expression includes another word or expression listed in Part II of the Schedule or the word "party"; and
- (b)   "already registered in the relevant part of the United Kingdom" means
  - (i)   in connection with the registration of the applicant party or a description in the Great Britain register, already registered in respect of the part of Great Britain in respect of which the applicant party is registered (in the case of an application under section 30 of the Political Parties, Elections and Referendums Act 2000) or is applying to be registered (in the case of an application under section 28B or section 28 of that Act);
  - (ii)   in connection with registration of the applicant party or a description in the Northern Ireland register, already registered in that register.

(4)   In this article, any reference to a word or expression listed in any Part of the Schedule

to this Order includes a reference to a word or expression which translates a word or expression so listed into a language other than English.

SCHEDULE
WORDS AND EXPRESSIONS WHICH MAY NOT BE INCLUDED IN THE REGISTERED NAME OR REGISTERED DECEPTION OF A PARTY EXCEPT WHERE ARTICLE 2(2) APPLIES

Part I
Words and Expressions which may only be so Included where Article 2(2)(A) Applies

Duke
Duchess
Her Majesty
His Majesty
King
Prince
Princess
Queen
Royal
Royalty

Part II
Words and Expressions which may only be so Included where Article 2(2)(B) Applies

Britain
British
combined region
England
English
Gibraltar
Gibraltarian
National
Scotland
Scots
Scottish
United Kingdom
Wales
Welsh

Part III
Words and Expressions which may only be so Included where Article 2(2)(C) Applies

Independent
Official
Unofficial

Part IV
Words and Expressions which may only be so Included where Article 2(2)(D) Applies

Ratepayers
Residents
Tenants

Part V
Prohibited Expressions

None of the above.

Representation of the People (Combination of Polls) (England and Wales) Regulations 2004 (SI 2004/294)

22nd March 2004

Citation, commencement and extent

1 (1) These Regulations may be cited as the Representation of the People (Combination of Polls) (England and Wales) Regulations 2004 and shall come into force on the day after the day on which they are made.

(2) These Regulations shall not extend to Scotland or Northern Ireland.

Interpretation

2 (1) For the purposes of these Regulations--

"1983 Act" means the Representation of the People Act 1983;

"1985 Act" means the Representation of the People Act 1985;

"2000 Act" means the Local Government Act 2000;

"2001 Regulations" means the Representation of the People (England and Wales) Regulations 2001;

"2002 Act" means the European Parliamentary Elections Act 2002;

"2011 Act" means the Police Reform and Social Responsibility Act 2011;

"2004 Regulations" means the European Parliamentary Elections Regulations 2004;

"GLRO" means the Greater London Returning Officer, being the person who is for the time being the proper officer of the Greater London Authority for the purposes of section 35(2C) of the 1983 Act;

"mayoral election" means an election conducted under the Local Authorities (Mayoral Elections) (England and Wales) Regulations 2007; and

"PCC election" means an election of a police and crime commissioner in accordance with Chapter 6 of Part 1 of the 2011 Act;

"referendum" means a referendum conducted under the Local Authorities (Conduct of Referendums) (England) Regulations 2012.

(2) In the case of a referendum, a reference to a returning officer shall be construed as a reference to a counting officer, within the meaning of regulation 2(1) of the Local Authorities (Conduct of Referendums) (England) Regulations 2012.

Revocation

3 The Representation of the People Regulations 1986 are hereby revoked.

Returning officers and polling stations

4 (1) Where the poll at a parliamentary general election is taken together with the poll at another election or referendum under a relevant enactment—

    (a) those functions of the returning officer at the poll at the other election or referendum which are specified in regulation 5 shall be discharged by the returning officer at the parliamentary election for such part of the electoral region, local government area, voting area or police area (as the case may be) as is situated in the parliamentary constituency; and

    (b) only polling stations used for the parliamentary election shall be used for the other election or referendum.

(2) Where the above paragraph does not apply and the poll at an ordinary Authority election is taken together with the poll at another election or referendum under a relevant enactment—

    (a) those functions of the returning officer at the poll at the other election or referendum which are specified in regulation 5 shall be discharged by the returning officer at the Authority election for such part of the electoral region, local government area, voting area or police area (as the case may be) as is situated in the area for which he acts; and

    (b) only polling stations used for the Authority election shall be used for the poll at the other election or referendum.

(3) Where neither of the above paragraphs applies and the poll at an ordinary county council election is taken together with the poll at another election or referendum under a relevant enactment—

    (a) those functions of the returning officer at the poll at the other election or referendum which are specified in regulation 5 shall be discharged by the returning officer at the county council election for such part of the electoral region, local government area, voting area or police area (as the case may be) as is situated in the county or county borough; and

    (b) only polling stations used for the county council election shall be used for the poll at the other election or referendum.

(4) Where none the above paragraphs applies and the poll at an ordinary principal area council election (other than a county council election) is taken together with the poll at another election or referendum under a relevant enactment—

    (a) those functions of the returning officer at the poll at the other election or referendum which are specified in regulation 5 shall be discharged by the returning officer at the principal area council election for such part of the electoral region, local government area, voting area or police area (as the case may be) as is situated in the principal area; and

    (b) only polling stations used for the principal area council election shall be used for the poll at the other election or referendum.

(5) Where none of the above paragraphs applies and the poll at a mayoral election is taken together with the poll at an election under a relevant enactment—

    (a) those functions of the returning officer at the poll at the other election which are specified in regulation 5 shall be discharged by the returning officer at the mayoral election for such part of the electoral region, local government area or police area (as the case may be) as is situated in the local government area as respects which the mayoral election is held; and

    (b) only polling stations used for the mayoral election shall be used for the poll at the other election.

(6) Where none of the above paragraphs applies and the poll at a referendum is taken

together with the poll at an election under a relevant enactment–

(a) those functions of the returning officer at the poll at the election which are specified in regulation 5 shall be discharged by the returning officer at the referendum for such part of the electoral region, local government area or police area (as the case may be) as is situated in the voting area; and

(b) only polling stations used for the referendum shall be used for the poll at the election.

(7) Where none of the above paragraphs applies and the poll at an ordinary parish or community council election is taken together with the poll at another election under a relevant enactment–

(a) those functions of the returning officer at the other election which are specified in regulation 5 shall be discharged by the returning officer at the parish or community council election for such part of the electoral region or police area as is situated in the area of the parish or community council; and

(b) only polling stations used for the parish or community council election shall be used for the poll at the other election.

(7A) Where none of the above paragraphs applies and the poll at a PCC election is taken together with the poll at a European Parliamentary election under a relevant enactment–

(a) those functions of the returning officer at the European Parliamentary election which are specified in regulation 5 shall be discharged by the returning officer at the PCC election for such part of the electoral region as is situated in the police area; and

(b) only polling stations used for the PCC election shall be used for the European Parliamentary election.

(8) Subject to paragraph (9), where the polls at an election and another election or referendum for related areas (within the meaning of section 15(3) of the 1985 Act) are taken together under section 15(2) of the 1985 Act (including by virtue of section 15(2) and (3) as applied by orders or regulations made under any of the listed provisions)–

(a) the returning officers for each election or referendum shall decide which returning officer shall discharge in the related area those functions of the other (or others) which are specified in regulation 5, but the returning officer at a European Parliamentary election shall not discharge those functions; and

(b) the only polling stations which shall be used at each election or referendum are the polling stations used at the election or referendum for which the returning officer who discharges the functions referred to in sub-paragraph (a) above acts as returning officer.

(9) Where the polls at two or more elections or referendums are taken together other than under a relevant enactment, but one or more such polls are also taken together with the poll at another election or a referendum under a relevant enactment, paragraphs (1) to (7A) above shall apply as if–

(a) each election (other than a mayoral election) were an ordinary election; and

(b) the polls at each election or referendum were taken together under a relevant enactment.

(10) In this regulation–

"county council election" mean an election of councillors of a county or county borough;

"the listed provisions" means–

(a) sections 52ZQ and 113 of the Local Government Finance Act 1992,

(b) sections 9HE and 105, 9MG and 105 or 44 and 105 of the 2000 Act,

(c) sections 58 and 154 of the 2011 Act;

"police area" means a police area listed in Schedule 1 to the Police Act 1996 (police areas outside London);

"principal area" means any of the following–

(a)   a county, district or London borough in England, or

(b)   a county or county borough in Wales;

"principal area council election" means an election of councillors or London Borough councillors (as the case may be) of a principal area; and

"relevant enactment" means any of the following–

(a)   section 15(1) of the 1985 Act; or

(b)   section 36(3), (3AB) or (3AC) of the 1983 Act,

and includes a reference to each section as applied in orders or regulations made under any of the listed provisions.

(11)   In this regulation, except the first reference in paragraph (8)(a), any reference to a returning officer which applies to–

(a)   the returning officer at a European Parliamentary election, shall be construed as including a reference to the local returning officer,

(b)   the returning officer at an Authority election, shall be construed as a reference to the constituency returning officer for the Assembly constituency in which the functions specified in regulation 5 are to be discharged,

(c)   the returning officer at a PCC election, shall be construed as including a reference to the police area returning officer.

Functions at combined polls

5 (1)   The functions referred to in regulation 4 are the functions conferred–

(a)   at a parliamentary election by those rules in the parliamentary elections rules in Schedule 1 to the 1983 Act which are specified in paragraph (2);

(b)   at a European Parliamentary election, by those rules in the regulations made under section 7 of the 2002 Act which correspond to the rules specified in paragraph (2);

(c)   at a local government election, by those rules in the rules made under section 36 of the 1983 Act which correspond to the rules specified in paragraph (2));

(d)   at a mayoral election, by those rules in regulations made under sections 9HE and 105, or 44 and 105 of the 2000 Act which correspond to the rules specified in paragraph (2);

(e)   at a mayoral referendum, by those rules in regulations made under sections 9MG and 105 of the 2000 Act which correspond to the rules specified in paragraph (2);

(f)   at a PCC election, by those rules in an Order made under sections 58 and 154 of the 2011 Act which correspond to the rules specified in paragraph (2);

and, where the proceedings on the issue and receipt of postal ballot papers at more than one election or referendum are taken together under regulation 65 of the 2001 Regulations, the functions conferred by Part 5 of those Regulations.

(2)   The rules referred to in paragraph (1) are–

(za)   unless sub-paragraph (zb) applies, rule 19A (corresponding number list), to the extent that it relates to ballot papers to be provided in pursuance of rule 29(1);

(zb)   where the proceedings on the issue and receipt of postal ballot papers at more than one election or referendum are taken together under regulation 65 of the 2001 Regulations, rule 19A (corresponding number list);

(a)   rule 23(2) (notice of situation of polling stations etc);

(b)   where the proceedings on the issue and receipt of postal ballot papers at more than one election or referendum are taken together under regulation 65 of the

2001 Regulations, rule 24 (postal ballot papers);

(c) rule 25 (provision of polling stations);

(d) rule 26(1) and (2) (appointment of presiding officers and clerks) to the extent that that rule concerns the appointment of presiding officers and clerks to assist them;

(e) rule 29 (equipment of polling stations);

(f) rule 31(a) (notification of requirement of secrecy at polling stations);

(fa) where the proceedings on the issue and receipt of postal ballot papers at more than one election or referendum are taken together under regulation 65 of the 2001 Regulations, rule 31A (return of postal ballot papers);

(g) rule 32(3) (signature of certificate as to employment);

(h) rule 33(2)(b) (authorisation to order removal of persons from polling station); and

(i) in rule 45 (the count), paragraph (1), as substituted by paragraph 22 of Schedule 2, and paragraph (5);

(j) where the proceedings on the issue and receipt of postal ballot papers at more than one election or referendum are taken together under regulation 65 of the 2001 Regulations, rule 45(1B)(d) (the count).

(3) In this regulation, references to regulation 65 and Part 5 of the 2001 Regulations include references to–

(a) the provisions in regulations made under section 7 of the 2002 Act which correspond to that regulation and that Part; . . .

(b) that regulation and that Part as applied by regulations made under sections 9HE and 105, 9MG and 105 or 44 and 105 of the 2000 Act; and

(c) the provisions in an Order made under sections 58 and 154 of the 2011 Act which correspond to that regulation and that Part.

Modification of provisions about expenses in the 1983 Act

6 (1) Where those functions of a returning officer at an election or referendum which are specified in regulation 5 are discharged by the returning officer at another election or referendum under regulation 4, references to the returning officer or his charges or expenditure in–

(a) subsections (3), (4), (4A), (4B), (5), (7) and (8) of section 29 (payments by and to returning officer) of the 1983 Act;

(b) section 30 (taxation of returning officer's account) of the 1983 Act; and

(c) subsections (4) to (6A) of section 36 (local elections in England and Wales) of the 1983 Act,

shall, to the extent that such functions are so discharged, be construed as references to the returning officer who discharges those functions and his charges or expenditure in respect of those functions.

(2) The reference in section 36(6) of the 1983 Act to the returning officer or a person acting as returning officer requesting an advance in respect of his expenses shall, to the extent that those expenses relate to the functions specified in regulation 5, include a reference to the returning officer who under regulation 4 discharges those functions at the local government election, mayoral election or referendum.

(3) In relation to elections and referendums the polls at which are taken together under section 15(1) or (2) of the 1985 Act the Secretary of State may under section 29(3) of the 1983 Act include special provision for services rendered and expenses incurred in respect of the functions specified in regulation 5 and in respect of the remuneration of presiding officers and clerks by the returning officer who discharges those functions by virtue of regulation 4.

(4)   In relation to elections and referendums the polls at which are taken together under section 15(1) or (2) of the 1985 Act or section 36(3), (3AB) or (3AC) of the 1983 Act–

(a)   the council for a county, county borough, district or London borough;

(b)   the Greater London Authority;

(c)   the council for the district in which a parish is situated;

(d)   the council for the county or county borough in which a community is situated,

may, in fixing a scale under subsections (4), (4B), (5) and (5A) respectively of section 36 of the 1983 Act include special provision for expenses incurred in respect of the functions specified in regulation 5 and in respect of the remuneration of presiding officers and clerks by the returning officer who discharges those functions by virtue of regulation 4.

(5)   In this regulation, references to any provision of an enactment include references to–

(a)   any provision in regulations made under section 7 of the 2002 Act which corresponds to that provision; . . .

(ab) any provision in Chapter 6 of Part 1 of the 2011 Act which corresponds to that provision; and

(b)   that provision as applied by orders or regulations made under any of the listed provisions.

7   *Repealed*

Modification of parliamentary elections rules

8 (1)   Where the poll at a parliamentary election is to be taken with–

(a)   the poll at an election under subsection (1) or (2) of section 15 of the 1985 Act; . . .

(b)   the poll at a mayoral election or a referendum in accordance with regulations made under section 9HE and 105, 9MG and 105 or 44 and 105 of the 2000 Act, or

(c)   the poll at a mayoral election, referendum or PCC election in accordance with orders or regulations made under any of the listed provisions

or two or more such polls, the parliamentary elections rules in Schedule 1 to the 1983 Act shall have effect subject to the provisions of Schedule 2.

9   *Repealed*

SCHEDULE 1

Repealed

SCHEDULE 2
MODIFICATIONS TO PARLIAMENTARY ELECTIONS RULES

Regulation 8

1   In the circumstances set out in regulation 8 of these Regulations, the parliamentary election rules in Schedule 1 to the 1983 Act shall have effect subject to the following modifications.

2   In this Schedule, and in any provision modified by this Schedule–

"Combination of Polls Regulations" means the Representation of the People

(Combination of Polls) (England and Wales) Regulations 2004;

"GLRO" means the Greater London Returning Officer, being the person who is for the time being the proper officer of the Greater London Authority for the purposes of section 35(2C) of the Representation of the People Act 1983;

"mayoral election" means an election conducted under the Local Authorities (Mayoral Elections) (England and Wales) Regulations 2007);

"police and crime commissioner election" means an election of a police and crime commissioner in accordance with Chapter 6 of Part 1 of the 2011 Act;

"referendum" means a referendum conducted under the Local Authorities (Conduct of Referendums) (England) Regulations 2012; and

"relevant election or referendum" means one or more of the following–
  (a) a European parliamentary election,
  (b) a local government election,
  (c) a mayoral election,
  (d) a referendum,
  (e) a police and crime commissioner election,
the poll at which is taken together with the poll at the parliamentary election.

3 In this Schedule, and in any provision modified by this Schedule, in the case of a referendum a reference to–
  (a) an election agent or counting agent shall be construed as a reference to a counting observer, within the meaning of regulation 2(1) of the Local Authorities (Conduct of Referendums) (England) Regulations 2012;
  (b) a polling agent shall be construed as a reference to a polling observer, within the meaning of that regulation; and
  (c) a returning officer shall be construed as a reference to a counting officer, within the meaning of that regulation.

4 At the end of paragraph (2) of rule 19 (the ballot papers) insert–
  "(d) shall be of a different colour from that of any ballot papers used at any relevant election or referendum.".

5 At the end of rule 23 (notice of poll) the following paragraph shall be inserted–
  "(3) The notice published under paragraph (2) above shall–
  (a) state that the poll at the parliamentary election is to be taken together with the poll at a relevant election or referendum;
  (b) specify the relevant local counting area, local authority or, as the case may be, voting area and, in the case of a local government election to fill a casual vacancy, the electoral area for which the election is held; and
  (c) where the polls are to be taken together in part of the constituency only, specify that part."

6 At the end of rule 28 (issue of official poll cards) the following paragraph shall be inserted–
  "(5) If the returning officer for each relevant election or referendum agrees, an official poll card issued under this rule may be combined with an official poll card issued at each relevant election or referendum, with necessary adaptations."

7 After paragraph (1) of rule 29 (equipment of polling stations) there shall be inserted the

following paragraphs–

"(1A) The same ballot box may be used for the poll at the parliamentary election and the poll at each relevant election or referendum.

(1B) Where the same ballot box is not used under paragraph (1A), each ballot box shall be clearly marked with–

(a)   the election or referendum to which it relates, as shown on the ballot papers for that election or referendum; and

(b)   the words "Please insert the *specify colour of ballot papers in question* coloured ballot papers in here." "

8   After paragraph (3A) of rule 29 (equipment of polling stations) insert the following paragraph–

"(3B)   The large version of the ballot paper referred to in paragraph (3A)(a) above shall be printed on paper of the same colour as that of the ballot papers for use at the parliamentary election."

9   For paragraph (5) of rule 29 (equipment of polling stations) substitute–

"(5) In every compartment of every polling station there must be exhibited the notice:

"PARLIAMENTARY ELECTION

(*Specify colour* ballot paper)

Vote for ONLY ONE CANDIDATE by putting a cross X in the box next to your choice.

*EUROPEAN PARLIAMENTARY ELECTION

(*Specify colour* ballot paper)

Vote ONLY ONCE by putting a cross X in the box next to your choice.

*Specify name of council COUNCIL ELECTION

(*Specify colour* ballot paper)

*Vote for NO MORE THAN ... CANDIDATES by putting a cross X in the box next to EACH of your choices.

*Vote ONLY ONCE by putting a cross X in the box next to your choice.

*ELECTION OF THE MAYOR OF LONDON

(*Specify colour* ballot paper)

#On the ballot paper for the election of the Mayor, vote ONCE for your first choice and ONCE for your second choice.

*ELECTION OF THE LONDON ASSEMBLY

#On the constituency members ballot paper (*specify colour*) vote for ONE candidate only.

#On the London members ballot paper (*specify colour*) vote for ONE party or individual candidate only.

*Specify other ELECTION/REFERENDUM

(*Specify colour* ballot paper)

Specify voting instructions in accordance with the legislation governing the election or referendum

PUT NO OTHER MARK ON THE BALLOT PAPER OR YOUR VOTE MAY NOT COUNT.

*PLEASE DO NOT FOLD THE BALLOT PAPERS FOR *specify the election(s) and/or referendum(s)* at which the votes are to be counted electronically. Post them, face downwards, in the *appropriate ballot box.

*Complete or omit as necessary.

#Alternatively, insert such information as the GLRO may decide."

10   At the end of paragraph (3) of rule 30 (appointment of polling and counting agents) there shall be inserted the following–

"Notices of the appointment of polling agents and counting agents which are required by this paragraph and paragraphs (4) and (5) below to be given to the returning officer shall be given to the returning officer who discharges the functions specified in Regulation 5 of the Combination of Polls Regulations."

11   At the end of paragraph (1)(h) of rule 32 (admission to polling stations) insert–
"(i)   persons entitled to be admitted to the polling station at a relevant election or referendum.".

12 (1)   Rule 35 (questions to be put to voters) is amended as follows.

(2)   In the questions specified in the second column of the table set out in rule 35–
(a)   for the words "at this election", wherever they appear, substitute "at this Parliamentary election";
(b)   in question 3(b) after the words "here or elsewhere" insert "at this Parliamentary election".

13   After paragraph (3) of rule 37 (voting procedure) insert the following–
"(3A)   The same copy of the register of electors or where paragraph (3) applies, the same copy of the notice issued under section 13B(3B) or (3D) of this Act may be used under paragraph (1) for each relevant election or referendum and–
(a)   one mark may be placed in that register or on that notice under paragraph (1)(c) or in the list of proxies under paragraph (1)(e) to denote that a ballot paper has been issued in respect of each election or referendum; and
(b)   where a ballot paper has not been issued in respect of a relevant election or referendum, a different mark shall be placed in the register, on the notice or in the list, so as to identify each election or referendum in respect of which the ballot paper was issued.".

14   At the end of paragraph (2) of rule 38 (votes marked by presiding officer) there shall be inserted–
"The same list may be used for each relevant election or referendum and, where it is so used, an entry in that list shall be taken to mean that the ballot papers were so marked in respect of each election or referendum, unless the list identifies the election or referendum at which the ballot paper was so marked."

15   At the end of paragraph (4) of rule 39 (voting by person with disabilities) there shall be inserted–
"The same list may be used for each relevant election or referendum and, where it is so used, an entry in that list shall be taken to mean the votes were so given in respect of each election or referendum, unless the list identifies the election or referendum at which the vote was so given."

16   At the end of paragraph (3) of rule 40 (tendered ballot papers) there shall be inserted–
"The same list may be used for each relevant election or referendum and, where it is so used, an entry in that list shall be taken to mean that tendered ballot papers were marked in respect of each election or referendum, unless the list identifies the election or referendum at which a tendered ballot paper was marked."

16A   At the end of rule 41A (correction of errors on day of the poll) insert the following–
"The same list may be used for each relevant election or referendum and, where it is

so used, an entry in that list shall be taken to mean that ballot papers were issued in respect of each election or referendum, unless the list identifies the election or referendum for which a ballot paper was issued.".

17 At the end of paragraph (1) of rule 42 (adjournment of poll in case of riot) there shall be inserted "who discharges the functions specified in regulation 5 of the Combination of Polls Regulations".

18 In paragraph (1) of rule 43 (procedure on close of poll), after the words "polling agents", in the first place where they occur, insert "appointed for the purposes of the parliamentary election and for each relevant election or referendum".

19 After paragraph (1) of rule 43 (procedure on close of poll) there shall be inserted the following paragraphs–

"(1A) The contents of the packets referred to in sub-paragraphs (b), (c) and (e) of paragraph (1) above shall not be combined with the contents of packets made under the corresponding rule that applies at each relevant election or referendum; nor shall the statement prepared under paragraph (3) below be so combined.

(1B) References to the returning officer in paragraph (1) above are references to the returning officer who discharges the functions specified in Regulation 5 of the Combination of Polls Regulations."

20 For paragraph (1) of rule 44 (attendance at counting of votes) there shall be substituted the following paragraphs–

"(1) Where the returning officer at the parliamentary election discharges the functions specified in Regulation 5 of the Combination of Polls Regulations, he shall–

(a) make arrangements for–

(i) discharging the functions under rule 45(1) below (as substituted by Regulation 8 of those Regulations) in the presence of the counting agents appointed for the purposes of the parliamentary election and for each relevant election or referendum, as soon as practicable after the close of the poll; and

(ii) thereafter counting the votes at the parliamentary election in the presence of the counting agents appointed for the purposes of that election; and

(b) he shall give to those counting agents notice in writing of the time and place at which he will begin to discharge the functions under rule 45(1) below (as so substituted).

(1A) Where the returning officer at the parliamentary election does not discharge the functions specified in Regulation 5 of the Combination of Polls Regulations, he shall–

(a) make arrangements for counting the votes in the presence of the counting agents as soon as practicable after the delivery of the ballot papers to him by the returning officer who does discharge those functions, and

(b) give to the counting agents notice in writing of the time after which he will begin to count the votes if by then he has received the ballot papers and of the place at which that count will take place.

(1B) No person other than a person entitled to be present at the counting of the votes at each relevant election or referendum may be present at the proceedings under rule 45(1) (as so substituted)."

21 In paragraph (3) of rule 44 (attendance at counting of votes) before the words
    "counting of votes", in the first place where they occur, there shall be inserted the
    words "proceedings under rule 45(1) below (as so substituted) or the" and before the
    words "the efficient" there shall be inserted the words "the efficient separating of the
    ballot papers or, as the case may be".

22 For paragraphs (1) to (1A) of rule 45 (the count) there shall be substituted the following
    paragraphs–
    "(1) Where the returning officer at the parliamentary election discharges the
        functions specified in Regulation 5 of the Combination of Polls Regulations, he
        shall–
        (a) in the presence of the counting agents appointed for the purposes of the
             parliamentary election and each relevant election or referendum, open
             each ballot box and record separately the number of ballot papers used in
             each election or referendum;
        (b) in the presence of the election agents appointed for the purposes of the
             parliamentary election and each relevant election or referendum verify
             each ballot paper account;
        (c) count such of the postal ballot papers as have been duly returned and
             record separately the number counted at each relevant election or
             referendum;
        (d) separate the ballot papers relating to the parliamentary election from the
             ballot papers relating to each relevant election or referendum;
        (e) make up into packets the ballot papers for each relevant election or
             referendum and seal them up in separate containers endorsing on each a
             description of the area to which the ballot papers relate; and
        (f) deliver or cause to be delivered to the returning officer at the relevant
             election or referendum to which the ballot papers relate–
             (i)   those containers, together with a list of them and of the contents of
                   each;
             (ii) the ballot paper accounts together with a copy of the statement as
                   to the result of their verification in respect of that election or
                   referendum; and
        (g) at the same time deliver or cause to be delivered to that officer packets
             that so relate containing–
             (i)   the unused and spoilt ballot papers,
             (ii) the tendered ballot papers, and
             (iii) the completed corresponding number lists of the used ballot papers
                   and the certificates as to employment on duty on the day of the poll.
    (1AA) Where separate ballot boxes have been used, no vote for any candidate shall
           be rendered invalid by the ballot paper being placed in the ballot box used at
           any relevant election or referendum.
    (1AB) The returning officer shall count the votes given on the ballot papers used at
           the parliamentary election, but shall not count–
           (a) the votes given on postal ballot papers until the proceedings under
                paragraph (1)(c) and (d) above have been completed in relation to
                those papers and they have been mixed with the ballot papers from at
                least one ballot box; or
           (b) the votes given on ballot papers from a ballot box until the
                proceedings under paragraph (1)(a), (b) and (d) have been completed

in relation to those papers and they have been mixed with the ballot papers from at least one other box.

(1AC) Where the returning officer at the parliamentary election does not discharge the functions specified in Regulation 5 of the Combination of Polls Regulations, he shall–

(a) on receipt of containers from the returning officer who does discharge those functions, and after the time specified in the notice given under rule 44(1A) above (as substituted by Regulation 8 of those Regulations) in the presence of the counting agents open each container;

(b) where the proceedings on the issue and receipt of postal ballot papers are not taken together with those proceedings at a relevant election or referendum under regulation 65 of the 2001 Regulations (including that regulation as applied by regulations made under sections 9HE and 105, 9MG and 105 or 44 and 105 of the Local Government Act 2000, count such of the postal ballot papers as have been duly returned and record the number counted; and

(c) count the votes given on the ballot papers, but shall not count–

(i) the votes given on postal ballot papers until they have been mixed with the ballot papers from at least one ballot box; or

(ii) the votes given on ballot papers from a ballot box until they have been mixed with the ballot papers from at least one other ballot box.

Paragraph (5) below does not apply to these proceedings."

23 In paragraph (1B) of rule 45 (the count) the reference to the constituency shall be construed as a reference to–

(a) the area in the parliamentary constituency common to the local counting area, electoral area or voting area (as the case may be) in which the polls at the parliamentary election and a relevant election or referendum are being taken together; and

(b) in respect of which polls the voter has been issued with a postal ballot paper.

24 In paragraph (6) of rule 45 (the count) omit the words ", in so far as he and the agents agree," and the words from "For the purposes" to the end.

24A In rule 50 (declaration of result), after paragraph (2) insert–

"(3) But the returning officer shall not declare a candidate to be elected under paragraph (1) or (2)–

(a) in a case where the returning officer discharges the functions specified in Regulation 5 of the Combination of Polls Regulations, until after the returning officer has completed proceedings under rule 45(1) (as substituted by Regulation 8 of those Regulations);

(b) in a case where the returning officer does not discharge the functions specified in Regulation 5 of the Combination of Polls Regulations, until after proceedings corresponding to those mentioned in sub-paragraph (a) have been completed by the returning officer who does discharge those functions ("the other returning officer").

(4) The corresponding proceedings referred to in paragraph (3)(b) are proceedings under provision corresponding to rule 45(1) (as substituted by Regulation 8 of the Combination of Polls Regulations) made by or under any enactment in relation to the election or referendum at which the other returning officer has functions.".

25 For paragraph (2) of rule 54 (sealing up of ballot papers) substitute–
"(2) The returning officer shall not open the sealed packets of–
(a) tendered ballot papers, or
(b) certificates as to employment on duty on the day of the poll.

(3) Where he is the returning officer who discharges the functions referred to in regulation 5 of the Combination of Polls Regulations, the returning officer shall not open the sealed packets of–
(a) the completed corresponding number lists, or
(b) marked copies of the register of electors (including any marked copy notices issued under section 13B(3B) or (3D) of this Act) and lists of proxies.".

26 At the end of paragraph (1) of rule 55 (delivery of documents to the registration officer) there shall be inserted–
"At an election where the returning officer does not discharge the functions referred to in Regulation 5 of the Combination of Polls Regulations, this paragraph shall have effect as if sub-paragraphs (c), (ca) and (e) were omitted."

27 In rule 60 (death of independent candidate) after paragraph (5) insert–
"(6) Neither the countermand of the notice of poll at the parliamentary election nor the direction that that poll be abandoned shall affect the poll at each relevant election or referendum.".

27A (1) Rule 63 (death of party candidate) is modified as follows.

(2) After paragraph (2) insert–
"(2A) Neither the countermand of the notice of poll at the parliamentary election nor the direction that that poll be abandoned shall affect the poll at each relevant election or referendum.".

(3) In paragraph (3) after "with reference to the" insert "parliamentary".

27B (1) Rule 64 (death of Speaker of the House of Commons seeking re-election) is modified as follows.

(2) After paragraph (2) insert–
"(2A) Neither the countermand of the notice of poll at the parliamentary election nor the direction that that poll be abandoned shall affect the poll at each relevant election or referendum.".

(3) In paragraph (3) after "with reference to the" insert "parliamentary".

27C For rule 65 (abandoned poll) substitute the following–
"65(1) This rule applies to–
(a) a poll at a parliamentary election which is abandoned in pursuance of rule 60(4)(b) as if it were a poll at a contested election;
(b) a poll at a parliamentary election which is abandoned in pursuance of rule 63(2)(b) or 64(2)(b).

(2) No further ballot papers at the parliamentary election shall be issued in any polling station.

(3) At the close of poll for each relevant election or referendum the presiding officer at a polling station must take the like steps (so far as not already

taken) for the delivery to the returning officer of ballot boxes and ballot papers and other documents as he would be required to do if the poll at the parliamentary election had not been abandoned.

(4)   The returning officer must dispose of ballot papers used at the parliamentary election and other documents in his possession as he is required to do on the completion of the counting of votes.

(5)   It is not necessary for a parliamentary ballot paper account to be prepared or verified.

(6)   Having separated the ballot papers relating to each relevant election or referendum, the returning officer must take no step or further step for the counting of the ballot papers used at the parliamentary election or of the votes cast at the parliamentary election.

(7)   The returning officer must seal up all the ballot papers used at the parliamentary election (whether the votes on them have been counted or not) and it is not necessary to seal up counted and rejected ballot papers in separate packets.

(8)   The provisions of these rules as to the inspection, production, retention and destruction of ballot papers and other documents relating to a poll at a parliamentary election apply subject to paragraphs (9) and (10).

(9)   Ballot papers on which the votes were neither counted nor rejected must be treated as counted ballot papers.

(10) No order is to be made for–
    (a) the production or inspection of any ballot papers, or
    (b) the opening of a sealed packet of the completed corresponding number list or of certificates as to employment on the day of the poll, unless the order is made by a court with reference to a prosecution.".

28   In the Appendix of forms, for the form of directions for the guidance of voters in voting substitute the form of those directions as set out in the Appendix of Forms to this Schedule.

29   In the Appendix of forms, for the form of declaration to be made by the companion of a voter with disabilities substitute the form of that declaration in the Appendix of Forms to this Schedule.

Forms not reproduced

SCHEDULE 3

Repealed

Representation of the People (Electoral Registration Data Schemes) Regulations 2011 (SI 2011/1467)

Made 9th June 2011

Citation, commencement and extent

1 These Regulations may be cited as the Representation of the People (Electoral Registration Data Schemes) Regulations 2011.

2 These Regulations come into force on the day after the day on which they are made.

3 These Regulations do not extend to Northern Ireland.

Supply of electoral register for comparison

4 For the purposes of a scheme included in an order made under section 35 of the Political Parties and Elections Act 2009 (schemes for provision of data to registration officers), a registration officer may supply a copy of the whole or a part of the full register to a person in Great Britain in order to enable that copy to be compared with information contained in records kept by a person who is authorised or required to provide information to that registration officer under the scheme.

5 Where a copy of the whole or a part of the full register is supplied to a person under regulation 4, regulation 96(2) of the Representation of the People (England and Wales) Regulations 2001 and regulation 95(2) of the Representation of the People (Scotland) Regulations 2001 (restriction on use of the full register, or information contained in it, supplied in accordance with enactments or obtained otherwise) are modified by inserting in each "with the consent of the registration officer and" after "other than".

Representation of the People (England and Wales) Regulations 2001
(SI 2001/341)

9th February 2001

PART I
GENERAL, INTERPRETATION AND MISCELLANEOUS

PART II
SERVICE AND OVERSEAS ELECTORS' DECLARATIONS

Service declarations

Overseas electors' declarations

PART III
REGISTRATION

Information about electors

PART IV
ABSENT VOTERS

PART V
ISSUE AND RECEIPT OF POSTAL BALLOT PAPERS

PART VI
SUPPLY OF REGISTER ETC

PART I

GENERAL, INTERPRETATION AND MISCELLANEOUS

Citation, commencement and extent

1 (1)   These Regulations may be cited as the Representation of the People (England and Wales) Regulations 2001 and shall come into force on 16th February 2001.

(2)   These Regulations shall not extend to Scotland or Northern Ireland.

Revocations

2   The instruments listed in column 1 of Schedule 2 to these Regulations (which have the references listed in column 2) are hereby revoked to the extent indicated in column 3 of that Schedule.

Interpretation

3 (1)   For the purposes of these Regulations, unless the context otherwise requires–
"1983 Act" means the Representation of the People Act 1983;
"1985 Act" means the Representation of the People Act 1985;
"2000 Act" means the Representation of the People Act 2000;
"available for inspection" means available for inspection during ordinary office hours;
"British Council employee" means a person employed by the British Council in a post outside the United Kingdom;
"candidate" has the same meaning as in section 118A of the 1983 Act;
"certificate of anonymous registration" means a certificate issued in pursuance of regulation 45G;
"Crown servant" means a person who is employed in a post falling within the class or description set out in regulation 14 below;
"data" means information which is recorded with the intention that it should be processed by means of equipment operating automatically in response to instructions given for that purpose;
"data form" means information which is in a form which is capable of being processed by means of equipment operating automatically in response to instructions given for that purpose;
"digital service" means the Individual Electoral Registration Digital Service, which is the digital service provided by the Chancellor of the Duchy of Lancaster for the purpose of processing online applications under section 10ZC and 10ZD of the 1983 Act and for the purpose of verifying information under regulation 29ZA;
"edited register" has the meaning given in regulation 93(1) below;
"European Parliamentary overseas elector" means a peer who has made a European Parliamentary overseas elector's declaration and is registered or is entitled to be registered in pursuance of it;
"European Parliamentary overseas elector's declaration" means a declaration made in pursuance of section 2 of the 1985 Act, as applied by regulation 13 of, and Schedule 4 to, these Regulations;
"full register" has the meaning given in regulation 93(1) below;
"list of overseas electors" means the list prepared under regulation 45 below;
"overseas elector" means a person who has made an overseas elector's declaration and is registered or entitled to be registered as a parliamentary elector in pursuance of it;
"register" means the register of electors;
"registration area" means the area for which a registration officer acts; and
"registration officer" means the electoral registration officer.

(2) A reference in these Regulations to a numbered rule in the elections rules shall be construed as a reference to–
  (a) the rule of that number in the parliamentary elections rules in Schedule 1 to the 1983 Act in the case of a parliamentary election, or
  (b) the corresponding rule in the rules made under section 36 of the 1983 Act in the case of a local government election.

(3) A reference in these Regulations to a form identified by means of a letter shall be construed as a reference to the form so identified in Schedule 3 to these Regulations.

(3A) For the purposes of regulations 26, 26A, 26B, 32ZC, 32ZD, 32ZE, 32ZF, 32ZG and 32ZH a document may be given to a person–
  (a) by delivering it to the person;
  (b) by leaving it at the person's address; or
  (c) by sending it to the person by post.

(4) In the application of these Regulations to the registers which are required to be published not later than 15th February 2001 by section 13(1) of the 1983 Act, as enacted, references to the publication of the revised version are to be read as references to the publication of the register.

Forms

4 (1) The registration officer shall supply free of charge as many forms for use in connection with–
  (a) applications made under sections 10ZC(1)(a) and 10ZD(1)(a) of the 1983 Act, and
  (b) applications made under Schedule 4 to the 2000 Act and Part IV of these Regulations,
  as appear to that officer reasonable in the circumstances to any person who satisfies that officer of his intention to use the forms in connection with an election.

(2) The forms set out in Schedule 3 to these Regulations or forms substantially to the like effect may be used with such variations as the circumstances may require.

Communication of applications, notices etc

5 (1) The requirement in these Regulations that any application, notice or representation should be in writing is satisfied where (apart from the usual meaning of that expression) the text of it–
  (a) is transmitted by electronic means,
  (b) is received in legible form, and
  (c) is capable of being used for subsequent reference.

(2) Paragraph (1) does not apply to notice of a requirement to register given under regulation 32ZE(1) or notice of a civil penalty given under regulation 32ZF(2).

Electronic signatures and related certificates

6 (1) A requirement in these Regulations for an application, notice or representation to be signed is satisfied (as an alternative to the signature given by hand) where there is–
  (a) an electronic signature incorporated into or logically associated with a particular electronic communication, and
  (b) the certification by any person of such a signature.

(2) For the purposes of this regulation an electronic signature is so much of anything in electronic form as–
  (a) is incorporated into or otherwise logically associated with any electronic communication or both; and

      (b) purports to be so incorporated or associated for the purpose of being used in establishing the authenticity of the communication, the integrity of the communication or both.

(3) For the purposes of this regulation an electronic signature incorporated into or associated with a particular electronic communication is certified by any person if that person (whether before or after the making of the communication) has made a statement confirming that–

      (a) the signature,

      (b) a means of producing, communicating or verifying the signature, or

      (c) a procedure applied to the signature,

is (either alone or in combination with other factors) a valid means of establishing the authenticity of the communication, the integrity of the communication or both.

Copies of documents

7 (1) Where a document is made available for inspection under these Regulations, any person may make a copy (whether hand-written or by other means) of the whole or any part of it.

(2) Paragraph (1) does not apply to the full register.

(3) A person inspecting the full register may not–

      (a) make copies of any part of it, or

      (b) record any particulars included in it,

otherwise than by means of hand-written notes.

(4) A person who inspects the full register and makes a copy of it or records any particulars included in it otherwise than by means of hand-written notes shall be guilty of an offence and liable on summary conviction to a fine not exceeding level 5 on the standard scale.

(5) In this regulation "full register" includes–

      (a) any part of it; and

      (b) any notice published under section 13A(2), 13AB(2) or 13B(3), (3B) or (3D) of the 1983 Act altering the register.

(6) Paragraph (1) does not apply to copies of information covered by regulation 61(1) or to any of the documents open to public inspection under regulation 118.

Time

8 (1) Where the day or last day of the time allowed by these Regulations for the doing of any thing falls on any of the days mentioned in paragraph (3) below, that time shall be extended until the next following day which is not one of those days.

(2) Subject to regulation 56(6) below, in computing any period of not more than 7 days for the purposes of these Regulations any of the days mentioned in paragraph (3) below shall be disregarded.

(3) The days referred to in paragraphs (1) and (2) above are a Saturday, Sunday, Christmas Eve, Christmas Day, Good Friday or a bank holiday.

(4) In paragraph (3) above "bank holiday" means a day which is a bank holiday under the Banking and Financial Dealings Act 1971 in England and Wales.

Official poll card and postal poll card at parliamentary elections

9 (1) For the purposes of rule 28(3) of the rules in Schedule 1 to the 1983 Act, the following forms are hereby prescribed.

(2) The official poll card issued to an elector shall be in Form A.

(3)   The official postal poll card issued to an elector shall be in Form A1.

(4)   The official poll card issued to the proxy of an elector shall be in Form B.

(5)   The official postal poll card issued to the proxy of an elector shall be in Form B1.

Return and declaration of election expenses

10 (1)   For the purpose of section 75(3) of the 1983 Act, the form of the return of election expenses shall be in Form C and the form of the declaration as to election expenses shall be in Form D.

(2)   *Repealed*

(3)   The price of a copy of any such return, declaration or any accompanying document shall be at the rate of 20p for each side of each page.

Interference with notices etc

11   If any person without lawful authority destroys, mutilates, defaces or removes any notice published by the registration officer in connection with his registration duties or any copies of a document which have been made available for inspection in pursuance of those duties, he shall be liable on a summary conviction to a fine not exceeding level 3 on the standard scale.

Device referred to in rule 29(3A)(b) of parliamentary elections rules

12 (1)   The device referred to in rule 29(3A)(b) of the rules in Schedule 1 to the 1983 Act shall be of the description set out in this regulation.

(2)   The device must be capable of being attached firmly to a ballot paper and of being removed from it after use without damage to the paper.

(3)   On the right-hand side of the device there shall be tabs of equal size which satisfy the conditions in paragraphs (4) to (7) below.

(4)   The tabs shall be capable of being positioned on the ballot paper so that each one is above one of the spaces to the right of the particulars of the candidates on which the vote is to be marked ("the relevant space").

(5)   Each tab shall be numbered so that, when the device is positioned over a ballot paper, the number of each tab corresponds to that of the candidate whose particulars are to the left of the relevant space covered by the tab in question.

(6)   Each number on a tab shall be in raised form so that it can be clearly identified by touch.

(7)   Each tab shall be capable of being lifted so as to reveal the relevant space and so that there is sufficient room to allow a voter to mark a cross on that space.

Registration of European Parliamentary overseas electors

13 (1)   A peer who, apart from the requirement of registration, is entitled by virtue of section 3 of the 1985 Act to vote as an elector at a European Parliamentary election in a particular electoral region is entitled to be registered in a register under section 3 of that Act, prepared and published by a registration officer in accordance with this regulation and the provisions applied by it.

(2)   It is the duty of the relevant registration officer appointed under section 8 of the 1983 Act to prepare and publish a register under section 3 of the 1985 Act (which under subsection (7) of that section shall so far as practicable be combined with the register of parliamentary and local government electors) in respect of any year for which any

peer to whom paragraph (1) above applies is entitled to be registered and to take reasonable steps to obtain information required by him for that purpose.

(3) For the purposes of paragraph (2) above, "the relevant registration officer" is the officer who acts for the area within which is situated the place specified in the declaration in accordance with section 2(4) of the 1985 Act, as applied by this regulation, as having been the address in respect of which the declarant was previously registered or, as the case may be, at which he was resident.

(4) The provisions of the 1983 Act and the 1985 Act which are set out in column 1 of Schedule 4 to these Regulations shall, subject to–
  (a) any modifications and exceptions specified in relation to those provisions in column 2 of that Schedule, and
  (b) paragraph (5) below,

apply for the purposes of the registration of peers who (subject to the requirement of registration) are entitled to vote at a European Parliamentary election as they apply for the purpose of the registration of parliamentary electors.

(5) Unless the context otherwise requires, in the provisions applied by Schedule 4 to these Regulations–
  (a) any reference to an overseas elector's declaration shall be construed as a reference to a European Parliamentary overseas elector's declaration;
  (b) any reference to a constituency shall be construed as a reference to an electoral region;
  (c) any reference to a register of parliamentary electors shall be construed as a reference to a register kept under section 3 of the 1985 Act and any reference to the register of local government electors shall be disregarded; and
  (d) any reference to a provision which is also applied by Schedule 4 to these Regulations shall be construed as a reference to such a provision as so applied.

(6) The regulations which are set out in column 1 of Schedule 4A to these Regulations shall, subject to–
  (a) any modifications specified in relation to those provisions in column 2 of that Schedule, and
  (b) paragraph (7) below,

apply to a European Parliamentary overseas elector's declaration and registration in pursuance of it as they apply to an overseas elector's declaration and registration in pursuance of it.

(7) For the purposes set out in paragraph (6) above, those regulations shall, unless the context otherwise requires, have effect as if–
  (a) any reference to a parliamentary elector is a reference to a peer entitled to vote at a European Parliamentary election under section 3 of the 1985 Act;
  (b) any reference to an overseas elector is a reference to a European Parliamentary overseas elector;
  (c) any reference to an overseas elector's declaration is a reference to a European Parliamentary overseas elector's declaration; and
  (d) any reference to a provision which is applied by Schedule 4 to these Regulations is a reference to that provision as so applied.

(8) A register under section 3 of the 1985 Act may be published by means of a notice making additions to the registers of parliamentary electors and of local government electors with which it must be combined.

PART II
SERVICE AND OVERSEAS ELECTORS' DECLARATIONS

Service declarations

Qualification for Crown servant

14   A person (not being a member of the forces within the meaning of section 59(1) of the 1983 Act) who is employed in the service of the Crown in a post outside the United Kingdom falls within the class or description referred to in section 14(1)(b) of the 1983 Act if he is required to devote his whole working time to the duties of that post and the remuneration of it is paid wholly out of money provided by Parliament.

Contents of service declaration

15 (1)   In addition to the matters specified in paragraphs (a) to (f) of section 16 of the 1983 Act, a service declaration shall state–
   (a)   the declarant's full name and present address,
   (b)   the grounds on which the declarant claims a service declaration, and
   (c)   such of the particulars specified in paragraph (2), (3) or (4) below as are relevant to the service qualification claimed by the declarant.

   (2)   Where the declarant claims a service qualification on the grounds that he is a member of the forces (within the meaning of section 59(1) of the 1983 Act) or the spouse or civil partner of such a member, the service declaration shall state–
   (a)   the service (whether naval, military or air forces) in which that member serves,
   (b)   the rank or rating of that member, and
   (c)   the service number of that member;
   and where that member serves in the military forces, the service declaration shall in addition state the regiment or corps in which he serves.

   (3)   Where the declarant claims a service qualification on the grounds that he is a Crown servant to whom regulation 14 above applies or the spouse or civil partner of such a servant, the service declaration shall state–
   (a)   the name of the Government department in which that servant works,
   (b)   a description of the post of that servant, and
   (c)   any staff number, payroll number or other similar identifying number of that servant.

   (4)   Where the declarant claims a service qualification on the grounds that he is a British Council employee or the spouse or civil partner of such an employee, the service declaration shall state–
   (a)   a description of the post of that employee, and
   (b)   any staff number, payroll number or other similar identifying number of that employee.

Transmission of service declaration

16   A service declaration–
   (a)   must be transmitted to the registration officer for the area within which is situated the address specified in the declaration in accordance with section 16(d) of the 1983 Act; and
   (b)   may be transmitted through the digital service.

Notification by registration officer in respect of service declarations

17(1)   Where the registration officer is satisfied that the service declaration is duly made he shall so notify the declarant.

(2) Where the registration officer rejects an application for registration in pursuance of a service declaration because it–

    (a) does not contain the particulars required in paragraphs (a) to (f) of section 16 of the 1983 Act and regulation 15 above, or

    (b) does not comply with the requirements of sections 14 and 15 of the 1983 Act or, where appropriate, regulation 14 or 16 above,

Overseas electors' declarations

Contents of overseas elector's declaration

18 (1) In addition to the information required by paragraphs (a) to (d) of subsection (3) and subsection (4) of section 2 of the 1985 Act, an overseas elector's declaration shall state the declarant's full name and present address and, where appropriate, the information required by paragraphs (2) to (7) below.

(2) If the declarant–

    (a) was last registered in pursuance of a service or other declaration, rather than actual residence at the address specified in pursuance of section 2(4)(b) of the 1985 Act, and

    (b) no longer had connection with that address at the time at which he was so registered,

  the declaration shall include a statement that the declarant was so registered.

(3) If the declarant claims that his name has changed since he was last registered in respect of the address specified in the overseas elector's declaration in accordance with section 2(4)(b) of the 1985 Act, that declaration shall–

    (a) set out the name in respect of which the declarant was last previously registered, and

    (b) give the reason for the change of name.

(4) Where a declarant–

    (a) has on a previous occasion been registered in a register of parliamentary electors in pursuance of an overseas elector's declaration, and

    (b) has not, since being so registered, been registered in such a register by virtue of being resident or treated for the purposes of registration as resident at an address in the United Kingdom,

  his overseas elector's declaration shall state those facts and indicate when he was last registered in pursuance of an overseas elector's declaration.

  For the purposes of the application of this paragraph by regulation 13(6) above, this paragraph shall have effect as if, in addition to the modifications made by that regulation, the words "a register of local government electors" were substituted for the words "such a register".

(5) Where a declarant has not made an overseas elector's declaration in pursuance of which he was registered in a register of parliamentary electors since being included in such a register by virtue of being resident or treated for the purposes of registration as resident at an address in the United Kingdom, or has never made such a declaration, his overseas elector's declaration shall state–

    (a) in the case of a declarant who is the bearer of a British passport which describes his national status as "British citizen", the number of that passport together with its date and place of issue; or

    (b) in the case of a declarant who is not the bearer of such a passport, but who was born in the United Kingdom before 1st January 1983, those facts; or

(c) in the case of a declarant who is not the bearer of such a passport and who was not born in the United Kingdom before 1st January 1983, when and how he acquired the status of British citizen, together with the date, place and country of his birth.

For the purposes of the application of this regulation by regulation 13(6) above, this paragraph shall have effect as if, in addition to the modifications made by that regulation, the words "a register of local government electors" were substituted for the words "such a register".

(6) Where, in the case of a declarant to whom regulation 19 below applies (and who is accordingly required to transmit a copy of his birth certificate together with his declaration), his name on his birth certificate is not the same as his name as given in his overseas elector's declaration, that declaration shall state the reason for the change of name.

(7) Where, in the case of a declarant to whom regulation 19 below applies, he relies on the registration of either–
   (a) a parent whose name in the register referred to in section 1(4)(c) of the 1985 Act is not the same as the name of that parent as given in either the declarant's birth certificate or overseas elector's declaration in accordance with section 2(4)(c)(iii) of the 1985 Act, or
   (b) a guardian whose name in the register referred to in section 1(4)(c) of the 1985 Act is not the same as the name of that guardian as given in the declarant's overseas elector's declaration in accordance with section 2(4)(c)(iii) of the 1985 Act,

that declaration shall state the name of the parent or, as the case may be, guardian as given in the register referred to in section 1(4)(c) and, where known, the reason for the change or, as the case may be, changes of name or, where such reason (or reasons) is not known, a statement to that effect.

For the purposes of the application of this regulation by regulation 13(6) above, this paragraph shall have effect as if, in addition to the modifications made by that regulation, the words "section 3(4)(c)" were substituted for the words "section 1(4)(c)", in each place where those words occur.

Certain declarants to supply copy of birth certificates

19 (1) This regulation applies to a person who has made an overseas elector's declaration in which he claims to be qualified as an overseas elector by virtue of the conditions set out in section 1(4) of the 1985 Act, and who has not on a previous occasion made an overseas elector's declaration in pursuance of which he was registered in a register of parliamentary electors.

For the purpose of the application of this regulation by regulation 13(6) above, this paragraph shall have effect as if, in addition to the modifications made by that regulation, the words "section 3(4)" were substituted for the words "section 1(4)".

(2) Where this regulation applies, a declarant shall transmit together with his overseas elector's declaration a copy of his birth certificate which shows the names of either or both of his parents as well as his date of birth.

20   *Repealed*

Transmission of overseas elector's declaration

21 An overseas elector's declaration shall be transmitted to the registration officer for that part of a constituency within which is situated the address specified in the declaration in accordance with section 2(4) of the 1985 Act.

Notification about registration as overseas elector

22 (1) Where the registration officer is satisfied that the declarant qualifies as an overseas elector under the provisions of sections 1 and 2 of the 1985 Act, he shall so notify the declarant.

(2) Where the registration officer rejects an application for registration in pursuance of an overseas elector's declaration because–

    (a) in his opinion the declarant does not qualify as an overseas elector under section 1 of the 1985 Act, or

    (b) the declaration does not satisfy the requirements of section 2 of the 1985 Act or regulation 18 or 20 above, or

    (c) in the case of a person to whom regulation 19 above applies, the requirement in that regulation has not been complied with,

he shall return the declaration to the declarant and set out his reasons for rejecting the application for registration.

(3) For the purposes of the application of this regulation by regulation 13(6) above, paragraphs (1) and (2) above shall have effect as if, in addition to the modifications made by that regulation–

    (a) in paragraph (1), for the words "sections 1 and 2" there were substituted the words "sections 2 and 3", and

    (b) in paragraph (2), for the words "section 1" there were substituted the words "section 3".

PART III
REGISTRATION

Information about electors

Power to require information

23 (1) A registration officer may require any person to give information required for the purposes of that officer's duties in maintaining registers of parliamentary and local government electors.

(1A) A registration officer may not use the power conferred by paragraph (1) to require a person who has made an application under section 10ZC or 10ZD of the 1983 Act to provide information to assist the registration officer in determining, in connection with that application, whether the applicant is the person named in the application or is entitled to be registered.

(2) A registration officer is under a duty to require persons to give information required for the purposes of that officer's duty under section 3(1) of the Juries Act 1974.

(3) If any person–

    (a) fails to comply with

    (b) *Repealed*

any such requisition of the registration officer as is mentioned in this regulation, he shall be liable on summary conviction to a fine not exceeding level 3 on the standard scale.

NOTES

Initial Commencement

Specified date

Specified date: 16 February 2001: see reg 1(1).

Amendment

Para (1A): inserted by SI 2013/3198, reg 7.

Date in force: 10 June 2014: see SI 2013/3198, reg 1(5)(b).

Date in force: 1 January 2007: see SI 2006/2910, reg 1(1).

Para (3): sub-para (b) and word omitted immediately preceding it revoked by SI 2006/2910, reg 3.

Evidence as to age and nationality

24 (1) Where a registration officer has doubts about a person's age or nationality, he may require that person to produce such evidence as is specified in paragraph (2) below for the purposes of registration.

(2) The evidence which the registration officer may require is as follows–

  (a) a birth certificate;

  (b) a certificate of naturalisation;

  (c) where a person has made an overseas elector's declaration, further evidence of his status as a British citizen including a document showing that he has become a British citizen by virtue of registration;

  (d) in any other case–

  (i) a document showing that he has become a Commonwealth citizen by virtue of registration; or

  (ii) a statutory declaration that he is a qualifying Commonwealth citizen or citizen of the Republic of Ireland or a relevant citizen of the Union.

(3) If any fee is payable in connection with the making of a declaration for the purposes of this regulation, the registration officer shall pay that fee and it shall be treated as part of his registration expenses within the meaning of section 54(1) of the 1983 Act.

(4) Any such declaration shall be made available for inspection at the registration officer's office until the determination of the application for registration and of any objections duly made to it.

(4A) Paragraph (4) does not apply where the declarant has, or has applied for, an anonymous entry.

(5) This regulation does not apply where an application for registration is made in pursuance of a service declaration.

(6) In this regulation "qualifying Commonwealth citizen" has the same meaning as in section 4 of the 1983 Act.

NOTES

Initial Commencement

Specified date

Specified date: 16 February 2001: see reg 1(1).

Amendment

Para (2): in sub-para (a) words omitted revoked by SI 2013/3198, reg 8.

Date in force: 10 June 2014: see SI 2013/3198, reg 1(5)(b).

Para (4A): inserted by SI 2006/2910, reg 4.

Date in force: 1 January 2007: see SI 2006/2910, reg 1(1).

See Further

See further, in relation to the application of this regulation, with modifications, in relation to extending the rights of citizens and nationals of Accession States to register and be registered as local government electors and European Parliamentary electors: the Local and European Parliamentary Elections (Registration of Citizens of Accession States) Regulations 2003, SI 2003/1557, reg 7, Sch 2, para 1(1), (3)(a).

Reminders to electors registered pursuant to a declaration

25 (1) This regulation applies in respect of a person registered in pursuance of–

  (a) a service declaration;

  (b) a declaration of local connection; and

  (c) an overseas elector's declaration.

(2) Subject to paragraph (4) below, the registration officer shall, during the relevant period, send to a person to whom this regulation applies a reminder of the need to make a fresh declaration if he wishes to remain registered as an elector in pursuance of such a declaration.

(3) In paragraph (2) "the relevant period" means–

    (a) except in cases to which sub-paragraph (b) applies, the period beginning nine months after the date when the existing entry in a register of the person in question first takes effect and ending ten months after that date, and

    (b) in the case of a person mentioned in section 14(1)(a) or (d) of the 1983 Act (members of the forces and their spouses or civil partners) who is registered in pursuance of a service declaration, the period beginning 57 months after the date when the existing entry in a register of the person in question first takes effect and ending 58 months after that date.

(3A) Subject to paragraph (4) below, the registration officer must send a second reminder not less than 21 nor more than 28 days after the date of the sending of the first reminder.

(4) Paragraphs (2) and (3A) above do not apply in respect of a person to whom this regulation applies where–

    (a) the registration officer has already received from that person a fresh declaration, or

    (b) information which the registration officer has received indicates that that person is no longer entitled to make the relevant declaration.

NOTES

Initial Commencement

Date in force: 19 March 2010: see SI 2010/882, art 1(2).

Specified date

Specified date: 16 February 2001: see reg 1(1).

Para (3A): inserted by SI 2014/3161, regs 2, 5(a).

Date in force: 9 December 2014: see SI 2014/3161, reg 1.

Amendment

Para (3): substituted by SI 2006/3406, art 3.

Date in force: 1 January 2007: see SI 2006/3406, art 1(2).

Para (3): sub-para (b) substituted by SI 2010/882, art 3.

Para (4): words "Paragraphs (2) and (3A) above do" in square brackets substituted by SI 2014/3161, regs 2, 5(b).

Date in force: 9 December 2014: see SI 2014/3161, reg 1.

Reminders to persons who have an anonymous entry

25A (1) This regulation applies to each person who has an anonymous entry.

  (2) Subject to paragraph (3), the registration officer must, during the relevant period, send to a person to whom this regulation applies a reminder that–

    (a) his entitlement to registration will terminate at the end of the period of 12 months beginning with the date on which his entry in the register first took effect;

    (b) if he wishes to remain entered in the register after that period, he must make a fresh application for registration in accordance with the requirements prescribed for the purposes of section 10ZC(1)(b) of the 1983 Act;

    (c) if he wishes to remain entered in the register anonymously, the application for registration must be accompanied by a fresh application for an anonymous entry.

  (3) Paragraph (2) does not apply where the registration officer has already received from that person a fresh application for registration made in accordance with the

requirements prescribed for the purposes of section 10A(1)(a) which is accompanied by a fresh application for an anonymous entry.

(4) In this regulation, "the relevant period" must be construed in accordance with regulation 25(3)(a).

NOTES

Amendment

Inserted by SI 2006/2910, reg 5.

Date in force: 1 January 2007: see SI 2006/2910, reg 1(1).

Para (2): in sub-para (b) words "section 10ZC(1)(b) of the

1983 Act" in square brackets substituted by SI 2013/3198, reg 9.

Date in force: 10 June 2014: see SI 2013/3198, reg 1(5)(b).

Applications for registration

26 (1) An application for registration as a parliamentary or local government elector (or both) under section 10ZC or an application for alteration in respect of address under section 10ZD of the 1983 Act ("an application") must be in writing and must state–
  (a) the applicant's full name;
  (b) except in the case of an application being made in pursuance of a service declaration or an overseas elector's declaration, the address in respect of which the applicant applies to be registered and at which they are resident on the date of the application;
  (c) any address at which the applicant has ceased to reside within 12 months before the date of the application and, where that address is not in the United Kingdom, an indication of whether the person was registered in pursuance of an overseas elector's declaration during this period;
  (d) an indication of whether the applicant is resident at any other address, including at any address in respect of which the applicant is currently registered as an elector and in respect of which the applicant claims to be entitled to remain registered;
  (e) the applicant's date of birth or, if they are not able to provide that information, the reason why they are not able to do so and a statement as to whether the applicant is under 18 years old or aged 76 or over;
  (ea) space for the applicant to provide their most recent previous name (if they have one) and an explanation that provision of this information is not mandatory but may assist the registration officer in verifying the applicant's identity, and that if the information is not provided then additional personal information may be required;
  (f) the applicant's national insurance number or, if they are not able to provide that information, the reason why they are not able to do so;
  (g) except in the case of a person applying to be registered in pursuance of an overseas elector's declaration, the applicant's nationality or nationalities or, if they are not able to provide that information, the reason why they are not able to do so;
  (h) an indication of whether the applicant requests that their name and address are omitted from the edited version of the register;
  (i) in the case of an applicant whose application is accompanied by an application for an anonymous entry, that fact;
  (j) a declaration by the applicant that the information provided in the application is true; and
  (k) the date of the application.

(2) In the case of a person applying to be registered as a parliamentary or local government elector (or both) in pursuance of a service declaration, a declaration of

local connection or an overseas elector's declaration, an application under paragraph (1) must include the appropriate declaration.

(3) The Electoral Commission must design a paper application form which requires the information and declarations in paragraphs (1) and (2) and includes–

    (a) a statement that the information provided in the application will be processed in accordance with the Data Protection Act 1998 and as to what information will appear on the electoral register;

    (b) a statement that persons without lawful immigration status are ineligible to register to vote, and that registration officers may request checks in relation to an applicant's immigration status against Home Office records;

    (c) a statement that it is an offence to provide false information to the registration officer, together with a statement of the maximum penalty for that offence;

    (d) space for a bar code, local authority reference number and security code unique to each form;

    (e) space for the email address and telephone number or numbers of the applicant and an explanation that provision of this information is not mandatory;

    (f) space for the registration officer to include local authority information and details of how the registration officer may be contacted;

    (g) an indication of whether the applicant wishes to be able to cast an absent vote;

    (h) an explanation of what the edited register is, using the short version of the form of words prescribed by regulation 45 of and Schedule 3 to the Representation of the People (England and Wales)(Description of Electoral Registers and Amendment) Regulations 2013; and

    (i) the web site address of the digital service.

(4) The paper application form for persons applying to be registered in pursuance of a service declaration must–

    (a) instead of the information required in paragraph (1)(b), request the applicant's correspondence address or British Forces Post Office Number;

    (b) in the case of an application in pursuance of a service declaration on the grounds that the applicant is a member of the forces (within the meaning of section 59(1) of the 1983 Act) or the spouse or civil partner of a member of the forces (within the meaning of section 59(1) of the 1983 Act), also include a statement that the applicant must renew their application for registration every 5 years but may cancel it at any time.

(5) The paper application form for persons applying to be registered in pursuance of an overseas elector's declaration must, instead of the information required in paragraph (1)(b), request–

    (a) the last address at which the applicant was registered as an elector; and

    (b) the address at which the applicant can be contacted.

(6) The Electoral Commission must obtain the approval of the Chancellor of the Duchy of Lancaster to the design of the application forms under paragraphs (3), (4) and (5) and must then make the forms available to registration officers.

(7) Where a registration officer gives a paper application form to a person resident in England or Wales, it must be accompanied by a pre-addressed reply envelope, return postage of which must be prepaid.

(8) A registration officer may authorise the applicant to provide the information required by paragraph (1) to the registration officer by telephone or in person and, where the officer does so, the registration officer must–

    (a) provide the applicant with an explanation of what the edited register is, using the short version of the form of words prescribed by regulation 45 of and Schedule 3 to the Representation of the People (England and

Wales)(Description of Electoral Registers and Amendment) Regulations 2013; and

    (b) transfer the information provided by the applicant into an application in writing.

(9) An application under paragraph (1) may be made through the digital service and, where it is, the Chancellor of the Duchy of Lancaster must request the applicant's email address and telephone number or numbers and provide an explanation of the purpose for which this information will be used.

(10) A registration officer may, but need not, accept an application in pursuance of an overseas elector's declaration through the digital service.

(11) The Chancellor of the Duchy of Lancaster must send to the registration officer any application he receives together with–

    (a) the applicant's email address and telephone numbers (if provided); and

    (b) a reference number unique to that application.

NOTES

Application for alteration of register in respect of name under section 10ZD

26A (1) An application for alteration in respect of name under section 10ZD of the 1983 Act must be in writing and must state–

    (a) the applicant's full name;

    (b) the full name in respect of which the applicant is currently registered;

    (c) the date of the change of name;

    (d) the address in respect of which the applicant is registered;

    (e) a declaration by the applicant that the information provided in the application is true;

    (f) the date of the application.

(2) The Electoral Commission must design a form for applications for alteration in respect of name under section 10ZD of the 1983 Act, which requires the information in paragraph (1) and includes–

    (a) a statement that the information provided in the application will be processed in accordance with the Data Protection Act 1998 and as to what information will appear on the electoral register;

    (b) space for a bar code, local authority reference number and security code unique to each form; and

    (c) space for the registration officer to include local authority information and details of how the registration officer may be contacted.

(3) The Electoral Commission must obtain the approval of the Chancellor of the Duchy of Lancaster to the design of the application form under paragraph (2) and must then make the form available to registration officers.

(4) A person making an application for alteration in respect of name under paragraph (1) must give to the registration officer as part of their application documentary evidence of the applicant's change of name.

(5) Where a person is unable to provide any documentary evidence, they must provide their date of birth and national insurance number as part of their application or, if they are not able to provide their date of birth or national insurance number, the reason why they are not able to do so.

(6) Where the registration officer considers it appropriate, the officer may require that the applicant provide the original of any copy document provided under paragraph (4) after the application has been made.

Power to request additional evidence where certain information is unavailable or where the registration officer considers it necessary

26B (1) This regulation applies where a registration officer considers additional evidence is necessary to verify the identity of a person or determine their entitlement to register in respect of their application under section 10ZC or 10ZD of the 1983 Act, including where that is necessary because the person is not able to state the information required by any of sub-paragraphs (e), (f) or (g) of regulation 26(1).

(2) The registration officer may require that the applicant give them a copy, or where the registration officer considers it appropriate, the original, of one of the following documents–

    (a) the applicant's passport;

    (b) the applicant's identity card issued in the European Economic Area;

    (c) the applicant's biometric immigration document issued in the United Kingdom in accordance with regulations made under section 5 of the Borders Act 2007;

    (d) the applicant's electoral identity card issued in Northern Ireland; or

    (e) the applicant's photocard driving licence granted in the United Kingdom or driving licence granted by a Crown Dependency, which bears a photograph of the applicant.

(3) Where an applicant is not able to give one of the documents in paragraph (2), the registration officer may require that the applicant give them a copy, or where the registration officer considers it appropriate, the original, of–

    (a) one of the following documents, which, except in relation to paragraph (vii), must have been issued in the United Kingdom or Crown Dependencies–

        (i) the applicant's birth certificate;

        (ii) the applicant's marriage or civil partnership certificate;

        (iii) the applicant's adoption certificate;

        (iv) the applicant's firearms certificate granted under the Firearms Act 1968;

        (v) the record of a decision on bail made in respect of the applicant in accordance with section 5(1) of the Bail Act 1976;

        (vi) the applicant's driving licence, which is not in the form of a photocard; or

        (vii) the applicant's driving licence granted other than in the United Kingdom or Crown Dependencies, which bears a photograph of the applicant and which must be valid for at least 12 months from the date the applicant entered the United Kingdom; and

    (b) two other documents, each of which may be either from sub-paragraph (a) or from paragraph (4).

(4) Where the applicant is not able to give documents in accordance with paragraph (3), the registration officer may require that the applicant give them a copy, or where the registration officer considers it appropriate, the original, of four documents, each of which may be any of the following kinds of evidence and which must bear the applicant's full name–

    (a) a financial statement, including but not limited to–

        (i) a mortgage statement;

        (ii) a bank or building society statement or a letter from a bank or building society confirming that the applicant has opened an account with that bank or building society;

        (iii) a credit card statement;

        (iv) a pension statement;

    (b) a council tax demand letter or statement;

    (c) a utility bill;

    (d)   a Form P45 or Form P60 issued to the applicant by their employer or former employer;

    (e)   a statement of benefits or entitlement to benefits, such as a statement of child benefit, within the meaning of section 141 of the Social Security Contributions and Benefits Act 1992, or a letter confirming that the applicant is entitled to housing benefit, within the meaning of section 130 of that Act.

(5)   If an applicant is unable to give the documentary evidence required under paragraphs (2) to (4), the registration officer may require that the applicant give an attestation as set out in paragraph (6).

(6)   An attestation must–

    (a)   confirm that the applicant is the person named in the application;

    (b)   state that the person signing the attestation is aware of the penalty for providing false information to a registration officer;

    (c)   be in writing and signed by a person–

        (i)   whom the registration officer is satisfied is of good standing in the community;

        (ii)   who is registered as an elector in the same local authority area as the applicant;

        (iii)   who is not the spouse, civil partner, parent, grandparent, brother, sister, child or grandchild of the applicant; and

        (iv)   who has not already signed attestations under this regulation for two applicants since the last revised version of the register was published under section 13(1) of the 1983 Act.

    (d)   state the full name, date of birth, address, electoral number and occupation of the person signing the attestation; and

    (e)   state the date on which it is made.

(7)   Paragraphs (2) to (6) do not apply where the application is made pursuant to the following declarations–

    (a)   a service declaration on the grounds that the applicant is a Crown servant (within the meaning of regulation 14) or the spouse or civil partner of a Crown servant (within the meaning of regulation 14);

    (b)   a service declaration on the grounds that the applicant is a member of the forces (within the meaning of section 59(1) of the 1983 Act);

    (c)   a service declaration on the grounds that the applicant is the spouse or civil partner of a member of the forces (within the meaning of section 59(1) of the 1983 Act); or

    (d)   an overseas elector's declaration.

(8)   In the case of an application in pursuance of a declaration within paragraph (7)(a) or (c), the registration officer may require that the applicant give them a copy, or where the registration officer considers it appropriate, the original, of one of the following documents, which has been certified by a Crown servant (within the meaning of regulation 14) or British Council employee or an officer of the forces (within the meaning of section 59(1) of the 1983 Act) who is not the applicant's spouse or civil partner–

    (a)   the applicant's passport; or

    (b)   the applicant's identity card issued in the European Economic Area.

(9)   In the case of an application in pursuance of a declaration within paragraph (7)(b), the registration officer may require that the applicant give an attestation which must–

    (a)   confirm that the applicant is the person named in the application;

    (b)   be in writing and signed by an officer of the forces (within the meaning of section 59(1) of the 1983 Act) who is not the spouse, civil partner, parent, grandparent, brother, sister, child or grandchild of the applicant;

(c)   state the full name, address and rank of the person signing the attestation and the service (whether naval, military or air forces) in which they serve; and

(d)   state the date on which it is made.

(10)   In the case of an application in pursuance of a declaration within paragraph (7)(d), the registration officer may require that the applicant give an attestation which must–

(a)   confirm that the applicant is the person named in the application;

(b)   be in writing and signed by a registered elector who is a British citizen living overseas and who is not the spouse, civil partner, parent, grandparent, brother, sister, child or grandchild of the applicant;

(c)   state the full name, address and occupation of the person signing the attestation;

(d)   state the attestor's British passport number together with its date and place of issue; and

(e)   state the date on which it is made.

(11)   Where a registration officer considers that additional evidence is necessary in order to determine whether the applicant is a qualifying Commonwealth citizen, the registration officer may require that the applicant provide evidence relating to the applicant's immigration status, including, if applicable, the applicant's biometric immigration document issued in the United Kingdom.

(12)   In this regulation–

(a)   "Crown Dependency" means the Bailiwick of Jersey, the Bailiwick of Guernsey or the Isle of Man;

(b)   "qualifying Commonwealth citizen" has the same meaning as in section 4 of the 1983 Act.

Objections to registration

27 (1)   Any objection to a person's registration shall state–

(a)   the name of the person against whom the objection is made;

(b)   in the case of an objection made before that person is entered in the register, the address of that person as given in the application for registration;

(ba)   in the case of an objection made after that person is entered in the register, the electoral number and qualifying address of that person contained in the register;

(c)   the grounds of the objection;

(d)   the name of the objector and his address as shown in the register (if so shown) together with the address to which correspondence should be sent if that address is different or if no address is shown in the register; and

(e)   the electoral number of the objector.

(2)   An objection shall be made in writing and be signed and dated by the person objecting.

(3)   In this Part of these Regulations "objection" includes representations made against an application for registration under section 13A(1)(za) of the 1983 Act.

Inspection of applications and objections

28 (1)   An entry on the list of applications for registration kept under regulation 29(2)(a) and any objection to a person's registration shall be made available for inspection at the registration officer's office until the application to which the entry relates or objection has been determined by the registration officer.

(2)   This regulation does not apply to an application for registration which is accompanied by an application for an anonymous entry.

Determination of applications and objections

Verification of information provided in an application

29ZA (1) On receipt of an application under section 10ZC or 10ZD of the 1983 Act made otherwise than through the digital service, a registration officer must disclose the name or names, date of birth and national insurance number given under regulation 26 or 26A to the Chancellor of the Duchy of Lancaster in such a format and through such a conduit system as the Chancellor of the Duchy may have notified to the registration officer in writing.

(2) Following receipt of the information from the registration officer or (in the case of an application made through the digital service) from the applicant, the Chancellor of the Duchy of Lancaster may disclose the information to the Secretary of State.

(3) Where information has been disclosed to the Secretary of State under paragraph (2), the Secretary of State may compare it against–
   (a) the name, date of birth and national insurance number of individuals appearing in the following types of databases kept by the Secretary of State–
      (i) databases kept for the purposes of functions relating to social security (including such information kept on behalf of the Department for Social Development); and
      (ii) databases relating to working tax credit, child tax credit and child benefit (being information kept on behalf of Her Majesty's Revenue and Customs); and
   (b) any other information contained in those databases which relates to the information disclosed under paragraph (2).

(4) The Secretary of State may disclose the results of the comparison to the Chancellor of the Duchy of Lancaster.

(5) On receipt of such results, the Chancellor of the Duchy of Lancaster may disclose them to the registration officer in whose register the applicant has applied to be registered.

(6) Where the Chancellor of the Duchy of Lancaster does so, the registration officer must take the results into account in determining the application.

(7) In this regulation–
   (a) "conduit system" has the same meaning as in paragraph 1 of Schedule 2 to the Telecommunications Act 1984;
   (b) "the Secretary of State" means the Secretary of State for the Department for Work and Pensions.

Processing of information provided in connection with an application under section 10ZC or 10ZD

29ZB (1) If a person provides an original document under regulation 26A(4), 26B(2) to (4) or 26B(8), the registration officer must make a copy of that document and return the original document to the person who provided it.

(2) In respect of any application under section 10ZC or 10ZD of the 1983 Act, the registration officer must retain until the application has been determined–
   (a) the application form or, in the case of an application made through the digital service, the information contained in the application;
   (b) any other information or documents provided to the registration officer in connection with the application or, in the case of original documents which are returned under paragraph (1), a copy of such documents.

(3) Subject to paragraph (4), the registration officer may retain the application form, information and documents in paragraph (2) after the application has been

determined but, if they do so, must delete the applicant's national insurance number from the application form, information and documents in paragraph (2) by no later than the date which is 13 months from the date on which the registration officer determined the application under section 10ZC or 10ZD.

(4)   The requirement to delete the national insurance number in paragraph (3) does not apply where the application, information and documents in paragraph (2) are required for the purpose of any civil or criminal proceedings.

(5)   Information disclosed under regulation 29ZA may not be disclosed to any other person, except–

      (a) for the purpose of determining the application in connection with which the information was disclosed; or

      (b) for the purpose of any civil or criminal proceedings.

(6)   A person who discloses information in breach of paragraph (5) is guilty of an offence and liable–

      (a) on conviction on indictment, to imprisonment for a term not exceeding two years, or to a fine, or to both;

      (b) on summary conviction, to imprisonment for a term not exceeding 12 months, or to a fine not exceeding the statutory maximum, or to both.

(7)   Any person who discloses information under regulation 29ZA must process it in accordance with any requirements as to the processing of information that may have been imposed by the Chancellor of the Duchy of Lancaster in writing, including requirements as to the transfer, storage, destruction and security of that information.

(8)   Any requirements, in accordance with which a person must process information, must be imposed by the Chancellor of the Duchy before a registration officer is required to disclose that information under regulation 29ZA(1).

(9)   "Copy" in this regulation includes an electronic copy.

Procedure for determining applications for registration and objections without a hearing

29 (1)   A registration officer shall discharge his functions of determining an application under section 10ZC(1)(a) or 10ZD(1)(a) of the 1983 Act or considering an objection under section 10ZC(2), 10ZD(2) or 10ZE(5)(a) of that Act in accordance with this regulation and regulations 30 to 31A below.

(2)   The registration officer must keep separate lists of–

      (a) applications for registration;

      (b) objections made before the person against whom the objection is made is entered in the register;

      (c) objections made after the person against whom the objection is made is entered in the register.

(2A)   On receipt of an application the registration officer must enter the name and nationality of the applicant and the address claimed as his qualifying address in the list he keeps in pursuance of paragraph (2)(a).

(2B)   Paragraph (2A) does not apply to an application accompanied by an application for an anonymous entry.

(2BA)   Where an application for registration has been made and that application is successful, the registration officer must give confirmation in writing to the applicant of that fact, before either–

      (a) publication of the revised register to which the applicant will be added under section 13(1) of the 1983 Act; or

(b) issue of a notice of alteration under section 13A(2) of that Act specifying that the applicant's name will be added to the register,
whichever is appropriate.

(2BB) Where confirmation is given under paragraph (2BA) in relation to an application for registration made in response to an invitation to register under section 9E(1) of the 1983 Act, the registration officer must give that confirmation either–
    (a) by delivering it to the applicant, leaving it at the applicant's address or sending it to the applicant's address by post; or
    (b) by electronic means.

(2BC) Where confirmation is given under paragraph (2BA) in relation to an application for registration made other than in response to an invitation to register under section 9E(1) of the 1983 Act–
    (a) the registration officer must give confirmation by delivering it to the applicant, by leaving it at their address or by sending it to them by post; and
    (b) the confirmation must give the registration officer's contact details and must request that any person who receives that confirmation inform the registration officer if the applicant is not resident at the address in respect of which the application was made.

(2BD) A confirmation given under paragraph (2BA) must–
    (a) contain the date on which the applicant's name will be published in the revised register under section 13(1) or in a notice of alteration under section 13A(2) of the 1983 Act; and
    (b) where–
        (i) the registration officer has information that the applicant is registered in respect of a different address from the one in respect of which they have applied to be registered; and
        (ii) in their application for registration, the applicant has identified that address as being an address at which they have ceased to reside in accordance with regulation 26(1)(c);
inform the applicant that their entry relating to that address will be removed from the register under section 10ZE(2) of the 1983 Act.

(2BE) In the case of an application to register in pursuance of a service declaration, or an overseas elector's declaration, the address to be used for the purposes of paragraph (2BB)(a) or (2BC)(a), is the address the applicant has given under regulation 26(4)(a) or 26(5)(b), as appropriate.

(2BF) The Electoral Commission must–
    (a) design the forms of confirmation to be used under paragraph (2BA);
    (b) obtain the approval of the Chancellor of the Duchy of Lancaster to the forms; and
    (c) then make them available to registration officers.

(2C) On receipt of an objection made before the person against whom the objection is made is entered in the register, the registration officer must enter–
    (a) in the list he keeps in pursuance of paragraph (2)(b), the name and qualifying address of the objector together with the particulars referred to in paragraph (2A), and
    (b) in the list he keeps in pursuance of paragraph (2)(a), the particulars of the objection.

(2D) On receipt of any other objection, the registration officer must enter the name and qualifying address of the objector together with the particulars referred to in paragraph (2A) in the list he keeps in pursuance of paragraph (2)(c).

(3) The registration officer may ask for further information and take no further action until such information is supplied, if he is of opinion that the particulars given in the application or objection are insufficient.

(4) Subject to paragraph (4A), the registration officer may allow an application without a hearing provided that no objection is made within the period of five days beginning with the day following the entry of the application in the list of applications.

(4A) In the case of an application for registration accompanied by an application for an anonymous entry, the registration officer may allow the former application without a hearing at any time.

(5) The registration officer may disallow an objection if he is of opinion that the objector is not entitled to object; and he shall so inform the objector.

(5A) The registration officer may disallow an objection without a hearing if he is of the opinion that the objection is clearly without merit.

(5B) Where the registration officer disallows an objection under paragraph (5A), he must send to the objector a notice stating that the application has been disallowed on that basis and the grounds for his opinion.

(5C) An objector may require the objection to be heard by giving notice to the registration officer within three days from the date of the notice given under paragraph (5B).

(5D) A notification under paragraph (5C) is not to prevent the application to which the objection relates from being allowed.

(6) The registration officer may send to the applicant or objector a notice stating his opinion that an application or objection cannot be allowed because–
    (a) the matter has been concluded by the decision of a court, or
    (b) the particulars given in the application or objection do not entitle the applicant or objector to succeed.

(7) In cases to which paragraph (6) applies, the registration officer shall state the grounds for his opinion and that he intends to disallow the application or objection unless that person gives the registration officer notice within three days from the date of the registration officer's notice that he requires the application or objection to be heard; and if he receives no such notice within that time, he may disallow the application or objection.

(8) In this regulation, "qualifying address" includes the address specified in an overseas elector's declaration in accordance with section 2(4)(b) or (c)(ii) of the 1985 Act.

Notice of hearing

30 (1) The registration officer shall, unless he allows or disallows the application or objection under regulation 29 above, send a notice–
    (a) in the case of an application, to the person making the application, and
    (b) in the case of an objection, to the objector and the person objected to, stating–
        (i) the time and place at which he proposes to hear the application or objection;
        (ii) the name and address of the objector and the grounds of the objection (in the case of a notice sent to a person objected to).

(2) The time fixed for the hearing of an application or objection shall not be earlier than the third day or later than the seventh day after the date of the notice referred to in paragraph (1) above.

Hearing of applications and objections

31 (1)   The persons entitled to appear and be heard are as follows–
    (a)   on an application, the applicant;
    (b)   on an objection, the objector and the person objected to;
    (c)   on an application or an objection, any other person who appears to the registration officer to be interested.

   (2)   The right to appear and be heard includes the right to make written representations.

   (3)   Any person entitled to appear and be heard may do so either in person or by any other person on his behalf.

   (4)   The registration officer may, at the request of any person entitled to appear and be heard or, if he thinks fit, without such a request, require that the evidence tendered by any person shall be given on oath and may administer the oath for the purpose.

Objections relating to applications that have been allowed, but before alterations to register have taken effect

31A (1)   This regulation applies where–
    (a)   an application for registration has been allowed (whether without or following a hearing), and
    (b)   either–
      (i)   an objection is later made to that application, or
      (ii)   an objector whose objection in respect of that application has been disallowed in pursuance of regulation 29(5A) notifies the registration officer, in accordance with regulation 29(5C), that he requires the objection to be heard, and
    (c)   no alteration to the register has yet taken effect in respect of that application by virtue of section 13(5), 13A(2), 13AB(2) or 13B(3) of the 1983 Act.

   (2)   Where the registration officer–
    (a)   is able to determine the objection before the alteration to the register is due to take effect, and
    (b)   allows the objection,
   the application is to be treated as if it had been disallowed.

   (3)   Where the registration officer is not able to determine the objection before the alteration to the register is due to take effect, the objection is to be treated as if it was made after the person against whom it is made is entered in the register.

   (4)   Where paragraph (3) applies, the registration officer must transfer the entry relating to the objection from the list he keeps in pursuance of paragraph (2)(b) of regulation 29 to the list he keeps in pursuance of paragraph (2)(c) of that regulation.

Other determinations by registration officer of entitlement to registration

31B (1)   A registration officer must discharge the functions specified in paragraph (2) in accordance with regulations 31C to 31FZA.

   (2)   The functions specified in this paragraph are–
    (a)   determining, under the following provisions, whether a person was entitled to be registered–
      (i)   sections 7(3)(aa), 7A(3)(aa), 7C(2)(aa), 10ZE(1)(a) and 15(2)(aa) of the 1983 Act, and
      (ii)   section 2(2)(aa) of the 1985 Act;
    (b)   determining, under the following provisions, whether a person was registered or their entry has been altered as a result of an application made by another person–

    (i)   sections 7(3)(ab), 7A(3)(ab), 7C(2)(ab), 10ZE(1)(c) and 15(2)(ab) of the 1983 Act; and

    (ii)   section 2(2)(ab) of the 1985 Act;

(c) determining under section 10ZE(1)(b) of the 1983 Act whether a person has ceased to be resident at the address or has otherwise ceased to satisfy the conditions for registration set out in section 4 of the 1983 Act.

Summary procedure for determining in specified circumstances person has ceased to satisfy conditions for registration

31C (1) In any of the circumstances specified in paragraph (2) the registration officer may make a determination under section 10ZE of the 1983 Act in respect of an elector without following the procedure set out in regulations 31D to 31FZA.

(2) The circumstances specified in this paragraph are where either–

    (a) the registration officer has received information either through the digital service or from another registration officer that–

       (i)   the elector has made an application under section 10ZC or 10ZD of the 1983 Act in respect of an address which is different from the one in respect of which they are registered; and

       (ii)   in that application the elector has in accordance with regulation 26(1)(c) identified the address in respect of which they are registered as being an address at which they have ceased to reside; and

      the relevant registration officer has determined that the person should be entered on the register maintained by that officer; or

    (b) the registration officer–

       (i)   has information from at least two sources that support such a determination;

       (ii)   has been provided with a death certificate in respect of the elector; or

       (iii) has been notified by the registrar of births and deaths that the elector has died.

(3) In this regulation "elector" means a person who is duly entered in a register in respect of an address.

Procedure for reviewing entitlement to registration

31D (1) A registration officer must, for the purposes of making a determination of the nature specified in regulation 31B(2), conduct a review in respect of a person entered in the register.

(2) Where the registration officer is not satisfied that the subject of the review is entitled to be registered, he must–

    (a) send to that person such notice, of a kind specified in paragraph (4), as he considers appropriate, and

    (b) enter the review in the list kept in pursuance of regulation 31E.

(3) Paragraph (2)(b) does not apply where the subject of a review has an anonymous entry.

(4) A notice is specified for the purposes of this paragraph if it–

    (a) states that the registration officer is of the opinion that the subject of the review is or was not entitled to be registered, or has an entry in the register which results from or was altered as the result of an application made by another person, and the grounds for his opinion,

    (b) states the reason for the review and requires the subject of the review to provide such further information as might be specified in the notice or requires him to make a declaration under regulation 24 or both, or

(c) states the reason for the review and that the registration officer intends to conduct a hearing of it.

(5) Where–

    (a) the registration officer sends to the subject of the review a notice in the form specified in paragraph (4)(a), and

    (b) that person does not, within 14 days beginning with the date of that notice, notify the registration officer that he requires the review to be heard,

the registration officer may determine without a hearing that the subject of the review was not entitled to be registered, that the subject of the review was registered and their entry has been altered as the result of an application made by another person, or, as the case may be, that the subject of the review has ceased to satisfy the conditions for registration set out in section 4 of the 1983 Act.

(6) Paragraph (7) applies where–

    (a) the registration officer sends to the subject of the review a notice in the form specified in paragraph (4)(b), and

    (b) that person does not respond to the registration officer's satisfaction, or at all, within the period of 28 days beginning with the date of that notice.

(7) The registration officer may send a notice to the subject of the review which states that he is not satisfied that that person is or was entitled to be registered, or that the person's entry in the register does not result from or has not been altered as the result of an application made by another person, and the grounds for his opinion.

(8) Where–

    (a) the registration officer sends to the subject of the review a notice in pursuance of paragraph (7), and

    (b) the subject of the review does not, within the period of 14 days beginning with the date of that notice, notify the registration officer that he requires the review to be heard,

the registration officer may determine without a hearing that the subject of the review was not entitled to be registered, that the subject of the review was registered and their entry has been altered as the result of an application made by another person, or, as the case may be, that the subject of the review has ceased to satisfy the conditions for registration set out in section 4 of the 1983 Act.

(9) In making a determination under paragraph (5) or (8), the registration officer must take into account any written representations made to him by the subject of the review and may take into account the written representations of any other person who appears to him to be interested.

(10) In this regulation and regulations 31E and 31F–

"review" must be construed in accordance with paragraph (1);

"the subject of the review" means the person in respect of whom the review is conducted.

List of reviews

31E (1) The registration officer must keep a list of reviews.

(2) The list must contain, in relation to each review, the following particulars–

    (a) the full name of the subject of the review,

    (b) his electoral number,

    (c) his qualifying address, and

    (d) the reason for the review.

(3) The list must be made available for inspection at the registration officer's office.

(4) This regulation does not apply to any review where the subject of the review has an anonymous entry.

Hearings of reviews

31F (1) Where the registration officer determines that a hearing of the review should be conducted, the notice given under regulation 31D(4)(c) must also state the time and place at which he proposes to hear the review.

(2) Where the subject of the review requires the review to be heard, the registration officer must send to that person a notice stating the time and place at which he proposes to hear the review.

(3) The time fixed for the hearing must not be earlier than the third day after the date of the notice in which that time is stated.

(4) The persons entitled to appear and be heard are–
   (a) the subject of the review;
   (b) any other person who appears to the registration officer to be interested.

(5) Paragraphs (2) to (4) of regulation 31 apply to the hearing of a review as they apply to the hearing of an application for registration or objection.

(6) The registration officer may determine that the subject of the review was not entitled to be registered, that the subject of the review was registered and their entry has been altered as the result of an application made by another person, or, as the case may be, that the subject of the review has ceased to satisfy the conditions for registration set out in section 4 of the 1983 Act, despite the failure of that person (or any other person entitled to appear and be heard) to attend.

(7) In making a determination under paragraph (6), the registration officer must take into account any written representations made to him by the subject of the review and may take into account the written representations of any other person who appears to him to be interested.

Notification of outcome of reviews

31FZA Where the registration officer is required to send the subject of the review a notice under regulation 31D(2), the registration officer must notify the subject of the review in writing of its outcome and when doing so–
   (a) state whether there is a right of appeal under section 56(1)(azd) or (aa) of the 1983 Act;
   (b) specify the time within which any notice of appeal under that section must be given (in accordance with regulation 32(2)); and
   (c) provide such other information about the appeal that the registration officer considers necessary.

Determinations of entitlement to remain registered during the annual canvass

31FA If a registration officer is required by section 10ZE(5)(b) of the 1983 Act to consider making a determination under section 10ZE(1) of that Act as a result of information received in response to the canvass conducted under section 9D of that Act, the registration officer must so far as reasonably practicable take any relevant steps under regulations 31D to 31FZA so as to enable the relevant determination to be made, and the subject of the review to be notified of the determination, before the registration officer publishes a revised version of the register under section 13(1)(a) of the 1983 Act.

Anonymous registration: applications and declarations

31G (1)   An application for an anonymous entry must state–
      (a)   the applicant's full name,
      (b)   the address given in accordance with regulation 26(1)(b),
      (c)   the reason for the application, and
      (d)   the date of the application.

  (2)   The application must be in writing and signed by the applicant.

  (3)   The application must be accompanied by evidence of the nature prescribed in regulation 31I or 31J.

  (4)   Where the evidence mentioned in paragraph (3) relates not to the applicant, but to another person of the same household as the applicant, the application must be accompanied by evidence that that person is of that household.

  (5)   The application must be accompanied by a declaration made by the applicant that–
      (a)   the particulars given in accordance with paragraph (1) are true,
      (b)   so far as he is aware, the evidence provided in pursuance of paragraph (3) is genuine, and
      (c)   where paragraph (4) applies–
         (i)   the person to whom the evidence relates is a person of the same household of the applicant, and
        (ii)   so far as he is aware, the evidence provided in pursuance of paragraph (4) is genuine.

  (6)   The application may give an address to which the registration officer must send correspondence, other than the address given in accordance with paragraph (1)(b).

Anonymous registration: determination of applications by registration officer

31 (1)   Paragraph (2) applies where–
      (a)   the registration officer determines that the applicant for an anonymous entry is entitled to be registered, and
      (b)   the application for an anonymous entry is made in accordance with regulation 31G(1), (2) and (5).

  (2)   The registration officer must determine that the safety test is satisfied (and accordingly allow the application for an anonymous entry) where he is satisfied–
      (a)   that the evidence provided in support of the application in pursuance of regulation 31G(3) constitutes evidence of the nature prescribed in regulation 31I or 31J, and
      (b)   in the case of an application where regulation 31G(4) applies, that the evidence provided in pursuance of that paragraph establishes that the person in question is a person of the same household as the applicant.

Anonymous registration: evidence consisting of relevant court orders or injunctions

31I (1)   Evidence which meets the following conditions is prescribed for the purposes of regulations 31G(3) and 31H(2)(a).

  (2)   The first condition is that the evidence is, or is a copy of, a relevant order or injunction.

  (3)   A relevant order or injunction is–
      (a)   an injunction for the purpose of restraining a person from pursuing any conduct which amounts to harassment granted in proceedings under section 3 of the Protection from Harassment Act 1997;
      (b)   an injunction granted under section 3A(2) of the Protection from Harassment Act 1997;

(c) a restraining order made under section 5(1) of the Protection from Harassment Act 1997;

(d) a restraining order on acquittal made under section 5A(1) of the Protection from Harassment Act 1997;

(e) a non-harassment order, interdict or interim interdict made under section 8 or 8A of the Protection from Harassment Act 1997;

(f) a non-harassment order made under section 234A(2) of the Criminal Procedure (Scotland) Act 1995;

(g) a non-molestation order made under section 42(2) of the Family Law Act 1996;

(h) an injunction for the purpose of restraining a person from pursuing any conduct which amounts to harassment granted in proceedings under article 5 of the Protection from Harassment (Northern Ireland) Order 1997;

(i) a restraining order made under article 7 of the Protection from Harassment (Northern Ireland) Order 1997;

(j) a restraining order on acquittal made under article 7A(1) of the Protection from Harassment (Northern Ireland) Order 1997;

(k) a non-molestation order made under article 20(2) of the Family Homes and Domestic Violence (Northern Ireland) Order 1998;

(l) a matrimonial interdict within the meaning of section 14 of the Matrimonial Homes (Family Protection) (Scotland) Act 1981;

(m) a domestic interdict within the meaning of section 18A of the Matrimonial Homes (Family Protection) (Scotland) Act 1981;

(n) a relevant interdict within the meaning of section 113 of the Civil Partnership Act 2004;

(o) an interdict that has been determined to be a domestic abuse interdict within the meaning of section 3 of the Domestic Abuse (Scotland) Act 2011;

(p) any interdict with an attached power of arrest made under section 1 of the Protection from Abuse (Scotland) Act 2001;

(q) a forced marriage protection order or interim forced marriage protection order made under any of the following provisions–

(i) Part 4A of the Family Law Act 1996;

(ii) section 2 of, and paragraph 1 of Schedule 1 to, the Forced Marriage (Civil Protection) Act 2007;

(iii) section 1 of the Forced Marriage etc (Protection and Jurisdiction) (Scotland) Act 2011; and

(iv) section 5 of the Forced Marriage etc (Protection and Jurisdiction) (Scotland) Act 2011.

(4) The second condition is that the relevant order or injunction is made for the protection, or otherwise for the benefit, of–

(a) the applicant for an anonymous entry, or

(b) another person of the same household as him.

(5) The third condition is that the relevant order or injunction is in force on the day on which the application for an anonymous entry is made.

Anonymous registration: evidence by attestation

31J (1) An attestation within the meaning of this regulation is prescribed for the purposes of regulations 31G(3) and 31H(2)(a).

(2) The attestation must–

(a) certify that the safety of the applicant, or of another named person of the same household as him, would be at risk if the register contained the name of the applicant or his qualifying address,

(b) state the date on which it is made, and

      (c)   be in writing and signed by a qualifying officer.

(3)   The attestation must state the period for which it has effect, being a period of between one and five years beginning with the date on which the attestation is made.

(4)   Qualifying officer means–

      (a)   a police officer of or above the rank of superintendent of any police force in England and Wales;

      (b)   a police officer of or above the rank of superintendent of the Police Service of Scotland;

      (c)   a police officer of or above the rank of superintendent of the Police Service of Northern Ireland;

      (d)   the Director General of the Security Service;

      (e)   the Director General of the National Crime Agency;

      (f)   any director of adult social services in England within the meaning of section 6(A1) of the Local Authority Social Services Act 1970;

      (g)   any director of children's services in England within the meaning of section 18 of the Children Act 2004;

      (h)   any director of social services in Wales within the meaning of section 6(1) of the Local Authority Social Services Act 1970;

      (i)   any chief social work officer in Scotland within the meaning of section 3 of the Social Work (Scotland) Act 1968;

      (j)   any director of social services of a Health and Social Services Board established under article 16 of the Health and Personal Social Services (Northern Ireland) Order 1972;

      (k)   any executive director of social work of a Health and Social Services Trust established under article 10 of the Health and Personal Social Services (Northern Ireland) Order 1991.

Registration appeals

32 (1)   This regulation makes provision in connection with the right of appeal under section 56(1)(a), (aza), (azb), (azc), (azd), (aa) and (ab) of the 1983 Act.

(2)   A person desiring to appeal must–

      (a)   give notice of appeal to the registration officer and to the opposite party (if any) when the decision is given, or within 14 days thereafter, and

      (b)   specify the grounds of appeal.

(3)   The registration officer shall forward any such notice to the appropriate county court in accordance with rules of court together, in each case, with–

      (a)   a statement of the material facts which in his opinion have been established in the case, and

      (b)   his decision upon the whole case and on any point which may be specified as a ground of appeal.

(4)   Where it appears to the registration officer that any notices of appeal given to him are based on similar grounds, he shall inform the appropriate county court of this to enable the court (if it thinks fit) to consolidate the appeals or select a case as a test case.

Annual canvass

32ZA (1)   The annual canvass required by section 9D(1) of the 1983 Act must be conducted in accordance with the following paragraphs.

(2)   The Electoral Commission must–

      (a)   design a canvass form;

(b) obtain the approval of the Chancellor of the Duchy of Lancaster to the form; and

(c) then make the form available to registration officers.

(3) The canvass form in paragraph (2) must–

(a) require the full name and nationality of each person aged 16 and over who is eligible to register and is residing at the address to which the form is given;

(b) require an indication as to whether–

(i) there is no one residing at the address;

(ii) the address is solely of business premises;

(iii) none of the people residing at the address is entitled to be registered by reason of their nationality, together with a statement of their nationalities;

(iv) none of the people residing at the address is entitled to be registered for any reason other than their nationality and a statement of why they are not so entitled;

(c) include space for a bar code, local authority reference number and security code unique to each form;

(d) include a statement that the occupier or (if there is no occupier or it is not reasonably practicable for the occupier to provide the required information) the person in charge of the premises, must provide the required information to the registration officer for the area which includes the address to which the form was delivered, and the manner in which they may do so;

(e) include an explanation of the requirements for entitlement to register to vote and state that this form is not an application to register;

(f) include a statement that the information provided in response to the form will be processed in accordance with the Data Protection Act 1998;

(g) include a statement that failure to provide the information required by the canvass form to the registration officer may be an offence and a statement of the maximum penalty for that offence;

(h) include a statement that it is an offence to provide false information to the registration officer, and a statement of the maximum penalty for that offence;

(i) include a declaration that the information provided is true, to be made by a named person at the address to which the form is given and include an indication, if the person who is making the declaration is not resident at the address, of the capacity in which they are making it;

(j) include space for the email address and telephone number or numbers of each person residing at the address who is entitled to register to vote and an explanation that provision of this information is not mandatory;

(k) include space for the registration officer to provide local authority information and details of how the registration officer may be contacted;

(l) include the web site address of the digital service; and

(m) require the date of completion of the form.

(4) Each registration officer must send a canvass form in the form designed by the Electoral Commission to each residential address in the area for which the officer acts and the canvass form must be accompanied by a pre-addressed reply envelope, the postage of which has been prepaid.

(5) Before sending a canvass form under paragraph (4), the registration officer must, if practicable print on the form–

(a) any information required by the canvass form which the officer already holds in respect of each person who is registered at the address to which the canvass form is provided, with the exception of persons registered as mentioned in section 9D(6) of the 1983 Act; and

(b) an indication as to whether each person who is registered at that address is aged 76 or over.

(6) Where the registration officer has printed on the canvass form information in accordance with paragraph (5) the registration officer must include on the canvass form–

    (a) an explanation of what the edited register is, using the short version of the form of words, which is prescribed in regulation 45 of, and Schedule 3 to, the Representation of the People (England and Wales)(Description of Electoral Registers and Amendment) Regulations 2013;

    (b) an indication of whether the name and address of each person, who is currently registered as an elector in respect of that address, are omitted from the edited register; and

    (c) an indication that the person should contact their registration officer if they wish to request that their name and address be included in or omitted from the edited register, as the case may be, and an explanation that return of the canvass form will not constitute a request for the purpose of regulation 93A.

Steps to be taken by a registration officer where no information in response to an annual canvass form is received in respect of a particular address

32ZB (1) If a registration officer has sent an annual canvass form to an address but has not received information in response to the annual canvass form in respect of that address within a reasonable time of sending the form, the officer must send a second canvass form to that address.

(2) If no information in response is received in respect of a second form sent under paragraph (1) within a reasonable time of sending the second form, the registration officer must send a third canvass form to that address.

(3) A registration officer may visit the address at any stage in order to obtain the information required by the canvass form and must make or have made one visit if no information has been received in response to a third canvass form sent under paragraph (2).

(4) The second and third canvass forms, if required, must be in the same form as the first canvass form.

(5) The registration officer must take the steps required by paragraphs (1) to (3) before publishing a revised register under section 13(1)(a) of the 1983 Act.

(6) This regulation does not apply where a registration officer, having inspected records under regulation 35, concludes that there is no-one residing at the address or that the address is solely of business premises.

Invitations to apply for registration

32ZC (1) The Electoral Commission must–

    (a) design an invitation to apply for registration;

    (b) obtain the approval of the Chancellor of the Duchy of Lancaster to the invitation; and

    (c) then make the invitation available to registration officers.

(2) The invitation in paragraph (1) must include–

    (a) the full name and address of the person to be invited;

    (b) an explanation of how to make an application for registration; and

    (c) a statement as to the circumstances in which a civil penalty may be imposed under section 9E of the 1983 Act, and the amount of the civil penalty.

(3) Where a registration officer is required by section 9E(1) of the 1983 Act to give a person an invitation to apply for registration–

(a) the registration officer must give the invitation as soon as reasonably practicable and in any event within 28 days of the conditions in section 9E(1) being satisfied;

(b) the invitation must be in the form designed by the Electoral Commission under paragraph (1);

(c) the invitation must be accompanied by an application form in the form designed by the Electoral Commission under regulation 26(3), on which the registration officer has, if practicable, printed the full name and address of the person to be invited; and

(d) the invitation, the application form and a pre-addressed reply envelope, return postage of which has been prepaid, must be given in an envelope on which is printed–

    (i) a direction requesting that the envelope is not redirected if it is incorrectly addressed; and

    (ii) a direction requesting that any other person who receives the envelope who is resident at the address to which the invitation is addressed inform the registration officer if the addressee is not resident at that address and the registration officer's contact details in order that they may do so.

Steps to be taken by a registration officer to encourage a person to make an application for registration in response to an invitation to do so

32ZD (1) If a registration officer has given a person an invitation to apply for registration under section 9E(1) of the 1983 Act and the person has not made an application to register within a reasonable time of receipt of the invitation, the registration officer must give the person a second invitation.

(2) If no application is received in respect of the second invitation within a reasonable time of receipt of the second invitation, the registration officer must give the person a third invitation.

(3) The registration officer may visit the address at which the first invitation was given in order to encourage the person to make an application for registration at any time and must make or have made one visit if no application has been received in response to the third invitation.

(4) The second and third invitations to apply for registration, if required, must be in the same form as the first invitation to apply for registration.

(5) Paragraphs (1) to (3) do not apply if the registration officer is satisfied that–

    (a) the person is not entitled to be registered at the address at which the invitation or invitations to register was or were given; or

    (b) the person is registered at a different address.

(6) Paragraphs (1) to (3) do not apply in relation to a person whom the registration officer has reason to believe would, if registered, be registered–

    (a) in pursuance of an application made by virtue of section 7(2) or 7A(2) of the 1983 Act;

    (b) in pursuance of a declaration of local connection, service declaration or overseas elector's declaration; or

    (c) with an anonymous entry.

Requiring a person to make an application for registration

32ZE (1) Where a registration officer requires a person to make an application for registration by a specified date under section 9E(4) of the 1983 Act, the registration officer must give the person notice in writing of the requirement.

(2) A registration officer may not require a person to apply for registration unless–
  (a) the registration officer has taken the last of the steps required by regulation 32ZD;
  (b) the registration officer has established that the person–
    (i) has received an invitation to apply for registration;
    (ii) has been informed how to make an application for registration; and
    (iii) has been informed that the registration officer may impose a civil penalty if the person is required to make an application but does not do so; and
  (c) the registration officer has established that the person is resident at the address at which the invitations to apply for registration were given.

(3) A notice under paragraph (1) must state–
  (a) the date by which the person must make an application for registration;
  (b) that, if the person does not make an application by that date, the registration officer may impose a civil penalty on that person;
  (c) the amount of any such civil penalty and the rate of interest payable if the penalty is not paid on time;
  (d) that, if the person is not entitled to be registered, they must, before the date in sub-paragraph (a), inform the registration officer of that fact and explain why they are not so entitled, and the person is not required to make an application for registration;
  (e) that, if the person is registered at another address, they must, before the date in sub-paragraph (a), inform the registration officer of that fact and provide that address, and the person is not required to make an application for registration;
  (f) that the person may make other representations before the date in sub-paragraph (a) as to why they should not be required to make an application to register by the specified date, or why a civil penalty should not be imposed if they do not do so.

(4) The registration officer must give with the notice an application form in the form designed by the Electoral Commission under regulation 26(3) on which the registration officer has, if practicable, printed the full name and address of the person.

(5) A registration officer must cancel a requirement to make an application for registration, and give the person concerned notice in writing of the cancellation, if–
  (a) the registration officer is satisfied that the person is not entitled to be registered at the address at which the invitations to register were given; or
  (b) the registration officer is satisfied that the person is registered at a different address; or
  (c) any of the requirements in paragraph (2) has not been met.

(6) A registration officer may cancel a requirement to make an application for registration if the registration officer considers it appropriate to do so and must give the person concerned notice in writing of the cancellation.

Notice of Civil Penalty

32ZF (1) The amount of the civil penalty, which a registration officer may impose under section 9E(7) of the 1983 Act, is £80.

(2) Where the registration officer imposes a civil penalty under that section, the registration officer must give the person notice in writing that the penalty has been imposed and specify the reasons for imposing it.

(3) The notice in paragraph (2) must state that the person must–
  (a) within 28 days of the date of the notice, make an application to register;

(b)   within 28 days of the date of the notice, pay the full amount of the civil penalty; or

(c)   within 14 days of the date of the notice, request a review of the decision to impose the civil penalty.

(4)   The notice in paragraph (2) must also state–
    (a)   the amount due;
    (b)   how to make payment;
    (c)   the rate of interest payable if the penalty is not paid on time; and
    (d)   that making an application to register within 28 days will prevent the person being liable to pay the civil penalty.

Payment, enforcement and cancellation of civil penalty

32ZG (1)   Subject to paragraph (2), a person on whom a civil penalty is imposed under section 9E(7) of the 1983 Act must pay the amount of the penalty to the registration officer who imposed it within 28 days of the date of the notice given under regulation 32ZF(2).

(2)   If a person on whom a civil penalty is imposed requests a review under regulation 32ZH(1) or brings an appeal under regulation 32ZI(1), the 28 day period in paragraph (1) ceases to run whilst that review or appeal is being considered, and in the calculation of that period–
    (a)   the day on which the review is requested or the appeal brought shall be excluded; and
    (b)   the day on which the review or appeal is concluded shall be included.

(3)   If the person does not pay the civil penalty as required by paragraph (1) or (2), interest at 8% per annum will be charged from the date payment becomes overdue to the date of payment.

(4)   A civil penalty not paid in accordance with paragraph (1) or (2) and any interest on the civil penalty is recoverable, if the county court so orders on the application of the registration officer, as if it were payable under an order of that court.

(5)   A registration officer must cancel a civil penalty, and give the person concerned notice in writing of the cancellation, if–
    (a)   the person makes an application for registration at any time before the time for payment of the civil penalty in paragraph (1) or (2) has elapsed;
    (b)   the registration officer is satisfied that–
        (i)   the person is not entitled to be registered at the address at which the invitations to register were given; or
        (ii)   the person is registered at a different address; or
    (c)   any of the requirements in regulation 32ZE(2) has not been met.

(6)   A registration officer may cancel the civil penalty if the registration officer considers it appropriate to do so and must give the person concerned notice in writing of the cancellation.

Review of registration officer's decision to impose a civil penalty

32ZH (1)   A person on whom a civil penalty has been imposed may request a review of the registration officer's decision to impose the penalty.

(2)   A request under paragraph (1) must be made in writing within 14 days of the date of the notice given under regulation 32ZF(2).

(3)   Where a person requests a review of the registration officer's decision under paragraph (1), the registration officer must within 7 days of receiving the request give notice in writing to the person–
    (a)   acknowledging the request;

    (b) informing the person that they may within 14 days of the date of the notice–
        (i) make representations explaining why they have not made an application to register or why the civil penalty should be cancelled;
        (ii) submit evidence in support of such representations; and
    (c) explaining how such representations may be made and such evidence may be submitted.

(4) The registration officer must carry out a review, and such review may not start before the earlier of–
    (a) the end of the fourteenth day after the date of the notice sent under paragraph (3); or
    (b) the receipt of any representations or evidence.

(5) Following a review under paragraph (4), the registration officer may–
    (a) uphold the decision to issue a civil penalty; or
    (b) cancel the civil penalty.

(6) The registration officer must inform the person in writing of the outcome of the review.

(7) If the registration officer upholds the decision to impose a civil penalty, the notice must also state that the person on whom the penalty has been imposed–
    (a) may appeal against that decision to the First-tier Tribunal, and how to make such an appeal; and
    (b) must pay the penalty by a specified date, which shall be the date on which the 28 day period in regulation 32ZG(1) or (2) expires.

Appeals to the First-tier Tribunal against a notice of civil penalty

32ZI (1) If a registration officer upholds the decision to issue a civil penalty under regulation 32ZH(5)(a), the person on whom the penalty was imposed may appeal to the First-tier Tribunal.

  (2) On an appeal under paragraph (1) the First-tier Tribunal may–
    (a) uphold the registration officer's decision to impose the civil penalty; or
    (b) cancel the civil penalty.

Representations regarding clerical errors

32A (1) For the purposes of section 13B(3C) of the 1983 Act a representation may be made orally or in writing.

  (2) Where a representation is made in a polling station to a presiding officer, the presiding officer must as soon as practicable communicate that representation to the relevant registration officer.

33   *Repealed*
34   *Repealed*

Registration officer's right to inspect certain records

35 (1) A registration officer is authorised to inspect, for the purpose of his registration duties, records kept (in whatever form) by–
    (a) an authority listed in paragraph (2) below, or
    (b) any person providing services to, or authorised to exercise any function of, any such authority.

  (2) Those authorities are–
    (a) the council by which he was appointed;
    (aa) where the council by which he was appointed is a council for a district in a county for which there is a county council, that county council; and

    (b) any superintendent registrar of births, deaths and marriages, registrar of births and deaths or registrar of marriages.

(3) A registration officer is authorised to make copies of information contained in such records.

Disclosure of certain local authorities' records

35A (1) A local authority listed in paragraph (2) may disclose to a registration officer information contained in records held by that authority, for any of the purposes mentioned in paragraph 1A(1) of Schedule 2 to the 1983 Act.

(2) The authorities are–
    (a) the authority by which the registration officer was appointed; and
    (b) where the council by which the registration officer was appointed is a council for a district in a county for which there is a county council, that county council.

(3) A disclosure under paragraph (1) may be made only in accordance with a written agreement between the authority and the registration officer regulating the processing of the information, including its transfer, storage, destruction and security.

(4) Where an authority refuses a request by a registration officer to disclose information under paragraph (1) it must give the registration officer written reasons for its refusal.

Notices in connection with registration

36 (1) A notice under section 13(3) of the 1983 Act must be published–
    (a) not less than 14 days before the publication of the revised version of the register to which it relates;
    (b) in a newspaper circulating in the area for which the registration officer acts, and
    (c) by posting a copy of it at his office and in some conspicuous place or places in that area.

(2) A notice under section 13A(2), 13AB(2) or 13B(3), (3B) or (3D) of that Act must be issued by–
    (a) making a copy of it available for inspection under supervision–
      (i) at his office, and
      (ii) at such places, if any, in his registration area as allow members of the public in that area reasonable facilities for that purpose;
    (aa) supplying copies of it in accordance with Part VI of these Regulations; and
    (b) except in a case falling within regulation 29(2BA), 31C and 31FZA above, sending a copy of it to any person affected by its contents.

(3) For the purposes of section 13B(3A) and (3C) of the 1983 Act the prescribed time on the day of the poll is 9pm.

36A Communication of notices made on polling day

(1) Where a notice is issued under section 13B(3B) or (3D) of the 1983 Act on the day of the poll, the registration officer must take reasonable steps to ensure that the notice comes to the attention of the relevant presiding officer.

(2) Such steps may include communicating the notice to the presiding officer by telephone.

(3) Where a notice issued under section 13B(3B) or (3D) of the 1983 Act is communicated to a presiding officer by telephone, the presiding officer must make a written record of that notice.

Notice by registration officer of a change of address

37 (1) This regulation applies where a registration officer receives an application for registration which includes a statement given in accordance with regulation 26(1)(c) above.

(2) Where the address given in the statement received by the registration officer ("the new registration officer") is in an area for which another registration officer ("the former registration officer") acts, the new registration officer shall as soon as practicable notify the former registration officer that the applicant no longer resides in his area.

The register

Separate part of a register for each parliamentary polling district

38 (1) The register shall be framed in separate parts for each parliamentary polling district.

(2) Where a parliamentary polling district is contained in more than one electoral area, there shall be a separate part of the register for each part of the polling district contained in each electoral area.

Different letter for each parliamentary polling district

39 There shall be a different letter or letters in the register for each parliamentary polling district and such letter or letters shall be deemed to form part of an elector's number in the register.

Qualifying addresses which are not included in the register

40 (1) Section 9(2)(b) of the 1983 Act (which requires each register of parliamentary or local government electors to contain the qualifying addresses of the persons registered in it) does not apply–

(a) to an address to which paragraph (2) or (3) below applies, or

(b) which is specified in an overseas elector's declaration in accordance with section 2(4)(b) or (c)(ii) of the 1985 Act.

(2) This paragraph applies to an address where it appears to the registration officer that–

(a) a service voter in his service declaration, or

(b) a person who has made a declaration of local connection,

has given that address in such a declaration as an address–

(i) at which he has resided, but

(ii) which is not an address at which he is or would be residing but for the circumstances entitling him to make such a declaration.

(3) This paragraph applies to an address given in a declaration of local connection in accordance with section 7B(4)(b) of the 1983 Act.

Order of names

41 (1) Subject to paragraphs (2) and (3) below, the names and addresses of each separate part of the register shall be arranged in street order.

(2) If the registration officer determines for any part of the register that street order is not reasonably practicable, the names and addresses shall be arranged in alphabetical order or partly in street order and partly in alphabetical order.

(3) The name of any person whose qualifying address is not contained in a register by virtue of regulation 40 above shall be grouped together in alphabetical order–

(a) at the end of that part of the register to which the address relates;

(b) beneath the heading "Other electors", and

(c) without giving that address.

Anonymous entries

41A (1) An anonymous entry of a person consists of that person's electoral number together with the letter "N".

(2) The entry is to be entered in the register–

   (a) at the end of the part of the register which relates to the qualifying address of the person entitled to the entry,

   (b) under the heading of "Other electors" as mentioned in regulation 41(3)(b), and

   (c) following the names grouped together under that heading in pursuance of that regulation.

Marking of names

42 (1) Paragraphs (3) to (7) below specify the marks to appear against a person's entry in the register to indicate that he is registered in one or more of the four registers (those of: parliamentary electors; local government electors; relevant citizens of the Union registered as European Parliamentary electors, and peers overseas registered as European Parliamentary overseas electors) which are required to be combined.

(2) Where no mark appears against a person's entry in the register of electors, this indicates that he is registered in the registers of parliamentary and local government electors.

(3) To indicate that a relevant citizen of the Union is registered only in the register of local government electors, the letter "G" shall be placed against his entry.

(4) To indicate that such a citizen is registered in both that register and the register of such citizens registered as European Parliamentary electors, the letter "K" shall be placed against his entry.

(5) To indicate that any other person is registered only in the register of local government electors, the letter "L" shall be placed against his entry.

(6) To indicate that an overseas elector is registered only in the register of parliamentary electors, the letter "F" shall be placed against his entry.

(7) To indicate that a European Parliamentary overseas elector is registered only in the register of such electors, the letter "E" shall be placed against his entry.

Publication of register

43 (1) The manner in which each revised version of the full register is to be published under section 13(1) and (3) of the 1983 Act is by the registration officer–

   (a) making a copy of it available for inspection under supervision–

      (i) at his office, and

      (ii) at such places, if any, in his registration area as allow members of the public in that area reasonable facilities for that purpose; and

   (b) supplying copies of it in accordance with Part VI of these Regulations.

(1A) Where a copy of the full register is made available pursuant to paragraph (1)(a) above by providing the register on a computer screen or otherwise in data form, the registration officer shall ensure that the manner in, and equipment on, which that copy is provided do not permit any person consulting that copy to–

   (a) search it by electronic means by reference to the name of any person; or

   (b) copy or transmit any part of that copy by electronic, or any other, means.

(2) The revised version of the register shall be kept published until the coming into force of the next revised version of it.

Information about register

44 (1)   As soon as practicable after the publication of a revised version of the register under section 13(1) of the 1983 Act, the registration officer shall supply to the Secretary of State a document setting out the information about electors which is required by paragraphs (2) to (4) and (6) below.

(2)   The document referred to in paragraph (1) above shall state the name of the constituency (and, if only part of the constituency is situated in the area for which the registration officer acts, that fact) and shall list the following total numbers of electors in that constituency or part thereof, namely–
  (a)   parliamentary electors (including those referred to in sub-paragraph (d) below);
  (b)   local government electors (including those referred to in sub-paragraph (d) below);
  (c)   those local government electors who are ineligible to vote at parliamentary elections; and
  (d)   those registered in pursuance of section 4(5) of the 1983 Act.

(3)   The document referred to in paragraph (1) above shall set out separately as respects those electors referred to in sub-paragraphs (a) and (d) of paragraph (2) above the following totals, namely–
  (a)   those registered by virtue of residence at a qualifying address;
  (b)   those registered in pursuance of a service declaration;
  (c)   those registered in pursuance of an overseas elector's declaration; and
  (d)   those registered in pursuance of a declaration of local connection.

(4)   The document referred to in paragraph (1) above shall in respect of each relevant area in the constituency state–
  (a)   its name or number;
  (b)   the letters referred to in regulation 39 above for each parliamentary polling district in each relevant area (or part thereof); and
  (c)   if only part of the relevant area is situated in the constituency, that fact;
  and shall list the following total numbers of electors in that area (or part thereof) namely–
    (i)   parliamentary electors (including those referred to in sub-paragraph (ii)) below;
    (ii)   those registered by virtue of section 4(5) of the 1983 Act; and
    (iii)   those local government electors who are ineligible to vote at parliamentary elections.

(5)   In paragraph (4) above "relevant area" means–
  (a)   in England, a ward of a district, of a London borough or of the City of London, and
  (b)   in Wales, an electoral division of a county or county borough.

(6)   The document referred to in paragraph (1) shall state the total number of electors who have an anonymous entry.

Preparation and publication of list of overseas electors

45 (1)   The registration officer shall prepare a list of the names of each person who appears to him to be entitled to be registered in pursuance of an overseas elector's declaration ("the list of overseas electors"); and shall include in that list the address specified in that declaration in accordance with section 2(4) of the 1985 Act and regulation 18(1) above.

(2) In respect of each constituency which is wholly or partly comprised in the area for which the registration officer acts there shall be a separate part of the list of overseas electors; and the names of the persons included in each part shall be listed in alphabetical order.

(3) At the time when the registration officer publishes a revised version of the register under section 13(1) of the 1983 Act, he shall publish the list of overseas electors by making a copy of it available for inspection under supervision at his office; and the list shall be kept so published until the next revised version of the register is published under section 13(1) of the 1983 Act.

(4) The name of a person appearing to the registration officer to be entitled to be registered in pursuance of a European Parliamentary overseas elector's declaration (and included in the list of overseas electors by virtue of regulation 13(6) above) shall be marked with the letter "E".

Record of anonymous entries

45A (1) The registration officer must keep a record of anonymous entries.

(2) The registration officer must enter in the record each person who is entered in the register with an anonymous entry.

(3) The entry in the record must contain the following particulars–
    (a) the full name of the person to whom the entry relates;
    (b) his electoral number;
    (c) his qualifying address;
    (d) where he has given in his application for an anonymous entry an address other than his qualifying address to which correspondence should be sent, that address;
    (e) the date on which the anonymous entry in the register took effect.

(4) Where the application of a person with an anonymous entry to vote by post is granted, the registration officer must also enter in the record the address to which the postal ballot paper should be sent as given in the application (in accordance with regulation 51(2)(d)).

Duties of registration officer and his staff in relation to record of anonymous entries

45B (1) This regulation applies to–
    (a) the registration officer,
    (b) any deputy registration officer, and
    (c) any person appointed to assist any such officer or who in the course of his employment is assigned to assist such officer in his registration duties.

(2) Where the registration officer is also the returning officer or acting returning officer at any election or counting officer at any referendum (and in consequence has access to the record of anonymous entries without being supplied with a copy of it), this regulation applies to–
    (a) the registration officer acting in that other capacity,
    (b) any deputy returning officer, deputy acting returning officer or deputy counting officer, and
    (c) any person appointed to assist any person mentioned in sub-paragraph (a) or (b) or who in the course of his employment is assigned to assist any such officer in his duties in respect of the election or referendum in question.

(3) No person to whom this regulation applies may–
    (a) supply to any person a copy of the record,
    (b) disclose information contained in it, or

(c)   make use of such information,

otherwise than in accordance with an enactment (including these Regulations) or the order of any court or tribunal made at any hearing or during the course of any proceedings.

(4)   Nothing in paragraph (3) applies to the supply or disclosure by a person to whom this regulation applies to another such person in connection with his registration duties or for the purposes of an election or referendum.

(5)   The persons to whom this regulation applies must take proper precautions for the safe custody of the record.

(6)   In this regulation and regulation 45C–
"counting officer" means the counting officer at a referendum held by or under any Act;
"enactment" has the same meaning as in section 17(2) of the 2000 Act.

Supply of record of anonymous entries to returning and counting officers

45C (1)   Paragraph (2) applies whenever the registration officer supplies a copy of the full register, or any part of it, to a returning officer or counting officer.

(2)   The registration officer must supply–
   (a)   together with the copy of the register, a copy of the record of anonymous entries;
   (b)   together with any part of the register, a copy of the record so far as it relates to that part.

(3)   A registration officer may supply a copy of the record to a returning officer or counting officer at any other time.

(4)   No person to whom a copy of the record has been supplied under this regulation may–
   (a)   supply a copy of the record,
   (b)   disclose any information contained in it, or
   (c)   make use of any such information,
   other than for the purposes of an election or referendum (as the case may be).

(5)   Each person supplied with a copy of the record under this regulation must take proper precautions for its safe custody.

Supply of record of anonymous entries in connection with summoning of juries

45D (1)   Paragraph (2) applies to any person to whom a copy of the full register has been supplied or to whom information contained in it has been disclosed for the purpose of summoning juries, other than a designated officer within the meaning of section 3(1) of the Juries Act 1974.

(2)   The registration officer must at the request in writing of a person to whom this paragraph applies supply to that person a copy of the record of anonymous entries.

(3)   Paragraphs (4) and (5) apply to–
   (a)   each person who has been supplied with a copy of the record of anonymous entries in accordance with section 3(1A) of the Juries Act 1974;
   (b)   each person who has been supplied with a copy of the record in accordance with paragraph (2).

(4)   No person to whom this paragraph applies may–
   (a)   supply a copy of the record,
   (b)   disclose any information contained in it, or
   (c)   make use of any such information,
   other than for the purpose of summoning juries.

(5)   The persons to whom this paragraph applies must take proper precautions for the safe custody of the record.

Supply of record of anonymous entries to the security services

45E (1)   This regulation applies where the registration officer supplies a copy of the full register to–
        (a) the Security Service;
        (b) the Government Communications Headquarters;
        (c) the Secret Intelligence Service.

(2)   The registration officer must supply a copy of the record of anonymous entries together with the register.

(3)   *Repealed*

(4)   *Repealed*

Supply of the record of anonymous entries to police forces and other organisations

45F (1)   The registration officer must supply a copy of the record of anonymous entries, at the request in writing of a senior officer, to–
        (a) any police force in Great Britain,
        (b) the Police Service of Northern Ireland or the Police Service of Northern Ireland (Reserve),
        (c) the Police Information Technology Organisation,
        (d) any body of constables established under an Act, or
        (e) the National Crime Agency.

(2)   Senior officer means–
        (a) in the case of the forces and organisations mentioned in paragraph (1)(a) to (d), an officer of a rank senior to that of superintendent;
        (b) in the case of the National Crime Agency, the Director General of that Agency.

(3)   No person serving whether as a constable, officer or employee of any of the forces and organisations mentioned in paragraph (1) may–
        (a) supply to any person a copy of the record,
        (b) disclose any information contained in it, or
        (c) make use of any such information,
otherwise than for the purposes specified in paragraph (4).

(4)   The purposes are–
        (a) the prevention and detection of crime and the enforcement of the criminal law (whether in England and Wales or elsewhere);
        (b) the vetting of a relevant person for the purpose of safeguarding national security.

(5)   Relevant person means–
        (a) a constable or officer or prospective constable or officer of the force or organisation;
        (b) an employee of, or applicant for employment by, the force or organisation.

(6)   Each person supplied with a copy of the record under this regulation must take proper precautions for its safe custody.

Certificate of anonymous registration

45G (1)   Where a registration officer enters a person in the record of anonymous entries, he must issue to that person a certificate of anonymous registration.

(2)   A certificate of anonymous registration must be in writing and signed by the registration officer.

(3)   A certificate for anonymous registration must state–
    (a)   the name of the area for which the registration officer acts;
    (b)   the name, electoral number and qualifying address of the person who has the anonymous entry;
    (c)   the date on which the anonymous entry took effect;
    (d)   that unless a fresh application for an anonymous entry is made, the entitlement to remain registered anonymously will terminate no later than at the end of the period of 12 months beginning with the date stated in accordance with sub-paragraph (c).

45H   *Repealed*

46   *Repealed*

47   *Repealed*

48   *Repealed*

49   *Repealed*

PART IV
ABSENT VOTERS

Interpretation of Part IV

50   In this Part of these Regulations–
"Schedule 4" means Schedule 4 to the 2000 Act;
"absent voter" means an elector who is entitled to vote by proxy or an elector or proxy who is entitled to vote by post;
"allotted polling station" has the meaning set out in regulation 53(7) below.

General requirements for applications for an absent vote

51 (1)   An application under Schedule 4 must comply with the requirements of this regulation and such further requirements in this Part of these Regulations as are relevant to the application.

(2)   The application must state–
    (a)   the full name of the applicant;
    (b)   the address in respect of which the applicant is registered or has applied to be (or is treated as having applied to be) registered in the register except in the case of an application under paragraph 7(4) or (7) of Schedule 4;
    (c)   in the case of such an application, the proxy's address, together with the name of the elector for whom he will act as proxy and the elector's address for the purposes of sub-paragraph (b) above;
    (d)   in the case of a person applying to vote by post, the address to which the ballot paper should be sent;
    (e)   in the case of an application to vote by proxy, the grounds on which the elector claims to be entitled to an absent vote;
    (f)   in the case of a person who is unable to provide a signature, the reasons for his request for waiver of any requirement under paragraph 3, 4 or 7 of Schedule 4 to provide a signature and the name and address of any person who has assisted him to complete his application, and
    (g)   where the applicant has, or has applied for, an anonymous entry, that fact.

(3)   The application shall be made in writing and shall be dated.

(3A) Where an application is required to contain a signature and date of birth, the information must be set out in a manner that is sufficiently clear and unambiguous as to be capable of electronic scanning into his record by configuring the information as follows–

    (a) the signature shall appear against a background of white unlined paper of at least five centimetres long and two centimetres high; and

    (b) the applicant's date of birth shall be set out numerically configured in the sequence of date, month and year, namely ddmmyyyy.

(3B) Where the application contains a request that the registration officer waive the requirement for a signature, sub-paragraph (a) of paragraph (3A) shall not apply.

(4) An application under Schedule 4 which is made for an indefinite period or the period specified in the application must state–

    (a) that it is so made, and

    (b) whether it is made for parliamentary elections, local government elections or both.

(5) An application under Schedule 4 which is made for a particular parliamentary or local government election must–

    (a) state that it is so made, and

    (b) identify the election in question,

but, where the poll at one election falls on the same day as the poll at another election, the same application may be used for both elections.

(6) Where an application is made to vote by proxy, it shall include an application for the appointment of a proxy which meets the requirements of regulation 52 below.

Additional provision concerning the requirement that an application for an absent vote must be signed by the applicant

51A The registration officer may satisfy himself–

    (a) that an application under Schedule 4 meets any requirements that it has been signed by the applicant and states his date of birth by referring to any signature and date of birth–

        (i) previously provided by the applicant to the registration officer or the returning officer; or

        (ii) previously provided by the applicant to the authority referred to in regulation 35(2)(a), which the registration officer is authorised to inspect for the purposes of his registration duties; and

    (b) as to whether the applicant is unable to provide a signature or a consistent signature due to any disability or inability to read or write.

Additional requirement for applications for ballot papers to be sent to different address from that stated in application

51AA (1) Paragraph (2) applies where–

    (a) in the case of an application to vote by post under paragraph 3(1) or (7) or 4(1) of Schedule 4, the addresses stated in accordance with regulation 51(2)(b) and (d) are different;

    (b) in the case of an application by a proxy to vote by post under paragraph 7(4) of Schedule 4, the proxy's address stated in accordance with regulation 51(2)(c) and the address stated in accordance with regulation 51(2)(d) are different.

(2) The application must set out why the applicant's circumstances will be or are likely to be such that he requires the ballot paper to be sent to the address stated in accordance with regulation 51(2)(d).

(3) This regulation does not apply where an applicant has, or has applied for, an anonymous entry.

Additional requirements for applications for ballot papers to be sent to different address from that shown in the record kept under paragraph 3(4) or 7(6) of Schedule 4

51B (1) An application under–

    (a) paragraph 4(3)(a) of Schedule 4 by a person shown as voting by post in the record kept under paragraph 3(4) of that Schedule; or

    (b) paragraph 7(7) of that Schedule by a person shown as voting by post in the record kept under paragraph 7(6) of that Schedule,

for his ballot paper to be sent to a different address from that shown in the record shall set out why the applicant's circumstances will be or are likely to be such that he requires his ballot paper to be sent to that address.

(2) This regulation does not apply where an applicant has, or has applied for, an anonymous entry.

Additional requirements for applications for the appointment of a proxy

52 An application for the appointment of a proxy under paragraphs 3 and 4 of Schedule 4 shall state the full name and address of the person whom the applicant wishes to appoint as his proxy, together with his family relationship, if any, with the applicant, and–

    (a) if it is signed only by the applicant, shall contain a statement by him that he has consulted the person so named and that that person is capable of being and willing to be appointed to vote as his proxy, or

    (b) if it is also signed by the person to be appointed, shall contain a statement by that person that he is capable of being and willing to be appointed to vote as the applicant's proxy.

Additional requirements for applications for a proxy vote for a definite or indefinite period on grounds of blindness or any other disability

53 (1) An application to vote by proxy for a particular or indefinite period under paragraph 3(3)(b) of Schedule 4 shall specify the disability by reason of which it is made.

(2) Subject to paragraph (3) below, such an application shall be attested and signed by–

    (a) a registered medical practitioner;

    (b) a nurse registered on the register maintained by the Nursing and Midwifery Council under article 5 of the Nursing and Midwifery Order 2001 by virtue of qualifications in nursing;

    (c) a registered dentist as defined by section 53(1) of the Dentists Act 1984;

    (d) a registered dispensing optician or a registered optometrist within the meaning of the Opticians Act 1989;

    (e) a registered pharmacist as defined by article 3(1) of the Pharmacy Order 2010;

    (f) a registered osteopath as defined by section 41 of the Osteopaths Act 1993;

    (g) a registered chiropractor as defined by section 43 of the Chiropractors Act 1994;

    (h) a Christian Science practitioner;

    (i) *Repealed*

    (j) a person registered as a member of a profession to which the Health and Social Work Professions Order 2001 for the time being extends;

    (k) the person carrying on a care home registered under Part 2 of the Care Standards Act 2000;

    (l)   the warden of premises forming one of a group of premises provided for persons of pensionable age or disabled persons for which there is a resident warden, where the applicant states that he resides in such premises;

   (m) a manager within the meaning of section 145(1) of the Mental Health Act 1983, or on behalf of such a manager; or

   (n) a person registered in the register for social workers maintained in accordance with section 56 of the Care Standards Act 2000.

(3)   A person who qualifies–

    (a) by virtue of any of sub-paragraphs (a) to (j) of paragraph (2) above, may not attest an application for these purposes unless–

       (i)   he is treating the applicant for the disability specified in the application; or

      (ii) the applicant is receiving care from him in respect of that disability; or

     (iii) the person is a social worker who qualifies by virtue of sub-paragraph (j) of paragraph (2), and has arranged care or assistance for the applicant in respect of that disability; or

    (b) by virtue of sub-paragraph (n) of paragraph (2) above, may not attest an application for these purposes unless–

       (i)   he is treating the applicant for the disability specified in the application;

      (ii) the applicant is receiving care from him in respect of that disability; or

     (iii) he has arranged care or assistance for the person in respect of their disability.

(4)   The person attesting the application shall state–

    (a) his name and address and the qualification by virtue of which he attests the application;

    (b) where the person who attests the application is a person referred to in paragraph (3)(a) above, that–

       (i)   he is treating the applicant for the disability specified in the application; or

      (ii) the applicant is receiving care from him in respect of that disability;

    (c) where the person who attests the application is a person referred to in paragraph (3)(b) above, that–

       (i)   he is treating the applicant for the disability specified in the application;

      (ii) the applicant is receiving care from him in respect of that disability; or

     (iii) he has arranged care or assistance for the applicant in respect of that disability;

    (d) that, to the best of his knowledge and belief, the applicant has the disability specified in the application and that he cannot reasonably be expected to go in person to his allotted polling station or to vote unaided there by reason of that disability; and

    (e) that, to the best of his knowledge and belief, the disability specified in the application is likely to continue either indefinitely or for a period specified by the person attesting the application.

(5)   Paragraphs (2) to (4) above shall not apply where–

    (a) the application is based on the applicant's blindness and the applicant is registered by the local authority which is specified in the application as–

       (i)   a blind person under section 29(4)(g) of the National Assistance Act 1948; or

      (ii) a person who is severely sight-impaired under section 77(1) of the Care Act 2014 (registers of sight-impaired adults); or

    (b) the application states that the applicant is in receipt of the higher rate of the mobility component of a disability living allowance (payable under section 73 of the Social Security Contributions and Benefits Act 1992), armed forces independence payment under the Armed Forces and Reserve Forces (Compensation Scheme) Order 2011 or the enhanced rate of the mobility component of personal independence payment (payable under section 79(2) of the Welfare Reform Act 2012) because of the disability specified in the application.

(5A) A person who qualifies by virtue of sub-paragraph (m) of paragraph (2) above, shall, instead of the matters specified in paragraph (4)(a) above, state in the attestation–

    (i)   his name;

    (ii) his position in the hospital at which the applicant is liable to be detained or at which he is receiving treatment;

    (iii) that he is a person authorised to make the attestation; and

    (iv) in the case of an applicant who is liable to be detained in hospital, the statutory provision under which the applicant is liable to be so detained.

(6) The fact that an applicant is registered with a local authority under section 29(4)(g) of the National Assistance Act 1948 or registered as severely sight-impaired by a local authority under section 77(1) of the Care Act 2014 (registers of sight-impaired adults) shall be deemed sufficient evidence that he is eligible to vote by proxy on the grounds set out in paragraph 3(3)(b) of Schedule 4.

(7) In this regulation and in regulations 54 and 55 below, "his allotted polling station", in relation to an elector means the polling station allotted or likely to be allotted to him under the appropriate rules (as defined in paragraph 1 of Schedule 4).

Additional requirements for applications for a proxy vote for a definite or indefinite period based on occupation, service, employment or attendance on a course

54 (1) An application to vote by proxy for a particular or indefinite period under paragraph 3(3)(c) of Schedule 4 shall state–

    (a) whether the occupation, service or employment in respect of which it is made is that of the applicant or his spouse or civil partner or, as the case may be, it is the applicant or his spouse or civil partner who is attending the course provided by an educational institution in respect of which the application is made;

    (b) the nature of the occupation, service or employment or course provided by an educational institution giving rise to the application;

    (c) where the person in respect of whose occupation, service or employment it is made (in this regulation referred to as "the employed person") is self employed, that fact; and in any other case the name of that person's employer;

    (d) the reason, relevant to the general nature of the employment, service or occupation in question or the course provided by an educational institution, why the applicant cannot reasonably be expected to go in person to his allotted polling station.

(2) Such an application shall be attested and signed–

    (a) where the person is self-employed, by a person who–

       (i)   is aged 18 years or over;

       (ii) knows the self-employed person; and

       (iii) is not related to him;

    (b) by the employer of the employed person or by another employee to whom this function is delegated by the employer; and

    (c) in the case of a course provided by an educational institution, by the director or tutor of that course or by the principal or head of that institution or an employee to whom this function is delegated by the head or principal.

(3) The person attesting an application made under paragraph (2) above shall–

    (a) where the applicant is the employed person or the person attending the course, certify that the statements required by sub-paragraphs (a) to (d) of paragraph (1) above to be included in the application are true; or

    (b) where the applicant is the spouse or civil partner of the employed person or the person attending the course, certify that the statements included in the application in accordance with the requirements of sub-paragraphs (a) to (c) of paragraph (1) above are true.

(4) The person attesting an application under paragraph (2) above shall also state–

    (a) his name and address, that he is aged 18 years or over, that he knows the employed person, self-employed person or person attending a course provided by an educational institution but is not related to him; and

    (b) if he is attesting as or on behalf of the employer of the employed person, that he is the employer or the position he holds in the employment of that employer; or

    (c) if he is attesting an application made on the grounds of attendance at a course provided by an educational institution, the post he holds at that institution.

(5) For the purposes of this regulation, one person is related to another if he is the spouse, civil partner, parent, grandparent, brother, sister, child or grandchild of the other.

Additional requirements for applications for a proxy vote in respect of a particular election

55 (1) An application under paragraph 4(2) of Schedule 4 to vote by proxy at a particular election shall set out why the applicant's circumstances on the date of the poll for that election in respect of which it is made will be or are likely to be such that he cannot reasonably be expected to vote in person at his allotted polling station.

(1A) Paragraph (1) does not apply where the applicant has an anonymous entry.

(2) Where an application under paragraph 4(2) of Schedule 4–

    (a) is made on the grounds of the applicant's disability; and

    (b) is made after 5 pm on the sixth day before the date of the poll at the election for which it is made,

  the requirements of regulation 53 as to the matters to be specified and the attestation shall apply.

(3) Where an application mentioned in paragraph (2) above is made, the person who attests the application shall state, in addition to those matters specified in regulation 53, to the best of his knowledge and belief, the date upon which the applicant became disabled.

(3A) Where an application under paragraph 4(2) of Schedule 4–

    (a) is made on grounds relating to the applicant's occupation, service or employment; and

    (b) is made after 5 pm on the sixth day before the date of the poll at the election for which it is made,

  the requirements of regulation 55A as to the matters to be specified and the attestation shall apply.

(4) Where an application under paragraph 4(2) of Schedule 4 is made by a person to whom paragraph 2(5A) of that Schedule applies after 5pm on the sixth day before the date of the poll at the election for which it is made, the requirements of paragraph (5) below as to the matters to be specified and as to attestation shall apply.

(5) Where an application mentioned in paragraph (4) above is made–

    (a) the application shall additionally state the name and address of the hospital at which the applicant is liable to be detained; and

    (b) the application shall be attested by or on behalf of a manager, within the meaning of section 145(1) of the Mental Health Act 1983, of the hospital at which the applicant is liable to be detained, and the attestation shall state–

        (i) the name of the person attesting the application;

        (ii) his position in the hospital at which the applicant is liable to be detained;

(iii) that he is a person authorised to make the attestation; and

(iv) the statutory provision under which the applicant is liable to be detained in the hospital.

(6) This regulation does not apply where an applicant has an anonymous entry.

Additional requirements for application for an emergency proxy vote in respect of a particular election

55A (1) This regulation sets out the requirements referred to in regulation 55(3A).

(2) The application must (in addition to providing the information required by regulation 55(1)) state–

(a) where the applicant is self-employed, that fact; and, in any other case, the name of the applicant's employer;

(b) that the reason provided in accordance with regulation 55(1) relates to the applicant's occupation, service or employment; and

(c) the date on which the applicant became aware of that reason.

(3) Paragraphs (4), (5) and (6) apply unless the applicant is or will be registered as a service voter.

(4) The application must be attested and signed–

(a) where the applicant is self-employed, by a person who–

(i) is aged 18 years or over;

(ii) knows the applicant; and

(iii) is not related to the applicant;

(b) where the applicant is not self-employed, by the applicant's employer or by another employee to whom this function is delegated by the employer.

(5) The person attesting an application under paragraph (4) (the "attestor") must certify that the statements required by paragraph (2) and the information required by regulation 55(1) are true to the best of their knowledge and belief.

(6) The attestor shall also state–

(a) the attestor's name and address; and

(b) if the attestor is attesting–

(i) where the applicant is self-employed, that the attestor is aged 18 years or over and that the attestor knows, but is not related to, the applicant; or

(ii) as or on behalf of the employer of the applicant, that the attestor is the employer, or the position the attestor holds in the employment of that employer.

(7) For the purposes of this regulation, one person ('A') is related to another ('B') if A is the spouse, civil partner, parent, grandparent, brother, sister, child or grandchild of B.

Closing date for applications

56 (1) An application under paragraph 3(1), (6) or (7), or 7(4) of Schedule 4 shall be disregarded for the purposes of a particular parliamentary or local government election and an application under paragraph 4(3) of Schedule 4 shall be refused if it is received by the registration officer after 5 pm on the eleventh day before the date of the poll at that election.

(2) An application under paragraph 3(2) or 6(7) of Schedule 4 shall be disregarded for the purposes of a particular parliamentary or local government election if it is received by the registration officer after 5 pm on the sixth day before the date of the poll at that election.

(3)   Subject to paragraph (3A), an application under paragraph 4(2) or 6(8) of Schedule 4 shall be refused if it is received by the registration officer after 5 pm on the sixth day before the date of the poll at the election for which it is made.

(3A)   Where an application made under paragraph 4(2) of Schedule 4 is made–

    (a)   on the grounds of the applicant's disability and the applicant became disabled after 5pm on the sixth day before the date of the poll at the election for which it is made; or

    (aa)   on grounds relating to the applicant's occupation, service or employment and the applicant became aware of those grounds after 5 pm on the sixth day before the date of poll at the election for which it is made; or

    (b)   by a person to whom paragraph 2(5A) of that Schedule applies,

the application, or an application under paragraph 6(8) of that Schedule made by virtue of that application, shall be refused if it is received after 5pm on the day of the poll at the election for which it is made.

(4)   An application under paragraph 4(1) or 7(7) of Schedule 4 shall be refused if it is received by the registration officer after 5 pm on the eleventh day before the date of the poll at the election for which it is made.

(5)   An application under–

    (a)   paragraph 3(5)(a) of Schedule 4 by an elector to be removed from the record kept under paragraph 3(4) of that Schedule, or

    (b)   paragraph 7(9)(a) of Schedule 4 by a proxy to be removed from the record kept under paragraph 7(6) of that Schedule,

and a notice under paragraph 6(10) of that Schedule by an elector cancelling a proxy's appointment shall be disregarded for the purposes of a particular parliamentary or local government election if it is received by the registration officer after 5 pm on the eleventh day before the date of the poll at that election.

(5A)   Any application or notice mentioned in this regulation shall be disregarded for the purposes of a particular parliamentary or local government election if, before the application or notice is considered by the registration officer, the elector or proxy has returned a postal ballot paper to the returning officer (except where it has been returned in accordance with regulation 77 or 78 (spoilt and lost postal ballot papers)).

(6)   In computing a period of days for the purposes of this regulation, Saturday, Sunday, Christmas Eve, Christmas Day, Good Friday or a bank holiday shall be disregarded.

(7)   In paragraph (6) above "bank holiday" means–

    (a)   in relation to a parliamentary general election, a day which is a bank holiday under the Banking and Financial Dealings Act 1971 in any part of the United Kingdom, and

    (b)   in relation to a parliamentary by-election or a local government election, a day which is a bank holiday under that Act in England and Wales;

except that where, at a parliamentary general election, any proceedings are commenced afresh by reason of a candidate's death, sub-paragraph (b), not (a), shall apply.

Grant or refusal of applications

57 (1)   Where the registration officer grants an application to vote by post, he shall notify the applicant of his decision.

(2)   Where the registration officer grants an application for the appointment of a proxy, he shall confirm in writing to the elector that the proxy has been appointed, his name and address, and the duration of the appointment.

(3)   The form of proxy paper (as amended for use also in respect of European Parliamentary elections) in Form E is hereby prescribed for the purposes of paragraph 6(9) of Schedule 4.

(4)   Where the registration officer refuses an application under Schedule 4, he shall notify the applicant of his decision and of the reason for it.

(4A) Where the registration officer grants an application made under–
   (a)   paragraph 4(3)(a) of Schedule 4 by a person shown as voting by post in the record kept under paragraph 3(4) of that Schedule; or
   (b)   paragraph 7(7) of that Schedule by a person shown as voting by post in the record kept under paragraph 7(6) of that Schedule,
   he shall notify the applicant of this.

(4B) Where a person is removed from the record kept pursuant to paragraph 3(4) or 7(6) of Schedule 4, the registration officer shall where practicable notify him of this and the reason for it.

(4C) Where the appointment of a proxy is cancelled by the elector or otherwise ceases to be in force, the registration officer shall where practicable notify the elector that the appointment has been cancelled or, as the case may be, notify him that the appointment has ceased and the reason for it.

(5)   Where, under regulation 56 above, a registration officer disregards an application for the purposes of any particular parliamentary or local government election, he shall notify the applicant of this.

(6)   At a parliamentary election where the registration officer is not the acting returning officer for any constituency or part of a constituency in the area for which he is the registration officer, he shall send to that officer details of any application to vote by post which he has granted as soon as practicable after doing so.

Notice of appeal

58 (1) A person desiring to appeal under section 56(1)(b) of the 1983 Act against the decision of a registration officer must give notice of the appeal to the registration officer within 14 days of the receipt of the notice given under regulation 57(4) above specifying the grounds of appeal.

(2)   The registration officer shall forward any such notice to the appropriate county court in the manner directed by rules of court together in each case with a statement of the material facts which in his opinion have been established in the case, of his decision upon the whole case and on any point which may be specified as a ground of appeal.

(3)   Where it appears to the registration officer that any notices of appeal given to him are based on similar grounds, he shall inform the county court of this to enable the court (if it thinks fit) to consolidate the appeals or select a case as a test case.

Cancellation of proxy appointment

59   Where the appointment of a proxy is cancelled by notice given to the registration officer under paragraph 6(10) of Schedule 4 or ceases to be in force under that provision or is no longer in force under paragraph 6(11)(b) of that Schedule, the registration officer shall–
   (a)   notify the person whose appointment as proxy has been cancelled, expired, ceases to be or is no longer in force, unless the registration officer has previously been notified by that person that he no longer wishes to act as proxy, and
   (b)   remove his name from the record kept under paragraph 3(4)(c) of Schedule 4.

Inquiries by registration officer

60 (1) The registration officer may, at such times as he thinks fit, make inquiries of a person–

(a) who is shown as voting by proxy in the record kept under paragraph 3(4) of Schedule 4 in pursuance of an application granted on the grounds set out in paragraph 3(3)(b) and (c) of that Schedule; or

(b) who immediately before the date of the commencement of Schedule 4 was entitled to vote by proxy for an indefinite period at parliamentary elections, local government elections or both in pursuance of an application granted on grounds corresponding to those set out in paragraph 3(3)(b) and (c) of Schedule 4 (physical incapacity, blindness, occupation, service or employment),

for the purpose of determining whether there has been a material change of circumstances.

(2) Where the grant of an application for a proxy vote for an indefinite or particular period was based on the grounds referred to in paragraph 3(3)(c) of Schedule 4 (or grounds corresponding to those grounds), the registration officer shall make the inquiries referred to not later than three years after the granting of the application or the last such inquiries, as the case may be.

(3) The registration officer may treat the failure by a person of whom inquiries have been made to respond to such inquiries within one month of the date on which they were made as sufficient evidence of a material change in circumstances.

Requirement to provide fresh signatures at five yearly intervals

60A (1) The registration officer shall every year by 31 January send every person who remains an absent voter and whose signature held on the personal identifiers record is more than five years old a notice in writing–

(a) requiring him to provide a fresh signature, and

(b) informing him of the date (six weeks from the date of sending the notice) on which he would cease to be entitled to vote by post or by proxy in the event of a failure or refusal to provide a fresh signature.

(2) The notice must be sent by the registration officer to the current or last known address of the absent voter.

(3) The registration officer must, if the absent voter has not responded to the notice within three weeks from the date on which the notice was sent, as soon as practicable send a copy of the notice to him.

(4) Where a notice or copy of a notice is sent by post, the registration officer may use–

(a) a universal postal service provider; or

(b) a commercial delivery firm,

and postage shall be prepaid.

(5) A notice or copy of a notice sent to an absent voter in accordance with paragraph (1) or (3) must be accompanied by a pre-addressed reply envelope and, in the case of any notice or copy of a notice sent to an address in the United Kingdom, return postage must be prepaid.

(6) Upon the expiration of the period specified in the notice sent to the absent voter the registration officer shall determine whether the absent voter has failed or refused to provide a fresh signature.

(7) Where the registration officer determines that the absent voter has refused or failed to provide a fresh signature within the specified period, he must remove that person's entry from the records kept pursuant to paragraph 3(4) or 7(6) of Schedule 4 and from

the postal voters list, list of proxies or proxy postal voters list (as the case may be) kept under paragraph 5(2), 5(3) or 7(8) of that Schedule.

(8) Where a registration officer removes an absent voter's entry in the circumstances to which paragraph (7) refers–

    (a) the registration officer shall inform the absent voter, where appropriate, of the location of the polling station allotted or likely to be allotted to him under the appropriate rules (as defined in paragraph 1 of Schedule 4);

    (b) regulation 57(4) and regulation 58 shall apply as if the registration officer were refusing an application under Schedule 4; and

    (c) in the case of an entry removed from the proxy postal voters list, the registration officer must also notify the elector who appointed the proxy whose entry has been removed.

(9) The registration officer shall include in the notice to be sent to an absent voter regarding their removal from the records kept pursuant to paragraph 3(4) or 7(6) of Schedule 4 and from the postal voters list, list of proxies or proxy postal voters list (as the case may be) kept under paragraph 5(2), 5(3) or 7(8) of that Schedule, information–

    (a) explaining the effect of such removal; and

    (b) reminding the absent voter that he may make a fresh application under Schedule 4 to vote by post or by proxy (as the case may be).

Requirement to provide fresh signatures following rejection of a postal voting statement

60B (1) Where an absent voter is notified under regulation 61C that the signature does not match the example held on the personal identifiers record, and the absent voter continues to be shown on the relevant record as voting by post, the registration officer may require the absent voter to provide a fresh signature for the personal identifiers record.

(2) In doing so the registration officer must–

    (a) issue a notice in writing to the absent voter, requiring the provision of a fresh signature, and

    (b) inform the absent voter of the date (six weeks from the sending of the notice) on which the absent voter would cease to be entitled to vote by post in the event of a failure or refusal to provide a fresh signature.

(3) The registration officer must, if the absent voter has not responded to the notice within three weeks from the date on which the notice was sent, as soon as practicable send a copy of the notice to the absent voter.

(4) The notice and any copy must be sent by the registration officer to the current or last known address of the absent voter.

(5) Where a notice or copy of a notice is sent by post, the registration officer may use–

    (a) a universal postal service provider; or

    (b) a commercial delivery firm,

and postage shall be prepaid.

(6) A notice or copy of a notice sent to an absent voter in accordance with paragraph (2) or (3) must be accompanied by a pre-addressed reply envelope and, in the case of any notice or copy of a notice sent to an address in the United Kingdom, return postage must be prepaid.

(7) Following the date specified in the notice sent to the absent voter, the registration officer must determine whether the absent voter has failed or refused to provide a fresh signature.

(8) Where the registration officer determines that the absent voter has refused or failed to provide a fresh signature, the registration officer must remove that person's entry from the records kept pursuant to paragraph 3(4) or 7(6) of Schedule 4 and from the postal voters list or proxy postal voters list (as the case may be) kept under paragraph 5(2) or 7(8) of that Schedule.

(9) Where a registration officer removes an absent voter's entry in the circumstances to which paragraph (8) refers–
    (a) the registration officer shall inform the absent voter, where appropriate, of the location of the polling station allotted or likely to be allotted to the voter under the appropriate rules (as defined in paragraph 1 of Schedule 4);
    (b) regulation 57(4) and regulation 58 shall apply as if the registration officer were refusing an application under Schedule 4; and
    (c) in the case of an entry removed from the proxy postal voters list, the registration officer must also notify the elector who appointed the proxy whose entry has been removed.

(10) The registration officer shall include in the notice to be sent to an absent voter regarding their removal from the records kept pursuant to paragraph 3(4) or 7(6) of Schedule 4 and from the postal voters list or proxy postal voters list (as the case may be) kept under paragraph 5(2) or 7(8) of that Schedule, information–
    (a) explaining the effect of such removal; and
    (b) reminding the absent voter that they may make a fresh application under Schedule 4 to vote by post or by proxy (as the case may be).

(11) Where an absent voter has provided a registration officer with a fresh signature in response to a notice issued by the registration officer under this paragraph, or in response to a notice issued by the registration officer under any other enactment following the rejection of the absent voter's postal voting statement at an election or referendum, the registration officer may use that signature and enter it in the records kept in accordance with regulation 61B and paragraphs 3(4), 4(6) and 7(12) of Schedule 4.

Records and lists kept under Schedule 4

61 (1) Any person entitled to be supplied in accordance with regulation 103, 105, 106 or 108 below with copies of the full register is also a person entitled, subject to this regulation and to regulation 61A, to request that the registration officer supply free of charge the relevant part (within the meaning of those regulations) of a copy of any of the following information which he keeps–
    (a) the current version of the information which would, in the event of a particular parliamentary or local government election, be included in the postal voters lists, the list of proxies or the proxy postal voters lists, which he is required to keep under paragraph 5 or 7(8) of Schedule 4;
    (b) the current or final version of the postal voters list, the list of proxies or the proxy postal voters lists kept under paragraph 5 or 7(8) of Schedule 4.

(2) A request under paragraph (1) shall be made in writing and shall specify–
    (a) the information (or the relevant parts of the information) requested;
    (b) whether the request is made only in respect of the current lists or whether it includes a request for the supply of any final list; and
    (c) whether a printed copy of the records or lists is requested or a copy in data form.

(3) A person who obtains any information under this regulation may use it only for the permitted purposes specified in regulation 61A, and any restrictions–
    (a) specified in that regulation, or

(b)   which would apply to the use of the full register under whichever of regulation 103, 105, 106 or 108 entitled that person to obtain that information,

shall apply to such use.

(4)   The registration officer shall supply a current copy of the information requested under paragraph (1), as soon as practicable after receipt of a request that is duly made.

(5)   The registration officer shall supply a final copy of the postal voters list kept under paragraph 5(2) of Schedule 4, as soon as practicable after 5pm on the eleventh day before the day of the poll, in response to a request under paragraph (1) that has been duly made.

(6)   As soon as practicable after 5pm on the sixth day before the day of the poll the registration officer shall–

(a)   make a copy of the lists kept under paragraphs 5 and 7(8) of Schedule 4 available for inspection at his office in accordance with paragraphs (10) to (15); and

(b)   at a parliamentary election, if he is not the acting returning officer for any constituency or part of a constituency in the area for which he is the registration officer, send to that officer a copy of those lists;

(c)   supply a final copy of the postal voters lists or the list of proxies in response to every request under paragraph (1) that has been duly made.

(6A) At a parliamentary election, the registration officer must, on a request made at any time, supply the acting returning officer for any constituency or part of a constituency for which he is the registration officer with so much of the lists kept under paragraphs 5 and 7(8) of Schedule 4 as relate to that constituency or part of a constituency.

(7)   The registration officer shall supply a final copy of the proxy voters list kept under paragraph 5(3) of Schedule 4, updated to include any additions to that list made in consequence of any applications granted in accordance with regulation 56(3A), as soon as practicable after 5pm on the day of the poll, to every person who received that list in accordance with paragraph (6)(c).

(8)   Any person who has obtained or is entitled to obtain a copy of information covered by paragraph (1) may–

(a)   supply a copy of the information to a processor for the purpose of processing the information, or

(b)   procure that a processor processes and supplies to them any copy of the information which the processor has obtained under this regulation,

for use in respect of the purposes for which that person is entitled to obtain such information.

(9)   Paragraphs (2) and (3) and the condition in paragraph (9) of regulation 92 shall be taken to apply to the supply and processing of information supplied under this regulation as they apply to the supply and processing of the full register under Part 6 of these Regulations.

(10) Any person is entitled to request that the registration officer make available for inspection a copy of any of the information specified in paragraph (1).

(11) A request under paragraph (10) shall be made in writing and shall specify–

(a)   the information (or relevant parts of the information) requested;

(b)   whether the request is made only in respect of the current lists or whether it includes a request for the inspection of any final list;

(c)   who will inspect the information;

(d)   the date on which they wish to inspect the information; and

(e)   whether they would prefer to inspect the information in a printed or data form.

(12) The registration officer shall make a copy of the information available for inspection under supervision as soon as practicable after the date of receipt of a request that has been duly made.

(13) Where inspection takes place by providing a copy of the information on a computer screen or otherwise in data form, the registration officer shall ensure that the manner in, and equipment on, which that copy is provided do not permit any person consulting that copy to–

    (a) search it by electronic means by reference to the name of any person; or

    (b) copy or transmit any part of that copy by electronic, or any other means.

(14) A person who inspects a copy of the information, whether a printed copy or in data form, may not–

    (a) make copies of any part of it, or

    (b) record any particulars in it,

otherwise than by means of hand-written notes.

(15) Subject to any direction by the Secretary of State under section 52(1) of the 1983 Act, any duty on a registration officer to supply a copy or make information available for inspection under this regulation, imposes only a duty to provide that information in the form in which he holds it.

(16) For the purposes of this regulation–

    (a) a "current copy" of records or lists is a copy of the records or lists as kept by the registration officer at 9am on the date it is supplied; and

    (b) any period of days shall be calculated in accordance with regulation 56(6) and (7).

(17) The registration officer shall ensure that where he supplies or discloses information covered by paragraph (1)(a) in accordance with this regulation, he does not supply or disclose any record relating to a person specified in paragraph (18).

(18) The persons specified in this paragraph are–

    (a) a person who has an anonymous entry;

    (b) the proxy of a person who has an anonymous entry.

Conditions on the use, supply and inspection of absent voter records or lists

61A The restrictions on the supply, disclosure and use of the full register in regulations 94 and 96 shall apply to information covered by regulations 61(1)(a) and (b), as they apply to the full register, except that the permitted purpose shall mean either–

    (a) research purposes within the meaning of that term in section 33 of the Data Protection Act 1998; or

    (b) electoral purposes.

The personal identifiers record

61B (1) The registration officer shall maintain a record ("the personal identifiers record"), apart from the other records and lists which he is required to keep under Schedule 4, of the signatures and dates of birth provided by persons whose applications under paragraph 3(1) or (2), paragraph 4(1) or (2) or paragraph 7(4)(a) or (b) of Schedule 4 were granted, until the expiry of twelve months from–

    (a) the date on which a person is removed from the record kept pursuant to paragraph 3(4) or 7(6) of Schedule 4; or

    (b) the date of the poll for the purposes of which the person's application for an absent vote was granted under paragraph 4(1) or (2) or 7(4)(b) of Schedule 4.

(2) The personal identifiers record shall contain the following information in respect of each absent voter on the postal voters list, list of proxies or proxy postal voters list–
   (a) his name;
   (b) his date of birth; and
   (c) his signature, or a record of the waiver by the registration officer of the requirement for a signature;

(3) The registration officer may disclose information held in the personal identifiers records to–
   (a) any candidate or agent attending proceedings on receipt of postal ballot papers, in accordance with and for the purposes referred to in regulation 85A;
   (b) any person attending proceedings on receipt of postal ballot papers, who is entitled to do so by virtue of any of sections 6A to 6D of the Political Parties, Elections and Referendums Act 2000, but only to the extent required to permit them to observe the proceedings.

Notification of a rejected postal voting statement

61C (1) Where an absent voter (whether an elector or a proxy), appears on the list created under regulation 87(4) then–
   (a) the registration officer responsible for the personal identifiers record that contains information in respect of the absent voter must notify them (and the elector if the absent voter is a proxy) that the ballot paper concerned was rejected because the returning officer was not satisfied that the postal voting statement was duly completed;
   (b) the registration officer must send the notification within the period of three months beginning with the date of the poll at which the ballot paper was rejected; and
   (c) the notification must include information as to which of the specified reasons referred to in regulation 87(5) applied to the absent voter's postal voting statement.

(2) The registration officer is not obliged to send a notification–
   (a) to any person who is no longer shown as voting by post in the relevant record at the time the registration officer proposes to send out the notification, or
   (b) where the returning officer suspects that an offence may have been committed in relation to the postal ballot paper, postal voting statement or the absent voter's registration as an elector.

(3) A notification issued under paragraph (1) may also include any other information that the registration officer considers appropriate, but a notification must not include information held on the personal identifiers record.

Marked register for polling stations

62 To indicate that an elector or his proxy is entitled to vote by post and is for that reason not entitled to vote in person, the letter "A" shall be placed against the entry of that elector in any copy of the register, or part of it, provided for a polling station.

Certificate of employment at a parliamentary election

63 (1) The form of certificate in Form F is hereby prescribed for the purposes of rule 32(3) of the elections rules in Schedule 1 to the 1983 Act.

(2) The prescribed officer of police for those purposes is one of or above the rank of inspector.

Corresponding number lists

63A (1) The form of the corresponding number list to be prepared by a returning officer under rule 19A of the rules in Schedule 1 to the 1983 Act shall be in Form L1.

(2) The form of the corresponding number list to be prepared by a returning officer for the purposes of rules 29(3)(e) and 37(1)(b) of the rules in Schedule 1 to the 1983 Act shall be in Form L2.

(3) The form of the corresponding number list to be prepared by a returning officer under rule 19A of the rules in Schedule 1 to the 1983 Act, when a parliamentary election is combined with another poll under section 15 of the Representation of the People Act 1985 or section 44 or 45 of the Local Government Act 2000 shall be in Form M1.

(4) The form of the corresponding number list to be prepared by a returning officer for the purposes of rules 29(3)(e) and 37(1)(b) of the rules in Schedule 1 to the 1983 Act, when a parliamentary election is combined with another poll under section 15 of the Representation of the People Act 1985 or section 44 or 45 of the Local Government Act 2000 shall be in Form M2.

PART V
ISSUE AND RECEIPT OF POSTAL BALLOT PAPERS

Interpretation of Part V

64 For the purposes of this Part of these Regulations, unless the context otherwise requires–

"agent" includes the election agent and a person appointed to attend in the election agent's place;

"ballot paper envelope" and "covering envelope" mean the envelopes referred to in regulation 74 below;

"postal ballot paper" means a ballot paper issued to a postal voter;

"postal voter" means an elector or proxy who is entitled to vote by post;

"postal voters' ballot box" means the ballot box referred to in regulation 81(1)(a);

"receptacle for ballot paper envelopes", and other references to specified receptacles, means the receptacles referred to in regulation 81(5) below;

"spoilt postal ballot paper" means a ballot paper referred to in regulation 77(1) below;

"universal postal service provider" has the meaning given in Part 3 of the Postal Services Act 2011 to a "universal service provider"; and

"valid postal voting statement" means a postal voting statement which, in accordance with regulation 85 or 85A, the returning officer is satisfied has been duly completed.

Issue of Postal Ballot Papers

Combination of polls

65 Where the polls at elections are taken together under–

(a) subsection (1) or (2) of section 15 of the 1985 Act (combination of polls at parliamentary, European Parliamentary and local government elections), or

(b) subsection (3) or (3AB) of section 36 of the 1983 Act (combination of polls at local elections),

the proceedings on the issue and receipt of postal ballot papers in respect of each election may, if the returning officers concerned agree, be taken together.

Form of postal voting statement

66   The form of the postal voting statement for the purposes of rule 24 of the rules in Schedule 1 to the 1983 Act shall be–
  (a)   in Form G at a parliamentary election taken alone;
  (b)   in Form H at a parliamentary election where the proceedings on the issue and receipt of postal ballot papers are taken together with those proceedings at another election;
  (c)   in Form J at a parliamentary election where the poll is taken together with the poll at another election, but where the proceedings on the issue and receipt of postal ballot papers are not.

Persons entitled to be present at proceedings on issue of postal ballot papers

67   Without prejudice to the provisions of section 6A, 6B, 6C, 6D, or 6E of the Political Parties, Elections and Referendums Act 2000, no person may be present at the proceedings on the issue of postal ballot papers other than the returning officer and his clerks.

Persons entitled to be present at proceedings on receipt of postal ballot papers

68   Without prejudice to the provisions of section 6A, 6B, 6C, 6D, or 6E of the Political Parties, Elections and Referendums Act 2000, no person may be present at the proceedings on the receipt of postal ballot papers other than–
  (a)   the returning officer and his clerks,
  (b)   a candidate,
  (c)   an election agent or any person appointed by a candidate to attend in his election agent's place or, at an election of parish or community councillors, any person appointed by the candidate to attend at those proceedings, and
  (d)   any agents appointed under regulation 69 below.

Agents of candidates who may attend proceedings on receipt of postal ballot papers

69 (1)   Each candidate may appoint one or more agents to attend the proceedings on the receipt of the postal ballot papers up to the number he may be authorised by the returning officer to appoint so, however, that the number authorised shall be the same in the case of each candidate.

  (2)   Notice in writing of the appointment stating the names and addresses of the persons appointed shall be given by the candidate to the returning officer before the time fixed for the opening of the postal voters' ballot box.

  (3)   Where postal ballot papers for more than one election are issued together under regulation 65 above, the returning officer to whom notice shall be given under paragraph (2) above and paragraphs (4) and (5) below is the returning officer who issues the postal ballot papers.

  (4)   If an agent dies or becomes incapable of acting, the candidate may appoint another agent in his place and shall forthwith give to the returning officer notice in writing of the name and address of the agent appointed.

  (5)   Agents may be appointed and notice of appointment given to the returning officer by the candidate's election agent instead of by the candidate.

  (6)   In this Part of these Regulations references to agents shall be taken as references to agents whose appointments have been duly made and notified and, in the case of agents appointed under paragraph (1) above, who are within the number authorised by the returning officer.

(7)   A candidate may himself do any act or thing which any agent of his, if appointed, would have been authorised to do, or may assist his agent in doing any such act or thing.

(8)   Where in this Part of these Regulations any act or thing is required or authorised to be done in the presence of the candidates or their agents, the non-attendance of any such persons or person at the time and place appointed for the purpose shall not, if the act or thing is otherwise duly done, invalidate the act or thing done.

Notification of requirement of secrecy

70   The returning officer shall make such arrangements as he thinks fit to ensure that every person attending the proceedings in connection with the issue of receipt or postal ballot papers has been given a copy in writing of the provisions of subsections (4) and (6) of section 66 of the 1983 Act.

Time when postal ballot papers are to be issued

71   Postal ballot papers (and postal voting statements) must be issued by the returning officer as soon as it is practicable to do so.

Procedure on issue of postal ballot paper

72 (1)   *Repealed*

(2)   The number of the elector as stated in the register shall be marked on the corresponding number list, next to the number and unique identifying mark of the ballot paper issued to that elector.

(3)   A mark shall be placed in the postal voters list or the proxy postal voters list against the number of the elector to denote that a ballot paper has been issued to the elector or his proxy, but without showing the particular ballot paper issued.

(4)   The number of a postal ballot paper shall be marked on the postal voting statement sent with that paper.

(5)   Where postal ballot papers for more than one election are issued together under regulation 65 above–
  (a)   one mark shall be placed in the postal voters list or the proxy postal voters list under paragraph (3) above to denote that ballot papers have been issued in respect of all those elections; except that, where ballot papers are not so issued, a different mark shall be placed in the absent voters list or proxy postal voters list to identify the election in respect of which the ballot paper was issued; and
  (b)   the number of each ballot paper shall be marked on the postal voting statement under paragraph (4) above.

(6)   Where the poll at one election is taken with the poll at another election (under the provisions referred to in regulation 65 above) but not the proceedings on the issue and receipt of postal ballot papers, the colour of the postal ballot paper shall also be marked on the postal voting statement sent with that paper.

(7)   Subject to paragraph (8), the address to which the postal ballot paper, postal voting statement and the envelopes referred to in regulation 74 below are to be sent is–
  (a)   in the case of an elector, the address shown in the postal voters list;
  (b)   in the case of a proxy, the address shown in the proxy postal voters list.

(8)   Where a person has an anonymous entry in the register, the items specified in paragraph (7) must be sent (as the case may be) to the address to which postal ballot papers should be sent–
  (a)   as shown in the record kept under paragraph 3(4) or 7(6) of Schedule 4, or

(b) as given in pursuance of an application made under paragraph 4(1) or 7(4)(b) of Schedule 4.

Refusal to issue postal ballot paper

73 Where a returning officer is satisfied that two or more entries in the postal voters list, or the proxy postal voters list or in each of those lists relate to the same elector, he shall not issue more than one ballot paper in respect of that elector at any one election.

Envelopes

74 (1) Paragraphs (2) and (3) below prescribe the envelopes which are to be issued to a postal voter in addition to the ballot paper and postal voting statement (which are issued under rule 24 of the elections rules).

(2) There shall be issued an envelope for the return of the postal ballot paper or, as the case may be, ballot papers and the postal voting statement (referred to as a "covering envelope") which shall be marked with the letter "B".

(3) There shall also be issued a smaller envelope (referred to as a "ballot paper envelope") which shall be marked with–
(a) the letter "A";
(b) the words "ballot paper envelope", and
(c) unless the envelope has a window through which the number on the ballot paper (or ballot papers) can be displayed, the number of the ballot paper or, as the case may be, ballot papers.

(4) Where polls are taken together (under the provisions referred to in regulation 65 above) but not the proceedings on the issue and receipt of postal ballot papers–
(a) the envelope referred to in paragraph (2) above shall also be marked "Covering envelope for the *insert colour of ballot paper* coloured ballot paper", and
(b) on the envelope referred to in paragraph (3) above, after the words "Ballot paper envelope" there shall be added the words "for the *insert colour of ballot paper* coloured ballot paper".

Sealing up of completed corresponding number lists and security of special lists

75 (1) As soon as practicable after the issue of each batch of postal ballot papers, the returning officer shall make up into a packet the completed corresponding number lists of those ballot papers which have been issued and shall seal such a packet.

(2) Until the time referred to in regulation 84(9), the returning officer shall take proper precautions for the security of the marked copy of the postal voters list and the proxy postal voters list.

(3) *Repealed*

76 Delivery of postal ballot papers

(1) For the purposes of delivering postal ballot papers, the returning officer may use–
(a) a universal postal service provider;
(b) a commercial delivery firm, or
(c) clerks appointed under rule 26(1) of the elections rules.

(2) Where the services of a universal postal service provider or commercial delivery firm are to be used, envelopes addressed to postal voters shall be counted and delivered by the returning officer with such form of receipt to be endorsed by that provider or firm as may be arranged.

(3) Postage shall be prepaid on envelopes addressed to the postal voters (except where paragraph (1)(c) above applies).

(4) Return postage shall be prepaid on all covering envelopes where the address provided by the postal voter for the receipt of the postal ballot paper is within the United Kingdom.

Spoilt postal ballot papers

77 (1) If a postal voter has inadvertently dealt with his postal ballot paper or postal voting statement in such a manner that it cannot be conveniently used as a ballot paper (referred to as "a spoilt ballot paper") or, as the case may be, a postal voting statement (referred to as "a spoilt postal voting statement") he may return (either by hand or by post) to the returning officer the spoilt ballot paper or, as the case may be, the spoilt postal voting statement.

(2) Where a postal voter exercises the entitlement conferred by paragraph (1), he shall also return–
   (a) the postal ballot paper or, as the case may be, the postal voting statement, whether spoilt or not;
   (b) where postal ballot papers for more than one election have been issued together under regulation 65, all other ballot papers so issued, whether spoilt or not; and
   (c) the envelopes supplied for the return of the documents mentioned in paragraph (1) or sub-paragraph (a) or (b).

(3) Subject to paragraph (3A) on receipt of the documents referred to in paragraph (1) and, where applicable paragraph (2) above, the returning officer shall issue another postal ballot paper or, as the case may be, ballot papers except where those documents are received after 5 pm on the day of the poll.

(3A) Where the returning officer receives the documents referred to in paragraph (1) and, where applicable paragraph (2), after 5 pm on the day before the day of the poll, he shall only issue another postal ballot paper or, as the case may be, ballot papers if the postal voter returned the documents by hand.

(4) Regulations 72 (except paragraph (3)), 74, 75 and, subject to paragraph (7) below, 76 above shall apply to the issue of a replacement postal ballot paper under paragraph (3) above.

(5) Any postal ballot paper or postal voting statement, whether spoilt or not, returned in accordance with paragraph (1) or (2) shall be immediately cancelled.

(6) The returning officer, as soon as practicable after cancelling those documents, shall make up those documents in a separate packet and shall seal the packet; and if on any subsequent occasion documents are cancelled as mentioned above, the sealed packet shall be opened and the additional cancelled documents included in it and the packet shall be again made up and sealed.

(7) Where a postal voter applies in person–
   (a) by 5 pm on the day before the day of the poll, the returning officer may hand a replacement postal ballot paper to him; or
   (b) after 5 pm on the day before the day of the poll, the returning officer may only hand a replacement postal ballot paper to him,
instead of delivering it in accordance with regulation 76.

(8) The returning officer shall enter in a list kept for the purpose ("the list of spoilt postal ballot papers")–

(a) the name and number of the elector as stated in the register (or, in the case of an elector who has an anonymous entry, his electoral number alone);

(b) the number of the postal ballot paper (or papers) issued under this regulation; and

(c) where the postal voter whose ballot paper is spoilt is a proxy, his name and address.

Lost postal ballot papers

78 (1) Where a postal voter claims either to have lost or not to have received–

    (a) his postal ballot paper, or

    (b) the postal voting statement, or

    (c) one or more of the envelopes supplied for their return,

by the fourth day before the day of the poll, he may apply (whether or not in person) to the returning officer for a replacement ballot paper.

(2) Such an application shall include evidence of the voter's identity.

(2A) Where a postal voter exercises the entitlement conferred by paragraph (1), he shall return–

    (a) the documents referred to in paragraph (1)(a) to (c); and

    (b) where postal ballot papers for more than one election have been issued together under regulation 65, all other ballot papers so issued,

which he has received and which have not been lost.

(2B) Any postal ballot paper or postal voting statement returned in accordance with paragraph (2A) shall be immediately cancelled.

(2C) The returning officer, as soon as practicable after cancelling those documents, shall make up those documents in a separate packet and shall seal the packet; and if on any subsequent occasion documents are cancelled as mentioned above, the sealed packet shall be opened and the additional cancelled documents included in it and the packet shall be again made up and sealed.

(3) Subject to paragraph (3A) where the application is received by the returning officer before 5 pm on the day of the poll and the returning officer–

    (a) is satisfied as to the voter's identity, and

    (b) has no reason to doubt that the postal voter has either lost or has not received the original postal ballot paper or the postal voting statement or one or more of the envelopes provided for their return,

he shall issue another postal ballot paper or, as the case may be, postal ballot papers.

(3A) Where the application is received by the returning officer after 5 pm on the day before the day of the poll, he shall only issue another postal ballot paper or, as the case may be, other ballot papers if the postal voter applied in person.

(4) The returning officer shall enter in a list kept for the purpose ("the list of lost postal ballot papers")–

    (a) the name and number of the elector as stated in the register (or, in the case of an elector who has an anonymous entry, his electoral number alone);

    (b) the number of the postal ballot paper issued under this regulation; and

    (c) where the postal voter is a proxy, his name and address.

(5) Regulations 72 (except paragraph (3)), 74, 75 and, subject to paragraph (6) below, 76 above shall apply to the issue of a replacement postal ballot paper under paragraph (3) above.

(6) Where a postal voter applies in person–

    (a) by 5 pm on the day before the day of the poll, the returning officer may hand a replacement postal ballot paper to him; or

(b) after 5 pm on the day before the day of the poll, the returning officer may only hand a replacement postal ballot paper to him,

instead of delivering it in accordance with regulation 76.

Cancellation of postal ballot papers

78A (1) Where, after the final nomination day at a parliamentary or local government election, an application under–

    (a) paragraph 3(5)(a) of Schedule 4 to the 2000 Act (application to be removed from record of absent voters),

    (b) paragraph 3(6) or 4(3)(b) of that Schedule (application to vote by proxy by a person recorded as voting by post),

    (c) paragraph 3(7) of that Schedule (application to vote by post by person recorded as voting by proxy),

    (d) paragraph 4(3)(a) of that Schedule (application for postal ballot paper to be sent to different address),

    (e) paragraph 6(7) or (8) of that Schedule (appointment of proxy),

    (f) paragraph 7(7) of that Schedule (application from postal proxy voter for postal ballot paper to be sent to a different address), or

    (g) paragraph 7(9)(a) of that Schedule (application by proxy to be removed from record of postal proxies),

is granted or a notice under paragraph 6(10) of that Schedule (cancellation of proxy appointment) is received, and the application or notice is not to be disregarded for the purposes of that election under regulation 56, the registration officer must notify the returning officer who must immediately cancel any postal ballot paper issued to the elector or proxy and, in the case of an application mentioned in sub-paragraph (d) or (f), must issue a replacement ballot paper.

(2) Where a person returns a postal ballot paper that has been or is to be cancelled in accordance with paragraph (1) (whether to the registration officer or the returning officer), it must be dealt with as follows–

    (a) the ballot paper, together with any other ballot papers, postal voting statements or covering envelopes which are returned to the registration officer, must be given by the registration officer to the returning officer;

    (b) any document returned in accordance with this paragraph but not cancelled in accordance with paragraph (1) must be immediately cancelled;

    (c) the returning officer, as soon as practicable after receiving and cancelling those documents, shall make up those documents in a separate packet and shall seal the packet, and if on any subsequent occasion documents are returned in accordance with this paragraph, the sealed packet shall be opened and the additional cancelled documents included in it and the packet shall be again made up and sealed.

(3) The returning officer must enter in a list kept for the purpose of recording postal ballot papers cancelled under this regulation ("the list of cancelled postal ballot papers")–

    (a) the name and number of the elector as stated in the register of electors (or, in the case of an elector who has an anonymous entry, their electoral number alone);

    (b) the number of the cancelled postal ballot paper;

    (c) the number of any replacement postal ballot paper issued under paragraph (1); and

    (d) where the postal voter is a proxy, their name and address.

(4) Regulations 72 (except paragraph (3)), 74, 75 and 76 apply to a replacement postal ballot paper issued under paragraph (1).

(5) In this regulation "the final nomination day" has the meaning given by section 13B(5) of the 1983 Act.

Receipt of Postal Ballot Papers

Alternative means of returning postal ballot paper or postal voting statement

79 (1) For the purposes of rule 45(1B) of the rules in Schedule 1 to the 1983 Act the manner in which a postal ballot paper or postal voting statement may be returned to a polling station is by hand.

(2) For these purposes, the manner in which such a paper or statement may be returned to the returning officer is by post or by hand.

(3) Subject to paragraph (4) the presiding officer of the polling station shall deliver, or cause to be delivered, any postal ballot paper or postal voting statement returned to that station to the returning officer in the same manner and at the same time as he delivers, or causes to be delivered, the packets referred to in rule 43(1) of the elections rules.

(4) The returning officer may collect, or cause to be collected, any postal ballot paper or postal voting statement which by virtue of paragraph (3) the presiding officer of a polling station would otherwise be required to deliver or cause to be delivered to him.

(5) Where the returning officer collects, or causes to be collected, any postal ballot paper or postal voting statement in accordance with paragraph (4) the presiding officer shall first make it (or them) up into a packet (or packets) sealed with his own seal and the seals of such polling agents as are present and desire to affix their seals.

Notice of opening of postal ballot paper envelopes

80 (1) The returning officer shall give to each candidate not less than 48 hours' notice in writing of each occasion on which a postal voters' ballot box and the envelopes contained in it is to be opened.

(2) Such a notice shall specify–
   (a) the time and place at which such an opening is to take place, and
   (b) the number of agents a candidate may appoint under regulation 69(1) above to attend each opening.

Postal ballot boxes and receptacles

81 (1) The returning officer shall provide a separate ballot box for the reception of–
   (a) the covering envelopes when returned by the postal voters ("postal voters' ballot box"), and
   (b) postal ballot papers ("postal ballot box").

(2) Each such ballot box shall be marked "postal voters' ballot box" or "postal ballot box", as the case may be, and with the name of the constituency or electoral area (or areas) for which the election (or elections) is held.

(3) The postal ballot box shall be shown to the agents present on the occasion of opening the first postal voters' ballot box as being empty.

(4) The returning officer shall then lock the ballot box and apply his seal in such manner as to prevent its being opened without breaking the seal; any of the agents present who wish to add their seals may then do likewise.

(5) The returning officer shall provide the following receptacles–
   (a) the receptacle for rejected votes;
   (b) *Repealed*

- (c) the receptacle for ballot paper envelopes;
- (d) the receptacle for rejected ballot paper envelopes;
- (e) the receptacle for rejected votes (verification procedure); and
- (f) the receptacle for postal voting statements (verification procedure).

(6) The returning officer shall take proper precautions for the safe custody of every ballot box and receptacle referred to in this regulation.

82 Receipt of covering envelope

(1) The returning officer shall, immediately on receipt (whether by hand or by post) of a covering envelope (or an envelope which is stated to include a postal vote) before the close of the poll, place it unopened in a postal voters' ballot box.

(2) Where an envelope, other than a covering envelope issued by the returning officer–
- (a) has been opened, and
- (b) contains a ballot paper envelope, postal voting statement or ballot paper,

the first-mentioned envelope, together with its contents, shall be placed in a postal voters' ballot box.

Opening of postal voters' ballot box

83 (1) Each postal voters' ballot box shall be opened by the returning officer in the presence of the agents.

(2) So long as the returning officer ensures that there is at least one sealed postal voters' ballot box for the reception of covering envelopes up to the time of the close of the poll, the other postal voters' ballot boxes may previously be opened by him.

(3) The last postal voters' ballot box and the postal ballot box shall be opened at the counting of the votes under rule 45 of the elections rules.

Opening of covering envelopes

84 (1) When a postal voters' ballot box is opened, the returning officer shall count and record the number of covering envelopes (including any envelope which is stated to include a postal vote and any envelope described in regulation 82(2)(above).

(1A) *Repealed*

(1B) He shall open separately each covering envelope (including an envelope described in regulation 82(2) above).

(2) The procedure in regulation 85A applies where a covering envelope (including an envelope to which regulation 82(2) above applies) contains a postal voting statement.

(3) Where the covering envelope does not contain the postal voting statement separately, the returning officer shall open the ballot paper envelope to ascertain whether the postal voting statement is inside.

(4) Where a covering envelope does not contain a postal voting statement (whether separately or not), the returning officer shall mark the covering envelope "provisionally rejected", attach its contents (if any) and place it in the receptacle for rejected votes.

(5) *Repealed*

(6) In carrying out the procedures in this regulation and regulations 85 to 88, the returning officer–
- (a) shall keep the ballot papers face downwards and shall take proper precautions for preventing any person from seeing the votes made on the ballot papers; and

      (b) shall not be permitted to view the corresponding number list used at the issue of postal ballot papers.

(7) Where an envelope opened in accordance with paragraph (1B) contains a postal voting statement, the returning officer shall place a mark in the marked copy of the postal voters list or proxy postal voters list in a place corresponding to the number of the elector to denote that a postal vote has been returned.

(8) A mark made under paragraph (7) shall be distinguishable from and shall not obscure the mark made under regulation 72(3).

(9) As soon as practicable after the last covering envelope has been opened, the returning officer shall make up into a packet the copy of the marked postal voters list and proxy postal voters list that have been marked in accordance with paragraph (7) and shall seal such a packet.

Confirming receipt of postal voting statements

84A (1) An elector or a proxy voter who is shown in the postal voters list or proxy postal voters list may make a request, at any time between the first issue of postal ballots under regulation 71 and the close of the poll, that the returning officer confirm–
      (a) whether a mark is shown in the marked copy of the postal voters list or proxy postal voters list in a place corresponding to the number of the elector to denote that a postal vote has been returned, and
      (b) whether the number of the ballot paper issued to the elector or his proxy has been recorded on either of the lists of provisionally rejected votes kept by the returning officer under paragraphs (2) and (3) of regulation 87.

(2) A request under paragraph (1) shall–
      (a) be made by any method specified, and
      (b) include any evidence of the voter's identity requested,
    by the returning officer.

(3) Where a request is received in accordance with paragraph (2) the returning officer shall satisfy himself that the request has been made by the elector or their proxy and where he is so satisfied provide confirmation of the matters under paragraph (1).

85   *Repealed*

Procedure in relation to postal voting statements: personal identifier verification

85A (1) This regulation applies in the circumstances described in regulation 84(2).

(2) The returning officer must satisfy himself that the postal voting statement is duly completed and as part of that process must compare the date of birth and the signature on the postal voting statement against the date of birth and signature contained in the personal identifier record relating to the person to whom the postal ballot paper was addressed.

(3) Where the returning officer is not so satisfied, he shall mark the statement "rejected", attach to it the ballot paper envelope, or if there is no such envelope but there is a ballot paper, the ballot paper, and, subject to paragraph (4), place it in the receptacle for rejected votes (verification procedure).

(4) Before placing a postal voting statement in the receptacle for rejected votes (verification procedure), the returning officer must show it to the agents and must permit them to view the entries in the personal identifiers record which relate to the person to whom the postal ballot paper was addressed, and if any of them object to his decision, he must add the words "rejection objected to".

(5) The returning officer shall then examine the number on the postal voting statement against the number on the ballot paper envelope and, where they are the same, he shall place the statement and the ballot paper envelope respectively in the receptacle for postal voting statements (verification procedure) and the receptacle for ballot paper envelopes.

(6) Where–
    (a) the number on a valid postal voting statement is not the same as the number on the ballot paper envelope, or
    (b) that envelope has no number on it (or only one number when the postal voting statement has more than one),
the returning officer shall open the envelope.

(7) Paragraph (8) applies where–
    (a) there is a valid postal voting statement but no ballot paper envelope; or
    (b) the ballot paper envelope has been opened under regulation 84(3) or paragraph (6) above.

(8) In the circumstances described in paragraph (7) above, the returning officer shall place–
    (a) in the postal ballot box, any ballot paper the number on which is the same as the number on the valid postal voting statement;
    (b) in the receptacle for rejected votes (verification procedure), any other ballot paper, with the valid postal voting statement attached and marked "provisionally rejected";
    (c) in the receptacle for rejected votes (verification procedure), any valid postal voting statement marked "provisionally rejected" where–
        (i) there is no ballot paper, or
        (ii) in the case of a statement on which the number of more than one ballot paper appears, there is not a sufficient number of ballot papers and, in such a case, shall mark the statement to indicate which ballot paper is missing;
    (d) in the receptacle for postal voting statements (verification procedure), any valid statement not disposed of under sub-paragraph (b) or (c) above.

85B   *Repealed*

Opening of ballot paper envelopes

86 (1) The returning officer shall open separately each ballot paper envelope placed in the receptacle for ballot paper envelopes.

(2) He shall place–
    (a) in the postal ballot box, any ballot paper the number on which is the same as the number (or one of the numbers) on the ballot paper envelope;
    (b) in the receptacle for rejected votes, any other ballot paper which shall be marked "provisionally rejected" and to which shall be attached the ballot paper envelope; and
    (c) in the receptacle for rejected ballot paper envelopes, any ballot paper envelope which shall be marked "provisionally rejected" because it does not contain either a ballot paper or, where more than one number appears on the ballot paper envelope, a sufficient number of ballot papers (and indicating, in such a case, the missing ballot paper).

Retrieval of cancelled postal ballot papers

86A (1) Where it appears to the returning officer that a cancelled postal ballot paper has been placed–

    (a) in a postal voters' ballot box;

    (b) in the receptacle for ballot paper envelopes; or

    (c) a postal ballot box,

    he shall proceed as follows.

(2) He shall, on at least one occasion on which a postal voters ballot box is opened in accordance with regulation 83, also open any postal ballot box and the receptacle for ballot paper envelopes and–

    (a) retrieve the cancelled ballot paper;

    (b) show the ballot paper number on the cancelled ballot paper to the agents;

    (c) retrieve the postal voting statement that relates to a cancelled ballot paper from the receptacle for postal voting statements (verification procedure);

    (d) attach any cancelled postal ballot paper to the postal voting statement to which it relates;

    (e) place the cancelled documents in a separate packet and deal with that packet in the manner provided for by regulation 77(6) or 78A(2); and

    (f) unless the postal ballot box has been opened for the purposes of the counting of votes under rule 45 of the elections rules, re-lock (if it has a lock) and re-seal the postal ballot box in the presence of the agents.

(3) Whilst retrieving a cancelled ballot paper in accordance with paragraph (2), the returning officer and his staff–

    (a) shall keep the ballot papers face downwards and shall take proper precautions for preventing any person seeing the votes made on the ballot papers, and

    (b) shall not be permitted to view the corresponding number list used at the issue of postal ballot papers.

Lists of rejected postal ballot papers

87 (1) In respect of any election, the returning officer shall keep three separate lists relating to rejected postal ballot papers.

(2) In the first list, he shall record the ballot paper number of any postal ballot paper for which no valid postal voting statement was received with it.

(3) In the second list, he shall record the ballot paper number of any postal ballot paper which is entered on a valid postal voting statement where that ballot paper is not received with the postal voting statement.

(4) In the third list, he shall record for every postal voting statement within the receptacle for rejected votes (verification procedure) immediately prior to sealing–

    (a) the elector's name and address (and the name and address of the proxy if the elector has a proxy),

    (b) the elector's number on the register of electors (and that of the proxy if the elector has a proxy),

    (c) the specified reason or reasons for the rejection of the postal voting statement, and

    (d) any other information relating to the rejection that the returning officer considers appropriate, but not the ballot paper number.

(5) The specified reasons that may be given under sub-paragraph (4)(c) for the rejection of a postal voting statement are as follows–

    (a) the signature does not match the example held on the personal identifiers record,

    (b)   the date of birth does not match the one held on the personal identifiers record,

    (c)   the signature field is blank, or

    (d)   the date of birth field is blank.

Checking of lists kept under regulation 87

88 (1)   Where the returning officer receives a valid postal voting statement without the postal ballot paper (or papers or, as the case may be, all of the papers) to which it relates, he may, at any time prior to the close of the poll, check the list kept under regulation 87(2) above to see whether the number (or numbers) of a postal ballot paper to which the statement relates is entered in that list.

  (2)   Where the returning officer receives a postal ballot paper without the postal voting statement to which it relates, he may, at any time prior to the close of the poll, check the list kept under regulation 87(3) above to see whether the number of that ballot paper is entered in that list.

  (3)   The returning officer shall conduct the checks required by paragraphs (1) and (2) above as soon as practicable after the receipt of packets from every polling station in the constituency or, as the case may be, electoral area under rule 43(1) of the elections rules.

  (4)   Where the ballot paper number in the list matches that number on a valid postal voting statement or, as the case may be, the postal ballot paper, the returning officer shall retrieve that statement or paper.

  (5)   The returning officer shall then take the appropriate steps under this Part of these Regulations as though any document earlier marked "provisionally rejected" had not been so marked and shall amend the document accordingly.

Sealing of receptacles

89 (1)   As soon as practicable after the completion of the procedure under regulation 88(3) and (4) above, the returning officer shall make up into separate packets the contents of–

    (a)   the receptacle of rejected votes,

    (b)   *Repealed*

    (c)   the receptacle of rejected ballot paper envelopes,

    (d)   the lists of spoilt, lost or cancelled postal ballot papers,

    (e)   the receptacle of rejected votes (verification procedure), and

    (f)   the receptacle of postal voting statements (verification procedure),

    and shall seal up such packets.

  (2)   Any document in those packets marked "provisionally rejected" shall be deemed to be marked "rejected".

Abandoned poll

90 (1)   Where a poll is abandoned or countermanded after postal ballot papers have been issued, by reason of the death of a candidate, the returning officer–

    (a)   shall not take any step or further step to open covering envelopes or deal with the contents in accordance with the provisions of this Part of these Regulations; and

    (b)   shall, notwithstanding regulations 84 to 86 above, treat all unopened covering envelopes and the contents of those that have been opened as if they were counted ballot papers.

  (2)   Paragraph (1) above shall not apply where postal ballot papers for more than one election have been issued together under regulation 65 above.

Forwarding of documents

91 (1)   The returning officer shall forward to the relevant registration officer determined in accordance with rule 55(1A) of the elections rules at the same time as he forwards the documents mentioned in rule 55 of the elections rules–

    (a)   any packets referred to in regulations 75, 77(6), 78(2C), 78A(2), 84(9) and 89 above, subject to regulation 90 above, endorsing on each packet a description of its contents, the date of the election to which it relates and the name of the constituency or electoral area (or areas) for which the election (or elections) was held, and

    (b)   a completed statement in Form K of the number of postal ballot papers issued.

(2)   *Repealed*

(3)   Where–

    (a)   any covering envelopes are received by the returning officer after the close of the poll (apart from those delivered in accordance with the provisions of regulation 79(3) above);

    (b)   any envelopes addressed to postal voters are returned as undelivered too late to be readdressed, or

    (c)   any spoilt postal ballot papers are returned too late to enable other postal ballot papers to be issued,

the returning officer shall put them unopened in a separate packet, seal up such packet and endorse and forward it at a subsequent date in the manner described in paragraph (1) above.

(3A)   A returning officer, shall at the same time as forwarding the documents mentioned in paragraph (1)–

    (a)   forward the list required to be compiled under regulation 87(4) to the relevant registration officer determined in accordance with rule 55(1A) of the election rules, and

    (b)   where the constituency comprises any part of the area of more than one local authority, the returning officer shall also forward a copy of such extracts of the list required to be compiled under regulation 87(4) as are relevant to each of the other registration officers concerned.

(4)   Rules 56 and 57 of the elections rules shall apply to any packet or document forwarded under this regulation except that in applying those rules to the list compiled under regulation 87(4), the list and any extracts from it are to be treated in the same manner as a counted ballot paper.

(5)   A copy of the statement referred to in paragraph (1)(b) above shall be provided by the returning officer to the Secretary of State and the Electoral Commission in the period which starts 10 days after the day of the poll and ends 15 days after that day.

PART VI
SUPPLY OF REGISTER ETC

Interpretation and edited register

Interpretation and application of Part VI etc

92 (1)   In this Part "register" includes–

    (a)   any part of the register referred to, and

(b) (except in regulations 93 and 93A and in the context of the supply by the registration officer of the register and notices altering the register), any notice altering the register which is published under section 13A(2), 13AB(2) or 13B(3), (3B) or (3D) of the 1983 Act.

(2) In this Part–

    (a) "enactment" has the same meaning as in section 17(2) of the 2000 Act,

    (b) "processor" means any person who provides a service which consists of putting information into data form or processing information in data form and any reference to a processor includes a reference to his employees;

    (c) "relevant conditions" has the same meaning as in section 33(1) of the Data Protection Act 1998, and

    (d) "research purposes" shall be construed in accordance with section 33(1) of the Data Protection Act 1998.

(3) In this Part, any reference to an employee of any person who has access to a copy of the full register shall be deemed to include any person working or providing services for the purposes of that person or employed by or on behalf of, or working for, any person who is so working or who is supplying such a service.

(4) Where any person has been supplied with a copy of a register of electors pursuant to the Representation of the People (Scotland) Regulations 2001, or the Representation of the People (Northern Ireland Regulations 2001, that person shall be under the same duties and obligations and subject to the same penalties in relation to the copy supplied as he would have been under had that copy been supplied to him pursuant to these Regulations (and, accordingly, where that copy is a copy of a full register he shall be under the same duties, obligations and penalties that he would have been under had he been supplied with a copy of a full register pursuant to these Regulations).

(5) Subject to any direction of the Secretary of State under section 52(1) of the 1983 Act, any duty on a registration officer to supply data under this Part imposes only a duty to supply data in the form in which he holds it.

(6) The registration officer shall not supply data which includes information not included in the printed version of the full register otherwise than under a provision in an enactment.

(7) Any person who has obtained or is entitled to obtain a copy of the full register under regulations 97(5), 97A(7), 98, 100, 101, 103, 105, 106, 109, 109A(9), 113 or 114 may–

    (a) supply a copy of the full register to a processor for the purpose of processing the information contained in the register,

    (b) procure that a processor processes and provides to them any copy of the register which the processor has obtained under these Regulations,

for use in respect of the purposes for which that person is entitled to obtain such copy or information (as the case may be).

(8) *Repealed*

(9) The processor may not disclose the full register or the information contained in it except to the person who supplied it to the processor or an employee of that person or a person who is entitled to obtain a copy of the full register under these Regulations or any employee of such a person.

(10) The restrictions contained in regulations 94(3), 95(2), 97(6), 97A(8), 98(9), 100(3), 101(6), 103(3), 104(3), 105(4), 106(3), 107(3), 107(8), 108(5), 109(3) and 109A(10) below apply to a person to whom the full register, or any information contained in it (that is not contained in the edited register) has been supplied or disclosed under those paragraphs as they apply to the person to whom those regulations apply.

Edited version of register

93 (1) At the time when the registration officer publishes a version of the register under section 13(1) or (3) of the 1983 Act, ("the full register"), he shall also publish a version of the register under this regulation ("the edited register").

(2) The edited register shall omit the name and address of any elector whose details are included in the full register, if a request has been duly made to the registration officer in accordance with regulation 26 or regulation 93A by that elector for his name and address to be excluded from the edited register.

(2A) The edited register shall omit all anonymous entries in the register, and any information relating to them.

(3) In other respects the edited register shall be identical to the full register (and, accordingly, shall include any mark or date which is required to be recorded against the name of any elector), except that it shall take account of alterations in respect of which the registration officer has issued a notice under section 13A of the 1983 Act.

(3A) The registration officer must publish a revised version of the edited register incorporating any alterations which are required to be made by virtue of a request under either regulation 26 or regulation 93A and any alterations to the edited register in respect of which the registration officer is required to issue a notice under section 13A of the 1983 Act.

(3B) The registration officer must publish the revised version of the edited register in accordance with paragraph (3A)–
  (a) on the first day of the month which follows the date the request was received or, if the first day of the month is less than 14 days after the date the request was received, on the first day of the month immediately following that month; or
  (b) on the day the registration officer is required to publish the notice of alteration in accordance with section 13A;
whichever is appropriate.

(3C) Where no alterations are required to be made the duty in regulation 93(3A) does not apply.

(4) Notwithstanding the omission of names and addresses in accordance with paragraph (2), regulation 41 above shall apply to the edited register as it applies to the full register.

(5) Unless the contrary intention appears, any reference in these Regulations to the register is to the full register.

(6) The manner in which each revised version of the edited register is to be published under this regulation is–
  (a) by the registration officer making a copy of it available for inspection at his office; and
  (b) by such other means (if any) as he thinks appropriate.

(7) Each revised version of the edited register shall be kept published until the coming into force of the next revised version of it.

Notifying registration officer of change to edited register preference

93A (1) A person must make a request to the registration officer for the area in which the person resides if that person wishes to be included in or omitted from the edited register otherwise than in accordance with an application under regulation 26.

(2)   A person making a request under paragraph (1) must provide the registration officer with the person's full name, address and an indication of whether the person wishes to be included in or omitted from the edited register.

(3)   A registration officer may not treat information received in response to a canvass form given under regulation 32ZA(4) or 32ZB(1), (2) or (3) as a request for the purpose of this regulation.

(4)   Where a person has made a request in accordance with paragraph (1), the registration officer must notify the person in writing of the following–
    (a)   confirmation that the person has requested that they are included in or omitted from the edited register;
    (b)   when a revised version of the edited register reflecting the request will be published under regulation 93(3A);
    (c)   the manner in which the person may contact the registration officer if this information is not correct.

Restrictions on supply of full register and disclosure of information from it by the registration officer and his staff

94 (1)   This regulation applies to–
    (a)   the registration officer;
    (b)   any deputy registration officer; and
    (c)   any person appointed to assist any such officer or who in the course of his employment is assigned to assist any such officer in his registration duties.

(2)   Where the registration officer is also the returning officer or acting returning officer at any election or the counting officer at a referendum held by or under an Act of Parliament (and thereby has access to the full register without being supplied with a copy of it), this regulation also applies to–
    (a)   the registration officer acting in that other capacity;
    (b)   any deputy returning officer, deputy acting returning officer or deputy counting officer; and
    (c)   any person appointed to assist any person mentioned in paragraph (a) or (b) or who in the course of his employment is assigned to assist any such officer in his duties in respect of the election or referendum in question.

(3)   No person to whom this regulation applies may–
    (a)   supply to any person a copy of the full register,
    (b)   disclose information contained in it (and not contained in the edited register), or
    (c)   make use of any such information,
otherwise than in accordance with an enactment, including these Regulations.

(4)   Nothing in paragraph (3) above applies to the supply or disclosure by a person to whom this regulation applies to another such person in connection with his registration duties or for the purposes of an election or referendum.

Restrictions on use of the full register supplied under section 3 of the Juries Act 1974 or information contained in it

95 (1)   This regulation applies to–
    (a)   any officer designated by the Lord Chancellor under section 3(1) of the Juries Act 1974; and
    (b)   any other person to whom a copy of the full register has been supplied or to whom information contained in it has been disclosed for the purpose of summoning jurors.

(2) No person to whom this regulation applies may–
  (a) supply a copy of the full register,
  (b) disclose any information contained in it (that is not contained in the edited register), or
  (c) make use of such information,
otherwise than for the purpose of summoning jurors.

Restriction on use of the full register, or information contained in it, supplied in accordance with enactments or obtained otherwise

96 (1) This regulation applies to–
  (a) any person to whom a copy of the full register has been supplied in pursuance of a relevant provision;
  (b) any person to whom information contained in the full register has been disclosed in pursuance of a relevant provision;
  (c) any person to whom a person referred to in sub-paragraph (a) or (b) has supplied a copy of the full register or information contained in it for the purposes (express or implied) of a relevant provision; and
  (d) any person who has obtained access to a copy of the full register or information contained in it by any other means.

(2) No person to whom this regulation applies may–
  (a) supply a copy of the full register,
  (b) disclose any information contained in it (that is not contained in the edited register), or
  (c) make use of any such information,
other than for a permitted purpose construed in accordance with paragraph (2A).

(2A) The "permitted purpose"–
  (a) where the copy was supplied or the information obtained in pursuance of a relevant provision, means the particular purpose for which the copy was supplied or the information disclosed to the person in question pursuant to the relevant provision;
  (b) where the copy was not supplied or the information was not disclosed in pursuance of a relevant provision–
    (i) in the case of a person to whom the copy of the full register was made available for inspection under supervision in accordance with regulations 43(1)(a), 97(2)(a) and (3), 97A(4)(a) and (b), 99(4)(a) and 109A(6)(a) and (b), does not include direct marketing within the meaning of section 11(3) of the Data Protection Act 1998; and
    (ii) in any other case, means any purpose for which the person to whom this regulation applies could have obtained a copy of the register or the information contained in it pursuant to any enactment, including these Regulations.

(3) In this regulation "relevant provision" means any enactment (except the Juries Act 1974 and these Regulations) under which a copy of the full register is to be supplied or information from that register disclosed for a particular purpose.

Supply on publication and specific restrictions

Supply of free copy of full register to the British Library and restrictions on use

97 (1) Each registration officer shall supply, free of charge and on publication–
  (a) one printed copy and one data copy of any revised version of the register published under section 13(1) or (3) of the 1983 Act, and

(b)   one printed copy of any list of overseas electors,
to the British Library.

(2)   Subject to paragraph (5) no person employed by the British Library may–
    (a)   supply a copy of the full register other than to another such person or to a person using the Library to inspect it under supervision;
    (b)   disclose any information contained in it (that is not contained in the edited register) otherwise than in accordance with paragraph (3); or
    (c)   make use of any such information.

(3)   Subject to paragraph (5) no information which is contained in the full register (that is not contained in the edited register) may be disclosed otherwise than by allowing a person using the British Library to inspect it under supervision.

(3A)   Where a copy of the full register is made available for inspection by providing the register on a computer screen or otherwise in data form, the British Library shall ensure that the manner in, and equipment on, which that copy is provided do not permit any person consulting that copy to–
    (a)   search it by electronic means by reference to the name of any person; or
    (b)   copy or transmit any part of that copy by electronic means.

(4)   A person who inspects the copy of the full register held by the British Library, whether a printed copy or in data form, may not–
    (a)   make copies of any part of it, or
    (b)   record any particulars included in it,
otherwise than by means of hand-written notes.

(5)   A person employed by the British Library is not prohibited from supplying a copy of, or disclosing information contained in, a version of the full register where–
    (a)   more than ten years have expired since that version of the register was first published in accordance with regulation 43; and
    (b)   the supply or disclosure is for research purposes in compliance with the relevant conditions.

(6)   No person who obtains a copy of the full register or to whom information contained in it that is not contained in the edited register is disclosed under the circumstances described in paragraph (5) may–
    (a)   supply a copy of it,
    (b)   disclose any such information, or
    (c)   make use of any such information,
otherwise than for research purposes in compliance with the relevant conditions.

Supply of free copy of full register to the National Library of Wales and restrictions on use

97A (1)   Each registration officer in Wales shall supply, free of charge and on publication–
    (a)   one printed copy and one data copy of any revised version of the register published under section 13(1) or (3) of the 1983 Act, and
    (b)   one printed copy of any list of overseas electors,
to the National Library of Wales.

(2)   Each registration officer in England shall supply, free of charge and on publication–
    (a)   one copy of any revised version of the register published under section 13(1) or (3) of the 1983 Act, and
    (b)   one printed copy of any list of overseas electors,
to the National Library of Wales.

(3)   In paragraph (2)(a), the duty to supply is a duty to supply a data copy unless, prior to publication, the National Library of Wales has requested in writing a printed copy instead.

(4)   Subject to paragraph (7), no person employed by the National Library of Wales may–
    (a)   supply a copy of the full register other than to another such person or to a person using the Library to inspect it under supervision;
    (b)   disclose any information contained in it (that is not contained in the edited register) otherwise than by allowing a person using the National Library of Wales to inspect it under supervision; or
    (c)   make use of any such information.

(5)   Where a copy of the full register is made available for inspection by providing the register on a computer screen or otherwise in data form, the National Library of Wales shall ensure that the manner in, and equipment on, which that copy is provided do not permit any person consulting that copy to–
    (a)   search it by electronic means by reference to the name of any person; or
    (b)   copy or transmit any part of that copy by electronic means.

(6)   A person who inspects a copy of the full register, whether a printed copy or in data form, may not–
    (a)   make copies of any part of it, or
    (b)   record any particulars included in it,
otherwise than by means of hand-written notes.

(7)   A person employed by the National Library of Wales is not prohibited from supplying a copy of, or disclosing information contained in, a version of the full register where–
    (a)   more than ten years have expired since that version of the register was first published in accordance with regulation 43; and
    (b)   the supply or disclosure is for research purposes in compliance with the relevant conditions.

(8)   No person who obtains a copy of the full register or to whom information contained in it that is not contained in the edited register is disclosed under the circumstances described in paragraph (7) may–
    (a)   supply a copy of it,
    (b)   disclose any such information, or
    (c)   make use of any such information,
otherwise than for research purposes in compliance with the relevant conditions.

Supply of free copy of full register to the National Library of Scotland

97B   Each registration officer in England and Wales shall supply, free of charge and on publication–
    (a)   one data copy of any revised version of the register published under section 13(1) or (3) of the 1983 Act; and
    (b)   one printed copy of any list of overseas electors,
to the National Library of Scotland.

Supply of free copy of full register for electoral purposes and restrictions on use

98 (1)   Each registration officer shall supply, free of charge and on publication, one copy of–
    (a)   any revised version of the register published under section 13(1) or (3) of the 1983 Act, and
    (b)   any notice setting out an alteration to the register published under section 13A(2), 13AB(2) or 13B(3), (3B) or (3D) of that Act,
to the persons listed in paragraph (2) below.

(2) Those persons are–
    (a) the returning officer for a non-metropolitan county;
    (b) the persons or officers who, under subsections (2B) and (2C) of section 35 of the 1983 Act are the returning officers at an election of members of the London Assembly and of the Mayor of London;
    (c) the returning officer appointed pursuant to section 35(1) or (1A) (as the case may be) of the 1983 Act for elections to each parish or community council within the electoral area.

(3) In paragraph (1) the duty to supply one copy of the register is a duty to supply it in data form unless, prior to publication, the officer or person to whom it is to be supplied has requested in writing a printed copy instead.

(4) As soon as practicable after the relevant event, a registration officer who is not the acting returning officer for a constituency wholly or partly in his registration area shall supply free of charge to that officer as many printed copies of–
    (a) the latest revised version of the register published under section 13(1) or (3) of the 1983 Act, as the case may be,
    (b) any notice setting out an alteration to that version of the register published under section 13A(2), 13AB(2) or 13B(3), (3B) or (3D) of that Act, and
    (c) the most recent list of overseas electors,
as the returning officer may reasonably require for the purposes of a parliamentary election.

(5) In paragraph (4) above–
    (a) "relevant event" means–
        (i) the dissolution of Parliament in accordance with section 3(1) of the Fixed-term Parliaments Act 2011, or
        (ii) the occurrence of a vacancy in the relevant constituency; and
    (b) the duty to supply as many printed copies of the register, notices and list of overseas electors as the returning officer may reasonably require includes a duty to supply one copy of each in data form.

(6) As soon as practicable after the relevant date, a registration officer who is not designated as a local returning officer for part of an electoral region which falls wholly or partly in his registration area shall supply free of charge to that officer as many printed copies of the documents referred to in paragraph (4)(a), (b) and (c) above as the local returning officer may reasonably require for the purposes of a European Parliamentary election.

(7) In paragraph (6) above–
    (a) "relevant date" means–
        (i) in the case of a general election of MEPs, the date which is two months before the day appointed by order of the Secretary of State for the poll, or
        (ii) where the Secretary of State has made an order appointing a day for the poll at a by-election, the date on which that order was made; and
    (b) the duty to supply as many printed copies of the register, notices and list of overseas electors as the local returning officer may reasonably require includes a duty to supply one copy of each in data form.

(8) Where a registration officer is not the returning officer for any election to the National Assembly for Wales in respect of any constituency or region wholly or partly within his registration area, he shall supply free of charge to that officer as many printed copies of the documents referred to in paragraph (4)(a) or (b) above, together with one copy of each in data form, as the returning officer may reasonably require for the purposes of such an election.

(9) No person to whom a copy of the register has been supplied under this regulation may–
   (a) supply a copy of the full register,
   (b) disclose any information contained in it (that is not contained in the edited register), or
   (c) make use of any such information,
other than for the purposes of an election.

Supply of free copy of full register etc to Statistics Board

99 (1) Each registration officer shall supply, free of charge and on publication, one copy of–
   (a) any revised version of the register published under section 13(1) or (3) of the 1983 Act,
   (b) any notice setting out an alteration to the register published under section 13A(2), 13AB(2) or 13B(3), (3B) or (3D) of that Act, and
   (c) any list of overseas electors,
to the Statistics Board (in this regulation referred to as "the Board").

(2) In paragraph (1) the duty to supply is a duty to supply in data form unless, prior to publication, the Board has requested in writing a printed copy instead.

(3) Subject to paragraph (6) no person employed by the Board may–
   (a) supply a copy of the full register other than to another such person;
   (b) disclose any information contained in it (that is not contained in the edited register) otherwise than in accordance with paragraph (4) below; or
   (c) make use of any such information other than for statistical purposes.

(4) Subject to paragraph (6) no information which is contained in the full register and not in the edited register may be disclosed otherwise than–
   (a) by allowing a person using the premises of the Board to inspect it under supervision, and
   (b) by publishing information about electors which does not include the name or address of any elector.

(4A) Where a copy of the full register is made available by providing the register on a computer screen or otherwise in data form, the Board shall ensure that the manner in, and equipment on, which that copy is provided do not permit any person consulting that copy to–
   (a) search it by electronic means by reference to the name of any person; or
   (b) copy or transmit any part of that copy by electronic means.

(5) A person who inspects the full register, whether a printed copy or in data form, may not–
   (a) make copies of any part of it, or
   (b) record any particulars included in it,
otherwise than by means of hand-written notes.

(6) A person employed by the Board is not prohibited from supplying a copy of, or disclosing information contained in, a version of the full register where–
   (a) more than ten years have expired since that version of the register was first published in accordance with regulation 43; and
   (b) the supply or disclosure is for research purposes in compliance with the relevant conditions.

(7) No person who obtains a copy of the full register or to whom information contained in it that is not contained in the edited register is disclosed under the circumstances described in paragraph (6) may–
   (a) supply a copy of it,

(b)   disclose any such information, or

(c)   make use of any such information,

otherwise than for research purposes in compliance with the relevant conditions.

Supply of free copy of full register etc to Electoral Commission and restrictions on use

100 (1)   Each registration officer shall supply, free of charge and on publication, one copy of–

(a)   any revised version of the register published under section 13(1) or (3) of the 1983 Act,

(b)   any notice setting out an alteration to the register published under section 13A(2), 13AB(2) or 13B(3), (3B) or (3D) of that Act, and

(c)   any list of overseas electors,

to the Electoral Commission (in this regulation referred to as "the Commission").

(2)   In paragraph (1) the duty to supply is a duty to supply in data form unless, prior to publication, the Commission has requested in writing a printed copy instead.

(2A)   Each registration officer shall, if the Commission has made a written request, supply the Commission free of charge with one copy of any revised version of the register created following the publication of a notice of alteration in the register under section 13A(2), 13AB(2) or 13B(3), (3B) or (3D) of the 1983 Act.

(2B)   In paragraph (2A) the duty to supply is a duty to supply in data form unless the Commission in the written request for the revised register has requested a paper copy instead.

(3)   Neither the Electoral Commissioners nor any person employed by the Commission may–

(a)   supply a copy of the full register other than to an Electoral Commissioner or another such person;

(b)   disclose any information contained in it that is not contained in the edited register otherwise than in accordance with paragraph (5) below; or

(c)   make use of any such information otherwise than in connection with their functions under, or by virtue of, the Political Parties, Elections and Referendums Act 2000.

(4)   In paragraph (3) "Electoral Commissioner" includes a Deputy Electoral Commissioner and an Assistant Electoral Commissioner.

(5)   The full register or any information contained in it and not in the edited register may not be disclosed otherwise than–

(a)   where necessary to carry out the Commission's duties in relation to the rules on permissible donors in the Political Parties, Elections and Referendums Act 2000; or

(b)   by publishing information about electors which does not include the name or address of any elector.

Supply of free copy of full register etc to certain Commissions and restrictions on use

101 (1)   Each registration officer in England shall supply, free of charge and on publication, one copy of each of the documents listed in paragraph (3) below to the Boundary Commission for England.

(2)   Each registration officer in Wales shall supply, free of charge and on publication, one copy of each of the documents listed in paragraph (3) below to the Boundary Commission for Wales and the Local Government Boundary Commission for Wales.

(3)   Those documents are–

(a)   any revised version of the register published under section 13(1) or (3) of the 1983 Act;

(b) any notice setting out an alteration to the register published under section 13A(2), 13AB(2) or 13B(3), (3B) or (3D) of that Act; and

(c) any list of overseas electors.

(4) In paragraphs (1) and (2) the duty to supply is a duty to supply in data form unless, prior to publication, the Commission to whom it is to be supplied has requested in writing a printed copy instead.

(5) In paragraph (6) below "a relevant person" means, in relation to each of the Commissions referred to in paragraphs (1) and (2) above–

(a) a member of the Commission in question;

(b) a person appointed to assist the Commission in question to carry out its functions; and

(c) a person employed by the Commission in question.

(6) A relevant person may not–

(a) supply a copy of the full version of the register, other than to another relevant person;

(b) disclose any information contained in it and not contained in the edited register, otherwise than by publishing information about electors which does not include the name and address of any elector; or

(c) process or make use of any such information, other than in connection with their statutory functions.

Supply on request and specific restrictions

Supply of full register etc under regulations 103 to 109

102 (1) The persons or organisations falling within regulations 103 to 109 below may request the registration officer to supply free of charge the relevant part (within the meaning of those regulations) of any of the following–

(a) a revised version of the register published under section 13(1) or (3) of the 1983 Act;

(b) any notice setting out an alteration to the register published under section 13A(2), 13AB(2) or 13B(3), (3B) or (3D) of that Act;

(c) a list of overseas electors.

(2) Such a request shall be made in writing and shall–

(a) specify the documents requested;

(b) subject to paragraph (5) below, state whether the request is made only in respect of the current documents or whether it includes a request for the supply of any subsequent document on publication for as long as the person making the request falls within the category of person entitled to receive such copies; and

(c) state whether a printed copy of any of the documents is requested instead of the version in data form.

(3) Unless a request has been made in advance of supply under paragraph (2)(c) above, the copy of a document supplied under this regulation shall be in data form.

(4) The registration officer shall supply the relevant part of the documents referred to in paragraph (1) above in accordance with a request that has been duly made.

(5) A person falling within regulation 108 below may not make the request for the supply of any subsequent document on publication.

(6) A person who obtains a copy of any document under paragraph (4) above may use it for any purpose for which that person would be entitled to obtain that document under these Regulations and any restrictions which apply under whichever of

regulations 103 to 108 or 109 entitles that person to obtain that document for that purpose shall apply to such use.

Supply of full register etc to elected representatives for electoral purposes and restrictions on use

103 (1)   This regulation applies to–

(a)   the Member of Parliament for any constituency wholly or partly within the registration area;

(b)   each Member of the European Parliament for an electoral region in which the registration area is situated;

(c)   each Member of the National Assembly for Wales for any constituency or region wholly or partly within the registration area;

(d)   each councillor for an electoral area falling within the registration area;

(e)   the Mayor of London and the London members of the London Assembly, where the registration area falls wholly or partly within Greater London;

(f)   the constituency members of the London Assembly, where the registration area falls wholly or partly within an Assembly constituency (within the meaning of the Greater London Authority Act 1999); and

(g)   an elected mayor within the meaning of section 39(1) of the Local Government Act 2000 where the registration area falls wholly or partly within the area of the local authority for which the mayor is elected.

(2)   For the purposes of regulation 102(1) above the relevant part of the documents listed in that provision–

(a)   in the case of a Member of Parliament or of the National Assembly for Wales, is so much of them as relates to the whole or any part of the constituency or region which he represents as falls within the registration area;

(b)   in the case of a Member of the European Parliament, is all parts of them;

(c)   in the case of a councillor for an electoral area, is so much of them as relates to that area;

(d)   in the case of the Mayor of London and a London member of the London Assembly, is so much of them as relates to the Greater London area;

(e)   in the case of a constituency member of the London Assembly, is so much of them as relates to any part of the Assembly constituency which he represents as falls within the registration area;

(f)   in the case of a mayor falling within paragraph (1)(g) above, is so much of them as relates to any part of the area of the local authority for which he is elected as falls within the registration area.

(3)   No person to whom this regulation applies who has been supplied with a copy of the register may–

(a)   supply a copy of the full register to any person,

(b)   disclose any information contained in it that is not contained in the edited register, or

(c)   make use of any such information,

otherwise than for purposes in connection with the office by virtue of which he is entitled to the full register or for electoral purposes.

Supply of full register to holders of relevant elective offices and candidates

104 (1)   This regulation applies to–

(a)   the holder of a relevant elective office within the meaning of paragraph 1(8) of Schedule 7 to the Political Parties, Elections and Referendums Act 2000;

(b)   a candidate for election at a Parliamentary, local government or Authority election.

(2) For the purposes of regulation 102(1) above, the relevant part of the documents listed in that provision is the whole of them.

(3) No person to whom this regulation applies who has been supplied with a copy of the register may–
    (a) supply a copy of the full register to any person,
    (b) disclose any information contained in it that is not contained in the edited register, or
    (c) make use of any such information,
otherwise than for the purpose set out in paragraph (4) below.

(4) That purpose is the purpose of complying with the controls on donations contained in Schedule 7 to, the Political Parties, Elections and Referendums Act 2000 or Schedule 2A of the Representation of the People Act 1983, as the case may be.

Supply of full register etc to local constituency parties and restrictions on use

105 (1) This regulation applies to any person nominated to act for the purposes of this regulation for a particular constituency by the registered nominating officer, (within the meaning of section 24 of the Political Parties, Elections Referendums Act 2000) of a registered political party.

(2) Not more than one person for the same constituency may be nominated under paragraph (1) above in respect of the same registered political party and registration area.

(3) In the case of a person to whom this regulation applies, the relevant part of the documents listed in regulation 102(1) above is so much of them as relates to the whole or any part of the constituency in question as falls within the registration area.

(4) No person to whom this regulation applies who has been supplied with a copy of the register may–
    (a) supply a copy of the full register to any person,
    (b) disclose any information contained in it (that is not contained in the edited register), or
    (c) make use of any such information,
otherwise than for electoral purposes or the purposes of electoral registration.

Supply of full register etc to registered political parties etc and restrictions on use

106 (1) This regulation applies to–
    (a) a registered political party other than a minor party, within the meaning of section 160(1) of the Political Parties, Elections and Referendums Act 2000;
    (b) a recognised third party within the meaning of section 85(5) of that Act, other than a registered political party; and
    (c) a permitted participant within the meaning of section 105(1) of that Act, other than a registered political party.

(2) In the case of the parties and participants to whom this regulation applies, the relevant part of the documents listed in regulation 102(1) above is the whole of them.

(3) No person employed by, or assisting (whether or not for reward) a party or participant to which this regulation applies and to which a copy of the register has been supplied may–
    (a) supply a copy of the full register to any person,
    (b) disclose any information contained in it (that is not contained in the edited register), or
    (c) make use of any such information,

otherwise than for the purposes set out in paragraph (4) below.

(4) Those purposes are–
    (a) in the case of a party falling within paragraph (1)(a) or (b),
        (i) electoral purposes, and
        (ii) the purpose of complying with the controls on donations under Part IV of or, as the case may be, Schedule 11 to, the Political Parties, Elections and Referendums Act 2000; and
    (b) in the case of a permitted participant within the meaning of section 105(1) of that Act,
        (i) purposes in connection with the campaign in respect of the referendum identified in the declaration made by the participant under section 106 of that Act, and
        (ii) the purposes of complying with the controls on donations in Schedule 15 to that Act.

Supply of full register etc to certain councils and restrictions on use

107 (1) Paragraphs (2) to (5) of this regulation apply to–
    (a) the local authority by which the registration officer was appointed, and
    (b) a local authority whose area falls wholly or partly within the registration area of that local authority, other than a parish council or community council (within the meaning of paragraph (6)).

(2) For the purposes of regulation 102(1) above, the relevant part of the documents listed in that provision is so much of them as relates to the area of the local authority concerned.

(3) Subject to paragraph (4) below, no councillor or employee of the local authority may–
    (a) supply a copy of the full register to any person other than to another councillor of or employee of the same local authority;
    (b) disclose any information contained in it that is not included in the edited register; or
    (c) make use of any such information.

(4) A councillor or employee of the local authority may supply a copy of the register, or disclose or make use of information contained in it that is not contained in the edited register–
    (a) where necessary for the discharge of a statutory function of the local authority or any other local authority relating to security, law enforcement and crime prevention, or
    (aa) for the purposes of a poll under section 116 (local polls) of the Local Government Act 2003, or
    (b) for statistical purposes, in which case no information shall be disclosed which includes the name and address of any elector (whether that name or address appears in the edited register or only in the full register).

(5) In this regulation, "local authority" has the meaning given by section 116 of the Local Government Act 2003.

(6) Paragraphs (7) and (8) of this regulation apply to parish councils, as established by sections 9(4) of the Local Government Act 1972 and community councils as referred to in section 27(2) of that Act.

(7) For the purposes of regulation 102(1) above, the relevant part of the documents listed is so much of them as relates to the parish or community concerned.

(8)   No parish or community councillor, person employed by or otherwise assisting (whether or not for reward) a parish or community council and to which a copy of the register has been supplied may–

    (a)   supply a copy of the full register to any person,

    (b)   disclose any information contained in it that is not included in the edited register, or

    (c)   make use of any such information,

otherwise than for the purpose of establishing whether any person is entitled to attend and participate in a meeting of, or take any action on behalf of, the parish or community, as the case may be or for the purposes of a poll under section 116 (local polls) of the Local Government Act 2003.

Supply of full register etc to certain candidates and restrictions on use

108 (1)   This regulation applies to a candidate at–

    (a)   a Parliamentary or European Parliamentary election,

    (b)   an election to the National Assembly of Wales,

    (c)   a local government election, and

    (d)   an election of a mayor under Part II of the Local Government Act 2000,

where any part of the area in respect of which the candidate stands for election includes the whole or part of a registration area.

(2)   In this regulation "candidate" includes–

    (a)   a candidate at an election of a mayor under Part II of the Local Government Act 2000; and

    (b)   an individual candidate at a European Parliamentary election or an election in an electoral region for the National Assembly for Wales.

(3)   In the case of a registered political party which submits a list of candidates at a European Parliamentary election, an election of the London members of the London Assembly or an election in an electoral region for the National Assembly for Wales, the entitlement otherwise conferred by this regulation on a candidate is conferred on the election agent of that party.

(4)   For the purposes of regulation 102(1) above, the relevant part of the documents listed in that provision is so much of them as relate to the area for which the candidate is standing.

(5)   No candidate or election agent to whom a copy of the register has been supplied by virtue of this regulation may–

    (a)   supply a copy of the full register to any person,

    (b)   disclose any information contained in it (that is not contained in the edited register), or

    (c)   make use of any such information,

other than for electoral purposes.

Supply of full register etc to the security services

108A (1)   This regulation applies to–

    (a)   the Security Service;

    (b)   the Government Communications Headquarters;

    (c)   the Secret Intelligence Service.

(2)   For the purposes of regulation 102(1) above the relevant part of the documents listed in that provision is the whole of them.

Supply of full register etc to police forces and other agencies,

109 (1) This regulation applies to–

   (a) any police force in Great Britain;

   (b) the Police Service of Northern Ireland and the Police Service of Northern Ireland (Reserve);

   (c) the National Crime Agency;

   (e) the Police Information Technology Organisation;

   (f) any body of constables established under an Act of Parliament;

   (g) *Repealed*

   (h) *Repealed*

   (i) *Repealed.*

   (2) For the purposes of regulation 102(1) above the relevant part of the documents listed in that provision is the whole of them.

   (3) No person serving whether as a constable, officer or employee in any of the forces and organisations to which this regulation applies may–

   (a) supply a copy of the full register to any person,

   (b) disclose any information contained in it (that is not contained in the edited register), or

   (c) make use of any such information,

   otherwise than for the purposes specified in paragraph (4).

   (4) The purposes referred to in paragraph (3) are–

   (a) *Repealed*

   (i) the prevention and detection of crime and the enforcement of the criminal law (whether in England and Wales or elsewhere);

   (ii) the vetting of a relevant person for the purpose of safeguarding national security;

   (b) *Repealed.*

   (5) In this Regulation "relevant person" means–

   (a) a constable or officer or prospective constable or officer of the force or organisation; or

   (b) an employee of, or applicant for employment by, the force or organisation.

Supply of full register to public libraries and local authority archives service, and restrictions on use

109A (1) A public library or a local authority archives service may request the registration officer to supply free of charge the relevant part (within the meaning of paragraph (2)) of any of the following–

   (a) a revised version of the register published under section 13(1) or (3) of the 1983 Act;

   (b) any notice setting out an alteration to the register published under section 13A(2), 13AB(2) or 13B(3), (3B) or (3D) of that Act;

   (c) a list of overseas electors.

   (2) For the purposes of paragraph (1) the relevant part of the documents listed in that provision is so much of them as a public library or local authority archives service has been given responsibility for keeping by a library authority or local authority respectively.

   (3) Such a request shall be made in writing and shall–

   (a) specify the documents requested;

(b) state whether the request is made only in respect of the current documents or whether it includes a request for the supply of any subsequent document on publication; and

(c) state whether a printed copy of any of the documents is requested instead of the version in data form.

(4) Unless a request has been made in advance of supply under paragraph (3)(c), the copy of a document supplied under this regulation shall be in data form.

(5) The registration officer shall supply the relevant part of the documents referred to in paragraph (1) in accordance with a request that has been duly made.

(6) Subject to paragraph (9), no person employed by the public library or the local authority archives service may–

(a) supply a copy of the full register other than to another such person or to a person using the library or the archives service to inspect it under supervision;

(b) disclose any information contained in it (that is not contained in the edited register) otherwise than by allowing a person using the library or the archives service to inspect it under supervision; or

(c) make use of any such information.

(7) Where a copy of the full register is made available for inspection in accordance with paragraph (6)(a) or (b) by providing the register on a computer screen or otherwise in data form, the library or the archives service shall ensure that the manner in, and equipment on, which that copy is provided do not permit any person consulting that copy to–

(a) search it by electronic means by reference to the name of any person; or

(b) copy or transmit any part of that copy by electronic means.

(8) A person who inspects a copy of the full register, whether a printed copy or in data form, may not–

(a) make copies of any part of it, or

(b) record any particulars in it,

otherwise than by means of hand-written notes.

(9) The public library or local authority archives service is not prohibited from supplying a copy of, or disclosing information contained in, a version of the full register where–

(a) more than ten years have expired since that version of the register was first published in accordance with regulation 43; and

(b) the supply or disclosure is for research purposes in compliance with the relevant conditions.

(10) No person who obtains a copy of the full register or to whom information contained in it that is not contained in the edited register is disclosed under the circumstances described in paragraph (9) may–

(a) supply a copy of it,

(b) disclose such information, or

(c) make use of any such information,

otherwise than for research purposes in compliance with the relevant conditions.

(11) In this regulation–

"library authority" has the same meaning as in section 206 of the Local Government Act 1972 and section 4 of the Public Libraries and Museums Act 1964;

"local authority archives service" means an archives service established by–

(a) a county council,

(b) a county borough council,

(c) a district council,

(d) a London Borough council,

    (e) the Common Council of the City of London, or

    (f) the Council of the Isles of Scilly,

in exercise of its functions under the Local Government (Records) Act 1962;

"public library" means a library maintained by a library authority.

Sale of edited and full registers and specified restrictions

Sale of edited register

110 (1) The registration officer shall supply a copy of the edited register to any person on payment of a fee calculated in accordance with paragraph (2) below.

  (2) In the case of the register–

    (a) in data form, the fee shall be at the rate of £20 plus £1.50 for each 1,000 entries (or remaining part of 1,000 entries) in it; and

    (b) in printed form, the fee shall be at the rate of £10 plus £5 for each 1,000 entries (or remaining part of 1,000 entries) in it.

Sale of full register etc: restrictions on supply, charges, etc

111 (1) The registration officer may not sell a copy of–

    (a) the full register,

    (b) any notice under section 13A(2), 13AB(2) or 13B(3), (3B) or (3D) of the 1983 Act altering the register ("a relevant notice"), or

    (c) the list of overseas electors,

except to a person who is entitled under regulation 113 or 114 below to purchase them.

  (2) The fee for such sale is to be calculated in accordance with paragraphs (3) to (6) below.

  (3) Where a person purchases the full register together with any relevant notices which are published at that time altering the register, the register and the notices shall be treated as the same document for the purposes of the calculations set out in paragraph (5) below; and any entry in the register which is deleted by a notice shall accordingly be ignored for the purposes of the calculation.

  (4) Where a person purchases a relevant notice separately from the full register, the calculations set out in paragraph (5) below shall be applied to that notice.

  (5) Subject to paragraph (3) above, in the case of the register or a relevant notice–

    (a) in data form, the fee shall be at the rate of £20 plus £1.50 for each 1,000 entries (or remaining part of 1,000 entries) in it; and

    (b) in printed form, the fee shall be at the rate of £10 plus £5 for each 1,000 entries (or remaining part of 1,000 entries) in it.

  (6) In the case of the list of overseas electors–

    (a) in data form, the fee shall be at the rate of £20 plus £1.50 for each 100 entries (or remaining part of 100 entries) in it; and

    (b) in printed form, the fee shall be at the rate of £10 plus £5 for each 100 entries (or remaining part of 100 entries) in it.

  (7) In any copy of the full register or any copy of a notice under section 13A(2), 13AB(2) or 13B(3), (3B) or (3D) of the 1983 Act which is sold in accordance with regulations 112 to 114 below, the letter "Z" shall be placed against the entry of any person whose entry is not included in the edited version of the register.

Sale of full register etc: general provisions

112 (1) This regulation applies in respect of the supply on payment of a fee of copies of the full register, including any notice published under section 13A(2), 13AB(2) or 13B(3), (3B) or

(3D) of the 1983 Act altering that register, in accordance with regulations 113 and 114 below.

(2) The registration officer shall not supply a printed copy of the full register under those regulations if to do so would result in his having insufficient copies of it for the purposes of any requirement made by or under any enactment.

(3) In those regulations, "the relevant restrictions" means the restrictions set out in paragraphs (4) and (5) below.

(4) No person in an organisation to which a copy of the register has been supplied under regulations 113 or 114 below may–
    (a) supply a copy of the full register to any person,
    (b) disclose any information contained in it (and not contained in the edited register), or
    (c) make use of any such information,
other than for the purpose set out in the regulation by virtue of which the full register has been supplied.

(5) The restrictions in paragraph (4) above apply to a person to whom a copy of the full register has been supplied in accordance with regulations 113 and 114 below or to whom information contained in it has been so disclosed as it applies to a person in the organisation to which the copy of the full register was supplied under the regulation in question.

(6) In regulations 113 and 114 below, "a relevant document" means–
    (a) the full register published under section 13(1) or (3) of the 1983 Act;
    (b) any notice published under section 13A(2), 13AB(2) or 13B(3), (3B) or (3D) of that Act amending it; and
    (c) the list of overseas electors.

(7) A request for a copy of the full register, or of any notice published under section 13A(2), 13AB(2) or 13B(3), (3B) or (3D) of the 1983 Act altering that register, as the case may be, must be made in writing and must–
    (a) specify the documents required;
    (b) state whether the request is made only in respect of the current documents or whether it includes a request for the supply of any subsequent documents on publication for as long as the person making the request pays for them; and
    (c) state whether a printed copy of any document is requested instead of the version in data form.

Sale of full register to government departments and other bodies

113 (1) Subject to regulation 112(2) above, the registration officer shall supply on request and on payment of a fee calculated in accordance with regulation 111 above a copy of a relevant document to–
    (a) a government department;
    (b) the Environment Agency;
    (c) the Financial Conduct Authority;
    (ca) the Prudential Regulation Authority; or
    (d) a body not falling within sub-paragraphs (a) to (ca) which carries out the vetting of any person for the purpose of safeguarding national security,
other than a department to which regulation 108A applies or a force or organisation to which regulation 109(1) applies.

(2) For the purposes of regulation 112(3), the relevant restrictions apply–
    (a) in the case of a body falling within sub-paragraphs (a) to (c) of paragraph (1), except for the purpose of–

        (i)   the prevention and detection of crime and the enforcement of the criminal law (whether in England and Wales or elsewhere);

        (ii) the vetting of employees and applicants for employment where such vetting is required pursuant to any enactment;

        (iii) the vetting of any person where such vetting is for the purpose of safeguarding national security; or

        (iv) supply and disclosure in accordance with paragraphs (3) to (6); and

   (b) in the case of a body falling within sub-paragraph (d) of paragraph (1), except for the purpose of the vetting of any person where such vetting is for the purpose of safeguarding national security.

(3) A government department, other than one mentioned in regulation 108A may supply (whether or not on payment) a copy of the full register to a person ("an authorised person"), who may only disclose information contained in it in accordance with paragraph (5) below.

(4) In this regulation any reference to an authorised person includes a reference to his employees.

(5) Information contained in the full register may not be disclosed by an authorised person except to any person falling within regulations 103 to 108 above; and for use for the purposes for which such a person could obtain a register under the regulation concerned.

(6) The restrictions in regulations 103 to 108 respectively apply to a person to whom information contained in the full register is disclosed under paragraph (5) as it applies to a person to whom a copy of the register is applied under those regulations.

Sale of full register to credit reference agencies

114 (1) Subject to regulation 112(2) above, the registration officer shall supply on request and on payment of a fee calculated in accordance with regulation 111 above copies of a relevant document to a person who has permission under the Financial Services and Markets Act 2000 to furnish persons with information relevant to the financial standing of other persons and which is carrying on the business of providing credit reference services.

(2) For the purposes of regulation 112(3) above, the relevant restrictions apply except for the purposes set out in paragraph (3) below.

(3) Those purposes are–

   (a) vetting applications for credit or applications that can result in the giving of credit or the giving of any guarantee, indemnity or assurance in relation to the giving of credit;

   (b) meeting any obligations contained in the Money Laundering Regulations 2007 or any rules made by the Financial Conduct Authority under section 137A of the Financial Services and Markets Act 2000 which relate to the prevention and detection of money laundering in connection with the carrying on of regulated activities by authorised persons; and

   (c) statistical analysis of credit risk assessment in a case where no person whose details are included in the full register is referred to by name or necessary implication.

(4) The registration officer may require a credit reference agency to provide such evidence that it is carrying on the business of providing credit reference services as he shall reasonably require.

(5) In this regulation–

"application for credit" includes an application to refinance or reschedule an existing credit agreement;

"credit" includes a cash loan and any other form of financial accommodation; and

"credit reference services" means the furnishing of persons with information relevant to the financial standing of individuals, which is information collected by the person furnishing it for the purpose of so furnishing it.

(6) Paragraph (1) must be read with–
    (a) section 22 of the Financial Services and Markets Act 2000,
    (b) any relevant order under that section, and
    (c) Schedule 2 to that Act.

Offences

Offences in respect of contravention of Part 3, Part 4 and Part 6 regulations

115 (1) A person is guilty of an offence–
    (a) if he contravenes any of the provisions specified in paragraph (2), or
    (b) if he is an appropriate supervisor of a person (P) who fails to comply with any of those provisions and he failed to take appropriate steps.

(2) Those provisions are regulations 45C(4), 45D(4), 45F(3), 61(3), 61(14), 92(9), 94(3), 95(2), 96(2), 97(2), (4) and (6), 97A(4), (6) and (8), 98(9), 99(3), (5) and (7), 100(3) and (5), 101(6), 103(3), 104(3), 105(4), 106(3), 107(3) and (8), 108(5), 109(3), 109A(6), (8) and (10), 112(4) and (5) and 113(5) and (6).

(3) P is not guilty of an offence under paragraph (1) if–
    (a) he has an appropriate supervisor, and
    (b) he has complied with all the requirements imposed on him by his appropriate supervisor.

(4) A person who is not P or an appropriate supervisor is not guilty of an offence under paragraph (1) if he takes all reasonable steps to ensure that he complies with the provisions specified in paragraph (2).

(5) In paragraphs (1)(b) and (3)–
    (a) an appropriate supervisor is a person who is a director of a company or concerned in the management of an organisation in which P is employed or under whose direction or control P is;
    (b) appropriate steps are such steps as it was reasonable for the appropriate supervisor to take to secure the operation of procedures designed to prevent, so far as reasonably practicable, the occurrence of a failure to comply with the provisions in paragraph (2).

(6) A person guilty of an offence as mentioned in paragraph (1) is liable on summary conviction to a fine not exceeding level 5 on the standard scale.

PART 7
ACCESS TO MARKED REGISTERS AND OTHER DOCUMENTS OPEN TO PUBLIC INSPECTION AFTER AN ELECTION

Interpretation of Part 7

116 (1) In this Part references to the "marked register or lists" means any part of the marked copies of–
    (a) the full register;

(aa) the notices amending the full register issued under section 13B(3B) or (3D) of the 1983 Act;

(b)   the postal voters list;

(c)   the list of proxies; and

(d)   the proxy postal voters list,

forwarded to the relevant registration officer under regulation 91 above or rule 55(1)(e) of the elections rules.

(2)   For the purposes of this Part any period of days shall be calculated in accordance with regulation 56.

(3)   Paragraphs (2) and (3), and the condition in paragraph (9), of regulation 92 shall be taken to apply to the supply and processing of information supplied under this Part as they apply to the supply and processing of the full register under Part 6 of these Regulations.

(4)   Subject to any direction by the Secretary of State under section 52(1) of the 1983 Act, any duty on a relevant registration officer to supply records or lists or make them available for inspection under this Part imposes only a duty to provide that information in the form in which he holds it.

Supply of marked registers and lists after an election

117 (1)   Any person entitled to be supplied in accordance with regulation 100, 103, 105, 106, 108, 109 or 113 above, with copies of the full register at a particular parliamentary or local government election, is also a person entitled, subject to this regulation and to regulation 119, to request that a relevant registration officer supply copies of the relevant part (within the meaning of those regulations) of the marked register or lists he is required to keep.

(2)   A person whose entitlement to request copies of the marked register or lists under paragraph (1) arises from being in a category of persons covered by regulation 103, 105, 106 or 108 before a particular election, shall be entitled to request those documents regardless of whether he remains in a entitled category after that election for which the marked register or list was prepared.

(3)   A request under paragraph (1) shall be made in writing and shall–

(a)   specify which of the marked register or lists (or the relevant part of the register or lists) are requested;

(b)   state whether a printed copy of the records or lists is requested or a copy in data form;

(c)   state the purposes for which the marked register or lists will be used and why the supply or purchase of a copy of the full register or unmarked lists would not be sufficient to achieve that purpose.

(4)   The relevant registration officer shall supply a copy of the relevant part of the marked register or lists where a request is duly made, and–

(a)   he is satisfied that the requestor needs to see the marks on the marked register or lists in order to achieve the purpose for which it is requested, and

(b)   he has received payment of a fee calculated in accordance with regulation 120 below.

(5)   If the relevant registration officer is not satisfied in accordance with paragraph (4)(a) he may treat the request for a marked register or list as a request for information in unmarked lists under regulation 61 or for the published copy of the full register in accordance with regulation 102, or both.

(6) A person who obtains a copy of any part of a marked register or list under this regulation may use it only for the permitted purposes specified in paragraph (2) of regulation 119, and any conditions–
  (a) specified in that paragraph, or
  (b) which would apply to the use of the full register under whichever of regulations 100, 103, 105, 106, 108, 109 or 113 entitled that person to obtain that document,
  shall apply to such use.

(7) The conditions in regulations 100(3), 103(3), 105(4), 106(3), 108(5) and 109(3) shall apply to a person to whom a marked register or list, or any information contained in it (that is not contained in the edited register) has been supplied or disclosed under those paragraphs as they apply to the person to whom those regulations apply.

(8) Any person who has obtained or is entitled to obtain a copy of the marked register or lists under this regulation may–
  (a) supply a copy of the marked register or lists to a processor for the purpose of processing the information contained therein, or
  (b) procure that a processor processes and supplies to them any copy of the information in the marked register or lists which the processor has obtained under this regulation,
  for use in respect of the purposes for which that person is entitled to obtain such copy or information (as the case may be).

Inspection of documents open to public inspection

118 (1) Any person is entitled to request that the relevant registration officer make available for inspection a copy of any of the following documents (referred to in this regulation and in regulation 119 as "the documents open to public inspection")–
  (a) the marked register or lists;
  (b) such other documents relating to an election as the relevant registration officer is required by or under any enactment to retain for any period except–
    (i) ballot papers
    (ii) completed corresponding number lists;
    (iii) certificates as to employment on the day of the election;
    (iv) the list required to be compiled under regulation 87(4), and any extracts produced from that list.

(2) A request under paragraph (1) shall be made in writing and shall specify–
  (a) which documents are requested;
  (b) the purposes for which the information in any document will be used,
  (c) where the request is to inspect the marked register or lists, any reason why inspecting the full register or unmarked lists would not be sufficient to achieve that purpose,
  (d) who will inspect the documents,
  (e) the date on which they wish to inspect the documents, and
  (f) whether they would prefer to inspect the documents in a printed or data form.

(3) Subject to paragraph (4), the relevant registration officer shall make the documents open to public inspection available for inspection under supervision not later than 10 days after the date of receipt of a request that has been duly made.

(4) Where a request has been made to inspect copies of the marked register or lists under paragraph (2) and the relevant registration officer is not satisfied that the purposes of the requestor cannot be met by inspection of the full register, he shall inform the requestor–
  (a) of his decision under this paragraph, and

(b) provide the requestor with information concerning the availability of the published full register for inspection in accordance with regulation 43.

(5) A person who obtains a copy of or information in any document open to public inspection under this regulation may use it only for the permitted purposes specified in regulation 119, and any conditions–
(a) specified in that regulation,
(b) specified in paragraph (7) below, or
(c) which would apply to the use of the full register under regulation 109 where such a person has obtained a copy of that document under paragraph (8),
shall apply to such use.

(6) Where inspection takes place by providing the records or lists on a computer screen or otherwise in data form, the relevant registration officer shall ensure that the manner in, and equipment on which that copy is provided do not permit any person consulting that copy to–
(a) search it by electronic means by reference to the name of any person; or
(b) copy or transmit any part of that copy by electronic, or any other means.

(7) Subject to paragraph (8) a person who inspects a copy of a document open to public inspection, whether a printed copy or in data form, may not–
(a) make copies of any part of it, or
(b) record any particulars in it,
except that a person who inspects a copy of the marked register or lists may make hand written notes.

(8) The relevant registration officer shall, on request, supply free of charge copies of any documents open to public inspection–
(a) to each of the departments mentioned in regulation 108A;
(b) to a person who has inspected those documents and who is entitled to be supplied with a copy of the marked register or lists by virtue of being a person to whom regulation 109 applies.

Conditions on the use, supply and disclosure of documents open to public inspection

119 (1) Subject to paragraphs (2) and (3) the restrictions on the supply, disclosure and use of information in regulations 94 and 96 shall apply to the documents open to public inspection as they apply to the full register.

(2) Where a person–
(a) obtains copies of the information in the marked register or lists in accordance with regulation 117(1), or
(b) a person inspects information in accordance with regulation 118(1),
the permitted purpose shall mean either–
(i) research purposes within the meaning of that term in section 33 of the Data Protection Act 1998; or
(ii) electoral purposes.

(3) Where a copy of any information was supplied in the circumstances to which regulation 118(8)(b) applies, the permitted purpose means the purposes set out in regulation 109(4).

Calculating the fee for supply of marked registers or lists

120 (1) The fee to be paid in accordance with regulation 117(4)(b) by a person making a request for a copy of the whole or of any part of the marked register or lists is set out in paragraph (2).

(2) The fee shall be the sum of £10, plus for a copy–

(a) in printed form, £2 for each 1,000 entries (or remaining part of 1,000 entries) covered by the request; and

(b) in data form, £1 for each 1,000 entries (or remaining part of 1,000 entries) covered by the request.

(3) For the purposes of this regulation, a request for a copy of the whole or the same part of the marked register or lists in both a printed and data form may be treated as two separate requests.

PART 8

ACCESS TO DOCUMENTS AFTER AN ELECTION TO THE NATIONAL ASSEMBLY FOR WALES

Interpretation of Part 8

121 In this Part–

(1) "the 2007 Order" means the National Assembly for Wales (Representation of the People) Order 2007;

"Assembly election" means an election to the National Assembly for Wales under Part 1 of the Government of Wales Act 1998 or under Part 1 of the Government of Wales Act 2006;

"the Assembly list of proxies" means the list kept under article 10(1) and (3) of the 2007 Order;

"the Assembly postal voters list" means the list kept under article 10(1) and (2) of the 2007 Order;

"the Assembly proxy postal voters list" means the list kept under article 12(8) of the 2007 Order;

"the National Assembly for Wales" means the National Assembly for Wales constituted by the Government of Wales Act 2006; and

"relevant Assembly election documents" means such documents relating to an Assembly election as the relevant registration officer is required to retain by rule 69(1) of Schedule 5 to the 2007 Order.

(2) "The marked Assembly register or lists" means any part of the marked copies of–

(a) the full register;

(aa) the notices amending the full register issued under section 13B(3B) or (3D) of the 1983 Act;

(b) the Assembly postal voters list;

(c) the Assembly list of proxies; and

(d) the Assembly proxy postal voters list,

forwarded to the relevant registration officer under paragraph 31 of Schedule 3 or rules 67(1)(h) and (2)(f) of Schedule 5 to the 2007 Order.

122 Subject to the modifications specified in regulations 123 to 126, Part 7 of these Regulations shall apply in respect of the marked Assembly register or lists and the other relevant Assembly election documents as it applies in respect of the marked register or lists and other documents open to inspection under that Part.

123 References in Part 7 to "the marked register or lists" shall be construed as references to the marked Assembly register or lists, and any like terms shall be similarly construed.

124 Regulation 116 shall apply as if–

(a) paragraph (1) were omitted;

(b) in paragraph (2) the reference to regulation 56 were a reference to paragraph 7 of Schedule 1 to the 2007 Order; and

(c) in paragraph (4), the reference to a direction by the Secretary of State under section 52(1) of the 1983 Act included a reference to a direction by the Secretary of State under article 28(1) of the 2007 Order.

125 Regulation 117 shall apply as if–

(a) references to "a particular parliamentary or local government election" and to "a particular election" include reference to a particular Assembly election; and

(b) the reference in paragraph (5) to regulation 61 were a reference to paragraph 13 of Schedule 1 to the 2007 Order.

126 Regulations 118 and 119 shall apply as if references to "documents open to public inspection" were a reference to–

(a) the Assembly marked register or lists; and

(b) the other relevant Assembly election documents except–

(i) ballot papers;

(ii) completed corresponding number lists;

(iii) certificates as to employment on the day of the election,

and any like terms shall be construed accordingly.

SCHEDULE 1
ENABLING POWERS

These Regulations are made under the following powers:

(a) sections 10A(7) and (9), 13A(6), 36(3C), 53 and 201(1) and (3) of, rule 24 of Schedule 1 and Schedule 2 to, the Representation of the People Act 1983 ("the 1983 Act");

(b) sections 3(5), (6) and (7) and 15(5) of the Representation of the People Act 1985 ("the 1985 Act");

(c) having regard to the definition of "prescribed" in section 202(1) of the 1983 Act, sections 4(4), 9(2), 10A(1), (3), (6) and (7), 13(3), 13A(2), 13B(3), 14(1), 16, 56(1) and (5), 75(3) and 89(1) of, rules 24, 28(3), 29(3A), 32(3) and 45(1B) in Schedule 1 to, and paragraph 8(1) of Schedule 4 to, that Act;

(d) having regard to the definition of "prescribed" in section 202(1) of the 1983 Act and section 27(2) of the 1985 Act, section 2(3) of the 1985 Act;

(e) having regard to the definition of "prescribed" in section 202(1) of the 1983 Act and paragraph 1(2) of Schedule 4 to the Representation of the People Act 2000, the following provisions in that Schedule, namely, paragraphs 3(1)(b) and (2)(c), 4(1)(b), (2)(c) and (4)(a), 6(7) and (8) and 7(5)(c) and (7);

(f) having regard to the designation of the Secretary of State for the purposes of section 2(2) of the European Communities Act 1972 in relation to measures relating to the rights of citizens of the Union to vote at European Parliamentary elections and local government elections in England and Wales, that section 2(2); and

(g) paragraph 2(4)(b) of Schedule 1 to the European Parliamentary Elections Act 1978.

Continuation

Following the consolidation of the European Parliamentary Elections Act 1978, Sch 1, para 2(4)(b), this Order has effect under para (g) above as if made under the European Parliamentary Elections Act 2002, s 7(4), by virtue of Sch 2, para 2 thereto.

SCHEDULE 2
REVOCATIONS

Not reproduced

SCHEDULE 3
FORMS

Not reproduced

SCHEDULE 4
APPLICATION WITH MODIFICATIONS OF PROVISIONS OF THE 1983 AND 1985 ACTS FOR REGISTRATION OF EUROPEAN PARLIAMENTARY OVERSEAS ELECTORS

Regulation 13

1 Provision applied	2 Modification
PART I: THE 1983 ACT	
Section 4(5) (attainers)	
Section 9 (register of electors)	In subsection (1)(a) omit "for each constituency or part of a constituency". In subsection (2) omit "Subject to section 9B(3) below,". Omit subsection (2)(b). Omit subsections (5) to (8).
Section 10A (maintenance of registers: registration of electors), subsections (1)(a), (3), (3A), (4) and (9)	In subsection (3) after "register in question" insert "or by a person entitled to vote as an elector at an election to the European Parliament by virtue of section 8 of the European Parliamentary Elections Act 2002". In subsection (4) for "Subsections (1) and (3) above" substitute "Subsections (1)(a) and (3) above". In subsection (4) omit paragraph (b). In subsection (9) omit the definition of "resident".
Section 13 (publication of registers)	For subsections (1) to (3) substitute: "(1) Where a register under section 3 of the 1985 Act is in force, a revised version of it shall be published when a revised version of the registers of parliamentary and local government electors is published under this section as it has effect for the purposes of such registers.".
Section 13A (alteration of registers)	In subsection (1)(b) for "by virtue of any provision of this Part of this Act" substitute "by virtue of any provision of the Representation of the People Act 1985". In subsection (1)(c) omit "or 58". In subsection (2)(b) for "sections 13B(1) and 13BA(1)" substitute "section 13B(1)". For subsection (3) substitute: "(3) Subsection (2) above does not require a registration officer to issue a notice under that subsection in a case where (apart from this subsection) that subsection would require the notice to be issued– (a) at the beginning of the month containing the date on which revised versions of the registers of parliamentary and local government electors are

1	2
Provision applied	Modification
	next due to be published in accordance with section 13(1) or (3) as it has effect for the purposes of such registers, or
	(b) at the beginning of either of the two months preceding that containing the date on which revised versions of the registers of parliamentary and local government electors are next due to be published in accordance with section 13(1)(a) as it has effect for the purposes of such registers,
	and in such a case the alteration in question shall be made in those revised versions of the registers.".
	In subsection (4) omit "or 13BA(3), (6) or (9)".
	In subsection (5) omit "or 13BA".
	In subsection (6) omit from "; and section 119 below shall apply" to the end.
Section 13AB (alteration of registers: interim publication dates)	For subsection (4) substitute:
	(4) This section applies to elections to the European Parliament.
Section 13B (alteration of register: pending elections)	For subsections (4) substitute:
	"(4) This section applies to elections to the European Parliament.".
	Omit subsection (6).
Section 50 (effect of misdescription)	For paragraphs (a), (b) and (c) substitute "in the register".
Section 52 (discharge of registration duties)	In subsections (1) and (4) after the word "Act" insert "and regulation 13 of the Representation of the People (England and Wales) Regulations 2001".
Section 54 (payment of expenses of registration)	In subsection (1) after the word "Act" in the first place where it occurs, insert "and regulation 13 of the Representation of the People (England and Wales) Regulations 2001".
	Omit subsection (3).
Section 56 (registration appeals: England and Wales)	In subsection (1) for paragraph (aa) substitute:
	"(aa) from any decision under section 2(2)(aa) of the Representation of the People Act 1985 of the registration officer that a person registered in a register of parliamentary electors in pursuance of a European Parliamentary overseas elector's declaration was not entitled to be registered.".
	In subsection (1) omit paragraphs (ab) and (b).
Section 63 (breach of official duty)	In subsection (3)–
	(a) for paragraphs (a) to (d) substitute: "(a) any registration officer,"; and
	(b) for the words from "relating to" to the end of the subsection substitute "relating to the registration of European Parliamentary overseas electors".

1 Provision applied	2 Modification
PART II: THE 1985 ACT	
Section 2 (registration of British citizens overseas)	In paragraph (a) of subsection (1) omit "constituency or" and in paragraph (b) after "of that" insert "part of the". In paragraph (c) of subsection (2) for the words from "parliamentary" to the end of that paragraph, substitute "local government electors". In subsection (4) for "section 1" substitute "section 3". In subsection (7) omit "constituency or". In subsection (8) for "section 1(1)(a)" substitute "section 3(1)(a)".
In section 12 (offences as to declarations etc), subsections (1), (2) and (4)	In subsection (1)(a) for the word "parliamentary" substitute "European Parliamentary".

SCHEDULE 4A
APPLICATION WITH MODIFICATIONS OF REGULATIONS
FOR REGISTRATION OF EUROPEAN PARLIAMENTARY OVERSEAS ELECTORS

Regulation 13

1 Regulation applied	2 Modification
Regulation 3	In paragraph (1) omit the definition of "certificate of anonymous registration".
Regulation 5	
Regulation 6	
Regulation 7	
Regulation 8	
Regulation 11	
Regulation 18	In paragraphs (4), (5) and (7) after "regulation 13(6) above" insert "and Schedule 4A to these Regulations" and for "modifications made by that regulation" substitute "modifications made by that Schedule".
Regulation 19	In paragraph (1) after "regulation 13(6) above" insert "and Schedule 4A to these Regulations" and for "modifications made by that regulation" substitute "modifications made by that Schedule".
Regulation 20	In paragraph (1) after "regulation 13(6) above" insert "and Schedule 4A to these Regulations" and for "modifications made by that regulation" substitute "modifications made by that Schedule".
Regulation 21	
Regulation 22	In paragraph (3) after "regulation 13(6) above" insert "and Schedule 4A to these Regulations" and for "modifications made by that regulation" substitute "modifications made by that Schedule".
Regulation 23	
Regulation 24	Omit paragraph (4A).
Regulation 25	
Regulation 27	

1	2
Regulation applied	Modification
Regulation 28	Omit paragraph (2).
Regulation 29	Omit paragraphs (2B) and (4A).
	In paragraph (4) omit "Subject to paragraph (4A),".
Regulation 30	
Regulation 31	
Regulation 31A	
Regulation 31B	In paragraph (1) for "regulations 31C to 31F" substitute "regulations 31D to 31F".
	For paragraph (2) substitute:
	"(2) The functions specified in this paragraph are determining under section 2(2)(aa) of the 1985 Act whether a person was entitled to be registered.".
Regulation 31D	Omit paragraph (3).
	In paragraphs (5) and (8) omit "or, as the case may be, has ceased to satisfy the conditions for registration set out in section 4 of the 1983 Act.".
Regulation 31E	In paragraph (2) omit sub-paragraph (c).
	Omit paragraph (4).
Regulation 31F	In paragraph (6) omit "or, as the case may be, has ceased to satisfy the conditions for registration set out in section 4 of the 1983 Act,".
Regulation 32	In paragraph (1) for sub-paragraph (b) substitute:
	"(b) under section 56(1)(aa) of the 1983 Act, from the decision of a registration officer made in accordance with regulations 31D to 31F that a person was not entitled to be registered;".
	In paragraph (1) omit sub-paragraph (c).
Regulation 36(2) and (3)	In sub-paragraph (2)(b) omit "except in a case falling within regulation 31C(2)(d) above,".
Regulation 38	
Regulation 39	
Regulation 40	For paragraph (1) substitute:
	"(1) Section 9(2)(b) of the 1983 Act (which requires each register of parliamentary or local government electors to contain the qualifying addresses of the persons registered in it) does not apply to an address which is specified in an overseas elector's declaration in accordance with section 2(4)(b) or (c)(ii) of the 1985 Act.".
	Omit paragraphs (2) and (3).
Regulation 41	
Regulation 42	
Regulation 43	In paragraph (1) omit "and (3)".
Regulation 45	In paragraph (4) after "regulation 13(6) above" insert "and Schedule 4A to these Regulations".

Returning Officers (Parliamentary Constituencies) (England) Order 2007 (SI 2007/2878)

Made 3rd October 2007

Citation, commencement and interpretation

1(1) This Order may be cited as the Returning Officers (Parliamentary Constituencies) (England) Order 2007.

(2) This Order comes into force
   (a) for the purposes of proceedings preliminary or relating to a parliamentary election to be held after the issue of a proclamation by Her Majesty summoning a new Parliament, on 5th October 2007; and
   (b) for all other purposes, on the issue of a proclamation by Her Majesty summoning a new Parliament.

(3) References to constituencies in this Order are references to those constituencies in England constituted by an Order in Council made under section 4 of the Parliamentary Constituencies Act 1986.

Revocations

2 Subject to article 1(2), the following Orders are revoked
   (a) the Returning Officers (Parliamentary Constituencies) (England) Order 1995;
   (b) the Returning Officers (Parliamentary Constituencies) (England) (Amendment) Order 1996;
   (c) the Returning Officers (Parliamentary Constituencies) (England) (Amendment) Order 1997; and
   (d) the Returning Officers (Parliamentary Constituencies) (England) (Amendment) Order 1999.

Designation of returning officers for borough constituencies

3 In the case of a borough constituency listed in the left-hand column of Schedule 1 to this Order (being a constituency which is not coterminous with or wholly contained in a district), the returning officer for a parliamentary election shall be the chairman of the council of the district listed in the righ-thand column of that Schedule opposite to the name of the constituency.

Designation of returning officers for London borough constituencies

4 In the case of a borough constituency listed in the left hand column of Schedule 2 to this Order (being a constituency which is situated partly in one London borough and partly in another), the returning officer for a parliamentary election shall be the mayor of the London borough listed in the right-hand column of that Schedule opposite to the name of the constituency.

5(1) Where a London borough council are operating executive arrangements which involve a mayor and cabinet executive or a mayor and council manager executive, article 4 shall have effect as if for the expression "mayor of a London borough" there were substituted "chairman of a London borough".

(2) In this article, "executive arrangements", "mayor and cabinet executive" and "mayor and council manager executive" have the same meaning as in Part 2 of the Local Government Act 2000.

Designation of returning officers for county constituencies

6   In the case of a county constituency listed in the left-hand column of Schedule 3 to this Order (being a constituency which is not coterminous with or wholly contained in a county, as defined by section 38 of the Sheriffs Act 1887), the returning officer for a parliamentary election shall be the chairman of the council of the district listed in the right-hand column of that Schedule opposite to the name of the constituency.

Designation of acting returning officers at parliamentary elections

7   In the case of a county constituency listed in the left-hand column of Schedule 4 to this Order, the duties of the returning officer for a parliamentary election shall be discharged, as acting returning officer, by the registration officer appointed by the council of the district listed in the right-hand column of that Schedule opposite to the name of the constituency.

SCHEDULE 1

RETURNING OFFICERS FOR CERTAIN BOROUGH CONSTITUENCIES OUTSIDE GREATER LONDON

Name of borough constituency	*District of which chair is returning officer*
Ashton-under-Lyne	Tameside
Blackley and Broughton	Manchester
Denton and Reddish	Tameside
Wythenshawe and Sale East	Manchester
Garston and Halewood	Liverpool
St Helens South and Whiston	St Helens
Jarrow	South Tyneside
Halesowen and Rowley Regis	Dudley
Wolverhampton South East	Wolverhampton
Luton South	Luton
Reading East	Reading
Bournemouth West	Bournemouth
Kingston upon Hull West and Hessle	Kingston upon Hull
Brighton, Kemptown	Brighton and Hove
Eastbourne	Eastbourne
Aldershot	Rushmoor
Gosport	Gosport
Broxbourne	Broxbourne
Watford	Watford
Blackpool North and Cleveleys	Blackpool
Hyndburn	Hyndburn
Rossendale and Darwen	Rossendale
Lincoln	Lincoln
Norwich North	Broadland
Norwich South	Norwich
StokeonTrent North	StokeonTrent
Epsom and Ewell	Epsom and Ewell
Worthing West	Worthing

SCHEDULE 2

RETURNING OFFICERS FOR CERTAIN BOROUGH CONSTITUENCIES IN GREATER LONDON

Name of borough constituency	London borough of which mayor or chair is returning officer
Dagenham and Rainham	Barking and Dagenham
Erith and Thamesmead	Bexley
Hampstead and Kilburn	Camden
Lewisham West and Penge	Lewisham
Chelsea and Fulham	Hammersmith and Fulham
Ruislip, Northwood and Pinner	Hillingdon
Richmond Park	Richmond upon Thames
Dulwich and West Norwood	Lambeth
Chingford and Woodford Green	Waltham Forest
Leyton and Wanstead	Waltham Forest
Cities of London and Westminster	Westminster

SCHEDULE 3
RETURNING OFFICERS FOR CERTAIN COUNTY CONSTITUENCIES

Name of county constituency	District of which chair is returning officer
Brigg and Goole	North Lincolnshire
Rutland and Melton	Melton

SCHEDULE 4
ACTING RETURNING OFFICERS FOR COUNTY CONSTITUENCIES

Name of county constituency	District of which registration officer is acting returning officer
Bolton West	Bolton
Hazel Grove	Stockport
Heywood and Middleton	Rochdale
Leigh	Wigan
Makerfield	Wigan
Oldham East and Saddleworth	Oldham
Rochdale	Rochdale
Stalybridge and Hyde	Tameside
Wigan	Wigan
Worsley and Eccles South	Salford
Sefton Central	Sefton
Wirral South	Wirral
Wirral West	Wirral
Barnsley East	Barnsley
Don Valley	Doncaster
Doncaster North	Doncaster
Penistone and Stocksbridge	Sheffield
Rother Valley	Rotherham
Sheffield, Hallam	Sheffield
Wentworth and Dearne	Rotherham
Meriden	Solihull
Calder Valley	Calderdale
Colne Valley	Kirklees
Dewsbury	Kirklees
Elmet and Rothwell	Leeds

Name of county constituency	District of which registration officer is acting returning officer
Hemsworth	Wakefield
Keighley	Bradford
Morley and Outwood	Leeds
Normanton, Pontefract and Castleford	Wakefield
Shipley	Bradford
Wakefied	Wakefield
North East Somerset	Bath and North East Somerset
Mid Bedfordshire	Mid Bedfordshire
North East Bedfordshire	Bedford
South West Bedfordshir	South Bedfordshire
Bracknell	Bracknell Forest
Maidenhead	Windsor and Maidenhead
Newbury	West Berkshire
Reading West	Reading
Windsor	Windsor and Maidenhead
Wokingham	Wokingham
Aylesbury	Aylesbury Vale
Beaconsfield	South Bucks
Buckingham	Aylesbury Vale
Chesham and Amersham	Chiltern
Wycombe	Wycombe
Huntingdon	Huntingdonshire
North East Cambridgeshire	Fenland
North West Cambridgeshire	Peterborough
South Cambridgeshire	South Cambridgeshire
South East Cambridgeshire	East Cambridgeshire
City of Chester	Chester
Congleton	Congleton
Crewe and Nantwich	Crewe and Nantwich
Eddisbury	Vale Royal
Ellesmere Port and Neston	Ellesmere Port
Halton	Halton
Macclesfield	Macclesfield
Tatton	Macclesfield
Weaver Vale	Vale Royal
Camborne and Redruth	Kerrier
North Cornwall	North Cornwall
South East Cornwall	Caradon
St Austell and Newquay	Restormel
St Ives	Penwith
Truro and Falmouth	Carrick
Barrow and Furness	BarrowinFurness
Copeland	Copeland
Penrith and The Border	Eden
Westmorland and Lonsdale	South Lakeland
Workington	Allerdale
Amber Valley	Amber Valley
Bolsover	Bolsover
Derbyshire Dales	Derbyshire Dales
Erewash	Erewash
High Peak	High Peak

Name of county constituency	District of which registration officer is acting returning officer
Mid Derbyshire	Derby
North East Derbyshire	North East Derbyshire
South Derbyshire	South Derbyshire
Central Devon	West Devon
East Devon	East Devon
Newton Abbot	Teignbridge
North Devon	North Devon
South West Devon	Plymouth
Tiverton and Honiton	Mid Devon
Torridge and West Devon	Torridge
Totnes	South Hams
Christchurch	Christchurch
Mid Dorset and North Poole	Poole
North Dorset	North Dorset
South Dorset	Weymouth and Portland
West Dorset	West Dorset
Bishop Auckland	Wear Valley
City of Durham	City of Durham
Easington	Easington
North Durham	ChesterleStreet
North West Durham	Derwentside
Sedgefield	Sedgefield
Beverley and Holderness	East Riding of Yorkshire
Cleethorpes	North East Lincolnshire
East Yorkshire	East Riding of Yorkshire
Haltemprice and Howden	East Riding of Yorkshire
Scunthorpe	North Lincolnshire
Bexhill and Battle	Rother
Hastings and Rye	Hastings
Lewes	Lewes
Wealden	Wealden
Braintree	Braintree
Brentwood and Ongar	Brentwood
Clacton	Tendring
Epping Forest	Epping Forest
Harlow	Harlow
Harwich and North Essex	Colchester
Maldon	Maldon
Rayleigh and Wickford	Rochford
Rochford and Southend East	SouthendonSea
Saffron Walden	Uttlesford
South Basildon and East Thurrock	Basildon
Witham	Braintree
Forest of Dean	Forest of Dean
Stroud	Stroud
Tewkesbury	Tewkesbury
The Cotswolds	Cotswold
East Hampshire	East Hampshire
Fareham	Fareham
Meon Valley	Winchester
New Forest East	New Forest

Name of county constituency	District of which registration officer is acting returning officer
New Forest West	New Forest
North East Hampshire	Hart
North West Hampshire	Test Valley
Romsey and Southampton North	Test Valley
Winchester	Winchester
Hereford and South Herefordshire	Herefordshire
North Herefordshire	Herefordshire
Hemel Hempstead	Dacorum
Hertford and Stortford	East Hertfordshire
Hertsmere	Hertsmere
Hitchin and Harpenden	St Albans
North East Hertfordshire	North Hertfordshire
South West Hertfordshire	Three Rivers
St Albans	St Albans
Stevenage	Stevenage
Welwyn Hatfield	Welwyn Hatfield
Isle of Wight	Isle of Wight
Ashford	Ashford
Canterbury	Canterbury
Chatham and Aylesford	Medway
Dartford	Dartford
Dover	Dover
Faversham and Mid Kent	Maidstone
Folkestone and Hythe	Shepway
Gravesham	Gravesham
Maidstone and The Weald	Maidstone
North Thanet	Thanet
Rochester and Strood	Medway
Sevenoaks	Sevenoaks
Sittingbourne and Sheppey	Swale
South Thanet	Thanet
Tonbridge and Malling	Tonbridge and Malling
Tunbridge Wells	Tunbridge Wells
Chorley	Chorley
Fylde	Fylde
Lancaster and Fleetwood	Lancaster
Morecambe and Lunesdale	Lancaster
Ribble Valley	Ribble Valley
South Ribble	South Ribble
West Lancashire	West Lancashire
Wyre and Preston North	Wyre
Bosworth	Hinckley and Bosworth
Charnwood	Charnwood
Harborough	Oadby and Wigston
Loughborough	Charnwood
North West Leicestershire	North West Leicestershire
South Leicestershire	Blaby
Boston and Skegness	Boston
Gainsborough	West Lindsey
Grantham and Stamford	South Kesteven
Louth and Horncastle	East Lindsey

Name of county constituency	District of which registration officer is acting returning officer
Sleaford and North Hykeham	North Kesteven
South Holland and The Deepings	South Holland
Middlesborough South and East Cleveland	Redcar and Cleveland
Milton Keynes North	Milton Keynes
Broadland	Broadland
Great Yarmouth	Great Yarmouth
Mid Norfolk	Breckland
North Norfolk	North Norfolk
North West Norfolk	King's Lynn and West Nrfolk
South Norfolk	South Norfolk
South West Norfolk	King's Lynn and West Norfolk
Corby	Corby
Daventry	Daventry
Kettering	Kettering
South Northamptonshire	South Northamptonshire
Wellingborough	Wellingborough
North Somerset	North Somerset
WestonSuperMare	North Somerset
BerwickuponTweed	Alnwick
Hexham	Tynedale
Wansbeck	Wansbeck
Harrogate and Knaresborough	Harrogate
Richmond (Yorks)	Hambleton
Scarborough and Whitby	Scarborough
Selby and Ainsty	Selby
Skipton and Ripon	Craven
Thirsk and Malton	Ryedale
Ashfield	Ashfield
Bassetlaw	Bassetlaw
Broxtowe	Broxtowe
Gedling	Gedling
Mansfield	Mansfield
Newark	Newark and Sherwood
Rushcliffe	Rushcliffe
Sherwood	Newark and Sherwood
Banbury	Cherwell
Henley	South Oxfordshire
Oxford West and Abingdon	Vale of White Horse
Wantage	Vale of White Horse
Witney	West Oxfordshire
Ludlow	South Shropshire
North Shropshire	North Shropshire
Shrewsbury and Atcham	Shrewsbury and Atcham
The Wrekin	Telford and Wrekin
Bridgwater and West Somerset	Sedgemoor
Somerton and Frome	South Somerset
Taunton Deane	Taunton Deane
Wells	Mendip
Yeovil	South Somerset
Filton and Bradley Stoke	South Gloucestershire
Thornbury and Yate	South Gloucestershire

Name of county constituency	District of which registration officer is acting returning officer
Burton	East Staffordshire
Cannock Chase	Cannock Chase
Lichfield	Lichfield
South Staffordshire	South Staffordshire
Stafford	Stafford
Staffordshire Moorlands	Staffordshire Moorlands
Stone	Stafford
Tamworth	Tamworth
Bury St Edmunds	St Edmundsbury
Central Suffolk and North Ipswich	Mid Suffolk
South Suffolk	Babergh
Suffolk Coastal	Suffolk Coastal
Waveney	Waveney
West Suffolk	Forest Heath
East Surrey	Tandridge
Guildford	Guildford
Mole Valley	Mole Valley
Runnymede and Weybridge	Runnymede
South West Surrey	Waverley
Surrey Heath	Surrey Heath
Woking	Woking
North Swindon	Swindon
South Swindon	Swindon
Kenilworth and Southam	Warwick
North Warwickshire	North Warwickshire
Nuneaton	Nuneaton and Bedworth
Rugby	Rugby
StratfordonAvon	Stratford on Avon
Arundel and South Downs	Horsham
Bognor Regis and Littlehampton	Arun
Chichester	Chichester
East Worthing and Shoreham	Adur
Horsham	Horsham
Mid Sussex	Mid Sussex
Chippenham	North Wiltshire
Devizes	Kennet
North Wiltshire	North Wiltshire
Salisbury	Salisbury
South West Wiltshire	West Wiltshire
Bromsgrove	Bromsgrove
Mid Worcestershire	Wychavon
Redditch	Redditch
West Worcestershire	Malvern Hills
Wyre Forest	Wyre Forest
York Outer	York

Returning Officers (Parliamentary Constituencies) (Wales) Order 2007 (SI 2007/171)

Made 23 January 2007

Citation and commencement

1(1) This Order may be cited as the Returning Officers (Parliamentary Constituencies) (Wales) Order 2007.

(2) This Order comes into force
   (a) for the purposes of parliamentary elections upon the next issue of a proclamation by Her Majesty summoning a new Parliament;
   (b) for the purposes of proceedings preliminary or relating to the next general election, on the day after the day on which it is made.

(3) References to constituencies in this Order are references to constituencies in Wales, which are established by the Parliamentary Constituencies and Assembly Electoral Regions (Wales) Order 2006 or any subsequent Order in respect of Wales under the Parliamentary Constituencies Act 1986.

Revocations

2 Subject to article 1(2), the following Orders are revoked
   (a) the Returning Officers (Parliamentary Constituencies) (Wales) Order 1996; and
   (b) the Returning Officers (Parliamentary Constituencies) (Wales) (Amendment) Order 2004.

Designation of returning officers at parliamentary elections

3 In the case of the county constituency of Merthyr Tydfil and Rhymney, being a county constituency which is not coterminous with or wholly contained in a preserved county as defined by section 64 of the Local Government (Wales) Act 1994, the sheriff of the preserved county of Mid Glamorgan shall be the returning officer at a parliamentary election.

4 In the case of the borough constituency of Cardiff South and Penarth, being a borough constituency which is not coterminous with or wholly contained in a county or county borough, the chairman of Cardiff County Council shall be the returning officer for a parliamentary election.

Designation of acting returning officers at parliamentary elections

5 In the case of a county constituency specified in column 1 of the Schedule to this Order, the duties of the returning officer for a parliamentary election shall be discharged, as acting returning officer, by the officer of the council appointed to be the electoral registration officer by the council of the county or county borough specified in column 2 of the Schedule opposite to the name of the constituency.

SCHEDULE
ACTING RETURNING OFFICERS FOR COUNTY CONSTITUENCIES

1	2
Name of county constituency	**County or county borough for which registration officer is acting returning officer**
Aberavon	Neath Port Talbot
Aberconwy	Conwy
Alyn and Deeside	Flintshire
Arfon	Gwynedd
Blaenau Gwent	Blaenau Gwent
Brecon and Radnorshire	Powys
Bridgend	Bridgend
Caerphilly	Caerphilly
Carmarthen East and Dinefwr	Carmarthenshire
Carmarthen West and South Pembrokeshire	Pembrokeshire
Ceredigion	Ceredigion
Clwyd South	Wrexham
Clwyd West	Conwy
Cynon Valley	Rhondda, Cynon, Taff
Delyn	Flintshire
Dwyfor Meirionnydd	Gwynedd
Gower	Swansea
Islwyn	Caerphilly
Llanelli	Carmarthenshire
Merthyr Tydfil and Rhymney	Merthyr Tydfil
Monmouth	Monmouthshire
Montgomeryshire	Powys
Neath	Neath Port Talbot
Newport East	Newport
Newport West	Newport
Ogmore	Bridgend
Pontypridd	Rhondda, Cynon, Taff
Preseli Pembrokeshire	Pembrokeshire
Rhondda	Rhondda, Cynon, Taff
Torfaen	Torfaen
Vale of Clwyd	Denbighshire
Vale of Glamorgan	The Vale of Glamorgan
Wrexham	Wrexham
Ynys Môn	Isle of Anglesey

Act of Sederunt (Rules of the Court of Session 1994)
SI 1994/1443

Part 5
Other proceedings in relation to statutory applications

69 Election Petitions

Interpretation of this Chapter

69.1   In this Chapter–

"the Act of 1983" means the Representation of the People Act 1983;

"the 2004 Regulations" means the European Parliamentary Elections Regulations 2004;

"election court" has the meaning assigned in section 123 of the Act of 1983;

"election petition" means a petition presented under—

(a)   section 121 of the Act of 1983 (whether or not the petition also includes any application under section 167 of the Act of 1983);

(b)   section 121 of the Act of 1983 as applied and modified by article 82 of and Schedule 6 to the Scottish Parliament (Elections etc.) Order 2015 (whether or not the petition also includes any application under section 167 of the Act of 1983, as so applied and modified); or

(c)   regulation 89 of the European Parliamentary Elections Regulations 2004[4] (whether or not the petition also includes any application under regulation 108 of those Regulations);

"region" means a region for the purposes of the Scotland Act 1998; and any reference in this Chapter to a constituency shall be construed as a reference to a constituency for the purposes of the said Act of 1998 where it is used in relation to a Scottish parliamentary election;

"Scottish parliamentary election" means an election for membership of the Scottish Parliament.

Form of election petitions

69.2(1)   An election petition shall be in Form 69.2.

(2)   Such a petition shall–

(a)   specify the name, designation and address of–

(i)   each petitioner, and

(ii)   each person referred to as, or deemed to be, the respondent by virtue of section 121(2) of the Act of 1983 or regulation 89(2) of the 2004 Regulations, as the case may be; and

(b)   set out in numbered paragraphs–

(i)   the title of the petitioner under section 121(1) of the Act of 1983 or regulation 89(1) of the 2004 Regulations to present the petition;

(ii)   the proceedings at, and the result of, the election; and

(iii)   the facts relied on in support of the prayer of the petition.

Presentation of petition

69.3   The election petition shall be lodged in the Petition Department with–

(a)   a process;

(b)   six copies of the petition; and

(c) a letter signed by or on behalf of the petitioner–

    (i) giving the name and address of a solicitor whom he authorises to act on his behalf or stating that he acts for himself, as the case may be; and

    (ii) specifying an address within Scotland at which notices addressed to him may be delivered.

Security for expenses

69.4(1) On presentation of an election petition, the petitioner shall apply by motion for–

    (a) an order for intimation and service of the petition within such period as the court thinks fit after the giving of security,

    (b) for an order for the respondent to lodge any objections in writing under section 136(4) of the Act of 1983 or regulation 94(4) of the 2004 Regulations (objections to form of security) within such period as the court thinks fit, and

    (c) the fixing of the amount of security for expenses;

and the petition shall be placed forthwith before the Lord Ordinary or the vacation judge, in court or in chambers, who shall fix the security to be given.

(2) A motion under paragraph (1) shall not be intimated to any person.

(3) Where the security to be given by the petitioner under section 136 of the Act of 1983 or regulation 94 of the 2004 Regulations is given in whole or in part by bond of caution, the bond shall be in Form 69.4.

Service and intimation of election petition

69.5(1) On serving the election petition on the respondent under subsection (3) of section 136 of the Act of 1983 or regulation 94(3) of the 2004 Regulations, the petitioner shall intimate a copy of each of the documents mentioned in that subsection to—

    (a) the Lord Advocate; and

    (b) the Advocate General for Scotland.

(2) The notice of presentation of the petition mentioned in section 136(3) of the Act of 1983 or regulation 94(3) of the 2004 Regulations shall be in Form 69.5.

(3) Within 5 days after serving the petition under section 136 of the Act of 1983 or regulation 94 of the 2004 Regulations, the petitioner shall lodge in process an execution copy of the election petition containing the certificate of service and a copy of the notice mentioned in that subsection which was served on the respondent.

(4) Where the court makes an order for intimation and service of an election petition, the Deputy Principal Clerk shall send a copy of the petition to the Electoral Commission.

Objections to form of security

69.6(1) Where the respondent makes an objection under section 136(4) of the Act of 1983 or regulation 94(4) of the 2004 Regulations (objection to form of security), he shall–

    (a) set out in writing the grounds of the objection;

    (b) lodge the objection in process; and

    (c) intimate a copy of the objection to the petitioner.

(2) As soon as possible after the lodging of an objection under paragraph (1), the Keeper of the Rolls shall–

    (a) fix a diet for a hearing on the objections before one of the judges on the rota for the trial of election petitions or the vacation judge; and

    (b) give written intimation of the time and place of the diet to the parties.

(3) The period within which the petitioner may, under section 136(7) of the Act of 1983 or regulation 94(6) of the 2004 Regulations, remove the objection shall be such period from the date of the decision on the objection as the court thinks fit.

Consequences of failure to give security etc.

69.7 If no security is given, or an objection to a security is allowed and not removed, the respondent may apply by motion to have the prayer of the petition refused.

List of election petitions

69.8(1) In preparing the list of election petitions in terms of section 138(1) of the Act of 1983, the Deputy Principal Clerk shall insert the names of the solicitors, if any, acting for the petitioner and respondent, and the addresses, if any, to which any notices may be sent.

(2) The list of election petitions may be inspected in the Petition Department at any time during its normal office hours.

Time and place of trial

69.9(1) The time and place of the trial of an election petition shall be fixed by the Keeper of the Rolls, who shall give written intimation of the date of the trial by post to–
  (a) the parties;
  (b) the Lord Advocate;
  (ba) the Advocate General for Scotland;
  (c) the returning officer for the relevant constituency or as the case may be, region ; and
  (d) the House of Commons shorthand writer.

(2) On receipt of intimation given under paragraph (1), the returning officer shall forthwith publish the date of the diet of trial in the constituency or as the case may be, region to which it relates.

Postponement of trial

69.10(1) The election court or any of the judges on the rota for the trial of election petitions, may, at its or his own instance or on the motion of a party, postpone the trial of a petition to such day as may be specified.

(2) Written intimation of such postponement shall be given by the Keeper of the Rolls to the returning officer who shall forthwith publish the postponement and its new date in the constituency or as the case may be, region.

Procedure where seat claimed

69.11(1) Where a petitioner claims the seat for an unsuccessful candidate, alleging that he had a majority of lawful votes, the party complaining of, and the party defending, the return, not less than 6 days before the date of the trial, shall each–
  (a) lodge in process a list of the voters intended to be objected to, and of the objections to each voter; and
  (b) intimate a copy of that list to–
    (i) every other party;
    (ii) the Lord Advocate ; and
    (iii) the Advocate General for Scotland.

(2) No evidence shall be allowed to be given against any vote or in support of any objection which is not specified in the list, except by leave of the election court or, on a motion heard before the date of the trial, of any of the judges on the rota for the trial of election petitions, on such terms as to amendment of the list, postponement of the trial and payment of expenses as may be ordered.

Evidence under section 139(5) of the Act of 1983

69.12(1) Where the respondent intends to give evidence permitted under section 139(5) of the Act of 1983 or regulation 96(4) of the 2004 Regulations (evidence to prove person not duly elected), he shall, not less than 6 days before the date of the trial–
    (a) lodge in process a list of the objections to the election on which he intends to rely; and
    (b) intimate a copy of that list to–
        (i) every other party;
        (ii) the Lord Advocate; and
        (iii) the Advocate General for Scotland.

(2) No evidence shall be allowed to be given on behalf of the respondent in support of any objection to the return not specified in the list, except with leave of the election court or, on a motion heard before the date of the trial, of any of the judges on the rota for the trial of election petitions, on such terms as to amendment of the list, postponement of the trial and payment of expenses as may be ordered.

Lodging of statement of evidence to be led

69.13(1) Subject to paragraph (2), any party shall, not less than 6 days before the date of the trial, lodge in process a statement of the matters on which he intends to lead evidence.

(2) Before lodging such a statement in process, the party proposing to lodge it shall intimate a copy of the statement to—
    (a) every other party;
    (b) the Lord Advocate ; and
    (c) the Advocate General for Scotland.

Evidence at trial

69.14(1) No evidence shall be led at the trial of an election petition other than matters contained in–
    (a) the list lodged under rule 69.11 (procedure where seat claimed) or 69.12 (evidence under section 139(5) of the Act of 1983),
    (b) the statement lodged under rule 69.13 (statement of evidence to be led), or
    (c) matters which have been sufficiently set out in the petition, except with the leave of the election court or one of the judges on the rota for the trial of election petitions, on such conditions as to postponement of the trial, payment of expenses or otherwise, as may be ordered.

(2) The admissibility of any evidence sought to be led on the matters referred to in paragraph (1) shall be within the discretion of the election court.

Warrant to cite witnesses

69.15 The warrant for the citation of a witness to the trial of an election petition shall be granted on the motion of any party and shall be in Form 69.15.

Clerk of court at trial

69.16 At an election court held for the trial of an election petition, a clerk of session nominated by the Principal Clerk and appointed by the court shall discharge the duties of clerk of court of the election court.

Expenses of witnesses

69.17(1)   The prescribed officer for the purposes of section 143(1) of the Act of 1983 or regulation 99(1) of the 2004 Regulations shall be the clerk of session appointed to act as clerk of court under rule 69.16.

(2)   The expenses of a witness permitted under section 143(1) of the Act of 1983 or regulation 99(1) of the 2004 Regulations shall be ascertained by the clerk of court.

(3)   The expenses allowed under section 143(1) of the Act of 1983 or regulation 99(1) of the 2004 Regulations shall, in the first instance, be paid by the party adducing that witness.

Applications for special case

69.18   An application under section 146(1) of the Act of 1983 or regulation 101(1) of the 2004 Regulations for a special case, shall be made by motion to the Inner House or the vacation judge.

Applications for leave to withdraw election petitions

69.19(1)   A notice of intention to withdraw an election petition under section 147(2) of the Act of 1983 or regulation 102(2) of the 2004 Regulations shall be in Form 69.19–A.

(2)   A copy of such notice shall be intimated by the petitioners to–
    (a)   the respondent;
    (b)   the Lord Advocate;
    (ba) the Advocate General for Scotland;
    (c)   the returning officer for the relevant constituency or as the case may be, region; and
    (d)   the Deputy Principal Clerk.

(3)   On receipt of a notice under paragraph (2), the returning officer shall publish it in the constituency or as the case may be, region to which it relates.

(4)   An application for leave to withdraw an election petition shall–
    (a)   be in Form 69.19–B;
    (b)   state the ground on which the application to withdraw is made;
    (c)   be signed by the person making the application and by the consenters, if any, or by their respective solicitors; and
    (d)   be lodged in the process of the election petition.

Applications to be substituted as petitioner on withdrawal

69.20(1)   A person who seeks to apply under section 150(1) of the Act of 1983 to be substituted as a petitioner, shall, within 5 days after the date on which the notice of intention to withdraw has been given under section 147(2) of the Act of 1983 and rule 69.19 (applications for leave to withdraw election petitions), give notice in writing signed by him or on his behalf to the Deputy Principal Clerk of his intention to apply, at the hearing of the application for leave to withdraw, to be substituted as the petitioner.

(2)   A copy of the notice given under paragraph (1) shall be intimated by the applicant to–
    (a)   the respondent;
    (b)   the Lord Advocate; and
    (ba) the Advocate General for Scotland;
    (c)   the returning officer for the relevant constituency.

(3)   Any informality in such a notice shall not defeat an application to be substituted as the petitioner if it is made at the hearing of the application to withdraw, subject to such order as to postponement of that hearing and expenses as the election court thinks fit.

Hearing of application for leave to withdraw

69.21(1) Subject to paragraph (2), the time and place for hearing an application for leave to withdraw an election petition shall be fixed by one of the judges on the rota for the trial of election petitions or by the vacation judge, who shall hear and determine the application unless he considers that the application should be determined by the Inner House.

(2) The time fixed under paragraph (1) shall not be earlier than 7 days after the expiry of the period specified in rule 69.20.

(3) The Keeper of the Rolls shall give written intimation of the diet fixed under paragraph (1) to–
   (a) the petitioner;
   (b) the respondent;
   (c) the Lord Advocate;
   (ca) the Advocate General for Scotland;
   (d) the returning officer for the relevant constituency; and
   (e) to any person who has given notice under rule 69.20 of his intention to apply to be substituted as the petitioner.

Security of substituted petitioner

69.22(1) The period within which security shall be given on behalf of a substituted petitioner before he proceeds with the petition shall be 5 days after the order of substitution.

(2) The substituted petitioner shall lodge the letter referred to in rule 69.3(name and address of solicitor etc.) within 5 days after the order of substitution.

Death of petitioner

69.23(1) In the event of the death of the petitioner or the surviving petitioner, the notice for the purpose of section 152(3) of the Act of 1983 (notice of abatement of petition by death) shall be intimated in Form 69.23 by the solicitor acting for the petitioner, the respondent, the returning officer or any other person interested to whose knowledge the death of the petitioner shall come, to, as the case may be–
   (a) the respondent;
   (b) the Lord Advocate;
   (ba) the Advocate General for Scotland;
   (c) the returning officer for the relevant constituency or as the case may be, region; and
   (d) the Deputy Principal Clerk.

(2) The returning officer shall, on receipt of such a notice, or, where he is giving notice under paragraph (1), on intimating such notice to those persons mentioned in that paragraph, publish the notice in the constituency or as the case may be, region to which it relates.

Applications to be substituted on death of petitioner

69.24(1) An application to be substituted as a petitioner on the death of the petitioner or surviving petitioner shall be made by motion within 5 days after the publication of the notice.

(2) A motion under paragraph (1) shall be intimated to–
   (a) the respondent;
   (b) the Lord Advocate; and
   (ba) the Advocate General for Scotland;

(c) the returning officer for the relevant constituency or as the case may be, region where he is not a respondent.

Notice that respondent does not oppose

69.25(1) A notice, for the purposes of section 153(1) of the Act of 1983, by a respondent other than a returning officer, that he does not intend to oppose an election petition shall be–

    (a) signed by him; and

    (b) lodged in process not less than 6 days before the date of the trial.

(2) Where a respondent lodges a notice under paragraph (1), he shall forthwith intimate a copy of it to–

    (a) the petitioner;

    (b) any other respondent;

    (c) the Lord Advocate; and

    (ca) the Advocate General for Scotland;

    (d) the returning officer for the relevant constituency.

(3) On receipt of a notice under paragraph (1), the returning officer shall publish it in the constituency to which it relates.

Death, peerage or resignation of respondent

69.26(1) Where, for the purposes of section 153(1) of the Act of 1983–

    (a) a respondent other than a returning officer dies,

    (b) in the case of a parliamentary election, a respondent other than a returning officer is summoned to Parliament as a Peer of Great Britain,

    (c) a respondent other than a returning officer has vacated his seat following a resolution by the House of Commons, or

    (d) a respondent resigns or otherwise ceases to be a member of the Scottish Parliament,

the agent for the respondent shall give notice of that fact in the constituency to which the election petition relates.

(2) Such a notice shall be published in at least one newspaper circulating in the constituency, and by intimating a copy of the notice, signed by him to–

    (a) the petitioner;

    (b) any other respondent;

    (c) the Lord Advocate;

    (ca) the Advocate General for Scotland;

    (d) the returning officer for the relevant constituency; and

    (e) the Deputy Principal Clerk.

Applications to be admitted as respondent

69.27 The period of time within which a person may apply to be admitted as a respondent under section 153 of the Act of 1983 shall be–

    (a) 5 days after the notice is intimated under rule 69.25 (notice that respondent does not oppose);

    (b) 10 days after the notice is intimated under rule 69.26 (death, peerage or resignation of respondent); or

    (c) such other period as the court thinks fit.

Expenses in election petitions

69.28   Where any expenses are awarded by the election court in the course of proceedings under the Act of 1983 or the 2004 Regulations, such an award shall be deemed equivalent to a finding of expenses in the Court of Session.

Motions in election petitions

69.29(1)   Subject to any other provision in this Chapter or the Act of 1983, all applications shall be dealt with by motion.

   (2)   Subject to the provisions of this Chapter, Chapter 23 (motions) shall apply to a motion in an election petition.

   (3)   A motion in an election petition shall be intimated to–
         (a) the Lord Advocate; and
         (aa) the Advocate General for Scotland;
         (b) the returning officer for the relevant constituency or as the case may be, region.

Intimation to Lord Advocate

69.30   All applications to the court in an election petition other than a motion under rule 69.4(1) (security for expenses) shall be intimated to—
         (a) the Lord Advocate; and
         (b) the Advocate General for Scotland;
         and the Lord Advocate and the Advocate General for Scotland shall be entitled to appear or be represented at the hearing of that application.

Evidence of publication by returning officer

69.31(1)   Where a returning officer publishes a notice in accordance with a provision in this Chapter or an order of the election court, he shall forthwith send to the Deputy Principal Clerk a letter–
         (a) certifying that the appropriate notice has been published; and
         (b) detailing the manner in which the publication has been made.

   (2)   Where publication has been made by inserting a notice in a newspaper or other publication, the letter under paragraph (1) shall be accompanied by–
         (a) a copy of the newspaper or other publication containing the notice; or
         (b) a certificate of publication by the publisher stating the date of publication and the text of the notice.

Town and Country Planning (Control of Advertisements) (England) Regulations 2007 (SI 2007/783)

Part 1
General

Citation, commencement and application

1(1) These Regulations may be cited as the Town and Country Planning (Control of Advertisements) (England) Regulations 2007 and shall come into force on 6th April 2007.

(2) These Regulations apply in relation to the display of advertisements on sites in England only.

(3) Parts 2 and 3 of these Regulations do not apply to the display of an advertisement of a description set out in column (1) of Schedule 1 to these Regulations so long as

    (a) the display complies with the conditions and limitations specified in column (2) of that Schedule as applicable to advertisements of that description; and

    (b) except in the case of an advertisement within Class F, all the conditions specified in Schedule 2 are complied with;

    (c) in the case of an advertisement within Class F, the requirements of paragraphs 1 to 3 and 5 of the standard conditions are complied with.

Interpretation

2(1) In these Regulations

    "the Act" means the Town and Country Planning Act 1990;

    "advertisement" does not include

        (a) anything employed wholly as a memorial or as a railway signal; or

        (b) a placard or other object borne by an individual or an animal;

    "advertiser", in relation to an advertisement, means

        (a) the owner of the site on which the advertisement is displayed;

        (b) the occupier of the site, if different; and

        (c) any other person who undertakes or maintains the display of the advertisement;

    and any reference in these Regulations to the person displaying an advertisement shall be construed as a reference to the advertiser;

    "amenity" includes aural and visual amenity;

    "Area of Outstanding Natural Beauty" means an area designated as such by an order made under section 82 of the Countryside and Rights of Way Act 2000;

    "area of special control" means an area designated by an order under regulation 20;

    "balloon" means a tethered balloon or similar object;

    "deemed consent" means consent granted by regulation 6;

    "discontinuance notice" means a notice served under regulation 8;

    "electronic communication" means an electronic communication within the meaning of the Electronic Communications Act 2000, the processing of which on receipt is intended to produce writing;

    "electronic communications code operator" means

        (a) a provider of an electronic communications network in whose case the electronic communications code applies by virtue of a direction given by OFCOM under section 106 of the Communications Act 2003; and

     (b) a person who, by virtue of paragraph 17(1) and (2) of Schedule 18 to that Act, is treated after the commencement of that section as a person in whose case that code applies by virtue of a direction given by OFCOM;

"electronically" means by electronic communication;

"express consent" has the meaning given by regulation 5;

"highway authority" has the meaning given by sections 1 to 3 of the Highways Act 1980;

"highway land" means any land within the boundaries of a highway;

"illuminated advertisement" means an advertisement which is designed or adapted to be illuminated by artificial lighting, directly or by reflection, and which is so illuminated (whether continuously or from time to time);

"local planning authority"

     (a) as regards land in a National Park, other than land within a metropolitan county, means the county planning authority for the area where the land is situated;

     (b) as regards land in the area of an urban development corporation, means (except in regulation 20) that corporation where it is the local planning authority for the purposes of sections 220 and 224 of the Act; and

     (c) as regards any other land, means the relevant district planning authority, metropolitan district or London borough council or urban development corporation;

"National Park" has the meaning given by section 5 of the National Parks and Access to the Countryside Act 1949;

"site" means any land or building, other than an advertisement, on which an advertisement is displayed;

"standard conditions" means the conditions specified in Schedule 2;

"statutory undertaker" includes, in addition to any person referred to in section 262(1) of the Act

     (a) any person deemed to be a statutory undertaker under subsection (3) or (6) of that section,

     (b) the British Airports Authority,

     (c) the Coal Authority or any licensed operator within the meaning of section 65(1) of the Coal Industry Act 1994,

     (d) any electronic communications code operator, and

     (e) any person who is a licence holder, or who has the benefit of a licence exemption, within the meaning of Part 1 of the Railways Act 1993,

and "statutory undertaking" shall be construed accordingly;

"traffic sign" has the meaning given by section 64(1) of the Road Traffic Regulation Act 1984;

"vehicle" includes a vessel on any inland waterway or in coastal waters; and

"working day" means a day which is not a Saturday or a Sunday, Christmas Day, Good Friday or a bank holiday in England and Wales under the Banking and Financial Dealings Act 1971.

(2) Except in Class 15 in Schedule 3, any reference in these Regulations to the building, the land, the premises or the site on which an advertisement is displayed includes, in the case of an advertisement which is displayed on, or which consists of, a balloon, a reference to the building, the land, the premises or the site to which the balloon is attached and to all buildings, land or premises normally occupied therewith.

3-5 *Not reproduced*

Part 2
Deemed Consent

Deemed consent for the display of advertisements

6(1)   Subject to regulations 7 and 8, and in the case of an area of special control also to regulation 21, consent is granted for the display of an advertisement of any class specified in Part 1 of Schedule 3, subject to

(a)   the standard conditions; and

(b)   in the case of any class other than Class 12, the conditions and limitations specified in that Part in relation to that class.

(2)   Part 2 of Schedule 3 applies for the interpretation of that Schedule.

7-29   *Not reproduced*

Contravention of Regulations

30(1)   Subject to paragraph (2), a person displaying an advertisement in contravention of these Regulations shall be liable, on summary conviction of an offence under section 224(3) of the Act, to a fine of an amount not exceeding level 4 on the standard scale and, in the case of a continuing offence, one tenth of level 4 on the standard scale for each day during which the offence continues after conviction.

(2)   Paragraph (1) does not apply to the Crown.

SCHEDULE 1
CLASSES OF ADVERTISEMENT TO WHICH PARTS 2 AND 3 DO NOT APPLY

Regulation 1(3)

(1) Description of advertisement	(2) Conditions, limitations and interpretation
CLASS A An advertisement displayed on enclosed land.	1 The advertisement is not readily visible from outside the enclosed land or from any place to which the public have a right of access. 2 For the purposes of Class A, "enclosed land" includes (a) any railway station (and its yards) or bus station, together with its forecourt, whether enclosed or not; but does not include any public park, public garden or other land held for the use or enjoyment of the public, or (except as specified above) any enclosed railway land normally used for the carriage of passengers or goods by rail; (b) any sports stadium; and (c) any shopping mall or covered shopping arcade other than an historic shopping arcade. 3 In paragraph 2(c) "historic shopping arcade" means a group of buildings (a) of which more than 50% (i) are listed buildings within the meaning of the Planning (Listed Buildings and Conservation Areas) Act 1990 (whether listed individually or for their group value); or (ii) are located within a conservation area within the

(1)	(2)
Description of advertisement	Conditions, limitations and interpretation
	meaning of that Act; and
	(b) in more than 50% of which at least 75% of the ground floor is used for retail purposes.
CLASS B An advertisement displayed on or in a vehicle normally employed as a moving vehicle.	The vehicle is not used principally for the display of advertisements.
CLASS E An advertisement relating specifically to a pending Parliamentary, European Parliamentary or local government election or a referendum under the Political Parties, Elections and Referendums Act 2000.	The advertisement shall be removed within 14 days after the close of the poll in the election or referendum to which it relates.
CLASS I An advertisement displayed inside a building.	1 The advertisement may not be illuminated. 2 No part of the advertisement may be within 1 metre of any external door, window or other opening, through which it is visible from outside the building.

SCHEDULE 2
THE STANDARD CONDITIONS

Regulation 2(1)

1 No advertisement is to be displayed without the permission of the owner of the site or any other person with an interest in the site entitled to grant permission.

2 No advertisement shall be sited or displayed so as to
   (a) endanger persons using any highway, railway, waterway, dock, harbour or aerodrome (civil or military);
   (b) obscure, or hinder the ready interpretation of, any traffic sign, railway signal or aid to navigation by water or air; or
   (c) hinder the operation of any device used for the purpose of security or surveillance or for measuring the speed of any vehicle.

3 Any advertisement displayed, and any site used for the display of advertisements, shall be maintained in a condition that does not impair the visual amenity of the site.

4 Any structure or hoarding erected or used principally for the purpose of displaying advertisements shall be maintained in a condition that does not endanger the public.

5 Where an advertisement is required under these Regulations to be removed, the site shall be left in a condition that does not endanger the public or impair visual amenity.